1 MONTH OF
FREE
READING

at
www.ForgottenBooks.com

By purchasing this book you are eligible for one month membership to ForgottenBooks.com, giving you unlimited access to our entire collection of over 1,000,000 titles via our web site and mobile apps.

To claim your free month visit:
www.forgottenbooks.com/free1321194

ISBN 978-0-428-87922-8
PIBN 11321194

This book is a reproduction of an important historical work. Forgotten Books uses
state-of-the-art technology to digitally reconstruct the work, preserving the original format
whilst repairing imperfections present in the aged copy. In rare cases, an imperfection in
the original, such as a blemish or missing page, may be replicated in our edition. We do,
however, repair the vast majority of imperfections successfully; any imperfections that
remain are intentionally left to preserve the state of such historical works.

THE

CANADIAN

NETARY TIMES

AND

INSURANCE CHRONICLE:

FINANCE, COMMERCE, INSURANCE, BANKS, RAILWAYS, NAVIGATION, MINES, VESTMENT, PUBLIC COMPANIES, AND JOINT STOCK ENTERPRISE.

VOLUME II.

TORONTO:

THE OFFICE OF "THE CANADIAN MONETARY TIMES," No. 60 CHURCH STREET

l for the Proprietors by Robertson & Cook, Daily Telegraph Publishing House, Bay Street, cor. King.

1868–69.

EX TO VOLUME II.

INDEX TO VOLUME II.

THE CANADIAN
MONETARY TIMES
AND
INSURANCE CHRONICLE.
EVOTED TO FINANCE, COMMERCE, INSURANCE, BANKS, RAILWAYS, NAVIGATION, MINES, INVESTMENT, PUBLIC COMPANIES, AND JOINT STOCK ENTERPRISE.

| C. II—NO. 1. | TORONTO, THURSDAY, AUGUST 20, 1868. | { SUBSCRIPTION, { $2 A YEAR. |

Mercantile.

W. Rowland & Co.,
)UCE BROKERS and General Commission Merants. Advances made on Consignments. Corner ck and Front Streets, Toronto.

C. P. Reid & Co.
RTERS and Dealers in Wines, Liquors, Cigars and f Tobacco, Wellington Street, Toronto.   28.

Childs & Hamilton.
UFACTURERS and Wholesale Dealers in Boots 1d Shoes, No. 7 Wellington Street East, Toronto.
,   28

John Fisken & Co.
: OIL and Commission Merchants, Yonge St., ronto, Ont.

Lyman & McNab.
)LESALE Hardware Merchants, Toronto, Ontario.

L. Coffee & Co.
UCE and Commission Merchants, No. 2 Manning's ek, Front St., Toronto, Ont. Advances made on ments of Produce.

W. D. Matthews & Co.
)UCE Commission Merchants, Old Corn Exchange, Front St. East, Toronto Ont.

R. C. Hamilton & Co.
UCE Commission Merchants, 119 Lower Water , Halifax, Nova Scotia.

J. & A. Clark,
Commission Merchants, Wellington Street nto, Ont.

John Boyd & Co.
.E Grocers and Commission Merchants, , Toronto.

W. & R. Griffith.
of Teas, Wines, etc. Ontario Chambers, 1 and Front Sts , Toronto.

illon.
Illington Street, Toronto,

& Co.
-Dealers in Groceries, outo, Ont.

stead.
lerchant. Hops bought 82 Front St., Toronto.

and Earthenware, .t.]

Sessions, Turner & Co.,
TURERS, Importers and Wholesale Dealers s and Shoes, Leather Findings, etc., 8 Wel- est, Toronto, Ont

Thos. Haworth & Co.
3 and dealers in Iron, Cutlery and general , King St., Toronto, Ont.

D. Crawford & Co.,
JFACTURERS of Soaps, Candles, etc., and dealers Petroleum, Lard and Lubricating Oils, Palace St., , Ont.

Meetings.

PROVINCIAL INSURANCE COMPANY.

The nineteenth annual general meeting of the shareholders of the Provincial Insurance Company, was held at their offices in this city, on the 11th August.

The following gentlemen were present: Hon. Malcolm Cameron, Hon. J. H. Cameron, W. J. MacDonnell, C. J. Campbell, A. M. Smith, H. S. Howland. John Duggan, T. C. Stephens, G. Barrett, G. Duggan, F. Paterson, James K. Ellis, A. Morrison, L. Moffatt. E. Goldsmith, H. Hartney, and J. McMurrich (representing the estate of John Reid).

The Hon. J. Hillyard Cameron, president, having taken the chair, the report of the Directors, as follows, was read :—

REPORT.

The statement of the affairs of the Company, in accordance with the Act of Incorporation, for the year ending June 30, 1868, is herewith submitted.

Statement of affairs for the year ending 30th June, 1868.

Capital subscribed	$470,760	00
" called in	89,738	00
Amount insured during the year ending 30th June, 1868 :		
Fire	5,806,583	00
Marine	3,023,953	00
Premiums received during the year ending 30th June, 1866 :		
Fire	98,966	66
Marine	100,366	16
Amount paid for losses on risks of the year :		
Fire	40,201	35
Marine	59,543	13
Amount liable to be paid for losses on risks of the year :		
Fire	12,299	41
Marine	7,605	11
Amount paid for losses of previous years :		
Fire	6,691	59
Marine	13,439	83
Funds and property.		
Balance at agencies	$35,065	01
Cash in Bank and Treasurer's hands	11,878	30
Debentures and Stock	5,250	00
Real estate	21,448	01
Personal property	860	07
Sundry debtors	40,013	24
Salvage claims and unpaid stock	19,425	75
Bills receivable	47,499	28
	$182,039	66
Less all unpaid liabilities	51,251	12
Balance in favor of the company	$130 788	54

The annual balance sheet and the account of income and expenditure, with explanatory schedules, together with the auditors' report thereon, are also submitted.

The income from premiums (less re-insurances), and from other sources, amounting during the year to	$197,329	12
The total losses in Marine and Fire Insurance	$119,579	05
The ordinary expenses for the year	24,553	36
The commission to agents	17,646	86
Together	161,779	27
Deduct from the above receipts show a net profit of	$35,549	85

Your Directors have again the pleasure of congratulating you on the result of the year's transactions. The business of the company has greatly increased, and shows the receipt of $44,735.98 in excess of the premiums obtained last year. A further reduction of capital has been made by the cancelling of three hundred and seventy-one shares. Your Directors beg to report the very satisfactory position of the agencies at Halifax and St. John, New Brunswick, both of which have lately been visited and inspected by the president of the Company. By the provisions of the Act of the last session of Parliament, Canadian proprietary insurance companies are requested to invest the sum of $50,000 in Dominion stock in three annual instalments. Although, according to the Statute, no instalment could be demanded by the Government until the 1st August 1869, the company, in common with the other Canadian companies, made the deposit of the first instalment of $16,666.67 on the 1st inst. Your Directors congratulate the shareholders on the satisfactory financial condition of the company, and the continued steady and successful progress of its business; and they have much pleasure in declaring a dividend of three per cent. for the past twelve months, out of the very handsome profit realized on the year's transactions. This dividend will be payable on the 20th inst., to which period the stock books of the Company will be closed.

The report was adopted. The thanks of the shareholders were then voted to the manager, officers, and agents of the company, for their exertions during the past year.

Messrs. J: Duggan and R. G. Barrett were appointed scrutineers and were voted $5 each for their services. The sum of $1,000 was also voted to the president for his services for the year. The meeting then adjourned.

The following gentlemen were elected Directors for the current year, viz :—Hon. J. Hillyard Cameron, C. J. Campbell, Esq., Angus Morrison, Esq., Hon. Malcolm Cameron, A. T. Fulton, Esq., A. R. McMaster, Esq., H. S. Howland, Esq., George Duggan, Esq., Lewis Moffatt, Esq., W. J. MacDonnell, Esq., and John Worthington, Esq.

The board of Directors, on the following day, elected the Hon. J. Hillyard Cameron president, and Lewis Moffatt, Esq., vice-president of the company.

BROCKVILLE AND OTTAWA RAILWAY COMPANY.

The general meeting of the stockholders and bondholders of the Brockville and Ottawa Railway took place on August 12th, at 12 noon, at the company's office. We are sorry more were not present at the meeting, and particularly sorry to notice the absence of Mr. R. F. Steele, who worked so hard for the organization and completion of the road. Those who were present, however, seem to have undoubted confidence in the management, and probably this confidence may be the reason why so few took the trouble of coming.

The report of the manager, Mr. Henry Abbott, was submitted to the meeting, and from it we gather the details following:—
The receipts from the 1st January, 1868, to the 1st July, 1868, inclusive, amounted to $73,348 71
Same period last year 52,598 63

Increase in six months $20,750 08
The working expenses proper amount to 98,950 05
(Or 51 1-10 per cent. of the income)
The whole expenses of operating the road, including all actual renewals, amount to $46,087 55
(Or 62 8-10 per cent of receipts.)
A result which has not been previously accomplished on this road, and which compares favorably with operations on any other railway in the Dominion.

This portion of the report is very satisfactory it shows a development in the country which few parts of Canada can boast, for those lines of railway are very few in this country whose "*traffic receipts*" increases in six months $20,000 or at the rate of 40,000 per year. Of course, this statement has reference to railways of the same length. While, therefore, we congratulate the company on the increased traffic, we propose now to look into the sources of Revenue.

The transportation of lumber is one of the chief sources, while the cattle, butter and pork, and the passengers formally make up the rest. Now, however, we have to notice a new source of income as mentioned in the report as follows:— "Iron ore which appears for the first time in the report is destined to form one of the chief sources of revenue." This iron ore is brought from the neighborhood of Perth and from Arnprior, the largest quantity coming from Arnprior. It consists of Red Hematite of good quality and will doubtless be a source of wealth to the present proprietors.

We wish now to notice the operating expenses. Last year the operating expenses were $28,974 63 For the first six months this year, they are.. 38 950 05
This increase in the operating expenses is chiefly due to the fact of a purchase of large quantities of fuel—there remaining at present on hand, 5,299½ —$8,392 23, and to some other small amounts, which by reference to the report will more fully appear.
We also wish to call the attention of those interested to the small amounts of renewals.
Bridge at Smith's Falls........$1,768 57
Bridge covering at Arprior..... 198 92
Ties 5,170 01
Re-organization 3,610 83
                 $10,748 33
Renewals last year.............. 38,375 28
If for the balance of the year only, as much more for renewals is calculated, the whole expenses this year would amount to nearly $18,000 less than last year.

It is proposed by the manager to build a new iron girder bridge at Carlton Place, as one of this year's renewals, and a turntable at Perth, which, it is expected, will be all the renewals necessary. Why these "repairs" should be called "renewals" and charged in a separate account we are not aware, unless it be to make the "operating expenses" smaller.

We also notice this statement : " Operating expenses 53 1-10 per cent for this half year, against 54 7-10 last year the difference being 1 6-10 in favor of this year's operations." We do not understand this statement, or rather, we think there may be a little inconsistency, inasmuch as Mr. C. F. Fraser, who acted as Secretary-Treasurer to the Company last year, stated in a letter to the Board of Directors as follows : "The gross receipts in cash for the year 1867 were $146,209.39. The per centage for operating expenses has been in the proportion of 48.11 per cent of such gross receipts."

Mr. Abbott in his reports says there were in proportion of 54 7-10. We think this arises from the renewals not being taken into consideration last year.
Cash on hand 1st of July is $24,479.02. Number of miles run to one cord of wood in 1867, 44.49; 1868, 45.45.
Speaking of " renewals" and operating expenses the report says :—
" It will be borne in mind also that the cost of all renewals of wheels, &c., to cars or engines were last year charged as " renewals," while this year they are included in operating expenses, thereby causing the article "wages" and "materials" to cars and engines to appear larger in this than in last year's statement. This also accounts for the increase in the cost of locomotive power per mile run."
It is with much satisfaction that we lay down this report of the Brockville and Ottawa Railway. We think so far as we could gather, that the Company has been well managed for the last half year, and that the road has been properly conducted in every department, and we congratulate Mr. Abcott and the public, the former for having been so efficient, and the latter for having such a courteous gentlemen to deal with.

We have heard of no complaints except, perhaps, the rate of freights for iron ore, and so far as the employees are concerned all are highly pleased.
We close with the hope that the road will always be conducted as well, with the wish that more would attend the meetings and hear the report read, and with the desire that some person well qualified would write a book called " The Art of reading and understanding Railway Bank and other reports."

ROYAL INSURANCE COMPANY.—The annual meeting of the Royal Insurance Company was held yesterday, the results disclosed being very satisfactory. The fire premiums received in 1867 were £460,553, against £447,271 in 1866. The fire claims incurred in 1867 were £292,125, or about 68 per cent. The result is a profit on the year of £56,373, after paying all losses and expenses; and it is announced that the lapsed months of the current year permit still more favorable results. In the life branch it appears that the recent decision of the company to increase the members' share of profits has produced a considerable effect on the business. The average annual amount of new life business for the last three years has been £801,000, against £688,000 in the preceding quinquennium, and in addition to this, the annual average amount declined on lives considered to be ineligible was £213,000. The company declared its usual dividend of 7s. per share, carrying forward a considerable addition to the reserve fund.

CANADA CENTRAL RAILWAY.—At a late meeting of the Shareholders of this company the following officers were elected:—John G. Richardson, President ; H. Habbott, Vice-President ; and Messrs. Scott, Powell, Ashworth, Lowe and Rivers, Directors. It is intended by means of this road to greatly facilitate communication between the west and Ottawa. At present the road will be built from Oitawa to Carleton Place, and ultimately to make it connect Montreal with the Georgian Bay. The first sod has been turned, and a good sum paid on a station in the city of Ottawa.

Insurance.

MONTREAL.

(From our own Correspondent.)

Montreal, August 18, 1868.
There has been a lull in fires this week, and our fire marshals have a respite in their arduous duties ; you will see by the papers that Messrs. A. Savage & Son have again been unfortunate.

This is their third fire in twelve months. The report of the oil works being burnt down is incorrect. The fire was in an old wooden building near Point St. Charles, used for making fuller soap out of refuse from the large works in St. Maurice Street. The whole plant, stock and all was not worth over $2,400 and they are insured in the Royal for $1,200, the total loss will not be over $1,000, and in no way interferes with the business. In Life Insurance, you will doubtle have seen the strong articles recently in the Dai. News respecting the Ætna Life Insurance Company of Hartford. The company, through the age here, threatened an action of damages against the News, but so far has done nothing.

FIRE RECORD.

TORONTO, August 16.— A fire broke out on Adelaide Street a little west of York, consuming the upper part of the house of JohnBell and number of houses belonging to Mr. Bowman. Mr. Bell was insured in the British American for $, the other property was insured in the Western ; the Company will have to pay about $1,750.

AUG. 19.—Residence of Mr. Hicks ; insured contents for $600 in the North British and Mercantile ; the building was owned by Mr. Mitchell, who resides in Quebec, insured for $8 in the Provincial.

QUEBEC, August 13.—Two houses fronting Augustin and Cross Streets were totally consumed including the rear buildings ; total loss, including contents, $10,000. The buildings destroyed were Powell's store, O'Connell's frame faced with brick Allen's, stone ; Allen's, frame ; Mrs. Fahey frame ; Ryan's, frame ; Campbell's, frame ; Cullin's, frame ; Grannery's, frame ; Bulger's a A. H. Murphy's slightly damaged. The co panies named lose as follows :—British American $2,800 ; Western of England, $2,000 ; Quebec Fire, $1,500 ; Provincial $415 ; total insuran $6,715. The fire broke out in McCullin's sta and burnt twenty minutes before it was discover by any one but the owner. He, instead of giv alarm, endeavored to save his property, so t the fire brigade were not notified for twenty-to thirty minutes after the fire commenced.

WHITBY, August 6.—Brown & Patterso Foundry ; loss $25,000 to $30,000 ; insurance ab $11,000 ; cause unknown.

GEORGETOWN, August 15.—This place had narrow escape from a sweeping conflagration fr extensive fires in the adjoining woods.

MATILDA, August 13.—Geo. Robinson's dw ing-house and outbuildings ; loss $2,000 ; no surance.

SENECA, August 8.—G. Powell and J Dalt houses and some other property ; Dalton was sured for $800 in the Victoria Mutual.

NASSAGEWAYA, August 15.—A fire wh ooiginated in the woods and did extensive dam in various places, reached the steam saw mill dwelling houses of Mr. Cargill and consumed th Messrs. Guffin & Hatton had 600,000 feet of lumber on the premises ; their loss will be $5,000 ; Cargill's loss not stated. A Mr. Mo lost a barn with 16 tons of hay by the same no particulars as to insurance.

HARRINGTON, Ont., Aug. 12.—Barn of J Ivenson totally destroyed, loss $800, no insura It is thought that the fire originated from smoking of a pipe.

MONO MILLS, Aug. 15.—Tannery of Camph Sons; loss $15,000 ; about one half the furni and a small quantity of leather were saved. insurance.

ST. CATHARINES, August 11.—Brick cottage of ames Heap; loss $150, covered by insurance in ie Liverpool and London, and Globe.

THE LATE FIRE AT STAYNER.—The insurances a the Northern Railway Station and the buildings :tached amounted to $4,650, which amount was ivided equally between the British America, the rovincial, the Imperial, the Phœnix of London id the Western of Canada. The loss to each will ? from $700 to $800, according to the result of ie adjustment now pending.

THE LATE FIRE ON VICTORIA STREET, To-ONTO.—Suspicion is pretty strongly fixed on a cer-.in party in connection with this fire; there is .lk of a fire inquest.

STRATFORD.—The Town Council of Stratford ave agreed to submit to the decision of the rate-ayers of the town the question, whether they will irchase a steam fire engine.

DANGEROUS.—Information has reached us that me of the Insurance Companies who have not mplied with the law, in respect to deposit, con-nue to take risks in a quiet way. This is a risky usiness—much more risky than fire insurance is dinarily supposed to be. It is also rumoured iat detectives are watching some of the repre-ntatives of these unlicensed Companies.

LOST.—On the 13th instant the schooner 'Notre ame de St. Louis, of Quebec, from Montreal to harlotte Town, P. E. I., with flour, ran ashore at ierce when attempting to get under weigh. A :id lamp in the cabin was overturned by the jock, and in a few minutes the cabin was in umes. The high wind rendered it impossible to :tinguish the fire, but a small part of the rigging id about 200 brls of flour were saved; the rest ' the cargo and the vessel were entirely destroyed. he schooner belonged to Mr. Miller of Kamour-ka.

CONDUCT AT FIRES.—The New York Insurance urnal referring to our remarks a few weeks nce upon the reckless conduct witnessed at the te ' fires in this city, says :—The Canadian In-rance Chronicle complains of a state of things in >ronto in reference to the conduct at fires similar that which existed in our city prior to the in-oduction of the paid fire department, when the ze companies were directed by officers who were iheeded and even defied in the reign of the volunteers." A destructive enthusiasm, more tal than the flames, seems to guide the action of iose who rush to the scene of disaster at the cry danger : and perhaps without any other design an that of being useful, these ardent men occa-on more mischief than the fire itself. In New ork, upon the discovery of a building on fire, a rdon is immediately formed in front of the house ' the police, inte which no one is admitted ex-pt those who have been previously privileged by badge worn upon the coat. Then the fire patrol nerally attend to the preservation of those arti-es that are in jeopardy, and everything thus pro-eds with as much order and as little violence as rcumstances will permit. The city of Toronto ight to be armed with similar resources, and the sees at their various conflagrations would be uch reduced.

INSURANCE IMPOSTS.—The insurance com-inies transacting business in the State of Ken-cky, who are taxed at the rate of five per cent. , their premium receipts, have united together r resistance. The companies are about forty in imber, and they propose submitting the ques-m to the Supreme Court, whether the citizens of ie State are entitled or not to the privileges of xe several States. It is torture enough to respond the current taxes of a State ; but that one ould be invented for the special punishment of ipanies that ought to be cherished for their use-lness, is an absolute outrage upon ordinary jus-e.—Insurance Journal.

AGRICULTURAL MUTUAL INS. CO.—The Secre-ry of this Company informs us that during the

month of July 7,632 policies were issued, and the number for June was 1,621, making a total of 3,253, against 2,665 last year—a number then considered an extraordinary large issue.

Railway News.

NOVA SCOTIA RAILWAYS.—The visit of the Minister of Public Works to Nova Scotia has already borne fruit. Tenders are asked for cer-tain works on the line between Halifax, Windsor and Truro. These works comprise the repair of several bridges, improvements in masonry, the substitution of solid earth embankments for exist-ing wooden structure, together with station accommodation at Richmond. Expenses are to be reduced by the dismissal of unnecessary em-ployees.

GREAT WESTERN RAILWAY.—Traffic for week ending 31st July, 1868.

Passengers	$28,183 30
Freight and live stock.....	33,054 16
Mails and sundries.........	2,187 75
	$63,425 21
Corresponding Week of '67·	66,419 61
Decrease.........	$2,994 40

NORTHERN RAILWAY.—Traffic Receipts for week ending 8th August, 1868.

Passengers......................	$2,549 68
Freight........................	5,343 08
Mails and sundries.........	233 86
Total receipts for week......	$8,126 62
Corresponding week 1867...	11,544 13
Decrease.........	$3,417 51

GRAND TRUNK.—Mr. Peter Clarke of Montreal writes to the Investors' Guardian, London, Eng-land, respecting the management of the Grand Trunk as follows :—

SIR,—One great source by which the income of this company may be improved is by an efficient control over the passenger fares. At present some of the passengers pay their fares to the clerk at the booking-office, while others pay them to the conductor (guard) when the train has started, and not a small number never pay their fares—they give a present (much less than their fare) to the conductor and then travel free. Between this city and Toronto there are six or eight of those con-ductors employed: all those, with the exception of one, follow the plan I have stated. I cannot speak with certainty about the conductors on the other parts of the railway. I have enquired of two parties who travel a good deal on the line between here and Toronto, and asked their opinion as to the extent to which this dead-head system is carried ; they estimate it at one-fifth of the entire number of passengers, say 20 per cent. Take it at one-half, or 10 per cent over the whole line. it would amount to £700 to £800 sterling per week, or £35,-000 to £40,000 per annum.

Mining.

MOISIC RIVER MINES.—A correspondent of the Hamilton Spectator visited these mines. He says that the ore is found at the very works in the form of a magnetic iron sand, and almost of pure metal. This is thrown into the first and brought out a mass of metal, ready for the hammers. For a distance of three miles down the coast this rich metal extends, and in some cases is six feet in depth. The Company has secured 12 miles of

wood land on each side of the Moisic River, by which they will have a supply of charcoal for many years. Mr. W. M. Molson of Montreal, is the President of the Company. It is intended to ship the iron sand to Cleveland, Chicago, New York and Philidelphia in its crude state in addition to the manufacture of iron on the Company's property.

PAID UP SHARES.—The case of the Imperial Silver Quarries Company has raised an important question about fully paid-up shares. Shares given to directors to qualify them for a seat at the board must now, according to Vice-Chancellor Malins, be considered as carrying a liability equal to the nominal value of the shares ; and shares allotted fully paid up, unless to a bona fide holder or for purchase-money, must, we presume, be regarded as still carrying the original liability. This doc-trine is somewhat startling at first, but when it is examined in the light of reason and common sense, it is seen to be conformable to both. For my own part, I hail it with considerable satisfac-tion. I could name more than one company in which people were induced to become shareholders on account of each of the directors having a stake of £1,000, when in reality they had not the value of the pen this is written with. Once let it be an understood thing that directors' and promoters' fully paid-up shares will in case of suspension or winding up be liable for the whole amount, and directors will not be as plenty as blackberries, as they have been for sometime past. Shareholders' eyes are being gradually opened, and they will perhaps not make such mistakes in the future as they have in the past.—Investors' Guardian.

PRODUCE OF COAL.

According to the latest returns which are at hand, it would seem that the total known produce of coal in the world is thus distributed over the chief nations:—

	Tons.
Great Britain..........................	101,630,000
United States..........................	25,800,000
Prussia and the Zollverein..........	20.610,000
France..................................	10,710,000
Belgium.................................	9,935,000
Austria.................................	4,500,000
British North America.................	1,500,000
Russia	1,500,000
Spain	300,000
New South Wales......................	250,000
Ireland.................................	123,500
Total	176,858,500

It would appear, then that of the total known produce of coal in the world, Great Britain raises more than half (57 per cent.), although it forms probably not more than one in forty of the popu-lation of the world. If to this coal produce we add that of the United States and the Colonies, we may conclude that the Teutonic race enjoys 73 per cent. or almost three parts out of four of the coal raised. It is hardly possible to over estimate the forces acting in our favor which are represented by this partial monopoly of the most powerful material agent of civilization.

TRADE OF THE UPPER LAKES.—The report of the American Bureau of Statistics for 1867 shows that the number of Western steamers has been nearly doubled, and that the tonage has more than trebled in fifteen years. In 1852 the total tonage of the Western lakes' and rivers was 432,021, against 902,500 in 1866. The sail navigation of the upper lakes alone increased 900 per cent. in fifteen years ending with 1866, when it was 305,-000 tons. In 1830 the whole tonage of the country was but 1,200,000 tons; in 1840 it was 2,200,000, and in 1866 4,340,000. That is, the inland navi-gation began only in 1830, when it amounted to no it is 22 per cent. In 1852 there were 687 steamers plying on the Western waters, of 171,153 tonnage, and in 1866 there were 1,312, with 364,964 tons.

☞ THE CANADIAN MONETARY TIMES AND
INSURANCE CHRONICLE is printed every Thursday
Evening, in time for the English Mail.

Subscription Price, one year, $2, or $3 in
American currency ; Single copies, five cents each.
Casual advertisements will be charged ten cents
per line of solid nonpareil each insertion. All
letters to be addressed, "THE CANADIAN MONE-
TARY TIMES, TORONTO, ONT." Registered letters
so addressed are at the risk of the Publishers.
Cheques should be made payable to J. M. TROUT,
Business Manager, who will, in future, issue all
receipts for money.

The Canadian Monetary Times.

THURSDAY, AUGUST 20, 1868.

VOLUME II.

The first year of the existence of this journal has closed and, as evidence of the success
that has attended our efforts to supply an
admitted want, we lay before our readers, at
the advent of a new volume, a paper of sixteen pages instead of the modest eight page
sheet that sufficed at the outset. The variety
of subjects with which we have been called
upon to deal, and the many important matters affecting joint stock enterprise that
engrossed public attention, have pressed
sorely on our limited space. Though disposed
to deal fairly by each interest we have been
compelled to administer what might be
termed scant justice. The result is that
necessity has forced an enlargement of our
borders. The support accorded to our undertaking has been generous and the sympathy
of those whose approval is worth the endeavor
to gain has not been with-held. We do not
pretend to furnish light reading ; our aim is
rather to collect and diffuse such statistics
and other information as will prove not only
of immediate service, but also of permanent
value to those interested in the subjects that
come within our scope. The class to which
we look for support is made up of those who
desire to keep themselves informed, at the
least in a general way, of the progress and
state of the material interests of Canada, of
the movements of capital, of the success or
failure of the many combinations whereby
enterprise seeks to accomplish its ends. The
theories of the speculative are hereto be found
along side the results achieved by the practical
man. Manager and agent are here brought
face to face, and he who supplies the moving
principle has a plat form which enables him to
see the whole machinery at work and compare
his own success or failure with that of his
neighbors. The Reports of public companies
which some may, and doubtless do, consider
dry reading are now found to be not only of

practical service to those immediately co
cerned in their statements, but also,
interest to a much wider circle. For instanc
the Report of an Insurance Company intere
agents and stockholders, but it also comman
the attention of those individuals whose p
perty is covered by its policies, of the bank
whose funds are occasionally sought to
used and the broker who traffics in its shar
'or advises this sale and that purchase.
Joint Stock Company whose stock pas
through many hands must, if it would gi
such stock a real ascertainable value, let t
public know what its position is. We ha
among us few men with large balances lyi
idle so that an enterprise of any magnitud
or even of ordinary dimensions, must nee
appeal at the set-out to the lawyer, the me
chant, the farmer and the mechanic, as well
to those who deal more directly in money
those technically called investors, for t
means of attaining its ends. Take the c
of our banks. They are not the private p
perty of a few individuals, such as the Rot
childs or the Glyns, but the result of unit
effort on the part of innumerable Brow
Jones' and Robinsons. Our banks and m
of our public companies are built on the ea
ings of the many not on the accumulatic
of the few. We have to stand by each oth
through lack of capital, and make t
pennies of the industrious and well-to
discharge that duty which the pounds of
rich perform elsewhere. When the prot
from our Board rooms are sneered at as
offspring of selfishness, and the opinions
bank managers show a particular schem
legislation to be mischievous, if not ruin
in its tendencies, some affect to reg
such as the utterances of "blood-suc
money lenders," forgetting that our ba
are not corporations sole, but institution
which are invested the surplus means
thousands of our fellow citizens of every cl
Injury to them implies injury wide-spr
and disastrous. Hence it is, not to div
too far from the subject in hand, that in
country especially, interests are so interl
as to act and react upon each other and h
the value of such a journal as this, to wi
scattered and seemingly unconnected cla

While, therefore, it is our duty as we
the best policy, to assist prospects of a pr
worthy character we, at the same time, c
the privilege of journalists in distingui
between the hollow, the pretentious and
misconducted, and such enterprises as
bine the opposites. Without malice or
tiality we have ventured to criticise f
that which provoked censure or desc
praise. Corporations are said to hav
souls ; in some cases there is noticeable

of body also. It shall be our object, as it has heretofore been, to endeavor to do justice and in exercising the prerogative of criticism we deprecate the imputation for improper motives until we have shewn ourselves recreant.

It is needless to say that our ideal of what a journal such as ours should be, has not yet been reached ; but while we fully appreciate our distance from the proper standard, we are certain that every effort will be made to increase the usefulness of the MONETARY TIMES, to surround ourselves with a staff of writers whose contributions will reflect credit on the journal and on the country, and to furnish such information as will be of service to the various interests we represent.

THE GORE BANK.

As was stated by Mr. Street at the late meeting of the shareholders of the Gore Bank, the practical question is, what is to be done with the institution. It is claimed that seventy-two and a half per cent. of the capital is intact. This estimate leaves $586,-710 available for future use. The liability to the public is :

Circulation	$201,512
Due to Banks	26,295
Deposits	268,666
	$496,473

To meet this the bank has

Coin and Prov. Notes	$192,350
Real Estate	82,007
Goverment Securities	82,733
Notes of other banks	17,608
Due from other banks	80,959
Notes and Bills Discounted	730,013
Other Debts	195,509
	$1,381,179

Of the value of this the following approximate estimate may be made, making allowances for contingencies :

Coin, &c.	$192,350
Real Estate	52,000
Government Securities	82,733
Other Banks	17,608
Due from Banks	60,959
	$405,650

We presume that the balances due from banks include the Bank of Upper Canada debt, and if such is the case the estimate we have given is near the truth. Of the $192,350 of coin and Provincial notes, we imagine that the largest part is Provincial notes which Mr. King doubtless insisted upon being held by the bank. However, after making every allowance and taking things at their worst, the bank has enough to pay all sums due to the public less $100,000, and still have $730,013 of notes and bills to the good.

Such being the state of the bank's affairs, it is natural to enquire what course should be pursued. It is proposed that the shareholders shall wait without dividends until sufficient is earned to replace the capital that has been lost. Another suggestion is that permission should be obtained from the Legislature to reduce the capital. The other alternatives are amalgamation or liquidation. But as amalgamation seems to have met with no advocates, it may be taken for granted that it is out of the question.

The bank has undoubtedly suffered by the withdrawal of public confidence. A comparative statement of deposits and circulation of 30th June, 1867, and of the same date in 1868, shows a decrease in deposits of $761,000 and in circulation of $335,000—total $1,096,-000. On that confidence rested the deposit account and the circulation. Any calculation of future profits must be toned by the knowledge that two important sources of profit are well nigh closed, and competition has to be expected with institutions in the full enjoyment of both. Small means imply small accounts and small profits. But the shareholders are for the most part individuals whose influence and wealth would tell greatly in favour of any institution which they chose to do business with. If they all determine to stand by the bank, and a thorough investigation, such as is now contemplated, reveals nothing worse than what is known, public confidence might be again commanded. The Bank of Montreal at one time was in as bad a position as that which the Gore Bank now occupies, yet it has become the largest and wealthiest bank in the country. The gross profit for the year ended June 30, 1868, is placed at $71,265. If such a profit was realized during a time of more than ordinary anxiety and trouble, when confidence in the bank was well nigh carried away in a panic, when every bank suffered to a greater or less extent from "runs," when bill holders were frightened and shareholders themselves grew timid, when ignorance prevailed regarding the bank's true position and the worst, of course, was imagined, it is not unreasonable to expect a greater degree of success in a state of circumstances infinitely more satisfactory. There is about $600,000 to work with, and the double liability of shareholders to fall back upon.

The fall in the market price of the stock can be easily understood. A local bank in a small city will always have trouble with its stock. A few thousand dollars worth of shares put on the market is not readily absorbed. It may not be sold from any desire to get rid of the stock, but rather on account of a necessity to use the proceeds. It will be found, we think, that the first noticeable decline in stock was occasioned by a few shareholders selling out, not through fear, but to procure funds for use elsewhere. When shares do not float lightly in Hamilton it cannot be expected that they will do so elsewhere and a fall is the consequence. We are inclined to think therefore, that if continuance in business be determined on, it would be well to bring the head office to Toronto—a central locality—establish a branch in Montreal and keep an agency in Hamilton. A reduction in capital would then be advisable, as it is a poor business keeping afloat an institution without dividends. There are two great centres of business in the provinces, Toronto and Montreal, and the best prospect is afforded to the Gore bank by migrating to Toronto.

There is no necessity for going into liquidation. The rejection of Mr. Street and others who are largely interested in the bank and whose assistance is invaluable, we conceive was unwise. It is said that the present Board advocate a winding up. Were the bank's doors closed to-morrow and the process of realization commenced it would take a length of time to complete the work and the expense incurred would necessarily be heavy, but not more so than it is at present to keep the institution open.

The circulation and deposits would at once commence to carry six per cent interest, and this, under present circumstances, would perhaps involve an expenditure of, say $10,-000 for the first year. Then a forced realization of the notes and bills would certainly cause a heavy loss, say from ten to twenty per cent. If liquidation be determined on it might be just as well to let the business go on, due caution being exercised and at the same time realization might continue in progress. If, at the end of a certain time, public confidence were not restored and success seemed distant, the whole business could be closed up at once. For these reasons we are inclined to agree with the late President, that business should be continued and a bold effort made to regain public favor. It is a pity to throw away a business, be it small or great, which it has taken long years to secure, to lose the money paid away to obtain a charter and to sacrifice an investment when the chances are rather in favor of than against improvement and the institution is perfectly solvent. As we take it, Hamilton is deeply interested in the existence of its only local bank ; its fall will be a loss of prestige which an ambitious city cannot safely stand. Much depends however, on the report of the Committee of investigation. Unless a full enquiry be made and a trustworthy report laid before the public, it will be better to realize the assets than to peril what is now on hand in a new career based on deception. We believe that the shareholders are bent on knowing their real position and when that knowledge is obtained it will be for them to take such measures as will be deemed most expedient.

PROVINCIAL INSURANCE COMPANY.

The report read to the shareholders at the last annual meeting of this Company, shows that a large increase has taken place in the business—the premiums for the year having exceeded those of the year previous by $44,735.98. The net profit realized is placed at $35,549, and a dividend of three per cent. was declared. In analysing the figures given in the report, we find that the per centage of loss to premiums (less re-insurance) is over 60 ; on the Fire business, nearly 53 ; and on the Marine, over 67. The average rate of premium on Fire risks is probably 1¼, and on Marine, 6 per cent.

In making the calculations we have taken the figures as they stand in the report, but, on reflection, we feel scarcely justified in allowing ourselves to be carried away by their specious appearance. Balance at agencies $36,655- On referring to the report of the British America, whose paid up capital is $200,000, we find they have out in agent's hands only about $19,000. We suppose that the $35,665 represents, for the most part, premium notes on the marine business. However the amount out in this way does seem large considering that the profits of the year are $35,549. The next item is Sundry Debtors $40,013. This mysterious generalization would be more intelligible if it were replaced by the designation "Bad and Doubtful debts." It looks so suspicious that we take the risk of advising the company not to rely upon it as an asset. On the heels of "Sundry Debtors," we see "Salvage claim and unpaid stock $19,425." Salvage claim and unpaid stock ! The in harmonious blending of the two reflects little credit on the analytical powers of the author of the report. Surely it would have been an easy thing to say Salvage so much, and Unpaid Stock so much. If the combination was intentional, then we beg to assure the Directors that transparent tricks of the kind are not harmless, but well calculated to beget suspicions in the minds of stockholders, and to stamp the report as unreliable. The books of the company are not open to the public, and seeming trifles are apt to do a great deal of harm. When a company with a paid up capital of only $89,-738, and no reserve carries risks to the amount of $8,000,000, a little trick may prove dangerous.

We do not think the Director's report is fair. It most certainly does not "exhibit a full and unreserved statement of the affairs" as the Act of Incorporation requires. We can easily understand why the annual meeting was harmonious, as it undoubtedly was, seeing that the report was merely read by the President instead of printed copies being in the hands of every one present. Its round numbers were pleasant to hear, and its announcement of a three per cent. dividend was not unwelcome. Dissatisfaction, if there were any, had no material. Somebody did ask if the $11,878 were actually in the bank, and the President assured the inquirer that such was actually the case. But no one asked, for we suppose that few knew, why the company's premises were lately mortgaged to a Building Society for $6000. Nobody asked why such a proceeding was necessary in the face of a net profit of $35,549. True, the deposit of $10,666 had to be made with the government, but the "net profit" exceeded by far the required amount.

However, a three per cent. dividend was declared. We hope that the clause in the Act of Incorporation which states "that no dividend or bonus shall be declared or paid out of the capital stock of the Company was kept in mind by the Directors. At all events, this declaration of a dividend has not brought Provincial Insurance Company stock up even to a quotation mark. Its increased business has not brought forward purchasers. Why? Its shareholders are for the most part substantial persons; its directors are men of worth, respectability and means; its prospects are seemingly good; it has realized $35,549 profits from one year's business ; and a dividend of three per cent. has been declared. Why then is its stock valueless. It is not for us to answer this question, we simply state the fact. What has become of the capital? Where is the reserve? Where is the reinsurance fund ? An Insurance Company is not an institution chartered to gamble. There are certain well understood principles which Insurance Companies find it necessary and expedient to apply, and certain fixed rules, the essence of experience, which they should not, if they value their existence, ignore. If such be disregarded, the shareholders feel the consequences in the loss of their investment.

But we are not without hope that the Directors of this Company will see how dangerous this hand-to-mouth, trust-to-luck system of doing business is, and make some effort to improve a state of affairs which they must know is unsatisfactory. We are aware that the present is an improvement on the past, but that is the strongest reason why an effort should now be made to understand how matters are with them. Let a President be got

who will give his attention to the affa the Company, and pay him well for doi for however able the present incumbent be, he certainly has not the requisite ti his disposal. Let this declaration of dends be put a stop to until the capi restored and a reserve formed. Let fu calls be made on the subscribed capita a fresh start had. A committee shou appointed to investigate the state of the pany and settle on some definite plan. things on a proper footing, the bu would increase ; a good profit be realized the stock would soon rise in the market. strongly advise the Directors to go office of the British America and h accept instructions in the art of revivi Insurance Company.

We use the word reviving advisedl we applied to the affairs of the Prov. the test to which the Insurance Commi ers of the State of New York subje Fire Insurance Companies of that Sta should find that the Provincial would pare far from favourably with similar rations. A reinsurance fund of fifty per of the premiums on unexpired fire risk one hundred on marine risks, is there i upon. The unpaid liabilities of the P cial are given at $51,251 ; a reinsuranc of (to place it at an absurdly low figur $110,000, should be available; the paid up is $89,738. The total liab would then be $250,989. Taking for g that the "Funds and property" rep cash assets of $181,039, there would be ciency of $68,950. But if we deduct fr sum total of "Funds and property" be doubtful debts the assets would be reduced, and the startling fact appea the paid up capital is lost. Howev submit these remarks to the Directors i faith, trusting some one will be found them with courage enough to insist on ing the truth.

NEW YORK LIFE.—An exchange says th Company has decided to deposit $100,000 Dominion, and otherwise to comply with Insurance Law. It is added that the dep be made without delay.

WITHDRAWALS.—The Secretary of the B Life Insurance Company of Massachusetts, us by a private letter of the fact that th pany has withdrawn from the Dominio reason assigned is that the Company under the State Laws of Massachusetts, with our law. The Western of Buffalo, Phoenix of B and Security of New York, all marine, ar the Companies that have withdrawn.

Mr. Young, of Georgetown, has been a the Stratford agent of the Royal Canada

W TO MAKE THE ST. LAWRENCE THE
MMERCIAL HIGHWAY OF THE WEST.

No. 3.

Halifax, N.S., Aug. 7, 1868.

efore dealing with the wider subject of our
ity to compete with the Erie Canal for the
e of the Western States, let us glance at a less
ortant point, but one that more immediately
:erns the present—the importance of the St.
'rence in developing our trade with the Mari-
e Provinces and with the West Indies. Our
orts to the latter are met by the products of
Western States, and of the western portions of
Dominion, of which New York becomes the
or. Our exports to the Maritime Provinces by
St. Lawrence have to contend with a formida-
competitor, the Grand Trunk Railway, to the
gy and enterprise of which we are under great
gations. It has now an advertisement in the
ifax newspapers, that it "will, at all times,
freight for Montreal or Toronto at the low-
ate for which any steamer then in the port of
ifax will sign bills of lading." This is an
naly that deserves enquiry. Either the
d Trunk must lose by such low rates of
ht, or the facilities for transport by the St.
rence must be very imperfect or greatly im-
d. It is manifest, at the outset, that a water
way which nature, without cost or charge,
ps in working order for seven months of the
, must, while navigation is open, be
sper than an iron road, built and maintained
heavy cost, which requires constant repairs,
should pay not only its working expenses, but
some return for the millions that were ex-
ied in its construction. *Every ton sent by
which could be conveniently forwarded by
r, represents a certain loss to the public—so
h deducted from the productive capital of a
try.* Somebody must pay for railways.
ebody must keep them in repair, and the ex-
e of railway traffic must fall ultimately on
body, the producer, the consumer, the mer-
t, or the railway company. But the results
e trade by the Grand Trunk are not as bene-
l as might be expected. The flour and other
ucts of Western Canada are forwarded by rail
Montreal to Portland, and thence to Halifax
steamer, which carries back but little in re-
. Hence the flour has to be paid for in cash,
he drain on the Lower Provinces is very heavy,
rade being altogether one-sided, and unsatis-
ry, in spite of the very low rates at which
is landed by the Grand Trunk at Halifax.
ould be slightly ungracious in any one except
ockholder in the Grand Trunk to enquire
her the public are not gaining more than the
any by this traffic. It is, however, perfectly
'that if facilities are afforded for transport by
propellers direct from Toronto to Picton, and
low down freights are lowered still more by
nerative return freights, the Grand Trunk,
ng the summer months at least, cannot pre-
to compete with our water highway ; and
an advertisement as that which I have
ed, would be simply an offer to do business on
proverbially unprofitable principle of "work-
or nothing and finding yourself." The pro-
to encourage return freights of fuel by tem-
rily giving a bounty on Nova Scotian coal,
taking off canal dues on provincial coal,

though at first sight it might appear to be simply
a boon to Nova Scotia, would have in the long
run proved of greater importance to the grain
grower and manufacturer of Canada West. Very
many public men in Ontario, Quebec and New
Brunswick, who opposed a duty most strenuously,
were favorable to the other proposition, holding,
not unreasonably, that any imposition for the general benefit should be equally borne by the Dominion at large. As the measure would have had
the support of Mr. Galt and other independent
members, it rested with the Government to say
whether it should be adopted or not. But there
were political considerations of the utmost urgency
that rendered the measure advisable, apart from
its commercial bearing. The Nova Scotians were
fretting under some real, and many imaginary
grievances, and were, with singular unanimity,
about to appeal to the Imperial Parliament to
dissolve the union. The adoption of the proposed
measure would have cut the ground from under
the feet of the Nova Scotian delegation, and
would have given the beleaguered friends of union
among us, a weapon by which they could have
defeated the opponents of confederation. On returning to Nova Scotia, after the public meeting
at Toronto, in April last, I urged most strongly
upon the Finance Minister my belief, that the
agitation in Nova Scotia was likely to increase in
intensity, and that the proposed concession, if
immediate, would shut the mouth of discontent,
but that it would come too late, if deferred until
another session. Time will show whether the
impression was erroneous or not. That the Nova
Scotian members did not urge a measure which
would have had the effect of stultifying themselves, was the strongest argument to spur the
Government on, and is certainly the last reason
which can be alleged for no action having been
been taken. Why nothing was done, is still a
mystery to us. The only parties who could, by any
possibility, be injuriously affected by it, were
Pennsylvanian coal owners, and the Grand Trunk
Railway. The former, though omnipotent in the
United States, are powerless here ; while even the
great ability and zeal of those who manage the
latter, can hardly have raised it to such a formidable position, as to render the peace and even the
permanence of the Dominion a matter of secondary consideration.

As we cannot find in either of these influential
interests a clue to the difficulty, we must assume
that it will be found in some urgent political
necessity not yet confided to the public.

Though there may appear to be a competition between the Grand Trunk and the St. Lawrence
route, it is only temporary, and arises from the
limited amount of business that is accommodated.
That the traffic has assumed even its present
dimensions, is due more to the energy and enterprise of the Grand Trunk, and to American legislation, than to our appreciation of the facilities
for trade which nature has bestowed upon us, in
our great water highway to the West. Were our
trade by the St. Lawrence developed, the Grand
Trunk would in time be equally the gainer. During seven months of the year it would secure most
of the passenger traffic, and even if the heavy freights
should be attracted by the St. Lawrence route,
the Grand Trunk would have a reversionary interest, which would for five months in the winter,
give it the monopoly of the trade, and enable it to
reap the benefit of any impulse which had during
the summer months been given to intercolonial
trade by way of the St. Lawrence. Whether the
Intercolonial Railway will prove not here a more troublesome competitor I need not here enquire. It is
difficult for the casual observer to see that the
Grand Trunk has anything to fear from it, and
even if it has, by the time that that formidable
undertaking is accomplished, the traffic to be
accommodated, if we put our shoulders to the
wheel, will tax the capabilities of all the outlets
for our trade.

There is, however, room enough for all, and
but little need for jealous rivalry, in that wider

field, the West Indian and South American trade.
Its capability for almost unlimited extension I
have imperfectly sketched in my pamphlet on
Intercolonial Trade. At present more than sixty
millions of dollars worth of products is exported
by the United States, most of which we could produce more cheaply than themselves. We have
been so long inured to being "hewers of wood
and drawers of water" to the Americans, that like
their bondsmen in the South, we prefer relying
upon our taskmasters for existence, and dread the
liberty of independence when it is bought at the
price of energy and self-reliance. We have
hitherto had but little ambition to rise to a more
lucrative and honorable position in the scale of
nations, and are now forced, by the repeal of the
Reciprocity Treaty, that commercial Emancipation
Act, to face the somewhat startling fact, that we
can compete on favorable terms with our overtaxed
neighbors. There are some markets in the West
Indies to which we export nothing, the Americans
enjoying a monopoly. How long they will be
able to remain our factors, purchasing our products in the face of a 20 per cent. duty, and
making a profit by exporting them to markets,
which are as open to us as to them must
depend upon time, or at least upon our capabilities for sedentary inaction. Our freedom from
taxation is a great advantage in our favour, and if
we supplement it by increasing our facilities for
moving our products cheaply to the seaboard, the
gains will be so plainly ours, as to preclude any
indifference on our part.

We have the necessary class of vessels, intelligent and reliable shipmasters, and merchants
familiar with the West Indian trade—all the
machinery that is required for developing this
field of enterprise, so soon as the manufactures
and producers of the West begin to covet the large
profits which reward the enterprise of our neighbors in the markets of the south.

The trade will be carried on by means of propellers running to Pictou. Mr. Patterson, the
Secretary of the Corn Exchange of Montreal, in
his very able and exhaustive report on the trade
of that city, suggests that the canals should be
deepened and improved, and that produce for
Europe should be transhipped at Montreal from
barges into sea-going vessels, while that intended
for the Maritime Provinces and the West Indies
should be carried direct to Pictou by propellers
from the lakes. This proposition, which is a very
sensible one, goes a good deal farther than he intended. If it is possible to send produce to Pictou
in lake propellers, it is equally practicable to send
the products intended for Europe to the same convenient point of transhipment. This proposal
opens up a more interesting and important field
than the West Indian and South American trade,
and that is the *possibility of making a port near
the eastern limits of the Dominion the point of
transhipment for the exports to Europe from the
Western States and from Western Canada,* a subject
which I will treat of in my next.

R. G. HALIBURTON.

WASTED INVESTMENTS.

Editor Canadian Monetary Times.

But two years ago Ontario had one of its remit-
tent speculative fevers. Oil had been discovered
in the township of Enniskillen a few years before;
prejudice had at last been overcome ; enthusiasts
proclaimed that a source of wealth had been
discovered which would enable this Province to
compete with any other country in the globe ;
money was being made, and everyone was determined to make it. The most stingy County
Councils voted bonuses to the companies that
would sink a deep shaft for oil. Many tried it,
and "rowed up Salt river." One or two, the
Goderich one for instance, were fortunate enough

to reach the salt. But in the counties of Kent and Lambton, what agreements were entered into, purchases made, and wells erected where the indications were promising. Unfortunately the fever and the price of oil reached their greatest height at one and the same time. The oil poured forth, the price went steadily down, and unwary speculators found themselves with unsaleable lands on their hands, investors with wells yielding rivers of oil, worth little more than the waters of the adjacent creek, hotel keepers had rats for boarders, and deserted villages to look upon from their front doors. Now the unhappy owners of real estate think of nothing but how to get rid of it, and so land in the western counties can be got at prices far below its actual worth as farming lands. So disgusted are they with their bargains that hardly any notice is taken of the announcement that Judge Higgins has been able to buy up all the oil in the market and what will be produced this fall, on such terms that by Christmas day the learned judge and his associates will probably be hundreds of thousands of dollars richer in consequence of this judicious investment.

In the oil regions of Pennsylvania, a similar revulsion took place. There, however, the people persevered until by this time a market has been found for the oil, and prosperity has rewarded the energy put forward. I have no statistics to show what the consumption of petroleum is in the United States, yet it must be an increasing one; but we have those published in the *New York Shipping and Commercial List*, and they show that this year, from the 1st of January up to the 8th of August, the petroleum exported was 53,280,000 gallons, against 36,139,000 during the corresponding period of last year. This increasing trade is not so much with England as the Continent; the exports up to the above date were respectively to the following ports: 1868, Bremen, 5,902,000 gals., 1867, 2,629,000 gals.; 1868, Antwerp, 3,850,000 gals., 1867, 827,000 gals. So that the United States, with an internal consumption at least as great as it ever was in the time of the wildest excitement, has developed an export trade which will reach, this year, probably 80,000,000 gals., and hardly existed three years ago.

The prices at which petroleum is quoted in New York are on the above date:

Crude oil in bulk 17½c. per gal., or $7 a barrel of 40 gallons; crude oil in shipping order 23¼c. per gal., or $9.30 a barrel; refined standard white 34½c, per gal. or $13.80 a barrel. In view of the comparisons I propose making, I may here mention that the difference of 5¾c., represented by the difference between the price of oil in "bulk" and shipping order," consists of the barrels and the cost of filling, &c. In quoting Canadian prices the barrels are always included unless specially excepted.

The effect this had upon the oil districts of Pennsylvania is thus given by a correspondent of the *N. Y. Tribune* writing from Oil City: "The "oil region has recuperated, and is now being "operated upon sound business principles. Lands "heretofore deemed worthless for oil boring pur"poses, are in good demand, and the extent of "territory now in course of development is fully "quadruple in extent of that of all previous "years. This development is being made by the "oil operators to a great extent, and in all "portions of the oil fields, oil is being obtained "in paying quantities from a larger per centage "of wells than many previous years. Lands that "were freely offered one year ago at prices ranging "from $10 to $100 per acre, are now held at $1000 "to $1,200, and $3000 per acre is being freely "paid at Pleasantville oil fields. The excitement "is intense, but has taken a decidedly practical "shape. Lands are bought for development not "for speculation. $5 per barrel for oil at the "wells pays the producer very handsomely for "producing and development. * * At present "the demand is fully equal to the supply, and "every effort is being made to keep up this "last to an average. Those versed in the statis"tical history of this business tell us that to keep "up the present daily production it is necessary "to have not less than 300 new wells going down, "or rather in process of drilling. * * Never, "to my recollection, has general business been in "a more prosperous state, or has the future of the "oil region looked so bright. * * Oil on the "creek and at the wells in different localities is "being sold at $4 to $6.75 per barrel, and com"mands at Oil city $6 per barrel. The demand "is good, and the tendency still upward."

How different have been the Canadian oil interests, they have been truly "killed off" by the supply exceeding the local demand. Several things have been against us, a strong prejudice in England, the difficulty of deodorizing our oil, and the fact that a great part of the capital invested came from the United States and the investors considering the first loss the best, have abandoned their money and the country together. It has been impossible to send oil to the States owing to the prohibitory duty; the only resource open was to export it to other countries, and this has not been done for the reasons I have just mentioned. Some time ago Mr. McCrae, a Liverpool oil broker, examined a sample of oil refined at London, Ont., and pronounced it equal to the best American standard white. Before Mr. Higgins' "corner" this oil was selling wholesale at 10 and 12c a gallon, including barrels and excluding the duty, which would not affect oil shipped for exportation. Crude oil was a complete drug and could be bought at from 25 to 35 cents a barrel at the wells—including the barrels. Surely there is a margin here for some one to take advantage of—an advantage which would be productive of the greatest benefit to the country generally. My only surprise has been that refiners have not attempted to create this trade themselves instead of joining, as they are said to have done, Judge Higgins in his operation which at best can only secure a temporary advantage to the parties to the transaction.

Yours, &c.,

OIL.

MONTREAL MONEY MARKET.

(From our own Correspondent.)

MONTREAL, Aug. 18, 1868.

The money market remains much the same as last week, if anything rather easier; loans of round sums, say $50,000 or over, could be obtained at six per cent. on undoubted security. The bank rates are from seven to eight per cent for good paper, very little is offering in the streets, and rates are uncertain; there are still more renewals on the market than usual, but when money begins to circulate freely, it is expected they will to a large extent disappear. For all building purposes, or for public improvements, there is abundance of capital at reasonable rates.

In the Auditor's statement of the condition of the banks in Quebec and Ontario on the 30th June last, the circulation is given at $7,286,588, against $8,404,377 same time last year, showing a decrease of $1,117,789, which is to be accounted for by the quantity of silver in use, not only in the country but also in the towns. I notice that the "silver nuisance" is attracting considerable attention in Western Canada, but I fear I shall prove a true prophet, and that the co nation will soon fall through. Here we have d nothing, putting up with the evil as incurable the Government takes same decided action in premises. The deposits in the banks 30th J 1868, are $30,167,534, against $28,704,326 year, an increase of $1,463,208; this shows steady increase in the material prosperity of country, which is further evidenced by the that the deposits are nearly $4,000,000 in ex of the paid up capital of the banks. Gold not fluctuated very materially this week, opinions here and in New York are very div as to the prospects of a rise or fall. For my I believe it will rise, especially if we look at fact that the imports into the States, 1st Jan to 1st Aug., are $145,173,534 specie, exclusiv freight and duty, and the exports for same pe $59,079,058 currency, the difference has to provided for either in *Gold* or by the sale of U Debentures, of which a large quantity, has l shipped to Europe, but it is believed on spec tion and not *bona fide* sales. There is at prese great amount of reckless gold speculation in York, chiefly short sales by weak parties, we l already seen one large failure, and need no surprised soon to hear of more.

Stocks of all sorts are buoyant, but busi has been limited. Sales of Bank of Montrea 134½, but buyers are asking 135. Our stock share lists will give full particulars of prices.

TORONTO STOCK MARKET.

(Reported by Pellatt & Osler, Brokers.)

There was a fair business done this week, demand for investment is greater than supply.

Bank Stock.—Montreal has again advanced, is to-day in demand at 133½ to 134. Brit nominal, at 103. There were transactions in tario at 99 and 98½; a limited demand exist the latter figure. Toronto sold at 114½ and 1 and is in demand at the latter rate. There considerable sales of Royal Canadian at 81½ to the latter rate is freely offered. Commerce i great demand at 103; very little offered. Gore in market. Merchants' is offered at 106 buyers at 105. Molsons in demand at 101, 1 offering. There were small sales of City at 101½ t and the stock is in demand. Buyers offer 10 Du Peuple and 105½ for Nationale; other b nominal.

Debentures.—Canada sterling fives and sixe in great demand. Toronto offering to pay 7 cent interest. There were considerable sale County at high rates.

Sundries.—Building Society stock is again h er; Canada Permanent sold early in the wee 115¼ to 115½, but buyers now offer 116 for it, there are no sellers; Western Canada is in demand, buyers are numerous and would adv but there is none in market; there are no s of Freehold, buyers would give 103 to 103½. of Canada Landed Credit stock, all calls took place at 62½. City gas sold at 105 and demand at that figure. No Montreal Teleg in market. Mortgages are readily placed at cent.; there is a fair demand for money.

BANK OF ENGLAND RETURNS.

The Bank Returns for the week ending, Satu 8th August, compared with the corresponding pe of 1867, 1866, are as follows:—

	1868.	1867.	18
Bank Bullion........	£21,371,060	£23,255,564	£13,6
Res've of Notes......	10,255,485	12,699,355	2,7
Notes in circu'n.......	24,963,380	24,343,480	25,0
Rate of Disco't.......	2 per cent.	2½ per cent.	10 per
Con's for money......	93⅜	94⅝	8

VINCIAL NOTES.—The following is a state-
of the Provincial Notes in circulation Wed-
/, the 5th August, 1866, and of the specie
gainst them at Montreal and Toronto:—

ucial notes in circulation pay-	
ble at Montreal...................	$2,612,727
le at Toronto....................	1,114,273
Total...................	$3,727,000
e held at Montreal......	$450,000
do Toronto.....:.........	400,000
Total...................	$950,000
tturef held by the Receiver Gen-	
ral under the Provincial Note	
ct......................	$3,000,000

NTERFEITS.—The Montreal *Witness* cau-
its readers against taking counterfeit
gs. It says that a number of English shil-
f the present reign are in circulation, which
akilfully executed that they would readily
en by an expert when tendered with num-
f the genuine, and the inexperienced would
y receive the single coin without suspicion.
ghtly slippery surface and a defect in the
g is the most conspicuous evidence by which
be detected.

OLVENTS.—The following insolvents were
ed last week:—John Hunter, London; L.
atson, Goderich; Thos. J. Leitch, Arnprior;
Meares, Seaforth; Wm. B. Hut, Brant-
John A Bolkingham, Cobourg; West Bro-
Montreal; W. F. Howell, do; Oliver Lop-
Sarnia; Stead and Crawford, Newmarket.
.. YOUNG, of Georgetown, has been appointed
tratford agent of the Royal Canadian Bank.

LL, IN PRICE.—Monetary affairs are at present
very depressed state in Liverpool. The fail-
f Zeigler, Meiss & Co., a large firm in the
n trade, with liabilities from £150,000 to
,000, and some minor stoppages in the corn
, have unsettled everything. I expect more
ulties in the cotton trade, and unless some
ges take place in prices, difficulties in the corn
are only what may be looked for.—*Investors'
dian,*

DUCTION OF TAXATION.—A reduction of taxa-
in the United States, to the extent of $164,-
vithin two years. By Act of Congress, July
1868, $60,000 were taken off. A law of the
farch, if filled, a further reduction of $4000,-
. the cotton tax repeal Bill reduced the load
23,769,000, and an Act of March last
led taxes to the amount of $44,500. Those
tions must tend strongly to relieve trade in
tates, and restore some of its lost vigor and
ity.

e Gore Bank wants to get rid of its Bank of
r Canada Certificates, and also its City of
ilton Debentures.

Commercial.

MONTREAL CORRESPONDENCE.

(From our own Correspondent.)

ice my last, the weather has been very change-
A good deal of rain has fallen; but as the
of the harvest is now housed, no harm has
done; on the contrary, the root crop and
rass have greatly benefitted. The days gen-
' are warm, but the nights are cool and ples-
Accounts from all parts of the Province
nue very cheering, and I see by an excellent
tary in the New York papers, that a very
yield in the States, especially of wheat, is

expected, whilst that of the coarser grains will be
fully up to an average. It is a great pity that our
Bureau of Agriculture has not a department
especially devoted to obtaining from all sections
of the Provinces reliable information respecting
the harvest, and making such information generally known through the official organs. At Washington the Bureau of Agriculture has its regular
correspondents in all sections of the States, who
report as to the yield, and also the probable value
of the crops. The utility of such statistics can
easily be perceived. It might be done at comparatively little trouble and expense; a form should
be sent round to all the country Reeves and
Mayors, and also Magistrates, to be filled up with
information respecting the crops in their immediate districts, which, coming from an official source,
would command attention; at present such gleaning is left either to the press or private individuals
interested in the grain trade, and is in most cases
far from reliable. I think it would be well for
you in Toronto, who are all deeply interested, to
urge the matter on the consideration of your local
Government.

I would strongly advise our farmers to hurry
their grain to market, and take advantage of the
present high prices. As a general rule, they seem
always reluctant to do so, fancying that prices
must rise if they hold off; the fallacy of such
reasoning must be apparent, instead of prices falling by degrees through the gradual bringing forward of their supplies, they are apt to come down
with a rush, when every one must sell; the markets are overcrowded; the means of transport run
short, or freight has to be engaged at much higher
rates, and both farmers and storekeepers suffer;
the latter especially in not receiving their money
in time to pay off old scores to the merchants,
and come forward in good time to lay in their fall
and winter supplies, before freight and insurance
rule high.

It certainly cannot be expected in the face of
news from all parts of the world, that prices can
remain at their present high scale, and I opine
that $1.68 for U. C. spring wheat will soon be a
thing of the past. Business in all branches continues very dull, in fact each week seems quieter
than the preceding. It is to be hoped a reaction
will soon set in, as this state of affairs is very discouraging. Groceries of every description are exceedingly quiet; there is some little talk of trying, when the tariff comes before the House, to
get the duties on wine altered, it being asserted
that the present way of levying them leads either
to prohibit the importation of fine wines or a considerable amount of falsifying invoices.

In *Dry Goods* the stocks are pretty well opened
out, but so far only few buyers have come forward.
Boots and Shoes seem the only articles in which
there is any liveliness, but even in them the trade
is only just beginning to move.

In *Produce*, on Friday and Saturday, the flour
market was brisk, but it has since subsided to its
usual dulness; good strong baker's flour of favorite brands sells as high as $8.50, and U. C. spring
wheat by the car load fetches $1.66; *long prices!*

TORONTO MARKET.

DRY GOODS.—Importations are now mostly to
hand and are being arranged for the inspection of
buyers, who, it is expected, will begin to come
forward in the course of a fortnight. A fair, but
not a large trade is expected. It is generally understood that country merchants are still pretty
well stocked with certain lines of goods, such as
Canadian woolens, and their requirements especially in such articles, will be small. Cottons are
generally light in stock and they will be required
to the usual amount. Country merchants complain of dreadfully slack times and say they are
taking in no money; as a consequence their remittances are unusually slow. The great quietness in trade just now may be accounted for
chiefly by the fact that the dry weather has

brought the crops to maturity almost at the same
time, crowding the harvest work into a much
smaller space than usual, this has had the effect
of keeping farmers and others close at home, and
delayed purchases of goods till a more convenient
season.

The demand for woolen goods is expected to be
slack, because (1) of the large supply in the
hands of country storekeepers, and (2) because of
the low prices of wool, which has the effect of
keeping this staple at home to a great extent, and
thus increasing the supply of home-made flannels
and cloths. Prices of woolen goods will open
about 10 per cent. lower than the quotations of
the spring trade. The importations of foreign
woolens have been very light and the prices are
firmer than for Canadian woolens. Cotton goods
have altered little since the spring trade; we do
not notice any material difference in the quotations of this market. In other articles there is
nothing important to note, the usual stock having
been laid in and a fair demand being anticipated.

GROCERIES.—*Sugar*—The market is dull and
a decline in prices will be noted on reference to
our quotations. The London *Produce Markets
Review* says that an increase of 40,000 tons in the
European crop is looked for; the Cuban crop is
expected to yield 100,000 tons more than last year
and an increase of 30,000 tons is looked for in the
British West Indies. There are also 1,600 tons
more afloat from the East to Great Britain, France,
&c., while there is an excess of 10,000 tons on its
way from Java to Holland. A probable increase of
the crop of Mauritius, Louisiana, &c., is placed at
30,000 tons, so that altogether an increased supply
of 220,000 tons may be looked for, an augmentation which would require an increased European
and American consumption of 8 to 10 per cent.
to exhaust during the twelve months, from June,
1868 to June, 1869. We need not say that we
look for no such result at present and higher prices
thus seem out of the question, which, unless a
considerable revival in trade takes place, a further
fall must be looked for. While there is much
force in these remarks, yet the known lightness of
stock in the principal markets is strong ground
for maintaining the opposite view of the question.

PRODUCE.—*Wheat.*—There is no business doing
of any consequence; the market is dull and lower
than last week and closed nominal at $1.45 to
$1.48 for both spring and fall. The quantities of
wheat imported into Great Britain during the
first six months of 1868, with the countries from
whence received were:—

	Cwt.
Russia...............................	4,489,880
Denmark.............................	249,385
Prussia..............................	2,213,473
Schleswig, Holstein and Lunenburg...	32,270
Mecklenberg.........................	371,416
Hanse Towns........................	381,837
France...............................	12,934
Illyria, Crotia and Dalmatia..........	615,861
Turkey, Wallachia and Moldavia......	1,915,656
Egypt...............................	2,264,611
Chili................................	442,342
United States........................	3,817,082
British North America................	154,376
Other Countries......................	704,900
Total cwts........ ....:.	17,696,508

Wheat has undergone a steady decline in the
English market, amounting to 12s. per quarter
since May 1. *Barley.*—The new crop has begun
to arrive; about 8,000 bush. having been taken
on the street within the past seven days; prices
opened at 97 to 99c., advanced to $1.08 and $1.12,
and declined, closing at $1.05 to $1.06. There is
a good demand for all that is offered; it is now
certain that our entire crop will meet with a ready
sale, and that the prices will average about as high
as in the years of the American war, when barley
growers obtained prices that makes that period a
memorable one to them. *Oats*—have been very

irregular and unsettled as to price. Sales were made of small lots as high as 80c., but at the close there were free sellers at 55c. but no buyers except for less money. The change does not result from any movement in outside markets, but is wholly the result of good supplies following extreme scarcity. *Peas.*—None.

FLOUR.—Receipts, 500 brls.; flour has ruled dull and closed fully 25 cents lower on superfine, the present quotation being nominally $6.75. During the week sales were made of 200 brls. at $6.50 on cars at Brantford, 100 brls. at $7.25 here, and 200 brls. from midge-proof wheat at $6.75; holders of strong bakers' flour ask $7.25, and probably could realize $7. Good extra is wanted at $7 for local use, and superior at $7.25; none of either grade offering. *Oatmeal*—firm; selling at retail at $6.50 to $6.75. *Bran*—$10 per ton by the carload.

PROVISIONS.—Little doing in any article. *Butter*—Is firm and scarce at 16 to 18c. for store packed; 18 to 22c. for dairy, and 26c. for small rolls for retailing. *Cheese*—Firm at 10 to 10½c. for export. *Eggs*—Selling in lots at 10 to 12c. In other provisions nothing doing.

LIVE STOCK.—The market is fairly supplied; beef cattle sell at $6. to $6.50 for medium to chice, and $4.50 to $5.50 for inferior and common; a lot of 20 cattle sold at 4¾c., live weight. Sheep $3 to $5 each; lambs $1.50 to $2.50. Calves $5 per head.

Petroleum Trade of Pennsylvania.

The Titusvills *Herald's* monthly Petroleum report for the month ending July 31st, says: The production has been unsteady during the month, and large variations have taken place. For the greater part of the first week it remained unchanged, but from about the 7th it commenced to decrease, and on the 19th the total reached scarcely over 10,700 or 10,900 barrels. From the latter date until the close there was quite a rapid increase from striking new wells and torpedoing old ones.

The following table shows the total production for the month of July, the average per day, the production previously this year, and the average since January 1st:

Total shipments of crude for July of barrels, of 45 gallons each, bbls......		327,413
Add to reduce to barrels of 43 gallons each, bbls..........		15,228
Total shipment of barrels of 43 gallons gach, bbls..........		342,641
Total stock, July 1st, bbls......	278,450	
Total stock August 1st, bbls...	267,450	
Deduct decrease on August 1st, bbls...		11,000
Total production during July, bbls....		331,641
Average per day for 31 days, bbls	10,688	
Production previously this year, bbls..		1,689,565
Total production from January 1st to August 1st, bbls..........		2,021,206
Average per day for 213 days, bbls	9,489	

The annexed table shows the daily production on the 7th of each month from November 7th, 1867, to April 8th, 1868, the average per day for the twenty-three days ending April 30th, for the thirty-one days ending May 31st, and the average per day during May 30th and 31st, June 29th and 30th, and August 30th and 31st:

November 7, 1867..........Bbls.	9,885
December 7, 1867..........	10,462
January 7, 1868..........	11,065
February 7, 1868..........	10,811
March 7, 1868..........	9,708
April 7, 1868..........	8,943
Average per day for the 31 days ending April 30th..........	8,650
Average per day for the thirty-one days ending May 31st..........	9,790
Average per day during May 30 and 31....	10,035
Average per day during June 29 and 30...	11,299
Average per day during July 30 and 31...	11,405

STOCK OF PETROLEUM IN THE MARKET.—The stock of petroleum in the producing regions on August 1st, was 267,450 barrels of forty-three gallons each. In this stock are included 231,450 barrels in iron tankage, five thousand in wooden storage tanks at Titusville and on the Hyde and Egbert Farm, and forty-one thousand in wooden tankage that are on the hands of producers, brokers, and shippers. Of the amount in iron takage, about sixty thousand barrels have been sold for delivery all this year, and thirty thousand are held by Cleveland refiners. Of the remainder about fifty-one thousand are in the hands of parties who tanked it, and seventy or eighty thousand are held by the different shippers in the tanks of the pipe companies and brokers.

As compared with the stock held on the 1st of July, that held on August 1st shows a reduction of eleven thousand barrels. The greater part of this reduction took place by shipments from iron tankage, the stock held at the wells having remained about the same as on July 1st.

The following table shows the total stock of petroleum and the amounts in iron tankage on the 7th of each month from November 7th to April 8th, and on May 1st, June 1st, and August 1st:—

	Am't in Iron Tankage.	Total Stock.
November 7, 1867, bbls	459,000	655,000
December 7, 1867, "	480,900	620,400
January 7, 1868, "	466,500	534,000
February 7, 1868, "	480,100	541,100
March 7, 1868, "	497,194	552,194
April 7, 1868, "	488,600	559,500
May 1, 1868, "	381,400	421,000
June 1, 1868, "	246,100	290,400
July 1, 1868, "	231,050	278,450
August 1, 1868, "	221,450	206,450

THE IRON TANKAGE.—The capacity of iron tankage remains unchanged since our last report. There is but very little doing in the way of constructing tanks, and work has been suspended on three or four of those that were commenced during June and July. The total capacity, which is now 1,064,539 barrels, is more than large enough to supply any storage demand that may arise during the next three or four months. The capacity of empty tankage has been enlarged by ten thousand barrels, and on the first the capacity reached 843,089 barrels.

THE DEVELOPMENT.—The number of drilling wells is steadily increasing, and on August first the total reached three hundred and twenty-seven, being an increase of twenty-eight from the same date last month, and of seventy from the first of June. About one-half these wells are situated in the Upper Cherry Run and Pleasantville districts. Of these, between twenty-five and forty will be completed within the next thirty days, and, probably, as many more within the next sixty or seventy days. In all parts of the region large numbers of leases have been given, and operations have been commenced upon many of them, but on account of a scarcity of material, the work of drilling has been delayed. All the machine shops in the region are worked to their greatest capacity in turning out the apparatus for drilling, but the supply of the necessary materials is wholly inadequate to meet the demand. From this cause the number of drilling wells on August first was from seventy-five to one hundred smaller than it would have been if there had been a sufficient supply of material.

RECAPITULATION.

Total amount of petroleum in iron and wooden storage tanks and on the hands of producers, brokers, and shippers..........bbls.	267,450
Total capacity of iron takage,......bbls.	1,064,539
Total amount of petroleum in iron tankage..........bbls.	221,450
Amount of iron tankage empty...bbls.	743,0
Number of new wells drilling..........	3
Daily production.......... bbls.	11,3

Fish and Fish Oils.

A late number of the Quebec *Gazette* has t following:—

FISH.—Several schooners have recently arriv from the lower St. Lawrence; but there are arrivals of round lots to report, and prices rem unchanged. Unusual activity prevails in maki preparations for prosecuting the trade in herrin &c., &c.; and several schooners and briganti have recently left this port and Montreal for t Labrador coast. The class of vessels employed this service is better than usual, and several cra of large carrying capacity, have been chartered remunerative rates to the owners.

FISH OILS.—Arrivals are confined to small l by each schooner, and all descriptions selling very fair rates; an impression prevailing that t supply this season will be below the average.

Albany Lumber Market Review.

The receipts have been large and stock is ac mulating considerably, particularly of gre lumber. The assortment in market is goo Sales have been fairly active, though but lit has yet been purchased for winter stock. Pri are well maintained on most kinds, and if t present price of goods continues or increases advance on pine is anticipated. Shipments ha been pretty large with no difference in freigh Clear pine is selling at $57 to $60, and fou quality $52 to $55.

Halifax Market.

Halifax, Aug. 12.

Since our last review we have no change to n in business. The past week has been the dull of this dull season. The imports are light a the exports extremely small. The political citement going on just now will militate agai business and have an injurious effect upon fall trade. Capitalists will be very cautious investing or speculating until this excitem subsides.

BREADSTUFFS.—Flour, a further advance taken place, and No. 1 Canada is worth $8. and holders are firm. Extra may be quoted $8 70 to $8.80. We quote Extra State at $8 $8.10. Baltimore (Howard Street) $8.30 to $8. Superfine $7.25 to $7.50. Common $6.25 to 50. Rye, quiet at $6.50 to $6.75. Cornmeal fair demand at $4.50 for Halifax Ground; $4 to $5 for Kiin dried. Oatmeal in fair dema at $8 per bbl. for Nova Scotia and Canada. I ports for the week, 4443 bbls. flour, 922 bl corn meal, 100 bbls. oatmeal.

EXCHANGE.—Bank Bills on London 60 d sight, 13½ per cent. prem.; Private Bills 12½ 12¾ per cent. prem.; Gold Drafts on New Yor sight 3¼ per cent. prem.; Currency Drafts 2 30 per cent discount. Sight Drafts on Mont 3½ per cent prem.; sight drafts on Newfoundla 5 per cent prem.

Demerara Sugar Market.

The following is from Sandbach, Parker & C Circular, dated Georgetown, Demerara, 8th Ju

SUGAR.—All offering has been bought up the American Market, but there has not bee much animation as during the previous mo the shipments for June were about equal betw America and the United Kingdom, viz., hhds. to each, the amount to come forwar July and August will be small, so that we ar opinion that rates will not go much lower it b likely that several buyers will be in the mar the quality has not been quite up to the mark past fortnight, the wet weather making the j much thinner, necessitating a longer perio

s, which always acts injuriously on the color.
nsactions have taken place during the fort-
t the following rates:

ARS (package included sold by 100 lbs:
, 10 per cent. tare F. O. B.
scavados, equal at No. 8 }
   Standard $4.10 ℔ 100 lbs.
|o. 10 do. $4.80   "
   " 12 do. $5.00   "   } In hhds.
um Pan No. 12 do. $5.75   } of about
   "   " 14 do.   6.00   } 1800 lbs. each.
   "   " 16 do.   6.00
   "   " 18 do.   6.59

LASSES. (package included, sold by Imperial
l.)
scovado, from 20 @ 26 cents, as } In puns
or sad density.   } of
num Pan from 26 @ 36 cents, as } 100 gals.
or and density
k (colored, package included, sold }
perial gal. from 35 per cent, @ 38
roof 38 @ to 40 cents.   } Ditto.
38 per cent. @ 40 overproof, 38
cents. "

The Wine Crop in France.

Salut Public of Lyons says :—" The wine
ffers a splendid aspect almost everywhere,
s magnificent in Burgundy, the Maçonnais
dmont, and Lyons country. In the vine-
of Beaujolais, the vine stocks literally bend
th the weight of the grapes, which at pre-
ave attained almost their full size, and have
. to redden for the last few days. The
s are in high spirits ; and if slight showers
feat heat should alternate, as hitherto, there
ounds for expecting a very superior yield. In
ity and in quality, as compared with that of
ear ; and, besides, the vintage ground can
de a month earlier. We cannot deny, how-
that the prolonged drought, and the extra-
ry heat, have caused some damage in certain
eps. In sandy and gravelly soils, many of
rapes have been roasted by the sun. The
ards of the Mount d'Or have particularly
ed in that respect, and rain is ardently long-
. In the South, the oidium comparatively
nsive in these districts, has caused serious

The Cattle Disease.

good deal of anxiety has been felt in connec-
with a disease which has destroyed a good
cattle in the Western States. It is there
l by some the "Black Water" disease. A
nent is also made on the authority of Hon.
aristie, of Paris, Ont., that the disease had
its appearance in that vicinity. We hope
may prove to be a mistake ; the Dominion
rnment have sent a special agent to examine
he facts of the case. Respecting its nature
eculiarities, the ollowi g statement of facts
een made to the Agricultural Department at
ington : —"First, that the disease is con-
ated from cattle from Texas, Florida, and
portions of the Gulf Coast. Third, that the
communicating it are not only apparently
hy, but are generally improving in condition
th—That while local herds receiving the in-
m, nearly all die ; they never communicate
isease to others. Fifth—That either a con-
able increase in elevation, or a distance of two
ree degrees of latitude from the starting point,
essary to develope the virus into activity and
ency ; and a further progress of two degrees
itude, and a few weeks in time, is sufficient
minate the poison from the system.—Sixth
at Texas cattle removed to other miasmatic
ous, as the Mississippi bottoms, up to the
y-sixth parallel communicate no infection to
herds. Seventh— Medication has thus far
of no avail ; it concludes that this disease
ot become general,—that it cannot exist only
the movements of Texas cattle, which should
gulated or suppressed, and that it does not
t from travel, but from climatic causes.

STATEMENT OF BANKS

ACTING UNDER CHARTER, FOR THE MONTH ENDING 31st JULY, 1868, ACCORDING TO RETURNS FURNISHED BY THE BANKS TO THE AUDITOR OF PUBLIC ACCOUNTS.

NAME OF BANK.	CAPITAL.		Promissory Notes in circulation not bearing Interest.	Balances due to other Banks.	Cash Deposits not bearing Interest.	Cash Deposits bearing interest.	TOTAL LIABILITIES.	Coin, Bullion, and Provincial Notes.	Landed or other Property of the Bank.	Government Securities.	Promissory Notes, or Bills of other Banks.	Balances due from other Banks.	Notes and Bills Discounted.	Other Debts due the Bank, not included under foregoing heads.	TOTAL ASSETS.
	Capital authorized by Act.	Capital paid up.													
ONTARIO AND QUEBEC.	$	$	$ c.	$ c.	$ c.	$ c.	$ c.	$ c.	$ c.	$ c.	$ c.	$ c.	$ c.	$ c.	$ c.
Montreal	6,000,000	6,000,000	528,146	604,467 58	5,095,613 09	5,464,481 77	19,828,897 19	9,901,796 60	350,000 00	3,372,906 67	571,884 11	852,924 34	12,463,344 98	341,849 80	36,651,436 40
Quebec	3,000,000	1,478,320	406,663	87,877 69	638,337 04	356,960 72	2,036,433 33	442,343 60	89,728 94	148,453 33	79,440 61	230,653 88	2,386,063 41	273,546 49	3,532,739 16
City	1,200,000	1,200,000	316,157	9,007 63	545,513 74	776,193 48	1,857,394 73	539,909 58	38,923 53	185,809 08	105,640 95	38,920 74	2,380,136 96	127,044 33	3,605,315 78
Gore	1,000,000	993,642	95,032	96,346 99	149,514 49	143,041 51	496,412 3	290,259 30	47,334 83	123,713 33	17,608	59,969 60	780,153 96	136,330	1,381,179 74
British North America			124,204	657 71	325,209 25	177,212 93	577,403 88	317,456 11	140,394 44	160,864 44	35,793 73	342,094 44	55,625 74	55,625 74	2,384,992 44
Banque du Peuple	1,600,000	1,600,000	491,534	54,492	173,444 62	431,997 94	959,390 43	431,097 94	43,730 70	8,473 38	4,775 72	47,507 44	37,015 39	273,580 17	765,200 17
Niagara District	1,000,000	901,738	61,766	114,561 62	208,809 10	507,147 05	782,029 79	974,902 62	90,075 15	74,285 53	39,834 67	34,850 67	1,357,105 01	47,737 18	2,116,415 95
Molson's	1,000,000	1,000,000	963,014	108,643 68	398,808 14	599,208 28	1,682,453 83	542,600 94	43,287 89	99,663 33	99,030 73	193,467 13	1,464,138 99	337,085 35	3,499,169 15
Toronto	2,000,000	2,000,000	961,955	1,002,413 84	96,434 59	72,234 90	3,114,788 10	719,399 08	14,000 00	164,185 68	32,028 22	43,600 17	477,633 84	5,000 00	1,761,254 47
Ontario	3,000,000	3,000,000	400,000	7,584 74	96,454 59	73,234 90	941,745 84	53,635 45	14,000 00	96,983 33	33,689 89	43,600 17	477,633 84	5,000 00	1,470,738 64
Eastern Townships	400,000	400,000	104,649	113,360 43	251,746 63	440,909 36	769,187 61	180,618 40		42,365	134,813 51	13,850 17	396,336 86		692,645 77
Banque Nationale	2,000,000	1,908,959	725,561	16,051 18	899,148 37	777,597 80	688,380 71	665,895 21		86,983 33	200,592 90	455,348 75	2,286,737 70	1,013,069 78	7,138,342 07
Banque Jacques Cartier	1,000,000	991,385	170,390	14,085 18	641,309 48	1,359,077 87	544,243 73	76,839 75		101,599 81	134,310 16	955,472 74	2,373,378 33	45,461 2	3,456,638 75
Merchants'	6,000,000	2,399,945	631,390	337,081 97	840,756 60	1,585,077 97	3,268,711 51	653,806 81	354,436 65	99,386 67	194,310 97	118,643 18	2,871,979 85	45,461 2	1,660,836 58
Royal Canadian	1,000,000	1,000,150	164,291	255,012 51	387,232 30	135,019 14	981,472 54	64,095 32	34,398 39	59,645 10	188 95	43,048 95	371,013 67	5,877 36	593,617 10
Union B'k Low. Canada	2,000,000	960,150	89,963	255,321 85	387,232 30	135,019 14	381,072 54	64,095 32					371,013 67		
Mechanics'	1,000,000	371,086		95,132 31	106,813 33	708,466 81	3,102,459 74	829,465 98	94,386 39	191,670 33	65,645 15	74,395 66	2,014,650 90		3,120,832 17
Bank of Canada		908,548													
NOVA SCOTIA.															
Bank Yarmouth															
Merchants' Bank															
People's Bank															
Union Bank															
Bank Nova Scotia															
NEW BRUNSWICK.															
Bank New Brunswick	600,000	600,000	312,356	54,165 92	298,703 38	17,605 41	671,493 46	82,380 63	32,000 00		8,053 00	62,193 78	1,068,007 79	39,840 00	1,292,454 60
Commercial Bank															
St. Stephen's Bank	200,000	200,000	323,303		13,997 88	29,169 16	365,332 54	29,076 20	4,484 40		45,187 32	32,895 31	345,361 81	96,603 00	560,700 04
People's Bank															
Totals.....															

CANADA

Life Assurance Company.

IN compliance with the Act respecting Insurance Companies, 31 Vic., chap. 48,

NOTICE IS HEREBY GIVEN,

THAT THE

CANADA LIFE ASSURANCE COMPANY,

Has been licensed by the

HONORABLE THE MINISTER OF FINANCE,

To transact the

Business of Life Assurance.

A. G. RAMSAY,
Manager.

August 1st, 1868. 1-1m

Edinburgh Life Assurance Company.

Founded 1823.

HEAD OFFICE—22 GEORGE STREET, EDINBURGH.

Capital, ... £500,000 *Ster'g.*
Accumulated and Invested Funds, £1,000,000 "

HEAD OFFICE IN CANADA:
WELLINGTON STREET, TORONTO.

SUB-AGENTS THROUGHOUT THE PROVINCE.

J. HILLYARD CAMERON,
Chairman, Canadian Board.

DAVID HIGGINS,
Secretary, Canadian Board.

Western Assurance Company.

NOTICE is hereby given that the Annual General Meeting of Shareholders of the Company will be held at the Company's Office, on

TUESDAY, THE 1ST DAY OF SEPTEMBER NEXT,

At 12 o'clock, noon, to receive the Annual Report, and for the election of Directors to serve during the ensuing year.

By order of the Board.

B. HALDAN,
Secretary.

50-td.

KERSHAW & EDWARDS,
IMPROVED PATENT
NON-CONDUCTING AND VAPORIZING
FIRE AND BURGLAR-PROOF SAFES,
139 & 141
ST. FRANCOIS XAVIER STREET,
MONTREAL.

AGENTS:
A. K. BOOMER, TORONTO.
J. W. MURTON, HAMILTON.
A. G. SMYTH, LONDON, ONT.

51-6m.

Insurance Act.

NOTICE is hereby given that the

COMMERCIAL UNION ASSURANCE COMPANY

Having complied with the Act 31st Vic., cap. 48, by depositing the sum of

100,000 Dollars,

have received the required license to transact the business of

FIRE AND LIFE INSURANCE
IN THE DOMINION OF CANADA.

MORLAND, WATSON & CO.,
General Agents for Canada.

W. M. WESTMACOTT,
Agent for Toronto. 51-4t.

TORONTO PRICES CURRENT.—August 20, 1868.

Name of Article.	Wholesale Rates.	
Boots and Shoes.	$ c.	$ c.
Mens' Thick Boots ...	2 20	2 50
" Kip........	2 45	3 20
" Calf	3 00	3 75
" Congress Gaiters..	2 00	2 40
" Kip Cobbourgs....	1 00	1 50
Boys' Thick Boots....	1 65	1 90
Youths' "	1 45	1 55
Women's Batts	95	1 20
" Congress Gaiters..	1 15	1 50
Misses' Batts.	0 75	1 00
" Congress Gaiters..	1 00	1 30
Girls' Batts	0 65	0 90
" Congress Gaiters..	0 80	1 10
Children's C. T. Cacks..	0 50	0 65
" Gaiters.........	0 65	0 90
Drugs.		
Aloes Cape.........	0 12½	0 16
Alum	0 02½	0 03
Borax	0 00	0 00
Camphor, refined.....	0 65	0 70
Castor Oil..........	0 18	0 28
Caustic Soda........	0 04½	0 05
Cochineal..........	0 90	1 00
Cream Tartar	0 00	0 00
Epsom Salts	0 03	0 04
Extract Logwood.....	0 09	0 11
Gum Arabic, sorts....	0 30	0 35
Indigo, Madras......	0 75	1 00
Licorice	0 14	0 45
Madder	0 13	0 16
Nutgalls	0 00	0 00
Opium..............	6 70	7 00
Oxalic Acid.........	0 28	0 35
Potash, Bi-tart......	0 25	0 28
" Bichromate...	0 15	0 20
Potass Iodide	3 80	4 50
Senna	0 12½	0 60
Soda Ash	0 03	0 04
Soda Bicarb	4 50	5 50
Tartaric Acid........	0 37½	0 45
Verdigris	0 35	0 40
Vitriol, Blue.........	0 09	0 10
Groceries.		
Coffees:		
Java, ℔ lb..........	0 23@0 25	
Laguayra, ...	0 17	0 18
Rio...............	0 16	0 18
Fish:		
Herrings, Lab. split..	0 00	0 00
" round......	0 00	0 00
" scaled......	0 00	0 00
Mackerel, small kitts..	1 00	1 25
Loch. Her. wh'e firks..	2 50	2 75
" half " ..	1 50	1 75
White Fish & Trout..	None.	
Salmon, saltwater....	16 00	17 50
Dry Cod, ℔ 112 lbs....	5 00	0 00
Fruit:		
Raisins, Layers	2 20	2 30
" M R.........	2 10	2 20
" Valentias new..	0 08½	0 09
Currants, new........	0 05	0 06
" old.........	0 03¾	0 04½
Figs..............	0 13	0 15
Molasses:		
Clayed, ℔ gal.........	0 37½	0 40
Syrups, Standard	0 46	0 47
" Golden	0 52	0 53
Rice:		
Arracan	4 75	5 00
Spices:		
Cassia, whole, ℔ lb...	0 35	0 40
Cloves	0 11	0 13
Nutmegs	0 50	0 65
Ginger, ground	0 16	0 25
" Jamaica, root..	0 25	0 30
Pepper, black........	0 09	0 10
Pimento	0 08	0 09
Sugars:		
Port Rico, ℔ lb......	0 08¾	0 09
Cuba "	0 08¾	0 09
Barbadoes (bright)...	0 08¾	0 08¾
Dry Crushed, at 60d...	0 11¾	0 11¾
Canada Sugar Refine'y, yellow No. 2, 60 ds..	0 08¾	0 08¾
Yellow, No. 2½.......	0 09	0 09¼
No. 3........	0 09¾	0 09½
Crushed X	0 10	0 10½
" A.........	0 11½	0 11¾
Ground............	0 11¾	0 12
Extra Ground........	0 12¾	0 13
Teas:		
Japan com'n to good..	0 40	0 55
" Fine to choicest..	0 55	0 65
Colored, com. to fine..	0 60	0 75
Congou & Souch'ng...	0 42	0 75
Oolong, good to fine..	0 50	0 65
Y. Hyson, com to gd..	0 45	0 55
Medium to choice	0 65	0 80
Extra choice	0 85	0 95
Gunpowd'r c. to med..	0 55	0 70
" med. to fine..	0 70	0 85

Name of Article.	Wholesale Rate.	
Groceries—*Contin'd*	$ c.	$ c.
" fine to fins't..	0 85	0 95
Hyson	0 45	0 80
Imperial	0 42	0 80
Tobacco, Manufact'd:		
Can Leaf, ℔ lb 5s & 10s..	0 26	0 30
Western Leaf, com..	0 25	0 26
" Good	0 27	0 32
" Fine	0 32	0 35
" Bright fine..	0 40	0 50
" " choice..	0 60	0 75
Hardware.		
Tin (net cash prices)		
Block, ℔ lb.........	0 25	0 26
Grain.............	0 26	0 27
Copper:		
Pig	0 24	0 25
Sheet.............	0 30	0 33
Cut Nails:		
Assorted ¼ Shingles, ℔ 100 lb.........	3 05	3 15
Shingle alone do	3 30	3 40
Lathe and 5 dy.......	3 55	3 65
Galvanized Iron:		
Assorted sizes........	0 00	0 10
Best No. 24.........	0 09	0 00
" 26.........	0 08¾	0 00
" 28.........	0 09¾	0 10
Horse Nails:		
Guest's or Griffin's assorted sizes......	0 19	0 20
For W. ass'd sizes...	0 19	0 20
Patent Hammer'd do..	0 18	0 19
Iron (at 4 months):		
Pig—Gartsherrie No1..	26 00	27 00
Other brands. No1..	22 00	23 00
" No2..	24 00	25 00
Bar—Scotch, ℔ 100 lb..	2 25	2 50
Refined	3 00	3 25
Swedes	5 00	5 50
Hoops—Coopers.......	3 00	3 25
Band	3 00	3 25
Boiler Plates.........	3 25	3 50
Canada Plates........	4 00	4 25
Union Jack	0 00	0 00
Pontypool..........	0 00	0 00
Swansea	0 00	0 00
Lead (at 4 months):		
Bar, ℔ 100 lbs...	0 07	0 07½
Sheet "	0 08	0 09
Shot............	0 07½	0 07¾
Iron Wire (net cash):		
No. 6, ℔ bundle....	2 70	2 80
" 9, "	3 10	3 20
" 12, "	3 40	3 50
" 16, "	4 30	4 40
Powder:		
Blasting, Canada....	3 50	3 75
FF " ...	4 50	4 75
FFF " ...	5 00	5 25
Blasting, English ...	5 00	5 50
FF loose..	5 50	6 00
FFF " ..	6 00	6 50
Pressed Spikes (4 mos):..		
Regular sizes 100.....	4 00	4 25
Extra " ..	4 50	5 00
Tin Plates (net cash):		
IC Coke	7 50	8 00
IC Charcoal.........	8 50	8 75
IX "	10 50	10 75
IXX "	12 50	0 00
DC "	7 50	9 00
DX "	0 50	10 00
Hides & Skins. ℔ lb		
Green rough	0 05½	0 06
Green, salt'd & insp'd..	0 00	0 07
Cured	0 07½	0 08½
Calfskins, green.......	0 00	0 10
Calfskins, cured.......	0 00	0 12
" dry........	0 18	0 20
Lambskins, ...	0 50	0 00
" pelts......	0 40	0 00
Hops.		
Inferior, ℔ lb.........	0 10	0 15
Medium...........	0 15	0 20
Good	0 20	0 25
Fancy	0 25	0 35
Leather, @ (4 mos.) In lots of less than 50 sides, 10 ℔ cent higher.		
Spanish Sole, 1st qual.. heavy, weights ℔ lb..	0 23	0 23½
Do. 1st qual middle do..	0 23	0 23½
Do. No. 2, all weights..	0 20	0 22
Slaughter heavy	0 28	0 29
Do. light.........	0 28	0 29
Harness, best	0 32	0 34
" No. 2.........	0 30	0 33
Upper heavy..........	0 34	0 36
" light..........	0 36	0 40

Name of Article.	Wholesale Rates.
Leather—*Contin'd.*	$ c.
Kip Skins, Patna	0 45
French	0 70
English	0 65
Hemlock Calf (30 to 35 lbs.) per doz....	0 75
Do. light	0 45
French Calf..........	1 05
Grain & Satn Clt ℔ doz..	0 00
Splits, large ℔ lb......	0 38
" small	0 20
Enamelled Cow ℔ foot..	0 20
Patent	0 21
Pebble Grain	0 17
Buff	0 17
Oils.	
Cod	0 55
Coconnut, ℔ lb.......	0 00
Lard, extra	0 00
" No. 1	0 00
" Woollen.......	0 00
Lubricating, patent...	0 00
Linseed, raw.........	0 77½
" boiled......	0 82½
Machinery...........	0 00
Olive, 2nd, ℔ gal......	1 45
" salad	2 00
" salad, in bots. qt. ℔ case....	3 00
Sesame salad, ℔ gal...	1 60
Seal, pale...	0 70
Spirits Turpentine....	0 65
Varnish	0 00
Whale.	0 75
Paints, &c.	
White Lead, genuine in Oil, ℔ 25lbs......	0 00
Do. No. 1 "	0 00
" 2 "	0 00
" 3 "	0 00
White Zinc, genuine..	3 00
White Lead, dry......	0 06
Red Lead...........	0 07
Venetian Red, Eng'h..	0 02
Yellow Ochre, Fren'h..	0 02
Whiting	0 90
Petroleum. (Refined ℔ gal.)	
Water white, car l'd..	0 31
" small lots....	0 35
Straw, by car load....	0 30
" small lots....	0 33
Amber, by car load..	0 30
" small lots	0 3
Benzine	0 35
Produce.	
Grain:	
Wheat, Spring, 60 lb..	1 4
" Fall 60 "..	1 4
Barley........ 48 "..	1 0
Peas...... 60 "..	0 8
Oats...... 34 "..	0 5
Rye .... 56 "..	0 0
Seeds:	
Clover, choice 60 "..	0 0
" com'n 68 "..	0 0
Timothy, cho'e 4 "..	0 0
" inf. to good 48 "..	0 0
Flax .... 56 "..	1 2
Flour (per brl.):	
Superior extra......	7 2
Extra superfine,......	7 0
Fancy superfine.......	0 0
Superfine No. 1......	7 0
" No. 2......	0 0
Oatmeal, (per brl.)....	6 2
Provisions.	
Butter, dairy tub ℔ lb..	0 1
" store packed..	0 1
Cheese, new	0 1
Pork, mess, per brl....	23 0
" prime mess......	16 0
" prime..........	14 0
Bacon, rough	0 0
" Cumberl'd cut...	0 1
" smoked	0 0
Hams, in salt.........	0 0
" sug. cur. & canv'd..	0 1
Shoulders, in salt	0 0
Lard, in kegs.........	0 1
Eggs, packed	0 1
Beef Hams	0 0
Tallow	0 0
Hogs dressed, heavy..	0 0
" medium.....	0 0
" light....	0 0
Salt, &c.	
American brls.........	1 5
Liverpool coarse	0 0
Plaster.............	1 0
Water Lime	1 5

Candles.	$ c.	$ c.
d & Co.'s ..		
ial.........	0 07½	0 08
n Bar	0 07	0 07½
Bar........	0 07	0 07½
....	0 05	0 05½
....	0 03¾	0 04
....	0 10	0 11

Liquors,
c.

er doz......	2 60	2 65
Dub Portr..	2 35	2 40
aica Rum...	1 80	2 25
r's H. Gin..	1 50	1 60
ld Tom.....	1 90	2 00
ses.........	4 00	4 25
ld Tom, c...	6 00	6 25
mon	1 00	1 25
old	2 00	4 00
ımmon	1 00	1 50
ium........	1 70	1 80
or golden ..	2 50	4 00

Brandy:	$ c.	$ c.
Hennessy's, per gal..	2 50	2 75
Martell's " ..	2 50	2 75
J. Robin & Co.'s " ..	2 10	2 75
Otard, Dupuy & Cos..	2 10	2 75
Brandy, cases........	8 50	9 00
Brandy, com. per c....	4 00	4 50
Whiskey:		
Common 36 u. p......	0 65	0 70
Old Rye	0 85	0 87½
Malt........	0 85	0 87½
Toddy...............	0 85	0 87½
Scotch, per gal.......	1 90	2 10
Irish—Kinnahan's c...	7 00	7 50
" Dunnville's Belf't..	6 00	6 25
Wool.		
Fleece, lb.............	0 26½	0 29
Pulled "............	0 00	0 00
Furs.		
Bear.................	3 00	10 00
Beaver..............	1 00	1 25
Coon	0 20	0 40
Fisher...............	4 00	6 00
Martin...............	1 40	1 60
Mink................	4 00	4 25
Otter................	5 75	6 00
Spring Rats..........	0 15	0 17
Fox.................	1 20	1 25

SURANCE COMPANIES.

ENGLISH.—*Quotations on the London Market.*

Last Dividend.	Name of Company.	Shares par val £	Amount paid.	Last Sale.
	Briton Medical and General Life ...	10	—	1⅝
7½	Commer'l Union, Fire, Life and Mar.	50	5	5½
8	City of Glasgow	25	2½	5
9½	Edinburgh Life	100	15	30⅝x
5—½ yr	European Life and Guarantee......	2½	11s6	4s 6d
10	Etna Fire and Marine............	10	1½	1
5	Guardian	100	50	52x
12	Imperial Fire..................	500	50	345
9½	Imperial Life	100	10	16¼
10	Lancashire Fire and Life..........	20	2	2⅞x
11	Life Association of Scotland.......	40	7½	23
5s. p. sh	London Assurance Corporation ..	25	12½	48
5	London and Lancashire Life	10	1	1
40	Liverp'l & London & Globe F. & L.	20	2	7⅞
5	National Union Life	5	1	1
12½	Northern Fire and Life	100	5	10⅝
12 '68, bo 5s.	North British and Mercantile	50	6¼	17½
50	Ocean Marine	25	5	20
£5 12s.	Provident Life...................	100	10	38
£4½ p. s.	Phœnix......................	....	....	136
2½—h. yr.	Queen Fire and Life	10	1	15-16
11⅝	Royal Insurance................	20	3	6¾
10	Scottish Provincial Fire and Life ..	50	2½	4⅞
25	Standard Life	50	12	65
5	Star Life	25	1¼	—
	CANADIAN.			⅌ c.
4	British America Fire and Marine ..	$50	$25	55
....	Canada Life	...	....	.....
12	Montreal Assurance	200	20	135
....	Provincial Fire and Marine........	60	11	.....
....	Quebec Fire..................	40	32½	£10½
8	" Marine...................	100	40	90-91
5 7 mo's.	Western Assurance.............	40	6	.....

RAILWAYS.	Sha's	Paid	Montr	London.
and St. Lawrence..................	£100	All.	....	56 58
nd Lake Huron	20½	"	....	3½ 3¾
do. Preference	10	"	....	5½ 6½
antf. & Goderich, 6⅌c., 1872-3-4.....	100	"	....	....
in and St. Lawrence	....	....	9½ 10½	....
do Pref. 10 ⅌ ct..........	....	....	50 70	....
runk	100	"	15 16	16½ 16¾
Eq.G. M. Bds. 1 ch. 6⅌c...........	100	"	....	78 82
First Preference, 5 ⅌ c	100	"	....	48 50
Deferred, 3 ⅌ ct..	100	"	....	....
Second Pref. Bonds, 5⅌c..........	100	"	....	37 40
do Deferred, 3 ⅌ ct...........	100	"	...	....
Third Pref. Stock, 4⅌ct...........	100	"	...	27 29
do. Deferred, 3 ⅌ ct..........	100	"	....	....
Fourth Pref. Stock, 3⅌c..........	100	"	....	19 20
do. Deferred, 3 ⅌ ct..........	100	"	....	....
estern	20½	"	....	13¼ 13¾
New	20½	18	16 17	....
6 ⅌ c. Bds, due 1873-76..........	100	All.	....	99 101
5½⅌c Bds. due 1877-78..........	100	"	....	91 93
Railway, Halifax, $250, all...........	$250	"	....	....
ı, of Canada, 6⅌c. 1st Pref. Bds........	100	"	.. .	77 82

EXCHANGE.	Halifax.	Montr'l.	Quebec.	Toronto.
ı London, 60 days or 75 days date	....	9¼ 9¾	9¾ 10¼	10¼
do.	....	8½ 9	8¾ 9	9½
with documents...........	....	8½ 9¼	....	....
. New York...............	....	32½ 33	30 30¼	68½
do.	....	33 33½	31 31½	....
afts do.	....	¼ dis to p.	par ½ dis.	par ½ dis.
....	....	4½ 4¾	....	4⅝ 7

STOCK AND BOND REPORT.

The dates of our quotations are as follows:—Toronto, Aug. 19; Montreal, Aug. 17; Quebec, August 17; London, Aug. 1.

NAME.	Shares.	Paid up.	Divid'd last 6 Months	Dividend Day.	CLOSING PRICES. Toronto.	Montre'l	Quebec.
BANKS.			⅌ ct.				
British North America.......	$250	All.	3	July and Jan.	102 103	102 103	103 105½
Jacques Cartier.............	50	"	4	1 June, 1 Dec.	106 107	105	104½103
Montreal	200	"	5	"	134 135	133¼134½	134 135
Nationale..................	50	"	4	1 Nov. 1 May.	105 106	105½	107 107½
New Brunswick	100	"	......	......	....	..	....
Nova Scotia	200	28	7&b$3½	Mar. and Sept.	....	....	....
Du Peuple..................	50	"	4	1 Mar., 1 Sept.	106 107	106½107½	106½107
Toronto	100	"	4	1 Jan., 1 July.	114 114½	113 115	113 114
Bank of Yarmouth..........	....	....	......	......	....	....	....
Canadian Bank of Com'e......	50	95	......	......	102½ 103	102	101¾102
City Bank Montreal	80	All.	4	1 June, 1 Dec.	101 102	100 100½	101 012
Commer'l Bank (St. John)....	100	"	⅌ ct.	......	....	...	....
Eastern Townships' Bank.....	50	"	4	1 July, 1 Jan.,	....	97	96 97
Gore	40	...	3½	1 Jan., 1 July.	46	46	45 46
Halifax Banking Company....	....	....	......	......	....	....	....
Mechanics' Bank............	50	70	4	1 Nov., 1 May.	94 96	93½ 95	93½ 94
Merchants' Bank of Canada....	100	70	4	1 Jan., 1 July.	105½106	105 105½	105 105¼
Merchants' Bank (Halifax)....	....	....	......	......	....	....	....
Molson's Bank..............	50	All.	4	1 Apr., 1 Oct.	109½110	108½109	109 110
Niagara District Bank...	100	70	3½	1 Jan., 1 July.	...	....	....
Ontario Bank...............	40	All.	4	1 June, 1 Dec.	98½ 99½	98½ 99½	98 99
People's Bank (Fred'kton)....	100	"	......	......	....	....	....
People's Bank (Halifax)	20	"	7 12 m	......	....	...	....
Quebec Bank	100	"	3½	1 June, 1 Dec.	97 98	98	97½ 97¾
Royal Canadian Bank	50	50	4	1 Jan., 1 July.	81½ 82½	80 85	82 85
St. Stephens Bank	100	All	.....	......	....	..	....
Union Bank	100	70	4	1 Jan., 1 July.	101 102	101 102	101¾102¼
Union Bank (Halifax)........	100	40	7 12mo	Feb. and Aug.	....	....	.. .
MISCELLANEOUS.							
British America Land........	250	44	2½	......	....	....	....
British Colonial S. S. Co......	250	32½	2½	......	...	50	...
Canada Company	32½	All.	5	......	....	....	....
Canada Landed Credit Co.....	50	$14	3½	......	61 62	....	....
Canada Per. B'ldg Society....	50	All.	5	......	115½116	....	....
Canada Mining Company.....	4	90	......	......	....	....	....
Do. Inl'd Steam Nav. Co.....	100	All.	20 12 m	......	....	106 108½	106 108
Do. Glass Company.........	100	"	12½ "	......	....	95	....
Canad'n Loan & Investm't....	25	2½	7	......	....	....	....
Canada Agency	10	½	......	......	....	....	....
Colonial Securities Co.......	...	....	......	......	....	....	....
Freehold Building Society....	100	All.	5	......	103 103½	....	....
Halifax Steamboat Co........	100	"	5	......	....	....	....
Halifax Gas Company........	....	....	......	......	....	....	....
Hamilton Gas Company......	....	....	......	......	....	....	....
Huron Copper Bay Co........	4	12	20	......	....	25 40	....
Lake Huron S. and C.........	5	102	......	......	....	....	....
Montreal Mining Consols	20	$15	......	......	....	2.15 2.50	...
Do. Telegraph Co...	40	All.	5	......	132½134	133	132½ 133
Do. Elevating Co...	00	"	15 12 m	......	....	....	....
Do. City Gas Co.........	40	"	4	15 Mar. 15 Sep.	....	135	134 135
Do. City Pass. R,. Co.....	50	"	5	......	....	107	106 107
Nova Scotia Telegraph	20	"	....	......	....	....	....
Quebec and L. S.	8	$4	......	......	.. ..	....	25 cts
Quebec Gas Co..............	200	All.	4	1 Mar., 1 Sep.	....	...	b'ks cl'd
Quebec Street R. R..........	50	25	3	......	....	....	96 97
Richelieu Navigation Co......	100	All.	7 p.a.	1 Jan., 1 July.	....	114 116¾	114 115
St. Lawrence Tow Boat Co.....	100	"	......	3 Feb.	....	...	45 50
Tor'to Consumers' Gas Co.....	50	"	2 3 m.	1 My Au Mar Fe	104½ 105	...	104 105
Trust & Loan Co. of U. C.....	20	5	3	......	....	....	.. .
West'n Canada Bldg Soc'y....	50	All.	5	......	108 109	....	....

SECURITIES.	London.	M'ntreal	Quebec.	Toronto.
Canadian Gov't Deb. 6 ⅌ ct. stg., due 1872........	....	100 101½	100½ 101	101 101½
Do. do. 6 do due Ja. & Jul. 1877-84........	103 105	99 100	100 100½	99½ 100
Do. do. 6 do. Feb. & Aug........	104 106	....	.. .	....
Do. do. 6 do. Mch. & Sep........	104 106	...	...	...
Do. do. 5 ⅌ ct. cur., 1883	91 93	90	90 90½	89 90
Do. do. 5 do. stg., 1885	....	92	90½ 91½	92 93
Do. do. 7 do. cur.,........	....	101 101½	100 100½	....
Dominion 6 p. c. 1878 cy.,........	....	99 100	......	100
Hamilton Corporation........	....	....	......	....
Montreal Harbor, 8 ⅌ ct. d. 1869........	..	....	......	....
Do. do. 7 do. 1870........	....	....	......	....
Do. do. 6½ do. 1875........	....	100 100½	......	....
Do. do. 6½ do. 1873........	....	....	......	....
Do. Corporation, 6 ⅌ c. 1891	....	92½ 93	92 93	90½ 91½
Do. 7 p. c. stock........	....	102¾103½	101 103	102½103½
Do. Water Works; 6 ⅌ c. stg. 1878........	....	....	......	90 91
Do. do. 6 do. cy. do.	....	92½ 93½	......	91 92
New Brunswick, 6 ⅌ ct., Jan. and July	102 104	....	......	....
Nova Scotia, 6 ⅌ ct., 1875........	101 103	...	......	....
Ottawa City 6 ⅌ c. d. 1880	....	90 91	......	...
Quebec Harbour, 6 ⅌ c. d. 1883.	....	....	60 70	....
Do. do. 7 do. do........	....	....	70 80	....
Do. do. 8 do. 1886........	....	....	85 90	....
Do. City, 6 ⅌ c. d. 9 years	....	80 90	86 87	80 90
Do. do. 7 do. 9 do.	....	....	90 91	....
Do. do. 7 do. 2½ do.	....	....	96 96½	....
Do. Water Works, 7 ⅌ ct., 4 years........	....	....	95 96	....
Do. do. 6 do. 2 do.	....	....	92½ 93½	....
Toronto Corporation	....	92½	...	....

Miscellaneous.

ntreal House, Montreal, Canada.

ONETARY MEN.—Merchants, Insurance Agents,
yers, Bankers, Railway and Steamboat Travellers,
Agents, Directors and Stockholders of Public Com
and other persons visiting Montreal for business
sure, are here by most respectfully informed that
iersigned proposes to furnish the best hotel accom-
on at the most reasonable charges. It is our study
ide every comfort and accommodation to all our
especially for gentlemen engaged as above. To
who have been accustomed to patronize other first-
otels, we only ask a trial; we have the same accom-
on and our table is furnished with every delicacy
eason.
H. DUCLOS.

22. 1867. 15-1?

Hurd, Leigh & Co.,

MPORTERS AND DECORATORS OF
FRENCH CHINA.
and families supplied with any pattern or crest
desired.
mmon goods always on hand. 72 Yonge Street,
), Ontario. 26y

Paper is printed from Messrs. Miller & Richards
tra hard metal Type, sold by
W. HALLEY,
83 Bay Street, Toronto.

Financial.

Pellatt & Osler.

K AND EXCHANGE BROKERS, Accountants
nts for the Standard Life Assurance Company and
ork Casualty Insurance Company.
TICE—86 King Street East, four Doors West of
Church Street, Toronto.

.Y PELLATT, EDMUND B. OSLER,
Notary Public. Official Assignee.

BROWN'S BANK,
(W. R. Brown. W. C. Chewett.)

KING STREET EAST, TORONTO,

'SACTS a general Banking Business, Buys and
ls New York and Sterling Exchange, Gold, Silver,
Bonds and Uncurrent Money, receives Deposits sub-
Cheque at sight, makes Collections and Discounts
ercial Paper.

s by Mail or Telegraph promptly executed at
most favourable current quotations.
Address letters, "BROWN'S BANK,
Toronto."

H. N. Smith & Co.,

1ST SENECA STREET, BUFFALO, N. Y., (corres-
ndent Smith, Gould, Martin & Co., 11 Broad Street,
Stock, Money and Exchange Brokers. Advances
on securities. 21-1y

Philip Browne & Co.,

NKERS AND STOCK BROKERS.

DEALERS IN

ILING EXCHANGE—U. S. Currency, Silver and
mds—Bank Stocks, Debentures, Mortgages, &c.
on New York issued, in Gold and Currency.
t attention given to collections. Advances made
urities.
No. 67 YONGE STREET, TORONTO.

BROWNE. PHILIP BROWNE, Notary Public.

Honore Plamondon,

TOM House Broker, Forwarder, and General Agent,
uebec. Office—Custom House Building. 17-1y

Candee & Co.,

KERS AND BROKERS, dealers in Gold and Silver
in, Government Securities, &c., Corner Main and
nge Streets, Buffalo, Y. N. 21-1y

Financial.

The Canadian Land and Emigration
COMPANY

Offers for sale at Cheap Rates, on condition of settle
ment,

FARM LOTS, IN DYSART,
And adjoining Townships, in the County of
Peterborough.

THE greater portion of the Company's block of nine
Townships is excellent farming land. The Judges at
the Provincial Exhibition at London, in 1865, awarded to
the Company a Special Prize, and at Kingston, in 1867,
a Diploma for the assortment of Farm Produce from their
settlements. The country is well watered, healthy and
picturesque. Dysart is a well settled Township, with
mills, schools, &c., while stores, post-office, boarding-
houses, &c., are established in the Village of Haliburton.
There is also a rising settlement in the Township of Harcourt; and along the Peterson road the settler has a choice
of good Farm Lots in no less than six Townships.
The communication to the Townships is good, a great
part of it by Railroad and Steamboat.
The Bobcaygeon, Opeongo, Peterson, Mississippi, and
Hastings Roads will all give access to the Company's
block, but other roads are being opened up, giving a more
direct communication with the County Town of Peterborough.
The Company has expended a considerable sum in the
construction of Roads to and through its Townships, and
has still a large appropriation for this purpose.
Dysart and adjoining Townships, the property of the
Company, form one Municipality which cannot fail to
make more rapid progress than any of the Municipalities
in that section of the country, on account of the large sum
levied every year from the Company.
For further information and particulars and conditions
of sale, apply to the Secretary,
CHARLES JAS. BLOMFIELD,
Bank of Toronto Buildings, Toronto.

Toronto, Jan. 21. 24-1y

Insurance.

J. T. & W. Pennock,

FIRE and Life Insurance Agents, Parliamentary and
Departmental Agents, Mining Agents, and Exchange
Brokers.
Ottawa, Dec. 21st, 1867. 10-1y

The Standard Life Assurance Company,

WITH which is now united the COLONIAL LIFE ASSU-
RANCE COMPANY.
Established 1825.
HEAD OFFICES—EDINBURGH and MONTREAL.
Accumulated Fund, upwards of $15,000,000.
Income, 1867 $3,285,000.
Manager—W. M. RAMSAY. Inspector—RICH'D BULL.
TORONTO—HENRY PELLATT, AGENT.
Agencies in every Town throughout the Dominion.
18-1y.

Fire and Marine Assurance.

THE BRITISH AMERICA
ASSURANCE COMPANY.
HEAD OFFICE:
CORNER OF CHURCH AND COURT STREETS.
TORONTO.

BOARD OF DIRECTION:
Hon G. W. Allan, M L C., A. Joseph, Esq.,
George J. Boyd, Esq., Peter Paterson, Esq.,
Hon. W. Cayley, G. P. Ridout, Esq.,
Richard S. Cassels, Esq., E H. Rutherford, Esq.,
Thomas C. Street, Esq.
Governor:
GEORGE PERCIVAL RIDOUT, Esq.
Deputy Governor:
PETER PATERSON, Esq.
Fire Inspector: Marine Inspector:
E. ROBY O'BRIEN. CAPT. R. COURNEEN.
Insurances granted on all descriptions of property
against loss and damage by fire and the perils of Inland
navigation.
Agencies established in the principal cities, towns, and
ports of shipment throughout the Province.
THOS. WM. BIRCHALL,
23-1y Managing Director.

Insurance.

Reliance Mutual Life Assurance
Society.
(Established, 1840,) OF LONDON, E. C.

Accumulated Funds, over $1,000,000.

Annual Income, $300,000
THE entire Profits of this long-established Society belong
to the Policy-holders.
HEAD OFFICE FOR DOMINION—MONTREAL.
T. W. GRIFFITH, Manager & Sec'y.
15-1y WM. HENDERSON, Agent for Toronto.

Etna Insurance Company of Dublin.

The number of Shareholders exceeds Five Hundred.
Capital, $5,000,000—Annual Income nearly $1,000,000.
THIS Company takes Fire and Marine Risks on the most
favorable terms.
T. W. GRIFFITH, Manager for Canada.
Chief office for Dominion— Corner St. Francois Xavier
and St. Sacrament Ste., Montreal.
15-1y WM. HENDERSON, Agent for Toronto.

Scottish Provincial Assurance Co.

Established 1825.
CAPITAL £1,000,000 STERLING.
INVESTED IN CANADA (1854) $300,000.
Canada Head Office, Montreal.

LIFE DEPARTMENT.
CANADA BOARD OF DIRECTORS:
HUGH TAYLOR, Esq., Advocate,
Hon. CHARLES WILSON, M. L. C.
WM. SACHE, Esq., Banker,
JACKSON RAE, Esq., Banker.
WM. FRASER, Esq. M. D., Medical Adviser.

The special advantages to be derived from Insuring in
this office are these:—Strictly Moderate Rates of Premium;
Large Bonus (intermediate bonus guaranteed ;) Liberal
Surrender Value, under policies relinquished by assured ;
and Extensive Limits of Residence and Travel. All business disposed of in Canada, without reference to parent
office.
A DAVIDSON PARKER,
Resident Secretary.
G. L. MADDISON,
15-1yr AGENT FOR TORONTO.

Lancashire Insurance Company.

CAPITAL, - - - - - - - - £3,000,000 Sterling.

FIRE RISKS
Taken at reasonable rates of premium, and
ALL LOSSES SETTLED PROMPTLY,
By the undersigned; without reference elsewhere.
S. C. DUNCAN-CLARK & CO.,
General Agents for Ontario,
N. W. Corner of King & Church Streets,
25-1y TORONTO.

Etna Fire & Marine Insurance Company.

INCORPORATED 1819. CHARTER PERPETUAL.

CASH CAPITAL, - - - - - $3,000,000.

LOSSES PAID IN 50 YEARS, 23,500,000 00.

JULY, 1868.
ASSETS.
(At Market Value.)
Cash in hand and in Bank $544,842 39
Real Estate 258,267,29
Mortgage Bonds, 982,945.00
Bank Stock 1,272,670 00
United States, State and City Stock, and other
Public Securities 2,049,855 51

Total $5,052,880 19

LIABILITIES.
Claims not Due, and Unadjusted $409,803 55
Amount required by Mass. and New York
for Re-Insurance 1,405,267 15
E. CHAFFEY & CO., Agents.
56-6m

THE CANADIAN
MONETARY TIMES
AND
INSURANCE CHRONICLE,

EVOTED TO FINANCE, COMMERCE, INSURANCE, BANKS, RAILWAYS, NAVIGATION, MINES, INVESTMENT,
PUBLIC COMPANIES, AND JOINT STOCK ENTERPRISE.

L. II—NO. 2.   TORONTO, THURSDAY, AUGUST 27, 1868.   { SUBSCRIPTION, 62 A YEAR.

Mercantile.

Meetings.

ROYAL INSURANCE COMPANY.

The annual meeting of the shareholders of the Royal Insurance Company was held on the 6th August, at the company's offices, Royal Insurance Buildings, Liverpool. C. Turner, Esq., M.P., Chairman of the Board of Directors, presided; and the following Directors and Shareholders were present:—W. Smith, John Torr, k. Brocklebank, M. Bonsfield, F. Maxwell, T. D. Hornby, Joseph Younghusband, Christopher Atkinson, C. J. Corbally, James Finlay, Robert Horsfall, D. Malcomson, C. Crittenden, W. Cliff, W. Ravenscroft, Robert Roberts, Henry Hargreaves, Wm. Whatham, John Grierson, W. O. Carter, A. Barucheson, K. Alexander, Isaac Kitchin, Colonel Mawdsley, W. F. Arnitt, James Holme, G. Moore, Wm. M'Quie, and Wm. J. Powell, &c., &c.

The Actuary (Mr. Dove), read the circular calling the meeting, and the report of the Directors, which was as follows:—

REPORT FOR THE YEAR 1867.

The experience of Fire Insurance Companies generally for the three years preceding the year 1867, the transactions of which form the subject of the present report of your Directors, has been with rare exceptions such a record of unusual calamities by fires, many purely accidental, and not a few undoubtedly designed, that the first pause in the heavy ratio of losses which has prevailed, and the first indications of a possibly favorable change in the anticipations of the future, bring with them a sensation of relief.

The Royal Insurance Company has benefitted in full proportion both in the advantages of the actually improved result of the past year, and in the reasonable prospects of the present one.

Before passing to the special experience of this office during the last year, it may briefly be stated that the causes which have acted favorably on the accounts of the larger number of Insurance Companies in the United Kingdom during that period may be considered as almost entirely included in the following, viz.:—

1. The continued convictions obtained in the criminal courts in cases of clear and well proven acts of incendiarism.

2. The establishment of a moderate increase in the charges for insurance, according to their respective hazards, which are capable of modulation from time to time, as necessity shows cause, and the marked improvement in certain classes of risks consequent on the defensive action of the Insurance Companies.

3. The late severe commercial lessons, which teach that the establishment of new offices of insurance furnish even less fields than others for success, unless there be exercised in their formation far more matured views, and far more practical experience, than have been exhibited by the careless originators of new companies of all kinds, which have been brought into existence, and have sunk into annihilation, within the limits of the last four years; and

4. The foreshadowing of a coming Act for Judicial Investigation into suspicious fires, which, there are grounds to conclude, will be passed by the new Parliament, in its first session.

These observations serve to introduce the statistics to be now presented to the Company's.

FIRE BRANCH

The premiums received in the year 1867 amount to the sum of £460,533 14s. being an increase on the preceding year of £13,282 12s.

As at the time these accounts were made up, viz., 31st December, 1867, the company had been established about 22½ years, it will be sufficient to show its unmatched progress to refer back to the year 1856, the mid period of the company's existence. The premiums for that year were only £151,733, less than one-third of the sum collected under the same head in 1867.

The losses which have accrued in the year 1867 reach the sum of £292,125 0s. 2d.

It will serve to exhibit in favorable contrast the result of this year with the preceding one, to announce that the losses of the latter year reached the sum of £379,405 (a difference of no less an amount than £87,280) against the smaller amount of premium collected therein. The ratio of claims, therefore, on the present occasion is less by upwards of 20 per cent. of the premiums received in comparison with the year 1866, and, so far as those two years are concerned, shows a very satisfactory transition from a disastrous experience to one which exhibits a fair and satisfactory amount of profit.

The result of the year at the close of the books leaves, on account of the British and Foreign business, including interest, an amount to the credit of profit and loss of £43,286 1s. 6d., while a separate amount of profit on the American branch has been realized of £13,087 0s. 2d.

It, moreover, inhances the significance of this favorable change to report further, that an estimate made of the transactions of the first six months of the present year exhibits, proportionately for the time, an equal if not a still more satisfactory result. The continuance, however, of this amount of success cannot consistently be reckoned on, as while on the one hand the same ratio of profits might by a certain degree of probability be continued through the year, on the other hand, there is at least an equal if not a greater probability, that at any time before its close undue anticipations of success may be rudely shaken, if not. indeed, wholly destroyed, by a series of losses which have happened in rapid succession many times in the late unpropitious years.

The report of the last year having indicated the remedial measures adopted by this company in consequence of the discovery of new elements of risk producing lamentable results to the country, and some portion of the present comparative exemption being fairly attributable thereto, a brief detail of the manner in which these measures have been carried out will not be unacceptable :

The increased rigour used in investigating proposals for insurance, then announced, has not been relaxed, and its advantageous results are now shown in a way that cannot well be controverted.

Almost every special risk in the company's books, old or new, has undergone a renewed and careful investigation, and the measure of risks involved has been tested by a fresh weighing of its relative importance.

It has been an equal object of desire in this laborious process to avoid in any one instance unnecessarily to raise the rate of premium, as it has been to provide that no risk of unusual danger should be kept on the books that would not yield to the shareholders some moderate probability of reasonable profit.

That both these designs have been successful, admits of conclusive proof.

With regard to the first it may safely be affirmed that the popularity of the company throughout the world remains undiminished, and has not been in the slightest degree undermined by impolitic harshness in carrying out the indispensable requirements which have been adverted to. So much has this been the case, that the risks which have been withdrawn by insurers, in consequence of the needful correction of the rates, have (so far as the exigencies of the long-continued commercial pressure and the large reduction in the value of produce permitted, which have told upon all insurance business alike) been more than compensated by the influx of fresh insurance. The Royal has never had a larger body of constituents than now.

The ratio of increase of premium during the last two years, notwithstanding the conservative policy adopted, and the diminished price of commodities, shows unmistakably that the favor of the public has grown with the growth of the Company, and has not suffered even a temporary diminution from any cause whatever.

No happier announcement can be made to the shareholders than that which is contained in the following statement—that, notwithstanding the considerable augmentation of the annual premiums collected, the entire amount of the Company's risk is very considerably less than what it has been. The total amount assured will, in all probability, improve with the improvement of commerce, whilst its effect will be still further to increase the revenue of the Company.

The beneficial effects of the new investigations made into the business, item by item, can be shown by the tabulated results which have been systematically carried on so far as has been practicable.

The difficulties in the way of making this record entirely complete are of course insurmountable; yet, like the plan originated by this Company of tracing declined lives, it may with all its unavoidable imperfections, because of great use in the conduct of the business. The value of any instance traced of a loss avoided by cautionary measures, is not in itself diminished in the slightest degree by the fact that there must necessarily be always many other like cases which escape observation altogether.

The shareholders will be gratified to learn that the amounts of loss by fire distinctly traced have been escaped by risks declined by this office since the last year's meeting, reach the large sum of £72,811. This, be it remembered, is in addition to an amount of £40,000 announced at that time to have been saved in like manner. This large amount may, however, be considered exceptional in some respects, as it is not probable that the most diligent scrutiny will suffice at all times to discover more than a moderate per centage of the amount of declined risks ultimately resulting in fire.

The following is the report from the different branches of losses which have occurred from 1st August, 1867, to 30th July, 1868, on risks declined by the Company :—

In the Agency Department		£53,901
" Home "		960
" Foreign "		13,700
" Guarantee "		4,250
		£72,811

LIFE BRANCH.

The measures announced at the last meeting of the Shareholders detailing the regulations with respect to the projected increase in the proportion to profits to be given to participating Assurers, have already had a considerable effect on the Life Branch of the Company's business.

The fact that new participating assurances will now receive three-fourths of the Profits, instead of two-thirds, as heretofore, cannot fail to induce a large influx of fresh business from this time forward.

Notwithstanding that the commercial depression referred to has considerably interfered with Life Assurance as well as Fire Insurance throughout Great Britain and its dependencies, of which this Company has shared in the effects, the progress of this department has independently of this temporary obstruction, been highly satisfactory.

The average annual amount of New Sums Assured during the three expired years of the present quinquennial period (1865, '66 and '67), is £801,000. The annual average amount of new business for last quinquennial period (1859 '64), during which the Life business had made a most remarkable spring in advance, was yet only about £688,000, whilst in the preceding like period (1854, '59) it was only £331,000.

The Lives declined during the same three years (1855, '57), number 1163, the aggregate sum proposed for Assurance thereon being £638,484, a sufficient proof of care in selection.

The mortality for the last year has been moderate.

The increase of the Life and Annuity Funds in the year 1867, after paying every claim and every expense, reaches the sum of £128,588 5s 10d. The total amount of these Funds, it will now be seen, exceeds One Million Sterling.

In 1864, after appropriating the portion of profits of the preceding five years to the shareholders, the funds stood at............£621,434 15 4
In 1865, the amount invested for the year, after paying all claims and expenses, was............ 103,116 7 4
In 1866,   do.   do.   124,165 7 5
In 1867,   do.   do.   128,583 5 10
Whilst an estimate of the first six months of 1868 shows a credit balance of about............ ......   54,000 0 0

Total sums now invested on the Life account £1,031,329 15 11

The annual increase, therefore, of the Life and Annuity Funds since the last Actuarial Report in 1864 is £118,631 14s 6d, a most satisfactory augmentation, so far, of the Actuary's estimate of £100,000 annually for the ten years immediately following that year.

DIRECTORS.

The following Directors now retire, and are eligible for re-election :—

Thomas D. Anderson, Esq., Ralph Brocklebank, Esq., Michael Bousfield, Esq., Thomas Dever, Esq., David Malcomson, Esq., William J. Marrow Esq., Francis Maxwell, Esq., M. Hyslop Maxwell, Esq.

DIVIDEND AND BONUS.

The Directors propose to the proprietors that a dividend be declared of 3s per share, and a bonus of 4s per share, together 7s per share free of income tax.

The statements contained in this report are so satisfactory that the Directors feel they need not add a single argument further to commend them to the attention of the shareholders.

CHARLES TURNER,
Chairman.

August 6, 1868.

The Chairman, after the reading of the Report made some explanatory remarks. He said that they then met under more favorable circumstances than at any time within the past three years. The accounts for 1867 gave a fairly remunerative but not an excessive profit, which in view of the adverse circumstances under which they had labored for the past three years, would be considered a very satisfactory state of affairs. After some further remarks of a general character,

he alluded to the statement for the past which he regarded as a most interesting one profit and loss account stood thus :—The the credit of the British and Foreign account 286, and American £13,987. Now the di and bonus which is the same that we have I if we deduct of paying will amount to £34,48 if we deduct that from the gross amount, w a balance of £21,892 which will stand to the of profit and loss, after we have paid out profits of 1867 a dividend and bonus of share. (Cheers.) Now, gentlemen, our Ar securities are on the whole in a pretty fair but we thought that, as this was a pros year, we should write off £4,000 as agai American securities, which would leave the of profit and loss £17,892 for the year But the reserve fund is increased by interest ed £5,261. Therefore, in the total result paying our dividend and bonus, the Royal since Company will be £23,153 better off at of 1867 than it was at the end of the yea (Applause.) Well, gentlemen, on the wl think that it is not an unsatisfactory state of With the profit and loss account as I have and with the reserve fund now standing at 174 that will make £140,066 as the am profit and loss and reserve fund, after makin deduction at the end of the year 1867. Thi an unsatisfactory result, but at the same don't wish to conceal from you at all tha reserves should be more—considerably mo they are at present. (Hear, hear.) But st are now mounting up ; we have improved o dition by £23,000 since the commencement ance Company last, besides paying the dividend. As resp Life business, the result is, I think, perhap than ordinarily encouraging. The course you have pursued on the advice of our ex actuary to give the old and new assurer fourths instead of two-thirds of our prof been attended with very favourable (Cheers.) We anticipated an increase of ti ness, and the report will show that the a tions of our excellent manager and a though they were thought rather sanguin time, have been more than fulfilled. The ago the actuary expressed his opinion that funds would be increased in the ratio of a year for the next ten years. We have i three years of that period, and the average in our life funds has been £118,316, excee estimate of our actuary by the amount of per annum. During the past year the inci been £128,000, while during the present far as it has gone, as you will see by the r the first six months of 1868, the present credit balance of £54,000. (Cheers.) think, gentlemen, is a very satisfactory affairs, and I don't think that anything any would increase your information on the The Chairman concluded by moving the and printing of the report and statemer counts.

Mr. John Torr (director), seconded the He thought they might attribute the su the Company to the steady, unwavering c tive policy they had adopted, and the un among the managers and agents of the Co which ever existed, tended strongly to th result.

The resolution, declaring a dividend an as mentioned in the report, was then adop The retiring directors were re-elected as —Thomas D. Anderson, Esq., Ralph bank, Esq., Michael Bousfield, Esq., Dever, Esq., David Malcomson, Esq., W Marrow, Esq., Francis Maxwell, Esq., M Maxwell, Esq.

The retiring auditors, Joseph Youngl Esq., and Christopher Atkinson, Esq., elected, and their yearly remuneration to £100 a year each.

Mr. Younghusband, in returning tha that they (the auditors) had examined ev ment, every account, and every vouc iking book and every security. There was not ingle doubtful or questionable security ; and y had not made a single bad debt—indeed, he ieved that they had not made a single bad debt ce the Company commenced business. (Cheers).

Mr, Atkinson, commented on the satisfactory angement and order that prevailed in the Company's office, and said that every security had sed through his hands, including the debts of 'erent properties in this country, and in Can-, and all their investments, loans, and securi- on policies, and he believed them to be all roughly sound and good. This must not only gratifying to the shareholders, but encouraging the customers of the Company, and to the pol--holders. He attributed the success of the mpany to its good management. (Cheers).

A resolution was then passed tendering the .nks of the meeting to the company's officers t agents at home and abroad for their valuable vices during the past year.

The Chairman then proposed the health of P. M. ve, Esq., the company's actuary.

Mr. Dove, after referring to the arduous period ough which the company had passed and the eps labor that had fallen to his lot during period of depression, continued—it is, how- r, well to understand that fire insurance will her now satisfy any enlarged expectations of fit, and it is better for the permanency of our titution that it should not do so. (Hear, hear.) e larger attention which is now paid to the tistics of fires will enable the offices to appor- n rates more closely to the true value of risks, i there is a general tendency in the whole body offices to protect insurers from extravagant rges. (Cheers.) The "Royal" will not forfeit now traditional character of liberality by fail- to support this principle. The prospects of Life Branch are of the most cheering charac- (Hear, hear.) This company now stands on same platform with the very best among the ny excellent institutions of the kind existing. sers.) The boon of an additional proportion the profits to the old assurers, which cannot ervise be regarded than as a voluntary act of erosity, has given a favorable feeling, not only the recipients, but likewise to assurers in all ts of the world, and this department will, I fidently hope, show happy results in the future. tory. (Cheers.) Indeed it only requires the manent adoption of the lessons of prudence ich have fallen from the Chair, and then, by d's help, the Company will not, I trust, pause its future career. (Cheers.)

he proceedings were concluded by a vote of nks to the chairman.

OMINION TELEGRAPH COMPANY.—The pros- tus of this Company is issued. At a late meet- the following gentlemen were chosen as officers the Company in Toronto :—Hon. W. Cayley, sident ; Hon. J. McMurrich, Treasurer ; Messrs. aeron & McMichael, Solicitors ; H. B. Reeve, retary ; Martin Ryan, General Superintendent.

irectors—Hon. J. McMurrich, of Bryce, Mc- rrich & Co. ; Hon. M. C. Cameron, Provincial retary ; A. R. McMaster, of McMaster & phews ; James Michie, of Fulton, Michie & Co., l George Michie & Co. ; L. Moffatt, of Moffatt, rray & Co. ; A. M. Smith, of A. M. Smith & ; Hon. W. Cayley, Toronto ; H. B. Reeve, ronto. Martin Ryan, Toronto. It is also con- plated to form local boards in Hamilton, St. tharines, &c.

$900,000 of seven per cent. Canada debentures turing 1st proximo, will be redeemed at the eceiver General's office on that date.

An elevator has just been completed in Belle- lle ; capacity, 45,000, and will load a vessel at s rate of 2,000 bushels per hour.

Mining.

MADOC GOLD DISTRICT.

(From our own Correspondent.)

Belleville, Aug. 24, 1868.

The record of the Quinte mining district, since the middle of May, contains little else than a melancholy chronicle of disappointment ; one dis- astrous failure succeeding another with such un- deviating regularity, that the thermometer of public confidence, like the mercurial thermometer in January, kept sinking until it has reached several degrees below zero. Men failed to do that which they confidently asserted they could and would do. Machinery failed to extract the gold, for the collection of which it was constructed. "Quartz leads" failed to bear out the assays, which ascribed to them rich contents of gold and silver ; and worst of all, mines failed to give pro- fitable returns to those who worked them in good faith.

First, the returns from the Richardson Mine sank from $140 per ton, (the result of the first experimental crushing in Daniels, Scott & Co.'s mill), to $4.00 per ton in their own mill, with a loss of mercury of more than double the value of the gold extracted. Next the Wyckoff process was found to be quite inadequate to deal with the refractory ores of this region, and Daniels & Co. shut up their establishment. Turley & Gilbert's mill in which the reduction effected by the pan or grind- ing process, gave for some time better results ; but having been sold to other parties, reports were circulated which impugned the authenticity of the results obtained, and insinuated a wholesale system of salting ; the consequence of which was that the mill lost the confidence of the miners, and came again into the possession of the original pro- prietors who are about removing it to another locality. Next the mill of the Bay State Com- pany, of which such great things were predicted by its projector, Dr. Otway, failed in extracting the colour of gold either from the Richardson ore, or that of their own shaft ; while scarcely a fraction of the quicksilver employed could be recovered. The mill of Mr. Berry, too, in the Township of Denbigh, although much superior in the com- pleteness of its arrangements to any of the others, gave very poor results, and is now closed. The mill erected for Severn & Co., by Mr. Caldwell, in the 11th Concession of the Township of Marmora, was at work for a few days, with every prospect of a satisfactory return, when the front plate of the boiler blew out, fortunately without doing much damage beyond the stoppage of the work. The cleaning up, so far as they had gone, gave $20.00 to the ton. A new boiler has been purchased, and the mill will be at work again in a few days. The Anglo-Saxon Company have got their works in running order at last. This is the most exten- sive concern yet established in the district. The machinery, which is a combination of the pan and Wyckoff apparatus, is of the most massive char- acter, and is worked by a 75 horse power engine. No returns have as yet been made public ; but I hear that some difficulty has been experienced from the clogging of the ore.

Several of the mines from which experimental crushings have been made in the Eldorado Mills, are loudly asserted to have been salted during the process ; returns of from $10.00 to $30.00 having been given from rock which will not yield above $1.00 to $3.00, even by fire assay. This unworthy deception is said to have been practised not so much by mining speculators, as by tradesmen and tavern-keepers in the neighborhood, in order to keep up the excitement, and bring visitors to the villages, and customers to their establishments. From all I can learn, I fear there is too much truth in these reports.

The consequence of all this is, that confidence in the mines and mills has sunk to so low an ebb, that no one here is disposed to venture another

dollar in mining stock, or mining adventure of any description.

As a climax to these mishaps, and to complete the general depression. The Richardson mine is now in the hands of the Sheriff, having been taken in execution last week. The debt of the Company exceeds $18,000.

Notwithstanding the prejudicial effect of these misfortunes, there are still some enterprising indi- viduals, chiefly from the United States, who are resolute in trying to secure the profits which they believe are to be obtained by properly conducted enterprise in this district. Among others, Messrs. Jones & Co., from Fond du Lac, Wisconsin, are about to put up works upon Lot 23, in the 12th Concession of Hungerford, in which they mean to use the Stevens Flux. Some of the existing com- panies are also making such alterations in and additions to their apparatus, as they think may enable them to get out the gold which they firmly believe to exist within the limits of their respec- tive claims ; while others are turning their atten- tion to the baser metals, and are forming Com- panies for working the veins of lead ores which are to be found in many places within the district.

Several new discoveries of gold-deposits of great apparent richness have also been made of late. In addition to those found in the 11th Concession of Marmora by Mr. Powell and Mr. Feigel, a mass of quartz has been developed on Lot 9, in the 6th Concession of the same Township which is said to exceed in richness all that has been yet found. Mr. W. Gilbert is about removing his mill from Eldorado to this Lot, and it will be worked at as early a date as possible. Mr. Jeremiah Loucks, of the same Township, has also got a quartz lead which has returned to assay by amalgamation $14.00 per ton. Quartz leads containing a pro- mising show of visible gold have also been found on Lots 6 and 9, in the 3rd Concession of Elzeyir.

In conclusion, though it has turned out exactly as I have always maintained, viz : that it is use- less to expect that every vein of quartz or dolo- mite shall contain gold ; or even that every true gold-bearing rock will yield the precious metal in paying quantity ; yet there is every reason to be- lieve that there do exist here and there in this dis- trict, beds of rock which contain deposits of ore of sufficient richness to afford a remunerative branch of industrial occupation to those who bring to their development the skill and the capital requisite to ensure commensurate returns.

NOVA SCOTIA GOLD MINING REVIEW.

We condense the following summary from the Halifax Mining Gazette for August :—

SHERBROOKE.—Work is being vigorously prose- cuted in this district. It is estimated that about 700 men are employed by the various companies. Steam mills (all Fifteen Stamps) are being erected by the Dominion, Wentworth, Canada and Meridian Companies ; and Mr. Snow has commenced a large water-mill for the mines, under his management. The Dominion mill has a highly finished appear- ance. These, when completed, will make the number in the district eleven. In addition to the older companies the following are carrying on work to a considerable extent : the Chicago, Meridian, Kingston and Sherbrooke, Crescent, Delta, Stanley, Blue Lead, Canada, Woodbine, Caledonia, Coborng and the Wentworth. The Crescent Company have found a new lead, 4½ feet thick, yielding 14 dwts. to the ton. Mr. Barnes is also sinking on the well-known "Root Hog" Lead.

The explorations on the Kingston and Sher- brooke Company's property, under Mr. Kirk- patrick's management, have brought to light a number of new leads. One of them, over a foot in thickness, shows visible gold in the various places in which it is being opened. A ton of quartz from the "Red Jacket" claims close to the west of the Russell, or Drysdale Block, yielded 12¾ ounces of gold.

Numerous gold-bearing leads have been opened on the northern part of the Wentworth property, and on five of them shafts are being sunk. Mr. Goodall is the manager of this Company.

The Woodbine Company are sinking several shafts, employing a large amount of labor and pressing on their works. A steam engine has been erected for the purpose of hoisting. Numerous buildings have also been erected.

The Caledonia property, which, with the Woodbine, is under the management of Mr. Brown, is also undergoing development.

The Cobourg Company are sinking shafts near the road on some promising leads.

The Meridian Company are pushing down their shaft on the Sears Lead—the manager, Mr. Goodall, intending, it is said, to cross out from this to the shafts further south, thus crossing the numerous leads of the Dominion Company.

The Metropolitan (formerly the Boulder), Dominion and Palmerston Companies, have resumed operations on the portions of that working which had been recently flooded. During the temporary stoppage, much new work has been done, and valuable developments made on different parts of their respective properties. Mr. Goodall, the manager of the Dominion mine, has sent to Montreal a bar of $7,000 and has yet on hand many hundred tons of rich ore, ready to be crushed.

The Wellington mine, under Mr. Snow, is sustaining its well-established reputation. A second shoot has been found in the main lead. This is another interesting proof that the ore shoots are repeated, and is of importance as shewing that the Nova Scotia gold-bearing quartz veins will be found productive to great depths.

The Hayden and Derby (also under Mr. Snow's management) and the New York and Sherbrooke, (under its experienced manager, Mr. Zwicker) continue to prosecute their operations with success.

The veins in the two deepest shafts at the Canada (formerly known as Nova Scotia) mine, are increasing in thickness. The Blue Lead is being worked at the east end of the property. Mr. Barnes, the manager, has completed the new wharf, and a good road leading to it.

The Blue Lead Company have resumed operations, and are working two newly discovered veins containing visible gold. This property gives promise of good results, and with the Blue Lead shaft again in operation, will contribute to the yield of the district.

The large property belonging to the Stanley Company is being rapidly developed, under the management of Mr. Cook, and judging from present appearances, bids fair to become a paying mine.

The Chicago Company, for the past three months, have been prospecting their valuable property, and with good results. Shafts are now being sunk on several rich leads. Their mill, formerly known as the English Company's, has been entirely remodelled by the manager, Mr. Goodall.

RENFREW.—We have no special advices, but find the Ophir Company and Colonel Allan have passed through Messrs. Huse & Lowell's hands 638 ozs. 16 dwt. 18 grs. since last publication—a sufficient proof that the district is still productive.

WINE HARBOR.—Our special report confirms the impression that this district is bound to revive, and the Commissioners returns show 367 ozs. 3 dwts. 14 grs. as the gold product of the past two months :—

The Provincial Company, under the management of Mr. Charles Eadiewriter, are employing about forty men, and are obtaining very satisfactory results. The mine has lately been visited by the President, William Workman, Esq., Mayor of Montreal. He took back with him two bars containing $2,400 worth of gold, produced during his stay at the mine. The net profits of the month preceding amounted to about $3,000. It has been discovered that a valuable lead exists close to the mouth of the Hattie lode, and as this can be easily worked by means of shafts already sunk, great profits from this source are likely to be realized for some time to come.

At the Eureka Mine the Barrasois lodes have been struck, and a shaft is being sunk upon one of them. Another shaft is being put down on what is believed to be the Major Norton Lead. The vein is of a very promising character, and is widening rapidly. The Eureka Lode is thicker in the new shaft than in the old, and here also shews gold freely. The tunnel connecting the two shafts is approaching completion. This Company is also under Mr. Eadiewriter's management.

In the Eldorado Company's tunnel, the new steam drill has got into operation, and is said to be quite successful, effecting a great saving in labor and time. All important lead has lately been discovered near the line between the property of this Company and that of the McIntosh. It comprises nearly ten feet of slate and quartz, the latter shewing many large specks of gold at the surface. Its position is north of the run of the Hattie lead.

The McIntosh and Stadacona Companies are carrying on operations on the Washington and Winsaast leads. These companies have purchased the Victoria mill and water power.

A new group of leads has been discovered north of those worked by the Orient Company. One of them contains three feet of quartz. Westward they strike into the areas belonging to the Hon. Mr. Patton. The mill of this company is being refitted, and will be running again in a short time.

OLDHAM.—This district is steadily improving owing to the perseverance of Mr. Shaffer. The last crushing from his mine gives over two ounces to the ton, and the quartz now being taken out is still improving. Other lodes in the same district are being opened and doing well.

The English Company's crusher is now in new hands, who are fitting up some novel arrangements for saving gold, so that we may soon look for new developments.

The Caledonia Company are making some alterations in their mill and preparing to mine. This property is situated in the centre of the Oldham district, and on the anticlinal axis, and when a perpendicular shaft is put down to a sufficient depth, they expect to open some good lodes. The property has changed hands and continues an average yield. Lot 595 on the Barrel Lode, belonging to L. & W. Hall, produced 12 ozs. 7 dwts. 7 grs. from a recent crushing of 8 tons.

MONTAGUE.—The Montreal association have been making explorations on their property adjoining the locations of the Albion and Union Companies, and have met with very gratifying success. The operations of the Union Company are confined to a few men working on the Belt lode. Last month's yield was 120 ounces.

UNIACKE.—The Uniacke Company of Boston have been getting 3 ounces to the ton from some of their quartz. The new boiler of the Alpha Company crusher has been fitted on its plan and the mill is again running. Another vein near the Mitchell Lead shewing a considerable amount of gold is being worked by this Company. Their twenty feet in depth. The Union Company are sinking on two large lodes within four feet of each other. The last crushing is said to have given two ounces to the ton. Mr. Barkner is still working an area adjoining, and continuing to raise equally good quartz. The Uniacke Central Company have some rich ore ready for crushing. The lead worked by the Prince of Wales Company is increasing at the rate of one inch for each five feet in going down.

The Queen Company are getting out a quantity of quartz shewing coarse gold for their new mill which is being pushed forward to completion. The building is up and the boiler and machinery already upon the ground. Since the late rains the mill of the Westlake Company has commenced running. The Company continue to add to their large stock of ore.

A new Company called the Eureka has been lately formed for working the property adjoining westward to the St Lawrence mine, and is placed under the management of Mr. S. D. Oakes.

In the property which Mr. A. Michel is interested in exploring belongs to a Company formed in Montreal. It comprises 288 areas in one block forming a perfect square, and is situated at the western extremity of the rich belt of the district being about a mile and a quarter distant from the main developments. The property is, in part limited to the Coxcomb Lake, and it is intersected to the west by the Windsor and Halifax road. I width it extends 3,600 feet on the course of the lodes, and 3,000 feet in depth or across. The work to date consists of 11,200 running feet of crosscut down to the bed-rock (consequently of varyin depth), and in 48 openings. The trenches traver the property from north to south, the principal one, which is the most easterly, having exposé 53 veins of quartz, of which the greater number have been retraced to the west by other trenches. Those 53 veins have been already all examined the depth of 5 to 6 feet by means of an excavation made upon each ; but as these veins are often di posed in groups a single excavation has sometimes sufficed for the examination of several. The quantity of rock extracted from the aforesaid excavations by means of powder, is 7,800 cut feet. These exploratory works, trenches and e cavations have required 985 days labor, the m being under the direct supervision of Mr. Tongouy, with whom we have reason to know M Michel is well pleased.

Some specimens taken from the first twent four veins, numbered from north to south, has been already submitted for tests to Dr. Dana Hay State Assayer of Boston, and a quantity of g per ton of $10, $12, $13, $20, $22, and $25, v the result of six assays, while three others o produced $2, $8, and $9. The results of the lo numbered from 25 to 53 are not yet known. A Michel is actively prosecuting the exploration by sinking further on the shafts which offer greatest inducements.

This same Montreal Company owns also 32 ar in Montague district, and 132 areas at Lawren town. The exploration of those properties entrusted to Professor H. Y. Hind, of Labra and Saskatchewan Survey fame.

LAWRENCETOWN.—This district is still attr ing a great deal of attention, and mining inter are looking up. The Shanghai property has b sold in New York for $40,000, and fresh operati are to be forthwith commenced.

The Werner property is reported to have b purchased by two parties in England, the p being $54,000. The quartz, which is being mi and put through the mill, shews gold freely. lead in Messrs. Glass and Strange's shaft is look very well.

Important discoveries have been made upon property of the Montreal Association, verifyin a remarkable manner Professor Hind's views in gard to the geological structure of this distri This property consists of 80 areas, and has l sufficiently developed to prove the existence of almost inexhaustible supply of gold-bearing qua

—A meeting was held at Ottawa a few c since to consider the expediency of building w works in that city. After a good deal of dis sion, it was resolved that it was inexpedien the present state of the city finances for the Council to undertake their construction.

THE CANADIAN MONETARY TIMES AND
INSURANCE CHRONICLE is printed every Thursday
Evening, in time for the English Mail.

Subscription Price, one year, $2, or $3 in
American currency ; Single copies, five cents each.
Casual advertisements will be charged ten cents
per line of solid nonpareil each insertion. All
letters to be addressed, "THE CANADIAN MONE-
TARY TIMES, TORONTO, ONT." Registered letters
so addressed are at the risk of the Publishers.
Cheques should be made payable to J. M. TROUT,
Business Manager, who will, in future, issue all
receipts for money.

The Canadian Monetary Times.

THURSDAY, AUGUST 27, 1868.

THE NORTHERN RAILWAY.

Toronto has a peculiar interest in the prosperity of this railway. While it brings timber, lumber, grain, flour and the etceteras of
traffic into the city and carries back into a
thriving section of country what our merchants have to sell, its steady increase of
earnings under prudent management affords
evidence from which success may be reasonably anticipated by the promoters of other
railway enterprises intended to serve the
splendid country lying to the north and west.
The Great Western and Northern keep alive
our faith in Canadian railways. We can
rejoice, therefore, in the success of the
Northern, for we know that a true spirit of
enterprise has characterised its operations.
Its increased earnings have furnished additional facilities to trade, and the efforts made
in that direction have justified anticipations.
The action of the London Board has been
liberal. The report for 1867 explained how
willingly sacrifices had been made by the
postponement of payments on account of
arrears of interest dividends, and how much
assistance had been rendered through the
negotiation of a temporary loan of £5,000
stg. Through this sacrifice the pressure of
traffic has been, to a certain extent, relieved
and although a great deal is yet to be done
in the way of addition and extension to prevent embarrassment, the schemes now well
in hand command themselves as most expedient. The line is chiefly dependent on
freight for its revenue, and considerations of
economy as well as the manifest wisdom of
serving a rapidly extending and elastic traffic
evidently impress the Management with the
importance of keeping pace with the times.
Such figures as these are refreshing :

Gross earnings—	
1859	$240,044 86
1860	332,067 01
1861	410,030 91
1862	406,238 02

Gross earnings—	
1863	406,606 55
1864	467,266 15
1865	506,748 58
1866	512,874 66
1867	561,370 25

In other words, the earnings have advanced
during the last eight years about 135 per cent.
But we do not stop at 1867. For the
half year ended June, 1868, the receipts
amounted to $275,073 34, as against $271,-
406 55, being an increase of 2.81 per cent.
over the corresponding period of 1867. The
revenue available for dividend has amounted
to $79,274, as against $75,335, and the interest dividends of both classes of bonds have
been paid and a balance of $29,567 carried
forward to credit of interest fund. It must
be remembered too, that the exceptional
security of last winter had an injurious effect
on the traffic, while it increased the working
expenses.

While we reflect on the progress made by
this railway, we should also consider how
fair its future seems. The Muskoka district,
the settlements on the north shore of the
Georgian Bay and the shores of Lake Huron
and Superior with their mineral treasures,
all young, all full of promise, will undoubtedly
develope into fruitful districts, and supply
ever increasing freights.

THE ROYAL INSURANCE COMPANY.

The report of this company for the year
1867, is given in another column with a synopsis of the proceedings at the late annual
meeting of shareholders. The premiums of
the year in the Fire branch amounted to the
sum of £460,533, being an increase of £13,-
282. Increased vigour has been used in investigating proposals for insurance. Though special risks
have been retested, and such rates exacted as
the unusual danger justified, yet the influx
of new business has more than compensated
for the effects of the conservative policy
adopted. Premiums have increased while
the company's risks have been considerably
lessened. The causes which have acted on
the accounts of the English Insurance Companies are traced to the convictions obtained
in cases of incendiarism, the establishment
of a moderate increase in rates, and the better
classes of risks thereby gained, the advantages enjoyed by staunch companies, over
evanescent and carelessly managed companies, and the foreshadowing of a coming
act for the judicial investigation into suspicious fires.

In the Life Branch the annual average
amount of new business for the period 1865-6
and 7, is £601,000. The increase in the Life
and Annuity Funds, after paying claims and
expenses, reached the sum of £128,583, and
the total amount of these funds exceeds one

million sterling. The mortality for the year has been moderate.

The satisfaction that pervaded the remarks made at the meeting, appears to have been fully justified. Soundness within the company, and activity and appreciation without were quite sufficient to provoke the brightest anticipations. The services of Mr. Dove, the highly esteemed Manager of the Company, were fittingly acknowledged, and a just tribute paid to his efforts in promoting the success of the institution.

WHO'S TO BLAME?

The water supply of Toronto for fire purposes has long been in an unsatisfactory state. It has at last degenerated into a tri-parte squabble—the parties to which are the City Council, the Fire department and the Water Company. Like an Irishman's feud which is revived on the occasion of subsequent spree, this quarrel breaks out anew after every fire. Fault-finding and recrimination are freely exchanged through the medium of the daily press, and then the matter again subsides into its wonted quiescence till the next conflagration gives fresh impetus to the "irrepressible conflict" between fire and water. But this matter has a serious—a very serious aspect. The question just now is, who is responsible for the burning of Bell's house on the 16th. The first engine that arrived on the spot was attached to a hydrant which was out of order, causing a delay of twenty minutes, and also causing, according to Mr. Ashfield, the Chief Engineer of the Fire Department, the destruction of Mr. Bell's building. The matter being clear thus far, the question arises: Who is responsible for keeping the hydrants in repair? Respecting this, the Water Company say over the signature of their Superintendent:

"The Water Company do not consider that "they have anything whatever to do with "the hydrants, and had so notified the city "authorities, shortly before the fire referred "to. The fact that several of the hydrants "were out of repair was specially brought "under the notice of the authorities by the "Company, but nothing has been done to "remedy this defect."

The statement of the company is perhaps correct that it is not its duty *now* to keep the hydrants in repair. An Alderman is reported to have admitted this at a late meeting of the City Council. Whose duty then is it to attend to this important matter? Very little public attention is just now directed to the subject, but in case of an extensive fire, the delinquents would be called sharply to account. We repeat the enquiry—Who's to blame?

This affair should be settled—definitely and permanently settled, and at once. Perhaps it is unreasonable, accepting the popular view, to expect an Aldermanic body to settle anything except themselves, still we venture to implore them to give a little attention to this water question, and at least relieve us of the dread uncertainty of being all burnt out through a misunderstanding! The present state of things has lasted long enough; a change cannot come too soon.

MINING RIGHTS AND PRIVILEGES.*

It is interesting to review the conflicting opinions among text writers respecting the rights of the Crown to mines and minerals. Among the Romans, gold, silver and other precious metals usually belonged to the State, under the Civil Law, whilst all other minerals, mines and quarries belonged to the owner of the soil. Blackstone says the right to mines has its original from the King's prerogative of coinage, in order to supply him with materials, and, therefore, those mines which are properly royal, and to which the King is entitled when found, are only those of silver and gold. The rights of the French Crown relatively to the rights of the proprietors, were settled by ordinance of Charles VI. The payment of ten per cent. as a regalian right was exacted, and the enactment embraced not only gold and silver, but all mines and minerals. The commissions of the Governors of Canada, granted by the French Crown, enjoined them to search carefully for mines and minerals, reserving the tenth part of gold and silver, and giving them, as regards the other mines, "what might belong to them of the rights thereto," to sustain the local government. This is taken to show that an exclusive right to gold and silver mines was not claimed, but that the Crown merely reserved a certain regalian right, not as an impost or duty, but as a recognition of the sovereign authority. About 1677 the French Government was very liberal, or took little interest in the mineral resources of Canada, for Letters Patent were presented by the King to one De Lagny des Brigandieres, and we suppose "Germain Davin, essayeur et affineur," and others, set to work pursuant thereto, "de faire ouvrir les mines, minieres et mineraux, et purifier les metaux qui se peuvent trouver en ce pays."

We have on our statute book an act relating to gold mining,—17 & 28 Vic., c. 9, and the act of 1865 amending it. These are said to be based on the theory that when the pro-

*Practical suggestions on Mining Rights and Privileges in Canada, by A. M. Hart, Barrister-at-Law of Lower Canada, and Counsellor-at-Law of New York.—Montreal: JOHN LOVELL.

prietor of the soil is either unable or unwilling to work the mines, which may be disclosed on his property, the Crown, from considerations of public policy, may concede the right to other persons. The part granted by the Crown, which form the l of all our western titles to land reser with very few exceptions, to the Crown mines and minerals. The Mining Act, pa by the Legislature of Ontario, at its re sitting, provides that the proprietors o private lands heretofore granted, or w hereafter may be granted, situate within mining divisions, shall have the right against the Crown, to mine for gold and ver upon such lands, subject to royalty the provisions of the act. The nominal propriation by the Crown of alluvial diggi has set at rest many questions that m have arisen with riparian proprietors. acts above referred to are still in force ir Province of Quebec, but in Ontario the passed last session substitutes new re tions in this province.

All necessary rights are comprised grant without which it would be useless lease of mines, or a proprietor's licens sink mines, carries with it a right to us much of the surface as may be necessary working the mines. Between a lease a license there is a difference in effect. former is exclusive of the rights of all oth the latter is not necessarily exclusive o rights of the grantor who retains the rig work himself for the same minerals, license others to do so. The interest th license purports to convey is what is k as an incorporeal freehold, and such an i est in land cannot be effectually create an instrument not under seal. Wh license has been granted under circumst which show that the personal skill or k edge of the grantee is a material ingredi the contract, the right cannot be assign

There are many other matters although of practical interest at the pr time when mining operations attract so a:tention we cannot notice, but for inf tion regarding such we refer inquirers t Hart's useful work. It embodies the of much study, yet its simplicity bring subject within the grasp of laymen of ord intelligence.

GRAND TRUNK RAILWAY.

A communication which we publish, by a merchant of this City, respecti freight arrangements of the Grand T collates a number of facts that are wor the attention of those proprietors of th in England who are now seeking to pla

s of the Company in a better position.
act that American freight was, and is,
carried *at a loss* is nothing new. Mr.
ges, we think, has stated that more than
in his reports. But we were not pre-
l for the extraordinary results which
figures point to. Working for nothing,
paying expenses is eschewed by most
e as an undesirable way of spending
time, but it seems to have fallen to the
f our great railway to carry American
actions nearly on these terms, trusting
her sources to make good the adverse
ce so created. This is justified by Mr.
ges in this way : it is necessary to carry
se low rates in order to get through
t at all : this through freight cannot be
ased with ; the business must be retain-
whatever cost, till the "temporary"
ciation of American currency disappears,
cannot be regained. Several questions
here ; are not the Company paying "too
for their whistle ?"—is the depreciation of
ican currency likely to be any more
porary" than the existence of the Grand
k itself, if its credit be not improved,
ould it not be better to do a small pay-
usiness, for the time being, with loss
g stock and reduced annual outlay for
lant and repairs to the permament way,
to do a large non-paying business, in
the increase of loss and of traffic go
er ? It is these heavy through trains
are experiencing a strong trying on the permanent
s well as on the rolling stock. More
is wanted on these points.

MONTREAL vs. TORONTO.

active efforts of the merchants of To-
to head off Montreal in the trade with
rn Canada, seem to have borne fruit.
leading commercial organ of the east,
Montreal *Herald* displays commendable
r in the following, which we extract
that paper of Saturday last :—

ur own Province will be in a decidedly
er position to meet its obligations than
as last year, on account of the crops
ing out so much superior, and although
er Canada must be fully as well off as
she was in 1867, it is very doubtful if
treal will benefit in future so much by
prosperity. It is quite natural for
se doing business in the West, to con-
as much of that trade as possible to
r own territory, and we confess to have
rved a most vigorous effort in Toronto
prevent so large a share of the trade so
essary to the maintainance of Montreal
coming beyond the first named place.
attempt has not by any means failed ;
the contrary, it has succeeded, perhaps
degree which at first was hardly looked
Lately Western merchants have been
mulated by the low rates of through
ght from Liverpool to Toronto ; in not

"a few cases, goods having been laid down
"at their doors for less than was being paid
"to this port. This, if only a comparatively
"small advantage is one which will be made
"use of against the trade of this port, and
"while business here has ruled with unusual
"quietness since last fall, it may be that what
"has been taken from Montreal by compe-
"tition has rendered it more depressing."

UNITED STATES CHAMBER OF LIFE INSUR-
ANCE.—An extra of the *Monitor* informs us
that the Chamber met at Saratoga, August 19.
Some discussion took place as to the propriety
of requiring the data of policies *seriatim*, it
being contended that a valuation by groups
would answer every purpose. The rule, however, was allowed to stand. A Committee
was appointed to nominate a suitable person
for ACTUARY-IN-CHIEF, and to name the salary
to be attached to the office. This Committee
will report in November. Some suggested
$5,000 and others $10,000 as proper sums.
After some other business the meeting adjourned.

PHENIX INSURANCE COMPANY.—In giving
a list of Companies, last week, which do not
intend to comply with the Insurance Act, we
included the Phenix of Brooklyn. This we
did from information furnished us which we
learn proves to be incorrect. We now
hear from the Toronto agent, Mr. C.
G. Fortier, that the Company has no intention of withdrawing from the Dominion.

Communications.

WOODEN RAILWAYS.

The Editor Monetary Times.

SIR,—Some correspondence on the subject of
" Wooden Railways," which was published in the
Peterborough *Review*, for the information of those
interested in opening up the rear of the County of
Peterborough, was noticed a short time ago in
your journal.

I have just returned from a visit to the Railway
particularly referred to by my correspondent, Mr.
Hulbert, and a short account of it may perhaps be
of interest to your readers. The party consisted
of Mr. Morris, M.P., Mr. Cartwright, M.P., Col.
D. E. Boulton, Mr. George Kirkpatrick, of Kingston, and myself. I mention these names merely
to shew that the subject of "Wooden Railways,"
for our undeveloped country, is now attracting
some attention in different parts of Ontario.

The Wooden Railway commences on the Water-
town Railway, 22 miles from Ogdensburgh, 2 miles
past the De Kalb Junction. Its length is 24 miles
to the Clifton Iron Mines, or mountain, which is
in the Adirondack range, and in what is known
as John Brown's Tract. In this distance it rises
no less than 1,100 feet. There is hardly any
cutting, but the road is carried clear up and over
the hills. There are three or four grades of 285
feet in the mile, and some short pitch even over
that. In place of earthwork, trasselwork is used
to a very great extent, and this generally of a rude
but strong construction—cross logs. The line is
a particularly difficult one, and considerable
engineering skill has been displayed, in the manner in which it has been carried over rapid streams
and rocky ravines. Many of the curves are very

sharp, and there is no great portion of the line—
at least the part that we traversed—at all straight.
We commenced our journey near the next little
village of Hermon, and had about 19 miles of
rail, and the chief rise in the road commences at
that point. We travelled at a considerable disadvantage, the engine being a miserable affair, of a
very weak constitution, with a small, upright
boiler, two cylinders facing it, one of which we
afterwards discovered was out of gear ; so with
one lung gone, we were not surprised at its *wheez-
ing* and panting as it breasted the tremendous
hills. However, with two cars loaded with bricks
and one with lime, we did manage to get safely up
to the Iron mountain. There we found large
steel works in the course of construction by a
Company prepared with capital to the extent of
$150,000. The ore, which contains from 65 to 70
per cent. of iron, is put in the furnaces, (like
long box stoves), where it is "treated" with charcoal and blasts of carbon, and is turned out the
purest steel. The Company expects to turn out
about 50 tons per day. A Steel Rail manufactory
is about to be erected shortly. These rails, which
will be sold at a moderate price, will, in the estimation of Mr. Hulbert, before very long, supersede iron rails ; and it is in contemplation in the
future to lay down the rails on the wooden road.
The Iron Mountain is all iron, nearly pure ; no
tunnelling or sinking shafts is necessary, the mountain has simply to be cut away. There are now
about six different branches of the road striking
into the mountain at various points. The upper
part of the road, about 2½ miles from the mountain to the youthful village of Clifton, was completed about a year ago to bring the iron down to
the smelting works which are there in full blast,
and along this portion trains were run nearly all
the winter. The furnace, which is of enormous
thickness, is filled with iron and charcoal, in due
proportions, to the height of 36 feet, where there
is a platform conveniently opening out on the top
of the bank, the furnace commencing at the bottom. The crusher is worked by water power ; it
is a heavy iron wedge working at an angle against
a fixed iron block. The wedge works on a pin, the
bottom always in the same position, nearly close
to the block, the top about a foot from the block,
oscillating forwards and backwards. The ore is
thrown in and is gradually crushed smaller and
smaller, dropping with its own weight, until it
falls out the right size—about that of a hen's egg.
It appeared to me to be the best principle for a
crusher, even for gold quartz, as it can be adjusted
to any degree of fineness. The cost is about $1200
U. S. currency, and the machine would be an
admirable one for crushing stones for macadamiz-
ing roads, saving time, money and human labor,
generally considered of a degrading character.
The "General" who was superintending the boiler
shewed as their enormous charcoal houses, where
they always keep a reserve of 300,000 bushels for
emergencies. If charcoal can be used with such
excellent results in both iron and steel works,
cannot our Canadian capitalists be induced to put
a little money into smelting works in this country ?
From Clifton we took with us about 25 tons of
ore ; the grades being of course chiefly down hill,
but some of them being ascents of 70 feet to the
mile. With the new engine which Mr. Hulbert
expects immediately, there is no doubt that he
can take 50 tons with safety and at a fair rate of
speed—eight or ten miles an hour. The day we
were there, the General Superintendent of the
Company authorised him to at once order several
new engines and cars, which will enable him to
take out 300 tons a day, besides the ore supplied
to the steel works on the mountain. A good deal
of ore is shipped by the Iron R. R. to different
points for smelting.

The Company own about 74,000 acres. They
supplied and are now supplying Mr. Hulbert with
funds for construction of road and purchase of
rolling stock ; Mr. Hulbert getting out the ore
himself under an arrangement with the Company,
paying a royalty and selling it himself.

We asked the Superintendents of the Steel Works and Iron Works, whether they were satisfied with the working of the road, they replied—"perfectly more powerful engines are only needed, and these are on their way."

The present engine, by the way, was hauled over a hilly country for 20 miles.

In the letters which you reprinted, a statement appeared giving a particulars of construction of the road to which I will refer your readers. The sleepers employed are not adzed. The notch for the rails is made by machine, the wedges; two at each notch, are made by an adapted shingle machine from the waste of the maple rails, which are easily sawn in an ordinary mill. Most of the rails that we saw were good, and the part that had been used for a year for heavy work had worn well. Mr. Hulbert gives the average "life" of a rail at five years. There is not the slightest difficulty in replacing the old rails with new. A few minutes suffice to unwedge the rail take it up and lay down and wedge up another. The mill cannot warp sideways being tightly notched in, every yard the wood being made to take the curve in a way that would be impossible with iron. The curves were pronounced to be beautifully laid. This road which was a particularly difficult and expensive one to make, was constructed at a cost of $7,000 U. S. currency, or $5,000 gold a mile, but in an ordinary country such a road can be laid down for much less. A short line of road which Mr. Hulbert made a few years ago was made for $4,000 a mile, and he is willing to contract to carry the Clifton road right through a mountainous country for 150 miles at $4,000 gold a mile. In a back country, where wood is only too plentiful, it seems probable that a Wooden Railway can be laid down at from $2,000 to $3,000 a mile. We were all satisfied that a considerable traffic can be carried over such a road, that steeper grades and sharper curves can safely be made use of, that freight may be taken at the rate of about 10 and passengers about 20 miles an hour, without more risk than over an Iron Road. I may add that the rough passenger car that we rode in had no springs but the bumping was by no means severe.

Wooden Railways appear to me to be the very thing that are wanted in this country. I do not think that they will ever take the place of Iron Railways where capital can be obtained for either, but as feeders to the main line, and for the purpose of opening up the country, I believe they will be found to be of the greatest benefit. In our back country all the material is there at hand, and nothing is required but superintendence and labour; the labour is not of a specially skilled description, but is of just the kind to suit the inhabitants of the country, and the care of the railway can safely be entrusted to them, the repairs requiring much the same kind of work that they are in the habit of doing every day.

I must now no longer trespass on your space, but what I have written may, I hope, help still further to direct the attention of the public to a subject which I, in common with others, believe will prove of vast importance to this Canada of ours.

I am sir, yours truly,
CHARLES JAS. BLOMFIELD.
Toronto, Aug. 25, 1868.

GRAND TRUNK RAILWAY.

Editor Canadian Monetary Times.

SIR,—There has been a good deal said and written, both here and in England, in reference to the present position and management of the Grand Trunk Railroad, and I see it noticed they intend applying, or have applied, to the Government of Ontario for a grant of land, and to the Dominion Government for other assistance. This being the case, I think it desirable the public should know before such aid is granted the unjust policy this Company are now and have been pursuing towards this country in favor of the United States, and now lay before them the following facts in reference to the rates of freight charged :—

Rate from Chicago to Boston on
  flour and meal, Am cy............... 95c
Out of which road pays,
Dockage and shipping in Chicago...   3c
Agent's wages, say...................   1c
Boat from Chicago to Sarnia 25 per
  cent............................... 24c
Portland to Boston................... 12c
                                      ——
                                      40c
Grand Trunk gets in Am cy.......... 55c
Which is equal to 38½c gold, from Sarnia to Portland 798 miles, or less than ½c per ton per mile.

Rate from Chicago to St. John, N.B. $1 15
Dockage and shipping on flour and
  meal...............................   3c
Agents wages.........................   1c
Boat from Chicago to Sarnia 25 per
  cent............................... 20c
Portland to St. John, 20c gold...... 28c
                                      ——
                                      61c
Grand Trunk gets in Am cy.......... 54c
Which is also less than ½c per ton per mile.

Rate from Chicago to Toronto on
  flour and meal..................... 50c
Dockage and shipping.................   3c
Agents' wages........................   1c
Boat from Chicago to Sarnia gets 49
  per cent........................... 24½c
                                      ——
                                      28½c
Grand Trunk gets in Am cy.......... 21½c
Which is equal to 14c gold, or less than 9-10c per ton per mile.

Rates from Chicago to Montreal on
  flour and meal..................... 79c
Out of which road pays,
Dockage and shipping................   3c
Agents' wages........................   1c
Boat from Chicago to Sarnia 29 per
  cent............................... 20 3-10
                                      ——
                                      24 3-10
Grand Trunk gets in Am cy.......... 45 7-10
Which is equal to 32c gold, or less than 65-100c per ton per mile.

Contrast the rates on Canadian productions to Toronto.

Sarnia to Toronto $35 per car, over 2c per ton per mile.

Stratford to Toronto, $28 per car, over 3c per ton per mile.

Guelph to Toronto, $21 per car, over 4½c per ton per mile.

Brampton to Toronto, $15 75 per car, over 7½c per ton per mile.

The summer rate per tariff to Montreal from all stations west of Toronto is about 1½c per ton per mile, but as a great compliment, if you will not mention it, they will take grain from Stratford to Montreal for 15 cents per bushel, which is 1½c per ton per mile, but to Toronto they can make no reduction from the tariff. I do not say that the through rates to Montreal and Portland in Canadian productions are too high, for it is an acknowledged fact that no railroad can pay working expenses that does not get 1½c per ton per mile ; but I do say the rates charged per ton per mile from all stations west to Toronto are exorbitant, and go to balance the loss on through freight from the United States.

Some time since they reduced these rates from here to Halifax and St. John, so they got about 1c per ton per mile to Portland ; but from stations west where there is no water competition, they are still, I believe, getting 1½c per ton per mile. The question is asked every day why so many emigrants pass through the West. The answer is "Land is cheaper there and the pr... tions are worth more," as the cost of trans... tion to the seaboard is less than from the Pr... of Ontario, and carried by railroads built British capital, and in which the producers United States have no interest except to get productions carried at a loss to the road of 1 cent, and to make this up they charge exor rates on the productions of Ontario. The Trunk freight trains from Sarnia to Portland sist of fourteen cars for which they get $38. car, or $532 per train ; distance 798 miles, the same number of cars from Sarnia to To... distance only 168 miles, they get $490, o less than to Portland.

I could continue these calculations, but I have given sufficient to satisfy all wh... Grand Trunk Railway is doing for Ontar... will now show you how it stimulates trad Halifax and St. John. I, among others sugar and molasses consigned to use for sale Halifax. The best rate of freight the Trunk would give was 37½c per 100 lbs., th... When in New York last month I called office, and enquired what they would take from New York to London, Ont., for, and surprise found that they would take it f... (American currency) per 100 lbs. and d lighterage themselves, which costs 5c per 1... which would leave the road 32c American rency, or 23c gold, which is 14c per 100 lbs. London from New York than to Toronto Halifax. No wonder our merchants canno West India produce [in Halifax, or the mer there ship it here for sale by the Grand Railway.

It is amusing to see the calculation m England, that a railroad should be work 60 per cent of its earnings. How can it costs 1½c per ton per mile, and the road ge than ½c per ton per mile ; or in other wor Grand Trunk gets 50c for what it costs then to earn. Notwithstanding all this, the bo ers think the road should be worked for cent of its earnings ; if so what an exo rate of freight they must get on the produc Ontario to make up the loss on American Ontario to make up the loss on American

Your obedient servant,
T. C. CHISH...

August 26, 1868.

PROVINCIAL INSURANCE COMPA

Editor of the Monetary Times.

SIR,—I have read your remarks on the statement of the "Provincial Insurance Co. much interest, and fully agree with your statement, "Capital Subscribed," is $470,760.

Referring to their advertisement in the Times of this City. I find their "Sub Capital" put down in large figures at $1,7 a difference of something over $1,272,000. Which figures are correct ? Can you your readers ?

Yours respectfully,
Enqu
Hamilton, August 22, 1868.

Financial.

MONTREAL MONEY MARKET

(From our own Correspondent.)

MONTREAL, AUGUST 25

Financial.—Money continues very e the banks are anxious to discount, but very little good paper offering, seven per the nominal price, but six has been taken instances for unobjectionable bills. Owin lightness of imports, a great part of tl usually employed in paying duties is no on the market, and as there is a total a ulation it is difficult to invest it for short s. As I predicted, your silver combination already pretty well fallen through; Hamilton Ottawa have both relapsed and I expect To- o will soon follow, these private combinations r last long. Stocks of all sorts rule high and n demand. Bank of Montreal has, however, ed to 133½. Full quotations of stocks and es will be found in our stock lists. The price ilver to-day is, buying 4½, selling 4¾. Green- s buying 31¼ to 31½, selling 31 dis. Gold ts, par. Exchange on New York, buying 31 1¼, selling 30¾ dis.

TORONTO STOCK MARKET.

(Reported by Pellatt & Osler, Brokers.)

here was a good average business done in ks this week; but the demand exceeds the ly.

ink Stock.—There were sales of Montreal at to 135 the market closing at 134½. British ering at 104, with buyers at 103. Transac- s in Ontario are reported at 98 to 98½, clos- with buyers and sellers at the latter rate. have to quote an advance of three per cent. in al Canadian; considerable sales having taken e at 85 to 85½. Commerce sold at 103½ to 103¾, is in great demand. Gore is held at 50. chants sold at 105 to 105½ and 106, and there good demand. Molson's is wanted at 110. City 102 would be paid; none in market. People closed at 107½; the books are now d for the payment of dividend on the 1st ember. No Nationale in Market. There are ers of Jacques Cartier at 106. Mechanics, on, and Quebec nominal.

ebentures.—There were sales of Currency 5 per s. at 90½, 90, and 89½. No sixes in market. minion Stock is offered at par. Toronto are l offering at rates to pay 7 per cent. interest. ere were considerable sale of County at rates to abont 6¼ per cent. interest.

'undries.—City Gas sold at 105 and is in de- nd. Building Society Stock is much sought for, none offered except some Freehold which sold 03 to 104. Montreal Telegraph is wanted at to 135. Canada Landed Credit sold at 62 to . A few good Mortgages were negociated at per cent. There is a fair supply of money good securities.

Insurance.

MONTREAL ASSURANCE COMPANY.

'he following correspondence between this upany and Mr. Harvey, of the Finance Depart- it, will explain itself:—

MONTREAL ASSURANCE OFFICE,
Montreal, 21st July, 1868.

HARVEY, Esq.,
Dept. of Minister of Finance, Ottawa.

SIR,—I duly received your circular letter, convey- copy of the Insurance Act of last Session. is Company was authorized to transact Fire urance business by the special ordinance of Province of Lower Canada, 3rd & 4th Vic., . 37; Life and Marine business by the Act of late Province of Canada, 6 Vic. cap. 22; and an Marine, by the Act 13 & 14 Vic., cap. 41. is Company has never transacted any Life In- ance business; it withdrew its Fire Insurance iness from the late Province of Canada West ee years ago, and that branch is now restricted the Province of Quebec. Its Inland Marine iness is confined to the Provinces of Ontario l Quebec, these forming the late Province of ada, by the Legislature of which it was author- d to transact that description of business. Un- these circumstances, I am advised that it is not necessary that this Company should take out a license under the Act referred to.

I am, sir, your obedient servant,
(Signed), WM. MURRAY, Manager.

AUDIT OFFICE, OTTAWA,
July 23rd, 1868.

DEAR SIR,—In reply to your favor of the 21st, I have the honor to state that you are without doubt correctly advised, and that it is not necessary that for the transaction of the Insurance business specified in your letter, you should take out a license under our new law. Will you, however, allow me to add that the four Chief Ontario offices have deposited $17,000 each, and will receive their license on the first prox., and that it would be very pleasing to this department, were your office, and indeed, all Canadian offices, to fall in with the insurance policy of the Government. This would stengthen our hands in dealing with foreign Companies, and, perhaps, conduce more than any other step to the building up of a sound and strong insurance interest among ourselves.

I have the honor, to be, dear sir,
Your obedient servant,
(Signed), ARTHUR HARVEY.

To Wm. Murray, Esq., Manager Montreal Assurance Office, Montreal.

MONTREAL ASSURANCE OFFICE,
Montreal, 8th August, 1868.

ARTHUR HARVEY, Esq., Audit Office, Ottawa.

DEAR SIR,—I duly received your favor of the 23rd ult., which would have had my earlier attention but for absence from the city. Had this Company been transacting any business at the time, requiring a compliance with the Act, the deposit would, of course, have been made; as it is it would afford the Directors pleasure to meet the views of the Department, could that be done without entailing the actual loss which would result from a transfer of the funds of the Company from present securities paying from eight to ten per cent into bonds returning but six per cent.

I observe that several foreign Companies have deposited various descriptions of securities, and if a similar course of proceeding on the part of this Company would be satisfactory to the Government, the directors would be happy to transfer the amount required, $50,000, in Montreal Bank stocks, reserving always power to draw the dividends on the same. Be good enough to advise me if this arrangement would be likely to answer, and oblige,

Dear sir, your obedient servant,
(Signed), WM. MURRAY, Manager.

REPORT OF THE CONNECTICUT INSURANCE COMMISSIONER.

We give below some extracts from this report which will be found interesting:

At the present time there are fifty-one Fire Insurance Companies incorporated by other States, doing business in this State under Certificates of Authority from this Department.

These institutions are sustained by capitals amounting to $18,400,000, and they have also in earned and unearned premiums, interest, &c., the further sum of $15,403,500, making in gross assets $33,808,590 all of which are held liable for insurances amounting to $1,921,481,127.

The severe losses of 1866 were not repeated in full measure last year, therefore Fire Insurance Companies now present a better state of finances, but losses are still very heavy, and some means should be devised to either diminish fires, or avoid insurances which seem now to be too freely taken.

It is now an established fact, that almost any city or compact town can establish water-works which will pay the interest on the cost, by furnishing water to water motors, for light machinery, leaving at the same time power by day, and especially by night, free for protection against fire, without cost.

In all cases where the water head creates power to a water hydrant, equal to a steam fire engine, such hydrant is equal to a fire engine, and better too, for it furnishes its own power and water, and saves the cost of the steamer, fuel, &c., besides the hydrant is always ready day or night, the instant the water is needed.

The gross receipts for premiums of the fifty-one Fire Insurance Companies doing business in this State, were for the year 1867, $21,425,764, and their losses paid amounted to $13,180,544.

The progress of life insurance is very rapid at the present time, indicating extraordinary activity on the part of solicitors and agents, to whom large allowances, as commissions and fees, for the services they render, are paid.

There are at the present time twenty-six life insurance companies incorporated by other States, doing business in this State, under certificates of authority from this department.

All but six have specific capitals, amounting to $2,390,000; their gross assets amount to the sum of $76,389,583, of which there is unrealized, in commuted commissions, dues from agents and premiums not yet collected, quarterly and semi-annual premiums not yet due, advance in the market value of U. S. securities and bonds and Stocks, in all, a sum not less than $24,748,200.

The liabilities of these companies for policies in force amount to $505,133,793, and their outstanding dividends, in various forms, amounts to over $20,000,000.

That these life insurance companies are sound and reliable, cannot be doubted: that they will prosper, is almost equally certain, but such policy holders as believe that life insurance companies can be conducted and perpetuated without absorbing, annually, a part of the premiums paid in, either deceive themselves or allow others to do it.

It is true, that now and then losses will favor the company, by falling below the expected annual average; but sooner or later losses will overtake the company, and each company should keep its accumulations advancing, in order to meet the mortality which time is sure to bring upon them.

The most favorable system of dividends for both the companies and the insured would seem to be that which leaves the dividends with the company, as an addition to the amounts insured, to become a part of the policy and payable with it.

In regard to the standard rates of interest to be adopted in making calculations for life insurance companies in the United States, but little need be said; for while it is well known that six per cent per annum is the lowest legal standard of any State, and runs up to 10 per cent and more in many States, it is a retrograde movement to introduce English standards, or to try and drive American life insurance companies down to English rates of interest.

There seems to be a determination to force upon American life insurance companies the low standard of English life insurance tables, based upon four or five per cent of interest. Such an effort indicates a singular theory of financial affairs in the United States; for though money is more plenty than ever before, the nation, the States, and most of the cities and towns are borrowers, and very little money is borrowed as low as six per cent per annum, and billions are and will be borrowed by the States, and by individuals on improved real estate, at rates varying from seven to ten per cent per annum: besides those who borrow at national banks pay at the rate of eight per cent per annum, including what is called exchange or undrawn deposits, and no moneyed corporation lends without the borrower pays the money taxes, be it lent to the State or to the individual borrower.

So long as the vast territory of the United States requires money, it will command a high rate of interest, and the attempt to adjust life insurance in this country on a basis of interest on money, common on the Island of Great Britain, where it is a drug, is as absurd as would be the attempt to adjust a republican form of government on the basis of crown titles and entailed estates.

It may be said comparatively, that while Great Britain is finished, the United States are but just commenced, and that money will command, for the next hundred years, on an average, not less than seven per cent per annum interest.

As a matter of course, the *less* the rates of interest, the *greater* the annual premium must be; and the *greater* the rate of interest, the *less* the premium fund, and the fund on which annuities rest.

Was not this last suggestion well founded, the largest life company in this State, and such companies as have followed (as far as they could) their example, could not practice life insurance so liberally. They avail themselves of the highest American standards and the best of security.

When the State of New York reduces its legal standard of interest down to five per cent per annum, and can fund its own debt at five per cent per annum, and other States and the nation can fund their debts at the same rate, it would seem reasonable to force life insurance companies down to that rate of interest in making computations, but such an event is so far in the future, as to exonerate any anxious official from all responsibility for the hereafter in this particular.

FIRE RECORD.

MONTREAL, Aug. 25.—I have only one fire to report, viz.: the out-buildings of three houses in St. Elizabeth Street; the back parts of two of the houses were seriously injured. The total damage will amount to about $4,000; the insurance was in the British America, but what that Office will lose is not yet ascertained.

INSURANCE DEPOSITS.—The Scottish Provincial Insurance Company has replaced the British three per cent. consolidated annuities, provisionally deposited with the Receiver General by a cash deposit of £10,309 5s sterling. A license has accordingly been issued bearing date July 31st. The London & Lancashire Life Assurance Company has a cash deposit of $50,171.93, and has received a license.

Railway News.

NORTHERN RAILWAY.—Traffic Receipts for week ending 15th August, 1868.

Passengers......................	$2,586 45
Freight.........................	5,647 04
Mails and sundries...........	260 54
Total receipts for week......	$8,494 03
Corresponding week 1867..	10,678 40
Decrease............	$2,184 37

GREAT WESTERN RAILWAY.—Traffic for week ending 7th August, 1868.

Passengers	$29,452 91
Freight and live stock......	25,460 89
Mails and sundries...........	2,042 75
	$56,956 55
Corresponding Week of '67·	62 652 20
Decrease............	$5,695 65

Commercial.

Montreal Correspondence.

(From our own Correspondent.)

MONTREAL, 25th Aug., 1868.

Since my last, business in some branches shews signs of awakening activity, but, with the exception of Dry Goods, the fall trade will scarcely set in before the end of next month, and although the volume of business done in Canada may be equal to that of last year, still, I doubt if Montreal individually will do its usual amount. This is caused by the direct importations to the west being larger than usual, and Toronto is trying its best to secure as much as possible of the country trade which has usually been transacted here; freights and money have both been cheap, and your large merchants have always been jealous of our monopoly, so it would seem that they have taken a more than usually strong stand to wrest the western trade from Montreal, and their efforts must affect us to a certain extent, still, Montreal being the great monetary centre, the bulk of business must be transacted here. The weather for the last week has been hot and dry. This will enable farmers to secure their late crops in splendid condition.

Our PRODUCE market has been very quiet. Buyers and sellers differing widely in their estimate of values. Strong baker's flour has receded to $7.50, and a sale of 1000 bbls., City brand, was made to-day, for September delivery at $5.75. Holders are anxious to work off their light stocks while prices continue high, having lost faith in their remaining so; the new flour, when brought forward, will find a comparatively empty market, and both buyers and sellers will be able to start from a new stand point, without any particular loss on either side in the way of accumulation of old stock. Nothing doing in wheat. Peas sell by the car at $1.50 per 60 lbs.; Oats at 53c. to 55c. per 32 lbs, and Corn at 81c. to 82c. per 56 lbs. for mixed western. These prices are nominal. For dairy produce, the demand for shipment continues. Butter is scarce, and commands readily 17c to 21c., according to quality; should the dry weather continue, I fear the market will rule high during the fall, as buyers from here have scoured most parts of the country, securing the farmer's present stocks, and also to a considerable extent their future make, at long prices. The demand for Cheese for shipment to England still continues, and all offering is readily picked up at 10 to 10½ for factory. Were it not for Ashes, Butter and Cheese, our steamers would have to go light to Quebec to load back, as there is nothing else in the way of freight offering. The rates of freight, at present are, to Liverpool—no grain—Pot ashes, 25s.; Pearls, 30s.; Butter, 45s.; Cheese, 35s.; to Glasgow, Butter and Cheese same as to Liverpool, Pots, 20s.; Pearls, 30s. I give receipts of flour here from 1st Jan. to 19th of August.

1867.	1868.	
280,256 brls.	207,536 brls.	Increase 17,280 brls.

Shipments of do. for same period.

1867.	1868.	
272,952 brls.	276,632 brls.	Increase 3,680 brls.

Groceries.—A lively business has been done in sugar, the demand falling chiefly on uncolored Japans of medium to fine qualities, good Young Hysons, Gunpowders and Twankays, of the latter there is scarcely any on the market and full prices would be paid. Sales during the week amount to between 2,500 to 3000, half chests all sorts, and prices are well maintained. Rather more doing in sugar, but prices are scarcely so firm, 100 hhds. good Barbadoes sold to-day at 7½c, 7 to 8c. is about the range for common to good grocers' qualities. The refineries have not altered their rates. Tobaccos are quiet, but very firmly held, manufacturers finding it impossible to turn out goods at last spring prices, owing to an advance of nearly 100 per cent on leaf. A New York company are erecting a very large factory here and promise to drive an extensive business. It will be in operation in October. The demand for most other staples has been fair, and prices generally are well maintained.

Fuel.—There is a strong feeling of anxiety as to the probable range of prices of this important article during the coming winter. Good U. C. maple is worth already $7 on the wharf, and although Lower Canada wood can be bought cheaper, still the quality is inferior and the length very irregular. It is to be hoped that the vast peat beds which exists in all parts of the province will ultimately reduce the price of fuel.

Dry Goods.—All the importers have now fully opened out their stocks, and although the importations have been comparatively light, still the assortment is excellent. I give the importations from 1st January to 30th June :

	1867.	1868.
Cottons..............	$2,082,397	$1,588,901
Woollens.............	1,791,824	1,183,861
Silks, &c.............	398,080	323,804
Total.........	$4,272,203	$3,096,566

Shewing a decrease of $1,175,732, or about 30 per cent. Could I give the figures for July and August the falling off would be still more marked. The trade is likely to be a healthy one, prices staples will rule firm, as they cannot be laid down below present rates. Prospects in England look bright for a large and healthy trade, which always the case when provisions rule low. The prices of cotton have also steadied, the market having recovered from its extreme depression and manufacturers feel more confidence in operating this will give a better tone to our market. The remittances have been by no means satisfactory of late, but after the harvest, when money circulate more freely, a change for the better may be expected.

Toronto Market.

Large receipts of barley during the week has given a good deal of activity to the produce trade and caused a freer circulation of money. The favorable effect on the general retail trade is especially noticeable. Judging from all the indications we have come to our notice, we think a more favorable view is taken of the prospects of the trade than was entertained a fortnight since. The early commencement made will favorably affect the aggregate result.

DRY GOODS.—Matters remain as reported last week. Very few buyers have yet visited the market; the trade must, however, soon commence.

PRODUCE.—*Wheat.*—There were no receipts of wheat of any consequence, and the market is not bare with only a small local demand. Midge-proof wax offered at $1.45, but loads of the same variety sold on the street at $1.32. Fall is offered at $1. no transactions. *Barley.*—A rough estimate places the receipts for the week, by teams and by rail, 60,000 bush.; the shipments were 39,000 bush Business has been principally confined to purchase of waggon loads on the street, where prices open at $1.04 to $105, and with slight fluctuations continued in the neighbourhood of these figures, finally closing at $1.05 to $1.06; several car lots sold at $1.05. *Oats*—Steady and dull at 50 to 55 sales of cars at 50c. for new. Receipts 1,190 bush There is an abundant supply in market with only a small demand. *Peas.*—No receipts or stock a small local business doing. There is no shipping demand. No. 1 superfine is nominal at $6.25 $6.50; extra $7; superior extra $7.25. *Oats.*—In small supply and selling in a retail way $6.50. *Bran*—$13 to $14 per ton at the mill.

PROVISIONS.—*Butter*—Is scarce but the demand for export has slackened owing to the high price asked by holders; from 17 to 20c. would now paid for good tub. *Cheese*—Firm with some demand at 10 to 10½c. with little doing. *Eggs*—In best supply and selling wholesale at 10c. *Oatmeal.*—No stocks; nominal.

FREIGHTS.—A number of vessels have been chartered to Oswego at 3½c. U. S. currency. Baltic was chartered for Toledo on private terms There is very little freights except barley lumber, moving just now. The steamers run to Montreal have had a dull season, and had to content with small profits. Freights by rail unchanged.

DETROIT AND MILWAUKEE RAILWAY.—first mortgage bonds of this Company falling May 15th, 1875, payable in New York, semi nual interest at seven per cent., are offered and interest.

STATEMENT OF BANKS

ACTING UNDER CHARTER, FOR THE MONTH ENDING 31st JULY, 1868, ACCORDING TO RETURNS FURNISHED BY THE BANKS TO THE AUDITOR OF PUBLIC ACCOUNTS.

NAME OF BANK	CAPITAL		LIABILITIES					ASSETS							
	Capital authorized by Act	Capital paid up	Promissory Notes in circulation not bearing Interest	Balances due to other Banks	Cash Deposits not bearing Interest	Cash Deposits bearing interest	TOTAL LIABILITIES	Coin, Bullion, and Provincial Notes	Landed or other property of the Bank	Government Securities	Promissory Notes, or Bills of other Banks	Balances due from other Banks	Notes and Bills Discounted	Other Debts due the Bank, not included under foregoing heads	TOTAL ASSETS
ONTARIO AND QUEBEC															
Montreal	6,000,000	6,000,000	968,146	684,457 33	5,695,611 00	5,564,451 77	12,929,607 10	2,401,738 60	350,000 00	3,379,396 67	371,894 11	898,194 34	12,465,944 98	341,349 59	20,691,486 40
Quebec	3,000,000	1,478,350	499,653	422,417 49	498,571 04	850,200 73	2,069,452 55	443,843 60		145,432 33	72,459 61	320,023 83	3,398,039 61	273,546 49	4,052,739 16
City	1,200,000	1,200,000	316,137	9,907 61	546,513 74	776,195 46	1,647,284 79	290,869 38		133,039 59	105,349 56	44,674 74	3,390,190 05	127,044 33	3,008,816 78
Gore	1,000,000	999,380	301,513	28,265 66	128,314 69	742,293 13	498,473 33	192,820 50		83,387 50	17,098 54	90,560 00	790,013 09	106,506 59	1,381,179 74
British North America	4,866,666	4,866,666	582,077	16,431 00	1,444,686 00	2,389,343 00	4,522,340 00	236,035 00		343,333 00	959,311 00	96,605 00	5,467,377 00	190,844 00	7,726,618 00
Banque du Peuple	1,600,000	1,600,000	64,534	667 71	335,399 25	372,315 92	497,403 68	317,455 11		160,864 44	36,782 70	39,605 00	1,896,842 76	-55,625 74	2,884,069 41
Niagara District	1,000,000	995,294	127,439	64,445 91	173,445 17	73,368 66	451,097 74	67,075 64		46,730 00	8,872 99	49,654 67	597,315 33	47,072 15	765,280 17
Molson's	1,000,000	1,000,000	91,392	114,561 02	590,869 18	567,147 35	860,339 43	274,950 02		107,353 33	74,288 33	94,982 67	1,367,125 60	357,056 35	2,156,413 66
Toronto	2,000,000	680,569	480,549	8,642 56	398,960 61	1,154,759 09	2,943,463 50	520,069 62		94,250 00	90,085 97	132,467 18	3,404,190 94	18,614 94	3,389,150 15
Ontario	3,000,000	993,014	295,014	182,537 43	1,682,411 34	818,642 10	3,113,798 10	155,555 38		300,000 00	128,983 31	239,983 31	3,971,473 67	117,005 00	6,432,018 57
Eastern Townships	600,000	480,000	124,649	7,784 74	66,424 30	73,384 80	341,124 10	38,023 46	14,000 00		25,428 59	48,559 17	477,680 54	-1,005 00	669,664 47
Banque Nationale	1,000,000	1,000,000	985,014	115,360 48	331,394 72	375,188 30	645,089 71	977,123 60		286,703 83	41,900 08	41,900 08	1,163,634 89	25,060 23	1,761,294 47
Banque Jacques Cartier	1,000,000	941,883	17,949 19	17,949 19	140,205 60	464,869 08	771,407 68	64,589 71		281,703 83	43,691 97	43,691 97	1,980,329 68	1,672,765 64	1,679,342 50
Merchants'	5,000,000	4,957,960	837,681 97	837,681 97	890,183 57	1,632,077 97	3,389,713 61	653,989 51	364,439 65	523,906 07	940,602 90	468,645 75	2,398,727 79	1,972,009 78	7,102,342 70
Royal Canadian	2,000,000	1,492,475	14,889 13	14,889 13	440,890 90	833,847 60	2,344,317 49	650,955 02		124,966 09	134,519 07	428,621 78	3,479,970 02	46,463 60	3,816,738 78
Union B'k Low. Canada	3,000,000	1,999,140	955,311	955,311	397,903 89	154,471 01	898,976 90	114,300 73		119,966 39	118,448 17	711,344 38	1,438,178 76		1,206,386 56
Mechanics'	1,000,000	371,296	636 07	636 07	106,318 33	125,019 14	231,072 54	44,065 23	34,898 20	529,966 67	39,945 10	138 96	373,012 87	5,877 15	1,590,417 10
Bank of Commerce	2,000,000	998,845	668,795	96,112 31	450,750 54	709,866 01	1,152,094 76	689,405 68	40,792 92	106,483 18	65,546 15	74,896 06	2,914,605 98		3,130,339 17
NOVA SCOTIA															
Bank of Yarmouth															
Merchants' Bank															
People's Bank	1,000,000	1,000,000	119,340	11,493 73	105,689 47	851,973 90	630,194 79	82,726 94	34,600 00	80,000 00	95,356 00	89,093 36	777,692 15	55,316 65	1,111,191 40
Union Bank															
Bank of Nova Scotia															
NEW BRUNSWICK															
Bank of New Brunswick	900,000	600,000	400,094	58,148 12	438,890 30	678,526 33	1,575,096 10	330,173 92	15,594 45		43,694 00	101,522 06	1,896,734 76	88,808 10	2,468,724 66
Commercial Bank	600,000	512,305	612,305	54,745 93	398,793 38	1,366 41	671,459 44	81,890 63	31,000 00		6,053 00	62,152 08	1,306,867 79	29,840 00	1,732,464 50
St. Stephen's Bank	390,000	390,000		13,987 38	13,987 38	38,163 16	430,551 91	29,043 00			55,187 33	345,261 81	345,261 81	85,560 00	1,465,700 54
People's Bank															
Totals	39,930,966	39,530,715	8,014,639	2,384,857 34	14,670,187 03	17,790,763 37	43,890,437 48	9,644,645 91	1,098,849 91	6,438,100 94	3,923,360 17	3,009,007 12	50,669,170 56	3,967,304 69	76,731,974 90

TORONTO PRICES CURRENT.—August 27, 1868.

Name of Article.	Wholesale Rates.	
	$ c.	$ c.
Boots and Shoes.		
Mens' Thick Boots	2 20	2 50
" Kip	2 45	3 20
" Calf	3 00	3 75
" Congress Gaiters	2 00	2 40
" Kip Cobourgs	1 00	1 50
Boys' Thick Boots	1 65	1 90
Youths' "	1 45	1 55
Women's Batts	95	1 20
" Congress Gaiters	1 15	1 50
Misses' Batts	0 75	1 00
" Congress Gaiters	1 00	1 30
Girls' Batts	0 65	0 90
" Congress Gaiters	0 80	1 10
Children's C. T. Cacks	0 50	0 65
" Gaiters	0 65	0 90
Drugs.		
Aloes Cape	0 12½	0 16
Alum	0 02½	0 03
Borax	0 00	0 00
Camphor, refined	0 65	0 70
Castor Oil	0 18	0 28
Caustic Soda	0 04½	0 05
Cochineal	0 90	1 00
Cream Tartar	0 00	0 00
Epsom Salts	0 03	0 04
Extract Logwood	0 00	0 11
Gum Arabic, sorts	0 30	0 35
Indigo, Madras	0 75	1 00
Licorice	0 14	0 45
Madder	0 13	0 16
Nutgalls	0 00	0 00
Opium	6 70	7 00
Oxalic Acid	0 28	0 35
Potash, Bi-tart	0 25	0 28
" Bichromate	0 15	0 20
Potass Iodide	3 80	4 50
Senna	0 12½	0 60
Soda Ash	0 03	0 04
Soda Bicarb	4 50	5 50
Tartaric Acid	0 37½	0 45
Verdigris	0 35	0 40
Vitriol, Blue	0 09	0 10
Groceries.		
Coffees:		
Java, ⅌ lb	0 23@	0 25
Laguayra	0 17	0 18
Rio	0 16	0 18
Fish:		
Herrings, Lab. split	0 00	0 00
" round	0 00	0 00
" scaled	0 00	0 00
Mackerel, small kitts	1 00	1 25
Loch. Her. wh'e firks	2 50	2 75
" half "	1 50	1 75
White Fish & Trout	None.	
Salmon, saltwater	16 00	17 50
Dry Cod, ⅌ 112 lbs	5 00	0 00
Fruit:		
Raisins, Layers	2 20	2 30
" M R	2 10	2 20
" Valentias new	0 08½	0 09
Currants, new	0 05	0 06
" old	0 03¾	0 04½
Figs	0 13	0 15
Molasses:		
Clayed, ⅌ gal	0 37½	0 40
Syrups, Standard	0 46	0 47
" Golden	0 52	0 53
Rice:		
Arracan	4 75	5 00
Spices:		
Cassia, whole, ⅌ lb	0 35	0 40
Cloves	0 11	0 13
Nutmegs	0 50	0 65
Ginger, ground	0 16	0 25
" Jamaica, root	0 25	0 30
Pepper, black	0 09	0 10
Pimento	0 08	0 09
Sugars:		
Port Rico, ⅌ lb	0 08¾	0 09
Cuba "	0 08¾	0 09
Barbadoes (bright)	0 08¾	0 08½
Dry Crushed, at 60 d	0 11¾	0 11½
Canada Sugar Refine'y, yellow No. 2, 60 ds	0 08¾	0 08¾
Yellow, No. 2½	0 09	0 09½
No. 3	0 09¾	0 09½
Crushed X	0 10	0 10½
" A	0 11½	0 11¾
Ground	0 11¾	0 12
Extra Ground	0 12¾	0 13
Teas:		
Japan com'n to good	0 40	0 55
" Fine to choicest	0 55	0 65
Colored, com. to fine	0 60	0 75
Congou & Souch'ng	0 42	0 75
Oolong, good to fine	0 50	0 65
Y. Hyson, com to gd	0 45	0 55
Medium to choice	0 65	0 80
Extra choice	0 85	0 95
Gunpowd'r c. to med	0 55	0 70
" med. to fine	0 70	0 85

Name of Article.	Wholesale Rate.	
Groceries—*Contin'd*	$ c.	$ c.
" fine to fins't	0 85	0 95
Hyson	0 45	0 80
Imperial	0 42	0 80
Tobacco, Manufact'd:		
Can Leaf, ⅌ lb 5s & 10s	0 26	0 30
Western Leaf, com	0 25	0 26
" Good	0 27	0 32
" Fine	0 32	0 35
" Bright fine	0 40	0 50
" " choice	0 00	0 75
Hardware.		
Tin (net cash prices)		
Block, ⅌ lb	0 25	0 26
Grain	0 26	0 27
Copper:		
Pig	0 24	0 25
Sheet	0 30	0 33
Cut Nails:		
Assorted ¼ Shingles, ⅌ 100 lb	3 05	3 15
Shingle alone do	3 30	3 40
Lathe and 5 dy	3 55	3 65
Galvanized Iron:		
Assorted sizes	0 09	0 10
Best No. 24	0 09	0 00
" 26	0 08¾	0 00
" 28	0 09¾	0 10
Horse Nails:		
Guest's or Griffin's assorted sizes	0 19	0 20
For W. ass'd sizes	0 19	0 20
Patent Hammer'd do	0 18	0 19
Iron (at 4 months):		
Pig—Gartsherrie No1	26 00	27 00
Other brands. No1	22 00	23 00
" No2	24 00	25 00
Bar—Scotch, ⅌ 100 lb	2 25	2 50
Refined	3 00	3 25
Swedes	5 00	5 50
Hoops—Coopers	3 00	3 25
Band	3 00	3 25
Boiler Plates	3 25	3 50
Canada Plates	4 00	4 25
Union Jack	0 00	0 00
Pontypool	0 00	0 00
Swansea	0 00	0 00
Lead (at 4 months):		
Bar, ⅌ 100 lbs	0 07	0 07½
Sheet "	0 08	0 09
Shot	0 07½	0 07¾
Iron Wire (net cash):		
No. 6, ⅌ bundle	2 70	2 80
" 9, "	3 10	3 20
" 12, "	3 40	3 50
" 16, "	4 30	4 40
Powder:		
Blasting, Canada	3 50	3 75
FF "	4 50	4 75
FFF "	5 00	5 25
Blasting, English	5 00	5 50
FF loose	5 50	6 00
FFF "	6 00	6 50
Pressed Spikes (4 mos):		
Regular sizes 100	4 00	4 25
Extra "	4 50	5 00
Tin Plates (net cash):		
IC Coke	7 50	8 00
IC Charcoal	8 50	8 75
IX "	10 50	10 75
IXX "	12 50	0 00
DC "	7 50	9 00
DX "	9 50	10 00
Hides & Skins, ⅌ lb		
Green rough	0 05½	0 06
Green, salt'd & insp'd	0 00	0 07
Cured	0 07½	0 08½
Calfskins, green	0 00	0 10
Calfskins, cured	0 00	0 12
" dry	0 18	0 20
Lambskins	0 50	0 00
" pelts	0 40	0 00
Hops.		
Inferior, ⅌ lb	0 10	0 15
Medium	0 15	0 20
Good	0 20	0 25
Fancy	0 25	0 35
Leather, @ (4 mos.) In lots of less than 50 sides, 10 ⅌ cent higher.		
Spanish Sole, 1st qual. heavy, weights ⅌ lb	0 23	0 23½
Do. 1st qual middle do	0 23	0 23½
Do. No. 2, all weights	0 20	0 22
Slaughter heavy	0 28	0 29
Do. light	0 28	0 29
Harness, best	0 32	0 34
" No. 2	0 30	0 33
Upper heavy	0 34	0 36
" light	0 36	0 40

Name of Article.
Leather—*Contin'd.*
Kip Skins, Patna
French
English
Hemlock Calf (30 to 35 lbs.) per doz
Do. light
French Calf
Grain & Satn Clt ⅌ doz
Splits, large ⅌ lb
" small
Enamelled Cow ⅌ foot
Patent
Pebble Grain
Buff
Oils.
Cod
Cocoanut, ⅌ lb
Lard, extra
" No. 1
" Woollen
Lubricating, patent
Linseed, raw
" boiled
Machinery
Olive, 2nd, ⅌ gal
" salad
" salad, in bot qt. ⅌ case
Sesame salad, ⅌ gal
Seal, pale
Spirits Turpentine
Varnish
Whale
Paints, &c.
White Lead, genuine in Oil, ⅌ 25 lbs
Do. No. 1 "
" 2 "
" 3 "
White Zinc, genuine
White Lead, dry
Red Lead
Venetian Red, Eng'h
Yellow Ochre, Fren'h
Whiting
Petroleum. (Refined ⅌ gal.)
Water white, car l'd
" small lots
Straw, by car load
" small lots
Amber, by car load
" small lots
Benzine
Produce.
Grain:
Wheat, Spring, 60 lb
" Fall 60 "
Barley 48 "
Peas 60 "
Oats 34 "
Rye 56 "
Seeds:
Clover, choice 60 "
" com'n 68 "
Timothy, cho'e 4 "
" inf. to good 48 "
Flax 56 "
Flour (per brl.):
Superior extra
Extra superfine
Fancy superfine
Superfine No. 1
" No. 2
Oatmeal, (per brl.)
Provisions.
Butter, dairy tub ⅌ lb
" store packed
Cheese, new
Pork, mess, per brl.
" prime mess
" prime
Bacon, rough
" Cumberl'd cut
" smoked
Hams, in salt
" sug. cur. & canv'
Shoulders, in salt
Lard, in kegs
Eggs, packed
Beef Hams
Tallow
Hogs dressed, heavy
" medium
" light
Salt, &c.
American brls
Liverpool coarse
Plaster
Water Lime

& Candles.	$ c.	$ c.
ford & Co.'s ..		
perial.........	0 07½	0 08
den Bar	0 07	0 07½
er Bar........	0 07	0 07½
....	0 05	0 05½
....	0 03¾	0 04
....	0 10	0 11
s, Liquors, &c.		
, per doz......	2 60	2 65
ss Dub Portr..	2 35	2 40
amaica Rum...	1 80	2 25
yper's H. Gin..	1 50	1 60
Old Tom.....	1 90	2 00
cases.........	4 00	4 25
Old Tom, c...	6 00	6 25
ommon	1 00	1 25
ne old	2 00	4 00
, common	1 00	1 50
edium........	1 70	1 80
pale or golden..	2 50	4 00

Brandy:	$ c.	$ c.
Hennessy's, per gal..	2 50	2 75
Martell's " ..	2 50	2 75
J. Robin & Co.'s " ..	2 10	2 75
Otard, Dupuy & Cos..	2 10	2 75
Brandy, cases........	8 50	9 00
Brandy, com. per c...	4 00	4 50
Whiskey:		
Common 36 u. p......	0 65	0 70
Old Rye	0 85	0 87½
Malt........	0 85	0 87½
Toddy...............	0 85	0 87½
Scotch, per gal.......	1 90	2 10
Irish—Kinnahan's c...	7 00	7 50
" Dunnville's Belf't..	6 00	6 25
Wool.		
Fleece, lb...........	0 25	0 27
Pulled "............	0 00	0 00
Furs.		
Bear............	8 00	10 00
Beaver...............	1 00	1 25
Coon	0 20	0 40
Fisher...............	4 00	6 00
Martin...............	1 40	1 60
Mink.................	4 00	4 25
Otter................	5 75	6 00
Spring Rats	0 15	0 17
Fox.	1 20	1 25

INSURANCE COMPANIES.

ENGLISH.—*Quotations on the London Market.*

Last Dividend.	Name of Company.	Shares parval £	Amount paid.	Last Sale.
	Briton Medical and General Life ...	10	—	1½
7½	Commer'l Union, Fire, Life and Mar.	50	5	5¼ 5¾
8	City of Glasgow	25	2½	5
9½	Edinburgh Life	100	15	30½x
5—½ yr	European Life and Guarantee......	2½	11s6	4s 6d
10	Etna Fire and Marine.............	10	1½	1
5	Guardian	100	50	52x
12	Imperial Fire....................	500	50	345
9½	Imperial Life	100	10	16½
10	Lancashire Fire and Life.........	20	2	2½x
11	Life Association of Scotland......	40	7¼	23
45s. p. sh	London Assurance Corporation ..	25	12½	48
5	London and Lancashire Life	10	1	1
40	Liverp'l & London & Globe F. & L.	20	2	7½
5	National Union Life	5	1	1
12½	Northern Fire and Life	100	5	10½
12 '68, bo 5s.	North British and Mercantile	50	6¼	17 18
50	Ocean Marine	25	5	20
£5 12s.	Provident Life...................	100	10	38
£4½ p. s.	Phœnix...........................			136
2½—h. yr.	Queen Fire and Life	10	1	15-16
3s. bo. 4s	Royal Insurance..................	20	3	6½
10	Scottish Provincial Fire and Life ..	50	2½	4½
25	Standard Life	50	12	65
5	Star Life	25	1½	—
	CANADIAN.			℘ c.
4	British America Fire and Marine ..	$50	$25	55
4	Canada Life			
12	Montreal Assurance	200	20	135
8	Provincial Fire and Marine........	60	11	
	Quebec Fire	40	32½	£19½
8	" Marine..................	100	40	90-91
5 7 mo's.	Western Assurance................	40	6	

RAILWAYS.	Sha's	Paid	Montr	London.
and St. Lawrence....................	£100	All.		56 58
nd Lake Huron	20½	"		3½ 3¾
do Preference	10	"		5½ 6½
antt. & Goderich, 6℘c., 1872-3-4....	100	"		
in and St. Lawrence			9½ 10½	
do Pref. 10 ℘ ct....			50 70	
runk	100	"	15 16	15¾ 16¼
Eq.G. M. Bds. 1 ch. 6℘c...........	100	"		78 82
First Preference, 5 ℘ c	100	"		45 48
Deferred, 3 ℘ ct..	100	"		
Second Pref. Bonds, 5℘c..........	100	"		35 37
do Deferred, 3 ℘ ct..........	100	"		
Third Pref. Stock, 4℘ct...........	100	"		25 27
do. Deferred, 3 ℘ ct........	100	"		
Fourth Pref. Stock, 3℘c...........	100	"		18¼ 19½
do. Deferred, 3 ℘ ct.	100	"		
estern	20½	"		12¾ 13½
New	20½	18	16 17	
6 ℘ c. Bds, due 1873-76...........	100	All.		100 102
5½℘c Bds. due 1877-78...........	100	"		91 93
Railway, Halifax, $250, all.......	$250	"		
, of Canada, 6℘c. 1st Pref. Bds...........	100	"		77 82

EXCHANGE.	Halifax.	Montr'l.	Quebec.	Toronto.
London, 60 days......				
r 75 days date...........	13½	9½ 9½	9½ 9¾	9½ 10
do.		8½ 9	8¾ 8¾	9½
with documents..........		8¾ 9½		
New York.............		30½ 31	30 30½	69½
do.		31 31½	31 31½	
fts do.		½ dis to p.	par ½ dis.	par ½ dis.
.. ..		4½ 4½		4½ 7

STOCK AND BOND REPORT.

The dates of our quotations are as follows:—Toronto, Aug. 25; Montreal, Aug. 24; Quebec, August 24; London, Aug. 7.

NAME.	Shares.	Paid up.	Divid'd last 6 Months	Dividend Day.	CLOSING PRICES. Toronto.	Montre'l	Quebec.
BANKS.			℘ ct.				
British North America	$250	All.	3	July and Jan.	102 103	102½ 103½	103 103½
Jacques Cartier..............	50	"	4	1 June, 1 Dec.	106 108	106 108	106 107
Montreal	200	"	5	"	134 135	133 133½	133½ 134
Nationale....................	50	"	4	1 Nov. 1 May.	106 107	105½	107 107½
New Brunswick	100	"					
Nova Scotia	200	28	7&b$3½	Mar. and Sept.			
Du Peuple....	50	"	4	1 Mar., 1 Sept.	Bksclo'd		
Toronto	100	"	4	1 Jan., 1 July.	191	113 115	114 115
Bank of Yarmouth............							
Canadian Bank of Com'e......	50	95			103 104	102	101½ 102
City Bank Montreal	80	All.	4	1 June, 1 Dec.	101½ 102	102	102 102½
Commer'l Bank (St. John)....	100	"	℘ ct.				
Eastern Townships' Bank.....	50	"	4	1 July, 1 Jan..		97	96 97
Gore	40	...	3½	1 Jan., 1 July.	46 50	46	45 46
Halifax Banking Company....							
Mechanics' Bank.............	50	70	4	1 Nov., 1 May.	94½ 96	94½ 96	94 95
Merchants' Bank of Canada....	100	70	4	1 Jan., 1 July.	105½ 106	105½ 106	105¼ 106
Merchants' Bank (Halifax)....							
Molson's Bank...............	50	All.	4	1 Apr., 1 Oct.	109½ 110	110	109 110
Niagara District Bank...	100	70	3½	1 Jan., 1 July.			
Ontario Bank................	40	All.	4	1 June, 1 Dec.	98 99	98 99	98 99
People's Bank (Fred'kton)....	100	"					
People's Bank (Halifax)	20	"	7 12 m				
Quebec Bank	100	"	3½	1 June, 1 Dec.	97½ 98	97 98	97½ 97¾
Royal Canadian Bank	50	50	4	1 Jan., 1 July.	84 85½	82½ 85	82 85
St. Stephens Bank	100	All					
Union Bank	100	70	4	1 Jan., 1 July.	101 102	101 102	102 102½
Union Bank (Halifax)........	100	40	7 12 mo	Feb. and Aug.			
MISCELLANEOUS.							
British America Land........	250	44	2½				
British Colonial S. S. Co.....	250	32½	2½			50	
Canada Company	32½	All.	5				
Canada Landed Credit Co.....	50	$14	3½		62½		
Canada Per. B'ldg Society....	50	All.	5		116		
Canada Mining Company.....	4	90					
Do. Inl'd Steam Nav. Co.....	100	All.	20 12 m			106 108	106 107
Do. Glass Company.........	100	"	12½ "			95	
Canad'n Loan & Investm't....	25	2½	7				
Canada Agency	10	¼					
Colonial Securities Co........							
Freehold Building Society....	100	All.	5		103 104		
Halifax Steamboat Co........	100	"	5				
Halifax Gas Company........							
Hamilton Gas Company.......							
Huron Copper Bay Co........	4	12	20			35 50p.s.	
Lake Huron S. and C.........	5	102					
Montreal Mining Co..........	20	$15				2.75 2.90	
Do. Telegraph Co...	40	All.	5		133 135	134 134½	133 135
Do. Elevating Co...	00	"	15 12 m				
Do. City Gas Co.........	40	"	4	15 Mar. 15 Sep.		134 134½	134 135
Do. City Pass. R,. Co.....	50	"	5			108 110	107 108
Nova Scotia Telegraph	20	"					
Quebec and L. S.	8	$4					25 cts
Quebec Gas Co...............	200	All.	4	1 Mar., 1 Sep.			b'ks cl'd
Quebec Street R. R..........	50	25	8				96 97
Richelieu Navigation Co......	100	All.	7 p.a.	1 Jan., 1 July.		114 116	113 114
St. Lawrence Tow Boat Co.....	100	"		3 Feb.			45 50
Tor'to Consumers' Gas Co.....	50	"	2 3 m.	1 My Au MarFe	104½ 105		104 105
Trust & Loan Co. of U. C.....	20	5	3				
West'n Canada Bldg Soc'y....	50	All.	5		108 109		

SECURITIES.	London.	M'ntreal	Quebec.	Toronto.
Canadian Gov't Deb. 6 ℘ ct. due 1872		100 101	100½ 102	101 101½
Do. do. 6 do due Ja. & Jul. 1877-84........	103 105	99 100	100 100½	99½ 100
Do. do. 6 do. Feb. & Aug.........	102 103			
Do. do. 6 do. Mch. & Sep.........	104 106			
Do. do. 5 ℘ ct. cur., 1883	91 93	90	90½ 91	89½ 90
Do. do. 5 do. stg., 1885		91	91 91½	90 91
Do. do. 7 do. cur., ...			100 100½	
Dominion 6 p. c. 1878 cy..........................		99½ 100		100
Hamilton Corporation.....				
Montreal Harbor, 8 ℘ ct. d. 1869..................				
Do. do. 7 do. 1870....................				
Do. do. 6½ do. 1875....................		99½ 100½		
Do. do. 6½ do. 1873....................				
Do. Corporation, 6 ℘ c. 1891		92½ 93	92 93	91½
Do. 7 p. c. stock..............................		103½ 105	101 103	103½ 105½
Do. Water Works, 6 ℘ c. stg. 1878..........				90 91
Do. do. 6 do. cy. do.		92½ 93½		91 92
New Brunswick, 6 ℘ ct., Jan. and July	102 104			
Nova Scotia, 6 ℘ ct., 1875........................	101 103			
Ottawa City 6 ℘ c. d. 1880		90 91		
Quebec Harbour, 6 ℘ c. d. 1883.			60 70	
Do. do. 7 do. do.......................			70 80	
Do. do. 8 do. 1886.....................			85 90	
Do. City, 7 ℘ c. d. 5 years		85 90	90 91	80 90
Do. do. 7 do. 9 do.			86 87	
Do. do. 7 do. 2½ do.			96 96½	
Do. Water Works, 7 ℘ ct., 4 years			95 96	
Do. do. 6 do. 2 do.			92½ 93½	
Toronto Corporation		90		

Financial.

The Canadian Land and Emigration COMPANY

Offers for sale at Cheap Rates, on condition of settlement,

FARM LOTS, IN DYSART,

And adjoining Townships, in the County of Peterborough.

THE greater portion of the Company's block of nine Townships is excellent farming land. The Judges at the Provincial Exhibition at London, in 1865, awarded to the Company a Special Prize, and at Kingston, in 1867, a Diploma for the assortment of Farm Produce from their settlements. The country is well watered, healthy and picturesque. Dysart is a well settled Township, with mills, schools, &c., while stores, post-office, boarding-houses, &c., are established in the Village of Haliburton. There is also a rising settlement in the Township of Harcourt, and along the Peterson road the settler has a choice of good Farm Lots in no less than six Townships.

The communication to the Townships is good, a great part of it by Railroad and Steamboat.

The Bobcaygeon, Opeongo, Peterson, Mississippi, and Hastings Roads will all give access to the Company's block, but other roads are being opened up, giving a more direct communication with the County Town of Peterborough.

The Company has expended a considerable sum in the construction of Roads to and through its Townships, and has still a large appropriation for this purpose.

Dysart and adjoining Townships, the property of the Company, form one Municipality which cannot fail to make more rapid progress than any of the Municipalities in that section of the country, on account of the large sum levied every year from the Company.

For further information and particulars and conditions of sale, apply to the Secretary,

CHARLES JAS. BLOMFIELD,
Bank of Toronto Buildings, Toronto.

Toronto. Jan. 21   24-1y

Insurance.

J. T. & W. Pennock.

FIRE and Life Insurance Agents, Parliamentary and Departmental Agents, Mining Agents, and Exchange Brokers.

Ottawa. Dec. 21st, 1867.   10-1y

The Standard Life Assurance Company,

WITH which is now united the COLONIAL LIFE ASSURANCE COMPANY.

Established 1825.

HEAD OFFICES—*EDINBURGH* and *MONTREAL.*

Accumulated Fund, upwards of $18,000,000.
Income, 1867............... $3,285,000.

Manager—W.M. RAMSAY.   Inspector—RICH'D BULL.

TORONTO—HENRY PELLATT, AGENT.

Agencies in every Town throughout the Dominion.

18-1y

Fire and Marine Assurance.

THE BRITISH AMERICA
ASSURANCE COMPANY.

HEAD OFFICE :

CORNER OF CHURCH AND COURT STREETS.

TORONTO.

BOARD OF DIRECTION :

Hon. G. W. Allan, M L C.,	A. Joseph, Esq ,
George J. Boyd, Esq ,	Peter Paterson, Esq.,
Hon. W. Cayley,	G. P. Ridout, Esq.,
Richard S. Cassels, Esq.,	E H. Rutherford,Esq.,
Thomas C. Street, Esq.	

Governor:

GEORGE PERCIVAL RIDOUT, ESQ.

Deputy Governor:

PETER PATERSON, ESQ.

Fire Inspector: Marine Inspector:

E. ROBY O'BRIEN.   CAPT. R. COURNEEN.

Insurances granted on all descriptions of property against loss and damage by fire and the perils of inland navigation.

Agencies established in the principal cities, towns, and ports of shipment throughout the Province.

THOS. WM. BIRCHALL,
Managing Director.

23-1y

Insurance.

Reliance Mutual Life Assurance Society.

(*Established*, 1840,) *OF LONDON, E. C.*

Accumulated Funds, over $1,000,000.

Annual Income, $300,00.

THE entire Profits of this long-established Society belong to the Policy-holders.

HEAD OFFICE FOR DOMINION—MONTREAL.

T. W. GRIFFITH, *Manager & Sec'y.*

15-1y   WM. HENDERSON, *Agent for Toronto.*

Etna Insurance Company of Dublin.

The number of Shareholders exceeds Five Hundred.

Capital, $5,000,000—*Annual Income nearly* $1,000,000.

THIS Company takes Fire and Marine Risks on the most favorable terms.

T. W. GRIFFITH, *Manager for Cana da*

Chief office for Dominion—Corner St. Francois Xavie and St. Sacrament Sts., Montreal.

15-1y   WM. HENDERSON, *Agent for Toronto.*

Scottish Provincial Assurance Co.

Established 1825.

CAPITAL ....£1,000,000 STERLING.
INVESTED IN CANADA (1834) ....$500,000.

Canada Head Office, Montreal.

LIFE DEPARTMENT.

CANADA BOARD OF DIRECTORS :

HUGH TAYLOR, Esq., Advocate,
Hon. CHARLES WILSON, M. L. C.
WM. SACHE, Esq., Banker,
JACKSON RAE, Esq., Banker.

WM. FRASER, Esq. M. D., Medical Adviser.

The special advantages to be derived from Insuring in this office are:—Strictly Moderate Rates of Premium; Large Bonus (intermediate bonus guaranteed ;) Liberal Surrender Value, under policies relinquished by assured ; and Extensive Limits of Residence and Travel. All business disposed of in Canada, without reference to parent office.

A DAVIDSON PARKER,
Resident Secretary.

G. L. MADDISON,

15-1yr   AGENT FOR TORONTO.

Lancashire Insurance Company.

CAPITAL, - - - - - - - - £2,000,000 Sterling.

FIRE RISKS

Taken at reasonable rates of premium, and

ALL LOSSES SETTLED PROMPTLY,

By the undersigned, without reference elsewhere.

S. C. DUNCAN-CLARK & CO.,

General Agents for Ontario,

25-1y   N. W. Corner of King & Church Streets,
TORONTO.

Etna Fire & Marine Insurance Company.

INCORPORATED 1819. CHARTER PERPETUAL.

CASH CAPITAL, - - - - - - - $3,000,000.

LOSSES PAID IN 50 YEARS, 28,500,000. 00.

JULY, 1868.

ASSETS:

(At Market Value.)	
Cash in hand and in Bank...........	$544,343 39
Real Estate.......................	255,267 29
Mortgage Bonds.	932,245 00
Bank Stock.......................	1,272,670 00
United States, State and City Stock, and other Public Securities	2,049,855 51
Total.................	$5,052,880 19

LIABILITIES.

Claims not Due, and Unadjusted	$499,803 55
Amount required by Mass. and New York for Re-Insurance....................	1,405,297 15

E. CHAFFEY & CO., Agents.

50-6m

THE CANADIAN
ONETARY TIMES
AND
INSURANCE CHRONICLE.

DEVOTED TO FINANCE, COMMERCE, INSURANCE, BANKS, RAILWAYS, NAVIGATION, MINES, INVESTMENT,
PUBLIC COMPANIES, AND JOINT STOCK ENTERPRISE.

VOL. II.—NO. 3.   TORONTO, THURSDAY, SEPTEMBER 3, 1868.   { SUBSCRIPTION, $3 A YEAR.

Mercantile.

W. Rowland & Co.,
PRODUCE BROKERS and General Commission Merchants. Advances made on Consignments. Corner Scott and Front Streets, Toronto.

C. P. Reid & Co.,
PORTERS and Dealers in Wines, Liquors, Cigars and leaf Tobacco, Wellington Street, Toronto.

Childs & Hamilton,
MANUFACTURERS and Wholesale Dealers in Boots and Shoes, No. 7 Wellington Street East, Toronto.

John Fisken & Co.,
COAL, OIL, and Commission Merchants, Yonge St., Toronto, Ont.

Lyman & McNab,
WHOLESALE Hardware Merchants, Toronto, Ontario.

L. Coffee & Co.,
PRODUCE and Commission Merchants, No. 2 Manning's Block, Front St., Toronto, Ont. Advances made on gnments of Produce.

W. D. Matthews & Co.,
PRODUCE Commission Merchants, Old Corn Exchange, 18 Front St., Toronto Ont.

R. J. Hamilton & Co.,
PRODUCE Commission Merchants, 119 Lower Water St., Halifax, Nova Scotia.

J. & A. Clark,
PRODUCE Commission Merchants, Wellington Street East, Toronto, Ont.

John Boyd & Co.,
WHOLESALE Grocers and Commission Merchants, Front St., Toronto.

W. & R. Griffith,
PORTERS of Teas, Wines, etc. Ontario Chambers, r, Church and Front Sts., Toronto.

Reford & Dillon,
PORTERS of Groceries, Wellington Street, Toronto, ntario.

Thos. Griffith & Co.,
PORTERS and Wholesale Dealers in Groceries, iquors, &c., Front St., Toronto, Ont.

J. B. Boustead,
VISION and Commission Merchant. Hops bought nd sold on Commission. 82 Front St., Toronto.

Hurd, Leigh & Co.,
DEALERS and Enamellers of China and Earthenware, 73 Yonge St., Toronto, Ont. [See advt.]

Parson Bros.,
PETROLEUM Refiners, and Wholesale dealers in Lamps, Chimneys, etc. Waterooms 51 Front St., Refinery cor. and Don Sts., Toronto.

Sessions, Turner & Co.,
MANUFACTURERS, Importers and Wholesale Dealers in Boots and Shoes, Leather Findings, etc., 4 Wellington St. West, Toronto, Ont.

Thos. Haworth & Co.,
PORTERS and dealers in Iron, Cutlery and general ardware, King St., Toronto, Ont.

D. Crawford & Co.,
MANUFACTURERS of Soaps, Candles, etc., and dealers of Petroleum, Lard and Lubricating Oils, Palace St., .to, Ont.

Meetings.

WESTERN ASSURANCE COMPANY.

The seventeenth annual meeting of the shareholders of this company was held at their offices, Church street, on Tuesday the 1st September. The report of the Directors for the seven months, from 1st December, 1867, to 30th June, 1868, is as follows:—

In compliance with the decision of shareholders at the annual meeting in December last, changing the time for closing the office accounts and holding the annual meetings for the future in midsummer, the President and Directors have now much pleasure in placing before the shareholders full and explicit statements of the company's affairs on the business for the seven months ending 30th June, comprising, viz., the usual general statements of assets and liabilities with balance sheet, also auditors' report, which the Directors feel assured will be received with no ordinary degree of satisfaction. And in submitting the following brief abstract of figures taken from the official statements on the table, congratulate their co-shareholders on the high position the company has attained as shown in the largely increased business of the office accomplished at same time with profitable results.

The business for the seven months is as follows:—

RECEIPTS.

Premium in the Fire Branch	$82,658 80
" " Marine Branch	43,746 64
Interest account	2,459 77
Total receipts	$128,865 21

DISBURSEMENTS.

Losses in the Fire Branch	$43,150 49
" Marine Branch	15,244 98
Total loss	$58,395 47

Which includes an appropriation of $4,000 00 on two marine claims standing over unsettled in closing the accounts. One, a loss reported three days before 30th June; the other, a claim ordered for payment, but unsettled, being held under seizure by creditors. In the fire branch there are no claims against the company.

Re-assurance on Fire and Marine	$6,650 25
General expenses, agents' commissions, and all other charges for the business	24,284 36
Total disbursements	$89,330 08
Leaving bal. in favor of Co.	$39,535 13

The assets of the company including $33,660 48 cash in bank, as per general statement, amount to $155,669 29

Less liabilities 6,759 51

$148,909 78

Which sum is represented by the following accounts:

Capital stock paid up	$75,100 00
Reserve Funds	50,000 00
Profit and loss account for bal at credit	23,809 78
	$148,909 78

A comparative statement submitted in last year's report for the past three years showed very forcibly the rapid increase of the company's business, and chiefly as in 1867, the premium receipts for that year amounting to $171,960 56.

Following up the comparison as between the past year and this for the corresponding period from 1st December to 30th June,

The premium receipts in 1867 were	$86,557 78
" " 1868 are	126,405 44

From these figures it will be seen that the anticipation of the Directors as to the progress of the company have been more than realized and the marked increase in the premium receipts is no doubt largely attributable to the prompt and liberal settlement of all claims, together with the good effect produced in the recent call on capital stock by affording additional security to the insured on the increased business.

Since closing the accounts at the 30th June, your Directors declared a dividend of 5 per cent, on the seven months business, and further withdrew from the cash funds in bank the sum of $25,000, appropriated as follows:—

$17,000, the first instalment of deposit with Government under the late Insurance Act of the Dominion Legislature; and $8,000 invested in Dominion stock. Your Directors are well satisfied that the Insurance Act referred to, though moderate in its requirements is a move in the right direction, and well calculated to place the insurance business in Canada on a much safer basis than formerly. The Directors in closing their report unhesitatingly express their conviction that under the same continued watchfulness and attention to the company's interests, the future holds out the prospect of still further increasing the business with satisfactory results.

JOHN McMURRICH, President.

Toronto, 1st September, 1868.

General Statement of the affairs of the Western Assurance Company of Canada for the period of seven months ending 30th June, 1868.

Assets.

Capital stock not called in	$300,000 00
Calls on stock, unpaid, due and maturing	24,900 00
Cash in Bank	33,660 48
Provincial and Municipal Debentures	35,791 82
Loans on Mortgages	28,656 37
Building Account and office furniture	16,000 00
Bills receivable	33,503 39
Interest unpaid and accrued	992 20
Agents' balances	7,048 28
Cash balance in office	16 75
	$480,569 29

Liabilities.

Capital stock, 10,000 shares of $40 each..		$400,000 00
Losses under adjustment......	$4,000 00	
Unpaid dividends	1,372 07	
Sundry accounts	1,387 44	
		$6,759 51
Surplus account...	50,000 00	
Profit and loss account......	23,809 78	
		$73,809 78
		$480,569 29

Profit and Loss Account.- Dr.

Expense account......... ...	$5,314 23	
Charges on Business:		
Directors' compensation	1,662 00	
Salaries account..........	4,899 85	
Law expense account......	256 33	
Agents' commission.......	11,362 31	
		23,494 72
Fire loss account..........................		43,150 49
Marine loss account......................		15,244 08
Re-assurance............................		6,650 25
Marine expense account....		711 06
Rent account balance.....................		77 08
Balance.................................		39,535 13
		$128,865 21

Cr.

Fire premium..............	$82,658 80	
Marine premium..........	43,746 64	
		$126,405 44
Interest account (balance at credit)...		2,459 77
		$128,865 21

Audited and approved—August 24th, 1868.—
G. A. Barber, John Maughan.

Auditors' Report.— To the President and Directors of the Western Assurance Company.

Gentlemen,—We have respectfully to report that our audit of the books and financial affairs of the company, for the period commencing 1st December, 1867, and ending 30th June, 1868, has been this day completed.

As the results of that audit, we beg leave to submit herewith a statement of the assets and liabilities of the company, together with a statement of the profit and loss account at the 30th June. We accompany these *general* statements with several subordinate statements of certain particular accounts, made out more in detail, all the same having been duly audited by the several books of the company, and verified by the proper corresponding vouchers.

And having, in the progress of our audit, enjoyed the opportunity of reviewing the business of the company for the period referred to, in the marine as well as the fire department, it affords us much pleasure to congratulate the company upon the very marked success which have attended the past term of its transactions.

We remain, gentlemen, your obedient servants.
G. A. Barber, and John Maughan, Auditors.
Toronto, August 24th, 1868.

---

1 The Chairman moved, seconded by Chas. Robertson, Esq.,—That the report now read be received and adopted. Carried.

2 Moved by George Duggan, Esq., seconded by J. T. Smith. Esq.—That the thanks of the shareholders be presented to the President and Directors for their services and attention to the company's interests during the past year. Carried.

3 Moved by W. J. Macdonell, Esq., seconded by John Duggan, Esq.—That the President be requested to accept of $500, and the Vice-President of $300, for their valuable services rendered to the company since the last annual meeting.—Carried.

4 Moved by John Duggan, Esq., seconded by Chas. Robertson, Esq.—That the thanks of the meeting be given to the Secretary, assistant Secretary and officers of the company for their assiduity in the interests of the shareholders. Carried.

5 Moved by Angus Morrison, Esq., seconded by T. G. Wallis, Esq.—That Messrs. Robertson, Barber and Macdonell be the scrutineers for taking the poll for election of Directors to serve for the current year, and that the same be opened at 2 o'clock, to close at 4 o'clock; or if, after 3 o'clock, fifteen minutes should lapse and no votes recorded the poll to be then closed; and that the scrutineers be paid $6 each for their services. Carried.

The meeting then adjourned, and at 4 o'clock the scrutineers handed the following report:—

The undersigned scrutineers beg to report the election of the undernamed gentlemen as directors of the Western Assurance company for the current year:—Hon. J. McMurrich, Chas. Magrath, Esq., A. M. Smith, Esq., Robert Beaty, Esq., James Michie, Esq., John Fisken, Esq., Alex. Manning, Esq., N. Barnhart, Esq., and R. J. Dallas, Esq.

Report received and adopted.

A vote of thanks was then passed to Hon. J. McMurrich for his courteous manner and able conduct as chairman of the day's proceedings.

The meeting then adjourned.

Mining.

MADOC GOLD DISTRICT.

(From our own Correspondent.)

Belleville, Sept. 1st, 1868.

The attention of the mining interest in this quarter has centered, during the past week, on the doings of Richardson Company, and the efforts they are making to retrieve their position. At an adjourned meeting, held on Saturday, two proposals were made to the stockholders, viz., either to increase their capital stock by $100,000, raising the total amount to $400,000, or to issue preference shares, or more properly, mortgage bonds to an amount sufficient to cover their present indebtedness of $18,000, and to raise an extra sum to put their works into better condition, and pay working expenses, until the mine could be put into a state to make returns. It was also proposed to apply to the Local Legislature for an Act to empower the Directors to make such assessments on the shares as might be found necessary for these purposes in future. An adjourned meeting is to be held this afternoon (Tuesday), to determine which of the above plans shall be adopted. A large majority of the stockholders has agreed to support the Directors in endeavoring to obtain satisfactory results from this hitherto unfortunate undertaking.

Beyond this I have nothing to communicate. The reports of recent discoveries in Marmora and Elzevir are confirmed by many persons who have visited the several localities where gold has been found, and the parties who have secured interests in the same are preparing to test their value by actual work, on a sufficient scale to ensure accurate and reliable results.

THE ASCOT MINES.

The Hartford Smelting Works, Ascot, are reported to be doing a very good business. They have two furnaces in operation, turning out two and a half tons of 40 to 50 per cent. copper *mat* per day, using 40 tons of ore, and employing at the smelting works and the mine over 100 hands. One of the shafts at the mine is now 280 feet deep, and the vein of copper ten feet in width. The ore increases in richness as the shaft is sunk.

The *North American Mining & Smelting Company* at Capleton are running but one furnace at present, making about one and a half tons of *mat*, of a quality similar to the *Hartford*. At the smelting works and the mine they employ 50 hands.

At the *Suffield* (silver) mine about 20 men at present employed in getting out and b ore. The works for separating the silver fr ore are not yet in operation.

At the Golconda (gold) mine nothing doing.

We understand that a practical miner an Sherbrooke last week, and has been for days engaged in examining the gold mine Magog River, in the interest of the stock of that company. This is the mine from Prof. Tuck announced the taking of over in about a week, a couple of years since. or two ago one of the proprietors from Ne visited the locality, and spent a day panning for gold with an experienced labor Chaudiere District, and we understand ex himself highly pleased with the result. has, no doubt, been a good deal of *salting* nection with this mine, but we have be perienced and reliable miners pronounce th of gold there as very rich. The company vested a good deal of capital in the conce if gold ore be found in paying quantities will be taken to obtain it.

Gen. Adams, who is at the head of th ford and Suffield Companies, with his tv deserves a great deal of credit for the peri and idomitable spirit which they have en in developing the mining interests in Ascot believe it may now be announced as a fact Hartford Mining and Smelting Compan decided success, and may be considered an of the success of other companies, and tension of the mining interest in this se the Province. We think there cannot be that Ascot, Orford and several other Town this District are rich in mineral wealth. require capital, skill and perseverance to d wealth from the bowels of the earth ; tv into circulation, and to encourage ever branch of industry. Heretofore, mining h been entered into principally as a spec and there is too much reason to believe scrupulous and unprincipled men, perfectly less of the means adopted to fill their own and to deplete the pockets of others. T been the character of mining operation where. Sherbrooke and vicinity is not suffering in its reputation from the reckless ters of a few adventurers, who have impo the credulity of the public in these s operations. While this has been the gre of injury to the mining interests here, it suffered from the operations of parties w entered into this business without skill little prudence, and without sufficient c authorize the hope of success. The r been that after spending a few thousand commencing operations, they have bec couraged, and abandoned the work, wealth which would have rewarded a ski persevering outlay, eluded their too eag Disappointed and disgusted they have, them, denounced all mining operation section as folly. So persistent and posit been the statements made and opinions by parties of this stamp that, were a r mine to be discovered, it would be very to get any attention paid to the subject however, will correct this evil. The working of one or two mines, will soc confidence. We believe the time is not when the copper and silver, if not go lies buried in the earth in the Township will be brought to the surface in immens ties, and prove a source of wealth and to the population of the surrounding t—*Sherbrooke Gazette.*

It is said that the Hon. John Rose wil Washington shortly, on business conne the negotiation of the Reciprocity Treat

Insurance.

RECORD.—Sunnidale, Aug. 29.—A most us fire occurred at this place. It originated the woods and spreading to the village of le committed great destruction. Among dings destroyed were the passenger and rouse of the Northern Railway, insured for hed and contents, $1,200; station agent's $250; total, $2,300. The loss is equally between the British America, Imperial, of London, Western and Provincial.

trham, Ont., Aug.—A Peterboro' paper t on the 15th inst., a house in Ashburned as a tavern, but not occupied at present ng of Mr. Mowry, but occupied by Mr. G. ind Mr. John Clarke's tannery, and the and sheds attached to all these buildings sumed by fire. The loss may be summed i :—The tavern stables and shed about ; owned by Joseph Sedgwick. Mr. l loss is about $1,500 ; insured for $1,000. rk's loss he considered about $3,000 ; insr. $1,400 in the Royal and Ætna. Total ut $6,000 ;—total insured, $2,400.

rton, Aug.—A large barn belonging to Mr. Goetz, was struck by lightning and onsumed, together with its entire contents, ng of the principal part of this season's and a lot of machinery and implements. spread with great rapidity, and no sooner dreadful crash heard by those near, than le barn was one sheet of flame. The processtroyed consisted of 500 bushels of fall 40 tons of hay; &c., &c. The loss is esti t over $3,000, and there is no insurance.

River, Ont., Aug. 31.—VanOrden's mill sroyed under very suspicious circumstances. two arrests have since been made. Loss insured in Commercial Union for $1,000, he Queen for $1,000.

hn, N.B., Aug.—The steam saw mill of Turtlott & Allingham was totally destroy e on Thursday evening. Insurance $8,000. is supposed to be the work of an incen

rich, Aug. 31.—The Press dispatch says, lay a fire broke out in a large wooden n West street belonging to Dr. Gordon, of h, and Thomas Robertson, of Dundas, and d by W. Moss, shoemaker, B. McCormick, Miss Taylor, milliner, Mr. Thompson, ker, and Mr. Sharp as a dwelling. The g being old and dry, the flames spread , and in a short time communicated with k North American hotel, kept by Andrew l, which too fell a prey to the devouring l. No water could be procured for the enat by the use of pails and zealous exertions itizens the Bank of Montréal building on b was saved. Several buildings on the op ide of the street were fired, but promptly ished. The North American hotel was fipr $1,600 on building in the Provincial ce company, and for $500 on furniture in b Mutual, which it is thought will fully fr. Donogh's loss. Mr. Gordon had $500 on wooden block, but I cannot ascertain mount, if any, Mr. Robertson has on his , the loss of occupants except Miss Taylor, small, as most of their goods were saved, course damaged. The fire is said to have led in Miss Taylor's shop, but how is yet en. She places her loss at $800, and has ge of $700. Fortunately the wind was not and happened to be in the right direction, eighth of the town would undoubtedly en burnt.

YORK LIFE.—The New York Life Insu 'ompany has made a deposit with the Go nt, and has, we are informed, obtained the ry license to transact Life Insurance busi the Dominion of Canada.

SCHOONER DUNDERBERG.—This vessel, which sunk off Point au Barques some time since, was insured for $35,000, as follows : Home, of New York, $5,000 ; Western, of Buffalo, $5,000 ; Underwriters' Agency, $5,000; Detroit Fire and Marine, $5,000; Ætna, $10,000, and James New Haven, $5,000. The cargo was covered as follows: Security, of New York, $15,000 ; Western, of Buffalo, $12,000; National, of Boston, $5,000; Republic, of Chicago, $5,000.

MONTREAL WATER WORKS.—A Committee of the City Council, at a late meeting, recommended that the sum of $25,900 be appropriated for the construction of certain engine houses according to plans and specifications approved by the Committee. A further sum of $4,000 was voted for defraying certain expenses, and the contract let to Mr. John Donnelly at $24,315. At the same meeting the contract for the construction of a central fire station was awarded to James Howley & Co., for the sum of $4,600.

HALIFAX FIRE DEPARTMENT.—The following figures, which we take from a Halifax paper, show the various amounts contributed by the Fire Insurance Companies to the revenue of, that city during the years 1863, '64, 65 and '66 ; as also the sums paid by the city in support of the Fire Department during the same periods :—

Assessment paid by the various Insurance Companies :

In 1863,	$3,739 00
1864,	4,278 57
1865,	2,786 70
1866,	2,944 84
Total,	$13,749 11

The average being $3,437 28.

City Expenditure on account of the Fire Department :

In 1863,	$2,948 55
1864,	3,092 93
1865,	4,000 00
1866,	3,540 00
Total,	$14,181 48

The average being $3,545 27. It will thus be seen that the Insurance Companies alone, nearly supported the Fire Department, the difference against them being only a little over $100.

IS FIRE UNDERWRITING A PROFITABLE BUSINESS.

Do fire insurance companies pay their stockholders remunerative dividends? Let us take the statistics of the New York insurance department. In the last three years the one hundred and sixty-four fire and fire-marine insurance companies which do business in that state, received $110,720,700.28 in premium receipts on fire and marine risks. Where did these one hundred and ten millions of dollars go? For payment of losses, $61,996,684.07 ; for agents' commissions, $13,091,936.49 ; for the tax iniquity, national, state and local, $5,986,870.97 ; for salaries and other management expenses, 15,650,210-33 ; total $111,519,470.70, or $798,769.93 *excess of disbursements over current receipts in a three years' busi ness* ! True, these companies paid $11,670,184 in dividends during this period—an average of $3,920,061 annually among one hundred and sixty-four companies. Now the total assets of these companies during these three years averaged $73,902,575, which, according to the figure just given, yielded only five and one-third per cent. in actual profits to stockholders. But these dividends were not obtained from the surplus earnings of the current business, the expenses of which exceeded the receipts from new transactions. They were only reached by appropriating the interest from the accumulated earnings of previous business, transacted during the period when fire underwriting was a prosperous occupa tion. In other words, in order to give the holders of insurance stock even a paltry interest upon the money invested therein, the directors of these companies had to borrow from the funds which legitimately belong to and should always remain in their reserved surplus. Increased business demands increased facilities. So it happens that insurance companies, to preserve themselves in safe condition, to afford adequate security to their policy holders, must either confine their business to fixed limits, or increase their surplus additions every year in the same ratios as they extend their operations. Companies which go on year after year, writing all the risks which they can get, without accumulating a corresponding increase of surplus assets, will very soon reach a crisis in their affairs when neither premium receipts nor interest receipts will suffice to liquidate their losses. It hardly requires the force of argument to prove that safety and prosperity alike urgently demand that not only shall past surplus reserves be preserved intact, but that the interest arising therefrom shall be applied every year to their further addition. The use of this interest fund to pay dividends can not be too severely reprehended. But when it is used, not only to pay dividends but to repair excess of current disbursements over current receipts, then we should hardly be able to find language to express our condemnation of the practice. A business so conducted as not to yield enough income to discharge current liabilities must be on the verge of immediate disaster. It is to this point that fire underwriting in the United States has finally reached, and, though there may be relief in a brief period of unusual prosperity, the law of average will soon assert itself, bringing, perhaps, untold and unparalleled disasters.

That we may be able, not less to bring the importance and necessity of reform to the notice of insurance companies, than to illustrate the absurdity of the public prejudice against the existing rates of insurance, we present herewith an original analysis of insurance receipts and disbursements for the last three years, as compiled by us from the returns of the one hundred and sixty-four fire and fire-marine companies doing business in the state of New York :

INCOME.

	1865.	1866.
Fire premiums	$25,419,589 55	$32,281,404 76
Marine and inland premiums	4,188,652 76	6,586,087 51
Interest and rents	4,785,639 39	4,476,944 94
Miscellaneous receipts	131,865 08	168,548 77
Total cash income	$34,525,746 80	$43,512,985 98
Fire premiums	$36,162,138 45	$93,883,132 76
Marine and inland premiums	6,082,827 23	16,837,567 52
Interest and rent	4,752,841 58	14,015,425 91
Miscellaneous receipts	219,979 17	520,393 02
Total cash income	$47,217,786 43	$125,256,519 21

DISBURSEMENTS.

	1865.	1866.
Fire losses	$17,264,618 33	$23,913,745 87
Marine losses	3,422,417 08	6,092,545 19
Dividends	4,616,607 11	3,369,250 70
Commissions	3,323,687 59	4,805,407 34
Salaries	2,401,339 69	2,812,866 30
National taxes	873,992 97	1,089,746 04
State and local taxes	909,755 97	955,844 19
All other expenses	2,020,782 70	2,321,327 70
Total disbursements	$34,833,201 44	$45,239,133 24
Total prem. receipts	$29,608,242 33	$35,867,492 27
Excess of disbursements, including dividends, over premium receipts	$5,224,959 11	$6,371,640 97
Dividends	$4,616,607 11	$3,369,250 70
Excess of losses and current expenses over prem. receipts	$1,608,352 00	$3,002,390 27

	1867.	Total.
Fire losses	$20,818,269 87	$61,996,634 07
Marine losses	5,350,456 17	14,793,818 35
Dividends	3,774,326 96	11,690,184 67
Commissions	4,962,842 56	13,091,936 49
Salaries	3,280,292 06	8,494,498 05
National taxes	1,209,259 42	3,122,998 43
State and local taxes,	998,272 38	2,863,872 54
All other expenses	2,813,601 88	7,155,712 28
Total disbursements	$43,207,320 30	$123,279,654 98
Total prem. receipts	$42,244,965 68	$110,720,700 28
Excess of disbursements, including dividends, over premium receipts	$962,354 62	$12,558,954 70
Dividends	3,774,326 96	11,760,184 77
Excess of losses and current expenses over prem. receipts		$798,769 93

The following calculation of per centages will be interesting in connection with the above tables:

Percentage of total losses to total premium receipts	9.93
Percentage of total commissions to total premium receipts	11.81
Percentage of total management expenses, exclusive of commissions and taxes, to total premium receipts	14.14
Percentage of total taxes to total premium receipts	5.14
Total	101.29
	100.00
Percentage of excess of current expenses to current receipts	1.29

Now the total average capital and surplus assets of these companies were $73,902,575.09. In calculating the per centage of dividend to stockholders we use these figures as principal. The total assets of a company are what that company uses in the transaction of its business. It is the amount of money employed for the protection of policy-holders, and, being actually thus used—the company liable constantly to its entire payment for losses—it is right that a calculation upon the basis of *total assets* should determine the per centage of dividend. A dividend may be declared upon mere capital, but the dividend so declared represents the earnings, not only of the chartered capital, but of all other funds reserved in connection with that capital. Applying this rule, we discover that the total capital (chartered and reserve) of insurance companies, during the three years covered by the above statistics, yielded an average annual dividend of only five and one-third per cent!

The great and startling facts brought out by these figures are these:

1. That one hundred and sixty-four principal American insurance companies doing a fire and fire-marine business paid out during the years 1865, 1866, and 1867, *twelve and a half millions of dollars more than their current premium receipts.*

2. That the premium receipts of insurance companies are not adequate to pay their current expenses.

3. That of one hundred and twenty-five million dollars of total income for three years, less than two millions were preserved for surplus additions.

4. That the profit of the capital actually employed in the business was only five and one-third per cent.

5. That nearly five and one-half per cent. of the premium receipts of fire insurance companies is absorbed by the tax imposition; in other words that the proportion of premium receipts saved for dividends is less than the amount thereof paid for taxes.

It is only by studying closely the experience of the past, and by applying the knowledge deducible from such study, that companies can fitly undertake future transactions. Their management involves greater skill and more constant prudence, because of greater hazard, than any other commercial or financial operation. Their business is subject to constantly varying conditions and the most powerful and sudden contingencies.

On the other hand their patrons are not less interested than are the companies themselves in the practical recognition of whatever demands shall be essential to the prosperity of insurance corporations. Insurance is valuable only when it is guaranteed by a company which adheres to safe methods of underwriting. It is obvious that a merchant can better afford to pay three or even four per cent. to a company which has always indemnified its policy-holders, and which possesses an unimpaired capital, than one or two per cent. to a company whose integrity and ability are not fully above suspicion. What the insured pays when he purchases a policy of insurance is recovery from loss, and his policy, to be worth anything, must carry with it the assured and absolute certainty of indemnity in case of damage. But against any and all contingencies, fire is the ever constant contingency to which every property holder is subject; and insurance is the single and only adequate preserver and conservator of his fortune. But there are degrees of insurance. Unfortunately nothing is too sacred for the rapacity of audacious mankind; and, therefore, we find hundreds of unloosed penitentiary subjects swarming the land in the sheep-guise of insurance agents, and insurance presidents and insurance secretaries, confusing the public by the allurement of what is called cheap rates. To any reflecting mind the term suggests sufficient condemnation to repel patronage. A commodity to be called *cheap* must be either less valuable than the same commodity sold at a higher price, must cost less, or must afford its dealer less profit. Now what are the facts in relation to cheap insurance? We pointed out last month that the earnings of legitimate and honest insurance companies are, and have been for many years, less than the earnings of capital in any other occupation; and we have again shown in the figures exhibited above, that the interest returns of insurance capital are ridiculously and absurdly low. Certainly no man, much less any liberal business man, will insist, after viewing the deduction we have enumerated, that insurance companies can afford to continue a business which does not yield sufficient to pay current expenses. Hence a reduction of the existing rates of insurance is wholly out of the question. Not only that, but insurance companies must at once either devise some means to largely lessen their losses by fire, or considerable increase their rates. While the ordinary management and agency expenses of all our principal fire insurance companies have already settled to the lowest point of economy consistent with their vast and widely extended operations, it might be possible, without a further increase of rates in most localities, to reform the business *in the more writing of risks* (accepting only those that are free from *moral* hazard) so as to make the premium receipts adequate to the payment not only of all losses and expenses, but also of fair dividends to stockholders, leaving the entire interest receipts from capital and surplus unimpaired for the further accumulaion of the companies' gross assets.

FAILURE OF A LIVE STOCK INSURANCE COMPANY.—The Hartford Live Stock Insurance Company, of Hartford, Conn., has been suspended. The company has sustained losses within the last twenty-two months of $410,000. The capital of the company is $150,000, $100,000 of which has been deposited with the Treasurer of Connecticut. The balance of $50,000 was kept by the company for working capital. The $100,000 in the Treasurer's hands will be used by the company for paying losses and unearned premiums. The Superintendent of the insurance department at Albany has notified the agents of the company in this State to take no more policies.

Railway News.

NORTHERN RAILWAY.—Traffic Rec[...]
week ending 22nd August, 1868.

Passengers	$2,85[...]
Freight	6,78[...]
Mails and sundries	29[...]
Total receipts for week	$9,94[...]
Corresponding week 1867	11,01[...]
Decrease	$1,07[...]

GREAT WESTERN RAILWAY.—Traffic [...]
ending 14th August, 1868.

Passengers	$29,9[...]
Freight and live stock	30,14[...]
Mails and sundries	2,1[...]
	$62,2[...]
Corresponding Week of '67.	66,9[...]
Decrease	$4,6[...]

TORONTO, GREY AND BRUCE RAILW[...]
town of Owen Sound has granted a bon[...]
000 to this enterprise. The vote on th[...]
for that purpose, stood 106 for the By[...]
13 against it.

The directors of this company ar[...]
meetings in various localities, along [...]
which the road is proposed to take. [...]
been favorably received and have obt[...]
mises of support from most of the mu[...]
who have not yet voted.

RAILWAY CONTRACT.—The contract [...]
ing the Massawippi Valley Railroad, an[...]
of the road for ninety-nine years to the P[...]
River Company, was signed on Friday w[...]
price paid for building the road is $8[...]
$23,500 per mile, the distance being [...]
miles. The road is to be completed [...]
July, 1870, in time to celebrate the [...]
Lennoxville on Dominion day and at [...]
the 4th July. The contractors, we u[...]
are to break ground on the 1st of next [...]

THE MASSAWIPPI VALLEY RAILR[...]
learn by the Stanstead *Journal* that ar[...]
have been completed between the Mass[...]
Passumpsic companies, which secure th[...]
struction of the above road. The [...]
corporation engage to build the lin[...]
boundary to Lennoxville, a distance of [...]
miles, by the 1st of July, 1870, for a C[...]
scription of $165,000, an equal amo[...]
furnished by parties south, $400,000 [...]
and $70,000 in stock, making a capi[...]
$800,000. The Passumpsic Company [...]
poration, then lease the road, agreeing [...]
same stock dividends that they do o[...]
road, pay the interest on the bonds, an[...]
bonds at maturity. The Passumpsic [...]
of course are to have a majority of t[...]
directors of the Massawippi Corpora[...]
road is constructed by the latter corpo[...]
cause it would be awkward for a foreig[...]
to undertake such a work in Canada. [...]
gratulate that flourishing section of th[...]
on the prospect of having so fine a r[...]
munication with the northern and south[...]
on such advantageous terms as the abo[...]
ments indicate. The Passumpsic Com[...]
of the most successful in New Englan[...]
dends of 3 per cent. having been decla[...]
the past year. Its stock will be greatl[...]
in value by the construction of the Can[...]
which will lessen the distance between [...]
and Quebec by 65 miles, and the Ca[...]
holders in the Massawippi stock comm[...]
to reap equal profits with the Passum[...]
pany.—*Montreal Witness.*

THE CANADIAN MONETARY TIMES AND
INSURANCE CHRONICLE is printed every Thursday
Evening, in time for the English Mail.
Subscription Price, one year, $2, or $3 in
American currency. Single copies, free cents each.
Casual advertisements will be charged ten cents
per line of solid nonpareil, each insertion. All
letters to be addressed, "THE CANADIAN MONE-
TARY TIMES," TORONTO, ONT. Registered letters
so addressed are at the risk of the Publishers.
Cheques should be made payable to J. M. TROUT,
Business Manager, who will, in future, issue all
receipts for money.

The Canadian Monetary Times.

THURSDAY, SEPTEMBER 3, 1868.

TORONTO AS AN EMPORIUM OF TRADE.

It is admitted that trade flows in certain
natural channels, and these it will seek despite every effort to divert it. Recognizing
this axiom the shrewd business-man always
seeks to place himself exactly in the current;
or, in other words, to locate himself at the
most favorable point for the successful prosecution of his operations. Success or failure
often hinge on mere location, and a mistake
in this respect has frequently terminated in
disaster in spite of the most vigilant economy,
perseverance and honesty.

New evidence is being daily afforded of the
correctness of a wide-spread impression that
Toronto is making marked progress in commercial importance. Many of these evidences
are, to a certain extent, intangible, but for
that none the less conclusive or convincing.
Our inland position renders it a work peculiarly complicated to collect the figures which
accurately represent our business and the
annual increase of it; but still enough are
forthcoming to point out unmistakably the
fact just stated.

As an export market, Toronto is favorably
situated. It is the point to which the surplus
products of Ontario flow as naturally as the
St. Lawrence to the Ocean. Once here these
products can be sent to a half dozen leading
markets on this continent with the greatest
facility, or to Europe by either of the competing routes via New York or Montreal as
the cost of freight and charges makes most
desirable. The immense bulk of grain,
lumber and timber that flows into this market,
especially in the fall, induces a fleet of schooners to collect in our harbour, the competition
among which cheapens freight to the lowest
paying point. This enables our dealers to
get what they have to ship laid down in
American markets at less cost than their
fellow dealers of the shipping towns either

east or west. This is one of the reasons why
higher prices are usually paid here for farm
produce than at other markets no further
distant from the great centres of population.
But it is not the only reason; much larger
lots are handled which permits of a smaller
per centage of profit; time and wages, bank
expenses, insurance and other charges are
proportionately less, and besides a greater
number of cargoes are turned over during
the course of the season which admits of an
aggregate profit large in amount. The sum
credited to us under the head of exports rose
steadily from $625,682 in 1858, to $2,478,292
in 1867, showing that our trade outward has
quadrupled within a decade. We speak of the
amount credited because a great part of our
exports do not appear in the official accounts
as exports from Toronto. Numerous large
rafts of timber, for instance, which are towed
down the lake and the St. Lawrence, are
credited in the export returns of Montreal,
or those of the Canadian Gibraltar a little
further down-stream. So that while our
export returns do not at all exhibit the entire volume of our trade, they do indicate
the rate of increase, for it is fair to presume
that the proportion credited in the way we
have pointed out, is relatively the same from
year to year.

The important flour trade with the markets
of the Lower Provinces, was more largely
done by Toronto last season than ever before.
The Grand Trunk and Great Western Railways
actively competed for this trade, (as they also
did for the carriage of produce destined for
Liverpool) one via Portland and the other
via Boston, and this competition resulted in
cheaper rates than had previously been obtained. Besides a steamer, Her Majesty,
running direct between Toronto and Halifax
and other ports of the Lower Provinces,
carried a large amount and at rates of freight
more favorable to shippers than are charged
by the regular lines.

In respect of our imports, the account is
not less flattering. They rose in value from
$3,768,934, in 1858, to $7,352,335, last year,
or nearly one hundred per cent. As in the
case of exports, these figures, which are from
the official returns, do not show the full value
of all the imported goods received in this
market. They merely represent the value
of goods entered at Toronto in the books of
the Custom House here, while it is, undisputed that a considerable portion of the
importations of Toronto merchants are passed
through the Custom House at Montreal,
and appear among the imports of that port.
There are various reasons for this, of a special character which it is not for us to point
out; they are well understood by those in
trade.

But the increase in our import trade is not more clearly shown by the figures just given than by the extension of our facilities for the storage and sale of all kinds of imported goods, and the marked increase in the number, and improvement in the commercial status of the houses engaged in this department. Some of the very best firms in London and Hamilton, whose names will at once recur to those at all familiar with the matter under notice, have permanently located themselves here; others whom we know of and of equally good standing, would do likewise only for a variety of obstacles connected with a change of situation. But the principal additions to our business firms have been from Montreal. Several leading establishments of that city have opened branches here; and others contemplate doing so as soon as our warehouse accommodation will permit.

It is because we intercept a large share of the trade which formerly went past us, that these changes are being made. We can now lay many classes of goods down from Liverpool as cheap as Montreal houses, and save distance, time and expenses to the Western dealer. These facts are indisputable. But those who want further proof can make enquiry of almost any country merchant, and they will soon be satisfied.

Frequent cases have come to our notice of dealers in Ontario who went to Montreal to make purchases, but returned to Toronto without buying a dollar's worth, and made their selections in our market. The bearing of such facts is unmistakable. They are deeply suggestive.

Toronto has made a long step in advance within the past twelvemonth. Real Estate has risen in value, and is now readily saleable at enhanced prices. Rents have risen 15 to 25 per cent., and houses are scarce. Should the proposed lines of railway leading into this city be constructed, as there is little reason to doubt they will be, we shall enter upon a period of progress of which the present is merely a foretaste. These roads will bring the productions of those fertile districts, intended to be served, directly into this market—a result which would give us daily receipts at least treble what they are now. Within five years. if all these enterprises go on, we expect our census returns to show a population of one hundred thousand. These grand results are plainly foreshadowed in the facts we have hinted at, and it is but for our citizens to show a liberal public spirit and exchange lethargy for enterprise to accelerate what must come at last—to give Toronto the position of the first city in the Dominion.

WESTERN ASSURANCE COMPANY.

A statement of the business of this Company for the seven months ended June 30th, appears in the report presented at the annual meeting held on the 1st instant. The gross fire premiums were $82,658.80 and the losses $43,150.49 or 52 per cent.; in the Marine Branch premiums $43,746.64, losses $15,244 or 34 2-5 per cent. The balance available was $39,535.13 out of which a dividend of five per cent was declared, and a sum of $25,000 was absorbed by the deposit of $17,000 with government and the investment of $8,000 in Dominion stock. The paid up capital is represented by Debentures $35,791.82, Mortgages $28,656.37, Building $16,000, which certainly are substantial looking assets. We are glad to notice that the Agents' Balances do not exceed $7,048.28, although, possibly, the Bills Receivable or the marine notes, are swollen in amount at the expense of the former item. We have already had occasion to notice a report of a company which professes to have $35,065 out in the precarious custody of agents, and we confess to little faith in such an asset.

A large increase in the business done, and a percentage of losses far below the average, justifies the Directors in hoping for continued prosperity, but an extended business requires greater security and we think it would have been well had the dividend of five per cent. been forgone. The present period of success should be made the best possible use of to fortify against darker days. The Company is undoubtedly doing too much business. We do not know whether this will be taken as complimentary or otherwise, but if the Directors desire to build up their interests on the broad basis of an unwavering public confidence they must adopt the spirit of the old adage, "cut your coat according to your cloth." The Company has back-bone, but it is quite possible to overload it. But we must defer further comment for the present.

THE HARVEST.

Returns, which have been published, from various parts of the country, east and west, indicate that the harvest now gathered in has, after all, been a fair average. Fall wheat suffered little damage from any cause and gives a large yield of excellent quality. Spring wheat suffered much, midge, weevil, rust, drought and the whole army of mishaps and nuisances have scourged it, so that we may not expect more than a two-thirds crop. Barley in many cases was stinted by heat and lack of moisture, but probably on the whole the thinness of the berry brought about in this way will be compensated

by its beautiful bright color and thin The color of this grain affects its val much as its weight. Oats are a crop in the aggregate, though in sections they were reported an entire ure; so dry was the weather that the not in some places grow higher than t inches, a few light grains making u head. Peas in many places fell a vict bugs; drought also did its share of da and there will only be half a crop. are quite a failure; late sown may do thing, if not potatoes will be a scarce modity before spring. Hay was a large having nearly advanced to maturity the drought set in. Apples, plums, &c., are doing fairly as is shewn by the supply now in the market at moderate p small fruits were a failure.

Altogether we ought to be satisfied wi season's ingathering. Notwithstandir shortness of the yield of some article high prices now obtainable for all farn duce secure ample profits to producers.

THE PROVINCIAL INSURANCE PANY.

As our statement respecting the mo given by this Company on its premise been questioned we now furnish some ulars which are the result of a pe investigation at the Registry office. stated that the mortgage was mad Building Society. It now appears t was first made by the Company to an dual and then assigned to a Building S The mortgage is dated 30th July, 18 by a strange coincidence, the assign also dated the 30th July, 1868. There error in the amount of the mortgag placed it at $6,000. We must apolog this error as the true amount was $8,0 yet remains to be explained what the sity was that occasioned such an extr ary proceeding in the face of a "net of $35,549.

TORONTO WATER SUPPLY

Some observations made a week reference to the question of water sup fire purposes in this city, has called letter from the Superintendent of th Company. For this letter we reques ful perusal by our citizens. It gives mary of the proceedings had in the n dispute between the Corporation an pany, and traces it down to its prese quo. The matter will, no doubt, further ventilation. As it is, the an the remuneration which the Compa receive, seems to be open and unsettl so far as we have looked into the m that in addition to the awkwardness er of the situation, the city is drift- a law-suit which will do no good o the lawyers who have the manage- the case. Why not settle the matter way now, and avoid the expense of irable an issue.

TO OUR READERS.

any interesting communications pub- our columns prove, from the inquiry ite, the advantage of collecting the ce of various localities and obtaining ts or suggestions from different in- ı. Such communications provoke and stimulate research, besides add- e general stock of information. We r obligations to the writers and we ir numbers will increase as there is ılination on our part to extend court- l seeking or communicating inform- common interest. There are many als connected with every department h our pages are devoted who are pable of instructing their cólaborers e endeavour to fulfil our mission we the same time, fairly ask the assist- those whose opportunities furnish th facts which it would benefit all to acquainted with, or whose studies solutions for problems in finance, in- and commerce which, as yet, are not ly settled. Our desire is to make per as interesting as possible. We e hope those friendly to our under- will manifest their friendliness by ng the objects we have in view.

nanager of the Ætna Insurance Com- Dublin writes us from that city in e to our quotations of the stock of pany, alleging that our figures are t. In explanation, we have merely hat we correct our stock list weekly rices given in the London *Economist* ers of the leading journals in Eng- ıich are regarded as reliable authori- matters of this kind, and we cannot he falsity of their quotations with- ıbitable proof. We, however, cheer- re the friendly letter of Mr. Innes in column that he may speak for himself.

Communications.

PROVINCIAL INS. CO.

he Monetary Times.

As a stockholder in the Provincial Insur- npany, I beg to thank you for your place this Company on a proper foot- r stock is not paid up and, like many am loth to throw good money after hat benefit is it to me to have affairs

go on as they are?' My liability is constantly staring me in the face. Were there any rea- sonable prospect of improvement I should not complain, but I am convinced, from the last Statement, that the present Management is wholly incompetent. If what I hear be true, respecting the delays in payment, the trivial excuses made from time to time, the complaints of agents and the old-fogy red tapeism that prevail, I say make a change or give up the ship. Mr. Crocker is not the man for the office he holds. I have heard some of the directors and many of the sharehold- ers express the greatest contempt for his business capacity. I think he is kept there out of sheer pity. Well, pity is to be cultivated, but I cer- tainly think that some consideration is due to those who have money invested in the concern. I, for one, want to know how I stand and endorse cordially your suggestion respecting an investiga- tion.

Yours, &c.,
A SHAREHOLDER.

Toronto, August 29.

[We have little pity to spare for the writer of the above. If he did not think it worth his while to attend the late meeting and there give vent to his grievances, he should take the conse- quences. We think that there is every hope for the Company, but when its members show them- selves neglectful, we are not prepared to do their work.—Ed. C. M. T.]

"WHO'S TO BLAME!"

To the Editor of the Monetary Times.

Sir,—Your paper of the 27th inst., under the above pertinent interrogatory, contains an article on the Water Supply of this City, for fire pur- poses.

Reference through the public press to this sub- ject has of late been so frequently made by me, I feel reluctant to again recur to it, but feeling the importance of the interests you represent, I am in- duced as briefly as possible to refer again to the history of the Water Company, in its relationship with the City Corporation, in respect to the supply of water for fires, &c.

At the construction of the Water Works of this City, when Toronto was confined to very narrow limits, the Water Company erected a certain num- ber of fire hydrants on their Works, which, up to the present time, have been used by the Fire De- partment. In an agreement of twenty-one years between the Water Company and the City (which agreement expired on the thirtieth June, 1864), the City was granted the right of erecting as many more additional hydrants as they saw necessary, at their own expense, on any new Mains to be laid down by the Company, and of which right the City availed themselves to the extent of the pre- sent establishment.

On the eve of the expiry of the above contract, namely, on the Twenty-ninth February, 1864, in answer to an enquiry of the Committee on Fire, Water and Gas, on the subject of the terms and conditions on which the Company would supply water for fires after the first of July of that year —when the old contract expired—a letter was ad- dressed to the City Clerk, by the Clerk of the Water Company, containing, amongst other provi- sions, the following paragraph, as the basis on which the Company were willing to enter into a further negotiation with the City :

"The City to purchase from the Company the hydrants now belonging to the latter, at a valua- tion, and to assume the entire *supervision, control,* and *repair* of all the hydrants."

An arbitration between the City and the Com- pany soon followed the above communication, but keeping in view only the amount of compensation which the Company should receive for fire purposes alone, the Arbitrators in naming a yearly sum for the service which could be determined by either party giving nine months' notice of their intention

so to do, clearly lost sight of the conditions quoted in the above paragraph, and on the fulfilment of which alone the Company were induced to go into arbitration at all.

Amongst other reasons, from the repetition of the frequent statements and rumours from interested pparties, and taken up by the press as true, (almost at every fire,) of the cry—"No water in the Hy- drants!"—no matter how long the service of turn- ing on the high pressure had been performed by the Company's turncock, before the arrival of any engine on the spot, the Company felt it necessary to deter- mine their agreement with the City on the 1st July last, and a letter, of which the following is a copy, was written by the Clerk of the Company to the Clerk of the City Council.

Office Metropolitan Water Co.,
Sept. 25, 1867.
John Carr, Esq., City Clerk.

Sir,—I am instructed to notify you that this Company will terminate the present arrangement with the city for water supply, for extinguishing fires, on the 30th day of June next.

I am, sir, yours, &c.,
(Signed), JOHN EVANS,
Clerk Water Company.

Up to the 29th June of this year no satisfactory reply was had from the city authorities, and on this date the Company's Solicitor wrote the City Clerk, stating the sum which the Company would charge for the supply of water for the ensuing year, referring to the following proviso, "That the city at once become the purchasers of the twenty- eight hydrants belonging to the Company, the re- maining sixty-one being already the property of the city, and assume the responsibility of turning the high pressure on and off as necessity may re- quire. The fact of the fire hydrants of a city not being within the entire control of the municipal authorities is exceptional, and in this instance, to make that control complete, the city must under- take the management of the high-pressure valve. The police station, where a responsible officer is on duty day and night, being adjacent to the valve, this service can be effected prompt, and effi- ciently by him. These two points are insisted upon, and will not be waived under any circum- stances, as they have heretofore, and will for all time to come, (if allowed to remain in their pres- ent position), prove a most fruitful source of com- plaint and irritation between the Company and the city officials."

In answer to the letter of the Company's Solici- tor, dated 29th June, and of which the above is a portion, the Company, on the 5th August, received a communication from the City Clerk, stating that the city were willing to refer the matter to arbitration. To this latter communication the Company's Solicitor had replied, viz : "That the Metropolitan Water Company are advised that the city authorities have, by their acts, (i.e.), by having, since the expiration of the contract, on several occasions used the water for fire purposes, accepted the terms contained in his letter of the 29th June, and that the same are binding upon them for the current year, and consequently so far as the terms are concerned, there is nothing to arbitrate about ; but with regard to the hydrants taken up by the city under the arrangement, the Company are prepared to name their arbitrator and proceed with the reference."

In order to avoid all collision with the city, or rather the Fire Department, I ask can anything be fairer on the part of the Water Company, or more compatible with the interests of the citizens at large, than the giving of the city authorities the entire control of their works, as far as it extends to fire purposes ? Can any honest set of men, de- siring that every inhabitant of this city should have the earliest and most ample supply of water in case of fire, through the hands of the paid offi- cials of the city, refuse to adopt a course, in itself so apparently beneficial in the activity which it is calculated to create in the Fire Department, which, in such case, would not, as heretofore, have the alleged delay or inefficiency of the Water Company's officials as a loophole to escape by.

In conclusion, I beg to say in reference to the bugbear "street watering," that the Company make no contracts with the city for watering streets. The city authorities advertise for tenders for watering various sections of the city in the season, the tenders are taken up by various carters in the city who have to provide securities to the satisfaction of the city for the proper fulfilment of their duties; and who, if the city required of them, would also give additional security for the repairs of the hydrants, when put out of order by them, they being the parties alone responsible for any damage. The Water Company simply sell the contractors the water, on the understanding that they have the permission of the city authorities to use the hydrants, and in getting this permission the ratepayers are well aware that their share of the assessment for street watering would be increased six-fold if such permission were denied to the contractors, and that they were compelled to fetch their water from the bay. I can find persons in this city who will undertake to keep the whole of the hydrants in repair for one dollar each per annum, and it is a great pity the City Council allow both themselves and the citizens to be so unduly exercised by so very paltry an affair.

I am, sir, your obedient servant,
L. G. BOLSTER,
Sup. Met. W. W. Co.
Water Work's Office, Toronto,
29th August, 1858.

AMERICAN SILVER.

To the Editor Monetary Times.

SIR,—For the last month the newspapers of this country have been flooded with communications on this subject. First, with a grand flourish as the merchants in each town came into the combination to put silver below its proper value, and secondly, recording the secessions from the scheme, as the parties thereto found out the absurdity and impracticability of carrying it out. Doctors are said to kill oftener than they cure, which evil report against the profession probably arises from the malpractice of quacks, who, wanting in proper knowledge, impose upon the soft heads of the community. In the same way the currency may be likened to a profession; but alas! the educated doctors in it are few. Every man thinks that he understands the silver question and can remedy the evil at once, summarily and forever. However, when the infallible plan is tried it simply unsettles value for a few days and then is dropped; the result of the experiment having been profit to the few and loss to the many. In the name of common sense I protest against these currency quacks being allowed to meddle any more with our silver circulation, which, if let alone, regulates itself according to supply and demand as justly and systematically as any other article of commerce.

The amount of silver capital in this country is estimated at $10,000,000, nearly all of which has been accumulated within the last five years. This amount, to a great extent, represents the profits that we made out of the necessities of the people of the United States during their war; the representative in fact of an extreme value for all our productions. Let me ask whether the country is less prosperous now than it was before we received this accession to our wealth. Does not the improved financial position of every branch of industry in the country answer no? The Americans, from whom we got this silver, have to rest content with a depreciated currency, worth only seventy cents in the dollar; while we wretched people complain of a currency which is depreciated only on account of its plentifulness; a currency, the value of which is contained in itself, being really better value to the holder than notes of the Bank of England.

It stands to reason that a country which owns a floating capital of specie out of the power of the banks, lending institutions or anything in that nature,—a capital which, like labour, only enriches by active and useful employment,—a capital which never lies dead in stocks or bonds, but which is always being employed by thousands of small holders in every description of investment and enterprise, must be richer than one whose capital may be almost entirely drawn in by banks or individuals in seasons of commercial or agricultural depression.

At certain periods of the year the banks call in the largest part of their loans, and their money is, for the time, withdrawn from use; but the silver is not withdrawn, but remains continually circulating without being influenced in any way by bank panics or withdrawals. People feel no uncertainty about the value which they own when they hold silver, but serious doubts sometimes arise in their minds about bank notes. Silver, at least, has the merit of being worth a certain absolute value, say ninety-five cents to the dollar, while bank bills, which compose the rest of the currency of our country, Canadian silver being but trifling in amount, are worth their face, or are not dependant altogether on the wisdom and prudence of managers and directors. Without in any way reflecting on the management of our banks, I hold that the $10,000,000 of absolute value in the hands of the people is better secured to the country than it would be if deposited in the banks, and the void filled by the promises to pay, of any chartered institution. I would strongly urge on the people of Canada to hold fast to their silver, which is worth so much an ounce all the world over, and is certainly better value than bank notes, which depend for their value on the uprightness and ability of managers and directors, and which may be rendered irredeemable any day by a panic in the commercial world.

Again, it is idle for any man to say that silver is not worth what it brings. Silver is its very excess, made an article of commerce, and is bought and sold as such. Each man who handles it receives it as a representative of a certain value to him, and if it is not the representative of the value he parted with, he was simply a fool to sell. Nothing can be clearer than this fact, and any man who states that he sells an article at a loss, because he is obliged to take silver at par, is a poor business man, to say the least of it, and would get his name in the Gazette if we had no other currency than gold.

The present silly attempt to set a value on an article of commerce like silver is almost entirely due to the retail merchants, and is simply an attempt to make more money than they are entitled to. If they have succeeded in getting, as in fact they are bound to get 10 per cent on all silver they receive, they have been simply making from 4 to 5 per cent. on all that people have been fools enough to give them at that rate. Some pretence was made when the movement was initiated, that the silver would be exported, but that blind is now dropped, and the storekeepers are actually selling the silver which they receive at 10 per cent. to the brokers at 5 per cent for large and 6½ per cent. for small. The brokers return the silver again to the country through the medium of the produce buyers, and the storekeepers expect that the farmers will give them another 4 or 5 per cent. profit on it. The wonder is that the dealers do not allow a little discount on their goods to any one that will pay them in silver. These facts need no comment.

The main evil with the storekeepers in this country is the long credit which they give and receive. A man commences business with a small capital, buys goods from the wholesale dealers at 4 or 6 months credit and sells them out again on an indefinite credit hoping to get his money, or rather the wholesale dealers money, back in time to meet his notes. The result generally is that their customers do not pay up in time, and then commences the "kicking against the pricks," which generally ends in the failure of the retail dealer

and loss to the wholesale dealer. The storekeeper of course glad to get silver or anything, it will give him ready money and is forced to goods too low for cash in order to stave off demands of his creditors. If the retail dealer in an independent position and could afford to cash for his goods, or at least a large portion them, he could then demand a price sufficient cover any loss incurred in taking silver, at. But until they do restrict themselves within capital, or near it, they will always be paying much for something, say butter, wheat, or a other article of produce for which they can cash, as they do now for silver.

The wholesale merchants are on a different footing; being independent they insist on receiving silver only at what it is worth to them, and suffer no loss by it. I feel satisfied that the which afflicts the retail merchant is not the silver which they take at par, but the practice they of pushing their business beyond their means, which they lose their independence, and put in the power of the wholesale merchants to overcharge them for their goods, and in the power their customers to underpay them for their classes. If the young generation of Canada be brought to see that labor is fully as honorable trade, and that independence as a farmer or a chanic is far preferable to the weary, ing dependence of the storekeeper. We we have fewer complaints about an excessive silver currency, and certainly no organized attempt an overcrowded occupation, to impose a tax on whole people for their sole profit and annoy and loss to all others. Especially let us have Government interference in this matter. Silver an article of commerce, and its value is determined by supply and demand. This is a free country and no man is forced to take silver at more than is worth, nor should he be forced to sell it at than it is worth. Government action or pa combinations will never settle the silver question It can only be settled between man and consumer Each person is at full liberty to take it or leave as he wills.

I am, &c.,
HARD MONEY.

INSURANCE QUOTATIONS.

Editor Canadian Monetary Times.

SIR,—I observe in your paper that the shares this Company are quoted at £1 10s., paid up, selling price £1. I beg to acquaint you tha quotation is incorrect, inasmuch as no such of our shares has taken place at that price, they have always been disposed of at par, sales have been effected.

Relying upon your kind offices to rectify mistake in the columns of your influential well conducted Journal,

I remain, Sir,
Yours faithfully,
JOHN INNES,
Manager
The Ætna Insurance Company (Limited),
46 & 47 Upper Sackville Street,
Dublin, 18th August, 1858.

Financial.

TORONTO STOCK MARKET.

(Reported by Pellatt & Osler, Brokers.)

Business in stocks was very limited last there being little of any class of securities on market.

Bank Stock—There are buyers of Montreal 133½ and sellers at 134; no sales. No British market. Sales of Ontario are reported at 98 and 99½, and it is now offering at the latter No Toronto in market; buyers would give There are buyers of Royal Canadian at 84

ttle offering. Sales of Commerce, particurred at 103 and of fully paid at 103½ yers offer 36 to 37 for more, but there are t these rates. Merchant's sold at 106 offered at 106, Quebec is offered at olson's in Market; buyers offer 110, uired for at 102 to 102½. Du Peuple laced at 105, ex dividend. Jacques offered at 198 with buyers at 104½, lle sold at 102. Other Banks nominal es.—No Canada Sterling Bonds in Market sixes are in demand at 100 to 100½; Stock is wanted at par, none offering. Toronto are offering at rates to pay cent interest. County are wanted ring at very high rates...

—City Gas sold at 104½ to 105, and it lemant at the latter rate. There were of British America Assurance at 56, eqrable at that figure. Canada Permanent Building Society is freely bid for at out inducing holders to sell. There sales of Western Canada at 109, and lot 110 would be paid. Freehold also still extent at 104; very little to be had telegraph is procurable at 134. Holders for Canada Landed Credit, ex dividend Mortgages are offering. Money is in and, and is readily obtainable on first

NTREAL MONEY MARKET.

(From our own Correspondent.)

Montreal, Sept. 1, 1868,

ery little to add to my remarks of last he money market is very easy, god paper, of which there is very ing, is freely taken by the banks per cent; street prices range from per cent. The comparatively light money paid for duties (owing to light as thrown a considerable amount of he market, seeking short date investch are difficult to find. Prices of bank high. Bank of Montreal, 133¾ to 134, 102. Peoples' Bank, sales at 105, asking 106. Merchants' sold at 106, more now asked. Ontario, steady at Bank of Toronto, 115. Gore Bank little doing in railroad and mining t prices are steady. You will have r. Jones, a money and exchange broker, onded. What his total liabilities are ascertained. I believe the Ontario he heaviest sufferer. Nearly all the kers are more or less bitten. Very little in gold, and no speculation for either Silver is unchanged. I see your orchants are wavering in their aile e combination. It has fallen through even I expected...

ntreal Correspondence.

(From our own Correspondent.)

Montreal, 1st Sept., 1868 now entering on the month in which le in every department of business may pected to commence. From the 20th end of September is the season of the dry goods trade, and from the September to the end of October is the of all other branches. Thanks to the nk railway, we have not the same hurry used to have before that line was built isiness closed with the close of navigation to a large extent. It can be carried on e winter. It is almost impossible to e benefits of this railroad to Montreal,

and much as we may cavil at the lavish expenditure incurred in building it and carp at the extravagant manner in which it is managed, still we cannot shut our eyes to the fact that it is now a necessity, and must be supported coûte qui coûte; the only question now is how it can be worked in the cheapest and yet most efficient manner. The faults of its management are patent to all, overpaid and over-numerous high officials, underpaid and insufficient staff of underlings, faulty system in the freight department, constant accumulations of freight waggons at stations where they are not wanted, and scarcity of them at points where they are required, general bathness of the track, dirty illventilated passenger cars, with a great insufficiency of vehicles suitable for carrying the number of emigrants constantly passing over the line, the utter want of attention to the respectability, comfort and cleanliness of poor travellers; these and other serious abuses are the defects in the management of the Grand Trunk, yet, still, as I said before, the line is a necessity and the public should insist that the present mismanagement be altered, or that Government, which had so much to do in building the line, should see to its proper working. The prevalent opinion in Montreal is that the next session of Parliament will be a very stormy one and a great number of important measures, such as those regarding the tariff, currency, railroads, immigration, &c., will be only cursorily touched upon and be then shoved on one side to make room for the paramount question, the consolidation of the Dominion.

The weather during the week has been very fluctuating, some very hot days and nights and some heavy rains, succeeded by cold; altogether it has been favorable for agricultural pursuits. In the county of Argenteuil, farmers have very long faces, the oats and peas, (the staple crops) being quite a failure. The different cheese factories are now closed for the season, the weather being cool enough to make butter for the market. In the country parts the price of really good butter is 20 cents per lb., and the views of the farmers as to its future range are high.

Our Produce Market continues very dull. Flour is gradually declining, and holders are slowly working off their stocks. In grain there is nothing doing; but as a considerable quantity will soon be brought forward, more activity and definite prices may be expected. As regards Provisions of all sorts, there is no special feature to note.

In Groceries the market has ruled quiet. As regards the prices of staples for the future, opinions are very divided, many hold that we will have a late fall trade and a lower range of prices in most articles, with the exception of teas; others maintain that, with a plentiful harvest in the West, light importations and no present overstocks, prices will rule firm, or if anything advance; a few weeks will decide which of the prophets are right, my opinion inclines to the latter view. There has been considerable speculation in Fish oils, especially cod, and the stock is now held in few hands.

Dry Goods, as mentioned in my last stocks are fairly opened out, and several large Western buyers are in the market. Prices of cottons rule firm, and holders are not pressing sales. Fancy goods are in ample supply, but, for the more expensive articles of these, and also of fine silks and velvets, the sale is so far slow. Spinners of the coarse qualities of Canadian manufactured woollens have had a hard time of it this season. They bought their wool when it was dear and have now to compete for the fall trade with those who purchased the raw material at greatly reduced prices; the markets too are overstocked and many descriptions of heavy woollens and coarse hosiery are a drug in the market. Makers of fine tweeds are in a better position and will realize a profit on their goods. A number of the factories depending on water-power are stopped owing to the lowness of the rivers, this will prevent any serious increase in stocks. There is a fair demand for imported

woollens, and the prices ruling last spring still obtain.

Montreal Manufactured Hardware.—The market continues dull but manufacturers are busy making stock for the fall and winter demand. The agricultural machine makers have had a busy season, and I believe a profitable one. The use of reaping and threshing machines is rapidly spreading in the Province of Quebec, even amongst the habitans, who are slowly beginning to see the great economy of their use, especially when labor is as dear as it has been this season.

The Boot and Shoe trade is lively, and old stocks are getting worked off, whilst new and good wares are in active demand. This increased activity will soon have an effect on the leather trade, which, up to the present moment has been very dull.

Miscellaneous.—Our trade with the River Plate is rapidly assuming considerable proportions. At present there are four vessels loading lumber for Monte Video, and from the excellent quality of timber in the course of shipment, so superior to what they have been in the habit of receiving from the Iowa ports, there is no doubt but that in future Brazil and the River Plate will draw the bulk of their supplies from Montreal, and we shall be able to reciprocate by getting return cargoes of dry and salted hides, instead of having, as at present, to buy them in New York.

There is a strong desire to get our principal streets repaved with the Nicholson pavement, and petition is before the council to commence with Great St. James' street.

The question of buying land for a public park comes before the Council to-morrow night. It is to be hoped some action will be taken.

[Toronto Market.

Produce.—Wheat.—Receipts very light; the market is dull and nominal, in the absence of receipts or stocks; one car in fair proof sold at $1.20 in store. New wheat is being offered at the stations west of this, at about $1.25. There is little demand and nothing doing yet. Barley.—Receipts by cars 26,104 bush., and on the street 45,000, making a total of 69,104 bush. against 60,000 bush. the previous week. The market closed a week ago at $1.05 to $1.06, but suddenly fell off to $1, and during the last few days has ranged between 90 and 95c, closing at 93 to 95c. Sales of car loads were made at 92 to 93c; a small cargo was offered at the close of the week at 96c, but that is above the market. The market opened unusually high, and it is not to be expected that prices will recover this season. A telegram from Oswego, of the 2nd September, quotes at $1.70, with sales of 25,000 bush. Oats.—Receipts 1,200 bush; the market is dull; a small lot sold at 45c, which is now the top of the market. Peas.—Some small lots of raw have been offered, 200 bush. sold at 95c.

Flour.—Receipts, 725 brls. and 500 brls. last week. Superfine is very dull, there is a small shipping demand for the Lower Provinces at about $5.90 with sales at $6; no sales reported. Extra is steady with a small demand at $7, a lot of 50 brls. selling at $7.25. Superior is nominal at quotations; none offering and no sales. Oatmeal—is selling in small lots to the retail trade at $6.50 to $6.75. Cornmeal—is selling at $4 to $4.50.

Provisions.—Butter is a little easier, there is, however, very little in market. The dry weather has greatly reduced the production of butter in the country. Cheese.—A traveller for one of our houses gives it as his opinion that the cheese crop will not be more than half of that of last year. This arises not merely from drouth and consequent decrease of food for cattle, but also from the unsatisfactory results of last year's business. Cheese moved slowly, sold at low prices and returns were a long time in coming in. Eggs.—There is a fair supply in market; from 10 to 11c is paid.

BOOTS & SHOES.—The fall trade is fairly opened up, and during the past week a good, lively, and at the same time healthy business has been done. The demand of course runs chiefly on heavy goods, which are now in season. Prices are unchanged.

DRY GOODS.—Now that it is definitely ascertained that the harvest has been about a fair average, more confidence has been imparted to the wholesale trade. Buyers are gradually coming in. The incoming week is expected to be a busy one.

LEATHER.—Trade is very quiet, and the market is rather weak at quotations.

HIDES.—A fair trade is reported at unchanged prices.

FREIGHTS.—Owing to the dulness of the Barley Market, there was very little done in freights by lake. The rate on grain to Oswego remains steady at 3¼ cts. American currency, with few engagements; to Toledo, 5 cts. Flour to Montreal, nominal at 20 cts.; plenty of tonnage but little freight. Railroad freights unchanged.

Halifax Market.

Halifax, 26th Aug.

Breadstuffs.—The demand for flour continues good for the season, and holders are firm at $8.25 to $8.50 for No. 1 Canada; $8.75 for extra; extra State $8 to $8.20; Baltimore superior $7.25 to $7.75; Baltimore extra $8.25 to $8.50. Rye, dull at $6.50 to $6.75. No change in meal, Kiln dried $4.80 to $5; fresh ground, $4.50. Oatmeal dull, at $8. Imports from 1st January to 25th August, 1867 and 1868.

	Brls. Flour.	Brls. Cornmeal.
1868	107,022	37,321
1867	104,598	27,957

West India Produce.—Without change. Holders firm at quotations. Market almost bare of Vaccuum Pan sugar. Porto Rico 6¼ to 6½c; Cuba 5¾ to 6c. Barbadoes 6 to 6¼c in bond. Molasses 30c early crop Cienfuegos. Rum Demerara 50 to 51c. St. Jago 43c in bond.

Financial.—Bank drawing rate on London 60 day bills 13¾ per cent prem.; Private 12½ to 12¾ per cent prem. New York gold drafts at sight, 3½ per cent prem. Currency drafts 27½ per cent discount. Montreal sight drafts 3¼ per cent prem. Newfoundland sight drafts 5 per cent prem.—*R. C. Hamilton & Co.'s Circular.*

The Wool Trade.

The *United States Economist*, in reviewing the wool market says:

It was said at the time the wool season commenced that wool was never so light as this year, but did any one ever know a time when it was extremely hot at the time of shearing that the wool was very light? It is true fleeces did not weigh heavy, but this was not on account of the wool being free from yolk, but because it was short in growth. Farmers are not getting a heavy growth of wool this year. Corn and grain was too high, and they was too poor to make good wool. This year we have a large amount of weak stapled wool, which will shrink heavily in working, and, on account of the hot weather, it will shrink heavily in scouring; but notwithstanding all these drawbacks, there are some very good and choice wools; and it is also true that the good wools bring in the market less comparatively than the poorer ones. One thing may be put down as a fact from which there is no getting away, goods are doing better.

Cotton has had its day for a time. Wool will now take the lead. Woolen goods, and every kind of goods into the manufacture of which wool enters, will better. Wool in six months will be scarce; in nine months it will be very scarce; manufacturers will run their machinery, and will wool be wanted. It is no use getting excited about it nor making reports to excite or stimulate consignments, the wool will all be wanted, and will be sold before next June.

Every grade will be wanted. Pulled will wool be in demand; it is wanted now; medium and coarse wools are wanted. Combing is wanted and is scarce, and as provisions decrease in price, wool will advance. It is no use to talk about pelts; England wants hay and corn. This will keep up the price to some extent, but it will stop the flow of gold, and may turn the tide this way. We need it; business of every description wants it, but most of all, wool and woolens; we should not be dependant. We have a large country, and a numerous people to cloth and feed, and we can do it. It is no use killing sheep before they are fat. Then we want them for food. but before that we want them for clothing.

St. Lawrence Canals.

The following was the amount of tolls collected on goods passing through the St. Lawrence canals for the month of July:

Tolls upwards	$3,267 09	$3,495 86
Tolls downwards	4,986 13	4,705 75
Other dues	983,81	1,711 82
Total	$9,237 03	$9,913 43
Free Produce downward	768 60	1,104 95

Trade with South America.

There is still a fair demand for vessels for the River Plate for sawn Lumber. The *Sir Richard MacDonnell* and *Ennerdale* have both been taken up, the former loading at Three Rivers on Canadian account, and the latter at the wharf, foot of the current, on New York account—both chartered by W. M. Freer & Co. The *St. Lawrence*, *Rivoli* and *Annie Logan* are also loading for South American ports.—*Montreal Herald.*

New Customs Regulations.

A difference of opinion appearing to prevail at several ports in reference to the definition of the word "periodical," mentionêd in the Tariff, the Customs Department has issued a circular to Collectors, stating that it comprises those publications which appear at regular intervals, such as newspapers, reviews, magazines, annual registers, etc., devoted to religion, politics, the sciences, arts, amusements, etc., which publications are entitled entry at five per cent. *ad valorem.* The Department has likewise decided that the interpretations of the "Tariff 1867," transmitted with circular of 24th January last, in regard to admission of machinery for mills and factories, are to be held to include all new machinery imported for the extension of manufacturing power, and not to replace or repair old articles of the same class.

Albany Lumber Market.

AUGUST 19.—The receipts for the week have been large and stock is accumulating in the market. The supply is good and well assorted. The sales have been good, and several large buyers have been purchasing for winter stock, and prices are considered as low as they will be this season.

Freights are without nominal change. We quote: To New York $1.50, to Bridgeport and New Haven $2.25, to Norwich and Middletown $2.75, to Providence $3.25, to Hartford $3.25, and to Philadelphia $3.50.

The receipts of board and scantling thus far exceeds those of last year 52,512,040 feet, shingles 12,024m, timber 60,450 c. ft., and staves 8,505,586.

The Thames River Channel.

Mr. Stephenson, member of the Ontario Parliament, a few days since addressed the Chatham Council respecting the dredging of the mouth the river. He stated that the Government h offered to appropriate $2,400 for that purpos provided the local authorities would raise a lil amount. Mr. Stephenson also read a letter fro Mr. Brown, offering to dredge a fifty-feet chann ten feet deep for $4,800; $2,400 to be paid wh completed, and balance after the close of navig tion next year, provided the town or count would guarantee the payment of such balance.

Liverpool Provision Market.

BACON—Continues in good request, both consumption and export; 1s. advance is now quired for Cumberland Cut and Short rib. Stoc are reducing fast.

LARD.—The sales about 100 tons at stea rates.

CHEESE.—The arrivals are considerable, whi sell freely at an advance of 1s. @ 2s. ℔ cwt. on quotations.

BUTTER.—New Canadian has just arrived. the quality and condition are good, it will bri our highest quotations.

Current rates are:—CHEESE—Extra, per cv 58s. @ 62s.; fine, 48s. @ 55.; middling, 20s. 40s. BUTTER.—U. S. and Canada, fine and ext per cwt. (new), 85s. to 110s.—*Circular, Aug.*

Imports of Dry Goods.

Imports of Dry Goods at Montreal from January to 30th June.

		1867.		186
Cottons,	Jan.	$145,018	...	$98,9
	Feb.	573,171	..	409,1
	Mar.	878,902	...	577,7
	April	210,708	...	226,
	May	170,978	...	182,7
	June.	103,617	...	94,
		$2,082,394		$1,588,
Woollens,	Jan.	$149,230	...	$84,
	Feb.	425 325	...	233,
	March	800,377	...	468,
	April	186,308	...	209,
	May	247,927	...	101,
	June	82,657	...	76,
		1,701,824	..	$1,183,
Silks, &c.,	Jan.	20,593	...	$8,
	Feb.	67,841	...	45,
	March	160,878	...	104,
	April	75,533	...	76,
	May	40,646	...	46,
	June	32,589	...	41,
		$398,080	...	$3

Recapitulation of totals 1st Jan. and to 30tl

	1867.		1
Cotton	$2,082,394	...	$1,5
Woolens	1,791,824	...	1,1
Silks, etc.	398,080	...	3
Total	$4,272,298	...	$3,09

Shewing a falling off of $1,175,732, or abot per cent.

INSOLVENTS.—The following is the new l insolvents, published in the *Canada Gazette* c 8th inst.:—Chester T. Card, Colborne; Joh Manning, Montreal; William and Adam Hu Brantford; Romaneo & Clark, hardware merch Brantford; John Bowers, Ingersoll; Wm. Gor North Williamsburg; Thomas Meares, (wri attachment), Goderich; Alfred Bourguignon, thier; Thomas Wilson, Mount Forest; Wil Tewksbury, Reach; Archibald McLean, Pendl Martin Nestor, Grantham; S. M. Sanderson & Toronto; Louis Roberge, La Presentation; phonse Guerin, Francis O'Hara, Cleophas St. J Montreal; Francois Cusson, Lachine; Ber Goldberg, Hamilton.

CEIPTS OF GRAIN.—The following will show omparative receipts of flour and grain at the of Milwaukee, Chicago, Toledo, Detroit and land, from January 1st to August 15, for and 1868 :

	1868.	1867.
.............brls	1,844,726	1,541,071
at..............bu	9,687,676	6,813,398
....	21,893,586	19,682,119
....	6,720,374	4,219,394
y	433,510	555,587
....	310,645	638,280
Total grain..	30,045,791	31,908,778

NKRUPTCY.—A Bill, which has for its object mendment of the Bankruptcy Act of 1861' een brought in by Mr. Moffatt, Mr. Craw-Mr. Ayrton, and Mr. Charles Foster. It is sed to repeal the 86th section of that Act, n lieu thereof to enact that any debtor may ion for an adjudication of bankruptcy against elf, the filing of which would be an act of ruptcy, without any previous declaration of vency. The petitioner would have to satisfy ourt that he could pay 5s. in the pound, or, g this, to prove that he had convened a meet-f all his creditors whose debts exceeded £10. eed made between a debtor and his creditors d be valid unless left at the office of the re-ar, with a list of his debts and liabilities, at time of signing the deed —*London Produce kets Review.*

ONTREAL, Sept. 1.—There was only one large which destroyed the provision store of W. & unn, situated close to the St. Ann's Market. exact loss is not yet fully ascertained. There been several alarms and some small fires, but ing of any moment during the week.

EPOSITS.— The New York and Connecticut , and the Ætna and Hartford Fire Insurance panies have paid their deposits into the hands e Finance Department, as required by the Act ast session.

SE OF PETROLEUM.—A petroleum establish-t in Leipsic, besides various forms of appara-for refining petroleum and producing petro-o gas, advertises the following chemical ducts : Alcanzine, for coloring fats and oils ; latine, for dyeing wool and silk, as well as for r printing of books and plates ; Petroleum er, for therapeutic and technological purposes ; zine of any degree of fluidity, clear as water perfectly free from smell ; Ligroin, for burn-in sponge lamps ; Artificial Oil of Turpentine, waxed cloth and varnished fabrics, as well as the cleansing of type and printers' form ; Re-al Petroleum, almost inodorous, and Petroleum idum for gas-making.

44 THE CANADIAN MONETARY TIMES AND INSURANCE CHRONICLE.

CANADA

Life Assurance Company.

IN compliance with the Act respecting Insurance Companies, 31 Vic., chap. 48,

NOTICE IS HERBY GIVEN,

THAT THE

CANADA LIFE ASSURANCE COMPANY,

Has been licensed by the

HONORABLE THE MINISTER OF FINANCE,

To transact the

Business of Life Assurance.

A. G. RAMSAY,
Manager.

August 1st, 1868. 1-1m

Edinburgh Life Assurance Company.

Founded 1823.

HEAD OFFICE—22 GEORGE STREET, EDINBURGH.

Capital, ... £500,000 *Ster'g.*
Accumulated and Invested Funds, £1,000,000 "

HEAD OFFICE IN CANADA:
WELLINGTON STREET, TORONTO.

SUB-AGENTS THROUGHOUT THE PROVINCE.

J. HILLYARD CAMERON,
Chairman, Canadian Board.

DAVID HIGGINS,
Secretary, Canadian Board.

Western Assurance Company.

NOTICE is hereby given that the Annual General Meeting of Shareholders of the Company will be held at the Company's Office, on

TUESDAY, THE 1ST DAY OF SEPTEMBER NEXT,

At 12 o'clock, noon, to receive the Annual Report, and for the election of Directors to serve during the ensuing year.

By order of the Board.

B. HALDAN,
Secretary.

50-td.

KERSHAW & EDWARDS,
IMPROVED PATENT
NON-CONDUCTING AND VAPORIZING
FIRE AND BURGLAR-PROOF SAFES,
139 & 141
ST. FRANCOIS XAVIER STREET,
MONTREAL.

AGENTS:
A. K. BOOMER, TORONTO.
J. W. MURTON, HAMILTON.
A. G. SMYTH, LONDON, ONT.

51-6m.

Insurance Act.

NOTICE is hereby given that the

COMMERCIAL UNION ASSURANCE COMPANY

Having complied with the Act 31st Vic., cap. 48, by depositing the sum of

100'000 Dollars,

have received the required license to transact the business of

FIRE AND LIFE INSURANCE

IN THE DOMINION OF CANADA.

MORLAND, WATSON & CO.,
General Agents for Canada.

W. M. WESTMACOTT,
Agent for Toronto.

51-4

TORONTO PRICES CURRENT.—September 3, 1868.

Name of Article.	Wholesale Rates. $ c.	$ c.
Boots and Shoes.		
Mens' Thick Boots	2 20	2 50
" Kip	2 45	3 20
" Calf	3 00	3 75
" Congress Gaiters	2 00	2 40
" Kip Cobourgs	1 00	1 50
Boys' Thick Boots	1 65	1 90
Youths' "	1 45	1 55
Women's Batts	95	1 20
" Congress Gaiters	1 15	1 50
Misses' Batts	0 75	1 00
" Congress Gaiters	1 00	1 30
Girls' Batts	0 65	0 90
" Congress Gaiters	0 80	1 10
Children's C. T. Cacks	0 50	0 65
" Gaiters	0 65	0 90
Drugs.		
Aloes Cape	0 12½	0 16
Alum	0 02½	0 03
Borax	0 00	0 00
Camphor, refined	0 65	0 70
Castor Oil	0 18	0 28
Caustic Soda	0 04½	0 05
Cochineal	0 90	1 00
Cream Tartar	0 00	0 00
Epsom Salts	0 03	0 04
Extract Logwood	0 09	0 11
Gum Arabic, sorts	0 30	0 35
Indigo, Madras	0 75	1 00
Licorice	0 14	0 45
Madder	0 13	0 16
Nutgalls	0 00	0 00
Opium	6 70	7 00
Oxalic Acid	0 28	0 35
Potash, Bi-tart	0 25	0 28
" Bichromate	0 15	0 20
Potass Iodide	3 80	4 50
Senna	0 12½	0 60
Soda Ash	0 03	0 04
Soda Bicarb	4 50	5 50
Tartaric Acid	0 37½	0 45
Verdigris	0 35	0 40
Vitriol, Blue	0 09	0 10
Groceries.		
Coffees:		
Java, ℔ lb.	0 23@0	25
Laguayra,	0 17	0 18
Rio	0 16	0 18
Fish:		
Herrings, Lab. split	0 00	0 00
" round	0 00	0 00
" scaled	0 00	0 00
Mackerel, small kitts	1 00	1 25
Loch. Her. wh'e firks	2 50	2 75
" half "	1 50	1 75
White Fish & Trout	None.	
Salmon, saltwater	16 00	17 50
Dry Cod, ℔ 112 lbs	5 00	0 00
Fruit:		
Raisins, Layers	2 20	2 30
" M R.	2 10	2 20
" Valentias new	0 08½	0 09
Currants, new	0 05	0 06
" old	0 03¾	0 04½
Figs	0 13	0 15
Molasses:		
Clayed, ℔ gal	0 37½	0 40
Syrups, Standard	0 46	0 47
" Golden	0 52	0 53
Rice:		
Arracan	4 75	5 00
Spices:		
Cassia, whole, ℔ lb.	0 35	0 40
Cloves	0 11	0 13
Nutmegs	0 50	0 65
Ginger, ground	0 16	0 25
" Jamaica, root	0 25	0 30
Pepper, black	0 00	0 10
Pimento	0 08	0 09
Sugars:		
Port Rico, ℔ lb.	0 08¾	0 00
Cuba "	0 08¾	0 00
Barbadoes (bright)	0 08¾	0 08¾
Dry Crushed, at 60 d.	0 11¾	0 11⅞
Canada Sugar Refine'y, yellow No. 2, 60 ds	0 08¾	0 08¾
Yellow, No. 2½	0 09	0 09½
No. 3	0 09⅜	0 09½
Crushed X	0 10	0 10½
" A	0 11½	0 11¾
Ground	0 11¾	0 12
Extra Ground	0 12¾	0 13
Teas:		
Japan com'n to good	0 40	0 55
" Fine to choicest	0 55	0 65
Colored, com. to fine	0 60	0 75
Congou & Souch'ng	0 42	0 75
Oolong, good to fine	0 50	0 65
Y. Hyson, com to gd	0 45	0 55
Medium to choice	0 65	0 80
Extra choice	0 85	0 95
Gunpowd'r c. to med	0 55	0 70
" med. to fine	0 70	0 85
Groceries—*Contin'd*		
" fine to fins't	0 85	0 95
Hyson	0 45	0 80
Imperial	0 42	0 80
Tobacco, Manufact'd:		
Can Leaf, ℔ lb 5s & 10s.	0 26	0 30
Western Leaf, com.	0 25	0 26
" Good	0 27	0 32
" Fine	0 32	0 35
" Bright fine	0 40	0 50
" " choice	0 60	0 75
Hardware.		
Tin (net cash prices)		
Block, ℔ lb	0 25	0 26
Grain	0 26	0 27
Copper:		
Pig	0 24	0 25
Sheet	0 30	0 33
Cut Nails:		
Assorted ¼ Shingles, ℔ 100 lb.	3 05	3 15
Shingle alone do	3 30	3 40
Lathe and 5 dy	3 55	3 65
Galvanized Iron:		
Assorted sizes	0 09	0 10
Best No. 24	0 00	0 00
" 26	0 08¾	0 09
" 28	0 09½	0 10
Horse Nails:		
Guest's or Griff'n's assorted sizes	0 10	0 20
For W. ass'd sizes	0 19	0 20
Patent Hammer'd do	0 18	0 19
Iron (at 4 months):		
Pig—Gartsherrie No1	26 00	27 00
Other brands. No1	22 00	23 00
" No2	24 00	25 00
Bar—Scotch, ℔ 100 lb	2 25	2 50
Refined	3 00	3 25
Swedes	5 00	5 50
Hoops—Coopers	3 00	3 25
" Band	3 00	3 25
Boiler Plates	3 25	3 50
Canada Plates	4 00	4 25
Union Jack	0 00	0 00
Pontypool	0 00	0 00
Swansea	0 00	0 00
Lead (at 4 months):		
Bar, ℔ 100 lbs	0 07	0 07½
Sheet "	0 08	0 09
Shot	0 07½	0 07¾
Iron Wire (net cash):		
No. 6, ℔ bundle	2 70	2 80
" 9, "	3 10	3 20
" 12, "	3 40	3 50
" 16, "	4 30	4 40
Powder:		
Blasting, Canada	3 50	3 75
FF "	4 50	4 75
FFF "	5 00	5 25
Blasting, English	5 00	5 50
FF loose	5 50	6 00
FFF "	6 00	6 50
Pressed Spikes (4 mos):		
Regular sizes 100	4 00	4 25
Extra "	4 50	5 00
Tin Plates (net cash):		
IC Coke	7 50	8 00
IC Charcoal	8 50	8 75
IX "	10 50	10 75
IXX "	12 50	0 00
DC "	7 50	9 00
DX "	9 50	10 00
Hides & Skins. ℔ lb		
Green rough	0 05½	0 06
Green, salt'd & insp'd	0 00	0 07
Cured	0 07½	0 08½
Calfskins, green	0 00	0 10
Calfskins, cured	0 00	0 12
" dry	0 18	0 20
Lambskins,	0 50	0 00
" pelts	0 40	0 00
Hops.		
Inferior, ℔ lb	0 10	0 15
Medium	0 15	0 20
Good	0 20	0 25
Fancy	0 25	0 35
Leather, @ (4 mos.) In lots of less than 50 sides, 10 ℔ cent higher.		
Spanish Sole, 1st qual. heavy, weights ℔ lb	0 23	0 23½
Do. 1st qual middle do	0 23	0 23½
Do. No. 2, all weights	0 20	0 22
Slaughter heavy	0 28	0 29
Do. light	0 28	0 29
Harness, best	0 32	0 34
" No. 2	0 30	0 33
Upper heavy	0 34	0 36
" light	0 36	0 40
Leather—*Contin'd.*		
Kip Skins, Patna	0 45	0 55
French	0 70	0 90
English	0 65	0 80
Hemlock Calf (30 to 35 lbs.) per doz	0 75	0 85
Do. light	0 45	0 50
French Calf.	1 05	1 25
Grain & Satn Clt ℔ doz	0 00	0 00
Splits, large ℔ lb	0 38	0 40
" small	0 20	0 30
Enamelled Cow ℔ foot	0 20	0 21
Patent	0 21	0 22
Pebble Grain	0 17	0 18½
Buff	0 17	0 19
Oils.		
Cod	0 55	0 60
Cocoanut, ℔ lb	0 00	0 00
Lard, extra	0 00	1 25
" No. 1	0 00	1 15
" Woollen	0 00	1 05
Lubricating, patent	0 00	0 00
Linseed, raw	0 77½	0 85
" boiled	0 82½	0 90
Machinery	0 00	0 00
Olive, 2nd, ℔ gal	1 45	1 60
" salad	2 00	2 30
" salad, in bots. qt. ℔ case	3 60	3 75
Sesame salad, ℔ gal	1 60	1 75
Seal, pale	0 70	0 75
Spirits Turpentine	0 65	0 70
Varnish	0 00	0 00
Whale	0 75	0 80
Paints, &c.		
White Lead, genuine in Oil, ℔ 25 lbs	0 00	2 50
Do. No. 1 "	0 00	2 25
" 2 "	0 00	2 00
" 3 "	0 00	1 75
White Zinc, genuine	3 00	3 50
White Lead, dry	0 06	0 09
Red Lead	0 07½	0 08
Venetian Red, Eng'h	0 02½	0 03
Yellow Ochre, Fren'h	0 02½	0 03
Whiting	0 90	1 25
Petroleum. (Refined ℔ gal.)		
Water white, car l'd	0 32	0 32
" small lots	0 35	0 36
Straw, by car load	0 31	0 32
" small lots	0 34	0 35
Amber, by car load	0 00	0 00
" small lots	0 00	0 00
Benzine	0 35	0 45
Produce.		
Grain:		
Wheat, Spring, 60 lb	1 35	1 4[illegible]
" Fall 60 "	1 42	1 4[illegible]
Barley 48 "	0 92	0 9[illegible]
Peas 60 "	0 94	0 9[illegible]
Oats 34 "	0 44	0 4[illegible]
Rye 56 "	0 00	0 0[illegible]
Seeds:		
Clover, choice 60 "	5 50	6 0[illegible]
" com'n 68 "	0 00	0 0[illegible]
Timothy, cho'e 4 "	2 00	2 5[illegible]
" inf. to good 48 "	1 50	2 0[illegible]
Flax 56 "	1 25	1 6[illegible]
Flour (per brl.):		
Superior extra	7 25	7 3[illegible]
Extra superfine,	7 00	7 2[illegible]
Fancy superfine	0 00	0 0[illegible]
Superfine No. 1	5 90	6 0[illegible]
" No. 2	0 00	0 0[illegible]
Oatmeal, (per brl.)	6 50	6 6[illegible]
Provisions.		
Butter, dairy tub ℔ lb	0 18	0 2[illegible]
" store packed	0 16	0 1[illegible]
Cheese, new	0 10½	0 1[illegible]
Pork, mess, per brl	23 00	24 0[illegible]
" prime mess	16 00	17 0[illegible]
" prime	14 00	15 0[illegible]
Bacon, rough	0 00	0 1[illegible]
" Cumberl'd cut	0 10½	0 1[illegible]
" smoked	0 00	0 0[illegible]
Hams, in salt	0 00	0 0[illegible]
" sug. cur. & canv'd	0 13	0 1[illegible]
Shoulders, in salt	0 09½	0 1[illegible]
Lard, in kegs	0 13½	0 1[illegible]
Eggs, packed	0 10	0 1[illegible]
Beef Hams	0 00	0 1[illegible]
Tallow	0 00	0 0[illegible]
Hogs dressed, heavy	0 00	0 0[illegible]
" medium	0 00	0 0[illegible]
" light	0 00	0 0[illegible]
Salt, &c.		
American brls.	1 58	1 6[illegible]
Liverpool coarse	0 00	0 0[illegible]
Plaster	1 05	1 1[illegible]
Water Lime	1 50	0 0[illegible]

STOCK AND BOND REPORT.

The dates of our quotations are as follows:—Toronto, Sept. 2; Montreal, Aug. 31; Quebec, August 31; London, Aug. 7.

NAME	Shares	Paid up.	Divid'd last 6 Months	Dividend Day	Toronto	Montreal	Quebec
BANKS.							
British North America	$250	All	3	July and Jan.	102 103	103 104	102½103
Jacques Cartier	50	"	4	1 June, 1 Dec.	106 108	106½ 106	106 107
Nationale	200	"	5		133 134	134 135	133 134
Nationals	50	"	4	1 Nov. 1 May.	109 105½	105½	107 107½
New Brunswick	100	"					
Nova Scotia	200	25	7&7&3½	Mar. and Sept.			
Du Peuple	50	"	4	1 Man., 1 Sept	106 105½xd		
Toronto	100	"	4	1 Jan., 1 July.	114½115	115	114 115
Bank of Yarmouth							
Canadian Bank of Com'e.	50	95			108 104	102 102½	101½102
City Bank Montreal	80	All	4	1 June, 1 Dec.	102 102½	102½	101½102
Commerl' Bank (St. John)	100	"	8½				
Eastern Townships' Bank	50	"	4	1 July, 1 Jan.		96	96 97
Gore	40	"	4	1 Jan., 1 July.		46	45 46
Halifax Banking Company							
Mechanics' Bank	50	70	4	1 Nov., 1 May	95 99	94½ 96½	94 96
Merchants'Bank of Canada	100	70	4	1 Man.,1 Sept	105½106	105½106½	105½ 106
Merchants' Bank (Halifax)							
Molson's Bank	50	All	4	1 Apr., 1 Oct.	109½110	110	109 110
Niagara District Bank	100	70	3½	1 Jan., 1 July.			
Ontario Bank	40	All	4	1 June, 1 Dec.	98½ 99½	98 99	98 99
People's Bank (Fred'kton).	100	"					
People's Bank (Halifax)	20	"	7 12 m				
Quebec Bank	100	"	3½	1 June, 1 Dec.			97½ 97
Royal Canadian Bank	50	50	4	1 Jan., 1 July.	84 85	83 ½ 82	82 85
St. Stephens Bank	100	All					
Union Bank	100	70	4	1 Jan., 1 July.	101 102		102 103
Union Bank (Halifax)	40	"	7 12 mo	Feb. and Aug.			
MISCELLANEOUS.							
British America Land.	250	44	2½				
British Colonial S. S. Co.	250	33½				50	
Canada Company	33½	All	2½				
Canada Landed Credit Co.	50	614			98½		
Canada Per. Bldg Society	50	All	5		115 116½		
Canada Mining Company	4	90					
Do. Int'd Steam Nav. Co.	100	All	20 12 m			107½109	106 107
Do. Glass Company	100	70	12½				
Canada Loan & Investm't.	25	2½	7				
Canada Agency	10	5					
Colonial Securities Co.							
Freehold Building Society	100	All	5		103 104		
Halifax Steamboat Co.	100	"					
Halifax Gas Company							
Hamilton Gas Company							
Huron Copper Bay Co.	4	12	90			52	
Lake Huron S. and C.	5	100					
Montreal Mining Co.	20	$15				8.60	
Do. Telegraph Co.	40	All	5		133 134	134 134	134 134½
Do. Elevating Co.	100	"	15 12 m				
Do. City Gas Co.	50	"		15 Mar, 15 Sept		136	134 135
Do. City Pass. R. Co.	50	"	5			107½109	107 108
Nova Scotia Telegraph	50	"					
Quebec and L. S.	100	"	8½				25 cts
Quebec Gas Co.	200	All	4	1 Mar., 1 Sep.			b'ks off'd
Quebec Street R. R.	25	25	5				96 97
Richelieu Navigation Co	100	All	7 p.a.	1 Jan., 1 July.		116 116½	112 113
St. Lawrence Nav. Co.	100	25	3	1 Feb.			45 50
Tor to Consumers' Gas Co.	50	"	2 3 m.	1 My at MarFe	104½ 105		104 105
Trust & Loan Co. of U. C.	20	5	8				
West'n Canada Bdg Soc'y.	50	All	5		109 110		

INSURANCE COMPANIES.

British.—Quotations on the London Market.

No. of Shares.	Last Dividend.	Name of Company.	Shares par val.	Amount paid.	Last
20,000	..	Briton Medical and General Life	10	1	½
50,000	7½	Commer'l Union, Fire, Life and Mar.	50	8	8½ 9
24,000	8	City of Glasgow	10	2	..
6,000	9½	Edinburgh Life	100	15	30¾
20,000	10	European Life and Guarantee	2½	11s6d	4s 6d.
20,000	10	Ætna Fire and Marine	100	10	11½
20,000	..	Guardian	100	50	62½
24,000	..	Imperial Fire	500	50	345
7,500	9½	Imperial Life	100	10	16½
20,000	10	Lancashire Fire and Life	20	2	4
10,000	22½	Life Association of Scotland	40	7	23
55,862	45s. p. sh	London Assurance Corporation	25	12½	48
10,000	..	London and Lancashire Life	50	5	
57,504	40	Liverp'l & London & Globe F. & L.	20	2	
80,000	5	National Union Life	5	1	
20,000	13½	Northern Fire and Life	100	5	109
1,000	12	"			
3,000	'58, bo	North British and Mercantile	50	6½	17 18
10,000	50	Ocean Marine	25	5	20
2,500	45s.	Provident Life	100	10	38
	£4½ p. s.	Phœnix			136
30,000	5s. h pr.	Queen Fire and Life	50	5	15-16
30,000	3s. 10d.	Royal Insurance	50	2½	4
20,000	10	Scottish Provincial Fire and Life	50	2½	
10,000	25	Standard Life	50	2½	103
4,000	5	Star Life	50	1	
		CANADIAN			
8,000	..	British America Fire and Marine	$50	$25	65
	12	Canada Life			
4000	12	Montreal Assurance	200	20	184
16,000	8	Provincial Fire and Marine	50	11	
	..	Quebec Fire	40	32½	
	..	Marine	100	40	
10,000	5 7 mo's.	Western Assurance	40	30	

RAILWAYS.	Sha's	Paid	Montr'l	London	Montreal	Quebec	Toronto
lantic and St. Lawrence	£100	All		56 58			
ffalo and Lake Huron				35½			
Do. Preference				81½			
fl., Brantf. & Goderich, 6%, 1873-3-4	100			91½			
amphin and St. Lawrence							
Do. do. Pref. 10 %			50				
and Trunk				16 16	103 104		
Do. Eq.G. M. Bds. 1 ch. 6%	100			78 82		89	
Do. First Preference, 5 %	100			45 48		90	
Do. Deferred, 3 %	100				100 100½	93	
Do. Second Pref. Bonds, 5%	100			85 87		100	
Do. do Deferred, 3 %	100						
Do. Third Pref. Stock, 4 %	100			25 27			
Do. Deferred, 3 % ct.	100						
Do. Fourth Pref. Stock, 3%c.	100			18½ 19½			
Do. do. Deferred, 3 % ct.	100						
eat Western			20½	102 12½			
Do. New			18 16 17				
Do. 6 % c. Bds. due 1879-76	100			100 102			
rine Railway, Halifax, $250, all	100			91 93			
rthern, of Canada, 6 % 1st Pref. Bds.				77 82			

SECURITIES	London	Montreal	Quebec	Toronto
Canadian Gov't Deb. 4 p ct. due 1872				
Do. do. 6 do due Ja. & Jul. 1877-84	103 105	100 101	100½ 102	99½ 100
Do. do. 6 do Feb. & Aug.	102 103	99 100	100 101½	
Do. do. 6 do Mch. & Sep.	104 106			
Do. do. 6 p.c. stg. 1883	91 92	90	90½ 91	89
Do. do. 6 do. stg.£ 4885		91	91 91½	93
Dominion 6 p.c. 1876		100 100½	100 100½	100
Hamilton Corporation		97½100		
Montreal Harbor, 8 % ct. d. 1869				
Do. do. 7 do. 1870		99½ 100½		
Do. do. 7 do. 1875		93 93½		
Do. do. 7 do. 1879				
Do. Corporation, 6 % c. 1891		92 92½	92 93	91½
Do. Water Works, 6 % c. stg. 1878		103 105	103 105	90 91
Do. do. 7 % ct. 4 years		91½ 92½		91 92
New Brunswick, 6 % ct., Jan. and July	102 104		94½ 95½	
Nova Scotia, 6 % ct., 1875	101 103		96 97	
Ottawa City 6 % ct.		90 91		
Quebec Harbour, 6 % c. d. 1863			60 70	
Do. do. 6 do. 1876			70 80	
Do. do. 6 do. 1886			85 90	
Do. City, 7 % c. d. 5 years	85 90		90 91	90 90
Do. do. 7 do. 10 years			95 97	
Do. Water Works, 7 % ct. 4 years			96 96½	
Do. do. 6 do. 2 do.			95 96	
Do. do. 6 do. 2 do.			92½ 93½	
Toronto Corporation		90		

EXCHANGE	Halifax	Montr'l	Quebec	Toronto
nk on London, 60 days	13½	9½	9½ 9¾	9½
ight or 75 days date	12½13½	9¾	9¾	9¾
vate do.		8¾	8¾	8¾
vate, with documents		8¾	8¾	
nk on New York		30½	30 30½	70
vate		38	31 31½	
ld Drafts &c.		½ dis to ¾	per ¼ dis.	par ½ dis.
ver		4½ 4½		8¾

(Grocery/liquor price list — left column, partially legible)

Miscellaneous.

ontreal House, Montreal, Canada.

MONETARY MEN.—Merchants, Insurance Agents, lwyers, Bankers, Railway and Steamboat Travellers, ig Agents, Directors and Stockholders of Public Com asure, are here by most respectfully informed that idersigned proposes to furnish the best hotel accommodation at the most reasonable charges. It is our study ovide every comfort and accommodation to all our s, especially for gentlemen engaged as above. To who have been accustomed to patronize other firsthotels, we only ask a trial; we have the same accommodation and our table is furnished with every delicacy : season.

H. DUCLOS.
v. 22, 1867. 15-1y

Hurd, Leigh & Co.,

IMPORTERS AND DECORATORS OF FRENCH CHINA.

ls and families supplied with any pattern or crest desired.
Jommon goods always on hand. 72 Yonge Street,
ato, Ontario. 26y

IS Paper is printed from Messrs. Miller & Richards Extra hard metal Type, sold by

W. HALLEY,
83, Bay Street, Toronto.

Financial.

Pellatt & Osler.

)CK AND EXCHANGE BROKERS, Accountants, gents for the Standard Life Assurance Company and York Casualty Insurance Company.
OFFICE—86 King Street East, four Doors West of Church Street, Toronto.

RY PELLATT, EDMUND B. OSLER,
Notary Public. Official Assignee.

BROWN'S BANK,

(W. R. Brown. W. C. Chewett.)
60 KING STREET EAST, TORONTO,

ANSACTS a general Banking Business, Buys and sells New York and Sterling Exchange, Gold, Silver, Bonds and Uncurrent Money, receives Deposits subto Cheque at sight, makes Collections and Discounts mercial Paper.

ers by Mail or Telegraph promptly executed at most favourable current quotations.
Address letters, "BROWN'S BANK,
y Toronto."

H. N. Smith & Co.,

EAST SENECA STREET, BUFFALO, N. Y., (correspondent Smith, Gould, Martin & Co., 11 Broad Street, .,) Stock, Money and Exchange Brokers. Advances e on securities. 21-1y

---

Philip Browne & Co.,

IANKERS AND STOCK BROKERS,

DEALERS IN

ERLING EXCHANGE—U. S. Currency, Silver and Bonds—Bank Stocks, Debentures, Mortgages, &c. 3s on New York issued, in Gold and Currency; apt attention given to collections. Advances made ecurities.

No. 67 YONGE STREET, Toronto.

2s BROWNE. PHILIP BROWNE, Notary Public.

Honore Piamondon,

ISTOM House Broker, Forwarder, and General Agent, Quebec. Office—Custom House Building. 17-1y

---

Candee & Co.,

.NKERS AND BROKERS, dealers in Gold and Silver Coin, Government Securities, &c., Corner Main and hange Streets Buffalo, Y. N. 21-1y

---

Financial.

The Canadian Land and Emigration COMPANY

Offers for sale at Cheap Rates, on condition of settle ment,

FARM LOTS, IN DYSART,
And adjoining Townships, in the County of Peterborough.

THE greater portion of the Company's block of nine Townships is excellent farming land. The Judges at the Provincial Exhibition at London, in 1866, awarded to the Company a Special Prize, and at Kingston, in 1867, a Diploma for the assortment of Farm Produce from their settlements. The country is well watered, healthy and picturesque. Dysart is a well settled Township, with mills, schools, &c., while stores, post-office, boardinghouses, &c., are established in the Village of Haliburton. There is also a rising settlement in the Township of Harcourt; and along the Peterson road the settler has a choice of good Farm Lots in no less than six Townships.
The communication to the Townships is good, a great part of it by Railroad and Steamboat.
The Bobcaygeon, Opeongo, Peterson, Mississippi, and Hastings Roads will all give access to the Company's block, but other roads are being opened up, giving a more direct communication with the County Town of Peterborough.
The Company has expended a considerable sum in the construction of Roads in and through its Townships, and has still a large appropriation for this purpose.
Dysart and adjoining Townships, the property of the Company, form one Municipality which cannot fail to make more rapid progress than any of the Municipalities in that section of the country, on account of the large sum levied every year from the Company.
For further information and particulars and conditions of sale, apply to the Secretary,

CHARLES JAS. BLOMFIELD,
Bank of Toronto Buildings, Toronto.
Toronto, Jan. 21. 24-1y

Insurance.

J. T. & W. Pennock,

FIRE and Life Insurance Agents, Parliamentary and Departmental Agents, Mining Agents, and Exchange Brokers.
Ottawa, Dec. 21st, 1867. 10-1y

The Standard Life Assurance Company,

WITH which is now united the COLONIAL LIFE ASSURANCE COMPANY.

Established 1825.
HEAD OFFICE—EDINBURGH and MONTREAL.
Accumulated Fund, nearly.... $19,000,000.
Income, 1867 .... $3,376,953.
Manager—W. M. RAMSAY. Inspector—RICH'D BULL.
TORONTO—HENRY PELLATT, AGENT.
Agencies in every Town throughout the Dominion.
18-1y.

Fire and Marine Assurance.

THE BRITISH AMERICA
ASSURANCE COMPANY.
HEAD OFFICE:
CORNER OF CHURCH AND COURT STREETS,
TORONTO.

BOARD OF DIRECTION:
Hon G. W. Allan, M.L.C., A. Joseph, Esq.,
George J. Boyd, Esq., Peter Paterson, Esq.,
Hon. W. Cayley, G. P. Ridout, Esq.,
Richard S. Cassels, Esq., E H.Rutherford,Esq.,
Thomas C. Street, Esq.

Governor:
GEORGE PERCIVAL RIDOUT, Esq.
Deputy Governor:
PETER PATERSON, Esq.

Fire Inspector: Marine Inspector:
E. ROBY O'BRIEN. CAPT. R. COURNEEN.

Agencies granted on all descriptions of property against loss and damage by fire and the perils of inland navigation.
Agencies established in the principal cities, towns, and ports of shipment throughout the Province.
THOS. WM. BIRCHALL,
23-1y Managing Director.

Insurance.

Reliance Mutual Life Assurance Society.

(Established, 1840,) OF LONDON, E. C.

Accumulated Funds, over $1,000,000.
Annual Income, $300,00.
THE entire Profits of this long-established Society belong to the Policy-holders.
HEAD OFFICE FOR DOMINION—MONTREAL.
T. W. GRIFFITH, Managers Sec'y.
15-1y WM. HENDERSON, Agent for Toronto.

Etna Insurance Company of Dublin.

The number of Shareholders exceeds Five Hundred.
Capital, $5,000,000—Annual Income nearly $1,000,000.
THIS Company takes Fire and Marine Risks on the most favorable terms.
T. W. GRIFFITH, Manager for Cana da
Chief office for Dominion—Corner St. Francois Xavie and St. Sacrament Sts., Montreal.
15-1y WM. HENDERSON, Agent for Toronto.

Scottish Provincial Assurance Co.

Established 1825.
CAPITAL ....£1,000,000 STERLING.
INVESTED IN CANADA (1866) ....$500,000.
Canada Head Office, Montreal.

LIFE DEPARTMENT.
CANADA BOARD OF DIRECTORS:
HUGH TAYLOR, Esq., Advocate,
Hon. CHARLES WILSON, M. L. C.
WM. SACHE, Esq., Banker,
JACKSON RAE, Esq., Banker.
WM. FRASER, Esq. M. D., Medical Adviser.

The special advantages to be derived from Insuring in this office are:—Strictly Moderate Rates of Premium; Large Bonus (intermediate bonus guaranteed ;) Liberal Surrender Value, under policies relinquished by assured ; and Extensive Limits of Residence and Travel. All business disposed of in Canada, without reference to parent office.

A DAVIDSON PARKER,
Resident Secretary.
G. L. MADDISON,
15-1yr AGENT FOR TORONTO.

Lancashire Insurance Company.

CAPITAL, - - - - - - - - £2,000,000 Sterling.

FIRE RISKS
Taken at reasonable rates of premium, and
ALL LOSSES SETTLED PROMPTLY,
By the undersigned, without reference elsewhere.
S. O. DUNCAN-CLARK & CO.,
General Agents for Ontario,
N. W. Corner of King & Church Streets,
25-1y TORONTO.

Etna Fire & Marine Insurance Company.

INCORPORATED 1819. CHARTER PERPETUAL.

CASH CAPITAL, - - - - - $3,000,000 :

LOSSES PAID IN 50 YEARS, 23,500,000 00.

JULY, 1868.
ASSETS.
(At Market Value.)
Cash in hand and in Bank.................. $544,842 39
Real Estate............................... 258,367,29
Mortgage Bonds.......................... 982,245,00
Bank Stock............................... 1,272,670 00
United States, State and City Stock, and other Public Securities 2,040,855 51

Total.................. $5,062,880 19

LIABILITIES.
Claims not Due, and Unadjusted $499,803 55
Amount required by Mass. and New York for Re-Insurance......................... 1,405,207 15
E. CHAFFEY & CO., Agents.
50-6ta

8

THE CANADIAN

MONETARY TIMES

AND

INSURANCE CHRONICLE.

'EVOTED TO FINANCE, COMMERCE, INSURANCE, BANKS, RAILWAYS, NAVIGATION, MINES, INVESTMENT, PUBLIC COMPANIES, AND JOINT STOCK ENTERPRISE.

| L. II—NO. 4. | TORONTO, THURSDAY, SEPTEMBER 10, 1868. | SUBSCRIPTION, 82 A YEAR. |

Mercantile.

J. B. Boustead.
VISION and Commission Merchant. Hops bought nd sold on Commission. 82 Front St., Toronto.

John Boyd & Co.
OLESALE Grocers and Commission Merchants, Front St., Toronto.

Childs & Hamilton.
{UFACTURERS and Wholesale Dealers in Boots and Shoes, No. 7 Wellington Street East, Toronto, io.   28

L. Coffee & Co.
DUCE and Commission Merchants, No. 2 Manning's lock, Front St., Toronto, Ont. Advances made en nments of Produce.

J. & A. Clark,
DUCE Commission Merchants, Wellington Street East, Toronto, Ont.

D. Crawford & Co.,
NUFACTURERS of Soaps, Candles, etc., and dealers in Petroleum, Lard and Lubricating Oils, Palace St., to, Ont.

John Fisken & Co.
OIL and Commission Merchants, Yonge St., ronto, Ont.

lery and general

nd Earthenware,

D. Matthews & Co.
nission Merchants, Old Corn Exchange, East, Toronto Ont.

C. Hamilton & Co.
nission Merchants, 119 Lower Water Nova Scotia.

Parson Bros.,
-finers, and Wholesale dealers in Lamps, . Warerooms 51 Front St. Refinery cor. ., Toronto.

wland & Co.,
and General Commission Mer- made on Consignments. Corner -ets, Toronto.

Peford & Dillon,
RTERS of Groceries, Wellington Street, Toronto, tario.

Sessions, Turner & Co.,
{UFACTURERS, Importers and Wholesale Dealers in Boots and Shoes, Leather Findings, etc., 8 Wel- St. West, Toronto, Ont

---

Meetings.

GRAND TRUNK RAILWAY.

Report of the Directors to the Bond and Stock-holders, for the Special Meeting to be held on Thursday, August 27, at the Cannon-street Hotel, at one o'clock, to consider whether lists of Bond and Stockholders shall be issued.

The following is the object for which the meeting will be held, viz. :—" For the purpose of submitting a resolution for authorising the Directors to supply to bond and stockholders, on application, a list of the registered proprietors of bonds and stocks of the Company ;" and as the hesitation of the directors to give to certain parties this list without such authority as that now sought to be obtained, has been made a ground of attack against them, they deem it proper to place before the proprietors the following statement :— On the 28th of April last the board received a letter from Mr. Heseltine, the chairman of the Buffalo Company, applying for a list of the registered proprietors of the Grand Trunk Company, and on the next day the following resolution was passed and sent to that gentleman :—" Resolved —That as this board have invariably (under legal advice) felt obliged to decline to furnish to individual Grand Trunk shareholders the list requested in Mr. Heseltine's letter, such request be not complied with. But that under the special circumstances of the Buffalo and Lake Huron Company's connection with the Grand Trunk, and of Mr. Heseltine as their representative, the secretary be directed to address and forward to the Grand Trunk shareholders (of course at Mr. Heseltine's expense) any communication which he may desire to make to them, if he thinks it proper to make such communication independently of this board. The board, it will be observed in this resolution, undertook, in fact, to forward to their proprietors matter which, from previous discussions with Mr. Heseltine, they could not but be aware would be altogether in the interest of the Buffalo Company, and opposed to the views of the Grand Trunk board. Mr. Heseltine refused to accept the offer thus made him. Following this, viz., on the 27th of May last, a similar application for a list of the registered proprietors was made by Messrs. Marshall, Paine & Co, on behalf of themselves and other bond and stockholders. Upon that requisition the board, on the same day on which it was received, passed the following resolution, viz :—" The request of Messrs. Marshall Paine, &c., having been read and considered, it was resolved that they be informed that (acting on legal advice) this board cannot comply with this request, especially as they have always hitherto declined compliance with similar requests ; but if at the next general meeting it be the pleasure of the shareholders to instruct the board to apply for further powers in this respect, such power shall forthwith · be applied for, this board personally having no objection whatever to comply with the wishes of the shareholders."

Subsequently the board ordered the following letter to be written to Messrs. Marshall Paine & Co., and the other requisitionists :—

"21, Old Broad street, London, E.C., "May 30. 1868.
"Gentlemen,—The Great Western Company of Canada labored under a similar disability as ourselves in regard to the issue of a list of the registered proprietors up to 1860, when a resolution was passed at the half-yearly meeting of that Company to the following effect :—' That any shareholder be permitted to inspect, on a payment of a fee of 2s. 6d., and an application in writing to be supplied with an alphabetical list of the shareholders and their respective addresses on paying for the cost of extracting the same from the books of the Company.' I am now desired to ask you to be good enough to state whether it is your wish to give notice of your intention to propose a similar resolution at our next half-yearly meeting, and if so, I am to add the Directors will embody the notice in the notice calling the meeting. I may here repeat what I yesterday mentioned to your Mr. Lewis Paine, that, as regards the application of Mr. Heseltine for a list of our proprietors, whilst the Company could not comply with the request, the Directors were nevertheless ready and willing and distinctly offered to send out from this office any communication which he or his Company desired to circulate amongst the Grand Trunk bond and stockholders.
"I am, Gentlemen, your obedient servant,
"J. M. GRANT.
"Messrs. Marshall Paine & Co., Stock Exchange.

Further, in a letter sent by the secretary on the 16th of June last to Mr. Creak and Mr. Hartridge, the conveners of the meeting held at the London Tavern on the 18th of that month, he, in accordance with the board's instructions, wrote that "any communication or statement which they may desire to circulate among the bond and stock holders the board will be happy at once to forward accordingly without delay ;" but this offer was not accepted by those gentlemen. At the meeting of the 18th June, besides a resolution calling upon the present board to resign, a resolution was passed requesting the Directors to furnish Mr. Creak and Mr. Hartridge with a list of the stock and bond-holders at the earliest possible period. To this application the Directors, on the 24th June, sent the following resolution in reply :—" That with respect to the application for a list of bond and stockholders, Mr. Creak be informed that, under present circumstances, the Board can only refer to their resolution of the 27th ult., and to the secretary's letter to Mr. John Marshall Paine, of the 30th ult., inviting that gentleman, and those acting with him, to take the necessary steps for obtaining for this Board authority from the ensuing general meeting to furnish the list requested, this board repeating that as far as they are concerned they will be happy to co-operate in asking for the necessary authority. Mr. Creak acknowledged the receipt of this resolution on the 25th, and the board hearing nothing further from him or from his colleagues for a week, they, on the 1st July, passed the following resolution :—" In reference to Mr. Creak and Mr. Hartridge's committee, it was decided that if no requisition be presented by the dissentient stockholders by Wednesday next, the board should itself call a meeting to consider the question of printing the list of registered proprietors, and then adjourn to the ordinary half-yearly meeting to be held in October, when the questions raised by that committee could be fairly submitted to the whole body of the proprietary." On the following day, viz., the 2nd of July, Mr. Creak sent in a resolution of his committee requesting the board to convene special meetings at the earliest legal period, and at their next board the directors resolved that the meetings referred to should be called for the earliest date at which they could be assembled, a choice of days being given to the committee. The 27th of the present month (August) was then fixed for the special meeting to consider the question of issuing the list of registered proprietors. The second meeting will be held in October on the same day as the ordinary half-yearly meeting, of which due notice will be given. Upon the general question of the right of shareholders in these railway undertakings to know who are their partners, and what are the respective interests of those partners, it is to be observed that there is but little analogy between these cases and the cases of ordinary mercantile partnerships, to which some persons have erroneously compared them. In truth, the rights and powers of the Shareholders in these undertakings are limited, and are defined by the several acts of Parliament, which give to the Directors only certain powers and to the shareholders only certain other powers. And, in point of fact, the Grand Trunk act (differing in this respect from most English acts) does not give the shareholders a right to have a list of their fellow shareholders, nor does it give the Directors the right to publish such list. The board have throughout shown every willingness, as far as they personally are concerned, for any class of stock and bondholders to communicate with their fellows; beyond this the Board have not felt at liberty to go, because, not only on former occasions, when they have refused lists of stockholders to applicants for them, has that refusal been sustained by the subsequent general meetings, but it is within the knowledge of the board that many bond and stockholders still object to the publication of their names. Under these circumstances, the board have all along considered that they have no right to publish such lists without, at least, the previous consent of a meeting of the Company. In favor of the publication of the list it may be urged that thereby all the stock and bondholders would be at once known to each other; but this is, perhaps, little more than an apparent advantage, since the same result (and without the attendant disadvantages of the publication of the list) would be attained by the circulation by the board (in accordance with their offer) amongst the stock and bondholders generally of any communication which any individual, or set of individuals, might desire to make to their fellows. Against the publication of the list it may, on the other hand be urged that many persons may consider it a serious disadvantage to have their names unnecessarily published to the world as being what some parties may choose to call speculators in Grand Trunk stocks. With these few observations *pro* and *con.*, the Board leave the matter entirely in the hands of the proprietors generally, they themselves not intending to vote upon it one way or the other. Herewith is enclosed a form of assent or dissent, which they request may be signed and returned before the day of meeting. In regard to the matters now in dispute between the Buffalo and Grand Trunk Companies, and which have doubtless a close connection with the present opposition, the Board feel that they need only refer to the following letter addressed by the Company's solicitor to the Buffalo Directors :—

"32, Great George Street, Westminster, July 1st, 1868.

"Sir,—The Grand Trunk Board have referred to me your letter of the 24th ultimo, because it is a mere repitition of your Board's previously answered proposals, and because my clients conceive that therefore, as well as because the whole matter has necessarily assumed a legal shape; they cannot themselves further interfere usefully. My

letters to your solicitors will show why a reference of the vague character now again proposed by you could lead to no practical result save delay. If your solicitors will either adopt my proposed form of reference or will suggest any definite form which would enable the Board of Trade to appoint an arbitrator, and enable the arbitrator to make an award on the points in dispute, or will leave it to Mr. Farrer, or Mr. Herbert, of the Board of Trade, to settle the form of reference, my instructions are to give the matter immediate attention, with a view to the earliest possible settlement. I am, Sir, your obedient servant,

"J. BREND BATTEN.

"Thos. Short, Esq., secretary, Buffalo and Lake Huron Company."

The offer contained in this letter was declined, Grand Trunk proprietors will see, however, that the Board have done all in their power to obtain a settlement of the pending disputes with the Buffalo Company consistently with a due regard to the interests of the undertaking of which they are trustees.—By order,

EDWARD W. WATKIN, *President.*

To the Bond and Stockholders of the Grand Trunk Railway Company.

Mr. E. Hesseltine has published a reply to the recent statement by Mr. Watkin, the chairman of the Grand Trunk Company, to the bond and stockholders. Mr. Hesseltine replies that on the 1st of May last he expressed his opinion that the affairs of the Company were mismanaged. It was his intention then, as it was now, to obtain a list of the proprietors, and to ask them, either personally or by proxy, to say yea or nay to the question, "Shall Mr. Watkin continue to manage our affairs ?" Nearly four months had elapsed, and he was afraid he would still have some time to wait before this list was obtained, unless the proprietors would speak out very plainly.

Mr. Hesseltine, after replying to some arguments by Mr. Watkin, states—"Gentlemen, I am satisfied, as I told you in my circular of the 1st of May, that a change of management is absolutely necessary. It is unwise, as I might almost say absurd, in us, the proprietors, to allow a gentleman like Mr. Watkin, so overwhelmed with business, to have almost the uncontrolled management of our affairs. Mr. Watkin, as I am told, has little or no interest as a shareholder in the Company, but he draws, I believe, something like £40 per week for the honor of sitting in the chair in Old Broad Street. In addition, I am told, the South-eastern chairmanship gives him £50 a week. From the Sheffield Company he enjoys about £20 a week. I set my face against this trade in Directorships. Let us say distinctly to Mr. Watkin that we are not satisfied with his management, and seek the services of a gentleman who can give us his entire time."

In another place Mr. Hesseltine says:—"I have no wish to use unnecessarily harsh language, but as representing an interest in the Grand Trunk property to the amount of £2,500,000, I cannot look on and be witness to the misery caused to hundreds by the mismanagement of this fine property, without making every effort in my power to effect a change. I have no connection with the Grand Trunk Committee, further than I believe we both aim at the same object; viz., a change in the mangement. Mr. Watkin's efforts to divert your attention from the subject of management, to his disputes with the Buffalo Company, will, I have no doubt, be estimated by you at their true value. I trust at the meeting on the 27th a large number of proprietors will attend, and insist on a list of the bond and stockholders (without the amount of their holdings) being printed, and accessible to the shareholders, on or before the 5th September next." He intends to abstain from attending the meeting on the 27th instant, in order that the bondholders', &c., "attention may not be diverted to Buffalo and Lake Huron affairs."

LONDON AND PORT STANLEY RAILW The annual meeting of the stockholders London and Port Stanley Railway took Aug. 3rd, when the report of the superint was read and adopted. The gentlemen wh elected on the Board this year are as f Messrs. M. Anderson, London; Thomas St. Thomas; and R. Thompson, Port St At an after meeting Mr. Anderson was President, and Mr. Thomas Arklee, of St. T Vice-President.

Mining.

NOVA SCOTIA GOLD MINING REV:

We condense the following from the *Gazette* :—

SHERBROOKE.—Considerable activity exist The Dominion Company expect to ret hundred ounces this week. The ore in the improves in depth, and the width of the vei the quantity of rock raised during the guarantee constant and profitable work f new mill.

The American Companies have reason to satisfied with their present prospects. Mr took up a large brick last week, and material for another in the battery. Mr. has now the management of the Stanley Mi Cook having taken an interest in a prop Oldham.

The Canadian purchases are being system explored. A new lode, showing gold at s has just been struck across the Chicago, worth and Woodbine lots.

Prospecting continued on the eastern side river, from McDaniel's lands down to Several lodes have been found on Mount Pr a property that offers capital facilities for by mining, but which the folks here do not kno or are afraid to attempt.

RENFREW.—"The returns of the Ophir for June, totalled 357 ounces; but owing want of water for crushing, the yield for the of July was only 247 ounces. During th part of this present month the water had its lowest level, but thanks to a heavy rai yesterday there is now sufficient water to crusher at full speed; so that Ophir will p new lode was discovered on the Ophir about 50 feet south of the old "Sout during the month of June. Two tons of crushed from shaft No. 1, taken from the producing 5 ounces. Since then it h opened in three other places, with the most ing indications of success. Colonel Allen posed of the Ives property to a Canadian C The Company under the management of Lockie, Esq., have commenced operati good prospects. They have already ta quite a number of tons of ore, showing vis very freely. It is to be hoped that their will be commensurate with their expe A large amount of prospecting has been d ing the summer. New lodes have been op look promising. New ground has been se mining purposes. New Companies ha formed, and ere the year closes Renfrew resumed its former activity and Nothing had been done at the Nine M washings, since last advice until this company having just been formed for th of sinking a shaft to the bed rock, wher pected that gold will be found in abunda

WINE HARBOR.—Times here are no improving, although the returns for th will not show a large amount of gold, ow fact of the "Victoria" and "Orient undergoing repairs. The only crusher this month is the "Machias," and the going through that is not very rich; a large lead on the north wall, which at one is not considered worth taking down, but lds from five to ten pennyweights—thus ; that our gold-saving machinery has im-

: has been a rich lead discovered on the lo Company's property, on what once d to; the Nova Scotia Land and Gold g and Gold Amalgamating Company, which prove (if further proof were necessary) at Company's business was mismanaged. lbrado Company are sinking a shaft on this d also repairing their crusher. This Com-1 future, will be under the management of eth Williams.

same lead is also being prospected for on Intosh property, and shows in the street 1 the McIntosh and Eldorado. The Eureka ent Companies have large crews of men to ut they will have no quartz crusher, as the mill is being repaired.

Eureka Company have no mill yet, but will ice building soon. One or two other pro-properties are expected to change hands which will still further improve the

hundred and forty-four areas have been applied for in August, besides some prospect-lications, thus showing that the interest in trict is not decreasing.

CKE.—The results from this district, quite the favor in which it is generally held by ho are not biassed by eastern interests. "Uniacke" Company is making a cross cut eet level, have opened an exceedingly rich iich improves at every foot of descent. 'Queen" Company are also taking down a le, rich in coarse gold, at 75 feet. They w 130 tons from previously opened veins, to be crushed by their own mill, which is dy. This lot is expected to give an average ounces. The last batch of ore from the e, consisting of 13 tons 15 dwt., crushed niacke Company's mill, gave 47 ozs. 11 grs. Some large and splendid specimens est Friday from the bottom of the shaft. rlew at the office of Mr. John Stairs, Hollis in early part of this week.

xplorations on the "St. Lawrence" Co.'s have met with good results, and we have own some pieces of quartz full of large tained near the surface. A detailed report ear in our next issue.

'Central" Company expect to derive the f the new lode discovered on the "Uniacke" y's areas.

xplorations of the large tract owned by the eal" Company is carefully conducted by quoy during the temporary absence of Mr. el. As the work proceeds the indications profitable development, become more and parent.

sociation has been formed under the title 'North Uniacke Mining Company" to ex-tract of 114 areas, immediately north of , and about half a mile north of the d gold band. The existence of paying that portion of the field has yet to be

CAN ASSOCIATION FOR THE AD-VANCEMENT OF SCIENCE.

T. S. Hunt, of Montreal, Canada, pre-views "On the chemico-geological rela-metals," the object being to sustain the f the aqueous origin of auriferous veins, stise gave rise to some discussion.

Silliman expressed his impression that veins are not contemporaneous with the ut that they have filled the fissures north, west, and which have, in some sense, owth like that of endiginous trees. He ceived, everywhere, a singular dualism on

the adjacent walls of the same fissure—if on the one side is pyrites, there is the same on the other side, exhibiting the deposit from a central place or axis, the spread of the walls being due to the crystallizing action demanding more space, the fissure showing the length of time of the deposit and the amount of matter. He could no longer hold that the fissure was as wide formerly, a line of force, geodesic in character, northeast and southwest, having determined the deposition, widening from fifty to one hundred, and in the Comstock lode to two hundred feet. These, as Dr. Hunt had shown, exhibit no evidence of in-filtration except seepage from the vein as slicken-sides, debris, etc. In the gold-bearing veins most constant in tenor, the metallic sulphides are always found, as of iron, copper, and more rarely lead, with sometimes zinc and arsenic. The con-dition of gold in the sulphides was a vexed ques-tion. Sometimes we see the gold, but not gener-ally, and it will not yield to amalgamation in any profitable degree ; hence the process of extraction must be chemical and not mechanical—the method of chlorination after roasting being the most ra-tional.

Mr. Bassnett, of Ottawa, asked if the Stanislaus lode at Carson's Creek did not negate, so far as itself was concerned, the proposition of Prof. Silli-man.

Prof. Silliman had examined it, and found it to exhibit no evidence of igneous origin.

Dr. Blaney asked if it was supposed that the brilliant iron and copper pyrites are precipitated from solution.

Prof. Silliman replied in the affirmative and denied that any man could put his finger upon any evidence of igneous origin in metallic veins. He had been a disciple of the igneous school, but his convictions had been changed after much toil in the field.

Dr. Hunt, in support of his proposition, men-tioned the effect of the thermal spring upon the pipes conducting it, the pipe being of bronze, in dissolving.

Dr. Blaney asked whether the Doctor believed that the materials held in solution were deposited by double decomposition.

Dr. Hunt replied that there was a difficulty in stating how substances existing in solution were deposited. Generally it was a mere question of temperature.

Professor Blake, of California, commended the manner and matter of the paper, remarking that its observations were confirmed by all that he had seen in California and Nevada. He understood that the deposits were brought up by hot waters or vapors, and deposited by reason of contact with the rocks, the water carrying the metal in solu-tion. He had observed that there was an out-flow of hot water, for example, in the Comstock lode, and the miners in Nevada first found the mineral adjacent to a spring. This was so in the great Ophir Mine, which, being followed down seven hundred feet, there was still hot water, charged with various salts.

Prof. Stoddard asked if the veins were richer as they descend, as would follow from the law of saturation, and release from pressure. If this were not so, he asked how it could be accounted for.

Prof. W. P. Blake, remarked that his observa-tions for several years upon the gold-bearing veins of California and other regions fully sustained the view of the aqueous origin of quartz veins, and the deposition of gold and silver from thermal waters ascending along fissures. In California there were several interesting confirmatory ex-amples. Gold had been found in visible grains in semi-opal, clearly the result of aqueous deposi-tion. He would even go farther than Prof. Hunt, and maintain the view that gold was even now rising to the surface in springs, and depositing in appreciable quantities, near or at the surface, either by diminution of pressure or of temperature, or by chemical decomposition by contact with in-filtrations from the surface, or from the sides of

the fissures. A fine example of the formation of quartz veins is found in the well known Steam-boat Springs of Nevada, where hot water rises along a fissure for half a mile, and is depositing quartz, and possibly gold and silver. Prof. Blake believed that future chemical investigation of thermal waters in such localities would show the presence of gold and silver, although perhaps in very small quantities. At the celebrated Ophir Mine of Nevada, from which such a flood of Silver had been sent forth, there was originally a spring of water at the service, and a flow of water had been found even at a great depth, and that there the water is hot, and holds various salts in solu-tion.

ORIGIN OF PETROLEUM.

Professor HUNT read a paper " On the Upper Silurian and Devonian Rocks of Ontario." He observed that the palæozoic rocks of the South-west Ontario region are covered by a thick layer of clay which have rendered examinations of them extremely difficult, but more recently borings for petroleum have greatly modified or entirely re-moved these obstacles. The stratification of the rocks was noticed at length. The Genesee black slate, the Hamilton group, the sandstone for-mations were specifically noticed. The distribu-tion of the gray Hamilton shales and black shales has been pretty clearly determined by the borings. The entire thickness of the Portgage group is 224 feet. The Hamilton group attains a thickness of 1,000 feet in some places. The calcareous forma-tions are from 200 to 400 feet thick. The Lower Devonian or corniferous limestone is from 60 to 275 feet in thickness, increasing towards the west. In the northwest the thickness is greatest. Here a boring of 700 or 800 feet was made before reach-ing a soft marl ; below was a layer of rock-salt forty feet thick. This salt formation measures nearly 1,000 feet in New York and on Lake Huron. Gypsum is also found in the lower soil. This shews a condition of very slight precipitation of moisture and of very great evaporation at that time. The petroleum was thought to originate in the lower Devonian limestones. An oilwell in Inniskillen was sunk to a depth of 776 feet. Other very deep wells were mentioned to confirm the theory of the origin of the oil. Similar wells occur in the corniferous limestones in Kentucky. Oil is also found in the lower Silurian. The borings show geological horizons far below the bottoms of the lakes, and that the southwest portions of lakes Erie and St. Clair have been excavated from the quartenary formations.

In the discussion that followed Professor New-berry remarked that the present bed of Lake Erie did not well represent the ancient basin either in extent or depth. The lake was there only a river , and rivers now running into it from the south have their beds one hundred feet above their ancient ones. The rock formations along the river valleys show the undisturbed geological order. He had a different theory from that of Professor Hunt con-cerning the genesis of petroleum. If it originat-ed in rocks then we can extract it from them. The Hamilton black shales are carbonaceous, and afford some oil. In the Chemung and other groups great oil reservoirs are found. The origin of it must be looked for above where it is found. He thought the black shales, and not the corni-ferous limestones furnished the petroleum. The carbonaceous matter is derived both from animal and vegetable organism. The lower Silurian lime-stone is highly carbonaceous, and affords oil in some regions. He showed that, a high tempera-ture was not essential to a production of oil from hydro-carbonaceous depositions ; a lower tempera-ture only retarded the process.

One member remarked that there was a dif-ference between the Canada and Pennsylvania oils.

Professor Hunt thought these differences of minor importance. He proceeded to review the remarks of Professor Newbury, rather confirming his former position. He would recognize different sources of oil in different regions. Even gravel beds have been found impregnated with oil. He thought a low temperature insufficient to effect the transformation of animal organisms into oil. He carefully described the chemical process of the of the conversion of vegetable and animal deposit-ions into liquid oil, showing very thorough inves-tigation and ably sustaining his theory for the genesis of oil, in the lower Silurian carbonaceous limestones. The question of temperature was more carfully considered and it was claimed that the chemical transformations producing oil could take place within certain limits of temperature.

Professor Newberry acknowledged that this was a chemical question, but that not all chemists agreed upon certain transformations in carbonace-ous substances. Carburetted hydrogen was a pro-duct of spontaneous decomposition, and he still thought that the theory presented in the paper was incorrect. He hoped chemists would make observations on spontaneous distillation of car-bonaceous substances so as to arrive at a correct theory.

Professor Winchell, remarked that he had spent considerable time in the Ontario region and had carfully examined the petroleum wells. He de-sired to present a paper referring to the Ontario region. He remarked at some length on the gene-sis of petroleum, regarding the shales as the true origin. He had examined a test well, and was assured that the corniferous limestones did not furnish the oil. There are dark shales at the bot-tom of the Hamilton group, but it is calcareous in most regions, although in others it is bituminous, and may furnish oil.

Professor Hunt had spent more time in the region than Professor Winchell, and had made wider observations. At Tillotson the oil is undoubtedly from the limestone, because there are no shales above it. Also at Thamesville oil was pumped from sixteen feet below the upper surface of lime-stone. He remarked further upon some very deep oils, and reservoirs of oil in rocks which do not produce it.

Professor Winchell rose to speak, but Professor Newberry rose to explain that in Pennsylvania the corniferous limestone was not thick enough to furnish oil.

Professor Winchell then said that he would not have Professor Hunt consider the difference a question of veracity, for he could not question the authenticity and veracity of the statements made. He proceeded to explain and defend his theory.

Insurance.

INSURANCE MATTERS IN MONTREAL.

(From a Correspondent.)

MONTREAL, Sept. 8, 1868.

I question if there is any occupation that affords a larger field for the practice of deception than that of the agency of a Fire Insurance Company, and more especially in the city of Montreal. Fire business in it has reached that pitch, that the insurers now name the rate of premium they will pay, and do business on their own terms ; and I regret to say that some of the leading British Com-panies afford the most ample proof of this fact. Once they get a customer inside their doors he is not allowed to leave till the risk is secured at any rate. A rather curious illustration of this fact has come to my knowledge, and I will briefly state the case. Some twelve months since a policy was taken out by the Grand Trunk Railroad Company with the "Royal" for $400,000 at 6 per cent., making the premium $24,000. During the period the policy was in force, overtures were made by the Grand Trunk Railway to some six leading insurance companies for a general policy to cover every imaginable property, whether their own or in trust, the amount required was $4,000,000, (including the $400,000 then covered by the Royal), several meetings of those six companies were held, involving the loss of a great deal of

time and trouble, and the rate was named by the following Companies, viz., Royal, Phœnix, Impe-rial, North British and Mercantile, Queen, and Liverpool, London and Globe, and communicated to the Grand Trunk Railroad Company. That Company was in no hurry in returning an answer, but kept the Insurance Companies in suspense as to what their final decision would be. Time wore on and some of the agents began to have misgiv-ings as to the good faith of others of their number. All professed to be bound to accept the risk only at the rate named, or do without it, and ample time was allowed them to advise with their princi-pals in England on the matter. So far all went on smoothly, and knowing that the Royal had already received $24,000 premium on their $400,-000, they all felt secure in acting in good faith. It appears, however, that they were soon doomed to disappointment for, as usual, one company broke faith in the most treacherous manner. Acting through its New York agent it made over-tures and secured the whole $4,000,000 policy, leaving the other five offices out in the cold. The Company, acting in this manner, is the Liverpool, London and Globe, and what adds still more to the bad look of the transaction, is the fact that the sun named as the premiums of that amount, is less than the amount paid the Royal for its $400,000 policy. It remains to be seen whether the head office of this Company will tol-erate such a transaction after they are fully in possession of the facts. On this point I may in-form you in a future communication. Meantime, however, the Company in question is not likely to make anything by the transaction. Many fires during the past six weeks along the line of the Grand Trunk Railroad have destroyed several bridges, culverts and quantities of cordwood, together with several cars loaded with freight.

To-day I noticed the prompt settlement made for passengers' baggage lost between Brockville and Kingston, the owners were highly gratified at the liberal and prompt payment which amounted to the aggregate to $1,600.

I think I am under the mark when I state that the claims for loss since the policy commenced (some eight weeks ago) already exceed $20,000. Should a fire occur at or near the General Offices, the wooden steam mills, or car shops at Point St. Charles, it might destroy over $2,000,000 ere it could be got under, these properties being situ-ated at the city limits, where there is only a small 3 or 4 inch waterpipe leading to it. Once let a fire begin at either of the above places designated and it will have made such headway before the city firemen can get at it, that some dozen of buildings would be certainly destroyed. In some of these buildings there are at times 30 to 35 loco-motives. I think it only requires to be brought to the notice of the stockholders of the Liverpool, London and Globe Company to prevent a repeti-tion of this style of doing business. Your remarks on the annual statement of the Provincial Insur-ance Company have been well received here. It is felt to be all-important that the press should closely watch the proceedings of all public com-panies and fearlessly expose anything that is wrong in their management. I shall be curious to see if the Provincial will submit their affairs to a thorough investigation. I fear not.

FIRE RECORD.—Toronto, Sept. 1.—A fire broke out on the premises of Thompson & Duff, King street, little damage done. The building and stock were insured in the Liverpool and London and Globe, British America and Provincial.

West Farnham, 2nd Sept.—A barn belonging to the Episcopal parsonage was burnt. Loss $500 ; partly insured.

Bowmanville, Aug. 23.—Cheese factory of John Joness, four miles west of this place, was totally destroyed. Loss estimated at $2,000 ; insurance $1,400 ; cause believed to be incendiarism.

Bathurst, Ont., August 29.—John Menzies' house and contents, on the 1st concession of this

township, no insurance. Originated from pipe.

Point Grosse, Sept. 2.—One of the ste rial, belonging to the Ottawa Transportation Co was burnt at Point Grosse on the 23rd.

St. John, N.B.—Two houses of John and one of James Addison, on the Lake road, were consumed. The latter only A young man named Maxwell Kennedy, be intoxicated, was caught by the fire and to death.

Prince Albert, Ont.—The barn, with season's crop, of J. Ackney, on the 8th cor Reach township, were consumed. Loss, of building, estimated at $1,600 ; insuran building owned by Moore of Brooklin, un

Kingston, Aug. 30.—Six houses occu soldiers of the Royal Canadian Rifles others seriously damaged. Loss to the Government $6,000.

STEAMERS BURNED AND DAMAGED BY Since the era of steamboat navigation on it is not a little surprising from the nu stroyed, the disasters have been often att great loss of life. The most eventful of currences was that of the steamer Erie, a craft, with a brief but unfortunate care Erie was built at Erie, Pennsylvania, in 1 commenced plying between Buffalo and during the latter part of that season. beautiful modelled or finished boat has n introduced on our inland seas or lakes, an of good speed. She was 600 tons burden cabins above the main deck. In August, burst her boiler, causing the death of si in Detroit River, and in 1841, on the August 9th, she became a total loss by Silver Creek, with 280 lives. Those rescued were taken on board the steame Clinton, Captain A. H. Squier, with m dead, and landed at Buffalo the follo The Erie was commanded from first to la tain T. J. Titus, who was subsequently on the coast of Lake Michigan. The ne loss of life by the burning of a steamer, boat G. P. Griffith, in Lake Erie, bel land, Captain C. C. Roby, of Perrysburg mand. A few days prior to this sad Griffith changed hands at Buffalo, and port on a Sunday morning, having on boa party of excursionists, of which numbe of 250 were either burned or drowned. Captain Roby, his wife and child. Th Washington No. 2 was burned off Silver the 2nd of June 1838, with the loss of She was commanded by Captain J. W The propellor Phœnix, Captain B. G. Swe for Chicago, on Lake Michigan, took fire night in November, 1846, a short dista Sheboygan, and was totally destroyed, lives. Captain Sweet happened to be his post at the time. The steamer Nia tain F. S. Miller, some years subsequ with a like fate, with the loss of upward lives. Of other steamers which trav lakes in those times, mention might which suffered damages or were total some means, not omitting the Sea Bird Michigan, the early part of the prese wtth 100 lives. The Great Western wa destroyed by fire at Windsor ; the Tham loss at Windsor ; the Little Western, a the Cynthia, near Malden ; the Daniel W Sandusky, at Buffalo ; also the W. F. The Detroit No. 2 was partially destroy at Newport. The steamer Vermillion destroyed in the same manner while lay dock in Huron, with five lives. The summary of no less than fifteen b destroyed, with nearly 1,000 lives in al loss.

A LAWSUIT.—A writ has been issu Superior Court, Montreal, in the suit of Life Insurance Company vs. the Daily that city, and served, and is returnable September.—Gazette.

☞ THE CANADIAN MONETARY TIMES AND INSURANCE CHRONICLE is printed every Thursday Evening, in time for the English Mail.

Subscription Price, one year, $2, or $3 in American currency ; Single copies, five cents each. Casual advertisements will be charged ten cents per line of solid nonpareil each insertion. All letters to be addressed, "THE CANADIAN MONETARY TIMES, TORONTO, ONT." Registered letters so addressed are at the risk of the Publishers. Cheques should be made payable to J. M. TROUT, Business Manager, who will, in future, issue all receipts for money.

The Canadian Monetary Times.

THURSDAY, SEPTEMBER 10, 1868.

RESPONSIBILITY IN MANAGEMENT.

The question of responsibility in the management of our banking institutions is one that requires definite settlement. There was a time in the history of this province when a looseness of management characterised our most wealthy corporations, the plainest dictates of prudence being ignored with an easy recklessness, and ordinary business principles treated with a contempt amazing in its audacity. But competition undermined these outrages on honesty and common sense and, one after another, institutions rotted away and tumbled helplessly to earth burying beneath their ruins the fortunes of deluded victims. Excavation brought to light the secret of their destruction and now fully warned by a hapless experience, the public look for guarantees against disaster that would have, in the old state of things, been deemed hair-brained and revolutionary. The real fact is that we have arrived at a period when business must be done on the strictest business principles.

For the sake of a practical application of our remarks we confine ourselves to the case of banks. How much blame is to be borne by the Manager or the Cashier of a bank and how much is fairly attachable to its Directors when the affairs of the institution become involved? The responsibility is undoubtedly divided ; the Cashier has his share and the Directors have theirs. Sometimes the Cashier shelters himself under the supposed larger responsibility of the Directors and not unfrequently, the latter clear their skirts at the expense of their chief executive officer. As long as prosperity prevailed, mutual congratulations, felicitous in phrase, were exchanged at intervals; but when the little cloud of trouble appeared on the horizon, the vote of thanks was less hyperbolical and on the bursting of the storm-cloud recrimination and

hostility extinguished every spark of thankfulness. Under such circumstances we naturally enquire where should justice place the responsibility.

In some cases, the Cashier is the only one cognizant of the facts out of which transactions arise, sometimes owing to their intricacy, at others, owing to the apathy, laziness, or trustfulness of the Directors. On the other hand, we meet with instances in which the Cashier is the mere special agent of those who are his superiors ; a machine moved by a will and guided by a discretion other than his own. His judgment is fettered by the caprice, partiality, or honest stubbornness of his Directors or some of them. Again the Cashier may have above him a Board to whom he is actually afraid to communicate everything that occurs, for it is a matter of notoriety that some Board rooms are leaky. We can hardly imagine anything more trying to a Cashier than the consciousness of having the whisperings of the innermost chamber of his institution proclaimed on the housetops or told in the strictest confidence at the market place or on the corners of the streets. Every bank has its secrets and many banks have before now profited largely by gleaning on their neighbor's fields. Although an accumulation of matters, requiring secresy for their success, is a dangerous heritage, still there is a judicious mean between blatant exposure and studied concealment which it becomes those engaged in the working of banks to respect. A Cashier compelled to labor under such disadvantages as result from a disclosure of his plans or a public explanation of the why and wherefore of his actions, has not a fair chance.

Under the infinite variety of circumstances that might be presented one finds it impossible to lay down strict rules. A Cashier without liberty of discretion is an automaton who heaps up wrath against himself. Any credit earned by the display of ability in the discharge of his duties is appropriated by his superiors. On the other hand where Directors yield a willing obedience to his demands ; accept his statements as axiomatic truths and act in the supposed discharge of a trust as if they had neither part nor lot in the matter, they not only expose themselves to legal liability but also justly incur public contempt.

The only way out of a labyrinth so much like an inextricable maze is likely to be found by gaining a clue to a proper, clearly defined dostribution of authority. Grant the Cashier or Manager a certain line of discretion within which he shall be absolute. In this we, of course take it for granted, that the individual who fills that position has been selected for his qualifications. If such is not the case the sooner he is got rid of the better, for no amount of checking, chectmaking, zeal or astutness on the part of Directors, will disguise his follies or repair his faults. There is no desire on our part to deprive Directors of their privileges or operations. On the contrary we would have them zealous and keen, not too timid to advance their opinions nor too confiding to shirk the trouble of acquainting themselves with what is essentially their business. Sometimes we find Cashiers not over endowed with ability but often times we discover directors utterly bankrupt as regards force of character or capacity for the intelligent comprehension of what passes before their eyes. But, withal, Directors have a certain duty to perform, and it is reasonably expected from them that they bring to bear on their deliberations, at least ordinary discretion.

In practice, a Cashier is supposed to lay before his Directors at their meetings the details of important transactions, and an outline of the whole business. In the case of accounts unduly swollen it is a proper thing to ascertain the nature of the business that requires increased accommodation and to prevent a few individuals, no matter who they may be, from monopolising the resources of the institution. Possibly reforms might be introduced of a useful character. For instance we believe it is not an unusual thing for a customer to increase the balance at his credit by drawing foreign bills, and depositing them in his bank. The bills are forthwith charged against the foreign agent of the bank, and the depositor credited with the proceeds. So that A. builds up his account by drawing bills say on England and the foreign agent of the bank appears on the bank's books to be the real debtor for the very amount which A. is using. Such a system is well calculated to deceive and we can understand how some persons have in this way been allowed to run up debts to a large amount, without the Directors knowing anything about it.

Without enlarging too much into detail we may safely assume the truth of the saying in this as in other matters that "what is everybody's business is nobody's business." Elementary principles as well as the lessons of experience drive us to the conclusion that the responsibilities of those concerned in the management of banks, where a certain amount of discretion has to be exercised are such that it is expedient to arrive at an understanding on the subject, and after a distict line of demarcation has been drawn the blameworthy can be punished, and the innocent saved from unjust imputation.

A bill has been filed in Chancery with the object of restraining the city of Hamilton from transferring the Great Western Railway stocks held by the city to the Wellington, Grey and Bruce Railway Company.

TELEGRAPHY.

The unusual activity, at this time, of Telegraph Companies in extending their wires and in enlarging their field of operations, and the appearance in our midst of a new Company, organized under the name of the Dominion Telegraph Company, prove how effectively the laws of supply and demand work, and confirm the opinions, already expressed in these column, that private competition is fully equal to the task of meeting the public wants as regards telegraphic communication. The action of the British Government in purchasing the telegraph lines of the United Kingdom, has not changed our views, for a great deal is to be said in favor of Government interference, where Companies, by virtue of their control of exclusive patents, imposed an oppressive tariff which prevented a general enjoyment of telegraphic facilities. The continued life of the patents upon the peculiar kind of instruments used in the United Kingdom required the strong arm of Goverment to accomplish a result generally acknowledged to be desirable. Here and in the United States where the Morse system has been adopted (that patent having expired), to bring about the same results of cheap rates and efficient service, nothing but a well-ordered competition need be invoked. The figures given in Mr. Scuddamore's report show how regular has been the annual increase of telegraphing in the United Kingdom. The history of the tariffs established there for the last few years is worthy of note. From 1860 to 1865 the tariff of English Companies, except for a short period of struggle between the United Telegraph Company and the London District Telegraph Company remained stationary, and during that time telegraphing increased from the ratio of one telegram to 296 letters in 1860 to one telegram to 169 letters in 1864. Early in 1865 an arrangement was arrived at between the owners of the various patents which excluded the possibility of competition and tariffs were advanced, and in some instances by the London Telegraph District Company, doubled. Notwithstanding this, the ratio of telegrams again increased in two years from 1 telegram to 169 letters in 1864 to 1 telegram to 121 letters in 1866. In Belgium the cheapening of rates caused an increase in the number of dispatches of 233 per cent., and that, too, upon wires managed solely by Government officials in the usual stolid style of that little kingdom. What it would have been had the additional stimulant of competing private interests, adopting new modes, multiplying new facilities, and dependent not on Government but the people, entered into the experience, we are left to conjecture.

No modern agency of science has de and is developing, so rapidly as the te Europe, Asia, the United States, a the North Coast of Africa, are ali schemes, having for their object the of its facilities ; continents are span oceans crossed by multiplying wires.

Within our own borders much re be done in the way of increasing the of offices and the cheapening of rate present rates are generally regarded and in some quarters this has car scheme of Government monopoly to l on with favor. To such a scheme country we are opposed for reasons made public. We believe in private tition, and entering upon a new era solidated material and political adv it is proper to encourage every legiti terprise whose prospects seem fair, especially such enterprises as will larged means of intercommunicat produce by a healthy rivalry increas ties and cheaper rates.

THE NEW ENGLISH BANKI ACT.

The Act amending the Bankrup passed at the last session of the Impe liament is one to amend the procee regard to arrangement deeds. The such deeds were found to be ma want of means to prevent sham cre senting, the power given to secured to vote in respect of their whole the want of means to compel inquir creditor suspected something wrong a stop to sham creditors simulating the provision is the deposit in cour tailed list of the creditors assenting of arrangement with their names, and the particulars of their debts w fication under oath. The list is borate in detail, showing the ti such debts or liabilities were cor incurred, and the considerations for the names, residences and occupat creditors, the respective amounts d and the securities held by them, timated value of such securities. and list are to be deposited at the It has been found that the interest creditors was often times dispropo the nominal amount of their debt little to lose in proportion to the creditor there was an antagonism o the secured creditor's great anxie procure a speedy settlement. It that secured creditors shall prove in the ordinary way and deduct, f pose of compensation, in assent deed of arrangement, the full va securities. The remaining object

ıe examination, as in bankruptcy,
:or, or any creditor, or any person
.ve information about the estate.

AL ASSURANCE COMPANY.

'ght ago we published some corre-
had between the manager of this
and the Finance Department re-
ıe question of deposit. As will be
ed, that correspondence shows that
ny is not required to deposit at all;
osit would have been made only
ı step would involve a considerable
of the annual income from invest-
reference to the statement, else-
ll make it plain that the securities
l not be exchanged for Dominion
:ing but six per cent., without a
or they are, with one or two excep-
he best class.
y say what is due to the manage-
the position of the Company, in
g it as one of the soundest con-
ıg insurance business in Canada.
anagers of Canadian Companies
ow a leaf from Mr. Murray's book
'.

---

eting of the Grand Trunk proprie-
London, called for the 27th August,
out an apparently trivial matter,
significance. The immediate ques-
ke is, shall the Directors be *required*
e a list of the bond and stockholders
ıd with their names and addresses.
Journal says the introduction of the
ıs a change of management. The
this meeting will therefore be looked
interest; and hence we have been
give the statement of the directors
at the matter may be placed fairly
r readers.

---

st English mails report the death
Matthew Dove, Esq., who held the
f Manager and Actuary of the Royal
Company from its origination. His
decease occurred on the 24th Aug.

's MAGAZINE FOR SEPT.—The contents
nth's number embrace an article on the
ı of the U. S. debt, statistics respecting
ıal Banks, reports on the Savings Banks,
usual amount of banking and financial

ERY OF SALT AT KINCARDINE.—Kin-
ept. 8.—Salt was struck here yesterday
th of 895 feet, being over 100 feet nearer
e than at Goderich. They drilled
ıirteen feet eight inches of solid salt.
ordinary glasses of the brine, one and
sses of pure white salt, the same in
that Goderich has produced. There is
l of excitement in town to-day, and the
re much elated at the success of their

Financial.

TORONTO STOCK MARKET.

(Reported by Pellatt & Osler, Brokers.)

We have to report another quiet week in stocks, the demand still exceeds the supply.

Bank Stock.—There are buyers of Montreal at 133½ and sellers at 134½. No transactions in British. Ontario sold at 98½ and 99 and there are now buyers at 98¾. For Toronto 115 would be paid; no sales. Royal Canadian sold at 87½ to 88 and is in demand. Commerce is asked for at 103 to 103½. Merchants' sold at 104¾ to 105¼; little offering. There are buyers of Molson's at 112; no sellers. City is wanted at 102; none on market. There are sellers of Du Peuple at 105 to 105½; and buyers of Nationale at 105½. There are sellers of Mechanics' at 98; no buyers at that rate. Union nominal at 101 to 102. Nothing doing in other banks.

Debentures.—There are buyers of Canada sterling fives at 90 to 91; sterling sixes are offering at 100¾; and Dominion stock at 101. There were sales of Toronto at about 6¾. No County in market.

Sundries.—There is very little doing in Building Society stock owing to its scarcity; there were several sales of Canada Permanent at 118 to 118½; buyers would give 110½ for Western Canada; and 104 to 105 for Freehold, but there are no sales. City Gas sold at 105 and is still offering at that price. Buyers would give 132½ for Montreal Telegraph; nothing doing. Sales of Canada Landed Credit occurred at 63, which is still offered. A few good mortgages were placed at 8 per cent. Money easy on good securities.

MONTREAL MONEY MARKET.

(From our own Correspondent).

MONTREAL, Sept. 8, 1868.

Money continues plentiful, and good paper is scarce and readily taken at the banks at 7 per cent. and at times for less. I see first-class short dated paper can be done in New York at 4 to 5 per cent. So far there is very little movement of money west, but as soon as the large buyers of produce fairly commence operations, we may look for increased activity in that direction. The supply here is more than ample for all probable wants, so that no tightening of the banks may be expected. The stock and share market has been quiet during the week, prices rule high. Bank of Montreal advanced to 135. British and City nominal, former at 102½, and latter at 102. Merchants' steady at 105 to 105½. Toronto enquired for at 115, but none offering. Jacques Cartier held at 108, buyers at 106. Ontario, 98 to 98¼. Holders of Champlain and St. Lawrence stock have advanced their pretensions to 10½, and those of Richelieu Co. to 115. but no buyers at those rates. Gold has ranged during the week from 145 to 143¾, closing to-day at 144½. Silver to-day buying at 3½, selling at 3¼ discount. This is a rise of fully 1 per cent. during the week. The demand is good, and a further advance is anticipated. The spring shipments of silver from here of about $1,200,000 are likely to tell favorably on the price during the next two months, as the stock cannot be increased from New York as in former years, the duty of 15 per cent on American silver being in effect prohibitory. Greenbacks—Selling price, 30½ to 30¾; buying do., 31 per cent. discount. Gold drafts on New York par to ½ discount.

NEW YORK MONEY MARKET.

August has been characterised by the usual ease in the money market. The banks have held large amounts of idle funds, the deposits of the Western banks having perhaps been unusually large; and, with but a moderate demand for discounts, the supply on call has been very abundant at 3 to 4 per cent, with a brief interval of 4 to 5 per cent. About the 10th of the month there was a very active demand from the West, which continued for two weeks, causing a loss of about $10,000,000 of currency, chiefly national bank notes. This demand was to provide for the moving of the earlier grain crop in the more southern sections of the West, and was followed by a suspension of remittances. The outflow of currency almost exhausted the supply of bank bills, but had little effect upon the loan market. The loanable resources of the banks, however, were undoubtedly largely curtailed, and the fact of the rate of interest on call loans not being enhanced was perhaps due to the banks anticipating a renewal of the westward outflow in September, and holding themselves prepared for such a movement whenever it may occur. In August of last year the movement corresponded closely with that of last month, the banks sending a large amount of currency West from the 10th to the 25th of the month, after which the shipments fell off, and the rate of interest declined one per cent. But in September the outflow of currency was renewed, with the loss of a large amount of legal tenders, and the advance of the rate of interest to seven per cent in gold toward the close of the month.—*New York Financial Chronicle.*

BANK OF ENGLAND.

The position of the bank at August 19th, 1868, was as follows:

Issue Department.	
Notes issued	£34,638,755
Government debt	£11,015,100
Other Securities	3,984,900
Gold coin and bullion	19,638,755
Silver bullion	
	£34,638,755
Banking Department.	
Proprietors' capital	£14,553,000
Rest	3,353,849
Public deposits (including Exchequer, Commissioners of National Debt, Savings' Banks, and Dividend Accounts)	2,864,234
Other deposits	20,172,244
Seven day and other bills	510,680
	£41,454,107
Government securities (including Dead Weight Annuity)	£13,790,131
Other securities	16,174,185
Notes	10,393,345
Gold and silver coin	1,096,446
	£41,454,107

COUNTERFEIT HALF AND QUARTER DOLLARS —The public should be on their guard against taking counterfeit American half and quarter dollars, of which large numbers are at present in circulation. The milling on the edge is rather defective, and the coin is considerably lighter than the genuine.

SILVER CIRCULATION.—Mr. D. Burn, of the Northumberland and Durham Savings' Bank, gives his views about the difficulty of a surplus of silver in circulation in these words:—"I have read attentively the communications which have appeared for some time past in many of our newspapers, on the subject of what is termed 'the silver nuisance,' and have come to the conclusion that the best remedy we could adopt to mitigate the evil, would be to authorize our chartered banks to issue "quarter dollar" bills, redeemable in precisely the same way as their other bills are at present. I cannot see the slightest objection in the present position of Canada, to the issue of a currency of this denomination. At present we are nearly all together dependent upon a foreign country for our smaller currency—a dependence which ought not to be allowed to exist; and the only way in which I think this evil can be removremoved is to give our chartered banks the power I have suggested. The banks, I am sure, would gladly undertake the issue of this smaller currency, for the business would be a profitable one to them, inasmuch as the circulation of bills of a quarter-dollar each could not fail to be much more extended, and continue, as the phrase is, 'longer out,' than the present circulation of bills of one dollar and upwards."

Railway News.

NORTHERN RAILWAY.—Traffic Receipts for week ending 29th August, 1868.

Passengers	$3,587 66
Freight	8,782 91
Mails and sundries	216 67
Total receipts for week	$12,587 24
Corresponding week 1867..	10,057 01
Increase	$2,530 23

Traffic Receipts for week ending Sept. 5, 1868 :

Passengers	$3,419 30
Freight	7,295 70
Mails and Sundries	1,168 04
Total Receipts for week	$11,883 04
Corresponding week 1867....	7,067 60
Increase	$4,815 44

GREAT WESTERN RAILWAY.—Traffic for week ending 21st August, 1868.

Passengers	$33,172 74
Freight and live stock	29,046 02
Mails and sundries	2,127 26
	$64,346 02
Corresponding Week of '67	63,052 45
Decrease	$1,293 57

WELLINGTON, GREY AND BRUCE RAILWAY.— The ratepayers of Hamilton, on the 2nd inst., voted on the by-law authorizing the transfer of the city stock in the Great Western Railway, amounting to $100,000, to the Wellington, Grey and Bruce. At the close of the polls the vote stood 720 for and 84 against.

Commercial.

Montreal Correspondence.

(From our own Correspondent.)

Montreal, 8th Sept., 1868.

Since my last an increased activity is discernable in business circles, not that there are many actual transactions to report, but the desire to do business is obviously more than it has been for sometime past. Merchants appear more cheerful, and instead of the hackneyed remark, "Nothing doing," is now heard, "Business is decidedly brisker." There are many causes which will tend to soon give an impetus to trade ; the certainty that the harvest is a success as far as regards the great crop, viz., wheat ; plenty of money, and though last, not least, the provincial rifle match and agricultural exhibition, both of which will attract large numbers of persons from all parts of the Dominion, most of whom will combine business with pleasure, so that in ten days or a fortnight we may look for considerable activity. So far, the preparations for the exhibition proceed very quietly and unostentatiously, and except in the immediate neighborhood of the buildings there is nothing to indicate that anything unusual is going on. I am glad to note that the harvest east of Quebec is safely housed, and bids fair to prove the largest yield for years past.

Our PRODUCE MARKET—Generally is dull, but for the last few days flour has been more active, prices have steadily receded since my last, considerable sales of city brands at $6, strong superfines have ranged from $6 15 to $6 35, fancy has realized in lots $6 25 and $6 45 for small parcels. The stock here is about 20,000 brls., being much the same that it was last year at this time. In grain the receipts are very light and prices not yet established ; U. C. spring ex cars worth $1 35, other qualities nominal. A cargo sale of mixed corn was made at 84c. Pork is very quiet. In dairy products, butter and cheese are in demand at high rates. Western butter is worth 19c to 20c, and choice dairy 21c to 22c. Cheese ranges from 10c to 11c.

The GROCERY market is reviving, and goods of all descriptions meet with more demand. Sugars have ruled very low, but I fancy the bottom has been touched, and as prices are rather better in New York and London, we may look for increased stiffness, if not a rise here. Some parcels of teas are selling chiefly for local trade, but large buyers and Western men will hold off till the cargo sales. A portion of the fall auctions are already advertised, they take place rather later this year than usual. The first will be held to-morrow. It is a cargo sale of Mediterranean goods on account of Messrs. Reuter, Lionnais & Co. I give you the names and dates of the other sales, as it will interest your Western subscribers :—September 29, Victor Hudon, and Rimmer, Gunn & Co. ; September 30, Buchanan, Leckie & Co. ; October 1, D. Torance & Co., and Chapman, Fraser & Co. ; September 2, A. Urquhart & Co. D. Torance & Co's is purely a tea sale, the others comprise all sorts of groceries, two of them chiefly of Mediterranean goods imported direct.

DRY GOODS.—Our importers are very busy. Next week I shall be able to write you more fully, as then the prices of the fall trade will be over, and I will be in a better position to draw a comparison between the amount of business done this year and the preceding ones.

HARDWARE.—Imported. — Generally speaking trade is more than usually dull at this period. Some few houses have, nevertheless, been fully employed. It is expected that there will be plenty of buyers in about a fortnight, and considerable activity. Imports have been light, and although prices during the last five weeks have run down, it is expected that a change will take place and the market will stiffen, if not advance. The assortment here is excellent.

Home Manufactured.—The mills have been running full time all summer, except some few that had to stop during the intense heat. A ready sale is expected for all produced, there being sufficient orders on hand to pretty well work off all that can be turned out before the close of the season. Prices generally have been well maintained, and the trade altogether is in a healthy state.

Toronto Market.

The past week has witnessed a general opening up of the fall trade in all the leading branches. A great many county and town buyers from the various sections of Ontario, have been or are now in market, and the principal houses are exceedingly busy.

DRY GOODS.—In this branch the season has begun well ; importers are looking hopeful, and now speak of a successful fall trade. A very considerable amount of goods has already been placed satisfactorily, and still the season is only fairly commenced. In view of the present hopeful views of buyers, and the early opening of the trade, we may fairly expect a good average business at least ; the state of the weather, and other unforeseen contingencies, may have a marked influence on the aggregate result. Woolen Goods are moving off freely at unchanged prices. Even Canadian Woollens, which it was expected would go slow, owing to the pretty full stock of these goods on

the shelves of country merchants, have m a fair demand ; but this may be largely acc for by the superior style and finish given tl compared with previous years. Cottons a and selling at full prices, the tendency bei ward. We give the importations of dry g the port of Toronto for the month of A These figures pretty well indicate the cours trade thus far. It will be seen that due has been exercised, and the probability ju is that we shall not have such an accumula stock to hold over the coming winter, as that of 1868. We have no desire for the rec of such a gloomy state of affairs as existed beginning of the current year in this branc

Imports of Dry Goods for August.

	1867.	18
Manufac. of Woollens	$304,785	$24
Do. Cottons	189,049	16
Do. Silks & Velv'ts	39,869	4
Do. Fancy Goods.	14,942	4
Wearing Apparel	1,092	
	$549,737	$45

BOOTS AND SHOES.—The houses in tl have had a busy week. Buyers are or freely in anticipation of good demand seasonable goods. Prices are a shade low last week.

GROCERIES.—Trade is also brisk in this Sugars—Continue to rule low, and import fits are now cut very fine. The market is in favor of buyers. Teas—Are steady in p without noticeable change. We give the tations entered at Toronto for August of a the leading articles.

Imports of Groceries for August.

	1867.	1
Sugar, lbs	482,124	32
Tea, lbs	20,749	7
Tobacco Manufactured, lbs.	4,690	
Coffee, lbs	10,839	1
Confectionery	45,839	

LIQUORS.—We have no change to note in a full trade is reported at quotations.

Imports of Liquors for August.

	1867.	
Wine, gallons	6,241	
Brandy, "	283	
Gin, "	207	
Rum, "	593	
Whiskey "	177	

LEATHER.—There is more doing tl though the trade is still quiet and price ary.

PRODUCE.—Owing to the dullness o markets for breadstuffs and barley, and off in the receipts, there was less business mediately in this market during the p days. Wheat—Has gradually recede quotations, and closed dull but steady. little demand and only small lots offeri of cars were offered at $1.20 to $1.25 and $1.30 for fall. Barley—The recei week from all sources would foot up to 000 bushels, being about 10,000 bus. les previous week. Prices opened at 93 t improved somewhat, closing at 95 to ? sales of car loads were reported within several cargo lots changed hands a to 98c.; there is a general dispotition to private. There are still sellers at 98c. port on the Bay of Quinte. Peas—A was offered at 98c. f.o.b. with 95½ offere Oats—A small trade was done in car l to 51c., the market closing with seller 51c. and buyers at 48c.

FLOUR.—Receipts light ; superfine d is a moderate demand for shipment to Provinces. A lot of 500 brls. choice sold at $6, and 1,000 brls. spring ext while 100 brl lots of ordinary sold superior and extra not much wanted as offered at $7.25 and only $6.50 bid. Only a local trade doing at quotations.

ARE.—There is more doing, but the not fully open before toward the end nth. Importations will be moderate, *Iron*—New stocks will be to hand in ten days, when the assortment will be 1 at present.

ONS.—*Butter*—Receipts are light and tle doing. The late rains will tend to e production which was unusually light season so far owing to the excessive nd the scarcity of pasture and green kinds. There are moderate stocks in y, but very little in first hands. It has ost wholly bought up by jobbers and s who hold ordinary store packed lots in firmly for 22 to 23 cts. per pound. res exporters will not pay at present, business has been confined within a ow compass. Not more than 18 to now offered. *Cheese*—There is very lit- country, and it is held for 10½ to 11½ to quality. The home market is just dull, and there is no disposition to export, especially at the high prices ed. Respecting the condition of the market the *Shipping List* says "The rket continues dull, with slight conces- ie inferior grades. Unlike butter the cheese continues large, and either enter to consumption or are taken by ex- While the make of butter in this State ely calculated at an increase of one-third of cheese is correspondingly decreased. drought in Europe—in largely reducing of dairy products—cheese particularly, ide additional demand for American er previous years, and with a smaller ow prices can hardly prevail during the season, and will be found difficult to r force." *Eggs* are quiet at 10 to 11 cts. s nominal. *Pork* no stock; market d.

TOCK—The receipts of cattle have been ring the week, and include heavy arrivals western part of Ontario. The most of ring have been taken up for shipment to and Quebec. First class have met with emand, being relatively scarce and sold s $6 50 including beef, hide and tallow. cond quality there was an abundant sup- for these we quote the average price iferior were also freely offered and met le demand. The bad state of the pas- ing the hot weather has caused an undue n of poor cattle to be brought into *Sheep* were plentiful, throughout the at the close there was a large supply we quote prices $4, $3 and $2 50 for ond and third qualities respectively. re also freely offered, selling at $1 50 to o quality. *Calves* are scarce being con- it of season, not much demand, they are to $6 each. *Hogs.*—In the market for we note a fair demand, a sale of a lot of numbering 77 head is reported at 6 cts. l live weight. Packers think the market e maintained at so high a point. At e-cured bacon is quoted at about 62 shil- Liverpool, but as the season approaches ssed hogs can be packed and shipped, ket must recede owing to the increased which will pour in.

—The new crop is beginning to arrive, samples are held for 30 cts.

EUM.—As the season advances and the ncreases, the market acquires firmness. llowing were the exports of petroleum principal United States ports from the nuary to the 1st September in the years

lons	65,747,702
"	40,615,172
"	38,849,974
"	11,955,029

Havana Sugar Market.

August 28.—SUGAR.—*Clayed.*—There has prevailed much more dullness during the week under review than of late, the same having been increased by the continued unfavorable quotations transmitted per cable from London and New York. The business of the week comprises the few sales we notice below, which have been closed for the greater part on the basis of 7½ to 7¾ rs. per arrobe for Number 12. To-day, however, buyer's offers do not exceed generally the former figure, but they continue to meet with very few sellers, as the majority of these seem to pay little attention to the adverse news received from abroad, according to which buyers cannot afford to grant higher prices than those they offer at present. The market, therefore, closes very dull, and in view of the last sales of good dry sugar our last quotations, based on 7¾ rls. for No. 12, must be reproduced to-day nominally, stating, however, that there are no buyers on that basis nor sellers at a lower one.

Trade in Chicago.

SEPT. 1.—The past week has shown an active business in all branches of trade centering here. The receipts of grain continue at a daily average of over four hundred thousand bushels of Corn, Wheat, Oats, Barley and Rye, which is about the full carrying capacity of the roads tapping the districts from which the crop is being marketed. The receipts from Wisconsin and Minnesota are, however, comparatively insignificant yet. During the week the movement of grain Eastward has been very free, preventing any accumulation here, to which fact is, in one respect, due the ease with which the banks have worked through such a heavy business. The business in Dry Goods, Groceries, Lumber, etc., is now more active than at any time since last summer. The increase of trade is reflected in the aggregate of the week's business at the Clearing House, which, as shown below, is nearly double what it was five weeks ago, being a little over ten millions for the week ending August 1st. The report for the week ending to-day is as below:

	Clearings.	Balances.
Aug. 31............	$2,787,489 41	$238,036 04
Sept. 1............	3,216,356 08	279,204 03
Sept. 2............	3,620,052 85	328,835 00
Sept. 3............	3,002,777 98	224,610 73
Sept. 4............	3,182,548 94	254,558 34
Sept. 5............	3,079,556 72	367,282 62
Total........	$18,888,781 98	$1,692,526 76
Last week	16,771,282 78	1,448,842 10

Money has worked close, but with more freedom during the latter part of the week. The increased promptness of country collections has relieved the necessities of merchants, so that they are calling for comparatively few accommodations, while at the same time an increase in deposits is noticed at the banks having the largest lines of mercantile accounts. The movement of currency to the country has been large during the whole week. Owing to large receipts from New York to-day there was a good supply, but large amounts are being paid out over the counter, to commission men, who are forwarding by express to grain buyers in the country. Orders from country banks also continue, so that, altogether, the estimate of two millions is a small one for the outflow of currency from this city, for the past week.

Demerara Sugar Market.

The following is from Sandbach, Parker & Co.'s Circular, dated Georgetown, Demerara, Aug. 7th:

We have had a wretched dull fortnight; complete stagnation in every branch of trade. Food of every kind is in excess, and the great decline in prices will entail heavy losses on importers. The arrivals since our last comprise seven vessels from United Kingdom, three from United States, seven from British Provinces, and eight schooners from the Islands.

IMPORTS—BREADSTUFFS.—Last mail we were called upon to report arrival of heavy stocks, including 5,500 brls. Flour, 1,100 brls. Bread, 800 brls. Meal, &c., &c., most of which remain unsold, this fortnight further supplies have come to hand to the extent of 3,500 brls. Flour, 1,100 brls. Bread, 700 brls. Meal, &c. The Market is very flat.

PROVISIONS.—We have received by the same vessels 400 brls. Pork, Rump, $24; P. Mess $20 to 22; Mess, $25 to $26; C. Mess, $27; 200 half brls. Beef $11.75 to $12.75; Cheese, $12 to $14; 800 pails Lard, $4 to $4.12; French Butter has sold in small lots at $18.

EXPORTS.—SUGAR—The amount offered for sale during the fortnight has not been large, and many Merchants holding orders have been afraid to operate for fear of falling short after vessels are chartered, up to yesterday from $6.50 to $6.75 was paid for choice samples V.P., but the news from America by the the mail this morning not being favorable, only $6.25 was bid at the public sale, the lots were all withdrawn; we do not expect any high range of prices during the coming fortnight.

MOLASSES—Is to day quite neglected, although sales were made previously at 30 to 32 cents.

RUM.—There have been some transactions for the British Provinces, but prices show no improvement.

SUGARS (package included) sold by 100 lbs. Dutch, 10 per cent. tare F. O. B., in hhds of 1,800 lbs.

Muscovadoes, equal to No. 8 Dutch Standard, $4 per 100 lbs.; No. 10, $4.25; No. 12, $4.50; Vacuum Pan, equal to No. 12, $5.75; No. 14, $6; No. 16, $6.20; No. 18, $6.40.

MOLLASSES (package included, by Imperial gal.) in puns. of 100 gals. Muscovado, from 20 to 26 cents, as to color and density; Vacuum Pan, from 26 to 30 cents.

RUM (colored, package included, sold by Imperial gallon, in puns. of 100 gals., from 35 per cent. to 38 overproof 38 to 40 cents; from 38 per cent. to 40 overproof 40 to 45 cents.

FREIGHTS.—Have been in a very depressed state, and have shown no animation since our last advices. 1s. 9d. is still the nominal shipping rate, but not over 1s. 3d. could be had on Charter, the quantity of Produce coming forward for the United Kingdom is so small, that one vessel on the birth for each Port is quite sufficient for present requirements.

WEATHER.—Has been much too dry, and if the wet season breaks up now Estates will suffer severely as the fall of rain has not been sufficient to enable them to stand the approaching dry season of four months duration.

Reciprocity.

An announcement was lately made in the pnblic prints to the effect that Mr. Seward had been for some time past in correpondence with Mr. Thornton, the British Ambassador at Washington. on the subject of a new Reciprocity Treaty, and it was also hinted that our Minister of Finance was about to preceed to Washington to consummate the understanding arrived at. The New York *Albion* thus refers to the subject:

We are now able to state, on the best authority, that there is not a word of truth in the report. What the object of this semi-official announcement was, it is not for us to even conjecture; but certain it is that the Republican party is held *responsible*, by more than one indignant community, for the crabbed and ill-tempered repeal of the late treaty; and now that the Presidential election is rapidly approaching, this announcement may have been made in the interests of *that party*. Be this however, as it may, we are persuaded that time alone is necessary to convince our American cousins that their Government did a very unwise act when it abrogated the old treaty; and it is not unlikely, by any means, that Mr. Seward is now actually contemplating the course now only *prematurely* attributed to him.

New York, Boston and Portland, all feel the loss of the trade which reciprocity gave them; as well as the interior cities of Chicago, Milwaukee, Detroit, Toledo, Cleveland, Buffalo, Oswego and Ogdensburgh; and whenever the boards of trade of those cities combined, choose to move in the matter, neither the Treasury Department or the State Department at Washington, can effectively resist the pressure. In fact this pressure is sure to come sooner or later; but now that the New Dominion has arranged its commercial affairs to meet the changed condition of things, it is perhaps as well that it should remain as it is until entire free trade with Europe can be adopted, when the United States may ask in vain for a new treaty.

Halifax Market.

Halifax, 1st Sept.

BREADSTUFFS.—Flour steady and in fair demand at $8.00 to $8.25 for No. 1 Canada; $8.75 for good extra; extra State $8 to $8.20; Baltimore superfine $7.25 to $7.75; Baltimore extra $8 to $8.50. Rye, dull at $6.50 to $6.75. Meal dull at $4.75 to $4.80 for kiln dried, $4.50 for fresh ground. Oatmeal dull, at $8.75. Imports from 1st January to September 1, 1867 and 1868.

	Brls. Flour.	Brls. Cornmeal.
1868	121,000	39,231
1867	109,460	28,557

FISH.—We have no material change to note in dry codfish. Large shore $3.80 to $4; small hard cured from store, $3.10 to $3.25. Haddock, $1.75 to $2. Salmon still continue dull at $15 to $16 for No. 1's; $14 for No. 2's, $9 50 to $10 for No. 3's. Mackerel—No. 3's improving; No 1's or 2's in market; No. 3 sold at $5.85, and some holders are asking as high as $6. Herrings quiet at $3 80 to $4 for shore split. Alewives $3.50 to $3 75.

OILS.—Cod has improved, and sales made during the week at 46c; prices are now firm at 45c to 47½c. Seal unchanged. Kerosene quiet, 38c to 40c for American.

WEST INDIA PRODUCE.—Without any change. Sugars—Holders asking 6¼c to 6½c for Porto Rico; 5½c to 6c for Cuba, and 6c to 6¼c for Barbadoes in bond. Molasses—Cienfuegos 29½c to 30c in bond. Rum—Demerara, 52c to 53c; St. Jago, 43c in bond.

FINANCIAL.—Bank drawing rate on London 60 day bills 13 per cent prem.; Private 12 to 12¼ per cent prem. New York gold drafts at sight, 4 per cent prem. Currency drafts 27 per cent discount. Montreal sight drafts 4 per cent prem. Newfoundland sight drafts 5 per cent prem.—*R. C. Hamilton & Co.'s Circular.*

Telegraphs.

A special report in connection with the Electric Telegraph Bill has just appeared, which includes, among other interesting particulars, a statement showing the mileage of railways under agreement with the Telegraph Companies, and the number of years which the agreements have to run, as well as the mileage of wires on such railways. A summary of the statement shows there are 1,280 miles of line and 4,226 of wire under a term of agreement of from six to ten years; 3,211½ miles of line and 13,397 of wire under a term of agreement of from 11 to 20 years; 340½ miles of line and 1,247 of wire under a term of agreement of from 21 to 30 years; and 4,650 miles of line and 1,556 of wire with a term of agreement of from 31 to 99 years—making a total of 13,470 miles of line and 54,744 of wire, under various terms of agreement with the telegraph companies, the average duration of these agreements being 26¾ years per mile of line, and 25¼ years per mile of wire.—*Herepath's Journal.*

Cable Telegrams.

The tariff on Atlantic cable telegrams from New Brunswick, has been changed as follows:—From any station in New Brunswick to any station in Great Britain and Ireland, for ten words, sixteen dollars and thirty-five cents; for each additional word, one dollar and sixty-three cents.

Grain Trade of Hamilton.

The following shows the receipts and stocks of grain at Hamilton up to the 5th September:—

	Receipts.	Stocks.
Barley, bushs....................	73,480	8,486
Wheat, red, bushs.............	10,466	10,466
" white, bushs...........	1,367	1,367
" spring, bushs..........	562	562
Peas, bushs....................	11,450	11,450

The only shipments to that date were 64,994 bushels barley.

Produce in New York.

The following table gives the stock of grain in warehouse in New York and Brooklyn, August 31, 1868:—

Wheat, bushels	....	290,512
Corn	"	2,089,480
Oats	"	336,654
Barley	"	585
Malt	"	101,603
Peas	"	37,786

The Customs Department has given notice that after the 1st October, forms for reports and entries will not be supplied gratuitously, as hitherto, to the public.

NEW INSOLVENTS.—The following insolvents were gazetted last week: Thos. H. Roffe, Stratford; Wm. Buchanan, Menzea; Chas. Penrose, Lindsay; J. A. Bawthinhimer, Brantford; Jacob Robbins, St. Catherines; John Bouskell, Port Hope; J. & P. Judge, Harveyhill Mines; John Northey, do; Geo Cochrane, Cobourg; Wm. Grafton, Blanshard; Adam Thompson, Kingston; Jos. Bradley, Guelph; John Dickson, Maryboro.

DAY'S

Commercial College and High School,

No. 82 KING STREET EAST,

(Near St. James' Cathedral.)

THE design of this institution is to prepare Young Men and others as Book-keepers, and for general business, and to furnish them with the facilities for acquiring an excellent

English and Commercial Education.

Mr. DAY is also prepared to give Private Instruction in the several subjects of his department, and to assist Merchants and others in the checking and balancing of books, adjusting their accounts and partnership affairs, &c.

For further information, please call on or address the undersigned.

JAMES E. DAY,
Accountant

Toronto, Sept. 3rd, 1868.

The Canadian Land and Emigration Company

Offers for sale on Conditions of Settlement,

GOOD FARM LANDS

In the County of Peterboro, Ontario,

In the well settled Township of Dysart, where there are Grist and Saw Mills, Stores, &c., at

ONE-AND-A-HALF DOLLARS AN ACRE.

In the adjoining Townships of Guilford, Dudley, Harburn, Harcourt and Bruton, connected with Dysart and the Village of Haliburton by the Peterson Road, at ONE DOLLAR an Acre.

For further particulars apply to

CHAS. JAS. BLOOMFIELD,
Secretary C. L. and E. Co., Toronto.

Or to ALEX. NIVEN, P.L.S.,
Agent C. L. & E. Co., Haliburton.

AUCTION SALES OF GROCERIE

IN MONTREAL,

FOR THE

Fall Season of 1868.

September 29th,

Sale by Auction, at the Stores of

Victor Hudon, Esq.,

Of MEDITERRANEAN GOODS, *Wines, Liquors, and Gene Groceries.*

J. G. SHIPWAY,
Auctioneer

September 29th,

Sale by Auction, at the Stores of

Messrs. Rimmer, Gunn & Co.,

Of Teas, Wines, Brandies, Tobaccos, and General Grocer

JOHN LEEMING & Co.,
Auctionee

September 30th,

Sale by Auction, at the Stores of

Messrs. Buchanan, Leckie & Co.,

Of 3,000 Packages *Green Teas, ex. Annie Braginton,* dire from Shanghai. Also, 2,000 Packages, *Uncolored Japa* and a large assortment of *Wines, Liquors, Fruit,* a *General Groceries.*

JOHN LEEMING & CO.,
Auctionee

October 1st,

Sale by Auction at the Stores of

Messrs. Chapman, Fraser & Tylee,

Of Fruit, Wines, Brandies, Oils, and General Grocer

JOHN LEEMING & CO.,
Auctionee

October 1st,

Auction Sales at the Stores of

Messrs. David Torrance & Co.,

Of 7,892 Packages Fine New Crop GREEN TEAS, *ex An Braginton,* direct from Shanghai. Also, 2,000 half che UNCOLORED JAPANS, in English order.

JOHN LEEMING & CO.,
Auctionee

October 2nd,

Sale by Auction at the Stores of

Messrs. Alex. Urquhart & Co.,

The Cargo of the *Western Ware,* from Marseilles. Als large assortment of ENGLISH GROCERIES.

JOHN LEEMING & CO.,
Auctione

Sylvester, Bro. & Hickman,

COMMERCIAL Brokers and Vessel Agents. Office—1 Ontario Chambers, [Corner Front and Church S Toronto.

THE QUEEN'S HOTEL

THOMAS DICK, Proprietor.

FRONT STREET, - - - TORONTO,

KERSHAW & EDWARDS

IMPROVED PATENT

NON-CONDUCTING AND VAPORIZING

FIRE AND BURGLAR-PROOF SAFE

139 & 141

ST. FRANCOIS XAVIER STREET,

MONTREAL.

AGENTS:

A. K. BOOMER, TORONTO.
J. W. MURTON, HAMILTON.
A. G. SMYTH, LONDON, ONT.

MINION TELEGRAPH COMPANY.

L STOCK . . . . . $500,000.

In 10,000 *Shares at* $50 *Each.*

PRESIDENT,
HON. WILLIAM CAYLEY.

TREASURER,
HON. J. McMURRICH.

SECRETARY,
H. B. REEVE.

SOLICITORS,
ESSRS. CAMERON & McMICHAEL.

GENERAL SUPERINTENDENT.
MARTIN RYAN.

DIRECTORS.

HON. J. McMURRICH,
Bryce, McMurrich & Co., Toronto.

A. R. McMASTER, Esq.,
A. R. McMaster & Brother, Toronto.

HON. M. C. CAMERON,
Provincial Secretary, Toronto.

JAMES MICHIE, Esq.,
Michie & Co., and George Michie & Co., Toronto.

HON. WILLIAM CAYLEY,
Toronto.

A. M. SMITH, Esq.,
A. M. Smith & Co., Toronto.

L. MOFFATT, Esq.,
Moffatt, Murray & Co., Toronto.

H. B. REEVE, Esq.,
Toronto.

PROSPECTUS.

DOMINION TELEGRAPH COMPANY has been anized under the act respecting Telegraph Com- hapter 67, of the consolidated Statutes of Canada. t is to cover the Dominion of Canada with a com- -work of Telegraph lines.

The Capital Stock.

00, divided into 10,000 shares of $50 each, 5 per e paid at the time of subscribing, the balance to by instalments, not exceeding 10 per cent per said instalments to be called in by the Directors as s progress. The liability of a subscriber is limited nount of his subscription.

---

e Business Affairs of the Company.

er the management of a Board of Directors, an- lected by the Shareholders, in conformity with the and By-Laws of the Company.

irectors are of opinion that it would be to the of the Stockholders generally to obtain subscrip- m all quarters of Canada, and with this view they to divide the Stock amongst the different towns s throughout the Dominion, in allotments suited pulation and business occupations of the different and the interest which they may be supposed to uch an enterprise.

Contracts of Connections.

ract, granting permanent connection and extraor- lvantages, has already been executed between this and the Atlantic and Pacific Company, of New ius, at the very commencement, as the Lines of this are constructed from the Suspension Bridge, at the point of connection) to any point in the Do- ll the chief cities and places in the States, touch- he Lines of the Atlantic and Pacific Telegraph , are brought in immediate connection therewith.

nanent connection has also been secured with the estern Telegraph Company, of Chicago, whereby pany will be brought into close connection with Lake Ports and other places through the North- States, and through to California.

4-3mos

TORONTO PRICES CURRENT.—September 10, 1868.

Name of Article.	Wholesale Rates.	
Boots and Shoes.	$ c.	$ c.
Mens' Thick Boots	2 20	2 50
" Kip..............	2 45	3 20
" Calf	3 00	3 75
" Congress Gaiters..	2 00	2 40
" Kip Cobourgs....	1 00	1 50
Boys' Thick Boots.....	1 65	1 90
Youths' "	1 45	1 55
Women's Batts	95	1 20
" Congress Gaiters..	1 15	1 50
Misses' Batts.	0 75	1 00
" Congress Gaiters..	1 00	1 30
Girls' Batts	0 65	0 90
" Congress Gaiters..	0 80	1 10
Children's C. T. Cacks..	0 50	0 65
" Gaiters	0 65	0 90
Drugs.		
Aloes Cape............	0 12½	0 16
Alum.................	0 02½	0 03
Borax	0 00	0 00
Camphor, refined......	0 65	0 70
Castor Oil.............	0 18	0 28
Caustic Soda..........	0 04½	0 05
Cochineal.............	0 90	1 00
Cream Tartar	0 00	0 00
Epsom Salts	0 03	0 04
Extract Logwood......	0 09	0 11
Gum Arabic, sorts.....	0 30	0 35
Indigo, Madras	0 75	1 00
Licorice	0 14	0 45
Madder	0 13	0 18
Nutgalls	0 00	0 00
Opium................	6 70	7 00
Oxalic Acid...........	0 28	0 35
Potash, Bi-tart........	0 25	0 28
" Bichromate....	0 15	0 20
Potass Iodide	3 80	4 50
Senna	0 12½	0 60
Soda Ash	0 03	0 04
Soda Bicarb	4 50	5 50
Tartaric Acid..........	0 37½	0 45
Verdigris	0 35	0 40
Vitriol, Blue...........	0 09	0 10
Groceries.		
Coffees:		
Java, ℔ lb............	0 22@0 24	
Laguayra, ...	0 17	0 18
Rio	0 15	0 17
Fish:		
Herrings, Lab. split..	0 00	0 00
" round......	0 00	0 00
" scaled......	0 00	0 00
Mackerel, small kitts..	1 00	0 00
Loch. Her. wh'e firks..	2 50	2 75
" half " ..	1 25	1 50
White Fish & Trout...	None.	
Salmon, saltwater.....	15 00	16 00
Dry Cod, ℔112 lbs.....	4 75	5 00
Fruit:		
Raisins, Layers	2 20	2 25
" M. R..........	2 10	2 20
" Valentias new..	0 08½	0 09
Currants, new.........	0 05	0 06
" old.........	0 03½	0 04½
Figs	0 12½	0 13
Molasses:		
Clayed, ℔ gal.........	0 00	0 35
Syrups, Standard	0 45	0 46
" Golden	0 50	0 51
Rice:		
Arracan	4 60	4 75
Spices:		
Cassia, whole, ℔ lb...	0 37½	0 40
Cloves	0 11	0 12
Nutmegs	0 50	0 60
Ginger, ground	0 15	0 25
" Jamaica, root..	0 22	0 25
Pepper, black.........	0 09	0 10
Pimento	0 08	0 09
Sugars:		
Port Rico, ℔ lb.......	0 08¾	0 08¾
Cuba "	0 08½	0 08½
Barbadoes (bright)...	0 08¾	0 08¾
Dry Crushed, at 60d...	0 11	0 00
Canada Sugar Refine'y, yellow No. 2, 60ds..	0 08¾	0 08½
Yellow, No. 2½.......	0 08¾	0 08¾
No. 3........	0 00	0 00
Crushed X	0 10	0 10½
" A............	0 11¼	0 11¾
Ground...............	0 11¾	0 12
Extra Ground.........	0 12¾	0 13
Teas:		
Japan com'n to good..	0 40	0 55
" Fine to choicest..	0 55	0 65
Colored, com. to fine..	0 60	0 75
Congou & Souch'ng...	0 42	0 75
Oolong, good to fine..	0 50	0 65
Y. Hyson, com to gd..	0 45	0 55
Medium to choice.....	0 65	0 80
Extra choice	0 85	0 95
Gunpowd'r c. to med..	0 55	0 70
" med. to fine	0 70	0 85

Name of Article.	Wholesale Rate.	
Groceries—*Contin'd.*	$ c.	$ c.
" fine to fine't..	0 85	0 95
Hyson	0 45	0 80
Imperial	0 42	0 80
Tobacco, Manufact'd.:		
Can Leaf, ℔ lb 5s & 10s.	0 26	0 30
Western Leaf, com..	0 25	0 26
" Good	0 27	0 32
" Fine	0 32	0 35
" Bright fine..	0 40	0 50
" " choice..	0 60	0 75
Hardware.		
Tin (net cash prices)		
Block, ℔ lb..........	0 25	0 26
Grain................	0 25	0 26
Copper:		
Pig	0 23	0 24
Sheet................	0 30	0 33
Cut Nails:		
Assorted ¼ Shingles, ℔ 100 lb.	3 05	3 15
Shingle alone do	2 25	2 35
Lathe and 5 dy.......	3 45	3 55
Galvanized Iron:		
Assorted sizes........	0 09	0 10
Best No. 24..........	0 09	0 00
" 26..........	0 08½	0 09
" 28..........	0 09½	0 10
Horse Nails:		
Guest's or Griffin's assorted sizes......	0 19	0 20
For W. ass'd sizes...	0 18	0 19
Patent Hammer'd do..	0 17	0 18½
Iron (at 4 months):		
Pig—Gartsherrie No1..	26 00	27 00
Other brands. No1..	22 00	23 00
" No2..	24 00	25 00
Bar—Scotch, ℔100 lb..	2 25	2 50
Refined..............	3 00	3 25
Swedes	5 00	5 50
Hoops—Coopers.......	3 00	3 25
Band	3 00	3 25
Boiler Plates.........	3 25	3 50
Canada Plates,.......	4 00	4 25
Union Jack	0 00	0 00
Pontypool...........	4 00	4 25
Swansea	0 00	0 00
Lead (at 4 months):		
Bar, ℔ 100 lbs.......	0 07	0 07½
Sheet "	0 08	0 09
Shot.................	0 07½	0 07¾
Iron Wire (net cash):		
No. 6, ℔ bundle....	2 70	2 80
" 9, "	3 10	3 20
" 12, "	3 40	3 50
" 16, "	4 30	4 40
Powder:		
Blasting, Canada.....	3 50	3 75
FF " ...	4 25	4 50
FFF " ...	4 75	5 00
Blasting, English ...	5 00	5 50
FF loose..	5 50	6 00
FFF " ..	6 00	6 50
Pressed Spikes (4 mos):		
Regular sizes 100....	4 00	4 25
Extra " ..	4 50	5 00
Tin Plates (net cash):		
IC Coke	7 50	8 00
IC Charcoal..........	8 50	8 75
IX "	10 50	10 75
IXX "	12 50	0 00
DC "	7 50	9 00
DX "	9 50	10 00
Hides & Skins, ℔ lb		
Green rough	0 05½	0 06
Green, salt'd & insp'd..	0 00	0 07
Cured	0 07½	0 08½
Calfskins, green......	0 00	0 10
Calfskins, cured......	0 00	0 12
" dry.........	0 18	0 20
Lambskins, ...	0 50	0 00
" pelts......	0 40	0 00
Hops.		
Inferior, ℔ lb.........	0 10	0 15
Medium..............	0 15	0 20
Good	0 20	0 25
Fancy	0 25	0 35
Leather, @ (4 mos.) In lots of less than 50 sides, 10 ℔ cent higher.		
Spanish Sole, 1st qual.. heavy, weights ℔ lb..	0 23	0 23½
Do. 1st qual middle do..	0 23	0 23½
Do. No. 2, all weights..	0 20	0 22
Slaughter heavy	0 28	0 29
Do. light............	0 28	0 29
Harness, best	0 32	0 34
" No. 2	0 30	0 33
Upper heavy..........	0 34	0 36
" light,..........	0 36	0 40

Name of Article,	Wholesale Rates.	
Leather—*Contin'd.*	$ c.	$ c.
Kip Skins, Patna	0 45	0 55
French	0 70	0 90
English	0 65	0 80
Hemlock Calf (30 to 35 lbs.) per doz....	0 75	0 85
Do. light	0 45	0 50
French Calf.	1 05	1 25
Grain & Satn Clt ℔ doz..	0 00	0 00
Splits, large ℔ lb......	0 38	0 40
" small	0 20	0 30
Enamelled Cow ℔ foot..	0 20	0 21
Patent	0 21	0 22
Pebble Grain	0 17	0 18½
Buff	0 17	0 19
Oils.		
Cod	0 55	0 60
Lard, extra..........	0 00	1 25
" No. 1	0 00	1 15
" Woollen........	0 00	1 05
Lubricating, patent...	0 00	0 00
" Mott's economic	0 50	0 00
Linseed, raw.........	0 77½	0 85
" boiled......	0 82½	0 90
Machinery...........	0 00	0 00
Olive, 2nd, ℔ gal......	1 45	1 60
" salad	2 00	2 30
" salad, in bots. qt. ℔ case....	3 60	3 75
Sesame salad, ℔ gal...	1 60	1 75
Seal, pale...........	0 70	0 75
Spirits Turpentine....	0 65	0 70
Varnish	0 00	0 00
Whale.	0 75	0 80
Paints, &c.		
White Lead, genuine in Oil, ℔ 25 lbs.....	0 00	2 50
Do. No. 1 "	0 00	2 25
" 2 "	0 00	2 00
" 3 "	0 00	1 75
White Zinc, genuine..	3 00	3 50
White Lead, dry......	0 06	0 09
Red Lead............	0 07½	0 08
Venetian Red, Eng'h..	0 02½	0 03½
Yellow Ochre, Fren'h..	0 02½	0 03
Whiting	0 90	1 25
Petroleum. (Refined ℔ gal.)		
Water white, car l'd..	0 32	0 32½
" small lots....	0 35	0 36
Straw, by car load.....	0 31	0 32
" small lots....	0 34	0 35
Amber, by car load..	0 00	0 00
" small lots	0 00	0 00
Benzine	0 35	0 45
Produce.		
Grain:		
Wheat, Spring, 60 lb..	1 20	1 26
" Fall 60 "..	1 30	1 32
Barley........ 48 "..	0 95	0 98
Peas......... 60 "..	0 95	0 96
Oats......... 34 "..	0 48	0 49
Rye .... 56 "..	0 00	0 80
Seeds:		
Clover, choice 60 "..	5 50	6 00
" com'n 68 "..	0 00	0 00
Timothy, cho'e 4 "..	2 00	2 50
" inf. to good 48 "..	1 50	2 00
Flax .... 56 "..	1 25	1 60
Flour (per brl.):		
Superior extra.......	6 75	7 00
Extra superfine,......	6 50	6 75
Fancy superfine	0 00	0 00
Superfine No. 1......	5 85	5 90
" No. 2......	0 00	0 00
Oatmeal, (per brl.)....	6 50	6 60
Provisions.		
Butter, dairy tub ℔ lb..	0 18	0 22
" store packed...	0 16	0 18
Cheese, new	0 10½	0 11½
Pork, mess, per brl....	23 00	24 00
" prime mess......	16 00	17 00
" prime	14 00	15 00
Bacon, rough	0 00	0 00
" Cumberl'd cut...	0 12	0 13
" smoked	0 00	0 00
Hams, in salt.........	0 00	0 00
" sug. cur. & canv'd..	0 00	0 00
Shoulders, in salt	0 00	0 00
Lard, in kegs........	0 13½	0 14
Eggs, packed	0 11	0 12
Beef Hams	0 00	0 13
Tallow	0 00	0 00
Hogs dressed, heavy..	0 00	0 00
" medium......	0 00	0 00
" light.......	0 00	0 00
Salt, &c.		
American brls........	1 58	1 60
Liverpool coarse	0 00	0 00
Plaster	1 05	1 10
Water Lime	1 50	0 00

Soap & Candles.		
	$ c.	$ c.
D. Crawford & Co.'s ..		
Imperial.........	0 07½	0 08
" Golden Bar	0 07	0 07½
" Silver Bar.........	0 07	0 07½
Crown	0 05	0 05½
No. 1	0 03½	0 03¾
Candles	0 10	0 10½
Wines, Liquors, &c.		
Ale:		
English, per doz......	2 00	2 65
Guinness Dub Portr..	2 35	2 40
Spirits:		
Pure Jamaica Rum...	1 80	2 25
De Kuyper's H. Gin..	1 50	1 60
Booth's Old Tom.....	1 90	2 00
Gin:		
Green, cases.........	4 00	4 25
Booth's Old Tom, c...	6 00	6 25
Wines:		
Port, common	1 00	1 25
" fine old	2 00	4 00
Sherry, common	1 00	1 50
" medium........	1 70	1 80
"old pale or golden..	2 50	4 00

Brandy:	$ c.	$
Hennessy's, per gal..	2 50	2 75
Martell's " ..	2 50	2 75
J. Robin & Co.'s " ..	2 10	2 75
Otard, Dupuy & Cos..	2 10	2 75
Brandy, cases........	8 50	9 00
Brandy, com. per c...	4 00	4 50
Whiskey:		
Common 36 u. p......	0 65	0 70
Old Rye	0 85	0 87½
Malt.......	0 85	0 87½
Toddy	0 85	0 87½
Scotch, per gal........	1 90	2 10
Irish—Kinnahan's c...	7 00	7 50
" Dunnville's Belf't..	6 00	6 25
Wool.		
Fleece, lb.............	0 25	0 27
Pulled ".............	0 00	0 00
Furs.		
Bear................	3 00	10 00
Beaver..............	1 00	1 25
Coon	0 20	0 40
Fisher................	4 00	6 00
Martin................	1 40	1 60
Mink..................	4 00	4 25
Otter..................	5 75	6 00
Spring Rats...........	0 15	0 17
Fox.	1 20	1 25

INSURANCE COMPANIES.

ENGLISH.—*Quotations on the London Market.*

No. of Shares.	Last Dividend.	Name of Company.	Shares parval £	Amount paid.	Last
20,000		Briton Medical and General Life...	10	—	1¾
50,000	7½	Commer'l Union, Fire, Life and Mar.	50	5	5½ 5¾
24,000	8	City of Glasgow	25	2½	5
5,000	9½	Edinburgh Life	100	15	30½x
400,000	5—½ yr	European Life and Guarantee......	2½	11s6	4s 6d
100,000	10	Etna Fire and Marine............	10	1½	1
20,000	5	Guardian	100	50	52x
24,000	12	Imperial Fire...................	500	50	345
7,500	9½	Imperial Life	100	10	16½
100,000	10	Lancashire Fire and Life..........	20	2	2⅜x
10,000	11	Life Association of Scotland.......	40	7¼	23
35,862	45s. p. sh	London Assurance Corporation ..	25	12½	48
10,000	5	London and Lancashire Life	10	1	1
87,504	40	Liverp'l & London & Globe F. & L.	20	2	7⅞
20,000	5	National Union Life	5	1	1
20,000	12½	Northern Fire and Life	100	5	10⅝
40,000	12 '68, bo 5s.	North British and Mercantile	50	6¼	16 16½
40,000	50	Ocean Marine	25	5	20
2,500	£5 12s.	Provident Life..................	100	10	38
....	£4½ p. s.	Phœnix.........................	....	....	136
200,000	2½—h. yr.	Queen Fire and Life	10	1	15-16
100,000	3s. bo. 4s	Royal Insurance.................	20	3	6¾
20,000	10	Scottish Provincial Fire and Life ..	50	2½	4⅝
10,000	25	Standard Life	50	12	65
4,000	5	Star Life	25	1¼	—
		CANADIAN.			₩ c.
8,000	4	British America Fire and Marine ..	$50	$25	56
....	4	Canada Life	...	....	.....
4000	12	Montreal Assurance	£50	£10	135
10,000	3	Provincial Fire and Marine........	60	11	.....
....	....	Quebec Fire	40	32½	£10¼
....	8	" Marine.....................	100	40	90-91
10,000	5 7 mo's.	Western Assurance..............	40	6	.....

RAILWAYS.	Sha's	Paid	Montr	London.
Atlantic and St. Lawrence....................	£100	All.	....	57 59
Buffalo and Lake Huron	20½	"	....	3¼ 3½
Do. do. Preference	10	"	....	5¼ 6½
Buff., Brantt. & Goderich, 6₩c., 1872-3-4....	100	"	....	....
Champlain and St. Lawrence	....	....	9 10	....
Do. do Pref. 10 ₩ ct....	....	....	62½	....
Grand Trunk	100	"	15 16	15½ 16
Do. Eq.G. M. Bds. 1 ch. 6₩c.............	100	"	....	78 82
Do. First Preference, 5 ₩ c	100	"	....	46 49
Do. Deferred, 3 ₩ ct..	100	"	....	....
Do. Second Pref. Bonds, 5₩c..........	100	"	....	36 39
Do. do Deferred, 3 ₩ ct..........	100	"	...	....
Do Third Pref. Stock, 4 ₩ct...........	100	"	...	25 27
Do. do. Deferred, 3 ₩ ct......	100	"	...	....
Do. Fourth Pref. Stock, 3₩c..........	100	"	....	18 19
Do. do. Deferred, 3 ₩ ct.........	100	"	....	....
Great Western	20½	"	....	13 13½
Do. New	20½	18	16 17	....
Do. 6 ₩ c. Bds, due 1873-76..........	100	All.	....	100 102
5½ ₩c Bds. due 1877-78....	100	"	....	92 94
Marine Railway, Halifax, $250, all......	$250	"	....	....
Northern, of Canada, 6₩c. 1st Pref. Bds...........	100	"	.. .	80 83

EXCHANGE.	Halifax.	Montr'l.	Quebec.	Toronto.
Bank on London, 60 days ...... sight or 75 days date	13½	9 9½	9¼ 9¾	9⅝
Private do.	12 12½	8 8½	8¼ 8½	9
Private, with documents..........	....	8¾ 9¼	....	....
Bank on New York...............	....	30½ 31	30 30½	69¾
Private do.	....	33 31½	31 31½	....
Gold Drafts do.	....	⅛ dis to p.	par ⅛ dis.	par ½ dis.
Silver	....	4¼ 4½	....	4½ 6¾

STOCK AND BOND REPORT.

The dates of our quotations are as follows:—Toronto, Sept. 9; Montreal, Sept. 8; Quebec, Sept. 7; London, Aug. 17.

NAME.	Shares.	Paid up.	Divid'd last 6 Months	Dividend Day.	CLOSING PRICES. Toronto.	Montre'l	Quebec.
BANKS.			₩ ct.				
British North America	$250	All.	3	July and Jan.	102 103	102	102½ 103
Jacques Cartier..........	50	"	4	1 June, 1 Dec.	106 108	106 108½	107 108
Montreal	200	"	5	"	133½ 134	134½	133½ 134½
Nationale....................	50	"	4	1 Nov. 1 May.	106 106½	105½ 108	107 107½
New Brunswick	100	"	....	......	....	...	....
Nova Scotia	200	28	7&b$3½	Mar. and Sept.	....	....	....
Du Peuple.....	50	"	4	1 Mar., 1 Sept.	105 105½	104 106	....
Toronto	100	"	4	1 Jan., 1 July.	114½ 115	115	114 115
Bank of Yarmouth...........	....	....	......	......	....	....	....
Canadian Bank of Com'e......	50	95	......	......	103 104	101½	101½ 102
City Bank Montreal	80	All.	4	1 June, 1 Dec.	102 102½	102	102 102½
Commer'l Bank (St. John)....	100	"	₩ ct.	. ...	....	...	....
Eastern Townships' Bank.....	50	"	4	1 July, 1 Jan..	....	96	96 97
Gore	40	...	3½	1 Jan., 1 July.	....	....	45 46
Halifax Banking Company....	..	....	......	. ....	....	....	....
Mechanics' Bank............	50	70	4	1 Nov., 1 May.	95 96	94 95	94 95
Merchants' Bank of Canada....	100	70	4	1 Jan., 1 July.	105 105½	105 106	105½ 106
Merchants' Bank (Halifax)....	....	....	......	......	....	....	....
Molson's Bank......	50	All.	4	1 Apr., 1 Oct.	110 112	112	110 111
Niagara District Bank...	100	70	3½	1 Jan., 1 July.	....	....	....
Ontario Bank................	40	All.	4	1 June, 1 Dec.	98½ 99	98 98½	98 99
People's Bank (Fred'kton)....	100	"	....	......	....	....	....
People's Bank (Halifax)......	20	"	7 12 m	......	....	....	....
Quebec Bank	100	"	3½	1 June, 1 Dec.	98 98½	97½ 98½	97½ 98½
Royal Canadian Bank	50	50	4	1 Jan., 1 July.	88 88½	87 89	86 87
St. Stephens Bank	100	All	.....	......	....	....	....
Union Bank	100	70	4	1 Jan., 1 July.	101 102	101½ 102½	102½ 103
Union Bank (Halifax)........	100	40	7 12 mo	Feb. and Aug.	....	....	.. .
MISCELLANEOUS.							
British America Land........	250	44	2½	......	....	....	....
British Colonial S. S. Co......	250	32½	2½	......	...	50	...
Canada Company	32½	All.	5	......	....	....	....
Canada Landed Credit Co.....	50	$14	3½	......	62½ 63	....	....
Canada Per. B'ldg Society....	50	All.	5	......	118 118½	....	....
Canada Mining Company.....	4	90		... ..	....	....	....
Do. Inl'd Steam Nav. Co.....	100	All.	20·12 m	......	....	106 109	107 108
Do. Glass Company.........	100	"	12½ "	......	....	95	. ....
Canad'n Loan & Investm't....	25	2½	7	......	....	....	....
Canada Agency	10	½	......	......	....	....	....
Colonial Securities Co........	...	....	......	......	....	....	....
Freehold Building Society....	100	All.	5	......	103 104	....	....
Halifax Steamboat Co........	100	"	5	......	....	....	....
Halifax Gas Company........	....	....	......	. .. .	....	...	....
Hamilton Gas Company......	....	....	.....	. ....	....	....	....
Huron Copper Bay Co........	4	12	20	. ....	....	3 50	....
Lake Huron S. and C........	5	102	......	......	....	....	....
Montreal Mining Co..........	20	$15	......	. ....	....	3 3.50	...
Do. Telegraph Co...	40	All.	5	......	133 134	133 133½	134 134½
Do. Elevating Co...	00	"	15 12 m	......	....	....	....
Do. City Gas Co.........	40	"	4	15 Mar. 15 Sep.	....	Bks. clod	135 136
Do. City Pass. R. Co....	50	"	5	......	....	108	108 109
Nova Scotia Telegraph	20	"	....	. ....	....	....	....
Quebec and L. S.	8	$4	......	.....	. ..	....	25 cts
Quebec Gas Co..............	200	All.	4	1 Mar., 1 Sep.	....	...	116 117
Quebec Street R. R..........	50	25	8	......	....	....	96 97
Richelieu Navigation Co......	100	All.	7 p.a.	1 Jan., 1 July.	....	112 115	112 114
St. Lawrence Tow Boat Co....	100	"	......	3 Feb.	...	...	45 50
Tor'to Consumers' Gas Co.....	50	"	2 3 m.	1 My Au Mar Fe	104½ 105	...	104 105
Trust & Loan Co. of U. C.....	20	5	3	......	....	....	.. .
West'n Canada Bldg Soc'y....	50	All.	5	......	109½ 110	....	....

SECURITIES.	London.	M'ntreal	Quebec.	Toronto.
Canadian Gov't Deb. 6 ₩ ct. due 1872	....	100 100½	100 102	99½ 100½
Do. do. 6 do due Ja. & Jul. 1877-84........	103 105	....	100 101½	....
Do. do. 6 do. Feb. & Aug...	102 103	....	.. .	....
Do. do. 6 do. Mch. & Sep.........	104 106	.. .	...	.. .
Do. do. 5 ₩ ct. cur., 1883	91 93	89	90½ 91	89
Do. do. 5 do. stg., 1885	....	90	91 91½	90 91
Do. do. 7 do. cur.,..................	....	....	100 100½	....
Dominion 6 p. c. 1878 cy....	....	99½ 100	101 101½	100½ 101
Hamilton Corporation.....	....	....	......	....
Montreal Harbor, 8 ₩ ct. d. 1869..................	..	....	......	....
Do. do. 7 do. 1870................	....	....	......	....
Do. do. 6½ do. 1875................	....	100½	......	....
Do. do. 6½ do. 1873................	....	....	......	....
Do. Corporation, 6 ₩ c. 1891	....	92½ 93	92 93	91½
Do. 7 p. c. stock..............................	....	103½ 105	103 105	103 105
Do. Water Works, 6 ₩ c. stg. 1878..........	....	....	......	90 91
Do. do. 6 do. cy. do.	....	92	......	91 92
New Brunswick, 6 ₩ ct., Jan. and July	102 104	....	......	....
Nova Scotia, 6 ₩ ct., 1875......................	101 103	...	......	....
Ottawa City 6 ₩ c. d. 1880	....	90 91	......	...
Quebec Harbour, 6 ₩ c. d. 1883.	....	....	60 70	....
Do. do. 7 do. do....................	....	....	70 80	....
Do. do. 8 do. 1886...................	...	....	85 90	....
Do. City, 7 ₩ c. d. 5 years	....	85 90	90 91	80 90
Do. do. 7 do. 9 do.	....	....	86 87	....
Do. do. 7 do. 2½ do.	....	....	96 96½	....
Do. Water Works, 7 ₩ ct., 4 years	....	....	95 96	....
Do. do. 6 do. 2 do.	....	....	92½ 93½	....
Toronto Corporation	....	90	...	....

MONTREAL ASSURANCE COMPANY.

(MARINE.)

Incorporated, - - - - - - - 1840.

HEAD OFFICE, - - - - - - - GREAT ST. JAMES STREET,

MONTREAL.

WILLIAM MURRAY,

MANAGER.

STATEMENT OF BANK AND OTHER STOCKS, REAL ESTATE AND OTHER ASSETS HELD by the Company, as security to the Assured, in addition to the Subscribed Capital as below:—

402 Shares	BANK OF MONTREAL,	Stock valued at		$108,540
470 "	CITY BANK,	" "		38,728
358 "	GORE BANK,	" "	cost $26,329	16,500
200 "	BANK OF COMMERCE,	" "		10,250
41 "	MERCHANTS' BANK.	" "		4,305
147 "	MONTREAL TELEGRAPH	" "		24,138
62 "	MONTREAL GAS COMP'Y	" "		3,398
49 "	CANADA SHIPPING COMP'Y		paid to date.	16,000
200 "	MONTREAL MINING COMP'Y		cost $3,500	1,000
25 "	MONTREAL & NEW YORK R.R.		cost 6,050	500
REAL ESTATE (Annual Rental, $5,800)				80,000
MORTGAGES				15,218
				$318,577

Accrued Dividends and Rents, Bills Receivable, Good Debts, Balances due by Agents, Cash in Bank and on hand exceed............ 25,000

$343,577

Subscribed Capital liable to call and held wholly by a Responsible Proprietory 720,000

TOTAL.. $1,063,577

NO LOSSES UNSETTLED.

TORONTO BRANCH OFFICE:

82 WELLINGTON STREET EAST,

Inland Hull and Cargo Risks, and Risks to and from the Lower Ports entered at Toronto and various Agencies, at moderate rates,

R. N. GOOCH,
Agent and Local Secretary.

CAPT. A. TAYLOR,
Marine-Inspector.

2t

Financial.

Pellatt & Osler,

OCK AND EXCHANGE BROKERS, Accountants, gents for the Standard Life Assurance Company and York Casualty Insurance Company.

OFFICE—86 *King Street East, four Doors West of Church Street, Toronto.*

IRY PELLATT, EDMUND B. OSLER, *Notary Public.* *Official Assignee.*

BROWN'S BANK,
)(**(W. R. Brown, W. C. Chewett.)**
30 *KING STREET EAST, TORONTO,*

ANSACTS a general Banking Business, Buys and Sells New York and Sterling Exchange, Gold, Silver, Bonds and Uncurrent Money, receives Deposits subject to Cheque at sight, makes Collections and Discounts mercial Paper.

ers *by Mail or Telegraph promptly executed at most favourable current quotations.*

☞ Address letters, "BROWN'S BANK, -y Toronto."

Insurance.

CANADA

Life Assurance Company.

·compliance with the Act respecting Insurance Companies, 31 Vic., chap. 48,

NOTICE IS HEREBY GIVEN,

THAT THE

ANADA LIFE ASSURANCE COMPANY,

Has been licensed by the

HONORABLE THE MINISTER OF FINANCE,

To transact the

Business of Life Assurance.

— A. G. RAMSAY,
— Manager.
ugust 1st, 1868. 1-1m

The Liverpool and London and Globe Insurance Company.

ital and Reserved Funds.......$17,005,000.
DAILY CASH RECEIPTS,....$20,000.

TICE IS HEREBY GIVEN, that this Company having deposited the sum of

150,000 Dollars,

ccordance with the Act, 31st Vic., cap. 48, has received License of the Finance Minister, to transact the business of Life and Fire Insurance in the Dominion of Canada.

G. F. C. SMITH, Chief Agent for the Dominion.

Hartford Fire Insurance Company.
HARTFORD, CONN.

h *Capital and Assets over Two Million Dollars,*

$2,026,220.29.

CHARTERED 1810.

IS old and reliable Company, having an established usiness in Canada of more than thirty years standing, complied with the provisions of the new Insurance and made a special deposit of

$100,000

the Government for the security of policy-holders, and continue to grant policies upon the same favorable s as heretofore.

pecially low rates on first-class dwellings and farm perty for a term of one or more years.

osses as heretofore promptly and equitably adjusted.
oronto, Ont. E. CHAFFEY & Co., AGENTS.

ROBERT WOOD, GENERAL AGENT FOR CANADA.
6m

Insurance.

J. T. & W. Peacock,

FIRE and Life Insurance Agents, Parliamentary and Departmental Agents, Mining Agents, and Exchange Brokers.
Ottawa. Dec. 21st, 1867. 10-1y

The Standard Life Assurance Company,

WITH which is now united the COLONIAL LIFE ASSURANCE COMPANY.

Established 1825.
HEAD OFFICES—EDINBURGH and MONTREAL.
Accumulated Fund, nearly.... $19,000,000.
Income, 1867........... $3,376,953.

·Manager—W. M. RAMSAY. Inspector—RICH'D BULL.
Toronto—HENRY PELLATT; AGENT.
Agencies in every Town throughout the Dominion.
18-1y.

Fire and Marine Assurance.

THE BRITISH AMERICA
ASSURANCE COMPANY.

HEAD OFFICE:
CORNER OF CHURCH AND COURT STREETS,
TORONTO.

BOARD OF DIRECTION:	
Hon. G. W. Allan, M.L.C.,	A. Joseph, Esq.,
George J. Boyd, Esq.,	Peter Peterson, Esq.,
Hon. W. Cayley,	G. P. Ridout, Esq.,
Richard S. Cassels, Esq.,	E. H. Rutherford, Esq.,
Thomas C. Street, Esq.	

Governor:
GEORGE PERCIVAL RIDOUT, Esq.
Deputy Governor:
PETER PATERSON, Esq.

Fire Inspector: Marine Inspector:
E. ROBY O'BRIEN. CAPT. R. COURNEEN.

Insurances granted on all descriptions of property against loss and damage by fire and the perils of inland navigation.

Agencies established in the principal cities, towns, and ports of shipment throughout the Province.

THOS. WM. BIRCHALL,
28-1y Managing Director.

Edinburgh Life Assurance Company.

Founded 1823.

HEAD OFFICE—22 GEORGE STREET, EDINBURGH.

Capital, ... £500,000 Ster'g.
Accumulated and Invested Funds, £1,000,000 "

HEAD OFFICE IN CANADA:
WELLINGTON STREET, TORONTO.

SUB-AGENTS THROUGHOUT THE PROVINCE.

J. HILLYARD CAMERON,
Chairman, Canadian Board.

DAVID HIGGINS,
Secretary, Canadian Board. 3-3m

Queen Fire and Life Insurance Company,
OF LIVERPOOL AND LONDON,

ACCEPTS ALL ORDINARY FIRE RISKS
on the most favorable terms.

LIFE RISKS

Will be taken on terms that will compare favorably with other Companies.

CAPITAL, - - - £2,000,000 Stg.

CHIEF OFFICES—Queen's Buildings, Liverpool, and Gracechurch Street London.
CANADA BRANCH OFFICE—Exchange Buildings, Montreal.
Resident Secretary and General Agent,
A. MACKENZIE FORBES,
13 St. Sacrament St., Merchants' Exchange, Montreal.
WM. ROWLAND, Agent, Toronto. 1-1y

Insurance.

Reliance Mutual Life Assurance Society.
(Established 1840,) OF LONDON, E. C.

Accumulated Funds, over $1,000,000.
Annual Income, $300,00.
THE entire Profits of this long-established Society belong to the Policy-holders.
HEAD OFFICE FOR DOMINION—MONTREAL.
T. W. GRIFFITH, Manager Sec'y.
15-1y WM. HENDERSON, Agent for Toronto.

Etna Insurance Company of Dublin.
The number of Shareholders exceeds Five Hundred.

Capital, $5,000,000—Annual Income nearly $1,000,000.
THIS Company takes Fire and Marine Risks on the most favorable terms.
T. W. GRIFFITH, Manager for Cana da
Chief office for Dominion—Corner St. Francois Xavie and St. Sacrament Sts., Montreal.
15-1y WM. HENDERSON, Agent for Toronto.

Scottish Provincial Assurance Co.
Established 1825.

CAPITAL, ...£1,000,000 STERLING.
INVESTED IN CANADA (1854) ....$500,000.

Canada Head Office, Montreal.

LIFE DEPARTMENT.
CANADA BOARD OF DIRECTORS:
HUGH TAYLOR, Esq., Advocate,
Hon. CHARLES WILSON, M. L. C.
WM. SACHE, Esq., Banker,
JACKSON RAE, Esq., Banker.
WM. FRASER, Esq. M. D., Medical Adviser.

The special advantages to be derived from Insuring in this office are:—Strictly Moderate Rates of Premium; Large Bonus (intermediate bonus guaranteed;) Liberal Surrender Value, under policies relinquished by assured; and Extensive Limits of Residence and Travel. All business disposed of in Canada, without reference to parent office.
A DAVIDSON PARKER,
Resident Secretary.
G. L. MADDISON,
AGENT FOR TORONTO.

Lancashire Insurance Company.
CAPITAL, - - - - - - - - £2,000,000 Sterling.

FIRE RISKS
Taken at reasonable rates of premium, and
ALL LOSSES SETTLED PROMPTLY,
By the undersigned, without reference elsewhere.
S. C. DUNCAN-CLARK & CO.,
General Agents for Ontario,
N. W. Corner of King & Church Streets,
25-1y TORONTO.

Etna Fire & Marine Insurance Company.

INCORPORATED 1819. CHARTER PERPETUAL.

CASH CAPITAL, - - - - $3,000,000

LOSSES PAID IN 50 YEARS, 23,500,000 00.

JULY, 1868.

ASSETS.
(At Market Value.)
Cash in hand and in Bank........................ $344,842 39
Real Estate.................................... 253,307 29
Mortgage Bonds............................... 982,245 00
Bank Stock.................................... 1,272,670 00
United States, State and City Stock, and other
Public Securities............................. 2,040,855 51
Total....................$5,052,880 19

LIABILITIES.
Claims not Due, and Unadjusted $499,803 55
Amount required by Mass. and New York
for Re-Insurance............................. 1,405,267 15
E. CHAFFEY & CO., Agents.
50-6m

THE CANADIAN
IONETARY TIMES
AND
INSURANCE CHRONICLE.
OTED TO FINANCE, COMMERCE, INSURANCE, BANKS, RAILWAYS, NAVIGATION, MINES, INVESTMENT,
PUBLIC COMPANIES, AND JOINT STOCK ENTERPRISE.

| [NO. 5. | TORONTO, THURSDAY, SEPTEMBER 17, 1868. | { SUBSCRIPTION, { $2 A YEAR. |

Mercantile.

J. B. Boustead.
ON and Commission Merchant. Hops bought
dd on Commission. 82 Front St., Toronto.

John Boyd & Co.
SALE Grocers and Commission Merchants,
4 St., Toronto.

Childs & Hamilton.
CTURERS and Wholesale Dealers in Boots
Shoes, No. 7 Wellington Street East, Toronto,
23

L. Coffee & Co.
& and Commission Merchants, No. 2 Manning's
Front St., Toronto, Ont. Advances made on
ale of Produce.

J. & A. Clark,
E Commission Merchants, Wellington Street
Toronto, Ont.

D. Crawford & Co.,
ACTURERS of Soaps, Candles, etc., and dealers
roleum, Lard and Lubricating Oils, Palace St.
nt.

John Fisken & Co.
IL and Commission Merchants, Yonge St.,
to, Ont.

Thos. Griffith & Co.
IRS and Wholesale Dealers in Groceries,
s, &c., Front St., Toronto, Ont.

W. & R. Griffith.
IRS of Teas, Wines, etc. Ontario Chambers,
ureh and Front Sts., Toronto.

Thos. Haworth & Co.
IRS and dealers in Iron, Cutlery and general
ire, King St., Toronto, Ont.

Hurd, Leigh & Co.
i and Enamellers of China and Earthenware,
nge St., Toronto, Ont. [See advt.]

Lyman & McNab.
SALE Hardware Merchants, Toronto, Ontario.

W. D. Matthews & Co.
E Commission Merchants, Old Corn Exchange,
nt St. East, Toronto Ont.

R. C. Hamilton & Co.
E Commission Merchants, 119 Lower Water
alifax, Nova Scotia.

Parson Bros.,
RUM Refiners, and Wholesale dealers in Lamps,
eys, etc. Warerooms 51 Front St. Refinery cor.
Don Sts., Toronto.

C. P. Reid & Co.
IRS and Dealers in Wines, Liquors, Cigars and
obacco, Wellington Street, Toronto. 28.

W. Rowland & Co.,
BROKERS and General Commission Mer-
Advances made on Consignments. Corner
d Fron t Streets, Toronto.

Reford & Dillon.
IRS of Groceries, Wellington Street, Toronto,

Sessions, Turner & Co.,
ACTURERS, Importers and Wholesale Dealers
ots and Shoes, Leather Findings, etc., 8 Wel-
West, Toronto, Ont

Meetings.

LONDON AND PORT STANLEY RAILWAY.

The report of the Directors read at the Annual
Meeting held on the 2nd Sept., is as follows:—
Your Directors, at the close of another financial
year, have the honor to present the following
statement of receipts and disbursements and other
returns in connection with the business of the
road:—
The total receipts from all sources is $41,704.62,
being a falling off from last year's revenue of
$981.72. This amount of deficit is less than
might have been expected from the very dull state
of trade consequent on the failure of the Commercial Bank and the general mistrust and stagnation that followed in its wake.
The revenue account is made up of the following
amounts, viz.:—Passenger traffic, $16,968.93 as
against $17,308.23 last year; a decrease of $339.30.
Freight traffic, $22,410.40, against $23,064.76
last year; a decrease of $633.36. The balance
of receipts, $2334.29, is from mails and sundries.
The total number of passengers carried was 42,-
704, a large proportion of which were excursionists, being a decrease as compared with the former
of 1,122 passengers. Total freight carried; 22,-
868 tons, against 25,542 in 1867; decrease of
1,674 tons.
The working expenses have been unnecessarily
high, as foreshadowed by the last annual report,
in which reference was made to the necessity of
large outlays for reconstruction of bridges, repairs to passenger and flat cars, and also to engines.
The working expenses, including all outlays for
rebuilding bridges, repairing and painting three
first-class passenger cars—a thorough repair,
amounting, in fact, to a rebuilding of the engine
Lawnason—new iron water tank at St. Thomas
and general traffic expenses, amount to $36,463
62, being about 87 per cent. of the gross earnings.
The expenses for the coming year will be proportionately as heavy as the last, as there will be a
considerable outlay to meet the following requirements: Say 200 tons of new iron, the strengthening of trestle bridges at Kettle and Mill Creeks,
and at Union, the renewal of cattle guards at the
level crossings, besides the ordinary wear and tear
on works, rolling stock, and fences.
The works and plant are in good ordinary
working order, as evidenced by the fact, that the
traffic has been worked without any accident or
detention during the year. We might note as
worthy of remark, that since the opening of the
line in October, 1856, all the trains have been
run with regularity with the exception of one,
which was withdrawn on account of the intense
severity of the weather, it being impossible for
the employees to work. The whole of which is
respectfully submitted.
(Signed), MURRAY ANDERSON, President.

GRAND TRUNK RAILWAY.

A special meeting of the bond and stockholders
was held in London, August 26; Mr. T. Baring,
M.P., in the absence of Mr. Watkin, in the chair.
The chairman said that certain queries in rela-

tion to the business of the meeting—namely, the
supplying of the list of the bond and stockholders
to any proprietor asking for the same—had been
sent out to the shareholders, and it was now his
duty to read a statement of the result. The first
question put was, " Shall a list of the proprietors
of stocks or of bonds, or both, be printed every
year ?" To this 416 persons, representing £918,-
050, said " nay," and 233 persons, representing
£965,000, said " yes." The second question was
" Shall a list of proprietors be supplied to any
bond or stockholder on payment of the cost of
copying the same, or of some small sum for covering the expense of printing." The answers were
425 persons representing £1,228,734 of stock, said
" yea,", and 199 persons, representing £423,946,
said " nay." The third question was, " Shall the
company abide by the board's offer of sending out
for any stock or bondholders circulars from the
office without supplying any list ?" To this 219
persons, representing £943,313, said " nay," and
244 persons, representing £475,655, said " yea."
In consequence of these answers, he now had the
honor to propose the following resolution: " That
a list of proprietors be supplied to any bond or
stockholder on payment of the cost of copying
the same."
A good deal of discussion followed in reference
to the expense of obtaining the list. The chairman said the cost would be about £3. Different
speakers made their views known to the meeting
in reference to the particular matter in hand, but
in regard to the entire management which some
critised with wich great severity. Sir R. Jarvis
at the conclusion of a somewhat lengthy speech,
moved an amendment to the effect that the Directors should prepare a list of the proprietors, and
that any shareholder or proprietor who might require a copy of it should be supplied with one on
the payment of a fee of half-a-crown.
In the remarks subsequently made, one of the
shareholders accused Mr. Watkin of assuming to
fill the office of President of the company, to
which Mr. Baring replied that there was always a
" president" of the company, the first being the
Hon. John Ross, of Canada, and no alteration had
ever taken place in that respect.
The amendment was finally put to the meeting
and carried unanimously, and on being put as a
substantive resolution was passed with a rider
appended. The resolution ultimately stood as
follows:—"That a printed list of proprietors be
immediately supplied to any bond or stockholder
on the payment of a sum of 2s. 6d. per copy, and
that a list of shareholders and bondholders, with
their addresses, as far as can be ascertained, be
printed and circulated once a year with the report."
After a vote of thanks to the chairman, Mr
Creak said that as the chairman of the committee,
through whose instrumentality the present meeting was called he wished to say that it was quite
possible that within a very short time the committee might be compelled to appeal to the proprietors, and when they did so he trusted they
would receive their most hearty support in trying
to improve the management of the company.
The proceedings then terminated.

Port Hope has decided to grant a bonus of $30,-
000 for the extension of the Port Hope and Lindsay Railway to Beaverton on Lake Simcoe.

Insurance.

INSURANCE MATTERS IN MONTREAL.

(From a Correspondent.)

MONTREAL, Sept. 15, 1868.

I wrote you last week the details of a very *peculiar* transaction in which the Liverpool, London and Globe Insurance Company prominently figured. I hear the amount of premium received on the $4,000,000 was $50,000. By way of further shewing the keenness of competition here, the country agent of an English Company took a risk on a saw mill at 10 per cent. premium, the office here not liking the risk, reinsured it in a good company for 3 per cent. It has often struck me as strange that we have not a good Marine Insurance office established in Canada. I am sure it would pay, as it is astonishing the large sums remitted to the States to pay for marine risks. Our present Canadian Offices have not the capital to do a tithe of the business, and thus large sums have to be sent out of the country, benefitting neither the community nor the Government, as the American Marine offices pay no taxes, nor have they to make any deposit the same as Fire and Life offices.

FIRE RECORD.—Goderich Sept. 9.—Another very destructive fire occurred here which consumed the tannery, with contents, of Messrs. Seegmiller, together with the dwelling house of J. Seegmiller. Most of the furniture was removed from the dwelling house. There was an insurance of $1100, which is far below the loss.

St. Johns, Sept. 2.—The St. Johns (Q.) *News* of a late date says:—"In the early part of the week, fires had been lighted in the woods adjoining the parish of St. Sebastien, and owing to the prevailing winds, spread rapidly over a vast area until it reached the farms of the Lamoureux range. Houses, barns, outhouses, fences, pickets and immense quantities of wood and grain were consumed. Twenty-five buildings of different kinds were destroyed. Among the sufferers are Messrs. Jules, Joseph and Julien Lamoureux, Bernard, Dupuis, Cyr, Dagenais and Choninard. Several of the victims were left totally destitute by the lamentable occurrence.

Arran, Grey Co., Ont., Aug. 28.—The barn of Mr. Fawcett, of 10th Concession of Arran, was destroyed. The exact loss is not known, but as there was a large quantity of hay in the building at the time, it is doubtless heavy. No insurance.

Shipley, Ont., Aug. 29.—House and barn of Thos. Mulvey, and contents, including proceeds of the harvest ; loss heavy ; no insurance.

Portsmouth, Ont., Sept. 9.—P. Quinn and R. Howard's houses. The origin of the fire is mysterious, the last tenants having left the day previous; the fire also commenced in a part of the house vacant for some time. The building is insured for $1,200, which is said to be above the value. The house destroyed belonged to Mr. Howard and was insured for $500. So certain are the neighbours that this fire was the work of an incendiary, that they have decided to demand a Coroner's investigation into the matter.

Owen Sound, Ont., Aug. 27.—During a heavy storm the lightning struck a large barn belonging to D. Davis, junr., of Sydenham, which, with two large frame sheds, was rapidly consumed with the crop of 145 acres—value $2,500 ; no insurance.

Harriston, Ont., Aug. 29.—The barn, stable and and sheds on the premises of Mr. Webb, occupied by Thomas Nevans, were totally destroyed with about 120 bushels or wheat, and Mr. Nevans' farming implements. Mr. Nevans' loss will be about $600—no insurance. It is not known whether the proprietor had the buildings insured or not. Origin of the fire unknown.

Wareham, Grey Co., Ont., Aug. 28.—Part of the outbuildings, crops and farm implements, of N. Battrick, were destroyed by fire, which origi-

nated from some burning stumps ; and had it not been for the arrival of assistance, the remainder of the crop, outhouses, and the dwelling house and store, etc., would have been consumed. His loss will be about $500, on which there was no insurance.

MARINE RECORD.—Picton, Sept. 10.—A small schooner, named the *Dolphin*, was capsized and sunk in the gale on Monday evening. There were four men on board at the time of the accident, two of whom were drowned.

FIRE ENGINE FOR STRATFORD, ONT.—A public meeting was held at Stratford a few days since, to consider the expediency of purchasing a new fire engine in place of the present one, which is considered inefficient. A large majority were in favor or the purchase if favorable terms could be made.

PEDDLAR vs. THE DAILY NEWS.—The *News*, of Montreal, in a recent article, confesses that it was led into the publication of the article complained of by the plaintiff respecting the Etna Life Insurance Company, of Hartford, by false representations, and makes an apology, which it is supposed will lead to a settlement of the affair.

OCEAN MARINE LOSSES FOR AUGUST.—The table of marine losses upon the ocean for the month of August, gives an aggregate of thirty-two vessels. Of this number three were ships, eight were barks, ten were brigs, and eleven schooners ; of the above three were missing, supposed lost, and two sunk after collision. The total value of the property lost and missing is estimated at $948,000.

The following table gives the losses from the 1st of January up to the present time, as compared with the three preceding seasons :—

	Vessels.	Tons.
Total losses for January	43	$2,479,400
Total losses for February	32	1,648,000
Total losses for March	30	1,478,800
Total losses for April	41	1,041,000
Total losses for May	22	519,000
Total losses for June	22	1,364,000
Total losses for July	6	202,000
Total losses for August	32	948,000
Total for eight months	228	$10,600,000
Same period in 1867	455	15,455,000
Same period in 1866	267	18,664,800
Same period in 1865	243	19,738,000

AN INCENDIARY FIRE MARSHAL.—In a recent number we mentioned that the city of Montreal, desirous to imitate our system of holding inquests upon conflagrations, appointed two fire marshals for the purpose—gentlemen who, being lawyers, had no other qualification for the appointment than that of being expert in matters of evidence. Thus to perform the rougher duties of the office a deputy was required, and it was thought that a proper person was found in a Mr. J. C. Davis, of whom it is now said that he fled from this city to avoid a charge of perjury, while employed here in the excise service. However little truth there may be in the latter allegation, he seems to have terribly overstepped the functions allotted to him in the former. He was of an enterprising character, and determined to supply the deficiencies that led to inactivity by promoting a crime that he was commissioned to suppress, so he became the incendiary as well as the deputy marshal.

It appears that this Mr. Davis has been adding to the conflagrations of the New Dominion by setting fire to the houses of Montreal, and then in virtue of his office entering upon inquiries into the cause of disaster as gravely as if he were a spotless judge. However great the energy with which the enquiry was affectedly pursued, the crime was not adroitly practiced; for the delinquent was detected, and it was found that many of the fires upon which he held a sort of judicial inquest were the work of his own hands, and he is now under arrest to answer for his guilt.

Thus, added to the disqualification of the two legal fire marshals for the discharge of the duties to which they were appointed by an indiscreet

Common Council, a still more unfortunate select was made in that of Davis, who with a deep sh upon his character, retreated from this city in hope of finding refuge amongst a people by wh he was unknown. Why this utter stranger sho have been preferred by the marshals to the m competent persons for the incumbent duties wh Montreal must contain is somewhat incom hensible, but we should hope that the resul which it has conducted will promote a compl reform in the original appointment, so that a marshal will be chosen who will be competen perform the duties without a deputy as his princi —*N. Y. Insurance Journal.*

INSURANCE DEPOSITS.

The *Post Magazine*, in reviewing Supt. Bar last report, and referring to the required dep of $100,000 for the protection of policy-holders new life Companies, says : "It would be a cap improvement of our own system of forming I rance Companies if a deposit of a like sum w enforced. The advantage of it, the Superintend says, has been abundantly justified by experie in the United States ; and he seems dispose recommend an increase of the amount."

THE PHILOSOPHY OF LIFE INSURAN

It is a distinguished characteristic of man l last report, and referring to the state of civilization that he takes some though the future—not living, like the American Ind careless of to-morrow's fire, content with the e and pleasures of the day. One of the necess of American society, as well as that of all ot highly civilized countries, is Life Insurance. man who has lived in such a country has lear the necessity of anticipating the future and viding against its contingencies—the period sickness, the affirmities of age, and the comfo those who depend upon him. Our male pop tion are emphatically a race of producers. fortunes and support of a great majority of families are in the productive brain or hand of paternal head. When that is taken away often does it follow that the widow and chil are suddenly reduced to want—dependent their own exertions for support! The first p office for the insurance of lives is said to originated with Rev. Wm. Anhott, D.D., of J dleton, in Lancashire, England, about 1698. The benefit of widows of clergymen and otl The poverty in which clergymen leave their f lies has become proverbial, and it is not a strange that the subject of Life Insurance sh first have been thought of in connection wit prominent class of unfortunate widows. were pre-eminently dependent upon their bands for support ; but no more so than the lies of every laboring man in this country to The life of every man has a value; not mer moral value, as weighed in the scale of soci fection and family ties, but a value which sured in money or productive capital. It replace the loss of such a resource that Lif surance was first thought of, and many a de ent family, which has been deprived of its has felt no emotion of gratitude toward great and good men who first conceived th of Life Insurance, and who, after much toi scientific research, gave an idea to the wor the form of a fact, at once available to all. inheritance secured by Life Insurance, wh the death of the husband, descends to his and children, confers a benefit not only o widows and orphans, but on society at lar preventing their dependence on the public, the breaking up of the family rel and the destruction of home. If every h and father would thus leave to his wife and l an inheritance, poverty would be confined l rower bounds. and the national prosperity be advanced.

That modern organization, known as the

ongress, which loves to discuss all questing to the present welfare and future of the human race, should not forget at meeting, to take up the subject of Life . How essentially it promotes the happiness of domestic life, how cheaply it secures an e to the poor, and how efficiently it protects against the caprices of fortune and fousness of wealth! How considerately ipport to old age, and the means of advy to youth. How vivifying it proves to undertakings, and how readily it immercial investments and enterprises a hich cannot be shaken by death itself. uty of all who are theoretically interactically concerned in the solution of politico-economical questions, to awake in the minds of the people an appreciate Insurance, and a disposition to profit antages. In all well-regulated communt is regarded as obligatory on a citizen his children, provide for his family, hise buildings against fire. We expect, it come when a man will be considered duty if he neglects to insure his life. y the money is saved, the same way as deposited in the savings bank; and begunth it confers on the family of the insured, it increases the accumulated stive capital of the country. Most of igs would be lost to the family and the for the motive held out by Life Insur-

lld take a broad view of the benificence uranced. It is more noble than public ecause it places those who receive its love the need of public charity. Familiarity foundation of a well-ordered society, elfare of families is the welfare of the efforts of the thoughtful, the unselfiq diligent, who devote their savings to ition, in the confidence and well-founded that their families, after their decease, he fullest benefit of their providence ry, should not go unrewarded; and it is hat such citizens as are not in the enaffluence, but who are able to show have insured their lives for the benefit niffice, shall have a certain percentage om their taxes by the Government, wide and humane proposition, and no grument will give it due consideration mmence to legislate for the benefit of . It is just as sensible to tax asylums ais, as to seek to gain a revenue from in which foresight and affection have set he protection of thousands of helpless

land, for more than a hundred years, ance has been an established system. untry it is still in its infancy, the first having been established in 1825, but e year 1845, comparatively few persons emselves of its advantages, and more ixths of all the policies now outstanden issued within the last five years. juence is, the benefits of Life Insurance y begun to be seen in this country, but e more fully realised when its present commence to pass away, and the vast money now in the treasuries of these flows out in a stream whose volume is ly equal to that of the incoming pre- t is estimated that a million and a half born and unborn, are already provided country by those who have availed of the benefits of Life Assurance. of the oldest companies of the land, obligations have just begun to mature, dispersed, during the past eight years, ty-one millions of dollars, and at the ae the annual outflow is more than five dollars.

id growth of the system of Life Insuris country during the last few years is ly to the civil war, which swallowed up so many valuable lives, making death and the danger of leaving domestic interests unprotected a present reality in every household. While the cost of everything else is advanced, the price of Life Assurance remains the same, and people who insure now, while a depreciated paper currency is abundant, have the prospect of having their security returnable at some day. In actual coin, after specie payments have been resumed. The amount which the Life Insurance Companies of this country have already promised to pay to the insured or their dependents, is nearly nine hundred millions of dollars. Of course the larger part of these obligations is contingent upon the continuance of the payment of an annual premium by the insured; but if the growth of this system receives no check, the pecuniary interests involved will exceed, within the lifetime of the present generation, those depending on the good faith and ability of the General Government to pay the national debt. And yet the growth of Life Insurance in this country, rapid as it is, is not false or unnatural. The conviction daily gains ground that it is the best plan which has yet been devised to provide against the uncertainty of human life; and therefore every enlightened man, in whom are wrapped up the lives and well-being of others, deems it his duty to provide for their protection and happiness.

In order to meet the various views and circumstances of persons desiring insurance, various kinds of policies are issued. One form of these is known as the whole life policy, which is payable after death to the legal representative of the person insured. Sometimes two or more persons get insured together, when the policy is called a joint-life policy, and is payable on the death of the persons named in the policy, in case he survives another person or persons named. Endowment policies are most commonly used to make a provision for children upon attaining a certain age, either with or without a return of the premiums paid, in case of death before the specified age is required. In endowment assurance policies it is agreed to pay the sum named to the insured himself in case he attains a specified age; otherwise to pay it to his heirs, as in the case of the ordinary life policy. Simple-term policies are for one, five or seven years, and are paid to the heirs, in case the holder dies within the term. This short-term policy does not seem to find much favor with those who insure, as they prefer to take out one for life.

In 1863, nineteen-twentieths of all policies were the whole life policies, with premiums payable annually during life. This form of policy provides most cheaply against the contingency of early death, and the annual premiums are smaller, having been distributed over all the probable years of life, but many people dislike the weary prospect of continual liability to pay an annual premium to the very end of life, especially as they reflect upon the possible inability at some future period in life, to meet the payment. The best way to surmount these objections is to pay for the policy wholly in advance by a single premium. This plan ignores the main inducement to insure—the hazard of death during the earlier years of the policy. Thus paying in advance for all the possible years of his life, he pays largely for insurances which he may never need. But the circumstances of many prevent them from paying so large a sum at one time, and it will be conceded that the single premium plan is not the best one for the largest number of people. The modification of this plan, termed Deposit Life Insurance, has been offered to the public, but it has no material advantage over this ordinary single plan, and does not seem to find much favor with the public. A happy compromise between these two plans is that of a limited number of annual payments. The number of payments is usually limited to ten, and if, after two or three payments, the party insured fails to make any further payment, he is then entitled to a paid up policy for as many tenths of the original sum insured as there have been full premiums paid. This plan is popular, and has been eagerly adopted by the public. The objections to this plan are the same in kind, though not in degree, as those which lie against the single premium plan, each of the ten payments being somewhat larger, but as it brings the payments within the productive period of life, it relieves the contract from the indefinite obligation to pay long after the ability may have ceased, and therefore it finds favor with the public.

Premiums on whole-life policies may be limited to any number other than ten, as the one who gets insured shall choose, with or without the non-forfeiture clause. In endowment policies the number of premiums is necessarily limited to the number of years in the term covered by the policy; in other words, as it is plain to be seen, the payments must cease with the maturity of the endowment. The ten or five years plan of payments can be applied to these policies if desired, and with some companies the policies become nonforfeitable as fast as the premiums are paid. The adoption of these features has done much to popularize the system of Life Insurance. The fear of forfeiting the policy if the annual payments are not promptly made, and thus losing the whole, deterred many from insuring their lives; but now, since each payment tells, securing a part of the total amount, the people do not hesitate to take advantage of this admirable institution. The fair and liberal spirit which now prevades most Life Insurance Companies is all that could be desired, and redounds much to the credit and success of the system. Philantrophy can afford to be just, and justice, as well as honesty, is the best policy.

Life Insurance is most a blessing to persons of small pecuniary means, and for them the ordinary annual premium is best adapted. To be sure, in order to secure the full benefit of his payments, it is necessary for the policy-holder to continue them; but if misfortunes overtake him, so that he is unable to make his annual payments, all he can fairly claim is, that he shall receive in insurance an equivalent for all the money he has paid. The plans of non-forfeiture adopted by Insurance Companies are concessions to the justice of this claim; and in some States, as Massachusetts, for example, the subject has become a matter of legislation, and the remedy is carried to the full extent of the evil; that is, it extends to all policies issued, of whatever kind; so that now whatever the form of policy taken out, the law secures to the holder, without the necessity of any action on his part, a fair equivalent for all the money he has paid. This end is accomplished by providing that, in case of a failure to pay his annual premium, his policy, instead of being absolutely forfeited (according to the old plan), shall stand good for a length of time equivalent to the amount of money he has already paid upon it. But when that time (which is fixed by a set of tables) has expired, the insurance ceases, and the money paid is for ever lost.

The business of Life Insurance is of a peculiar nature, and there is great opportunity for fraud or false error, unless some system of public supervision is instituted, which shall ascertain the actual value of the policies issued by every company. In Life Insurance, the profits come first and the expenditure afterwards, which reverses all the laws of commercial enterprise and investments. This will be readily seen, when we state that in the first years of a Life Insurance Company, its treasury overflows with the incoming premiums, while its liabilities are postponed for the lifetime of a generation. Under these circumstances, its condition must be probed by some decisive test. A considerable portion of the annual payments received from policyholders must be sacredly set apart, and allowed to accumulate at compound interest, as a fund to pay the future losses. One of the duties of this public supervision is to ascertain if enough has been so reserved and securely invested. The necessity of this acumulation is apparent to the most casual reflection.

About one-quarter of the policies now issued are on the ten annual payment plan. The effect of this large infusion of limited premium policies is to increase very perceptibly the ratio of the required reserve to the amount insured. It does not increase the hazards of the business, but adds to its resources and strength; but at the same time it enhances the moral hazards, and imposes upon the guardians of these funds the duty of more carefully husbanding their resources to meet the liabilities of the future. There should be a frequent comparison of the required reserve with the actual accumulation.

The term *valuation*, is applied to a policy, either to its value or worth to the Company, or to the insured. For finding the valuation of a policy, it is only necessary to compute the premium reserve, or ascertain the amount required to reinsure all the outstanding risks of the Company. There should always be funds enough on hand to reinsure with another sound Company all its outstanding risks.

Life Insurance proceeds upon the law of mortality and the rate of interest on money. With these two principal assumptions, it is not difficult to ascertain the exact average cost or premium for insuring a life at any given age. To meet the probable expenses of the business, there is added to this premium a margin varying from ten to forty per cent., making the gross or actual premium charged. But it must be assumed that this margin will be used up year by year in expenses, and no profit from this source can be safely anticipated, as present assets. Consequently, the valuation must be based on the net or mathematical premium without the margin. If it can once be fairly believed that there is no mystery surrounding the process technically called valuation, its importance will be more generally understood.

Next to the introduction of policies on the limited premium and non-forfeiture plans, the advance in the number and proportion of endowment assurance policies is worthy of notice. The effect of a large number of term insurance policies combined with endowment, upon the business and stability of companies, is unquestionably salutary. It diminishes the actual hazards so far as they depend on the correctness of the assumption of mortality, the one feature acting as a counterpoise to the other. To the insured this kind of policy changes somewhat the motive and effect of insurance. The whole-life policy provides only for those who survive the person insured while the endowment combined with insurance provides for the dependants of the insured and contingently for the insured himself. It also has something of the attractions of an investment. Endowment assurance is more like an investment than insurance of the whole life, because it provides contingently for a return to the insured himself. If a man were sure of living to the average age of mankind, or living out the full term of an endowment assurance policy, he would deposit his money with the savings bank; but as he is not and cannot be sure of this, he invests with the Insurance Company. In that view (of possibly *not* living out his expectations), the Life Insurance is the best possible investment; for it promises and performs what the savings bank is too slow to accomplish. It reverses the laws which govern investments. To get the benefit of the latter, the depositor must live, or his survivors must wait; but the sooner the holder of a Life Insurance policy dies, the larger the instant return, relatively to the money he has paid.

This is one of the beauties of Life Insurance, that while death shortens the period during which industry may provide for the weak, it does not cut short the provision which the policy secures, but makes the benefit larger as measured by its cost. The wise will ever regard Life Insurance as a security against the uncertainty of an individual life, and there is no safer plan of deposit than a well managed Insurance Company.—*N. S. Northern Monthly.*

Financial.

MONTREAL MONEY MARKET.

(From our own Correspondent.)

MONTREAL, Sept. 15, 1868.

Our Money Market continues the same that it has done for some weeks back, and I have no new features to note. There has been a rather heavier demand at the Banks for accommodation, but this is not owing to any demand for money to remit West, but rather from the shortness of the usual remittances from the country. Good paper continues scarce, and is readily taken up at low rates; in the street the terms are 12 to 16 per cent. for ordinary paper, and 3 to 4 per cent. for really good. Gold has fluctuated very little since my last, the range being about 144. Silver remains steady at a slight decline on my last quotations. Mr. Weir, a money broker in this city, has issued a circular, according to which he agrees to buy up all American silver at 2½ per cent. discount, and export it on a guarantee of a certain sum to be paid him monthly as indemnification for any loss; said money, as I understand it, to be raised by the different towns in the two Provinces. He estimates by this plan he would be able to relieve the market of fully $1,000,000, and that gradually the price would rise to par. I only had a hasty glance over his circular, but will send you one when they are fairly before the public. The stock market has been inactive, the high price of first-class securities having checked operations. Dominion stock has attracted attention, and sold largely at 101.

BANK OF ENGLAND.

The following statement shows the condition of the bank for the week ending Wednesday, August 26, 1868:—

Issue Department.

Notes issued	£34,617,335
Government debt.	£11,015,100
Other securities......................	3,984,900
Gold coin and bullion..................	19,617,335
Silver bullion..........................	
	£34,617,335

Banking Department.

Proprietors' capital................	£14,553,000
Rest	3,331,497
Public deposits (including Exchequer, Commissioners of National Debt, Savings' Banks, and Dividend Accounts)..........................	2,979,410
Other deposits.........................	19,838,830
Seven day and other Bills..............	502,953
	£41,205,680
Government securities (including Dead Weight Annuity)...............	£13,790,131
Other securities..	15,597,078
Notes.................................	10,661,705
Gold and silver coin...................	1,156,766
	£41,205,680

TORONTO STOCK MARKET.

(Reported by Pellatt & Osler, Brokers.)

Bank and Building Society stocks have been freely dealt in this week, and the market closed firm.

Bank Stock.—There are buyers of Montreal at 134 and sellers at 135. Ontario is offered at 99, with buyers at 98½. Considerable sales of Toronto at 116 to 116½. There were sales of Royal Canadian at 88 and 89, and is in demand at the latter rate. Buyers offer 103 for Commerce, sellers at 104. Merchant's sold at 105¼; sellers now demand 106. There are buyers of Molson's at 112; none

in market. City is offered at 102¼. Sellers 108 for Jacques Cartier, with buyers at Union could be placed at 101¾; sellers ask Other Banks nominal.

Debentures.—There were sales of Canada st five per cents. at 90½ and 91, and of Sterling at 100¼ and 101. Currency sixes are offered at There were small sales of Toronto at rates about 7 per cent. interest. County are in de and very scarce.

Sundries.—Building Society stock higher. ada Permanent sold at 119 and 119¼; which are still offered. For Western Canada 111 t is freely bid. Freehold sold at 105¼ and 106 ing with purchasers at the latter rate. Cit sold at 105 and 105½, and in demand. E America Assurance is held at 56, with buy 5. Canada Landed Credit sold at 63 and demand at that rate. Very few Mortgages off Money is easy on good short date paper.

PROVINCIAL NOTES.—The following is a ment of the Provincial Notes in circulation 2nd of September, and of the Specie held a them at Montreal, Toronto and Halifax, a ing to the returns of the Commissioners the Provincial Note Act:

Provincial Notes in Circulation, payable at Montreal....	$2,8!
Payable at Toronto......................	1,2
Payable at Halifax......................	
Specie held at Montreal	4,
" " Toronto.................	4
" " Halifax	
Debentures held by Receiver-General under the Tender Act.............	3,0

STATEMENT of the Revenue and Expendi the Dominion of Canada, for the month 31st August, 1868:—

REVENUE :—Customs................	$891,1
Excise..................	144,1
Post Office.............	52,1
Bill Stamps...........	4,1
Public Works including Railways........	100,
Miscellaneous	185,
Total..............	$1,377,
EXPENDITURE........................	$964,

Railway News.

GREAT WESTERN RAILWAY.—Traffic fo ending 28th August, 1868.

Passengers	$36,206
Freight and live stock......	38,009
Mails and sundries..........	2,212
	$76,428
Corresponding Week of '67·	77,539
Decrease........	$1,111

RAILWAY TRAFFIC.—In the railway t turns for August, the Great Western Rai turns were $260,017 against $270,183 in last year; Grand Trunk, $627,713 $600,799 last year; the Northern Railwa a decrease of $10,000 as compared with la Brockville and Ottawa, $14,115 against and the St. Lawrence and Ottawa, $9,349 $9,518.

DEPOSITS.—The New York Life Insuran pany's deposit consists of $75,000 in U. bonds. The Atlantic Mutual of Albany has made a deposit of $50,000 in U. bonds.

TELEGRAPH EXTENSION.—The Montr graph Company have this week opened Frenchman's Bay and Odessa, which ready for business.

THE CANADIAN MONETARY TIMES AND
INSURANCE CHRONICLE is printed every Thursday
Evening, in time for the English Mail.
Subscription Price, one year, $2, or $3 in
American currency ; Single copies, five cents each.
Casual advertisements will be charged ten cents
per line of solid nonpareil each insertion. All
letters to be addressed, "THE CANADIAN MONE-
TARY TIMES, TORONTO, ONT.:" Registered letters
so addressed are at the risk of the Publishers.
Cheques should be made payable to J. M. TROUT,
Business Manager, who will, in future, issue all
receipts for money.

The Canadian Monetary Times.

THURSDAY, SEPTEMBER 17, 1868.

DUTIES AND RESPONSIBILITIES OF DIRECTORS OF COMPANIES.

The want of discrimination sometimes shewn in selecting directors of companies, and the readiness with which persons accept office, wholly indifferent to the duties and responsibilities thus incurred, is surprising. The gentlemen appointed are too often nominated for their respectability alone, are frequently among the smallest shareholders of the concern, live possibly hundreds of miles away from headquarters, and unwilling, even if capable, of exercising any discriminating control over the management of the common property. The embarrassments or total ruin to which so many companies are brought through the carelessness or criminality of the officers in whose hands the entire management is allowed passively to remain is properly chargeable to the men who are or ought to be the shareholders' trustees, the directors. Although directors are so often culpable, still all the blame does not properly rest on their shoulders, it primarily and chiefly rests on those of the shareholders themselves, who seldom attend general meetings and vote ignorantly for whatever name is proposed for the direction. Can it be wondered at, then, that the supervision of such boards should be little more than nominal, that the directors should practically consider the purposes for which they are appointed that of attracting business by their individual position, and that their duties are limited to attending board meetings when called upon, and discussing there such subjects as the manager or secretary may choose to bring before them.

We desire, as shortly as possible, to describe the responsibility which directors incur. Towards the public, the board of direction represents—is, indeed, the company; all contracts are entered into by their authority, and they can render the company liable on

contracts to enormous amounts. But considering the magnitude of the interests and number of the persons for whom they are trustees, and to prevent reckless dealing with money not their own, the joint stock acts declare them jointly and severally liable for all debts of the company in case they declare a dividend when the company is insolvent, or the payment of which would render the company insolvent, or have the effect of reducing its capital stock, and also that they shall be jointly and severally liable for the amount of any loan made by them of the company's funds to any shareholder.

As regards the shareholders, even without any special agreement, the mere acceptance of office implies an undertaking on the part of directors with them to use their best exertions fairly and honestly to advance the interests of the company, not to acquire any interest adverse to such duty, and not to make any profit from their office.

It has sometimes occurred when actions have been prosecuted against directors for false or misleading statements contained in reports, or other official documents, that they were entirely ignorant of the incorrectness of such statements; sometimes through passive inattention, in other cases through the falsifications of the company's servants this has proved to be the case. But the language of the Judges is, in all cases, that it is the bounden duty of directors to know the real state of the company, and it is also their duty to take care that the books are kept in such a way that this state can be readily and correctly ascertained by others. It is the duty of courts of justice to prevent men from gaining advantages by representations of that which is false or suppression of truth. In many cases a true statement of the affairs of companies, if as honestly published as the law requires, would bring the concern into public disrepute, while there is every probability that if confidence be retained for a few months, all difficulties will be overcome. If directors choose to make false statements for this purpose, they themselves run the risk. They are not at liberty to do evil that good may come, even for a corporation without a soul to be saved.

The directors are also responsible for another reason. Shareholders, however induced to become members of the company, are liable, according to the terms of the corporate agreement, for the debts of the company. If through the false statements of outsiders, they have been induced to make the bad investment, their only resource is, to pay the amount of their liability and then bring an action against the persons who have caused the loss. A company is in no way responsible for damage caused by unauthorised statements. It is a different matter when the fraudulent representations are made by the directors or by the documents issued by or under the sanction of the general body of the shareholders. In such case, the parties becoming shareholders have no valid ground as against creditors for resisting the liability attached to ownership of shares. Parties having taken shares cannot repudiate them as against creditors. But they may successfully resist contribution to the company's debts by shewing that they have been misled by statements made by the authority and issued under the sanction of the company.

INSURANCE COMPANIES' RESERVES.

A good story is told of a prominent lawyer who attended a meeting of the shareholders of a local Insurance Company, at which the propriety of having a reinsurance fund was suggested, and succeeded in defeating a proposition to establish such a fund by asserting, with all the effrontery of ignorance, that the idea of such a thing was wholly without precedent. Of course insurance business was not very well understood here at the time, or the intense absurdity of the assertion would have brought down on the facile advocate an avalanche of ridicule. But it seems that ignorance on the subject still holds sway, and we ask the pardon of the better informed in now venturing to refer to some of the elementary principles which the veriest tyro in insurance should have at his finger-ends. In a prior issue, we gave the substance of an article that appeared in the Chicago *Spectator*, an excellent insurance journal, reviewing the Fire Insurance business of the State of New York. It appeared from the statistics there collected, that the Directors of many companies have borrowed from the funds which legitimately belonged to the reserved surplus, to pay dividends. We are prepared to go a little farther than our contemporary, and adduce instances in which a company has gone on paying dividends without having a reserved surplus at all. The earnings that should have gone to form a reserve were divided amongst the delighted shareholders, and luck being in the ascendant, the whole affair was considered very jolly. Of course a day of reckoning came, when fourteen per cent. dividends were exchanged for five and ten per cent. calls, and stock at a premium wilted into an unsaleable liability. So long as the amount of premiums received exceeded the amount of losses, affairs were considered satisfactory, but a time arrived when losses increased in magnitude, and there being no adequate provision for such an emergency, the result was as we have stated.

The insurance laws of Massachusetts are explicit in prescribing a basis of dividends. One section reads as follows :—

" At each annual meeting, the directors shall cause to be furnished to the stockholders a statement of the condition of the company, and in making dividends, shall not consider any part of the premium moneys divisible until the risks for which the same was paid have absolutely been terminated. But in making up their annual statement, they shall be required to charge the company only such portions of the cash or notes received on policies which are unexpired, as would be requisite to reinsure all outstanding risks."

The first point for consideration is the restraint upon the division of premiums until the risk for which such premiums were paid have been absolutely terminated. In other words, the premiums must be first earned before they can be divided. The next point is, the company must be charged such portion of the premiums on unexpired policies as would be required to reinsure all outstanding risks. That is, the amount requisite to reinsure outstanding risks is to be considered just as much a liability as the unpaid losses. We desire to make these two positions clearly understood, for we are prepared to give instances where, in the management of some of our local Fire Insurance Companies, they have been overlooked. Suppose a company insures a certain number of individuals for against loss or damage by fire ; that in the middle of the year an account is taken of the gross premiums received ; and that the amount is divided by way of dividend among the stockholders in that company. How do matters stand? The half year yet to run may be fruitful in losses, and if the premiums have been paid away, where is the money to come from to meet the company's engagements. It must come out of other premiums or out of the reserve. In either event, it is manifest that the shareholders have received what they were not entitled to. If the reserve is not adequate, a great injustice is done to the policy holders. Why do banks go on accumulating heavy reserves? as a matter of precaution, against a possible time of disaster. With Insurance Companies, a reserve is a strict matter of justice to those whom it undertakes to insure.

The journal to which we have already referred, puts the matter in a clear light. "What the insured pays when he purchases a policy of insurance is recovery from loss, and his policy to be worth anything must carry with it the assured and absolute certainty of indemnity in case of damage." When we consider that "164 principal American Insurance Companies doing a fire and fire-marine business, paid out during the years 1865, 1866 and 1867, twelve and a half millions of dollars more than their current

premium receipts," we can appreciate necessity of a reserve.

But a reserve is technically distinct f a reinsurance fund. Mr. Superinten Barnes in his last report says : "excep cases of companies holding a very large of premium, a reserve is needed also in a tion to an ordinary capital and reinsur fund." A reinsurance fund is a liabi while a reserve is rather a wise provi against uncertainties. In the Annual St ments of New York Joint Stock Fire In ance Companies, an abstract of which Barnes published with his report, we fin the list of liabilities, immediately follo the amount of losses, this item, " Am required to reinsure all outstanding fire at an average of 50 per cent. of unexp premiums." If this requirement is of much importance in the United States, su it is of equal importance here. In fact, true state of a company cannot be ascerta without information as to the amount n sary to reinsure its outstanding risks, an statement is correct that does not inc among the liabilities of a company such item. One might as well accept as a pr balance sheet a statement of the assets v out any reference at all to liabilities.

In Barnes' Report for 1865, we find following :—

" The repeated efforts of the Superir dent for several years to compel an ade fire reserve for reinsurance and continge have been partially effective, but the re at the session of 1865, of the Act of requiring a reserve of the full amo premiums received on unexpired risk resulted disastrously both to the comp and the public, by its tendency to r premiums below the standard of safety also by diverting funds to the payme dividends which in several cases at least needed for the payment of losses. however, quite probable that the only f cal method of teaching these truths w the crucial test of actual experience, has now been severely applied to so companies."

On the subject of a reinsurance on M business, it is remarked :—

" The question of what amount shou charged as a liability to a Marine Con as a reinsurance fund for outstanding ri is very important in stating the condit such a company. In accordance wit recommendation of the Board of U writers, and the opinions of the sounde most experienced marine underwriter reinsurance reserve has been fixed at 1 cent. of the full amount of premiums re on unexpired risks or policies not mari as terminated. All the Marine Com are now charged with this amount, an the Fire Companies engaged in Marine ance, on their marine and inland risks.

As we are now writing more partic for those who do not make insurance m the subject of special attention, we ma make ourselves better understood by an ple, and with that object we give the ment of the American Branch of the British and Mercantile Insurance Com-As it appears in Mr. Barnes' Report:

Stock of the Company, $1,215,666.66

I. ASSETS.

and Bonds owned by the Company:—		
	Par value.	Market value.
30 bonds......	$200,000	$216,750
of cash on hand in the Company's		$216,750 00
off, and cash deposited with Dabney,		
rgan & Co.......... $108,481 15		
the hands of Agents received for		
miums during the year..	334 22	
amount of cash items.............		108 815 47
egate amount of all actual available sets...........................		$325,565 46

II. LIABILITIES.

adjusted, but not due ..	$20,208 33	
unadjusted............	9,750 00	$29,953 33
amount of losses unpaid............		
t required to re-insure all outstanding		
s risks at an average of fifty per cent.		
unexpired premiums (estimated by		
Company at 40 per cent., $88,536.75		73,170 98
t of all other claims against the Com-		
ny, consisting of U. S. taxes on pre-		
ums not due.................		1,276 96
egate amount of liabilities.........		$106,306 27

III. INCOME.

sh premiums received on fire risks ..	$162,475 26
nd dividends received from all	
urces..............	871,42
regate income received during the	
ar in cash................	$163,346 68

IV. EXPENDITURES.

mount paid for fire losses during the	
ar..............	$21,569 74
or commissions on premiums	28,930 70
nt paid for salaries, fees, and all other	
arges of officers, directors, agents,	6,451 39
erks and other employés	
nt paid for national, state and local	3,823 70
xes, stamps, &c........	
nt of all other payments, consisting of	
e following items—rent, exchange,	5,200 89
stage, printing, stationery, &c......	
regate Expenditures during the year	
cash..............	$63,976 42

V. MISCELLANEOUS.

mount of fire risks written during the	
ar..............	$14,405,922 00
st of fire risks in force Dec. 31, 1867,	
ving less than 1 year to run $11,031,142	
g more than one and not	
er three years $11,800	
g more than 3 years to run 60,800	
l amount of risks in force Dec. 31,	
67..............	$11,303,742 00
nt deposited in different states and	
untries for the security of policy-	
lders........	200,000 00
ss in the State of New York during the year:	
nt of fire risks written	$8,726,699 00
fire premiums received	76,384, 33
fire losses incurred	17,079 99
taxes paid to various fire depart-	
ents in the state of New York during	
e year..............	707 27

e above is a simple and intelligible out-of affairs. If we compare it with the ments of some of our local companies as telligible document, the difference be-n them will tell greatly against us.

few weeks ago we gave the Annual State-of the Provincial, and, certainly, a "extraordinary jumble could not be cted, if the sole object were to confuse. Statement of the Western was far more ligible, and much more full in detail.

While congratulating the latter company on its success in business, we considered that the declaration of a dividend was unwise under the circumstances, and we know that some of its most clear-headed shareholders coincided in our opinion. It is a great mistake to suppose that the mere declaration of a dividend is necessary to strengthen public confidence in a company. The fact of increasing the reserve and providing a reinsurance fund is much more likely to command business. It is idle to say that the capital, liable to be called in, answers the purpose of a reserve or reinsurance fund, for no one can tell how much of it is or ever will be available. The difficulty of getting it in through small calls is evidence enough to establish this point. At any rate we have the experience of other countries to guide us in the matter, and to affect a contempt for that experience indicates sheer stupidity.

A HOWLING COMPANY AND A BLOODY PERORATION.

The *Monitor* is greatly mistaken if it supposed that our Insurance Act of last session, by which insurance companies doing business in Canada are required to make a deposit for the protection of Canadian policy holders, is a "Kanuck trick," or that "the law will be repealed as soon as all the Dominion stock is taken that can be forced off through that channel." The Berkshire is making quite too much fuss about its withdrawal.

About thirty American and British Companies have complied with the law without any childish howling, and we doubt not that they find their business profitable. If they did not do so, we take it for granted that they would join the Berkshire in an exodus. The Act may not be perfect; no one says it is; but at the same time it is not such a dreadful thing as some affect to regard it. Those who wait for its repeal will have to possess themselves in patience for a considerable length of time. We are uncertain whether our contemporary is not "poking fun" at the Berkshire. Hark!

"The Berkshire alludes to the laws of Massachusetts under which it is organized, its deposits, the character of its investments, and says, 'These facts should remove any doubt of the safety of the Company or of its ability at all times to pay its claims,' just as if any one had any right to entertain such a doubt ; just as if every one did not know that a policy in the Berkshire was a thousand times as secure, a thousand times as desirable, from every point of view, as any that could be issued by a company doing business in Canada that has not complied with the laws of New York or Massachusetts."

If this is not satire, it certainly is a puff that savors of Brobdignag. Being charitably

---

disposed towards our iron-clad contemporary, we adopt the former view and extend our sincere sympathy to the Berkshire. The peroration of the paragraph we have under consideration is good :

"Our Yankee blood rebels against unnecessary condescension or seeming apology to our cousins across the lake who are trying to cheat us and mean, bye and bye, to laugh at us for falling into their trap."

We hope that the recent hot weather did not provoke this rebellion of "Yankee blood." If it did, Dr. Sangrado's services are required in and about New York.

INSURANCE COMMISSIONERS,

THE opinion seems to be gaining ground in England that State supervision is productive of benefit in insurance business. It has proved so in the United States, and testimony is borne by no partial authority to the many advantages apparently incidental to its adoption. We have at various times touched on the subject, and, though we have not a very great number of Insurance Companies doing business in our country, still we cannot close our eyes to the fact that some check should be placed on the operations of those to whom are entrusted interests so important as those involved in Fire, Life and Marine Insurance. There are those to whom novelty is much the same as crime. But, in addition to a share of the haters of new things, we are blessed with a goodly company of fellow citizens whose likes and dislikes are balanced with the most accurate nicety on patriotic prejudices. We hear with equanimity of "unreliable Yankee companies," of "old-fogy English companies," and of "unsound Canadian companies," for we make allowances for exuberance of imagination and excess of patriotic ardour, and we know that some insurance agents are not over-particular in their expressions when they scent business. The epithets are bandied almost with a recklessness worthy of a better cause, and their adroit use may be considered tricks of the trade.

We have heard objection made to the appointment of Insurance Commissioners, on the ground that the practice is un-English. Of course the objector was one of a class who consider anything that is unknown or not practiced in England as not worth knowing or doing. Perhaps the day is not far distant when they will have in England government officers to discharge duties similar to those performed in some of the United States by Insurance Commissioners or Superintendents. When that day arrives, perhaps we shall venture to step out of the beaten track and accept the appointment as a signal for us to think about following the example.

ENGLISH Newspapers exchanging with this Journal will oblige by directing all papers *via* Canadian steamer.

A correspondent enters fully into the practical question as to the profitable export of Canadian Petroleum. His letter contains interesting facts, which go to show that we might share in the extensive trade done with Europeans by the Americans in this article, had we only the necessary enterprise. We cannot do more than refer to the matter this week, reserving our observations on the subject to a future issue.

THE Equitable Life Insurance Society of New York is expected to make a deposit next week.

Communications.

THE EXPORTATION OF CANADIAN PETROLEUM.

To the Editor of the Monetary Times.

SIR,—Some short time ago a letter appeared in your valuable journal under the head of "Wasted Investments," which referred to the deplorably dull state of the Canadian oil trade; many valuable facts were brought out in that letter, but as the oil business in Canada is, or ought to be, one of the most important branches of industry in the Dominion, I may be excused for bringing forward the subject again.

It has been a matter of surprise to many that Petroleum, which is intrinsically one of the most valuable articles bestowed upon us by Providence, should for nearly the last two years have been almost valueless to the producer in Canada; for when crude oil is sold for 25 cents a barrel, or little more than half a cent a gallon, it is almost equivalent to giving it away, and at this price numbers of barrels have been sold in Enniskillen since 1866. The crude being in this state it is not to be wondered at that refined oil has been, until recently, sold at ridiculously low prices; for instance large quantities of excellent refined oil were sold by the car load at ten cents a gallon (barrels *included*); and notwithstanding the trouble of handling and storing, was sold retail as low as 17 cents a gallon. I well remember when, about eight years ago, refined oil was first introduced here the price was $1.25 per gallon retail, which was readily given, and it was considered then by far the cheapest light to be had. On reflection it will be seen how marvelously cheap refined oil is at 10 cents a gallon, or $4 per barrel; the barrel itself is worth $2, which leaves only $2 for the 40 gallons of oil, or 5 cents per gallon wholesale for what we used to consider cheap at $1.25 per gallon retail, or 25 times the price which it pays the refiner to sell it at now. The prices mentioned so far, are as they were before the recent duty upon refined petroleum was imposed, but that makes no difference as to the matter under consideration, for the duty of 5 cents a gallon recently imposed is merely an excise duty for home consumption, and does not affect the question of export. Nor does the increased price of oil in Canada for the last few weeks make any difference, for that is only the consequence of Judge Higgins having bought up most of the oil and virtually controlling the market for the present. In a few months Mr. Higgins' reign will be over, and prices will again recede as low as they have previously been, unless some effort is made to place the Oil Trade of Canada upon a firm and permanent basis.

This cannot be done unless an export trade is established for our oil; nothing but exportation will really relieve the market, and the reason is obvious. We are now in the somewhat peculiar position of having an article of real and acknowledged intrinsic value, almost a drug upon our hands. At present only the Canadian market is open for the sale of Canadian oil, and probably one or two of the large wells in Enniskillen could, if regularly worked, supply sufficient oil for the whole of Canada. What, then, are the other wells to do? Are dozens of wells to remain idle because one or two can supply the Canadian demand? In most cases the necessities of the owners drive them to work their wells and sell the oil at any price, and hence the reason that the price has been as low as 25 cents, and I believe even 15 cents a barrel. The great complaint of oil men has been that there is too much oil. Can there be too much of a valuable article? The oil men will answer in the affirmative, and tell you that when a large well is struck it is one of the greatest misfortunes for the oil interest generally. Now is not all this contrary to reason? Has there not been something radically wrong in the way of canvassing this matter? We have not far to go for the true answer and the real explanation of these questions. If we look across the border and see what has been done in the United States in this same oil busines, we shall find an example worthy to be followed. In 1865 the oil business of the United States was in nearly as low a state as the Canadian oil trade is now; great quantities of oil being produced, the price went rapidly down, the bubble Companies that had been started on bogus principles collapsed, no export trade of any consequence had been established and general stagnation was the result. Did matters long remain thus in the American oil regions? Did the oil men all agree that too much oil was being produced, and endeavour to make combinations (as our people have done) to keep the price up to a certain figure? No, our neighbours have a different way of getting over a difficulty; they looked the evil full in the face and set to work to apply the remedy. They saw that such an exceedingly valuable product as petroleum was never destined to remain hidden in the ground, for the reason that there was too much of it, but that if there was too great an abundance for home consumption the surplus was given them to export to other countries, that the rest of the civilized world might share in the valuable article so profusely bestowed upon them, and they accordingly went to work in real earnest to find the most suitable markets in which to dispose of their oil. And with most triumphant success have their efforts been crowned; the extent of the import trade of Petroleum from the United States is something marvellous, when we take into consideration the exceedingly short space of time it has taken to establish that trade, and it still appears to be increasing at a wonderfully rapid rate.

To illustrate this, let us look at a few facts as taken from the "New York Shipping and Commercial List;" the Petroleum exported from the United States to foreign ports from January 1st, 1868, to September 8th, 1867, amounts to 67,167,432 gallons, against 41,590,031 gallons for the same time in 1867. The amount exported for the same time in 1865, was only 12,536,485 gallons; so that the export of 1868 is more than fifty per cent. in advance of 1867, and more than five times that of 1865. What other trade has increased in anything like this proportion? The great increase has taken place in the continent of Europe, although a considerable amount has been shipped to Central and South America, the West Indies, and Australia, and some to India and Japan. Havre takes five times as much this year as in 1867; Marseilles more than twice as much; Antwerp six times as much; Bremen, Hamburg, Cronstadt, Konisberg and Stettin, more than three times as much. Alexandria in Egypt takes more than three times the amount of last year; many ports in Spain and Portugal, and Ge-

noa and Leghorn, more than five times; Naples and Palermo, nearly a million gallons this year against 62,000 last year; Trieste, 900,000 against 37,600; Constantinople 308,000 against 24,800 last year, while the trade with Brazil and Mexico has increased more than double, and with Chili and Peru more than threefold; and this year considerable shipments have been made to various ports for the first time.

What a contrast is this to the Canadian Trade; there is no complaining in the States of superabundance of oil; no grumbling at Providence for giving them too much of a good thing Canadian oil dealers can surely take a lesson from this. What is to prevent refined oil being exported in the same way that it is from the States? The Canadian Oil Region has every advantage in this respect. Petrolia, the great producing region capable probably of producing more oil than any other region of its size in the world, is situate upon the Great Western Railway, and is within about 20 miles by Railway from Sarnia, from whence if desired, the oil can be shipped to any part of the world, or it could be sent by rail to Hamilton and shipped from thence. As we have previously stated, refined oil has been sold as $4 per barrel wholesale, and it may be concluded that the refiner made a profit of not less than 50 cents per barrel, this then shows that the refiner, if he had wells his own, could always produce refined oil at a cost of not more than $3.50 per barrel, including barrel; for if he had good wells he could produce the crude oil as cheaply as it has ever been sold, for 25 cents per barrel. The following is a computation made by a practical refiner from actual experience of the cost of shipping oil to Liverpool. Cost of barrel of refined oil at Petrolia, inclusive of barrel (provided refiner has his own wells)................................$3

Freight per G. W. R. to Hamilton.	0
Freight by vessel from Hamilton to Quebec	0
Expenses of coopering barrels, &c., at Quebec	0
Ocean freight from Quebec to Liverpool....	1
Insurance, 20 cents ; Expenses at Liverpool, 30 cents	0
Commission	0
	$7

Thus making a total cost of $7.00 per barrel when delivered in Liverpool ready for sale at present price at which refined petroleum is quoted in Liverpool is 1s 6d sterling per imperial gallon one of our barrels of refined oil contains 33 imperial gallons, and the market value of the barrel would therefore be £2 9s 6d stg., or a little better than $12 ; from this deduct the cost of the barrel of oil laid down in Liverpool, $7.00, and a profit of $5.00 per barrel remains, which sum shows a larger margin of profit than the exportation of any other Canadian article, and far larger profit than any ordinary business will yield. A refinery capable of turning out 100 barrels refined oil daily, would make according to the above calculation, a clear profit of $500 per day by exporting the oil, which would probably net several hundred per cent. per annum upon the capital invested in wells, refinery, and every outlay. Upon a large scale it is believed that the cost of barrels and freights could be considerably reduced; a large establishment making its barrels would save at least 25 cents upon each barrel, on each barrel. In the above estimate the oil is transshipped at Hamilton and Quebec ; but there is no reason, if the exporter used vessels of his own, why the oil should not be shipped direct from Sarnia to Liverpool, and have only 20 miles of land carriage altogether. Should we be told that the present price of refined oil in Liverpool, (1s 6d per gallon), is higher than price at which it is likely to continue ; but posing it to be so, a very handsome, profit would be made if the price were two pence per gallon less than it is now. If our people were to commence the exportation of refined oil and find out from actual experience how profitable

: is every reason to suppose that the
d increase as rapidly as in the United
n the American oil districts, good oil
lands are more valuable and bring
ces to-day for actual development than
s of the greatest oil excitement, and I
d of prices as high as $8,000 an acre
m lately paid for oil land in some parts
vania. A large Canadian export trade
e a most wonderful effect upon the value
our oil districts; it would make them
e for their actual intrinsic value than
st speculator would formerly have asked
vhen everything was prosperous in Oil-
e price of crude oil at the wells in Penn-
s from $5.00 to $6.00 per barrel, Amer-
ney; this is equal to from $3.50 to $4.20
in gold, and let the price in the Canadian
only get up to that figure and stay there
tly, as it would do. If a large export
established, and the amount of business
l be done would be perfectly marvel-
e present price of refined oil in New
t cents, American currency, per gallon,
of barrels, which is equivalent to $8.88
r barrel, and at this price immense quan-
ought for exportation.
as formerly much prejudice against Can-
n account of its smell. This prejudice
ly from badly refined oil being shipped
ada, but principally in consequence of
icans shipping quantities of inferior
oil, which they passed off as Canadian,
Canadian oil for a time obtained a very
. The truth is, however, that the Can-
roleum is capable of being quite as thor-
eodorized, as American, and has been
possess greater illuminating power than
Oil. After due investigation, I mainly and without fear of contradiction, that
oil can be rendered completely odorless,
samples of refined American and Cana-
are placed side by side, they are so nearly
t it is impossible to make any distinction
them.
es of petroleum for illuminating purposes
been referred to, and space does not per-
w to enter upon the question of petroleum
but it is the opinion of many scientific
for steam vessels, liquid fuel is destined
fuel of the future.
Yours, &c.,   PETROLEUM.
o, Sept. 14, 1868.

MADOC GOLD DISTRICT.

(From our own Correspondent).

BELLEVILLE, Sept. 14, 1868.
ipression which has so seriously impeded
ncement of the mining interests of this
s beginning to give way before the influ-
ounder and better conducted enterprise.
a of charlatanism and deception is over
resent, and the development of the mine-
s which really exist is being attempted
e direction of science and common sense.
sterswivel tribe, who persuaded every man
iad a rich gold or silver mine in his well
and who pretended to extract buttons of
d globules of gold from the stones by the
, have been routed out of the district;
practical men, who reduced every lead of
ous limestone to the California or Nevada
, and misled by similarity of appearance,
ancied, uniformly mistook titanic, specu-
rsenical iron, marcasite, molybdenite, and
mbago, for pres of silver, are beginning to
their mistake, and to look for those lodes
omise to be permanently remunerative,
as or deposits of true vitreous quartz, con-
old in visible particles, and of sufficient
warrant the erection of the expensive
ry requisite for its extraction. Under this
olesome regime, several promising discov-
e already been made; some of which I have

indicated in former letters, but which I shall now
recapitulate.

Lot 16, in the eleventh concession of the township of Marmora. This is known as the Feigel
mine. The material is a vitreous quartz, crystal-
ized on the surface, and enclosing micaceous per-
oxide of iron within the crystals and in the inter-
stices or seams of the massive part. This lode
has assayed from $73 to $154 per ton.

On an adjacent lot is the quartz vein discovered
some months ago by Mr. D. N. Powell. This
vein has also turned out some very rich specimens;
but I do not know its extent, or how much it will
assay.

Numbers 6, 7 and 8, in the ninth concession of
the same township, have also yielded some good
shows of gold in vitreous quartz, which appears
to be as rich as the Feigel mine.

Numbers 6, 7 and 8, in the eighth concession,
also contain veins from which gold-bearing quartz
has been taken; and I saw but last week, in the
Hon. R. Read's office, a slab of quartz over a foot
square by three inches thick, on both sides of
which gold was plainly visible in several places;
this was from No. 10, in the eighth concession.

On lot 6, in the third concession of Elzevir,
Messrs. Coe & McPherson have found a vein of
quartz from which they have got out several rich
specimens. On lot 9, in the same concession,
known as the Langley lot, a vein of auriferous
quartz also exists, a specimen of which is now
before me. This quartz appears very impure, presenting a dull, greasy-looking fracture, and being
intersected with blackish stripes. It is encased
above and below with dark mica schist, encrusted
with iron oxide, and shows gold in several places.
A striking peculiarity of this quartz is, that it
possesses a rhomboidal fracture, almost amounting
to a distinct cleavage.

Another very rich specimen was brought in for
assay last week from the vicinity of Bannockburn,
in the township of Madoc; but as I expect to visit
the locality in which it occurs to-morrow, I shall
reserve any further details until my next.

Existing mines and mills are much in the same
position as at the date of my last letter. The
Seven mill, in the eleventh concession of Marmora,
the boiler of which exploded soon after it commenced running, has been repaired, and has been
working for three or four days. It is said to work
in a very satisfactory manner.

The Anglo-Saxon mill has been running about
a month, with a few intermissions; but they have
not cleaned up yet, and will not do so until 500
tons have been put through.

The Merchants' Union Company are making
slow progress in setting up their machinery. It
will be recollected that this Company bought
Daniels & Co.'s mill, to which I believe they intend to make some additions.

The Hepburn pan, for the Barry mine, in Elzevir, are being got up at Messrs. G. & I. Brown's
factory, but it will be some weeks before they will
be in working order.

The Richardson Company are doing nothing in
the way of working either mine or mill. I hear
that they have found another vein of rock, which
yields $10 per ton. The sale is to take place on
Tuesday, (to-morrow), after which operations will
probably be resumed.

The Bay State mine and mill are still shut up.
I have heard nothing of the doings of the Victoria, the Toronto and Whitby, or the Madoc and
Toronto Companies; but as I shall be in the vicinity of their mines to-morrow, I shall be likely
to get some information respecting them.

QUEBEC AND GOSFORD RAILWAY.—At a recent
meeting of the Council of the Quebec Board of
Trade, the following resolution was passed unanimously:—"That in the opinion of this Council a
Wooden Railway from Quebec to Gosford would
be an enterprise likely to be of great benefit to the
city of Quebec, in providing cheap firewood, as
well as employment for a large number of laboring men and good lands for settlement."

Commercial.

Montreal Correspondence.

(From our own Correspondent.)

Montreal, 15th Sept., 1868.
The weather during the week has been very variable. For the present, this part of the country
has had rain enough, and warmth is wanted to
bring forward the aftergrass. Fodder is likely to
be exceedingly scarce in the districts around Montreal, the oat, pea, and barley straw being very
short, and in many parts not worth cutting, consequently farmers are extremely anxious to sell
stock, and the Americans have agents buying up
in all directions. One drover told me that he had
already purchased 620 horned cattle, paying on an
average $10 per head, a most losing price for the
farmer, yet better than attempting to hold over,
as we well know the expense of wintering cattle in
Lower Canada when fodder has to be bought.

OUR PRODUCE MARKET continues quiet, prices
not yet having reached the bottom. There is no
doubt that our market has been damaged by the
unnaturally high prices which ruled at an earlier
period of the season, and that drove a large proportion of our trade elsewhere; but we trust that
when prices recede to their natural level to get it
back again. There would be a good export demand for flour and wheat, were prices here suffi-
ently low to justify our merchants in operating.
From present indications they will soon reach
that limit, as speculators in the great grain centres in the west, can hardly keep up present rates
in the face of the large supplies that will soon be
poured in upon them; and as English gold will
be needed to move the grain, the English markets
will necessarily determine prices.

	1867.	1868.	Incr's.
	brls.	brls.	brls.
Receipts of flour 1st January to 9th Sept......	412,777	430,459	17,682
Shipments of flour 1st Jan. to 9th Sept......	305,837	289,735	7,291

For the coarse grains there seems a speculative
movement in the country for barley, and long
prices have been paid, but I scarcely think that
farmers can calculate on the present extreme rates
being maintained. The market for peas is in an
interesting position, as little doubt can be entertained of the shortness of the crop, some rating
it at only one-half, so that farmers are looking for
exceptional prices, but whether they will obtain
them or not is at present a question, though there
cannot be any doubt but that rates will rule high.

IN GROCERIES, the chief activity is confined to
teas and molasses; considerable transactions having taken place in both articles, there have also
been fair sales of U. C. Highwines at $1.45. Other
staples are quiet. Our first arrivals of the fall
fleet are now daily expected, and that will give an
impetus to our market.

HARDWARE keeps dull; but several buyers being down to attend the Exhibition, more activity
may be expected towards the close of the week.

DRY GOODS still continue in brisk demand,
especially cottons and prints, and a much larger
quantity has been moved off than anticipated at
the commencement of the season. Woollens continue dull owing to the heavy stocks in the country.

There have been a large number of strangers in
town to be present at the Exhibition and Rifle
Match; but so far they have been too much taken
up with sight-seeing to pay much attention to
business; but towards the end of the week I expect they will devote their time to the more practical part of their visit.

Toronto Market.

As the fall advances trade grows steadily better,
and in all the different departments an increased
business is spoken of during the past week.
Remittances from country merchants have been
better, showing that the proceeds of the harvest is
passing into their hands.

DRY GOODS.—An active trade which extended to all classes of goods is reported, there being no striking feature calling for particular notice. Prices have a firm tendency, but we are not aware of any quotable change.

GROCERIES.—As will be observed by reports elsewhere, sugar is quoted higher in the leading markets, the advance in New York being three-eighths of a cent per pound. This has given rise to a firm feeling here, and holders are stiff at quotations.

BOOTS AND SHOES.—Orders from country dealers continue to pour in faster than they can be filled. We are now in the height of the season which, however, is expected to continue brisk for a month or six weeks yet. Goods are held with rather more firmness, but manufacturers' prices remain the same.

LEATHER—More active at quotations. The demand runs chiefly on Spanish sole and French calf.

PETROLEUM.—The combination continue to hold entire control of the market. The export question is being revived, and seems now certain to take a tangible shape.. A Company, having its headquarters on the other side of the Atlantic in London or Glasgow, and having a representative at Petrolia, is preparing to export a cargo, and there is little doubt of the success of the venture. Others are also preparing to take a similar step. Meantime the combination intend retaining control of the market, preparations being made for an extension of the present pact beyond the period named in the existing arrangement. There is a small local trade doing at our quotations.

PRODUCE.—*Wheat*—Receipts 1,650 bush. The market is dull and nominal. *Barley*—Receipts by rail 12,518 bush.; by teams 20,000 bush.—total, 32,518 bush., against 20,000 bush the previous week. We expect good receipts for some time to come now that the fall seeding is over. The market opened at 93c to 95c, and steadily advanced to $1 to $1.02 at the close, holders asking $1.03 to $1.04; sales of car lots at $101½ to $102, the tendency is upwards; there is a general feeling that barley will not go lower. *Peas.*—Receipts small; sale, 6,500 bushs. at 97c. f.o.b. at Hamilton; street prices here 95 to 96c. *Seeds.*—Timothy firm and in good demand at $2.50 to $2.75.

FLOUR.—Receipts 1,650 brls.; market dull and lower; sales of superfine occurred at $5.85 to $5.90, the market closing with free sellers at $5.75, and no buyers above $5.65. A lot of extra was placed at $5.85; 100 brls. fancy found a buyer at $6.25. *Meal*—Nominal.

PROVISIONS.—*Butter*—Dull; selected lots offering at 21c.; no sales. *Cheese*—Scarce and in demand, chiefly for the local trade, at 10c. to 11c.; makers want 11c. to 11½c. *Eggs*—Quiet at 11c. to 12c. *Pork*, nominal. *Dressed Hogs*—A few selling at $7 to $8 per cwt.

LIVE STOCK.—*Cattle*, a little lower, at $4 to $6, according to quality. *Sheep* $3 to $4 each. *Lambs* selling at $1.50 to $2.50 each. *Calves* $5 to $6 a head.

FREIGHTS.—A steady business is dolng in lumber to Oswego at $1.50 to $1.75 greenbacks. A few lots of flour have gone to Montreal by steamer at 20c. Barley to Oswego pays 3½c. per bushel American currency.

MONEY.—Sterling 60 day bills, 9¼. Gold drafts on New York, par to ¼ premium. Silver bought and sold by the brokers at 4½ to 5½ discount.

Drawbacks on Sugar.

Our English exchanges inform us that a conference of the powers who are parties to what is known, as the Drawback Convention, (entered into for the purpose of regulating the sugar trade), was held at the Hague recently. The alterations made in the terms of the Convention are said to be unimportant, and simply consist in a somewhat greater approximation to a fair treatment of the English refiners. The official account will shortly be published.

The Fur Trade.

The London sales took place in the beginning of the month. The bidding was spirited, and in no case was there a decline in price. Mink, Musquash and Fisher advanced slightly. Beaver, Lynx, and Marten advanced 15 to 20 per cent. on previous sales. Inferior Beaver advanced 40 per cent., and Otter 20 per cent. Red Fox brought 15 per cent. more than at the March sales. The advances in the cases of Marten, Mink, and Beaver were discontinued here and will not affect the market. Before advices were received Beaver changed hands at $2 per lb. The impression is general that these high prices will not be sustained through the Fall and Winter.—*Montreal Herald.*

New York Grocery Market.

SUGARS.—Sept. 11.—Imports for the week were light. The market steadily improved; increasing both in firmness and activity closing at an advance of 3-8 on the opening prices of the week, with more firmness on the part of holders. The business has been confined to refining grades.

TEAS.—The imports include two cargoes of Japans and Greens, making a total of 988,549 lbs. There is an improved feeling in the market for all kinds, and a more active enquiry for Greens and Japans, with considerable sales at full prices.

TOBACCO.—The market has been somewhat irregular; Kentucky leaf was more active at a shade lower prices. Crop prospects are excellent, and holders are more disposed to realize.

Halifax Market.

SEPT. 8.—BREADSTUFFS.—Flour in fair demand and prices tending downward. Canada No. 1 $7.80 to $8.10; extra $8.50 to $8.75; extra State $7.75 to 7.90; Baltimore super. $7 to 7.25; extra $8 to 8.25; rye without change and dull at $6.50 to 6.60. Cornmeal in fair enquiry at $4.60 to 4.70 for kiln dried, fresh ground at $4.40 to 4.50. Oatmeal dull at $7.85. Imports from Jan. 1st to Sept. 8th, 1867 and 1868:

	Brls. Flour.	Brls. Cornmeal.
1868	123,389	39,381
1867	112,549	29,133

WEST INDIA PRODUCE.—Sugars dull, and quotations may be considered nominal. Porto Rico 6¼ to 6¾c.; Cuba 5¾ to 6c.; Barbadoes 6 to 6¼c. Molasses firm at 29½ to 30c. for Cienfuegos in bond, Rum—Demerara 52 to 53c.; St. Jago 43c.

Stock in Warehouse 31st of August, 1867 and 1868:

1868. Malasses, 2,843 puns., 243 tres., 209 bbls.; sugar, 2,483 hhds., 219 tres., 1,083 bbls., 343 boxes; rum, 606 puns., 1 hhd. 1867. molasses, 4,582 puns., 541 tres., 328 bbls.; sugar, 2,302 hhds., 62 tres., 987 bbls.; rum, 1,003 puns., 15 hhds., 21 bbls.

FINANCIAL.—Bank drawing rate on London 60 day sight bills 13 per cent. prem.; private 12 to 12½ per cent. prem. New York gold drafts at sight, 4 per cent. prem. Currency drafts 27½ per cent. discount. Montreal sight drafts 4 per cent. prem. Newfoundland sight drafts 5 per cent. prem.—*R. C. Hamilton & Co.'s Circular.*

Reciprocity Treaty.

The Quebec Board of Trade have decided to petition His Excellency in Council respecting the proposed treaty. They urge:—That during the past seventeen years, vessels built in the United States have been admitted to registry in all ports of the British Empire upon the same terms and conditions as vessels built in these Colonies, and they have also been admitted to the coasting trade of Great Britain on equally favorable terms. That the principal industry of the city of Quebec is that of shipbuilding, which is now in a very depressed state, and the artizans and laborers connected therewith, almost totally deprived of employment, for want of new markets for shippers. Your Petitioners therefore humbly pray that no Treaty of Reciprocity be concluded without a provision giving the vessels built or owned in the Dominion of Canada the right of registration in the United States, as is now enjoyed by the vessels of that nation in all the ports of the British Empire.

NION TELEGRAPH COMPANY.

STOCK - - - - $500,000.

10,000 *Shares at $50 Each.*

PRESIDENT,
HON. WILLIAM CAYLEY.

TREASURER,
HON. J. McMURRICH.

SECRETARY,
H. B. REEVE.

SOLICITORS,
SSRS. CAMERON & McMICHAEL.

GENERAL SUPERINTENDENT,
MARTIN RYAN.

DIRECTORS.

HON. J. McMURRICH,
Bryce, McMurrich & Co., Toronto.

A. R. McMASTER, Esq.,
R. McMaster & Brother, Toronto.

HON. M. C. CAMERON,
Provincial Secretary, Toronto.

JAMES MICHIE, Esq.,
hie & Co., and George Michie & Co., Toronto.

HON. WILLIAM CAYLEY,
Toronto.

A. M. SMITH, Esq.,
A. M. Smith & Co., Toronto.

L. MOFFATT, Esq.,
Moffatt, Murray & Co., Toronto.

H. B. REEVE, Esq.,
Toronto.

PROSPECTUS.

MINION TELEGRAPH COMPANY has been zed under the act respecting Telegraph Com-ter 67, of the consolidated Statutes of Canada. to cover the Dominion of Canada with a com-rk of Telegraph lines.

The Capital Stock

divided into 10,000 shares of $50 each, 5 per aid at the time of subscribing, the balance to instalments, not exceeding 10 per cent per t instalments to be called in by the Directors as rogress. The liability of a subscriber is limited nt of his subscription.

Business Affairs of the Company.

the management of a Board of Directors, an-ed by the Shareholders, in conformity with the By-Laws of the Company.

tors are of opinion that it would be to the he Stockholders generally to obtain subscrip-ll quarters of Canada, and with this view they divide the Stock amongst the different towns roughout the Dominion, in allotments suited lation and business occupations of the different d the interest which they may be supposed to ı an enterprise.

ontracts of Connections.

t, granting permanent connection and extraor-ntages, has already been executed between this nd the Atlantic and Pacific Company, of New , at the very commencement, as the Lines of this re constructed from the Suspension Bridge, at point of connection) to any point in the Do-the chief cities and places in the States, touch-Lines of the Atlantic and Pacific Telegraph re brought in immediate connection therewith.

nent connection has also been secured with the ern Telegraph Company, of Chicago, whereby ny will be brought into close connection with e Ports and other places through the North-tes, and through to California.

4-3mos

TORONTO PRICES CURRENT.—September 10, 1868.

Name of Article.	Wholesale Rates.	
	$ c.	$ c.
Boots and Shoes.		
Mens' Thick Boots	2 20	2 50
" Kip	2 45	3 20
" Calf	3 00	3 75
" Congress Gaiters	2 00	2 40
" Kip Cobourgs	1 00	1 50
Boys' Thick Boots	1 65	1 90
Youths' "	1 45	1 55
Women's Batts	95	1 20
" Congress Gaiters	1 15	1 50
Misses' Batts	0 75	1 00
" Congress Gaiters	1 00	1 30
Girls' Batts	0 65	0 90
" Congress Gaiters	0 80	1 10
Children's C. T. Cacks	0 50	0 65
" Gaiters	0 65	0 90
Drugs.		
Aloes Cape	0 12½	0 16
Alum	0 02½	0 03
Borax	0 00	0 00
Camphor, refined	0 65	0 70
Castor Oil	0 18	0 28
Caustic Soda	0 04½	0 05
Cochineal	0 90	1 00
Cream Tartar	0 00	0 00
Epsom Salts	0 03	0 04
Extract Logwood	0 09	0 11
Gum Arabic, sorts	0 30	0 35
Indigo, Madras	0 75	1 00
Licorice	0 14	0 45
Madder	0 13	0 16
Nutgalls	0 00	0 00
Opium	6 70	7 00
Oxalic Acid	0 28	0 35
Potash, Bi-tart	0 25	0 28
" Bichromate	0 15	0 20
Potass Iodide	3 80	4 50
Senna	0 12½	0 60
Soda Ash	0 03	0 04
Soda Bicarb	4 50	5 50
Tartaric Acid	0 37½	0 45
Verdigris	0 35	0 40
Vitriol, Blue	0 09	0 10
Groceries.		
Coffees:		
Java, ₩ lb.	0 22@	0 24
Laguayra,	0 17	0 18
Rio	0 15	0 17
Fish:		
Herrings, Lab. split	0 00	0 00
" round	0 00	0 00
" scaled	0 00	0 00
Mackerel, small kitts	1 00	0 00
Loch. Her. wh'e firks	2 50	2 75
" half "	1 25	1 50
White Fish & Trout	None.	
Salmon, saltwater	15 00	16 00
Dry Cod, ₩112 lbs.	4 75	5 00
Fruit:		
Raisins, Layers	2 20	2 25
" M. R.	2 10	2 20
" Valentias new	0 08½	0 09
Currants, new	0 05	0 06
" old	0 03½	0 04½
Figs	0 12½	0 13
Molasses:		
Clayed, ₩ gal.	0 00	0 35
Syrups, Standard	0 45	0 46
" Golden	0 50	0 51
Rice:		
Arracan	4 60	4 75
Spices:		
Cassia, whole, ₩ lb.	0 37½	0 40
Cloves	0 11	0 12
Nutmegs	0 50	0 60
Ginger, ground	0 15	0 25
" Jamaica, root	0 22	0 25
Pepper, black	0 09	0 10
Pimento	0 08	0 09
Sugars:		
Port Rico, ₩ lb.	0 08½	0 08¾
Cuba "	0 08½	0 08⅝
Barbadoes (bright)	0 08⅝	0 08⅝
Dry Crushed, at 60 d.	0 11	0 00
Canada Sugar Refine'y, yellow No. 2, 60 ds.	0 08½	0 08¼
Yellow, No. 2½	0 08⅝	0 08¾
" No. 3	0 00	0 00
Crushed X	0 10	0 10½
" A	0 11½	0 11¾
Ground	0 11¾	0 12
Extra Ground	0 12½	0 13
Teas:		
Japan com'n to good	0 40	0 55
" Fine to choicest	0 55	0 65
Colored, com. to fine	0 60	0 75
Congou & Souch'ng	0 42	0 75
Oolong, good to fine	0 50	0 65
Y. Hyson, com to gd.	0 45	0 55
Medium to choice	0 65	0 80
Extra choice	0 85	0 95
Gunpowd'r c. to med.	0 55	0 70
" med. to fine	0 70	0 85

Name of Article.	Wholesale Rate.	
	$ c.	$ c.
Groceries—*Contin'd*		
" fine to fins't	0 85	0 95
Hyson	0 45	0 80
Imperial	0 42	0 80
Tobacco, Manufact'd:		
Can Leaf, ₩ lb 5s & 10s.	0 26	0 30
Western Leaf, com.	0 25	0 26
" Good	0 27	0 32
" Fine	0 32	0 35
" Bright fine	0 40	0 50
" " choice	0 60	0 75
Hardware.		
Tin (net cash prices)		
Block, ₩ lb.	0 25	0 26
Grain	0 25	0 26
Copper:		
Pig	0 23	0 24
Sheet	0 30	0 33
Cut Nails:		
Assorted ¼ Shingles, ₩ 100 lb.	3 05	3 15
Shingle alone do	2 25	2 35
Lathe and 5 dy.	3 45	3 55
Galvanized Iron:		
Assorted sizes	0 09	0 10
Best No. 24	0 09	0 00
" 26	0 08½	0 09
" 28	0 09½	0 10
Horse Nails:		
Guest's or Griffin's assorted sizes	0 19	0 20
For W. ass'd sizes	0 18	0 19
Patent Hammer'd do	0 17	0 18½
Iron (at 4 months):		
Pig—Gartsherrie No1	26 00	27 00
Other brands, No 1	22 00	23 00
" No 2	24 00	25 00
Bar—Scotch, ₩100 lb.	2 25	2 50
Refined	3 00	3 25
Swedes	5 00	5 50
Hoops—Coopers	3 00	3 25
Band	3 00	3 25
Boiler Plates	3 25	3 50
Canada Plates	4 00	4 25
Union Jack	0 00	0 00
Pontypool	4 00	4 25
Swansea	0 00	0 00
Lead (at 4 months):		
Bar, ₩ 100 lbs.	0 07	0 07½
Sheet "	0 08	0 09
Shot	0 07½	0 07¾
Iron Wire (net cash):		
No. 6, ₩ bundle	2 70	2 80
" 9, "	3 10	3 20
" 12, "	3 40	3 50
" 16, "	4 30	4 40
Powder:		
Blasting, Canada	3 50	3 75
FF "	4 25	4 50
FFF "	4 75	5 00
Blasting, English	5 00	5 50
FF loose	5 50	6 00
FFF "	6 00	6 50
Pressed Spikes (4 mos):		
Regular sizes 100	4 00	4 25
Extra "	4 50	5 00
Tin Plates (net cash):		
IC Coke	7 50	8 00
IC Charcoal	8 50	8 75
IX "	10 50	10 75
IXX "	12 50	0 00
DC "	7 50	9 00
DX "	9 50	10 00
Hides & Skins. ₩lb		
Green rough	0 05½	0 06
Green, salt'd & insp'd	0 00	0 07
Cured	0 07½	0 08½
Calfskins, green	0 00	0 10
Calfskins, cured	0 00	0 12
" dry	0 18	0 20
Lambskins,	0 50	0 00
" pelts	0 40	0 00
Hops.		
Inferior, ₩ lb.	0 10	0 15
Medium	0 15	0 20
Good	0 20	0 25
Fancy	0 25	0 35
Leather, @ (4 mos.) In lots of less than 50 sides, 10 ₩ cent higher		
Spanish Sole, 1st qual. heavy, weights ₩ lb.	0 23	0 23½
Do. 1st qual middle do	0 23	0 23½
Do. No. 2, all weights	0 20	0 22
Slaughter heavy	0 28	0 29
Do. light	0 28	0 29
Harness, best	0 32	0 34
" No. 2	0 30	0 33
Upper heavy	0 34	0 36
" light	0 36	0 40

Name of Article.	Wholesale Rates.	
	$ c.	$ c.
Leather—*Contin'd.*		
Kip Skins, Patna	0 45	0 55
French	0 70	0 90
English	0 65	0 80
Hemlock Calf (30 to 35 lbs.) per doz.	0 75	0 85
Do. light	0 45	0 50
French Calf	1 05	1 25
Grain & Satn Clt ₩ doz.	0 00	0 00
Splits, large ₩ lb.	0 38	0 40
" small	0 20	0 30
Enamelled Cow ₩ foot	0 20	0 21
Patent	0 21	0 22
Pebble Grain	0 17	0 18½
Buff	0 17	0 19
Oils.		
Cod	0 55	0 60
Lard, extra	0 00	1 25
" No. 1	0 00	1 15
" Woollen	0 00	1 05
Lubricating, patent	0 00	0 00
" Mott's economic	0 50	0 00
Linseed, raw	0 77½	0 85
" boiled	0 82½	0 90
Machinery	0 00	0 00
Olive, 2nd, ₩ gal.	1 45	1 60
" salad	2 00	2 30
" salad, in bots. qt. ₩ case	3 60	3 75
Sesame salad, ₩ gal.	1 60	1 75
Seal, pale	0 70	0 75
Spirits Turpentine	0 65	0 70
Varnish	0 00	0 00
Whale.	0 75	0 80
Paints, &c.		
White Lead, genuine in Oil, ₩ 25 lbs.	0 00	2 50
Do. No. 1 "	0 00	2 25
" 2 "	0 00	2 00
" 3 "	0 00	1 75
White Zinc, genuine	3 00	3 50
White Lead, dry	0 06	0 09
Red Lead	0 07½	0 08
Venetian Red, Eng'h	0 02½	0 03½
Yellow Ochre, Fren'h	0 02½	0 03
Whiting	0 90	1 25
Petroleum. (Refined ₩ gal.)		
Water white, car l'd	0 32	0 32½
" small lots	0 35	0 36
Straw, by car load	0 31	0 32
" small lots	0 34	0 35
Amber, by car load	0 00	0 00
" small lots	0 00	0 00
Benzine	0 35	0 45
Produce.		
Grain:		
Wheat, Spring, 60 lb.	1 20	1 26
" Fall 60 "	1 30	1 32
Barley 48 "	0 95	0 98
Peas 60 "	0 95	0 96
Oats 34 "	0 48	0 49
Rye 56 "	0 00	0 80
Seeds:		
Clover, choice 60 "	5 50	6 00
" com'n 68 "	0 00	0 00
Timothy, cho'e 4 "	2 00	2 50
" inf. to good 48 "	1 50	2 00
Flax 56 "	1 25	1 60
Flour (per brl.):		
Superior extra	6 75	7 00
Extra superfine,	6 50	6 75
Fancy superfine	0 00	0 00
Superfine No. 1	5 85	5 90
" No. 2	0 00	0 00
Oatmeal, (per brl.)	6 50	6 60
Provisions.		
Butter, dairy tub ₩lb.	0 18	0 22
" store packed	0 16	0 18
Cheese, new	0 10½	0 11½
Pork, mess, per brl.	23 00	24 00
" prime mess	16 00	17 00
" prime	14 00	15 00
Bacon, rough	0 00	0 00
" Cumberl'd cut	0 12	0 13
" smoked	0 00	0 00
Hams, in salt	0 00	0 00
" sug. cur. & canv'd	0 00	0 00
Shoulders, in salt	0 00	0 00
Lard, in kegs	0 13½	0 14
Eggs, packed	0 11	0 12
Beef Hams	0 00	0 13
Tallow	0 00	0 00
Hogs dressed, heavy	0 00	0 00
" medium	0 00	0 00
" light	0 00	0 00
Salt, &c.		
American brls.	1 58	1 60
Liverpool coarse	0 00	0 00
Plaster	1 05	1 10
Water Lime	1 50	0 00

Soap & Candles.

D. Crawford & Co.'s ..	8 c.	8 c.
Imperial....	0 07½	0 08
" Golden Bar	0 07	0 07½
" Silver Bar......	0 07	0 07½
Crown	0 05	0 05½
No. 1	0 03½	0 03½
Candles	0 10	0 10½

Wines, Liquors, &c.

Ale:
English, per doz......	2 00	2 05
Guinness Dub Portr..	2 35	2 40

Spirits
Pure Jamaica Rum...	1 80	2 25
De Kuyper's H. Gin..	1 50	1 60
Booth's Old Tom, c...	1 90	2 00

Gin:
Green, cases........	4 00	4 25
Booth's Old Tom, c. .	6 00	6 25

Wines:
Port, common	1 00	1 25
" fine old	2 00	4 00
Sherry, common	1 00	1 50
" medium......	1 70	1 90
"old pale or golden ..	2 50	4 00

Brandy:
Hennessy's, per gal..	2 50	2 75
Martell's " ..	2 50	2 75
J. Robin & Co.'s " ..	2 10	2 75
Otard, Dupuy & Cos..	2 10	2 75
Brandy, cases........	8 50	9 00
Brandy, com. per c. ..	4 00	4 50

Whiskey:
Common 36 u. p......	0 65	0 70
Old Rye	0 85	0 87½
Malt...............	0 85	0 87½
Toddy..............	0 85	0 87½
Scotch, per gal......	1 90	2 10
" DunnVille's Belf't..	7 00	7 50
" DunnVille's Belf't..	6 00	6 25

Wool.

Fleece, lb............	0 25	0 27
Pulled "............	0 00	0 00

Furs.

Bear................	3 00	10 00
Beaver..............	1 00	1 25
Coon	0 20	0 40
Fisher..............	4 00	6 00
Martin..............	1 40	1 60
Mink................	4 00	4 25
Otter...............	5 75	6 00
Spring Rats	0 13	0 17
Fox................	1 20	1 25

INSURANCE COMPANIES.

ENGLISH.—Quotations on the London Market.

No. of Shares.	Last Dividend.	Name of Company.	Shares per val'e	Amount paid.	Last
20,000		Briton Medical and General Life ...	10		1½
50,000	7½	Commer'l Union, Fire, Life and Mar.	50	5	5½ 5⅜
24,000	5	City of Glasgow	25	2½	
5,000	9½	Edinburgh Life	100	15	30⅝x
400,000	5—⅝ yr	European Life and Guarantee......	2½	11s6	4s 6d
100,000	10	Etna Fire and Marine	10	1½	1
20,000	5	Guardian	100	50	52x
24,000	12	Imperial Fire..................	500	50	345
7,500	9½	Imperial Life	100	10	10½
100,000	10	Lancashire Fire and Life	20	2	15½
10,000	11	Life Association of Scotland......	40	7½	23
33,862	45s. p. sh	London Assurance Corporation ...	25	12½	48
10,000	5	London and Lancashire Life	10	1	1
87,504	40	Liverp'l & London & Globe F. & L.	20	2	7⅜
20,000	5	National Union Life	2	1	1
20,000	12½	Northern Fire and Life	100	5	10½
40,000	'68,no 5s.	North British and Mercantile	50	6½	16 16½
40,000	50	Ocean Marine	25	5	20
2,500	£5 12s.	Provident Life	100	10	28
	£4½ p. s.	Phœnix........................			136
200,000	3½–½. yr.	Queen Fire and Life	10	1	15-16
100,000	3s. 6d.4s	Royal Insurance.................	20	3	6½
20,000	10	Scottish Provincial Fire and Life ..	50	2½	4½
10,000	25	Standard Life	50	12	65
4,000	1½	Star Life	25	1½	

CANADIAN.

					₹ c.
8,000	4	British America Fire and Marine ..	850	825	55½
	4	Canada Life			
4000	12	Montreal Assurance	£50	£10	135
10,000	3	Provincial Fire and Marine	60	11	
		Quebec Fire	40	32½	£.19
	8	" Marine................	100	40	90-91
10,000	5 7 mo's.	Western Assurance..............	40	6	...

RAILWAYS.

	Sha's	Paid	Montr	London.
Atlantic and St. Lawrence	£100	All.		57 59
Buffalo and Lake Huron	20½	"		3⅛ 3½
Do. do Preference	10	"		5½ 6½
Buff., Brantf. & Goderich, 6½e., 1872-3-4	100	"		
Champlain and St. Lawrence			9 10	
Do. do Pref. 10 ₹ ct.			62½	
Grand Trunk	100	"	15 16	15¼ 16
Do. Eq. G. M. Bds. 1 ch. 6⅝e........	100	"		78 82
Do. First Preference, 5 ₹ c	100	"		46 49
Do. Deferred, 3 ₹ ct.............	100	"		...
Do. Second Pref. Bonds, 5½e........	100	"		...
Do. do Deferred, 3 ₹ ct........	100	"		...
Do. Third Pref. Stock, 4 ₹ct........	100	"		25 27
Do. do. Deferred, 3 ₹ ct........	100	"		...
Do. Fourth Pref. Stock, 3 ₹e........	100	"		...
Do. do. Deferred, 3 ₹ ct........	100	"		13 19
Great Western	20½	"		13 13½
Do. New	20½	18	16 17	
Do. 6 ₹ c. Bds, due 1873-76.......	100	All.		100 102
" 5½e Bds. due 1877-78.........	100	"		92 94
Marine Railway, Halifax, $250, all	$250	"		...
Northern, of Canada, 6½e. 1st Pref. Bds	100	"		80 83

EXCHANGE.

	Halifax.	Montr'l.	Quebec.	Toronto.
Bank on London, 60 days...	13½	9 9½	9½ 9½	9½
sight or 75 days date......	12 12½	8 8½	8½ 8½	9½
Private do.		8½ 0½	...	...
Private, with documents.......		8½ 8½	...	...
Bank on New York........		30½ 31	30 30½	60½
Private do.	33	31½ 31½	31½	...
Gold Drafts do.		½ dis to p.	par ½ dis.	par ½ dia.
Silver		4½ 4½	...	4½ 6½

STOCK AND BOND REPORT.

The dates of our quotations are as follows:—Toronto, Sept. 17; Montreal, Sept. 16; Que Sept. 15; London, Aug. 17.

NAME.	Shares.	Paid up.	Divid'd last 6 Months	Dividend Day.	Toronto.	Montre'l
BANKS.			₹ ct.			
British North America	$250	All.	3	July and Jan.	102½ 103	102
Jacques Cartier.........	50	"	4	1 June, 1 Dec.	106 108	106 108
Montreal	200	"	5	"	134 135	134 135
Nationale..............	50	"	4	1 Nov. 1 May.	106	106 108
New Brunswick	100	"	...		...	...
Nova Scotia............	200	28	7½ b 3½	Mar. and Sept.	104 106	105 106
Du Peuple.............	50	"	4	1 Mar., 1 Sept.	113 116	114 116
Toronto...............	100	"	4	1 Jan., 1 July.	116 116½	116 116½
Bank of Yarmouth.......					...	...
Canadian Bank of Com'e...	50	95	...		103 103½	101½ 102½
City Bank Montreal	80	All.	4	1 June, 1 Dec.	102 102½	102 102½
Commer'l Bank (St. John)..	100	"	₹ ct.		...	...
Eastern Townships' Bank..	50	"	4	1 July, 1 Jan.	...	96 98
Gore	40	"	3½	1 Jan., 1 July.	...	...
Halifax Banking Company..					...	...
Mechanics' Bank.........	50	70	4	1 Nov., 1 May.	94½ 95½	94 96
Merchants' Bank of Canada..	100	79	4	1 Jan., 1 July.	105 106	105 105½
Merchants' Bank (Halifax)..					...	...
Molson's Bank..........	50	All.	4	1 Apr., 1 Oct.	111 112	112
Niagara District Bank.....	100	70	3½	1 Jan., 1 July.	...	...
Ontario Bank...........	40	All.	4	1 June, 1 Dec.	98½ 99	98 98½
People's Bank (Fret'kton)...	100	"	...		...	...
People's Bank (Halifax)....	20	"	7 12 ni		98 99	97½ 98½
Quebec Bank	100	"	3½	1 June, 1 Dec.	89 90	88 91
Royal Canadian Bank	50	50	4	1 Jan., 1 July.	...	...
St. Stephens Bank	100	All.	...		...	...
Union Bank	100	70	4	1 Jan., 1 July.	101½ 101½	102 103
Union Bank (Halifax).....	100	40	7 12 mo	Feb. and Aug.	...	...
MISCELLANEOUS.						
British America Land......	250	44	2½		...	...
British Colonial S. S. Co....	250	32½	2½		...	50
Canada Company	33½	All.	5		...	...
Canada Landed Credit Co....	50	31½	3½		62½ 63	...
Canada Per. B'l'dg Society...	50	All.	5		119 119½	...
Canada Mining Company...	4	00	...		...	...
Do. Inl'd Steam Nav. Co...	100	All.	20 12 m		...	107½ 109
Do. Glass Company......	100	"	12½		...	95
Canad'n Loan & Investm't...	25	2½	7		...	...
Canada Agency	10	½	...		...	...
Colonial Securities Co.					...	...
Freehold Building Society...	100	All.	5		105 105	...
Halifax Steamboat Co......	100	"	5		...	...
Halifax Gas Company......					...	...
Hamilton Gas Company....					...	...
Huron Copper Bay Co.....	4	12	20		...	33 50c ps
Lake Huron S. and C......	5	1½0	...		...	...
Montreal Mining Co.......	20	$15	...		...	3.75 3.50
Do. Telegraph Co...	40	"	15 12 m		133 134	133 134½
Do. Elevating Co...	00	"			...	...
Do. City Gas Co...	50	All.	5	15 Mar. 15 Sep.	...	Bks.clod
Nova Scotia Telegraph	20	"			...	108
Quebec and L. S.	8	$4	...		...	...
Quebec Gas Co.	200	All.	4	1 Mar., 1 Sep.	...	...
Quebec Street R. R.......	50	25	3		...	116 118
St. Lawrence Tow Boat Co..	100	All.	7 p.a.	1 Jan., 1 July.	...	...
Tor'to Consumers' Gas Co...	100	"	2 3 m.	1 My Au Mar Fe	104½ 105	...
Trust & Loan Co. of U. C...	20	5	3		...	...
West'n Canada Bldg Soc'y..	50	All.	5		111 112	...

SECURITIES.

	London.	Montreal.	Quebec.
Canadian Gov't Deb. 6 ₹ ct. due 1872		100 100½	100½ 101½
Do. do. 6 do due Ja.& Jul. 1877-84	103 105		
Do. do. 6 do. Feb. & Aug.	103 103		
Do. do. 6 do. Meh. & Sep.	104 106		
Do. do. 5 ₹ ct. cur., 1883	91 93	90	90 90½
Do. do. 5 do. stg., 1885		90	90½ 91
Do. do. 7 do. cur., ...		...	...
Dominion 6 p. c. 1878 cy'.		99½ 100	100½ 101½
Hamilton Corporation......................		...	...
Montreal Harbor, 8 ₹ ct. d. 1869............		...	...
Do. do. 7 do. 1870.................		100½	...
Do. do. 6½ do. 1875.................		...	...
Do. do. 6½ do. 1878.................		...	...
Do. Corporation, 6 ₹ c. 1891........		92 98	92 93
Do. 7 p. c. stock...................		103 100	103 105
Do. Water Works, 6 ₹ c. stg. 1878..		...	...
Do. do. 6 do. cy. do.		92 93	...
New Brunswick, 6 ₹ ct., Jan. and July....	102 104	...	...
Nova Scotia, 6 ₹ ct., 1875................	101 103	...	...
Ottawa City 6 ₹ c. d. 1880		90 91	...
Quebec Harbour, 6 ₹ c. d. 1883		...	70 80
Do. do. 8 do. 1886.		...	70 80
Do. City, 7 ₹ c. d. 5 years		85 90	85 90
Do. do. 7 do. 9 do.		...	90 91
Do. do. 7 do. 6 do.		...	88 87
Do. Water Works, 7 ₹ ct., 4 years...		...	90 95½
Do. do. 6 do. 2 do.		...	95 96
Toronto Corporation.......................		90	92½ 93½

9

Financial.

Pellatt & Osler.

ND EXCHANGE BROKERS, Accountants,
r the Standard Life Assurance Company and
asualty Insurance Company.
-86 *King Street East, four Doors West of*
Church Street, Toronto.

LLATT, EDMUND B. OSLER,
tary Public. *Official Assignee.*

OWN'S BANK.

(. R. Brown. W. C. Chewett.)

NG STREET EAST, TORONTO,

TS a general Banking Business, Buys and
ew York and Sterling Exchange, Gold, Silver,
s and Uncurrent Money, receives Deposits sub-
que at sight, makes Collections and Discounts
l Paper.

Mail or Telegraph promptly executed at
iost favourable current quotations.

ress letters, "BROWN'S BANK,
Toronto."

.dian Land and Emigration Company

rs for sale on Conditions of Settlement,

OD FARM LANDS

n the County of Peterboro, Ontario,

l settled Township of Dysart, where there are
Grist and Saw Mills, Stores, &c., at

D-A-HALF DOLLARS AN ACRE.

idjoining Townships of Guilford, Dudley, Harcourt and Bruton, connected with Dysart and
f Haliburton by the Peterson Road, at ONE
an Acre.

her particulars apply to

CHAS. JAS. BLOOMFIELD,
Secretary C. L. and E. Co., Toronto.
ALEX. NIVEN, P.L.S.,
Agent C. L. & E. Co., Haliburton

Insurance.

Liverpool and London and Globe
Insurance Company.

and Reserved Funds........$17,005,000.

DAILY CASH RECEIPTS.....$20,000.

S IS HEREBY GIVEN, that [this Company
ng deposited the sum of

150,000 Dollars,

ance with the Act, 31st Vic.) cap. 48, has received
ise of the Finance Minister, to transact the busi-
ife and Fire Insurance in the Dominion of Canada.

G. F. C. SMITH,
Chief Agent for the Dominion.

artford Fire Insurance Company.

HARTFORD, CONN.

ipital and Assets over Two Million Dollars.

$2,026,220.29.

CHARTERED 1810.

ld and reliable Company, having an established
ess in Canada of more than thirty years standing,
lied with the provisions of the new Insurance
made a special deposit of

$100,000

Government for the security of policy-holders, and
inue to grant policies upon the same favorable
heretofore.

ly low rates on first-class dwellings and farm
for a term of one or more years.

as heretofore promptly and equitably adjusted.

E. CHAFFEY & CO., AGENTS.
,o, Ont.

iERT WOOD, GENERAL AGENT FOR CANADA

Insurance.

The Standard Life Assurance Company,
Established 1825,
WITH WHICH IS NOW UNITED
THE COLONIAL LIFE ASSURANCE COMPANY.

Head Office for Canada:
MONTREAL—STANDARD COMPANY'S BUILDINGS,
No. 47 GREAT ST. JAMES STREET.

Manager—W. M. RAMSAY. *Inspector*—RICH'D BULL,

THIS Company having deposited the sum of ONE HUN-
DRED AND FIFTY THOUSAND DOLLARS with the Receiver-
General, in conformity with the Insurance Act passed last
Session, Assurances will continue to be carried ont at
moderate rates and on all the different systems in practice.

AGENT FOR TORONTO—HENRY PELLATT,
KING STREET.
AGENT FOR HAMILTON—JAMES BANCROFT.
6-6mos.

Fire and Marine Assurance.

THE BRITISH AMERICA
ASSURANCE COMPANY.
HEAD OFFICE:
CORNER OF CHURCH AND COURT STREETS.
TORONTO.

BOARD OF DIRECTION:
Hon. G. W. Allan, M.L.C., | A. Joseph, Esq.,
George J. Boyd, Esq , | Peter Paterson, Esq.,
Hon. W. Cayley, | G. P. Ridout, Esq.,
Richard S. Cassels, Esq.,, | E.H. Rutherford, Esq.,
Thomas C. Street, Esq.,

Governor:
GEORGE PERCIVAL RIDOUT, Esq.
Deputy Governor:
PETER PATERSON, Esq.

Fire Inspector: | Marine Inspector:
E. ROBY O'BRIEN. | CAPT. R. COURNEEN.

Insurances granted on all descriptions of property
against loss and damage by fire and the perils of inland
navigation.
Agencies established in the principal cities, towns, and
ports of shipment throughout the Province.

THOS. WM. BIRCHALL,
25-1y *Managing Director.*

Edinburgh Life Assurance Company.

Founded 1829.

HEAD OFFICE—22 GEORGE STREET, EDINBURGH.

Capital, ... £500,000 *Ster'g.*
Accumulated and Invested Funds, £1,000,000 "

HEAD OFFICE IN CANADA:
WELLINGTON STREET, TORONTO.

SUB-AGENTS THROUGHOUT THE PROVINCE.

J. HILLYARD CAMERON,
Chairman, Canadian Board.

DAVID HIGGINS,
Secretary, Canadian Board. 3-3m

Queen Fire and Life Insurance Company,
OF LIVERPOOL AND LONDON,
ACCEPTS ALL ORDINARY FIRE RISKS
on the most favorable terms.

LIFE RISKS
Will be taken on terms that will compare favorably with
other Companies.

CAPITAL, - - - £2,000,000 Stg.

CHIEF OFFICES—Queen's Buildings, Liverpool, and
Gracechurch Street London.
CANADA BRANCH OFFICE—Exchange Buildings, Montreal.
Resident Secretary and General Agent,
A. MACKENZIE FORBES,
13 St. Sacrament St., Merchants' Exchange, Montreal.
WM. ROWLAND, Agent, Toronto. 1-1y

Insurance.

Reliance Mutual Life Assurance
Society.
(*Established,* 1840,) OF LONDON, E. C.

Accumulated Funds, over $1,000,000.

Annual Income, $800,00.
THE entire Profits of this long-established Society belong
to the Policy-holders.
HEAD OFFICE FOR DOMINION—MONTREAL.
T. W. GRIFFITH, Manager & Sec'y.
15-1y WM. HENDERSON, Agent for Toronto.

Etna Insurance Company of Dublin.
The number of Shareholders exceeds Five Hundred.

Capital, $5,000,000—Annual Income nearly $1,000,000.
THIS Company takes Fire and Marine Risks on the most
favorable terms.
Chief office for Dominion—Corner St. Francois Xavier
and St. Sacrament Sts., Montreal.
15-1y WM. HENDERSON, Agent for Toronto.

Scottish Provincial Assurance Co.
Established 1825.
CAPITAL, ...£1,000,000 STERLING.
INVESTED IN CANADA (1854) ....$500,000.
Canada Head Office, Montreal.

LIFE DEPARTMENT.
CANADA BOARD OF DIRECTORS:
HUGH TAYLOR, Esq., Advocate,
Hon. CHARLES WILSON, M.L.C.,
WM. SACHE, Esq., Banker,
JACKSON RAE, Esq., Banker.
WM. FRASER, Esq. M. D., Medical Adviser.

The special advantages to be derived from Insuring in
this office are :—Strictly Moderate Rates of Premium;
Large Bonus (intermediate bonus guaranteed ;) Liberal
Surrender Value, unless policies relinquished by assured ;
and Extensive Limits of Residence and Travel. All business disposed of in Canada, without reference to parent
office.

A DAVIDSON PARKER,
Resident-Secretary.
G. L. MADDISON,
15-1yr AGENT FOR TORONTO.

Lancashire Insurance Company.
CAPITAL, - - - - - - £2,000,000 Sterling.

FIRE RISKS
Taken at reasonable rates of premium, and
ALL LOSSES SETTLED PROMPTLY,
By the undersigned, without reference elsewhere.
S. C. DUNCAN-CLARK & CO.,
General Agents for Ontario,
N. W. Corner of King & Church Streets,
25-1y TORONTO.

Etna Fire & Marine Insurance Company.
INCORPORATED 1819. CHARTER PERPETUAL.
CASH CAPITAL, ... $3,000,000
LOSSES PAID IN 50 YEARS, 23,500,000 00.

JULY, 1868.
ASSETS.
(At Market Value.)
Cash in hand and in Bank $844,842 39
Real Estate.............................. 255,267,29
Mortgage Bonds.......................... 982,345,00
Bank Stock.............................. 1,372,670 00
United States, State and City Stock, and other
Public Securities 2,049,855 51

Total $5,052,880 19

LIABILITIES.
Claims not Due, and Unadjusted $499,803 55
Amount required by Mass. and New York
for Re-Insurance.......................... 1,405,267 15
E. CHAFFEY & CO., Agents.
50-6m

Insurance.

The Liverpool and London and Globe Insurance Company.

INVESTED FUNDS:

FIFTEEN MILLIONS OF DOLLARS.

DAILY INCOME OF THE COMPANY:

TWELVE THOUSAND DOLLARS.

LIFE INSURANCE,

WITH AND WITHOUT PROFITS.

FIRE INSURANCE
On every description of Property, at Lowest Remunerative Rates.

JAMES FRASER, Agent,
5 King Street West.

Toronto, 1868. 35-1y

Briton Medical and General Life Association,

with which is united the

BRITANNIA LIFE ASSURANCE COMPANY.

Capital and Invested Funds............£750,000 Sterling.

ANNUAL INCOME, £220,000 Sterling.
Yearly increasing at the rate of £25,000 Sterling.

THE important and peculiar feature originally introduced by this Company, in applying the periodical Bonuses, so as to make Policies payable during life, without any higher rate of premiums being charged, has caused the success of the BRITON MEDICAL AND GENERAL to be almost unparalleled in the history of Life Assurance. *Life Policies on the Profit Scale become payable during the Lifetime of the Assured, thus rendering a Policy of Assurance a means of subsistence in old age, as well as a protection for a family,* and a more valuable security to creditors in the event of early death; and effectually meeting the often urged objection, that persons do not themselves reap the benefit of their own prudence and forethought.

No extra charge made to members of Volunteer Corps for services within the British Provinces.

TORONTO AGENCY, 5 KING ST. WEST.
oct 17—9-1yr   JAMES FRASER, Agent.

Phenix Insurance Company,
BROOKLYN, N. Y.

PHILANDER SHAW,   EDGAR W. CROWELL,
Secretary.   Vice-President.
STEPHEN CROWELL, President.
Cash Capital, $1,000,000. Surplus, $666,416.02. Total,
1,666,416.02. Entire Income from all sources for 1866 was
$2,131,830.82.

CHARLES G. FORTIER, Marine Agent.
Ontario Chambers, Toronto, Ont.   19-1y.

ÆTNA
Live Stock Insurance Company,
OF
HARTFORD, CONN.

DIRECTORS:

E. A. BULKELEY,   C. C. KIMBALL,
SAMUEL WOODRUFF,   T. O. ENDERS,
AUSTIN DUNHAM,   ROBT. E. DAY,
L. J. BASSETT,   EDWD. KELLOGG,
J. S. WOODRUFF,   ALVAN P. HYDE.

This Company Insures
HORSES AND CATTLE
AGAINST DEATH
BY FIRE,
ACCIDENT,
OR DISEASE.
Also,
AGAINST THEFT,
And the
HAZARDS OF TRANSPORTATION.

C. C. KIMBALL, President.
T. O. ENDERS, Vice President.
J. B. TOWER, Secretary.

Parties desiring Local Agencies will apply to
E. L. SNOW, GENERAL AGENT,
Montreal.

SCOTT & WALMSLEY,
67nov1ly   Agents, Ontario.

Insurance.

The Victoria Mutual
FIRE INSURANCE COMPANY OF CANADA.

Insures only Non-Hazardous Property, at Low Rates.

BUSINESS STRICTLY MUTUAL.

GEORGE H. MILLS, President.
W. D. BOOKER, Secretary.
HEAD OFFICE ....HAMILTON, ONTARIO
aug 15-1yr

The Ætna Life Insurance Company.

AN attack, abounding with errors, having been made upon the Ætna Life Insurance Co. by the editor of the Montreal *Daily News*; and certain agents of British Companies being now engaged in handing around copies of the attack, thus seeking to damage the Company's standing, —I have pleasure in laying before the public the following certificate, bearing the signatures of the Presidents and Cashiers who happened to be in their Offices) of *every Bank in Hartford*; also that of the President and Secretary of the old Ætna Fire Insurance Company :—

"To whom it may concern:—.
"We, the undersigned, regard the Ætna Life Insurance Company, of this city, as one of the most successful and prosperous Insurance Companies in the States,— entirely reliable, responsible, and honourable in all its dealings, and most worthy of public confidence and patronage."

Lucius J. Hendee, President Ætna Fire Insurance Co.,
and late Treasurer of the State of Connecticut.
J. Goodnow, Secretary Ætna Fire Insurance Co.
C. H. Northam, President, and J. B. Powell, Cashier
National Bank.
C. T. Hillyer, President Charter Oak National Bank.
E. D. Tiffany, President First National Bank.
G. T. Davis, President City National Bank.
F. S. Riley, Cashier, do. do. do.
John C. Tracy, President of Farmers' and Mechanics'
National Bank.
M. W. Graves, Cashier Conn. River Banking Co.
H. A. Redfield, Cashier Phenix National Bank.
O. G. Terry, President Ætna National Bank.
J. R. Redfield, Cashier National Exchange Bank.
John G. Root, Assistant Cashier American National Bank.
George F. Hills, Cashier State Bank of Hartford.
Jas. Potter, Cashier Hartford National Bank.
Hartford, Nov. 26, 1867.

Many of the above-mentioned parties are closely connected with other Life Insurance Companies, but all unhesitatingly commend our Company as "reliable, responsible, honorable in all its dealings, and most worthy of public confidence and patronage.

JOHN GARVIN,
General Agent, Toronto Street.
Toronto, Dec. 3. 1867.   16-1y

Life Association of Scotland.

INVESTED FUNDS
UPWARDS OF £1,000,000 STERLING.

THIS Institution differs from other Life Offices, in that the
BONUSES FROM PROFITS
Are applied on a special system for the Policy-holder's
*PERSONAL BENEFIT AND ENJOYMENT
DURING HIS OWN LIFETIME,*
WITH THE OPTION OF
LARGE BONUS ADDITIONS TO THE SUM ASSURED.

The Policy-holder thus obtains
A LARGE REDUCTION OF PRESENT OUTLAY
OR
*A PROVISION FOR OLD AGE OF A MOST IMPORTANT
AMOUNT IN ONE CASH PAYMENT,
OR A LIFE ANNUITY,*
Without any expense or outlay whatever beyond the ordinary Assurance Premium for the Sum Assured, which remains in tact for Policy-holder's heirs, or other purposes.

CANADA—MONTREAL—PLACE D'ARMES.

DIRECTORS:
DAVID TORRANCE, Esq., (D. Torrance & Co.)
GEORGE MOFFATT, (Gillespie, Moffatt & Co.)
ALEXANDER MORRIS, Esq., M.P., Barrister, Perth.
SIR G. E. CARTIER, M.P., Minister of Militia.
PETER REDPATH, Esq., (J. Redpath & Son).
J. H. R. MOLSON, Esq., (J. H. R. Molson & Bros.)
Solicitors—Messrs. TORRANCE & MORRIS.
Medical Officer—R. PALMER HOWARD, Esq., M.D
Secretary—P. WARDLAW.
Inspector of Agencies—JAMES B. M. CHIPMAN. 7

Insurance.

North British and Mercantile Insurance Company.

Established 1809.

HEAD OFFICE, - - CANADA - - MONT[

TORONTO BRANCH:
Local Offices, Nos. 4 & 6 WELLINGTON STREE
Fire Department, ...R. N. GOO

Life Department, ... H. L. HIM[
29-1y

Phenix Fire Assurance Compan

LOMBARD ST. AND CHARING CROSS,
LONDON, ENG.

Insurances effected in all parts of the Wo[
Claims paid
WITH PROMTITUDE and LIBERALIT
MOFFATT, MURRAY & BEATTIE,
Agents for Toronto
36 Yonge St[
28

The Commercial Union Assurau Company,

19 & 20 CORNHILL, LONDON, ENGLAND.

Capital, £2,500,000 Stg.—Invested over $2,000,00

FIRE DEPARTMENT.—Insurance granted on [scriptions of property at reasonable rates.

LIFE DEPARTMENT.—The success of this b has been unprecedented—NINETY PERCENT. o[miums now in hand. First year's premiums wer[$100,000. Economy of management guaranteed I e curity. Moderate rates.

OFFICE—385 & 387 ST PAUL STREET, MONTRE

MORLAND, WATSON & C[
General Agents for C[

FRED. COLE, Secretary.
Inspector of Agencies—T. C. LIVINGSTON, [
                      W. M. WESTMACOTT, Agent at Tor[
16-1y

Phenix Mutual Life Insurance C[
HARTFORD, CONN.

Accumulated Fund, $2,000,000, Income, $60[

THIS Company, established in 1851, is one of the reliable Companies doing business in the countr[has been steadily prospering. The *Massachusetts Ins[Reports* show that in nearly all important matter[superior; o the general average of Companies. It of[intending assurers the following reasons, amongst o[for preferring it to other companies:

It is purely Mutual It allows the Insured to and reside in any portion of the United States and E It throws out almost all restriction on occupation fr[Policies. It will, if desired, take a note for part [Premium, thus combining all the advantages of a no[all cash company. Its Dividends are declared an[and applied in reduction of Premium. Its Dividen[in every case on Premiums paid. The Dividends [PHENIX have averaged fifty per cent. yearly. settlement of Policies, a Dividend will be allowed fo[year the policy has been in force. The number o[dends will always equal the outstanding Notes. Pa[losses promptly—during its existence never havin[tested a claim. It issues Policies for the benefit o[ried Women beyond the reach of their husband's cre[Creditors may also insure the lives of Debtors. Its P[are all *Non-forfiting*, as it always allows the assur[surrender his Policy, should he desire, the Compa[ing a paid-up Policy therefor. This important [will commend itself to all. The inducements now [by the PHENIX are better and more liberal than th[any other Company. Its rate of Mortality is excee[low and under the average.

Parties contemplating *Life Insurance* will find it t[interest to call and examine our system. Policie[payable either in *Gold* or *American* currency.

ANGUS R. BETHUNE,
General Manager,
Dominion of C[

Office: 104 ST. FRANÇOIS XAVIER ST., MONTRE[

Active and energetic Agents and Can[wanted in every town and village, to whom liberal [ments will be given. I[

PRINTED AT THE DAILY TELEGRAPH PRIN
HOUSE, BAY[ST., COR. KING.

THE CANADIAN
ONETARY TIMES
AND
INSURANCE CHRONICLE.
TED TO FINANCE, COMMERCE, INSURANCE, BANKS, RAILWAYS, NAVIGATION, MINES, INVESTMENT, PUBLIC COMPANIES, AND JOINT STOCK ENTERPRISE.

6.   TORONTO, THURSDAY, SEPTEMBER 24, 1868.   { SUBSCRIPTION, $3 A YEAR.

Insurance.

INSURANCE MATTERS IN MONTREAL.

(From a Correspondent.)

MONTREAL, Sept. 23, 1868.

We have had only two fires during the past week, both of livery stables, and both attended with the loss of valuable horses. The first was in Rapin's stables, where three horses belonging to the Beauharnois Agricultural Society, were destroyed. The total loss is estimated at $4,000; no insurance. The second fire was in the stables belonging to the Glasgow Hotel, where two horses were burnt; loss about $700, also no insurance.

You will see that an amalgamation has taken place between the Citizen's Company (a local company which, so far, has not been required to pay the Government deposit, but must now do so) and the European Guarantee and Life Co., Messrs. H. Allen, C. J. Brydges, and W. Workman, Directors of the European, take their places on the Board of Directors of the Citizens.

FIRE RECORD.—Waterloo, Sept. 13—Mr. Newton's hop house, with its contents, was totally destroyed. The fire caught at one of the kilns, and for want of water, could not be stopt. Although there were soon a great many citizens present, for want of proper management, very little stock was saved, though it is the opinion of many that a large quantity of hops could have been saved, had the people known what to do. Mr. Newton loses his whole year's crop, the product of 35 acres, which he values at about $5,000, together with the building, worth between $2,000 and $3,000. He has an insurance of $4,000 in the Waterloo Mutual, and $2,000 in the Western. The uselessness of the fire engine, without a company, will certainly convince the council and people of the importance of having another company at once.—*Exchange.*

Sept. 17—A brick house owned by Mr. Jackson, of Berlin; loss on house estimated at $600; Hackett, the occupant, loses a like sum on furniture, tools, &c. ; no insurance.

MULMUR, Sept. 5—The premises of John Hare, merchant, in the Township of Mulmur, were completely destroyed by fire on the morning of the 5th inst. Loss over $3,000; insured for only $600. Fire was accidental and the cause unknown.

THOROLD, Sept. 11th.—Barn of F. McMahon, filled with oats and hay; no particulars as to insurance.

QUEBEC, Sept.—A fire was set in a caleche under the porch of one Claude Caron, carter, St. Roch's. A portion of the inside of the vehicle was destroyed. On the previous evening a wooden box, the property of the same man, was set on fire. Both are the act of an incendiary, who has adopted this fiendish method of revenging some private grievance. The Fire Marshal has instituted an enquiry which will probably lead to the arrest of the guilty party.

MONTREAL, Sept. 15—Stables in rear of Rapin's hotel, St. Joseph street; three valuable horses were destroyed; "Emigrant," imported at a cost of $1,700, "Old Beauharnois," valued at

$1,100, and another horse, valued at $900. Why were they not insured in some good Live Stock Company?

ELMA, Ont.—A barn, with its contents, belonging to a Mr. Gabiel, of Elma, was entirely consumed on the night of Sunday week. It was a clear case of incendiarism, and the guilty party, a man named Beaken, has confessed that he did it through spite. Gabiel's loss is over $1,000.

ERIN, Ont., Sept. 13.—The barn on the farm of Mr. Sandford, of Erin, was destroyed by fire, together with the wheat which grew on twenty-five acres, worth $400, some hay, peas, etc., the product of 100 acres. Cause supposed to be incendiarism.

—The Ottawa Agency of the Provincial has been transferred to the Hon. Malcolm Cameron.

LAMBETH, Sept. 17—Barn of Mr. S. Reynolds; insurance $200. Incendiarism the cause.

GRAND TRUNK BOND INTEREST.—Notice is given, that a dividend on the postal and military service bonds, at the rate of £1 7s. 10d. ($6.77 currency) per £100 bond, having been declared for the half-year ending 8th August, 1868, the same will be paid on presentation of the bonds at Montreal.

NEW WATER WORKS.—At a late meeting of the Toronto City Council, a resolution was passed requiring the City Clerk to give notice, that application will be made at the next session of the Legislature for an act to erect new water works in the city.

THE LATE MR. PERCY M. DOVE.—With deep regret we have to record the death of Mr. Percy M. Dove, the actuary and manager of the Royal Insurance Company; who, to the great loss of his family and many attached friends, has this week passed away. Mr. Dove's knowledge of fire insurance business was very considerable, and he was examined before the Select Committee on Fire Protection, and some suggestions of his were recommended for adoption by the House of Commons. Mr. Dove made his last appearance in public at the annual meeting of the Royal Insurance Company, three weeks ago. His health was then in a precarious state, and on Monday last he expired at Claughton, near Birkenhead, at the age of sixty-four. Mr. Dove took the greatest interest in philanthropic and religious subjects, and his loss as an eminent actuary and man of deep religious principle will be extensively felt; but he has left behind him, in the highly success-ful position of the Royal Insurance Company, a lasting monument of his talents. Assisted by Mr. M'Laren in Liverpool, who will doubtless succeed to his post, and by his able coadjutors in London, Mr. Johnston and Mr. Fothergill, he brought the Royal Assurance Company to a point of success which entitles it to be recognized as one of the first institutions in Europe. Mr. Dove's name will ever live in the memory of those who have been associated with the growth of this most successful Insurance Company—*Investor's Guardian.*

ENGLISH OPINION OF THE AMERICAN INSURANCE SYSTEM.—The advantages accruing to the several branches of the Insurance business, through State supervision, which enforces normal development through healthful publicity, have been for many years manifest enough, in American experience. Even our egotistical Uncle John on the other side is now willing to admit its superiority, and English insurance journals in late years have earnestly urged upon Parliament the expediency of similar legislation for their offices. But every attempt thus far made in that direction has been met and defeated by the combined opposition of close corporations. Aversion to change of any kind is characteristic of the Anglo-Saxon temperament. Reforms, the need of which is patent and urgent, are secured by slow and painful processes, and sometimes under threats of revolution.

The London Journal of Actuaries and Assurance Magazine, in a complimentary review of Superintendent Barnes' Eighth Annual Report, expresses its conviction that the appointment of a "Government Inspector, with power to order Insurance Companies to publish Balance Sheets, would be productive of much good, and tend greatly to the protection of the public" in England. But even so intelligent an organ seems to be dazed by the idea of a really radical change. "We are of opinion, however, that the functions of such an officer should be strictly limited to obtaining and making public a true statement of the business transactions and the financial position of each company." That is to say, the "Government Inspector," who of all men connected with the business would necessarily be best qualified to offer, annually, useful suggestions and recommendations, should have no public opinions. In America, where corporations grow and prosper by abundant light and ventilation, there is no dread of official opinion, which is accepted on its merits only.

With respect to new and peculiar modes of transacting Life business, recently introduced by young American offices, such as the reduced Homœopathic premium rate, and the arbitrary modification of the average expectation of life, according to supposed special laws governing individual cases of vitality, as adopted by the American Popular Life Ins. Co., and noticed in the Superintendent's Report, the Assurance Magazine says:—"The experience of this country gives no encouragement to such novelties as these; for whenever anything of the kind has been attempted, it has been invariably abandoned after a few years' trial."

In footing up the aggregate of American Life businessfor 1866, our contemporary is not a little surprised: "The magnitude of the American Life offices far surpass anything that this country can show. It appears to be a law of nature that everything in the New World, whether in the realm of nature or art, shall be on a larger scale than in the Old World." And the qualifying caveat is well put, and deserves the especial attention of not a few young offices, now paying 25 to 40 per cent. for business. "It seems doubtful whether the assured receive any advantage from the magnitude of the offices; for the expenses of management appear to bear as large a proportion to the premiums as in England; if indeed the proportion be not larger."—Insurance Monitor.

ANNUAL REPORT OF THE INSURANCE COMMISSIONER FOR MASSACHUSETTS.—Mr. Sanford, the able Commissioner of Massachusetts, comes before us with his Annual Report; one remarkable for much of view, and vigor of statement. The number of companies made the subject of his report is 47, showing an increase of 3 in 1867, and this year 3 more have been admitted. The growth of Life Insurance is strikingly shown. No less than 62½ million dollars were paid to the 47 companies, in all 1867, by 430,000 policy holders, of which 9½ millions were paid out for claims on death. 40,000 policies are stated to have been allowed to lapse by policy holders, involving them in a heavy loss, but the Massachusetts laws appropriate this money to the insurance of those who paid it. The Commissioner raises the question whether these 47 companies are all funding enough to meet their enormous future obligations, or whether, between the ambitious struggle to pay large dividends to the assured on the one hand, and the temptation to pay large commissions to

agents, large salaries and perquisites to officers, and large royalties to stockholders, on the other; the bottom of the fund may not be reached at a day more or less distant, with a few hundred million dollars unprovided for. In this young country no such precedent has occurred, but there are many such in England. The Commissioner points out that that the great necessity of Life Insurance is accumulation at every period of its existence, a life company must have a fund growing with its growth, increasing with its age and business, devoted to coming obligations. So long as a company can respond to the great law of accumulation and reserve, stability is secured. The legislature of Massachusetts, which recognizes the importance of an effective supervision, applies a test by an "annual valuation of policies." This valuation has been made by aid of the tables published by Elizur Wright.

The only test of stability is the reserve or accumulation fund. The fundamental laws or assumptions on which life insurance proceeds, are a rate of mortality sufficiently high, and a rate of interest sufficiently low.

The Commissioner adheres to the Actuaries' table of mortality, and 4 per cent. on the rate of interest. In the State of New York, the rate of interest established by law for the valuation of Life Insurance Companies is 5 per cent., and the mortuary table used, is the combined experience or Actuaries' table. The Commissioner's next discussion is the question of assets. What is to be considered a legitimate present asset deserving to be counted as a part of the solid reserve fund? Real Estate is allowed to be good investment, and U. S. securities which form about two-thirds of the gross assets, and about four-fifths of the aggregate reserve fund. All accrued interest is admitted to be a good asset. Unpaid and deferred premiums, if including only the balances of annual premiums on policies in force, the first instalment of which fall due during the year, and that these premiums or balances not having been collected or received by the company, do not appear elsewhere among its assets, are likewise good assets, as in making the valuation of policies to which these premiums attach, it is assumed that the premiums have been all received. The premium notes and loans are next discussed as to their being good assets. They are admitted to be safe for the company, and may be, therefore, counted among its legitimate or realized assets. The note system is thus made to appear as not bad for the company, though not so apparently for the policy holders who are deluded by it. Some companies have returned "commuted commissions," loans to agents, purchase of agents' annuities, &c., as assets. These are disallowed as not being real assets.

The question of expenses is next discussed, as one of the utmost importance.

The mortuary record as shown in the experience of the companies is passed over, and instead thereof, is presented Mr. Levi M. Meech's life tables of the United States, prepared at the Commissioner's request.

The last subject discussed is that of the distribution of surplus.

The old per centage system is condemned, and the new system devised by Messrs. Shepherd Homans, and D. P. Fackler, shown to be the most equitable, which secures to each insurer a return of premium according to the amount of premium he has paid.

The contribution plan recognizes the constant sources of surplus—a higher rate of interest than was assumed, a lower rate of mortality than was expected, and a less per centage of expense than was provided for in establishing the premiums and reserve of the company. These resources yield a surplus which varies with the reserve on each policy, with the age of the insured, and with all the terms and conditions of the insurance. The system adapts itself to the incidents of each policy, and returns the surplus earnings from interest, and the excess of the payments for mor-

tality and expenses which belong to it. In brief, it seeks to give to each of the insured surplus which his money has earned or created. It requires no other statement than this to demonstrate its theoretical equity. The actual adation of the plan is demonstrated by the fact, its formulas are deduced from and harmonize the fundamental processes of life insurance, no mathematics either suggest or justify the centage plan.

In the appendix to the report, are communications from various officers of the companies whom the Commissioner had applied for information as to their opinions on the best mode of tribution.

PERSONAL APPLICATION.

It is a false delicacy which induces Agents to abstain from speaking to their friends and neighbours on the subject of Insurance. It is a matter of regret that too many are content to be silent on the subject, and to trust alone to the sending of bills, books, boards and brass plates.

If by any ingenious method short of a personal application persons can be induced to propose, these agents are quite willing to adopt it. But to call on a man and explain to him the assurance is a highly beneficial scheme which possibly be of inestimable future value to him, to urge upon a decision which heis more than persuaded to, is infra dig. This delicacy would in no way suffer, should he press upon the advantage of assuring his life or goods.

It not unfrequently happens that the solicitation to a man to assure saves the necessity would otherwise afterwards exist of soliciting charitable assistance on behalf of his children. Which is the more preferable? To ask a man to assure out of his own independent resources or to beg the favour of numerous votes and interest of the voters, on behalf of his son or daughters? No delicacy is felt about the latter. Surely none should be felt about the former. There should be no hesitation about personal application in as good a service.

In no business is it more necessary than surance wants explaining. To many it is a mystery of mysteries, a something which is expensive, and which people in good circumstances indulge in, a luxury for those who eat early peas and the first peas. They are not at all how it is obtainable. Some seem to have an impression that the entrance is a shadow rites of free masonry. As to whether it cost pound or twenty pounds, what the conditions and as to the mode of procedure, there are to be found everywhere who are perfectly ignorant. Nor are they limited to any class.

But even where a knowledge is possessed personal application is not the less necessary. Nine out of ten are indisposed to assure at once unwilling to do it without an infinite delay; is the one transaction of all others, about which there is no hurry. Tomorrow will serve as well to day, and next year will suit as well at present one.

Again, so much depends in Assurance ability of the issuers of the contract to fulfil a future day. The quality of the Assurance pends, as it were upon this, and personal exertion is eminently necessary to show the value of the commodity offered. A circular will convince a man of the soundness of an Office fully as viva voce replies to all his interrogatories. If then an Agent desires to be successful, make up his mind for "personal application" on an extended scale. All the ways for overwork an Agency which have ever been practised are before this.

In no business is it more successful every day. It is seen in town and city, almost every hamlet. It is in the records of every Insurance Office.

very little business is procured without a by Agents. So great has been the the the Agency system of Insurance Comring the last fifty years, that trading ll kinds have imitated it and planted icies in every direction. e mountain will not come to Mahomet, must go to the mountain." And so it hat as the people have not flocked to be 1e Agents have taken Assurance to them. s been the personal contact, the active n, the forcible illustration, the lucid n, the urgent persuasion of the Agent nversation with the people, that have 1e success. No other class of institu- no section of commerce, can show so é incomes permanently obtained as the ost solely of personal application. BUSINESS IS IT MORE EXCUSED.—Insur- its are always freely excused for seeking even from comparative strangers. The s they present of their being the repre- of a well-established and prosperous "known to fame," is a passport for f there no commission attaching to the n, the act would be the essence of ilanthropy but the benefit which an likely to reap from a policy is so much a any the Agent can possibly derive from dssion, that the invitation to propose the aspect of a personal service. On d the proofs have been multiplied of late 1e sterling advantages which Insurance d this has paved the way for a courteous of the subject when presented by a Agent. Many another representative d be shown the door, while the Agent of nce Office is received with respect. Some sound Companies have let loose on so- ar and untutored men—impecunious and less ; and these often meet with the fate ays deserve. It would be the same if s in any position. For the worthy Agent tantial Company, there is always a ready en for some intrusion in a personal appli-

1 who have tried this system need no urg- peat it. But to all who have never yet ed to establish an Agency we say em- y, try methodically and for a season, on 2rable scale; *Personal Application.—In- Agent.*

Railway News.

WESTERN RAILWAY.—Traffic for week th Sept., 1868.

engers	$38,480 53
ght and live stock	45,434 45
s and sundries	1,767 98
	$85,682 91
esponding Week of '67.	78,645 30
Decrease	$7,037 61

:ERN RAILWAY.—Traffic Receipts for ing Sept. 12, 1868.

engers	$3,475 26
ght	7,915 77
s and Sundries	260 82
l Receipts for week	$11,651 85
esponding week 1867	9,909 13
:crease	$1,742 72

:NGTON, GREY and BRUCE RAILWAY.— ilton papers say that the tender of Messrs. Hill, for the construction of the first f this road has been accepted, and that will be gone on with at once.

RAILWAY BONUSES.—The Township of West Whitby passed a by-law on the 19th inst., grant- ing a bonus of $15,000 to aid in the building of the Whitby & Port Perry Railway. On the same day, the Township of Uxbridge passed a by-law granting $50,000 to aid the construction of the Toronto & Nipissing Railway.

RAILWAY APPOINTMENTS.—The Windsor *Record* says, several important changes took place in the staff of the Great Western Railway officials at this station. Mr. Craft, superintendent of the through traffic, removed his office and the whole corps of clerks to Detroit, which will, hereafter, be his head quarters. Mr. Dow will remain station-master here, and will, in addition to these duties, act as local freight agent ; Mr. Stonier will be cashier of the local freight; and Mr. Jones, who has heretofore had charge of the freight department in Detroit, will shortly be promoted —most likely to be general western agent.

A NEW PROPOSITION.—A gentleman writing from Quebec to the *Investor's Guardian,* London, England, under date of 14th August, after some introductory remarks, makes the following sug- gestion :—

"I now come to the real point on which I wish to address you, and this has reference to your inquiry, on behalf of several shareholders, whether "an American railroad company or companies could not be got to lease or work the Grand Trunk, and leave a sufficient amount to cover certain bonds and the other preferences on the other side ?"

To this really important question I, with some practical leading railway parties in Montreal, have not only devoted some time and attention, but we have gone so far as to lay it before gentle- men intimately associated with very important railroad interests connected with Boston, U. S.

We first of all proceeded to work out what was at present stated by the directors to be the annual net revenue of the whole Grand Trunk system, and assuming this net revenue at £1,400,000, and comparing their present outgoings or expenses, which amount really to about 80 per cent., we showed them that on this amount 10 per cent. we the very least can be saved—say ...... £140,000 Ditto, by working in unison with these American railroad lines connected prin- cipally with the outside agencies 15,000

£155,000

Ditto salaries of chief officers in Canada, of president and other officers in Eng- land ...... 10,000 Improvement to net revenue by working under this proposed system 40,000

£205,000

These statements were given them of course in detail, and, through these figures, a knowledge of which these gentlemen were almost as conversant with as ourselves, we fully satisfied them of the safety of embarking their interests with such an almost bankrupt concern as the Grand Trunk.

The result has been that, concurring in these views, a gentleman, intimately acquainted with these railroad parties, and with all the details as to how the American railroads are worked, will go home by the steamer 'Nestorian' on the 22nd from here, and on arriving at Liverpool will im- mediately proceed to London, prepared with an offer to rent certain portions of the Grand Trunk, or the whole, on certain terms and conditions, the principles on which the offer is based being a lease or rent of the whole line, backed by capitalists of Boston, who could produce guarantees for one *million dollars* if required, they agreeing or bind- ing themselves to pay over (over and above what- ever the net revenue may be on 30th June last) a clear sum of upwards of two hundred thousand pounds—a result which, I feel sure, without some such combination in connection with these rail- roads in the States connected with Boston, will not be obtained under the present system.

Mr. H——, the gentleman named, will have letters of introduction to several railway author- ities.

I am satisfied that the more any one looks at the "past" of the Grand Trunk, and takes in a review of its connection with the great trades or traffic of this Continent, the more he must be im- pressed with the actual necessity of engrafting it more and more into the present great American system of railways. Without them it is entirely at their mercy, and *per se,* it may go on for years trying to carry their traffic at "through" compet- itive rates, and it will continue to fail ; but con- nect it with these interests "thoroughly," and before many years are over it would be paying a dividend on the whole £100 stock *now worth £16 to the £100 !"*

GRAND TRUNK.

Let us suppose that the traffic on the line is worked at 60 per cent. This we believe is ample to pay all working expenses, including renewals for fully keeping the line in repair, if the line throughout were in good order. 40 per cent. as the fair working profit would be about £550,000 a year. All the interest, &c., charges prior to the 1st preference are about £200,000 a year, leaving say £350,000 for the 1st, 2nd, 3rd, and 4th pre- ferences, as far as it would go in meeting those claims. Now the 1st preference interest is some £125,000 a year, the 2nd preference £68,000, the 3rd preference £28,000, and the 4th £150,000.

	Per Annum.
1st preference	£125,000
2nd "	68,000
3rd "	28,000
4th "	150,000
	£371,000

It follows that if the profits were only 40 per cent. of the traffic, if the working expenses were as high as 60 per cent., the present profits would be nearly equal to paying the 4th preference in full after discharging every claim of 1st, 2nd, and 3rd preferences.

But the Company want to renew large portions of their line within better rails, &c., so as to have a first-class road. How are they to do it? They can't raise further capital.

If the £350,000 be employed in renewing the road, &c., the renewals may be done all the sooner, but the 1st preference cannot be paid in cash. The 1st preference, however, are crying out lustily for their cash dividends, and if they cannot (and we believe they cannot) have any for the past June half-year they will try for some in the current December half-year.

Under the Arrangements Act the 1st and 2nd preference Bondholders are really nothing more than preference Shareholders to the end of 1872. After that, from the beginning of 1873, they are Bondholders, and then their interest (and that of the 2nd preference bonds) must be paid, but until that time arrives if the management uses their money in renewals they cannot prevent it. The only thing they can do is to change the manage- ment.

A large and important section of the Grand Trunk Proprietors are dissatisfied with the management of the line. They believe that results widely dif- ferent from the present could be obtained by better management; that the working expenses could be materially economised, and a much larger revenue balance left either for renewals or for preference dividends. Out of a gross revenue of £1,350,000 a year we think at least £550,000 profit may be had. This would leave the working expenses at about 60 per cent., or nearly £600 per mile per annum. Speaking recently with a railway authority who had travelled over the line, he agreed with us that about £600 per mile per annum, or 60 per cent. of the present traffic, ought to be very ample to cover all working expenses in respect of the present traffic, including a large sum for maintenance.

Besides ordinary maintenance no doubt the line requires most extensive renewing, in fact rails, &c., which it never had, new stations, sidings, fish-platings, signals, trimming and draining of the slopes of cuttings, wharfage, completion of ballasting &c. Undoubtedly the Company require a large sum to expend in completing and perfecting their great line. This circumstance seems to us to amount to additional evidence of the importance of working the traffic with the greatest economy, so as to extract from it the largest amount of profit, or this profit could either be applied to doing the renewals, &c., or to paying the preference dividends. If employed in finishing the line it would be advantageously used, for this would enable the Company to carry more traffic, to earn a larger profit, and when the 1st 2nd, 3rd, and 4th preference holders knew that the money to pay their dividends was earned but spent in the line, they receiving paper dividends in lieu thereof, they would know that it could only last for a comparatively short period; that it was for the good of the Company, and ultimately for their own benefit. If, on the other hand, the money was paid away in dividends upon the 1st, 2nd, 3rd, and 4th preferences the credit of the Company would be so improved that they could easily raise the required additional capital on a second equipment mortgage. There would clearly be an advantage to the Company in the enlargement of the working profits. It is a perfectly legitimate and highly useful proceeding on the part of the Proprietors to closely investigate the affairs of the Company, with a view to a thorough reform in the management. If they find that a different system of management would place at their disposal a much larger amount of working profit they are entitled to carry the reform.

It is important to place the Grand Trunk railway, at the earliest moment, in the best condition for carrying traffic. Canada is a rising country. The population and business of Montreal have nearly doubled in the last few years, and the great towns of the Dominion generally are "looking up" with a bright aspect. The Intercolonial railway is carried, and this will do the Grand Trunk much good, always provided they do not lose by its working (if they work it)—which seems to us a further reason for the Proprietors to closly attend to their affairs. As it is the Grand Trunk traffic has greatly increased. In the last report of the Directors it is stated—"In 1861 the gross traffic of the line was £920,579, whilst in 1866, on the same mileage, it was £1,356,795, or an increase of 47½ per cent." Without another mile of line it will, we believe, be £2,000,000 by 1873, if the Intercolonial is then in operation, and if the full working powers of the line are brought to bear. We say, then, that there is something substantial to get by good management, and we should consider it the worst of management, to neglect placing the line in the best order and the rolling stock in full supply and condition.

£2,000,000 a year gross income, from which probably the net would be £1,000,000, would render the Grand Trunk a highly successful undertaking.—*Herepath's Journal.*

Financial.

MONTREAL MONEY MARKET.

(From our own Correspondent.)

MONTREAL, Sept. 22, 1868.

Very little is doing in money circles and the tone of the market is unchanged; so far, very little accommodation is asked at the banks for money to remove grain; good paper is scarce and there is to alteration in rates either at the banks or in the street. Stocks are scarce, but the enquiry is moderate. Bank of Montreal would sell freely at 135½. British in demand at 103, but none in the market. Ontario a shade better. Merchants' dull and heavy. Peoples' in light request at 105½. For City 102 is offered without attracting sellers. Toronto held at 117, but no buyers over 115½. Miscellaneous stocks are generally held for high figures but not much movement in them. Gold has slowly declined during the week, the market closing at 142⅝, this is owing to the low rate of sterling exchange in New York, which is only worth 8¾; so far the Presidential contest has not affected the gold market, to what extent it will remains to be seen. Greenbacks buyiug price 30¼, selling 29¾ to 30 dis. Gold drafts in New York par to ⅛ dis. Silver in good supply at 3½ buying, and 3 selling. Sterling exchange dull at 9 to 9¼ for bank.

The *silver nuisance.*—As promised in my last letter I now give you a synopsis of Mr. Weir's Circular on this subject. Last spring Mr. Weir made an effort to abate the nuisance, but it was not sufficiently comprehensive to affect its object, and lately, he has been delayed in taking any action, being unwilling to interfere with the movement in the Province of Ontario, which at one time promised considerable success. He goes on the basis that the duty of 15 per cent. on American silver is prohibitory, therefore, if the surplus silver can be exported from the country, and kept out of it, the evil will be removed. The total amount of silver in the country has little to do with the rate of discount, it is only the quantity not required for *change*, which accumulates in the banks and broker's hands, this sum he estimates at $1,000,000 and another million in the hands of the public which could be spared. *He proposes to export two million dollars, say $50,000 per week for forty weeks, commencing the 15th October next.* The removal of that amount would leave little more than is required for small change and reduce the discount permanently to one or two per cent., causing the volume of business to be transacted in gold and bank notes. The cost of exporting $50,000 silver, purchased at 2½ per cent. dis. will be (including commissions, interest, &c.) about $3,000, which amount he proposes to raise in accordance with a form of contract, but should the support tendered fall short of the amount required to insure him against loss, of course the movement falls to the ground.

TORONTO STOCK MARKET.

(Reported by Pellatt & Osler, Brokers.)

Very little doing in the stock market owing to the scarcity of securities.

Bank Stock.—Very few transactions in Montreal stock; buyers offer 134½. Sellers ask 98 for Ontario, and sales occurred during the week at 98¼ and 98¾. Small lots of Toronto offer at 116 to 116½. There are buyers of Royal Canadian at 91 for paid up stock. Buyers offer 104 for paid up Commerce. Sellers ask 105½ for Merchants', buyers offer 105. There are sellers of City at 102½ and buyers at 101½. Du Peuple is held at 105½. Buyers offer 106 for Jacques Cartier. Sellers ask 97 for Mechanics', buyers offering 94½. There are buyers of Union at 102, and sellers at 103. In other banks nothing to report.

Debentures.—Canada are in great demand. No sterling six per cents in market. Five per cents offering at 91, and Dominion stock at 101½. There were sales of short date Toronto bonds to pay 7 per cent. interest. A few County are offering at high rates, and small lots have been taken.

Sundries.—Building Society Stock is again up and is now saleable at rates never before reached; the last sales of Canada Permanent were at 119½. Buyers offer 112½ for Western Canada; no sellers. Freehold sold at 105½ and 106¼, and is in demand. There were sales of Montreal Telegraph at 134 to 134½. Buyers offer 62½ to 63 for Canada Landed Credit, $20 paid. City Gas sold at 105 to 105½, and is offered at 105, ex dividend due 1st October. British America was offering at 56; no sales. Mortgages, none to be had. Money continues very easy, and offers at low rates on good security.

AMERICAN SECURITIES HELD IN EUROPE... *N. Y. Financial Chronicle* gives the fo... table of the amount of American Railw... Canal Stocks owned in Europe:—

Atlantic and St. Lawrence Railroad sterling bonds		$
Eastern R.R. (Mass) sterling bonds		
Western R.R. (Mass.)	do. ...	4,
Erie Railroad	do. ...	4,
Panama Railroad	do. ...	1,
Camden and Amboy R.R.	do. ...	1,
South Carolina Railroad	do. ...	2,
Pennsylvania Railroad	do. ...	2,
Philadelphia and Reading Railroad, sterling bonds		
Baltimore and Ohio Railroad (Md. guar.) sterling bonds		3,
Eaton and Hamilton Railroad		
Marietta and Cincinnati R.R. ...about		
Detroit and Milwaukee Railroad		
Michigan Central Railroad		
Chicago, Burlington and Quincy Railroad bonds (Frankford)		1,
Illinois Central Railroad, ster'g bonds		3,
Troy and Greenfield Railroad		
Mobile and Ohio Railroad		4,
Total		$33,

Sterling Canal and Water Bonds:—

Boston Water bonds	$1,949,000	
Chesapeake & Ohio Canal bonds	1,949,000	
Susquehanna and Tide-water Canal bonds	816,000	
Illinois Canal bonds	1,850,000	
		$8,9
Total Canal ster'g bonds		8,9
Add further for dollar bonds, railroad and other, including $35,000,000 Illinois Central		60,0

Add further for Railroad stocks:—

Atlantic & Great Western	$15,000,000	
Erie	6,000,000	
Illinois Central	17,500,000	
Philadelphia & Reading	10,000,000	
All other roads	7,500,000	
Total Railroad stock		56,
Total transportation securities		$158,

The issues of the five-twenties of 1862 i... 000,000; and from the extreme scarcity ... bonds it is very generally conceded that t... nearly all held abroad. Of the sixes of 18... are $283,000,000 outstandingr which also ... cipally in the hands of foreigners. The p... for ten-forties, on acoount of the specific... for the payment of the principal in gold, have drawn out of the country less than $... 000 of those bonds; while the minor am... all other issues combined cannot be estin... less than $50,000,000. So that the total of United State bonds held abroad must ... nearly $700,000,000, or possibly more. ... together, then, the foregoing items, we ... following result, as the amount of all ... American securities held in Europe:—

United States bonds	$700
Sterling bonds issued by railroad companies	33
Sterling bonds issued by canal and water companies	8
Dollar bonds of railroad and other companies	60
Railroad Stocks	56
State Stocks	60
Municipal and miscellaneous stocks,	22
Total estimated amount of American securities held abroad	$938

—It is stated that the Ontario Legisla... meet on the 3rd of November.

☞ THE CANADIAN MONETARY TIMES AND INSURANCE CHRONICLE *is printed every Thursday Evening, in time for the English Mail.*

Subscription Price, one year, $2, or $3 in American currency; Single copies, five cents each. Casual advertisements will be charged ten cents per line of solid nonpareil each insertion. All letters to be addressed, "THE CANADIAN MONE-TARY TIMES, TORONTO, ONT." Registered letters so addressed are at the risk of the Publishers. Cheques should be made payable to J. M. TROUT, Business Manager, who will, in future, issue all receipts for money.

The Canadian Monetary Times.

THURSDAY, SEPTEMBER 24, 1868.

BANK STATEMENTS AND STERLING BILLS.

In directing attention to the duties and responsibilities of Bank directors, we urged the necessity of a careful and intelligent supervision of the bank affairs, free, on the one hand from mere prying curiosity and injudicious interference with the rights of the cashier, and on the other, from passive inattention to the banks' position and interests. We also condemned a too careless acceptance of mere general information, as if that were all which is entailed upon directors by their office. It is true that a cashier has a great deal of power, and if his character and ability be such as to command respect, his suggestions and advice will have the greatest weight with his directors. The latter being selected for their respectability or business knowledge, are supposed to bring to bear supervisory powers which derive value from their experience in business, but their acquaintance with banking principles is, of course, limited, and their knowledge of detail in the bank's operations must of necessity be imperfect. They have not time to examine every transaction thoroughly even if they had the opportunity. They express opinions and adopt resolutions as to future action, and the cashier has upon his shoulders the onus of working out their wishes. Such being the case, one can easily understand how important it is to have carefully prepared statements submitted to them. In some banks the statements are of such a character that the directors can at once appreciate the nature of the business done, not only in the aggregate, but in elaborate details which their business experience can grasp and dissect. It is for them to insist upon such statements as convey the necessary information being produced by the cashier, and it is for the cashier to devise such forms of statement as will place affairs in the clearest light. When we remember that directors are not only called upon to give judgment on the advisability of increasing or decreasing accommodation to individual customers, but also to understand the bank's relative powers and position in the ever changing aspects of the trade of the country, and even its safety in times of financial difficulty, we can estimate the value of full and accurate information.

It may fairly enough be assumed that no better or truer statement of a bank's position could be desired by a director, than the general balance sheet with a synopsis of the particular accounts which appear on it. To that one would naturally look for information, and probably no better guide could be suggested for acquiring a general knowledge of how the bank's affairs really stand. There is, however, an important particular in the preparation of those balance sheets which renders them an unreliable guide without explanation from the cashier. They are supposed to show the whole of the bank's liabilities and the whole of its assets, but we contend that they do not serve that purpose. By a strange anomaly, bills discounted which happen to be drawn payable in Europe, never appear on the balance sheet at all. No matter what may be their number, their character, or their amount, not one of them is seen under the proper heading of "Bills Discounted," in the bank's statements. They are rigidly excluded from that, the most striking asset in the balance sheet. In referring to this practice, in a former article, we were not aware that the point had been made before, but we find in the answers to the Senate questions the following:

"Many if not all the banks charge sterling bills of exchange to their English correspondents, the moment they are purchased or sent off by mail, although they may have 60' 90, or even 120 days to run before maturity. By doing so, these bills disappear from the balance sheet of the bank, notwithstanding its liability for their endorsement. They ought in all cases to appear amongst the assets of the bank until paid, being as much 'bills discounted' as any other bills cashed by them."

This extract will be found in the evidence of Mr. Morton, whose experience in the Bank of Upper Canada doubtless taught him how dangerous such a practice as that we complain of might prove. As we have said, we were not aware when the previous article was written that we were but following in Mr. Morton's footsteps; and while we apologise to that gentleman for the seeming appropriation of his idea, we are glad to be able to cite a gentleman of his ability and practical banking experience as an authority in our favour.

The practice complained of, is manifestly wrong. It is surely absurd to suppose that a bill drawn at 90 days on Montreal, New York or Baltimore, ought to be charged to

"Bills Discounted" and looked upon as an asset until paid, but that a bill in all respects similar which happens to be drawn on a house in Europe should not be regarded at all as an asset by the bank although it cashed it! Yet such is the case practically, for there is this difference in the treatment of these two classes of advances on bills, viz., that while a bill drawn payable in America is held on the balance sheet as an advance carrying with it a certain risk until paid, no matter how good the names may be; a bill drawn payable in Europe is treated as if it were actual cash, no matter how weak the names to it may be.

We are fully aware of the causes which have given rise to this reprehensible practice. We know that bankers in England receive mercantile bills of exchange from Canadian bankers who keep accounts with them as if they were so much cash, to this extent, that when indorsed by the bank sending them they are looked upon as a credit to be drawn against. This being the case the Canadian banks are in the habit of charging these mercantile bills to their English correspondents as if they actually were cash remitted, while, by way of balancing the charge, they credit their English correspondents with such bills as they themselves may draw. The practice has undoubtedly its conveniences. It saves some little trouble in bookkeeping. But the mere fact that a London banker accepts the exchange of a Canadian bank against the hypothecation of indorsed mercantile bills, does not render such mercantile bills cash. If unpaid, they are returned upon the bank in the same way as any other unpaid bills, and, therefore, they ought to appear amongst the assets under their proper heading until paid or until it can reasonably be supposed they are paid. Let them be charged to that account till then. Exactness of accounts, which we are entitled to expect in a bank, demands this. If the bank desire that its statements should have a good appearance and be, at the same time, perfectly correct, no great harm would be done if it were to include among the "cash deposits" these bills of exchange which have not matured, drawn by itself on its English correspondents. This latter is, however, a matter of little consequence and may be safely left to the bank's discretion.

Some banks include their English bills in a memorandum book purporting to shew the liabilities of customers, but this is not enough. It does not fully meet the case. The custom of charging these sterling bills purchased, or, in other words, discounted to English bankers, when mailed instead of when paid is one which, we believe, prevails with almost all the banks in Canada and, we repeat, that it

is a custom open to the greatest objections. It practically amounts to a re-discounting of customers' paper without recording on the balance sheet the amount of such re-discounts, and is a use of the bank's credit which may, at any moment, merge into an abuse. So long as such a system prevails, so long will there be a risk of false impressions as to the true position of a bank's affairs, when the concealment of imprudent advances becomes desirable. Under such a practice, indeed, it becomes an easy matter, or, at least, quite possible to conceal a bad debt from the balance sheet, and keep it out of sight perhaps for years, by merely transforming it into a sterling bill of exchange, and keeping it constantly renewed. But even if there were no danger of such an extreme result flowing from the practice, the fact that it enables a Cashier to make heavy advances to a certain class of customers without in the least degree swelling the item of "bills discounted" is sufficient to condemn it.

TRADE MARKS.

Of late years reputation as a marketable commodity has greatly increased in importance, the measure of it has been ascertained and the value enhanced. In speaking of reputation we mean that intangible ideal property founded on the tendency of mankind to follow each others' lead, to lodge where they have lodged before, "the probability of the old custom reverting to the old place," which is commonly called good-will. For many years the good-will of inns and taverns has been recognized, bought and sold and protected by the courts. It grew up at the time when the means of locomotion were scanty and slow, and lodgings at way-side inns were large items of expense to the traveler. At that time trade was stationary and goods were to a great extent sold in the locality where they were manufactured. Railways came and swept the country hostelries away, good-will and all, killed off local industries and centralised production in large manufactures, whence goods were sent at prices and of a quality with which it was useless to compete. And with the new life and new modes of doing business, good-will assumed another phase and is now commonly called trade marks. The food we eat, the wines, beer, and spirits we drink, the clothes we wear, the needles and thread with which they are put together, everything in fact comes from large factories, are sent wholesale to every part of the world, and are compounded and prepared by companies, managed with unwearied energy, skill and care. Consequently it becomes of the utmost importance to both the vendor and purchaser that the goods sold should be what

they pretend to be and that imitation well-known names, marks and labels, sh be prevented.

Accordingly, a branch of mercantile la being consolidated, defining what are t marks, what are imitations, where courts interfere against, and what restrictions be placed on and damages awarded ag imitators.

Trade marks may for general purpos defined as a peculiar name, design, w or arrangements of words by which a ce quality of goods or a certain proprietor become widely known and acquired a ma able value, and such a marked name that nary buyers using the name would at get the article required.

Imitations consist of such a general larity of form, color, or name, as to h direct tendency to mislead ordinary bu Where ordinary attention on the pa purchasers would enable them to observ imitation, it is not, in the eyes of the la infringement of the trade mark, but i ordinary mass of purchasers, paying attention which people would usually p purchasing the articles in question, probably be deceived, then courts interfere. It must appear, however, there is such a distinctive individuali the mark or name employed by the cou feiter, as to procure him the benefit deception resulting from the general blance between the genuine and the terfeit.

The name or designation must, ho have a distinctive peculiarity. In th brated essence of anchovies case, wher gess, the son, used the same name father, viz: "Burgess' essence of anch and the father tried to restrain hin doing so, an eminent judge remarked "no man can have any right to repres goods as the goods of another, but those cases it must be made out that fendant is selling his own goods as the of another." In another case, a manuf had applied for protection against using the name " white soft soap," by his own wares had become known, but a person making white soap would ha entitled to call it by the same nam application was refused. To illustra principle, the use of the name "imperia with the addition of a star, was for even when the name bibassic was in on the ground that it was an infringe the chief part of a name or label b the plaintiff's goods were well known, the use of which, by the defendant, tl lic were deceived.

Trade marks which contain false re tations will not be protected.

tain the assistance of the courts, the seeking it must apply promptly on ning the infringement; indolent obn of the public advertisement of the ment or the display of the labels, is as acquiescence, and good ground for relief when the application is made ne afterwards.

on as a case of infringement of trade s proved, the courts will interfere by on, restraining the imitator from r selling the counterfeit, and cong him in expenses, and thereafter, e defendant and all other persons wilsing it will be liable to an action for s at the suit of the true owner.

ry simple and inexpensive system of tion of trade marks has been for some in force in Canada, England, and s, and this system is eminently useful preventing innocent imitations by dealers, and in enabling proprietors ve their own trade marks, and the of time during which they have been

OTTON CROP OF THE STATES.

ral American journals publish stateof the crop and the course of the trade for the year ending Sept. 1st of sent year. From these it appears that ole crop amounted to 2,498,895 bales, 2,019,774 bales last year. The exrom the United States were 1,657,015 and the stock on hand at the close of r 38,130 bales. In the interior towns ok of cotton at the above date was ales, against 5,703 bales the previous . The total receipts at the Atlantic lf shipping ports were 2,240,282 bales, 1,965,774 bales last year. If we add e figures the amount shipped directly ufacturers, we have the total crop as given.

the different cotton-growing States, ana stands first in the quantity of cotised, the total being 534,240 bales, 702,131 bales last year; then come a, Tennessee, Alabama, South Caro-Virginia, Texas, etc., in the order

yield of cotton steadily increased from 0 bales in 1820-21, to 4,669,770 bales in 9—the largest crop ever raised. Due war no record was kept, but since r the amount produced has increased half a million of bales, showing clearly is important interest is reviving. The f Sea Island cotton was 21,275 bales, an average of about 45,000 bales in years immediately preceding the war,

Prices in Liverpool ranged from 10½ to 15¾ in 1866-67, and from 7¼ to 12⅜ in 1867-8, showing a much lower range of prices in the latter year.

NOVA SCOTIAN FINANCES.

The Estimates for 1868 have been laid before the Nova Scotia Legislative Assembly. The expenditure up to the 31st December is estimated at $563,880, and the income $551,088 76, leaving a probable deficit of 12,791 24 made up as follows :—

ESTIMATED EXPENDITURE.

Civil List.	$41,800
Criminal Prosecutions................. ...	2,000
Coroners' Inquests........................	2,000
Education	165,000
Immigration	800
Legislative Expenses......	34,000
Miscellaneous...........	18,520
Deaf and Dumb Institutions............	2,000
Agriculture	6,000
Department of Works....................	65,000
Navigation Securities....	10,000
Poor's Asylum............	2,000
Poor's Asylum (New)...................	3,000
Public Printing.........................	8,000
Relief.................................	3,000
Road Compensation......................	500
Roads and Bridges.......	100,000
Transient Poor.........................	3,400
Steamboats, Packets and Ferries........	3,860
Provincial Exhibition..................	3,000
New Provincial Building.................	41,000
Total............................	$563,880

ESTIMATED INCOME.

Assets 1st January, 1868:—

Balance in hand of Treasurer	$38,700 50	
Education.......................	22,885 77	
Immigration	1,000 00	
Arrears........	119,509 29	
		$183,135 58

Probable Revenue for 1868:—		
Department of Mines...	$90,000 00	
Hospital for Insane...	20,000 00	
Crown Lands..............	22,000 00	
Balance of Subsidy....	235,953 18	
		$367,953 18

Total.......................		$551,088 76

Estimated Expenditure for 1868.. ...	$563,880 00
Income for 1868...................	551,088 76

Probable Deficit.................	$12,791 24

Taking for granted that this estimate is fair, we really cannot see where the proposed $50,000 secret service money is to come from. It is not likely that a loan for bringing about a dissolution of the Confederation could be floated in London.

THE NORTH WEST.

It is announced that the Privy Council at Ottawa have appointed the Hon. Messrs. McDougall and Cartier, as a delegation to England in the matter of the ownership of the vast tract of country known as the North West Territory. That huge monopoly, the Hudson's Bay Company, is determined to

fight stoutly for its preserves, and its influence, both in and out of Parliament, is anything but despicable. Its position is favorable for defensive purposes, not only length of possession but also present occupation and enjoyment being a formidable weapon against the party compelled to attack. The maxim, *nullum tempus occurrit regi* may be perfectly sound but as between Canada, claimant and the Hudson's Bay Company, tenant, it will not be accepted as conclusive. A considerable number of influential Englishmen have a direct pecuniary interest in sustaining the Company's claims, and we may rest assured that no stone will be left unturned by them to secure the best possible bargain for the interest they represent. The situation is undoubtedly understood and appreciated by our Government, and those delegated to sustain our cause before the Imperial Government will, we are confident, do well whatever can be done to prevent advantage being taken of our expressed intention and manifest willingness to become purchasers. Although the matter is of great importance to the Dominion, it is of special interest to the Province of Ontario, and should Mr. McDougall and his colleagues succeed in their mission, they will have earned for themselves the gratitude of every western Canadian. The fact is, we must annex the North West. Between Lake Superior and the Red River settlement, the country is in a state of nature, but a line of communication is projected, which, when completed, will render the country accessible. The trade of the North West Territories may be drawn to Canada. The people of Red River at present purchase their goods in St. Paul, and take them thence full six hundred miles overland to the settlement, and the cost of freight is from four and a half to five dollars per 100 lbs. Mr. Dawson, whose report has been published, is confident that if communication with Canada were opened, the cost of transport from Lake Superior to Red River would not exceed $1.75 per 100 lbs. It is estimated that even now a trade amounting to several millions of dollars annually, would be transferred to Canada. The state of Minesota is doing a good deal to facilitate intercourse with the settlement, and it becomes our authorities to be up and doing before our opportunity has gone by.

SUGAR DUTIES.

As mentioned in our issue of last week, a conference of the four contracting powers to what is known as the Drawback Convention—England, France, Holland and Belgium—has been held at The Hague. No account of the proceedings has yet appeared. The discussion was, according to the Paris *Moniteur*, in reference to Article 13, which had the effect of protecting the French refiners as against the refiners of the other countries named, to the extent of 2 shillings per cwt. This article has been so remodelled as to remove this anomaly. It is not thought that this change will benefit the English refiners, as English refines are not saleable in France, they being, according to the *Produce Markets Review*, made with a large crystal, to chop well and look brilliant, whereas French sugar is sawn into squares, and to prevent waste, is made with as small a grain as possible. Instead of being benefitted, the journal just quoted thinks that the change in the terms of the Convention will operate to the detriment of the English refiners, inasmuch as it will strengthen the hands of their Dutch and Belgian competitors. It is complained, too, that the French refiners adopt in practice only two rates of duty on raw sugar, while by the terms of the Convention they should have a graduated scale of four duties, thus giving them a great advantage, by enabling them to use as rich a sugar as possible. An understanding has been arrived at with France to do away with the bounty of five francs on the import of French Colonial sugar, and also the bounty on the import in French ships. It is not known whether a bounty of four per cent. on the import of Java sugar into Holland, which has been hitherto paid, has been stopped, but this is regarded by the English refiners as a flagrant violation of the principle of the treaty.

The *Produce Markets Review* concludes an article on the subject in the following words: —" For ourselves, we have all along regarded the Drawback Convention as a piece of waste paper, fit only for the rubbish shelves of Downing Street. The system of buying by analysis, by which, as we have shown elsewhere, the French refiners can obtain a bounty of 8d. to 1s. per cwt., has for ever destroyed all systems founded on color, and this bounty is in no way affected by the changes made at Hague. We are of opinion that nothing can keep foreign sugar out of England except an even duty, which would force our refiners to work from fine sugar, and to separate entirely the manufacture of Pieces and Loaves."

WOODEN RAILWAYS.

Notice has been given that application will be made at the next session of Parliament for a charter to construct a wooden Railway from North Douro, County of Peterboro, to Haliburton, one of the townships owned by the Canadian Land and Emigration Company. It is expected that the Port Hope and Peterboro' Railway will be extended to North Douro, and that a conjunction of the lines will be formed there.

Communications.

MADOC GOLD DISTRICT.

(From our own Correspondent.)

Belleville, Sept. 21st. 1868.

As I hinted in my last week's letter I went on Tuesday to inspect the quartz vein newly discovered on lot 30, in the sixth concession of Madoc, a specimen said to be taken from which yielded the handsome assay rate of $378.00 to the ton; and as it is nearly typical of those lately found in the district, I shall give a somewhat detailed account of what I observed.

The place where it is opened is about three quarters of a mile from the village of Bannockburn in a northeasterly direction. The vein runs along the gently sloping side of a small valley where a clearing of a few acres in extent has been made, and has only about a foot of loose earth on the top. The lode consists of a vein of massive quartz of a porcelain like appearance, with a rather greasy thin glassy fracture, and running in the direction of N. 30° E. by compass. It is enclosed by two well-defined wall rocks, that on the west side being of mica-schist, dipping at an angle of about 87 degrees to the west, while that on the east is of a soft talc-schist, dipping towards the east with an inclination of about 80 degrees, so that the vein appears to widen as it goes downwards at an angle of perhaps 12 degrees. Besides gold, the veinstone contains a few scattered crystals of iron sulphurets, scales and plates of titanic iron, and a distinct, though interrupted vein of galena (sulphide of lead) runs along the middle part, with an average thickness of about half an inch. It has only been exposed for some ten feet along the lead, but has been traced across nearly the whole of lot No. 29, and for some 50 rods on lot No. 30, where it enters the side of a piece of rising ground under the cover of the woods, where the discoverer ceased to follow it any further.

On arriving at the spot, my first care was to ascertain whether I could discern any gold *in situ*; and I succeeded in fishing up from the bottom of the hole, which is about two feet deep, and then contained a few inches of water from the late rains, a few fragments of quartz containing shews of gold. I then chipped off a few pieces from the solid quartz of the vein, and found the precious metal in some of them, which satisfied me of the genuineness of the discovery, and of the good faith of the fortunate finder.

On leaving, I brought away a quantity of quartz with me, and since my return, I have made an assay of 5 lbs., selecting such rock as did not show any gold on the surface of the pieces. From this I obtained by simple amalgamation a return of gold at the rate of $13.64 per ton.

It is the opinion of some of the practical men who are prospecting in that neighborhood, that this is an extension of some of the gold-bearing veins lately found in the township of Marmora, to which I alluded in my last letter, and indeed, the magnetic bearing being nearly the same, and the quartz closely agreeing with the Marmora type, even to the presence of the galena, which occurs in some of the Marmora veins in a disseminated form, that I scarcely wonder at their drawing the inference, though I had rather not express an opinion as to its correctness.

The chattel sale at the Richardson mine took place on Tuesday, 15th inst. The ore on hand, 100 tons, was sold at 50 cents per ton. The furniture of the agent's house and other movables were bought in on behalf of the Company.

On my way I visited the mill of the Anglo-Saxon Company. It consists of a Blake crusher to prepare the ore for the stamps, which are 30 in number, divided into three batteries of ten stamps each, to each battery is a grinding pan of some seven feet in diameter, and a row of ten Wyckoff cylinders, 30 in all, the batteries are so arranged as to work independently of each other. When I was there, the only parts in motion were the

breaker and one row of oscillating cylinders. T whole of the machinery is of the most mass description, and has been got up without reg to expense; but it does not meet the approbati of the California men, who do not approve of Wyckoff system of amalgamating, preferring pans throughout.

The mill of the Toronto and Whitby Comp is being erected close to the village of Bann burn. Mr. March, their very gentlemanly sup intendent, informs me that he expects to have running by Christmas, he is quite sanguine as the success of the Company's enterprise.

Intelligence has been received from the Sev Mill in the eleventh concession of Marmora, wh has been working on rock from the Feigel mi 32 tons have been put through, and the return stated at $608 in gold, or at the rate of $19 ton. I hear, however, that a chancery suit been entered, and an injuction issued to prev the present holders to take any more quartz f the mine till the question of title shall have b determined.

THE ENGLISH TELEGRAPH ACT.

The statute to enable the Postmaster-Genera England to acquire, work, and maintain elec telegraphs is an important measure, and of wh the following is a summary: In 24 sections preamble affirms that the means of commun tion within the United Kingdom are insufficie and that many districts are without; that it we be attended with great advantage to the State well as to merchants and traders, and to the pu generally, if a cheaper, more widely extended, more expeditious system of telegraphy were es lished, and to that end the Postmaster-Genera empowered to work telegraphs in connection v the Post-office. The uniform rate, subject to ulation, of messages throughout the United K dom, and without regard to distance, is to be rate not exceeding 1s. for the first 20 words, not exceeding 3d. for each additional five w or part of five words. The Postmaster-Gener now authorised, with the consent of the Treas "out of any moneys which may be from tim time appropriated by act of Parliament, and at his disposal for that purpose, to purchase whole or such parts as he shall think fit of undertaking of any Company." Telegraph panies are empowered to sell their underta under certain conditions specified, with a prov as to the appointment of their servants b Government, or compensation by way of ann The Postmaster-General is to enter into cont with certain Railway Companies mentioned i act, and very specific directions are given such acquisition, to transmit all messages Railway Company in any way relating t business of the Company in the United Kin free of charge. All matters of difference bet the Postmaster-General and Railway Comp are to be settled by arbitration. The sum t received by Reuter's Telegraph Company is applied in the first instance to the payment o debts and liabilities of the Company. The provisions in the statute to enable the Postm to acquire the right of way over canals. S agreements may be made with newspaper pr tors and with the occupiers of news-rooms, or exchange rooms, to transmit messages at a not exceeding 1s. for every 100 words betwe a.m. and 6 p.m., and special use of a wire obtained under regulations, without undue pri or preference; messages having priority are specially marked, and all messages are to be by means of stamps, which are to be kept for to the public at offices under the control o Postmaster-General, to be appointed for that pose. It is a misdemeanor in any person h official duties to disclose or to intercept mess Copies of all contracts and agreements made the act are to be laid before Parliament. I schedule annexed to the act, thirteen agreer with Railways and Telegraph Companies are

ect to the approbation of Parliament, res it to be expedient that agreements ade with other railways set forth, in- metropolitan districts. Three months' be given by the Postmaster-General panies. The Postmaster-General, with t of the Treasury, can purchase the gs of Telegraph Companies, but no agreement to purchase is to be binding ame has been laid for one month on f both Houses of Parliament without . The last enactment is that if no act in the recent or next session of Parlia- ng at the disposal of the Postmaster- th moneys as may be requisite for car- the act, then the agreements made to d the Postmaster to pay the expenses

OF THE BANK OF ENGLAND AND FRANCE.—The return of the Bank of or the week ending September 2nd, ollowing results, when compared with is week :—

.........£3,611,437 Increase...£279,950
posits. 3,274,415 Increase... 295,005
osits..19,577,780 Decrease .. 271,100

ther side of the account:
it Se-
.........£13,790,131 No change.
rities. 16,239,930 Increase..£642,852
ploy'd10,422,460 Decrease.. 239,255
unt of notes in circulation is £24,307,- an increase of £351,475 ; and the stock in both departments is £20,846,653, increase of £72,552, when compared receding return.
in the present return is £3,611,437, ld admit of a dividend of 4 per cent., to £582,120, and leave the "rest" 7. The dividend will probably be de- the above rate of 4 per cent. The last half year was 4 per cent., and in r, 1867, it was to 4½ per cent.
ined is a comparison of the present posi- he Bank of England and the price of ith the corresponding week of last year:

	At present.	Same week last year.
.............£20,846,653	£24,072,282	
.... 11,539,548	15,009,342	
circulation... 24,307,105	24,062,940	
scount......... 2 per cent.	2 per cent.	
.... 94	94¾	

ekly return of the Bank of France to the , shows the following changes (the ex- en taken at 25 francs to the pound):

bullion	.. Increase......	£176,000
ounted	Decrease......	1,300,000
circulation.....	Increase......	752,000
eposits	Decrease......	1,160,000
balance.........	Decrease......	1,300,006
....	Decrease......	200,000

ther large falling off in the discount indi- ontinuance of stagnation and distrust in of France, which is lamentable, seeing auous additions to the stock of bullion. t, by the present addition, holds no less ,472,000.

COMPANIES INCORPORATED IN NOVA -Among the bills assented to at the pre- on of the Nova Scotia Legislative Assem- he following to incorporate :

ington and Sherbrooke Gold Mining

utario Gold Mining Company of Nova

anada Gold Mining Company of Nova

ureka Gold Mining Company of Nova

lpha Gold Mining Company of Mount Nova Scotia.

The Wentworth Gold Mining Company of Nova Scotia.
The Gladstone Mining Company.
Hayden and Derby Mining Company.
The Uniacke Union Gold Mining Company.
The Imperial Gold Mining Company.
The Prince of Wales Gold Mining Company.
The Orient Gold Mining Company.
The Meridian Gold Mining Company of Nova Scotia.
The Crescent Gold Mining Company of Nova Scotia.
The Delta Gold Mining Company of Nova Scotia.
The Westlake Company.
The Chicago Gold Mining Company of Nova Scotia.
The Montreal Gold Mining Association.
The Scotia Coal Company.
The Stanly Gold Company.
The Royal Gold Company of Nova Scotia.
The North Saint Lawrence and Mount Uniacke Gold Company.
The North American Mining Company.
The Strawberry Hill Gold Mining Company.
The following Companies had their charters amended :
The Block House Mining Company.
The Blue Lead Gold Mining Company.
The Dominion Gold Mining Company.
The Provincial Gold Mining Company.

Commercial.

Montreal Correspondence.

(From our own Correspondent.)

Montreal, 22nd Sept. 1868.

During the past week the town has been very lively, owing to the large influx of strangers from all parts of the Dominion. Hotels and cabs have been driving a large business, but I regret to say actual trade has received but a slight impetus, and we have not witnessed the activity generally expected. The Exhibition has been a success but it has on the whole hardly come up to previous ones. The great value of these Exhibitions con- sists in this that they are milestones, shewing the progress made in the arts and manufactures of a country and by them we are enabled to compute the rate at which we advance in material civili- zation. Viewed from this point the exhibition just closed has been in every way most satisfactory and we can congratulate ourselves in having made considerable strides in the last few years. As our papers have recently been filled almost ad nauseam with the subject I need write nothing more.
There has been increased liveliness in business circles, and the fall trade has fairly set in, great activity cannot be expected till the arrival of the fall fleet, which promises to be unusually late this year. Our harbour looks nearly as deserted as it did in midsummer nor do we expect the usual number of vessels, this is owing to the very bad home freights that ruled during the spring, in fact we had nothing to fill up sailing vessels, the bulk of which had either to go home light or go to Three Rivers or Quebec to load lumber. This en- tailed so heavy a loss on shipowners that a good many even of the regular traders have been taken off the route. So far it is lucky that the fall fleet is late, as produce is coming forward slowly, but we trust next month to have ample supplies to fill all the vessels that will be here and at rates which will help to make up the spring losses.
OUR PRODUCE MARKET still continues very dull, receipts are light and prices rule 'too high to enable speculators to operate, the anxious question is not yet solved, is the bottom reached ? or how much more will prices recede before that is the case. My opinion is unaltered that the bottom is by no means reached, and that present rates are only maintained by the long purses and tenacity of Western speculators and that as soon as the great volume of the harvest is brought forward fur-

ther steady decline must be expected ; the large Eastern Markets on this contenent can only take a tithe of the large surplus west, and prices in Europe leave no margin for profit on shipments made at present rates in the West. Flour has scarcely altered in price during the week, super No. 1 ranging from $5.80 to $5.85 for good brands and $6 to $6.10 for strong bakers flour, but the tone of the market is dull and drooping. Wheat is coming forward more freely, but buyers are oper- ating very cautiously, U.C. Spring sells ex cars at $1.30, and Chicago No. 2 Spring has sold by the cargo at $1.28. Corn nominally remains the same as last week 83 to 84c. for mixed, but the sales are not sufficient to form a quotation. In coarse grain there is absolutely nothing doing, farmers expect long prices and operators are un- willing to move till they can see their way somewhat more clearly. In wheat we know that there will be a large surplus, but what the deficiency will be in Peas, Oats, and Barley it is impossible to predict ; the crops of Oats and Peas are certain to be very short, and barley will be a very partial crop, in some districts abundant, but in others small and in all good in color but light in weight.
IN GROCERIES, I have to report greatly increased activity, and next week we expect still further life, as notwithstanding your having rival auction sales to ours, we know that a great many Western buyers will be here. I notice that in your adver- tising columns you give the list of all our large sales so far as they are announced. Stocks of all staples are not heavy either in town or country and fall importations are generally expected to be light, we may safely anticipate that a large quan- tity of goods will be placed. Our first cargo sale of fish took place to-day and high prices were realized.
DRY GOODS.—Our importers continue exceed- ingly busy, but the number of buyers expected down during the exhibition has been much smaller than anticipated ; but travelers have brought in more than the usual number of orders and a great many round lots have been placed. Cottons have been very active at full prices, the demand falling chiefly on Prints and fancy goods ; heavy shirtings are slower of sale. Woolens,—All the finer quali- ties of cloths and tweeds are enquired for, prices range about 20 per cent. less than last fall ; this decline is caused by the fall in wool and the over- production of most woolens ; the heavier and causse qualities are dull of sale at very uneven prices. Hosiery generally is in good demand. I am glad to say that for the last ten days there has been a marked improvement in remittances.

Toronto Market.

We are now in the most active part of the fall season, and fortunately the condition of the weather has been highly favorable to business operations. Barley has poured into the City in immense quan- tities ; the aggregate for the week exceeding in quantity anything within our recollection for years past. On the street market the receipts, which have been very large all week, have fallen off within the last four days, owing chiefly to the absence of many farmers at the Provincial Fair at Hamilton.
DRY GOODS.—The leading houses report an active business in all leading articles. Remit- tances from country merchants are spoken of as very satisfactory during the week. There is no change in prices.
BOOTS AND SHOES.—There is no abatement of the brisk demand reported last week for seasonable goods. Our houses have more business than they can do. Prices are firm and unchanged.
HATS, CAPS AND FURS.—The trade in raw furs is not yet commenced, as the Ontario game law, passed last Session of Parliament, prohibits trap- ping till the end of November. This measure is much complained of by the dealers in furs. For all the purposes of the trade a skin taken off in the end of October is equally good with that taken in November or December. This regulation prevents

the trade opening up at the usual time, and hence prices are nominal and business inactive. There is a great demand for silk hats for the country stores. Some of our manufacturers inform us that they cannot keep the trade supplied much less accumulate a stock of these goods. The late cool weather has stimulated the retail trade, and now a good lively business is reported in all kinds of seasonable goods.

GRAIN.—*Wheat.*—Receipts by cars 1,871 bush., light arrivals on the street. The market has ruled dull, there is very little offered and prices are stationary at the quotations of last week. A lot of 400 bush. spring sold at $1.20 and on the street $1.18 was paid; for midge-proof the street buyers pay $1.20 to $1.22; fall is scarce and firm at $1.30 for car loads, $1.32 was paid on the street for waggon loads. *Barley.*—Receipts by cars for the week 41,058 bush. and on the street 120,000 bush. making a total of 181,058 bush. from all sources. The market has ruled firm and steadily advanced from $1.02 to $1.03 at the opening to $1.09 to $1.10 at the close, the tendency being still upwards. About twenty car loads in all were reported sold during the week at current rates. Some cargo lots also changed hands, but mostly on p. t.; $1.10 was readily obtainable at the end of the week. *Peas.*—Receipts light; car loads are offered at 99c. to $1.00 and there are buyers at 97c., a sale having occurred at that price. On the street there were moderate receipts and prices ranged from 95c. to 96c. *Oats* are steady with a small demand and not many offering, the market closing at 50c. to 52c.; on the street, no sales of car loads reported. *Rye.*—None selling, nominal at about 80c.

FLOUR.—Receipts 1,575 brls. against 1,250 brls. the previous week. The market continues dull and nominal with a downward tendency on superfine; a lot sold early in the week at $5.65 but there are now free sellers at $5.50 and some late sales have occurred but terms are kept private. In extra and superior there were no transactions.

PROVISIONS.—*Butter* continues dull at 17c. to 22c. for tub; no sales of lots reported. *Eggs* are scarce and as high as 17c. was paid for a small quantity. *Cheese* continues scarce and firm, holders asking 11¼ to 12c. Dressed hogs sell at $5.00 to 8.50.

LIVE STOCK.—There were a great many transactions in choice animals at the Fair and fancy prices were paid; one large steer brought $400 for this market. Live hogs have sold to a considerable extent at $6.00 per 100 lbs. Beef cattle ordinary sell at $5.00 to $6.00; and sheep at $3.00 to $4.00.

The Cotton Market.

The Charleston *Courier* gives place to the following carefully prepared estimate of the probable supply of cotton for the years 1868-69 :

The elements that determine the question of supply are, first the area of land planted in cotton ; second, the quantity and efficiency of the labor employed in the culture. The Bureau of Agriculture at Washington, in its report of July 1, 1868, estimates the diminished quantity of land laid down in cotton the present year at ten per cent. This we deem to be below the average, which appears to have been higher. But adopting this estimate with regard to the area of cotton cultivation, the average reduction would be equivalent to 250,000 bales on an assumed supply of 2,250,000 bales. If we suppose the increased production to have been ten per cent. on an assumed basis of 2,250,000 bales, the aggregate product would be 2,250,000 bales.

As regards the other element—the quantity and effectiveness of the labor, applied to the culture—comparing this year with the last, it is still more difficult to arrive at a satisfactory conclusion. From all concurrent testimony that there has been an increased and a more effective application of labor to the culture of cotton, comparing this year with the preceding, seems indisputable, from the consciousness of the laborers that they were to

derive increased advantages from their self-imposed tasks. This has not only added to the quantity, but contributed to the greater efficiency of labor, subjected to the deduction connected with their presence at elections and political meetings. Against this, again, is to be placed the fact that the land has been less productive than it would have been had fewer fertilizers than usual had not been purchased from the comparative want of the means of purchase by the planters. If we assume as the crop of 1867-68 the figure of 2,250,000 bales, and admit the diminished area of land cultivated in cotton to have been ten per cent. as compared with the previous year, and allow ten per cent for increased productiveness, the crop of 1868-69 may be fairly estimated at 2,250,000 bales. Another mode of estimating the crop would be, supposing the working force to be 500,000 hands, and the average product per hand 4½ bales, we would arrive at the same result— 2,250,000 bales.

The question, however, of the probable extent of the crop of 1868-69 does not depend simply on the capacity to grow cotton, but on the combined power to grow and gather in the produce of that and every other crop. The extent of land planted in cotton and the ability to pick out the crop after it is made, is the measure of that power. We do not think that the physical ability exists to produce a larger crop than 2,500,000 bales with our present working force.

As regards the other sources of supply, the probable conclusion is that they have reached their maximum, under the present state of prices. The imports of raw cotton into England from the East Indies, Egypt and Brazil increased in 1868 only 8,000 bales as compared with 1867, while the average deliveries for consumption increased to 171,000 bales. If, under a moderate stimulus to prices, and such an increased consumption the imports had augmented only 8,000 bales, the probable inference is that a maximum of increase in the supply from these sources had been obtained. A Liverpool circular of the 1st of August, from the house of Edwards, Smith & Co., states that "from India" the exports are very trifling, say 46,000 bales from Bombay to all Europe in the first three weeks of July, and from all we can learn we think they will continue small for the remainder of the year." This strengthens this conclusion is the fact that both in the East Indies and Egypt the necessity of greater attention to cereals and less to cotton has been made manifest from the increasing tendency to famines in those countries.

The same journal, after discussing also the questions of consumption and future prices, arrives at the following conclusions :—

1. That the American supply will be at least equal to that of the year just closed.

2. That the foreign supply under prevailing prices has reached its maximum.

3. That the consumption will, in all probability, be increased from 10 to 15 per cent. during the present year, should there be continued peace in Europe, but that it is checked when middling uplands exceed 10d.

4. That the price of this description will, after some fluctuation, settle at about 10d., as affording remuneration to the manufacturer and the planter.

To Resume.

The Maitland Distillery will soon be in operation again, the necessary preparations for running being nearly completed. The name of the new firm is Fletcher, Hoag & Co. Mr. Halliday will take a leading part in its management.

Changed Hands.

The Factory of Messrs. Edward Miall & Co., Oshawa has resumed work under the control and ownership of Messrs. Gibbs & Bro. of that place. Important additions and improvements are contemplated.

What is Petroleum ?

Professor Hitchcock, of New York, sta petroleum is unquestionably of organic ori his opinion, the great mass of it has been from plants; it has been thought by sol derived from the animal kingdom, bein a fish oil or a substance related to adipo tillation of coal, since its chemical compo different from the oil manufactured from nels, containing neither aniline nor nitro Moreover, petroleum occupied fissures in urian and Devonian strata of America lon the trees of the coal period were growing native forests. Brine is generally associat petroleum, and the fact of the slight solu hydrocarbon in fresh water, but insolub salt water, excites the inquiry whether so of primæval lagoons may not have prevex escape of the vegetable gases beneath, a densed them into liquid. The immense t in North America, several hundred squa in extent, underlaid by certain geologica tions in an unaltered state, implies that th leum of the New World, like its coal, is p inexhaustible. In a paper by Professor cock, read before the British Association i America produced more than 300,000,000 of petroleum. The average daily yield in 1866 was at least 12,000 barrels. The l of collecting, transporting, and refining ployed as many hands as either the coal trade. The most prolific of all the pe regions is Western Pennsylvania. The oil i beneath each of three sandstones, or sets of vious strata. Petroleum may occur in and fissures in the strata. The existen cavity is inferred from the prodigious an fluid spouting out of the ground; at the well at Pitt Hole the produce was at the 1800 barrels of petroleum per day. There less than fourteen different formations in America from which petroleum has been ob

English Tea Market.

The arrival of the first of the clippers w season's Tea was looked for some time nex but the trade was rather surprised on ' with the announcement that the *Ariel* wa Channel and would be in dock the followi on which day (September 2) the *Spindlh* reported, the two having run the distance an hour or two, making the swiftest pas record for sailing ships. The steamers and *Agamemnon* were fully expected t first, although they were two or three wee starting, but the *Agamemnon* only turned the 3rd, and the *Achilles* has not yet p appearance. The *Sir Lancelot, Teeping* an *Will* followed, and to-day (Friday) the *L* signalled off the Lizard. The samples ha freely put out, and sales have been mo moderate extent, according to quality, at to 2s. 5d. for Kaisow, 1s. 11d. to 2s. 1d. f chests and 2s. 5d. to 2s. 9d. for boxes I The reports received from China regard generally inferior quality are fully borne o being very little, so far, that can be call The medium and finer sorts are badly mad mixed in leaf and dusty, having all the ap of old leaves being thrown in with the n At the public sales held on the last and 2 several large parcels of new season's assorted Pekoe, brought overland, were put up "; reserve." They were quite unsuited for i ket, being hastily prepared and thin, an very little favor with buyers, the prices from 1s. 2½d. to 1s. 5½d. per lb., which ma a heavy loss, as the expenses of transit c are necessarily exceptional. Some scente sold privately at fair rates, being more in and better prepared than the Pekoes. I same sales common Congou went about lb. easier than at the sales a fortnight pre other descriptions unchanged. Fine Gree wanted.—*Grocer, Sept. 6.*

hip Building at St. John.

ine in the ship building business has
commercial prosperity of St. John,
ed the hopes of those citizens who ex-
e this one of the most thriving cities
erican seaboard. Some of our most
builders have manfully struggled against
se circumstances which have come up
em like a rising tide, hoping by brave
effort to overcome these circumstances.
turned their attention to the construc-
nce ships, they have built vessels to be
heir own account, and they have sought
eans to avert the evil days that gathered
hem. But their success has not been
rate with their labors, with their enter-
their capital or skill. The same amount
invested in other ways, or in other
would have yielded far more generous
As a last resource they will probably try
ships, concerning which much has
en written. The manufacture of these
quires very heavy capital; a capital so
o tax the resources of the individual
r beyond his strength, and, indeed, to
ix the resources of any combination of
that might be made. The general
of the Province depends so largely upon
ng, and the decline of this branch of
being so general, the people seem to be
ing that out of the Provincial funds aid
granted to those willing to try to keep
important industry, in the shape of
o composite ships built here. Although
ature has not yet responded to what ap-
e the general wish, we think it cannot
o so at its next session.

Demeara Sugar Market.

lowing is from Sandbach, Parker & Co's.
ated Aug. 24.
—About 2,000 hhds. have been sold
e month ; Muscovados are neglected, and
tity offering very small; for Vacuum Pan
nd is good, but buyers are not inclined
e high: prices lately ruling, the rates at
les have been made during the fortnight
better than the English quotations ; about
f September the bulk of the Estates will
k and a large quantity will be offering
when the capacity of the American market
anufacture will be fully tested.
ses.—The demand has been small and
rates ruling in New York have for the
lmost put a stop to shipments of any but
finest qualities.
—About 50 puncheons were offered for
ug the fortnight and sold for Halifax.

Halifax Market.

STUFFS.—Flour—stocks light, with fair
at slightly lower prices; Canada No. 1
$7.90 ; Extra $8.30 to $8.40 ; Extra State
7.70 to $7.80 ; Baltimore Super. $7.00 to
xtra $7.75 to $8.00 ; Rye dull. Corn
at $4.60 to $4.70 for kiln dried ; $4.40
for fresh ground. Oatmeal dull at $7.75
eady than usual at $7.75

Imports from January 1st to September
67 and 1868 :

	Brls. Flour.	Brls. Cornmeal.
3.	125,389	40,381
7	120,576	29,583

INDIA PRODUCE.—Sugars dull, and prices
nal at our quotations ; sales made of a
good grocery Cuba at 5½c. in bond, and
ommon Cuba at 5⅛c. in bond. Molasses
l in good demand at 29½c. to 30c. for
os in bond. Rum—Demerara 52c. to
Jago 43c. in bond.
CIAL.—Bank drawing rate on London 60
t bills 13 per cent. premium ; Private 12
er cent. premium. New York Gold drafts
4 per cent. premium. Currency drafts
nt. discount. Montreal sight drafts 4 per
mium. Newfoundland sight drafts 5 per
mium.—R. C. Hamilton & Co's. Circular.

NEW INSOLVENTS.—Hiram Albert Grannis,
Hillier ; Anna S. Miller, Hamilton ; James Per-
sullivan and David Wells, Barrie ; John J. Shanly,
Caro, Three Rivers ; Emernie Couvrette, Mon-
treal ; Thomas Goffatt, Jr., Barrie ; R. Collins &
Sons, St. John ; Henry Parsons, Montreal ; A.
Zariesbeer, Bowmanville ; David Huston, Mary-
boro ; John Ainlay, Hope.

INSOLVENTS.—The following Insolvents were
gazetted on the 19th :—P. Sinclair & Son, Quebec;
Archibald McLean, Pendleton ; A. S. Hart, Three
Rivers ; David Parish, Port Stanley ; Benjamin
Connor, Orangeville ; Jas. Connor, Peterboro' ; Jno.
Hamson, do ; Hy. Spencer, Hamilton ; Jno. Fer-
guson, Buckingham ; Andrew Cowen, Ottawa ;
Robert Hammond, Amaranth ; Jas. Russ, St.
Catharines ; Wm. Johnson, Montreal ; Charles
Crawford, Thorold ; Jno. Farquharson, Whitby ;
Jno. McMahon, do ; Jno. Herd, Biddulph.

GODERICH SALT.—During the month of August
3,500 bbls. of salt were shipped from Goderich by
lake. The Signal says this amount would have
been larger had there been salt to supply the
demand.

AUCTION SALES OF GROCERIES
IN MONTREAL,
FOR THE
Fall Season of 1868.

September 29th,
Sale by Auction, at the Stores of
Victor Hudon, Esq.,
Of MEDITERRANEAN GOODS, *Wines, Liquors, and General Groceries.*
J. G. SHIPWAY,
Auctioneer.

September 29th,
Sale by Auction, at the Stores of
Messrs. Rimmer, Gunn & Co.,
Of Teas, Wines, Brandies, Tobaccos, and General Groceries
JOHN LEEMING & Co.,
Auctioneers.

September 30th,
Sale by Auction, at the Stores of
Messrs. Buchanan, Leckie & Co.,
Of 3,000 Packages *Green Teas, ex. Annie Braginton*, direct from Shanghai. Also, 2,000 Packages *Uncolored Japans* and a large assortment of *Wines, Liquors, Fruit, and General Groceries.*
JOHN LEEMING & CO.,
Auctioneers.

October 1st,
Sale by Auction at the Stores of
Messrs. Chapman, Fraser & Tylee,
Of Fruit, Wines, Brandies, Oils, and General Groceries.
JOHN LEEMING & CO.,
Auctioneers.

October 1st,
Auction Sales at the Stores of
Messrs. David Torrance & Co.,
Of 7,802 Packages Fine New Crop GREEN TEAS, ex *Annie Braginton*, direct from Shanghai. Also, 2,000 half chests UNCOLORED JAPANS, in English order.
JOHN LEEMING & CO.,
Auctioneers.

October 2nd,
Sale by Auction at the Stores of
Messrs. Alex. Urquhart & Co.,
The Cargo of the *Western Wave*, from Marseilles. Also, a large assortment of ENGLISH GROCERIES.
JOHN LEEMING & CO.,
Auctioneers.

Brown Brothers,
ACCOUNT-BOOK MANUFACTURERS,
Stationers, Book-Binders, Etc.,
66 *and* 68 *King Street East, Toronto, Ont.*

ACCOUNT Books for Banks, Insurance Companies, Merchants, etc., made to order of the best materials, and for style, durability and cheapness unsurpassed.

A large stock of Account-Books and General Stationery constantly on hand.

September 1, 1868. 3-1y

Philip Browne & Co.,
BANKERS AND STOCK BROKERS.
DEALERS IN
STERLING EXCHANGE—U. S. Currency, Silver and Bonds—Bank Stocks, Debentures, Mortgages, &c. Drafts on New York issued, in Gold and Currency. Prompt attention given to collections. Advances made on Securities.
No. 67 YONGE STREET, TORONTO
JAMES BROWNE. PHILIP BROWNE, *Notary Public.*
y

Honore Plamondon,
CUSTOM House Broker, Forwarder, and General Agent, Quebec. Office—Custom House Building. 17-1y

TORONTO PRICES CURRENT.—September 24, 1868.

Name of Article.	Wholesale Rates.	
Boots and Shoes.	$ c.	$ c.
Mens' Thick Boots	2 20	2 50
" Kip	2 45	3 20
" Calf	3 00	3 75
" Congress Gaiters	2 00	2 40
" Kip Cobourgs	1 00	1 50
Boys' Thick Boots	1 65	1 90
Youths' "	1 45	1 55
Women's Batts	95	1 20
" Congress Gaiters	1 15	1 50
Misses' Batts	0 75	1 00
" Congress Gaiters	1 00	1 30
Girls' Batts	0 65	0 90
" Congress Gaiters	0 80	1 10
Children's C. T. Cacks	0 50	0 65
" Gaiters	0 65	0 90
Drugs.		
Aloes Cape	0 12½	0 16
Alum	0 02½	0 03
Borax	0 00	0 00
Camphor, refined	0 65	0 70
Castor Oil	0 18	0 28
Caustic Soda	0 04½	0 05
Cochineal	0 90	1 00
Cream Tartar	0 00	0 00
Epsom Salts	0 03	0 04
Extract Logwood	0 09	0 11
Gum Arabic, sorts	0 30	0 35
Indigo, Madras	0 75	1 00
Licorice	0 14	0 45
Madder	0 13	0 16
Nutgalls	0 00	0 00
Opium	6 70	7 00
Oxalic Acid	0 28	0 35
Potash, Bi-tart	0 25	0 28
" Bichromate	0 15	0 20
Potass Iodide	3 80	4 50
Senna	0 12½	0 60
Soda Ash	0 03	0 04
Soda Bicarb	4 50	5 50
Tartaric Acid	0 37½	0 45
Verdigris	0 35	0 40
Vitriol, Blue	0 09	0 10
Groceries.		
Coffees:		
Java, ℔ lb.	0 22@0 24	
Laguayra,	0 17	0 18
Rio	0 15	0 17
Fish:		
Herrings, Lab. split	0 00	0 00
" round	0 00	0 00
" scaled	0 00	0 00
Mackerel, small kitts	1 00	0 00
Loch. Her. wh'e firks	2 50	2 75
" half "	1 25	1 50
White Fish & Trout	None.	
Salmon, saltwater	15 00	16 00
Dry Cod, ℔ 112 lbs	4 75	5 00
Fruit:		
Raisins, Layers	2 20	2 25
" M R	2 10	2 20
" Valentias new	0 08¾	0 09
Currants, new	0 05	0 06
" old	0 03½	0 04½
Figs	0 12½	0 13
Molasses:		
Clayed, ℔ gal	0 00	0 35
Syrups, Standard	0 45	0 46
" Golden	0 50	0 51
Rice:		
Arracan	4 60	4 75
Spices:		
Cassia, whole, ℔ lb.	0 37½	0 40
Cloves	0 11	0 12
Nutmegs	0 50	0 60
Ginger, ground	0 15	0 25
" Jamaica, root	0 22	0 25
Pepper, black	0 09	0 10
Pimento	0 08	0 09
Sugars:		
Port Rico, ℔ lb.	0 08½	0 08¾
Cuba "	0 08¼	0 08½
Barbadoes (bright)	0 08¾	0 08¾
Dry Crushed, at 60 d.	0 11	0 00
Canada Sugar Refine'y, yellow No. 2, 60 ds	0 08¼	0 08½
Yellow, No. 2½	0 08⅝	0 08¾
" No. 3	0 00	0 00
Crushed X	0 10	0 10½
" A	0 11¼	0 11½
Ground	0 11¾	0 12
Extra Ground	0 12½	0 13
Teas:		
Japan com'n to good	0 40	0 55
" Fine to choicest	0 55	0 65
Colored, com. to fine	0 60	0 75
Congou & Souch'ng	0 42	0 75
Oolong, good to fine	0 50	0 65
Y. Hyson, com to gd	0 45	0 55
Medium to choice	0 65	0 80
Extra choice	0 85	0 95
Gunpowd'r c. to med	0 55	0 70
" med. to fine	0 70	0 85

Name of Article.	Wholesale Rate.	
Groceries—*Contin'd*	$ c.	$ c.
" fine to fins't	0 85	0 95
Hyson	0 45	0 80
Imperial	0 42	0 80
Tobacco, Manufact'd:		
Can Leaf, ℔ lb 5s & 10s.	0 26	0 30
Western Leaf, com	0 25	0 26
" Good	0 27	0 32
" Fine	0 32	0 35
" Bright fine	0 40	0 50
" " choice	0 60	0 75
Hardware.		
Tin (net cash prices)		
Block, ℔ lb	0 25	0 26
Grain	0 25	0 26
Copper:		
Pig	0 23	0 24
Sheet	0 30	0 33
Cut Nails:		
Assorted ¼ Shingles, ℔ 100 lb.	3 05	3 15
Shingle alone do	2 25	2 35
Lathe and 5 dy	3 45	3 55
Galvanized Iron:		
Assorted sizes	0 09	0 10
Best No. 24	0 00	0 00
" 26	0 08¾	0 09
" 28	0 09¼	0 10
Horse Nails:		
Guest's or Griffin's assorted sizes	0 19	0 20
For W. ass'd sizes	0 18	0 19
Patent Hammer'd do	0 17	0 18½
Iron (at 4 months):		
Pig—Gartsherrie No1	26 00	27 00
Other brands. No1	22 00	23 00
" No2	24 00	25 00
Bar—Scotch, ℔ 100 lb	2 25	2 50
Refined	3 00	3 25
Swedes	5 00	5 50
Hoops—Coopers	3 00	3 25
Band	3 00	3 25
Boiler Plates	3 25	3 50
Canada Plates	4 00	4 25
Union Jack	0 00	0 00
Pontypool	4 00	4 25
Swansea	0 00	0 00
Lead (at 4 months):		
Bar, ℔ 100 lbs	0 07	0 07½
Sheet "	0 08	0 09
Shot	0 07½	0 07¾
Iron Wire (net cash):		
No. 6, ℔ bundle	2 70	2 80
" 9, "	3 10	3 20
" 12, "	3 40	3 50
" 16, "	4 30	4 40
Powder:		
Blasting, Canada	3 50	3 75
FF "	4 25	4 50
FFF "	4 75	5 00
Blasting, English	5 00	5 50
FF loose	5 50	6 00
FFF "	6 00	6 50
Pressed Spikes (4 mos):		
Regular sizes 100	4 00	4 25
Extra "	4 50	5 00
Tin Plates (net cash):		
IC Coke	7 50	8 00
IC Charcoal	8 50	8 75
IX "	10 50	10 75
IXX "	12 50	0 00
DC "	7 50	9 00
DX "	9 50	10 00
Hides & Skins, ℔ lb		
Green rough	0 05½	0 06
Green, salt'd & insp'd	0 00	0 07
Cured	0 07½	0 08½
Calfskins, green	0 00	0 10
Calfskins, cured	0 00	0 12
" dry	0 18	0 20
Lambskins,	0 50	0 00
" pelts	0 40	0 00
Hops.		
Inferior, ℔ lb	0 10	0 15
Medium	0 15	0 20
Good	0 20	0 25
Fancy	0 25	0 35
Leather, @ (4 mos.) In lots of less than 50 sides, 10 ℔ cent higher.		
Spanish Sole, 1st qual heavy, weights ℔ lb	0 23	0 23½
Do. 1st qual middle do	0 23	0 23½
Do. No. 2, all weights	0 20	0 22
Slaughter heavy	0 28	0 29
Do. light	0 28	0 29
Harness, best	0 32	0 34
" No. 2	0 30	0 33
Upper heavy	0 34	0 36
" light	0 36	0 40

Name of Article.	Wh… R…
Leather—*Contin'd.*	$ c
Kip Skins, Patna	0 4
French	0 7
English	0 6
Hemlock Calf (30 to 35 lbs.) per doz	0 7
Do. light	0 4
French Calf	1 0
Grain & Satn Clt ℔ doz	0 0
Splits, large ℔ lb	0 3
" small	0 2
Enamelled Cow ℔ foot	0 2
Patent	0 2
Pebble Grain	0 1
Buff	0 1
Oils.	
Cod	0 5
Lard, extra	0 0
" No. 1	0 0
" Woollen	0 0
Lubricating, patent	0 0
" Mott's economic	0 5
Linseed, raw	0 7
" boiled	0 8
Machinery	0 0
Olive, 2nd, ℔ gal	1 4
" salad	2 0
" salad, in bots. qt. ℔ case	3 6
Sesame salad, ℔ gal	1 6
Seal, pale	0 7
Spirits Turpentine	0 6
Varnish	0 0
Whale	0 7
Paints, &c.	
White Lead, genuine in Oil, ℔ 25lbs	0 0
Do. No. 1 "	0 0
" 2 "	0 0
" 3 "	0 0
White Zinc, genuine	3 0
White Lead, dry	0 0
Red Lead	0 0
Venetian Red, Eng'h	0 0
Yellow Ochre, Fren'h	0 0
Whiting	0 9
Petroleum. (Refined ℔ gal.)	
Water white, car l'd	0 3
" small lots	0 3
Straw, by car load	0 3
" small lots	0 3
Amber, by car load	0 0
" small lots	0 0
Benzine	0 3
Produce.	
Grain:	
Wheat, Spring, 60 lb	1 1
" Fall 60 "	1
Barley 48 "	1
Peas 60 "	0
Oats 34 "	0
Rye 56 "	0
Seeds:	
Clover, choice 60 "	5
" com'n 68 "	0
Timothy, cho'e 4 "	2
" inf. to good 48 "	1
Flax 56 "	1
Flour (per brl.):	
Superior extra	6
Extra superfine,	6
Fancy superfine	0
Superfine No. 1	5
" No. 2	0
Oatmeal, (per brl.)	6
Provisions.	
Butter, dairy tub ℔ lb	0
" store packed	0
Cheese, new	0
Pork, mess, per brl	23
" prime mess	16
" prime	14
Bacon, rough	0
" Cumberl'd cut	0
" smoked	0
Hams, in salt	0
" sug. cur. & canv'd	0
Shoulders, in salt	0
Lard, in kegs	0
Eggs, packed	0
Beef Hams	0
Tallow	0
Hogs dressed, heavy	0
" medium	0
" light	0
Salt, &c.	
American brls	1
Liverpool coarse	0
Plaster	1
Water Lime	1

…andles.		
… & Co.'s ..	$ c.	$ c.
…l.	0 07½	0 08
… Bar	0 07	0 07½
…ar.	0 07	0 07½
…	0 05	0 05½
…	0 03½	0 03¾
…	0 10	0 10½
Liquors,		
…r doz.	2 60	2 65
…ub Portr..	2 35	2 40
…ica Rum...	1 80	2 25
…'s H. Gin..	1 50	1 60
…d Tom.	1 90	2 00
…es.	4 00	4 25
…d Tom, c...	6 00	6 25
…non.	1 00	1 25
…ld.	2 00	4 00
…mmon.	1 00	1 50
…um.	1 70	1 80
…or golden..	2 50	4 00

Brandy:	$ c.	$ c.
Hennessy's, per gal..	2 0	2 75
Martell's " ..	2 0	2 75
J. Robin & Co.'s " ..	2 10	2 75
Otard, Dupuy & Cos..	2 10	2 75
Brandy, cases.	8 50	9 00
Brandy, com. per c...	4 00	4 50
Whiskey:		
Common 36 u. p.	0 65	0 70
Old Rye	0 85	0 87½
Malt	0 85	0 87½
Toddy	0 85	0 87½
Scotch, per gal.	1 90	2 10
Irish—Kinnahan's c...	7 00	7 50
" Dunnville's Belf't..	6 00	6 25
Wool.		
Fleece, lb.	0 27	0 30
Pulled "	0 00	0 00
Furs.		
Bear.	8 00	10 00
Beaver	1 00	1 25
Coon	0 20	0 40
Fisher	4 00	6 00
Martin	1 40	1 60
Mink	4 00	4 25
Otter	5 75	6 00
Spring Rats	0 15	0 17
Fox.	1 20	1 25

…NSURANCE COMPANIES.

ENGLISH.—*Quotations on the London Market.*

…ast Dividend.	Name of Company.	Shares par val £	Amount paid.	Last
	Briton Medical and General Life	10	—	1⅜
7½	Commer'l Union, Fire, Life and Mar.	50	5	5¼ 5¾
8	City of Glasgow	25	2½	5
9½	Edinburgh Life	100	15	30⅜x
…—½ yr	European Life and Guarantee	2½	11s6	4s 6d
10	Etna Fire and Marine	10	1½	1
5	Guardian	100	50	52x
12	Imperial Fire	500	50	345
9½	Imperial Life	100	10	16¼
10	Lancashire Fire and Life	20	2	2⅞x
11	Life Association of Scotland	40	7¼	23
…s. p. sh	London Assurance Corporation	25	12½	48
5	London and Lancashire Life	10	1	1
40	Liverp'l & London & Globe F. & L.	20	2	7⅜
5	National Union Life	5	1	1
12½	Northern Fire and Life	100	5	10⅝
12 …8, bo 5s.	North British and Mercantile	50	6¼	16 16½
50	Ocean Marine	25	5	20
…25 12s.	Provident Life	100	10	38
…4½ p. s.	Phœnix	....	....	136
…½—h. yr.	Queen Fire and Life	10	1	15-16
…s. bo. 4s	Royal Insurance	20	3	6⅞
10	Scottish Provincial Fire and Life	50	2½	4⅞
25	Standard Life	50	12	65
5	Star Life	25	1¼	—
	CANADIAN.			₩ c.
4	British America Fire and Marine	$50	$25	55½
4	Canada Life	...	.....	.....
12	Montreal Assurance	£50	£10	135
3	Provincial Fire and Marine	60	11	.....
....	Quebec Fire	40	32½	£19
8	" Marine	100	40	90-91
7 mo's.	Western Assurance	40	6	.....

RAILWAYS.	Sha's	Paid	Montr	London.
…nd St. Lawrence	£100	All.	....	57 59
…d Lake Huron	20½	"	....	3 3½
do Preference	10	"	....	5½ 6½
…att. & Goderich, 6₩c., 1872-3-4	100	"	....	....
… and St. Lawrence	....	....	9 10	....
do Pref. 10 ₩ ct.	....	....	62½	....
…ank	100	"	15 16	15¾ 16¼
Eq. G. M. Bds. 1 ch. 6₩c.	100	"	....	80 83
First Preference, 5 ₩ c	100	"	....	47 50
Deferred, 3 ₩ ct.	100	"	....	....
Second Pref. Bonds, 5₩c.	100	"	....	37 30
do Deferred, 3 ₩ ct.	100	"	....	....
Third Pref. Stock, 4₩ct.	100	"	....	26 28
do. Deferred, 3 ₩ ct.	100	"	....	....
Fourth Pref. Stock, 3₩c.	100	"	....	18½ 19½
do. Deferred, 3 ₩ ct.	100	"	....	....
…stern	20½	"	....	13¾ 14
New	20½	18	16 17	....
6 ₩ c. Bds, due 1873-76.	100	All.	....	100 102
5½ ₩c Bds. due 1877-78.	100	"	....	93 95
…ilway, Halifax, $250, all	$250	"	....	....
… of Canada, 6₩c. 1st Pref. Bds.	100	"	....	80 83

…CHANGE.	Halifax.	Montr'l.	Quebec.	Toronto.
London, 60 days				
75 days date	13½	8⅝ 8⅞	9 9¼	9¼
do.	12 12½	8 8½	8¼ 8⅝	8⅜
…ith documents	....	8⅞ 9¼	....	....
…ew York	....	30½ 31	30 30½	70
do.	....	33 31½	31 31½	....
…ts do.	....	1-32 dis.	par ½ dis.	par ½ dis.
…	....	4¼ 4½	....	4⅜ 6⅜

STOCK AND BOND REPORT.

The dates of our quotations are as follows:—Toronto, Sept. 23; Montreal, Sept. 21; Quebec, Sept. 21; London, Sept. 7.

NAME.	Shares.	Paid up.	Divid'd last 6 Months	Dividend Day.	CLOSING PRICES. Toronto.	Montre'l	Quebec.
BANKS.			₩ ct.				
British North America	$250	All.	3	July and Jan.	102 102½	108	102½ 103
Jacques Cartier	50	"	4	1 June, 1 Dec.	106 108	106 108	106 107
Montreal	200	"	5		134 135	134¼ 134¾	134 134½
Nationale	50	"	4	1 Nov. 1 May.	106	106½ 108	107½ 108
New Brunswick	100	"	......	......	....	...	....
Nova Scotia	200	28	7&b$3½	Mar. and Sept.	....	....	....
Du Peuple	50	"	4	1 Mar., 1 Sept.	104 106	105½ 106	105 106
Toronto	100	"	4	1 Jan., 1 July.	116 116½	115	115 116
Bank of Yarmouth	....	....	......	......	....	....	....
Canadian Bank of Com'e	50	95	......	......	103½ 104	101½	101½ 102
City Bank Montreal	80	All.	4	1 June, 1 Dec.	102 102½	102	102 103
Commer'l Bank (St. John)	100	"	₩ ct.	......	....	...	....
Eastern Townships' Bank	50	"	4	1 July, 1 Jan..	....	95	96 97
Gore	40	...	3½	1 Jan., 1 July.	....	....	40 45
Halifax Banking Company	...	....	......	......	....	....	....
Mechanics' Bank	50	70	4	1 Nov., 1 May.	94½ 95½	94 97	94 95
Merchants' Bank of Canada	100	70	4	1 Jan., 1 July.	105 105½	104¾ 105½	105 105½
Merchants' Bank (Halifax)	....	....	.....	......	....	....	....
Molson's Bank	50	All.	4	1 Apr., 1 Oct.	111 112	Bks. clod	Bks. clod
Niagara District Bank	100	70	3½	1 Jan., 1 July.	....	....	....
Ontario Bank	40	All.	4	1 June, 1 Dec.	98¼ 98¾	98 98½	97½ 98½
People's Bank (Fred'kton)	100	"	......	......	....	....	....
People's Bank (Halifax)	20	"	7 12 m	......	....	....	....
Quebec Bank	100	"	3½	1 June, 1 Dec.	98 99	97½ 98½	98 98½
Royal Canadian Bank	50	50	4	1 Jan., 1 July.	90 91	88½ 91	88 90
St. Stephens Bank	100	All	.....	......	....	....	....
Union Bank	100	70	4	1 Jan., 1 July.	102½ 103	102½ 103	102 102½
Union Bank (Halifax)	100	40	7 12 mo	Feb. and Aug.	....	....	..
MISCELLANEOUS.							
British America Land	250	44	2½	......	....	....	....
British Colonial S. S. Co	250	32½	2½	......	...	50	...
Canada Company	32½	All.	5	......	....	....	....
Canada Landed Credit Co.	50	$20	3½	......	62½ 63	....	....
Canada Per. B'ldg Society	50	All.	5	......	119 119½	....	....
Canada Mining Company	4	90	......	......	....	....	....
Do. Inl'd Steam Nav. Co.	100	All.	20 12 m	......	....	108 109	108 109
Do. Glass Company	100	"	12½ "	......	....	95	....
Canad'n Loan & Investm't	25	2½	7	......	....	....	....
Canada Agency	10	½	......	.....	....	....	....
Colonial Securities Co	...	....	......	.....	....	....	....
Freehold Building Society	100	All.	5	......	105 106	....	....
Halifax Steamboat Co.	100	"	5	......	....	....	....
Halifax Gas Company	....	....	......	...	....	...	....
Hamilton Gas Company	....	....	.....	.....	....	....	....
Huron Copper Bay Co	4	12	20	.....	....	25 50cps	....
Lake Huron S. and C.	5	102	......	......	....	....	....
Montreal Mining Co	20	$15	......	.....	....	3 3.50	...
Do. Telegraph Co.	40	All.	5	......	134 134½	133½ 135	134½ 134¾
Do. Elevating Co.	00	"	15 12 m	......	....	....	....
Do. City Gas Co.	40	"	4	15 Mar. 15 Sep.	....	Bks. clod	Bks. cl'd
Do. City Pass. R. Co.	50	"	5	......	....	108 110	108 109
Nova Scotia Telegraph	20	"	....	.....	....	....	....
Quebec and L. S.	8	$4	......	.....	....	....	25 cts
Quebec Gas Co	200	All.	4	1 Mar., 1 Sep.	....	...	117 118
Quebec Street R. R	50	25	8	......	....	....	96 97
Richelieu Navigation Co.	100	All.	7 p.a.	1 Jan., 1 July.	....	Bks. clod	116 117
St. Lawrence Tow Boat Co.	100	"	......	3 Feb.	....	...	40 45
Tor'to Consumers' Gas Co.	50	"	2 3 m.	1 My Au Mar Fe	104½ 105	...	108 104
Trust & Loan Co. of U. C.	20	5	3	......	....	....	..
West'n Canada Bldg Soc'y	50	All.	5	......	111 112	....	....

SECURITIES.	London.	Montreal.	Quebec.	Toronto.
Canadian Gov't Deb. 6 ₩ ct. due 1872	....	100 100½	100 101	99½ 101
Do. do. 6 do due Ja. & Jul. 1877-84	103 105	....	....	....
Do. do. 6 do. Feb. & Aug.	103 106	....	....	....
Do. do. 6 do. Mch. & Sep.	102 104	....	....	....
Do. do. 5 ₩ ct. cur., 1883	90 92	89	89½ 90	90
Do. do. 5 do. stg., 1885	....	90	90 90½	90 91
Do. do. 7 do. cur.,	....	....	......	....
Dominion 6 p. c. 1878 cy.	....	99½ 100	100½ 101½	100 101
Hamilton Corporation	....	....	......	....
Montreal Harbor, 8 ₩ ct. d. 1869	..	....	......	....
Do. do. 7 do. 1870	...	....	......	....
Do. do. 6½ do. 1875	....	100½	......	....
Do. do. 6½ do. 1873	....	....	......	....
Do. Corporation, 6 ₩ c. 1891	....	02	92	91½ 92
Do. 7 p. c. stock	....	105 105½	103 105	105 105½
Do. Water Works, 6 ₩ c. stg. 1878	...	....	......	91 92
Do. do. 6 do. cy. do.	....	92	......	92 93
New Brunswick, 6 ₩ ct., Jan. and July	102 104	....	......	....
Nova Scotia, 6 ₩ ct., 1875	100 102	...	......	....
Ottawa City 6 ₩ c. d. 1880	....	90 91	......	...
Quebec Harbour, 6 ₩ c. d. 1883	....	....	60 70	....
Do. do. 7 do. do.	....	....	70 80	....
Do. do. 8 do. 1886	...	....	85 90	....
Do. City, 7 ₩ c. d. 5 years	....	80 90	90 91	....
Do. do. 7 do. 9 do.	....	....	86 87	....
Do. do. 7 do. 2½ do.	....	....	96 96½	....
Do. Water Works, 7 ₩ ct., 4 years	....	....	95 96	....
Do. do. 6 do. 2 do.	....	....	92½ 93½	....
Toronto Corporation	....	90	...	....

Insurance.

The Liverpool and London and Globe Insurance Company.

INVESTED FUNDS:
FIFTEEN MILLIONS OF DOLLARS.

DAILY INCOME OF THE COMPANY:
T WELVE THOUSAND DOLLARS.

LIFE INSURANCE,
WITH AND WITHOUT PROFITS.

FIRE INSURANCE
On every description of Property, at Lowest Remunerative Rates.

JAMES FRASER, AGENT,
5 King Street West.

Toronto, 1868　　　38-1y

Briton Medical and General Life Association,

with which is united the
BRITANNIA LIFE ASSURANCE COMPANY.

Capital and Invested Funds............£750,000 Sterling.

ANNUAL INCOME, £220,000 STG. :
Yearly increasing at the rate of £25,000 Sterling.

THE important and peculiar feature originally introduced by this Company, in applying the periodical Bonuses, so as to make Policies payable during life, without any higher rate of premiums being charged, has caused the success of the BRITON MEDICAL and GENERAL to be almost unparalleled in the history of Life Assurance. *Life Policies on the Profit Scale become payable during the Lifetime of the Assured, thus rendering a Policy of Assurance a means of subsistence in old age, as well as a protection for a family,* and a more valuable security to creditors in the event of early death ; and effectually meeting the often urged objection, that persons do not themselves reap the benefit of their own prudence and forethought.
No extra charge made to members of Volunteer Corps for services within the British Provinces.

☞ TORONTO AGENCY, 5 KING ST. WEST.
oct17—9-1yr　　　JAMES FRASER, Agent.

Phenix Insurance Company,
BROOKLYN, N. Y.

PHILANDER SHAW,　　EDGAR W. CROWELL,
Secretary.　　　　　Vice-President.
STEPHEN CROWELL, President.
Cash Capital, $1,000,000.　Surplus, $666,416.02.　Total, 1,666,416.02.　Entire Income from all sources for 1866 was $4,131,830.82.

CHARLES G. FORTIER, Marine Agent.
Ontario Chambers, Toronto, Ont.　　19-1y.

ÆTNA
Live Stock Insurance Company,
OF
HARTFORD, CONN.

DIRECTORS:
R. A. BULKELEY,　　　C. C. KIMBALL,
SAMUEL WOODRUFF,　T. O. ENDERS,
AUSTIN DUNHAM,　　ROBT. E. DAY,
E. J. BASSETT,　　　EDWD. KELLOGG,
J. S. WOODRUFF,　　ALVAN P. HYDE.

This Company Insures
HORSES AND CATTLE
AGAINST DEATH
BY FIRE,
ACCIDENT,　　　　OR DISEASE.
Also,
AGAINST THEFT,
And the
HAZARDS OF TRANSPORTATION.

C. C. KIMBALL, President.
T O. ENDERS, Vice President.
J. B. TOWER, Secretary.

Parties desiring Local Agencies will apply to
E. L. SNOW, GENERAL AGENT,
Montreal

SCOTT & WALMSLEY,
d7nov11y　　　　　Agents, Ontario.

Insurance.

The Victoria Mutual
FIRE INSURANCE COMPANY OF CANADA.

Insures only Non-Hazardous Property, at Low Rates.

BUSINESS STRICTLY MUTUAL.

GEORGE H. MILLS, President.
W. D. DOOKER, Secretary.
HEAD OFFICE ....　......HAMILTON, ONTARIO
aug 15-1yr

The Ætna Life Insurance Company.

AN attack, abounding with errors, having been made upon the Ætna Life Insurance Co. by the editor of the Montreal *Daily News* : and certain agents of British Companies being now engaged in handing around copies of the attack, thus seeking to damage the Company's standing,—I have pleasure in laying before the public the following certificate, bearing the signatures of the Presidents and Cashiers who happened to be in their Offices) of *every Bank* in *Hartford* ; also that of the President and Secretary of the old Ætna Fire Insurance Company :—
" *To whom it may concern :—*
" We, the undersigned, regard the Ætna Life Insurance Company, of this city, as one of the most successful and prosperous Insurance Companies in the States,— entirely reliable, responsible, and honourable in all its dealings, and most worthy of public confidence and patronage."

Lucius J. Hendee, President Ætna Fire Insurance Co., and late Treasurer of the State of Connecticut.
J. Goodnow, Secretary Ætna Fire Insurance Co.
C. H. Northam, President, and J. B. Powell, Cashier National Bank.
C. T. Hillyer, President Charter Oak National Bank.
E. D. Tiffany, President First National Bank.
G. S. Riley, Cashier,　do.　do.　do.
John C. Tracy, President of Farmers' and Mechanics' National Bank.
M. W. Graves, Cashier Conn. River Banking Co.
H. A. Redfield, Cashier Phœnix National Bank.
O. G. Terry, President Ætna National Bank.
J. R. Redfield, Cashier National Exchange Bank.
John G. Root, Assistant Cashier American National Bank.
George F. Hills, Cashier State Bank of Hartford.
Jas. Potter, Cashier Hartford National Bank.
Hartford, Nov. 26, 1867.

Many of the above-mentioned parties are closely connected with other Life Insurance Companies, but all unhesitatingly commend our Company as " reliable, responsible, honorable in all its dealings, and most worthy of public confidence and patronage.

JOHN GARVIN,
General Agent, Toronto Street.
Toronto, Dec. 3. 1867.　　　16-1y

Life Association of Scotland.

INVESTED FUNDS
UPWARDS OF £1,000,000 STERLING.

THIS Institution differs from other Life Offices, in that the
BONUSES FROM PROFITS
Are applied on a special system for the Policy-holder's *PERSONAL BENEFIT AND ENJOYMENT DURING HIS OWN LIFETIME,*
WITH THE OPTION OF
LARGE BONUS ADDITIONS TO THE SUM ASSURED.

The Policy-holder thus obtains
A LARGE REDUCTION OF PRESENT OUTLAY
OR
A PROVISION FOR OLD AGE OF A MOST IMPORTANT AMOUNT IN ONE CASH PAYMENT, OR A LIFE ANNUITY,
Without any expense or outlay whatever beyond the ordinary Assurance Premium for the Sum Assured, which remains in tact for Policy-holder's heirs, or other purposes.

CANADA—MONTREAL—PLACE D'ARMES.

DIRECTORS:
DAVID TORRANCE, Esq., (D. Torrance & Co.)
GEORGE MOFFATT, (Gillespie, Moffatt & Co.)
ALEXANDER MORRIS, Esq., M P., Barrister, Perth.
Sir G. E. CARTIER, M.P., Minister of Militia.
PETER REDPATH, Esq., (J Redpath & Son)
J. H. R. MOLSON, Esq., (J. H. R. Molson & Bros.)
Solicitors—Messrs. TORRANCE & MORRIS.
Medical Officer—R. PALMER HOWARD, Esq., M.D
Secretary—P. WARDLAW.
Inspector of Agencies—JAMES B. M. CHIPMAN.　　y

Insurance.

North British and Mercantile Insur Company.

Established 1809.

HEAD OFFICE, - - CANADA - - MON

TORONTO BRANCH:
Local Offices, Nos. 4 & 6 WELLINGTON STR
Fire Department, ... R. N. Go

Life Department, ... H. L. HI
29-1y

Phenix Fire Assurance Compa
LOMBARD ST. AND CHARING CROSS,
LONDON, ENG.

Insurances effected in all parts of the P

WITH PROMTITUDE and *LIBERAL.*
MOFFATT, MURRAY & BEATTI
Agents for Tor
36 Yonge !

The Commercial Union Assura Company,
19 & 20 CORNHILL, LONDON, ENGLAND.
Capital, £2,500,00 Stg.—Invested over $2,000,

FIRE DEPARTMENT.—Insurance granted on scriptions of property at reasonable rates.
LIFE DEPARTMENT.—The success of this has been unprecedented—NINETY PER CENT. mums now in hand. First year's premiums we $100,000.　Economy of management guaranteed e curity.　Moderate rates.
OFFICE—386 & 387 ST PAUL STREET, MONTI
MORLAND, WATSON &
General Agents for
FRED. COLE, Secretary.
Inspector of Agencies—T. C. LIVINGSTON
W. M. WESTMACOTT, Agent at T
16-1y

Phœnix Mutual Life Insurance
HARTFORD, CONN.

Accumulated Fund, $9,000,000, Income, $1,0

THIS Company, established in 1851, is one of reliable Companies doing business in the coun has been steadily prospering.　The *Massachusetts l Reports* show that in nearly all important matt superior; o the general average of Companies.　T intending assurors the following reasons, amongs for preferring it to other companies:
It is purely Mutual　It allows the Insured and reside in any portion of the United States and It throws out almost all restriction on occupation Policies.　It will, if desired, take a note for par Premium, thus combining all the advantages of a all cash company.　Its Dividends are declared and applied in reduction of Premium.　Its Divi in every case on Premiums paid.　The Dividend Phœnix have averaged fifty per cent. yearly. settlement of Policies, a Dividend will be allowe year the policy has been in force.　The numbe dends will always equal the outstanding Notes. loses promptly—during its existence never ha tested a claim.　It issues Policies for the benefi ried Women beyond the reach of their husband's Creditors may also insure the lives of Debtors. It are all *Non-forfeiting,* as it always allows the as surrender his Policy, should he desire, the Com ing a paid-up Policy therefor.　This importan will commend itself to all.　The inducements no by the PHŒNIX are better and more liberal than any other Company.　Its rate of Mortality is ex low and under the average.
Parties contemplating *Life Insurance* will find i interest to call and examine our system.　Polici payable either in *Gold* or American currency.
ANGUS R. BETHUN
General Manager
Dominion o

Office: 104 ST. FRANÇOIS XAVIER ST. MONTI

☞ Active and energetic Agents and C wanted in every town and village, to whom liber ments will be given.

PRINTED AT THE DAILY TELEGRAPH PR
HOUSE, BAY, ST., COR. KING.

THE CANADIAN
MONETARY TIMES
AND
INSURANCE CHRONICLE.
'OTED TO FINANCE, COMMERCE, INSURANCE, BANKS, RAILWAYS, NAVIGATION, MINES, INVESTMENT,
PUBLIC COMPANIES, AND JOINT STOCK ENTERPRISE.

| II—NO. 7. | TORONTO, THURSDAY, OCTOBER 1, 1868. | { SUBSCRIPTION, { $2 A YEAR. |

Mercantile.

Mining.

MADOC GOLD DISTRICT.

Some interesting details respecting mining
matters, are afforded in the following correspondence which, coming from a thoroughly reliable
source, we take pleasure in publishing :—

Belleville, Ont., Sept., 25, 1868.

DEAR SIR,—According to your request, I visited, on Wednesday, 16th inst., the Quartz-lead
discovered by D. B. Johnston, on Lot No. 30, in
the sixth concession of the township of Madoc,
and now beg to hand you the result of my observations.

Leaving the waggon at the village of Bannockburn, we followed a bye-road leading through the
woods in a north-easterly direction, for about
three-fourths of a mile, which brought us to the
place where the vein had been exposed, a few
yards within the boundary of the lot.

The lode runs along the gently sloping side of a
little valley, where a clearing of a few acres in
extent has been made, across which it has been
traced for about 40 rods, to where it enters the
base of a piece of rising ground covered with thick
woods, beyond which it has not been followed ;
the bearing by compass being N. 30 E.

The lode consists of a distinct vein of semi-
opaque crystalline quartz of a whitish color, and
possessing a rather oleaginous than glassy lustre
on the surface of fracture. It is about four feet
wide, and is enclosed between well defined wall-
rocks; that on the west side consisting of mica-
schist, dipping to the west with an inclination of
about 87 degrees ; and that on the east side of
talc-schist, dipping to the east at an angle with
the horizon of about 80 degrees, so that the vein
appears to widen downwards at an angle of about
1½ degrees, The whole is covered with only a
few inches of loose soil, which had been removed
for a space of 12 feet in length by 7 feet broad.

Having taken notes of these points, I proceeded
to search for gold in situ, and succeeded in bringing up from the bottom of the hole made by
blasting, which is nowhere more than two feet
deep, and then contained a little water from recent
rains, a few pieces of quartz in which gold was
plainly discernable. I then broke off from the
solid rock of the vein a few fragments which contained visible particles of gold. Some of the
larger pieces which lay about, apparently just as
thrown out by the explosion, also showed gold on
their surfaces.

I also observed that the quartz contains a few
scattered nodules and scales of titanic and magnetic iron ore, and crystals of common pyrites
(bisulphuret of iron), and has an interrupted vein
of galena (sulphide of lead), about half an inch in
thickness, running along the middle.

On leaving, I selected portions of the clean
vein-stone ; of earthy debris, containing fragments of the wall-rocks and surface quartz; of
the decomposed quartz forming the cap of the
vein ; and of the central part, containing the
galena—over 25 lbs. in all ; from which, since
my return, I have made the following tests :—

No. 1. Clean vein-stone, shewing no gold to
the eye ; 5 lbs. yielded by amalgamation (mill

process) 0·82 grains gold = 13 dwts. 16 grs., value
$13.64 per ton of 2,000 lbs.

No. 2. Earthy debris, containing fragments of
wall rocks and vein-stone ; 5 lbs. gave by mill
process, 0·07 grs. gold = 1 dwt. 4 grs. per ton.

No. 3. Ferruginous decomposed quartz from
surface of lode : 5 lbs. gave, by mill process, a
small quantity of gold.

No. 4. Same as last ; 5 lbs. gave a similar
return.

No. 5. Fire assay of sulphurets concentrated
from the tailings of the above four assays—425
grains yielded 0·11 grains alloy, containing 0·075
silver, and 0·085 gr. gold=

Silver, 5 oz. 2 dwt. 22 gr. } Value, { $ 6.58 } =$54.58 ℔ ton.
Gold, 2 " 8 " .00 } { 48.00 }

No. 6. Quartz from middle of vein, including
galena, &c., 5 lbs. concentrated to 1,116 grains,
of which 69 grains was magnetic iron. The 1,116
grains yielded by fire assay, 805 grains lead, or
72·148 per cent. ; which, by cupellation, gave
2·13 grains of silver alloyed with about 1-700th
part of gold = 77 ozs. 3 dwts. 11 grs.—value
$98.64 per ton.

From the above results I draw the following
deductions :—

First—That the discovery is genuine and valuable.

Second—That if properly worked, the vein is
likely to prove richly remunerative.

Third—That so far as I can judge from the
present limited exposure, the gold appears to be
disseminated throughout the whole width of the
vein ; but that it occurs chiefly in the immediate
vicinity of the wall-rocks, especially on the west
side of the lode ; and that the silver accompanies
the galena.

Fourth—That the proper mode of working such
a vein would be, to separate the portion containing the galena, and work the remainder by amalgamation, saving the sulphurets. The portion containing the galena to be crushed and
concentrated, and reduced by smelting along with
the sulphurets from the other part of the vein,
when the alloy of silver and gold would be obtained by Pattinson's process, and afterwards
by solution and precipitation.

I am, dear Sir,

Yours very truly,

JAMES T. BELL,
Practical Mineralogist & Assayer.

W. H. PONTON, Esq.

NOVA SCOTIA COAL MINES.

The Albion Mines near New Glasgow, cover an
area of four square miles, in which several pits
have been bored and mining continued at a depth
of 400 feet in all directions. The thickness of
the coal seams heretofore mined has been enormous
—nearly forty feet ; but of this not more than
twelve feet has been of a good quality of coal.
At present only two pits are being worked, others
having been abandoned, and one, the largest,
having taken fire within a year, involving the
necessity of permitting the river to flow in and
submerge it in order to extinguish the flames.
At present, however, the company have a new pit
900 feet in depth, where, as they claim, a much

better quality of coal can be obtained, and to work which they have imported heavy machinery from England at an enormous cost, looking forward to a new reciprocity treaty, and consequent increase of business.

The new machinery is certainly wonderful for its massiveness and strength. A walking-beam which I saw is composed of wrought iron, and weighs seventeen tons. The cages for the shaft are made of steel by the Bessmere process, and are models of strength. The building for the engine is of solid masonry, and the engine itself is of enormous power and weight. Indeed weight, ponderosity, seems to be the necessary elements of British strength. A railroad extends from the mines to the loading-ground on Pictou Harbor, where vessels can readily come up to get their loading.

The Albion Mines formerly employed as many as 800 to 900 men, but this number is now reduced by the slackness of trade to 300 or 500. The village where the miners live is laid out with some attempt at regularity, but the houses present a poverty-stricken and dilapidated appearance, and want of neatness in their surroundings, painful to the American eye. This Company last year mined about one hundred thousand tons of coal, selling at $2.25 (gold) per ton.

The coal is bituminous, and best suited for gas purposes; much of it is used by the New York and Boston Gas Companies; it makes a very superior coke. Contiguous to the Albion Mines are those of the Acadia Company. This Company is, with one exception (Hugh Allan, Esq., Montreal), made up of New York men. Its officers are as follows: J. W. Clendennin, President and Treasurer; Cambridge Livingstone, Secretary; Jesse Hoyt, General Agent. Directors: J. W. Clendennin, E. S. Sanford, Cyrus W. Field, C. B. Hoffman, Marshall Lefferts, New York, Hugh Allen Montreal. The property was originally purchased by Mr. Cyrus W. Field from a citizen of Pictou for the sum of $52,000 (gold) Mr. Field considered it a good investment, and with his usual liberality divided it among his friends on his return to New York. General Lefferts was the first President of the Company, and Jesse Hoyt, Esq., Superintendent of the Nova Scotia Telegraph Company, General Agent. General Lefferts, however, was unable to give the the time and attention to the enterprise which its importance required, and resigned about a year since, being succeeded by Mr. Clendennin, who has exhibited great energy and judgment in his management, being ably assisted by Mr. Hoyt, who has the entire local charge, and whose efficient and judicious superintendence will make this one of the richest mines in the country. The first borings brought to light a seam of coal of the same character as at the Albion mines, and probably a portion of the same, in which the coal, though a fair quality, was interseamed with foreign matter, detracting much from its value. But two years since a new seam was discovered, twenty feet in thickness, of the finest quality of rich bituminous coal, the best discovered in the Province; this discovery so enhanced the value of the adjoining property, that a similar area has been sold to the Incorcolonial Company for $150,000.

The Territory of the Acadia Company comprises in mining area, four square miles, and in surface and woodland, 1,400 acres; this is held on a lease of 80 years, paying a royalty on coal sold of five per cent. ad valorem.

The two collieries at present in operation are the McGregor, having a slope (or inclined entrance shaft) of 700 feet, and a seam of 12 feet; and the Acadia with a slope of 400 feet, and a seam of 20 feet. The Acadia coal crops out absolutely on the surface only a few feet below the grass; the entrance down an inclined plane of 350 feet leads you to transverse passages, one extending 1,600, the other 700 feet, these being again intersected by cross-passages, or galleries of various lengths An air shaft conveys air into the mine, and at the base, in a chamber showing the whole depth of the seam, are two furnaces, kept constantly burning

for purification; the effect in the huge, black coal chamber, with its mysterious galleries made more mysterious by the flashing of the furnace fires; the smart pitmen, with their little stars of lamps fastened to their hats; and the general impression that you are in the depths of the earth gives you a curious and not altogether agreeable sensation, which is not improved by your progression through those black and inscrutable galleries, guided by one of the sooty pitmen aforesaid, and lighted by a little tin apology for a lamp with which you are provided. I breathed more freely, in all senses of the word, when I reached the surface of the earth again. The coal is really beautiful; it resembles anthracite in its brilliance, but is soft and easily broken in the hand; as a domestic coal it is better than the Liverpool, and not very inferior to the channel; it burns with a clear, brilliant flame and throws out no flakes, being exceedingly clean to handle.

The price of the coal is $2.25 per ton at the wharf, the same at the Albion, which is far inferior; add duties, premium on gold, and freight, and it costs in Boston about $8.50 per ton; with free trade it could be delivered in New York for $7 per ton, while Liverpool is $14 to $15, and Channel $18 to $20. For steam purposes treatment of iron, and domestic uses this coal is the best in the Province.

The Acadia Company commenced operations in 1866, and its capacity is about one thousand tons per day. A branch railway, 3½ miles long, connects the mines with the Nova Scotia Railway to Halifax and Windsor, and the Company possesses a loading-ground on the harbor of Pictou; so its facilities for transportation are unexcelled. About three hundred men are employed, who earn from $1.50 to $2.50 per day each.

Stores containing all necessary commodities are already in full operation. The new machinery for hauling coal, pumping, &c., is now being erected, having been made at the Novelty Works, New York, and also contrasts with the English work, in its lightness and evident strength, combined with elegance of appearance.

The amount of coal shipped for the present year will be about 75,000 tons, as they are getting out about 300 to 400 tons a day at present.

When it is taken into consideration that the carboniferous system of Nova Scotia occupies a large portion of ten out of the eighteen counties, and that what I have described is merely the workings of eight square miles, and those in their infancy, it will be seen how much room there is for speculation on the Nova Scotia coal trade of the future. As these coal-measures contain iron ores of the richest character, producing bar-iron of a better quality than any manufactory elsewhere in the British Dominions, and steel only equalled by that of the Dannemora mines of Sweden, something may be hereafter looked for in this industry.
—*Cor. N. Y. World.*

THE UTILIZATION OF PEAT FOR SMELTING PURPOSES.

The use of peat in the smelting of iron ores has been frequently attempted on many French and German metallurgical works. It has, however, generally proved that, for the most part, insuperable difficulties have stood in the way of attaining the end in view. The chief difficulty to contend with in the use of peat in blast furnaces seems to be the ease with which it crumbles into small pieces, thereby choking up the furnace, and, in the end, rendering it necessary to blow out. We are told of an occasional exception to this, in case of the use of very rich peats—the furnaces, under such circumstances, having given very satisfactory results. We are glad to learn that an attempt is now being made in this country to utilize the peat beds of the Lake Superior region for the purpose of smelting the rich ores of iron so abundant in that locality.

B. M. Peirce, Sr., Metallurgist and Mining

Engineer of the French School, is attemp prove, beyond all question, the adaptab this kind of fuel to the smelting of ores i furnaces. Should his efforts be crowned w cess it will be a fine thing for the Superior r Bituminous coal from the deposits of Penns or Ohio would no longer be a matter of ne There would, in all probability, be a savin least one-half in the cost of fuel. That indeed, be an item of no small consideratio it to come to the chances of success, as t two rival metallurgical districts. An allus made in our last issue, in the Mining Su article upon the the Copper District of Vermont, to the attempt made there, a she ago, to utilize the peat in the smelting of ore. Should the attempt to prepare it, so can be used successfully in the iron fur Lake Superior, succeed, we shall conside other things being equal, the problem is l solved for the Vermont copper furnace may, then, fairly consider that the expe now going on are, in point of fact, not Lake Superior region alone, but rather regions where peat and ore beds are round proximity, with, of course, a scarcity of a kinds of fuel.

We hope soon to learn of the complete of Mr. Peirce's attempts in the utilization as fuel in the running of blast furnaces.— *of Mining.*

SILVER ORE.—A Chicago paper says:— nificent specimen of dog tooth spar was ex on 'Change, taken from the Shunian (Silver of Thunder Bay, on the northern shore o Superior, and presented by Messrs. N. C and J. E. Withers, of the Mining Comp the Chicago University. It is a rarity in a beauty, and will, we doubt not, be highly by all connected with the institution ch the recipient.

—Iron works have been established at M on the southern shore of Lake Superior, w is expected, will produce pig iron at less c is done at Pittsburg.

—Perhaps the best evidence of the perm of the mines of the precious metals may b in the fact that, after more than three centuries of operation, more or less acti silver mines of Mexico remain as her gre dustrial resource, the basis of her commer the best security she can offer for the cos improvement she may contemplate.

Railway News.

GREAT WESTERN RAILWAY.—Traffic ending 11th Sept., 1868.

Passengers	$30,09
Freight and live stock	42,67
Mails and sundries	1,83
	$83,50
Corresponding Week of '67	83,49
Decrease	8

NORTHERN RAILWAY.—Traffic Rec week ending Sept. 19, 1868.

Passengers	$2,08
Freight	8,00
Mails and Sundries	...
Total Receipts for week	$12,17
Corresponding week 1867	10,91
Increase	$1,2

—Hon. M. Carling has been chosen of the Great Western, in the room of T. resigned.

/AY COMMISSIONERS.—Aquila Walsh,
. P. for Norfolk, has been appointed
. Commissioner for Ontario; C. J. Brydges
anaging director of the Grand Trunk
, for Quebec; the Hon. E. B. Chandler,
Brunswick; and Mr. Meredith, for Nova
. Under the Independence of Parliament
ercolonial Railway Acts passed last session,
not be necessary for Mr. Walsh to go back
onstituency for re-election.

W. G. AND B. RAILWAY.—An exchange
he first section of this road was let on the
st., to contractors, at a figure below the
s, ($15,500 per mile.) The township of
by which lately withdrew the By-law
[a bonus to the narrow gauge has now
sed one to give a bonus of $50,000 to the
and B. road.

D TRUNK.—We hear that a satisfactory
ment has been come to, during the week,
. the Committee, headed by Mr. Ritter and
ak, and the Board, by which three or four
mbers will be introduced into the Board,
ig Mr. Ritter and Mr. Creak, to whom the
tors are deeply indebted for the exertions
m the management.

omy in working is to be the order of the
uture, and this being so, we tell the Pro-
that in the Grand Trunk they have a much
roperty than most of them think.

ourse, under the circumstances of the
e and fair arrangement made between
Creak and Ritter's Committee and the
there will be no necessity for the formation
and Trunk Proprietor's Association. Agi-
will cease, and its expense be avoided.—
th's Journal.

WAY TRAFFIC.—The railway returns for
show as follows:—The Great Western
7 in 1868 against $270,183 for the same
last year; Grand Trunk, $627,713 in 1868
$800,779; Brockville and Ottawa, $14,-
ainst $10,213; St. Lawrence and Ottawa,
against $9,518; New Brunswick and Cana-
),837, against $7,459; European and North
au $18,560 against $15,517; Nova Scotia,
8 against $22,006.

ANTIC AND GREAT WESTERN RAILWAY.—
ral meeting of the stockholders was held
r York on Sept. 21. After James McHenry
en voted to the chair and the minutes of
vious meeting adopted, a report from the
of Directors was read, congratulating the
olders on the improved aspect of affairs,
. that arrangements had been completed
he English creditors, which were being
y carried out, and recommending that the
olders should ratify the terms of the agree-
with the creditors, and should formally
ize the issue of seven million (7,000,000)
of second consolidated mortgage bonds, to
a similar amount of debentures. .
lutions carrying these recommendations
ect were adopted, and the thanks of the
g were voted to the President, the Directors
Mr. McHenry for their exertions in behalf
Company.

LVENTS.—The following new Insolvents
gazetted last week:—Louis Roverge, La
tation; Jas. Christie, Elora; Henry Winter,
a; John H. Bartlett, Granby; Calvin Hall,
rs; Moïse Duquette, Montreal; Pierre Du-
hillips, Montreal; Thomas J. Jones, St. Mary's;
Phillips, Montreal; Prosper Archombault,
of St. Vincent de Paul; Anthony and
w Walsh, Montreal; Wm. Hilton & Co.,
al; Ephraim Cronk, Aylmer Village Co.
Thomas L. Lewis, Innisfil; Charles Can-
Plessisville, Somerset; Edward Fawcett,
George Wilson, M. D., St. Mary's; W. B.
& Co., Montreal; Pierre Beique, Granby;
n Adna Bates, Mitchell; Thomas McFane,
; Octave Brisettes, St. Bridgette; J. B.
& Co., Oshawa.

Insurance.

INSURANCE MATTERS IN MONTREAL.
(From a Correspondent.)

MONTREAL, Sept. 30, 1868.

Since my last the incendiary has been actively
at work, and we have had three fires, all in stables,
in one of which three horses were destroyed. The
total loss will be under $800. The city authori-
ties are going to offer a reward of $1000 to detect
the authors, but I question if it will be any use.
It is a positive fact that from the day our local
goveanment appointed two of their *hangers-on*
(both briefless barristers, and in every respct most
incompetent) we have had nothing but incendiarism. One of the employees of these marshals has
been accused of being the author of many of these
fires.

If I were to say that the Insurance Agents are
becoming alarmed at the existing state of affairs, I
might do them an injustice. Owing to the want
of honest dealing one with another, and the universal distrust they exhibit towards their confreres,
no united action in any way pertaining to their
common interests can be expected. Mr. Perry of
the "Royal," seems the only person who takes an
interest in exposing the existing state of affairs.
He is the author of the existing Fire Marshal's
bill, an excellent one, if worked by an honest and
efficient Fire Marshal. Unfortunately, however,
this is not the case, and the number of fires is
rapidly increasing, as the following table of fires
for the two months the Marshals have been in
office, compared with those of previous years, will
plainly show.

No. of Fires,	1865.	1866.	1867.	1868.
July	6	11	14	18
" August	10	12	14	18
Totals	16	23	28	36

Of the 16 fires for the two months of 1865, 13
were accidental and 3 unaccounted for. Of the 23
for same period, 1866, 21 were accounted for and 2
not ascertained. Of the 28 for same period, 1867,
21 were accidental and 7 not known. Of the 36
in same time, 1868, being the two months during
which the Fire Marshals have held sway, 24 are
known to be acts of wilful incendiarism. During
the present month of September, we have already
had fourteen fires, eleven of which were purposely
set. So much for the operation of our new system
of fire marshalship under the Chauveau & Dunkin Government.

FIRE RECORD.—London, Ont.—The boiler of
Messrs. M. & E. Anderson, exploded, killing one
man, seriously injuring a number of others, and
greatly damaging the building.

Wellington Square, Sept. 21.—Stable of Thos.
L. White, at Hillbridge, partially consumed;
the whole of his extensive premises had a narrow
escape; cause supposed to be heated manure.

Black Creek, Sept.—Dwelling-house, barn and
outbuildings and live stock of Mr. Roundtree;
particulars as to insurance, not given; believed
to be incendiary.

The Grist Mill and Distillery belonging to Mr.
George Privat, Enniskillen, were totally consumed.

Aineyville, Sept.—Store and contents of Mr.
George R. Ross; very little saved. Loss heavy;
partially insured; no satisfactory account of the
fire can be given.

Lambeth, Sept.—Barn of S. Reynolds, and
contents; insured for $200; loss heavy. The
fire is thought to be the work of an incendiary,
and the suspected party has left the neighborhood;
four valuable horses in the barn were roasted to
death.

St. John, Sept. 12.—Premises of Joseph Fair-
weather, Market Avenue, totally destroyed; loss
chiefly covered by insurance.

Richmond, Quebec, Sept. 22.—House and store
of Mr. E. F. Miller, with contents; loss about
$8,000 partially insured; cause unknown.

Ancaster, September 27.—Hotel of J. Crann,
and adjoining building of A. Raymond; total loss
about $5,000; Crann was insured for $600; Raymond no insurance.

North Norwich, Township, Ont., Sept. 1.—
Barn of M. M. Kiff, and contents; loss heavy;
partial insurance.

Port Dalhousie, Sept. 28.—The light-house at
this place caught fire, but was saved.

MARINE RECORD.—Port Rowan, Ont., Sept. 28.
—The schooner *Florida* and barque *Grace Greenwood* went ashore last night on Long Point, near
the old cut. The barque was got off this morning.
The schooner is hard on, loaded with 19,000 bus.
of corn from Chicago to Oswego.

OSWEGO, Sept. 21.—The schooner *Resolute*,
from Belleville, Ont., for this port, with barley,
in attempting to enter the harbor last night,
struck the west pier, and is going to pieces.
Crew saved.

Newcastle, Sep. 28.—The schooner *Ariadne*, of
Port Newcastle, went ashore on Saturday, at 11
P. M., a little to the west of Port Granby. The
vessel was loaded with barley, for Oswego, and
had just left the harbor, when, owing to the heavy
swell, she struck the ground outside. The crew
endeavoured to pull her off by the anchor, which
dragged, the wind being very high, and blowing
from the sixth. She beached about one hundred
and fifty yards west of the pier. There is about
three feet water now in the hold. The vessel and
cargo are partially insured.

—The Equitable Life Insurance Company has
made a deposit with the Government.

—The Ætna Life has adopted the contribution
method of distributing surplus applicable only to
dividends to policy holders making their payments
under new tables of low cash rates.

—Under the English system of granting small
government insurances and annuities through the
medium of the Post Office, the number of life
policies issued at the end of 1867 were 1485, covering £111,437. The success thus far is not considered a justification of the anticipations formed
respecting government schemes.

HARTFORD LIVE STOCK Co.—The failure and
winding up of the Hartford Live Stock Company
is said to be owing to claims amounting to $80,000
which had never been reported to the Directors,
and an immense volume of bad risks. Profiting
by this failure the Ætna has increased its rates 30
per cent., inaugurated a new system of inspection
and reduced the risks to two classes. The liabilities of the Hartford are placed at $180,000, to
pay which it has $100,000 in hand and $20,000
other assets.

PREMIUM NOTES.—In discussing the question of assets the Massachusetts Commissioner, in
his recent report, says:—The merit of the premium
note plan involves two questions: *First*, Is the
plan a good one for the insured? and *second*, Is it
a safe one for the company? With the first question we have nothing to do here, except so far as
it is involved in the second, and shall, therefore
find no occasion to say anything upon it.

Are premium notes or loans a safe investment
for the company, and may they properly be counted among its legitimate or realized assets as against
its reserve fund? There is no mystery about the
matter because it involves a transaction between a
life insurance company and a policy-holder. If
John Doe has given his bond to pay a sum of
money to Richard Roe, and at the same time
holds the note of Richard running to himself, the
note of Richard is just as good as legal tender to
John, *under certain limitations*. The limitations
are these: The amount due on the note must
always be less than the liability on the bond, and
John Doe must always have his affairs so well in
hand that he can take care of all his other debts

without having to resort to Richard's note for that purpose. So long as he can afford to hold the note to pay *pro tanto* this particular bond, he need not trouble himself about the solvency of the maker.

Applying the same sort of common sense to life insurance, we fail to see why policy-holders' notes, *under similar limitations*, are not a perfectly safe investment, and a perfectly good asset *for the purposes of the company.* The amount of the note or loan on any policy must always be less than the unearned premium or self-insurance under the policy, so that whenever and however the policy is terminated, the insured will owe as much as or more to the company than the company can lose by the non-payment of the note. In other words, the balance on each policy as it stands must always be in favor of the company. All of the note companies have, accordingly, in answer to an enquiry directed to this point, distinctly responded that the premium-note or other credit on any policy, with a few exceptional cases, is never allowed to exceed its net present value, Actuaries' four per cent.

It is also evident that a company cannot sell insurance wholly upon credit. It must have a cash working capital ample enough to pay all of its current losses and expenses without resorting to its notes, or, in other words, it must not be under the necessity of using A's notes to discharge its obligations to B. Without attempting to indicate the precise limit beyond which the proportion of premium notes cannot safely go, we exhibit in the table on another page the actual ratio of the premium notes and loans held by each company, including all loans secured by the policy, to its computed premium reserve, and also to its net assets or actual premium reserve. By the latter is meant the gross assets diminished by all liabilities except the computed premium reserve and guaranteed capital.

Probably no one will seriously contend upon this showing, that any company has passed the absolute limit of safety, unless we are to assume that the company is liable to an experience which upsets the fundamental assumption of an average mortality, and this has the absurdity of begging the whole question. No one, certainly, will say that these notes are a barren investment for the company. Bearing interest from the moment the premium is due, there is also no risk, within the limitations indicated, of their non-payment. If the policy-holder expects that he, or his money, is not bound to pay them to the last cent of principal and interest, he simply allows himself to be defrauded. It will not be claimed that they are unrealized assets simply because they are unpaid notes. If so, unpaid mortgage notes must be put in the same category.

DAMAGES BY REMOVAL.—A writer in the *Monitor* gives some valuable hints on the subject of adjustment when "damages by removal" are claimed. Such claims are often paid in full, the condition as to the amount payable, viz: such proportion as the sum insured bears to the whole value of the goods, being ignored. He says—"The contract is for indemnity against loss and damage by fire. The insurer agrees to give a certain measure of indemnity, on certain clearly defined conditions, for a certain consideration. One of these conditions is, that in case the property insured is exposed to loss or damage by fire, the assured shall use his best endeavors to save and protect the same, and unless he shall do so, he shall not recover at all ; but right here the insurer agrees that in condition to the actual loss and damage by fire, he will also *contribute* to the damage on such proportion of the property saved as shall be caused in saving the same. In the absence of this latter clause in the contract, I insist that the insured could not sustain any claim against the insurer for damages caused solely by removal. That would be a risk which the insurer did not assume, as would be indicated by the condition requiring the owner to remove and save the

property from burning, if possible, and he agreed to do it. * * * * * * * I am aware of the various notions of agents and others on this point ; many supposing that in cases where the building ignites or is totally consumed, or where a portion of the goods insured are burned, the insurer is liable for all loss and damage up to the full sum insured. But there is no reason or authority for such notions. There are no legal adjudications that favor such views, where the condition in question prevails in the contract. The case of Case *vs.* Hartford Fire Ins. Co., in 13 Ill., 376 does not favor the doctrine that the insurer is liable for the whole damages caused by removal under certain circumstances, but simply settles the question whether the assured could recover at all in that particular case, leaving the contract to govern as to the *extent* of such recovery. It was similar to the case of Hillier vs. Allegheny County Mutual Ins. Co., in 3 Penn St., 470, in which it was held that, under the circumstances of that case, the insured could not recover at all. But in the case of Wilson vs. Peoria M. & F. Ins. Company in 5 Minnesota, the whole subject was deliberately considered, and it was decided, that although one tenement of the building containing the property insured was on fire, and part of the insured stock was burnt, and balance removed, the amount of loss and damage on goods removed, must be borne by insured and insurer in such proportion as the whole value of the property at the time of the loss. The reasoning of the learned judge in this case is so cogent and logical, I cannot better close this article than by commending the full opinion to the careful examination of all who call themselves underwriters or adjusters.

The true rule in such cases may be stated as follows : A stock of merchandize valued at $10,000 is insured for 5,000. A fire occurs, and $7,000 of the goods are removed, but the damage by such removal is $8,000 and $3,000 of the goods are consumed. The loss should be adjusted thus :—

Goods totally consumed or destroyed		$3,000
Underwriters pay for same		3,000
Damage by removal of goods saved, say total value $7,000 00		
damages	800 00	
Underwriter's pay on 2,000 00 being balance of policy, 2–7	228 57	
Owners. on uninsured portion, $5,000, 5–7.	571 43	
		$800
Total claim under the policy		$3,228 57

Law Report.

EASTERN TOWNSHIPS BANK vs. HUMPHREY, *et al.*—This case was lately tried in the Queen's Bench, (appeal side), Montreal. Mr. Justice Badgley said, John Humphrey, a trader in business at Barnston, needing money accommodation, applied to the Eastern Townships Bank, at Sherbrook, in May, 1862, for discount for a year for $1,000, and was refused, the Bank not discounting at the time. He afterwards proposed to take United States notes. The Bank having received these notes at par, would not part with them except at the same value. This was agreed to, and for the note of $1,000 he received $982, the discount of $18 being retained for three months' interest, at the legal Provincial Bank interest of 7 per cent., Humphrey to be permitted to renew the note every three months and have it extended over a year. After the transaction had been effected another transaction took place between Mr. Farwell, cashier of the Bank, and Humphrey, by which the latter paid to the former $10 as a commission for working through the arrangements and renewals of liability during the year. This seems to have been a private bargain between them in no way connected with the discounting of the note, etc. * * * * * * *

Mr. Farwell, in his deposition, says th a separate transaction, and not a stipulati discount,—*and the evidence shows that h ciation of Humphrey's irregularity an were abundantly justified.*

Now looking at the transaction as p can scarcely be termed a discount or a loan the meaning of the Bank charter, 18 Vi 20, sec. 20, which authorizes the Bank only in gold and silver bullion, bills of e discounting of promissory notes and n securities, and in such trade generally mately appertains to the business of B the 21st section refers to discounts and made on commercial paper or securities, 22nd authorizes the Bank to take disc promissory notes or other negotiable discounted. Discount is in effect lending but in practice money does not pass, but receive notes of the Bank, which are the eq of money from their convertibility int by the issuing Bank. In this sense the to have been really no discounting so far a the discounted proceeds in money, but agreement to take or purchase from the *the discounted note this foreign bank pa* prepayment of the three months' intere question then turns upon the value of t modity given to him for the proceeds of t and as to the United States notes giv sufficiently established that these very n been taken by the Bank at their par value nominally in some cases at a discount of 3 such notes were the chief currency at th ship at the time, and passed generally thro country at their par value, and Humphr specially for such notes and received them value and actually disposed of them in of his own indebtedness at their par valu seems therefore manifest that they had p value at the time.

Now usury is the taking a rate of int yond that allowed by the law, and to tute the usury, there must not only be to take illegal interest that is a corrupt ag to take it in violation of the law, or by vice or shift to reserve or to take it. And though it is said that the notes rece Humphrey were depreciated, it does no that the owner was not entitled to den require a higher price, namely, their cu value before he consented to part with * * No disguise was used; the tr was in good faith, and there could be because the thing loaned was of full val lender and was so received and used by rower. * * Nor is there anythin Bank Charter which brings this transact in a possible contravention of the Ch trading illegally beyond what appertai business of banking.

The second ground in support of th usury is the payment of $10.00 as a shift to increase the rate of interest. Th foundation; in fact it formed no part of t al transaction, nor with the original co parties, who were the Bank itself and H.

MARINE INSURANCE — UNSEAWORTH In a policy of insurance on a vessel to plaintiff, insured only against peril one of the conditions was that the defend not to be liable for loss or damage ari unseaworthiness. The vessel in quest fifteen minutes after leaving port, begu and in some five hours went down. Bot and water, it appeared, were at the time calm, and no actively adverse cause co was assigned for the accident, nor wa dence given by plaintiff to rebut the pr which, it was contended, therefore arose loss was not occasioned by perils of the

Held, that plaintiff was bound to gi dence, and that the absence of it disen to recover.—*Coons vs. the Ætna Insuran C. P.*, 305.

THE CANADIAN MONETARY TIMES AND
INSURANCE CHRONICLE is printed every Thursday
Evening, in time for the English Mail.
Subscription Price, one year, $2, or $3 in
American currency ; Single copies, five cents each.
Casual advertisements will be charged ten cents
per line of solid nonpareil each insertion. All
letters to be addressed, "THE CANADIAN MONE-
TARY TIMES, TORONTO, ONT." Registered letters
so addressed are at the risk of the Publishers.
Cheques should be made payable to J. M. TROUT,
Business Manager, who will, in future, issue all
receipts for money.

The Canadian Monetary Times.

THURSDAY, OCTOBER 1, 1868.

CANADIAN SHIPPING.

An Official Return, just published, furnishes us with statistics respecting the mercantile navy of the Dominion. The figures
are not unpleasant to contemplate and, while
affording satisfaction to us Canadians, they
may possibly give to those outside our boundaries who affect to despise us, some reason to
change their opinions.

	Tons.	No. of Men.	Value.	No.
Ontario	66,959	3,192	2,787,800	481
Quebec	155,090	8,548	4,632,945	1,428
New Brunswick	200,777	6,207	5,904,505	826
Nova Scotia..........	362,917	19,288	10,256,812	3,087
Total............	756,843	37,235	$23,588,062	5,822

Were Prince Edward Island and Newfoundland members of our Confederacy, as
they undoubtedly will be, we should be able
to show such totals as would give the Dominion rank as the third maritime power in
the world.

In spite of obstacles thrown wantonly in
our path by our enterprising cousins across
the lines, our Marine is making some headway, and we have good reason to congratulate ourselves on the fact that the carrying
trade which our aforesaid cousins were kind
enough to do for us is likely to be efficiently
performed by home-made, home-owned and
home-manned vessels. But our ship-owners
have grounds of complaint which it is the
bounden duty of our Government to examine into. A branch of industry so important
as our shipping interest which gives employment to so many, in a country where the
want of a variety of employment tells fearfully against an increase of population ;
which represents a value of twenty-three and
a-half millions of dollars; and which is capable of immense development to our immediate profit; is one entitled to the greatest
consideration and a fostering care. At the
least our ship owners are entitled to receive
fair play.

Our navigation laws tell against ourselves.
On the sea board, a Canadian vessel is not

allowed to participate in the American coasting trade while, on the lakes, American vessels
enter and leave our ports as freely as Canadian vessels do. On the other hand, a Canadian vessel in an American port is viewed as
a safe victim for the most outrageous exactions and annoyances. The American Custom House officials at the lake ports seem to
be constantly on the alert to seize upon
unfortunate Canadian skippers and the pet-
tiest infraction of their thousand-and-one
laws is the signal for an explosion of rapacity
and greed. While our laws are interpreted
with a foolish liberality, the whole drift of
American legislation is antagonistic to our
interests and their regulations seem prompted by a malicious desire to keep us back as
much as possible. An American vessel cannot purchase so much as a spar in a Canadian
port without danger of seizure on her return.
A Canadian vessel, when she touches an
American port, is charged, in addition to a
tonnage due of 30 cents per ton, from 75c.
to $1.20 for a clearance and this too, often,
when nothing is landed or received, whereas
American vessels are permitted to land passengers and freight free of any charge for
entry or clearance. American vessels are
allowed to carry timber from the Canadian
ports to the Quebec market, landing it at
Clayton, New York, while Canadian vessels
are prohibited from carrying grain from any
American to a Canadian port, even if its
ultimate destination be an American port.
Canadian vessels are not permitted to enter
any American inland stream or canal, whereas American vessels and tugs are allowed to
enter Canadian canals and rivers. Even
a Canadian steamer will not be allowed to go
to the American side of the St. Clair river to
take in tow an American vessel which has
got a permit here nor Customs authorities
to carry bricks from our Canadian landing
to another. American steamboats are allowed to carry passengers from one Canadian
port to another evading the strict requirement of the law by touching at an American
port previous to landing those passengers.
Americans monopolise the ferries to the
manifest disadvantage of Canadians, as they
make it necessary for a Canadian ferryboat
to enter and clear every time she touches an
American landing; whereas American ferry-
boats are permitted to cross to and fro without any charge or restriction. American
citizens are allowed to command Canadian
vessels, but no Canadian is permitted to
command an American vessel, the same privilege being extended to American engineers
on Canadian steamers, but denied to Canadian engineers on Canadian boats unless
they become American citizens.

Is this list of grievances long enough or

shall we go on giving chapter and verse for an endless number of annoyances intended to build up the American Marine at the expense of our own? The object the Americans have in view is to prevent Canadian vessels doing any business whatever to or from American ports. They make no secret of their intent. It is for our legislators to say whether we are to yield ourselves willing victims to their schemes. The Province of Ontario has vessels to the value of $2,787,-800 and the Province of Quebec, $4,633,945, engaged in trade for the most part on our lakes and rivers. Is that interest of sufficient magnitude and importance to be worth some little attention from our Government? Surely, the smallest consideration for the present if not a decent respect for the future should prompt us to follow the dictates of ordinary prudence. The progress made by our shipping interests has been achieved in spite of difficulties innumerable and when the appeal is made for fair play by our ship owners our Government should not be slow to recognise their claims and see that they are justly dealt with. Our excessive liberality in this matter towards our neighbors procures us no thanks; on the contrary, it seems but an incentive to renewed exactions and more wily schemes for getting the better of us. We cannot blame the Americans for taking advantage of our folly on this side, nor do we wonder that they put on the screws on the other. Business is business, and if they can dishearten our ship-owners, secure our carrying trade and, at the same time, retain their own, so much the better for them. Our loss is their gain. But we do wonder that our legislators are so indifferent to the country's prosperity as to ignore practical grievances which injure us at present and may do still more injury in the future. Our pride and our interests are alike concerned in this matter, and if we hope to attain that position which every Canadian should desire, we must take such measures as men of ordinary discretion would adopt under the circumstances to relieve our ship owners from unfair rivalry. The remedy lies in our own hands, and we are worse than fools if we delay to apply it. We need appeal to no one outside our boundaries for either sympathy or redress.

MOVEMENT OF GRAIN.

It is now about four weeks since the crop of 1868 began to move in this section, and during that time an amount of business has been done in receiving and shipping grain, which is creditable alike to our facilities for such operations and to the activity and enterprise of our dealers. Barley, so far, has engrossed attention, it being always brought first into market. During the limited time mentioned nearly 600,000 bushels of this cereal alone have been received and about 400,000 exported and sold in a foreign country. Oswego has, as formely been the chief receptacle of all this grain, but Toledo has taken a large share. As to the prices realized nothing could be more satisfactory. They are equal to the figures (then thought fabulous) which were paid during the American war. Forty-eight pounds of barley represent about as much money as sixty pounds of wheat. Realising such prices it is easy to understand that the conversion of 600,000 bushels of barley into more than that number of dollars has had an immense influence on trade in all its branches.

While the barley trade is thus active, the wheat crop has not yet begun to move to any important extent and will not till the barley is got out of the way; besides the price is such as to give the farmer no special inducement to bring it out.

This late movement of the wheat crop has disappointed the anticipations of the Montreal dealers. The *Herald* thus deprecates their loss of trade,—" At a much earlier date we " had anticipated increased buoyancy in the " market for all descriptions of cereals; but " the disappointment which has been and is " continuing to stare us in the face, is assum- " ing a somewhat serious nature, and, we " fear, injuring this port to an extent which " may not be realized until sufficient mischief " is done to destroy the position which Mon- " treal has attained as a receiving point for " grain. If the produce was not in the coun- " try, the cause would be easily explained " away; but when the reverse is the case, and " this is the season at which stuff should be " coming forward freely, it is a difficult pro- " blem to solve. Whatever the causes are, " we hope they are natural ones."

In the United States the new crop of cereals is moving to the shipping ports finely. At the principal five western lake ports there were received from the 1st August to the 19th September, 832,513 barrels of flour against 722,055 brls. last year, showing an increase of nearly one hundred thousand barrels over 1867, and three hundred thousand brls. over 1866. The receipts of grain were three and a half millions larger for the same period—or twenty-five per cent. The shipments from the same ports show a considerable increase also. These facts go to confirm the largest estimates made of the crop. A careful writer puts the total yield of wheat at 200,000,000 bushels, and of corn at 1,000,000,000 bushels —quantities of which it is difficult to have a practical conception. Of the total wheat it is expected that there will be 40,000,000 bushels of an exportable surplus, or 30 per cent more than last year; a greater quantity of corn will also be than in any previous year.

These facts could not fail to influenc as they have done, bringing wheat d shillings per quarter in the English It may be that this marked decline more than the facts would justify; if will be a sharp reaction. In any ca is no longer room for doubt that the supply of breadstuffs is abundant a cost consumers less than for several years.

LEGAL RESPONSIBILITY DIRECTORS.

Recently in treating of the respon of shareholders, we shewed that in shareholders misled by false statemen by the company, although responsib debts, could still set up such fraud fence in an action brought by the against them for contribution on the remaining unpaid upon their liabili company itself. Very often no cont is required from shareholders of i companies, but unfortunate individ themselves a few months after ha good faith, bought their shares rely the glowing statements contained in reports, possessors of worthless p such cases the private fortunes of tors guilty of such fraud are resp make good the amount lost by their d This responsibility is so lightly th that very often boards of manager sider themselves justified in pu favorable an aspect on the affairs pany, in the hope that it may co command public confidence and we storm for some time until someth up.

A very valuable judgment wa delivered in England, by Lord Ro Master of the Rolls, containing, b judgment upon the particular cas very valuable statements of the law the responsibilities of directors to ers in general. The case was reg late Herefordshire Bank in proces ation and was brought by the offic tor appointed under the winding- law, as yet, not passed by our L against directors, and represen deceased directors, on behalf of t body of shareholders, to recover siderable sums of money under th circumstances: The Banking Co been losing money for several yea directors, contrary to the charter, to call a meeting of the shareh inform them at the time of the c pany, and had lent money to one of lves without taking further security. case made by the official liquidator st. That the directors had in the s, &c., of the company, stated the a of the company too favorably. 2nd. rying on of the business when in fact the ly was practically insolvent. And 3rd. erly sanctioning loans to one of them.

Upon the first ground, the Court at the action could not be maintained. tual shareholders who had lost money equence of the false statements of the rs, could prove that they had been ed and could consequently recover, but ld not be taken for granted that the l body of shareholders had been so. case, in order to succeed for such a must stand upon its own merits.

he second ground, his Lordship went nto the evidence, which showed that ole of the surplus fund, and one-fourth capital had been lost, that false reports lance sheets had been published, that nad been allowed to stand over unpaid, at the directors had carried on the ss of the bank long after the capital had ntirely lost. It was proved that the ing directors were aware of the true n of affairs, and that the other direc- ere not so, but it was held that such unce was no excuse and did not avoid gal liability. Directors who assumed lce were bound to know the position of company, and the ordinary shareholders right to look to them for compensation sses suffered in consequence of their ot of duty. The third ground was also d, and these his Lordship held were nes of trust, for which, during the ears they had continued, the directors able to make good any loss which the any had sustained in consequence, and rtunes of the directors, both of those ed and those surviving, were liable to good the losses which the company had ned by reason of their having failed in uty.

are sorry to find that the articles which ecently appeared in this journal have, ie quarters, been erroneously supposed e been levelled at particular companies. were this the case, no animus on our ould either alter the position of a com- or the liabilities of a single director. re far from stating that we consider the statements of law which have recently red in these pages, either ill-timed or ed for. Corporations in Canada are the same as in England, both good and In the case of Insurance Companies istence of the Government deposit is small security for shareholders; but

inspection by a Government superintendent and the existence of a simple and compara- tively inexpensive winding-up act would save the general body of shareholders from unnecessary loss, and by increasing public confidence put the institutions themselves on a sounder basis and give their shares a better market value.

RED RIVER TRADE.

The opening of this new channel of trade, this spring, and the prospect of greatly en- larged operations with the Red River settlers next year, render it of importance to circulate some facts regarding the extent of the com- merce which may be drawn to Ontario from this source, and the facilities that exist for carrying it on.

The entire business of the country east of the mountains has been, until this spring, done by Minnesota and England. The Hudson's Bay Company have been in the habit of annually importing from London in their own vessels from $300,000 to $400,000 worth of goods for the use of the inhabitants of the Red River settlement, and for the supply of the fur trade in the interior— from which fur trade outfit alone, it has been stated, their annual sales have amounted some years to as much as $1,000,000 to $1,500,000. But in addition to the Hudson's Bay Company, there are numerous traders, small and great, who also dabble in this trade, and the main part of their outfits hitherto, has come to hand via the Hudson's Bay route, in a specially chartered vessel, or has been imported from St. Paul, Minnesota, with an occasional sprinkling of goods from New York and Chicago. Of late years the increase of these traders in Red River, com- bined with the general prosperity of the settlement, its enlargement by natural in- crease and additions from the outside world —very limited though these latter be— resulted, as a matter of course, in an exten- sion of the imports and exports. In addition to the traffic by the ice-bound regions of Hudson's Bay, thousands of carts have been despatched semi-annually to St. Cloud, (the head of navigation on the Mississippi,) or to St. Paul, loaded with some of the ex- portable products of the country, furs and hides; and, reloading at the latter towns, have returned to Selkirk with half a ton of goods, or more, on each cart. A portion of the stuff thus brought back to the settlement is usually, English goods, sent out in bond; but, in great part, the loads are purchased in St. Paul, or its rival for this trade, St. Cloud. Groceries, hardware, dry goods, clothing and agricultural implements, form the bulk of the loading—all of which supplies brought the

merchants of Minnesota such handsome pro- fits that many years ago they commenced assiduously to cultivate the trade. Through these efforts, seconded by the State Legisla- ture, four horse coaches were run through the wilderness as far as Fort Abercrombie, on the Red River, some 250 miles from St. Paul; a fine steamer was built and placed on the Red River to run from Abercrombie to Fort Garry; and, in addition, a mail went through from St. Paul to Pembina,—on the boundary line—twice a week all the year round. Pem- bina, we may state, is only some sixty odd miles from Fort Garry. In making these efforts the people and legislature of Minne- sota had one grand object in view—an object frequently and openly avowed—and that was the securing the rich and promising trade of the North-West, and the peaceable annexa- tion of that country, if possible. The efforts to keep the route open, and make the trade of that region tributary to Minnesota, worked to a charm. Whether or not the other part of their programme will be carried out, remains to be seen.

Our readers may ask, how was all this ac- complished? Easily enough. The Post Office department gave out a contract for carrying the mails, and the company who took it, in conjunction with companies having contracts to Government Forts, and other business in the interior, had to see to it that the roads were in passable trim, and that the rivers were bridged, be the bridging ever so rude. If any of their rough log crossings were swept away, as sometimes happened by a spring freshet, they were replaced by a few hours work; particularly bad spots on any of the roads—and such places are few and far between—were mended, and then, when some heavier work was needed, such as cut- ting through fifteen or twenty miles of forest, State aid came in to supplement the efforts made by these contractors. Any little bal- ance needed to make travelling more secure, falls to the lot of the several brigades of carts passing to and from Selkirk. The labor and expense divided over so many is continuously and cheerfully performed, and a really good road, some 500 miles long, is kept open between St. Cloud, the present terminus of the North Pacific Railway, and Fort Garry. With the exception of the fifteen or twenty miles nearest the latter post, this highway is so level and in such good order for a road through the wilderness, that any Canadian travelling over it would be astonished. Few of the roads in the vicinity of Toronto, mac- adamized though they be, are half so good and free from danger to freight and passen- gers.

While the Red River steamboat was in the hands of the mail contractors, Benbank &

Co., of St. Paul, their charge for forwarding goods from St. Paul was $6 in gold, per 100 lbs. But for the last three years merchants preferred sending for their freight from the settlement, either with their own carts and waggons, horses and oxen, or else hiring such transport in Red River, and in this way their freight from St. Cloud comes to $4 and $5 per 100 lbs. By either of these last-mentioned modes of transit, there is really little or no danger or loss to be apprehended to horses or oxen. Both start together from Fort Garry in long trains, hundreds of carts at a time, make the round trip in from four or five weeks, and come back, with good management as fat, and in as good order as they left. They have the best prairie grass to feed on by the way, abundance of water, and with easy drives of twenty or twenty-five miles a day—an ox cannot safely be driven faster—this tremendous business of going 1000 or 1,200 miles to market, is not very hard on the animals hauling.

A little of this trade, somewhere about $50,000 worth, was done by Canada this spring. Groceries, clothing, hardware, dry goods, and many other lines of business being represented in the Canadian exports to Red River—and all of these goods were brought and landed in the settlement at rates with which the Minesota traders were utterly unable to compete. Before reaching St. Paul they had to be sent over 1000 miles, and yet they were landed in the Apostolic city at rates which defied competition from that quarter. Next season four or five times the above mentioned amount of trade will be done with Canada; but see under what disadvantages we enter into the competition. Taking Mr. Dawson's report, recently issued as a basis of comparison, we find that the probable rate of freight from the head of Lake Superior to the settlement by the projected Canadian route, would not exceed $1,80 to $2 per 100 lbs., and this, even making the most liberal allowance for the expense of transit. But in the absence of any such road, Canadian goods must find their way round through Michigan, Wisconsin and Minnesota, before they even get to a starting point, from whence to Red River the freight will be at least double what it would cost were the Canadian route in use. The entire cost of opening up a route to this country, a channel through which Canada might draw a trade of a couple of millions annually, is estimated by Mr. Dawson to be $166,500, a comparatively insignificant outlay to secure so rich a trade as the North West opens up to us.

Under the circumstances, it is with pleasure we notice the intention of the Dominion Government, as announced by the Commissioner of Public Works, to commence this fall opening that portion of the road between Fort Garry and Lake of the Woods. Though partially adapted as a means of affording work and relief to some of the distressed settlers in Red River—the movement is a bold one—it looks business-like, and it is to be hoped it will not be abandoned until the road to Fort William is fully constructed.

THE INTERCOLONIAL RAILWAY.

The appointment under the Act of last Session, of Mr. Walsh as Railway Commissioner for Ontario, Mr. Brydges for Quebec, and Mr. Chandler for New Brunswick, has created considerable discussion. It is urged that the position of Mr. Brydges as Manager of the Grand Trunk, and his alleged shortcomings in that capacity, should have stood in the way of his receiving an appointment of such importance. As the appointments are made, it is useless to discuss the questions raised on that issue. The office of Commissioner is held during pleasure. The Chief Engineer is to be appointed by the Governor, and act under instructions of the Commissioners. The latter are empowered to employ a secretary, engineers and surveyors, agents and workmen; to cause a survey to be made; and to purchase land and assess damages to property. With respect to tenders and contracts, section 16 provides—"The Commissioners shall build such Railway by tender and contract after the plans and specifications therefor shall have been duly advertised, and they shall accept the tenders of such contractors as shall appear to them to be possessed of sufficient skill, experience and resources to carry on the work or such portions thereof as they may contract for; provided always that the Commissioners shall not be obliged to accept the lowest tender, in case they should deem it for the public interest not to do so; provided also that no contract under this section involving an expense of ten thousand dollars or upwards shall be concluded by the Commissioners until sanctioned by the Governor in Council."

It will be seen, therefore, that the Government will be responsible for the contracts, and that the office of Commissioner is not one in which very great power is centred.

LIVE STOCK INSURANCE.

We know of no reason why a large business should not be done in this province in the insurance of live stock, if the proper exertions be made to make known its advantages. Most of our farmers are, to a greater or less extent, engaged in stock raising, and we cannot see why they should not insure stock as freely and as readily as they do their houses or barns. Valuable animals are consta imported from abroad; and such accid as that which occurred recently in Mont where three horses worth respectively $ $1,100 and $1,700, were destroyed, sh the importance of effecting an insuran such property in a live stock company. ing the cattle plague in England, associa were formed for insurance against that ease, and there are now, we believe, at fifteen or sixteen companies in England insure cattle. In 1864 a plan was subm to the British Government for a Nat Live Stock Insurance organization on compulsory principle, but it was foun practicable. The Ætna Live Stock, reputation is unquestioned, is the only pany doing this class of insurance throu the Dominion. We need scarcely add we hope our farming population, for own sake, will take advantage of the p tion it affords.

THE Quebec and Riviere Du Loup s of the Grand Trunk Railway is order be closed forthwith.

Financial.

TORONTO STOCK MARKET.

(Reported by Pellatt & Osler, Brokers.)

We have to report a very dull week, few actions having taken place.

Bank Stock.—There are buyers of Mont 134½, sellers asking 135¼. Ontario would at 98¾; no sellers under 99¼; no trans There are buyers of Toronto at 117; no s market. Fully paid Royal Canadian offer and partially paid at 91. There were cons sales of Commerce at 103½ to 104. Gore i at 46. Buyers offer 105¼ for Merchants sellers at 106. 98 would be paid for Small sales of City were reported at 102¾, offer 102 freely. For Du Peuple 105 w paid; no late sales. There are sellers of Cartier at 108, buyers offering only 106. ask 97 for Mechanics' with buyers at 95. banks nominal.

Debentures.—Canada very scarce; 101 i for sterling six per cents, 100½ for currenc and 101 for Dominion stock. There wer sales of Toronto at rates to pay about 7 interest. County in demand to yield 6½ interest.

Sundries.—Building Society Stock Holders ask 120 for Canada Permanent; r There were sales of Western Canada at 113, and in demand. No Freehold in ma is wanted at 106½. Montreal Telegraph 135. There were small sales of British Assurance at 56. City Gas sold at 10 rate is freely offered. Considerable sales ada Landed Credit took place, owing holders selling out to avoid the call d October. Some good mortgages have bee at 8 per cent. Money continues easy security.

—B. H. LeMoine and Geo. S. Brush h admitted members of the Corporation Banque du Peuple.

—An interim dividend of five per been declared by the Richelieu Company, on 5th October.

ONTREAL MONEY MARKET.

(From our own Correspondent).

Montreal, 28th Sept. 1868.

oney market is unusually quiet for this the year; so far there has been scarcely und on the banks for the movement of e only call being for the purchase of heese and pork. The imports having much short of last year a far less amount needed for the payment of freights, c. This amount if therefore thrown on the and seeks short dated investments, thus creased ease to the markets. Bank rates m 7 to 7½ for first class and 8 to 10. d to third class paper. There is not per offering on the street, and the rate om 12½c. to 14 per cent. on warehouse and other securities. Holders of stocks prices, which restricts business. Bank eal is firmly held at 135½; but buyers give over 134½. For British 103, and a shade over without inducing sellers. k last sales were at 102½. Considerable ons in Ontario at 98½, and firmly held at . Bank of Toronto 115. Gore Bank t 40, sellers holding for 42½. Fair sales ants at 105½. Books of the Richelieu y closed, a half yearly dividend of 5 per clared payable on the 5th prox. City r railroad 110. New City Gas Co. t 125; but holders demand 132½. Gov- s are strong. Gold here is 142½; silver t 3½, selling at 3 to 3½ dis.; Greenbacks t 30, selling at 29¼ to 29½ dis.

LTON DEBENTURES.—The London *Times* 8th Sept. says:—The corporation of the Hamilton, Canada, has forwarded to the ak the usual remittance to provide for the maturing on the 1st of October, upon rling debentures. The bonds are of two the water works and ordinary, bearing in- 4½ and 4 per cent. respectively, increas- per cent.. They were created under the g circumstances:—In 1861 the coupons on inal 6 per cent. debentutres of the Cor- became unpaid, and so remained until hen an Act of the Provincial Parliament ed the old bonds and the accrued interest and constituted the existing issue. his arrangement was made the coupons en punctually provided for.

OF ENGLAND.—The half-yearly general f the Bank of England was held on the stant, Thomas Newman Hunt, Esq., the r, presiding. The net profits for the half- ling the 31st of August amount to £584,- 9d., making the amount of rest on that 610,596 17s. 1d., and after providing a d of 4 per cent. the rest will stand at £3,- 17s. 1d.. The dividend was declared on the 12th of October without deduction ne-tax.

TERED BANKS.—A Blue book is out, con- returns from the several chartered banks, the name and place of residence of each lder, with the number and nominal value shares held by them. It comprises the g banks:—British North America; La Nationale, Molson's Bank, Gore Bank, que Du Peuple, City Bank, Montreal; Bank, Ontario Bank, Commercial Bank of unswick, the People's Bank of New Bruns- Niagara District Bank, St. Catharines; St. 's Bank, St. Stephen, N. B.; La Banque Cartier, Bank of Montreal, the People's f Halifax, Eastern Townships Bank, Mer- Bank of Canada, Bank of Yarmouth, N.S.; Toronto, Royal Canadian Bank, Commer- k of Windsor, N. S.

e Permanent Building Society of the Dis- Montreal have declared a dividend, for year, of 5 per cent., payable 1st October.

Commercial.

Montreal Correspondence.

(From our own Correspondent.)

Montreal, Sept. 29, 1868.

The weather during the past week has been exceedingly wet and cold; a quantity of rain has fallen which will help to fill up the streams, and must prove a great boon to millers.

PRODUCE.—As I anticipated, the bottom has not yet been reached, and flour during the week declined considerably. Up to Saturday last, the decline was very gradual, but on that day prices gave way considerably, and large sales were made for shipment to the lower ports at $5.50 for supers. At this decline the market is for the present steady; but I should not be astonished to see a further fall, as it can hardly be expected that the English markets will remain at their present point long enough to enable shipments from here to reach them, and thus realize the small profit which they shew now on our present rates of flour and freights. Wheat has followed in the wake of flour, but not to the same extent, the fall being at the outside, 3 cts. per bush.; but prices are purely nominal. U. C. spring being $1.27 to $1.30, and No. 2 Chicago spring $1.26 to $1.28. The market for coarse grains is quiet and unchanged, no wholesale transactions being reported in peas, oats or barley. In provisions, the stock of mess pork is ample, and prices have rather declined; but there is no stock of thin mess, prime mess or prime, which tends to keep up prices. Mess sells at $24.

Large droves of hogs and cattle of all descriptions are being brought rapidly to market, farmers being anxious to dispose of as much as possible of their stock before the winter sets in, as fodder will run very short; the bulk of the cattle, however, are in poor condition, and bring low prices. Good fat cattle would sell rapidly, and at full prices. Dairy produce continues very high; a round lot of Eastern Township butter sold at 24 cts., and a further advance is anticipated. The shipping demand has fallen off, present rates leaving no margin. The steamers for Liverpool take weekly between 1,500 and 2,000 packages of cheese, the price of which is 10½ cts., to 11 cts., for fair to good factory, and 11 cts. to 11¼ for choice.

GROCERIES.—The market is completely unsettled; but the large auction sales this week will have the effect of steadying prices. There have been considerable transactions in fish, oils and teas; the former chiefly for the American market. Messrs. D. Torrence & Co. having disposed of the cargo of the "Annie Braginton," it is of course withdrawn from their catalogue; they will, however, have a good assortment to offer. The sales commenced to-day, Messrs. Rimmer, Gunn & Co.'s being the first. The audience consisted chiefly of city buyers, and the sale generally was a failure, very few goods being placed at low prices. At Victor Hudon's in the afternoon there was an excellent assembly, including a large sprinkling of western buyers. Although the competition was not keen, still there was enough to give animation, and a large quantity of goods were placed. Prices generally ruled low; but not sufficiently so to depress the market. Wines, brandies, and Mediterranean goods constituted the bulk offered. To-morrow, Buchanan, Leckie & Co., offer a large quantity of teas and other groceries; in fact, with the exception of Saturday, we have one or two sales every day.

HARDWARE.—Business has been very brisk; orders from the West being numerous, and several large buyers having come down. The tone of the market has been very firm, and on most qualities of iron an advance of 5 cents per cwt. has been obtained; several sizes of bar and hoop iron have run nearly out of stock, but the fall fleet, part of which is near at hand, will speedily remedy any deficiency. The combination of the cut-nail manufacturers having broken down, the market for them is unsettled, and prices have receded. Stocks are heavy, and holders do not wish to carry over extra quantities during the winter; ordinary brands have sold to a considerable extent at $2.70, and best do. at $2.80 to $2.85. Shelf goods are in good assortment, and sell readily at full rates.

Toronto Market.

The fall trade is making satisfactory progress and promises well. Merchants are generally satisfied with results so far.

DRY GOODS.—A good active business was done during the past week, many houses report sales largely in advance of the same period of last year. There are some complaints of the backwardness of retailers in making payments; but during the week money has come forward more freely, and importers are better satisfied.

HARDWARE.—Trade has improved, and is now fairly active: such changes in prices as have occurred are noted in our Price List.

BOOTS AND SHOES.—Demand active without change in prices.

FANCY GOODS.—Though there has been an important increase of the number of houses engaged in this branch within a year or two, yet they all, so far at least as our enquiries have extended, report a good trade. The best of the season is, however, yet to come, when the assortment, in the wholesale dry goods houses, of many small articles will become broken; dealers will then have to seek the fancy goods stores to sort up. Importations in this branch show an increase on last year.

HOOP SKIRTS.—This trade is actively competed for by not only the principal cities, but the towns have each their manufactories, the product of which comes in competition with the yield of our factories and those of Montreal, as well as the imported also. Prices remain about the same as last fall, but if anything a shade lower. In the early part of the season a tardiness on the part of country merchants in making remittances was complained of, but within the past week there is an improvement in this respect.

GROCERIES.—Business during the last week has been more than ordinarily brisk, many dealers having visited the city and left orders before proceeding to the Provincial Fair at Hamilton. The fall trade is opening up well, and payments are on the whole quite satisfactory. *Sugars*—Are quiet and firm; an advance of ⅛ to ¼ of a cent is quoted in the New York market, and this in face of a decline in gold. The stock in New York is 42,063 boxes, 71,575 hhds., 86,481 Manilla bags, against 65,529 boxes, 50,765 hhds. and 35,281 bags at the same date in 1867. *Molasses*—Are firm; the New York market is quoted 2 to 3c. higher. *Teas*—Steady and unchanged; we note a sale in the New York market of 900 half chests, greens, English orders, shipped to Canada and sold on Canadian account. *Tobacco*—The market for leaf is fairly active at weakening prices.

HOPS.—Our crop is now coming forward freely, but meets with a very slow demand. Holders of good hops would accept 20 cts. gladly owing to the heavy look of the market; so far there have been only retail sales at about that figure. The Wisconsin crop is reported good, and will amount to 18,000 to 20,000 bales, and is a very fine sample. Any lots brought into this market yet are spoken of as generally good.

PETROLEUM.—A meeting of refiners and dealers was held at Hamilton on Tuesday week, and it was agreed to extend the existing combination beyond the first of December, though to what period is not stated. There is a good demand for consumption at steady prices.

LEATHER.—The demand is steady but not so large as might be expected at this season, though next month is expected to be better. There is little variation in prices, but the tendency is upwards.

GRAIN.—*Wheat.*—Receipts 900 bushels, and 1760 bush. last week. In the present dull state of the market farmers have very little inducement to bring their wheat forward ; the demand is limited to the requirements of local mills. It is doubtful even if prices were better that any quantity would be moved, so long as the barley lasts, and is as eagerly sought for and saleable at such long prices as at present. Speculators will not take hold of breadstuffs until they are satisfied that they have touched bottom, which, notwithstanding the greatly reduced prices reached, is still uncertain. It is thought by many that the favorable crops have had an undue influence on prices ; that the general anticipation of a decline has led to a much more rapid movement of wheat to market than is usual; that the increased receipts so induced have tended to the belief that the yield was greater than it will shortly prove to be, and that then—say in the latter part of October or in November—will come a reaction. Be this as it may, no one buys just now except on orders or for immediate use, the chances being considered on the side of still lower prices. Spring has settled down to $1.15 and $1.18 ; midge-proof is worth $1.20. *Barley.*—Receipts for the week by rail38,000 bush. against 41,058 bush. last week ; receipts by teams 130,000 bush. and 120,000 bush. for the previous week. This day week the market opened at ½1.10 to $1.12, and gradually advanced to $1.20 and $1.21, on the street ; but owing to a break in Oswego, fell off to the opening prices of the week ; within the last two days an improvement has taken place ; the market closing at the quotations in our price list. The total receipt of barley from all sources are estimated at nearly 600,000 bush., and the shipments at 350,000 to 400,000 bush. The following vessels cleared with barley during the six days ending with Saturday last :—The "Australia," with 7,000 bush. ; "H. P. Murray," 9,921 bush. ; "John A. Macdonald," 9,268 bush., and the "Defiance," 5,839 bush., all for Oswego ; the "Cecelia," with 10,000 bush., the " Jessic," 14,000, the " Annie Mulvey," 17,000 bush. the "Eureka," 8,000 bush. and the "Paragon," 11,522 bush. all for Toledo. A careful estimate of the movements from the commencement of the season puts the total receipts at 451,000 bush. ; shipments, 287,000 ; in store, 200,000 bush. The shipments were :—To Oswego, 179,000 bush ; to Toledo, 80,000 bush. ; to Ogdensburg, 18,000 bush. ; to Cleveland, 10,000 bush. *Oats.*—Car loads are arriving in sufficient numbers to supply the local trade, and are selling at 51c to 51½c. *Peas* are dull and nominal ; very little of the new crop has been offered in this market yet. *Rye* is selling in small lots at 80 to 85c.

Flour.—Receipts for the week 900 barrels and 1,260 barrels last week. There is a quiet demand on orders for shipment to the Lower Provinces and for local use ; but there are more sellers than buyers. No. 1 Superfine has sold during the week at $5.50 to $5.60 ; at the close there were sellers of ordinary brands at $5.50, while, for favorite, higher figures are demanded. There were some sales of Fancy at $5,85. Superior and Extra nominal, as quoted.

Halifax Market.

Sept. 22.—*Breadstuffs.*—Flour in steady demand, stocks rather heavy; Canada No. 1 $7.40 to $7.50; Extra $8.40 to $8.50; Extra State dull at $7.25 to $7.50; Baltimore Supr. $7.25; Rye in little demand. Corn meal, kiln dried $4.60 to $4.75; fresh ground $4.40 to $4.50. Oatmeal, Canada $7.75 to $7.85. Imports from January 1st to Sept 22nd, 1867 and 1868:

	Brls. Flour.	Brls. Cornmeal.
1868	130,143	40,881
1867	127,624	29,742

West India Produce.—The importation of sugar and molasses having almost entirely ceased for this year's crop, and the New York market having recovered to a large extent, holders of sugars are very firm. The only sales reported are 50 hhds. common anceery Cuba at 5½c; 70 hhds. fair Barbadoes at 5½c in bond for export. We quote Porto Rico 6c to 6¾; Barbadoes 5¾ to 6c; Cuba 5¼ to 5½; Centrifugal Cuba 6c in bond.

Financial.—Bank drawing rate on London 60 day sight bills 13 per cent prem.; Private 12 to 12½ per cent prem. New York gold drafts at sight, 4 per cent prem. Currency drafts 27 per cent discount.

Graduated Sugar Duties.

We have had our experience in this country of the difficulty in working a graduated scale of sugar duties. Similar difficulties are met with elsewhere. We take a paragraph bearing on this point from the London *Produce Markets Review* of Sept. 17th :

It has long been remarked as an extraordinary thing, that if part of a cargo of Sugar were sent to the Clyde, and part to London, the Sugar sent to the Clyde was generally assessed at a lower rate of duty to that levied on what was sent to London. As the difference in favor of the Clyde would amount to 1s. 7d. per cwt. on the 8s. duty, and to 11d. on the 9s. 7d. rate, it is somewhat strange that the refiners had never looked into so probable an explanation of the extraordinary cheapness of Sugar on the Clyde, under which London was completely losing the Pieces trade. We understand, however, that the question has now been taken up, and the extraordinary discovery arrived at, that by the system of sampling carried on in London the " foots " are never touched by the " borer ;" while on the Clyde, on the contrary, the " footy" part of the hogshead is always included in the samples drawn. Naturally, the Sugar drawn in London would be lighter in color than on the Clyde, and, as a matter of course, if it happened to be near the Duty Standards in color, a Sugar paying 9s. 7d. in London would pay 8s. on the Clyde. The sins of the fathers are certainly visited on the children in this case, for the dishonest system of sampling introduced in London by a former generation of merchants, and maintained up to the present day in spite of the continued protests of the trade, has thus recoiled on the heads of their representatives by driving the trade away from London. The refiners also have paid dearly for supporting the system on the ground that a slight uncertainty in color made no difference to them, while it would make a great difference to grocers, so that the uncertainty of the turn-out of Raw Sugar would force the trade to buy Pieces. We are of opinion not only that a fair mode of sampling should be enforced, but that fairness in this respect should be necessarily inserted among the conditions of sale, and also that no Sugar should be offered for sale without samples being redrawn from the hogsheads not later than a week from the date of contract. We have so often described our present vicious system of sampling that we need not enlarge upon it further, except as a moral to show the absurdity of graduated Sugar duties, for if these were logically carried out, every few inches in a hogshead of Raw Sugar ought to be assessed at a different rate.

Mercantile.

John Boyd & Co.,
WHOLESALE GROCERS AND COMMISSION MERCHANTS,

61 AND 63 FRONT STREET'
TORONTO.

NOW in store, direct from the European and West India Markets, a large assortment of General Groceries, comprising

Teas, Sugars, Coffees, Wines and Liquors,
AND
GENERAL GROCERIES.

Ship Chandlery, Canvas, Manilla and Tarred Rope, Oakum, Tar, Flags, &c., &c.,
DIRECT FROM THE MANUFACTURERS.

JOHN BOYD.   ALEX. M. MONRO.   C. W. BUNTING.
Toronto, Oct. 1st, 1868.   7 1y

STATEMENT OF BANKS

ACTING UNDER CHARTER, FOR THE MONTH ENDING 31st AUGUST, 1888, ACCORDING TO RETURNS FURNISHED BY THE BANKS TO THE AUDITOR OF PUBLIC ACCOUNTS.

NAME OF BANK	CAPITAL		LIABILITIES.					ASSETS							
	Capital authorized by Act	Capital paid up	Promissory Notes in circulation not bearing interest	Balances due to other Banks	Cash Deposits not bearing interest	Cash Deposits bearing interest	TOTAL LIABILITIES	Coin, Bullion, and Provincial Notes	Landed or other Property of the Bank	Government Securities	Promissory Notes, or Bills of other Banks	Balances due from other Banks	Notes and Bills Discounted	Other Debts due the Bank, not included under foregoing heads	TOTAL ASSETS
ONTARIO AND QUEBEC.	$	$	$	$ c.	$ c.	$ c.	$ c.	$ c.	$ c.	$ c.	$ c.	$ c.	$ c.	$ c.	$ c.
Montreal	6,000,000	6,000,000	327,407	475,674 91	5,871,871 00	6,365,290 32	13,080,043 25	2,436,144 95	350,000 00	3,045,368 33	413,327 85	1,723,759 61	12,096,143 08	380,096 33	21,012,653 40
Quebec	3,000,000	1,478,350	543,070	39,317 91	620,557 49	807,823 34	2,066,047 64	331,174 37	69,723 94	146,483 33	88,488 83	876,504 06	2,546,010 56	374,893 23	3,713,444 31
City	1,200,000	1,200,000	357,089	31,746 73	382,713 37	827,843 07	1,745,384 77	318,760 88	32,929 59	188,609 99	81,701 66	36,075 32	2,383 00 31	117,311 66	3,148,402 68
Gore	1,000,000	800,000	202,032	11,978 34	61,596 63	119,723 69	414,855 56	176,043 70	83,007 60	83,738 83	12,437 85	16,932 35	678,019 09	239,582 71	1,397,675 73
British North America	4,866,666	4,866,666	981,729	19,937 00	1,145,967 00	3,435,546 00	4,536,059 00	856,574 00	83,333 00	563,333 00	138,679 00	35,875 00	5,408,325 00	122,256 00	7,712,943 00
Banque du Peuple	1,600,000	1,600,000	611,110	1,316 97	343,683 91	160,717 73	672,932 00	381,108 07	60,960 19	706,364 44	33,107 99	75,318 77	1,792,397 87	64,889 78	2,887,932 61
Niagara District	440,000	936,224	137,015	69,094 90	144,107 02	70,596 08	419,813 61	51,328 47	13,579 72	44,730 00	8,443 07	47,690 91	546,637 08	45,655 55	783,168 81
Molsons	1,000,000	1,000,000	88,492	56,053 73	217,154 25	468,661 48	885,001 76	135,989 63	90,573 15	107,553 32	109,080 02	18,473 00	1,380,052 93	212,071 42	2,037,269 98
Toronto	3,000,000	765,601	765,601	13,987 70	289,140 71	1,373,133 18	2,397,169 59	680,214 41	42,668 84	96,280 00	11,313 65	132,777 79	9,517,044 64	18,793 29	5,392,057 56
Ontario	3,000,000	2,000,000	902,439	123,601 60	997,828 29	945,339 89	2,990,166 98	607,705 69	154,007 11	906,592 69	140,023 17	134,738 71	3,994,327 95	116,411 84	5,434,714 07
Eastern Townships	440,000	440,000	107,603	6,355 09	84,071 87	68,301 72	297,500 26	40,177 91	16,000 00	68,025 51	83,235 44	49,800 09	473,879 59	5,000 00	686,006 90
Banque Nationale	1,000,000	1,000,000	124,640	99,448 09	318,411 41	173,414 31	692,176 05	182,919 40	23,518 00	115,480 00	85,375 89	54,407 79	1,187,382 77	65,596 22	1,717,493 77
Banque Jacques Cartier	1,000,000	992,610	77,855	8,573 77	318,884 48	498,196 51	830,359 56	98,297 64		101,236 07	24,987 56	50,355 62	1,040,089 92		1,918,935 90
Merchants'	5,000,000	3,113,590	790,112	388,907 09	838,555 73	1,577,988 06	3,594,575 73	788,338 63		525,966 67	211,518 54	646,907 58	3,890,067 93	1,871,513 96	7,373,728 63
Royal Canadian	9,000,000	1,108,350	1,119,093	37,014 61	619,940 87	828,726 09	2,597,773 17	665,431 27		129,333 33	112,632 99	335,543 46	2,711,012 56	65,579 05	3,589,818 48
Union B'k Lower Canada	2,000,000	980,390	940,085	940,085 59	308,455 96	224,391 85	865,932 61	116,408 98		129,193 83	69,914 83	73,498 11	1,315,969 79		1,995,407 97
Mechanics'	2,000,000	375,390	83,039	1,203 94	114,101 73	106,037 98	215,125 67	40,179 59	84,309 19	120,396 66	67,064 11	3,546 30	961,822 94	3,369 00	1,111,864 66
Bank of Commerce	1,000,000	936,185	784'033	84,394 72	493,597 12	789,369 75	2,772,365 59	896,595 13	40,842 43	106,906 30	70,643 97	64,723 63	3,185,799 79		3,275,573 34
NOVA SCOTIA.															
Bank of Yarmouth	....	....	....	....	....	....	....	....	....	....	....	....	....	....	....
Merchants' Bank	....	....	....	....	....	....	....	....	....	....	....	....	....	....	....
People's Bank	....	....	....	....	....	....	....	....	....	....	....	....	....	....	....
Union Bank	....	....	....	....	....	....	....	....	....	....	....	....	....	....	....
Bank of Nova Scotia	....	....	....	....	....	....	....	....	....	....	....	....	....	....	....
NEW BRUNSWICK.															
Bank of New Brunswick	500,000	500,000	409,653	69,844 06	495,063 75	714,196 35	1,455,476 05	329,097 08	16,574 45		33,546 00	368,387 35	1,818,380 37	84,550 13	3,892,971 93
Commercial Bank	300,000	300,000	325,127		91,801 44	24,997 20	362,015 64	44,547 60	4,464 00		85,043 62	18,513 30	347,613 36	96,605 00	669,717 83
St. Stephen's Bank															
People's Bank															
Totals	38,306,666	29,463,717	8,601,920	1,710,299 75	13,600,909 69	13,859,737 05	49,101,843 49	8,697,541 08	1,845,978 05	5,957,196 39	1,911,086 66	5,902,695 21	49,306,054 38	3,505,799 41	75,349,661 81

AUCTION SALES OF GROCERIES
IN MONTREAL,
FOR THE
Fall Season of 1868.

September 29th,
Sale by Auction, at the Stores of
Victor Hudon, Esq.,
Of MEDITERRANEAN GOODS, *Wines, Liquors, and General Groceries.*
J. G. SHIPWAY,
Auctioneer.

September 29th,
Sale by Auction, at the Stores of
Messrs. Rimmer, Gunn & Co.,
Of Teas, Wines, Brandies, Tobaccos, and General Groceries
JOHN LEEMING & Co.,
Auctioneers.

September 30th,
Sale by Auction, at the Stores of
Messrs. Buchanan, Leckie & Co.,
Of 3,000 Packages *Green Teas, ex. Annie Braginton*, direct from Shanghai. Also, 2,000 Packages *Uncolored Japans* and a large assortment of *Wines, Liquors, Fruit, and General Groceries.*
JOHN LEEMING & CO.,
Auctioneers.

October 1st,
Sale by Auction at the Stores of
Messrs. Chapman, Fraser & Tylee,
Of Fruit, Wines, Brandies, Oils, and General Groceries.
JOHN LEEMING & CO.,
Auctioneers.

October 1st,
Auction Sales at the Stores of
Messrs. David Torrance & Co.,
Of 7,892 Packages Fine New Crop GREEN TEAS, *ex Annie Braginton*, direct from Shanghai. Also, 2,000 half chests UNCOLORED JAPANS, in English order.
JOHN LEEMING & CO.,
Auctioneers.

October 2nd,
Sale by Auction at the Stores of
Messrs. Alex. Urquhart & Co.,
The Cargo of the *Western Wave*, from Marseilles. Also, a large assortment of ENGLISH GROCERIES.
JOHN LEEMING & CO.,
Auctioneers.

Brown Brothers,
ACCOUNT-BOOK MANUFACTURERS,
Stationers, Book-Binders, Etc.,
66 *and* 68 *King Street East, Toronto, Ont.*

ACCOUNT Books for Banks, Insurance Companies, Merchants, etc., made to order of the best materials, and for style, durability and cheapness unsurpassed.

A large stock of Account-Books and General Stationery constantly on hand.

September 1, 1868. 3-1y

Philip Browne & Co.,
BANKERS AND STOCK BROKERS.
DEALERS IN
STERLING EXCHANGE—U. S. Currency, Silver and Bonds—Bank Stocks, Debentures, Mortgages, &c. Drafts on New York issued, in Gold and Currency. Prompt attention given to collections. Advances made on Securities.
No. 67 YONGE STREET, TORONTO
JAMES BROWNE. PHILIP BROWNE, *Notary Public.*
y

Honore Plamondon,
CUSTOM House Broker, Forwarder, and General Agent, Quebec. Office—Custom House Building. 17-1y

TORONTO PRICES CURRENT.—October 1, 1868.

Name of Article.	Wholesale Rates. $ c.	$ c.
Boots and Shoes.		
Mens' Thick Boots	2 20	2 50
" Kip	2 45	3 20
" Calf	3 00	3 75
" Congress Gaiters	2 00	2 40
" Kip Cobourgs	1 00	1 50
Boys' Thick Boots	1 65	1 90
Youths' "	1 45	1 55
Women's Batts	95	1 20
" Congress Gaiters	1 15	1 50
Misses' Batts	0 75	1 00
" Congress Gaiters	1 00	1 30
Girls' Batts	0 65	0 90
" Congress Gaiters	0 80	1 10
Children's C. T. Cacks	0 50	0 65
" Gaiters	0 65	0 90
Drugs.		
Aloes Cape	0 12½	0 16
Alum	0 02½	0 03
Borax	0 00	0 00
Camphor, refined	0 65	0 70
Castor Oil	0 18	0 28
Caustic Soda	0 04½	0 05
Cochineal	0 90	1 00
Cream Tartar	0 00	0 00
Epsom Salts	0 03	0 04
Extract Logwood	0 09	0 11
Gum Arabic, sorts	0 30	0 35
Indigo, Madras	0 75	1 00
Licorice	0 14	0 45
Madder	0 13	0 16
Nutgalls	0 00	0 00
Opium	6 70	7 00
Oxalic Acid	0 28	0 35
Potash, Bi-tart	0 25	0 28
" Bichromate	0 15	0 20
Potass Iodide	3 80	4 50
Senna	0 12½	0 60
Soda Ash	0 03	0 04
Soda Bicarb	4 50	5 50
Tartaric Acid	0 37½	0 45
Verdigris	0 35	0 40
Vitriol, Blue	0 09	0 10
Groceries.		
Coffees:		
Java, ₽ lb.	0 22@	0 24
Laguayra,	0 17	0 18
Rio	0 15	0 17
Fish:		
Herrings, Lab. split	0 00	0 00
" round	0 00	0 00
" scaled	0 35	0 40
Mackerel, small kitts	1 00	0 00
Loch. Her. wh'e firks	2 50	2 75
" half "	1 25	1 50
White Fish & Trout	3 25	3 50
Salmon, saltwater	14 00	15 00
Dry Cod, ₽112 lbs.	4 75	5 00
Fruit:		
Raisins, Layers	2 20	2 25
" M R	2 10	2 20
" Valentias new	0 08¾	0 09
Currants, new	0 05	0 05½
" old	0 03¾	0 04½
Figs	0 11	0 12½
Molasses:		
Clayed, ₽ gal.	0 00	0 35
Syrups, Standard	0 43	0 44
" Golden	0 49	0 50
Rice:		
Arracan	4 50	4 65
Spices:		
Cassia, whole, ₽ lb.	0 37½	0 40
Cloves	0 11	0 12
Nutmegs	0 45	0 55
Ginger, ground	0 15	0 25
" Jamaica, root	0 22	0 25
Pepper, black	0 09	0 10
Pimento	0 08	0 09
Sugars:		
Port Rico, ₽ lb.	0 08½	0 08¾
Cuba "	0 08¼	0 08½
Barbadoes (bright)	0 08¾	0 08¾
Dry Crushed, at 60 d.	0 11	0 11¼
Canada Sugar Refine'y, yellow No. 2, 60 ds.	0 08¾	0 08¼
Yellow, No. 2½	0 08¾	0 08¾
No. 3	0 09	0 09½
Crushed X	0 10	0 10½
" A	0 10¾	0 11
Ground	0 11	0 11½
Extra Ground	0 12½	0 12¾
Teas:		
Japan com'n to good	0 40	0 55
" Fine to choicest	0 55	0 65
Colored, com. to fine	0 60	0 75
Congou & Souch'ng	0 42	0 75
Oolong, good to fine	0 50	0 65
Y. Hyson, com to gd	0 45	0 55
Medium to choice	0 65	0 80
Extra choice	0 85	0 95
Gunpowd'r c. to med	0 55	0 70
" med. to fine	0 70	0 85

Name of Article.	Wholesale Rate. $ c.	$ c.
Groceries—*Contin'd*		
" fine to fins't	0 85	0 95
Hyson	0 45	0 80
Imperial	0 42	0 80
Tobacco, Manufact'd:		
Can Leaf, ₽ lb 5s & 10s.	0 26	0 30
Western Leaf, com	0 25	0 26
" Good	0 27	0 32
" Fine	0 32	0 35
" Bright fine	0 40	0 50
" " choice	0 60	0 75
Hardware.		
Tin (net cash prices)		
Block, ₽ lb.	0 25	0 26
Grain	0 25	0 26
Copper:		
Pig	0 23	0 24
Sheet	0 30	0 33
Cut Nails:		
Assorted ¼ Shingles, ₽ 100 lb.	2 90	3 00
Shingle alone do	3 15	3 25
Lathe and 5 dy	3 30	3 40
Galvanized Iron:		
Assorted sizes	0 00	0 10
Best No. 24	0 09	0 00
" 26	0 08	0 08½
" 28	0 09	0 09½
Horse Nails:		
Guest's or Griffin's assorted sizes	0 19	0 20
For W. ass'd sizes	0 18	0 19
Patent Hammer'd do	0 17	0 18
Iron (at 4 months):		
Pig—Gartsherrie No1	26 00	27 00
Other brands. No1	22 00	24 00
" No2	24 00	25 00
Bar—Scotch, ₽100 lb.	2 25	2 50
Refined	3 00	3 25
Swedes	5 00	5 50
Hoops—Coopers	3 00	3 25
Band	3 00	3 25
Boiler Plates	3 25	3 50
Canada Plates	4 00	4 25
Union Jack	0 00	0 00
Pontypool	4 00	4 25
Swansea	3 90	4 00
Lead (at 4 months):		
Bar, ₽ 100 lbs.	0 07	0 07½
Sheet "	0 08	0 09
Shot	0 07½	0 07¾
Iron Wire (net cash):		
No. 6, ₽ bundle	2 70	2 80
" 9, "	3 10	3 20
" 12, "	3 40	3 50
" 16, "	4 30	4 40
Powder:		
Blasting, Canada	3 50	3 75
FF "	4 25	4 50
FFF "	4 75	5 00
Blasting, English	5 00	5 50
FF loose	5 50	6 00
FFF "	6 00	6 50
Pressed Spikes (4 mos):		
Regular sizes 100	4 00	4 25
Extra "	4 50	5 00
Tin Plates (net cash):		
IC Coke	7 50	8 00
IC Charcoal	8 50	8 75
IX "	10 50	10 75
IXX "	12 50	0 00
DC "	7 50	9 00
DX "	9 50	10 00
Hides & Skins, ₽ lb		
Green rough	0 05½	0 06
Green, salt'd & insp'd	0 00	0 07
Cured	0 07½	0 08½
Calfskins, green	0 00	0 10
Calfskins, cured	0 00	0 12
" dry	0 18	0 20
Lambskins,	0 50	0 00
" pelts	0 40	0 00
Hops.		
Inferior, ₽ lb.	0 10	0 15
Medium	0 15	0 20
Good	0 20	0 25
Fancy	0 25	0 35
Leather, @ (4 mos.) In lots of less than 50 sides, 10 ₽ cent higher.		
Spanish Sole, 1st qual. heavy, weights ₽ lb.	0 23	0 23½
Do. 1st qual middle do.	0 23	0 23½
Do. No. 2, all weights	0 20	0 22
Slaughter heavy	0 28	0 29
Do. light	0 28	0 29
Harness, best	0 32	0 34
" No. 2	0 30	0 33
Upper heavy	0 35	0 40
" light	0 40	0 45

Name of Article.	Wholesale Rates. $ c.	$
Leather—*Contin'd.*		
Kip Skins, Patna	0 45	0
French	0 70	0
English	0 65	0
Hemlock Calf (30 to 35 lbs.) per doz.	0 75	0
Do. light	0 45	0
French Calf	1 05	1
Grain & Satn Clt ₽ doz.	0 00	0
Splits, large ₽ lb.	0 38	0
" small	0 20	0
Enamelled Cow ₽ foot	0 20	0
Patent	0 21	0
Pebble Grain	0 17	0
Buff	0 17	0
Oils.		
Cod	0 55	0
Lard, extra	0 00	1
" No. 1	0 00	1
" Woollen	0 00	1
Lubricating, patent	0 00	0
" Mott's economic	0 50	0
Linseed, raw	0 77½	0
" boiled	0 82½	0
Machinery	0 00	0
Olive, 2nd, ₽ gal.	1 45	1
" salad	2 00	2
" salad, in bots. qt. ₽ case	3 60	3
Sesame salad, ₽ gal.	1 00	1
Seal, pale	0 70	0
Spirits Turpentine	0 65	0
Varnish	0 00	0
Whale	0 75	0
Paints, &c.		
White Lead, genuine in Oil, ₽ 25lbs.	0 00	2
Do. No. 1 "	0 00	2
" 2 "	0 00	2
" 3 "	0 00	1 7
White Zinc, genuine	3 00	3 5
White Lead, dry	0 06	0
Red Lead	0 07½	0
Venetian Red, Eng'h	0 02½	0
Yellow Ochre, Fren'h	0 02¾	0
Whiting	0 90	1 2
Petroleum. (Refined ₽ gal.)		
Water white, car l'd	0 31	
" small lots	0 34	
Straw, by car load	0 30	
" small lots	0 33	0
Amber, by car load	0 00	0
" small lots	0 00	0
Benzine	0 35	0
Produce.		
Grain:		
Wheat, Spring, 60 lb.	1 15	1
" Fall 60 "	1 30	1
Barley 48 "	1 16	1
Peas 60 "	0 92	0
Oats 34 "	0 50	0
Rye 56 "	0 80	0
Seeds:		
Clover, choice 60 "	5 50	6
" com'n 68 "	0 00	0
Timothy, cho'e 4 "	2 50	2
" inf. to good 48 "	1 50	2
Flax 56 "	1 25	1
Flour (per brl.):		
Superior extra	6 75	7
Extra superfine,	6 50	6
Fancy superfine	0 00	0
Superfine No. 1	5 45	5
" No. 2	0 00	0
Oatmeal, (per brl.)	6 25	6
Provisions.		
Butter, dairy tub ₽ lb.	0 18	0
" store packed	0 16	0
Cheese, new	0 10½	0
Pork, mess, per brl.	23 00	24
" prime mess	16 00	17
" prime	14 00	15
Bacon, rough	0 00	0
" Cumberl'd cut	0 12	0
" smoked	0 00	0
Hams, in salt	0 00	0
" sug. cur. & canv'd	0 00	0
Shoulders, in salt	0 00	0
Lard, in kegs	0 13½	0
Eggs, packed	0 14	0
Beef Hams	0 00	0
Tallow	0 00	0
Hogs dressed, heavy	0 00	0
" medium	0 00	0
" light	0 00	0
Salt, &c.		
American brls	1 58	1
Liverpool coarse	0 00	0 0
Plaster	1 05	1 1
Water Lime	1 50	0 0

ap & Candles.	$ c.	$ c.
Crawford & Co.'s ..		
Imperial........	0 07½	0 08
Golden Bar	0 07	0 07½
Silver Bar........	0 07	0 07½
wn	0 05	0 05½
o. 1	0 03½	0 03¾
dles	0 10½	0 11
Vines, Liquors, &c.		
glish, per doz......	2 60	2 65
inness Dub Portr..	2 35	2 40
rits:		
re Jamaica Rum...	1 80	2 25
Kuyper's H. Gin..	1 55	1 65
oth's Old Tom.....	1 90	2 00
een, cases.........	4 00	4 25
oth's Old Tom, c...	6 00	6 25
nes:		
rt, common	1 00	1 25
fine old	2 00	4 00
erry, common	1 00	1 50
medium........	1 70	1 80
old pale or golden..	2 50	4 00

Brandy:	$ c.	$ c.
Hennessy's, per gal..	2 40	2 50
Martell's " ..	2 40	2 50
J. Robin & Co.'s " ..	2 25	2 35
Otard, Dupuy & Cos..	2 25	2 85
Brandy, cases........	8 50	9 00
Brandy, com. per c...	4 00	4 50
Whiskey:		
Common 36 u. p......	0 62½	0 5
Old Rye	0 85	0 7½
Malt	0 85	0 7½
Toddy	0 85	0 7½
Scotch, per gal........	1 90	2 60
Irish—Kinnahan's c...	7 00	7 50
" Dunnville's Belf't..	6 00	6 25
Wool.		
Fleece, lb............	0 27	0 30
Pulled "............	0 00	0 00
Furs.		
Bear................	3 00	10 00
Beaver..............	1 00	1 25
Coon	0 20	0 40
Fisher..............	4 00	6 00
Martin..............	1 40	1 60
Mink................	4 00	4 25
Otter...............	5 75	6 00
Spring Rats.........	0 15	0 17
Fox.................	1 20	1 25

INSURANCE COMPANIES.

ENGLISH.—*Quotations on the London Market.*

o. of ares.	Last Dividend.	Name of Company.	Shares par val £	Amount paid.	Last
,000		Briton Medical and General Life...	10	—	1¼
,000	7½	Commer'l Union, Fire, Life and Mar.	50	5	5½ 5¾
,000	8	City of Glasgow	25	2½	5
,000	9½	Edinburgh Life	100	15	30½x
,000	5—½ yr	European Life and Guarantee......	2½	11s6	4s 6d
,000	10	Etna Fire and Marine..........	10	1½	1
,000	5	Guardian	100	50	52x
,000	12	Imperial Fire................	500	50	345
,500	9½	Imperial Life	100	10	16½
,000	10	Lancashire Fire and Life........	20	2	2½x
,000	11	Life Association of Scotland......	40	7½	23
,862	45s. p. sh	London Assurance Corporation ..	25	12½	48
,000	5	London and Lancashire Life	10	1	1
,504	40	Liverp'l & London & Globe F. & L.	20	2	7¾
,000	5	National Union Life	5	1	1
,000	12½	Northern Fire and Life	100	5	10⅝
000	12 '68, bo 5s.	North British and Mercantile	50	6¼	16 16½
,000	50	Ocean Marine	25	5	20
,500	£5 12s.	Provident Life................	100	10	38
.....	£4½ p. s.	Phœnix......................	....	....	136
,000	2½—h. yr.	Queen Fire and Life	10	1	15-16
,000	3s. bo. 4s	Royal Insurance................	20	3	6¾
,000	10	Scottish Provincial Fire and Life ..	50	2½	4½
,000	25	Standard Life	50	12	65
,000	5	Star Life	25	1¼	—
		CANADIAN.			℘ c.
,000	4	British America Fire and Marine ..	$50	$25	56
.....	4	Canada Life	...	....	.....
4000	12	Montreal Assurance	£50	£10	135
,000	8	Provincial Fire and Marine.......	60	11	.....
.....	....	Quebec Fire	40	32½	£19
.....	8	" Marine..................	100	40	90-91
,000	5 7 mo's.	Western Assurance..............	40	6	.....

RAILWAYS.	Sha's	Paid	Montr	London.
antic and St. Lawrence.........................	£100	All.	....	56 58xd
ffalo and Lake Huron	20½	"	....	3 3½
Do. do. Preference	10	"	....	5½ 6½
ff., Brantt. & Goderich, 6℘c., 1872-3-4....	100	"	....	----
amplain and St. Lawrence	....	....	9 10	....
Do. do Pref. 10 ℘ ct...........	....	....	62½	....
and Trunk	100	"	15 16	16¾ 17¼
Do. Eq. G. M. Bds. 1 ch. 6℘c...........	100	"	....	80 83
Do. First Preference, 5 ℘ c	100	"	....	50 52
Do. Deferred, 3 ℘ ct..	100	"	....	....
Do. Second Pref. Bonds, 5℘c..........	100	"	....	40 42
Do. do Deferred, 3 ℘ ct...........	100	"	...	....
Do. Third Pref. Stock, 4 ℘ct...........	100	"	...	28 30
Do. do. Deferred, 3 ℘ ct.....	100	"	....	....
Do. Fourth Pref. Stock, 3℘c...........	100	"	....	19½ 20
Do. do. Deferred, 3 ℘ ct...........	100	"	....	....
eat Western	20½	"	....	14½ 14⅝
Do. New	20½	18	16 17	....
Do. 6 ℘ c. Bds, due 1873-76...........	100	All.	....	101 103
5½ ℘c Bds. due 1877-78...........	100	"	....	93 95
rine Railway, Halifax, $250, all.......	$250	"	....	....
rthern, of Canada, 6℘c. 1st Pref. Bds..........	100	"	.. .	80 83

EXCHANGE.	Halifax.	Montr'l.	Quebec.	Toronto.
nk on London, 60 days......				
ight or 75 days date	13½	8¾ 8⅞	8¾ 9	99½
ivate do.	12 12½	8 8½	8 8¼	8½
ivate, with documents.........	....	7½ 8	....	....
nk on New York...............	....	30½ 31	30 30½	71½
ivate do.	....	31 31½	31 31½	....
ld Drafts do.	....	1-32 dis.	par ½ dis.	par ½ dis.
ver	....		....	3½ 5

STOCK AND BOND REPORT.

The dates of our quotations are as follows:—Toronto, Sept. 30; Montreal, Sept. 28; Quebec, Sept. 28; London, Sept. 17.

NAME.	Shares.	Paid up.	Divid'd last 6 Months	Dividend Day.	CLOSING PRICES. Toronto.	Montre'l.	Quebec.
BANKS.			℘ ct.				
British North America.......	$250	All.	3	July and Jan.	102½ 103	103 104	102½ 103
Jacques Cartier.............	50	"	4	1 June, 1 Dec.	106 108	106 108	106 107
Montreal	200	"	5	"	134½ 135½	135 136	134 135
Nationale..................	50	"	4	1 Nov. 1 May.	106	107 108	107½ 108
New Brunswick	100	"	......	......	....	...	....
Nova Scotia	200	28	7&b$3½	Mar. and Sept.	....	....	....
Du Peuple..................	50	"	4	1 Mar., 1 Sept.	105 106	105½ 106	105 106
Toronto	100	"	4	1 Jan., 1 July.	116½ 117	115 117	115 116
Bank of Yarmouth...........	....	....	......	......	....	....	....
Canadian Bank of Com'e......	50	95	......	......	103½ 104	101½ 103	101½ 102
City Bank Montreal	80	All.	4	1 June, 1 Dec.	102 102½	102½ 103	102 103
Commer'l Bank (St. John)....	100	"	℘ ct.	......	....	...	....
Eastern Townships' Bank.....	50	"	4	1 July, 1 Jan..	....	95 97	96 97
Gore	40	...	3½	1 Jan., 1 July.	....	....	39 40
Halifax Banking Company....	...	....	......	.....	...	...	...
Mechanics' Bank............	50	70	4	1 Nov., 1 May.	95 97	95 97	95 96
Merchants' Bank of Canada....	100	70	4	1 Jan., 1 July.	105 105½	105 105½	105 105½
Merchants' Bank (Halifax)....	....	....	.....	.....	....	.. ..	....
Molson's Bank..............	50	All.	4	1 Apr., 1 Oct.	Bksclo d	Bks. clod	Bks. clod
Niagara District Bank...	100	70	3½	1 Jan., 1 July.	...	....	....
Ontario Bank...............	40	All.	4	1 June, 1 Dec.	98½ 99½	98 99	98 98½
People's Bank (Fred'kton)....	100	"	......	......	....	....	....
People's Bank (Halifax)	20	"	7 12 m	......	....	...	. ..
Quebec Bank	100	"	3½	1 June, 1 Dec.	97½ 98	98 99	98 98½
Royal Canadian Bank	50	50	4	1 Jan., 1 July.	90 91½	90 92	90 91
St. Stephens Bank	100	All	.....	......	....	..	....
Union Bank	100	70	4	1 Jan., 1 July.	102 102½	102 102½	102½ 103
Union Bank (Halifax)........	100	40	7 12 mo	Feb. and Aug.	....	....	. .
MISCELLANEOUS.							
British America Land........	250	44	2½	------	....	----	....
British Colonial S. S. Co......	250	32½	2½	------	...	50	....
Canada Company	32½	All.	5	......	....	----	....
Canada Landed Credit Co.....	50	$20	3½	......	62 63	----	....
Canada Per. B'ldg Society....	50	All.	5	......	119 119½	....	....
Canada Mining Company.....	4	90	......	--- --	....	....	....
Do. Inl'd Steam Nav. Co.....	100	All.	20 12 m	......	----	107 109	107 108
Do. Glass Company.........	100	"	12½ "	......	....	95	....
Canad'n Loan & Investm't....	25	2½	7	......	....	....	----
Canada Agency	10	½	......	......	....	....	----
Colonial Securities Co........	...	....	.....	.....	....	....	....
Freehold Building Society....	100	All.	5	......	106 106½	----	....
Halifax Steamboat Co........	100	"	5	------	....	....	....
Halifax Gas Company........	....	----	------	.. .. .	....	...	....
Hamilton Gas Company......	----	----	-----	. ...	.....	....	....
Huron Copper Bay Co........	4	12	20	. ....	....	35 50cps	....
Lake Huron S. and C.........	5	102	......	......	....	....	....
Montreal Mining Co..........	20	$15	......	......	....	2.90 3.15	...
Do. Telegraph Co...	40	All.	5	......	134 135	134 135	134½ 134¾
Do. Elevating Co...	00	"	15 12 m	......	....	100 103	....
Do. City Gas Co.........	40	"	4	15 Mar. 15 Sep.	....	127½ 132½	128 130
Do. City Pass. R. Co.....	50	"	5	......	....	110 112	110 112
Nova Scotia Telegraph	20	"	....	. ....	....	....	....
Quebec and L. S.	8	$4	......	......	. .	....	25 cts
Quebec Gas Co..............	200	All.	4	1 Mar., 1 Sep.	....	...	117 118
Quebec Street R. R..........	50	25	8	......	....	....	96 97
Richelieu Navigation Co......	100	All.	7 p.a.	1 Jan., 1 July.	....	113 x d	113 x d
St. Lawrence Tow Boat Co.....	100	"	......	3 Feb.	....	...	40 45
Tor'to Consumers' Gas Co.....	50	"	2 3 m.	1 My Au Mar Fe	104½ 105	...	103 104
Trust & Loan Co. of U. C.....	20	5	3	......	....	....	.. .
West'n Canada Bldg Soc'y....	50	All.	5	......	112½ 113	....	----

SECURITIES.	London.	Montreal.	Quebec.	Toronto.
Canadian Gov't Deb. 6 ℘ ct. due 1872	....	100 101	100 101	100 101
Do. do. 6 do due Ja. & Jul. 1877-84........	104 106	....	....	....
Do. do. 6 do. Feb. & Aug..........	103 105	....	.. .	....
Do. do. 6 do. Mch. & Sep..........	103 105	.. .	...	.. .
Do. do. 5 ℘ ct. cur., 1883	91 93	89 90	89½ 90	90
Do. do. 5 do. stg., 1885	....	89 90	90 90½	90 90½
Do. do. 7 do. cur.,...................	....	....	......	....
Dominion 6 p. c. 1878 cy.....	....	100 101	100½ 101½	100 101
Hamilton Corporation.....	. ..	....	......	....
Montreal Harbor, 8 ℘ ct. d. 1869.................	..	....	......	....
Do. do. 7 do. 1870.................	....	....	......	....
Do. do. 6½ do. 1875.................	....	100 100½	......	....
Do. do. 6½ do. 1878.................	....	....	......	....
Do. Corporation, 6 ℘ c. 1891	....	92	92 93	92 93
Do. 7 p. c. stock...........................	....	105 106	103 105	105 105½
Do. Water Works, 6 ℘ c. stg. 1878..........	....	....	......	92 93
Do. do. 6 do. cy. do.	....	92½ 93	......	92 93
New Brunswick, 6 ℘ ct., Jan. and July	102 104	....	......	....
Nova Scotia, 6 ℘ ct., 1875......................	100 102	...	......	....
Ottawa City 6 ℘ c. d. 1880	....	90 91	......	...
Quebec Harbour, 6 ℘ c. d. 1883.	....	....	60 70	....
Do. do. 7 do. do.....................	....	....	70	....
Do. do. 8 do. 1886..................	...	....	85	....
Do. City, 7 ℘ c. d. 5 years	....	80 90	90 91	....
Do. do. 7 do. 9 do.	....	....	86 87	....
Do. do. 7 do. 2½ do.	....	....	96 96½	....
Do. Water Works, 7 ℘ ct., 4 years............	....	....	95 96	....
Do. do. 6 do. 2 do.	....	....	92½ 93½	....
Toronto Corporation	....	90 92½	...	......

Financial.

Pellatt & Osler.

STOCK AND EXCHANGE BROKERS, Accountants, Agents for the Standard Life Assurance Company and York Casualty Insurance Company.
OFFICE—86 *King Street East, four Doors West of Church Street, Toronto.*

HENRY PELLATT,   EDMUND B. OSLER,
Notary Public.   *Official Assignee.*

BROWN'S BANK,
(W. R. Brown. W. C. Chewett.)

60 *KING STREET EAST, TORONTO.*

TRANSACTS a general Banking Business, Buys and Sells New York and Sterling Exchange, Gold, Silver, U.S. Bonds and Uncurrent Money, receives Deposits subject to Cheque at sight, makes Collections and Discounts Commercial Paper.
Orders by Mail or Telegraph promptly executed at most favourable current quotations.
☞ Address letters,   "BROWN'S BANK,
5-y   Toronto."

The Canadian Land and Emigration Company

Offers for sale on Conditions of Settlement,
GOOD FARM LANDS

In the County of Peterboro, Ontario,

the well settled Township of Dysart, where there are Grist and Saw Mills, Stores, &c., at

TWO-AND-A-HALF DOLLARS AN ACRE,

In the adjoining Townships of Guilford, Dudley, Harburn, Harcourt and Bruton, connected with Dysart and Village of Haliburton by the Peterson Road, at ONE DOLLAR an Acre.

For further particulars apply to
CHAS. JAS. BLOMFIELD,
Secretary C. L. and E. Co., Toronto.
Or to   ALEX. NIVEN, P.L.S.,
Agent C. L. & E. Co., Haliburton.

Insurance.

The Liverpool and London and Globe Insurance Company.

Capital and Reserved Funds........$17,005,000.
DAILY CASH RECEIPTS,......$20,000.

NOTICE IS HEREBY GIVEN, that this Company having deposited the sum of
150,000 Dollars,

in accordance with the Act, 31st Vic., cap. 48, has received a License of the Finance Minister, to transact the business of Life and Fire Insurance in the Dominion of Canada.

G. F. C. SMITH,
-4t   Chief Agent for the Dominion.

Hartford Fire Insurance Company.
HARTFORD, CONN.

With Capital and Assets over Two Million Dollars.

$2,026,220.29.

CHARTERED 1810.

THIS old and reliable Company, having an established business in Canada of more than thirty years standing, is complied with the provisions of the new Insurance Act, and made a special deposit of
$100,000

with the Government for the security of policy-holders, and will continue to grant policies upon the same favourable terms as heretofore.

Specially low rates on first-class dwellings and farm property for a term of one or more years.
Losses as heretofore promptly and equitably adjusted.
E. CHAFFEY & CO., AGENTS.
Toronto, Ont.

ROBERT WOOD, GENERAL AGENT FOR CANADA
04-6m

Insurance.

The Standard Life Assurance Company,
Established 1825.

WITH WHICH IS NOW UNITED
THE COLONIAL LIFE ASSURANCE COMPANY.

Head Office for Canada:
MONTREAL—STANDARD COMPANY'S BUILDINGS,
No. 47 GREAT ST. JAMES STREET.

Manager—W. M. RAMSAY.   Inspector—RICH'D BULL.

THIS Company having deposited the sum of ONE HUNDRED AND FIFTY THOUSAND DOLLARS with the Receiver-General, in conformity with the Insurance Act passed last Session, Assurances will continue to be carried out at moderate rates and on all the different systems in practice.

AGENT FOR TORONTO—HENRY PELLATT,
KING STREET.

AGENT FOR HAMILTON—JAMES BANCROFT.
0-6mos.

Fire and Marine Assurance.

THE BRITISH AMERICA
ASSURANCE COMPANY.

HEAD OFFICE:
CORNER OF CHURCH AND COURT STREETS.
TORONTO.

BOARD OF DIRECTION:
Hon. G. W. Allan, M.L.C.,   A. Joseph, Esq.,
George J. Boyd, Esq.,   Peter Paterson, Esq.,
Hon. W. Cayley,   G. P. Ridout, Esq.,
Richard S. Cassels, Esq.,   E. H. Rutherford, Esq.,
Thomas C. Street, Esq.

Governor:
GEORGE PERCIVAL RIDOUT, ESQ.
Deputy Governor:
PETER PATERSON, ESQ.

Fire Inspector: Marine Inspector:
E. ROBY O'BRIEN.   CAPT. R. COURNEEN.

Insurances granted on all descriptions of property against loss and damage by fire and the perils of inland navigation.
Agencies established in the principal cities, towns, and ports of shipment throughout the Province.
THOS. WM. BIRCHALL,
23-ly   Managing Director.

Edinburgh Life Assurance Company.

Founded 1823.

HEAD OFFICE—22 GEORGE STREET, EDINBURGH.

Capital,....................£500,000 Ster'g.
Accumulated and Invested Funds, £1,000,000 "

HEAD OFFICE IN CANADA:
WELLINGTON STREET, TORONTO.

SUB-AGENTS THROUGHOUT THE PROVINCE.

J. HILLYARD CAMERON,
Chairman, Canadian Board.

DAVID HIGGINS,
Secretary, Canadian Board.   3-3m

Queen Fire and Life Insurance Company,
OF LIVERPOOL AND LONDON,
ACCEPTS ALL ORDINARY FIRE RISKS
on the most favorable terms.

LIFE RISKS
Will be taken on terms that will compare favorably with other Companies.

CAPITAL,   £2,000,000 Stg.

CHIEF OFFICES—Queen's Buildings, Liverpool, and Gracechurch Street London.
CANADA BRANCH OFFICE—Exchange Buildings, Montreal.
Resident Secretary and General Agent,
A. MACKENZIE FORBES,
13 St. Sacrament St., Merchants' Exchange, Montreal.
WM. ROWLAND, Agent, Toronto.   1-ly

Insurance.

Reliance Mutual Life Assurance Society.
(Established, 1840,) OF LONDON, E. C.

Accumulated Funds, over $1,000,000.
Annual Income, $300,00.
THE entire Profits of this long-established Society belong to the Policy-holders.
HEAD OFFICE FOR DOMINION—MONTREAL.
T. W. GRIFFITH, Manager & Sec'y.
15-ly   WM. HENDERSON, Agent for Toronto.

Etna Insurance Company of Dublin.
The number of Shareholders exceeds Five Hundred.

Capital, $5,000,000—Annual Income nearly $1,000,000.
THIS Company takes Fire and Marine Risks on the most favorable terms.
T. W. GRIFFITH, Manager for Canada
Chief office for Dominion—Corner St. Francois Xavier and 87. Sacrament Sts., Montreal.
15-ly   WM. HENDERSON, Agent for Toronto.

Scottish Provincial Assurance Co.
Established 1825.

CAPITAL, ...£1,000,000 STERLING.
INVESTED IN CANADA (1854)..............$500,000.
Canada Head Office, Montreal.

LIFE DEPARTMENT.
CANADA BOARD OF DIRECTORS:
HUGH TAYLOR, Esq., Advocate,
Hon. CHARLES WILSON, M.L.C.
WM. SACHE, Esq., Banker,
JACKSON RAE, Esq., Banker.
WM. FRASER, Esq., M. D., Medical Adviser.

The special advantages to be derived from Insuring in this office are:—Strictly Moderate Rates of Premium; Large Bonus (Intermediate bonus guaranteed;) Liberal Surrender Value, under policies relinquished by assured; and Extensive Limits of Residence and Travel. All business disposed of in Canada, without reference to parent office.

A. DAVIDSON PARKER,
Resident Secretary
G. L. MADDISON,
15-1yr   AGENT FOR TORONTO.

Lancashire Insurance Company.

CAPITAL, - - - - - - - - £2,000,000 Starling.

FIRE RISKS
Taken at reasonable rates of premium, and
ALL LOSSES SETTLED PROMPTLY,
By the undersigned, without reference elsewhere.
S. C. DUNCAN-CLARK & CO.,
General Agents for Ontario,
N. W. Corner of King & Church Streets,
25-ly   TORONTO.

Etna Fire & Marine Insurance Company.

INCORPORATED 1819. CHARTER PERPETUAL.

CASH CAPITAL,   - - - - : $3,000,000

LOSSES PAID IN 50 YEARS, 23,500,000 00.

JULY, 1868.
ASSETS.
(At Market Value.)
Cash in hand and in Bank................ $544,842 29
Real Estate.................................. 255,207,29
Mortgage Bonds............................ 982,345.00
Bank Stock................................. 1,272,670 00
United States, State and City Stock, and other Public Securities..................... 2,049,855 51
Total................ $5,052,380 19

LIABILITIES.
Claims not Due, and Unadjusted........... $499,803 55
Amount required by Mass. and New York for Re-Insurance,...................... 1,405,287 15
E. CHAFFEY & CO., Agents.
50-6m

Insurance.

ÆTNA
Live Stock Insurance Company.

LICENSED BY THE DOMINION GOVERNMENT TO
DO BUSINESS IN CANADA.

THE following Accidents, this month, show the importance of Insuring your Horses and Cattle against Death
from any cause, or Theft, in the ÆtnaInsurance Company:

MONTREAL, September 16, 1868.
At a fire last night, in the sheds behind Ripin's Hotel,
St. Joseph Street, three valuable Stock Horses were destroyed, "Young Clydesdale" and "Emigrant," belonging
to the Huntingdon Agricultural Society—the former worth
$900, and the latter $1,700; and "Old Beauharnois" cost
$1,000, belonging to the Beauharnois Society.

PORT COLBORNE, September 18, 1868.
Horses DROWNED.—Two horses belonging to Mr. Briggs,
of Port Colborne, and four owned by Mr. Julion, of Port
Dalhousie, were drowned in the Canal, near the Junction,
early this morning.

A fire at the Glasgow Hotel, Montreal, this morning, destroyed two horses. The fire was caused by drunkenness
on the part of the stable man.

MONTREAL, September 24, 1868.
A fire in F. X. Cusson's stables, St. Joseph Street, last
night, destroyed three horses.

E. L. SNOW, GENERAL AGENT,
Montreal
Agents for Ontario:—
SCOTT & WALMSLEY,
67nov11y   Ontario Hall, Church Street, Toronto.

The Liverpool and London and Globe
Insurance Company.

INVESTED FUNDS:
FIFTEEN MILLIONS OF DOLLARS.

DAILY INCOME OF THE COMPANY:
TWELVE THOUSAND DOLLARS.

LIFE INSURANCE,
WITH AND WITHOUT PROFITS.

FIRE INSURANCE
On every description of Property, at Lowest Remunerative
Rates.

JAMES FRASER, AGENT,
5 King Street West.
Toronto, 1868.   38-1y

Briton Medical and General Life
Association,
with which is united the
BRITANNIA LIFE ASSURANCE COMPANY.

Capital and Invested Funds..............£750,000 Sterling.

ANNUAL INCOME, £220,000 STG. :
Yearly increasing at the rate of £25,000 Sterling.

THE important and peculiar feature originally introduced by this Company, in applying the periodical
Bonuses, so as to make Policies payable during life, without
any higher rate of premiums being charged, has caused
the success of the BRITON MEDICAL and GENERAL to be
almost unparalleled in the history of Life Assurance. *1¼*
*Policies on the Profit Scale become payable during the lifetime
of the Assured, thus rendering a Policy of Assurance a
means of subsistence in old age, as well as a protection for a
family, and a more valuable security to creditors in the
event of early death; and effectually meeting the often
urged objection, that persons do not themselves reap the
benefit of their own prudence and forethought.*
No extra charge made to members of Volunteer Corps
for services within the British Provinces.

☞ TORONTO AGENCY, 5 KING ST. WEST.
oct17—9-1yr   JAMES FRASER, Agent.

Phenix Insurance Company,
BROOKLYN, N. Y.

PHILANDER SHAW, EDGAR W. CROWELL,
Secretary.   Vice-President.
STEPHEN CROWELL, President.
Cash Capital, $1,000,000. Surplus, $666,416.02. Total,
1,666,416.02. Entire Income from all sources for 1866 was
$2,131,530.82.

CHARLES G. FORTIER, Marine Agent.
Ontario Chambers, Toronto, Ont.   19-1y.

Insurance.

The Victoria Mutual
FIRE INSURANCE COMPANY OF CANADA.

Insures only Non-Hazardous Property, at Low Rates.

BUSINESS STRICTLY MUTUAL.

GEORGE H. MILLS, President.
W. D. BOOKER, Secretary.
HEAD OFFICE ....HAMILTON, ONTARIO
aug 15-1yr

The Ætna Life Insurance Company.

AN attack, abounding with errors, haVing been made
upon the Ætna Life Insurance Co. by the editor of the
Montreal Daily News : and certain agents of British
Companies being now engaged in handing around copies of
the attack, thus seeking to damage the Company's standing,
—I haVe pleasure in laying before the public the following
certificate, bearing the signatures of the President and
Cashiers who happened to be in their Offices) of every Bank
in Hartford; also that of the President and Secretary of
the old Ætna Fire Insurance Company :—
"To whom it may concern...
"We, the undersigned, regard the Ætna Life Insur-
ance Company, of this city, as one of the most successful
and prosperous Insurance Companies in the States,—
entirely reliable, responsible, and honourable in all its
dealings, and most worthy of public confidence and
patronage."
Lucius J. Hendee, President Ætna Fire Insurance Co.,
and late Treasurer of the State of Connecticut.
J. Goodnow, Secretary Ætna Fire Insurance Co.
C. H. Northam, President, and J. B. Powell, Cashier
National Bank.
C. T. Hillyer, President.Charter Oak National Bank.
E. D. Tiffany, President First National Bank.
G. T. Davis, President City National Bank.
F. S. Riley, Cashier, do. do. do.
John C. Tracy, President of Farmers' and Mechanics'
National Bank.
M. W. Graves, Cashier Conn. River Banking Co.
H. A. Redfield, Cashier Phœnix National Bank.
O. G. Terry, President Ætna National Bank.
J. R. Redfield, Cashier National Exchange Bank.
John G. Root, Assistant Cashier American National Bank.
George F. Hills, Cashier State Bank of Hartford.
Jas. Potter, Cashier Hartford National Bank.
Hartford, Nov. 26, 1867.
Many of the above-mentioned parties are closely con-
nected with other Life Insurance Companies, but all un-
hesitatingly commend our Company as "reliable, respon-
sible, honorable in all its dealings, and most worthy of pub-
lic confidence and patronage.
JOHN GARVIN,
General Agent, Toronto Street.
Toronto, Dec. 3. 1867.   16-1y

Life Association of Scotland.

INVESTED FUNDS
UPWARDS OF £1,000,000 STERLING.

THIS Institution differs from other Life Offices, in that
the
BONUSES FROM PROFITS
Are applied on a special system for the Policy-holder's
*PERSONAL BENEFIT AND ENJOYMENT
DURING HIS OWN LIFETIME,*
WITH THE OPTION OF
LARGE BONUS ADDITIONS TO THE SUM ASSURED.

The Policy-holder thus obtains
A LARGE REDUCTION OF PRESENT OUTLAY
OR
*A PROVISION FOR OLD AGE OF A MOST IMPORTANT
AMOUNT IN ONE CASH PAYMENT,
OR A LIFE ANNUITY,*
Without any expense or outlay whatever beyond the
ordinary Assurance Premium for the Sum
Assured, which remains in tact for
Policy-holder's heirs, or other
purposes.

CANADA—MONTREAL—PLACE D'ARMES.

DIRECTORS:
DAVID TORRANCE, Esq., (D. Torrance & Co.)
GEORGE MOFFATT, (Gillespie, Moffatt & Co.)
ALEXANDER MORRIS, Esq., M.P., Barrister, Perth.
SIR G. E. CARTIER, M.P., Minister of Militia.
PETER REDPATH, Esq., (J. Redpath & Son).
J. H. R. MOLSON, Esq., (J. H. R. Molson & Bros.)
Solicitors—Messrs. TORRANCE & MORRIS.
Medical Officer—R. PALMER HOWARD, Esq., M.D
Secretary—P. WARDLAW.
Inspector of Agencies—JAMES D. M. CHIPMAN.
             y

Insurance.

North British and Mercantile Insurance
Company.

Established 1809.

HEAD OFFICE, - - CANADA. - - MONTRE

TORONTO BRANCH:
LOCAL OFFICES, Nos. 4 & 6 WELLINGTON STREET.
Fire Department, ... R. N. GOOCH
                Ag
Life Department, ... H. L. HIME,
29-1y   Ag

Phœnix Fire Assurance Company.
LOMBARD ST. AND CHARING CROSS,
LONDON, ENG.

Insurances effected in all parts of the World

Claims paid
WITH PROMTITUDE and LIBERALITY
MOFFATT, MURRAY & BEATTIE,
Agents for Toronto,
36 Yonge Stree
                28-1

The Commercial Union Assurance
Company,
19 & 20 CORNHILL, LONDON, ENGLAND.
Capital, £2,500,000 Stg.—Invested over $2,000,000

FIRE DEPARTMENT.—Insurance granted on all
scriptions of property at reasonable rates.
LIFE DEPARTMENT.—The success of this bra
has been unprecedented—NINETY PERCENT. of
miums now in hand. First year's premiums were i
$100,000. Economy of management guaranteed Pe
c curity. Moderate rates.
OFFICE—385 & 387 ST PAUL STREET, MONTREAL
MORLAND,
General Agents for Can
FRED. COLE, Secretary.
Inspector of Agencies—T. C. LIVINGSTON, P.
W. M. WESTMACOTT, Agent at Toron
16-1y

Phœnix Mutual Life Insurance Co.
HARTFORD, CONN.

Accumulated Fund, $3,000,000, Income, $1,000,

THIS Company, established in 1851, is one of the
reliable Companies doing business in the country,
has been steadily prospering. The Massachusetts Insu
Reports show that in nearly all important matters
superior; to the general average of Companies. It offe
intending assurers the following reasons, amongst ot
for preferring it to other companies :
It is purely Mutual It allows the Insured to t
and reside in any portion of the United States and Eu
It throws out almost all restriction on occupation fro
Policies. It will, if desired, take a note for part of
Premium, thus combining all the advantages of a note
all cash company. Its Dividends are declared ann
and applied in reduction of Premium. Its Dividend
in every case on Premiums paid. The Dividends o
year the policy has been in force. The number of
dends will always equal the outstanding Notes. It pa
losses promptly—during its existence never having
tested a claim. It issues Policies for the benefit of
ried Women beyond the reach of their husband's cred
Creditors may also insure the lives of Debtors. Its Pol
are all Non-forfeiting, as it always allows the assur
surrender his Policy, should he desire, the Compan
ing a paid-up Policy therefor. This important fea
will commend itself to all. The inducements now of
by the Phœnix are better and more liberal than tho
any other Company. Its rate of Mortality is exceed
low and under the average.
Parties contemplating Life Insurance will find it to
interest to call and examine our system. Policies i
payable either in Gold or American currency.
ANGUS R. BETHUNE,
General Manager,
Dominion of Can

Office: 104 ST. FRANÇOIS XAVIER ST. MONTREA

☞ Active and energetic Agents and Canva
wanted in every town and village, to whom liberal ts
ments will be given.   16

PRINTED AT THE DAILY TELEGRAPH PRINT
HOUSE, BAY ST., COR. KING.

THE CANADIAN
ONETARY TIMES
AND
INSURANCE CHRONICLE.
DEVOTED TO FINANCE, COMMERCE, INSURANCE, BANKS, RAILWAYS, NAVIGATION, MINES, INVESTMENT, PUBLIC COMPANIES, AND JOINT STOCK ENTERPRISE.

| OL. II—NO. 8. | TORONTO, THURSDAY, OCTOBER 8, 1868. | { SUBSCRIPTION. $2 A YEAR. |

Mercantile.

Gundry and Langley,
CHITECTS AND CIVIL ENGINEERS, Building Surveyors and Valuators. Office corner of King and Jordan ts, Toronto.
THOMAS GUNDRY.   HENRY LANGLEY.

J. B. Boustead.
OVISION and Commission Merchant. Hops bought and sold on Commission. 82 Front St., Toronto.

John Boyd & Co.
HOLESALE Grocers and Commission Merchants, Front St., Toronto.

Childs & Hamilton.
NUFACTURERS and Wholesale Dealers in Boots and Shoes, No. 7 Wellington Street East, Toronto, rio.

L. Coffee & Co.
ODUCE and Commission Merchants, No. 2 Manning's Block, Front St., Toronto, Ont. Advances made on ignments of Produce.

J. & A. Clark,
ODUCE Commission Merchants, Wellington Street East, Toronto, Ont.

D. Crawford & Co.,
ANUFACTURERS of Soaps, Candles, etc., and dealers in Petroleum, Lard and Lubricating Oils, Palace St., nto, Ont.

John Fisken & Co.
CK OIL and Commission Merchants, Yonge St., Toronto, Ont.

W. & R. Griffith.
ORTERS of Teas, Wines, etc. Ontario Chambers, or. Church and Front Sts., Toronto.

Thos. Haworth & Co.
ORTERS and dealers in Iron, Cutlery and general Hardware, King St., Toronto, Ont.

Hurd, Leigh & Co.
LDERS and Enamellers of China and Earthenware, 72 Yonge St., Toronto, Ont. [See advt.]

Lyman & McNab.
HOLESALE Hardware Merchants, Toronto, Ontario.

W. D. Matthews & Co.
ODUCE Commission Merchants, Old Corn Exchange, 16 Front St. East, Toronto Ont.

R. C. Hamilton & Co.
ODUCE Commission Merchants, 119 Lower Water St., Halifax, Nova Scotia.

Parson Bros.,
TROLEUM Refiners, and Wholesale dealers in Lamps, Chimneys, etc. Warerooms 51 Front St. Refinery cor. r and Don Sts., Toronto.

C. P. Reid & Co.
ORTERS and Dealers in Wines, Liquors, Cigars and eaf Tobacco, Wellington Street, Toronto.   28-

W. Rowland & Co.,
UCE BROKERS and General Commission Merants. Advances made on Consignments. Corner ch and Front Streets, Toronto.

Reford & Dillon.
ORTERS of Groceries, Wellington Street, Toronto, ntario.

Meetings.

BANK OF ENGLAND.

The half-yearly court of the governor and proprietors of the Bank of England was held on September 17.

The Governor said that the directors had carefully gone through the accounts, and he had to report that the net profit for the year ending August 30 amounted to £584,369, making the amount of rest or undivided profits on that day £3,610,596. After providing for a dividend of 4 per cent. for the half-year, the rest would amount to £3,028,476. The court of governors therefore proposed that a half-years dividend be made of 4 per cent., being at the rate of 8 per cent. per annum, and that the dividend be payable on the 10th October next.

The Governor, in replying to various questions, put by Mr. Jones and other proprietors, said that the capital of the Bank upon which dividend had to be paid was £14,553,000. All the rest of the property belonging to the Bank were the profits arising out of the Bank's operations, and it was commonly called "rest." The rest was the undivided profits which the court of proprietors long since decided should never be allowed to fall below £3,000,000. The building in which they were assembled occupied rather over three acres of ground, and its value was not included in the capital, but the branch establishments were. With regard to the rate of discount being different on long and short loans, gentlemen of experience must know that a discount was a short transaction for a short time, and a loan might extend over a series of years, and the rate must be different. In 1836 the discount was 10 per cent., but the Consols were only 2¾; railway debentures, in some cases, were at 5. There were deposits of a permanent character, which the board knew how to deal with, and there were also short deposits, which they might be called upon to pay, and must be prepared to pay, at any moment. As to the Bank not having deposits, he believed the deposits had never been so large as—not, perhaps, at that moment of speaking—but over an average of the last six months. No doubt the country would be benifitted by money being lent to farmers, but it was not the province of this bank to lend it to them. It could only safely be done by the local bankers, and even to them it was a question fraught with grave difficulty. With regard to the rate of discount the explanation was simple. Every one remembered that five or six years ago, that was a period auto the crisis of 1866, there was a very great extension of credit, but those sudden and excessive extensions of credit were not always wise. The first effect of it was this, that those who embarked in business were suddenly called upon to pay their debts, and to do that they had to withdraw money from the legitimate operations they were engaged in, and that produced a crisis. What took place in 1866 had been miscalled a panic. It was a crisis arising from and following naturally upon too wide an extension of credit, and this crisis out of its convulsions produced panic. Upon 12th May it was a banking panic, who people were seized with unreasoning fear for the safety of their when they had it in their possession. Then came, a railway panic, when people thought that railway debentures of all kinds were not worth buying. This was succeeded by a commercial panic, when the trade came almost to a standstill; but, through all, this corporation had steered one steady course. With regard to the rate of discount, it, of course, depended very much upon supply and demand. If there was a large sum of money to lend and a few borrowers, the money must go at a lower rate than if the number of borrowers were greater. Whether the Bank had too much money to lend, or too few borrowers, the result was the same. Some said that the Bank might invest upon some other securities, but they forget that the Bank had to pay on demand, and it would be useless to tell a man asking for his money that it had been invested in a safe and snug security.

The report was approved and the dividend declared.

Mining.

NOVA SCOTIA GOLD MINING REVIEW.

Bad weather has slightly interfered with prospecting; but sheltered works have made good progress during the past fortnight. Sales have taken place of properties at Renfrew, Uniacke, and Wine Harbor. Good developed tracts still command high prices. Mining stocks general ly are dull.

SHERBROOK—A critical, but very conscientious, writer—"Wentworth"—reports :—" The original grounds of the Canada Co. are, so far, innocent of gold, but some new purchases have been added, which may turn the scale. The Wecdbine Co., under Mr. Brown, are developing their grounds in a very safe and commendable manner. The Wentworth Co. are doing some work and of all the new companies, this looks the brightest, and under proper management will be a success. The Chicago Co. have not advanced their works sufficiently for one to judge of their prospects.

The Meridian Co. will pay at great depth and after much outlay. The Dominion Co. have an excellent property and people wonder that it has not payed a dividend before this. The Metropolitan Co. is purely Haligonian. The Palmerston, Hayden & Derby and Wellington take out a great deal of gold. The New York and Sherbrooke property maintains its average yield. The Kingston and Sherbrooke mine has yet a record to make. The Delta and Crescent properties have a good future before them. The Stanley and Red Jacket are still classed as outsiders.

The Union mill is considered the "active principle" here, and justly so. The New York and Sherbrooke Companies and the Hayden mills have seen their best days. The Wellington and Palmerston are in good order and fully at work. The Dominion is now going on: it is much on the same principle as the Chicago. The Meridian mill is in want of ore. The Canada mill will soon stamp water mill. The Wentworth, building by Mr. Wilson, is nearly finished and will be the

also the Provincial and Orient Companies' mines. The Orient mill has been refitted by Mr. E. Leedham with Windsor mortars and cams, and it is now "the Mill of Wine Harbor." The Provincial mill of 8 stamps is working steadily. This company well soon erect a 15-stamp mill with a 60 h.p. engine, and combine pump and hoisting gear under one action. The Eldorado Co. are putting 10 stamps in the old English mill, the original machinery of which has been torn out to make room for them. The steam mill on the Eldorado property is a great success, but through the negligence of a workman some portions of the machinery were injured, and it is now idle pending repairs which have to be done at Boston.

UNIACKE.—The reports from this district continue favorable. The mills are all going and we expect to have a large bullion supply in next issue. A lot of 22 tons from Mr. Burkner's wide lode, reduced at the Alpha mill, gave 12 ozs. 11 dwts. The North St. Lawrence Co. report a small but exceedingly rich lode.

INDIAN PATH.—Messrs. Waddelow and Macdonald are working two lodes (one from 6 to 7 ft. the other about 8 inches wide), which show gold freely. This field is likely to prove of great importance.

ECUM SECUM.—Mr. F. S. Andrews has favored us with an interesting report of this district, and the works of the Atlantic Co. which he has gone down to manage. The prospects of this district, too, are very bright. Mr. Andrews' report will appear in next issue.

WAGAMATCOOK.—Mr. D. Y. Estey has recently visited this district and speaks encouragingly of the future of this field for placer mining.—*Mining Gazette*

THE SMELTING OF COPPER ORES IN CANADA.

Some facts from trustworthy sources have lately come to our knowledge in regard to the present manufacture of copper from a pyritous ore in the Province of Quebec, about eighty miles distant from the city of that name, upon the Grand Trunk Railway. They are of a very cheering character, and coming to us as they do, at a time when the copper interest generally is in a very depressed condition, we feel inclined to make them the basis of a few editorial lines. They may serve to encourage those who are engaged in similar undertakings, but unfortunately not with the same success. At all events we have good testimony to the effect that even at the present unprecedently low rates of ingot copper in the market it is possible to utilize low grade ores, and that too at a fair rate of profit. The facts as given to us by one of the gentlemen who assisted in inaugurating the enterprise run about as follows:—

Through the talcose and chloritic slates of the region of the country alluded to, cuts a vein of copper ore, having an average width of ten feet. The vein yields a low grade pyritous ore, assaying only about four per cent. of copper. The conditions of the vein are, however, such that it can be easily worked, the expense of the mining the ore amounting to some $2.15 per ton in gold. The ores are broken, sorted, and roasted in heaps in the open air, at a cost in gold of seventy-five cents per ton. This work is done by contract; the contractor preparing the fuel necessary, a great abundance of timber being near at hand upon the lands of the company. Thus much for the mining and preparation of the ore for the following process of smelting. This is done upon the works erected near at hand, consisting of four furnaces supplied with a cold air blast, a steam engine furnishing the necessary power. We understand that the furnaces were modelled after those in use upon the works of the Revere Copper Company, at Point Shirley, near Boston,

but have since undergone some slight modifications, in order to adapt them more perfectly to the nature of the ore, and to bring out the most practical results. The fuel used for smelting the ore is of the very best. It is imported from New Castle on the Tyne, and costs delivered at the works thirteen dollars in gold per ton. The gangue mass in the vein is of such a nature as to render the use of a flux necessary. We have now to speak of some of the results of the practical working of these furnaces. We confess to no little surprise when our attention was called to them, and are of the opinion that copper men generally are quite as little prepared for them as we were, for, in point of successful copper smelting they really go beyond the precedent. Two furnaces running at the same time, produce nearly five tons of matt per day. Each furnace has a capacity of about twenty-three tons of ore in one day of twenty-four hours. They run, of course, day and night. The consumption of fuel is remarkably light, and the amount of concentration proportionally great. We are informed that every ten tons of ore produce one ton of matt, containing nearly forty per cent. of copper. This is as it should be, when we remember that it is a four per cent. ore that is taken from the mine. As we have it in our notes, the average percentage of the matt produced in the last six months amounts to thirty-seven and nine-tenths per cent. The cost per ton of ore all told, for smelting, amounts to the sum of four and a quarter dollars in gold. This copper matt is subjected to no further treatment upon the works, but shipped to Liverpool and there sold in the market at the ruling rates. The cost of shipment, including freight, insurance, commission, etc., amounts to twelve dollars in gold. At the present market rates of copper, the matt sells in the Liverpool market for some $130 in gold per ton. In connection with the manufacture of copper matt, there is one point of peculiar interest that we must not fail to mention, as to the success of these works is in a great measure due. In the smelting of pyritous copper ores it is generally necessary to blow out at the expiration of a few days, or at the most, in a couple of weeks, and rebuild the interior portions of the furnaces, they having become meanwhile so eaten away and changed in form as to render it impossible to bring about the desired metallurgical results without such reconstruction. But, in this instance, by some slight modifications of the furnaces, together with a certain peculiar management, it has been possible to largely overcome this difficulty. It seems that when the fire brick lining of the furnaces is eaten away, a certain peculiar course of procedure on the part of the smelter causes a new lining to form in place, composed of the slag from the smelted ores. It certainly a very anomalous course of procedure, but as long as it brings about the required results at the lowest rate of cost, nothing could be better. At the time of our interview with our informant, one furnace had entered upon its tenth week of work, and appeared good for two or three weeks more before it would be necessary to refit. It is evident that for the smelting of this kind of ore, under the above conditions, there has been a great improvement made—an improvement that may, perhaps, be made to serve the interest of others engaged in a similar work. If the price of copper in the market is going to remain at this present low figure, there must be a proportional decrease in the cost of its production, if not, our copper mines will have to remain unworked and our smelting mills stand still. We are only too glad amid the general stagnation that now prevails among the copper industries of the country, to be able to record what we have of an enterprise that has sprung up in our midst during the past year, and by means of a proper application of enterprise and skill been brought to such a good degree of success. We hope to obtain in the future, still further information in regard to the enterprise, that will be of general interest to our readers.—*American Jour. of Mining.*

GEOLOGICAL SURVEY OF NOVA SCOTIA.—understand that the survey of the Provin being vigorously prosecuted. Sir W. E. I has been for some time at New Glasgow wit assistant, Mr. Hartley, making researches of numerous coal mines of that vicinity. Dr. son, we believe, has also been observing in same district, as well as at Mount Uniacke in Cape Breton. Professor How has been en during the summer in Digby and Ann Counties, and has forwarded large collectio specimens to the office of the Survey at Mot Dr. Honeyman has been occupied in the C of Antigonishe, and is now, we understand Cape Breton. As no official reports can pected for some time, the exact scenes of the of the officers of the Survey will not, of c be always accurately known, and, with the re can only be conjectured in the meantime. survey, it will be remembered, is geologica not merely mineralogical. We believe som interesting additions have already been m the large amount of paleontological ma accumulated by previous observers. Thes whatever discoveries of useful minerals are will be duly announced in the official r which will not probably be issued more freq than once every year or two.—*Mining Gaz*

Insurance.

INSURANCE MATTERS IN MONTRI

(From a Correspondent.)

MONTREAL, Oct. 6, 1

Incendiarism is still the order of the day city. Since my last we have had seven fi of which were in exposed stables, all pur fired. Five of them were insured with the al," the loss on which, will not, however, $1500. The only accidental fire occurred i way's Ready Relief medical establishment, by the man in charge putting the hot as box in one of the upper flats of the b The firemen speedily got the fire under, loss will not exceed two hundred dollars. Radway & Co. have presented the Brigade numbers only 32 men) with one hundred for their exertions.

The corporation have not yet offered th reward for the arrest of the gang or any of t of incendiaries, but the matter is on the the day for the first meeting of the Coun surance Agents here are rather nettled remarks in my last, as to their inactiv yesterday they had a meeting, and it is str they intend offering a reward of $1000. however, no faith that such a step will b There has been a meeting of the Corpor which the question of petitioning the Loc ernment to do away with the present offic Marshal, was debated and finally passe vote of 14 to 6; this, however, will not effect of abolishing the office, though it n the removal of the present incumbents can be no question, that the bill is not worked, and it can only be done so by so who can attend each fire on its first disc

I hear it rumoured that it is in contem remove the present agent of the "Pi here and replace him by Mr. T. Hart. not improve the business, as it is only a ago, that a judgment for a few hundre against the company was offered on the s by one of our brokers. No agent can ness for a company when such facts known.

The Western, of England, have paid degree of the £ to those who had claim losses with they also offer 15s. in full to any who may prefer that to waiting for th up and final dividend.

About one o'clock this morning, when about 20 miles of Pultneyville, we were called up and found the propellor on fire. The fire commenced near the smoke pipe, and in less than fifteen minutes the boat was burned to the water's edge. The two mates, porter, wheelsman and myself launched a life boat, and were picked up by the propellor 'Enterprise,' about five o'clock this morning. The crew consisted of seventeen men and two women, fourteen of whom were lost, including the captain. I think none of the others made any effort to save themselves. I don't know the names of any of the crew. Both vessel and cargo were insured.

EQUITABLE LIFE.—The Equitable Life Assurance Society of New York has deposited $75,000 in U. S. 5-20 bonds. The deposit is for the general benefit of all the policy holders in the Company. It does business on the mutual principle, so as to be unable legally to make a deposit for the security of policy holders resident in Canada.

BRITON MEDICAL.—The Briton Medical and General Life Association of London, England, has made a cash deposit of $100,343.68.

EDINBURGH LIFE INSURANCE CO.—A statement appeared in the *Canada Gazette* of the 1st August respecting this Company, to the effect that a deposit of British 3 per cents had been made, pending an examination of the charter by the law officers of the crown. We were made aware of the incorrectness of this statement at the time, but preferred leaving it to the *Gazette* to make the required correction. It is as follows:
"The statement in the *Gazette* of the 1st August, that the Edinburgh Life Insurance Company had deposited 3 per cent. British Consolidated Annuities, pending an examination of the special terms of their charter, was based on erroneous information. The deposit was originally made in cash, of the amount and at the date specified in the *Gazette* of the 15th of August, viz: $150,000 deposited on the 27th July."

PERTH MUTUAL INSURANCE CO.— Some one who signs himself Nicklin, alleges unfair treatment by this Company, and is writing hard things against the management in the Stratford papers. He says the Company cheated him out of $200, because he was late in paying his assessment, while they paid other losses where the sufferers stood in a similar position. There is probably little foundation for the charges made.

RETIREMENT.—Mr. Wm. Murray, the Assistant Secretary of the Provincial Insurance Company, has been compelled, through failing health, to resign his post. He was a most efficient and obliging officer, and his withdrawal will be a serious loss to the Company.

U. S. OCEAN MARINE LOSSES FOR SEPT.— During the past month 29 vessels were lost, valued at $1,098,000. The total losses for nine months, 1868, to Oct. 1st, were 257 vessels, valued at $11 698,500. The loss for corresponding period in

	No. Vessels.	Aggregate loss.
1867	388	$16,876,100
1866	389	19,680,800
1865	275	20,549,800

—Thirty-two Insurance Companies have made deposits with the government, under the new insurance act.

—A lawsuit was had in Yarmouth with the Insurance Companies respecting the *Eliza Young*, lost at St. John some time since; about 30 witnesses were examined; result not yet known.

DAMAGES BY REMOVAL

The remarks of an adjuster respecting damages by removal, which we gave last week, are thus criticised in the September number of the *Monitor*.

His positions are undoubtedly correct as to general principles, and as to the reprehensible loose practice, of which most companies are guilty, in adjusting this sort of claim, but he falls into an arithmetical absurdity when he pays the *total* loss *first* and then proceeds, by a separate calculation, to fix the amount due for damages. The point, not visible to my eye, is this. The Company's liability for a pro rata share of the damages being admitted, by what right is the amount of the policy reduced before the calculation for contribution is made? That is to say, is the claim for one portion of the loss of greater virtue than for another portion, and if so, why?

Suppose we invert the order of adjuster's calculations and pay the *damages first*, and the total loss afterwards, thus:—

Value of damaged goods,	$7,000 00
Amount of policy	5,000 00
Amount of damages	800 00

Underwriter's pay on $5,000 5-7 of $800	$571 40
Underwriter's pay for goods totally destroyed	3,000 00

Total claim under policy	$3,571 40

Being a difference of $352 83 in favor of claimant over the amount of adjuster's award.

Will adjuster have the kindness to show wherein the above arithmetic is defective, and explain by what principle he exalts one portion of the same claim, arising at the same fire, upon the same policy, over another portion so as to give it precedence in payment, to the prejudice of that other portion, under a contract that specifically provides for payment in proportion as the sum assured bears to the whole value of the goods.

INTERNATIONAL LIFE ASSURANCE SOCIETY.

A letter appears in the *Post Magazine* of the 26th September, signed by R. Thomson, accountant, respecting the affairs of this company, which it will be remembered was swallowed up very unceremoniously by the Hercules Company a short time since. From this letter we make an extract:—

Sir—A client of mine eleven years ago obtained a profit policy in this society on his own life, and has regularly paid up his accruing premiums. In May last, he received a letter from the Hercules Insurance Company (Limited), informing him that the business of the International was transferred to that company and requesting the policy to be forwarded to the Hercules for indorsement to that effect. The International Society have always advertized their "individual capital" at £500,000 of which at least £200,000 ought now to be "under investment" as a reserve guarantee fund for payment of policies as they fall due. Judge of my surprise on reading a report dated 13th May, 1868, signed "E. S. Symes, chairman," notifying the interest realized on International investments as "£5,471 6s. 3d." per annum, an amount I apprehend "totally insufficient" to pay interest on the "proprietors paid up capital," who by "the way have received no interest whatever for many years past." I know little of the financial position of either society, but am somewhat at a loss to understand how it happens that the International subscribed capital before May, 1868, was £500,000, and the Hercules subscribed capital advertized at £500,000, whilst it now appears the Hercules advertise their "subscribed capital and funds invested " at only £373,869. This it may be observed is after they profess to have taken the International liabilities upon themselves. The International by such report of 13th May, 1868, allege they have received in premiums during the last year of their existence "£34,601 16s. 0d." and paid in claims "£33,432 8s. 0d.!!!," whilst Directors of the International are dragooning the Proprietors to pay calls, some of which as it plainly appears were enforceable (if at all) several years since. Both companies are "perfectly silent " as regards the "conditions for the amalgamation " and the amount of consideration passing in respect of it. So far as I have been able to learn, and I "have made ever possible enquiry" neither Proprietors or Policyholders in either company were supplied with sufficient data from which to judge as to the prudence of the important step about to be taken, although the two companies are "differently constituted" and for "widely different" objects.

[This company has some policies here but we presume the holders will scarcely throw away any more money on so shaky a concern.—Ed. C. M. T.]

LIFE INSURANCE.

A passage bearing upon this point by a recent writer is sound in the fullest degree. He urges that "one of the most important benefits to be derived from Life Insurance is, that it enables the man of large means, but of extended and varied business, to provide an amount of ready cash immediately after his death, to be used by his family either to meet their daily necessities or to aid in closing up the estate to the best advantage. To this end some of the richest men in the country have made large insurance on their lives, and the results are always satisfactory. Thousands of dollars have been saved in the closing of estates by means of a small amount of ready money. The records of our Probate Courts will attest to the truth of this statement, and that, on the other hand, thousands and tens of thousands of dollars have been lost, and estates utterly ruined, for the want of a small sum of ready money. Life Insurance provides a remedy for all this; and a policy of insurance on the life of the husband, payable, as the law directs, to the wife and children, does not wait the law's delay, but comes up promptly to the rescue of the hard-earned estate of the deceased. When a house is discovered to be on fire, the first inquiry made is, 'Is it insured?' If not, the carelessness or neglect of the owner is severely reprobated. How much more censurable is it in a father or husband to die, leaving his family unprovided for, when they could have been secured against poverty by Life Insurance. Let every man ponder on this."

The enormous growth of the business of Life Insurance is a strong presumptive argument in favor of its usefulness and the equitable adjustment of its details. If time did not attest and make good their pretensions to benefit the community, the great companies, instead of becoming richer and more respected as they grow older, would fall into disrepute. An enterprise may be conducted on a fallacious basis for a time and may succeed in duping the public to a certain extent, but no such concern will run decades into generations, meeting its engagements on every hand, continually strengthening its hold on public confidence, unless its foundations are stable, healthful and secure. We believe that the great companies are among the staunchest and most trustworthy monetary institutions in the world. Indeed, conducted upon the principles that most of them are, their failure would be as near impossibility as that of any sublunary thing. They are always growing, and they take no risks which are dependent on commercial accidents or monetary revulsions; and hence in the most troublous times they may confidently be expected to stand firm.

We make no scruple, then, in saying to our friends, both in public and in private, insure your lives. None can tell what an hour may bring forth. None can be certain, however prosperous in appearances his affairs, of not leaving those nearest and dearest to suffer a long life of trouble and penury through a negligence which has no excuse. None will die the sooner by being insured, for a prudent and manly regard to a high obligation is rather likely, by setting the conscience and the heart at rest, to protract life than to shorten it. And apart from, and independent of, all this, if only on purely selfish grounds, a careful study of the offers and principles of our best companies will show that Life Insurance pays; a consideration which should be of supreme and conclusive weight with our thrifty and far seeing community.

Law Report.

LIFE ASSURANCE—INTEREST ON AMOUNT INSURED.—The assignee of a person upon whose life a policy of insurance has been effected, is not entitled to claim interest on the amount of the policy, until he is in a position to give assurers a full legal discharge upon payment of the claim.—*Toronto Savings Bank vs. the Canada Life, 14 Ch. Rep. 509.*

INSURANCE INTEREST—INCREASE OF RISK:— In an action on a policy of insurance by A., brought for the benefit of B., an incorporated bank, to whom the policy had been assigned, on a traverse of any insurable interest in B. Held, that a warehouse receipt for wheat, the property of A., a warehouseman, signed by a clerk of A., in his own name, was sufficient under 24 Vic. chap. 23, sec. 1, to pass the property in the wheat so as to confer an insurable interest on B.

The policy was subject to a condition that in the event of any alteration, etc., whereby the risk should be increased and a consequent additional premium required, the policy should be void unless notice of such alteration etc., should be given to defendants and allowed by indorsement on the policy, and consequent additional premium paid. It appeared in evidence that at the time the policy was effected by A., he was told by the agent of the defendants that if an elevator were erected on the premises, without informing the defendants, his policy would be avoided, as in that case he would have to pay an additional premium, but this was not inserted in the policy. A. erected an elevator and did not give notice to the defendants. Held, on a plea setting out the condition and alleging the erection of the elevator, that the risk was thereby increased, and that a consequent additional premium would have been thereby required, that the jury not having found any increase of risk, the facts afforded no defence.—*Todd vs. Liverpool, London and Globe Insurance Co., 18 C. P., 192.*

TROVER—PROPERTY AFTERWARDS BURNED—RECEIPT BY PLAINTIFFS OF INSURANCE MONEY.— Plaintiffs had a large quantity of wheat in the warehouse of one T., for which they held his receipt, and defendants also held T.'s receipt for wheat in the same place, on which they had made advances; but there was not enough wheat to satisfy both. T. having left the country, gave R., defendants' agent, a letter to C., who was in charge of the warehouse, directing him to give R. possession of the warehouse and all grain in it belonging to him, T. On receiving this letter, C. gave R. the key, went with him into the warehouse and pointed out T.'s wheat, and received back the key, agreeing to hold possession. On the same day R. again got the key to go into the place with one M., and again returned it to C., who said he considered he still had possession of the store, and that he would not have given up the wheat to the plaintiffs if R. had so directed him. Plaintiffs demanded their wheat from R., who, as they alleged, answered, "I won't do so at present," but almost immediately after defendants' attorney served a written disclaimer on plaintiffs, informing them that defendants disclaimed all possession of the storehouse and wheat therein. On the same day plaintiffs brought trover.

Held, assuming the facts most favorably for the plaintiffs, that it should have been left to the jury to say whether R. entertained a bona fide doubt as to the plaintiffs' right to the wheat, and whether a reasonable time had elapsed for clearing it up; and Quære, whether the facts could legally suffice to establish a conversion.

Evidence was rejected that the plaintiffs had insured the wheat sued for and had received the insurance money, the fire having taken place two days after the alleged conversion. Semble, that such evidence should have been received, as shewing the plaintiffs' conduct and dealing with regard to the property after the alleged conversion, and thus being relevant to the issue.—*Gilpin et al. v. the Royal Canadian Bank. 27 Q.B. 310.*

LINDSAY VS. NIAGARA MUTUAL FIRE INSURANCE COMPANY.—This case was tried at the Woodstock assizes. It was an action to recover the amount of a policy of insurance on a dwelling in Princeton, Totten & J. H. Cameron for plaintiff, C. Brown & Hon. M. C. Cameron for defendant; verdict for plaintiff, $1,201.37½.

MARINE INSURANCE—TOTAL LOSS—NOTICE ABANDONMENT.—In marine insurance notice of abandonment is indispensably necessary in cases where the insured elects to abandon.

In this case the vessel insured ran upon rocks on the 11th October, and the defendant agent was informed of it by the insured on 16th October, but he was not informed of abandonment as for a total loss until he made protest before the agent on the 17th October, nor formal abandonment in writing, under terms of the policy, was made until 27th December following, when the vessel had been floated off utterly lost by the carelessness of the insured. Held, that the notice was too late to be available even if there had been such a loss as would entitled the insured to abandon.

Whether a loss is to be considered a total depends on the fact whether the vessel, as injured, is useless to the owner, unless at an expense no prudent man, if uninsured, would incur, an expense exceeding the value of the ship when repaired. In this case it appeared that on the 1st day after the vessel went upon the rocks, the captain, on returning to her, found her in as good a state as on the second day, and that she remained between two and three weeks on the rocks, then floated two or three miles below. It further appeared that there was not the slightest attempt made to get her off or recover her, or even to mine her, while all the witnesses said they had tried to get her off, and it seemed beyond doubt that there were eight days during which from the calm state of the weather, an attempt could have been successfully made for work of three days after she first ran on she floated without any assistance, and there was evidence that even one man could have hauled her off the captain, a witness stated, intimated to that he did not mean to do anything with the vessel. Held, that the evidence wholly disproved total loss, either actual or constructive.

Held, also, that the fact of the plaintiff not having made any exertion to get the vessel off ground for a new trial, as, if the vessel got off rocks by perils of the sea and was injured, plaintiff was entitled to be indemnified for that; but if he was not obliged to take her off, but could leave her on the rocks until she went to pieces, though he could not recover for the destruction thus voluntarily suffered.—*Harkley v. the Provincial Insurance Co., 18 C. P. Rep. 335.*

THE PRODUCTION OF GOLD AND SILVER.— Bankers' Magazine contains an elaborate article on the "Past and Present Production of Gold and Silver throughout the world." The production since the discovery of America. The production in the Nineteenth Century to the year. The production since the discovery of California. The present annual production of countries. Annual report of the General Office, U. S., on Gold and Silver. Special report of Mr. J. Rosse Browne, on the Pacific Coast. Special report of Mr. James W. Taylor. The relative supply of both metals, past and present.—The annual and aggregate supply in and South Carolina, Georgia, Virginia, Texas, California, Mexico, Canada, South America, and total America, Bolivia, Peru, Buenos Ayres, gray, Chili, New Grenada, Europe, Great France, Spain, Scandinavia, Austria, Prussia, Saxony, Italy, Asia, Siberia, Africa, Australia, &c., with the views of Jacob, Newmarch and Chevalier, and Also a list of 360 Savings Banks in New York, number of depositors and of deposits in each.

☞ THE CANADIAN MONETARY TIMES AND
NSURANCE CHRONICLE is printed every Thursday
Evening, in time for the English Mail.

Subscription Price, one year, $2, or $3 in
American currency ; Single copies, five cents each.
Casual advertisements will be charged ten cents
per line of solid nonpareil each insertion. All
letters to be addressed, "THE CANADIAN MONE-
TARY TIMES, TORONTO, ONT." Registered letters
so addressed are at the risk of the Publishers.
Cheques should be made payable to J. M. TROUT,
Business Manager, who will, in future, issue all
receipts for money.

The Canadian Monetary Times.

THURSDAY, OCTOBER 8, 1868.

THE INTERCOLONIAL RAILWAY.

The appointment of Commissioners under
the Act of last session, relating to the construction of the Intercolonial Railway, the
signification by the Imperial Government of
their approval of the route selected, and the
advertisement for tenders, show that a long
talked of scheme is approaching realization.
The Duke of Buckingham's despatch, dated
22nd July, is as follows:—

"I have received your Lordship's tele-
graphic message that the route by the Bay of
Chaleur has been selected by the Canadian
Government, as the one to connect Truro
with Riviere du Loup, and thus complete the
Intercolonial Railway.

"I understand three routes to have been
under the consideration of the Government
of Canada, namely : one crossing the St. John
River, either at Woodstock or Fredericton ;
the second in a more central direction through
New Brunswick, and the third following the
line selected by Major Robinson in 1848.
The route crossing the St. John River, either
at Woodstock or Fredericton, is one to which
the assent of Her Majesty's Government could
not have been given ; the objections on military grounds to any line on the south side of
St. John River are insuperable. One of the
main advantages, sought in granting an Imperial Guarantee for constructing the railway,
would have been defeated if that line had
been selected. The remaining lines were the
central line, and that following the general
course of the route surveyed by Major Robinson ; and Her Majesty's Government have
learned, with much satisfaction, that the latter
has been selected by the Canadian Government. The communication with this line
affords with the Gulf of St. Lawrence at
various points, and its remoteness from the
American Frontier, are conclusive considerations, in its favor, and there can be no doubt
that it is the only one which provides for the
national objects involved in the undertaking."

For the sake of presenting at one view the
comparative distances (of the different lines
projected) from Riviere du Loup to St. John
and Halifax, and the number of miles of
railway already built, we give this table :—

Frontier Routes.

No. of line.	TO ST. JOHN. Rail-way Built.	TO ST. JOHN. Not Built.	Total.	TO HALIFAX. Rail-way Built.	TO HALIFAX. Not Built.	Total.
1	27	292	319	184	401	585
2	45	305	350	202	414	507
3	00	301	301	187	410	561

Central Route.

	TO ST. JOHN.			TO HALIFAX.		
4	..	326	326	157	435	592
5	..	328	328	157	437	594
6	87	343	380	1n0	462	572
7	77	349	426	80	458	588
8	87	307	344	190	416	586
9	77	313	390	80	422	502
10	96	326	422	61	435	496
11	87	323	360	190	432	562
12	77	330	406	60	458	618

Bay Chaleurs Routes.

	TO ST. JOHN.			TO HALIFAX.		
13	87	387	434	190	488	618
14	96	377	473	61	486	547
15	96	390	486	61	499	560

The shortest Frontier route to St. John is
301 miles, and to Halifax, 567 miles ; the
shortest Central route to St. John is 326
miles, and to Halifax, 496 miles ; the
shortest Bay Chaleurs route to St. John is
424 miles, and to Halifax, 547 miles. The
average number of inhabitants for each mile
of railway by the different routes is given as
follows :—

Frontier line.... 260 per mile of railway.
Central........... 122   "   "
Bay Chaleurs ... 235   "   "

The route recommended by Major Robinson as the best general direction for the proposed railway is from Halifax to Truro, at
the head of the Bay of Fundy, passing over
the Cobequid Hills, and on near to Amherst and Bay Verte, crossing from these
over to the River Richibucto and Miramichi ;
then by the valley of the north-west Miramichi and Nipisiguit River to Bathurst ; then
along the shore of the Bay Chaleurs to the
Restigouche River ; then by the valley of
the Matapedia over the River Metis ; then
along the banks of the St. Lawrence, at a
distance of eight or twelve miles from the
south shore to Riviere du Loup. The line
is No. 15 in the above table. The distance
to St. John and Halifax by this line are estimated as follows :—

Railway from R. du Loup to St. John.

	Con-structed.	Not con-structed.	Total.
From River du Loup, by Metis and Matapedia, to Dalhousie.	..	196	196
From Dalhousie to Bathurst...	..	53	53
From Bathurst to E. & N. A. Railway	..	141	141
Along E. & N. A. Railway to St. John	..	96	96
Total..............	96	300	486

Railway to Halifax.

	Con-structed.	Not sr, ucted.	Total.
From River du Loup, by Metis, Matapedia, Dalhousie, and Bathurst, to Moncton	..	390	390
From Moncton to Truro	..	109	100
From Truro by Railway to Ha. lifax..................	61	..	61
Total..............	61	400	500

As the Imperial Government is in favor of
the Major Robinson line, and disinclined to
adopt any other, and as the Imperial guaran-

tee is a *sine qua non* in the matter, we have to make the best of what many consider rather a bad bargain. The scheme for a railroad between Quebec and Halifax was brought before the Canadian public by a Nova Scotian about the year 1845, addresses were adopted which led to the offer from the Imperial Secretary of State to cause a survey to be made by an officer of the Royal Engineers, provided Canada, Nova Scotia and New Brunswick would bear the expense. This offer was accepted, and Major Robinson's report was the result. In subsequent negotiations with the Imperial Government, the Robinson route was insisted on by them. New Brunswick refused to adopt it, Nova Scotia naturally preferred it, and Canada seemed willing to accept either it or the line by the valley of the St. John; but conflicting interests brought about the failure of that attempt to secure an Intercolonial Railway. Earl Derby's government decided against the St. John route, basing their decision on the advantage to be derived from security in case of hostilities. It has been stated that Mr. Hincks and some of the English railway contractors, who afterwards had so much to do with the Grand Trunk, were at the bottom of the disagreement, but this has been denied by Mr. Hincks over his own signature, and the failure of negotiations attributed to New Brunswick. At least two members of the present Cabinet at Ottawa were in favor of the Central Route, but it seems that the longest and most expensive, and the least valuable (in a commercial point of view) route carried the day. The estimate made by Mr. Sanford Fleming of the cost of the line is $20,000,000. The British Government guarantees interest on the loan of $15,000,000.

The next question that presents itself is the probable returns for such an expenditure. Halifax is 550 miles nearer to Liverpool than New York, 357 nearer than Boston, 373 nearer than Quebec, and 316 nearer than Portland. It is said the Robinson route will best secure the largest European passenger traffic, the carriage of mail matter and express freight, and could accommodate, next to the Frontier line, the largest amount of "local" traffic. The favourable position of New York and Portland renders them the convenient winter outlets for freight from the Provinces that constituted old Canada. The nearest United States port to Toronto is New York, 540 miles; the nearest to Montreal is Portland, 297 miles; while the distance from Toronto to St. John, by Riviere du Loup, is 913 miles, and from Montreal to the same place 583 miles. However, should the United States prevent our freight from passing through their territory, all we have to do

is take it round another way, and the Intercolonial would carry during winter all the freight to and from the seaboard which would bear the cost of transportation..

Toronto is distant from Halifax over 1,168 miles. It costs two cents a ton per mile to move freight by rail, and it would cost $2.23 per barrel to move flour from Toronto to Halifax, while a barrel of flour can now be sent via the St. Lawrence at 50 cents. The fact is, and we may as well admit it, the Intercolonial is a sentimental railway. The money to be spent on it forms the consideration on which the Confederation contract rests. It is rather pleasant to think that Ontario, a Province deriving little or no immediate advantage from the concern, is sufficiently patriotic to shoulder the twelve millions of dollars of debt for the benefit of Nova Scotia, but it is not so pleasant to reflect on the small share of thanks we receive for the sacrifice.

REINSURANCE FUNDS.

The annual statements to be furnished to the Minister of Finance by Fire Insurance Companies whose deposits are under one thousand dollars, embrace two items, namely: "Amount of premiums earned for the past year," and "Amount of premiums unearned for the past year," which will enable one to calculate what the amount of the Reinsurance Fund of such companies should be, and to determine their solvency or insolvency. The statements heretofore made public by some of our home companies have lacked in this particular, so that an outsider could only guess at the probable condition of a company. So much ignorance has prevailed on the subject of a Reinsurance Fund that we were led to explain its object, and to show how in Massachusetts and New York a provision of the kind was rendered obligatory by statutory enactment. We have every reason to consider that our remarks were not lost on some of the Directors of home companies, and that greater attention will be given, for the future, to the subject.

THE PACKING TRADE.

The packing season is now commencing; live hogs are being bought up to a considerable extent. One packing house took, during the last week, 350 head at prices ranging from 5¾ to 5¾c. live weight. Dressed hogs will not begin to come in freely for three or four weeks yet, and not then unless the weather becomes cold. Should the weather be favourable, there is every reason to anticipate an early commencement and a short season. The high prices of peas, potatoes, and almost every kind of farm produce renders it unprofitable to farmers to feed their hogs long; for this reason also, and on account of the dry sum-

ner, we may expect a good many hogs i condition. We anticipate a pretty lively here, and think prices must rule high. supply of money will be forthcoming and tition will be keen. The present high figu which pork rules, is an element of dang should not be lost sight of. This will ma drain on the funds of our banks heavier, tending to make the more cautious deale back, may check to a wholesome extent th of speculation. Stocks of cutmeats of all are run very low. Our lumbermen had to themselves lately almost wholly from the (market, where very considerable operation taken place recently on Canadian account of these purchases were no doubt made in pation of a scarcity at the commencement bering operations and prospective high pr Canadian markets.

From the carefully written circular of Henry Milward & Co., published elsew good idea may be formed of the prospects Western trade. The season there will op A careful estimate shows that there will increase of consequence in the number of the West. In Canada we think there has t increase whatever, but it is probable that th ber of hogs marketed will be much the s last season. A private letter from a leadi in Dublin, Ireland, estimates a decrease of in the number of hogs in that country as co with last year. Our dealers, while general ing the necessity of caution, take a hopefu of the trade. So far as the Toronto ma concerned, there will be a considerable ex of this already important and growing br industry.

Communications.

WOODEN AND IRON HULLS.

To the Editor Monetary Times.

The occasional though serious disasters have befallen the Royal Mail Line of Stea descending the River St. Lawrence, betwee ston and Montreal, during the past three years, and the severe losses sustained in quence of these disasters, render it, I t matter worthy the consideration of under whether hulls built wholly of iron are adapted for the navigation of our inland w those built of wood. For ocean-going craft have not to encounter the hidden dangers navigation, I am prepared to admit the sup water, such as often prevails on that part St. Lawrence to which I have made referen the slightest error in judgment of the pr command, the momentary inattention of the men, or the trifling derangement of any po the machinery, causes ever so slight a deviati the proper channel, and the vessel at all those hidden enemies, a shock, which might cause the starting of a plank or two a displacement of one or two timbers of a hull, may possibly result in fatal injury iron vessel. As an example of this I may n I think the "Grecian," some three months though her encounter with the sharp poi rock created, at the moment, no undue amongst those on board, yet, so rapid was mersion, that she was run aground at the s Island, and, on being raised some few weeks quently, it was found that for upwards of ty feet her bottom had been ripped along, as gh it had been done by a pair of shears. The re and extent of the casualties to other vessels is line, tend also, I think, upon the whole, to out the opinion that the advantages possessed on over wood, in the construction of hulls—ring, of course, to the navigation of our inland rs—are, in a great measure, imaginary. As ds the insuring of these vessels, I cannot see these supposed advantages—even with the iling excessive competition—should be suffi- to force underwriters into a breaking away some of those principles which they have laid as a rule and safeguard. This, I conceive, have done from year to year hitherto, by sub- ng to a too low valuation, the application of policy under fire conditions during the winter n, and the ignoring of that most important ition, the deduction on the hull of one-third for old in case of partial loss, to say nothing naterial reduction on tariff rates of premium. e subject upon which I have ventured these emarks is, perhaps, deserving of attention, from those without the insurance pale. I however, that in the preparations by under- rs for the business of another season, it will be ed worthy of their consideration.

Yours, most truly,

INSURER.

ronto, 7th Oct., 1868.

TORONTO STOCK MARKET.

(Reported by Pellatt & Osler, Brokers.)

iere was considerable activity in the stock ket this week, and prices are well maintained.

ank Stock.—There is a great demand for Mon- l at 135, holders asking 135½. Sales of ario occurred at 98½ to 99, which latter figure eely offered. Toronto is in demand at 116½ 17. Holders generally ask 92 for Royal Can- n, small sales occurring from 91 to 92. Paid Commerce is offered at 103¾. There were small sactions in Gore at 40. Buyers offer 105 for chants', sellers asking 105½. City could be ed at 102½, holders asking 102¾. There are ers of Du Peuple at 105½. For Jacques Car- buyers offer 106, holders demanding 108. ers would give 96½ for Mechanics'. In other s nothing doing.

ebentures.—Sales of Canada six per cents oc- ed at 100½. Sterling five per cents are offered 0½. Toronto are offered to pay 7 per cent. rest. Considerable amounts of County changed ds at rates to pay 6½ per cent. interest.

undries.—Building Society stock active and ier. There were considerable sales of Canada nanent at 120½ and 121, and there are still ers at these rates. Western Canada has been t in freely at 113 to 113½, and is still procur- at the latter rate. City Gas sold at 104½ to There are buyers of British America Assur- at 55 to 56. Considerable transactions in ada Landed Credit occurred at 63 to 64 for k, $20 paid. Mortgages are much asked for, very few offering. Money is readily procur- on good paper.

MONTREAL MONEY MARKET.

(From our own Correspondent).

Montreal, Oct. 6, 1868.

he money market remains very quiet, and I no special feature to note; there is a steady and for accommodation at the Banks, but much less than last year; this, with the inac- y of the Produce trade, and the general quiet- of business, has led to a considerable accumulation of idle capital at some of our leading institutions. The rates at the Banks are 7 to 8 per cent. for first class Commercial paper, and 8½ to 10 for other, according to names. Advances on warehouse receipts are made at exceptional rates. On the street, business is dull, the bulk of paper offering being less desirable than usual; discount ranges from 12 to 16 per cent. The Stock Exchange exhibits a marked improvement, favourite securities having advanced; Bank of Montreal is offered at 135½, with buyers at 134¾. British wanted at 103½. City sold at 102¾, and is now wanted at 103. Ontario, small sales at 99½ to par. People's 105½. Other stocks and shares firm at the quotations given in our daily lists. Large sales of Dominion stock at 101, and buyers still at that rate, but sellers want 102.

Mr. Weir continues to push forward his proposition for the exportation of silver coin, but owing to the magnitude of the enterprise, he has found it necessary to extend the time for receiving the contracts to the 5th day of November next. This is now of less importance, as the discount has already fallen to about three per cent. and will likely remain low until the result of his movement is made known. It will be unfortunate if the present exceptionally low rate of discount should lead those interested to treat his proposal with indifference till it is too late, as in that case the rate of discount must again advance to four and one half per cent.

The details of Mr. Weir's proposition have been submitted to the public. I understand that he has also secured the services of a gentleman well known in Ontario, to visit the principal cities and towns in the west in connection with the movement.

BANK OF ENGLAND.

The following statement shows the condition of the bank for the week ending Wednesday, Sept. 16, 1868:—

Issue Department.

Notes issued	£34,612,035
Government debt	£11,015,100
Other securities	3,984,900
Gold coin and bullion	19,612,035
Silver bullion	
	£34,612,035

Banking Department.

Proprietors' capital	£14,553,000
Rest	3,615,980
Public deposits (including Exchequer, Commissioners of National Debt, Savings' Banks, and Dividend Accounts)	3,975,728
Other deposits	19,309,767
Seven day and other Bills	590,204
	£42,044,688
Government securities (including Dead Weight Annuity)	£13,790,131
Other securities	16,124,020
Notes	10,966,580
Gold and silver coin	1,163,927
	£42,044,688

The return continues to attest the slackness of the demand for money. The private securities have fallen off until they stand at little more than £16,000,000, while the unemployed reserve has enlarged considerably, so that it now exceeds twenty millions. The private deposits are lower, but only to an inconsiderable amount, and the public deposits are increasing. The bullion has increased nearly £40,000.

COUNTERFEITS.—Counterfeit $4 notes of the Niagara District Bank have been circulated in St. Catharines. A local paper says they are a close imitation of the genuine, and are likely to deceive those not initiated in the detection of counterfeits. The notes are darker colored, shorter and wider, as well as softer in texture, than the genuine. The easiest method of detection is in the portrait of the Hon W. H. Merritt, whose features have a sharp, contracted expression, and the eyes are unnatural. Bills of the same denomination of the Gore Bank have also been passed off to a considerable extent. The figures indicating the number of the bill are much larger than in the genuine.

REVENUE AND EXPENDITURE.—The revenue of Canada for September was as follows:

Customs	$935,114
Excise	161,845
Post Office	16,495
Bill Stamps	11,558
Public Works (including railways)	106,793
Miscellaneous	614,559
	$1,846,364
Expenditure	$2,294,409

SALE OF STOCKS IN ST. JOHN.—At a sale of Stocks by J. D. Nash the following prices were realized:—Ninety shares in the Union Bank $53. 75 at $54; one share Bank B. N. A., £66 1s. 3d; one share Horticultural Gardens $41; one Provincial Railway Debenture £100 stg., £102 stg.; $2,500 School Debentures $96; $800 City Prison do $95; ten shares Salt Company $20.25; £100 stg. Windsor and Annapolis Railway Bond, 6 per cent., Coupons attached, £87 10s. stg. asked, £50 stg. offered. The following Gold Stocks were offered at the following prices, but no sales effected: —Imperial 20 cts.; Uniacke Union 9 cts.; Uniacke Central 9 cts.; Prince of Wales 12 cts.; Eureka 5 cts.; Brunswick 12 cts.

At a recent sale of stock in Halifax, the following prices were realized: Sixteen shares in the Halifax Gas Co., £65 5s.; eight Halifax Fire Ins. Co., $37 50; and shares in the Queen's Gold Mining Company at Mount Uniacke, 55 cents; Westlake Gold Co. at do., 50 cents; Dominion Gold Stock, 75 cents offered, $1 40 asked; Mount Uniacke do., 12½ cents asked; Central Gold do., 7 cents offered, 13 asked; Nova Scotia Marine Ins. Co., shares were offered at £42, £37 10s. bid.

UNITED STATES ASSAY OFFICE FOR AUGUST.—Below we give the statement of business at the United States Assay Office at New York for the month ending August 31, 1868:—

DEPOSITS OF GOLD.

Foreign coin	$8,900 00	
Foreign bullion	144,100 00	
United States bullion	1,302,500 00	—$1,455,500 00

DEPOSITS OF SILVER, INCLUDING PURCHASES.

Foreign coins	$4,000 00	
Foreign bullion	13,500 00	
United States bullion (contained in gold)	12,500 00	
Montana	3,500 00	
Colarado	16,500 00	
Lake Superior	2,000 00	
Nevada	18,500 00	— $,70,500 00
Total deposits, payable in bars	1,426,000 00	
Total deposits, payable in coins	100,000 00	—1,526,000 00
Gold bars stamped		1,142,785 25

CATTLE DISEASE.—The order prohibiting the transportation of American cattle over our railways has, we believe, been revoked, all restrictions to cease on and after Oct 1st.

—A Quebec paper has reason to believe that the Local Government has ceded 1200 acres of land to the Gosford Railway Company, at the rate of 30c. per acre, and the company has therefore undertaken to lay down firewood in Quebec at $2.50 to $3 per cord.

—Work on the European and North American Railway is being pushed on with vigor.

Railway News.

GREAT WESTERN RAILWAY.—Traffic for week ending 18th Sept., 1868.

Passengers	$41,722 12
Freight and live stock	38,974 06
Mails and sundries	2,243 75
	$82,939 93
Corresponding Week of '67	82,452 36
Increase	$487 57

NORTHERN RAILWAY.—Traffic Receipts for week ending Sept. 26, 1868.

Passengers	$4,163 35
Freight	8,876 41
Mails and Sundries	274 74
Total Receipts for week	$13,314 50
Corresponding week 1867	13,287 78
Increase	$26 72

WOODEN RAILWAYS.—Application will be made to the Quebec Legislature, at its next session, for an act "to revise, continue and amend the charter of the Drummond and Arthabaska Counties Railway Company." If we mistake not, this is the first practical step towards the construction of a wooden railway from Arthabaska to the line of the Grand Trunk Railway, at or near Upton. Some of the interested municipalities have undertaken to promote the work, which was projected on its new basis by Mr. Hemming, M.P.P. for Drummond and Arthabaska.

GRAND TRUNK.—A little sunshine we hope is about to be felt by this Company. We are unable to say precisely whence it will come or in what degree it will be produced, but we believe all down to and including the 4th Preference will experience the warmth of its rays.

It is said that within the last few years Montreal has doubled in importance and business, and bids fair to do better in future. The railway seems to have kept pace with the great City of Canada in progress, and if it should do so in future in a few years' time the Grand Trunk will earn £50,000 a week traffic.—*Herapath's Journal.*

Commercial.

Montreal Correspondence.

(From our own Correspondent.)

Montreal, Oct. 6, 1868.

After cold and wet, the weather has now set in fine and bright, though cool, with every chance of having a spell of it. This is most favorable for housing the root crops, which takes place about the end of this month, with the exception of potatoes. ; I fear the housing of the others will take little time or trouble as they are very short.

The fall fleet is now dropping in, the "Anglesea," "Gleniffer," "Queen of the Clyde" "Shandon," "Florence Lee," "Island Queen," "Thistle," "La Plata" and "Abeona," having arrived, and are busily discharging their cargoes, consisting of heavy goods. Of these the "Gleniffer," "Shandon," and "Abeona," are here on their third voyage this season. So far, we have little or nothing in the way of return cargoes for them : and it is to be hoped that produce will shortly come forward in sufficient supplies, and selling at such prices as will enable us to fill them up speedily, causing no detention. Should such not be the case, the shipping interest of Montreal will be seriously damaged, as shippers will hardly risk sending vessels here, to be either detained till the dangerous season for navigating the Gulf sets in, or the insurance rates rule so high as naturally to affect

profits. The Allan's steamers have lately been winning golden opinions by the shortness of their passages—(the average having been less than ever before made. We Montrealers feel great pride in this fine line, especially of late, since accidents of any sort have been of rare occurrence ; and all Canada ought to join with us in wishing success to a line which is, emphatically, the national one of the Dominion, and nearly the only one that has competed successfully with the Cunard line.

PRODUCE MARKET.—Business continues very quiet ; small sales of flour on the spot ; some sales of round lots of ordinary to good supers., in shipping order, at $5.45 to $5.50. There is no tendency towards speculation ; but the light stocks—only 16,607 brls. on 1st October, against 24,892 brls. last year—have, for the present, checked the downward tendency. Several small cargoes of wheat sold during the week to local operators. Prices are : U. C. Spring and red winter, $1.25 ; Chicago No. 2, nominal Imports : 1st January to 30th September, 1,229,773 bushels, against 1,066,800 bushels in 1867, showing an increase of 152,673 bushels. Coarse grains remain unchanged. A cargo of 10,000 bush. peas sold at $1.06¼ per 66 lbs.

PROVISIONS.—Pork and cut meats are very quiet, and unchanged in price. Receipts of butter during the last few days have been heavy, but prices are fully maintained—choice dairy selling at 24c. for shipment. Cheese in moderate enquiry, at 10½c. to 11c.

GROCERIES.—Our first batch of fall sales are over. The attendance of buyers was large, and a considerable amount of business was done. At Buchanan, Leckie & Co.'s tea sale only a few hundred packages were left unsold, the trade being anxious to stock themselves, in the finer qualities, and sellers were willing to meet their views. The prices were hardly up to expectation, but, still, good and remunerative. At D. Torrance & Co.'s sale the quality was not so good, and buyers were not so anxious. Messrs. Torrance were, however, very stiff, and the consequence is about one-half offered was withdrawn. The sale of their portion of the "Annie Braginton's" cargo, and also another on joint account of two houses here, in New York, strengthen the market greatly, and dealers who have not stocked themselves will, I expect, have to pay higher rates. A considerable quantity of wines and Mediterranean goods were also placed, prices ranging pretty much the same as they did in the spring. As prices on the continent have advanced during the spring and summer, our fall imports have cost more ; and those prices which left a profit here last spring, barely clear importers this fall. I give you the imports here of the leading groceries, from the 1st January to the 30th June ; they having been only just made up :

Coffee, lbs.	543576	874917	lbs. 564623	870526
Fruit, lbs.	4450090	210966	lbs. 6517617	300533
Brandy, gals.	149170	106152	gls. 97175	102701
Gin, gals.	155650	76213	gls. 251938	109618
Rum, gals.	61508	28281	gls. 55593	24858
Molasses, lbs.	9069701	161561	lbs. 5311298	101791
Tea, lbs.	4830216	1679424	lbs. 4575637	1550094
Tobacco, lbs.	405261	57902	lbs. 357411	56451
Sugar, raw, lbs.	38047748	1372505	lbs. 31904468	1595073
Cane Juice, lbs.	5475308	115700	lbs. 7406533	197509
Common Soap, lbs.	877400	20927	lbs. 321505	12307

I give the total imports of the port for the same period :—

1867.	1868.	Decrease.
$29,213.067	$24,836,208	$4,376,859.

The bulk of this decrease occurs in dutiable goods.

Total value of dutiable goods imported for—

1867.	1868.	Decrease.
$21,851,103	$19,237,977	$2,613,126

Do. Free Goods :

1867.	1868.	Decrease.
$7,361,964	$5,598,231	$1,763,733.

DRY GOODS.—Although the great rush is over, we have had a very steady trade during the week, which I expect will last nearly the whole month.

There are a fair amount of orders coming in, several considerable buyers are in town. The porters have done a better business than they expected, and the season will most probably with light stocks of staples, especially cotto prices have ruled firm, and now remittances coming in more freely, so that the business gether is in a healthy state.

Toronto Market.

The weather of the past week has been favo to business. The same is true of the past weeks which have elapsed since the commence of the fall trade. It is seldom, indeed, that mers have so favorable an opportunity, on sec of the dryness of the roads and the mod amount of rain, to get their produce to ma This fact is telling favorably on the deman dry goods, groceries, hardware, &c., and its ence is being felt in an increase of money in lation, and greater promptness in payment o part of country merchants.

DRY GOODS.—Importations continue Stocks are being steadily worked off, and reach at least a safe point, if, indeed, the a ment does not become badly broken, befo season closes. Payments are getting better season advances.

GROCERIES.—Trade for the week is re quite up to the mark, and everything is m along satisfactorily. Sugars are steady at quotations ; Redpath's prices were advance a cent on Tuesday. Teas.—A considerab bing business has been done ; but, as usual, have been kept strictly private. Fruit.—C kinds of raisins are advanced, owing to lig of stock. Tobaccos.—Only a very moderate ar of business doing, at quoted prices.

GRAIN.—Wheat. Receipts for the week b 15,291 bushels, against 900 bushels the pr week. The demand is strictly limited to re requirements, and with good receipts and markets abroad, our market has not only ru but is quotably lower than last week. The now free sellers at $1.15, and some buyers at for good spring. Fall is somewhat scarce, accounts for the few lots which have been the market going off at good prices ; $1.35 to would be paid for prime samples. Barley. ceipts by cars for the week 41,103 bushel 38,000 bushels last week. Shipments for th 75,121 bushels, and 94,550 bushels the pr week. Total shipments since the commenc of the season, 393,848 bushels, to October which 110,971 bushels were shipped in A and the balance in September. The fol vessels cleared with cargoes of barley duri week ended with Saturday last :—

Schooners "New Dominion," with 13,62 the "Mary Taylor," with 9,200 bush ; the ney Lass," with 16,000 bush.; and the Beard," with 10,007 bush., all for Toled "Whaling," for Milwaukee, with 15,025 the "Eveleen," with 5,944 bush., and the lington," with 5,321 bush., for Oswego.

The market opened a week ago at $1.16 t and moved up to $1.38 and $1.40 at the numerous sales occurred during the week, which was a lot 40,000 bush. at $1.25 f.o.b —Receipts by cars, 3,671 bush.; the m dull and 3 cents lower, closing at 48 c. . Receipts by cars, 2,944 bush.; the market ir at 90c. to 92c.; sales of several car lots o at these prices. Rye selling at 80c.

FLOUR.—Receipts by cars 3,700 brls., 900 brls. for the previous week. The der very slack, and there are free sellers but fe ers. Superfine has declined 30c. to 50c. quotations of last week, closing nominal a $5.00; sales during the week ranged from to $5.25. Fall wheat flour has latterly m a better demand, but was this week dull an ing without enquiry at $6.50 to $6.75.

PROVISIONS.—Butter is more active and demand at steady prices; a round lot of 45 airy and store-packed mixed sold at 21¾c. cars; another lot of 150 packages is offer- 22½c. *Chese* is firm. A lot of 400 boxes orted sold at 11¾c.; Holders generally ask o 12½c. *Pork*—Holders of mess are very t $25 for small lots. There is a general n that there will be a great scarcity before w hog crop comes into market; live hogs are at 5⅝c. to 5¾c. to packers.

s.—There is no demand above 16c. for good ut this figure holders refuse to accept, ask- c., which is now an outside price in view quotations given in the American markets. e unpleasant fact that our market is open ericans while theirs, by a five cent duty, is to us. This is an unwise and unsatisfactory ement, and unfair to our dealers and grow- We have previously given our objections to ng the present state of matters to exist, and that if vigorous and united efforts were by those most interested, a change might cted.

E STOCK.—*Cattle.*—The market has been supplied with first-class cattle, but there is t abundance of inferior; prices range from $6.50, according to quality. *Sheep* were lentiful, and sell at $2 to $5 each. *Lambs* rth $1.50 to $3. *Hogs*—$5.37½ to $5.75, eight.

LES—Selling at $1 to $2.50 per barrel.

ROLEUM. — The Combination, it now ap- has been extended to January 1st. There gns of weakness visible, and it cannot be ted that so unadhesive a concern as an oil ould stick long together. Possibly the first nuary may dissolve the organization. In ase what about prices? They may go lower, s stocks will have been pretty well worked s we will be in the middle of the season the demand is greatest, and as, by every pro- ity, good arrangements will have been com- d for the exportation of our own surplus oil e stocks can again accumulate, their seems reason to anticipate a return to low prices. his market the demand is good, though in l lots, and prices are unchanged.

The Packing Season.

e condense the following respecting the pros- of the in-coming season from Henry Milward .'s Circular, dated Chicago, Oct. 1st:

t of ninety-two points in Illinois, Indiana, , Missouri and Kansas, from which reports been received, the number of hogs in the try returned as more than last year sum up y-one; as about the same, twenty-six; and s, thirty-five. Personal investigation through siderable region of country in the States of ois and Iowa would lead us to the belief that of the hogs at all fit for slaughter have been eted; that the stock hogs constitute the ipal number now remaining, and that these ot be made fit for market before the middle ose of the ensuing packing season. Of the ition of hogs in Indiana, Missouri and Kan- we have had no opportunity of judging per- lly, but from the reports received we assume they are in the same condition as in the States e mentioned. Our approaching packing sea- will probably commence very late, as the ent prices for hogs are quite sufficient to appal the most venturesome among packers. We ot expect to be in full work much earlier than 1st of January, at which time last year packers talking of closing their houses. It is diffi- to predict the probable range of prices, so y unlooked for contingencies may arise. Last some 80,000 hogs were packed in this city ng the months of August and September, and ice-cured products were, about the present coming into competition with the winter- d. This year no hogs have been packed, and e is little chance of any parties engaging in business, as apart from the danger of spoiled meat, the price now ruling for hogs would preclude the possibility of furnishing products at anything like the rates at which winter-cured can be obtained. The stock of provisions in our market a week ago, by the most careful personal investigation, was: Mess pork, 9,820 brls; prime mess, 275 brls; extra prime, 175 brls; total, 10,270 brls. Lard, 6,607 tcs; bulk shoulders, 2,700,000 lbs; bulk sides, 95,000 lbs; Cumberland middles, 117,000 lbs; clear sides 800,000 lbs; short ribs, 700,000 lbs; total cut meats, 4,412,000 lbs. The shipments since then to the present date have been as follows: Pork, 3,440 brls; lard, 2,600 tcs; cured meats, 1,626,177 lbs—leaving as the present stock, pork, 6, 830 brls; lard, 4,007 tcs; cured meats, 2,785,823 lbs. The shipments from here for the last month have averaged each week, pork, 1,786 brls; lard, 1,685 tcs; cut meats, 1,312,114 brls; and as they seem to be increasing rather than diminishing, we shall be entirely bare of stocks before the expiration of the month of October, while from present appearances as to the price of early hogs, we can have no meat cured fit for smoking before the 29th of December. The shipments of products for the month of October last year summed up as follows: Cured meats, 1,934,-487 lbs; and for November, 3,510,859 lbs; total 5,445,346 lbs. Of pork in October, 5,852 brls; in November, 11,134 brls; total, 16,885 brls. Of lard in October, 12,276 tcs; in November, 12,988 tcs; total, 25,264 tcs. Last year we had an early spring, and a large amount of autumn packing was carried over in salt till far in December and January. The packers show little disposition to make contracts for the sale of stuff for forward delivery, as they find it utterly impossible to make any forward purchases of hogs. There has been some inquiry for English meats, and offers have been made to sell Cumberlands, 25 to 30 days in salt, delivered here in the first fifteen days in January, at 11c. per lb. Short rib could probably be had at 12¼c to 12½c, same delivery. The English buyers, however, wish the delivery to be as early as possible in December, which the packers do not dare to accede to, knowing the season must be late. It is probable that but few sales will be made until the packers have ascertained that they can obtain hogs at prices likely to afford them some remuneration, as from present appearances the opening rates are likely to be high. Some sales of lard for December and January delivery here, have been made at 13¾c and 14c; but it is now held higher.

Exportation of Cattle.

The St. John's (Quebec) *News* says:—Large quantities of cattle are still being exported from Canada to the States. A drove of some 500 head brought, we believe, from the vicinity of Lachute was sent out from St. Johns on Monday. The prices paid, we are told, are not high, in the present instance the average for two year olds being only $11 per head. Other stock is also steadily purchased for the American markets, the demand for fowls being particularly brisk. Fodder in Western Canada being scarce, we learn that much live stock will be sent to this Province for wintering.

Petroleum.

The quantities of Petroleum exported from the United States to foreign ports from January 1st to 2nd October, were:

FROM	1868.	1867.
Boston	1,924,498	1,567,087
Philadelphia	28,401,987	20,981,989
Baltimore	2,042,775	1,234,726
Portland	558,970	
New York	43,154,013	22,297,443
Total gallons	76,092,243	46,081,245
Corresponding period, 1866, gallons		45,182,022
Corresponding period, 1865, gallons		15,574,295

Receipts at New York, Jan. 1st to Oct, 2nd, 1868, 746,115 bbls.; corresponding period in 1867, 982,164 barrels.

Demerara Sugar Market.

The following is from Sandbach, Parker & Co.'s circular, dated Georgetown, 7th September, 1868:

SUGARS.—On the 1st inst. intelligence was received of a decline in the New York market, and parcels which commanded $6.30 to $6.40 the day before fell to $6 to $6.10; no change for the better has shown itself, and a good many holders are accepting current rates in preference to shipping. Towards the end of this month almost every estate will be manufacturing, and produce will then be plentiful.

MOLASSES.—Vacuum Pan has followed sugar, and 24 to 25c. is now difficult to obtain for some qualities that before commanded 30 to 32c. Muscovado is in better demand for Lisbon and B. Provinces, and good samples fetch 24 to 26c.

RUM.—There have been some transactions for Halifax and Bermuda at 40 to 42c.

Transactions have taken place during the fortnight at the following rates:

SUGARS (package included) sold by 100 lbs. Dutch, 10 per cent. tare F.O.B.

Muscavadoes, equal at No. 8 Dutch Standard $3.60 ℔ 100 lbs.	In hhds. of about 1800 lbs. each.
No. 10 do. $4.00 "	
" 12 do. $4.25 "	
Vacuum Pan No. 12 do. $5.50	
" " 14 do. 5.75	
" " 16 do. 6.00	
" " 18 do. 6.10	

MOLASSES (package included, sold by Imperial gallon.)

Muscovado, from 20 @ 26 cents, as to color and density	In puns of 100 gals.
Vacuum Pan from 20 @ 25 cents, as to color and density	
RUM (colored, package included, sold by Imperial gal. from 35 per cent, @ 38 overproof 38 @ 40 cents.	Ditto.
From 38 per cent. @ 40 overproof, 40 @ 42 cents.	

FREIGHTS—Are in a wretched state, nominal at 1s. 9d.; an unclassed vessel is offering to take sugar freight free to London. The shipments to America last month were 2,100 hhds. against 1,700 to the United Kingdom, and a like proportion is likely to be the case this month; no charters have been effected since our last.

WEATHER—Has been intensely hot and dry. Water is beginning to run short both in town and country, and many estates are taking in salt water for navigation purposes. The Lamaha Canal is too low for estates to use, and serious fears are entertained for the young canes if we are not soon relieved by copious showers.

St. John Market.

BREADSTUFFS.—Sept. 30.—Receipts for the week are as follows:—Grand Trunk Railway, steam and sailing vessels, 4,700 barrels of flour. Via Gulf of St. Lawrence and E. & N. A. Railway—none since 1407 barrels Flour on 17th inst. From New York per sailing vessel, 439 bbls. flour, 100 bbls. oatmeal; from Boston by sailing vessel 95 bbls flour and 25 sacks California do.

Our flour market, which has been very bare for the last few weeks, has been largely replenished during the past week, and the prices which a week ago for Canada flour were relatively high, have dropped to a level more in accordance with rates in Toronto and Montreal. The decline within the week has been about thirty-five cents per bbl. for all grades. The stock of flour now in the city is moderate, and as the fall trade will soon commence, we look to a brisk demand and fairly remunerative prices for the miller and consigner. We quote Canada super. $6.90 to $7.00, choice $7.25. Cornmeal very firm at $4.60.—*News.*

Copyrights.

The Copyright Act, imposing 12½ per cent. duty *ad valorem* on British copyrights reprinted in foreign countries and imported into Canada, came in force on the 28th Sepcember.

Halifax Market.

BREADSTUFFS.—Sept. 29.—Flour market dull and depressed. Canada No. 1 offered at $7.25, but we think could be bought a shade lower. Extra $3.25 to$3.30; Extra State $6.75 to $7.25. Rye dull. Corn Meal dull at $4.60 to $4.75; Fresh Ground $4.40 to $4.50. Oatmeal dull at $7.75 to $8. Imports from January 1st to September 29th, 1867 and 1868 :—

	Brls. Flour.	Brls. Cornmeal.
1868	132,265	41,107
1867	134,139	29,951

WEST INDIA PRODUCE.—Prices of both Sugar and Molasses are without change. Holders are firm, and are looking forward for an advance, as the markets in Boston and New York are steadily improving. Sales of small lots by retail, but we have no sales of cargoes to report. Porto Rico 6 to 6¾c.; Barbadoes 5¾ to 6c.; Cuba 5¼ to 5½c.; Centrifugal Cuba 6c. in bond.

FINANCIAL.—Bank drawing rate on London 60 day sight bills 13 per cent. prem.; private 12 to 12½ per cent. prem. New York Gold drafts at sight, 4 per cent. prem. Currency drafts 25¼ per cent discount. Montreal sight drafts 4 per cent. prem. Newfoundland sight drafts 5 per cent. prem.—R. C. Hamilton & Co.'s Circular.

St. John Market.

Sept. 22.—Breadstuffs.—Since our last week's report flour has commenced coming in from Canada and prices have declined. The arrivals for the week have only been about 4,500 barrels, but the decline in Ontario and Montreal has met with a ready response here. We hear of some sales of very choice flour at $7.25 to $7.40 and in all probability No. 1 Super. could be bought in round lots at $7. The trade still keeps rather dull although a slight improvement has taken place during the week. We look for a brisk demand during the ensuing two months. Canada flour is driving American brands entirely out of the market.—News.

The Cotton Crop.

The very large receipts which we are now reporting from week to week by telegraph, cannot be taken as a fair indication of the total crop. They show, however, what we have all along stated, that cotton is more forward than usual. This is certainly a favourable fact. Up to this date probably much more has been secured than at the same period last year. When we hear, therefore, of damage from worms and rust, and rain, it is well to remember that the start is better than in 1867, and if we have a return of fair weather, with a late fall the prospect is still good for an increased yield. Reports this week continue, however, unfavorable. Less rain has fallen, but the weather is still unsettled. We hear fewer complaints of worms, except in South Carolina and Georgia, where they are reported in sections hitherto free of them. The accounts from Texas are better.—Financial Chronicle.

The New Ship "Lake Ontario."

This fine new clipper ship. the first of a fleet of vessels now being built on the Clyde for the Canada Shipping Co., of which Mr. Wm. Murray, of this city, is President, arrived in port yesterday morning, and is now lying in the Metcalf Basin, almost opposite the Royal Insurance Buildings. The Lake Ontario sailed from the Tail of the Bank at Greenock, at half-past two on the afternoon of the 11th ult., and after making a very unusual run, entered the straits of Belle Isle on Tuesday, the 22nd, reaching Bic on the 30th, and Quebec on the 5th October. She is a handsome vessel, and of somewhat greater capacity than the general class of ships entering this port. Her length is 210 feet, keel and forerake; beam 34½ feet, tonnage 1,060, and is capable of carrying 1,500 tons burden. The Lake Ontario is constructed with the latest improvements in ship building, and carries what few vessels do, viz., a Donkey Engine, which is a very great assistance in driving the pumps, warping, discharging cargo,

and otherwise taking the place of a vast amount of manual labor. The crew is 30 in number, commanded by Captain Ritchie, who can boast of having brought out one of the finest sailing vessels that ever arrived at this port. She was built by Messrs. Barclay, Curle & Co., Glasgow. Messrs. Thompson, Murray & Co. are the agents of the Company here.—Herald

---

Consumers' Gas Company.

THE Annual Meeting of the Stockholders of the Consumers'Gas Company of Toronto, to receive the Report of the Directors, and for the election of Directors for the ensuing year, will be held at the Company's Office, on Toronto Street, on

Monday, the 26th October inst.,

At seven o'clock p.m.

H. THOMPSON,

Manager.

Consumers' Gas Company,

Toronto, October 3, 1868.   .8-3t

BEAVER

Mutual Insurance Association.

HEAD OFFICE—20 TORONTO STREET,

TORONTO.

INSURES LIVE STOCK against death from any cause. The only Canadian Company having authority to do this class of business.

R. L. DENISON,

President.

W. T. O'REILLY,

Secretary.   8-1y-25

HOME DISTRICT

Mutual Fire Insurance Company.

OFFICE:

North-West Corner of Yonge and Adelaide Streets,

TORONTO.—(UP STAIRS.)

INSURES Dwelling Houses, Stores, Warehouses, Merchandise, Furniture, &c.

PRESIDENT—The Hon. J. McMURRICH.

VICE-PRESIDENT—JOHN BURNS, Esq.

JOHN RAINS, Secretary.

AGENTS:

DAVID WRIGHT, Esq., Hamilton; FRANCIS STEVENS, Esq., Barrie; Messrs. GIBBS & BRO., Oshawa.   8

UNRIVALLED!

THE BRITISH AMERICAN COMMERCIAL COLLEGE,

Consolidated with the

Bryant, Stratton and Odell Business College

AND TELEGRAPHIC INSTITUTE,

STANDS Pre-eminent and Unrivalled. It is the LARGEST and MOST EFFICIENT. It employs the largest staff of Teachers, among whom are the two BEST PENMEN OF CANADA.

The TUITION FEE is the same as in other Iustitutions having a similar object.

The PRICE OF BOARD is the same as in other Canadian Cities.

In an EDUCATIONAL point of view, there is no other Institution in the country that has equal advantages and facilities.

YOUNG MEN intending to qualify themselves for business, will find it to their advantage to send for a Circular, or call at the College Rooms, corner of King and Toronto streets.

Scholarships good in Montreal and throughout the United States.

ODELL & TROUT,

Principals and Proprietors.

October 2.   8

STATEMENT OF BANKS

ACTING UNDER CHARTER, FOR THE MONTH ENDING 31st AUGUST, 1865, ACCORDING TO RETURNS FURNISHED BY THE BANKS TO THE AUDITOR OF PUBLIC ACCOUNTS.

NAME OF BANK	CAPITAL — Capital authorized by Act.	Capital paid up.	LIABILITIES — Promissory Notes in circulation not bearing Interest.	Balances due to other Banks.	Cash Deposits not bearing Interest.	Cash Deposits bearing Interest.	TOTAL LIABILITIES.	ASSETS — Coin, Bullion, and Provincial Notes.	Landed or other Property of the Bank.	Government Securities.	Promissory Notes, or Bills of other Banks.	Balances due from other Banks.	Notes and Bills Discounted.	Other Debts due the Bank and included under foregoing heads.	TOTAL ASSETS.
ONTARIO AND QUEBEC.															
Montreal	6,000,000	6,000,000	327,407	475,574	5,671,571	6,380,390	13,099,343	2,436,114	850,000	3,045,309	413,327	1,733,760	12,698,142	356,000	21,013,628
Quebec	1,475,000	1,473,090	247,670	86,517	398,057	997,928	2,008,047	331,174	89,733	146,433	38,936	376,404	2,390,016	574,668	3,713,644
City	1,500,000	1,200,000	257,680	81,161	631,713	907,862	2,145,284	218,780	80,675	163,900	30,173	104,996	3,048,780	127,311	3,446,402
Gore	1,000,000	889,269	362,653	111,878	233,112	776,445	1,174,843	176,443	91,477	85,728	91,477	28,710	2,463,269	122,588	1,997,978
British North America	4,866,666	4,866,666	902,663	110,728	1,143,467	2,406,144	4,329,903	666,514	343,333	761,671	153,476	56,772	5,406,205	159,988	7,715,843
Banque du Peuple	1,600,000	1,600,000	90,719	1,810	1,410,683	78,990	4,579	44,976		160,964	32,447	75,384	84,566	45,655	84,066
Niagara District	1,000,000	1,000,000	61,118	137,015	144,107	75,000	419,513	40,940	12,679	180,289	33,450	17,234	640,017	22,937	733,152
Molsons	1,000,000	895,524	85,468	68,098	217,134	465,584	696,861	131,128	42,678	907,785	71,833	47,600	1,381,296	18,759	1,932,930
Toronto	2,000,000	800,000	765,561	63,887	330,140	1,278,138	2,367,192	989,214	25,475	97,359	106,000	18,478	3,007,044	18,788	4,208,627
Ontario	3,000,000	3,000,000	125,061	997,889	946,310		2,009,166	697,765	61,738	906,983	71,193	16,475	3,994,227	116,411	6,424,714
Eastern Townships	1,000,000	800,000	107,989	84,671	98,361	200,000	691,192	49,677	42,679	80,389	140,083	40,900	1,091,517	66,000	683,650
Banque Nationale	1,000,000	1,000,000	134,846	99,448	394,473	174,414	603,176	138,510	29,118	115,488	86,578	64,487	1,187,808	65,000	1,778,467
Banque Jacques Cartier	1,000,000	700,000	77,161	6,373	318,884	436,281	835,689	88,987		101,326	34,962	44,557	1,649,989	61,000	1,918,828
Merchants'	6,000,000	3,000,000	733,111	97,014	610,949	388,785	2,594,879	655,431		123,730	112,852	123,733	2,717,017		3,893,874
Royal Canadian	5,000,000	1,118,530	1,112,983		339,455	224,981	2,577,893	116,488		130,388	99,414	225,347	1,915,569		3,926,437
Union B'k Lower Canada	1,000,000	975,900	58,639	43,453	306,585	96,533	855,833	46,179	34,300	130,355	87,864	37,488	1,931,983		1,884,666
Mechanics'	1,000,000	955,185		84,594	639,997	763,390	2,372,865	896,960	40,842	106,200	70,543	64,733	1,156,799		3,375,713
NOVA SCOTIA.															
Bank of Nova Scotia	660,000	630,000	406,668	60,444	469,288	714,196	1,655,476	322,867	15,374		33,546	398,157	1,638,360	84,556	2,649,271
People's Bank					21,901	34,087	363,115	44,547	4,604		58,043	19,815	347,319	96,605	569,717
NEW BRUNSWICK.															
Bank of New Brunswick	660,000	630,000	255,177												
Commercial Bank															
St. Stephen's Bank															
People's Bank															
Totals	58,300,000	39,951,117	8,601,599	1,710,399	13,600,398	18,469,737	42,120,541	8,827,541	1,646,113	5,987,196	1,911,868	5,902,965	49,203,694	5,300,790	74,349,651

TORONTO PRICES CURRENT.—October 8, 1868.

Name of Article.	Wholesale Rates.	
Boots and Shoes.	$ c.	$ c.
Mens' Thick Boots	2 20	2 50
" Kip	2 45	3 20
" Calf	3 00	3 75
" Congress Gaitors	2 00	2 40
" Kip Cobourgs	1 00	1 50
Boys' Thick Boots	1 65	1 90
Youths' "	1 45	1 55
Women's Batts	95	1 20
" Congress Gaiters	1 15	1 50
Misses' Batts	0 75	1 00
" Congress Gaiters	1 00	1 30
Girls' Batts	0 65	0 90
" Congress Gaiters	0 80	1 10
Children's C. T. Cacks	0 50	0 65
" Gaiters	0 65	0 90
Drugs.		
Aloes Cape	0 12½	0 16
Alum	0 02½	0 03
Borax	0 00	0 00
Camphor, refined	0 65	0 70
Castor Oil	0 18	0 28
Caustic Soda	0 04½	0 05
Cochineal	0 90	1 00
Cream Tartar	0 00	0 00
Epsom Salts	0 03	0 04
Extract Logwood	0 09	0 11
Gum Arabic, sorts	0 30	0 35
Indigo, Madras	0 75	1 00
Licorice	0 14	0 45
Madder	0 13	0 16
Nutgalls	0 00	0 00
Opium	6 70	7 00
Oxalic Acid	0 28	0 35
Potash, Bi-tart	0 25	0 28
" Bichromate	0 15	0 20
Potass Iodide	3 80	4 50
Senna	0 12½	0 60
Soda Ash	0 03	0 04
Soda Bicarb	4 50	5 50
Tartaric Acid	0 37½	0 45
Verdigris	0 35	0 40
Vitriol, Blue	0 09	0 10
Groceries.		
Coffees:		
Java, ℔ lb.	0 22@	0 24
Laguayra,	0 17	0 18
Rio	0 15	0 17
Fish:		
Herrings, Lab. split	0 00	0 00
" round	0 00	0 00
" scaled	0 35	0 40
Mackerel, small kitts	1 00	0 00
Loch. Her. wh'e firks	2 50	2 75
" half "	1 25	1 50
White Fish & Trout	3 25	3 50
Salmon, saltwater	14 00	15 00
Dry Cod, ℔ 112 lbs	4 75	5 00
Fruit:		
Raisins, Layers	2 20	2 25
" M. R.	2 10	2 20
" Valentias new	0 08¼	0 08½
Currants, new	0 05	0 05½
" old	0 04¼	0 04½
Figs	0 11	0 12½
Molasses:		
Clayed, ℔ gal	0 00	0 35
Syrups, Standard	0 43	0 44
" Golden	0 49	0 50
Rice:		
Arracan	4 50	4 65
Spices:		
Cassia, whole, ℔ lb.	0 37½	0 40
Cloves	0 11	0 12
Nutmegs	0 45	0 55
Ginger, ground	0 20	0 25
" Jamaica, root	0 22	0 25
Pepper, black	0 09½	0 10
Pimento	0 08	0 09
Sugars:		
Port Rico, ℔ lb.	0 08½	0 08¾
Cuba "	0 08¼	0 08¾
Barbadoes (bright)	0 08¼	0 08¾
Dry Crushed, at 60d.	0 11	0 11½
Canada Sugar Refine'y, yellow No. 2, 60ds.	0 08¾	0 08¼
Yellow, No. 2½	0 08¾	0 08½
" No. 3	0 09½	0 09¾
Crushed X	0 10	0 10½
" A	0 10¾	0 11
Ground	0 11	0 11¼
Extra Ground	0 12½	0 12¾
Teas:		
Japan com'n to good	0 40	0 55
" Fine to choicest	0 55	0 65
Colored, com. to fine	0 60	0 75
Congou & Souch'ng	0 42	0 75
Oolong, good to fine	0 50	0 65
Y. Hyson, com to gd	0 45	0 55
Medium to choice	0 65	0 80
Extra choice	0 85	0 95
Gunpowd'r c. to med	0 55	0 70
" med. to fine	0 70	0 85

Name of Article.	Wholesale Rate.	
Groceries—*Contin'd*	$ c.	$ c.
" fine to fins't	0 85	0 95
Hyson	0 45	0 80
Imperial	0 42	0 80
Tobacco, Manufact'd:		
Can Leaf, ℔ lb 5s & 10s.	0 26	0 30
Western Leaf, com	0 25	0 26
" Good	0 27	0 32
" Fine	0 32	0 35
" Bright fine	0 40	0 50
" " choice	0 00	0 75
Hardware.		
Tin (net cash prices)		
Block, ℔ lb	0 25	0 26
Grain	0 25	0 26
Copper:		
Pig	0 23	0 24
Sheet	0 30	0 33
Cut Nails:		
Assorted ½ Shingles, ℔ 100 lb.	2 90	3 00
Shingle alone do	3 15	3 25
Lathe and 5 dy	3 30	3 40
Galvanized Iron:		
Assorted sizes	0 00	0 10
Best No. 24	0 09	0 00
" 26	0 08	0 08½
" 28	0 09	0 09½
Horse Nails:		
Guest's or Griffin's assorted sizes	0 19	0 20
For W. ass'd sizes	0 18	0 19
Patent Hammer'd do	0 17	0 18
Iron (at 4 months):		
Pig—Gartsherrie No1	26 00	27 00
Other brands. No1	22 00	24 00
" No2	24 00	25 00
Bar—Scotch, ℔ 100 lb	2 25	2 50
Refined	3 00	3 25
Swedes	5 00	5 50
Hoops—Coopers	3 00	3 25
Band	3 00	3 25
Boiler Plates	3 25	3 50
Canada Plates	4 00	4 25
Union Jack	0 00	0 00
Pontypool	4 00	4 25
Swansea	3 90	4 00
Lead (at 4 months):		
Bar, ℔ 100 lbs	0 07	0 07½
Sheet "	0 08	0 09
Shot	0 07½	0 07¾
Iron Wire (net cash):		
No. 6, ℔ bundle	2 70	2 80
" 9, "	3 10	3 20
" 12, "	3 40	3 50
" 16, "	4 30	4 40
Powder:		
Blasting, Canada	3 50	3 75
FF "	4 25	4 50
FFF "	4 75	5 00
Blasting, English	5 00	5 50
FF loose	5 50	6 00
FFF "	6 00	6 50
Pressed Spikes (4 mos):		
Regular sizes 100	4 00	4 25
Extra "	4 50	5 00
Tin Plates (net cash):		
IC Coke	7 50	8 00
IC Charcoal	8 50	8 75
IX "	10 50	10 75
IXX "	12 50	0 00
DC "	7 50	9 00
DX "	9 50	10 00
Hides & Skins, ℔ lb		
Green rough	0 05½	0 06
Green, salt'd & insp'd	0 00	0 07
Cured	0 07½	0 08½
Calfskins, green	0 00	0 10
Calfskins, cured	0 00	0 12
" dry	0 18	0 20
Lambskins,	0 50	0 00
" pelts	0 40	0 00
Hops.		
Inferior, ℔ lb	0 10	0 15
Medium	0 15	0 20
Good	0 20	0 25
Fancy	0 25	0 35
Leather, @ (4 mos.) In lots of less than 50 sides, 10 ℔ cent higher.		
Spanish Sole, 1st qual heavy, weights ℔ lb	0 23	0 23½
Do. 1st qual middle do	0 23	0 23½
Do. No. 2, all weights	0 20	0 22
Slaughter heavy	0 28	0 29
Do. light	0 28	0 29
Harness, best	0 32	0 34
" No. 2	0 30	0 33
Upper heavy	0 35	0 40
" light	0 40	0 45

Name of Article.
Leather—*Contin'd.*
Kip Skins, Patna
French
English
Hemlock Calf (30 to 35 lbs.) per doz.
Do. light
French Calf.
Grain & Satn Clf ℔ doz
Splits, large ℔ lb
" small
Enamelled Cow ℔ foot
Patent
Pebble Grain
Buff
Oils.
Cod
Lard, extra
" No. 1
" Woollen
Lubricating, patent
" Mott's economic
Linseed, raw
" boiled
Machinery
Olive, 2nd, ℔ gal
" salad
" salad, in bots. qt. ℔ case
Sesame salad, ℔ gal
Seal, pale
Spirits Turpentine
Varnish
Whale.
Paints, &c.
White Lead, genuine in Oil, ℔ 25 lbs.
Do. No. 1 "
" 2 "
" 3 "
White Zinc, genuine
White Lead, dry
Red Lead
Venetian Red, Eng'h
Yellow Ochre, Fren'h
Whiting
Petroleum. (Refined ℔ gal.)
Water white, car l'd
" small lots
Straw, by car load
" small lots
Amber, by car load
" small lots
Benzine
Produce.
Grain:
Wheat, Spring, 60 lb
" Fall 60 "
Barley 48 "
Peas 60 "
Oats 34 "
Rye 56 "
Seeds:
Clover, choice 60 "
" com'n 68 "
Timothy, cho'e 4 "
" inf. to good 48 "
Flax 56 "
Flour (per brl.):
Superior extra
Extra superfine,
Fancy superfine
Superfine No. 1
" No. 2
Oatmeal, (per brl.)
Provisions.
Butter, dairy tub ℔ lb
" store packed
Cheese, new
Pork, mess, per brl
" prime mess
" prime
Bacon, rough
" Cumberl'd cut
" smoked
Hams, in salt
" sug. cur. & canv'd
Shoulders, in salt
Lard, in kegs
Eggs, packed
Beef Hams
Tallow
Hogs dressed, heavy
" medium
" light
Salt, &c.
American brls.
Liverpool coarse
Plaster
Water Lime

ndles.		
Co.'s ..	$ c.	$ c.
....	0 07½	0 08
ar	0 07	0 07½
r........	0 07	0 07½
....	0 05	0 05½
....	0 08½	0 08¾
....	0 11	0 11½
iquors,		
doz......	2 60	2 65
b Portr..	2 35	2 40
a Rum...	1 80	2 25
H. Gin..	1 55	1 65
Tom.....	1 90	2 00
i.........	4 00	4 25
Tom, c...	6 00	6 25
on	1 00	1 25
l	2 00	4 00
mon	1 00	1 50
m........	1 70	1 80
r golden..	2 50	4 00

Brandy:	$ c.	$ c
Hennessy's, per gal..	2 40	2 50
Martell's " ..	2 40	2 50
J. Robin & Co.'s " ..	2 25	2 35
Otard, Dupuy & Cos..	2 25	2 35
Brandy, cases.........	8 50	9 00
Brandy, com. per c...	4 00	4 50
Whiskey:		
Common 36 u. p.......	0 62½	0 65
Old Rye	0 85	0 87½
Malt........	0 85	0 87½
Toddy	0 85	0 87½
Scotch, per gal........	1 90	2 10
Irish—Kinnahan's c...	7 00	7 50
" Dunnville's Belf't..	6 00	6 25
Wool.		
Fleece, lb.............	0 27	0 30
Pulled "............	0 00	0 00
Furs.		
Bear.......	3 00	10 00
Beaver..	1 00	1 25
Coon	0 20	0 40
Fisher................	4 00	6 00
Martin....	1 40	1 60
Mink..................	4 00	4 25
Otter..................	5 75	6 00
Spring Rats...........	0 15	0 17
Fox.	1 20	1 25

SURANCE COMPANIES.

ENGLISH.—*Quotations on the London Market.*

Di- d.	Name of Company.	Shares parval £	Amount paid.	Last
	Briton Medical and General Life ...	10	—	1½
7½	Commer'l Union, Fire, Life and Mar.	50	5	5½ 5¾
8	City of Glasgow	25	2½	5
9½	Edinburgh Life	100	15	30½x
—½ yr	European Life and Guarantee......	2½	11s6	4s 6d
10	Etna Fire and Marine..............	10	1½	1
5	Guardian	100	50	52x
12	Imperial Fire......................	500	50	345
9½	Imperial Life	100	10	16¼
10	Lancashire Fire and Life..........	20	2	2¾x
11	Life Association of Scotland.......	40	7½	23
s. p. sh	London Assurance Corporation ..	25	12½	48
5	London and Lancashire Life	10	1	1
40	Liverp'l & London & Globe F. & L.	20	2	7⅞
5	National Union Life	5	1	1
12½	Northern Fire and Life	100	5	10⅝
12 8, bo 5s.	North British and Mercantile	50	6¼	16 16½
50	Ocean Marine	25	5	20
5 12s.	Provident Life......................	100	10	38
4½ b. s.	Phœnix................................	....	....	136
—h. yr.	Queen Fire and Life	10	1	15-16ths
. bo. 4s	Royal Insurance.....................	20	3	6⅞
10	Scottish Provincial Fire and Life ..	50	2½	4½
25	Standard Life	50	12	65
5	Star Life	25	1¼	—
	CANADIAN.			₩ c.
4	British America Fire and Marine ..	$50	$25	56
4	Canada Life	...	....	.....
12	Montreal Assurance	£50	£5	135
3	Provincial Fire and Marine........	60	11	.....
....	Quebec Fire	40	32½	£19
8	" Marine........................	100	40	90-91
7 mo's.	Western Assurance..................	40	6	.....

RAILWAYS.	Sha's	Paid	Montr	London.
d St. Lawrence........................	£100	All.	....	56 58xd
l Lake Huron	20½	"	....	3 3½
do. Preference	10	"	....	5½ 6½
tt. & Goderich, 6₩c., 1872-3-4....	100	"	....	----
and St. Lawrence	....	....	10 11	....
do Pref. 10 ₩ ct....	....	....	65 72½	....
nk	100	"	15 16	16¼ 16¾
Eq. G. M. Bds. 1 ch. 6₩c..........	100	"	....	84 86
First Preference, 5 ₩ c	100	"	....	49 51
Deferred, 3 ₩ ct..	100	"	....	....
Second Pref. Bonds, 5₩c...........	100	"	....	39 41
do Deferred, 3 ₩ ct..........	100	"	...	....
Third Pref. Stock, 4₩ct...........	100	"	...	28 30
do. Deferred, 3 ₩ ct......	100	"	....	....
Fourth Pref. Stock, 3₩c...........	100	"	....	19 20
do. Deferred, 3 ₩ ct..........	100	"	....	....
tern	20½	"	....	13¾ 14
New	20½	18	----	....
6 ₩ c. Bds, due 1873-76..........	100	All.	....	101 103
5½₩c Bds. due 1877-78...........	100	"	....	93 95
lway, Halifax, $250, all......	$250	"	....	....
f Canada, 6₩c. 1st Pref. Bds...........	100	"	.. .	80 83

CHANGE.	Halifax.	Montr'l.	Quebec.	Toronto.
London, 60 days......				
75 days date	13½	8¾ 8⅞	8⅞ 9	9⅛
o.	12 12½	8 8½	8 8¼	8¾
th documents..........	....	7½ 8	....	....
ew York...............	....	30½ 31	30 30½	72
do.	....	31 31½	31 31½	....
s do.	....	1-32 dis.	par ½ dis.	par ½ dis.
....	....		....	3½ 5

STOCK AND BOND REPORT.

The dates of our quotations are as follows:—Toronto, Oct. 7; Montreal, Oct. 6; Quebec, Oct. 6; London, Sept. 23.

NAME.	Shares.	Paid up.	Divid'd last 6 Months	Dividend Day.	CLOSING PRICES. Toronto.	Montre'l	Quebec.
BANKS.			₩ ct.				
British North America........	$250	All.	3	July and Jan.	103½ 105	103 104	102½ 103
Jacques Cartier..............	50	"	4	1 June, 1 Dec.	106 108	107 108	106½ 107½
Montreal	200	"	5	"	135 135½	135 135½	135 135½
Nationale....................	50	"	4	1 Nov. 1 May.	106	107 108	107½ 108
New Brunswick	100	"	....	......	....	...	....
Nova Scotia	200	28	7&b$3½	Mar. and Sept.	....	....	....
Du Peuple....	50	"	4	1 Mar., 1 Sept.	105 106	105½ 106	105 105½
Toronto	100	"	4	1 Jan., 1 July.	116½ 117	116 117	116 116½
Bank of Yarmouth...........	....	....	......	......	....	....	....
Canadian Bank of Com'e......	50	95	......	......	103 103½	102 103	102 103
City Bank Montreal	80	All.	4	1 June, 1 Dec.	102½ 103	103 104	102½ 103½
Commer'l Bank (St. John)....	100	"	₩ ct.	....	....	...	....
Eastern Townships' Bank.....	50	"	4	1 July, 1 Jan..	....	95 97	96 96½
Gore	40	...	3½	1 Jan., 1 July.	....	....	39 40
Halifax Banking Company....	...	....	......	.....	....	....	....
Mechanics' Bank.............	50	70	4	1 Nov., 1 May.	95 97	95 97	95½ 96½
Merchants' Bank of Canada....	100	70	4	1 Jan., 1 July.	105 105½	105 105½	105 105½
Merchants' Bank (Halifax)....	....	....	.....	.....	....	....	....
Molson's Bank......	50	All.	4	1 Apr., 1 Oct.	108 109	108 109	107 107½
Niagara District Bank...	100	70	3½	1 Jan., 1 July.	....	....	....
Ontario Bank.................	40	All.	4	1 June, 1 Dec.	99 100	99½ 100	98½ 99½
People's Bank (Fred'kton)....	100	"	......	......	....	....	....
People's Bank (Halifax)	20	"	7 12 m	......	....	...	....
Quebec Bank	100	"	3½	1 June, 1 Dec.	97½ 98	98½ 99	98½ 99
Royal Canadian Bank	50	50	4	1 Jan., 1 July.	91 92	90½ 91½	90 91
St. Stephens Bank	100	All	.....	......	....	..	...
Union Bank	100	70	4	1 Jan., 1 July.	102 102½	102 103	102½ 103
Union Bank (Halifax)........	100	40	7 12 mo	Feb. and Aug.	....	....	. .
MISCELLANEOUS.							
British America Land........	250	44	2½	......	....	----	....
British Colonial S. S. Co.....	250	32½	2½	......	...	50	....
Canada Company	32½	All.	5	......	....	----	....
Canada Landed Credit Co.....	50	$20	3½	......	62 63	----	....
Canada Per. B'ldg Society....	50	All.	5	......	120½ 121	....	....
Canada Mining Company.....	4	90	......	......	....	....	....
Do. Inl'd Steam Nav. Co....	100	All.	20 12 m	......	----	107 109	108 109
Do. Glass Company.........	100	"	12½ "	......	....	95	....
Canad'n Loan & Investm't....	25	2½	7	......	....	....	----
Canada Agency	10	¼	......	......	....	....	----
Colonial Securities Co.......	...	....	.....	.....	....	....	....
Freehold Building Society....	100	All.	5	......	106 106½	----	....
Halifax Steamboat Co........	100	"	5	------	....	....	....
Halifax Gas Company........	....	----	------	. .. .	....	...	....
Hamilton Gas Company......	....	....	.....	. ....	....	....	....
Huron Copper Bay Co........	4	12	20	. ....	....	25 50cps	....
Lake Huron S. and C.........	5	102	......	......	....	....	....
Montreal Mining Co..........	20	$15	......	. ....	....	2.90 3.15	...
Do. Telegraph Co...	40	All.	5	......	132 133	130 133	130 132
Do. Elevating Co...	00	"	15 12 m	......	....	100 103	....
Do. City Gas Co........	40	"	4	15 Mar. 15 Sep.	....	132½ 135	133 134
Do. City Pass. R,. Co....	50	"	5	......	....	106 110	106 110
Nova Scotia Telegraph	20	"	....	. ....	....	....	....
Quebec and L. S.	8	$4	......	......	....	....	25 cts
Quebec Gas Co...............	200	All.	4	1 Mar., 1 Sep.	....	...	117 118
Quebec Street R. R.........	50	25	8	......	....	....	96 97
Richelieu Navigation Co......	100	All.	7 p.a.	1 Jan., 1 July.	....	110 113	113 114
St. Lawrence Tow Boat Co....	100	"	......	3 Feb.	....	...	40 45
Tor'to Consumers' Gas Co....	50	"	2 3 m.	1 My Au MarFe	104½ 105	...	103 104
Trust & Loan Co. of U. C....	20	5	3	......	....	....	.. .
West'n Canada Bldg Soc'y....	50	All.	5	......	113 113½	....	----

SECURITIES.	London.	Montreal	Quebec.	Toronto.
Canadian Gov't Deb. 6 ₩ ct. due 1872	....	100 101	100½ 101	100 101
Do. do. 6 do due Ja. & Jul. 1877-84.........	104 106	....	....	....
Do. do. 6 do. Feb. & Aug....	103 105	....	.. .	....
Do. do. 6 do. Mch. & Sep.........	103 105	....	....	....
Do. do. 5 ₩ ct. cur., 1883	91 93	89½ 91	89½ 90	90 90½
Do. do. 5 do. stg., 1885	....	89½ 91	90 90½	90 90½
Do. do. 7 do. cur.,........................	....	....	......	....
Dominion 6 p. c. 1878 cy.....	....	100 101	100½ 101½	100½ 101
Hamilton Corporation.....	. ..	....	......	....
Montreal Harbor, 8 ₩ ct. d. 1869......................	..	....	......	....
Do. do. 7 do. 1870........................	....	....	......	....
Do. do. 6½ do. 1875........................	....	100 100½	......	....
Do. do. 6½ do. 1873........................	....	....	......	....
Do. Corporation, 6 ₩ c. 1891	....	92	92 93	92 93
Do. 7 p. c. stock..................................	....	105 106	104 105	105 105½
Do. Water Works, 6 ₩ c. stg. 1878............	....	....	......	92 93
Do. do. 6 do. cy. do.	....	92½ 93	......	92 93
New Brunswick, 6 ₩ ct., Jan. and July	102 104	....	......	....
Nova Scotia, 6 ₩ ct., 1875..............................	100 102	...	......	....
Ottawa City 6 ₩ c. d. 1880	....	90 91	......	...
Quebec Harbour, 6 ₩ c. d. 1883.	....	....	60	....
Do. do. 7 do. do..............................	....	....	70	....
Do. do. 8 do. 1886............................	...	....	85	....
Do. City, 7 ₩ c. d. 5 years	....	80 90	90½ 91	....
Do. do. 7 do. 9 do.	....	....	87 88	....
Do. do. 7 do. 2½ do.	....	....	96½ 97	....
Do. Water Works, 7 ₩ ct., 4 years..............	....	....	95 96	....
Do. do. 6 do. 2 do.	....	....	92½ 93½	....
Toronto Corporation	....	90 92½	....	....

Miscellaneous.

DOMINION TELEGRAPH COMPANY.

CAPITAL STOCK   -   - $500,000.
In 10,000 Shares at $50 Each.

PRESIDENT,
HON. WILLIAM CAYLEY.

TREASURER,
HON. J. McMURRICH.

SECRETARY,
H. B. REEVE.

SOLICITORS,
MESSRS. CAMERON & McMICHAEL.

GENERAL SUPERINTENDENT,
MARTIN RYAN.

DIRECTORS.

HON. J. McMURRICH,
Bryce, McMurrich & Co., Toronto.

A. R. McMASTER, Esq.,
A. R. McMaster & Brother, Toronto.

HON. M. C. CAMERON,
Provincial Secretary, Toronto.

JAMES MICHIE, Esq.,
Fulton, Michie & Co., and George Michie & Co., Toronto

HON. WILLIAM CAYLEY,
Toronto.

A. M. SMITH, Esq.,
A. M. Smith & Co., Toronto.

L. MOFFATT, Esq.,
Moffatt, Murray & Co., Toronto.

H. B. REEVE, Esq.,
Toronto.

MARTIN RYAN, Esq.,
Toronto.

PROSPECTUS.

THE DOMINION TELEGRAPH COMPANY has been organized under the act respecting Telegraph Companies, chapter 67, of the consolidated Statutes of Canada. Its object is to cover the Dominion of Canada with a complete net-work of Telegraph lines.

The Capital Stock

Is $500,000, divided into 10,000 shares of $50 each, 5 per cent to be paid at the time of subscribing, the balance to be paid by instalments, not exceeding 10 per cent per month—said instalments to be called in by the Directors as the works progress. The liability of a subscriber is limited to the amount of his subscription.

The Business Affairs of the Company.

Are under the management of a Board of Directors, annually elected by the Shareholders, in conformity with the Charter and By-Laws of the Company.
The Directors are of opinion that it would be to the interest of the Stockholders generally to obtain subscriptions from all quarters of Canada, and with this view they propose to divide the Stock amongst the different towns and cities throughout the Dominion, in allotments suited to the population and business occupations of the different localities, and the interest which they may be supposed to take in such an enterprise.

Contracts of Connections.

A contract, granting permanent connection and extraordinary advantages, has already been executed between this Company and the Atlantic and Pacific Company, of New York ; thus, at the very commencement, as the Lines of this Company are constructed from the Suspension Bridge, at Clifton (the point of connection) to any point in the Dominion, all the chief cities and places in the States, touched by the Lines of the Atlantic and Pacific Telegraph Company, are brought in immediate connection therewith.
A permanent connection has also been secured with the Great Western Telegraph Company, of Chicago, whereby this Company will be brought into close connection with all the Lake Ports and other places through the Northwestern States, and through to California.
                                                   4-3mos

Miscellaneous.

GOLD &   [image]   SILVER
STEAM   STAMP
QUARTZ   CRUSHER,
(JAMES'   PATENT).

Dickey, Neill & Co.,
ENGINEERS AND BOILER MAKERS,
SOHO FOUNDRY, TORONTO, ONT.,
Sole Manufacturers for the Dominion.

THIS Machine is warranted for two-thirds the price, to do the work of any ordinary Ten Stamp Mill, and is the most perfect Crushing Machine in the world.
Engines and Boilers of all sizes, and Mill Machinery
OF EVERY DESCRIPTION ON HAND.
Send for Circular and Price List.   31-6m

Extract of Hemlock Bark—Extract of Oak Bark.

Important to Tanners, Merchants, Machinists, Lumbermen and Capitalists seeking for a Remunerative and Profitable Investment in Canada.

THE IRVING BARK EXTRACT COMPANY OF BOSTON have succeeded in perfecting a Machine for obtaining by compression from unground Bark, all the astringent and Tanning properties of Hemlock and Oak Bark.
By the operation of this Machine, which can be taken into the forests of Canada, on the spot where the Bark is peeled, the actual Tanning principle of the Bark is extracted by compression, and is produced in so concentrated and so small a bulk, that it can be conveyed to market, ready for use, at a mere fractional part of the expense required to freight the crude Bark ; 40 galls. of this Extract, weighing 400 lbs., can be obtained from one cord of first quality of Hemlock Bark, and this is worth for home use or for eXportation $20 per barrel.
We are now ready to grant licenses or to receive orders for these Machines.
☞ Any further information may be obtained by addressing
THOR. W. JOHNSON,
At American House,
Boston, Massachusetts.
nov21—14-1yr

The Mercantile Agency,
FOR THE
PROMOTION AND PROTECTION OF TRADE
Established in 1841.
DUN, WIMAN & Co.
Montreal, Toronto and Halifax.
REFERENCE Book, containing names and ratings of Business Men in the Dominion, published annually.   24-1y

The St. Lawrence Glass Company
ARE now manufacturing and have for sale,
COAL OIL LAMPS,
Various styles and sizes.
LAMP CHIMNEYS,
of extra quality for ordinary Burners also, for the 'Comet' and 'Sun' Burners.
SETS OF
TABLE GLASSWARE, HYACINTH GLASSES,
STEAM GUAGE TUBES, GLASS RODS, &c.,
or any other article made to order, in White or Colored Glass.
KEROSENE BURNERS, COLLARS and SOCKETS, will be kept on hand.
DRUGGISTS' FLINT GLASSWARE, and
PHILOSOPHICAL INSTRUMENTS,
made to order.
OFFICE—388 ST. PAUL STREET, MONTREAL.
A. McK. COCHRANE,
8-1y   Secretary.

Miscellaneous.

Western Canada Permanent Buil Savings Society.
OFFICE—No 70 CHURCH STREET, TO
SAVINGS BANK BRANCH,
DEPOSITS RECEIVED DAILY.   INTEREST P YEARLY.

ADVANCES
Are made on the security of Real Estate, rep most favourable terms, by a Sinking I
WALTER S
35-1y   Se

Canada Permanent Building and Society.

Paid up Capital .... $
Assets ....
Annual Income ....

Directors:—JOSEPH D. RIDOUT, Presi
PETER PATERSON, Vice-President
J. G. Worts, Edward Hooper, S. Nordhein
Chewett, E. H. Rutherford, Joseph Rot
Bankers:—Bank of Toronto ; Bank of Mon
Canadian Bank.
OFFICE—Masonic Hall, Toronto Street.
Money Received on Deposit bearing five cent. interest.
Advances made on City and Country Property i of Ontario.
J. HERBERT
36-y   S.

STAMP MILLS,
WHEELER PANS,
And other amalgamating Apparat:
SETTLERS, &c.
STEAM ENGINES, BOI
And all sorts of
GOLD MINING MACHINERY,
Of the most approved description,
G. & I. Brown's
Machine Shop and Agricultural
BELLEVILLE.

PROSPECTING MILLS
Worked by Hand, Horse, or Machine
Parties going into Gold Mining in the Qui will do well to have their machinery on the spot and save freight.
Belleville, April, 1868.

J. H. Boyce,
NOS. 63 and 65, Great James Street, Mor and Importer of all kinds of TOYS and FA J. R. B. is the only manufacturer of La Cro the new Indian Game of LACROSSE, and has hand a large supply, with the printed Rule He also manufactures all the requisites for all other Parlour and Lawn Games. Beskets and every variety of Hair Work, Wigs, Curls Dress and Theatrical Wigs, for sale. Wholesa Parties engaged in forming new La Crosse well to apply direct to the above address.

The Albion Hotel
MONTREAL,
ONE of the oldest established houses in th under the personal management of
Mr. DECKER,
Who, to accommodate his rapidly increasin adding Eighty more Rooms to the hous ALBION one of the Largest Establishments in
June, 1868.

Geo. Girdlestone,
FIRE, Life, Marine, Accident, and Sto Agent
Very best Companies represent
Windsor, Ont. June, 1868

Financial.

Pellatt & Osler,

ND EXCHANGE BROKERS, Accountants,
or the Standard Life Assurance Company and
auality Insurance Company.
— 86 *King Street East, four Doors West of
Church Street, Toronto.*

ELLATT,   EDMUND B. OSLER,
otary Public.   *Official Assignee.*

OWN'S BANK.

F. R. Brown.   W. C. Chewett.)

NG STREET EAST, TORONTO,

7TS a general Banking Business, Buys and
ew York and Sterling Exchange, Gold, Silver,
s and Uncurrent Money, receives Deposits sub-
que at sight, makes Collections and Discounts
l Paper.

*Mail or Telegraph promptly executed at
ost favourable current quotations.*

ress letters,   "BROWN'S BANK,
Toronto."

dian Land and Emigration Company

rs for sale on Conditions of Settlement,

OD FARM LANDS

n the County of Peterboro, Ontario,

l settled Township of Dysart, where there are
Grist and Saw Mills, Stores, &c., at

DA-HALF DOLLARS AN ACRE.

idjoining Townships of Guilford, Dudley, Harcourt and Bruton, connected with Dysart and
l of Haliburton by the Peterson Road, at ONE
in Acre.

her particulars apply to

CHAS. JAS. BLOMFIELD,
     Secretary C. L. and E. Co., Toronto.
ALEX. NIVEN, P.L.S.,
     Agent C. L. & E. Co., Haliburton]

Insurance.

**Liverpool and London and Globe
Insurance Company.**

and Reserved Funds......$17,005,000.
DAILY CASH RECEIPTS,....$20,000.

.E. IS HEREBY GIVEN, that 'this Company
'ing deposited the sum of

150,000 Dollars,

iance with the Act, 31st Vic., cap. 48, has received
nse of the Finance Minister, to transact the busi-
ife and Fire Insurance in the Dominion of Canada.

G. F. C. SMITH,
     Chief Agent for the Dominion.

lartford Fire Insurance Company.

HARTFORD, CONN.

'apital and Assets over Two Million Dollars.

$2,026,220.29.

CHARTERED 1810.

old and reliable Company, having an established
iness in Canada of more than thirty years standing,
iplied with the provisions of the new Insurance
d made a special deposit of

$100,000

e Government for the security of policy-holders, and
itinue to grant. policies upon the same favorable
s heretofore.

ally low rates on first-class dwellings and farm
y for a term of one or more years.

is as heretofore promptly and equitably adjusted.

E. CHAFFEY & Co., AGENTS.
ato, Ont.

'BERT WOOD, GENERAL AGENT FOR CANADA

Insurance.

The Standard Life Assurance Company,

Established 1825.

WITH WHICH IS NOW UNITED

THE COLONIAL LIFE ASSURANCE COMPANY.

Head Office for Canada :
MONTREAL—STANDARD COMPANY'S BUILDINGS,
No. 47 GREAT ST. JAMES STREET.

Manager—W. M. RAMSAY.   *Inspector*—RICH'D BULL.

THIS Company having deposited the sum of ONE HUN-
DRED AND FIFTY THOUSAND DOLLARS with the Receiver-
General, in conformity with the Insurance Act passed last
Session, Assurances will continue to be carried out at
moderate rates and on all the different systems in practice.

AGENT FOR TORONTO—HENRY PELLATT,
KING STREET.

AGENT FOR HAMILTON—JAMES BANCROFT.

6-6mos.

Fire and Marine Assurance.

THE BRITISH AMERICA

ASSURANCE COMPANY.

HEAD OFFICE :

CORNER OF CHURCH AND COURT STREETS.

TORONTO.

BOARD OF DIRECTION :

Hon G. W. Allan, M. L. C.,	A. Joseph, Esq
George J. Boyd, Esq.,	Peter Paterson, Esq.,
Hon. W. Cayley,	G. P. Ridout, Esq.,
Richard S. Cassels, Esq.,	E. H. Rutherford, Esq ,

Thomas C. Street, Esq.

Governor:

GEORGE PERCIVAL RIDOUT, Esq.

Deputy Governor:

PETER PATERSON, Esq.

Fire Inspector: Marine Inspector:
E. ROBY O'BRIEN.   CAPT. R. COURNEEN.

Insurances granted on all descriptions of property
against loss and damage by fire and the perils of inland
navigation.

Agencies established in the principal cities, towns, and
ports of shipment throughout the Province.

THOS. WM. BIRCHALL,
23-1y   Managing Director.

Edinburgh Life Assurance Company.

Founded 1823.

HEAD OFFICE—22 GEORGE STREET, EDINBURGH.

Capital, ... £500,000 Ster'g.
Accumulated and Invested Funds, £1,000,000 "

HEAD OFFICE IN CANADA:

WELLINGTON STREET, TORONTO.

SUB-AGENTS THROUGHOUT THE PROVINCE.

J. HILLYARD CAMERON,
Chairman, Canadian Board.

DAVID HIGGINS,
Secretary, Canadian Board.   3-3m

Queen Fire and Life Insurance Company,

OF LIVERPOOL AND LONDON,

ACCEPTS ALL ORDINARY FIRE RISKS
on the most favorable terms.

LIFE RISKS

Will be taken on terms that will compare favorably with
other Companies.

CAPITAL,   •   •   •   **£2,000,000** Stg.

CHIEF OFFICES—Queen's Buildings, Liverpool, and
Gracechurch Street London.
CANADA BRANCH OFFICE—Exchange Buildings, Montreal.
Resident Secretary and General Agent,
A. MACKENZIE FORBES,
13 St. Sacrament St., Merchants' Exchange, Montreal.
WM. ROWLAND, Agent, Toronto.   1-1y

Insurance.

**Reliance Mutual Life Assurance
Society.**

(Established, 1840,) OF LONDON, E. C.

Accumulated Funds, over $1,000,000.

Annual Income, $300,00.

THE entire Profits of this long-established Society belong
to the Policy-holders.

HEAD OFFICE FOR DOMINION—MONTREAL.

T. W. GRIFFITH, Manager& Sec'y.
15-1y   WM. HENDERSON, Agent for Toronto.

Ætna Insurance Company of Dublin.

The number of Shareholders exceeds Five Hundred.

Capital, $5,000,000—Annual Income nearly $1,000,000.

THIS Company takes Fire and Marine Risks on the most
favorable terms.

T. W. GRIFFITH, Manager for Canada.
Chief office for Dominion—Corner St. Francois Xavier
and St. Sacrament Sts., Montreal.
15-1y   WM. HENDERSON, Agent for Toronto

Scottish Provincial Assurance Co..

Established 1825.

CAPITAL, ...£1,000,000 STERLING.
INVESTED IN CANADA (1864) ....$500,000.

Canada Head Office, Montreal.

LIFE DEPARTMENT.

CANADA BOARD OF DIRECTORS:

HUGH TAYLOR, Esq., Advocate,
Hon. CHARLES WILSON, M. L. C.
WM. SACHE, Esq., Banker,
JACKSON RAE, Esq., Banker.
WM. FRASER, Esq. M. D., Medical Adviser.

The special advantages to be derived from Insuring in
this office are :—Strictly Moderate Rates of Premium ;
Large Bonus (intermediate bonus guaranteed ;) Liberal
Surrender Value, under policies relinquished by assured ;
and Extensive Limits of Residence and Travel. All business disposed of in Canada, without reference to parent
office.

A DAVIDSON PARKER,
     Resident Secretary
G. L. MADDISON,
15-1yr   AGENT FOR TORONTO.

Lancashire Insurance Company.]

CAPITAL, • • • • • • • £2,000,000 Sterling

FIRE RISKS

Taken at reasonable rates of premium, and

ALL LOSSES SETTLED PROMPTLY,

By the undersigned, without reference elsewhere.

S. C. DUNCAN-CLARK & CO.,
     General Agents for Ontario,
N. W. Corner of King & Church Streets,
25-1y   TORONTO.

Ætna Fire & Marine Insurance Company.

INCORPORATED 1819.   CHARTER PERPETUAL.

CASH CAPITAL,   •   •   • $3,000,000

LOSSES PAID IN 50 YEARS, 23,500,000 00.

JULY, 1868.

ASSETS.

(At Market Value.)

Cash in hand and in Bank..........	$544,842 39
Real Estate.................................	253,967 99
Mortgage Bonds........................	932,945 00
Bank Stock...............................	1,272,670 00
United States. State and City Stock and other	
Public Securities	2,049,855 51
Total.................	$5,052,580 19

LIABILITIES.

Claims not Due, and Unadjusted	$499,808 55
Amount required by Mass. and New York	
for Re-Insurance.........................	1,455,267 15

E. CHAFFEY & CO., Agents.
50-6m

THE CANADIAN

IONETARY TIMES

AND

INSURANCE CHRONICLE.

OTED TO FINANCE, COMMERCE, INSURANCE, BANKS, RAILWAYS, NAVIGATION, MINES, INVESTMENT, PUBLIC COMPANIES, AND JOINT STOCK ENTERPRISE.

II—NO. 9.   TORONTO, THURSDAY, OCTOBER 15, 1868.   { SUBSCRIPTION $2 A YEAR.

Mercantile.

Meetings.

NARROW GAUGE RAILWAYS.

A Public Meeting was held in the St. Lawrence Hall, Toronto, on the 13th inst., and for the purpose of considering the propriety of granting a bonus of $250,000 towards the construction of the Toronto, Grey and Bruce Railway, and $15,000 to the Toronto and Nipissing Railway. The Mayor occupied the chair, Mr. Chas. Robertson acted as Secretary. There was a large attendance of the citizens.

Mr. Jas. G. Worts, President of the Board of Trade, rose and moved the first resolution affirming the desirability of the proposed roads in the interests of this City, the districts through which they are to pass, and the Province at large. Mr. Worts proceeded to refer to the gradual growth of the city from a muddy little village to its present proportions. He also dwelt upon the advantage of the existing railways to the trade of the city, and the sums voted by Toronto for their construction, and for building the Esplanade. The city could well afford to give the sums asked, and in proof of that he pointed to the rapid progress in building and the steady increase in the value of property. Hamilton had agreed to give $112,000 in Great Western Railway stock to build a railroad, not into Hamilton, but from Guelph to Elora, and the nearest point of that road would be 40 miles from Hamilton. If, then, Hamilton could afford to give that sum for such a purpose, what could Toronto afford to give for 70 miles of railway north-east and 70 miles north-west, and both terminating in the city? It was estimated that the increase of taxes, resulting from granting the proposed bonuses, would amount to only $1.50 on every $1,000 of assessment. Though the amount was large he, as the largest tax-payer in the city, was willing and glad to give it. He thought the smaller ratepayers would say the same. The money could be raised in Canada, excepting that they would have to go to England for the railroad iron. As a consequence they would not have to send large sums out of the country every year to pay interest, as was the case with other public works. He pointed out, in concluding, that it was the railways of Chicago that made her what she is, giving her such facilities for bringing forward the produce of the country to a shipping port. This trade largely contributed to make her what she was—the largest grain market in the world.

Ald. Manning seconded the resolution, and ably supported it at considerable length. It was then put to the meeting and unanimously carried.

Mr. Wm. Gooderham moved the second resolution, specifying the amount of the bonus, and requesting the Council to submit By-laws to the people, authorizing the appropriation.

Mr. John Crawford seconded the resolution, and argued in support of it at some length.

Mr. John Gordon, of Gordon & McKay, also supported the resolution. One reason he did so, was because the city would be directly benefitted to an incalculable extent, and because the control of them would be left among themselves: to all intents and purposes the roads would be Canadian, raised of money in Canada, for the good of Can-

ada, and managed by Canada men, in Canada. He concluded by urging them to aid the scheme with the subscription asked.

Ald. Medcalf and Mr. John Nasmith spoke in support of the revolution, and Mr. A. Fleming and James Beaty, M. P., against, when, on being put to the meeting, it was carried unanimously.

After three cheers for the Queen the assemblage dispersed.

Mining.

THE STEVENS FLUX.

A correspondent of the Chicago *Tribune* writes as follows :—

Fluorine, one of the components of fluor, and likewise of the residuum from the cryolite, is a gaseous materal. Its usefulness in smelting quartz ores has been known in Freiberg for many years, and has been there turned to practical account. Flour spar is found in quite a number of veins in Saxony, and in particular abundance in the royal mine Chur Prinz, near Freiberg. The boys, who break and sort the ores raised from this mine, receive 2½ groschen, about 5 cents of our money, for each hundred weight of fluor spar separated pure from the mineral and gangue. The fluor spar thus obtained is used in smelting, simply and solely in order to volatilize a portion of the quartz in the form of fluor silicic acid ; while the calcium remaining, combines with another portion of quartz and forms a slag, which runs or is tapped off. The residuum from cryolite would act in a precisely similar manner and might be used with advantage in smelting certain quartz ores, provided it cost little or nothing ; for many ores it would be worse than useless. Even if it were as useful as its advocates claim, it could not be used with profit, for the simple reason that the cost per ton of its transportation to any of our new territories would alone be greater than the average yield of the quartz. For example, a ton of the flux laid down here in Montana would cost not less than $40, and we can, with such a yield of gold, return a clear profit of at least $25 per ton of ore, and, further, smelting is a process adapted only to those localities where labour fuel and all materials are attainable at the lowest prices, and solely for lead and copper ores. In England, in Germany, and, in general, on the continent of Europe, common labor receives twenty-five cents to fifty cents of our money for a full day's work of twelve hours at the furnaces. In Mexico, likewise, the common laborer is content with 25 cents to 37½ cents per day; good miners receive in the lowlands 50 cents per day; or for three holes, each sixteen inches in depth, and in the mountains 62½ cents, and in rare instances 75 cents for a like amount of work. In none of the above mentioned localities is the cost of living excessive. On the other hand, in California and Nevada miners and mill hands receive from $2.50 to $4 coin per day, and are often hard to be got even at the latter figure. Here in Montana $5 currency is the ordinary per diem, except during winter, when good hands are forced to work at prices varying from $40 to $60 per month and board. Hence it is that all successful mining and reduction have, up to the present time, been confined to such ores as are workable without excessive handling. That is to say, amalgamation has been successful, and smelting, except for the very richest ores, unsuccessful. California has expended thousands in attempting to smelt such of her ores as could not be amalgamated, and the result has been, in an economical point of view, uniformly unfavorable; technically, the smelting has been all that could be wished for —the metal or regulus has separated cleanly from the slag, and the precious or useful metals have been obtained as perfectly as in any of the European works, but it has always failed to pay. And why? For the simple reason that in smelting, too much handling, too much manual labor was required. This is an obstacle which time will overcome, but in a manner the reverse of agreeable to the laborer. The amalgamation, on the other hand, is almost entirely accomplished by machinery; a few attendants only being required to overlook the tireless stamps and the obedient grinders in the pans. Mines yielding free gold may be worked to a profit in California, under favorable conditions as to size of vein, proximity to lines of easy communication with the great cities, etc., when the yield per ton is only $5; and on the average, in the State, when the ores contain about $15 per ton. Free gold in Montana may, also, be worked to a profit where the average yield is about $15 per ton.

If the metal be locked up in sulphurets of iron, (pyrites), it may be very satisfactorily extracted by roasting and by Plattner's chlorination process, which would not cost, under average conditions, to exceed $20 per ton.

Amalgamating silver ores must contain at least $30 per ton to cover the cost of extraction, and that only where a preliminary roasting is not required. When the latter is the case they may cost from $6 to $10 per ton extra for calcining.

Lead ores, which contain silver, can only be reduced by the smelting process, and must contain at least $60 per ton to pay expenses under the now existing conditions. In the new Territories, the lead now produced is practically valueless, since the cost of transportation to a market renders competition with the lead regions of the West impossible. This, more than any other circumstance, renders smelting the least desirable. It is true that, by the fire process, there is saved a greater percentage of the precious metals contained in the ore, but, as an offset, there is required a far greater expenditure of labor and a more frequent reworking of the by-products. The amalgamation has, we may say, no by-products which require a reworking. The tailings are frequently of sufficient value to warrant a rehandling, particularly where the ore is rich in sulphurets. These, by the action of the moisture and oxygen of the atmosphere, aided frequently by a small addition of common salt, become decomposed and the contained precious metal or metals then readily lend themselves to the process of amalgamation.

To return, however, to the flux of Stevens. It is stated " that sulphuretted ores, which, by common process, yielded $300 per ton, were by amalgamating with the cryolite residuum, made to yield $1,400 per ton." The report is not sufficiently definite ; it does not state what the common process was ; it does not state in what form the gold was reduced nor in what metal, probably lead, the reduced gold was collected. That the gold was obtained at once in a button of the pure metal is improbable, not to say impossible, and the same or greater advantage as a flux might, with better reason, be conceded to pure soda, litharge or borax. Most absurd and illogical of all is the statement in regard to the 2,500 lbs. of Ackworth ore from the State of Georgia. According to the mint assay, there was contained the sum of $22 per ton, and this miraculous flux succeeded in extracting $481 per ton. In such a case we have a choice between two conclusions ; that is either the mint assay was incorrect, or that Colonel Stevens has discovered the true philosopher's stone, and can put gold where nature has not been so accommodating; or to make use of an expressive vulgarism, Colonel Stevens is able to "extract blood from a turnip."

It is worse than absurd to credit the flux with these superhuman capabilities, and the conditions of the experiment are not stated in sufficient detail to render it worthy of more than passing criticism. The report further states that "the flux is efficacious in detaching the gold from the sulphurets of iron and copper, and that to the presence of fluorine is due the remarkable fluidity of the melted mass, which allows the unoxydized metals to sink to the bottom of the crucible in clean detached globules." All this is entirely an error. If the gold be free there is no need or smelting, and if in combination, the fluorine of the flux will not separate it. On the contrary, the fluorine attacks the quartz preferable to the sulphurets, and eliminating one portion of the quartz as fluor silicic acid sets the calcium free to unite with another portion of the quartz to form a slag. The metals, whether free or combined with sulphur, will sink to the bottom, and in the latter case, will form a matter which must be subjected to a new treatment before the precious metals can be obtained free. To bolster up the flux, the name of Dr. A. A. Hays, of Boston is introduced, who indulges in some glittering metallurgical generalities in regard to smelting with the flux, with or without common salt. Dr. Hays is doubtless a good practical chemist ; but his remarks in regard to smelting with salt shew an entire misconception of the uses of that material. Salt has been used in smelting sulphurets, and then only with a view to making the matter more easily breakable ; the sulphide of calcium formed in the process of reduction, is a deliquescent body ; draws water from the atmosphere, and, as a result, the matter crumbles to powder, at the same time omitting sulphuretted hydrogen. It has always been found too expensive an adjunct to be at all universally introduced ; and if too costly where labor is very cheap, it would be still more applicable to our territories, where labor is so high.

In fine, whatever may be the merits of the cryolite residuum, salt, &c., as a laboratory flux, they have only a very circumscribed applicability, and even then would certainly yield the preference to borax or litharge, which, in a far wider sense, may be nominated universal fluxes. Sulphuret, yielding gold well up in the hundreds, are quite the exception, and for such Plattner's chlorination process affords the best and speediest method of reduction. Quite a number of such works are now in operation in California with uniformly favorable results.

Colonel Stevens has made a "mountain of a mole hill," and his so-called discovery might as well, for all practical purposes, be at once "consigned to the tomb of the Capulets."

THE CHLORINATION PROCESS.—This process, which is spreading rapidly in California, and has proved profitable in every case where there was a good supply of sulphurets and management by competent men, is to be introduced in Arizona. A gentleman familiar with the process has gone to erect a furnace at the Sterling mine, near Prescott, and it is reported that a contract has been made that if the rock yields well to chlorination, certain gentlemen of San Francisco shall buy the mine for $80,000. There is a lode, ten feet thick, full of metalliferous sulphurets, and near the surface it yielded a large amount of free gold, as much according to rumour, as $500 per ton. A mill, however, with the common apparatus for amalgamation failed to pay after the decomposed quartz had been worked, and all the attempts made to extract the gold from deep-lying sulphurets have failed. If chlorination succeeds with one it is supposed that Arizona will come right up, for there is more quartz in one county of that territory, than half of California. The gold, however, is found in connection with the sulphurets of lead and Antimony, and will not be caught by the copper plate or quicksilver. The quartz lodes have the same general character throughout the Territory, being highly mineralized.

MINING LAWS.—As the Gold Mines b[...] come an acknowledged branch of indus[...] one of the main sources of revenue to t[...] vince, it behoves the Goverment to foster every way by protecting the rights of miners and giving increased security and agement to investors. Among the impro[...] which suggest themselves or from time have been suggested to us, we enume[...] following, though some of them have been noticed :

In order to test the depth to which qua[...] ing may be extended, the Government mig[...] half the expense of carrying down a [...] eight hundred feet ; the other half being [...] the principal Gold Mine proprietors in t[...] vince.

Now, with an accumulation of evidenc[...] favour, the prosecuting a deep search country is no lottery, but rather a duty o[...] science and investors ; it is more than [...] that good paying ore would be met wit[...] descent which would cover the whole cos[...] experiment ; and, even, if it did not, the[...] ledge to what depth the quartz veins safely followed is one of such pressing im[...] that it can hardly be too dearly purchas[...] areas. Again, one company's means may be absorbed in machinery, building dams, &c., and oth[...] work ; and yet the excess of labour bey[...] statute requirements will not be taken in sideration in the next year's account w[...] Dominion. Not to issue a prospecting for private lands, until the owner has had day's notice of the application. Not to receipt for mining leases or to private land the application can show the owner's cons encourage prospecting and substantially[...] discoverers. The single free claim is [...] better than a white elephant. To abolish areas. To have lithographed maps for trict. To appoint a registrar in every p[...] district, and in the unproclaimed to hav an acting deputy commissioner. To pu[...] tistics regularly and frequently. To m[...] form of statistics so as to give fuller info[...] To compel mining records. To institut[...] search or enquiry at the Mines Departme[...] To purchase the best quartz specimens t[...] be found, and to preserve them in the To engage the professors of Geology at vincial Colleges occasionally to visit a[...] upon the districts.—From Heatheringto[...] to the Gold Fields of Nova Scotia.

COAL MINING.—The Montreal Gazette A company is being formed in this cit[...] purpose of developing and working a new eral coal deposit at Picton. This deposi[...] examined and favourably reported on by LIAN LOGAN, and lies along the track of extension railway, in the immediate vicin[...] intercolonial mine. The capital of the pany, which is to be called "The Picton, fixed at $50,000, and a considerable por amount has already been subscribed for.

—The Huron Copper Bay Company h[...] a dividend of 15 per cent for the half ye[...] 45 per cent for the year, payable on Nov[...] Transfer books will be closed from 12th to the 4th November.

—New fish rails are being laid on sou[...] of the Port Hope and Beaverton Rail[...] embankment at Galloway Bridge is a [...] pleted.

URANCE MATTERS IN MONTREAL.

(From a Correspondent.)

MONTREAL, Oct. 13, 1868.

Quebec press and the *Daily News* of this
re engaged in a controversy respecting the
farshalship of Montreal, arising out of the
taken by the Corporation following on the
nce agents petitioning the Local Govern-
to abolish the office. I send you the pro-
gs taken at a meeting of the Insurance
nies held on Thursday. There were present:
ood, of the Ætna, (Hartford,) in the chair;
. Routh, Royal; Johnson, North British
rcantile; Rose, Commercial Union; Forbes,
; Stephens, London; Hobbs, Lancashire;
Liverpool and London and Globe; Be-
Home and Western; and Muir, of the
. It having been explained that the object
meeting was to consider whether some com-
action should not be taken by the Insurance
nies to discover the cause of the recent
ous incendiary fires, and to endeavour to
stop to the same. After the consideration
subject, it was

lved,—That a reward of $500 be offered by
surance Companies doing business in this
r such information as will lead to the arrest
nviction of the party or parties who have
ilty of the late acts of incendiarism.

lved,—That a petition be sent to the Corpo-
of this city praying that early action be
by them on Dr. Benard's motion relative to
re Marshal passed by the City Council on
d instant.

lved,—That, in view of the recent numer-
idently incendiary fires which have taken
n this city, and the total failure of the in-
itious under the Fire Marshal Act to discover
icendiaries, the Insurance Companies do
n the Legislature of Quebec, praying that
ice of Fire Marshal for the City of Montreal
lished.

ssrs. Wood, Forbes, Johnson and Smith
iamed a Committee to carry out the above
ions.

action of the Corporation in this matter
e excused, but that of the Insurance Agents
ither be excused or justified. I feel certain,
er, that the Government will not stultify
at the instigation of those who have them-
done so. I believe a change will soon be
by Mr. Austin's retiring from the office he
ind himself so incompetent to fill. Should
r the case, I believe that Mr. Perry and the
e of our fire brigade, are disposed to assist
xoming man, which they certainly have not
rith the present incumbent.

e my last, incendiarism has not been so fre-
one stable only, containing 9 horses, was
n Tuesday, 6th inst., but was extinguished
.ight loss; the same premises were attempted
like result on the 7th, and on the 8th a
iccessful attempt was made, by which the
was burned, but the horses were all got out.
owever, before several of them were injured
smoke.

Friday a fire occurred on the premises of the
L. B. Smith, a crockery store on St. Paul
at first it was feared it would be a total
but thanks to the efficient Water and Fire
ments, it was got under with a loss of less
$4000. The stock was insured with the
and some other American company, and the
rn, of Canada. The Citizens' lose about
on the building. The executors of the
were so pleased with the exertion of the Fire
e that they sent them a cheque for $100.
ondon and Liverpool and Globe, with the
British, suffered to the extent of $2000
on a small steamer, *St. Marie,* partly burnt

a few days ago near Quebec. The "Royal" and
"Commercial Union" had a narrow escape from
being in for a heavy loss at J. Hudson & Co.'s,
wholesale grocers, on the night of the 9th instant.
It appears the gas bracket got out of order, by
which the light communicated to the connecting
pipe, which melted and receded, burning up between the lath and plaster partition. Fortunately
it was early discovered, and by the timely arrival
and exertions of the Fire Brigade, it was got under
at a loss of about $100. The stock of goods on
the premises was valued at over $100,000.

Insurance business suffers much from unfair
competition and want of principle on the part of
the agents of some Companies. A risk of $20,000
cleared for Muskegon for a cargo of lumber, but
one Company by another at a reduction of premium amounting to over $40. This is a sample
of the way business is generally done here.

Our Fire Department have completed the monument in the Mount Royal Cemetery. I will
furnish you with some particulars of it in my
next. The Corporation have followed the course
of the Insurance Companies, and offer $500 reward
for the detection and conviction of the perpetra-
tors of the late acts of incendiarism. To my
mind, the Insurance Companies would have done
something in earnest, had they employed one or
two efficient detectives to fish out the parties; but
this might have interfered with the per centages
of some agents who have to pay all their expenses
out of their commission.

MARINE RECORD.—Kingston, October 8.—The
Schooner Defiance, lumber laden, from Toronto,
bound to Ogdenburg, went ashore on Snake Island
reef near this city, during the gale this morning.
The tug has gone to her assistance, and it is
thought she will be rescued from her present
dangerous position with but slight damage. It has
since been learned that she will prove a total loss,
and is insured.

PICTOU, Oct. 8.—The schooner Fulton, from
Toledo to Ogdensburg, loaded with 220,000 feet of
black walnut lumber, sprang a leak and was water-
logged abreast of Nicholson's Island in the gale of
last night. She is now at anchor in South Bay.
A tug and lighter, and steam pump, have been sent
for.

PORT COLBORNE, Oct. 8.—The barque Arabia,
of Kingston, loaded with wheat, for Kingston,
went ashore, during the gale this morning, behind
the east pier. There are two feet of water in her
hold now: the prospects of getting her off are good.
This vessel has been got off without serious damage.

DUNNVILLE, ONT. Oct. 8.—Schooner A. P. Wait
will be a total loss; cannot get to her assistance
with a tug. She will pound to pieces on the reef.
She was coal laden, from Cleveland to Toronto.

COLLINGWOOD, Oct. 10.—The schooner John
Drake, with cargo of corn from Chicago, W. H.
Brice commander, reports that to the eastward of
the Ducks, about 15 miles, a black fore-and-aft
schooner steering for Love Island is supposed to
have founded on Wednesday morning during a
heavy westward gale. She was within half a mile
of the Drake, carrying away bulwarks and boats,
and in an hour after daylight appearing nothing
could be seen of her from the mast-head with the
glass. She carried three jibs, and was about a
13,000 bushel vessel: appeared heavily laden.

PROPELLER PERSEVERANCE.—The propellor
Perseverance, which was destroyed by fire off Put-
neyville, on the morning of the 6th inst., some
particulars of which we gave last week, was a craft
of 632 tons burthen, old style, being built in 1864,
at St. Catharines, by L. Shickluna, rated A 2,
valued at $40,000 and was the property of the
Welland Railroad Company.

MARINE DISASTERS.—The following list of disasters to American shipping on the lakes we clip
from some of our American exchanges :—

The schooner Coaster is reported ashore at Grand
Haven.

A Milwaukee telegram says that the schooner

Glen Cuyler was struck by a propeller and sunk
on Thursday night. She was freighted with wood.

The schooner W. C. Grant, grain loaded, had
her small boat, topsail-yard, mainboom and mainsail carried away when about sixty miles from
Milwaukee. She put back to the latter port.

The schooner Colonel Glover, bound from Muskegon to Racine, lost about 20,000 feet of her deck
load of lumber during the passage across the lake.
The Captain entered a protest at Milwaukee, and
then cleared for his destination.

The schooner Jennie Mutlen a few days ago in
the Chicago river was slightly damaged. She
cleared for Muskegon for a cargo of lumber, but
returned minus her mainboom and mainsail. Her
centre-board was also damaged,—the result of
heavy weather.

The Milwaukee *Sentinel* of the 9th has the
following disasters :— "The schooner Wm. Arbuckle, of Racine, lay at the Wolfe River pier
during the storm, and was severely injured. Her
starboard quarter got caught under the pier and
was so badly wrenched that it has dropped fully
one foot; several holes were stove through the
outside planking, and several frames and every
stanchion on the starboard side broken; her stern
timbers are also started from the transom. She
arrived here yesterday morning in a leaky condition. Her damages are upwards of $1,000.

"The new schooner Bessie Boalt weathered the
gale at the same pier. She lost some timber heads,
and had her rudder post started and the rudder
broken from its fastenings.

"Another vessel, whose name is not given, lost
some timber heads and a portion of her rail at the
same place. The pier, of course, did not escape
without severe injury.

"The schooner Spy, bound from Sheboygan to
this port with a hole full of wheat and a deck load
of pork barrels, commenced making bad weather
when off our north point, Tuesday night, and was
obliged to jettison the barrels, 500 in number,
after which she succeeded in finding a lee and
weathered the storm without further mishap. She
arrived here on Wednesday evening. Her grain
sustained no damage. The barrels were worth upwards of $700. All efforts to release this vessel
from her unpleasant position just inside of the
harbor piers have thus far proved fruitless. The
united efforts of the powerful tugs Admiral Porter
and American Union, yesterday afternoon, failed
to start her an inch. Several hawsers were parted
in the attempt to pull her off. Last evening a
dredge was at work digging a channel alongside
of the vessel.

"The propeller Idaho, bound down with a full
cargo, undertook to leave our harbor about midnight, Wednesday, and run aground in the jaws
of the piers. The sea soon swung her athwartships
the harbor, her bow heading north and her stern
pounding heavily against the South Pier. Her
rudder, shoe, and stern-post were carried away,
and had it not been for the timely assistance rendered by the tug Tiffit she would no doubt have
pounded a whole into her hull and sunk. She
was brought into the river about 2 a.m. yesterday."

A despatch received from Buffalo states that the
bark H. P. Baldwin has arrived at that port with
about one-half of her cargo of corn in a damaged
condition.

The bark Golden Fleece, which got aground at
Chicago is still hard on. The schooner Champion
was keeping her company. The schooner Annie
Vaught, which was aground near these vessels,
was got off and towed to her dock, for the purpose
of discharging her cargo of lumber.

The bark Homer in endeavouring to make the
Chicago harbor on the 10th went on the bar, but
was got off in the afternoon by the tug Geo. W.
Wood without damage.

The schooner Blue Bell, which went ashore at
Grand Haven, on Tuesday night, is well up on the
beach, and it is thought she has broken in two.
She measures one hundred and fifty tons, old style
was built at Huron, by Bates, in 1844, received
large repairs in 1861, and rates C. 1.

The schooner Forfar, which went ashore off Muskegon at an early hour on the 8th, was a craft of 170 tons burden, rated B. 2 was built in the year 1855, received a general overhauling in 1865, and was the property of James Bowen, of Chicago. She was valued at $600, and insured for $3,500.

The bark City arrived at Marquette on Oct. 9th, in tow of the tug J, C. Morse, with her jib-boom, dolphin-striker and a spritsail-yard carried away. She was run into by the Morse in the De our Passage, a heavy gale blowing at the time. The tug was but slightly injured.

The Detroit Free Press of Thursday, says : "The owner of the schooner Glad Tidings received intelligence of that vessel being ashore on the north side of Lake Erie and near the Rond Eau. The Tidings, at the time of the disaster was taking on a cargo at a landing near that place, and had completed her load, but while attempting to get under way was driven on the beach. This shore there, abouts is favorable for getting her off, which will doubtless be the result without damage to the vessel. She is owned by D. Whitney, Jr., in this city, and is comparatively a new vessel. Some miles further down the lake a vessel is reported also ashore and full of water, supposed to be a Canadian craft. Her name we could not definitely ascertain, no further than that she hails from Lake Ontario, and, at the time, was loading timber. What her prospects are for getting afloat was not stated. The Magnet has gone to the schooner Tidings.

"The propeller Fountain City, which grounded on Beach Island, was got off yesterday morning by the propeller Atlantic, and arrived here. The nature of the damages sustained we were not informed. The schooner Juliet, by an awkward display of seamanship, mistayed yesterday, and came foul of Pittman's dock, doing more or less damage. The wrecker which left here a day or two since to visit the wrecks of the schooners Byphen and Contest, returned yesterday with the steam pump recovered from the former vessel, and the outfit of the latter craft. No bodies were discovered, though it is apprehended they have come to the surface and drifted out into the lake."

FIRE RECORD.—Thornhill, Oct. 3.—The house occupied by Mr. Gordon, in the village of Thorn hill, was consumed, together with the premises on the north adjoining, occupied by Archibald Campbell, tinsmith. Mr. Campbell had no insurance on his property, and will lose considerable ; both the shop and dwelling house were his own property, and were entirely consumed.

Augusta, Ont., Oct. 3.—A fire originating in an out-house extended to the two barns, hophouse and stable of Mr. Shoecroft, near this village, which with their contents were consumed. Partially insured, and loss heavy. The cause is supposed to be incendiarism.

St. John, N. B., Oct. 2.—Two houses on Pond Street owned by Mr. McCarthy and Mr. O'Keefe, and occupied by themselves and tenants, were destroyed by fire ; and the building adjoining, on the corner of Pond and George Streets, owned by Mr. Campbell, was considerably damaged.

Whitby, Ont., Oct. 7.—Mr. James Forsythe lost by fire two hundred loads of straw. Another large stack owned by Michael Tierney, was also burned at the same time. Total loss about $400 ; no insurance. It is said that a little boy thoughtlessly set the stacks on fire.

Toronto, Oct. 13.—A fire originated in the outhouses of Richardson's grocery store, corner of Teraulay and Albert streets, but was extinguished before much damage was done to the store. The property, which was the property of Mr. C. Fisher, weighmaster, was damaged to the extent of $400 weighmaster. Insured in the Liverpool and Home District for $2,000.

Lindsay, Oct. 12.—About half-past ten o'clock on Sunday night, Mr. Cullis' flour mill and house in Mariposa, were destroyed by fire. Loss about $10,000. The origin of the fire is unknown.

DANGERS OF LAKE INSURANCE.

The season of 1868, even so far, has not been a favorable one, and the great bulk of the lake losses are yet to come. October, and specially November are the disastrous months ; n our inland seas, against which the summer should have laid up its accumulated profits, on which to draw for the heavy losses that invariably attend the closing season. No such accumulations have been garnered this year, and there is no human probability that the companies can end the season without serious average loss. We beg leave, therefore, to suggest a few conservative ideas, which, if heeded, may break the force of the blow that is in reserve for the companies doing a lake business.

The Presidents themselves should take this matter in charge, and with a strong hand overrule agents whose tendencies are at all towards mal' practice. The points needing particular attention are Lines, Re-insurance, and rates :

1. LINES.—There is a large amount of property to be transported before the end of the season, and there will be plenty of business for every company (although there never is enough for every agent.) Lines, therefore, should be rigidly restricted to such minimum as each company may fix, and no departure from that sum permitted under any circumstances.

11. RE-INSURANCE.—The practice of accepting large amounts and re-insuring excesses is a pernicious one. It is opposed to all principles of sound underwriting, and is one of the most fruitful causes of grasping competition among agents. It should be broken up at any cost, and the rule adhered to without deviation, that each company will accept only such lines as it can carry alone. It is absurd to assert that the business cannot be conducted on this plan ; a schooner afloat can be managed quite as readily as a warehouse ashore ; and it will be, as soon as each company will say resolutely that it will neither grant nor accept re-insurance.

111. RATES.—There is no safety in cutting the rates at any time, and particularly in October and November. The printed tariff of the late Lake Association should be inflexibly adhered to, and, even at those figures, it is not probable that the premiums of the coming sixty days will equal the losses.

Nevertheless, as before remarked, the force of the November gales upon the companies may be broken by an adherence to full rates, moderate lines, and direct insurances. Will they heed the warning!—Monitor.

Railway News.

GREAT WESTERN RAILWAY.—Traffic for week ending 25th Sept., 1868.

Passengers......	$59,935 14
Freight and live stock......	41,633 03
Mails and sundries......	2,115 65
	$103,683 82
Corresponding Week of '67·	90,393 29
Increase......	$13,290 53

NORTHERN RAILWAY.—Traffic Receipt for week ending Oct. 3, 1868.

Passengers......	$4,989 16
Freight......	9,150 27
Mails and Sundries......	1,552 63
Total Receipts for week......	$15,692 06
Corresponding week 1867....	16,271 66
Decrease......	$579 60

CONTRACT.—The Witness learns that the proprietors of the Montreal Car Wheel Works have received a contract for nearly 800 wheels for a New Brunswick railway, of the kind called "change gauge," because they can be shifted on their axles to suit either the broad or narrow gauge railways.

MERCHANTS' UNION EXPRESS.—We learn f the Cincinnati Commercial that, after four w spent in negotiations, the Merchants' Union the American Express Companies were rece consolidated. The new company is to draw same percentage from the general revenue both do now. The object of the consolidatio to reduce competition and economize in man ment. It is claimed that this arrangement bring dividends to the stockholders—somet they have not seen for the past two years.

RIVERE DU LOUP RAILWAY.—The Mon Gazette refers to the rumor about closing Rivere du Loup railway, as follows :—The Ga Quebec papers, both French and English, been very much exercised about some state that the Quebec and Richmond and River Loup sections of the G. T. R. are to be c during the coming winter. We have never anything about this, and what is more, we if the managing officers of the railway have ei The excitement is in fact all about nothing if not about nothing, it may arise from the aciousness of our friends in the sister city the portion of road referred to is the least pr tive of the whole of the Grand Trunk system does not pay for the expense of keeping it op winter. But now that something is to be to the extreme eastern end, it should occur contemporaries that this is not a time at wh should be closed.

THE SOUTHERN RAILWAY.—The St. T Dispatch says : We believe that those inte in the construction of the Great Southern l railway will shortly hear good news respecti negotiations carried out for organizing an co influential enough to secure the co-operat American companies, and the subscription sufficient capital in the English market t struct the road and equip it with stock.

—New Station buildings have been erected Great Western at Paris. It is the intent establish a wood and water depot at the sta lot of land having already been purchased that view, reaching down to Smith's whence the water will be thrown by hy power into tanks at each end of the yard ; in the event of a fire occuring at any future there will be an abundance of water on h extinguish it, as well as to supply the engi

NOTICE TO SHIPPERS OF SEAMEN.—Mr. Starr, Ship Broker and Commission Ag Halifax, writes to the press to warn partie ested against the practice of getting seamen ping from Colonial ports to ports in the States and thence to any other port for wh vessel might get a charter, to sign shipping on board the vessel. The U. S. Courts ho articles so signed are not binding. Mr. the case of a Pictou vessel which shipped at that port for a round voyage. On the of the vessel at Portland, U. S., one man c and secured his discharge owing to the f he had signed articles on board the vessel. decision of the Courts is for the purpose venting Captains from getting men on los vessels while intoxicated, and obliging sign articles for a voyage and on terms, when sober they would not bind themselv Exchange.

LAUNCHES.—The Owen Sound Adver marks :—On the 17th of September the ne steam tug Okours, built and owned by M of this town, was successfully launched. intended for rafting and general purp Georgian Bay. On Saturday, the 28th made a trial trip, which gave entire satis her two and a half miles in ten Her dimensions are sixty-five feet length thirteen feet beam, depth of hold three fe is propelled by a sixteen-inch direct-acti pressure engine.

THE CANADIAN MONETARY TIMES AND
INSURANCE CHRONICLE *is printed every Thursday
Evening, in time for the English Mail.*

Subscription Price, one year, $2, *or* $3 *in
American currency ; Single copies, five cents each.
Casual advertisements will be charged ten cents
per line of solid nonpareil each insertion. All
letters to be addressed,* "THE CANADIAN MONE-
TARY TIMES, TORONTO, ONT." *Registered letters
so addressed are at the risk of the Publishers.
Cheques should be made payable to* J. M. TROUT,
*Business Manager, who will, in future, issue all
receipts for money.*

The Canadian Monetary Times.

THURSDAY, OCTOBER 15, 1868.

INSURANCE COMPANIES AND LITI-
GATION.

One of the morning journals recently published some remarks which reflected on Insurance Companies for taking advantage of
technical objections to defeat claims under
their policies, and made a few vague comments
on a case in which the BEAVER MUTUAL was
concerned at the Barrie assizes. There is no
reason why public companies should not be
allowed the same privileges as individuals in
our Courts of Law ; but this we do know,
that a prejudice exists against Corporations
of all kinds, so strong that juries do oftentimes stretch a good many points to favor
an individual when the contest lies between
him and a Corporation. In fact, a Corporation when it does battle against an individual,
need expect no mercy. A great many reasons
might be urged against the cultivation of such
an unjust prejudice, and public journals
should not lend themselves to the unworthy
task of encouraging and strengthening it. We
are prepared to admit that some Companies,
or rather Managers, have a morbid taste for
technicalities, but such supplies its own cor-
rective. The reputation acquired by those
who are fond of plunging into litigation is
neither enviable nor profitable, and Insurance Companies properly managed rarely
find themselves called on to exercise acute-
ness in discovering holes out of which to
creep. An Insurance Company cannot, for
its own sake, afford to become litigious, as it
has not only a deep rooted prejudice on the
part of juries to contend against, but also the
keen watchfulness and tell-tale tongues of its
rivals. Much less can it afford to be given

to technicalities, for what it gains from success on questionable grounds it loses tenfold
in popular estimation. The real fact is that
no institutions are so liberal, or so often called upon to waive technical objections as Insurance Companies. The despotic terrorism
under which they exist restrains them from
construing their contracts with too great
nicety. The nature of the business they do,
their dependence on public favor, and the
desire on the part of their agents to extend
operations, are so many preventives of undue
harshness. Of course there are exceptions in
this particular as in every other, but the
general rule is as we have stated.

Insurance Companies may be a great boon,
or a great curse to a country. It is hard to
say whether the advantages they confer in
the protection of the honest and industrious,
are not counterbalanced by the great temptations to crime they are the means of begetting.
Their readiness to yield their rights amounts
to a positive fault in many instances, and has
given rise to a species of despotic exaction
which has attained, through custom, almost
the dignity of law. The alarming increase in
the number of cases of incendiarism and arson
of late years, can be traced to no other cause
than the facilities afforded for escape from
the consequences of such crimes by the conduct of Insurance Companies themselves.

Their inconsiderate settlement of losses
without adequate inquiry; their patient submission to palpable fraud; their rash haste to
acquire a name for "prompt payment;" their
timid shrinking from the maintenance of their
rights; their supineness in securing the
punishment of crime, have produced evils
which should alarm every lover of his
country. When fraud obtains the upper
hand, and crime runs riot without check,
public morality must suffer. Viciousness
overawes virtue, and the honest poor, seeing
their less conscientious neighbours grow rich
by crimes in which large Corporations apparently acquiesce, are only too apt to give
way to that kind of logic which now obtains in the jury room, when a Corporation
attempts to defend itself against a demand
of any kind; whether just or unjust. The
degeneracy of the times is a source of frequent complaint on the part of the social
philosopher. The rapid increase of incendiarism and arson is terrible to think of. The
stab of the assassin may seal the doom of one
victim, but who can sum up in a word the
awful guilt of the wretch who, at dead of
night, applies the torch to his own or his
neighbour's dwelling; who exposes to the
most terrible of deaths the innocent and the
harmless; who, at one swoop, devours wife,
child and home, and leaves a broken-hearted
desolate one to go through life heavy-laden

with the woes brought upon him by a fellow-being whom he never wronged. He who stands between such a criminal and swift punishment does injustice to himself, to his family, to his neighbour and to his country.

That many of the fires which occur are the result of deliberate intent, we firmly believe, and to frustrate the designs of such as become criminals with that intent is, we hold, not only the duty of Insurance Companies but the interest of the public. If another man's house adjoins mine I have to pay more for insurance than I would have to do if my house were isolated. The connection of the two renders the risk the greater. If my neighbour sets fire to his house to secure his insurance money he may gain his object, but it will be doubtless by destroying my property. Have I no interest, then, in keeping him honest? The object of punishing crime is to deter others from attempting it. Is it not a duty I owe to myself, therefore, not to take any higher ground, to assist in furthering the ends of justice to the utmost of my power?

The ends of justice are certainly not furthered by pandering to popular prejudice, the offspring of ignorance, or laying blame on a class when one member only may be at fault. Nor are the ends of justice furthered by condemning a company for taking a certain line of defense, the reasons for which are unknown. In this very Beaver case, the real defence was, that plaintiff had set fire to his own premises, after having encumbered both real estate and chattels beyond their value, without notice to the company, and the defendants, if convinced that their grounds of suspicion were good, were perfectly justified in resorting to every means to defeat the claim; not only so but they were, we consider, bound to do so. However, as the counsel for the company has explained he did intend to go fully into the merits of the case were it not that the cause was at the foot of the docket and the presiding Judge, having to adjourn the assizes, could not spare so much time as a full examination of witnesses would have occupied. As the defendants were thus cornered up, they were driven to insist on objections of a technical character which placed the plaintiff out of court.

It will be found in nine cases out of ten in which insurance companies are concerned when technical objections are taken, that there is good and sufficient reason for so doing owing to the injustice of the claim. Often times a company cannot fasten the crime on a claimant although there is not a shadow of a doubt that he wilfully destroyed his premises. In such cases what are the companies to do? Are they to pay the claim and set a premium

on crime, or are they to muster courage enough to resist payment and thereby be heralded before the public as litigious? Even judges do sometimes give utterance to comments on cases in which insurance companies are concerned, which comments are not only uncalled for, but also unjust if all the facts were known. A case came within our own observation in which a Judge soundly berated a company for defending an action, and only stayed his criticism when informed by a learned brother by his side, that the plaintiff had been sent to the Penitentiary by that learned brother's own sentence for the crime of arson. In that case the objections relied upon by the defendants were technical, but their real defence was, that the plaintiff had set fire to the house covered by the policy. The gist of the matter is this. We have no excuse to offer for a company taking an undue advantage under a technicality where there is no bona fide defence, or litigating a claim where escape from liability would be unjust. But we do say, that to condemn a class for pursuing the opposite course, or to injure the many for the faults of one, or even a few, is not expedient, from a public point of view, nor just from a private one.

If the form of monthly statement returned to the Government were to distinguish between loans effected and maturing in Canada, from those maturing in the United States and England on some such plan as that indicated by Mr. Hogan, of the Bank of Toronto, in his elaborate and able answers to the inquiries of the Senate Committee last session, we should have full information as to the Bank of Montreal's operations in New York.

THE MONTREAL FIRE MARSHALS.

The Montreal City Council has decided to petition the Local Legislature for the abolition of the office of Fire Marshal, and the repeal of the Act creating it. We do not wonder that public indignation has been aroused by the improper use that has been made of the Act in the appointment of incapable officials, and the large increase of incendiary fires since the marshals were installed. No one supposes that these officers are guilty of fire raising though opinion is not so favourable to their deputy but it seems to be generally conceded that a more useless pair could not be secured for love or money than the two men who enjoy the dignity and emoluments of the Fire Marshalship. If the act is defective, and it is acknowledged on all hands, that it is, let it be amended; if the present incumbents are useless or worse let them be removed but to repeal the Act altogether does seem to savor of absurdity.

CANADIAN MONEY IN NEW YO[

At this season, when the circulation o banks is at its highest point, it is usua those institutions to remit to England i ticipation of January balances. This c is the safest, and ordinarily the most p able, as exchange is lowest in the fal highest in the winter. The Toronto *graph*, in a telling article, draws attentic the authority of the New York *Post*, · startling fact that Canadian Banks are funds, to the extent of six millions of d in the New York Gold Market. Th Canadian bank likely to engage in such ulations is the Bank of Montreal. Som ago we traced this practice home to bank, and pointed out how it was ind in at a time when the other Canadian were contracting their discounts to the imum by reason of the working of the vincial Note Act, and when the needs o country were the greatest. The Ba Montreal is the financial agent of the ernment of Canada, and if the people's i is to be withdrawn from this countr used for speculative purposes in the York Gold Room, Canada is certainly b and may consider itself fortunate in enabled thus to contribute to the div declared by the Bank of Montreal. bank's charter was intended to cover a mate banking business in Canada. being the case, these speculations in York are certainly without its true sph

We suppose the bank lends gold speculators in the Gold Room, to be within a certain period, United State being received as security, with a p sell, and a margin allowed for a fal rate given by operators for the use varies, of course, with the demand, from one-eighth to even three-quar cent. a day. This is rather a heavy interest, and the fact of its being paid that this class of customers is not to sired by a bank wishing to do a leg banking business.

PEAT AS FUEL.

There are three primary necessa human existence—meat, drink and In a civilized state of society all the to be produced by human skill and It is true, our flocks, herds and the tions of the field give us the first; n its countless springs, streams, and riv second; and the forests, coal depo of man is required to utilize the al resources that nature provides.

In primitive times the forests su sufficiency of fuel for the wants of

at the lowest cost ; as civilization ex-
ded, they gradually disappeared rendering
er and cheaper substitutes for wood neces-
y. In England, coal has chiefly supplied
place of wood, for there it exists in such
ndance as to force all other articles of fuel
of the market. But in those countries,
are coal is not indigenous, peat has, gener-
r, been found in large quantities. For hun-
ds of years the vast peat beds of Ireland
l the north of Germany have supplied fuel
o cheap a rate, that searching for coal has
n a needless task, even supposing that
h existed. In Canada, where the highest
horities have denied the existence of coal
osits, it has become a work of imperative
essity to cultivate the resources that
ure has kindly given us. There is not
slightest doubt of the existence of vast
s of peat in many sections of the Province,
l that it will take little time and trouble
discover them. But how are these to be
ned to profitable account ? This import-
problem is being solved ; in various parts
the country Peat Companies have sprung
o existence, and if they prove successful
may look for many more.

here are at present three organized com-
ies for the manufacture and sale of peat
fuel, the oldest and most extensive of
ch is the "Canada Peat Manufacturing
npany," next comes the " Anglo Ameri-
Peat Company," and lastly, a company
ned at Sorel.

'eat is undoubtedly the parent of coal,
latter having been formed by the pressure
superincumbent layers of heavy strata of
s on the once soft beds of peat, which
ain over a large portion of the earth's sur-
; pressure and the internal heat of the
h gave to the coal beds their hardness,
at the same time condensed. the com-
tible gases within certain prescribed lim-
This transformation took place especially
hose countries which have been exposed
igh volcanic action ; but, in other sections,
re the operations of nature have been
er, the result has been the formation of
vast peat beds which we find distributed
most parts of the world, and which
ess, in a diffuse degree, the chemical
position of coal.

eat is a sponge-like substance composed
quatic plants, mosses, grasses, and a
sty of shrubs and low trees, with the
s, leaves and branches in a state of deposition, exactly in the same place and
:ion in which they have grown and accu-
ted for ages. It is therefore an entirely
table compound, containing no extra-
s matter, except such as may have been
ied into it by floods and rains. There
wo sorts of peat.. One called the Black,

which is found on the sides of hills and
mountains in Ireland, which, when cut and
dried, becomes exceedingly hard, and without
any manufacturing process whatsoever, makes
excellent fuel. The other sort is Red peat;
which is the only description found on this
continent ; it grows abundantly in all shallow
pools, lakes or basins, where there is no outlet for the water. When cut from the bog
and dried, red peat is very light and loses
only some forty per cent. of its bulk by
shrinkage, but by evaporation it parts with
about eighty to ninety per cent. of its weight.
As cut from an undrained bog, peat contains
but very little solid matter ; and to manufacture one ton of fuel, it is necessary to dig
from six to eight tons of the raw material
The great difficulty consists in getting rid of
the immense quantity of water ; and from
the earliest times of peat manufacture, all
sorts of mechanical contrivances have been
resorted to, but so far without fully accomplishing the object, or if successful in doing
so, it has been at a cost, which has prohibited
its general manufacture as an article of commerce. But to thoroughly prepare it for the
market, a further process than the mere
expulsion of the water, is required, as
red peat still retains its sponge-like character, has a great tendency to expand, readily
absorbs moisture, and would not stand the
blast of a furnace. The further process is
performed by pulping, so as to entirely destroy the fibre or tube-like character of the
innumerable rootlets of which it is principally
composed, and this must be done before it is
subjected to the action of the atmosphere, or
dried to any considerable extent. When this
operation is properly performed, the pulped
mass is left to dry by natural evaporation,
and it becomes dense and hard in proportion
to the quality of the bog from whence it is
obtained. The result is a fuel of the purest
character, equal to the best and hardest burned
coke, in fact in some respects preferable, as peat
fuel, when well manufactured and dried, does
not readily absorb moisture, even when exposed for some days to the wet ; this has been
proved by the immersion of a piece of peat in
a pail of water for two hours, when the absorption was only 3½ per cent., not equal to
that of coke if exposed to a heavy shower of
rain, and little more than that of small
coal.

The material question with which we have
to deal is the cheapness with which it can be
supplied in comparison with wood and coal.
It is established beyond a doubt that for
every practical purpose of heating it can be
used to advantage. Firstly, for railways.
As locomotives are at present constructed, the
waste of steam power to create a blast or
draft is enormous, it being estimated that

about two-fifths of the whole quantity of fuel
is expended for that purpose. Now, well
dried peat requires but very little draft
through the furnace bars ; owing to the immense quantity of gas it evolves, it is necessary
for its complete combustion to admit the air
through the furnace door, and when the
furnaces are altered to meet the requirements
of peat fuel, at least twenty per cent. additional power will be given to all peat burning engines, or a corresponding decrease in
the quantity of fuel used, will be effected.
In proof of this we may state that the Grand
Trunk R. R. experiments have all proved so
satisfactory, as to result in a contract with
the Canada Peat Company, extending over
five years or seasons, during the first of which
the G. T. R. are to take 100 tons per day,
and during the four succeeding seasons 300
tons per day. That all railways will eventually
use peat is certain, as it is found by experiment to be cheaper and better than any fuel
at present in use, and the only reason they
have not more generally adopted it is, the
difficulty of making it in sufficient quantities.
One ton of well dried peat is fully equal in
heating power to one cord of best hard wood.
Another great advantage is that no sparks
issue from the smoke stack of a locomotive,
even with the present enormous blast, and
when the furnaces are specially adapted for
it, fires from sparks will be unknown ; a most
important consideration in our hot and dry
summers. For many years, even at a very increased rate of production, the railroads will
absorb the bulk manufactured, so that it may
be some time before it becomes an article of
general domestic use. But even supposing
such should not be the case for years, the
effect of its large production will be to decrease the price of other fuel, especially wood,
as every ton of peat used by either railway or
steamboat is the saving of one cord of wood.
If we estimate the enormous consumption
of wood for railway and steamboat purposes,
and the rapid way in which the forests are
cleared in the neighbourhood of all stations,
we can estimate the advantage the introduction of any new and cheap fuel will be.
Take Montreal, for instance ; the consumption
for domestic purposes alone, per annum, is
about 100,000 cords of wood, and 60 to 70,-
000 tons of coal. Every year our wood dealers
eave to go further and further back to obtain
their supplies at a greatly enhanced cost, and
the railroads which we at first welcomed as
the means of giving us cheap fuel (they
running through large wood districts), have
proved the very means of enhancing the value.
They will not bring it cheaply to market as
that would ultimately increase the price for
themselves, and therefore every ton of peat
consumed by them represents a cord of wood

set free for the markets of our towns. So much for the advantages accruing to the country generally by the use of peat on railroads. There is another branch of business for which it is admirably suited, viz., in all iron and smelting works. A trial was made at the Rolling Mills of Messrs. Morland, Watson & Co., and the specimen bar was equal to the very best Swedish iron. This trial was made in a furnace adapted to the use of coal, without any alteration; had such been made a large saving of fuel could have been effected. With the blast furnaces as at present constructed, peat could not be used alone, but by mixing it with Pictou coal an iron could be produced equal to the best charcoal iron, and superior to any description at present imported. With the extension of the manufacture of peat, this important use of it will doubtless attract the attention of our large iron workers. Of the value of peat as a domestic fuel the experience of centuries certifies in its favor, and its large introduction is a mere question of time.

This article is already so long as not to admit of any further remarks as to its mode of manufacture, or the quantities at present made.

WOODEN RAILWAYS.

There are many parts of the country that suffer from a lack of railway facilities, without any prospect of bettering their condition in that respect, unless they can secure a road less costly than an iron railway. The advantages to be derived from wooden railways seem to have impressed themselves very forcibly on the minds of such as have taken the trouble either to inspect the wooden railways at work near the United States' border or to go through the estimates and calculations furnished respecting their cost, working expenses and earnings. Lines of wooden railway are "projected" in both Provinces, Quebec and Ontario; in the former, there are three in embryo— from Lennoxville to Lake Megantis; from Arthabaska to Upton, and from Quebec to Gosford ; in the latter, from Meaford to Collingwood, and from North Douro to Haliburton.

Some time ago, we published an interesting letter from Mr. C. J. Bloomfield, the representative of the Canadian Land and Emigration Company, giving the result of a personal inspection by himself and others of the wooden railway which runs to the Clifton Iron Mines, near Ogdensburgh, a distance of twenty-four miles.

These gentlemen are of opinion that such railways would be of great service to Canada as feeders to main lines, and likely to prove active agencies in the development of remote settlements, or such sections of country as

do not enjoy the advantage of lines running near them. In the back country the material is ready to hand. A saw mill, a blacksmith shop, plenty of maple, and a comparatively small amount of capital are all the requisites. As to the cost, estimates, of course, must be based on the character of the country through which a line would run and the price of timber. At any rate, from two to four thousand dollars per mile may be taken as about the probable cost. The solid maple rails 4 × 6 inches, are wedged every three feet into heavy notched ties, the notch being made by machinery, and the wedges, two at each otch, from the waste of the maple rails. An few minutes suffice to unwedge the rails and lay down new ones. Being tightly notched in, the rails cannot warp sideways. It is said that the wood is made to make a curve in a way that would be found impossible with iron. Fine sand and dust which get on the rails are soon crushed into the wood by the car wheels and form a hard and gritty surface, which does not wear, and greatly facilitates the traction. The maple rail, if sound, will last a number of years, the average life being, according to a good authority, five years, as the wet weather does not materially affect it. Good, broad wheels are essential; where the rolling stock is heavy, the wheels have a rim five inches in width. The sleepers are not adzed. A speed of ten miles an hour for freight trains, and twenty miles an hour for passenger trains, may be attained on these roads without any more risk, where the road is properly built, than would be incurred by running at the same speed on iron rails. This rate is higher than is generally supposed as capable of attainment on wooden railways, and certainly is as much as is realized on some of our iron railways. One of the requisites for the successful working of wooden railways is that the locomotive shall be light, and also the goods carried. We have already given the estimate per mile for cost of superstructure, but we reproduce it now for the sake of those who may not have subscribed the subject attention:

1760 ties delivered at 10 cents	$176 00
21,120 feet b. m. maple rails	316 00
Wedges, say	40 00
Notching ties and track laying	468 00
	$1000 00

It is to be hoped that the present time will be taken advantage of by those interested in the development of the country to push forward schemes so fraught with benefit as are those for the construction of railways. Money is abundant, and the farmers and settlers were never in a better position to render assistance to such undertakings. Every one feels instinctively that this country has taken a fresh start, and if the opportunity be al-

lowed to slip by unimproved, we shall lay ourselves open to the charge of w enterprise, which our Yankee neighb frequently cast in our teeth. If we v retain our population and get our fair of foreign immigration, we must be doing, for we have a neighbor whose tells seriously upon our prosperity, energy is undaunted, and whose nai gone abroad throughout the earth. but do justice to ourselves and to Can shall have no reason to fear the mos getic competition. There is plenty of to be done here, let us give industry a to do it. There are lands to be cleare homes to be hewn out of the forest, a soil to be cultivated, and mineral tr to be unearthed, let us clear the way ling hands. If we cannot have broad let us have narrow gauges ; if iron r are beyond our reach, let us at lea wooden railways.

MARINE LOSSES.

Under the proper heading will be fo unusually long list of marine disasters. occurred mainly in American shipping seems to have had rough usage in the lat Our underwriters have been pretty fo so far, and now that the equinoctial s storms that usually follow immediate wake are passed they begin to feel co of a profitable season's business. W their expectations will be realized.

NEW PUBLICATIONS.

EXCHANGE TABLES, by H. Morton Festin Com. Gen. to H. B. M. Forces. G. E. Desbarats.

This book, which is very creditable in ance to the publisher, Mr. Desberats of contains tables for the conversion of Ster Dollars and Cents, and vice versâ. The contains 100 tables, rising by 8ths from also a table of differences at 1-16. The systematic and complete, and should place of Oates' tables, which have been l generally used. The testimonials from missary General, Mr. Sterling, of the Un of Halifax, Mr. Vezina, of La Banque N Mr. Woodside, of the Royal Canadian, vey, of the Audit Department, and othe in no measured terms in its favour, and great pleasure in expressing our satisfac the system on which the tables are b the admirable manner in which the com are devised. We commend this work to tion of Bankers, Brokers, and Merchant

ADJUSTMENT OF FIRE LOSSES, by J. Insurance Monitor Office, New York

We acknowledge, with thanks, the rec C. C. Hine, Esq., of New York, of a cop useful book. It is written evidently by djuster. The examples given are lucid, and r intricate losses in which both concurrent specific policies were concerned. The law ting to points likely to arise in adjustment is marized in an intelligible manner under opriate heads. By the way, it is stated, t "transfer of insured property to an assignee er a decree of bankruptcy is alienation." This it is not fully settled here, and we should like ee a legal decision on the subject. We com- id the following extract to Insurance Com- ies :—

All adjustments should be made without un- ssary or vexatious delays; no merely technical ivolous objections should be made; but honest ns, fairly established, should in all cases be as y met and liberally construed; and the insured ıld receive the full indemnity contemplated by contract. No responsible Company having care for its good name in the community ıld sanction any short-comings of its adjusters hese particulars. Any other course would be olitic, unjust, and highly reprehensible, and tend to add to the prejudices already engen- d in the minds of quite a portion of the com- ity against Insurance Companies, in conse- nce of the dishonest practices of many unprin- ed adjusters in the settlement of claims for k or restless institutions."

Ir. Griswold's compendium will prove a useful d-book to adjusters and fire underwriters erally.

RACTICAL TREATISE ON SAVINGS BANKS, by Arthur Scratchley, M.A. London: Longman. Toronto: Scott & Walmsley.

RACTICAL TREATISE ON BUILDING SOCIETIES, by Arthur Scratchley, M.A.

EATISE ON LIFE ASSURANCE AND REVERSIONS, by Arthur Scratchley, M.A.

NUAL OF CHURCH PROPERTY, by Arthur Scratchley, M.A.

We need say nothing in praise of Mr. Scratch- 's works. His abilities as an author and his inence as an actuary, have been recognised at ne and abroad. The books mentioned may be ained from Messrs. Scott & Walmsley, whom Scratchley has appointed his special agent for ierica.

T OF POST OFFICES IN CANADA. Hunter, Rose & Co., Ottawa.

This list is complete, up to 1st July, 1858, and braces the names of Postmasters, as well as a of Officers.

Mr. Thomas Drewry has been appointed assist- Secretary of the Provincial Insurance Compa- in place of Mr. William Murray, resigned.

The Stratford agency of the Western, of Can- , has been transferred to Mr. Hayward, late of Royal Canadian Bank.

MADOC GOLD DISTRICT.

(From our own Correspondent.)

Belleville, Oct. 12, 1868.

The confidence which was beginning to be par- lly resuscitated in our gold region, has suffered other severe shock in the failure of the Anglo- con mill. After six weeks' work, with thirty mps, three pans and thirty Wyckhoff oscillators, quantity of gold collected amounted to a mere le, while a loss of over 600 lbs of mercury was tained. This denouement has all along been dicted by most of our practical men, who have constantly averred that the company had no indications of the existence of a mineral vein in the locality where they chose to erect their works, and from the cursory examination I had the opportunity of making, I must say that I quite concur in that opinion. How the managers happened so far to be misled, I cannot explain, but no doubt they must have had some "big" assays to induce them to spend their money so freely as they have done.

The effect of these disappointments is, that the opinion is rapidly spreading among our mining men, that the amalgamating process will not answer for the successful treatment of the ores of this region,—that the gold is not in a form in which it can be collected by the use of mercury, and that some other method must be applied in order to get a remunerative return from our mines. It is also currently reported that the actual result of the crushing lately done at the Caldwell (Severn) mill was only $8.00 per ton, instead of $19.00, as given out, and that the latter figures were taken from a calculation as to what the return would have been if the work had been done upon clean veinstone, instead of a mixture of wall rock and other dead matter with the gangue, of which the auriferous quartz constituted only one-third.

The Fiegel mine, from which the above return was obtained, is now under an injunction, a suit in chancery having been entered on the subject of title.

The Richardson company have raised money to set their works in motion again, and are about to make another trial as to whether they can recover their lost lode.

The Merchants' Union company have had a meeting, and have determined to make some additions to their machinery, and to give their ore a practical trial.

Messrs. Jones & Robbins are pressing forward their reduction works to completion. When finished we shall have a fair trial of the effect of the much talked of Stevens flux. Much doubt is expressed by the initiated in mining matters as to the result both practically and financially, but the gentlemen principally interested are quite confident in the efficiency of the material, as well as the quantity of gold contained in the ores they are about to work, which are chiefly of the pyriteous class. I sincerely hope they may be right, and that the spirit they have shown may be suitably rewarded. If this process fails, there is only one other which can be brought into operation with any hope of success, and that is Chlorination, which has not yet been tried here, but which if used in connection with good concentrating machinery, and an efficient desulphurizing apparatus, such as Whelpley & Stover's water-furnace, may yet enable our miners to remunerate themselves for their labor and outlay in developing the mineral riches which exist in the rocks of the district; from the mills as at present constructed and worked, we have little to hope.

Financial.

MONTREAL MONEY MARKET.

(From our own Correspondent.)

Montreal, Oct. 13, 1868.

In the present state of the money market it is difficult to strike on any new feature. The great ease still continues, there is little demand for funds to send to the West. The banks hold large accumulations of moneys belonging to parties who usually at this season have plenty of employment in trade for it, but that being the case only to a limited extent, the difficulty arises how to employ it for short dates. The consequence is, in the absence of speculation, a wish to get hold of good commercial paper, and also an active inquiry for all eligible stocks and bonds. To-day there is rather a better demand at the banks for funds, and prices of favorite securities are steady at full prices. Bank of Montreal is stiff at 135, sellers asking more; British, nominal at $103\frac{1}{2}$ to 105; City, sellers at 104, buyers $103\frac{1}{2}$. A glance at our weekly stock and share table will show how high prices rule.

Gold closes at $137\frac{1}{2}$. Silver buying $3\frac{3}{8}$, selling 3 to $3\frac{1}{4}$ dis. Greenbacks buying $27\frac{1}{2}$, selling 27 to $27\frac{1}{4}$ dis. Gold drafts on New York, par to $\frac{1}{8}$ dis. Bank exchange on New York buying $27\frac{1}{4}$, selling 27 dis. The silver movement is at present very slack.

TORONTO STOCK MARKET.

(Reported by Pellatt & Osler, Brokers.)

The stock market which opened with some activity is again very dull in consequence of the scarcity of securities.

Bank Stock.—There are buyers of Montreal at 135 and sellers at $135\frac{1}{2}$. British is offered at $105\frac{1}{2}$. Ontario has advanced 2 per cent. on last week's quotations; no sellers now under $101\frac{1}{2}$. There are buyers of Toronto at 117, no stock in market. Royal Canadian offers at 92 with buyers at $91\frac{1}{2}$. Sales of Commerce occurred at $103\frac{3}{4}$ for all paid, partially paid stock offering at 103 to $103\frac{1}{4}$. Gore, nominal and lower. Buyers offer 105 for Merchants, with no sellers under 106. No Quebec in market, buyers would give $98\frac{1}{2}$. Buyers would give $108\frac{1}{2}$ for Molson's, but no sales occurred since the books opened. City is asked for at $103\frac{1}{2}$. Du Peuple is offered at $105\frac{1}{2}$. Buyers offer 107 for Jacques Cartier, no sellers under 108. For Mechanics 97 would be paid. Other banks nominal.

Debentures.—Short dated Canada sixes (currency) offer at $100\frac{3}{4}$, and Dominion stock at $101\frac{1}{2}$. No Sterling bonds in market. Little doing in Toronto, a few small sales occurred at rates to pay about 7 per cent. interest. There were considerable sales of County at rates to pay about $6\frac{3}{8}$ per cent. interest.

Sundries.—City Gas is much asked for at 105. There were sales of Canada Parmanent Building Society at 121, very little to be had. Western Canada sold at $113\frac{1}{2}$, and is much asked for at that rate. Buyers will only give $127\frac{1}{2}$ for Montreal Telegraph. There are buyers of Canada Landed Credit at 70 to 72 for stock with all calls paid. Little doing in British America Assurance sellers at 56. No mortgages offering; they can be readily placed at 8 per cent. Money is offered freely on good paper.

Commercial.

Montreal Correspondence.

(From our own Correspondent).

Montreal, Oct. 13, 1868.

The autumnal weather noted in my last still continues, open days and cold nights, with now and then a sprinkling of rain, the weather is most favorable for fall ploughing, and all farmers of any experience know, that an acre ploughed in the fall is worth two ploughed in the spring, the soil is turned over and exposed to the autumn suns and rains, which penetrates well into the earth and the snow which is undoubtedly an excellent irrigator has a better chance of percolating into the soil.

Business during the week has been rather below an average, this is chiefly caused by the tardy arrival of the fall fleet, only some four vessels having arrived from Europe during the week, one of these is from London, one from Liverpool, one from Greenock, and one from the Continent. The number of arrivals by sea from opening of navigation to date are 361 exactly the same as during the same period last year. Several vessels are at Quebec ready to come up, but we have nothing to load them with; so far the prospect looks very discouraging, and unless a great change takes place within the next fortnight, we may regard our fall export trade as a failure. The persistance with which the farmers and grainholders in the west have held on to their grain is almost unparalelled, and I much fear that they will be heavy sufferers, as speculators in the east have held back, plainly seeing that prospects did not warrant, their embarking in any speculation at the rates which have ruled during the fall.

The PRODUCE MARKET here is exceedingly dull and prices have a downward tendency, thus showing that the bottom is not yet reached. Flour has declined 5c. to 10c. per bl. with very little doing, the impression being that supers will touch $5 before any rally is made. Choice brands of strong bakers' flour are in demand and keep well up in price, but the general feeling is one of depression. Wheat has also declined and with the exception of a few not important shipments the market has been very dull, prices in the west are so high that buyers here cannot operate. U.C. Spring sells slowly at $1.20. $1.22½. and Chicago No. 1 $1.18. Some cargo sales have been made of Peas, and prices continue firm say $1.07 per bush. Owing to the speculation west in Barley, prices here have ran up, but the rates are nominal. As I have always predicted, the prices both of Barley and Oats will rule high during the winter, the great shortness in the crops in Eastern Canada falling on the coarse grains. Ashes, the market for which is of great interest to your country storekeepers west, have commanded a ready sale at First Pots $5.65 $5.75, seconds $5.05 $5.10. Pearls $5.55. $5.60. For Provisions the market is fairly active, and the prices of Pork are maintained. Beef has declined owing to the large quantity imperfectly fattened being brought forward ; farmers are anxious to press off as much stock as they can before the winter, as fodder is certain to run so very short. Dairy produce continues to command very high rates, the shipping demand for England being almost as active as ever, best dairy butter would command as high as 25c. Cheese sells at 10¼c, 11½c. We need not look for any permanent reduction of prices during the winter.

Total Receipts of Flour 1st Jan. to 7th Oct.

1867.	1868.	Increase.
Bus. 1,199,346.	Bus. 1,348,856.	Bus. 149,510.

GROCERIES.—As to be expected after our large fall sales, there has been somewhat of a lull, this is especially the case in Teas, the buyers not yet having sorted out their new stocks and consequently will not for the present enter the market. The trade is not however over stocked; the high prices at recent sales having deterred many timid buyers from operating. We may therefore safely expect a good fall trade at full prices, as the state of the New York and London markets do not warrant any idea of a decline. In sugars there has been considerable stir, some 2000 hds. having changed hands during the week, the Refiners have been large operators, their purchases have been made chiefly on private terms, the market has stiffened considerably. The Refiners have advanced their rates ¼ on yellow and ⅜ on white refined sugars. Molasses have followed the sugar market, but the sales have not been extensive, prices are very firm. Salt in which there has been a great deal of speculation during the fall, appears to have touched the highest point, viz. : $1. $1.05 for Liverpool coarse ; it has now receded to 95c. and as some arrivals are shortly expected and the demand for Chicago has fallen off, a further decline may be looked for. Fish Oils still continue very high, the demand for the Eastern States being active All Cod Oil here is held on speculation, and as the yield especially of Cod is reported very light, a high range of prices may be expected. Of Fish there have been two sales on the wharf and prices ruled higher than they have done for years back and if our advices from the Lower Ports are correct we may look for a very high range of prices of fish during the season. I would advise your western buyers to watch narrowly the market here, and seize the earliest opportunity of supplying their wants.

DRY GOODS AND HARDWARE call for no special notice this week, trade is brisk and so far favorable ; in a short time I will be able to give you a better idea of the trade in these articles during the fall.

Toronto Produce Market.

GRAIN.—*Wheat*—Receipts 15,780 bush. and 15 291 bush. last week. The market is dull but steady. Spring is offered freely at $115 with a small demand at $112 to $113. There were one or two orders for good fall in market, and sales of several car loads occurred at $131 to $136 ; inferior almost unsaleable. *Barley*—Receipts are growing less, 35,474 came in by cars during the week against 41.103 bush. for the previous week, street receipts 20,000 to 30,000 bushels. The market opened at $1.38 to $1.40, and advanced closing steady and firm at $1.48 to $1.50 ; sales for the week 85,000 bushels at current rates, shipments about 65,000 bush. of which one cargo went to Chicago. PEAS—Receipts by cars for the week 4,564 and 2,944 bush. the previous week ; market dull, sales of car loads at 90 to 91½, and a lot of 10,000 bush. at Port Stanley at 85 cents per bush.

OATS.—Receipts 6,081 bush. and 3,671 bush. for the previous week ; market dull at quotations.

FLOUR.—Receipts 1.825 bush. and 3,700 bush. last week. There is no demand of consequence for any grade No. 1 is offered at $5.15 and one or two small lots of favorite brands have been taken at that figure. Prices are kept at so high a point that Boston and New York shippers have had the lion's share of the business lately. In the higher grades there is nothing doing.

PROVISIONS—*Butter* is firmer and several lots have been placed for export at 22 cents, at which figure their is a fair demand for good lots. *Dressed Hogs*—A few light hogs are arriving and sell at quotations. Buyers are prepared to pay a good figure for mess hogs, one dealer offers to take 1000 mess hogs between the 1st and 14th Nov. at $8. *Pork*—Mess is firm, and held at $25, with a good supply of Chicago Standard in market. There are considerable orders in market for November delivery. *Cheese*—Offering by the car load at 11¼. *Eggs*—good receipts and a fair demand at 16 cents.

SALT.—American barrelled salt $1.60. Liverpool coarse, is firm and higher, at $1.20 ; sales at $1.15.

LIVE STOCK.—*Cattle* are selling at $4.50 to $6.50 according to quality; there is a good demand for first-class. *Sheep* $2.50 to $3.50 each. *Lambs* $2 to $2.50 each.

The Cotton Crop.

Our crop reports this week are a trifle more favourable. The telegraph informs us of one storm passing up from the Gulf along the Atlantic coast, but our advices show that it was almost entirely a coast storm and did not extend far into the interior. From the West and Southwest the reports are better, the weather being good and complaints of worms, &c., being less frequently heard. Almost everywhere the freedmen appear to be working well.

Annexed is a statement showing the stocks of cotton in Liverpool and London, inclnding the snpplies of American and Indian produce ascertained to be afloat to those ports :

	1867.	1868.
Stock in Liverpool,...bales	820,520	422,140
" London............	110,810	74,360
American cotton afloat	10,000	3,200
Indian	336,280	83,950
Total.....	1,277,610	1,183,650

—*Financial Chronicle.*

Halifax Market.

BREADSTUFFS.—Oct. 6.—We have a further decline in prices of Flour to note, and holders are anxious to sell. We quote Montreal brands of No. 1 at $6.90 to $7 ; Toronto brands from Canada Wheat $7 to $7.25; Extra $8 to $8.25; Extra State $6.25 to $7! Corn Meal dull at $4. $4.70c, for kiln dried ; $4.40 to $4.50 for Ground. Oatmeal $7.75 to $7.85. Imports January 1st to October 6th, 1868 and 1868 :

	Brls. Flour.	Brls. Cornm
1868.........	135,147	41,945
1867.........	141,584	29,951

WEST INDIA PRODUCE.—The prices of and Molasses remain the same as last weel cargo of grocery Cuba Sugar was offered at a during the week, and sales were effected at 7 8c., duty paid, equal to 5½c. to 5⅝c. in Sales continue in lots at our quotations. stock of Vacuum Pan being entirely exha renders the holders of the better grades of Rico very firm in their prices. Porto Rico 6⅜c. in bond

FINANCIAL.—Bank drawing rate on Lond days sight 13 per cent. prem. : Private 1 12½c. prem. New York Gold drafts at si per cent, prem. Currency drafts 25 per cen count. Montreal sight drafts 4 per cent. Newfoundland sight drafts 5 per cent. pr

R. C. Hamilton & Co.'s Circular.

Buffalo Robes.

BUFFALO ROBES.—The Hudson Bay Com first consignment of Buffalo Robes has this been disposed of by private sale to the purc at the auction sales of last year. A tariff wa mitted to each purchaser, and the distributi each was stated to be made in proportion previous year's purchases. The collection an ed to about 8000 robes, and the Company g teed that the whole collection to be sold thi should not exceed 10,000 robes, i.e. : 2000 that to be sold in addition to the 8000 of tl sent consignment. The whole lot at p offered has been taken up, and is, we belief, cipally in the hands of four of the princip houses. One of the larger houses has, ho not bought any—a circumstance which exci mark, as the collection outside the Comp this year very small. Last year the Co sold at two sales about 17,000 robes. The ing is the Tariff :—No. 1 Prime, 12½c ; No 9⅝c; No. 3 do, 7c : No. 1 Summer, 6½c ; do, 4½c ; No. 1 Calf, 5¼c ; No. 2 do, 3½c ; do, 1¼c.

A New Feature in Ship Building.

A firm in Boston is building a new desc of vessel suited to the importation of molas other liquid matter in bulk. This mode of will save much expense, and would as create considerable business in cooperage port of reception.

Gore Bank.

THE Adjourned Annual Meeting of the Shareho receive the Report of the Committee appointe meeting held on the 3rd day of August last, will be the Banking House,

On MONDAY, the 2nd of NOVEMBER next, at

By order of the Board,

W. G. CASS

C

GORE BANK,
Hamilton, 12th Oct., 1868.

THE PRINCE EDWARD COUNTY

Mutual Fire Insurance Com

HEAD OFFICE,—PICTON, ONTARIO.

President, L. B. STINSON; *Vice-President*, W. A. R

Directors : H. A. McFaul, James Cavan, James N. S. DeMill, William Delong.—*Treasurer*, David *Secretary*, John Twigg ; *Solicitor*, R. J. Fitzgerald

THIS Company is established upon strictly Mu ciples, insuring farming and isolated proper hazardous,) *in Townships only*, and offers great ad to insurers, at low rates for *five years*, without the of a renewal. This Company has existed 12 years which period it has adjusted all losses in a sat manner. It is managed with strict economy, an an opportunity of insuring with safety and relia very little expense, which accounts for its long and the successful business which it has been an doing.

Picton, June 15, 1868.

Montreal House, Montreal, Canada.

H. N. Smith & Co.,

Hurd, Leigh & Co.,

IMPORTERS AND DECORATORS OF

FRENCH CHINA.

DAY'S

Commercial College and High School,

No. 82 KING STREET EAST,

(Near St. James' Cathedral.)

J. T. & W. Pennock,

Brown Brothers,

ACCOUNT-BOOK MANUFACTURERS,

Stationers, Book-Binders, Etc.,

66 and 68 King Street East, Toronto, Ont.

Philip Browne & Co.,

BANKERS AND STOCK BROKERS.

DEALERS IN

Candee & Co.,

TORONTO PRICES CURRENT.—October 15, 1868.

Name of Article.	Wholesale Rates.		Name of Article.	Wholesale Rate.		Name of Article.	
Boots and Shoes.	$ c.	$ c.	**Groceries**—Contin'd	$ c.	$ c.	**Leather**—Contin'd.	
Mens' Thick Boots ...	2 20	2 50	" fine to fine't..	0 85	0 95	Kip Skins, Patna	0
" Kip............	2 45	3 30	Hyson	0 45	0 80	French	0
" Calf	3 00	3 75	Imperial	0 42	0 80	English	0
" Congress Gaiters..	2 00	2 40	Tobacco, Manufac'd:			Hemlock Calf (30 to	
" Kip Cobourgs....	1 00	1 50	Can Leaf, ♭ ♭5s & 10s.	0 26	0 30	35 lbs.) per doz....	0
Boys' Thick Boots....	1 55	1 90	Western Leaf, com..	0 25	0 26	Do. light	0
Youths' "	1 45	1 55	" Good......	0 27	0 32	French Calf.........	1
Women's Balts	95	1 20	" Fine	0 32	0 35	Grain & Satn Clf 9 doz..	0
" Congress Gaiters..	1 15	1 50	" Bright fine..	0 40	0 50	Splits, large ♭ ♭....	0
Misses' Balts........	0 75	1 00	" choice..	0 60	0 75	" small	0
" Congress Gaiters..	1 00	1 30				Enamelled Cow ♭ foot..	0
Girls' Balts	0 65	0 90	**Hardware.**			Patent	0
" Congress Gaiters..	0 80	1 10	Tin (net cash prices)			Pebble Grain	0
Children's C. T. Cacks..	0 50	0 65	Block, ♭ ♭........	0 25	0 26	Buff.................	0
" Gaiters	0 65	0 90	Grain...............	0 25	0 26		
Drugs.			Copper:			**Oils.**	
Aloes Capin	0 12½	0 16	Pig	0 23	0 24	Cod	0
Alum................	0 02½	0 03	Sheet	0 30	0 33	Lard, extra	0
Borax	0 00	0 00	Cut Nails:			" No. 1	0
Camphor, refined.....	0 85	0 70	Assorted	Shingles,		" Woollen	0
Castor oil............	0 18	0 28	♭ 100 ℔..	2 90	3 00	Lubricating, patent...	0
Caustic Soda.........	0 04½	0 06	Shingle alone do	3 15	3 25	" Mott's economic	0
Cochineal............	0 90	1 40	Lathe and 5 dy.....	3 30	3 40	Linseed, raw........	0
Cream Tartar	0 00	0 00	Galvanized Iron:			" boiled........	0
Epsom Salts	0 03	0 04	Assorted sizes......	0 00	0 10	Machinery...........	0
Extract Logwood.....	0 09	0 11	Best No. 24	0 08	0 08½	Olive, 2nd, ♭ gal....	1
Gum Arabic, sorts....	0 30	0 35	" 26......	0 08	0 09¼	" salad	2
Indigo, Madras......	0 75	1 00	" 28........	0 09	0 09¾	" salad, in bots,	
Licorice	0 14	0 45	Horse Nails:			qt. ♭ case....	3
Madder	0 13	0 16	Guest's or Griffin's			Sesame salad, ♭ gal...	1
Nutgalls	0 00	0 00	Assorted sizes......	0 19	0 20	Seal, pale	0
Opium..............	8 70	7 00	For W axe'd sizes..	0 18	0 19	Spirits Turpentine...	0
Oxalic Acid	0 35	0 35	Patent Hammer'd do..	0 17	0 18	Varnish	0
Potash, Bi-tart......	0 25	0 28	Iron (at 4 months)			Whale...............	0
" Bichromate...	0 15	0 20	Pig—Gartsherrie No1..	26 00	27 00	**Paints, &c.**	
Potass Iodide	3 80	4 50	Other brands. No1..	24 00	25 00	White Lead, genuine	
Senna	0 12½	0 09	No 2..	24 00	25 00	in Oil, ♭ 25 lbs....	3
Soda Ash	0 03	0 04	Bar—Scotch, ♭100 ℔..	2 25	2 50	Do. No. 1 "	3
S:da Bicarb	4 50	5 50	Refined	3 00	3 25	" 2 "	3
Tartaric Acid........	0 37½	0 45	Swedes	5 00	5 50	White Zinc, genuine..	3
Verdigris	0 35	0 40	Hoops—Coopers.....	3 50	3 75	Hoop's Lead, dry.....	3
Vitriol, Blue........	0 09	0 10	" Band.......	3 00	3 25	Red Lead............	0
Groceries.			Boiler Plates........	3 25	3 50	Venetian Red, Eng'h..	0
Coffees:			Canada Plates.......	4 00	4 25	Yellow Ochre, Fren'h..	0
Java, ♭ ℔........	0 27½	0 34	Union Jack	0 00	0 00	Whiting	0
Laguayra,..........	0 17	0 18	Pontypool	4 00	4 25	**Petroleum**	
Rio.................	0 15	0 17	Swansea	3 90	4 00	(Refined ♭ gal.)	
Fish:			Lead (at 4 months)			Water white, car'd..	0
Herrings, Lab. split..	0 00	0 00	Bar, ♭ 100 ℔s......	0 07	0 07½	" small lots...	0
" round	0 00	0 00	Sheet " ..	0 08	0 09	Straw, by car load...	0
" scaled	0 85	0 40	Shot	0 07½	0 07¾	" small lots...	0
Mackerel, smallkitts..	1 00	0 00	Iron Wire (net cash):			Amber, by car load..	0
Loch. Her. wh'e ßrks..	1 50	2 75	No. 6, ♭ bundle.....	2 70	2 80	" small lots ...	0
" " half " ..	1 25	1 50	" 9, "	3 10	3 20	Benzine	0
White Fish & Trout...	3 25	3 50	" 12, "	3 40	3 50		
Salmon, saltwater....	10 00	15 00	" 16, "	4 30	4 40	**Produce**	
Dry Cod, ♭112 ℔s..	4 75	5 00	Powder:			Grain:	
Fruit:			Blasting, Canada ...	3 50	3 75	Wheat, Spring, 60 ℔..	1
Raisins, Layers	2 20	2 25	FF	4 25	4 50	" Fall	1
" M. R.	2 10	2 20	FFF	4 75	5 00	Barley,....... 48 "	0
" Valentias new..	0 08½	0 08½	Blasting, English ...	5 00	5 50	Peas,......... 60 "	0
Currants, new........	0 05	0 05½	FFF loose...	5 50	6 00	Oats.......... 34 "	0
" old........	0 04½	0 04½	Pressed Spikes (4 mos):			Rye .... 56 "	0
Figs	0 11	0 12	Regular sizes 100....	4 00	4 25	Seeds:	
Molasses:			Extra	4 50	4 75	Clover, choice 60 "	0
Clayed, ♭ gal	0 00	0 35	Tin Plates (net cash):			com'n 68 "	0
Syrups, Standard ...	0 43	0 44	IC Coke	7 50	8 00	Timothy, choi'e 4 "	0
" Golden	0 40	0 50	IC Charcoal.........	8 50	8 75	" inf. to good 48 "	0
Rice :			IX "	10 50	10 75	Flax .... 56 "	0
Arracan	4 50	4 65	IXX "	12 50	0 00	Flour (per brl.)	
Spices:			DC "	7 50	8 00	Superior extra.......	0
Cassia, whole, ♭ ℔..	0 37½	0 40	DX "	9 50	10 00	Extra superfine,.....	0
Cloves	0 11	0 12				Fancy superfine......	0
Nutmegs	0 45	0 55	**Hides & Skins.**♭℔			Superfine No. 1	0
Ginger, ground	0 20	0 25	Green rough	0 05½	0 06	No. 2.........	0
" Jamaica, root..	0 22	0 25	Green, salt'd & insp'd..	0 07	0 00	Oatmeal (per brl.)	
Pepper, black........	0 09½	0 10	Cured	0 07½	0 08½		
Pimento	0 08	0 09	Calfskins, green	0 00	0 10	**Provisions.**	
Sugars:			" cured......	0 12	0 12	Butter, dairy tub ♭℔..	0
Port Rico, ♭ ℔......	0 08½	0 08½	" dry........	0 18	0 20	" store packed..	0
Cuba "	0 08½	0 08½	Lambskins, ...	0 40	0 60	Cheese, new	0
Barbadoes (bright)..	0 08½	0 08½	" pelts....			Pork, mess, per brl....	24
Dry Crushed, at 60d...	0 11	0 11½				" prime mess,...	
Canada Sugar Refin'y,			**Hops.**			" prime......	
yellow No. 2, 60 da..	0 08½	0 08½	Inferior, ♭ ℔........	0 10	0 12	Bacon, rough	0
Yellow, No. 2½.....	0 09½	0 09½	Medium	0 12	0 15	" Cumberl'd cut..	
No. 3.....	0 09½	0 09½	Good	0 15	0 20	" smoked	0
Crushed X	0 10	0 10½	Fancy	0 00	0 00	Hams, in salt........	0
A	0 10½	0 11				" sug.cur.8melar'd	
Ground	0 11	0 11½	**Leather;** @ (4 mos.)			Shoulders, in salt	0
Extra Ground........	0 12½	0 12½	In lots of less than			Lard, in kegs	0
Teas:			50 sides, 10 ♭ cent			Eggs, packed	0
Japan com'n to good..	0 40	0 55	higher.			Beef Hams	
" fine to choicest,.	0 55	0 65	Spanish Sole, 1st qual..			Tallow	0
Coloured, com. to fine,.	0 60	0 75	heavy, weights ♭ ℔..	0 23	0 23½	Hogs dressed, heavy	0
Congou & Souch'ng..	0 42	0 75	Do. but qual middle..	0 23	0 23¼	" medium...	0
Oolong, good to fine...	0 50	0 65	Do. No. 2, all weights..	0 20	0 22	" light......	0
Y. Hyson, com to g'd..	0 45	0 55	Slaughter heavy	0 28	0 29		
Medium to choice	0 55	0 90	Do. light............	0 30	0 32	**Salt, &c.**	
Extra choice	0 55	0 95	Harness, best	0 32	0 34	American brls........	0
Gunpowd'rc. to med...	0 55	0 70	" No. 2	0 30	0 33	Liverpool coarse	0
" med. to fine	0 70	0 85	Upper heavy	0 35	0 40	Plaster	0
			" light........	0 40	0 45	Water Lime	0

			Brandy:	$ c.	$ c.
ndles.			Hennessy's, per gal.	2 40	2 50
Co.'s ..	$ c.	$ c.	Martell's "	2 40	2 50
....	0 07½	0 08	J. Robin & Co.'s "	2 25	2 35
ar	0 07	0 07½	Otard, Dupuy & Cos	2 25	2 35
....	0 07	0 07½	Brandy, cases	8 50	9 00
....	0 05	0 05½	Brandy, com., per c.	4 00	4 50
......	0 08½	0 08¾	*Whiskey:*		
....	0 11	0 11½	Common 36 u. p.	0 62½	0 65
quors,			Old Rye	0 85	0 87½
			Malt	0 85	0 87½
			Toddy	0 85	0 87½
loz......	2 60	2 65	Scotch, per gal.	1 90	2 10
o Portr..	2 35	2 40	Irish—Kinnahan's c.	7 00	7 50
			" Dunnville's Belf't.	6 00	6 25
. Rum...	1 80	2 25	**Wool.**		
H. Gin..	1 55	1 65	Fleece, lb.	0 27	0 30
Com.....	1 90	2 00	Pulled "	0 00	0 00
			Furs.		
			Bear	8 00	10 00
....	4 00	4 25	Beaver	1 00	1 25
Com, c...	6 00	6 25	Coon	0 20	0 40
			Fisher	4 00	6 00
n.......	1 00	1 25	Martin	1 40	1 60
....	2 00	4 00	Mink	4 00	4 25
non.....	1 00	1 50	Otter	5 75	6 00
....	1 70	1 80	Spring Rats	0 15	0 17
golden..	2 50	4 00	Fox	1 20	1 25

INSURANCE COMPANIES.

ENGLISH.—*Quotations on the London Market.*

Di-nd.	Name of Company.	Shares par val £	Amount paid.	Last
	Briton Medical and General Life	10	—	1¾
7½	Commer'l Union, Fire, Life and Mar.	50	5	5½ 5¾
3	City of Glasgow	25	2½	5
9½	Edinburgh Life	100	15	30½x
½ yr	European Life and Guarantee	2½	11s6	4s 6d
0	Etna Fire and Marine	10	1½	1
5	Guardian	100	50	52x
2	Imperial Fire	500	50	345
9½.	Imperial Life	100	10	16½
0	Lancashire Fire and Life	20	2	2½x
1	Life Association of Scotland	40	7½	23
p. sh	London Assurance Corporation	25	12½	48
5	London and Lancashire Life	10	1	1
0	Liverp'l & London & Globe F. & L.	20	2	7½
5	National Union Life	5	1	1
2½	Northern Fire and Life	100	5	10½
2 0 s.	North British and Mercantile	50	6¼	16 16½
0	Ocean Marine	25	5	20
12s,	Provident Life	100	10	38
p. s.	Phœnix	....	....	136
.yr.	Queen Fire and Life	10	1	15-16ths
0.4s	Royal Insurance	20	3	6¾
0	Scottish Provincial Fire and Life	50	2½	4½
5	Standard Life	50	12	65
5	Star Life	25	1¼	—
	CANADIAN.			₱ c.
4	British America Fire and Marine	$50	$25	56
4	Canada Life	....	....	.....
2	Montreal Assurance	£50	£5	135
3	Provincial Fire and Marine	60	11	.....
....	Quebec Fire	40	32½	£19½
8	" Marine	100	40	90-91
no's.	Western Assurance	40	6	.....

RAILWAYS.	Sha's	Paid	Montr	London.
St. Lawrence	£100	All.	....	56 58xd
ake Huron	20½	"	....	3 3½
do Preference	10	"	....	5½ 6½
& Goderich, 6 ₱c., 1872-3-4	100	"	....	----
d St. Lawrence	....	....	10 12	....
do Pref. 10 ₱ ct.	....	....	65 72½	....
....	100	"	16 17	16½ 16¾
Eq. G. M. Bds. 1 ch. 6 ₱c.	100	"	....	84 86
First Preference, 5 ₱ c	100	"	....	49 51
Deferred, 3 ₱ ct.	100	"	....	....
Second Pref. Bonds, 5 ₱c	100	"	....	39 41
do Deferred, 3 ₱ ct.	100	"	...	....
Third Pref. Stock, 4 ₱ct.	100	"	...	28 30
do. Deferred, 3 ₱ ct.	100	"	....	....
Fourth Pref. Stock, 3 ₱c	100	"	....	19 20
do. Deferred, 3 ₱ ct.	100	"	....	....
n	20½	"	13 14	13¾ 14
New	20½	18	----	....
6 ₱ c. Bds, due 1873-76	100	All.	....	101 103
5½ ₱c Bds. due 1877-78	100	"	....	93 95
ay, Halifax, $250, all	$250	"	....	....
Canada, 6 ₱c. 1st Pref. Bds.	100	"	.. .	80 83

ANGE.	Halifax.	Montr'l.	Quebec.	Toronto.
ndon, 60 days				
days date	18½	9½ 9½	9½	9¾
....	12 12½	8½ 9	8½ 8½	9
documents	....	7½ 8½	....	....
York	....	27 27½	27 27½	73
do.	....	27½ 28	27½ 28	....
do.	....	par	par ½ dis.	par ½ dis.
....	....	3 3½	....	3½ 5

STOCK AND BOND REPORT.

The dates of our quotations are as follows:—Toronto, Oct. 14; Montreal, Oct. 13; Quebec, Oct. 12; London, Sept. 23.

NAME.	Shares.	Paid up.	Divid'd last 6 Months	Dividend Day.	CLOSING PRICES. Toronto.	Montre'l.	Quebec.
BANKS.			₱ ct.				
British North America	$250	All.	3	July and Jan.	103 104	104 105½	102½ 103
Jacques Cartier	50	"	4	1 June, 1 Dec.	106 108	107½ 108½	106½ 107
Montreal	200	"	5	"	135 135½	135 135½	135 136½
Nationale	50	"	4	1 Nov. 1 May.	106	107 108	135 136
New Brunswick	100	"	......	......	....	...	....
Nova Scotia	200	28	7&b$3½	Mar. and Sept.	....	....	....
Du Peuple	50	"	4	1 Mar., 1 Sept.	105 105½	105 105½	105 106
Toronto	100	"	4	1 Jan., 1 July.	116½ 117	116 117	116 117
Bank of Yarmouth	....	....	......	......	....	....	....
Canadian Bank of Com'e	50	95	......	......	103 103½	102 103	102 103
City Bank Montreal	80	All.	4	1 June, 1 Dec.	103 103½	103½ 104	102½ 103
Commer'l Bank (St. John)	100	"	₱ ct.	......	....	...	....
Eastern Townships' Bank	50	"	4	1 July, 1 Jan.	....	95 96	96 96½
Gore	40	...	3½	1 Jan., 1 July.	....	35 37½	37 39
Halifax Banking Company	...	....	......	......	...	....	....
Mechanics' Bank	50	70	4	1 Nov., 1 May.	95 97	97 98	95½ 96½
Merchants' Bank of Canada	100	70	4	1 Jan., 1 July.	105 105½	105 105½	105 105½
Merchants' Bank (Halifax)	....	....	.....	......	....	....	....
Molson's Bank	50	All.	4	1 Apr., 1 Oct.	108 108½	106 106½	107 107½
Niagara District Bank	100	70	3½	1 Jan., 1 July.	....	....	....
Ontario Bank	40	All.	4	1 June, 1 Dec.	100½ 101½	100½ 101	99 99½
People's Bank (Fred'kton)	100	"	......	......	....	....	....
People's Bank (Halifax)	20	"	7 12 m	......	....	...	...
Quebec Bank	100	"	3½	1 June, 1 Dec.	97½ 98½	98½ 99	98½ 99
Royal Canadian Bank	50	50	4	1 Jan., 1 July.	91 92	91 91½	90 91
St. Stephens Bank	100	All	.....	......	....	..	....
Union Bank	100	70	4	1 Jan., 1 July.	102 102½	102 103	103 104
Union Bank (Halifax)	100	40	7 12 mo	Feb. and Aug.	....	....	...
MISCELLANEOUS.							
British America Land	250	44	2½	......	....	....	....
British Colonial S. S. Co	250	32½	2½	......	...	45 50	....
Canada Company	32½	All.	5	......	....	....	....
Canada Landed Credit Co.	50	$20	3½	......	62 63	....	....
Canada Per. B'ldg Society	50	All.	5	......	120½ 121	....	....
Canada Mining Company	4	90	......	......	....	....	....
Do. Inl'd Steam Nav. Co.	100	All.	20 12 m	......	----	107½ 108½	108 109
Do. Glass Company	100	"	12½ "	......	....	95	....
Canad'n Loan & Investm't	25	2½	7	......	....	....	....
Canada Agency	10	½	......	......	....	....	....
Colonial Securities Co.	...	....	.....	......	....	....	....
Freehold Building Society	100	All.	5	......	106 106½	....	....
Halifax Steamboat Co.	100	"	5	......	....	....	....
Halifax Gas Company	....	....	......	......	....	...	....
Hamilton Gas Company	....	....	......	......	....	....	....
Huron Copper Bay Co	4	12	20	......	....	25 50cps	....
Lake Huron S. and C.	5	102	......	......	....	....	....
Montreal Mining Consols	20	$15	......	......	....	2.50 3.00	...
Do. Telegraph Co.	40	All.	5	......	132 133	127½ 130	130 132
Do. Elevating Co.	00	"	15 12 m	......	....	100 103	....
Do. City Gas Co.	40	"	4	15 Mar. 15 Sep.	....	132½ 135	132 134
Do. City Pass. R. Co.	50	"	5	......	....	106 110	106 110
Nova Scotia Telegraph	20	"	....	......	....	....	....
Quebec and L. S.	8	$4	......	......	...	....	25 cts
Quebec Gas Co.	200	All.	4	1 Mar., 1 Sep.	...	...	117 118
Quebec Street R. R.	50	25	8	......	....	....	96 97
Richelieu Navigation Co.	100	All.	7 p.a.	1 Jan., 1 July.	....	110 112	110 113
St. Lawrence Tow Boat Co.	100	"	......	3 Feb.	....	...	35 40
Tor'to Consumers' Gas Co.	50	"	2 3 m.	1 My Au MarFe	104½ 105	...	103 104
Trust & Loan Co. of U. C.	20	5	3	......	....	....	...
West'n Canada Bldg Soc'y	50	All.	5	......	113 113½	....	....

SECURITIES.	London.	Montreal	Quebec.	Toronto.
Canadian Gov't Deb. 6 ₱ ct. due 1872	....	100 101	100½ 101	100 101
Do. do. 6 do due Ja. & Jul. 1877-84	104 106	....	....	....
Do. do. 6 do. Feb. & Aug.	103 105	....	....	....
Do. do. 6 do. Mch. & Sep.	103 105	....	...	....
Do. do. 5 ₱ ct. cur., 1883	91 93	89½ 91	89½ 90	90 90½
Do. do. 5 do. stg., 1885	....	89½ 91	90 90½	90 90½
Do. do. 7 do. cur.,	....	....	......	....
Dominion 6 p. c. 1878 cy	....	100½ 102	100½ 101½	100½ 101
Hamilton Corporation	....	....	......	....
Montreal Harbor, 8 ₱ ct. d. 1869	..	....	......	....
Do. do. 7 do. 1870	....	....	......	....
Do. do. 6½ do. 1875	....	100 100½	......	....
Do. do. 6½ do. 1873	....	....	......	....
Do. Corporation, 6 ₱ c. 1891	....	92½ 93½	92 93	92 93
Do. 7 p. c. stock	....	105 105½	104 105	105 105½
Do. Water Works, 6 ₱ c. stg. 1878	....	....	......	92 93
Do. do. 6 do. cy. do.	....	92½ 93½	......	92 93
New Brunswick, 6 ₱ ct., Jan. and July	102 104	....	......	....
Nova Scotia, 6 ₱ ct., 1875	100 102	....	......	....
Ottawa City 6 ₱ c. d. 1880	....	91½ 92½	......	...
Quebec Harbour, 6 ₱ c. d. 1883	....	....	60	....
Do. do. 7 do. do.	....	....	70	....
Do. do. 8 do. 1886	...	....	85	....
Do. City, 7 ₱ c. d. 5 years	....	80 90	90½ 91	....
Do. do. 7 do. 9 do.	....	....	87 88	....
Do. do. 7 do. 2½ do.	....	....	96½ 97	....
Do. Water Works, 7 ₱ ct., 4 years	....	....	95 96	....
Do. do. 6 do. 2 do.	....	....	92½ 93½	....
Toronto Corporation	....	90 92½	...	....

Miscellaneous. | Miscellaneous. | Miscellaneous.

Financial.

Pellatt & Osler.

'D EXCHANGE BROKERS, Accountants,
r the Standard Life Assurance Company and
wuality Insurance Company.
86 King Street East, four Doors West of
Church Street, Toronto.

LLATT,   EDMUND B. OSLER,
tary Public.   Official Assignee.

OWN'S BANK,

. R. Brown. W. C. Chewett.)

'G STREET EAST, TORONTO.

'S a general Banking Business, Buys and
w York and Sterling Exchange, Gold, Silver,
and Uncurrent Money, receives Deposits sub-
ue at sight, makes Collections and Discounts
Paper.
Mail or Telegraph promptly executed at
at favourable current quotations.
ass letters,   "BROWN'S BANK,
Toronto."

Iian Land and Emigration Company

s for sale on Conditions of Settlement,

OD FARM LANDS

the County of Peterboro, Ontario,

settled Township of Dysart, where there are
Grist and Saw Mills, Stores, &c., at

A-HALF DOLLARS AN ACRE.

Joining Townships of Guilford, Dudley, Har-
bart and Bruton, connected with Dysart and
of Haliburton by the Peterson Road, at ONE
. Acre.

ir particulars apply to

CHAS· JAS. BLOMFIELD,
Secretary C. L. and E. Co., Toronto.

ALEX. NIVEN, P.L.S.,
Agent C. L. & E. Co., Haliburton]

Iverpool and London and Globe Insurance Company.

d Reserved Funds.........$17,005,000.

ILY CASH RECEIPTS,......$20,000.

IS HEREBY GIVEN, that this Company
deposited the sum of

150,000 Dollars,

e with the Act, 31st Vic., cap. 48, has received
of the Finance Minister, to transact the busi-
of Fire Insurance in the Dominion of Canada.

G. F. C. SMITH,
Chief Agent for the Dominion.

tford Fire Insurance Company,

HARTFORD, CONN.

ital and Assets over Two Million Dollars.

$2,026,220.29.

CHARTERED 1810.

and reliable Company, having an established
s in Canada of more than thirty years standing,
ad with the provisions of the new Insurance
ade a special deposit of

$100,000

overnment for the security of policy-holders, and
ue to grant policies upon the same favorable
retofore.

low rates on first-class dwellings and farm
r a term of one or more years.
heretofore promptly and equitably adjusted.

E. CHAFFEY & CO., AGENTS.
Ont.

RT WOOD, GENERAL AGENT FOR CANADA

Insurance.

The Standard Life Assurance Company,

Established 1825.
WITH WHICH IS NOW UNITED
THE COLONIAL LIFE ASSURANCE COMPANY.

Head Office for Canada:
MONTREAL—STANDARD COMPANY'S BUILDINGS,
No. 47 GREAT ST. JAMES STREET.

Manager—W. M. RAMSAY.   *Inspector*—RICH'D BULL.

THIS Company having deposited the sum of ONE HUN-
DRED AND FIFTY THOUSAND DOLLARS with the Receiver-
General, in conformity with the Insurance Act passed last
Session, Assurances will continue to be carried out at
moderate rates and on all the different systems in practice.

AGENT FOR TORONTO—HENRY PELLATT,
KING STREET.

AGENT FOR HAMILTON—JAMES BANCROFT.
8-6mos.

Fire and Marine Assurance.

THE BRITISH AMERICA
ASSURANCE COMPANY.
HEAD OFFICE:
CORNER OF CHURCH AND COURT STREETS.
TORONTO.

BOARD OF DIRECTION:

Hon G. W. Allan, M L C.,   A. Joseph, Esq ,
George J. Boyd, Esq ,   Peter Paterson, Esq.,
Hon. W. Cayley   G. P. Ridout, Esq.,
Richard S. Cassels, Esq ,   E H. Rutherford, Esq ,
    Thomas C. Street, Esq.

Governor:
GEORGE PERCIVAL RIDOUT, ESQ.
Deputy Governor:
PETER PATERSON, ESQ.

Fire Inspector: Marine Inspector:
E. ROBY O'BRIEN.   CAPT. R. COURNEEN.

Insurances granted on all descriptions of property
against loss and damage by fire and the perils of inland
navigation.
Agencies established in the principal cities, towns, and
ports of shipment throughout the Province.

THOS. WM. BIRCHALL,
28-ly   Managing Director.

Edinburgh Life Assurance Company.

Founded 1823.

HEAD OFFICE—22 GEORGE STREET, EDINBURGH.

Capital, ... £500,000 *Ster'g.*
Accumulated and Invested Funds, £1,000,000 "

HEAD OFFICE IN CANADA:
WELLINGTON STREET, TORONTO.

SUB-AGENTS THROUGHOUT THE PROVINCE.

J. HILLYARD CAMERON,
Chairman, Canadian Board.

DAVID HIGGINS,
Secretary, Canadian Board.   3-3m

Queen Fire and Life Insurance Company,

OF LIVERPOOL AND LONDON,

ACCEPTS ALL ORDINARY FIRE RISKS
on the most favorable terms.

LIFE RISKS

Will be taken on terms that will compare favorably with
other Companies.

CAPITAL,   -   -   £2,000,000 Stg.

CHIEF OFFICES—Queen's Buildings, Liverpool, and
Gracechurch Street London.
CANADA BRANCH OFFICE—Exchange Buildings, Montreal.
Resident Secretary and General Agent,
A. MACKENZIE FORBES,
13 St. Sacrament St., Merchants' Exchange, Montreal.
WM. ROWLAND, Agent, Toronto.   1-1y

Insurance.

Reliance Mutual Life Assurance Society,

(Established, 1840,) OF LONDON, E. C.

Accumulated Funds, over $1,000,000.

      Annual Income, $900,000.
THE entire Profits of this long-established Society belong
to the Policy-holders.

HEAD OFFICE FOR DOMINION—MONTREAL.

    T. W. GRIFFITH, *Manager & Sec'y.*
15-1y   WM. HENDERSON, *Agent for Toronto.*

Ætna Insurance Company of Dublin.

The number of Shareholders exceeds Five Hundred.

Capital, $5,000,000—*Annual Income nearly* $1,000,000.

THIS Company takes Fire and Marine Risks on the most
favorable terms.
T. W. GRIFFITH, *Manager for Canada.*
Chief office for Dominion—Corner St. Francois Xavier
and St. Sacrament Sts., Montreal.
15-1y   WM. HENDERSON, *Agent for Toronto*

Scottish Provincial Assurance Co.

Established 1825.

CAPITAL, ...£1,000,000 STERLING.
INVESTED IN CANADA (1864) ....$600.000.

Canada Head Office, Montreal.

LIFE DEPARTMENT.

CANADA BOARD OF DIRECTORS:

HUGH TAYLOR, Esq., Advocate,
Hon. CHARLES WILSON, M. L. C.
WM. SACHE, Esq., Banker,
JACKSON RAE, Esq., Banker.
WM. FRASER, Esq. M. D., Medical Adviser.

The special advantages to be derived from Insuring in
this office are:—Strictly Moderate Rates of Premium;
Large Bonus (Intermediate bonus guaranteed); Liberal
Surrender Value, under policies relinquished by assured;
and Extensive Limits of Residence and Travel. All business disposed of in Canada, without reference to parent
office.
A. DAVIDSON PARKER,
Resident Secretary
G. L. MADDISON,
15-1yr   AGENT FOR TORONTO.

Lancashire Insurance Company.

CAPITAL, - - - - - - - £2,000,000 Sterling

FIRE RISKS

Taken at reasonable rates of premium, and
ALL LOSSES SETTLED PROMPTLY,

By the undersigned, without reference elsewhere.
S. C. DUNCAN-CLARK & CO.,
General Agents for Ontario,
N. W. Corner of King & Church Streets,
25-1y   TORONTO.

Ætna Fire & Marine Insurance Company.

INCORPORATED 1819. CHARTER PERPETUAL.

CASH CAPITAL, - - - - - $3,000,000

LOSSES PAID IN 50 YEARS, 23,500,000 00.

JULY, 1868.

ASSETS.
(At Market Value.)

Cash in hand and in Bank................... $544,842 39
Real Estate................................ 258,267 79
Mortgage Bonds............................. 982,245 00
Bank Stock................................. 1,273,670 08
United States, State and City Stock, and other
Public Securities......................... 2,049,855 51
      Total................... $5,052,880 19

LIABILITIES.
Claims not Due, and Unadjusted $409,808 55
Amount required by Mass. and New York
for Re-Insurance 1,405,267 13

E. CHAFFEY & CO., Agents.
50-6m

Insurance.

ÆTNA
Live Stock Insurance Company.

LICENSED BY THE DOMINION GOVERNMENT TO
DO BUSINESS IN CANADA.

THE following Accidents, this month, show the importance of Insuring your Horses and Cattle against Death
from any cause, or Theft, in the Ætna Insurance Company:

MONTREAL, September 16, 1868.
At a fire last night, in the sheds behind Ripin's Hotel,
St. Joseph Street, three valuable Stock Horses were destroyed. "Young Clydesdale" and "Emigrant," belonging
to the Huntingdon Agricultural Society—the former worth
$900, and the latter $1,700; and "Old Benuharnois" cost
$1,000, belonging to the Beauharnois Society.

PORT COLBORNE, September 18, 1868.
HORSES DROWNED.—Two horses belonging to Mr. Briggs,
of Port Colborne, and four owned by Mr. Julien, of Port
Dalhousie, were drowned in the Canal, near the Junction,
early this morning.

A fire at the Glasgow Hotel, Montreal, this morning, destroyed two horses. The fire was caused by drunkenness
on the part of the stable man.

MONTREAL, September 24, 1868.
A fire in F. X. Cusson's stables, St. Joseph Street, last
night, destroyed three horses.

E. L. SNOW, GENERAL AGENT,
Montreal
Agents for Ontario:—
SCOTT & WALMSLEY,
67nov11y   Ontario Hall, Church Street, Toronto.

The Liverpool and London and Globe
Insurance Company.

INVESTED FUNDS:
FIFTEEN MILLIONS OF DOLLARS.

DAILY INCOME OF THE COMPANY:
TWELVE THOUSAND DOLLARS.

LIFE INSURANCE,
WITH AND WITHOUT PROFITS.

FIRE INSURANCE
On every description of Property, at Lowest Remunerative
Rates.
JAMES FRASER, AGENT,
5 King Street West.
Toronto, 1868.   88-1y

Briton Medical and General Life
Association,

with which is united the
BRITANNIA LIFE ASSURANCE COMPANY.

Capital and Invested Funds............£750,000 Sterling.

ANNUAL INCOME, £220,000 STG. :
Yearly increasing at the rate of £25,000 Sterling.

THE important and peculiar feature originally introduced by this Company, in applying the periodical
Bonuses, so as to make Policies payable during life, without
any higher rate of premiums being charged, has caused
the success of the BRITON MEDICAL AND GENERAL to be
almost unparalleled in the history of Life Assurance. *Life
Policies on the Profit Scale become payable during the lifetime
of the Assured, thus rendering a Policy of Assurance a
means of subsistence in old age, as well as a protection for a
family, and a more valuable security to creditors in the
event of early death; and effectually meeting the often
urged objection, that persons do not themselves reap the
benefit of their own prudence and forethought.*

No extra charge made to members of Volunteer Corps
for services within the British Provinces.

☞ TORONTO AGENCY, 5 KING ST. WEST.
oct17—9-1yr   JAMES FRASER, Agent.

Phenix Insurance Company,
BROOKLYN, N. Y.

PHILANDER CROWELL,   STEPHEN CROWELL,
Secretary.   President.

Cash Capital. $1,000,000. Surplus, $666,416.02. Total,
1,666,416.02. Entire income from all sources for 1866 was
$2,131,839.82.

CHARLES G. FORTIER, Marine Agent.

Ontario Chambers, Toronto, Ont.   19-1y.

Insurance.

The Victoria Mutual
FIRE INSURANCE COMPANY OF CANADA.

Insures only Non-Hazardous Property, at Low Rates.

BUSINESS STRICTLY MUTUAL.

GEORGE H. MILLS, President.
W. D. BOOKER, Secretary.
HEAD OFFICE .... HAMILTON, ONTARIO

aug 15-1yr

The Ætna Life Insurance Company.

AN attack, abounding with errors, having been made
upon the Ætna Life Insurance Co. by the editor of the
Montreal *Daily News* : and certain agents of British
Companies being now engaged in handing around copies of
the attack, thus seeking to damage the Company's standing,
—I have pleasure in laying before the public the following
certificate, bearing the signatures of the Presidents and
Cashiers who happened to be in their Offices) of *every Bank
in Hartford*; also that of the President and Secretary of
the old Ætna Fire Insurance Company :—

"*To whom it may concern* :—

"We, the undersigned, regard the Ætna Life Insurance Company, of this city, as one of the most successful
and prosperous Insurance Companies in the States,—
entirely reliable, responsible, and honourable in all its
dealings, and most worthy of public confidence and
patronage."

Lucius J. Hendee, President Ætna Fire Insurance Co.,
and late Treasurer of the State of Connecticut.
J. Goodnow, Secretary Ætna Fire Insurance Co.
C. H. Northam, President, and J. B. Powell, Cashier
National Bank.
C. T. Hillyer, President Charter Oak National Bank.
E. D. Tiffany, President First National Bank.
G. T. Davis, President City National Bank.
F. S. Riley, Cashier,   do.   do.   do.
John C. Tracy, President of Farmers' and Mechanics'
National Bank.
M. W. Graves, Cashier Conn. River Banking Co.
H. A. Redfield, Cashier Phœnix National Bank.
O. G. Terry, President Ætna National Bank.
J. R. Redfield, Cashier National Exchange Bank.
John G. Root, Assistant Cashier American National Bank.
George F. Hills, Cashier State Bank of Hartford.
Jas. Potter, Cashier Hartford National Bank.
Hartford, Nov. 26, 1867.

Many of the above-mentioned parties are closely connected with other Life Insurance Companies, but all unhesitatingly commend our Company as "reliable, responsible, honorable in all its dealings, and most worthy of public confidence and patronage.
JOHN GARVIN,
General Agent, Toronto Street.
Toronto, Dec. 3. 1867.   16-1y

Life Association of Scotland.

INVESTED FUNDS
UPWARDS OF £1,000,000 STERLING.

THIS Institution differs from other Life Offices, in that
the
BONUSES FROM PROFITS
Are applied on a special system for the Policy-holder's
*PERSONAL BENEFIT AND ENJOYMENT
DURING HIS OWN LIFETIME,*
WITH THE OPTION OF
LARGE BONUS ADDITIONS TO THE SUM ASSURED.

The Policy-holder thus obtains
A LARGE REDUCTION OF PRESENT OUTLAY
OR
*A PROVISION FOR OLD AGE OF A MOST IMPORTANT
AMOUNT IN ONE CASH PAYMENT,
OR A LIVE ANNUITY,*

Without any expense or outlay whatever beyond the
ordinary Assurance Premium for the Sum
Assured, which remains in fact for
Policy-holder's heirs, or other
purposes.

CANADA—MONTREAL—PLACE D'ARMES.

DIRECTORS:
DAVID TORRANCE, Esq., (D. Torrance & Co.)
GEORGE MOFFATT, (Gillespie, Moffatt & Co.)
ALEXANDER MORRIS, Esq., M.P., Barrister, Perth.
Sir G. E. CARTIER, M.P., Minister of Militia.
PETER REDPATH, Esq., (J. Redpath & Son).
J. H. R. MOLSON, Esq., (J. H. R. Molson & Bros.)
Solicitors—Messrs. TORRANCE & MORRIS.
Medical Officer—R. PALMER HOWARD, Esq., M.D
Secretary—P. WARDLAW.
Inspector of Agencies—JAMES B. M. CHIPMAN.
y

Insurance.

North British and Mercantile Insura
Company.

Established 1809.

HEAD OFFICE, - - CANADA. - - MONT

TORONTO BRANCH:
LOCAL OFFICE, NOS. 4 & 6 WELLINGTON STRE
Fire Department, ... R. N. GO

Life Department, ... H. L. HIM
29-1y

Phœnix Fire Assurance Compa
LOMBARD ST. AND CHARING CROSS,
LONDON, ENG.

Insurances effected in all parts of the Wo

Claims paid
WITH PROMTITUDE and LIBERALI
MOFFATT, MURRAY & BEATTIE
Agents for Toron
36 Yonge St
2

The Commercial Union Assuran
Company,
19 & 20 CORNHILL, LONDON, ENGLAND.

Capital, £2,500,000 Stg.—Invested over $2,000,0

FIRE DEPARTMENT.—Insurance granted on
scriptions of property at reasonable rates.

LIFE DEPARTMENT.—The success of this
has been unprecedented—*NINETY PERCENT.* o
miums now in hand. First year's premiums wer
$100,000. Economy of management guaranteed
e curity. Moderate rates.
OFFICE—385 & 387 ST PAUL STREET, MONTRE
MORLAND, WATSON & C
General Agents for Ca
FRED. COLE, Secretary.
Inspector of Agencies—T. C. LIVINGSTON,
W. M. WESTMACOTT, *Agent at Tor*
16-1y

Phœnix Mutual Life Insurance C
HARTFORD, CONN.

Accumulated Fund, $2,000,000, Income, $1,000,0

THIS Company, established in 1851, is one of the
reliable Companies doing business in the countr
has been steadily prospering. The *Massachusetts Ins*
Reports show that in nearly all important matters
superior: o the general average of Companies. It of
intending insurers the following reasons, amongst
for preferring it to other companies:
It is purely Mutual It allows the Insured to
and reside in any portion of the United States and E
It throws out almost all restriction on occupation fr
Policies. It will, if desired, take a note for part
Premium, thus combining all the advantages of a no
all cash company. Its Dividends are declared an
and applied in reduction of Premium. The Dividen
in every case on Premiums paid. The Dividends
PHŒNIX have averaged fifty per cent. yearly.
settlement of Policies, a Dividend will be allowed t
year the policy has been in force. The number o
dends will always equal the outstanding Notes. It
losses promptly—during its existence never havi
tested a claim. It issues Policies for the benefit o
ried Women beyond the reach of their husband's cre
Creditors may also insure the lives of Debtors. Its P
are all *Non-forfiting*, as it always allows the assu
surrender his Policy, should he desire, thus Comp
ing a paid-up Policy therefor. This important
will commend itself to all. The inducements now
by the PHŒNIX are better and more liberal than th
any other Company. Its rate of Mortality is exce
low and under the average.
Parties contemplating *Life Insurance* will find it i
interest to call and examine our system. Policies
payable either in *Gold* or American currency.
ANGUS R. BETHUNE
General Manager,
Dominion of C

Office: 104 ST. FRANÇOIS XAVIER ST. MONTRE

☞ Active and energetic Agents and Can
wanted in every town and village, to whom liberal i
ments will be given.

PRINTED AT THE DAILY TELEGRAPH PRI
HOUSE, BAY ST., COR. KING.

THE CANADIAN
MONETARY TIMES
AND
INSURANCE CHRONICLE.

VOTED TO FINANCE, COMMERCE, INSURANCE, BANKS, RAILWAYS, NAVIGATION, MINES, INVESTMENT,
PUBLIC COMPANIES, AND JOINT STOCK ENTERPRISE.

II—NO. 10.   TORONTO, THURSDAY, OCTOBER 22, 1868.   { SUBSCRIPTION, $2 A YEAR.

Mercantile.

Gundry and Langley,
TECTS AND CIVIL ENGINEERS, Building Surveyors and Valuators. Office corner of King and Jordan, Toronto.
AS GUNDRY.   HENRY LANGLEY.

J. B. Boustead.
TION and Commission Merchant. Hops bought and sold on Commission. 82 Front St., Toronto.

John Boyd & Co,
ESALE Grocers and Commission Merchants, ont St.. Toronto.

Childs & Hamilton.
FACTURERS and Wholesale Dealers in Boots Shoes, No. 7 Wellington Street East, Toronto, 28

L. Coffee & Co.
CE and Commission Merchants, No. 2 Manning's k, Front St., Toronto, Ont. Advances made on ents of Produce.

J. & A. Clark,
ICE Commission Merchants, Wellington Street t, Toronto, Ont.

D. Crawford & Co.,
FACTURERS of Soaps, Candles, etc., and dealers Petroleum, Lard and Lubricating Oils, Palace St., Ont.

John Fisken & Co.
OIL and Commission Merchants, Yonge St, onto, Ont.

W. & R. Griffith.
ERS of Teas, Wines, etc. Ontario Chambers, Church and Front Sts , Toronto.

Thos. Haworth & Co.
ERS and dealers in Iron, Cutlery and general ware,King St., Toronto, Ont.

Hurd, Leigh & Co.
RS and Enamellers of China and Earthenware, onge St., Toronto, Ont. [See advt.]

Lyman & McNab.
ESALE Hardware Merchants, Toronto, Ontario.

W. D. Matthews & Co.
CE Commission Merchants, Old Corn Exchange, ront St. East, Toronto Ont.

R. C. Hamilton & Co.
CE Commission Merchants, 119 Lower Water Halifax, Nova Scotia.

Parson Bros.,
LEUM Refiners, and Wholesale dealers in Lamps, neys, etc. Wareroooms 51 Front St. Refinery oor. . Don Sts., Toronto.

C. P. Reid & Co.
ERS and Dealers in Wines, Liquors, Cigars and Tobacco, Wellington Street, Toronto.   28.

W. Rowland & Co.,
CE BROKERS and General Commission Mer-. Advances made on Consignments. Corner nd Front Streets, Toronto.

Reford & Dillon.
ERS of Groceries, Wellington Street, Toronto, to.

Sessions, Turner & Co.,
FACTURERS, Importers and Wholesale Dealers oots and Shoes, Leather Findings, etc., 8 Wel- West, Toronto, Ont

Meetings.

MOLSON'S BANK.

The annual general meeting of the shareholders of this Bank was held at its Banking House, in Montreal, on Monday, 12th October, 1868.

William Molson, Esq., President, having taken the chair, the Cashier read the following report:

GENTLEMEN,—A statement of the affairs of the Bank for the past year is now submitted.

The profits for the year amount to.............$90,083 43

Which were appropriated
To payment of dividend No. 25..............$40,000 00
Do.   do.   No. 26..............40,000 00
Bad debts written off........................10,083 43
                                    $90,083 43

In consequence of the business of the Bank, at present, being entirely local, and from the large amount of American silver in the country, the circulation still continues very contracted.

The Directors will have much pleasure in giving any information required by stockholders, regarding the affairs of the Bank.

(Signed),   WILLIAM MOLSON, President.
Molson's Bank, Montreal, Oct. 12, 1868.

1st. It was moved by Thomas Workman, Esq., seconded by John Ogilvy, Esq., That the report now read be adopted and printed for distribution among the shareholders.—Carried.

2nd. It was moved by G. W. Warner, Esq., sconded by F. X. St. Charles, Esq., That the thanks of the shareholders are due, and are hereby tendered to the President and Directors for their efficient management of the Bank during the past year and that the President be requested to accept the sum of $2,000, in consideration of his valuable services during that period.—Carried unanimously.

Messrs G. W. Warner and F. X. St. Charles having been appointed scrutineers, reported the undermentioned gentlemen re-elected Directors for the ensuing year, viz., William Molson, Esq., John H. R. Molson, Esq., Ephrem Hudon, Esq., Thomas Workman, Esq., John Ogilvy, Esq.

General Statement of the Affairs of the Molson's Bank, on the 30th September, 1868.

LIABILITIES.

Capital............................	$1,000,000 00
Bank Notes in circulation.........	101,970·00
Deposits $244,905 13	
Do. bearing interest.. 529,571 02	774,476 15
Balances due to other Banks.....	86,369 01
Twenty-sixth Dividend	40,000 00
Dividends uncalled for..........	290·00
Rest	100,000 00
Exchange, etc., reserved.........	9,374 09
	$2,172,479 25

ASSETS.

Coin, Bullion and Provincial Notes...............	225,734 79
Bills and Checks of other Banks,	136,471 33
Balance due by other Banks.....	41,268 30
Government Securities..........	107,553 32
Bank Premises and other Real Estate..............	90,865 15
Notes and Bills Discounted	1,365,645 56
Other debts due the Bank not included under the foregoing heads......................	204,939 80
	$2,175,479 25

The average amount of paper under discount during the year has been....................$1,561,009 58
The average Government securities 107,553 32
The average Deposits 684,830 37
The average Circulation........ 92,618 00
The average Specie and Provincial Notes 174,542 38

A meeting of the new Board of Directors was afterwards held, when Wm. Molson, Esq., was re-elected President, and John H. R. Molson, Esq., Vice-President.
(Signed),   WILLIAM SACHE, Cashier.

STANSTEAD AND SHERBROOKE MUTUAL FIRE INSURANCE COMP'Y.—The Annual Meeting of the Stanstead and Sherbrooke M. F. I. Co. took place on the 5th inst., R. W. Heneker, Esq., in the Chair, and A. G. Woodward, Esq., acting as Secretary. The President, Hon. Edward Hale, presented the Annual Report, which was read and adopted.

The following gentlemen were re-elected Directors : Edward Hale, A. A. Adams, Wm. Fling, Eros. Leborveau and C. Allan ; Henry G. Pierce was elected to fill the place of Elisha Gustin, deceased, and with J. Griffith, B. T. Morris, and G. K. Foster, who remains in office, constitute the board of Directors for the ensuing year.

A resolution was adopted instructing the Auditors to examine the deposit notes to see if they are correct as represented in the statement submitted to the Directors ; and a vote of thanks was passed to the President and Directors for their able management of the affairs of the company.

On motion of F. W. Terrill, seconded by R. W. Heneker, it was voted to recommend an increase of salary to the Secreary-Treasurer, which may be considered as evidence of approval of Mr. Woodward's services. After a vote of thanks to the Chairman the meeting adjourned.

We learn from the annual report that the number of policies issured is 4079, an increase of 866 during the year ; the value of property at present insured is $3,700,318, an increase of $863,170 for the year ; Deposit notes, being capital of the company, $273,364, an increase of $65,040 35. The amount of assessments due is $6,638, being a reduction since last report of $1,853. There has been an increase in the company's liabilities during the year of about $3.251. Amount of losses $10,764, an increase of a little over $3,000. The increase in liabilities is attributed to the increased losses, which have been met by current receipts,) and the writing off of a considerable number of bad claims. The losses of the year though large, are, as compared with the whole amount insured, about the same as last year, or 3½ per ct., and will be met together with the liabilities, by the assessment of 6 per cent laid by the Directors.

The report alludes to the case in litigation against A. W. Kendrick, Esq., involving to $1691, " which the Directors with much regret felt it their duty to institute, and which by the decision of the Board and the advice of their Counsel is now under appeal in the Court of Review."—*Sherbrooke Gazette.*

TORONTO AND NIPPISING RAILWAY.—The Brock township council have adopted a by-law granting $58,000 as a bonus to the Toronto and Nippissing railway.

Mining.

NOVA SCOTIA GOLD MINING REVIEW.

The weather has again interfered with open air operations, but the reports from underground works continue encouraging. There is less demand for new investment, either in stocks or land, and prices of both have a falling tendency.

SHERBROOKE.—"Wentworth" reports:—The explorations of the Canada Co. are still perseveringly prosecuted. The Woodbine Co. have suspended operations, but it is understood only for a brief period, pending a meeting of the shareholders. The New York and Sherbrooke Companies staff is being lessened, Mr. Zwickel contemplating a return to Europe, while new machinery is being prepared for the mine. The Stanley Company have stopped work altogether. The Meridian Co. are prosecuting a shaft on the line of the Dominion lode, and their mill is going to work in a day or two on their own rock. The Metropolitan Co., which owe their success mainly to the good management of Captain James Warren, an English miner, have sent up 102 ozs. 7 dwts. of gold. A bar of 84 ozs., sent up in July, was not reported in the Gazette. They are now working on the south shaft, in which they have about two feet of pay ore. The Dominion mill is working satisfactorily.

WINE HARBOR.—The new developments in this district promise well.

ISAAC'S HARBOR.—The Mulgrave Co. represented by Mr. Balcam, sent up $3000 worth of gold on the 20th ult.

ECUM SECUM.—The Atlantic Co. are pushing forward their works and have commenced erecting their crusher. They have thus far exposed twenty-nine lodes, and have sunk three shafts, two on the North lode, which is two feet thick and shows fine gold, and one on a fourteen inch lode running between walls of slate. A band of quartz seven feet wide, containing nine lodes, two showing gold, forms part of the exposed ground. They employ a force of twenty men at present, but as the work proceeds will increase their staff. The batteries have been supplied by Montgomery & Co., of Halifax, and the mill is being put up by Mr. McPherson, of Sherbrooke. The soil averages from two to six feet, and the road to the western field is in good condition. The journey from Halifax can be accomplished in two days. Mr. F. S. Andrews, the manager for the Atlantic Co., reports encouragingly of the prospects of alluvial washings being found in this district, and, having had experience in California, his opinion is entitled to some weight.

TANGIER.—The Strawberry Hill Co. have cleared up 108 oz. 12 dwts. from 31 tons of quartz, as the product of last month's work.

RENFREW.—The Ophir Co. are opening up the new lode lately spoken of, which still improves in depth. The Andrews lot is being worked to advantage. An experimental crushing from the Macdonald and Thomas lot gave 1 oz., 14 dwts., 15 grs. to the ton, and the lode shows well the deeper it is sunk upon. The Carnarvon Co. have about twenty men at work, and have laid bare several new lodes, which will soon be tested.

MONTAGUE.—The works of the Montreal Exploration Co. have been suspended for the season. The Albion Co. have not furnished any report.

LAWRENCETOWN.—The works of the Montreal Exploration Co. in this district, too, have been suspended for the winter. A property, consisting of forty-nine areas, belonging to Mr. E. M. Strange, and offering an extent of nearly half-a-mile on the lodes, worked by Messrs. Chapel & Werner, is placed in the market, or rather $15,000 are sought to be raised for its proper development.

UNIACKE.—The Montreal Exploration Co. have suspended operations for the winter; not from any discouragement met with, but because the sum voted for preliminary work on their various properties at Uniacke, Lawrencetown, and Montague has been spent, and the season is unfavorable for

further prospecting. The Mayflower Co. have been industriously trenching, and exposed several veins of moderate size. The Westlake Co.'s mill is again running. The Queen Co. show the quality of their ore and the capabilities of the district by some handsome specimens at the Exhibition. The Brunswick Co. report a new lode, supposed to be the Macintosh. The Uniacke, Central, Prince of Wales, North St. Lawrence, and Montreal Companies have not reported. Mr. Burkner's large lode gave 9 oz., 12 dwts., 3 grs., from a crushing of 17½ tons. The Alpha Co. have ceased explorations, but the mill is fully employed on custom work, and next week will be fitted with a third battery.

THE OVENS.—Captain Cornwall and Mr. Clarke, of Boston, are trying to retrieve the character of this district. The former is going to some expense in the erection of a smelting furnace. The latter has bought up the Macdonald claims. Work on Mr. McCulloch's property is also spoken of as about to be resumed before winter sets in.

GOLD RIVER.—The property of the late Chester Co. will, we understand, be taken hold of and worked this fall by Canadian capitalists, and a mill put in operation forthwith.

MUSQUODOBOIT.—Rich specimens full of fine gold from this district, from the lode, were brought to town by Mr. Burkner, who has just returned from the district. Most of the veins run in slate. Three lodes are already opened : one 15 in., one 7 in., and one 6 inches in width. The slate shows fine gold freely. The present drawback to prospecting on this field is the great depth of soil.—Halifax Mining Gazette.

COPPER.—The proprietors of the Tilt Cove Mine, Newfoundland, estimate their shipments for this year at 8,000 tons.

OIL DISCOVERIES.—A reliable informant, just returned from an exploration tour in Cape Breton, relates the discovery of an oil spring there, but for reasons which can be appreciated, does not at present wish the precise locality to be named.

QUICKSILVER VS. MELTED ZINC.

Successful gold mining comprises the possession of sufficiently rich gold quartz to pay the extraction and working, and the ability to extract the gold from the quartz economically and perfectly, in a few operations, and with as simple machinery as possible, requiring the presence of only such conditions as are anywhere at hand.

When we fairly examine the retentive faculty of quicksilver for gold, we find it very limited, indeed ;—that the affinity acts on the perfectly pure surface of both—a minority of cases in reality and that a reduction in temperature so greatly—reduces the affinity, that it hardly exists below a temperature of 42° Fah. The result is that on an average only one half, or thereabout, of the gold is extracted by quicksilver from the ore ; the rest is either carried away as flat-gold, by the water required for the batteries, or remains in the tailings. This fact, known to every intelligent operator, should alone be sufficient to point out the imperative necessity of devising other extracting agents for that great majority of ore, containing more than $20 to $25 per ton ; but not rich enough to leave a profit by direct chlorination. Concentration of the sulphurets, for chlorination is at best a great loss in float-gold. Many localities, with rich quartz veins, have insufficient water for batteries within convenient distance, and for the greater part of the year the ore has to be hauled long distances, with heavy expenditure, to a mill-site with water, or the mine must be abandoned and lie idle.

The case therefore stands thus : What is required, is an extracting agent, that does the work complete, cheaper than chloride, and requiring no water to reduce the ore, except such as is needed for the engine.

Zinc, of all substances in existence, chloride not excepted, has the greatest affinity to gold. Its

action, in a melted state, on gold, is to in eously dissolve the same in any proporti specific gravity, about 7, is sufficiently float all debris, not expecting sulphurets the constant companion of gold. It me comparatively low temperature, and requ little heat to retain its melted state. It is a ly volatile to permit of retorting, as in th quicksilver, but by a covered surface and perature below a dark red heat the loss tilization and burning is hardly appreciabl the metal is obtained at a low price and quantity required. Thus we have in[...] manageable and fulfilling the conditions of a gold extracting agent in a high degre than any other known.

The mode of applying it for this purp patented, April 7th, 1868, by the undersi[gn] many years engaged in gold mining. It simply in gradually introducing the gold pulverized substance, below the surface bath of melted zinc, which will immediate and dissolve nearly or every particle of gol the debris rises to the surface to be taken mechanism is very simple and durable. sulphurets, in which particles of gold are imbedded so as not to offer any contact eve smallest point, prevent the extraction t degree, that it will pay to work it over by tration, roasting and chlorination, it may But all the gold, in the other lost as fi and much more, is certainly already save zinc. Dry crushers to be used in prefere Millions of tons of tailings, now worthl might thus be worked profitably, and tl of good mines not capable of profitable wo amalgamation or chlorination, could be yield fair profits. Millions of dollars would thus be saved to the country.

Gold mining throughout the country la for the want of such a radical improveme additional cost of extraction by zinc may as about $8 to $12 per ton, or less than chlorination while it does the work fully as effectually, certainly infinitely quicker St. Journal.

THE INTERCOLONIAL COAL, CO.—The of the railway of the Drummond Collier works of the Intercolonial Coal Co. River, County Pictou, was celebrated o October. Sir Wm. E. Logan, the Honora Jackson, U. S. Consul at Halifax, Majo U. S. Consul at Pictou, and the Honorab Howe, Keith, Robertson, and other dis guests, honored the occasion with their The Citizen says :—" Operations were c in November, 1867, and since that time pany have sunk a double slope on the se depth of 730 feet, with lateral galleries of from 200 to 300 feet, from which ab tons of coal have been brought to th where it is ready for shipment—they h railroad over seven miles long, on whic several large and costly structures and tings—and have built a wharf 750 feet 'shoots' at which five ships can be sin ly loaded, and capable of putting on b tons a day ; the whole being accom eleven months, and at a cost of about fo thousand dollars. The railway was contract by Mr. Moore, of Montreal mining works have been conducted by pany's manager, Mr. Dunn—two gent seem to thoroughly understand thei Stevenson was loaded with coal for the company's wharf."

HOW TO SAVE QUICKSILVER.—G. proposes to save the mercury wasted in of amalgamation ; he entertains the o 300,000 tons of that metal has been l process. It escapes in the form of a calomel, as it is called. He advises

soluble residue with nitrate of soda and oric acid, in order to convert the insoluhloride of mercury into the soluble bichcorrosive sublimate. This solution is to d with sulphide of calcium, which is a winter product by the final reduction The mercury will be changed thereby ick sulphide. After drying the sulphide placed in retorts, with the proper amount d lime. The mercury is then obtained lation, and is caught in a receptacle conrater, connected with the retorts. The of calcium residue in the retort is then changing the sublimate into the black —*Journal of Mining.*

Insurance.

RECORD.—Stratford, Oct. 12.—A building Jas. McCulloch, known as the old flac fire and was consumed; the flames spread ing and fulling mill adjoining but were hed, by the fire engine; no insurance. mill is believed to have been set on fire low characters who frequented it. harines, Oct. 15.—May'e tavern, partially 1; loss, $300; no insurance. 1n, N.B., Oct. 6.—House of J. McIntosh; for $100: cause defective stove pipes, corners, near Stratford, Oct. 9.—Barn of e and contents wholly consumed; loss 800; insurance on building $150. It was r some drunken fellows going into the barn and lighting their pipes there; they were and committed for trial. town, Wentworth Co. Ont. Oct. 12.—A ly destroyed the dwelling house of James and store and dwelling house of Jno. Furniture and contents of Clark's store he buildings were owned by Jno. Howard; ; no insurance. The fire originated in pipe or chimney of Lunnon's house. 1n, N.B., Oct. 16.—A telegram says :— ctive fire took place this morning at Blacky and Candle Factory and Peters Tannery, ere partially destroyed. The estimate 0,000; only partially insured. mia, Oct. 20.—Between three and four his morning the Victoria foundry, belongristopher Young, Esq., was destroyed by nearly all its contents. Loss between four thousand dollars. Stock and tools n the Provincial Insurance Company for ndred dollars; building insured in the merica for three hundred dollars. Origin e unknown.

E RECORD.—Kingston. The schooner has been got off.

Oct. 12.—The schooner Advance went Grand Haven this morning. She is Captain D. Dell, of Chicago, and insured public, of Chicago. opeller Merchant, of the Evans Line of struck a wreck near Malden, and sunk. b consisted of about 5,000 barrels of flour 0 bushels of oats from Chicago. gram from Milwaukee, bearing date of the i, says, the iron steamship Milwaukee, ff the Grand Haven bar on Friday morne Milwaukee left this port at 8 o'clock on evening with a full passenger list, and ons of freight. The night was dark when and a furious storm arose, owing to the kness she missed the harbour and ran und on the bar, and soon drifted broadie beach. After being exposed to a tere i sea for upwards of four hours, the fine arted amidships and became a total loss. ngers, forty in number, were all safely

Milwaukee was built in the year 1860, at orming with the latter, the Milwaukee d Haven Steamship Line. She measured

700 tons, and cost $150,000. She was fully insured."

The schooner Clipper City went ashore at Grand Haven in a gale about ten days since, was got off, and was being towed into the harbor, when it was found necessary to scuttle her. She was a craft of 185 tons burden, having been built at Manitowoc, in the year 1854, rated B. 2, and her approximate gold value was $4,000. She was owned by Chicago parties.

The schooner Australia, bound for Chicago with cedar posts from Green Bay, sprung a leak off North Bay, and was obliged to put into Bailey's Harbour.

The bark Superior, upwards bound, coal laden, got ashore below Sandwich on Wednesday night, and on Thursday was being lightered off.

The schooner Fulton, bound from Toledo to Ogdensburgh, with a cargo of black nut, waterlogged off Nicholson Inang.

A late Chicago paper says :—The schooner Albatross reached here yesterday in tow of the propeller Ottawa, in a leaking condition. She will be docked for repairs as soon as her cargo of lumber is discharged.

The tug Union, came into port yesterday, having in tow of the schooner Australia, which sprung a leak off North Bay a few days since.

The schooner Hattie Earl is reported ashore on the east shore.

The schooner Thos. Simms was caught on this lake during the gale of Wednesday last, and reached the anchorage at the South Manitouninus, her foresail, mainsail and flying jib were lost.

An unknown bark—apparently grain-laiden—is reported ashore on the south point of the South Manitou Island.

The Canadian schooner Suffel is ashore on East Point. Put-in Bay.

The propeller City of Madison got aground in the Nebash Rapids, Saul St. Marie River, on Thursday, and had to be lightered off.

At Whitehall there are three vessels ashore—two white fore-and-aft schooners, and a topsail, scow, which is painted lead color. One of the schooners is full of water and apparently in bad shape.

Two vessels are on the beach at Muskegon. One of them is the scow Eugene, out high and dry; the other the schooner Wayne, which was sunk by the scow Monitor. The Monitor lies inside at Muskegon with a large hole stove in her bow above light water mark. The collision occurred just outside of the piers, while both vessels were endeavouring to reach the harbour.

The bark Fame, while lying in the River St. Clair, on Thursday, lost her bowsprit, jibboom and head gear, the result of a collision with an unknown craft.

The schooner U. S. Grant is ashore near Squaw Island.

The schooner David Stewart, which cleared from Chicago, for Escanaba, for iron ore, went ashore on Sunday, at Pilot Island.

The scow, William A. Parker, is ashore near Manistee. She is loaded with lumber for Chicago.

A despatch from Grand Haven states that the schooner Advance is ashore at that point. She can be got off without much trouble.

The schooner Eagle Wing reached Detroit on Saturday, with most of her cargo gone.

The sch. Chas. Hinckley was dismasted off Conneaut, Ohio, and is now undergoing repairs at Erie.

The schooner William Tell ran into the pier at Racine on Wednesday last, carrying away everything forward, and smashing in her bow badly. In turning into the harbor she had her small boat smashed.

In addition to the steamship Milwaukee, three vessels were beached at Grand Haven on Friday—two schooners and a scow. One of the schooners lies inside of the Milwaukee. The others stranded nearer the harbor, and were pulled off by a tug without having sustained any injury.

The schooner Glen Cuyler has been docked at Milwaukee to repair the damages sustained in the recent collision with the propeller City of Boston.

The schooner Sailor Boy was the other day chartered at Chicago to carry a cargo of Oats to Boston, direct via the St. Lawrence and around the coast, the first cargo of Oats ever shipped to Boston by this route from Chicago. On arriving at Boston this vessel will engage in the grain carrying trade between that port and New Orleans.

The schooner Defiance which went ashore on Snake Island Reef has been got off.

SOUTHAMPTON, Oct. 17.—The steamer Silver Spray dragged he anchor last night or this morning, and is ashore under the light house at Chantry Island. She is supposed to be damaged very much.

WATERLOO MUTUAL INSURANCE COMPANY.— We find the following correspondence respecting this Company in an exchange:—

ARTHUR HARVEY, ESQ.—SIR,—Your letter of the 37th May has been received, and in reply I beg to say, that it is the opinion of our Directors that our Company can take risks both on the Mutual and Cash system without making a deposit. Our Company was organized under the Act Chap. 52, Con. Stat. Upper Canada. And then we have a Special Act from the Ontario Legislature, authorizing us to take risks on the cash principle. Our business is confined to the Province of Ontario, and hence we think it comes under the exemption of Sec. 25 of the Insurance Act. Please let us know if this is the view taken by you and your Department. Signed. C.M. TAYLOR, Secretary.

Waterloo, June 6th, 1868.

To C. M. TAYLOR, Esq., Secretary of the Waterloo County Mutual Fire Insurance Company.— DEAR SIR,—Your enquiry as to whether the Waterloo Mutual Fire Insurance Company can take risks on the Cash System without making a deposit admits of an easy reply. If the Company is incorporated by any Act of the Ontario Legislature, and transacts no business outside the limits of Ontario, no deposit is required by the present Act. Signed. ARTHUR HARVEY.

AUDIT OFFICE, Ottawa, June 10, 1868.

Railway News.

GREAT WESTERN RAILWAY.—Traffic for week ending Oct. 2, 1868.

Passengers	$41,157 49
Freight and live stock	47,513 09
Mails and sundries	2,331 44
	$91,002 02
Corresponding Week of '67.	90,948 63
Increase	$53 39

NORTHERN RAILWAY.—Traffic Receipt for week ending Oct. 10, 1868.

Passengers	$3,222 29
Freight	8,285 20
Mails and Sundries	284 23
Total Receipts for week	$11,791 72
Corresponding week 1867	14,373 67
Decrease	$2,581 95

GREAT WESTERN RAILWAY.—The half-yearly meeting of the Great Western Railway Company, will be held in London, on the 21st Oct. current to receive the report and statement of accounts and for the election of officers. The transfer books will be closed from the 7th to 21st October, both days inclusive.

From the accounts of the half-year ending July 31 last, the board have decided on recommending a dividend at the rate of 2 per cent. per annum, free of income tax, reserving £2,000 for the renewal of ferry steamers and carrying forward to the current half-year the sum of £1,129 5s. This rate is just half that paid for the corresponding period last year.

RAILWAY TRAFFIC.—The official returns of Railway traffic for the month of September compare as follows:

	1868.	1867.
Great Western	$355,810	$334,988
Grand Trunk	624,108	603,632
Northern	49,019	41,175
Welland	13,101	12,459
London and Port Stanley	4,404	5,219
Port Hope, Lindsay, and B. with P. Branch	30,110	31,190
Brockville and Ottawa	17,085	14,893
St. Lawrence and Ottawa	8,732	8,628
NewBrunswick and Canada	8,541	7,185
European and North American	16,167	14,028
Nova Scotia (approximate)	29,179	23,913
Total	$1,156,265	$1,098,110

Financial.

TORONTO STOCK MARKET.

(Reported by Pellatt & Osler, Brokers.)

There has been rather more activity in the stock market this week, and some large transactions in County Debentures at high prices have taken place.

Bank Stock.—Montreal has again advanced, closing with buyers at 135¾. Nothing doing in British. There are buyers of Ontario at 100½; no sellers. Toronto is asked for at quotations. Paid up Royal Canadian stock is procurable at 92. Sales of partially paid Commerce occurred at 103. Nothing doing in Gore. Buyers are offering 105 and 105½ for Merchants'. No Quebec offering. City in demand at 103 to 103½. Du Peuple is offered at 105¼. No sellers of Jacques Cartier under 108. Other banks nominal.

Debentures.—Sales of Dominion Stock occurred at 102½. Sterling five per cents are offered at 91 to 91½. Sales of Toronto occurred during the week to pay 7 per cent. There were large transactions in County to pay 6½ per cent. interest.

Sundries.—Sales of Canada Permanent Building Society occurred at 121½. Western Canada inquired for at 114. Freehold offering at 106½. There are no buyers of Montreal Telegraph at over 127½. City Gas is in demand at 105 to 105½. Mortgages are readily placed to pay 8 per cent. Money continues easy on first-class paper.

MONTREAL MONEY MARKET.

(From our own Correspondent.)

Montreal, Oct. 19, 1868.

The abundance of money still continues, and the banks are ready to give accommodation at cheap rates. Round amounts have been lent on call at 4 per cent., and short dated transactions have taken place at 5 per cent. Good paper has been freely done at 6½ to 8. Really good bills are very scarce, and very few offering in the open market. Remittances from the country have much improved of late, thereby enabling the banks to better extend their accommodation. Stocks are active, the demand for some classes being greater than the supply, and outside prices are asked by holders for all favorite securities. Bank of Montreal would readily bring 135½ to 135¾, but there is none offering; Merchants tend upwards, there being buyers at 106¼; but sellers demand 106¾. City in demand at 104, but none offering. People's have been placed at 105¼. Ontario has advanced to ½ prem., but sellers now demand ¾. Toronto, quiet. Jacques Cartier, 109, but buyers not offering over 107½. Royal Canadian in demand at 91½, but sellers want 92. Of our leading stocks Richelieu Navigation Company are in demand at 111. Telegraph Co. dull, at 128, but buyers will not give over 125. New City Co., active, but the difference between buyers and sellers is too wide to admit of operations. Montreal Mining Consols are dull at $2.50 to $2.90, former the views of buyers, latter of sellers. Not much doing in other stock. The silver market has ruled very quiet. You will perceive that Mr. Weir has extended his time for commencing the exportation of silver to the 10th January prox. The reasons he gives in a letter to the *Gazette*, which I enclose. Present price here is 3c. 3¼. Gold is 137½, showing a very slight decline on last week's rates.

PROVINCIAL NOTES.—The amount of Provincial notes in circulation with the specie held for their redemption was as follows on Oct. 7th :—

Notes in circulation—	
Payable in Montreal	$3,264,589
Payable in Toronto	1,202,411
Payable at Halifax	136,000
Total	$4,603,000
Specie held—	
At Montreal	$550,000
At Toronto	450,000
At Halifax (estimated)	30,000
Total	$1,030,000
Debentures held under the Act.	$3,000,000

POST OFFICE SAVINGS BANKS.—The amount received from depositors during Sept. was $63,209, interest paid, $22.26; amount of withdrawal cheques, $13,227 67. Total deposits in hands of Receiver-General on 30th Sept., $357,958 87; of this amount $219,907 87 bears interest at 4 per cent., and $135,800 at 5 per cent.

BANK ITEMS.—A bag containing $5,000 in gold is said to have been abstracted from the safe of the Bank of Montreal at Hamilton, in a mysterious manner; there is no clue to the thief—Mr. Park late manager of the Gore Bank in Woodstock, has absconded and he is said to be a defaulter to a large amount. Mr. Park's sureties are believed to be good for the deficiency. Mr. Smith, late manager of the Gore Bank at Guelph has been appointed manager of the Branch of that Bank in Woodstock.

LIVE STOCK IN GREAT BRITAIN.

In Ireland the returns are made up to July 31, dating back to the year 1855, and in England to June 25, for 1867 and 1868 only, and these generally become known about the month of September. We have in consequence thought from the first week in October to the first week in April the most suitable periods to ascertain the results. We begin by giving in a tabular form the number of cattle, sheep and pigs, as furnished by Government from the Irish returns, beginning with the year 1855. In the next column we give the yearly increase or decrease, and in the last column we give the average price for the twenty-seven weeks. This average is from the highest price of best singed Waterford bacon; and, strangely enough, to show the little effect the Government returns have had upon prices, it will be seen that the highest rates have been current in the years 1856-57 and in 1865-66, both of which showed a considerable increase in the quantity of pigs over those of the previous years, and the highest average 69s. per cwt., being in the year that showed the largest number of pigs; then the lowest average prices for bacon were 58s. in 1858-59, and 59s. per cwt. in the years 1862-63 and 1863-64, in each of which years a decrease was shown in the return of pigs.

These remarks will, we think, tend to show that we must carry our ideas a little beyond one particular branch of business, For instance, although we have this year, when compared with last, a falling off of more than one million of pigs, we have an increase of about 340,000 head of cattle and 1,750,000 sheep; then we have to almost yearly increase of foreign suppl stock and provisions. Again, we have the laboring classes are well employed an —in fact, there are a variety of things t to be looked into before we come to a ju sion on the subject. As most of the l pers of the day have noticed this ye returns, but as none of them have show produced in former years, we think the we now publish will interest and be ac our readers. The following are the r live stock in Ireland for each year fro 1868 inclusive:

Years.	No. of Cattle.	No. of Sheep.	No. of Pigs.	Increase or decrease in Pigs with previous year. Increase.	Decrease.	Average prices of Bacon from first week in October to first week in April, say 27 weeks.
						cwt.
1856	3,587,858	3,694,294	918,525	......	......	
1857	3,620,054	3,452,252	1,255,186	337,661	......	1856-57..68s. 6d.
1858	3,667,304	3,494,993	1,409,883	154,707	......	1857-58..60s. 0d.
1859	3,815,958	3,592,804	1,265,751	......	144,132	1858-59..58s. 0d.
1860	3,606,374	3,542,080	1,271,072	5,321	......	1859-60..62s. 0d.
1861	3,471,688	3,556,060	1,102,042	......	169,030	1860-61..66s. 6d.
1862	3,254,890	3,456,132	1,154,324	52,282	......	1861-62..63s. 6d.
1863	3,144,231	3,308,204	1,067,458	......	86,686	1862-63..59s. 0d.
1864	3,262,294	3,366,941	1,058,480	......	8,973	1863-64..59s. 0d.
1865	3,497,548	3,694,356	1,305,953	247,473	......	1864-65..63s. 6d.
1866	3,746,157	4,274,282	1,497,274	191,321	......	1865-66..69s. 0d.
1867	3,702,378	4,826,015	1,233,893	......	263,381	1866-67..63s. 0d.

Total Number of Live Stock in Great
June 25.

	No. of Cattle.	No. of Sheep.
1867	4,993,034	28,919,101
1868	5,416,154	30,685,980
" Increase	423,120	1,766,879
" Decrease	—	—

—*Lon*

INSOLVENTS.—The following named were gazetted on Saturday last:—H Joseph Octave, Mercier Alexis, Norma Cready, Hilton & Co., David Sweet, W & Co., Montreal; Robert Hammond, Connor, Orangeville; Edward Kniffe C. B. Taylor & Co., Stratford; George St Catharines; Joseph Gervais, Labie Alex. Warwick, Woodstock; William ville; William Ferguson, Goderich; Richmond; Henry Reid Bell, Bowman ren Botsford, Brockville; Percy Bush ville; James Hodgert, Guelph; Sam Morrisburg.

CARRIAGE OF GOODS—NECESSITY DELIVERY.—In an action by plaintiff fendants for damages, occasioned delivery of a certain article of mac tracted to be delivered by them for appeared that no notice had been time of the contract to the defendants sity for a prompt delivery of the mach the use it was to be put to.

Held, that plaintiff could only reco of the missing article, and was no the loss of profits arising from its or the wages of certain workmen em the building in which the machine used.—*Ruthven Woolen Co.* v. *G. W* C. P. 316.

☞ THE CANADIAN MONETARY TIMES AND
NSURANCE CHRONICLE is printed every Thursday
Evening, in time for the English Mail.
Subscription Price, one year, $2, or $3 in
American currency ; Single copies, five cents each.
Casual advertisements will be charged ten cents
per line of solid nonpareil each insertion. All
letters to be addressed, "THE CANADIAN MONE-
TARY TIMES, TORONTO, ONT." Registered letters
so addressed are at the risk of the Publishers.
Cheques should be made payable to J. M. TROUT,
Business Manager, who will, in future, issue all
receipts for money.

The Canadian Monetary Times.

THURSDAY, OCTOBER 22, 1868.

THE GRAND TRUNK AND FREIGHT FACILITIES.

At a late meeting of the Montreal Board of Trade, the Hon. John Young complained that "the railroad. freight to Toronto was very much less, proportionably, than that to Montreal, the consequences being, of course, very detrimental to Montreal." The President said, "the Council had not lost sight of the subject, nor did it underrate its importance; but there was great difficulty in obtaining a remedy. The freight by the Allan line and the Grand Trunk to Toronto, for example, during the winter, was quoted remarkably low, for the reason that, except at very low rates, no business could be obtained. That arose from the fact that Toronto had several lines of steamers and railways available from New York; while Montreal had only the one line of steamers to Portland, and the Grand Trunk Railway." To a certain extent, Toronto is saved by its position from the effects of a monopoly of the carrying trade. But no thanks are due for this either to Montreal or the Grand Trunk. There being two routes from the seaboard, one via Montreal and the other via New York, any disposition on the part of the Grand Trunk to take an undue advantage would prejudice itself. As matters now stand, one of the reasons why the Grand Trunk commands this trade is, because the cost of handling goods by the New York route is heavy. If it were necessary, Toronto could make arrangements that would do away with this difficulty. The adoption of a policy which secures a trade that would otherwise take other channels, seems to be considered in Montreal a favour to Toronto.

There is no doubt that Montreal men look keenly after their own interests, and we cannot blame them for striving to keep the Western Province in bondage to their enterprising city. The energy with which they pushed their business deserved success and secure it. But with all their tact, with all their enterprise, they cannot neutralize the natural advantages that have hitherto sustained Toronto nor can their success close their eyes to the fact that Toronto has become a great distributing depôt, whose importance is daily on the increase. A splendid country lies to the rear of Toronto, and as the more remote sections become settled and developed there will arise increase demands upon the trading facilities of this city, and their necessary consequence, increased supplies. The railways now in existence and those about to be constructed will discharge into this reservoir, such streams as will distend to the utmost the channels of commerce. Already have the chains which bound Toronto in unwilling servitude to Montreal been shaken off and the Queen City of the West is securing a great share of the trade which rightly should fall to her, and seems determined not to rest content until she shall not only have regained it but added to its volume by levying on new districts.

The Grand Trunk Company is aware that the portion of its railway which runs through the Province of Ontario, makes the largest returns as will be seen from the following averages for the half year ended Dec., 1866.

Sarnia and Toronto	$128 68
Toronto and Kingston	140 24
Kingston and Montreal	132 51
Montreal and Richmond.	116 34
Richmond and Point Levi. . .	40 55
Richmond and Island Pond.	80 13
Chaudiere & Rivière du Loup	14 12

The Revière du Loup section, over 118 miles, was built at a cost of $3,000,000, and worked at a loss placed by some at $70,000 per annum. Mr. Brydges in one of his letters said, "We have to work 250 miles of railway east of Richmond, which yield no profit whatever. In the course of debate in Parliament, Mr. Simpson stated on the authority of Mr. Freer, the lessee of the Rivière du Loup section that while receiving a subsidy of $18,000 per annum for running it, and with a suitable equipment of rolling stock and the free use of four engines, it would have ruined him had he continued to work the line even on these apparently favorable terms.

The political influence of the Province of Ontario is confessedly great and will assuredly increase in magnitude, so that the time will come, if it has not already arrived, when deference must be paid to the interests and wishes of this section of the Dominion. If it can be shown that the Grand Trunk management does gross injustice to Toronto and to Ontario, a strong feeling of antagonism to the Company must spring up and react upon the welfare of the Company. The Montreal people, or some of them, complain that Toronto is favored in railway freights. So far from being favored the contrary is the case. Any grace shown to Toronto by the Grand Trunk has been a matter of necessity, not of favor. Montreal interests have swayed the traffic legislation; Montreal influence, political and otherwise, has directed the whole unfortunate career of the Company. The political influence which centres in Montreal forced the Company to build miles of unprofitable road, and in many other ways has proved its bane. This secret was learned at great cost, and the Company, awakened to a consciousness of its real position, freed itself of the load. Another secret has to be learned and that is, the gross injustice done to Toronto trade by freight arrangements which discriminate against Toronto and Western Canada generally and favor Montreal on the one hand and the Western States on the other. For the purpose of explaining this, we avail ourselves of calculations made by Mr. Chisholm, a prominent Toronto merchant, who has given a good deal of attention to its elucidation. The unjust policy pursued towards Canada in favor of the United States is thus shown. The rate of freight on flour and meal from Chicago to Boston is 55 cents, equal to 38½c. gold, from Sarnia to Portland, 798 miles, or less than ½c. a ton per mile ; from Chicago to Toronto 21½c. equal to 14c. gold or less than 9–10c. a ton per mile ; Chicago to Montreal 45 7-10 equal to 32c. gold or less than 65-100c a ton per mile. If we contrast the rates on Canadian productions to Toronto we can appreciate the extent of the injustice which we have to submit to. Sarnia to Toronto 2c. a ton per mile ; Stratford to Toronto over 3c. ; Guelph to Toronto over 4⅔c. ; Brampton to Toronto over 7¼c. Freight trains from Sarnia to Portland, consist of fourteen cars for which the Grand Trunk gets $38.50 per car or $539 per train, the distance being 798 miles. For the same number of cars from Sarnia to Toronto, distance only 168 miles, the Company gets $490 or $49 less than to Portland. Is it to be wondered at that Western Canada complains of the Grand Trunk not only when inducements are offered to immigrants to go beyond our boundaries as "through freight," but also when the cost of transportation to the sea-board from the Western States is less than from the Province of Ontario, and Western Yankees get their business done at a loss to the Grand Trunk of 150 per cent., which loss has to be made good by us Canadians in the payment of a tax in the way of extra charges on our own productions.

The freight arrangements, which brought about the state of affairs referred to, operate prejudicially to the whole of this Province. We shall now proceed to explain how Toronto is affected directly by the imposition of discriminating rates :—

	Miles.	Grain.	Flour
Cornwall to Montreal	67	10c	20n
Peterboro' to Toronto	68	16	24
		—	—
In favor of Montreal		6	4
Prescott to Montreal	112	14	28
Seaforth to Toronto	112	16	32
		—	—
In favor of Montreal		2	4
Kingston to Montreal	172	18	35
Sarnia to Toronto	168	20	40
		—	—
Four miles nearer in favor of Montreal	2	5	
Belleville to Montreal	220	20	40
Sarnia to Toronto	168	20	40
		—	—
		52	
Sarnia to Toronto and Toronto Montreal	501	45	90
Sarnia to Montreal direct	501	37	76
		—	—
In favor of Montreal		8	16

	Miles.	2nd Class Goods per 100 lbs.	3rd Class Goods per 100 lbs
Montreal to Cobourg	260	25c	22c
Toronto to Cobourg	72	20	15
	188	—	—
		5	7
Montreal to Bowmanville	290	25	22
Toronto to Bowmanville	43	17	14
		—	—
		8	8
Montreal to Kingston	198	16	15
Toronto to Kingston	165	28	22
	33	—	—
		12	7
Montreal to Whitby	304	25	22
Toronto to Whitby	29	14	12
	275	—	—
		11	10
Montreal to Lucan	446	35	31
Toronto to Lucan	113	25	20
		—	—
	333	10	11
Montreal to Seaforth	445	39	34
Toronto to Seaforth	112	25	20

It requires no great skill to discover why it is that the Grand Trunk Railway Company has so many enemies throughout the length and breadth of this Province. It has been wearing out its rails and locomotives in carrying through freight at a loss and taxing the local freight to make up for it. It has been carrying through freight and either neglecting local freight or transporting it so slowly as to drive business men into using every other available means of getting their goods. No time could be more opportune than the present for an inquiry into the character of the internal legislation of the Grand Trunk. The English stockholders are bent on knowing if there are ills to complain of. For their own sakes, as well as for the sake of the country, it is to be hoped that an immediate investigation will be had.

The editor of *Herapath's Journal* has directed great attention to the affairs of the company, and what we commend to his careful consideration what we have set out about. If the Riviere du Loup section does not pay,

close it, rather than compel this P bear an extra tax to make good tha the people of Quebec want that se open, let them pay for it. If the of Montreal wish props for their them pay for them. What Toron a fair field and no favor.

THE PREMIUM NOTE SYS

A letter from the Hon. Elizur Massachusetts, to S. Pedlar & Co. real, has been published in pamp As it may be regarded as the late to the literary pile which the Pre controversy has been the means o together, we are prompted to m subject of a review.

We are not admirers of the Pre system; we discussed it fully in al ings a few months ago, and beg t readers to Nos. 27, 28 and 30 of th Since then we have seen no reason our opinion, and need not, ther enlarge upon it. Our present re be confined to reviewing the arg Mr. Wright, whose defence is p best that has been written. We once, that we are quite at one w the conclusion that, financially, th perfectly sound ; in fact, we go a ther, and believe that, as a syste be so, so long as the cash portion mium in each year is sufficient t risk for that year, and so long as t charged on the notes is equal to (which in practice it always is) tha rial rate upon which the premiu We believe further, as we showed cles above mentioned, that there i difference, far less than is general between the note and all cash s that, if there is a slight advantag doubt) in the former in respect of amount of cash which is paid in years, it is far more than counter the uncertainty as to the rate of future and as to the sum which ceived at death, so that our obje the system, though financially s an advisable one for Life Insu Wright (p. 9) casts much ridicu Barnes for assuming that the ju premium notes is their being m dividends. As a matter of histo Mr. Barnes is probably right, f the origin of the note system t that when it was found that co declaring annual dividends of 5(upwards, the question naturall pay cash for the purpose of havi in a year or two why not give a Mr. Wright justifies the note way :

he annual premium to insure $1000 for the age of 40, is usually $32. If the ies' Mortality at 4 per cent. is adopted rule of reserve, this premium consists net $23.68, and the loading for expenc., of $8.32. By the same rule the emium to insure $1000 for one year at 9.96. But when the company is paid than that, it does not really insure but $1000, less what will be on hand end of the year to help pay the loss, it occur. This, in case $23.67 is paid, $14.41, and the company really insures 985.59, whether the insured pays all or part cash and a note, which, at 4 per will amount to $14.41 at the end of r. He has fully paid for the mathe-l value of the risk by the $9.82 cash. lance of the net premium, $13.86, the al of the net value of the policy or at the end of the year, may more be in the hands of the insured than are, and as profitably, if it brings as nterest. And if we could be certain e working expenses of the year would ceed $6.18, as the share of the policy, is note might be taken safely for the f the loading, or $2.14, making half year's premium, or $16." (pp. 10, 11.) , though perfectly true and proving learly the financial soundness of the , is not a correct explanation of its but rather a comparatively recent in-n to justify its continued existence; as e consider it a poor one, the note sys-ing an exceedingly clumsy and unsci-method of effecting what is thus avowed bject. It seems to be a natural infirm-the Anglo-Saxon mind to adhere to a le, whether good or bad, as long as e, and rather than adopt a better but nt one to obviate the pernicious conse-s of the old and bad one by various artifices and fictions. The history of h law, from Magna Charta downwards, mmentary on and corroboration of this It is similar in regard to the question now discussing. The obnoxious prin-in the evasion of which Mr. Wright he justification of the note system) hich Life Insurance has hitherto, that nearly two hundred years, been con-is the payment of equal annual pre-nium. The defect is that the same paid for a varying and unequal risk, a man insures at 25 for $1000; he pays an annual premium of about $20 ugh, whether at age 25 or 60, though after age the risk is nearly four times s as at the former. It follows of course more is paid in the earlier years than ssary to cover the risk then. This ience is now attempted to be evaded ng loans upon the policy by the decla-f dividends and bonuses, and, accord-Mr. Wright, by the adoption of the stem; in short, by any means rather e adoption of a different, though principle, that of charging only a

sufficient premium in each year to exactly cover the risk for that year, the premium of course increasing each year in exact propor-tion to the risk. This method was pointed out in a former number (28, p. 249) of this journal. The rates upon such a policy would be about the following, on a life aged 25, for $1000:

Year.	Amount.	Year.	Amount.	Year.	Amount.
1	$9 30	13	$13 00	25	$18 50
2	9 40	14	13 40	26	18 70
3	9 50	15	14 10	27	19 20
4	10 10	16	15 60	28	19 30
5	11 00	17	16 20	29	20 00
6	11 40	18	16 60	30	21 00
7	11 70	19	16 90	31	22 40
8	11 90	20	17 10	32	23 70
9	12 00	21	17 50	33	24 30
10	12 30	22	17 70	34	29 00
11	12 50	23	17 90	35	31 80
12	12 60	24	18 30	36	36 00

These are the Ætna term rates for an insu-rance for one year at the different ages from 25 to 60: we think they are larger than neces-sary. Of course, on a policy covering the whole life, a small percentage would have to be added to cover the extra risk of being obliged in the years after the first, to insure whether sick or well. We think the above rates are more than sufficient to cover this. Now in the same company the rate for a life aged 25 for $1000 is $20.52. Half of this being given in note, the cash half would be $10.26; add to this the interest on the note, 62 cents, and we get $10.88 as the cash pay-ment in the first year, being $1.58 more than the above.

The advantages of a policy of this kind over the note system would be the following: 1st. Less cash would have to be paid through-out for the same insurance. 2nd. The annual premium and the sum to be paid at death would be known and certain. 3rd. The in-sured could allow his policy to lapse at any time without loss, the payments made being exactly sufficient to cover the risk and no more. 4th. The payments would be ex-tremely small in the earlier years when the insured was least able to pay, and would only increase as (on the average) his ability to pay increased.

Mr. Wright concludes his letter with the following remarkable sentences: "The 'note system' can only be successfully attacked on the assumption that all men squander every-thing which they do not lay up in some savings bank from which they cannot with-draw it. The 'cash system,' as distinguished from the 'note system,' adds to Life Insu-rance a sort of compulsory savings bank. If a man insures $10,000 for life at 40 in a com-pany, which reserves by the Actuaries' Mor-tality at 4 per cent., and dies at 80, he has in deposit with the company, at the time of his death, $7,103.88. This, if it is in cash, his widow or heir gets, because it was his own money. In the mean time the sum really insured under the contract has dwindled from $9,855.88, in the first year, to $2,896.12 in

the last; and this last sum is all that the widow or heir gets of the Insurance Company as such. With perfect safety to itself the company might have taken and held his interest-bearing notes up to the amount of $7,103.88. If the insured could have made his money always earn one per cent. per an-num more than the rate of interest on his notes, he would have gained during 40 years by giving his notes, instead of cash, $1,451 55; and if these gains had been compounded at 6 per cent. from their receipt till the ter-mination of the policy, they would have amounted to $3,575.60. So that, though the widow and children should receive from the company, on the policy of $10,000, the sum of $7,103.88 in promissory notes of the de-ceased, of no use to them, they would be comforted by the receipt of $10,679.48 from his estate, which would not have been there if he had paid the company all cash." (pp. 15 16.)

We demur to the quiet assumption that the insured would make one per cent. more than he pays to the company on his notes. The rate on the notes allowing for its being paid in advance is 6 4-10 per cent.; we question much if men on the average make so much as this on a small sum, such as $60, which is half the average premium. We think the stockholders of the Grand Trunk Railway, for instance, would be glad to get even a sixth part of this rate of interest on their invest-ment. We should like to have seen the cal-culations by which Mr. Wright arrives at his figures, as without them we are obliged to guess. We presume then that the $7,103.88 is the amount which the insured pays beyond what is necessary to cover the risk from year to year during the 40 years. If so, it is curi-ous that so acute an actuary as Mr. Wright should fail to see that a properly conducted all cash company would have returned this sum, except the last three or four premiums, in the shape of dividends, so that the insured would have had the control of it, just as under the note system. It is this fact which assimi-lates the two systems and which seems to be systematically ignored, so that it is generally imagined that there is far greater difference between them than is actually the case. If, however, the $7,103.88 is not payment beyond the risk value, but is a portion of what goes to pay for the risk, so that the notes would be outstanding at death, then to this extent there will have been a failure of insurance during the 40 years, and the insured will get only $2,896.12 at death—the cash payments made being sufficient only to insure to that extent. If this be what Mr. Wright intends, then it is even more curious that he should not perceive that his argument, push-ed to its logical extreme, is utterly destructive of life insurance; for if it be so advantageous for the insured to keep the $7,103.88, and invest it himself, why ask him for any cash payment? Why not let him keep the rest, and comfort his widow with the additional compound 1 per cent on that also? In short, why insure at all? To this Mr. Wright would probably answer, that the object of insurance is to cover the risk of an early death; this we deny, and reply, that the case of an early death is an exceptional one, and that life insurance, is intended to provide not for exceptional but for average cases. The upholders of the note system seem to us involved in this dilemna. Either the notes given will be paid by dividends or they will not; in other words, the notes are necessary or they are not. If necessary, then they will be outstanding at death, and to the amount of them the life will not have been insured; if not necessary, then why go through the farce of giving them for the purpose of cancelling them in a year or two, by dividends.

We have always been under the impression that one of the main objects of Life Insurance was the very one which Mr. Wright appears to think so absurd, viz.; as a sort of Savings Bank, and that those who had once entered into an insurance contract should feel partly bound in honor to carry it on to the end for the sake of their families or others who might be dependent upon them, their creditors &c. and partially to prevent them from spending their means wastefully and extravagantly which, in spite of Mr. Wright, we believe that the majority of men are somewhat apt to do. A commoner case even than these, is that of a man with a family, having about enough to live upon, and who without an insurance, would infallibly live up to his income, but who on insuring his life would probably pinch himself so as to keep up the policy. We freely admit that there are cases when it would be a boon to a policy-holder to be allowed to withdraw partially or wholly from his bargain, as where he becomes too poor to keep it up or where his family have died and no one remains dependent upon him but such cases are exceptional and besides are not Life Insurance, and are therefore beside the question under discussion, which is not what beneficial bargains of any kind men may enter into, but which is the more or less beneficial mode of Life Insurance, in other words, the securing of a certain specified and ascertained sum of money at death.

Communications.

THE EXPORT OF CANADIAN PETROLEUM.

To the Editor of the Monetary Times.

SIR,—In a letter which appeared in your valuable Journal of the 17th September, I endeavoured to show some of the advantages to be derived from the export of Canadian Petroleum, and since then it is pleasing to note that a movement has commenced in that direction. The Canadian Land and Mineral Company operating at Petrolia, advertised last month for a vessel to carry 2,500

barrels of refined petroleum from Hamilton, Ont., to London, England, and have, I believe, since made a considerable shipment. A contemporary of the 10th inst. says, that "a few of the refiners are making a very superior article of refined oil for exportation to Europe. An effort has lately been made to open up a market in Europe for the crude article. The prospects of opening up a market there for both crude and refined, were never better than at the present moment." Mr. Macrea, the Oil Broker in Liverpool, an acknowledged authority upon the subject, recently published a letter with regard to Canadian petroleum, in which he advised the exportation of the best refined oil, but did not encourage the shipment of crude. There may, however, shortly arise a large demand for the crude oil, in consequence of the marked success of experiments lately made in Europe for burning crude petroleum on locomotives in the place of coal. The last *Illustrated Times* contains an illustration of the Emperor Napoleon riding on the engine of a railway train, for the purpose of personally examining the apparatus for using petroleum as fuel. On this occasion the train travelled a distance of 18 miles, and the method of raising steam by means of liquid fuel, was pronounced to be completely successful. The importance of these experiments cannot be overestimated, for should petroleum be generally adopted as fuel for locomotives, it would be found still more advantageous for steam vessels, and the demand for these purposes would be enormous.

Objections have been urged to the shipment of oil direct from Sarnia to Europe, but it would seem that the difficulties are more imaginary than real. The Cleveland *Herald* gives an account of a cargo of oil sailing direct from Cleveland to Liverpool. It says, "The Etowah, of Liverpool, is now loading with refined petroleum direct for Liverpool, at the dock of Thomas Walton. The cargo will consist of 2,000 barrels of oil, manufactured in Cleveland—this is the third or fourth cargo of oil that has been shipped direct to Liverpool from Cleveland. The previous ventures of this kind have proved profitable, and we have no doubt the present one will result the same way." If oil can be shipped profitably from Cleveland, how much more profitably from Sarnia? There are no more difficulties of navigation to contend with from Sarnia than there are from Cleveland, and a cargo of oil for Europe could be dispatched just as easily from one place as the other. The difference in price, however, in favour of Canadian oil is so great that it is surprising no business has hitherto been done in exporting from Sarnia. A refiner, provided he had his own wells, could lay down refined oil in Sarnia, ready for shipment, at $4 per barrel (including the barrels). I have not statistics to show what the exact price of refined oil would be in Cleveland, but it cannot be very much less than in New York, where the present price per barrel is equal to $9.50 in gold. Supposing the price in Cleveland to be $8, this would be double the cost of oil at Sarnia, which is only a day's sail further than Cleveland. Under these circumstances, it is astonishing that Canadians have so long allowed the whole export trade of petroleum to be monopolized by the United States, but it is hoped they are becoming more alive to their interests, and that a new era is about to dawn on the Canadian oil trade. The American oil regions, in consequence of their immense export trade, are flourishing beyond all precedent. Pleasantville, which is now one of the best producing districts of Pennsylvania, has grown into a city within the last few months. The Cleveland *Leader* says: "that mammoth hotels, theatres, boarding houses, restaurants, stores and saloons, have sprung up in every direction, and the building of the city still goes on. It is very fascinating, this oil business. Fortunes are made in a month, a week, sometimes a day. Territory sells from $500 to $2,500 per acre, according to location. Town lots for building purposes rent from $200 to $1,000 per year." The villages, in Enniskillen, present a sad contrast to this picture of

prosperity, but no other conclusion can be arrived at but that the difference is owing only to the want of enterprise in our country, and should the attention be given to our oil regions, there is reason why they should not be as flourishing as those in Pennsylvania. The Titusville *Herald* the following excellent remarks upon the petroleum trade:—

"While cotton, grain, tobacco, and other leading agricultural staples of the country combined, are universally regarded as the basis of industry and commerce, little is said of petroleum in same connection, notwithstanding the fact that there is probably as much money involved in last mentioned commodity as in any other article of home production. Petroleum, in reality, has become a product, not only of the first necessity, but of the first importance, at home and abroad; each succeeding year since it became a considerable article of commerce, witnessing increased consumption in every civilized portion of the world; and every year seems to develop new methods for its utilization. It is not only a universally employed as an illuminator, but in the manufacture of soap, candles, wax, lubricating substances and dye-stuffs, and as a motor, become of essential use. After the first flush of excitement attending the discovery of petroleum in Pennsylvania, grave fears were entertained that there might be, sooner or later, an exhaust of the supply, but these fears have been dispelled; succeeding years, during which there has been increase of production commensurate with increase of consumption. Petroleum has been discovered in various parts of the world, but far the wants of commerce have been mainly supplied by the United States, which has a practical monopoly of the trade. The exports of petroleum from New York, since the first of January, are, in round numbers, 43 million gallons, against 23 millions for the corresponding period last. From the whole of the United States the exports to date from first of January, are, 79 million gallons against 49 millions for the same period last year, being an increase of about sixty-three per cent. The great bulk of the exports are from New York and Philadelphia, though most of the business at the latter port is on New York account. The increase of exports this year is mainly Continental Europe. Leaving out France, which takes crude almost exclusively, most of the ports to Europe consist of refined article, it is not only safer to transport (as may be gathered from the fact that vessels carrying crude are subject to an extra insurance premium of 3 per cent.), but is really cheaper to the foreign consumer.

As to the risks incident to the transports of petroleum, there appears to be a great diversity of opinion, though as between crude and refined it is obvious that the former is by far the most flammable, and therefore more dangerous; very; but if the fear of accident was allowed to operate to the prejudice of common carriers, a severe blow would be inflicted upon commercial interests. Considering the immense comfort afforded by petroleum, the accidents directly or indirectly chargeable to the article, it must be confessed, have been proportionately small. Petroleum and its products may be safely transported when not exposed to heat beyond a certain normal degree, and when carried under proper regulations of packing."

It is hoped that before another year, Canada will take care to secure for themselves a fair share at least of this great trade.

Yours, &c.,
PETRO

—The schooner *Sailor Boy* was the one chartered at Chicago to carry a cargo of oats to Boston direct, via the St. Lawrence and the coast—the first cargo of oats ever shipped to Boston by this route from Chicago. On her arrival at Boston this vessel will engage in the carrying trade between that port and New York.

Commercial.

Montreal Correspondence.

(From our own Correspondent).

Montreal, Oct. 19, 1868.

Trade has been quiet during the week. I regret to notice the failure of two well-known jobbing firms in the grocery trade, Jeffrey Bros., and Forster, Moir & Co., and McCulloch, Jack & Co., in the dry goods trade. There are, as usual, rumors of other firms, but it would be impolitic to give any credence to them till a failure actually happens. It only unsettles confidence, does no good, but on the contrary, often produces much mischief. Since my last there has been the annual meeting of the members of the Corn Exchange. The report did not contain anything of a striking character, being chiefly composed of statistics of the movements of produce, here, in the States, and England; as these figures have been published before they will be of very little interest to your readers. I give the stocks of flour and wheat in the hands of millers and in store here on the 1th October:—

	1868.	1867.	1866.
Flour, brls,.........	40,331	29,972	27,802
Wheat, bu,.	111,854	84,155	39,900

Quantity of flour inspected 1st January to 1st October:—

	1868.	1867.	1866.
Barrels...	274,330	279,926	139,569

Our produce market has been very dull during the week, and the tendency of flour and wheat is still downwards. Strong bakers' flour has sold at $5.25 to $5.40, ordinary to good supers range from $5.10 to $5.20. There has been a tendency to speculate, but it is checked by the feeling that the lowest point has not yet been touched, and therefore till such is the case any purchases for the future would be dangerous. The same remarks apply to wheat. Latest quotations are: Upper Canada spring, $1.19 to $1.20; Red Western, $1.25; Chicago No. 2 is nominal. In coarse grains there is some stir in barley, and the price paid is $1.43 to $1.45, according to quality. In provisions and dairy produce not much is doing; the price of butter has fallen owing to a great cessation in the shipping demand, good shipping parcels have sold at 21¾c to 22c, but choice dairy for family use remain nominally at late high prices.

GROCERIES.—Our market has been quiet with the exception of teas and sugars, in both of which a fair business has been done. Salt and fish oils, in which recently there has been considerable speculation, have quieted down, and prices have receded from the highest point. Some large auction sales are advertised for the end of the month, which may impart some activity into the trade. I give the imports of the leading articles from 1st January to 1st August, our Custom-House returns only being made up to that period:—

	1867.		Val.	1868.		Val.
Cheese.....	248,552	lbs.	$37,483	233,013	lbs.	$20,387
Fruit.....	2,161,387	"	95,549	1,900,681	"	74,268
Brandy...	145,571	gal.	152,251	128,700	gal.	144,609
Gin......	156,886	"	66,633	153,684	"	70,486
Rum......	28,566	"	10,234	36,425	"	14,487
Molasses..	1,069,016	"	14,986	1,412,217	"	27,646
Sugars....	17,131,283	lbs.	654,687	21,048,570	lbs.	933,228
Tea......	2,288,083	"	1,131,747	1,981,901	"	638,658

DRY GOODS.—The fall trade is pretty well over and buyers are chiefly engaged in sorting up stocks. Our importers have hardly yet made up their sale books so as to arrive at drawing an average of the business done as it compares with former years. Taking generally they speak of it as a healthy trade, which though light is still in excess of the anticipations held during the summer. The most unsatisfactory branch has been that of Canadian manufactures. Our markets have been overstocked with heavy descriptions of woollens, and as we have no outlet for them out of Canada manufacturers have had to put up with considerable losses to push off their surplus stocks; this state of things will soon remedy itself, but for the present, the losses are in many cases severe. Fine Canadian manufactured woollens, such as fine tweeds, cloths, &c., have found ready sale at remunerative prices, the great falling off of the imports of these goods having given an expansion to our home trade.

HARDWARE.—Contrary to the activity usually noticeable at this period of the year, the past week has been very quiet, but as the fall fleet has now mostly arrived, and stocks are ample and well assorted, we may look for increased activity till the close of the navigation. Prices remain very firm.

BOOTS AND SHOES AND LEATHER.—There has been a good business doing in all these branches. The manufacturers of boots and shoes are comparatively active, and the bulk of their heavy stocks are by this time worked off. Prices of all staples have not receded, as it was at one time feared would be the case; this has caused greater liveliness in the leather market.

Toronto Market.

For the week past the weather has been fine, considering the stage of the season. Indeed, ever since the fall trade commenced, there has been nothing to complain of on this score. To this circumstance and the fine state of the country roads, the now undoubted success of the fall trade may, in a great measure, be attributed.

DRY GOODS.—The season is now pretty well over, and both importers and manufacturers express themselves satisfied with the results attained. Sales of all classes of goods have been fully up to expectations, which has had the effect of reducing stocks to a point that rids importers of any anxiety or inconvenience. A still better feature of the trade is found in the fact that payments from country merchants are now very good, and have been so since the commencement of the current month. It is said that the remittances for October will fully double those of September, which were not considered at all up to the mark. Importations show a large falling off on last year, and it seems now probable that importers have rather underestimated, if anything, the wants of the country.

GROCERIES.—Trade is unsettled, owing to the serious failures in Montreal. There is little change in prices from last week.

BOOTS AND SHOES.—Business continues very active, taxing to the fullest extent the resources of Manufacturers. Prices remain about the same. A gratifying feature in the trade is the steady acquisition of new customers, a great many names having been added to those on the books of our manuafcturers, since the commencement of the present season.

LEATHER.—The market is rather dull. *Hemlock calf*—None offering, and there is no demand for lots; small parcels have been taken at 50 to 60c. *Splits*—A large sale occurred on Tuesday at 20c. For further quotations see our price list.

GRAIN.—*Wheat*—Receipts 36,984 bushels, and 15,780 bushels the previous week. There is a good supply offering, and the market is dull and steady. Sales of 12 car loads spring were made at $1 13 to $1 14, and of fall at $1 18 to $1 35 according to quality. *Barley.*—Receipts by cars 38,000 bushels, and 35,474 bushels the previous week, and 15,000 on the street. Market irregular and unsettled, opening at $1 48 to $1 50 and closing dull at $1 40 to $1 43; sales about 50,000 bushels at current rates. *Peas* dull at quotations, no sales. *Oats* firmer, offering at 52 and buyers at 49½.

FLOUR.—Receipts for the week 2,150 barrels, and 1,825 barrels the previous week. Market dull; superfine offering freely at $5 to $5 15, with buyers at $5 to $5.10; sales two or three lots at $5.10, 100 barrels extra sold at $6 25.

PROVISIONS.—*Butter*—Quiet at 22c. sale one car-load at that price. *Cheese* offering at 11¼c. by the car-load. *Eggs* selling at 15c. to 17c. *Mess Pork* is held firmly at $24 50 to $25. *Hogs*, live sold to a considerable extent at 5½c. *Potatoes* selling at 50c. to 60c. by the car-load.

FREIGHTS.—The rate on flour to Montreal by steamer has advanced to 25c. and is firm, with plenty of down freight offering. Grain by steamer pays 8c; the propeller St. Lawrence is loading for Montreal at that figure. The steam barge Dromedary is loading at Hamilton with barley for Quebec at 10c; this is the first barley we believe that has gone east by vessel this season. Provisions to Europe pay about 56s. sterling; barley to Oswego 3½c. American currency, to Toledo 5c., to Chicago 7c; lumber to Oswego $1 50 to $1 75.

Halifax Market.

BREADSTUFFS.—Oct. 13.—The flour market still continues dull and depressed. Some holders forcing sales Canada No. 1 $6.75 to 6.80; we have heard of sales under quotations; (we note sale of city brands of No. 1 at Montreal at $5.25 to 5.30 for delivery within a short time. Extra Canada $8 to 8.20; extra State $6 to 7. Cornmeal dull at $4.60 to 4.70 for kiln dried; $4.50 for fresh ground. Oatmeal $7.75 to 7.80. Imports from January 1st to October 13th, 1867 and 1868:—

	Bbls. Flour.	Bbls. Cornmeal.
1868.	138,807	41,945
1867.	146,439	30,566

FISH.—We have no change to note in fish this week. Codfish may be quoted at $4 for large, and $2,80 to 3.20 for small. Labrador, a small lot in unsold. Bank and Bay none. Haddock $1.70 to $2. Herring, good Shore and Labrador in demand at $4 to 4.50. Mackerel, Mo. 1 $9 to 10; No. 2 $8 to 8.50; No. 3 large $6.25. Salmon unchanged at $14 for No. 1; $12 for No. 2, and $9.50 for No. 3.

WEST INDIA PRODUCE.—The stock of sugar is becoming reduced by shipments to Canada and United States, and sales of Cuba have been made at 5¾c in bond. An advance of ⅛c was reported in Canada the latter part of the week, and holders here are firm at our quotations. Vacuum Pan none; Porto Rico 6¼ to 6⅜c; Barbadoes 5¾ to 5⅞c; Cuba 5½ to 5¾c; Centrifugal Cuba 6c in bond.

FINANCIAL.—Bank drawing rate on London 60 day sight bills 13 per cent. prem.; Private 12 to 12½ per cent. prem. New York Gold drafts at sight, 4 per cent. prem. Currency drafts 25¼ per cent. discount. Montreal sight drafts 4 per cent. prem. Newfoundland sight drafts 5 per cent. prem.—*R. C. Hamilton & Co.'s Circular.*

St. John Market.

BREADSTUFFS.—Oct. 13.—Receipts—From New York, 1,199 bbls. flour, 150 bbls. cornmeal, 25 bbls. rye flour; from Ontario, per Grand Trunk Railway, steamers and sailing vessels, 5415 bbls. flour; by Gulf of St. Lawrence steamers and E. & N. A. Railway, 2,407 bbls. of flour, 874 of which are for A. Gibson, Esq., Nashwaak, and are being reshipped from the railway wharf to Fredericton. This will make a total of 6,948 bbls. flour, 150 bbls. cornmeal, and 25 bbls. rye flour for the merchants of this city. We have to report a slight decline from last week's rates. Pretty large receipts, and a weak market in the West, have tended to depress prices here. Holders seem anxious to effect sales, and buyers hold off in the anticipation of a still further decline. We hear of few large lots changing hands, purchasers, for the most part, confining their orders to small parcels. Buyers from the country districts have not yet commenced to lay in their winter stock, and all these circumstances combine to render the trade dull. We quote, $6.60 to $6.75 for supers., $7 for choice. Cornmeal has declined and is now held at $4.50.

SUGAR AND MOLASSES.—We have no arrivals to report the past week. In molasses there have been several transactions, and this article enjoys a brisk competition. At an auction sale of Barbadoes one or two small lots were sold on a basis of 36½c to 37c., and the balance withdrawn. This quality suffered a slight decline, but has again rallied, and is now held firmer. It becomes more evident, as the season advances, that the stock of strictly prime grocery molasses is barely sufficient for the demand, but the market is well supplied with cheaper qualities. For sugars there has been a steady demand without much competition, and we repeat our quotations which are maintained. Advices from the States report a further slight advance in sweets, and from Halifax we hear of still further purchases, more particularly of Barbadoes sugar, for the Canadian market.—*News*

The Cotton Crop.

The reports, with regard to the crop, which reach us this week, are most favourable. It is thought that there has been much less injury done in almost every section of the South by the rain and worms than was anticipated. Parties who have just travelled over the South-western and Gulf States report to us more encouragingly than we had expected. One usually well informed person, who has been over the field, sends a statement showing an excess in the crop this year over last year of 250,000 bales. This we are aware is above the present generally received estimate at this point, and cannot be fully credited until confirmed by reports from other sources. We think, however, there can be but little doubt but that with continued favourable weather, and a late fall, the exportable surplus will equal that for the season just closed. Some portions of the cotton growing States will evidently yield less, but the increase in others will at least make good the loss in those quarters.

Annexed is a statement showing the stocks of cotton in Liverpool and London, including the supplies of American and Indian produce ascertained to be afloat to those ports :

	1867.	1868.
Stock in Liverpool... Bales	795,680	424,180
" London..........	106,180	72,818
American cotton afloat......	10,000	6,000
Indian "	342,490	610,240
Total......................	1,254,350	1,113,238

Of the present stock of cotton in Liverpool, 25 per cent is American, against 29¾ per cent last year. Of Indian cotton the proportion is 42½ per cent against 34 per cent.

Oil Trade of Pennsylvania.

The Titusville *Herald's* Monthly Petroleum Report, for the month ending September 30th, 1868, says:

Toward the close of the first week of the period under review, the production began to decline, and during the latter part of the third week, there were days when it scarcely exceeded 11,500 or 11,600 barrels. Early in the last week the decline was checked by the production of two or three new wells which were then struck, and by that of several older ones which were resuscitated. A very material increase was occasioned during the last three days, by the striking of four new wells, the production of one of which reached 400 barrels per day. The average on the 30th and 31st reached 12,529 barrels, by gauge tank measurement at the wells, or an increase of 182 barrels from the daily average of the last two days of the previous month, and of 124 barrels over that during July 30th and 31st.

During the month there were from forty to forty-five wells completed and tested. Of these but seven were failures; one produced four hundred barrels per day, and each of five others averaged from fifty to one hundred barrels, the remainder from five to forty barrels per day.

The actual production during September of forty-three gallons to the barrel, as shown by the shipments from the region by the Alleghany river and the railroad and transportation lines and from the decrease in stock on October 1st, was 344,292 barrels, or an average of 11,486 barrels. As compared with last month, the daily average shows a decrease of 495 barrels.

The following table shows the total production for September, the average per day, the production

previously reported, and the average per day from January 1st to September 1st :

Total shipments of Crude for September
bbls of 45 gallons each, bbls.......... 360,032
Add to reduce to bbls. of 43 gallons each, bbls...................................... 16,745

Total shipment of bbls. of 43 gallons
each, bbls............................... 376,777
Stock on hand Sept. 1st, bbls....295,993
Stock on hand Oct. 1st, bbls. 263,898
　　　　　　　　　　　　　　　　　　——————
Deduct decrease on October 1st, bbls 32,185
Total production during Sept., bbls... 344,592
Average per day for 30 days, bbls 11,436
Production previously reported, bbls....2,392,779
Total production from January 1st to
October 1st, bbls....... 2,747,371
Average per day for 274 days, bbls. 10,023.

Stock of Petroleum.

The stock of Petroleum in the region continued without any considerable change until during the last three days, when it was decreased by large shipments. On the 1st instant it reached 263,898 barrels of 43 gallons each. This stock includes 175,608 barrels in iron tankage, 1000 in wooden storage tanks at Titusville, 1200 on the Hyde and Egbert Farm, 4000 at Oil City, and 2000 at Tidioute, and the stock at the wells on the hands of producers, dealers and shippers, which reached 80,000 on the 1st. The stock at the wells was increased principally by some of the producers holding for a rise. Fully 60,000 bbls of it, however, were owned by dealers and shippers.

As compared with last month, the total stock shows a decrease of 35,165 barrels, and that in iron tankage a decrease of 51,988 barrels. The stock in iron tankage shows the largest reduction on account of unusually large quantities having been delivered into tank cars from many of the iron tanks during the last two days of the month. The following table shows the total stock and the amount in iron tankage on the dates named :

	Am't in iron tankage.	Total stock.
November 7th, 1867, bbls..459,000		655,000
December 7th.....................480,900		620,400
January 7th 1868.............466,500		534,600
February 7th.....................430,100		541,100
March 7th......................497,194		552,194
April 7th.........................486,600		559,000
May 1st..........................381,400		421,600
June 1st..........................246,100		290,400
July 1st..........................231,050		258,450
August 1st......................221,450		267,450
September 1st..................227,573		295,973
October 1st......................175,608		253,808

The Iron Tankage.

The capacity of iron tankage has been enlarged by the completion of six thousand barrels at Miller's Farm, and on the 1st it reached a total of 1,070,539 barrels. The capacity of tankage was increased 893,981 barrels. On the 1st of October, 1867, the total capacity of tankage was a little over 600,000 barrels. This shows an increase during the year ending the 1st inst. of nearly one hundred per cent. The decline in the price of Petroleum has favored the erection of additional tankage, and during the month contracts have been effected for the construction of fully one hundred thousand barrels capacity. Of this capacity about fifty thousand barrels is located at Miller and the remainder at Oil City and Titusville.

Recapitulation.

Total amount of Petroleum in iron and
wooden storage tanks and in the hands
of producers, brokers and shippers,
bbls.. 263,898
Total capacity of iron tankage, bbls.....1,070,539
Total amount of Petroleum in iron tank-
age, bbls............................... 175,608
Amount of iron tankage empty, bbls 894,931
Number of new wells drilling.............. 278
Daily production, bbls. 12,529

Sale of Canadian Ships in England.

By advances received by a late English ma[il] learn that the following sales of Canadian vessels have recently taken place in Liver viz. :—Quorn, 1228 tons register, built at Q 926 tons register, built at St. John in 1865, cl A. 17 years, $5800. In 1865, classed A. 17 years, £5600. DeCo 926 tons register, built at St. John in 1865, cl A. 17 years, $5800. Aberdeen, 374 tons reg built at Quebec in 1868, classed 3-3ds, in B Veritas 7 years, £3000.

Valentia Raisins.

Respecting the yield of Valencia, the *Pr Markets Review* publishes the following letter a prominent firm in Valencia, dated Sept. Our Raisin crop is, as you are aware, drawing close, and although the total yield is estimat various persons to be about 17,000 tons, we, selves, from information received, do not be it will far exceed 15,000 tons. On account o great drought experienced this season, the fr not so fine nor so even as in some previous y but, nevertheless, it is a good, sound, kei fruit. Up to the 11th inst, the date of our advices, 138,705 quintals had been shipped, distributed as follows :—112,937 to the U Kingdom, 16,578 to the United States, 6,2 Montreal, 1,200 to Marseilles, 1,000 to Sw and 750 to Malaga. Owing to the late rain, a tion of the fruit has been slightly affected, an greater part of that now remaining is of a lov inferior quality. Good, dry, sound fruit, costs 3½ dollars and upwards.

How the "Corner" in Oil Works.

An Oil Springs correspondent of the *Cha Planet*, a week ago said that several new refin were building at that place, and he then thou stand would be made against the oil combin formed under Judge Higgins. In a latter l he says the new refiners appear to have succ owing to threats of the combination to throw oil on the market and ruin all concerned, appears they have succeeded in bringing the men into harness, with the understanding they draw from the Combination wareho weekly, half the quantities of oil that they manufacture—paying for the same just wh would actually cost them to make it. This arr ment will be mutually advantageous, for th finers will have half the quantity that they in have in case they persisted in running withou risk, and the Combination work off the large of oil they were compelled to purchase in or control the market ; and it will be to the in both to keep prices up.

Gore Bank.

THE Adjourned Annual Meeting of the Shareholders
　　receive the report of the Committee appointed meeting held on the 3rd day of August last, will be the Banking House,

On MONDAY, the 2nd of NOVEMBER next, at :

By order of the Board,

W. G. CASSEL[S]
Cas[hier]

Gore Bank,
Hamilton, 12th Oct., 1868.

THE PRINCE EDWARD COUNTY

Mutual Fire Insurance Comp[any]

Head Office,—PICTON, ONTARIO.
President, L. B. Stinson ; Vice-President, W. A. Ric[hards]

Directors : H. A. McFaul, James Cavan, James J. N. B. DeMill, William Delong. Treasurer, David Secretary, John Twigg ; Solicitor, R. J. Fitzgerald.

THIS Company is established upon strictly Mutu
　　ciples, insuring farming and isolated proper hazardous ; Townships only, and offers great advan insurers, at low rates for five years, without the ex; a renewal This Company has existed 1¾ years, which period it has adjusted all losses in a sati manner. It is managed with strict economy, and a opportunity of insuring with safety and reliance, a little expense, which accounts for its long stan the successful business which it has been and is no Picton, June 15, 1868.

Montreal House, Montreal, Canada.

TO MONETARY MEN.—Merchants, Insurance Agents, Lawyers, Bankers, Railway and Steamboat Travellers, Mining Agents, Directors and Stockholders of Public Companies, and other persons visiting Montreal for business or pleasure, are here by most respectfully informed that the undersigned proposes to furnish the best hotel accommodation at the most reasonable charges. It is our study to provide every comfort and accommodation to all our guests, especially for gentlemen engaged as above. To those who have been accustomed to patronize other first-class hotels, we only ask a trial; we have the same accommodation and our table is furnished with every delicacy of the season.

H. DUCLOS.

Nov. 22, 1867. 15-1y

H. N. Smith & Co.,

2, EAST SENECA STREET, BUFFALO, N. Y., (correspondent Smith, Gould, Martin & Co., 11 Broad Street, N.Y.,) Stock, Money and Exchange Brokers. Advances made on securities. 21-1y

Hurd, Leigh & Co.,

IMPORTERS AND DECORATORS OF

FRENCH CHINA.

Hotels and families supplied with any pattern or crest desired.

Common goods always on hand. 72 Yonge Street, Toronto, Ontario. 26y

DAY'S

Commercial College and High School,

No. 82 KING STREET EAST,

(Near St. James' Cathedral.)

THE design of this institution is to prepare Young Men and others as Book-keepers, and for general business, and to furnish them with the facilities for acquiring an excellent

English and Commercial Education.

Mr. DAY is also prepared to give Private Instruction in the several subjects of his department, and to assist Merchants and others in the checking and balancing of books, adjusting their accounts and partnership affairs, &c.

For further information, please call on or address the undersigned.

JAMES E. DAY,
Accountant

Toronto, Sept. 3rd, 1868.

J. T. & W. Pennock,

FIRE and Life Insurance Agents, Parliamentary and Departmental Agents, Mining Agents, and Exchange Brokers.

Ottawa, Dec. 21st, 1867. 10-1y

Brown Brothers,

ACCOUNT-BOOK MANUFACTURERS,

Stationers, Book-Binders, Etc.,

66 *and* 68 *King Street East, Toronto, Ont.*

ACCOUNT Books for Banks, Insurance Companies, Merchants, etc., made to order of the best materials, and for style, durability and cheapness unsurpassed.

A large stock of Account-Books and General Stationery constantly on hand.

September 1, 1868. 3-1y

Philip Browne & Co.,

BANKERS AND STOCK BROKERS.

DEALERS IN

STERLING EXCHANGE—U. S. Currency, Silver and Bonds—Bank Stocks, Debentures, Mortgages, &c. Drafts on New York issued, in Gold and Currency. Prompt attention given to collections. Advances made on Securities.

No. 67 YONGE STREET, TORONTO

JAMES BROWNE. PHILIP BROWNE, *Notary Public.*
y

Candee & Co.,

BANKERS AND BROKERS, dealers in Gold and Silver Coin, Government Securities, &c., Corner Main and Exchange Streets Buffalo, Y. N. 21-1v

TORONTO PRICES CURRENT.—October 22, 1868.

Name of Article.	Wholesale Rates.	
Boots and Shoes.	$ c.	$ c.
Mens' Thick Boots ...	2 20	2 50
" Kip	2 50	3 25
" Calf	3 20	3 70
" Congress Gaiters	2 00	2 40
" Kip Cobourgs	1 00	1 50
Boys' Thick Boots	1 65	1 90
Youths' "	1 45	1 55
Women's Batts	95	1 30
" Congress Gaiters	1 15	1 50
Misses' Batts	0 75	1 00
" Congress Gaiters	1 00	1 30
Girls' Batts	0 65	0 85
" Congress Gaiters	0 80	1 10
Children's C. T. Cacks	0 50	0 65
" Gaiters	0 65	0 90
Drugs.		
Aloes Cape	0 12½	0 16
Alum	0 02½	0 03
Borax	0 00	0 00
Camphor, refined	0 65	0 70
Castor Oil	0 18	0 28
Caustic Soda	0 04½	0 05
Cochineal	0 90	1 00
Cream Tartar	0 00	0 00
Epsom Salts	0 03	0 04
Extract Logwood	0 09	0 11
Gum Arabic, sorts	0 30	0 35
Indigo, Madras	0 75	1 00
Licorice	0 14	0 45
Madder	0 13	0 16
Nutgalls	0 00	0 00
Opium	6 70	7 00
Oxalic Acid	0 28	0 35
Potash, Bi-tart	0 25	0 28
" Bichromate	0 15	0 20
Potass Iodide	3 80	4 50
Senna	0 12½	0 60
Soda Ash	0 03	0 04
Soda Bicarb	4 50	5 50
Tartaric Acid	0 37½	0 45
Verdigris	0 35	0 40
Vitriol, Blue	0 09	0 10
Groceries.		
Coffees:		
Java, ℔ lb.	0 22@	0 24
Laguayra,	0 17	0 18
Rio	0 15	0 17
Fish:		
Herrings, Lab. split	6 75	7 00
" round	0 00	0 00
" scaled	0 35	0 40
Mackerel, small kitts	1 00	0 00
Loch. Her. wh'e firks	2 50	2 75
" half "	1 25	1 50
White Fish & Trout	3 25	3 50
Salmon, saltwater	14 00	15 00
Dry Cod, ℔112 lbs	5 00	5 00
Fruit:		
Raisins, Layers	2 20	2 25
" M. R.	2 10	2 20
" Valentias new	0 03½	0 08½
Currants, new	0 05	0 05½
" old	0 04¼	0 04½
Figs	0 11	0 12½
Molasses:		
Clayed, ℔ gal.	0 00	0 35
Syrups, Standard	0 43	0 44
" Golden	0 52	0 55
Rice:		
Arracan	4 50	4 75
Spices:		
Cassia, whole, ℔ lb.	0 42	0 45
Cloves	0 11	0 12
Nutmegs	0 45	0 55
Ginger, ground	0 20	0 25
" Jamaica, root	0 20	0 25
Pepper, black	0 09½	0 10
Pimento	0 08	0 09
Sugars:		
Port Rico, ℔ lb.	0 08½	0 08¾
Cuba "	0 08¼	0 08¾
Barbadoes (bright)	0 08¼	0 08¾
Dry Crushed, at 60d.	0 11¼	0 11½
Canada Sugar Refine'y, yellow No. 2, 60ds.	0 08¾	0 08½
Yellow, No. 2½	0 08¾	0 09¼
No. 3	0 09¾	0 09¾
Crushed X	0 10	0 10½
" A	0 10¾	0 11
Ground	0 11¼	0 11½
Extra Ground	0 12½	0 12¾
Teas:		
Japan com'n to good	0 40	0 55
" Fine to choicest	0 55	0 65
Colored, com. to fine	0 60	0 75
Congou & Souch'ng	0 42	0 75
Oolong, good to fine	0 50	0 65
Y. Hyson, com to gd.	0 45	0 55
Medium to choice	0 65	0 80
Extra choice	0 85	0 95
Gunpowd'r c. to med.	0 55	0 70
" med. to fine	0 70	0 85

Name of Article.	Wholesale Rate.	
Groceries—*Contin'd*	$ c.	$ c.
" fine to fins't	0 85	0 95
Hyson	0 45	0 80
Imperial	0 42	0 80
Tobacco, Manufact'd:		
Can Leaf, ℔ lb 5s & 10s.	0 26	0 30
Western Leaf, com.	0 25	0 26
" Good	0 27	0 32
" Fine	0 32	0 35
" Bright fine	0 40	0 50
" " choice	0 60	0 75
Hardware.		
Tin (net cash prices)		
Block, ℔ lb.	0 25	0 26
Grain	0 25	0 26
Copper:		
Pig	0 23	0 24
Sheet	0 30	0 33
Cut Nails:		
Assorted ¼ Shingles, ℔ 100 lb.	2 90	3 00
Shingle alone do	3 15	3 25
Lathe and 5 dy	3 30	3 40
Galvanized Iron:		
Assorted sizes	0 09	0 10
Best No. 24	0 00	0 00
" 26	0 08	0 08½
" 28	0 00	0 09½
Horse Nails:		
Guest's or Griffin's assorted sizes	0 19	0 20
For W. ass'd sizes	0 18	0 19
Patent Hammer'd do	0 17	0 18
Iron (at 4 months):		
Pig—Gartsherrie No1	26 00	27 00
Other brands. No1	22 00	24 00
" No2	24 00	25 00
Bar—Scotch, ℔100 lb	2 25	2 50
Refined	3 00	3 25
Swedes	5 00	5 50
Hoops—Coopers	3 00	3 25
Band	3 00	3 25
Boiler Plates	3 25	3 50
Canada Plates	4 00	4 25
Union Jack	0 00	0 00
Pontypool	4 00	4 25
Swansea	3 90	4 00
Lead (at 4 months):		
Bar, ℔ 100 lbs.	0 07	0 07½
Sheet "	0 08	0 09
Shot	0 07½	0 07¾
Iron Wire (net cash):		
No. 6, ℔ bundle	2 70	2 80
" 9, "	3 10	3 20
" 12, "	3 40	3 50
" 16, "	4 30	4 40
Powder:		
Blasting, Canada	3 50	3 75
FF "	4 25	4 50
FFF "	4 75	5 00
Blasting, English	5 00	5 50
FF loose	5 50	6 00
FFF "	6 00	6 50
Pressed Spikes (4 mos):		
Regular sizes 100	4 00	4 25
Extra "	4 50	5 00
Tin Plates (net cash):		
IC Coke	7 50	8 00
IC Charcoal	8 50	8 75
IX "	10 50	10 75
IXX "	12 50	0 00
DC "	7 50	0 00
DX "	9 50	10 00
Hides & Skins. ℔ lb		
Green rough	0 05½	0 06
Green, salt'd & insp'd	0 00	0 07
Cured	0 07½	0 08½
Calfskins, green	0 00	0 10
Calfskins, cured	0 00	0 12
" dry	0 18	0 20
Lambskins,	0 70	0 00
" pelts	0 60	0 00
Hops.		
Inferior, ℔ lb	0 10	0 12
Medium	0 12	0 15
Good	0 15	0 20
Fancy	0 00	0 00
Leather, @ (4 mos.) In lots of less than 50 sides, 10 ℔ cent higher.		
Spanish Sole, 1st qual. heavy, weights ℔ lb.	0 20	0 21
Do. 1st qual middle do.	0 22	0 23
Do. No. 2, all weights	0 15	0 19
Slaughter heavy	0 25	0 26
Do. light	0 50	0 00
Harness, best	0 32	0 34
" No. 2	0 30	0 33
Upper heavy	0 44	0 38
" light	0 36	0 40

Name of Article.	Wholesale Rates.	
Leather—*Contin'd.*	$ c.	$
Kip Skins, Patna	0 30	0
French	0 70	0
English	0 65	0
Hemlock Calf (30 to 35 lbs.) per doz.	0 75	0
Do. light	0 45	0
French Calf.	0 98	1
Grain & Satn Clt ℔ doz.	0 00	0
Splits, large ℔ lb.	0 30	0
" small	0 20	0
Enamelled Cow ℔ foot	0 17	0
Patent	0 18	0
Pebble Grain	0 17	0
Buff	0 17	0
Oils.		
Cod	0 60	0
Lard, extra	0 00	1
" No. 1	0 00	1
" Woollen	0 00	1
Lubricating, patent	0 00	0
" Mott's economic	0 50	0
Linseed, raw	0 77½	0
" boiled	0 82½	0
Machinery	0 00	0
Olive, 2nd, ℔ gal.	1 45	1
" salad	2 00	2
" salad, in bots. qt. ℔ case	3 00	3
Sesame salad, ℔ gal.	1 00	1
Seal, pale	0 70	0
Spirits Turpentine	0 65	0
Varnish	0 00	0
Whale.	0 75	0
Paints, &c.		
White Lead, genuine in Oil, ℔ 25lbs.	0 00	2
Do. No. 1 "	0 00	2
" 2 "	0 00	2
" 3 "	0 00	1
White Zinc, genuine	3 00	3
White Lead, dry	0 06	0
Red Lead	0 07½	0
Venetian Red, Eng'h	0 02½	0
Yellow Ochre, Fren'h	0 02½	0
Whiting	0 90	1
Petroleum. (Refined ℔ gal.)		
Water white, car l'd	0 31	
" small lots	0 34	
Straw, by car load	0 30	
" small lots	0 33	
Amber, by car load	0 00	
" small lots	0 00	
Benzine	0 35	
Produce.		
Grain:		
Wheat, Spring, 60 lb.	1 12	
" Fall 60 "	1 20	
Barley 48 "	1 40	
Peas 60 "	0 90	
Oats 34 "	0 49	
Rye 56 "	0 82	
Seeds:		
Clover, choice 60 "	5 50	
" com'n 68 "	0 00	
Timothy, cho'e 4 "	2 50	
" inf. to good 48 "	1 50	
Flax 56 "	1 40	
Flour (per brl.):		
Superior extra	6 25	
Extra superfine,	6 00	
Fancy superfine	0 00	
Superfine No. 1	5 00	
" No. 2	0 00	
Oatmeal, (per brl.)	6 00	
Provisions.		
Butter, dairy tub ℔ lb.	0 20	
" store packed	0 16	
Cheese, new	0 10½	
Pork, mess, per brl.	24 50	2
" prime mess	0 00	
" prime	0 00	
Bacon, rough	0 00	
" Cumberl'd cut	0 00	
" smoked	0 00	
Hams, in salt	0 00	
" sug. cur. & canv'd	0 00	
Shoulders, in salt	0 00	
Lard, in kegs	0 13½	
Eggs, packed	0 15	
Beef Hams	0 00	
Tallow	0 00	
Hogs dressed, heavy	6 50	
" medium	6 00	
" light	6 00	
Salt, &c.		
American brls.	1 58	
Liverpool coarse	1 20	
Plaster	1 05	
Water Lime	1 50	

Candles.		
...rd & Co.'s ..	$ c.	$ c.
...rial	0 07½	0 08
...m Bar	0 07	0 07½
...: Bar	0 07	0 07½
...	0 05	0 05½
...	0 03½	0 03¾
...	0 11	0 11½
..., Liquors, &c.		
...per doz.	2 60	2 65
... Dub Portr..	2 35	2 40
...aica Rum	1 80	2 25
...er's H. Gin..	1 55	1 65
...Old Tom	1 90	2 00
...ases	4 00	4 25
...Old Tom, c.	6 00	6 25
...nmon	1 00	1 25
... old	2 00	4 00
...ommon	1 00	1 50
...dium	1 70	1 80
...le or golden..	2 50	4 00

Brandy:	$ c.	$ c
Hennessy's, per gal..	2 30	2 0
Martell's " ..	2 30	2 0
J. Robin & Co.'s " ..	2 25	2 5
Otard, Dupuy & Cos..	2 25	2 5
Brandy, cases	8 50	9 0
Brandy, com. per c...	4 00	4 50
Whiskey:		
Common 36 u. p.	0 62½	0 65
Old Rye	0 85	0 87½
Malt	0 85	0 87½
Toddy	0 85	0 87½
Scotch, per gal.	1 90	2 10
Irish—Kinnahan's c...	7 00	7 50
" Dunnville's Belf't..	6 00	6 25
Wool.		
Fleece, lb.	0 27	0 30
Pulled "	0 00	0 00
Furs.		
Bear	3 00	10 00
Beaver	1 00	1 25
Coon	0 20	0 40
Fisher	4 00	6 00
Martin	1 40	1 60
Mink	4 00	4 25
Otter	5 75	6 00
Spring Rats	0 15	0 17
Fox	1 20	1 25

INSURANCE COMPANIES.

ENGLISH.—*Quotations on the London Market.*

Last Dividend.	Name of Company.	Shares parval £	Amount paid.	Last
	Briton Medical and General Life	10	—	1¼
7½	Commer'l Union, Fire, Life and Mar.	50	5	5½
8	City of Glasgow	25	2½	5
9½	Edinburgh Life	100	15	30½x
5—½ yr	European Life and Guarantee	2½	11s6	4s 6d
10	Etna Fire and Marine	10	1½	1
5	Guardian	100	50	51½
12	Imperial Fire	500	50	345
9½	Imperial Life	100	10	16½
10	Lancashire Fire and Life	20	2	2½x
11	Life Association of Scotland	40	7½	23
45s. p. sh	London Assurance Corporation	25	12½	48
5	London and Lancashire Life	10	1	1
40	Liverp'l & London & Globe F. & L.	20	2	7⅞
5	National Union Life	5	1	1
12½	Northern Fire and Life	100	5	10⅝
12 '68, bo 5s.	North British and Mercantile	50	6½	16 16½
50	Ocean Marine	25	5	20
£5 12s.	Provident Life	100	10	38
£4½ p. s.	Phœnix	....	....	136
2½—h.yr.	Queen Fire and Life	10	1	15-16ths
3s. bo. 4s	Royal Insurance	20	3	6¼
10	Scottish Provincial Fire and Life	50	2½	4½
25	Standard Life	50	12	65
5	Star Life	25	1½	—
	CANADIAN.			⅌ c.
4	British America Fire and Marine	$50	$25	56
4	Canada Life	...	....	.....
12	Montreal Assurance	£50	£5	135
3	Provincial Fire and Marine	60	11	.....
....	Quebec Fire	40	32½	£19½
8	" Marine	100	40	90-95
5 7 mo's.	Western Assurance	40	6	.....

RAILWAYS.	Sha's	Paid	Montr	London.
...and St. Lawrence	£100	All.	....	56 58xd
...nd Lake Huron	20½	"	....	3 3½
do Preference	10	"	....	5½ 6½
...antf. & Goderich, 6⅌c., 1872-3-4	100	"	....	....
...n and St. Lawrence	....	....	10 12	....
do Pref. 10 ⅌ ct.	....	....	65 72½	....
...runk	100	"	16 17	16½ 16¾
Eq.G. M. Bds. 1 ch. 6⅌c.	100	"	....	84 86
First Preference, 5 ⅌ c	100	"	....	49 51
Deferred, 3 ⅌ ct.	100	"	....	....
Second Pref. Bonds, 5⅌c.	100	"	....	39 41
do Deferred, 3 ⅌ ct.	100	"	...	....
Third Pref. Stock, 4⅌ct.	100	"	....	28 30
do. Deferred, 3 ⅌ ct.	100	"	....	....
Fourth Pref. Stock, 3⅌c.	100	"	....	19 20
do. Deferred, 3 ⅌ ct.	100	"	....	....
...stern	20½	"	13 14	13¾ 14
New	20½	18	....	....
6 ⅌ c. Bds, due 1873-76	100	All.	....	101 103
5½ ⅌c Bds. due 1877-78	100	"	....	93 95
...ailway, Halifax, $250, all	$250	"	....	....
..., of Canada, 6⅌c. 1st Pref. Bds.	100	"	....	80 83

...XCHANGE.	Halifax.	Montr'l.	Quebec.	Toronto.
London, 60 days				
...r 75 days date	13½	9¾ 9⅞	9¾ 10	9½
do.	12 12½	8½ 9	8¾ 9	8¼
...with documents	....	7½ 8½	....	....
New York	....	26½ 27½	27 27½	73¼
do.	....	27½ 27½	27½ 28	....
...fts do.	....	par	par ¼ dis.	par ½ dis.
...	....	3 3½	....	3½ 5

STOCK AND BOND REPORT.

The dates of our quotations are as follows:—Toronto, Oct. 21; Montreal, Oct. 20; Quebec, Oct. 20; London, Oct. 1.

NAME.	Shares.	Paid up.	Divid'd last 6 Months	Dividend Day.	CLOSING PRICES. Toronto.	Montre'l	Quebec.
BANKS.			⅌ ct.				
British North America	$250	All.	3	July and Jan.	103 104	104 105½	103 104
Jacques Cartier	50	"	4	1 June, 1 Dec.	106 108	108 108½	106½ 107
Montreal	200	"	5	"	135 135½	135½ 136	135½ 136
Nationale	50	"	4	1 Nov. 1 May.	106 108	107 108	Bks. clos
New Brunswick	100	"	......	......	....	...	....
Nova Scotia	200	28	7&b$3½	Mar. and Sept.	....	....	....
Du Peuple	50	"	4	1 Mar., 1 Sept.	105 105½	105 105½	105½ 106
Toronto	100	"	4	1 Jan., 1 July.	116½ 117	116 117	116 117
Bank of Yarmouth	....	....	......	......	....	....	....
Canadian Bank of Com'e	50	95	......	......	103 103½	103½ 104½	102 103
City Bank Montreal	80	All.	4	1 June, 1 Dec.	103 103¾	103 103½	103 103½
Commer'l Bank (St. John)	100	"	⅌ ct.	......	....	...	....
Eastern Townships' Bank	50	"	4	1 July, 1 Jan..	....	95½ 96	96 96½
Gore	40	...	3½	1 Jan., 1 July.	....	35 37½	35 37
Halifax Banking Company	....	....	......	.....	...	....	...
Mechanics' Bank	50	70	4	1 Nov., 1 May.	95 97	Bks. clos	Bks. clos
Merchants' Bank of Canada	100	70	4	1 Jan., 1 July.	105 105½	106½ 106½	105½ 106½
Merchants' Bank (Halifax)	....	....	......	......	....	...	....
Molson's Bank	50	All.	4	1 Apr., 1 Oct.	108 108½	108 109	107½ 108
Niagara District Bank	100	70	3½	1 Jan., 1 July.	....	....	....
Ontario Bank	40	All.	4	1 June, 1 Dec.	100½ 101½	100 101	99½ 100
People's Bank (Fred'kton)	100	"	......	......	....	....	....
People's Bank (Halifax)	20	"	7 12 m	......	....	...	....
Quebec Bank	100	"	3½	1 June, 1 Dec.	97½ 98½	98½ 100	99½ 100
Royal Canadian Bank	50	50	4	1 Jan., 1 July.	91 92	91	90 91
St. Stephens Bank	100	All	.....	......	....	..	....
Union Bank	100	70	4	1 Jan., 1 July.	102 102½	102½ 103½	103 104
Union Bank (Halifax)	100	40	7 12 mo	Feb. and Aug.	....	....	...
MISCELLANEOUS.							
British America Land	250	44	2½				
British Colonial S. S. Co.	250	32½	2½	......	....	....	....
Canada Company	32½	All.	5	......	...	45 50	...
Canada Landed Credit Co.	50	$20	3½	......	62 63	....	....
Canada Per. B'ldg Society	50	All.	5	......	121 121½	....	....
Canada Mining Company	4	90	......	......	....	....	....
Do. Inl'd Steam Nav. Co.	100	All.	20 12 m	......	....	108½ 110	107 109
Do. Glass Company	100	"	12½ "	......	....	95	....
Canad'n Loan & Investm't	25	2½	7	......	....	....	....
Canada Agency	10	¼	......	......	....	....	....
Colonial Securities Co.	...	....	......	......	....	....	....
Freehold Building Society	100	All.	5	......	106 106½	....	....
Halifax Steamboat Co.	100	"	5	......	....	....	....
Halifax Gas Company	....	....	......	......	....	....	....
Hamilton Gas Company	....	....	......	......	....	...	....
Huron Copper Bay Co.	4	12	20	......	....	25 50cps	....
Lake Huron S. and C.	5	102	......	......	....	....	....
Montreal Mining Consols	20	$15	......	......	....	2.50 2.90	...
Do. Telegraph Co.	40	All.	5	......	127 127½	127 129	130 132
Do. Elevating Co.	00	"	15 12 m	......	....	100 103	....
Do. City Gas Co.	40	"	4	15 Mar. 15 Sep.	....	132½ 135	132 134
Do. City Pass. R. Co.	50	"	5	......	....	110 112	104 105
Nova Scotia Telegraph	20	"	....	......	....	....	....
Quebec and L. S.	8	$4	......	......	....	....	25 cts
Quebec Gas Co.	200	All.	4	1 Mar., 1 Sep.	....	...	117 118
Quebec Street R. R.	50	25	8	......	....	....	96 97
Richelieu Navigation Co.	100	All.	7 p.a.	1 Jan., 1 July.	....	111½ 112½	110 112
St. Lawrence Tow Boat Co.	100	"	......	3 Feb.	....	...	35 40
Tor'to Consumers' Gas Co.	50	"	2 3 m.	1 My Au Mar Fe	105 105½	...	103 104
Trust & Loan Co. of U. C.	20	5	3	......	....	....	..
West'n Canada Bldg Soc'y	50	All.	5	......	113½ 114	....	....

SECURITIES.	London.	Montreal.	Quebec.	Toronto.
Canadian Gov't Deb. 6 ⅌ ct. due 1872	....	100 101	100½ 101	100 101
Do. do. 6 do due Ja. & Jul. 1877-84	104 106	....	....	....
Do. do. 6 do. Feb. & Aug.	103 105	....	.. .	....
Do. do. 6 do. Mch. & Sep.	103 105	....	....	....
Do. do. 5 ⅌ ct. cur., 1883	91 93	89½ 91	89½ 90	91 91½
Do. do. 5 do. stg., 1885	....	89½ 91	90 90½	91 91½
Do. do. 7 do. cur.,	....	....	......	....
Dominion 6 p. c. 1878 cy.	....	102 103	100½ 101½	102½ 103
Hamilton Corporation	....	....	......	....
Montreal Harbor, 8 ⅌ ct. d. 1869	..	....	......	....
Do. do. 7 do. 1870	....	....	......	100 101
Do. do. 6½ do. 1875	....	100 100½	......	....
Do. do. 6½ do. 1873	....	....	......	....
Do. Corporation, 6 ⅌ c. 1891	....	92½ 93½	92 93	92 93
Do. 7 p. c. stock	....	105 105½	104 105	105 105½
Do. Water Works, 6 ⅌ c. stg. 1878	....	....	......	92 93
Do. do. 6 do. cy. do.	....	92½ 93½	......	92 93
New Brunswick, 6 ⅌ ct., Jan. and July	102 104	....	......	....
Nova Scotia, 6 ⅌ ct., 1875	100 102	....	......	....
Ottawa City 6 ⅌ c. d. 1880	....	91½ 92½	......	...
Quebec Harbour, 6 ⅌ c. d. 1883	....	....	60	....
Do. do. 7 do. do.	....	....	70	....
Do. do. 8 do. 1886	...	....	85	....
Do. City, 7 ⅌ c. d. 5 years	....	80 90	90½ 91	....
Do. do. 7 do. 9 do.	....	....	87 88	....
Do. do. 7 do. 2½ do.	....	....	96½ 97	....
Do. Water Works, 7 ⅌ ct., 4 years	....	....	95 96	....
Do. do. 6 do. 2 do.	....	....	92½ 93½	....
Toronto Corporation	....	90 92½	....	....

Miscellaneous.

DOMINION TELEGRAPH COMPANY.

CAPITAL STOCK - - - $500,000.

In 10,000 Shares at $50 Each.

PRESIDENT,
HON. WILLIAM CAYLEY.

TREASURER,
HON. J. McMURRICH.

SECRETARY,
H. B. REEVE.

SOLICITORS,
MESSRS. CAMERON & McMICHAEL.

GENERAL SUPERINTENDENT,
MARTIN RYAN.

DIRECTORS.

HON. J. McMURRICH,
Bryce, McMurrich & Co., Toronto.

A. R. McMASTER, Esq.,
A. R. McMaster & Brother, Toronto.

HON. M. C. CAMERON,
Provincial Secretary, Toronto.

JAMES MICHIE, Esq.,
Fulton, Michie & Co., and George Michie & Co., Toronto

HON. WILLIAM CAYLEY,
Toronto.

A. M. SMITH, Esq.,
A. M. Smith & Co., Toronto.

L. MOFFATT, Esq.,
Moffatt, Murray & Co., Toronto.

H. B. REEVE, Esq.,
Toronto.

MARTIN RYAN, Esq.,
Toronto.

PROSPECTUS.

THE DOMINION TELEGRAPH COMPANY has been organized under the act respecting Telegraph Companies, chapter 67, of the consolidated Statutes of Canada. Its object is to cover the Dominion of Canada with a complete net-work of Telegraph lines.

The Capital Stock

Is $500,000, divided into 10,000 shares of $50 each, 5 per cent to be paid at the time of subscribing, the balance to be paid by instalments, not exceeding 10 per cent per month—said instalments to be called in by the Directors as the works progress. The liability of a subscriber is limited to the amount of his subscription.

The Business Affairs of the Company.

Are under the management of a Board of Directors, annually elected by the Shareholders, in conformity with the Charter and By-Laws of the Company. The Directors are of opinion that it would be to the interest of the Stockholders generally to obtain subscriptions from all quarters of Canada, and with this view they propose to divide the Stock amongst the different towns and cities throughout the Dominion, in allotments suited to the population and business occupations of the different localities, and the interest which they may be supposed to take in such an enterprise.

Contracts of Connections.

A contract, granting permanent connection and extraordinary advantages, has already been executed between this Company and the Atlantic and Pacific Company, of New York: thus, at the very commencement, as the Lines of this Company are constructed from the Suspension Bridge, at Clifton (the point of connection) to any point in the Dominion, all the chief cities and places in the States, touched by the Lines of the Atlantic and Pacific Telegraph Company, are brought in immediate connection therewith.

A permanent connection has also been secured with the Great Western Telegraph Company, of Chicago, whereby this Company will be brought into close connection with all the Lake Ports and other places through the North-western States, and through to California.

-6-3mos

Miscellaneous.

GOLD &   **SILVER**

STEAM   STAMP

QUARTZ   *CRUSHER,*

(JAMES'   PATENT).

Dickey, Neill & Co.,
ENGINEERS AND BOILER MAKERS,
SOHO FOUNDRY, TORONTO, ONT.,
Sole Manufacturers for the Dominion.

THIS Machine is warranted for two-thirds the price, to do the work of any ordinary Ten Stamp Mill, and is the most perfect Crushing Machine in the world.

Engines and Boilers of all sizes, and Mill Machinery
OF EVERY DESCRIPTION ON HAND.

Send for Circular and Price List.   31-6m

Extract of Hemlock Bark—Extract of Oak Bark

Important to Tanners, Merchants, Machinists, Lumbermen and Capitalists seeking for a Remunerative and Profitable Investment in Canada.

THE IRVING BARK EXTRACT COMPANY OF BOSTON have succeeded in perfecting a Machine for obtaining by compression from unground Bark, all the astringent and Tanning properties of Hemlock and Oak Bark.

By the operation of this Machine, which can be taken into the forests of Canada, on the spot where the Bark is peeled, the actual Tanning principle of the Bark is extracted by compression, and is produced in so concentrated and so small a bulk, that it can be conveyed to market, ready for use, at a mere fractional part of the expense required to freight the crude Bark; 40 galls. of this Extract, weighing 400 lbs., can be obtained from one cord of first quality of Hemlock Bark, and this is worth for home use or for exportation $20 per barrel.

We are now ready to grant licenses or to receive orders for these Machines.

☞ Any further information may be obtained by addressing

THOS. W. JOHNSON,
At American House,
Boston, Massachusetts.
nov21—14-1yr

The Mercantile Agency,

FOR THE
PROMOTION AND PROTECTION OF TRADE
Established in 1841.

DUN, WIMAN & Co.
Montreal, Toronto and Halifax.

REFERENCE Book, containing names and ratings of Business Men in the Dominion, published semi-annually.   24-1y.

The St. Lawrence Glass Company

ARE now manufacturing and have for sale,

COAL OIL LAMPS,
various styles and sizes.
LAMP CHIMNEYS,
of extra quality for ordinary Burners also, for the 'Comet' and 'Sun' Burners.

SETS OF
TABLE GLASSWARE, HYACINTH GLASSES, STEAM GUAGE TUBES, GLASS RODS, &c., or any other article made to order, in White or Colored Glass.

KEROSENE BURNERS, COLLARS and SOCKETS, will be kept on hand.

DRUGGISTS' FLINT GLASSWARE, and PHILOSOPHICAL INSTRUMENTS, made to order.

OFFICE—388 ST. PAUL STREET, MONTREAL.
A. McK. COCHRANE,
3-1y   Secretary.

Miscellaneous.

Western Canada Permanent Building a Savings Society.

OFFICE—No. 70 CHURCH STREET, TORONTO.

SAVINGS BANK BRANCH,

DEPOSITS RECEIVED DAILY. INTEREST PAID HA: YEARLY.

ADVANCES
Are made on the security of Real Estate, repayable most favourable terms, by a Sinking Fund.

WALTER S. LEE,
36-1y   Sec'y. & Tr

Canada Permanent Building and Savi Society.

Paid up Capital	$1,000,0
Assets	1,700,0
Annual Income	400,0

Directors:—JOSEPH D. RIDOUT, President.
PETER PATERSON, Vice-President.
J. G. Worts, Edward Hooper, S. Nordheimer, W. Chewett, E. H. Rutherford, Joseph Robinson.
Bankers:—Bank of Toronto; Bank of Montreal; 1 Canadian Bank.

OFFICE—Masonic Hall, Toronto Street, Toron

Money Received on Deposit bearing five and six cent. interest.

Advances made on City and Country Property in the Pro of Ontario.
J. HERBERT MASON
36-y   Sec'y & T

STAMP MILLS,

WHEELER PANS,
And other amalgamating Apparatus,
SETTLERS, &c.

STEAM ENGINES, BOILERS
And all sorts of
GOLD MINING MACHINERY,
Of the most approved description, at

G. & I. Brown's
Machine Shop and Agricultural Works,
BELLEVILLE.

PROSPECTING MILLS,

Worked by Hand, Horse, or Machine Power.

Parties going into Gold Mining in the Quinte Dist will do well to have their machinery made on the spot and save freight.

Belleville, April, 1868.   33-

J. R. Boyce,

NOS. 63 and 65, Great James Street, Montreal, and Importer of all kinds of TOYS and FANCY G R. B. is the only manufacturer of La Crosse Stic the new Indian Game of LACROSSE, and has constat hand a large supply, with the printed Rules of the He also manufactures all the requisites for Croqu all other Parlour and Lawn Games. Baskets, of all and every variety of Hair Work, Wigs, Curls, Beard Dress and Theatrical Wigs, for sale, Wholesale and Parties engaged in forming new La Crosse Clubs, well to apply direct to the above address.

The Albion Hotel,

MONTREAL,

ONE of the oldest established houses in the City ! under the personal management of
Mr. DECKER,

Who, to accommodate his rapidly increasing bush adding Eighty more Rooms to the house, maki ALBION one of the Largest Establishments in Canada.
June, 1868.

Geo. Girdlestone,

FIRE, Life, Marine, Accident, and Stock In: Agent
Very best Companies represented.
Windsor, Ont. June, 1868

Financial.

Pellatt & Osler,

OK AND EXCHANGE BROKERS, Accountants, gents for the Standard Life Assurance Company and York Casualty Insurance Company.

OFFICE—86 *King Street East, four Doors West of Church Street, Toronto.*

HENRY PELLATT,   EDMUND B. OSLER,
Notary Public.   *Official Assignee.*

BROWN'S BANK,

(W. Brown. W. C. Chewett.)

10 KING STREET EAST, TORONTO,

TRANSACTS a general Banking Business, Buys and Sells New York and Sterling Exchange, Gold, Silver, Bonds and Uncurrent Money, receives Deposits subject to Cheque at sight, makes Collections and Discounts mercial Paper.

Orders by Mail or Telegraph promptly executed at most favourable current quotations.

For Address letters,   "BROWN'S BANK,
-y   Toronto."

Canadian Land and Emigration Company

Offers for sale on Conditions of Settlement,

GOOD FARM LANDS

In the County of Peterboro, Ontario,

the well settled Townships of Dysart, where there are Grist and Saw Mills, Stores, &c., at

AND-A-HALF DOLLARS AN ACRE.

In the adjoining Townships of Guilford, Dudley, Harburn, Harcourt and Bruton, connected with Dysart and Village of Haliburton by the Peterson Road, at ONE DOLLAR an Acre.

For further particulars apply to

CHAS. JAS. BLOMFIELD,
Secretary C. L. and E. Co., Toronto.

Or to ALEX. NIVEN, P.L.S.,
Agent C. L. & E. Co., Haliburton.

The Liverpool and London and Globe Insurance Company.

Capital and Reserved Funds........$17,005,000.

DAILY CASH RECEIPTS,......$20,000.

NOTICE IS HEREBY GIVEN, that this Company having deposited the sum of

150,000 Dollars,

in accordance with the Act, 31st Vic., cap. 48, has received License of the Finance Minister, to transact the business of Life and Fire Insurance in the Dominion of Canada.

G. F. C. SMITH,
Chief Agent for the Dominion.

Hartford Fire Insurance Company.

HARTFORD, CONN.

Cash Capital and Assets over Two Million Dollars.

$2,026,220.29.

CHARTERED 1810.

THIS old and reliable Company, having an established business in Canada of more than thirty years standing, complied with the provisions of the new Insurance Act, and made a special deposit of

$100,000

with the Government for the security of policy-holders, and I continue to grant policies upon the same favorable terms as heretofore.

Especially low rates on first-class dwellings and farm property for a term of one or more years.

Losses as heretofore promptly and equitably adjusted.

E. CHAFFEY & CO., AGENTS.
Toronto, Ont.

ROBERT WOOD, GENERAL AGENT FOR CANADA.
6m

Insurance.

The Standard Life Assurance Company,
Established 1825.

WITH WHICH IS NOW UNITED
THE COLONIAL LIFE ASSURANCE COMPANY.

Head Office for Canada:
MONTREAL—STANDARD COMPANY'S BUILDINGS,
No. 47 GREAT ST. JAMES STREET.

Manager—W. M. RAMSAY.   *Inspector*—RICH'D BULL.

THIS Company having deposited the sum of ONE HUNDRED AND FIFTY THOUSAND DOLLARS with the Receiver-General, in conformity with the Insurance Act passed last Session, Assurances will continue to be carried out at moderate rates and on all the different systems in practice.

AGENT FOR TORONTO—HENRY PELLATT,
KING STREET.

AGENT FOR HAMILTON—JAMES BANCROFT.
6-6mos.

Fire and Marine Assurance.

THE BRITISH AMERICA
ASSURANCE COMPANY.
HEAD OFFICE:
CORNER OF CHURCH AND COURT STREETS,
TORONTO.

BOARD OF DIRECTION:

Hon. G. W. Allan, M.L.C.,   A. Joseph, Esq.,
George J. Boyd, Esq.,   Peter Paterson, Esq.,
Hon. W. Cayley,   G. P. Ridout, Esq.,
Richard S. Cassels, Esq.,   B.H. Rutherford, Esq.,
Thomas C. Street, Esq.

Governor:
GEORGE PERCIVAL RIDOUT, Esq.

Deputy Governor:
PETER PATERSON, Esq.

Fire Inspector: Marine Inspector:
E. ROBY O'BRIEN.   CAPT. R. COURNEEN.

Insurances granted on all descriptions of property against loss and damage by fire and the perils of inland navigation.

Agencies established in the principal cities, towns, and ports of shipment throughout the Province.

THOS. WM. BIRCHALL,
22-1y   *Managing Director.*

Edinburgh Life Assurance Company.

Founded 1823.

HEAD OFFICE—22 GEORGE STREET, EDINBURGH.

Capital, ... £500,000 *Ster'g.*
Accumulated and Invested Funds, £1,000,000 "

HEAD OFFICE IN CANADA:
WELLINGTON STREET, TORONTO.

SUB-AGENTS THROUGHOUT THE PROVINCE.

J. HILLYARD CAMERON,
Chairman, Canadian Board.

DAVID HIGGINS,
Secretary, Canadian Board.   3-3m

Queen Fire and Life Insurance Company,
OF LIVERPOOL AND LONDON,

ACCEPTS ALL ORDINARY FIRE RISKS
on the most favorable terms.

LIFE RISKS

Will be taken on terms that will compare favorably with other Companies.

CAPITAL - - - £2,000,000 Stg.

CHIEF OFFICES—Queen's Buildings, Liverpool, and Gracechurch Street London.
CANADA BRANCH OFFICE—Exchange Buildings, Montreal. Resident Secretary and General Agent,
A. MACKENZIE FORBES,
13 St. Sacrament St., Merchants' Exchange, Montreal.
WM. ROWLAND, Agent, Toronto.   1-1y

Insurance.

Reliance Mutual Life Assurance Society.
(*Established, 1840,*) *OF LONDON, E. C.*

Accumulated Funds, over $1,000,000.

Annual Income, $300,000.

THE entire Profits of this long-established Society belong to the Policy-holders.

HEAD OFFICE FOR DOMINION—MONTREAL.
T. W. GRIFFITH, *Managed Sec'y.*
15-1y   WM. HENDERSON, *Agent for Toronto.*

Etna Insurance Company of Dublin.

The number of Shareholders exceeds Five Hundred.

Capital, $5,000,000—Annual Income nearly $1,000,000.

THIS Company takes Fire and Marine Risks on the most favorable terms.

T. W. GRIFFITH, *Manager for Canada.*

Chief office for Dominion—Corner St. Francois Xavier and St. Sacrament Sts., Montreal.
15-1y   WM. HENDERSON, *Agent for Toronto*

Scottish Provincial Assurance Co.

Established 1825.

CAPITAL ....£1,000,000 STERLING.
INVESTED IN CANADA (1864) ....$500,000.

Canada Head Office, Montreal.

LIFE DEPARTMENT.

CANADA BOARD OF DIRECTORS:

HUGH TAYLOR, Esq., Advocate.
Hon. CHARLES WILSON, M. L. C.
WM. SACHE, Esq., Banker,
JACKSON RAE, Esq., Banker.
WM. FRASER, Esq. M. D., Medical Adviser.

The special advantages to be derived from Insuring in this office are—Strictly Moderate Rates of Premium; Large Bonus (intermediate bonus guaranteed;) Liberal Surrender Value, under policies relinquished by assured; and Extensive Limits of Residence and Travel. All business disposed of in Canada, without reference to parent office.

A DAVIDSON PARKER,
Resident Secretary.
G. L. MADDISON,
15-1yr   AGENT FOR TORONTO.

Lancashire Insurance Company.

CAPITAL, - - - - - - - £2,000,000 Sterling

FIRE RISKS

Taken at reasonable rates of premium, and ALL LOSSES SETTLED PROMPTLY,

By the undersigned, without reference elsewhere.

S. C. DUNCAN-CLARK & CO.,
General Agents for Ontario,
N. W. Corner of King & Church Streets,
25-1y   TORONTO.

Etna Fire & Marine Insurance Company.

INCORPORATED 1819. CHARTER PERPETUAL.

CASH CAPITAL, - - - - $3,000,000

LOSSES PAID IN 50 YEARS, 23,809,000 00.

JULY, 1868.

ASSETS.
(At Market Value.)

Cash in hand and in Bank............	$544,842 39
Real Estate..........................	255,527 29
Mortgage Bonds......................	932,245 09
Bank Stock..........................	1,272,670 90
United States, State and City Stock, and other	
Public Securities....................	2,049,855 51
Total.........................	$5,052,880 19

LIABILITIES.

Claims not Due, and Unadjusted........	$499,903 55
Amount required by Mass. and New York	
for Re-Insurance....................	1,405,267 15
	E. CHAFFEY & CO., Agents.
	30-6m

Insurance.

ÆTNA
Live Stock Insurance Company

LICENSED BY THE DOMINION GOVERNMENT TO DO BUSINESS IN CANADA.

THE following Accidents, this month, show the importance of Insuring your Horses and Cattle against Death from any cause, or Theft, in the Ætna Insurance Company:

MONTREAL, September 16, 1868.
At a fire last night, in the sheds behind Ripin's Hotel, St. Joseph Street, three valuable Stock Horses were destroyed, "Young Clydesdale" and "Emigrant," belonging to the Huntingdon Agricultural Society—the former worth $900, and the latter $1,700; and "Old Beauharnois" cost $1,000, belonging to the Beauharnois Society.

PORT COLBORNE, September 18, 1868.
HORSES DROWNED.—Two horses belonging to Mr. Briggs, of Port Colborne, and four owned by Mr. Julien, of Port Dalhousie, were drowned in the Canal, near the Junction, early this morning.

A fire at the Glasgow Hotel, Montreal, this morning, destroyed two horses. The fire was caused by drunkenness on the part of the stable man.

MONTREAL, September 24, 1868.
A fire in F. X. Cusson's stables, St. Joseph Street, last night, destroyed three horses.

E. L. SNOW, GENERAL AGENT, Montreal
Agents for Ontario:—
SCOTT & WALMSLEY,
67nov11y   Ontario Hall, Church Street, Toronto.

The Liverpool and London and Globe Insurance Company

INVESTED FUNDS:
FIFTEEN MILLIONS OF DOLLARS.

DAILY INCOME OF THE COMPANY:
TWELVE THOUSAND DOLLARS.

LIFE INSURANCE,
WITH AND WITHOUT PROFITS.

FIRE INSURANCE
On every description of Property, at Lowest Remunerative Rates.
JAMES FRASER, AGENT,
5 King Street West.
Toronto, 1868.   38-1y

Briton Medical and General Life Association,
with which is united the
BRITANNIA LIFE ASSURANCE COMPANY.

Capital and Invested Funds............£750,000 Sterling.

ANNUAL INCOME, £220,000 STG. :
Yearly increasing at the rate of £25,000 Sterling.

THE important and peculiar feature originally introduced by this Company, in applying the periodical Bonuses, so as to make Policies payable during life, without any higher rate of premiums being charged, has caused the success of the BRITON MEDICAL AND GENERAL to be almost unparalleled in the history of Life Assurance. Life Policies on the Profit Scale become payable during the lifetime of the Assured, thus rendering a Policy of Assurance a means of subsistence in old age, as well as a protection for a family, and a more valuable security to creditors in the event of early death ; and effectually meeting the often urged objection, that persons do not themselves reap the benefit of their own prudence and forethought.

No extra charge made to members of Volunteer Corps for services within the British Provinces.
☞ TORONTO AGENCY, 5 KING ST. WEST.
oct17—9-1yr   JAMES FRASER, Agent.

Phenix Insurance Company,
BROOKLYN, N. Y.

PHILANDER SHAW,   STEPHEN CROWELL,
Secretary.   President.
Cash Capital, $1,000,000. Surplus, $666,416.02. Total, $1,666,418.02. Entire Income from all sources for 1866 was $2,131,839.82.
CHARLES G. FORTIER, Marine Agent.
Ontario Chambers, Toronto, Ont.   19-1y

Insurance.

The Victoria Mutual
FIRE INSURANCE COMPANY OF CANADA.

Insures only Non-Hazardous Property, at Low Rates.

BUSINESS STRICTLY MUTUAL.

GEORGE H. MILLS, President.
W. D. BOOKER, Secretary.
HEAD OFFICE ....HAMILTON, ONTARIO
aug 15-1yr

The Ætna Life Insurance Company.

AN attack, abounding with errors, having been made upon the Ætna Life Insurance Co. by the editor of the Montreal Daily News : and certain agents of British Companies being now engaged in handing around copies of the attack, thus seeking to damage the Company's standing, —I have pleasure in laying before the public the following certificate, bearing the signatures of the Presidents and Cashiers who happened to be in their Offices) of every Bank in Hartford; also that of the President and Secretary of the old Ætna Fire Insurance Company :—

" To whom it may concern :—

"We, the undersigned, regard the Ætna Life Insurance Company, of this city, as one of the most successful and prosperous Insurance Companies in the States,— entirely reliable, responsible, and honourable in all its dealings, and most worthy of public confidence and patronage."

Lucius J. Hendee, President Ætna Fire Insurance Co., and late Treasurer of the State of Connecticut.
J. Goodnow, Secretary Ætna Fire Insurance Co.
C. H. Northam, President, and J. B. Powell, Cashier National Bank.
C. T. Hillyer, President Charter Oak National Bank.
E. D. Tiffany, President First National Bank.
G. F. Davis, President City National Bank.
P. S. Riley, Cashier,   do.   do.   do.
John C. Tracy, President of Farmers' and Mechanics' National Bank.
M. W. Graves, Cashier Conn. River Banking Co.
H. A. Redfield, Cashier Phoenix National Bank.
O. G. Terry, President Ætna National Bank.
J. R. Redfield, Cashier National Exchange Bank.
John G. Root, Assistant Cashier American National Bank.
George F. Hills, Cashier State Bank of Hartford.
Jas. Potter, Cashier Hartford National Bank.
Hartford, Nov. 26, 1867.

Many of the above-mentioned parties are closely connected with other Life Insurance Companies, but all unhesitatingly commend our Company as "reliable, responsible, honorable in all its dealings, and most worthy of public confidence and patronage.
JOHN GARVIN,
General Agent, Toronto Street.
Toronto, Dec. 3. 1867.   16-1y

Life Association of Scotland.

INVESTED FUNDS
UPWARDS OF £1,000,000 STERLING.

THIS Institution differs from other Life Offices, in that the
BONUSES FROM PROFITS
Are applied on a special system for the Policy-holder's
PERSONAL BENEFIT AND ENJOYMENT DURING HIS OWN LIFETIME,
WITH THE OPTION OF
LARGE BONUS ADDITIONS TO THE SUM ASSURED.

The Policy-holder thus obtains
A LARGE REDUCTION OF PRESENT OUTLAY
OR
A PROVISION FOR OLD AGE OF A MOST IMPORTANT AMOUNT IN ONE CASH PAYMENT, OR A LIFE ANNUITY,
Without any expense or outlay whatever beyond the ordinary Assurance Premium for the Sum Assured, which remains in tact for Policy-holder's heirs, or other purposes.

CANADA—MONTREAL—Place D'Armes.

DIRECTORS:
DAVID TORRANCE, Esq., (D. Torrance & Co.)
GEORGE MOFFATT, (Gillespie, Moffatt & Co.)
ALEXANDER MORRIS, Esq., M.P., Barrister, Perth.
Mr G. E. CARTIER, M.P., Minister of Militia.
PETER REDPATH, Esq., (J. Redpath & Son).
J. H. R. MOLSON, Esq., (J. H. R. Molson & Bros.)
Solicitors—Messrs. TORRANCE & MORRIS.
Medical Officer—R. PALMER HOWARD, Esq., M.D
Secretary—P. WARDLAW.
Inspector of Agencies—JAMES B. M. CHIPMAN.   y

Insurance.

North British and Mercantile Insur Company.

Established 1809.

HEAD OFFICE. - CANADA. - - MON

TORONTO BRANCH:
LOCAL OFFICES, NOS. 4 & 6 WELLINGTON STR
Fire Department, ... R. N. OC

Life Department, ... H. L. HI
29-1y

Phœnix Fire Assurance Compa
LOMBARD ST. AND CHARING CROSS,
LONDON, ENG.

Insurances effected in all parts of the W

Claims paid
WITH PROMTITUDE and LIBERAL:
MOFFATT, MURRAY & BEATTI
Agents for Toro
36 Yonge 1

The Commercial Union Assura Company,
19 & 20 CORNHILL, LONDON, ENGLAND.

Capital, £2,500,000 Stg.—Invested over £2,000,

FIRE DEPARTMENT.—Insurance granted on scriptions of property at reasonable rates.

LIFE DEPARTMENT.—The success of this has been unprecedented—NINETY PERCENT. miums now in hand. First year's premiums we $100,000. Economy of management guaranteed 6 surety. Moderate rates.
OFFICE—385 & 387 ST PAUL STREET, MONT
MORLAND, WATSON &
General Agents for
FRED. COLE, Secretary.
Inspector of Agencies—T. C. LIVINGSTON
W. M. WESTMACOTT, Agent at To
16-1y

Phœnix Mutual Life Insurance
HARTFORD, CONN.

Accumulated Fund, $2,000,000, Income, $1,00

THIS Company, established in 1851, is one of reliable Companies doing business in the cou has been steadily prospering. The Massachusetts I Reports show that in nearly all important matt superior to the general average of Companies. I intending assurers the following reasons, amongs for preferring it to other companies :

It is purely Mutual It allows the Insured and reside in any portion of the United States an It throws out almost all restriction on occupation Policies. It will, if desired, take a note for pa Premium, thus combining all the advantages of a all cash company. Its Dividends are declared and applied in reduction of Premium. Its Divi in every case on Premiums paid. The Dividen PHŒNIX have averaged fifty per cent. yearly. settlement of Policies, a Dividend will be allowe year the policy has been in force. The numbe dends will always equal the outstanding Notes. losses promptly—during its existence never ha tested a claim. It issues Policies for the benefi ried Women beyond the reach of their husband's Creditors may also insure the lives of Debtors. It are all Non-forfeiting, as it always allows the su surrender his Policy, should he desire, the Com ing a paid-up Policy therefor.   This importan will commend itself to all. The inducements no by the PHŒNIX are better and more liberal than any other Company. Its rate of Mortality is ex low and under the average.

Parties contemplating Life Insurance will find Interest to call and examine our system. Poli payable either in Gold or American currency.
ANGUS R. BETHUN
General Manage
Dominion

Office: 104 ST. FRANÇOIS XAVIER ST. MONT
☞ Active and energetic Agents and wanted in every town and village, to whom liber ments will be given.

PRINTED AT THE DAILY TELEGRAPH P. HOUSE, BAY ST., COR. KING.

THE CANADIAN
ⅼONETARY TIMES
AND
INSURANCE CHRONICLE.

VOTED TO FINANCE, COMMERCE, INSURANCE, BANKS, RAILWAYS, NAVIGATION, MINES, INVESTMENT, PUBLIC COMPANIES, AND JOINT STOCK ENTERPRISE.

| . ⅼⅠ—NO. 11. | TORONTO, THURSDAY, OCTOBER 29, 1868. | { SUBSCRIPTION. {$2 YEAR. |

Mercantile.

Gundry and Langley.
TECTS AND CIVIL ENGINEERS, Building Sur-
s and Valuators. Office corner of King and Jordan
Toronto.
ⅼAS GUNDRY.   HENRY LANGLEY.

J. B. Boustead.
SION and Commission Merchant. Hops bought
sold on Commission. $2 Front St., Toronto.

John Boyd & Co.
ⅼESALE Grocers and Commission Merchants,
ont St., Toronto.

Childs & Hamilton.
FACTURERS and Wholesale Dealers in Boots
 Shoes, No. 7 Wellington Street East, Toronto.

L. Coffee & Co.
ⅼCE and Commission Merchants, No. 2 Manning's
k, Front St., Toronto, Ont. Advances made on
ents of Produce.

J. & A. Clark,
ⅼCE Commission Merchants, Wellington Street
t, Toronto, Ont.

D. Crawford & Co.,
ⅼFACTURERS of Soaps, Candles, etc., and dealers
Petroleum, Lard and Lubricating Oils, Palace St.,
Ont.

John Fisken & Co.
OIL and Commission Merchants, Yonge St.,
onto, Ont.

W. & R. Griffith.
ⅼERS of Teas, Wines, etc. Ontario Chambers,
Church and Front Sts., Toronto.

Thos. Haworth & Co.
ⅼERS and dealers in Iron, Cutlery and general
ware, King St., Toronto, Ont.

Hurd, Leigh & Co.
RS and Enamellers of China and Earthenware,
Yonge St., Toronto, Ont. [See advt.]

Lyman & McNab.
ⅼESALE Hardware Merchants, Toronto, Ontario.

W. D. Matthews & Co.
ⅼCE Commission Merchants, Old Corn Exchange,
ront St. East, Toronto Ont.

R. C. Hamilton & Co.
ⅼCE Commission Merchants, 119 Lower Water
Halifax, Nova Scotia.

Parson Bros.,
ⅼLEUM Refiners, and Wholesale dealers in Lamps,
mneys, etc. Warerooms 51 Front St. Refinery cor.
f Don Sts., Toronto.

C. P. Reid & Co.
ⅼERS and Dealers in Wines, Liquors, Cigars and
Tobacco, Wellington Street, Toronto.   28.

W. Rowland & Co.
ⅼCE BROKERS and General Commission Mer-
t. Advances made on Consignments. Corner
and Front Streets, Toronto.

Reford & Dillon.
ⅼERS of Groceries, Wellington Street, Toronto,
ri.

Sessions, Turner & Co.,
FACTURERS, Importers and Wholesale Dealers
Boots and Shoes, Leather Findings, etc., 8 Wel-
t West, Toronto, Ont

Meetings.

GRAND TRUNK RAILWAY.

The Report for the half-year ended June 30th,
1868, is as follows :

June half of 1867. £		June half of 1868. £
	The gross receipts upon the whole undertaking, including the Buffalo and Champlain lines, have	
609,121	...been........	646,797
	Deduct— The ordinary working expenses (being at the rate of 65·93 per cent., against 70·53 of the corresponding half of last	
529,792	...year) £426,477	
179,329		
	The renewals of the permanent way and works in the half-year debited	
54,973	...to revenue	36,020
124,356		
	Amounts paid on account for loss by fires at Sarnia	
10,274	...and Toronto..............	4,110
		——466,607
	Leaving an available net balance	
114,082	...earned in the half-year of........	180,190
	Deduct loss on American currency ...	
21,554	...rency	18,882
92,528		161,308
	Or an increase over the corresponding half-year of £68,780.	
	But from this balance of..............	161,308
	Must be deducted the renewal suspense debit from last half-year of ....:.......	31,383
		129,925
	And the amount of postal revenue for the half-year to the postal and military Bondholders:.......................	17,829
		Leaving the balance of £112,096

Applicable for the following payments, viz.:
Interest, &c., paid on lands..................	£1,579
do. on mortgage to Bank of Upper Canada	4,424
do. on loans, bankers' balances, promissory notes, European exchange, &c...	4,441
do. on British American Land Company's debentures	616
do. on Montreal Seminary debentures ..	616
do. on Island Pond debentures	2,700
Half-yearly instalment on Portland sinking fund	2,312
Atlantic and St. Lawrence lease (in full)...	31,692
Detroit line lease (in full)...................	11,250
Montreal & Champlain Railway Company	10,807
Buffalo and Lake Huron "	22,045
Equipment bond interest "	10,779
Balance carried to next half-year's account	8,835
	£112,096

Comparing the results of the half-year with the
corresponding period of 1867, there is an increase
in the gross receipts of £37,676, and a decrease in
the ordinary working expenses of £3,215, in
renewals of £18,953, and in the amount of the
damages paid on account of the Toronto and
Sarnia fires of £6,164. The rate of ordinary
working expenses for the past half-year being as
above stated 65·93 against 70·53 per cent. in
1867. The charges for renewals, adding £31,383
placed to "Suspense Account" last December,
which has now been wiped off, amount to £67,403.
The loss on American currency shows a decrease
of £2,672, being £18,882 against £21,554; so that
the net revenue balance, after deducting this loss
on the conversion of the American ·"greenbacks,"
amounts to £161,308 sterling, against £92,528 in
the corresponding period of 1867. The average
receipts from passengers in the half-year was
6s. 8¼d. per head, against 6s. 8d. in 1867; and the
average receipt per ton of freight was 16s. 6d.,
against 15s. 8d. in the corresponding period of last
year. The debit to the capital account for the
half-year amounts only to £4,083, but as the
capital account is in debt to revenue, this sum,
unless new capital is raised, will have to be written
off against the balance of £8,834. The charges
hitherto made against capital for extra weight of
rails and ballasting are now included under the
head of renewals, and brought against revenue.
The importance of completing the works of ballasting and improvement as soon as possible can hardly
be overrated. With regard to the loss on American currency, viz., £18,882, it may be stated that
the price of gold fluctuated during the half-year
between 133½ and 143½. The total loss on American currency since 1865 has amounted to £370,203.
The following statement shows the net earnings,
from 1861 to June of the present year, in mixed
currency and also in sterling, and also the half-
yearly and total expenditure in renewals, and the
half-yearly and total loss in American currency:

Date.	Miles open.	Gross earnings.	Ordinary working expenses.	Renew- ai.	Rev. balance.
	No.	£	£	£	£
1861, June	1,090	847,110	300,324	....	46,785
" Dec.	"	419,459	323,761	....	95,707
1862, June	"	383,902	319,556	....	63,436
" Dec.	"	439,361	262,308	·70,256	106,797
1863, June	1,174	456,222	239,970	32,962	183,280
" Dec.	"	510,580	291,796	37,037	181,747
1864, June	"	528,501	315,031	31,489	181,791
" Dec.	1,335	618,235	369,002	*51,540	197,695
1865, June	1,337	614,876	422,739	*51,533	139,602
" Dec.	"	714,780	448,619	*89,699	176,472
1866, June	"	637,495	403,490	20,285	207,720
" Dec.	"	719,371	413,608	72,392	233,371
1867, June	"	609,121	†440,007	54,973	114,081
" Dec.	"	704,379	‡403,470	85,819	165,089
1868, June	"	646,797	‡430,587	107,403	180,190
					£762,380

* Add to these sums the further amount of £79,657
carried in the first instance to suspense account, and subsequently paid out of revenue, making the total amount
charged against revenue for renewals between 1862 and
June, 1868, £781,037.
† Including the losses by the Toronto and Sarnia fires.
‡ Including £31,383 carried to suspense account in the
previous accounts.

Date.	Miles total.	Yearly total.	Loss on American currency.	Half-yr'r. sterling profit af'r Total loss on Am. cur.	Yearly Total profit on sterling.
	No.	£	£	£	£
1861, June	1,000	.....	.....	.....	......
" Dec.	"	142,492	.....	887	142,492
1862, June	"	.....	887	62,549	
" Dec.	"	170,233	13,672	93,125	155,674
1863, June	1,174	.....	6,589	126,700	
" Dec.	"	315,036	20,053	161,714	288,414
1864, June	"	.....	*	181,701	
" Dec.	1,335	349,487	78,413	89,383	271,074
1855, June	1,237	.....	35,849	103,753	
" Dec.	"	316,074	56,848	117,624	221,377
1866, June	"	.....	14,264	190,456	
" Dec.	"	441,091	61,828	171,543	364,999
1867, June	"	.....	21,554	92,537	
" Dec.	"	279,170	80,384	125,704	218,231
1868, June	"	.....	18,892	†161,308	161,30.
			£370,203		£1,823,500

Out of this total profit of £1,823,500, averaging £243,142 per annum, there has been paid in cash on leased lines £874,000, and for interest and other claims £624,500, and since 1862 on the 1st, 2nd, and 3rd preference bonds and stocks £325,000.

The figures of this table exhibit in a short compass both the progress and the real nature of the special difficulties which have beset the Grand Trunk Company since 1862. The direct loss on American currency has been no less than £370,203, or equal to say three years full dividend on the first preference bonds, and besides this direct and positive loss there have been, as a consequence of the American war, indirect losses by increased wages and cost of materials, perhaps, as large as the loss on the "greenbacks" themselves, after deducting any increased receipts from higher rates for freight. The expenditure on renewals, apart from ordinary maintenance, charged against revenue, has been £781,037, with the effect, of course, of greatly improving the road. Of the 25 engines lately ordered from Messrs. Neilson & Co., of Glasgow, 21 have, at the dates of the last letters received from Montreal, arrived in Canada. The remaining four are on the way. Seventeen of the engines are now ready for work on the line, and the whole of them, it is expected, will be ready for the anticipated heavy autumn traffic. The reports received of these engines are very satisfactory. A loan to effect the purchase of them has been arranged with the Company's bankers on favorable terms, the leaders having been willing to accept a hypothecation of the engines by way of collateral security. Every effort that the Directors have made to bring about an amicable settlement of the differences of account with the Buffalo Company has hitherto failed. The Buffalo Board will neither agree upon nor allow an impartial officer of the Board of Trade to settle a deed of arbitration. Recent further negotiation through Messrs. Creak & Ritter has ended in nothing, as while the President of the Company signed a memorandum of settlement of all matters, as Mr. Creak suggested, the representative of the Buffalo Company has refused to do the same. In the meantime, the amount stated in the accompanying accounts, as being the proportion due to that Company, must be taken as rendered without prejudice. The Directors have much satisfaction in announcing that negotiations have again been re-opened for the renewal of the Reciprocity Treaty. Every effort has been made, and with considerable suc-

cess, during the cessation of this treaty to open up new channels for the traffic formerly consigned to the States.

The newly developed traffic with the maritime provinces is gradually extending. For example during the past half-year the increase in the Halifax traffic is $28,256, and in the St. John traffic $26,604. The stoppage of trade with the United States has augmented largely the loss upon the Buffalo section, which, if independent, would hardly have paid its working expenses. The bonds issued by the City of Portland twenty years ago in the construction of the Atlantic and St. Lawrence railroad, amounting in the aggregate to $1,500,000, begin to fall due in December next. The amount then maturing is $200,000, of which sum it is expected there will be about one-half provided by the sinking fund attached to the loan ; the other half will have to be provided by the Grand Trunk Company. The balance of the above debt, viz., $1,300,000, falls due at various periods between December next and January, 1871. As the sinking funds will, in the aggregate, only be capable of providing about one-half of the whole amount, it follows that the remainder will have to be found by the Grand Trunk. To meet this amount of say $750,000, it will be necessary to issue new bonds, either in American currency or in sterling. The latter mode would of course be preferable in consequence of the high rate of premium now paid for gold in the United States. The bonds, whenever they are issued, will be protected by a sinking fund—they form part of the working expenses of the Grand Trunk Company—and the only mortgage that takes precedence of them is one for $1,500,000. The bonds bear 6 per cent interest, per annum, payable half-yearly. The Directors as owners (themselves and their immediate connections) of more than one-fifth of the total capital of the undertaking, feel entitled to urge, most seriously, upon their co-partners that recent divisions have done much to weaken and disorganise the executive management, and to paralyse efforts to restore the property. The Directors have done all that was possible to meet unexampled difficulties, and they believe that their policy and proceedings will be found, after the full enquiry which they court, in every way worthy of approval. They have preserved the property by successfully resisting its forfeiture in Canada. They have carried the Company through the periods of American war and Fenian raids, and they now see the Intercolonial railway secured, a renewal of the Reciprocity Treaty under negotiation, and the traffic and net profit in those more quiet times resuming the rate of developement which distinguished both up to 1866, when the Fenian troubles commenced and the Reciprocity Treaty was repealed.

THE ROCKLAND SLATE COMPANY.

The annual meeting of this company was held on the 20th, at its office in Montreal. The report presented by the retiring directors showed that during the year operations at the quarry, in the Township of Melbourne had so far advanced, that next spring the company would be in a position to manufacture roofing slate upon an extensive scale. The upper tunnel has been driven a distance of 315 feet, chiefly through solid rock, meeting the slate at a depth of 81 feet, and a shaft 56 feet in depth to connect this tunnel with the pit above is nearly completed. The surface of the quarry has also been largely cleared and prepared for manufacturing operations next season. The slate met with has a beautiful bluish black hue, splits with great facility, is free from cracks, and has no indications of being crossed by veins of quartz or other minerals which might diminish its extent. Operations are now performed entirely by contract. The present contractor has been working by night as well as by day on the overlying rock.

The quantity of slate manufactured during the year has not been large, as the chief object of the directors has been the preparation for large manu-

facturing operations next season. Rega quality, the slate from this quarry has a un bluish black colour, is free from lime and which would on exposure cause deterioratio an even cleavage, is very light and from it absorbing water, is unaffected by frost. A ing preference is being evinced for slate as a ing material.

The officers and directors of the compa the ensuing year are : President, Peter Red Esq.; Directors, Messrs. T. Sutherland St (Toronto), W. C. Baynes, Geo. A. Drumm and Thos. Frizzle (Melbourne) ; Secretary-1 urer, A. T. Drummond.

TORONTO CONSUMERS' GAS COMPANY.—A annual meeting of the stockholders of this pany, held on the 26th October, the foll gentlemen were elected directors for the en year :—Messrs. E. H. Rutherford, J. Austi C. Gilmour, J. T. Smith, L. W. Smith, J Mead, J. Henderson, Hon. W. McMaster, Rec Duggan, W. Cawthra, John Eastwood, an Lepper. At a subsequent meeting of the Bo Directors, Mr. E. H. Rutherford was re-el President, and Mr. James Austin, Vice-Presi

Financial.

THE GORE BANK.

The report of the Committee appointed t vestigate the affairs of the Gore Bank, authority of the resolution of the shareho passed at their annual meeting of 3rd Augu as follows :—

In assuming the office assigned to them b foregoing resolution, your Committee felt they were undertaking a very difficult an sponsible duty, and while resolving to perfe faithfully, to the best of their ability, they very anxious not to lay themselves justly op the charge of having exceeded it.

2. It would, therefore, have been satisfact their minds, had that clause in the reso which requires them, in addition to the val of the assets, and the preparation of a sta of losses, to report upon "the condition Bank's affairs in general," been accompan some intimation of the points, to which th tention was expected to be specially directe the absence, however, of any such specific in tions, they have felt themselves bound to and exhibit such information, and such ot seemed in their judgment to be necessa enable the shareholders to obtain an inte view of their actual position, and to assis in deciding upon their future course.

3. Three of the agencies, namely, L Guelph, and Paris, having been closed sh fore your Committee commenced their they proceeded, in the first instance, to the remaining three, namely, Simcoe, Ga Woodstock.

4. The cash, bills, and accounts were fo be correct, with the single exception deposit receipt account at Woodstock, the a of which, through the non-production of the receipts entered as paid, could not satisfactorily ascertained.

5. Had a regular and efficient system of in of the Agencies been in operation, an irr of this nature could scarcely have occur great trouble would have been spared.

6. The business of Simcoe and Galt app your Committee to be conducted with ma and judgment. The Agencies not havi rate circulation of their own, and the accruing from cash deposits not appearing books, it is impossible to come to a very conclusion as to the results of their operat so far as under the circumstances they ca your Committee are of opinion that, from establishments just mentioned, the Bank i

mitted to the annual meeting on the 3rd August last, and which still remains to be disposed of.

17. And that the final result of their labours may appear, in as compendious and intelligible a form as possible, they have furnished a statement of Liabilities and Assets, made up in accordance with what they believe to be the present position of the Bank.

18. It would have afforded them the most unfeigned satisfaction, could they have conscientiously been able to present that statement in a shape more favorable to the shareholders.

19. Your Committee are well aware how easy it is to be wise after the event, and how extremely difficult properly to estimate the merits of transactions, which were negotiated under circumstances that have ceased to exist. Some points, however, of mistaken judgment appear to them so singular and inexplicable, that it would be wrong to pass them without notice.

20. While, therefore, they deem it just to remark that a large proportion of the losses incurred is to be ascribed to the errors and misfortunes of a comparatively remote period, they consider that they ought not to conceal the fact that some of those errors have been perpetuated by the Directors to a recent date, and followed by disastrous consequences, through their failing to maintain a prudent proportion between the capital of the Bank and the extent of its individual risks, and also through the want, in some instances, of a sufficient regard on their part, to the adequacy and the available character of the securities, upon which important advances were made.

21. In concluding their report, your Committee feel that they would be evading a grave, though very painful obligation, were they not to express their decided opinion that very much of what is now, for the first time, known to be lost to the Bank, ought to have been long since written off as bad, and that a great part of the remainder should have been treated as of extremely doubtful value. And they deem it to be a subject for the deepest regret that the late Directors should not have seen it to be their imperative duty, both for their own sakes, and in the interest of all concerned, fairly to confront the difficulties with which the institution has been long beset, and to bring their published statements into harmony with the actual facts of the case.

All of which is respectfully submitted.—George Taylor, F. M. Willson, W. F. Findlay.

General Statement of the Affairs of the Gore Bank as on the 31st August, 1868.

LIABILITIES.	
Capital	$809,280 00
Circulation	212,712 00
Deposits bearing interest	110,902 34
Deposits not bearing interest	74,121 88
Balance due to other banks, &c.	14,328 64
Unpaid dividends	187 60
Adjusting exchange account	1,029 50
	$1,222,561 96

ASSETS.	
Gold and silver coin and Provincial notes	$164,594 97
Cheques and notes of other Banks	15,325 26
Balances due by other Banks	12,666 57
Government and Municipal debentures	153,118 89
Mortgages	40,979 69
Real estate	23,691 49
Bank of Upper Canada certificates	24,715 01
Bank premises, office furniture and stationery	12,600 00
Notes and bills discounted, and other debts due the Bank not included under the foregoing heads	450,245 54
Adjusting interest account, after reserving rebate on bills current	258 52
Profit and loss	315,466 57
	$1,222,561 96

Hamilton, Oct. 17, 1868.

The Director's report is as follows:

The Directors, in forwarding the report of the committee appointed by the Shareholders at the annual meeting held on the 3rd August last, at the same time transmit a report from themselves upon the present condition of the affairs of the Bank. It was found advisable to close the agencies at Guelph, London, and Paris, which has been done accordingly, and all outstanding accounts transferred to the office here. The Directors regret that the affairs of the Woodstock Branch were found in an unsatisfactory state; they therefore relieved Mr. Park, the Manager, from his position. After this occurred, it was ascertained that he had misappropriated the funds of the Bank; the loss, however, will be recovered from his sureties. The cash in the treasury has been counted by your Directors, and found correct; the cash at all the Agencies, including those closed, was also found correct. Your Directors have considered the question of Staff carefully, and concluded that a reduction of four officers at the head office could be made without impairing the proper management, which has been done. Your Directors have gone carefully over the assets and liabilities of the Bank, which, it will be seen, substantially agrees with what has been furnished by the committee—the difference, in a great measure, being accounted for by subsequent collections, of which explanation will be given at the meeting. The balance of $500,000 (in round numbers) is actually available to the Bank, without taking into account the gain which will accrue to the Bank by the loss of its notes in circulation, which, it is thought, will be very considerable.

Every debt considered bad has been written off, and ample allowance made where any doubt existed as to the value of an asset. The paper discounted at the other banks, referred to in the report of the late Board, amounting to $73,000, has been paid at maturity, without assistance from this Bank. The disposal of the properties held by the Bank has been vigorously prosecuted, with very satisfactory results, the sales amounting to $18,975, at the valuations given in our statement, the funds being made available for banking purposes. Your Directors have every reason to hope that after public confidence has been restored, (which, it is fully expected, will result from the publication of your committee's report,) to regain much of the lost business, which was of the best character, and to open a wider field for agricultural loans in small amounts, in addition to their ordinary business. In view of the reduction of the capital to its present amount of—say $500,000—it will be necessary for the shareholders to consider what course they will adopt, as the charter prevents the payment of dividends, until the amount of subscribed capital shall be fully made up. The Board having elected Mr. Æ. Irving, President, and that gentleman having resigned shortly afterwards, the Hon. Samuel Mills was unanimously elected President. Mr. W. G. Cassels having sent in his resignation to the Board, which they accepted, it is not their intention to continue the office of cashier, which duty will be performed by the party to be hereafter selected to fill the office of Manager. Mr. Cassels, however, has consented to retain office in the meantime. In conclusion, your Directors consider it will be to the interest of the shareholders to take the necessary steps to alter the name of the Bank to that of The Bank of Hamilton. Edward Martin, President, T. McIlwrath, Vice President, C. McQuesten, Wm. Hendrie, Samuel Mills, Wm. McMillan, John Waldie.

TORONTO STOCK MARKET.

(Reported by Pellatt & Osler, Brokers.)

Although money has been easy for the past week, little business has been done in stocks or bonds, in consequence of so few investments offering.

Bank Stock.—There were sales of Montreal at 135¾. Ontario is in demand at 101. Toronto sold at 117. Partially paid up Royal Canadian is offering at 89½ to 90, and paid up at 91½ to 92. Commerce is enquired for, but none in market. There were sales of Gore at 30 during the week; sellers now asking 35. Merchants is in demand at 106 to 107. For City, 104 is offered. There are buyers of Du Peuple at 105 and under. Jacques Cartier sold at 108. Other banks nominal.

Debentures.—Dominion stock and sterling five and six per cents are in great demand at quotations. Toronto are offering to pay 6¾ to 7 per cent. interest. Short dated, first class County are offering to pay 6½ per cent.

Sundries.—Canada Permanent Building Society is in demand at 121½; Western sold at 114½; Freehold not offered. Montreal Telegraph is again lower; buyers now only offer 125. British America Assurance sold at 56. First class mortgages are much enquired for. Money is freely offered, but very little first class paper is to be had.

MONTREAL MONEY MARKET.

(From our own Correspondent.)

Montreal, Oct. 27, 1868.

There still continues an abundant supply of money, and the Banks are discounting all good paper freely; good business paper ranges from 6½ per cent. to 8 per cent. according to the names and length of time to run. On the street very little is offering. The Banks have ample means to meet present wants of trade, they being lighter than usual, and remittances from the Country having lately been more abundant, our merchants are not pressed either to force sales of goods, or to demand any extra accommodation from the Banks. On the contrary during the winter months when business is dull, it will be somewhat difficult for the Banks to find investments for their surplus funds at the rates now current. The amount of stocks offered during the week has been small, and generally placed on the market at rates above the ideas of buyers. There exists a steady demand but the prices of favorite stock are so high as to cause very limited sales. Bank of Montreal sells at 136 to 136½, but now buyers ask 137½. Merchants, in demand at 106¾, but sellers firm at 107 Peoples has fallen and buyers only offer 104½. Ontario asked for at 101, but held firm for 102. Toronto nominal at 117. The books of the Banks National and Mechanics' are closed, and the Ontario offers a dividend of 4 per cent for the half-year.

THE NEW YORK MONEY MARKET.

At the beginning of the week money suddenly assumed an extreme stringency. On Tuesday, brokers found it difficult to supply their wants within the legal limit of interest, and for the last three days the rate outside the banks has been very generally 7 per cent. in gold, and even as high as ⅛ per cent. per day has been paid by needy borrowers. Yesterday and to-day stocks have been very generally purchaseable at ½ per cent. lower for immediate delivery than upon regular terms, which fairly indicates the scarcity of money. The movements at the Clearing House have very plainly indicated that efforts have been made by speculative combinations for holding money off the market, in order to break down the prices of securities; and other collateral evidence goes to establish that conclusion beyond question. It is impossible to form any satisfactory estimate as to the extent to which these operations have been carried. It is, however, to be remembered that, when they were commenced, the market was in a condition to be much affected by slight interference. This artificial meddling with the market has caused considerable feeling among the banks, especially as their own reputation is indirectly affected by the fact of certain bank managers having at least tacitly concurred in the operations. It was suggested in some quarters that the associated banks take combined action by formally agreeing to use their legal reserve in order to defeat the movement, and in that way make a practical protest against the proceedings. This proposal, however, appeared likely to create some unpleasant opposition in the Clearing House association, and was consequently abandoned. Nevertheless, some of the banks have, for the sake of protecting their customers, fallen back upon their legal tender reserve. This action has, to some extent, counteracted the "tying up" operations; and a contraction has also come from speculators desirous of protecting their stocks, by placing money upon the market. The fact, however, that notwithstanding these counteractions, money remains very stringent shews that, apart from artificial causes, the market is in a condition affording poor promise of an early return to ease. No relief of importance is to be expected from outside sources, the money markets of the interior cities being in a condition little different from our own.—*Financial Chronicle*, Oct. 23.

BANK OF ENGLAND.

	Oct. 10, 1868.	Oct. 11, 1867.
Bank rate of discount	2 per cent.	2 per cent.
Bank reserve............	£11,060,030	£14,581.999
Bank stock of bullion	30,707,945	24,109,034
Price of Consols	94¼	94¼

The Bank return exhibits a considerable decrease in the stock of specie, as well as in the reserve; the falling off in the former case is £293,191, and in the latter £559,836. The other deposits have undergone a considerable diminution.

The following are the particulars as compared with the preceding week:

Rest	£3,622,719
Increase	999
Public Deposits	5,306,623
Decrease	78,672
Other deposits	18,022,446
Decrease..............................	712,671
On the other side of the account:—	
Government Securities	£15,039,716
Increase	99,585
Other Securities	16,054,128
Increase	312,564
Notes unemployed	10,045,020
Decrease	460,785

The amount of notes in circulation is £24,647,912, being an increase of £256,642.

REVENUE OF CANADA.—The following is a statement of the Revenue and Expenditure of the Dominion of Canada for the nine months, from the 1st January to the 1st October, 1868. The result goes to confirm Mr. Rose's prediction, that there will be a surplus on the financial year:—

	REVENUE.	EXPENDITURE.
January	$ 856,903	$1,063,627
February..............	597,942	782,529
March..................	1,321,182	950,327
April	1,342,881	1,134,721
May	1,344,068	906,696
June...........	1,074,077	1,156,890
July.....................	1,375,722	1,801,622
August	1,377,933	964,293
September	1,846,360	2,294,409
Totals	$11,137,068	$11,055,114

Railway News.

GREAT WESTERN RAILWAY.—Traffic for week ending Oct. 9, 1868.

Passengers	$39,703 36
Freight and live stock......	53,065 93
Mails and sundries..........	2,462 80
	$95,232 09
Corresponding Week of '67·	87,843 41
Increase..........	$7,388 68

NORTHERN RAILWAY.—Traffic Receipt for week ending Oct. 17, 1868.

Passengers	$4,070 04
Freight..........................	10,074 53
Mails and Sundries............	296 06
Total Receipts for week......	$14,440 63
Corresponding week 1867....	15,724 68
Decrease....	$1,284 05

SHIPBUILDING AT QUEBEC.—The C
appointed by the Federal Government to
consideration the subject of ship-build
reported the evidence, from which several
appear in the *Journal de Quebec*, though
the names of the witnesses examined.
dence goes to show that ship-building h
diminished at Quebec, chiefly on accoun
preference now given to iron ships, and
the kind called mixed—half iron and ha
Last year, moreover, the difficulties of the
were increased by the strike, which was
far more general and better organized t
previously been known. The cause of
doubtless, it is said, to be found in par
high cost of living, but it was really inst
an organization in New York. Quel
builders, it is said, require no protectio
sense opposed to free trade, but no new re
treaty ought to be concluded with the
States without the free registration of
vessels being permitted in the Unite
The drawback of duties on articles em
the construction of ships is thought to b
the builders ought to expect. As to
assistance, there was no reason to bel
Banks would make advances on ships on t
if they were even allowed to do so. A
differences in favour of iron or mixed ove
ships, they are said to be these: that
classed for Liverpool for twenty at Lloyd
teen or fifteen years; that they last lo
their yearly depreciation is less; and th
stronger and less liable to leak, they of c
better. In order to build such ships at
it is said that at first it would be well t
all the iron and even the teak necessar
purpose ready for use. The cost would
ceed $2.50 or $3 per ton and with the f
there would be a net profit to the builder
ton after paying these charges. No pro
wanted; but it is desirable that Que
should be able to sell in all the marke
world. Those of France are already thu
but many are closed, especially that of t
States, which, if accessible, would assure
perity of the shipbuilding trade at Que
shipbuilders of Quebec believe themse
entitled to that market, since American
now admitted to registry in England a
rate as English and Colonial ships. Th
builders, however, fear to begin the co
of mixed ships because of the losses wh
attend upon the first experiments. Th
would be made by those who built the f
of the class, and the men who hold a
profit by their experience. In order, t
prevent this loss being saddled upon so
benefit of all, it is proposed that a bou
$4 to $6 per ton should be granted f
four or five mixed ships that shall be b
cost at Quebec of a good ship of 500 to
classed for seven years, would be, say,
per ton; in the United States, £13 s
England, £10 or £11 sterling, and one
years, £15 or £16. A mixed ship wou
or £18 per ton in England; but they
high as £22 per ton. In France,
Italy, ships of oak will cost a little mo
England. In all cases the equipment
more complicated elsewhere than in Que
times there are complaints of the treat
Quebec shipbuilders receive in Englan
said these could be avoided if builders w
take to do no more than they can do
own resources, and then would load
themselves, if they did not find freigh
would then save two-thirds of the
which they now pay.—*Exchange.*

—In the Insurance suit at Yarm
Scotia, between the owners of the
Young," and the Yarmouth Marin
Company, a verdict was given in fa
defendant.

☞ The Canadian Monetary Times and Insurance Chronicle *is printed every Thursday Evening, in time for the English Mail.*

Subscription · *Price, one year, $2, or $3 in American currency ; Single copies, five cents each. Casual advertisements will be charged ten cents per line of solid nonpareil each insertion. All letters to be addressed,* "The Canadian Monetary Times, Toronto, Ont." *Registered letters so addressed are at the risk of the Publishers. Cheques should be made payable to* J. M. Trout, *Business Manager, who will, in future, issue all receipts for money.*

The Canadian Monetary Times.

THURSDAY, OCTOBER 29, 1868.

INSURANCE COMPANIES AND LITIGATION.

To argue for the sake of proving that it is discreditable· on the part of Insurance Companies to evade the payment of just claims, by taking advantage of technical objections, is one way of wasting words. Ordinary people would take that conclusion for granted. Yet the Toronto *Globe* seems to consider it necessary to approach it cautiously and by slow stages lest, we suppose, the Companies themselves or the public should be taken by surprise. We imagine that the writer of the observations to which we now refer, who has toiled severely to rear a fabric of logic for the support of one of the most ordinary truisms, is not beyond the reach of prejudice, and perhaps has not succeeded in ridding his mind of that antipathy to Corporations, which obtains among the ignorant, whose imaginations conjure up spectral organizations preying on the vitals of the community, having neither bowels of compassion nor yet souls to be affected by the disregard of ethical rules. Every one knows that juries are merciless to Companies, and many are aware that a most improper advantage is taken of a well understood prejudice, which has its origin in a misconception of the objects of Companies as well as of their nature. Take the case of Insurance Companies. Instead of being the victims of an unreasoning antagonism they should have a standing presumption in their favour. Sir James Parke puts the matter in a clear light when he states: "Insurances give greater security to the fortunes of private people, and by dividing amongst many that loss which would ruin an individual, make it fall light and easy upon the whole society." The large amount of business done by these Companies affords ample evidence of the value placed upon the protection they afford to industry ; the benefits they confer in the advancement of trade and navigation, and the blessings they shower in the path of the widow and orphan. There is impartiality, however, in prejudice Railroad Companies as well as Insurance Companies, small Companies and large Companies may all shake hands and confess themselves to be in the same box.

It is said that "a great many absurd and some impracticable conditions" are printed on the policy but never read, and that to take advantage of such loop-holes in order to evade payment of "claims, which at any rate cannot be proved unjust," is a discreditable proceeding. Fire Insurance is a contract to indemnify against loss in a certain event and on certain conditions. These conditions are sneered at by our critic. In a case before the House of Lords, on appeal, Lord St. Leonards, certainly a high authority, said: "The Court, observing how very often Companies of this nature have been subjected to frauds, will carefully guard them against fraud, and will give effect to any part of the contract which has this object. Nay, more, *it is from the very advice given in Courts of Law that the Companies have endeavoured to protect themselves, by those stringent provisions which we so usually find in policies of insurance.*" If the insured don't think it worth their while to read the conditions on which their contract rests, they are themselves to blame. It is admitted that Insurance Companies have a right to protect themselves from fraud and imposition, and that it is for the interest of the community that all attempted frauds in the way of misrepresentation and fire raising should be put down ; but all claims that cannot be proved by legally admissible evidence to be unjust, must be paid under penalty of the condemnation of our critic. The experience of every insurance man in the country, the experience of almost every business man of any kind, will suggest instances in which arson has been committed without legal evidence being obtainable to bring the crime home to the culprit, but yet the circumstances left no doubt on the mind that the crime was committed. The fire-raiser does not usually take witnesses along with him. When the Directors of an Insurance Company are convinced that a claim made upon them is unjust, in that the loss in respect of which it arose, was the result of a wilful act on the part of the claimant, and yet the evidence which established the conviction in their minds cannot be given in a court of law, by reason of a want of elasticity in the rules of evidence ; or in case it be good and legally admissable, are they, or are they not, justified in standing strictly on their rights, and accepting from the Court the legal interpretation of their contract? Our critic says "to fight fraud by fraud and set off quirk against quirk will never do." To set off quirk against quirk will do, and does do ; as for fighting fraud by fraud, no one is foolish or wicked enough to propose it. If the writer means that Insurance Companies act fraudulently in standing on their strict rights under their contract, to ward off a fraudulent claim, nonsense has got the better of him. The following sentence has an air of innocent wisdom about it which enables one to gauge our critic's qualifications for the position of mentor: "There is no doubt that Insurance Companies are very liable to be victimized, but their great protection is simply greater carefulness in accepting risks." Carefulness in accepting risks is a good thing, and a necessary thing; but no amount of care in a country where people move about so much as they do here, where personal antecedents are not so closely followed up as, say, in England would suffice as "the great protection" to Companies, in the absence of those "absurd" conditions on the back of the policy, which are intended to be, and have proved themselves, if not "the great protection," at least the nearest thing to it. An eminent writer on law says: "The Companies intend to pay any just claim without taking advantage of any technical objection, and to make use of their defence only against what they may believe to be a fraud, although they may not be able to prove it." The Directors of an Insurance Company are a jury, and they are expected to satisfy themselves, before paying a claim, that it is just. The ill effects of an opposite course, we have already pointed out.

Well, then, what guarantees have the insured that an undue use will not be made of the power that is reserved by the Insurance Companies, and that individuals will not be harrassed from captious or improper motives? Our courts of law afford redress. Insurance companies as a rule are averse to litigation. Juries never strain presumptions in their favor. As a rule the directors who have to decide on the line of defence to be adopted, have no immediate personal interest to serve, and in most cases have no acquaintance with a claimant; hence it is unlikely that personal motives sway their decisions. They are usually men of high standing in the community, whose names alone are sufficient to command public confidence. The business of Insurance is of such a nature that a disposition to take an unworthy advantage of technicalities cannot long be concealed, and when once made known, soon reacts upon a company's welfare. Fair dealing is part of a company's reputation, and no company is so strong as to set public opinion at defiance. The probabilities are, therefore, greatly in favor of honorable treatment in dealing with Insurance Compa-

nies, and, in practice, expectation in this respect is fully realized. There may arise exceptions, but such exceptions, from the antagonism they excite, only prove the rule. To blame all for the faults of one is about as just as to rail at mankind for the malpractices of the dishonest. When we reflect on the evils that have sprung from looseness of management, and the fear of being branded as litigious, all honest men should strengthen the hands of the companies, and, as a matter of public policy, insist on every means being taken to prevent fraud obtaining the upper hand.

THE GRAND TRUNK.

The half-year's report presented at the meeting held in London, England, on the 20th instant, will be found in another column. It appears that the receipts up to June 30th amounted to £646,797, showing an increase of £37,676 over the corresponding period of last year. The ordinary working expenses were reduced from 70.53 per cent. to 65.93 per cent. of the receipts. Permanent way renewals absorbed £36,000. The available net balance earned amounted to £180,190, against £114,082 in the corresponding half of last year; the gross revenue for the whole year being £1,351,176. Taking the capital at £17,500,000, this revenue represents an earning of 7¾ per cent. on the investment. The loss on American currency, £18,882, being deducted, left £161,308. From this was deducted £31,333, the revenue suspense debt from last year, £17,829 for postal and military bond-holders, £16,688 interest charges, £31,692 rent of Atlantic and St. Lawrence lease, £11,250 rent on Detroit lease, £10,807 for Montreal and Champlain Railway, £22,045 for Buffalo and Lake Huron Railway, £10,779 for equipment bond interest, leaving a balance of £8,834. The capital account being in debt to revenue to the amount of £4,083, this latter sum had to be deducted from the revenue balance of £8,834 in the absence of additional capital. The average receipts from passengers was 6s 8½d per head, against 6s 8d in 1867 ; and the average receipt per ton of freight was 16s 6d, against 15s 8d. From 1861 to 1868 the total profit on working was £1,823,569 ; the loss on American currency, £370,203 ; the total renewals, £781,037 ; the amount paid in cash £874,500 ; for interest, &c., £624,500, and since 1862, on preference bonds and stocks, £325,000.

Certain of the bond and stock-holders, dissatisfied with the present management, having called upon the Directors to resign, a resolution was passed inviting the dissatisfied to call a special general meeting and submit

the matter to the proprietors. In reply, Croak and Mr. Ritter recommended—

" The appointment of a Managing Director in London, whose whole time and energies are to be consecrated to the interests of Grand Trunk. He should be prepared to visit Canada whenever required, and secure for the Board at home the thorough control over the whole undertaking. He should be disconnected with any other business or profession, and receive a salary of (say) £1,500 a year till the 1st, 2nd, and 3rd preferences are paid. That the existing arrangements in Canada should be revised at an early date. That publicity and economy should be carefully maintained, both in all our supplies may be satisfactory in quality and in price. That as a pledge and guarantee of the adoption of this policy the Board should agree to receive at once, subject to confirmation at the October meeting, five gentlemen, at least, to be nominated by the committee, without, however, adding to the number of the Board in England."

The Board offered to make room for two members of the complainants' committee and one bond-holder from Scotland, who held considerable amount of the property in this. This concession was the result of a desire to secure harmony in entering upon negotiations with the Canadian Government respecting the Intercolonial, in the settlement of the International Bridge question, without which the undertaking would be an "unbourgot in the hands of the Anti-Grand Trunk party in Canada." It was subsequently concluded to refer the whole matter to the general meeting. That meeting has been held, it is stated that the present management been endorsed, but the particulars have course not yet arrived.

BREADSTUFFS.

Now that the barley crop is pretty well out of the way, and the handsome proceeds of farmers' pockets, it is opportune to glean facts and suggestions regarding the wheat, which has not yet found its way to of the granaries of producers to any important extent. So far as the crop has been offered, it has met with a dull reception. Buyers and sellers cannot agree ; they adhere as closely as possible to form prices, which, owing to the low quotations abroad, exporters cannot pay, and they refuse to touch the article at the rates demanded. As a consequence, the wheat market has been maintained at exceedingly high rates. This could not have occurred only that a local milling demand has absorbed the most that has yet come forward. As stocks accumulate, the market must come down to a point which will admit of even a small margin on shipments to foreign markets.

The English crop of wheat is an good authority equal to the crop t so good as that of 1863. Mr. ird, writing in the London *Times*, the opinion that the average will two bushels per acre, or about five er the yearly average yield of the ngdom. He estimates in harmony gricultural returns, that there were res more under wheat this season or an increase in the average of twelfth. Taking, then, the average cre as above given, he figures up ield at 15,700,000 quarters, leaving y of 5,000,000 quarters to be supforeign sources. That deficiency ver, be increased by circumstances the foreign supply required fully a-half millions. The English ve had, as in this country, exceedrable weather for fall seeding, n a large breadth being sown with er most propitious circumstances, onnection we may notice the incks in store at various points. In there were on the 15th, 111,854 st 84,155 in 1867 and 39,900 in Chicago on the 20th there were nush. against 754,100 last year, and 1866; in Milwaukee there were at ate 618,000 bush., against 455,000 year; and 281,000 in 1866; in Bufwere, on the 19th, 764,000 bush., ,000 bush. last year; and in New were 760,652 bush., against 258,- ar. These increased stocks arise n an earlier movement of the crop nd the prevailing mania for specestern markets has kept back a that should have reached New ince.

ext the receipts at the five princilake ports—Chicago, Milwaukee, ledo and Cleveland—we have an wheat receipts from 21,203,118 ear to 24,470,164 bush. this year, ꞓ and a half millions of bushels in the same period of the previous . At the same time the increase arge, rising from 2,772,996 brls. 3,194,756 brls. this year, an inetty nearly half a million barrels. pts at New York tell another tale. arison of them it appears that 375 bushels were received from ꞓer up to to the 20th inst., against ꞓr the same time last year, showase of close on 700,000 bushels. of nearly 80,000 barrels in flour parent by a similar comparison. es corroborate the statement bethat western speculators are holdop for prices which shippers at not pay, in the hope of forcing hipment and consumption to make

the necessary concessions. Whether they they will succeed or succumb depends on the extent of supplies and the money resources of those who are interested in upholding the market.

GORE BANK.

A meeting of the shareholders of this bank will be held on Monday next, to receive the report of the committee appointed some time ago to examine the Bank affairs. This report and the report of the Directors, which accompanied it, are given elsewhere. For the sake of presenting at one view the state of affairs on 31st August last, we give the balance sheet annexed to the Directors' report:

LIABILITIES.		
Circulation		$212,712 00
Deposits at Interest..........	$116,902 34	
" not at Interest........	74,121 88	
		185,024 22
Balance due to other Banks......		14,328 04
Unpaid Dividends..............		187 60
Allowed for Adjusting Exchange ..	1,000 00	
" Law and other Expen's	3,000 00	
" Rebate of Interest on		
" Current Bills Disc'ted	3,851 75	
" Incidentals..........	5,000 00	
		12,851 75
Balance to Cr. of Capital Account.		500,479 87
		$925,584 08

ASSETS.		
Gold, Silver and Provincial Notes..		$194,594 97
Cheques and Notes of other Banks		15,325 26
Balance due by other Banks.....		12,666 67
Bank of U. C. Certificates, (Market		
Value).....................		24,715 00
$92,783 83-100 of Government De-		
bentures, (Market Value)........		76,114 66
$118,800 of Hamilton Debentures,		
(Market Value).............		77,831 00
Mortgages, (Market Value		40,963 00
Real Estate, "		22,861 00
Bank Premises, "		12,000 00
Safes and Office Furniture at Ham-		
ilton and Branches, (Market val.)		1,000 00
Interest on Debentures to date....		1,400 87
Other debts		7,650 00
Notes and Bills discounted Current $410,151 19		
Less allowed for Loss........	80,041 54	
		330,069 65
Notes and Bills discounted—past		
due.........................	279,997 28	
Allowed for Loss..............	142,235 28	
		137,762 10
		$925,584 08

At the time the investigation committee was appointed, we dwelt upon the necessity of a careful examination and a faithful report, and we are glad to be able to express the belief that that line of duty has been followed out.

The bank has been over thirty years in existence and has had its share of the vicissitudes of fortune. Adverse circumstances affected it in 1847, but it recovered and afterwards paid good dividends. It now finds itself with about $500,000 available. The Committee attribute a large portion of the losses "to the errors and misfortunes of a remote period;" in other words, during the Dark Ages of banking in this Province its means were misused. The most serious fault of recent times has been the perpetuation of some of the errors which experience has shown to lie at the root of the difficulties with which our oldest banking institutions were beset. Bad debts which should have

been written off long ago, were allowed to continue on the balance sheet, thus giving a delusive appearance to the affairs of the bank. The Committee charge the Directors with neglect of duty, in not boldly encountering the difficulties which beset the institution, and bringing "their published statements into harmony with the actual facts of the case." It came out at the last meeting that the Directors have been, all along, furnished with information as to the state of accounts which has proved the great source of trouble, and, such being admitted, we are not at a loss in placing the responsibility on the proper shoulders. If the Cashier had either acted independently of his Board, or concealed from them what was necessary to a proper understanding of what was being done, we should unhesitatingly charge him with fault. But the facts are otherwise, and the shareholders must hold their Directors answerable under the charges so distinctly made by the committee. We do not say and no one imagines that the Directors have used the bank funds for their own purposes, or that there has been intentional dishonesty on their part in publishing statements from time to time, but that they have been guilty of neglect and carelessness we take to be fully established. As to the valuation of assets, there has been much to complain of and this case may be taken as evidence of the necessity that exists for a more perfect system of audit than at present prevails.

It remains to be decided whether the bank should continue in business or go into liquidation. Taking the committee's report and all the circumstances into consideration, we hesitate not to reiterate the conclusion expressed in these columns, some time ago, that it is for the interest of the shareholders, as well as that of the public, that the proprietary should not give up the ship. The position seems to be such that the bank could at present pay off all its liabilities in thirty days. Every dollar of circulation could at once be redeemed over the counter.

The assets are of such a character that they might be realized at once. The paper held by the bank seems to be good if we may judge from the fact that the portion of it on which $350,000 were advanced by the other banks by way of assistance at a time of emergency, has been fully and promptly met at maturity. The amount of capital intact is respectable. An examination of great strictness has revealed the state of affairs, and this will be found much less "desperate" than was anticipated. On the whole, we believe that the proprietors will find it to their advantage to let the bank go on. Under careful management they may reasonably hope to regain public confidence.

Insurance.

INSURANCE MATTERS IN MONTREAL.

(From a Correspondent.)

MONTREAL, Oct. 27, 1868.

There was a large fire attended with loss of life at the Steam Mills and Lumber yard of L. Charbonneau, corner of Craig and St. Charles Borromie streets. The buildings were very much injured, and a large quantity of lumber was destroyed, the watchman named A. Vian was burnt to death, he is supposed to have fallen asleep. The fire caught from the engine. The loss is estimated at $25,000 without insurance. Mr. Charbonneau always stated that it was cheaper to insure himself than pay the high rates the offices charge on such premises ; he has now found out his mistake.

Since my loss there has been a marked decrease in the number of fires in this City, which to a certain extent may be attributed to the offering of rewards by the Insurance Companies and the City Corporation, nothing however has been elicited with regard to the late numerous acts of incendiarism. A few weeks ago an advertisement appeared in some of our City papers signed by Gillespie, Moffatt & Co., asking for applications for the Agency of an Insurance Company. A large number of applicants handed in their papers and one gentleman preferring to "deal with principals only," took first steamer to England to secure the prize. I learn that Mr. Jas. Davison, the manager of the Phœnix, was an applicant for the office, but afterwards withdrew his proposals. The 'Phœnix' will therefor retain the services of one of our most careful and reliable managers in this City.

Mr. Perry has gone west on business of the 'Royal,' and will probably be away for some months, the *double-headed* Fire Marshal will therefore enjoy peace and quietness for a time ; let us fondly hope he may enjoy it.

APPOINTMENTS.—Mr. C. J. Bloomfield has been named as the Toronto agent of the London and Lancashire Life Assurance Company. Mr. Evans, of the firm of Evans, Elmsley & Co. of this city, will represent the New York Life Insurance Company here. Both first-class men.

FIRE RECORD.—Belleville.—A fire broke out in the brick building of R. Price, grocer. The fire was confined to the second story, in which were Dr. Potts, and Mr. Bate, tailor. Potts was insured for $600 in the Lancashire which would not cover his loss. Price was insured for $2,000, also in the Lancashire, and there was an additional insurance of $2,000 on the building which, a Belleville paper says, will cover the loss.

Amherstburgh, October 22.—A telegram says : Thomas' grist and saw mill took fire this morning at five o'clock. Loss, $10,000. No insurance. It is supposed to have taken from some dry lumber that was over the boiler. Borrowman's factory was, with difficulty, saved.

Morrisburg, October 22.—Barn of Alpheus Cook, in the township of Matilda, and contents, consisting of season's crop. Loss, $1,000. No insurance.

Mariposa, Victoria Co., Ont., Oct. 11.—The Alma Mills and contents, and dwelling house of Jno. Cullis were destroyed by fire; no particulars as to insurance.

—The sum of $200 was recently sent to the Treasurer of the Vermont Mutual Insurance Co. from a confessor, through a Catholic priest.

BUILDING SOCIETIES.—Forfeiting shares. When after the death of a member of a Building Society, his shares were permitted to run in arrear.

Held, that in the absence of a personal representative, the Society could not take any steps to forfeit the shares any more than they could have enforced their claim by action, by debt, as provided by the statutes. Glass v. Hope, 14 Ch. Rep. 484.

Communications.

Montreal Correspondence.

(From our own Correspondent).

Montreal, Oct. 27, 1868.

Since my last we have had a heavy fall of snow, accompanied by frost and high winds, and the snow has not yet wholly disappeared. Rain is wanted, the country being nearly as dry as in mid-summer; up the Ottawa freight boats can scarcely carry half their usual freight; should winter set in before the small rivers, creeks, and swamps are filled, we may look for a very disastrous season for the lumbermen. A few weeks of open, warm weather, with considerable rain, will be of immense benefit to every part of Lower Canada.

PRODUCE.—Our produce market has been tolerably active, fair sales of flour for export and local consumption at about last week's rates; several shipments have been made to England, arrivals is by no means overstocked ; the prices remain much the same as last week. Wheat is unchanged, 20,000 bush. Chicago No. 2 sold on the spot at $1.14 and 10,000 do. to arrive at $1.11. U. C. spring remains at $1.19 to $1.20. The coarse grains are very scarce and high, and likely to continue so. Peas are worth about $1 per 66 lbs. Oats as high as 50c. per 32 lbs. has been paid for lots to supply our local millers, Lower Canada oats are exceedingly light, and in many parts of the country the farmers have preferred feeding them down to the horses in the straw in preference to threshing them. Barley here, as in Toronto, is exceedingly high and quotations are nominal. In Beauharnois county, the farmers have been paid as high as 84c. per minot, the Americans being in the market. The quality generally is good, the color being white but the weight is deficient. Some information respecting our Montreal retail markets may not be without interest to your readers. We possess six city markets under the control of our corporation and subject to very severe restrictions, as a large proportion of our city revenue is derived from them. We have consequently no private butcher shops nor green groceries, though most of our general grocers sells vegetables, pork, hams, &c., to their customers, but by a strange anomaly are prohibited from selling fresh meat and fish. This is often the cause of great inconvenience to the citizens and I think might easily be remedied by the corporation granting licences outside of the market.

PROVISIONS.—The supplies of Lower Canada cattle have been rather less than usual, especially hogs, which generally have been high. The farmers are bringing forward all their horned cattle fearful of the supply of fodder running short; consequently meat of all descriptions, excepting pork, is cheap, but the quality is inferior, such as your butchers would scarcely like to offer; the price of beef ranges from $5.50 to $8, according to quality, the fattest bringing as high a $9. The bulk of our supply for retail uses from Western Canada so far, very few of our Canadian farmers have turned their attention to grazing, which in many districts would prove most profitable. Writing on agricultural matters my attention was attracted by an article in your paper of the 16th, intitled "Peat vs. Fuel," in which the value of peat has been prominently brought forward. The writer has omitted to recognize its great value for agricultural purposes. Mr. A. Young, a distinguished English agriculturalist, in his "Farmer's Tour through England," published in the year 1812, states that the value of peat ashes is hardly known in the farming districts. Ten bushels applied to one acre bearing clover will fully double the crop, and the same result may be expected on all hay lands. On the Bellevue farm, situated on the Ottawa river, they have been used instead of soot, &c., to turnip fields with the most successful results and peat dust is most valuable for protect-

ing onions from their enemies and for eradic. thistles.

GROCERIES.—The market has been com tively active during the week, dried fruits, cially Valentia raisins, having sold freely on the spot and to arrive. Teas have been but there have been considerable transacti sugars. There are only three large auction advertized, viz.: Rimmer, Gunn & Co., A quhart & Co., and T. & F. Ross & Co., (a firm having a branch here); several Western b are in town and more are expected by to-n train, but the general impression is that very business will be done, your large grocers have direct importers to so large an extent tha not worth their while to attend our sales. matter is often discussed in Montreal as t advisability of auction sales, except for cargoes. It is true they enable individual chants to move off considerable quantities of but on the other hand it is agreed that it da not only the private sales of the merchant interferes most seriously with the busines large and useful class of the mercantile comm viz., the jobbers. Small country buyer attend our large sales can buy small lots of at prices fully equal, if not in many cases le the jobber, both buying in the same mark under similar advantages. In New York, Liverpool, and all other large commercial men or jobbers enter the market, and there established a distinctive *wholesale* and *whole retail price*. The question is this, has advanced sufficiently for such a distinction is an open one and much debated in our co cial circles. I give no positive opinion eith way or another but leave it to your readers.

Toronto Market.

Trade in the various departments has bee quiet this week, but considering the stage season a good deal is being done.

HARDWARE.—The fall stocks are now to hand, and the assortment, as a whole though some lines of heavy goods are runn owing to a pretty active demand. We red quotations of a number of articles.

GRAIN.—Wheat receipts by cars, 41,35 and 36,984 bush. last week. The mar Spring is dull, with a downward tenden closed at a decline of 1 to 2 cents on las prices. Sales include 5,700 bush. at $11 and a number of car loads at $1.11 to $1.12 is some demand for midge proof wheat ; bush. sold at $1.14½ f.o.b., and several $1.14. For the better qualities of Fall, t fair demand, and Choice sells at $1.30 t About twenty car loads in all sold at thes tions, and several cars inferior at $1.20 to there is no demand except for the best. Receipts by cars for the week 24,750 bu 38,000 bush. for the previous week. Th receipts have been light amounting only 10,000 to 12,000 bushels. The shipm water to the 26th were 634,000 bush. $81,675 bush. were shipped last week ; quantity 6,789 bush. went to Erie ; 8,0 to Toledo, and the balance to Oswego. T In store here is about 150,000 bush., decreased about 50,000 bush. within t The market opened at $1.40 to $1.43, adv $1.44, and closed unsettled at $1.35 t Sales during the week were two cars a three cars at $1.44 ; 2,500 bush. at $1.4 bush. at $1.42 ; one car at $1.38, and c $1.35. *Peas*—Receipts by cars for the we bush. ; stock about 35,000 bush. ; there ited demand at 90c. to 91c., holders as No sales reported. *Oats*.—Receipts by c bush. ; there is a moderate demand market is quiet at 51c. to 52c., with sale cars at quotations. *Rye*.—The distill paying 93c. per 60 lbs. *Seeds*.—There demand for timothy at $2.25 to $2.75

Barbadoes, 5¼ to 5¾c.; Cuba ,5¼ to 5½c.; Centrifugal Cuba, 6c., in bond.

FINANCIAL.—Bank drawing rate on London 60 day sight bills 13 per cent. prem.; private 12 to 12½ per cent. prem. New York gold drafts at sight, 3¾ per cent. prem. Currency drafts 28½ per cent. discount. Montreal sight drafts 3¾ per cent. prem. Newfoundland sight drafts 5 per cent. premium.

St. Clair Flats Canal.

The improvement of the St. Clair Flats, which is now being made, after the plans and under the direction of General T. J. Cram, of the United States Corps of Engineers, cannot but be of interest not only to commercial men, but citizens of the Western States ; for the deepening of the channel will facilitate to a great extent the shipment of the produce from the lakes so as to enhance the value of all cereals. The canal will be one and a half miles in length by 300 feet in width and will be dredged so as to allow vessels drawing thirteen feet to pass through at the lowest stage. It is to be so constructed that it can be deepened to admit vessels drawing eighteen feet whenever the demands of commerce shall render it necessary. It is being furnished with timber dykes, one on each side, running the entire length, which will be filled from the channel. The banks, besides, are being made fifty-eight feet wide and five feet above water.

The Suez Canal.

The completion of the Suez Canal, which it is expected will be open for the passage of vessels during the present month, marks an important era in Oriental affairs ; in fact, its influence reacts upon commercial matters throughout the world. This wonderful work of engineering skill and patient labor, costing about $30,000,000, is capable of carrying upon its bosom vessels of the largest class engaged in the European and Indian trade, and will shorten the distance about one half. It is owned by a French Company, and its chief-engineer, to whose genius its construction is chiefly due, is M. Ferdinand de Lesseps, a grandson of the Marquis de Lafayette. Thus another link in the great chain of civilization and progress is forged, binding nations with bonds more enduring than steel.

The Tea Trade.

The tea movement in London and Liverpool from the 1st January to the 30th September, is shown by the following figures :

	1867.	1868.
London—	lbs.	lbs.
Foreign imports	79,345,218	92,564,687
Coastwise imports	133,200	239,040
Duty paid deliveries	103,700,053	102,631,951
Exports—coastwise	27,755,636	24,391,018
Exports—foreign	23,141,549	28,261,539
Stock	60,307,495	58,173,060
Liverpool—		
Foreign imports	460,792	600,232
Coastwise imports	2,773,007	1,956,047
Duty paid deliveries	4,209,548	3,487,362
Exports—foreign	451,710	316,989
Exports—coastwise	751,286	564,941
Stock	1,326,184	743,183

The shipments from Hong Kong to Sept. 17th 1868, were 95,000,000 lbs; to Sept. 28th, 1867, 71,000,000 lbs.

Cotton.

A statement showing the stocks of cotton in Liverpool and London, including the supplies of American and Indian produce ascertained to be afloat to those ports, is as follows:—

	1867.	1868.
Stock in Liverpool, bales	737,000	427,100
„ London	103,580	62,770
American cotton afloat	14,000	11,000
Indian	323,460	526,920
Total	1,178,040	1,047,790

Of the present stock of cotton in Liverpool 20¼ per cent. is American against 29 per cent. last year. Of Indian cotton the proportion is 53 per cent. against 46¾ per cent.

Prince Edward Island.

P. E. Island has imported this year— say up to the 20th Sept.—12,188 tons of coal, 21,759 bbls. flour, 6,000 bbls. cornmeal. In the same time it has exported 10,685 bbls. mackerel, the greater portion, however, having been taken in U. S. bottoms, more than 3,000 bbls. of which have been sent through New Brunswick by rail to the States. The fishermen are availing themselves more than heretofore of the Island as a fishing station ; instead of returning with their fares as soon as taken, they ship them homeward from Charlottetown or land them at Shediac.

Newfoundland Fisheries.

The results of codfishing on the eastern coast of Newfoundland this season are most disastrous. In order that the expenses may be covered, it is necessary that every vessel employed should take at least 160,000 cod ; but this year many have only caught 20,000, 25,000, or 30,000. Accordingly, discouragement is general; and many of the owners of vessels have determined to fish no more. The resolution will deprive of occupation a large number of seamen of France. So says a letter from French St. Peters.

Imports of Wheat.

Imports of Wheat into the United Kingdom during the seven months ending July 31st, 1866, 1867 and 1868 :

WHEAT.	1866.	1867.	1868.
Russia.............cwts.	3,988,969	6,464,815	5,371,682
Prussia	2,450,902	4,071,707	2,402,419
Mecklenburg	455,922	552,821	425,566
Hanse Towns	489,720	451,615	402,449
Illyria, Crotia, and Dalmatia	1,191,619	249,074	762,992
Turkey, Moldavia, and Wallachia	300,973	1,528,421	2,367,044
Egypt	8,738	204,124	2,528,211
United States	323,160	1,408,736	4,357,616
Chili	34,344	1,271,197	772,686
British North America	5,789	27	247,762
Total, including other countries	13,784,485	17,744,178	20,706,791
FLOUR.	1866.	1867.	1868.
Hanse Towns	160,477	258,559	313,272
France	2,074,122	1,013,626	344,706
United States	166,949	141,709	428,222
Total, including other countries	3,452,822	2,055,521	1,689,447

PORTAGE LAKE AND LAKE SUPERIOR SHIP CANAL COMPANY.—This Company was incorporated by the Legislature of Michigan as early as 1854. The canal will be about three miles in length, thirteen feet deep, one hundred feet wide at bottom and top, and will shorten the distance between the two points about two hundred miles of dangerous lake navigation. The Company was originally organized in 1861, with a land grant of 200,000 acres. After a careful survey, this grant not being deemed sufficient to build the canal, it was increased last year to 400,000 acres. This work is now in active progress, and is being pushed with such vigor by the Company that this great project will be an accomplished fact in a few short months. Of the marsh excavation over one-half mile has been completed, which, with a few hundred feet further, connecting with a small lake of over a half a mile in length, will leave about three-fourths of a mile of clear sand digging to bring the two great lakes together. The dredges are at work night and day.—*Chicago Jour. of Com.*

PETROLEUM SHIPMENTS.—The *Etowah*, of Liverpool, is now loading with Refined Petroleum, direct for Liverpool, at the dock of Thos. Walton. The cargo will consist of 2000 barrels of oil, manufactured in Cleveland, mostly by the Walton Brothers, and is owned by Messrs. Cunningham, Shaw & Co., of Liverpool. The tunnage will consist of staves and boat oars. This is the third or fourth cargo of oil that has been shipped direct to Liverpool from Cleveland. The previous ventures of this kind have proved profitable, and we have no doubt the present one will result the same way.—*Cleveland Herald, Sept. 29th.*

COMPETING ROUTES.

The *Chicago Tribune* says:—"The elevator at New Orleans is now nearly completed, and will have a storing capacity of 750,000 bushels, which it is proposed to utilize by towing Grain down the Father of Waters in fleets of boats built for the purpose, and thence shipping it in ocean vessels to Europe, or even to the Atlantic cities, which, it is claimed, can be accomplished at a much cheaper rate than, as now, by rail, lake and canal, from the farming districts within a few miles of the Mississippi River. It is well known that past experience in shipping corn round through the Gulf has not been peculiarly profitable, loss by heating having occurred in almost every instance, the warm humidity of the Gulf streambeing found more detrimental in producing precocious germination than the transit of the equatorial zone outside of that stream. But there are not wanting arguments in favor of the route, or well-posted men who believe that the passage can be made in the winter months without risk. The New Orleans merchants have determined to try it, and are aided by capital from outside, which at least assures a fair trial, which they claim has not yet been made. Connected with this is the proposition to supply the North-west, and especially Chicago, with many of the products which now come by way of New York. It is stated to be in contemplation to establish a line of vessels to the Isthmus of Panama, by which heavy freight can be brought from California much more cheaply than by the overland route, with the Pacific Railroad in its favor, and it is believed that the opening of that route "across the continent," will so increase the traffic between the Pacific seaboard and the (now called) Western States, as to make such a line an absolute necessity for the transit of the heavier classes of goods which will move in upon us in rapidly increasing abundance—too great for the facilities of the railroad, even though the question of expense did not interfere in favor of the scheme. The same course is proposed with regard to goods from New York and Europe, designed for the trans-Mississippi region.

Canada Life Assurance Company.

CAPITAL AND CASH ASSETS,
OVER $2,000,000.

SUMS ASSURED,
$5,000,000.

A COMPARISON of the rates of this Company with others cannot fail to demonstrate the advantage of the low premiums, which, by the higher returns from its investments, it is enabled to offer.

IF PREFERRED, ASSURERS NEED ONLY
PAY ONE-HALF OF EACH YEAR'S PREMIUM IN CASH,

during the whole term of policies on the 10 payment plan, or for seven years on the whole life plan.

For the unpaid portion of premiums,
"NOTES" ARE NOT REQUIRED BY THIS COMPANY,

so that assurers are not liable to be called upon for payment of these, nor for assessments upon them, as in the case of Mutual companies.
Every facility and advantage which can be afforded are offered by this Company.

A. G. RAMSAY, Manager.
E. BRADBURNE, Agent,
3n11   Toronto Street.

Lyman & McNab,

Importers of, and Wholesale Dealers in,
HEAVY AND SHELF HARDWARE,
KING STREET,
TORONTO, ONTARIO.

London Assurance Corporation,
FOR
FIRE AND LIFE ASSURANCE.

INCORPORATED BY ROYAL CHARTER,
A. D. 1720.

No. 7, Royal Exchange, London, England.

ROMEO H. STEPHENS,
AGENT FOR CANADA.
Office 56, St. Francois Xavier Street,
MONTREAL.

ISAAC C. GILMOR,
AGENT FOR TORONTO,
Office—Western Assurance Buildings,
50 Colborne Street.   11-1m

Ontario Bank.
DIVIDEND No. 23.

NOTICE is hereby given, that a Dividend of Four per cent. upon the Capital Stock of this Institution for the current half year, has this day been declared, and that the same will be payable at the Bank and its Branches, on and after
Tuesday, the First day of December next.
The Transfer Books will be closed from the 15th to the 30th November, both days inclusive.
By order of the Board.
D. FISHER, Cashier.
Ontario Bank,
Bowmanville, 24th Oct., 1868.}   11-td

Gore Bank.

THE Adjourned Annual Meeting of the Shareholders to receive the report of the Committee appointed at the meeting held on the 3rd day of August last, will be held at the Banking House,
On MONDAY, the 2nd of NOVEMBER next, at noon,
By order of the Board,
W. G. CASSELS,
Cashier.
GORE BANK,
Hamilton, 12th Oct., 1868.   9.td

THE PRINCE EDWARD COUNTY
Mutual Fire Insurance Company.

HEAD OFFICE,—PICTON, ONTARIO.
President, L. B. STINSON ; *Vice-President,* W. A. RICHARDS. *Directors :* H. A. McPaul, James Cavan, James Johnson, N. S. DeMill, William Delong. *Treasurer,* David Barker. *Secretary,* John Twigg ; *Solicitor,* R. J. Fitzgerald.

THIS Company is established upon strictly Mutual principles, insuring farming and isolated property, (not hazardous,) *Townships only,* and offers great advantages to insurers, at low rates for *fire* years, without the expense of a renewal This Company has existed 12 years, during which period it has adjusted all losses in a satisfactory manner. It is managed with strict economy, and affords an opportunity of insuring with safety and reliance, and very little expense, which accounts for its long standing and the successful business which it has been and is now doing.
Picton, June 15, 1868.   9-1y

UNRIVALLED!

THE BRITISH AMERICAN COMMERCIAL COLLEGE,
· Consolidated with the ·
Bryant, Stratton and Odell Business College
AND TELEGRAPHIC INSTITUTE,

STANDS Pre-eminent and Unrivalled. It is the LARGEST and MOST EFFICIENT. It employs the largest staff of Teachers, among whom are the two BEST PENMEN OF CANADA.
The TUITION FEE is the same as in other Institutions having a similar object.
The PRICE OF BOARD is the same as in other Canadian Cities.
In an EDUCATIONAL point of view, there is no other Institution in the country that has equal advantages and facilities.
YOUNG MEN intending to qualify themselves for business, will find it to their advantage to send for a Circular, or call at the College Rooms, corner of King and Toronto streets.
Scholarships good in Montreal and throughout the United States.
ODELL & TROUT,
October 2.   Principals and Proprietors.   8

BEAVER
Mutual Insurance Associ:

HEAD OFFICE—20 TORONTO STREET,
TORONTO.

INSURES LIVE STOCK against death from : The only Canadian Company having authorit: class of business.
R. L. DENISO
W. T. O'REILLY,   P.
Secretary.

HOME DISTRICT
Mutual Fire Insurance Com

OFFICE:
North-West Corner of Yonge and Adelaid
TORONTO.—(UP STAIRS.)

INSURES Dwelling Houses, Stores, Wareho chandise, Furniture, &c.

PRESIDENT—The Hon. J. McMURRIC:
VICE-PRESIDENT—JOHN BURNS, Esq.
JOHN RAINS, S:

AGENTS:
DAVID WRIGHT, Esq., Hamilton ; FRANCIS STE\
Barrie ; Messrs. GIBBS & BRO., Oshaw:

John Boyd & Co.,
WHOLESALE GROCERS AND COMM
MERCHANTS,
61 AND 63 FRONT ST
TORONTO.

NOW in store, direct from the European and Markets, a large assortment of Genera comprising
Teas, Sugars, Coffees, Wines and Li
AND
GENERAL GROCERIES.
Ship Chandlery, Canvas, Manilla and Ta Oakum, Tar, Flags, &c.,
DIRECT FROM THE MANUFACTU
JOHN BOYD.   ALEX. M. MONRO.   C. :
Toronto, Oct. 1st, 1868.

John Ross & Co.,
QUEBEC.

T. & F. Ross & Co.,
GENERAL WHOLESALE GR
PRODUCE AND COMMISSION MERCH
361 Commissioner Street,
MONTREAL.

W. McLaren & Co.,
WHOLESALE
BOOT AND SHOE MANUFAC
18 ST. MAURICE STREET,
MONTREAL.
June, 1868.

Honore Plamondon
CUSTOM House Broker, Forwarder, an Quebec. Office—Custom House Bu

STATEMENT OF BANKS

ACTING UNDER CHARTER, FOR THE MONTH ENDING 30th SEPTEMBER, 1866, ACCORDING TO RETURNS FURNISHED BY THE BANKS TO THE AUDITOR OF PUBLIC ACCOUNTS.

NAME OF BANK	Capital authorized by Act.	Capital paid up.	Promissory Notes in circulation not bearing interest.	Balances due to other Banks.	Cash Deposits not bearing Interest.	Cash Deposits bearing Interest.	TOTAL LIABILITIES.	Coin, Bullion, and Provincial Notes.	Landed or other Property of the Bank.	Government Securities.	Promissory Notes, or Bills of other Banks.	Balances due from other Banks.	Notes and Bills Discounted.	Other Debts due the Bank, not included under foregoing heads.	TOTAL ASSETS.
ONTARIO AND QUEBEC.															
Montreal	6,000,000	6,000,000													
Quebec	3,000,000	1,478,350													
City	1,200,000	423,095													
British North America	4,866,666	4,866,666													
Banque du Peuple	1,600,000	1,600,000													
Niagara District	1,000,000														
Molson's	1,000,000	1,000,000													
Toronto	2,000,000														
Ontario	3,000,000														
Eastern Townships	446,000	400,000													
Banque Nationale	1,000,000	1,000,000													
Banque Jacques Cartier	1,000,000	1,000,000													
Merchants'	6,000,000														
Royal Canadian	1,110,465														
Union B'k. Low. Canada	3,000,000														
Mechanics'	1,000,000	377,675													
Bank of Commerce		965,958													
NOVA SCOTIA.															
Bank of Yarmouth															
Merchants' Bank															
People's Bank															
Union Bank															
Bank of Nova Scotia															
NEW BRUNSWICK.															
Bank of New Brunswick	600,000	600,000													
Commercial Bank	300,000	300,000													
St. Stephen's Bank															
People's Bank															
Totals	86,966,666	92,760,000													

TORONTO PRICES CURRENT.—October 29, 1868.

Name of Article.	Wholesale Rates.	
Boots and Shoes.	$ c.	$ c.
Mens' Thick Boots	2 20	2 50
" Kip	2 50	3 25
" Calf	3 20	3 70
" Congress Gaiters	2 00	2 40
" Kip Cobourgs	1 00	1 50
Boys' Thick Boots	1 65	1 90
Youths' "	1 45	1 55
Women's Batts	95	1 30
" Congress Gaiters	1 15	1 50
Misses' Batts	0 75	1 00
" Congress Gaiters	1 00	1 30
Girls' Batts	0 65	0 85
" Congress Gaiters	0 80	1 10
Children's C. T. Cacks	0 50	0 65
" Gaiters	0 65	0 90
Drugs.		
Aloes Cape	0 12½	0 16
Alum	0 02½	0 03
Borax	0 00	0 00
Camphor, refined	0 65	0 70
Castor Oil	0 18	0 28
Caustic Soda	0 04½	0 05
Cochineal	0 90	1 (0
Cream Tartar	0 00	0 00
Epsom Salts	0 03	0 04
Extract Logwood	0 09	0 11
Gum Arabic, sorts	0 30	0 35
Indigo, Madras	0 75	1 00
Licorice	0 14	0 45
Madder	0 13	0 16
Nutgalls	0 00	0 00
Opium	6 70	7 00
Oxalic Acid	0 28	0 35
Potash, Bi-tart.	0 25	0 28
" Bichromate	0 15	0 20
Potass Iodide	3 80	4 50
Senna	0 12½	0 60
Soda Ash	0 03	0 04
Soda Bicarb	4 50	5 50
Tartaric Acid	0 37½	0 45
Verdigris	0 35	0 40
Vitriol, Blue	0 09	0 10
Groceries.		
Coffees:		
Java, ℔ lb.	0 22@0 24	
Laguayra,	0 17	0 18
Rio	0 15	0 17
Fish:		
Herrings, Lab. split	6 75	7 00
" round	0 00	0 00
" scaled	0 35	0 40
Mackerel, small kitts	1 00	0 00
Loch. Her. wh'e firks	2 50	2 75
" half "	1 25	1 50
White Fish & Trout	3 25	3 50
Salmon, saltwater	14 00	15 00
Dry Cod, ℔ 112 lbs	5 00	5 00
Fruit:		
Raisins, Layers	2 20	2 25
" M. R.	2 10	2 20
" Valentias new	0 08½	0 08½
Currants, new	0 05	0 05½
" old	0 04½	0 04½
Figs	0 11	0 12½
Molasses:		
Clayed, ℔ gal.	0 00	0 35
Syrups, Standard	0 43	0 44
" Golden	0 52	0 55
Rice:		
Arracan	4 50	4 75
Spices:		
Cassia, whole, ℔ lb.	0 42	0 45
Cloves	0 11	0 12
Nutmegs	0 45	0 55
Ginger, ground	0 20	0 25
" Jamaica, root	0 20	0 25
Pepper, black	0 09½	0 10
Pimento	0 08	0 09
Sugars:		
Port Rico, ℔ lb.	0 08½	0 08¾
Cuba "	0 08½	0 08¾
Barbadoes (bright)	0 08½	0 08¾
Dry Crushed, at 60 d.	0 11½	0 11½
Canada Sugar Refine'y, yellow No. 2, 60 ds.	0 08¾	0 08¾
Yellow, No. 2½.	0 08¾	0 09¼
No. 3.	0 09¾	0 09¾
Crushed X	0 10	0 10½
" A	0 10½	0 11
Ground	0 11½	0 11½
Extra Ground	0 12½	0 12¾
Teas:		
Japan com'n to good	0 40	0 55
" Fine to choicest	0 55	0 65
Colored, com. to fine	0 60	0 75
Congou & Souch'ng	0 42	0 75
Oolong, good to fine	0 50	0 65
Y. Hyson, com to gd	0 45	0 55
Medium to choice	0 65	0 80
Extra choice	0 85	0 95
Gunpowd'r c. to med	0 55	0 70
" med. to fine	0 70	0 85

Name of Article.	Wholesale Rate.	
Groceries—*Contin'd*	$ c.	$ c.
" fine to fins't	0 85	0 95
Hyson	0 45	0 80
Imperial	0 42	0 80
Tobacco, Manufact'd:		
Can Leaf, ℔ lb 5s & 10s.	0 26	0 30
Western Leaf, com	0 25	0 26
" Good	0 27	0 32
" Fine	0 32	0 35
" Bright fine	0 40	0 50
" " choice	0 60	0 75
Hardware.		
Tin (net cash prices)		
Block, ℔ lb.	0 25	0 26
Grain	0 25	0 26
Copper:		
Pig	0 23	0 24
Sheet	0 30	0 33
Cut Nails:		
Assorted ¼ Shingles, ℔ 100 lb.	2 00	3 00
Shingle alone do	3 15	3 25
Lathe and 5 dy	3 30	3 40
Galvanized Iron:		
Assorted sizes	0 09	0 10
Best No. 24	0 09	0 00
" 26	0 08	0 08½
" 28	0 09	0 09½
Horse Nails:		
Guest's or Griffin's assorted sizes	0 19	0 20
For W. ass'd sizes	0 18	0 19
Patent Hammer'd do	0 17	0 18
Iron (at 4 months):		
Pig—Gartsherrie No1	26 00	27 00
Other brands. No1	22 00	24 00
" No2	24 00	25 00
Bar—Scotch, ℔ 100 lb	2 25	2 50
Refined	3 00	3 25
Swedes	5 00	5 50
Hoops—Coopers	3 00	3 25
Band	3 00	3 25
Boiler Plates	3 25	3 50
Canada Plates	4 00	4 25
Union Jack	0 00	0 00
Pontypool	4 00	4 25
Swansea	3 90	4 00
Lead (at 4 months):		
Bar, ℔ 100 lbs.	0 07	0 07½
Sheet "	0 08	0 09
Shot	0 07½	0 07¾
Iron Wire (net cash):		
No. 6, ℔ bundle	2 70	2 80
" 9, "	3 10	3 20
" 12, "	3 40	3 50
" 16, "	4 30	4 40
Powder:		
Blasting, Canada	3 50	3 75
FF "	4 25	4 50
FFF "	4 75	5 00
Blasting, English	5 00	5 50
FF loose	5 50	6 00
FFF "	6 00	6 50
Pressed Spikes (4 mos):		
Regular sizes 100	4 00	4 25
Extra "	4 50	5 00
Tin Plates (net cash):		
IC Coke	7 50	8 00
IC Charcoal	8 50	8 75
IX "	10 50	10 75
IXX "	12 50	0 00
DC "	7 50	9 00
DX "	9 50	10 00
Hides & Skins, ℔ lb		
Green rough	0 05½	0 06
Green, salt'd & insp'd	0 00	0 07
Cured	0 07½	0 08½
Calfskins, green	0 00	0 10
Calfskins, cured	0 00	0 12
" dry	0 18	0 20
Lambskins,	0 70	0 00
" pelts	0 60	0 00
Hops.		
Inferior, ℔ lb.	0 10	0 12
Medium	0 12	0 15
Good	0 15	0 20
Fancy	0 00	0 00
Leather, @ (4 mos.) In lots of less than 50 sides, 10 ℔ cent higher.		
Spanish Sole, 1st qual. heavy, weights ℔ lb.	0 20	21
Do. 1st qual middle do.	0 22	23
Do. No. 2, all weights	0 15	19
Slaughter heavy	0 25	26
Do. light	0 50	00
Harness, best	0 32	34
" No. 2	0 30	33
Upper heavy	0 44	0 38
" light	0 36	0 40

Name of Article.
Leather—*Contin'd.*
Kip Skins, Patna
French
English
Hemlock Calf (30 to 35 lbs.) per doz
Do. light
French Calf.
Grain & Satn Clt ℔ doz.
Splits, large ℔ lb.
" small
Enamelled Cow ℔ foot.
Patent
Pebble Grain
Buff
Oils.
Cod
Lard, extra
" No. 1
" Woollen
Lubricating, patent
" Mott's economic
Linseed, raw
" boiled
Machinery
Olive, 2nd, ℔ gal.
" salad
" salad, in bots. qt. ℔ case
Sesame salad, ℔ gal.
Seal, pale
Spirits Turpentine
Varnish
Whale.
Paints, &c.
White Lead, genuine in Oil, ℔ 25lbs
Do. No. 1 "
" 2 "
" 3 "
White Zinc, genuine
White Lead, dry
Red Lead
Venetian Red, Eng'h
Yellow Ochre, Fren'h
Whiting
Petroleum. (Refined ℔ gal.)
Water white, car l'd
" small lots
Straw, by car load
" small lots
Amber, by car load
" small lots
Benzine
Produce.
Grain:
Wheat, Spring, 60 lb
" Fall 60 "
Barley 48 "
Peas 60 "
Oats 34 "
Rye 56 "
Seeds:
Clover, choice 60 "
" com'n 68 "
Timothy, cho'e 4 "
" inf. to good 48 "
Flax 56 "
Flour (per brl.):
Superior extra
Extra superfine,
Fancy superfine
Superfine No. 1
" No. 2
Oatmeal, (per brl.)
Provisions.
Butter, dairy tub ℔ lb.
" store packed
Cheese, new
Pork, mess, per brl.
" prime mess
" prime
Bacon, rough
" Cumberl'd cut
" smoked
Hams, in salt
" sug. cur. & canv'd
Shoulders, in salt
Lard, in kegs
Eggs, packed
Beef Hams
Tallow
Hogs dressed, heavy
" medium
" light
Salt, &c.
American brls.
Liverpool coarse
Plaster
Water Lime

dles.			*Brandy:*	$ c.	$ c
			Hennessy's, per gal..	2 30	2 0
Jo.'s ..	$ c.	$ c.	Martell's " ..	2 30	2 0
....	0 07½	0 08	J. Robin & Co.'s " ..	2 25	2 5
....	0 07	0 07½	Otard, Dupuy & Cos..	2 25	2 5
....	0 07	0 07½	Brandy, cases........	8 50	9 0
....	0 05	0 05½	Brandy, com. per c...	4 00	4 50
....	0 03½	0 03¾	*Whiskey:*		
....	0 11	0 11½	Common 36 u.p.......	0 62½	0 5
uors,			Old Rye	0 85	0 7½
			Malt	0 85	0 7½
			Toddy	0 85	0 7½
z......	2 60	2 65	Scotch, per gal......	1 90	2 10
Portr..	2 35	2 40	Irish—Kinnahan's c...	7 00	7 50
			" Dunnville's Belf't..	6 00	6 25
Rum...	1 80	2 25	**Wool.**		
. Gin..	1 55	1 65	Fleece, lb...........	0 27	0 30
m.....	1 90	2 00	Pulled "...........	0 00	0 00
			Furs.		
....	4 00	4 25	Bear................	8 00	10 00
m, c...	6 00	6 25	Beaver..............	1 00	1 25
			Coon	0 20	0 40
			Fisher..............	4 00	6 00
....	1 00	1 25	Martin..............	1 40	1 60
....	2 00	4 00	Mink................	4 00	4 25
m....	1 00	1 50	Otter...............	5 75	6 00
....	1 70	1 80	Spring Rats.........	0 15	0 17
olden..	2 50	4 00	Fox.................	1 20	1 25

SURANCE COMPANIES.

ENGLISH.—*Quotations on the London Market.*

Di- d.	Name of Company.	Shares parval £	Amount paid.	Last
	Briton Medical and General Life ...	10	—	1⅝
	Commer'l Union, Fire, Life and Mar.	50	5	5½
	City of Glasgow	25	2¼	5
	Edinburgh Life	100	15	30⅝x
yr	European Life and Guarantee......	2½	11s6	4s 6d
	Etna Fire and Marine............	10	1½	1
	Guardian	100	50	51½
	Imperial Fire..................	500	50	345
	Imperial Life	100	10	16¼
	Lancashire Fire and Life........	20	2	2⅞x
	Life Association of Scotland.....	40	7¼	23
sh	London Assurance Corporation ..	25	12½	48
	London and Lancashire Life	10	1	1
	Liverp'l & London & Globe F. & L.	20	2	7⅞
	National Union Life	5	1	1
	Northern Fire and Life	100	5	10⅝
	North British and Mercantile	50	6¼	16 16½
	Ocean Marine	25	5	20
ts.	Provident Life..................	100	10	38
. s.	Phœnix.........................	....	....	136
pr.	Queen Fire and Life	10	1	15-16ths
.4s	Royal Insurance.................	20	3	6¾
	Scottish Provincial Fire and Life ..	50	2½	4¾
	Standard Life	50	12	65
	Star Life	25	1¼	—
	CANADIAN.			℘ c.
	British America Fire and Marine ..	$50	$25	56
	Canada Life	...	....	.....
	Montreal Assurance	£50	£5	135
	Provincial Fire and Marine........	60	11	.....
...	Quebec Fire	40	32½	£19½
	" Marine...................	100	40	90-95
's.	Western Assurance...............	40	6	.....

RAILWAYS.	Sha's	Paid	Montr	London.
. Lawrence........................	£100	All.	....	56 58xd
ke Huron	20½	"	....	8 8½
do Preference	10	"	....	5½ 6½
:Goderich, 6℘c., 1872-3-4....	100	"	....	....
. St. Lawrence	....	....	10 12	....
do Pref. 10 ℘ ct............	....	....	65 72½	....
....	100	"	16 17	16¼ 16¾
Eq.G. M. Bds. 1 ch. 6℘c............	100	"	....	84 86
First Preference, 5 ℘ c	100	"	....	49 51
Deferred, 3 ℘ ct..	100	"	....	....
Second Pref. Bonds, 5℘c............	100	"	....	39 41
do Deferred, 3 ℘ ct...........	100	"	...	....
Third Pref. Stock, 4℘ct............	100	"	....	28 30
do. Deferred, 3 ℘ ct...........	100	"	....	....
Fourth Pref. Stock, 3℘c............	100	"	....	19 20
do. Deferred, 3 ℘ ct...........	100	"	....	....
....	20½	"	13 14	13¾ 14
New	20½	18	....	....
6 ℘ c. Bds, due 1873-76............	100	All.	....	101 103
5½℘c Bds. due 1877-78..............	100	"	....	93 95
y, Halifax, $250, all..............	$250	"	....	....
anada, 6℘c. 1st Pref. Bds..........	100	"	.. .	80 83

ANGE.	Halifax.	Montr'l.	Quebec.	Toronto.
don, 60 days......				
ays date..........	13½	9½ 9¾	9½ 10	10½
....	12 12½	8½ 9	8¾ 9	9½
ocuments..........	....	7½ 8½	....	....
York..............	....	25½ 26	26 26½	75
....	....	26½ 26½	26½ 27	....
....	....	par	par ½ dis.	par ½ dis.
....	....	3½ 3½	....	3½ 5

STOCK AND BOND REPORT.

The dates of our quotations are as follows:—Toronto, Oct. 28; Montreal, Oct. 26; Quebec, Oct. 26; London, Oct. 1.

NAME.	Shares.	Paid up.	Divid'd last 6 Months	Dividend Day.	CLOSING PRICES. Toronto.	Montre'l	Quebec.
BANKS.			℘ ct.				
British North America	$250	All.	3	July and Jan.	103 105	104 105	103 104
Jacques Cartier..............	50	"	4	1 June, 1 Dec.	106 108	108 109	108 108½
Montreal	200	"	5	"	135¾	136½ 137½	135¾ 136½
Nationale....................	50	"	4	1 Nov. 1 May.	106 108	Bks.clos	Bks.clos
New Brunswick	100	"	....	......	....	...	....
Nova Scotia	200	28	7&b$3¼	Mar. and Sept.	....	....	....
Du Peuple....................	50	"	4	1 Mar., 1 Sept.	105 106	105 105½	105½ 106
Toronto	100	"	4	1 Jan., 1 July.	116½ 117	117 118	116 117
Bank of Yarmouth.............	....	....	......	......	....	....	....
Canadian Bank of Com'e.......	50	95	......	......	103½ 104	103½ 104½	103 104
City Bank Montreal	80	All.	4	1 June, 1 Dec.	102 102½	104 105	103½ 104½
Commer'l Bank (St. John).....	100	"	℘ ct.	.....	....	....	....
Eastern Townships' Bank......	50	"	4	1 July, 1 Jan..	....	95 96	96 96½
Gore	40	...	3½	1 Jan., 1 July.	35 40	33 35	30 32½
Halifax Banking Company......	...	....	......	.....	...	....	...
Mechanics' Bank..............	50	70	4	1 Nov., 1 May.	95 97	Bks.clos	Bks.clos
Merchants' Bank of Canada....	100	70	4	1 Jan., 1 July.	105½ 106	106½ 107	106½ 106½
Merchants' Bank (Halifax)....	....	....	.....	.....	....	....	....
Molson's Bank................	50	All.	4	1 Apr., 1 Oct.	....	106½ 109	106½ 108
Niagara District Bank........	100	70	3½	1 Jan., 1 July.	....	....	....
Ontario Bank.................	40	All.	4	1 June, 1 Dec.	101 101½	101 102	101 102
People's Bank (Fred'kton)....	100	"	......	......	....	....	....
People's Bank (Halifax)......	20	"	7 12 m	......	....	...	....
Quebec Bank	100	"	3½	1 June, 1 Dec.	97½ 98	99 100	99½ 100
Royal Canadian Bank	50	50	4	1 Jan., 1 July.	90 91½	91½ 92½	90 91
St. Stephens Bank	100	All	.....	......	....	..	....
Union Bank	100	70	4	1 Jan., 1 July.	102 102½	102½ 103½	103 104
Union Bank (Halifax).........	100	40	7 12mo	Feb. and Aug.	....	....	. .
MISCELLANEOUS.							
British America Land.........	250	44	2½	......	....	....	....
British Colonial S. S. Co....	250	32½	2½	......	...	45 50	....
Canada Company	32½	All.	5	......	....	....	....
Canada Landed Credit Co......	50	$20	3½	......	62 63	....	....
Canada Per. B'ldg Society....	50	All.	5	......	121½	....	....
Canada Mining Company........	4	90	......	.....	....	....	....
Do. Inl'd Steam Nav. Co..	100	All.	20 12 m	......	....	108½ 110	108 109
Do. Glass Company........	100	"	12½ "	......	....	95	....
Canad'n Loan & Investm't.....	25	2½	7	......	....	....	....
Canada Agency	10	½	......	......	....	....	....
Colonial Securities Co.......	...	....	......	.....	....	....	....
Freehold Building Society....	100	All.	4	......	106 106½	....	....
Halifax Steamboat Co.........	100	"	5	......	....	....	....
Halifax Gas Company..........	....	....	......	.....	....	...	....
Hamilton Gas Company.........	....	....	.....	.....	....	....	....
Huron Copper Bay Co..........	4	12	20	.....	....	35 50c ps	....
Lake Huron S. and C..........	5	102	......	......	....	....	....
Montreal Mining Consols......	20	$15	......	......	....	2.50 2.90	...
Do. Telegraph Co.........	40	All.	5	......	125	122½ 125	125 127
Do. Elevating Co.........	00	"	15 12 m	......	....	100 103	....
Do. City Gas Co..........	40	"	4	15 Mar. 15 Sep.	....	132 134	132½ 134
Do. City Pass. R. Co.....	50	"	5	......	....	109 110½	107 110
Nova Scotia Telegraph	20	"	....	.....	....	....	....
Quebec and L. S.	8	$4	......	.....	....	....	25 cts
Quebec Gas Co................	200	All.	4	1 Mar., 1 Sep.	....	...	118 119
Quebec Street R. R...........	50	25	8	......	....	....	96 97
Richelieu Navigation Co......	100	All.	7 p.a.	1 Jan., 1 July.	[illegible]	111½ 113	111½ 112
St. Lawrence Tow Boat Co.....	100	"	......	3 Feb.	...	...	35 40
Tor'to Consumers' Gas Co.....	50	"	2 3 m.	1 My Au Mar Fe	106 106½	...	103 104
Trust & Loan Co. of U. C.....	20	5	3	......	....	....	.. .
West'n Canada Bldg Soc'y.....	50	All.	5	......	114 114½	....	....

SECURITIES.	London.	Montreal.	Quebec.	Toronto.
Canadian Gov't Deb. 6 ℘ ct. due 1872	....	100 101	100½ 101	100 101
Do. do. 6 do due Ja. & Jul. 1877-84	104 106	....	....	....
Do. do. 6 do. Feb. & Aug.	103 105	....	.. .	....
Do. do. 6 do. Mch. & Sep.	103 105	.. .	...	...
Do. do. 5 ℘ ct. cur., 1883	91 93	90 91	89½ 90	90 91
Do. do. 5 do. stg., 1885	....	90 91	90 90½	91 91½
Do. do. 7 do. cur., ...	....	....	......	....
Dominion 6 p. c. 1878 cy..........	....	102 103	102½ 103	102½ 103
Hamilton Corporation..........	....	....	......	....
Montreal Harbor, 8 ℘ ct. d. 1869..........	..	....	......	....
Do. do. 7 do. 1870..........	....	....	......	100 101
Do. do. 6½ do. 1875..........	....	100 100½	......	....
Do. do. 6½ do. 1873..........	....	....	......	....
Do. Corporation, 6 ℘ c. 1891	....	92½ 93½	92 93	92 93
Do. 7 p. c. stock..........	....	105 105½	104 105	105 105½
Do. Water Works, 6 ℘ c. stg. 1878..........	....	....	......	92 93
Do. do. 6 do. cy. do.	....	92½ 93½	......	92 93
New Brunswick, 6 ℘ ct., Jan. and July	102 104	....	......	....
Nova Scotia, 6 ℘ ct., 1875..........	100 102	...	......	....
Ottawa City 6 ℘ c. d. 1880	....	92 93	......	...
Quebec Harbour, 6 ℘ c. d. 1883..........	....	....	60	....
Do. do. 7 do. do..........	....	....	70	....
Do. do. 8 do. 1886..........	....	....	85	....
Do. City, 7 ℘ c. d. 5 years	....	80 90	95 96	....
Do. do. 7 do. 9 do.	....	....	88 89	....
Do. do. 7 do. 2½ do.	....	....	97 98	....
Do. Water Works, 7 ℘ ct., 4 years	....	....	96 97	....
Do. do. 6 do. 2 do.	....	....	93½ 94	....
Toronto Corporation	....	90 92½	...	....

Financial.

Pellatt & Osler.

D EXCHANGE BROKERS, Accountants,
the Standard Life Assurance Company and
nality Insurance Company.
16 King Street East, four Doors West of
Church Street, Toronto.

LATT,　　　　　EDMUND B. OSLER,
ary Public.　　　　Official Assignee.

OWN'S BANK,
E. Brown.　W. C. Chewett.)
G STREET EAST, TORONTO,

s a general Banking Business, Buys and
York and Sterling Exchange, Gold, Silver,
nd Uncurrent Money, receives Deposits sub-
s at sight, makes Collections and Discounts
aper.

Mail or Telegraph promptly executed at
d favourable current quotations.
s letters,　　　　"BROWN'S BANK,
　　　　　　　　　Toronto."

ian Land and Emigration Company

for sale on Conditions of Settlement,

D FARM LANDS

the County of Peterboro, Ontario,

ettled Township of Dysart, where there are
rist and Saw Mills, Stores, &c., at

A-HALF DOLLARS AN ACRE.

oining Townships of Guilford, Dudley, Har-
art and Bruton, connected with Dysart and
Haliburton by the Peterson Road, at ONE
Acre.

particulars apply to
　　CHAS. JAS. BLOMFIELD,
　　Secretary C. L. and E. Co., Toronto.
　　　ALEX. NIVEN, P.L.S.,
　　Agent C. L. & E. Co., Haliburton?

Insurance.

HE PRINCE EDWARD COUNTY
Fire Insurance Company.

AD OFFICE,—PICTON, ONTARIO.
B. STINSON; Vice-President, W. A. RICHARDS.

H. A. McFaul, James Cavan, James Johnson,
William Delong.—Treasurer, David Barker
an Twigg; Solicitor, R. J. Fitzgerald.

pany is established upon strictly Mutual prin-
nsuring farming and isolated property, (not
n Townships only, and offers great advantages
at low rates for five years, without the expense
This Company has existed 12 years, during
it has adjusted all losses in a satisfactory
is managed with strict economy, and affords
ty of insuring with safety and reliance, and
xpense, which accounts for its long standing
ssful business which it has been and is now
ne 15, 1868.　　　　　　　　　9-1y

ford Fire Insurance Company.
HARTFORD, CONN.

al and Assets over Two Million Dollars.

$2,026,220.29.

HARTERED 1810.

nd reliable Company, having an established
in Canada of more than thirty years standing,
with the provisions of the new Insurance
le a special deposit of

$100,000

ernment for the security of policy-holders, and
a to grant policies upon the same favorable
stofore.

ow rates on first-class dwellings and farm
a term of one or more years.
aretofore promptly and equitably adjusted.
　　　E. CHAFFEY & Co., AGENTS.
nt.

WOOD, GENERAL AGENT FOR CANADA?

Insurance.

The Standard Life Assurance Company,
Established 1825.
WITH WHICH IS NOW UNITED
THE COLONIAL LIFE ASSURANCE COMPANY.

Head Office for Canada:
MONTREAL—STANDARD COMPANY'S BUILDINGS,
No. 47 GREAT ST. JAMES STREET.
Manager—W. M. RAMSAY.　Inspector—RICH'D BULL.

THIS Company having deposited the sum of ONE HUN-
DRED AND FIFTY THOUSAND DOLLARS with the Receiver-
General, in conformity with the Insurance Act passed last
Session, Assurances will continue to be carried out at
moderate rates and on all the different systems in practice.

AGENT FOR TORONTO—HENRY PELLATT,
　　　KING STREET.
AGENT FOR HAMILTON—JAMES BANCROFT.
6-6mos.

Fire and Marine Assurance.

THE BRITISH AMERICA
ASSURANCE COMPANY.
HEAD OFFICE:
CORNER OF CHURCH AND COURT STREETS,
TORONTO.

Hon. G. W. Allan, M.I.C.,	A. Joseph, Esq.
George J. Boyd, Esq.,	Peter Paterson, Esq.,
Hon. W. Cayley,	G. P. Ridout, Esq.,
Richard S. Cassels, Esq.,	E. H. Rutherford, Esq.,
Thomas C. Street, Esq.	

Governor:
GEORGE PERCIVAL RIDOUT, Esq.
Deputy Governor:
PETER PATERSON, Esq.

Fire Inspector:　　　　Marine Inspector:
E. ROBY O'BRIEN.　　CAPT. R. COURNEEN.

Insurances granted on all descriptions of property
against loss and damage by fire and the perils of inland
navigation.

Agencies established in the principal cities, towns, and
ports of shipment throughout the Province.

　　THOS. WM. BIRCHALL,
23-1y　　　　Managing Director.

Edinburgh Life Assurance Company.

founded 1823.

HEAD OFFICE—22 GEORGE STREET, EDINBURGH.

Capital, ... £500,000 Ster'g.
Accumulated and Invested Funds, £1,000,000 "

HEAD OFFICE IN CANADA:
WELLINGTON STREET, TORONTO.

SUB-AGENTS THROUGHOUT THE PROVINCE.

J. HILLYARD CAMERON,
Chairman, Canadian Board.

DAVID HIGGINS,
Secretary, Canadian Board.　3-3m

Queen Fire and Life Insurance Company,
OF LIVERPOOL AND LONDON,

ACCEPTS ALL ORDINARY FIRE RISKS
on the most favorable terms.

LIFE RISKS
Will be taken on terms that will compare favorably with
other Companies.

CAPITAL, - - - £2,000,000 Stg.

CHIEF OFFICES—Queen's Buildings, Liverpool, and
Gracechurch Street London.
CANADA BRANCH OFFICE—Exchange Buildings, Montreal.
Resident Secretary and General Agent,
　　A. MACKENZIE FORBES,
13 St. Sacrament St., Merchants' Exchange, Montreal.
WM. ROWLAND, Agent, Toronto.　　1-1y

Insurance.

Reliance Mutual Life Assurance
Society.
(Established, 1840,) OF LONDON, E. C.

Accumulated Funds, over $1,000,000.
　　　　　　Annual Income, $300,000.
THE entire Profits of this long-established Society belong
to the Policy-holders.

HEAD OFFICE FOR DOMINION—MONTREAL.
　　T. W. GRIFFITH, Manager & Sec'y.
15-1y　　WM. HENDERSON, Agent for Toronto.

Etna Insurance Company of Dublin.
The number of Shareholders exceeds Five Hundred.

Capital, $5,000,000—Annual Income nearly $1,000,000.
THIS Company takes Fire and Marine Risks on the most
favorable terms.
　　　T. W. GRIFFITH, Manager for Canada.
Chief office for Dominion—Corner St. Francois Xavier
and St. Sacrament Sts., Montreal.
15-1y　　WM. HENDERSON, Agent for Toronto

Scottish Provincial Assurance Co.
Established 1825.

CAPITAL,......................£2,000,000 STERLING.
INVESTED IN CANADA (1864) ....$500,000.
Canada Head Office, Montreal.

LIFE DEPARTMENT.
CANADA BOARD OF DIRECTORS:
HUGH TAYLOR, Esq., Advocate,
　　Hon. CHARLES WILSON, M. L. C.
　　　　WM. SACHE, Esq., Banker,
　　　　　JACKSON RAE, Esq., Banker.
WM. FRASER, Esq. M. D., Medical Adviser.

The special advantages to be derived from Insuring in
this office are:—Strictly Moderate Rates of Premium;
Large Bonus (intermediate bonus guaranteed ;) Liberal
Surrender Value, under policies relinquished by assured ;
and Extensive Limits of Residence and Travel. All business disposed of in Canada, without reference to parent
office.

　A DAVIDSON PARKER,
　　　Resident Secretary
　　G. L. MADDISON,
15-1yr　　AGENT FOR TORONTO.

Lancashire Insurance Company.

CAPITAL, - - - - - - - £2,000,000 Sterling

FIRE RISKS
Taken at reasonable rates of premium, and
ALL LOSSES SETTLED PROMPTLY,
By the undersigned, without reference elsewhere.
　S. C. DUNCAN-CLARK & CO.,
　　　General Agents for Ontario,
25-1y　N. W. Corner of King & Church Streets,
　　　　TORONTO.

Etna Fire & Marine Insurance Company.

INCORPORATED 1819.　CHARTER PERPETUAL.

CASH CAPITAL, - - - - - $3,000,000

LOSSES PAID IN 50 YEARS, 23,500,000 00.

JULY, 1868.
ASSETS.
(At Market Value.)

Cash in hand and in Bank....................	$644,842 39
Real Estate............................	205,267 19
Mortgage Bonds..........................	932,945 00
Bank Stock............................	1,273,670 00
United States, State and City Stock, and other	
Public Securities......................	2,046,855 51
Total..................	$5,052,880 19

LIABILITIES.

Claims not Due, and Unadjusted	$409,808 55
Amount required by Mass. and New York	
for Re-Insurance........................	1,405,267 15
E. CHAFFEY & CO., Agents.	
	50-6m

Insurance.

ÆTNA
Live Stock Insurance Company

LICENSED BY THE DOMINION GOVERNMENT TO
DO BUSINESS IN CANADA.,

THE following Accidents, this month, show the importance of Insuring your Horses and Cattle against Death
from any cause, or Theft, in the Ætna Insurance Company:

MONTREAL, September 16, 1868.
At a fire last night, in the sheds behind Ripin's Hotel,
St. Joseph Street, three valuable Stock Horses were destroyed, "Young Clydesdale" and "Emigrant," belonging
to the Huntingdon Agricultural Society—the former worth
$900, and the latter $1,700; and "Old Beauharnois" cost
$1,000, belonging to the Beauharnois Society.

PORT COLBORNE, September 18, 1868.
HORSES DROWNED.—Two horses belonging to Mr. Briggs,
of Port Colborne, and four owned by Mr. Julien, of Port
Dalhousie, were drowned in the Canal, near the Junction,
early this morning.

A fire at the Glasgow Hotel, Montreal, this morning, destroyed two horses. The fire was caused by drunkenness
on the part of the stable man.

MONTREAL, September 24, 1868.
A fire in F. X. Cusson's stables, St. Joseph Street, last
night, destroyed three horses.

E. L. SNOW, GENERAL AGENT,
Montreal
Agents for Ontario:—
67nov11y   SCOTT & WALMSLEY,
            Ontario Hall, Church Street, Toronto.

The Liverpool and London and Globe
Insurance Company

INVESTED FUNDS:
FIFTEEN MILLIONS OF DOLLARS.

DAILY INCOME OF THE COMPANY:
T WELVE THOUSAND DOLLARS.

LIFE INSURANCE,
WITH AND WITHOUT PROFITS.

FIRE INSURANCE
On every description of Property, at Lowest Remunerative
Rates.
JAMES FRASER, AGENT,
5 *King Street West.*
Toronto, 1868.   38-1y

Briton Medical and General Life
Association,
with which is united the
BRITANNIA LIFE ASSURANCE COMPANY.

Capital and Invested Funds............£750,000 Sterling.

ANNUAL INCOME, £220,000 STG. :
Yearly increasing at the rate of £25,000 Sterling.

THE important and peculiar feature originally introduced by this Company, in applying the periodical
Bonuses, so as to make Policies payable during life, without
any higher rate of premiums being charged, has caused
the success of the BRITON MEDICAL AND GENERAL to be
almost unparalleled in the history of Life Assurance. *Life
Policies on the Profit Scale become payable during the lifetime
of the Assured, thus rendering a Policy of Assurance a
means of subsistence in old age, as well as a protection for a
family,* and a more valuable security to creditors in the
event of early death; and effectually meeting the often
urged objection, that persons do not themselves reap the
benefit of their own prudence and forethought.

No extra charge made to members of Volunteer Corps
for services within the British Provinces.

☞ TORONTO AGENCY, 5 KING ST. WEST.
oct17—9-1yr   JAMES FRASER, Agent.

Phenix Insurance Company,
BROOKLYN, N. Y.

PHILANDER SHAW,   STEPHEN CROWELL,
Secretary.   *President,*

Cash Capital, $1,000,000. Surplus, $600,416.02. Total,
1,666,416.02. Entire income from all sources for 1866 was
$2,131,839.82.
CHARLES G. FORTIER, *Marine Agent.*

Ontario Chambers, Toronto, Ont.   19-1y

Insurance.

The Victoria Mutual
FIRE INSURANCE COMPANY OF CANADA.

Insures only Non-Hazardous Property, at Low Rates.

BUSINESS STRICTLY MUTUAL.

GEORGE H. MILLS, *President.*
W. D. BOOKER, *Secretary.*

HEAD OFFICE ....HAMILTON, ONTARIO

aug 15-1yr

The Ætna Life Insurance Company.

AN attack, abounding with errors, having been made
upon the Ætna Life Insurance Co. by the editor of the
Montreal Daily News : and certain agents of British
Companies being now engaged in handing around copies of
the attack, thus seeking to damage the Company's standing,
—I have pleasure in laying before the public the following
certificate, bearing the signatures of the Presidents and
Cashiers who happened to be in their Offices) *of every Bank
in Hartford;* also that of the President and Secretary of
the old Ætna Fire Insurance Company :—
" To whom it may concern: ..
"We, the undersigned, regard the Ætna Life Insurance Company, of this city, as one of the most successful
and prosperous Insurance Companies in the States,—
entirely reliable, responsible, and honourable in all its
dealings, and most worthy of public confidence and
patronage."

Lucius J. Hendee, President Ætna Fire Insurance Co.,
and late Treasurer of the State of Connecticut.
J. Goodnow, Secretary Ætna Fire Insurance Co.
C. M. Northum, President, and J. B. Powell, Cashier
National Bank.
C. T. Hillyer, President Charter Oak National Bank.
E. D. Tiffany, President First National Bank.
G. T. Davis, President City National Bank.
F. S. Riley, Cashier,   do.   do.   do.
John C. Tracy, President of Farmers' and Mechanics'
National Bank.
M. W. Graves, Cashier Conn. River Banking Co.
H. A. Redfield, Cashier Phœnix National Bank.
O. G. Terry, President Ætna National Bank.
J. R. Redfield, Cashier National Exchange Bank.
John G. Root, Assistant Cashier American National Bank.
George F. Hills, Cashier State Bank of Hartford.
Jas. Potter, Cashier Hartford National Bank.
Hartford, Nov. 26, 1867.

Many of the above-mentioned parties are closely connected with other Life Insurance Companies, but all unhesitatingly commend our Company as "reliable, responsible, honorable in all its dealings, and most worthy of public confidence and patronage.
JOHN GARVIN,
General Agent, Toronto Street.
Toronto, Dec. 3. 1867.   16-1y

Life Association of Scotland.

INVESTED FUNDS
UPWARDS OF £1,000,000 STERLING.

THIS Institution differs from other Life Offices, in that
the
BONUSES FROM PROFITS
Are applied on a special system for the Policy-holder's
*PERSONAL BENEFIT AND ENJOYMENT
DURING HIS OWN LIFETIME,*

WITH THE OPTION OF
LARGE BONUS ADDITIONS TO THE SUM ASSURED.

The Policy-holder thus obtains

A LARGE REDUCTION OF PRESENT OUTLAY
OR
A PROVISION FOR OLD AGE OF A MOST IMPORTANT
AMOUNT IN ONE CASH PAYMENT,
OR A LIFE ANNUITY,

Without any expense or outlay whatever beyond the
ordinary Assurance Premium for the Sum
Assured, which remains in tact for
Policy-holder's heirs, or other
purposes.

*CANADA—MONTREAL—*PLACE D'ARMES.

DIRECTORS:
DAVID TORRANCE, Esq., (D. Torrance & Co.)
GEORGE MOFFATT, (Gillespie, Moffatt & Co.)
ALEXANDER MORRIS, Esq., M.P., Barrister, Perth.
Sir G. E. CARTIER, M.P., Minister of Militia.
PETER REDPATH, Esq., (J. Redpath & Son).
J. H. R. MOLSON, Esq., (J. H. R. Molson & Bros.)
*Solicitors—*Messrs. TORRANCE & MORRIS.
*Medical Officer—*R. PALMER HOWARD, Esq., M.D
*Secretary—*P. WARDLAW.
*Inspector of Agencies—*JAMES B. M. CHIPMAN.   y

Insurance.

North British and Mercantile Insu
Company.

Established 1809.

HEAD OFFICE, - - CANADA - - MO

TORONTO BRANCH :
LOCAL OFFICE, Nos. 4 & 6 WELLINGTON ST
Fire Department, ... R. N. G

Life Department, ... H. L. H
29-1y

Phenix Fire Assurance Comp
LOMBARD ST. AND CHARING CROS
LONDON, ENG.

Insurances effected in all parts of the

Claims paid
WITH PROMTITUDE and *LIBERAL*
MOFFATT, MURRAY & BEATT
Agents for To
36 Yonge

The Commercial Union Assura
Company,
19 & 20 CORNHILL, LONDON, ENGLAND.

Capital, £2,500,000 Stg.—Invested over $2,00

FIRE DEPARTMENT.—Insurance granted o
scriptions of property at reasonable rates.

LIFE DEPARTMENT.—The success of thi
has been unprecedented—NINETY PERCENT.
niums now in hand. First year's premiums w
$140,000. Economy of management guaranteed
curity. Moderate rates.

OFFICE—385 & 387 ST PAUL STREET, MON
MORLAND, WATSON &
General Agents for

FRED. COLE, *Secretary.*
*Inspector of Agencies—*T. C. LIVINGSTO
W. M. WESTMACOTT, *Agent at '*
16-1y

Phœnix Mutual Life Insurance
HARTFORD, CONN.

Accumulated Fund, $2,000,000, Income, $1,0

THIS Company, established in 1851, is one o
reliable Companies doing business in the co
has been steadily prospering. The *Massachusetts
Reports* show that in nearly all important ma
superior to the general average of Companies.

It is purely Mutual It allows the Insure
and reside in any portion of the United States a
It throws out almost all restriction on occupatio
Policies. It will, if desired, take a note for p
Premium, thus combining all the advantages of
all cash company. Its Dividends are declare
and applied in reduction of Premium. Its Di
in every case on Premiums paid. The Divide
PHŒNIX have averaged fifty per cent. yearl
settlement of Policies, a Dividend will be allow
year the policy has been in force. The num
dends will always equal the outstanding Notes.
losses promptly—during its existence never h
tested a claim. It issues Policies for the bene
ried Women beyond the reach of their husband
Creditors may also insure the lives of their Debtors
are all *Non-forfeiting,* as it always allows the
surrender his Policy, should he desire, the Co
ing a paid-up Policy therefor. This importi
will commend itself to all. The inducements
by the PHŒNIX are better and more liberal th
any other Company. Its rate of Mortality is
low and under the average.

Parties contemplating *Life Insurance* will fin
interest to call and examine our system. Pol
payable either in *Gold* or American currency.
ANGUS R. BETH
General Mana
Dominio.

Office: 104 ST. FRANÇOIS XAVIER ST. MON

☞ Active and energetic Agents and
wanted in every town and village, to whom lib
ments will be given.

PRINTED AT THE DAILY TELEGRAPH
HOUSE, BAY ST., COR. KING.

THE CANADIAN
MONETARY TIMES
AND
INSURANCE CHRONICLE.
VOTED TO FINANCE, COMMERCE, INSURANCE, BANKS, RAILWAYS, NAVIGATION, MINES, INVESTMENT, PUBLIC COMPANIES, AND JOINT STOCK ENTERPRISE.

II—NO. 12.   TORONTO, THURSDAY, NOVEMBER 5, 1868.   { SUBSCRIPTION. $2 YEAR.

Mercantile.

Mining.

MADOC GOLD DISTRICT.

(From our own Correspondent.)

Belleville, Nov. 2, 1868.

The high hopes respecting the richness of this region in the precious metals, which were so prevalent eighteen months ago, have been slowly giving way before the repeated disappointments which have attended the efforts of Companies and individuals to realize the expectations excited by the undoubted richness of some of the deposits, and the reported value of others. Instead of the general haste to become rich, by monopolizing every lot where gold was said to have been found, the holders of mining property, so called, are for the most part only desirous of finding a chance to *hedge*, or in other words, to get rid of their lands, stock, etc., with the least possible loss ; while the question of the day has resolved itself into this, "Does gold exist in Hastings in paying quantities?"

To this momentous query, the reply of the great majority of those who have been stung by the golden *Ignis* would be, if they spoke their real sentiments, a decided "NO!" And yet there is no doubt that gold does exist in appreciable quantities in many of the rocks of the district,—that it is not confined to a few localities, or to any particular stratum, but that it is diffused over a large extent of country, and is to be found in several varieties of rock, of very different chemical composition and mechanical structure. In short, it is at once enticingly common, and provokingly scarce. Upon the right solution of this question, however, depends the future prosperity of the district, and the wellbeing of a large number of its population; and it is therefore worthy of serious consideration and demands a close examination to discover, if possible, the real causes of the general want of success which has thrown such a gloom over ourmining prospects.

The first appears to be the rash confidence with which men, totally ignorant of the requisites for success in mining operations, invested their means in the purchase of land and the construction of machinery, on the mere report of interested parties and of *soi disant* assayers, who were either ignorant of the business, or so dishonest as to give false certificates for the purpose of attracting customers and increasing their receipts. Next, the utter inadequacy of the machinery employed to deal with the peculiar conditions under which the gold of these formations is associated with other metals and minerals. Third, the difficulty of obtaining persons qualified to work such machinery as was in use to the best advantage. Fourth, the want of that determined energy which perseveres to the end, and submits to no discouragement so long as a chance of success remains, but when one method fails, sets about to try another. Lastly, in many instances, the want of sufficient capital to carry out the expensive alterations which would be necessary to pursue their object to a satisfactory conclusion.

Having thus presented the dark side of the picture, let us inquire what inducements there are to persevere in the attempt to realize the advantages promised by the presence of the precious metals. First, only one method of reduction has been tried, namely, mercurial amalgamation, which, as is well known, can only be successfully applied to ores in which the metal exists, not only in a free or native, but also in a clean state. Now, most of the gold of this region is found in combination with other matters which impede, and in some cases totally prevent the action of the quicksilver. In many cases which have come under my own observation, particles of gold, distinctly visible to the naked eye, some of them over a grain, or even several grains in weight, have been submitted to the action of mercury for an hour or more, without any amalgamation being effected, even after being boiled with salt, soda, etc., though after being submitted to the roasting action of the blow-pipe, the mercury seized upon the same particles with avidity. I have also frequently observed several particles of gold in the tailings of an amalgamation assay, partially coated with quicksilver; from which it appears that the action of mercury is at best only partial and uncertain, and that we must expect considerable loss from its employment as the agent for the collection of gold.

Second, no attempt has yet been made to get rid of any part of the dead matter, (lime, magnesia, silex, alumina, and other comparatively worthless minerals), previous to submitting the ore to the action of the mercury; yet the metallurgists of Europe have found that the net returns of their mines have been largely increased by well managed concentration with improved apparatus, and that by this means they have been enabled to reduce profitably many ores which were formerly considered too poor to pay working expenses, and even to work over again the refuse of former operations. There is, however, an objection to these modes of concentration, viz., that they operate through the medium of water, which causes a loss of a certain portion of the valuable matter of the ore, varying according to the friability and gravity of the substance; though, in the case of gold, I believe the loss to be over stated. This difficulty seems likely to be overcome, as I read lately an account of a machine exhibited in Montreal, which separates the various substances contained in an ore by the application of centrifugal force, and the resistance of the atmosphere, according to their several specific gravities. After their separation, the valuable portions can either be melted with proper fluxes, or roasted and submitted to the action of mercury or chlorine.

The last mentioned agent has not been hitherto introduced in this district, though it is being used with great success in the Pacific States for the reduction of gold-bearing sulphurets, and I am strongly of opinion that it may be profitably employed in the treatment of the similar substances which abound in the Hastings mines, and which has so far proved the chief difficulty in our reduction works.

Two other processes are about to be tried here. One is the Stevens flux, in which very few of our mining men appear to have any confidence. The works of Messrs. Jones & Robbins, in Hungerford township, have been ready for two weeks past, and their operations have only been delayed by the absence of the flux, which was shipped from Boston on the 10th ult, but has been unaccountably delayed in its transit.

The other is the thermo-electric process of Dr. Rae, of Syracuse, the apparatus for which he is now engaged in fitting up in the mill of the Merchants Union Company, in the village of Maeloe, and which will shortly be in operation.

A telegram to the *Intelligencer*, of Friday last, announced the cleaning up of a crushing of 70 tons of rock from the Feigel mine, township of Marmora, the result of which is stated to be $1,330 in gold, or at the rate of $19 per ton.

NOVA SCOTIA GOLD MINING REVIEW.

The continued wetness of the season has seriously affected both surface and underground operations. Work has wholly ceased on several shafts until machinery can be procured for draining them, and there has been a consequent falling off in the produce of some of the best mines.

The following quantities of bar gold have been reported in Halifax between the 10th and 22nd October:—

Co.	District.	Oz.	Dwt.	grs.
Shaffer	Oldham	74	17	0
Queen	Uniacke	58	0	0
North St. Lawrence	"	28	0	0
Wellington	Sherbrooke	83	15	0
Palmerston	"	115	1	18
Hayden & Derby	"	25	11	1
El Dorado	Wine Harbor	23	3	6
Ophir	Renfrew	163	2	0
Uniacke	Uniacke	96	12	11
Waverley	Waverley	16	3	13
Boston & Nova Scotia	"	17	6	12
Not stated		3	12	0
		11	6	10
		716	11	3

The Mines Department Returns for the last quarter of 1867 and the first six months of 1868 have just been issued. The yield for 1867 shows an increase of 2090 oz. 5 dwts. 20 grs. over that of 1866; and the yield for the first quarter of 1868 is 67 oz. 5 dwts. 4 grs. in excess of the same period in 1867; but the same quarter, from the causes above referred to, shows a falling off, compared with that of the previous year, of 2548 oz. 18 dwts. 7 grs. It is gratifying to see Lawrencetown again resume the rank of a producing district, although at present it is but in a small way, the returns for the half-year being only 192 oz. 13 dwts. 17 grs.

SHERBROOKE.—Mr. Carnie, of Boston, has started the works of the Stanley Co. A rich boulder or great width has been found on the property of the New York & Sherbrooke Co., and they are now searching for the lode, which the depth of soil and extremely wet weather render a somewhat arduous task. The Palmerston, Wellington, and Hayden and Derby Companies have sent up substantial results, described in the bullion report; and the Canadian Companies are making good and hopeful progress.

WINE HARBOR.—Under date the 8th inst., "A Miner" writes:—"Times are first-rate here at present, any amount of men of all sizes, grades, and professions to work, the picture of content stamped upon every lineament of their features; quite the contrary to what it has been here for the last two or three autumns, when every person appeared to be anxious to know which pit was likely to work longest, or all winter, so that they could secure a winter's job. This autumn, however, there are no doubts or uncertainties. The Orient Co. are pushing on their work with a strong battalion, fully armed and equipped with all the necessities for a long winter's campaign. The manager has just let a contract to David Murray & Co., which, when completed, will come to nearly four thousand dollars. It is calculated said contract will turn out 400 tons of quartz or thereabouts. There are also two other contracts going on on two other leads. The Eureka Co. have let a contract which, when completed, will, it is calculated, turn out 240 tons or thereabouts. The Provincial Co. are pressing forward towards

the prize which even former unbelievers now allow they will yet receive. The El Dorado Co. is all right. They have just cleared up 58 tons, which they had crushed at the Victoria mill (out of the new lode they have been sinking on, which is fourteen feet wide,) and which yielded 21 oz. retorted gold. When it is taken into consideration that where they are sinking is on their extreme western line, and that said belt runs through the whole breadth of their property, I think every one else might come to the decided conclusion that they are all right. The McIntosh Co. are to work on the same belt, about 400 feet to the westward of the El Dorado shaft, taking out quartz at almost a tremendous rate, and showing some beautiful specimens of gold. They have just commenced to crush out of said lode, and the manager purposes to run two batteries on it for the remainder of this month, after which it will speak for itself. The Stalsacoua Co. are, to use a common expression, 'going in big licks,' and turning out a great pile of crushing material. They have not cleaned up any yet, consequently I cannot give a correct or decided account of what has been taken out, or the yield thereof. It will, however, speak for itself shortly."

The Provincial Co. have had a portable stamp mill of one battery, for prospecting purposes, built by Messrs. Symonds & Co., of this city. It is a most complete arrangement, and attracted much notice at the late Exhibition.

UNIACKE.—The Queen Co., besides taking a prize at the Exhibition, have sent up nearly 60 ounces within the fortnight, and are now passing through their mill ore of very excellent quality. The North St. Lawrence Co. have contributed a small bar, and the Uniacke Co. have remitted 96 oz. 12 dwts. 11 grs.

OLDHAM.—Messrs Cook & Belding are working with good prospects; and Mr. Shaffer has worked with good results, 74 oz. 17 dwts. being his medium for the past fortnight.

RENFREW.—The Ophir tells its progress by a brick of 163 oz. 2 dwts.; the Andrews shaft continues to give satisfaction; the Colonial Co. report some promising lodes; the Carnarvon Co., when not impeded by weather, have made good headway in prospecting; and Messrs. Thomas and Macdonald are working a lode that shows both coarse and fine gold.

ECUM SECUM.—The machinery for the mill of the Atlantic Co. has all arrived, and Mr. Andrews continues to report favorably.—*Halifax Mining Gazette.*

THE SALT WELLS OF GODERICH.

The discovery of Salt was quite unlooked for, the result following the search for oil. A well having been sunk there with the expectation of getting petroleum, turned out a blank. It was then suggested that, by going deeper, salt might possibly be reached, especially as the water obtained at a depth of 500 feet was rather salty in flavour. The drilling was resumed, and at the depth of between one thousand and eleven hundred feet heavy brine was reached, which it was thought would yield salt in paying quantities. Before going further a chemical analysis of the brine was obtained, to discover if the properties contained would render the salt valuable for pickling purposes, and also to see if a sufficient per centage of solid salt could be obtained from a given quantity of brine to render the industry profitable. The samples were referred to competent chemists, and their reports being highly satisfactory, it was determined by the Goderich Salt and Petroleum Company—the enterprising pioneers of the salt interest—to erect the necessary works for the manufacture of salt. These works have for about a year been in active operation, and so far have proved a financial success, and notwithstanding the competition offered by the Americans, who seek to swamp the infant enterprise, the works are run to a profit. Other companies, following the example of this

company, have gone to work and sunk wells, there is no question that Goderich is now in a position to supply all the salt required by Onta The wells finished and partly in operation num eight, as follows:—

	Cap
Goderich Salt and Petroleum Co.	$15,
Tecumseh	5,
Dominion	20,
Huron (in operation)	10
Victoria (do)	10
Maitland	10
Prince Well (now boring)	10
Ontario	15

Of the above, the first named is the lar operating with 104 kettles; the Tecumseh is ing till spring; the Ontario commenced in making 60 kettles; Dominion 60 kettles; Huron 120 kettles, in full operation; Victori kettles; Maitland, drilled to salt, operation the present suspended, with a view to experi on some cheaper method of evaporation; P well down 600 or 700 feet. We will now att to describe the process of salt making. The machinery is precisely the same as that by oil wells. The "well" is a round hole of four to five inches in diameter, drilled perf straight down over a thousand feet into earth, and lined or cased with iron casing to vent the surrounding earth from "caving in filling it up. Down this well is fixed the tubing, about three inches in diameter, w descends to about 600 feet. At the end of b of the tubing is fixed the pump, and insi pump tubing are wooden rods connected b couplings, which work the pump valves and the brine up the tubing to the surface. In Goderich Company" they use a 20 horse engine, which, by the aid of connecting machi works the pump. The brine, which is pum at the rate of 560 barrels in 24 hours, flow large vat, where it is held till wanted, an nected with the vat are pipes leading to the kettles. In the "Goderich Company's" there are four rows of these kettles, to the n of 104, each holding 140 gallons of brine. occupy a space of 120 feet long and 24 wid are, of course, built in brick-work, and heath are the furnaces to heat the brine and off the vapour. One long furnace runs each row of kettles, so that four furnaces a ployed, each using about four cords of wo day. When the furnaces are in full blas kettles are "drawn" or emptied every four and then the yield is generally a bushel half of salt to each charge. The kettles cleaning once a day, the process being th ping off the calcined salt which adheres sides, and is only valuable for manure, and to the farmers at $2 a ton. The quality salt depends much upon the cooking of th as the faster it boils the finer becomes th Another item of absorbing the water is by ation by solar heat; but this process requ ventive works, produces a coarse salt, and yet been introduced into Canada. The cordwood at the wells is about $2 to $2. some of the works are about to try coal as economical fuel, as it can be be laid down erich for $4.50 per ton. The number of r ployed at the "Goderich Company's" wo prise fourteen, including engineer and The workmen state that the action of has a singular effect upon their clothes, rotting all cotton garments, rendering it for them to wear woollen clothes, which affected by the brine.

Taking the experience of the "Goderi pany," the manufacture of salt costs abo barrel, including the package, which is station or wharf is 44c. per barrel, and to Goderich $24 per car load, and to Lon The amount turned out by the company about from 90 to 100 barrels per day, 28 salt comprising a barrel. For purity and ɡn substances, the Goderich salt is unfor dairy and pork packing it is proɔꞏbe all that is needed, its preserving ranking high in the estimation of those used it. As an illustration of this fact, stated that a shipment of from 400 to ls has already been made, to Chicago, s, duty. of 70c. in gold per barrel is n its importation to the United States. derich salt makers argue that, as the ıt has placed a duty of 6 cents per galimportation of American crude oil, and er gallon against American refined oilding the theory of protection—it is but the growing salt interests should also elping hand. Nor could objection be he Provinces of Quebec, New Brunsʋva-Scotia to such a course, for American ot reach those places, the cheap rate at ʋerpool. salt is offered excluding the article: No Goderich salt, could, with ent farther east than Kingston. ıe from which the salt is made is of a gravity, averaging from 90° to 100° in s tested by the salometer. It is free ın and any bitter flavor, and possesses ꞅ degree the peculiar properties which ıeat from decay. Some salts, it may sually known, are destitute of this, and used in the dairy or for pork-packing. briue reaches the density of 200°, by ter, (the fluid being heated to 60° Fah. fair test) the water can absorb no more ʜıghest standard of absorption having ed ; if more salt is added to brine which ae strength of 100° it will not be taken ls to the bottom of the vessel. With ıation the reader can readily understand ı salt the Goderich brine is. We have sample from the "Dominion Salt ʜıch is remarkable for its snowy purity, ꞅıce of flavor; indeed, all the Goderich ı the same qualifications. In order to new enterprises the public can do much ; terest of dealers still prompts them to urtheat Oswego salt because a few cents ʌdditional profits to be made on its sale. ʜıe wish to help the salt works of Onꞅery one who is a consumer ASK FOR SALT, and accept no other. Directly and and persistent demand springs up Ꞌdict, storekeepers will provide themsꞋ it, and the American article, imported ʌl cost of $130,000, will be excluded, ꞌney annually paid out for its purchase ıt at home, and give employment to the of willing workers. We hope that the ıtizens of Ontario will sustain "home ꞇes," without which we should be a poor ꞇountry indeed!—*Free Press.*

PRODUCT OF NOVA SCOTIA.

		Ozs.	Dwts.	Grs.
0 to 31 Dec. 1861 (est'd)	6000	0	0
1 Dec. 1862 { officially reported	7275	0	0
1 Dec. 1863		14001	14	17
1 Dec. 1864 "	20022	18	13
1 Dec. 1865 "	25454	4	8
1 Dec. 1866 "	25204	13	2
1 Dec. 1867 "	27294	11	11
June, 1869 "	10411	9	12
		135664	11	15
ꞅold stolen and not re- ꞇ, at least		135	8	9
		135800	0	0

ꞇesents, a gross value of $2,716,000 ıs currency.—*Mining Gazette.*

AR FROM THE SIERRA NEVADA.—We ꞇ *Enterprise*) were yesterday shown a from the mine of the Sierra Nevada Company. The bar contained $2·118 47 in gold, and $101 65 in silver—total, $4,221 12. It is the ꞅroduct of 280 tons of ore, worked by the ꞅrocess common in California for gold quartz—that is, no amalgamating pans are used. The lot of 280 tons was run through the batteries in seven days, being at the rate of 40 tons per day. The whole cost of working does not exceed $2 per ton, whereas the yield per ton is nearly $8, leaving a clear profit of $240 per day for the mill.

EXTENSIVE MINING.—The Report of the Yellow Jacket Company of Nevada, shows that their total receipts for the fiscal year ending June 30, including a balance of $116,087 on hand at the commencement, were $1,240,585. Three assessments were collected during the year, amounting to $390,000. The amount of bullion produced was $670,861 from 24,719 tons of ore, showing an average yield of 19 50. The disbursements for the year amounted to $1,191,326, leaving a balance to the credit of the Company over all liabilities of $49,249. Only one dividend of $50,000 was disbursed. The amount expended for labor at the mine was $294,833, and for reduction of ore $517,643, of which $254,228 was paid to outside mills. The liabilities of the Company were stated at $66,823, and the assets at $116,071, showing, as already remarked, a surplus of 49,249. Included in the assets are $104,724 cash in the Bank of California.

Railway News.

GREAT WESTERN RAILWAY.

The Directors report that the receipts on capital account during the half-year amounted to £321 4s. 2d., and the total receipts to the 31st July, 1868, to £6,260,529 4s. 9d. The aggregate expenditure to the same date amounted to £5,382,594 3s. 10d., leaving a balance to the debit of capital acco·nt of £121,764 19s· 1d. The outlay on capital a·count during the half-year has been 20,788 11s. 11d. This expenditure includes a proportion of the cost of rebuilding in stone the bridge over twenty-mile creek at Jordan: sundry additions to stations; cost of raising the level of track at Prarie Siding, (a station between Chatham and Baptiste creek), as a protection : gainst floods; payment on account of building a new warehouse at Detroit for the better concentration of the freight business; proportion of the cost of rebuilding in brickwork the passenger station at Paris, originally of wood, cost of five new locomotive engines; and ten new composite cars for the accommodation of emigrant traffic and mixed trains on the b·ranch lines. The receipts and expenditure on revenue account were as follows:—

	£
Gross receipts	356,649
Working expenses, including renewals	208,462
	£148,187

From which there has to be deducted:—

	£
Interest on bonds, loan, &c.	£52,270
Loss on conversion of American funds	54,749
Loss on working Erie & Niagara rai·way	520
Do. Galt and Guelph railway	476
Detroit fire claims, final charge	4,110
Amount set aside for renewal of feriy steamers	2,000
	114,134
Net profit on half-year's operations	34,054
Add surplus from last half-year	2,725
Available for Dividend	£6,776

From this amount the Directors recommend a dividend at the rate of two per cent. per annum, free of income tax, which will absorb £35,649 11s. 6d., and leave a surplus of £1,129 2s. to be carried to the credit of next half-year. The renewal fund for the ferry steamers now amounts with interest to £7,125. The loss on conversion of American funds for the half-year amounts to £54,748 12s. 5d., as compared with £52,820 10s. for the corresponding half-year of 1867. The average rate of conversions made during the half-year was 139⅗, the average price of gold for the same period having been 140⅖. The unconverted American funds in hand at 31st July, 1868, amounted to $153,146,24. The following table exhibits the receipts and expenses for six corresponding half-years:—

	RECEIPTS.				
Half-year ending	Passengers, mails, and sundries.	Freight and live stock.	Rents.	Total.
	£	£	£	£
July, 1863	111,671	146,772	625	259,067
July, 1864	125,382	119,381	577	214,940
July, 1865	139,821	144,028	716	284,565
July, 1866	178,781	165,577	864	345,162
July, 1867	163,367	198,221	1,116	320,704
July, 1868	155,082	200,619	543	356,649

	EXPENSES.		
	Including renewals.	Per cent. of gross receipts.
	£	
July, 1863	171,262	50·44
July, 1864	171,452	58·44
July, 1865	158,334	55·81
July, 1866	175,747	51·21
July, 1867	182,768	49·93
July, 1868	208,462	58·45

The total traffic receipts show a decrease of £3,887 2s. 6d. as compared with the corresponding period of 1867.

This decrease arises as follows:—

Decrease in local passenger traffic	£3,785
" foreign ditto	5,297
" local freight traffic	7,424
" mails and sundries	3,708
	£20,214
Increase in foreign freight traffic £8,822	
" emigrant ditto 2,505	
	11,327
Total decrease	£8,887

The decrease in the receipts is owing to the diminished rates adopted by the parallel routes for through passengers and freight, and to the total interruption of the traffic on three separate occasions during several days, by snow storms and floods, over our own and connecting lines, at the commencement of the half-year. The low rates and fares which competition has forced upon the Company for through traffic have had a material effect upon the per centage of working expenses; this, including, renewals, has amounted to 58.45 per cent. as compared with 49·98 for the corresponding half-year. If the tariff of through rates and fares in force at the corresponding period had been maintained during the past half-year the receipts for this traffic would have been augmented by upwards of $100,000, without incurring any increase in the working expenses. The increase in the amount of working expenses is £25,593 4s 9d compared with the corresponding period. This increase has been a matter of serious concern to the Directors, and has engaged the attention of a deputation of the Board which visited Canada during the summer upon the business of the Company. It is chiefly attributed to the extraordinary severity of last winter, and the damage to the rolling-stock and roadway by the intense frost, which exceeded all previous experience. The reports of the engineer and the mechanical superintendent hereto annexed, refer to this expenditure, and also to the increased cost of fuel. The General Manager also specially reports, that making proper allowance for diminished earnings, increased mileage, and extra cost involved by the causes above referred to, he has reason to believe that the ordinary working expenses of the half-year would n t have exceeded those of the corresponding period. It will be seen in the Mechanical Superintendent's report that two new and powerful freight lo.co-motives have, during the half-year, been constructed at the cost of revenue and set to work, to replace the same number of an inferior class of passenger engines, and that satisfactory progress has been made in the renewal of others of the same secondary description, by the substitution of new ones of a greatly improved construction ; and the Board have every reason to be satisfied with the general efficient condition of the plant and rolling stock. Future prospects from the improved condition of the Dominion are encouraging, and from the recent abundant harvest an increased traffic for the current half-year may reasonably be looked for. It is satisfactory to learn from later advices, that the increased rates the deputation advocated when in Canada, have to some extent been carried into effect. The gross earnings of the Detroit and Milwaukee railroad for the half year ending June 30th, 1868, were £153,204 14s. 5d., and the working expenses, including taxes and insurance, amounted to £98,150 2s., leaving a net revenue of £55,054 12s. 5d. It is satisfactory to be able to state that in consequence of arrangements made by the deputation of the Board to relieve the finances of the Detroit and Milwaukee Company if its increasing prosperity does not meet with any unforseen reverses, there is every reason to expect the Company will be able. at an early period, to commence liquidating the claims for interest so long overdue to this Company. Mr. Thomas C. Street, M.P., having resigned his seat at the Canadian Board, the Honorable John Carling, M.P., has been nominated to fill up the vacancy.

Signed on behalf of the Board of Directors,
THOMAS DAKIN, President.

London, October 5, 1868.

The following is the New Board of Directors :—President, Alderman Dakin, London ; Thomas Faulconer, London ; John Fikes, M. P., Manchester ; Francis Head, London ; Alex. Hoyes, Southampton ; Charles Hunt, London, Canada ; Donald MacInnes, Hamilton, Canada ; Hon. Wm. McMaster, Senator, Toronto, Canada ; Paul Margetson, George Smith, London ; Hon. John Carling, M.P., London, Canada.

BUFFALO AND LAKE HURON RAILWAY.

The report of the Directors states that it would be seen from the Grand Trunk report that the gross revenue for the half-year, ending the 30th June last, was £646,797 ; the ordinary working expenses, £426,477 ; the renewals of permanent way, £36,030 ; and the loss by fires, £4,110—leaving a net available balance of £180,190. From this was deducted £31,383 transferred from suspense account, £10,807 for Montreal and Champlain proportion, £18,882 loss on American currency—leaving a balance of £119,118 divisible between the two companies, in the proportion of 84½ per cent. to the Grand Trunk Company, and 15½ per cent. to the Buffalo and Lake Huron Company ; thus making the latter Company's share £18,456, and not £22,045 as published in the Grand Trunk report. In partial explanation of this discrepancy the directors referred to their previous report, in which the proprietors would see that the amount due to the Buffalo Company for the half-year ending the 31st of December, 1867, was £18,429, although the Trunk Company only made the amount £12,284. This was done by dealing with the £31,284, then carried to the debit of suspense account. The amount really due for the half-year ending December, 1867, was £18,429, and for June, 1868, £18,456, making the figures at £34,329. Of this amount the Directors of the Buffalo Company regretted that they had not received any portion. On comparing the Trunk revenue with the corresponding period last year it had increased by £37,876, the ordinary working expenses had decreased £3,915, and the sum expended on renewals of permanent way was £18,953, less £6,164 charged to the Sarnia and Toronto fires—£66,103, deducting from the suspense account the £31,383, leaving the actual gain on the previous half-year £34,725. In the Trunk report was the following paragraph :—"Every effort that the directors had made to bring

about an amicable settlement of the differences of account with the Buffalo Company had hitherto failed. The Buffalo Board would neither agree upon nor allow an impartial officer of the Board of Trade to settle a deed of arbitration. Recent further negotiations through Messrs. Creak and Ritter had ended in nothing, as while the President of the Company signed a memorandum of settlement of all matters, as Mr. Creak suggested, the representatives of the Buffalo Company had refused to do the same." On this statement the Board would only remark that the chairman did certainly refuse to sign a document put before him by Mr. Creak, having the signature of Sir E. Watkins, because it was drawn up in a loose and inexact manner, leaving blank spaces for amounts to be afterwards settled, and still proposing to refer most points to arbitration. There was also introduced a fresh claim which until that moment had never been heard of. This also was to go to the arbitrators. To evince, however, the desire for peace, Mr. Heseltine, with refusing to sign Sir E. Watkin's paper, put into Mr. Creak's possession a carefully drawn up memorandum based upon the verbal recommendations of Messrs. Creak and Ritter, which paper left nothing open, no point unsettled, but disposed of all subjects in dispute without arbitration. The directors had heard nothing more of this paper. It stated that Sir E. Watkin had lost no opportunity of impressing upon his shareholders the small value to them of the Buffalo line, urging an alteration of the lease. The Board uniformly replied that they would be surprised, indeed, if the line did pay, seeing the manner in which the traffic was conducted. Loud complaints were made all along the line of the want of accommodation. The directors were ready, however, as soon as the Grand Trunk Company would fairly carry out the present agreement, and pay, or make arrangements for paying, the balance due to this company, to discuss terms for an alteration in the lease. They did not intend, however, to be coerced into any fresh agreement by Sir E. Watkin withholding the balance due. Although prepared to discuss terms for an alteration of the lease, the Board would prefer to entertain the question of cancelling it entirely. The directors had no hesitation in saying the value of the property was worth all and more than the Grand Trunk Company had given for it, and if the line were in other hands, and the power over its contributories of local traffic and "through" United States traffic were cut off from the Grand Trunk system, their loss would be much more than this company's present share of joint revenue. In conclusion, the directors regretted their inability to make any payment to the bondholders. The Board hoped that before long they might have to deal with some other gentleman rather than Sir E. Watkin in the settlement of these disputes.

ORANGEVILLE TRAMWAY CO.

The Orangeville Sun says the Tramway Directors have decided to leave their claims against the Corporation of Orangeville in abeyance and unite in an effort to secure the early construction of the Toronto, Grey and Bruce Railway. If the latter road is built to Orangeville within two years, the tramway claims will be altogether abandoned ; the shareholders receiving a bond of indemnity for their paid-up stock. The agreement will be submitted for ratification to a special meeting of the tramway shareholders to be held on Thursday next. There is no doubt but the agreement will be ratified, and the only obstacle to the Orangeville grant of $15,000 to the Toronto, Grey and Bruce Railway thereby removed.

It is announced that the Government of Ontario has appointed Hon. George W. Allan to be a trustee of the subsidies voted by the municipalities in aid of the Toronto and Nipissing Railway, and that A. W. Lauder, Esq., M.P.P. for South Grey, has been appointed trustee of the subsidies voted in aid of the Toronto Grey and Bruce Railway.

NORTHERN RAILWAY.—Traffic Receipt ending Oct. 24, 1868.

Passengers	$3,07·
Freight	8,24
Mails and Sundries	22·
Total Receipts for week	$11,54
Corresponding week 1867	14,94
Decrease	$3,39
Total traffic from 1 Jan. '68	$188,91
Corresponding period '67	211,97
Decrease	$23,06

GREAT WESTERN RAILWAY.—Traffic ending Oct. 16, 1868.

Passengers	$35,47
Freight and live stock	52,79
Mails and sundries	2,57
	$90,17
Corresponding Week of '67·	89,67
Increase	$45

NEW ROUTES.—A convention was recently held at Norfolk Va. to take such steps as would secure a portion of the trade of the West to that city. It is proposed to build a line of railway from to connect that city with the fertile valleys of the Ohio and Mississippi. The distance from Norfolk to Louisville is 351 miles less than from that city to New York ; to Cincinnatti 237 miles and to Cairo 400 miles less. In connection with this scheme it is proposed to establish a line of steamers between Norfolk and Liverpool.

CUTTING IN RAILWAY FREIGHTS.—A rate war is now in progress between the three trunk lines from New York to the West. The immense amount of wealth and capital represented by each, the contest is likely to be a hot one. The war which has been carried on for some time between the New York Central and Erie has at last extended to the Pennsylvania Central, and now all three lines are contending for the patronage of the public by cutting rates. It is stated that the Erie takes freights of freight to and from Chicago and New York at nail the entire distance, for 40c per 100 lbs, or $8 per ton, whereas the previous rate for freight was $1.88, for second class $1.60, class $1.27, and for fourth class $4.08, a reduction in freights on the New York Central great, and the Pennsylvania Central has in like manner compelled to cut down freights.—Chicago Journal of Commerce.

—The ramie plant, whose fibre is a sort of cross between cotton and linen, is harvested in the Southern States. A satisfaction to the planters, and it may down as an important substitute for one that will take gradual preference... cotton planters.

BALANCE SHEET

ntees of the Bank of Upper Canada,
1st November, 1868.

LIABILITIES.

circulation	$126,610 00
lors on old accounts......	116,008 01
ors on Trustees' Certificates	256,171 37
Co...... $266,811 42	
...ands of Glyn	
...ers, and remit-	
...em for lands	
.... 94,448 56	
	172,362 84
...ment	1,133,430 75
	$1,896,582 97
...ts....................	
...of Profit and Loss Account	635,019 72
	$2,441,602 69

ASSETS.

...ances with Banks	$14,962 12
Securities, new	
.... $09,903 43	
...ouse of comple-	
.... 28,760 47	
account	98,663 92
	54,707 43
...d, but deeds not completed	1,186,950 70
...s., Debentures, &c	38,000 00
...ate, &c....................	12,811 67
	1,035,506 45
....	$2,441,602 69
	$2,441,602 69

—The above does not include interest ac-
... not been added either to the assets or
...bove assets are held in the Balance Sheet,
...tions at which they were handed over by
...yr Canada to the Trustees.
...ETON, (Signed) P. PATERSON,
Secretary. Chairman.

...on Debentures for Sale

...0 DOLLARS,

IN SUMS OF

...'s and 1,000 dollars each,

ISSUED ON ACCOUNT OF

...nts on Church and Sherbourne Streets.
...y to the undersigned,
A. T. McCORD,
. Chamberlain.
Office,
...ov. 2, 1868. 12tf

...n Assurance Society.

...1......................A. D. 1849.

...ed ....A. D. 1854.

.... £1,000,000 ....: Sterling.
Income, over £330,000 Sterling.

NAVAL AND MILITARY LIFE DE-
...is under the Special Patronage of
...Her Most Gracious Majesty
THE QUEEN.

...AN is one of the largest LIFE ASSU-
...s, (independent of its Guarantee Branch),
... It has paid over Two Millions Sterling,
...Bonuses, to representatives of Policy

...ve appointed the undersigned to be their
...minion of Canada.
...equested to pay their Renewal Life Pre-
...io, either to him direct, or through any of
...ts of the Society in the country.
EDWARD RAWLINGS.
...nt European Assurance Society, Montreal.

...to,
W. T. MASON,
ONTARIO HALL.

☞ THE CANADIAN MONETARY TIMES AND
INSURANCE CHRONICLE *is printed every Thursday
Evening, in time for the English Mail.*

Subscription Price, one year, $2, *or* $3 *in
American currency ; Single copies, five cents each.
Casual advertisements will be charged ten cents
per line of solid nonpareil each insertion. All
letters to be addressed,* "THE CANADIAN MONE-
TARY TIMES, TORONTO, ONT." *Registered letters
so addressed are at the risk of the Publishers.
Cheques should be made payable to* J. M. TROUT,
*Business Manager, who will, in future, issue all
receipts for money.*

The Canadian Monetary Times.

THURSDAY, NOVEMBER 5, 1868.

THE PACIFIC RAILROAD.

The progress already made in the construction of the two lines of Railroad, known
as the Union Pacific, and the Central Pacific,
and the energy with which the work is being
pushed on, justifies the hope that Railway
communication between St. Louis and San
Francisco will be complete early next spring.
The Union Pacific is working from the Eastern
side, and runs trains to Point of Rocks eight
hundred and thirty miles west of Omaha and
two hundred and thirty-four miles from Salt
Lake. The Central Pacific has its track laid
for three hundred and forty-eight miles east
of Sacramento, or within three hundred and
three miles of Salt Lake. So that about five
hundred miles remain to be constructed before the two lines will connect. The distance
between Sacramento and Omaha is one
thousand seven hundred and twenty-five
miles. The Editor of the American Journal
of Mining says, he was at the end of the
Central Pacific on the 19th of August, during
which day six miles and a half of track were
laid along the level valley of the Humboldt.
According to a California paper that Company
employs about ten thousand workmen and
over three thousand teams, and the track is
being extended at the rate of two and a
quarter miles per day.

THE COLONIAL SOCIETY.

A Society bearing the above name has been
formed in London, England, with Viscount
Bury as President, and a large number of
noblemen and influential gentlemen as Vice-
Presidents, Trustees and directors. Its objects are thus summarized :—

"To provide a place of meeting for all
gentlemen connected with the Colonies and
British India, and others taking an interest
in Colonial and Indian affairs ; to establish a
reading-room and a library, in which recent
and authentic intelligence upon Colonial subjects may be constantly available, and a
museum for the collection and exhibition of
Colonial productions ; to facilitate interchange
of experiences amongst persons representing
all the Dependencies of Great Britain ; to
afford opportunities for the reading of papers,
and for holding discussions upon Colonial
subjects generally ; and to undertake scientific,
literary, and statistical investigations in connection with the British Empire."

It is hardly necessary to enlarge upon the
many advantages connected with the existence of a Society of the character alluded to.
Complaint has been made time and again of
the gross ignorance prevailing in London respecting Canada, and though we may be able
to excuse it, we are none the less hurt that a
country so large, so full of resources, so likely to make itself a place among nations, should
attract but little serious attention and excite
but little interest at the world's great centre.
When Canadians visit London they necessarily incur obligations to private friends and
acquaintances, which might be avoided to a
certain extent if there were some place in
the nature of a club, where they could go as
a matter of right. Any number of Canadians
may be in the great Metropolis without being
aware of each other's presence, unless they
happen to meet while sauntering on Regent
Street, or catch one another stealing a night's
amusement at the Alhambra. A "Colonist"
is shewn a great deal of kindness by individual Londoners, but a Colonist as a Colonist
merely finds it difficult to secure official recognition. Instances are not rare in which Canadians have gone to the United States Minister for favours rather than risk a snubbing
at the Colonial Office, or go through the
ordeal of question and answer at some of the
other Public Departments. Selfishness alone
should prompt many of our merchants and
professional men to assist in establishing the
Colonial Society. Mr. A. R. Roche is Secretary, and such as wish to join should communicate with him at 80 Lombard St., E. C.

THE BANK OF UPPER CANADA.

The meeting of shareholders and creditors
held yesterday brings to mind the deeds,
good and bad, which the old Bank of Upper
Canada bore on its much burdened shoulders,
and, as one glances over the balance sheet
presented by the Trustees, the inclination is
irresistible to compare the present with the
past. On the 13th November, 1866, after
the suspension of the Bank, the following
was the state of affairs :

LIABILITIES.

Circulation......................	$722,086 00
Due to depositors, &c............	401,190 76
Due to Glyn & Co.................	299,300 00
Government debt.................	1,149,430 75
Total $2,572,007 51	

ASSETS.	
Specie and Bank balances.....	$47,394 85
Mortgages........................	62,580 85
Real estate......................	1,673,623 37
Railway stock, debentures......	35,282 52
Bills, judgments, &c............	2,225,469 30
Government debentures..........	17,591 99
Total.....................	$4,061,941 88

The balance to credit of profit and loss was, therefore, $1,489,034.37. The statement laid before the meeting of Wednesday, as of November 1st, 1868, places the present balance at $635,019.72. While the liabilities have been reduced by $765,424.54, the assets has been diminished by $1,620,359.19, showing, thus far, a loss of $854,914.65.

Since 1866 the liabilities have been reduced as follows :

On circulation and deposits.........	$622,487
Glyn & Co.......................	126,938
Government debt...................	16,000
Total	$765,425

On the other hand, the assets have been reduced in this way :

Cash and Bank balances	$32,131
Government Securities	17,502
Bonds and Debentures	23,471
Real Estate	148,673
Bills, Judgments, &c.	1,180,963
	$1,711,130
Mortgages increased	90,790
Total	$1,620,340

Of this sum of $1,620,340, about $630,000 have been written into debts irrecoverable. This would leave assets realized to the extent of $1,000,060 by a reduction in liabilities of $765,425. The difference between these two amounts, or $244,235, represents the net loss on realization. Losses on real estate sold have probably footed up to $180,000. Within the last six months, $50,000 have been lost in the compounding of doubtful debts. The loss on real estate has been very heavy, proving how absurd was the valuation placed upon the lands owned by the bank. In fact, the real estate asset may be taken to represent a value between forty and fifty per cent. below that at which it was handed over to the Trustees.

Owing to the pressure upon our space, we are compelled to leave over till next week an account of the proceedings of the meeting of the shareholders of the Gore Bank, at Hamilton, as well as other interesting matter.

SCHOONER BURLINGTON.—In the gale of Saturday last, the 30th ult., this vessel, when about four miles off Grimsby, became unmanageable, and sunk in eighty feet of water. Her crew were not off her more than three minutes before she went under. Her cargo consisted of 6000 bushels of white wheat, valued at $8,10 . Hull and spars are both a total loss. She was rated P. 1, and valued at $2,200. The cargo was insured in the Montreal Assurance Company for $3000.

Insurance.

INSURANCE MATTERS IN MONTREAL.

(From a Correspondent.)

MONTREAL, Nov. 3rd, 1868.

Since my last, two or three incendiary fires have occurred. A stable in St. Monique St., was burned, and a most impudent attempt was made to set fire to the premises of Messrs. Evans, Mercer & Co., on Notre Dame St. In broad day light by some scoundrel, who has little fear of fire marshal or coroner's inquest rewards before his eyes. Talking of fire marshals that functionary has got into hot water again. This time however he is forced into good company. It appears that the Sheriff by order of the Attorney-General of Quebec gave him possession of a jury room in the Court House for the purpose of carrying on his investigations. His Honor Judge Berthelot objected to this proceeding, and ordered the Sheriff to resume the room for its legitimate purposes ; instead of doing so, the Sheriff gave his reasons and showed a written authority from Attorney-General Ouimette. His Honor fined the Sheriff £25 for contempt and issued a fresh order for ejection of the parties. The matter stands thus at present, both parties are obstinate and determined to carry their point, so there is no saying how the affair may end. This is one of the first conflicts between local and federal governments, let us hope that the struggle for State Rights may not eventuate as in the States a few years ago and lead to a rebellion.

FIRE RECORD—A barn owned by a man named Maguire, north of Duffin's Creek, was destroyed. No insurance.

Quebec.—There were two unimportant fires here recently ; one in a house on the corner of St. Louis and St. Ursula streets, and the other on Nouvelle street. Not much damage was done.

St. John, N. B., Nov. 2.—The residence of Mr. Perkins, Rothsay, was destroyed by fire this morning. Insurance, $5,390.

Nictaux, N. B.—The saw mill, grist mill, and carding machine, owned by Mr. Samuel McKeown, at Nictaux Falls, were totally destroyed by fire. The loss is estimated at $4,000. No insurance.

Some wretches attempted to fire the steam mills of Mr. Merrill, in the south-west part of Burford, county of Brant. Fortunately the attempt was detected in time to frustrate the fiendish purpose. A reward of $100 has been offered for the apprehension and conviction of the parties.

MARINE RECORD.—The Steamer Grecian struck in the Gallop Rapids, River St. Lawrence ; she was run into a cove and sunk in fourteen feet of water. Insured for about $32,000. The passengers and freight all saved ; her place on the route will be supplied by the "Champion " of the same line. The "Grecian" will be raised, brought to Kingston and placed in dry dock.

The schooner Lady Moulton, of Montreal, downward bound, arrived at Detroit on Saturday in a disabled condition. While sailing into the Detroit river, and just about Hog Island, she was met with by a tow of two vessels bound up, the forward one being the schooner Minnie Slatnson, struck her, carrying away her bowsprit, jibboom, and headgear, besides minor damage to her bows. She succeeded in reaching port, and is now repairing. She has a cargo of walnut lumber, from Chatham for Buffalo.

The schooner Frances, Captain William Parker, Master, left St. John, the 19th inst., for Granville, Nova Scotia, where she belonged. The snow was raging when she left, and as she proceeded it increased to be a perfect tempest. The darkness of night came on. She missed the Gut, and went ashore about ten miles above Digby, and soon became a perfect wreck. She had on board goods to

a considerable amount, shipped for Bridge and other ports, which were considerably injured, if not a total loss. Fortunately, all on board ill-fated vessel reached the shore safely.

A Quebec letter reports the total loss of schooner Marie Louise, from Quebec, at mouth of the Miramichi river. She was with flour. The ship Napier is also reported aground near Batiscan. The Deodara and crew have arrived.

PORT ROWAN, Nov. 2.—The schooner Bavarian, bound from Chicago to Oswego, 12,000 bushels wheat, went ashore about ten above this place, at 4 p.m. on the 30th ult. vessel sunk in twelve feet of water, and is a wreck. The crew and the Captain's wife the rigging and remained there until yesterday, when they were rescued in an exhausted condition.

DETROIT, Oct. 30.—The propeller "Cortez," from Buffalo for Chicago, loaded with railroad and salt, was totally destroyed by fire on the near Thunder Bay. Crew saved. She was at thirty thousand dollars and insured for thousand dollars.

PORT COLBORNE, Nov. 2.—The captain "Grace Whitney " reports passing a vessel, off Port Burwell, on Saturday early. Three men were at the mast-head, Whitney could render no assistance, owing gale and high sea.

—The schooner Defiance, which went ashore Snake Island reef, has been got off.

The captain of the "Mountaineer " report a large black barque, supposed to be with lumber, water-logged, about forty miles west of Long Point. There were four men on the quarter-deck. He tried for over two to get them off, but could do nothing as was so high. He also saw the sunken vessel there was only one man then on her.

The captain of schooner " Light Guard seeing two barges, the "Empire " and the land," loaded with lumber, water-logged middle of the lake. There were no person It is supposed they were taken off by the t had them in tow.

Captains say that on the night of the 30th Oct. they had the heaviest weather experienced.

The brig H. Roney, of Kingston, arrived the entire board and top-sail gone.

The schooner Annakeng lost her jib.

The " Caroline," of Coburg, lost her She saw a large barque run under Long P all her canvas gone. Several other vessels arrived yesterday and to-day were damaged less.

The steamer Leeds struck on a rock ning the Chute at Blandeau, in the Ottawa and sunk in forty feet of water. No one is expected to be raised at once.

WRECKING UNDER DIFFICULTIES.—We following curious story, from the Buffalo cial Advertiser, for what it may be worth Canadian bark Arabia, with a cargo of wheat Chicago to Montreal, was stranded at borne, head of Welland Canal, on the night 7th, in the severe storm then raging. bounded over one reef, and finally broke a deep bight on the edge of and between shoal reefs of rocks. The cargo was insured National Insurance Company of Boston American companies. The vessel was Canadian companies. Captain John Ried patched by the agents of the National Co. from Buffalo, with tug-pump and barges to the relief of the cargo and vessel. Inspector of the Canadian company, inspected the hull, being also at the wreck, and authority commenced. The master of the declining to take any positive position much delay. The insurers on the hull permit the pump to be placed on board vessel did not leak much, or the cargo

ie vessel would be in danger of driving t the reef. He looked to the interest of the vessel only, and having saw the ship's crew, and the ports being t delayed, Captain Rice in his efforts urgo as well as the vessel. Rice persever, and having the able assistance of asey Brown, and his powerful tug nanaged to get the Canadian inspector seizing the opportunity lightered the it 19,000 bushels on the night of the ; her off and into port during a strong before daylight, without damage to or cargo, much to the chagrin of the inspector and his sympathizers. The dispatched to St. Catharines to be the cargo in the lighter had to be forwarded over the Welland Railway at Port Dalhousie. Here the sample another point, and refused to take of the lighter by the elevator except housand for shovelling, and several Rice managed to get the lighter elevator, however, and letting go and the centreboard of the lighter, im from moving and forced them to , after a hand-to-hand fight with the f American underwriters and shippers eet to such dog-in-the-manger policy as evinced in this case by Cana-and carriers, they had better in is insuring cargoes per Canadian

AMICABLE.—We understand that the er and Actuary to the *Scottish Amiurance Society*, vacant by the death has been conferred on Mr. Stott, the tary of that Institution. Mr. Stott, Secretary at the Head Office in Glasfellow of the Institute of Actuaries a well as of the Faculty of Actuaries

NATIONAL.—At the Meeting of the nal Insurance Company at Edinburgh at, the new policies of the year were ve been 597, for £274,265. A bonus nade to the policies at the rate of £1, per annum for the four years since 00 was added to the paid-up capital and a dividend declared of 10 per im.

ATISTICS.]—The number of deaths in 1st January to 30th September, 6. The number above 20 years of 3. Accidents produced 13 deaths ; ; sunstroke, 4 ; intemperance, 3 ; were shot; 2 burned ; 3 killed by oned ; and 1 frightened to death. ine months 12 died whose united .9, and the average was 77 7-12. men died whose united ages reached taining 100, and another 102. An atio of deaths in the city is given 864, one in 49 ; 1865, one in 49 ; 63-7 ; 1867, one in 69.

'e understand that the appointment r to the *Royal Insurance Company* nt by Mr. McLaren's accession to ormerly held by the late Mr. Dove, red upon Mr. C. G. Fothergill, the tary to the London office. While t London loses so courteous and able a Mr. Fothergill, we are pleased to cessor Mr. T. Septimus Marks, for ief clerk of the London office, a ibently adapted for the post he has ion to occupy.—*Insurance Record.*

AY.—Hudson Bay Company's shares cely purchased, on a report that it to be brought into the Canadian mbly for the purpose of buying the e Company.—*Herepath's Journal.*

MAIDEN INSURANCE.

One people in Europe has, for some generations, attempted a novel form of assurance which is or the girls of the middle and higher classes. In Denmark, among the nobility, there has existed for some time what may be called "Maiden Assurance Companies." The basis of these were property belonging to the old cloisters, afterward secularized. A Danish gentleman, who should wish to secure his daughter against the contingencies of fortune, deposits at her birth, we will suppose, $2,000 in one of these companies. The child receives during her minority four per cent. interest annually ; at eighteen she comes into a higher income, regulated according to the property of the company ; at twenty-five she receives a still higher premium, and rooms and appointment in the buildings of the former cloister, if she desire, and again at thirty-five a still more liberal income, based again on profits.

If she die or marry, the deposit reverts to the funds of the association. In certain cases, however, if she marry and become a widow, she receives an annual stipend. The probabilities are so great that a given female child will either die or marry, that the company can afford to pay liberal interest (for Europe) on the deposit of the father, and will soon accumulate funds for the survivors who live as single women. A class of persons who are most exposed to hardship in modern society—unmarried women of the cultivated ranks—are thus ingeniously guarded against poverty and loneliness, having a sure income after a certain age, and respectable quarters with others of like position and tastes.

We see not why some similar assurance to these Danish companies might not be started in this country. The evil exists painfully in the older States—of the unprotected condition of daughters in the middle classes. The worst poverty ever known is of cultivated young women who are not strong enough for manual labor, and not clever enough to strike out new professions. Woman at the best, in artificial society, is at a disadvantage with men, in the "struggle for existence." She ought to have the help of an assured income ; and in this, as in all insurance, why should not the fortunate who marry, help the unprotected who do not happen to find a husband to their liking ? Why should not a father take advantage of the chances of death and marriage to secure his daughter against possible poverty and hardship ? If it be urged in objection that such security would tend to discourage marriage, already too infrequent, we would reply that nature is stronger than any pecuniary motive, and few women could be found to reject a husband, because they sacrifice thereby a few hundreds a year. Or, if it be urged, that better than assurance is education of woman, we answer that a man's insurance of his family does not prevent his educating them, and that the certainty of a small income would not deter from, but rather aid, young girls in training themselves thoroughly.

There are two elements in the insurance proposed easily calculated—the ratio of death of female children, and the ratio of marriages under certain years. Surely some of the ingenious brains who are now contriving insurance for every possible object might frame a sound system of insurance on this basis.

IMPORTANT MEETING AT LLOYD'S.

A meeting was held in London in the committee room of Lloyd's, to consider the relative position of underwriters and merchants as ascertained by the recent judgment in the case of "Dickinson v. Jardine." The judgment of the Court of Common Pleas in this case determined that where goods insured are jettisoned—that is, thrown overboard in the hope of saving the remainder of the cargo—the assured, if the goods are totally lost, according to the other conditions of the policy, is en-

titled to immediate settlement as for a total loss notwithstanding that the assured can recover the arrival value of the goods jettisoned by general contribution from the owners of all property arriving safe after the jettison. The following resolution were passed :—"1. That, in the opinion of this meeting, it is not desirable that the responsibility of collecting general average from the contributories to the same should fall upon the underwriter." "2. That it is therefore advisable that policies of assurance should be so framed that in case of any loss to the subject matter of insurance by a general average act, the claim upon the other contributing interests be recovered by the assured in general average as heretofore." "3. That, in order to carry out the decision in 'Dickinson v. Jardine,' and at the same time to preserve the legitimate rights of the underwriter, it is advisable to insert a clause in all goods and freight policies to the effect that in cases of loss to the subject matter of insurance by a general average act, the underwriters thereon could pay the difference between any amount payable by the contributory interests and the insured value, except in those cases where the underwriter is, by terms of the policy and the events which have happened free from any claim for particular average." The following further resolution was submitted and agreed to :—

"4. That in order to carry out the feeling of the meeting, the following clause be recommended for insertion in all policies :—'Should the property, hereby insured, be injured or destroyed by a general average act, any claim the assured is entitled to make in respect thereof, by way of particular average or total loss, shall be subject to the deduction of the sum payable to the assured by the other contributory interests of ship, freight and cargo.'"

"That, in the opinion of this meeting, it is desirable that, immediate steps should be taken to obtain an act of parliament for the purpose of most clearly defining and regulating the duty of the shipowners to collect general average from the contributories and to distribute the same.

A vote of thank was accorded to Mr. Goschen for taking the chair, and for the manner in which he had conducted the business ; and it was arranged that a copy of the proceedings should be sent to every chamber of commerce, and be circulated as widely as possible.

Financial.

MONTREAL MONEY MARKET.

(From our own Correspondent.)

Montreal, Nov. 3, 1868.

Money continues very easy, in fact the difficulty is, how to invest it, more especially on short dates. There is a great scarcity of good bills. There is no speculative feeling as regards produce of any sort. The demand for money for the ordinary purposes of trade is less than usual; the imports having been light, consequently the requirements for the payment of duties has been small. On the other hand, the remittances from the country have been heavier than for years past, and constantly increasing, so that funds here are readily in excess of all demands. The question now arises, how to employ the surplus. We have invested a very large amount in buildings and public improvements. Our stocks and shares of all sorts are held at exceedingly high rates; in fact, above their positive value, and yet money is accumulating and seeking investment. What will be the outlet? I think the solution of the question not so difficult but it requires some sounding of the financial waters before committing myself to a decided expression of opinion.

There is a speculative enquiry for Bank of Montreal stock, and the price has gone up to 140. I cannot give the reason for this rise, except that should the Provincial Bank note system be carried out, the Bank of Montreal will to a certain extent stand in the same position to Canada that the Bank of England does to Great Britain. As will be seen by your list of Montreal stocks, &c., there is a decided advance in all good securities, and holders are not anxious to enter the market except at extreme rates. *Silver.*—The discount on silver has fallen to three per cent., being a lower rate than it has reached during the last four years, and showing that the export of over a million dollars last spring must have had a favourable influence on the market. This low rate is operating rather against the export movement, and I understand it is Mr. Weir's intention to delay the shipments until the close of the fall trade permits silver to return and the discount to advance. I give price of gold 133⅜. Greenbacks, buying 25¼, selling 24⅞ discount. Silver, buying 3, selling 2½ to 2⅞ dis. Drafts on New York, 25 buying, 24½c. to 24¾c. selling.

TORONTO STOCK MARKET.

(Reported by Pellatt & Osler, Brokers.)

The stock market has been rather more lively during the past week, and closed firm with an upward tendency in quotations.

Bank Stock.—There were several small sales of Montreal at 135¾, and buyers now offer 136¼. Ontario has again advanced, buyers to-day offer 103 and no sellers under 103½. Toronto is wanted nominally at 117, but there is no stock in market and buyers would pay an advance on that quotation. There were sales of Royal Canadian paid-up at 92½, and small lots are still be had at that figure. Commerce is in demand at 101; very little offering. Gore has advanced 5 per cent., buyers now offer 40 with no sellers. Merchants' sold at 107 to 107½, and is in demand. Quebec is offered at 101, and there are buyers at par. For City 104 would be paid. There are sellers of Du Peuple at 104½; no buyers. Jacques Cartier sold at 108. In other banks nothing doing.

Debentures.—Canada sterling five per cents are offered at 91½; no six per cents to be had. Dominion stock readily commands 103. Toronto are in rather more demand, and are readily taken to pay 7 per cent. interest. There were small sales of County at rates to pay about 6½ per cent. interest.

Sundries.—City Gas is in demand at 105 to 105½, none offering. Building Society stock is again higher. Canada Permanent sold to-day (3rd Oct.) at 122½ to 123. Western Canada sold in small parcels at 115, which rate is now freely offered. Freehold is wanted at 107 to 108. British America Assurance offers at 56 with buyers at 55. Montreal Telegraph dull and in no demand at 120. Canada Landed Credit is wanted at 72½ for stock all paid. Few good mortgages offering. Money continues plentiful on undoubted security.

INTERNATIONAL COINAGE.

The report of the Royal Commission appointed to consider the possibility of establishing an International Coinage, together with the Minutes of evidence, has just been issued in London. The following are the conclusions at which the Commission arrived:

"The adoption of the proposal of the Paris Conference of merely reducing the value of the pound to that of 25 f., would facilitate the comparison of sums stated in large coins, but the difficulty would remain of comparing sums expressed in pence in England, in centimes in France, or in cents in the United States, and it is seldom that statements of prices, or statistical returns do not contain sums expressed in these small denominations. The reduction of the value of the pound would disturb all existing obligations, and would cause the many and serious difficulties which we have stated in the earlier part of this Report; while if at any future time a more complete assimilation of coins should be determined upon, a further change would be required, in many respects more difficult of application. The measure is, after all, only a partial measure, and although advocated by some witnesses as good in itself, and as a step to further assimilation, the object sought for by the witnesses connected with the trade and with the scientific bodies of this country would not be fully attained by anything less than a complete assimilation of the currencies of different countries. Several witnesses who took this view deprecated any change unless a complete assimilation of currency of moneys of account as well as of coins were made, and it is a serious objecpion that by this step all the admitted evils of the change in the value of the pound would be incurred, while the advantages by which it is anticipated that those evils would be compensated would not be attained. Upon full consideration of all these circumstances, we do not recommend that this country should merely adopt a gold coin of the value of 25 f. to be substituted for the sovereign. We have felt it to be our duty to state the grounds on which with a view to the general interest of the commerce of the world, the English sovereign and pound might form a convenient basis for international currency. The consideration of such a question, however, leads to one of a much more important character,—namely, that of a complete assimilation of the currencies of at least the principal commercial countries. We entertain no doubt that an uniform system of coins, bringing into harmony the various standards of value and moneys of account, alike in their higher denominations and their lower subdivisions, as well as an uniform system of weights and measures, would be productive of great general advantage. The latter proposal, however, is not referred to us; and we will only say, therefore, that we do not consider it necessary that any measures for the assimilation of the currency of the principal countries of the world should be postponed until steps are also taken for the assimilation of weights and measures. We are not insensible of the many and serious difficulties which must attend any attempt to effect a general assimilation of the currencies of different countries. Under any circumstances, great inconvenience must be encountered by many, if not by all, the countries joining in any monetary convention for such purposes; but the arrangement is one in which all commercial countries are interested, and none more deeply than our own. It would obviously conduce to a probable agreement that the burden of inconvenience should not press very unequally on any of them. What should be the common basis of their currencies, what international coin should be adopted, what proportion of alloy it should contain, what should be its sub-divisions or multiples, are all matters on which an agreement must be arrived at before any assimilation can be attained. On all these points widely different opinions may be held in different countries; and on the determination of them depends the degree of inconvenience to be sustained by each country. To what extent of inconvenience any country may be willing to submit for the sake of establishing a common international system of currency can only be ascertained by communication with the Government of each country. It is obvious that before any agreement can be concluded very difficult and complicated questions will have to be settled, concessions will have to be made on one part and on the other, and it will also be an important matter for consideration how far an agreement may be facilitated by making the changes which are necessary bear on any country as lightly as is consistent with the attainment of the common object. The assembling of some general international conference on the subject seems to have been looked forward to by many members of the Conference at Paris; and we are disposed to think that all the various questions might be best considered, the various interests of different countries di and their conflicting views reconciled by au representatives of the different countries in such a Conference.

"Halifax, C. P. Villiers, Stephen C Wilson Patten, M. Longfield, John L Thomas Baring, L N. de Rothschild, J. B. Thomson Hankey, John G. Hubbard, Th Hunt, G. B. Airy, Thomas Graham, C. Wilson, Secretary.

"July 25th, 1868."

Mr. J. B. Smith, Sir John Lubbock a Hubbard have made supplementary report

BANK OF ENGLAND.

Returns for the week ending October 14

Issue Department.

Notes issued	£34,
Government debt	£11,
Other securities	3,
Gold coin and bullion	19,
Silver bullion	
	£34,

Banking Department.

Proprietors' capital	£14,
Rest	3,
Public deposits (including Exchequer, Commissioners of National Debt, Savings' Banks, and Dividend Accounts)	3,
Other deposits	20,
Seven day and other Bills	
	£42,
Government securities (including Dead Weight Annuity)	£15,
Other securities	15,
Notes	9,
Gold and silver coin	1,
	£42,

LONDON MONEY MARKET.

The Money Market has shewn a rather tendency this week. The supply of capit the payment of the dividends comme Wednesday, has much increased, whilst mand for money has remained extremely consequently the rates of discount rule ing 1⅝ to 1¾ per cent. for first-class pap open market, whilst advances on British ment securities are offered at 1 per cen Stock Exchange without finding many *Investor's Guardian, Oct. 16.*

Boston Prices of Nova Scotia Gol —A Circular gives the following quotati

	Bid.
Boston and Nova Scotia	40
California	
El Dorado	55
Hayden and Derby	15
Uniacke	40
North American	03
Ophir	90
Orient	20
Palmerston	59
Renfrew	03
Sherbrooke and New York	15
Wellington	30

Ophir is in good demand at 90c. P looks strong; also El Dorado. Wel weak. Orient is offered at 25., and There seems to be a disposition to buy u and Boston and Nova Scotia at from per share. Money has been scarce, b easier.

INT-STOCK COMPANIES.—The num-
. companies in England is 393; and
companies 12. In Ireland there
d within the same period 29; and in
imited and 4 unlimited companies.
rhich is appended to the return is
:resting as showing the decline in
liability fever during the last five
63 there were 783 companies regis-
proposed capital of £139,982,249, in
year the number increased to 992,
sed capital of £237,437,083 14s.
e falling off has been rapid, as shown
ng figures:

Companies.	Capital.
.... 1,013...£205,391,818	
.... 752... 76,724,823	
.... 469... 31,444,982	
n l to May 31) 201... 13,896,182	

EXPRESS COMPANY.—At a meeting
bers of the Dominion Express Com-
Montreal, the following gentlemen
Provisional Directors :—Ira Gould,
rlane, Victor Hudon, A. W Ogilvie,
liam McNaughton, George D. Fer-
er McGibbon, George Heubach, and
Messrs. Carter, Pominville, and
re appointed Solicitors to the Com-
ription books will immediately be
other parts of the Dominion.

) AND SILVER CURRENCY.—More
s ago a correspondent, writing on the
cy, said that if our shillings were
oluan would be 80 miles high. The
Brown, M.P. for South Lancashire,
.ject interested in connexion with the
.age, was staggered at this. So a
the Bank of England made a more
oning, and trumped our correspon-
sion by a result of 87½ miles. Had
een quite new, the pile would have
.es high. The 87½ was got from the
ordinary use. New shillings have
ch ; the average in actual circul-
m 19 to 20. When they come down
inch, the Mint send them to the
Many persons were not—perhaps
e that our silver pieces are not coins ;
.lses to pay, like bank-notes ; only
ar the promise in value that actual
.ald not yield a sufficient profit. The
es to pay a sovereign for 20 of them,
; much worn, just as the Bank will
for a note, no matter how much
.mpled. So those who think it a
a deduction should be made for light
ne is made for light silver, may see
themœum.

treal Correspondence,

om our own Correspondent,

Montreal, Nov. 3, 1868.
ast very little of interest has trans-
is the commencement of the dull
all trade being pretty well over, and
ade not having commenced. Taken
e business has not been very dull,
ery sales having caused some stir in
s besides groceries. We have had a
rain, but, in spite of that, the water
e canal is so low that it is scarcely
pply the different factories, and the
.ted propellers, &c., have difficulty in
gh ; such is the lowness of the water
our manufacturies on the canal in-
large tanks and employing engines
water from the river into them, so
the inconvenience experienced last
regards the supply for the city, the

prospect looks gloomy ; the new improvements
have scarcely progressed beyond the foundation of
the new engine-house, and fully two months must
elapse before the works are in working order. As
regards our different factories this short supply is
of most serious account, they calculating for their
motive power on an unlimited supply ; the only
means by which such can be secured is by deepening the Lachine canal, which could easily be
done, considering the rise is about forty-five feet.
The mill sites are too valuable to the Government
to run the risk of losing, if a small sum will render them serviceable all the year round.

OUR PRODUCE market has been quiet. Prices
have not materially fluctuated since my last.
The shipments continue light ; apparently shippers
in the West are not disposed to give in to the
prices which must rule in Great Britain. The
wheat harvest there shows a surplus of some
fifty-eight millions of bushels over last year, and
that taken against the amount annually required, will show such a comparatively slight deficit in the amount required for consumption
that prices must materially decline and our shippers must accept the situation. Sales of flour have
been considerable during the week, prices ranging
firm for strong supers at $5,45 to $5,50, and other
brands at $6,15 to $5,30. For No. 2 the sales
have been considerable at $4,85 to $4,90. Wheat
has been dull, U.C. Spring worth $1,20 ex cars,
and $1,15 by the cargo ; prices are however too
undertain to give reliable quotations. U. C.
Red winter sold as high as $1.20 to $1.22½ ex cars.
Coarse grains continue very high, and are likely
to remain so. I notice that the crops throughout
Great Britain of barley, oats and peas, are exceedingly light, and as the supplies from this side will
fall short, we can hardly look for any reduction
in prices here. In provisions, pork continues
dull, the large quantity of hogs thrown on the
market having kept down the prices, and also a
large import of barrelled pork from the West,
induced by the high prices that ruled during the
summer and beginning of autumn. In butter
there has been an active demand, and large
shipping parcels have been sold at 22½c. to 24c.,
a long price for this time of the year, but which
fully bears out my remarks made as far back as
July. Cheese and lard are about stationary in
price, with a fair demand. Ashes sell freely at
1st pots $5.92½ to $6, according to tares ; 2nd,
$5.15 to $5.26; 3rd, $4.60 to $4.65. Pearls,
$5.55 to $5.70.

GROCERIES.—As stated in my last the sales were
not satisfactory, the audiences were moderate and
the bidding slow. At the same time, neither
section of the Province is overstocked, the only
fear has been that in overbuying, the merchants ran
a great risk, although the crops were generally
good, still there were liabilities outstanding on the
part of the farmers and country storekeepers, that
rendered any great extension of credit unwise.
Here in Montreal we are not overstocked, the only
extra supply being of fruits and light wines. As
far as concerns the first, we feel certain that owing to the short supply of green fruits and the
scarcity of home made provisions, all imported
fruit will sell readily during the winter, and that
our (at present) superabundant stocks will be
worked off at full rates. For all fish there has
been an active demand, and extreme prices have
been obtained at auction as well as at private sale.
The old question of fish inspection is agitated. I
shall have something to say concerning it in my
next. Sugar is lively, but molasses more especially
so, as the high price of butter always has a great
effect on this article.

MANUFACTURES.—The manufacturing interests
have lately been more active, and sales beyond
general expectations. A fair amount of dry goods
have been worked off, the fall business closing up
with more buoyancy than was generally looked for.
Hardware has been active and for some time an
active trade may be looked for, as the heavy staples
must be shipped before the close of navigation. In
the boot and shoe trade more activity has been

experienced than for some weeks past ; the late
wet weather has given an impetus to the demand
for heavy wares, and all our manufactories are
working on full time. Prices which were expected to rather recede, remain firm, and the
tendency is, if anything, towards a rise. This
activity has had the effect of causing more animation in the leather trade, and an advance in
the price of the heavy staples.

Toronto Market.

Trade for the week has been good considering
the stage of the season. Though the bulk of the
full trade is quite over there is a good deal doing
with the country merchants in the way of sorting
up stocks which have been broken.

BOOTS AND SHOES.—A fair demand from the
retail trade keeps manufacturers well employed,
so that there is no accumulation of stock.

GROCERIES.—Sugars—Are about a quarter of a
cent better in consequence of a corresponding rise
in the New York market. The *Financial Chronicle* of the 13th says : "The unsettled condition of
affairs in Cuba continues to operate with force
upon the market. From this cause, immediately
after the date of our last report, there was a sharp
advance of a quarter of a cent upon the goods
taken by refiners, who were the active operators.
The excitement, however, ended in a reaction
which is but just passing away. Sugars receded
¼ cent again, and closed at ½ advance on the last
week's prices. The imports of the week were
small." Teas.—There is good enquiry for teas of
every grade, and a good many lots are moving
within the range of quotations. Fruits—Are
much firmer, owing to a considerable advance in
prices in England, and New York and places of
growth. Importers have been selling large lots
of Valencia raisins at 7c. to 7½c., and they are
now held for 7½c. to 8c. in jobbing lots. Fish—
Of every kind are very fine, and likely to be
higher, owing to a heavy demand and light supplies. Rice—Firm and steady. Tobaccos—are
without change.

APPLES.—A considerable trade is being done in
shipping apples eastward, where there appears to
be a large demand for them. One line of vessels
here has contracts to carry 6,000 barrels, a portion of which have already gone down. They are
worth $1.75 to 2.75 per barrel.

GRAIN,—Barley—Receipts by cars for the week
19,685 bush., against 24,750 bush. last week.
The shipments across the lake for the week ending
with Saturday last were 61,986 bush., and 81,985
for the previous week. Of these shipments, 7,548
bush. went to Erie, 24,670 bush. to Toledo, and
41,360 bush. to Oswego. Total shipments as per
Customs' returns,' by lake, since the commencement of the season, 595,743 bush. The following
vessels cleared with barley during the week named :
the schooner Todman, with 7,600 bush., the
Phœbe Catherine with 7,571 bush., the Jessie
Macdonald with 4,222 bush., the H. P. Murray
with 9,875 bush., all for Oswego ; the Antelope
with 10,868 bush., the Sea Gull with 13,892 bush.
for Toledo ; the J. G. Beard with 7,548 bush. for
Erie. The market opened unsettled at $1.35 to
$1.40, and owing to a semi-panic in the American
markets tumbled to $1.15, from which it after-
wards recovered, closing firmer at $1.20 to $1.25.
Few sales reported.

WHEAT.—Receipts for the week 32,686 bush.,
and 51,358 bush. last week. Shipments for the
week 11,392 bush.; the schooner J. J. Hill took
5,100 bush.; and the Wanderer 6,292 bush., both
for Oswego. Fall opened with a fair demand at
$1.30 to $1.35 for fair samples, but after the cargoes shipped by the above vessels were made up
the demand fell off, so that there were no buyers
at the close of the week ; sellers ask $1.32 to
$1.35. Midge proof is nominal at $1.10 to
$1.12. There is more demand for Spring, and
sales of small lots were made at $1.09 to $1.11.
Peas.—Receipts by cars for the week 4,160
bush., and 2,907 bush. last week. Considerable
shipments have been made eastward by steam,

The market is lower, closing dull at 85c. to 88c. *Oats.*—Receipts by cars 3,720 bush., and 4,000 bush. last week. The market has fluctuated somewhat, closing with buyers at 50c. to 51c., sellers asking 52c. to 53c.; no sales. *Rye.*—Nominal. *Seed.*—Timothy is worth $2.25 to $2.75. *Clover.*—$6.00 to $6.50.

FLOUR.—Receipts for the week 2,400 bls., and 1,090 bls. last week: there were good shipments eastward and by Grand Trunk. There is some demand for lots of superfine and very little offering. Holders ask $5.00 to $5.10; some transactions occured at $5.00. Extra is offered at $6.50, but is only worth about $6.00 · Superior is held at $6.50.

PROVISIONS—*Butter*—Is held firmly at 22½c to 23c, no sales; pound rolls, 26c to 27c. *Mess Pork*—Nominal at quotations. *Dressed Hogs*—Selling at $6.50 to $7.50; not a great many have come forward. *Lard*—Quiet, at 14½c. *Bacon*—Held at 11c. *Hams*—11¼c to 12c asked for lots. *Eggs*—Selling at 18c for packed.

LIVE STOCK.—The cattle market is well supplied; lots selling at $6 for first-class, and down to $4.50 for inferior. *Sheep*—$2.50 to $3 each. *Hogs*—One firm put down 6,000 hams during the past week. Live hogs are selling at $5 to $5.50. The average weight of live hogs to date was 191 lbs.

PETROLEUM.—There is good demand for consumption at quotations.

HIDES.—There were some large transactions in hides during the week at about 6c.

FREIGHTS.—Rates by steamer to Montreal are 30c. per brl. on flour and apples; on grain 7c. to 8c.; to Kingston, 2c.; grain to Chicago, by vessel, 3½c.; to Erie, 4c. U. S. cy.; lumber, to Oswego, $1.75, U. S. cy. Rates per Grand Trunk, to Montreal, 35c. on flour; to Halifax, 95c.; to St. John, 85c. Rates to Liverpool are by the Grand Trunk, via Portland—boxed meats, gross ton, 67s. 6d.; lard and butter, 77s. per ton; beef per tierce, 11s. stg.; pork per brl. 9s.

The Chicago *Tribune* of the 30th says: The movement in grain vessels at this point to-day was a large one, and rates were firm on the basis of 9½ to 10c. for wheat, and 8½c. for corn to Buffalo, by sail craft; 15¾c. for wheat to Kingston; 16c. for corn to Brockville; 16c. for corn to Prescott; 7c. for oats to Erie; 7½c. for corn to Windsor; 16c. for wheat to Oswego; and 13½c. for oats to Ogdensburg. In all there were sixteen charters. The number of vessels awaiting cargoes is comparatively light.

The Wine Trade.

SHERRY.—The vintage in Spain has at the last moment proved rather disappointing; the heavy rains coming upon the ripe fruit will, it is feared, have the effect of deteriorating the quality somewhat. This is unfortunate, as just before the gathering the vines looked everything that could be desired. The market demand is for good sound cheap descriptions; the lowest-priced wines are the scarcest. Quotations: Sound common, 14*l.* to 18*l.*; Cadiz wines, 20*l.* to 25*l.*; middling stout, 26*l.* to 36*l.*; fair to good, 38*l.* to 50*l.*; superior to fine old, 54*l.* to 90*l.*; very fine choice, 100*l.* to 250*l.* per butt in bond.

PORT.—The Douro vintage has resulted in excellent quality, but the great heat and drought has shortened the quantity. Dealers are stated to have made large purchases of the new wine, and prices at Oporto have been well maintained, the general impression being that the vintage will take a high rank.

FRENCH.—The transactions in this market are of a limited nature; nevertheless prices are firmly supported, the large business done at Bordeaux causing holders here to show no disposition to sell except at advanced rates. That sound low to middling Clarets are good value there is no doubt from the very fact of the Germans buying so largely at Bordeaux of the present vintage.

The gathering for red wines finished on the 3rd instant; the vintage is said to be less than an ordinary average in quantity, but of superior quality. More business has been done in this year's wines than probably ever was known so early in the season; consequently prices are advancing.

CHAMPAGNE.—The vintage in Champagne terminated about the 24th ult. The produce is good in quality, and in this respect, and also as to quantity, is decidedly above the average of ordinary years. The prices have been even higher than the celebrated year 1865. Never have champagne houses shown themselves so eager to purchase. Such, indeed, was the rivalry, that the whole of the grapes of the principal vineyards were bought before the gathering; and this haste on the part of the buyers has been a little to the disadvantage of the quality of some of the wines, for the proprietors assured of the sale of their crops, began to gather several days before the maturity of the grapes was complete. The result of this will be that generally the wines of 1868, whilst preserving a high character for delicacy and bouquet, will not possess the fullness and richness of the wines of 1865. The quantity of wine made is very large; in spite of this, there is not now a single cask of wine in the hands of the proprietors. In less than three days the whole of this year's production was sold. Very high prices were paid, which must be attributed to the eagerness of buyers rather than to the wonderful superiority of the wine.

BRANDY.—This market has lately exhibited firmness—in fact, sellers pretend to slightly higher prices, the reasons for which are reports from Charente of a greater deficiency in the crop than was anticipated; one-third of an average vintage is reported as the probable yield. This is expected to influence opening prices in an upward degree, which will in its turn probably give stability to quotations for old brandy, but must, or rather ought to, limit speculation in new spirit, considering the present large stock on hand. From our advices we should calculate one-half to be nearer than one-third of an average as the probable result, which would show a very respectable total in actual figures.—*London Grocer.*

Halifax Market.

BREADSTUFFS.—Oct. 27.—Flour without change and dull. No. 1 Canada $6.25 to $6.40. Strong Bakers $6.65 to $6.75. Extra Canada $7.50 to $8. Extra State dull at $6 to $6.40; No. 2 in good demand at $5 to $5.50. Cornmeal dull at $4.50 for kiln dried, and $4.40 for fresh ground. Oatmeal $7.70 to $7.80. Imports from January 1st to October 27th, 1867 and 1868:

	Bbls. Flour.	Bbls. Cornmeal.
1868.	149,307	42,145
1867.	159,999	30,566

WEST INDIA PRODUCE.—Sugars and Molasses remain without change. Large lots are being shipped out of our market and must soon affect prices here. Porto Rico, 6¼ to 6¾; Barbadoes, 5¾ to 5⅞c.; Cuba, 5¼ to 5¾c.; Centrifugal Cuba, 6c., in bond. Rum scarce and in demand at 62½c. for Demerara and 51 to 52½c. for St. Jago.

St. John Market.

Oct. 25.—We have to report a further decline in our flour market. Receipts have been liberal, and as the demand has kept small, stocks have been accumulating. Holders are very anxious to sell, and almost any price that buyers would name would be accepted. In the absence of sales prices are nominal. Good No. 1 Super, is offering at $6.25 and some sales are reported under that.

The Transportation of Petroleum.

While cotton, grain, tobacco, and other leading agricultural staples of the country combined, are universally regarded as the basis of industry and commerce, little is said of Petroleum in the same connection, notwithstanding the fact that there is probably as much money involved in the last mentioned commodity as in any other single article of home production. Petroleum, indeed, has become a product, not only of the first necessity, but of the first importance, at home and abroad, each succeeding year since it became a considerable article of commerce, witnessin increased consumption in every civilized p the world; and every year seems to develop methods for utilization. It is not only al universally employed as an illuminator, bu the manufacture of soap, candles, wax, lubric substances, and dye-stuffs, and as a motor, i become of essential use. After the first flu excitement attending the discovery of Petrol in Pennsylvania, grave fears were entertained there might be, sooner or later, an exhaustio the supply; but these fears have been expelle succeeding years, during which there has bee increase of production commensurate with increase of consumption. It is true oil wells constantly being exhausted, but for each one proves unproductive, a new one, or more, is s and thus the supply is kept up, and may no said to be all but inexhaustible. Petroleum been discovered in various parts of the world, thus far the wants of commerce have been ma supplied by the United States, which has a p tical monopoly of the trade. The export Petroleum from New York since the 1st of Jan are, in round numbers, 40,000,000 gallons, ag 20,000,000 gallons for the corresponding pe last year. From the United States the ex to date are, in round numbers, 70,000,000 gal against 42,000,000 the corresponding period year, an increase of about sixty per cent. great bulk of the exports are from New York Philadelphia, though most of the business o latter port is on New York account. The inc of exports this year is mainly to Continental rope, as will be seen by the exports, a glan which cannot fail to prove highly instructi those who take an interest in the march of pro in this important branch of commerce. Lea out France, which takes crude almost exclusi most of the exports to Continental Europe co of the Refined article, which is not only saf transport, as may be gathered from the fact vessels carrying Crude are subject to an extra rance of three or four per cent., but is cheaper to the foreign dealer and consumer was with a view to retaining the entire busin refining Petroleum in this country that so st ous an effort was made at the last session of gress to have the tax on the Refined pr reduced, and which, though it met with p success, will, it is thought, ultimately be a plished, since a monopoly of the refining p must necessarily add some millions of dolla nually to the wealth of the country.

As to the risks incident to the transportat Petroleum there appears to be a great divers opinion, though, as between Crude and Re it is obvious that the former is by far the inflammable, and therefore more dangerous. liquid or product that will throw off exp vapor, must, to a certain extent, be danger convey; but if the fear of accident were al to operate to the prejudice of common carr severe blow would be inflicted upon comm interests. Considering the immense con afforded by Petroleum, the accidents dire indirectly chargable to the article, it must b fessed, have been proportionately small. leum and its products may be safely trans when not exposed to heat beyond a certain nized degree and when carried under proper lations of packing, but if these regulations observed, they may become exceedingly dan from their liability to explode from expansi heat. This opinion is borne out by a recen munication to the British Academy of Sc by M. Henri Deville, who stated that the product called petroleum increases in bu one-hundredth of its volume for every ten of heat; and that if this expansion we allowed for, explosions must take place. Petroleum has come to be an article of un necessity, it is safe to say that ingenuity v vise means for the safety of its transpo storage and handling, as it has done in t of all other extra hazardous commodities.

New Advertisements.

THE AGRICULTURAL
Mutual Assurance Association of Canada.

OFFICE............................ LONDON, ONT.

rely Farmers' Company. Licensed by the Government of Canada.

al, 1st January, 1868...................... $220,121 25
and Cash Items, over...................... $65,000 00
' Policies in force.......................... 28,764

18 Company insures nothing more dangerous than
larm property. Its rates are as low as any well-established Company in the Dominion, and lower than those
charge many. It is largely patronised, and continues
to win public favor.
Insurance, apply to any of the Agents, or address
secretary, London, Ontario.
ndon, 2nd Nov., 1868. 13-1y

J. C. Small,
mitive BANKER AND BROKER,
ccountant, General Agent, &c.,
No. 34 King Street East, Toronto, Ontario.

NK Stock, Debentures and other Securities bought
and sold.
ans by way of Mortgage negotiated.
ober, 1868. 12-1y

Ontario Bank.

DIVIDEND No. 23.

TICE is hereby given, that a Dividend of Four per
cent. upon the Capital Stock of this Institution for
current half year, has this day been declared, and that
ame will be payable at the Bank and its Branches,
nd after

Tuesday, the First day of December next.

e Transfer Books will be closed from the 15th to the
November, both days inclusive.
order of the Board.
                            D. FISHER, *Cashier.*
rio Bank,
wmanville, 24th Oct., 1868. 11-td

Miscellaneous.

HE QUEEN'S HOTEL.

THOMAS DICK, Proprietor.

NT STREET, - - - TORONTO, ONT
                                           8-1y

ontreal House, Montreal, Canada.

MONETARY MEN.—Merchants, Insurance Agents,
awyers, Bankers, Railway and Steamboat Travellers,
ng Agents, Directors and Stockholders of Public Com
es, and other persons visiting Montreal for business
easure, are here by most respectfully informed that
undersigned propose to furnish the best hotel accommodation at the most reasonable charges. It is our study
provide every comfort and accommodation to all our
ts, especially for gentlemen engaged as above. To
e who have been accustomed to patronise other first-
hotels, we only ask a trial; we have the same accommodation and our table is furnished with every delicacy
season.
                            H. DUCLOS.
v. 22, 1867. 15-1y

The Albion Hotel,
MONTREAL,

E of the oldest established houses in the City is again
nder the personal management of
                  Mr. DECKER.

to accommodate his rapidly increasing business, is
g Eighty more Rooms to the house, making the
ow one of the Largest Establishments in Canada.
ae, 1868. 42-6ms

Mercantile.

Hurd, Leigh & Co.,
IMPORTERS AND DECORATORS OF
FRENCH CHINA.

Hotels and families supplied with any pattern or crest
desired.
Common goods always on hand. 72 Yonge Street,
Toronto, Ontario. 26y

John Boyd & Co.,
WHOLESALE GROCERS AND COMMISSION
MERCHANTS,

61 AND 63 FRONT STREET
TORONTO.

NOW in store, direct from the European and West India
Markets, a large assortment of General Groceries,
comprising

Teas, Sugars, Coffees, Wines and Liquors,
AND
GENERAL GROCERIES.

Ship Chandlery, Canvas, Manilla and Tarred Rope,
Oakum, Tar, Flags, &c., &c.,
DIRECT FROM THE MANUFACTURERS.

JOHN BOYD.   ALEX. M. MONRO.   C. W. BUNTING.
Toronto, Oct. 1st, 1868. 7-1y

John Ross & Co.,
QUEBEC.

T. & F. Ross & Co.,
GENERAL WHOLESALE GROCERS,
PRODUCE AND COMMISSION MERCHANTS,
361 *Commissioner Street,*
MONTREAL. 6

W. McLaren & Co.,
WHOLESALE
BOOT AND SHOE MANUFACTURERS,
18 ST. MAURICE STREET,
MONTREAL.

June, 1868. 42-1y

Brown Brothers,
ACCOUNT-BOOK MANUFACTURERS,
Stationers, Book-Binders, &c.,
66 and 68 King Street East, Toronto, Ont.

ACCOUNT Books for Banks, Insurance Companies,
Merchants, etc., made to order of the best materials,
and for style, durability and cheapness unsurpassed.
A large stock of Account-Books and General Stationery
constantly on hand.
September 1, 1868. 3-1y

Philip Browne & Co.,
BANKERS AND STOCK BROKERS,
DRALERS IN

STERLING EXCHANGE—U S. Currency, Silver and
Bonds—Bank Stocks, Debentures, Mortgages, &c.
Drafts on New York issued, in Gold and Currency.
Prompt attention given to collections. Advances made
on Securities.
          No. 67 YONGE STREET, TORONTO
JAMES BROWNE.   PHILIP BROWNE, *Notary Public.*
y

Candee & Co.,
BANKERS AND BROKERS, dealers in Gold and Silver
Coin, Government Securities, &c., Corner Main and
Exchange Streets, Buffalo, Y. N. 21-1y

Honore Plamondon,
CUSTOM House Broker, Forwarder, and General Agent,
Quebec. Office—Custom House Building. 17-1y

Sylvester, Bro. & Hickman,
COMMERCIAL Brokers and Vessel Agents. Office—No.
1 Ontario Chambers, [Corner Front and Church Sts.]
Toronto. 2-6m

Mercantile.

TEAS. Reford & Dillon **TEAS.**

HAVE just received ex. steamships "*St. David* and
Nestorian :"

1000 hlf. chests new season TEAS !
      Comprising Twankays, Young Hysons, Imperials,
      Gunpowders, colored and uncolored Japans,
      Congous, Souchongs, and Pekoes.
500 hlf. bxs. new Valentia Raisins (selected fruit).
500 bags cleaned Arracan and Rangoon Rice.
500 bgls. choice Currants.

—ALSO, IN STORE :—

250 hhds. bright Barbadoes and Cuba Sugars.
250 brls. Portland, Standard, Golden & Amber Syrups.
100 bags Rio, Jamaica, Laguayra, and Java Coffees.
200 bxs. 10s Tobacco, "Queen's Own" and "Prince of
      Wales" brands.

WITH A GENERAL AND
WELL SELECTED STOCK OF GROCERIES;
All of which they offer to the Trade low.
12 & 14 WELLINGTON STREET, TORONTO.
                                           7-1y

Robert M. Gray,
Manufacturer of Hoop Skirts
AND
CRINOLINE STEEL,
IMPORTER OF
HABERDASHERY, TRIMMINGS
AND
GENERAL FANCY GOODS,
43, YONGE STREET, TORONTO, ONT. 6-1y

Lyman, Elliot & Co.,
Chemists and Druggists.

OFFICE AND SAMPLE ROOMS, ... 157 *King Street East.*
RETAIL DEPARTMENT, ... 155 *King Street East.*
WAREHOUSES, ... 83 & 85 *Front Street.*
MILLS, ... *Palace Street.*

IMPORTERS and Manufacturers of every requirement o
the RETAIL DRUG TRADE. A full assortment of the following classes of Goods always on hand :—

Drugs and Chemicals	Patent Medicines.
Corks.	Perfumery.
Dye Stuffs.	Preparations.
Furniture.	Soaps.
Surgical Instruments and	Bronze, Gold Leaf, &c
Appliances.	Colors, Dry.
Spices.	Colors, in Oil.
Sundries.	Varnishes.

DRUGGISTS' EARTHENWARE and GLASSWARE, in whole
Packages, at Factory Rates.
Enquiries and orders by mail will receive prompt and
careful attention.

Teas! Teas!! Teas!!!

FRESH ARRIVALS

NEW CROP TEAS,
WINES, AND GENERAL GROCERIES,

Special Inducements given to
PROMPT PAYING PURCHASERS.

All Goods sold at very Lowest Montreal Prices!
W. & R. GRIFFITH,
ONTARIO CHAMBERS,
Corner of Front and Church Streets,
                            TORONTO,
                                  ONTARIO

Mercantile.

DOMINION TELEGRAPH COMPANY.

CAPITAL STOCK   -   - $500,000.

In 10,000 Shares at $50 Each.

PRESIDENT,
HON. WILLIAM CATLEY.

TREASURER,
HON. J. McMURRICH.

SECRETARY,
H. B. REEVE.

SOLICITORS,
MESSRS. CAMERON & McMICHAEL.

GENERAL SUPERINTENDENT,
MARTIN RYAN.

DIRECTORS.

HON. J. McMURRICH,
Bryce, McMurrich & Co., Toronto.

A. R. McMASTER, Esq.,
A. R. McMaster & Brother, Toronto.

HON. M. C. CAMERON,
Provincial Secretary, Toronto.

JAMES MICHIE, Esq.,
Fulton, Michie & Co., and George Michie & Co., Toronto

HON. WILLIAM CAYLEY.
Toronto.

A. M. SMITH, Esq.,
A. M. Smith & Co., Toronto.

L. MOFFATT, Esq.,
Moffatt, Murray & Co., Toronto.

H. B. REEVE, Esq.,
Toronto.

MARTIN RYAN, Esq.,
Toronto.

PROSPECTUS.

THE DOMINION TELEGRAPH COMPANY has been organized under the act respecting Telegraph Companies, chapter 67, of the consolidated Statutes of Canada. Its object is to cover the Dominion of Canada with a complete net-work of Telegraph lines.

The Capital Stock

Is $500,000, divided into 10,000 shares of $50 each, 5 per cent to be paid at the time of subscribing, the balance to be paid by instalments, not exceeding 10 per cent per month—said instalments to be called in by the Directors as the works progress. The liability of a subscriber is limited to the amount of his subscription.

The Business Affairs of the Company.

Are under the management of a Board of Directors, annually elected by the Shareholders, in conformity with the Charter and By-Laws of the Company.

The Directors are of opinion that it would be to the interest of the Stockholders generally to obtain subscriptions from all quarters of Canada, and with this view they propose to divide the Stock amongst the different towns and cities throughout the Dominion, in allotments suited to the population and business occupations of the different localities, and the interest which they may be supposed to take in such an enterprise.

Contracts of Connections.

A contract, granting permanent connection and extraordinary advantages, has already been executed between this Company and the Atlantic and Pacific Company, of New York ; thus, at the very commencement, as the Lines of this Company are constructed from the Suspension Bridge, at Clifton (the point of connection) to any point in the Dominion, all the chief cities and places in the States, touched by the Lines of the Atlantic and Pacific Telegraph Company, are brought in immediate connection therewith.

A permanent connection has also been secured with the Great Western Telegraph Company, of Chicago, whereby this Company will be brought into close connection with all the Lake Ports and other places through the North-western States, and through to California.

6-3mos

Mercantile.

UNRIVALLED!

THE BRITISH AMERICAN COMMERCIAL COLLEGE, Consolidated with the

Bryant, Stratton and Odell Business College
AND TELEGRAPHIC INSTITUTE.

STANDS Pre-eminent and Unrivalled. It is the Largest and Most Efficient. It employs the largest staff of Teachers, among whom are the two BEST PENMEN OF CANADA.

The TUITION FEE is the same as in other Institutions having a similar object.

The PRICE OF BOARD is the same as in other Canadian Cities.

In an EDUCATIONAL point of view, there is no other Institution in the country that has equal advantages and facilities.

YOUNG MEN intending to qualify themselves for business, will find it to their advantage to send for a Circular, or call at the College Rooms, corner of King and Toronto streets.

Scholarships good in Montreal and throughout the United States.

ODELL & TROUT,
Principals and Proprietors.

October 2.   8

The Mercantile Agency,

FOR THE
PROMOTION AND PROTECTION OF TRADE
Established in 1841.

DUN, WIMAN & Co.,
Montreal, Toronto and Halifax.

REFERENCE Book, containing names and ratings of Business Men in the Dominion, published semi-annually.   14-1y.

The St. Lawrence Glass Company

ARE now manufacturing and have for sale,

COAL OIL LAMPS,
various styles and sizes.

LAMP CHIMNEYS,
of extra quality for ordinary Burners also, for the 'Comet' and 'Sun' Burners.

SETS OF
TABLE GLASSWARE, HYACINTH GLASSES,
STEAM GUAGE TUBES, GLASS RODS, &c.,
or any other article made to 'order, in White or Colored Glass.

KEROSENE BURNERS, COLLARS and SOCKETS, will be kept on hand.

DRUGGISTS' FLINT GLASSWARE, and
PHILOSOPHICAL INSTRUMENTS,
made to order.

OFFICE—388 ST. PAUL STREET, MONTREAL.
A. McK. COCHRANE.
8-1y   Secretary.

J. R. Boyce,

NOS. 63 and 65, Great James Street, Montreal, Dealer and Importer of all kinds of TOYS and FANCY GOODS. J. R. B. is the only manufacturer of La Crosse Sticks for the new Indian Game of LACROSSE, and has constantly on hand a large supply, with the printed Rules of the Game. He also manufactures all the requisites for Croquet, and all other Parlour and Lawn Games. Baskets, of all kinds, and every variety of Hair Work, Wigs, Curls, Beards, &c.; Dress and Theatrical Wigs, for sale. Wholesale and Retail Parties engaged in forming new La Crosse Clubs, will do well to apply direct to the above address.

Lyman & McNab,

Importers of, and Wholesale Dealers in,

HEAVY AND SHELF HARDWARE,
King Street,
TORONTO, ONTARIO.

H. N. Smith & Co.,

2 EAST SENECA STREET, BUFFALO, N. Y., (correspondent Smith, Gould, Martin & Co., 11 Broad Street, N.Y.,) Stock, Money and Exchange Brokers. Advances made on securities.   21-1y

Mercantile.

DAY'S
Commercial College and High School
No. 82 KING STREET EAST,
(Near St. James' Cathedral.)

THE design of this institution is to prepare Young and others as Book-keepers, and for general business and to furnish them with the facilities for acquiring excellent

English and Commercial Education.

Mr. Day is also prepared to give Private Instruction the several subjects of his department, and to assist merchants and others in the checking and balancing of adjusting their accounts and partnership affairs, &c.

For further information, please call on or address the undersigned.

JAMES E. DAY,
Accountant

Toronto, Sept. 3rd, 1868.

Financial.

Canada Permanent Building and Savings Society.

Paid up Capital	$1,000
Assets	1,700
Annual Income	400

Directors:—JOSEPH D. RIDOUT, President.
PETER PATERSON, Vice-President.
J. G. Worts, Edward Hooper, S. Nordheimer, W. Chewett, E. H. Rutherford, Joseph Robinson.
Bankers:—Bank of Toronto ; Bank of Montreal ; Canadian Bank.

OFFICE—Masonic Hall, Toronto Street, Toronto

Money Received on Deposit bearing five and six cent. interest.

Advances made on City and Country Property in the P of Ontario.

36-y
J. HERBERT MASON
Sec'y &

Pellatt & Osler.

STOCK AND EXCHANGE BROKERS, Accountants Agents for the Standard Life Assurance Company New York Casualty Insurance Company.
OFFICE—86 King Street East, four Doors West Church Street, Toronto.

HENRY PELLATT,   EDMUND B. C
1y   Notary Public.   Official Assign

The Canadian Land and Emigration Company

Offers for sale on Conditions of Settlement,

GOOD FARM LAND
In the County of Peterboro, Ontario,

In the well settled Township of Dysart, where there Grist and Saw Mills, Stores, &c., at

ONE-AND-A-HALF DOLLARS AN A

In the adjoining Townships of Guilford, Dudley, burn, Harcourt and Bruton, connected with Dysart the Village of Haliburton by the Peterson Road,

DOLLAR an Acre.

For further particulars apply to
CHAS. JAS. BLOMFIELD,
Secretary C. L. and E. Co., T
Or to
ALEX. NIVEN, P.L.S.,
Agent C. L. & E. Co., Halib

Western Canada Permanent Building Savings Society.

OFFICE—No 70 CHURCH STREET, TORONTO

SAVINGS BANK BRANCH,

DEPOSITS RECEIVED DAILY. INTEREST PAID Yearly.

ADVANCES

Are made on the security of Real Estate, repayable most favourable terms, by a Sinking Fund.

WALTER S. LEE
36-1y   Secy. &

Name of Article.	Wholesale Rates.		Name of Article.	Wholesale Rates.		Name of Article.	Wholesale Rates.	
Boots and Shoes.	$ c.	$ c.	**Groceries**—*Contin'd*	$ c.	c.	**Leather**—*Contin'd.*	$ c.	$ c.
Mens' Thick Boots	2 30	2 50	" fine to fins't..	0 85	95	Kip Skins, Patna	0 30	0 40
" Kip............	2 50	3 25	Hyson	0 45	0 80	French	0 70	0 90
" Calf	2 20	2 70	Imperial	0 42	0 80	English	0 65	0 80
" Congress Gaiters...	2 00	2 40	Tobacco, manufac'd :			Hemlock Calf (30 to		
" Kip Cobourgs....	1 10	1 50	Can Leaf, ⅌ ℔ 5s & 10s.			35 lbs.) per doz...	0 75	0
Boys' Thick Boots.....	1 70	1 90	Western Leaf, com..	0 20	30	Do. light	0 45	0
Youths'	1 45	1 50	" Good ...	0 25	29	French Calf.	0 95	1
Women's Batts	95	1 30	" Fine ...	0 27	32	Grain & Satn Clf ⅌ doz..	2 00	3 30
" Congress Gaiters...	1 15	1 50	" Bright, fine..	0 32	35	Splits, large ⅌ ℔....	0 30	0
Misses' Batts...........	0 75	1 00	" choice.	0 40	0 50	" small	0 20	0
" Congress Gaiters	1 00	1 30		0 60	0 75	Enamelled Cow ⅌ foot..	0 17	0
Girls' Batts	0 60	0 85	**Hardware.**			Patent	0 18	0
" Congress Gaiters	0 80	1 10	Tin *(net cash prices)*			Pebble Grain	0 17	0
Children's C. T. Cacks...	0 50	0 65	Block, ⅌ ℔...........	0 25	0 26	Buff	0 17	0 18½
" Gaiters....	0 65	0 90	Grain...............	0 25	0 26			
Drugs.			*Copper:*			**Oils.**		
Aloes Capo.	0 12½	0 15	Pig.................	0 22	0 24	Cod	0 00	0 65½
Alum	0 02½	0 03	Sheet...............	0 30	0 33	Lard, extra	0 00	1 25
Borax	0 00	0 00	*Cut Nails:*			" No. 1	0 00	1 15
Camphor, refined.....	0 65	0 70	Assorted ¼ Shingles,			" Woollen	0 00	1 05
Castor Oil............	0 18	0 28	⅌ 100 ℔............	2 90	3 00	Lubricating, patent...	0 00	0 00
Caustic Soda..........	0 04½	0 05	Shingle alone do ...	3 15	3 25	" Mott's economic	0 50	0 60
Cochineal.............	0 95	1 10	Lathe and 5 dy...	3 30	3 40	Linseed, raw	0 77½	0 85
Cream Tartar	0 00	0 00	*Galvanised Iron:*			" boiled.......	0 82½	0 90
Epsom Salts	0 03	0 04	Assorted sizes....	0 08	0 09	Machinery	0 00	0 00
Extract Logwood......	0 00	0 11	Best. No. 24.......	0 09	0 00	Olive, 2nd, ⅌ gal....	1 45	1 60
Gum Arabic, sorts....	0 30	0 35	" 26.........	0 08	0 08½	" salad	2 00	3 30
Indigo, Madras........	0 75	1 00	" 28.........	0 09	0 09½	" salad, in lots.		
Licorice	0 14	0 45	*Horse Nails:*			qt. ⅌ case...	3 00	3 75
Madder	0 12	0 16	Guest's or Griffin's			Sesame salad, ⅌ gal..	1 60	1 75
Nutgalls	0 00	0 00	assorted sizes....	0 08	0 09	Seal, pale.........	0 70	0 75
Opium	6 70	7 00	For W., ass'd sizes...	0 18	0 19	Spirits Turpentine...	0 65	0 70
Oxalic Acid...........	0 25	0 35	Patent Hammer'd do..	0 17	0 19	Varnish	0 00	0 00
Potash, Bi-tart, ...	0 25	0 28	*Iron (at 4 months):*			Whale...........	0 75	0 80
" Bichromate,	0 15	0 20	Pig—Gartsherrie No1.	24 00	25 00			
Potass Iodide	3 90	4 50	Other brands. No1..	25 00	24 00	**Paints, &c.**		
Senna	0 12½	0 60	No2..	0 00	0 00	White Lead, genuine		
Soda Ash	0 05	0 04	Bar—Scotch, ⅌100 ℔..	2 25	2 50	in Oil, ⅌ 25℔s.....	0 00	2 50
Soda Bicarb	4 50	5 50	Refined	3 00	3 25	Do. No. 1 " ...	0 00	2 25
Tartaric Acid.........	0 37½	0 45	Swedes	5 00	5 50	" 2 " ...	0 00	1 75
Verdigris	0 35	0 40	Hoops—Coopers....	3 00	3 25	" 3 " ...	0 00	1 50
Vitriol, Blue	0 09	0 10	Band	3 00	3 25	White Zinc, genuine..	3 00	3 50
			Boiler Plates.......	3 25	3 50	White Lead, dry......	0 00	0 99
Groceries.			Canada Plates......	4 00	4 25	Red Lead.........	0 07½	0 08½
Coffees:			Union Jaok	0 00	0 00	Venetian Red, Eng'h..	0 02½	0 08½
Java, ⅌ ℔.	0 22@0 24		Pontypool.........	4 00	4 25	Yellow Ochre, Fren'h..	0 02½	0 02
Laguayra, ...	0 17	0 18	Swansea	3 00	4 00	Whiting	0 90	1 25
Rio...................	0 15	0 17	*Lead (at 4 months):*					
Fish:			Bar, ⅌ 100 ℔s.....	0 07	0 07½	**Petroleum.**		
Herrings, Lab. split...	6 75	7 00	Sheet "	0 08	0 00	*(Refined ⅌ gal.)*		
" rouu......	0 00	0 00	Shot..............	0 07½	0 07½	Water white, car'd ...	0 31	
" scaled.....	0 35	0 40	*Iron Wire (net cash):*			" small lots ...	0 00	0 33½
Mackerel, small kitts...	1 00	0 00	No. 6, ⅌ bundle ..	2 70	2 90	Straw, by car load	0 30	—
Loch. Her. wh's frks..	2 20	2 75	" 12, "	3 10	3 30	" small lots....	0 31	0 32
" half "	1 25	1 50	" 13, "	3 40	3 50	Amber, by car load....	0 00	0 00
White Fish & Trout...	3 25	3 50	" 16, "	4 30	4 40	" small lots	0 00	0 00
Salmon, saltwater.....	14 00	15 00	*Powder:*			Benzine	0 00	0 00
Dry Cod, ⅌112 ℔s....	5 00	5 00	Blasting, Canada....	3 50	3 75			
Fruit:			FF "	4 25	4 50	**Produce.**		
Raisins, Layers	2 20	2 25	FFF "	4 75	5 00	*Grain:*		
" M. R. ...	2 20	2 25	Blasting, English ...	4 00	5 00	Wheat, Spring, 60 ℔..	1 00	1 11
" Valentiasnew.	0 08½	0 08½	FF loose.	5 00	6 00	" Fall 60 "	1 20	1 30
Currants, new.........	0 05	0 05½	FFF "	6 00	6 50	Barley .... 48 "	1 25	1 30
" old.........	0 04½	0 04½	*Pressed Spikes (4 mos):*			Peas......... 60 "	0 85	0 89
Figs	0 11	0 12½	Regular sizes 100..	4 00	4 25	Oats .... 34 "	0 51	0 53
Molasses:			Extra "	4 50	5 00	Rye .... 56 "	0 88	0 90
Clayed, ⅌ gal.	0 00	0 35	*Tin Plates (net cash):*			*Seeds:*		
Syrups, Standard ...	0 43	0 44	IC Coke "	7 50	8 00	Clover, choice 60 "..	6 25	6 50
" Golden ...	0 52	0 55	IC Charcoal.......	8 25	8 75	" com'n 68 " ..	6 00	6 25
Rice :			IX "	10 25	10 75	Timothy, cho'e 4 "..	3 50	3 75
Arracan	4 50	4 75	IXX "	12 50	0 00	" inf. to good 48 "	2 00	2 40
Spices:			DC "	7 50	9 00	Flax .... 56 "	1 40	1 60
Cassia, whole, ⅌ ℔...	0 42	0 45	DX "	9 50	10 00	*Flour (per brl.):*		
Cloves	0 11	0 12				Superior extra.......	6 25	6 50
Nutmegs	0 45	0 55	**Hides & Skins ⅌℔**			Extra superfine......	5 00	6 10
Ginger, ground	0 20	0 25	Green rough	0 05½	0 06	Fancysuperfine......	0 00	0 00
" Jamaica, root..	0 20	0 25	Green, salt'd & insp'd..	0 00	0 07	Superfine No. 1......	5 00	5 05
Pepper, black.........	0 09½	0 10	Cured	0 07½	0 08½	" No. 2......	0 00	0 00
Pimento	0 08	0 09	Calfskins, green.....	0 00	0 19	*Oatmeal, (per brl.)*..	5 00	5 25
Sugars:			Calfskins, cured.....	0 00	0 14			
Port Rico, ⅌ ℔......	0 08½	0 08½	" dry	0 18	0 27	**Provisions.**		
Cuba	0 08½	0 08½	Sheepskins, ...	0 70	0 00	Butter, dairy tub ⅌ ℔..	0 23	0 24
Barbadoes (bright)....	0 08½	0 08½	" country....	0 60	0 65	" store packed...	0 21	0 22
Dry Crushed, at 60 d...	0 11½	0 11½				Cheese, new	0 11	0 12
Canada Sugar Refine'y,			*Hops.*			Pork, mess, per brl....	24 42	24 75
yellow No. 2, 60 ds..	0 08½	0 09½	Inferior, ⅌ ℔.......	0 30	0 12	" prime mess....	0 00	0 00
Yellow, No. 2½.......	0 08½	0 09½	Medium............	0 12	0 15	" pume	0 00	0 00
" No. 3.......	0 04½	0 09½	Good	0 15	0 00	Bacon, rough	0 00	0 00
Crushed X :	0 10	0 10½	Fancy	0 00	0 00	" Cumberl'd cut..	0 11	0 12
A	0 05	0 11				" smoked	0 00	0 00
Ground..............	0 00½	0 11½	**Leather,** @ (4 mos.)			Hams, in salt........	0 00	0 00
Extra Ground........	0 05½	0 12½	In lots of less than			" sug. cur. & canv'd..	0 00	0 00
Teas:			50 sides, 10 ⅌ cent			Shoulders, in salt	0 00	0 00
Japan com'n to good ..	4	55	higher.			Lard, in kegs	0 00	0 15
" Fine to choicest..	5	65	Spanish Sole, 1st qual...			Eggs, packed	0 18	0 19
Colored, com. to fine ..	4	75	heavy, weights ⅌ ℔...	0 20	21	Beef Hams	0 00	0 00
Congou & Soueh'ng ...	4	75	Do. 1st qual middle do..	0 22	23	Tallow	0 00	0 09
Oolong, good to fine...	5	65	Do. No. 2, all weights..	0 15	19	Hogs dressed, heavy..	6 50	7 50
Y. Hyson, com to gd ..	4	55	Slaughter heavy	0 25	30	" medium...	0 00	0 00
Medium to choice	6	8	Do. light...........	0 50	00	" light.....	0 00	0 00
Extra choice	8	83	Harness, best	0 32	34			
Gunpowd're. to med...	5	70	" No. 2	0 30	33	**Salt, &c.**		
" med. to fine	0 70	80	Upper heavy........	0 44	38	American brls........	1 48	1 60
			" light.........	0 90	40	Liverpool coarse	1 30	0 40
						Plaster	1 05	1 10
						Water Lime	1 50	0 00

Soap & Candles.

	$ c.	$ c.
D. Crawford & Co.'s ..	8 c.	8 c.
Imperial	0 07¼	0 08
" Golden Bar	0 07	0 07¼
" Silver Bar........	0 07	0 07½
Crown	0 63	0 05½
No. 1	0 03½	0 0.3
Candles	0 09	0 11½

Wines, Liquors, &c.

Ale:		
English, per doz......	2 60	2 65
Guinness Dub Portr..	2 25	2 40
Spirits:		
Pure Jamaica Rum....	1 80	2 25
De Kuyper's H. Gin..	1 45	1 65
Booth's Old Tom......	1 90	2 00
Gin:		
Green, cases..........	4 00	4 25
Booth's Old Tom, c...	6 00	6 25
Wines:		
Port, common	1 00	1 25
" fine old	2 00	4 00
Sherry, common	1 00	1 50
" medium	1 70	1 80
old pale or golden..	2 50	4 00

Brandy:

	8 c.	8 c.
Hennessy's, per gal..	2 30	2 50
Martell's	2 20	2 30
J. Robin & Co.'s "	2 25	2 25
Otard, Dupuy & Cos..	2 25	2 35
Hennely, cases......	8 50	9 00
Brandy, crun. per c..	4 00	4 50
Whiskey:		
Gooderm 36 u. p.....	0 62½	0 65
Old Rye	0 85	0 87
Malt	0 85	0 87½
Toddy	0 85	0 87½
Scotch, per gal.......	1 00	2 10
Irish—Kinnahan's v..	7 00	7 50
" Dunville's Holf'l..	6 00	6 25

Wool.

Fleece, lb.............	0 23	0 25
Pulled "	0 22	0 25

Furs.

Bear...................	3 00	10 00
Beaver................	1 00	1 25
Coon	0 20	0 40
Fisher.................	4 00	6 00
Martin	1 40	1 60
Mink..................	4 00	4 25
Otter..................	4 75	6 00
Spring Rats	0 15	0 17
Fox....................	1 20	1 25

STOCK AND BOND REPORT.

The dates of our quotations are as follows:—Toronto, Nov. 3; Montreal, Nov. 2; Q
Nov. 2; London, Oct. 16.

NAME.	Shares	Paid-up	Divid'd last 6 Months	Dividend Day.	CLOSING PRI	
					Toronto.	Montre'l
BANKS.						
British North America...	82½0	All.	U ct. 3	July and Jan.	104 104½	103½104½
Jacques Cartier..........	50	"	4	1 June, 1 Dec.	104 109	108 109
Montreal	200	"	5		137½ 138	137½137½
Nationale................	50	"	4	1 Nov. 1 May.	....	105 106½
New Brunswick	100	"			....	....
Nova Scotia..............	200	28	7½b6½	Mar. and Sept.	....	....
Du Peuple................	50	"	4	1 Mar., 1 Sept.	104½ 105	104½105½
Toronto	100	"	4	1 Jan., 1 July.	117 117	117 118
Bank of Yarmouth........	....	"			....	....
Canadian Bank of Com'n..	50	95			163½101	163½104½
City Bank Montreal	80	All.	4	1 June, 1 Dec.	102 104	104 105
Commer'l Bank (Md. John)..	100	"	3½ ct.		....	....
Eastern Townships' Bank..	50	"	4	1 July, 1 Jan.	....	95½ 96
Gore	40	....	3½	1 Jan., 1 July.	....	95½ 95
Hal'fax Banking Company..	....	....			....	....
Mechanics' Bank	50	75	4	1 Nov., 1 May.	95 97	....
Merchants Bank of Canada..	100	70	4	1 Jan., 1 July.	106½107	107½ 108
Merchants' Bank (Halifax)..	....	....			....	....
Molson's Bank	50	All.	4	1 Apr., 1 Oct.	107 109	107 109
Niagara District Bank....	100	70	3½	1 Jan., 1 July.	108 108½	102 102½
Ontario Bank	40	All.	4	1 June, 1 Dec.	....	....
People's Bank (Fred'kton)..	100	"			....	....
People's Bank (Halifax) ..	20	"	7 12 m		....	....
Quebec Bank	100	"	3½	1 June, 1 Dec.	99 101	100 101
Royal Canadian Bank	50	50	4	1 Jan., 1 July.	92 92½	93½ 92½
St. Stephens Bank	100	All.			....	....
Union Bank	100	70	4	1 Jan., 1 July.	102½108½	103 104
Union Bank (Halifax).....	100	40	7 12mo	Feb. and Aug.	....	....
MISCELLANEOUS.						
British American Land...	220	44	2½		....	....
British Colonial S. S. Co...	260	22½	2½		....	45 50
Canada Company	22½	All.	5		....	....
Canada Landed Credit Co...	50	$20	3½		72 73	....
Canada Per. B'ldg Society..	50	All.	5		122 123	....
Canada Mining Company...	4	20			....	....
Do. In'l'd Steam Nav. Co...	100	All.	20 12 m		....	107½108½
Do. Glass Company......	100	"	12½		....	9½ ..
Canad'a Loan & Investm't..	25	2½	7		....	....
Canada Agency	10½	4			....	....
Colonial Securities Co.....	....	....			....	....
Freehold Building Society...	100	All.	5		100½ 107½	....
Halifax Steamboat Co.....	100.	"	5		....	....
Halifax Gas Company.....	....	....			....	....
Hamilton Gas Company...	....	....			....	....
Huron Copper Bay Co.....	4	13	20		....	25 50 pm
Lake Huron S. and Co....	4	10¼			....	....
Montreal Mining Compch...	20	8 15			....	2.50 2.90
Do. Telegraph Co.......	40	All.	5		118 120	120 125
Do. Elevating Co.......	60	"	15 12 m		....	160 168
Do. City Gas Co........	40	"	4	15 Mar. 16 Sep.	....	132½ 138
Do. City Pass. R. Co...	50	"	5		....	100½110½
N'v'g Scotia Telegraph ...	100	"			....	....
Quebec and L. S.	8	8½			....	....
Quebec Gas Co...........	200	All.	4	1 Mar., 1 Sep.	....	....
Quebec Street R. R.......	50	25	8		....	114 116
Richelieu Navigation Co...	100	All.	7 p.a.	1 Jan., 1 July.	....	....
St. Lawrence Tow Boat Co...	100	"	5	3 Feb.	....	....
Trust & Loan Co. of U. C...	50	5	3	1 My Au MarFe	105 105½	....
Trust & Loan Co.	20	5	3		....	....
West'n Canada Bldg Soc'y..	50	All.	5		114½ 115	....

INSURANCE COMPANIES.

ENGLISH.—*Quotations on the London Market.*

No. of Shares.	Last Dividend.	Name of Company.	Shares per cal.	Amount paid.	Last
20,000		Briton Medical and General Life....	10	..	5½
50,000	7½	Commer'l Union, Fire, Life and Mar.	50	5	5½
24,000	8	City of Glasgow	25	2¼	..
5,000	9½	Edinburgh Life	100	15	30½x
400,000	5—½ yr	European Life and Guarantee.....	27	11s6	4s 6d
100,000	10	Rtna Fire and Marine	10	1½	..
20,000	5	Guardian	100	50	51½
24,000	12	Imperial Fire....................	500	50	34½
7,500	9½	Imperial Life	100	10	10½
100,000	10	Lancashire Fire and Life	20	2	2½s
10,000	11	Life Association of Scotland	40	7½	23
35,862	45s. p.sh	London Assurance Corporation ...	25	12½	48
10,000	5	London and Lancashire Life	10	1	1
87,504	40	Liverp'l & London & Globe F. & L.	20	2	7½
20,000	5	National Union Life	5	1	..
20,000	12½	Northern Fire and Life..........	100	5	10½
40,000	'08,l0s 5s.	North British and Mercantile ...	50	6½	16 16½
40,000	50	Ocean Marine	25	5	20
2,500	£5 12s.	Provident Life...................	100	10	38
	4½ p.s	Phoenix	..	..	130
200,000	2½—h. yr.	Queen Fire and Life	10	1	15–16ths
100,000	3s. 1os.4d	Royal Insurance.................	20	3	4¾
90,000	10	Scottish Provincial Fire and Life ..	50	2½	4½
14,000	25	Standard Life	50	12	65
4,000	5	Star Life	25	1	..

CANADIAN.

8,000	4	British America Fire and Marine..	$50	$25	96
......	4	Canada Life	..	..	56
4000	7½	Montreal Assurance	£50	£5	135
10,000	3	Provincial Fire and Marine......	60	11	....
......		Quebec Fire	40	32½	ä 19½
......	8	" Marine	100	40	59-95
10,000	5 7 no's.	Western Assurance	40	6	....

RAILWAYS.

	Sha's Paid	Montr'l	London.
Atlantic and St. Lawrence.............	£100	All.	50 57
Buffalo and Lake Huron..............	20½	"	..
Do. do Preference........	10	"	5½ 6½
Buff., Brantb & Goderich, 6%n, 1872-3-4..	100	"	60 70
Champlain and St. Lawrence	..	0 11	..
Do. do Pref. 10 ℔ ct......	..	80	..
Grand Trunk	10½	16 17	16 16½
Do. Eq. G. M. Ids. 1 ch. 6%n.......	100	"	81 82
Do. First Preference, 5 ℔c	100	"	49 51
Do. Deferred, 3 ℔ ct..............	100	"	..
Do. Second Pref. Bonds 5%n........	10½	"	38 40
Do. do Deferred, 3 ℔ ct.......	100	"	..
Do. Third Pref. Stock, 4 ℔ct......	100	"	25 30
Do. " Deferred, 2 ℔ ct.........	100	"	..
Do. Fourth Pref. Stock, 3pc........	100	"	12 20
Do. " Deferred, 3 ℔ ct.........	100	"	..
Great Western	20½	13 14	13½ 14½
Do. New	25	28	..
Do. 6 ℔ c. Bds, due 1873-76.......	100	All.	132 132½
Do. 5½ ℔c. Ids, due 1877-78......	100	"	92 94
Marine Railway, Halifax, $250, all	$250	"	..
Northern, of Canada, 6½n 1st Pref Bds....	100	"	90 93

EXCHANGE.

	Halifax	Montr'l.	Quebec.	Toronto.
Bank on London, 60 days	13½	9½ 9½	9½ 9¾	9½ 9½
sight or 75 days date	12 12½	9½ 9	9 9½	....
Private do.	....	7½ 8½	....	....
Private, with documents.....	....	25¼ 26	25 26	75½
Bank on New York...........	....	20½ 26½	25 27	....
Private do.	....	par	par ½ dis.	par ½ dis.
Gold Drafts do.	....	3½ 3½	....	3½ 4
Silver	....	....	....	....

SECURITIES.	London.	Montreal.	Quebeo.
Canadian Gov't Deb. 6 ℔ ct. stg.......	....	103 101	100½ 101
Do. do. 6 do due Ja. & Jul. 1877-84.......	103 107	....	....
Do. do. 6 do. Feb. & Aug.........	104 106	....	....
Do. do. 6 do. Mch. & Sep.........	104 106	....	....
Do. do. 5 ℔ ct. cur., 1883	91 93	90 91	83½ 90
Do. do. 5 do. stg. 1885..........	....	90 91	90 90½
Do. do. 6 do. cur...............	....	....	....
Dominion 6 p. c. 1878 cy...........	....	103 104	102½ 103
Hamilton Corporation..............	....	....	....
Montreal Harbor, 6 ℔ ct. d. 1800.......	....	....	....
Do. do. 7 do. 1870........	....	100 100½	....
Do. do. 6½ do. 1873........	....	....	....
Do. do. 6 do. 1875........	....	92½ 93½	....
Do. Corporation, 6 ℔ c. 1801......	....	105 105½	104 105
Do. 7 p. c. stock	....	....	....
Do. Water Works, 9 ℔ c. stg. 1878..	....	95½ 93½	....
New Brunswick, 6 ℔ ct., jan. and July..	102 104	....	....
Nova Scotia, 6 ℔ ct., July, 1875......	100 102	....	....
Ottawa City 6 ℔ c. d., 1880	....	92½ 93½	....
Quebec Harbour, 6 ℔ c. d. 1882.......	....	....	60
Do. do. 8 do. 1883..........	....	....	79
Do. do. 8 do. 1884..........	....	....	85
Do. City, 7 ℔ p.s. d. 5 years	....	80 90	95 96
Do. do. 6 do. 2 do.	....	....	88 89
Do. do. 7 do. 2½ do.	....	....	97 98
Do. Water Works, 7 ℔ ct., 4 years ..	....	....	96 97
Do. do. 6 do. 3 do.	....	....	103½ 94
Toronto Corporation	....	99 99½	....

Insurance.

BEAVER
Mutual Insurance Association.

HEAD OFFICE—20 TORONTO STREET,
TORONTO.

ES LIVE STOCK against death from any cause.
only Canadian Company having authority to do this
business.

R. L. DENISON,
President.

P'REILLY,
  at Secretary.   8-1y-25

HOME DISTRICT
al Fire Insurance Company.

OFFICE:

West Corner of Yonge and Adelaide Streets,
TORONTO.—(UP STAIRS.)

tES Dwelling Houses, Stores, Warehouses, Merdise, Furniture, &c.

PRESIDENT—The Hon. J. McMURRICH.
VICE-PRESIDENT—JOHN BURNS, Esq.
JOHN RAINS, Secretary.

AGENTS:

WRIGHT, Esq., Hamilton: FRANCIS STEVENS, Esq.,
Barrie; Messrs. GIBBS & BRO., Oshawa.
8-1y

THE PRINCE EDWARD COUNTY
ual Fire Insurance Company.

HEAD OFFICE.—PICTON, ONTARIO.
id, L. B. STINSON; Vice-President, W. A. RICHARDS.
tors; H. A. McPaul, James Cavan, James Johnson,
eMill, William Delong.—Treasurer, David Barker
y, John Twigg; Solicitor, B. J. Fitzgerald.

Company is established upon strictly Mutual prin-
les, insuring farming and isolated property, (not
ns,) in Townships only, and offers great advantages
rers, at low rates for five years, without the expense
ewal. This Company has existed 12 years, during
eriod it has adjusted all losses in a satisfactory
. It is managed with strict economy, and affords
rtunity of insuring with safety and reliance, and
ttle expense, which accounts for its long standing
successful business which it has been and is now

n, June 15, 1866   9-1y

Hartford Fire Insurance Company.

HARTFORD, CONN.

Capital and Assets over Two Million Dollars.

$2,026,220.29.

CHARTERED 1810.

old and reliable Company, having an established
 dness in Canada of more than thirty years standing,
pplied with the provisions of the new Insurance
nd made a special deposit of

$100,000

te Government for the security of policy-holders, and
utinue to grant policies upon the same favorable
as heretofore.

ially low rates on first-class dwellings and farm
ty for a term of one or more years.

ross as heretofore promptly and equitably adjusted.
E. CHAFFEY & CO., AGENTS.
uto, Ont.

OBERT WOOD, GENERAL AGENT FOR CANADA?

Geo. Girdlestone,
, Life, Marine, Accident, and Stock Insurance
gent

Very best Companies represented.
or, Ont. June, 1868

Insurance.

The Standard Life Assurance Company,
Established 1825.

WITH WHICH IS NOW UNITED

THE COLONIAL LIFE ASSURANCE COMPANY.

Head Office for Canada:

MONTREAL—STANDARD COMPANY'S BUILDINGS,
No. 47 GREAT ST. JAMES STREET.

Manager—W. M. RAMSAY. *Inspector*—RICH'D BULL.

THIS Company having deposited the sum of ONE HUN-
DRED AND FIFTY THOUSAND DOLLARS with the Receiver-
General, in conformity with the Insurance Act passed last
Session, Assurances will continue to be carried out at
moderate rates and on all the different systems in practice.

AGENT FOR TORONTO—HENRY PELLATT,
KING STREET.

AGENT FOR HAMILTON—JAMES BANCROFT.
6-6mos.

Fire and Marine Assurance.

THE BRITISH AMERICA

ASSURANCE COMPANY.

HEAD OFFICE:

CORNER OF CHURCH AND COURT STREETS.

TORONTO.

. BOARD OF DIRECTION :

Hon. G. W. Allan, M.L.C.,	A. Joseph, Esq.,
George J. Boyd, Esq.,	Peter Paterson, Esq.,
Hon. W. Cayley,	G. P. Ridout, Esq.,
Richard S. Cassels, Esq.,	E. H. Rutherford, Esq.,

Thomas C. Street, Esq.

Governor:

GEORGE PERCIVAL RIDOUT, Esq.

Deputy Governor:

PETER PATERSON, Esq.

Fire Inspector: Marine Inspector:
E ROBY O'BRIEN.   CAPT. R. COURNEEN.

Insurances granted on all descriptions of property
against loss and damage by fire and the perils of inland
navigation.

Agencies established in the principal cities, towns, and
ports of shipment throughout the Province.

THOS. WM. BIRCHALL,
22-1y   Managing Director.

Edinburgh Life Assurance Company.

Founded 1823.

HEAD OFFICE—22 GEORGE STREET, EDINBURGH.

Capital, ... £500,000 *Ster'g.*
Accumulated and Invested Funds, £1,000,000 "

HEAD OFFICE IN CANADA :

WELLINGTON STREET, TORONTO.

SUB-AGENTS THROUGHOUT THE PROVINCE.

J. HILLYARD CAMERON,
Chairman, Canadian Board.

DAVID HIGGINS,
Secretary, Canadian Board.   3-3m

Queen Fire and Life Insurance Company,
OF LIVERPOOL AND LONDON,

ACCEPTS ALL ORDINARY FIRE RISKS

on the most favorable terms.

LIFE RISKS

Will be taken on terms that will compare favorably with
other Companies.

CAPITAL,   £2,000,000 Stg.

CHIEF OFFICES—Queen's Buildings, Liverpool, and
Gracechurch Street London.
CANADA BRANCH OFFICE—Exchange Buildings, Montreal.
Resident Secretary and General Agent,
A. MACKENZIE FORBES,
13 St. Sacrament St., Merchants' Exchange, Montreal.
WM. ROWLAND, Agent, Toronto.   1-1y

Insurance.

Reliance Mutual Life Assurance
Society.
(Established, 1840,) OF LONDON, E. C.

Accumulated Funds, over $1,000,000.

Annual Income, $900,000.

THE entire Profits of this long-established Society belong
to the Policy-holders.

HEAD OFFICE FOR DOMINION—MONTREAL.
T. W. GRIFFITH, Managerd Sec'y.
15-1y   WM. HENDERSON, Agent for Toronto.

Ætna Insurance Company of Dublin,
The number of Shareholders exceeds Five Hundred.

Capital, $5,000,000—Annual Income nearly $1,000,000.

THIS Company takes Fire and Marine Risks on the most
favorable terms.

. T. W. GRIFFITH, Manager for Canada.
Chief office for Dominion—Corner St. Francois Xavier
and St. Sacrament Sts., Montreal.
15-1y   WM. HENDERSON, Agent for Toronto

Scottish Provincial Assurance Co.
Established 1825.

CAPITAL .... £1,000,000 STERLING.
INVESTED IN CANADA (1854) .... $500,000.

Canada Head Office, Montreal.

LIFE DEPARTMENT.

CANADA BOARD OF DIRECTORS:
HUGH TAYLOR, Esq., Advocate,
Hon. CHARLES WILSON, M. L. C.
WM. SACHE, Esq., Banker,
JACKSON RAE, Esq., Banker.

WM. FRASER, Esq. M. D., Medical Adviser.

The special advantages to be derived from Insuring in
this office are :—Strictly Moderate Rates of Premium ;
Large Bonus (intermediate bonus guaranteed ;) Liberal
Surrender Value, under policies relinquished by assured ;
and Extensive Limits of Residence and Travel. All business disposed of in Canada, without reference to parent
office.

A DAVIDSON PARKER,
Resident Secretary
G. L. MADDISON,
15-1yr   AGENT FOR TORONTO.

Lancashire Insurance Company.

CAPITAL, - - - - - - - - £2,000,000 Sterling

FIRE RISKS
Taken at reasonable rates of premium, and'
ALL LOSSES SETTLED PROMPTLY,
By the undersigned, without reference elsewhere.
S. C. DUNCAN-CLARK & CO.,
General Agents for Ontario,
N. W. Corner of King & Church Streets,
25-1y   TORONTO.

Ætna Fire & Marine Insurance Company.

INCORPORATED 1819. CHARTER PERPETUAL.

CASH CAPITAL, - - - - $3,000,000

LOSSES PAID IN 50 YEARS, 23,500,000 00.

JULY, 1868.

ASSETS.
(At Market Value.)

Cash in hand and in Bank	$544,842 30
Real Estate	258,267 29
Mortgage Bonds	925,245 06
Bank Stock	1,272,670 00
United States, State and City Stock, and other Public Securities	2,049,855 51

Total $5,052,880 19

LIABILITIES.

Claims not Due, and Unadjusted	$409,803 55
Amount required by Mass. and New York for Re-Insurance	1,405,267 15

E. CHAFFEY & CO., Agents.
50-8m

Insurance.

ÆTNA
Live Stock Insurance Company

LICENSED BY THE DOMINION GOVERNMENT TO DO BUSINESS IN CANADA.

THE following Accidents, this month, show the importance of Insuring your Horses and Cattle against Death from any cause, or Theft, in the Ætna Insurance Company:

MONTREAL, September 16, 1868.
At a fire last night, in the sheds behind Ripin's Hotel, St. Joseph Street, three valuable Stock Horses were destroyed, "Young Clydesdale" and "Emigrant," belonging to the Huntingdon Agricultural Society—the former worth $900, and the latter $1,700; and "Old Beauharnois" cost $1,000, belonging to the Beauharnois Society.

PORT COLBORNE, September 18, 1868.
HORSES DROWNED.—Two horses belonging to Mr. Briggs, of Port Colborne, and four owned by Mr. Julien, of Port Dalhousie, were drowned in the Canal, near the Junction, early this morning.

A fire at the Glasgow Hotel, Montreal, this morning, destroyed two horses. The fire was caused by drunkenness on the part of the stable man.

MONTREAL, September 24, 1868.
A fire in F. X. Cusson's stables, St. Joseph Street, last night, destroyed three horses.

E. L. SNOW, GENERAL AGENT, Montreal

Agents for Ontario:—
SCOTT & WALMSLEY,
67nov11y   Ontario Hall, Church Street, Toronto.

The Liverpool and London and Globe Insurance Company

INVESTED FUNDS:
FIFTEEN MILLIONS OF DOLLARS.

DAILY INCOME OF THE COMPANY:
TWELVE THOUSAND DOLLARS.

LIFE INSURANCE,
WITH AND WITHOUT PROFITS.

FIRE INSURANCE
On every description of Property, at Lowest Remunerative Rates.
JAMES FRASER, AGENT,
5 King Street West.
Toronto, 1868.   58-1y

Briton Medical and General Life Association,
with which is united the
BRITANNIA LIFE ASSURANCE COMPANY.

Capital and Invested Funds............£750,000 Sterling.

ANNUAL INCOME, £220,000 STG. ;
Yearly increasing at the rate of £25,000 Sterling.

THE important and peculiar feature originally introduced by this Company, in applying the periodical Bonuses, so as to make Policies payable during life, without any higher rate of premiums being charged, has caused the success of the BRITON MEDICAL AND GENERAL to be almost unparalleled in the history of Life Assurance. *Life Policies on the Profit Scale become payable during the lifetime of the Assured, thus rendering a Policy of Assurance a means of subsistence in old age, as well as a protection for a family,* and a more valuable security to creditors in the event of early death; and effectually meeting the often urged objection, that persons do not themselves reap the benefit of their own prudence and forethought.

No extra charge made to members of Volunteer Corps for services within the British Provinces.
☞ TORONTO AGENCY, 5 KING ST. WEST.
oct17—9-1yr   JAMES FRASER, Agent.

Phœnix Insurance Company,
BROOKLYN, N.Y.

PHILANDER SHAW,   STEPHEN CROWELL,
Secretary.   President.
Cash Capital, $1,000,000. Surplus, $666,416.02. Total, $1,666,416.02. Entire Income from all sources for 1866 was $2,191,839.82.

CHARLES G. FORTIER, *Marine Agent.*
Ontario Chambers, Toronto, Ont.   19-1y

Insurance.

The Victoria Mutual
FIRE INSURANCE COMPANY OF CANADA.

Insures only Non-Hazardous Property, at Low Rates.

BUSINESS STRICTLY MUTUAL.

GEORGE H. MILLS, *President.*
W. D. BOOKER, *Secretary.*

HEAD OFFICE ....HAMILTON, ONTARIO
aug 15-1yr

The Ætna Life Insurance Company.

AN attack, abounding with errors, having been made upon the Ætna Life Insurance Co. by the editor of the *Montreal Daily News* ; and certain agents of British Companies being now engaged in handing around copies of the attack, thus seeking to damage the Company's standing, —I have pleasure in laying before the public the following certificate, bearing the signatures of the Presidents and Cashiers who happened to be in their Offices of *every Bank in Hartford;* also that of the President and Secretary of the old Ætna Fire Insurance Company :
"*To whom it may concern.*:
"We, the undersigned, regard the Ætna Life Insurance Company, of this city, as one of the most successful and prosperous Insurance Companies in the States,— entirely reliable, responsible, and honourable in all its dealings, and most worthy of public confidence and patronage."

Lucius J. Hendee, President Ætna Fire Insurance Co., and late Treasurer of the State of Connecticut.
J. Goodnow, Secretary Ætna Fire Insurance Co.
C. H. Northam, President, and J. B. Powell, Cashier National Bank.
C. T. Hillyer, President Charter Oak National Bank.
E. D. Tiffany, President First National Bank.
G. T. Davis, President City National Bank.
F. S. Riley, Cashier,   do.   do.   do.
John C. Tracy, President of Farmers' and Mechanics' National Bank.
M. W. Graves, Cashier Conn. River Banking Co.
H. A. Redfield, Cashier Phœnix National Bank.
O. G. Terry, President Ætna National Bank.
J. R. Redfield, Cashier National Exchange Bank.
John G. Root, Assistant Cashier American National Bank.
George F. Hills, Cashier State Bank of Hartford.
Jas. Potter, Cashier Hartford National Bank.
Hartford, Nov. 26, 1867.

Many of the above-mentioned parties are closely connected with other Life Insurance Companies, but all unhesitatingly commend our Company as "reliable, responsible, honorable in all its dealings, and most worthy of public confidence and patronage.
JOHN GARVIN,
General Agent, Toronto Street.
Toronto, Dec. 3. 1867.   16-1y

Life Association of Scotland.

INVESTED FUNDS
UPWARDS OF £1,000,000 STERLING.

THIS Institution differs from other Life Offices, in that the

BONUSES FROM PROFITS
Are applied on a special system for the Policy-holder's
PERSONAL BENEFIT AND ENJOYMENT DURING HIS OWN LIFETIME,
WITH THE OPTION OF
LARGE BONUS ADDITIONS TO THE SUM ASSURED.

The Policy-holder thus obtains
A LARGE REDUCTION OF PRESENT OUTLAY
OR
A PROVISION FOR OLD AGE OF A MOST IMPORTANT AMOUNT IN ONE CASH PAYMENT, OR A LIFE ANNUITY.

Without any payment or outlay whatever beyond the ordinary Assurance Premium for the Sum Assured, which remains in fact for Policy-holder's heirs, or other purposes.

CANADA—MONTREAL—Place d'Armes.

DIRECTORS:
DAVID TORRANCE, Esq., (D. Torrance & Co.)
GEORGE MOFFATT, (Gillespie, Moffatt & Co.)
ALEXANDER MORRIS, Esq., M.P., Barrister, Perth.
Sir G. E. CARTIER, M.P., Minister of Militia.
PETER REDPATH, Esq., (J. Redpath & Son).
J. H. R. MOLSON, Esq., (J. H. R. Molson & Br. s.)
Solicitors—Messrs. TORRANCE & MORRIS.
Medical Officer—H. PALMER HOWARD, Esq., M.D
Secretary—P. WARDLAW.
Inspector of Agencies—JAMES B. M. CHIPMAN.   y

Insurance.

North British and Mercantile Insu Company.

Established 1809.

HEAD OFFICE, - - CANADA - - MO

TORONTO BRANCH:
Local Offices, Nos. 4 & 6 WELLINGTON ST
Fire Department, ... R. N. C

Life Department, ... H. L. H
29-1y

Phœnix Fire Assurance Comp
LOMBARD ST. AND CHARING CROS
LONDON, ENG.

Insurances effected in all parts of the '

Claims paid
WITH PROMPTITUDE and LIBERAL
MOFFATT, MURRAY & BEATT
Agents for To
36 Yonge

The Commercial Union Assur Company,
19 & 20 CORNHILL, LONDON, ENGLAND.
Capital, £2,000,000 Stg—Invested over $2,00

FIRE DEPARTMENT.—Insurance granted o scriptions of property at reasonable rates.

LIFE DEPARTMENT.—The success of th has been unprecedented—*NINETY PERCENT,* miums now in hand. First year's premiums w $100,000. Economy of management guaranteed security. Moderate rates.

OFFICE—383 & 387 ST PAUL STREET, MONT
MORLAND, WATSON &
General Agents for
FRED. COLE, *Secretary.*
Inspector of Agencies—T. C. LIVINGSTO
W. M. WESTMACOTT, *Agent at*
16-1y

Phœnix Mutual Life Insurance
HARTFORD, CONN.

Accumulated Fund, $2,000,000, Income, $1,6

THIS Company, established in 1851, is one of reliable Companies doing business in the co has been steadily prospering. The *Massachusetts Reports* show that in nearly all important ma superior to the general average of Companies. intending assurers the following reasons, amon for preferring it to other companies :

It is purely Mutual It allows the Insured and reside in any portion of the United States a It throws out almost all restriction on occupatio Policies. It will, if desired, take a note for p Premium, thus combining all the advantages of all cash company. Its Dividends are declare and applied in reduction of Premiums. In every case on Premiums paid. The Divide Phœnix have averaged fifty per cent. yearly settlement of Policies, a Dividend will be allow year the policy has been in force. The numb demds will always equal the outstanding Notes. losses promptly—during the existence never l texted a claim. It issues Policies for the ben ried Women beyond the reach of their husband Creditors may also insure the lives of Debtors. are all *Non-forfeiting,* as it always allows the surrender his Policy, should he desire, the Co ing a paid-up Policy therefor. This import will commend itself to all. The Inducements by the Phœnix are better and more liberal th any other Company. Its rate of Mortality is low and under the average.
Parties contemplating *Life Insurance* will fin interest to call and examine our system. Po payable either in Gold or American currency.
ANGUS R. BETH
General Mana
Dominio

Office: 104 ST. FRANÇOIS XAVIER ST. MON
☞ Active and energetic Agents and wanted in every town and village, to whom lib ments will be given.

PRINTED AT THE DAILY TELEGRAPH HOUSE, BAY ST., COR. KING

THE CANADIAN
MONETARY TIMES
AND
INSURANCE CHRONICLE.

'EVOTED TO FINANCE, COMMERCE, INSURANCE, BANKS, RAILWAYS, NAVIGATION, MINES, INVESTMENT, PUBLIC COMPANIES, AND JOINT STOCK ENTERPRISE.

L. II—NO. 13.   TORONTO, THURSDAY, NOVEMBER 12, 1868.   { SUBSCRIPTION   82 YEAR.

Mercantile.

Meetings.

THE GORE BANK.

The adjourned general meeting of the shareholders of the Gore Bank was held in Hamilton on the 2nd November, Mr. Edward Martin, the President in the chair. The report of the committee appointed on the 3rd of August last, to examine and report upon the affairs of the bank, also a special report from the President and Directors, were read by the Secretary, Mr. McCracken. (Both those documents were published in No. 11.) Before the adoption of the Report should be moved, the Chairman desired to afford any information which should be additionally desired on the part of the shareholders, and he would be prepared to answer any enquiries to be put by gentlemen present. The statements presented in both reports were very complete, and covered nearly all the ground for enquiry. They showed a loss of $80,000 on note and bill transactions; but it was fair to explain that this had occurred upon only two or three special transactions, and that therefore it was not to be assumed that the general character of their bank business had been unremunerative. The exceptional instances he would not define by name, as a portion of the paper was still recoverable, and it would not be prudent to refer in precise terms to unclosed business. The main question, however, was what was best to be done to meet these losses, and their proposition had been to reduce the value of their stock to, say, sixty cents on the dollar. Legislation would be required for the various alterations proposed to be effected in their position, and that they (the directors) desired to take authority to seek for.

Some questions were put by stockholders concerning a discrepancy in the Statements of the value of the assets, which the President explained amounted to only about $6,000, which was further reduced by $3,000. Several stockholders expressed gratification that the discrepancy was so small.

It was moved by A. T. Wood, Esq., seconded by Colonel Martin, "That the report of the committee be adopted."

Mr. Street was in favour of the adoption of the report, with the exception of the clause for changing the name of the bank. He could see no good reason for this change, while there were, he considered, several weighty reasons against it. A large expense would be incurred, for no benefit that he could see. Some of the assets of the Bank, he thought, were undervalued in the statement. They had Government debentures amounting to $82,000 odd, face value, and these were put down at present market value, $86,000 or so less. The Government compelled the bank to hold these securities; why, therefore, should they be reckoned at less than par value? He thought there was an inconsistency here.

Mr. Irving said that the adoption of the report would not bind the meeting to change the name of the Bank, as it must rest with an Act of Parliament. The adoption of the report would not bind the shareholders to act upon the recommendation of the Directors. He had heard the reasons assigned for the change of name : 1st, That under the name of the Bank of Hamilton, the institution would rise above a feeling which had been raised

in connection with the name of the Gore Bank ; 2nd, That the bills of the Gore Bank at present were executed in a style to invite counterfeiting. A considerable gain was anticipated from the past destruction of their current circulation, and that could not be correctly estimated without some such step as calling it in. He believed that a remodelling of their note plates was necessary in any case. He did not like the idea of amending a report that would in no way compromise the meeting. The matter of changing the name would be an after consideration.

Mr. Street thought the adoption of the report would be binding upon the meeting to procure the changing of the name of the Bank.

Dr. Clark said that the Bank had nothing to thank the City of Hamilton for; the people of Hamilton were the first to labor for its embarrassment when it fell into difficulty. He did not see the ground for the proposed change of name of this old established institution. The change of name was mainly of interest to Hamilton folk. Agencies had been closed where they were more profitable than Hamilton. At Guelph, for example, there had not been $2,000 lost in 25 years.

Mr. McMillan stated the recommending of a change in the name of the Bank, and a new issue of bills, was based mainly on the fact that the bills were counterfeited, and that the Bank had recently received eighty four bills that were counterfeit.

It was then moved in amendment by T. C. Street, Esq., seconded by D. Thompson, Esq., that when the report of the Directors is adopted, the last clause be omitted."—Lost.

A second amendment, moved by Dr. Wm. Clarke, seconded by Dr. W. L. Billings, to the effect— "That the report of the Directors now read be not adopted as a whole ; but that it be read clause by clause," was also lost.

Dr. Billings having strongly urged the desirability winding up their affairs, a long discussion ensued as to how votes were to be taken upon such a vital matter, and the Chairman having finally stated that he would put Dr. Billings' resolution after the business in hand, and would count votes by shares, the Report was adopted without further discussion.

Dr. Billings then moved, seconded by Dr. Clarke, a resolution affirmatory of the advisability of winding up the affairs of the Bank, and empowering the Board to take the necessary steps for doing so. He was actuated by no feeling of hostility in bringing forward such a measure, but hitherto their transactions had been very unfortunate and their capital had been lost without any proper account having been given of it. Shares had been maintained at quotations of fictitious value, and shareholders had been induced to accept moderate dividends on the understanding that a surplus was being devoted to the creation of a Rest. That confidence had been undeserved, and moreover, he doubted if expenses of management would be any less upon a capital of $500,000 than upon one of $1,000,000. The same staff would be required. [No, no. A Shareholder— Reduction of the staff has commenced already.] It would be found very much more difficult to reduce an existing establishment than to originate a new one on an economical basis. Repeating the previously offered arguments against the cost of alteration, he declared himself prepared to accept the 60 cents which his dollar was said to be worth, in preference to running further risk in connection with it. He did not of course propose that any less sum than that estimated by the valuators should be accepted, but this he should be pleased to realize, knowing that he could employ it at seven per cent. without either risk or trouble.

Mr. Irving said that any resolution now passed would only take the form of a recommendation, which would have to be considered before the Legislature. He was in favour of carrying the Bank on, as he believed that would be the most effective method for shareholders to realize their investments. He did not wish to press the project of a change of name, but thought unanimity of purpose and feeling was the first object to be attained among shareholders. He spoke at length in explaining his method of re-establishing the Bank on a new basis, and submitted the draft of a Bill he proposed to have presented to to the Legislature.

Moved by Mr. Irving, seconded by Mr. Winer,— "Whereas, by the report of the committee appointed at the annual meeting of the shareholders, held on the 3rd day of August last, to enquire into the affairs of the Bank, it appears that the balance at credit of the capital account on 31st August last was $493,813 43, and it being expedient that the shares in the capital stock now paid up should be reduced to meet the losses made on capital, be it

Resolved: That it is expedient to amend the charter of this Bank in the following particulars:
1. To reduce the shares now issued from $40 to $24 each share.
2. To increase the qualification of a director to the number of shares which shall be equal to $1,000 of capital stock wholly paid up.

And the president and directors are hereby authorized and instructed to procure the passage of a Bill by the Legislature of Canada, embodying the foregoing provisions, and are further empowered to insert such provisions therein as may seem best to obtain or preserve the right of issuing the stock to the previously authorized amount of one million of dollars, to determine the amount in which the share capital can most conveniently be divided, and to change the day for the annual meeting of shareholders."

Mr. Triller asked when the sixty cents could be realized. From past experience he would be rather disposed to take this amount if he could get it. Their charter would expire in 1870, and they might meanwhile liquidate gradually.

The Chairman said that it would be impossible to announce exactly how long it would take to collect and distribute a million of money, nor could losses be avoided where sales were forced. To let the charter expire was merely to let the bank bleed to death, as nobody could be expected to continue dealing with an institution that was doomed, when they might as easily do business with its competitors.

Mr. McMillan having pointed out the fact that the business of the bank was generally lucrative, notwithstanding some individual losses,

A Shareholder remarked that the value of their stock had risen five to ten per cent. in a few days, which he attributed mainly to the determination of the Board to recommend going on. Many of these gentlemen who desired to wind up, and who spoke so feelingly of their prospective losses, would not lose so much if they lost all they had invested (laughter), and he did not think it was fair for them, or others whose wealth could afford a sacrifice, to force the property of poorer men to whom it was comparatively of greater value.

Several other shareholders expressed satisfaction at the Report, and confidence in the position of the Institution. An opinion was expressed that if their temporary difficulties had not been published there would have been no necessity for very extraordinary efforts to meet them.

In reply to an assertion that assets forced upon the market would necessarily be sacrificed,

Dr. Clarke enquired what reliance was to be placed upon a statement of account representing as tangible property, assets which it seemed were only hypothetically serviceable. He would allow those who desired to carry on the Bank to do so.

A shareholder suggested that Dr. Clarke should sell his shares.

The Chairman pointed out that their resources were by no means insufficient for progress. They had not merely their capital of $500,000, but the disposal of $400,000 public money. And surely no one would say that a million was not enough to work with. He thought the suggestion regarding the over-estimate of their debentures a very just one. He showed also that the bank premises had been set down at only $12,000, while the ordinary rate of office rent in Hamilton justified them in standing at a considerably higher figure. They had thus seen that their circumstances had been stated at the worst, but even Dr. Clarke himself was inclined to estimate their property at 75 cents on the dollar, and this could surely be considered as no adequate reason for winding up their business. It was not business like to give up on account of losses, and they have found themselves at the bottom of their loss. Winding up was an expensive and tedious proceeding, and would be conducted without any incoming to sustain its drain. It was admitted that the business in Galt and Simcoe had been profitable, and lately that in Hamilton had been altogether profitable. Their business had been generally of the best character, and, although much of it had been lost, the cream of it was still recoverable. They had here prosperity at their doors. Errors of the past need not be repeated. There were rocks ahead to be easily avoided, and the lesson against too many eggs in one nest was not one to be readily forgotten.

After some further desultory conversational discussion the question was put on Mr. Irving's amendment (seconded by Mr. Winer), 40 hands were held up for the amendment and 12 against it. Dr. Billings and Dr. Clarke consenting thereupon to withdraw their proposition in deference to the views of the majority (applause), Mr. Irving's amendment was put as a substantive motion and carried unanimously, the result being received with enthusiasm.

A conversation took place regarding the sale of some bank property to a son of the Hon. S. Mills (a director) which the latter desired to have approved by the meeting. The matter had been brought up by letter from Mr. Thompson to the Board, Mr. Thompson having Mr. Chas. Magill's authority for stating that he (C. M.) would have purchased it at a higher figure had he been permitted. Mr. Cassels being called upon by the chairman, an elaborate explanation was offered.

It was thereupon moved by James Bain, Esq., of Galt, seconded by John Triller, Esq. of Wellington Square,—"That whereas the Shareholders, at the present Meeting, have been informed that the Directors have lately entered into a contract with Jas. H. Mills Esq., of Hamilton, for the sale to him of the property in Hamilton formerly owned by the late Colin C. Ferrie, and containing about nine acres, at the sum of nine thousand dollars, and having learnt from the President and Directors the particulars and circumstances of the sale,

Be it Resolved,—That it is the opinion of this Meeting that the Directors have exercised a proper discretion in making the said sale; and that in so far as the same can be effectual, the Shareholders now assembled confirm and ratify the same."—Carried.

Dr. Billings moved, seconded by Mr. Winer, a resolution authorizing an application to Parliament for change of title to that of Bank of Hamilton. He thought every facility should be afforded the Board for carrying on the business of the Institution profitably.

A general discussion ensued, Dr. Clarke suggesting the Wellington, Grey and Bruce as the new name. The proposal was then put, declared lost, and, by permission withdrawn.

It was then moved by Mr. Irving, seconded Col. Martin, and resolved:—
"The shareholders present at this adjourned meeting, having received the report presented to them by the directors, and having heard the planations of the President upon the situation of the Bank, the circumstances attendant upon securing certain debts due to the Bank, and disposal of unproductive property, desire to press the great obligations which have been referred upon the entire body of the shareholders the labour and attention which the Board bestowed in placing the affairs of the Bank a sound basis.

Be it therefore resolved: That a vote of the be offered to the Directors for the care given the general interests of the Bank, and that expression of full confidence in their management be recorded on the minutes of the meeting."

The President having been requested to the chair, and Mr. Street to take the same, resolution was put and carried unanimously.

The President, for himself and the Directors acknowledged the compliment. He said the Cassels desired to make a statement with regard a matter which they had all heard talked of.

Mr. Cassels said that one of the Directors, McQuesten, had intimated something to the that the former, as Cashier, had misinformed otherwise given an erroneous impression to the latter, as to the amount of certain large advances which had been made by the Bank, under his C.'s) management. The books were, at meeting, regularly placed before the Directors and the standing of each account was there in tail, in a form the simplest and easiest for reference that had yet been devised. If Dr. McQuesten not examined the books, it was his own fault (Mr. Cassels,) distinctly denied that he had kept back information from the Board, or any member of it.

Since his accession to office, full and regular returns had invariably been made of all applications for discount, and no discount had at any been granted without the approval of the directors. Large discounts had been permitted his absence in England, for which he could not any way be considered responsible.

Dr. McQuesten said he had never intimated any one that erroneous information had been given him by Mr. Cassels, or that he had ever any to doubt the fact that the books, regularly mitted, showed the true estimate of each account. What he had said was that certain advances were largely beyond what he had understood to be.

A Shareholder present said it was not that no wrong information was actually meant. The question was—Did Mr. Cassels, know, one or more of the Directors were under impression as to certain debts due to the Bank, believing them to be much less than they were, still omit to set these Directors right should have done? This was an important to be determined for the guidance of future tors and managers.

Mr. Street protested against any attempt shift responsibility fairly devolving on the to the shoulders of its officer. In the doings which took place Mr. Cassels was fully exonerated from any negligence of accountancy, and tion was expressed regarding his fidelity established procedure of his office.

THE GRAND TRUNK.

The half-yearly meeting was held in on the 22nd October; Sir E. W. Watkins chair.

The Chairman said this term of expiring. He had always said that he intend to remain in the direction beyond time, as his other engagements would of it. He had ventured to state on a former sion that the difficulties of the company

y. . The increase in the net traffic was the past half-year over the corresponding 1867. The gross traffic receipts in half-year had nearly reached an increase of £20,000. The expenses had been re- he thought if things continued to pro- would be a surplus to pay interest on ference bonds at the end of this year, now present in the room about 200 out of between 3,000 and 4,000 stockholders present having interests ; Western of Canada and Buffalo and n. They would agree that none of the railways were in a satisfactory state. Western of Canada, which was pro- undest of all, only paid a dividend at wo per cent. per annum for the past though the proprietors had been as- it was projected that it would pay ; 10 or 15 per cent. per annum. The Lake Huron was estimated when pro- y in the first seven years a dividend at., which would afterwards rise to 25 ent., and those hopes had been field irm of Messrs. Hesseltine and Powell estimated capital of £410,000 would ded; but the railway had eventually ng more than £100,000,000. The work- were not to exceed 50 per cent., al- had since cost the Grand Trunk 108 istead of the 50 per cent originally Those calculations had misled every ied. The low class of the bulk fic on those lines from agricultural similar to the mineral traffic car- lish lines, not paying much for car- there was the adverse effect of cli- rails, and other matters which ren- esult of working unsatisfactory. In eport he made to the proprietors in the Grand Trunk, in July, 1862, he understand that the working of rail- ada was not like the working of rail- land. The Grand Trunk was then miles in length, and he had told ey might travel along the line for 20 ithout getting a passenger. Their ad over long lengths of railway, and comparatively small. The original Grand Trunk had not been com- did not believe that it would be worked until it was extended to Hali- tlantic, so as to convey traffic from ral States in America to a convenient Various opinions had been expressed the rates charged on the railway n who had visited Canada had ad- vering of the rates, while another ad recommended the raising of the lirectors had not, however, reduced The Government Commission ap- year 1861 reported that the traffic y was not sufficient to pay the work- ; that during two and a half years it its working expenses, and that the not an adequate supply of plant. ms situate two miles from Montreal; the railway could not approach the ad no elevation for the grain traffic, was unpopular with the people, and had no credit when he first went to 1861, and the trains did not keep It was proposed that the capital duced, and that the railway should y its debts. He assured the proprie- t were not for his exertions to protect soon after he arrived in Canada, in ld have been sold in the course of a auction. No doubt some mistakes le, but he could assure them that ad been made by the present board l improve the property. In 1862 on the working amounted to £142,- 868 to £287,000, showing an increase f one hundred per cent. They had in 1862, and 298 engines in 1868.

In 1862 each engine earned 1,687l in the year, while in 1868 each engine earned on the average 2,107l. They had 3,084 cars in 1862, each of which earned on the average, 124l., while in 1868 they had 4,104 cars that earned 133l. each, shew- ing an increase in the earnings of the engines of 420l. each, and in the cars an increase of 29l. each. He then adverted to the proceedings of Messrs. Creak & Ritter's Committee, with a view to show that the line had been more carefully managed as to economy of fuel than they had represented.

(To be continued.)

Mining.

MINING ON LAKE SUPERIOR.

(From our own Correspondent.)

BRUCE MINES, Nov. 2nd, 1868.

I send you some facts as to the present position of mining matters in this vicinity, and shall keep your readers regularly advised hereafter of all movements hereabouts.

BRUCE MINE.

The position of this mine is pretty well known to Canadians, and I do not think it necessary to enter into a geographical description of it. The property containing the Bruce and Wellington Mines was purchased from the Montreal Mining Company by the present holders—the West Can- ada Mining Co., represented by the celebrated firm of Messrs. John Taylor & Sons, London, England. The property contains 6,400 acres, and is on the whole very valuable. Several large veins run through it, on the chief of which are workings, named respectively the Bruce Mine and the Wellington Mine. The Bruce Mine has been in operation since the year 1848, and the adven- ture has been more or less successful. The pros- pects of the mine are at present rather gloomy, all the workings being stopped, owing to the con- tinued depression in the price of copper ore, which is having a most disastrous effect on copper min- ing, both on this continent and in Europe.

The veins which, near the surface, were very rich and productive have, at their present depth, (300 feet) somewhat fallen off in quality and this coupled with the depreciated value of the metal have caused the company, after the most energetic efforts, to abandon the thing for the time being.

The contemplation of this noble old mine, the pioneer of mining in Canada, has a very sadden- ing effect. The once busy dressing houses, filled with men and boys, the hum and whirr of the powerful machinery, hauling, crushing, cleansing, and the various other operations and append- ages of a rich mine, gave the whole affair a look of life and prosperity, which contrasted with the present desolate appearance of everything, fills the observer with sorrow, and the desire for the good old time of "high prices" to return.

WELLINGTON MINE.

Here the state of affairs is more cheerful. This mine is working vigorously. The deepest sink- ings have reached 248 feet, and the vein at that depth shows itself rich and well defined. A por- tion of this mine is suspended, but it is at all times available, and will be worked when the price of copper will warrant it. The exploratory works are at present confined to one shaft and one level or drift. The ore returns are chiefly made from 5 stopes as they are technically termed, and will amount to 65 or 70 tons per month. This is mined by a force of 36 men. The average yield of the vein is about two tons per lineal fathom.

HURON COPPER BAY MINE.

This mine is wrought on a continuation of the Wellington vein, which runs through the property of the Huron Copper Bay Mining Co., and is held on lease by the West Canada Mining Co. This is undoubtedly a splendid property and

its producing capabilities are very great, but like the rest, has not escaped the scathing effects of the low markets and portions of it are suspended temporarily. The chief workings are on one large and leading vein, in some places 24 feet wide with a N.E. and S.W. bearing. It has two or three tributaries on which very little has been done. The deepest point reached is 320 feet from the surface, at this point the vein fell off in quality, but as this is only one small opening on several hun- dred fathoms in length it is not a fair test of the value of the whole, and even here the vein is pro- ductive enough to work. The ore raised in this mine is about 240 tons of 18% per month. The number of men employed underground is 71, and the average yield of the vein is about 3 tons per lineal fathom.

The ore produced by all these mines is a yellow sulphuret, having a matrix of quartz, calc spar and wall rock, which is greenstone. When dis- covered at the surface, the ore is generally a rich "grey," with portions of "horse flesh," these two kinds sometimes producing as high as 60%; but as the ore descends it lessens in quality, but in many cases increases in quantity.

Insurance.

INSURANCE MATTERS IN NEW YORK.

(From our own Correspondent.)

NEW YORK, Nov. 6, 1868.

You will probably recognize the recent spirited and decisive action of the Executive Committee of the National Board of Fire Underwriters at Chicago, as the "newest feature" in the fire busi- ness. When the National Board was organized some years ago, a half years ago, the Fire business of the States was undergoing a rapid demoraliza- tion. The "cut throat" system of rate compe- tition prevailed generally ; risks of corresponding hazard, in different sections of the country were taken, figures at various rates their locations, and, unscrupulous agents not only put reputable Companies into unnecessary expense ; but in the general scramble for cheap insurance, which the mercantile classes had been educated to seek and expect, were enabled to get many weak corpora- tions into an amount of business they had not the pecuniary responsibility to carry. Hence under- writing was being done at a loss to the Companies generally, and but for the pause then made, the better class of Companies would soon have been obliged to retire their capital.

How serious the lesson, how imminent the danger, is shown in the unanimity and alacrity with which extraordinary powers have been con- ferred on the Committee. Heretofore no suffi- cient number of leading offices have been willing to invest an Executive with sufficient authority to secure that prestige which would give weight to its pronunciamentos. But the present spirit of combination is a thoroughly determined one, inspired by a sense of common danger. Once, inspire it by a sense of common danger. Com- panies and Local Boards show no tendency to " secession." It would be proclamation of a pur- pose to renew insurance guerillaism, that could only disgrace the recalcitrants. Dismissal of the agent is now the penalty of the cutting rates. The report of the Rating Committee shows much hard work done in the Great West. The report of the Committee on Legislation and Taxation affords hopeful assurance that the several States will speedily be induced to revise many invidious, inequitable and oppressive laws, several of them having already taken such action. Especially with reference to taxation; it is clear that it should be based upon net earnings, and not upon the gross premium receipts. The recommenda- tion for a repeal of all deposit laws, or making them reciprocal is equally important. Such legis- lation is however opposed to that free trade for which the " Mother Country," of both the Dominion and the States, so stoutly contends. Another recommendation by this Committee, that each State require of its home and agency Companies an implicit annual statement of uniform character to be made in the month of January, is important. The time is not far distant when all the States must follow the example of Massachusetts, New York, Ohio, California and Iowa. especially if they hope to decentralize the insurance business, and keep premiums at home.

The broker war, like Ætna and Vesuvius, has its periodic eruptions, and is just now in full flame. Twenty-for y o fices, including several of such A 1 corporatio s as the Home, Continental, Royal, Manhattan, Washington and Republic, have united in a league, and after the manner of the fathers in 1776, have issued a declaration of independence. They will no longer pay brokerage, and will, without charge, place risks for their customers. You will not care to have me discuss this vexed question in your columns. There are some hundred and twenty brokers on the Brokers' Board, beside scores of semi-occasional fellows. This eager crowd of middlemen strive to skim 15 to 25 per cent. from the office premiums, though the statistics show that the New York offices, as a whole, have made no money for the past five years. Dividends have been merely interest dividends, and generally made at the expense of needed reserve. Allow me to express my conviction that if the New York fire brokers ever were a useful "institution," they have survived that usefulness. Many efforts have been made during the last 15 years to strike them off, but there has always been enough young and sturdy offices not "in combination," to keep them in countenance. Any movement to be effectual must be unanimous or nearly so.

The rapidity with which "Co-operative" Life Insurance Companies are springing up in different parts of the Union, revives the reflection that there is very little now under the sun. New York, Chicago, Cincinnatti, Philadelphia, Baltimore, Charleston, Enfaula, (Ala.), and other cities, are supplied with one or more. New York has three and may soon have ten or twenty. They are substantially like the insurance "little goes" that infested London at the commencement of the eighteenth century, and which were suppressed by a penal statute in Queen Anne's reign.

For a mere trifle, say $3 to $6 initiation fee, and $1 on the death of a member, the *insured's* family is to get $5000 at his demise. Such highly benevolent concerns need and have no charter, or authority for doing business. There is no guarantee or any possibility that the obscure and impecunious " promoters " will be able or likely to continue them, *nem con* the fact, that the obligations which they propose to assume are expected to run from one to thirty years. No notice is taken of the decrement or deterioration of life, or rate of interest, and there is no provision or assurance that the accumulated fund, if one is ever got, will be accessible to the family of a deceased member. The Insurance *Monitor* has been handling the Manhattan National Union, United States, and others of this ilk, without gloves, and I notice that these swindles are receiving attention in Chicago, Baltimore, and other quarters. If our Superintendent of the Insurance Department at Albany, has no power under existing laws to suppress them, an "enabling" statute will be passed when the Legislature meets in January. Meantime some hundreds of mechanics and labourers may be cheated out of hard earnings. Of course the business classes are not to be caught by the contemptible "shysters" who are pushing their 'little goes" redivivus.

Prominent among the causes which have secured for life insurance such great popularity, and the unprecedented growth in the American Union, is the general application of the mutual principle, and the half premium note. You, on the other side of Jordan have seen enough of the irrepressible and acquisitive "Yank" to know that he is pretty shrewd. When he had got sufficiently

well planted in business to give some attention to life insurance (about twenty years ago), he quickly saw that its "mission" was with the sentiments and affections in co-operation with the advancing spirit of a high Christian civilization, and that it could not live in the atmosphere of sordid gain. Hence the "proprietary" or English system has never been favoured by our people, and of forty-three companies doing business in this State last year, but four, strictly, were stock companies, having 4,975 policies in force, with ,380,963 premium receipts in 1867, as against thirty-nine companies, mutual, with 295,105 policies, and $50,052,546 premium receipts in 1867, and total assets of $123,025,818, as compared with 52,523,137 in stock companies. There should be no such word as gain or profit in life insurance, commercially speaking.

The recent organization of a proprietary company with $1,000,000 capital, and all the profits or return premiums to be paid to the stockholders, has brought the question of the mutual vs. the stock plan, sharply before the public. The mutuals have combined in some liberal expenditures for discussing this question. I know of one publication 25,000 copies of which are going into the hands of merchants, bankers, brokers, and other professional and tradespeople. As the readers of the *Monetary Times* do not require its publishers to be responsible for the views of correspondents, I will take the liberty of "guessing" that the stock plan never will be popular in the future, as it has always been unpopular in the past. The million dollar company deducts about 25 per cent off ordinary premium rates, in consideration of the policies being non-participating, but as most of the well established mutuals return 50 per cent of premiums to policy holders, besides in many cases paying six and seven for it on small capitals, it is obvious that Mr. Milledol. expects to make about 25 net profit on the premium receipts, which will be a decidedly good thing for the stockholders, but not so funny for the insured. The introduction of capital into life insurance for merely speculative purposes, is not only not necessary, but is to be regretted as it will tend to unsettle and demoralize the system devised for a purely benevolent and unselfish purpose.

M. A. C.

INSURANCE MATTERS IN MONTREAL.

(From a Correspondent.)

MONTREAL, Nov. 10th, 1868.

The recent judgement by Mr. Justice MacKay *in re* Henry Chapman & Co., vs. the Lancashire Insurance Company, is exciting a good deal of attention and not a little indignation from business men here. The claim is for a loss by fire that occurred in 1864. The judgement was given upon the following pleas, fyled in opposition to the claim:—1st. Some informality in the award of arbitrators appointed to assess the damage caused by the fire. 2nd. Neglect on the part of the assured to notify the office of the occupation by a tenant of part of the premises in which the fire was covered, and also a failure to notify a further insurance on the same property. All of which was held to invalidate the claim.

Incendiarism is still rampant here. On Wednesday night some sheds in rear of a house on Radegonde Street were fired, but put out with but little damage.

On Thursday night the stable in rear of the dwelling occupied by Mr. Edward Hilton, in St. Genevieve Street, was fired, and in consequence of delay in the supply of water was totally destroyed, two horses and a cow were destroyed in the stable.

On Saturday night about 10.30 a fire broke out in a stable in rear of Bonaventure Street, it was about three-quarters of an hour before the water was let on, and then with so little force that the brigade had to use engines to force a stream, consequently

a whole nest of wooden outbuildings we destroyed.

It is somewhat curious to note the form of these acts of incendiarism; with we have had four fires within a stone each other, in the western section of w..list some three or four weeks ago we seven or eight fires within the same gr und in the eastern part of the city. not be well if some of our scientific would (say after the style of DeQuincy') " murder on one of the Fine Arts,") tree essay on the causes of this curious in fact, let him go into the subject in all th bearings, ascertain whether it may be malarious influences, or, if not, what? I would suggest that *one-half* of our or double-barreled fire-marshal should this literary task, and thus earn the gr the scientifically inclined, as well as easily earned fees of the office.

CANADA LIFE.—The business of this for the past half year, shows an increase same period of last year of 59.33 per ce number of new policies issued ; an ii 54.01 per cent. in the new premiums, per cent. in the sum assured.

FIRES AND ALARMS IN QUEBEC.—Mr. guson, Chief Engineer of the Fire De furnishes the following statement of th of fires and alarms of fire in that city d six months ending the 31st October, 186 corresponding period of 1867, viz: 18 37, alarms, 36 ; 1867—fires, 35, alarms.

—The Union Mutual Life Assuran Maine, has received license to transac in Canada, on depositing U.S. 6's of 81- B. B. Corwin, general agent, St. John,

—A petition has been introduced into t Legislature praying for an act of incorp the "Ontario Mutual Life Insurance Co

FIRE RECORD.—St. John, N. B., Harrington's saw mill at the Shediac totally destroyed by fire. Bateman's alongside also burnt; loss $4,000; no los Wyoming, Ont., Oct. 30.—Clark & saw, carding and falling mill, and ski chine, all totally destroyed; loss ea $7,000; no insurance. A barn belong Convoy, across the road from the m the flames and was consumed with it loss $1,000; no insurance. Windham Township, Ont., Oct. 1 James Cosey, and contents; took fire family were at church and believed to of an incendiary; no insurance. Quebec, Oct.—Mr. Hayes' groc Amoth and D'Artigny street; origin a insurance on building; stock insured in the British America. Also, grocery store of Mr. Le Bel, Notre Dame street; caused by a ligt falling into some highwines; the fire guished with little damage; stock ins Quebec Fire and Home Insurance Con Hamilton Township, Ont., Oct. 2 B. Harris and contents totally dest unknown; no information as to insura Kingston Road, Ont.—Stacked s insured in the Provincial for $600.

MARINE DISASTERS ON THE LAKE named Jas. Blessington was lost off tl *Gale*, near Point Pelee, a few days sin The scow, *A. P. Waite*, which sa Colborne recently, was washed ashore by the recent hea*vy* gale. The schooner *Tom Martin* arrived borne on Saturday, the 30th Oct., i condition. Both mast-heads were and some of her sails gone. The schooner *Fred. L. Wells*, of wrecked on the 2nd inst., off Port I

re of Lake Erie, and is a total loss.
ilt at St. Catharines, in 1849, by L.
measured 150 tons, rated B 1, and
about $1,800.

oner *Kate Kelley*, grain loaded, went
Sand Hills, seven miles below Clay
e Erie, on the 2nd inst., and will prove

ty vessels entered Buffalo on the 2nd
l protests—most of the damages to the
g comparatively light, and confined to
f upper works. Quite a quantity of
ret.

oner *Sweepstakes* lost all her canvas
t sails.

oner *Frontier City* was struck by the
ntabula. She put back, and reached
s leaky condition. She has discharged

oner *C. C. Trowbridge* lay four hours
ea making a clean sweep athwart her
her port bulwarks completely stove.
MuKee, of the schooner *J. Beigler*, re-
g, Saturday noon, the barges *Empire*
in, water-logged and abandoned, about
s off shore, near Grand River. The
Empire remained intact, but both were
pidly toward the north shore, where
stand a very small chance of hanging
ng in the storm that was then raging.
William Fisk came into Buffalo with
badly damaged, as did also the bark
sell.

y, on 31st ult., the schr *H. N. Todman*,
on, while running into harbor for shelter
the wrong way and went behind the
where she pounded considerably. For-
r her, the gale subsided, and she got

oner *St. Paul*, with a cargo of coal,
n the 31st Oct. in the river below De-
vas got off by the tug *Hector*, under
s detention.

oner *Kelly*, grain loaded, was driven
t miles below Port Burwell during the
id has gone to pieces. The *Kelly* had
15,800 bushels of wheat, shipped by
parties and consigned to Oswego. It
n the Ætna and Home Companies for
according to the register, the measure-
Kelly is 350 tons, rate A 2, and value
She is owned in Oswego by Messrs.
Kelly—the latter commanding her.

IAL UNION ASSURANCE CO'Y.

.... $12,500,000
) FUNDS, UPWARDS OF ... 2,600,000

is:—19 & 20 *Cornhill, London, England.*
r *Canada:—385 & 587 St. Paul St., Montreal*
AGENTS:—MORLAND, WATSON & Co.

SPECIAL NOTICE.

effected this year will have a full Bonus
he next declaration of Profits.

*dy are Examples of Bonus declared at
ion of Profits, 31st December, 1857:*

cted the ar.	Age at Entry	Sum Assured.	Bonus Added.	Annual Premium.
165	20	$1,000	$65	$19 61
163	30	5,000	545	122 54
165	40	25,000	1,655	802 95
163	50	15,000	1,650	657 56

he Policy-holders had the option of
lieu of the above Reversionary Bonus,

(2) an equivalent in Cash, (3) of having a large
accumulated Bonus payable if the expected average age be attained, or (4) of having the Policy
payable on attaining a certain deferred age, although effected at the ordinary rate of premium:
thus, the holder of Policy No. 297 had the offer
of £173, 10s. ($867.50) cash paid down in lieu of
the bonus of $1,650 added to his policy, or of
having a Bonus of $3,800 added to his Policy if
he lived 16 years and attained the age of 71; the
holder of Policy 570 had the offer of having his
Policy payable on attaining the age of 72½, in
respect of the 1867 Bonus only:—at each successive division of profits an earlier age would be
named for the payment to him of the sum assured.

The following are the advantages offered by the
Commercial Union.—(1) PERFECT SECURITY.—
The Life Policies in addition to their own separate
Trust Fund amounting on the 31st December,
1867, to £169,623 (848,115.00) have the security
of a guaranteed Capital of upwards of £2,000,000
($10,000,000), and the invested assets of the Com-
pany, irrespective of the Life Funds, amounts to
upwards of £350,000, (1,750,000.00). (2) LARGE
RESERVES.—The valuation of the Commercial
Union was made on safer principles than that of
any other office doing business in Canada. The
rate of interest for the future investments of the
Life Branch was assumed in the calculations at
only 3 per cent., whereas an average of 5 per cent.
had been made of the Life Funds during the previous 5 years. The net or risk premiums only
were assumed, and the value of the margin reserved for future expenses and profits, was nearly 3
times as large as the bonus declared. The rate of
future mortality assumed was higher than by the
Carlisle Table although the previous experience
of the office was more than 50 per cent. under the
Carlisle, showing the first class character of the
business transacted by the Company. (3) BONUS.
—A greater number of ways of receiving the
Bonus are offered for the option of Policy holders
than by any other Company. The above table
giving examples of Bonuses at various ages speaks
for itself. No other Company can produce so good
a table. (4) ECONOMY.—The maximum expenses
of management are guaranteed by the Company
not to exceed a small per centage of the premium
income. The average rate of expenses, including
commission paid to Agents, was under 13 per cent.
for the last 5 years. (5) PROMPT SETTLEMENTS.
—Claims are paid one month after proof, instead
of three months, the usual time stipulated for by
other offices. (6) CURRENCY.—All settlements
are made in Sterling.

Remarks on the advantages offered by the Commercial Union contrasted with other Institutions.—
(1) AMERICAN OFFICES.—The rapid growth of
these offices is well known, but as the Hon. J. E.
Sanford, the Insurance Commissioner of Massachusetts, remarks in his report for 1867, the magnitude of these offices enforces the enquiry—one
which is, of profound interest to their Policy-
holders. "Whether these companies are, after
all, funding enough to meet their enormous future
obligations, or whether—between the ambitious
struggle to pay large dividends to the assured, on
the one hand, and the temptations, to pay large
commissions to agents, large salaries and perquisites to officers, and large Royalties to Stockholders, on the other,—the bottom of the fund may
not be reached at some day, more or less distant,
with a deficiency of a few hundred millions of
dollars unprovided for!"

That these offices are open to doubt may be inferred from the condemnation of the practice of
some of them by Mr. Barnes, the Insurance Commissioner of New York, and Mr. Sandford before
referred to. It appears that in the assets are sometimes included commissions paid to
agents. Mr. Barnes speaks of such assets as of a
"fictitious character;" Mr. Sanford terms them
"*unreal* assets."

Mr. Barns draws attention with regret to the
tendency to accumulate a considerable portion of

the assets in premium notes, and points out the
serious diminution of the cash reserve of realized
assets held by note companies. If the accounts
of the American Office be examined, the object of
these remarks by the American Commissioners
will clearly appear; take for instance the Ætna
Office:—

The gross assets are given as...... $7,599,898.

But of this amount the sum of... 4,171,883,
is represented by premium notes or unrealizable
assets. Only $316,450, less than 1-20, are in-
vested in loans on mortgages (first liens), while
upwards of $700,000, are invested in various
Bank stocks. Considering the large number of
Banks which fail in any long period of time, such
investments can scarcely be considered safe for
money held in trust to meet payments which may
not become due for 30 or 40 years. But there are
other objections to which American Offices are
open. Since the suspension of specie payments,
the sum assured by policies has been reduced 30
per cent and upwards. Those who effected policies for $1,000 previous to the war, and paid the
corresponding premium, would in the event of
death, now receive $1,000 in Greenbacks, which
are only equal to about $700 Canadian currency.
During the war between the North and South, it
is well known that the policies of the Southerners,
no matter how old their standing, were forfeited,
and their premiums, paid over many years, were
sacrificed. If war should ever arise between Great
Britain or Canada and the United States, is it
probable "Britishers" would be treated differently
by the American Offices? Policies upon which,
it may be, 20 or 30 years premiums had been
paid, would be liable to forfeiture.

(2.) ENGLISH OFFICES.—The rates of the Commercial Union will be found somewhat lower than
most of the English offices. The valuation was
made according to principles which give a larger
reserve than the method used by other offices.
The accounts and balance sheet are published,
and more information is given than by any other
English Life Office.

(3.) CANADIAN OFFICES.—The Canada Life
Office gives in its prospectus a comparison between
the rates charged by English offices and themselves, but omits to compare the bonuses. We
propose to supply the deficiency: To compare
policies of the same standing : Canada Life Policy
No. 3376, effected in 1861 for $8000, obtained in
1865 a bonus of $433,21.— Commercial Union
Policy, No. 570, effected in 1863 for $5000; ob-
tained in 1867 a bonus of $545,00, that is to say,
a larger bonus than a policy in the Canada Life,
effected for $3000 more in amount. If both poli-
cies had been for $10,000, the Canada Life bonus
would have been $541,51, while the Commercial
Union bonus would have been $1,090,00, more
than double that of the Canada Life. If the
premiums be compared it will be found that at
age 30 the premium for $10,000 is $223,00 in the
Canada Life; in the Commercial Union, $247,08—
a difference in *premium* on the five years of
$120,40, while the difference in *bonus* was $548 ;
or, to deal with present values, the Commercial
Union would give for their bonus $385,00 cash,
while the bonus of the Canada Life, at the same
rate—a liberal assumption we venture to believe—
would realize $191,27—a difference in favour of
the Commercial Union of $193.73 ; thus the
policy holder in the Commercial Union would be
the gainer, in five years, of $73.33 (cash) over the
holder of the Canada Life policy.

The Canada Life Office states that its funds,
while yielding more remunerative returns, are yet
invested with equal security. It is true the interest realized by that Company last year was six
per cent. as compared with five per cent. of the
Commercial Union, but if the account published
this year be referred to, it will be seen that a large
sum had to be written off for losses by investments.
But this difference in the rate of interest is not,
even if the investments were equally safe, as far
as the bonus is concerned, of such importance as

would at first appear. It is the surplus interest realized, beyond the assumed ra,e, which gives the profit. The Commercial Union reserve for its existing engagements is based on the assumption that only three per cent. compound interest will be realized. The excess beyond that rate will be profit. Has the Canada Life Office also assumed three per cent, or has it assumed four or four and a half per cent, or even five per cent, as some of the American offices have assumed!. The Canada Life Office is worked at a greater relative expense, The expenditure last year exceeded 20 per cent of the premium income. The capital is a very small one, only $125,000 paid up.

If the foregoing remarks be carefully considered, it will be seen the *Commercial Union* is entitled to the support of all thinking Canadians.

☞ THE CANADIAN MONETARY TIMES AND INSURANCE CHRONICLE *is printed every Thursday Evening, in time for the English Mail.*

*Subscription Price, one year, $2, or $3 in American currency ; Single copies, five cents each. Casual advertisements will be charged ten cents per line of solid nonpareil each insertion. All letters to be addressed, "*THE CANADIAN MONETARY TIMES, TORONTO, ONT." *Registered letters no addressed are at the risk of the Publishers. Cheques should be made payable to* J. M. TROUT, *Business Manager, who will, in future, issue all receipts for money.*

The Canadian Monetary Times.

THURSDAY, NOVEMBER 12, 1868.

INSURANCE LEGISLATION.

It has been stated that Insurance Companies doing business in Canada have been harshly dealt with by our legislators. However, when we compare the enactment in force here with the laws respecting Insurance Companies which are in existence in the United States, we may find fewer grounds on which to envy our neighbours. A report presented by the Committee on Legislation and Taxation at the late meeting of the Executive Committee of the U. S. National Board of Fire Underwriters furnishes us with some interesting facts relating to the various State Insurance laws. It appears that Iowa, although it has repealed its Deposit law, imposes a grievous tax of two per cent. upon the gross premiums received in that State; Missouri, besides requiring payment of taxation on the gross premiums at the same rate as is levied upon the citizens of the State, for State license fee of $400 for St. Louis; $300 for Counties of 150,000 population, $60 for Counties of smaller population, &c. Maryland exacts a license fee from representatives of Companies of other States from $200 to $400 per annum, and has enacted that agents of Companies of other States shall be empowered to settle losses without the interference of officers of other Companies. Pennsylvania exacts $500 to $600 for State licenses. Minnesota requires a tribute of two per cent. upon gross premiums. West Virginia requires a deposit of $25,000. Tennessee requires a deposit of $20,000 ; exacts license fees, and State, County, and Municipal taxes. Massachusetts exacts from other State Companies a tax of two per cent. upon all premiums, and four per cent. from foreign Companies. A national tax of one and a-half per cent. on gross premiums, caps the climax. The Chicago *Spectator* recently published a compilation of the returns of 164 Fire, and Fire and Marine Companies doing business in the State of New York, which showed that these Companies disbursed in 1867, for national taxes, $1,209,259, and for State and local taxes, $998,272. A calculation of per centages, covering the business of three years, gave 5.14 as the percentage of total taxes to total premium receipts. The report to which we have referred states,—"Results show that the Government receives about one-half of the net proceeds of the business of fire insurance in the form of taxes."

In England the Companies are subject to duties of 1s 6d and 3s per cent. per annum on insurances against fire. In 1866, the sum of £867,961 stg. was paid by fifty-four Companies, as the gross amount of duty, into the Inland Revenue Office.

Under the Canadian Act respecting Insurance Companies, all Companies desirous of doing business here must obtain a license, and deposit the sum of at least $50,000 for each branch of business, subject to certain exceptions to be increased under certain conditions, in the case of foreign Companies to $100,000 or $150,000. Certain clauses of the Act provide for substituting in special cases for this deposit, either the investments already made of the securities of the Government of which provisions the Companies interested are at liberty to avail themselves. The deposit, if made in money, draws interest at six per cent. and will be repaid if the Company withdraw from business here. The Dominion Government imposes no taxes, and the charge for a license to do business is either nothing at all, or a mere nominal sum. Home Companies are, it seems, subjected to a Municipal tax in the nature of an income tax, which is rather based on capital. Montreal charges $300 a year for allowing Companies to do business there ; and Quebec, which has caused more loss to Insurance Companies than any other place in Canada, professes to charge $500 ; but we understand that this imposition has been successfully resisted. Toronto does not demand a license fee. So far as foreign Companies are concerned they are wholly exempt from taxes, except on their buildings. They merely pay the license in localities where it is imposed upon in common with all other companies. It be seen, therefore, that Foreign Companies are actually in this respect in a better position than Home Companies. The holders in a Home Company pays his of taxes as such, and is at the same time pelled to pay his private income tax. is another matter which may be appropriate referred to in this connection. Home panies are appealed to for aid whenever companies are to be raised, or fire e procured ; not only is this the case locality where their head office is situated all over the country wherever they agencies. Foreign Companies invariably escape this "tax," by referring the matter their head offices.

It is apparent, therefore, that all there are grounds of complaint, yet C nies doing business in Canada are heavily burdened as are Companies s

If any one will take the trouble to c the attitude of this country towards ance Companies with that assumed b countries toward their own and Foreig panies, it will be seen that our leg appreciate the injustice done to the and the embarrassments imposed on in capital by unwise enactments. Th source of annoyance and wrong is the cious action of certain Municipalities.

THE GRAND TRUNK AND BRYDGES.

There is no doubt that Mr. Brydge pies a position in many respects une At least, he is exposed and subjected tematic attacks which he is comp endure at a disadvantage. Were his as a railway manager, merely, called tion, he could join issue with assaila meet the matter fairly on its merit might as any officer of a company, res to them and them alone, is entitle appeal to the fact of his retention in the best evidence of the value plac his services. Messrs. X, Y, and eve disapprove of Mr. Brydges' admini but, if his employers, the Grand Tru way Company choose to keep him Manager in Canada, they are at lib so, although X, Y and Z become en what they consider their stupidity. Brydges is subjected to attacks mu difficult to deal with. His honest pugned, and as his position necessari enemies, the pack at his heels is as r and relentless as any man could we collect. Newspapers have taken side against him, and he has the que

s of seeing his reputation tossed back-
and forwards like a shuttlecock, in an
contest between contending factions.
we have, at various times, pointed
at we consider errors in his manage-
l the Grand Trunk, we are none the
sposed to condemn those whose per-
r political motives lead them into a
exsecution of the man ; to deprecate
tacks as are unfair ; and to disregard
iticisms as wear on their face malice
e. It is an easy thing for Mr. Nelson
Any-body-else to put together in
let form the gossip of the streets, or
inuations of the disappointed and the
us ; and it is, unfortunately, no less
procure publicity for all the charges
uing charges that can be concocted.
ve no authority, if we had the wish,
ertake a defence of Mr. Brydges ; he
able to stand up for himself. But as
m man and man, we think it grossly
that he should be persecuted by the
tion through the columns of public
ls of charges of personal dishonesty,
have not been carried to the proper
al, or if they have been so carried,
ither been disbelieved or disproved.
hould the public be pestered with this
able iteration." If Mr. Nelson has
s to make against Mr. Brydges, charges
involve the latter's honesty as a man,
is faithfulness as a servant, there is
er place where, and a proper time
hey can be made, so as to secure not
xamination but suitable action on the
Why, in the name of common sense,
e persist in raving through Canada
atters with which the Canadian public
power to deal ? Those directly inter-
n what he has to say are the proprie-
the Grand Trunk Railway, and surely
lson is at liberty to take his stock of
, grievances, insinuations and advice,
proper quarter, and there appeal for
estigation. He casts his illegitimate
gs at our doors, and then rushes off.
ere so dreadfully anxious about the
of the Grand Trunk, he could easily
urnished some of those who attended
e meeting in London with a copy of
rges, and the evidence he relies on to
them. We have read over the pro-
s of the meeting, but we do not find
r. Nelson is referred to. It does not
that he asked for a chance to make
s allegations, or volunteered a state-
f affairs. Although he knew that a
g was coming off in London, that a
opposition had been organized against
sent management of the Grand Trunk,
t blazing away in Canada against
rydges, and wasted no inconsiderable

amount of pens, ink, and paper, in his zealous
crusade. We are not acquainted with Mr.
Nelson's peculiarities, but we do certainly
think that his conduct would justify the
issue of a writ de lunatico inquirendo. Had
he applied for an investigation and been refused, then there might be some excuse for
troubling us out here with his columns of
charges. As it is, Mr. Brydges is perfectly
justified in treating such effusions with silent
contempt. He is the servant and agent of
the board of direction, and, while continued
as such, is entitled to shelter himself behind
them. They are responsible for his acts,
and upon them should be laid the burden ;
were such not the case every servant of a
company might be held personally liable even
where his superiors have endorsed his acts
and assumed the responsibility of them.
The report of the meeting in London shews
that Mr. Brydges was called to account there
by some of the proprietors, and our readers
may judge for themselves as to the strength
of the defence. The Railway Times says ;
"Mr. Brydges spoke out clearly, resolutely,
but not defiantly, so much so in fact, that he
gained the ear, conquered the antipathy and
acquired the confidence of his auditory." So
far as we can see, it must be taken for granted
that Mr. Brydges has successfully defended
himself against charges of unfaithfulness and
dishonesty ; that his employers accept his
explanations ; and that something more will
be required from Mr. Nelson than mere insinuations or assertions, before the public
can be expected to lend credence to his
letters or pamphlets. Opinions may differ as
to the judgment displayed by Mr. Brydges
in his management, but as regards his honesty the verdict thus far is in his favour.
At the adjourned meeting, Mr. Brydges
was fully exculpated. Mr. Hodgson said
that he thought Mr. Brydges had fairly and
fully answered the questions put to him at
the previous meeting, and he thought that it
was only just to acknowledge it. Mr. Heseltine said that the charges he had made
against the Canadian officials did not apply
in all cases to Mr. Brydges, and for his own
part he was perfectly satisfied as to the
honour and integrity of the man. Mr.
Creek said that while there were some of the
answers to his questions which he should like
to have had more in detail, yet, on the whole,
he was perfectly satisfied with Mr. Brydges'
explanation.

REGISTRATION OF BIRTHS AND DEATHS.

We are pleased to observe that there is
every probability that legislation will be had
on this subject during the present Session of

the Ontario Assembly. Two members of the
Opposition, Messrs. Boyd and Pardee, each
gave notice of motion last week for leave to
bring in a bill upon the subject. That of Mr.
Boyd was read a first time on Friday last,
but not yet being printed, we have been
unable to ascertain its contents ; Mr. Pardee
brought in his bill on Monday, but we presume
he intends to incorporate it with that of his
colleague. We, some time ago, (in vol. 1 p.
274 of this Journal), pointed out the necessity
and urged the adoption of a law of this nature,
and predicted that the introduction of one
could not be much longer delayed. The promoters of the scheme are both able men, and
the Act will therefore doubtless be well drawn ;
when it appears we shall carefully consider it
and hope to see it as perfect as possible. A
badly drawn act which would not attain the
desired end of a complete registration, would,
for the purpose we have in view, viz : that of
Life Insurance, be worse than useless ; as the
returns under it, instead of being a guide,
would mislead. An act of the kind has been
in force in Nova Scotia for several years ; but
it is only now, after two or three amendments, that registration under it is becoming
anything like as full and complete as it
should be. If a good Act be passed here, in a
few years we shall be able, from the returns
made under it, to frame insurance tables of
mortality, similar to the celebrated ones of
Dr. Farr, accurately representing the value
of life in this Province, and which, therefore,
will be, in every respect, more satisfactory
than those based upon English lives, which
Canadian Companies are now compelled to
use.

In compliance with the request of our
enterprising friends of the Commercial Union
Assurance Company, we give place to a circular setting forth the advantages, all and
sundry, that are to arise to insurers from
placing their risks with that particular Company. If this document shall be the means
of inducing any to take the steps necessary to insure their families or dependants
against poverty and want, whether it is done
through the excellent agency of the Commercial or any other sound Company, we are
satisfied. There is no harm done by any
Company giving the greatest prominence to
its "peculiar" inducements," or even comparing its terms and rates with those of other
Companies in a fair and friendly spirit. By
this sort of discussion the public are enlightened ; attention is drawn to the subject of
life insurance ; opportunities are offered for
impressing its advantages, and good may be
done. We have no doubt that the "Circular"
under notice will be generally read, and at
some future time we may have something to
say as to the merits of the questions raised.

Financial.

MONTREAL MONEY MARKET.

(From our own Correspondent.)

Montreal, Nov. 10, 1868.

The ease in the money market still continues, and those seeking accommodation have better times generally than for years past. I have often tried to explain the causes of this ease. Short imports during the fall; small demands on the banks for grain operations; unwillingness of capitalists to embark in any of the new schemes presented to the public, and the large accumulation of profits on business some years back, a considerable proportion of which has been invested in real estate, buildings, &c.; but there is still a large amount of capital seeking investment, consequently the high price of all good securities; the ease with which all good bills are discounted, even if they have only one name. The pressure in the New York money market has had no effect here, as we are in more or less of an independent position. Bank stocks have risen, and sales of Montreal reported at 142. Merchant's have also advanced, sales being made at $108\frac{1}{2}$, and now hold for 109. British and City are both out of the market. Ontario has risen to $102\frac{3}{4}$ to 103, at which prices it sells freely. Toronto, if offered, would bring $118\frac{1}{2}$, and Jacques Cartier, $108\frac{1}{2}$; but holders do not care to sell at those prices. Gore Bank has risen, and would readily bring 40. Under new and proper management, it doubtless will to a great extent recover its position, but that will depend greatly on the new Board, and whether the Hamiltonians will support it. Of miscellaneous stocks, City Railroad are in demand at $110\frac{1}{4}$, but none offering. Richelieu wanted at $114\frac{1}{8}$, but sellers ask much more. Gas steady at 133 to 135. Corporation Bonds and Stocks firm. Mining Consols dull at $2.60, but no buyers over $2.50.

NEW YORK MONEY MARKET.

Nov. 6.—The excessive stringency in money has been continued throughout the past week without abatement. The week ended with a bank statement showing a loss of $5,100,000 in legal tenders, and $4,100,000 in currency deposits, and with but a nominal decrease in loans. This exhibit added to the uneasy feeling among lenders, naturally induced unusual caution. The balances at the Clearing House book ceased to show the irregularities apparent last week at banks holding accounts of parties known to be engaged in operations for breaking the stock market; and from this it was inferred that there was a suspension of the artificial efforts to tighten money. However this may have been tried, there has been an increased difficulty in borrowing; and outside the banks the rate of interest on call loans has ranged from $\frac{1}{8}$ to $\frac{1}{6}$ per cent. per day, which the difference between cash and regular sales of stocks has been generally $\frac{1}{4}$ per cent. To-day the pressure resulted in a general break in the stock market, and at the close, money was offered more freely in many cases at 7 per cent.; which may possibly be the beginning of the relaxation of the artificial means for embarrassing the market, or the offers may have been made for the purpose of drawing parties into stocks with a view to again purchasing them. The money market and the stock market are entirely in the hands of a knot of unprincipled speculators, and the consequent feeling of demoralization exceeds anything experienced since the panic of 1857.—*Exchange.*

—A Woodstock paper says: "We are gratified to learn that the late manager of the agency of the Gore Bank here, who lately left the Province under mental excitement, has accounted for the money supposed to be in default. This will give much satisfaction to his friends, although it is no more than was expected would be the case."

TORONTO STOCK MARKET.

(Reported by Pellatt & Osler, Brokers.)

Business still contiues limited, owing to the scarcity of securities. Nearly all stocks show an advance on last week's quotations.

Bank Stock.—Montreal has again advanced, closing with buyers at 140, and no sellers under 142. Ontario is active and in demand at 103 to $103\frac{1}{2}$. Toronto has advanced with small sales at 119, which rate is freely offered. Small lots of Royal Canadian are offering at 92; little doing. Commerce is in demand; there are buyers at $104\frac{3}{4}$, and sellers at $105\frac{1}{2}$. Gore is in demand at 41; none on market. There were sales of Merchants' at 107 to 108. Quebec is active; there are buyers at par, and sellers at 101. No Molson's in Market. Buyers offer $104\frac{1}{2}$ for City; none in market. There are sellers of Du Peuple at $105\frac{1}{4}$ and buyers at 105. Jacques Cartier sold at 109. Union could be placed at $103\frac{1}{2}$. Other Banks nominal.

Debentures.—There were sales of Canadian Stirling five per cents. at $91\frac{1}{2}$. and of Dominion Stock at 102 to $104\frac{1}{2}$. No six per cents. in market. There were considerable sales of Toronto at rates to pay 7 per cent. interest to purchasers. County are in great demand and very scarce.

Sundries.—City Gas is in great demand, but none in market; buyers would pay an advance. Canada Permanent Building Society is in demand at $122\frac{1}{2}$ to 123; none in market. Western Canada sold at 115 and is in demand; there are buyers of Freehold at 107 to $107\frac{1}{4}$; holders asking 108. Buyers offer 127 for Montreal Telegraph; sellers ask 130. Canada Landed Credit is enquired for at 70; none in market. A few large mortgages were placed at 8 per cent. interest. Money is easy on undoubted security.

French and English Savings' Banks.—The annual report concerning the operations of the savings' banks in France during the year 1867 was lately presented to the general meeting of the managers and directors. The *Débats* now makes the following observations on the general results. In making some comments upon it, it contrasts, the savings' banks of France with those of England: "England had in 1861, 640 establishments, 1,580,359 depositors for 937,430,000f., whilst France possessed 683, 1,300,521, and 401,313,151f. respectively. In 1866, England had no less than 4054—in consequence of the opening of the post offices (which receive from one shilling up to the limit for one year, namely, £30 sterling), 2,123,-124, and 1,049,031, 775f. In France the figures were 993; 1,748,944, and 528,917,299f. During that period the number of banks and accounts has therefore increased in a much larger proportion, in Great Britain, while the progression of the deposits has been more considerable on this side of the Channel. "England," the authors say, "has gained 81 millions, while France has improved by 127, a balance in favour of the latter of 46 millions." This result is doubtless satisfactory; but would it not be more so if the same facilities had been accorded here for the deposit of small sums which exist in England in the post office branches. The fact must not be forgotten that the British savings' banks contain more than a thousand millions of francs, although the mutual aid societies and co-operative associations form an increasing competition with them, while the French establishments only possess a little more than half that total. If it is borne in mind that the population of the United Kingdom does not reach 30 millions, while that of France approaches very slowly, it is true, 40, the conclusion must be come to that the contingent of small accounts put by, of which those institutions are the reservoirs, form little more in France than two fifths of that of England."

—A wooden railway is projected from Kingston into Loughborough and the township adjoining.

Railway News.

Northern Railway.—Traffic Receipt fo
ending Oct. 31, 1868.

Passengers	$3,865
Freight	9,717
Mails and Sundries	1,918
Total Receipts for week	$15,501
Corresponding week 1867	14,330
Increase	$1,171
Total traffic from 1 Jan. '68	$204,415
Corresponding period '67	226,308
Decrease	$21,893

Great Western Railway.—Traffic fo
ending Oct. 23, 1868.

Passengers	$34,272
Freight and live stock	50,637
Mails and sundries	2,427
	$87,337
Corresponding Week of '67	86,979
Increase	$358

Averages of New York State Railw
We are indebted to John Worthington, E
copies of the Report for 1866 and 1867,
State Engineer and Surveyor of the State
York. The following deductions from the
of about sixty companies will be found i
ing:—

	1866.	
Average number of miles traveled by each passenger	37.44	
Average number of passengers in each train	69.72	
Average number of miles each ton of freight was transported	113.95	
Average number of tons in each freight train	74.85	
Aggregate movement of passenger trains is equivalent to passing over the road	3,898 times	2,
Aggregate movement of freight trains is equivalent to passing over the road	5,570 times	4,
Average number of trains passing daily over the road, about	20	
Average cost, per mile of road, for maintaining roadway	$4,577 35	
Average cost, per mile of road, for repairs of machinery	2,991 70	
Average cost, per mile of road, for operating road	6,287 24	
Average cost, per mile of single track, for maintaining roadway	2,789 82	
Average cost, per mile of single track, for repairs of machinery	1,823 40	
Average cost, per mile of single track, for operating road	3,882 04	
Average sum received for carrying one passenger one mile	2.42 cents	2
Average sum received for transporting one ton of freight one mile	2.353 cents	2
Average cost, per mile, for carrying each passenger	1.863 cents	
Average cost, per mile, for carrying each ton of freight	1.952 cents	
Average number of miles of travel for each passenger killed	40,203,823	
Average number of miles of travel for each passenger either killed or injured	6,387,523	
Average number of passengers carried for each one killed	1,073,804	
Average expense per cent. of all the earnings	75.99	

Railway Accidents.—Statistics rece
lished respecting English railways show th
ing accidents to passengers in 1866: kil
causes beyond their own contol, one
eighteen millions carried; injured. ditto
every half of a million carried; killed fr
own misconduct or want of caution, one
seventeen millions; injured, ditto, one
thirty-nine millions.

—The tenth call upon the capital sto
European and North American Railway,
sion from St. John's westward, has be
The call is 10 per cent., payable 19th N

Commercial.

Montreal Correspondence.

(From our own Correspondent.)

Montreal, Nov. 10, 1868.

Il fleet has now pretty well all arrived, maps come two or three exceptions, but cs of heavy goods, which we receive by vessels, are now landed and the merchants ied with their winter stocks.

local markets are dull and the tendency is ds; this is owing to a slight rise of water anals, which has made the supplies more has for some little time past. I give the lotations for the leading articles: Extra 65, fancy $5.50 to 5.65, strong supers. $5.35 up to $5.55 for very strong bakers, ng of 100 brl. lots; good supers. from wheat $5.20 to 5.25. Sales of Welland it lies at $5.20. No. 2 super has sold at of oatmeal, a sale of good U. C. was 6.25 per brl. Wheat—Ranges still high, pring being nominally $1.19 to 1.20; U. nter $1.20; Chicago spring No. 2 $1.12, e of No. 3 at $1.05; but buyers and e so apart in their views that quotations nominal. Of coarse grains sales of Peas s made at $1.05 to 1.06, but only in retail s. Corn—Has sold at 83c. to 84½c. 1.10 to 1.20, and Oats 48c. to 50c. dly say that the quantities offering and tese prices are no criterion.

OVISIONS there is a lull. Pork both in ind barrelled is very dull. Beef has been k, and the English markets have offered ement for b-re.led. Butter, as I have sadly, has been held for high prices, the y depression having given way to the real he country markets. Ordinary to fair lots at 20½c to 21c for Eastern; Western 22c ad choice dairy very scarce at 23½c to 24c, Grocers willingly paying 25c for extra Cheese—Is in fair shipping demand at ½c for good factory.

RIES.—There are several considerable auction announced for next week; these ie closing one of the season, and it is to will produce more activity than the last It is generally presumed that stocks are y in the west, and if so we may look for inter's trade. Everything will depend ancial position of our Western customers; indications point to ease.

VARE.—These is still an active business nd orders are coming forward freely. e much reduced especially bar and pig l prices are very firm with, if anything, al tendency. I have no change to note articles, some of which range at lower n is remunerative, but with the present mand and rapidly lessening stocks it may ed that all descriptions of hardware will elgre the close of the navigation.

RADE.—A few words on this may be e to your western readers. There is a or for local manufacture, which keeps up of Otter, Mink, and Beaver. Shipping dull. Buffalo, robes moving off pretty men hat near last year's prices.

Toronto Market

; the week trade has been pretty quiet, r amount of general business is reported jason.

oods.—Grains are moving off steadily, ay a fair demand from country merchants g up stocks. Travellers who have visited t to the east of this city say that country ers have still pretty fully shelves, yet few complaints of dullness. On the astate of the country trade in that direc-onounced quite satisfactory. There is a ly, demand for goods from dealers in the west, showing that the season's business is pro-gressing satisfactorily in that quarter also. Fancy Goods—Orders from the country have been coming in steadily until within the past few days since when there has been some falling off owing pro-bably to the state of the weather and the roads. Wool goods were sold pretty freely, such as Nubias, hoods, &c., but the stock is still well main-tained. Indeed it may be said of every depart-ment of the dry-goods business that stocks though reduced are well-assorted, showing that our im-porters have pretty well estimated the wants of the country in each particular line. While this is the case, there is no over stock in any depart-ment; in this respect especially the fall trade this year compares favorably with last year. Montreal houses have in many instances, as we are inform-ed, brought goods in excess of the demand that has been made upon them, so that some houses there will have to repeat the operation of last year and previous years, of carrying over winter stocks of inconvenient magnitude. Payments—there are some complaints of slowness on the part of country merchants just lately, from some cause. We give a statement showing the imports of dry goods at this port for the month of October:—

	1867.	1868.
Manufactures of woollens............	$65,996	$54,523
do cottons...............	47,600	44,097
do silks & velvets	11,986	10,714
do furs..............	1,507	984
Wearing apparel.............	647	198
	$127,736	$110,516

GROCERIES—Sugars—are firm and have under-gone a further advance of ½ per cent on all grades of raw, and refiners have put up their prices in the same proportion. Teas—There is a good enquiry; some job lots selling at full prices. We note also some sales of low grade Greens for export to the United States. Fish—firm, with a little more offering, several cargoes of new herrings having ar-rived in Montreal during the week. Fruit—There is considerable enquiry for fruit this week but no change in prices as yet. Two fruit ships, one with a cargo of Valencia raisins and the other with an assortment, are daily expect to arrive, and the market is in suspense till they are heard from. Should they not come to hand soon firmer prices may be looked for. There is very little fine fruit to be had this year, the great bulk being inferior. The imports of leading groceries at the port of Toronto for October were as follows :—

		1867.		1868.
		quant. value.		quant value.
Coffee, green, lbs.............	40061	$37750	34561	$4091
Tea, green and Japan, lbs...	181315	34211	161517	29405
Tea, black, lbs..............	...	...	9198	3272
Tobacco, manufactured, lbs...	5120	1262	3552	1143
Sugars	...	338891	37236	440079	21053
Cane Juice	...	42530	996	...	...
Mace and Nutmegs		2317	922	2919	777
Dried Fruits and Nuts	...	...	16920	...	6480

BOOTS AND SHOES.—Manufacturers have still more orders on hand than they can supply, and prices are firm and unchanged.

GRAIN—Wheat—Receipts by cars 20,773 bush. and 32,655 bush. last week. The market is very dull; and there are few buyers. Cars of spring were offered at $1.10 to $1.14, and some small sales to local millers were reported at these prices. There is no enquiry for export. Midge proof is nominal at about the same prices. Fall is ex-tremely dull, and may be quoted nominal at $1.10 to $1.20. Barley—Receipts by cars 5,034 bush. and 19,635 bush. last week. Shipments by water for the week called with Saturday last, 20,720 bush. and 31,675 bush. the previous week. Total shipments by water since the commence-ment of the season, 616,448 bush. The following vessels cleared with barley during the week : the schooner St. Ann, with 7,225 bushels; the Kate with 5,629 bush.; Ontario, with 2774 bush; Jessie Macdonald with 5,092 bush. (and 3392 bush. of wheat) all for Oswego. The market has ruled dull and unsettled, closing nominal at $1.30. Oats—Receipts by car 6000 bush. and 3720 last

week ; the market is dull at 50c to 51c. Peas—Receipts by cars 2400 bush. and 4760 bush. last week. There is little demand, and not much doing ; quotations nominal. Rye—Receipts for the week ended Saturday last by vessel 22,659 bush. all from local ports. Market dull at 85c.

FLOUR.—Receipts for the week 2320 bush. and 2400 bush. last week. The market is exceedingly dull, and tending lower. Superfine is now offered freely at $5.00, with some demand at $4.75 to 4.80 ; a sale occurred yesterday at $4.80. For other grades there is no demand, and no sales to report.

PROVISIONS—Butter—A large lot of tub sold a point west on the G. T. R. at 22½c.; and the same price was offered for another lot at Peterboro and refused ; holders demand 23½. Dressed Hogs —supply moderate, selling at $6.00 to 7.25. Live Hogs—There were some 700 to 800 bought in from the States, and will be packed here in bond for export to Europe. This is a new feature in the trade that we would be glad to see much extended. Cheese—offering at 11½ to 1 1½. Mess Pork—offering at $24.50 ; demand slack.

FREIGHTS—Rates by steamer to Montreal on flour 80c ; on wheat, &c.; barley to Oswego 3½c. to Erie 4c. ; Lumber to Oswego $1.75 per M feet ; coal Erie to Toronto $1.30 to 1.35, currency. Rates per Grand Trunk—Flour to Montreal; 65c bond meats to Liverpool per gross ton 67s. 6d ; lard and butter 77s.; Beef per ton 11s.; pork per bbl 9s.

The Grain Trade

We collect a few figures showing the movement in wheat and flour, and the stocks at different points. The receipts at New York for the week ended Nov. 6 were :

	1867.		1868.	
	For the week.	Since Jan. 1.	For the week.	Since Jan. 1.
Flour, brls.........	12,000	3,061,720	130,095	2,544,00
Wheat, bush...	1,123,200	7,425,740	621,120	5,145,765
Barley, bush...	218,880	589,550	345,545	1,995,45

The exports from New York to foreign ports were, since Jan. 1st:

	1867.	1868.
Flour, brls...............	663,380	820,622
Wheat, bush...	2,714,508	4,555,731
Barley, bush.............	886,833	90

The receipts of the same articles at five Western lake ports, Chicago, Milwaukee, Toledo, Detroit and Cleveland, for the week, and since January 1st, were:

	1867.		1868.	
	For the week.	Since Jan. 1.	For the week.	Since Jan. 1.
Flour, brls........	135,905	3,048,550	138,974	3,560,02
Wheat, bush...	1,428,370	20,290,168	1,591,585	27,442,954
Barley, bush...	73,892	2,052,580	137,607	2,351,939

The stocks in store at the following points, at the dates mentioned, were:

At New York

	Oct. 30, 1868.	Nov. 2, 1868.	Nov. 4, 1867.
Wheat, bush...	1,023,704	1,410,322	687,617
Barley, bush...	126,877	238,144	329,384
Oats, bush...	1,771,011	2,065,974	1,669,294
Peas, bush...	65,333	95,177	7,114
Malt, bush...	41,612	14,327	62,502

At Buffalo.

	Oct. 30, 1868.	Nov. 2, 1868.	Nov. 4, 1867.
Wheat, bush...	775,000	476,000	447,000
Oats, bush...	1,000,000	500,000	216,000
Barley, bush...	90,000	73,000	170,000
Peas, bush...	1,800	1,800	14,700

At Chicago.

Oct. 31.—Flour, 73,328 brls.; wheat, 1,252,-384 bush.; barley, 564,780 bush.; Rye 214,043 bush.

At Milwaukee.

Oct. 31.—Wheat, 476,000 bush., against 347,-000 bush. in store at same time in 1867.

Beet Root Sugar.

A Beet Root Sugar Manufactory is about to be established in Buena Vista County Town. The re-quisite machinery is to be brought from France at a cost of $100,000. Five thousand acres of land have been purchased on which to grow the Beets.

Demerara Sugar Market.

The following is from Sandbach, Parker & Co.'s circular, dated Georgetown, 8th October, 1868:

BREADSTUFFS.—Early in the fortnight the market was languid and sales were made at rates quoted in our last. A demand for export having sprung up, an advance of 50c. on Flour and Meal was established at which rates considerable business was done. The mail yesterday bringing advices of short shipments for this place, and low stocks in the Islands, holders are to-day firm ; and although we have not heard of any sales, yet we look for an advance in prices.

PROVISIONS.—By the above vessels we have received 537 brls. Pork, Rump $24 prime Mess $22, Mess $27, clear Mess $29 ; 500 half brls. Beef $11. 50, 1500 Tins Lard $4 20, for New York $4 50, for Baltimore : 225 Boxes Cheese 18 cents ; 42 Tieroes Hams 15 cents : 150 Firkins French Butter $18.

RICE.—The "Lincelles," with 9000 Bags has arrived from Calcutta ; as the stocks estimated at 60,000 Bags, are in the hands of no less than six houses, with the unusually dull market for the article, no advance in price can be obtained. The abundance of native provisions, still continues, and the sales of Rice for the fortnight have been on the smallest possible scale.

OATS, BRAN, CORN, &c.—There has been some slight enquiry for Irish Oats, but prices are not remunerative. Canadian are almost unsaleable.

SUGARS.—Almost every Estate in the Colony is fairly at work, the demand for America for good samples is steady at $6 to $6 10 for V.P., but as a rule the quality-offering for sale is not up to the usual standard ; this is the more unaccountable as the juice is sweetening every day with such hot weather. American advices lead us to think that the demand for that country will be active the next few months ; very little doing in Muscava- does,-purchasers not feeling inclined to purchase at the limits of holders.

MOLASSES.—There has been but few transactions for Vacuum Pan and the sales have rarely exceeded 25 cts. Planters are unwilling to accept the low rates and are re-boiling to a great extent, if prices improve orders to a very large extent could be filled ; the demand for Muscavado has been good, and bright samples have commanded better rates than Vacuum Pan.

Transactions have taken place during the fortnight at the following rates :

SUGARS (package included) sold by 100 lbs. Dutch, 10 per cent. tare F.O.B.

Muscavadoes, equal at No. 8 Dutch Standard $3.00 ₩ 100 lbs.	
No. 10 do. $4.00 "	In hhds. of about 1800 lbs. each.
" 12 do. $4.25 "	
Vacuum Pan No. 12 do. $5.50	
" 14 do. 5.75	
" 16 do. 6.00	
" 18 do. 6.10	

MOLASSES (package included, sold by Imperial gallon.)

Muscovado, from 20 @ 26 cents, as to color and density	In puns of 100 gals.
Vacuum Pan from 20 @ 25 cents, as to color and density	
Rum (colored, package included, sold by Imperial gal. from 35 per cent, @ 38 overproof 38 @ 40 cents.	Ditto.
From 38 per cent. @ 40 overproof, 40 @ 42 cents.	

Halifax Market.

BREADSTUFFS.—No. v 3.—Flour.—The demand for flour during the past week has been quite brisk, but owing to the large supply there has been no advance in prices. Canada No. 1 ranges from $6.25 to $6.50. Strong Bakers $6.65 to $6.70. Extra Canada $7.50 to $8. Extra State still continues dull at $6 to $6.40, according to quality ; No. 2 in good demand at $5 to $5.50. Cornmeal without change at $4.50 for kiln dried, and $4.40 for fresh ground. Oatmeal $7.70 to

$7.80. Imports from January 1st to October 27th, 1867 and 1868 :

	Bbls. Flour.	Bbls. Cornmeal.
1868.	152,507	42,545
1867.	162,699	30,766

FISH.—Codfish scarce and in good demand without change in price, at $4.15 to $4.25 for good large shore. Labrador $2.25 to $2.50. Bank and Bay none. Good hand cure Arichat Haddock $2 to $2.10 ; Eastern Shore $1.80 to $1.90 ; Western $1.60 to $1.65 ; Pollock $1.50. Herring in good demand at $5 for Labrador and $4.75 for shore. Mackerel scarce at $12.50 for No. 1, $11 for No. 2, and $6.75 to $7 for No. 3. Salmon $14 for No. 1, $12 for No. 2, and $9.50 for No. 3.

WEST INDIA PRODUCE.—Sugars and Molasses remain without change. Large lots are being shipped out of our market and must soon affect prices here. Porto Rico 5½ to 6½c. ; Barbadoes 5¾ to 5½c. ; Cuba 5¼ to 5½c. Centrifugal Cuba 6c., in bond. Rum scarce and in demand at 62c. for Demerara, and 51 to 52½c. for St. Jago.

Exports of Petroleum.

The following were the exports of petroleum from the United States to foreign countries, from January 1st to October 30 :

From	1868.	1867.
Boston	2,100,619	1,710,412
Philadelphia	31,075,836	23,436,494
Baltimore	2,417,315	1,303,675
Portland	571,370	300
New York	47,614,237	26,227,777
Total, gallons	83,779,268	52,679,068
Corresponding period 1866, gallons		52,783,617
Corresponding period 1865, gallons		18,618,603

	Barrels.
Receipts at New York, Jan. 1 to Oct. 30, 1868	807,990
Receipts at New York, Jan. 1 to Oct. 30, 1867	1,075,780

U. S. NATIONAL BOARD OF UNDERWRITERS.— The executive committee met in Chicago on the 22nd October. The following resolutions as to rates of premiums were passed:—

Resolved, That when undoubted evidence is received by the officers of the Executive Committee that the rates in any given locality are so high, low, or unequal in their operations, that no business can be secured by companies comprising this Board, it shall be their duty to send at the earliest moment, a proper committee to revise the rates, and that immediate notice shall be given to all companies belonging to this Board of any change therein ; but rates so revised shall not be in effect until five days after publication and notification to such Board.

Resolved, That any agent of companies belonging to the National Board who does not adhere with all the companies which he represents to the rates established by authority of the committee, or who shall negotiate for or obtain elsewhere any insurance at less than tariff rates, shall not continue to represent any company of this Board.

The Committee on Form of Policies reported the following resolutions, which were adopted :—

Resolved, That our mercantile policies, as printed and ordinarily filled up, to wit: "On merchandise —their own or held by them in trust or on commission, or sold but not delivered," are intended to protect and do fully protect the interest of owners, of commission merchants and factors who have advanced on the goods to the entire value of the goods they have in charge, not exceeding the amount insured thereon.

Resolved, That when the party or parties insured have sold and delivered the goods, and thereby their responsibility for preservation of the goods has ceased, they cannot take the required oath of interest in the goods in case of a loss therein, and consequently have no claim under the policy.

Resolved, That the requirement in the policy that consent of the company in writing must be obtained before the interest can pass to cover a party not originally insured is of sound, practical value ; and we take warning to ourselves and give it to our brother underwriters of this and other

cities that it is dangerous to use written words or our policies which might be construed into a waiver of vital printed "conditions."

Resolved, That claims for the loss of goods as it is truly set forth in the "proof of loss," in the sale note or contract of sale there writing the following words, or others to the effect:—"Deliverable at the option of the at any time within —— days ;" or if an order the warehouse has been given and such order made to read, "Deliver to A. B. & Co." purchasers), at any time within —— days words to that effect, the insurance comp members of the New York Board of Fire Underwriters, will recognize the assured in the named as the owner of the goods within at to the time of such limitation, provided the number of days is fixed at the time of sale and written in the contract on order, and provided the buyer shall not have presented his order had the goods placed to his or other accou the store.

The Committee on Statistics presented the following report:

Number of Companies	States.	Combined Capital.	Gross Income from Fire Insurance.	Expenses.	Losses.
12	New York	$94,661,136	$21,527,664	$7,609,727	$14,352,797
13	Mass.	4,000,000	1,537,417	497,484	982,517
5	Conn.	2,100,000	1,093,210	303,316	641,954
6	Pennsylvania	2,150,000	1,958,997	294,842	5,773,590
6	Maryland	1,095,382	1,445,021	432,412	166,810
5	Ohio	726,000	378,991	72,315	214,090
3	Illinois	1,000,333	279,397	118,488	248,095
3	California	904,000	406,063	145,900	411,995
4	Ontario, Can.	2,988,392	940,661	96,857	1,076,440
170	Total.	$68,603,617	$29,391,716	$13,176,703	$22,406,577

STEAMER GRECIAN.—This steamer has raised, and having transhipped her cargo, has to Montreal to go into dry dock.

—The Greenock Advertiser understands Messrs. Allan, of Glasgow, have contracted Messrs. Robert Steele & Company, for a screw steamer of about 3,000 tons, for the between the Mersey and the St. Lawrence. is to be a fac simile of the Austrian. Her en of 300 horse-power, are to be supplied by Rankin & Blackmore, Eagle Foundry.

—It is said that the National Steamship pany have made a proposal to the British office Department to carry letters to Ameri greatly reduced rate. Last year they were stood to have offered to carry letters to New at a penny per ounce.

Gore Bank.

New Advertisements.

Miscellaneous.

Mercantile.

Mercantile.

Mercantile.

DOMINION TELEGRAPH COMPANY.

CAPITAL STOCK   -   - $500,000.

In 10,000 Shares at $50 Each.

PRESIDENT,
HON. WILLIAM CAYLEY.

TREASURER,
HON. J. McMURRICH.

SECRETARY,
H. B. REEVE.

SOLICITORS,
MESSRS. CAMERON & McMICHAEL.

GENERAL SUPERINTENDENT.
MARTIN RYAN

DIRECTORS.

HON. J. McMURRICH,
Bryce, McMurrich & Co., Toronto.

A. R. McMASTER, Esq.,
A. R. McMaster & Brother, Toronto.

HON. M. C. CAMERON,
Provincial Secretary, Toronto.

JAMES MICHIE, Esq.,
Fulton, Michie & Co., and George Michie & Co., Toronto

HON. WILLIAM CAYLEY,
Toronto.

A. M. SMITH, Esq.,
A. M. Smith & Co., Toronto.

L. MOFFATT, Esq.,
Moffatt, Murray & Co., Toronto.

H. B. REEVE, Esq.,
Toronto.

MARTIN RYAN, Esq.,
Toronto.

PROSPECTUS.

THE DOMINION TELEGRAPH COMPANY has been organized under the act respecting Telegraph Companies, chapter 67, of the consolidated Statutes of Canada. Its object is to cover the Dominion of Canada with a complete net-work of Telegraph lines.

The Capital Stock

Is $500,000, divided into 10,000 shares of $50 each, 5 per cent to be paid at the time of subscribing, the balance to be paid by instalments, not exceeding 10 per cent per month—said instalments to be called in by the Directors as the works progress. The liability of a subscriber is limited to the amount of his subscription.

The Business Affairs of the Company.

Are under the management of a Board of Directors, annually elected by the Shareholders, in conformity with the Charter and By-Laws of the Company.

The Directors are of opinion that it would be to the interest of the Stockholders generally to obtain subscriptions from all quarters of Canada, and with this view they propose to divide the Stock amongst the different towns and cities throughout the Dominion, in allotments suited to the population and business occupations of the different localities, and the interest which they may be supposed to take in such an enterprise.

Contracts of Connections.

A contract, granting permanent connection and extraordinary advantages, has already been executed between this Company and the Atlantic and Pacific Company, of New York ; thus, at the very commencement, as the Lines of this Company are constructed from the Suspension Bridge, at Clifton (the point of connection) to any point in the Dominion, all the chief cities and places in the States, touched by the Lines of the Atlantic and Pacific Telegraph Company, are brought in immediate connection therewith.

A permanent connection has also been secured with the Great Western Telegraph Company, of Chicago, whereby this Company will be brought into close connection with all the Lake Ports and other places through the North western States, and through to California.

4-3mos

Mercantile.

UNRIVALLED!

THE BRITISH AMERICAN COMMERCIAL COLLEGE,
Consolidated with the

Bryant, Stratton and Odell Business College
AND TELEGRAPHIC INSTITUTE.

STANDS Pre-eminent and Unrivalled. It is the LARGEST and MOST EFFICIENT. It employs the largest staff of Teachers, among whom are the two BEST PENMEN OF CANADA.

The TUITION FEE is the same as in other Institutions having a similar object.

The PRICE OF BOARD is the same as in other Canadian Cities.

In an EDUCATIONAL point of view, there is no other Institution in the country that has equal advantages and facilities.

YOUNG MEN intending to qualify themselves for business, will find it to their advantage to send for a Circular, or call at the College Rooms, corner of King and Toronto streets.

Scholarships good in Montreal and throughout the United States.

ODELL & TROUT.
October 2.   Principals and Proprietors.
8

The Mercantile Agency,
FOR THE
PROMOTION AND PROTECTION OF TRADE
Established in 1841.
DUN, WIMAN & Co.
Montreal, Toronto and Halifax.

REFERENCE Book, containing names and ratings of Business Men in the Dominion, published semi-annually.   24-1y

The St. Lawrence Glass Company

ARE now manufacturing and have for sale,

COAL OIL LAMPS,
various styles and sizes.

LAMP CHIMNEYS,
of extra quality for ordinary Burners also, for the 'Comet' and 'Sun' Burners.

SETS OF
TABLE GLASSWARE, HYACINTH GLASSES,
STEAM GUAGE TUBES, GLASS RODS, &c.,
or any other article made to order, in White or Colored Glass.

KEROSENE BURNERS, COLLARS and SOCKETS, will be kept on hand.

DRUGGISTS FLINT GLASSWARE, and
PHILOSOPHICAL INSTRUMENTS,
made to order.

OFFICE—368 ST. PAUL STREET, MONTREAL.
A. McK. COCHRANE.
8-1y   Secretary.

J. R. Boyce,

NOS. 63 and 65, Great James Street, Montreal, Dealer in and Importer of all kinds of TOYS and FANCY GOODS. J. R. B. is the only manufacturer of La Crosse Sticks for the new *Indian Game of LACROSSE*, and has constantly on hand a large supply, with the printed *Rules of the Game*. He also manufactures all the requisites for Croquet, and all other Parlour and Lawn Games. Baskets, of all kinds, and every variety of *Hair Work, Wigs, Curls, Beards*, &c. ; *Dress and Theatrical Wigs*, for sale, Wholesale and Retail Parties engaged in forming new La Crosse Clubs, will do well to apply direct to the above address.

Lyman & McNab,
Importers of, and Wholesale Dealers in,
HEAVY AND SHELF HARDWARE,
KING STREET,
TORONTO, ONTARIO.

H. N. Smith & Co.,

2, EAST SENECA STREET, BUFFALO, N. Y., (correspondent Smith, Gould, Martin & Co., 11 Broad Street, N.Y.,) Stock, Money and Exchange Brokers. Advances made on securities.   21-1y

Mercantile.

DAY'S
Commercial College and High Sch
No. 82 KING STREET EAST,
(*Near St. James' Cathedral.*)

THE design of this institution is to prepare Y and others as Book-keepers, and for general and to furnish them with the facilities for acc excellent

English and Commercial Education.

Mr. DAY is also prepared to give Private Inst. the several subjects of his department, and to a chants and others in the checking and balancing adjusting their accounts and partnership affairs,

For further information, please call on or ac undersigned.
JAMES E. D
Acc
Toronto, Sept. 3rd, 1868.

Financial.

Canada Permanent Building and S
Society.

Paid up Capital $1,
Assets 1,
Annual Income ....

Directors:—JOSEPH D. RIDOUT, *Presiden*
PETER PATERSON, *Vice-President.*
J. G. Worts, Edward Hooper, S. Nordheimer
Chewett, E. H. Rutherford, Joseph Robin
Bankers:—Bank of Toronto; Bank of Montre
Canadian Bank.

OFFICE—*Masonic Hall, Toronto Street,*

Money Received on Deposit bearing five a
cent. interest.

Advances made on City and Country Property in f
of Ontario.
J. HERBERT M
36-y   Ser

Pellatt & Osler.

STOCK AND EX HANGE BROKERS, A
Agents for the Standard Life Assurance Co
New York Casualty Insurance Company.
OFFICE—86 *King Street East, four Doors*
Church Street, Toronto.
HENRY PELLATT,   EDMUND
1y   Notary Public.   Official A

The Canadian Land and Emigration

Offers for sale on Conditions of Settlem
GOOD FARM LAN
In the County of Peterboro, Ontari

In the well settled Township of Dysart, whe
Grist and Saw Mills, Stores, &c., a
ONE-AND-A-HALF DOLLARS AN

In the adjoining Townships of Guilford, I
burn, Harcourt and Bruton, connected with
the Village of Haliburton by the Peterson Ro
DOLLAR an Acre.

For further particulars apply to
CHAS. JAS. BLOMFIELD,
Secretary C. L. and E. C
Or to   ALEX. NIVEN, P.L.S.,
Agent C. L. & E. Co., E

Western Canada Permanent Build
Savings Society.

OFFICE—No 70 CHURCH STREET, TOR

SAVINGS-BANK BRANCH,

DEPOSITS RECEIVED DAILY. INTEREST P
YEARLY.

ADVANCES
Are made on the security of Real Estate, rep
ment favourable terms, by a Sinking F
WALTER S
36-1y   Se

TORONTO PRICES CURRENT.—November 12, 1868.

Name of Article.	Wholesale Rates.	Name of Article.	Wholesale Rate.	Name of Article.	Wholesale Rates.
Boots and Shoes.	$ c. $ c.	**Groceries**—Contin'd	$ c. $ c.	**Leather**—Contin'd	$ c. $ c.
Mens' Thick Boots ...	2 20 2 50	" fine to fins't..	0 85 0 95	Kip Skins, Patna ..	0 50 0 40
" Kip	2 50 3 25	Hyson	0 45 0 80	French	0 70 0 90
" Calf	3 20 3 70	Imperial	0 42 0 80	English	0 65 0 90
" Congress Gaiters..	2 00 2 40	Tobacco, Manufac'd:		Hemlock Calf (30 to	
" Kip Cobourgs...	1 10 1 50	Can Leaf, ⅌ ℔ 5 & 10s.	0 25 0 30	35 lbs.) per doz..	0 75 0 85
Boys' Thick Boots...	1 70 1 90	Western Leaf, com..	0 25 0 26	Do. light	0 45 0 50
Youths'	1 45 1 50	" Good	0 27 0 32	French Calf.	0 96 1 15
Women's Batts	95 1 30	" Fine	0 32 0 35	Grain & Satn Cl'⅌ doz.	0 00 0 00
" Congress Gaiters..	1 15 1 50	" Bright fine..	0 40 0 50	Splits, large ⅌ ℔..	0 30 0 38.
Misses' Batts	0 75 1 00	" choice..	0 60 0 75	" small ..	0 29 0 32
" Congress Gaiters,,	1 00 1 30	**Hardware.**		Enamelled Cow ⅌ foot..	0 17 0 18
Girls' Batts	0 00 0 85	Tin (net cash prices)		Patent	0 18 0 20
" Congress Gaiters,.	0 80 1 10	Block, ⅌ ℔.......	0 25 0 26	Pebble Grain	0 17 0 18½
Children's C. T. Cacks...	0 50 0 65	Grain............	0 25 0 26	Buff	0 17 0 18
" Gaiters ..	0 65 0 90	Copper:		**Oils.**	
Drugs.		Pig	0 23 0 24	Cod	0 60 0 62½
Aloes Cape.	0 12½ 0 16	Sheet.............	0 20 0 33	Lard, extra	0 00 1 25
Alum..............	0 02½ 0 06	Cut Nails :		" No. ..	0 00 1 15
B rax	0 00 0 00	Assorted ¼ Shingles,		" Woollen ...	0 00 1 05
Camphor, refined....	0 65 0 70	⅌ 100 ℔........	2 90 3 00	Lubricating, patent..	0 00 0 00
Castor Oil..........	0 18 0 33	Shingle alone do ...	3 15 3 25	" Moti's economic	0 80 0 00
Caustic Soda........	0 04½ 0 05	Lathe and 5 dy..	3 30 3 40	Linseed, raw	0 77½ 0 85
Cochineal...........	0 00 1 0	Galvanized Iron:		" boiled.....	0 82½ 0 90
Cream Tartar	0 00 0 00	Assorted sizes......	0 08 0 09	Machinery	0 00 0 00
E₂son Salts	0 02 0 04	Best No. 24.......	0 00 0 00	Olive, 2nd. ⅌ gal..	1 40 1 60
Extract Logwood....	0 00 0 11	" 26.......	0 08 0 08¼	" salad	2 00 2 30
Gum Arabic, sorts....	0 20 0 35	" 28.......	0 00 0 09½	" salad, in bota.	
Indigo, Madras......	0 75 1 00	Horse Nails:		qt. ⅌ case .	3 50 3 75
Liocrice	0 14 0 45	Guest's or Griffin's		Sesame salad, ⅌ gal..	1 60 1 75
Madder............	0 13 0 15	assorted sizes......	0 00 0 00	Seal, pale	0 75 0 75
Nutgalls	0 00 0 35	For W. ass'd sizes	0 18 0 19	Spirits Turpentine..	0 65 0 70
Opium.............	6 70 7 00	Patent Hammer'd do	0 17 0 18	Varnish	0 00 0 00
Oxalic Acid.........	0 23 0 35	Iron (at 4 months):		Whale............	0 75 0 80
Potash, Bi-tart......	0 25 0 25	Pig—Gartsherrie No1..	24 00 25 00		
" bichromate..	0 15 0 20	Other brands. No1..	22 00 24 00	**Paints, &c.**	
Potass Iodide	3 80 4 50	No2..	0 00 0 00	White Lead, genuine	
Senna	0 12½ 0 60	Bar—Scotch, ⅌100 ℔..	2 25 2 50	in Oil, ⅌ 25℔s....	0 00 2 50
Soda Ash	0 03 0 04	Refined..........	3 00 3 25	Do. No. 1	0 00 2 25
S da Bicarb	0 06 0 07	Swedes	5 00 5 50	" 2	0 00 1 75
Tartaric Acid.......	0 37½ 0 45	Hoops—Coopers.....	3 00 3 25	White Zinc, genuine	3 10 3 50
Verdigris	0 35 0 40	Band	3 00 3 25	White Lead, dry	0 05 0 09
Vitriol, Blue........	0 09 0 10	Boiler Plates.......	3 25 3 50	Red Lead	0 07½ 0 08
Groceries.		Canada Plates......	4 00 4 25	Venetian Red, Eng'h.	0 02 0 09½
Coffees :		Union Jack	0 00 0 00	Yellow Ochre, Fren'h..	0 02½ 0 03
Java, ⅌ ℔..........	0 22 0 24	Pontypool.........	4 00 4 25	Whiting	0 90 1 25
Laguayra...........	0 17 0 18	Swansea	3 90 4 00		
Rio................	0 15 0 17	Lead (at 4 months):		**Petroleum.**	
Fish :		Bar, ⅌ 100 ℔s.....	0 07 0 07½	(Refined ⅌ gal.)	
Herring, Lab. split..	6 75 7 00	Sheet "	0 08 0 09	Water white, car'l'd..	0 31 —
" round......	0 00 0 00	Shot.............	0 07½ 0 07½	" small lots...	0 00 0 32½
" scaled.....	0 85 0 40	Iron Wire (net cash):		Straw, by car load...	0 30 —
Mackerel, small kitts..	1 00 0 00	No. 6, ⅌ bundle ...	2 70 2 80	" small lots...	0 31 0 32
Louh. Her. wt e firks..	2 35 2 75	" 9	3 10 3 20	Amber, by car load..	0 00 0 00
" half "	1 25 1 50	" 12, "	3 40 3 50	" small lots	0 00 0 00
White Fish & Trout...	3 25 3 50	" 10, "	4 30 4 40	Benzine	0 00 0 00
Salmon, saltwater.....	14 00 15 00	Powder :			
Dry Cod, ⅌112 lbs...	5 00 5 00	Blasting, Canada....	3 50 3 75	**Produce.**	
Fruit :		FF	4 25 4 50	Grain :	
Raisins, Layers	2 20 2 25	FFF	4 75 5 00	Wheat, Spring, 60 ℔..	1 09 1 11
" M R.........	2 10 3 20	Blasting, English ...	4 00 5 00	" Fall 60 "	1 20 1 30
" 'valentianes".	0 08½ 0 08½	FF loose..	5 00 6 00	Peas........ 60 "..	0 85 0 89
Currants, new	0 05 0 06½	FFF "	6 00 6 50	Oats........ 34 "..	0 51 0 52
" old........	0 11 0 12½	Pressed Spikes (4 mos).:		Rye .... 56 "..	0 88 0 90
Molasses :		Regular sizes 100....	4 00 4 25	Seeds:	
Clayed, ⅌ gal........	0 00 0 35	Extra	4 50 5 00	Clover, choice 60 "..	6 25 6 50
Syrups, Standard	0 45 0 44	Tin Plates (net cash):		" com'n 68 "..	0 00 0 00
" Golden	0 52 0 55	IC Coke	7 50 8 00	Timothy, cho'e 4 "..	2 50 2 75
Rice :		IC Charcoal.......	8 25 8 75	" inf. to good 48 "	2 00 2 40
Arracan	4 50 4 75	IX "	10 25 10 75	Flax " .. 56 "	1 40 1 50
Spices :		IXX "	12 50 12 75	Flour (per brl.) :	
Cassia, whole, ⅌ ℔.	0 42 0 45	DC "	7 50 9 00	Superior extra.....	6 25 6 50
Cloves	0 11 0 12	DX "	9 50 10 00	Extra superfine,....	5 90 6 10
Nutmegs	0 45 0 55	**Hides & Skins⅌℔**		Fancy superfine	0 00 0 00
Ginger, ground	0 20 0 25	Green rough	0 05½ 0 06	Superfine No. 1.....	5 00 5 05
" Jamaica, root..	0 20 0 25	Green, salt'd & insp'd...	0 00 0 00	" No. 2.....	0 00 0 00
Pepper, black........	0 45 0 55	Cured	0 07½ 0 08½	Oatmeal, (per brl.)..	6 00 6 25
Pimento	0 08 0 00	Calfskins, green.....	0 00 0 21		
Sugars :		" cured.....	0 00 0 12	**Provisions.**	
Port Rico, ⅌ ℔......	0 08½ 0 08½	" dry.......	0 18 0 20	Butter, dairy tub ⅌℔..	0 23 0 24
Cuba "	0 08½ 0 08½	Sheepskins, ...	0 70 0 00	" store packed..	0 21 0 22
Barbadoes (bright)..	0 08½ 0 08½	" country...	0 60 0 85	Cheese, new	0 11 0 12
Dry Crushed, at 60d.	0 11½ 0 11½			Pork, mess, per brl...	24 62 24 75
Canada Sugar Refine'y,		**Hops.**		" prime mess....	0 00 0 00
yellow No. 2, 60 ds..	0 08½ 0 08½	Inferior, ⅌ ℔.......	0 10 0 12	Bacon, rough	0 00 0 00
Yellow, No. 2½......	0 08½ 0 09½	Medium...........	0 12 0 15	" Cumber'd out..	0 11 0 12
" No. 3...	0 09½ 0 09½	Good	0 15 0 00	" smoked	0 00 0 00
Crushed X ...	0 09 0 11	Fancy	0 00 0 00	Hams, in salt.......	0 00 0 00
" A	0 00 0 00			" sug. cur &canv'd ..	0 00 0 00
Ground............	0 09½ 0 11½	**Leather,** ⅌ (4 mos.)		Shoulders, in salt ...	0 00 0 00
Extra Ground.......	0 09½ 0 12½	In lots of less than		Lard, in kegs	0 15 0 16
Teas :		50 sides, 10 ⅌ cent		Eggs, packed	0 18 0 19
Japan com'n to good..	0 40 0 55	higher.		Beef Hams	0 00 0 00
" Fine to choicest..	0 55 0 60	Spanish Sole, 1st qual..		Tallow	0 00 0 00
Colored, com. to fine...	0 00 0 75	heavy, weights ⅌℔..	0 20 0 21	Hogs dressed, heavy..	6 50 7 00
Congou & Souch'ng..	0 42 0 75	Do. No. 1, cut middle do..	0 15 0 19	" light.......	5 00 6 00
Oolong, good to fine..	0 50 0 65	Do. No. 2, all weights..	0 15 0 19		
Y. Hyson, com to gd..	0 45 0 55	Slaughter heavy ...	0 23 0 30	**Salt, &c.**	
Medium to choice ...	0 55 0 80	Do. light..........	0 50 0 00	American hds.......	1 55 1 00
Extra choice	0 85 0 06	Harness, best	0 31 0 34	Liverpool coarse	1 30 - 0 40
" med. to fine	0 55 0 70	" No. 2	0 30 0 33	Pluster	1 05 1 10
" med. to fine	0 70 0 85	Upper heavy	0 44 0 38	Water Lime	1 50 0 00
		" light.......	0 36 0 40		

Soap & Candles.	$ c.	$ c.
D. Crawford & Co.'s ..		
Imperial........	0 07½	0 08
" Golden Bar	0 07	0 07½
" Silver Bar........	0 07	0 07½
Crown :..............	0 05	0 05½
No. 1	0 03½	0 03¾
Candles	0 00	0 11½
Wines, Liquors, &c.		
Ale:		
English, per doz......	2 60	2 65
Guinness Dub Portr..	2 35	2 40
Spirits:		
Pure Jamaica Rum...	1 80	2 25
De Kuyper's H. Gin..	1 55	1 65
Booth's Old Tom.....	1 90	2 00
Gin:		
Green, cases.........	4 00	4 25
Booth's Old Tom, c...	6 00	6 25
Wines:		
Port, common	1 00	1 25
" fine old	2 00	4 00
Sherry, common	1 00	1 50
" medium	1 70	1 80
"old pale or golden..	2 50	4 00

Brandy:	$ c	$ c
Hennessy's, per gal..	2 30	2 50
Martell's " ..	2 30	2 50
J. Robin & Co.'s " ..	2 25	2 35
Otard, Dupuy & Cos..	2 25	2 35
Brandy, cases........	8 50	9 00
Brandy, com. per c...	4 00	4 50
Whiskey:		
Common 36 u. p......	0 62½	0 65
Old Rye	0 85	0 87½
Malt	0 85	0 87½
Toddy	0 85	0 87½
Scotch, per gal.......	1 90	2 10
Irish—Kinnahan's c...	7 00	7 50
" Dunnville's Belf't..	6 00	6 25
Wool.		
Fleece, lb.............	0 28	0 35
Pulled "............	0 22	0 25
Furs.		
Bear........	3 00	10 00
Beaver..	1 00	1 25
Coon	0 20	0 40
Fisher..............	4 00	6 00
Martin...	1 40	1 60
Mink................	4 00	4 25
Otter................	5 75	6 00
Spring Rats	0 15	0 17
Fox.	1 20	1 25

INSURANCE COMPANIES.

ENGLISH.—*Quotations on the London Market.*

No. of Shares.	Last Dividend.	Name of Company.	Shares par val £	Amount paid.	Last
20,000		Briton Medical and General Life...	10	....	1⅜
50,000	7½	Commer'l Union, Fire, Life and Mar.	50	5	5½
24,000	8	City of Glasgow	25	2½	5
5,000	9½	Edinburgh Life	100	15	30½x
400,000	5—½ yr	European Life and Guarantee......	2½	11s6	4s 6d
100,000	10	Etna Fire and Marine.............	10	1½	1
20,000	5	Guardian	100	50	51½
24,000	12	Imperial Fire.....................	500	50	345
7,500	9½	Imperial Life	100	10	16½
100,000	10	Lancashire Fire and Life..........	20	2	2⅜x
10,000	11	Life Association of Scotland.......	40	7½	23
35,862	45s. p. sh	London Assurance Corporation ..	25	12½	48
10,000	5	London and Lancashire Life	10	1	1
87,504	40	Liverp'l & London & Globe F. & L.	20	2	7⅝
20,000	5	National Union Life	5	1	1
20,000	12½	Northern Fire and Life	100	5	10⅜
40,000	12 '68, bo 5s.	North British and Mercantile	50	6¼	16 16½
40,000	50	Ocean Marine	25	5	20
2,500	£5 12s.	Provident Life.....................	100	10	38
....	£4½ p. s.	Phœnix...........................	....	....	136
200,000	2½—h. yr.	Queen Fire and Life	10	1	15-16ths
100,000	3s. bo. 4s	Royal Insurance..................	20	3	6½
20,000	10	Scottish Provincial Fire and Life ..	50	2½	4½
10,000	25	Standard Life	50	12	65
4,000	5	Star Life	25	1½	—
		CANADIAN.			℔ c.
8,000	4	British America Fire and Marine ..	$50	$25	56
....	4	Canada Life	..	....	.....
4000	12	Montreal Assurance	£50	£5	135
10,000	3	Provincial Fire and Marine........	60	11	.....
....	....	Quebec Fire	40	32½	£19½
....	8	" Marine..........................	100	40	90-95
10,000	5 7 mo's.	Western Assurance................	40	6	.....

RAILWAYS.	Sha's	Paid	Montr	London.
Atlantic and St. Lawrence........................	£100	All.	....	59 57
Buffalo and Lake Huron	20½	"	....	3 3½
Do. do Preference	10	"	....	5½ 6½
Buff., Brantt. & Goderich, 6℔c., 1872-3-4....	100	"	....	60 70
Champlain and St. Lawrence	....	....	9 11	....
Do. do Pref. 10 ℔ ct....	...	....	80	....
Grand Trunk	100	"	16 17	16 16½
Do. Eq.G. M. Bds. 1 ch. 6℔c...........	100	"	...	81 83
Do. First Preference, 5 ℔c	100	"	....	49 51
Do. Deferred, 3 ℔ ct..	100	"	....	....
Do. Second Pref. Bonds, 5℔c..........	100	"	....	38 40
Do. do Deferred, 3 ℔ ct..........	100	"	...	....
Do. Third Pref. Stock, 4 ℔ct...........	100	"	...	28 30
Do. do. Deferred, 3 ℔ ct......	100	"	...	....
Do. Fourth Pref. Stock, 3℔c..........	100	"	....	19 20
Do. do. Deferred, 3 ℔ ct.........	100	"	....	....
Great Western	20½	"	13 14	13½ 14½
Do. New	20½	18	....	....
Do. 6 ℔ c. Bds, due 1873-76..........	100	All.	....	102 104
5½ ℔c Bds. due 1877-78....	100	"	....	92 94
Marine Railway, Halifax, $250, all.	$250	"	....	....
Northern, of Canada, 6℔c. 1st Pref. Bds..........	100	"	.. .	80 83

EXCHANGE.	Halifax.	Montr'l.	Quebec.	Toronto.
Bank on London, 60 days......				
sight or 75 days date	13½	9¼ 9¾	9⅝ 9	9½
Private do.	12 12½	8½ 9	8½ 9	9
Private, with documents........	....	7½ 8½	....	....
Bank on New York..............	....	25 25½	24¾ 25¼	75
Private do.	....	25½ 26	25½ 26	....
Gold Drafts do.	....	par	par ½ dis.	par ½ dis.
Silver	....	2½ 3½	....	3½ 5

STOCK AND BOND REPORT.

The dates of our quotations are as follows:—Toronto, Nov. 10; Montreal, Nov. 2; Q Nov. 9; London, Oct. 16.

NAME.	Shares.	Paid up.	Divid'd last 6 Months	Dividend Day.	CLOSING PR Toronto.	Montre'
BANKS.			℔ ct.			
British North America	$250	All.	3	July and Jan.	103½ 104½	103½ 104½
Jacques Cartier.........	50	"	4	1 June, 1 Dec.	108 109	108½ 11
Montreal	200	"	5	"	140 142	140 141
Nationale....................	50	"	4	1 Nov. 1 May.	....	105 105½
New Brunswick	100	"	......	......	....	...
Nova Scotia	200	28	7&b$3½	Mar. and Sept.	....	....
Du Peuple...	50	"	4	1 Mar., 1 Sept.	105 105½	105½ 105¾
Toronto	100	"	4	1 Jan., 1 July.	119 119½	118 119
Bank of Yarmouth...........	....	....	......	......	....	....
Canadian Bank of Com'e......	50	95	......	......	104½ 105½	103½ 104½
City Bank Montreal	80	All.	4	1 June, 1 Dec.	134 135	105 105½
Commer'l Bank (St. John)....	100	"	℔ ct.	. ...	....	...
Eastern Townships' Bank.....	50	"	4	1 July, 1 Jan..	....	95½ 96
Gore	40	...	3½	1 Jan., 1 July.	40 42	40 41
Halifax Banking Company....	.	....	......	. ....	....	....
Mechanics' Bank............	50	70	4	1 Nov., 1 May.	94	94 95
Merchants' Bank of Canada....	100	70	4	1 Jan., 1 July.	108 108½	108½ 109
Merchants' Bank (Halifax)....	....	....	......	.....	....	....
Molson's Bank......	50	All.	4	1 Apr., 1 Oct.	107 109	107½ 109
Niagara District Bank...	100	70	3½	1 Jan., 1 July.	....	....
Ontario Bank...............	40	All.	4	1 June, 1 Dec.	103 103½	102½ 103½
People's Bank (Fred'kton)....	100	"	......	......	....	....
People's Bank (Halifax)	20	"	7 12 m	......	....	...
Quebec Bank	100	"	3½	1 June, 1 Dec.	100 101	100 101
Royal Canadian Bank	50	50	4	1 Jan., 1 July.	92 92½	91 92
St. Stephens Bank	100	All	.....	......	....	..
Union Bank	100	70	4	1 Jan., 1 July.	103½ 104½	103½ 104½
Union Bank (Halifax)........	100	40	7 12 mo	Feb. and Aug.	....	....
MISCELLANEOUS.						
British America Land........	250	44	2½	......	....	....
British Colonial S. S. Co......	250	32½	2½	......	...	45 50
Canada Company	32½	All.	5	......	....	....
Canada Landed Credit Co.....	50	$20	3½	......	72 75	....
Canada Per. B'ldg Society....	50	All.	5	......	122½ 123	....
Canada Mining Company.....	4	90	......	......	....	....
Do. Inl'd Steam Nav. Co.....	100	All.	20 12 m	......	....	106 108½
Do. Glass Company.........	100	"	12½ "	......	....	95
Canad'n Loan & Investm't....	25	2½	7	......	....	....
Canada Agency	10	¼	......	......	....	....
Colonial Securities Co........	...	....	......	.....	....	....
Freehold Building Society....	100	All.	4	......	107½ 108	....
Halifax Steamboat Co.........	100	"	5	......	....	....
Halifax Gas Company........	....	....	......	. .. .	....	...
Hamilton Gas Company......	....	....	......	. ....	....	....
Huron Copper Bay Co........	4	12	20	. ....	....	25 50cp
Lake Huron S. and C.........	5	102	......	......	....	....
Montreal Mining Consols......	20	$15	......	......	....	2.50 3.0
Do. Telegraph Co....	40	All.	5	......	128 130	129 13
Do. Elevating Co...	00	"	15 12 m	......	....	100 10
Do. City Gas Co.........	40	"	4	15 Mar. 15 Sep.	....	100 102
Do. City Pass. R. Co....	50	"	5	......	....	110 111
Nova Scotia Telegraph	20	"	....	. ....	....	....
Quebec and L. S.	8	$4	......	.....	.. ..	....
Quebec Gas Co..............	200	All.	4	1 Mar., 1 Sep.	....	...
Quebec Street R. R..........	50	25	8	......	....	....
Richelieu Navigation Co......	100	All.	7 p.a.	1 Jan., 1 July.	....	115 116
St. Lawrence Tow Boat Co....	100	"	......	3 Feb.	...	...
Tor'to Consumers' Gas Co....	50	"	2 3 m.	1 My Au Mar Fe	105 106½	...
Trust & Loan Co. of U. C.....	20	5	3	......	....	....
West'n Canada Bldg Soc'y....	50	All.	5	......	114½ 115	....

SECURITIES.	London.	Montreal.	Quebec.
Canadian Gov't Deb. 6 ℔ ct. stg..................	...	101 102	100½ 101
Do. do. 6 do due Ja. & Jul. 1877-84........	105 107	....	....
Do. do. 6 do. Feb. & Aug..	104 106	. ....	.. .
Do. do. 6 do. Mch. & Sep..........	104 106	.. .	...
Do. do. 5 ℔ ct. cur., 1883	91 93	91 92	89½ 90
Do. do. 5 do. stg., 1885	....	91 92	89½ 90
Do. do. 7 do. cur.,......................	....	....	......
Dominion 6 p. c. 1878 cy.....	....	103 104	103 104
Hamilton Corporation.....	. ..	....	......
Montreal Harbor, 8 ℔ ct. d. 1869...............	..	....	......
Do. do. 7 do. 1870.................	...	....	......
Do. do. 6½ do. 1875...	....	101 101	......
Do. do. 6½ do. 1873.................	....	....	......
Do. Corporation, 6 ℔ c. 1891	....	94 95	93 93½
Do. 7 p. c. stock...........................	....	105 106	105½ 106
Do. Water Works, 6 ℔ c. stg. 1878......... ..	...	....	......
Do. do. 6 do. cy. do.	....	95 96	......
New Brunswick, 6 ℔ ct., Jan. and July	102 104	....	.. ...
Nova Scotia, 6 ℔ ct., 1875.......................	100 102	...	......
Ottawa City 6 ℔ c. d. 1880	....	92½ 93½	......
Quebec Harbour, 6 ℔ c. d. 1883.	....	....	55 60
Do. do. 7 do. do....................	....	....	65 70
Do. do. 8 do. 1886..................	...	....	75 85
Do. City, 7 ℔ c. d. 5 years	....	94 95	94 95
Do. do. 7 do. 9 do.	....	....	88 89
Do. do. 7 do. 2½ do.	....	....	97 98
Do. Water Works, 7 ℔ ct., 4 years...........	....	....	96 97
Do. do. 6 do. 2 do.	....	....	93½ 94
Toronto Corporation	....	90 92½	...

Insurance.

BEAVER
Mutual Insurance Association.

HEAD OFFICE—20 TORONTO STREET,
TORONTO.

INSURES LIVE STOCK against death from any cause.
The only Canadian Company having authority to do this
class of business.

R. L. DENISON,
President.

O'REILLY,
Secretary.   8-1y-25

HOME DISTRICT
Mutual Fire Insurance Company.

OFFICE:
North-West Corner of Yonge and Adelaide Streets,
TORONTO.—(UP STAIRS.)

INSURES Dwelling Houses, Stores, Warehouses, Merchandise, Furniture, &c.

PRESIDENT—The Hon. J. McMURRICH.
VICE-PRESIDENT—JOHN BURNS, Esq.
JOHN RAINS, Secretary.

AGENTS:
Wright, Esq., Hamilton; FRANCIS STEVENS, Esq.,
Barrie; Messrs. GIBBS & BRO., Oshawa.   8-1y

THE PRINCE EDWARD COUNTY
Mutual Fire Insurance Company.

HEAD OFFICE,—PICTON, ONTARIO.
President, L. B. STINSON; Vice-President, W. A. RICHARDS.
Directors: H. A. McFaul, James Cavan, James Johnson,
DeMill, William Delong.—Treasurer, David Barker
Secretary, John Twigg; Solicitor, R. J. Fitzgerald.

THIS Company is established upon strictly Mutual principles, insuring farming and isolated property, (not towns,) in Townships only, and offers great advantages to insurers, at low rates for five years, without the expense of renewal. This Company has existed 12 years, during which period it has adjusted all losses in a satisfactory manner. It is managed with strict economy, and affords the opportunity of insuring with safety and reliance, and at little expense, which accounts for its long standing and the successful business which it has been and is now doing.
Picton, June 1^, 1868.   9-1y

Hartford Fire Insurance Company.
HARTFORD, CONN.

Capital and Assets over Two Million Dollars.

$2,026,220.29.

CHARTERED 1810.

An old and reliable Company, having an established business in Canada of more than thirty years standing, has complied with the provisions of the new Insurance Act, and made a special deposit of

$100,000

with the Government for the security of policy-holders, and continue to grant policies upon the same favorable terms as heretofore.

Specially low rates on first-class dwellings and farm property for a term of one or more years.

Losses as heretofore promptly and equitably adjusted.
H. J. MORSE & Co., AGENTS.
Toronto, Ont.

ROBERT WOOD, GENERAL AGENT FOR CANADA.

Geo. Girdlestone,
Fire, Life, Marine, Accident, and Stock Insurance
Agent.

Very best Companies represented.
Barrie, Ont. June, 1868 }

Insurance.

The Standard Life Assurance Company,
Established 1825.
WITH WHICH IS NOW UNITED
THE COLONIAL LIFE ASSURANCE COMPANY.

Head Office for Canada:
MONTREAL—STANDARD COMPANY'S BUILDINGS,
No. 47 GREAT ST. JAMES STREET.
Manager—W. M. RAMSAY.   Inspector—RICH'D BULL.

THIS Company having deposited the sum of ONE HUNDRED AND FIFTY THOUSAND DOLLARS with the Receiver-General, in conformity with the Insurance Act passed last Session, Assurances will continue to be carried out at moderate rates and on all the different systems in practice.

AGENT FOR TORONTO—HENRY PELLATT,
KING STREET.
AGENT FOR HAMILTON—JAMES BANCROFT.
6-6mos.

Fire and Marine Assurance.
THE BRITISH AMERICA
ASSURANCE COMPANY.
HEAD OFFICE:
CORNER OF CHURCH AND COURT STREETS.
TORONTO.

BOARD OF DIRECTION:
Hon G. W. Allan, M. L. C.,   A: Joseph, Esq.,
George J. Boyd, Esq.,   Peter Paterson, Esq.,
Hon. W. Cayley,   G. P. Ridout, Esq.,
Richard S. Cassels, Esq.,   E. H. Rutherford, Esq.,
        Thomas C. Street, Esq.,
Governor:
GEORGE PERCIVAL RIDOUT, Esq.
Deputy Governor:
PETER PATERSON, Esq.
Fire Inspector: Marine Inspector:
E. ROBY O'BRIEN.   CAPT. R. COURNEEN.

Insurances granted on all descriptions of property
against loss and damage by fire and the perils of inland
navigation.
Agencies established in the principal cities, towns, and
ports of shipment throughout the Province.
THOS. WM. BIRCHALL,
28-1y   Managing Director.

Edinburgh Life Assurance Company.

Founded 1823.

HEAD OFFICE—22 GEORGE STREET, EDINBURGH.

Capital, ... £500,000 Ster'g.
Accumulated and Invested Funds, £1,000,000 "

HEAD OFFICE IN CANADA:
WELLINGTON STREET, TORONTO.

SUB-AGENTS THROUGOUT THE PROVINCE.

J. HILLYARD CAMERON,
Chairman, Canadian Board.

DAVID HIGGINS,
Secretary. Canadian Board.   3-3m

Queen Fire and Life Insurance Company,
OF LIVERPOOL AND LONDON.

ACCEPTS ALL ORDINARY FIRE RISKS
on the most favorable terms.

LIFE RISKS
Will be taken on terms that will compare favorably with
other Companies.

CAPITAL, - - - - £2,000,000 Stg.

CHIEF OFFICES—Queen's Buildings, Liverpool, and
Gracechurch Street London.
CANADA BRANCH OFFICE—Exchange Buildings, Montreal.
Resident Secretary and General Agent,
A. MACKENZIE FORBES,
13 St. Sacrament St., Merchants' Exchange, Montreal.
WM. ROWLAND, Agent, Toronto.   1-1y

Insurance.

**Reliance Mutual Life Assurance
Society.**
(Established, 1840,) OF LONDON, E. C.

Accumulated Funds, over $1,000,000.

Annual Income, $300,000.

THE entire Profits of this long-established Society belong
to the Policy-holders.
HEAD OFFICE FOR DOMINION—MONTREAL.
T. W. GRIFFITH, Managerd Sec'y.
15-1y   WM. HENDERSON, Agent for Toronto.

Ætna Insurance Company of Dublin.
The number of Shareholders exceeds Five Hundred.

Capital, $5,000,000—Annual Income nearly $1,000,000.

THIS Company takes Fire and Marine Risks on the most
favorable terms.
T. W. GRIFFITH, Manager for Canada.
Chief office for Dominion—Corner St. Francois Xavier
and St. Sacrament Sts., Montreal.
15-1y   WM. HENDERSON, Agent for Toronto

Scottish Provincial Assurance Co.
Established 1825.

CAPITAL .... £1,000,000 STERLING.
INVESTED IN CANADA (1854) .... $500,000.

Canada Head Office, Montreal.

LIFE DEPARTMENT.
CANADA BOARD OF DIRECTORS:
HUGH TAYLOR, Esq., Advocate,
Hon. CHARLES WILSON, M. L. C.
WM. SACHE, Esq., Banker,
JACKSON RAE, Esq., Banker,
WM. FRASER, Esq., M. D., Medical Adviser.

The special advantages to be derived from insuring in
this office are:—Strictly Moderate Rates of Premium,
Large Bonus (intermediate bonus guaranteed;) Liberal
Surrender Value, under policies relinquished by assured;
and Extensive Limits of Residence and Travel. All business disposed of in Canada, without reference to parent
office.
A. DAVIDSON PARKER,
Resident Secretary
15-1yr   G. L. MADDISON,
AGENT FOR TORONTO.

Lancashire Insurance Company.
CAPITAL, - - - - - - £2,000,000 Sterling

FIRE RISKS
Taken at reasonable rates, of premium, and
ALL LOSSES SETTLED PROMPTLY,
By the undersigned, without reference elsewhere.
S. C. DUNCAN-CLARK & CO.,
General Agents for Ontario,
25-1y   N. W. Corner of King & Church Streets,
TORONTO.

Ætna Fire & Marine Insurance Company.

INCORPORATED 1819.   CHARTER PERPETUAL.

CASH CAPITAL $3,000,000

LOSSES PAID IN 50 YEARS, 23,500,000 00.

JULY, 1868.
ASSETS.
(At Market Value.)
Cash in hand and in Bank $544,842 39
Real Estate 285,207.29
Mortgage Bonds 935,245.00
Bank Stock 1,272,670 00
United States, State and City Stock and other
Public Securities 7,049,855 51

Total $5,053,890 19

LIABILITIES.
Claims not Due, and Unadjusted $499,403 55
Amount required by Mass. and New York
for Re-Insurance 1,405,267 15
E. CHAFFEY & CO., Agents.
50-6m

Insurance. | ## Insurance. | ## Insurance.

ÆTNA
Live Stock Insurance Company

LICENSED BY THE DOMINION GOVERNMENT TO DO BUSINESS IN CANADA.

THE following Accidents, this month, show the importance of Insuring your Horses and Cattle against Death from any cause, or Theft, in the Ætna Insurance Company.

MONTREAL, September 16, 1868.
At a fire last night, in the sheds behind Ripin's Hotel, St. Joseph Street, three valuable Stock Horses were destroyed, "Young Clydesdale" and "Emigrant," belonging to the Huntingdon Agricultural Society—the former worth $900, and the latter $1,700; and "Old Beauharnois" cost $1,000, belonging to the Beauharnois Society.

PORT COLBORNE, September 18, 1868.
HORSES DROWNED.—Two horses belonging to Mr. Briggs, of Port Colborne, and four owned by Mr. Julien, of Port Dalhousie, were drowned in the Canal, near the Junction, early this morning.

A fire at the Glasgow Hotel, Montreal, this morning, destroyed two horses. The fire was caused by drunkenness on the part of the stable man.

MONTREAL, September 24, 1868.
A fire in F. X. Cusson's stables, St. Joseph Street, last night, destroyed three horses.

E. L. SNOW, GENERAL AGENT,
Montreal;
Agents for Ontario:—
SCOTT & WALMSLEY,
87nov11y   Ontario Hall, Church Street, Toronto.

The Liverpool and London and Globe Insurance Company

INVESTED FUNDS:
FIFTEEN MILLIONS OF DOLLARS.

DAILY INCOME OF THE COMPANY:
TWELVE THOUSAND DOLLARS.

LIFE INSURANCE,
WITH AND WITHOUT PROFITS.

FIRE INSURANCE
On every description of Property, at Lowest Remunerative Rates.
JAMES FRASER, AGENT,
5 King Street West.
Toronto, 1868.   38-1y

Briton Medical and General Life Association,
with which is united the
BRITANNIA LIFE ASSURANCE COMPANY.

Capital and Invested Funds...........£750,000 Sterling.

ANNUAL INCOME, £290,060 STG. :
Yearly increasing at the rate of £25,000 Sterling.

THE important and peculiar feature originally introduced by this Company, in applying the periodical Bonuses, so as to make Policies payable during life, without any higher rate of premiums being charged, has caused the success of the BRITON MEDICAL AND GENERAL to be almost unparalleled in the history of Life Assurance. *Life Policies on the Profit Scale become payable during the lifetime of the Assured, thus rendering a Policy of Assurance a means of subsistence in old age, as well as a protection for a family,* and a more valuable security to creditors in the event of early death; and effectually meeting the often urged objection, that persons do not themselves reap the benefit of their own prudence and forethought.

No extra charge made to members of Volunteer Corps for services within the British Provinces.
TORONTO AGENCY, 5 KING ST. WEST.
oct17—q-1yr   JAMES FRASER, Agent.

Phenix Insurance Company,
BROOKLYN, N. Y.

PHILANDER SHAW,   STEPHEN CROWELL,
Secretary.   President.
Cash Capital, $1,000,000. Surplus, $666,416.02. Total, 1,666,416.02. Entire Income from all sources for 1866 was $2,151,539.82.
CHARLES G. FORTIER, Marine Agent.
Ontario Chambers, Toronto, Ont.   10-1y,

The Victoria Mutual
FIRE INSURANCE COMPANY OF CANADA.

Insures only Non-Hazardous Property, at Low Rates.

BUSINESS STRICTLY MUTUAL.

GEORGE H. MILLS, President.
W. D. BOOKER, Secretary.
HEAD OFFICE ....HAMILTON, ONTARIO
aug 15-1yr

The Ætna Life Insurance Company.

AN attack, abounding with errors, having been made upon the Ætna Life Insurance Co. by the editor of the Montreal *Daily News* : and certain agents of British Companies being now engaged in handing around copies of the attack, thus seeking to damage the Company's standing, —I have pleasure in laying before the public the following certificate, bearing the signatures of the Presidents and Cashiers who happened to be in their Offices of every Bank in Hartford; also that of the President and Secretary of the old Ætna Fire Insurance Company :—
"*To whom it may concern :*—
" We, the undersigned, regard the Ætna Life Insurance Company, of this city, as one of the most successful and prosperous Insurance Co. panies in the States,—entirely reliable, responsible, and answourable in all its dealings, and most worthy of public confidence and patronage."

Lucius J. Hendee, President Ætna Fire Insurance Co., and late Treasurer of the State of Connecticut.
J. Goodnow, Secretary Ætna Fire Insurance Co.
C. H. Northam, President, and J. B. Powell, Cashier National Bank.
C. T. Hillyer, President Charter Oak National Bank.
E. D. Tiffany, President First National Bank.
G. T. Davis, President City National Bank.
F. S. Riley, Cashier,   do.   do.   do.
John C. Tracy, President of Farmers' and Mechanics' National Bank.
M. W. Graves, Cashier Conn. River Banking Co.
H. A. Redfield, Cashier Phœnix National Bank.
O. G. Terry, President Ætna National Bank.
J. R. Redfield, Cashier National Exchange Bank.
John G. Root, Assistant Cashier American National Bank.
George P. Hills, Cashier State Bank of Hartford.
Jas. Potter, Cashier Hartford National Bank.
Hartford, Nov. 26, 1867.

Many of the above-mentioned parties are closely connected with other Life Insurance Companies, but all unhesitatingly commend our Company as "reliable, responsible, honorable in all its dealings, and most worthy of public confidence and patronage.
JOHN GARVIN,
General Agent, Toronto Street.
Toronto, Dec. 3. 1867.   16-1y

Life Association of Scotland.

INVESTED FUNDS
UPWARDS OF £1,000,000 STERLING.

THIS Institution differs from other Life Offices, in that the
BONUSES FROM PROFITS
Are applied on a special system for the Policy-holder's
PERSONAL BENEFIT AND ENJOYMENT DURING HIS OWN LIFETIME,
WITH THE OPTION OF
LARGE BONUS ADDITIONS TO THE SUM ASSURED.

The Policy-holder thus obtains
A LARGE REDUCTION OF PRESENT OUTLAY
OR
A PROVISION FOR OLD AGE OF A MOST IMPORTANT AMOUNT IN ONE CASH PAYMENT, OR A LIFE ANNUITY,
Without any expense or outlay whatever beyond the ordinary Assurance Premium for the Sum Assured, which remains in tact for Policy-holder's heirs, or other purposes.

CANADA—MONTREAL—PLACE D'ARMES.

DIRECTORS:
DAVID TORRANCE, Esq., (D. Torrance & Co.)
GEORGE MOFFATT, (Gillespie, Moffatt & Co.
ALEXANDER MORRIS, Esq., M.P., Barrister, Perth.
Sir G. E. CARTIER, M.P., Minister of Militia.
PETER REDPATH, Esq., (J. Redpath & Son).
J. H. R. MOLSON, Esq., (J. H. R. Molson & Bros.)
Solicitors—MESSRS. TORRANCE & MORRIS.
Medical Officer—R. PALMER HOWARD, Esq., M.D
Secretary—P. WARDLAW.
Inspector of Agencies—JAMES B. M. CHIPMAN.   y

North British and Mercantile Insur Company.

Established 1809.

HEAD OFFICE. - - CANADA - - MC

TORONTO BRANCH:
LOCAL OFFICES, Nos. 4 & 6 WELLINGTON St.
Fire Department, ... R. N.

Life Department, ... H. L. F
29-1y

Phœnix Fire Assurance Comp
LOMBARD ST. AND CHARING CROS
LONDON, ENG.

Insurances effected in all parts of the
Claims paid
WITH PROMTITUDE and LIBERA.
MOFFATT, MURRAY & BEAT
Agents for To
36 Yonge

The Commercial Union Assur Company,
19 & 20 CORNHILL, LONDON, ENGLAN
Capital, £2,500,000 Stg.—Invested over £2,00

FIRE DEPARTMENT.—Insurance granted scriptions of property at reasonable rates.

LIFE DEPARTMENT.—The success of th has been unprecedented—*NINETY PERCENT* niums now in hand. First year's premiums $1,0,005. Economy of management guaranteed c surity. Moderate rates.
OFFICE—385 & 387 ST PAUL STREET, MON
MORLAND, WATSON &
General Agents fo
FRED. COLE, Secretary.
Inspector of Agencies—T. C. LIVINGST
W. M. WESTMACOTT, Agent at
16-1y

Phœnix Mutual Life Insuranc
HARTFORD, CONN.

Accumulated Fund, $2,000,000, Income, $1,

THIS Company, established in 1851, is one reliable Companies doing business in the c has been steadily prospering. The *Massachuset Reports* show that its nearly all important in superior to the general average of Companies intending assurers the following reasons, amon for preferring it to other companies:

It is purely Mutual. It allows the Insure and resite in any portion of the United States a it throws out almost all restriction on occupatic Policies. It will, if desired, take a note for $\frac{1}{2}$ Premium, thus combining all the advantages of all cash company. Its Dividends are declared and applied in reduction of Premium. Its Di in every case on Premiums paid. The Divide PHŒNIX have averaged fifty per cent. yearly settlement of Policies, a Dividend will be allow year the policy has been in force. The num dends will always equal the outstanding Notes. losses promptly—during its existence never I tested a claim. It issues Policies for the ben ried Women beyond the reach of their husband Creditors may also insure the lives of Debtors. are all *Non-forfeiting,* as it always allows the surrender his Policy, should he desire, the U ing a paid-up Policy therefor. This import will commend itself to all. The inducements by the PHŒNIX are better and more liberal th any other Company. Its rate of Mortality is low and under the average.

Parties contemplating *Life Insurance* will fin interest to call and examine our system. Po payable either in *Gold* or American currency.
ANGUS H. HEUL
General Mana
Dominio.

Office: 104 ST. FRANÇOIS XAVIER St. MON
*Active and energetic Agents and wanted in every town and village, to whom lib ments will be given.

PRINTED AT THE DAILY TELEGRAPH
HOUSE, BAY ST., COR. KING.

THE CANADIAN

IONETARY TIMES

AND

INSURANCE CHRONICLE,

)TED TO FINANCE, COMMERCE, INSURANCE, BANKS, RAILWAYS, NAVIGATION, MINES, INVESTMENT,
PUBLIC COMPANIES, AND JOINT STOCK ENTERPRISE.

| —NO. 14. | TORONTO, THURSDAY, NOVEMBER 19, 1868. | { SUBSCRIPTION. |
| | | { $2 YEAR. |

Mercantile.

Meetings.

THE GRAND TRUNK.

(Proceedings at the Annual Meeting Continued.)

The total average of the cost of wood to the
G.T. was $2.57; to the Great Western, $2.54.
But deducting the discount for greenbacks, 26
cents, showed that the comparison would be 19½
cents, in favour of the G. T. He though peat, for
many purposes a most admirable and useful fuel.
Canada had not throughout its length and breadth
an ounce of coal, and Mr. Hodges, the gentleman
who built the Victoria bridge, and, who had a large
bog in Canada, thought that he would be doing a
great thing for Canada if he could convert it into
coal. He had patented machinery for that purpose, by which he was enabled to make a contract
with the Grand Trunk Company to supply
them at Montreal at the rate of $3.20, or
12s. 9d. per ton. Mr. Ritter's view was that
that was an extravagant contract. He (the chairman) looked upon the supply of fuel in Canada not
altogether as a question of price, but as a question
of getting it. They had required some means of
competition with the daily increase in price by
the wood contractors, something to show that if
they did not deal at their shop, there was another
to which they could go. Having looked into the
matter, he was convinced Mr. Brydges had tried
his utmost, and obtained the best terms he possibly could, therefore he was to be praised rather
than blamed. What was required was to encourage the production of a fuel to compete with wood,
which could not be obtained by running down
every man's price and refusing him a fair profit.
It was not wise to deal in twopences, but it was
wise to give a man that had a peat bog a fair price,
to enable him to set up machinery and manufacture peat, in order to lower the price of fuel.. Mr.
Trevethick, who had been to Bavaria, the only
place where peat was used for railways, had put
the cost of it at from 10s. to 11s. per ton, whereas
the Grand Trunk Company were paying 12s. 9d.
But he had also said that the wages and labour to
produce it were only 1s. 8d. per day in Bavaria,
whereas the labour employed in Canada was a
dollar a day, besides which, the peat in Canada
was worth from 15 to 25 per cent. more than the
peat in Bavaria. The experiments made by Mr.
Trevethick showed that a cord of peat of 240 lbs.
was equal to a cord of wood. With peat a train
would run 328 miles—with wood, it would only
run 35. The contract which had been made with
Mr. Hodges was on sufferance, and it rested with
them to terminate it when they pleased, but he
thought it would be a great mistake if they did so.
His official connection with the company would
soon cease, and that his only connection in future
would be as a holder of property, but he would be
ever ready to give any gratuitous advice that the
existing board may ask of him. A good deal had
been said of his receiving £2,000 a year from the
company for his services as chairman. Though
he received that sum, it did not come out of the
profits of the company. By the Consolidation Act
of the company a certain sum was fixed for management. When he joined the board in 1862 he
was requested to take the chair, and he was asked
what remuneration he thought he should receive.

His reply was that whatever sum he received he
would not consent that the shareholders would
have to pay anything additional to the charges
laid down by the Act of Parliament on his account.
He was at that time making £1,500 a year by his
own business, and taking that into consideration
and the fact also that as chairman of the company
he should keep a house in London, it was decided
that he should get £3,000 a year for his time and
services. To make up the sum without adding to
the charges laid down by the Act of Parliament,
Mr. Baring, M. P., and Mr. Glyn, M. P., said
that they would take no remuneration, and Mr.
Potter, (another of the directors) suggested, and t
was agreed to, that these three gentlemen would
only take their remuneration nominally, and the
whole of the three amounts should go towards
making up the £2,000 which he had been in the
habit of receiving as chairman. The shareholders
would, therefore, see that he was not the cormorant that he was represented to have been.

Mr. K. D. Hodgson having seconded the mo
tion for the adoption of the report—

Mr. Albert Creak said they must remember that
the present Board were responsible for the present
condition of the company. He looked upon Mr.
Baring when he was chairman as the author of all
their difficulties.

The Chairman explained the reason of Mr. Bar-
ings absence. .

Mr. Creak—Though Mr. Baring was not absolutely at the head of the concern, yet they all looked upon him as its head, and accordingly treated
him as responsible for its safe conduct and prosperity. Any statement brought forward with his
name carried enormous weight in the city of London. The line was handed over to the directors
by the contractors when it was in an unfinished
condition, and now every half-year they had to ·
pay for what to have been done at first. Mr. Baring may say that he trusted to the engineer to
ascertain that the line was in a satisfactory state.
He had nothing to do with that. He still looked
to the board. He complained of the way in which
it had been renewed ; but Sir Edward Watkin
said that the board had done they best that they
could. They were told that rails did not last so
long in Canada ·as in other parts of the world.
But some rails had lasted in Canada for no less
than twenty years, and still would last for five
years longer. If bad rails had been laid down,
who was to blame for it but the board ? The
directors told them that they were innocent, and
that they had done the best in their power for the
shareholders, and that they were the most immac-
culate board ever created. If they could not rely
on the estimates sent out by the board, on what
what were they to put their trust ! In 1863 the
directors had told them that a sum of £70,000 a
year for five years would be required to pay for
their renewals. . Now, what were the facts ! Instead of £350,000 being sufficient, £572,000 had
been expended. The sum which had during this
period been paid for renewals was more than 40
per cent. in excess of the estimated amount.
They had spent thousands, and yet had left the
line unballasted. They had the company without
a single shilling in its locker, and where they
were going to get a shilling at the present moment
he did not know. They should have said to them,
let the road be put in order, and have asked for

the bill. No doubt the American war, and especially the Reciprocity Treaty, had contributed to
their difficulties, but not to the extent which the
board represented they had. They had been told
at their last meeting, "Only wait until October."
Their chairman had pledged himself if their traffic
was not largely increased and their expenditure
greatly diminished that Mr. Brydges should resign. They were promised very large reductions
in three great points, viz.: in wages, materials,
and fuel. Mr. Creak went on to give figures
showing that for a rise of 6 per cent. in the traffic
there had been a rise of 6 per cent. in wages. If
they were to pay thus for every increase in the
traffic, what was the benefit of the increase? The
cost of materials was reduced only 4 per cent.,
while the cost of fuel was £2,000 extra. This
was not the amendment they were told to expect.
He asked the board to fulfil their pledge, and
withdraw Mr. Brydges from the management;
and as that gentleman had come across the
Atlantic to be present at that meeting, he would
ask him a few questions. One was as to the condition of the road and what percentage was in good
working order? What was the condition of the
rolling stock, and what number of engines and
cars were useless, and what was the number of
the remainder? 90 of the 298 of their engines
were in hospital, and a large number of their cars
were useless. He would also ask Mr. Brydges
what was the amount likely to be yet required to
put the line in good order. He contended that
no one should leave the room that day without
they knew what they had yet to pay on this score.
He had been told that £100,000 after this would
do it; but he never had yet seen an estimate of
the Grand Trunk verified. What was the number of free passes granted last year? how many of
these passes were for officials, and how many were
complimentary? How the loss arose on greenbacks? How was it, however, he would ask, that
they could only get 35½ miles out of a cord of
wood, when the Great Western of Canada could
get 45½ miles? They paid as much for fuel in
Canada as the London and North Western did in
this country. How was it that while coal was 19s
a ton in Quebec, that it would not be better than
wood, as it was cheaper, as wood cost them 17s a
cord. Mr. Yates was the engineer of the line for
some time, but no one of them knew who were
the engineers now. Now, when Mr. Yates came
to this Company he had a patent, and he would
ask Mr. Brydges if, while that gentleman was
engineer, he had certified the work of which he
got the business? Mr. Brydges himself admits
that he was connected with the Kingston Locomotive Works, out of which several engines had
been supplied to the Grand Trunk. He would
ask Mr. Brydges whether he or any of the officials
on the line were connected with any company who
did work for the Grand Trunk, or to his knowledge
any official had received commissions for work
done?

Mr. Brydges said that he would state deliberately, as man to man ought to state, that there
was not one single word of truth in the allegation,
and he was not in any way connected with any
company supplying materials to the Grand Trunk,
with the exception of the Kingston Ironworks, nor
to the best of his knowledge was any officer connected with the company, and that neither they
nor he received commissions for any materials
which had been supplied.

Mr. A. Creak said that he was very glad to have
received that declaration from Mr. Brydges, and
he did not think that gentleman would blame
him for giving him an opportunity of distinctly
stating the facts. The committee of which he had
been chairman, had been called very hard names.
It had been said that they had been overcome by
the soft sawder and the blandishments of the chairman (Sir E. Watkin). They had, he assured them,
done nothing of the kind, but they would carry
out the wishes of the meeting that appointed
them. The committee had been willing to agree
to anything which would produce peace, and he

was sorry that such a compromise had been agreed
to. He had received, on Saturday last, by the
latest post, a letter saying that two members of
the shareholders' committee should be appointed
to the board, and that two members of another
committee should also be appointed—viz. Messrs.
Fearon and Hodgkinson. He looked upon this as
a departure from the understanding which had
been arrived at with the board. He was no party
to it, and he repudiated it. Mr. Fearon was not
a holder of stock in this company, but merely represented another company who held a stake in
the Grand Trunk. Both Mr. Ritter and himself
held a moderate interest, about £35,000 or £40,-
000. He did not think that they ought to receive
a nominee of another company. He was going to
move an amendment to the effect that the report
and accounts not being satisfactory, the directors
be requested to resign, and that a committee be
appointed to represent the board. If the board
had not repudiated the arrangement that had been
made he would not have taken the course which
he now recommended. He believed that 600
proxies had been received in favour of a new
board, and there was a large amount of the proprietors determined for a change, and that change
must and ought to come.

Mr. Hesseltine, in seconding the amendment
of Mr. Creak, said that the remark of the chairman that his connection with the company would
soon cease, removed all his objections to him. He
had received the proxies of 598 proprietors, with
a view of reorganizing the board. He would say
to the proprietors and to the chairman, that the
well-being of that company was the well-being of
the Buffalo, and if he could see the interest on
the Buffalo bonds paid, he would be satisfied. Sir
Edward had said that he had received something
from him in the shape of an apology. If he looked upon that in the light of an apology, he would
let him do so. He was, however, sorry that he
had used the strong statements that he had done.
He was extremely sorry that he had gone the
length that he had done. He hoped that the
chairman would pass the question by and consider
the difficulty with which it was settled. He also
thought that Sir Edward Watkin would consider this statement satisfactory. He begged to second Mr.
Creak's motion.

Sir E. Watkin said that if Mr. Hesseltine meant
that he was sorry for having charged him with
doing that which, as an honorable man, he must
have known him to be incapable of doing, he
should be perfectly willing to accept the apology.

Mr. Hesseltine said that such was his intention.

Sir E. Watkin said that from that time bygones
would be bygones.

Mr. France said it now devolved upon them to
set about reforming their board. He did not wish
to lose the services of the board as a body, as he
should be sorry to see Messrs. Baring and Glyn
unrepresented on the board, not only in the interests of the shareholders, but in the interests of
the Canadian Government, as without the assistance of that Government he did not see how they
were to pull together. They wished, if possible,
to make the Canadian hopes and feelings identical
with their own. Although he did not think that
they had treated the Company well, or in a fair
manner, yet he was anxious that they should do
everything in their power to conciliate the Government of Canada. He would also wish to have the
presence of Mr. K. Hodgson on the board, but
thought they could dispense with the services of
Mr. Brydges as a managing Director, because he
was too ambitious to suit the Company.

Mr. Ritter was sorry that the chairman had alluded to the patent question, as it was not his own
intention to have done so. He had gone very
deeply into it, and he would give them the benefit
of his labours. He had found that there was a
large quantity of bog land along the line, and the
sole reason which had induced him to largely increase his holding was, because he believed he
could make every economy in the fuel question.
That which he had now referred to as a patent was

no patent at all. He had proved to
Watkin that the machinery was twelv
years old, and that was the reason
particularly insisted on the contract [
end to. The contract rate was also
whereas, he maintained that peat co
easily by the Company at the rate
or 6s. That would not be a two-peni
would involve a sum of about £10,00(
He would go further and say that a C
the Grand Trunk, that could not pay i
might have made great use of tha
might have supplied the various tow
along the line. He did not think
treated as a twopenny affair, because
to be anticipated that £1,400 a yea
been realised. In Canada they could
the year—they could not work in th
so it would be some months before th
used to work at tids. There was an
sentence with reference to the conti
never be executed. What they had
was half mud. They had been payi
13s. 4d., but Mr. Trevethick had
report that they were actually payi
Handyside had also gone out to Can
expense, and had brought back a re[
peat would come ultimately to 24s.,
that one cord of wood would go as fa
of peat. It was a very painful thin
gentleman like Mr. Brydges with g
but it appeared to him that inform
have been obtained in France, have
before the contract had been entere
Handyside had brought home docum
given a short report, and he would n
Secretary of the Company to allow
as the facts contained in it were mos
[The Secretary then read the r
Handyside.]

Mr. Brydges said that a distinct st
been made that he and others come
Grand Trunk Company had entere
contract for the supply of wheels aga
rests of the Company. He begg
allowed to state on his honour that
was an entire fabrication. The n
that letter was a Mr. Scovill of
Scovill was a wheel manufacturer,
ago the Company bought wheels of
of the Three Rivers Company. Th
Rivers Company failed, and so v
make any more wheels for the Gran
moment that this happened, Mr. B
Company notice that he would re
dollar for every wheel, supposing
have all the market to himself. B
proceeded to take some steps to
competition, and so bring down th
went to Montreal and said that th
in Toronto making wheels, but who
price than they wished to give.
parties contracted to supply wheel
—a dollar and a half less than
force upon them, and that man da
ward and tried to accuse him of
duty to the Company.

To be Continued.

ERIE AND NIAGARA EXT
WAY COMPAN

At a meeting of the Provision
Company held at the Court Ho
on Tuesday, the 10th day of N
the following were present:—W
Esq., President of the Erie and
Colin Munro, Esq., Sheriff o
Elgin; John Duck, Esq., Ward
of Kent; Thomas M. Nairn, Es
County of Elgin; Richard Gra
Erie; John Smith, Esq., Tilsonb
Esq., Colchester, County of E
Farrel, Registrar of Haldiman
taken by Mr. Sheriff Munro, an

inted Secretary to the meeting. The lutions were then passed :—
A. Thompson be elected President; Nairn, Vice-President, and Nicol , Secretary and Treasurer. That ae immediately opened in accordance of Incorporation, and that the Secertise a meeting of the Directors to riptions of Stock, to be held at the Company at Fort Erie, on the 16th . D. 1868. That application be Board to the various municipalities the construction of the proposed .n appropriation of the right of way aid to the undertaking as to them et. · That the Board having heard g statement made by Mr. Thompson ; and progress on behalf of this tender to him their sincere thanks and would express their confidence and integrity carrying it to a suecetion. That the Ontario Bank be : the Bankers of the Company. Crooks, Kingsmill and Cattanach be Solicitors of the Company.
thanks to Sheriff Munro was then efficient conduct in the chair, and was adjourned to Wednesday, the ar, next, to meet at the office of the Port Erie. ·

3EC AND GOSFORD WOODEN RAILWAY.

of the shareholders and others in-he construction of this railway was ee, for the purpose of hearing Mr. engineer from the United States. arneau had introduced Mr. Nicoll ig, the latter gentleman explained en engaged at Clifton in the conwooden railway, which had turned iiary point of view, as a complete ive general satisfaction. They were locomotives and 60 cars, and the proposed to add four additional id 100 cars. He had passed over inder consideration with Mr. Fitzid come to the conclusion that it much cheaper than the lines he had
He was surprised to hear that we out the cost of cordwood, with such a available within 25 miles of our mpossible for him to give the meetfigures of the cost of construction, : it could it could be put in workor about $200,000. These railways speed of 16 miles in 60 minutes. at rate in Clifton, but from 8 to 10 me time was sufficient for all prac-
The locomotive on this line could a-day, forty cords each load, which h four locomotives running, 540
The width of way required was nore, he believed, than at first con-he shareholders—Mr. Hulbert then led description of the grade which railways can attain, which is as et on the mile, and also upon the of the property through which the ss. With fair usage, he thought a ade of maple—for he found it the pose—would last at least five years. ide of the rail was worn out, it ed. He here showed the requirement of a rail such as is used in wooden road as he proposed is 66 feet t require cattle guards, and they with fencing. He also stated astruction, not one pound of iron . Mr. Fitzgerald here said that el for the rails could be obtained conceded by the Government. ued his explanations stating that onsulted by certain gentlemen in

Ontario, who proposed building a similar road. These gentlemen had visited the road he had lately built, and expressed themselves highly satisfied. He thought for cheapness it was undoubtedly the best thing they could get up. It was also suggested as an encouragement to persons to buy stock, that each shareholder be entitled to a cord of wood for each share they held, at cost price. This idea appeared to meet with the general approval of the meeting. The next question taken up, in which nearly all the gentlemen present expressed their opinion, was the cost of labor. Mr. H. said that the ordinary unskilled laborer† or navvy in the United States was paid $1.50 currency per day. Mr. Garneau was of opinion that unskilled labor here could be obtained for four shillings a day, and perhaps less. As the road had to be built in the summer season, labor would, of course, be higher. Mr. Henry Fry said that in the winter season they could obtain as much labor here as they required at their own price, for the people were going round the soup-kitchens for subsistence. Mr. Hulbert said in his experience he found that when there was a large demand for labor, the wages generally increased. After some further conversation upon the probable competition that would arise between the batteaux carrying wood from the lower St. Lawrence and the Gosford Road, the meeting adjourned for a few days, to allow Mr. Hulbert an opportunity to prepare certain plans and specifications, which would give them a more definite idea of the probable cost at which the road could be constructed.—*Chronicle.*

RAMA TIMBER TRANSPORTATION COMPANY.— A meeting of this company was held on the 17th inst., in the office of Messrs. Strong, Edgar and Grahame, Jordan street. The object of the company is to cut a canal for the floating of timber from the waters of the Black River, in the County of Ontario, to Lake St. John, and through to Lake Couchiching, so as to facilitate the transportation of timber from the extensive forests on the Black River. Heretofore it has been passed through the River Severn, Georgian Bay, and three of the great lakes with their connections, before arriving here. It will, after the completion of the canal, be brought down Lake Simcoe and shipped by the Northern Railway to Toronto. The whole of the stock, amounting to $40,000 has been subscribed, and $10,000 of it paid up. The following gentlemen were appointed directors for the ensuing year :—Messrs. F. W. Cumberland, M.P.P., H. W. Sage, Thompson Smith, John Thompson and Clarence Moberly. ·

ROSSIN HOUSE—The annual meeting of the Rossin House Company took place at that hotel on the 17th. The President, Mr. Gzowski occupied the chair. The annual report of the Directors was submitted to the meeting and showed the business of the past year to have been very satisfactory on the whole. The Directors thought that for several years to come the receipts from the renting of the stores in the building would likely be required to pay the principal and interest. In the report the Directors recommended the opening of the second flat. The following gentlemen were elected Directors for the coming year, viz:— Messrs. Jno. McDonald, W. C. Chewett, Adam Crooks, C. S. Gzowski, and B. Dickson. Mr. Gzowski was re-elected President, and Mr. W. C. Chewett managing director.

Mining.

GOLD MINING REVIEW.

NOVA SCOTIA.—The sale of two large properties in the eastern districts had taken place within the fortnight, but the enquiry for lands is declining, and for stock has almost ceased.
UNIACKE.—The Queen Company has sent up 114 ounces as the product of 36 tons.

ISAAC'S HARBOR.—The prospects of the north lode are very good. The mill, containing at present two 5-stamp batteries, has commenced running, and gives satisfaction.
The alleged alluvial · discoveries were, as . surmised, much exaggerated. It has long been known that pay dirt could be washed at Dunn Cove and Hurricane Point. Dunn Cove offers certain facilities for sluicing; but at neither are the deposits so rich or so extensive as to warrant even the least excitement, or to give them at- present any marked superiority over other districts in the Province where. alluvial washings have already been tried.
ECUM SECUM.—The mill of the Atlantic Co, will not be started until next week, owing to the delay in the receipt of some essential part of the machinery, which was before reported on the spot and complete. Mr. Andrews speaks encouragingly of the progress of the works and the general prospects of the company.
INDIAN PATH.—The mill of Messrs. Waddelow and MacDonald commenced running on the 26th October, and is said to work satisfactorily. It has at present two batteries, each of five stamps, but there is room for two more batteries if required. The stamps are driven by an 18 ft. overshot wheel. The supply of water is abundant and has a good fall. The shafts of this company are still sending up rich looking ore, and its quality will soon be tested *en gross*, as they have now about 500 tons on the surface, which will be put through the batteries so soon as the stamps have had proper play. Twenty-six men are now employed on these works.
THE OVENS.—The furnace of Captain Cornwall is being fast completed, and satisfactory progress is still reported of his works and those of Mr. Clarke. The two companies employ about 20 men.
MUSQUODOBOIT.—The following results are reported from Mr. Burkner from experimental crushings conducted by himself:
1450 lbs. quartz, from which half an ounce of specimens had been taken, gave in the battery 2 ozs. 7 dwts.
1000 lbs. from a three feet lode, half quartz and half slate, reduced in the stamp mill, yielded 4 dwts.
Mr. Tuoguoy, who has just returned from the district, has also brought specimens with him, visibly rich in gold.
The following quanties of bar gold have been reported in Halifax between 23rd October and 5th November:

Co.	District.	Oz.	dwts.	grs.
Ophir,	Renfrew,	172	11	0
......	do.,	3	9	0
......	do.,	1	11	0
Mulgrave,	Isaac's Harbor,	92	17	9
North American,	Waverley,	24	1	22
Macintosh,	Wine Harbor, ‚	12	13	21
Queen,	Uniacke;	134	10	0
Caledonia, ·	Oldham,	34	6	0
North St. Lawrence,	Uniacke,	14	5	0
	Total,	490	4	15

—*Halifax Mining Gazette.*

THE TAXES ON THE PRODUCTION OF THE PRECIOUS METALS IN MEXICO.

We have received a printed copy of the report submitted to the Mexican Congress in May last, recommending a reduction of the taxes on precious metals, and a perusal of the document fills us with astonishment that a Government can exist with taxes so oppressive, that the mining industry continues to support a large portion of the population, and the mines should be found to produce $20,000,000 annually (the manifested exportation is $15,000,600) with a considerable profit, after submitting to such terrible exactions. The taxes amount to 24,.66 per cent. or nearly one-fourth of the total production.

The Committee suppose that a miner takes from his mill a bar containing 1,000 mares of silver worth $9,416.36. He must pay on this $270, or 3 per cent. of the tax called the quinto; $135, or 1¼ of the mineria; $22.50, or ½ for assay; $22.50, or ½ for State tax; 1½c. for additional tax; $461.85, more than 5 per cent., for coining; 2½ per cent. for circulation, and 7½ per cent. for exportation; so that of the $9,415.36 with which he started, he pay out $1,863.45 of tax, and has $7,551.91 left for himself. The charge for coining is ostensibly less than 5 per cent., but the law allows a certain variation from the standard coins in fineness and weight, and this variation is managed to the loss of the miner, who gets only so much as the Mint officers are compelled to deliver to him. Two and a half per cent. have been taken off since this report was made, but 22 per cent. still remain, and the Committee recommend the entire abolition of all taxes on the precious metals. The adoption of their recommendation would prove the wisest official act in the history of Mexico. The ores must be very rich, or the cost of extraction very small, to permit any productions under such burthens. The imposition of such a tax in California and Nevada would reduce the annual productions of these two States from $50,000,000 to $10,000,000, or less. The mines of note which produce more than 20 per cent. met in this State can be counted up on the fingers, and yet our mines are regarded as the richest in the world.

The report estimates the annual production of the mines at $20,000,000, and says this amount is extracted from 600,000 tons of selected ore, picked from 5,000,000 tons of vein-stone, making an average of $33 to the ton of selected ore, and 4 to the ton of vein-stone broken down in the mine. At the Valenciana mine 3,100 laborers were at one time employed, and at the Proano 3,400, in extraction and the work directly or indirectly connected therewith, leaving the amalgamators and packers out of the count. At Fresnillo while the Proano mine was most productive, the richest ore yielded five times as much to the ton as the poorest; but the poorest was so much more abundant that its total production was seven times as great as that of the richest. The average yield of Proano was thirty-one ounces per ton in 1836, and only nine and a half ounces in 1862; and of Real del Monte forty-nine ounces in 1843 and twenty-nine ounces in 1852. At Proano the extraction cost $45 and the reduction 31 65 per ton in 1836, and in 1853 the expense had been reduced to $10 85 for extraction, and 11 17 for reduction.

PLUMBAGO IN ST. JOHN.—A plumbago mine is worked at St. John, the product of which is sent to New York, prepared by a simple process and returned in the manufactured state. Already 2,000 barrels of 300 pounds each have been raised. Another mine is to be sunk shortly beside it.

Insurance.

FIRE RECORD.—Galt, Nov. 9.—Barn of James Casey; insured in the Waterloo Mutual.

Wingram Township, near Galt, Ont., Oct. 30.—Building of Thos. Agnew and contents; loss estimated at $2,500; insured in the Provincial for $1,500; also Thos. Birkeley's building adjacent; contents saved; loss $800; no insurance.

Stratford, Nov. 6.—Stable of A. Smith and one horse; no insurance; fire thought to be incendiary.

Bowmanville, Nov. 17.—The worst fire that has occurred in Bowmanville for many years took place last night. It was evident at once that the whole block would go. This consisted of McClung's dry goods and grocery store; McArthur's dry goods, and Murdoch's grocery, being four large and commodious brick stores. Most unfortunate-

ly our fire engine was comparatively useless, owing to the bursting of the hose. Great exertions were made by the inhabitants to get the goods removed; this was done in the case of McArthur and Murdoch systematically, much of their stock being got out in good order. It was feared at one time that the whole street west would go, but the next building to Murdoch's was a small frame one, and this circumstance enabled them to keep the fire in check. All the parties who were burned out have got places to go into. McClung's stores are insured for $4,500, the stock for $18,000; McArthur's store insured for $3,000; stock fully; Murdoch's store $2,500, stock fully.

Grantham, Ont.—House and barn of McGuire, with all his season's crops; no insurance.

MARINE LOSSES.—The amount of property lost to shipping interests on the Canadian coasts of Lakes Erie and Huron for the past ten years is upwards of $2,251,364, besides a vast number of lives. A good harbor of refuge on each of those lakes, according to the above figures, is much needed.

Port Stanley, Nov. 11.—The propeller *East*, on attempting to enter the harbor this morning, struck the bar and drifted off to the east of the pier, where she now lies hard aground in a hopeless condition, and unless assistance is sent to her she is in danger of becoming a wreck.

— The *Frances Smith* got aground in the river on Saturday evening, and remained fast until noon on Sunday, when she reached her wharf. Again, on Monday evening, while endeavoring to pass the *Acadia* at the mouth of the river, she got aground and was obliged to remain in that position till morning.

MARINE BUSINESS.—The statements of 16 Boston Marine Companies for 1866 and 1867, show a net loss over premiums of 20 per cent.

MUNICIPAL INSURANCE.—The new project of Municipal Insurance is one of the principal topics of talk at Hamilton at present. Its advocates say that no City in Canada is as safe against large fires (within the limits of the water supply) as Hamilton is, and that the Insurance Companies, are drawing large sums annually for a supposed risk, which is next to no risk at all. They contrast Hamilton in this respect with London, Brantford, and other places and affirm that Hamilton does not receive from the insurance companies, anything like a fair reduction on rates paid, according to decreased risk. We are paying a heavy annual charge, say they for the cost of the water works, and why not realize all the benefit therefrom that we may. It is conceded that only by some altogether extraordinary combination of circumstances can a fire now spread beyond the building it originates in. Meantime, conjectures —very far apart, indeed—are hazarded as to the probable amount paid annually in insurance premiums. Some say it cannot be over $25,000 per annum, while others think $100,000 nearer the correct figure.—*Globe Cor.*

SENSIBLE.—We learn that a Committee of citizens of New Haven have been appointed to investigate the cause of fires. This committee is now examining the heating apparatus, flues, &c., of buildings.—*N. E. Insurance Gazette.*

WHAT LIFE INSURANCE IS AND DOES.

Life insurance is a method of becoming instantaneously wealthy, as to one of the noblest purposes of wealth.

He whose labor supports himself and others in comfort may feel poor—and that is almost as bad as to be poor—in his dread of the poverty which would overtake those he loves, were he to die suddenly.

Here are one hundred healthy, active men, with pleasant homes and happy families. It is almost certain that one of them—no one can tell which—

will die this very year. And yet not one of can die without leaving his family straighten the means of a desirable life, if not dead. Hence every one of them feels poor, and is be suddenly better off. Oh, for a lucky ticket, a lucky idea to be patented, the dear rich uncle reminiscent in his will, or some supernatural windfall to put one in possession fund of at least two or three thousand d *Life Insurance* steps in, and, with a stroke pen, converts those one hundred poor men hundred rich ones—rich, every one the short, if he should die before to-morrow, he leave enough to do perhaps all that money to prolong the happiness of his family—rich without being dependent.

If one was to die this year, it is plain eno has bought this wealth cheap.

If he is to live a long life, it is worth all to feel so rich all the while.

The value of human life, we all understand not to be measured by money. The end is be replaced by the means. Yet the end exist without the means. Therefore, the en not be honored without honoring the means complished without considering the means.

A true life is not ended by death. That in fact, too mean to live, which does not l and in those that live after it.

There are cases enough of a sort of savage civilization, where the individual amasse rosely or otherwise, for those who are to li him, the means of living, with little or no to their existent life. Wife, children, depe of all sorts, as to their present life, are left half starved, mentally if not physically, p in character and humanity, in order that a gr tate may be left when the husband and fath This case may get along without life insu The premature death of such a man can ha considered a loss to his heirs, so great is the bility that wealth left to heirs unqualified it would prove a curse.

A wiser style of man does not thus mista means for the end. He aims to create che secure future by present happiness, and le heirs, at all events, rich in themselves and memories of him. But in doing this, in nine cases out of ten in America, he must fearful risk, which life insurance, and the can take off his hands. Life insurance, slays like lion in his path of well and liberal He may be sure now that a good part money-value of his life, as well as that v immeasurable in money, will live after his

In point of fact, the life insurance comp the United States last year distributed to t of the deceased, on about 3,000 policies, no $8,000,000. On very few of these could miums received by the company have amo one-tenth of the sum received from it. benefit, vast as it is, can be considered onl part of that which results from life in The surviving 297,000 policy-holders, it be forgotten, have all enjoyed the satis feeling that, by their own prudence and se the welfare of their families is provided fo fatal dart strike when it will.

How far this satisfaction goes to accou demonstrated fact that insured lives do t fast as the mortality tables lead us to ex impossible to say, but so far as it does go, rance really insures life beyond the pecuni

No matter, if a man's ancestral tree v up of Methuselahs, inasmuch as taking a two too slow in crossing the street, or a of that sort, *might* terminate his earl tenor, a policy, while he lives, must b received, day by day and hour by hour—by his poor—in his dread on his pillow, a morning, when he wishes his darlings go *Elizur Wright.*

—A Company is to be organized with capital to work the Joliette gold min north of Montreal, owned by Mr. Dupr gave from $8.41 to $31.75 to the ton.

ERN RAILWAY.—Traffic receipts for week ov. 7, 1868.

engers....	$3,434 36
ght........................ ...	6,976 76
ıs and Sundries............	316 95
l Receipts for week......	$10,728 07
esponding week 1867....	10,973 32
ecrease....	$245 25
l traffic from 1 Jan. '68..	$215,143 07
esponding period '67....	237,281 80
	$22,138 73

WESTERN RAILWAY.—Traffic for week ct. 30, 1868.

engers......................	$33,928 18
ght and live stock......	42,272 70
s and sundries..........	2,537 26
	$78,738 14
esponding Week of '67·	83,312 11
Increase............	$4,573 97

'N RAILWAYS.—Sherbrooke has express- lingness to subscribe $25,000 to the pro- oden railway, should it start from that

C AND GOSFORD RAILWAY.—By an Council, dated 7th October, the Local ent have granted the Quebec and Gosford Company 61 lots of land, constituting an of 12,141 acres, at the rate of 30 cents payable when the road is built, and goes into operation. This substantial e will tell most favorably upon the pros- the undertaking. It is satisfactory to at the authorities consider the railway to encouragement, for this among other -that one of its objects is the supply of vith firewood. Should the line not be peration before the first of January, 1872, re land will revert to the Government indemnity. The Company is empowered ll the land wanted for the construction of off these lots.

Financial.

ONTREAL MONEY MARKET.

(From our own Correspondent.)

Montreal, Nov. 17, 1868.

still to notice a plethora of money and a fficulty in disposing of it, especially on ıted investments; the amount of paper is very light, and is readily taken up at y rates. Bank stocks are so high that s do not care about investing any heavy not knowing what some mercantile or change may produce; the consequence is, ant question is asked—*How can I invest my* The answer is difficult. Mortgages and stantial style of security are eagerly taken tes, which a few years ago would have sidered absurd, namely, 7 and 8 per cent, the general price for a mortgage on real ed to be 10 to 12 per cent; but capitalists ommodate their ideas the modern charges. ocks and Government debentures offer a , but the rates are so high that the inter- ıot come up to the mark. In fact, every *acknowledged stock* stands above its fair The only solution therefore to the problem Canada contain sources of wealth, as yet developed or only partially so? Undoubt- *does.* In her vast agricultural, mineral ıfacturing resources there are elements ly require fostering to give rise to a pros- ıich will quickly absorb all our surplus capital. This is rather too large a field to open upon in this letter, but I may revert to it more fully in a future communication. The prices of Bank stocks and other securities show the state of our market.

TORONTO STOCK MARKET.

(Reported by Pellatt & Osler, Brokers.)

The Market has been rather freer this week, but the demand for securities still greatly exceeds the supply, and nearly all stocks show a further advance.

Bank Stock.—There were sales of Montreal at 140½, 141 and 141¼; holders now ask 142½. Buyers offer 104 for British; none in market.. The last sales of Ontario were made at 104; buyers offer par ex dividend. No Toronto in market; there are buyers at 119 to 119½. Royal Canadian sold at 91½, and may still be had at that rate. Very little Commerce in market; small sales occurred at 105½. There are buyers of Gore at 40, and sellers at 41. Merchants' closed firm at 109½ to 110. For Quebec 101 is offered; none in market. Molson's is asked for at 107, but there are no sellers. Holders ask an advance on city; buyers offer 105. Sales of Du Peuple occurred at 105¼, at which rate there are still buyers. Jacques Cartier is held at 110, with buyers at 109. For Mechanics' 95½ is offered; no sellers. Union is held at 105, with buyers at 103½.

Debentures.—Canada are in great demand, but none of any kind offering. There were considerable sales of Toronto at rates to pay 7 per cent. interest. County in demand; none in market.

Sundries.—City Gas is not to be had, though buyers offer an advance. Canada Permanent Building Society is in demand and valued at 123, but higher would be paid. No Western Canada in market, buyers offer 115½; there were considerable sales of Freehold at 107½ to 108; books now closed. Montreal Telegraph is readily saleable at 130. There were several sales of Canada Landed Credit at 72 to 73, at which figures there are still buyers. A few large mortgages were placed at 8 per cent, but buyers are not willing now to pay more than 7¾ interest on first-class mortgages. Money is abundant on good security.

BANK OF FRANCE.

Stock of Bullion, October 22nd, 1868........	£48,903,568
" September 17th, 1868......	51,959,542
Rate of Discount..............................	2½ per cent.

BANK OF ENGLAND.

The returns for the week ending October 28th, give the following results when compared with last month's return:

Rest..............................	£3,091,978
Decrease	538,200
Public Deposits............ ...	4,129,038
Decrease.........................	1,065,801
Other Deposits............... ..	19,919,524
Increase	719,344
On the other side of the account:—	
Government Securities... ...	£15,985,874
Increase..........................	1,195,743
Other Securities	15,705,432
Decrease..........................	293,263
Notes unemployed............	9,574,350
Decrease...	1,623,135

The amount of notes in circulation is £24,175,880, showing an increase of £605,535, and the stock of bullion in both departments is £19,844,861, being a decrease of £1,119,979 when compared with the preceding return.

Rate of Discount............... 2 per cent.

MONTREAL, 17 Nov.—(Our own correspondent writes)—Since my last have nothing to report of any consequence. Some few trifling fires; but nothing sufficient to disturb the rest of our fire marshals, who, doubtless, will be more troubled at the sudden and unexpected return from Chicago of Mr. Perry, than at any fire.

THE COTTON MARKET.

We have had a falling market this week, and yet under the circumstances it has really exhibit- considerable strength. Prices at Liverpool have been drooping, receipts at our ports have continued large, more favorable estimates of the crop are becoming general, and the money market, though at the close easier, yet is feverish and sensitive; still, in spite of all these adverse influences, prices this afternoon are only about one cent off from last week. Great confidence still arises from the condition of the stocks in Europe and the continued high rate of consumption there. Our cable despatches to-day give the week's consumption and export at Liverpool at 56,000 bales, and the total stock at 405,000 bales, of which 44,000 bales are American, with 291,000 bales afloat, of which 55,000 bales are American. These figures (although for the week the consumption has fallen off, probably through the use of Egyptian or Brazilian cotton) show that the immediate future is the critical point in the market, and it is believed by many that either short time must be resorted to at Manchester, or the amount afloat for Liverpool from this side must be rapidly increased if we are to see much lower prices. On the other hand, we cannot lose sight of the fact that the stock of American has decreased only very slightly this week, and that in the present state of our money market advances upon cotton are difficult to be made, and should the amount afloat for Liverpool increase materially, the sales there to arrive will have an adverse influence on present rates. Besides it is claimed that Manchester is now producing goods at a loss, and as it is becoming evident that our crop is a good one, small stocks at Liverpool during the next two months would not be likely to create uneasiness. We give these opposing views of the market that our readers may judge for themselves as to the probabilities of the future. The sales for forward delivery still indicate confidence in the maintenance of high rates. During the week the transactions of this description have been numerous. On last Saturday we note sales of 100 bales Middlings for January, and 100 bales for February at 23½c; on Monday, 200 bales for December at the same figure; on Tuesday, 500 bales for January and February at the same price; on Wednesday, 200 bales for January and February, and 100 bales for February at 23c, also 100 bales for December and 150 bales for January at 22 5-8c. To-day 400 bales are reported, of which 100 bales for January and the same for December were on private terms, 100 bales for December were at 22¼c, and 100 bales for December and January at 22 5-8, all Middlings.—*N. Y. Financial Chronicle.*

GRAIN IN STORE.

The following quantities of grain were in store at the points mentioned, on given dates:—

At New York.

		Nov. 9. 1868.	Nov. 2. 1868.	Nov. 11. 1867.
Wheat ...	bush.	1,821,057	1,410,322	942,129
Corn	"	2,778,307	2,873,017	1,954,706
Oats	"	2,072,798	2,065,974	2,246,752
Barley	"	371,055	238,144	361,053
Rye.........	"	123,248	85,106	134,543
Peas	"	70,588	95,177	21,662
Malt........	"	23,694	14,327	52,155
Total ...	"	7,260,747	6,782,067	5,712,010

At Chicago.

	1866.	1867.	1868.
Grain in store, Nov. 9, bush.	647,900	991,200	1,416,000

At Milwaukee.

	1866.	1867.	1868.
Grain in store, Nov. 9, bush.	383,000	562,000	413,000

	At Buffalo.		
	Nov. 2. 1868.	Nov. 9. 1868.	Nov. 11. 1867.
Wheat ...bush.	476,000	402,000	550,000
Corn ...... "	603,000	532,000	200,000
Oats...... "	500,000	300,000	400,000
Barley.... "	73,000	100,000	134,000
Rye .... "	210,000	155,000	30,000
Total...	1,862,000	1,549,000	1,314,000

☞ THE CANADIAN MONETARY TIMES AND INSURANCE CHRONICLE *is printed every Thursday Evening, in time for the English Mail.*

*Subscription Price, one year, $2, or $3 in American currency ; Single copies, five cents each. Casual advertisements will be charged ten cents per line of solid nonpareil each insertion. All letters to be addressed, "*THE CANADIAN MONETARY TIMES, TORONTO, ONT.*" Registered letters so addressed are at the risk of the Publishers. Cheques should be made payable to J. M. TROUT, Business Manager, who will, in future, issue all receipts for money.*

The Canadian Monetary Times.

THURSDAY, NOVEMBER 19, 1868.

LIFE ASSURANCE.

An article on "Life Assurance in the United States," appeared in the *Globe* of Saturday last, which, professing to be a review of the last report made by Mr. Sandford, the Massachusetts Insurance Commissioner, with malicious obliqueness strikes at all American Life Companies. In the course of the article the outrageous statement is made, that in the 46 Companies under review the average of deaths amongst new assurances taken out during the past year, 1867, [was 23 per cent. upon the sum assured. Our co₁emporary has probably not had so much experience in Life Insurance matters as was desirable before putting its ideas upon paper, otherwise it would not have been guilty of the absurdity of writing about an average of "*deaths* upon *sums* assured," or of the ridiculous blunder of stating such average as 23 per cent., or nearly one death to every four assurances. What it intended to say was that the average of *death claims* was 23-100ths of one per cent upon the sums assured. This would give $1 loss for every $435 insured. During the same time the per centage of deaths among the new assurances was 21-100th of one per cent., or about one in every 476 assurances. Our contemporary further says, it has seen "similar returns in reference to one of the Life Companies of this country," and finds " that during the last 20 years there were 16 in which it never lost a life taken during the financial year's currency." In view of the above figures and in the absence of any particulars respect-

ing this, "one of the Life Companies of this country," we see nothing wonderful in this fact. At the above mentioned ratio, a Company effecting 47 new insurances a year would run an even chance of not suffering a loss of this description for ten years, twice as good a per centage as that of "one of the Life Companies of this country," which, according to the figures in the *Globe*, undergoes such a loss in four years out of every twenty.

In truth, however, the only thing which gives figures of this kind any worth at all, is a comparison of them with those of other years, and as those above given are for one year only, they are, for that reason, quite valueless. As our contemporary appears to stand in need of some enlightenment on this subject, we give for its edification the following figures, which will enable it to arrive at a conclusion in respect to the care exercised by American Companies in the selection of lives, somewhat different from, and nearer the truth, than the one indicated in its article :—

Table showing the amount of Policies in force and the Losses of Companies doing business in the State of New York, from the year 1859 to 1867, inclusive.

Year.	Amount of Policies in force.	Losses.	Per centage of Losses to Amount in force.
1859	$141,497,977	$1,388,170	·9811
1860	163,703,455	1,438,578	·8787
1861	164,256,052	1,535,791	·9350
1862	183,962,577	1,740,294	·9460
1863	267,658,677	2,490,617	·9305
1864	395,603,054	3,266,724	·8255
1865	580,882,253	4,304,017	·7409
1866	865,105,877	6,423,668	·7425
1867	1,161,729,776	8,241,582	·7094

So that, on the whole, the per centage of loss has decreased from ·9811 in 1859, to ·7094 in 1867. This scarcely shows a decrease of care in the selection of lives. We commend these figures to the intelligence of the would-be actuary of the *Globe*, and, in conclusion, recommend that paper to stick to its proper business of abusing politicians of the opposite party, and not to meddle with matters which it does not understand. *Ne sutor ultra crepidam.*

THE DOMINION TELEGRAPH COMPANY.

When it was announced that a Telegraph Company was being organised to compete with the Company now in possession of the field, we expressed satisfaction that a hope was afforded of a reduction in rates of telegraphing, and of the enjoyment of all those advantages which the public derive from a wholesome rivalry for their patronage. We believe that an opposition Telegraph Com-

pany, with properly constructed lir capital not inflated by contractor's p and managed by men of character who a practical knowledge of the business, ₁ made to pay, not enormous profits, bₜ dividends to shareholders. Several att have been made to establish competing in Canada, but so far they have been fai and it is because we would be glad successful competition that we are di₁ to view with favor new enterprises 1 that object before them. Competition business of telegraphy signifies, so Canada is concerned, competition fullest sense. The Montreal Comp₁ beyond doubt a strong one. The Di₁ are men of wealth, and business shrew with a sufficient interest in the Comp induce them to look well after its ₁ The business of the Company, and it ₁ just to say it, is managed by able and tical men, who have not only the cont of the directors, but also of the public. facilities are extensive and means ampl thus far their Company have gobbl rivals, and found them very small mout All this must be taken into account competition is talked of, and a successf₁ petitor must start from a solid foun₁ But there is no reason why a rival Co₁ should not be managed just as well Montreal Company is ; no reason ₁ should not command its share of patr₁ no reason why it could not be worked · and no reason why such a Company not have its head quarters at Toronto before satisfactory results can be ob certain conditions must be compliе₁ and the ordinary chances of success m be overlooked.

A Montreal paper has atacked wi siderable vigour the promoters of the ion Telegraph Company, and after rec the story of the Grand Trunk Telegra₁ pany, of unhappy memory, charges Dominion Company has as its origin. Snow of sixteen years ago ; it gives M the about-to-be Superintendent, a c which, if inuendo can be regarde least indifferent and ferrets out a rela between Snow and the Messrs. Josiah T. Snow, did certainly victi Canadians, in the matter of the Trunk abortion, and no Canadian, w would feel anxious to assist him in r his attempt to build a telegraph lin territory.

The question, then, presents itsel tlement at the outset of this enterp there a nigger in the fence," (to use classic across the lines) ; and is Snow that troublesome customer. tory of Josiah is thus epitomized :

ry Snow came into Canada from the representing himself as an extensive graph Contractor, &c. He succeeded in several most respectable business men onto and other towns to permit the use of their names as Directors. Having succeeded in this, he and his agents went about the country, holding meetings, and parading names, and getting stock taken very actively for his lines. Directorships without number were urged upon prominent in different places, many of whom found names on the list without their authority, on the strength of which names, many people were induced to subscribe, held meetings all through the country, telling the people that it was a most favourable time for establishing a new Telegraph Company; that the business was merely in its infancy; that the profits were immense, and of room for two Companies: Assessments were to be very light, &c., &c. The shareholders being very numerous, and not any holding enough stock to take an interest in the affairs of the Company, taking for granted that the *very respectable* Directors or somebody was looking after the management in a proper manner, a thousand miles or more of lines were hastily built. And Mr. Snow, who manipulated the business, then went about, gathered a balance of his subscriptions, and *ately returned to the States.* The lines went into a state of premature decay, the business seemed likely to come to an end together. An attempt, however, was made to revive the concern. A number of "fees" were appointed, and funds borrowed to start again under a new management. The lines worked on for a year or so and again got into a state of chronic decay and were sold out to Mr. Wm. Weller, of Cobourg. After endeavoring with his means and energy to carry on the business soon again failed, and the old material line was finally sold for a mere nominal sum. Snow, it was reported, made 0 out of the operation, but not a single of the original shareholders ever got back of their money in any shape."

I do not vouch for the accuracy of this eventful history, but of Snow's return to the States, and of the death and burial of the Company, we are certain. The evidence of Snow thus proceeds. The Dominion Company calls the Great Western Telegraph Company of Chicago its "right bower." Snow is secretary and director to the Great Western Company. In the Western circular his name appears; in that circular as reprinted in Canada this name is kept out. This, however, is merely minus. The next charge is that Mr. Reeve Secretary of the Dominion Company, is a son of Snow's. This, too, we consider suspicious. The next charge is that somebody is working up a similar speculation in the States, in connection with the Dominion Company. This may be quite true, and yet it may not be directly interested on this

It appears that the Montreal Telegraph Company and Mr. Snow had some communication so late as last spring. It is stated by Mr. Dwight, the Toronto manager of the Montreal Company, that overtures were made to his Company by Mr. Snow, with the object of arriving at a mutual agreement "that neither company should reduce rates." This mysterious appearance of Snow had a mysterious opportuneness about it. The Dominion is started here with the proclaimed object of reducing rates, and if it can be proved that its promoters first tried to fasten high rates on our people by a preconcerted arrangement with a company which it proposes to compete with, we can can only say that deception at the outset augurs a bad ending.

As we have said, we are by no means disposed to take as proved all the allegations alluded to; and we should be loth to injure an enterprise by condemning it without a full examination of the evidence on both sides. So far a strong *prima facie* case of suspicion is made out, and before the public can be reasonably called upon to further or take stock in the Dominion Company it should and must clear itself. The names on the board of direction are of the highest character, and we call on the board to come forward and let us know what the true state of the case really is. Did those gentlemen whose names appear there accept gifts of stock, or are they *bona fide* subscribers to the concern? Did they examine into the enterprise or take every statement for granted? Has Snow anything to do with them? Who obtained the contract for building the road? What prices are to be paid for doing it? No object is to be gained by concealment. Questions such as those we have put are in everybody's mouth; and the sooner they are answered the better for the reputation of those who lent the enterprise the use of their names, and the better for the Dominion Telegraph Company. We have already heard of parties who talk not only of declining to pay future instalments on this stock, but also of demanding back what they have paid, simply because they consider that the statements made, under which they were induced to subscribe, overshot the bounds of truth.

THE NARROW GAUGE RAILWAYS.

It is indisputably desirable that the districts lying to the north-east and north-west of Toronto should have railway service connecting them with this city. There is direct mutuality between the city and the country in this matter, and as the advantage is alike to both, it is reasonable that both should contribute in the measure of their ability and interest. The townships interested have already, to a considerable extent, pledged

their means in support, and the city of Toronto is now invited to adopt by-laws authorizing aid to these lines to the amount of $400,000. The aggregate of bonuses for the first division of each of the projected railways is $5,000 per mile, in sums of from $20,000 to $60,000. The time seems, therefore, to have arrived when we should take a careful survey of the situation in order to ensure the fullest success at the least possible cost, and to the avoidance of those errors which, in past times, have overclouded promising enterprises by the rashness, imprudence, and corruption by which they were promoted.

The Toronto, Grey and Bruce Railway has three divisions. The first division starts from Toronto on a right of way reserved by the city for railway purposes, runs along the bank of the Humber for a short distance, thence north-west *via* Caledon East and Charleston to Orangeville, thence in a westerly direction to some point in Arthur, and thence to Mount Forest. The second division embraces a line through Bruce to Southampton, and a branch from Mount Forest to Owen Sound. The whole length of railway will be about 300 miles; the first division being 85 to 90 miles long. The territory to be served is estimated at 435,000 square miles of the richest and most fertile lands in Canada, leaving a corresponding extent of country tributable to the other railroads. The trade immediately available is estimated as equal to that done by the Northern, for although the Northern does a very large export business in pine lumber and timber, which would not be expected by this railroad, yet the import traffic of pine lumber, and the export of square timber and staves, together with a much larger cattle, grain, provision, produce and passenger traffic, should make the total business exceed that of the Northern so soon as the trade shall have adopted this new channel of communication.

The route of the Toronto and Nipissing Railway is in a direct north-easterly course from the city of Toronto, through Scarboro, Markham, Uxbridge, Brock and Eldon to a point on the Gull River, at or near Coboconck, thence northerly to a point on Lake Nipissing. The first division of the road extends about 100 miles, and is all that the Company undertakes to build on its own responsibility, according to present arrangements. The remaining 150 miles of road would be through new and unsettled country, and it is not contemplated to build it without a Government subsidy, either of land or money.

The grain and passenger traffic to be secured by this road to Lake Nipissing will not, it is considered, exceed half that of the Northern, but the practically inexhaustible supplies of pine and other kinds of timber will afford a business durable and profitable. Unlike the railroads now in operation, the Toronto and Nipissing cannot expect to share in the North-west lake trade, but this disadvantage is compensated for by the lumber trade, which the latter will have control of in the absence of· competition. A Government grant should and will, undoubtedly, be forthcoming when the road reaches the boundary of Eldon. A grant of alternate lots of 200 acres each would be sufficient to sell the bonds of the Company at par, so that with the proceeds the railroad could be built, within three or four years, to the shores of Lake Nipissing.

There are two principles involved in the scheme for the construction of these railways, which are somewhat novel in Canada. The first is that the gauge is limited to 3 feet 6 inches, such as has been worked in Norway, which is alleged to have a carrying capacity of over 800,000 tons per annum, and a speed of 20 to 30 miles per hour. The highest traffic returns of the Northern give a total of 200,000 tons, thus apparently showing that both the capacity and speed of the 3 ft. 6 in. gauge are ample for the local Canadian business likely to be secured. The other novel feature is the system of bonuses which the people have adopted and sanctioned.

The financial programme is founded on the receipt of bonuses to the extent of $5,000 per mile. $5,000 per mile will represent the amount to be paid for iron and a first mortgage on the road will be given to secure its payment. The proposal to confine the expenditure to $15,000 per mile rests mainly on the division of the work into very small contracts, economy in the purchase of the right of way, checking commissions on the purchase of iron, the construction of timber bridges with stone abutments, the possession of plain and efficient rolling stock, the erection of stations inexpensive and simple, and the obtaining of nothing on credit but the iron.

The object which Toronto has at heart, and which is worth every legitimate effort she can put forth, is to attract to herself a perpetuity of the traffic of the districts which these lines are designed to serve and in a secondary sense, to do this with the least possible burden to herself. To meet these conditions she should see that the location is made so as to command new traffic throughout (or as nearly as possible throughout) the entire length of new construction. It is not her interest or her object to compete with lines already doing her business and promoting her trade ; it is her object to get new trade and new customers by connecting herself with new districts. To intrude com-

petition upon lines already engaged in her trade is to divert her strength and means to less profitable purposes. It is, moreover, certain that new enterprises demanding large investments are much more easily and quickly handled if backed, rather than opposed, by existing and powerful interests. The Hamilton people in seeking the support of the Great Western Railway have illustrated this principle, indeed, without such aid, it is probable they could scarcely move at all. For the benefit of all interested in the success of these roads, we advise a careful consideration of this view of the case. It is said that both roads will come direct into Toronto. If it is essential to their independence that it should be so, the proposal is quite legitimate. But two railways may use one track just as freely as two stages can traverse one road, and to multiply railways with a mere view to independence is simply a fallacy and extravagance. The first 25 miles of a railway out of a city, as is well known, are unproductive of local traffic and the multiplication of such unproductive mileage is a palpable folly, unless it is absolutely unavoidable—more especially so when we have to pay out of our own pockets for the gratification of the propensity. It is peculiar to the schemes about to be subsidized that no professional guidance has been appealed to in placing them before us in detail. We want to know, and we suppose every tax-payer would like to know if twenty-five or thirty miles of the most unproductive and difficult portions of these roads might be saved by adopting King as a common point of departure, utilizing the Northern Railway to that extent under the security of Parliamentary enactment, giving independent running power on an equitable payment or toll for the privilege. It is asserted that such a saving in mileage would be more than equivalent to the whole contribution that Toronto is invited to make, and the companies in such case would be enabled either to use the subsidy in constructing that twenty-five or thirty miles into absolutely new territory (in Bruce or Victoria) or at any rate so as to strengthen their financial position as by such a saving of length they would be enabled to make the construction of their lines a positive and immediate certainty. To our minds twenty-five or thirty miles additional of railway in Bruce and Victoria would be vastly more profitable in new trade to this city than the like length in the townships of York, Peel, and Ontario, which are now in as complete connection with this City, as is possible. If we have money to give we, at least, have none to waste; and while we should exercise a wise liberality towards legitimate enterprises promoted in our interest, we should be jealous to see that it is applied to the best purpose and with a

certainty of the best returns of wh[...] capable. It can be of little advan[...] Toronto to put a fourth railway thro[...] townships of York and Peel. To d[...] necessarily or under the mere influ[...] hostility to the three existing lines is [...] less and unprofitable appropriation o[...] which, at the least, will represent a [...] burden upon our resources, and w[...] applied in new districts as yet bey[...] reach would ensure us an earlier an[...] compensation for our efforts. What [...] ultimate decision may be on the p[...] have raised, no one will venture to [...] they are not worthy of every attenti[...]

Leaving this part of the subject, [...] to the criticism of experts and co[...] ourselves with simply directing publ[...] tion to its importance, it becomes ou[...] duty to look somewhat more closely [...] financial operations arising out of tl[...] enterprises. It is proposed that [...] shall issue debentures in aid of these [...] amounting in the aggregate to £[...] Assuming that the city can do this [...] over-weighting its resources and [...] also that it may be done with le[...] there can, we fancy, be no question [...] advantage and propriety of the meas[...] are all agreed on the immense ben[...] would accrue from the constructio[...] projected railways. Though unani[...] vail on that point, it is the duty [...] the interest of every citizen to exam[...] and understand the financial positi[...] city before agreeing to assume fur[...] dens. Truth will out, and it is [...] should out at the beginning than b[...] out at the end to our discomfiture.

The debt of Toronto, on the 1st of [...] 1868, as returned by the Chambe[...] $2,114,853 44. To meet the liab[...] that debt and to provide for curren[...] an annual income is necessary to tl[...] of $404,500, in addition to receipts [...] sources, to raise which, the ass[...] perty being $24,614,000, would [...] gross rate of 1¾ cents in the doll[...] moderate allowance for probable [...] made. By law it is rendered obl[...] the city to levy rates in each yea[...] for the payment of all accruing in [...] (by a sinking fund) for the ultima[...] tion of the debt at maturity. [...] past six or seven years a consider[...] of the City's liabilities has been [...] and the sinking fund is said to [...] default from $320,000 to $400,0[...] city was able to pay and yet di[...] faith has been broken with the city [...] If there was absolute inability, [...] city going to face its creditors [...] burden voluntarily assumed. W[...] fore us as a statement of the Sin[...]

it only gives one side of the account, does not show the amount accrued e by-laws. During the past four there has been an annual suspense Sinking Fund. If, then, it be s default exists, the city should, ies new debentures, measure its l see that it does not involve v engagements entirely beyond

s is not to make any declaration he enterprises which we all are d, and which we all desire to see n the contrary it is friendly to ts, for if they ask for bread it is iry to give them a stone. The has sought to make us honest in selves, and to enforce a limit to iture of municipalities by an enohibitory of the issue of new when the annual rate that the ll levy in any year exceeds two dollar. Would the rate exceed n the dollar if the Council levied which it is legally bound, and ompelled to levy this year? The e in Toronto is 1½ cents in the h produces less than $370,000. were compelled to raise $125,000 it would require a rate in excess ts in the dollar. The Sinking rs, as we have seen, amount to $300,000. Such being the case, doubt that holders of debentures ir by-laws which provide for the a sinking fund by a special annual i be entitled to an injunction in) restrain the city from issuing : debentures until all arrears of fund are made up. Not only so, benture holders have the right to Corporation to assess and levy ient to cover the portions of the d not provided for in former he city be in such a position that cess of two cents in the dollar of value of the whole rateable proessary to provide for all engagebenture-holder or a rate-payer quity, restrain the issue of new

It does not require great legal understand why it should be so. is a correct one, the promoters of wises should look to it that they ved, and our city Council should at they do not involve themselves If we are mistaken we shall be i to be convinced that such is the know of nothing more likely to nto, and the back country than f the two railways under con-

sideration. The promoters are entitled to the thanks of the community for the energy and perseverance they have displayed in bringing their schemes to maturity. But it is worse than folly for any well-wisher of the enterprises to disguise from himself the real state of affairs.

THE NEW YORK LIFE INSURANCE COMPANY.

There is something wonderful in the increase of Life Assurance business on this Continent during the past few years. In 1862 the total amount of policies in force, of companies doing business in the State of New York, was $183,962,577. In 1867, the total was $1,161,729,776, being more than five times the former amount, and still the work goes bravely on.

In our advertising columns appears the annual statement of the Company whose name stands at the head of this article, for 1867. During the period now mentioned the amount of its policies in force increased from $22,293,864 to $69,406,477, more than threefold in five years ; in the same time its annual premiums increased from $759,567 to $3,104,051, or upward of four times, and what is even more satisfactory, as it evidences the increased safety of the concern, is the augmentation of its assets during that period from $2,592,633 to $9,159,753, or nearly fourfold, being greater than that of the policies in force, so that while in 1862 the ratio of assets to the amount of policies in force was about 11½ per cent, in 1867 it was over 13 per cent. The liabilities at the latter date were $7,517,328, leaving a divisible surplus of $1,642,425. The company is a premium note one, 40 per cent of the premiums being payable by note. Out of the above-mentioned sum of assets, $1,601,015 is held in the shape of premium notes, to which if we add the deferred and unpaid premiums, &c., we get a total of $2,361,852 of unrealized assets, being about 25½ per cent of the whole assets. This is considerably under the average, which for the year 1867, for companies doing business in New York State was over 36 per cent. This is satisfactory, and shows that the company possesses the elements of stability, provided always of course that the assets are invested in reliable securities. On this head we find that a considerable proportion are like those of all American companies invested in United States Bonds and Treasury Notes, probably as safe a security as could be selected.

This company is a purely mutual one, so that as in all companies of that description, the whole of the profits made go to the insured. Since starting about 20 years ago,

the company has paid in this way dividends amounting in 1867 to about $1,400,000. The New York Life, we believe, claims as an additional fact to its credit, that it was the first which adopted the principle of the ten year non-forfeiture plan, the general adoption of which, as a matter of common justice to policy-holders, we have strenuously urged in these columns, and shall continue to urge as opportunity occurs. This is a step in the right direction, that of non-forfeiture. We do not doubt but that much of its popularity is attributable to this fact, thus affording an inducement to other companies to follow its example in this respect.

A NEW EXPRESS COMPANY.

If the commercial community of Canada have a grievance which galls them more harshly than any other, it is found in their enforced slavery to the present express monopoly. Incivility and exorbitant charges go hand in hand, and certainly if half of what we hear be true, it is time that a remedy were found for the evils complained of. Merchant after merchant has assured us that the charges of this monopoly are simply outrageous, and the impudence of its understrappers intolerable. It is the old story over again. Monopoly has got fat and kicked. That the profits must be enormous we are convinced. Before the establishment of the Merchant's Union of New York the stock of the other combination was not to be had at any price. The nominal quotations ranged from 250 to 400. The profits of the Canadian Express carrying trade have all gone to swell the dividends of foreign companies, and it is not their fault if the Canadian branch of their business has not yielded handsome returns. An opportunity is now afforded to secure relief from a grevious burden by an union among merchants for the establishment of a Canadian Company, having Canadian interests to serve. If our merchants will only take the matter in hand themselves the remedy is within easy reach. The prospectus of the new company, (whose provisional directors are excellent men) states that the terms of subscription are that no payment on account of stock shall be required until after $250,000 shall have been subcribed. This is a guarantee of a useful character. A provision in the charter takes away all power to sell out to any other company or to amalgamate. All this looks like business, and we wish the company every success.

THE WESTERN OF ENGLAND.

We learn from a circular issued by the Agent of this Insurance Company, that the Company's business was taken over by the

Provincial of Toronto on 30th June last. We are also informed that the Provincial bound itself to satisfy all claims arising in respect of policies of the Western current on 1st July, 1868, and to save harmless the Western from all claims, liability and loss, as well as costs, damages and expenses that arise out of such policies. We suppose that parties in the position of claimants under policies issued by the Western will be settled with by the Provincial. It is gratifying to know that the Western people did not leave their policy-holders in the lurch.

COMMERCIAL BANK OF NEW BRUNSWICK.

On the 10th instant, this Bank suspended specie payments. An uneasy feeling has prevailed for some time past respecting its circumstances, and the action of its shareholders in getting rid of stock has, doubtless, contributed greatly to the present result. On the 8th, three lots were sold at $16, $17 and $18, respectively ; their par value being $100. It is generally conceded that the Bank's circulation, about $200,891, is perfectly secure, as the charter provides not only for a treble liability, but also for the continuance of that liability for a year after the shares are parted with. The paid up capital is $600,000.

The Toronto *Leader* and the Ottawa *Times* have made this suspension yield the deduction that "the Government should now step in and take out of the hands of the Banks their power to issue notes." A letter has appeared in the *Leader* in reply to the remarks of that journal, on the desirableness of the circulation of the country being in the hands of the Government. The writer, after showing that the circulation of the Commercial Bank was not large in proportion to its capital, that a Government issue would lead to a depreciated currency, that nearly every Government currency throughout the world is at a discount, that a Government issue would lead to the severest curtailment of discounts that has been known, points out the consequent crippling of commerce, and that the notes of the only bank which has not paid its creditors in Canada are worth nearly as much at this moment as those of the United States.

— The formation of a Joint Stock Company, called the Elgin Manufacturing Company, is announced in the St. Thomas (Ontario) papers, with a capital of $50,000, divided into 2,000 shares of $25 each, for the purpose of manufacturing Agricultural Implements in that town. Thos. Arkell is President.

Owen Sound Harbor.—The *Advertiser* says—The propellor *Acadia*, with 200 tons of merchandise for this port, was unable to go up the river, because of the low water. She remained all day Monday at the new Wharf of the North West Forwarding Company, where she would have been glad to have discharged her freight had the wharf been ready for its accommodation.

Commercial.

Montreal Correspondence.

(From our own Correspondent).

Montreal, Nov. 17, 1868.

During the past week the weather has been cold and our streets are thinly covered with snow. We have now four steamships in the harbour—the *St. David*, with a large cargo now discharging ; the *St. George*, loading for Glasgow ; the *Nova Scotian*, for Liverpool, and the *Cleopatra*, for London. All these vessels are chartered and busily engaged taking in their return cargoes of produce. The *St. George* brought out a large quantity of malt from Glasgow, this being a more favorable market than either the Scotch or English ones. Hops on the contrary are dull of sale, and there are several hundreds of bales offering for which no price is obtainable. As the bulk of hops sold here are received from the west, this information may be of value to intending shippers. Our full fleet of sailing vessels have now nearly gone, and our wharves are getting deserted except by steamers and small lower port craft, which generally remain to peddle out their cargoes, till they are forced to take winter quarters at Boucherville or Three Rivers. It would seem that nothing can teach the captains of the small coasting craft the value of time. To my knowledge they are constantly offered a fair lump sum for their cargoes, but prefer dealing it out in a few barrels, and not only losing time, but running the risk of being detained all winter.

Produce Market.—The tendency of flour has been downwards. In the beginning of the week holders were very stiff, but the accumulation of stocks and the falling off in shipments forced them to give way. Supers have consequently declined from $5.30 to $5.15 ; for strong lots of Baker's flour, $5.30 to $5.35 is the price. The receipts from 1st January to the 13th inst. are :

1867.	1868.	Increase.
611,835 brls.	649,606 brls.	37,771 brls.

Shipments for same date :

1867.	1868.	Increase.
455,013 brls.	460,068 brls.	4,994 brls.

The stock of flour in store and in the hands of millers, on the 16th, was 31,515 brls. ; on the 2nd, 22,107 brls. ; on the 15th Nov. last year 52,330 brls.

In wheat, the market has fluctuated, the supply from the west having been more attracted to the eastern American shipping ports than here ; New York and Boston dealers have offered rates that we could not afford, and consequently the trade has gone past us. I believe that this will be to the benefit of Montreal, as I feel convinced that heavy losses will result in all grain shipments this year. I have steadily expressed my opinion on this subject, and now find it sustained by the leading journals of New York and Great Britain.

The stock of wheat on the 16th was 114,160 bush., and 179,704 bush. last year.

In coarse grains there is a fair business doing. Cargo sales of peas have been made at $1.01¼ per 66 lbs. Corn at 83½c to 84c. Barley rules high, and is likely to advance, bright samples bringing up to $1.37½. Oats have sold up to 48c and 49c per 32 lbs, according to sample. Provisions—Pork is very dull, the supply of both live and dressed hogs is greatly in excess of the demand, consequently prices are down, and any large lots are hard of sale. Dressed hogs are worth $9.75 to $7.25 ; mess pork $23.75 to $24, other qualities in proportion. Butter continues very high, and for reasons stated in my former letters is likely to continue so. Best dairy is very scarce and would bring readily 24c to 24½c ; shipping parcels 20½ to 21½, and good western 22c to 23c.

Groceries.—I mentioned in my last that some late fall sales were to come off this week. A. Urquhart & Co. was the first ; the attendance was

below an average, only some few Western being present, and they not being an purchase. I do not think that the otl will meet with more success, except that rance's of teas, as there is no doubt that tions of the Province is low in stock, esp the finer qualities, and at present Montre cheapest market. For fish the compet been active, and at Shipway's sales on t yesterday and to-day, over six thousand l Labrador, and $3½ for round herrings. have advanced their prices, and in vie short stocks and active demand, they likely carry their point.

Hardware.—The fall shipments havir and being much reduced by sales, made i pation of them, we can safely look for business, and at more satisfactory prices. are coming in freely, and buyers are a get them promptly executed, as the clo inland navigation is rapidly drawing t The advices from England also indicate able activity and an advancing market, s tone of our market is much firmer.

Dry Goods are exceedingly dull, the the present being over ; there is gener revival when sleighing fairly sets in. S glad to say that remittances have been l usual, and the trade taken altogethe healthy condition.

Toronto Market.

During the week the weather wa mostly wet, and therefore unfavorable The country roads are almost i in many places.

Grain.—*Wheat*—Receipts by cars 15 and 20,773 bush. Very little of the ne been marketed yet so that millers have scant supplies. This fact has also limite idly of flour, causing that article to be eer scarce. With a view of meeting th millers between now and the commen sleighing, one of our city dealers is br cargo of Western wheat which is now arrive. This wheat can, we believe, b here so as to sell for less than $1.00, fair profit. In the present state of t market, buyers can operate to good a there seems to be little faith in th wheat, and besides the tightness o market renders holding a difficult an operation. We hear that the miller Rochester, and other points on the have not laid in their usual supplies fall grinding, owing to the state of market. This fact may shortly giv improvement in our wheat trade. S at $1.00 and $1.05 ; no sales. Midg to 1.08. Fall sold to some extent at ing from $1.03 to 1.18, according Barley—Receipts by cars 6,000 l 5,034 bush. last week. The shipm week ended with Saturday last, were and 20,720 bush. the previous week. ments by water since the opening 648,440 bush., as per Custom's retu a fair demand for good samples at $8 sales of a few cars at these prices. P by cars 550 bush. and 2,400 bus market nominal, no sales. Oats—P bush. and 6,000 bush., according. Ne held at 51c to 52c. Rye—lower at

Flour.—Receipts 1,560 brls., an last week. Superfine is offered spar at $4.80, with little demand; sub lots at $4.75. Extra sold at $5.50.

Provisions.—*Butter.*—A lot of sold at 23½c here, and a lot of 1 point some distance out of the city cars. Rolls in boxes sell at 23 to is offered at 11½c by the car load. 100 brls. new, sold at $23.50. I Little doing, at quotations. *Eggs*

E STOCK.—Two or three lots of live hogs t 5½c.; a great quantity of our packers' supare now brought in from Chicago. In cattle keep the usual local trade is doing, at unded prices.

rs.—Lower and dull of sale; 15 bales prime t 11¼c., and a small lot, fair, at 7c.

EIGHTS.—Rates by steamer to Montreal on 30c; on wheat, 8c; barley to Oswego, 3½., to 4c; Lumber to Oswego, $1.75 per M feet; Erie to Toronto, $1.30 to $1.35 currency, per Grand Trunk—Flour to Montreal, 35c; meats to Liverpool per gross ton 67s. 6d; and butter 77s.; Beef per ton 11s.; pork per s.

Halifax Market.

BREADSTUFFS.—Nov. 10.—Flour still continues od demand without change in price. Canada ranges from $6.25 to $6.50; strong bakers, to $6.70; extra Canada, $7.50 to $8; extra still continues dull at $6 to $6.40, according ality. No. 2 in good demand at $5 to $5.50. neal without change at $4.50 for kild dried, $4.40 for fresh ground. Oatmeal $7.70 to Imports from January 1st to October 27th, and 1868:

	Brls. Flour.	Brls. Cornmeal.
1868.	155,003	42,919
1867.	169,191	32,316

SH.—The weather the past week has operated 1st transactions in dry Codfish. Prices remain out change at $4.15 to $4.25 for good large s; $3.20 to $3.30 for for good small shore; ador $2.25 to $2.50; Bank and Bay none. 1 hard cure Arichat Haddock $2 to $2.10; ern Shore $1.80 to $1.90; Western $1.60 to 5; Pollock $1.50. Herring in good demand .50 to 5 for Labrador, and $4.25 to 4.50 for Mackerel scarce at $12.50 to 12.75 for 1; $11 for No. 2, and $6.75 to 7 for No. 3. on $14 to 15 for No. 1; $12 to 13 for No. 2, $9.50 to 10 for No. 3.

Furs and Skins.

f Sea Otter there are two kinds—the Siberian Alaskan. The difference between them is the Siberian is more downy, bushy and thick, also of a dark brown, almost black color interd with grey hair, which gives it a silvery apance; whereas the Otter from Alaska is not so k and of a lighter shade, giving it the yellow cloudy color. The difference of the color, ever, is frequently disguised by dyeing, and i the silvery hair is counterfeited by false light hair, inserted through it by means of a needle. tampered with, it requires a very experienced to detect an Alaskan Sea Otter from a Siberian price in this market, of the former, ranges $30 to $40, whereas the latter ranges from to $250, according to quality. Russia presents best market for the Sea Otter, where good is are scarce, and the demand being very great, securetimes fetch enormous prices. Fur is—The Russian American Company killed in 7, on the whole territory, 127,000 of these mals, whereas the different American Conies have already killed 164,000 up to this date. er the Fur Seals are killed, the skins are either d or salted. The dried skins are considered rior; saleable at $1.50 each. The salted skins ng softer and better adapted for cleaning and ssing, the salt, keeping the natural grease of skin from evaporation, command $3 a skin. highest price paid this year in the Alaska ritory for Seals was 25 cents each. Ermines- Alaska is not very white, and is inferior to nine, and as there is a good demand for it in country, the best kinds are imported from ssia. As far as can be ascertained, the value of Skins and Furs exported from Alaska in 1868 ounts to $1,000,000. The quotations which low are much below those recently ruling here reason of heavy importations from the North, all of which, by the way, are entered at our stom House, but are recently sold in the open rket. List of prices of Furs in San Francisco

at date: Bear, Black, Prime, Fine $3 to $5 per skin; do. Heavy, $1 to $2.50; do. Seconda, $1 to $2; do. Cubs, 50c to $1.50; do. Brown and Grizzly, about 20 per cent. less than black. Badger 50c to $1 per skin. Fisher, Prime, Dark, $2 to $3; do. Pale, $1 to $2; do. Seconds, 50c to $1 per skin. Fox—Silver, $2 to $15; do. Cross, $2 to $3; do. Red, 50c to $1; do. Kitt 20c to 30c; do. White, 50c to $1; do. Gray 50c to 60c. Lynx, $1 to $1.50. Marten, Prime Dark, $2 to $4; do. Pale, $1 to 2; do. Seconds, $1 to 1.50; do. Thirds, 25c to 75c. Mink—Dark, Northern, Prime, $1.50 to $2.25; do. Seconds, 50c to 75c; do. Thirds, 20c to 25c per skin. Muskrats 10c to 15c. Otter—Sea, Prime, Dark, Silvery, $50 to 60; do. Prime, $20 to 30; do Brown, $15 to 20; do. Pups, 50c to $3. Otter—Land, Prime, Dark, Northern, $1 to 2; do. Southern, 75c to $1.50; do. Seconds, 50c to $1; do. Thirds, 20c to 50c. Raccoon, 20c to 25c. Wolf large, $2 to 3; do. Small, $1 to 50; do. Seconds, 50c to 75c. Wolverine—Firsts, $3 to 4; do. Seconds, $2 to 2.50. Wild Cat— First 30c to 40c; do. Seconds, 10c to 20c. Skunks, 10c to 15c. Seal—Fur, $1 to 2.50; do. Hair, 10c to 20c. Beaver—Northern, 50c to $1; do. Southern, 75c to 90c. Deer Skins—Indian Dressed, (Smoked preferred) $1 to 1.25; do. Raw, 20c to 25c; do. Winter, 15c to 18c. Ermine— Alaskan, 5c to 15c; do. Siberian, 25 to 50c.—*San Francisco Com. Herald.*

Reduction in Telegraph Rates.

We are informed that the Montreal Telegraph Company will, from 1st January, send telegrams from Toronto to any point in Ontario, and as far east as Montreal for 25cts. The tariff to more distant points in the Lower Provinces will be correspondingly reduced.

Insurance.

BEAVER
aal Insurance Association.

HEAD OFFICE—20 TORONTO STREET,
TORONTO.

ES LIVE STOCK against death from any cause.
only Canadian Company having authority to do this
business.

R. L. DENISON,
President.

'REILLY,
Secretary.   8-1y-25

HOME DISTRICT
al Fire Insurance Company.

OFFICE:

West Corner of Yonge and Adelaide Streets,
TORONTO.—(UP STAIRS.)

RES Dwelling Houses, Stores, Warehouses, Merdise, Furniture, &c.

PRESIDENT—The Hon. J. McMURRICH.
VICE-PRESIDENT—JOHN BURNS, Esq.
JOHN RAINS, Secretary.

AGENTS:

WRIGHT, Esq., Hamilton ; FRANCIS STEVENS, Esq.,
Barrie; Messrs. GIBBS & BRO., Oshawa.   8-1y

THE PRINCE EDWARD COUNTY
ual Fire Insurance Company.

HEAD OFFICE.—PICTON, ONTARIO.
nt, L. B. STINSON; Vice-President, W. A. RICHARDS.
tors: H. A. McPaul, James Cavan, James Johnson,
aMill, William Delong.—Treasurer, David Barker
y, John Twigg; Solicitor, R. J. Fitzgerald.

Company is established upon strictly Mutual prin-
les, insuring farming and isolated property, (not
ns,) in Townships only, and offers great advantages
rers, at low rates for five years, without the expense
ewal. This Company has existed 12 years, during
eriod it has adjusted all losses in a satisfactory
. It is managed with strict economy, and affords
rtunity of insuring with safety and reliance, and
ttle expense, which accounts for its long standing
successful business which it has been and is now

n, June 15, 1868.   9-1y

lartford Fire Insurance Company.
HARTFORD, CONN.

apital and Assets over Two Million Dollars.

$2,026,220.29.

CHARTERED 1810.

old and reliable Company, having an established
iness in Canada of more than thirty years standing,
pplied with the provisions of the new Insurance
al made a special deposit of

$100,000

e Government for the security of policy-holders, and
itinue to grant policies upon the same favorable
s heretofore.

ally low rates on first-class dwellings and farm
y for a term of one or more years.
s as heretofore promptly and equitably adjusted.
H. J. MORSE & CO., AGENTS.
ato, Ont.

BERT WOOD, GENERAL AGENT FOR CANADA]

Geo. Girdlestone,
, Life, Marine, Accident, and Stock Insurance
ent

Very best Companies represented.
r, Ont.; June, 1868.

Insurance.

The Standard Life Assurance Company,
Established 1825.
WITH WHICH IS NOW UNITED
THE COLONIAL LIFE ASSURANCE COMPANY.

Head Office for Canada:
MONTREAL—STANDARD COMPANY'S BUILDINGS,
No. 47 GREAT ST. JAMES STREET.
Manager—W. M. RAMSAY.   Inspector—RICH'D BULL.

THIS Company having deposited the sum of ONE HUN-
DRED AND FIFTY THOUSAND DOLLARS with the Receiver-
General, in conformity with the Insurance Act passed last
Session, Assurances will continue to be carried out at
moderate rates and on all the different systems in practice.

AGENT FOR TORONTO—HENRY PELLATT,
KING STREET.

AGENT FOR HAMILTON—JAMES BANCROFT.
6-6mos.

Fire and Marine Assurance.

THE BRITISH AMERICA
ASSURANCE COMPANY.
HEAD OFFICE :
CORNER OF CHURCH AND COURT STREETS.
TORONTO.

BOARD OF DIRECTION :

Hon G. W. Allan, M L C.,   A. Joseph, Esq ,
George J. Boyd, Esq ,   Peter Paterson, Esq.,
Hon. W. Cayley,   G. P. Ridout, Esq.,
Richard S. Cassels, Esq.,   E H. Rutherford, Esq ,
      Thomas C. Street, Esq.

Governor:
GEORGE PERCIVAL RIDOUT, Esq.

Deputy Governor:
PETER PATERSON, Esq.

Fire Inspector: Marine Inspector:
E ROBY O'BRIEN.   CAPT. R. COURNEEN.
Insurances granted on all descriptions of property
against loss and damage by fire and the perils of inland
navigation.

Agencies established in the principal cities, towns, and
ports of shipment throughout the Province.
THOS. WM. BIRCHALL,
23-1y   Managing Director.

Edinburgh Life Assurance Company.

Founded 1823.

HEAD OFFICE—22 GEORGE STREET, EDINBURGH.

Capital, ... £500,000 Ster'g.
Accumulated and Invested Funds, £1,000,000 "

HEAD OFFICE IN CANADA:
WELLINGTON STREET, TORONTO.

SUB-AGENTS THROUGHOUT THE PROVINCE.

J. HILLYARD CAMERON,
Chairman, Canadian Board.

DAVID HIGGINS,
Secretary, Canadian Board.   3-3m

Queen Fire and Life Insurance Company,
OF LIVERPOOL AND LONDON,
ACCEPTS ALL ORDINARY FIRE RISKS
on the most favorable terms.

LIFE RISKS
Will be taken on terms that will compare favorably with
other Companies.

CAPITAL, - - - £2,000,000 Stg.

CHIEF OFFICES—Queen's Buildings, Liverpool, and
Gracechurch Street London.
CANADA BRANCH OFFICE—Exchange Buildings, Montreal.
Resident Secretary and General Agent,
A. MACKENZIE FORBES,
13 St. Sacrament St., Merchants' Exchange, Montreal.
WM. ROWLAND, Agent, Toronto.   1-1y

Insurance.

Reliance Mutual Life Assurance
Society.
(Established, 1840,) OF LONDON, E. C.

Accumulated Funds, over $1,000,000.
Annual Income, $800,000.
THE entire Profits of this long-established Society belong
to the Policy-holders.
HEAD OFFICE FOR DOMINION—MONTREAL.
T. W. GRIFFITH, Manager& Sec'y.
15-1y   WM. HENDERSON, Agent for Toronto.

Etna Insurance Company of Dublin.
The number of Shareholders exceeds Five Hundred.

Capital, $5,000,000—Annual Income nearly $1,000,000.
THIS Company takes Fire and Marine Risks on the most
favorable terms.
T. W. GRIFFITH, Manager for Canada.
Chief office for Dominion— Corner St. Francois Xavier
and St. Sacrament Sts., Montreal.
15-1y   WM. HENDERSON, Agent for Toronto

Scottish Provincial Assurance Co.
Established 1825.

CAPITAL ....£1,000,000 STERLING.
INVESTED IN CANADA (1866) ....$500,000.

Canada Head Office, Montreal.

LIFE DEPARTMENT.
CANADA BOARD OF DIRECTORS:
HUGH TAYLOR, Esq., Advocate,
Hon. CHARLES WILSON, M. L. C.
WM. SACHE, Esq., Banker,
JACKSON RAE, Esq., Banker.
WM. FRASER, Esq. M. D., Medical Adviser.
The special advantages to be derived from Insuring in
this office are :—Strictly Moderate Rates of Premiums ;
Large Bonus (intermediate bonus guaranteed ;) Liberal
Surrender Value, under policies relinquished by assured ;
and Extensive Limits of Residence and Travel. All busi-
ness disposed of in Canada, without reference to parent
office.
A DAVIDSON PARKER,
Resident Secretary
G. L. MADDISON,
15-1yr-   AGENT FOR TORONTO.

Lancashire Insurance Company.]

CAPITAL, - - - - - - - - £2,000,000 Sterling

FIRE RISKS
Taken at reasonable rates of premium, and
ALL LOSSES SETTLED PROMPTLY,
By the undersigned, without reference elsewhere.
S. C. DUNCAN-CLARK & CO.,
General Agents for Ontario,
N. W. Corner of King & Church Streets,
25-1y   TORONTO.

Etna Fire & Marine Insurance Company.

INCORPORATED 1819. CHARTER PERPETUAL.

CASH CAPITAL, - - - - - $3,000,000

LOSSES PAID IN 50 YEARS, 23,500,000 00.

JULY, 1868.
ASSETS.
(At Market Value.)
Cash in hand and in Bank............. $544,842 29
Real Estate............................ 268,207 29
Mortgage Bonds........................ 932,245.00
Bank Stock............................. 1,272,070 00
United States, State and City Stock, and other
Public Securities..................... 2,040,855 61
          Total.................... $5,052,880 19

LIABILITIES.
Claims not Due, and Unadjusted............ $499,808 55
Amount required by Mass. and New York
for Re-Insurance........................ 1,405,267 15
E. CHAFFEY & CO., Agents.
50-6m

Insurance.

ÆTNA
Live Stock Insurance Company

LICENSED BY THE DOMINION GOVERNMENT TO DO BUSINESS IN CANADA.

THE following Accidents, this month, show the importance of Insuring your Horses and Cattle against Death from any cause, or Theft, in the Ætna Insurance Company:

MONTREAL, September 16, 1868.
At a fire last night, in the sheds behind Riplu's Hotel, St. Joseph Street, three valuable Stock Horses were destroyed, "Young Clydesdale" and "Emigrant," belonging to the Huntingdon Agricultural Society—the former worth $800, and the latter $1,700; and "Old Beauharnois" cost $1,000, belonging to the Beauharnois Society.

PORT COLBORNE, September 18, 1868.
HORSES DROWNED.—Two horses belonging to Mr. Briggs, of Port Colborne, and four owned by Mr. Julion, of Port Dalhousie, were drowned in the Canal, near the Junction, early this morning.

A fire at the Glasgow Hotel, Montreal, this morning, destroyed two horses. The fire was caused by drunkenness on the part of the stable man.

MONTREAL, September 24, 1868.
A fire in F. X. Cusson's stables, St. Joseph Street, last night, destroyed three horses.

E. L. SNOW, GENERAL AGENT,
Montreal.

Agents for Ontario:—
67nov11y   SCOTT & WALMSLEY,
Ontario-Hall, Church Street, Toronto.

The Liverpool and London and Globe Insurance Company

INVESTED FUNDS:
FIFTEEN MILLIONS OF DOLLARS.

DAILY INCOME OF THE COMPANY:
TWELVE THOUSAND DOLLARS.

LIFE INSURANCE,
WITH AND WITHOUT PROFITS.

FIRE INSURANCE
On every description of Property, at Lowest Remunerative Rates.

JAMES FRASER, AGENT,
8 King Street West.

Toronto, 1868.   28-1y

Britou Medical and General Life Association,

with which is united the
BRITANNIA LIFE ASSURANCE COMPANY.

Capital and Invested Funds............£750,000 Sterling.

ANNUAL INCOME, £220,000 STG.:
Yearly increasing at the rate of £25,000 Sterling.

THE important and peculiar feature originally introduced by this Company, in applying the periodical Bonuses, so as to make Policies payable during life, without any higher rate of premiums being charged, has caused the success of the BRITON MEDICAL AND GENERAL to be almost unparalleled in the history of Life Assurance. *Life Policies on the Profit Scale become payable during the lifetime of the Assured, thus rendering a Policy of Assurance a means of subsistence in old age, as well as a protection for a family,* and a more valuable security to creditors in the event of early death; and effectually meeting the often urged objection, that persons do not themselves reap the benefit of their own prudence and forethought.

No extra charge made to members of Volunteer Corps for services within the British Provinces.

☞ TORONTO AGENCY, 5 KING ST. WEST.
oct17—9-1yr   JAMES FRASER, *Agent.*

Phenix Insurance Company,
BROOKLYN, N. Y.

PHILANDER SHAW,   STEPHEN CROWELL,
Secretary.   *President.*

Cash Capital, $1,000,000. Surplus, $666,416.02. Total, 1,666,416.02. Entire Income from all sources for 1866 was $2,131,839.82.

CHARLES G. FORTIER, *Marine Agent.*

Ontario Chambers, Toronto, Ont.   19-1y;

Insurance.

The Victoria Mutual
FIRE INSURANCE COMPANY OF CANADA.

Insures only Non-Hazardous Property, at Low Rates.

BUSINESS STRICTLY MUTUAL.

GEORGE H. MILLS, *President.*
W. D. BOOKER, *Secretary.*

HEAD OFFICE ....HAMILTON, ONTARIO
aug 15-1yr

The Ætna Life Insurance Company.

AN attack, abounding with errors, having been made upon the Ætna Life Insurance Co. by the editor of the *Montreal Daily News*; and certain agents of British Companies being now engaged in handing around copies of the attack, thus seeking to damage the Company's standing, —I have pleasure in laying before the public the following certificate, bearing the signatures of the Presidents and Cashiers who happened to be in their Offices *of every Bank in Hartford*, also that of the President and Secretary of the old Ætna Fire Insurance Company :—

"*To whom it may concern :*—
"We, the undersigned, regard the Ætna Life Insurance Company, of this city, as one of the most successful and prosperous Insurance Companies in the States,— entirely reliable, responsible, and honourable in all its dealings, and most worthy of public confidence and patronage."

Lucius J. Hendee, President Ætna Fire Insurance Co., and late Treasurer of the State of Connecticut.
J. Goodnow, Secretary Ætna Fire Insurance Co.
C. H. Northam, President, and J. B. Powell, Cashier National Bank.
C. T. Hillyer, President Charter Oak National Bank.
K. D. Tiffany, President First National Bank.
G. T. Davis, President City National Bank.
F. S. Riley, Cashier, do. do. do.
John C. Tracy, President of Farmers' and Mechanics' National Bank.
M. W. Graves, Cashier Conn. River Banking Co.
H. A. Redfield, Cashier Phœnix National Bank.
O. G. Terry, President Ætna National Bank.
J. R. Redfield, Cashier National Exchange Bank.
John G. Root, Assistant Cashier American National Bank.
George F. Hills, Cashier State Bank of Hartford.
Jas. Potter, Cashier Hartford National Bank.
Hartford, Nov. 26, 1867.

Many of the above-mentioned parties are closely connected with other Life Insurance Companies, but all unhesitatingly commend our Company as "reliable, responsible, honourable in all its dealings, and most worthy of public confidence and patronage."

JOHN GARVIN,
General Agent, Toronto Street.
Toronto, Dec. 3. 1867.   16-1y

Life Association of Scotland.

INVESTED FUNDS
UPWARDS OF £1,000,000 STERLING.

THIS Institution differs from other Life Offices, in that the
BONUSES FROM PROFITS
Are applied on a special system for the Policy-holder's
PERSONAL BENEFIT AND ENJOYMENT DURING HIS OWN LIFETIME,
WITH THE OPTION OF
LARGE BONUS ADDITIONS TO THE SUM ASSURED.

The Policy-holder thus obtains
A LARGE REDUCTION OF PRESENT OUTLAY
OR
A PROVISION FOR OLD AGE OF A MOST IMPORTANT AMOUNT IN ONE CASH PAYMENT, OR A LIFE ANNUITY.

Without any expense or outlay whatever beyond the ordinary Assurance Premium for the Sum Assured, which remains in tact for Policy-holder's heirs, or other purposes.

CANADA—MONTREAL—PLACE D'ARMES.

DIRECTORS:
David Torrance, Esq., (D. Torrance & Co.)
George Moffatt, (Gillespie, Moffatt & Co.)
Alexander Morris, Esq., M.P., Barrister, Perth.
Sir G. E. Cartier, M.P., Minister of Militia.
Thomas Redpath, Esq., (J. Redpath & Son).
J. H. R. Molson, Esq., (J. H. R. Molson & Bro.)
Solicitors—Messrs. TORRANCE & MORRIS.
Medical Officer—H. PALMER HOWARD, Esq., M D
Secretary—P. WARDLAW.
Inspector of Agencies—JAMES F. M. CHIPMAN.   y

Insurance.

North British and Mercantile Insurance Company.

Established 1809.

HEAD OFFICE, - - CANADA - - MONTR

TORONTO BRANCH:
LOCAL OFFICES, Nos. 4 & 6 WELLINGTON STREE
Fire Department, ... R. N. GOO

Life Department, ... H. L. HIM
29-1y

Phœnix Fire Assurance Compan
LOMBARD ST. AND CHARING CROSS,
LONDON, ENG.

Insurances effected in all parts of the Wo

Claims paid
WITH PROMITUDE and LIBERALI
MOFFATT, MURRAY & BEATTIE
Agents for Toron
36 Yonge St
2

The Commercial Union Assuran
Company,

19 & 20 CORNHILL, LONDON, ENGLAND.

Capital, £2,500,000 Stg.—Invested over $2,000,0

FIRE DEPARTMENT—Insurance granted on scriptions of Property at reasonable rates.

LIFE DEPARTMENT—The success of this has been unprecedented—NINETY PERCENT. miums now in hand. First year's premiums we $100,000. Economy of management guaranteed security. Moderate rates.

OFFICE—385 & 387 ST PAUL STREET, MONTR
MORLAND, WATSON & C
General Agents for

FRED. COLE, Secretary.
*Inspector of Agencies—T. C. LIVINGSTON
W. M. WESTMACOTT, Agent at Tor*

16-1y

Phœnix Mutual Life Insurance
HARTFORD, CONN.

Accumulated Fund, $2,000,000. Income, $1,00

THIS Company, established in 1851, is one of reliable Companies doing business in the coun *Reports* show that in nearly all important matt has been steadily prospering. The *Massachusetts R* superior to the general average of Companies. It intending assurers the following reasons, among for preferring it to other companies :

It is purely Mutual. It allows the Insured and ratio in any portion of the United States and It throws off almost all restriction on occupation tabilies. It will, if desired, take a note for par Premium, thus combining all the advantages of a all cash company. Its Dividends are declared and applied in reduction of Premium. Its Divi in every case on Premiums paid. The Dividend Phœnix have averaged fifty per cent. yearly, settlement of Policies, a Dividend will be allowed year the policy has been in force. The numbe dends will always equal the outstanding Notes leaves promptly—during the existence never ha tested a claim. It issues Policies for the bene ried Women beyond the reach of their husband's Creditors may also insure the lives of Debtors. It are all *Non-forfeiting*, as it always allows the s surrender his Policy, should he desire, the Com ing a paid-up Policy therefor. This importar will commend itself to all. The inducements m by the Phœnix are better and more liberal than any other Company. Its rate of Mortality is ex low and under the average.

Parties contemplating *Life Insurance* will find luterest to call and examine our system. Polic payable either in *Gold* or *American* currency.

ANGUS D. SETHU
*General Manage
Dominion*

Office: 104 ST. FRANÇOIS XAVIER ST. MONT

☞ Active and energetic Agents and wanted in every town and village, to whom libe ments will be given.

PRINTED AT THE DAILY TELEGRAPH P
HOUSE, BAY ST., COR. KING.

TORONTO PRICES CURRENT.—November 19 1868.

Name of Article.	Wholesale Rates.		Name of Article.	Wholesale Rate.		Name of Article.	Wholesale Rates.	
Boots and Shoes.	$ c.	$ c.	**Groceries**—Contin'd	$ c.	$ c.	**Leather**—Contin'd.	$ c.	$ c.
Mens' Thick Boots ...	2 20	2 50	" fine to fine't..	0 85	0 95	Kip Skins, Patna ...	0 30	0 40
" Kip	2 50	3 25	Myson	0 45	0 80	French	0 76	0 90
" Calf	3 20	3 70	Imperial	0 42	0 80	English	0 85	0 90
" Congress Gaiters..	2 00	2 40	Tobacco, Manufact'd:			Hemlock Calf (30 to		
" Kip Cobourgs...	2 10	1 50	Can Leaf, ℔ 5s & 10s.	0 26	0 30	35 lbs.) per doz...	0 75	0 85
Boys' Thick Boots...	1 70	1 90	Western Leaf, com..	0 25	0 26	Do. light	0 45	0 80
Youths'	1 45	1 6	" Good ...	0 27	0 32	French Calf....	0 08	1 15
Women's Batts ...	95	1 8	" Fine ...	0 32	0 35	Grain & Satn Clf ℔ doz.	0 00	0 00
" Congress Gaiters..	1 15	1 5	" Bright fine..	0 40	0 50	Splits, large ℔ lb...	0 30	0 35
Misses' Batts	0 7	1 0	" choice..	0 60	0 75	" small	0 20	0 30
" Congress Gaiters..	1 0	1 2	**Hardware.**			Enamelled Cow ℔ foot..	0 17	0 18
Girls' Batts	0 68	0 8	Tin (net cash prices)			Patent	0 18	0 20
" Congress Gaiters..	0 80	1 1	Block, ℔ lb.	0 25	0 26	Pebble Grain ...	0 17	0 18¼
Children's C. T. Cacks..	0 50	0 6½	Grain	0 25	0 26	Buff	0 17	0 18
" Gaiters ...	0 65	0 08	Copper:—			**Oils.**		
Drugs.			Pig	0 23	0 24	Cod	0 00	0 02½
Aloes Cape.	0 12½	0 16	Sheet............	0 30	0 33	Lard, extra	0 00	1 25
Alum	0 02¼	0 03	Cut Nails:			" Woollen	0 00	1 05
Borax	0 07	0 15	Assorted ¼ Shingles,			" No. 1	0 00	1 15
Camphor, refined....	0 45	0 70	℔ 100 lb... ...	2 90	3 00	Lubricating, patent...	0 00	0 00
Castor Oil..........	0 18	0 26	Shingle alone do	3 15	3 25	" Mott's economist	0 50	0 00
Caustic Soda........	0 04½	0 05	Lathe and 5 dy...	3 00	3 40	Linseed, raw	0 77½	0 85
Cochineal	1 00	1 10	Galvanised Iron:			" boiled...	0 82½	0 00
Cream Tartar	0 00	0 00	Assorted sizes ..	0 08	0 09	Machinery	0 00	0 00
Epsom Salts	0 00	0 04	Best No. 24..	0 09	0 00	Olive, 2nd, ℔ gal...	1 45	1 80
Extract Logwood.....	0 09	0 11	" 26	0 08	0 08½	" salad	2 00	2 80
Gum Arabic, sorts...	0 80	0 85	" 28........	0 09	0 00½	" salad, in bots.		
Indigo, Madras......	0 75	1 00	Horse Nails:			qt. ℔ case..	2 50	3 75
Licorice	0 14	0 45	Guest's or Griffin's			Scamne salad, ℔ gal..	1 60	1 75
Madder	0 13	0 16	assorted sizes.....	0 00	0 00	Seal, pale........	0 70	0 75
Nutgalls	0 22	0 00	For W. ass'd sizes...	0 18	0 19	Spirits Turpentine....	0 62	0 70
Opium	6 70	7 00	Patent Hammer'd do..	0 17	0 18	Varnish	0 00	0 00
Oxalic Acid........	0 28	0 35	Iron (at 4 months):			Whale........	0 75	0 80
Potash, Bi-tart......	0 55	0 58	Pig—Gartsherrie No1..	24 00	25 00			
" Bichromate..	0 15	0 30	Other brands. No1..	22 00	24 00	**Paints, &c.**		
Potass Iodide	3 80	4 80	" No2..	0 00	0 00	White Lead, genuine		
Senna	0 13½	0 60	Bar—Scotch, ℔ 100 ℔..	2 25	2 50	in Oil, ℔ 25lbs...	0 00	2 50
Soda Ash	0 03	0 04	Refined	3 00	3 25	Do. No. 1	0 00	2 25
Soda Bicarb	4 50	5 50	Swedes	5 00	5 50	" 2 "	0 00	2 00
Tartaric Acid.......	0 37½	0 45	Hoops—Coopers .	3 00	3 25	" 3 "	0 00	1 75
Verdigris	0 35	0 40	" Band	3 00	3 25	White Zinc, genuine..	3 50	3 50
Vitriol, Blue	0 09	0 10	Boiler Plates.......	3 25	3 50	White Lead, dry	0 00	0 00
Groceries.			Canada Plates......	4 00	4 25	Red Lead........	0 07½	0 08
Coffees:			Union Jack	0 00	0 00	Venetian Red, Eng'h..	0 02½	0 03¼
Java, ℔ lb.	0 22	0 24	Pontypool........	4 00	4 25	Yellow Ochre, Fren'h..	0 02½	0 03
Laguayra, ...	0 17	0 18	Swanson	3 90	4 00	Whiting	0 90	1 25
Rio, ...	0 15	0 17	Lead (at 4 months):					
Fish:			Bar, ℔ 100 lbs...	0 07	0 07½	**Petroleum.**		
Herrings, Lab. split..	5 75	7 00	Sheet "	0 08	0 00	(Refined ℔ gal.)		
" round	0 00	0 00	Shot. "	0 07½	0 07½	Water white, car'l'd..	0 31	
" scaled...	0 55	0 40	Iron Wire (net cash):			" small lots..	0 00	0 32
Mackerel, small kitts..	1 00	0 00	No. 6, ℔ bundle...	2 70	2 80	Straw, by car load..	0 21	
Loch. Her. ℔ h'f brls..	2 00	2 75	" 9 "	3 10	3 00	" small lots ..	0 21	0 32
half "	1 25	1 50	" 12, "	3 40	3 50	Amber, by car load..	0 00	0 07½
White Fish & Trout...	3 25	3 50	" 16, "	4 30	4 40	" small lots ..	0 00	0 00
Salmon, saltwater....	14 00	15 00	Powder:			Benzine	0 00	0 00
Dry Cod, ℔ 112 lbs....	5 00	5 00	Blasting, Canada.....	3 50	3 75			
Fruit:			FF "	4 25	4 50	**Produce.**		
Raisins, Layers ...	2 20	2 25	FFF "	4 75	5 00	Grain:		
" M "	2 60	2 80	Blasting, English ...	4 00	5 00	Wheat, Spring, 60 lb...	1 00	1 05
" Valentians new..	0 08½	0 08½	FF " loose.	8 00	0 00	" Fall "	1 00	1 20
Currants, new	0 05	0 06½	FFF "	6 00	6 50	Barley.. 48 "	1 20	1 25
" old.....	0 05	0 04½	Prussed Spikes (4 mos):			Peas..... 60 "	0 84	0 86
Figs	0 11	0 12½	Regular sizes 100....	4 00	4 25	Oats..... 34 "	0 56	0 58
Molasses:			Extra	4 50	5 00	Rye..... 56 "	0 00	0 75
Clayed, ℔ gal........	0 00	0 35	Tin Plates (net cash):			Seeds:		
Syrups, Standard	0 43	0 44	IC Coke	7 50	8 00	Clover, choice 60 "..	6 25	6 50
" Golden	0 52	0 55	IC Charcoal........	8 25	8 75	" com'n 60 "..	6 00	6 25
Rice:			IX "	10 25	10 75	Timothy, cho's 4 "..	2 60	2 75
Arracan	4 50	4 75	IXX "	12 50	0 00	" inf. to good 48 "	2 00	2 00
Spices:			DC "	7 50	9 00	Flax .... 56 "	1 40	1 60
Cassia, whole, ℔ lb..	0 42	0 45	DX "	9 50	10 00	Flour (per brl.):		
Cloves	0 11	0 13				Superior extra..	5 75	6 00
Nutmegs	0 45	0 55	**Hides & Skins ℔ lb**			Extra superfine,......	5 50	5 75
Ginger, ground	0 30	0 35	Green rough ...	0 06	0 06½	Fancy superfine	0 00	0 00
" Jamaica, root..	0 20	0 25	Green, salt'd & insp'd..	0 00	0 07	Superfine No. 1...	4 70	4 80
Pepper, black........	0 09½	0 10	Cured	0 08	0 08½	" No. 2..	0 00	0 00
Pimento	0 08	0 09	Calfskins, green....	0 00	0 11	Oatmeal, (per brl.)...	6 00	6 25
Sugars:			Calfskins, cured......	0 00	0 12			
Port Rico, ℔ lb......	0 08½	0 08½	" dry.....	0 18	0 20	**Provisions.**		
Cuba "	0 08½	0 08½	Sheepskins, "	0 00	0 00	Butter, dairy tub ℔ lb..	0 22	0 24
Barbadoes (bright)...	0 08	0 08½	" country...	0 80	0 80	" store packed...	0 21	0 22
Dry Crushed, at 80 d..	0 11	0 11½				Cheese, new	0 11	0 12
Canada Sugar Refine'y,			**Hops.**			" prime	0 00	0 00
yellow No. 2, 60 lbs..	0 08½	0 08½	Inferior, ℔ lb.......	0 05	0 07	Bacon, rough	0 00	0 00
Yellow, No. 2½	0 08½	0 09½	Medium	0 07	0 09	" Cumberl'd cut..	0 11	0 12
No. 3..	0 08½	0 09½	Good	0 09	0 12	" smoked	0 00	0 00
Crushed X "	0 10	0 10½	Fancy	0 00	0 00	Hams, in salt........	0 00	0 00
" A "	0 09	0 11				" sug.cur.&canv'd.	0 00	0 00
Ground.........	0 09½	0 11½	**Leather.** @ (4 mos.)			Shoulders, in salt ...	0 00	0 00
Extra Ground........	0 09½	0 12½	In lots of less than			Lard, in kegs.......	0 00	0 15
Teas:			50 sides, 10 ℔ cent			Eggs, packed	0 00	0 22
Japan com'n to good..	0 40	0 55	higher.			Beef Hams	0 00	0 00
" fine to choicest..	0 55	0 65	Spanish Sole, 1st qual..			Tallow	0 00	0 00
Colored, com. to fine..	0 00	0 75	heavy, weights ℔ lb..	0 21	0 22	Hogs dressed, heavy..	7 50	7 60
Congou & Souch'ng..	0 50	0 75	No. 2, qual middle do..	0 22	0 23	" medium...	0 50	7 00
Oolong, good to fine..	0 50	0 65	Do. No. 2, all weights.	0 20	0 21	" light	6 05	0 00
Y. Hyson, com to gd..	0 45	0 55	Slaughter heavy ...	0 20	0 25			
Medium to choice	0 55	0 65	Do. light.......	0 00	0 00	**Salt, &c.**		
" Extra choice	0 55	0 65	Harness, best	0 32	0 34	American brls.......	1 58	1 60
Gunpowd'r c. to med..	0 55	0 70	No. 2........	0 30	0 33	Liverpool coarse ...	1 25	1 35
" med. to fine	0 70	0 85	Upper heavy	0 44	0 38	Plaster	1 05	1 10
			" light........	0 36	0 40	Water Lime	1 50	0 00

Soap & Candles.	$ c.	$ c.
D. Crawford & Co.'s ..		
Imperial..........	0 07½	0 08
" Golden Bar	0 07	0 07½
" Silver Bar........	0 07	0 07½
Crown	0 05	0 05½
No. 1	0 03½	0 03¾
Candles	0 00	0 11½
Wines, Liquors, &c.		
Ale:		
English, per doz......	2 60	2 65
Guinness Dub Portr..	2 35	2 40
Spirits:		
Pure Jamaica Rum...	1 80	2 25
De Kuyper's H. Gin..	1 55	1 63
Booth's Old Tom.....	1 90	2 00
Gin:		
Green, cases..........	4 00	4 25
Booth's Old Tom, c...	6 00	6 25
Wines:		
Port, common	1 00	1 25
" fine old	2 00	4 00
Sherry, common	1 00	1 50
" medium........	1 70	1 80
"old pale or golden..	2 50	4 00

Brandy:	$ c.	$ c.
Hennessy's, per gal..	2 30	2 50
Martell's " ..	2 30	2 50
J. Robin & Co.'s " ..	2 25	2 35
Otard, Dupuy & Cos..	2 25	2 35
Brandy, cases.........	8 50	9 00
Brandy, com. per c...	4 00	4 50
Whiskey:		
Common 36 u. p......	0 62½	0 65
Old Rye	0 85	0 87½
Malt	0 85	0 87½
Toddy	0 85	0 87½
Scotch, per gal........	1 90	2 10
Irish—Kinnahan's c...	7 00	7 50
" Dunnville's Belf't..	6 00	6 25
Wool.		
Fleece, lb.............	0 28	0 35
Pulled ".............	0 22	0 25
Furs.		
Bear...................	3 00	10 00
Beaver................	1 00	1 25
Coon	0 20	0 40
Fisher................	4 00	6 00
Martin................	1 40	1 60
Mink..................	4 00	4 25
Otter..................	5 75	6 00
Spring Rats..........	0 15	0 17
Fox...................	1 20	1 25

INSURANCE COMPANIES.

ENGLISH.—*Quotations on the London Market.*

No. of Shares.	Last Dividend.	Name of Company.	Shares parval £	Amount paid.	Last
20,000		Briton Medical and General Life ...	10	....	1⅜
50,000	7½	Commer'l Union, Fire, Life and Mar.	50	5	5½
24,000	8	City of Glasgow	25	2½	5
5,000	9½	Edinburgh Life	100	15	30⅞x
400,000	5—½ yr	European Life and Guarantee......	2½	11s6	4s 6d
100,000	10	Etna Fire and Marine.............	10	1½	1
20,000	5	Guardian	100	50	51½
24,000	12	Imperial Fire......................	500	50	345
7,500	9½	Imperial Life	100	10	16½
100,000	10	Lancashire Fire and Life..........	20	2	2⅞x
10,000	11	Life Association of Scotland.......	40	7½	23
35,862	45s. p. sh	London Assurance Corporation ..	25	12½	48
10,000	5	London and Lancashire Life	10	1	1
87,504	40	Liverp'l & London & Globe F. & L.	20	2	7⅜
20,000	5	National Union Life	5	1	1
20,000	12½	Northern Fire and Life	100	5	10⅝
40,000	12 '68, bo 5s.	North British and Mercantile	50	6¼	16 16½
40,000	50	Ocean Marine	25	5	20
2,500	£5 12s.	Provident Life......................	100	10	38
....	£4½ p. s.	Phœnix..............................	....	....	136
200,000	2½—h.yr.	Queen Fire and Life	10	1	15-16ths
100,000	3s. bo.4s	Royal Insurance...................	20	3	6⅞
20,000	10	Scottish Provincial Fire and Life ..	50	2½	4⅜
10,000	25	Standard Life	50	12	65
4,000	5	Star Life	25	1½	—
		CANADIAN.			℘ c.
8,000	4	British America Fire and Marine ..	$50	$25	56
....	4	Canada Life	...	....	.....
4000	12	Montreal Assurance	£50	£5	135
10,000	3	Provincial Fire and Marine........	60	11	.....
....	....	Quebec Fire	40	32½	£10½
....	8	" Marine......................	100	40	90-95
10,000	5 7 mo's.	Western Assurance................	40	6	.....

RAILWAYS.	Sha's	Paid	Montr	London.
Atlantic and St. Lawrence......................	£100	All.	....	58 60
Buffalo and Lake Huron	20½	"	....	3 3½
Do. do Preference	10	"	....	5½ 6½
Buff., Brantt. & Goderich, 6℘c., 1872-3-4....	100	"	....	....
Champlain and St. Lawrence	....	....	0 11	....
Do. do Pref. 10 ℘ ct....	....	....	70 75	....
Grand Trunk	100	"	16 17	16 17
Do. Eq.G. M. Bds. 1 ch. 6℘c..........	100	"	....	83 86
Do. First Preference, 5 ℘ c	100	"	....	52 53
Do. Deferred, 3 ℘ ct..	100	"	....	....
Do. Second Pref. Bonds, 5℘c..........	100	"	....	41 43
Do. do Deferred, 3 ℘ ct..........	100	"	...	....
Do. Third Pref. Stock, 4 ℘ct..........	100	"	...	28 30
Do. do. Deferred, 3 ℘ ct.....	100	"	....	....
Do. Fourth Pref. Stock, 3℘c..........	100	"	....	18½ 19½
Do. do. Deferred, 3 ℘ ct..........	100	"	....	....
Great Western	20½	"	13 14	14½ 14½
Do. New	20½	18	....	....
Do. 6 ℘ c. Bds, due 1873-76..........	100	All.	....	102 104
5½ ℘c Bds. due 1877-78....	100	"	....	93 94
Marine Railway, Halifax, $250, all......	$250	"	....	....
Northern, of Canada, 6℘c. 1st Pref. Bds..........	100	"	.. .	80 83

EXCHANGE.	Halifax.	Montr'l.	Quebec.	Toronto.
Bank on London, 60 days......				
sight or 75 days date	13½	9½ 9½	9½ 9¾	9½
Private do.	12 12½	8 8½	9 9½	8¾ 9
Private, with documents........	....	7½ 8½	....	....
Bank on New York...............	....	25½ 26	23 24	74½
Private do.	....	26 26½	23½ 24½	....
Gold Drafts do.	....	par	par ½ dis.	par ½ dis.
Silver	....	3 8½	....	3½ 5

STOCK AND BOND REPORT.

The dates of our quotations are as follows:—Toronto, Nov. 17; Montreal, Nov. 16; Nov. 16; London, Oct. 30.

NAME.	Shares.	Paid up.	Divid'd last 6 Months	Dividend Day.	CLOSING Toronto.	CLOSING Mon
BANKS.			℘ ct.			
British North America	$250	All.	3	July and Jan.	103½ 104½	103
Jacques Cartier...........	50	"	4	1 June, 1 Dec.	109 110	106
Montreal	200	"	5	"	141 142	140
Nationale......................	50	"	4	1 Nov. 1 May.	....	.
New Brunswick	100	"	......	......	....	..
Nova Scotia	200	28	7&b$3½	Mar. and Sept.	....	..
Du Peuple...	50	"	4	1 Mar., 1 Sept.	105¼ 106	105¼
Toronto	100	"	4	1 Jan., 1 July.	119 119½	118
Bank of Yarmouth.............	....	....	......	......	....	..
Canadian Bank of Com'e......	50	95	......	......	104½ 105½	104½
City Bank Montreal	80	All.	4	1 June, 1 Dec.	104 105	101
Commer'l Bank (St. John)....	100	"	℘ ct.	. ...	....	.
Eastern Townships' Bank.....	50	"	4	1 July, 1 Jan..	....	97
Gore	40	...	3½	1 Jan., 1 July.	40 41	40
Halifax Banking Company....	...	....	......	. ....	...	..
Mechanics' Bank..............	50	70	4	1 Nov., 1 May.	94½ 96	95
Merchants' Bank of Canada....	100	70	4	1 Jan., 1 July.	109 111	111
Merchants' Bank (Halifax)....	....	....	.....	......	....	..
Molson's Bank......	50	All.	4	1 Apr., 1 Oct.	107½ 109	107½
Niagara District Bank...	100	70	3½	1 Jan., 1 July.	...	...
Ontario Bank................	40	All.	4	1 June, 1 Dec.	103½ 104	100
People's Bank (Fred'kton)....	100	"	......	......	....	...
People's Bank (Halifax)	20	"	7 12 m	......	....	...
Quebec Bank	100	"	3½	1 June, 1 Dec.	101 102	..
Royal Canadian Bank	50	50	4	1 Jan., 1 July.	91 91½	91
St. Stephens Bank	100	All	.....	......	....	..
Union Bank	100	70	4	1 Jan., 1 July.	104 105½	103½
Union Bank (Halifax)........	100	40	7 12 mo	Feb. and Aug.	....	...
MISCELLANEOUS.						
British America Land.........	250	44	2½	......	....	...
British Colonial S. S. Co......	250	32½	2½	......	...	45
Canada Company	32½	All.	5	......	....	...
Canada Landed Credit Co.....	50	$20	3½	......	72 73	...
Canada Per. B'ldg Society....	50	All.	5	......	122½ 123	...
Canada Mining Company.....	4	90	......	... ..	....	..
Do. Inl'd Steam Nav. Co.....	100	All.	20 12 m	......	....	106
Do. Glass Company.........	100	"	12½ "	......	....	40
Canad'n Loan & Investm't....	25	2½	7	......	....	...
Canada Agency	10	¼	......	......	....	...
Colonial Securities Co........	...	....	......	......	....	...
Freehold Building Society....	100	All.	4	......	107½ 108	...
Halifax Steamboat Co........	100	"	5	......	....	...
Halifax Gas Company.........	....	....	......	. .. .	....	..
Hamilton Gas Company.......	....	....	.....	. ....	....	..
Huron Copper Bay Co........	4	12	20	. ....	....	25 5
Lake Huron S. and C.........	5	102	......	......	....	..
Montreal Mining Consols.....	20	$15	......	. ....	....	2.50
Do. Telegraph Co...	40	All.	5	......	130 132	132½
Do. Elevating Co...	00	"	15 12 m	......	....	100
Do. City Gas Co.........	40	"	4	15 Mar. 15 Sep.	....	133
Do. City Pass. R., Co....	50	"	5	......	....	110
Nova Scotia Telegraph	20	"	....	. ....	....	..
Quebec and L. S.	8	$4	......	......	. ..	..
Quebec Gas Co...............	200	All.	4	1 Mar., 1 Sep.	....	..
Quebec Street R. R..........	50	25	8	......	....	..
Richelieu Navigation Co......	100	All.	7 p.a.	1 Jan., 1 July.	....	115
St. Lawrence Tow Boat Co.....	100	"	......	3 Feb.	....	.
Tor'to Consumers' Gas Co.....	50	"	2 3 m.	1 My Au Mar Fe	105½ 106½	.
Trust & Loan Co. of U. C.....	20	5	3	......	....	..
West'n Canada Bldg Soc'y....	50	All.	5	......	114½ 115	.

SECURITIES.	London.	Montreal.	Que
Canadian Gov't Deb. 6 ℘ ct. stg............	....	101 102	101 1
Do. do. 6 do due Ja.& Jul. 1877-84.......	107 108	....	...
Do. do. 6 do. Feb. & Aug.........	104 106	....	..
Do. do. 6 do. Mch. & Sep.........	104 106	.. .	..
Do. do. 5 ℘ ct. cur., 1883	93 94	91 92	90
Do. do. 5 do. stg., 1885	....	91 92	90½
Do. do. 7 do. cur.,.....................	....	....	....
Dominion 6 p. c. 1878 cy...............	....	103½ 104½	103
Hamilton Corporation..................	. ..	....	....
Montreal Harbor, 8 ℘ ct. d. 1869.........	..	....	....
Do. do. 7 do. 1870...............	....	....	....
Do. do. 6½ do. 1875...............	....	101 101½	....
Do. do. 6½ do. 1873...............	....	....	....
Do. Corporation, 6 ℘ c. 1891	....	93 96	93 9
Do. 7 p. c. stock........................	....	105½ 107	105½
Do. Water Works, 6 ℘ c. stg. 1878.........	....	....	....
Do. do. 6 do. cy. do.	....	94 96	....
New Brunswick, 6 ℘ ct., Jan. and July	103 105	....	....
Nova Scotia, 6 ℘ ct., 1875..................	103½ 104½	...	....
Ottawa City 6 ℘ c. d. 1880	....	92½ 93½	....
Quebec Harbour, 6 ℘ c. d. 1883.	....	....	6
Do. do. 7 do. do..................	....	....	65
Do. do. 8 do. 1886................	...	....	75
Do. City, 7 ℘ c. d. 5 years	....	90 91½	94
Do. do. 7 do. 9 do.	....	....	9
Do. do. 7 do. 2½ do.	....	....	97
Do. Water Works, 7 ℘ ct., 4 years	....	....	96
Do. do. 6 do. 2 do.	....	....	93½
Toronto Corporation	....	90 92½	..

ION TELEGRAPH COMPANY.

TOCK - - - $500,000.

10,000 *Shares at $50 Each.*

PRESIDENT,
HON. WILLIAM CAYLEY.

TREASURER,
HON. J. McMURRICH.

SECRETARY,
H. B. REEVE.

SOLICITORS,
IRS. CAMERON & McMICHAEL.

GENERAL SUPERINTENDENT,
MARTIN RYAN

DIRECTORS.

HON. J. McMURRICH,
yce, McMurrich & Co., Toronto.

A. R. McMASTER, Esq.,
R. McMaster & Brother, Toronto.

HON. M. C. CAMERON,
Provincial Secretary, Toronto.

JAMES MICHIE, Esq.,
ie & Co., and George Michie & Co., Toronto]

HON. WILLIAM CAYLEY,
Toronto.

A. M. SMITH, Esq.,
A. M. Smith & Co., Toronto.

L. MOFFATT, Esq.,
Ioffatt, Murray & Co., Toronto.

H. B. REEVE, Esq.,
Toronto.

MARTIN RYAN, Esq.,
Toronto.

PROSPECTUS.

NION TELEGRAPH COMPANY has been
l under the act respecting Telegraph Com-
r 67, of the consolidated Statutes of Canada.
cover the Dominion of Canada with a com-
of Telegraph lines.

The Capital Stock

vided into 10,000 shares of $50 each, 5 per
l at the time of subscribing, the balance to
atalments, not exceeding 10 per cent per
astalments to be called in by the Directors as
gress. The liability of a subscriber is limited
of his subscription.

usiness Affairs of the
Company.

a management of a Board of Directors, an-
l by the Shareholders, in conformity with the
y-Laws of the Company.
rs are of opinion that it would be to the
Stockholders generally to obtain subscrip-
quarters of Canada, and with this view they
ride the Stock amongst the different towns
ughout the Dominion, in allotments suited
ion and business occupations of the different
the interest which they may be supposed to
u enterprise.

itracts of Connections.

granting permanent connection and extenor-
ages, has already been executed between this
the Atlantic and Pacific Company, of New
t the very commencement, as the Lines of this
constructed from the Suspension Bridge, at
ohut of connection) to any point in the Do-
o chief cities and places in the States, touch-
ines of the Atlantic and Pacific Telegraph
brought in immediate connection therewith.
at connection has also been secured with the
n Telegraph Company, of Chicago, whereby
will be brought into close connection with
Ports and other places through the North-
s, and through to California.

4-3mos

Ontario Bank.

DIVIDEND No. 23.

NOTICE is hereby given, that a Dividend of Four per
cent. upon the Capital Stock of this Institution for
the current half year, has this day been declared, and that
the same will be payable at the Bank and its Branches,
on and after

Tuesday, the First day of December next.

The Transfer Books will be closed from the 15th to the
30th November, both days inclusive.

By order of the Board.

D. FISHER, *Cashier.*

Ontario Bank,
Bowmanville, 24th Oct., 1868.   11-td

THE QUEEN'S HTEL.

THOMAS DICK, Proprietor.

FRONT STREET,   - - -   TORONTO, ONT
3-1y

Montreal House, Montreal, Canada.

TO MONETARY MEN.—Merchants, Insurance Agents,
Lawyers, Bankers, Railway and Steamboat Travellers,
Mining Agents, Directors and Stockholders of Public Com
panies, and other persons visiting Montreal for business
or pleasure, are have by most respectfully informed that
the undersigned proposes to furnish the best hotel accommodation at the most reasonable charges. It is our study
to provide every comfort and accommodation to all our
guests, especially for gentlemen engaged as above. To
those who have been accustomed to patronize other first-
class hotels, we only ask a trial; we have the same accommodation and our table is furnished with every delicacy
of the season.

H. DUCLOS.

Nov. 22, 1867.   15-1y

The Albion Hotel,

MONTREAL,

ONE of the oldest established houses in the City is again
under the personal management of

Mr. DECKER,

Who, to accommodate his rapidly increasing business, is
adding Eighty more Rooms to the house, making the
ALBION one of the *Largest Establishments in Canada.*

June, 1868.   42-6ms

BY-LAW No. .

A By-Law to aid and assist the Toronto, Grey and
Bruce Railway Company, by giving $250,000
to the Company by way of bonus, and to issue
debentures therefor, and to authorize the levying
of a special rate for the payment of the deben-
tures and interest.

WHEREAS, by the Act of the first session of the Legislature of the Province of Ontario, passed in the thirty-
first year of Her Majesty's reign, incorporating the Toronto,
Grey and Bruce Railway Company, it is provided as follows: "And it shall further be lawful for any Municipality
or Municipalities through any part of which, or near which,
the Railway or Works of the said Company shall pass, or
be situated, to aid and assist the said Company by loaning
or guaranteeing, or giving, money by way of bonus or other
means to the Company or issuing Municipal Bonds to or in
aid of the Company, and otherwise, in such manner, and
to such extent, as such Municipalities, or any of them,
shall think expedient: provided always, that no such aid,
loan, bonus, or guarantee shall be given except after the
passing of by-laws for the purpose, and the adoption of
such by-laws by the ratepayers, as provided in the Railway
Act."

And whereas, by the seventy-seventh section of the Railway Act, chapter sixty-six of the Consolidated Statutes of
the late Province of Canada, it is provided that no Municipal Corporation shall subscribe for stock, or incur any
debt or liability, under the said Railway Act, or the Special
Act, unless and until a By-law to that effect has been duly
made and adopted, with the consent first had of a majority
of the qualified electors of the Municipality in the manner
determined by the By-law, after public advertisement
thereof containing a copy of the proposed By-law, inserted
at least four times in each newspaper printed within the
limit of the Municipality, or if none be printed therein,
then in some one or more newspapers printed in the nearest
city or town thereto, and circulated therein, and also put
up in at least four of the most public places in each Municipality.

And whereas the Municipality of the Corporation of the
City of Toronto has determined to aid and assist the said
Toronto, Grey and Bruce Railway Company by giving
thereto the sum of $250,000 by way of bonus, under the
authority conferred by the said Act first in recital.

And whereas, to carry the last recited object into effect,
it is necessary for the said Municipality to raise the said
sum of $250,000, in the manner hereinafter mentioned.

And whereas it will require the sum of $27,500 to be
raised annually by special rate for paying the said debt of
$250,000 and interest on the debentures to be issued there-
for as hereinafter mentioned.

And whereas the amount of the whole ratable property
of the said Municipality, irrespective of any future increase
of the same, and also irrespective of any income to be
derived from the temporary investment of the sinking fund
hereinafter mentioned, or any part thereof, according to the
last revised assessment roll of the said Municipality, being
for the year one thousand eight hundred and sixty-eight,
was $24,078,673.

And whereas the amount of the existing debt of the said
Municipality is the sum of $2,144,853 44.

And whereas, for paying the interest and creating an
equal yearly sinking fund for paying the said debt of
$250,000, as hereinafter mentioned, it will require an equal
annual special rate of one mill and one-eighth of a mill in
the dollar, in addition to all other rates to be levied in each
year.

Therefore the Council of the Corporation of the City of
Toronto enact as follows:

I. That it shall and may be lawful for the said Municipality to aid and assist the Toronto, Grey and Bruce Railway Company, by giving thereto the sum of $250,000 by
way of bonus.

II. That it shall be lawful, for the purpose aforesaid, for
the Mayor of the said City to cause any number of debentures to be made for such sums of money as may be required
for the said purpose, not less than twenty dollars each, and
not exceeding in the whole the amount of $250,00`, which
said debentures shall be sealed with the seal of the said
City, and be signed by the Mayor and Chamberlain thereof.

III. That the said debentures shall be made payable in
twenty years from the day hereinafter mentioned for this
by-law to take effect, at the Bank of Toronto, in Toronto,
and shall have attached to them coupons for the payment
of interest at the rate and in the manner hereinafter mentioned.

IV. That the said debentures will bear interest at and
after the rate of six per cent. per annum from the date
thereof, which interest shall be payable half-yearly on the
first day of May and November in each year, at the Bank
of Toronto, in Toronto.

V. That for the purpose of forming a sinking fund for
payment of the said debentures, and the interest thereon,
at the rate aforesaid, an equal special rate of one mill and
one-eighth of a mill in the dollar shall, in addition to all
other rates, be raised, levied, and collected in each year
upon all the ratable property in the said Municipality
during the said term of twenty years from the coming into
effect of this By-law, unless such debentures shall be sooner
paid.

VI. That this By-law shall take effect on, from and after
the first day of January, in the year of our Lord, 1869.

VII. That the debentures to be signed and issued as
aforesaid shall be delivered to the Mayor of the said City to
the Trustees appointed (or to be appointed) in accordance
with the tenth section of the said Act incorporating the
said Toronto, Grey and Bruce Railway Company.

VIII. And it is further enacted, by the Municipal Council
aforesaid, that the votes of the electors of the said Municipality will be taken on the said proposed By-law at the
following places, that is to say:

For Saint Lawrence Ward at the City Hall in rooms heretofore used as a Police Court.

For Saint George's Ward, at No. 171 King Street west

For first electoral division of Saint John's Ward, at the
Engine House, Elizabeth Street.

For second electoral division of Saint John's Ward, at the
house on Hayter Street, where the last Municipal Election
was held.

For first electoral division of Saint Andrew's Ward, at
the Bay Street Fire Hall.

'For second electoral division of Saint Andrew's Ward, at
the Temperance Hall, Brock Street.

For first electoral division of St. James' Ward, at the
Police Court, Court Street.

For second electoral division of St. James' Ward, at the
house on Yonge Street where the last Municipal Election
was held.

For first electoral division of Saint Patrick's Ward, at St.
Patrick's Market, on Queen Street.

For second electoral division of St. Patrick's Ward, at
No. 485, on the north side of Queen Street, west.

For first electoral division of Saint David's Ward, at the
Berkley Street Fire Hall.

For second electoral division of Saint David's Ward, at
the house on the north east corner of Parliament and Beech
Streets, on the 8th day of December, at the hour of nine
o'clock in the forenoon and closing at five o'clock in the
afternoon of the same day.

And that the following will be the Returning Officers for taking the said votes:—

For Saint Lawrence Ward, Mr. James Tilt.

For Saint George's Ward, Mr. R. B. Miller.

For first electoral division of Saint John's Ward, Mr. Andrew Fleming.

For second electoral division of Saint John's Ward, Mr. John Downey.

For first electoral division of Saint Andrew's Ward, Mr. Henry Sproatt.

For second electoral division of Saint Andrew's Ward, Mr. Andrew Riddell.

For first electoral division of James' Ward, Mr. James Crowther.

For second electoral division of Saint James' Ward, Mr. Robert Frazer.

For first electoral division of Saint Patrick's Ward, Mr. H. W. Murray.

For second electoral division of Saint Patrick's Ward, Mr. W. A. Lee.

For first electoral division of Saint David's Ward, Mr. John Burns.

For second electoral division of Saint David's Ward, Mr. Robert H. Trotter.

Take notice that the above is a true copy of a proposed By-law which will be taken into consideration by the Council of the Corporation of the City of Toronto after one month from the first publication in the *Christian Guardian, Daily Telegraph, Daily Globe, Irish Canadian, Daily Leader, Patriot, Watchman, Canadian Freeman, Canadian Monetary Times, Christian Baptist, Spirit of the Age, British Canadian.*

The date of which first publication was the 13th day of December, A. D. 1868, and that the votes of the electors of the said Municipality will be taken thereon at the following places in the said Municipality:

For St. Lawrence Ward, in rooms heretofore used as the Police Court, City Hall, Mr. James Tilt, Returning Officer.

For St. George's Ward, at No. 171 King Street west, Mr. R. B. Miller, Returning Officer.

For first electoral division of St. John's Ward, at the Engine House, Elizabeth Street, Mr. Andrew Fleming, Returning Officer.

For second electoral division of St. John's Ward, at the house on Hayter Street where the last Municipal election was held, Mr. John Downey, Returning Officer.

For first electoral division of St. Andrew's Ward, at the Bay Street Fire Hall, Mr. Henry Sproatt, Returning Officer.

For the second electoral division of St. Andrew's Ward, at the Temperance Hall, Brock Street, Mr. Andrew Riddell, Returning Officer.

For first electoral division of St. James' Ward, at the Police Court, in said Ward, Mr. James Crowther, Returning Officer.

For second electoral division of St. James' Ward, at the house on Yonge Street, where the last Municipal election was held.

For first electoral division of St. Patrick's Ward, at St. Patrick's Market, Queen Street, Mr. H. W. Murray, Returning Officer.

For second electoral division of St. Patrick's Ward, at 438, north side of Queen Street, Mr. W. A. Lee, Returning Officer.

For first electoral division of St. David's Ward, at Berkley Street Fire Hall, Mr. John Burns, Returning Officer.

For second electoral division of St. David's Ward, at the building at the north east corner of Parliament and Beech Streets, Mr. Robert H. Trotter, Returning Officer.

On the 8th day of December, A. D. 1868, commencing at nine o'clock in the forenoon, and closing at five o'clock in the afternoon of the same day.

JOHN CARR,
City Clerk.

CITY CLERK'S OFFICE,
Toronto, Nov. 13, 1868.

BY-LAW No. .

A By-Law to aid and assist the Toronto and Nipissing Railway Company, by giving $150,000 to the Company by way of bonus, ond to issue debentures therefor, and to authorize the levying of a special rate for the payment of the debentures and interest.

WHEREAS, by the Act of the first session of the Legislature of the Province of Ontario, passed in the thirty-first year of Her Majesty's reign, incorporating the Toronto and Nipissing Railway Company, it is provided as follows: "And it shall further be lawful for any Municipality or Municipalities through any part of which, or near which, the Railway or Works of the said Company shall pass, or be situated, to aid and assist the said Company by loaning or guaranteeing, or giving money by way of bonus or other means to the Company, or issuing Municipal bonds to or in aid of the Company, and otherwise, in such manner, and to such extent, as the Municipalities, or any of them, shall think expedient; provided always, that no such aid, loan, bonus or guarantee shall be given except after the passing of by-laws for the purpose, and the adoption of such by-laws by the ratepayers, as provided in the Railway Act.

And whereas, by the seventy-seventh section of the Railway Act, chapter sixty-six of the Consolidated Statutes of the late Province of Canada, it is provided that no Municipal Corporation shall subscribe for stock, or incur any debt or liability, under the said Railway Act or the Special Act, unless and until a By-law to that effect has been duly made and adopted, with the consent first had of a majority of the qualified electors of the Municipality in the manner determined by the By-law, after public advertisement thereof containing a copy of the proposed By-law, inserted at least four times in each newspaper printed within the limit of the Municipality, or if none be printed therein, then in some one or more newspapers printed in the nearest city or town thereto, and circulated therein, and also put up in at least four of the most public places in each Municipality.

And whereas the Municipality of the Corporation of the City of Toronto has determined to aid and assist the said Toronto and Nipissing Railway Company by giving thereto the sum of $150,000 by way of bonus, under the authority conferred by the said Act first in recital.

And whereas, to carry the last recited object into effect, it is necessary for the said Municipality to raise the said sum of $150,000 in the manner hereinafter mentioned.

And whereas it will require the sum of $16,500 to be raised annually by special rate for paying the said debt of $150,000 and interest on the debentures to be issued therefor as hereinafter mentioned.

And whereas the amount of the whole ratable property of the said Municipality, irrespective of any future increase of the same, and also irrespective of any income to be derived from the temporary investment of the sinking fund hereinafter mentioned, or any part thereof, according to the last revised assessment roll of the said Municipality, being for the year one thousand eight hundred and sixty-eight, was $24,673,678.

And whereas the amount of the existing debt of the said Municipality is the sum of $2,144,863.44.

And whereas, for paying the interest and creating an equal yearly sinking fund for paying the said debt of $150,000, as hereinafter mentioned, it will require an equal annual special rate of two-thirds of a mill in the dollar, in addition to all other rates to be levied in each year.

It is therefore enacted, by the Council of the Corporation of the City of Toronto,

I. That it shall and may be lawful for the said Municipality to aid and assist the Toronto and Nipissing Railway Company, by giving thereto the sum of $150,000 by way of bonus.

II. That it shall be lawful, for the purpose aforesaid, for the Mayor of the said Municipality to cause any number of debentures to be made for such sums of money as may be required for the said purpose, not less than twenty dollars each, and not exceeding in the whole the amount of $150,000, which said debentures shall be sealed with the seal of the said City, and be signed by the Mayor and Chamberlain thereof.

III. That the said debentures shall be made payable in twenty years from the day hereinafter mentioned for this By-law to take effect at the Bank of Toronto, in the City Toronto, and shall have attached to them coupons for the payment of interest at the rate and in manner hereinafter mentioned.

IV. That the debentures shall bear interest at and after the rate of six per cent. per annum, from the date thereof, which interest shall be payable half-yearly on the first day of January and June in each year, at the Bank of Toronto, in the said City of Toronto.

V. That for the purpose of forming a sinking fund for payment of the said debentures, and the interest thereon, at the rate aforesaid, an equal special rate of two-thirds of a mill in the dollar shall, in addition to all other rates, be raised, levied and collected in each year upon all the ratable property in the said Municipality during the said term of twenty years from the coming into effect of this By-law, unless such debentures shall be sooner paid.

VI. That this By-law shall take effect on, from and after the first day of January, in the year of our Lord 1869.

VII. That the debentures to be signed and issued as aforesaid shall be delivered by the Mayor of the said City to the Trustees appointed (or to be appointed) in accordance with the eleventh section of the said Act incorporating the Toronto and Nipissing Railway Company.

VIII. And it is further enacted, by the Municipal Council aforesaid, that the votes of the electors of the said municipality will be taken on the said proposed By-law at the following places, that is to say:

For St. Lawrence Ward, in rooms heretofore used as a Police Court, City Hall.

For St. George's Ward, at No. 171 King Street West.

For First Electoral Division of Saint John's Ward, at the Engine House, Elizabeth Street.

For Second Electoral Division of Saint John's Ward, at the house on Hayter Street, where the last Municipal Election was held.

For the First Electoral Division of Saint Andrew's Ward, at the Bay Street Fire Hall.

For the Second Electoral Division of St. Andrew's Ward, at the Temperance Hall, Brock Street.

For First Electoral Division of St. James' Ward, Police Court, Court Street.

For Second Electoral Division of St. James' Ward, House on Yonge Street where the last Municipal El was held.

For First Electoral Division of St. Patrick's W Saint Patrick's Market on Queen Street.

For Second Electoral Division of St. Patrick's, 438 on the North side Queen Street west.

For First Electoral Division of Saint David's Wa the Berkeley Street Fire Hall.

For Second Electoral Division of Saint David's W the House on the north-east corner of Parliament and Streets—said Divisions being set out in a By-law di the said City of Toronto into Electoral Divisions for cipal purposes—on the 8th day of December, A.D. commencing at the hour of Nine o'clock in the for and closing at five o'clock in the afternoon of the sam and that the following persons shall be the Returning for taking the said votes:

For St. Lawrence Ward, Mr. James Tilt.

For Saint George's Ward, Mr. R. B. Miller.

For First Electoral Division of Saint John's War Andrew Fleming.

For Second Electoral Division of Saint John's Wa John Downey.

For First Electoral Division of Saint Andrew's Wa Henry Sproatt.

For Second Electoral Division of Saint Andrew's Mr. Andrew Riddell.

For First Electoral Division of Saint James' Wa James Crowther.

For Second Electoral Division of Saint James' Wa Robert Fraser.

For First Electoral Division of Saint Patrick's W H. W. Murray.

For Second Electoral Division of Saint Patrick's Mr. W. A. Lee.

For First Electoral Division of Saint David's W John Burns.

For Second Electoral Division of Saint David's Mr. Robt. H. Trotter.

TAKE NOTICE

That the above is a true copy of a proposed By-la will be taken into consideration by the Council of of Toronto, after one month from the first public the *Daily Globe, Daily Leader, Daily Telegraph, C Guardian, Irish Canadian, Patriot, Watchman, C Freeman, Canadian Monetary Times, Christian Spirit of the Age, and British Canadian*: the date first publication was the 13th day of November, A. and that the votes of the electors of the said Mun will be taken thereon:

For St. Lawrence Ward, in rooms heretofore use Police Court, City Hall, for which Mr. James Tilt is ing Officer.

For Saint George's Ward, at No. 171 King Street which Mr. R. B. Miller is Returning Officer.

For First Electoral Division of Saint John's War Engine House, Elizabeth Street, for which Mr. Fleming is Returning Officer.

For Second Electoral Division of Saint John's the House on Hayter Street, where the last M Election was held, for which Mr. John Downey is ing Officer.

For First Electoral Division of St. Andrew's Wa Bay Street Fire Hall, for which Mr. Henry Sproa turning Officer.

For Second Electoral Division of St. Andrew's the Temperance Hall, Brock Street, for which Mr. Riddell is Returning Officer.

For First Electoral Division of Saint James Wa Police Court, Court Street, for which Mr. James s Returning Officer.

For Second Electoral Division of Saint James' the House on Yonge Street, where the last Munic tion was held, for which Mr. Robert Fraser is I Officer.

For First Electoral Division of Saint Patrick's St. Patrick's Market on Queen Street, for which M Murray is Returning Officer.

For Second Electoral Division of St. Patrick's No. 438 on the North side of Queen Street west, Mr. W. A. Lee is Returning Officer.

For First Electoral Division of St. David's Wa Berkeley Street Fire Hall, for which Mr. John Returning Officer.

For Second Electoral Division of Saint David's the house on the north east corner of Parliament Streets, for which Mr. Robert H. Trotter is Officer.

On the 8th day of December, A. D. 1868, comm Nine o'clock in the forenoon, and closing at Five the afternoon of the same day.

JOHN CAR

CITY CLERK'S OFFICE,
Toronto, Nov. 13, 1868.

PROSPECTUS

OF THE

OMINION EXPRESS COMPANY OF CANADA.

ORGANIZED UNDER THE JOINT STOCK COMPANIES' ACTS.

CAPITAL STOCK, • • • • • • $1,000,000,

In $10,000 Shares, $100 each.

is proposed to organize a DOMINION EXPRESS COMPANY, to meet the present and prospective demand for increased facilities of general transportation. It is the interest of Canadians to do their own work, and *accumulate* cash capital, and one of the objects of this scheme is the retention his country of the profits arising from the business done.

Express Companies obtain "four-fifths" of their business from merchants and bankers, and no reason exists why they cannot transport their own ls, by their *own Agents, economically* and *efficiently*, and by a *union of capital* and *effort*, they hereby resolve so to do. Being thus united, and ging to it their business and influence, secures to this Company certain and complete success.

This organization, like the mail system, is to extend, under *one general management*, to all cities, towns and villages in the Dominion, and to connect ll parts of the United States, and being but "one Company," will secure *unity, despatch* and *accuracy.*

It is proposed to distribute the stock widely, throughout the Dominion, in limited sums, apportioned as nearly as practicable to the business of the scribers. The capital Stock of the Company to be not less than $1,000,000, in 10,000 shares of $100 each.

Ten per cent. of the stock subscribed will be required to be paid after the subscription shall have reached the sum of $250,000, and after a Charter l have been obtained, of which due notice will be given to the subscribers; the subsequent calls, not exceeding *ten per cent. at any one time,* to be es at convenient intervals, as the demands on the Company may require. But the aggregate of all calls to be made will, it is believed, not exceed *ity per cent.* of the Capital Stock.

This business to be done strictly on *cash principles.* With a paying business assured from the start, by *interested* and *reliable* Stockholders, it will s be seen that a small per centage *only* of the subscriptions will be required to put the Company in working order, and it is confidently and reasonably eved that the receipts will thereafter maintain and extend it. And in order to secure an equitable voice in its management, t'e principal commercial res will be represented at the Board, by Directors recommended by Stockholders of their own localities, who will also recommend to the Direction local Agents, and thus secure a general influence in its management, as well as its business.

All Express enterprises, both in this country and the United States, have been decidedly successful, resulting from the profits of the business itself; having an organization and a share list—such as are now proposed—with energy and economy in the direction, no doubt can be entertained of the it satisfactory results.

With such prospects, the Merchants of the Dominion, Capitalists and others interested in the success of this enterprise, are invited to become ckholders.

The following shall be included in the By-Laws to be hereafter framed for the Government of the Company:

1. The Company shall be known by the name or title of "THE DOMINION EXPRESS COMPANY OF CANADA."
2. The Capital Stock of the Company shall be *One Million of Dollars,* divided into *Ten Thousand Shares of One Hundred Dollars each.*
3. Each Shareholder shall be liable only for the amount of Stock subscribed by him, her, or them.
4. The Shares of Stock of the Company shall be transferable; but no transfer shall be valid without the consent of the Directors, in writing, unless shares shall be paid up in full.
5. It shall be lawful for the Stockholders, so soon as the sum of two hundred and fifty thousand dollars shall have been subscribed, to call a General ting of the subscribers, to be held at the office of the Company, in the City of Montreal, and proceed to elect nine qualified persons to be Directors he Company, each of whom to be a proprietor of not less than ten Shares of Stock of the said Company, and three of whom shall form a quorum, i all the powers of the Directors. The said Directors shall also, at their first General Meeting, elect a President, Secretary, Treasurer, and General erintendent or Managing Director, from amongst themselves.
6. The said Directors so elected shall proceed, without delay, to frame all necessary By-laws to govern the Company, and shall have power to alter amend the same as circumstances may require.
7. The Directors shall not have power either to *sell out* the said Company to any other Express Company or organization now in existence, or her.- r to be incorporated, or to amalgamate with any other Express Company.
8. No Stockholder shall be at liberty to hold in his, her, or their name, more than one hundred shares of the Capital Stock of the said Company, iont the consent of the Directors, in writing, first having been obtained.

PROVISIONAL DIRECTORS.

MESSRS. IRA GOULD, WALTER MACFARLAN, VICTOR HUDON,	MESSRS. WM. McNAUGHTON, DUNCAN MACDONALD, JOSEPH BARSALOU,	MESSRS. ALEXANDER McGIBBON, GEORGE HEUBACH, J. T. KERBY.

OFFICERS.

PRESIDENT:	VICE-PRESIDENT:	TREASURER:	SECRETARY:
WALTER MACFARLAN.	WM. McNAUGHTON.	JOSEPH BARSALOU.	GEORGE HEUBACH.

MESSRS. CARTIER, POMINVILLE, & BETOURNAY, SOLICITORS.   J. T. KERBY, GENERAL AGENT.

e following are among the prominent firms in Montreal who have subscribed to the original Stock List at the formation of the Company:—

srs. Ira Gould, President Corn Exchange.	Messrs. W.McNaughton, Messrs. Sincennes & McNaughton.	Messrs. Boyer, Hudon, & Co.
" Walter McFarlan, (Messrs. Walter McFarlan & Baird).	" A. W. Ogilvie & Co., Glenora Mills.	" %. Benoit, Wholesale Merchant.
" James Donelly, Wholesale Dry Goods.	" Beaning & Barsalou, Auctioneers.	" Evans & Evans, Wholesale Hardwar).
" Luke Moore, (Messrs. Moore, Lemple & Hatchette).	" AleX McGibbon, China House.	" James Smith, M.P.
" Duncan Macdonald.	" T. Baillie & Co., Wholesale Dry Goods.	" Andrew Watson.
" A. Shannon & Co., Wholesale Grocers.	" Alex. Walker, Wholesale Dry Goods.	" A. Freeman & Co.
" Lewis, Kay & Co., Wholesale Dry Goods.	" Geo. Winks & Co., Wholesale Dry Goods, Albert Buildings.	" John Rhynas,
" George Brush, Eagle Foundry.	" W. P. Ryan, M.P.	" Cartier, Pominville & Betournay, Solicitors.
	" Victor Hudon & Co., Wholesale Grocer.	" Cassels & Cameron, Wholesale Dry Goods.
		" Ferrier & Co., Wholesale Hardware.

TWENTY-THIRD ANNUAL REPORT

OF THE

NEW YORK LIFE INSURANCE COMPAN

Accumulated Capital, over $10,000,000. · · Divisible Surplus, Jan. 1, 1868, $1,642,425 5

Annual Statement, January 1st, 1868.

AMOUNT OF NET CASH ASSETS, January 1st, 1867		$6,727,816 65
AMOUNT OF PREMIUMS RECEIVED DURING 1867	$3,104,051 34	
AMOUNT OF INTEREST RECEIVED AND ACCRUED, INCLUDING PREMIUMS ON GOLD, &c.	487,339 94	
		3,591,391 28
		$10,319,207 93

DISBURSEMENTS.

Paid Losses by Death	$561,921 45	
Paid for Redemption of Dividends, Annuities, and surrendered and cancelled Policies	485,851 36	
Paid Salaries, Printing, Office and Law Expenses	98,032 55	
Paid Commissions and Agency Expenses	333,207 43	
Paid Advertising and Physician's Fees	46,518 77	
Paid Taxes and Internal Revenue Stamps	19,291 26	
		1,544,861 92
		$8,774,326 01

ASSETS.

Cash on hand, in Bank, and in Trust Company	$575,236 54	
Invested in United States Stocks, (Market value, $3,150,506 87) cost	2,978,907 49	
Invested in New York City Bank Stocks (Market value, $45,855), cost	41,549 00	
Invested in New York State Stocks (Market value, $836,050), Cost	806,306 60	
Invested in other Stocks (Market value, $151,225), cost	149,337 01	
Loans on Demand, secured by U. S. and other Stocks, (Market value, $311,497)	237,700 00	
Real Estate (Market value, $709,125 66)	528,234 53	
Bonds and Mortgages (Secured by Real Estate, valued at $2,260,000)	1,072,800 00	
Premium Notes on existing Policies, bearing interest	1,556,837 47	
Quarterly and semi-annual Premiums due subsequent to January 1, 1868	346,285 81	
Interest accrued to January 1, 1868	52,402 83	
Rents accrued to January 1, 1868	2,401 96	
Premiums on Policies in hands of Agents and in course of transmission	406,326 77	
		$8,774,326 01
And excess of market value of securities over cost		385,427 90
Cash Assets, Jan. 1, 1868		$9,159,753 91

LIABILITIES OF THE COMPANY.

Amount of Adjusted Losses, due subsequent to Jan. 1, 1868	$134,800 00	
Amount of Reported Losses awaiting proof, &c.	38,214 32	
Amount reserved for Re-insurance on existing Policies (valuations, Carlisle table four per cent. interest, net premium)	6,283,635 49	
Return Premium, declared prior to 1866, payable on demand	72,572 51	
Return Premium, 1866 (now to be paid)	422,638 00	
Return Premium, 1867 (present value)	565,468 00	
		$7,517,328 32
Divisible Surplus		$1,642,425 59

During the Year, 6,597 Policies have been issued, insuring $22,541,940.

The Progress of the Company for the Past Four Years will be seen in the following Statement:—

Assets.		Increase of Assets over previous year.		Assets.	Increase of Assets over previous year.
1864	$3,658,755 55	$1,005,217 63	1866	6,727,816 65	1,845,896 95
1865	4,881,919 70	1,223,164 15	1867	8,774,326 01	2,046,509 36
			Total increase	$6,120,788 69.	

One of the special features of this Company is the TEN YEAR NON-FORFEITURE PLAN.

The system popularly termed "The Non-Forfeiture Plan," was originated and first presented to the public by this Company, in their well-"TEN YEAR NON-FORFEITURE POLICY," in the year 1860; and its perfect adaptation to the wants of every class in the community, ob every reasonable objection to Life Insurance, is shown from the fact that every other American Company has been compelled, in deference to olinion, to adopt it, although in many cases it is done in such a way as considerably to impair its value. It has received the *unqualified approva gest business men of the land*, large numbers of whom have taken out policies under it, simply as an investment.

By the Table on which this class of Policies is based, a person incurs no risk in taking out a policy. Insuring to-day for $10,000, if he should die to-morrow, th immediately becomes a claim ; and if he shall live ten years, and make ten annual payments, his policy will be paid for, and his dividends *still continue*, making

HIS LIFE POLICY A SOURCE OF INCOME TO HIM WHILE LIVING.

By the specific terms of these policies, and not by vague and indefinite statements made in circulars, a party after the second year does not forfeit what he has paid in pa Thus, if one insuring by this plan for $10,000 discontinues after the second year, he is entitled to a PAID-UP POLICY, according to the number of full years paid in, as foll

Second year, two-tenths of $10,0 0 (amount insured), amounting to... $2,000 | Fourth year, four-tenths of $10,000 (amount insured), amounting to.... $4,000
Third year, three-tenths of $10,000 (amount insured), amounting to... 3,000 | Fifth year, five-tenths of $10,000 (amount insured), amounting to.... 5,000

And so on, until the tenth annual payment, *when all is paid*. The paid up policies, for the proportionate partial payments, as well as for the full amount, participa Dividends of the Company during the whole existence of the policies. ☞ This being a purely mutual Company, ALL ITS PROFITS ARE DIVIDED AMONG THE AS

MORRIS FRANKLIN, PRESIDENT.
WILLIAM H. BEERS, VICE-PRES'T & ACTUARY.

EVANS, ELMSLEY & CO., Agents for To

THE CANADIAN

ONETARY TIMES

AND

INSURANCE CHRONICLE,

ED TO FINANCE, COMMERCE, INSURANCE, BANKS, RAILWAYS, NAVIGATION, MINES, INVESTMENT, PUBLIC COMPANIES, AND JOINT STOCK ENTERPRISE.

NO. 15. TORONTO, THURSDAY, NOVEMBER 26, 1868. { SUBSCRIPTION $2 YEAR.

Mercantile.

Meetings.

THE GRAND TRUNK.

(Proceedings at the Annual Meeting Continued.)

Mr. Grant, the Secretary, by permission of the Chairman, read a statement by Mr. Handyside in reference to the management in Canada, especially with regard to the supply, quality and state of the rails used on the line. One man told him that if he dared to work as he could his earnings would be £3 a day. The original rails had been rolled with soft iron and put on the road again. He was told that some of the English rails had not lasted above twelve months. He found there were no inspectors of rails on the line. He was also told at the Rolling Mills at Toronto that many of the rails did not last above four years. Iron twice heated in order to work up with other iron became too soft, and unfit for rails. The re-rolling cost £6 per ton at Toronto; the soft iron rails were worn out in one year. In respect of the effect of climate good rails had been laid down for seventeen years, and were good now, he had had some of his information from Mr. Scovill, a manufacturer. The evil system was contracting without having proper stipulations and conditions to compel the contractor to do his duty to the Company. The contracts let were too large, and the term of the contract was too long. Above all, there was not an efficient mode of testing the quality of the rails before they were laid down on the track. So that their qualities were never known till after being tested on the line by the rolling stock passing over them. He also stated that the Company never accepted the lowest tender.

Mr. Brydges reiterated his contradiction.
Sir Raymond Jarvis remarked that he did not see in the list of share and bondholders the names of any Canadian shareholders.
The Chairman said that the reason was, that the Canadian list was not published.
The Secretary then went on with the reading of Mr. Handyside's documents. He recommended that the present plant should be put in good and efficient repair before any more money was ex-pended on new rolling stock. The management of the Grand Trunk was very unfortunate. The information given by Mr. Scovill was signed by him in the form of letters. Mr. Handyside had also visited the wheel works at Toronto, and stated that he had received every facility from the Chairman of the company, Mr. Brydges, and Mr. Hickson, the secretary in Canada. It was the opinion of Mr. Handyside that Mr. Brydges had too much work to do, he had to direct every kind of work, whether he understood it or not, and although it entailed a great deal of unnecessary labor on Mr. Brydges, he did not think such a system either so efficient or so economical as it might be made by a proper division of labor. He considered that the passenger-train service was badly managed, trains were sometimes three hours behind owing to the track being a single one. The goods trains retarded the passenger trains, and that was felt in the receipts. He thought the Directors should endeavor to pay the interest on the first, second, and third preference bonds, and leave the improvement of the line to come out of

the surplus. The population and wealth were in-creasing, all along the western portion of their line cottages were being taken down in many places to make room for larger and more substan-tial buildings.

Mr. Handyside said that some people might have a very poor opinion of the Grand Trunk, but he had been over the railway and had great faith in the resources of the line. He had an idea of those resources, but he believed, from the way the company was managed, whatever the traffic might be, the shareholders would never get a farthing. He would tell them from the evidence he had got from the people on the line, that the line was badly managed. He assured them that that was the opinion that he had got from the people working on the line. In coming to Mon-treal and Toronto, he had traveled with the super-intendent of the line, and he had said, when he (Mr. Handyside) was speaking about the short time the rails lasted, that he could show him iron rails that had been laid down on the track only two months, which were entirely worn out. He had found out that the reason of these rails so soon wearing out was that they were made of soft and old iron rails, which were rolled again. He had gone to the mills where they were rolling rails, and he assured the meeting that there was no inspector there, notwithstanding all that had been said about the bad iron. He bore no ill-feeling to Sir Edward Watkin, nor to Mr. Brydges, but he laid all the trouble that had fallen on the company to their charge. Iron lost, it is well known, 25 per cent. in re-rolling, and he had seen people in the mills who were buying soft iron and putting it in the middle of the rails. They had heard a great deal about the wear and tear of rails in Canada, but he believed that rails, if properly made, would last as long in that country as in England. There was not a single testing engine from one end of the line to the other, and he could prove it.

Mr. Rokeby Price said that the line he chalked out to produce peace and harmony to the Grand Trunk was the resignation of the chairman and the board. Anything short of that would not do.

Mr. Maxwell Heslop, was an unfortunate bond-holder in both companies, the Buffalo and Lake Huron and the Grand Trunk. Therefore, it was to him doubly unfortunate to see the warfare between the two companies.

Mr. Molesworth thought their attention should be directed to the present and future, and let every one retire from the new board. It appeared that Mr. Brydges had answered all the questions, and they should now see how those tests were to be applied in respect of the rails, and some practi-cal man to carry them out.

Mr. Brydges said from some of the observa-tions he had heard, he hoped the meeting would give him fair play. He had devoted the whole of his time to the service of the Company, and all his exertions and ability, and he could do no more. He had answered Mr. Scovill's letters. Mr. Handyside had acknowledged that he received every facility in his inquiries from the general manager in Canada, but he did not stop long enough in the country to get all the requisite in-formation. Captain Tyler had reported that better rails were made in Toronto than those that came from England. Corruption did exist no doubt, and it was difficult to get contracts carried out properly. Tenders were invited, and those offered at the lowest price were always accepted provided the materials, &c., were as good as others could supply. Mr. Creak's first question was about the rails. On the 30th June, 1868, there were 1,377 miles of railway open, of which 808½ consisted of T rails fished, 232 miles of T rails not fished, leaving 336¼ miles of original U rails. There were 113 miles of the old rails on the Rivière du Loup line; nearly 200 miles on the Portland section, which would have to be renewed in about three years. The T rails were in good order. The T rails, 68 miles, on the Buffalo line would be renewed. As to the rolling stock it was all in good condition. The number of cars under repair was about 3 or 4 per cent. of the whole, not more than that. They had constructed from 60 to 70 which were charged to working expenses. They had 298 engines, including those of the other two Companies. There were 33 engines not in use when Mr. Trevethick made his report, because after the effects of the winter they had always a larger number of repairs. From 20 to 25 per cent. of the whole engine stock in England were generally out of use or under repair. During the east four years they had built in their shops at Montreal 21 engines of large size out of revenue, to replace other engines wearing out. With regard to the stock of engines they had 7 more than they had bought or broken up. The average cost of renewals of way from the 1st January, 1860, to January, 1867, was $468 80 per mile, while on the Great Western of Canada the cost had been $646.49 per mile. The Great Western had expended $1,715,000 for maintenance and renewals, and they had now commenced renewing their line over again. The proprietors must bear in mind that there must always be renewing the line in one place or another. The extent of the renewals would depend upon the amount of the traffic, the effects of climate and the nature of the materials used. It was impossible to state what the renewals would cost, $646 a mile was enough at one time, but they had since cost more. He was reminded by Mr. Creak that he had reported to the board about three years ago what would be required for the next ensuing three years, and that the estimate had been exceeded. The average cost of renewals in the years 1867 had been £139,000 for the whole 1,377 miles, or say £140,000 for renewals per annum. They never could stop renewals, they would always go on so long as the railway was worked. They could do the renewals only during the months when the climate permitted, in the other part of the year the permanent way was frozen up. As to the question of ballasting there were considerable portions of the line that had never been ballasted at all. They had spent between £30,000 and £35,000 in ballasting in three years, and he wished they could have spent more. The free passes was another question. There could be no greater boon to him than taking away the power to issue free passes. Other Companies issued free passes to parties having goods traffic on the line, to members of the press, and to the officials of other Companies having connecting lines with their line. They only had complied with the usual rule in respect to free passes all over America, and they must do the same as other railway Companies did. He had New York passes sent to him, and piles of them for other lines in the United States. They issued them only to persons engaged in the Company or to the members of the press, and the railway officials of other lines. He could say distinctly that they restricted to the utmost possible extent the issue of those passes.

Mr. Creak wished to know whether Mr. Brydges desired a resolution from the shareholders prohibiting him from granting these passes.

Mr. Brydges said no; it was the practice of the country to grant these passes, and it was impossible to do otherwise than follow it. The next question referred to the greenbacks. He was asked how they got them, and why they did not charge up the fares or rates in greenbacks so as to cover the loss on exchange. The receipt of greenbacks arose from traffic passing from the United States over their line. They must recollect that there were four or five competing lines to their line from east to west, and if the Grand Trunk refused to take the current rates in greenbacks the consequence would be that the passengers and freighters would not pay more than on the American lines, and the Grand Trunk Company would lose the traffic thus obtained.

Mr. Spencer Herapath understood it to mean that if the traffic of the Grand Trunk were confined to purely Canadian traffic, there would be no greenbacks to exchange; but as the interchange of traffic between American and Canadian lines involved payment in greenbacks, they must accept them in payment and incur the loss in exchange, or abandon that portion of through traffic.

Mr. Brydges then proceeded with his reply to the questions of Mr. Creak. He was asked why was not coal cheaper than wood to burn, and why was not the wood used on the Grand Trunk as effective as that used on the Great Western of Canada. The contract for wood let this year was a little under 16s. per cord, and at that price it would not be economy to use coal. In addition to the price of coal at Quebec it would have to be carried in barges to Montreal, which would add a dollar more to the price of it; then about 99 per cent. of their locomotives had iron fire boxes, which would soon be destroyed by burning coal fuel. As to the patent by Mr. Yates for mending rails, it had been sold in 1865, and was now in other hands. The Company's road was frozen up to the middle of May in each year. He had come to the last of Mr. Creak's questions, and he had stated what was perfectly true. He hoped if there were any more questions to answer or charges to make against him they would be made now, as he was there to answer them.

Mr. Prance asked if Mr. Brydges had not a Government commission for the Intercolonial Railway.

Mr. Brydges said he had not any Government commission, and gave the whole of his time to the service of the Company.

Another report puts it in this way:

Mr. Prance wished to know whether it was not a fact that Mr. Brydges had been appointed to the Intercolonial. How was it possible for him to give his whole time and attention to the affairs of the Grand Trunk in this case ?

Mr. Brydges had never been offered the appointment, and therefore had not accepted it.

The Chairman said that it had been intimated some time ago that Mr. Brydges might be appointed to the Intercolonial, and it had been a matter of discussion with them whether it would not be advisable for Mr. Brydges to accept that post.

After some further remarks Mr. Creak's amendment, on being put to the meeting, was declared carried on a show of hands, but a poll was demanded by the chairman. Mr. Batten and Mr. Creak were appointed scrutineers, and a poll was ordered.

THE CANADA SALT WORKS COMPANY OF GODERICH.

At a meeting of the Directors, held at Windsor, on November 21st, 1868, the President made the following report:

"GENTLEMEN,—It is with infinite pleasure I beg to inform you of the entire success of our enterprise thus far, and the healthy condition of our finances. Our well is completed, having passed through 38 feet of solid salt at a depth of 997 feet, and obtained the strongest brine yet found. Everything is now in perfect order, and the work of the most substantial nature, and nothing remains to be done except building the blocks for evaporating ; and, in one sense, it is fortunate our well was not sooner finished, as, from recent experiments, a much cheaper mode of evaporation has been discovered.

"Although our capital stock is fourtee sand dollars, we closed the stock-book wi thousand seven hundred dollars had be scribed, and as soon as sixty per cent. on mentioned sum has been paid in by the holders the Company will be entirely fr debt and have a balance of one hund eighty-three dollars to their credit, so I f ranted in hoping that the stock subscrib finish the works and commence the man of salt.

"I have every reason to believe that vestment will be a most profitable one fi following facts:—Although our well is finished, and no others have been comme Canada, the manufacturers have been u fill their orders, and the price obtained thirty to forty cents per barrel advance other salt, which advance is also obtained Western States, and leaves a margin fo after paying the gold duty of seventy-fiv so that should the Reciprocity Treaty course of negotiation be consummated, wi estimate the value of our property, while such treaty it is most valuable."

Moved by Hiram Walker, Esq., secon Wm. McGregor, Esq., That the President is most satisfactory and be adopted.—Carr

Moved by Henry Kennedy, Esq., secon G. W. Girdlestone, Esq., That a call of cent. be made, payable on December 10ti to cover all expenses to date.—Carried.

Moved by Henry Prince, Esq., secon Hiram Walker, Esq., That Messrs. Kenn McGregor do proceed at once to Goderic ceive the well from the contractor, and to th ly examine the different modes of evap deciding upon the best and most economic to receive tenders from contractors for buil same, and to report to the Directors at a to be called immediately after their r Carried.

Moved by G. W. Girdlestone, Esq., secon Hiram Walker, Esq., That the proceeding meeting be printed and forwarded to the c shareholders.—Carried.

Railway News.

NORTHERN RAILWAY.—Traffic receipt ending Nov. 14, 1868.

Passengers	$3,34	
Freight	6,65	
Mails and Sundries............	31	
Total Receipts for week......	$10,	
Corresponding week 1867....	9,	
Increase...........	$1,20	

GREAT WESTERN RAILWAY.—Traffic ending Nov. 6, 1868.

Passengers	$32,21	
Freight and live stock......	41,97	
Mails and sundries...........	2,81	
	$76,99	
Corresponding Week of '67	80,60	
Decrease............	$3,61	

—The Richmond *Guardian*, speaki St. Francis Valley Railway, says: "The Compton County have already set the b and it is to be hoped that by union and ise on the part of both parties concerned er company will at once be formed."

—Three residents of Port Perry ha $10,000 each of stock in the Port I Whitby road.

—The Massawippi railway, to connec sumpsic and Grand Trunk was commenc 16th.

'AY TRAFFIC RETURNS

MONTH OF OCTOBER, 1868.

Grand Trunk Railway	282293	25500	518760	826553	769974	1377	1377
London and Port Stanley Railway	1179	143	3673	4995	5942	25	25
Welland Railway	1315	1082	8988	11383	16792	25	25
Northern Railway	19221	4280	45473	68974	75641	97	97
Port Hope, Lindsay, and Beaverton Railway, and Peterborough Branch	......	......	......	......	......	......	......
Cobourg, Peterborough and Marmora Railway	......	......	......	......	......	......	......
Brockville and Ottawa Railway	4722	1121	16018	21861	17750	86	86
St. Lawrence and Ottawa Railway	6568	713	4935	12234	11546	54	54
Carillon and Grenville Railway*	......	......	......	......	......	......	......
Stanstead, Shefford & Chambly Raily*	......	......	......	......	......	......	......
St. Lawrence and Industry Railway*	489	......	940	1429	1884	12	12
New Brunswick and Canada Railway	......	......	......	......	......	......	......
European & North American Railway	7360	1152	11567	20479	19782	108	108
Nova Scotia Railway	......	......	......	......	......	......	......
Total	......	......	......	......	......	......	......

JOHN LANGTON,
Auditor.

, 1868.

Financial.

'TO STOCK MARKET.

d by Pellatt & Osler, Brokers.)

of securities still continues very
oks of several of the Banks are
payment of dividends due on 1st

Montreal is offered at 140 ex-divi-
yers at 137. Nothing doing in
uld be paid. There are sellers of
ex-dividend. No Toronto to be
eely offered. Royal Canadian is
nd no buyers. There are buyers
105; none in market. Gore is in
rith sellers at 48. Merchants' has
last sale was made at 112. There
olson's at 108½; no sales. City is
ex dividend. Buyers would give
ple. Jacques Cartier is offered at
d. Sales of Mechanics' occurred
buyers of Union at 104. Nothing
anks.

The market is quite cleared of Can-
minion Stock offered at 104½.
siderable sales of Toronto at rates
per cent. interest. No County in
ould readily be taken at rates to

ty Gas continues in great demand
rket. There were several sales of
ent Building Society at 124 and
latter price would now be paid.
a would command 115½; none in
were sales of Freehold at 104 to
l, and buyers still offer the latter
treal Telegraph in market; 132
would be paid. There were sales of Canada Landed Credit at 73, at which rate there are buyers. Mortgages are in demand to pay 8 per cent. interest. Money is readily obtainable on good paper.

MONTREAL MONEY MARKET.

(From our own Correspondent.)

Montreal, Nov. 24, 1868.

As reported in my last there is a plethora of money, and the Banks have rather reduced their rates of discount; the amount of good bills offering is very light, and readily taken at 6 to 6½ per cent., and on the street fair commercial paper is taken at 10 to 12½. Stocks still rule high, latest quotations being, Bank of Montreal, 136 ex div.: but holders are firm at 140, the demand is active, and clearly points to the feeling, that this Bank will have the management of the Government issue. City Bank easier at 102, but buyers will not give over 101. Ontario is also easier, with buyers at 97. Peoples are wanted at 106. Merchants, several transactions at 112, the closing rates being sellers 112½, buyers 111½. Toronto enquired for at 118½. No great change in other Banks, but the prices generally are very stiff. In other stocks Telegraph are wanted at 133 but none offering. Gold 132½ to 134. Richelieu stock holders have advanced their views, sellers wanting 120, buyers offering 115. Corporation bonds (6 per cent.) active at 94 at 95. Mining Consols offering at $2.75, with buyers at $2.25. Dominion Stock 105.

I give latest prices—Gold buying 4¼, selling 3¾ Greenbacks buying at 26, selling at 25½ to 25¾. Gold drafts on New York, par. Bank Exchange buying 25¼, selling 25½.

PROVINCIAL NOTES.—The following is a statement of the Provincial Notes in circulation, the 4th Nov., and of the Specie held against them at Montreal, Toronto, and Halifax, according to the Returns of the Commissioners under the Provincial Note Act:

Provincial Notes in Circulation—		
Payable at Montreal	$3,738,593	
Payable at Toronto*	1,266,407	
* Including $76,000 marked St. John.		
Payable at Halifax.........	206,000	
		$5,211,000
Specie held—		
At Montreal..................	$593,333	
At Toronto	500,000	
At Halifax†..................	42,000	
† Estimated, the return not being received.		
		$1,135,333
Debentures held by the Receiver General under the Provincial Note Act		$3,000,000

POST OFFICE SAVINGS' BANK.—The following is a statement of the Post Office Savings' Bank Account, for the month of October, 1868, published in accordance with the Act 31 Vic., chap. 10, sec. 72:—

In hands of the Receiver General as per last Statement (Sept. 30th)..			$357,953.87
Amount received from depositors during Oct'r...	$76,074.00		
Interest paid on closed accounts	57.35		
		$76,131.35	
Withdrawal cheques paid during October		20,018.98	
			55,212.38
In hands of Receiver General Oct. 31..........			413,171 24
Bearing interest at 4 per cent		$244,088.39	
Bearing interest at 5 per cent		167,200.00	
Bearing no interest, being the amount in the hands of the Receiver General to meet outstanding cheques		1,882.85	
			$413,171.24

Insurance.

FIRE RECORD.—Plattsville, Ont., Nov. 17.—J. B. Sorley's tannery and contents; loss from $5,000 to $6,000; insured for $2,500 in the Western and $2,500 in the Provincial; total insurance, $5,000.

Gananoque, Ont., Nov. 20.—The woollen factory of R. P. Colton, part of which was occupied by Gordon & Kirkham, took fire in the fourth story from a shoddy machine and was totally destroyed. The machinery, amounting to $500, was saved. Loss of Mr. Colton about $9,000; insured in the Western for $2,100 and in the Provincial for $4,000. Gordon & Kirkham's loss about $2,000; partly insured. Also, the nail factory of Corwin & Britton was severely damaged; loss about $1,000; no insurance.

Almonte, Ont., Nov. 19.—Two large frame buildings, a grist mill, and a woollen mill, owned by Mr. Henry, of Ottawa, were destroyed by fire early this morning. Loss, $16,000; insurance $8,000.

St. Vincent Township, Grey Co., Nov. 16.—House of James Arthur, 9th con., totally destroyed; loss $650; insurance $300; part of the furniture was saved.

Owen Sound, Ont., Nov. 12.—Store of H. Taylor, Division street, totally destroyed; loss $5,000; insurance $2,000. House of Mr. Gordon adjoining somewhat damaged, also furniture. The fire engine prevented the fire spreading further.

Quebec, Nov. 20.—A number of small fires have recently occurred here, but nothing of consequence.

North Oxford, 16th Oct.—Barn of Mr. Francis Box; origin of fire unknown; no insurance.

— The Western Insurance Company of this city have presented Capt. G. W. Rounds of Buffalo with an elegant silver tea set, in acknowledgment of the services of that gentleman, in rescuing the schooner *Ionia* from peril, that vessel being stranded off Silver Creek.

— The hail insurance companies of France insured in 1867 about $50,000,000 against the hazards of hail in the departments of France. The loss was about seventy cents for each hundred dollars insured.

OIL TRADE OF PENNSYLVANIA.

The Titusville *Herald's* Monthly Petroleum Report for the month ending October 31st, 1868, shows the total production for that month, the average per day, and from January 1st to Nov. 4.

Total shipments of crude for October of brls. of 45 galls. each..................		325,666
Add to reduce to brls. of 43 galls. each		15,147
Total shipments of brls. of 43 galls. each		340,813
Stock on hand, Oct. 1st, brls.	266,888	
Stock on hand, Nov. 1st, brls.	266,180	
Add increase on Nov. 1st..................		2,372
Total production during October, brls.		343,185
Average per day for 31 days......	10,133	
Production previously reported, brls....		2,747,371
Total production from January 1st to November 1st, brls........................		3,090,556
Average ℔ day for 305 days, brls.	10,133	

The average daily proportion at the wells on farms and in districts is given during the last two days of the month, for the purpose of showing whether the reduction is receding or enlarging.

The following table shows the production as taken from the guage tanks at the wells during days and periods named:

November	7th,	1867,	brls.	9,885
December	"	"	"	10,462
January	"	1868,	"	11,035
February	"	"	"	10,811
March	"	"	"	9,768
April	"	"	"	8,943

Average per day for the twenty-three days ending April 30th, bbls..........................	8,650
Average per day for the thirty-one days ending May 31st, bbls......................	9,790
Average per day during May 30th and 31st, bbls.	10,035
Average per day during June 29th and 30th bbls.	11,299
Average per day during July 30th and 31st, bbls.......	11,405
Average per day during August 30th and 31st, bbls	12,347
Average per day during September 29th and 30th, bbls..............................	12,527
Average per day during October 30th and 31st, bbls	11,113

THE DEVELOPMENT AND THE TERRITORY.

The number of new wells being drilled on November 1st, was 435, an increase of fifty-seven from the 1st of the previous month. This increase is a large one and was unlooked for at this season of the year. The number of wells drilling on the 1st inst., was forty-four greater than at any previous date during 1868, and one hundred and ninety more than at the same date in 1867. Of these 435 wells drilling on the 1st, 213 were located in the Pleasant district. In this district the known producing territory has again been greatly extended by the finding of several large producing wells. It now embraces from three to four square miles, and is much the largest tract of producing territory over discovered.

On Cherry Tree Run the development has been very unsatisfactory, six or seven new wells having been tested that did not produce more than from three to twenty barrels per day. On Charley Run, near Oil City, there is some demand for leases, and it is probable that several wells will be commenced in that district during November. On Upper Cherry Run the known producing territory has been found to be but a few acres in extent, and the number of drilling wells has fallen off. To the east of this district a vein of black petroleum, like that found in the whole of the Pleasantville district, has been discovered, and it is almost certain that it is but a continuation of the vein found in that district.

From the experience of the past eight years, there is no reason to believe but that the territory in Pennsylvania can, for at least a century, supply any demand which may arise. Although on a general survey of the whole territory, there now appears to be little that, by development, is known to be of the producing order, that has not been drawn upon more or less largely, yet there is no doubt but that there are still large tracts which remain undeveloped, and the territory that has been abandoned can, by exhausting the water from it, again be made to produce. The work of exhausting the water from abandoned territory has been actively commenced, and the result has already proved that by further prosecution of it, the territory can be made to produce, although not so largely as at first.

THE STOCK OF PETROLEUM.

The stock of petroleum in the region has remained without material change, having amounted on November 1st to 266,180 barrels, of forty-three gallons each. This stock shows an increase of but 2,372 barrels. The amount in iron tankage has been increased by 1,272 barrels. Compared with November 1st, 1867, the total stock shows a decrease of 338,820 barrels.

In the total stock are included the amount in iron tankage throughout the region, 5,000 barrels, at Titusville, 500 on the Hyde & Egbert Farm, 1,300 at Oil City, and 1,500 barrels at Tidioute, all in wooden storage tanks, and the amount in tanks at the wells which was 81,000 barrels. This latter amount is owned by producers, dealers, and shippers, the latter parties owning two-thirds. Of the stock at the wells 32,000 barrels were held at Pleasantville.

The following recapitulation gives in small space the condition of affairs at the end of the month:—

Total amount of petroleum in iron and wooden storage tanks and on the hands of producers, brokers, and shippers, bbls...............................	266,180
Total capacity of iron tankage, bbls...	1,070,539
Total amount of petroleum in iron tankage, bbls	176,880
Amount of iron tankage empty, bbls...	893,659
Number of new wells drilling............	435
Daily production, bbls.....................	11,113

☞ THE CANADIAN MONETARY TIMES AND INSURANCE CHRONICLE *is printed every Thursday Evening, in time for the English Mail.*

*Subscription Price, one year, $2, or $3 in American currency ; Single copies, five cents each. Casual advertisements will be charged ten cents per line of solid nonpareil each insertion. All letters to be addressed, "*THE CANADIAN MONETARY TIMES, TORONTO, ONT.*" Registered letters so addressed are at the risk of the Publishers. Cheques should be made payable to J. M. TROUT, Business Manager, who will, in future, issue all receipts for money.*

The Canadian Monetary Times.

THURSDAY, NOVEMBER 26, 1868.

NEW MINING LAWS.

The discussion evoked by the Act of last session respecting mines and minerals, the manifest impolicy of putting in force its provisions, and the repeated failures in Madoc to extract gold in paying quantities, not to speak of the personal examination by the Commissioner of Crown Lands of the mineral region to the north-west, have brought about a change in the mineral policy of the Government of Ontario. This change is embodied in the following resolutions introduced last week in the Assembly :

1. *Resolved*, That, in the opinion of this House, all royalties, taxes or duties, which by any patents heretofore issued are reserved, or made payable upon or in respect of any ores or minerals extracted from the land granted by such patent, and situated within this Province, should be repealed and abandoned, and that such lands and ores and minerals should be henceforth exempt from every such royalty, tax or duty.

2. That the proprietors of all private lands heretofore granted by the Crown, situated within this Province, and their assigns, should, as against Her Majesty, her heirs and successors, have the right to mine for gold and silver upon such lands, for their own benefit and advantage.

3. That it is expedient that the unoccupied Crown Lands of this Province should be declared free and open to explorations for mines and minerals, and that persons should, under proper regulations, be allowed to mine upon such lands, for their own benefit and advantage, free from any charge or royalty.

The system of royalties has undoubtedly obtained a place in our legislation from time immemorial, as part and parcel of which, so far as the furtherance of terests is concerned, has only wonder at its intense stupidity. regulations first in force in the Huron mineral region, parties mig and secure locations of ten square four shillings per acre. Those remained in force until 1853. change was the imposition of an c fee of £25 ; the quantity of land to 400 acres ; and the price per raised to seven shillings and sixp 1861 the price was fixed at $1 per the locations were subject to the that the patent should not issu had been shown that the mine worked for one year. But these not apply to gold and silver mines. the provision respecting the working was abolished, and in lieu of it a $2\frac{1}{2}$ per cent. was imposed. In 186 of a royalty, a fixed duty was exc per ton of ore extracted. In 1865, cided to waive the gold clause, in mining lands on Lake Superior wer ed. In 1866, all royalties were In 1868, royalties were reimposed. of 1868 was passed under the impre the mines of Thunder Bay were rich, and that their product would value of silver throughout the wor scarcely necessary to say that it enforced. It is now proposed, and very sensibly, to repeal the act o sion, and to abolish all royalties, open the Crown Lands free of ch out depriving any parties of a rig chase. Those who do not desire t will be allowed to occupy a claim they continue to work, and to d charge or royalty. The policy o ernment will commend itself to al in the progress of the country calculated to develope our minera

ETNA INSURANCE COMP DUBLIN.

We have received a circular in stated that this Company has a transfer its business to "The U and General Insurance Company pany which has just been orga circular also states that the Canad will be continued.

In our English exchanges we lowing paragraph relating to the

The ETNA.—A petition for the windin Court of Chancery, of the Etna In pany was presented to the Master of Tuesday last by Ferdinand Philip F berg, of 13 Cockspur street, and su directed to be heard on Saturday n instant.

N TELEGRAPH COMPANY.

last week the charges made Company, and this week we in- from the President and one from y of the Company in reply. The xcited a good deal of public at- . no doubt these communications with interest.

NANCIAL CRISIS IN NEW BRUNSWICK.

nsion of the Commercial Bank, a great deal of trouble on the few Brunswick. This bank has onthly returns to the Auditor of ints, but we find in the Bank ir July last, the following returns:

up $600,000

Liabilities.

.... 312,305
es 54,745
.... 304,368

.... $671,418

Assets.

.... $82,360
.... 32,000
er banks............... 8,053
ies........................ 62,193
ills discounted 1,008,007
.... 29,840

$1,222,454

Stephen's Bank Statement for nishes the following particulars:
up..............:.......... $200,000

Liabilities.

.... 249,548
.... 56,079

.... $305,627

Assets.

........................: $39,866
.... 4,394
ir banks.................... 45,517
as 61,973
lls discounted .:.......... 344,353
.... 96,605

$592,710

a flight of the cashier leaving a),000 is rather a serious matter tors of the Commercial Bank. on has been very unlucky, and on the sufferance of the other nths past, and although it held a ($100,000) on behalf of the ment, its credit was exhausted. Montreal refused its paper and n followed suit. The Dominion came to the rescue of the Local and expressed its readiness to es to prevent embarrassment.

Mr. Tilley stated in a telegram that there is a supply of gold in St. John. On this the *Freeman* makes the following comments:

"The other banks complained bitterly some time ago that the Bank of Montreal abused its position as the Government agency to force specie from them, merely for the purpose of hoarding it, and it was said at one time that over Three Hundred Thousand Dollars had accumulated in the possession of the Montreal Bank. But the amount of Savings' Bank deposits on July 1st, 1867, was $777,-259. If gold to that amount, or half that amount has been kept lying idle in St. John, while the Dominion Government was borrowing from the very same Bank of Montreal at 7 per cent. and commission, the House of Commons should certainly endeavor to know "the reason why."

The *Morning News* points this moral :— "Meanwhile there is one great lesson to be gathered from the record of the disasters which have befallen the Commercial Bank, that in all financial and industrial associations the co-operators at large should see to it that frequent, exact and exhaustive examinations should be made. No namby pamby talk about having confidence in Directors, Managers, Treasurers, Secretaries, and so forth, should for one moment be listened to, if confidence is intended as a substitute for scrutiny frequent and severe. Many and many a disastrous failure would have been avoided had this been done, and infinite suffering averted from those not deserving of it and but ill able to endure it."

THE CRISIS IN NEW BRUNSWICK.

(From Our Own Correspondent.)

St. John, N. B., Nov. 26, 1868.

Our community is in the midst of a terrible commercial and monetary panic, which for duration and intensity has never been equalled in the Province. Indeed, it seemed at one time as though the whole monetary system of the country was about to be overturned, and everything reduced to chaos. So wild was the excitement, as disclosure after disclosure burst upon the public ear, that men stood aghast, and asked each other,—What next? As I am sure our friends in the Western Provinces must feel anxious to learn the history of our troubles, I will endeavour to give something like a connected narrative of the events of the last fortnight. The first mutterings of the coming storm were heard on Monday, the 9th, when some sales by auction of Commercial Bank Stock took place, the price realized being only $16 per $100 share. Towards the close of the day, it began to be rumoured that the bank had had large amounts of English Exchange returned. It was surmised that these were connected with the failure of the absconded some weeks since,) and the House of Mackay Brothers, of Liverpool, also bankrupt. This rumour gained strength, and after bank hours the various broker's offices were besieged by applicants anxious to get rid of their notes. They were of course rejected, and when Tuesday morning came and the bank doors remained closed, the worst fears were confirmed. Still as the bank was known to have a good deal of outstanding commercial paper falling due, for which their own notes would be available, it was thought that the

inconvenience would be but temporary, and Tuesday and Wednesday passed off comparatively quiet. Thursday and Friday an impression got abroad (it is impossible to say how) that the St. Stephen's Bank was unsafe, and a run for gold commenced on the agency here. This agency was conducted by Mr. S. J. Scovil, who very imprudently charged 1 per cen. for cashing the notes, which had the effect of inducing the other banks to throw them out, and from this hour the fate of the St. Stephen's Bank was sealed. The panic spread, and on Saturday Mr. Scovil's office was closed, and a placard intimated that the notes would only be redeemed by the bank itself at St. Stephen. It seems remarkable that up to this time the Directors of the bank at St. Stephen were ignorant of the imminent danger which threatened their institution, and indeed only heard of it by chance. This brings us up to Saturday the 14th, and it is here proper to describe the position occupied by Mr. Scovil. He was the recognized agent at St. John of the St. Stephen's Bank, both for the circulation and redemption of its paper; but in addition to that he did a large brokerage, exchange and insurance business, and received money on deposit, for which he allowed 6 per cent. interest.

To resume my narrative :—On Monday morning it was discovered that the cashier of the Commercial Bank (Mr. George F. Sancton) had absconded, a defaulter to the amount of, it was stated, $90,000. This did not mend matters, but still people were far even then from guessing the whole extent of the impending disaster. Tuesday brought the startling discovery was made that Mr. Scovil was a defaulter to the Bank, in $60,000, and that the whole of the vast amounts deposited with him, had been swept away in gold speculations in New York. It is impossible to ascertain at present the exact amount of the deposits held by Mr. Scovil; but general consent seems to place it as high as $150,000 to $200,000. The St. Stephen Directors went manfully to work, and when they left St. John on Tuesday, it was generally understood that the Bank would keep up, and it was thought and hoped that the crisis was past. Later in the day, however, the Cashier, (who had been left to watch matters in St. John,) had another interview with Scovil, and telegraphed the Directors at St. Stephen to suspend payment. Universal distrust took possession of the community. Prince Edward Island notes, Nova Scotian notes; Commercial and St. Stephen Bank notes, all were refused, and travellers from the north shore, P. E. Island, and parts of Nova Scotia, found themselves with pockets full of useless bank notes. A run for gold commenced on the other banks, but it was principally for small sums ; and as it was well known in the commercial community that they were well prepared, it scarcely extended in their case beyond the numerous, though not wealthy class, who can scarcely distinguish one bank note from another. Some of this class could scarcely be made to believe that the gold they were receiving was genuine, and some amusing episodes occurred which will be long remembered. Thus passed Thursday and Friday, the days of the height of the panic. On Saturday a telegram was sent to all the city papers from the President of the St. Stephen's Bank, which had the effect of greatly restoring confidence, and the notes of his bank, which had been as low as 60 cents to the dollar, went up to 80 and 90 cents. As I write, the feeling is decidedly improved, and hopes are confidently entertained that the worst is past. Such is a brief sketch of the greatest financial disaster which ever befel this city or perhaps any state now to speak ; neither shall I give currency to the many rumours of failure in the mercantile community which have been set afloat. It seems almost impossible that such a crisis should not produce a plentiful crop, but as yet none have actually transpired.

THE DOMINION TELEGRAPH COMPANY.

We copy the following communication from the President of the Dominion Telegraph Company, addressed to the Editor of the Montreal *Gazette:*

SIR,—May I ask the privilege of replying, through your columns, to an article which appeared in a Montreal paper, *The Trade Review*, of the 13th instant, assailing the Dominion Telegraph Company, and impeaching the good faith of those who are promoting that enterprise.

When my attention was first called to the article in question, I hastily drew the conclusion that it had emanated from the head quarters of the Montreal Telegraph Company, and I frankly confess to having been pained at the thought that the President of that Company, a gentleman occupying a prominent position in the commercial world, towards whom, in former days, I stood in no unfriendly relations, had sanctioned a resort to personalities as an effectual means of damaging a rival Company. I was soon satisfied, that in entertaining this impression I had done Mr. Allan a wrong, as later in the day a printed paper was handed to me, headed "Private Circular," written by Mr. Dwight, an employee of the Montreal Company, and addressed to its agents. This circular, less the personalities, forms the sum and substance of the article in the *Trade Review*. I am not disposed to quarrel with Mr. Dwight's circular, far less with the embellishments it has received at the hands of the *Trade Review*. No doubt those gentlemen are satisfied that they have done good service to their masters. I am more than satisfied that they have done yeemen's service to the Dominion Company in furnishing us with an opportunity which we might long have sought for in vain, of meeting our opponents face to face, and of exposing the misrepresentations which, by private circulars and the command of the wires, have been so secretly and diligently spread throughout Western Canada. Before entering upon the main subject, I must allude, passingly, to the attack on Mr. Ryan, a gentleman associated with the Company. That attack is so personal, and reflects so strongly on the character of the party assailed, that I may not attempt in his absence to anticipate the course which he may think it right to pursue for his own vindication. This much I am authorized to say, that the Directors are unaware of anything which would justify them in attaching the slightest credit to the aspersions put forth in the *Trade Review*. To the Messrs. Reeve, also, I shall leave the task of throwing light on their supposed relationship to Mr. Snow, an individual not known even by name to the resident Directors of the Toronto Board. My sole object in entering into print is to clear the Dominion Telegraph Company from the suspicions attempted to be cast upon it, to show that it is no *humbug*, as Mr. *Trade Review* is pleased to suggest, and to expose the real and dishonest design of the writer, while professing to recognize the irreproachable character of such men as McMurrich, Moffatt, Michie and McMaster, to covertly convey the insinuation that they contemplate the perpetration of a *vast swindle* on the public.

We have a right to ask of the public to accept our Prospectus as a plain and honest outline of our scheme, until our actions speak otherwise. In that Prospectus, while giving a sketch of the career of Telegraphy from its infancy on this continent down to this period, when it has assumed gigantic proportions, we have stated our reasons for viewing the present opportunity as favorable to a still further extension of its usefulness in Canada. By way of reply our opponents, those who seek to retain the monopoly of the whole field for the Montreal Company, point to the failure of the Grand Trunk Telegraph Company in 1852.

We deny that there is any analogy in the surrounding circumstances. Then, the telegraph was but occasionally resorted to, now it is in universal request. Then, through the close connection formed between the Western Union of the State of New York and the Montreal, the field was closed against all others. Now, through the more recently established Companies, the Atlantic and Pacific, and the Great Western, with whom we have entered into engagements, the whole field is open to both.

Is the Montreal Company prepared to endorse the allegations put forth by Mr. Dwight, or the imputations cast upon our motives by his backer, the *Trade Review?* Both Mr. Dwight and the *Trade Review* roundly assert that the Dominion Company is simply a second edition of an alleged old swindle, the Grand Trunk Telegraph Company of sixteen years ago, and that the same prominent actor, Mr. Snow, is again at work behind the scenes. We, the Toronto Board, have stated, and repeat the statement, that we are not even aware of the existence of such a personage. It is hinted that Mr. Reeve is a relative of his; of that fact, if it be one, we are ignorant. Nor can it affect the question if it be true. Have we given the Montreal Company any grounds for the charges of bad faith and intended fraud imputed to us by their Agents? Have we, the Board of Directors, the only competent authority which the Dominion Company recognizes, approached the Montreal Company with any propositions that could give color to such charges? Have we attempted to intimidate, or suggested that we were ready to be bought out, or made any proposal of a combination against the public? We have pointed to what we considered objectionable features in the Montreal Company's scale of rates and system of adjustment. Would that be a defensible ground for its attempts to discredit us? On both these points Mr. Dwight, in his circular, confirms our view, for he informs his agents that the Company is about to make a second reduction of rates, lower than ever, and make reforms so as to embrace whole sections of country under a new system of classification. The professed object of Mr. Dwight's circular is thus stated: "It is of course impossible for us to "meet and expose all the extraordinary statements "made by these Agents, and it is hardly necessary for "us to do so, as the truth will in due time appear. In "fact, anxious enquiries are already being made as to "these representations by parties who have through "them, been induced to subscribe for stock. There "are, however, some facts regarding our own Com"pany's affairs, which it is as well you should know, "in order that you may answer intelligently such "enquiries as may be made of you, and inform your "friends whenever called upon to do so." On reading this I fully expected to find matters treated of with regard to which the Montreal Company felt that they had been injuriously misrepresented by the Dominion Company. No such thing. Nearly one half of the circular was devoted to proving that the Montreal Company was not doing half as well as was supposed, and possessed nothing like the capital which had been represented. The pains that Mr. Dwight takes to explain to his agents, in order tha they might be able to explain again how none but the initiated could understand stock quotations is somewhat amusing. By far the larger portion of the sheet is taken up with the Snow story, in order, I suppose, that the Agents might be able to explain it *intelligently* to their friends and the subscribers for Dominion Stock. Much labor is bestowed upon this portion of his circular in order to prove that the Dominion Telegraph scheme is to "all appearance a precisely similar operation." Only one short paragraph is devoted to the subject of rates, explaining what changes and reductions they were about to make, to which I have already alluded. I must not omit to notice another passage in Mr. Dwight's circular, in which he endeavours to connect Mr. Snow with the Dominion Company, and to hold up both in anything but a credible light. He states that early last spring (It must be borne in mind that the Dominion Charter was not obtained till the 25th June, and that the present Board of Directors was not organized till late in July, and issued their Prospectus in August) Mr. Dwight states that early last spring the Montreal Company was approached by Mr. Snow with a proposition that *neither Company should reduce rates*. In whose behalf was Mr. Snow supposed to speak? Surely not the Dominion Company, which came into existence some months later? And yet this impression is most distinctly intended to be conveyed, although Dr. Dwight has not the hardihood to state it in express terms. We learn, however, from Dr. Dwight that Snow is manipulating other companies in the States. Was it in their name that he made the proposition? Nothing more probable than that the companies recently organized in the States should seek to extend their field of operation to Canada, and propose a reciprocity treaty with the Montreal Company, leaving the latter to adjust its own rates. And it is equally certain that such a proposition, if made, would be at once rejected. What! lend a hand to break down monopoly and introduce the wedge for the reduction of rates? However the fact, nothing is more clear than that the Dominion Company, whose central Board was organized in the latter end of July, put forth its Prospectus, announcing its policy of *low* rates, with the view to encourage a more general use of the Telegraph.

Turning to the *Trade Review*, I find several statements, admissions I might call them, to wh
to call the attention of our subscribers. S
No, 1: "We honestly believe in the encou
of anything that will tend to increase te
facilities, and think that a competition
existing company, who have a monopoly
facilities, would be desirable."

The question naturally suggests itself l
should not the Dominion Telegraph Compar
"*anything*" which it is so desirable to e
in order to break down the great monop
there anything in the composition of its
Management calculated to disqualify it f
forming that service to the public. What
Trade Review on this point. He enters
detail, and has evidently bestowed pains
himself master of the subject. The port
gives of the writer is more graphic than
A wornout politician—very needy. Th
clause "but respectable," enables him to
ter, and the *Review*-er pronounces his fiat
Directors, asa Board, are,, unimpeachab
then it is objected, "their utter ignoran
work in hand." Well, there is Mr. Alle
practical operator!—is he a sufficiently goo
to select the best materials for a good
Would he venture, on his own judgment, t
bundle of wire? Mr. Allan owns a fleet of
is he a practial engineer? And yet he is at
of two of the most successful companies on
tinent. What is the reason! He knows how
the right man for the right place—to appoi
commanders to his ships, competent office
several posts. Mr. Dwight is a very
energetic officer in his proper department
little too much zeal, perhaps. I again
Review:—"The scheme, so far, has met
"cess. A large amount of stock has be
"for, and the chances are that the new li
"built, and a good thing made by some o
the stockholders, we confidently believe. H
we have these very important facts admitt
who writes with no friendly pen. That t
monopoly which should be broken up. Th
Company in the interest of the public s
encouraged. That the Board of Directo
Dominion Company is irreproachable, and
of men of honor. That so far the scheme as
great success, with every probability of its
ried through. I shall not stop to enquire
Dwight has been at such pains to unde
success, and be-little the standing of his c
pany. What he has raked up the skelet
old Grand Trunk Telegraph Company, ar
its foul shroud about the shoulders of t
nion Company, to scare away intendin
bers. Or why the *Trade Review*, so anxi
something and *anything* to break up
monopoly, should be so suspicious of th
of the irreproachable Board. I shall n
with either Mr. Dwight or the *Trade R*
giving us the opportunity of having the
scheme thoroughly ventilated.

The winding up of the *Trade Review* ar
thoroughly marked with good sound s
one can readily overlook all else that is
irrelevant, or unfriendly. I reiterate hi
and address to the stockholders as well a
tors—"All we have to say in conclusion i
directors owe it to the public, and especi
shareholders, who are beguiled into the
on the faith of their respectability, to ex
than the ordinary vigilance; and if the
go on, to call to their aid men of reli
practical knowledge." Let the stockho
that while they have proved their confide
Board, they will expect from them an
charge of the duties they have assumed,
time a full account of their trust; and le
tors shew that they are keenly alive to
sibilities of their position. It is not i
of any man to command success; it is i
of every one to deserve it. Your obd't

W. CAYLEY,

No portion of the work has yet been
from the contractors, nor will be until it
gone a rigid inspection by thoroughly cor
ties. The aid of the local board will a
in, to see that this inspection is satisfa
in their respective districts. The Ins
also be required here and there, to take
the Montreal Company's line, as a test f
to pass nothing which does not, at le
to that standard of excellence.—W. C.

TORONTO, Nov. 16, 1868.
IR,—In reply to the accusations pub-
1e *Trade Review* of the 13th instant,
to say that the statements therein con
the Secretary, Mr. H. B. Reeve, is a rela-
loyee of Josiah T. Snow, IS UNTRUE.
Secretary has any interest in the Do-
graph Company, (except as a subscriber
d a moderate compensation for services),
RUE.
. Martin Ryan was employed by Josiah
work the oracle, or for any purpose, at
ALSO UNTRUE.
. Snow or his son ever signed any ap-
the Government to obtain the Charter
inion Telegraph Company IS ALSO UN-

r. Josiah T. Snow, or his son, are the
r in any way connected with the Do-
graph Company, or ever had at any time
authority to negotiate concerning the
established by the Company, is ALSO

a liberal use of stock, the necessary
rization was procured, (which means, I
at the stock has been given away,) IS
E. Not a single share has ever been
promised for services, or for any purer. Every subscriber is to pay $50 per
ding to the terms of the subscription.

"Very truly yours,
"H. B. REEVE."

Commercial.

ntreal Correspondence.

(From our own Correspondent).

Montreal, Nov. 24, 1868.

last, we have had some heavy snow
the sleighing is excellent, both in the
rrounding country.
DUCE trade has been quiet, and the
t present in a very uncertain state; the
still downwards. If it were possible
ly a reasonable prospect for a short crop
, there are plenty of speculators anxi-
rate, notwithstanding the many that
bitten at previous times; but when all
stances of the markets have been con-
is scarcely to be wondered at, that there
o little spirit in the operations in bread-
peculators have therefore acted with
nd considering the point, that markets
world have reached, I think, the pre-
e is not only a necessary action, but
hings into consideration, *the bottom has*
reached. I know that my ideas may
palatable to your Western readers, but
accept the situation, and my advice to
v, as it has been for a good many weeks
lurry forward your produce as fast as
ailst prices are high!" The fact is this,
rn farmers have too much relied upon
rices, instead of using their own good
thus making themselves the tools of spe-
the East, who have tried all sorts of *cor-*
ter up prices, and stave off the evil day.
rices of flour have rather stiffened
e large shipments to Quebec and to the
; though, owing to the present wintery
is doubtful if they will be able to get
ter quarters. I quote Fancy at $5.40
Strong Supers very weak, the stock
and the demand light—price $5.20 to
pers from western wheat, $5.10; ditto
ands, $5.05 to $5.10. No. 2, $4.65
ith but little demand; this quality is
aired for, for shipment to the lower
flour, which has a large country sale,
2.50 to $2.62½, according to quality.
ere is very little doing; the receipts
ing almost nil, and all sea-going ves-
left the port; the only requirements
local trade, or for shipment via Port-
e you our last quotations—Wheat, U.C.
Spring, nominal at $1.12½ to $1.14. Red Winter, $1.16. Peas, no sales; prices nominal. Corn mixed, 83c to 85c. Barley, several bright samples have recently been brought forward and have sold at extreme rates say $1.20 to $1.25. Oats are scarce and stiff at 52c to 53c per 32 lbs. *Provisions.*—Pork remains dull; the large importation of hogs from the country, and also from the west, induced by recent high prices, has for the time being broke down our market; barrelled pork, and both live and dressed hogs are very dull of sale, and I would advise the western men not to hurry forward their supplies as I have no doubt but that there will be a reaction in the beginning of the year. Butter rules very high and is likely to continue to do so. A large number of milch cows have been pressed on the market during the summer and fall, and the supply in the agricultural districts during the winter is consequently likely to fall short, so that all descriptions of dairy produce *must* rule high. To a large extent we have to look to the west for our supplies of both cheese and butter, and I therefore think that the making an excellent article would be of great benefit to the farmers. I know you have cheese factories, such as "*Morton's*," which compete successfully with the English cheese makers, and why should not butter do the same thing.

GROCERIES.—As predicted in my last, the late fall sales went off very dull. The only branch in which there is animation is the fish trade, several sales on the wharf having taken place, and very full prices have been paid. The stocks here and in the West are not large, and consequently prices must remain high. Your Western buyers have been nervous, and must now pay for it. I give you the imports of different leading articles from 1st Jan. to 1st Oct.:

	1867.	1868.
Fruit..........	2,469,492 lbs.	2,394,671 lbs.
Brandy.........	147,193 gals.	126,854 gals.
Gin............	174,947 "	168,192 "
Rum............	28,483 "	32,893 "
Molasses.......	3,120,513 "	6,372,694 "
Sugar..........	23,752,895 lbs.	25,601,296 lbs.
Teas...........	3,457,856 "	2,920,190 "

The market for teas and sugars recently has been very quiet; but, as far as I can learn, the markets in the West, and, to my knowledge, our local ones, are not overstocked, buyers having operated with great caution; so that we may safely look for a fair, steady winter trade.

DRY GOODS and HARDWARE are both very quiet, and now likely to rule so for some time to come, though both have an impetus given them when the winter roads have fairly set in.

The LEATHER TRADE here, as throughout the Province, has fallen considerably short of general expectancy. Prices have advanced, from the short supply of the raw material. I shall give you in my next a full list of prices, but to-day my space, is rather circumscribed.

The BOOT AND SHOE TRADE is one not only of great importance here, but also in Toronto. Here there has been no unusual rush, but business has been steadily and well maintained, the competition has been active, and manufacturers have had to cut down their prices to the lowest possible paying figure, chiefly from the fact that a large amount of inferior stocks had been held over from last spring, which had to be forced off before any new stock could be placed. All fine descriptions of goods were worked off rapidly, and sold at full prices. Prices now, for all sorts, are firm. Montreal must, for many reasons, I think, remain at the head of this branch of manufacture, and my reasons are the following: Our manufacturers possess a large capital, thus enabling them to not only buy up every improvement that can be brought forward in the manufacture of boots and shoes, but also enables them to give time to those who buy from them; a very important feature in every trade. Their assortments of goods are larger than smaller manufacturers can afford to keep, and therefore buyers can have a better selection in their purchases. The most modern improvements in style is carefully consulted and complied with regardless of cost, and last, though not least, they possess the advantage of cheaper labor, that being always more procurable at the centre of a manufacturing point than at the extreme ends. I do not make these remarks so much as a Montrealer as from a general knowledge as to how trade must flow.

The Cotton Crop.

Our reports with regard to the crop contain nothing new this week. Picking has progressed so favorably, that the generally received estimate of the total yield is, in this market, raised to about 2,700,000 bales, the figures we gave several weeks since. There is an evident inclination, at almost all points, to increase estimates though at some of the Atlantic ports, where the receipts will show a decrease, the merchants and planters are rather less sanguine. We hear of no killing frost as yet in any portion of the South.

Annexed is a statement showing the stocks of cotton in Liverpool and London, including the supplies of American and Indian produce ascertained to be afloat to those ports:

	1867.	1868.
Stock in Liverpool...Bales	571,800	426,810
" London...........	111,184	127,711
American cotton afloat....	25,000	35,000
Indian.......................	222,880	272,720
Total.......................	930,864	862,241

Halifax Market.

BREADSTUFFS.—Nov. 17.—Flour still continues to arrive freely from Canada and United States, the supply being equal to the demand. We have no change to note in prices from last week's quotations. Canada No. 1 ranges from $6.25 to 6.50; strong bakers $6.65 to 6.70; extra Canada $7.50 to 8; extra State still continues dull at $6 to 6.40, according to quallity. No. 2 in good demand at $5 to 5.50. Cornmeal without change at $4.50 for kiln dried, and $4.40 for fresh ground. Oatmeal $7.50 to 7.80. Imports from January 1st to November 17th, 1867 and 1868:

	Brls. Flour.	Brls. Cornmeal.
1868.	161,756	42,919
1867.	173,289	33,041

FISH.—Codfish is arriving slowly, and holders are firm at quotations. Fat Mackerel are in request and prices have advanced this week. Herrings quiet. We quote Codfish at $4.15 to 4.25 for good large shore; $3.20 to 3.30 for good small shore; Labrador $2.25 to 2.50. Bank and Bay none. Good hard cure Arichat Haddock $2 to 2.10; Eastern shore $1.80 to 1.90; Western $1.60 to 1.65; Pollock $1.40 to 1.50. Herring in demand at $4.50 for Labrador, and $4 for shore. Mackerel scarce at $13 to 13.50 for No. 1; $11 for No. 2, and $6.75 to 7 for No 3. Salmon $14.15 for No. 1; $12.13 for No. 2, and $9.50 to 10 for No. 3.

OILS.—Cod dull at 50c. No change in seal. Kerosene, 44c. for American.

PRODUCE.—Butter continues steady at 24c. for good dairy; 23c. for shipping. Lard without change. Oats, 55 to 60c. for P. E. I. prime mess. Canadian white nominal.

PROVISIONS.—Pork has been arriving from the Island, and sales made at auction yesterday at $22.25 for mess, and $17.75 for P. E. I. prime mess. Beef dull and unchanged.

WEST INDIA PRODUCE.—Sugars and Molasses remain without change. Porto Rico, 6¼ to 6⅜c.; Barbadoes, 5¾ to 5⅞c.; Cuba, 5½ to 5¾c.; Centrifugal Cuba, 6c. in bond. Rum scarce and in demand at 65 to 67½c for Demerara, and 57½ to 60c for St. Jago.

FINANCIAL.—Bank drawing rate on London 60 day sight bills 13 per cent. prem.; private 12 to 12½ per cent prem. New York Gold drafts at sight 3½ per cent. prem. Currency drafts 22 per cent. discount. Montreal sight drafts 3½ per cent. prem. Newfoundland sight drafts 5 per cent. prem.

Toronto Market.

GROCERIES.— *Sugars.*—Are firm ; prices of both raw and refined are again higher as quoted. *Teas.*—There has been a considerable movement of fine greens to the American market at full prices. *Fish.*—Are still scarce and firm.

BOOTS AND SHOES.—Trade is good, but not quite so lively as for the past two or three weeks. Retailers are meeting their engagements very fairly. Altogether the country dealers seem to be in a better position, and are likely to do a better trade the coming winter than for the past two years.

GRAIN—*Wheat*—Receipts 9,430 bush., and 15,000 bush. last week. Fall wheat has met with a good demand, and about 20,000 bush. changed hands at prices ranging from $1.18 to $1.24. There are now no stocks in market. Several cars of Spring sold at $1.07. to $1.49, and holders now ask $1.06 to 1.10, with buyers at $1.04 to $1.05. An exchange points out the fact that the crop of the Western States is being held back this year to a greater extent than ever before. The receipts at the five principal western lake ports from the 1st of January to the 14th Nov. this year were 29,000,000 bushels more than last year, and twelve millions larger than in 1866. The stock in store in Buffalo on the 23rd Nov. was 377,000 bush., on the 16th 371,000 bush., against 114,000 bush. in 1867, and 178,296 bush. in 1866. *Barley.*—Receipts by cars, 3,794 bush., nd 6,000 bush. for the previous week. Shipments for the week ended Saturday last, 31,966 bush., and 32,000 bush. the previous week. Total shipments by lake since the commencement of the season, 680,000 bush. There is a good demand and little offering, and the market is higher. There are buyers at $1.28 to 1.30 and few sellers. *Oats.*—Receipts by cars, 3,600 bush., and 6,100 bush. last week. A cargo of Chicago oats arrived during the week, per schooner *Jno. Weedon.* Car loads of Canadian are selling at 51 to 52c. *Peas.*—Receipts by cars, 900 bush., and 350 bush. last week. Market dull. Car loads offering at 85 to 88c.; no sales.

FLOUR.—Receipts 1,622 brls., and 1,500 brls. last week. There is some demand for superfine, and sales of two or three lots occurred at $4.75. A lot of extra sold at $5.40. Nothing doing in other grades.

PROVISIONS.—*Butter*—There is a good enquiry for round lots of butter at 23½ to 24c.; holders asking 25c.; no sales. Rolls sell at 23½ to 24c. *Dressed Hogs*—In fair supply and selling readily at quotations. *Lard*—Firm at quotations. Little doing in other provisions.

The Gore District Mutual Fire Insurance Company

GRANTS INSURANCES on all description of Property against Loss or Damage by FIRE. It is the only Mutual Fire Insurance Company which assesses its Policies yearly from their respective dates ; and the average yearly cost of insurance in it, for the past three and a half years, has been nearly

TWENTY CENTS IN THE DOLLAR

less than what it would have been in an ordinary Proprietary Company.

THOS. M. SIMONS,
Secretary & Treasurer.

ROBT. McLEAN,
Inspector of Agencies.

Galt, 25th Nov., 1868. 15-1y

The Waterloo County Mutual Fire Insurance Company.

HEAD OFFICE : WATERLOO, ONTARIO.

ESTABLISHED 1863.

THE business of the Company is divided into three separate and distinct branches, the

VILLAGE, FARM, AND MANUFACTURES.

Each Branch paying its own losses and its just proportion of the managing expenses of the Company.
C. M. TAYLOR, Sec.   M. SPRINGER, M.M.P., Pres.
J. HUGHS, Inspector. 15-yr

STATEMENT OF BANKS

ACTING UNDER CHARTER, FOR THE MONTH ENDING 31st OCTOBER, 1868, ACCORDING TO RETURNS FURNISHED BY THE BANKS TO THE AUDITOR OF PUBLIC ACCOUNTS.

NAME OF BANK	CAPITAL		LIABILITIES					ASSETS								
	Capital authorized by Act.	Capital paid up.	Promissory Notes in circulation not bearing Interest.	Balances due to other Banks.	Cash Deposits not bearing Interest.	Cash Deposits bearing Interest.	TOTAL LIABILITIES.	Coin, Bullion, and Provincial Notes.	Landed or other Property of the Bank.	Government Securities.	Promissory Notes, or Bills of other Banks.	Balances due from other Banks.	Notes and Bills Discounted.	Other Debts due the Bank, not included under foregoing heads.	TOTAL ASSETS.
ONTARIO AND QUEBEC.	$	$	$	$	$	$	$	$	$	$	$	$	$	$	$
Montreal	6,000,000	6,000,000	382,706	111,367 66	5,718,774 75	7,528,482 19	13,902,300 97	1,013,344 92	330,600 00	972,082 67	528,687 98	4,910,315 16	13,185,073 91	311,256 96	22,171,229 49
Quebec	3,000,000	1,474,350	679,696	56,387 88	609,824 82	785,565 34	2,740,178 18	236,020 57	41,470 62	85,425 14	44,155 19	84,195 75	1,241,724 15	144,434 53	3,201,679 29
City	1,200,000	1,200,000	435,485	5,665 98	607,261 84	730,169 07	1,790,880 44	119,600 71	67,977 50	186,969 99	110,730 45	99,873 32	2,293,831 41	157,924 25	3,163,271 82
Gore	1,000,000	800,000	298,286	5,065 98	72,699 03	418,423 70	834,180 16	82,733 93		12,967 93	34,538 30	34,538 30	693,682 32	193,462 44	1,894,710 48
British North America	4,866,666	4,866,666	1,186,982	171,288 37	571,530 69	325,051 54	6,076,241 49	197,096 92	34,199 81	193,338 00	125,666 40	470,086 69	5,039,008 24	47,881 81	1,480,446 80
Banque du Peuple	1,600,000	1,600,000	365,234	84,614 00	971,598 69	472,838 99	476,623 99	160,384 44	34,199 81	160,864 44	37,152 86	573,189 40	573,189 42	49,982 60	2,367,141 07
Niagara District	440,000	440,000	190,796	160,144 84	31,861 13	11,967 81	476,623 99	99,601 43		46,726 80	9,342 61	145,064 47	143,064 47	317,219 47	811,814 23
Molson's	1,000,000	1,000,000	108,749	18,788 53	226,548 03	654,489 67	1,059,568 28	232,394 61	42,530 08	107,263 63	82,533 57	71,820 29	1,144,985 82	318,408 47	2,107,319 38
Toronto	2,000,000	2,000,000	1,116,849	19,788 53	367,556 33	1,098,691 49	3,006,537 76	453,035 19		99,700 00	72,021 73	533,500 85	2,944,985 82	18,396 62	4,104,299 25
Ontario	2,000,000	2,000,000	859,485	98,638 44	1,163,373 03	1,062,543 70	3,096,977 76	943,312 18	154,242 16	906,902 93	195,564 18	369,875 75	4,259,875 75	135,781 87	6,067,108 52
Eastern Townships	2,000,000	900,000	559,264	7,379 09	238,243 03	866,883 92	585,611 55	341,512 16	174,862 66	191,061 07	18,284 69	148,582 87	1,134,582 87	4,430 00	1,698,275 65
Banque Nationale	1,000,000	1,000,000	129,782	34,080 31	232,989 04	585,485 56	585,611 55	147,079 49	23,218 90	120,039 00	75,790 43	169,815 63	1,198,582 87	90,082 82	2,111,879 73
Banque Jacques Cartier	1,000,000	994,310	113,116	1,782 15	965,885 56	668,482 97	988,556 94	157,150 61		191,130 67	49,150 66	64,150 67	2,111,879 67		6,826,679 64
Merchants'	4,000,000	3,331,577	1,395,276	8,589 64	1,678,895 18	1,678,897 81	4,538,194 15	1,004,674 95		129,996 61	142,017 09	731,723 09	3,114,979 18		4,734,644 64
Royal Canadian	2,000,000	1,110,468	1,773,923	38,559 40	725,979 45	830,786 29	3,386,961 15	123,643 74		129,431 76	156,651 55	158,985 55	1,271,300 23		6,918,539 33
Union B'k Low. Canada	2,000,000	988,488	99,099	178,929 60	411,865 69	239,138 02	953,489 14	129,743 74		120,393 49	117,954 59	117,954 59	962,572 53	70,435 36	522,084 29
Mechanics'	1,000,000	275,193	1,150,466	80,784 33	116,001 27	18,381 67	343,501 57	243,464 18	34,386 10						
Bank of Commerce	1,000,000	972,593			654,947 34	940,784 04	2,542,401 76	986,561 42	40,319 31	120,396 66	83,637 19	190,040 68	2,883,365 30	11,534 43	3,906,053 79
NOVA SCOTIA															
Bank of Yarmouth															
Merchants' Bank															
People's Bank	1,000,000	400,000	134,560	45,614 59	139,928 83	345,991 00	667,104 42	125,845 30	21,000,00	53,000,00	9,433 60	13,183 16	116,734 64	136,735 63	1,114,051 73
Union Bank															
Bank of Nova Scotia															
NEW BRUNSWICK.															
Bank of New Brunswick	600,000	600,000	432,313	110,948 48	512,005 01	706,885 89	1,853,401 88	191,658 95	15,414 45	53,000,00	82,463 00	488,853 65	1,889,173 80	64,946 76	2,726,434 74
Commercial Bank											4 994 00	43,557 41	61,973 81	344,333 37		992,710 55

Bank of Toronto.

DIVIDEND No. 25.

ICE is hereby given that a dividend of FOUR per ... for the current half year, being at the rate of ... per cent. per annum upon the paid-up capital of ... ank, has this day been declared, and that the same ... payable at the Bank or its branches, on and after

RDAY, THE SECOND DAY OF JANUARY NEXT

transfer books will be closed from the sixteenth to ... day of December next, both days inclusive.

order of the Board.

G. HAGUE,

Cashier.

...to, Nov. 26, 1868.   15-td

Royal Canadian Bank.

DIVIDEND No. 7.

ICE is hereby given that a Dividend of Four per nt. upon the paid-up Capital of this Bank for the ... year, has this day been declared, and that the ... be payable at the Bank, or its agencies, on and SATURDAY, the SECOND DAY OF JANUARY. The Transfer Books will be closed from the 16th 31st December, both days inclusive.

order of the Board.

T. WOODSIDE, Cashier.

al Canadian Bank, Nov. 25, 1868.   15-td

The Canadian Bank of Commerce.

DIVIDEND No. 3.

ICE is hereby given, that a Dividend at the rate of)UR per cent. on the paid up Capital Stock of this tion has been declared for the current half year, at the same will be payable at its Banking House in ly, and at its branches, on and after sturday, the Second day of January next.

Transfer Books will be closed from the 15th to the ecember, both days inclusive.

order of the Board.

R. J. DALLAS,

Cashier.

nte, Nov. 23.   15-td

Ontario Bank.

DIVIDEND No. 23.

CE is hereby given, that a Dividend of Four per t. upon the Capital Stock of this Institution for rent half year, has this day been declared, and that se will be payable at the Bank and its Branches, after

esday, the First day of December next.

'ransfer Books will be closed from the 15th to the vember, both days inclusive.

der of the Board.

D. FISHER, Cashier.

Bank,

anville, 24th Oct., 1868.   11-td

mentary and d Exchange

10-ly

eneral Agent, g.   17-ly

J. R. Boyce,

53 and 65, Great James Street, Montreal, Dealer Importer of all kinds of TOYS and FANCY GOODS. is the only manufacturer of La Crosse Sticks for Indian Game of LACROSSE, and has constantly on large supply, with the printed Rules of the Game. manufactures all the requisites for Croquet, and r Parlour and Lawn Games. Baskets, of all kinds. ry variety of Hair Work, Wigs, Curls, Beards, &c.; nd Theatrical Wigs, for sale, Wholesale and Retail engaged in forming new La Crosse Clubs, will do apply direct to the above address.

DAY'S

Commercial College and High School,

No. 82 KING STREET EAST,

(Near St. James' Cathedral.)

THE design of this institution is to prepare Young Men and others as Book-keepers, and for general business, and to furnish them with the facilities for acquiring an excellent

English and Commercial Education.

Mr. DAY is also prepared to give Private Instruction in the several subjects of his department, and to assist Merchants and others in the checking and balancing of books, adjusting their accounts and partnership affairs, &c.

For further information, please call on or address the undersigned.

JAMES E. DAY,

Accountant

Toronto, Sept. 3rd, 1868.

John Ross & Co.,

QUEBEC.

T. & F. Ross & Co.,

GENERAL WHOLESALE GROCERS,

PRODUCE AND COMMISSION MERCHANTS,

361 Commissioner Street,

MONTREAL.   6

W. McLaren & Co.,

WHOLESALE

BOOT AND SHOE MANUFACTURERS,

18 ST. MAURICE STREET,

MONTREAL

June, 1868.   42-1y

Lyman & McNab,

Importers of, and Wholesale Dealers in,

HEAVY AND SHELF HARDWARE,

KING STREET,

TORONTO, ONTARIO.

THE QUEEN'S HOTEL.

THOMAS DICK, Proprietor.

FRONT STREET,   -   -   -   TORONTO, ONT

3-1y

Montreal House, Montreal, Canada.

TO MONETARY MEN.—Merchants, Insurance Agents, Lawyers, Bankers, Railway and Steamboat Travellers, Mining Agents, Directors and Stockholders of Public Companies, and other persons visiting Montreal for business or pleasure, are here by most respectfully informed that the undersigned proposes to furnish the best hotel accommodation at the most reasonable charges. It is our study to provide every comfort and accommodation to all our guests, especially for gentlemen engaged as above. To those who have been accustomed to patronize other first-class hotels, we only ask a trial; we have the same accommodation and our table is furnished with every delicacy of the season.

H. DUCLOS.

Nov. 22, 1867.   15-1y

The Albion Hotel,

MONTREAL,

ONE of the oldest established houses in the City is again under the personal management of

Mr. DECKER,

Who, to accommodate his rapidly increasing business, is adding Eighty more Rooms to the house, making the ALBION one of the Largest Establishments in Canada.

June, 1868.   42-6ms

DOMINION TELEGRAPH COMPANY.

CAPITAL STOCK   -   -   - $500,000.

In 10,000 Shares at $50 Each.

PRESIDENT,

HON. WILLIAM CAYLEY.

TREASURER,

HON. J. McMURRICH.

SECRETARY,

H. B. REEVE.

SOLICITORS,

MESSRS. CAMERON & McMICHAEL.

GENERAL SUPERINTENDENT.

MARTIN RYAN.

DIRECTORS.

HON. J. McMURRICH,

Bryce, McMurrich & Co., Toronto.

A. R. McMASTER, Esq.,

A. R. McMaster & Brother, Toronto.

HON. M. C. CAMERON,

Provincial Secretary, Toronto.

JAMES MICHIE, Esq.,

Fulton, Michie & Co., and George Michie & Co., Toronto.

HON. WILLIAM CAYLEY,

Toronto.

A. M. SMITH, Esq.,

A. M. Smith & Co., Toronto.

L. MOFFATT, Esq.,

Moffatt, Murray & Co., Toronto.

H. B. REEVE, Esq.,

Toronto.

MARTIN RYAN, Esq.,

Toronto.

PROSPECTUS.

THE DOMINION TELEGRAPH COMPANY has been organized under the act respecting Telegraph Companies, chapter 67, of the consolidated Statutes of Canada. Its object is to cover the Dominion of Canada with a complete net-work of Telegraph lines.

The Capital Stock

Is $500,000, divided into 10,000 shares of $50 each, 5 per cent to be paid at the time of subscribing, the balance to be paid by instalments, not exceeding 10 per cent per month—said instalments to be called in by the Directors as the works progress. The liability of a subscriber is limited to the amount of his subscription.

The Business Affairs of the Company.

Are under the management of a Board of Directors, annually elected by the Shareholders, in conformity with the Charter and By-Laws of the Company.

The Directors are of opinion that it would be to the interest of the Stockholders generally to obtain subscriptions from all quarters of Canada, and with this view they propose to divide the Stock amongst the different towns and cities throughout the Dominion, in allotments suited to the population and business occupations of the different localities, and the interest which they may be supposed to take in such an enterprise.

Contracts of Connections.

A contract, granting permanent connection and extraordinary advantages, has already been executed between this Company and the Atlantic and Pacific Company, of New York ; thus, at the very commencement, as the Lines of this Company are constructed from the Suspension Bridge, at Clifton (the point of connection) to any point in the Dominion, all the chief cities and places in the States, touched by the Lines of the Atlantic and Pacific Telegraph Company, are brought into immediate connection therewith.

A permanent connection has also been secured with the Great Western Telegraph Company, of Chicago, whereby this Company will be brought into close connection with all the Lake Ports and other places through the Northwestern States, and through to California.

4-3mos

The Standard Life Assurance Company,

Established 1825.

WITH WHICH IS NOW UNITED

THE COLONIAL LIFE ASSURANCE COMPANY.

Head Office for Canada:

MONTREAL—STANDARD COMPANY'S BUILDINGS,

No. 47 GREAT ST. JAMES STREET.

Manager—W. M. RAMSAY.   *Inspector*—RICH'D BULL.

THIS Company having deposited the sum of ONE HUN-DRED AND FIFTY THOUSAND DOLLARS with the Receiver-General, in conformity with the Insurance Act passed last Session, Assurances will continue to be carried out at moderate rates and on all the different systems in practice.

AGENT FOR TORONTO—HENRY PELLATT,
King Street.

AGENT FOR HAMILTON—JAMES BANCROFT.

6-6mos.

Fire and Marine Assurance.

THE BRITISH AMERICA

ASSURANCE COMPANY.

HEAD OFFICE:

CORNER OF CHURCH AND COURT STREETS.

.TORONTO.

BOARD OF DIRECTION:

Hon G. W. Allan, M L C.,	A. Joseph, Esq ,
George J. Boyd, Esq ,	Peter Paterson, Esq.,
Hon. W. Cayley,	G. P. Ridout, Esq.,
Richard S. Cassels, Esq.,	E H. Rutherford, Esq ,

Thomas C. Street, Esq.

Governor:

GEORGE PERCIVAL RIDOUT, ESQ.

Deputy Governor:

PETER PATERSON, ESQ.

Fire Inspector: Marine Inspector:

E. RODY O'BRIEN.   CAPT. R. COURNEEN.

Insurances granted on all descriptions of property against loss and damage by fire and the perils of inland navigation.

Agencies established in the principal cities, towns, and ports of shipment throughout the Province.

THOS. WM. BIRCHALL,
Managing Director.

23-1y

Edinburgh Life Assurance Company.

Founded 1829.

HEAD OFFICE—22 GEORGE STREET, EDINBURGH.

Capital, ... £500,000 Ster'g.

Accumulated and Invested Funds, £1,000,000 "

HEAD OFFICE IN CANADA:

WELLINGTON STREET, TORONTO.

SUB-AGENTS THROUGHOUT THE PROVINCE.

J. HILLYARD CAMERON,
Chairman, Canadian Board.

DAVID HIGGINS,
Secretary, Canadian Board.   3-2m

Queen Fire and Life Insurance Company,

OF LIVERPOOL AND LONDON,

ACCEPTS ALL ORDINARY FIRE RISKS

on the most favorable terms.

LIFE RISKS

Will be taken on terms that will compare favorably with other Companies.

CAPITAL,-   -   -   £2,000,000 Stg.

CHIEF OFFICES—Queen's Buildings, Liverpool, and Gracechurch Street London.

CANADA BRANCH OFFICE—Exchange Buildings, Montreal. Resident Secretary and General Agent,

A. MACKENZIE FORBES,

13 St. Sacrament St., Merchants' Exchange, Montreal.

WM. ROWLAND, Agent, Toronto.   1-1y

Reliance Mutual Life Assurance Society.

(Established, 1840,) OF LONDON, E. C.

Accumulated Funds, over $1,000,000.

Annual Income, $300,000.

THE entire Profits of this long-established Society belong to the Policy-holders.

HEAD OFFICE FOR DOMINION—MONTREAL.

T. W. GRIFFITH, *Manager Sec'y.*

15-1y   WM. HENDERSON, *Agent for Toronto.*

Etna Insurance Company of Dublin.

The number of Shareholders exceeds Five Hundred.

Capital, $5,000,000—Annual Income nearly $1,000,000.

THIS Company takes Fire and Marine Risks on the most favorable terms.

T. W. GRIFFITH, *Manager for Canada.*

Chief office for Dominion— Corner St. Francois Xavier and St. Sacrament Sts., Montreal.

15-1y   WM. HENDERSON, *Agent for Toronto*

Scottish Provincial Assurance Co.

Established 1825.

CAPITAL ....£1,000,000 STERLING

INVESTED IN CANADA (1854) ....$500,000.

Canada Head Office, Montreal.

LIFE DEPARTMENT.

CANADA BOARD OF DIRECTORS:

HUGH TAYLOR, Esq., Advocate,

Hon. CHARLES WILSON, M. L. C.

WM. SACHE, Esq., Banker,

JACKSON RAE, Esq., Banker.

WM. FRASER, Esq. M. D., Medical Adviser.

The special advantages to be derived from Insuring in this office are :—Strictly Moderate Rates of Premium; Large Bonus (intermediate bonus guaranteed ;) Liberal Surrender Value, under policies relinquished by assured ; and Extensive Limits of Residence and Travel. All business disposed of in Canada, without reference to parent office.

A DAVIDSON PARKER,
Resident Secretary

G. L. MADDISON,

15-1yr   AGENT FOR TORONTO.

Lancashire Insurance Company.]

CAPITAL,-   -   -   -   £2,000,000 Sterling

FIRE · RISKS

Taken at reasonable rates of premium, and

ALL LOSSES SETTLED PROMPTLY,

By the undersigned, without reference elsewhere.

S. C. DUNCAN-CLARK & CO.,

General Agents for Ontario,

N. W. Corner of King & Church Streets,

25-1y   TORONTO.

Etna Fire & Marine Insurance Company.

INCORPORATED 1819.   CHARTER PERPETUAL.

CASH CAPITAL,   -   -   -   - $3,000,000

LOSSES PAID IN 50 YEARS, 23,500,000 00.

JULY, 1868.

ASSETS.

(At Market Value.)

Cash in hand and in Bank....................	$544,842 39
Real Estate................................	253,267 29
Mortgage Bonds.............................	932,245,00
Bank Stock.................................	1,272,670 00
United States, State and City Stock,and other Public Securities ··········	3,049,855 61
Total..................	$6,052,880 19

LIABILITIES.

Claims not Due and Unadjusted	$499,808 55
Amount required by Mass. and New York for Re-Insurance.......................	1,405,267 15

THOS. R. WOOD,

50-6   Agent for Toronto.

TORONTO PRICES CURRENT.—November 26, 1868.

Name of Article.	Wholesale Rates.		Name of Article.	Wholesale Rate.		Name of Article.	Wholesale Rates.	
Boots and Shoes.	$ c.	$ c.	**Girls'**—*Contin'd*	$ c.	$ c.	**Leather**—*Contin'd.*	$ c.	$ c.
Mens' Thick Boots ...	2 05	2 80	" fine to fins't .	0 85	0 95	Kip Skins, Patna	0 30	0 40
" Kip	2 50	3 25	Hyson	0 45	0 80	French	0 70	0 90
" Calf	3 20	3 70	Imperial	0 42	0 80	English	0 65	0 80
" Congress Gaiters..	2 00	3 40	Tobacco, *Manufac'd;*			Hemlock Calf (30 to		
" Kip Cobourgs ...	1 10	1 50	Can Leaf, ℔ 5s & 10s..			35 lbs.) per doz...	0 75	0 85
Boys' Thick Boots....	1 70	1 90	Western Leaf, com..	0 20	0 30	Do. light	0 45	0 60
Youths' "	1 45	1 50	" Good ..	0 25	0 26	French Calf.	0 98	1 15
Women's Batts	.95	1 30	" Fine ..	0 27	0 32	Grain & Satn Clf ℔ doz.	0 00	0 00
" Congress Gaiters..	1 15	1 50	" Bright fine..	0 32	0 35	Splits, large ℔ ℔....	0 30	0 38
Misses' Batts.	0 75	1 00	" small ..	0 40	0 50	" small	0 30	0 30
" Congress Gaiters	1 00	1 30	" choice..	0 60	0 75	Enamelled Cow ℔ foot..	0 17	0 18
Girls' Batts	0 60	0 85	**Hardware.**			Patent	0 18	0 20
" Congress Gaiters	0 80	1 10	*Tin (net cash prices)*			Pebble Grain	0 17	0 18½
Children's C. T. Cacks..	0 50	0 55	Block, ℔ ℔.	0 25	0 26	Buff	0 17	0 18
" Gaiters ...	0 05	0 90	Grain	0 25	0 26	**Oils.**		
Drugs.			*Copper:*			Cod	0 60	0 62½
Aloes Caps.	0 12½	0 16	Pig	0 23	0 24	Lard, extra	0 00	1 25
Alum	0 02½	0 03	Sheet	0 30	0 32	" No. 1	0 00	1 15
Borax	0 09	0 09	*Cut Nails:*			" Woollen	0 00	1 05
Camphor, refined....	0 55	0 70	Assorted ¾ Shingles,			Lubricating, patent...	0 00	0 00
Castor Oil..........	0 18	0 28	℔ 100 lb...........	2 00	3 00	" Mott's economic	0 80	0 90
Caustic Soda........	0 04½	0 05	Shingle alone do	2 15	3 25	Linseed, raw.........	0 77½	0 85
Cochineal...........	0 90	1 10	Laths and 5 dy......	3 30	3 40	" boiled........	0 82½	0 90
Cream Tartar	0 00	0 00	*Galvanised Iron:*			Machinery	0 00	0 00
Epsom Salts	0 02	0 04	Assorted sizes.......	0 08	0 09	Olive, 2nd, ℔ gal. ...	1 43	1 60
Extract Logwood....	0 09	0 11	Best No. 24.........	0 09	0 00	" salad	2 00	2 30
Gum Arabic, sorts...	0 30	0 35	" 26..........	0 08	0 08½	" salad, in bots.		
Indigo, Madras......	1 75	1 00	" 28..........	0 09	0 09½	qt. ℔ case...	3 00	3 75
Licorice	0 14	0 45	*Horse Nails:*			Sesame salad, ℔ gal.	1 00	1 75
Madder.............	0 13	0 15	Gnest's or Griffin's			Seal, pale..........	0 70	0 75
Nutgalls	0 20	0 28	assorted sizes.......	0 00	0 00	Spirits Turpentine...	0 00	0 00
Opium	6 70	7 00	For W. ass'd sizes...	0 18	0 19	Varnish	0 00	0 00
Oxalic Acid	0 28	0 35	Patent Hammer'd do..	0 17	0 18	Whale.............	0 75	0 80
Potash, Bi-tart.....	0 25	0 28	*Iron (at 4 months):*					
" Bichromate..	0 15	0 20	Pig—Gartsherrie No1..	24 00	25 00	**Paints, &c.**		
Potass Iodide	0 80	0 85	Other brands. No1..	22 00	24 00	White Lead, genuine		
Senna	0 12½	0 60	" No.2..	0 00	0 00	in Oil, ℔ 25lbs...	0 00	2 50
Soda Ash	0 03	0 04	Bar—Scotch, ℔ 100 ℔..	2 35	2 50	Do. No. 1 " ..	0 00	2 35
Soda Bicarb	0 08	0 11	Refined	3 00	3 25	" 2 " ..	0 00	2 00
Tartaric Acid.......	0 40	0 50	Swedes	5 00	5 50	" 3 " ..	0 00	1 75
Verdigris	0 37½	0 45	Hoops—Coopers....	3 00	3 25	White Zinc, genuine.	3 00	3 50
Vitriol, Blue........	0 35	0 40	" Band	3 00	3 25	Do. No. 1, best....	0 00	3 00
	0 09	0 10	Boiler Plates.......	3 25	3 50	Red Lead..........	0 07½	0 08
Groceries.			Canada Plates......	0 00	4 25	Venetian Red, Eng'h..	0 02½	0 08½
Coffees:			Union Jack	0 00	0 00	Yellow Ochre, Fren'h..	0 02½	0 03½
Java, ℔ lb..........	0 22½	0 24	Pontypool..........	4 00	4 25	Whiting	0 90	1 25
Laguayra;	0 17	0 18	Swansea	3 90	4 00			
Rio.................	0 15	0 17	*Lead (at 4 months):*			**Petroleum.**		
Fish:			Bar, ℔ 100 lbs......	0 07	0 07½	(Refined ℔ gal.)		
" Herrings, Lab. split..	5 75	7 00	Sheet "	0 08	0 09	Water white, car'l'd..	0 31	—
" round ..	0 00	0 00	Shot "	0 07	0 07½	" small lots...	0 00	0 32
" scaled...	0 35	0 40	*Iron Wire (net cash):*			Straw, by car load...	0 30	—
" Mackerel,smallkits..	1 00	0 00	No. 6, ℔ bundle......	2 70	2 80	" small lots...	0 31	0 33
" Loch. Her. wh'e fples.	3 50	3 75	" 9, "	3 20	3 30	Amber, by car load...	0 00	0 00
" half " ..	1 25	1 50	" 12, "	3 40	3 50	" small lots ..	0 00	0 00
" White Fish & Trout..	3 50	3 75	" 16, "	4 20	4 40	Benzine	0 00	0 00
Salmon, saltwater....	14 00	15 00	*Powder:*					
Dry Cod, ℔ 112 lbs..	5 00	5 25	Blasting, Canada....	3 50	3 75	**Produce.**		
Fruit:			FF "	4 25	4 50	*Grain;*		
" Raisins, Layers	2 15	2 20	FFF "	4 75	5 00	Wheat, spring, 60 lb..	1 05	1 08
" M. R........	2 10	2 15	Blasting, English ...	4 00	5 00	" Fall .. ℔	1 15	1 24
" Valentians new..	0 08½	0 08½	FFF loose.	5 00	6 00	Barley......... 48 "	1 20	1 25
Currants, now	0 05	0 05½	FFF "	0 00	0 60	Peas......... 60 "	0 84	0 85
" old...	0 04½	0 04½	*Pressed Sptes (4 mos):*			Oats......... 34 "	0 50	0 51
Figs	0 10	0 11	Regular sizes 100....	4 00	4 25	Rye.......... 50 "	0 00	0 00
Molasses:			Extra	4 50	5 00	*Seeds:*		
Clayed, ℔ gal.......	0 00	0 40	*Tin Plates (net cash):*			Clover, choice 60 "	6 25	6 50
Syrups, Standard ...	0 00	0 50	IC Coke	7 50	8 00	" scm'n 68 "	6 00	6 25
" Golden ..	0 54	0 55	IC Charcoal.........	8 25	8 75	Timothy, cho'e 4 "	2 50	2 75
Rice:			IX "	10 25	10 75	" Int. to good 48 "	2 00	2 50
Arracan	4 50	4 75	IXX "	12 00	0 00	Flax......... 56 "	1 40	1 60
Spices:			DC "	7 50	9 00	*Flour* (per brl.):		
Cassia, whole, ℔ ℔..	0 42	0 45	DX "	9 80	10 00	Superior extra.......	0 00	0 00
Cloves	0 11	0 12				Extra superfine......	5 60	5 85
Nutmegs	0 45	0 55	**Hides & Skins, ℔ lb**			Fancy superfine	0 00	0 00
Ginger, ground	0 20	0 25	Green rough	0 00	0 00½	Superfine No. 1	4 70	4 80
" Jamaica, root..	0 20	0 25	Groom, salt'd & inap'd..	0 00	0 00	" No. 2.....	0 00	0 00
Pepper, black........	0 09	0 10	Cured	0 00	0 08½	*Oatmeal,* (per brl.)...	6 00	6 25
Pimento	0 08	0 09	Calfskins, green......	0 00	0 10			
Sugars:			" cured......	0 00	0 08	**Provisions.**		
Port Rico, ℔ lb.......	0 08½	0 08	" dry.........	0 13	0 30	Butter, dairy tub ℔ lb..	0 23	0 24
" Cuba	0 08½	0 08½	Sheepskins, ...	0 90	0 00	" store packed..	0 21	0 22
Barbadoes (bright)..	0 08½	0 08½	" country....	0 90	0 00	Cheese, new	0 11	0 12
Dry Crushed, at 60 d..	0 11½	0 11½				Pork, mess, per brl...	22½ 25	00
Canada Sugar Refine'y,			**Hops.**			" prime mess...	0 00	0 00
yellow No. 2, 60 ds..	0 08½	0 00	Inferior, ℔ ℔........	0 05	0 07	" puine	0 00	0 00
Yellow, No. 2½.......	0 06½	0 00½	Medium	0 07	0 00	Bacon, rough	0 00	0 00
No. 3......	0 08½	0 00	Good	0 00	0 12	" Cumberl'd cut...	0 10	0 11
Crushed X	0 10	0 10½	Fancy	0 00	0 00	" smoked	0 00	0 00
A	0 11	0 11½				Hams, in salt........	0 00	0 00
Ground.............	0 11	0 11½	**Leather,** @ (4 mos.)			" sug. cur. &canv'd..	0 00	0 00
Extra Ground	0 12½	0 12½	In lots of less than			Shoulders, in salt ...	0 00	0 00
Teas:			higher.			Lard, in kegs........	0 00	0 14
Japan com'n to good..	0 40	0 55	Spanish Sole, 1st qual..			Eggs, packed........	0 00	0 00
" Fine to choicest..	0 55	0 55	heavy, weights ℔ ℔..	0 21	0 22	Beef Hams	0 00	0 00
Colored, com. to fine..	0 60	0 75	Do,1st qual middle do..	0 22	0 23	Tallow	0 00	0 00
Congou & Souch'ng...	0 48	0 75	Do. No. 2, all weights..	0 20	0 21	Hogs dressed, heavy.	7 00	7 25
Oolong, good to fine ..	0 52	0 55	Slaughter heavy	0 25	0 26	" medium ...	6 50	6 50
Y. Hyson, com to gd..	0 45	0 55	Do, light............	0 00	0 00	" light.....	6 00	6 50
Medium to choice	0 65	0 80	Harness, best	0 30	0 34			
Extra choice	0 85	0 95	" No. 2	0 30	0 33	**Salt, &c.**		
Gunpowd're. to med..	0 55	0 70	Upper heavy	0 44	0 38	American bris.......	1 58	1 60
" mod. to fine	0 70	0 85	" light.....	0 36	0 40	Liverpool coarse	1 25	1 35
						Plaster	1 15	1 10
						Water Lime	1 50	0 00

Soap & Candles.

	$ c.	$ c.
D. Crawford & Co.'s ..		
Imperial.........	0 07½	0 08
" Golden Bar	0 07	0 07½
" Silver Bar........	0 07	0 07½
Crown	0 05	0 05½
No. 1	0 03½	0 03¾
Candles	0 00	0 11½
Wines, Liquors, &c.		
Ale:		
English, per doz......	2 60	2 65
Guinness Dub Portr..	2 35	2 40
Spirits:		
Pure Jamaica Rum...	1 80	2 25
De Kuyper's H. Gin..	1 55	1 65
Booth's Old Tom.....	1 90	2 00
Gin:		
Green, cases.........	4 00	4 25
Booth's Old Tom, c...	6 00	6 25
Wines:		
Port, common	1 00	1 25
" fine old	2 00	4 00
Sherry, common	1 00	1 50
" medium........	1 70	1 80
"old pale or golden..	2 50	4 00

	$ c.	$ c.
Brandy:		
Hennessy's, per gal..	2 30	2 50
Martell's " ..	2 30	2 50
J. Robin & Co.'s " ..	2 25	2 35
Otard, Dupuy & Cos..	2 25	2 35
Brandy, cases........	8 50	9 00
Brandy, com. per c...	4 00	4 50
Whiskey:		
Common 36 u. p......	0 62½	0 65
Old Rye	0 85	0 87½
Malt........	0 85	0 87½
Toddy	0 85	0 87½
Scotch, per gal........	1 90	2 10
Irish—Kinnahan's c...	7 00	7 50
" Dunnville's Belf't..	6 00	6 25
Wool.		
Fleece, lb............	0 23	0 35
Pulled "............	0 22	0 25
Furs.		
Bear..................	3 00	10 00
Beaver................	1 00	1 25
Coon	0 20	0 40
Fisher................	4 00	6 00
Martin................	1 40	1 60
Mink..................	4 00	4 25
Otter.................	5 75	6 00
Spring Rats	0 15	0 17
Fox.	1 20	1 25

INSURANCE COMPANIES.

ENGLISH.—*Quotations on the London Market.*

No. of Shares.	Last Dividend.	Name of Company.	Shares par val £	Amount paid.	Last Sale.
20,000		Briton Medical and General Life ...	10	....	1½
50,000	7½	Commer'l Union, Fire, Life and Mar.	50	5	5½
24,000	8	City of Glasgow	25	2½	5
5,000	9½	Edinburgh Life	100	15	30½x
400,000	5—½ yr	European Life and Guarantee......	2½	11s6	4s 6d
100,000	10	Etna Fire and Marine	10	1½	1
20,000	5	Guardian	100	50	51½
24,000	12	Imperial Fire........................	500	50	345
7,500	9½	Imperial Life	100	10	16½
100,000	10	Lancashire Fire and Life..........	20	2	2¾x
10,000	11	Life Association of Scotland.......	40	7½	23
35,862	45s. p. sh	London Assurance Corporation ..	25	12½	48
10,000	5	London and Lancashire Life	10	1	1
87,504	40	Liverp'l & London & Globe F. & L.	20	2	7¾
20,000	5	National Union Life	5	1	1
20,000	12½	Northern Fire and Life	100	5	10¾
40,000	12 '68, bo 5s.	North British and Mercantile	50	6¼	16 16½
40,000	50	Ocean Marine	25	5	20
2,500	£5 12s.	Provident Life........................	100	10	38
....	£4½ p. s.	Phœnix................................	....	....	136
200,000	2½—h. yr.	Queen Fire and Life	10	1	15-16ths
100,000	3s. bo. 4s	Royal Insurance.....................	20	3	6¾
20,000	10	Scottish Provincial Fire and Life ..	50	2½	4½
10,000	25	Standard Life	50	12	65
4,000	5	Star Life	25	1¼	—
		CANADIAN.			℘ c.
8,000	4	British America Fire and Marine ..	$50	$25	56
....	4	Canada Life	...	....	.....
4000	12	Montreal Assurance	£50	£5	135
10,000	3	Provincial Fire and Marine........	60	11	.....
....	....	Quebec Fire	40	32½	x 20
....	8	" Marine.........................	100	40	95
10,000	5 7 mo's.	Western Assurance.................	40	6	.....

RAILWAYS.	Sha's	Paid	Montr	London.
Atlantic and St. Lawrence........................	£100	All.	....	58 00
Buffalo and Lake Huron	20½	"	....	3 3½
Do. do Preference	10	"	....	5½ 6½
Buff., Brantt. & Goderich, 6℘c., 1872-3-4....	100	"	....	....
Champlain and St. Lawrence	....	....	9 11	....
Do. do Pref. 10 ℘ ct....	....	....	71½75	....
Grand Trunk	100	"	15 17	16 17
Do. Eq. G. M. Bds. 1 ch. 6℘c............	100	"	....	83 86
Do. First Preference, 5 ℘ c	100	"	....	52 53
Do. Deferred, 3 ℘ ct..	100	"	....	....
Do. Second Pref. Bonds, 5℘c..........	100	"	....	41 43
Do. do Deferred, 3 ℘ ct..........	100	"	....	....
Do. Third Pref. Stock, 4℘ct..........	100	"	...	28 30
Do. do. Deferred, 3 ℘ ct......	100	"	...	....
Do. Fourth Pref. Stock, 3℘c..........	100	"	....	18½ 19½
Do. do. Deferred, 3 ℘ ct...........	100	"	....	....
Great Western	20½	"	13 15	14¼ 14½
Do. New	20½	18	....	....
Do. 6 ℘ c. Bds, due 1873-76............	100	All.	....	102 104
5½ ℘c Bds. due 1877-78....	100	"	....	93 94
Marine Railway, Halifax, $250, all......	$250	"	....	....
Northern, of Canada, 6℘c. 1st Pref. Bds..........	100	"	.. .	80 83

EXCHANGE.	Halifax.	Montr'l.	Quebec.	Toronto.
Bank on London, 60 days......				
Sight or 75 days date	13½	9¼ 9½	9¾ 9¾	9¾
Private do.	12 12½	8 9	8¾ 9	9
Private, with documents....	....	....	....	....
Bank on New York..................	....	24½ 25	24½ 25	74¾
Private do.	....	25 25½	25 25½	....
Gold Drafts do.	....	par	par ¼ dis.	par ¼ dis.
Silver	....	3 3½	....	3½ 5

STOCK AND BOND REPORT.

The dates of our quotations are as follows:—Toronto, Nov. 24; Montreal, Nov. 23; Quebe Nov. 23; London, Oct. 30.

NAME.	Shares.	Paid up.	Divid'd last 6 Months	Dividend Day.	CLOSING PRICE Toronto.	Montre'l	Qu
BANKS.			℘ ct.				
British North America	$250	All.	3	July and Jan.	103½ 104½	104 105	103
Jacques Cartier..........	50	"	4	1 June, 1 Dec.	105½ 107	105 107	Bk
Montreal	200	"	5	"	137 140	136 140	Bk
Nationale.....................	50	"	4	1 Nov. 1 May.	....	...	105
New Brunswick	100	"	......	......	....	...	.
Nova Scotia	200	28	7&b$3½	Mar. and Sept.	....	....	.
Du Peuple...	50	"	4	1 Mar., 1 Sept.	105½ 107	106 106½	105
Toronto	100	"	4	1 Jan., 1 July.	119 119½	118 119	118
Bank of Yarmouth..........	....	....	......	......	....	....	.
Canadian Bank of Com'e.....	50	95	......	......	104½ 105½	104½ 105½	104
City Bank Montreal	80	All.	4	1 June, 1 Dec.	102 103	100 102	Bk
Commer'l Bank (St. John)....	100	"	℘ ct.	.....	....	...	.
Eastern Townships' Bank....	50	"	4	1 July, 1 Jan..	....	97½ 98½	96
Gore	40	...	3½	1 Jan., 1 July.	42 43	40 43½	41
Halifax Banking Company....	...	....	......	.....	....	....	.
Mechanics' Bank..............	50	70	4	1 Nov., 1 May.	94½ 96	95 96	9
Merchants' Bank of Canada....	100	70	4	1 Jan., 1 July.	111 112	111½ 112½	111
Merchants' Bank (Halifax)....	....	....	.....	.....	....	....	.
Molson's Bank......	50	All.	4	1 Apr., 1 Oct.	107½ 109	108 109	107
Niagara District Bank...	100	70	3½	1 Jan., 1 July.	....	....	.
Ontario Bank................	40	All.	4	1 June, 1 Dec.	99½ 100	97¾ 100	Bk
People's Bank (Fred'kton)....	100	"	......	......	....	....	.
People's Bank (Halifax)	20	"	7 12 m	......	....	...	.
Quebec Bank	100	"	3½	1 June, 1 Dec.	97½ 100	....	.
Royal Canadian Bank	50	50	4	1 Jan., 1 July.	91 91½	90 92	90
St. Stephens Bank	100	All	.....	......	....	...	
Union Bank	100	70	4	1 Jan., 1 July.	103½ 104	103½ 104	104
Union Bank (Halifax).........	100	40	7 12 mo	Feb. and Aug.	....	....	.
MISCELLANEOUS.							
British America Land........	250	44	2½	......	....	....	.
British Colonial S. S. Co......	250	32½	2½	......	...	....	.
Canada Company	32½	All.	5	......	....	....	.
Canada Landed Credit Co.....	50	$20	3½	......	72 73	....	.
Canada Per. B'ldg Society....	50	All.	5	......	124 124½	....	.
Canada Mining Company.....	4	90	......	......	....	....	.
Do. Inl'd Steam Nav. Co.....	100	All.	20 12 m	......	....	105 108	106
Do. Glass Company.........	100	"	12½ "	......	....	40 70	.
Canad'n Loan & Investm't....	25	2½	7	......	....	....	.
Canada Agency	10	¼	......	......	....	....	.
Colonial Securities Co........	....	....	.....	.....	....	....	.
Freehold Building Society....	100	All.	4	......	103¾ 104½	....	.
Halifax Steamboat Co.........	100	"	5	......	....	....	.
Halifax Gas Company.........	....	....	......	.....	....	...	.
Hamilton Gas Company.......	....	....	.....	.....	....	....	.
Huron Copper Bay Co........	4	12	20	.....	....	25 40c ps	.
Lake Huron S. and C.........	5	102	......	......	....	....	.
Montreal Mining Consols......	20	$15	......	......	....	225 275	
Do. Telegraph Co...	40	All.	5	......	130 132	133 136	131
Do. Elevating Co...	00	"	15 12 m	......	....	101 103	.
Do. City Gas Co.........	40	"	4	15 Mar. 15 Sep.	....	132½ 135	133
Do. City Pass. R.. Co.....	50	"	5	......	....	110 110½	100
Nova Scotia Telegraph	20	"	....	.....	....	....	.
Quebec and L. S.	8	$4	......	......	....	....	2
Quebec Gas Co...............	200	All.	4	1 Mar., 1 Sep.	....	...	119
Quebec Street R. R..........	50	25	8	......	....	....	90
Richelieu Navigation Co......	100	All.	7 p.a.	1 Jan., 1 July.	....	115 120	11
St. Lawrence Tow Boat Co....	100	"	......	3 Feb.	....	...	4
Tor'to Consumers' Gas Co.....	50	"	2 3 m.	1 My Au Mar Fe	105½ 105½	...	10
Trust & Loan Co. of U. C.....	20	5	3	......	....	....	
West'n Canada Bldg Soc'y....	50	All.	5	......	115 115½	....	

SECURITIES.	London.	Montreal.	Quebec.	Tor
Canadian Gov't Deb. 6 ℘ ct. stg..................	....	101 102	101 101½	10
Do. do. 6 do due Ja. & Jul. 1877-84.........	107 108	....	....	.
Do. do. 6 do. Feb. & Aug.........	104 106	....	...	.
Do. do. 6 do. Mch. & Sep..........	104 106	....	...	
Do. do. 5 ℘ ct. cur., 1883	93 94	91 92	90 91	9
Do. do. 5 do. stg., 1885	....	91 92	90½ 91½	91
Do. do. 7 do. cur.,........................	....	....	......	
Dominion 6 p. c. 1878 cy..........................	....	103 105	103½ 104	10
Hamilton Corporation..............................	....	....	......	
Montreal Harbor, 8 ℘ ct. d. 1869..................	..	....	......	
Do. do. 7 do. 1870......................	....	....	......	10
Do. do. 6½ do. 1875......................	....	101 101½	......	
Do. do. 6½ do. 1873......................	....	....	......	
Do. Corporation, 6 ℘ c. 1891	....	93 96	94 95	9
Do. 7 p. c. stock................................	....	105½ 107	105½ 106½	10
Do. Water Works, 6 ℘ c. stg. 1878...........	....	....	......	9
Do. do. 6 do. cy. do.	....	94 96	......	9
New Brunswick, 6 ℘ ct., Jan. and July	103 105	....	......	
Nova Scotia, 6 ℘ ct., 1875.........................	103½ 104½	....	......	
Ottawa City 6 ℘ c. d. 1880	....	....	......	
Quebec Harbour, 6 ℘ c. d. 1883....................	....	....	60	
Do. do. 7 do. do..........................	....	....	65 70	
Do. do. 8 do. 1886..........................	...	....	75 85	
Do. City, 7 ℘ c. d. 5 years	....	90 91½	94 95	
Do. do. 7 do. 9 do.	....	....	90	
Do. do. 7 do. 2½ do.	....	....	97 98	
Do. Water Works, 7 ℘ ct., 4 years	....	....	96 98	
Do. do. 6 do. 2 do.	....	....	93½ 94	
Toronto Corporation	....	90	....	

PROSPECTUS

OF THE

)MINION EXPRESS COMPANY OF CANADA

ORGANIZED UNDER THE JOINT STOCK COMPANIES' ACTS.

CAPITAL STOCK, $1,000,000,

In $10,000 Shares, $100 each.

proposed to organize a DOMINION EXPRESS COMPANY, to meet the present and prospective demand for increased facilities of general trans- rtation. It is the interest of Canadians to do their own work, and *accumulate* cash capital, and *one* of the objects of this scheme is the retention country of the profits arising from the business done.

xpress Companies obtain "four-fifths" of their business from merchants and bankers, and no reason exists why they cannot transport their own by their *own Agents, economically* and *efficiently,* and by a *union of capital* and *effort,* they hereby resolve so to do. Being thus united, and ng to it their business and influence, secures to this Company certain and complete success.

his organization, like the mail system, is to extend, under *one general management,* to all cities, towns and villages in the Dominion, and to connect parts of the United States, and being but "one Company," will secure *unity, despatch* and *accuracy.*

is proposed to distribute the stock widely, throughout the Dominion, in limited sums, apportioned as nearly as practicable to the business of the ibers. The capital Stock of the Company to be not less than $1,000,000, in 10,000 shares of $100 each.

'en *per cent.* of the stock subscribed will be required to be paid after the subscription shall have reached the sum of $250,000, and after a Charter have been obtained, of which due notice will be given to the subscribers ; the subsequent calls, not exceeding *ten per cent. at any one time,* to be t convenient intervals, as the demands on the Company may require. But the aggregate of all calls to be made will, it is believed, not exceed *per cent.* of the Capital Stock.

he business to be done strictly on *cash principles.* With a paying business assured from the start, by *interested* and *reliable* Stockholders, it will e seen that a small per centage *only* of the subscriptions will be required to put the Company in working order, and it is confidently and reasonably d that the receipts will thereafter maintain and extend it. And in order to secure an equitable voice in its management, the principal commercial s will be represented at the Board, by Directors recommended by Stockholders of their own localities, who will also recommend to the Direction al Agents, and thus secure a general influence in its management, as well as its business.

ll Express enterprises, both in this country and the United States, have been decidedly successful, resulting from the profits of the business itself; ‹ving an organization and a share list—such as are now proposed—with energy and economy in the direction, no doubt can be entertained of the atisfactory results.

'ith such prospects, the Merchants of the Dominion, Capitalists and others interested in the success of this enterprise, are invited to become. olders.

The following shall be included in the By-Laws to be hereafter framed for the Government of the Company :

The Company shall be known by the name or title of "THE DOMINION EXPRESS COMPANY OF CANADA."

The Capital Stock of the Company shall be *One Million of Dollars,* divided into *Ten Thousand Shares of One Hundred Dollars each.*

Each Shareholder shall be liable only for the amount of Stock subscribed by him, her, or them.

The Shares of Stock of the Company shall be transferable; but no transfer shall be valid without the consent of the Directors, in writing, unless ares shall be paid up in full.

It shall be lawful for the Stockholders, so soon as the sum of two hundred and fifty thousand dollars shall have been subscribed, to call a General g of the subscribers, to be held at the office of the Company, in the City of Montreal, and proceed to elect nine qualified persons to be Directors Company, each of whom to be a proprietor of not less than ten Shares of Stock of the said Company, and three of whom shall form a quorum, 1 the powers of the Directors. The said Directors shall also, at their first General Meeting, elect a President, Secretary, Treasurer, and General tendent or Managing Director, from amongst themselves.

The said Directors so elected shall proceed, without delay, to frame all necessary By-laws to govern the Company, and shall have power to alter- end the same as circumstances may require.

The Directors shall not have power either to *sell out* the said Company to any other Express Company or organization now in existence, or here- o be incorporated, or to amalgamate with any other Express Company.

No Stockholder shall be at liberty to hold in his, her, or their name, more than one hundred shares of the Capital Stock of the said Company, t the consent of the Directors, in writing, first having been obtained.

PROVISIONAL DIRECTORS.

MESSRS. IRA GOULD, WALTER MACFARLAN, VICTOR HUDON,	MESSRS. WM. McNAUGHTON, DUNCAN MACDONALD, JOSEPH BARSALOU,	MESSRS. ALEXANDER McGIBBON, GEORGE HEUBACH, J. T. KERBY.

OFFICERS.

PRESIDENT :	VICE-PRESIDENT :	TREASURER :	SECRETARY :
ALTER MACFARLAN.	WM. McNAUGHTON.	JOSEPH BARSALOU.	GEORGE HEUBACH.

MESSRS. CARTIER, POMINVILLE, & BETOURNAY, SOLICITORS.   J. T. KERBY, GENERAL AGENT.

ollowing are among the prominent firms in Montreal who have subscribed to the original Stock List at the formation of the Company:—

Ira Gould, President Corn Exchange.
Walter McFarlan, (Messrs. Walter McFarlan & Baird).
James Donelly, Wholesale Dry Goods.
Luke Moore, (Messrs. Moore, Lemple & Hat-chette).
Duncan Macdonald.
A. Shannon & Co., Wholesale Grocers.
Lewis, Kay & Co., Wholesale Dry Goods.
George Brush, Eagle Foundry.

Messrs. W.McNaughton, Messrs. Sincennes & McNaughton.
" A. W. Ogilvie & Co., Glenora Mills.
" Denning & Barsalou, Auctioneers.
" Alex. McGibbon, China House.
" T. Baillie & Co., Wholesale Dry Goods.
" Alex. Walker, Wholesale Dry Goods.
" Geo. Winks & Co., Wholesale Dry Goods, Albert Buildings.
" W. P. Ryan, M.P.
" Victor Hudon & Co., Wholesale Grocer.

Messrs. Boyer, Hudon, & Co.
" Z. Benoit, Wholesale Merchant.
" Evans & Evans, Wholesale Hardware.
" James Smith, M.P.
" Andrew Watson.
" A. Freeman & Co.
" John Rhá nan.
" Cartier, Pominville & Betournay, Solicitors.
" Cassels & Cameron, Wholesale Dry Goods.
" Ferrier & Co., Wholesale Hardware.

TWENTY-THIRD ANNUAL REPORT

OF THE

NEW YORK LIFE INSURANCE COMPAN

Accumulated Capital, over $10,000,000. - - **Divisible Surplus, Jan. 1, 1868, $1,642,425 5**

Annual Statement, January 1st, 1868.

AMOUNT OF NET CASH ASSETS, January 1st, 1867		$6,727,816 65
AMOUNT OF PREMIUMS RECEIVED DURING 1867	$3,104,051 34	
AMOUNT OF INTEREST RECEIVED AND ACCRUED, INCLUDING PREMIUMS ON GOLD, &c.	487,339 94	
		3,591,391 28
		$10,319,207 93

DISBURSEMENTS.

Paid Losses by Death	$561,921 45	
Paid for Redemption of Dividends, Annuities, and surrendered and cancelled Policies	485,851 36	
Paid Salaries, Printing, Office and Law Expenses	98,032 55	
Paid Commissions and Agency Expenses	333,207 43	
Paid Advertising and Physician's Fees	46,518 77	
Paid Taxes and Internal Revenue Stamps	19,291 26	
		1,544,861 92
		$8,774,326 01

ASSETS.

Cash on hand, in Bank, and in Trust Company	$575,236 54	
Invested in United States Stocks, (Market value, $3,150,506 87) cost	2,978,907 49	
Invested in New York City Bank Stocks (Market value, $45,855), cost	41,549 00	
Invested in New York State Stocks (Market value, $836,050), cost	806,306 00	
Invested in other Stocks (Market value, $151,225), cost	149,337 01	
Loans on Demand, secured by U. S. and other Stocks, (Market value, $311,497)	257,700 00	
Real Estate (Market value, $709,125 66)	528,234 53	
Bonds and Mortgages (Secured by Real Estate, valued at $2,260,000)	1,072,800 00	
Premium Notes on existing Policies, bearing interest	1,556,637 47	
Quarterly and semi-annual Premiums due subsequent to January 1, 1868	340,285 81	
Interest accrued to January 1, 1868	52,402 83	
Rents accrued to January 1, 1868	2,401 96	
Premiums on Policies in hands of Agents and in course of transmission	406,326 77	
		$8,774,326 01
And excess of market value of securities over cost		385,427 90
Cash Assets, Jan. 1, 1868		$9,159,753 91

LIABILITIES OF THE COMPANY.

Amount of Adjusted Losses, due subsequent to Jan. 1, 1868	$134,800 00	
Amount of Reported Losses awaiting proof, &c.	38,214 32	
Amount reserved for Re-insurance on existing Policies (valuations, Carlisle table four per cent. interest, net premium)	6,283,635 49	
Return Premium, declared prior to 1866, payable on demand	72,572 51	
Return Premium, 1866 (now to be paid)	422,638 00	
Return Premium, 1867 (present value)	565,468 00	
		$7,517,328 32
Divisible Surplus		$1,642,425 59

During the Year, 6,597 Policies have been issued, insuring $22,541,940.

The Progress of the Company for the Past Four Years will be seen in the following Statement:—

	Assets.	Increase of Assets over previous year.				Increase of Assets previous year.
1864	$3,658,755 55	$1,005,217 63		1866	6,727,816 65	1,845,896 95
1865	4,881,919 70	1,223,164 15		1867	8,774,326 01	2,046,509 36
		Total increase	$6,120,788 69.			

One of the special features of this Company is the TEN YEAR NON-FORFEITURE PLAN.

The system popularly termed "The Non-Forfeiture Plan," was originated and first presented to the public by this Company, in their well "TEN YEAR NON-FORFEITURE POLICY," in the year 1860; and its perfect adaptation to the wants of every class in the community, ob every reasonable objection to Life Insurance, is shown from the fact that every other American Company has been compelled, in deference to opinion, to adopt it, although in many cases it is done in such a way as considerably to impair its value. It has received the *unqualified approva best business men of the land*, large numbers of whom have taken out policies under it, simply as an investment.

By the Table on which this class of Policies is based, a person incurs no risk in taking out a policy. Insuring to-day for $10,000, if he should die to-morrow, the immediately becomes a claim ; and if he shall live ten years, and make ten annual payments, his policy will be paid for, and his dividends *still continue*, making

HIS LIFE POLICY A SOURCE OF INCOME TO HIM WHILE LIVING.

By the specific terms of these policies, and not by vague and indefinite statements made in circulars, a party after the second year does not forfeit what he has paid in p Thus, if one insuring by this plan for $10,000 discontinues after the second year, he is entitled to a PAID-UP POLICY, according to the number of full years paid in, as foll

Second year, two-tenths of $10,000 (amount insured), amounting to.. $2,000 | Fourth year, four-tenths of $10,000 (amount insured), amounting to.. $4,000
Third year, three-tenths of $10,000 (amount insured), amounting to.. 3,000 | Fifth year, five-tenths of $10,000 (amount insured), amounting to.... 5,000

And so on, until the tenth annual payment, *when all is paid*. The paid up policies, for the proportionate partial payments, as well as for the full amount, participa Dividends of the Company during the whole existence of the policies. ☞ This being a purely mutual Company, ALL ITS PROFITS ARE DIVIDED AMONG THE AE

MORRIS FRANKLIN, PRESIDENT.
WILLIAM H. BEERS, VICE-PRES'T & ACTUARY.

Medical Examiners :
HENRY H. WRIGHT, ESQ., M.D.,
JOHN E. KENNEDY, ESQ., M.D.,

EDWYN EVANS,

Agent for Toronto, 15 Wellington Street

ptsmaspk
THE CANADIAN
ONETARY TIMES
AND
INSURANCE CHRONICLE.
ED TO FINANCE, COMMERCE, INSURANCE, BANKS, RAILWAYS, NAVIGATION, MINES, INVESTMENT,
PUBLIC COMPANIES, AND JOINT STOCK ENTERPRISE.

| NO. 16. | TORONTO, THURSDAY, DECEMBER 3, 1868. | { SUBSCRIPTION. $3 YEAR. |

Mercantile.

Mining.

PLUMBAGO.

Among the the most refractory substances in nature is the mineral plumbago, which is called black lead, graphite, and carburet of iron. Its name, plumbago, is derived from the Latin "plumbum ago," meaning, "I act like lead ;" the name carburet of iron is more appropriate, as the mineral consists of ninety odd per cent. of carbon, and a fair per cent. of iron. The Brazilian plumbago, however, is pure carbon. It is quite soft, has a specific gravity of 2.09, a metallic lustre, a shining streak, and an iron-black to steel-gray color. It is opaque, soils paper, and feels greasy. When of laminated structure, its laminæ are flexible ; but it also occurs massive and granular. Its regular crystal form is a rhombohedron, but hexagonal tabular crystals are also found. It burns at a high temperature, without flame or smoke ; is insurable before the blow-pipe, and not affected by acids. Its geological position is in the primary rocks or altered rocks lying at the base of the palæozoic series. It is mostly disseminated in calcareous or argillaceous shales. Extensive formations of plumbago occur in the Laurentian series of rocks in the north-eastern part of the State of New York, near the head of Lake Champlain, at Ticonderoga, Lake George, and in the range across the lake in Canada West ; in the metamorphic region of Massachusetts, at Sturbridge. In the gneiss of North Carolina there is an extensive formation ; large blocks have been quarried from this locality a few weeks ago. England boasts of the first known and best locality, at Borrowdale, in Cumberland, discovered in the year 1564 during the reign of Queen Elizabeth. It is found there in a greenstone rock, in nests and beds of clay. From the date of this discovery, a new epoch in the industrial operations of domestic economy was opened ; and its importance was manifested by the mandate of the English Government prohibiting the exportation of graphite. In Bavaria, Germany, and Bolivia large deposits have been worked. Ceylon has furnished immense quantities of the best laminated graphite. In addition to those above mentioned, the United States furnishes many localities, among which we may mention Morristown, N. J., Concord, N. H., Brandon, Vt., Amity and Hillsboro, N. Y. An extensive deposit has been lately discovered near Saco, Me. California has exported a thousand tons of superior graphite. Greenland, Spain, Mexico, Norway and Siberia have of late years supplied the world with excellent material. Canada has furnished beautiful specimens of laminated graphite from Burgess and Grenville, and much of it has been disposed of in this market. Other localities could be mentioned where plumbago has, from time to time been obtained in greater or less abundance. New York, Ceylon, Siberia and Bavaria are, however, the main sources of supply.

The principal uses made of plumbago in the arts are as follows:

The lead pencil, made from the best quality of graphite, has contributed more to the spread of the arts and sciences in modern times than any other article that can be mentioned among the contrivances in daily use. The black lead crucible is of immense benefit to the brass-founder, assayer and steel manufacturer. Graphite is valuable as a lubricator, to prevent friction in machinery, the journals of engines, etc. To impart lustre to iron, especially stoves. In the process of electrotyping or depositing metals by galvanism, this material is useful to coat the wax of the moulds, and render it a conductor of the electric current. In the manufacture of green glass wine bottles, called hock bottles. In the manufacture of gunpowder, for glazing the grains. For "facing " in iron foundries. For lubricating the action in piano-fortes.

The discovery of the Borrowdale mine, in Cumberland, dispelled all other contrivances for writing, and the manufacture of lead pencils became quite universal. The mineral, as it came from the mine, was sawed into thin slabs and these again into long strips of the requisite size, which were, without further preparation, glued into the wood. These pencils are not surpassed in delicacy or smoothness, and to this day are made in the same manner as they were three hundred years ago. The black lead mine at Borrowdale had a yearly revenue of £40,000 sterling, from the monthly public sales. The mine was only allowed to be open six weeks in a year, that the market might not be overstocked. This great mine is now exhausted, and nothing but impure refuse is obtained from that celebrated locality. English manufacturers and men of science, have been searching for new supplies, but the discoveries in Spain, Ceylon, Greenland, California, France, Italy, Canada and the Atlantic States, made from time to time, have not yet produced a complete substitute for the Borrowdale mineral. Long before the final exhaustion of that mine, processes were invented for cleaning and refining the impure refuse which had been cast away, and improving coarser and less valuable minerals by its use.

In this way, although the Borrowdale lead could not be had in its palmy days, for less than $10, gold, per pound, many manufacturers could obtain fair materials for 10 cents per pound.

It is, however, a remarkable fact that the Borrowdale graphite owed its fine quality rather to its peculiar style of aggregation than to its purity, as it was ascertained to contain more foreign matter than Ceylon and Canadian graphites. The attempts to refine and clear the impure graphite were carried on by the English mechanics, Baudie and Brockedon, who contrived methods of overcoming the difficulties of the case. Brockedon was long occupied in render the powdered graphite coherent by submitting it to enormous pressure. It operated in vacuo, and the difficulty of introducing apparatus under the receiver of an air-pump was avoided by an arrangement of simple character. The powdered graphite was compacted by moderate pressure, and enclosed in very thin paper, which was glued over the whole surface, except a small hole for the air to escape from within. The block thus prepared was placed under an exhausting receiver, the air removed, and the orifice closed with a small piece of paper ; and in this state it was left for twenty-four hours. It was then submitted to a regulated pressure once more ; the different particles become agglomerated, and a black graphite was produced as solid as the natural mineral.

In 1795 an important discovery was made in France, which proved a great success, and has become the basis of the present manufacture of pencils. It was the admixture of fine clay with the purified graphite ; it not only restored to the graphite the necessary consistency, without material ly diminishing the writing qualities, but also any degree of hardness or softness, a result that could not be obtained from the pure Borrowdale. The German black lead has been used for a century past in the manufacture of crucibles and for small furnaces for assayers and chemists, while the finest varieties of graphite for pencils have been furnished from Cumberland and Siberia. The Ceylon and German, as likewise the Ticonderoga graphite furnish the sole material for crucibles. All other localities yield materials for lustres, lubricators and other purposes. Argillaceous matters are not prejudicial to the manufacture of crucibles ; but the presence of carbonate of lime is very objectionable, since the lime forms a fusible compound at the great heat to which the crucibles are exposed, and the object is defeated.

The German Bavarian crucibles, which stood in high estimation for centuries past, are composed of very impure materials, not half of their constituents containing black lead ; while the American crucible, first introduced in the United States by that pioneer, JOSEPH DIXON, contains nearly three parts of black lead and one part clay. He began manufacturing the black lead crucibles in 1837, and drove the triangular pots out of this market. This firm consumes at the present day more plumbago than any other one concern in the world. Their crucibles are now introduced all over the civilized world, where the precious metals, steel, or alloys, as brass, German silver, are made or melted. They consume 40 tons of it per week; they procure their supplies principally from Ceylon and Ticonderoga, in New York. The consumption of crucibles for pyro-chemical operations is very considerable; I saw last year, in Pittsburgh, in one establishment, 200 large black lead crucibles, in the furnaces at the same time; considering the number of ten or twelve crucible manufactories in the United States, the amount of plumbago consumed in the country cannot be less than 10,000 tons per annum. This quantity of graphite is not used up for the manufacture of crucibles alone, a very large amount is wanted for the lustre, so-called British or Mexican lustre, which forms a very considerable branch of industry ; there are no less than fifty manufacturers of lustre in the United States, of which DIXON & Co, put up 150 gross, or 20,000 packages of the lustre per day. Large establishments exist in Philadelphia, Boston, Cleveland, and in New York, so that we may compute the amount manufactured in the U. S. at 1,000 gross per day.

In conclusion, a few remarks on the great American locality of graphite situated at Ticonderoga, may give an idea of the extent to which this branch of industry is now carried on. The mining property of the American Graphite Company is comprised in the Arthur and Joes Mountains, at Ticonderoga, on Lake Champlain, and at Warrensburgh, on Lake George ; the latter contains veins of the granular or compact graphite, which, after having been purified, furnishes excellent pencil lead, while the Ticonderoga mines have only the foliated graphite containing disseminated carbonate of lime, which requires to be concentrated by proper machinery. This is done in the most practical manner, so that from five to ten tons per day are forwarded ready for crucible-makers. Not less than 150 veins or deposits have already been discovered ; some of them have been worked to the depth of several hundred feet ; parallel veins are constantly discovered at a distance of 12 feet.—*American Journal of Mining.*

— Mr. E. A. C. Pew has purchased 1,400 acres of Peat land, in the County of Welland, for a joint stock Company about being organized. It is to be called the Ontario Peat Company. It is stated that Peat can be manufactured and put on the bank of the Welland Canal for $1 per ton.

THE NEW MINING ACT.

We give below the most important clauses of the new Act relating to mining, now before the Legislature of Ontario.

3. All Royalties, Taxes or Duties which by any patent or patents heretofore issued, are reserved, imposed or made payable upon, or in respect of any ores or minerals extracted from the lands granted by such patents, and lying within this Province, are hereby repealed and abandoned, and such lands, ores, and minerals shall henceforth be free and exempt from every such Royalty, Tax or Duty.

4. All reservations of gold and silver mines contained in any patent or patents heretofore issued, granting in fee simple any land or lands situate within this Province, are hereby rescinded and made void, and all such mines in or upon any such lands shall henceforth be deemed to have been granted in fee simple as part of such lands, to the subsequent and present proprietors or owners thereof in fee simple.

5. No reservation or exception of gold, silver, iron, copper, or other mines or minerals, shall hereafter be inserted in any patent from the crown granting any lands in the Province known as mining lands.

6. Any person or persons may explore for mines or minerals in any unsold Crown lands, surveyed or unsurveyed, not in the actual use or occupation of the Crown or of any public Department, and not under lease or license from the Crown or the Commissioner of Crown Lands, and not for the time being marked or staked out and occupied as hereinafter mentioned.

7. Crown Lands supposed to contain mines or minerals may be sold as mining lands, or may, when situate within any mining division, be occupied and worked as "Mining Claims," under miners' licenses, as hereinafter provided.

8. Such lands, so sold when situate in unsurveyed territory, or in townships surveyed in sections, shall be sold in blocks to be called "Mining Locations."

9. Mining Locations under this Act shall conform to the following requirements:

1st. In the unsurveyed lands in the Territory to the north or north-west of the River Mattawa, Lake Nipissing and the French River (and which includes the territory bordering with Lakes Superior and Huron, and the River St. Mary), every regular Mining Location shall be rectangular in shape, eighty chains in length by forty in width, containing three hundred and twenty acres, and the bearings of the outlines of each location shall be due north and south, and due east and west astronomically, the length to be run north and south.

2nd. When a Mining Location in the unsurveyed lands in the territory aforesaid borders upon a lake or river, an allowance of one chain in width shall be reserved along the margin of such lake or river, and the width of the location shall front on said road.

3rd. In the Townships in said territory surveyed, or hereafter to be surveyed in sections, every Mining Location, after such survey, shall consist of half of a section, divided by a line run north and south, except when the section borders on a lake or river, when the section shall be divided north and south, or east and west, whichever will give the narrowest frontage on such lake or river.

4th. In all patents for such Mining Locations in the territory aforesaid, there shall be a reservation for roads of five per cent. of the quantity of land professed to be granted.

5th. In the unsurveyed lands not situate within the limits of the territory aforesaid, Mining Locations shall be, as may be defined by any Order in Council hereafter to be made.

10. Mining Locations in unsurveyed territory shall be surveyed by a Provincial Land Surveyor, and be connected with some known point in previous surveys (so that the tract may be laid down

on the office maps of the territory in the Lands Department), at the cost of the applicant who shall be required to furnish with the application the surveyor's plan, field notes and tions thereof, showing a survey in accordance this Act, and to the satisfaction of the Commissioner of Crown Lands.

Section 12 provides that patents shall contain a reservation of pine trees ; ... mining divisions may be declared by in Council ; 14, that an Inspector is appointed for each division, with power to settle disputes as to claims, &c., subject to 16, that the Inspector shall issue licenses ; 17, that a miner's license in force one year, have only one name therein, and not be transferable, may be renewed ; 19, that the licensee have the right to stake out and work mining claim.

20. Each mining claim shall be of the following dimensions, viz :

For any one person, two hundred feet vein or lode, by one hundred feet at either end thereof, measuring from the centre of the lode.

Companies of two or more persons, who hold a miner's license, may take out an additional feet along a vein or lode by the width in the proportion of one hundred additional feet in length to every additional miner ; but not exceed one thousand feet in length altogether work the claim jointly.

21. Mining claims shall be laid out possible, uniformly, and in quadrilateral or angular shapes ; measurements of all claims shall be horizontal ; and the grounds included in every such claim shall be deemed bounded under the surface by lines vertical to the horizon.

22. A mining claim shall be deemed forfeited and abandoned, and to be open to location by any licensee, or subject to any disposition by the Crown, when the same shall have been unworked for the space of two weeks, unless by the Inspector for the division be satisfied of the justness or other reasonable cause to the satisfaction of the Inspector for the division be satisfied cause the licensee has neglected or failed to comply with the requirements of this Act, and allegations to be made under it, or has not renewed his license.

23. No person shall occupy at the same time more than one mining claim on Crown Lands, except in the cases hereinafter provided for registration of claims rendered temporarily workable.

25. The discoverer of any new mineral entitled to two mining claims of the kind described by this Act, or by any regulations may be based under it and in force discovery may be made ; provided the discovery shall have been immediately reported to the Inspector of the division ; and at immediately reporting such a discovery he allowed to mine on any Crown Lands one year.

26. No person shall be considered the discoverer of a new quartz mine, unless the alleged discovery shall be distant, if at vein or lode, at least three miles from any known mine on the same vein or lode, or one mile at right angles from the centre of the nearest known vein or lode.

30. Any person occupying a mining Crown Lands, which, in consequence occupies water or other unavoidable reasons as the Inspector for the division, cannot worked, may, upon payment of one certain fee for his right to such claim in the office of the inspector for the division, in a book to be kept for that purpose, and may then proceed where; but in case such person do so occupy the claim so registered, within after the surrounding claim or claim

orkable, he shall forfeit all right and aim; provided that every person so :laim shall be held to plant a wooden : in the centre thereof as possible, hall be cut or painted, in legible gistration number of said claim. eutenant-Governor in Council may, ;ims, make all and every such regu- ulations as he may deem necessary for the appointment of Arbitrators ards to hear and determine appeals ions of Inspectors of Divisions, and ibing, defining and establishing the i, and mode of procedure of such Mining Boards; for the construction ince of roads through the Mining l generally for the purpose of carry- ;ct; and such regulations, after pub- ie *Ontario Gazette*, shall have the it of law.

Insurance.

.D.—Askin's tavern in the township ut nine miles west of Owen Sound, by fire on the 27th ult. A child, in and a man were burned to death, rs, including the father and mother etor, were so severely injured that pes are entertained of their recovery. .n, Nov. 24.—Akins' hotel situated s from this place, took fire at two morning and was destroyed. Two rned to death, and the proprietor s were so badly injured that they ed to recover.

ec. 1.—About one o'clock this morn- ke out in Messrs. W. & J. Work- use, and the staßles of A. T. Argo, Messrs. Workman's hardware store, rican and Canadian Express office. l iron house were entirely destroyed, ir or more the brick block, from the vestward, was in imminent danger, rtions of the firemen and citizens evented from spreading.

ov.—A fire was discovered in the . Disbrow, Wellington Row. It ippressed before much damage was

c. 2.—A serious fire occurred at i particulars not yet received. Some further particulars of the place have come to hand. Three d by J. Hearvey of Ottawa were in- 0 :—" A part of the large mill was vi C. Northup, as a grist mill ; n ind Northrop, cloth manufacturers; t by W. Tennaut & Co., also in the . Northrop's stock in the grist d for $1,000, which will not cover loss of the firm of Bragg & North- ery heavy, they being insured for id having lost all their machinery, tion of one loom. W. Tennaut & ieir machinery, upon which their nnce, their estimated loss being machinery owned by Gilbert North- ugle mill, was all safely removed. furniture would received some ig so hastily taken out, but upon insurance. The fire is supposed to . from the stovepipes in the second

ORD.—Quebec, Dec. 1.—An upper m Kingston to this port, with i of wheat for Ross & Whithall, lay, when tide ebbed she grounded side, drew from cross beams and oing, into which the return tide ng the whole of her cargo. The it $6,000. No insurance. atch announces the loss of the ship hich sailed from Quebec for Liver-

pool on the 26th October, with a cargo of timber and phosphate of lime. Her owners, Irving & Webster, had the ship fully insured by shippers D. D. Young & Co., in the Quebec Marine Insur- ance Company.

OWEN SOUND, Nov. 29.—The steamer Francis Smith went on shore near Byng Inlet last Wed- nesday, on her way to Byng Inlet. She had a load of hay and provisions for the mills there. The crew came to Owen Sound this morning by the steamer Bonnie. They were unable to get her off. They say she is damaged a great deal. They filled her with water to make her lay easy. Loss estimated at $50,000 insured for $20,000 to $25,000 in the Phœnix, British American, Pro- vincial, and we think another office.

CLEVELAND, Nov. 28.—The steamer Boston is reported to have been sunk in Lake Michigan by the steamer Milwaukie. They are both of the Northern Transportation Company's Line. There are no lives lost.

Montreal, Nov.—The schooner 'Indian Queen,' bound for Pictou to the Moisie, with a cargo of coals for Mr. Molson; was lost going into the Moisie River on the 11th inst. She will be a total loss, only three feet of her stern being visible at low water. Crew saved. Molson's steamer, em- ployed at the mines, broke adrift during the gale and was rescued with great difficulty. Several scows were lost at the same time, which were em- ployed in carrying sand to the mines.

— The steamers Grecian and Magnet are going into dry dock for the winter—the former to repair damages sustained in the collision near Kingston, and the laҭer to have a new engine and boilers put in.

— The Life Association of Scotland is about erecting a splendid stone building on the Place d'Armes, Montreal. The demolition of a portion of their former offices by the City Corporation in widening Little St. James Street, has rendered the erection of new offices a necessity to the Association.

— $300,000 worth of property were destroyed by fire in New York last week. Incendiarism is rampant throughout the United States.

— It was proposed in the Hamilton City Coun- cil, some time since, to obtain power from the Legislature to insure property along the line of water pipes, as the rates of insurance are so high that it has become the cause of complaint. The proposition met with favor, and it was intended to have gone on with the matter, but it was found impossible to arrange a bill for this session, of the Legislature of Ontario, and it has accordingly been abandoned for the present.

THE UNITED PORTS AND GENERAL.— The United Ports and General" Insurance Company is another newly registered project. The capital is fixed at £500,000, in 500,000 shares of £1 each, and the objects for which it is associated are—To carry on in Great Britain, or elsewhere, the busi- ness of fire, life, and marine insurance in all its branches, as well as of underwriters and insurers, and insurance brokers. To make loans and ad- vances, acquire land and buildings, grant an- nuities, endowments, and loans, and every des- cription of insurance business which may be legally undertaken. To amalgamate with, pur- chase, or otherwise acquire the business of, or to make any arrangements with any underwriters, insurers, insurance brokers, or insurance companies in Great Britain or elsewhere ; and to do all other things that may conduce or be incidental to car- rying into effect the objects of the company. The promoters and directors are—Charles Ellis, Port- land-place, underwriter ; Peter Pyne, 4 Parlia- ment-street, Hull, West India merchant ; Athur Wellesly Joyce, 4 Parliament-street, Hull, mer- chant ; W. N. Goodlath, 8 Eden Quay, Dublin, merchant ; D. J. Wake, 3 Mark-lane, merchant ; Thomas A. N. Goodlath, Malahide, Dublin, gen- tleman ; William Thomas Procktor, 74 Cowper-

road, South Hornsey, merchant ; and Thomas Gregg, 13 Upper Sackville-street, Dublin, mer- chant.—*Insurance Record.*

INSURANCE STOCKS IN HARTFORD.—The fol- lowing are the latest quotations :

	Bid.	Asked.
Ætna	190	197½
Hartford	190	200
Connecticut	113	116
Phœnix	195	200
Charter Oak	50	51
City	135	145
Putnam	55	85
Travellers'	117	122
Ætna Live Stock	40	50

REAL ESTATE INSURANCE.—The *News* of London, proposes, in view of the vexatious delay and uncertainty attendant upon the conveyance of real estate in England, and the consequent em- barrassment to owners and buyers, the establish- ment of a "Landed Title Estate Insurance Company," to secure land owners against the consequences of a defective title. Commenting upon the evils which such an organization would remedy, it says :

Our system of conveyancing, the obsolete coin- age of an age when the investment of capital in land was almost a thing unknown, operates as a deterring influence, paralyzes the motive which should be the mainspring of all traffic in land, compelling its retention in the hands that are unable to make the best use of it, and would willingly part with it, and denying it to those who have capital to invest in it, and are able to employ labour in its improvement.

PORK-HOUSE RISKS.

The Pork season is upon us, and large lines on Hog Products will soon be in demand. Special pleas for this and that establishment will be laid before Insurance Officers, and they will be ex- pected to reduce a rate or enlarge a privilege, be- cause the construction or policy of a particular establishment is near what it ought to be. Owners and agents are sometimes so overcome with the superiority of a new brick pork-house, over the old wooden shell that burned last season, that they suppose no such paragon ever before adorned the footstool, and the clamor, equal to their inex- perience, is raised for the Companies, who were blistered when the old one burned, to gape with admiration and then reduce the rate ; the popular notion being that THE RATE is' made for the poorest risks, and that whatever grades above the worst is entitled to a reduction ! Would it not be good practice for the Companies to accept only the best at THE RATE and reject all others unconditionally ?

The principal processes of a pork establishment, and those out of which its inherent perils arise, are four ; SLAUGHTERING, PACKING, RENDERING and SMOKING.

Slaughtering and slaughter-houses are always nuisances ; not only during the season of killing, but particularly in the summer ; and are often burned by those living adjacent. Annual risks on or in slaughter houses, specially in thickly inhabited neighborhoods, are a ticklish business. Short risks that expire before warm weather may do better.

Cutting and packing are not, of themselves, dangerous ; but they are usually done in a hurried manner, and often at night. *Pieces of meat are often used as candlesticks*, and sconces and ricketty tin lanterns are apt to abound.

Lard-rendering is very hazardous at the best, and should only be done by experienced and trusty hands. Kettles should be well set, and the top of the furnaces covered with an iron plate having a flange around the edge. A metal *extinguisher* should be hung on a pulley so as to be let down over the kettle instantly when the lard takes fire. *Water will not quench burning grease, it can only* be done by smothering. Steam rendering generates an explosive gas that takes fire from a lighted candle. No lights of any kind, open or closed, should ever be permitted about lard tanks.

Smoking is undoubtedly the great peril of the business, and the arrangements should be of the best character. A slatted floor—iron is better than wood—ten feet or more above the fire, to prevent meat from falling into it, is indispensable. The smudge should be in a stove or under a brick arch, or conveyed from an outside fire, and great watchfulness should prevail over this department.

City establishments have a great advantage over those in the country, in the superior fire department; the extra care of the city police, in addition to private watchmen, and the better average experience of men who work in large concerns over those in small. It is a great error to suppose that country pork-houses are better risks than those in the city, where they have these advantages.

Pork-houses should be reviewed by the travelling agents of the companies with great care, and their notations carefully heeded. Many a concern that meets the requirements of a printed application, will from its untidy or ill-managed features, be rejected by the vigilant supervisor of risks on a personal inspection.—*Monitor.*

☞ THE CANADIAN MONETARY TIMES AND INSURANCE CHRONICLE *is printed every Thursday Evening, in time for the English Mail.*

Subscription Price, one year, $2, or $3 in American currency ; Single copies, five cents each. Casual advertisements will be charged ten cents per line of solid nonpareil each insertion. All letters to be addressed, "THE CANADIAN MONETARY TIMES, TORONTO, ONT." *Registered letters so addressed are at the risk of the Publishers. Cheques should be made payable to* J. M. TROUT, *Business Manager, who will, in future, issue all receipts for money.*

The Canadian Monetary Times.

THURSDAY, DECEMBER 3, 1868.

THE AUDIT OF PUBLIC INSTITUTIONS.

The greatest success seems to attend the operations of those joint-stock companies whose management takes the form of Executive individuality, as Mr. Scratchley calls it. The greater the concentration in power, the greater are the chances of working out efficiently and successfully the end in view, more especially so where promptness in decision and a speedy use of opportunities are rendered necessary by circumstances. No one underrates the advantage of judicious management ; it is of the greatest importance so far as prosperity is concerned. But there is a tendency to ignore in practice the advantage of an effective audit and a close supervision which dearly bought experience now shows us to be essential to safety. As has been well said— "For one Company that fails by dishonesty or from want of skill on the part of the chief official, ten come to grief from careless supervision." The fact that the natural tendency

in management is towards concentration of power, suggests of itself a necessity for supervision ; not a supervision of a formal character ; not a mere hasty glance over totals ; not a take-for-granted purview of details, but all that is meant by the words—an effective audit. Directors, in too many instances, are either too much engrossed in their own affairs, or possessed of too little knowledge of the details of the Company they profess to govern, and too careless to pay that attention necessary to acquire the necessary knowledge, to understand very clearly its actual financial condition. Directors who meet, perhaps, once or twice a week, for an hour or two, cannot be expected to acquire a very detailed knowledge of a Company ; a want of regularity in their attendance leads to a want of unity in their deliberations ; and the absence through accident or design, of a seemingly trifling bit of information, may thwart their most carefully considered resolves. We do not need to go back to the old Bank of Upper Canada for evidence to sustain our statements; unfortunately cases are still fresh in the memory of us all which would support all we have to say on the subject, and a great deal more.

A few weeks ago, the Committee appointed to investigate the affairs of the Gore Bank, told us that " they would be evading a grave though very painful obligation, were they not to express their decided opinion that very much of what is now, for the first time known to be lost to the Bank, ought to have been long since written off as bad, and that a great part of the remainder should have been treated as of extremely doubtful value. And they deem it to be a subject for the deepest regret that the late Directors should not have seen it to be their imperative duty, both for their own sakes and in the interest of all concerned fairly to confront the difficulties with which the institution has been long beset, and to bring their published statements into harmony with the actual facts of the case."

The recent crisis in New Brunswick furnishes the latest case in point. The cashier of the Commercial Bank was allowed to follow his own devices by his Directors, and at the close of his career, left a deficit of $90,000 in his accounts. On his sudden departure, it is at once admitted that he had managed the Bank without the slightest restraint or check. The St. John's *News* hit the nail on the head when it said "the corporators in all financial and industrial associations should see to it that frequent, exact and exhausting examinations are made."

However, it must not be supposed that Banks are the only corporations that suffer from the lack of efficient supervision. Our remarks apply with equal force to all public or private companies, and it would

be easy to illustrate our position by c[...] which companies of various kinds hav[...] familiarized with trouble through l[...] simple precautions. The superficial[...] jump at the conclusion when a Ban[...] pends payment, that our system of b[...] is a wrong one. But the system is n[...] responsible for the failures than it is [...] failures of the crops. The most perfe[...] tem of banking that could be devised[...] be liable to the same contingencies[...] real responsibility rests upon those w[...] to work the system properly. That it[...] well worked is proved by the fact th[...] worked well by many institutions[...] names will readily occur to the read[...] system may, of course, be improved [...] ters of detail. Before measures reve[...] ary are adopted, it would seem expec[...] try measures remedial. The answer[...] to the Senate Committee on Bankin[...] and contained many useful suggestion[...] guarding against the abuse of a system[...] in theory and practice, is the best ada[...] the circumstances of the country. S[...] the bankers who made answers went[...] as to suggest a periodical inspection[...] per officers to be appointed by Gover[...] We do not think that such an ins[...] would be necessary if a more perfect[...] of audit were inaugurated.

Mr. Scratchley, in his book on[...] Building Societies, puts the matter i[...] light, and we cannot do better than[...] own words :

"The generality of Auditors el[...] Shareholders are persons having no[...] for experience in matters of finar[...] their audits, in consequence, are lit[...] than an illusion. Auditors, to b[...] real value, should be in the cha[...] Committees of Surveillance, and sh[...] be expected to content themselv[...] checking the vouchers for payments,[...] accuracy of the items entered in tl[...] books. As long as it is considered a[...] interference on the part of the Au[...] they desire to extend their investiga[...] yond the accounts of a company,[...] give no guarantee either to the Sha[...] or to the Creditors that all the tra[...] of the Directors and officials hav[...] record in the books.

"Hence the present system of au[...] the highest degree pernicious, for it[...] create the idea of security where[...] really given.

"The public mind is perplexed[...] fraud can be prevented. It is un[...] when a concern is not managed e[...] one proprietor, somebody must[...] ed, and that auditors would not [...] prevent forgery or the falsificati[...] counts. This objection is groun[...] fraud begins when neglect of supe[...] the management commences ; and[...] way to prevent fraud is to introduce[...] which will create a fear of detection[...]

al source of the disease is the in-
of the system of audit now in force.
emen appointed are too often the
of the Directors, even where they
be elected by the Shareholders,
heir election, not so much to their
estigating accounts, as to their be-
s of the managing officials. Not
tly do they take their first lesson
g books at the company which
ppointed to investigate.

ndeed, is it sufficient for an Audi-
merely an honourable man, for it
pecial experience to know where
of the "cook" may be traced in a
counts."

proposes the following plan :
vide, then, a sufficient bar to dis-
r curative to lack of principle, a
of two professional Inspectors
ppointed, whose duty it should be
a surveillance over the Execu-
ittee, without interfering in the
agement, except to report what is
to the constituents of the Com-
areholders. The Inspectors should
simply accountants : one at least
required to possess some legal, as
fessional knowledge, of the matters
to the particular class of business
alled upon to supervise. They
required to test the accuracy of
a from time to time submitted by
ers ; and to watch that all their
aken are in strict accordance with
f Settlement, and the objects and
of the Society. These Inspectors
nen of fair position in life, and be
paid. Their tenure of office
limited, and fresh Inspectors
ppointed—under a Rotation sys-
two or three years. They should,
ularly, *not be permitted to send
to do the work* which they have
, and for which they have been
elected.

ld they have the strongest incen-
aithful discharge of their duties,
ay neglect, they would not only
ticular appointment they hold in
but render themselves ineligible
a in other institutions.

bjected, that in some recent no-
res the management was intrusted
pposed superior position in life,
that in those very instances the
deceived by an apparently respect-
of Directors placed over the com-
ials, who, while they were not
draw large remuneration out of
ere yet too indolent to exercise a
d wholesome supervision over its
s would not have occurred had
nspectors attached to the associa-
l of a large body of Directors,
such special experience as would
to detect the irregularities that
ng.

glad to observe in the Chicago
nnouncement, that the publishers
urnal "a complete and positive
t is edited with great ability and
ocess. We may also add that it
y printed.

MINING EXTRAORDINARY.

Enterprise has, sometimes, an odd way of
shewing what it can do. It is sanguine and
self confident. It despises small things for
its visions are golden; it sets natural laws
at defiance for its spirit is unquenchable.
Devious are its ways; oftentimes past finding
out. Stimulated by the *auri sacra fames*, it
soars on venturesome wing into the regions
of imagination, and, from loftiest eyry, out-
stares the noonday sun. Fledglings are
sorely tempted by its hair-brained feats and
like Icarus of classic story dare to trust to
unproven pinions on a voyage through space,
and, with a like luck, end their ambitious
career amid the waves of trouble.

It has been said that Canadians are not an
enterprising people. If we are not, we are
certainly nearing the proper standard. We
have in our midst those whose eyes are full of
speculation. Madoc has been worked out by
promoters of companies, and though the
experience gained is anything but pleasant
to reflect on, it has not been lost on some individuals. There were some, however, who
despised Madoc gold, whose caution prevented them from sinking their money in gold
mines so near home. Although little gold
has been brought from Madoc, a quantity
not inconsiderable has been waylaid on its
road thither. Some of those who resisted
successfully the seductions of Madoc remembered this and in an unguarded moment fell
victims to Nova Scotia. Although we are
ready to condole with the unfortunate, we
are ready to concede that a nice thing may
be made by starting a company. Being in a
communicative mood, we are prepared to tell
how the nice thing may be made. Suppose
A and B own a tract in Nova Scotia worth
$9,000. They start a company (let us call
it the Honeysuckle) and stock it for $125,-
000. A and B retain as proprietors and
promoters half the stock, $62,500, and sell
the other half, $62,500, at eighty cents in
the dollar. Two calls of 20 per cent realize
$25,000, which A and B pocket and then
make a further call of 10 per cent for working
capital.

Take another case. C and D delighted
with the undertaking just spoken of, determine to try their hands at forming a company.
They also journey to Nova Scotia, secure
two acres worth $2,000 and some government
areas worth $15. On their return they may
bring out the Scotch Thistle Gold Mining
Company of Nova Scotia—capital $50,000.
Of the 50,000 shares the promoters realize
three-eighths, or 18,750, leaving 31,250 to
be sold. The latter are sold at 80 cents per
share, realizing $25,000. Of this the pro-
moters retain $20,000 for their land and their

trouble, and generously allow $5,000 to go
as working capital. If the laws of Nova
Scotia do not permit a company to obtain a
charter unless its capital is $100,000, it is an
easy thing to issue 50,000 new shares and
distribute them gratis among the shareholders. The only effect of this manœuvre
is to double the shareholders' liability, and
as it occurs after they have been drawn into
the scheme, they can only grumble a little.
By forming companies in the way indicated, it it quite possible for promoters to
make considerable sums of money, and as the
plan has been tried here with great success, we
are justified in concluding that all Canadians
are not deficient in enterprise. The promoters are rewarded, and if the shareholders are not satisfied they can tune their
voices and chant in chorus the Rev. Mr.
Punshon's verses :

We grasp at grains of shining dust,
  But in the grasp they perish.
We put in men's applause our trust ;
  It cheats the hopes we cherish.

Remorse, a ghostly shadow blights
  Each wreath we weave for pleasure ;
But restless still we scale the heights,
  Or search the mines for treasure.

BEET ROOT SUGAR.

The trade in sugar has, as all are aware, assumed large proportions. Sugar is produced
now in nearly every country, and enters so
largely into our social wants that it will be interesting to our readers if we can show how
the trade is to be developed in the New
Dominion, and not only the consumers benefitted, but also several other industries encouraged, chief among which is the agricultural
one. We purpose, therefore, in this article,
to point out as briefly as possible the probable
advantages to the Dominion of erecting factories for the manufacture of sugar from beet
roots, after first having taken a slight retrospective glance at the sugar trade. In the
year 1148 sugar cane was first introduced into
Europe from Asia, and cultivated in Cyprus,
and afterwards introduced by the Moors into
Spain ; but the production was very limited
and the chief mode of sweetening food was
with honey and syrups. In 1506 the cane
was first imported into the West Indies,
which, with the East Indies, supplied the
European world until recently.
This trade rapidly developed itself till the
time of the Continental blockade, when
Napoleon sought to cripple England by ob-
structing her Colonial trade. In 1747 a
German, named Margraaf, commenced a
series of experiments on extracting sugar
from different roots, especially beets; but
beyond drawing the attention of the scientific
world to it, nothing practical resulted. During Napoleon's reign the matter was brought

to a working issue, and many manufactories were built. After his fall the business languished, till 1825, when a new impetus was given to it in France. It was introduced into Germany also, and so rapidly has the trade progressed that nearly every Continental country manufactures its own sugar, and it is not improbable that, twenty years hence, the consumption of cane sugar in Europe, except in Great Britain, Spain, and Turkey, will be a thing of the past.

It is a well-known fact that the productive capabilities of the cane-growing countries are not equal to supply the enormous and still rapidly increasing demand for sugar all over the world, and the question naturally arises, What is the cheapest and best substitute for cane. This is solved in Europe by the extensive use of beets. To prove this we give the quantities produced in the following countries in the year 1865:

France..................510,000,000 lbs.
Germany ....370,000,000 "
Austria...................190,000,000 "
Prussia...................100,000,000 "
Belgium ....35,000,000 "
Sweden ....30,000,000 "
Holland ....10,000,000 "

From this it will be seen that France is a long way ahead in the manufacture, making not only enough to supply her own wants, but also to export, since in that year she exported 100,000,000 lbs to Great Britain, thus proving that beet sugar can compete with that produced from cane. The question arises, Can we in Canada, where labor is so dear, raise beets cheap enough to make such a factory a paying concern? By the aid of a few figures we are enabled to frame an answer to this. In the first place, the soil and climate of Canada are admirably suited for the growth of beets. An acre of land will produce eighteen tons, which, at $4 per ton, is $72 per acre. The cost of planting, harvesting, &c., we may estimate at $50, certainly not more, showing a profit to the farmer of $22 per acre, which would well repay him. So much for the raw material. Now for the cost of manufacture—and we may state that the figures we give are derived from a gentleman thoroughly and practically acquainted with the manufacture of beet-root sugar in Germany:

Estimating that the factory is capable of converting 1,500 cwt. of raw beets into sugar each day during the season (say 150 days), we have—

225,000 cwt. of beets at 20c. $45,000
Fuel 13,000
Wages—20 skilled men at $400 8,000
100 unskilled men at $1 per day 15,000
Manager 2,000
Office expenses................................. 7,000
Wear and tear of machinery, &c........... 10,000

Total $100,000

225,000 cwt gives 9 per cent.
of raw sugar..................20,250 cwt
Loss in refining, say 25 per
cent.............................. 5,062¼ cwt

Amount of refined sugar ...15,187¼ cwt
Worth, at lowest, 8c per lb..................$121,500

Profit $21,500

This is the profit on the sugar, but to it must be added the syrup made from the waste in refining, and also the refuse, which makes a very wholesome and nutritious food for cattle. The calculation then stands—

Profit as above.... ....$21,500
2,530 cwt of syrup at $1.25............... 3,162
10,000 cwt of refuse at 50c.......... 5,000

Total profit................................$29,662

We notice that in California and many parts of the Western States, the subject has attracted the attention of monied men, and that many factories have been erected. Canada alone could support over a score of such establishments, which would add very materially to our wealth, and enable us to retain and use in the country the money we now sent out to pay for the raw article. The agricultural interest would be materially benefitted, as at least 20,000 acres would be required to raise the necessary amount of beets to supply twenty factories, thus giving a great impetus to farming, and the works themselves would give employment to nearly 3,000 laborers for at least half a year, and that at a season when the demand for labor is slack ; as the crushing process is carried on from about the end of October till towards the middle of March, at which time the beets begin to lose their saccharine element. On the Continent of Europe the erection of new factories is constantly going on, and, in many places, by the small farmers clubbing together, on the same principle as our cheese factories, they furnishing not only the raw material, but also, to a great extent, the labor. The only capital required is a sufficiency for erecting the building and getting the necessary machinery. As regards the latter, our large machine shops can readily furnish it—the models could be brought from Germany. Thus a great benefit would accrue to our manufacturing interests. So that, regarded from every point, the establishment of sugar factories would be of general benefit to the Dominion.

The best kind of beet suitable for the purpose, the mode of cultivation, and also the last improved modes of making sugar will be discussed hereafter.

—A meeting of Mr. Scovill's depositors and creditors took place in St. John on the 23rd Nov. A committee was appointed to investigate the bankrupt's affairs.

DOMINION NOTES FROM HALI

Complaint has been made by some in this Province that the "Dominion N issued payable in Halifax are subjec a discount of four per cent. by the ag the Bank of Montreal here. The fi these so-called Dominion Notes issue able in Halifax have certain peculiariti discredit them to the name of D₂ Notes. The Act under which they are says: "Such of the said notes as ar payable at Halifax, shall so long as t rency of Nova Scotia remains such as is, be redeemable in that currency at t of £1 sterling, English, for every $5 full value and shall be a legal tender i Scotia only."

We do not suppose that notes pay Halifax have been issued by the B Montreal in this Province but if the it would be well for business men to b ful, lest they find on their hands Do Notes which are not legal tenders Nova Scotia, and are only received banks at a discount of four per cent £1 sterling is equal to $5 in Nova Sco this Province it is equal to $4.80.

—We learn from the Chicago S₂ that Superintendent Barnes has dete to make a thorough investigation of th ness affairs of the Etna Live Stoc pany. The failure of the Hartford I dently started the enquiry. The jou which we have referred says, "we l reason to doubt that the Company vent, so far as ability to pay all its l are concerned ; but the question n arises, in view of the fact that then other Company in which to insure, the good of a re-insurance fund unle fund is kept constantly equal to amount of its unearned premiums. then, that it is plainly the duty Company, if it cannot keep its cash to the full amount of all its unear miums, to abandon the business wh able to do so honorably."

Some statements made by us in two weeks ago, respecting the N Life Insurance Company require exp We mentioned that this was a prem company, which is true, but for a g past it has done business strictly o cash system. The statement of pany's assets shows a considerabl be held in the shape of premium these were nearly all taken at period of the company's existence twenty-seven years since its organi New York Life has earned amounting to $2,545,022.52, a por of which was credited to the Comp former reference to its statement.

e Publishing Office of THE CANA- ONETARY TIMES AND INSURANCE E is removed to No. 60, Church doors north cf Court Street.

Railway News.

RN RAILWAY.—Traffic receipts for week v. 21, 1868.

igers	$3,684 54
it........................ ...	5,293 61
and Sundries...........	218 55
Receipts for week......	$9,196 70
sponding week 1867....	8,241 73
Increase..........	$954 97

WESTERN RAILWAY.—Traffic for week v. 13, 1868.

igers	$33,269 72
it and live stock......	41,520 39
and sundries..........	1,862 69
	$76,652 80
ponding Week of '67.	76,153 93
Increase.............	$498 87

MATION OF EXPRESS COMPANIES.—On ult., at a meeting of the Merchants' d American Express Companies held in , a consolidation of the two companies lly agreed upon. Under the arrange- de, the capital of the American was its present amount, while that of the ' Union was counted at one-half its nount, viz., $9,000,000, so that the the consolidated company will be $18,- It appears to have been assumed that companies would accept the new cor- a part of the working combination of panies, with an interest proportioned of its stock to the total capital of the ompanies, viz., 53 per cent.; but we that the Adams Company objects to f consolidation between the American ants' Union, and also demand a redis- f interest in the general combination, upon the proportion of capital. As w stand, there appears to be some pro- a breaking up of the present joint ar- s of the several companies, with a opposition.

AND PORT PERRY RAILROAD.—The r the building of the Whitby and Port way has been given to Messrs. Kestevan t, their tender having been regarded as vourable of about half a dozen tenders received. The contractors agree "to nd equip the road for the round sum of and to accept in payment the $95,000, the bonuses of Reach, and of the Town hip of Whitby; $55,000, cash; to take ock themselves, and the bonds of the n the road for $140,000." The Com- ver is to find the right of way. The to be upon the broad or five feet six . The subsidies from the Municipali- oted some time since, and the directors $75,000 in stock to raise. The Whitby ompany has agreed to return as a bonus pany, one-fourth of all the tolls col- manufactured lumber from the north, r the road for ten years. A preliminary s been completed, which makes the rom Port Perry to Whitby Harbor 20½ is expected that the railway will be d by the first of August next.

Financial.

TORONTO STOCK MARKET.

(Reported by Pellatt & Osler, Brokers.)

There were rather more securities on the market this week, but they all find ready sale at advancing rates. Bonds and Debentures are much sought after.

Bank Stock—There are buyers of Montreal at 139 ex. dividend, and sellers at 140. For British American 104 would be paid, no sellers. Ontario is offering at 99½ to par. There are buyers of Toronto at 120—no sellers. Royal Canadian has declined, there being sellers at 90½ and no buyers over 90. Considerable sales at 105, which rate is freely offered for stock bearing full dividend. Gore continues to improve; large sales occurred at 43½, at which rate there are buyers. There are buyers of Merchants' at 112½, and no sellers under 113. Quebec nominal at 109, with buyers at 108½ ex. dividend—no sellers under 103. Molson's is offered at 109, with buyers at 108½. City is asked for at 102½ ex. dividend—no sellers under 103. Buyers offer 106 for Du Peuple—none in market. Sellers ask 106½ for Jacques Cartier, with buyers at 106. Sales of Mechanics, took place at 95½ to 96. No Union in market—104½ would be paid.

Debentures—Canada sterling 5 per cents sold at 93¼. and Dominion stock at 104½; no 6 per cents in market. Large sales of Toronto occurred at rates to pay 6¾ per cent. to purchasers. County are in great demand—none in market.

Sundries—City gas is much asked for, and an advance would be paid but there are no sellers. Canada Permanent Building Society sold at 124½ to 125, closing with buyers at the latter rate. No Western Canada in market for some time past, 106 would be paid. Freehold sold at 104½, and is enquired for at that rate. There are sellers of British America Assurance at 57, and buyers at 54 to 55. Buyers offer 135 for Montreal Telegraph without leading to business. Sales of Canada Landed Credit occurred at 72 to 73, and there buyers at the latter rate. Some small mortgages have been placed at 8 per cent. Good paper is readily discounted at reasonable rates.

MONTREAL MONEY MARKET.

(From our own Correspondent.)

Montreal, DEC. 24, 1868.

I have nothing new to report. It is a relief to us that the panic in New Brunswick is subsiding; the stocks of both the Commercial and the St. Stephen's Banks have risen considerably. Here the money market is very easy, the difficulty is how to invest capital at anything like profitable rates, there are very few good bills offering, and the Banks readily take them up at from 6½ to 7 per cent. for good trade paper. Even one name bills, with collaterals can be passed at 6 to 7 per cent. There is not much second class paper on the market, which is a noticeable feature, and presupposes a healthy state of trade. The transactions in stocks and shares of all sorts are very light owing to the ideas of buyers and sellers being so far apart that sales have been few and far between. For a full report of prices I refer to our stock and share list. I enclose latest gold and silver quotations:—Gold 35½; Silver 4⅛ to 4¼; Greenbacks 26¼; Exchange 25¾ to 26; Sterling in N. Y. 9½.

THE BUILDING SOCIETIES OF ENGLAND have been deprived of a great privilege by the late Parliament, which they have enjoyed since their establishment, upwards of thirty years ago. The bill was disguised under the title of "An act to amend the laws relating to the Inland Revenue," and therefore the offensive provision was not detected until it was matured. It provides, that "the exemption from stamp duty conferred by the acts of the sixth and seventh years of King William the Fourth, for the regulation of benefit building societies, shall not extend to any mortgage to be made after the passing of this act." As these documents have always been exempt from stamps, it is scarcely possible to anticipate what effect this future heavy charge will have upon those associations; for it was a boon which encouraged the workingmen in habits of providence.

UNITED STATES BANKS.—Total capital invested in National Banks, $422,804,666; taxes paid to the United States, $2,525,607; average rate of tax on capital paid to the United States, 2¼ per cent.; taxes paid to and assessed by State authorities, $8,812,127; average rate per cent. of State taxation, $2¼; total tax paid United States and State authorities, $18,338,734; rate per cent. of United States and State tax on capital, 4⅓, and on deposits, 3½.

THE GORE BANK.—Mr. G. J. Forster, wholesale grocery merchant, at Hamilton, has been elected a Director of the Gore Bank, in the room of Dr. McQuesten, who has resigned.

Commercial.

Montreal Correspondence.

(From our own Correspondent).

Montreal, Dec. 2, 1868.

Our harbor is now deserted, with the exception of river craft and some few schooners. What I may term "the water season," has been remarkably open, and vessels have gone down to Quebec and the Gulf with comparative safety. It may be of interest to your readers to have some few shipping statistics of our port for the past few years, and to note the gradual change in the style of vessels employed; the fluctuations have been in sea-going craft engaged in the European trade, firstly from small ships to those of large size and lately those of a large aize to steamers; the tonnage of the latter this last year being one-third of the tonnage arrived at this port. I have no doubt that in a few years the greatest bulk of our shipping will consist of steam vessels.

The navigation of the St. Lawrence requires steam power to ensure speed and safety, and when those elements are combined, the bulk of business must fall to their share. In 1865, the arrivals by sea were 272 vessels, with a total tonnage of 134,735 tons; in 1866 the arrivals increased to 438 vessels, and 189,254 tons. For this year, the arrivals are 409 vessels, and 188,557 tons. Now, to show the increase of steam vessels ten years ago, we had 10 steamers arrived only; 59 in 1866, representing a tonnage of 69,228; whilst in this year the number increased to 67 vessels, with 84,906 tons. The capacity and regularity of the steamers has and will materially effect the business of sailing ships. With proper facilities for better opening up the St. Lawrence to the west, Montreal might safely aspire to rank as one of the largest shipping ports on this continent; it only requires a certain amount of energy to open some of the many new routes constantly brought under the notice of the public. Will Montreal have the courage to do it? is the question.

Our PRODUCE MARKET is very dull, and prices of flour have declined. There are still some shipments to Quebec, but they are so slight as not to affect prices. Extra, $5.50 to $5.75; Fancy, $5 to $5.10; Supers range from $4.80 to $4.90 for No. 1, and $4.40 to $4.50 for No. 2; Strong Bakers' range as high as $5.05 for very choice brands; the stocks here are not heavy, but the demand from this out will be purely local. Little doing in grain of any description, and prices are purely nominal; say U. C. Spring Wheat $1.10 to $1.12½; Peas, 92½c to 95c; Corn, 83c to 85c; Barley, $1.20 to $1.30; Oats, 47½c to 48½. Provisions rule in the general dulness, and no change is to be noted in prices. Butter has rather declined, but is still very high for this season of the year.

GROCERIES. — This market has ruled very quiet, there not being the slightest speculative movement in any article, but fair sales have been made to the trade at full rates. The late fall sales being so unsatisfactory, merchants have preferred holding over their stock, which, with the exception of Fruit and Wine (especially light French), are small; and although a fair amount of goods were placed at the early fall sales, still, from all the reports I can hear from the West, the country storekeepers are decidedly understocked, and that is the general impression here, so that, the money market being exceedingly easy, there is no necessity to force goods forward, or in any way sacrifice them. Such firms as have done so during the spring and summer have been so rudely shaken that they have not repeated the experiment this fall. We may look for a fair and healthy business during the winter.

In DRY GOODS.—The trade is, for the present, over, and many merchants are already beginning to take stock. After New Year's we generally have more liveliness, but till then dull times must be expected.

HARDWARE.—With the close of the Canal the trade in heavy Hardware generally closes, the extra freight charged during the winter by the Grand Trunk Railroad operating against it. The demand for shelf goods has also, for the present, fallen off; but the trade, though light, is steady during the winter, the rise in freight not much affecting the cost.

Toronto Market.

During the past week snow has fallen to the depth of a few inches, and the weather has been cold and freezing. There is no sleighing yet, though in Montreal and other places east of that city, the roads are in first-rate condition, there being an abundance of snow. Navigation is now closed, with the exception of a few vessels which are engaged in the coal and wood trade. The St. Lawrence Canals and the Erie Canal are all closed for the season. As a consequence there has been no export business done. Stocks of produce left at the principal ports are pretty large. A comparative statement of the quantities in store, in Toronto, on the 1st Dec., is a follows:—

	1867.	1868.
Fall, bbls..	1,781	2,426
Fall Wheat, bushls.	8,619	16,246
Spring Wheat "	40,986	15,500
Oats "	6,600	23,400
Barley "	25,900	85,500
Peas "	12,796	11,492

GRAIN.—*Wheat.*—Receipts light, market dull, holders of Spring ask $1.05 to 107 without buyers. Fall dull and nominal. *Barley.*—There is a fair demand at $1.25 to 128, and $1.30 was offered for a lot, winter storage paid; sales of cars at quotations. *Peas.*—Quiet at 80c. to 82c. for fair to good Grand Trunk peas; sales of three cars at these prices. *Oats.*—Steady at 50c. to 52c.

FLOUR.—Receipts light, there is some demand for Superfine for shipment at $4.65, holders asking $4.75 to 4.80; sales at $4.70. Better grades nominal.

PROVISIONS.—*Butter.*—A lot of 100 tubs sold at 24c. Market closed dull at 23c. to 24½; large rolls sold at 20c. to 22c. *Mess Pork.*—Nominal and unchanged. *Hams.*—A lot of 100 smoked sold at 11¾c. *Bacon.*—Lots of new are held at 10c., no sales. *Lard.*—Steady at 14c. *Dressed Hogs.*—The market was fairly supplied; prices steady as quoted. *Potatoes.*—Plenty, and offering by the car load at 45c. to 55c. *Apples.*—Lots are offering at $2.50 for good winter.

LIVE STOCK.—The best cattle are scarce at $6.50 to 7.00; other kind plenty at $3.50 to 5.00 per 100 lbs. dressed weight. *Live Hogs*, $5.00 to $5.40. *Sheep*—$5.00 to 6.00 each.

HIDES AND SKINS.—Sheep skins have advanced to $1.25 and $1.30; no change in other articles.

Demerara Sugar Market.

The following is from Sandbach, Parker & Co.'s Circular, dated Georgetown, Demerara, Nov. 7:

We last Mail advised a severe drought from which the country had been suffering for some weeks. This has continued up to the present time, and not only is the young cultivation on the Estates seriously injured, but Sugar-making has been much retarded, owing to the scarcity of water in the navigable canals. The inhabitants have also been reduced to great straits for want of drinking water. Trade has likewise suffered severely, and we have to report a dull and inanimate market. The arrivals consist of twelve Vessels from the United Kingdom, four from United States, four from British Provinces, and ten from neighboring Colonies.

SUGAR.—The demand for Vacuum Pan, for America, has been steady during the fortnight; prices ranging from $6 to $6.10 for good samples up to $6.20 for very choice. The quality of the produce during the fortnight has improved, and considerable quantities have changed hands, eleven vessels having cleared for North America since our last. Muscovado sugar is held for better rates than purchasers feel inclined to give. The shipments to America last month were larger than they have ever been.

MOLASSES.—There has been a decided improvement in this article; the demand good, and prices of Vacuum Pan have advanced; for Muscovado we have but little change to note.

RUM.—No transactions in our Market.

TIMBER.—One charter during the fortnight to load in Demerara River, but no animation whatever in the trade.

Transactions have taken place during the fortnight at the following rates:

SUGARS (package included) sold by 100 lbs. Dutch, 10 per cent. tare F.O.B.

Muscavadoes, equal at No. 8 Dutch Standard	$3.80 ℔ 100 lbs.	In hhds. of about 1800 lbs. each.
No. 10 do.	$4.00 "	
" 12 do.	$4.25 "	
Vacuum Pan No. 12 do.	$5.50	
" " 14 do.	5.75	
" " 16 do.	6.00	
" " 18 do.	6.10	

MOLASSES (package included, sold by Imperial gallon.)

Muscovado, from 20 @ 28 cents, as to color and density	In puns of 100 gals.
Vacuum Pan from 24 @ 30 cents, as to color and density	
RUM (colored, package included, sold by Imperial gal. from 35 per cent, @ 38 overproof 38 @ 40 cents. From 38 per cent. @ 40 overproof, 40 @ 42 cents.	Ditto.

Halifax Market.

BREADSTUFFS.—Nov. 24.—Flour continues to arrive freely, supply being equal to the demand. We have no change to note in prices from last week's quotations. Canada No. 1 ranges from $6.25 to 6.50; Strong Bakers $6.65 to 6.70; Extra Canada $7.50 to 8.00, Extra State still continues dull at $6.00 to 6.40, according to quality.; No. 2 in good demand at $5.00 to 5.50. Corn Meal without change at $4.50 for kiln dried, and $4.40 for Fresh Ground. Oatmeal $7.70 to 7.80. Imports from January 1st to November 24th, 1867 and 1868:—

	Bbls. Flour.	Bbls, Cornmeal,
1868	167,252	43,119
1867	178,340	33,925

PROVISIONS.—Pork $22 50.

WEST INDIA PRODUCE.—Sugars and Molasses continue in fair demand at quotations. At auction a lot of about 70 hhds, choice Vacuum Pan Sugar sold at 9½c. and 9¾c. duty paid. We quote Porto Rico 6¼ to 6¾. Barbadoes 5¾ to 5¼c. Cuba 5½ to 5¾. Centrifugal Cuba 6c. in Bond. Rum scarce and in demand at 70 to 75c. for Demerara and 60 to 65 for St. Jago.

FINANCIAL.—Bank drawing rate on Lon
days sight, 3¼ per cent prem. Currency
22 per cent. discount. Montreal sight dr
per cent. prem. Newfoundland sight draft
cent. prem.

NEW INSOLVENTS.—The following ins
are gazetted—Louis Forget, St. Janvier; J. C
Orillia; J. T. Beech, Washago; Dame R. S.
Montreal; George Wilson, Montreal; John
ton, Petrolia; William Griffin, Nottaw
John Sutherland, Toronto; Augustus H
Napanee; W. Silver, Hamilton; David
Aylmer; Charles Connevy, Inverness; R
Radcliff, Goderich; Wm. Kennedy, Buckin
Joseph Griffin, Bronte; Remenes V. Clark,
ford; Thomas L. L. Ferris, Innisfil; David
Nottwa village; John S. Munroe, Wellan
Robert Waller, Tilsonburg, and Jasper Su
Nottawasaga.

Bank of Toronto.
DIVIDEND No. 25.

NOTICE is hereby given that a dividend of FOUR per cent, for the current half year, being at the rate of 8 per cent. per annum upon the paid up capital of bank, has this day been declared, and that the same is payable at the Bank or its branches, on and after FRIDAY, THE SECOND DAY OF JANUARY NEXT transfer books will be closed from the sixteenth to thirty-first day of December next, both days inclusive.
order of the Board.

G. HAGUE,
Cashier.
nto, Nov. 26, 1868.　　　　15-td

Royal Canadian Bank.
DIVIDEND No. 7.

NOTICE is hereby given that a Dividend of Four per cent. upon the paid-up Capital of this Bank for the half year, has this day been declared, and that the will be payable at the Bank, or its agencies, on and SATURDAY, the SECOND DAY OF JANUARY next. The Transfer Books will be closed from the 16th 31st December, both days inclusive.
order of the Board,

T. WOODSIDE, Cashier.
Canadian Bank, Nov. 25, 1868,　　15-td

The Canadian Bank of Commerce.
DIVIDEND No. 3.

NOTICE is hereby given, that a Dividend at the rate of FOUR per cent. on the paid up Capital Stock of this tion has been declared for the current half year, at the same will be payable at its Banking House in ty, and at its branches, on and after Saturday, the Second day of January next.

Transfer Books will be closed from the 15th to the December, both days inclusive.
order of the Board.

R. J. DALLAS,
Cashier.
nto, Nov. 23.　　15-td

Ontario Bank.
DIVIDEND No. 28.

NOTICE is hereby given, that a Dividend of Four per nt. upon the Capital Stock of this Institution for rent half year, has this day been declared, and that me will be payable at the Bank and its Branches, after

Tuesday, the First day of December next.

Transfer Books will be closed from the 15th to the November, both days inclusive.
order of the Board.

D. FISHER, Cashier.
o Bank, manville, 24th Oct., 1868.　11-td

Geo. Girdlestone,
, Life, Marine, Accident, and Stock Insurance gent

Very best Companies represented.
or, Ont , June, 1868

J. T. & W. Pennock,
and Life Insurance Agents, Parliamentary and partmental Agents, Mining Agents, and Exchange rs.
wa, Dec. 31st, 1867.　　10-1y

Honore Plamondon,
TOM House Broker, Forwarder, and General Agent, uebec. Office—Custom House Building.　17-1y

Sylvester, Bro. & Hickman,
MERCIAL Brokers and Vessel Agents. Office—Ne. Ontario Chambers, [Corner Front and Church Sts.] o　　2-6m

Waterloo County Mutual Fire Insurance Company.
HEAD OFFICE : WATERLOO, ONTARIO.

ESTABLISHED 1863.
business of the Company is divided into three parate and distinct branches, the
AGE, FARM, AND MANUFACTURES.

Branch paying its own losses and its just proportion managing expenses of the Company.
TAYLOR, Sec.　M. SPRINGER, M.M.P., Pres.
J. HUGHES, Inspector.　　15-yr

DAY'S
Commercial College and High School,
No. 82 KING STREET EAST,
(Near St. James' Cathedral.)

THE design of this institution is to prepare Young Men and others as Book-keepers, and for general business, and to furnish them with the facilities for acquiring an excellent

English and Commercial Education.

Mr. DAY is also prepared to give Private Instruction in the several subjects of his department, and to assist Merchants and others in the checking and balancing of books, adjusting their accounts and partnership affairs, &c.

For further information, please call on or address the undersigned.

JAMES E. DAY,
Accountant
Toronto, Sept. 3rd, 1868.

John Ross & Co.,
QUEBEC.

T. & F. Ross & Co.,
GENERAL WHOLESALE GROCERS,
PRODUCE AND COMMISSION MERCHANTS,
361 Commissioner Street,
MONTREAL,　　6

W. McLaren & Co.,
WHOLESALE
BOOT AND SHOE MANUFACTURERS,
18 St. MAURICE STREET,
MONTREAL
June, 1868.　　42-1y

Lyman & McNab,
Importers of, and Wholesale Dealers in,
HEAVY AND SHELF HARDWARE,
KING STREET,
TORONTO, ONTARIO.

THE QUEEN'S HOTEL.
THOMAS DICK, Proprietor.
FRONT STREET,　　-　　TORONTO, ONT
3-1y

Montreal House, Montreal, Canada.

TO MONETARY MEN:—Merchants, Insurance Agents, Lawyers, Bankers, Railway and Steamboat Travellers, Mining Agents, Directors and Stockholders of Public Companies, and other persons visiting Montreal for business or pleasure, are here by most respectfully informed that the undersigned proposes to furnish the best hotel accommodation at the most reasonable charges. It is our study to provide every comfort and accommodation to all our guests, especially for gentlemen engaged as above. To those who have been accustomed to patronize other first-class hotels, we only ask a trial; we have the same accommodation and our table is furnished with every delicacy of the season.

H. DUCLOS.
Nov. 22, 1867.　　15-1y

The Albion Hotel,
MONTREAL,

ONE of the oldest established houses in the City is again under the personal management of
Mr. DECKER,
Who, to accommodate his rapidly increasing business, is adding Eighty more Rooms to the house, making the ALBION one of the Largest Establishments in Canada.
June, 1868.　　42-6ms

DOMINION TELEGRAPH COMPANY.

CAPITAL STOCK　-　-　$500,000
In 10,000 Shares at $50 Each.

PRESIDENT,
HON. WILLIAM CAYLEY.

TREASURER,
HON. J. McMURRICH.

SECRETARY,
H. B. REEVE.

SOLICITORS,
MESSRS. CAMERON & McMICHAEL.

GENERAL SUPERINTENDENT,
MARTIN RYAN.

DIRECTORS.
HON. J. McMURRICH,
Bryce, McMurrich & Co., Toronto.

A. R. McMASTER, Esq.,
A. R. McMaster & Brother, Toronto.

HON. M. C. CAMERON,
Provincial Secretary, Toronto.

JAMES MICHIE, Esq.,
Fulton, Michie & Co., and George Michie & Co., Toronto.

HON. WILLIAM CAYLEY,
Toronto.

A. M. SMITH, Esq.,
A. M. Smith & Co., Toronto.

L. MOFFATT, Esq.,
Moffatt, Murray & Co., Toronto.

H. B. REEVE, Esq.,
Toronto.

MARTIN RYAN, Esq.,
Toronto.

PROSPECTUS.

THE DOMINION TELEGRAPH COMPANY has been organized under the act respecting Telegraph Companies, chapter 67, of the consolidated Statutes of Canada. Its object is to cover the Dominion of Canada with a complete net-work of Telegraph lines.

The Capital Stock
Is $500,000, divided into 10,000 shares of $50 each, 5 per cent to be paid at the time of subscribing, the balance to be paid by instalments, not exceeding 10 per cent per month—said instalments to be called for by the Directors as the works progress. The liability of a subscriber is limited to the amount of his subscription.

The Business Affairs of the Company.
Are under the management of a Board of Directors, annually elected by the Shareholders, in conformity with the Charter and By-Laws of the Company.

The Directors are of opinion that it would be to the interest of the Stockholders generally to obtain subscriptions from all quarters of Canada, and with this view they propose to divide the Stock amongst the different towns and cities throughout the Dominion, in allotments suited to the population and business occupations of the different localities, and the interest which they may be supposed to take in such an enterprise.

Contracts of Connections.
A contract, granting permanent connection and extraordinary advantages, has already been executed between this Company and the Atlantic and Pacific Company, of New York ; thus, at the very commencement, as the Lines of this Company are constructed from the Suspension Bridge, at Clifton (the point of connection) to any point in the Dominion, all the chief cities and places in the States, touched by the Lines of the Atlantic and Pacific Telegraph Company, are brought into immediate connection therewith.

A permanent connection has also been secured with the Great Western Telegraph Company, of Chicago, whereby this Company will be brought into close connection with all the Lake Ports and other places through the North western States, and through to California.
4-3mos

Insurance.

BEAVER
Insurance Association.

EAD OFFICE—29 TORONTO STREET,
TORONTO.

IVE STOCK against death from any cause.
Canadian Company having authority to do this
ness.

R. L. DENISON,
President.
LLY,
Secretary.   8-1y-25

HOME DISTRICT
Fire Insurance Company.

th–West Cor. Yonge & Adelaide Streets,
TORONTO.—(UP STAIRS.)

Dwelling Houses, Stores, Warehouses, Mer-
Furniture, &c.

IDENT—The Hon. J. McMURRICH.
-PRESIDENT—JOHN BURNS, Esq.
JOHN RAINS, Secretary.
AGENTS:
IT, Esq., Hamilton; FRANCIS STEVENS, Esq.,
rie; Messrs. GIBBS & BRO., Oshawa.   8-1y

HE PRINCE EDWARD COUNTY
Fire Insurance Company.

EAD OFFICE,—PICTON, ONTARIO.
B. STINSON; Vice-President, W. A. RICHARDS.
H. A. McPAUL, James Cavan, James Johnson,
William Delong.—Treasurer, David Barker
an Twigg; Solicitor, R. J. Fitzgerald.

nany is established upon strictly Mutual prin-
nsuring farming and isolated property, (not
n Townships only, and offers great advantages
at low rates for five years, without the expense

ne 15, 1868.   9-1y

---

ford Fire Insurance Company.
HARTFORD, CONN.

al and Assets over Two Million Dollars.

$2,026,220.29.

CHARTERED 1810.

and reliable Company, having an established
in Canada of more than thirty years standing,
i with the provisions of the new Insurance
de a special deposit of

$100,000

ernment for the security of policy-holders, and
e to grant policies upon the same favorable
tofore.

low rates on first-class dwellings and farm
a term of one or more years.
eretofore promptly and equitably adjusted.
H. J. MORSE & Co., AGENTS.
int.

T WOOD, GENERAL AGENT FOR CANADA.

THE AGRICULTURAL
. Assurance Association of Canada.

E .... LONDON, ONT.

armers' Company. Licensed by the Government of Canada.

January, 1868 .... $220,121 25
ah Items, over $65,000 00
ce in force 28,76

npany insures nothing more dangerous than
roperty. Its rates are as low as any well-es-
ompany in the Dominion, and lower than those
any. It is largely patronised, and continues
ublic favor.

ance, apply to any of the Agents, or address
y, London, Ontario.
2nd Nov., 1868.   12-1y.

Insurance.

The Standard Life Assurance Company,
Established 1825.
WITH WHICH IS NOW UNITED
THE COLONIAL LIFE ASSURANCE COMPANY.

Head Office for Canada:
MONTREAL—STANDARD COMPANY'S BUILDINGS,
No. 47 GREAT ST. JAMES STREET.
Manager—W. M. RAMSAY.   Inspector—RICH'D BULL.

THIS Company having deposited the sum of ONE HUN-
DRED AND FIFTY THOUSAND DOLLARS with the Receiver-
General, in conformity with the Insurance Act passed last
Session, Assurances will continue to be carried out at
moderate rates and on all the different systems in practice.

AGENT FOR TORONTO—HENRY PELLATT,
KING STREET.

AGENT FOR HAMILTON—JAMES BANCROFT.
6-6mos.

Fire and Marine Assurance.

THE BRITISH AMERICA
ASSURANCE COMPANY.
HEAD OFFICE:
CORNER OF CHURCH AND COURT STREETS.
TORONTO.

BOARD OF DIRECTION:
Hon. G. W. Allan, M.L.C.,   A. Joseph, Esq.,
George J. Boyd, Esq.,   Peter Paterson, Esq.,
Hon. W. Cayley,   G. P. Ridout, Esq.,
Richard S. Cassels, Esq.,   E. H. Rutherford, Esq.,
Thomas C. Street, Esq.,

Governor:
GEORGE PERCIVAL RIDOUT, Esq.

Deputy Governor:
PETER PATERSON, Esq.

Fire Inspector: Marine Inspector:
E. ROBY O'BRIEN.   CAPT. R. COURNEEN.

Insurances granted on all descriptions of property
against loss and damage by fire and the perils of inland
navigation.

Agencies established in the principal cities, towns, and
ports of shipment throughout the Province.
THOS. WM. BIRCHALL,
22-1y   Managing Director.

Edinburgh Life Assurance Company.

Founded 1829.

HEAD OFFICE—22 GEORGE STREET, EDINBURGH.

Capital, ... £500,000 Ster'g.
Accumulated and Invested Funds, £1,000,000 "

HEAD OFFICE IN CANADA:
WELLINGTON STREET, TORONTO.

SUB-AGENTS THROUGHOUT THE PROVINCE.

J. HILLYARD CAMERON,
Chairman, Canadian Board.

DAVID HIGGINS,
Secretary, Canadian Board.   8-3m

Queen Fire and Life Insurance Company,
OF LIVERPOOL AND LONDON,
ACCEPTS ALL ORDINARY FIRE RISKS
on the most favorable terms.

LIFE RISKS
Will be taken on terms that will compare favorably with
other Companies.

CAPITAL, - - - £2,000,000 Stg.

CHIEF OFFICES—Queen's Buildings, Liverpool, and
Gracechurch Street London.
CANADA BRANCH OFFICE—Exchange Buildings, Montreal.
Resident Secretary and General Agent,
A. MACKENZIE FORBES,
13 St. Sacrament St., Merchants' Exchange, Montreal.
WM. ROWLAND, Agent, Toronto.   1-1y

Insurance.

Etna Fire and Marine Insurance Company of Dublin.

AT a Meeting of the Shareholders of this Company,
held at Dublin, on the 18th ult., it was agreed that
the business of the "ETNA" should be transferred to the
"UNITED FORTS AND GENERAL INSURANCE COMPANY."
In accordance with this agreement, the business will hereafter be carried on by the latter Company, which assumes
and guarantees all the risks and liabilities of the "ETNA."

The Directors have resolved to continue the CANADIAN
BRANCH, and arrangements for resuming FIRE AND MA-
RINE business are rapidly approaching completion.
T. W. GRIFFITH,
16   MANAGER.

Etna Insurance Company of Dublin.
The number of Shareholders exceeds Five Hundred.

Capital, $5,000,000—Annual Income nearly $1,000,000.

THIS Company takes Fire and Marine Risks on the most
favorable terms.
T. W. GRIFFITH, Manager for Canada.
Chief office for Dominion—Corner St. Francois Xavier
and St. Sacrament Sts., Montreal.
15-1y   WM. HENDERSON, Agent for Toronto

Scottish Provincial Assurance Co.
Established 1825.

CAPITAL, ...£1,000,000 STERLING.
INVESTED IN CANADA (1854) ....$600,000.

Canada Head Office, Montreal.

LIFE DEPARTMENT.
CANADA BOARD OF DIRECTORS:
HUGH TAYLOR, Esq., Advocate,
Hon. CHARLES WILSON, M.L.C.
WM. SACHE, Esq., Banker,
JACKSON RAE, Esq., Banker.
WM. FRASER, Esq. M.D., Medical Adviser.

The special advantages to be derived from insuring in
this office are:—Strictly Moderate Rates of Premium;
Large Bonus (intermediate bonus guaranteed;) Liberal
Surrender Value, under policies relinquished by assured ;
and Extensive Limits of Residence and Travel. All business disposed of in Canada, without reference to parent
office.

A. DAVIDSON PARKER,
Resident Secretary.
G. L. MADDISON,
15-1yr   AGENT FOR TORONTO.

Lancashire Insurance Company.
CAPITAL, - - - - - - - £2,000,000 Sterling

FIRE RISKS
Taken at reasonable rates of premium, and
ALL LOSSES SETTLED PROMPTLY,
By the undersigned, without reference elsewhere.
S. C. DUNCAN-CLARK & CO.,
General Agents for Ontario,
N. W. Corner of King & Church Streets,
25-1y   TORONTO.

Etna Fire & Marine Insurance Company.

INCORPORATED 1819. CHARTER PERPETUAL.

CASH CAPITAL, - - - - $3,000,000

LOSSES PAID IN 50 YEARS, 23,500,000 00.

JULY, 1868.
ASSETS.
(At Market Value.)
Cash in hand and in Bank.............. $544,842 39
Real Estate................................. 255,267 39
Mortgage Bonds............................ 932,845 00
Bank Stock................................. 1,372,679 00
United States, State and City Stock, and other
Public Securities 2,049,855 51

Total................... $5,052,880 19

LIABILITIES.
Claims not Due, and Unadjusted $490,803 55
Amount required by Mass. and New York
for Re-Insurance.......................... 1,405,267 15
THOS. R. WOOD,
50-6   Agent for Toronto.

Insurance.

ÆTNA
Live Stock Insurance Company

LICENSED BY THE DOMINION GOVERNMENT TO DO BUSINESS IN CANADA.

THE following Accidents, this month, show the importance of Insuring your Horses and Cattle against Death from any cause, or Theft, in the Ætna Insurance Company:

MONTREAL, September 16, 1868.
At a fire last night, in the sheds behind Ripin's Hotel, St. Joseph Street, three valuable Stock Horses were destroyed, "Young Clydesdale" and "Emigrant," belonging to the Huntingdon Agricultural Society—the former worth $900, and the latter $1,700; and "Old Beauharnois" cost $1,900, belonging to the Beauharnois Society.

PORT COLBORNE, September 18, 1868.
HORSES DROWNED.—Two horses belonging to Mr. Briggs, of Port Colborne, and four owned by Mr. Jollou, of Port Dalhousie, were drowned in the Canal, near the Junction, early this morning.

A fire at the Glasgow Hotel, Montreal, this morning, destroyed two horses. The fire was caused by drunkenness on the part of the stable men.

MONTREAL, September 24, 1868.
A fire in F. X. Cusson's stables, St. Joseph Street, last night, destroyed three horses.

E. L. SNOW, GENERAL AGENT, Montreal

Agents for Ontario:—
     SCOTT & WALMSLEY,
67novlly   Ontario Hall, Church Street, Toronto.

The Liverpool and London and Globe Insurance Company

INVESTED FUNDS:
FIFTEEN MILLIONS OF DOLLARS.

DAILY INCOME OF THE COMPANY:
TWELVE THOUSAND DOLLARS.

LIFE INSURANCE,
WITH AND WITHOUT PROFITS.

FIRE INSURANCE
On every description of Property, at Lowest Remunerative Rates.

JAMES FRASER, AGENT,
5 King Street West.
Toronto, 1868.   38-1y

Briton Medical and General Life Association,
with which is united the
BRITANNIA LIFE ASSURANCE COMPANY.

Capital and Invested Funds ....£750,000 Sterling.

ANNUAL INCOME, £220,000 STG. ;
Yearly increasing at the rate of £25,000 Sterling.

THE important and peculiar feature originally introduced by this Company, in applying the periodical Bonuses, so as to make Policies payable during life, without any higher rate of premiums being charged, has caused the success of the BRITON MEDICAL AND GENERAL to be almost unparalleled in the history of Life Assurance. *Life Policies on the Profit Scale become payable during the lifetime of the Assured, thus rendering a Policy of Assurance a means of subsistence in old age, as well as a protection for a family,* and a more valuable security to creditors in the event of early death; and effectually meeting the often urged objection, that persons do not themselves reap the benefit of their own prudence and forethought.

No extra charge made to members of Volunteer Corps for services within the British Provinces.

☞ TORONTO AGENCY, 5 KING ST. WEST.

oct17—9-1yr   JAMES FRASER, Agent.

Phenix Insurance Company,
BROOKLYN, N. Y.

PHILANDER SHAW,   STEPHEN CROWELL,
     Secretary.   President,

Cash Capital, $1,000,000. Surplus, $666,416.02. Total, 1,666,416.02. Entire Income from all sources for 1866 was $2,131,839.82.

CHARLES G. FORTIER, Marine Agent.

Ontario Chambers, Toronto, Ont.   19-13†

Insurance.

The Victoria Mutual
FIRE INSURANCE COMPANY OF CANADA.

Insures only Non-Hazardous Property, at Low Rates.

BUSINESS STRICTLY MUTUAL.

GEORGE H. MILLS, *President.*
W. D. BOOKER, *Secretary.*

HEAD OFFICE ....HAMILTON, ONTARIO

aug 15-1yr

The Ætna Life Insurance Company.

AN attack, abounding with errors, having been made upon the Ætna Life Insurance Co. by the editor of the Montreal *Daily News* ; and certain agents of British Companies being now engaged in handing around copies of the attack, thus seeking to damage the Company's standing,—I have pleasure in laying before the public the following certificate, bearing the signatures of the Presidents and Cashiers who happened to be in their Offices) of *every Bank in Hartford* ; also that of the President and Secretary of the old Ætna Fire Insurance Company :—
"To whom it may concern :—
"We, the undersigned, regard the Ætna Life Insurance Company, of this city, as one of the most successful and prosperous Insurance Companies in the States,—entirely reliable, responsible, and honourable in all its dealings, and most worthy of public confidence and patronage."

Lucius J. Hendee, President Ætna Fire Insurance Co., and late Treasurer of the State of Connecticut.
J. Goodnow, Secretary Ætna Fire Insurance Co.
C. H. Northam, President, and J. B. Powell, Cashier National Bank.
C. T. Hillyer, President Charter Oak National Bank.
E. D. Tiffany, President First National Bank.
G. T. Davis, President City National Bank.
F. S. Riley, Cashier,   do.   do.   do.
John C. Tracy, President of Farmers' and Mechanics' National Bank.
M. W. Graves, Cashier Conn. River Banking Co.
H. A. Redfield, Cashier Phœnix National Bank.
O. G. Terry, President Ætna National Bank.
J. R. Redfield, Cashier National Exchange Bank.
John G. Root, Assistant Cashier American National Bank.
George F. Hills, Cashier State Bank of Hartford.
Jas. Potter, Cashier Hartford National Bank.
Hartford, Nov. 20, 1867.

Many of the above-mentioned parties are closely connected with other Life Insurance Companies, but all unhesitatingly commend our Company as "reliable, responsible, honourable in all its dealings, and most worthy of public confidence and patronage.

JOHN GARVIN,
General Agent, Toronto Street.
Toronto, Dec. 3. 1867.   16-1y

Life Association of Scotland.

INVESTED FUNDS
UPWARDS OF £1,000,000 STERLING.

THIS Institution differs from other Life Offices, in that the

BONUSES FROM PROFITS
Are applied on a special system for the Policy-holder's
PERSONAL BENEFIT AND ENJOYMENT DURING HIS OWN LIFETIME,

WITH THE OPTION OF
LARGE BONUS ADDITIONS TO THE SUM ASSURED.

The Policy-holder thus obtains
A LARGE REDUCTION OF PRESENT OUTLAY
OR
*A PROVISION FOR OLD AGE OF A MOST IMPORTANT AMOUNT IN ONE CASH PAYMENT,
OR A LIFE ANNUITY,*

Without any expense or outlay whatever beyond the ordinary Assurance Premiums for the Sum Assured, which remains in tact for Policy-holder's heirs, or other purposes.

CANADA—MONTREAL—PLACE D'ARMES.

DIRECTORS:
DAVID TORRANCE, Esq., (D. Torrance & Co.)
GEORGE MOFFATT, (Gillespie, Moffatt & Co.)
ALEXANDER MORRIS, Esq., M.P., Barrister, Perth.
Sir G. E. CARTIER, M.P., Minister of Militia.
PETER REDPATH, Esq., (J. Redpath & Sons).
J. H. R. MOLSON, Esq., (J. H. R. Molson & Bros.)
Solicitors—Messrs. TORRANCE & MORRIS.
Medical Officer—R. PALMER HOWARD, Esq., M.D
     Secretary—P. WARDLAW.
Inspector of Agencies—JAMES P. M. CHIPMAN.   y

Insurance.

North British and Mercantile Ins Company.

Established 1809.

HEAD OFFICE,   -   CANADA   -   M

TORONTO BRANCH:
LOCAL OFFICES, Nos. 4 & 6 WELLINGTON S
Fire Department, ... R. N.

Life Department, ... H. L.
29-1y

Phenix Fire Assurance Com
LOMBARD ST. AND CHARING CRO
LONDON, ENG.

Insurances effected in all parts of the

WITH PROMITUDE and LIBERA
MOFFATT, MURRAY & BEA
     Agents for 1
     36 Yong

The Commercial Union Assu Company,
19 & 20 CORNHILL, LONDON, ENGLA
Capital, £2,500,000 Stg.—Invested over $2,0

FIRE DEPARTMENT.—Insurance granted scriptions of property at reasonable rates.

LIFE DEPARTMENT.—The success of has been unprecedented—*NINETY PER CE* miums now in hand. First year's premiums $100,000. Economy of management guarantee security. Moderate rates.

OFFICE—385 & 387 ST PAUL STREET, MO
MORLAND, WATSON
     General Agents

FRED. COLE, Secretary.
     Inspector of Agencies—T. C. LIVINGS
     W. M. WESTMACOTT, Agent n
19-1y

Phenix Mutual Life Insuranc
HARTFORD, CONN.

Accumulated Fund, $2,000,000, Income, $1

THIS Company, established in 1851, is one reliable Companies doing business in the c has been steadily prospering. The *Massachusett Reports* show that in nearly all important m superior to the general average of Companies, intending assurers the following reasons, among for preferring it to other companies :
It is purely Mutual   It allows the Insur and reside in any portion of the United States It throws out almost all restriction on occupati Policies. It will, if desired, take a note for Premium, thus combining all the advantages of all cash company. Its Dividends are declared and applied in reduction of Premium. Its Di in every case on Premiums paid. The Divid Phœnix have averaged fifty per cent. year settlement of Policies, a Dividend will be allo year the policy has been in force. The num dends will always equal the outstanding Notes losses promptly—during the existence never testled a claim. It boasts Policies for the ben fited Women beyond the reach of their husband Creditors may also insure the lives of Debtors are all Non-forfeiting, as it always allows the surrender his Policy, should he desire, the C ing a paid-up Policy therefor. This Import will commend itself to all. The inducements by the Phœnix are better and more liberal th any other Company. Its rate of Mortality is low and under the average.
Parties contemplating *Life Insurance* will fin interest to call and examine our system. Po payable either in Gold or American currency.
     ANGUS R. BETH
     General Agent
     Dominio

Office : 104 ST. FRANÇOIS XAVIER ST. MON
☞ Active and energetic Agents and wanted in every town and village, to whom lib ments will be given.

PRINTED AT THE DAILY TELEGRAPH HOUSE, BAY ST., COR. KING.

TORONTO PRICES CURRENT.—December 3' 1868.

Name of Article.	Wholesale Rates.	Name of Article.	Wholesale Rate.	Name of Article.	Wholesale Rates.
Boots and Shoes.	$ c. $ c.	**Groceries**—*Contin'd*	$ c. $ c.	**Leather**—*Contin'd.*	$ c. $ c.
Mens' Thick Boots ..	1 05 1 50	" fine to fins't..	0 85 0 95	Kip Skins, Patna	0 20 0 40
" Kip	2 50 3 25.	Hyson	0 45 0 80	French	0 70 .0 90
" Calf	3 20 3 70	Imperial	0 42 0 80	English	0 65 0 80
" Congress Gaiters..	2 00 2 40	Tobacco, *Manuf'ct'd:*		Hemlock Calf (30 to	
" Kip Coburgs....	1 10 1 50	Can Leaf, ℔ 5s & 10s.	0 26 0 30	35 lbs.) per doz..	0 75 0 85
Boys' Thick Boots....	1 70 1 90	Western Leaf, com	0 25 0 26	Do. light	0 45 0 50
Youths'	1 45 1 50	" good	0 27 0 32	French Calf..	0 96 1 15
Women's Batts	95 1 30	" Fine	0 32 0 35	Grain & Satn Clr ℔ doz..	0 00 0 00
" Congress Gaiters..	1 15 1 50	" Bright fine..	0 40 0 50	Splits, large ℔, ℔....	0 30 0 48
Misses' Batts..	0 75 1 00	" choice..	0 60 0 75	" small	0 20 0 30
" Congress Gaiters..	1 00 1 30	**Hardware.**		Enamelled Cow ℔ foot..	0 17 0 18
Girls' Batts	0 60 0 85	Tin *(net cash prices)*		Patent	0 18 0 20
" Congress Gaiters..	0 80 1 10	Block, ℔ ℔..........	0 25 0 26	Pr.de Gralin	0 17 0 18½
Children's C.T. Cacks..	0 50 0 65	Grain..........	0 25 0 26	Buff	0 17 0 18
" Gaiters	0 65 0 90	*Copper:*		**Oils.**	
Drugs.		Pig	0 23 0 24	Cod	0 60 0 62½
Aloes Cape............	0 12½ 0 16	Sheet..........	0 30 0 33	Lard, extra	0 00 1 25
Alum	0 02½ 0 03	*Cut Nails:*		" No. 1	0 00 1 15
Borax	0 00 0 00	Assorted ½ Shingles,		" Woollen	0 50 0 95
Camphor, refined....	0 65 0 70	℔ 100 ℔s.........	2 90 3 00	Lubricating, patent..	0 00 0 00
Castor Oil............	0 18 0 38	" Mott's economic	0 00 0 00	" No 2	0 00 0 00
Caustic Soda........	0 04½ 0 05	Shingle alone do ..	3 15 3 25	Linseed, raw	0 77½ 0 85
Cochineal............	0 90 1 10	Lathe and 5 dy ..	3 30 3 40	" boiled......	0 82½ 0 90
Cream Tartar........	0 00 0 00	*Galvanized Iron:*		Machinery	0 00 0 00
Epsom Salts	0 03 0 04	Assorted sizes.....	0 08 0 09	Olive, 2nd, ℔ gal. ..	1 43 1 00
Extract Logwood....	0 09 0 11	Best No. 24....	0 09 0 00	" salad	2 00 2 30
Gum Arabic, sorts....	0 30 0 35	" 20......	0 08 0 08½	" salad, in bots.	
Indigo, Madras........	0 75 1 00	" 28........	0 09 0 09½	qt. ℔ case ..	3 60 3 75
Licorice	0 14 0 42	*Horse Nails:*		Sesame salad, ℔ gal.,	1 60 1 75
Madder	0 13 0 16	Griest's or Griffin's		Seal, pale........	0 70 0 75
Nutgalls	0 00 0 00	assorted sizes......	0 00 0 00	Spirits Turpentine..	0 65 0 70
Opium............	6 70 7 00	For W. ass'd. sizes..	0 18 0 10	Varnish	0 00 0 00
Oxalic Acid........	0 28 0 33	Patent Hammer'd do..	0 17 0 18	Whale............	0 75 0 80
Potash, Bi-tart........	0 25 0 28	*Iron (at 4 months):*		**Paints, &c.**	
" Bichromate..	0 15 0 20	Pig—Gartsherrie No1..	24 00 25 00	White Lead, genuine	
Potass Iodide	3 80 4 60	" No 2....	23 00 24 00	in Oil, ℔ 25 lbs....	0 00 2 50
Senna	0 12½ 0 60	" No 3....	0 00 0 00	Do. No. 1	0 00 2 25
Soda Ash	0 03 0 04	Bar—Scotch, ℔100 ℔s..	2 25 2 50	" 2	0 00 2 00
Soda Bicarb	4 50 5 50	Refined	3 00 3 25	" 3	0 00 1 75
Tartaric Acid........	0 87½ 0 45	Swedes	3 50 3 60	White Zinc, genuine	3 00 3 50
Verdigris	0 35 0 40	Hoops—Coopers....	3 00 3 25	White Lead, dry	0 00 0 00
Vitriol, Blue............	0 09 0 10	Band	3 90 3 25	Red Lead..........	0 07½ 0 08
Groceries.		Boiler Plates........	3 25 3 60	Venetian Red, Eng'h..	0 03 0 03½
Coffee:		Canada Plates	4 00 4 25	Yellow Ochre, Fren'h..	0 03½ 0 04
Java, ℔ lb............	0 22@0 24	Union Jack	0 00 0 00	Whiting	0 90 1 25
Laguayra, ...	0 17 0 18	Pontypool	4 00 4 25	**Petroleum.**	
Rio............	0 15 0 17	Swansea	3 90 4 00	*(Refined ℔ gal.)*	
Fish:		Lead (at 4 months):		Water white, car'l'd..	0 31 —
Herrings, Lab. split..	0 75 7 00	Bar, ℔ 100 ℔s...	0 07 0 07½	" small lots..	0 00 0 32
" round...	0 00 0 00	Sheet "	0 08 0 09	Straw, by car load..	0 30 —
" scaled......	0 35 0 40	Shot..........	0 07½ 0 07½	" small lots....	0 31 0 32
Mackerel, small kitts..	1 00 0 00	*Iron Wire* (net cash):		Amber, by car load..	0 00 0 00
Loch. Har. w'h'sfrks..	2 50 2 75	No. 6, ℔ bundle...	2 70 2 80	" small lots....	0 00 0 00
" half "	1 25 1 50	" 9, "	3 10 3 30	Benzine	0 00 0 00
White Fish & Trout...	3 50 3 75	" 12, "	3 40 3 50	**Produce.**	
Salmon, saltwater....	14 00 15 00	" 16, "	4 30 4 40	*Grain:*	
Dry Cod, ℔112 lbs....	5 00 5 25	*Powder:*		Wheat, Spring, 60 ℔..	1 00 1 06
Fruit:		Blasting, Canada....	3 50 3 75	" Fall 60 "	1 10 1 30
Raisins, Layers	2 15 2 20	FF	4 25 4 50	Barley .... 48 "	1 22 1 30
" M H	2 10 2 15	FFF	4 75 5 00	Peas.... so 60 "	0 84 0 86
" Valentias new..	0 08½ 0 08½	Blasting, English ..	4 50 5 00	Oats.... 34 "	0 50 0 51
Currants, new......	0 05 0 05½	FF loose..	5 00 6 00	Rye .... 56 "	0 00 0 75
" old........	0 04½ 0 04½	FFF "	0 00 0 00	*Seeds:*	
Figs	0 10 0 11	*Pressed Spikes* (4 mos):		Clover, choice 60 "..	6 25 6 50
Molasses:		Regular sizes 100....	4 00 4 25	" com'n to gd "..	5 50 6 00
Clayed, ℔ gal	0 00 0 40	Extra "	4 50 5 00	Timothy, cho'e 48 "..	2 50 2 75
Syrups, Standard	0 00 0 50	*Tin Plates* (net cash):		" inf. to good 48 "..	2 00 2 50
" Golden	0 54 0 56	IC Coke	7 50 8 00	Flax (per brl.):..	1 00 1 00
Rice:		IC Charcoal......	8 25 8 75	Superior extra....	0 00 0 00
Arracan	4 50 4 75	DC "	9 50 10 00	Extra superfine,....	5 30 5 40
" "		IX "	10 25 10 75	Fancy superfine....	0 00 0 00
Spices:		IXX "	12 50 0 00	Superfine No. 1....	4 60 4 75
Cassia, whole, ℔ ℔..	0 42 0 45	DX "	7 50 9 00	" No. 2....	5 30 5 40
Cloves	0 11 0 12	DX "	9 50 10 00	*Oatmeal,* (per brl.)....	5 00 6 25
Nutmegs	0 45 0 55	**Hides & Skins,℔℔**			
Ginger, ground	0 20 0 25	Green rough ..	0 06 0 06½	**Provisions.**	
" Jamaica, root..	0 20 0 25	Green, salt'd & insp'd..	0 00 0 07	Butter, dairy tub ℔ lb..	0 23 0 24
Pepper, black......	0 09½ 0 10	Cured	0 08 0 08½	" store packed..	0 21 0 22
Pimento	0 08 0 00	Calfskins, green......	0 00 0 10	Cheese, new	0 11 0 12
Sugars:		Calfskins, cured......	0 00 0 13	" old	0 23½23 60
Port Rico, ℔ lb........	0 08½ 0 09	" dry....	0 12 0 00	Pork, mess, per brl..	0 00 0 00
Cuba	0 08½ 0 08½	Sheepskins, com....	0 00 0 00	" prime mess ..	0 00 0 00
Barbadoes (bright)..	0 09½ 0 10½	" country....	0 60 0 80	" prime	0 00 0 00
Dry Crushed, at 60 d..	0 11½ 0 11½			Bacon, rough	0 00 0 00
Canada Sugar Refine'y,		**Hops.**		" Cumberl'd cut..	0 10 0 11
yellow No. 2, 60 ds..	0 08½ 0 00	Inferior, ℔ ℔........	0 05 0 07	" smoked	0 00 0 00
Yellow, No. 2½..	0 09½ 0 09½	Medium	0 07 0 09	Hams, in salt........	0 00 0 00
" No. 3..	0 09½ 0 04½	Good	0 09 0 11	" sug.cur &canv'd..	0 00 0 00
Crushed X....	0 10 0 10½	Fancy	0 00 0 00	Shoulders, in salt....	0 00 0 00
" "	0 11 0 11½			Lard, in kegs	0 00 0 14
Ground..........	0 11 0 11½	**Leather,** ℔ (4 mos.)		Eggs, packed	0 18 0 20
Extra Ground......	0 12½ 0 12½	In lots of less than		Beef Hams	0 00 0 00
Teas:		50 sides, 10 ℔ cent		Tallow	0 00 0 00
Japan com'n to good..	0 40 0 55	higher.		Hogs dressed, heavy..	7 00 7 25
" Fine to choicest..	0 50 0 95	Spanish Sole, 1stqual..		" medium..	6 60 7 35
Colored, com. to fine..	0 50 0 75	heavy, weights ℔ ℔..	0 21 0 22	" light	6 00 6 50
Congou & Souch'ng..	0 42 0 75	Do.1st qual midd'e do..	0 21 0 22	**Salt, &c.**	
Oolong, good to fine..	0 50 0 65	Do. No. 2, all weights..	0 23 0 26	American best,..	1 55 1 60
Y. Hyson, com to gd..	0 45 0 55	Slaughter heavy	0 25 0 26	Liverpool coarse ..	1 25 1 35
Medium to choice	0 50 0 85	Do. light........	0 50 0 00	Plaster	1 01 1 10
Extra choice	0 85' 0 95	Harness, best	0 32 0 34	Water Lime	1 50 0 00
Gunpowd're. to med..	0 55 0 70	" No. 2	0 30 0 33		
" med. to fine	0 70 0 85	Upper heavy	0 44 0 38		
		" light......	0 35 0 40		

Soap & Candles.	$ c.	$ c.
D. Crawford & Co.'s ..		
Imperial.........	0 07¼	0 08
" Golden Bar	0 07	0 07½
" Silver Bar........	0 07	0 07½
Crown	0 05	0 05½
No. 1	0 03½	0 03¾
Candles	0 00	0 11½
Wines, Liquors, &c.		
Ale:		
English, per doz......	2 60	2 65
Guinness Dub Portr..	2 35	2 40
Spirits:		
Pure Jamaica Rum...	1 80	2 25
De Kuyper's H. Gin..	1 55	1 65
Booth's Old Tom.....	1 90	2 00
Gin:		
Green, cases.........	4 00	4 25
Booth's Old Tom, c...	6 00	6 25
Wines:		
Port, common	1 00	1 25
" fine old	2 00	4 00
Sherry, common	1 00	1 50
" medium.........	1 70	1 80
"old pale or golden..	2 50	4 00

Brandy:	$ c.	$ c
Hennessy's, per gal..	2 30	2 50
Martell's " ..	2 30	2 50
J. Robin & Co.'s " ..	2 25	2 35
Otard, Dupuy & Cos..	2 25	2 35
Brandy, cases........	8 50	9 00
Brandy, com. per c...	4 00	4 50
Whiskey:		
Common 36 u. p......	0 62½	0 65
Old Rye	0 85	0 87½
Malt........	0 85	0 87½
Toddy	0 85	0 87½
Scotch, per gal........	1 90	2 10
Irish—Kinnahan's c...	7 00	7 50
" Dunnville's Belf't..	6 00	6 25
Wool.		
Fleece, lb.............	0 28	0 35
Pulled ".............	0 22	0 25
Furs.		
Bear..................	3 00	10 00
Beaver................	1 00	1 25
Coon	0 20	0 40
Fisher................	4 00	6 00
Martin................	1 40	1 60
Mink..................	4 00	4 25
Otter.................	5 75	6 00
Spring Rats	0 15	0 17
Fox...................	1 20	1 25

INSURANCE COMPANIES.

English. – *Quotations on the London Market.*

No. of Shares.	Last Dividend.	Name of Company.	Shares par val £	Amount paid.	Last Sale.
20,000		Briton Medical and General Life...	10	....	1⅞
50,000	7½	Commer'l Union, Fire, Life and Mar.	50	5	5¼
24,000	8	City of Glasgow	25	2½	5
5,000	9½	Edinburgh Life	100	15	30½x
400,000	5—½ yr	European Life and Guarantee......	2½	11s6	4s 6d
100,000	10	Etna Fire and Marine.............	10	1½	1
20,000	5	Guardian	100	50	51½
24,000	12	Imperial Fire.....................	500	50	345
7,500	9½	Imperial Life	100	10	16½
100,000	10	Lancashire Fire and Life..........	20	2	2⅞x
10,000	11	Life Association of Scotland.......	40	7½	23
35,862	45s. p. sh	London Assurance Corporation ..	25	12½	48
10,000	5	London and Lancashire Life	10	1	1
87,504	40	Liverp'l & London & Globe F. & L.	20	2	7⅛
20,000	5	National Union Life	5	1	1
20,000	12½	Northern Fire and Life	100	5	10⅝
40,000	12 '68, bo 5s.	North British and Mercantile	50	6¼	16 16½
40,000	50	Ocean Marine	25	5	20
2,500	£5 12s.	Provident Life....................	100	10	38
....	£4½ p. s.	Phœnix...........................	....	....	136
200,000	2½—h. yr.	Queen Fire and Life	10	1	15-16ths
100,000	3s. bo. 4s	Royal Insurance..................	20	3	6¾
20,000	10	Scottish Provincial Fire and Life ..	50	2½	4⅞
10,000	25	Standard Life	50	12	65
4,000	5	Star Life	25	1¼	—
		CANADIAN.			℘ c.
8,000	4	British America Fire and Marine ..	$50	$25	56
....	4	Canada Life	...	....	.....
4000	12	Montreal Assurance	£50	£5	135
10,000	3	Provincial Fire and Marine........	60	11	.....
....	....	Quebec Fire	40	32½	£ 20
....	8	" Marine........................	100	40	95
10,000	5 7 mo's.	Western Assurance.................	40	6	.....

RAILWAYS.	Sha's	Paid	Montr	London.
Atlantic and St. Lawrence.......................	£100	All.	....	58 60
Buffalo and Lake Huron	20½	"	....	3 3½
Do. do Preference	10	"	....	5½ 6½
Buff., Brantf. & Goderich, 6℘c., 1872-3-4....	100	"	....	....
Champlain and St. Lawrence	....	....	9 11	....
Do. do Pref. 10 ℘ ct....	....	...	71½75	....
Grand Trunk	100	"	15 17	16 17
Do. Eq. G. M. Bds. 1 ch. 6℘c..........	100	"	....	83 86
Do. First Preference, 5 ℘ c	100	"	....	52 53
Do. Deferred, 3 ℘ ct..	100	"	....	....
Do. Second Pref. Bonds, 5℘c..........	100	"	....	41 43
Do. do Deferred, 3 ℘ ct..........	100	"	...	....
Do Third Pref. Stock, 4 ℘ct..........	100	"	...	28 30
Do. do. Deferred, 3 ℘ ct.....	100	"	....	....
Do. Fourth Pref. Stock, 3℘c..........	100	"	....	18½ 19½
Do. do. Deferred, 3 ℘ ct...........	100	"	....	...
Great Western	20½	"	13 15	14¼ 14½
Do. New	20½	18	....	....
Do. 6 ℘ c. Bds, due 1873-76...........	100	All.	....	102 104
5½ ℘c Bds. due 1877-78....	100	"	....	93 94
Marine Railway, Halifax, $250, all......	$250	"	....	....
Northern, of Canada, 6℘c. 1st Pref. Bds..........	100	"	...	80 83

EXCHANGE.	Halifax.	Montr'l.	Quebec.	Toronto.
Bank on London, 60 days......				
Sight or 75 days date	13½	9½ 9½	9⅝ 9⅝	9⅝
Private do.	12 12½	8 9	8¾ 9	9¼
Private, with documents..........	....	....	....	....
Bank on New York...............	....	25½ 26	24½ 25	74¼
Private do.	....	26 26½	25 25½	....
Gold Drafts do.	....	par	par ½ dis.	par ½ dis.
Silver	....	3 3½	....	3½ 5

STOCK AND BOND REPORT.

The dates of our quotations are as follows:—Toronto, Dec. 3; Montreal, Dec. 2; Dec. 1; London, Oct. 30.

NAME.	Shares.	Paid up.	Divid'd last 6 Months	Dividend Day.	CLOSING PRICES Toronto.	Montr
BANKS.			℘ ct.			
British North America	$250	All.	3	July and Jan.	104 105	103½10
Jacques Cartier........	50	"	4	1 June, 1 Dec.	106 106½	105½10
Montreal	200	"	5	"	138 139	138 14
Nationale....................	50	"	4	1 Nov. 1 May.	....	105 10
New Brunswick	100	"	......	......	....	...
Nova Scotia	200	28	7&b$3¼	Mar. and Sept.	....	....
Du Peuple.....	50	"	4	1 Mar., 1 Sept.	106 106½	106 10
Toronto	100	"	4	1 Jan., 1 July.	119½120	119 12
Bank of Yarmouth..........	....	....	......	......	....	....
Canadian Bank of Com'e......	50	95	......	......	105 105½	105 10
City Bank Montreal	80	All.	4	1 June, 1 Dec.	102 102½	104½10
Commer'l Bank (St. John)....	100	"	℘ ct.	. ...	....	...
Eastern Townships' Bank.....	50	"	4	1 July, 1 Jan..	....	98 9
Gore	40	...	3½	1 Jan., 1 July.	43 43½	42 4
Halifax Banking Company....	..	....	......	. ....	...	....
Mechanics' Bank.............	50	70	4	1 Nov., 1 May.	95½ 96	95 9
Merchants'Bank of Canada....	100	70	4	1 Jan., 1 July.	112 113	112 11
Merchants' Bank (Halifax)....	....	....	.....	.....	....	. ..
Molson's Bank......	50	All.	4	1 Apr., 1 Oct.	108½ 109	109 11
Niagara District Bank...	100	70	3½	1 Jan., 1 July.	...	....
Ontario Bank.................	40	All.	4	1 June, 1 Dec.	99½ 100	98½ 99
People's Bank (Fred'kton)....	100	"	......	......	....	....
People's Bank (Halifax)......	20	"	7 12 m	......	....	...
Quebec Bank	100	"	3½	1 June, 1 Dec.	97¼100	....
Royal Canadian Bank	50	50	4	1 Jan., 1 July.	90 91	89 9
St. Stephens Bank	100	All	.....	......	....	..
Union Bank	100	70	4	1 Jan., 1 July.	104 105	104½ 1
Union Bank (Halifax)........	100	40	7 12 mo	Feb. and Aug.	....	....
MISCELLANEOUS.						
British America Land........	250	44	2½	......	....	....
British Colonial S. S. Co......	250	32½	2½	......	...	45 5
Canada Company	32½	All.	5	......	....	....
Canada Landed Credit Co.....	50	$20	3½	......	72 73	....
Canada Per. B'ldg Society....	50	All.	5	......	124½125	....
Canada Mining Company.....	4	90	......	......	....	....
Do. Inl'd Steam Nav. Co.....	100	All.	20 12 m	......	....	106 10
Do. Glass Company.........	100	"	12½ "	......	....	50 75
Canad'n Loan & Investm't....	25	2½	7	......	....	....
Canada Agency	10	¼	......	......	....	....
Colonial Securities Co.........	...	....	.....	.....	....	....
Freehold Building Society....	100	All.	4	......	103¾104½	....
Halifax Steamboat Co........	100	"	5	......	....	....
Halifax Gas Company........	....	....	......	. .. .	....	...
Hamilton Gas Company......	....	....	.....	. ....	....	....
Huron Copper Bay Co........	4	12	20	. ....	....	25 40c
Lake Huron S. and C.........	5	102	......	......	....	....
Montreal Mining Consols.....	20	$15	......	......	....	2.25 2.
Do. Telegraph Co...	40	All.	5	......	133 136	135 13
Do. Elevating Co...	00	"	15 12 m	......	....	100 10
Do. City Gas Co.........	40	"	4	15 Mar. 15 Sep.	....	132½ 1
Do City Pass. R,. Co.....	50	"	5	......	....	110 11
Nova Scotia Telegraph	20	"	....	. ....	....	....
Quebec and L. S.	8	$4	......	......	. ..	....
Quebec Gas Co...............	200	All.	4	1 Mar., 1 Sep.	....	...
Quebec Street R. R..........	50	25	8	......	....	....
Richelieu Navigation Co......	100	All.	7 p.a.	1 Jan., 1 July.	....	118 12
St. Lawrence Tow Boat Co....	100	"	......	3 Feb.	....	...
Tor'to Consumers' Gas Co....	50	"	2 3 m.	1 My Au Mar Fe	106 106½	...
Trust & Loan Co. of U. C.....	20	5	3	......	....	....
West'n Canada Bldg Soc'y....	50	All.	5	......	115½116	....

SECURITIES.	London.	Montreal	Quebec.
Canadian Gov't Deb. 6 ℘ ct. stg..................	....	102 103	101 101½
Do. do. 6 do due Ja. & Jul. 1877-84........	107 108	....	....
Do. do. 6 do. Feb. & Aug.........	104 106	....	...
Do. do. 6 do. Mch. & Sep.........	104 106	...	...
Do. do. 5 ℘ ct. cur., 1883	93 94	92½ 93	93 93
Do. do. 5 do. stg., 1885	....	92½ 93½	93 93
Do. do. 7 do. cur....................	....	....	......
Dominion 6 p. c. 1878 cy.....	....	104½ 105½	104½ 104
Hamilton Corporation.....	. ..	....	......
Montreal Harbor, 8 ℘ ct. d. 1869.................	..	....	......
Do. do. 7 do. 1870....	...	....	......
Do. do. 6½ do. 1875......................	....	101 102	......
Do. do. 6½ do. 1873......................	....	....	......
Do. Corporation, 6 ℘ c. 1891	....	95½ 96½	94 95
Do. 7 p. c. stock.................................	....	106 107½	106 107
Do. Water Works, 6 ℘ c. stg. 1878......... ..	....	....	......
Do. do. 6 do. cy. do.	....	96 96½	......
New Brunswick, 6 ℘ ct., Jan. and July	103 105	....	......
Nova Scotia, 6 ℘ ct., 1875.........................	103½ 104½	....	......
Ottawa City 6 ℘ c. d. 1880	....	....	......
Quebec Harbour, 6 ℘ c. d. 1883.	....	....	60
Do. do. 7 do. do..........................	....	....	65 70
Do. do. 8 do. 1886.......................	....	....	75 85
Do. City, 7 ℘ c. d. 5 years	....	90 91	94 95
Do. do. 7 do. 9 do.	....	....	90
Do. do. 7 do. 2½ do.	....	....	97 98
Do. Water Works, 7 ℘ ct., 4 years.............	....	....	96 98
Do. do. 6 do. 2 do.	....	....	93½ 94
Toronto Corporation	....	90 92½	...

PROSPECTUS

OF THE

MINION EXPRESS COMPANY OF CANADA

ORGANIZED UNDER THE JOINT STOCK COMPANIES' ACTS.

CAPITAL STOCK, $1,000,000,

In $10,000 Shares, $100 each.

proposed to organize a DOMINION EXPRESS COMPANY, to meet the present and prospective demand for increased facilities of general transportation. It is the interest of Canadians to do their own work, and *accumulate* cash capital, and *one* of the objects of this scheme is the retention country of the profits arising from the business done.

press Companies obtain "four-fifths" of their business from merchants and bankers, and no reason exists why they cannot transport their own by their *own Agents, economically* and *efficiently*, and by a *union of capital* and *effort*, they hereby resolve so to do. Being thus united, and g to it their business and influence, secures to this Company certain and complete success.

is organization, like the mail system, is to extend, under *one general management*, to all cities, towns and villages in the Dominion, and to connect arts of the United States, and being but "one Company," will secure *unity, despatch* and *accuracy*.

is proposed to distribute the stock widely, throughout the Dominion, in limited sums, apportioned as nearly as practicable to the business of the ibers. The capital Stock of the Company to be not less than $1,000,000, in 10,000 shares of $100 each.

n per cent. of the stock subscribed will be required to be paid after the subscription shall have reached the sum of $250,000, and after a Charter ave been obtained, of which due notice will be given to the subscribers; the subsequent calls, not exceeding *ten per cent. at any one time,* to be t convenient intervals, as the demands on the Company may require. But the aggregate of all calls to be made will, it is believed, not exceed *per cent.* of the Capital Stock.

e business to be done strictly on *cash principles.* With a paying business assured from the start, by *interested* and *reliable* Stockholders, it will s seen that a small per centage *only* of the subscriptions will be required to put the Company in working order, and it is confidently and reasonably d that the receipts will thereafter maintain and extend it. And in order to secure an equitable voice in its management, the principal commercial will be represented at the Board, by Directors recommended by Stockholders of their own localities, who will also recommend to the Direction al Agents, and thus secure a general influence in its management, as well as its business.

l Express enterprises, both in this country and the United States, have been decidedly successful, resulting from the profits of the business itself; ving an organization and a share list—such as are now proposed—with energy and economy in the direction, no doubt can be entertained of the tisfactory results.

ith such prospects, the Merchants of the Dominion, Capitalists and others interested in the success of this enterprise, are invited to become olders.

The following shall be included in the By-Laws to be hereafter framed for the Government of the Company:

The Company shall be known by the name or title of "THE DOMINION EXPRESS COMPANY OF CANADA."

The Capital Stock of the Company shall be *One Million of Dollars,* divided into *Ten Thousand Shares of One Hundred Dollars each.*

Each Shareholder shall be liable only for the amount of Stock subscribed by him, her, or them.

The Shares of Stock of the Company shall be transferable; but no transfer shall be valid without the consent of the Directors, in writing, unless ares shall be paid up in full.

It shall be lawful for the Stockholders, so soon as the sum of two hundred and fifty thousand dollars shall have been subscribed, to call a General g of the subscribers, to be held at the office of the Company, in the City of Montreal, and proceed to elect nine qualified persons to be Directors Company, each of whom to be a proprietor of not less than ten Shares of Stock of the said Company, and three of whom shall form a quorum, ll the powers of the Directors. The said Directors shall also, at their first General Meeting, elect a President, Secretary, Treasurer, and General ntendent or Managing Director, from amongst themselves.

The said Directors so elected shall proceed, without delay, to frame all necessary By-laws to govern the Company, and shall have power to alter nend the same as circumstances may require.

The Directors shall not have power either to *sell out* the said Company to any other Express Company or organization now in existence, or here-e to incorporated, or to amalgamate with any other Express Company.

No Stockholder shall be at liberty to hold in his, her, or their name, more than one hundred shares of the Capital Stock of the said Company, it the consent of the Directors, in writing, first having been obtained.

PROVISIONAL DIRECTORS.

MESSRS. IRA GOULD,	MESSRS. WM. McNAUGHTON,	MESSRS. ALEXANDER McGIBBON,
WALTER MACFARLAN,	DUNCAN MACDONALD,	GEORGE HEUBACH,
VICTOR HUDON,	JOSEPH BARSALOU,	J. T. KERBY.

OFFICERS.

| PRESIDENT: | VICE-PRESIDENT: | TREASURER: | SECRETARY: |
| WALTER MACFARLAN. | WM. McNAUGHTON. | JOSEPH BARSALOU. | GEORGE HEUBACH. |

MESSRS. CARTIER, POMINVILLE, & BETOURNAY, SOLICITORS.   J. T. KERBY, GENERAL AGENT.

ollowing are among the prominent firms in Montreal who have subscribed to the original Stock List at the formation of the Company:—

Ira Gould, President Corn Exchange.	MESSRS. W. McNaughton, Messrs. Sincennes & McNaughton.	MESSRS. Boyer, Hudon, & Co.
Walter McFarlan, (Messrs. Walter McFarlan & Baird)	" A. W. Ogilvie & Co., Glenora Mills.	" Z. Benoit, Wholesale Merchant.
James Donelly, Wholesale Dry Goods.	" Benning & Barsalou, Auctioneers.	" Evans & Evans, Wholesale Hardware.
Luke Moore, (Messrs. Moore, Lemple & Hatchette).	" Alex. McGibbon, China House.	" James Smith, M.P.
Duncan Macdonald.	" T. Baillie & Co., Wholesale Dry Goods.	" Andrew Watson.
A. Shannon & Co., Wholesale Grocers.	" Alex. Walker, Wholesale Dry Goods.	" A. Freeman & Co.
Lewis, Kay & Co., Wholesale Dry Goods.	" Geo. Winks & Co., Wholesale Dry Goods, Albert Buildings.	" John Rhynas.
George Brush, Eagle Foundry.	" W. F. Ryan, M.P.	" Cartier, Pominville & Betournay, Solicitors.
	" Victor Hudon & Co., Wholesale Grocer.	" Cassels & Cameron, Wholesale Dry Goods.
		" Ferrier & Co., Wholesale Hardware.

TWENTY-THIRD ANNUAL REPORT

OF THE

NEW YORK LIFE INSURANCE COMPANY

Accumulated Capital, over $10,000,000. - - Divisible Surplus, Jan. 1, 1868, $1,642,425 59

Annual Statement, January 1st, 1868.

AMOUNT OF NET CASH ASSETS, January 1st, 1867		$6,727,816 65
AMOUNT OF PREMIUMS RECEIVED DURING 1867	$3,104,051 34	
AMOUNT OF INTEREST RECEIVED AND ACCRUED, INCLUDING PREMIUMS ON GOLD, &c.	487,339 94	
		3,591,391 28
		$10,319,207 93

DISBURSEMENTS.

Paid Losses by Death	$561,921 45	
Paid for Redemption of Dividends, Annuities, and surrendered and cancelled Policies	485,851 36	
Paid Salaries, Printing, Office and Law Expenses	98,032 55	
Paid Commissions and Agency Expenses	333,207 43	
Paid Advertising and Physician's Fees	46,518 77	
Paid Taxes and Internal Revenue Stamps	19,291 26	
		1,544,861 92
		$8,774,326 01

ASSETS.

Cash on hand, in Bank, and in Trust Company	$575,236 54	
Invested in United States Stocks, (Market value, $3,150,506 87) cost ...	2,978,907 49	
Invested in New York City Bank Stocks (Market value, $45,855) cost ...	41,549 00	
Invested in New York State Stocks (Market value, $836,050), cost ...	806,306 60	
Invested in other Stocks (Market value, $151,225), cost	149,337 01	
Loans on Demand, secured by U. S. and other Stocks, (Market value, $311,497)...	257,700 00	
Real Estate (Market value, $709,125 66)	528,234 53	
Bonds and Mortgages (Secured by Real Estate, valued at $2,260,000) ...	1,072,800 00	
Premium Notes on existing Policies, bearing interest	1,556,837 47	
Quarterly and semi-annual Premiums due subsequent to January 1, 1868 ...	346,285 81	
Interest accrued to January 1, 1868	52,402 83	
Rents accrued to January 1, 1868	2,401 96	
Premiums on Policies in hands of Agents and in course of transmission ...	406,326 77	
		$8,774,326 01
And excess of market value of securities over cost		385,427 90
Cash Assets, Jan. 1, 1868		$9,159,753 91

LIABILITIES OF THE COMPANY.

Amount of Adjusted Losses, due subsequent to Jan. 1, 1868	$134,800 00	
Amount of Reported Losses awaiting proof, &c.	38,214 32	
Amount reserved for Re-insurance on existing Policies (valuations, Carlisle table four per cent. interest, net premium) ...	6,283,635 49	
Return Premium, declared prior to 1866, payable on demand	72,572 51	
Return Premium, 1866 (now to be paid)	422,638 00	
Return Premium, 1867 (present value)	565,468 00	
		$7,517,328 32
Divisible Surplus		$1,642,425 59

During the Year, 6,597 Policies have been issued, insuring $22,541,940.

The Progress of the Company for the Past Four Years will be seen in the following Statement:—

Assets.		Increase of Assets over previous year.			Increase of Assets over previous year.
1864 .... $3,658,755 55		$1,005,217 63	1866 .... 6,727,816 65		1,845,896 95
1865 .... 4,881,919 70		1,223,164 15	1867 .... 8,774,326 01		2,046,509 36
		Total increase .... $6,120,788 09.			

One of the special features of this Company is the TEN YEAR NON-FORFEITURE PLAN.

The system popularly termed "The Non-Forfeiture Plan," was originated and first presented to the public by this Company, in their well-known "TEN YEAR NON-FORFEITURE POLICY," in the year 1860; and its perfect adaptation to the wants of every class in the community, obviate every reasonable objection to Life Insurance, is shown from the fact that every other American Company has been compelled, in deference to public opinion, to adopt it, although in many cases it is done in such a way as considerably to impair its value. It has received the *unqualified approval* of the *best business men of the land*, large numbers of whom have taken out policies under it, simply as an investment.

By the Table on which this class of Policies is based, a person incurs no risk in taking out a policy. Insuring to-day for $10,000, if he should die to-morrow, the policy immediately becomes a claim; and if he shall live ten years, and make ten annual payments, his policy will be paid for, and his dividends *still continue*, making

HIS LIFE POLICY A SOURCE OF INCOME TO HIM WHILE LIVING.

By the specific terms of these policies, and not by vague and indefinite statements made in circulars, a party after the second year does not forfeit what he has paid in premium. Thus, if one insuring by this plan for $10,000 discontinues after the second year, he is entitled to a PAID-UP POLICY, according to the number of full years paid in, as follows:—

Second year, two-tenths of $10,000 (amount insured), amounting to.. $2,000 | Fourth year, four-tenths of $10,000 (amount insured), amounting to... $4,000
Third year, three-tenths of $10,000 (amount insured), amounting to... 3,000 | Fifth year, five-tenths of $10,000 (amount insured), amounting to.... 5,000

And so on, until the tenth annual payment, *when all is paid*. The paid up policies, for the proportionate partial payments, as well as for the full amount, participate in the Dividends of the Company during the whole existence of the policies. ☞ This being a purely mutual Company, ALL ITS PROFITS ARE DIVIDED AMONG THE ASSURED.

MORRIS FRANKLIN, President,
WILLIAM H. BEERS, Vice-Pres't & Actuary.

Medical Examiners :
HENRY H. WRIGHT, ESQ., M.D.,
JOHN E. KENNEDY, ESQ., M.D.,

EDWYN EVANS,

Agent for Toronto, 15 Wellington Street E

THE CANADIAN
ONETARY TIMES
AND
INSURANCE CHRONICLE.

D TO FINANCE, COMMERCE, INSURANCE, BANKS, RAILWAYS, NAVIGATION, MINES, INVESTMENT, PUBLIC COMPANIES, AND JOINT STOCK ENTERPRISE.

| ̃O. 17. | TORONTO, THURSDAY, DECEMBER 10, 1868. | { SUBSCRIPTION. { $2 YEAR. |

Mercantile.

Meetings.

THE TRUST AND LOAN COMPANY OF UPPER CANADA.

The following is the report of the Directors submitted to the Proprietors on the 30th Sept. :

"The following report and statement of accounts for the six months ending the 30th of September of the current year is submitted to the proprietors. The balance at credit of revenue, including £3,359 5s. 6d. brought forward from March last, is £17,156 12s. 1d. The Directors recommend that out of this balance a dividend at the rate of 8 per cent. per annum, less income tax, be declared on the paid-up capital stock of the Company ; £3,920 18s. will be carried to the reserve fund, in accordance with the provisions of the Royal Charter of Incorporation, and the balance then remaining to the credit of the next half-year's accounts will be £3,255 14s. 1d. During the period embraced by these accounts, the reserve fund has been charged with the sum of £1,277 15s. 4d for losses on realization of securities in default. The balance at credit of this fund, after adding the £3,920 18s. above referred to, will be £68,391 13s. 6d. The Directors have pleasure in stating that the debentures of the Company are again in request, and that the renewal of bonds maturing during the present year—including a large proportion of those issued at 6 per cent., and which have been continued at 5 per cent.—have been very satisfactory. The demand for loans at present in Canada is not as active as the Directors could wish, but they trust that the recent abundant harvest will shortly have a beneficial effect on the operations of the Company.

DIRECTORS.—The Rt. Hon. Edward Pleydell Bouverie, M.P., president; Charles Morrison, Esq., deputy-chairman. Ashley Carr Glyn, Esq. ; Jas. Hutchinson, Esq. ; William Gordon Thomson, Esq. ; T. M. Weguelin, Esq., M.P., Secretary— F. Fearon, Esq.

THE GRANBY RED SLATE COMPANY.

From the Annual Report of the Directors we condense the following :

Up to September 12, 1867, operations had been carried on in opening the quarry upon the Company's property, for a period of about three months, and an expenditure incurred of about $1,500. Soon after this time, they had purchased an adjoining property, consisting of a farm of 100 acres, whereon were indications of a deposit of good workable green slate of great extent, for $1,900. The terms of payment were $1,000 payable within thirty days, the remaining $900 in the ensuing month of May. These payments were duly made, and the deed of transfer executed. This purchase, added to the 200 acres previously owned, gives a domain of 300 acres of good land. With respect to the slate itself, it is found, upon test of working, to be equal its quality to that of the best quarries in the States, and the supply is inexhaustible. The workable bands of slate have a smaller overburthen to be removed, and are more free from other substances than is usually the case with slate quarries. The slate upon the new purchase proving

to be good, the workmen were all put upon the opening commenced thereon, which was prosecuted vigorously through the winter, and has been continued till the present time. There has been discovered also a very valuable band of purple slate lying alongside of the green, so that the two bands can be worked together. A large quantity of overburthen has been removed, so that a sufficiency of good workable slate is easily obtained ; and during the ensuing winter a small number of quarrymen will be sufficient to supply the factory. The works are now fully equipped, with the exception of stone-cutters, for doing carved work upon mantels, &c. It has been found exceedingly difficult to obtain this class of workmen.

There are some $2,000 worth of mantels, &c., partly finished, which would have been completed by the present time if stone-cutters could have been obtained. Arrangements are now nearly completed for a full supply in this department of labour.

The property of the company is all paid for, and free from mortgage or claim of any kind. There is still sufficient treasury stock remaining to pay off all the indebtedness of the company, leaving 2,000 shares unsold. The last sales have been made at $3 per share, at which price several hundred shares have been sold. A limited number of shares are still offered at that price.

It is estimated that the present equipment of machinery and scale of operations will be sufficient to turn out manufactures to the average amount of $2,000 per month for the ensuing year, which, from the experience of similar establishments in the States, the directors believe will yield a remunerative profit. From the orders already received, and from correspondence had with dealers in this class of manufactures in different parts of Canada, it is considered pretty certain that there will be found a ready sale in Canada for all articles the company can produce.

The Directors feel that they should not conclude this report without alluding to the valuable services rendered by their Secretary, Mr. E. L. Snow, to whose good judgment and untiring efforts they attribute, in a large measure, the sound and prosperous condition in which the company's affairs are found at the close of its first year's operations.

ANOTHER WOODEN RAILWAY PROJECT.—A meeting was held in Montreal, on the 1st December, for the purpose of considering the propriety of promoting the construction of a wooden railway from Montreal to some point to the North of St. Jerome, in the county of Terrebonne.

The following gentlemen were present: The hon. Edouard Masson, of Terrebonne; Dr. LaChaine, of St. Adele; Godefroi Laviolette, L. Villemure, of St. Jerome; A. W. Ogilvie, M.P.P., Lewis Beaubien, M.P.P., Duncan Macdonald, P. S. Murphy, Chas. Legge, and several other influential citizens.

Moved by Louis Beaubien, Esq., seconded by Dr. Lachaine, and unanimously resolved, That the meeting is of opinion that it is expedient to build a wooden railway from Montreal to the Northern part of the district of Terrebonne, in order to encourage the colonization of that part of the country.

It was then decided that a committee should drive out to St. Jerome, and inspect the country north of that village so as to be in a position to report at a future meeting on the best route to be adopted.

QUEBEC AND GOSFORD RAILWAY.—A full meeting of the provisional directors was held on Monday evening in the Mayor's room, City Hall. Some time was passed in discussing a proposition made by Mr. Hulbert in a letter received that day, and a sub-committee was appointed to examine and report on estimates, &c. The proposition to give each shareholder annually one cord of first quality three-foot wood for every share of paid-up stock was fully considered and resolved on by the Board. It was resolved also that each share should carry with it one vote, and that as soon as $60,000 of stock shall have been subscribed, a general meeting of the shareholders should be called to elect their own Board of Directors. Several gentlemen of the Committee were named, who will call upon the citizens with lists, for the purpose of getting the stock taken up as soon as possible.—*Chronicle.*

Insurance.

INSURANCE MATTERS IN MONTREAL.

(From Our Own Correspondent.)

MONTREAL, Dec. 8th, 1868.

There have been few fires in Montreal for the past two or three weeks ; the only heavy one in the city (until to-day) being that at Graham's Stationery Store, on St. Francis Xavier Street, by which the Royal and Scottish Provincial will lose some $10,000, and the Citizen about $1,000 on the building. This morning, at about 6 a.m., a fire was discovered in the Custom's Examining Warehouse, on Common Street ; the alarm was promptly given, and the fire subdued after a sharp fight. The loss will probably range from $7,000 to $8,000. The goods were insured by the Custom House authorities for $152,000, in several of the leading English Offices here. There has, evidently, been foul play in the case, and the supposed criminal is in the hands of the police, for, upon investigation immediately after the extinction of the fire, desks and drawers were found to have been broken open and the contents tumbled about in great disorder. A robbery has evidently been committed—by whom is a question for our indefatigable Fire Marshals to decide. These gentlemen, however, are much more zealous in the collection of their fees than in the rather more diligent inquiry into origins of fires. The first session of our Local Legislature will, it is hoped, make a radical change in that office.

There is little or no news of an interesting nature in Insurance matters transpiring here at present, the usual break-neck competition for business still prevails to a considerable extent. Perry, the Inspector of the "Royal," has returned from his tour in the Western States, and has completed his very clear and voluminous report on the state of Insurance matters in the far West.

FIRE RECORD.—Brooklin, Ont., Dec. 4.—Last night the barn on Thos. Lumsden's farm, about a mile east of Brooklin, and rented by Henry Knight, caught fire. 200 bushels of wheat, a lot of oats, and three head of cattle were burned in the barn. Probable loss, $1,500 to 2,000—insured for $600.

Ingersoll, Dec. 7.—A fire broke out in the parsonage occupied by the Rev. J. P. Hincks, incumbent of St. James's Church, which, with the barn and building adjoining, was totally destroyed. Most of the library and furniture were saved. Loss $1,000 ; insured in the Western for $500.

Simcoe, Nov. 27.—The grist and woollen mills belonging to Jacob Soveren, township of Middleton, County Norfolk, with all their contents, were entirely destroyed by fire. The Simcoe *Reformer*

says the fire is supposed to have originated from a lamp hanging near the ceiling. Mr. Soveren, who had lain down to sleep for a while, had a narrow escape, and was considerably scorched. There was a large quantity of wool, cloth, &c., in the mill, but nothing whatever was saved. The loss will amount to $10,000, which is only partially covered by an insurance of $2,000 in the Gore Mutual.

Quebec, Dec. 1.—An alarm of fire was raised but no damage done. Subsequently a fire started in a shop in St. John Street, next to the store of Loger & Rinfret, occupied by Maurice, dealer in general merchandise. When an entrance was effected by the brigade, it was found that the fire proceeded from a large wooden box under the counter. It was extinguished without much damage.

Montreal, Dec. 3.—The dwelling house of Mr. Ward, situated off the St. Catharine road, about half a mile from the residence of the late Sheriff Boston, was totally destroyed by fire. The property, we understand, was insured for $8,000.

Kingston, Dec. 3.—A fire broke out in the bakehouse of McCammon, William street, but was extinguished before any serious damage was done.

Trenton, Dec. 2.—This fire, which was mentioned last week, originated in the millinery shop of Mrs. Wicks on Water street, and extended to the stores of Mr. Losey and the harness shop of Reeves & McEwen ; these buildings which formed one block were consumed, only a portion of the stock saved. The fire extended to two municipal frame shops, owned by Geo. Reeves, and the dwelling house adjoining, owned by Geo. Young and occupied by Irish, dentist, and McCready, tailor. A good deal of damage was done to goods by removal, and the total loss is unknown, but will range from $10,000 to $14,000; no particulars as to insurance.

Mitchell, Ont., Dec. 1.—The saw mill on 5th concession of Logan township, owned by Thos. Matheson, of Mitchell, and worked by Cyrus Allan, was totally consumed by fire. Allan, it appears, placed a can of oil upon the stove, and, having left the mill for a short time, in his absence the fluid boiled over, and from the heat of the stove, ignited. The flames soon reached the building, causing the destruction of the property. Loss, about $1000; no insurance.

Maryboro' Township, Ont., Nov. 17.—Patterson's saw mill, on the 7th concession, was totally consumed. No insurance. The fire is supposed to have been caused by sparks blown from the furnace during a high wind.

Orillia, Ont., Dec. 1.—The residence of T. W. George, Postmaster, Falkenburg, was destroyed by fire. We have no particulars.

Toronto, Dec. 3.—An alarm was given, and the engines turned out, but only a chimney was on fire.

Nictaux, N. S., Nov.—The saw mill, grist mill and carding machine, owned by Samuel McCeown, at Nictaux Falls, were totally destroyed by fire. The loss is estimated at $4,000. No insurance.

Plattsville, Ont., Nov. 27.—Park's tannery, in this village, was totally destroyed. The steam engine and the hides in the vats were saved ; no particulars as to insurance : cause unknown.

Inverhuron, Ont., Nov. 25.—An extensive fire occurred at this village. The following particulars are received:—Alex. McLellan, building entirely consumed; supposed to be fully insured. L. Oliver, building insured; a lot of tools, a quantity of finished and unfinished work, all his household goods. Hugh Matheson, building, a quantity of lumber and some tools; some insurance. P. McRae, building, and about $400 in goods; no insurance. P. & N. McInnis, pearl ashes, value about $500. J. H. Coulthard Underwood, goods about $400. John McDonald, do., $200. W. McFarlane, do., $150. Mrs. Turner, Tiverton,

do., $70. Also, a quantity of fish and f tackle, the property of fishermen.

Ingersoll, Dec. 3.—Mr. S. P. Lodges' factory was entirely destroyed by fire this ing. It is supposed to have been the work incendiary. A reward of $100 is offered f apprehension and conviction of the par parties.

Stratford, Dec. 1.—Some account of th in Workman's hardware store was given last the loss is about $4,000; insurance $2,600 supposed it to be the work of an incen while others affirm that it was purely accide

Windsor, Nov. 27.—A fire occurred at W ton, a few miles from Windsor, which des several cooper shops and their contents, c ing of tools, barrel staves and barrels, the p ty of Mr. Hiram Walker, of Detroit. The ings were so combustible, that althoug Windsor steam engine was conveyed to th the fire swept the whole range.

Napanee, Ont., Dec. 3.—Last night, abo miles from this place, a fire broke out, a o'clock, in a house, formerly a tavern star owned by Patrick McAmbridge, which wast together with a quantity of grain, whic stored in the house. The fire was cause defective stove pipe. Loss about $1,C00; surance.

Stratford, Dec. 5.—A dispatch says night, about nine o'clock, a fire broke out stables in the rear of the old "Union The whole centre of the town, for a time, danger, but by the exertions of the people suppressed. It was the work of an incend Carleton County, N.B., Nov. 27.—The d of Mr. Arch. Good, of Williamstown, was to the ground, with the greater portion contents, such as furniture, household goo visions, &c. Mr. Good was absent from and the inmates of the house had hardly escape. No insurance.

MARINE RECORD.—The following i have occurred to lake shipping, as repo American papers :

Schooner Condor, of Montreal, Capt. from Montreal to St. John's, Newfoundla being in collision off Cape Ray, went ash Point-au-Basque, and is expected to be loss.

The schooner Minnesota, loaded wit went ashore about seventeen miles north minster, and will prove a total loss.

The schooner Mercer, of Port Huro went ashore at Port au Basque, had no late accounts, been got off, and it is now she will prove a total loss. She cam 1849, and was formerly a United States cutter, but for the past four years has in the merchant service. She was 130 measurement.

The schooner J. G. Beard, bound fr Elgin, Canada, to Oswego, with a cargo ran ashore on Charity Island, soon afte port, and was obliged to jettison 2,000 b her corn in order to get off.

The schooner M. F. Johnson lies ir fathoms of water under Erie Peninsula. bound from Detroit to Erie. The ves sured for $8,000—$4,000 of which is in th

The schooner Northerner pounded hea the bottom while loading with wood at at Amsterdam, and after getting out lake was discovered to be leaking badly. he could not keep her free, the captai her alongside the pier at Port Washingto the deck load was discharged in order t her. This done, the services of the Cuyahoga were secured to tow the disab to Milwaukee. She filled with water sized off Port Uloa, and had to be ad the Cuyahoga picked up her crew anc them to port.

ner Jennie Mullen is at Port Huron, boom, bowsprit, and everything for- Probably the result of a collision.

ler W. T. Emery, a few days since, tact with the tug Jessie, just outside ell harbor, resuling in damaging the of the latter and the head gear of The total damage will probably

ler Billy Doran, a small vessel bound er to Cobourg, on the 10th instant., of 150 barrels of salt, has not been and apprehensions are felt for her crew consisted of Captain George es Estes, son of Captain Estes, and

th the schooner Clyde, bound from with hay and supplies, on the way llet, ran afoul of the steamer Francis Cape Commodore. The latter was ed, but the Clyde had her larboard in and sprung a leak. She was towed id.

m a resident of Stony Point, a short Monroe, on Lake Erie, states that inst. a vessel supposed to belong to unknown, foundered near that place, c load, hatches, etc., were washed he crew nothing is known.

id despatch says: Theodore Cham dent of the Northern Transportation es up the City of Boston, sunk in au, as a total loss. She was valued isured for $20,000.

Juayle brought into Cleveland the t, owned there, that had capsized in She was laden with lumber. Her l lost, also the spars and sails; very te.

ler Mazeppa, which went ashore on rse Bay is a total loss. She was iongo, and worth $10,000, partially

ler Josephine Horn went to pieces e; insured for $1,500, and cargo for

ler Arbuckle ashore in Sister Bay ain, will likely prove a total loss; l,500; she is owned in Racine. Iechanic struck the pier at Racine ashed in; loss $3,000; insurance had in hour before.

DEPOSITS.—The Guardian Fire and e Company of London, England, has cash $100,346.86 with the Govern not yet appointed. The Star Life iciety of England has deposited Joseph Gregory, agent, Toronto.

Brigade of Sarnia entertained their en of Port Huron,—together with of the Sarnia Corporation,—to a evening of the 26th ult., about two all, assembling to take part in the

milton exchanges say that a special le Victoria Mutual Insurance Com d in Hamilton on Monday last, "to racticability of establishing a branch take risks within the range of the nter works." The project was favor ed, and a committee was appoint reliminary steps for carrying out the

FIRE INSURANCE ASSOCIATION.— y, the registration of which was paper of September 19th, is now fully inaugurated for business with half a million, in £10 shares, with sse to one million. Medical and General Life Associa e connection the Britannia Fire As enjoy the advantage—has an annual

premium income of upwards of £230,000, the new premiums exceeding £25,000 a year, and possesses upwards of 2,700 agents, with branch offices in Edinburgh, Glasgow, Dublin, Manchester, Liver pool, Birmingham, Leeds, Nottingham, Swan sea, Bristol, Plymouth, Southampton, and Ham burg. The share and Policy holders of the com pany number over 25,000 persons, and in addition, the society, from its peculiar constitution, has an extensive connection amongst a very large num ber of the medical profession throughout the king dom. The whole of this large representative and connectional influence will, under the above arrangements, be used for the benefit of the Bri tannia Fire Association, and from the valuable organization thus formed, a large and remunera tive business may be safely anticipated. It is not difficult to predicate a large amount of success, considering that Mr. Messent, of the Briton Med ical and General Life Association, has accepted the responsible duties of manager of the Britannia Fire Association.—*Investors' Guardian.*

THE POWERS AND DUTIES OF FIRE INSURANCE AGENTS.

THE AGENT.—By common law, any person or persons having power to do a thing, in his or their own right, may do it by an agent. A com pany can not be affected by any act of an agent not within the scope of his authority. A com pany can not be discharged by *private* instructions to agents, the insured being ignorant of such in structions at the time of making the contract. When an agent has no written appointment, the jury must decide as to the extent of his authority, from what he testifies and did, coupled with the acts of the company recognizing him. No per son can act as agent in a transaction in which he has an adverse interest or employment. An agent can not receive an application from himself, and insure his own property under it so as to bind the company. An agent cannot delegate his authority to another. Policies which are valid only when countersigned by an agent duly au thorized, must not be signed by another party for him. An agent for two or more companies takes a risk in one of them and reinsures it in a second for which he is also agent; held, that such re assurance is not binding on such said company until approved by the parent office. Agents hav ing no power to issue policies, cannot consent to transfer of policies, or make other valid endorse ments. Knowledge by agents of facts forfeiting a policy, is not binding upon his company, unless communicated to him by the insured,—rumor or street talk is not notice. An application is held to be the act of an applicant, and where the con ditions of the policy require that the applicant shall be bound by his application, he is affected by any omissions in it by the agent, even when the latter is agent of both parties. But when an agent omits from an application facts stated by applicant, and which agent promised to insert, the agent must not suffer for the omission. An applicant entrusting an application in blank to a sub-agent, not empowered to issue policies, with permission to fill up the same, is responsible for statements subsequently inserted by the sub agent. If either party must suffer by the mistake of an agent, it must be the party whose agent he is. When an agent surveys premises and inserts the value as given by applicant, such value binds the insured, but not the company. An agent has no authority to issue a policy *after a loss occurs,* if known to him, though in receipt of an application for same, but not acted upon. And if a verbal contract for the insurance had been previously distinctly made, the agent should nevertheless decline to issue the policy until the facts have been communicated to his company. In a part nership agency, each partner has all the powers of the firm. *Duty of an Agent.*—In cases of loss by fire, in the absence of a special adjuster, the local agent

must identify himself heartily with his company, and act upon the defensive, so far as necessary, until he can hear from the parent office. He should fully comprehend that *he is the representa tive of his company,* and *not of the insured:* "a man cannot serve two masters." He should also understand that while it is *not* expected that he will seek to take undue advantage of any party, it *is* confidently that he will watch closely to pre vent any party from taking improper advantage of his company, either by accident or design. And, as such representative, he should be espe cially careful, in doubtful cases, that he does not commit himself or his company to a recognition of any claim, or to any definite line of policy as to its adjustment, without especial instructions from the parent office; for inasmuch as the laws are the only safeguard for the underwriter against unjust and fraudulent claims, so no legal point in favor of the company should be unadvisedly waived or surrendered, either by act or by impli cation, until the proof submitted shall have been made entirely satisfactory in all its details, or the claim may have been compromised. If the loss be a just one, it cannot be injured by scrutiny. Undue haste, on the part of a claimant, is sug gestive that something behind needs investiga ting; whilst feverish anxiety on the part of the agent to hurry up the closing of the claim, be cause other companies have paid, indicates want of experience and lack of judgment. *Notice of Loss.*—Where a case of loss or damage under a policy of his company, whether large or small, comes to his knowledge, the local agent is required to notify the parent office immediately, by telegram when the amount is large, giving number of the policy, probable amount of loss, partial or total ; with the gross amount of other insurance, if any ; to be followed, with as little delay as possible, by letter giving particulars more fully ; as to whether knowledge of such loss was obtained directly from the insured, or his agent, in accordance with the conditions of the policy, or from other sources ; also the names of the com panies interested in the loss, and amounts covered by each ; together with such other information touching the loss or damage as may be known or suspected at the time. This is imperative ! In cases involving large amounts, or likely to prove intricate in the settlement, a special adjuster is usually sent from the office ; but smaller and simple cases may be left to the local agent, whose mind will be much enlightened as to his own duties and the reserved rights of his company, by an attentive study of the printed "*Conditions of In surance,*" as given by the policy, and by corre spondence with the parent office, when necessary. *Preservation of the Property.*—After notice of the loss has been promptly forwarded to the com pany, and until advised by the parent office, the local agent will look after the interest of his com pany. He will see that the owner, whose duty it is to do so, under the conditions of the policy, makes proper and timely efforts to preserve from further injury or deterioration the property saved, whether sound or in a damaged condition. If necessary, it should be removed to another build ing. Should the owner refuse or delay, to the evident detriment of the property, to have it pro perly attended to, he will do so at his own peril. The agent will at once notify the parent office of the fact, by telegram in special cases, and await advices. Should delay, however, involve no im mediate injury to the property, action by the local agent may be deferred until the arrival of an adjuster, or definite advices be received from the company. Especial attention should be paid to shelf hardware, cutlery, stove and tinware, and similar stocks which rust quickly. *Wet goods,* millinery stocks and such like, should be opened and spread out to dry, so as to prevent mildew, stain or mold, arising from heat. Any perishable property, which would materially injure by delay, should be submitted to appraisers as soon as pos sible, and when appraised, turned over to the claimant, as every day's delay adds to the damage;

or if delay would render it likely to be totally destroyed, it should at once be sold at auction, or at private sale, by agreement with the claimant, for cash, "*for and on account of whom it may concern.*" As the representatives of the insurers, agents have the right of access to, and a general supervisory interest over the property covered by their companies, which *should always be exercised when necessary* for its preservation against further damage by loss or theft. Further instructions upon the duty of local agents, in regard to damaged goods, will be found under the head of "Appraisement of damaged goods."

Investigation of the Origin of the Fire.—While attending to the proper preservation of the goods or other property, the local agent should make diligent inquiry as to the origin of, and circumstances attendant upon the fire; the more especially if originating upon the premises of the insured, so as to be prepared to communicate the result of his investigations either to the adjuster on his arrival, thus giving him a clue to work upon, or by letter to the company.

Examination of the risk, at the time of the fire, with reference to the terms of the contract.—Agent should carefully read the written portions of the policy, and the representations as made in the survey and application, to discover if any changes *material* to the risk had been made since the policy was issued; either by changes in occupancy, by additions or alterations, or other causes affecting the insurance. The conditions of the policy should be carefully scanned, for the purpose of detecting any *wilful* violation by the insured. Any information gained by this investigation of the policy and conditions should be carefully noted, ready for use at the proper time, should occasion require. Having made all these preliminary investigations, the agent is ready to proceed with the adjustment of the loss; and the more thoroughly the investigation has been thus made, the more satisfactory and easy will the final adjustment be.—*Griswold's Handbook of Adjustments.*

MATHEWSON *v.* THE ROYAL INSURANCE COMPANY.—The following judgment was given in the Supreme Court, Montreal, by Judge Berthelot:—In this case, which has been tried before a jury, there were two motions—one by plaintiffs for judgment, and one by defendant for a new trial. The plaintiffs sued as the purchasers and owners of a quantity of coal oil, which had been stored in Middleton's warehouse and burned at the fire which took place there some time ago. There were various pleas; among the rest some raising the question whether the ownership of the oil was in the plaintiff, and whether there was as large a quantity as the latter claimed for. His Honour now said that the verdict of the Jury was doubtful upon the first question submitted to them; as they merely said they believe that the plaintiffs were the proprietors of the oil; and positive on the second question that all the oil claimed for was destroyed by fire. Neither party was satisfied with the ruling of the learned Judge Monk. The plaintiffs had excepted to his statement that there was no evidence as to the quantity of the oil in the warehouse, and the defendant to the statement that there was evidence that the oil belonged to the plaintiffs. Graham on new trials, who was the best authority on the subject, said that in cases of verdict against evidence, the power to order a new trial was intended to give a remedy against the ignorance, prejudice, and carelessness of juries, and that the Judge was to exercise an effective control. The fact that there was some evidence on both sides did not exclude the power, and if the Judge conscientiously believed the verdict to be against the weight of evidence, he was bound to grant a new trial. Moreover, great attention was to be given to the opinion of the Judge who presided at the trial, for if he were dissatisfied with the verdict, it would be a great inducement to send the case to another jury. Now in this case neither party was satisfied with the Judge's charge; but the learned Judge had distinctly stated his opinion that there was no proof as to the quantity of oil that was burned. For his own part he not only thought that there was no proof on that point, but he also doubted whether there was any sufficient proof of the proprietorship being in the plaintiff. As to the evidence about the quantity of the oil it was of the vaguest and most uncertain character. There was no evidence on which it was possible to rest for a determination on that head. Under these circumstances there was no other course than to reject the motion for the judgment, and to grant the application for a new trial.

☞ The Publishing Office of THE CANADIAN MONETARY TIMES AND INSURANCE CHRONICLE is removed to No. 60, Church Street, 4 doors north of Court Street.

The Canadian Monetary Times.

THURSDAY, DECEMBER 10, 1868.

THE DOMINION TELEGRAPH CO.

We have placed our readers in possession of the charges made against the promoters of the Dominion Telegraph Company, as well as the reply of the President of that Company. As the President puts it in his letter, the sum of the accusation is that "the Dominion Company is simply a second edition of an alleged old swindle, the Grand Trunk Telegraph Company of sixteen years ago, and that the same prominent actor, Mr. Snow, is again at work behind the scenes." The President denies that the Toronto Board are aware of the existence of Mr. Snow, and affirm that they are ignorant of any relationship existing between Mr. Snow and Mr. Reeve. After referring to the charge that "early last spring the Montreal Company was approached by Mr. Snow with a proposition that neither Company should reduce rates," he states the Dominion Company's charter was not obtained till the 25th of June, and the present Board was not organized till July. He assures the public that no portion of the work has yet been taken over from the contractors, nor will be until it has undergone a rigid inspection by thoroughly competent parties.

So far as we can learn it is admitted on all hands that competition in the telegraph business is likely to prove beneficial to the public, and were even Mr. Snow, with all his disagreeable associations, to build a line with his own money, no one would say a word against his doing so. But inasmuch as the Canadian public are asked to furnish the money necessary to secure the competition spoken of, it is incumbent upon us to prevent, if possible, an unworthy advantage being taken of public spirit, if such is attempted. We have no hesitation in saying we believe that Snow's operation of six... years ago was an enormous swindle. If Toronto Board of the Dominion Comp... are not aware of the transaction with w... he had to do, we can refer them to plent... people who are fully competent to enligh... them. We further believe that those ...ronto gentlemen who constitute the Boar... the Dominion Company are thorou... honest, and unlikely to take part in anyt... that is a swindle or a sham, if aware ... such is the character of an enterpris... which they lend the sanction of their na... They would not and could not afford to ... pear as partners in a swindle. But, as g... charges have been made; as the Board ... fess their ignorance of Snow and his tri... as some of the directors have even conf... an utter want of knowledge as to the a... of the Company, and as a great many C... dians have become shareholders in the C... pany, we are forced to examine the m... of the charges and the evidence adduc... their support.

In so far as the shareholders are conce... the question to be settled is, has Mr. ... any connection with the Company? in ... words, is the enterprise undertaken in ... faith? A second article in the Mon... journal which made the attack on the ... minion Company is more explicit tha... first that appeared. Fully conscious o... benefits likely to accrue from compet... duly appreciating the reduction in rate ... has been already brought about by th... pearance of a rival, and not a little ... picious of the quarter whence the ... came, we feel disposed to make allow... for bias, and are all the more determi... test as far as possible the truth of the ... ments made.

With this object in view, therefor... have instituted inquiries, and have be... liably informed as to the following ... On the 5th of February, 1868, a Cert... and Articles of Association was exec... Clifton, preparatory to the incorpora... a company, to be called the Dominio... graph Company. The Certificate state...

"The names of the shareholders, an... number of shares held by each respe... at this time, are as follows, viz :

Josiah Snow	100
Wm. D. Snow	100
Thomas Wilson	5
E. W. Bromley	10
Zenas B. Lewis	5
W. W. Woodruff	5
G. W. Mastin	10

This document was witnessed by S... It would seem, however, that it v... acted upon, or perhaps was withdraw...

On the 28th of May, another Ce... and Articles of Association were exec...

ecting the Dominion Company, that—

ames and places of residence of lders, and the number of shares h respectively, at this time are viz. :

lson, Clifton	5	shares
nley "	10	"
ewis "	5	"
druff "	5	"
tin "	10	"
e, New York	150	"
ve "	100	"

informalities in this document, ted by the Department at Ottawa. h June, a third application was a new Certificate, in which the peared :

mes of the Shareholders and the shares held by each respectively , are as follows, viz. :

an	10	shares
s	100	"
e	9,890	"

in a position to sum up the case ecution. In the first application ration by the Dominion Tele-paay the names of Josiah Snow Snow appear. In the second ap-heir names are omitted, and lah Reeve and H. B. Reeve take . In the third application the eholders is reduced to three per-ose three are Messrs. Ryan, S. . B. Reeve.

nce, which by the way is circum-ws, we think, that Snow had to e starting of the Company. connection has ceased or not he directors and stockholders to or themselves. There are the for believing that none of the ectors were aware of the real they allowed their names to be t Mr. Cayley assures the public ard did not know such a man as by name. Such an admission ounded very strangely in all the vns in Canada, where the name still a household word, and is remembered for some time to an admission must in itself uch to shake confidence in Mr. city and acquaintance with such s that with which he has allied e have reason to believe that the at last enlightened as to the affairs, and are puzzling their d the solution of a rather diffi-. In the meantime they are experience the very useful lesson permitting their names to be nection with any public enter-hould be careful to see that they er directly or indirectly, aiding

adventurers to impose on the community. At various times we have called the attention of those whose names go forth to the public as endorsers for embryo enterprises or full-fledged companies, to the grave responsibilities they incur. The gentlemen on the Board of this Company cannot be considered as in fault to any greater degree than are many others occupying equally influential positions and equally honest. Their unwitting culpability is but the result of a practice which has had too many supporters, and if the lesson now learned produce its legitimate fruits, it will, though purchased by an unpleasant experience, have not been too dear.

BANK OF BRITISH NORTH AMERICA V. TORRANCE.

The action brought by the Bank of British North America against the Messrs. Torrance of Montreal, has given rise to a good deal of newspaper controversy which may justly be considered ill-timed, while legal proceedings are pending. The defendants have been induced to publish a letter explaining their position, and the manager of the Bank has also published a reply. The Messrs. Torrance state that in 1867, they employed a Mr. Yarwood to purchase grain for them in Ontario, on commission, and opened a credit for him of $45,000 with the Bank of Montreal at London. At the opening of Navigation orders were given to Mr. Yarwood to ship the grain purchased, but he informed the Messrs. Torrance that he had hypothecated a large portion of it to the British Bank "for his own private purposes." Being asked to assist in extricating him, the Messrs. Torrance accepted one bill for $10,000, and another for $9,000, which Yarwood undertook to provide for as they were for his accommodation. The day before the first bill became due, an accepted cheque for $10,000 was received from him, and a letter stating that it was to retire the draft, and advising that he had drawn upon the Messrs. Torrance, at three months, for $10,000. The remittance was put to Yarwood's credit in payment of the acceptance, and he was telegraphed that the draft would not be accepted. The Messrs. Torrance say:

"It subsequently appeared that the agent of the Bank of British North America had discounted Mr. Yarwood's bill upon us without knowing or asking whether we would honour it, carrying the proceeds to his credit, and accepting his cheque for $10,000, which he remitted to cover his engagement. The Bank now seeks to recover from us the money they thus gave to Mr. Yarwood, but which we consider no liability of ours, and we have also refused to accept a draft we never, directly or indirectly, came under the slightest obligation to honour."

"As our private affairs have thus been partially disclosed, we will finish the story by giving the financial results of the whole transaction. In order to get possession of our property, we had to pay in addition to the whole cost and value of it, the sum of $9,000 to the Bank of British North America, and we narrowly escaped having to pay the institution $10,000 more, which it is now endeavouring to collect by legal process. What success will attend such an attempt remains to be seen."

Mr. Hooper, the manager of the British Bank at Montreal, gives his side of the case thus : the evidence established that the drawing by Yarwood of the drafts for $10,000 and $9,000, was the result of an arrangement privately made between Yarwood and the Messrs. Torrance, to the effect that the latter would accept his drafts to the extent of $25,000, on the sole security of a life policy for $25,000 which Yarwood promised to send them. The immediate effect of the discounting of these drafts was to enable the Messrs. Torrance to get possession of grain to the value of $19,000. When the discount was given the Bank knew nothing of the arrangement referred to. When the $10,000 draft was near maturity, the Bank discounted a new draft for Yarwood, and accepted a check for $10,000, payable in Montreal to the order of D. Torrance & Co., on the faith of Yarwood's representation and undertaking that the Messrs. Torrance would accept the new draft. Yarwood forwarded the accepted cheque to the Messrs. Torrance. Instead of depositing the cheque in bank, as is customary, the Messrs. Torrance cashed it, at the same time keeping the draft in their possession for twenty-four hours and concealing from the Bank their predetermination not to accept it. Before the proceeds of the cheque were applied to retire the draft the Messrs. Torrance were notified by the Bank of all the circumstances, and forbidden to use the proceeds of the cheque without accepting the draft. The financial result of the transaction was that the Messrs. Torrance received payment at the expense of the Bank of $10,000 of bad debts due them by Yarwood, and by the payment of only $9,000 secured possession of grain of the value of $19,000. Mr. Hooper considers that the Messrs. Torrance "were both legally and morally bound to accept the draft in question, or restore to the Bank the money which they received from it on the faith that they would duly accept the draft."

The Messrs. Torrance allege that, out of courtesy to the bank, they did give early intimation of their probable refusal to accept the draft, and that if Yarwood had offered any good security for his new draft, they would have accepted it.

ENGLISH MONEY MARKET.

A change has at length come over the English money market. After continuing at 2 per cent. for sixty-nine weeks, the rate of discount at the Bank of England advanced to 2½ per cent. and subsequently to 3 per cent., as the cable dispatches inform us. The rate was never longer than thirty-seven weeks continuously at 2 per cent. in the previous history of the Bank. This fact goes to strengthen the statement that the panic of 1866 was more severe than any of its predecessors.

This anxiously expected change has not arisen from an increase in the demand for money for the purposes of trade, but resulted from a large withdrawal of gold for Russia, the amount of which is, it is said, almost unprecedented in a single transaction. During the week ending on the 18th November, the stock of coin and bullion in the bank was withdrawn to an amount exceeding one million pounds.

MINING IN NOVA SCOTIA.

We did not intend that our remarks in the last number of this Journal should be construed as depreciatory of gold mining in Nova Scotia. The fact that gold has been found there in quantities is proved beyond a doubt. Dr. Sterry Hunt, in his report on that region, states : "It may be affirmed that the average yield of gold to the ton in Nova Scotia, and also to each miner, is greater in Nova Scotia than in any other auriferous region known." What we did intend to convey was, that parties desirous of investing in gold mining enterprises should make themselves fully acquainted with the preliminary arrangements attendant upon the formation of the Companies they go into.

THE NARROW GAUGE RAILWAYS.

The By-Laws authorising the issue of debentures in aid of the Toronto, Grey and Bruce, and the Toronto and Nipissing Railways, were sanctioned by a vote of the property owners of Toronto, on the 8th inst. The opposition was trifling, as it is generally conceded that the construction of these roads would be of immense benefit to the City. We are glad to see that steps are being taken to legalize the By-Laws passed to aid these undertakings and to obviate the difficulties which we pointed out in a previous number.

—Mr. McCracken, of the Gore Bank, has resigned his situation and accepted an engagement from the Royal Canadian.

CLOSE OF NAVIGATION.

All the channels of navigation are now closed, and vessels, with few exceptions, have been dismantled for winter. The past season has been a very unsuccessful one for vessel property in general. Where vessel owners handled their own cargoes, a little money may have been made ; all others have lost. A great deal of disappointment has been occasioned by the speculative policy of Western grain dealers in holding back the produce of the west from finding its way to the seaboard. This illegitimate kind of business has been carried to a greater extent this year than probably ever before, and must be attended by correspondingly augmented losses ; this, and other causes, ha e made the past few seasons most unsatisfactory to vessel owners; so that they are now fairly disheartened, and until a change for the better occurs, we need not expect to see any increase in the tonnage of our lake marine.

—Mr. Fitzgerald, of the Royal Canadian Agency at Brampton, has been appointed to the Kingston Agency.

—We notice among our exchanges the *Chronicle*, of Chicago, an insurance journal, which seems to be flourishing, and has lately increased its size by four pages. Our enterprising contemporary has our best wishes for its success.

ÆTNA LIFE INSURANCE CO.—The following paragraph from the Montreal *News* should prove a warning to newspapers disposed to plunge into insurance matters without being possessed of the information necessary to sustain their conclusions :

"As articles derogatory to this Company have at various times appeared in these columns, which were written without a full knowledge of all the facts discussed, and would not have been published had we possessed the data now within our reach, we feel it due to that Company, and our own character for truthfulness, to state that we are not aware of anything in the standing or business of the Ætna Life Assurance Company which the public could have cause to distrust."

Financial.

MONTREAL MONEY MARKET.

(From our own Correspondent.)

Montreal, Dec. 8, 1868.

The fourth of the month (the day on which bills generally fall due) passed off without any pressure on the banks, and the market is still very easy. The old difficulty remains as how to invest money at short dates with the chance of any profitable return. Stocks are high and all available securities command such rates that they offer but low interests. There is also plenty of money on the look-out for good permanent investments, but capitalists are very cautious in their investments, hence the large amount at the credit of the "deposit account" in

the banks. Before spring we will assuredly plenty of schemes to tempt the cupidity of moneyed men. I give the latest quotation our leading stocks : Bank of Montreal scarce 138½ to 139; City firm at 102 to 102½; People demand at 107, with considerable sales at rate; Merchants' inquired for at 112½, but hol ask 113½; British nominally 101, and To 120, which price would be readily paid; C nominal at 104½ to 106; Molson's has been p at 110; Jacques Cartier quiet at 106 to 107. other stocks: Telegraph is easier, seller's at 1 but buyers at 135; Richelieu Co. dull at 1 118½; City Railroad, 110 to 110½; Cana Navigation Co. have sold at 108; Mon mining consols, $2 25 to $3.

TORONTO STOCK MARKET.

(Reported by Pellatt & Osler, Brokers.)

Considerable business has been done in stocks this week, and prices have been well tained with the exception of Royal Cana which has declined ¼ per cent.

Bank Stocks.—Montreal has been sold a but closed with buyers at 138 and sell 138½. No British in market—buyers give 105. There were large transactio Ontario at 99½, 100, and 100½, closing firm No Toronto in market, buyers give 120½, but none in market. Royal Can has been sold during the week at 85½, 86 and 87 ; sellers generally asking the latte Numerous sales of Commerce occurred at 1 and 105½, the latter rate is freely offered. are sellers of Gore at 42½, and no buyers o Merchants is offered at 113½, and buyer 113. Buyers offer 109½ for Molson's, an for City, but no sellers of either. The buyers of Du Peuple at 106½, and of Natio 105, no sellers. There are sellers of J Cartier at 107, and buyers at 106. Sell 106 for Union, with buyers at 104½.

Debentures.—Sales of Dominion stock o at 105, no sterling bonds on market. T have been sold to pa* 67 per cent. to pur County have been almost entirely withdraw the market, but would command high rat

Sundries.—City Gas is much enquired fo in market. There were transactions in Permanent Building Society at 124½ to 125 are now buyers at the latter rate. No V Canada in market : 116 would readily b Several sales of Freehold occurred at 104 and the latter price would still be paid offer 136 for Montreal Telegraph, with s 140. Small sales of Canada Landed Cr curred at 71 to 72. There are buyers of America Ass. at 54 to 55, and sellers at 5 Mortgages are readily taken at 8 per cent. is freely offered on good security.

AUDIT OF BANKING BALANCE SHEE have frequently called attention to the n of providing a specified form of balance s all banking Companies, and have also poi that shareholders have no security wit efficient and independent audit.—*Investor dian.*

QUEBEC CITY REVENUE.—Comparativ ment of the receipts of the Corporation city of Quebec, for the seven months end November in each year:

	1867.	
Assessments: receipts..	133,899 36	19
Water Works, do. ..	38,646 75	5
	$172,543 11	$24
		1
More in 1868..	....	$7

BANK OF ENGLAND.

ℯ the week ending November 18th:—

Issue Department.

.... £33,202,620

debt	£11,015,100
ties..............................	3,984,900
i bullion....................	17,202,620
n..............................	

£32,202,624

Banking Department.

:apital.,..................	£14,553,000
....	3,091,457
its (including Exchequer, sioners of National Debt, Banks, and Dividend	
s)........	5,030,529
ts..............................	18,762,567
d other Bills......	605,325

£42,042,878

securities (including eight Annuity)............	£15,301,437
ties...........................	16,873,882
....	8,713,520
ver coin.....................	1,154,089

£42,042,878

BANKING.—A crisis similar to our rienced in Canada in 1866, and gave lative inquiry. In answer to cer- s of the Committee of the Senate, ie, cashier of the Bank of Toronto, s powers of legislation in reference tion of the business of the banker. n it would be impossible to devise ould prevent bank failures. These from bad management, which can- ined by Act of Parliament, and which : its natural effect in the end. One important measures within reach require frequent returns, exhibiting of the business, which would exer- ctive and restraining influence upon nnselves, and would be a great benefit ℐ the customers, and the shareholders. ould be furnished in such detail as to ligible, the model taken in this in- the accounts of the Bank of France. Hague recommends for Canada we ite at home. Our banking system iced on the footing of the Bank of this respect, but the greater detail of f France would be necessary. The i carried on under constant public in- he open light of day, could in future chinations of the evil-minded, who ℐeed by mystery and darkness. Our em would by this means attain a ℐafety which might even reconcile the ℐland directors. It would prove as ℐtection to credit in its latest form as 844 has been in another way.—*Bul-* ℐ

ℐAUTIOUS OLD LADY.—During the v Brunswick, a customer of one of ℐ banks declined to take American s on the ground that it was always ℐd down." The good lady demanded

ℐTOCKS.—The following stocks were ℐx last week at the prices mentioned : ℐalifax Fire Insurance

ℐny............................	£10 17 6
nk of Nova Scotia......	65 0 0
Water Stock............	150 15 0
ℐlt Company............	$ 10 50
ℐv. Building Society...	271 00
ℐion Bank...	53 50
" "	53 00
" "	52 50
ℐchool Debentures......	98 50

Railway News.

NORTHERN RAILWAY.—Traffic receipts for week ending Nov. 28, 1868.

Passengers.....	$3,330 68
Freight........................	3,474 71
Mails and Sundries...........	441 99

Total Receipts for week....	$7,247 38
Corresponding week 1867....	8,013 00

Decrease...........	$765 62

GREAT WESTERN RAILWAY.—Traffic for week ending Nov. 20, 1868.

Passengers ..../..........	$31,644 40
Freight and live stock......	41,024 52
Mails and sundries..........	1,339 92

	$74,008 84
Corresponding Week of '67.	73,734 17

Increase.............	$274 67

— The Township of Markham has passed a by-law granting $30,000 to the Toronto and Nipissing Railway. In Brock Township, a by-law granting $58,000 to the same road, has been defeated.

OVERLAND ROUTE THROUGH BRITISH AMERICA.—Mr. Waddington's pamphlet advocates a line from Ottawa into Hudson's Bay Territory to the north of Lake Superior to the Red River Settlement, whence it branches to the north through a belt of fertile country, and reaches British Columbia near the site of the gold diggings at the source of the Fraser. The cost of a single line from Ottawa to Head of Bute Inlet, 2,385 miles, 4ft. 8½in. gauge, he estimates at $130,150,000, or say 27 millions sterling but if with a 3ft. 6in. gauge it would be less. This he proposes should be carried out by a company, the Government issuing bonds guaranteed a fix rate of interest in much the same way as the Union Pacific is being carried out.

CANADA CENTRAL RAILWAY.—We are glad to learn says the Ottawa *Citizen*, that Mr. Abbott, who went some short time ago to England on business connected with this road, has returned, after successfully carrying out the objects of his journey. The work on the line will now be pushed forward with all celerity towards completion.

NEW BRIDGE ON THE BUFFALO AND LAKE HURON RAILWAY AT PARIS.—The new bridge for Buffalo and Lake Huron Railway across the Grand River at Paris, which has been in course of erection for more than a year, is completed. It is built of wood, on the Howe Truss principle, supported on stone piers 66 feet high, and spans the river with five arches. The total length is 775 feet 1 inch ; the width 18 feet 6 inches, and the height from the stonework to the rails 24 feet 9 inches, so that the rails are 90 feet above the water. The spans vary somewhat in length, the dimensions being as follows : commencing at the east end—No. 1. 158 feet 5 inches; No. 2. 165 feet; No. 3. 156 feet 5 inches; No. 4. 162 feet 3 inches, and No. 5. 126 feet. On each side of the track there is a sidewalk 5 feet high, and a chain on each side of the bridge, supported in iron pillars, to protect passengers from falling over.

The bridge rests upon the place which supported the one it replaces, and the trains had to be kept running during the whole process of reconstruction. In order to effect this, one span was only operated on at a time. A tressel bridge was first erected from one pier to another to support the ℐtrack, the old timbers were then taken down, and the new ones put in their places, lastly ; the tressels were taken down. The same process was pursued with each successive span till the whole was renewed.

Mr. Yates, of Brantford, was the contractor, and Mr. James Finney superintended the work.

The bridge just completed is the fourteenth bridge on the Buffalo and Lake Huron line, which has been rebuilt since the railway was eased by the Grand Trunk Railway Company.

Commercial.

Montreal Correspondence.

(From our own Correspondent).

Montreal, Dec. 8, 1868.

The winter is fairly upon us, and our merchants have begun to reckon the profits or losses on the year's operations.

DRY GOODS.—Taken altogether, a fair trade was done in this branch ; not equal in extent to former years, but larger than the most sanguine anticipated. For some years past Montreal has almost had a monopoly of this particular branch of business, few purchases being made in the States ; the style of goods suitable for Canada, differing essentially from those imported by the Americans. Toronto and the western towns purchased sparingly at home, finding Montreal, as a general rule, a better market, so that our merchants have been led to import heavily, in fact more than the country could bear ; profits for the years 1864, '65 and '66 being large, consequently, as always the case after three successful years, in 1867, the imports were so entirely in excess of the requirements, that our merchants found themselves hampered at the close of that year with very heavy stocks. Those who had capital held on to their goods, but others were obliged to realize. The losses were very heavy. Another element, on which they did not sufficiently calculate, came into play. The west had gradually been creeping up from its many disastrous years of short crops, over land speculation, and over trading ; and your Toronto merchants, never favorable to Montreal, seeing the profits of dry goods men, bought largely in the English markets, and entered into a lively competition in our best district, viz : the western section of Canada, so that it was only by forcing off our goods, and by dint of superior capital, enabling us to give long credits, and renew notes falling due, in many cases in full, that we have been enabled to work off our stocks.

The experience of 1867 taught wisdom to our importers, and consequently our imports during this year were very light, and sales were made with not only a due regard to profits, but also to the standing of the parties to whom they were made, so that the business, although much less in amount, has left a larger profit to our merchants than for some two years back. During the fall country remittances have been better than usual; the season closed with light stocks and a healthy tone of the market. I note that the Toronto Dry Goods men have imported considerably, but seemingly have not worked off their stocks so successfully, as I see that one large firm has offered a large quantity of goods by auction, which sale by your papers has proved a great success, thus shewing that the country merchants are not overstocked. Some few years ago Geo. Winks & Co., of this city, tried the experiment of selling their then large stock of dry goods by auction, but the result was not such as to warrant the attempt being repeated ; in England such sales are of daily occurrence, but here they are regarded as an expedient for raising the wind, and any house loses cast that attempts them. Why it should be so I cannot say, for I see no difference between placing a cargo of groceries at auction and disposing of a heavy stock of silks, cottons, &c., however, we must bend the neck to the laws of custom. To-day I have only space to touch lightly on the dry goods trade. In my future letters I shall deal with hardware and our local manufactures. In the latter I feel sure that I can find many topics of interest to your western readers.

PRODUCE.—Business in Produce is very dull, and prices of Flour rule much the same as last week, Extras being $5.50 to $5.75; Fancy, $5 to $5.10, and Supers, No. 1, $4.80 to $4.90, while Strong Bakers have ranged from $5 to $5.05; but the trade is pretty well supplied, and the demand is consequently light. Supers No. 2, $4.40 to $4.50. No demand for the lower grades, and no lots of any description pressing on the market. The market for grain of all descriptions is very dull, and prices are purely nominal. Wheat, U.C. Spring, $1.08 to $1.10; U.C. Red Winter, $1.10; Chicago No. 2, $1.08. Peas, 60 lbs—92c to 94c. Corn, 56 lbs—Mixed Western, 87½c to 90c. Barley, 48 lbs—$1.20 to $1.30 for ordinary. Oats, 32 lbs—47c to 48c. No Rye. Provisions are also very quiet, and it is difficult to give quotations. In Pork, little is doing, and our Ottawa lumbermen are not yet in the market, the winter roads to the shanties not being opened out; we want more cold weather and snow to make them passable. The swamps are barely frozen over, and in the woods the snow is not deep enough to cover the inequalities of the usual rough bush roads. Mess Pork is worth $23.75 to $24; Thin Mess, $21 to $22; Prime Mess and Prime nominal. Dressed Hogs, for which there is a fair demand, are worth, heavy, $7.50 to $8; medium, $7 to $7.50; light, $6.87½ to $7. Dairy produce remains very quiet. Butter, best quality, would sell readily to the grocers, but shipping lots are in no demand; the price is purely nominal. Factory Cheese sells at 11c to 12c for best brands. Ashes are very dull at, first Pots, $5.62½ to $5.65; seconds, $4.80 to $4.85; Pearls, $5.50 for firsts, and no seconds offering.

Petroleum.

Receipts at New York for the week ending Dec. 1 ....pkgs. 11,701
Exports from New York for the week ending Nov. 24..................galls. 733,348
Exports from N. York, Jan. 1. galls. 48,929,001
same time last year ....galls. 30,171,060

The following is the quantity exported from other ports, Jan. 1 to Nov. 28:

FROM	1868.	1867.
Boston ....galls.	2,302,330	2,109,661
Philadelphia..............	36,003,973	25,886,317
Baltimore..............	2,420,482	1,314,157
Portland..............	636,850	100
Total gallons........	41,473,635	30,311,535
Total exports from the United States........	91,803,052	60,726,970
Same time in 1866 ...		61,396,808
Same time in 1865 ...		24,724,283

Toronto Market.

Snow has fallen liberally, and winter has fairly set in.

BOOTS AND SHOES.—Trade continues good; quotations are slightly altered, as shown in our price list.

GROCERIES.—Sugars are steady and without change. There is more demand for raw Sugars, owing to small local supplies, and a number of job lots have been readily placed. There is a steady demand for refined at unchanged prices. Teas are very lively, in consequence of a good demand for both city and country trade. The export demand noticed a few weeks since has entirely ceased, the supplies in the New York market having increased, and so lessened the demand on this and other Canadian markets. Were it not for the American differential duty of 10 per cent., our dealers could still ship to that market, and make a fair profit. There is a specially large demand for uncolored Japans, and several job lots have been placed at 57c to 58c. A Tea that is good value at these prices is constantly in demand. We note some enquiry for the higher grades of Japan Teas for the Province of Quebec. Fruit—

The enquiry is good, as is usual at this season; prices unchanged. There is a speculative demand for Layer Raisins in Montreal, and two lots of 4,000 and 5,000 boxes changed hands at $1.85. Fish—Fish seem to be going more generally into consumption, and consequently a larger trade has been done this year than for a long time before. Split Labrador Herrings are worth $5.75 to 6.50, and round, $4 to $4.75. Rice is 5c to 10c higher per 100 pounds, and in good demand. Syrups—The better quality of Molasses and Syrups are in good demand; refinery Syrups are up 2c per gallon since last week. Tobacco—4's have advanced at the factories 1c per pound on last week, and the demand is very good. Coffees—Not much doing; the demand seems to grow less every year. We give imports of groceries and liquors at Toronto for November:

Imports of Groceries.

		1867.		1868.	
Coffee, green ......lbs	38,913	(3,582	51,622	85,482
Chicory, ground........	1,139	51	10,013	482
Common Soap..........	2,000	121	.....	....
Starch	.....	.....	544	54
Tea, Green and Japan.	57,909	27,739	147,778	57,893
Tea, Black	.....	.....	17,000	5,981
Tobacco, manuf'd....	12,969	5,764	2	2
Sugar..............	353,541	28,029	160,735	7,748
Sugar Candy, &c....	3,656	833	7,285	1,397
Mace and Nutmegs..	849	269	9,542	7,843
Dried Fruits and Nuts	17,260	8,953	.....	19,099

Imports of Liquors.

		1867.		1868.	
Brandy..........gals	1,856	1,021	107	341
Gin.............gals	2,837	1,650	2,451	1,272
Rum.............gals	4,671	2,008	988	225
Whiskey.........gals	1,904	710	3,894	3,073
Ale, Beer and Porter, in casks ...gals	285	110	.....	.....
Ale, Beer and Porter, in bottles ......doz	5,328	1,735	2,508	1,311
Wines..........gals	4,697	4,731	8,509	7,572

DRY GOODS.—The trade sale at the stores of Messrs. Gordon & McKay is the only occurrence of the week worthy of notice. At that sale there was a large attendance of buyers, the bidding was spirited, and a very considerable quantity of goods was placed at fair prices. As the first venture of the kind in Toronto for a long time, we are glad to be able to report it such a success. The imports of Dry Goods at this port for November were:—

Imports of Dry Goods.

	1867.	1868.
Manufactures of Woolens.............$31,344		$36,527
Do. Cottons..............	38,472	52,821
Do. Silks and Velvets....	10,587	13,634
Do. Furs..............	1,019	3,050
Wearing Apparel..............	521	95

GRAIN.—Wheat—Receipts light; Spring nominal at $1 to $1.06, and fall at $1.05 to $1.15. Barley—There is a fair demand, but little offering; $1.16 was paid for waggon loads. Peas dull at 80c. Oats steady at 52c to 53c.

FLOUR.—No. 1 Superfine is offered at $4.70, with buyers at $4.50 to $4.65; there is some demand for the Lower Provinces; nothing doing in Extra or any of the other grades.

PROVISIONS.—Dressed Hogs are now coming in pretty freely, and the market is 50c. better at quotations. Butter nominal, only a retail business doing. Cheese offering at 11c to 11½c. Pork nominal at $22 to $22.50; prime Mess, $18; Extra Prime, $16 to $17. Live Hogs nominal at $5.20 to $5.40.

PETROLEUM.—There is a steady demand at quotations. The market is a little lower.

LEATHER.—The trade is quiet, at unchanged prices.

FREIGHTS.—Navigation is now closed. Rates by Grand Trunk Railway—Flour to all stations from Belleville to Lynn, inclusive, 35c.; grain per 100 lbs 18c; flour to Brockville and Cornwall, inclusive, 43c; grain 22c; flour to Montreal 50c, grain 25c; flour to all stations between Island Pond and Portland, inclusive, 85c; grain 43c; flour to Boston $1.15 U.S. currency; flour to Halifax 75c, grain —v; flour to St. John, 85c. Boxed meats and butter to Liverpool per gross ton, 80s; lard

or butter in tinnets, 85c; pork, 10s 6d per ton; flour, 6s 6d per barrel; grain, 12s 6d per [?] pounds. Rates by Great Western Railway, Flour, Toronto to Suspension Bridge, 25c.; thence to New York, 76c U.S. currency per [?] to Boston, 86c. Rates from Toronto to [?] pool are—Beef, bacon and pork, 90s, go [?] 100 lbs; lard, in barrels and tierces, 98c do; in kegs or tinnets, $1.00 do; butter and [?] $1.28 do.

Halifax Market.

BREADSTUFFS.—Dec. 1.—Flour still con [?] to arrive freely, and the demand is good, v [?] change in price. Canada No. 1 ranges from to $6.50; Strong Bakers, $6.65 to $6.70; Canada, $7.50 to $8.00; Extra State st [?] times dull at $6.00 to $6.40, according to c [?] No. 2 in good demand at $5.90 to $5.50, meal without change, at $4.50 for kiln dri [?] $4.25 for Fresh Ground. Oatmeal, $8.00 [?] and 1868:—

	Blds Flour.	Bbls. O [?]
1868..............	169,327	48,
1867..............	179,940	33,

FISH.—Codfish firm and in demand at $ [?] $4.24 for good large shore; $3.20 to $3.30 f [?] small shore; Labrador, $2.25 to $2.50. [?] and Bay none. Good hard cure Arich [?] dock, $2.00 to $2.19; Eastern Shore, $ [?] $1.90; Western, $1.60 to $1.65; Pollock [?] to $1.50. Herring in demand at $4.50 t [?] for Labrador, and $4.00 to $4.50 for shore. [?] erel scarce and in demand. No shore. B [?] to $10 for No. 1; $13 to $14 for No. 2; $ [?] for No. 3. Salmon, $15 for No. 1; $13 [?] 2, and $10 for No. 3.

WEST INDIA PRODUCE.—Sugars and [?] continue in fair demand at quotations. W [?] Porto Rico 6¼c to 6½c; Barbadoes, 3¼c [?] Cuba, 5¼c to 5½c; Centrifugal Cuba, 6c [?] Rum scarce and in demand at 70c to 75c [?] merara, and 60c to 65c for St. Iago.

COMPANIES INCORPORATED.—Letters [?] have been issued incorporating the Ki [?] Salt Prospecting Company, with a nomina [?] of $5000, and the Anglo-American Peat ([?] of Welland, with a nominal capital of $ [?]

SHIPBUILDING.—It is said that altho [?] about 18,000 are ships building at O [?] the extent of tons, the work is proceedi [?] quietly, in great contrast to the season of [?] when about 60,000 tons were built.

—Application will be made to the Que [?] islature for a grant of land along the St. [?] in aid of the Pictou railway.

Canadian Express Company,

**HAL EXPRESS FORWARDERS, CUSTOM-HOUSE
BROKERS,**

AND

SHIPPING AGENTS.

DS and VALUABLES forwarded by all principal
.asenger Trains.

aced rates for all large consignments.

aced rates on Poultry, Butter, and other produce, to
al markets in Canada and the United States.

perishable articles guaranteed against damage by
without extra charge, nature of goods at all times
stipulated in receipt at time of shipment.

signments for Lower Provinces taken to Portland,
sbec, and from thence by Steamer or Express, as
ad securing quick dispatch.

ekly Express is made up for Europe, for which
should be sent forward in time to reach Portland on
each week.

a. messed facilities as shipping agents in Liverpool.

seed rates on large Consignments from the Steamer
ding.

particulars, inquire at any of the principal offices.

signments solicited.

G. CHENEY,
Superintendent.

Bank of Toronto.

DIVIDEND No. 25.

ICE is hereby given that a dividend of FOUR per
ent. for the current half year, being at the rate of
F per cent. per annum upon the paid up capital of
ank, has this day been declared, and that the same
payable at the Bank or its branches, on and after
RDAY, THE SECOND DAY OF JANUARY NEXT
transfer books will be closed from the sixteenth to
rty-first day of December next, both days inclusive.
rder of the Board,

G. HAGUE,
Cashier.
nto, Nov. 26, 1868.   15-td

Royal Canadian Bank.

DIVIDEND No. 7.

ICE is hereby given that a Dividend of Four per
nt. upon the paid-up Capital of this Bank for the
t half year, has this day been declared, and that the
vill be payable at the Bank, or its agencies, on and
SATURDAY, the SECOND DAY OF JANUARY
. The Transfer Books will be closed from the 16th
31st December, both days inclusive.
order of the Board,

T. WOODSIDE, Cashier.
al Canadian Bank, Nov. 25, 1868.   15-td

The Canadian Bank of Commerce.

DIVIDEND No. 3.

ICE is hereby given, that a Dividend at the rate of
)UR per cent. on the paid up Capital Stock of this
ation has been declared for the current half year,
at the same will be payable at its Banking House in
ty, and at its branches, on and after
iturday, the Second day of January next.
Transfer Books will be closed from the 15th to the
ecember, both days inclusive.
order of the Board,

R. J. DALLAS,
Cashier.
nto, Nov. 23.   15-td

J. T. & W. Pennock,

i and Life Insurance Agents, Parliamentary and
parimental Agents, Mining Agents, and Exchange
's.

wa, Dec. 21st, 1867.   10-1y

Honore Plamondon,

TOM House Broker, Forwarder, and General Agent,
uebec. Office—Custom House Building.   17-1y

Sylvester, Bro. & Hickman,

MERCIAL Brokers and Vessel Agents. Office—No.
Ontario Chambers, [Corner Front and Church Sts.]
o.   2-6m

DAY'S

Commercial College and High School,

No. 82 KING STREET EAST,

(Near St. James' Cathedral.)

THE design of this institution is to prepare Young Men
and others as Book-keepers, and for general business,
and to furnish them with the facilities for acquiring an
excellent

English and Commercial Education.

Mr. Day is also prepared to give Private Instruction in
the several subjects of his department, and to assist Merchants and others in the checking and balancing of books,
adjusting their accounts and partnership affairs, &c.

For further information, please call on or address the
undersigned.

JAMES E. DAY,
Accountant
Toronto, Sept. 3rd, 1868.

John Ross & Co.,

QUEBEC.

T. & F. Ross & Co.,

GENERAL WHOLESALE GROCERS,

PRODUCE AND COMMISSION MERCHANTS,

361 *Commissioner Street,*

MONTREAL.   6

W. McLaren & Co.,

WHOLESALE

BOOT AND SHOE MANUFACTURERS,

18 ST. MAURICE STREET,

MONTREAL

June, 1868.   42-1y

Lyman & McNab,

Importers of, and Wholesale Dealers in,

HEAVY AND SHELF HARDWARE,

KING STREET,

TORONTO, ONTARIO.

THE QUEEN'S HOTEL.

THOMAS DICK, Proprietor.

FRONT STREET,   -   -   TORONTO, ONT
                                      3-1y

Montreal House, Montreal, Canada.

TO MONETARY MEN.—Merchants, Insurance Agents,
Lawyers, Bankers, Railway and Steamboat Travellers,
Mining Agents, Directors and Stockholders of Public Com
panies, and other persons visiting Montreal for business
or pleasure, are here by most respectfully informed that
the undersigned proposes to furnish the best hotel accommodation at the most reasonable charges. It is our study
to provide every comfort and accommodation to all our
guests, especially for gentlemen engaged as above. To
those who have been accustomed to patronize other first-
class hotels, we only ask a trial; we have the same accommodation and our table is furnished with every delicacy
of the season.

H. DUCLOS.
Nov. 22, 1867.   15-1y

The Albion Hotel,

MONTREAL,

ONE of the oldest established houses in the City is again
under the personal management of

Mr. DECKER,

Who, to accommodate his rapidly increasing business, is
adding Eighty more Rooms to the house, making the
Albion one of the *Largest Establishments in Canada.*

June, 1868.   42-6ms

DOMINION TELEGRAPH COMPANY.

CAPITAL STOCK   -   -   - $500,000

In 10,000 Shares at $50 Each.

PRESIDENT,

HON. WILLIAM CAYLEY.

TREASURER,

HON. J. McMURRICH.

SECRETARY,

H. D. REEVE.

SOLICITORS,

MESSRS. CAMERON & McMICHAEL.

GENERAL SUPERINTENDENT.

MARTIN RYAN,

DIRECTORS.

HON. J. McMURRICH,
Bryce, McMurrich & Co., Toronto.

A. R. McMASTER, Esq.,
A. R. McMaster & Brother, Toronto.

HON. M. C. CAMERON,
Provincial Secretary, Toronto.

JAMES MICHIE, Esq.,
Fulton, Michie & Co., and George Michie & Co., Toronto.

HON. WILLIAM CAYLEY,
Toronto.

A. M. SMITH, Esq.,
A. M. Smith & Co., Toronto.

L. MOFFATT, Esq.,
Moffatt, Murray & Co., Toronto.

H. B. REEVE, Esq.,
Toronto.

MARTIN RYAN, Esq.,
Toronto.

PROSPECTUS.

THE DOMINION TELEGRAPH COMPANY has been
organized under the act respecting Telegraph Companies, chapter 67, of the consolidated Statutes of Canada.
Its object is to cover the Dominion of Canada with a complete net-work of Telegraph lines.

The Capital Stock

Is $500,000, divided into 10,000 shares of $50 each, 5 per
cent to be paid at the time of subscribing, the balance to
be paid by instalments, not exceeding 10 per cent per
month—said instalments to be called in by the Directors as
the works progress. The liability of a subscriber is limited
to the amount of his subscription.

The Business Affairs of the Company.

Are under the management of a Board of Directors, an
nually elected by the Shareholders, in conformity with the
Charter and By-Laws of the Company.

The Directors are of opinion that it would be to the
interest of the Stockholders generally to obtain subscriptions from all quarters of Canada, and with this view they
propose to divide the Stock amongst the different towns
and cities throughout the Dominion, in allotments suited
to the population and business occupations of the different
localities, and the interest which they may be supposed to
take in such an enterprise.

Contracts of Connections.

A contract, granting permanent connection and extraor-
dinary advantages, has already been executed between this
Company and the Atlantic and Pacific Company, of New
York; thus, at the very commencement, as the Lines of this
Company are constructed from the Suspension Bridge, at
Clifton (the point of connection) to any point in the Do-
minion, all the chief cities and places in the States, touch-
ed by the Lines of the Atlantic and Pacific Telegraph
Company, are brought in immediate connection therewith.

A permanent connection has also been secured with the
Great Western Telegraph Company, of Chicago, whereby
this Company will be brought into close connection with
all the Lake Ports and other places, through the North
western States, and through to California.

4-3mos

Insurance.

Insurance.

Insurance.

BEAVER
Mutual Insurance Association.

Head Office—50 Toronto Street,
TORONTO.

INSURES LIVE STOCK against death from any cause, only Canadian Company having authority to do this business.

R. L. DENISON,
President.
REILLY,
Secretary.
8-1y-25

HOME DISTRICT
Mutual Fire Insurance Company.

North-West Cor. Yonge & Adelaide Streets, TORONTO.—(Up Stairs.)

INSURES Dwelling Houses, Stores, Warehouses, Merdise, Furniture, &c.

President—The Hon. J. McMURRICH.
Vice-President—JOHN BURNS, Esq.
AGENTS:
ENGHT, Esq., Hamilton; FRANCIS STEVENS, Esq., Barrie; Messrs. GIBBS & BRO., Oshawa. 8-1y

THE PRINCE EDWARD COUNTY
Mutual Fire Insurance Company.

Head Office,—PICTON, ONTARIO.
R., L. B. STINSON; Vice-President, W. A. RICHARDS.
Secy. H. A. McFaul, James Caven, James Johnson,
John William DeLong.—Treasurer, David Barker.
y, John Twigg; Solicitor, R. J. Fitzgerald.

Company is established upon strictly Mutual principles, insuring farming and isolated property, (not villages,) in Townships only, and offers great advantages to insurers, at low rates, for five years, without the expense of renewal.
Picton, June 15, 1868.
9-1y

Hartford Fire Insurance Company.
HARTFORD, CONN.

Capital and Assets over Two Million Dollars.

$2,026,220.29.

CHARTERED 1810.

This old and reliable Company, having an established business in Canada of more than thirty years standing, complied with the provisions of the new Insurance Act made a special deposit of

$100,000

with Government for the security of policy-holders, and continue to grant policies upon the same favorable terms heretofore.

Usually low rates on first-class dwellings and farm property for a term of one or more years.

Losses as heretofore promptly and equitably adjusted.

H. J. MORSE & Co., AGENTS.
Picton, Ont.

BERT WOOD, GENERAL AGENT FOR CANADA
13-1y

THE AGRICULTURAL
Mutual Assurance Association of Canada.

OFFICE..................................LONDON, ONT.

The only Farmers' Company Licensed by the Government of Canada.

Fire, 1st January, 1868................. $220,121 23
Cash Items, over.................... $65,000 00
Policies in force.....................26,76

This Company insures nothing more dangerous than farm property. Its rates are as low as any well-managed Company in the Dominion, and lower than those in many. It is largely patronised, and continues in public favor.

For insurance, apply to any of the Agents, or address the Secretary, London, Ontario.
London, 2nd Nov., 1868.
12-1y

The Gore District Mutual Fire Insurance
Company

GRANTS INSURANCES on all description of Property against Loss or Damage by FIRE. It is the only Mutual Fire Insurance Company which assesses its Policies yearly from their respective dates; and the average yearly cost of insurance in it, for the past three and a half years, has been nearly

TWENTY CENTS IN THE DOLLAR

less than what it would have been in an ordinary Proprietary Company.

THOS. M. SIMONS,
Secretary & Treasurer.
ROBT. McLEAN,
Inspector of Agencies.
Galt, 26th Nov., 1868.
15-1y

Geo. Girdlestone,

FIRE, Life, Marine, Accident, and Stock Insurance Agent

Very best Companies represented.
Windsor, Ont. June, 1868

The Standard Life Assurance Company,
Established 1825.

WITH WHICH IS NOW UNITED
THE COLONIAL LIFE ASSURANCE COMPANY.

Head Office for Canada:
MONTREAL—STANDARD COMPANY'S BUILDINGS,
No. 47 GREAT ST. JAMES STREET.

Manager—W. M. RAMSAY. Inspector—RICH'D BULL.

THIS Company having deposited the sum of ONE HUNDRED AND FIFTY THOUSAND DOLLARS with the Receiver-General, in conformity with the Insurance Act passed last Session, Assurances will continue to be carried out at moderate rates and on all the different systems in practice.

AGENT FOR TORONTO—HENRY PELLATT,
KING STREET.

AGENT FOR HAMILTON—JAMES BANCROFT.
6-6mos.

Fire and Marine Assurance.

THE BRITISH AMERICA
ASSURANCE COMPANY.
HEAD OFFICE:
CORNER OF CHURCH AND COURT STREETS.
TORONTO.

BOARD OF DIRECTION:
Hon. G. W. Allan, M.L.C., | A. Joseph, Esq.,
George J Boyd, Esq., | Peter Paterson, Esq.,
Hon. W. Cayley, | G. P. Ridout, Esq.,
Richard S. Cassels, Esq., | E. H. Rutherford, Esq.,
| Thomas C. Street, Esq.
Governor:
GEORGE PERCIVAL RIDOUT, Esq.,
Deputy Governor:
PETER PATERSON, Esq.,
Fire Inspector: | Marine Inspector:
E. ROBY O'BRIEN. | CAPT. R. COURNEEN.
Insurances granted on all descriptions of property against loss and damage by fire and the perils of inland navigation.
Agencies established in the principal cities, towns, and ports of shipment throughout the Province.
THOS. WM. BIRCHALL,
23-1y
Managing Director.

Queen Fire and Life Insurance Company,
OF LIVERPOOL AND LONDON.

ACCEPTS ALL ORDINARY FIRE RISKS
on the most favorable terms.

LIFE RISKS

Will be taken on terms that will compare favorably with other Companies.

CAPITAL, - - £2,000,000 Stg.
CHIEF OFFICE—Queen's Buildings, Liverpool, and Gracechurch Street London.
CANADA BRANCH OFFICE—Exchange Buildings, Montreal.
Resident Secretary and General Agent,
A. MACKENZIE FORBES.
12 St. Sacrament St., Merchants' Exchange, Montreal.
WM. ROWLAND, Agent, Toronto.
1-1y

The Waterloo County Mutual Fire Insurance
Company.

HEAD OFFICE: WATERLOO, ONTARIO.

ESTABLISHED 1863.
THE business of the Company is divided into three separate and distinct branches, the

VILLAGE, FARM, AND MANUFACTURES.

Each Branch paying its own losses and its just proportion of the managing expenses of the Company.
C. M. TAYLOR, Sec. M. SPRINGER, M.M.P., Pres.
J. HUGHES, Inspector. 15-yr

Etna Fire and Marine Insurance Company of
Dublin,

AT a Meeting of the Shareholders of this Company, held at Dublin, on the 13th ult., it was agreed that the business of the "ETNA" should be transferred to the "UNITED PORTS AND GENERAL INSURANCE COMPANY." In accordance with this agreement, the business will hereafter be carried on by the latter Company, which assumes and guarantees all the risks and liabilities of the "ETNA."
The Directors have resolved to continue the CANADIAN BRANCH, and arrangements for resuming FIRE and MARINE business are rapidly approaching completion.
T. W. GRIFFITH,
16
MANAGER.

Scottish Provincial Assurance Co.
Established 1825.

CAPITAL ....£1,000,000 STERLING.
INVESTED IN CANADA (1864) ....$500,000.

Canada Head Office, Montreal.

LIFE DEPARTMENT.

CANADA BOARD OF DIRECTORS:
HUGH TAYLOR, Esq., Advocate,
HON. CHARLES WILSON, M.L.C.
WM. SACHE, Esq., Banker,
JACKSON RAE, Esq., Banker.
WM. FRASER, Esq., M. D., Medical Adviser.

The special advantages to be derived from Insuring in this office are:—Strictly Moderate Rates of Premium; Large Bonus (intermediate bonus guaranteed); Liberal Surrender Value, under policies relinquished by assured; and Extensive Limits of Residence and Travel. All business disposed of in Canada, without reference to parent office.

A DAVIDSON PARKER,
Resident Secretary.
G. L. MADDISON,
15-1yr
AGENT FOR TORONTO.

Lancashire Insurance Company.

CAPITAL, - - - - - £2,000,000 Sterling

FIRE RISKS
Taken at reasonable rates of premium, and
ALL LOSSES SETTLED PROMPTLY,
By the undersigned, without reference elsewhere.
S. C. DUNCAN-CLARK & CO.,
General Agents for Ontario,
N. W. Corner of King & Church Streets,
25-1y
TORONTO.

Etna Fire & Marine Insurance Company.

INCORPORATED 1819. CHARTER PERPETUAL.

CASH CAPITAL, - - - - $3,000,000

LOSSES PAID IN 50 YEARS, 23,500,000 00.

JULY, 1868.
ASSETS.
(At Market Value.)
Cash in hand and in Bank............... $544,842 39
Real Estate.......................... 253,267 59
Mortgage Bonds...................... 932,245,00
Bank Stock........................... 1,272,679 00
United States, State and City Stock, and other Public Securities.................... 2,049,855 51
_____
Total..................... $5,052,880 19

LIABILITIES.
Claims not Due, and Unadjusted............ $499,803 55
Amount required by Mass. and New York for Re-Insurance...................... 1,405,267 15
THOS. R. WOOD,
50-6
Agent for Toronto.

Insurance.

ÆTNA
Live Stock Insurance Company

LICENSED BY THE DOMINION GOVERNMENT TO DO BUSINESS IN CANADA.

THE following Accidents, this month, show the importance of Insuring your Horses and Cattle against Death from any cause, or Theft, in the Ætna Insurance Company:

MONTREAL, September 16, 1868.
At a fire last night, in the sheds behind Ripin's Hotel, St. Joseph Street, three valuable Stock Horses were destroyed, "Young Clydesdale" and "Emigrant," belonging to the Huntingdon Agricultural Society—the former worth $600, and the latter $1,700; and "Old Beauharnois" cost $1,000, belonging to the Beauharnois Society.

PORT COLBORNE, September 13, 1868.
HORSES DROWNED.—Two horses belonging to Mr. Briggs, of Port Colborne, and four owned by Mr. Julien, of Port Dalhousie, were drowned in the Canal, near the Junction, early this morning.

A fire at the Glasgow Hotel, Montreal, this morning, destroyed two horses. The fire was caused by drunkenness on the part of the stable man.

MONTREAL, September 24, 1868.
A fire in F. X. Cusson's stables, St. Joseph Street, last night, destroyed three horses.

E. L. SNOW, GENERAL AGENT,
Montreal;

Agents for Ontario:—
    SCOTT & WALMSLEY,
67nov11y   Ontario Hall, Church Street, Toronto.

The Liverpool and London and Globe Insurance Company

INVESTED FUNDS:
FIFTEEN MILLIONS OF DOLLARS.

DAILY INCOME OF THE COMPANY:
TWELVE THOUSAND DOLLARS.

LIFE INSURANCE,
WITH AND WITHOUT PROFITS.

FIRE INSURANCE
On every description of Property, at Lowest Remunerative Rates.
JAMES FRASER, AGENT,
5 King Street West.

Toronto, 1868.   28-1y

Briton Medical and General Life Association,
with which is united the
BRITANNIA LIFE ASSURANCE COMPANY.

Capital and Invested Funds············£750,000 *Sterling*.

ANNUAL INCOME, £220,000 STG. :
Yearly increasing at the rate of £25,000 Sterling.

THE important and peculiar feature originally introduced by this Company, in applying the periodical Bonuses, so as to make Policies payable during life, without any higher rate of premiums being charged, has caused the success of the BRITON MEDICAL AND GENERAL to be almost unparalleled in the history of Life Assurance. *Life Profits on the profit Scale become payable during the lifetime of the Assured, thus rendering a Policy of Assurance a means of subsistence in old age, as well as a protection for a family,* and a more valuable security to creditors in the event of early death; and effectually meeting the often urged objection, that persons do not themselves reap the benefit of their own prudence and forethought.

No extra charge made to members of Volunteer Corps for services within the British Provinces.

☞ TORONTO-AGENCY, 5 KING ST. WEST.
oct17—9-1yr   JAMES FRASER, Agent.

Phenix Insurance Company,
BROOKLYN, N. Y.

PHILANDER SHAW,   STEPHEN CROWELL,
Secretary.   *President.*

Cash Capital, $1,000,000. Surplus, $606,416.02. Total, 1,606,416.02. Entire Income from all sources for 1866 was $2,131,839.82.

CHARLES G. FORTIER, *Marine Agent.*
Ontario Chambers, Toronto, Ont.   19-1y;

Insurance.

The Victoria Mutual
FIRE INSURANCE COMPANY OF CANADA.

Insures only Non-Hazardous Property, at Low Rates.

BUSINESS STRICTLY MUTUAL.

GEORGE H. MILLS, *President.*
W. D. BOOKER, *Secretary.*

HEAD OFFICE ·············· HAMILTON, ONTARIO
aug 15-1yr

The Ætna Life Insurance Company.

AN attack, abounding with errors, having been made upon the Ætna Life Insurance Co. by the editor of the *Montreal Daily News* : and certain agents of British Companies being now engaged in handing around copies of the attack, thus seeking to damage the Company's standing,—I have pleasure in laying before the public the following certificate, bearing the signatures of the Presidents and Cashiers who happened to be in their Offices of *every Bank in Hartford*; also that of the President and Secretary of the old Ætna Fire Insurance Company :—

"*To whom it may concern.*—
"We, the undersigned, regard the Ætna Life Insurance Company, of this city, as one of the most successful and prosperous Insurance Companies in the States,—entirely reliable, responsible, and honourable in all its dealings, and most worthy of public confidence and patronage."

Lucius J. Hendee, President Ætna Fire Insurance Co., and late Treasurer of the State of Connecticut.
J. Goodnow, Secretary Ætna Fire Insurance Co.
C. H. Northam, President, and J. B. Powell, Cashier National Bank.
C. T. Hillyer, President Charter Oak National Bank.
E. D. Tiffany, President First National Bank.
G. T. Davis, President City National Bank.
F. S. Riley, Cashier, do. do. do.
John C. Tracy, President of Farmers' and Mechanics' National Bank.
M. W. Graves, Cashier Conn. River Banking Co.
H. A. Redfield, Cashier Phenix National Bank.
O. G. Terry, President Ætna National Bank.
J. R. Redfield, Cashier American Exchange Bank.
John G. Root, Assistant Cashier American National Bank.
George F. Bills, Cashier State Bank of Hartford.
Jas. Potter, Cashier Hartford National Bank.
Hartford, Nov. 26, 1867.

Many of the above-mentioned parties are closely connected with other Life Insurance Companies, but all unhesitatingly commend our Company as "reliable, responsible, honorable in all its dealings, and most worthy of public confidence and patronage."
JOHN GARVIN,
General Agent, Toronto Street.
Toronto, Dec. 3. 1867.   16-1y

Life Association of Scotland.

INVESTED FUNDS
UPWARDS OF £1,000,000 STERLING.

THIS Institution differs from other Life Offices, in that the
BONUSES FROM PROFITS
Are applied on a special system for the Policy-holder's
PERSONAL BENEFIT AND ENJOYMENT DURING HIS OWN LIFETIME,
WITH THE OPTION OF
LARGE BONUS ADDITIONS TO THE SUM ASSURED.

The Policy-holder thus obtains
A LARGE REDUCTION OF PRESENT OUTLAY
OR
A PROVISION FOR OLD AGE OF A MOST IMPORTANT AMOUNT IN ONE CASH PAYMENT, OR A LIFE ANNUITY,
Without any expense or outlay whatever beyond the ordinary Assurance Premium for the Sum Assured, which remains in tact for Policy-holder's heirs, or other purposes.

CANADA—MONTREAL—PLACE D'ARMES.

DIRECTORS:
DAVID TORRANCE, Esq., (D. Torrance & Co.)
GEORGE MOFFATT, (Gillespie, Moffatt & Co.)
ALEXANDER MORRIS, Esq., M.P., Barrister, Perth.
Sir G. E. CARTIER, M.P., Minister of Militia.
PETER REDPATH, Esq., (J. Redpath & Son).
J. H. R. MOLSON, Esq., (J. H. R. Molson & Bros.)
Solicitors—Messrs. TORRANCE & MORRIS.
Medical Officer—R. PALMER HOWARD, Esq., M.D.
Secretary—P. WARDLAW.
Inspector of Agencies—JAMES P. M. CHIPMAN.   7

Insurance.

North British and Mercantile Insuran Company.

Established 1809.

HEAD OFFICE, - - CANADA. - - MONTR

TORONTO BRANCH :
LOCAL OFFICES, NOS. 4 & 6 WELLINGTON STREE
Fire Department, ·················· R. N. GOO

Life Department, ·················· H. L. HIME
29-1y

Phenix Fire Assurance Compan;
LOMBARD ST. AND CHARING CROSS,
LONDON, ENG.

Insurances effected in all parts of the Wor

Claims paid
WITH PROMITUDE AND LIBERALIT
MOFFATT, MURRAY & BEATTIE,
Agents for Toront
36 Yonge Str
28

The Commercial Union Assuran Company,
19 & 20 CORNHILL, LONDON, ENGLAND.
Capital, £2,500,000 *Stg.—Invested over* $2,000,00

FIRE DEPARTMENT.—Insurance granted on a scriptions of property at reasonable rates.

LIFE DEPARTMENT.—The success of this b has been unprecedented—NINETY PER CENT. of niums now in hand. First year's premiums were $100,000. Economy of management guaranteed P security. Moderate rates.

OFFICE—385 & 387 ST PAUL STREET, MONTREA
MORLAND, WATSON & Co
General Agents for Ca
FRED. COLE, *Secretary.*

Inspector of Agencies—T. C. LIVINGSTON,
W. M. WESTMACOTT, *Agent at Toro*
16-1y

Phenix Mutual Life Insurance C
HARTFORD, CONN.

Accumulated Fund, $2,000,000, *Income,* $1,000,

THIS Company, established in 1851, is one of th reliable Companies doing business in the countr has been steadily prospering. The *Massachusetts In Reports* show that in nearly all important matter superior to the general average of Companies. It a intending assurers the following reasons, amongst for preferring it to other companies :

It is purely Mutual. It allows the Insured to and reside in any portion of the United States and E It throws out almost all restriction on occupation fr Policies. It will, if desired, take a note for part Premium, thus combining all the advantages of a no all cash company. Its Dividends are declared an and applied in reduction of Premium. Its Divider in every case on Premiums paid. The Dividends PHENIX have averaged fifty per cent. yearly. settlement of Policies, a Dividend will be allowed fc year the policy has been in force. The number o dends will always equal the outstanding Notes. It losses promptly—during its existence never havin tested a claim. It issues Policies for the benefit o ried Women beyond the reach of their husband's cre Creditors may also insure the lives of Debtors. Its P are all *Non-forfeiting,* as it always allows the assu surrender his Policy, should he desire, the Compa ing a paid-up Policy therefor. This important f will commend itself to all. The inducements now r by the PHENIX are better and more liberal than th any other Company. Its rate of Mortality is excee low and under the average.

Parties contemplating *Life Insurance* will find it t interest to call and examine our rates. Policies payable either in *Gold* or American currency.
ANGUS R. BETHUNE,
General Manager,
Dominion of C
Office: 104 ST. FRANÇOIS XAVIER ST. MONTRE.

☞ Active and energetic Agents and Can wanted in every town and village, to whom liberal l ments will be given.

PRINTED AT THE DAILY TELEGRAPH PRI. HOUSE, BAY ST., COR. KING.

TORONTO PRICES CURRENT.—December 10, 1868.

Name of Article.	Wholesale Rates.		Name of Article.	Wholesale Rate.		Name of Article.	Wholesale Rates.	
Boots and Shoes.	$ c.	$ c.	**Groceries**—*Contin'd*	$ c.	$ c.	**Leather**—*Contin'd.*	$ c.	$ c.
Mens' Thick Boots ...	2 05	2 50	" fine to fins't..	0 85	0 95	Kip Skins, Patna ...	0 30	0 40
" Kip... ...	2 50	3 25	Hyson	0 45	0 80	French	0 70	0 90
" Calf ...	3 00	3 70	Imperial	0 62	0 80	English	0 65	0 90
" Congress Gaiters..	2 00	2 50	Tobacco, *Manufac'd:*			Hemlock Calf (30 to		
" Kip Cobourgs..	1 15	1 45	Can Leaf, ¢ ℔ 5 & 10s.	0 26	0 30	35 lbs.) per doz.	0 75	0 85
Boys' Thick Boots....	1 00	1 80	Western Leaf, com..	0 25	0 26	Do. light	0 45	0 50
Youths'	1 45	1 50	" Good ...	0 27	0 32	French Calf..	0 98	1 15
Women's Batts	95	1 30	" Fine ..	0 32	0 35	Grain & Satn Clf ℔ doz..	0 00	0 00
" Congress Gaiters	1 15	1 45	" Bright fine..	0 40	0 50	Splits, large ℔ ℔...	0 30	0 38
Misses' Batts..	0 75	1 00	" choice ..	0 60	0 75	" small ...	0 20	0 30
" Congress Gaiters..	1 00	1 30				Enamelled Cow ℔ foot..	0 17	0 18
Girls' Batts	0 60	0 85	**Hardware.**			Patent	0 18	0 20
" Congress Gaiters..	0 80	1 10	*Tin (net cash prices)*			Pebble Grain	0 17	0 18½
Children's C. T. Cacks..	0 50	0 65	Block, ℔ ℔........	0 25	0 26	Buff	0 17	0 18
"	0 65	0 90	Grain	0 25	0 26	**Oils.**		
Drugs.			*Copper:*			Cod	0 60	0 68½
Aloes Cape.	0 12½	0 16	Pig	0 23	0 24	Lard, extra	0 40	1 25
Alum..........	0 02½	0 03	Sheet..........	0 30	0 33	" No. 1	0 00	1 15
Borax	0 00	0 00	*Cut Nails:*			" Woollen ...	0 00	1 05
Camphor, refined....	0 65	0 70	Assorted ℔ Shingles,			Lubricating, patent..	0 00	0 00
Castor Oil..........	0 18	0 28	℔ 100 ℔........	2 90	3 00	" Mott's economic	0 50	0 00
Caustic Soda........	0 04½	0 05	Shingle alone do	3 15	3 25	Linseed, raw	0 77½	0 85
Cochineal..........	0 90	1 10	Lathe and 5 dy...	3 30	3 40	" boiled..	0 82½	0 90
Cream Tartar	0 00	0 00	*Galvanized Iron:*			Machinery	0 00	0 00
Epsom Salts	0 02	0 04	Assorted sizes	0 08	0 09	Olive, 2nd, ℔ gal ...	1 45	1 50
Extract Logwood....	0 09	0 11	Best No. 24	0 09	0 00	" salad	2 00	2 30
Gum Arabic, sorts ..	0 30	0 35	" 26..........	0 08	0 08½	" salad, in bots.		
Indigo, Madras......	0 75	1 00	" 28..........	0 09	0 09½	qt. ℔ case...	3 60	3 75
Licorice	0 14	0 45	*Horse Nails:*			Sesame salad, ℔ gal...	1 60	1 75
Madder..........	0 13	0 16	Guest's or Griffin's			Seal, pale..	0 70	0 75
Nutgalls	0 00	0 20	assorted sizes	0 00	0 00	Spirits Turpentine...	0 00	0 70
Opium..........	6 70	7 00	For W. nsa'd sizes..	0 18	0 19	Varnish	0 00	0 00
Oxalic Acid..........	0 28	0 35	Patent Hammer'd do..	0 17	0 18	Whale..........	0 75	0 80
Potash, Bi-tart..	0 25	0 28	Cut (4 months):			**Paints, &c.**		
" Bichromate ..	0 15	0 20	Pig—Gartsherrie No1..	24 00	25 00	White Lead, genuine		
Potass Iodide	3 80	4 50	Other brands. No 1..	22 00	24 00	in Oil, ℔ 25lbs...	0 00	2 50
Senna	0 12½	0 60	" No 3..	0 00	0 00	Do. No. 1 "	0 00	2 25
Soda Ash	0 02	0 04	Bar—Scotch, ℔100 ℔..	2 25	2 50	" 2 "	0 00	2 00
Soda Bicarb	4 50	5 50	Refined	3 00	3 50	" 3 "	0 00	1 75
Tartaric Acid..........	0 37½	0 45	Swedes	5 00	5 50	White Zinc, genuine..	3 00	3 50
Vertigris	0 35	0 40	Hoops —Coopers...	3 00	3 25	White Lead, dry......	0 6½	0 00
Vitriol, Blue..........	0 09	0 10	" Band ..	3 00	3 25	Red Lead	0 07½	0 08
Groceries.			Boiler Plates..	3 25	3 50	Venetian Red, Eng'h..	0 02½	0 03½
Coffees:			Canada Plates..	4 00	4 25	Yellow Ochre, Fren'h..	0 02½	0 03½
Java, ℔ ℔..........	0 22@0 24		Union Jack	0 00	0 00	Whiting	0 90	1 25
Laguayra, "	0 17	0 18	Pontypool	4 00	4 25			
Rio	0 15	0 17	Swansea	3 90	4 00	**Petroleum.**		
Fish:			*Lead (at 4 months):*			(Refined ℔ gal.).		
Herrings, Lab. split..	5 75	6 50	Bar, ℔ 100 ℔s..	0 07	0 07½	Water white, carl'd..	0 27½	
" round..	4 50	0 00	Sheet "	0 08	0 09	" small lots..	0 00	0 30
" scaled..	0 35	0 40	Shot..........	0 07½	0 07½	Straw, by car load ..	0 27	
Mackerel, small kitts..	1 00	0 00	*Iron Wire* (net cash):			" small lots ..	0 29	0 80
Loch. Her. wh'e frks..	3 50	3 75	No. 6, ℔ bundle...	2 70	2 80	Amber, by car load..	0 00	0 00
" half "	1 25	1 50	" 8, "	3 10	3 20	" small lots ..	0 00	0 00
White Fish & Trout...	3 50	3 75	" 14, "	3 40	3 50	Benzine	0 00	0 00
Salmon, saltwater..	14 00	15 00	" 16, "	4 30	4 40			
Dry Cod, ℔112 ℔s..	5 00	5 25	*Powder:*			**Produce.**		
Fruits:			Blasting, Canada....	3 50	3 75	*Grain.*		
Raisins, Layers	2 15	2 20	FF "	4 25	4 50	Wheat, Spring, 60 ℔..	1 03	1 06
" M R..........	2 10	2 15	FFF "	4 75	5 00	" Fall "	1 05	1 15
" Valentiasnew..	0 05	0 05½	Blasting, English ..	4 50	5 00	Barley .... 60 ".	1 25	1 30
Currants, new	0 05	0 05½	FF loose..	5 00	6 00	Peas .... 60 ".	0 80	0 83
" old..........	0 04½	0 04½	FFF "	6 00	6 50	Oats .... 34 ".	0 58	0 58
Figs .... "	0 10	0 11	*PressedSpikes* (4 mos):			Rye .... 56 ".	0 65	0 75
Molasses:			Regular sizes 100...	4 00	4 25	*Seeds:*		
Clayed, ℔ gal..........	0 00	0 40	Extra	4 50	5 00	Clover, choice 60 ".	6 25	6 50
Syrups, Standard ..	0 00	0 50	*Tin Plates* (net cash):			" com'n 60 "	0 00	0 00
" Golden ..	0 54	0 55	IC Coke	7 50	8 00	Timothy, choc 4 "...	2 50	2 75
Rice:			IC Charcoal..........	8 25	8 75	" inf. to good 48 ".	2 00	2 50
Arracan .... "	4 60	4 80	IX "	10 25	10 75	Flax .... 56 ".	1 40	1 60
Spices:			IXX "	12 50	0 00	*Flour* (per brl.):		
Cassia, whole, ℔ ℔...	0 42	0 45	DC "	7 50	9 00	Superior extra..	0 00	0 00
Cloves	0 11	0 12	DX "	9 50	0 00	Extra superfine,..	0 00	0 00
Nutmegs	0 45	0 55				Fancy superfine	0 00	0 00
Ginger, ground	0 20	0 25	**Hides & Skins/** ℔			Superfine No. 1..	4 50	4 65
" Jamaica, root..	0 20	0 25	Green rough	0 06	0 06½	" No. 2..	0 00	0 00
Pepper, black..........	0 09½	0 10	Green, salt'd & insp'd..	0 00	0 07	*Oatmeal,* (per brl.)..	6 00	6 25
Pimento	0 05	0 09	Cured	0 08	0 08½			
Sugars:			Calfskins, green......	0 00	0 13	**Provisions.**		
Port Rico, ℔ lb...	0 08½	0 08½	Calfskins, cured	0 00	0 12	Butter, dairy tub ℔ ℔...	0 23	0 24
Cuba "	0 08½	0 08½	" dry..	0 16	0 20	" store packed..	0 21	0 22
Barbadoes (bright) ..	0 08½	0 09	Sheepskins, ...	0 00	0 00	Cheese, new	0 11	0 11½
Dry Crushed, at 60d...	0 11½	0 11½	" country ...	0 60	0 80	Pork, mess, per brl...	22 00	22 50
Canada Sugar Refine'y,						" prime mess,..		
yellow No. 2, 60ds...	0 09	0 09½	**Mops.**			" prime	0 00	0 00
Yellow, No. 2½ ...	0 09½	0 00	Inferior, ℔ ℔..........	0 05	0 07	Bacon, rough	0 00	0 00
" No. 3..	0 00	0 09½	Medium..........	0 09	0 10	" Cumberl'd cut..	0 10	0 11
Crushed A	0 00	0 10½	Good	0 09	0 12	" smoked ...	0 11	0 11
" A	0 11	0 11	Fancy	0 00	0 00	Hams, in salt..	0 00	0 00
Ground..........	0 11	0 11½				" sug. cur & canv'd..	0 00	0 00
Extra Ground..........	0 12½	0 12½	**Leather.** ℔ (4 mos.)			Shoulders, in salt	0 00	0 00
Teas:			In lots of less than			Lard, in kegs	0 00	0 16
Japan com'n to good..	0 40	0 55	50 sides, 10 ℔ cent			Eggs, packed	0 18	0 20
" Fine to choicest..	0 55	0 65	higher.			Beef Hams	0 00	0 13
Colored, com. to fine..	0 65	0 75	Spanish Sole, 1st qual..			Tallow	0 09	0 00
Congou & Souch'ng...	0 42	0 75	" heavy, weights ℔ ℔..	0 21	0 22	Hogs dressed, heavy..	7 50	7 00
Oolong, good to fine..	0 50	0 65	No.1st qual middle do..	0 22	0 23	" light..........	6 50	7 00
Y. Hyson, com to gd..	0 45	0 65	No. 2, all weights..	0 20	0 21			
Medium to choice ..	0 65	0 80	Slaughter heavy ...	0 25	0 26	**Salt, &c.**		
Extra choice	0 65	0 95	Do. light..........	0 24	0 25	American brls..........	1 58	1 60
Gunpowd'r. to med..	0 55	0 70	Harness heavy	0 32	0 34	Liverpool coarse	1 25	1 35
" med. to fie.e	0 70	0 85	" No. 2 ..	0 30	0 32	Plaster	1 05	1 10
			Upper heavy	0 44	0 38	Water Lime	1 50	0 00
			" light..........	0 36	0 40			

	$ c.	$ c.
Soap & Candles.		
D. Crawford & Co.'s ..		
Imperial.........	0 07½	0 08
" Golden Bar	0 07	0 07½
" Silver Bar........	0 07	0 07½
Crown	0 05	0 05½
No. 1	0 03¼	0 03¾
Candles	0 00	0 11½
Wines, Liquors, &c.		
Ale:		
English, per doz......	2 60	2 65
Guinness Dub Portr..	2 35	2 40
Spirits:		
Pure Jamaica Rum...	1 80	2 25
De Kuyper's H. Gin..	1 55	1 65
Booth's Old Tom.....	1 90	2 00
Gin:		
Green, cases.........	4 00	4 25
Booth's Old Tom, c...	6 00	6 25
Wines:		
Port, common	1 00	1 25
" fine old	2 00	4 00
Sherry, common	1 00	1 50
" medium........	1 70	1 80
" old pale or golden..	2 50	4 00

	$ c.	$ c.
Brandy:		
Hennessy's, per gal..	2 30	2 50
Martell's " ..	2 30	2 50
J. Robin & Co.'s " ..	2 25	2 35
Otard, Dupuy & Cos..	2 25	2 35
Brandy, cases........	8 50	9 00
Brandy, com. per c...	4 00	4 50
Whiskey:		
Common 36 u. p.......	0 62½	0 65
Old Rye	0 85	0 87½
Malt........	0 85	0 87½
Toddy	0 85	0 87½
Scotch, per gal........	1 90	2 10
Irish—Kinnahan's c...	7 00	7 50
" Dunnville's Belf't..	6 00	6 25
Wool.		
Fleece, lb.............	0 28	0 35
Pulled "............	0 22	0 25
Furs.		
Bear..................	3 00	10 00
Beaver................	1 00	1 25
Coon	0 20	0 40
Fisher................	4 00	6 00
Martin................	1 40	1 60
Mink..................	4 00	4 25
Otter.................	5 75	6 00
Spring Rats...........	0 15	0 17
Fox...................	1 20	1 25

INSURANCE COMPANIES.

ENGLISH.—*Quotations on the London Market.*

No. of Shares.	Last Dividend.	Name of Company.	Shares par val £	Amount paid.	Last Sale.
20,000		Briton Medical and General Life ...	10	....	1¾
50,000	7½	Commer'l Union, Fire, Life and Mar.	50	5	5½
24,000	8	City of Glasgow	25	2½	5
5,000	9½	Edinburgh Life	100	15	30¾x
400,000	5—½ yr	European Life and Guarantee......	2½	11s6	4s 6d
100,000	10	Etna Fire and Marine............	10	1½	1
20,000	5	Guardian	100	50	51½
24,000	12	Imperial Fire................	500	50	345
7,500	9½	Imperial Life	100	10	16½
100,000	10	Lancashire Fire and Life.........	20	2	2¾x
10,000	11	Life Association of Scotland.......	40	7¼	23
35,862	45s. p. sh	London Assurance Corporation ..	25	12½	48
10,000	5	London and Lancashire Life	10	1	1
87,504	40	Liverp'l & London & Globe F. & L.	20	2	7¼
20,000	5	National Union Life	5	1	1
20,000	12½	Northern Fire and Life	100	5	10¾
40,000	12 '68, bo 5s.	North British and Mercantile	50	6¼	16 16½
40,000	50	Ocean Marine	25	5	20
2,500	£5 12s.	Provident Life................	100	10	38
....	£4½ p. s.	Phœnix	....	....	136
200,000	2½--h. yr.	Queen Fire and Life	10	1	15-16ths
100,000	3s. bo. 4s	Royal Insurance...............	20	3	6¾
20,000	10	Scottish Provincial Fire and Life ..	50	2½	4¼
10,000	25	Standard Life	50	12	65
4,000	5	Star Life	25	1¼	—
		CANADIAN.			℘ c.
8,000	4	British America Fire and Marine ..	$50	$25	56
....	4	Canada Life	...	....	.....
4000	12	Montreal Assurance	£50	£5	135
10,000	3	Provincial Fire and Marine.......	60	11	.....
....	....	Quebec Fire	40	32½	£ 20
....	8	" Marine................	100	40	95
10,000	5 7 mo's.	Western Assurance.............	40	6	.....

RAILWAYS.	Sha's	Paid	Montr	London.
Atlantic and St. Lawrence..................	£100	All.	....	58 60
Buffalo and Lake Huron	20½	"	....	3 3½
Do. do Preference	10	"	....	5½ 6½
Buff., Brantt. & Goderich, 6℘c.,1872-3-4....	100	"	....	60 70
Champlain and St. Lawrence	....	....	9 12	....
Do. do Pref. 10 ℘ ct....	....	....	65 80	....
Grand Trunk	100	"	16 17	15½ 16½
Do. Eq.G. M. Bds. 1 ch. 6℘c..........	100	"	....	84 86
Do. First Preference, 5 ℘ c	100	"	....	50 52
Do. Deferred, 3 ℘ ct..	100	"	....	....
Do. Second Pref. Bonds, 5℘c..........	100	"	....	41 43
Do. do Deferred, 3 ℘ ct...........	100	"	...	....
Do. Third Pref. Stock, 4℘ct...........	100	"	...	27 29
Do. do. Deferred, 3 ℘ ct......	100	"	...	....
Do. Fourth Pref. Stock, 3℘c...........	100	"	....	18½ 19½
Do. do. Deferred, 3 ℘ ct..........	100	"	....	...
Great Western	20½	"	13 14	13½ 14
Do. New	20½	18	....	....
Do. 6 ℘ c. Bds, due 1873-76.........	100	All.	....	102 104
5½ ℘c Bds. due 1877-78....	100	"	....	93 94
Marine Railway, Halifax, $250, all......	$250	"	....	....
Northern, of Canada, 6℘c. 1st Pref. Bds.........	100	"	.. .	80 83

EXCHANGE.	Halifax.	Montr'l.	Quebec.	Toronto.
Bank on London, 60 days......				
Sight or 75 days date...........	13¼	9¼ 9½	9¾ 9¾	9⅝
Private do.	12 12½	8 9	8½ 9	9
Private, with documents....	....	....	....	....
Bank on New York...............	....	25½ 26	24½ 25	74
Private do.	....	26 26½	25 25½	....
Gold Drafts do.	....	par	par ½ dis.	par ½ dis.
Silver	....	4 4½	....	3½ 5

STOCK AND BOND REPORT.

The dates of our quotations are as follows:—Toronto, Dec. 10; Montreal, Dec. 8; Dec. 7; London, Nov. 21.

NAME.	Shares.	Paid up.	Divid'd last 6 Months	Dividend Day.	CLOSING PI Toronto.	Montr
BANKS.			℘ ct.			
British North America	$250	All.	3	July and Jan.	105 106½	103¾10
Jacques Cartier..........	50	"	4	1 June, 1 Dec.	106 106½	106 10
Montreal	200	"	5	"	138½ 139	138¾ 1
Nationale..................	50	"	4	1 Nov. 1 May.	....	105 10
New Brunswick	100	"	......	......	....	...
Nova Scotia	200	28	7&b$2¼	Mar. and Sept.	....	....
Du Peuple...	50	"	4	1 Mar., 1 Sept.	106½ 107	106½10
Toronto	100	"	4	1 Jan., 1 July.	120 120½	119 12
Bank of Yarmouth...........	....	....	......	......	....	....
Canadian Bank of Com'e......	50	95	......	......	105½ 106	105 10
City Bank Montreal	80	All.	4	1 June, 1 Dec.	102 102½	102 10
Commer'l Bank (St. John)....	100	"	℘ ct.	. ...	....	...
Eastern Townships' Bank.....	50	"	4	1 July, 1 Jan..	....	98 9
Gore	40	...	3½	1 Jan., 1 July.	42 43	43 4
Halifax Banking Company....	..	....	......	. ....	...	....
Mechanics' Bank............	50	70	4	1 Nov., 1 May.	95½ 96	95 9
Merchants' Bank of Canada....	100	70	4	1 Jan., 1 July.	113 113½	112¾11
Merchants' Bank (Halifax)....	....	....	.....	.....	....	....
Molson's Bank......	50	All.	4	1 Apr., 1 Oct.	109 110	109¾11
Niagara District Bank...	100	70	3½	1 Jan., 1 July.	...	....
Ontario Bank................	40	All.	4	1 June, 1 Dec.	100 100½	99¾ 10
People's Bank (Fred'kton)....	100	"	......	......	....	....
People's Bank (Halifax)	20	"	7 12 m	......	....	...
Quebec Bank	100	"	3½	1 June, 1 Dec.	98 100	....
Royal Canadian Bank	50	50	4	1 Jan., 1 July.	85½ 87	85 8
St. Stephens Bank	100	All	.....	......	....	..
Union Bank	100	70	4	1 Jan., 1 July.	104 106	104½ 1
Union Bank (Halifax)........	100	40	7 12 mo	Feb. and Aug.	....	....
MISCELLANEOUS.						
British America Land........	250	44	2½	......	....	....
British Colonial S. S. Co......	250	32½	2½	......	...	40 6
Canada Company	32½	All.	5	......	....	....
Canada Landed Credit Co.....	50	$20	3½	......	72 73	....
Canada Per. B'ldg Society....	50	All.	5	......	124½125	....
Canada Mining Company.....	4	90	......	... ..	....	....
Do. Inl'd Steam Nav. Co.....	100	All.	20 12 m	......	....	106 10
Do. Glass Company.........	100	"	12½ "	......	....	50 60
Canad'n Loan & Investm't....	25	2½	7	......	....	....
Canada Agency	10	¼	......	......	....	....
Colonial Securities Co.......	...	....	.....	.....	....	....
Freehold Building Society....	100	All.	4	......	104 104½	....
Halifax Steamboat Co........	100	"	5	......	....	....
Halifax Gas Company.......	....	....	......	... .	....	...
Hamilton Gas Company......	....	....	.....	. ....	....	....
Huron Copper Bay Co........	4	12	20	. ....	....	25 40c
Lake Huron S. and C.........	5	102	......	......	....	....
Montreal Mining Consols.....	20	$15	......	. ....	....	2.25 2.
Do. Telegraph Co...	40	All.	5	......	136	136 13
Do. Elevating Co...	00	"	15 12 m	......	....	100 10
Do. City Gas Co.........	40	"	4	15 Mar. 15 Sep.	....	134 13
Do. City Pass. R., Co....	50	"	5	......	....	110 11
Nova Scotia Telegraph	20	"	....	. ....	....	....
Quebec and L. S.	8	$4	......	.....	. ..	....
Quebec Gas Co..............	200	All.	4	1 Mar., 1 Sep.	....	...
Quebec Street R. R..........	50	25	8	......	....	....
Richelieu Navigation Co......	100	All.	7 p.a.	1 Jan., 1 July.	....	118 12
St. Lawrence Tow Boat Co....	100	"	......	3 Feb.	...	...
Tor'to Consumers' Gas Co....	50	"	2 3 m.	1 My Au MarFe	106½ 107	...
Trust & Loan Co. of U. C.....	20	5	3	......	....	....
West'n Canada Bldg Soc'y....	50	All.	5	......	115½116	....

SECURITIES.	London.	Montreal.	Quebec.
Canadian Gov't Deb. 6 ℘ ct. stg.....................	....	102 103	101½ 102½
Do. do. 6 do due Ja. & Jul. 1877-84........	107½ 108½	....	....
Do. do. 6 do. Feb. & Aug..	105 107	....	.. .
Do. do. 6 do. Mch. & Sep.........	105 107	.. .	...
Do. do. 5 ℘ ct. cur., 1883	94 95	92½ 93	92 92
Do. do. 5 do. stg., 1885	94 95	92½ 93½	92½ 93
Do. do. 7 do. cur.,.....................	....	....	.....
Dominion 6 p. c. 1878 cy.....	....	105 106	105 105
Hamilton Corporation....	. ..	....	......
Montreal Harbor, 8 ℘ ct. d. 1869..................	..	....	......
Do. do. 7 do. 1870......................	...	....	......
Do. do. 6½ do. 1875......................	....	101 102	......
Do. do. 6½ do. 1878......................	....	....	......
Do. Corporation, 6 ℘ c. 1891	....	95½ 96½	95½ 96½
Do. 7 p. c. stock..........................	....	106 107½	106 107
Do. Water Works, 6 ℘ c. stg. 1878........	....	....	......
Do. do. 6 do. cy. do.	....	96 96½	......
New Brunswick, 6 ℘ ct., Jan. and July	104 106	....	.. ...
Nova Scotia, 6 ℘ ct., 1875.......................	104½ 105½	...	......
Ottawa City 6 ℘ c. d. 1880	....	....	......
Quebec Harbour, 6 ℘ c. d. 1883.	....	....	60
Do. do. 7 do. do......................	....	....	65 70
Do. do. 8 do. 1886....................	...	....	75 85
Do. City, 7 ℘ c. d. 5 years	....	90 91	95 96
Do. do. 7 do. 9 do.	....	....	90 92
Do. do. 7 do. 2½ do.	....	....	97 98
Do. Water Works, 7 ℘ ct., 4 years	....	....	96 98
Do. do. 6 do. 2 do.	....	....	93½ 94
Toronto Corporation	....	90 92½	...

PROSPECTUS

OF THE

)MINION EXPRESS COMPANY OF CANADA

ORGANIZED UNDER THE JOINT STOCK COMPANIES' ACTS.

CAPITAL STOCK, ... $1,000,000,

In 10,000 Shares, $100 each.

proposed to organize a DOMINION EXPRESS COMPANY, to meet the present and prospective demand for increased facilities of general trans-
-tation. It is the interest of Canadians to do their own work, and *accumulate* cash capital, and one of the objects of this scheme is the retention
country of the profits arising from the business done.
press Companies obtain "four-fifths" of their business from merchants and bankers, and no reason exists why they cannot transport their own
by their *own Agents, economically* and *efficiently*, and by a *union of capital* and *effort*, they hereby resolve so to do. Being thus united, and
ng to it their business and influence, secures to this Company certain and complete success.
iis organization, like the mail system, is to extend, under *one general management*, to all cities, towns and villages in the Dominion, and to connect
arts of the United States, and being but "one Company," will secure *unity, despatch* and *accuracy*.
is proposed to distribute the stock widely, throughout the Dominion, in limited sums, apportioned as nearly as practicable to the business of the
ibers. The capital Stock of the Company to be not less than $1,000,000, in 10,000 shares of $100 each.
m *per cent.* of the stock subscribed will be required to be paid after the subscription shall have reached the sum of $250,000, and after a Charter
ave been obtained, of which due notice will be given to the subscribers; the subsequent calls, not exceeding *ten per cent. at any one time*, to be
t convenient intervals, as the demands on the Company may require. But the aggregate of all calls to be made will, it is believed, not exceed
per cent. of the Capital Stock.
ie business to be done strictly on *cash principles*. With a paying business assured from the start, by *interested* and *reliable* Stockholders, it will
, seen that a small per centage *only* of the subscriptions will be required to put the Company in working order, and it is confidently and reasonably
d that the receipts will thereafter maintain and extend it. And in order to secure an equitable voice in its management, the principal commercial
will be represented at the Board, by Directors recommended by Stockholders of their own localities, who will also recommend to the Direction
al Agents, and thus secure a general influence in its management, as well as its business.
l Express enterprises, both in this country and the United States, have been decidedly successful, resulting from the profits of the business itself;
ving an organization and a share list—such as are now proposed—with energy and economy in the direction, no doubt can be entertained of the
atisfactory results.
ith such prospects, the Merchants of the Dominion, Capitalists and others interested in the success of this enterprise, are invited to become
olders.

The following shall be included in the By-Laws to be hereafter framed for the Government of the Company:

The Company shall be known by the name or title of "THE DOMINION EXPRESS COMPANY OF CANADA."
The Capital Stock of the Company shall be *One Million of Dollars*, divided into *Ten Thousand Shares of One Hundred Dollars each*.
Each Shareholder shall be liable only for the amount of Stock subscribed by him, her, or them.
The Shares of Stock of the Company shall be transferable; but no transfer shall be valid without the consent of the Directors, in writing, unless
ares shall be paid up in full.
It shall be lawful for the Stockholders, so soon as the sum of two hundred and fifty thousand dollars shall have been subscribed, to call a General
g of the subscribers, to be held at the office of the Company, in the City of Montreal, and proceed to elect nine qualified persons to be Directors
Company, each of whom to be a proprietor of not less than ten Shares of Stock of the said Company, and three of whom shall form a quorum,
l the powers of the Directors. The said Directors shall also, at their first General Meeting, elect a President, Secretary, Treasurer, and General
tendent or Managing Director, from amongst themselves.
The said Directors so elected shall proceed, without delay, to frame all necessary By-laws to govern the Company, and shall have power to alter
end the same as circumstances may require.
The Directors shall not have power either to *sell out* the said Company to any other Express Company or organization now in existence, or here-
be incorporated, or to amalgamate with any other Express Company.
No Stockholder shall be at liberty to hold in his, her, or their name, more than one hundred shares of the Capital Stock of the said Company,
t the consent of the Directors, in writing, first having been obtained.

PROVISIONAL DIRECTORS.

MESSRS. IRA GOULD,	MESSRS. WM. McNAUGHTON,	MESSRS. ALEXANDER McGIBBON,
WALTER MACFARLAN,	DUNCAN MACDONALD,	GEORGE HEUBACH,
VICTOR HUDON,	JOSEPH BARSALOU,	J. T. KERBY.

OFFICERS.

| PRESIDENT: | VICE-PRESIDENT: | TREASURER: | SECRETARY: |
| ALTER MACFARLAN. | WM. McNAUGHTON. | JOSEPH BARSALOU. | GEORGE HEUBACH. |

MESSRS. CARTIER, POMINVILLE, & BETOURNAY, SOLICITORS.   J. T. KERBY, GENERAL AGENT.

llowing are among the prominent firms in Montreal who have subscribed to the original Stock List at the formation of the Company:—

Ira Gould, President, Corn Exchange.	Messrs. W. McNaughton, Messrs. Sincennes & McNaughton.	Messrs. Boyer, Hudon, & Co.
Walter McFarlan, (Messrs. Walter McFarlan & Baird)	" A. W. Ogilvie & Co., Glenora Mills.	" Z. Benoit, Wholesale Merchant.
James Donelly, Wholesale Dry Goods.	" Benning & Barsalou, Auctioneers.	" Evans & Evans, Wholesale Hardware.
Luke Moore, (Messrs. Moore, Lemple & Hat-	" Alex. McGibbon, China House.	" James Smith, M.P.
chette).	" T. Baillie & Co., Wholesale Dry Goods.	" Andrew Watson.
Duncan Macdonald.	" Alex. Walker, Wholesale Dry Goods.	" A. Freeman & Co.
A. Shannon & Co., Wholesale Grocers.	" Geo. Winks & Co., Wholesale Dry Goods, Albert Buildings.	" John Rhynas.
Lewis, Kay & Co., Wholesale Dry Goods.	" W. P. Ryan, M.P.	" Cartier, Pominville & Betournay, Solicitors.
George Brush, Eagle Foundry.	" Victor Hudon & Co., Wholesale Grocer.	" Cassels & Cameron, Wholesale Dry Goods.
		" Ferrier & Co., Wholesale Hardwar .

TWENTY-THIRD ANNUAL REPORT

OF THE

NEW YORK LIFE INSURANCE COMPAN

Accumulated Capital, over $10,000,000. - - Divisible Surplus, Jan. 1, 1868, $1,642,425

Annual Statement, January 1st, 1868.

AMOUNT OF NET CASH ASSETS, January 1st, 1867		$6,727,816 65
AMOUNT OF PREMIUMS RECEIVED DURING 1867	$3,104,051 34	
AMOUNT OF INTEREST RECEIVED AND ACCRUED, INCLUDING PREMIUMS ON GOLD, &c.	487,339 94	
		3,591,391 28
		$10,319,207 93

DISBURSEMENTS.

Paid Losses by Death	$561,921 45	
Paid for Redemption of Dividends, Annuities, and surrendered and cancelled Policies	485,851 36	
Paid Salaries, Printing, Office and Law Expenses	98,032 55	
Paid Commissions and Agency Expenses	333,207 43	
Paid Advertising and Physician's Fees	46,518 77	
Paid Taxes and Internal Revenue Stamps	19,291 26	
		1,544,861 92
		$8,774,326 01

ASSETS.

Cash on hand, in Bank, and in Trust Company	$375,236 54	
Invested in United States Stocks, (Market value, $3,150,506 87) cost	2,978,907 49	
Invested in New York City Bank Stocks (Market value, $45,555), cost	41,549 00	
Invested in New York State Stocks (Market value, $836,650), cost	806,306 60	
Invested in other Stocks (Market value, $151,225), cost	149,337 01	
Loans on Demand, secured by U. S. and other Stocks, (Market value, $311,497)	237,700 00	
Real Estate (Market value, $709,125 66)	528,234 33	
Bonds and Mortgages (Secured by Real Estate, valued at $2,260,000)	1,072,800 00	
Premium Notes on existing Policies, bearing interest	1,556,837 47	
Quarterly and semi-annual Premiums due subsequent to January 1, 1868	346,285 81	
Interest accrued to January 1, 1868	52,402 83	
Rents accrued to January 1, 1868	2,401 96	
Premiums on Policies in hands of Agents and in course of transmission	406,326 77	
		$8,774,326 01
And excess of market value of securities over cost		385,427 90
Cash Assets, Jan. 1, 1868		$9,159,753 91

LIABILITIES OF THE COMPANY.

Amount of Adjusted Losses, due subsequent to Jan. 1, 1868	$134,800 00	
Amount of Reported Losses awaiting proof, &c.	38,214 32	
Amount reserved for Re-insurance on existing Policies (valuations, Carlisle table four per cent. interest, net premium)	6,283,635 49	
Return Premium, declared prior to 1866, payable on demand	72,572 51	
Return Premium, 1866 (now to be paid)	422,638 00	
Return Premium, 1867 (present value)	565,468 00	
		$7,517,328 32
Divisible Surplus		$1,642,425 59

During the year, 6,597 Policies have been issued, insuring $22,541,940.

The Progress of the Company for the Past Four Years will be seen in the following Statement:

	Assets.	Increase of Assets over previous year.				Increase of Assets previous year.
1864	$3,658,755 55	$1,005,217 63		1866	6,727,816 65	1,843,896 95
1865	4,881,919 70	1,223,164 15		1867	8,774,326 01	2,046,509 36
		Total increase	$6,120,788 69.			

One of the special features of this Company is the TEN YEAR NON-FORFEITUR PLAN.

The system popularly termed "The Non-Forfeiture Plan," was originated and first presented to the public by this Company, in their well-"TEN YEAR NON-FORFEITURE POLICY," in the year 1860; and its perfect adaptation to the wants of every class in the community, ob every reasonable objection to Life Insurance, is shown from the fact that every other American Company has been compelled, in deference to opinion, to adopt it, although in many cases it is done in such a way as considerably to impair its value. It has received the *unqualified approva best business men of the land,* large numbers of whom have taken out policies under it, simply as an investment.

By the Table on which this class of Policies is based, a person incurs no risk in taking out a policy. Insuring to-day for $10,000, if he should die to-morrow, th immediately becomes a claim; and if he shall live ten years, and make ten annual payments, his policy will be paid for, and his dividends *still continue,* making

HIS LIFE POLICY A SOURCE OF INCOME TO HIM WHILE LIVING.

By the specific terms of these policies, and not by vague and indefinite statements made in circulars, a party after the second year does not forfeit what he has paid in pe Thus, if one insuring by this plan for $10,000 discontinues after the second year, he is entitled to a PAID-UP POLICY, according to the number of full years paid in, as foll

Second year, two-tenths of $10,0 0 (amount insured), amounting to.. $2,000 | Fourth year, four-tenths of $10,000 (amount insured), amounting to.. $4,000
Third year, three-tenths of $10,000 (amount insured), amounting to.. 3,000 | Fifth year, five-tenths of $10,000 (amount insured), amounting to.... 5,000

And so on, until the tenth annual payment, *when all is paid.* The paid up policies, for the proportionate partial payments, as well as for the full amount, participa Dividends of the Company during the whole existence of the policies. ☞ This being a purely mutual Company, ALL ITS PROFITS ARE DIVIDED AMONG THE AS

MORRIS FRANKLIN, President.
WILLIAM H. BEERS, Vice-Pres't & Actuary.

Medical Examiners :
HENRY H. WRIGHT, ESQ., M.D.,
JOHN E. KENNEDY, ESQ., M.D.,

EDWYN EVANS,
Agent for Toronto, 15 Wellington Street

THE CANADIAN

[M]ONETARY TIMES

AND

INSURANCE CHRONICLE.

[DEVO]TED TO FINANCE, COMMERCE, INSURANCE, BANKS, RAILWAYS, NAVIGATION, MINES, INVESTMENT,
PUBLIC COMPANIES, AND JOINT STOCK ENTERPRISE.

—NO. 18.   TORONTO, THURSDAY, DECEMBER 24, 1868.   { SUBSCRIPTION, $2 YEAR.

Mercantile.

Financial.

PRINCIPLES OF BANKING.

(Continued.)

The function of Government in the creation of
a symbolic currency is almost equally restricted.
The test of value of such a currency is that of the
loanable capital it represents. Now the only
parties capable of deciding whether paper currencies represent an adequate amount of capital,
are those parties who are to receive them. It
would be very ridiculous for Government to attempt, by legislative enactment, to secure the
more certain payment of bills of exchange drawn
in commerce between nations. None are so able
to secure such provision as the parties to them.
If currencies were the representative of gold and
silver only, and not (as is the fact) of all kinds of
loanable property, then the functions of Government would be plain. All it would have to do
would be to restrict the issue of banks to the coin
in their vaults. But who shall decide whether it
is proper for a bank to make a loan by an issue of
its notes and credits to a party offering it a bill
given for a thousand barrels of flour? Of course,
those only who, from their intimate connection
with the trade, commerce and industry of the
country, are in a position to determine whether
the purchaser of the flour will be probably able to
sell the same and collect the proceeds before the
maturity of his note. Government can have no
such intelligence or functions as these—in fact,
it does not attempt to assume any control over
the greater portion of the symbolic currency in
use—the credits which banks write on their books.
Only a very small proportion of the transfers of
property are effected by bank notes. Outside of
these, the amount of currency that may be issued
is left, as it should be, to the discretion of banks.
The operation of natural laws will secure the conditions necessary to a perfect currency far more
effectually and completely than they can possibly
be secured by any act or oversight of Government.
If Government assumes to interfere with the
currency, its most important function would be
the restriction of loans to bills redeemable soon to
mature, and given for loanable property. With
such provision, rigidly enforced, there never could
be an inflation. But unfortunately, the action of
Government is always sought in a contrary direction—to authorize an expansion, which sooner or
latter must be followed by a corresponding revulsion ; but often not before society is so exhausted
that years are required to repair the losses sustained. The Bank of England, for example, is
authorized to issue notes to the amount of
$75,000,000 upon the strength of having the pos-
session of a corresponding amount of Government
debt, redeemable only at the pleasure of the latter.
This vast sum, although not the representative of
loanable capital, exerts, from the circulation obtained for the notes issued, precisely the effect,
for the time being, of so much capital. An extraordinary stimulus is given to every kind of
investment and expenditure, without the addition
of a penny to the means of consumption. It
gradually comes to be seen that the inflation has
led to the construction of too many ships and
railroads ; to the manufacture of too much iron
and cloth ; that too much money had been in-

vested in schemes which never should, and never
would, have been entertained, but for the disproportion created between the instruments and
means of expenditure. As soon as people get
their eyes open, each one endeavors to protect
himself by converting his means into money.
The bank puts up its rate of interest and calls in
its loans, which only serve to increase the alarm
and the drain upon it for gold, and the interposition of Government has to be invoked to allow
the bank to transcend its chartered powers, by
making loans irrespective of the amount of means
it may possess. But all this does not prevent
a crisis, which drives no small proportion of the
community into liquidation. With the consequent prostration of business, money becomes a
drug ; the rate of interest is reduced to a minimum, to stimulate its use, when the past experience of inflation and contraction is repeated with
all its attendant evils, but unfortunately, without
teaching any useful lesson.

Now, if the $75,000,000 issued on Government
securities, had represented loanable capital, either
in its vaults or in the hands of its borrowers, there
could have been no currency inflation, consequently no excessive contraction. The enterprises
which this sum had set in motion would have
rested on a solid basis—would have measured the
ability of the people to consume, and would have
exerted none other than a beneficent influence in
the channels of business and trade.

The amount of reserves of loanable capital necessary to be kept on hand by banks to meet the
calls to which they are constantly liable is a matter of experience, rather than of theoretical calculation. It will depend very much upon the character of the loans made. As the balance of indebtedness between the banks and the public is
always in favor of the former to the extent of their
capital, it follows that if their loans are made to
solvent parties, they can always place themselves
in funds from the payment of their bills. The
reserves in such case will have to be only nominal.
But as improper loans will always be made, involving corresponding disturbances in industries
and commerce, reserves must be maintained to
considerable amounts to meet such contingencies.

As the foreign commerce of a people is quite as
much to be considered in making loans, as their
domestic trade, reserves should be chiefly maintained in the great entrepôts of such commerce.
The rule of the New York banks, before the suspension of specie payments, was to maintain
reserves in coin equal to twenty-five per cent. of
their immediate liabilities. The coin held by the
country banks was much less, their reserves being
made up chiefly of balances against the city banks.
The great majority of the country banks held an
amount of coin only necessary for ordinary payments by way of change. Banks are not necessarily strong in proportion to the amount of coin
they may hold, but in ratio to the amount of promises of solvent parties to pay gold on demand.
But as before remarked, the amount of reserves
must be a matter of experience with banks, as
with merchants. When there is no Government
interference, and when perfect freedom of action
is accorded, reserves will always be in a proper
ratio to the demands likely to be made. People
have only to be left alone, to adopt the best means
to given ends, whether such be the construction
of a steamboat, a railroad, or any other contriv-

ance, the object of which is to facilitate the exchange of property, or promote their own welfare. Symbolic currencies will be good just in ratio as they express the business transactions of a people. There is great probability that they will be had just in ratio to the degree of governmental interference with them. Like all commercial contrivances—such as bills of exchange, steamships, and railways—their creation should be left entirely to the parties who are to use them.

The most perfect system of currency yet devised is that which so long prevailed in the New England States, and known as the Suffolk system. The parties to it were the banks of that section, which, without any legal enactment, agreed to make all their issues equal to gold at the commercial metropolis of those States—Boston; and to which, by necessary attraction, flowed all the currency issued that was not wanted for local purposes. With such a provision, there could not only be no excessive issues, but there was no motive to make them, as all such involved a direct loss of credit, and often of pecuniary loss. The result was that the unsecured notes of the New England banks, being always at par in one of the great monetary centers of the nation, were only at a very slight discount in every other portion of it. They were not at one-half of the discount in the city of New York, than the bills of the country banks of the latter State were, the ultimate redemption of which was fully secured by a deposit of bonds, but for the present redemption of which, no provision was made. A similar system, extended to the whole country, with New York as the central point, would give the nation as good a currency as could be devised by the wisdom of man. Such a system would compel every bank, no matter where situated, to limit its issues to its capital. Such restriction is the sole condition of a perfect currency.

The laws of currency, which have been elucidated in the preceding pages, effectually dispose of the theories of Bullionists, who for every dollar of currency issued, would compel the banks to maintain in their vaults a corresponding amount coin. They overlook the vital fact that merchandise of all kinds is symbolized as a means of transferring or loaning the same, precisely as is gold, and that such currencies when issued against such merchandise, are just as valuable and as convertible as when issued against gold; and that as mediums of exchange, they perform all the functions of gold. There is the same sense in their theories, and no more, that there would be in a proposition to return to the primitive condition in which all exchanges were effected in kind.

(To be continued,)

TORONTO STOCK MARKET.

(Reported by Pellatt & Osler, Brokers.)

Business in stocks during the past week was very limited ; many of the transfer books are closed, and little improvement may be expected till after the holidays.

BANK STOCK.—Buyers offer 138 for Montreal, with sellers at 138½. British would command 105 but there is none in market. Sales of Ontario occurred at 99¾, 100 and 100¼. No demand for Gore at 40. Buyers offer 97¼ for Quebec; no sellers under par. Molson's could be placed at 110 ; very limited amount in market. There were sales of City at 102½, which rate continues to be asked. No sellers of Du Peuple ; buyers at 107½. Jacques Cartier is nominally worth 106¼ to 107. Books of other banks closed.

DEBENTURES.—The only Canada Government security on the market is Dominion Stock, which is procurable at 105. Toronto are saleable to pay 6¼ per cent. interest. Large sales of County occurred during the week at rates to pay barely 6½ per cent. interest.

SUNDRIES. City Gas is much sought after, but not a share has been offered in the market for weeks. The books of the Canada Permanent and Western Canada Building Societies are closed. Freehold sold at 104½ to 105, and a few shares may still be had at the latter rate. There are buyers of Montreal Telegraph at 135, and no sellers. Canada Landed Credit is offered in small amounts at 73. There are buyers of British America Assurance at 55, and sellers at 57. Mortgages are in demand to pay 8 per cent. interest. Money is readily obtainable at reasonable rates on good paper.

BANK OF ENGLAND.

The returns for the week ending the 2nd Dec., give the following results when compared with the previous week:—

On the one side of the account :—	
Rest...............................	£3,068,636
Decrease..........................	25,867
Public Deposits....................	5,575,464
Increase..........................	148,668
Other Deposits.....................	18,685,878
Decrease..........................	17,490

On the other side of the account :—

Government Securities.............	£15,074,874
No change.	
Other Securities..................	17,193,379
Increase..........................	531,299
Notes unemployed..................	8,497,315
Decrease..........................	296,755

The amount of notes in circulation is £23,510,-112, being an increase of £266,857, and the stock of bullion in both departments is £18,087,448, showing a decrease of 169,180, when compared with the preceding return.

BANK OF COMMERCE.—The Directors of the Canadian Bank of Commerce have resolved to apply to Parliament for power to increase the capital stock of their institution from one million to two millions of dollars.

SALE OF STOCKS IN HALIFAX.—The following prices for Stocks were realized on the 10th, at W. M. Gray's sale of Stocks:—10 Shares Union Bank, $55; 10 do. $43; 7 do. 43.50; 15 do. $43.25; 13 do. $43; £200 Street Debenture, 5 per cent. £28 per £100; £500 do., £37 per £100; 100 shares Cape Canso Marine Railway. $2.50; 1 share Halifax Library, $6.00.

SOUND AND SENSIBLE.—In the Annual Report of the United States Secretary of the Treasury, occurs this passage:—" What is now required, as has been already intimated, are measures which will tend not only to prevent further exportation of our bonds, and in the regular course of trade to bring back to the country those that have been exported, but which will also tend to restore those important interests that are now languishing, as the result of the war and adverse legislation. The first and most important of these measures are those which shall bring about, without unnecessary delay, the restoration of the specie standard. The fiscal difficulties under which the country is labouring may be traced directly to the issue and continuance in circulation of irredeemable promises as lawful money. The country will not be really and reliably prosperous until there is a return to specie payments. The question of a solvent, convertible currency underlies all other financial and economical questions. It is, in fact, a fundamental question; and until it is settled, and settled in accordance with the teachings of experience, all attempts at other financial and economical reforms will either fail absolutely or be but partially successful. A sound currency is the life-blood of a commercial nation. If this is debased the whole current of its commercial life must be disordered and irregular. The starting point in reformatory legislation must be here. Our debased currency must be retired or raised to the par of specie, or cease to be lawful money, before substantial progress can be made with other reforms."

THE ARREST OF MR. SAMSON.—The New York Sun says :—Mr. George P. Samson, Cashier of the Commercial Bank of New wick, was taken into custody on Tuesday by Dep. Sheriff Jas. Campbell, on the being a defaulter to the amount of having absconded, as alleged, on 14th with the above sum in his possession. was made under an order of the King Supreme Court, at the suit of A. McL. President of the bank, on the affidavits Prescott, cashier, Jas. McArthur and W. tellers, and the President, Mr. Seely. M. swears that the accused while acting in th of cashier, appropriated to his own use o 090, for which he gave no account. Mr. swears that on 14th Nov., he gave the a sum of $76,000 for deposit in the safe. N was made of the money, nor had it been Mr. Magee swears that on 16th Nov. h accused $10,680 for deposit, but he sal ascertained that the money had not bee in the book kept by the prisoner, nor do the vault. The accused, who appears to 50 years of age, was committed in defau He refused to see or converse with any appears to be considerably shaken by t

GONE DOWN.—The "New England Company, after a brief but honorable c a loss of $20,000, has gone down.

Insurance.

FIRE RECORD.—Windsor, Dec. 12.— discovered in the store of Mr. Moore, wich street, and the store, with most o tents, and a residence adjoining, were It was owned by Mr. Johnson, whose probably reach $5,000. Johnson was in $1,300, and Moore, whose loss would $2,500, had an insurance of $1,800. known.

Halifax, Dec. 10.—A house belongi occupied by Henry Fredericks, on t West Arm road. No particulars.

Goderich, Dec. 11.—Grassi's blacks: caught fire, and both the blacksmith a shop were burned to the ground with Also Mr. Simond's dwelling house; saved. No insurance. Mr. Grassi is tie Gore Mutual for $1,200, but this cover the loss it is said. Cause unknown

Shediac, N. B., Dec. 8.—The res Joseph C. Weldon was destroyed by f about $1,800.

Sherbrooke, Dec. 15.—The dwelling Mr. Bailey Clough, near Sawyerville, l burned to the ground. Loss about insurance.

The Owen Sound Comet reports the of Mr. Claudius Ekins, Saugeen river t ship of Derby, was burnt by fire. Th Mr. Wm. Little, Miss Case, and Jane D a grand-child of Mr. Ekins, perished in Mr. Ekins, his father, mother, wife, s rietta, brother George, Mr. Case, Wm. John Dowd, were so severely burned recovery is doubtful.

Wellesley Township, Ont. Dec. 18.— place in River & Hickney's woole Wellesley, on Friday morning last, but i before it could make much headway, it w The loss will not be over $400 which covered by insurance.

Halifax, Dec. —.—A house near t station was destroyed.

Cayuga, Dec. 15.—Saloon of Al caught fire, but was saved with a los $75; no insurance.

Halifax, Dec. 7.—A severe storm southeast swept over Halifax, causi many disasters to the shipping in the l fences, blowing over chimney tops, unroofing houses on shore. The ed through the night. No less than shooners were seriously injured; in aving their masts, jibbooms, bow- nd bulwarks carried away, and the less stove in. The steamer Delta by a schooner and lost her fore-yard appeared to pass over the whole s feared that much damage was sus- iels along the whole coast.

old fire company had their annual and ball on Wednesday last; 150 tlemen were present.

ABIA.—The barque Maria, McKeu- on Quebec for Port Medoc, Wales, on the Newfoundland coast, and ew drowned. Six of the survivors it Halifax, N. S., on the 10th inst. s 285 tons register, and sailed from 5th of November, for Port Medoc, of spruce timber, deals, staves and

L.—Wm. Richardson, representing Assurance Company, Mr. Haldan, tna, and G. Rumball & Co., of the nited Captain Rowan, of the steamer with a token of their appreciation on the occasion of that vessel being off Chantry Island, by which the vere saved from a heavy loss.

Barclay, Curis & Co., of Greenock, hed the Lake Erie, a fine iron sail- 150 tons register, intended for the an trade. The vessel has been Canada Shipping Company of this rs of the Lake Ontario. The com- ntracted, it is said, for seven other ssels.—[Montreal Gazette.

FRANCIS SMITH.—This vessel will remain in her present position in the She is considered safe till that is said she can be got off without e loss is estimated at $8,000.

CTIVE INCIDENT—The following actual occurrence:—In one of our entative of an insurance company merchant in the vigor of a healthy rrently highly prosperous, who was This gentleman listened to the le with some interest, but finally is compelled, just then, to use his antile operations, but should soon e out a $10,000 policy. The agent his very circumstances were an ar- at immediate protection for his insurance alone could secure, and ble to give no more than $5,000 or gut prove of great benefit to them. he force of the reasoning; and was rid of the agent. The result was for a policy of $3,000. The two ner to die within ten days from a f fever, the latter to forward the h gave his widow three thousand vas all she had.

UTUAL INSURANCE COMPANY.— the report of the committee ap- Board of the Victoria Mutual In- iy on the subject of establishing a ring buildings on the line of the pipes: e with a resolution of the Board, nst., directing us to take such ac- it deem advisable towards the es- a branch in this city, to meet the y way of insurance) of those whose rotected by the line of water pipe,

22, Victoria Cap. 22, under which as incorporated, amply provides u of its business into two branches upon the following conditions:

1. That the Directors prepare a scale of risks for each department.

2. That they direct separate and distinct ac- counts to be kept.

3. That members shall only be liable for claims against the department in which they are insured, and not the one for the other.

4. That all necessary expenses incurred in the management and conducting of such departments, shall be assessed and divided between each in proportion to the amounts insured in each.

To afford complete security to policy holders for the payment of probable loss, it is the opinion of your committee that promises for insurance to the extent of $100,000 should be obtained before issuing a policy from the proposed branch.

That in lieu of cash, premium notes be ac- cepted, a small per centage of which should be paid in cash to meet the expense of management. The balance subject to assessment for the payment of loss.

That on account of the extra security of this district, afforded by the hydrants, no risk ac- cepted by the proposed branch should be reinsured in other companies; inasmuch as the money paid for premiums would probably exceed the whole amount assessable for loss in this district.

By following principally the foregoing princi- ples the Victoria, in the short space of five years, has attained a substantial position amongst in- surance companies, having issued during that time 7,153 policies, and now possessing in avail- able assets for the payment of loss, a sum exceed- ing $100,000.

It is, therefore, the intention of your committee to ascertain the views of such as are interested in the proposed object, by calling upon them without delay. (Signed,) Geo. H. Mills, T. McIlwraith, A. T. Wood, P. Carroll.

Risks to the extent of $114,000 have since been obtained.

INSURANCE COMPANIES.

The following are the Insurance Companies which have received licenses to transact the busi- ness of Insurance in the Dominion, viz.:—

I.—Canadian Companies.

The British America Assurance Company, de- posit $16,166 Cash—Fire and Inland Marine.

The Canada Life Assurance Co., $17,000 Cash— Life.

The Western Assurance Co., $17,000 Cash—Fire and Marine.

The Provincial Insurance Co., $16,666 Cash— Fire and Inland Marine.

The Agricultural Mutual Assurance Association, $12,000 Cash—Fire.

II.—British Companies.

The North British and Mercantile Insurance Co., $50,000 Cash; $100,258 Cash—Fire and Life.

The Liverpool and London and Globe Insurance Co., $50,000 Cash; $62,293 Canada 5's; $38,400 Canada 6's—Fire and Life.

The Royal Insurance Co., $96,982 Cash; $53,- 533 Canada 5's—Fire and Life.

The Reliance Mutual Life Assurance Society, $50,000 Cash—Life.

The Imperial Insurance Company $54,993 Bri- tish 3 per cts.; $48,667 Canada 5's; $1400 Canada 6's.

The Northern Assurance Co., $37,196 Cash; $12,166 Canada 5's; $2,000 Canada 6's—Fire.

The Lancashire Insurance Co., $33,383 Cash; $13,666 Canada 5's.

The Phenix Fire Insurance Co., $50,171 Cash; $50,126 Canada 5's—Fire.

The Commercial Union Assurance Co., $51,171 Cash; $50,618 Canada 5's—Fire.

The Life Association of Scotland $150,000 Cash —Fire and Life.

The Standard Life Assurance Co., $150,000 Cash —Life.

The Queen Insurance Co., $50,000 Cash; $51,- 100 Canada 5's—Fire and Life.

The Edinburgh Life Assurance Co., $150,515 Cash—Fire and Life.

The London Assurance Corporation, $150,000 British 3 per cts.—Life.

The Scottish Provincial Assurance Co., $50,171 Cash; $50,446—Fire and Life.

The London and Lancashire Insurance Co., $50,- 171 Cash—Life.

The Briton Medical and General Life Associa- tion, $100,343 —Life.

The Star Life Assurance Society, of England, $100,643.86 Cash—Life.

The Guardian Insurance Company, of England, $100,643.86 cash—Fire and Life.

III.—American Companies.

The Home Insurance Company of New Haven, Conn., $70,000 U.S. 5-20's—Fire.

The Ætna Insurance Company, of Hartford, Conn., $1,490 Cash; $48,510 Bank Stock—Fire.

The Hartford Insurance Company, of Hartford, Conn., $130,000 U.S. 5-20's—Fire.

The Phœnix Mutual Life Insurance Co., of Hartford, Conn., $70,000 U.S. 5-20's—Life.

The Connecticut Mutual Life Insurance Co., of Hartford, Conn., $140,000 U.S. 5-20's—Life.

The Travelers' Insurance Co., of Hartford, Conn., $140,000 U.S. 5-20's—Life and Accident.

The Ætna Life Insurance Co., of Hartford, Conn., $140,000 U.S. 5-20's—Life.

The New York Life Insurance Co., $75,000 U.S. 5-20's—Life.

The Atlantic Mutual Life Insurance Co., of Albany, N. Y., $50,000 U.S. 10-40's—Life.

The Equitable Life Insurance Co., of New York, $75,000 U.S. 5-20's—Life.

The Union Mutual Life Insurance Co., of Maine, 50,000 U.S. 6's of '81—Life.

MONTREAL FIRE BRIGADE.

We believe the Fire Department of no city in America is so economically managed as that of Montreal. Certainly none is more efficient; there- fore, to speak commercially, we have the best article at the lowest price. This is no doubt due to the perfection of discipline in the department, and the admirable general working of the fire-alarm telegraph. Strong indeed must be the wind, in- flammable the materials, and nearly absolute the want of water, if a fire should now be allowed to gain such head as to become serious. This being the case, let us see how we compensate the members of this efficient fire brigade of ours, as compared with the wages paid in, say, five of the principal cities of the Union, The subjoined figures show the annual cost per head of the fire departments, respectively, of the following cities:—

	Cost.	Population.
Chicago	$276,720	250,000
Detroit	63,000	85,000
Louisville	82,000	140,000
St. Louis	137,000	250,000
Baltimore	66,000	250,000
Montreal(gold)	18,125	120,000

From this it will be seen that Chicago pays $1.10 per head; Baltimore, $0.27; Detroit, $0.74; Louisville, $0.60; St. Louis, $0.55; and Montreal only $0.15, equal to $0.23 U. S. funds. So that our most efficient fire department is maintained at a rate of only about one-fifth of the cost of the fire department of Chicago; and the difference of rate between that of Montreal and the fire depart- ments of the four other cities of the Union which we have cited our readers can calculate for them- selves; but in every instance, except Baltimore, it is very great indeed.

The difference, too, between the rate of pay of the members of the fire brigade of the American cities just enumerated, and those of the Montreal fire brigade, is also striking. Our fire brigade has 16 men at $300, or $408 in U. S. funds; 9 men at $400, or $544 U. S. funds; 9 men at $500, or $680 U. S. funds; whilst the American firemen receive $1,000 each, and the drivers and horsemen $924 each.—Witness.

THE CANADIAN MONETARY TIMES
AND
INSURANCE CHRONICLE.

THE publishers will have the pleasure of sending this week to each Canadian subscriber of THE MONETARY TIMES, the first number of the REAL ESTATE JOURNAL, which will be sent regularly in future every fortnight, the subscription price being included in the $2.00 charged for THE MONETARY TIMES. In these days of cheap newspapers the publishers find this step to be necessary in order to keep pace with the times. The business public may now get the two papers for the price of one—each of which is worth more than the subscription price to any business man.

BANKING.

THE CANADIAN MONETARY TIMES AND INSURANCE CHRONICLE is the only paper in the Province which makes banking a specialty.

INSURANCE.

It is the only insurance journal in Canada. Every one who desires to know the character and standing of the Insurance Companies doing business in Canada can only get the information in its columns.

MINING.

It is the only journal which keeps regular correspondents in the principal mining districts, and affords strictly reliable information respecting mining matters.

COMMERCE.

Everything of interest in trade and commerce is carefully noted in the markets of Toronto, Montreal and the Maritime Provinces, making it more valuable in this department than purely commercial journals.

STOCKS AND SHARES.

The market prices of stocks, shares and debentures of every class in which our people are interested, as quoted in the centres of trade, are always to be found in the Stock and Share list.

PUBLIC COMPANIES.

The proceedings of all public companies in the country are reported, including banks, insurance, railway, mining, and other companies, building societies, &c., thus affording the only complete record of the doings of public companies to be obtained in the Province. These and other features make it invaluable to the Banker, Merchant, Insurance Agent, Miner, Capitalist, Manufacturer, and all business men.

SUBSCRIPTION PRICE—The MONETARY TIMES and REAL ESTATE JOURNAL, only $2.00 a year in advance.
Address,   THE MONETARY TIMES,
Toronto, Ont.

☞ The Publishing Office of THE CANADIAN MONETARY TIMES AND INSURANCE CHRONICLE is removed to No. 60, Church Street, 4 doors north of Court Street.

The Canadian Monetary Times.

THURSDAY, DECEMBER 24, 1868.

MR. WILMOT, OF NEW BRUNSWICK, ON THE CURRENCY?

This gentleman has responded to a series of questions on the currency by a committee of the House of Commons, and has published his replies in the New Brunswick papers. They seem to have excited some considerable attention, partly from their bold and confident assertions, and partly from the semilogical air which seems to pervade them, in which, to say the truth, there are as many fallacies and foolish fancies covered up as it has ever been our lot to meet within the same limits.

These fallacies and fancies are all branches of one fundamentally false notion, namely, that it is not desirable, or necessary, to have any fixed standard of value. Mr. Wilmot does not believe that a dollar should mean the same thing to-morrow as it does to-day, and he would have a currency which would fluctuate, not only in amount, but in value, with the necessities of the government, and the circumstances of the times.

It is somewhat cool, we must confess, at this time of day, for a gentleman professing to have financial ability to denounce the monetary system of Canada because it rests on a gold basis, and deliberately to advocate an irredeemable currency. When universal experience tells us that gold and silver are the only solid basis of monetary operations; when writers on finance, almost without exception, however widely they may differ on other matters, agree in the same conclusion; when the trade between every nation under heaven, is, and always has been, conducted on the same principle; when countries which have been forced by pressure of circumstances to deviate from this standard have invariably suffered such intolerable evils as to be willing to endure the most painful sacrifices in order to reach the path of safety again, it is idle to talk of a fixed price for gold being a relic of barbarism.

The man who can ascribe panics to this cause rather than to extravagance an l overtrading is not to be reasoned with. Throughout the whole of Mr. Wilmot's answers the notion crops up again and again, that the true remedy for financial evils is plenty of irredeemable paper money. He does not seem to have the slightest notion that a country, at this time of day, cannot isolate itself from the rest of the world, and, as respects other countries, may run into debt just as an individual may with other individuals. When a merchant runs into debt, all goes along smoothly enough so long as his creditors are willing to trust him. His expenditure may be over-running his profits by thousands a year, yet if he can only keep up his credit, and his correspondents continue to supply him with goods, he finds no difficulty in getting along. We have had plenty of examples of this kind of thing in every commercial community, and the end is invariably the same, namely, a break up of credit, a stoppage of supplies, an insisting on payments, law suits, bankruptcy, and poverty. The crash is a painful affair, and causes misery to the individual, to his creditors, his bankers, his family, and everybody that had any relations with him.

Now supposing this gentleman, in the midst of his bankruptcy, to reason in this manner:—What scandalous laws and customs these are which compel a man to pay his debts!— If I had never been pressed to *pay*, all would have been right.—Why could not my paper be kept afloat, as usual? Why could not things go on smoothly, as they did before? It would have been far better for all parties. I was a good customer to the foreign merchant. I was a capital customer to labouring tradesmen. All of their paper, and paper answered their purpose well. What madness then it was is my creditors, who are such fools, all our trading by insisting on my turned into miserable dirty gold.

Stripped of specious phraseology cisely thus that Mr. Wilmot reasons ing the panics which sweep period the commercial world. Everybody studied them is aware that they precede l by a period of extrava spending, recklessness and folly responding to the overspending vent trader, and that the panics same thing to the country as st ment is to a merchant. It is the sense to blame the gold basis as the panic, just as it is idle none trader to blame his creditors for h The panic is the natural result o vagance, and its counterpart is over and over again in private li speak of a trader, how often it is t a private individual spends more come, gets into debt, his creditor and he is sued; after a world of anxiety he manages to get time, of severe economy comes round awhile, and pays all he owes.

Now the trade of a country, whole, with other countries, is p lagous to the dealings of an indi individuals. When the balance against it, continuously, from reign importations, it simply ind vagance, overspending, and gettir The sure result is tightness of is it is with any man who spend ais income. People of that sor "hard up;" and a country may b and must be when extravagan spending produce their natural

Mr. Wilmot's remedy for t things is to issue more paper, sisely the same as for a spendt more of his promissory notes reditors, if they are so simp them. Common sense says th medy would be to economise and Let the country produce more —that would bring things r loubt. In private life this wo sally conceded, but in dealing affairs people are apt to get eave common sense altogether.

It cannot, however, be too o hat the laws of credit and fina able and irresistible. A nati scape their operation than i *Promises to pay, if never fu* r who is the promisor. Mr. have the country flooded with ontaining promises which are be fulfilled, and he is insane ose that such rubbish would igance and overspending from natural results.

does not say all this in ex- it no one can read his answers ut perceiving that this is the sm.

tice other points in these an- y.

ESTERN RAILWAY.

us to delight in paying its res- reat Western Railway. No tory exhausted than another ts place. The last is a state- ect that the New York Cen- to lease the Great Western. nas addressed a letter on the President of the Stock Ex- York in which he denies that us been received by the Great

MUTUAL LIFE.—The general mpany for Ontario has been re- y. It is under the management s. Mr. Fee will have the local

GOLD DISTRICT.

our own Correspondent).

BELLEVILLE, Dec. 21, 1868.
xistence of gold in the rocks or icular district, the most advan- separating the metal from the stances in which it is contained, is combined, is the subject which t importance to the miner. I in the absence of other matter, he processes by which sanguine e to enrich the fortunate holders claims, and themselves. As the us flux is that which has been world with the greatest flourish all pass it first in review, giving of the flux itself, and detailing its working in this quarter. given by the proprietors of the flux is shortly as follows: A cer- phens, (who is represented as both of practical mining and of nce, and therefore a most unlikely problem which has taxed the ablest scientific men of many le confined in a distant prison secession, heard much conversa- fellow prisoners respecting the ating the gold from the sulphur- s) often contained. These con- l a strong desire in his mind to ble method of extracting the om its baser accompaniments. he happened to get possession y of this, to him, unknown ma- it to Mr. Guild, an assayer in s requested to make an assay ld-bearing ore he might have in

his possession. Mr. Guild accordingly smelted with a portion of this flux a sample of ore which he knew to yield by "mint assay" $300 to the ton, and obtained therefrom no less a result than $2,400 per ton. Suspecting some error, as well he might, the assayer repeated the process, and again obtained the same result, $2,400 per ton.

The Colonel then had a furnace erected, in which he treated 2,500 pounds of ore, which had never yielded by other processes more than $22 per ton; but from which he extracted at a single melting, gold to the value of $539.58, or at the rate of $431 per ton. This is his own account; but there are not wanting those who say that the flux used on that occasion was heavily "salted." The experience we have had of the flux and its vendors is as follows: Early in the present year, two gentlemen from Wisconsin, Messrs. Jones and Robbins, visited the district, and took from a mine in the township of Hungerford a quantity of pyritiferous ore, which they took to Boston, and had it assayed by Mr. Guild, who gave them a return of $40 per ton. On the faith of this they returned to Canada, purchased the mine, put up reduction works according to plans, etc., fur- nished them by the Stephens Company, who agreed to send one of the partners to instruct them in the whole process of reduction by their method. When the works were finished, one of the Boston gentlemen came accordingly, and un- der his directions they smelted about three tons of ore, from which, instead of the pure metal they expected, they got about a ton and a half of "matt," i. e., a combination of crude metallic matter which might or might not contain gold as one of its component parts, but in which it was quite as intangible as in its original matrix. On being requested to go on and complete the process, the Boston man refused to do so, telling them that it would be necessary for them to send the matt to Boston to be refined, offering to do it for ten cents on the dollar of gold value. This they re- fused to do; and so the matter stands between them and the Boston Company at present. Messrs. Jones and Robbins have since dispatched a portion of said matt and also of the crude ore to Swansea, Wales, to be reduced, so that its value may be tested in a satisfactory manner.

The readers of THE MONETARY TIMES will of course draw their own inferences from the above related facts. My own I must candidly say, are not very favorable to the flux as a medium for the economical reduction of gold ores, or to the straightforwardness of its "proprietors." Even if it were all they assert, it could not, at its present price, be applied to the working of poor ores, as the expense attending its use could not be less than $25 to $30 per ton.

The Richardson Company have had another lot of twenty-five tons of their ore reduced, the pro- duce of which, though not yet melted down, is estimated by their manager at $150, or $6 per ton. Another lot, which was being operated upon at the time his message was sent off, promises, from the appearances of the amalgam which was forming, to give a better result than the foregoing. The mine at Mallorytown still continues to give good assay results. The machinery is rap- idly approaching completion. The building is ready for its reception, and the owners expect to be able to start work as soon as the spring sets in.

SILVER ON LAKE SUPERIOR.—Mr. Thomas Macfarlane has assayed the silver ores from the veins discovered by him at Mhunder Cape last summer, and we are authorized to state that the result of his assay is most satisfactory, showing a result of more than 1,900 ounces of silves to the ton of ore. The samples assayed were carefully taken under the supervision of Professor Dawson as exhibiting a fair average of the productive por- tion of the vein at Thunder Cape. Similar sam- ples have been sent fer assay to an assayer in the United States, the details of which assay, as well as Mr. Macfarlane's, will shortly be published.

PEAT.—An American Company has been formed in the State of Connecticut for the extraction and manufacture of peat after the process patented in Canada and the United States by Mr. Aubin, of Montreal. The capital of the Company is $250,- 000, in which the patent right goes in for $125,- 000. Mr. A. Hibbard, of Montreal, is one of the directors, and Mr. Aubin consulting engineer of the Company. Three other companies under the same patents will, we understand, begin or continue operations in Lower Canada, one at Sorel, one at Valleyfield, and another at Bolœil.

—On or about the 15th day of January next, S. P. Mansfield of Detroit, Alex. Dearborn, and G. B. Nichols of Boston, J. B. Hills of Newton, Mass., and J. W. W. Ward of Ottawa, will peti- tion the Lieutenant Governor in Council to in- corporate the "McNab Iron Company," whose purpose is the mining for iron and other metals, and the washing and smelting of ores in the town- ship of McNab, county of Renfrew, with a nom- inal capital of $50,000; stock subscribed, $30,000; and the amount to be paid in before granting the charter, $10,000, to be invested in mineral lands held by trustees for the company.

Railway News.

GREAT WESTERN RAILWAY.—Traffic for week ending Dec. 4, 1868.

Passengers	$30,825 34
Freight and live stock......	35,826 42
Mails and sundries...........	2,284 45
	$68,936 21
Corresponding Week of '67.	67,934 86
Increase.............	$1,001 35

NORTHERN RAILWAY.—Traffic receipts for week ending Dec. 19, 1868.

Passengers	$2,302 55
Freight.....................	5,296 16
Mails and Sundries..........	291 90
Total Receipts for week.....	$7,890 63
Corresponding week 1867....	6,385 61
Increase...........	$1,504 98

THE INTERCOLONIAL RAILWAY.—The Railway Commissioners have issued the following notice: —'The Commissioners appointed to construct the Intercolonial Railway, give public notice that they intend to let four sections of the line at once.

"Sections Nos. 1 and 2 embrace about 40 miles from a junction with the Grand Trunk Railway, near Riviere Du Loup, and each section will be about 20 miles in length.

"Section No. 3 will be about 26 miles in length, and lies between the east side of the Restigouch, River to near Dalhousie in New Brunswick.

"Section No. 4 will be about 24 miles in length and lies between Amherst and River Phillip in Nova Scotia.

"Plans and profiles, with specifications and terms of contract will be exhibited at the offices of the Commissioners in Ottawa, Riviere du Loup, Dalhousie, St. John and Halifax, on and after the 11th January, 1869, and sealed tenders addressed to the Commissioners of the Intercolonial Railway will be received at their office in Ottawa, up to 4 o'clock on the 8th February, 1869.

"Tenders will shortly be called for other section of the line as soon as the plans are sufficiently advanced."

The Commissioners are to assemble at St. John, N. R., on the 29th instant, where Mr. Fleming, Intercolonial Engineer, is to meet them. The Commissioners intend to make a local examination of the portions for which tenders will be asked on Monday.

About 90 miles are to be put under contract,

part of which is in each Province. It is divided into four sections, so that only four tenders can be accepted. Tenders will be addressed to the Commissioners here. The Commissioners will not decide, but will recommend to the Privy Council the tenders to be accepted.

The Commissioners have made the following appointments:—C. S. Ross, of Kingston, Secretary; J. B. Martel, of Quebec, Assistant Secretary; Wm. Wallace, of Simcoe, Accountant.

—It is reported that Mr. Ross and the Great Western Railway Company have come to an agreement for the liquidation of the debt due to the Canadian Government by the road.

PEAT MAKER.—*La Perys* says that a peat-making machine, the invention of Mr. Aubin, was put into operation at Sorel and Valleyfield last summer, and worked so satisfactorily that some American capitalists are about to form companies to develop the new industry. One of these companies is about to be organized for the State of Connecticut, and will have a capital of $25,000, of which amount $10,000 will be paid for the patent. Mr. Ashley Hibbard has been elected one of the directors, and Mr. Aubin, consulting engineer of this company.

THE PLATTSBURGH AND WHITEHALL ROAD—MASSAWIPPI RAILWAY—MISSISQUOI CENTRE ROUTE.—We see by the Plattsburgh *Republican* that the grading for the Whitehall and Plattsburgh Railway is nearly completed from Fort Henry to Ticonderoga, and the rails about to be laid down. This new route along the Western bank of Lake Champlain will give Montreal still another direct line of communication to New York, and by 1869, there will therefore be no less than three in operation.

WOODEN RAILWAYS.—Mr. Henning, M. P. P. for Drummond and Arthabaska, who has a Wooden Railway project on foot, for connecting the back towns of his own County with the Grand Trunk Railway, has been to New York State to see the Clifton Wooden Railroad, and in a letter describing his visit, says:—

"There was no appearance of the wheels cutting into the rails, even at the sharpest curves, neither did I find a single rail that had the appearance of being crushed. In fact the rails were so level and smooth that I walked the whole distance on the rail itself, at a pretty smart pace, and I have no pretension to being a "Blondin." We arrived at the train a little before sundown, which consisted of a ten ton locomotive, made expressly for the line—four trucks, carrying between five and six tons of iron ore each, and a car-load of lumber; the whole train weighing between forty and fifty tons. I should add that one of the trucks containing the ore was front of the engine. We now started in good earnest at a rate of about twenty miles an hour, and soon came to a part of the road which was nearly all supported on trestlework, there being no less than five viaducts, varying from 124 to 400 feet in length, and from 25 to 35 feet from the level of the ground, in a distance of half a mile. Imagine my surprise, when I found that the engine driver on arriving at this trestlework, so far from slackening his speed, actually increased it to thirty miles an hour!

The grading of course is the same as for an iron, except that stiffer grades can be ascended on the wooden road. The ties are of the ordinary description, but are not squared on any side, and on the Clifton road are placed at the usual distance of three feet apart, except on the trestles, where there are three ties to every two yards. In future, however, Mr. Hurlburt proposes to put the three ties to every two yards, as he proposes running heavier engines. The rails on the Clifton road are of maple, six inches by four; Mr. Hurlburt intends in future to alter their shape a little without increasing the quantity of timber, making them three and half inches on top, by seven inches deep, so as to be better adapted to the increased weight of engines, (fourteen tons instead of

ten.) Notches are cut in the round ties to such a depth as to keep the bottom of the rail about two inches from the ground after the road is ballasted, and the rail projects sufficiently above the notched tie to allow the flange of the wheel to pass. The rails are fastened to the ties by a couple of hard-wood wedges, driven in opposite directions on the outside of the rail, within the notch. This has the effect of making the whole superstructure one solid mass without the addition of any spikes or ties. In making the curves the rail itself is bent to the required shape, so that there is no angularity whatever in the line of rails. The trestles are of the simplest description. They consist of two upright sticks of square timber immediately under the rails, let into a transverse stick, which are braced to the sticks of timber laid lengthwise from one trestle to another, immediately under the line of rails in each direction. This is further supported by a similar stick of timber at each side, from the head of the trestle to the base, in a slanting direction, the whole of which is let into a squared leg at the base. The wooden rail is not, I believe a new invention, but Mr. Hurlburt has succeeded in making it available without using a particle of iron in the whole structure, and has, moreover, demonstrated that such railways can be used for long distances at a moderate cost, and this through a country where an iron line, as ordinarily constructed, would be practically an engineering impossibility. Mr. Hurlburt says that he is willing to contract to lay the superstructure of a wooden railway of his own improved construction at the rate of fifteen hundred dollars, American currency, a mile where maple and hemlock can be obtained at reasonable rates."

THE GOVERNMENT AND THE TELEGRAPH.

The discussion in England, both in and out of Parliament, in favor of the government controlling the telegraph by buying up all the existing lines in that country, has extended to the United States and the government at Washington is urged, in certain quarters, to place the telegraph system under the management of the Postmaster General by similar means. It seems to us almost as reasonable for the government to undertake the purchase and management of all the railways as all the telegraph lines in the country. The one kind of enterprise being not dissimilar to the other. That a government stops out of its legitimate sphere when it embarks in any such business can not be denied, while there are grave objections to government interference with the telegraph apart from the mere question of principle. In a country governed by parties as this is, it will never do to have the government of the day controlling the means of telegraph communication, and the same argument applies to England, where it has been already advanced with convincing effect, and inasmuch as party spirit runs higher here than there the danger would be correspondingly greater. The telegraph would, it may be accepted as a certainty, be used as a political machine by the party in power, and this of itself is sufficient to condemn government interference with it. There is no knowing how far the rights of the press and the people might be trampled upon in this particular by unscrupulous partizans in office, and consequently they should never be invested with the power for mischief which privileges of this kind would give them.

The advocates of the proposed scheme will, before much progress is made towards the desired end, have to show that the existing telegraph companies have failed to meet the wants of the people, and are, moreover, incapable of meeting them. Further, it will be also incumbent upon them to prove that the government will be better enabled to meet these requirements than the telegraph companies, and that there would be no drawbacks or inconveniences to the public to counterbalance any advantages arising from govern-

mental administration. That the telegraph panies have a stronger incentive to improve in everything connected with their business the government would have to achieve, enterprise they have shown in the past is a motive for the future. The English telegraph panies have been fully as active as those United States in their efforts to improve, and cheapen telegraphic communication. insulation by means of gutta percha was adopted and in 1857, and again in 1862, further improvements in insulation were effected. In Hughes' "type printers" were introduced, 1863, Caselli's for single telegraphy, while same year "printing instruments" and stone's automatic system," as also Hasseth's of working without wire were tried. I country, the Atlantic and Pacific, the Fr and other lines worked in opposition, Western Union Co. are being rapidly extended and in proportion as their business increase charges for the transmission of messages decreed. Competition is the life of trade, people should encourage it in the business graphing as much as in anything else, would, of course, be an end to this if the government monopolized the wires, and what government employees did their work then or the reverse, there would be no redress, a provements travel slowly through official channels while red tape, in this country as well where, interposes a vexatious bar to progress Albion.

CONTRACT.—An exchange says that Walter and Frank Shanley have contracted the State of Massachusetts to build the tunnel on the Troy and Boston Railway. be four and a half miles long and has partially completed, but the company which tempted it failed to carry it through Messrs. Shanley have taken the contract $5,000,000.

NIAGARA SHIP CANAL.—The Niagar Canal was brought up in the United States of Representatives on Monday; and made a order of the day for the 11th prox. by a 109 to 40. Some members voted for the out of good-will to the mover, but the vote strong that the friends of the measure have can be carried through. The bill proved the work shall be done as a military and mercial necessity by the Government, and direction of the Secretary of War; that it begun within one year after the passage finished as speedily as possible, and control of it shall be retained by the United The engineer's estimate as to the cost of the is about $12,000,000.

—The preliminary survey of the rout wooden railway, from Sherbrooke, Q., e has been commenced by Robinson Oughtr

ONTARIO LEGISLATION.

Prior to the adjournment of the Ontario lature the following bills passed a second
No. 118, to grant certain powers to the Farmers' Mutual Insurance Company.
No. 84, to incorporate the Ontario T Investment Company.
No. 83, to incorporate the Presque Belmont Railway Company.
No. 108, to incorporate the Simcoe and Railway Company.
No. 109, to incorporate the Norfolk Company.
No. 163, to amend the Act to incorporate Port Whitby and Port Perry Railway
No. 72, to amend and confirm the of the Ottawa and Gloucester Road Compan
No. 95, to incorporate the Mutual Fire Company of Hamilton.
No. 120, to incorporate the Caledon Manufacturing and Smelting Company.
The following passed its third reading

to amend the Act passed in the 28th
ving the granting of charters of into manufacturing, mining and other

the bills assented to by the Governor
Act for the incorporation of the Ontario
Assurance Company. An Act to ex-
16 sec. of Hamilton Debenture Act of
legalize the application of the rates
re City of Hamilton under the By-law
n that section.

Law Report.

SURANCE—FORFEITURE—WAIVER.—
case of the Supreme Court of Iowa,
g judgment was given:
a policy for insurance provides that
f fine to the building insured shall be
a change of occupation or other means
control of the insured, without the
sent of the insurers, the policy "shall
his condition being inserted for the
e insurers—they may dispense with
therewith, or waive a forfeiture of the
red by a breach of the condition, and
shade themselves from setting up the
r such breach thereof, as a defense to
r a loss subsequently occurring. And
nation or waiver need not be in writing
on any one consideration.
ts, declarations, or course of dealing
rers, with notice of the facts consti-
ich of a condition in the policy, re-
d treating the policy as still in force,
f premium, given consent of the coin-
the insured to regard himself as still
ereby, will amount to a waiver, of a
reason of such breach, and prevent
from setting up the same as a defense
or a subsequent loss.

agent for a foreign insurance com-
ciisal to effect insurances, and entrust-
blank policies of the company, with
fill up, countersign, and issue them,
f premium, give consent of the com-
ige of occupation and risk, assignment
and other things which by the
policy require such consent, and to
es in his discretion for increase of risk
ies is to be regarded as the general
company, authorised to transact the
surance for them at the place of his
has power, in the absence of a limi-
authority, known to those with whom
waive forfeitures of policies, by reason
f conditions therein, and to dispense
ulticus, and the acts and declarations
t, recognizing and treating a policy as
bsisting, with knowledge of facts con-
reach of its conditions, will be bind-
isurers.
ent by the insurers to the occupation
d building for a certain manufactory,
it a consent to the keeping and use or
of any article necessary to the manu-
mmodity used therein, although the
mb articles without the written con-
nsurers is expressly prohibited in the
l such consent to the occupation for
turer operates to waive or dispense
ohibition in the policy.
the agent of the insurers, after a change
ition of the insured building, involv-
ise of risk, consented to the continu-
policy, on condition that an iron door
t into the building, but without limit-
ific time within which this should be
ured was entitled to a reasonable time
door, and its being put in was not a
ecedent to the continuance of the
l if, after the exercise of reasonable
get the door put in, but before it was in
the building was destroyed by fire,
cannot resist payment of the loss on
f the door not having been put in.

JETTISON—LIABILITY OF INSURER.—If goods
are thrown overboard in order to save a vessel from
some danger, there arises a right on the part of the
owner of these goods to claim general average from
the owners of the ship, freight, and of the rest of
the cargo—that is, the owner of the goods jettisoned having been deprived of his goods for the
benefit of the owners of the rest of the cargo and
of the ship, is entitled to claim from these latter
compensation for the loss thus sustained. The
owner of the jettisoned goods does not recover the
whole of the value of his goods, as it is but right
that he, as well as others, should contribute to
make good the loss. All the owners of ship,
freight and cargo, including the owners of the
jettisoned goods, pay in proportion to the value
they had at stake when the jettison took place.
In Dickinson v. Jardine, 16 W. R. 1169, goods
had been properly jettisoned, and the ship and
cargo had consequently come safe to port, and
were therefore liable to a claim for general average.
The jettisoned goods were insured, and their owner
(the plaintiff), instead of first claiming payment of
the general average to which he was undoubtedly
entitled, and then claiming from the underwriters
the amount of his actual loss, claimed directly
from the underwriters the whole value of the
goods, and contended that it was for the underwriters, and not for him, to obtain payment of
the general average. The underwriters refused to
pay the whole loss actually suffered, they were
not bound to pay more, and that the plaintiff must
obtain payment of the general average contribution
for himself; and that the underwriters were only
liable for the amount of loss that remained after
deducting the amount so due to the plaintiff, as
that was really the amount of his loss.
It was held by the Court of Common Pleas that
the plaintiff was entitled to recover directly from
the underwriters the whole value of his goods, and
that it was for the underwriters to obtain payment
of the general average.
There seems to have been no reported case in
the English courts which decided this point, although there were several American authorities
upon the question. Bovill, C. J., cites a passage
from Phillips on Insurance, to the following effect:
—"It is not a condition that the assured on goods
must claim contribution by the other parties for a
jettison before he can demand indemnity from his
underwriters. He may demand it of them in the
first instance." The Court decided in accordance
with this passage, which now, therefore, correctly
states the English law on the subject. We believe
it has generally been the practice in London to
consider the underwriters in such circumstances
as those in Dickinson v. Jardine liable only for
the actual loss caused by jettison after debiting
the owner of the jettisoned goods with the amount
due for the general average contribution. This is,
however, quite opposed to the general principles
of insurance law, and although it may be a convenient way of settling accounts between insurers
and insured, it can have no legal force unless perhaps an unvarying custom to this effect could be
proved. It is, however, of course competent to
underwriters to insert in their policies an express
stipulation limiting their liability in these cases,
and there is no legal objection to such a course.

Commercial.

Montreal Correspondence.
(From our own Correspondent.)

Montreal, Dec. 15, 1868.
Our river is nearly frozen across, and all traffic
has ceased except such as comes through the Victoria Bridge. We now see the importance of that
vast, though expensive, structure. Our communication with the States and the south side of
the river remain unbroken; usually at this period,
till the ice bridge took, all connection with the opposite side ceased, or was carried on by canoes at

very considerable risk to life and property. The
same as with the Grand Trunk, we every year
more and more appreciate the great advantages
we derive from it; true we have paid rather
dearly for our whistle, but now we could not do
without it.
Our produce market remains very quiet, and
flour has not materially changed from my
last week's quotations. The sales are merely for
local wants, nor do we now look for any export
trade. The Grand Trunk Railroad brings us
down our necessary supplies, and all shipped goes
direct to Portland, so that we in Montreal have
not the handling of it. Grain is nominal in price
for all descriptions, and the same remark applies
to provisions.
In my last week's letter to you I gave a short
resume of the dry goods trade. Now I will give
you a sketch of the grocery market for the fall
season:
GROCERIES—The trade generally during the
fall has been satisfactory. Some of our large
jobbing firms have been operating beyond their
means, and forcing goods off to all sorts of buyers
in the West; others, not content with a good
healthy business, have speculated in gold and
other tempting things, and the consequence has
been that some of our leading jobbers have gone
down, but this by no means shows anything
wrong in the general business. On the contrary,
greater caution has been exercised than usual, and
the losses have been lighter.
CHEMICALS have sold largely but at almost a
nominal profit: this is owing to the large quantity,
especially of soda ash, sent here on consignment,
and therefore forced off at any price that will clear
cost, thus leaving the importers a small chance
of making a profit. Prices have ruled low.
COFFEE—Owing to the low prices which have
ruled during the last few months, a considerable
business has been done, but I doubt if sales have
been satisfactory to importers.
FISH have sold freely during the fall, and prices
have ruled high; the catch generally has been
light and consequently our supplies have been
light. The fish market here is very much regulated by the price of pork, and when that is high
the price of salted fish always rules proportionately
high. The exception has been in dry cod, of
which there has been a good supply, and prices
are rather easier. Of good mackerel there are
none on the market, and the stock of fish generally is light.
FRUIT (imported)—The result to importers has
been disastrous as regards raisins, but this has
been the experience of the last two years. Our
merchants have steadily over-imported. This
year it was considered that the comparative failure
of green fruit here would justify a larger import
than usual, but such has not been the case, and
importers have been the losers. In currants on
the contrary an active business has been done at
remunerative rates.
In NUTS, SARDINES, &c., the usual amount of
business has been done at fair prices.
MOLASSES—The business in this article is
mostly regulated by the price of butter. This
fall the price of molasses has ruled very low, and
that of butter very high, consequently a very
large business has been done. The market closes
low but active.
NAVAL STORES—A fair business has been done,
prices having followed the fluctuations of the
New York market.
OILS—In Cod and Seal the rapid increase of
price early in the fall restricted the amount of
business; at the end of the season the market
closed easier, and there was more disposition to
realize on the part of holders. Stocks are light.
In Linseed Oil business has been light, chiefly
owing to the decline in England, which has
caused buyers here to operate only from hand to
mouth. From what I can hear prices of linseed
oil have touched the bottom in England, and consequently we may look for a safe trade here.

RICE—In this staple the ordinary amount of business has been done; stocks are light, but importers are timid, owing to the low price of wheat, which materially interferes with the price o. rice.

SALT—A large business has been done during the fall and speculation has been rife; prices have fluctuated considerably, but the tendency has been upward. The market closes with light stocks, not more than sufficient for our requirements before the spring importations.

SUGAR—In raw sugar a large business has been done, chiefly with the refiners, although several in the trade have sold largely to their country customers, of good grades. I may here remark that the lower qualities of refined sugars are rapidly superseding even the higher styles of imported. They are got up in more convenient packages, and not the same loss by drainage. I hear that the importers are satisfied with the result of the fall's operations; stocks are moderate and held for high rates. This is owing to the state of the New York market. Refiners have advanced their prices for all descriptions.

TEAS—The business has been large and satisfactory to all interested. Stocks generally were only moderate, and of good grades very light. Good Japans are rapidly getting into favor.

TOBACCO—In manufactured the business has been to the usual extent, and prices have been remunerative. The season closes with very light stocks. The "Prince of Wales" brand has become in such favor that the manufacturers have not been able to make it in sufficient quantity to meet the demand. I hear of some orders which they have had in hand for five to six weeks and not completed. Leaf Tobacco has ruled dull and prices low. The market closed without animation.

Toronto Market.

The general trade of the city is still quiet, and will remain so until after the holidays.

GROCERIES.—Teas.—Are quiet, and there is little doing except that some few lines have been placed with the city trade. The stock of teas in London on the 30th Nov. was 73,652,061 lbs., and in Liverpool 1,084,907 lbs. against 61,954,- 760 lbs., and 1,731,619 lbs. respectively. A telegram from Hong Kong, dated 2nd, gives the exports of tea from China up to that date at 112,- 000,000 lbs., being an increase of about 29½ millions of pounds on the exports to the same date last year. Sugars.—Our market is quiet ; the New York market has fluctuated a good deal owing to the unsettled state of affairs in Cuba. Fish.—Quiet, and prices unchanged. Fruit.— There is a good demand for all kinds of fruit at steady prices. Rice—Unchanged.

HARDWARE.—Trade in heavy goods is a little better, and quotations are fully maintained.

PRODUCE.—Wheat.— Receipts for the week by cars 10,000 bush. ; there is a fair demand for Spring wheat for milling purposes at $1.00 to $1.03, and all that offers at these prices is readily taken, but most holders ask more money. Some 8 or 10 cars sold at $1.01 to $1.03. Midge proof is also in good demand at the same quotations. Fall, prime white, is enquired for, and some few cars of choice have been placed for shipment at $1.13 to $1.20. Medium sold at $1.11 to $1.12, and there are few buyers above these figures. Barley.— Receipts by car 1,300 bush. There is little offered, and the demand is quiet at $1.25-; sales of cars occurred at $1.22½ to $1.25. Oats.—Receipts 2,400 bush. ; there is a good local demand at 52c. to 54c. and sales occurred at 54c. Peas.—Nominal, no receipts.

FLOUR.—Receipts for the week 2,677 brls. No. 1 superfine is offered at $4.60, and there are buyers at choice brands at that price, while ordinary is nominal at $4.50 to $4.55. Extra is held at $5.50, with buyers at $5.25 to $5.30.

PROVISIONS.—Dressed Hogs. The market has closed brisk at higher prices ; receipts light.— Pork.—Mess is in good demand both for Canadian and old American. Provisions nominal.

FREIGHTS.—The following are the present rates via Great Western Railway from Toronto to Liverpool, London and Glasgow, per William & Gowan's line of steamers : Beef, bacon, pork, hams, lard and tallow, in lots not less than one car load and upwards, $1.03 gold per 100 lbs.; grain in bags, in lots of five car loads and upwards, 3s 4d sterling per 100 lbs.; flour, 6s 9d per bbl.. To Liverpool via National line: Beef, bacon and pork, $1 per 100 lbs.; lard, in barrels and tierces, $1.06 per 100 lbs.; in kegs and tinnets, $1.17 per 100 lbs.; butter and cheese, $1.43 per 100 lbs. Through bills of lading granted.

The winter rates of the Grand Trunk Railroad to the Maritime Provinces came into force on the 1st inst., and are as follows: From Toronto to St. John, N. B., general merchandise, per 100 lbs., first class, 90c; second class, 65c; third class, 55c; flour, per bbl., 95c; grain, per 100 lbs., 48c. From Stratford, London, or St. Mary's—flour, $1.10; grain, 55c. From Brantford—flour, $1.10; grain, 58c. From Guelph—flour, $1.05; grain, 53c. From Oshawa, Newcastle and Bowmanville—flour, 89c; grain, 45c. From Montreal—flour, 62c; grain, 30c. From Toronto to Halifax, N. S.—general merchandise, per 100 lbs., first class, 90c; second class, 65c; third class, 55c; flour, per bbl., $1.05; grain, per 100 lbs., 53c. From Guelph—flour, $1.15; grain, 58c. From Brantford, London and St. Mary's—flour, $1.20; grain, 60c. From Oshawa, Newcastle and Bowmanville—flour, 99c; grain, 50c. From Montreal—70c for flour, and 35c for grain.

The Cotton Trade.

The Liverpool cotton statement of to-day, as received by cable, shows the following condition of supply compared with the two previous statements:

	Dec. 18.	Dec. 11.	Dec. 5.
Total stock of cotton, bales...	354,000	365,000	367,000
Total stock of American...	51,000	40,000	44,800
Total afloat....................	258,000	238,000	254,000
American afloat..............	119,000	95,000	78,000
Total of all kinds stock and afloat................	609,000	603,000	621,360

We have here a slightly improving condition of supply, especially in view of the late large shipments to the Continent from this country, the total Continental shipments since September date reaching about 175,000 bales, against about 85,000 bales last year. The Bombay movement indicates that the shipments since October 1 to January 1 will show an increase this year of about 40,000 bales over the total for the same period last season. With regard to consumption, the probabilities are not clearly marked. Our own manufacturers certainly show no disposition to reduce their time. The stock of goods are very light, while prices have advanced considerably during the month, and the indications of a healthy, active trade for the spring are becoming extremely promising. The European consumption, however, is more uncertain. Private cable advices to-day claim that the mills will soon be, and are in fact now being put on half time. We should place more confidence in these rumors if something to the same effect had not been sent to this side before during the month. Besides, the foreign goods movement of Great Britain has been in no amount very favorable. The Board of Trade returns for October, just issued, and given in our London correspondent's letter, published to-day, show a continued increase in the exports of cotton goods. Still there is a point at which the high price of cotton will check the European consumption. Liverpool circulars received this week all claim it is now reached, and strongly advise the immediate, further and decided reduction of time at the mills. It is to be hoped that the raw material will not reach such a price as to make this resort necessary. It is the key to the position, and, if adopted for even a few weeks, could not fail to affect our market very unfavorably. But, on the other hand, with a living price for the raw material to the manufacturer, it is pretty clear that the total world's supply of

cotton this year will be needed.—F. Chronicle.

Halifax Market.

BREADSTUFFS.—Dec. 15, 1868.—We change to note in flour market. Receipt week 5,254 bbls. Canada No. 1 ranges fro to $6.40; strong bakers $6.65 to $6.70 Canada $7.50 to $8 ; extra State still co dull at $6 to $6.40, according to quality. in good demand at $5 to $5.50. Cornmeal dried scarce at $4.75 ; fresh ground, sound unsound $4.15 to $4.25. Rye flour $5.25 Oatmeal $8. Imports from December 8 1867 and 1868 :

	Brls. Flour.	Brls. Co
1868.	181,890	48,
1867.	186,507	35,

WEST INDIA PRODUCE.—Molasses i stock though no quotable advance i Sugars dull except Vacuum Pan, which c to be in good demand at 9¼c duty paid, stock in first hands. We quote: Porto to 6¾c., Barbadoes 5¾ to 5½c., Cuba 5¼ Centrifugal Cuba 6c., in bond. Rum ve at quotations ; 75c for Demerara and C5 Jago.—R. C. Hamilton & Co.'s Circular.

Petroleum.

The following were the exports of P from the United States, from January 1st 2nd :—

FROM	1868.	
New York........galls.	$1,072,351	32
Boston	2,320,486	2
Philadelphia........	30,710,012	27
Baltimore...........	2,583,021	1
Portland............	704,997	
Cleveland	270,000	
Total gallons........	91,660,777	63
Same time in 1866		62
Same time in 1865		26

Reduction in Charges for Telegra

The following are examples of the c which reductions have been made in t charged by the Montreal Telegraph Comp

	FORMER TARIFF.
Montreal to Father Point and Cacouna........	50c & 4c
" Portland........	50c " 4c
" Whitchall......	50c " 5c
" Pembroke and Perth......	35c " 3c
" Picton and Peterboro'.......	40c " 4c
" Hamilton	40c " 4c
" St. Catharines & London	50c & 5c
" Buffalo..........	50c " 6c
" Port Colborne...	70c " 7c
" Chatham.........	70c & 7c
" Detroit.........	75c " 7c

From Sackville to Detroit....$1.50 "14 Arrangements have also been made Western Union Company, by which th tariffs of the Companies have been redu following points:—

From Montreal to Boston	$0 6c
" " New York	0 75
" " Chicago........	1 50
" " St. John, N. B.	1 00
" " Halifax, N.S...	1 05

And from other places in nearly like p

British Wheat Trade.

The wheat trade during the week has acterized by much inactivity, and the probability that a series of dull market's until at least the turn of the year. A crop, and importations which are very sidering the heavy fall which has take prices during the last few months, wi to induce the miller to purchase only t to-mouth. As our importations are

re been expected, any hope of a perma-
rovement must, for the present, be dis-
Winter wheats are already in the blade,
weeks of frost would perhaps be desira-
ler to prevent them from becoming, in
ral parlance, "too proud."
llowing return shows the imports into the
Kingdom in November, and during the
onths ending November 30:

Imports in November.

	1866.	1867.	1868.
..cwt.	1,995,106	3,903,760	2,888,544
......	1,009,618	536,300	875,555
....	545,280	875,279	560,396
....	312,599	160,602	238,885
orn ...	786,876	282,194	956,547
....	402,897	389,426	273,116

Imports in Eleven Months.

....	20,547,038	30,877,923	30,303,752
....	7,053,423	5,315,127	6,397,883
....	8,017,291	8,678,021	7,602,915
....	1,008,957	1,281,946	874,802
....	1,017,534	1,856,585	2,446,981
orn...	13,936,499	8,087,252	10,528,478
....	4,403,133	3,040,350	2,698,725

turns for the ten months show that during od the imports were somewhat in excess rresponding period in 1867, but not to rtant extent. The receipts from Russia eduction of 3,250,000 cwt.; from Prussia 000 cwt.; from Chili, of 530,000 cwt.; the other hand, they have increased from ed States to the extent of 2,730,000 cwt.; ypt 2,150,000 cwt.; and from the Dan- rincipalities to the extent of 1,698,250 regards flour, the October importation increase of about 110,000 cwt.; but in months there is a diminution of 165,000

AILWAY TRAFFIC RETURNS

R THE MONTH OF NOVEMBER, 1868.

	Pa	M	Fr	To	To	Io	Io
		$	$	$	$		
Great Western Railway	125626	7508	162761	295890	296946	251½	251½
Grand Trunk Railway	202595	22500	389361	614456	573259	1377	1377
London and Port Stanley Railway	1128	150	2144	3422	3645	24½	24½
Welland Railway	1172	700	7655	9251	8448	25	25
Northern Railway	13797	1292	22398	37487	36336	97	97
Port Hope, Lindsay, and Beaverton Railway, and Peterborough Branch	3492	247	10095	13834	19712	56	56
Cobourg, Peterborough and Marmora Railway	21	......	864	885	1278	22	22
Brockville and Ottawa Railway	3616	209	14046	17871	16190	86	86
St. Lawrence and Ottawa Railway	4103	575	3974	8652	10162	54	54
Carillon and Grenville Railway*	......	......	......	......	......	....	....
Stanstead, Shefford & Chambly Rail'y*	......	......	......	......	......	....	....
St. Lawrence and Industry Railway*	301	......	1101	1402	2047	12	12
New Brunswick and Canada Railway	1349	......	8008	9357	7725	116	107
European & North American Railway	6526	847	9950	17323	15617	108	108
Nova Scotia Railway	10030	542	16612	27184	23503	145	145
Total	373756	34565	648969	1057290	1014868	2374	2305

rns.

JOHN LANGTON,
Auditor.

Office,
Nov. 13, 1868.

STATEMENT OF BANKS

ACTING UNDER CHARTER, FOR THE MONTH ENDING 30TH NOVEMBER, 1868, ACCORDING TO RETURNS FURNISHED BY THE BANKS TO THE AUDITOR OF PUBLIC ACCOUNTS.

NAME OF BANK	CAPITAL.		LIABILITIES.					ASSETS							
	Capital authorized by Act.	Capital paid up.	Promissory Notes in circulation not bearing interest.	Balances due to other Banks.	Cash Deposits not bearing Interest.	Cash Deposits bearing interest.	TOTAL LIABILITIES	Coin, Bullion, and Provincial Notes.	Landed or other Property of the Bank.	Government Securities.	Promissory Notes, or Bills of other Banks.	Balances due from other Banks.	Notes and Bills Discounted.	Other Debts due the Bank, not included under foregoing heads.	TOTAL ASSETS.
ONTARIO AND QUEBEC.	$	$	$	$ c.	$ c.	$ c.	$ c.	$ c.	$ c.	$ c.	$ c.	$ c.	$ c.	$ c.	$ c.
Montreal	6,000,000	6,000,000	322,794	811,701 68	6,317,891 71	9,096,591 23	16,548,978 62	3,517,485 27	350,000 00	838,887 67	504,277 72	5,854,718 75	13,442,987 60	308,557 25	24,816,944 26
Quebec	3,000,000	1,478,350	577,447	47,344 81	688,535 36	976,258 93	2,289,586 10	397,069 67	89,489 07	148,433 33	106,434 51	202,504 47	2,687,358 32	283,367 35	3,914,656 72
City	1,200,000	1,200,000	435,491	7,339 80	507,261 02	790,169 07	1,740,260 89	331,451 57	41,470 02	158,939 99	116,730 45	99,873 83	2,286,881 41	127,924 25	3,163,271 52
Gore	1,000,000	809,280	195,861	1,761 92	73,489 08	96,628 53	367,740 48	145,572 28	67,027 50	82,733 33	13,478 19	31,591 68	508,887 35	306,678 43	1,245,968 76
British North America	4,866,666	4,866,666	1,038,911	11,149 00	1,098,154 00	2,548,134 00	4,696,348 00	838,422 00	243,333 00	751,840 00	142,694 00	31,169 00	5,582,025 00	190,874 00	7,780,357 00
Banque du Peuple	1,600,000	1,600,000	86,539	2,153 50	320,668 63	252,987 28	662,348 41	174,342 31	54,199 01	160,364 44	43,120 60	31,412 05	1,940,897 27	40,954 90	2,445,290 58
Niagara District	400,000	305,224	192,345	7,159 86	159,292 75	107,596 25	466,393 86	82,756 39	12,879 72	46,720 00	8,594 80	34,582 45	570,000 76	52,558 34	808,092 46
Molson's	1,000,000	1,000,000	110,590	264,751 27	260,254 25	495,557 50	1,131,153 52	343,210 89	91,038 50	103,973 32	66,936 69	93,284 49	1,379,665 18	231,226 89	2,309,215 96
Toronto	2,000,000	800,000	1,029,122	45,859 66	385,964 21	1,483,099 74	2,944,045 61	493,059 30	42,327 08	99,280 00	98,042 16	180,173 32	3,193,914 53	18,695 48	4,125,491 87
Ontario	2,000,000	2,000,000	1,378,133	114,654 45	1,116,535 32	1,042,545 92	3,651,868 69	861,682 09	156,436 73	206,892 69	161,805 46	247,846 27	4,285,025 38	122,713 73	6,042,402 35
Eastern Townships	400,000	400,000	124,561	8,161 63	59,735 11	70,165 01	262,622 75	63,740 28	18,000 00	67,983 33	25,471 90	34,703 25	511,708 36	5,000 00	726,607 12
Banque Nationale	1,000,000	1,000,000	136,005	32,622 45	280,613 24	226,608 77	675,849 46	112,496 12	23,518 00	114,190 00	109,972 27	102,831 97	1,258,051 90	33,886 57	1,749,946 83
Banque Jacques Cartier	1,000,000	994,310	100,801	1,326 89	270,579 37	632,747 41	1,005,354 67	200,873 89	....	101,226 67	25,606 63	104,353 53	1,710,601 35	....	2,142,662 07
Merchants'	6,000,000	3,329,080	1,420,579	153,020 46	1,054,644 10	1,881,686 23	4,509,929 79	666,385 51	356,233 73	528,966 67	280,356 79	907,357 32	4,096,001 72	1,814,698 31	8,650,500 10
Royal Canadian	2,000,000	1,130,783	1,662,119	45,497 15	708,192 38	927,837 19	3,343,695 72	1,162,530 99	....	128,911 10	119,673 96	209,163 55	3,029,548 86	94,668 05	4,744,496 51
Union B'k Low. Canada	2,000,000	1,012,265	83,520	240,816 51	392,955 09	212,952 56	930,244 16	138,020 81	....	120,206 66	58,538 28	80,334 75	1,653,788 46	....	2,051,388 96
Mechanics'	1,000,000	285,423	....	554 79	112,351 43	127,559 32	240,465 54	42,226 31	34,308 19	....	59,682 11	6,265 52	379,352 52	16,623 76	538,458 44
Bank of Commerce	1,000,000	979,562	1,091,952	25,980 34	727,901 03	1,044,803 94	2,890,637 31	884,087 81	49,329 44	104,818 80	103,307 49	267,707 63	2,586,856 06	....	3,996,107 29
NOVA SCOTIA.															
Bank of Yarmouth	....	....	....	....	....	....	....	....	....	....	....	....	....	....	....
Merchants' Bank	....	....	....	....	....	....	....	....	....	....	....	....	....	....	....
People's Bank	....	....	....	....	....	....	....	....	....	....	....	....	....	....	....
Union Bank	....	....	....	....	....	....	....	....	....	....	....	....	....	....	....
Bank of Nova Scotia	....	....	....	....	....	....	....	....	....	....	....	....	....	....	....
NEW BRUNSWICK.															
Bank of New Brunswick	600,000	600,000	433,848	77,409 46	574,524 72	784,739 74	1,870,522 42	240,465 86	14,095 45	....	28,779 00	431,753 45	1,965,765 43	80,827 56	2,761,686 75
Commercial Bank	....	....	....	....	....	....	....	....	....	....	....	....	....	....	....
St. Stephen's Bank	....	....	....	....	....	....	....	....	....	....	....	....	....	....	....
People's Bank	....	....	....	....	....	....	....	....	....	....	....	....	....	....	....
Totals ....$	38,066,666	29,790,955	10,420,619	1,899,265 63	15,109,542 75	22,798,618 62	50,228,046 00	10,696,379 35	1,643,685 49	3,764,298 06	2,073,503 01	8,952,077 28	53,154,317 46	3,729,284 87	84,013,545 52

Mercantile.

DOMINION TELEGRAPH COMPANY.

PITAL STOCK . . . $300,000

In 10,000 Shares at $50 Each.

PRESIDENT,
HON. WILLIAM CAYLEY.

TREASURER,
HON. J. McMURRICH.

SECRETARY,
H. B. REEVE.

SOLICITORS,
MESSRS. CAMERON & McMICHAEL.

GENERAL SUPERINTENDENT.
MARTIN RYAN

DIRECTORS.

HON. J. McMURRICH,
Bryce, McMurrich & Co., Toronto.

A. R. McMASTER, Esq.,
R. McMaster & Brother, Toronto.

HON. M. C. CAMERON,
Provincial Secretary, Toronto.

JAMES MICHIE, Esq.,
ltan, Michie & Co., and George Michie & Co., Toronto;

HON. WILLIAM CAYLEY.
Toronto.

A. M. SMITH, Esq.,
A. M. Smith & Co., Toronto.

L. MOFFATT, Esq.,
Moffatt, Murray & Co., Toronto.

H. B. REEVE, Esq.,
Toronto.

MARTIN RYAN, Esq.,
Toronto.

PROSPECTUS.

HE DOMINION TELEGRAPH COMPANY has been organized under the act respecting Telegraph Companies, chapter 67, of the consolidated Statutes of Canada. object is to cover the Dominion of Canada with a complete net-work of Telegraph lines.

The Capital Stock

$500,000, divided into 10,000 shares of $50 each, 5 per t to be paid at the time of subscribing, the balance to paid by instalments, not exceeding 10 per cent per th—and instalments to be called in by the Directors as works progress. The liability of a subscriber is limited he amount of his subscription.

The Business Affairs of the Company.

under the management of a Board of Directors, an lly elected by the Shareholders, in conformity with the arter and By-Laws of the Company.
he Directors are of opinion that it would be to the rest of the Stockholders generally to obtain subscriptions from all quarters of Canada, and with this view they pose to divide the Stock amongst the different towns cities throughout the Dominion, in allotments suited the population and business occupations of the different lities, and the interest which they may be supposed to be in such an enterprise.

Contracts of Connections.

contract, granting permanent connection and extraordinary advantages, has already been executed between this mpany and the Atlantic and Pacific Company, of New rk; thus, at the very commencement, as the Lines of this mpany are constructed from the Suspension Bridge, at tion, (the point of connection) to any point in the Dominion, all the chief cities and places in the States, touched by the Lines of the Atlantic and Pacific Telegraph mpany, are brought in immediate connection therewith. permanent connection has also been secured with the of Western Telegraph Company, of Chicago, whereby Company will be brought into close connection with the Lake Ports and other places through the North tern States, and through to California.

4-8mos

Mercantile.

Teas! Teas!! Teas!!!

FRESH ARRIVALS

NEW CROP TEAS,

WINES, AND GENERAL GROCERIES,

Special Inducements given to

PROMPT PAYING PURCHASERS.

All Goods sold at very Lowest Montreal Prices!

W. & R. GRIFFITH,

ONTARIO CHAMBERS,
Corner of Front and Church Streets,

6-1y   TORONTO
                                               ONTARIO

TEAS.   Reford & Dillon   TEAS.

HAVE just received ex. steamships "*St. David* and *Nestorian :*"

1000 hlf. chests new season Teas!
   Comprising Twankays, Young Hysons, Imperials, Gunpowders, colored and uncolored Japans, Congous, Souchongs, and Pekoes.

500 hlf. bxs. new Valentia Raisins (selected fruit).
500 bags cleaned Arracan and Rangoon Rice.
500 brls. choice Currants.

—ALSO IN STORE:—

250 hhds. bright Barbadoes and Cuba Sugars.
250 brls. Portland, Standard, Golden & Amber Syrups.
100 bags Rio. Jamaica, Laguayra, and Java Coffees.
250 bxs. 10z Tobacco, "Queen's Own" and "Prince of Wales" brands.

WITH A GENERAL AND

WELL SELECTED STOCK OF GROCERIES;

All of which they offer to the Trade low.

12 & 14 WELLINGTON STREET, TORONTO.

7-1y

Robert H. Gray,

Manufacturer of Hoop Skirts

AND

CRINOLINE STEEL,

IMPORTER OF

HABERDASHERY, TRIMMINGS

AND

GENERAL FANCY GOODS,

43, YONGE STREET, TORONTO, ONT.   6-1y

John Boyd & Co.,

WHOLESALE GROCERS AND COMMISSION MERCHANTS,

61 AND 63 FRONT STREET

TORONTO.

NOW in store, direct from the European and West India Markets; a large assortment of General Groceries, comprising

Teas, Sugars, Coffees, Wines and Liquors,

AND

GENERAL GROCERIES.

Ship Chandlery, Canvas, Manilla and Tarred Rope, Oakum, Tar, Flags, &c., &c.,

DIRECT FROM THE MANUFACTURERS.

OHN BOYD.   ALEX. M. MONRO.   C. W. BUNTING.

Toronto, Oct. 1st; 1868.   7-1y

Mercantile.

UNRIVALLED!

THE BRITISH AMERICAN COMMERCIAL COLLEGE,
Consolidated with the

Bryant, Stratton and Odell Business College
AND TELEGRAPHIC INSTITUTE,

STANDS Pre-eminent and Unrivalled. It is the LARGEST and MOST EFFICIENT. It employs the largest staff of Teachers, among whom are the two BEST PENMEN OF CANADA.

The TUITION FEE is the same as in other Institutions having a similar object.

The PRICE OF BOARD is the same as in other Canadian Cities.

In an EDUCATIONAL point of view, there is no other Institution in the country that has equal advantages and facilities.

YOUNG MEN intending to qualify themselves for business, will find it to their advantage to send for a Circular, or call at the College Rooms, corner of King and Toronto streets.

Scholarships good in Montreal and throughout the United States.

ODELL & TROUT,
October 2.   Principals and Proprietors.
                                                     8

The Mercantile Agency,

FOR THE

PROMOTION AND PROTECTION OF TRADE
Established in 1841.

DUN, WIMAN & Co.

Montreal, Toronto and Halifax.

REFERENCE Book, containing names and ratings of Business Men in the Dominion, published semi-annually.   24-1y.

The St. Lawrence Glass Company

ARE now manufacturing and have for sale,

COAL OIL LAMPS,
various styles and sizes.

LAMP CHIMNEYS,
of extra quality for ordinary Burners also, for the 'Comet' and 'Sun' Burners.

SETS OF
TABLE GLASSWARE, HYACINTH GLASSES,
STEAM GUAGE TUBES, GLASS RODS, &c.,
or any other article made to order, in *White* or *Color* of
Glass.

KEROSENE BURNERS, COLLARS AND SOCKETS, will be kept on hand.

*DRUGGISTS FLINT GLASSWARE, and
PHILOSOPHICAL INSTRUMENTS,*
made to order.

OFFICE—388 ST. PAUL STREET, MONTREAL.
A. McK. COCHRANE.
6-1y   Secretary.

Financial.

BROWN'S BANK,
(W. R. Brown. W. C. Chewett.)

60 KING STREET EAST, TORONTO,

TRANSACTS a general Banking Business, Buys and Sells New York and Sterling Exchange, Gold, Silver, U. S. Bonds and Uncurrent Money, receives Deposits subject to Cheque at sight, makes Collections and Discounts Commercial Paper.

Orders by Mail or Telegraph promptly executed at most favourable current quotations.

Address letters;   "BROWN'S BANK,
33-y   Toronto."

Candee & Co.,

BANKERS AND BROKERS, dealers in Gold and Silver Coin, Government Securities, &c., Corner Main and Exchange Streets Buffalo, N. N.   21-1v

H. N. Smith & Co.,

2, EAST SENECA STREET, BUFFALO, N. Y., (Correspondent Smith; Gould, Martin & Co., 11 Broad Street, N.Y.,) Stock, Money and Exchange Brokers. Advances made on securities.   21-1y

TORONTO PRICES CURRENT.—December 23, 1868.

Name of Article.	Wholesale Rates.		Name of Article.	Wholesale Rate.		Name of Article.	Whole Rate.
Boots and Shoes.	$ c.	$ c.	**Groceries—Contin'd**	$ c.	$ c.	**Leather**—Contin'd.	$ c.
Mens' Thick Boots	2 05	2 50	" fine to fine's..	0 85	0 95	Kip Skins, Patna ...	0 30
" Kip........	2 50	3 25	Hyson	0 45	0 80	French	0 70
" Calf........	3 00	3 70	Imperial	0 42	0 80	English	0 65
" Congress Gaiters..	3 00	3 50	Tobacco, *Manufac'd:*			Hemlock Calf (30 to	
" Kip Cobourgs..	1 15	1 45	Can Leaf, ♥ lb.5s & 10s.	0 26	0 30	35 lbs.) per doz..	0 75
Boys' Thick Boots....	1 60	1 80	Western Leaf, com..	0 25	0 28	Do. light	0 45
Youths'	1 35	1 50	" Good....	0 27	0 32	French Calf, ...	0 98
Women's Balts	95	1 30	" Fine	0 22	0 35	Grain & Setn Cit'♥ doz ..	0 00
" Congress Gaiters..	1 15	1 45	" Bright fine..	0 40	0 50	Splits, large ♥ lb....	0 30
Misses' Balts..	0 75	1 00	" choice..	0 60	0 75	" small ..	0 29
" Congress Gaiters..	1 00	1 30				Enamelled Cow ♥ foot ..	0 17
Girls' Balts	0 60	0 85	**Hardware.**			Patent	0 20
" Congress Gaiters..	0 80	1 10	*Tin (net cash prices)*			Pebble Grain	0 17
Children's C. T. Clocks..	0 60	0 65	Block, ♥ lb...	0 25	0 26	Buff	0 17
" Gaiters	0 65	0 00	Grain........	0 25	0 26		
Drugs.			Copper:			**Oils.**	
Aloes Cape..	0 12½	0 15	Pig	0 22	0 24	Cod	0 60
Alum.........	0 02½	0 03	Sheet........	0 30	0 33	Lard, extra	0 90
Borax	0 00	0 00	*Cut Nails:*			" No. 1	0 00
Camphor, refined....	0 65	0 70	Assorted ¼ Shingles,			" Woollen....	0 00
Castor Oil..	0 18	0 28	♥ 100 lbs.. ...	2 90	3 00	Lubricating, patent..	0 00
Caustic Soda........	0 04½	0 05	Shingle alone do ...	3 15	3 25	" Mott's economic	0 50
Cochineal......	0 90	1 10	Lathe and 5 dy...	3 30	3 40	Linseed, raw.....	0 77½
Cream Tartar	0 25	0 30	*Galvanised Iron:*			" boiled..	0 83½
Epsom Salts	0 03	0 04	Assorted sizes	0 08	0 09	Machinery	0 00
Extract Logwood....	0 09	0 11	Best No. 24..	0 08	0 09	Olive, bid, ♥ gal....	1 45
Gum Arabic, sorts ..	0 30	0 35	" 26........	0 08	0 08½	" salad	2 00
Indigo, Madras......	0 75	1 00	" 28........	0 09	0 09½	" salad, in lots.	
Liquorice	0 14	0 45	*Horse Nails:*			qt ♥ case...	3 60
Madder	0 16	0 18	Guest's or Griffin's			Sesame salad, ♥ gal.	1 60
Nutgalls	0 00	0 00	assorted sizes....	0 00	0 00	Seal, pale.....	0 70
Opium........	0 70	7 00	For ♥, saw'd sizes..	0 18	0 19	Spirits Turpentine..	0 62
Oxalic Acid........	0 28	0 35	Patent Hammer'd do..	0 17	0 18	Varnish	0 00
Polash, Bi-tart......	0 25	0 28	*Iron (at 4 months):*			Whale..	0 75
" Bichromate..	0 15	0 20	Pig—Gartsherrie No1..	24 00	25 00	**Paints, &c.**	
Potass Iodide	3 80	4 50	Other brands. No 1..	22 00	24 00	White Lead, genuine	
Rhubarb	0 15	0 60	No 2..	0 00	0 00	in Oil, ♥ 25 lbs....	0 00
Senna	0 12½	0 60	Bar—Scotch, ♥ 100 lb..	2 25	2 60	Do. No. 1 " ...	0 00
Soda Ash	0 03	0 04	Refined	3 00	3 25	" 2 " ...	0 00
Soda Bicarb	4 50	5 50	Swedes	5 00	5 50	White Zinc, genuine..	3 00
Tartaric Acid......	0 37½	0 45	Hoops—Coopers....	3 00	3 25	White Lead, dry......	0 06
Ventigris	0 35	0 40	Band	3 00	3 25	Red Lead........	0 08½
V. tri il, Blue......	0 09	0 10	Boiler Plates....	3 25	3 50	Venetian Red, Eng'h..	0 02½
Groceries.			Canada Plates....	4 00	4 25	Yellow Ochre, Fren'h..	0 02½
Coffees:			Union Jack	0 00	0 00	Whiting	0 90
Java, ♥ lb.	0 22	0 24	Pontypool......	4 00	4 25	**Petroleum.**	
Laguayra, ...	0 17	0 18	Swanses	3 90	4 00	(Refined ♥ gal.)	
Rio..........	0 15	0 17	*Lead (at 4 months):*			Water white, car'd ..	0 37
Fish:			Bar, ♥ 100 lb.. ...	0 07	0 07½	" small lots..	0 00
Herrings, Lab. split..	4 75	5 50	Sheet	0 08	0 09	Straw, by car load..	0 37
" round..	4 00	4 75	Shot........	0 07½	0 07½	" small lots..	0 00
" scaled......	1 00	0 00	*Iron Wire (net cash):*			Amber, by car load..	0 00
Mackerel, small kitts..	2 50	2 75	No. 6, ♥ bundle...	2 70	2 80	" small lots ..	0 00
Louh. Her. wh'e firks..	1 25	1 50	" 9, "	3 10	3 20	Benzine	0 00
" half	3 50	3 75	" 12, "	3 40	3 50		
White Fish & Trout..	14 00	15 00	" 16, "	4 30	4 40	**Produce.**	
Salmon, saltwater ...	5 00	5 25	*Powder:*			*Grain:*	
Dry Cod, ♥112 lbs....			Blasting, Canada...	3 50	4 00	Wheat, Spring, 60 ℔..	1 00
Fruit:			FF "	4 25	4 50	" Fall "	1 05
Raisins, Layers	2 10	2 20	FFF "	4 75	5 00	Barley.. 48 "	1 25
" M R.......	1 90	2 10	Blasting, English ..	4 50	5 00	Peas.. 60 "	0 80
" Valentias new..	0 07	0 07½	FF " loose.	5 00	6 00	Oats.. 34 "	0 62
Currants, new......	0 05	0 05½	FFF "	6 00	6 50	Rye.. 56 "	0 00
" old.......	0 04½	0 04½	*Pressed Spldns (4 mos):*			*Seeds:*	
Figs	0 14	0 00	Regular sizes 100....	4 00	4 25	Clover, choice 60 " ..	6 25
Molasses:			Extra	4 50	5 00	" com'n 60 "	6 00
Clayed, ♥ gal.	0 00	0 25	*Tin Plates (net cash):*			Timothy, cho'e 4 " ..	3 00
Syrups, Standard ..	0 49	0 50	IC Coke	7 50	8 00	" inf. to good 48 "	2 50
" Golden	0 54	0 55	IC Charcoal...	8 25	8 50	Flax.. 56 "	1 40
Rice:			DX "	10 25	10 75	*Flour (per brl.):*	
Arracan	4 50	4 75	1XX "	12 25	0 00	Superior extra....	0 00
Spices:			DC "	7 25	9 00	Extra superfine,....	3 35
Cassia, whole, ♥ lb...	0 00	0 45	DX "	9 50	0 00	Fancy superfine	0 00
Cloves	0 11	0 12				Superline No. 1	0 00
Nutmegs	0 45	0 55	**Hides & Skins. ♥℔**			" No. 2....	0 00
Ginger, ground	0 20	0 25	Green rough	0 06	0 00	*Oatmeal, (per brl.)..*	0 00
" Jamaica, root..	0 20	0 25	Green, salt'd & insp'd..	0 00	0 08½		
Pepper, black......	0 09	0 10	Cured	0 08	0 08½	**Provisions**	
Pimento	0 08	0 09	Calfskins, green....	0 00	0 11	Butter, dairy tub ♥ lb..	0 2
Sugars:			" cured	0 18	0 10	" store packed..	0 2
Port Rico, ♥ lb.......	0 08½	0 08½	" dry......	0 18	0 90	Cheese, new	0 1
Cuba "	0 08½	0 08½	Sheepskins, ...	1 00	1 25	Pork, mess, per brl...	22 0
Barbadoes (bright)..	0 09	0 00	" country....	0 60	0 80	" prime mess ..	20 0
Dry Crushed, at 6 d.	0 11	0 11½				" prime	0 0
Canada Sugar Refine'y,			**Hops.**			Bacon, rough......	0 8
yellow No. 2, 60 ds..	0 09	0 09½	Inferior, ♥ lb.......	0 05	0 07	" Cumberl'd cut..	0 9
Yellow, No. 2........	0 09½	0 09½	Medium	0 00	0 00	" smoked	0 9
" No. 3........	0 09½	0 09½	Good	0 09	0 12	Hams, in salt......	0 1
Crushed X........	0 11	0 11½	Fancy	0 00	0 00	" sug'ar & canv'd..	0 1
" A	0 11	0 11½				Shoulders, in salt ..	0 0
Ground........	0 11	0 11½	**Leather.** ♥ (4 mos.)			Lard, in kegs.....	0 1
Extra Ground......	0 12½	0 12½	In lots of less than			Eggs, packed	0 1
Teas:			50 sides, 10 ♥ cent			Beef Hams	0 0
Japan com'n to good..	0 40	0 55	higher.			Tallow	0 0
" fine to choicest..	0 55	0 65	Spanish Sole, 1st qual..			Hogs dressed, heavy..	7 1
Colored, com. to fine..	0 60	0 75	heavy, weights ♥ ℔..	0 00	0 23	" medium...	6 0
Congou & Souch'ng..	0 42	0 75	Do.1st qual.middle do..	0 22	0 23	" light	6 0
Oolong, good to fine..	0 45	0 70	Do. No. 2, all weights..	0 20	0 26		
Y. Hyson, com to gd..	0 45	0 55	Slaughter heavy ..	0 50	0 00	**Salt, &c.**	
Medium to choice ..	0 65	0 80	Do. light......	0 22	0 34	American bris.....	1 1
Extra choice	0 85	0 95	Harness, best	0 30	0 33	Liverpool coarse....	1 0
Gunpowd'r, to med..	0 55	0 70	" No. 2	0 30	0 33	Plaster	0 0
" med. to fine	0 70	0 85	Upper heavy.......	0 40	0 00	Water Lime	1 1
			" light.......	0 36	0 40		

Candles.		
d & Co.'s ..	$ c.	$ c.
ial.........	0 07½	0 08
ı Bar	0 07	0 07½
Bar........	0 07	0 07½
....	0 05	0 05½
....	0 03½	0 03½
....	0 00	0 11½
Liquors, c.		
er doz......	2 60	2 65
Dub Portr..	2 35	2 40
aica Rum...	1 80	2 25
r's H. Gin..	1 55	1 65
ld Tom.....	1 90	2 00
ses.........	4 00	4 25
ld Tom, c...	6 00	6 25
mon	1 00	1 25
old	2 00	4 00
ommon	1 00	1 50
ium........	1 70	1 80
e or golden..	2 50	4 00

Brandy:	$ c.	$ c
Hennessy's, per gal..	2 30	2 50
Martell's " ..	2 30	2 50
J. Robin & Co.'s " ..	2 25	2 35
Otard, Dupuy & Cos..	2 25	2 35
Brandy, cases........	8 50	9 00
Brandy, com. per c...	4 00	4 50
Whiskey:		
Common 36 u. p......	0 62½	0 65
Old Rye	0 85	0 87½
Malt	0 85	0 87½
Toddy	0 85	0 87½
Scotch, per gal.......	1 90	2 10
Irish—Kinnahan's c...	7 00	7 50
" Dunnville's Belf't..	6 00	6 25
Wool.		
Fleece, lb.............	0 28	0 35
Pulled ".............	0 22	0 25
Furs.		
Bear..................	8 00	10 00
Beaver................	1 00	1 25
Coon	0 20	0 40
Fisher................	4 00	6 00
Martin................	1 40	1 60
Mink..................	4 00	4 25
Otter.................	5 75	6 00
Spring Rats...........	0 15	0 17
Fox...................	1 20	1 25

INSURANCE COMPANIES.

ENGLISH.—*Quotations on the London Market.*

ast Dividend.	Name of Company.	Shares parval £	Amount paid.	Last Sale.
	Briton Medical and General Life...	10	....	1¾
7½	Commer'l Union, Fire, Life and Mar.	50	5	5½
8	City of Glasgow	25	2½	5¾
9½	Edinburgh Life	100	15	31¾
5—½ yr	European Life and Guarantee.......	2½	11s6	5s
10	Etna Fire and Marine..............	10	1½	0
5	Guardian	100	50	51½
12	Imperial Fire.....................	500	50	0
9½	Imperial Life	100	10	15½
10	Lancashire Fire and Life..........	20	2	2⅞
11	Life Association of Scotland......	40	7½	25
5s. p. sh	London Assurance Corporation ..	25	12½	49
5	London and Lancashire Life	10	1	19s
40	Liverp'l & London & Globe F. & L.	20	2	6 15-16ths
5	National Union Life	5	1	0
12½	Northern Fire and Life	100	5	11½
12 / 38, bo / 5s.	North British and Mercantile	50	6¼	19¾
50	Ocean Marine	25	5	19¾
5 12s.	Provident Life....................	100	10	0
4½ p. s.	Phœnix............................	....	....	148
½--h. yr.	Queen Fire and Life	10	1	17s
s. bo. 4s	Royal Insurance..................	20	3	6
10	Scottish Provincial Fire and Life ..	50	2½	5
25	Standard Life	50	12	65½
5	Star Life	25	1¼	—
	CANADIAN.			₱ c.
4	British America Fire and Marine ..	$50	$25	56
4	Canada Life	....	....	.....
12	Montreal Assurance	£50	£5	135
3	Provincial Fire and Marine........	60	11	.....
....	Quebec Fire	40	32½	£21½
8	" Marine..................	100	40	95
7 mo's.	Western Assurance................	40	6	.....

RAILWAYS.	Sha's	Paid	Montr	London.
d St. Lawrence....................	£100	All.	....	58 60
l Lake Huron	20½	"	....	3 3½
do Preference	10	"	....	4½ 6
tl. & Goderich, 6₩c., 1872-3-4..........	100	"	....	65 00
and St. Lawrence	....	....	10 11	....
do Pref. 10 ₩ ct............	....	....	72 75	....
nk	100	"	15 16	15½ 17
Eq.G. M. Bds. 1 ch. 6₩c............	100	"	....	84 86
First Preference, 5 ₩ c	100	"	....	50 53
Deferred, 3 ₩ ct..................	100	"	....	....
Second Pref. Bonds, 5₩c............	100	"	....	39 42½
do Deferred, 3 ₩ ct...........	100	"	...	....
Third Pref. Stock, 4₩ct............	100	"	....	27 30
do. Deferred, 3 ₩ ct..............	100	"	....	....
Fourth Pref. Stock, 3₩c............	100	"	....	18½ 19¾
do. Deferred, 3 ₩ ct..............	100	"	....	....
tern	20½	"	13 14	13⅝ 14¾
New	20½	18	....	....
6 ₩ c. Bds, due 1873-76............	100	All.	....	100 104
5½₩c Bds. due 1877-78............	100	"	....	93 94
ilway, Halifax, $250, all..........	$250	"	....	....
of Canada, 6₩c. 1st Pref. Bds........	100	"	.. .	80 83

CHANGE.	Halifax.	Montr'l.	Quebec.	Toronto.
London, 60 days.......				
75 days date	12½	9½ 9¾	9½ 9¾	9¾
lo.	11½ 12	7½ 8	8⅞ 9¼	8¾
ith documents..........	....	....	....	....
ew York...............	....	25½ 26	25½ 25¾	74½
do.	....	23½ 23¾	25½ 25¾	....
s do.	....	par	par ½ dis.	par ½ dis.
....	....	4 4½	....	3½ 5

STOCK AND BOND REPORT.

The dates of our quotations are as follows:—Toronto, Dec. 23; Montreal, Dec. 22; Quebec, Dec. 21; London, Nov. 28.

NAME.	Shares.	Paid up.	Divid'd last 6 Months	Dividend Day.	CLOSING PRICES. Toronto.	Montre'l	Quebec.
BANKS.			₩ ct.				
British North America........	$250	All.	3	July and Jan.	105 106	105 106	104 105
Jacques Cartier..............	50	"	4	1 June, 1 Dec.	106 107	106½ 107½	105¾ 106¾
Montreal	200	"	5	"	138 138½	138 138½	138 138½
Nationale....................	50	"	4	1 Nov. 1 May.	....	105 106	106 106½
New Brunswick	100	"	......	......	....	...	....
Nova Scotia	200	28	7&b$3½	Mar. and Sept.	....	....	....
Du Peuple....................	50	"	4	1 Mar., 1 Sept.	106½ 107½	107½ 108	107 107½
Toronto	100	"	4	1 Jan., 1 July.	Bks cl'd	Bks cl'd	Bks cl'd
Bank of Yarmouth.............	....	....	......	......	....	....	....
Canadian Bank of Com'e.......	50	95	......	......	Bks cl'd	Bks cl'd	Bks cl'd
City Bank Montreal...........	80	All.	4	1 June, 1 Dec.	102 102½	101½ 102½	102 102½
Commer'l Bank (St. John).....	100	"	₩ ct.	......	....	....	....
Eastern Townships' Bank......	50	"	4	1 July, 1 Jan..	....	99 100	Bks cl'd
Gore	40	...	none.	1 Jan., 1 July.	39½ 40	40 42	41 42
Halifax Banking Company......	....	....	......	......	....	....	....
Mechanics' Bank..............	50	70	4	1 Nov., 1 May.	95½ 97	95 96	95 96
Merchants' Bank of Canada....	100	70	4	1 Jan., 1 July.	Bks cl'd	107 109	Bks cl'd
Merchants' Bank (Halifax)....	....	....	......	......	....	....	....
Molson's Bank................	50	All.	4	1 Apr., 1 Oct.	110 110½	109½ 110	109 110
Niagara District Bank........	100	70	3½	1 Jan., 1 July.	....	....	....
Ontario Bank.................	40	All.	4	1 June, 1 Dec.	100 100½	100	99 99½
People's Bank (Fred'kton)....	100	"	......	......	....	....	....
People's Bank (Halifax)......	20	"	7 12 m	......	....	....	....
Quebec Bank	100	"	3½	1 June, 1 Dec.	98 100	98 100	99½ 100
Royal Canadian Bank..........	50	50	4	1 Jan., 1 July.	Bks cl'd	Bks cl'd	Bks cl'd
St. Stephens Bank	100	All	......	......	....	....	....
Union Bank	100	70	4	1 Jan., 1 July.	Bks cl'd	Bks cl'd	Bks cl'd
Union Bank (Halifax).........	100	40	7 12mo	Feb. and Aug.	....	....	....
MISCELLANEOUS.							
British America Land.........	250	44	2½	......	....	....	....
British Colonial S. S. Co....	250	32½	2½	......	...	50 60	....
Canada Company	32½	All.	5	......	....	....	....
Canada Landed Credit Co......	50	$20	3½	......	72 73	....	....
Canada Per. B'ldg Society....	50	All.	5	......	124½ 125	....	....
Canada Mining Company........	4	90	......	......	....	....	....
Do. Inl'd Steam Nav. Co......	100	All.	20 12 m	......	....	106 109	105 107
Do. Glass Company............	100	"	12½ "	......	....	46 60	....
Canad'n Loan & Investm't.....	25	2½	7	......	....	....	....
Canada Agency	10	½	......	......	....	....	....
Colonial Securities Co.......	...	....	......	......	....	....	....
Freehold Building Society....	100	All.	4	......	104½ 105	....	....
Halifax Steamboat Co.........	100	"	5	......	....	....	....
Halifax Gas Company..........	....	....	......	......	....	....	....
Hamilton Gas Company.........	....	....	......	......	....	....	....
Huron Copper Bay Co..........	4	12	20	......	....	25 40cps	....
Lake Huron S. and C..........	5	102	......	......	....	....	....
Montreal Mining Consols......	20	$15	......	......	....	3.10 3.20	....
Do. Telegraph Co........	40	All.	5	......	135 137	135 136	135 138
Do. Elevating Co........	00	"	15 12 m	......	....	100 102½	....
Do. City Gas Co.........	40	"	4	15 Mar. 15 Sep.	....	135 136	133 134
Do. City Pass. R. Co....	50	"	5	......	....	110 110½	110 110½
Nova Scotia Telegraph	20	"	....	......	....	....	....
Quebec and L. S.	8	$4	......	......	....	....	25 cts
Quebec Gas Co................	200	All.	4	1 Mar., 1 Sep.	....	....	115 117
Quebec Street R. R...........	50	25	8	......	....	....	90 95
Richelieu Navigation Co......	100	All.	7 p.a.	1 Jan., 1 July.	....	117 118	116 117
St. Lawrence Tow Boat Co.....	100	"	......	3 Feb.	....	...	40 45
Tor'to Consumers' Gas Co.....	50	"	2 3 m.	1 My Au Mar Fe	106½ 107	...	105½ 106½
Trust & Loan Co. of U. C.....	20	5	3	......	....	....	....
West'n Canada Bldg Soc'y.....	50	All.	5	......	116 117	....	....

SECURITIES.	London.	Montreal.	Quebec.	Toronto.
Canadian Gov't Deb. 6 ₩ ct. stg..............	....	102 103	102½ 103	103 105
Do. do. 6 do due Ja. & Jul. 1877-84........	107½ 108½	....	....	....
Do. do. 6 do. Feb. & Aug...........	106 107	....	....	....
Do. do. 6 do. Mch. & Sep...........	106 107	....	....	....
Do. do. 5 ₩ ct. cur., 1883	94 95	92½ 93½	92 92½	93 93½
Do. do. 5 do. stg., 1885	94 95	92½ 93½	92½ 93	93 93½
Do. do. 7 do. cur., ...	....	....	......	....
Dominion 6 p. c. 1878 cy..................	....	104½ 105	104½ 105	104½ 105
Hamilton Corporation......................	....	....	......	....
Montreal Harbor, 8 ₩ ct. d. 1869..........	..	....	......	....
Do. do. 7 do. 1870......................	....	....	......	100 101
Do. do. 6½ do. 1875....................	....	101 102	......	....
Do. do. 6½ do. 1873....................	....	....	......	....
Do. Corporation, 6 ₱ c. 1891	....	95½ 96½	96 96½	94 96
Do. 7 p. c. stock.........................	....	106 107½	106 107	107½ 108
Do. Water Works, 6 ₱ c. stg. 1878..........	....	....	......	94 96
Do. do. 6 do. cy. do.	....	96 96½	......	94 96
New Brunswick, 6 ₩ ct., Jan. and July	104 106	....	......	....
Nova Scotia, 6 ₩ ct., 1875.................	104 105½	....	......	....
Ottawa City 6 ₩ c. d. 1880	....	92½ 93½	......	....
Quebec Harbour, 6 ₱ c. d. 1883.............	....	....	60	....
Do. do. 7 do. do......................	....	....	65 70	....
Do. do. 8 do. 1886.....................	....	....	75 80	....
Do. City, 7 ₱ c. d. 5 years	....	80 90	95 96	....
Do. do. 7 do. 9 do.	....	....	91 92	....
Do. do. 7 do. 2 do.	....	....	97 98	....
Do. Water Works, 7 ₱ ct., 4 years	....	....	96 97	....
Do. do. 6 do. 2 do.	....	....	94 95	....
Toronto Corporation	....	87½ 92½	....	....

Financial.

Pellatt & Osler.

STOCK AND EXCHANGE BROKERS, Accountants, Agents for the Standard Life Assurance Company and New York Casualty Insurance Company.

OFFICE—86 *King Street East, four Doors West of Church Street, Toronto.*

HENRY PELLATT,   EDMUND B. OSLER,
1y   *Notary Public.*   *Official Assignee.*

Philip Browne & Co.,

BANKERS AND STOCK BROKERS.

DEALERS IN

STERLING EXCHANGE—U. S. Currency, Silver and Bonds—Bank Stocks, Debentures, Mortgages, &c. Drafts on New York Issued, in Gold and Currency. Prompt attention given to collections. Advances made on Securities.

No. 67 YONGE STREET, TORONTO

JAMES BROWNE.   PHILIP BROWNE, *Notary Public.*
y

James C. Small,

BANKER AND BROKER,

No. 34 KING STREET EAST, TORONTO.

Sterling Exchange, American Currency, Silver, and Bonds, Bank Stocks, Debentures and other Securities, bought and sold. Collections promptly made. Drafts on New York in Gold and Currency issued.

Western Canada Permanent Building and Savings Society.

OFFICE—No 70 CHURCH STREET, TORONTO.

SAVINGS BANK BRANCH.

Deposits Received Daily. Interest Paid Half-Yearly.

ADVANCES

Are made on the security of Real Estate, repayable on the most favourable terms, by a Sinking Fund.

WALTER S. LEE,
56-1y   *Secy. & Treas.*

The Canadian Land and Emigration Company

Offers for sale on Conditions of Settlement,

GOOD FARM LANDS

In the County of Peterboro, Ontario,

In the well settled Township of Dysart, where there are Grist and Saw Mills, Stores, &c., at

ONE-AND-A-HALF DOLLARS AN ACRE.

In the adjoining Townships of Guilford, Dudley, Harburn, Harcourt and Bruton, connected with Dysart and the Village of Haliburton by the Peterson Road, at ONE DOLLAR an Acre.

For further particulars apply to

    CHAS. JAS. BLOMFIELD,
      Secretary C. L. and E. Co., Toronto.

Or to   ALEX. NIVEN, P.L.S.,
      Agent C. L. & E. Co., Haliburton.

Canada Permanent Building and Savings Society.

Paid up Capital	$1,000,000
Assets	1,700,000
Annual Income	400,000

Directors:—JOSEPH D. RIDOUT, *President.*
PETER PATERSON, *Vice-President.*
J. G. Worts, Edward Hooper, S. Nordheimer, W. C. Chewett, E. H. Rutherford, Joseph Robinson.
Bankers:—Bank of Toronto; Bank of Montreal; Royal Canadian Bank.

OFFICE—*Masonic Hall, Toronto Street, Toronto.*

Money Received on Deposit bearing five and six per cent. interest.

Advances made on City and County Property in the Province of Ontario.

J. HERBERT MASON,
30-y   *Sec'y & Treas.*

Insurance.

Montreal Assurance Company.

DIVIDEND NOTICE.

NOTICE is hereby given that a Dividend of TWELVE PER CENT. on the paid-up stock of the Company has been declared for the past year, and will be payable at the office, Great St. James Street, on and after MONDAY, the 14th inst.

WM. MURRAY,
      Manager.
Montreal, December 4, 1868.   17-2

The Victoria Mutual

FIRE INSURANCE COMPANY OF CANADA.

Insures only Non-Hazardous Property, at Low Rates.

BUSINESS STRICTLY MUTUAL.

GEORGE H. MILLS, *President.*
W. D. LOOKER, *Secretary.*

HEAD OFFICE .... HAMILTON, ONTARIO
aug 15-1yr

Life Association of Scotland.

INVESTED FUNDS

UPWARDS OF £1,000,000 STERLING.

THIS Institution differs from other Life Offices, in that the

BONUSES FROM PROFITS

Are applied on a special system for the Policy-holder's *PERSONAL BENEFIT AND ENJOYMENT DURING HIS OWN LIFETIME,*

WITH THE OPTION OF

LARGE BONUS ADDITIONS TO THE SUM ASSURED.

The Policy-holder thus obtains

A LARGE REDUCTION OF PRESENT OUTLAY

OR

A PROVISION FOR OLD AGE OF A MOST IMPORTANT AMOUNT IN ONE CASH PAYMENT, OR A LIFE ANNUITY,

Without any expense or outlay whatever beyond the ordinary Assurance Premium for the Sum Assured, which remains in tact for Policy-holder's heirs, or other purposes.

*CANADA—MONTREAL—*PLACE D'ARMES.

DIRECTORS:

DAVID TORRANCE, Esq., (D. Torrance & Co.)
GEORGE MOFFATT, (Gillespie, Moffatt & Co.)
ALEXANDER MORRIS, Esq., M.P., Barrister, Perth.
Sir G. E. CARTIER, M.P., Minister of Militia.
PETER REDPATH, Esq., (J. Redpath & Son).
J. H. R. MOLSON, Esq., (J. H. R. Molson & Bros.)
Solicitors—Messrs. TORRANCE & MORRIS.
Medical Officer—H. PALMER HOWARD, Esq., M.D
      Secretary—P. WARDLAW.
Inspector of Agencies—JAMES P. M. CHIPMAN.
              y

North British and Mercantile Insurance Company.

Established 1809.

HEAD OFFICE,   -   CANADA   -   MONTREAL.

TORONTO BRANCH:

LOCAL OFFICES, NOS. 4 & 6 WELLINGTON STREET.
Fire Department, ... R. N. GOOCH,
              Agent.
Life Department, ... H. L. HIME,
29-1y   *Agent.*

Phœnix Fire Assurance Company.

LOMBARD ST. AND CHARING CROSS,

LONDON, ENG.

Insurances effected in all parts of the World

Claims paid

WITH PROMPTITUDE and LIBERALITY.

MOFFATT, MURRAY & BRATTIE,
      Agents for Toronto,
           36 Yonge Street.
                  28-1y.

Insurance.

Canada Life Assurance Company.

CAPITAL AND CASH ASSE

OVER $2,000,000.

SUMS ASSURED

$5,000,00).

A COMPARISON of the rates of this Company others cannot fail to demonstrate the advantages, the low premiums, which, by the higher returns from investments, it is enabled to offer.

IF PREFERRED, ASSURERS NEED ONLY

PAY ONE-HALF OF EACH YEAR'S PREMIUM CASH,

during the whole term of policies on the 10 payment or for seven years on the whole life plan.

For the unpaid portion of premiums,

"NOTES" ARE NOT REQUIRED BY THIS COMPANY

so that assurers are not liable to be called upon for payment of these, nor for assessments upon them, as is the case of Mutual Companies.

Every facility and advantage which can be afforded offered by this Company.

A. G. RAMSAY, *Manager*
      E. BRADBURNE, *Agent*
3m11   Toronto St.

The Liverpool and London and Globe Insurance Company

INVESTED FUNDS:

FIFTEEN MILLIONS OF DOLLARS.

DAILY INCOME OF THE COMPANY:

TWELVE THOUSAND DOLLARS

LIFE INSURANCE,

WITH AND WITHOUT PROFITS.

FIRE INSURANCE

On every description of Property, at Lowest Remunerative Rates.

JAMES FRASER, Agent
      5 King Street
Toronto, 1868.

Briton Medical and General L Association,

with which is united the

BRITANNIA LIFE ASSURANCE COMPANY

Capital and Invested Funds,............£750,000 Stg.

ANNUAL INCOME, £220,000 STG. :

Yearly increasing at the rate of £85,000 Sterling

THE important and peculiar feature originally introduced by this Company, in applying the peculiar Bonuses, so as to make Policies payable during life, any higher rate of premiums being charged, has the success of the Briton Medical and General Policies on the Profit Scale become payable during the life of the Assured, thus rendering a Policy of Assurance of subsistence to old age, as well as a protection for family, and a more valuable security to creditors event of early death; and effectually meeting the urged objection, that persons do not themselves reap the benefit of their own prudence and forethought.

No extra charge made to members of Volunteers for services within the British Provinces.

☞ TORONTO AGENCY, 5 KING ST. WEST.

oct 17—9-1yr   JAMES FRASER.

Phœnix Insurance Company

BROOKLYN, N.Y.

PHILANDER SHAW,   STEPHEN CROWEL
      Secretary.   *Pres.*

Cash Capital, $1,000,000. Surplus, $666,416.02.
1,000,416.02. Entire Income from all sources for 1
$2,151,820.82.

      CHARLES G. FORTIER, Manager
Ontario Chambers, Toronto, Ont.

PROSPECTUS

OF THE

OMINION EXPRESS COMPANY OF CANADA

ORGANIZED UNDER THE JOINT STOCK COMPANIES' ACTS.

CAPITAL STOCK, • • • • • • $1,000,000,

In 10,000 Shares, $100 each.

is proposed to organize a DOMINION EXPRESS COMPANY, to meet the present and prospective demand for increased facilities of general transortation. It is the interest of Canadians to do their own work, and *accumulate* cash capital, and *one* of the objects of this scheme is the retention is country of the profits arising from the business done.

Express Companies obtain "four-fifths" of their business from merchants and bankers, and no reason exists why they cannot transport their own by their *own Agents, economically* and *efficiently*, and by a *union of capital* and *effort*, they hereby resolve so to do. Being thus united, and ing to it their business and influence, secures to this Company certain and complete success.

this organization, like the mail system, is to extend, under *one general management*, to all cities, towns and villages in the Dominion, and to connect parts of the United States, and being but "one Company," will secure *unity, despatch* and *accuracy*.

t is proposed to distribute the stock widely, throughout the Dominion, in limited sums, apportioned as nearly as practicable to the business of the ribers. The capital Stock of the Company to be not less than $1,000,000, in 10,000 shares of $100 each.

Ten per cent. of the stock subscribed will be required to be paid after the subscription shall have reached the sum of $250,000; and after a Charter have been obtained, of which due notice will be given to the subscribers; the subsequent calls, not exceeding *ten per cent. at any one time*, to be at convenient intervals, as the demands on the Company may require. But the aggregate of all calls to be made will, it is believed, not exceed y per cent. of the Capital Stock.

The business to be done strictly on *cash principles*. With a paying business assured from the start, by *interested* and *reliable* Stockholders, it will be seen that a small per centage *only* of the subscriptions will be required to put the Company in working order, and it is confidently and reasonably ed that the receipts will thereafter maintain and extend it. And in order to secure an equitable voice in its management; the principal commercial es will be represented at the Board, by Directors recommended by Stockholders of their own localities, who will also recommend to the Direction cal Agents, and thus secure a general influence in its management, as well as its business.

All Express enterprises, both in this country and the United States, have been decidedly successful, resulting from the profits of the business itself; aving an organization and a share list—such as are now proposed—with energy and economy in the direction, no doubt can be entertained of its satisfactory results.

With such prospects, the Merchants of the Dominion, Capitalists and others interested in the success of this enterprise, are invited to become holders.

The following shall be included in the By-Laws to be hereafter framed for the Government of the Company:

. The Company shall be known by the name or title of "THE DOMINION EXPRESS COMPANY OF CANADA."
. The Capital Stock of the Company shall be *One Million of Dollars*, divided into *Ten Thousand Shares of One Hundred Dollars each*.
. Each Shareholder shall be liable only for the amount of Stock subscribed by him, her, or them.
. The Shares of Stock of the Company shall be transferable; but no transfer shall be valid without the consent of the Directors, in writing, unless hares shall be paid up in full.
. It shall be lawful for the Stockholders, so soon as the sum of two hundred and fifty thousand dollars shall have been subscribed, to call a General ng of the subscribers, to be held at the office of the Company, in the City of Montreal, and proceed to elect nine qualified persons to be Directors Company, each of whom to be a proprietor of not less than ten Shares of Stock of the said Company, and, three of whom shall form a quorum, all the powers of the Directors. The said Directors shall also, at their first General Meeting, elect a President, Secretary, Treasurer, and General intendent or Managing Director, from amongst themselves.
. The said Directors so elected shall proceed, without delay, to frame all necessary By-laws to govern the Company, and shall have power to alter mend the same as circumstances may require.
. The Directors shall not have power either to *sell out* the said Company to any other Express Company or organization now in existence, or here. to be incorporated, or to amalgamate with any other Express Company.
. No Stockholder shall be at liberty to hold in his, her, or their name, more than one hundred shares of the Capital Stock of the said Company, at the consent of the Directors, in writing, first having been obtained.

PROVISIONAL DIRECTORS.

| MESSRS. IRA GOULD, WALTER MACFARLAN, VICTOR HUDON, | MESSRS. WM. McNAUGHTON, DUNCAN MACDONALD, JOSEPH BARSALOU, | MESSRS. ALEXANDER McGIBBON, GEORGE HEUBACH, J. T. KERBY. |

OFFICERS.

| PRESIDENT: | VICE-PRESIDENT: | TREASURER: | SECRETARY: |
| WALTER MACFARLAN. | WM. McNAUGHTON. | JOSEPH BARSALOU. | GEORGE HEUBACH. |

MESSRS. CARTIER, POMINVILLE, & BETOURNAY, SOLICITORS.   J. T. KERBY, GENERAL AGENT.

following are among the prominent firms in Montreal who have subscribed to the original Stock List at the formation of the Company:—

. Ira Gould, President Corn Exchange.
Walter McFarlan, (Messrs. Walter McFarlan & Baird)
James Donelly, Wholesale Dry Goods.
Luke Moore, (Messrs. Moore, Lemple & Hatchette).
Duncan Macdonald.
A. Shannon & Co., Wholesale Grocers.
Lewis, Kay & Co., Wholesale Dry Goods.
George Brush, Eagle Foundry.

Messrs. W. McNaughton, Messrs. Sincennes & McNaughton.
" A. W. Ogilvie & Co., Glenora Mills.
" Benning & Barsalou, Auctioneers.
" Alex. McGibbon, China House.
" T. Baillie & Co., Wholesale Dry Goods.
" Alex. Walker, Wholesale Dry Goods.
" Geo. Winks & Co., Wholesale Dry Goods, Albert Buildings.
" W. P. Ryan, M.P.
" Victor Hudon & Co., Wholesale Grocer.

Messrs. Boyer, Hudon, & Co.
" Z. Bendt, Wholesale Merchant.
" Evans & Evans, Wholesale Hardware.
" James Smith, M.P.
" Andrew Watson.
" A. Freeman & Co.
" John Rhynas.
" Cartier, Pominville & Betournay, Solicitors.
" Cassels & Cameron, Wholesale Dry Goods.
" Ferrier & Co., Wholesale Hardware.

Insurance.

BEAVER
Mutual Insurance Association.

HEAD OFFICE—20 TORONTO STREET,
TORONTO.

INSURES LIVE STOCK against death from any cause. The only Canadian Company having authority to do this class of business.

R. L. DENISON,
President.

W. T. O'REILLY,
Secretary.   8-1y-25

HOME DISTRICT
Mutual Fire Insurance Company.

Office—North-West Cor. Yonge & Adelaide Streets, TORONTO.—(UP STAIRS.)

INSURES Dwelling Houses, Stores, Warehouses, Merchandise, Furniture, &c.

PRESIDENT—The Hon. J. McMURRICH.
VICE-PRESIDENT- JOHN BURNS, Esq.
JOHN RAINS, Secretary.

AGENTS:
DAVID WRIGHT, Esq., Hamilton; FRANCIS STEVENS, Esq., Barrie; Messrs. GIBBS & BRO., Oshawa.   8-1y

---

THE PRINCE EDWARD COUNTY
Mutual Fire Insurance Company.

HEAD OFFICE.—PICTON, ONTARIO.
President, L. B. STINSON; Vice-President, W. A. RICHARDS.
Directors : H. A. McFaul, James Cavan, James Johnson, N. S. DeMill, William Delong.—Treasurer, David Barker
Secretary, John Twigg ; Solicitor, R. J. Fitzgerald.

THIS Company is established upon strictly Mutual principles, insuring farming and isolated property, (not hazardous,) in Township only, and offers great advantages to insurers, at low rates for five years, without the expense of a renewal.
Picton, June 1½, 1868.   9-1y

Hartford Fire Insurance Company.
HARTFORD, CONN.

Cash Capital and Assets over Two Million Dollars.

$2,026,220.29,

CHARTERED 1810.

THIS old and reliable Company, having an established business in Canada of more than thirty years standing, has complied with the provisions of the new Insurance Act, and made a special deposit of
$100,000
with the Government for the security of policy-holders, and will continue to grant policies upon the same favorable terms as heretofore.

Specially low rates on first-class dwellings and farm property for a term of one or more years.
Losses as heretofore promptly and equitably adjusted.
H. J. MORSE & CO., AGENTS.
Toronto, Ont.

ROBERT WOOD, GENERAL AGENT FOR CANADA
58-6m

THE AGRICULTURAL
Mutual Assurance Association of Canada.

HEAD OFFICE .... LONDON, ONT.

A purely Farmers' Company. Licensed by the Government of Canada.

Capital, 1st January, 1868 .... $220,121 25
Cash and Cash Items, over $65,000 00
No. of Policies in force 28,76

THIS Company insures nothing more dangerous than Farm property. Its rates are as low as any well-established Company in the Dominion, and lower than those of a great many. It is largely patronised, and continues to grow in public favor.
For Insurance, apply to any of the Agents, or address the Secretary, London, Ontario.
London, 2nd Nov., 1868.   12-1y

Insurance.

The Gore District Mutual Fire Insurance Company

GRANTS INSURANCES on all description of Property against Loss or Damage by FIRE. It is the only Mutual Fire Insurance Company which assesses its Policies yearly from their respective dates ; and the average yearly cost of insurance in it, for the past three and a half years, has been nearly
TWENTY CENTS IN THE DOLLAR
less than what it would have been in an ordinary Proprietary Company.
THOS. M. SIMONS,
Secretary & Treasurer.
ROBT. McLEAN,
Inspector of Agencies.
Galt, 26th Nov., 1868.   15-1y

Geo. Girdlestone,

FIRE, Life, Marine, Accident, and Stock Insurance Agent

Very best Companies represented.
Windsor, Ont. June, 1868

The Standard Life Assurance Company,
Established 1825.
WITH WHICH IS NOW UNITED
THE COLONIAL LIFE ASSURANCE COMPANY.

Head Office for Canada :
MONTREAL—STANDARD COMPANY'S BUILDINGS,
No. 47 GREAT ST. JAMES STREET.
Manager—W. M. RAMSAY.   Inspector—RICH'D BULL.

THIS Company having deposited the sum of ONE HUNDRED AND FIFTY THOUSAND DOLLARS with the Receiver-General, in conformity with the Insurance Act passed last Session, Assurances will continue to be carried out at moderate rates and on all the different systems in practice.

AGENT FOR TORONTO—HENRY PELLATT,
KING STREET.
AGENT FOR HAMILTON—JAMES BANCROFT.
6-6mos.

Fire and Marine Assurance.

THE BRITISH AMERICA
ASSURANCE COMPANY.
HEAD OFFICE :
CORNER OF CHURCH AND COURT STREETS.
TORONTO.

BOARD OF DIRECTION :
Hon G. W. Allan, M.L.C.,   A. Joseph, Esq.,
George J. Boyd, Esq ,   Peter Paterson, Esq.,
Hon. W. Cayley,   G. P. Ridout, Esq.,
Richard S. Cassels, Esq.,   E. H. Rutherford, Esq ,
         Thomas C. Street, Esq.
Governor:
GEORGE PERCIVAL RIDOUT, Esq.
Deputy Governor:
PETER PATERSON, Esq.
Fire Inspector: Marine Inspector:
E. ROBY O'BRIEN.   CAPT. R. COURKNEN.

Insurances granted on all descriptions of property against loss and damage by fire and the perils of inland navigation.
Agencies established in the principal cities, towns, and ports of shipment throughout the Province.
THOS. WM. BIRCHALL,
Managing Director.
23-1y

Queen Fire and Life Insurance Company,
OF LIVERPOOL AND LONDON,

ACCEPTS ALL ORDINARY FIRE RISKS
on the most favorable terms.

LIFE RISKS
Will be taken on terms that will compare favorably with other Companies.

CAPITAL,   •   •   •   £2,000,000 Stg.

CHIEF OFFICES—Queen's Buildings, Liverpool, and Gracechurch Street London.
CANADA BRANCH OFFICE—Exchange Buildings, Montreal.
Resident Secretary and Manager,
A. MACKENZIE FORBES,
13 St. Sacrament St., Merchants' Exchange, Montreal.
WM. ROWLAND, Agent, Toronto.   1-1y

Insurance.

The Waterloo County Mutual Fire I
Company.

HEAD OFFICE : WATERLOO, ONTARI

ESTABLISHED 1863.
THE business of the Company is divided separate and distinct branches, the
VILLAGE, FARM, AND MANUFA
Each Branch paying its own losses and its just of the managing expenses of the Company.
C. M. TAYLOR, Sec.   M. SPRINGER, M.M
J. IICOHES, Inspector.

Etna Fire and Marine Insurance Con
Dublin.

AT a Meeting of the Shareholders of this held at Dublin, on the 13th ult., it was the business of the "ETNA" should be transf "UNITED PORTS AND GENERAL INSURANCE In accordance with this agreement, the busines after be carried on by the latter Company, whi and guarantees all the risks and liabilities of th
The Directors have resolved to continue the BRANCH, and arrangements for resuming Fir rine business are rapidly approaching comple
T. W. GRI
16   )

The Commercial Union Assu
Company,

19 & 20 CORNHILL, LONDON, ENGLA

Capital, £2,500,000 Stg.—Invested over $2,

FIRE DEPARTMENT.—Insurance granted scriptions of property at reasonable rates.
LIFE DEPARTMENT.—The success of has been unprecedented—NINETY PER CE. miums now in hand. First year's premiums $160,000. Economy of management guarantee security. Moderate rates.

OFFICE—383 & 387 ST PAUL STREET, M
MORLAND, WATSON
General Agents
FRED. COLE, Secretary.
Inspector of Agencies—T. C. LIVINGS
W. M. WESTMACOTT, Agent a
10-1y

Lancashire Insurance Com

CAPITAL, · · · · · · · £2,000,

FIRE RISKS
Taken at reasonable rates of premiu
ALL LOSSES SETTLED PROMP
By the undersigned, without reference
S. C. DUNCAN-CLARK &
General Agents for O
N. W. Corner of King & Chu
25-1y   TORONTO.

Etna Fire & Marine Insurance C

INCORPORATED 1819. CHARTER PERPI

CASH CAPITAL,   -   -   -   -

LOSSES PAID IN 50 YEARS, 23,50

JULY, 1868.
ASSETS.
(At Market Value.)
Cash in hand and in Bank ....
Real Estate ....
Mortgage Bonds ....
Bank Stock ....
United States, State and City Stock, and othe
Public Securities ....

   Total ....

LIABILITIES.
Claims not Due, and Unadjusted ....
Amount required by Mass. and New Yor
   for Re-Insurance ....
                                THOS. R. W
50-6   Agent

PRINTED AT THE DAILY TELEGRAP
HOUSE, BAY ST., COR. KIN

THE CANADIAN
MONETARY TIMES
AND
INSURANCE CHRONICLE.
DEVOTED TO FINANCE, COMMERCE, INSURANCE, BANKS, RAILWAYS, NAVIGATION, MINES, INVESTMENT, PUBLIC COMPANIES, AND JOINT STOCK ENTERPRISE.

| OL. II—NO. 1 | TORONTO, THURSDAY, DECEMBER 24, 1868. | { SUBSCRIPTION. } |

Mercantile.

Financial.

PRINCIPLES OF BANKING.

(Continued.)

The function of Government in the creation of a symbolic currency is almost equally restricted. The test of value of such a currency is that of the loanable capital it represents. Now the only parties capable of deciding whether paper currencies represent an adequate amount of capital, are those parties who are to receive them. It would be very ridiculous for Government to attempt, by legislative enactment, to secure the more certain payment of bills of exchange drawn in commerce between nations. None are so able to secure such provision as the parties to them. If currencies were the representative of gold and silver only, and not (as is the fact) of all kinds of loanable property, then the functions of Government would be plain. All it would have to do would be to restrict the issue of banks to the coin in their vaults. But who shall decide whether it is proper for a bank to make a loan by an issue of its notes and credits to a party offering it a bill given for a thousand barrels of flour? Of course, those only who, from their intimate connection with the trade, commerce and industry of the country, are in a position to determine whether the purchaser of the flour will be probably able to sell the same and collect the proceeds before the maturity of his note. Government can have no such intelligence or functions as these—in fact, it does not attempt to assume any control over the greater portion of the symbolic currency in use—the credits which banks write on their books. Only a very small proportion of the transfers of property are effected by bank notes. Outside of these, the amount of currency that may be issued is left, as it should be, to the discretion of banks. The operation of natural laws will secure the conditions necessary to a perfect currency far more effectually and completely than they can possibly be secured by any act or oversight of Government.

If Government assumes to interfere with the currency, its most important function would be the restriction of loans to bills receivable soon to mature, and given for loanable property. With such provision, rigidly enforced, there never could be an inflation. But unfortunately, the action of Government is always sought in a contrary direction—to authorize an expansion, which sooner or later must be followed by a corresponding revulsion; but often not before society is so exhausted that years are required to repair the losses sustained. The Bank of England, for example, is authorized to issue notes to the amount of $75,000,000 upon the strength of having the possession of a corresponding amount of Government debt, redeemable only at the pleasure of the latter. This vast sum, although not the representative of loanable capital, exerts, from the circulation obtained for the notes issued, precisely the effect, for the time being, of so much capital. An extraordinary stimulus is given to every kind of investment and expenditure, without the addition of a penny to the means of consumption. It gradually comes to be seen that the inflation has led to the construction of too many ships and railroads; to the manufacture of too much iron and cloth; that too much money had been in-

vested in schemes which never should, and never would, have been entertained, but for the disproportion created between the instruments and means of expenditure. As soon as people get their eyes open, each one endeavors to protect himself by converting his means into money. The bank puts up its rate of interest and calls in its loans, which only serve to increase the alarm and the drain upon it for gold, and the interposition of Government has to be invoked to allow the bank to transcend its chartered powers, by making loans irrespective of the amount of means it may possess. But all this does not prevent a crisis, which drives no small proportion of the community into liquidation. With the consequent prostration of business, money becomes a drug; the rate of interest is reduced to a minimum, to stimulate its use, when the past experience of inflation and contraction is repeated with all its attendant evils, but unfortunately, without teaching any useful lesson.

Now, if the $75,000,000 issued on Government securities, had represented loanable capital, either in its vaults or in the hands of its borrowers, there could have been no currency inflation, consequently no excessive contraction. The enterprises which this sum had set in motion would have rested on a solid basis—would have measured the ability of the people to consume, and would have exerted none other than a beneficent influence in the channels of business and trade.

The amount of reserves of loanable capital necessary to be kept on hand by banks to meet the calls to which they are constantly liable is a matter of experience, rather than of theoretical calculation. It will depend very much upon the character of the loans made. As the balance of indebtedness between the banks and the public is always in favor of the former to the extent of their capital, it follows that if their loans are made to solvent parties, they can always place themselves in funds from the payment of their bills. The reserves in such case will have to be only nominal. But as improper loans will always be made, involving corresponding disturbances in industries and commerce, reserves must be maintained to considerable amounts to meet such contingencies.

As the foreign commerce of a people is quite as much to be considered in making loans, as their domestic trade, reserves should be chiefly maintained in the great entrepôts of such commerce. The rule of the New York banks, before the suspension of specie payments, was to maintain reserves in coin equal to twenty-five per cent. of their immediate liabilities. The coin held by the country banks was much less, their reserves being made up chiefly of balances against the city banks. The great majority of the country banks held an amount of coin only necessary for ordinary payments by way of change. Banks are not necessarily strong in proportion to the amount of coin they may hold, but in ratio to the amount of promises of solvent parties to pay gold on demand. But as before remarked, the amount of reserves must be a matter of experience with banks, as with merchants. When there is no Government interference, and when perfect freedom of action is accorded, reserves will always be in a proper ratio to the demands likely to be made. People have only to be left alone, to adopt the best means to given ends, whether such be the construction of a steamboat, a railroad, or any other contrivance.

ance, the object of which is to facilitate the exchange of property, or promote their own welfare. Symbolic currencies will be good just in ratio as they express the business transactions of a people. There is great probability that they will be bad just in ratio to the degree of govermental interference with them. Like all commercial contrivances —such as bills of exchange, steamships, and railways—their creation should be left entirely to the parties who are to use them.

The most perfect system of currency yet devised is that which so long prevailed in the New England States, and known as the Suffolk system. The parties to it were the banks of that section, which, without any legal enactment, agreed to make all their issues equal to gold at the commercial metropolis of those States—Boston; and to which, by necessary attraction, flowed all the currency issued that was not wanted for local purposes. With such a provision, there could not only be no excessive issues, but there was no motive to make them, as all such involved a direct loss of credit, and often of pecuniary loss. The result was that the unsecured notes of the New England banks, being always at par in one of the great monetary centers of the nation, were only at a very slight discount in every other portion of it. They were not at one-half of the discount in the city of New York, that the bills of the country banks of the latter State were, the ultimate redemption of which was fully secured by a deposit of bonds, but for the present redemption of which, at their par value in the city of New York, no provision was made. A similar system, extended to the whole country, with New York as the central point, would give the nation as good a currency as could be devised by the wisdom of man. Such a system would compel every bank, no matter where situated, to limit its issues to its capital. Such restriction is the sole condition of a perfect currency.

The laws of currency, which have been elucidated in the preceding pages, effectually dispose of the theories of Bullionists, who for every dollar of currency issued, would compel the banks to maintain in their vaults a corresponding amount coin. They overlook the vital fact that merchandise of all kinds is symbolized as a means of transferring or loaning the same, precisely as is gold, and that such currencies when issued against such merchandise, are just as valuable and as convertible as when issued against gold; and that as mediums of exchange, they perform all the functions of gold. There is the same sense in their theories, and no more, that there would be in a proposition to return to the primitive condition in which all exchanges were effected in kind.

(To be continued,)

TORONTO STOCK MARKET.

(Reported by Pellatt & Osler, Brokers.)

Business in stocks during the past week was very limited; many of the transfer books are closed, and little improvement may be expected till after the holidays.

BANK STOCK.—Buyers offer 138 for Montreal, with sellers at 138½. British would command 105 but there is none in market. Sales of Ontario occurred at 99¾, 100 and 100½. No demand for Gore at 40. Buyers offer 97½ for Quebec; no sellers under par. Molson's could be placed at 110; very limited amount in market. There were sales of City at 102½, which rate continues to be asked. No sellers of Du Peuple; buyers at 107½. Jacques Cartier is nominally worth 106½ to 107. Books of other banks closed.

DEBENTURES.—The only Canada Government security on the market is Dominion Stock, which is procurable at 105. Toronto are saleable to pay 6¾ per cent. interest. Large sales of County occurred during the week at rates to pay barely 6¼ per cent. interest.

SUNDRIES. City Gas is much sought after, but not a share has been offered in the market for weeks. The books of the Canada Permanent and Western Canada Building Societies are closed. Freehold sold at 104½ to 105, and a few shares may still be had at the latter rate. There are buyers of Montreal Telegraph at 135, and no sellers. Canada Landed Credit is offered in small amounts at 72. There are buyers of British America Assurance at 55, and sellers at 57. Mortgages are in demand to pay 8 per cent. interest. Money is readily obtainable at reasonable rates on good paper.

BANK OF ENGLAND.

The returns for the week ending the 2nd Dec., give the following results when compared with the previous week:—

Rest	£3,068,636
Decrease	25,897
Public Deposits	5,575,694
Increase	148,098
Other Deposits	18,085,878
Decrease	17,130

On the other side of the account:—

Government Securities	£15,074,874
No change.	
Other Securities	17,198,379
Increase	531,209
Notes unemployed	8,497,315
Decrease	396,785

The amount of notes in circulation is £23,510,112, being an increase of £266,857, and the stock of bullion in both departments is £18,087,448, showing a decrease of 169,189, when compared with the preceding return.

BANK OF COMMERCE.—The Directors of the Canadian Bank of Commerce have resolved to apply to Parliament for power to increase the capital stock of their institution from one million to two millions of dollars.

SALE OF STOCKS IN HALIFAX.—The following prices for Stocks were realized on the 10th, at W. M. Gray's sale of Stocks:—10 Shares Union Bank, $55; 10 do. $43: 7 do. 43.50; 15 do. $43.25; 13 do. $43; £200 Street Debenture, 5 per cent. £88 per £100; £500 do., £87 per £100; 100 shares Cape Canso Marine Railway. $2.50; 1 share Halifax Library, $6.00.

SOUND AND SENSIBLE.—In the Annual Report of the United States Secretary of the Treasury, occurs this passage:—"What is now required, as has been already intimated, are measures which will tend not only to prevent further exportation of our bonds, and in the regular course of trade to bring back to the country those that have been exported, but which will also tend to restore those important interests that are now languishing, as the result of the war and adverse legislation. The first and most important of these measures are those which shall bring about, without unnecessary delay, the restoration of the specie standard. The fiscal difficulties under which the country is labouring may be traced directly to the issue and continuance in circulation of irredeemable promises as lawful money. The country will not be really and reliably prosperous until there is a return to specie payments. The question of a solvent, convertible currency underlies all other financial and economical questions. It is, in fact, a fundamental question; and until it is settled, and settled in accordance with the teachings of experience, all attempts at other financial and economical reforms will either fail absolutely or be but partially successful. A sound currency is the life-blood of a commercial nation. If this is debased the whole current of its commercial life must be disordered and irregular. The starting point in reformatory legislation must be here. Our debased currency must be retired or raised to the par of specie, or cease to be lawful money, before substantial progress can be made with other reforms."

THE ARREST OF MR. SANCTON.—The N York *Sun* says:—Mr. George P. Sancton, l Cashier of the Commercial Bank of New Bru wick, was taken into custody on Tuesday even by Dep. Sheriff Jas. Campbell, on the charge being a defaulter to the amount of $100,0 having absconded, as alleged, on 14th of N with the above sum in his possession. The ar was made under an order of the King's Cour Supreme Court, at the suit of A. McL. Seely, President of the bank, on the affidavits of Geo Prescott, cashier, Jas. McArthur and W. L. Mag tellers, and the President, Mr. Seely. Mr. Pres swears that the accused while acting in the capa of cashier, appropriated to his own use over $10 000, for which he gave no account. Mr. McArtl swears that on 14th Nov, he gave the accused sum of $76,000 for deposit in the safe. No acco was made of the money, nor had it been deposit Mr. Magee swears that on 10th Nov. he gave accused $10,080 for deposit, but he subsequen ascertained that the money had not been ente in the book kept by the prisoner, nor deposited the vault. The accused, who appears to be ab 50 years of age, was committed in default of b He refused to see or converse with any one, a appears to be considerably shaken by his arr

GONE DOWN.—The "New England" Expr Company, after a brief but honorable career, a a loss of $20,000, has gone down.

Insurance.

FIRE RECORD.—Windsor, Dec. 12.—A fire v discovered in the store of Mr. Moore, on Sa wich street, and the store, with most of the c tents, and a residence adjoining, were destroy It was owned by Mr. Johnson, whose loss w probably reach $3,000. Johnson was insured $1,300, and Moore, whose loss would be ab $2,500, had an insurance of $1,800. Cause known.

Halifax, Dec. 10.—A house belonging to a occupied by Henry Fredericks, on the No West Arm road. No particulars.

Goderich, Dec. 11.—Grassi's blacksmith sl caught fire, and both the blacksmith and wa shop were burned to the ground with conte Also Mr. Simond's dwelling house; furnit saved. No insurance. Mr. Grassi is insure the Gore Mutual for $1,200, but this will cover the loss it is said. Cause unknown.

Shediac, N. B., Dec. 8.—The residence Joseph C. Weldon was destroyed by fire. I about $1,600.

Sherbrooke, Dec. 15.—The dwelling hous Mr. Bailey Clough, near Sawyerville, Eaton, burned to the ground. Loss about $600. insurance.

The Owen Sound *Comet* reports that the h of Mr. Claudius Ekins, Saugeen river road, to ship of Derby, was burnt by fire. The inma Mr. Wm. Little, Miss Case, and Jane Drumm a grand-child of Mr. Ekins, perished in the fla Mr. Ekins, his father, mother, wife, sister I rietta, brother George, Mr. Case, Wm. Bikell, John Dowd, were so severely burned that t recovery is doubtful.

Wellesley Township, Ont. Dec. 18.—A fire place in Riner & Hickney's woolen fact Wellesley, on Friday morning last, but fortun before it could make much headway, it was sto The loss will not be over $400 which was covered by insurance.

Halifax, Dec. —.—A house near the rai station was destroyed.

Cayuga, Dec. 15.—Saloon of Abel Y caught fire, but was saved with a loss of $75; no insurance.

Halifax, Dec. 7.—A severe storm from southeast swept over Halifax, causing a many disasters to the shipping in the harbor rwn fences, blowing over chimney tops, art unroofing houses on shore. The tinued through the night. No less than 'e schooners were seriously injured; in s having their masts, jibbooms, bow- ils and bulwarks carried away, and the e or loss stove in. The steamer Delta nto by a schooner and lost her fore-yard' corm appeared to pass over the whole it is feared that much damage was sus- vessels along the whole coast.

Thorold fire company had their annual pper and ball on Wednesday last; 150 gentlemen were present.

t. MARIA.—The barque Maria, McKen- r, from Quebec for Port Medoc, Wales, lost on the Newfoundland coast, and te crew drowned. Six of the survivors led at Halifax, N. S., on the 10th inst. i was 285 tons register, and sailed from the 5th of November, for Port Medoc, rgo of square timber, deals, staves and

DNIAL.—Wm. Richardson, representing real Assurance Company, Mr. Haldan, e Ætna, and G. Rumball & Co'., of the rrepted Captain Rowan, of the steamer ay, with a token of their appreciation duct on the occasion of that vessel being iore off Chantry Island, by which the ers were saved from a heavy loss.

a. Barclay, Curls & Co., of Greenock, unched the Lake Erie, a fine iron sail- of 950 tons register, intended for the nerican trade. The vessel has been the Canada Shipping Company of this wners of the Lake Ontario. The com- e contracted; it is said, for seven other ie vessels.—[Montreal Gazette.

R FRANCIS SMITH.—This vessel will to remain in her present position in the ring. She is considered safe till that it is said she can be got off without The loss is estimated at $8,000.

TRUCTIVE INCIDENT.—The following an actual occurrence:—In 'one of our presentative of an insurance company a merchant in the vigor of a healthy apparently highly prosperous, who was d. This gentleman listened to the made with some interest, but finally e was compelled, just then, to use his iercantile operations, but should soon take out a $10,000 policy. The agent hat his very circumstances were an ar- r that immediate protection for his ch insurance alone could secure, and alt able to give no more than $5,000 or t might prove of great benefit to them. lt the force of the reasoning; and was get rid of the agent. The result was tion for a policy of $3,000. The two former to die within ten days from a ick of fever, the latter to forward the vhich gave his widow three thousand l it was all she had.

a MUTUAL INSURANCE COMPANY.— ng is the report of the committee ap- the Board of the Victoria Mutual In- opany on the subject of establishing a insuring buildings on the line of the 'ater pipes: iance with a resolution of the Board, th inst., directing us to take such ac- might deem advisable towards the es- of a branch in this city, to meet the s (by way of insurance) of those whose re protected by the line of water pipe, port,

Act 22, Victoria Cap. 22, under which ay was incorporated, amply provides ation of its business into two branches nts, upon the following conditions:

1. That the Directors prepare a scale of risks for each department.

2. That they direct separate and distinct ac- counts to be kept.

3. That members shall only be liable for claims against the department in which they are insured, and not the one for the other.

4. That all necessary expenses incurred in the management and conducting of such departments, shall be assessed and divided between each in proportion to the amounts insured in each.

To afford complete security to policy holders for the payment of probable loss, it is the opinion of your committee that promises for insurance to the extent of $100,000 should be obtained before issuing a policy from the proposed branch.

That in lieu of cash, premium notes be ac- cepted, a small per centage of which should be paid in cash to meet the expense of management. The balance subject to assessment for the payment of loss.

That on account of the extra security of this district, afforded by the hydrants, no risk ac- cepted by the proposed branch should be reinsured in other companies; inasmuch as the money paid for premiums would probably exceed the whole amount assessable for loss in this district.

By following principally the foregoing princi- ples the Victoria, in the short space of five years, has attained a substantial position amongst in- surance companies, having issued during that time 7,153 policies, and now possessing in avail- able assets for the payment of loss, a sum exceed- ing $100,000.

It is, therefore, the intention of your committee to ascertain the views of such as are interested in the proposed object, by calling upon them without delay. (Signed,) Geo. H. Mills, T. McIlwraith, A. T. Wood, P. Carroll.

Risks to the extent of $114,000 have since been obtained.

INSURANCE COMPANIES.

The following are the Insurance Companies which have received licenses to transact the busi- ness of Insurance in the Dominion, viz.:—

I.—Canadian Companies.

The British America Assurance Company, de- posit $16,166 Cash—Fire and Inland Marine.

The Canada Life Assurance Co., $17,000 Cash— Life.

The Western Assurance Co., $17,000 Cash—Fire and Marine.

The Provincial Insurance Co., $16,666 Cash— Fire and Inland Marine,

The Agricultural Mutual Assurance Association, $12,000 Cash—Fire.

II.—British Companies.

The North British and Mercantile Insurance Co., $50,000 Cash; $100,258 Cash—Fire and Life.

The Liverpool and London and Globe Insurance Co., $50,000 Cash; $62,293 Canada 5's; $33,400 Cash—Fire and Life.

The Royal Insurance Co., $96,982 Cash; $53,- 538 Canada 5's—Fire and Life.

The Reliance Mutual Life Assurance Society, $50,000 Cash—Life.

The Imperial Insurance Company $54,993 Bri- tish 3 per cts.; $48,667 Canada 5's; $1400 Canada 6's.

The Northern Assurance Co., $97,198 Cash; $12,166 Canada 5's; $2,000 Canada 6's—Fire.

The Lancashire Insurance Co., $33,383 Cash; $13,666 Canada 5's.

The Phœnix Fire Insurance Co., $50,171 Cash; $50,126 Canada 5's—Fire.

The Commercial Union Assurance Co., $51,171 Cash; $50,613 Canada 5's—Fire.

The Life Association of Scotland $150,000 Cash —Fire and Life.

The Standard Life Assurance Co., $150,000 Cash —Life.

The Queen Insurance Co., $50,000 Cash; $51,- 100 Canada 5's—Fire and Life.

The Edinburgh Life Assurance Co., $150,515 Cash—Fire and Life.

The London Assurance Corporation, $150,600 British 3 per cts.—Life.

The Scottish Provincial Assurance Co., $50,171 Cash; $50,446—Fire and Life.

The London and Lancashire Insurance Co., $50,- 171 Cash—Life.

The Briton Medical and General Life Associa- tion, $100,343—Life.

The Star Life Assurance Society, of England, $100,643.86 Cash—Life.

The Guardian Insurance Company, of England, $100,643.86 cash—Fire and Life.

III.—American Companies.

The Home Insurance Company of New Haven, Conn., $70,000 U.S. 5-20's—Fire.

The Ætna Insurance Company, of Hartford, Conn., $1,490 Cash; $48,510 Bank Stock—Fire.

The Hartford Insurance Company, of Hartford, Conn., $130,000 U.S. 5-20's—Life.

The Phœnix Mutual Life Insurance Co., of Hartford, Conn., $70,000 U.S. 5-20's—Life.

The Connecticut Mutual Life Insurance Co., of Hartford, Conn., $140,000 U.S. 5-20's—Life.

The Travelers' Insurance Co., of Hartford, Conn., $140,000 U.S. 5-20's—Life and Accident.

The Ætna Life Insurance Co., of Hartford, Conn., $140,000 U.S. 5-20's—Life.

The New York Life Insurance Co., $75,000 U.S. 5-20's—Life.

The Atlantic Mutual Life Insurance Co., of Albany, N. Y., $50,000 U.S. 10-40's—Life.

The Equitable Life Insurance Co., of New York, $75,000 U.S. 5-20's—Life.

The Union Mutual Life Insurance Co., of Maine, 50,000 U.S. 6's of '81—Life.

MONTREAL FIRE BRIGADE.

We believe the Fire Department of no city in America is so economically managed as that of Montreal. Certainly none is more efficient; there- fore, to speak commercially, we have the best article at the lowest price. This is no doubt due to the perfection of discipline in the department, and the admirable general working of the fire-alarm telegraph. Strong indeed must be the wind, in- flamable the materials, and nearly absolute the want of water, if a fire should now be allowed to gain such head as to become serious. This being the case, let us see how we compensate the members of this efficient fire brigade of ours, as compared with the wages paid in, say, five of the principal cities of the Union. The subjoined figures show the annual cost per head of the fire departments, respectively, of the following cities:—

	Cost.	Population.
Chicago	$276,720	250,000
Detroit	63,000	85,000
Louisville	82,000	140,000
St. Louis	137,000	250,000
Baltimore	66,000	250,000
Montreal (gold)	18,125	120,000

From this it will be seen that Chicago pays $1.10 per head; Baltimore, $0.27; Detroit, $0.74; Louisville, $0.59; St. Louis, $0.55; and Montreal only $0.15, equal to $0.33 U. S. funds. So that our most efficient fire department is maintained at a rate of only about one-fifth of the cost of the fire department of Chicago; and the difference of rate between that of Montreal and the fire depart- ments of the four other cities of the Union which we have cited our readers can calculate for them- selves; but in every instance, except Baltimore, it is very great indeed.

The difference, too, between the rate of pay of the members of the fire brigade of the American cities just enumerated, and those of the Montreal fire brigade, is also striking. Our fire brigade has 16 men at $300, or $408 in U. S. funds; 9 men at $400, or $544 U. S. funds; 9 men at $500, or $680 U. S. funds; whilst the American firemen receive $1,000 each, and the drivers and horsemen $924 each.—Witness.

THE CANADIAN MONETARY TIMES
AND
INSURANCE CHRONICLE.

THE publishers will have the pleasure of sending this week to each Canadian subscriber of THE MONETARY TIMES, the first number of the REAL ESTATE JOURNAL, which will be sent regularly in future every fortnight, the subscription price being included in the $2.00 charged for THE MONETARY TIMES. In these days of cheap newspapers the publishers find this step to be necessary in order to keep pace with the times. The business public may now get the two papers for the price of one—both of which is worth more than the subscription price to any business man.

BANKING.
THE CANADIAN MONETARY TIMES AND INSURANCE CHRONICLE is the only paper in the Province which makes banking a specialty.

INSURANCE.
It is the only insurance journal in Canada. Every one who desires to know the character and standing of the Insurance Companies doing business in Canada can only get the information in its columns.

MINING.
It is the only journal which keeps regular correspondents in the principal mining districts, and affords strictly reliable information respecting mining matters.

COMMERCE.
Everything of interest in trade and commerce is carefully noted in the markets of Toronto, Montreal and the Maritime Provinces, making it more valuable in this department than purely commercial journals.

STOCKS AND SHARES.
The market prices of stocks, shares and debentures of every class in which our people are interested, as quoted in the centre of trade, are always to be found in the Stock and Share list.

PUBLIC COMPANIES.
The proceedings of all public companies in the country are reported, including banks, insurance, railway, mining, and other companies, building societies, &c., thus affording the only complete record of the doings of public companies to be obtained in the Province.
These and other features make it invaluable to the Banker, Merchant, Insurance Agent, Miner, Capitalist, Manufacturer, and all business men.

SUBSCRIPTION PRICE—The MONETARY TIMES and REAL ESTATE JOURNAL, only $2.00 a year in advance.
Address,   THE MONETARY TIMES,
                        Toronto. Ont.

☞ The Publishing Office of THE CANADIAN MONETARY TIMES AND INSURANCE CHRONICLE is removed to No. 60, Church Street, 4 doors north of Court Street.

The Canadian Monetary Times.

THURSDAY, DECEMBER 24, 1868.

MR. WILMOT, OF NEW BRUNSWICK, ON THE CURRENCY!

This gentleman has responded to a series of questions on the currency by a committee of the House of Commons, and has published his replies in the New Brunswick papers. They seem to have excited some considerable attention, partly from their bold and confident assertions, and partly from the semilogical air which seems to pervade them, in which, to say the truth, there are as many fallacies and foolish fancies covered up as it has ever been our lot to meet within the same limits.

These fallacies and fancies are all branches of one fundamentally false notion, namely, that it is not desirable, or necessary, to have any fixed standard of value. Mr. Wilmot does not believe that a dollar should mean the same thing to-morrow as it does to-day, and he would have a currency which would fluctuate, not only in amount, but in value, with the necessities of the government, and the circumstances of the times.

It is somewhat cool, we must confess, at this time of day, for a gentleman professing to have financial ability to denounce the monetary system of Canada because it rests on a gold basis, and deliberately to advocate an irredeemable currency. When universal experience tells us that gold and silver are the only solid basis of monetary operations ; when writers on finance, almost without exception, however widely they may differ on other matters, agree in the same conclusion ; when the trade between every nation under heaven, is, and always has been, conducted on the same principle ; when countries which have been forced by pressure of circumstances to deviate from this standard have invariably suffered such intolerable evils as to be willing to endure the most painful sacrifices in order to reach the path of safety again, it is idle to talk of a fixed price for gold being a relic of barbarism.

The man who can ascribe panics to this cause rather than to extravagance an l overtrading is not to be reasoned with. Throughout the whole of Mr. Wilmot's answers the notion crops up again and again, that the true remedy for financial evils is plenty of irredeemable paper money. He does not seem to have the slightest notion that a country, at this time of day, cannot isolate itself from the rest of the world, and, as respects other countries, may run into debt just as an individual may with other individuals. When a merchant runs into debt, all goes along smoothly enough so long as his creditors are willing to trust him. His expenditure may be over-running his profits by thousands a year, yet if he can only keep up his credit, and his correspondents continue to supply him with goods, he finds no difficulty in getting along. We have had plenty of examples of this kind of thing in every commercial community, and the end is invariably the same, namely, a break up of credit, a stoppage of supplies, an insisting on payments, law suits, bankruptcy, and poverty. The crash is a painful affair, and causes misery to the individual, to his creditors, his bankers, his family, and everybody that had any relations with him.

Now supposing this gentleman, in the midst of his bankruptcy, to reason in this manner : —What scandalous laws and customs these are which compel a man to pay his debts !— If I had never been pressed to *pay*, all would have been right.—Why could not my paper be kept afloat, as usual ? Why could not things go on smoothly, as they did before : It would have been far better for all parties. I was a good customer to the foreign merchant. I was a capital customer to the neighbouring tradesmen. All of them I paid paper, and paper answered their purpose well. What madness then it was to bring this crash. It is not I who am to blame is my creditors, who are such fools as to turned into miserable dirty gold.

Stripped of specious phraseology, it is cisely thus that Mr. Wilmot reasons respecting the panics which sweep periodically the commercial world. Everybody that studied them is aware that they are always preceded by a period of extravagance, of spending, recklessness and folly exactly responding to the overspending of an individual trader, and that the panics are just same thing to the country as stopping ment is to a merchant. It is the idlest sense to blame the gold basis as the cause panic, just as it is idle nonsense of trader to blame his creditors for his stoppage. The panic is the natural result of the extravagance, and its counterpart is to be found over and over again in private life. No speak of a trader, how often it is the case a private individual spends more than his come, gets into debt, his creditors press and he is sued ; after a world of trouble anxiety he manages to get time, and by of severe economy comes round again awhile, and pays all he owes.

Now the trade of a country, taken whole, with other countries, is precisely lagous to the dealings of an individual individuals. When the balance of trade against it, continuously, from excessive reign importations, it simply indicates extravagance, overspending, and getting into The sure result is tightness of money, as it is with any man who spends more his income. People of that sort are always "hard up ;" and a country may be "hard and must be when extravagance and 'pending produce their natural fruit.

Mr. Wilmot's remedy for this state of things is to issue more paper, which is precisely the same as for a spendthrift to nore of his promissory notes to conceal creditors, if they are so simple as to them. Common sense says the proper nedy would be to economise and work hard. Let the country produce more and spend —that would bring things round by doubt. In private life this would be sally conceded, but in dealing with national affairs people are apt to get mystified cave common sense altogether.

It cannot, however, be too often repeated that the laws of credit and finance are able and irresistible. A nation can no scape their operation than a mere *Promises to pay*, if never fulfilled,

o matter who is the promisor. Mr.
would have the country flooded with
)aper containing promises which are
eant to be fulfilled, and he is insane
to suppose that such rubbish would
extravagance and overspending from
ag their natural results.

course does not say all this in ex-
rms, but no one can read his answers
/ without perceiving that this is the
t of them.

all notice other points in these an-
· and by.

EAT WESTERN RAILWAY.

ur seems to delight in paying its res-
the Great Western Railway. No
s one story exhausted than another
take its place. The last is a state-
the effect that the New York Cen-
e offered to lease the Great Western.
nyard has addressed a letter on the
to the President of the Stock Ex-
n New York in which he denies that
offer has been received by the Great

---

cricut Mutual Life.—The general
: this Company for] Ontario has been re-
this City. It is under the management
). L. Sills. Mr. Fee will have the local

A DO'C GOLD DISTRICT.

(From our own Correspondent).

BELLEVILLE, Dec. 21, 1868.

to the existence of gold in the rocks or
any particular district, the most advan-
mode of separating the metal from the
neral substances in which it is contained,
which it is combined, is the subject which
: greatest importance to the miner. I
refore, in the absence of other matter,
few of the processes by which sanguine
: propose to enrich the fortunate holders
nd silver claims, and themselves. As the
Stephens flux is that which has been
into the world with the greatest flourish
ets, I shall pass it first in review, giving
account of the flux itself, and detailing
rience of its working in this quarter.
ccount given by the proprietors of the
· of the flux is shortly as follows: A cer-
onel Stephens, (who is represented as
gnorant both of practical mining and of]
gical science, and therefore a most unlikely
: solve a problem which has taxed the
of the ablest scientific men of many
ns,) while confined in a Southern prison
le war of secession, heard much conversa-
ing his fellow prisoners respecting the
ef separating the gold from the sulphur-
ich it is s> often contained. These con-
s excited a strong desire in his mind to
le profitable method of extracting the
metal from its baser accompaniments.
release, he happened to get possession
l quantity of this, to him, unknown ma-
ld took it to Mr. Guild, an assayer in
whom he requested to make an assay
: any gold-bearing ore he might have in

---

his possession. Mr. Guild accordingly smelted
with a portion of this flux a sample of ore which
he knew to yield by "mint assay" $300 to the
ton, and obtained therefrom no less a result than
$1,400 per ton. Suspecting some error, as well
he might, the assayer repeated the process, and
again obtained the same result, $1,400 per ton.

The Colonel · then had a furnace erected, in
which he treated 2,500 pounds of ore, which had
never yielded by other processes more than $22
per ton; but from which he extracted at a single
melting, gold to the value of $539.58, or at the
rate of $431 per ton. This is his own account;
but there are not wanting those who say that the
flux used on that occasion was heavily "salted."

The experience we have had of the flux and its
vendors is as follows: Early in the present year,
two gentlemen from Wisconsin, Messrs. Jones and
Robbins, visited the district, and took from a
mine in the township of Hungerford a quantity
of pyritiferous ore, which they took to Boston, and
had it assayed by Mr. Guild, who gave them a
return of $40 per ton. On the faith of this they
returned to Canada, purchased the mine, put up
reduction worl a according to plans, etc., furnished them by the Stephens Company, who
agreed to send one of the partners to instruct
them in the whole process of reduction by their
method. When the works were finished, one of
the Boston gentlemen came accordingly, and under his directions they smelted about 'three tons
of ore, from which, instead of the pure metal they
expected, they got about a ton and a half of
"matt," i. e., a combination of crude metallic
matter which might or might not contain
gold as one of its component parts, but
in which it was quite as intangible as in
its original matrix. On being requested to
go on and complete the process, the Boston
man refused to do so, telling them that it
would be necessary for them to send the matt to
Boston to be refined, offering to do it for ten
cents on the dollar of gold value. This they refused to do; and so the matter stands between
them and the Boston Company at present.
Messrs. Jones and Robbins have since dispatched
a portion of said matt and also of the crude ore to
Swansea, Wales, to be reduced, so that its value
may be tested in a satisfactory manner.

The readers of THE MONETARY TIMES will of
course draw their own inferences from the above
related facts. My own I must candidly say, are
not very favorable to the flux as a medium for the
economical reduction of gold ores, or to the
straightforwardness of its "proprietors." Even if
it were all they assert, it could not, at its present
price, be applied to the working of poor ores, as
the expense attending its use could not be less
than $25 to $30 per ton.

The Richardson Company have had another lot
of twenty-five tons of their ore reduced, the produce of which, though not yet melted down, is
estimated by their manager at $150, or $6 per
ton. Another lot, which was being operated upon
at the time his message was sent off, promises,
from the appearances of the amalgam which was
forming, to give a better result than the foregoing.
· The mine at Mallorytown still continues to
give good assay results. · The machinery is rapidly approaching completion. The building is
ready-for its reception, and the owners expect to
be able to start work as soon as the spring sets in.

SILVER ON LAKE SUPERIOR.—Mr. Thomas
Macfarlane has assayed the silver ores from the
veins discovered by him at Mhunder Cape last
summer, and we are authorized to state that the
result of his assay is most satisfactory, showing a
result of more than 1,900 ounces of silver to the
ton of ore. The samples assayed were carefully
taken under the supervision of Professor Dawson
as exhibiting a fair average of the productive portion of the vein at Thunder Case. Similar samples have been sent for assay to an assayer in the
United States, the details of which assay, as well
as Mr, Macfarlane's, will shortly be published.

PEAT.—An American Company has been formed
in the State of Connecticut for the extraction and
manufacture of peat after the process patented in
Canada and the United States by Mr. Aubin, of
Montreal. The capital of the Company is $250,-
000, in which the patent right goes in for $125,-
000. Mr. A. Hibbard, of Montreal, is one of the
directors, and Mr. Aubin consulting engineer of
the Company. Three other companies under the
same patents will, we understand, begin or continue
operations in Lower Canada, one at Sorel, one at
Valleyfield, and another at Beloeil.

—On or about the 15th day of January next,
S. P. Mansfield of Detroit, Alex. Dearborn, and
G. B. Nichols of Boston, J. B. Hills of Newton,
Mass., and J. W. W. Ward of Ottawa, will petition the Lieutenant Governor in Council to incorporate the "McNab Iron Company," whose
purpose is the mining for iron and other metals,
and the washing and smelting of ores in the township of McNab, county of Renfrew, with a nominal capital of $50,000; stock subscribed, $30,000;
and the amount to be paid in before granting the
charter, $10,000, to be invested in mineral lands
held by trustees for the company.

Railway News.

GREAT WESTERN RAILWAY.—Traffic for week
ending Dec. 4, 1868.

Passengers	$30,825 34
Freight and live stock	35,826 42
Mails and sundries	2,284 45
	$68,936 21
Corresponding Week of '67	67,934 86
Increase	$1,001 35

NORTHERN RAILWAY.—Traffic receipts for week
ending Dec. 19, 1868.

Passengers	$2,302 55
Freight	5,296 16
Mails and Sundries	291 90
Total Receipts for week	$7,890 62
Corresponding week 1867	6,385 61
Increase	$1,504 98

THE INTERCOLONIAL RAILWAY.—The Railway
Commissioners have issued the following notice :
—"The Commissioners appointed to construct the
Intercolonial Railway, give public notice that they
intend to let four sections of the line at once.

"Sections Nos. 1 and 2 embrace about 40 miles
from a junction with the Grand Trunk Railway,
near Riviere Du Loup, and each section will be
about 20 miles in length.

"Section No. 3 will be about 26 miles in length,
and between the east side of the Restigouch,
River to near Dalhousie in New Brunswick.

"Section No. 4 will be about 24 miles in. length
and lies between Amherst and River Phillip in
Nova Scotia.

"Plans and profiles, with specifications and
terms of contract will be exhibited at the offices
of the Commissioners in Ottawa, Riviere du Loup,
Dalhousie, St. John and Halifax, on and after the
11th January, 1869, and sealed tenders addressed
to the Commissioners of the Intercolonial Railway
will be received at their office in Ottawa, up to 4
o'clock on the 8th February, 1869.

"Tenders will shortly be called for other section
of the line as soon as the plans are sufficiently
advanced."

The Commissioners are to assemble at St. John,
N. B., on the 29th instant, where Mr. Fleming,
Intercolonial Engineer, is to meet them. The
Commissioners intend to make a local examination
of the portions for which tenders will be asked on
Monday.

About 50 miles are to be put under contract,

part of which is in each Province. It is divided into four sections, so that only four tenders can be accepted. Tenders will be addressed to the Commissioners here. The Commissioners will not decide, but will recommend to the Privy Council the tenders to be accepted.

The Commissioners have made the following appointments:—C. S. Ross, of Kingston, Secretary; J. B. Martel, of Quebec, Assistant Secretary; Wm. Wallace, of Simcoe, Accountant.

—It is reported that Mr. Ross and the Great Western Railway Company have come to an agreement for the liquidation of the debt due to the Canadian Government by the road.

PEAT MAKER.—*Le Pays* says that a peat-making machine, the invention of Mr. Aubin, was put into operation at Sorel and Valleyfield last summer, and worked so satisfactorily that some American capitalists are about to form companies to develop the new industry. One of these companies is about to be organized for the State of Connecticut, and will have a capital of $25,000, of which amount $10,000 will be paid for the patent. Mr. Ashley Hibbard has been elected one of the directors, and Mr. Aubin, consulting engineer of this company.

THE PLATTSBURGH AND WHITEHALL ROAD—MASSAWIPPI RAILWAY—MISSISQUOI CENTRE ROUTE.—We see by the Plattsburgh *Republican* that the grading for the Whitehall and Plattsburgh Railway is nearly completed from Fort Henry to Ticonderoga, and the rails about to be laid down. This new route along the Western bank of Lake Champlain will give Montreal still another direct line of communication to New York, and by 1869, there will therefore be no less than three in operation.

WOODEN RAILWAYS.—Mr. Hemming, M. P. P. for Drummond and Arthabaska, who has a Wooden Railway project on foot, for connecting the back towns of his own County with the Grand Trunk Railway, has been to New York State to see the Clifton Wooden Railroad, and in a letter describing his visit, says :—

"There was no appearance of the wheels cutting into the rails, even at the sharpest curves, neither did I find a single rail that had the appearance of being crushed. In fact the rails were so level and smooth that I walked the whole distance on the rail itself, at a pretty smart pace, and I have no pretension to being a "Blondin." We arrived at the train a little before sundown, which consisted of a ten ton locomotive, made expressly for the line—four trucks, carrying between five and six tons of iron ore each, and a car-load of lumber; the whole-train weighing between forty and fifty tons. I should add that one of the trucks containing the ore was front of the engine. We now started in good earnest at a rate of about twenty miles an hour, and soon came to a part of the road which was nearly all supported on trestlework, there being no less than five viaducts, varying from 124 to 400 feet in length, and from 25 to 35 feet from the level of the ground, in a distance of half a mile. Imagine my surprise, when I found that the engine driver on arriving at this trestlework, so far from slackening his speed, actually increased it to thirty miles an hour!

The grading of course is the same as for an iron, except that stiffer grades can be ascended on the wooden road. The ties are of the ordinary description, but are not squared on any side, and on the Clifton road are placed at the usual distance of three feet apart, except on the trestles, where there are three ties to every two yards. In future, however, Mr. Hurlburt proposes to put the three ties to every two yards, as he proposes running heavier engines. The rails on the Clifton road are of maple, six inches by four ; Mr. Hurlburt intends in future to alter their shape a little without increasing the quantity of timber, making them three and a half inches on top, by seven inches deep, so as to be better adapted to the increased weight of engines, (fourteen tons instead of

ten.) Notches are cut in the round ties to such a depth as to keep the bottom of the rail about two inches from the ground after the road is ballasted, and the rail projects sufficiently above the notched tie to allow the flange of the wheel to pass. The rails are fastened to the ties by a couple of hardwood wedges, driven in opposite directions on the outside of the rail, within the notch. This has the effect of making the whole superstructure one solid mass without the addition of any spikes or pins. In making the curves the rail itself is bent to the required shape, so that there is no angularity whatever in the line of rails. The trestles are of the simplest description. They consist of two upright sticks of square timber immediately under the rails, let into a transverse stick, which are braced to the sticks of timber laid lengthwise from one trestle to another, immediately under the line of rails in each direction. This is further supported by a similar stick of timber at each side, from the head of the trestle to the base, in a slanting direction, the whole of which is let into a squared log at the base. The wooden rail is not, I believe a new invention, but Mr. Hulbert has succeeded in making it available without using a particle of iron in the whole structure, and has, moreover, demonstrated that such railways can be used for long distances at a moderate cost, and this through a country where an iron line, as ordinarily constructed, would be practically an engineering impossibility. Mr. Hulbert says that he is willing to contract to lay the superstructure of a wooden railway of his own improved construction at the rate of fifteen hundred dollars, American currency, a mile where maple and hemlock can be obtained at reasonable rates."

THE GOVERNMENT AND THE TELEGRAPH.

The discussion in England, both in and out of Parliament, in favor of the government controlling the telegraphy by buying up all the existing lines in that country, has extended to the United States and the government at Washington is urged, in certain quarters, to place the telegraph system under the management of the Postmaster General by similar means. It seems to us about as reasonable for the government to undertake the purchase and management of all the railways as all the telegraph lines in the country. The one kind of enterprise being not dissimilar to the other. That a government steps out of its legitimate sphere when it embarks in any such business can not be denied, while there are grave objections to government interference with the telegraph apart from the mere question of principle. In a country governed by parties as this is, it will never do to have the government of the day controlling the means of telegraph communication, and the same argument applies to England, where it has been already advanced with convincing effect, and inasmuch as party spirit runs higher here than there the danger would be correspondingly greater. The telegraph would, it may be accepted as a certainty, be used as a political machine by the party in power, and this of itself is sufficient to condemn government interference with it. There is no knowing how far the rights of the press and the people might be trampled upon in this particular by unscrupulous partizans in office, and consequently they should never be invested with the power for mischief which privileges of this kind would give them.

The advocates of the proposed scheme will, before much progress is made towards the desired end, have to show that the existing telegraph companies have failed to meet the wants of the people, and are, moreover, incapable of meeting them. Further, it will be also incumbent upon them to prove that the government will be better enabled to meet these requirements than the telegraph companies, and that there would be no drawbacks or inconveniences to the public to counterbalance any advantages arising from govern-

mental administration. That the telegraph companies have a stronger incentive to improvement in everything connected with their business than the government would have is obvious, and enterprise they have shown in the past is a guarantee for the future. The English telegraph companies have been fully as active as those of the United States in their efforts to improve, extend and cheapen telegraphic communication. In 1851 insulation by means of gutta percha was adopted and in 1857, and again in 1862, further improvements in insulation were effected. In 1858 Hughes' "type printers" were introduced, and in 1863, Caselli's fac-simile telegraph, while in the same year, printing instruments and "Wheatstone's automatic system," as also Hawath's system of working without wires were tried. In this country, the Atlantic and Pacific, the Franklin and other lines worked in opposition to the Western Union Co. are being rapidly extended and in proportion as their business increases charges for the transmission of messages are reduced. Competition is the life of trade, and people should encourage it in the business of telegraphing as much as in anything else. The would, of course, be an end to this if the government monopolized the wires, and whether government employees did their work thoroughly or the reverse, there would be no redress, and improvements travel slowly through official channels while red tape, in this country as well as elsewhere, interposes a vexatious bar to progress. *Albion.*

CONTRACT.—An exchange says that Messrs. Walter and Frank Shanley have contracted with the State of Massachusetts to build the Hoosac tunnel on the Troy and Boston Railway. It is be four and a half miles long and has been partially completed, but the company which attempted it failed to carry it through. Messrs. Shanley have taken the contract $5,000,000.

NIAGARA SHIP CANAL—The Niagara Ship Canal was brought up in the United States House of Representatives on Monday, and made a special order of the day for the 11th prox. by a vote of 109 to 40. Some members voted for the consideration of the bill out of good-will to the mover, but the vote was so strong that the friends of the measure believe it can be carried through. The bill provides the work shall be done as a military and commercial necessity by the Government, under the direction of the Secretary of War; that it shall begun within one year after the passage of the act and finished as speedily as possible, and that the control of it shall be retained by the United States. The engineer's estimate as to the cost of the work is about $12,000,000.

—The preliminary survey of the route for wooden railway, from Sherbrooke, Q., eastward has been commenced by Robinson Oughtred.

ONTARIO LEGISLATION.

Prior to the adjournment of the Ontario Legislature the following bills passed a second reading:—

No. 174, to grant certain powers to the Ontario Farmers' Mutual Insurance Company.

No. 84, to incorporate the Ontario Trust and Investment Company.

No. 88, to incorporate the Presque Isle and Belmont Railway Company.

No. 108, to incorporate the Simcoe and Muskoka Railway Company.

No. 109, to incorporate the Norfolk Railway Company.

No. 100, to amend the Act to incorporate the Port Whitby and Port Perry Railway Company.

No. 72, to amend and confirm the charter of the Ottawa and Gloucester Road Company.

No. 95, to incorporate the Mutual Fire Insurance Company of Hamilton.

No. 120, to incorporate the Caledonia Manufacturing and Smelting Company.

The following passed its third reading :

112, to amend the Act passed in the 28th respecting the granting of charters of intion to manufacturing, mining and other ies.

ng the bills, assented to by the Governor -An Act for the incorporation of the Ontario Life Assurance Company. An Act to exhe '36 sec. of Hamilton Debenture Act of ad to legalize the application of the rates y the City of Hamilton under the By-law to in that section.

Law Report.

INSURANCE—FORFEITURE—WAIVER. — ent case of the Supreme Court of Iowa, owing judgment was given:

here a policy for insurance provides that sk of fire to the building insured shall be d by a change of occupation or other means the control of the insured, without the consent of the insurers, the policy "shall '—this condition being inserted for the of the insurers—they may dispense with nee therewith, or waive a forfeiture of the neurred by a breach of the condition, and preclude themselves from setting up the m, or such breach thereof, as a defense to n for a loss subsequently occurring. And pensation or waiver need not be in writing ided on any new consideration.

y acts, declarations, or course of dealing insurers, with notice of the facts consti- breach of a condition in the policy, re- g and treating the policy as still in force, lling the insured to regard himself as still d thereby, will amount to a waiver, of a re by reason of such breach, and prevent rers from setting up the same as a defense ied for a subsequent loss.

local agent for a foreign insurance com- ithorised to effect insurances, and entrust- the blank policies of the company, with y to fill up, countersign, and issue them, tes of premium, give consent of the com- change of occupation and risk, assignment ies, and other things which by the the policy require such consent, and to slides in his discretion for increase of risk causes is to be regarded as the general the company, authorised to transact the of insurance for them at the place of his and has power, in the absence of a limi- his authority, known to those with whom to waive forfeitures of policies, by reason es of conditions therein, and to dispense a conditions, and the acts and declarations gent, recognizing and treating a policy as subsisting, with knowledge of facts con- a breach of its conditions, will be bind- e insurers.

onsent by the insurers to the occupation sured building for a certain manufactory, ith it a consent to the keeping and use on ises of any article necessary to the manu- r commodity used therein, although the f such articles without the written con- ne insurers is expressly prohibited in the And such consent to the occupation for nfacturer operates to waive or dispense prohibition in the policy.

ere the agent of the insurers, after a change nupation of the insured building, involv- crease of risk, consented to the continu- he policy, on condition that an iron door put into the building, but without limit- pecific time within which this should be insured was entitled to a reasonable time the door, and its being put in was not a prevelent to the continuance of the And if, after the exercise of reasonable to get the door put in, but before it was in in, the building was destroyed by fire, ers cannot resist payment of the loss on id of the door not having been put in.

JETTISON—LIABILITY OF INSURER.—If goods are thrown overboard in order to save a vessel from some danger, there arises a right on the part of the owner of these goods to claim general average from the owners of the ship, freight, and of the rest of the cargo—that is, the owner of the goods jetti- soned having been deprived of his goods for the benefit of the owners of the rest of the cargo and of the ship, is entitled to claim from these latter compensation for the loss thus sustained. The owner of the jettisoned goods does not recover the whole of the value of his goods, as it is but right that he, as well as others, should contribute to make good the loss. All the owners of ship, freight and cargo, including the owners of the jettisoned goods, pay in proportion to the value they had at stake when the jettison took place.

In Dickinson v. Jardine, 16 W. R. 1169, goods had been properly jettisoned, and the ship and cargo had consequently come safe to port, and were therefore liable to a claim for general average. The jettisoned goods were insured, and their owner (the plaintiff), instead of first claiming payment of the general average to which he was undoubtedly entitled, and then claiming from the underwriters the amount of his actual loss, claimed directly from the underwriters the whole value of the goods, and contended that it was for the under- writers, and not for him, to obtain payment of the general average. The underwriters refused to do this, and argued that although they were liable to pay the whole loss actually suffered, they were not bound to pay more, and that the plaintiff must obtain payment of the general average contribution for himself; and that the underwriters were only liable for the amount of loss that remained after deducting the amount so due to the plaintiff, as that was really the amount of his loss.

It was held by the Court of Common Pleas that the plaintiff was entitled to recover directly from the underwriters the whole value of the goods, and that it was for the underwriters to obtain payment of the general average.

There seems to have been no reported case in the English courts which decided this point, al- though there were several American authorities upon the question. Bovill, C. J., cites a passage from Phillips on Insurance, to the following effect: —"It is not a condition that the assured on goods must claim contribution by the other parties for a jettison before he can demand indemnity from his underwriters. He may demand it of them in the first instance." The Court decided in accordance with this passage, which now, therefore, correctly states the English law on the subject. We believe it has generally been the practice in London to consider the underwriters in such circumstances as those in Dickinson v. Jardine liable only for the actual loss caused by jettison after debiting the owner of the jettisoned goods with the amount due for the general average contribution. This is, however, quite opposed to the general principle of insurance law. and although it may be a con- venient way of settling accounts between insurers and insured, it can have no legal force unless per- haps an unvarying custom to this effect could be proved. It is, however, of course competent to underwriters to insert in their policies an express stipulation limiting their liability in these cases, and there is no legal objection to such a course.

Commercial.

Montreal Correspondence.

(From our own Correspondent.)

Montreal, Dec. 15, 1868.

Our river is nearly frozen across, and all traffic has ceased except such as comes through the Vic- toria Bridge. We now see the importance of that vast, though expensive, structure. Our com- munication with the States and the south side of the river remain unbroken; usually at this period, till the ice bridge took, all connection with the op- posite side ceased, or was carried on by canoes at

very considerable risk to life and property. The same as with the Grand Trunk, we every year more and more appreciate the great advantages we derive from it; true we have paid rather dearly for our whistle, but now we could not do without it.

Our produce market remains very quiet, and flour has not materially changed from my last week's quotations. The sales are merely for local wants, nor do we now look for any export trade. The Grand Trunk Railroad brings us down our necessary supplies, and all shipped goes direct to Portland, so that we in Montreal have not the handling of it. Grain is nominal in price for all descriptions, and the same remark applies to provisions.

In my last week's letter to you I gave a short resume of the dry goods trade. Now I will give you a sketch of the grocery market for the fall season:

GROCERIES—The trade generally during the fall has been satisfactory. Some of our large jobbing firms have been operating beyond their means, and forcing goods off to all sorts of buyers in the West; others, not content with a good healthy business, have speculated in gold and other tempting things, and the consequence has been that some of our leading jobbers have gone down, but this by no means shows anything wrong in the general business. On the contrary, greater caution has been exercised than usual, and the losses have been lighter.

CHEMICALS have sold largely but at almost a nominal profit: this is owing to the large quantity, especially of soda ash, sent here on consignment, and therefore forced off at any price that will clear cost, thus leaving the importers a small chance of making a profit. Prices have ruled low.

COFFEE—Owing to the low prices which have ruled during the last few months, a considerable business has been done, but I doubt if sales have been satisfactory to importers.

FISH have sold freely during the fall, and prices have ruled high; the catch generally has been light and consequently our supplies have been light. The fish market here is very much regu- lated by the price of pork, and when that is high the price of salted fish always rules proportionately high. The exception has been in dry cod, of which there has been a good supply, and prices are rather easier. Of good mackerel there are none on the market, and the stock of fish gen- erally is light.

FRUIT (imported)—The result to importers has been disastrous as regards raisins, but this has been the experience of the last two years. Our merchants have steadily over-imported. This year it was considered that the comparative failure of green fruit here would justify a larger import than usual, but such has not been the case, and importers have been the losers. In currants on the contrary an active business has been done at remunerative rates.

In NUTS, SARDINES, &c., the usual amount of business has been done at fair prices.

MOLASSES—The business in this article is mostly regulated by the price of butter. This fall the price of molasses has ruled very low, and that of butter very high, consequently a very large business has been done. The market closes low but active.

NAVAL STORES—A fair business has been done, prices having followed the fluctuations of the New York market.

OILS—In Cod and Seal the rapid increase of price early in the fall restricted the amount of business; at the end of the season the market closed easier, and there was more disposition to realize on the part of holders. Stocks are light. In Linseed Oil business has been light, chiefly owing to the decline in England, which has caused buyers here to operate only from hand to mouth. From what I can hear prices of linseed oil have touched the bottom in England, and con- sequently we may look for a safe trade here.

RICE—In this staple the ordinary amount of business has been done; stocks are light, but importers are timid, owing to the low price of wheat, which materially interferes with the price o, rice.

SALT—A large business has been done during the fall and speculation has been rife; prices have fluctuated considerably, but the tendency has been upward. The market closes with light stocks, not more than sufficient for our requirements before the spring importations.

SUGAR—In raw sugar a large business has been done, chiefly with the refiners, although several in the trade have sold largely to their country customers, of good grades. I may here remark that the lower qualities of refined sugars are rapidly superseding even the higher styles of imported. They are got up in more convenient packages, and not the same loss by drainage. I hear that the importers are satisfied with the result of the fall's operations; stocks are moderate and held for high rates. This is owing to the state of the New York market. Refiners have advanced their prices for all descriptions.

TEAS—The business has been large and satisfactory to all interested. Stocks generally were only moderate, and of good grades very light. Good Japans are rapidly getting into favor.

TOBACCO—In manufactured the business has been to the usual extent, and prices have been remunerative. The season closes with very light stocks. The "Prince of Wales" brand has become in such favor that the manufacturers have not been able to make it in sufficient quantity to meet the demand. I hear of some orders which they have had in hand for five to six weeks and not completed. Leaf Tobacco has ruled dull and prices low. The market closed without animation.

Toronto Market.

The general trade of the city is still quiet, and will remain so until after the holidays.

GROCERIES.—Teas.—Are quiet, and there is little doing except that some few lines have been placed with the city trade. The stock of teas in London on the 30th Nov. was 73,652,061 lbs., and in Liverpool 1,084,907 lbs. against 61,954,-710 lbs., and 1,731,619 lbs. respectively. A telegram from Hong Kong, dated 2nd, gives the exports of tea from China up to that date at 112,-100,000 lbs., being an increase of about 29½ millions of pounds on the exports to the same date last year. Sugars.—Our market is quiet ; the New York market has fluctuated a good deal owing to the unsettled state of affairs in Cuba. Fish.—Quiet, and prices unchanged. Fruit.—There is a good demand for all kinds of fruit at steady prices. Rice—Unchanged.

HARDWARE.—Trade in heavy goods is a little better, and quotations are fully maintained.

PRODUCE.—Wheat.—Receipts for the week by cars 10,000 bush. ; there is a fair demand for Spring wheat for milling purposes at $1.00 to $1.03, and all that offers at these prices is readily taken, but most holders ask more money. Some 8 or 10 cars sold at $1.01 to $1.03. Midge proof is also in good demand at the same quotations. Fall, prime white, is enquired for, and some few cars of choice have been placed for shipment at $1.1 · to $1.20. Medium sold at $1.11 to $1.12, and there are few buyers above these figures. Barley.—Receipts by car 1.300 bush. There is little offered, and the demand is quiet at $1.25 ; sales of cars occurred at $1.22½· to $1.25. Oats.—Receipts 2,400 bush. ; there is a good local demand at 52c. to 54c. and sales occurred at 54c. Peas.—Nominal, no receipts.

FLOUR.—Receipts for the week 2,677 brls. No. 1 superfine is offered at $4.60, and there are buys s of choice brands at that price, while ordinary is nominal at $4.50 to $4.55. Extra is held at $5.50, with buyers at $5.25 to $5.30.

PROVISIONS.—Dressed Hogs. The market has closed briskly at higher prices ; receipts light.—Pork.—Mess is in good demand both for Canadian and old American. Provisions nominal.

FREIGHTS.—The following are the present rates via Great Western Railway from Toronto to Liverpool, London and Glasgow, per Williams & Gowan's line of steamers : Beef, bacon, pork, hams, lard and tallow, in lots not less than one car load and upwards, $1.03 gold per 100 lbs.; grain in bags, in lots of five car loads and upwards, 3s 4d sterling per 100 lbs.; flour, 6s 9d per bbl. To Liverpool via National line: Beef, bacon and pork, $1 per 100 lbs.; lard, in barrels and tierces, $1.06 per 100 lbs.; in kegs and tinnets, $1.17 per 100 lbs.; butter and cheese, $1.43 per 100 lbs. Through bills of lading granted.

The winter rates of the Grand Trunk Railroad to the Maritime Provinces came into force on the 1st inst., and are as follows: From Toronto to St. John, N. B., general merchandise, per 100 lbs., first class, 66c; second class, 65c; third class, 55c; flour, per bbl., 95c; grain, per 100 lbs., 48c. From Stratford, London, or St. Mary's—flour, $1.10; grain, 55c. From Brantford—flour, $1.10; grain, 58c. From Guelph—flour, $1.05; grain, 53c. From Oshawa, Newcastle and Bowmanville—flour, 89c; grain, 45c. From Montreal—flour, 62c; grain, 30c. From Toronto to Halifax, N. S.—general merchandise, per 100 lbs., first class, 90c; second class, 65c; third class, 55c; flour, per bbl., $1.05; grain, per 100 lbs., 53c. From Guelph—flour, $1.15; grain, 58c. From Brantford, London and St. Mary's—flour, $1.20; grain, 60c. From Oshawa, Newcastle and Bowmanville—flour, 99c; grain, 50c. From Montreal—70c for flour, and 35c for grain.

The Cotton Trade.

The Liverpool cotton statement of to-day, as received by cable, shows the following condition of supply compared with the two previous statements:

	Dec. 18.	Dec. 11.	Dec. 5.
Total stock of cotton, bales...	354,000	365,000	367,000
Total stock of American...	51,000	49,000	44,890
Total afloat...	255,000	298,000	254,000
American afloat...	116,000	95,000	78,009
Total of all kinds stock and afloat...	609,000	603,000	621,390

We have here a slightly improving condition of supply, especially in view of the late large shipments to the Continent from this country, the total Continental shipments since September to date reaching about 175,000 bales, against about 85,000 bales last year. The Bombay movement indicates that the shipments since October 1 to January 1 will show an increase this season of about 40,000 bales over the total for the same period last season. With regard to consumption, the probabilities are not clearly marked. Our own manufacturers certainly show no disposition to reduce their time. The stock of goods are very light, while prices have advanced considerably during the month, and the indications of a healthy, active trade for the spring are becoming extremely promising. The European consumption, however, is more uncertain. Private cable advices to-day claim that the mills will soon be, and are in fact now being put on half time. We should place more confidence in these rumors if something to the same effect had not been sent to this side before during the month. Besides, the foreign goods movement of Great Britain has been in no amount very favorable. The Board of Trade returns for October, just issued, are given in our London correspondent's letter, published to-day, show a continued increase in the exports of cotton goods. Still there is a point at which the high price of cotton will check the European consumption. Liverpool circulars received this week all claim it is now reached, and strongly advise the immediate, further and decided reduction of time at the mills. It is to be hoped that the raw material will not reach such a price as to make this resort necessary. It is the key to the position, and, if adopted for even a few weeks, could not fail to affect our market very unfavorably. But, on the other hand, with a living price for the raw material to the manufacturer, it is pretty clear that the total world's supply of

cotton this year will be needed.—Finan Chronicle.

Halifax Market.

BREADSTUFFS.—Dec. 15, 1868.—We have change to note in flour market. Receipts week 5,254 bbls. Canada No. 1 ranges from $ to $6.40; strong bakers $6.65 to $6.70 ; e Canada $7.50 to $8 ; extra State still conti dull at $6 to $6.40, according to quality. N in good demand at $5 to $5.60. Cornmeal—I dried scarce at $4.75 ; fresh ground, sound, n unsound $4.15 to $4.25. Rye flour $5.25 to 5 Oatmeal $3. Imports from December 8 to 1 1867 and 1868 :

	Brls. Flour.	Brls. Corn
1868.	181,890	48,294
1867.	186,507	35,125

WEST INDIA PRODUCE.—Molasses in a stock though no quotable advance in p Sugars dull except Vacuum Pan, which conti to be in good demand at 9½c duty paid, wit stock in first hands. We quote: Porto Ric to 6½c., Barbadoes 5½ to 5½c., Cuba 5½ to t Centrifugal Cuba 6c., in bond. Rum very so at quotations ; 75c for Demerara and 65c fo Jago.—R. C. Hamilton & Co.'s Circular.

Petroleum.

The following were the exports of Petrol from the United States, from January 1st to 2nd :—

FROM	1868.	186
New York...........galls.	51,072,351	32,049
Boston...................	2,320,486	2,163
Philadelphia............	30,710,012	27,672
Baltimore................	2,583,021	1,315
Portland................	704,997	
Cleveland...............	270,000	
Total gallons........	91,660,777	63,201
Same time in 1866		62,671
Same time in 1865		25,192

Reduction in Charges for Telegraping

The following are examples of the exten which reductions have been made in the charged by the Montreal Telegraph Company

	FORMER TARIFF.	RE
Montreal to Father Point and Cacouna......	50c & 4c	
" Portland........	50c · 4c	
" Whitehall.......	50c · 5c	
" Pembroke and Perth...	35c · 3c	25
" Picton and Peterboro'.............	40c · 4c	
" Hamilton	40c · 4c	
" St. Catharines & London.......	50c & 5	
" Buffalo..........	65c · 6c	40
" Port Colborne...	70c · 7c	
" Chatham	70c & 7c	
" Detroit.........	75c · 7c	
From Sackville to Detroit...$1.50 · 14c..7		

Arrangements have also been made wi Western Union Company, by which the th tariffs of the Companies have been reduced following points :—

From Montreal to Boston...........$0 60c..	
" " New York ... 0 75c ·	
" " Chicago........ 1 50c...	
" " St. John, N. B. 1 00c...	
" " Halifax, N.S... 1 05c...	

And from other places in nearly like prope

British Wheat Trade.

The wheat trade during the week has bee acterized by much inactivity, and there is probability that a series of dull markets wil until at least the turn of the year. An ab crop, and importations which are very larg sidering the heavy daily arrivals that have p prices during the last few months, will c to induce the miller to purchase only from to-mouth. As our importations are larg

ve been expected; any hope of a perma-
provement must, for the present, be dis-
Winter wheats are already in the blade,
weeks of frost would perhaps be desir-
der to prevent them from becoming, in
ural parlance, "too proud."

llowing return shows the imports into the
Kingdom in November, and during the
onths ending November 30:

Imports in November.

	1866.	1867.	1868.
...cwt.	1,995,106	3,903,780	2,888,544
......	1,009,613	536,300	875,555
......	545,280	875,279	560,396
......	312,599	160,602	238,885
orn...	786,876	282,194	956,547
......	402,897	389,426	273,116

Imports in Eleven Months.

......	20,547,038	30,877,923	30,303,752
......	7,053,423	5,315,127	6,397,883
......	8,017,291	8,678,021	7,602,915
....	1,008,957	1,281,946	874,802
......	1,017,534	1,856,585	2,446,981
corn...	13,936,499	5,087,252	10,525,478
......	4,405,133	3,040,350	2,698,725

eturns for the ten months show that during
iod the imports were somewhat in excess
orresponding period in 1867, but not to
ortant extent. The receipts from Russia
reduction of 3,250,000 cwt.; from Prussia
,000 cwt.; from Chili, of 530,000 cwt.;
the other hand, they have increased from
ted States to the extent of 2,730,000 cwt.;
gypt 2,150,000 cwt.; and from the Dan-
rincipalities to the extent of 1,693,250
s regards flour, the October importation
a increase of about 110,000 cwt.; but in
months there is a diminution of 165,000

RAILWAY TRAFFIC RETURNS
OR THE MONTH OF NOVEMBER, 1868.

Great Western Railway	864	14946	15 97
Grand Trunk Railway		2974	
London and Port Stanley Railway			
Welland Railway			
Northern Railway	1101	11492	98 54
Port Hope, Lindsay, and Beaverton Railway and Peterborough Branch	6698	5617	
Cobourg, Peterborough and Marmora Railway	9050	17303	12 108
Brockville and Ottawa Railway	16012	57154	118 145
St. Lawrence and Ottawa Railway			
Carillon and Grenville Railway			
Stanstead, Shefford & Chambly Railway			
St. Lawrence and Industry Railway			
New Brunswick and Canada Railway			
European & North American Railway			
Nova Scotia Railway			
Total...	648969	1067790	1014868

uras.

JOHN LANGTON, *Auditor.*

t Office,
, Nov. 13, 1868.

STATEMENT OF BANKS

ACTING UNDER CHARTER, FOR THE MONTH ENDING 30th NOVEMBER, 1868, ACCORDING TO RETURNS FURNISHED BY THE BANKS TO THE AUDITOR OF PUBLIC ACCOUNTS.

NAME OF BANK	CAPITAL — Capital authorized by Act	Capital paid up	LIABILITIES — Promissory Notes in circulation not bearing Interest	Balances due to other Banks	Cash Deposits not bearing Interest	Cash Deposits bearing Interest	TOTAL LIABILITIES	ASSETS — Coin, Bullion, and Provincial Notes	Landed or other Property of the Bank	Government Securities	Promissory Notes, or Bills of other Banks	Balances due from other Banks	Notes and Bills Discounted	Other Debts due the Bank not included under foregoing heads	TOTAL ASSETS
ONTARIO AND QUEBEC.															
Montreal	6,000,000	6,000,000													
Quebec	3,000,000	1,474,300													
City	1,500,000	1,200,000													
Gore	4,000,000	800,200													
British North America	4,866,666	4,866,666													
Banque du Peuple	1,600,000	1,600,000													
Niagara District	1,000,000	1,000,000													
Molson's	1,000,000	1,000,000													
Toronto	2,000,000	2,000,000													
Ontario	3,000,000	2,000,000													
Eastern Townships	400,000	400,000													
Banque Nationale	1,000,000	994,319													
Banque Jacques Cartier	6,000,000	3,329,696													
Merchants'	2,000,000	1,230,783													
Royal Canadian	2,000,000	1,912,965													
Union B'k Lower Canada	1,000,000	295,423													
Mechanics'															
Bank of Commerce		879,562													
NOVA SCOTIA.															
Bank of Yarmouth															
Merch'nts' Bank															
People's Bank															
Union Bank															
Bank of Nova Scotia															
NEW BRUNSWICK.															
Bank of New Brunswick	600,000	600,000													
Commercial Bank															
St. Stephen's Bank															
People's Bank															
Totals	38,966,666	32,790,965													

Mercantile.

DOMINION TELEGRAPH COMPANY.

TAL STOCK. - - - - - $500,000

In 10,000 Shares at $50 Each.

PRESIDENT,
HON. WILLIAM CAYLEY.

TREASURER,
HON. J. McMURRICH.

SECRETARY,
H. B. REEVE.

SOLICITORS,
MESSRS. CAMERON & McMICHAEL,

GENERAL SUPERINTENDENT.
MARTIN RYAN

DIRECTORS.

HON. J. McMURRICH,
Bryce, McMurrich & Co., Toronto.

A. R. McMASTER, Esq.,
A. R. McMaster & Brother, Toronto.

HON. M. C. CAMERON,
Provincial Secretary, Toronto.

JAMES MICHIE, Esq.,
on, Michie & Co., and George Michie & Co., Toronto.

HON. WILLIAM CAYLEY.

A. M. SMITH, Esq.,
A. M. Smith & Co., Toronto.

L. MOFFATT, Esq.,
Moffatt, Murray & Co., Toronto.

H. B. REEVE, Esq.,
Toronto.

MARTIN RYAN, Esq.,
Toronto.

PROSPECTUS.

E DOMINION TELEGRAPH COMPANY has been organized under the act respecting Telegraph Companies, chapter 67, of the consolidated Statutes of Canada. ect is to cover the Dominion of Canada with a complete network of Telegraph lines.

The Capital Stock

0,000, divided into 10,000 shares of $50 each, 5 per to be paid at the time of subscribing, the balance to id by instalments, not exceeding 10 per cent per —said instalments to be called in by the Directors as orks progress. The liability of a subscriber is limited amount of his subscription.

The Business Affairs of the Company.

nder the management of a Board of Directors, an elected by the Shareholders, in conformity with the r and By-Laws of the Company.
Directors are of opinion that it would be to the st of the Stockholders generally to obtain subscrip- from all quarters of Canada, and with this view they to to divide the Stock amongst the different towns ies throughout the Dominion, in allotments suited population and business occupations of the different ies, and the interest which they may be supposed to a such an enterprise.

Contracts of Connections.

ntract, granting permanent connection and extraor- advantages, has already been executed between this ny and the Atlantic and Pacific Company, of New York, at the very commencement, as the Lines of this ny are constructed from the Suspension Bridge, at (the point of connection) to any point in the Do- , all the chief cities and places in the States, touch- the Lines of the Atlantic and Pacific Telegraph ny, are brought in immediate connection therewith. rmanent connection has also been secured with the Western Telegraph Company, of Chicago, whereby mpany will be brought into close connection with Lake Ports and other places through the North n States, and through to California.
4-3mos

Mercantile.

Teas! Teas!! Teas!!!

FRESH ARRIVALS

NEW CROP TEAS,
WINES, AND GENERAL GROCERIES,

Special Inducements given to

PROMPT PAYING PURCHASERS.

All Goods sold at very Lowest Montreal Prices!

W. & R. GRIFFITH,

ONTARIO CHAMBERS,
Corner of Front and Church Streets,

TORONTO

6-1y
ONTARIO

TEAS. Reford & Dillon **TEAS,**

HAVE just received ex. steamships "*St. David*" and "*Nestorian:*"

1000 hlf. chests new season TEAS!
Comprising Twankays, Young Hysons, Imperials, Gunpowders, colored and uncolored Japans, Congous, Souchongs, and Pekoes.
500 hlf. bxs. new Valentia Raisins (selected fruit).
500 bags cleaned Arracan and Rangoon Rice.
500 brls. choice Currants.

—ALSO IN STORE:—

250 hhds. bright Barbadoes and Cuba Sugars.
250 brls. Portland, Standard, Golden & Amber Syrups.
100 bags Rio, Jackinta, Laguayra, and Java Coffees.
250 bxs. 10s Tobacco, "Queen's Own" and "Prince of Wales'" brands.

WITH A GENERAL AND

WELL SELECTED STOCK OF GROCERIES;

All of which they offer to the Trade low.

12 & 14 WELLINGTON STREET, TORONTO,
7-1y

Robert H. Gray,

Manufacturer of Hoop Skirts
AND
CRINOLINE STEEL,

IMPORTER OF
H A B E R D A S H E R Y, T R I M M I N G S
AND
GENERAL FANCY GOODS,

43, YONGE STREET, TORONTO, ONT.
6-1y

John Boyd & Co.,

WHOLESALE GROCERS AND COMMISSION MERCHANTS,

61 AND 63 FRONT STREET
TORONTO.

NOW in store, direct from the European and West India Markets, a large assortment of General Groceries, comprising

Teas, Sugars, Coffees, Wines and Liquors,
AND
GENERAL GROCERIES.

Ship Chandlery, Canvas, Manilla and Tarred Rope, Oakum, Tar, Plugs, &c., &c.,

DIRECT FROM THE MANUFACTURERS.

OHN BOYD.   ALEX. M. MONRO.   C. W. BUNTING.

Toronto, Oct, 1st, 1868,
7-1y

Mercantile.

UNRIVALLED!

THE BRITISH AMERICAN COMMERCIAL COLLEGE,
Consolidated with the

Bryant, Stratton and Odell Business College.
AND TELEGRAPHIC INSTITUTE,

STANDS Pre-eminent and Unrivalled. It is the LARGEST and MOST EFFICIENT. It employs the largest staff of Teachers, among whom are the two BEST PENMEN OF CANADA.

The TUITION FEE is the same as in other Institutions having a similar object.

The PRICE OF BOARD is the same as in other Canadian Cities.

In an EDUCATIONAL point of view, there is no other Institution in the country that has equal advantages and facilities.

YOUNG MEN intending to qualify themselves for business, will find it to their advantage to send for a Circular, or call at the College Rooms, corner of King and Toronto streets.

Scholarships good in Montreal and throughout the United States.

ODELL & TROUT,
Principals and Proprietors.
October 1.
8

The Mercantile Agency,

FOR THE
PROMOTION AND PROTECTION OF TRADE
Established in 1841.

DUN, WIMAN & Co.

Montreal, Toronto and Halifax.

REFERENCE Book, containing names and ratings of Business Men in the Dominion, published semi-annually.
24-1y.

The St. Lawrence Glass Company

ARE now manufacturing and have for sale,

COAL OIL LAMPS,
Various styles and sizes.

LAMP CHIMNEYS,
of extra quality for ordinary Burners also, for the '*Comet*' and '*Sun*' Burners.

SETS OF
TABLE GLASSWARE, HYACINTH GLASSES,
STEAM GUAGE TUBES, GLASS BODS, &c.,
or any other article made to order, in *White* or *Color Glass,*

KEROSENE BURNERS, COLLARS and SOCKETS, will be kept on hand.

DRUGGISTS FLINT GLASSWARE, and
PHILOSOPHICAL INSTRUMENTS,
made to order.

OFFICE—388 ST. PAUL STREET, MONTREAL.

A. McK. COCHRANE,
8-1y
Secretary.

Financial.

BROWN'S BANK,
(W. R. Brown. W. C. Chewett.)
60 KING STREET EAST, TORONTO.

TRANSACTS a general Banking Business, Buys and Sells New York and Sterling Exchange, Gold, Silver, U. S. Bonds and Uncurrent Money, receives Deposits subject to Cheque at sight, makes Collections and Discounts Commercial Paper.

Orders by Mail or Telegraph promptly executed at most favourable current quotations.

Address letters,   "BROWN'S BANK,
36-y   Toronto."

Candee & Co.,

BANKERS AND BROKERS, dealers in Gold and Silver Coin, Government Securities, &c., Corner Main and Exchange Streets. Buffalo, Y. N.
21-1v

H. N. Smith & Co.,

2, EAST SENECA STREET, BUFFALO, N. Y., (corres- pondent Smith, Gould, Martin & Co., 11 Broad Street, N.Y.,) Stock, Money and Exchange Brokers. Advances made on securities.
21-1y

TORONTO PRICES CURRENT.—December 23, 1868.

Name of Article.	Wholesale Rates.		Name of Article.	Wholesale Rate.		Name of Article.		
Boots and Shoes.	$ c.	$ c.	**Groceries**—Contin'd	$ c.	$ c.	**Leather**—Contin'd.		
Mens' Thick Boots	2 05	2 50	" fine to fine't.	0 85	0 95	Kip Skins, Patna		
" Kip.	2 50	3 25	Hyson	0 45	0 80	French		
" Calf	3 00	3 70	Imperial	0 45	0 80	English		
" Congress Gaiters...	2 00	2 50	Tobacco, Manufac'd u:			Hemlock Calf (3½ to		
" Kip Cobourgs....	1 15	1 45	Can Leaf, ♥ ℔ 5s & 10s.	0 26	0 30	35 lbs.) per doz....		
Boys' Thick Boots	1 60	1 80	Western Leaf, com...	0 25	0 26	Do. light		
Youths'	1 35	1 50	" Good....	0 27	0 28	French Calf.		
Women's Batts	96	1 30	" Fine	0 32	0 35	Grain & Satn Clt'd dor.		
" Congress Gaiters..	1 15	1 45	" Bright fine...	0 40	0 50	Splits, large ♥ ℔....		
Misses' Batts......	0 75	1 00	" choice..	0 60	0 75	" small		
" Congress Gaiters	1 00	1 30				Enamelled Cow ♥ foot.		
Girls' Batts	0 60	0 85	**Hardware.**			Patent		
" Congress Gaiters	0 80	1 10	Tin (net cash prices)			Pebble Grain		
Children's C. T. Cacks.	0 50	0 65	Block, ♥ ℔........	0 25	0 26	Buff		
" Gaiters	0 65	0 90	Grain	0 25	0 26	**Oils.**		
Drugs.			Copper:			Cod		
Aloes Cape.	0 12½	0 16	Pig...............	0 23	0 24	Lard, extra		
Alum...........	0 05½	0 03	Sheet............	0 30	0 33	" No. 1		
Borax	0 00	0 00	Cut Nails:			" Woollen		
Camphor, refined.....	0 65	0 70	Assorted ¼ Shingles,			Lubricating, patent..		
Castor Oil..........	0 18	0 28	♥ 100 ℔...	2 00	3 00	" Mott's economical		
Caustic Soda........	0 04½	0 05	Shingle alone do	3 15	3 25	Linseed, raw		
Cochineal..........	0 90	1 00	Lathe and 5 dy.	3 30	3 40	" boiled......		
Cream Tartar	0 25	0 30	Galvanized Iron:			Machinery		
Epsom Salts........	0 03	0 04	Assorted sizes......	0 08	0 09	Olive, 2nd, ♥ gal....		
Extract Logwood.....	0 09	0 10	Best No. 24.......	0 09	0 00	" salad, in bots.		
Gum Arabic, sorts....	0 30	0 35	" 26.	0 08	0 08½	" salad, in botn.		
Indigo, Madras......	0 75	1 00	" 28.	0 09	0 09½	qt. ♥ case...		
Licorice	0 14	0 45	Horse Nails:			Sesame salad, ♥ gal..		
Madder	0 16	0 18	Guests or Grifin's			Seal, pale......		
Nutgalls	0 00	0 00	assorted sizes......	0 00	0 00	Spirits Turpentine..		
Opium...........	0 70	7 00	For W. ass'd sizes...	0 18	0 19	Varnish		
Oxalic Acid.........	0 28	0 35	Patent Hammer'd do..	0 17	0 18	Whale..........		
Potash, Bi-tart......	0 25	0 28	Iron (at 4 months):			**Paints, &c.**		
" Bichromate..	0 15	0 20	Pig—Gartsherrie No1..	24 00	25 00	White Lead, genuine		
Potass Iodide	3 60	4 60	Other brands. No 1..	22 00	24 00	in Oil, ♥ 25lbs.....		
Senna	0 12½	0 00	No 2..	0 00	0 00	Do. No. 1 "		
Soda Ash	0 03	0 04	Bar—Scotch, ♥100 ℔..	2 25	2 50	" 2 "		
Soda Bicarb	4 50	5 50	Refined	2 00	2 25	" 3 "		
Tartaric Acid........	0 37½	0 45	Sweden	5 00	5 50	White Zinc, genuine..		
Ventligris	0 35	0 40	Hoops—Coopers......	3 00	3 25	White Lead, dry......		
Vitriol, Blue........	0 09	0 10	Band	3 00	3 25	Red Lead		
Groceries.			Boiler Plates.......	3 25	3 50	Venetian Red, Eng'h.		
Coffees:			Canada Plates......	4 00	4 25	Yellow Ochre, Fren'h.		
Java, ♥ ℔.	0 22½	0 24	Union Jack	0 00	0 00	Whiting		
Laguayra........	0 17	0 18	Puntypool........	4 00	4 25	**Petroleum.**		
Rio...........	0 15	0 17	Swansea	3 90	4 00	(Refined ♥ gal.)		
Fish:			Lead (at 4 months):			Water white, car'd ..		
Herrings, Lab. split..	5 75	6 60	Bar, ♥ 100 ℔s.....	0 07	0 07½	" small lots ..		
" round...	4 00	4 75	Sheet "	0 07	0 07½	Straw, by car load ..		
" scaled.......	0 35	0 40	Shot "	0 07½	0 07½	" small lots..		
Mackerel, small kitts...	1 00	0 00	Iron Wire (net cash):			Amber, by car load..		
Loch. Her. wh'drks...	2 60	2 75	No. 6, ♥ bundle..	2 70	2 80	" small lots..		
" half "	1 25	1 50	" 9, "	3 10	3 20	Benzine		
White Fish & Trout...	3 60	4 50	" 12, "	3 40	3 50			
Salmon, saltwater....	14 00	15 00	" 16, "	4 30	4 40	**Produce.**		
Dry Cod, ♥112 ℔s...	5 50	6 00	Powder:			Grain:		
Fruit:			Blasting, Canada...	3 50	0 00	Wheat, Spring, 60℔..		
Raisins, Layers	2 10	2 20	FF "	4 25	4 50	" Fall 60 "		
" M R......	1 90	2 10	FFF "	4 75	5 00	Barley........ 48 "		
" Valentiasew..	0 07	0 07½	Blasting, English ...	4 50	4 75	Peas......... 60 "		
Currants, new........	0 05	0 05½	FFF loose..	5 00	6 00	Oats......... 34 "		
" old......	0 04½	0 04½	FFF "	6 00	6 50	Rye .... 56 "		
Figs...........	0 14	0 09	Pressed Spikes (4 mos):..			Seeds:		
Molasses:			Regular sizes 100....	4 00	4 25	Clover, choice 60 " ..		
Clayed, ♥ gal.......	0 00	0 35	Extra "	4 50	5 00	com'n 68 " ..		
Syrups, Standard ...	0 49	0 50	Tin Plate (net cash):			Timothy, cho'e "		
" Golden ...	0 54	0 55	IC Coke	7 50	8 50	" inf. to good 48 "..		
Rice:			IC Charcoal......	8 25	8 50	Flax .... 54 "		
Arracan	0 54	4 75	IX "	10 25	10 75	Flour (per brl.):		
Spices:			IXX "	12 25	0 00	Superior extra........		
Cassia, whole, ♥ ℔..	0 00	0 45	DC "	7 25	9 00	Extra superfine,....		
Cloves	0 11	0 12	DX "	9 50	0 00	Fancysuperfine		
Nutmegs	0 45	0 55				Superfine No. 1		
Ginger, ground	0 30	0 35	**Hides & Skins.**			" No. 2....		
" Jamaica, root...	0 20	0 25	Green rough	0 06	0 00	Oatmeal, (per brl.)...		
Pepper, black........	0 09½	0 10	Green, salt'd & insp'd..	0 00	0 07			
Pimento	0 05	0 09	Cured	0 00	0 00	**Provisions.**		
Sugars:			Calfskins, green......	0 00	0 11	Butter, dairy tub ℔..		
Port Rico, ♥ ℔......	0 08½	0 08½	Calfskins, cured......	0 18	0 20	" store packed..		
Cuba "	0 08½	0 08½	" dry.......	1 00	1 25	Cheese, new		
Barbadoes (bright)...	0 08½	0 00	Sheepskins,	0 60	0 80	Pork, mess, per brl..		
Dry Crushed, at 60 d...	0 11½	0 11½	" country....			" prime mess..		
Canada Sugar Refine'y,						" prime		
yellow No. 2, 60 ds..	0 09	0 09½	**Hops.**			Bacon, rough		
Yellow, No. 1......	0 09	0 09½	Inferior, ♥ ℔......	0 05	0 07	" Cumberl'd cut..		
No. 3......	0 09	0 09½	Medium......	0 07	0 09	" smoked........		
Crushed X	0 10	0 10½	Good	0 09	0 12	Hams, in salt........		
" A	0 11	0 11½	Fancy	0 00	0 00	" sug. cur. & can'd.		
" Ground........	0 11	0 11½				Shoulders, in salt ..		
Extra Ground........	0 12½	0 12½	**Leather.** ♥ (4 mos.)			Lard, in kegs........		
Teas:			In bulk of less than			Eggs, packed		
Japan com'n to good..	0 40	0 55	50 sides, 10 ♥ cent			Beef Hams		
" Fine to choicest..	0 55	0 65	higher.			Tallow		
" Colored, com. to fine..	0 55	0 65	Spanish Sole, 1st qual..			Hogs dressed, heavy..		
" Congou & Souch'ng..	0 42	0 75	heavy, weights ♥ ℔..	0 23	0 23	" medium...		
" Oolong, good to fine..	0 50	0 68	Do.1st qual middle do..	0 22	0 23	" light........		
" Y. Hyson, com to gd..	0 65	0 00	Do. No. 2, all weights..	0 20	0 21			
" Medium to choice ...	0 65	0 80	Slaughter heavy	0 25	0 36	**Salt, &c.**		
" Extra choice	0 65	0 90	Do. light........	0 50	0 00	American brls.		
" Gunpowd're. to med..	0 55	0 70	Harness, best	0 32	0 34	Liverpool coarse		
" med. to fine	0 70	0 85	" No. 2........	0 30	0 32	Plaster		
			Upper heavy	0 44	0 38	Water Lime		
			" light........	0 36	0 40			

adles.			*Brandy:*	$ c.	$ c
			Hennessy's, per gal..	2 30	2 50
Co.'s ..	$ c.	$ c.	Martell's " ..	2 30	2 50
....	0 07½	0 08	J. Robin & Co.'s " ..	2 25	2 35
ır	0 07	0 07½	Otard, Dupuy & Cos..	2 25	2 35
....	0 07	0 07½	Brandy, cases........	8 50	9 00
....	0 05	0 05½	Brandy, com. per c...	4 00	4 50
......	0 03½	0 03¾	*Whiskey:*		
....	0 00	0 11½	Common 36 u. p......	0 62½	0 65
			Old Rye	0 85	0 87½
quors,			Malt	0 85	0 87½
			Toddy	0 85	0 87½
loz......	2 60	2 65	Scotch, per gal........	1 90	2 10
› Portr..	2 35	2 40	Irish—Kinnahan's c...	7 00	7 50
			" Dunnville's Belf't..	6 00	6 25
Rum...	1 80	2 25	**Wool.**		
H. Gin..	1 55	1 65	Fleece, lb............	0 28	0 35
'om.....	1 90	2 00	Pulled "............	0 22	0 25
			Furs.		
....	4 00	4 25	Bear............	3 00	10 00
'om, c...	6 00	6 25	Beaver............	1 00	1 25
			Coon	0 20	0 40
			Fisher............	4 00	6 00
a.......	1 00	1 25	Martin............	1 40	1 60
....	2 00	4 00	Mink............	4 00	4 25
ıon.....	1 00	1 50	Otter............	5 75	6 00
ı........	1 70	1 80	Spring Rats............	0 15	0 17
golden..	2 50	4 00	Fox............	1 20	1 25

ISURANCE COMPANIES.

ENGLISH.—*Quotations on the London Market.*

Di-nd.	Name of Company.	Shares parval £	Amount paid.	Last Sale.
	Briton Medical and General Life ...	10	....	1¾
	Commer'l Union, Fire, Life and Mar.	50	5	5½
	City of Glasgow	25	2½	5⅝
	Edinburgh Life	100	15	31½
yr	European Life and Guarantee......	2½	11s6	5s
	Etna Fire and Marine............	10	1½	0
	Guardian	100	50	51½
	Imperial Fire............	500	50	0
	Imperial Life	100	10	15½
	Lancashire Fire and Life........	20	2	2⅜
	Life Association of Scotland........	40	7½	25
. sh	London Assurance Corporation ..	25	12½	49
	London and Lancashire Life	10	1	19s
	Liverp'l & London & Globe F. & L.	20	2	6 15-16ths
	National Union Life	5	1	0
	Northern Fire and Life	100	5	11½
	North British and Mercantile	50	6¼	19¾
	Ocean Marine	25	5	19¾
ts.	Provident Life............	100	10	0
. s.	Phœnix............	....	....	148
yr.	Queen Fire and Life	10	1	17s
.4s	Royal Insurance............	20	3	6
	Scottish Provincial Fire and Life ..	50	2½	5
	Standard Life	50	12	65½
	Star Life	25	1½	—
	CANADIAN.			₩ c.
	British America Fire and Marine ..	$50	$25	56
	Canada Life	...	....	.....
	Montreal Assurance	£50	£5	135
	Provincial Fire and Marine........	60	11	.....
...	Quebec Fire	40	32½	£ 21½
	" Marine............	100	40	95
o's.	Western Assurance............	40	6	.....

RAILWAYS.	Sha's	Paid	Montr	London.
. Lawrence............	£100	All.	....	58 60
te Huron	20½	"	....	3 3½
do Preference	10	"	....	4½ 6
Goderich, 6₩c., 1872-3-4....	100	"	....	65 00
St. Lawrence	....	....	10 11	....
do Pref. 10 ₩ ct............	....	....	72 75	....
....	100	"	15 16	15½ 17
Eq.G. M. Bds. 1 ch. 6₩c............	100	"	....	84 86
First Preference, 5 ₩ c	100	"	....	50 53
Deferred, 3 ₩ ct..	100	"	....	....
Second Pref. Bonds, 5₩c............	100	"	....	39 42½
do Deferred, 3 ₩ ct............	100	"	....	....
Third Pref. Stock, 4₩ct............	100	"	....	27 30
do. Deferred, 3 ₩ ct............	100	"	....	....
Fourth Pref. Stock, 3₩c............	100	"	....	18½ 19½
do. Deferred, 3 ₩ ct.	100	"	....	....
....	20½	"	13 14	13⅝ 14¼
New	20½	18	....	....
6 ₩ c. Bds, due 1873-76............	100	All.	....	100 104
5½₩c Bds. due 1877-78............	100	"	....	93 94
y, Halifax, $250, all............	$250	"	....	....
ınada, 6₩c. 1st Pref. Bds............	100	"	....	80 83

ANGE.	Halifax.	Montr'l.	Quebec.	Toronto.
don, 60 days......				
ays date	12½	9½ 9¾	9½ 9¾	9¾
....	11½ 12	7½ 8	8½ 9½	8¾
ocuments............	....	....	....	....
fork............	....	25½ 26	25½ 25¾	74½
....	....	23½ 23¾	25½ 25¾	....
....	....	par	par ½ dis.	par ½ dis.
....	....	4 4½	....	3½ 5

STOCK AND BOND REPORT.

The dates of our quotations are as follows:—Toronto, Dec. 23; Montreal, Dec. 22; Quebec, Dec. 21; London, Nov. 28.

NAME.	Shares.	Paid up.	Divid'd last 6 Months	Dividend Day.	CLOSING PRICES. Toronto.	Montre'l	Quebec.
BANKS.			₩ ct.				
British North America	$250	All.	3	July and Jan.	105 106	105 106	104 105
Jacques Cartier............	50	"	4	1 June, 1 Dec.	106 107	106½107½	105¾106¾
Montreal	200	"	5	" "	138 138½	138 138½	138 138½
Nationale............	50	"	4	1 Nov. 1 May.	....	105 106	106 106½
New Brunswick	100	"	......	......	....	....	....
Nova Scotia	200	28	7&b$3½	Mar. and Sept.	....	....	....
Du Peuple............	50	"	4	1 Mar., 1 Sept.	106½107½	107½108	107 107½
Toronto	100	"	4	1 Jan., 1 July.	Bks cl'd	Bks cl'd	Bks cl'd
Bank of Yarmouth............	....	....	......	......	....	....	....
Canadian Bank of Com'e............	50	95	......	......	Bks cl'd	Bks cl'd	Bks cl'd
City Bank Montreal	80	All.	4	1 June, 1 Dec.	102 102½	101½102½	102 102½
Commer'l Bank (St. John)............	100	"	₩ ct.	......	....	....	....
Eastern Townships' Bank............	50	"	4	1 July, 1 Jan..	....	99 100	Bks cl'd
Gore	40	...	none.	1 Jan., 1 July.	39½ 40	40 42	41 42
Halifax Banking Company............	....	....	......	......	....	....	....
Mechanics' Bank............	50	70	4	1 Nov., 1 May.	95½ 97	95 96	95 96
Merchants' Bank of Canada............	100	70	4	1 Jan., 1 July.	Bks cl'd	107 109	Bks cl'd
Merchants' Bank (Halifax)............	....	....	......	......	....	....	....
Molson's Bank............	50	All.	4	1 Apr., 1 Oct.	110 110½	109½110	109 110
Niagara District Bank............	100	70	3½	1 Jan., 1 July.	....	....	....
Ontario Bank............	40	All.	4	1 June, 1 Dec.	100 100½	100	99 99½
People's Bank (Fred'kton)............	100	"	......	......	....	....	....
People's Bank (Halifax)	20	"	7 12 m	......	....	....	....
Quebec Bank	100	"	3½	1 June, 1 Dec.	98 100	98 100	99½100
Royal Canadian Bank	50	50	4	1 Jan., 1 July.	Bks cl'd	Bks cl'd	Bks cl'd
St. Stephens Bank	100	All	.....	......	....	....	....
Union Bank	100	70	4	1 Jan., 1 July.	Bks cl'd	Bks cl'd	Bks cl'd
Union Bank (Halifax)............	100	40	7 12mo	Feb. and Aug.	....	....	....
MISCELLANEOUS.							
British America Land............	250	44	2½	......	....	....	....
British Colonial S. S. Co............	250	32½	2½	......	....	50 60	....
Canada Company	32½	All.	5	......	....	....	....
Canada Landed Credit Co............	50	$20	3½	......	72 73	....	....
Canada Per. B'ldg Society............	50	All.	5	......	124½125	....	....
Canada Mining Company............	4	90	......	......	....	....	....
Do. Inl'd Steam Nav. Co............	100	All.	20 12 m	......	....	106 109	105 107
Do. Glass Company............	100	"	12½ "	......	....	40 60	....
Canad'n Loan & Investm't............	25	2½	7	......	....	....	....
Canada Agency	10	1	......	......	....	....	....
Colonial Securities Co............	....	....	......	......	....	....	....
Freehold Building Society............	100	All.	4	......	104½105	....	....
Halifax Steamboat Co............	100	"	5	......	....	....	....
Halifax Gas Company............	....	....	......	......	....	....	....
Hamilton Gas Company............	....	....	......	......	....	....	....
Huron Copper Bay Co............	4	12	20	......	....	25 40cps	....
Lake Huron S. and C............	5	102	......	......	....	....	....
Montreal Mining Consols............	20	$15	......	......	....	3.10 3.20	....
Do. Telegraph Co............	40	All.	5	......	135 137	135 136	135 136
Do. Elevating Co............	00	"	15 12 m	......	....	100 102½	....
Do. City Gas Co............	40	"	4	15 Mar. 15 Sep.	....	135 136	133 134
Do. City Pass. R. Co............	50	"	5	......	....	110 110½	110 110½
Nova Scotia Telegraph	20	"	....	......	....	....	....
Quebec and L. S.	8	$4	......	......	....	....	25 cts
Quebec Gas Co............	200	All.	4	1 Mar., 1 Sep.	....	....	115 117
Quebec Street R. R............	50	25	8	......	....	....	90 95
Richelieu Navigation Co............	100	All.	7 p.a.	1 Jan., 1 July.	....	117 118	116 117
St. Lawrence Tow Boat Co............	100	"	......	3 Feb.	....	...	40 45
Tor'to Consumers' Gas Co............	50	"	2 3 m.	1 My Au MarFe	106½ 107	...	105½106½
Trust & Loan Co. of U. C............	20	5	3	......	....	....	....
West'n Canada Bldg Soc'y............	50	All.	5	......	116 117	....	....

SECURITIES.	London.	Montreal.	Quebec.	Toronto.
Canadian Gov't Deb. 6 ₩ ct. stg............	....	102 103	102½ 103	103 105
Do. do. 6 do due Ja. & Jul. 1877-84............	107½ 108½	....	....	....
Do. do. 6 do. Feb. & Aug............	106 107	....	....	....
Do. do. 6 do. Mch. & Sep............	106 107	....	....	....
Do. do. 5 ₩ ct. cur., 1883	94 95	92½ 93½	92 92½	93 93½
Do. do. 5 do. stg., 1885	94 95	92½ 93½	92½ 93	93 93½
Do. do. 7 do. cur.,............	....	....	....	....
Dominion 6 p. c. 1878 cy............	....	104½ 105	104½ 105	104½ 105
Hamilton Corporation............	....	....	....	....
Montreal Harbor, 8 ₩ ct. d. 1869............	..	....	....	....
Do. do. 7 do. 1870............	....	....	....	100 101
Do. do. 6½ do. 1875............	....	101 102	....	....
Do. do. 6½ do. 1873............	....	....	....	....
Do. Corporation, 6 ₩ c. 1891	....	95½ 96½	96 96½	94 96
Do. 7 p. c. stock............	....	106 107½	106 107	107½ 108
Do. Water Works, 6 ₩ c. stg. 1878............	....	....	....	94 96
Do. do. 6 do. cy. do.	....	96 96½	....	94 96
New Brunswick, 6 ₩ ct., Jan. and July	104 106	....	....	....
Nova Scotia, 6 ₩ ct., 1875............	104 105½	....	....	....
Ottawa City 6 ₩ c. d. 1880	....	92½ 93½	....	....
Quebec Harbour, 6 ₩ c. d. 1883............	....	....	80	....
Do. do. 7 do. do............	....	....	65 70	....
Do. do. 8 do. 1886............	....	....	75 80	....
Do. City, 7 ₩ c. d. 5 years	....	80 90	95 96	....
Do. do. 7 do. 9 do.	....	....	91 92	....
Do. do. 7 do. 2 do.	....	....	97 98	....
Do. Water Works, 7 ₩ ct., 4 years............	....	....	96 97	....
Do. do. 6 do. 2 do.	....	....	94 95	....
Toronto Corporation	....	87½ 92½	....	....

Financial.

Pellatt & Osler.

STOCK AND EXCHANGE BROKERS, Accountants, Agents for the Standard Life Assurance Company and New York Casualty Insurance Company.

OFFICE—86 *King Street East, four Doors West of Church Street, Toronto.*

HENRY PELLATT,　　　EDMUND B. OSLER.
1y　　*Notary Public.*　　　*Official Assignee.*

Philip Browne & Co.,

BANKERS AND STOCK BROKERS.

DEALERS IN

STERLING EXCHANGE—U. S. Currency, Silver and Bonds—Bank Stocks, Debentures, Mortgages, &c. Drafts on New York issued, in Gold and Currency. Prompt attention given to collections. Advances made on Securities.

No. 67 YONGE STREET, TORONTO

JAMES BROWNE.　　　PHILIP BROWNE, *Notary Public.*
y

James C. Small.

BANKER AND BROKER,

No. 34 KING STREET EAST, TORONTO.

Sterling Exchange, American Currency, Silver, and Bonds, Bank Stocks, Debentures and other Securities, bought and sold.
Deposits received. Collections promptly made. Drafts on New York in Gold and Currency issued.

Western Canada Permanent Building and Savings Society.

OFFICE—No 70 CHURCH STREET, TORONTO.

SAVINGS BANK BRANCH,

DEPOSITS RECEIVED DAILY. INTEREST PAID HALF-Yearly.

ADVANCES

Are made on the security of Real Estate, repayable on the most favourable terms, by a Sinking Fund.

WALTER S. LEE,
86-1y　　　*Secy. & Treas.*

The Canadian Land and Emigration Company

Offers for sale on Conditions of Settlement,

GOOD FARM LANDS

In the County of Peterboro, Ontario,

In the well settled Township of Dysart, where there are Grist and Saw Mills, Stores, &c., at

ONE-AND-A-HALF DOLLARS AN ACRE.

In the adjoining Townships of Guilford, Dudley, Harburn, Harcourt and Bruton, connected with Dysart and the Village of Haliburton by the Peterson Road, at ONE DOLLAR an Acre.

For further particulars apply to

CHAS. JAS. BLOMFIELD,
Secretary C. L. and E. Co., Toronto.
Or to　ALEX. NIVEN, P.L.S.,
Agent C. L. & E. Co., Haliburton.

Canada Permanent Building and Savings Society.

Paid up Capital $1,000,000
Assets 1,700,000
Annual Income 400,000

Directors:—JOSEPH D. RIDOUT, *President.*
PETER PATERSON, *Vice-President.*
J. G. Worts, Edward Hooper, S. Nordheimer, W. C. Chewett, E. H. Rutherford, Joseph Robinson.
Bankers—Bank of Toronto; Bank of Montreal; Royal Canadian Bank.

OFFICE—*Masonic Hall, Toronto Street, Toronto.*

Money Received on Deposit bearing five and six per cent. interest.

Advances made on City and Country Property in the Provia of Ontario.

J. HERBERT MASON,
86-y　　　*Sec'y & Treas.*

Insurance.

Montreal Assurance Company.

DIVIDEND NOTICE.

NOTICE is hereby given that a Dividend of TWELVE PER CENT. on the paid-up stock of the Company has been declared for the past year, and will be payable at the Office, Great St. James Street, on and after MONDAY, the 14th inst.

WM. MURRAY,
Manager.
Montreal, December 4, 1868.　　　17-2

The Victoria Mutual
FIRE INSURANCE COMPANY OF CANADA.

Insures only Non-Hazardous Property, at Low Rates.

BUSINESS STRICTLY MUTUAL.

GEORGE H. MILLS, *President.*
W. D. BOOKER, *Secretary.*

HEAD OFFICE .... HAMILTON, ONTARIO
aug 15-1yr

Life Association of Scotland.

INVESTED FUNDS
UPWARDS OF £1,000,000 STERLING.

THIS Institution differs from other Life Offices, in that the
BONUSES FROM PROFITS
Are applied on a special system for the Policy-holder's *PERSONAL BENEFIT AND ENJOYMENT DURING HIS OWN LIFETIME,*
— WITH THE OPTION OF
LARGE BONUS ADDITIONS TO THE SUM ASSURED.

The Policy-holder thus obtains
A LARGE REDUCTION OF PRESENT OUTLAY
OR
A PROVISION FOR OLD AGE OF A MOST IMPORTANT AMOUNT IN ONE CASH PAYMENT, OR A LIFE ANNUITY,
Without any expense or outlay whatever beyond the ordinary Assurance Premium for the Sum Assured, which remains in tact for Policy-holder's heirs, or other purposes.

CANADA—MONTREAL.—PLACE D'ARMES.

DIRECTORS:
DAVID TORRANCE, Esq., (D. Torrance & Co.)
GEORGE MOFFATT, (Gillespie, Moffatt & Co.)
ALEXANDER MORRIS, Esq., M.P., Barrister, Perth.
Sir G. E. CARTIER, M.P., Minister of Militia.
PETER REDPATH, Esq., (J. Redpath & Son)
J. H. R. MOLSON, Esq., (J. H. R. Molson & Bros.)
Solicitors—Messrs. TORRANCE & MORRIS.
Medical Officer—R. PALMER HOWARD, Esq., M.D.
Secretary—P. WARDLAW.
Inspector of Agencies—JAMES P M. CHIPMAN. y

North British and Mercantile Insurance Company.

Established 1809.

HEAD OFFICE, - - CANADA. - - MONTREAL,

TORONTO BRANCH:
LOCAL OFFICES, NOS. 4 & 6 WELLINGTON STREET.
Fire Department, ... R. N. GOOCH,
Agent.
Life Department, ... H. L. HIME,
29-1y　　　*Agent.*

Phœnix Fire Assurance Company.
LOMBARD ST. AND CHARING CROSS,
LONDON, ENG.

Insurances effected in all parts of the World

Claims paid
WITH PROMTITUDE and LIBERALITY.
MOFFATT, MURRAY & BEATTIE,
Agents for Toronto,
36 Yonge Street.
28-1y.

Insurance.

Canada Life Assurance Company

CAPITAL AND CASH AS:
OVER $2,000,000.

SUMS ASSURED
$5,000,000.

A COMPARISON of the rates of this Comp others cannot fail to demonstrate the adve the low premiums, which, by the higher returns investments, it is enabled to offer.

IF PREFERRED, ASSURERS NEED ONLY
PAY ONE-HALF OF EACH YEAR'S PREMI CASH,
during the whole term of policies on the 10 paym or for seven years on the whole life plan.

For the unpaid portion of premiums,
"NOTES" ARE NOT REQUIRED BY THIS CO
so that assurers are not liable to be called upon ment of these, nor for assessments upon them, case of Mutual Companies.
Every facility and advantage which can be aff offered by this Company.

A. G. RAMSAY, Man.
E. BRADBURNE, A
3m11　　　Toronto

The Liverpool and London and G1 Insurance Company

INVESTED FUNDS:
FIFTEEN MILLIONS OF DOLLA

DAILY INCOME OF THE COMPANY:
TWELVE THOUSAND DOLI

LIFE INSURANCE,
WITH AND WITHOUT PROFITS.

FIRE INSURANCE
On every description of Property, at Lowest Rem Rates.
JAMES FRASER, A
5 King S
Toronto, 1868.

Briton Medical and General Association,
with which is united the
BRITANNIA LIFE ASSURANCE COM

Capital and Invested Funds £750,00

ANNUAL INCOME, £220,000 STG.
Yearly increasing at the rate of £25,000 St

THE important and peculiar feature origin duced by this Company, in applying the Bonuses, so as to make Policies payable during life any higher rate of premiums being charged, h the success of the BRITON MEDICAL AND GEN almost unparalleled in the history of Life Assur Policies on the Profit Scale become payable during of the Assured, thus rendering a Policy of A means of subsistence in old age, as well as a prot family, and a more valuable security to credit event of early death; and effectually meeting urged objection, that persons do not themselv benefit of their own prudence and forethought.

No extra charge made to members of Volun for services within the British Provinces.

TORONTO AGENCY, 5 KING ST. WEST.
oct 17—9-1yr　　　JAMES FRASE

Phenix Insurance Compa
BROOKLYN, N. Y.

PHILANDER SHAW,　　STEPHEN CRO
Secretary.
Cash Capital, $1,000,000. Surplus, $666,416
1,666,416.02. Entire Income from all sources :
$2,151,839.82.
CHARLES G. FORTIER, M
Ontario Chambers, Toronto, Ont,

PROSPECTUS

OF THE

)MINION EXPRESS COMPANY OF CANADA

ORGANIZED UNDER THE JOINT STOCK COMPANIES' ACTS.

CAPITAL STOCK, ... $1,000,000,

In 10,000 Shares, $100 each.

proposed to organize a DOMINION EXPRESS COMPANY, to meet the present and prospective demand for increased facilities of general trans. gation. It is the interest of Canadians to do their own work, and *accumulate* cash capital, and *one* of the objects of this scheme is the retention country of the profits arising from the business done.

press Companies obtain "four-fifths" of their business from merchants and bankers, and no reason exists why they cannot transport their own by their *own Agents, economically* and *efficiently*, and by a *union of capital* and *effort*, they hereby resolve so to do. Being thus united, and g to it their business and influence, secures to this Company certain and complete success.

iis organization, like the snail system, is to extend, under *one general management*, to all cities, towns and villages in the Dominion, and to connect arts of the United States, and being but "one Company," will secure *unity, despatch* and *accuracy.*

is proposed to distribute the stock widely, throughout the Dominion, in limited sums, apportioned as nearly as practicable to the business of the ibers. The capital Stock of the Company to be not less than $1,000,000, in 10,000 shares of $100 each.

m *per cent.* of the stock subscribed will be required to be paid after the subscription shall have reached the sum of $250,000, and after a Charter iave been obtained, of which due notice will be given to the subscribers ; the subsequent calls, not exceeding *ten per cent. at any one time,* to be t convenient intervals, as the demands on the Company may require. But the aggregate of all calls to be made will, it is believed, not exceed *per cent.* of the Capital Stock.

ie business to be done strictly on *cash principles.* With a paying business assured from the start, by *interested* and *reliable* Stockholders, it will : seen that a small per centage *only* of the subscriptions will be required to put the Company in working order, and it is confidently and reasonably + that the receipts will thereafter maintain and extend it. And in order to secure an equitable voice in its management, the principal commercial will be represented at the Board, by Directors recommended by Stockholders of their own localities, who will also recommend to the Direction :l Agents, and thus secure a general influence in its management, as well as its business.

l Express enterprises, both in this country and the United States, have been decidedly successful, resulting from the profits of the business itself, ving an organization and a share list—such as are now proposed—with energy and economy in the direction, no doubt can be entertained of the atisfactory results.

ith such prospects, the Merchants of the Dominion, Capitalists and others interested in the success of this enterprise, are invited to become iolders.

The following shall be included in the By-Laws to be hereafter framed for the Government of the Company :

The Company shall be known by the name or title of "THE DOMINION EXPRESS COMPANY OF CANADA."
The Capital Stock of the Company shall be *One Million of Dollars,* divided into *Ten Thousand Shares of One Hundred Dollars each.*
Each Shareholder shall be liable only for the amount of Stock subscribed by him, her, or them.
The Shares of Stock of the Company shall be transferable; but no transfer shall be valid without the consent of the Directors, in writing, unless ares shall be paid up in full.
It shall be lawful for the Stockholders, so soon as the sum of two hundred and fifty thousand dollars shall have been subscribed, to call a General g of the subscribers, to be held at the office of the Company, in the City of Montreal, and proceed to elect nine qualified persons to be Directors Company, each of whom to be a proprietor of not less than ten Shares of Stock of the said Company, and three of whom shall form a quorum, l the powers of the Directors. The said Directors shall also, at their first General Meeting, elect a President, Secretary, Treasurer, and General atendent or Managing Director, from amongst themselves.
The said Directors so elected shall proceed, without delay, to frame all necessary By-laws to govern the Company, and shall have power to alter end the same as circumstances may require.
The Directors shall not have power either to *sell out* the said Company to any other Express Company or organization now in existence, or here. be incorporated, or to amalgamate with any other Express Company.
No Stockholder shall be at liberty to hold in his, her, or their name, more than one hundred shares of the Capital Stock of the said Company, the consent of the Directors, in writing, first having been obtained.

PROVISIONAL DIRECTORS.

MESSRS. IRA GOULD, WALTER MACFARLAN, VICTOR HUDON,	MESSRS. WM. McNAUGHTON, DUNCAN MACDONALD, JOSEPH BARSALOU,	MESSRS. ALEXANDER McGIBBON, GEORGE HEUBACH, J. T. KERBY.

OFFICERS.

PRESIDENT :	VICE-PRESIDENT :	TREASURER :	SECRETARY :
ALTER MACFARLAN.	WM. McNAUGHTON.	JOSEPH BARSALOU.	GEORGE HEUBACH.

MESSRS. CARTIER, POMINVILLE, & BETOURNAY, SOLICITORS.　　　　J. T. KERBY, GENERAL AGENT.

---

lowing are among the prominent firms in Montreal who have subscribed to the original Stock List at the formation of the Company :

Ira Gould, President Corn Exchange.	Messrs. W. McNaughton, Messrs. Sincennes & McNaughton.
Walter McFarlan, (Messrs. Walter McFarlan & Baird)	" A. W. Ogilvie & Co., Glenora Mills.
James Donelly, Wholesale Dry Goods.	" Benning & Barsalou, Auctioneers.
Luke Moore, (Messrs. Moore, Lemple & Hat-chette).	" Alex. McGibbon, China House.
Duncan Macdonald.	" T. Baillie & Co., Wholesale Dry Goods.
A. Shannon & Co., Wholesale Grocers.	" Alex. Walker, Wholesale Dry Goods.
Lewis, Kay & Co., Wholesale Dry Goods.	" Geo. Winks & Co., Wholesale Dry Goods, Albert Buildings.
George Brush, Eagle Foundry.	" W. P. Ryan, M.P.
	" Victor Hudon & Co., Wholesale Grocer.

Messrs. Boyer, Hudon, & Co.
" Z. Benoit, Wholesale Merchant.
" Evans & Evans, Wholesale Hardware.
" James Smith, M.P.
" Andrew Watson.
" A. Freeman & Co.
" John Rhynas.
" Cartier, Pominville & Betournay, Solicitors.
" Cassels & Cameron, Wholesale Dry Goods.
" Ferrier & Co., Wholesale Hardware.

Insurance.

BEAVER
Mutual Insurance Association.

HEAD OFFICE—20 TORONTO STREET,
TORONTO.

INSURES LIVE STOCK against death from any cause. The only Canadian Company having authority to do this class of business.

R. L. DENISON,
President.
W. T. O'REILLY,
Secretary.   8-1y-25

HOME DISTRICT
Mutual Fire Insurance Company.

Office—North-West Cor. Yonge & Adelaide Streets,
TORONTO.--(UP STAIRS.)

INSURES Dwelling Houses, Stores, Warehouses, Merchandise, Furniture, &c.

PRESIDENT—The Hon. J. McMURRICH.
VICE-PRESIDENT—JOHN BURNS, Esq.
JOHN RAINS, Secretary.
AGENTS:
DAVID WRIGHT, Esq., Hamilton; FRANCIS STEVENS, Esq., Barrie; Messrs. GIBBS & BRO., Oshawa.   8-1y

THE PRINCE EDWARD COUNTY
Mutual Fire Insurance Company.

HEAD OFFICE,—PICTON, ONTARIO.
President, L. B. STINSON; *Vice-President,* W. A. RICHARDS.
Directors : H. A. McFAUL, James CAVAN, James Johnson, N. S. DeMILL, William DeLong.—*Treasurer,* David Barker Secretary, John Twigg; *Solicitor,* R. J. Fitzgerald.

THIS Company is established upon strictly Mutual principles, insuring farming and isolated property, (not hazardous,) in *Townships only*, and offers great advantages to insurers, at low rates for *fire years*, without the expense of a renewal.
Picton, June 15, 1868.   9-1y

Hartford Fire Insurance Company.

HARTFORD, CONN.

Cash Capital and Assets over Two Million Dollars.

$2,026,220.29.

CHARTERED 1810.

THIS old and reliable Company, having an established business in Canada of more than thirty years standing, has complied with the provisions of the new Insurance Act, and made a special deposit of

$100,000

with the Government for the security of policy-holders, and will continue to grant policies upon the same favorable terms as heretofore.
Specially low rates on first-class dwellings and farm property for a term of one or more years.
Losses as heretofore promptly and equitably adjusted.
H. J. MORSE & Co., AGENTS.
Toronto, Ont.

ROBERT WOOD, GENERAL AGENT FOR CANADA]
56-6m

THE AGRICULTURAL
Mutual Assurance Association of Canada.

HEAD OFFICE .... LONDON, ONT.

A purely Farmers' Company. Licensed by the Government of Canada.

Capital, 1st January, 1868 .... $220,121 25
Cash and Cash Items, over $65,000 00
No. of Policies in force...................... 26,76

THIS Company insures nothing more dangerous than Farm property. Its rates are as low as any well-established Company in the Dominion, and lower than those of a great many. It is largely patronised, and continues to grow in public favor.
For Insurance, apply to any of the Agents, or address the Secretary, London, Ontario.
London, 2nd Nov., 1868.   12-1y

Insurance.

The Gore District Mutual Fire Insurance Company

GRANTS INSURANCES on all description of Property against Loss or Damage by FIRE. It is the only Mutual Fire Insurance Company which assesses its Policies yearly from their respective dates ; and the average yearly cost of insurance in it, for the past three and a half years, has been nearly
TWENTY CENTS IN THE DOLLAR
less than what it would have been in an ordinary Proprietary Company.
THOS. M. SIMONS,
Secretary & Treasurer.
ROBT. McLEAN,
Inspector of Agencies.
Galt, 26th Nov., 1868.   15-1y

Geo. Girdlestone,

FIRE, Life, Marine, Accident, and Stock Insurance Agent

Very best Companies represented.

Windsor, Ont. June, 1868.

The Standard Life Assurance Company,
Established 1825.
WITH WHICH IS NOW UNITED
THE COLONIAL LIFE ASSURANCE COMPANY.

Head Office for Canada :
MONTREAL—STANDARD COMPANY'S BUILDINGS,
No. 47 GREAT ST. JAMES STREET.
Manager—W. M. RAMSAY.   *Inspector*—RICH'D BULL.
THIS Company having deposited the sum of ONE HUNDRED AND FIFTY THOUSAND DOLLARS with the Receiver-General, in conformity with the Insurance Act passed last Session, Assurances will continue to be carried out at moderate rates and on all the different systems in practice.

AGENT FOR TORONTO—HENRY PELLATT,
KING STREET.

AGENT FOR HAMILTON—JAMES BANCROFT.
6-8mos.

Fire and Marine Assurance.

THE BRITISH AMERICA
ASSURANCE COMPANY.
HEAD OFFICE:
CORNER OF CHURCH AND COURT STREETS.
TORONTO.

BOARD OF DIRECTION :
Hon G. W. Allan, M L C.,   A. Joseph, Esq.,
George J. Boyd, Esq ,   Peter Paterson, Esq.,
Hon. W. Cayley,   G. P. Ridout, Esq.,
Richard S. Cassels, Esq.,   E H. Rutherford, Esq ,
Thomas C. Street, Esq.

Governor:
GEORGE PERCIVAL RIDOUT, Esq.
Deputy Governor:
PETER PATERSON, Esq.
Fire Inspector: Marine Inspector:
E. ROBY O'BRIEN.   CAPT. R. COURNEEN.
Insurances granted on all descriptions of property against loss and damage by fire and the perils of inland navigation.
Agencies established in the principal cities, towns, and ports of shipment throughout the Province.
THOS. WM. BIRCHALL,
Managing Director.
23-1y

Queen Fire and Life Insurance Company,
OF LIVERPOOL AND LONDON.

ACCEPTS ALL ORDINARY FIRE RISKS
on the most favorable terms.

LIFE RISKS
Will be taken on terms that will compare favorably with other Companies.

CAPITAL,   -   -   -   £2,000,000 Stg.

CHIEF OFFICES—Queen's Buildings, Liverpool, and Gracechurch Street London.
CANADA BRANCH OFFICE—Exchange Buildings, Montreal.
Resident Secretary and General Agent,
A. MACKENZIE FORBES,
13 St. Sacrament St., Merchants' Exchange, Montreal.
WM. ROWLAND, Agent, Toronto.   1-1y

Insurance.

The Waterloo County Mutual Fire Insu Company.

HEAD OFFICE : WATERLOO, ONTARIO.

ESTABLISHED 1863.
THE business of the Company is divided in separate and distinct branches, the
VILLAGE, FARM, AND MANUFACT
Each Branch paying its own losses and the just pr of the managing expenses of the Company.
C. M. TAYLOR, Sec.   M. SPRINGER, M.M.P.,
J. HUGHLE, Inspector.

Ætna Fire and Marine Insurance Comp
Dublin.

AT a Meeting of the Shareholders of this Co held at Dublin, on the 13th ult., it was agr the business of the "ETNA" should be transferre "UNITED PORTS AND GENERAL INSURANCE Co In accordance with this agreement, the business w after be carried on by the latter Company, which and guarantee all the risks and liabilities of the '
The Directors have resolved to continue the C BRANCH, and arrangements for resuming FIRE r RINE business are rapidly approaching completion
T. W. GRIFFI
16   MAN

The Commercial Union Assura
Company,
19 & 20 CORNHILL, LONDON, ENGLAND.

Capital, £2,500,000 Stg.—*Invested over* $2,000,
FIRE DEPARTMENT.—Insurance granted on scriptions of property at reasonable rates.
LIFE DEPARTMENT.—The success of this has been unprecedented—NINETY PER CENT. miums now in hand. First year's premiums we 100,000. Economy of management guaranteed security. Moderate rates.
OFFICE—385 & 387 ST PAUL STREET, MONT
MORLAND, WATSON &
General Agents for
FRED. COLE, Secretary.
Inspector of Agencies—T. C. LIVINGSTON
W. M. WESTMACOTT, *Agent at T*
16-1y

Lancashire Insurance Comp

CAPITAL, - - - - - - - - £2,000,000

FIRE RISKS
Taken at reasonable rates of premium,
ALL LOSSES SETTLED PROMPTL
By the undersigned, without reference ele
S. C. DUNCAN-CLARK & CO
General Agents for Ont
25-1y   N. W. Corner of King & Church
TORONTO.

Ætna Fire & Marine Insurance Com

INCORPORATED 1819. CHARTER PERPETC

CASH CAPITAL,   -   -   -   -   -

LOSSES PAID IN 50 YEARS, 23,500,0

JULY, 1868.
ASSETS.
(At Market Value.)
Cash in hand and in Bank...............
Real Estate.............................
Mortgage Bonds.........................
Bank Stock.............................
United States, State and City Stock, and other
Public Securities......................

Total................$

LIABILITIES.
Claims not Due, and Unadjusted ....
Amount required by Mass. and New York
for Re-insurance..........................
THOS. R. WO
50-6   Agent fo

The Canadian Monetary Times

AND INSURANCE CHRONICLE,

DEVOTED TO FINANCE, COMMERCE, INSURANCE, BANKS, RAILWAYS, NAVIGATION, MINES, INVESTMENT, PUBLIC COMPANIES, AND JOINT STOCK ENTERPRISE.

VOL. I, NO. 20.   TORONTO, THURSDAY, JAN. 2, 1868.   { SUBSCRIPTION, $2 A YEAR.

Mines.

THE MADOC GOLD REGIONS.

From our own Correspondent.

BELLEVILLE, Dec. 31, 1867.

The weather of the present winter has so far been very favorable for the prosecution of miners' work. The unusual mildness of the temperature, and the comparative absence of snow, have hitherto allowed the prospectors to pursue their investigations almost without interruption, and most of the persons so engaged have been working with redoubled energy, so as to make the most of the time when they had the field to themselves, and so to anticipate the rush of would-be discoverers, whom they expect to swarm into our now well established mineral region in the spring.

Nor have their exertions been altogether without reward. Several additional deposits have been found, and the ore assayed, and if they yield in the gross anything like the amounts found in the assays made in the small quantities, (rarely exceeding five pounds) in which they are generally manipulated, the expectations of the most sanguine among our mining population will be fully realized.

The mine discovered by Mr. Powell, in the township of Marmora, is likely to turn out of great importance, as other specimens of equal richness to those first exhibited by him have been found.

As the nature of the country, and the lay of the gold-bearing ridges begin to be better understood, those persons who are engaged in prospecting go to work more systematically and with a better likelihood of success in their still somewhat precarious occupation. A reef, leading from the Barry mine, has thus been traced across several lots to a place on No. 8, the first concession of Elzevir, known as Smith's Falls, on Black Creek, where visible gold has been found in the rock, at a small depth below the surface.

The Wellington Mining Company, whose shaft is located on the west half of lot 18, in the 6th concession of Madoc, on the east half of which lot the Richardson mine is situated, have had a preliminary survey of a small lot of quartz made by Messrs. Scott & Co., which yielded gold at the rate of $148 per ton.

Another assay by the same firm of a portion of rock from a mine in the north-east corner of the township of Rawdon, gave $150 to the ton; which was confirmed by another assay from the same place, made by Mr. Smith, of Madoc, yielding $160 per ton.

I have already mentioned the Empire mine, in the village of Madoc, as one of our first-class mines. The owners have had two samples of their ore reduced by Messrs. Daniels & Co. The first of one ton returned $34.76 in gold. The second, of 14 tons, yielded at the rate of $21.40 per ton. This, I believe, is the largest sample of ore yet assayed at one operation, and cannot fail to be regarded as a most satisfactory return. The rock was not selected with a view of getting a large yield, as the proprietors do not intend to "stock" the mine, but was taken at various depths from the surface downwards, so as to give them as correct a view as possible of the value of their property.

Something has also been done in the way of silver, though the many reported discoveries of silver, though the many reported discoveries of silver ore have by no means been substantiated. One assay, however, by J. E. Morrison, of Toronto, has produced six grains of silver from one ounce of quartz taken from lot 12, in the 5th Con. of Tudor, or at the rate of $489 37 per ton.

Many of those fallacious silver reports have unquestionably arisen from pure ignorance on the part of some of our "practical miners," who, being unacquainted with the discrimination of the metals, or the proper tests to which they should be subjected, unhesitatingly pronounced every white "button" they obtained by their insufficient smelting to be silver; whereas the said buttons were generally alloys of lead, antimony, bismuth, copper, &c. For instance, a person brought to me, on Saturday, three beautiful buttons, which he confidently believed to be "pure silver;" but on being tested they proved to be tin, of great purity. An assay is to be made of ten pounds of the rock from which they were taken, and as the proportion of ore gangue appears to be large, I hope to be able to announce in my next the discovery of a valuable mine of tin.

SILVER MINE IN NEW BRUNSWICK.—We are informed on what appears to be reliable authority, that the silver mine discovered in Prince Wm., is capable of producing silver ore to the value of $10,000 per day, and that the antimony extracted from the ore is sufficiently valuable to pay all the expenses of mining. We have been further told that Mr. Lawrence, the owner of the mine, has refused $200,000 for a single acre of this silvery soil. He owns, it is said, a thousand acres, thinks the mine inexhaustible, and supposes himself to be the richest man on this continent.—Visitor, St. John.

THE DELERY GOLD MINES.—It appears that the General Manager, Mr. Winchell, resigned his office on the first of last month, and that Professor Hind, well and favorably known in connection with our provincial scientific commissions, has received the appointment ad interim. Professor Hind's recent explorations in the No. 1 section of the company's territory have resulted in two important discoveries. The one being an extensive deposit of iron mineral, and the other some very rich veins of gold, bearing granite. The latter discovery is of the utmost importance, as rock in this condition is far richer in gold than that known as quartz. The experiments made already demonstrate exceeding richness, and a vast body of "the mass."

DUBUQUE LEAD MINES.—The amount of lead mineral raised from January 1st to Dec. 15, 1867, from the Dubuque Lead Mines, aggregates 4,000,000 pounds, equal to 50,000 pigs of lead, valued at $48 per 1,000 lbs, and the pig lead at $3.50 per cental.—Exchange.

Insurance.

SURRENDER VALUE OF LIFE POLICIES.—The Amicable Mutual Life Assurance Society, recently established in the three cities of London, Dublin and Glasgow, has adopted as a new feature a liberal table of surrender values, so that any person insuring under its whole life table can learn how much the company will allow him for his policy, providing he should at any period be compelled to abandon further payments. For example, a person aged twenty-five years who had paid a premium of £10, could, at the end of this year, resign his policy and receive back £3 6s. 8d., or one-third of this payment. At the end of ten years he could retire with £4 2s. 1d. for every £10 paid, or £41 0s. 10d. of his £100. This is the same in principle as the much cherished non forfeiture clause of this country, but upon a rather less liberal basis, for in the States, although on

money is returned to the insured upon his withdrawal, upon payment of two premiums he is furnished with a life policy for the full amount, paid in premiums, less five per cent. interest, and no further premium is charged.—Insurance Journal.

FIRE RECORD. — Stratford, Dec. 24. The Stratford Woolen Mills; total loss estimated at $8,000; insurance $1,500.

Cornwallis, N. S., Dec. 10. Barn of David Ellsley; loss about $400.

Toronto, December 31. Beard's Foundry; loss heavy. Insured in Ætna, of Dublin, for $4,000; in the Lancashire for 2,000. Total $6,000.

DISASTERS ON THE LAKES IN 1867.—The Detroit papers published a list of the disasters which have occurred on the lakes during the past season of navigation. The list is very long, the total number of casualties far exceeding the number in any former year. Instances of vessels having grounded at various points where the expense of getting off has varied from ten to $50 and numbering ninety-four cases, those being secondary in importance have been omitted. With those recited they swell the grand total of disasters for the season of 1867 to 931. Seven propellers and thirty-three grain vessels have been lost, to which may be added thirty more which were engaged exclusively in the lumber trade. Fifteen vessels engaged in the grain traffic the past year have been condemned, and unless re-built, will have to fall back to the stave or lumber freighting.

The number of lives lost on the lakes and in ports during the season, is 182, being rather below the average fatality. By far the greater number of casualties in any one month, occurred in November, when 288 vessels of all classes met with disaster. The total tonnage lost is shown by the following recapitulation:

	Number.	Tonnage.
Steamers	3	450
Propellers	6	3,143
Tugs	6	565
Barks	9	4,121
Brigs	2	624
Schooners	25	11,196
Barges	1	462
Scows	7	509
Total	56	21,070

The following were the disasters for the last eight years:—Total number of disasters in 1860, 277; in 1861, 275; in 1862, 200; in 1863, 300; in 1864, 329; in 1865, 421; in 1866, 621; in 1867, 931.

NEW RATES IN FIRE INSURANCE.—The local Board of Underwriters have abandoned the rates established about ten months ago. It is said they have been but faithlessly adhered to, and this lack of integrity amongst its members has led to the dissolution of the combination. The magnitude of their prevailing losses by fire by no means justify the resumption of competing rates, and we trust that no company will attempt to transact business below remunerative premiums.—Real Estate Journal.

GREEK FIRE.—Which is regarded as one of the most terrible of incendiaries, because it is inextinguishable by water, is discovered to possess no such quality. Instead of its having rather an appetite for water, as stated by those who love the marvellous, it is found to succumb readily to that element, and is no more to be dreaded in that respect than a box of lucifer matches.

Financial.

RENEWALS.—The Directors of the Halifax Banks have come to the determination that from and after the 1st January to the 1st July, renewals of notes falling due shall not be for more than two-thirds of original, and from the 1st July to the 31st December one half shall be the minimum, and after that the system of renewing shall forever cease. This is likely to press hard on a good many persons at first, but it is a step in the right direction, as, if persevered in, it must eventually bring about the cash system of trade in all kinds of business.

NEW PUBLICATION.—We have received an ably written pamphlet, by Mr. John McLean, on the subject of Free Trade and Protection. It is written in the interest of protection, and worthy of careful perusal.

STATISTICS OF SAVINGS BANKS AND BUILDING SOCIETIES.
Condition of Savings Banks in 1866.

Name	Head Office	Assets	Liabilities	No. of Deposit'rs	Rate of Interest	Amount paid depos. 1866	Amount withdrawn
Providential	Quebec	$74,181	$619,353	3,321	4 & 5	$427,304	56,968
Caisse D'Economie	Quebec	265,130	720,500	5,491	4	1,214,554	56,821
City and District	Montreal	1,193,239	1,062,790	29,001	4	1,677,164	74,849
Northumberld & Durham	Cobourg	164,113	156,703	1,228	4	149,639	13,235
Home District	Toronto	270,250	225,724	739	5 & 6	142,301	13,273
Toronto	Toronto	149,796	114,582	709		145,528	65,381
Total		$2,276,803	$2,901,794	13,329		$4,027,583	$418,698

Provident, L. & I.	Kingston	263,596		396	5, 6 & 7	81,892	
Western C. P. I.	Toronto	74,181		189	6	83,510	
Freehold	Toronto	89,151		285	6	78,396	
Union Bldg.	Toronto	10,186		29	4, 5 & 6	1,704	
Provincial Bldg.	Toronto	1,264		13		146,810	
Canada Permanent	Toronto	318,907		783	4 & 6	61,116	
Commercial Bldg.	Toronto	31,770		44		113,279	
Huron & Erie S. & L.	London	50,755		235		65,381	
		$920,734		1,3500		$403,100	

(Bankers Societies — Transacting Savings Bank Business — Provident and)

Statistics of Permanent Building Societies, 1866.

NAME	Assets	Amount declared
Quebec	138,684	
Montreal	204,119	10 p ct.
Montreal Dis.	343,560	10
Kingston	16,876	
Frontenac L. & B.	179,390	10
Freehold	470,242	10
Union	61,489	10
Commercial	110,855	10
Canada Permanent	1,479,580	10
Metropolitan	64,009	10
Provincial	50,854	8
Toronto	11,938	
Western Canada	287,349	10
Guelph		
Oxford	4,888	...
Huron and Erie	228,889	9
Hand-in-hand	6,452	...
Ottawa	8,558	...
Civil Service	5,586	8
Total	3,608,327	

Comparative Recapitulation.

	1864.	1865.	1866.
Amounts due Depositors	$2,781,701	$2,904,147	$2,941,761
Savings Banks proper	488,310	855,929	629,733
Savings Branches Bldg. S.	$3,270,011	$3,459,876	$3,571,40x
Moneys in hands of Permanent Bldg. Societies	$2,629,703	$3,233,983	$3,068,327
Terminable Bldg. Societies	602,803	642,399	302,493
Total	$3,232,506	$3,876,381	$3,910,829

BANK FAILURE.—The Farmers and Mechanics' Bank of Burlington, Vermont, having failed a short time since, all the effects have been disposed of and a final dividend declared to the stockholders, of $7.40 per share, or 20 per cent. One hundred and five per cent. having been previously divided, the stockholders have had their entire capital returned them and a surplus of a little over twenty-seven per cent. Cause of failure—heavy losses in 1854.

"THE CANADIAN MONETARY TIMES."—Dr. Kempson, of the CANADIAN MONETARY TIMES AND INSURANCE CHRONICLE, a well conducted and valuable paper, published in Toronto, is in town canvassing in the interest of that journal. Mr. Cochrane has been appointed agent for this city and neighborhood. The MONETARY TIMES is highly spoken of by the American as well as the Canadian press, and we are glad to learn that, so far, Dr. Kempson has been most successful in his canvass.—Ottawa Times.

Law Report.

CURIOUS MARINE INSURANCE CASE.—The case of Dabney vs. the New England Life Mutual Insurance Company, was an action of contract upon a policy of insurance on the bark Fredonia, issued to the plaintiff by the defendant, to recover a sum of money, as general average for a jettison of a part of a cargo of oranges thrown overboard from the Fredonia and belonging to the plaintiff. In December, 1865, the bark Fredonia landed at this port about three hundred emigrants, who were taken from the ship Gratitude, which the captain of the bark found in a sinking condition. In order to make room for the passengers and crew of the ship the captain was obliged to throw overboard a part of his cargo of fruit, or leave the passengers and crew of the Gratitude to go down with the ship. The action was brought in the Superior Civil Court of Mass., and judgment ordered for the plaintiff. Exceptions were taken by the defendant and the case was carried to the Supreme Court. The following are the grounds upon which the Court ordered judgment for the defendant:—"The facts show that the immediate motive and cause of the jettison were not to preserve or restore the navigability of the vessel insured, but to make room for and receive on board the passengers and crew of another vessel, which was in imminent danger of foundering at sea with all on board. The jettison cannot, therefore, be deemed to have been before sacrifice of a part of the cargo for the purpose of obtaining safety from a peril impending over the vessel and cargo and freight. There was not a general average loss entitling the owner of cargo to contribution."

CONTRACT MADE IN CHICAGO.—A contract for the sale of goods to the plaintiffs at a certain price, payable in Toronto, was made by the defendant at Chicago, through his agent there the goods to be shipped by the G. T. R. from Toronto. No sold note was signed by the broker until after action brought for the non delivery: but it was proved that the 17th section of the Statute of Frauds was not in force in Illinois. It was held by the Court that the contract being valid when it was made could enforced here, though not in writing.—Gre v. Lewis, 26 Q. B. Reports.

Official Notices.

Notice is given that the Montreal Ci Passenger Railway Company will apply to t Legislature of Quebec for an Act grant amendments to its charter.

Notice is given that application will be ma to the Legislature of Quebec, for an amen ment to the Act incorporating "The Sh brooke Manufacturing Company," so as admit of an early election of Directors, and other purposes.

The annual general meeting of the Brockvi and Ottawa Railway Company will be held the "Campbell House," in Brockville, Wednesday, the fifth of February next.

Application will be made to the Legislatu of Quebec, for an Act to incorporate a co pany for the purpose of manufacturing boo shoes and other goods.

Notice is given that application will be ma to Parliament for an Act to amend the J chaptered 106, 29th and 30th Victoria, is tuled, an Act to incorporate the Ottawa C Passenger Railway Company.

Notice is given that application will made to the Lieutenant Governor of Ontar for a charter of incorporation, by the followi persons, viz.: Alpheus Field Wood, of Mad merchant; Richard Sparling, of Madoc, min Thomas Scram McGlashan, of Madoc, min Mahlon Burwell McGregor, of Madoc, liv keeper; Thomas Alexander Mitchell, of Mad miner, all in the county of Hastings; Jc Joseph Vickers, of Toronto, agent; Jar Edwin Ellis, of Toronto, jeweller. The h office of the company is to be at the village Madoc, and the operations of the company to be carried on in the township of Madoc, the county of Hastings, in the Province Ontario, and elsewhere in Canada. The c tal stock of the company is $72,000. ' number of shares is 2,400, and the value each is $30. The amount of stock paid i $47,310, which has been invested in min issue numbers 61, 62, 63, and 64, and number in the 5th concession of the township of Mac designated Eldorado.

Notice is given that application will made by petition to the Governor General Council for a Charter of Incorporation letters patent, by William Dow, gentle Benjamin Hutchins, merchant. William lace Stuart, merchant, Alexander Wal merchant, and James Moir, merchant, a the city of Montreal. The proposed corpo name of the company is "The Anglo-S Gold Mining Company." The head offic the company is to be at Montreal, and operations of the company are to be carrie in the township of Madoc. The nom capital of the company is $25,000 curre The number of shares is 25,000, and the v of each share is $5 currency. The amour stock subscribed is $100,000 currency.

— Shipbuilding on the Merrimack is al given up at present, two ships and two sel ers being all the vessels now on the st Cause: protective tariff.

FISHING LICENCES.—From a return ma the fishing licenses issued, the followi gleaned:—Issued from Nova Scotia ports, —341 vessels at 50 cents per ton, $9,368 1867—277 vessels, at $1. per ton, $1 Canada, on schooner "La Canadienne," 1 10 vessels 50 cents per ton, $2.96. New B wick, 1866—1 vessel at 50 cents per ton, Total, $23,109 50.

ADVANCE ON BEER.—The Toronto br advanced the price of beer, ale, and p five cents per gallon, on the 20th inst.

MONTREAL OCEAN STEAMSHIP COMPANY.—We notice that the Montreal Ocean Steamship company is building two new vessels of 3,000 tons each, to be respectively called the "European" and "Abyssinian." It may not be generally known, but it is nevertheless a fact, that the Messrs. Allans are now the largest steamship owners on the continent. Their Liverpool line may now be said to comprise 11 vessels, of a total of 27,188 tons, and their Glasgow line é vessels, of 5,757, or together 15 splendid full powered two screw steamers, of an aggregate of 32,925 tons. No other company in this side of the Atlantic can show such a large and fine fleet, for it may be said to be principally owned in this city. There is another fact in this connection which we would draw attention to. These 3,000 ton vessels are intended to come up to Montreal. Ship owners abroad may therefore form some idea of our harbour and the channel which leads up to.—*Montreal Gazette.*

GRAIN TRADE OF BUFFALO.—The receipts of grain at Buffalo for the last 18 years are shown by the following figures:

Years	Grain, bu.	Years	Grain, bu.
1849	11,986,690	1858	23,686,374
1850	11,585,649	1859	18,049,798
1851	16,762,673	1860	41,729,100
1852	18,588,876	1861	62,275,951
1853	19,816,019	1862	74,811,877
1854	23,796,038	1863	66,713,000
1855	21,613,904	1864	47,683,270
1856	30,798,225	1865	51,400,100
1857	16,142,310	1866	51,670,100
		1877	56,798,300

In 1866 the receipts are only to December 8th ; in 1867 the receipts are only to November 30th.

FAILURE.—John C. Fox, the piano-forte makers of Kingston, have failed for $66,000.

C. K. Remington,
266 MAIN STREET, BUFFALO, N. Y.

MUSIC Publisher, and dealer in all kinds of Musical Instruments and Merchandise.
All orders promptly attended to Orders from the Dominion of Canada solicited.
ly

J. T. & W. Pennock,
FIRE and Life Insurance Agents, Parliamentary and Departmental Agents, Mining Agents, and Exchange Brokers.
Ottawa, Dec. 31st, 1867.   10-1y

Western Assurance Company,
(OF CANADA.)

HEAD OFFICE:
COR. CHURCH AND COLBORNE STREETS,
TORONTO.

FIRE AND MARINE INSURANCE.

CAPITAL STOCK, ... $400,000.

STOCK paid in $96,351 03
Surplus account 36,736 01

Total (being investments at estimated value and Cash in Bank at 30th November, 1867).......$103,789 61

Premium Receipts for the year ending 30th November, 1867 ...... $171,300 56

PRESIDENT:
HON J. McMURRICH:

VICE-PRESIDENT:
CHARLES MAGRATH, Esq.

DIRECTORS:
Robert Beaty, Esq.   James Michie, Esq.
Noah Lewis, Esq.   Charles Magrath, Esq.
Archie J. McMurrich.   Thomas Haworth, Esq.
M. P. Smith, Esq.   John Fisken, Esq.
A. Manning, Esq.

W. W. Blight, ... *Fire Inspector.*
Capt. J. T. Douglas,.....*Marine Inspector.*

BERNARD HALDAN,
Secretary.

Western Assurance Company's Office,
Toronto, Dec 28, 1867.   }   20-tf : 19-3m

The Standard Life Assurance Company,
WITH which is now united the COLONIAL
ASSURANCE COMPANY.
Established 1825.

HEAD OFFICE—*EDINBURGH and MONTREAL.*
Accumulated Fund, upwards of $8,000,000.
Income, 1867 .... $3,385,000.
Manager—W. M. RAMSAY. *Inspector*—RICH'D BULL.
TORONTO—HENRY PELLATT, AGENT. .
Agencies in every Town throughout the Dominion.
18-1y

The St. Lawrence Glass Company
ARE now manufacturing and have for sale,

COAL OIL LAMPS,
various styles and sizes.
LAMP CHIMNEYS,
of extra quality for ordinary Burners
also, for the '*Comet*' and '*Sun*' Burners
— SIZES OF —
TABLE GLASSWARE, HYACINTH GLASSES;
STEAM GUAGE TABLES, GLASS RODS, &c.,
or any other article made to order., in *White* or
Colored Glass.

KEROSENE BURNERS, COLLARS and SOCKETS,
will be kept on hand.

DRUGGISTS' FLINT GLASSWARE, and
PHILOSOPHICAL INSTRUMENTS,
made to order.

OFFICE—388 ST. PAUL STREET, MONTREAL.
A. McK. COCHRANE,
18-1y   *Secretary.*

Phœnix Insurance Company,
BROOKLYN, N. Y.

PHILANDER SHAW,   EDGAR W. COWELL,
Secretary.   *Vice-President*
STEPHEN CROWE, *President.*

Capital, $1,000,000. Surplus, $666,416.62. To tal, $1,666,416.02. Entire Income from all sources for 1866 was $2,151,839.82. .

CHARLES G. FORTIER, *Marine Agent,*
Ontario Chambers, Toronto, Ont.   10-1y.

Honore Plamondon,
CUSTOM House Broker, Forwarder, and General
Agent, Quebec.
Office—*Custom House Building.*
Quebec, 9th December, 1867.   .   17-1y

Western Canada Permanent Building
AND SAVINGS SOCIETY.

NINTH HALF-YEARLY DIVIDEND.

NOTICE is hereby given, that a Dividend of 5 per cent on the capital stock of this institution has been declared for the half-year ending 31st inst., and the same will be payable at the office of the Society No. 70 Church St., on and after

WEDNESDAY, 8th DAY OF JANUARY NEXT.

The transfer books will be closed from the 10th to 31st December inclusive.
By order of the Board.
WALTER S. LEE,
Sec and Treasurer.
Toronto, Dec. 21.   19-tf

Canada Life Assurance Company.

ESTABLISHED IN 1847.

Incorporated under Special Act of Parliament.

Amount of Capital and Funds, over...... $1,300,000
Assurances in force, over................... $4,000,000
Number of Policies in force, over 3,000
Annual Income, over $170,000
Claims paid for Deaths since commencement of Company, over........... $450,000
This Company was specially established for the purpose of granting to assurers every security, advantage and facility which prudence or liberality can suggest; and that course has resulted in a larger amount of Life Assurance in Canada than any other Institution there.
Table of Rates for the more general form of Life Assurance, and every information, may be obtained at the Head Office, Hamilton, or at any of the Agencies.
A. G. RAMSAY,
Manager.

Office in Toronto, Toronto Street.
E. BRADBURNE,
Agent

J. R. Boyce,
NOS. 63 and 65, Great James Street, Montreal,
Dealer and Importer of all kinds of TOYS and
FANCY GOODS. J. R. B. is the only manufacturer
of La Crosse Sticks for the new *Indian Game of LA
CROSSE*, and has constantly on hand a large supply,
with the printed *Rules of the Game.* He also manufactures all the requisites for Croquet, and all other
Parlour and Lawn Games. Baskets, of all kinds, and
every variety of *Hair Work, Wigs, Curls, Beards,
&c. ; Dress and Theatrical Wigs,* for sale, Wholesale
and Retail. Parties engaged in forming new La
Crosse Clubs, will do well to apply direct to the
above address.
Nov. 30, 1867.   16-1y

The Commercial Union Assurance
Company,
19 & 20 CORNHILL, LONDON, ENGLAND.
Capital, £2,500,000 Stg.—*Invested over $2,000,000.*

FIRE DEPARTMENT.—Insurance granted on all descriptions of property at reasonable rates.
LIFE DEPARTMENT.—The success of this branch has been unprecedented—*NINETY PER CENT.* of premiums now in hand . First year's premiums were over $100,000 . Economy of management guaranteed. Perfect security. Moderate rates.
OFFICE—385 & 387 ST. PAUL STREET, MONTREAL.
MORLAND, WATSON & CO.,
General Agents for Canada.
FRED. COLE, *Secretary.*
Inspector of Agencies—T. C. LIVINGSTON, F.L.S.
W. M. WESTMACOTT, *Agent at Toronto.*
16-1y

Phœnix Mutual Life Insurance Co.
HARTFORD, CONN.

Accumulated Fund, $2,000,000, Income, $1,000,000

THIS Company, established in 1851, is one of the most reliable Companies doing business in the country, and has been steadily prospering. The *Massachusetts Insurance Reports* show that in nearly all important matters it is superior to the general average of Companies. It offers to intending assurers the following reasons, amongst others, for preferring it to other companies :
It is purely Mutual. It allows the Insured to travel and reside in any portion of the United States and Europe. It throws out almost all restriction on occupation from its Policies. It will, if desired, take a note for part of the Premium, thus combining all the advantages of a note and all cash company. Its Dividends are declared annually, and applied in reduction of Premium. Its Dividends are in every case on Premiums paid. The Dividends of the PHŒNIX have averaged fifty per cent. yearly. In the settlement of Policies, a Dividend will be allowed for each year the policy has been in force. The number of Dividends will always equal the outstanding Notes. It pays its losses promptly—during its existence never having contested a claim. It issues Policies for the benefit of Married Women beyond the reach of their husband's creditors. Creditors may also insure the lives of Debtors. Its Policies are all *Non-forfeiting*, as it always allows the assured to surrender his Policy, should he desire, the Company giving a paid-up Policy therefor. This important feature will commend itself to all. The inducements now offered by the PHŒNIX are better and more liberal than those of any other Company. Its rate of Mortality is exceedingly low, and under the average.
Parties contemplating *Life Insurance* will find it to their interest to call and examine our system. Policies issued payable either in Gold or American currency.
ANGUS R. BETHUNE,
General Manager,
Dominion of Canada.
Office 104 ST. FRANÇOIS XAVIER ST. MONTREAL.
Active and energetic Agents and Canvassers wanted in every town and village, to whom liberal inducements will be given.   16-1y

---

Reliance Mutual Life Assurance
SOCIETY, (*Established, 1840,*) OF LONDON, E. C.

Accumulated Funds, over $1,000,000.
Annual Income, over $300,000
THE entire Profits of this long-established Society belong to the Policy-holders.
HEAD OFFICE FOR DOMINION—MONTREAL.
15-1y   T. W. GRIFFITH, *Managers Sec'y.*

Ætna Insurance Company of Dublin.
The number of Shareholders exceeds Five Hundred

Capital, $2,500,000—Annual Income nearly $1,000,000
THIS Company takes Fire and Marine Risks on the most favorable terms.
T. W. GRIFFITH, *Manager for Canada.*
Chief office for Dominion—Corner St. François Xavier and St. Sacrament Sts., Montreal   15-1y

The Canadian Monetary Times.

THURSDAY, JAN. 2, 1868.

WESTERN ASSURANCE COMPANY.

The annual meeting of the shareholders
of this company was held at their offices in
this city, on the 27th inst. From a statement submitted by the Directors, it appears
that the total premiums received during the
year amounted to $171,960.56. After pro-
viding for losses adjusted and unadjusted,
footing up to $81,489 on fire and $17,739 on
marine risks, or a total of $99,228, a bal-
ance of $36,017.75 is carried to the credit of
profit and loss account. A dividend at the
rate of 8 per cent per annum was
declared on the half year, absorbing the
sum of $2,395. The report is considered
satisfactory.

THE GRAND TRUNK RAILWAY.

We have noticed at various times in
Herepath's Railway Journal, articles respecting the treatment the Grand Trunk Company received from Canada, whose tenor is
very unfair to us. Little credit is given for

what we have done, and our motives are
misconstrued. We are all willing to admit
that the road has been and is of the greatest
service to our country, and we all regret that
owing to a variety of circumstances it has
not been profitable as an investment. But
we do not use the language that our influential contemporary puts into our mouths,
nor are we so avaricious as we are represented to be. If those Englishmen who
put their money into the enterprise have
suffered and lost, we, Canadians, have suffered and lost likewise. But if all that we
have done has been forgotten, we take the
liberty of recalling a few suggestive facts.

When the prospectus of the Grand Trunk
Company was issued, the sum advanced and
to be advanced by the Province was fixed by
legislative enactment at £2,211,500 sterling
in Provincial debentures, secured by the
first hypothec on these particular works to
which the guarantee was supplied. These
constituted the inducements as far as the
Canadian Government was concerned, held
out in the prospectus to capitalists to invest.
In 1854, by the Grand Trunk Act, the
Government lien was declared to. apply to
the whole railway and its work.

In May, 1855, additional aid was grant-
by loan of £900,000 sterling, pursuant to
Act of Parliament. This was made a fir.
charge, payable in twenty years with inte
est. In July, 1856, the Province surrender
its first hypothec on the road, to the exte
of £2,000,000 sterling. In 1857 addition
relief was afforded by granting an extension of one year of time to complete t
Company's works. In 1858 the issue
additional preferential bonds was allowe.
The Government itself came to the assi-
ance of the Company, by making loans
advances through the Bank of Upper Cana
and thereby enabled the Company to t
over its financial difficulties. In 1862, po
was given to issue equipment mortg
bonds, a first charge on the road, to the
tent of £500,000.

Although the responsibility of the Pr
ince on behalf of the Company at the ou
was £2,211,500 sterling, yet additional
to the amount of £900,000 stg. was gran
The first hypothec of the Province s
diminished by the issue of two mill s
preferential bonds. An additional liabi s
was incurred by the Government of mee g
the obligations of the Company for inte
for a period of five years, in respect of e
whole £3,111,500, accepting in repayt ic
of this further advance, an equal am in
of stock in the share capital of the Comp.
Afterwards the Province gave up all c n
to interest from the Company until ts
earnings would be sufficient to pay al -
terest, with a dividend of six per cent t r
shareholders. Subsequently, as we
seen, the Company was empowered to m
an additional debt of half a million, w
privilege of priority of repayment w
any of the obligations of the Company.

Now, what proportion of the amount invested or lost do we Canadians bear?

Provincial bonds..................	$15,142,633
Municipal bonds.................	1,500,000
Stock held privately.............	250,000
Local loans......................	1,000,000
Interest to December, 1862......	6,368,947
Interest from 1862 to 1867; say	5,500,000
	$29,761,580

It cannot be said with justice that our Legislature has not acted in a liberal spirit towards the Grand Trunk Company, from its inception to the present time ; and considering the great expenditures rendered necessary by the opening up of the country and promoting its commercial interests, we are not ashamed of the amount we have put into the enterprise. The financial agents of this Province in London, great English contractors and their friends in Canada, have been the gainers. During the past seven years the earnings paid in cash out of its net earnings for dividends and interest the sum of $7,844,965 ; but we got none of the money. We have undertaken to build the Intercolonial Railway, which will directly benefit the Grand Trunk, and we are decided on the subject of further assistance to a Company which has taxed our resources heavily and will do so for years to come.

SUSPENSION.

A telegraphic despatch informs us of the failure of Browne, Gillespie & Co., wholesale grocers of Hamilton. Losses arising in connection with the failure of Havilland, Routh & Co., of Montreal, and unfortunate speculations in produce are assigned as the cause. It is hoped the firm may be enabled to resume business.

CAPT. TYLER'S REPORT.

Captain Tyler, who was sent out to examine and report upon the condition of the Grand Trunk Railway, has presented to the Board of that Company a voluminous and elaborate report. The editor of *Herepath's Journal* says with respect to it—

"We rise from a perusal of this honest and able report with the conviction that all our notions of the Grand Trunk are right—that it is a property, and, with good management, a little further assistance and those comparatively small completing works executed, it will be a very valuable property at a future time." Capt. Tyler refers to the competition to which the Grand Trunk system, comprising a total length of 1377 miles, is subjected ; the employment of "agencies" which this competition rendered necessary, and the modification of rates by the competition against water navigation for six or seven months in the year, he finds that the maintenance and renewals of way and works averaged in 1866,11¼ per mile against 5½ for railways in the United Kingdom.

He estimates that when the line is in good working order, 6¾ will be enough, and under such circumstances a saving would be effected of £115,000 a year in the department of working expenses. He analyses the traffic thus :

		30th June, 1867.	31st Dec., 1866.	
	Miles.	Dols.	Dols.	Dols.
(Grand Trunk Proper	72.47	87.20	97.07	
Atlantic District	101.38	135.21	142.33	
Montreal & Champlain	83	122.58	68.83	
Buffalo and Goderich	84	48.47	62.42	
Detroit & Port Huron	61	63.83	60.47	
	89	68.83	69.09	
	7	90.01	113.34	
	22	42.71	22.77	
Three Rivers Branch	45.82	11.98	8.53	
	14.38			
Total.	1377			
Average of the whole.		82.19	89.39	96.81

And the following are similar averages for certain portions of the above districts :—

Half-year ending Dec., 1862.	Dec. 31st. 1866 1865
$.c.	$. c. $. c.
63-64...Sarnia and Toronto...	120-68...114-70
106-12...Toronto and Kingston	140-24...130-42
104-82...Kingston and Montreal	132-52...126-58
100-96...Montreal & Richmond	143-34...114-97
87-87...Richmond & Point Levi	40-55... 39-88
87-40...Richmond and Island Pond...	86-13... 98-43
12-66...Chaudière Junction and Rivière du Loup...	14-12... 15-77

The steel rail question is disposed of very summarily. Capt. Tyler states his conviction to be, that iron rails of appropriate form, good quality and sufficient hardness in the heads, may be made to last on most parts of the line for 15 years, and on the average of the railway for very much more. There are rails now in the track which have carried a heavy traffic for periods varying from 10 up to even 20 years. The real question to be solved is how to obtain suitable material from the manufacturers. He considers that the climate of Canada has been made to bear more than its share of blame for the failure of rails that would not have been durable in any climate. He states that the railway is better sleepered than many of the railways in England, but the road was not well ballasted originally, and that the original rails were not of good quality, and their joints were badly fastened by light chairs. From the use of peat fuel he expects a saving of £40,000 a year or more as the traffic increases. He deprecates the expense of laying down a third rail from Fort Erie to Sarnia, but recommends that the Detroit and Port Huron road should be made a broad gauge line. He insists upon the importance of constructing, with the least possible delay, the Intercolonial Railway at Buffalo. He doubts the prospects of the Great Western and Grand Trunk working harmoniously under the present agreement, and recommends a complete amalga-

mation. He considers that the Managing Director and officers of the Grand Trunk in Canada have been ably and honestly doing their best for the line.

He sums up the amounts which will require to be raised on capital account as follows :

(1.) Bridge over Niagara River at Buffalo, with connections on both sides of the river, to be commenced as soon as possible......£250,000	
(2.) Expense consequent on, and incurred in, widening gauge on Detroit and Port Huron railway —to be carried out at once— broad gauge engines being supplied from other parts of the system	20,000
(3.) Additional steam ferry boat at Sarnia, with wharfage, berths, &c., to be ready on completion of the Buffalo bridge............	25,000
(4.) 20 engines (including 25 now under construction), 10 passenger cars, 300 freight cars, required in the course of next year	125,000
(5.) Buildings for engines,—much required,............	15,000
(6.) Completion of ballasting,—say, in 5 years, if possible..........	60,000
(7.) Trimming, draining, and turfing slopes of cuttings..........	10,000
(8.) Improvements for three years in stations, sidings, extra weights of rails and flat-plating.......	60,000
(9.) Completion of system of signals	6,000
(10.) Arrangements for changing trucks of cars at Buffalo and Detroit, to obviate inconvenience of break of gauge, and an expenditure of £175,000 for third rail between Sarnia and Fort Erie,— say	5,000
	£576,000

A further expenditure must be contemplated of :

30 engines, 10 passengers' cars, 300 freight cars, perhaps for 1868-9, but at all events to be ready before the Buffalo Bridge is completed	£125,000
Buildings for engines, by the same time..............	15,000
Further "improvement" in way and works..........	30,000
Further for cuttings..........	10,000
Permanent passengers' station, and extra freight accommodation at Toronto............	5,000
General offices, freight, warehouse, and passenger station at Bonaventure street, Montreal........	25,000
Altogether £215,000	

Of these last mentioned works the freight accommodation for extra traffic at Montreal and Toronto are the most pressing. The above two amounts form a total of £780,000; and it may be considered roughly that £500,000 of this sum would be spent for the Grand Trunk, and £286,000 for the purposes of the Buffalo and Lake Huron Railway. But inasmuch as greatly increased traffic, such as may be expected from the above developments, always requires increasing expenditure, and as the Intercolonial Railway may now be expected to be rapidly proceeded with, a further sum of £114,000 would be a moderate amount to be added for contingencies extending over the next six or eight years. And a total expenditure of £900,000 should therefore be anticipated, to do justice to the property, and to Canada.

THE CANADIAN GRAPHITE COMPANY.

From a Correspondent.

Through the courtesy of the agent of the above named company I was enabled to gather some few items as to their mines and works, and the mineral products of the lands adjacent. I find that gold, iron, and plumbago have been found in Buckingham Township, in the County of Ottawa. The works and mines belonging to this company are situated about 30 miles from the Capital. The mines have been in operation only since last Spring. When the first shafts were sunk and veins of the metal tested, they were found to be rich in plumbago in a pure state, and in large masses or blocks. There is one piece which I examined in the office of the agent, of pure plumbago, which had been just brought from the mine ; it weighed upwards of 250 pounds, and was about three feet long and one foot in diameter. The vein from which this piece was taken varied in width from 8 to 10 feet, gradually extending in width. As you descend the mine these veins of plumbago crop out on the ground for a length of 100 feet. On the same lot, and near to this lot, there are five other veins of plumbago, cropping out and giving equal promise. No shafts have as yet been sunk to work these veins. All these strata are situated upon ground elevated about 100 feet above the level of the ground adjacent ; thus allowing every facility for drainage. All the above described are on the north half of lot No. 21, on the seventh range of Buckingham Township. Upon the south half of lot No. 20, on the eighth range, a vast bed of disseminated plumbago is found, 230 feet in width and 60 feet in depth. This bed runs right up the face of a mountain, and at present it is impossible to say what is its extent ; but the ore is said to be rich, and to contain on an average from 20 to 30 per cent of pure plumbago. Average specimens of the ores obtained from these mines have been scientifically tested, both in England and Scotland, by chemical assayists, and the plumbago is pronounced equal to the best obtained from Ceylon for crucible purposes. Gold also is said to have been found in a creek on lot No. 19 in the eighth range ; and traces of sulphuret of silver are found in close proximity to the plumbago veins above alluded to. Gold has also been found in the adjoining Township of Templeton. The ore has been assayed and tested by Dr. Girdwood, and been found to yield an average of $17 of gold and $2 of silver to the ton.

Railway News.

GREAT WESTERN RAILWAY.—Traffic for the week ending Dec. 13, 1867 :—

Passengers.....................	$25,857 20
Freight and live stock.....	40,485 62
Mails and sundries...........	4,522 88
Total........................	70,865 70
Corresponding week, 1866.	47,011 13
Increase........................	23,854 57

NORTHERN RAILWAY.—Traffic receipts for the week ending Dec. 21, 1867 :—

Passengers	$2,385 84
Freight..........................	3,802 33
Mails and sundries	107 41
Total receipts for week...	6,385 63
Corresponding week, 1866...	5,446 55
Increase........................	939 08

EUROPEAN & N. AMERICAN RAILWAY.— The following were the traffic receipts for the month ended Nov. 30, of this and last year :—

	1867	1866
Passengers...............	$5,821 07	$5,602 47
Freight..................	8,903 46	8,430 00
Mails and Sundries...	721 00	898 00
Totals..........	$15,465 53	$14,930 50
Increase, $535 03.		

NEW ENGLAND INSURANCE GAZETTE.—We have received the last number of this excellent representative of insurance interests of New England, and we are sorry that our space will not allow us to borrow some of its reading matter. However, we take this opportunity of recording our sincere thanks to the editor for kindness and attention to our representative during his recent visit to Boston.

TONNAGE OF THE UNITED STATES.—The entire registered tonnage of the United States in the year ending with June, 1861, was 5,539,-843 tons—last June 30th, it was only 3,868,-615. The registered steam tonnage has increased from 102,608 tons to 175,520 tons, but there is a lamentable falling off in sailing vessels.

CULTIVATION OF GRAPES IN OHIO.—3,000 acres of grapes are under cultivation in Erie and Ottawa counties, Ohio, including the islands of Lake Erie, from which it is estimated that 200,000 gallons of wine were produced the past year. Growers have established a standard price at one mill per pound for each degree of specific gravity of must. The average production of grapes on the islands this year has been about one and a half tons per acre. The Kelly Island Wine Company purchased the grapes from about 225 acres, and have manufactured about 65,000 gallons of wine. Other parties have made at least 45,000 gallons, being a total of 100,000 gallons that is now stored on that island. Bass Island, it is estimated, had also in store 45,000 gallons in wine. Bass Island has sold more fruit for table purposes, in proportion to the ground in cultivation, than Kelley's Island. Additional attention is being given to the culture of new varieties of grapes. This is occasioned by a slight want of confidence in the Catawbas. Among those being most planted are Concords, Delawares Hartfords, Rogers,. Ives. Norton's Virnia, &c.

DUTIES ON BREADSTUFFS.—The Halifax (N. S.) Colonist states that a petition is being very generally signed, praying the General Government to remit the duty on Corn, Cornmeal and Rye Flour, on the ground that these articles enter largely into the consumption of the Fishery class, which, owing to the failure of fish and land crops, are now reduced to a state of great distress.

The Legislature of Nova Scotia has been called together for the despatch of business on the 30th January.

Market Review.

TORONTO, January 2, 1868.

In our local market but a small business has been done during the week, owing to the presence of the holidays.

Grain.—Receipts of wheat continue moderate, but so soon as sleighing becomes general they must increase, as there is undoubtedly a fair amount of stock still left in the hands of farmers and dealers at the various points distributed throughout the country. Our market continues very firm, with a good demand for milling purposes. At present prices of flour the margin on grinding wheat, at the rates now paid for it, is unprofitably small, but a rise in the former article seems to be confidently anticipated. This was shown during the week, by purchases for future delivery, at prices which would not be justified in the present state of the market. Fall wheat seems very scarce, and the few little lots that are put on the market

are held at $1.70 to $1.75, with buyers at $1.65 for choice. The receipts of wheat, up to date, at this point, are much the same as last year; but at Montreal an increase of 1,854,220 bush. is shown by the returns. The total shipments by sea-going vessels from the latter port during season of navigation were 1,459,622 bushels. Barley is very scarce and dear, the supply at the principal points seeming to have been found quite inadequate. Quotations in this market are nominal at $1.05. Oats, firm, with a good local demand, and fair receipts at 52 to 55c. Peas, no wholesale movement ; nominal at 72 to 74c. for small lots.

Flour.—Receipts light, shipments being generally made direct from the principal milling points on the Grand Trunk to Montreal and Portland. All the principal Canadian markets are firm, but lacking American markets show a downward tendency. There is little demand for the higher grades, nearly the whole business done being restricted to No. 1 superfine and inferior kinds. For No. 1 the market is nominal at $6.75 to $6.80 for good brands; in Montreal, the same grade is quoted at $7.25 to $7.35. Extra nominal at $7.30 to $7.40.

Provisions.—The market for dressed hogs continues moderately active at $4.75 to $6.00, according to weight and quality. Among the receipts we notice a large preponderance of thin hogs, fit only for roll bacon ; very few are fit for mess pork. Packers are putting down a good deal, and there is a free shipping movement to Montreal. In barrelled pork, no business is being done, and the inquiry is very limited. Mess is firm at $18. In cut meats and hog products generally, there is nothing doing to notice. The number of hogs packed at the places mentioned below, thus far this season, to the 18th inclusive, compared with last year, were as follows :—

	1867.	1866.
Cincinnati....................	248,129	179,486
Louisville...................	129,839	91,876
Detroit......................	14,667	3,615
St. Louis....................	150,500	38,000
Chicago.....................	806,800	308,800

Butter is firm, and good to choice is scarce, buyers having scoured the country in vain for lots ; inferior to medium is in fair supply, but there is no doubt of an immense falling off in the production, owing to the dryness of the season. Dairy packed has been sold in round lots, in one or two cases at 18c., holders now asking 19c.; store packed is held at 12 to 15c. cheese nominal at 8 to 9c.

Freights.—Tariff rates by Grand Trunk to the following points are: flour to all stations from Belleville to Lynn, inclusive, 35c., grain for 100 lbs. 18c.; flour to Brockville and Corn wall, inclusive, 43c., grain 22c.; flour to Montreal 50c., grain 25c.; flour to Montreal 50c., grain 25c.; flour to all stations between Island Pond and Portland, inclusive, 85c., grain 43c. flour to Halifax $1 05c., grain 53c.; flour to St John 95c.; Marine Insurance, Portland to Halifax 1¼ on flour, and to St. John 1 per cent. Dressed hogs, Torronto to Montreal, $70 per car load of 20,000 lbs., in less quantities 40c. per 200 lbs. Toronto to Liverpool, by Grand Trunk via Portland—boxed meats, per 100 lb. 90c.; lard and butter $1; beef, per tierce, 15 6d. stg.; pork, per brl. 11s. 6d.; flour and oatmeal 7s. Rates by Great Western—flour Suspension Bridge 25c.; Suspension Bridge Boston 90c., American currency.

HALIFAX MARKET, Dec. 26.—Business has been quiet during the week, the weather being stormy fish operations in consequence have been retarded There has been some activity in Breadstuffs owing to the increased duty on Corn, Cornmeal, and Rye flour. The imports are light ; the exports are about an average but fall far short of last week especially to West Indies.

Breadstuffs.—Flour has advanced, owing to the lightness of importations, No. 1 Canada being scarce, this quality has advanced and is worth $8 65 a $7 5, holders are firm, prices are likely keep up, as there is an upward tendency in Canada Extra Canada may be quoted 89 a $9 25 ; Extra State $8 40 a $8 50 ; Rye $7 a $7 25, and likely advance ; Corn Meal in active request, $6 50 Kiln dried ; Halifax ground nominal, this market bare at present ; Oatmeal scarce and wanted, may be quoted $3 75 a $4 for Canadian. Imports on the week : From United States, 1264 bbls Flour 638 bbls Cornmeal, 205 bags Corn : From P. E. Island, 16 bbls Oatmeal.—R. C. Hamilton & Co Circular.

STOCK AND BOND REPORT.

The dates of our quotations are as follows:—Toronto, Jan. 2; Montreal, Dec. 30; Quebec, Dec. 30; Halifax, Dec. 0; St. John, Dec. 0; London (Eng.), Dec. 14.

NAME.	Head Office.	Capital.	Shares.	Paid up.	Dividend last Six Months.	Dividend Day.	Closing Prices. Toronto.	Montre'l	Quebec.	St John	Halifax.	London, (Eng.)
BANKS.		$										
Bank of British North America....	London, Eng	4,866,666	£50 Stg.	All.	4½ ℘ ct.	July and Jan.	....	bks clo'd	bks clo'd	....	....	47 49
Banque Jacques Cartier	Montreal,	1,000,000	$ 50	"	4 "	1 June, 1 Dec.	....	105½ 106½	106 106½	....	....	....
Bank of Montreal	"	6,000,000	200	"	5 "	"	128	129 130	128½ 129½	....	....	....
Banque Nationale	"	1,000,000	50	"	4 "	1 Nov. 1 May.	....	106 107	106½ 106¾	....	....	....
Bank of New Brunswick	St. John.	600,000	100	"	......	......	....	....	....	....	....	....
Bank of Nova Scotia	Halifax,	2,000,000	200	28 ℘ ct.	7 & b $3 50	Mar. and Sept.	....	....	....	....	....	....
Banque du Peuple	Montreal,	1,600,000	50	"	4 ℘ ct.	1 Mar., 1 Sept.	....	107 107½	107 107½	....	....	....
Bank of Toronto	Toronto.	2,000,000	100	"	4 "	1 Jan., 1 July.	112	bks clo'd	bks clo'd	....	....	....
Bank of Yarmouth	Yarmouth,	2,000,000	....	....	......	......	....	....	....	....	....	....
Canadian Bank of Commerce	Toronto,	1,000,000	50	20 p. ct.	none yet.	......	103	bks clo'd	bks clo'd	....	....	....
City Bank of Montreal	Montreal,	1,200,000	80	All.	4 ℘ ct.	1 June, 1 Dec.	....	98½ 99½	99 100	....	....	....
Commercial Bank of Canada	Kingston,	4,000,000	100	"	3 "	1 Jan., 1 July.	30	29 31	29 30	....	....	....
Commercial Bank	St. John,	......	100	"	......	......	....	....	....	....	....	....
Eastern Townships' Bank	Sherbrooke,	400,000	50	"	4 ℘ ct.	1 July, 1 Jan.	....	bks clo'd	bks clo'd	....	....	....
Gore Bank	Hamilton,	1,000,000	40	....	3½ "	1 Jan., 1 July.	81	do	bks clo'd	....	....	....
Halifax Banking Company	Halifax,	......	....	....	......	......	....	....	....	....	....	....
Mechanics' Bank	Montreal,	1,000,000	50	30 ℘ ct.	4 ℘ ct.	1 Nov., 1 May.	....	97½	96 97½	....	....	....
Merchants' Bank	"	2,000,000	100	All.	4 "	1 Jan., 1 July.	....	104 105	....	....	....	....
Merchants' Bank	Halifax,	......	....	....	......	......	....	....	....	....	....	....
Molson's Bank	Montreal.	1,000,000	50	All.	4 ℘ ct.	1 Apr., 1 Oct.	....	110 111	109 110	....	....	....
Niagara District Bank	St. Catharn's	400,000	100.	70 ℘ ct.	3½ "	1 Jan., 1 July.	....	....	....	....	....	....
Ontario Bank	Bowmanv'le	2,000,000	40	All.	4 "	1 June, 1 Dec.	99 100	98 98½	98½ 99	....	....	....
People's Bank	Fredericktn	......	100	"	......	......	....	....	....	....	....	....
People's Bank of Halifax	Halifax,	400,000	20	"	7 ℘ ct. 12m	......	....	....	....	....	....	....
Quebec Bank	Quebec,	3,000,000	100	"	3½ "	1 June, 1 Dec.	....	98½ 99½	99 99½	....	..	....
Royal Canadian Bank	Toronto,	2,000,000	50	30 ℘ ct.	4 "	1 Jan., 1 July.	98½	bks clo'd	bks clo'd	....	....	....
St. Stephens Bank	St. Stephens	......	100	All.	......	......	....	....	....	....	....	....
Union Bank	Quebec,	2,000,000	100	50 ℘ ct.	4 ℘ ct.	1 Jan., 1 July.	....	100½ 101½	....	....	....	....
Union Bank of Halifax	Halifax,	1,000,000	100	40 "	7 " 12 mo	Feb. and Aug.	..	....	....	....	....	....
MISCELLANEOUS.												
British America Land	....	......	£50 Stg.	44	2½ ℘ ct.	......	....	....	....	....	....	17 21
British America Insurance Company	Toronto.	......	50	50 ℘ ct.	4 p. ct.	......	57½	....	....	....	....	....
British Colonial Steamship Company	....	......	£50 Stg.	32½	2½ "	......	....	50	....	....	....	....
Canada Company	....	......	32½	All.	5 "	......	....	....	....	....	....	64 68
Canada Landed Credit Company	Toronto,	......	50	$14	......	......	40	....	....	....	....	....
Canada Permanent Building Society	"	......	50	All.	5 "	......	117½	....	....	....	....	....
Canada Mining Company	Montreal,	......	4	90 ℘ ct.	......	......	....	....	....	....	....	....
Do. Inland Steam Navigation Co.	....	......	100	All.	14 ℘ ct. 12m	......	....	128 128½	....	....	....	....
Do. Glass Company	....	......	100	"	12½ "	......	....	96 98	....	....	....	....
Canadian Loanand Investment	....	......	25	2½ ℘ ct.	7 ℘ ct.	......	....	....	....	....	....	2 1 dis.
Canada Agency	....	......	10	½ "	......	......	....	....	....	....	....	....
Colonial Securities Company	....	......	....	....	......	......	....	....	....	....	....	....
Freehold Building Society	Toronto.	......	100	All.	5 "	......	102	....	....	....	....	....
Halifax Steamboat Company	Halifax.	......	100	"	5 "	......	....	....	....	....	....	....
Halifax Gas Company	"	......	....	....	......	......	....	....	....	....	....	....
Hamilton Gas Company	Hamilton,	......	....	....	......	......	....	....	....	....	....	....
Huron Copper Bay Company	....	......	4	12 cts.	20 ℘ ct.	......	....	45 50	....	....	....	....
Lake Huron S. and C.	....	......	5	102 cts.	......	......	....	....	....	....	....	....
Montreal Mining Consols	Montreal.	......	20	$15 10	......	......	....	2.00 2.25	....	....	....	....
Do. Telegraph Company	"	......	40	All.	5 ℘ ct.	......	....	133 133½	133½ 133¾	....	....	....
Do. Elevating Company	"	......	100	"	15 " 12m	......	....	100 102½	....	....	....	....
Do. City Gas Company	"	......	40	"	4 ℘ ct.	15 Mar. 15 Sep.	....	136	136 137	....	....	....
Do. City Passenger Railway Co.	"	......	50	"	5 "	......	....	99 101	....	....	....	....
Nova Scotia Telegraph	Halifax.	......	20	"	......	......	....	....	....	....	49¾ dis.	....
Quebec and L. S.	....	......	8	$4 10	......	......	....	....	25c.	....	....	....
Quebec Gas Co.	Quebec.	......	200	All.	4 ℘ ct.	1 Mar., 1 Sep.	....	....	118 119	....	....	....
Quebec Street R. R.	"	......	50	25 ℘ ct.	8 "	......	....	....	100 100½	....	....	....
Richelieu Navigation Company	....	......	100	All.	7 ℘ ct. p. a.	1 Jan., 1 July.	....	104 106	103 105	....	....	....
St. Lawrence Tow Boat Co.	Quebec.	......	100	"	......	3 Feb.	...	...	50 55	....	....	....
Toronto Consumers' Gas Company	Toronto.	......	50	"	2 ℘ ct. 3 m.	1 My Au Mar Fe	105	...	103 103½	....	....	....
Trust and Loan Company of U. C.	....	......	20	5 ℘ ct.	3 "	......	....	....	...	....	....	¾ ½ dis.
Western Canada Building Society	"	......	50	All.	5 p. ct.	......	108	....	....	....	....	....

SECURITIES.	London.	M'ntreal	Quebec	Toronto.	Halifax.	St. John.
Canadian Gov't Deb., 6 ℘ ct. stg., due 1872.	....	100	100 100½	100 101	....	....
Do. do. 6 do due Ja. & Jul. 1877-84	103 105	100 101	100 100½	...	....	....
Do. do. 6 do. Feb. & Aug.	101 103	....	....	....	....	....
Do. do. 6 do. Mch. & Sep.	101 103	....	....	....	....	....
Do. do. 5 ℘ ct. cur., 1883	90 92	88½ 89	88 89	88 89	....	....
Do. do. 5 do. stg., 1885	89 91	88 88½	88 89	....	....	....
Do. do. 7 do. cur.,	....	100 100½	100½ 101	....	....	....
Halifax Corporation	....	....	....	....	....	....
Hamilton Corporation	....	....	....	....	....	....
Do. Water Works	....	....	....	....	....	....
Montreal Harbor, 8 ℘ ct. d. 1869	..	....	....	....	....	....
Do. do. 7 do. 1870	...	102 103	....	....	....	....
Do. do. 6½ do. 1875	....	....	....	....	....	....
Do. do. 6½ do. 1873	....	....	....	....	....	....
Do. Corporation, 6 ℘ c. 1885	....	90½ 91	....	....	....	....
Do. Water Works, 6 ℘ c. stg. 1878	...	91 92	....	....	....	....
Do. do. 6 do. cy. do.	....	....	....	....	....	....
New Brunswick, 6 ℘ ct., Jan. and July	103 105	....	....	....	....	....
Nova Scotia, 6 ℘ ct., 1875	103 105	....	....	...	....	....
Ottawa City 6 ℘ c. d. 1888	....	90 91	....	...	....	....
Quebec Harbour, 6 ℘ c. d. 1883.	....	....	79 80	....	....	....
Do. do. 7 do. do.	....	....	89 90	....	....	....
Do. do. 8 do. 1886	...	....	98½ 99	....	....	...
Do. City, 6 ℘ c. d. 10 years	....	80 90	80 82	....	....	....
Do. do. 7 do. 10 do.	....	....	93 94	...	....	....
Do. do. 7 do. 3½ do.	....	....	96 97	....	....	....
Do. Water Works, 7 ℘ ct., 5 years	....	....	95 96	....	....	....
Do. do. 6 do. 3½ do.	....	....	95 95½	....	....	....
Toronto Corporation	....	91 95	....	7 7½	....	....

RAILWAYS.	Sh's	Paid	Montr	London
Atlantic and St. Lawrence	£100	All.	....	54 56
Buffalo and Lake Huron	20½	"	....	3 3½
Do. do. Preference	10	"	....	5½
Buff., Brantf. & Goderich, 6℘c., 1872-3-4	100	"	....	65 69
Champlain and St. Lawrence	....	....	11½ 13	....
Do. do. Pref. 10 ℘ ct.	....	....	74 80	....
Grand Trunk	100	"	16 17	16½ 17
Do. Eq. G. M. Bds. 1 ch. 6℘c.	100	"	....	80 82
Do. First Preference, 5 ℘ c	100	"	....	44 47
Do. Deferred, 3 ℘ ct.	100	"	....	....
Do. Second Pref. Bonds, 5℘c	100	"	....	33 36
Do. do. Deferred, 3 ℘ ct.	100	"	....	....
Do. Third Pref. Stock, 4℘ct.	100	"	....	28 30
Do. do. Deferred, 3 ℘ ct.	100	"	....	....
Do. Fourth Pref. Stock, 3℘c.	100	"	....	18 20
Do. do. Deferred, 3 ℘ ct.	100	"	....	....
Great Western	20½	"	....	16½ 17
Do. New	20½	18	16 17	....
Do. 6 ℘ c. Bds, due 1873-76.	100	All.	....	98 100
Do. 5½ ℘c. Bds. due 1877-78.	100	"	....	89 91
Marine Railway, Halifax, $250, all	$250	"	....	....
Northern, of Canada, 6℘c. 1st Pref. Bds.	100	"	....	79 81

EXCHANGE.	Halifax.	Montr'l.	Quebec.	Toronto.
Bank on London, 60 days sight or 75 days date	....	10½ 10½	110½ 110½	10½
Private do.	....	9½ 10	9½ 9¾	....
Private, with documents	....	9 9½	....	....
Bank on New York	....	25½ 26	24 25	24½
Private do.	....	26 26½	24½ 25½	....
Gold Drafts do.	....	par	par ½ dis	½ prem.
Silver.	..	4½ 4¾	....	5 4¾

THE CANADIAN
ONETARY TIMES
AND
INSURANCE CHRONICLE.
DEVOTED TO FINANCE, COMMERCE, INSURANCE, BANKS, RAILWAYS, NAVIGATION, MINES, INVESTMENT, PUBLIC COMPANIES, AND JOINT STOCK ENTERPRISE.

OL. II—NO. 21.   TORONTO, THURSDAY, JANUARY 7, 1869.   { SUBSCRIPTION, $2 YEAR. }

Mercantile.

Insurance.

INSURANCE MATTERS IN NEW YORK.

(From Our Own Correspondent.)

NEW YORK, Jan. 4, 1869.

The year just passed into the "eras and the centuries," though not signalized by any great event, has not died without a sign. The Presidential election has permanently settled the political status of affairs with us, and determined the policy of the country for some years to come, while affairs abroad show that the democratic principle continues to work towards the surface, and that progress continues to be the law of human society.

Finally, the outlook is encouraging. Our bank statements promise an easy money market for the spring's business, which is expected to be active. The general dividends are large. For this point, $52,000,000 are distributed in January, including about $1,000,000 by our insurance companies, and $14,000,000 at Boston. Our railroad development has been active—3,000 miles having been constructed in 1868. The general domestic trade and consumption have been largely stimulated by abundant crops, especially at the South. The import trade has not been excessive, nor particularly profitable, but it has been free from the disastrous losses of 1866-67.

This is the season of dividends and annual reports by the insurance offices. The New York Life offices have sixty days from January 1st to file returns, and statements by the Fire offices must be in by February 1st, proxime. The fire statements undergo many revisions at the Department; items in the "asset" and "liability" columns being frequently disallowed. It will, therefore, be some weeks before a general "synopsis" can be had.

It is the opinion of several experienced underwriters with whom I have conversed, that the fire losses of 1868 will not equal those of 1867. True, there have been many large fires of late, such as those of Bangor and Lynn, but no great conflagrations, such as, by times, were experienced at St. Louis, Chicago and Portland. The losses, too, have been pretty generally distributed among the agencies, so that very few companies of any character are likely to be seriously crippled. Of 98 New York Companies, 20 passed their dividends in January, 1868, and 13 in July following. The dividends for January, 1869, will mostly be announced during the present week, and will, undoubtedly, show a general improvement over the results of 1867.

The everlasting and irrepressible brokerage question has again been revived. The desire to get rid of the brokers is manifestly strengthening and widening; but, on account of the "guerilla" operations of the agencies of out of town Companies, it is almost impossible to secure unanimity of action among the New York Companies. The National Board of Fire Underwriters is opposed to any rebate to customers. If the New York Board shall fail to sustain the views of the National Board, and allow such rebate, other cities, such as Boston, Hartford, Chicago, &c., will follow the example, the authority of the National Board will be overthrown, and, practically, the rebate will only amount to ten per cent. more

commission out of the premiums and to the country agents. In two largely attended meetings, recently held, the New York Board have failed to come to any agreement on the question.

Superintendent Barnes's Report for 1869 is to contain a (first) valuation of the policies of all life companies reporting to him. It will be a great labor and his Report, "you bet," will not be out very early, as the time to which valuations are now made is the same in Massachusetts and New York (December 31). The public would have an excellent means of checking, by the two valuations, but for the unfortunate fact, that the New York Department is on the basis of 4½ per cent. interest, and the "American" table of expectation, while Commissioner Sanford, of Massachusetts, adheres to 4 per cent. interest and the "Combined Experience". table. Uniformity in these departments would be a great desideratum, and should be reached by adequate legislation.

You will have noticed that "out West," the English fashion of amalgamation has recently been introduced among the life companies. The Widows and Orphans of St. Louis has recently "gone over" to the Life Association of America, same city; but whether the transaction cost, $55,000, as in the recent affair between the British Mutual and the Prudential, this deponent saith not. Most likely not, as it seems the widows and orphans started with only $10,000 cash capital, six months before the "annexation." These consolidations cannot, however, become general in America. In the States having Departments, the law provides for the winding up of life companies, with insufficient assets on complaint of the Superintendent to the Att'y-General. And all States as they come to have any considerable number of respectable companies, must provide for Insurance Departments, since experience has shown that the business classes will not patronize companies that have not undergone official supervision. Companies like the North Western Life, of Milwaukee, come East for the purpose mainly of getting an official vise. This St. Louis occurrence is the beginning of a bad business. Not more than two or three of the dozen odd life companies in that city, are managed by men of experience, and the requisite actuarial skill. Of these companies several have only nominal note capitals, and very few enjoy a large public confidence. Their future is not doubtful. A few years of sickly existence and then—what? How can they hope to obtain a paying business. Two thirds of the fire and life business in the State of Missouri is done by the agency companies. They bring into the field the prestige of age, strength, and the success of experienced and skilful management, and hence command the business. The local cry about keeping premiums at home does not avail. A poor article of insurance will not be purchased or used when positive indemnity can be had at the same price.

We are beginning to see the effect of a too rapid multiplication of life companies. Forty-five have been organized in the past four years, which surpasses the worst speculative period of English experience. The waste of premiums attending the start of so many crude and unnecessary schemes for merely speculative purposes is monstrous and positively disgraceful. The business is thereby inflated. The losses, surrenders, and policies not taken, now amount to about 30 per cent. of the annual business done. The effect of this must soon be to disgust a large portion of the community with the whole business. Too many persons, who never could continue policies, have been induced to take them under all sorts of plausible, if not positively deceitful, representations.

Many of the old companies do not expect that the life business for 1868 will aggregate as favorably as it did in 1867. The Presidential election is always a disturbing element, diverting men's minds from domestic affairs, and entailing extraordinary expenses. The occasional stringency in the money market for the past few months, and many failures have also had a bad influence. The mercantile classes as a body have not had a profitable year, and surplus funds for such purposes as life assurance have not been so abundant. Besides, the extravagant commissions paid by many young offices have compelled the older offices to extend their expense account, which will be likely to tell against the years' accumulations.

A few office transfers have recently occurred here in connection with the changes incidental to the New Year. Mr. Edward A. Lambert, ex-Mayor of Brooklyn, succeeds Mr. Coe Adams as President of the Craftsmen's Life ; O. Del Mildgerger, late of Security Fire, is the new Secretary of Fireman's Trust. The Corn Exchange, which has been in trouble for some time, gets an efficient officer in the new Secretary, Geo. W. Hoffman, who brings twenty years' experience to his post.

A new insurance monthly, *The Review*, is announced for January 15, to be conducted by Mr. Jas. R. Hosmer. It was also rumored that the Chicago *Spectator* was to be transferred to this city, but it is now understood that the project has been abandoned. New York has seven professedly insurance sheets of more or less merit, besides the score of other publications largely patronized by insurance companies. The companies complain that there are too many insurance publications, but they seem nevertheless to secure the desired patronage.   M. A. C.

FIRE RECORD.—Almonte, Dec. 24.—The Roman Catholic Church was burned to the ground through a defective stovepipe. There was an insurance in the Beaver Mutual for $1,600.

Guelph, Jan. 1.—A fire this morning destroyed the bakery and warehouse of John Harris, Jr. Probable loss about $3,000; partially insured.

Pembroke, Dec. 24.—The tavern of Mrs. McCracken, widow of the late A. Pembroke, lumber merchant, took fire and was consumed. The origin of the fire is said to have been from the stovepipes. Very little of the furniture saved, and no insurance on either building or contents.

Ottawa, Jan. 1.—A fire was discovered in a building occupied by Dufour as a carriage shop, on Rideau street, which, with its contents, consisting of carriages, cutters, tools, and a large quantity of seasoned lumber, was entirely consumed. Dufour's loss will be heavy, as he had no insurance. The fire is supposed to have been the work of an incendiary.

Halifax, Dec. 12.—An unoccupied dwelling house on the Northwest Arm Road, owned by H. Fredericks, carpenter, was destroyed by fire. The fire brigade were promptly on the ground, but were unable to save the building in consequence of the want of water in that vicinity.

St. Catharines, Jan. 3.—J. Thomas, saloon, opposite the Custom House, was burned to the ground. Loss $1,000; no insurance. The Custom House caught fire, but was saved.

—The London fire has been settled by the insurance companies for $15,000 on the stock.

MONTREAL FIRE DEPARTMENT.—Chief Bertram of the Fire Department, reports that for the year

ending 31st December, 1868, he regrets there has been more fires than has ever occurred in Montreal in any previous year. The Department has been called out 222 times on the whole, or in part for 175 fires and 47 alarms. Five of the fires were beyond the city limits ; but a portion of the Fire Police went out to them.

INSURANCE DEPOSITS.—In our statement of the deposits made by the Insurance Companies given a fortnight ago, an error appeared in that of the Northern Assurance Company. Their deposit is as follows:—

Deposit in Cash	$85,834
" in Canada 5's	12,166
" in Canada 6's	2,000
Total	$100,000

ÆTNA LIVE STOCK CO.—The Chicago *Spectator* contains the following :—It is due to the Ætna Live Stock Insurance company, to say that the later and more authentic information has satisfied us that there is no truth in the report that that company's affairs had been made the subject of a second official investigation by Superintendent Barnes. Our correspondent at Hartford informed us, soon after the failure of the Hartford Live Stock company, that Mr. Barnes, after a thorough investigation of the Ætna's affairs, had commended the " responsibility and management" of the latter company, and moreover had complimented its officers for " keeping their business so well in hand." That information was entirely correct,—in fact could not have been otherwise, considering the eminent character and undoubted responsibility of our correspondent. We made editorial mention of the fact at the time, and considered ourselves justified in warmly defending the Ætna from the damage of an unfounded and untimely suspicion which was certain to follow the failure of its predecessor and rival. Subsequently there appeared the report that something in the later experience and business of the Ætna had occurred to shake the confidence of Superintendent Barnes in the company's stability. We are now permitted to state that these reports were entirely unfounded ; that no investigation of the company's affairs is making by Mr. Barnes ; and that Mr. Barnes does not, at present, entertain any change of the opinion which he expressed in his last letter to the company, of which the following is a copy, duly certified :

ALBANY, N. Y., August 14, 1868.

J. B. TOWER, Secretary Ætna Live Stock Insurance Co., Hartford, Conn.:

SIR,—Yours of the 12th inst. received, and also the special statement of your assets and exhibits as of August 1st, 1868.

The statement received is satisfactory, and the promptness with which it was made after request, is unprecedented in this department. I trust that your business will always be held so well in hand.

Very respectfully,
(Signed)   WM. BARNES, Superintendent.

HARTFORD, November 27, 1868.

Personally appeared H. T. Sperry and made oath that the above is a true copy of a letter received by J. B. Tower from Mr. Barnes. Mr. Sperry further states that he is familiar with the hand-writing of Mr. Barnes, and knows it to have been written by him.

(Certified)   JUSTIN SNOW, Notary Public.

The above letter, and positive information that the sentiments therein expressed have not been changed since the letter was written, justifies fully the opinion which we published in September—that the Ætna Live Stock Insurance Company is fully entitled to public confidence. We are glad to know that the management of the company's affairs is conducted with skill and prudence.

LIFE COMPANIES AND THEIR AGE[?]

It is now pretty generally admitted throug the broad field of life underwriting in this la try, that that company which secures and i the best agents is most successful. The tena of this position was, a few years ago, a subje debate. In many quarters, particularly a life officers, and also among general agent solicitors, it was thought that success was de dant on distinguishing characteristics of a c pany,—some wonderful alchemy for conve premium receipts into fabulous dividends, advantages of half note, or the merits of all t or things of kindred ilk,—that these consti the savory bait for business, and that such s points were altogether irresistable to the h hordes seeking insurance. The agent of th cash system looked down from a towering nence on the growling solicitor for the half and wondered how he obtained his bread ; t the sleek official, beside his cozy grate, count the gross amount of the morning's applica and solaced himself with the thought, tha days of the note system were number And the agent of the note plan looked with pity on the all cash advocate, wondering men could be " so foolish as to pay double for insurance," convinced in his own mind were they to listen to his arguments, su system could not exist for a day, and a applications came pouring in each day a home office, the officers laughed in happy and said, Behold ! this is the great ba which we have bottled. The officers o panies did attribute their success to the sup fact that their plans and practice were p able to the plans and practice of other comp In the year 1860 there came a gleam of The discovery was made by a young office young company, that honesty and faith, ho and cunningly devised plans, are the true pla for a life company to stand upon, and that all comes through heroic workers, and that by e in good faith with agents, paying them libe furnishing them every facility for accompl their arduous tasks, and protecting them in rights, any well organized company may How thoroughly that young officer understo work let the grand successes of some young panies testify. Other men followed in his t not immediately, but as early as 1863 ; our ers can name companies readily whose suc have been wonderful, and in every instance successes are attributable to agents in the fie

Now, that the fight for business among th companies is so fierce, let them consider thi ject of their duties to agents. It is all w talk about mutuality, and obligations to p holders ; but it is equally well to conside rights of agents. It is very natural as a com grows in power and influence, and its busine creases, for officers to assume undue auth become irrascible, grow dissatisfied with an an of work which would at another time have highly gratifying ; in short, deal curtly and i riously with a man whom once they courted coveted. The fact that an agent may have a list of renewals at the mercy of the com which he represents, renders him more or les sitive. Then again, who are these old agen the field ! They are the veterans. men who borne the burden and heat of the day, any c whom is worth a half dozen new recruits.

The point we desire to make is this : the justice cannot be too careful in establishing a tation for honorable and generous dealing agents. We are fast coming to a time when matter will assume a significance which it not now. Agents no longer stand aloof from each other as they did a few years since, but the s of rival companies throughout the country ciate together and are intimate with each o Any unwarrantable liberty on the part of a pany with an agent is regarded as a direct t at the rights of every other agent. Now we

·ative manœuvering among agents, and present no necessity for any movement .nd ; but the companies may as well t as last, that they are in the hands of ʋho have made them, and they should ways a peaceful and conciliatory spirit there exists difficulty ; avoiding recourse ꞏenever possible, and, indeed, we think ꞏaused in saying it does not look well for ꞏany to advertise that it has never littꞏ ꞏalm, when it is ready, on the slightest ꞏn, to take up the tomahawk against an pectatur.

[E DANGER FROM WITHIN.

ꞏlieved by some that we have too many ꞏnce companies in the country, and that ꞏss in which they are engaged is already This impression is derived from a conꞏ ꞏn of the inherent feebleness of some comꞏ ꞏhich never ought to have been organꞏ the hungry and fierce competition of ꞏlich bid too high for public patronage. ꞏes must, however, elapse before the full ꞏf life insurance is attained. It has ꞏbeen retarded by prejudice, ignorance, ꞏstition ; but, although they will always ꞏbstacle to the advancement of this and ꞏr liberal system of benificence, their opꞏ ꞏlas of late grown comparatively faint ꞏctive, and the progress of life insurance ꞏably be henceforth more impeded by its ꞏ but false friends, than by its open The latter are fast disappearing, and life insurance has received the approval benediction of the Pope himself, the ꞏ intolerance against the institution will ꞏd, and bigotry itself will be compelled to ꞏ ecclesiastical thunders against some ꞏt scientific improvement.

ꞏerefore, from within, and not from withꞏ life insurance is threatened with serious ꞏd dissolution. The trouble from this ꞏource is more to be dreaded than the ꞏng from every other cause, for it, strikes of the institution, saps its foundation, ꞏens public confidence in its worth and

ꞏound, honorable and skilfully managed ꞏny, confirms, increases and perpetuates ꞏerity of the land. In its operation, ꞏ than in its profession, it is the most ꞏadvocate of its own doctrines. It is ꞏfiot only by its own policy holders, but ꞏir friends and by the public. The reꞏ of its promises to the insured is the best ꞏn its favor. No eloquence can surpass ꞏngs of the widow and orphan. When ꞏhielded by life insurance from want and ꞏwho can witness the timely relief it ꞏem without being converted to its doctꞏ ꞏese doctrines teach economy, foresight ꞏlence. · They inculcate the duties of the ꞏrd the future, and more than fulfil the ꞏerforming, and even anticipating, the ꞏf genuine love and wisdom.

ꞏlife company makes good citizens. Its ꞏders, and their children, who benefit by ꞏstion, learn from its teachings the true ꞏof government, that there is no certain ꞏss all combine for the protection of each, there is no oppression where all alike another's burdens. It makes good and ꞏespected husbands and fathers ; good, ꞏd grateful wives, sons and daughters, practical christians. It would, indeed, ꞏible to enumerate the good a sound and ꞏucted life insurance company actually ꞏelps to do, for its blessiꞏgss, like the ꞏ solar light, penetrates and are reflected ꞏirection.

ꞏsolvent life insurance corporations, howꞏ ꞏing where they are not compelled to reꞏ ꞏactual condition, are yet young and

apparently flourishing · and able to hide their rottenness from the world. But the day of reck. oning and exposure must eventually arrive to them all, sooner or later If it be long delayed, the results will proꞏe only the more disastrous to the policy holders and injurious to life insurance. Every day's continuance of such hollow impositions multiplies the evils they will inflict. Every public journalist or private individual, cognizant of their unsoundness and ultimately inevitable failure, who shrinks from denouncing them tacitly, helps them to defraud our worthiest citiꞏ ꞏzens, and to make beggars of their widows and orphans.

Here no compromise ought to be made. The public should be warned against every unreliable insurance company, no matter how plausible and imposing its claims, or how seductive the array of names that endorse· its pretensions. We are blamed, abused, and threatened for exposing deꞏ lusive life companies, new· and old, British and American, but shall not suffer ourselves to be driven, either by slander or menaces, from the path of manifest duty.

No life insurance company has any claim to public confidence which does not annually make and publish a full, reliable, and exact exposition of its condition. A company may have essential reasons for not doing this, but they are such as should prevent the public from entrusting the maꞏnagement with its savings. We cannot accept less than an explicit statement of its description and ample security for the fulfilment of its pledges as a justification of tolerating the existence of any life company, and the time will come when none will be suffered to do business in America or Great Britain, whose policies, liabilities, reserves and assets are not annually valued by a government actuary, and pronounced by him to be corꞏrespondent and ample. Then we shall not have too many life companies, though they treble the existing number; for the perfect confidence of the public in life insurance will render its practice almost universal. We have a superfluity now, because many life companies which are not subꞏjected to a searching government supervision, are irresponsible, reckless or insolvent. These hollow and consumptive organizations form at present the principal impediment to the growth and spread of life insurance, which will never prosper as it might and should do, till all of them are legally, thoroughly, and permanently extirpated. Let every one who can hasten the consummation so devoutly to be wished.—*Insurance Times.*

Mining.

MADOC GOLD DISTRICT.

(From our own Correspondent).

BELLEVILLE, Jan. 4, 1869.
The following is an abstract of the report of Mr. John H. Dunstan, Superintendent of the Richardson mine, Eldorado, Madoc, addressed to the President and Directors of the company, dated Dec. 30, 1868 :

Aftꞏr congratulating the Board upon the faꞏvorable report which he has been able to make, Mr. Dunstan goes on to say: "On my appointꞏment last May to the management of the Richꞏardson Gold Mining Company's property, I exꞏamined the mill, and found it to be in so very unfit a state that I declined working it until parꞏtially refitted. On entering the mine I saw it had·been worked without judgment, even the first principles of mining had been ignored; and that it would not be safe to work it; until thoroughly timbered. On reporting this to the directors then in office, they concluded not to proceed with the work until after the general meeting of the shareꞏholders. From the new Board of Directors I reꞏceived instructions to get the mill put in working order and make a test of the ore, which was done in August; the ore treated being some left in the

rock-house of the mill by the former manager. After seven tons had been crushed the Sheriff seized and closed the works. On cleaning up, the result showed $9 per ton. The works then reꞏmained closed until October, when I received orders to put men to work in search of other veins, and to find out more about the property. After working about two weeks, a very promising vein of auriferous rock, 2 feet ·wide, was discovered ; although it does not show much gold, yet the inꞏdications are very favorable. On Nov. 17th I again started the mill on refuse rock, the cullings of all previous crushings, taking the first from the outside of the shaft-house, of·which I crushed 35 tons. I next commenced on the ore from the inꞏside of the house, and crushed 175 tons, in all 210 tons, which yielded from $1.50 to $7 per ton, average $4 per ton: I then took a few tons from the mine, 20 to 25 feet from the surface, without sorting, and got a return of $7 per ton. The whole cost of crushing, including hauling, cordꞏwood, &c., has been less than $1.50 per ton.

Mr. Dunstan then proceeds to show that these amounts per ton, though apparently small, are sufficient under a good system of mining to pay at least 100 per cent. upon the total cost of workꞏing, and adduces several statistical items, taken from the *American Journal of Mining*, Congresꞏsional Reports, and the record of some of the most successful mining enterprises, to prove that a much smaller tonnage, return will, on ·a large scale of working, under efficient management, pay ample dividends on the capital invested, even where the rate of wages and the price of cordwood are much higher than in Madoc.

The report is accompanied by plans and secꞏtions, showing the extent and direction of the auriferous deposit, with its divarications and peꞏculiarities so far as they have been developed, joꞏgether with the adjacent stratified and massive rocks; and such additional works as· in 'Mr. Dunstan's opinion will conduce to the more efꞏfective working of the mine.

Mr. Dunstan states the expenditure of the comꞏpany up to the present time at $80,000, a large proportion of which has been unnecessarily exꞏpended through the incompetence of the persons to whom the management of the works has been entrusted, while the rich deposit of gold found in the first instance, which ought to have repaid this expenditure and placed the company's affairs on a sound basis, has been totally lost to them for the want of an efficient supervision to restrain the pilfering propensities of their own employes and of the numerous visitors to the locality; for as the report avers, with·truth, "nearly every city, town and village in Canada, and very many in the United States, contain specimens, showing gold from the Richardson mine."

"In conclusion," writes Mr. Dunstan, "allow me to state that although the present shareholders may fail to reap the benefit of their investments, there is no doubt that there are other parties willing to carry on the works, and give the mine a thorough test; and although we are not certain of anything in mining, yet in my opinion, every indication shows that the Richardson mine will, at some future period, be one of the best paying mines in the world."

I have only to add to ·the above, that I saw on Thursday last an ingot of gold, value about $320, the produce of the last crushing mentioned in Mr. Dunstan's report; and that I was shown this morning a specimen of gold-dust, worth, I should judge, about 50 cents, washed from a sinꞏgle pan of crevice matter taken from one of the newly discovered veins in the ninth concession of the township of Marmora.

LAKE SUPERIOR MINES.—The Superior (Wis.) *Gazette*, Dec 12, gives an account of the progress and prospects of mining on the North Shore of Lake Superior. It says: "The Thunder Bay Mining Co., near Fort William, Lake Superior, Canada, are pushing ahead their mining operations with commendable energy, with a working force of about forty men ; they are working day and night sinking two shafts. Shaft A is down some seventy feet ; shaft B, about sixty feet ; commenced cross-cutting ; both shafts look promising. A good show of silver-glance at present depth. With an experienced superintendent, lately from the silver mines of Norway, and a wealthy English Canadian Company to back him, we shall expect early next summer to hear of some big runs from their eight-stamp mill, which was gotten up and sent over last season from England. Early next spring they will complete the erection of this mill, and have out sufficient ore to keep it constantly crushing. We do not know what process they will adopt after crushing, but would suggest that they take a look at our 'Tindall process,' which will be in operation at Vermillion Lake by spring. The Crown-land Commissioners visited this section of Canada last fall, and after seeing for themselves the many difficulties and great expense attendant upon the opening of mining enterprises in a new country, promised for the future a much more liberal policy. We hope they now see the folly of their 'Gold and Silver Mining Act,' passed last winter at Toronto. Many scientific and experienced mining men visited this section last summer and were very favorably impressed. On Thunder Cape, and at the mouth of Pigeon River, on the Montreal Mining Company's lands, some very rich discoveries were made, the vein at Thunder Cape carrying native silver and silver glance very rich, together with cobalt, graphite and galena. For 'surface shows,' so far as developed, this section surpasses anything heretofore found in our western territories. Of course we allude only to silver lodes. With a branch of the Northern Pacific Railroad to the mouth of Pigeon River, an American enterprise untrammelled by any such restrictions as were imposed by the passage of the late act termed the 'Gold and Silver Mining Act' of Canada, we firmly believe that this region of country (to the north and northeast of Lake Superior) would soon be developed into another Montana, or even California. So far as regards rich mineral bearing lodes, during a residence of eight years in Colorado or Montana we have never seen in either so many or so rich surface indications. The Vermillion Lake Mineral veins are undoubtedly an extension almost due west, of those."

HARVEY HILL COPPER MINES.—The Quebec News says :—" We are happy to learn that the new and improved machinery in connection with the extensive works erected by Dr. Douglas at these mines, are approaching rapidly to completion. We are also pleased to know that the operations below ground, which have been suspended since the disastrous fire of last year, have been lately resumed, and that last week a very fine lode of purple ore was struck, the promises of which are very encouraging, and there is now every reason to believe that the promoter of this great enterprise is about to reap the reward which his untiring efforts, under so many discouragements and difficulties, so well deserve."

LEAD MINING.

A recent number of the London Mining Journal, under this head, says : "Of the public-dividend lead mines in England and Wales, nearly one-half are situated in the Principality, while they yield considerably more than one-half of the aggregate amount paid in dividends. As an evidence of the progress of public estimation in favor of lead mines as an investment, it may be remarked that in 1862 there were 13 public lead mining companies, which divided during the year £70,500 ; but in 1867 the number had been increased to 18, which divided £127,280. The paid-up capital amounts to £468,073 ; the sum paid in dividends £1,263,587 ; and the current aggregate market value £1,372,657."

From the same authority we learn that the value of lead obtained in the United Kingdom in

1867 amounted to £1,337,509, while that of tin and copper, for which Britain has always been famous, amounted to only £799,203, and £831,-761, respectively. The last number of the Journal (dated Dec. 12) says :—"Lead Mining in Wales is being profitably and extensively prosecuted, and, though unostentatiously, is imperceptibly filling up the gaps created by the falling off in our Cornish mines. Large fortunes have been and are being made, and losses the exception. The Principality bids fair to take the first place in lead, as it is now doing in coal. Fresh districts are being discovered, and good discoveries are being made in old and neglected fields. Flintshire, long celebrated for founding county families from its mineral wealth, is again manifesting signs of activity." Lead has been gradually rising in price for nearly a century, and now commands a higher rate than at any former time. In England it is selling at £20, and in New York at $130, gold, per ton.

These, says the Kingston News, are encouraging facts for the Frontenac Company, which have now above ground upwards of 5,000 tons of ore. It is expected that several times this amount will be stoped during the winter, and the extensive dressing and smelting works of the company will be put into operation as soon as the cold weather is over. The above amount of ore has all been obtained from mere exploratory work, namely, sinking and driving, which in ordinary mining is not expected to pay expenses. But counting it at only $8 a ton, which is less than half the average of the estimates of Professors Dawson, Hunt, and Chapman, and Messrs. Robb, McDonald and Plummer (mining engineers), the value of the ore thus far raised is over $40,000. We understand the company has now a large quantity of rich ground ready for stoping out. As soon as this process is commenced, the ore, owing to the great breadth of the vein (12 feet), will accumulate even many times more rapidly than hitherto.

COPPER MINING IN QUEBEC.

The Sherbrooke Gazette furnishes some information regarding the Hartford copper mine, which is being worked in the township of Ascot, about six miles from Sherbrooke. There are about 130 men employed at the works:

The ore at present is mined at a distance underground from the surface of about 370 feet, from whence it is drawn to the surface of the ground by a railway propelled by horsepower; there are several slopes or levels at different depths, where there are various parties at work—altogether there is an area of some 150 by 120 feet entirely blasted out, the rock being supported by pillars of stone and huge posts of wood. The vein of copper is of unlimited extent and quantity so far as known. After the copper rock is brought to the surface it is carted to short distances and piled up in piles from 30 to 60 feet in length by say 15 to 20 feet wide, and about 8 feet in the centre, gradually sloping to the bottom. In the sides and ends there are small places left where wood is placed, and this when ignited soon communicates to the sulphur, with which the rock is largely impregnated, when the whole mass is heated and fused together, the sulphur furnishing sufficient material to feed the fire when once set agoing till the whole pile is soon a mass of red hot material. This process, which is technically called "roasting," separates the sulphur from the rock and renders it for smelting.

There are several buildings near the mines, houses, store, office, blacksmith and carpenter shops, and a large building partly finished near the mouth of the shaft, in which it is intended to place superior machinery to that now in use, for raising the rock from the bottom of the mine to the surface. This will be in operation in about two weeks.

We next visited the smelting works, where there are four large furnaces erected for smelting

the ore. Three of these were in full opero and smelting about 50 tons of ore daily. T is a large steam engine used for blowing the and other purposes. The furnaces are condu on a new principle introduced by General Ada The fuel, (of which it takes about one-eight quantity to seven-eighths of ore,) and the o thrown into the furnaces about twelve feet i the bottom, the blasts being introduced in res about four feet from the bottom. The furn are kept going day and night by relays of w men, and the refuse when melted pours out stream from every furnace and is carried of iron pots placed on wheels outside of the build In front of the furnaces there is a vessel sir to a large potash kettle, lined with "steep," i posed of coke, burnt alloy, charcoal, etc., which the metals when passed fall—the r rising to the top and running off over the si taken away. When the reservoir or kettle is of the copper "matt" or "regulus," as it is ca it is dipped out and laid aside, cooled, an ready for shipment. These furnaces have in operation, some of them, since the 1st of last, and have been, with the exception of days, kept going night and day, a fact un cedented in co per smelting operations. percentage of the rock in copper is about i cent., and when manufactured into "matt" from 30 to 40 per cent. of pure copper. 7 works were intended for use in connection another mine owned by the same company w half a mile of the works; but the present being partially developed, and proving of grade copper, has alone as yet been worked. estimated that there are 25,000 tons of ce rock now in sight.

Should the price of copper rise, (it now 1 very low,) both mines belonging to the Har Company will be worked.

There is another set of smelting works er at a short distance from the "Hartford," in nection with the "Capel" mine, owned p nolly by parties in Montreal, called the 2 American Smelting Works, under the ma ment of Mr. Bennett, an experienced m engineer, which we hope will prove highl numerative to the proprietors. We unde from General Adams that his mine is also well.

GOLD AT RAWDON.

A correspondent of the Montreal Gazette, w respecting certain gold mines in the towns Rawdon and Chertsey, and assays made l Girdwood, says :

In the townships of Rawdon and Chartse on rocks taken from the lands of Mr. Ba Cahill, by that gentleman's certificates, the 27th August last, it is found that some rock contain gold and silver to the ton as fo Gold, $29.12; silver, $3.79, which makes $ another specimen, dated 15th August, conta

Gold, 1 oz. 13 dwt. 1 gr., equal.	.$32
Silver, 1 oz. 9 dwt. 3 gr. " ...	1 .
Equal to......	.$35 (

Other rock taken from the surface is fo contain from $7 to $13 per ton.

In your paper of the 7th inst. I see by tract from the Belleville Intelligencer the from the Hastings gold region from the Ri son mines, the proceeds of one weeks' cru which yielded over $7 per ton, from 25 rock; the expense of extracting the same per ton, leaving a net profit of $5 75 p Now, sir, if there is within the distance (miles from Montreal, with all its acknow wealth, gold mines that yield four tim quantity of gold to the ton than the H mines do, with such easy access, why is su bounded wealth allowed to be unsought for!

f this rock are on their way to Phila-
: a new process of analysis and others
low shortly, but capital is wanted to
the full result of this feature. The
this is not much instructed in the
t when I have seen the excitement here-
; existed in going to the wilds of Cali-
stralia, and to other mines in Canada,
ising that such great wealth should be
lie dormant so near the greatest com-
y in the Dominion.
ie letter of the Mayor of Montreal some
o from the gold regions of Nova Scotia
plated localities of the crushing mills at
, and the difficulty of access thereunto;
no doubt, be pleased so know that
ilities and richer mines exist within six
e of Montreal. Adding to this facility
ous rivers and extensive water power
ld be used for the crushing purposes,
voiding the more expensive mode of
by steam. The writer, although no
ngineer, has made a short calculation
bable cost and expenses in establishing
mill, with its probable results.

ing Mill, by steam.........	$5000 00
ng for do....................	400 00
en to mine and crush the	
: at $1.00 per day.........	10 00
eer, $1.50 per do.........	1 50
st on capital, $400 do.....	4 00
ie time working	5 50
and incidental costs......	19 00

ppose a mill to crush ten tons per day,
:k to yield only $10 per ton, the result
'100 from $21—expenses would leave a
of $79 per day.

—

—

WESTERN RAILWAY.—Traffic for week
ec. 18, 1868.

ngers	$24,156 48
ht and live stock......	52,289 40
and sundries..........	2,998 17
	$79,444 05
sponding Week of '67.	74,445 03
Increase............	$4,999 02

ERN RAILWAY.—Traffic receipts for week
d January, 1869.

ngers	$2,871 89
ht........................ ...	3,416 45
and Sundries	362 36
Receipts for week......	$6,650 10
ponding week, 1887...	6,389 77
Increase............	$260 93

ANADA CENTRAL RAILWAY.—This road,
o connect Ottawa City with the Brock-
Ottawa Railroad at Carleton Place, is
g, the cutting out and grading is going
y.

. A. RAILWAY.—Captain Gitt, engineer
ilway on the American side, has been
me information to the Houlton *Pioneer*
progress of the work. It appears that
on is not proceeding very rapidly. From
ge of Winn, in Maine, to the Boun-
, there are three routes under considera-
e survey of one of these is now being
Mr. Ramsay. This line runs six miles
oulton than any of the others. The
ys that if the work is not pressed on
ily, Houlton will be compelled to seek
n with the St. Andrews Road. It was
l impression that the determination of
e of Houlton in this respect had been
some time; but the inference to be drawn from this observation of the *Pioneer* is that when they held those town meetings for the purpose of voting aid to a branch connecting Houlton with the St. Andrews Road, they were only coquetting, with the object of stirring up the Bangor folks, and really never had any intention of assisting the Houlton Branch.

On this side of the boundary the work is proceeding as rapidly as could be expected, although very little noise is made. The track is now laid from Brundage's Point to a point upwards of two miles beyond Wood's, a distance of eighteen miles or so.

PITTSBURGH AND LAKE RAILWAY.—On the 29th Dec., the Pittsburgh and Lakefield Railway was opened. The event was celebrated by a dinner, at which about 140 persons were present. The chair was occupied by the Rev. V. Clinton, supported on the right by Mr. Grover, M.P., Judge Denniston, and Mr. Clinton, and on the left by Messrs. Covert, Carnegie, M.P.P, Read, M.P.P., and Mayor Scott. Among those who made speeches on the occasion were Major Beamish, of Port Hope, Mr. Blomfield, of Toronto, and Mr. T. White, of Hamilton. This railway, it is expected, will command the trade of Douro, Dummer, and other townships in the east, and Smith, Ennismore, and other townships in the west. The cry is—Onward to Mud Lake, and thence by a wooden railway to Haliburton.

KINGSTON, PITTSBURGH AND GANANOQUE ROAD COMPANY.—A meeting of the Directors took place on the 28th Dec. After some conversation upon the question of retaining the present Secretary, and an idea of suspending that officer for a time, it was moved by Mr. Knight, seconded by Mr. Baxter, and carried, that all books and papers relating to the business of the Kingston, Pittsburg and Gananoque Railroad Company be herewith required to be delivered up to the Board for its inspection, and that they be placed under the control of the President, if required, and in his absence, that of the Vice-President.

It was moved by Mr. Baxter, seconded by Mr. Livingston, that the salary of the Secretary and Treasurer of the Board, whose duties should also include the superintendence of the road and of Cataraqui Bridge, should be £42 10s ($170).

Mr. Hope moved in amendment, seconded by Mr. Kinghorn, that the salary of the secretary, treasurer, &c., be £50 ($200), instead of the amount in the last resolution.

The amendment was carried.

It was moved by Mr. Baxter, seconded by Mr. Livingston, that the money collected by the treasurer of the company be paid into the Bank of British North America, and drawn therefrom when required by the check of the President or Vice-President. Carried.

It was moved by Mr. Kinghorn, seconded by Mr. Baxter, and carried, that the secretary be instructed to sell the toll-gate near Mr. Strachan's to Mrs. Burke for $320, a sum it is understood she is willing to pay, Mr. Brownley not having complied with the conditions of the sale of the gate to him.

The meeting, after instructing that a copy of the minutes be forwarded to Mr. Ferguson, adjourned.

— The Great Western Railway have, it is said, notified that a settlement due by the Company to the Government has been proposed to the Board, and accepted by them, subject to the consent of the shareholders.

INSOLVENTS.—The following insolvents are gazetted:—W. F. Howell, Montreal; Frank Owens, Montreal; West Brothers, Montreal; G. T. Marston, Hull; Calvin C. Barks, Hamilton; Robert Park, Goderich; W. C. Carlisle, Montreal; Donald McDonald, Orangeville; Edwin S. Cummer, Toronto; Peter Irish, Cramahe; John Judge, Whitby; James Stephens, Peterboro; W. B. Johnson, Simcoe.

THE NEW SUSPENSION BRIDGE AT NIAGARA.

It is 900 feet below the Falls on the American side, and on the Canada side about 300 feet below the Clifton House, and half a mile from the Horse Shoe Fall.

The cables, two in number, are each composed of seven twisted wire ropes, laid, one in the centre and six surrounding it. They are anchored on the Canada side in the solid limestone rock, 18 feet below the surface, and on the New York side in a mass of solid masonry, commencing at the same depth. The anchor chains are made of Low Moor iron, in four sections of flat links. The three first sections are each 10 feet in length, two of eight links by $\frac{7}{8}$ inchef, and one of seven links by 1 inch. The last section is composed of seven links of varying lengths, to favour the attachment and adjustment of the cable strands. The attachments are made by cast iron "yokes," of a novel but most reliable coustruction. The towers are constructed of white pine timber. Each tower at the base is in two parts, 28 feet square, diminishing to four feet at the top, with a space between them for a roadway 13 feet wide. At a convenient distance above the roadway, they are united by a system of girths and braces extending to the top. The angles of each tower are formed by four timbers, 12x12 inches, firmly bolted together, and these angles are connected together by ties and braces. The bottoms stand in cast iron shoes on the solid rock. These sixteen angle timbers meet at the top, and are housed in a heavy iron casting, on which the saddles supporting the cables and stays rest, with wrought iron rollers between. The floor beams are of white pine, each in two pieces, 3x10 inches, suspended 5 feet from centres. There are two side trusses, of the Howe pattern, which give stiffness to the structure and form the protecting railing to the railway. The floor is also stiffened by horizontal braces attached to the beams. The flooring is of Norway pine, in two thick masses, $1\frac{1}{4}$ inch each. The long suspenders are of wire rope, $\frac{5}{8}$ of an in diameter. The short ones are of $\frac{3}{4}$ round iron. There are twelve overfloor stays on each quarter of the floor, which are united in seven at the towers, and these are secured in the main anchorage. Some fifty wire rope guys, attaching the floor to the rocks of the cliffs and river banks, will secure the structure against the winds. Length of roadway between centres of towers, 1,268 feet; height above the water, 185 to 190 feet; length of central portion supported by the cables, between the outermost stays, 635 feet; length supported by stays and cables, 605 feet. Total length of the suspended platform, 1,240 feet. Defluction of cables in summer, 91 feet; difference in winter, 3 feet less. Full length of cables between anchorages, 1,828 feet. Height of towers—Canada, 105 feet; do. New York, 100 feet above the rock. Width of roadway, 10 feet; depth of side truss, $6\frac{1}{2}$ feet. The bottom cord of the truss is placed under the beams. It is 6 inches wide and 8 inches deep at the centre of the bridge, increasing to 12 inches in width at the towers. Diameter of cable, 7 inches; number of wires in each, 931; size of wire, No. 9. Weight of cables per lineal foot, 63 lbs.; aggregate breaking strain of cables, 1,680 tons net; do. of 48 stays, 1,320 tons net; total of cables and stays, 3,000 tons net. Number of suspenders, 480; strength, 10 tons each. Weight of suspended roadway, including weight of cables and stays, 250 tons. Ordinary working load, 50 tons; maximum load, 100 tons; permanent and transitory load, 350 tons.

This work has been designed by, and executed under the direction of Mr. Samuel Keefer, one of the oldest civil engineers in the Dominion of Canada. Over twenty years ago, when suspension work was in its infancy, Mr. Keefer erected a wire suspension bridge over the Ottawa river, just below the Chaudiere Rapids.

The superintendence of construction was allotted to Mr. E. F. Farrington, formerly of the Covington and Cincinnati Suspension Bridge.

It is owned by a Joint Stock Company, chartered by New York and Canada, with the following named gentlemen as principals: John J. Bush, President; Hollis White, Vice President; Delos De Wolfe, Treasurer; V. W. Smith, Secretary; and W. G. Fargo, Superintendent.

☞ The Publishing Office of THE CANADIAN MONETARY TIMES AND INSURANCE CHRONICLE is removed to No. 60, Church Street, 4 doors north of Court Street.

The Canadian Monetary Times.

THURSDAY, JANUARY 7, 1869.

LIFE INSURANCE IN THE UNITED STATES.

An American paper having asserted that all the New York Life Companies, but two, are actually every year by their excessive expenditures alone, eating into their substance and preparing themselves for irredeemable insolvency, the Chicago *Spectator* has undertaken to refute this "wilful libel" by presenting an analysis of the receipts and disbursements during the last three years of all the insurance companies doing business in New York. The aggregates are as follows:

	1865.	1866.	1867.
Receipts....	$24,897,010.24	$40,375,065.86	$56,481,996.74
Total receipts....			$121,754,681.81
Exp'ditures..	$10,562,796.73	$17,058,804.64	$23,650,876.42
Total expenditures....			$54,272,477.79

Excess of receipts .. $14,334,222.51 $23,316,861.22 $30,831,120.20
Total excess $93,482,204.0

Per centage of expenditure to receipts.....	1865.	1866.	1867.	Total
	.4178	.4224	.4541	.4376

These aggregates include payments of losses on account of death claims and surplus distributions to policy holders, items not purely chargeable to current expenses. The aggregate payments of death claims and dividends amounted to $25,334,690.13, which being deducted from the total disbursements, $53,272,477.79, leaves $25,334,690.13 as the actual current expenses. Taking the receipts for the three years at $121,754,681.81, and the actual current expenses for the same period at $27,939,887.66, there is left surplus of $93,816,794.15—the per centage of expenses to receipts being .2294. The conclusion arrived at is that these companies "in the last three years, after paying all expenses, disbursing over eighteen millions of dollars among the families of deceased policy-holders, and distributing nearly seven million dollars in cash dividends to surviving policy-holders, saved from their business more than seventy-seven per cent. of their current receipts."

An examination of the assets and liabilities gives the following aggregates :

	1865.	1866.	1867.
Assets.......	$64,232,123.24	$01,586,027.07	$125,548,051.40
Liabilities....	50,439,699.26	70,979,122.76	94,875,022.36
Surplus assets	$13,792,423.98	$20,606,905.21	$30,673,928.04
Per centage of assets to liabilities.	127	127	132

The liabilities increased from $50,000,000 in 1865 to $94,000,000 in 1867 ; the assets in the same period increased from $64,000,000 to $125,000,000; the rate of increase in liabilities in two years being 88 per cent. and in assets 95 per cent. These figures present in all its magnitude the development of life insurance, and as they are culled from official sources may be relied upon as correct. The *Spectator* says: "Looking thus at the balance sheet of these enormous operations in life contingencies, we can scarcely admit a doubt that the companies in this country are to-day in better, stronger and safer position, than they occupied before."

THE HURON AND ONTARIO SHIP CANAL.

We give up a large portion of our space to the discussion of this subject by Mr. Laidlaw, of Toronto, who has shown himself so earnest and successful an advocate of the narrow guage railways. His letter will be found full of argument, and worthy of every consideration. At another time we hope to be able to enter into the merits of the questions raised, and give both sides an impartial hearing.

PETROLEUM.

Despite the prophecies of the nervous, and the loudly expressed fears of the timid, that portion of our business community known as "Oilmen" still cherish faith in the future of oil, and are little disposed to relax their efforts to put the oil trade of Canada on a proper footing. During the first six months of the year the production at the refineries was largely in excess of the wants of the home market. In fact the competition among refiners was ruinous, and a stock of 50,000 barrels accumulated on their hands. The price of oil opened at 15 cents per gallon, and went as low as 10 cents. The Higgins scheme was a happy hit. A combination was entered into, to extend from July to January, the refineries were leased, 3,000 barrels, at an average price of 18 cents, were bought up with Canadian capital, and no oil was produced, except for export. The effect was that the oil went up in price, and holders, not in the combination, received the benefit of a rise to 35 cents a gallon. The export to Liverpool during the season was 6,000 barrels ; part of which was sold at satisfactory prices. The

Canadian Land and Mineral Company shipped 3,000 barrels. It has a still capacity manufacturing 2,500 barrels per week.

The beneficial results of the first combination suggested continued joint action, and Oil Refiners Association of Canada formed, whose operations will date from 1st of January. The terms of agreement pretty much the same as before. Prices been fixed, for one to five carloads, at 35 per gallon in London, Ontario ; five carlo and upwards, 32½ cents, cash on deliver The well owners have also formed an association, which embraces in the member the owners of producing wells in Petrol They purpose to sell only to the refiners sociation ; to limit the proportion to actual needs of the country, and to every possible encouragement to the ex trade.

Communications.

GEORGIAN BAY CANAL.

To the Editor Canadian Monetary Times.

SIR,—The agitation for ten million acres of in aid of the Georgian Bay Canal scheme is damaging the genuine commercial interests moral and political influence of the citizen Toronto. When it is threatened, with cheer present circumstances to consider the merit demerits of the proposed canal scheme, it is and the duty of those who dissent from the position advocated, to express their disbelief i practical necessity for, the possibility of obta money to make, and the inutility to Canadi the canal, if it were finished.

Unless their irregular and exorbitant dem are complied with, certain gentlemen, us conservative in their opinions, talk rather v of what must be done to effect their purpose servative, practically makes a very liberal, called for proposition as to the course he will it his duty to pursue in certain eventualitie

Now, sir, the country has been watchin conduct of the people of Toronto towards th gislature, and have felt, not untutored by its sufficient jealousy of its influence. If the G ment were to appeal to the country on this tion, and call for defenders of the public and domain against the incapacity and rapae Toronto canal and railway companies, ver friends of the city would find their way i our Legislative halls.

Really genuine and practicable schemes, vanced in preparation, might then share the dreams.

No doubt the Government feel if they ha millions of acres of land to donate, and i land, under certain contingencies, would l a source of credit, and a means to create works, their first duty would be to conside public works would do the greatest good greatest number of the present generation tario tax-payers. It will not probably b tended that Ontario should give away 250 ships of land for the almost exclusive ben a rival people, who fence us out of their with a tariff averaging 20 per cent. in heig

The Government would probably ask selves, how this wholesale donation of ten larger than many kingdoms renowned in l

armonize with the free grant, or rather kled system" already established. wernment would consider whether the in acres of land were to be made accessible by the construction of the if any hitherto unnavigated waters were ed to our system of navigation ; and he proposed Niagara ship canal is to be al, and would, in consequence, cause the of all invested in the Georgian Bay the Georgian Bay and in the Humber hy millions would be required in both ake artificial harbors capable of floating sels of one thousand tons burden, the rejected canal is to accommodate. How sels of such size are to reach Lake Ontario where they are to load and unload, or orage, has not yet been indicated. Is it that there are no vessels drawing over can come up the St. Lawrence !—equivalent to a lading of 800 tons.

a harbor on Lake Ontario, except Kingthe mouth of the Niagara River or a ship on the upper lakes, to which a vessel drawing over 11 feet !

ill ocean vessels of even 800 tons registered 13 feet !

otal freight shipped from the north shore orgian Bay, the Manitoulin Islands (for a an acre), and the Canadian shore of perior, equivalent to the lading of six 1,000 tons each ?

noteworthy still, vessels of 500 and 600 en do, and have, loaded, whenever a ed at any port on our coast line, from ed to Fort William, and have sailed via nd Canal to Kingston or Europe.

n ore from the American side of Lake s carried by vessels of 700 and 800 tons the smelting works at Detroit, and Therefore, of what necessity is the Bay Canal to Canada, or even American

ntained that the Great West will fill ied canal with cereals, &c. If so, why t fill the Welland Canal ?

enue from our existing canals has only nd one and a half per cent. on their

ricultural community would have just complaint against a government that e away one-third of the public domain to a canal company calculating to bring Canadian but United States produce, to a all our markets at home and abroad, roducts of their farms. The odds against ady are too great and unavoidable.

om 300 miles beyond Chicago is being lown in competition with Canadian ce-oronto, in large quantities at 60c per 56 Does not that fact affect the prices of and barley ? As to reducing the cost of s to the "starving millions" at home, ly used as an argument for the canal ; ed on the average as cheap in London nto ! And are they not now feeding wheat in England ? There is no use of rgument on false premises, if the Canal hed on the 1st of May it would not re-est of freight from Chicago to Liverpool, by 24 hours the average voyage of ves-Chicago to Kingston.

tance, a vessel leaving the head of Lake proceeding down through Lake Erie, at o rate of speed of sailing vessels, 5 miles would, via the Welland Canal, reach about in the same time, as if she had ugh the Georgian Bay Canal, at canal ed, 2 miles an hour, and the detention it upon the extra locking ; so that if the e built, and toll free, it would not be to st of vessel owners to send their vessels hat canal.

ury of twelve Lake Captains be got to e statements over their signatures ?

What is really wanted and needed, is the enlargement of the Welland Canal, so that the largest sailing and steam vessels used on the upper lakes could go through easily.

To accomplish that useful and rational purpose —not requiring the thirtieth or fortieth part of the proposed cost of the Georgian Bay Canal, a very large amount of canal debentures payable in tolls could be sold in the United States.

No system of carrying from Kingston to Montreal can be devised cheaper than that now in operation, provided the Welland Canal be enlarged, and an increase of business obtained, which would stimulate and sustain competition. The enlargement of the Welland Canal would not only pay, if American commerce were tolled, but Montreal would then have a "fair field" in which to compete with New York for the Northwestern United States trade. It is the low freights in large vessels to Buffalo, as compared with the high freights in small vessels to Kingston, from the upper lakes, that embarrasses and disables Montreal in her competition for the trade with New York.

WATER SUPPLY.

The Grand River scantily feeds the Welland Canal, and will the Severn supply two canals, with locks double the size of those in the Welland Canal ? There are two canals in the Georgian Bay Canal scheme, one to lift up vessels to the level of Lake Simcoe, and the other to lower them down to the level of Lake Ontario. Yet the Severn in summer affords little enough water for a couple of large sawmills. It is said, in reply to this objection, that some huge hydraulic power is to be used to supplement the natural supplies. If there is a profit in raising water to let it fall again, why advocate the Georgian Bay Canal; to get the water power for Toronto, why. not commence to pump our Bay, it will last as long as the Georgian Bay ?

Very few people, not engineers, can comprehend the magnitude of the proposed work. I have heard it said, ignorant of its fact or falsehood, that the earth from the nine mile cut would cover four township six feet thick, and that in this way the Holland Marsh is to be reclaimed ! Would it not be better and cheaper to try hydraulics for that purpose ! One authority alleges that the nine mile cut would cost more than the estimate for the whole canal ; and another, that the estimates are all based on twenty-five cents per cubic yard for earth work, supposing no rock to be met with ; while the actual cost of much of the earth work would exceed $3 per yard, especially that spread on the Holland Marsh.

It was tempting to the Egyptian ruler to canal the Isthmus of Suez, having a nation of serfs to labor for him ; because with the Suez Canal finished, he could toll the entire trade of Asia half of Africa, and all of Australasia. His canal affects the ultimate fate of British power and commerce in the east, because a saving of nearly two months on each voyage would be made, and a proportionate saving of wages and interest, while the cost of transporting troops and munitions of war would be greatly reduced ; yet, not one guinea have the Government, the Merchants, or the Engineers of England, given publicly to aid that gigantic and important enterprise.

The Isthmus of Panama is similarly situated as regards the United States, the Pacific coast of America and Australia, a canal through it would also save a two months' voyage, yet the nations interested, and capitalists shrink from the cost of such an undertaking. And shall we, to save one day's voyage, at most two days time from Chicago to Liverpool, undertake a work of nearly double the magnitude ?

Some members of our Board of Trade refer to the water power to be created, forgetting that any quantity of power is available on the Welland and St. Lawrence canals, at two or three hundred dollars for each manufactory. The western trade,

if it were to pass through such a canal, would do the ratepayers of Ontario no more good than is now done by the American vessel passing through the Welland Canal. We would see them and the trade we now do in lumber and cereals from the Northern Railway sailing from the mouth of the Humber past the back of the island, while the Northern Railway dock would be pasture for sheep; instead of a source of bread for a thousand mouths.

Niagara was not more effectually ruined by the Welland, than Toronto would be by the Georgian Bay Canal.

There is one, and only one argument, which, in the mouths of the gentlemen who advocate the canal, suffices as an answer to all objections.

It is alleged that Toronto, i. e., its present merchants, would make fortunes while the canal is building. It is contended by respectable, but unthinking men, that Canada has nothing to do with the matter ; give ten million, acres of land, and if the English invest their money and lose it, that is their look out ; we will get their money into this country and be merry over our gains, and the cons iousness that our kinsmen, our fellow Britons, our protectors, have been sacrificed to our ruthless greed. This contemplated raid on the small and great hoards of prudence and self denial in England, unblushingly advocated for the foregoing reason, involves larger pecuniary losses, and is much more culpable than that made under a belief that returns would be got for the money by the projectors of the Grand Trunk Railway. Yet what a howl has been raised about our ears for our share in that scheme ! Are the widows and orphans, said to be our victims, so soon to be fogotten ?

While the Government, bankers and capitalists are succeeding so well in establishing Canadian credit in Britain, for practicable and judicious enterprise, this system of advocating an impracticable scheme is demoralizing public opinion here, and elsewhere is destroying confidence in Canadian enterprise, and is certain not only to defeat the ends sought, but utterly to ruin the value of Canadian endorsement on any scheme whatever.

As to the American private capital said to be available to the extent of $20,000,000, on condition that 10,000,000 acres of land are obtained, I have only to say, that, probably, the Government would sell these capitalists ten million acres of mineral lands, north of Lake Superior, for half the money, without requiring them to put a dollar in the canal, if these capitalists would agree to settle the tenth of the land every five years.

Twelve millions of dollars only are asked to build the Niagara Ship Canal, seven miles in length. Congress has not, but may grant the money. But where, meantime, are the men with the twenty millions, ready for the Georgian Bay Canal ? Surely, the shortest canal is the best investment.

The proposed Ottawa Canal route is the shortest and most feasible outlet for American commerce from the upper lakes to the sea. It may be practicable, whether it is or not there will need to be double four millions of people in the Dominion before it is undertaken. Canals are so expensive that the cost of one would build 20 railroads of the same length.

The cost of the Georgian Bay Canal at the lowest estimate—forty millions—would build a railway from Ottawa, north of Lake Nipissing, south of the coast range of mountains on the north side of Lake Superior along the table, at the height of land, straight to the Red River country. If ten, or even twenty, millions acres of land are a basis of credit for forty million dollars, then our Ontario Government might give five millions, the Quebec Government five millions, and the Dominion Government ten millions acres, (of the Hudson's Bay Territory)—in all twenty million acres under proper checks, to build a railway from Ottawa to a suitable entrepot in the Red River district, there to build a second Moscow. Let us have four millions of good Britons, with a sprinkling of Scandinavians, along the line of that railway and in the Red River country, and with plenty of coals, iron, and Britons, we may—those will who live to see it—bid defiance to all the military power thence to Cape Horn.

I am, sir, your obedient servant,

G. LAIDLAW.

Financial.

TORONTO STOCK MARKET.

(Reported by Pellatt & Osler, Brokers.)

Since the New Year the stock market has been very brisk, transactions numerous and prices well maintained.

Bank Stock—There were transactions in Montreal at 138¼, with very little offering. Sellers are now asking ½ per cent. prem. for Ontario; large sales at par. Toronto is in great demand; none offering. Sales of Royal Canadian are reported at 87, ex-dividend; small lots offering at 86. Sellers are asking 101½ and 102, ex-dividend, for Commerce, with buyers at 101. Gore offering at 40, with no buyers at over 35. Transactions in Merchants' occurred at 106, ex-dividend; little doing. Quebec is nominal at 98½ to 99½. Sales of Molson's occurred at 110; little offering. City is offered at 101½. There are buyers of Du Peuple at 108. Sales of Jacques Cartier occurred at 107½; sellers asking 108. There are buyers of Union at 103, and no sellers under 104. Nothing doing in other banks.

Debentures—No Canada debentures in market; they would command a high price. No Toronto in market; the last sales were at rates to yield 6¾ per. cent. to purchasers. There were small sales of County during the week; they are eagerly sought after to pay 6½ per cent. interest.

Sundries—There were transactions in Canada Permanent Building Society at 120, ex-dividend; sellers now ask 121. Sales of Western Canada occurred at 113½, ex-dividend; little offering. Freehold enquired for none in market; 105½ would be paid. Sales of Montreal Telegraph occurred at 139; a half-yearly dividend of 5 per cent. is declared, payable on the 8th inst. A small sale of Canada Landed Credit occurred at 72; little in market. Several transactions occurred in British America Assurance at 57. City Gas in great demand; none offering. Mortgages—none offering. Money remains much the same as last week.

PAPER MONEY.

In his report for 1867, the Secretary of the United States Treasury makes the following remarks respecting paper money:

The Government of Austria, during the wars with Napoleon, resorted to the issue of its own notes to circulate as money. From time to time, as expenditure demanded, the volume was augmented, until in 1809, the amount outstanding reached a sum equivalent in our money to six hundred million dollars. In 1811 this paper was called in and replaced by "notes of redemption," as they were termed, at the rate of twenty cents on the dollar. After the return of peace in 1815, these "notes of redemption," together with a large amount of subsequent issues which had been depreciated, were taken up, partly in Bank of Austria notes and partly by conversion into Bank stock, at the rate of forty cents on the dollar. This disposed of the original issue at the rate of eight cents on the dollar.

Russia tried the experiment, and issued Government notes in making disbursements, which, at first, while the amount was small, circulated at par; but the "fatal facility," was fatal here as elsewhere.

There is not a single explanation on record of the power of creating money out of cheap materials having been exercised by a sovereign state for any length of time, or through any season of public difficulty, without having been abused. * * * The temptation to substitute issues for taxation, to relieve the wants of the treasury, * * * becomes too strong to be resisted. The career of debasement once entered upon, it has no pause till there is scarcely any value left to be destroyed.—Fullerton on the Regulation of Currencies, p. 24. "There has never been a Government yet, of the many which have issued irredeemable paper, which had the wisdom and firmness to resist, for any great length of time, the strong temptation to over issues. * * When once the press is set at work, it must work on with livelier speed; because, just in the ratio of the depreciation is the greater amount required."—Perry's Elements of Political Economy.

The advocates of a currency composed exclusively of Government paper, and that in augmented volume, cannot claim even the merit of originality; the experiment has been tried over and over again, and with but one result: the paper goes down until it becomes so nearly worthless that it is taken out of the way at some nominal rate, or repudiated altogether. There is no good reason to believe that it would fare any better now. On the contrary, the experience of the last five years in this country is but the counterpart of the earlier stages of the experiment in other countries and in other times.

In view of all the circumstances surrounding the public debt, the conditions under which, and the purposes for which it was contracted, the only rational course which can be pursued is the one that would suggest itself to every honorable business man; the careful husbanding of the national resources by strict economy in every branch of expenditure, and a plain recognition of the character of the national obligations. Floating indebtedness is always the most embarrassing. A wise policy would remove it, so that it should not be an element of uncertainty or of obstruction in the way of national credit.

COMMERCIAL BANK OF NEW BRUNSWICK.

A telegram dated January 5 says:—An adjourned meeting of the Stockholders of the Commercial Bank was held to-day, when the Directors presented an amended and more detailed report, which differs but slightly from the former. Total assets estimated at $765,671; liabilities, $630,958. Much of the assets consists of landed and other property difficult to realize. It is generally understood that nearly the entire capital has been lost. The Directors, in submitting the report, protested against further scrutiny into the accounts as prejudicial to the interests of the Stockholders, and a violation of the Bank Charter. Should the meeting still insist on fuller information they would retire. After a long discussion the report was referred back to the Directors, and the meeting adjourned to the 9th of March. This virtually leaves the Directors to wind up the bank, as the charter expires on Friday.

INTERNATIONAL CURRENCY.—The French Government has called in all the two and one-franc, half-franc, and four-sou pieces, as well as certain Belgian, Italian, and Swiss silver coins lately current in France. After the last day of the present year, no French or Italian coin of the above denominations will be received which bears date earlier than 1864; the silver Belgian pieces of Leopold I., and the Swiss pieces coined previously to 1860, will also be withdrawn at the same period. The public currency of these coins actually ceased on the 1st of October, but they will be received or exchanged at the postoffice and public *caisses* until the end of the year. T object of this arrangement is, to carry out t terms of a convention between France, Ital Belgium and Switzerland, by which the coins each country become current in the other, on t condition that they contain one uniform quant of silver—namely, 835 parts in 1,000. Some them at present contain 900 parts of silver, a others not more than 800. A similar conventi is being made with the Papal Government; when all these regulations are in force, the sm money, as well as the gold, of these five countr will be current without difference of exchan and without margin for speculation and export *Produce Markets Review, Dec. 5.*

DEATH OF MR. CONVERSE.—The news of death of Mr. Converse, accountant of the Bank Montreal, has excited much sympathy and re from all who were brought into contact with h in business relations. His long connection w the Bank of Montreal had made him gener known, and his quiet and attentive discharg his duties made him a universal favorite. By managers and directors of the Bank he was hig esteemed and respected, and the utmost confide was felt in his management of the important partment more immediately under his care, loss being felt as one that will not be easily paired. His personal friends, of whom he many, were warmly attached to him.

WHY THE BANK OF FRANCE IS LOSING GOLD.—The value of the wheat imported France in the first seven months of this year £10,520,784, as compared with £2,770,416 in corresponding period of 1867, and £59,171 in corresponding period of 1866. Of the sum for wheat imported by the French in the first se months of this year £277,220 went to the Un Kingdom, £336,672 to Belgium, £1,486,94 Russia, £1,431,784 to the Zollverein, £650,38 to Italy, and £4,530,960 to Turkey and Danubian Principalities. It will be seen that year's figures showed a considerable expansio compared with 1867 and 1866; but while Fr paid £10,520,784 for the wheat which she im ed to July 31 this year, the corresponding ment made by Great Britain in the same p was no less than £15,320,539.

BANK OF B. N. A. *vs.* TORRANCE.—Judg was delivered in this case on the 31st Decen in favour of the plaintiffs.

GAS EXPLOSION.

From a recent article in the 'Monitor,' we the following extract:—Coal gas is lighter the atmosphere, and leaking in a cellar or room, where most of these accidents occur, tendency to rise and diffuse itself througho house, escaping, and at the same time givin tice of its presence by its offensive odor. line is heavier than the atmosphere and fa the ground, rising only as water would rise, room fills. It does not send its odor to the parts of the house, but lurks, an unsuspecte for the approach of the fatal candle or n On the other hand, it may be said that the ten burners in the upper parts of the rooms there is one light near the floor, makin chances ten to one that coal gas will be ig sooner that the other, and equalizing to son tent the dangers arising from the different ties; but it is equally true that the diffusive ity of the coal gas sends it away, or so dilute the atmosphere as to render it measurably less, while the other, in a still room or cell mains comparatively solid, and hence more ble of mischief.

Both articles emit an offensive odor, bu of gasoline is similar to the smell of ker and, while familiar to all who have used oil" lamps, is not generally regarded as a of danger, while the "smell of gas" inv suggests a leak, and is a recognized war something wrong.

does not condense. Some of the gaso-
ituses are reported to have overcome
icy in that article, but so far as we
edge of the various processes, they re-
other in this, that the gasoline gas is
orced through the liquid, and impreg-
its vapor. This evaporation, if made
nperature, is not liable to condensation
i, but taking off only the more volatile
liquid, it leaves a portion of the gaso-
tank, and, being wasteful and expen-
s a temptation to employ artificial heat
o the whole. If evaporated at a high
i, it will inevitably condense in the
ng changed from its liquid state by
urally becomes liquid again as soon as
from the heat. This is the source of
n danger ; a match is lighted and the
d on," but, instead of gas, a stream of
spirts out, which is instantly ignited,
on the person or furniture in the
iid fire, burns with an unquenchable
several buildings and lives have thus
Economy demands the evaporation of
line ; safety demands only such evapo-
n be made at a low temperature. The
ns radical and irreconcilable. Until
e been overcome, safety and economy
ombined in the use of gasoline.
differences above stated, we conclude
.s is safer than gasoline.
less, we do not understand that ex-
spirts on," but, instead of gas, a stream
, so far, conclusive against the use
Many of the accidents that have
rom it might have occurred with
Leaky pipes, defective meters, care-
all these are incident to the use of
d productive of danger from both
ho would think for a moment of
coal gas generator under his draw-
is cellar ? Yet either would be as
s to keep gasoline, or to manufac-
ras, on one's premises. This seems
be the point that has been ignored.
he gas at a distance of not less than 50
ny building, run to your house through
es as you would city gas from the street
ithing but pipes, and those only such
ity gas, enter your premises; see, also
have been well put up and properly
i that no leaks exist, and we do not un-
hat the average danger of one kind of
ter than the other. When we say "pro-
up, we mean with grades, and traps,
ts, to provide for condensation and
We mean that no fire or artificial heat
roach the gasoline, or the apparatus.
he gasoline on one's ground is as dan-
bringing the same amount of powder.
perfectly harmless as long as no fire
r them, but there is little choice between
n once the fire touches either.
ild not, under any consideration, insure
are one of these infernal machines was
kling, or within burning distance of it.
e, so far, we regard as conclusive on that
l we again call the attention of Under-
the encroachments of these machines,
at that they be forewarned, and decline
ontaining them, or influenced by their

annual meeting of the shareholders of
wrence Warehouse and Dock Company
eld in Quebec on the first Monday in

—Mr. Alexander Gibson, of New Bruns-
iped during seven months, 77,942,511
feet of deals and battens, and 769,505
Liverpool.

a. Copp and Proctor, of Hamilton, have
he Directorships of the Dominion Tele-
npany, vacated by Messrs. McInnis &

MADERIA WINES.—According to a report of
Messrs. Richard Symonds and Son, the Maderia
vintage for 1868 shows a very considerable increase
on recent years, and may attain about 4,000
pipes—a quantity still very small compared with
that produced in the prosperous days of the Island
before 1851. About nine-tenths were grown on
the south side of the Island, where the best "Ma-
derias" were formerly produced, and will probably be good wines, taking into consideration the
youth of the plants ; the remaining tenth, grown
on the north side, will be very inferior. Of the
total about three-fourths will be required for
island consumption and for conversion into brandy, so that only about 1,000 pipes will ultimately
be available for exportation. These will be the
best wines of the year, but, before they are
shipped, should be allowed some five years to
attain thorough maturity. The progress of renewed vine culture is slow, but it is nevertheless
marked as regards both quantity and quality.

FLAG STONE.—The Brampton flagstone quarries will be worked vigorously next spring. The
quarries are situate on Lot 26, in the 4th Concession of Brampton, on the main road from Melbourne, close to the Grand Trunk Railway. The
flag stone rises abruptly from the road to an elevation of 126 feet, and extends along the highway
about a quarter of a mile, affording great facilities
for quarrying, and space for the employment of a
large number of gangs of men to work at the
same time. The stone is of a hard, tough and
non-absorbing nature, with a perfect cleavage,
splitting through the bed into any thickness required, and easily dressed with hammer or saw.
Unlike slate it is capable of standing fire and
frost without injury, as has been proved by many
years trial.

Commercial.

Montreal Correspondence.

(From our own Correspondent.)

Montreal, Jan. 5, 1869.
Having been absent from the city during our
Christmas holidays, I cannot give the details of
business that I am in the habit of sending you,
and can only state that in all the wholesale departments matters have been exceedingly flat.
Of course our merchants are prepared for this state
of thing, as during the large fall sales, retailers
both in town and in the country lay in their supplies of staples, and after that only buy to keep
assortments complete. I have already informed
you that our fall sales went off unsatisfactorily,
although a fair amount was placed. This arises
from a diffidence on the part of the Western buyers to operate till they practically realized the result of the good harvest, and from the keen competition of Toronto and other western cities,
whose merchants have imported direct and are
naturally anxious to secure what they consider
their legitimate business direct through themselves
instead of its passing through Montreal. This
city possesses a large connection in all sections of
the two Provinces, commands an immense capital
and most of the western men are well prepared and
can get better accommodation, if hard pressed,
here than in any other city. Our stocks are larger
and more varied, because they have to be suited
to a larger range of customers, and we can sell at
prices, if anything, lower than the wholsale
western men.

In Produce the market has been very dull, so
much so that it is difficult to give more than
nominal quotations—the business done bring only
from hand to mouth. This applies especially to
flour, grain and provisions. Butter has hardly
held its own, though very fine fresh butter is
scarce and would command almost any price.
Taken generally, the trade of Montreal for 1868
has been satisfactory ; in the spring everything
was dull and the prospects were anything but in-

viting ; during the summer this state of things
continued but with a distant breaking of the
clouds, as the prospects of the coming harvest appeared more and more bright. Our hopes in that
direction were verified to a large extent in Western
Canada, especially in the great staple of wheat ;
and the farmers, after realizing, to a great extent
found themselves in a position to pay off outstanding liabilities and yet be well forward with future
payments. In Lower Canada, to which my personal observations have chiefly been restricted,
the result of the harvest has not been so fortunate, as the leading grains, such as barley, oats,
peas, &c., have been almost a total failure ; our
crops of wheat have been good, but we do not
grow sufficient for our own consumption.

Toronto Market.

Trade is steadily improving since the holidays
and a general opinion seems to be, that the winter
trade promises well. In some of the leading
branches, attention has been chiefly directed to
stock-taking and the balancing of books.

PRODUCE.—*Wheat.*—Receipts for the week,
10,050 bush.; the market for Spring is steady at
$1 to $1.03 in store; there is a moderate demand
and not much offering. Midge proof is worth the
same prices as Spring, but there is little doing.
Fall is quiet at $1.10 to $1.12 for the best samples.

The following were the receipts and shipments
of wheat at the Toronto warehouses in the years
named:—

1868.	Fall Wheat.	Spring Wheat.
Receipts,.....bush.	252,589	364,174
Shipments... "	240,191	354.523
1867.		
Receipts,.....bush.	268,116	485,983
Shipments... "	303,152	478,435
1866.		
Receipts,.....bush.	534,272	493,197
Shipments... "	529,027	406,907
1865.		
Receipts,....bush.	587,688	238,000
Shipments... "	486,904	358,044

Barley.—Receipts by cars, 780 bush.; holders ask
$1.27 to $1.30, and buyers offer $1.25 to $1.27 ;
no sales. The total receipts of barley at the port
of Toronto, for the years named, were—

Receipts in 1868,	.............bu	988,410
Receipts in 1867,	....	1,025,455
Receipts in 1866,	....	1,278,767
Receipts in 1865,	....	1,197,126

Peas—No receipts, and market is dull and nominal at quotations. *Oats*—Receipts by cars, 2,400
bush. Under increased receipts, the market is
duller, and cars are now worth 51c. to 52c. ; sales
at 52c.

FLOUR.—Receipts for the week, 3,200 barrels.
There is not much offering ; sellers ask $4.55 to
$4.60 for No. 1 Superfine, with no buyers above
$4.50 ; sale one lot at $4.52 ; Extra is nominal at
$5.25, and fancy at $4.90 to $5.00. There is no
demand for the grades above No. 1 Superfine.

PROVISIONS.—*Dressed Hogs*—The market is
active and firm, and closed at considerable advance on last week's quotations. Hogs dividing
on 200 lbs are now worth $7.90, and good to heavy
Hogs bring $8 to $8.25. *Butter*—The stock is
light, and nothing doing except in the home
trade. Other provisions we have nothing reliable
to report.

PETROLEUM.—The new combination have now
entire control of the market, and prices are fixed
at 32½ to 35, according to quantity purchased.
The lowest quantity that the Association will sell
is one carload. In our market a fair business has
been done for consumption at the quotations elsewhere given. Benzine is falling into disuse, as
turpentine is said to be largely substituted
for it.

— It is said that peat has been discovered in
Hamilton, in St. Lawrence Ward, during the
course of making excavations for a sewer.

Produce in Store.

Stocks of grain in New York at the close of

	1866.	1867.	1868.
Wheat...bu	1,715,302	1,778,533	3,433,281
Corn	3,000,042	1,526,021	1,633,381
Rye	492,308	194,830	275,943
Barley	1,680,375	357,866	326,301
Oats	2,430,434	2,769,482	2,760,482
Peas	.....	8,200	66,608
Malt	.....	92'502	104,172

In store at Milwaukee, Dec. 21, 1868:

Wheat	bu 622,761
Corn	5,660
Oats	65,056
Barley	1,699
Rye	16,657
Total	731,833

Flour and grain in store at Chicago:

	Dec. 26, 1868.	Dec. 19, 1868.	Dec. 26, 1867.
Wheat....bu	1,079,562	1,005,173	741,971
Corn	430,892	383,482	564,167
Oats	462,288	442,468	388,190
Barley	312,571	328,574	145,126
Rye	157,694	152,466	21,283
Total	2,430,907	2,311,853	1,660,746

California Wheat Market.

The San Francisco Market Review of December 22, says: It has been estimated by the best authorities that, over and above all domestic requirements, California produced this harvest year, 8,000,000 centals for export, or nearly 3,000,000 more than last year. Of this surplus we have already exported 3,600,000 centals, divided as follows:—to Great Britain 1,600,000 centals ; to domestic Atlantic ports, chiefly to New York, 1,000,000 centals ; and to all other countries, 1,000,000 centals—leaving us with a surplus still on hand of 4,400,000 centals. These figures represent wheat, and flour reduced to wheat. In all of last year we shipped 4,312,000 centals, so that the surplus of this year, yet to be marketed, is within 712,000 centals of the whole of last year's export. No account is taken of the Oregon crop in this statement. It will require two hundred and twenty ships of a thousand tons each to carry away the remaining surplus wheat of California alone.

Losses on the Lakes—Harbors of Refuge.

The season of 1868, as has been shown by the reports already published, was attended by a far greater loss to the shipping than any preceding one in the annals of navigation, while a fearful loss of life has occurred. Sixteen disasters occurred during the month of March ; 110 in April ; 118 during May ; 101 in June ; 94 in July ; 126 in August ; 208 in September ; 233 in October ; 174 in November, and 12 in December. A large majority of the disasters on Lake Erie have taken place on the northern or Canadian coast, and in one particular instance no less than five shipwrecks are recorded within a distance extending only about one hundred miles. Vessels destined through that lake invariably pursue that route, being not only the most direct but more contiguous to various leas, which are interspersed at various points. These points of refuge alluded to, however, being located under the shelter of points or peninsular of land extending well out into the lake, are very hazardous in resorting to when vessels are suddenly overtaken by a sudden squall or gale of wind from an opposite quarter, and it is chiefly on such occasions that vessels are driven upon the beach and in numerous instances suffer complete and total shipwreck. The same views may also be applied to a greater or less extent with reference to Lake Huron. For the want of a reliable as well as an accessible point of shelter on that lake two fine steamers have been driven on a rock-bound coast and narrowly escaped total loss, while for the same reason the disasters to the sailing vessels on that lake have

been beyond precedent. As the Government of the neighboring Dominion of Canada have, as we are informed, been making surveys quite recently, with the view of locating a harbor of refuge on both of the above lakes, and doubtless will soon determine as to the feasibility of a proper site, a deep interest is felt on the part of our ship owners and ship masters at all our lake ports, where those harbors, if established, are to be located. On Lake Huron, Goderich will, without doubt, be decided on, and is unquestionably the most fit of all seeking that end. On Lake Erie, the location, as we have urged on repeated occasions, should be about half way distant between Buffalo and the Detroit river, or midway between the canal and the islands, and not less than fifty miles to the westward of Long Point. The selection should be at a point where a stream or river puts out into the lake, that can without an unreasonable outlay be converted into a harbor of sufficient width, and having also a wide entrance or mouth, not less than 150 feet. With these facilities, which should be of easy approach, with a light elevated and piers of proper extension in the lake, there can be no doubt that a harbor of refuge on either of the above lakes would be the means of saving many lives and much property, and ere long would be more than self-sustaining. On Lake Erie, so far as American ship owners and masters are interested in the above undertakings, and they are, as we have already stated, largely so, Port Burwell is the more preferable of all which have been spoken of, and without doubt such will be the decision of the Canadian Government.

The Pork Trade.

A recent St. Louis circular says: "The South is consuming meat of the new crop, while the old stock was consumed long before the new cure could be got forward. In the face of this fact, we have the evidence that there is at least an even chance for a small crop of hogs to give us the meat for the coming wants. Could we come up to last year's crop we should then be deficient, for that only met the necessities, which were cramped by the lack of means to pay. Now, with increased facilities for payment, and a consumption, so far, of the new crop, astonishing and unusual, and yet legitimate, the "Hog Product" is to be short this year in any event that can now occur. Some writers are descanting upon the fact that the present high prices are checking the exportations. To our mind this is of but little concern, for, from present appearances, the West will have no provisions to send out of the country. The home consumption will be as much as we can meet, and we may not be able to even do that if the hogs do not come forward in larger supply than they have thus far, and than a majority predict they will. One thing is palpable, either hogs must come down in price or the product must go higher than any prices we have yet seen. It is estimated that at the present time the stock of Lard is only about half and that of Pork only about one quarter of the stock of last year at Chicago, and other points also short."

London Barley Market.

Dec. 2.—The firmness of the barley trade noticed last month has been maintained, and high prices have again been realised for malting produce. Larger supplies of barley have, however, been received, and the maltsters have operated with a greater degree of caution ; nevertheless, 53s. and 54s. per quarter have been obtained for fine qualities of barley, being quite equal to the prices current at this period last month. The quality of the English barley is still very fine, and the high quotations have brought larger quantities to market than had been expected. As, however, the crop is a small one, it is evident that although our supplies may be tolerably good now, there will be a great scarcity of English barley later in the season, and, consequently, a continuance of high prices may be expected, unless, indeed, which is somewhat improbable, our importations should be very materially increased.

From abroad, the imports of barley have good. In October they amounted to 755,798 c against 463,368 cwt. last year, 839,612 cw 1866, and 726,167 cwt. in 1865. The increa our foreign supply is due,- in a great measur a large importation from France. From Germ very moderate supplies have been received, w as regards America, rather an importing coun a considerable quantity of produce has been chased here for shipment to New York. American demand is just now a feature in trade ; about 40,000 quarters have been purch in London and in other parts of the country, as a considerable fall took place in the val barley at New York on Monday, the deman been much less active during the last few day

The English Hop Crop of 1868.

The past season has been one of the mos riable and precarious known to hop grower many years, for at the period of the vine cal off the young hop shoots there was the promi one of the finest and heaviest hop crops of n years ; there was an entire absence of mildew insects, which invariably infest the young crops and deteriorate the produce, and the growers very reasonably estimated an unus heavy yield. In Kent and other well cultiv hop districts the hops were unprecedentedly l and there was every reasonable prospect tha picking time a prolific season would be the re tinued drought set in, which very fearfully tated against the consummation of the hop i throughout the country; but the want of moi to the hop roots had an injurious effect- foliage of the hops expanded and became and chaffy, and the aroma so essential to qualities was lost; and after gathering, the pr of kiln drying was almost superfluous, an hops trod into the pockets bulky and light the present year a far larger acreage of hop was gathered and cured than at any pre period. In 1855 hop cultivation in this cou had attained its highest standard, and 5 acres of land were devoted to the cultivati hops, and a sum of £398,365 was paid as ol duty (with additional imposts) to the I Revenue; but from that year many hop ga ware grubbed up, and in the next four years under hop cultivation had been diminishe 14,028 acres; in 1859 the hop yield was h and the old duty amounted to £328,070 o growth of 43,729 acres of hops, but on the abolition of the hop duty growers commence tending hop plantations which have annual creased, and this year 63,500 acres of hops been gathered and cured. Kent is the h hop county, and comprises nearly 30,000 a hop garden. Sussex is a large hop county Worcestershire is a more extensive and imp hop growing locality, and the hop garden being increased. Herefordshire cultivates a section of hop land. Hants and Berks cou hop growing districts. Surrey has at celebrity for its produce of hops of peculia superior rich flavor, and possessing proper high caste, the hops of this county (Farnl have hitherto attained the highest value; b year they were surpassed by Kent, and were most decidedly the best qualities. has grown from 7 to 14 cwt. an acre, b qualities are of a low standard. Kent pr an average yield of 8 cwt. an acre; and varied from 7 to 12 cwt ; and country (var to 11 cwt. per acre.—Morgan's Trade Jour

Petroleum.

Crude in bulk is coming forward a little freely, but there is no disposition to giv further in prices, although the demand is ate ; we quote at 17½c. Refined standard w trade is a little better to-day. The demand ever, is wholly speculative. Prices are a half cent per gallon higher, closing at 31½c sales are 1,500 bbls. at 31c. ; 500 bbls. at and 1,000 bbls. on private terms. For Pi

ery the demand is more active, mostly
ate' with a little steadier tone in the
the close. The sales are 3,000 bbls.
andard white, for the balance of the
; 80c. ; 3,000 bbls. do. for January,
and March delivery, at 80c., and 1,000
for March at 30¼c.

for the week ending Dec. 29..pkgs   19,609
for the week ending Dec. 28..galls.   765,999
from Jan. 1...............galls.   51,247,789
same time last year........galls.   33,481,778

llowing is the quantity exported from
z, Jan. 1 to Dec. 26.

	1868.	1867.
ston.............galls.	2,367,965	2,224,007
ladelphia	38,481,157	28,587,809
timore	2,587,207	1,513,209
tland	705,107	900
veland	270,000	
	44,414,236	32,317,916
orts from the United		
t.............	87,024,722	65,737,080
e in 1866		66,139,730
e in 1855		26,226,725

St. John Market.

9.—The banks are discounting rather
rly this week, although the paper taken
lly of unexceptionable character. In
circles we hear a good deal of surprise
hat the directors of the St. Stephen's
not bestirring themselves to make
ons for the opening of an agency here.'
oost certain that if a move is not im-
made in this direction, the ground will
d by a Canadian bank. Bank 60 days'
ills continue in fair demand on the basis
short sight 110½; Bankers latest quota-

rates—Sterling bills, 60 days, 8¾ prem.;
ills, 90 days, 8½ prem. ; drafts on Cana-
to par; drafts on Halifax, 3¼ dis.; gold
New York and Boston, ½ dis to par;
drafts on New York and Boston, 25½
a Scotia notes, 3¾ dis.; Prince Edward
tes, 5 dis. ; St. Stephen's Bank notes,

rates—On London, 30 days, 9 ¼prem.
k and Boston, sight (gold), ⅜ prem.;
sight, 2¼ dis.; Canadian cities, ¼ prem.;
drafts on New York and Boston, 25¼

-The prices, which during the past week
ve kept low, now show a disposition to
. The demand, however, is limited, and
call is for small lots to meet the local
nts. Superfine commands $6 and choice
6.25. There are no large arrivals and
ow look for prices to advance. Meal is
asier.

ropean Consumption of Cotton.
appears to be considerable misapprehen-
hink, with regard to the probable supply
umption of cotton in Europe this year.
ear to claim that there is not sufficient
meet the anticipated demand. We have
therefore, the following table, which
actual consumption for the last two years
imate for this year, which estimate will,
e, be looked upon as rather an under
. than an over statement of the probable

CONSUMPTION OF COTTON IN EUROPE.

	1866-7. (Actual.)	1867-8. (Actual.)	1868-9. (Est'd.)
ning of year..	1,143,000	1,092,500	614,000
m America..	1,495,000	1,676,000	1,659,000
" India...	1,524,000	1,312,000	*1,500,000
" Brazil...	481,000	675,000	750,000
" Egypt ...	228,000	235,000	270,000
" All others..	868,000	330,000	330,000
ly	5,239,000	5,318,000	5,144,000
se of year....	1,092,000	614,000	840,000
on during year.	4,147,000	4,604,000	4,274,000
y consumption.	80,000	85,500	84,000

Cotton was shipped late last year by reason of
and the Abyssinian war, and hence 250,000
ome into this year's supply—*Financ'l Chronicle.*

TORONTO PRICES CURRENT.—JANUARY 7, 1869.

Name of Article.	Wholesale Rates.		Name of Article.	Wholesale Rate.		Name of Article.	
Boots and Shoes.	$ c.	$ c.	**Groceries**—Contin'd	$ c.	$ c.	**Leather**—Contin'd.	
Mens' Thick Boots ...	2 05	2 50	" fine to fine't..	0 65	0 05	Kip Skins, Patna	0
" Kip........	2 50	3 25	Hyson	0 45	0 90	French	0
" Calf	3 00	3 70	Imperial	0 42	0 80	English	0
" Congress Gaiters..	2 00	2 50	Tobacco, Manufact'd:			Hemlock Calf (30 to	
" Kip Cabourgs...	1 14	1 46	Can Leaf, ⅌ ℔ 5s & 10s.	0 26	0 30	35 lbs.) per doz...	0
Boys' Thick Boots	1 60	1 80	Western Leaf, com..	0 25	0 30	Do. light	0
Youths'	1 25	1 50	" Good ...	0 27	0 32	French Calf........	0
Women's Batts	95	1 30	" Fine ...	0 32	0 35	Grain & Satn Clf ⅌ doz.	0
" Congress Gaiters..	1 15	1 45	" Bright fine...	0 40	0 50	Splits, large ⅌ ℔.....	0
Misses' Batts..........	0 75	1 00	" choice..	0 60	0 75	" small	0
" Congress Gaiters..	1 00	1 30				Grain & Satn Clf ⅌ doz.	
Girls' Batts	0 60	0 85	**Hardware.**			Enamelled Cow ⅌ foot..	0
" Congress Gaiters..	0 80	1 10	Tin (net cash prices)			Patent	0
Children's C. T. Cacks.	0 50	0 65	Block, ⅌ ℔.......	0 25	0 26	Pebble Grain	0
" Gaiters........	0 65	0 90	Grain	0 25	0 26	Buff	0
			Copper:			**Oils.**	
Drugs.			Pig	0 23	0 24	Cod	0
Aloes Cape..........	0 12½	0 16	Sheet..............	0 30	0 32	Lard, extra	0
Alum	0 02½	0 03	Cut Nails:			" No. 1	0
Borax	0 00	0 00	Assorted ¼ Shingles,			" Woollen.......	0
Camphor, refined....	0 65	0 70	⅌ 100 ℔.	3 90	4 00	Lubricating, patent...	0
Castor Oil	0 18	0 28	Shingle alone do ..	3 14	3 25	" Mott's economic	0
Caustic Soda........	0 04½	0 05	Lathe and 5 dy ...	3 30	3 40	Linseed, raw	2
Cochineal	0 65	1 10	Galvanized Iron:			" boiled.......	0
Cream Tartar	0 35	0 30	Assorted sizes	0 08	0 09	Machinery	0
Epsom Salts	0 03	0 04	Best No. 24.......	0 09	0 00	Olive, 2nd, ⅌ gal...	1
Extract Logwood.....	0 09	0 11	" 26.......	0 08	0 09½	" salad	2
Gum Arabic, sorts...	0 30	0 35	" 28.......	0 09	0 09½	" salad, in bots.	
Indigo, Madras	0 75	1 00	Horse Nails:			qt. ⅌ case......	4
Licorice	0 14	0 45	Gnest's or Griffin's			Sesame salad, ⅌ gal..	1
Madder	0 16	0 18	assorted sizes....	0 00	0 00	Seal, pale..........	0
Nutgalls	0 00	0 00	For W ass'd sizes...	0 18	0 19	Spirits Turpentine...	0
Opium	0 70	7 00	Patent Hammer'd do.	0 17	0 18	Varnish	0
Oxalic Acid..........	0 28	0 30	Iron (at 4 months):			Whale..............	0
Potash, Bi-tart......	0 25	0 28	Pig—Gartsherrie No 1.	24 00	23 00	**Paints, &c.**	
" Bichromate..	0 15	0 20	Other brands. No 1..	22 00	24 00	White Lead, genuine	
Potass Iodide	3 80	4 50	No 2..	0 00	0 00	in Oil, ⅌ 25℔s...	0
Senna	0 12½	0 60	Bar—Scotch, ⅌100 ℔..	2 25	2 50	Do. No. 1 " "	0
Soda Ash	0 03	0 04	Refined	3 00	3 25	" 2 " "	0
Soda Bicarb	0 60	5 50	Swedes	5 00	5 50	" 3 " "	0
Tartaric Acid........	0 37½	0 45	Hoops—Coopers....	3 00	3 25	White Zinc, genuine..	1
Verdigris	0 35	0 40	Band.............	3 50	3 75	White Lead, dry......	0
Vitriol, blue	0 09	0 10	Boiler Plates.......	3 75	3 90	Red Lead...........	0
			Canada Plates......	4 00	4 25	Venetian Red, Eng'h..	0
Groceries.			Union Jack	0 00	0 00	Yellow Ochre, Flen'h..	0
Coffees:			Pontypool	4 00	4 25	Whiting	0
Java, ⅌ ℔........	0 27@0 24		Swansea	3 90	4 00		
Laguayra, "....	0 17	0 18	Lead (at 4 months):			**Petroleum.**	
Rio................	0 15	0 17	Bar, ⅌ 100 ℔s.. ..	0 07	0 07½	(Refined ⅌ gal.)	
Fish:			Sheet	0 08	0 09	Water white, car'd..	0
Herrings, Lab. split...	5 75	6 50	Shot..............	0 07½	0 07½	" small lots...	0
" round....	4 00	4 75	Iron Wire (net cash):			Straw, by car load ..	
" scaled.......	0 35	0 40	No. 6 ⅌ bundle...	2 70	2 80	" small lots...	
Mackerel, small kitts..	1 00	0 00	" 7 ...	2 10	2 20	Amber, by car load..	U
Loch. Her. wh'e firks..	2 50	2 75	" 8, " ...	2 30	2 40	" small lots..	
" half "	1 25	1 50	" 9, " ...	2 40	2 50	Benzine	0
White Fish & Trout...	3 50	3 75	" 10, " ...	4 30	4 40	**Produce.**	
Salmon, saltwater....	14 00	15 00	Powder:			Grain:	
Dry Cod, ⅌112 ℔s....	0 00	8 25	Blasting, Canada....	3 50	4 00	Wheat, Spring, 60 ℔b..	1
Fruit:			FF "	4 00	0 00	" Fall 60 " ..	1
Raisins, Layers	2 10	2 20	FFF "	4 75	5 00	Barley .... 48 " .	1
" M H.......	1 90	2 10	Blasting, English ...	4 00	5 00	Peas............ 60 " .	0
" Valentians new "	0 07	0 07½	FF loose..	5 90	6 00	Oats............ 34 " .	0
Currants, new	0 05	0 05½	FFF "	6 00	6 50	Rye............. 56 " .	0
" old......	0 04½	0 04½	Pressed Spikes (4 mos):			Seeds:	
Figs................	0 14	0 00	Regular sizes 1½0...	4 00	4 25	Clover, choice 60 " ..	6
Molasses:			Extra	4 50	5 00	" com'n 68 " ..	5
Clayed, ⅌ gal.......	0 00	0 55	Tin Plates (net cash):			Timothy, cho'e 4 " ..	4
Syrups, Standard ...	0 40	0 50	IC Coke	7 50	8 50	" inf. to good 48 " ..	2
" Golden ...	0 54	0 55	IC Charcoal........	8 25	8 60	Flax .... 56 " ..	1
Rice:			IX "	10 25	10 75	Flour (per brl.):	
Arracan	4 50	4 75	IXX "	12 25	0 00	Superior extra......	4
Sugars:			DC "	7 25	9 00	Extra superfine......	4
Cassia, whole, ⅌ ℔..	0 00	0 45	DX "	9 50	0 00	Fancy superfine	4
Cloves	0 11	0 12				Superfine No. 1.....	4
Nutmegs	0 45	0 55	**Hides & Skins.⅌℔**			" No. 2	4
Ginger, ground	0 20	0 25	Green rough	0 06	0 00	Oatmeal brl.)....	
" Jamaica, root..	0 20	0 26	Green, salt'd & insp'd..	0 00	0 07	**Provisions.**	
Pepper, black.......	0 00	0 00	Cured	0 08	0 08½	Butter, dairy tub ⅌ ℔..	
Pimento............	0 09	0 09	Calfskins, green	0 00	0 10	" store packed..	
Sugars:			Calfskins, cured.....	0 00	0 12	Cheese, new	
Port Rico, ⅌ ℔.....	0 08½	0 08½	" dry ...	0 16	0 20	Pork, mess, per brl...	2
Cuba "	0 06½	0 06½	Sheepskins, ...	1 00	1 25	" prime mess....	
Barbadoes (bright)..	0 08½	0 09	"	0 60	0 90	" prime mess....	
Dry Crushed, at 60d..	0 11½	0 11½				Bacon, rough	
Canada Sugar Refine'y,			**Hops.**			" Cumberl'd cut..	
yellow No. 2, 60ds..	0 09	0 09½	Inferior, ⅌ ℔......	0 05	0 07	" sm'k'd	
Yellow, No. 2½.....	0 09½	0 09½	Medium............	0 07	0 09	Hams, in salt.......	
" No. 3....	0 00	0 00	Good	0 09	0 12	" sug'r cur'd canv's'd..	
Crushed X	0 10	0 10½	Fancy	0 09	0 00	Shoulders, in salt ...	
" A	0 11	0 11½				Lard, in kegs........	
Ground.. "	0 11	0 11½	**Leather, ⅌ ℔ (4 mos.)**			Eggs, packed........	
Extra Ground	0 12½	0 12½	In lots of less than			Beef Hams	
Teas:			50 sides, 10 ⅌ cent			Tallow	
Japan com'n to good..	0 40	55	less.			Hogs dressed, heavy..	
" Fine to choicest..	0 55	65	Spanish Sole, Istqual...			" medium ...	
Colored, com. to fine..	0 60	75	heavy, weights ⅌ ℔..	0 00	0 23	" light	
Congou & Souch'ng ..	0 43	70	Do.1st qual middle do...	0 22	0 23	**Salt, &c.**	
Oolong, good to fine..	0 60	65	Do. No. 2, all weights..	0 20	0 21	American bria........	
Y. Hyson, com to gd..	0 45	55	Slaughter heavy	0 25	0 26	Liverpool coarse.....	
Medium to choice	0 65	80	Do. light...........	0 50	0 00	Plaster	
Extra choice	0 85	95	Harness, best	0 32	0 34	Water Lime	
unpowd'r'd, to med..	0 55	70	" No. 2 ...	0 30	0 33		
" med. to fine	0 70	85	Upper heavy........	0 46	0 38		
			" light......	0 30	0 40		

ndles.		
Co.'s ..	$ c.	$ c.
....	0 07½	0 08
ar	0 07	0 07½
r.......	0 07	0 07½
....	0 05	0 05½
....	0 03½	0 03½
....	0 00	0 11½
quors,		
dos......	2 60	2 65
b Portr..	2 35	2 40
Rum...	1 80	2 25
H. Gin..	1 55	1 65
Tom.....	1 90	2 00
....	4 00	4 25
Tom, c...	6 00	6 25
n	1 00	1 25
....	2 00	4 00
non	1 00	1 50
n........	1 70	1 80
golden..	2 50	4 00

Brandy:	$ c.	$ c.
Hennessy's, per gal..	2 30	2 50
Martell's " ..	2 30	2 50
J. Robin & Co.'s " ..	2 25	2 35
Otard, Dupuy & Cos..	2 25	2 35
Brandy, cases........	8 50	9 00
Brandy, com. per c...	4 00	4 50
Whiskey:		
Common 36 u. p......	0 62½	0 65
Old Rye	0 85	0 87½
Malt	0 85	0 87½
Toddy	0 85	0 87½
Scotch, per gal.......	1 90	2 10
Irish—Kinnahan's c...	7 00	7 50
" Dunnville's Belf't..	6 00	6 25
Wool.		
Fleece, lb...........	0 28	0 35
Pulled "...........	0 22	0 25
Furs.		
Bear..................	8 00	10 00
Beaver................	1 00	1 25
Coon	0 20	0 40
Fisher................	4 00	6 00
Martin................	1 40	1 60
Mink..................	4 00	4 25
Otter.................	5 75	6 00
Spring Rats...........	0 15	0 17
Fox...................	1 20	1 25

INSURANCE COMPANIES.

ENGLISH.—*Quotations on the London Market.*

Di- end.	Name of Company.	Shares par val £	Amount paid.	Last Sale.
	Briton Medical and General Life ...	10	....	1½
7½	Commer'l Union, Fire, Life and Mar.	50	5	5½
8	City of Glasgow	25	2½	5¾
9½	Edinburgh Life	100	15	31½
½ yr	European Life and Guarantee......	2½	11s6	5s
0	Etna Fire and Marine,............	10	1½	0
5	Guardian	100	50	51½
2	Imperial Fire....................	500	50	0
9½	Imperial Life	100	10	15½
0	Lancashire Fire and Life.........	20	2	2½
1	Life Association of Scotland......	40	7½	25
p. sh	London Assurance Corporation ..	25	12½	49
5	London and Lancashire Life.......	10	1	19s
0	Liverp'l & London & Globe F. & L.	20	2	6 15-16ths
5	National Union Life	5	1	0
2½	Northern Fire and Life	100	5	11½
2 … 00 … s.	North British and Mercantile	50	6¼	19¾
0	Ocean Marine	25	5	19¾
12s.	Provident Life...................	100	10	0
p. s.	Phœnix...........................	....	....	148
.yr.	Queen Fire and Life	10	1	17s
0.4s	Royal Insurance..................	20	3	6
0	Scottish Provincial Fire and Life ..	50	2½	5
5	Standard Life	50	12	65½
5	Star Life	25	1½	—
	CANADIAN.			℘ c.
4	British America Fire and Marine ..	$50	$25	57½
4	Canada Life	...	....	.....
2	Montreal Assurance	£50	£5	135
8	Provincial Fire and Marine........	60	11	.....
....	Quebec Fire	40	32½	£ 21½
8	" Marine..................	100	40	95
no's.	Western Assurance................	40	9	.....

RAILWAYS.	Sha's	Paid	Montr	London.
St. Lawrence......................	£100	All.	....	58 60
ake Huron	20½	"	....	3 3½
do Preference	10	"	....	5½ 6½
& Goderich, 6℘c., 1872-3-4....	100	"	....	65 68
d St. Lawrence	....	....	10	....
do Pref. 10 ℘ ct...........	....	....	73	....
....	100	"	15 16	15½ 16
Eq.G. M. Bds. 1 ch. 6℘c...........	100	"	....	84 86
First Preference, 5 ℘ c	100	"	....	50 52
Deferred, 3 ℘ ct..	100	"	....	....
Second Pref. Bonds, 5℘c...........	100	"	....	39½ 40½
do Deferred, 3 ℘ ct............	100	"	...	....
Third Pref. Stock, 4 ℘ct...........	100	"	....	27 29
do. Deferred, 3 ℘ ct............	100	"	....	....
Fourth Pref. Stock, 5℘c...........	100	"	....	18 19
do. Deferred, 3 ℘ ct............	100	"	....	....
rn	20½	"	13 14	13¾ 14½
New	20½	18	....	....
6 ℘ c. Bds, due 1873-76...........	100	All.	....	100 101
5½ ℘c Bds. due 1877-78...........	100	"	....	93 94
ay, Halifax, $250, all...........	$250	"	....	....
Canada, 6℘c. 1st Pref. Bds.........	100	"	.. .	80 83

HANGE.	Halifax.	Montr'l.	Quebec.	Toronto.
ondon, 60 days.......				
days date	12½	9¾ 9⅞	9½ 9¾	9¾
....	11½ 12	8 9	8¾ 9	9
documents............	....	7½ 8	....	....
York.................	....	25½ 26	25 25½	74½
do.	....	26 26½	25½ 26	....
do.	....	par	par ¼ dis.	par ¼ dis.
....	....	4 4½	....	8½ 5

STOCK AND BOND REPORT.

The dates of our quotations are as follows:—Toronto, Jan. 5; Montreal, Jan. 4; Quebec, Jan. 4; London, Dec. 5.

NAME.	Shares.	Paid up.	Divid'd last 6 Months	Dividend Day.	CLOSING PRICES. Toronto.	Montre'l.	Quebec
BANKS.			℘ ct.				
British North America	$250	All.	3	July and Jan.	102 x.d	Bks cl'd	Bks cl'd
Jacques Cartier..............	50	"	4	1 June, 1 Dec.	107 107½	107 108	106 107
Montreal	200	"	5	"	138 138½	138 138½	138 138½
Nationale....................	50	"	4	1 Nov. 1 May.	105 106	105 106½	106 106½
New Brunswick	100	"	......	......	....	...	....
Nova Scotia	200	28	7&b$3½	Mar. and Sept.	....	....	....
Du Peuple....................	50	"	4	1 Mar., 1 Sept.	108 108½	108	107 108
Toronto	100	"	4	1 Jan., 1 July.	118 x.d	115 117	116 117
Bank of Yarmouth.............	....	....	......	......	....	....	....
Canadian Bank of Com'e.......	50	95	......	......	101 102	Bks cl'd	101 102
City Bank Montreal	80	All.	4	1 June, 1 Dec.	101½ 102	100 102	101 102
Commer'l Bank (St. John)....	100	"	℘ ct.	......	....	...	....
Eastern Townships' Bank.....	50	"	4	1 July, 1 Jan..	....	96 100	95 96
Gore	40	...	none.	1 Jan., 1 July.	35 40	40 42	35 40
Halifax Banking Company......	...	....	......	......	...	....	....
Mechanics' Bank..............	50	70	4	1 Nov., 1 May.	95 96	94 96	94 95
Merchants' Bank of Canada....	100	70	4	1 Jan., 1 July.	106	104½ 106	107 108
Merchants' Bank (Halifax)....	....	....	.....	......	....	....	....
Molson's Bank................	50	All.	4	1 Apr., 1 Oct.	100 100½	109½ 110½	109 110
Niagara District Bank........	100	70	3½	1 Jan., 1 July.	...	....	....
Ontario Bank.................	40	All.	4	1 June, 1 Dec.	100¼ 100½	99 99½	99 99½
People's Bank (Fred'kton)....	100	"	......	......	....	....	. ..
People's Bank (Halifax)	20	"	7 12 m	......	....	...	....
Quebec Bank	100	"	3½	1 June, 1 Dec.	98 100	98½ 99½	99½ 10
Royal Canadian Bank	50	50	4	1 Jan., 1 July.	86 87	83 85	85 97
St. Stephens Bank	100	All	.....	......	....	..	....
Union Bank	100	70	4	1 Jan., 1 July.	103 104	103 105	103½ 104½
Union Bank (Halifax).........	100	40	7 12mo	Feb. and Aug.	....	....	. .
MISCELLANEOUS.							
British America Land.........	250	44	2½	......	....	....	....
British Colonial S. S. Co....	250	32½	2½	......	...	....	....
Canada Company	32½	All.	5	......	....	....	....
Canada Landed Credit Co......	50	$20	3½	......	70 72	....	....
Canada Per. B'ldg Society....	50	All.	5	......	120 120½	....	....
Canada Mining Company........	4	90	......	......	....	....	....
Do. Inl'd Steam Nav. Co.	100	All.	20 12 m	......	....	106½ 107½	107 108
Do. Glass Company........	100	"	12½ "	......	....	...	....
Canad'n Loan & Investm't....	25	2½	7	......	....	....	....
Canada Agency	10	½	......	......	....	....	....
Colonial Securities Co.......	...	....	......	......	....	....	....
Freehold Building Society....	100	All.	4	......	104½ 105½	....	....
Halifax Steamboat Co.........	100	"	5	......	....	....	....
Halifax Gas Company..........	....	....	......	......	....	...	....
Hamilton Gas Company.........	....	....	.....	......	....	....	....
Huron Copper Bay Co..........	4	12	20	......	....	25 40cps	....
Lake Huron S. and C..........	5	102	......	......	....	....	....
Montreal Mining Consols......	20	$15	......	......	....	3.00 3.20	...
Do. Telegraph Co........	40	All.	5	......	139 140	Bks cl'd	136 138
Do. Elevating Co........	00	"	15 12 m	......	....	100 102½	....
Do. City Gas Co.........	40	"	4	15 Mar., 15 Sep.	....	136	134 135
Do. City Pass. R., Co...	50	"	5	......	....	110½ 111½	110 110½
Nova Scotia Telegraph	20	"	....	......	....	....	....
Quebec and L. S.	8	$4	......	......	....	....	25 cts
Quebec Gas Co................	200	All.	4	1 Mar., 1 Sep.	....	...	119 120
Quebec Street R. R...........	50	25	3	......	....	....	90 95
Richelieu Navigation Co......	100	All.	7 p.a.	1 Jan., 1 July.	....	116½ 117½	116 117
St. Lawrence Tow Boat Co.....	100	"	......	3 Feb.	....	...	40 45
Tor'to Consumers' Gas Co.....	50	"	2 3 m.	1 My Au Mar Fe	106½ 107	...	105½ 106½
Trust & Loan Co. of U. C.....	20	5	3	......	....	....	.. .
West'n Canada Bldg Soc'y.....	50	All.	5	......	113½	....	....

SECURITIES.	London.	Montreal.	Quebec.	Toronto.
Canadian Gov't Deb. 6 ℘ ct. stg................	....	102 103	102½ 103	103 105
Do. do. 6 do. due Ja. & Jul. 1877-84......	107½ 108½	....	....	....
Do. do. 6 do. Feb. & Aug..........	105 107	....	.. .	....
Do. do. 6 do. Mch. & Sep..........	105 107	.. .	...	. .
Do. do. 5 ℘ ct. cur., 1883	95 96	92½ 93½	92 92½	93 93½
Do. do. 5 do. stg., 1885	94 96	92½ 93½	92½ 93	93 93½
Do. do. 7 do. cur.,....................	....	....	......	....
Dominion 6 p. c. 1878 cy.....................	....	104½ 105	104 104½	104½ 105
Hamilton Corporation.........................	....	....	... ..	....
Montreal Harbor, 8 ℘ ct. d. 1869...............	..	....	......	....
Do. do. 7 do. 1870..................	....	....	......	100 101
Do. do. 6½ do. 1875..................	....	101 102	......	....
Do. do. 6½ do. 1873..................	....	....	......	....
Do. Corporation, 6 ℘ c. 1891	....	95 95½	95½ 95¾	94 96
Do. 7 p. c. stock	....	107½	104 106½	107½ 108
Do. Water Works, 6 ℘ c. stg. 1878..........	....	....	......	94 96
Do. do. 6 do. cy. do.	....	95 96½	......	94 96
New Brunswick, 6 ℘ ct., Jan. and July	104 106	....	......	....
Nova Scotia, 6 ℘ ct., 1875.....................	105 106	...	......	....
Ottawa City 6 ℘ c. d. 1880	....	92½ 93½	......	...
Quebec Harbour, 6 ℘ c. d. 1883..................	....	....	60	....
Do. do. 7 do. do..................	....	....	65 70	....
Do. do. 8 do. 1886................	...	....	80 85	....
Do. City, 7 ℘ c. d. 5 years	....	80 90	95 96	....
Do. do. 7 do. 9 do.	....	....	91 92	....
Do. do. 7 do. 2 do.	....	....	98 98½	....
Do. Water Works, 7 ℘ ct., 4 years	....	....	96 97	....
Do. do. 6 do. 2 do.	....	....	94 95	....
Toronto Corporation	....	87½ 92½	...	....

Financial.

Niagara District Bank.

DIVIDEND No. 30.

NOTICE is hereby given that a dividend of Four per cent. on the capital stock of this institution, has this day been declared for the current half year, and that the same will be payable at the Bank, on and after Saturday, the 2nd January next.

The transfer books will be closed from the 20th to the 31st December, both days inclusive.

Also, that a GENERAL MEETING of the Shareholders, for the election of Directors to serve during the ensuing year, will be held at the Bank on MONDAY, the 11th day of January next, at noon.

By order of the Board,
C. M. ARNOLD, Cashier.

Niagara District Bank,
St. Catherines, Nov. 26, 1868.   16-td

Canada Permanent Building and Savings Society.

17TH HALF YEARLY DIVIDEND.

NOTICE is hereby given, that a dividend of FIVE per cent. on the capital Stock of this institution has been declared for the half year ending 31st inst., and the same will be payable at the Office of the Society, on and after Friday, the 8th day of January next.

The Transfer Books will be closed from the 20th to the 31st December, inclusive.

By order of the Board.
J. HERBERT MASON,
Secretary and Treasurer.
Toronto, December 9th, 1868.   17-td.

Western Canada Permanent Building and Savings Society.

11TH HALF YEARLY DIVIDEND.

NOTICE is hereby given, that a Dividend of FIVE per cent. on the Capital Stock of this Institution has been declared for the half year ending 31st day of December, inst., and that the same will be payable at the Office of the Society, No. 70 Church Street, on and after Friday, the 8th day of January next.

The Transfer Books will be closed from the 20th to the 31st December, inclusive.

By order of the Board.
WALTER S. LEE,
Secretary and Treasurer.
Toronto, Dec. 14, 1868.   17-td.

BROWN'S BANK,
(W. R. Brown. W. C. Chewett.)
60 KING STREET EAST, TORONTO,

TRANSACTS a general Banking Business, Buys and Sells New York and Sterling Exchange, Gold, Silver, U. S. Bonds and Uncurrent Money, receives Deposits subject to Cheque at sight, makes Collections and Discounts Commercial Paper.

Orders by Mail or Telegraph promptly executed at most favourable current quotations.

☞ Address letters,   "BROWN'S BANK,
35-y   Toronto."

Honore Plamondon,

CUSTOM House Broker, Forwarder, and General Agent, Quebec. Office—Custom House Building.   17-1y

Sylvester, Bro. & Hickman,

COMMERCIAL Brokers and Vessel Agents. Office—No. 1 Ontario Chambers, [Corner Front and Church Sts.] Toronto.   2-6in

Candee & Co.,

BANKERS AND BROKERS, dealers in Gold and Silver Coin, Government Securities, &c., Corner Main and Exchange Streets Buffalo, Y. N.   21-1y

H. N. Smith & Co.,

2 EAST SENECA STREET, BUFFALO, N. Y., (correspondent Smith, Gould, Martin & Co., 11 Broad Street, N.Y.,) Stock, Money and Exchange Brokers. Advances made on securities.   21-1y

Hurd, Leigh & Co.,

IMPORTERS AND DECORATORS OF FRENCH CHINA.

Hotels and families supplied with any pattern or crest desired.

Common goods always on hand.   72 Yonge Street,
Toronto, Ontario.   36y

Mercantile.

Teas! Teas!! Teas!!!

FRESH ARRIVALS

NEW CROP TEAS,
WINES, AND GENERAL GROCERIES,

Special Inducements given to

PROMPT PAYING PURCHASERS.

All Goods sold at very Lowest Montreal Prices!
W. & R. GRIFFITH,

ONTARIO CHAMBERS,
Corner of Front and Church Streets,
6-1y   TORONTO
                                               ONTARIO

TEAS.   Reford & Dillon   TEAS.

HAVE just received ex. steamships "St. David and Nestorian:"

1000 hlf. chests new season TEAS!
Comprising Twankays, Young Hysons, Imperials, Gunpowders, colored and uncolored Japans, Congous, Souchongs, and Pekoes.
500 hlf. bxs. new Valentia Raisins (selected fruit).
500 bags cleaned Arracan and Rangoon Rice.
500 bris. choice Currants.

—ALSO IN STORE :—

250 hhds. bright Barbadoes and Cuba Sugars.
250 brls. Portland, Standard, Golden & Amber Syrups.
100 bags Rio, Jamaica, Laguayra, and Java Coffees.
250 bxs. 10s Tobacco, "Queen's Own" and "Prince of Wales'" brands.

WITH A GENERAL AND

WELL SELECTED STOCK OF GROCERIES;

All of which they offer to the Trade low.

12 & 14 WELLINGTON STREET, TORONTO.
                                               7-1y

Robert H. Gray,
Manufacturer of Hoop Skirts
AND
CRINOLINE STEEL,
IMPORTER OF
HABERDASHERY, TRIMMINGS
AND
GENERAL FANCY GOODS,

43, YONGE STREET, TORONTO, ONT.   6-1y

John Boyd & Co.,
WHOLESALE GROCERS AND COMMISSION MERCHANTS,

61 AND 63 FRONT STREET
TORONTO.

NOW in store, direct from the European and West India Markets, a large assortment of General Groceries, comprising

Teas, Sugars, Coffees, Wines and Liquors,
AND
GENERAL GROCERIES.

Ship Chandlery, Canvas, Manilla and Tarred Rope, Oakum, Tar, Flags, &c., &c.,

DIRECT FROM THE MANUFACTURERS.

OHN BOYD.   ALEX. M. MONRO.   C. W. BUNTING.

Toronto, Oct. 1st, 1868.   7-1y

Mercantile.

UNRIVALLED!

THE BRITISH AMERICAN COMMERCIAL CO
Consolidated with the
Bryant, Stratton and Odell Business C
AND TELEGRAPHIC INSTITUTE,

STANDS Pre-eminent and Unrivalled. It is the l and Most Efficient. It employs the largest Teachers, among whom are the two BEST PENM CANADA.

The TUITION FEE is the same as in other Inst having a similar object.

The PRICE OF BOARD is the same as in othe dian Cities.

In an EDUCATIONAL point of view, there is Institution in the country that has equal advant facilities.

YOUNG MEN intending to qualify themselves ness, will find it to their advantage to send for a c or call at the College Rooms, corner of King and streets.

Scholarships good in Montreal and throughout th States.
ODELL & TRO
October 2.   Principals and Propri

The Mercantile Agency,
FOR THE
PROMOTION AND PROTECTION OF TR.
Established in 1841.
DUN, WIMAN & Co.
Montreal, Toronto and Halifax.

REFERENCE Book, containing names and re Business Men in the Dominion, publishe annually.

The St. Lawrence Glass Company

ARE now manufacturing and have for sale,

COAL OIL LAMPS,
Various styles and sizes.

LAMP CHIMNEYS,
of extra quality for ordinary Burn for the 'Comet' and 'Sun' Burners.

SETS OF
TABLE GLASSWARE, HYACINTH GLASSES,
STEAM GUAGE TUBES, GLASS RODS,
or any other article made to order, in White o Glass.

KEROSENE BURNERS, COLLARS and SOCKI be kept on hand.

DRUGGISTS' FLINT GLASSWARE, and PHILOSOPHICAL INSTRUMENTS, made to order.

OFFICE—388 ST. PAUL STREET, MONTR
A. MoK. COCHR.
8-1y   S

Canadian Express Company,
GENERAL EXPRESS FORWARDERS, CUSTO BROKERS,
AND
SHIPPING AGENTS.

GOODS and VALUABLES forwarded by all Passenger Trains.

Reduced rates for all large consignments.
Reduced rates on Poultry, Butter, and other p principal perishable articles in Canada and the United Stat
All perishable articles guaranteed against d frost, without extra charge, nature of goods at to be stipulated in receipt at time of shipment.
Consignments for Lower Provinces taken t at low rates, and from thence by Steamer or E required, securing quick dispatch.
A Weekly Express is made up for Europe, f goods should be sent forward in time to reach P Friday each week.
Unsurpassed facilities as shipping agents in Li Reduced rates on large Consignments from the at Portland.
For particulars, inquire at any of the principal Consignments solicited.
G. CHENEY,
16-3t   Superint

Financial.

Pellatt & Osler,

AND EXCHANGE BROKERS, Accountants, &c. for the Standard Life Assurance Company.

OR—86 King Street East, four Doors West of Church Street, Toronto.

PELLATT,   EDMUND B. OSLER,
Notary Public.   Official Assignee.

Philip Browne & Co.,

BANKERS AND STOCK BROKERS.

DEALERS IN

FOREIGN EXCHANGE—U. S. Currency, Silver and Gold—Bank Stocks, Debentures, Mortgages, &c. On New York issued, in Gold and Currency. Attention given to collections. Advances made on Securities.

No. 67 Yonge Street, Toronto

BROWNE.   PHILIP BROWNE, Notary Public.

James C. Small.

BANKER AND BROKER,

No. 34 King Street East, Toronto.

Foreign Exchange, American Currency, Silver, and Bank Stocks, Debentures and other Securities, bought and sold.

Notes received. Collections promptly made. Drafts on New York in Gold and Currency issued.

Western Canada Permanent Building and Savings Society.

OFFICE—No. 70 Church Street, Toronto.

SAVINGS BANK BRANCH,

DEPOSITS Received Daily. Interest Paid Half Yearly.

ADVANCES

Made on the security of Real Estate, repayable on the most favourable terms, by a Sinking Fund.

WALTER S. LEE,
Secy. & Treas.

Canadian Land and Emigration Company

Offers for sale on Conditions of Settlement,

GOOD FARM LANDS

In the County of Peterboro, Ontario,

Well settled Townships of Dysart, where there are Grist and Saw Mills, Stores, &c., at

TWO-AND-A-HALF DOLLARS AN ACRE.

Adjoining Townships of Guilford, Dudley, Harcourt and Bruton, connected with Dysart and Village of Haliburton by the Peterson Road, at ONE Dollar an Acre.

Further particulars apply to
CHAS. JAS. BLOMFIELD,
Manager, C. L. and E. Co.,
Toronto Bank Buildings, Toronto.
ALEX. NIVEN, P.L.S.,
Agent C. L. & E. Co., Haliburton

Canada Permanent Building and Savings Society.

Paid up Capital $1,000,000
Assets 1,700,000
Annual Income 400,000

Directors—JOSEPH D. RIDOUT, President.
PETER PATERSON, Vice-President.
Forts, Edward Hooper, S. Nordheimer, W. C. Matthewett, E. H. Rutherford, Joseph Robinson.
Bank of Toronto; Bank of Montreal; Royal Canadian Bank.

Office—Masonic Hall, Toronto Street.

Received on Deposit bearing five and six per cent. interest.

Advances made on City and Country Property in the Province of Ontario.

J. HERBERT MASON
Sec'y & Treas.

Insurance.

J. T. & W. Pennock.

FIRE and Life Insurance Agents, Parliamentary and Departmental Agents, Mining Agents, and Exchange Brokers.

Ottawa, Dec. 21st, 1867.   10-1y

The Victoria Mutual
FIRE INSURANCE COMPANY OF CANADA.

Insures only Non-Hazardous Property, at Low Rates.

BUSINESS STRICTLY MUTUAL.

GEORGE H. MILLS, President.
W. D. BOOKER, Secretary.

HEAD OFFICE .... HAMILTON, ONTARIO
aug 15-1yr

Life Association of Scotland.

INVESTED FUNDS

UPWARDS OF £1,000,000 STERLING.

THIS Institution differs from other Life Offices, in that the

BONUSES FROM PROFITS

Are applied on a special system for the Policy-holder's

PERSONAL BENEFIT AND ENJOYMENT
DURING HIS OWN LIFETIME,

WITH THE OPTION OF

LARGE BONUS ADDITIONS TO THE SUM ASSURED.

The Policy-holder thus obtains

A LARGE REDUCTION OF PRESENT OUTLAY

OR

A PROVISION FOR OLD AGE OF A MOST IMPORTANT AMOUNT IN ONE CASH PAYMENT, OR A LIFE ANNUITY,

Without any expense or outlay whatever beyond the ordinary Assurance Premium for the Sum Assured, which remains in tact for Policy-holder's heirs, or other purposes.

CANADA—MONTREAL—PLACE D'ARMES.

DIRECTORS:
DAVID TORRANCE, Esq., (D. Torrance & Co.)
GEORGE MOFFATT, (Gillespie, Moffatt & Co.)
ALEXANDER MORRIS, Esq., M.P., Barrister, Perth.
Sir G. E. CARTIER, M.P., Minister of Militia.
PETER REDPATH, Esq., (J. Redpath & Son).
J. H. R. MOLSON, Esq., (J. H. R. Molson & Bros.)
Solicitors—Messrs. TORRANCE & MORRIS.
Medical Officer—R. PALMER HOWARD, Esq., M.D
Secretary—P. WARDLAW.
Inspector of Agencies—JAMES P. M. CHIPMAN.   7

North British and Mercantile Insurance Company.

Established 1809.

HEAD OFFICE, - - CANADA - - MONTREAL,

TORONTO BRANCH:

LOCAL OFFICES, Nos. 4 & 6 Wellington Street.
Fire Department, ... R. N. GOOCH,
Agent.
Life Department, ... H. L. HIME,
29-1y   Agent.

Phœnix Fire Assurance Company.

LOMBARD ST. AND CHARING CROSS,
LONDON, ENG.

Insurances effected in all parts of the World

Claims paid
WITH PROMPTITUDE and LIBERALITY.
MOFFATT, MURRAY & BEATTIE,
Agents for Toronto,
86 Yonge Street.
25-1y.

Insurance.

Canada Life Assurance Company.

CAPITAL AND CASH ASSETS

OVER $2,000,000.

SUMS ASSURED

$5,000,000.

A COMPARISON of the rates of this Company with others cannot fail to demonstrate the advantage of the low premiums, which, by the higher returns from its investments, it is enabled to offer.

IF PREFERRED, ASSURERS NEED ONLY

PAY ONE-HALF OF EACH YEAR'S PREMIUM IN CASH,

during the whole term of policies on the 10 payment plan, or for seven years on the whole life plan.

For the unpaid portion of premiums,

"NOTES" ARE NOT REQUIRED BY THIS COMPANY, so that assurers are not liable to be called upon for payment of these, nor for assessments upon them, as in the case of Mutual Companies.

Every facility and advantage which can be afforded are offered by this Company.

A. G. RAMSAY, Manager.
E. BRADBURNE, Agent,
3ull1   Toronto Street.

The Liverpool and London and Globe Insurance Company

INVESTED FUNDS:

FIFTEEN MILLIONS OF DOLLARS.

DAILY INCOME OF THE COMPANY:

TWELVE THOUSAND DOLLARS.

LIFE INSURANCE,

WITH AND WITHOUT PROFITS.

FIRE INSURANCE

On every description of Property, at Lowest Remunerative Rates.

JAMES FRASER, Agent,
5 King Street West.
Toronto, 1868.   36-1y

Briton Medical and General Life Association,

with which is united the
BRITANNIA LIFE ASSURANCE COMPANY.

Capital and Invested Funds............£750,000 Sterling.

ANNUAL INCOME, £220,000 Stg. ;
Yearly increasing at the rate of £25,000 Sterling.

THE important and peculiar feature originally introduced by this Company, in applying the periodical Bonuses, so as to make Policies payable during life, without any higher rate of premiums being charged, has caused the success of the BRITON MEDICAL AND GENERAL to be almost unparalleled in the history of Life Assurance. Life Policies on the Profit Scale become payable during the lifetime of the Assured, thus rendering a Policy of Assurance a means of subsistence in old age, as well as a protection for a family, and a more valuable security to creditors in the event of early death; and effectually meeting the often urged objection, that persons do not themselves reap the benefit of their own prudence and forethought.

No extra charge made to members of Volunteer Corps for services within the British Provinces.

TORONTO AGENCY, 5 King St. West.
oct17—9-1yr   JAMES FRASER, Agent.

Phenix Insurance Company,
BROOKLYN, N.Y.

PHILANDER SHAW,   STEPHEN CROWELL,
Secretary.   President.

Cash Capital, $1,000,000. Surplus, $666,616.02. Total, 1,666,416.02. Entire income from all sources for 1866 was $3,151,839.82.

CHARLES G. FORTIER, Marine Agent.

Ontario Chambers, Toronto, Ont.   19-1y

Insurance.

BEAVER
Mutual Insurance Association.

HEAD OFFICE—20 TORONTO STREET,
TORONTO.

INSURES LIVE STOCK against death from any cause.
The only Canadian Company having authority to do this
class of business.

R. L. DENISON,
President.
W. T. O'REILLY,
Secretary.   8-1y-28

HOME DISTRICT
Mutual Fire Insurance Company.

Office—North-West Cor. Yonge & Adelaide Streets,
TORONTO.—(UP STAIRS.) .

INSURES Dwelling Houses, Stores, Warehouses, Merchandise, Furniture, &c.

PRESIDENT—The Hon. J. McMURRICH.
VICE-PRESIDENT—JOHN BURNS, Esq.
JOHN RAINS, Secretary.
AGENTS:
DAVID WRIGHT, Esq., Hamilton; FRANCIS STEVENS, Esq.,
Barrie; Messrs. GIBBS & DRO., Oshawa.   8-1y

THE PRINCE EDWARD COUNTY
Mutual Fire Insurance Company.

HEAD OFFICE,—PICTON, ONTARIO.
President, L. D. STINSON; *Vice-President,* W. A. RICHARDS.
Directors: H. A. McFaul, James Cavan, James Johnson,
N. S. DeMill, William Delong.—*Treasurer,* David Barker
Secretary, John Twigg; *Solicitor,* R. J. Fitzgerald.

THIS Company is established upon strictly Mutual principles, insuring farming and isolated property, (not
hazardous,) in Townships only, and offers great advantages
to insurers, at low rates for *five years,* without the expense
of a renewal.
Picton, June 15, 1868.   9-1y

Hartford Fire Insurance Company.
HARTFORD, CONN.

Cash Capital and Assets over Two Million Dollars.

$2,026,220.29.

CHARTERED 1810.

THIS old and reliable Company, having an established
business in Canada of more than thirty years standing,
has complied with the provisions of the new Insurance
Act, and made a special deposit of

$100,000

with the Government for the security of policy-holders, and
will continue to grant policies upon the same favorable
terms as heretofore.
Specially low rates on first-class dwellings and farm
property for a term of one or more years.
Losses as heretofore promptly and equitably adjusted.
H. J. MORSE & Co., AGENTS.
Toronto, Ont.

ROBERT WOOD, GENERAL AGENT FOR CANADA]
50-6m

THE AGRICULTURAL
Mutual Assurance Association of Canada.

HEAD OFFICE .... LONDON, ONT.

A purely Farmers' Company. Licensed by the Government of Canada.

Capital,1st January, 1868................. $220,121 25
Cash and Cash Items, over................. $65,000 0
No. of Policies inforce................... 26,760

THIS Company insures nothing more dangerous than
Farm property. Its rates are as low as any well-established Company in the Dominion, and lower than those
of a great many. It is largely patronised, and continues
to grow in public favor.
For Insurance, apply to any of the Agents, or address
the Secretary, London, Ontario.
London, 2nd Nov., 1868.   12-1y.

Insurance.

The Gore District Mutual Fire Insurance Company

GRANTS INSURANCES on all description of Property
against Loss or Damage by FIRE. It is the only Mutual Fire Insurance Company which assesses its Policies
yearly from their respective dates; and the average yearly
cost of insurance in it, for the past three and a half years,
has been nearly

TWENTY CENTS IN THE DOLLAR

less than what it would have been in an ordinary Proprietary Company.
THOS. M. SIMONS,
Secretary & Treasurer.
ROBT. McLEAN,
Inspector of Agencies.
Galt, 25th Nov., 1868.   15-1y

Geo. Girdlestone,

FIRE, Life, Marine, Accident, and Stock Insurance
Agent
Very best Companies represented.
Windsor, Ont. June, 1868

The Standard Life Assurance Company,
Established 1825.
WITH WHICH IS NOW UNITED
THE COLONIAL LIFE ASSURANCE COMPANY.

Head Office for Canada:
MONTREAL—STANDARD COMPANY'S BUILDINGS,
No. 47 GREAT ST. JAMES STREET.

Manager—W. M. RAMSAY.   *Inspector*—RICH'D BULL.
THIS Company having deposited the sum of ONE HUNDRED AND FIFTY THOUSAND DOLLARS with the Receiver-
General, in conformity with the Insurance Act passed last
Session, Assurances will continue to be carried out at
moderate rates and on all the different systems in practice.

AGENT FOR TORONTO—HENRY PELLATT,
KING STREET.

AGENT FOR HAMILTON—JAMES BANCROFT.
6-6mos.

Fire and Marine Assurance.

THE BRITISH AMERICA
ASSURANCE COMPANY.
HEAD OFFICE:
CORNER OF CHURCH AND COURT STREETS.
TORONTO.

BOARD OF DIRECTION :

Hon G. W. Allan, M L C.,	A. Joseph, Esq.,
George J Boyd, Esq ,	Peter Paterson, Esq.,
Hon W. Cayley,	G. P. Ridout, Esq.,
Richard S. Cassels, Esq.,	E H.Rutherford,Esq.,
Thomas C. Street, Esq.,	

Governor:
GEORGE PERCIVAL RIDOUT, ESQ.
Deputy Governor:
PETER PATERSON, Esq.
Fire Inspector: Marine Inspector:
E. ROBY O'BRIEN.   CAPT. R. COURNEEN.
Insurances granted on all descriptions of property
against loss and damage by fire and the perils of inland
navigation.
Agencies established in the principal cities, towns, and
ports of shipment throughout the Province.
THOS. WM. BIRCHALL,
22-1y   Managing Director.

Queen Fire and Life Insurance Company,
OF LIVERPOOL AND LONDON,
ACCEPTS ALL ORDINARY FIRE RISKS
on the most favorable terms.

LIFE RISKS
Will be taken on terms that will compare favorably with
other Companies.

CAPITAL,   -   -   -   £2,000,000 Stg.

CHIEF OFFICES—Queen's Buildings, Liverpool, and
Gracechurch Street London.
CANADA BRANCH OFFICE—Exchange Buildings, Montreal.
Resident Secretary and General Agent,
A. MACKENZIE FORBES,
12 St. Sacrament St., Merchants' Exchange, Montreal.
WM. ROWLAND, Agent, Toronto.   1-1y

Insurance.

The Waterloo County Mutual Fire Insurance Company.

HEAD OFFICE : WATERLOO, ONTARIO.

ESTABLISHED 1863.
THE business of the Company is divided in
separate and distinct branches, the
VILLAGE, FARM, AND MANUFACT
Each Branch paying its own losses and its just p
of the managing expenses of the Company.
C. M. TAYLOR, Sen.   M. SPRINGER, M.M.P
J. HUGHES, Inspector.

Etna Fire and Marine Insurance Com]
Dublin.

AT a Meeting of the Shareholders of this C
held at Dublin, on the 13th ult., it was ag
the business of the "ETNA" should be transferr
"UNITED PORTS AND GENERAL INSURANCE C
In accordance with this agreement, the business w
after be carried on by the latter Company, which
and guarantees all the risks and liabilities of the
The Directors have resolved to continue the C
BRANCH, and arrangements for resuming FIRE
RINE business are rapidly approaching completio
16   T. W. GRIFF
Ma:

The Commercial Union Assure
Company,
19 & 20 CORNHILL, LONDON, ENGLAND.
Capital, £2,500,000 Stg.—Invested over $2,000

FIRE DEPARTMENT.—Insurance granted a
scriptions of property at reasonable rates.
LIFE DEPARTMENT.—The success of thi
has been unprecedented—*NINETY PER CENT*
miums now in hand. First year's premiums w
$140,000. Economy of management guaranteed
security. Moderate rates.
OFFICE—383 & 387 ST PAUL STREET, MONT
MORLAND, WATSON &
General Agents for
FRED. COLE, Secretary.
Inspector of Agencies—T. C. LIVINGSTO
W. M. WESTMACOTT, Agent at T
16-1y   —

Lancashire Insurance Comp

CAPITAL, - - - - - - - £2,000,00

FIRE RISKS
Taken at reasonable rates of premium,
ALL LOSSES SETTLED PROMPTL
By the undersigned, without reference els
S. C. DUNCAN-CLARK & CO
General Agents for Ont
25-1y   N. W. Corner of King & Church
TORONTO.

Etna Fire & Marine Insurance Com
INCORPORATED 1919. CHARTER PERPETU
CASH CAPITAL, - - - - -
LOSSES PAID IN 50 YEARS, 23,500,0

JULY, 1868.
ASSETS.
(At Market Value.)
Cash in hand and in Bank..................... $
Real Estate.................................
Mortgage Bonds.............................
Bank Stock................................. 1,
United States, State and City Stock,and other
Public Securities..........................

Total..................... $

LIABILITIES.
Claims not Due, and Unadjusted..............
Amount required by Mass. and New York
for Re-insurance.......................... 1

THOS. R. WOC
50-6   Agent for

PUBLISHED AT THE OFFICE OF THE M
TIMES, No. 60 CHURCH STREET
PRINTED AT THE DAILY TELEGRAPH PRINTIN
BAY STREET, CORNER OF KING.

THE CANADIAN
MONETARY TIMES
AND
INSURANCE CHRONICLE.

VOTED TO FINANCE, COMMERCE, INSURANCE, BANKS, RAILWAYS, NAVIGATION, MINES, INVESTMENT, PUBLIC COMPANIES, AND JOINT STOCK ENTERPRISE.

| I—NO. 22. | TORONTO, THURSDAY, JANUARY 14, 1869. | { SUBSCRIPTION, $2 YEAR. |

Mercantile.

Gundry and Langley,
TECTS AND CIVIL ENGINEERS, Building Surveyors and Valuators. Office corner of King and Jordan Toronto.
AS GUNDRY.   HENRY LANGLEY.

J. B. Boustead.
TION and Commission Merchant. Hops bought sold on Commission. 82 Front St., Toronto.

John Boyd & Co.
ESALE Grocers and Commission Merchants, Front St., Toronto.

Childs & Hamilton.
ACTURERS and Wholesale Dealers in Boots Shoes, No. 7 Wellington Street East, Toronto. 28

L. Coffee & Co.
CE and Commission Merchants, No. 2 Manning's Front St., Toronto, Ont. Advances made on ents of Produce.

J. & A. Clark,
CE Commission Merchants, Wellington Street Toronto, Ont.

D Crawford & Co.
ACTURERS of Soaps, Candles, etc., and dealers etroleum, Lard and Lubricating Oils, Palace St., Ont.

John Fisken & Co.
OIL and Commission Merchants, Yonge St., oto, Ont.

W. & R. Griffith.
ERS of Teas, Wines, etc. Ontario Chambers, hurch and Front Sts., Toronto.

H. Nerlich & Co.,
ERS of French, German, English and American foods, Cigars, and Leaf Tobaccos, No. 2 Adelaide st, Toronto.   15

Hurd, Leigh & Co.
S and Enamellers of China and Earthenware, nge St., Toronto, Ont. [see advt.]

Lyman & McNab,
SALE Hardware Merchants, Toronto, Ontario.

W. D. Matthews & Co.
CE Commission Merchants, Old Corn Exchange, ont St. East, Toronto Ont.

R. C. Hamilton & Co.
CE Commission Merchants, 119 Lower Water falifax, Nova Scotia.

Parson Bros.,
EUM Refiners, and Wholesale dealers in Lamps, neys, etc. Warerooms 51 Front St. Refinery cor. Don Sts., Toronto.

C. P. Reid & Co.
ERS and Dealers in Wines, Liquors, Cigars and obacco, Wellington Street, Toronto.   28.

W. Rowland & Co.,
E BROKERS and General Commission Merchants. Advances made on Consignments. Corner d Front Streets. Toronto.

Reford & Dillon.
LRS of Groceries, Wellington Street, Toronto,

Sessions, Turner & Co.,
ACTURERS, Importers and Wholesale Dealer oots and Shoes, Leather Findings, etc., 5 Wel- West, Toronto, Ont

Meetings.

BANK JACQUES CARTIER.

The general meeting was held in Montreal at the office of the Bank, on the 17th December, 1868, Hon. J. L. Beaudry, President of the Bank, having been called to the chair, and Mr. Cotté requested to act as Secretary, the President read the following—the seventh annual report of the Bank :

GENTLEMEN,—The Directors of the Bank Jacques Cartier, in submitting to you the report of the Bank for the year just ended, cannot state that the amount of profits is equal to that of preceding years, but the result of its operations has been relatively satisfactory.

All amongst you must have witnessed the serious fluctuations during the past year in general business, and the trade of Lower Canada appears to have suffered the most.

Failures have become in some way or other a matter of custom, and have succeeded each other with alarming rapidity. In other words commercial morality appears so singularly debased that a large portion of the community seem to consider it as not dishonorable to become bankrupt, or even fraudulently bankrupt, as a means to enrich themselves at the expense of others. Added to this the result of the harvest has been below an average, and you will have a faint idea of the trouble and anxiety of the Directors of the Bank, in order to arrive at the following results :

Balance of profit and loss to 30th Nov.
1867, ... $4,914 24
Net profit of last year to 30th Nov.
1868 .... 89,901 16
                                      ─────────
Total 94,815 40
Dedrct dividend 4 per cent. 1st June,
1868 .... $39,012 25
Deduct dividend 4 per cent. 1st Dec.
1868 .... $39,693 57, 78,705 83
                                      ─────────
Balance $16,109 57
From this balance is deducted for the
Reserve Fund 5,000 00
                                      ─────────
Balance to cover probable losses and
doubtful debts $11,109 57

The Reserve Fund now amounts to $90,000, equal to 9 per cent on the capital of the Bank.

Here, as elsewhere, after many years of prosperity, an annoying reaction has made itself felt, and confidence strongly shaken, in paralyzing business, has produced an unproductive accumulation of capital. To such an extent is this the case that never in Canada was so much capital seeking employment. To convince one of this fact, it is sufficient to look at the balance sheet attached to this report and you will there see that the Bank has in convertible assets $4 to $1 on its circulation, and $1 to $2½ due on its liabilities. This state of affairs although very reassuring to the holders of our notes and the depositors, is not satisfactory to your Directors, who desired to see the funds of the Bank employed in a more active manner.

Let us hope that there will soon be a change for the better, and that the Bank will obtain its fair allowance of the business accruing from any such change.

The books and other vouchers of the Bank have, as usual, received the attention of your Directors, and have been found to be perfectly correct.

The retiring Directors are Messrs. C. S. Rodin, J. L. Beaudry, and L. J. Beliveau. They are eligible for re-election.

In conclusion, your Directors have pleasure in noticing the scrupulous assiduity to their business, of the cashier and the other officers of the Bank. All of which is respectfully submitted,

J. L. BEAUDRY, President.
Montreal, Dec. 17, 1868.
Balance sheet to 30th November, 1868 :

ASSETS.

Bullion and Government notes......	$200,873 89
Government debentures...............	101,226 67
Notes and cheques of other banks...	25,606 63
Balances due by other banks........	104,353 53
	───────────
	$432,060 72
Notes discounted........................	$1,710,601 35
	───────────
	$2,142,662 07

LIABILITIES.

Paid up capital......................	$994,310 00
Reserve Fund........................	90,000 00
Profit and loss......................	11,109 57
Circulation..........................	100,801 00
Due other banks.....................	1,326 89
Deposits bearing interest...........	632,647 46
Deposits not bearing interest.......	269,535 97
Dividend payable 1st December.....	39,693 57
Unclaimed dividends.................	3,287 66
	───────────
	$2,142,662 07

H. COTTE, Cashier.
The usual vote of thanks to the President and Directors of the Bank was then proposed and carried.

Messrs. C. S. Rodin, J. B. Beaudry, and L. J. Beliveau, were re-elected Directors.

HURON AND ONTARIO SHIP CANAL.

A meeting of the Toronto Board of Trade was held on the 13th in the Mechanics' Institute, for the purpose of considering the prospects of the proposed Georgian Bay Ship Canal.

The meeting was very largely attended—in fact, it was the largest meeting of the Board for some years. A number of spectators were in the Board-room, to listen to the discussion. Among others, there were present the President, Mr. J. G. Worts, who occupied the chair, Messrs. Wm. Gooderham, sen., W. Gooderham, jun., T. C. Chisholm, G. Laidlaw, Wm. Ramsay, William Thompson, J. Burns, T. D. Harris, S. Spreull, James Young, W. F. McMaster, James Stock, N. Barnhart, F. W. Coate W. J. McDonnell, W. Myles, A. M. Smith, R. Wilkes, — Robertson, G. Gooderham, J. Adamson, H. Scott, J. Harris, F. A. Rolph, H. Gooderham, A. V. Delaporte, J. Nelson, J. Campbell, G. H. Wyatt, and many others.

After explaining the object of the meeting the Chairman called upon Mr. T. C. Chisholm, who moved, seconded by Mr. Gooderham, the following resolution:

"That the shipping and commercial interests of the Dominion of Canada, or the Province of Ontario do not require the construction of the Georgian Bay Canal."

In moving the resolution, Mr. Chisholm stated that he had been opposed to the construction of the canal ever since the subject was first broached, as being antagonistic to the interests of the country. He found that Mr. Capreol, in his pamphlet, set down the distance which would be saved in the carrying of grain from Chicago to New York, by the proposed canal, at 460 miles. The speaker, to refute this statement, gave the distances between the several points on the Welland Canal route, and between points on the route which would have to be travelled in passing through the projected Georgian Bay Canal, showing that the distance saved would only be 240 miles.

The total amount of grain which could possibly be shipped through the projected canal in a year would be as follows:

One vessel each way every hour, night and day for 7 months—26 days to the month, or 182 days —24 vessels each day down, gives 4368 vessels; estimate each vessel at 25,000 bush., give 109,- 200,000 bush., or 3,276,000 tons at 80c. per ton, the proposed toll would produce...... $2,620,800

Canal to cost $40,000,000
Interest on that sum at

7% would be..........	2,800,000	
Add working expenses and repairs	600,000	
		3,400,000

Annual loss.................. 779,200
This calculation is based on Mr. Capreol's figures, but all lake captains say the canal would not be used if the toll was over 20c. per ton—the same as on the Welland Canal—the result would be as follows:—

3,276,000 tons at 20c..................		$655,200
Less interest..................	$2,800,000	
Working expenses and repairs	6,00,000	
		3,400,000

Annual loss................. $2,744,800
In order to ascertain what were the feelings of captains of vessels on the subject of constructing the canal, the speaker had written the following letter :—

"TORONTO, Jan. 11, 1869.

"DEAR SIRS,—IN Mr. Capreol's proposition to build the Georgian Bay Canal, he proposes to charge 80 cts. per ton on grain, which is 2 cts. and 4 mills per bushel on wheat. Will you give me your opinion as to the number of steamers and vessels that would pass through it in preference to the Welland Canal, where the toll is 20c. per ton or 6 mills per bushel ; also your opinion as to the number of steamers and vessels that would pass through in preference to the Welland Canal, provided the tolls were the same, 20c. per ton ? The Georgian Bay Canal will be 100 miles long, have 42 locks, 31 of which are to have an average lift of 15 feet 2 inches ; 6 a lift of 15 ft, ; and 5 a lift of 8 ft. Will you give me your opinion as to the average time it would take to lock a steamer or vessel of 1,000 tons through these locks.

"Yours truly,
"THOS. C. CHISHOLM."

The following was the answer which he received, signed by a number of captains of vessels and steamboats :—

T. C. CHISHOLM.

DEAR SIR—In reply to your letter of the 11th, we, the undersigned steamboat and vessel captains beg leave to say that, at the toll of 80c. per ton on the Georgian Bay Canal, not one steamboat or vessel would pass through it. If the tolls were the same as on the Welland Canal 20c. per ton, we would decide as to which route we would take on arrival at the Straits of Mackinaw. We

consider 30 minutes for each lock a low estimate."

Captain Frank Jackman,
"   S. Sylvester,
"   J. Jackson,
"   Arch. Taylor,
"   Henry Jackman,
"   Jno. McCann,
"   S. S. Hamilton,
"   J. Jackman,
"   Joseph Kennedy,
"   G. B. Chisholm,
"   Jno. Kemp,
"   Geo. Coot,
"   M. C. Thompson,
"   Wm. Coot,
"   Hiram Williams,
"   Duncan Chisholm,
"   J. T. Douglass,
"   Robt. Thomas.

After reading the above, the speaker went on to say that grain was carried on the Northern Railway. a distance of 94 miles, at the rate of one cent and five mills per bushel per mile ; the rate from Chicago to Toronto in last December was only one cent and one mill. Mr. Capreol proposed to carry it at one cent and one mill per bushel per mile. Then there was a railway, building, direct from Oswego to New York, and intended for carrying grain, which would be another rival to the proposed canal. The speaker closed by adverting to the fact that, during six months of last year, grain was carried from Chicago to Buffalo at three cents and sometimes even as low as two cents per bushel, while Mr. Capreol proposed to charge two cents and one mill for the passage through the canal.

Mr. Wm. Gooderham, jr. had great pleasure in seconding the resolution.

Mr. Chisholm further pointed out the absurdity of the Company's statements in reference to the immense water power that they allege the canal would give to Toronto, and showed that the head of water spoken of could not be obtained without laying a pipe all the way to Lake Simcoe.

Mr. Wm. Gooderham, sen., seconded the resolution. Messrs. Thompson, McDonell, F. C. Capreol and Coate objected to the proceedings of the meeting and defended the canal project; and Mr. A. M. Smith, Mr. G. Laidlaw, Mr. J. G. Worts, and Mr. R. Wilkes spoke against it, some of them very forcibly and at considerable length. The resolution on being put to the meeting was carried —no one voting against it.

A resolution was subsequently put and carried to the effect that the Toronto Board of Trade be requested to enter into communication with the Boards in the principal cities of the Province, for the purpose of obtaining from the Dominion Government the enlargement of the Welland Canal.

COMMERCIAL BANK OF N. B.

The adjourned meeting of shareholders was held in St. John on the 5th. The Directors submitted the following supplementary report :—

"The President and Directors of the Commercial Bank of New Brunswick beg leave to submit herewith to the stockholders a detailed statement of the assets and liabilities of the bank, prepared pursuant to the resolution adopted at the last meeting. In submitting this statement they have given such details as can, in their opinion, be at present submitted by them consistently with the interest of the stockholders and their own duties as Directors to the customers of the bank whose accounts are expressly protected by the Bank Charter. The Directors are unwilling, after mature consideration, to take upon themselves the responsibility of giving at present further details, and believe that to do so would prove most injurious to the Stockholders, but should it be the wish of the Stockholders that such details should be given, the present Directors are prepared cheerfully to retire in favor of

such persons as shall be duly nominated by Stockholders, from a position in which they h no desire to continue except with the confiden of those whose property they have to control."

The total liabilities as on 23rd Novemb amounted to $630,958 85, and the assets to $76 671. The changes in assets and liabilities to January, were—

	Nov. 23.	Jan. 2.	Decrea
Circulation	$261,490 00	$131,020 00	$130,470
Bills discounted	269,932 00	162,239 00	107,692
Miramichi debt	100,000 00	53,311 00	46,688
Woodstock debt	60,000 00	57,999 00	2,001
Running acct	53,340 00	34,998 00	18,342
Other banks & agencies	193,709 00	139,021 00	54,688

The latter decrease is owing to the payment certain collaterals lodged before the suspension the Bank.

Deposits have increased	$31,491
Assets on hand, being part of amounts received from Miramichi, and in running accounts,	21,058

After the adoption of the report had be moved, Mr Reed, one of the new Directors, sai The figures showing the estimated surplus wa compromise of three several statements—c of them being made by Mr. Seeley and the Directors, and another by Mr. Jarvis, and third by myself, that the affairs of the bank w so far as it was possible under the circumstan to do, minutely gone into, and that each par estimated the realiable value of the various its honestly to the best of their judgment and in mation. In very many instances our opini differed as to the values, but the net results the several statements only varied a few thous dollars. The statement was got up in good fai and as the meeting was not a meeting of cre ors, and as the debts of the Bank must be pa it was deemed imprudent to expose the affa further than to assure you, over our signatures, The moral certainty that by judicious managem on the part of the Directors, and by forbeara on the part of the creditors that the assets wo not only, in our opinion, pay the liabilities, leave something to be divided amongst the Sto holders.

I consider it of the utmost importance t the Board of Directors, on whom at the exp tion of sixty days from the date of suspensi will fall the duty of winding up the affairs of Bank in accordance with the charter, shall h your entire confidence, because if they are supported by the Stockholders unanimou or nearly so, it will be impossible them to wind up the concern in the most adv tageous and economical way. Therefore the sing paragraph of the report puts the matte question, have you confidence in the discreti the judgment and the honesty of purpose of present Directors, or have you not ? If you h not, then we retire in favor of five gentlen qualified, who may be duly nominated by Stockholders to take our place.

Nearly all of you are in favor of the conc being wound up by the Directory, and not t Curator. The Central and Westmoreland Ba furnish illustrators of the two modes. The C tral was wound up under the Board of Direct the assets of which, not only paid the debts, a balance wrs left to be divided amongst Stockholders, whereas the Westmoreland b wound up by a Curator, under the direction the Supreme Court, the assets have been esti swamped, and a call of fifty per cent has alre been made upon the Stockholders, and I have very best authority for stating that another of a similar amount will shortly be made.

Mr. Milligan wanted to know where the $5 000 deficit above the losses by Sancton and J ley had gone to.

Mr. Kerr wished to see a more detailed settlement of the assets than had been presented. He alleged the Bank had violated its charter by using so largely in real estate, by which means the working energies of the Bank had been crippled and brought to its present position. The mortgages instead of being permitted to lie over, would have been made available, and the property converted into a working medium. From the returns to the Legislature from 1852 to 1862 it would appear, that the position of the Bank was good, when in reality amounts were it in as assets which were utterly worthless. The stockholders had never had an opportunity seeing how the returns were made up, and had information of the real situation of things. In 1862 Mr. McLaughlin and Mr. Sancton made th to the Legislature, that the stock was full, and the assets all good, and yet before the annual meeting in May following, the Directors struck £20,000 from the assets for which they gave a reason, and the stockholders could gain no information on the matter. With regard to the matter between him and Mr. Jack, he would now say that, although Mr. Jack had stated in the papers that he was not liable for the case he lost, that gentlemen had told Mr. Jarvis and Mr. ely and himself, that Mr. Hazen was liable for at amount, and yet that £500 had been put to the bad debt list. The Bank, moreover, in 1861 broken their own bye-laws, in hand £1500 over the counter to Mr. John Morrison, the Bank taking mortgage on his Mill property Fredericton, on which the Central Bank had a previous mortgage of £3500. Mr. Parks explained that when he went to the ward, Mr. Morrison owed the Bank £25,000, of which by great labors he had got covered, and then he told Mr. Morrison that all future accommodation must be done through the Board. He got leave of absence to go to Canada, and while he was gone the Board handed Morrison 000. Mr. Milligan spoke at some length on the departures from the terms of the Charter, and on the liability of the Directors as Trustees for the stockholders. Messrs. Reed and Jarvis were approved of to the vacancies at the Board, and the further consideration of the report was postponed till the second Tuesday in March.

—A meeting of the subscribers for stock in the rt Whitby and Port Perry Railway Company ll be held in Whitby on the 27th of January, the purpose of electing directors.

—The annual meeting of the shareholders of Nova Scotia Marine Insurance Company will held on the 18th January.

IRE RECORD.—Petrolia, Jan. 8.—A fire occurred here by which three houses were burned to the und. That in which the fire originated belonged to Mr. Lloyd, and was occupied by Sidney alters. It appears that Mrs. Walters made a in the stove after dinner, and went to a neigh's house, intending to stay a short time; and was not long gone when the fire was discovered. The fire doubtless originated from the stove, in what way, no one can tell, for when the door was burst open, the whole house was in nes. Mr. Walters and his family lost all their thing except what they had on, and all their niture; also $300 in bills. Mr. W. rushed in ough the flames, and brought out a small nk containing $100 in gold and silver; and at back and brought out the stand, in the wer of which was deposited the $300 in bills; by this time the top of the stand was burned ough, and the money destroyed. Mr. Lloyd, owner of the house, lost all his clothing; $30 ash; and a gold watch worth about $50. Of

the other two houses burned, one belonged to W. H. McGarvey, and was occupied by Michael Parker, but before the fire communicated to it, all the furniture, &c., was removed. The other house belonged to Mr. Wm. Dundas, of Enniskillen, and was occupied by Mr. John Hall, and its contents were likewise saved before the building itself caught fire. The loss, as far as the buildings are concerned, is complete, none of them having been insured; nor was their any insurance on any portion of Mr. Walters' or Mr. Lloyd's goods.

Windsor, July 2.—A fire broke out in a stable in the east end of the town, owned by Henry Offitt and was burned to the ground, with all its contents, including four horses. Loss $700; insured for $500. The wind was blowing quite fresh at the time, and there being no water to supply the engine, the fire soon communicated to the building owned by P. T. Worthington, of London, and occupied by Rev. Hugh Johnston, and it being of wood, was soon so far in flames as to preclude any hope of saving it. Mr. Johnston lost a great deal of his clothing and many of his books by theft, and much of his furniture was badly damaged by hasty removal. The most of the loss will, however, be made good by the insurance on it. This house was fully insured. The cause of the fire is involved in mystery.

Egremont, Co. Grey, Dec. 31.—The store and dwelling house owned by John Hunt; and occupied by Mrs. Jane Hunt, on the 14th concession of Egremont, was destroyed by fire. How the fire originated is not known. The total loss in goods, furniture, &c., will be about $1,500, and incudes $75 in cash, which was in one of the drawers. No insurance.

St. John, N. B.—Store of P. Connelly, on King street consumed, no particulars.

London, Jan. 7.—About eleven o'clock on Wednesday night a fire broke out in the tailors' department of Finlayson and Co.'s dry goods and clothing store, which threatened to destroy the principal part of the brick block on Dundas street, between Talbot and Richmond streets, the rear portions of the buildings where the fire originated being principally old wooden structures. By great exertions on the part of the fire brigade the fire was almost entirely confined to the premises which it broke out. The whole interior of Finlayson's including the stock is destroyed. The loss on stock is estimated at $23,000, $5,000 to 8,000 saved, insured for $16,000—$6,000 in the London Assurance; $2,500 in the Ætna, of Hartford; $2,500 in the North British Mercantile; $5,000 in the Northern, of England. The store is owned by Mr. D. Stirling, of Hamilton, and is fully insured. The adjoining store, occupied by Westlake, dry goods, received considerable damage by smoke and water. The loss is fully covered by an insurance settled for $1,002. Mr. Conachie's dry goods store on the other side also suffered loss through removal. It is insured and settled for $60.

Durham, Ont., Dec. 26.—The Carding Mill, Woollen Factory and Stockhouse, belonging to Peter Patterson, was destroyed by fire. Loss estimated at about $15,000. About $5,000 worth of cloth was destroyed, a portion of which belonged to customers, who will sadly miss the material intended for family wear. Insurance $2,000.

Montreal, Jan. 11th.—A fire broke out in a building situated on Wellington street, occupied as a farmers' tavern, by A. Ryan. The building is a brick one, covered with wood. One of the inmates, a German who was sleeping in the upper story, was at one time in great danger, but through the praiseworthy exertions of Mr. Alfred Ferry and the firemen, he was rescued and taken to the General Hospital in an insensible condition where he now lies in a very low state. The other inmates narrowly escaped uninjured. The loss on the building is about $5,000, insured in the Liverpool and London; on the contents about $1400, insured in the Royal.

Smithtown, King's Co., N. B., Dec. 31.—The Carding, Fulling and Dyeing Mills of J. McC.

Snow, were destroyed by fire. There was no insurance on the Mills, and Mr. Snow lost his books and papers, which were in his desk in the Mill at the time. A large quantity of Wool and Woollen Goods were also destroyed.

Lakelet, Co. Huron, Ont.—The house of Peter Neleny was burned down. The furniture was all saved. There was no insurance on the house, which was owned by R. Young.

Buctouche, N. B.—The dwelling-house and store of Mr. Alex. Johnson and the dwelling-house and store of Mr. John Keswick, both of Buctouche, were destroyed. The house of Mr. Keswick, in which the fire broke out was insured; Mr. Johnson was not insured, but he saved all his household effects.

Cobourg, January.—A fire occurred at Cobourg Station, G. T. R., by which about 400 cords of wood were burnt, the property of the railway company. A large steam sawing machine, owned by C. J. Starling, of Belleville, and which cost about $1,400 was almost completely destroyed.

Waterford, Jan. 12.—Last evening the barn and its contents belonging to Dr. Bowly was consumed. The fire was discovered about 8 P. M., and spread so rapidly that the effort to save anything was impossible. Four horses and two cows were in the building destroyed, together with a large amount of wheat. Loss about $2,500; partially covered by an insurance of $1,000 in the Waterloo Insurance Company.

FIRES IN HALIFAX.—There have been during the year 1863, in Halifax and vicinity, 49 fires and alarms, most of which have happened at night or between the hours of 6 p. m. and 5 a. m.

No. of actual fires in Halifax	26	
do. do. Dartmouth	1	27
No. of alarms in Halifax	21	
do. do. Dartmouth	1	22
Total		49

THE INTERNATIONAL LIFE ASSURANCE.—The case of the International Life Assurance Society came before the Equity Courts of Wednesday, in suit under a petition filed by a Mr. White, the holder of eighty-five shares, with £7 each paid, which, it appears from the evidence, he bought at an auction sale in Lothbury for the nominal sum of £11. The case was argued at great length, and Dr. Symes, the chairman of the International, and Mr. Shrubb, manager of the Hercules, were examined viva voce, before the court with a view of proving the inability of the Hercules to take over the transfer. The evidence went to show that the transfer was a valid one, and that the Hercules was a good and responsible company. It appeared also that £105,000 of mortgages, Government securities and other assets had been absolutely transferred to the Hercules in July last, and that about £15,000 in money had also been paid to them. It also appeared that more than 1,700 policyholders out of the 2,000 or thereabouts had actually accepted the Hercules in the place of the International, and had their policies transferred by endorsement or exchange. The Vice Chancellor gave judgment, the effect of which went to show that the petition must be dismissed unless a suit could be instituted by bill to assert the validity of the transfer-deed, which appeared from the tenor of his honor's remarks to be next to impossible.—Investors' Guardian.

TAXATION OR INSURANCE IN NOVA SCOTIA.—A correspondent writes to a Halifax paper as follows:—By the laws of our Province, we very properly provided, for the public security, that every company is obliged to make an annual return the first of each year, showing the amount of property insured—the gross amount of premiums charged thereon—with the net profit of the business for the year just finished; and on this return the City Assessor makes up his annual assessment. Knowing there was a good deal of dissatisfaction at the manner in which this wholesome law had been disregarded, I have taken the trouble to procure a correct statement up to the present time, which I must ask you kindly to publish with this, for the information of the general public, so that each man may form his own opinion, and judge for himself as to how many of the agencies comply with the requirements of the statute referred.

Memo. City Assessment on Fire Insurance Companies:

	1863.	1864.	1865.
Acadia	....	$232 30	$773 67
Halifax	$717 90	727 26	176 17
Liverpool & London.	985 84	1,540 80	193 40
Royal	453 32	385 84	695 32
Phœnix	nil	260 64	264 68
Queen	685 80	716 10	342 90
N. B. & Mercantile.	....	....	61 04
Lon. & Lancashire..	....	160 00	353 48
Imperial	....	....	....
American Offices (3).	427 50	230 73	....
Total	**$2310 16**	**$4253 61**	**$2760 36**

	1866.	1867.	1868.
Acadia	$642 85	$1024 38	$1055 50
Halifax	19 40	216 21	825 23
Liverpool & London.	1427 53	nil	nil
Royal	139 65	856 64	nil
Phœnix	337 19	431 34	375 25
Queen	nil	529 57	nil
N. B. & Mercantile.	60 52	145 75	350 35
Lon. & Lancashire..	231 00	185 27	nil
Imperial	....	15 80	99 05
American Offices (3).	....	....	20 57
Total	**$2858 14**	**$3354 97**	**$2726 28**

The agents of some of these companies have, as will be seen, generally complied with the law, and it is because there are others who have not, as well as in justice to those who do, that I have ventured to direct public attention to the matter. The statement also shows that the London and Liverpool, although doing a large business, made no general returns for 1867, and paid no taxes for 1867-68. The Royal, generally punctual, made returns, but paid no taxes either for current year. The Queen made no return for two years, and escaped taxes for 1868 and 1866 and 1878, and the London and Lancashire paid nothing for the current year, while at the same time, the Acadia and Halifax, doing a much smaller business, in consequence of being restricted by their charters, than most of the companies referred to, have, by a compliance with the laws of the land, which others have disregarded, taken a large amount annually from their shareholders to pay the city assessment made on their entirety, in consequence of their having made the necessary returns. My object now, Mr. Editor, is to inquire if this cannot and should not at once be looked into and remedied. If we have a law on our statute book requiring returns to be made under a penalty of $20 per month, whether some steps should not be at once taken to bring these refractory agents to book. It is manifestly unfair that foreign Companies should escape taxation, while the local ones, doing a much smaller amount of business, are called upon to contribute so largely to the city funds. I hope the Attorney General may consider it his duty to take the matter in hand, as he will find, if he looks sharply after it, that a very considerable amount in the shape of penalties may now be recovered, which, in the present impoverished condition of the Provincial Treasury, would, I presume, be very acceptable.

—A curious "accident insurance" case has just been decided in Chicago. A fireman insured for $2,000 in the Travellers' Insurance Company, was so injured at a fire that he afterward became delirious. During his delirium he took poison and died. The company provides in its policies that nothing can be collected in case of suicide, whether the party be sane or insane when the act is committed. The insurance in this case was claimed on the ground that the real cause of death was the accident which produced the fireman's insanity. The court decided that the direct and not the remote chance of death was the one insured against.

HARTFORD FIRE INSURANCE COMPANIES.—The following is a statement of the assets of the Hartford Fire Insurance Companies, January 1, 1869:

	Capital.	Surplus.	Total Assets.
Ætna	$3,000,000	$2,150,031.71	$5,150,031.71
Hartford	1,000,000	1,113,556.22	2,113,556.22
Phœnix	600,000	867,855.60	1,467,855.60
North American	300,000	149,859.65	449,859.65
Merchants'	200,000	246,900.00	446,900.00
Connecticut	200,000	142,613.49	342,613.50
City Fire	250,000	250,000.00	500,000.00
Putnam	400,000	150,000.00	550,000.00
Charter Oak	150,000	75,000.00	225,000.00
	$7,500,000	$5,146,796.68	$11,145,796.68

The Ætna has $259,553.98 of outstanding losses unpaid; the Phœnix, $131,970.62, and the Hartford about $100,000. The remainder have net assets as above. Dividends have been declared during the year as follows:

Ætna	16 per cent.	$480,000
Hartford	16 "	160,000
Phœnix	16 "	96,000
North American	12 "	36,000
Merchants'	12 "	24,000
Connecticut	12 "	24,000
City Fire	12 "	30,000
Charter Oak	10 "	15,000
Total		**$865,000**

OCEAN MARINE LOSSES IN 1868.—The following capitulation shows the number of vessels lost during each month of 1868, and their estimated value :

Months.	No. of Vessels.	Value.
January	38	$1,141,000
February	33	930,000
March	44	1,158,000
April	41	800,000
May	23	640,000
June	14	560,000
July	14	185,000
August	31	598,000
September	26	582,000
October	25	587,000
November	27	890,000
December	41	992,000
Total	**362**	**$10,080,000**

—A young man named John Robertson, who for about three years had been insurance agent in Galt, absconded last week.

LOSSES BY FIRE IN THE UNITED STATES.

Total losses in 1856	$21,150,000
" " 1857	15,792,000
" " 1858	11,561,000
" " 1859	16,058,000
" " 1860	15,597,000
" " 1861	18,020,000
" " 1862	17,640,000
" " 1863	14,060,000
" " 1864	28,522,000
" " 1865	43,130,000
" " 1866	66,410,000
" " 1867	36,905,000
" " 1868	34,757,000
Total losses in thirteen years	**$338,811,000**

Railway News.

GREAT WESTERN RAILWAY.—Traffic for week ending Dec. 26, 1868.

Passengers	$27,599 42
Freight and live stock.	52,259 18
Mails and sundries.	2,849 39
	$82,807 99
Corresponding Week of '67	72,560 09
Increase.	$10,247 90

THE ST. STEPHENS BRANCH RAILWAY, N. B, has been doing a prosperous business during the past season. The receipts for the year ending 81st Dec., 1868, are $110,000, while those of the year previous only amounted to $79,000. The up freights still continue good, as the lumber operators and St. John River merchants use this road to forward supplies. The down freight is now very small as the St. Croix is closed and it is difficult to ship lumber.

THE SHERBROOKE AND EASTERN TOWNSHIPS RAILWAY.

Mr. R. Oughtred who was engaged in the preliminary survey to Westbury, for the proposed Wooden Railway from this place to Weedon reported to the Town Council, the result of his explorations, from which we make a few extracts if

He says, the first two and three quarter miles from the Grand Trunk Depot, can be graded to about 80 feet to the mile, but will be very expensive on account of the long deep cut required through the high bank on the easterly side of the St. Francis. If, however, the Railway was to start at or near the top of the bank of the river the grade would be easy and the expense only ordinary. For the next two and a half miles there is a descent of about 124 feet, and can be graded to 50 feet per mile, the first mile and a half rather expensive, the ground being ledgy and broken, the remaining mile of the section being very easy to make. For the next section of three and a half miles there is a rise in the whole distance of about 49 feet and will only require a road-bed to be built, no cutting or filling being necessary. For the next section of one and three quarter miles the grade descends in that direction 53 feet, and will only require a road bed, with no cutting or filling. The next section on the Winslow brook of about half a mile can easily be graded to about 40 feet per mile at ordinary expense by descending gradually down the slope to the banks of said brook and bank of the River St. Francis for about a mile and a quarter from the beginning of the last mentioned section. The whole distance, surveyed and levelled, being about eleven miles from Sherbrooke. The route on the whole is more favorable than Mr. Oughtred or any one else expected, as to the grade, and can be shortened a good deal if more expense is incurred in cutting off some small angles and fill up some small hollows.

The route thus established will be seen to be favorable to laying down by and by iron rails instead of wood, and in the whole distance surveyed the principal expense will be in the grading for iron rails the first three or three and a half miles. At first for the wooden rails the greater part of this expense need not be incurred, and the wooden track can be used for doing the extra grading required, whenever the business of the road calls for iron instead of wood rails. Owing to the great depth of snow it is not thought advisable to continue the survey further at present, nor is it necessary, as it is known no impediments exist up the St. Francis beyond the point now reached, the supposed difficulties being to go from the Grand Trunk Depot across the height of land on the east side of the St. Francis. It is now demonstrated that these difficulties were more imaginary than real, and can be easily overcome. It might be well for the inhabitants in Dudswell, Weedon and other Townships interested to get up petititions to Parliament in favor of the charter being granted. We may add that the proposed line goes into the Township of Stoke in two places and if finally established it will be of great advantage to the settlers there, and tend to induce others to locate in that township, a thing much to be desired. It will also be a great service to this Town in opening up land from which great quantities of fire wood can be brought by the Railway at small expense.—*Sherbrooke Gazette.*

A NEW RAILWAY PROJECT IN NOVA SCOTIA.

It is proposed to extend the railway now in course of construction between Windsor and Annapolis, to Yarmouth, in the western part of the Province. Windsor is already connected with Halifax by rail, and the line from Windsor to Annapolis will doubtless be completed next summer. The distance from Halifax to Annapolis by this route is 130 miles, and it is computed that about 70 miles of rail will connect Annapolis and Yarmouth—making the whole distance from the latter place to Halifax about 200 miles. It is claimed for this route that, besides giving Western Nova Scotia railway connection with Halifax, it will afford a direct route for through travel to the West. The distance from Halifax to Yarmouth could be made by train in ten hours, and it is asserted that steamers could make the trip from Yarmouth to Portland in twelve hours—the distance being but 170 miles. This would enable the people of Halifax to reach the eastern terminus of the Grand Trunk within twenty-four hours—saving, at least, twelve hours, as compared with either of the existing routes.

The Government at Halifax have promised to put into their next estimates an appropriation of $2,000 for the survey of the route from Annapolis to Yarmouth. Mr. Sandford Fleming has, with the consent of the authorities at Ottawa, undertaken to make the survey for the money, and thinks such a survey may be made by March next.

—Notice is given that application will be made to the Legislature of Ontario, during the present session, for an Act to revive the charter of the Hamilton and Port Dover Railway Company, for the limited purpose of realizing their assets to pay debts.

—Proprietors of shares in the capital stock of the Ottawa City Railway Passenger Company are to pay a further call of 50 per cent. on the subscribed stock, at the Ontario Bank, before the 1st day of February.

ENTERPRISE IN QUEBEC.—Progress is the order of the day in Quebec as well as in Ontario, New Brunswick and Nova Scotia.

L'Evenement asserts that a company is now in process of formation with the object of building a narrow gauge railway from Point Levis to the Maine frontier, passing through the counties of Levis, Dorchester and Beauce, a route which would place the American terminus of the road near the headwaters of that old entrance to Canada, the Kennebec. It also states that the success of the enterprise is assured owing to the influential political men and wealthy capitalists who are at its head. Are the Halls, Forsyths, Chauveaus, Blanchets, Cauchons, etc., of the ancient capital seeking for a short outlet to the United States seaboard and a market for Quebec manufactured lumber? Time will tell.

The first actual year under Confederation has, to say the least, witnessed a great advance in the industrial enterprise of this Province. Among the greater and lesser works projected, most of which will eventuate into realities, a retrospective glance will disclose the following: 1. The St. Louis Hydraulic Company, a scheme designed to utilize about ten million horse-power now literally going to waste at our very doors, and calculated, with enterprise and good management, to make Montreal the greatest manufacturing centre on this continent. 2. The extension of the Massawippi, a work which will give Montreal and Quebec another almost direct route to Boston. 3. The extension of the Stanstead and Shefford Railway to Chambly and thence, ultimately to Longueil, opposite Montreal, an extension which, when completed, will still further shorten the route to the seaboard. 4. Construction of a railway through the county of Missisquoi, giving

many of the Eastern townships' farmers and traders direct access to New York, Boston and Montreal. 5. Wooden railway from Quebec to the township of Gosford, opening up the country to the northward for settlement, and furnishing a cheap and almost inexhaustible supply of firewood to the people of Quebec city and vicinity. 6. Wooden railway through the counties of Drummond and Arthabaska, opening portions of them up for settlement, and giving access to the St. Lawrence, Richmond and Sherbrooke. 7. Wooden railway along the valley of the St. Francis. 8. Wooden railway from Montreal to St. Jerome, and thence north, if we please, to the Pole, opening up an enormous district for colonization, and providing an inexhaustible supply of cheap firewood. 9. Revival of the Piles railway project, a scheme intended to give the settlers access to the Upper St. Maurice, and provide an outlet for the valuable lumber of that equally enormous valley. 10. Proposed canal between the rivers rivers Richiliea and Yamaska. 11. Proposed narrow gauge railroad between the St. Lawrence and the head waters of the Kennebec. Many other projects were mooted, but the above list comprises the principal ones—half of which, we confidently repeat, will begin to bear fruit before the present year has expired. Who can say, in view of the above array of intelligent, well-grounded schemes for the development of the resources of the Province of Quebec, that it has not prospered, or will not prosper under Confederation?

ASHBRIDGE'S BAY CANAL.—A scheme to open a harbour at Leslieville has been started by the inhabitants of the locality, and notice has been given of a bill to sanction the project. The object designed in the construction is, to become independent of the local market for fuel; and, with the canal constructed, wood can be brought in at as much less cost to the inhabitants than at present. It is computed that the parties who would benefit, use at least 7,000 cords per annum; and a very small amount, on the total cost of that quantity of fuel would construct the canal. Besides, there are large quantities of lime, plaster and other articles imported, which could be cheapened in cost of carriage by the proposed canal. Its length is estimated at about a mile, and it will strike across the bar a short distance east of Mr. Leslie's nurseries, near Toronto.

—The Lieutenant Governor of Ontario has authorized the issue of letters patent, incorporating the "Church Printing and Publishing Company," with a head office at Toronto or Hamilton, and with power to establish agencies in other cities and towns. Nominal capital $6,000.

—Some enterprising country projectors speak of making a canal between St. Hyacinthe and St. Charles, so as to connect the Richelieu with the Yamaska—a distance of about thirteen miles. This would enable the people of St. Hyacinth to get access to the St. Lawrence at Sorel, and thereby shorten the water way to Montreal.

NEW INSOLVENTS.—The following new insolvents were gazetted on Saturday, the 9th inst.: Paul Tasvrin, parish of Montreal; Joseph Nodeau, township of Stanfold; F. D. Crummen, Toronto; Lewis T. Cole, Napanee; David Dean, Bayham; Timothy McCarthy, Bayham; Guelph Packing Company, Guelph; Robert Armstrong, Allas Craiger, Joseph, St. Johns, Thomas Robinson, Esquesing; Joseph Mann, London; P. O'Brien, Belleville; D. L. Carsdallen, Belleville; James Flynn, Orangeville; John Wylie, Iroquois; M. Findley, Ingersoll; Wm. Gilmore, Toronto; Grant & Henderson, Ottawa; Donald Matheson, Toronto; A. T. Boucher, Montreal; William Riddle, London; D. D. Chesbro, Belleville; John Clements, Berthier; Edward Ward White, Kingston; Edward Wilmot, Kingston; Thomas Coe, Ashburnham; Monteath, London; L. P. Profontaine, Boloctal, Buckland, Howell & Co., Montreal.

THE MUNICIPAL LOAN FUND.

It appears that the municipalities of the Province of Ontario borrowed from the Government, under the Municipal Loan Fund Act, $7,300,000. Of this amount, $5,867,400 were spent on railways, and $1,482,600 on local improvements. Of the entire amount invested in railways $3,229,400 was by way of loan and $2,638,000 in stock.

Municipalities. Counties.	Railroads.	Local Improvements.
Grey	......	$16,000
Northumberland and Durham	......	460,000
Perth	200,000	88,000
Oxford	......	20,000
Lincoln	......	48,000
Lambton	......	16,000
Lanark and Renfrew	800,000	......
Elgin	80,000	......
Hastings	......	157,000
Essex	......	32,000
Huron and Bruce	300,000	8,000
Total counties	**$1,380,000**	**$845,600**
Townships.		
Hope	$60,000	......
Bertie	40,000	......
Brantford	50,000	......
Wainfleet	20,000	......
Canborough	8,000	......
Moulton and Sherbrooke	20,000	......
Middleton	......	5,000
Stanley	......	10,000
Woodhouse	80,000	......
Norwich	200,000	......
Opa	80,000	......
Windham	100,000	......
Elizabethtown	154,000	......
Total townships	**$812,000**	**$15,000**
Cities.		
Ottawa	$200,000	......
London	375,000	......
Total cities	**$575,400**	......
Towns.		
Port Hope	$680,000	$180,000
Niagara	280,000	......
Cobourg	500,000	......
Brantford	500,000	......
Paris	40,000	......
Prescott	100,000	......
St. Catherines	100,000	......
Woodstock	100,000	......
Cornwall	......	12,000
Belleville	......	20,000
Simcoe	100,000	......
Brockville	400,000	......
Stratford	100,000	......
Goderich	......	100,000
Barie	......	12,000
Chatham	......	100,000
Dundas	......	52,000
Guelph	80,000	......
Peterboro	100,000	......
Total towns	**$3,980,000**	**$548,000**
Villages.		
Chippawa	$20,000	$6,000
Total	**$5,867,400**	**$1,482,600**
Total	......	**$7,300,000**

Port Hope, which gave its entire $680,000 to two railways, the Peterboro and Port Hope, and the Port Hope, Lindsay and Beaverton, owes over a million and a half to the Fund, which is $40,000 more than the entire assessed value of the real and personal property of the town! Cobourg is in the next worst state, owing $971,400, whilst its assessment is but a million and a quarter.

The Canadian Monetary Times.

THURSDAY, JANUARY 14, 1869.

THE HURON AND ONTARIO SHIP CANAL.

The agitation raised by the Huron and Ontario Ship Canal Company respecting the non-reception, by the Ontario Legislature, of the petitions asking a grant of 10,000,000 acres of land in aid of the proposed scheme to connect lakes Huron and Ontario by a canal, calls for an examination of the grounds of such refusal. Ten millions of acres make, certainly, a large tract of country. One can understand what the expression means when we call to mind that there were in 1863 only a little over six million acres under cultivation in the province of Ontario. It means a tract of country equal, according to the number of acres assessed in 1866, to the counties of Huron, Bruce, Simcoe, Grey, Wellington, York, Peel, Elgin, Haldimand, Halton, Kent, Lambton, Middlesex, Norfolk, Waterloo, Wentworth, Oxford and Ontario—eighteen counties, the largest in the Province of Ontario—put together. Our experience of land monopolies in this country has been not such as to cause the creation of a new one to be viewed with popular favour; and any scheme which demands the donation of so much territory as that we have indicated must present extraordinary inducements before the Canadian people will consent to assist it in such a way. It is all very well to say that the land the Company would accept is of no value. If such be the case we should be lending ourselves to a fraud in tempting men to invest their means by pretending to give them something substantial when what we give is, in reality, of no value. If the land is sufficient in value to induce those to whom it would be given to invest $40,000,000 in a canal, then the question arises, Are we making the best of it?

The proposed canal would connect Lake Ontario (234 feet above the sea) with Lake Huron (574 feet above the sea), and have Lake Simcoe (704 feet above the sea) for its summit level and feeder. The estimated length is 100 miles, of which 24 miles are deep water navigation through Lake Simcoe, and 16 miles slack water navigation, there being 60 miles of canal proper, of which 30 miles would be summit level, and 30 miles interrupted by lockage. The total lockage is placed at 600 feet. The number of locks is 42. The width of the canal would be 100 feet at the water suface, and 80 feet in the bottom, and its depth 13 feet. The time required for passing through the canal is computed at 42 hours, thus:—

24 miles Lake navigation at 8 miles per hour... 3
52¼ "   River and Canal, long reaches 3½ m.p.h. 15
20   "   "   "   short   " 2 " " 10
3¼   "   42 locks, at 20 minutes each.......... 14
                                               ——
    Total.. 42

The estimated cost of all the works is $36,000,000, to which must be added the interest on expenditure during construction, which, together, would absorb the capital of $40,000,000.

The following advantages are claimed for the canal by its promoters:

1. The intricacies and dangers of the shoals and flats of Lakes Erie and St. Clair avoided, and a saving of about 500 miles affected.

2. Cargoes of 1000 or 1200 tons may be taken from Chicago, or other Lake ports, to tide water, or across the Atlantic, without transhipment.

3. Instead of 350 miles distance, and 14 days of time, on the warm and shallow water of the Erie Canal (exposing grain to risk of heating), the Huron and Ontario Canal and the St. Lawrence Canals, together, will have only 120 miles of length, with 14 feet of water, the rest of the navigation being equal to any in the world.

4. Quebec being 500 miles nearer than New York to Liverpool, there will be a saving of that distance in the sea voyage.

5. A cargo of 1,000 or 1,200 tons shipped at Chicago for Liverpool, via H. & O. Canal, would under ordinary circumstances, and whether transhipped at Quebec or not, reach Liverpool before another cargo shipped at same time, via Buffalo and Erie Canal, could reach New York.

6. With the advantages of the great saving of time and distance, and the passage of large cargoes without transhipment, the transportation charges as well between Chicago and Oswego as between Chicago and Liverpool, may be reduced nearly 50 per cent.

It is assumed that at least 5,275,000 tons of freight between the West and the East

would be commanded by the canal, yielding 80 cents per gross ton.

The advantages claimed as likely to accrue to this Province are "the creation of an almost unlimited water power along the first 24 miles of the canal," the expenditure of large sums of money, and the employment of a large amount of labor, the stimulation of ship building and the trade in ship-chandlery, and the developement of the vast and rich region west of Georgian Bay. As a national work, it is considered that it would supply the population of Great Britain with breadstuffs at a reduced rate, and constitute a powerful bond of peace with the United States.

The question to be decided by the people of Ontario is not whether the canal can be constructed—the Company's Engineers have answered that affirmatively—or whether, if constructed, would it pay dividends to the Stockholders in the Company—the Company must satisfy themselves on that,—but rather, Would the advantages to accrue to Ontario from the construction of the canal be equal to the advantages that might be secured from the giving of 10,000,000 acres of land, if they are to be given away, to aid other enterprises such as railways, which would assuredly benefit our own country directly and immediately? Would we derive greater benefit from building a canal by which the so-called "starving masses" in Europe might, or might not, get their bread cheaper than they do now, than we would by building railways and opening up new and fertile districts by which these "starving masses" might be induced to come here and feed themselves? A capacious mouth and a willing pair of hands in Canada are worth more to us than a great many mouths and hands in Europe. We consider, therefore, that Mr. Laidlaw has hit upon the true answer to those who ask us to lavish our means upon a canal, when the same assistance would build several railways and open up millions of acres to cultivation and settlement. But it may be said, let us do both; let us build canals and railways also. Very well. With all due deference to the energetic promoters of the canal scheme we assert that railways are entitled to precedence. If ten millions of acres are a sufficient inducement to the investment of forty millions of dollars in a canal, and our canals have no paid one and a half per cent. on their cost they should be a powerful temptation to capitalists to build a good many railways for us and that, too, through these very lands.

We need not be in too great a hurry with this canal project. The canal, if built, might be, (which is disputed) of great service to Chicago and the Western States. But in the present state of affairs, it would be of little use to us Canadians. Our American neigh irs shew little consideration for our interest in imposing a high tariff on everything sell to them. In a previous number of a journal (No. 7—Vol. 2) we pointed out outrageous treatment our Canadian mass-receivers at the hands of American legislators, and American Custom-house officials; by use every means to destroy our carrying de. They won't allow our vessels to enter American inland stream or canal; they n't even allow a Canadian steamer to go to American side of the St. Clair river to e in tow an American vessel; they have nepolized all the ferries, by making it essary for a Canadian ferry boat to enter clear every time she touches an American landing; they won't allow a Canadian to mand an American vessel, or to be an incan on one; they won't allow a Canadian sel to touch at any American port without ment of tonnage dues and a charge for urance; they wont allow our vessels to ticipate in their coasting trade at all; and lly, they won't allow a Canadian vessel carry grain from any American port to a adian port.

Vhat is the proclaimed object of the ron and Ontario Ship Canal? Why, to rd an additional outlet "to the teeming ducts of the great west"; in fact, to bene Chicago and the Western States. Who is ave the carrying trade? Assuredly not adians, for our friends across the lines 't allow our vessels to carry grain from American port to another. It is not sant to think of giving 10,000,000 acres and to build a canal which we could not They would exclude us from their ls and prevent us from using our own. er such circumstances, we say, we are likely to give away large blocks of our tory for their benefit, and we can afford sit until they manifest a more friendly t to us, in the meantime using our rees for our own benefit. Charity begins ome.

UR AND GRAIN TRADE OF 1868.

he trade in the natural products of the soil climate is primarily deserving of atten, in that it forms the basis of operations very branch of business. The importer the manufacturer frame their estimates ales and purchases with an eye chiefly to prosperity of agriculture; this is the baeter which unfailingly indicates the future he commercial horizon. Such being well erstood principles, the deductions of observon and experience, we need not explain great consequence to the whole country, every individual interest in it, of the

trade in the great agricultural staples of Canada—breadstuffs and grain.

In Ontario a good crop of wheat was gathered in last harvest. Fall sown was unusually favorable, and Spring did very well, taken as a whole, though the uncommonly dry summer weather ruined it in many localities, especially the late sown. The year opened with high prices, but the prolific production of nature was an overmatch for the resources of speculators, and the demands of consumers, so that a fall came—"and what a falling off was there!" Fall wheat sold in April last at $1 85, and in December at $1 10, for the same quality of sample—75 cents down; Spring was worth $1 65 on the first of April, and slipped down to $1 02; No. 1 superfine flour was worth $7 15 per barrel on the 1st. of August, and by the end of December sold for $4 50. Such a reduction in values, as may be supposed, kept millers and dealers at their wits end to keep from making ruinous losses—the profits of the grain, wheat and flour trade are very little talked of.

The movement through the Toronto warehouses is shown by the following figures :—

	Fall Wheat.	Spring Wheat.
1868.		
Receipts, bush.	252,589	364,174
Shipments, bush.	249,191	854,523
1867.		
Receipts, bush.	268,116	485,983
Shipments, bush.	302,152	478,435
1866.		
Receipts, bush.	534,272	468,197
Shipments, bush.	529,027	406,907
1865.		
Receipts, bush.	687,088	338,000
Shipments, bush.	586,904	358,000

It should be explained that the circumstances of the trade, within a few years, are such as induce a reduction, rather than an increase, in the receipts of wheat, at Toronto. Since our flour trade with the Lower Provinces was established in its present magnificent proportions, our milling interests have been more prosperous, and a great portion of our wheat, which passed through the city warehouses, and was shipped to American markets, there to be ground and mixed with their own wheat, of an inferior quality, and the product shipped to the Provinces, is now converted into flour at the mills along our lines of railway, and shipped direct to the Maratime markets. In other words the flour trade has increased, partly at the expense of the wheat trade. The shipments to Montreal, and the lower ports, were 184,770 bush. and 409,944 to Oswego and other American markets.

The movement in wheat in Montreal, in 1868, appears by the following statement :—

	1867.	1868.
Receipts, bush.	2,426,822	2,881,667
Shipments, bush.	1,141,673	1,575,346

Our flour trade with the Maratine ports has become of great service to the terri

tory tributary to Toronto. A half dozen firms—Messrs. Howland, W. D. Matthews, & Co., Gibbs & Bro., of Oshawa, T. C. Chisholm, Gooderham & Worts, and W. Marshall, of Stratford ; sent forward not less than 200,000 brls. to those markets. It is very interesting to notice the way in which the trade with St. John has been transferred from American to Canadian hands, since the demolition of the tariffs, and the establishment of closer political relations. A statement of receipts of flour at St. John for several years is :

1865.
Total Flour received from the
United States, barrels............ 205,373
Do. do. from Canada............ 28,000
_____
233,373

1866.
Total Flour received from the
United States, barrels............ 89,915
Do. do. from Canada............ 144,399
_____
234,314

1867.
Total Flour received from the
United States, barrels............ 32,000
Do. do. from Canada............ 220,000
_____
252,000

1868.
Total Flour received from the
United States, barrels............ 55,000
Do. do. from Canada............ 234,000
_____
259,000

The movement of flour at the Toronto warehouses is shewn by the following statement of receipts and shipments for the years named ;

	Receipts.	Shipments.
1868.—Barrels	56,120	51,930
1867.—Barrels	66,793	61,891
1866.—Barrels	125,089	108,852
1865.—Barrels	61,197	57,781

To the above receipts should be added about 50,000 barrels each year, being the estimated consumption of the city annually ; it need scarcely be added that these figures handled by our dealers.

Receipts and shipments of flour at Montreal during the years named were :

	1867.	1868.
Receipts, barrels	643,154	789,041
Shipments, barrels	561,047	510,847

The barley trade ranks next in importance. About 4,000,000 of bushels are estimated to have been produced in Ontario in 1868, yielding producers about $5,000,000. The dry weather greatly lessened our crop, but high prices more than compensated. The trade of the port of Toronto for several years is shown as follows :

	Receipts.	Shipments.
1868.—Bushels	988,410	895,380
1867.—Bushels	1,225,455	943,803
1866.—Bushels	1,278,767	1,247,708
1865.—Bushels	1,197,126	1,187,626

The receipts of barley at Oswego, from Canada, in the years named, were
Receipts at Oswego in 1865........bu. 2,992,432
" " 1866............ 4,094,889
" " 1867............ 2,528,447
" " 1868............ 2,031,885

To show the American ports to which our shipments go, we give the following statement of the receipts of barley from Ontario at the lake ports named, during 1868:—

Chicago, bush	92,017
Milwaukee, bush	15,013
Detroit, bush	113,060
Toledo, bush	593,227
Cleveland, bush	104,851
Buffalo, bush	544,195
Oswego, bush	2,031,385
Cape Vincent, bush	30,800
Ogdensburgh, bush	54,293
	3,578,841
Deduct Canada barley shipped from Oswego to western lake ports	79,184
Total receipts at above named ports	3,499,707

The market opened on the 13th of August, fully three weeks earlier than the average date of previous seasons. Beginning at 95 to 97c., and advancing to $1 50 in the middle of November, it closed at $1 25 to $1 30. Large profits were made by every one who handled the crop.

It is supposed that prices were greatly influenced, if not controlled, by a ring of speculators on both sides of the lakes, and the sudden drop in the early part of November is attributed to a breaking up of this organization by a severe monetary pressure. If a ring existed, its operations were carried on with unusual prudence and secrecy, and was managed by those who understood better the prospective requirements of the market than the great majority of dealers.

The whole course of the market is most extraordinary, and tends to enhance the great relative importance that this crop has assumed among the cereal products of Canada.

Communications.

GEORGIAN BAY CANAL.

Editor Canadian Monetary Times.

SIR,—The state of international law between the United States and Canada prevents Canadian ship owners from carrying wheat or other cargo from Chicago or any other United States port through the *Welland Canal*, Oswego, or other American port. Worse yet! If a cargo arrives in a Canadian bottom, at Port Colborne, and transhipped by rail or canal to Port Dalhousie? *No Canadian vessel is permitted* by the United States Government to carry such cargo to Oswego or other American port!

No Canadian bottom would be allowed to carry produce from an American to an American port *through the Georgian Bay Canal* if it was now ready for work.

Shall we, therefore, give ten million acres of land to build canals for the sole benefit of a people who will not allow us to carry *their trade through our own Canals with our own vessels!*

Before the Welland Canal is enlarged, or any other proposed, a treaty should be made, securing to Canadian, equal rights with American vessels in the upper lake carrying trade.

Much cannot be expected from a people who strain their construction of international coasting laws to such an extent as to declare it coasting for a *British vessel* to carry a cargo from New York, round Cape Horn, to San Francisco!

Pretty fellows they are, for which to ruin our kindred in building canals! England allows American vessels to carry coals from Newcastle to London or other British ports.

The Huron and Ontario Canal Company having absurdly proposed to commence a ship canal in *the middle* of our inland system of navigation, discovered, (when taught), the uselessness of their proposed work, unless the St. Lawrence canals were deepened and enlarged to correspond with the size of their proposed canal. I understood that the liberal leaders at the inception of Confederation, stipulated for the enlargement of the canals, and suppose the Dominion Government have, in consequence, a canal policy, to be developed after the Intercolonial Railway is built, or building.

If, however, the Huron and Ontario Canal Company assume the functions of the Dominion Government, and make the "enlargement of the St. Lawrence Canal part and parcel of their '*little business*' no doubt, although the enlargement is not necessary, it will be done forthwith.

Vessels of 500 tons could come to Montreal one hundred years ago. The mere deepening of the Clyde for a short distance has cost I believe over $10,000,000. The unnecessary deepening of the St. Lawrence and the Canals, to carry ocean vessels of 1,000 tons, would cost thirty or forty millions of dollars—the bed of the river and canals being mainly rock.

How much did the dredging of a channel through the mud of Lake St. Peter cost? Chicago harbor might be deepened; but all the harbors of refuge would also need to be deepened.

WATER SUPPLY.

The only stream running out of Lake Simcoe is the Severn, which, therefore, represents the surplus water of that lake. Its volume being a great deal less than that of the Grand river, which does not suffice to supply the small locks of the Welland Canal; how, therefore, with double-sized locks are the *two canals* from Lake Simcoe, one to the Georgian Bay and the other to Lake Ontario, to be supplied with water? By hydraulic power! The Severn after leaving Lake Simcoe, or rather the arm of it, Lake Couchichiug, receives many large affluents, one about as large as itself; yet in summer, when canals are required, these combined waters are barely sufficient to drive a couple of saw mills.

Some gain would accrue from the canal, if built, to the farmers of the county of Simcoe, and such business places as Newmarket, Bradford, Barrie, &c.; these places gaining what Toronto would lose, but at a cost unworthy of a moment's consideration.

Is it supposed by citizens of Toronto advocating the canal that vessels would load lumber and wheat at Barrie, for instance, and bring their cargoes to Toronto, discharge and reload again? No! Vessels would clear from Newmarket, Barrie, &c., for Oswego and Montreal, as they now do from St. Catharines or Thorold and would load back from Oswego and Montreal, to these places instead of loading for Toronto.

Toronto would, therefore, be *stripped of the whole Northern trade* by the very men and means employed to enhance its prosperity.

Does the state of the Welland Railway, alongside the Welland Canal, foreshadow the fate of the Northern Railway, with a canal as its rival!

I am, Sir,

Your obed't serv't,

G. LAIDLAW.

SALT.—Goderich salt is beginning to assume a much more prominent position in our market; the demand is increasing. We quote Goderich salt $1.65, American do. $1.50, Liverpool coarse, bag $1.30, do. fine do. $1.40.

Financial.

TORONTO STOCK MARKET.

(Reported by Pellatt & Osler, Brokers.)

The improvement in stocks noticed in our report has been well maintained; the busi done this week has been large and at advan rates.

Bank Stock—Several sales of Montreal occu at 138 to 138½; at the latter rate the market c ing firm, with a good demand at 138½. Tl have been no late transactions in British. L sales of Ontario occurred at 100, 100½ and 1(and closed firm at the latter rate. No Toront market. There are no buyers of Royal Cana over 84; sellers ask 86. Large sales of Comm occurred at 101½ and 102; there are now bu and sellers at the latter rate. Buyers offer 3 Gore; no sellers under 39. Merchants has l sold for 105 and 105½; small lots are now off at 106. Buyers offer 110 for Molson's, sellers at 110½. Sales of City occurred at 1 and 101; there are no sellers now under 1 Buyers offer 108 freely for Du Peuple; no sel There are sellers of National at 106½ and bu at 105. Jacques Cartier is not procurable u 108; buyers generally offer 107. Other b nominal.

Debentures—There have been no debenture the market for some time; buyers would adv on quotations. Sales of Toronto occurred at to pay 6¾ per cent. interest. County are in demand, and there were buyers at high rates.

Sundries—107 would readily be paid for Gas. there has been no stock in market for months. Sales of Canada Permanent Buil Society occurred at 120½, 121, 121½ and closing firm at the latter price. No We Canada in market; buyers offer 114 without tracting sellers. There are buyers of Freeho 105½; no sellers. Buyers would pay 133 for treal Telegraph, ex dividend; no sales. Sal Canada Landed Credit accurred at 71½ and and there are buyers at the latter rate. gages are readily sold to pay 8 per cent. int Money is very plentiful on good security.

U. S. NATIONAL BANKS.—The United S Comptroller of the Currency reports that th six of the National Banks are in volu liquidation, and fifteen have failed durin year. The aggregate capital of the 1629 Nat Banks in operation on 30th September, 1868 $426,159,111, an average of $261,000 to The taxes paid by them to government equ 4.332 per cent. The Comptroller recomme general redeeming agency at New York fo whole National Banks in operation, in lieu o nineteen cities at present.

GORE BANK.—Notice is given that applic will be made to the Parliament of the Dom next session for an Act to amend the char the Gore Bank by reducing the capital stock fully paid up, from $40 to $24 each, and l creasing the number of shares requisite fo qualification of its directors, and by autho the issue of new shares to an amount whic gether with the amount of share capital n sued when so reduced will make the capital Bank amount to one million dollars, an changing the time now fixed for holding th nual meeting of shareholders.

DOMINION REVENUE AND EXPENDITURE DECEMBER.—Revenue—Customs, $479,8 excise, $272,292.34; postoffice, $19,890.76 stamps, $5,480.60; public works, includin ways, $85,551.49; miscellaneous, $140,0 total, $1,002,610.33. Expenditure, $956,7

—The barque Grace E. Cram, which arri Winterport, Me., a few days since, brough tons of rails for the European and North A can Railroad. About 500 tons will be hau Bangor for immediate use.

BANK OF ENGLAND.

	Dec. 24, 1868.	Dec. 27, 1867.
te of discount	3 per cent.	2 per cent.
serve...........	£10,433,640	£13,578,182
ock of bullion	18,158,315	21,941,047
Consols.........	92⅝ x d	92 ¼ x d

ual just before the close of the year more for money has been experienced this nd in the open market 2⅝ per cent. is paid best three months paper. Some tightness market will probably be experienced next On the Stock Exchange the rate for ad- on British Government securities is 2 to ent.

BANKING IN FRANCE.

first bank of circulation in France was hed by John Law, a Scotchman, who in otained from the Duke of Orleans, the egent, the privilege of establishing a l bank" to receive deposits, discount com- paper, and issue bills payable to bearer and. In spite of the very small capital hich it was started, its beginnings were e; but the visionary theories of its , and the passions of a necessitous and ulous government, plunged it into specu- which speedily occasioned its downfall, nly four years of existence, it was com- o suspend operations. Fifty years elapsed ny further attempt was made to establish of circulation in France. In 1776, under nistry of Turgot, a bank of discount was hed at Paris. Its original capital was ven and a half million of francs, con- by its shareholders. In 1779, by an in council, its capital was increased to millions. The rate of discount was fixed per cent. on bills of exchange having two ee months to run. Shortly afterward it bank bills, and by this means doubled its In consideration of its public utility, stitution was authorized, by an order in of November 28, 1781, to assume a coat , which should serve both as a seal for the and an official stamp for its stock certifi- Such was the activity it imparted to the tion during the war which ended in 1783, the opinion of the most enlightened mer- of the time, commerce could not have d itself with silver, even at the rate of six nt., which was the uniform rate which it nded during the latter years of the war. ring the revolution which ensued, the em- ments of the bank were so great that it was ssed in March, 1793, by a decree of the ition. Various associations were subse- y formed at Paris for carrying on the dis- business, the most distinguished of which e "Caisse des Comptes Courants," or bank rent accounts, which was founded in 1800, s almost immediately afterward merged in nk of France.

he law of April 14, 1803, the monopoly of nk was declared, and the other establish- of like character, of which the "Comptoir ercial" was the most important, either up or were united with it. The same law ized it to issue bills, payable to bearer on d, of the denominations of 500 and 1,000

By the law of March 25, 1841, issues of ancs were authorized; by that of June 10, of 200 francs; and by that of March, 1848, francs.

he provisions of articles ten and eleven of t of April 14, 1803, the whole body of olders is represented at the annual meeting two hundred of them holding the largest r of shares; but each of these representa- has only one vote, whatever may be the r of shares which he holds.

chief direction of the bank is intrusted to rnor and two Deputy Governors, who are appointed by the executive government of the empire; and to fifteen regents and three censors apaointed by the shareholders in general meeting. The management of funds, amounting annually to eight thousand million francs ($1,600,000,000), is therefore directed by these twenty-one functionaries. On the 31st of December, 1866, the number of chief managers, directors of branches, managers, clerks, and inferior agents, was 1,193, of whom 574 were at Paris, and 619 at the branches.

The original capital was thirty millions of francs. The surplus fund having been used to purchase shares of the bank, its capital, in 1812, had been reduced to 67,900,000 francs, by the cancellation of 22,100 shares. It remained at this figure till 1848. On the 1st of January, 1849, the capital was increased by the addition of twenty-three and a half millions, resulting from the union of the provincial banks with the Bank of France, pursuant to the decrees of April 27 and May 2, 1848. With this addition it became 91,250,000 francs. The law of June 9, 1857, doubled that figure, and stipulated that out of the proceeds of 91,250 new shares to be issued, 100 millions of francs should be deposited in the public treasury in exchange for an inscription of inalienable three per cent. rentes of four millions a year. This transaction was completed on the 31st of December. 1860. This portion of the capital constitutes the reserve, necessary for the redemption, over the counter, of the bills which the bank puts into circulation. The limit of the circulation was fixed by three decrees of 1848 to an issue of 452 million francs; by the law of December 22, 1849, it was raised to 525 millions; but by that of April 6, 1850, all restrictions upon the amount of it were removed.

The law of June 9, 1857, required that within ten years from that date, the bank should have a branch in each of the departments. At the end of 1866 there were fifty-five branches established, and their united operations in that year amounted to 5,069½ millions of francs.

The principal business of the bank is the discount of commercial paper, bearing three signatures and not having more than ninety days to run. Instead of a third signatnre, the decree of January 16, 1808, authorizes the bank to receive collateral security of public stocks, or corporate shares of adequate value. Formerly, it discounted only twice a week, but since 1837 paper is disconnted every day the bank is open for business, and the proceeds of the discount are paid over immediately, whereas formerly they were held over till the following day.

The progress of discounts at Paris since the establishment of the bank has been as follows:

In 1800 the amount of commercial paper discounted did not exceed 112 millions of francs; in 1805 it had risen to 631 millions; but in 1814 it had fallen again to 85 millions, from which point it rose, till in 1817, it stood at 547¼ millions.

The bank pays no interest on deposits, but it makes collections for the depositors without charge.

The amount of the note circulation and of the specie reserved at corresponding dates is one of the facts most worthy of observation. The following figures show the maximum in millions of francs, for the years indicated:

Years.	Circulation.	Reserve.
1807	167·6	83·6
1817	96·2	94
1827	303·5	193·8
1837	216·9	248·2
1847	288·8	107·5
1848	390·4	141·5
1852	525·8	513·9
1856	589	132·9
1860	801·2	549·2
1862	869	431·3
1864	839·6	367·5
1866	1,029	748·7
1867 (Dec. 5)	1,142	987
1868 (Oct. 26)	1,266	1,207

These losses from bad debts are very inconsiderable, in fact, and especially so when the amount of business is considered. Up to 1833, inclusive, the sums carried to profit and loss to cover eventual losses of discounted paper did not reach two millions of francs ($400,000). After the Revolution of 1848 the suspended debt of the bank and its branches amounted to eighty-four and a half millions of francs ($17,000,000), but the whole of this debt was paid in the course of the two following years. Up to 1856 the sum charged off for bad debts slightly exceeded three millions of francs ($600,000), out of a total of sixty thousand millions ($12,000,000,000) discounted 1-200 of one per cent.—*Translator.* On the 24th of December, 1861, the suspended debt amounted to only 291,021 francs ($60,000), but at the same date in 1866 it had risen to 3,124,140 francs ($625,000). This increased figure was due to the crisis of 1866 in England, which had stricken down many of the English banks and caused the suspension of French houses having relations with them.

It was from the outset provided that the stockholders should receive a dividend of 5 per cent., and that the surplus should constitute a reserve fund to secure the maintenance of a uniform rate of interest, the reserve to accumulate till it reached a certain per centage. The minimum dividend was 10 francs (1 per cent.), in 1814; the maximum 272 francs (27 per cent.), in 1856; in 1859 it was 115 francs; in 1860, 140 francs; in 1864, 154 francs; and in 1866, 156 francs for the 133d and 134th dividends since the creation of the bank.

In the sixty-seven years of its existence the total of its operations has reached the sum of 133,390 million francs ($26,680,000,000), which is thus divided:

1. Discount of commercial paper, 75,357 millions; of bonds of the Mint, the Treasury, and the Bakers' Bank, and orders for cutting timber, 2,954 millions. Total, 78,311 millions.

2. Advances on treasury bonds, canal shares, and other securities, 990 millions; on rentes, 3,940 millions; on bullion, 2,304 millions; on obligations of railways, and of the Credit Mobilier, 4,434 millions. Total, 11,668 millions.

3. Operations in bullion and premiums on gold, 556 millions; operations with the Treasury and the city of Paris, 6,267 millions.

The total of these three classes is 96,762 millions of francs. The residue of 36,628 millions must be referred to operations of the bank and its branches other than discounts and advances.

The gross profits derived from all these operations, including the increase of rentes which the bank holds from the State, have amounted to 902 millions, of which 717 millions have been distributed in dividends; and the balance has been applied to the various expenses of the bank and its branches.—*Banker's Magazine.*

SPEEDY PROCESS FOR RECOVERING DEBTS.—Mr. McColl of Norfolk has introduced into the Legislative Assembly of Ontario a Bill entitled: "An Act to facilitate the recovery of debts acknowledged in writing, and to lessen the cost on their collection." It provides that all debts settled by note or acknowledged in writing, if unpaid for twenty-five days, shall become judgments against the debtor without the usual process of law, "provided such note or other written evidence of debt is undisputed." Such debts before becoming judgments "shall be placed in the hands" of the Clerk of the Court having jurisdiction, with an affidavit of the debt being paid and unpaid for twenty-five days, and the Clerk shall register it as a judgment. Judgments so obtained shall "hold the real and personal estate (now liable by law to be seized under execution for debt) of the debtor until such judgments are satisfied. If the note or other evidence of debt be disputed, the debtor may "on the day of the maturity of such debt, or within ten days thereafter notify the Clerk when such judgments are to be entered," of his intention to contest payment, setting forth his grounds of defence. Thereupon the Clerk shall notify immediately the the Judge presiding in such court, then, "in that event the usual process of law shall be followed as in all disputed suits." If the defence is frivolous or vexatious the defendant shall be liable to all costs and damages incurred. On all judgments obtained under this Act no execution shall issue until after the expiration of thirty days, and then only on Judge's order.

DeLery Gold Mines.—The action in the case of John O'Farrell and others against Alexander R. C. DeLery, now before the Court, was brought, says the Quebec *Chronicle*, to revoke the instrument known as the patent granted to the DeLery family as seignior and proprietors of the Fief and Seignory of Rigaud-Vaudreuil, giving the patentee the exclusive privilege to search, dig for and work all gold mines found in the seigniory, and to recover $250,000 damages.

Railway—Receipt Note for Freight.— Plaintiff's correspondents in Chicago delivered there to the Michigan Southern Railway Company certain articles of merchandize, to be transported to Toronto for plaintiff, that company at the time of delivery giving a receipt note to the effect that they had received from plaintiff's correspondents the merchandize in question, consigned to plaintiff at Toronto, to be transported over their line of road to their terminus, and delivered to the company whose line might be considered a part of the route, to be carried to the place of destination; the Michigan Company not to be liable as common carriers for the goods whilst at any of their stations awaiting delivery to the Company which was to forward them; with the further proviso, that no company or carrier forming part of the line, over which the freight was to be carried, should be responsible for demurrage or detention at its terminus, or beyond or on any part of the line, arising from any accumulation or over pressure of business ; and that "the Company" should not be liable for the destruction or damage of the freight from any cause whilst in the depot of the company, or for any loss or damage from "Providential" causes, or from fire, whilst in transit or at the stations.

It appeared that there was an arrangement between the Michigan Company and the defendants that the latter should carry their freight from the terminus of their line to certain points in Canada, and that the freight in question here arrived in Detroit, the terminus of the Michigan Company, who telegraphed defendants' agent, the day before its destruction by fire, that it was in store, and requested them to forward it. It also appeared that at this time defendants had such an accumulation of freight on hand that they could not transport, it all over their line, and could not therefore receive plaintiff's goods which were destroyed by fire at the Michigan Company's Station in Detroit the day after the defendants were advised of their arrival. In an action against defendants for the value of the goods, charging a refusal on their part to receive them, in consequence of which they became lost to plaintiff, *Held*, that plaintiff could not recover for that the receipt-note given by the Michigan Company, formed the basis of the contract to carry, and that they became the carriers ; but that they only undertook to carry over their line of road, and were plaintiff's agents to deliver over the merchandize to defendants to be carried to Toronto; but that the understanding between the Michigan Company and defendants, that the latter would, on certain terms, carry on the former's freight to Canada, created no privity between defendants and plaintiff, so as to enable him to sue defendants for not carrying out that arrangement; and that, even if defendants were bound to receive the merchandize at Detroit, for carriage to Toronto, the evidence shewed that they were not liable for not receiving, owing to

the overcrowded state of their premises, and the pressure of freight upon them.

Held, also, that plaintiff could not, in any case, recover more than nominal damages, if even that, as the value of the goods, which had been destroyed by fire, would not be the damages which would naturally flow from a breach of contract, or refusal to carry, in disregard of defendants' common law obligation to do so ; for that the loss by fire arose from the omission to insure, and it would by no means follow that, even if defendants had received the property, it might not have been on the express condition of exemption from liability in that event.

Held, also, that the condition that "the Company" should not be liable for loss from Providential causes, or from fire from any cause what-ever, &c., applied to the Michigan Company alone, and not to defendants also.—*Crawford v. G. W. R. Co.*, 18 *C. P.* 511.

Commercial.

Toronto Market.

Trade has improved somewhat since the beginning of the new year ; but there is not much activity in any branch.

Groceries.—Business, since the beginning of the week, has been a little more brisk ; there is a good deal doing with city buyers. *Teas.*—Several lines of medium have met with a better enquiry from jobbers. Considerable sales of half-chests greens have been made in New York on English orders. *Sugars*.—Quiet and unchanged.

Produce.—*Wheat.*—Receipts 8,360 bushels, and 10,050 bushels last week. There is more demand for Spring, chiefly of a local character, and sales of several carloads occurred at $1 02 to $1 03. Midge proof would bring the same figures but is not offered. *Fall*, there is a fair demand for good samples, which are worth $1 10 to $1 12. Nothing prime could be bought below $1 14 to $1 15, owing to its scarcity and to the fact that it is held in few hands. *Barley.*—Receipts by cars 959 bushels and 870 bush. last week. The market is unchanged at $1 25 to $1 27 ; we notice greater activity in the New York market. There are one or two large holders here who are confident of a rise to a point far above present quotations before our Winter is over. *Peas.*—Receipts, slight.— The market is quiet at quotations. *Oats.*—Receipts 4,800 bush. and 2,400 bush. last week. Sales of eight to ten cars occurred at 53 to 54c. delivered in the city, the market closing at 52c. on the track.

Flour.—Receipts, 1,225 bbls, and 3200 bbls. last week. There are buyers of No. 1 superfine at $4.50 to $4.55, and sales of 500 barrels occurred at $4.55, and 400 bbls. at $4.60. Other grades nominal and not quoted.

Provisions.—*Dressed Hogs*—The market was active throughout the week, and closed from 75c. to $1 higher than last week. One or two lots sold at $9.50, and medium lots brought $9 freely. Some very light sold as low as $8.62½. In other provisions nothing doing.

St. John Markets.

Breadstuffs—The demand continues to be very light, and there is no change in prices. Superfine continues to rate at $5.90 to $6 for ordinary brands of Canada, favorite qualities bringing 10c to 15c above the outside rate. Arrivals are in excess of sales, and the stock is not diminishing.

Flour and Meal—Duty : free, except oatmeal, 15 per cent.

Extra State, per brl	$5.75 to 6.00
Canada Superfine	5.90 to 6.00
Canada Choice	6.00 to 6.15
Family and Pastry	7.25 to 7.50
Rye Flour	6.00 to 6.25
Oatmeal	7.50 to 7.55
Cornmeal	4.50 to 4.50

Arrivals of flour have kept up late in the year and the stock now on hand is estimated at 20,000 to 25,000 barrels. Of course, as usual at this date, the demand is small, and will continue for two months to come, hence there is not much to encourage holders in looking for high prices. The year has been an unprofitable one to millers and dealers in flour, there being very little indeed who will go out of the year 1868 without loss. A new feature in the flour trade of the past year has been the opening of some trade with the distant port of Milwaukee; some thousands of barrels having been received from there. We believe this trade has been without profit to the importers. Present appearances indicate that low prices will prevail during the winter and spring.

A Duty on Salt.

A petition has been gotten up by W. T. Hayes, Esq., M.P.P., which has been already signed by sixty-four members of the Local Legislature, for presentation to the House of Commons when it meets. It runs as follows:

"We the undersigned members of the Local Legislature of Ontario, would most respectfully represent to your Honorable body, that the discovery of salt at Goderich, in the county of Huron is an event of great importance not only to the Province but to the whole Dominion of Canada, and we also most respectfully wish to represent to your Honorable body, that salt manufactured in the United States of America, is permitted to be imported into this Province free from duty, and that the Government of the United States exact a duty of seventy cents in gold on every barrel of salt exported from this Province into the said United States. That we look upon this state of affairs as unjust in the extreme, and hope that your Honorable body will take the matter into your serious consideration, and give such relief the premises as to your Honorable body in your wisdom may seem meet."

Petroleum.

The movement at New-York for the period mentioned was—

Receipts for week ending Jan. 5....pkgs.	16,1
Exports " " ....galls.	203,7
Exports from Jan. 1 ....galls.	203,7
Exports same time last year....galls.	342,0

The following is the quantity exported from other ports :

	1868.	1867
From Boston....galls.	2,410,114	2,241,4
Philadelphia. "	32,921,691	29,083,0
Baltimore.... "	2,587,707	1,514,0
Portland...... "	705,107	
Cleveland.... "	270,000	
Total...... "	45,894,619	32,840,4
Total exports from United States....	98,697,821	66,674,0
Same time in 1866.		66,919,0
Same time in 1865.		29,072,0

Stock in yard January 1 :

	1869.	186.
Crude ....bbls.	9,900	32,0
Refined .... "	*49,000	3,0
Nepha .... "	300	3,0
Residum .... "		
Total.................... "	59,200	40,0
Stock December 1....................		26,

Halifax Market.

Breadstuffs—San. 5.—Flour: There has been no activity in the market the past week, and without quotable change ; prices have been unfavorable to buyers. The receipts for the week have been large, are in excess of the demand. Canada No. 1 ordinary Supers, $6.25 ; choice $6.35 to $6.40 ; Strong Bakers', $6.50 to $6.75 ; Extra, $7.25 to $7.75 ; Extra State dull at $6.00 to $6.40 ; No. 2, $5.00 to $5.30. Corn Meal Kiln dried unchanged at $4.75 to $5.00 ; Fresh Ground, dull. Oatmeal, $8.00. Imports from January 1st to December 31st, 1867 and 1868

	Bbls. Flour.	Bbls. Oatmeal.
68	191,941	48,698
37	190,563	48,680

,—All the descriptions remain firm at our
ons, although the market shares the gene-
liness prevailing during the holidays.
Cod, large hard cured, $4.00 to $4.25 ;
$3.20 to $3.30 ; Bay and Bank none ;
or, $2.25 to $2.50. Haddock—Good hard
Arichat, $2.00 to $2.10 ; Eastern Shore,
o $1.90 ; Western, $1.60 to $1.65. Her-
'ithout change; Bay Island Bank selling
) to $2.30 ; Split, $3.50 to $4.00 ; Round,
o $3.25. Bay, $16.25 to $16.50 for No. 1;
to 14.50 for No. 2 ; $7.80 for No. 3.
nchanged.

sh—

Tres.	Drums.	Boxes.	Hf-boxes.
36,641	19,821	26,982	18,905
36,710	20,203	23,713	12,381

Fish—

12,493	5,791	1,231	530
7,848	9,800	1,043	562

Salmon, Mackerel, Herring, Alewives

bbls.	bbls.	bbls.	bbls.
8,897	43,514	69,396	7,771
9,927	58,511	58,643	9,522

† INDIA PRODUCE.—Without change ;
very small, and in one or two hands.
goe Molasses, 29½c to 30c per gal. Sugars
ged ; demand small, and only for local
Rum—Stocks very light ; quotations
l Imports from January 1st, to December
67 and 1868 :
ses, 1868—11,030 puns., 1,112 trcs., 843
807—10,068 puns., 965 trcs., 1,052 bbls.
1868—9,096 hhds; 984 trcs., 4,591 bbls.,
es; 1867—6,340 hhds., 340 trcs., 3,263
Rum, 1868—1,153 puns. ; 1867—2,345

s in wareyouse, December 31, 1867 and

ses, 1868—200 puns., 14 trcs., 10 bbls. ;
572 puns., 7 trcs. Sugar, 1868—760 hhds.,
294 bbls., 26 boxes ; 1877—179 hhds.,
s, 7 boxes. Rum, 1868—94 puns., 1
bbls ; 1867—561 puns., 4 hhds.
NCIAL.—Bank drawing rates, London 60
2½ percent premium. New York, Gold
d' Sight, 3½ per cent premium. Currency
'23 per cent discount. Montreal Sight
3½ per cent premium. New Brunswick
Drafts, 3 per cent, premium. Newfund-
gilt Drafts, 5 per cent. premium. Private
to 1 per cent. lower than bank rates.
t on American Invoices at Customs tells
) per cent.—R. C. Hamilton & Co.'s Cir-

Refiners' Association of Canada.

sove Association hereby give notice that an Office
been opened

AT LONDON, ONTARIO,

FOR THE SALE OF ALL

REFINED PETROLEUM OIL,

by the Association, at the following Rates and
ns :

OF ONE TO FOUR CAR LOADS, INCLUSIVE, AT
35 CENTS PER GALLON.

OF FIVE CAR LOADS AND UPWARDS, AT 32 CENTS
PER GALLON.

erms—Cash, free on board, at London.

l sold to be received at the place of shipment by
haser ; and in the event of his failing to appoint
to inspect and receive the oil, it must be under-
t it will in all cases be subject to the Inspector's
d by the Association ; and after shipment is
o drawbacks on account of quality, quantity,
, or otherwise, will be allowed.
lers to be addressed to the Secretary, and all
ces to be made to the Treasurer.

SAMUEL PETERS, President.
WM. DUFFIELD, Vice-President.
L. C. LEONARD, Secretary.
CHARLES HUNT, Treasurer.

Ont., Jan. 5, 1869.　22-tf

THE CONNECTICUT MUTUAL

LIFE INSURANCE COMPANY,

HARTFORD, CONNECTICUT.

WOODBRIDGE S. OLMSTEAD, SECRETARY,　GUY R. PHELPS, PRESIDENT,
EDWIN W. BRYANT, ACTUARY,　ZEPHANIAH PRESTON, VICE PRESIDENT.
LUCIAN S. WILCOX, MEDICAL EXAMINER.

Organized in 1846.　Charter Perpetual.

The Largest Mutual Life Insurance Company.　Numbering Over 75,000 Members.

BEING A PURELY MUTUAL COMPANY, ITS ASSETS BELONG EXCLUSIVELY TO ITS MEMBERS.

ASSETS, $21,000,000.—Acquired by prudent and economical management of twenty-two years, without the aid of
a single dollar of original capital.
SURPLUS ASSETS, $6,861,967.—All profits divided among the members. Each policy holder is a member. There are
no stockholders.
ITS DIVIDENDS—Have averaged over 50 per cent. annually.　Total amount of dividends paid the members since its
organization, $4,897,142.
ITS SUCCESS UNPARALLELED—It has arrived at the extraordinary condition where the income from annual interest
alone is more than sufficient to pay all the losses. Total amount of losses paid by the Company, $6,866,623.
ITS RESPONSIBILITY—For every $1.0 of liabilities it has $154 of assets.
LAST YEAR'S PROSPEROUS BUSINESS.
Amount insured fiscal year, 1867 ..... $45,647,191 00 | Income received fiscal year, 1867..... $7,586,886 19
During its last fiscal year this Company paid to its living members, and to the families of deceased members,
nearly $2,000,000, and at the same time added more than four millions to its accumulated capital.
The whole record of this Company has been one of prudent management and prosperous advancement. Among the
older and leading Life Insurance Companies the average ratio of expenses to income has, throughout its entire history, been
the lowest of any.
ITS LIBERALITY—It accommodates the insured by giving credit for part premium, and grants insurance to meet
all the contingencies and wants to which Life Insurance is applicable.
It issues policies on a single life from $100 to $15,000.
MEDICAL REFEREES—J. WIDMER ROLPH, M.D.; H. H. WRIGHT, M.D.

OFFICE —— No. 90 King Street East, Toronto.
J. D. FEE, AGENT, TORONTO.　DANIEL L. SILLS, GENERAL MANAGER FOR CANADA.
Toronto, December 24, 1868.　12-1y

INTERESTING TO LIFE AGENTS.

AGENT'S

MONETARY LIFE

AND

VALUATION TABLES,

WITH VALUABLE EXPLANATIONS.

A New Work by D. PARKS FACKLER, Esq.,
CONSULTING ACTUARY.

THIS is an interesting and valuable work. Every Life
Agent should have a copy.

For sale at the office of the MONETARY TIMES, No. 60
Church street.

GRISWOLD'S

Handbook of the Adjustment of Fire Losses,

The most complete Manual of Adjustment ever published. Handsomely gotten up in blue cloth.

For sale at the office of THE MONETARY TIMES, No. 60
Church street.

Toronto, Jan. 7, 1869.　21-tf

Montreal Telegraph Company.

NOTICE IS HEREBY GIVEN, that the Annual General Meeting of the Shareholders will be held at the
Company's Office in Montreal, on FRIDAY, the 8th day of
January next, at ONE o'clock P.M., to elect Directors for
the ensuing year, and generally to transact the business of
the Company.
A Dividend of FIVE per cent. for the Half-year ending
30th November has been declared upon the Capital Stock,
which will be payable at the Offices of the Company on
and after FRIDAY, the 8th January.
The Transfer Books will be closed from the 31st December till after the General Meeting.

By order of the Board.
JAMES DAKERS,
Secretary.
December 24, 1868.　8-20.

TORONTO PRICES CURRENT.—JANUARY 14, 1869.

Name of Article.	Wholesale Rates.		Name of Article.	Wholesale Rate.		Name of Article.	
	$ c.	$ c.	**Groceries**—Contin'd	$ c.	$ c.	**Leather**—Contin'd	
Boots and Shoes.			" fine to fan't ..	0 85	0 95	Kip Skins, Patna	
Mens' Thick Boots ...	2 00	2 50	Hyson	0 45	0 80	French	
" Kip	2 50	3 25	Imperial	0 42	0 80	English	
" Calf	3 60	3 70	Tobacco, Manufac'd:			Hemlock Calf (30 to	
" Congress Gaiters..	2 00	2 50	Can Leaf, ⅌ lb 5s & 10s..	0 26	0 30	35 lbs.) per doz....	
" Kip Cobourgs..	1 15	1 45	Western Leaf, com...	0 25	0 26	Do. light	
Boys' Thick Boots.....	1 60	1 90	" Good	0 27	0 32	French Calf	
Youths' "	1 35	1 50	" Fine	0 32	0 35	Grain & Sat'n Cit'dins.	
Women's Baits	95	1 30	" Bright fine..	0 40	0 50	Splits, large ⅌ lb....	
" Congress Gaiters..	1 15	1 45	" choice ..	0 00	0 75	" small	
Misses' Baits	0 75	1 00	**Hardware.**			Enamelled Cow ⅌ foot..	
" Congress Gaiters.	1 00	1 30	Tin (retail prices)			Patent	
Girls' Baits	0 60	0 85	Block, ⅌ lb	0 25	0 26	Pebble Grain	
" Congress Gaiters..	0 80	1 10	Grain	0 25	0 26	Buff	
Children's C.T. Caeks,.	0 50	0 65	Copper:			**Oils.**	
" Gaiters	0 65	0 90	Pig	0 23	0 24	Cod	
Drugs.			Sheet	0 30	0 33	Lard, extra	
Aloes Cape. .,...	0 12½	0 16	Cut Nails:			" No. 1	
Alum	0 02½	0 03	Assorted ½ Shingles,			" Woollen	
Borax	0 00	0 00	⅌ 100 lbs.........	2 90	3 00	Lubricating, patent...	
Camphor, refined.....	0 65	0 70	Shingle alone do	3 15	3 25	" Moll's economic	
Castor Oil...........	0 18	0 28	Lath> and 5 dy.....	3 30	3 40	Linseed, raw.........	
Caustic Soda.........	0 04½	0 05	Galvanized Iron:			" boiled.....	
Cochineal...........	0 90	1 00	Assorted sizes........	0 08	0 09	Machinery	
Cream Tartar........	0 25	0 30	Best No. 24.........	0 23	0 00	Olive, 2nd, ⅌ gal....	
Epsom Salts	0 03	0 04	" No. 26......	0 08	0 09	" salad	
Extract Logwood.....	0 00	0 11	" 28........	0 00	0 09½	" salad, in bots.	
Gum Arabic, sorts....	0 30	0 35	Horse Nails:			qt. ⅌ case...	
Indigo, Madras.......	0 75	1 00	Guest's or Griffin's			Sesame salad, ⅌ gal.	
Licorice	0 14	0 45	assorted sizes.......	0 00	0 00	Seal, pale...........	
Madder.............	0 16	0 18	Fox W. ass'd sizes....	0 18	0 19	Spirits Turpentine ...	
Nutgalls	0 00	0 00	Patent Hammer'd do..	0 17	0 18	Varnish	
Opium..............	6 70	7 00	Iron (at 4 months):			Whale	
Oxalic Acid.........	0 28	0 85	Pig—Gartsherrie No 1..	24 00	25 00	**Paints, &c.**	
Potash, Bi-cart......	0 25	0 38	Other brands. No 1..	23 00	24 00	White Lead, genuine	
" Bichromate...	0 15	0 20	No 2..	0 00	0 00	in Oil, ⅌ 25 lbs....	
Potass Iodide	3 80	4 50	Bar—Scotch, ⅌ 100 lb..	2 25	2 50	Do. No. 1 "	
Senna	0 12½	0 60	Refined	2 35	3 25	" 2 "	
Soda Ash	0 03	0 04	Swedes	3 60	3 50	" 3 "	
Soda Bicarb	4 50	5 50	Hoops—Coopers...	3 00	3 25	White Zinc, genuine..	
Tartaric Acid........	0 37½	0 45	Band	3 05	3 25	White Lead, dry......	
Verdigris...........	0 35	0 40	Boiler Plates	3 25	3 50	Red Lead............	
Vitriol, Blue.........	0 09	0 10	Canada Plates......	4 00	4 25	Venetian Red, Eng'h..	
Groceries.			Union Jack	0 00	0 00	Yellow Ochre, Fren'h..	
Coffees:			Pontypool.........	4 00	4 25	Whiting	
Java, ⅌ lb...........	0 22	0 24	Swansea	3 90	4 00	**Petroleum.**	
Laguayra, ...	0 17	0 18	Lead (at 4 months):			(Refined ⅌ gal.)	
Rio, ...	0 13	0 17	Bar, ⅌ 100 lbs......	0 07	0 07½	Water white, car'd ..	
Fish:			Sheet "	0 00	0 00	" small lots..	
Herrings, Lab. split..	5 75	6 50	Shot.	0 07½	0 07½	Straw, by car load...	
" round...	4 00	4 75	Iron Wire (net cash):			" small lots...	
" souled....	0 35	0 40	No. 6, ⅌ bundle ...	2 70	2 80	Amber, by car load...	
Mackerel, small kitts...	1 90	0 00	" 8, " ...	3 10	3 20	" small lots	
Loch. Her. wh'brks..	2 50	2 75	" 9, " ...	3 40	3 50	Benzine	
" half " ..	1 25	1 50	" 10, " ...	4 30	4 40		
White Fish & Tront...	3 50	3 75	Powder:			**Produce.**	
Salmon, saltwater.....	14 00	15 00	Blasting, Canada....	3 50	6 00	Grain:	
Dry Cod, ⅌112 lbs...	5 00	5 25	FF "	4 25	4 60	Wheat, Spring, 60 lb..	
Fruit:			FFF "	4 75	5 00	" Fall " ..	
Raisins, Layers	2 00	2 10	Blasting, English ...	4 10	5 00	Barley.... 48 " ..	
" M. R......	1 90	2 10	FF louse..	5 00	6 00	Peas........ 60 " ..	
" Valentias new..	0 0½	0 7	FFF " ..	6 00	6 50	Oats........ 34 " ..	
Currants, new	0 07	0 07½	Pressed Spikes (4 mos):..			Rye......... 56 " ..	
" old......	0 04½	0 04½	Regular sizes 10¢....	4 00	4 25	Seeds:	
Figs	0 14	0 00	Extra "	4 50	5 00	Clover, choice 60 " ..	
Molasses:			Tin Plates (net cash):			" com'n " ..	
Clayed, ⅌ gal......	0 00	0 35	IC Coke	0 49	0 50	Timothy, cho'e 4 " ..	
Syrups, Standard	0 49	0 50	IC Charcoal........	8 25	8 50	" inf. to good 48 " ..	
" Golden ...	0 55	0 57½	IX "	10 25	10 75	Flax....... 56 " ..	
Rice:			IXX "	12 25	0 00	Flour (per brl.):	
Arracan	4 50	4 75	DC "	7 25	9 00	Superior extra.......	
"			DX "	9 50	0 00	Extra superfine,.....	
Spices:			**Hides & Skins ⅌lb**			Fancysuperfine	
Cassia, whole, ⅌ lb...	0 00	0 43				Superfine No 1	
Cloves	0 11	0 12	Green rough	0 06	0 06½	" No. 2..	
Nutmegs	0 45	0 55	Green, salt'd & insp'd..	0 00	0 07	Oatmeal, (per brl.)...	
Ginger, ground	0 20	0 25	Cured	0 08	0 08½	**Provisions.**	
" Jamaica, root..	0 20	0 25	Calfskins, green......	0 00	0 10	Butter, dairy tub ⅌ lb.	
Pepper, black........	0 09½	0 10	Calfskins, cured	0 00	0 12	" store packed..	
Pimento	0 08	0 09	" dry......	0 18	0 20	Cheese, new	
Sugars:			Shoepskins, ...	1 00	1 20	Pork, mess, per brl...	
Port Rico, ⅌ lb......	0 08½	0 08½	" country...	0 00	0 89	" prime mess...	
Cuba "	0 08½	0 08½				" prime......	
Barbadoes (bright)..	0 08½	0 09	**Hops.**			Bacon, rough	
Dry Crushed, at 60d...	0 11½	0 11½	Inferior, ⅌ lb........	0 05	0 07	" Cumberld cut..	
Canada Sugar Refine'y,			Medium	0 07	0 09	" smoked	
yellow No. 2, 60 ds..	0 09	0 00	Good	0 09	0 12	Hams, in salt.......	
Yellow, No. 2½.......	0 09½	0 00	Fancy	0 00	0 00	" sug'r cur & sm'd,,	
" No. 3.....	0 09½	0 00				Shoulders, in salt	
Crushed X	0 10	0 10½				Lard, in kegs........	
" A	0 11½	0 00	**Leather,** @ (4 mos.)			Eggs, packed........	
Ground.............	0 11½	0 11½	Spanish Sole, 1st qual..			Tallow	
Dry Crushed	0 11	0 11½	heavy, weights ⅌ lb...	0 00	0 23	Hogs dressed, heavy...	
Extra Ground........	0 12½	0 12½	Do. 1st qual middle do..	0 00	0 23	" medium...	
Teas:			Do. No. 2, all weights..	0 23	0 21	" light......	
Japan, com'n to good..	0 40	0 55	Slaughter heavy	0 25	0 26	**Salt, &c.**	
" Fine to choicest..	0 55	0 65	Do. light...........	0 24	0 25	American bris........	
Colored, com. to fine..	0 60	0 75	Harness, best	0 32	0 34	Liverpool coarse	
Congou & Souch'ng..	0 42	0 75	" No. 2	0 30	0 33	Plaster	
Oolong, good to fine..	0 50	0 65	Upper heavy........	0 44	0 49	Water Lime	
Y. Hyson, com to gd..	0 45	0 55	" light.......	0 36	0 40		
Medium to choice ..	0 65	0 80					
Extra choice	0 85	0 95					
unpowd'r c. to med...	0 55	0 70					
" med. to fine.	0 70	0 84					

Candles.	$ c.	$ c.
ord & Co.'s ..		
erial........	0 07½	0 08
len Bar	0 07	0 07½
er Bar........	0 07	0 07½
....	0 05	0 05½
....	0 03½	0 03½
....	0 00	0 11½
s, Liquors, &c.		
, per doz.......	2 60	2 65
ss Dub Portr..	2 35	2 40
maica Rum....	1 80	2 25
per's H. Gin..	1 55	1 65
Old Tom......	1 90	2 00
cases.........	4 00	4 25
Old Tom, c...	6 00	6 25
mmon	1 00	1 25
e old	2 00	4 00
common	1 00	1 50
dium........	1 70	1 80
ale or golden..	2 50	4 00

	$ c.	$ c.
Brandy:		
Hennessy's, per gal..	2 .0	2 50
Martell's " ..	2 30	2 50
J. Robin & Co.'s " ..	2 25	2
Otard, Dupuy & Cos..	2 25	2
Brandy, cases........	8 50	9 00
Brandy, com. per c...	4 00	4 50
Whiskey:		
Common 36 u. p.......	0 62½	0 65
Old Rye	0 85	0 87½
Malt	0 85	0 87½
Toddy	0 85	0 87½
Scotch, per gal........	1 90	2 10
Irish—Kinnahan's c...	7 00	7 50
" Dunnville's Belf't..	6 00	6 25
Wool.		
Fleece, lb..............	0 28	0 35
Pulled "	0 22	0 25
Furs.		
Bear....................	3 00	10,00
Beaver..................	1 00	1 25
Coon	0 20	0 40
Fisher..................	4 00	6 00
Martin..................	1 40	1 60
Mink....................	4 00	4 25
Otter...................	5 75	6 00
Spring Rats.............	0 15	0 17
Fox.....................	1 20	1 25

SURANCE COMPANIES.

ENGLISH.—*Quotations on the London Market.*

Last Dividend.	Name of Company.	Shares parval £	Amount paid.	Last Sale.
	Briton Medical and General Life...	10	....	1½
7½	Commer'l Union, Fire, Life and Mar.	50	5	5½
8	City of Glasgow	25	2½	5½
9½	Edinburgh Life	100	15	31½
5—½ yr	European Life and Guarantee.......	2½	11s6	5s
10	Etna Fire and Marine..............	10	1½	0
5	Guardian	100	50	51½
12	Imperial Fire.....................	500	50	0
9½	Imperial Life	100	10	15½
10	Lancashire Fire and Life..........	20	2	2½
11	Life Association of Scotland......	40	7½	25
45s. p. sh	London Assurance Corporation ..	25	12½	49
5	London and Lancashire Life	10	1	19s.
40	Liverp'l & London & Globe F. & L.	20	2	6 15-16ths
5	National Union Life	5	1	0
12½	Northern Fire and Life............	100	5	11½
12 '63, bo 5s.	North British and Mercantile	50	6½	19½
50	Ocean Marine	25	5	19½
£5 12s.	Provident Life....................	100	10	0
£4½ p. s.	Phœnix............................	....	....	148
2½—h. yr.	Queen Fire and Life	10	1	17s
3s. bo. 4s	Royal Insurance...................	20	3	6
10	Scottish Provincial Fire and Life ..	50	2½	5
25	Standard Life	50	12	65½
5	Star Life	25	1½	—
	CANADIAN.			℘ c.
4	British America Fire and Marine ..	$50	$25	57½
4	Canada Life	....	....	....
12	Montreal Assurance	£50	£5	135
3	Provincial Fire and Marine........	60	11	......
5	Quebec Fire	40	32½	23½
8	" Marine..........................	100	40	90
5 7 mo's.	Western Assurance.................	40	9	......

RAILWAYS.	Sha's	Paid	Montr	London.
and St. Lawrence................	£100	All.	....	58 60
nd Lake Huron	20½	"	....	3 3½
do Preference	10	"	....	5½ 6½
antt. & Goderich, 6℘c., 1872-3-4...	100	"	....	65 69
in and St. Lawrence	....	....	10	....
do Pref. 10 ℘ ct.	....	....	73	....
runk	100	"	15 16	15½ 16
Eq. G. M. Bds. 1 ch. 6℘c........	100	"	....	84 86
First Preference, 5 ℘ c	100	"	....	49 51
Deferred, 3 ℘ ct.	100	"	....	....
Second Pref. Bonds, 5℘c.........	100	"	....	38 40
do Deferred, 3 ℘ ct	100	"	....	....
Third Pref. Stock, 4 ℘ct........	100	"	....	26 28
do. Deferred, 3 ℘ ct.	100	"	....	....
Fourth Pref. Stock, 3℘c.........	100	"	....	17½ 18½
do. Deferred, 3 ℘ ct.	100	"	....	....
estern	20½	"	13 14	14½ 14½
New	20½	18	....	....
6 ℘ c. Bds, due 1873-76.........	100	All.	....	99 101
5½ ℘c Bds. due 1877-78..........	100	"	....	93 94
Railway, Halifax, $250, all.....	$250	"	....	....
, of Canada, 6℘c. 1st Pref. Bds...	100	"	....	80 83

EXCHANGE.	Halifax.	Montr'l.	Quebec.	Toronto.
London, 60 days				
r 75 days date	12½	9½ 9½	9½ 9½	9½
do.	11½ 12	8 9	8½ 9	9
with documents........	....	7½ 8	....	....
New York..............	....	25½ 26	24½ 25	74½
do.	....	26 26½	25 25½	....
fts do.	....	par	par ½ dis.	par ½ dis.
....	....	4 4½	....	8½ 5

STOCK AND BOND REPORT.

The dates of our quotations are as follows:—Toronto, Jan. 12; Montreal, Jan. 4; Quebec, Jan. 11; London, Dec. 24.

NAME.	Shares.	Paid up.	Divid'd last 6 Months	Dividend Day.	CLOSING PRICES. Toronto.	Montre'l	Quebec
BANKS.			℘ ct.				
British North America	$250	All.	3	July and Jan.	101½ 102	....	101 101½
Jacques Cartier..............	50	"	4	1 June, 1 Dec.	107 108	107 108	106 107
Montreal	200	"	5	"	138½ 139	138½	137½ 138½
Nationale....................	50	"	4	1 Nov. 1 May.	105 106	105 106½	106½ 106½
New Brunswick	100	"	......	......	....	...	....
Nova Scotia	200	28	7&b$3½	Mar. and Sept.	....	....	....
Du Peuple....................	50	"	4	1 Mar., 1 Sept.	108 108½	108½	108 108½
Toronto	100	"	4	1 Jan., 1 July.	118 x.d	115 117	116 117½
Bank of Yarmouth.............	....	....	....				
Canadian Bank of Com'e.......	50	95	......	......	101½ 102	102 103	101 102
City Bank Montreal	80	All.	4	1 June, 1 Dec.	101 101½	100 101½	101½ 102½
Commer'l Bank (St. John).....	100	"	℘ ct.		....		....
Eastern Townships' Bank......	50	"	4	1 July, 1 Jan.	....	96½ 100	96 96½
Gore	40	...	none.	1 Jan., 1 July.	35 40	40 42	35 40
Halifax Banking Company......	...	...	......	.....	...	....	....
Mechanics' Bank..............	50	70	4	1 Nov., 1 May.	94 96	94 96	94 95
Merchants' Bank of Canada....	100	70	4	1 Jan., 1 July.	105½ 106	106 106½	105 106
Merchants' Bank (Halifax)....	....	....	.....				....
Molson's Bank................	50	All.	4	1 Apr., 1 Oct.	110 110½	110½ 110½	109 110
Niagara District Bank........	100	70	3½	1 Jan., 1 July.	...	....	....
Ontario Bank.................	40	All.	4	1 June, 1 Dec.	100 100½	99½ 100½	99 100
People's Bank (Fred'kton)....	100	"	......	......	....	....	. ..
People's Bank (Halifax)......	20	"	7 12 m	......	....	...	....
Quebec Bank	100	"	3½	1 June, 1 Dec.	98 100	....	99½ 100
Royal Canadian Bank	50	50	4	1 Jan., 1 July.	84 86	....	85 87
St. Stephens Bank	100	All	.....	.....			
Union Bank	100	70	4	1 Jan., 1 July.	103 103½	102½ 103½	103½ 104½
Union Bank (Halifax).........	100	40	7 12mo	Feb. and Aug.	....		
MISCELLANEOUS.							
British America Land.........	250	44	2½	......	....	....	....
British Colonial S. S. Co....	250	32½	2½	......	...	....	....
Canada Company	32½	All.	5	......	....	....	....
Canada Landed Credit Co......	50	$20	3½	......	70 72	....	....
Canada Per. B'ldg Society....	50	All.	5	......	121 122	....	....
Canada Mining Company........	4	90	......	......	....	....	....
Do. Inl'd Steam Nav. Co.....	100	All.	20 12 m	......	....	106½ 107½	107 108
Do. Glass Company...........	100	"	12½ "	......	....	....	....
Canad'n Loan & Investm't.....	25	2½	7	......	....	....	....
Canada Agency	10	½	......	......	....	....	....
Colonial Securities Co.......	....	....	......	......	....	....	....
Freehold Building Society....	100	All.	4	......	105½ 106	....	....
Halifax Steamboat Co.........	100	"	5	......	....	....	....
Halifax Gas Company..........	....	....	......	......	....	....	....
Hamilton Gas Company.........	....	....	......	......	....	....	....
Huron Copper Bay Co..........	4	12	20	......	....	25 40cps	....
Lake Huron S. and C..........	5	102	......	......	....	....	....
Montreal Mining Consols......	20	$15	......	......	....	3.00 3.05	...
Do. Telegraph Co............	40	All.	5	......	134 135	132xd.	Bks cl'd
Do. Elevating Co............	00	"	15 12 m	......	....	100 102½	....
Do. City Gas Co.............	40	"	4	15 Mar. 15 Sep.	....	136	134 135
Do. City Pass. R. Co........	50	"	5	......	....	110 111	110½ 111
Nova Scotia Telegraph	20	"	......	......	....	....	....
Quebec and L. S..............	8	$4	......	......	...	....	25 cts
Quebec Gas Co................	200	All.	4	1 Mar., 1 Sep.	....	....	119 120
Quebec Street R. R...........	50	25	8	......	....	....	90 95
Richelieu Navigation Co......	100	All.	7 p.a.	1 Jan., 1 July.	....	114 116	116 117
St. Lawrence Tow Boat Co.....	100	"	......	3 Feb.	....	....	40 45
Tor'to Consumers' Gas Co.....	50	"	2 3 m.	1 My Au Mar Fe	106½ 107	....	105½ 106½
Trust & Loan Co. of U. C.....	20	5	3	......	....	....	...
West'n Canada Bldg Soc'y.....	50	All.	5	......	113½ 114	....	....

SECURITIES.	London.	Montreal.	Quebec.	Toronto.
Canadian Gov't Deb. 6 ℘ ct. stg............	....	103	102½ 103	103 105
Do. do. 6 do due Ja. & Jul. 1877-84........	106½ 107½	....	....	....
Do. do. 6 do. Feb. & Aug...................	105 107	....	....	....
Do. do. 6 do. Mch. & Sep...................	105 107	....	....	....
Do. do. 5 ℘ ct. cur., 1883	94½ 95½	92½ 93½	92½ 93	93 93½
Do. do. 5 do. stg., 1885	94 96	92½ 93½	92 93½	93 93½
Do. do. 7 do. cur..........................	....	....	......	....
Dominion 6 p. c. 1878 cy...................	....	104½ 105	104 104½	104½ 105
Hamilton Corporation.......................	....	....	......	....
Montreal Harbor, 8 ℘ ct. d. 1869...........	....	....	......	....
Do. do. 7 do. 1870.........................	....	....	......	100 101
Do. do. 6½ do. 1875........................	....	101 102	......	....
Do. do. 6½ do. 1873........................	....	....	......	....
Do. Corporation, 6 ℘ c. 1891	....	94 95	95½ 95½	93 94
Do. 7 p. c. stock..........................	....	107 110	106½ 107½	107½ 108
Do. Water Works, 6 ℘ c. stg. 1878..........	....	....	......	94 96
Do. do. 6 do. cy. do.......................	....	95 96½	......	94 96
New Brunswick, 6 ℘ ct., Jan. and July	104 106	....	......	....
Nova Scotia, 6 ℘ ct., 1875.................	105 106	....	......	....
Ottawa City 6 ℘ c. d. 1880	....	....	......	....
Quebec Harbour, 6 ℘ c. d. 1883.............	....	....	60	....
Do. do. 7 do. do...........................	....	....	65 70	....
Do. do. 8 do. 1886.........................	....	....	80 85	....
Do. City, 7 ℘ c. d. 5 years	....	....	95 96	....
Do. do. 7 do. 9 do.........................	....	....	91 92	....
Do. do. 7 do. 2 do.........................	....	....	98 98½	....
Do. Water Works, 7 ℘ ct., 4 years..........	....	....	96 97	....
Do. do. 6 do. 2 do.........................	....	....	94 95	....
Toronto Corporation	....	....	...	....

Financial.

Niagara District Bank.

DIVIDEND No. 30.

NOTICE is hereby given that a dividend of Four per cent. on the capital stock of this institution, has this day been declared for the current half year, and that the same will be payable at the Bank, on and after Saturday, the 2nd January next.

The transfer books will be closed from the 20th to the 31st December, both days inclusive.

Also, that a GENERAL MEETING of the Shareholders, for the election of Directors to serve during the ensuing year, will be held at the Bank on MONDAY, the 11th day of January next, at noon.

By order of the Board,
C. M. ARNOLD, *Cashier.*

Niagara District Bank,
St. Catherines, Nov. 26, 1868.   16-td

Canada Permanent Building and Savings Society.

17TH HALF YEARLY DIVIDEND.

NOTICE is hereby given, that a dividend of FIVE per cent. on the capital Stock of this institution has been declared for the half year ending 31st inst., and the same will be payable at the Office of the Society, on and after Friday, the 8th day of January next.

The Transfer Books will be closed from the 20th to the 31st December, inclusive.

By order of the Board.
J. HERBERT MASON,
Secretary and Treasurer.

Toronto, December 9th, 1868.   17-td.

Western Canada Permanent Building and Savings Society.

11TH HALF YEARLY DIVIDEND.

NOTICE is hereby given, that a Dividend of FIVE per cent. on the Capital Stock of this Institution has been declared for the half year ending 31st day of December, inst., and that the same will be payable at the Office of the Society, No. 70 Church Street, on and after Friday, the 8th day of January next.

The Transfer Books will be closed from the 20th to the 31st December, inclusive.

By order of the Board.
WALTER S. LEE,
Secretary and Treasurer.

Toronto, Dec. 14, 1868.   17-td.

BROWN'S BANK,

(W. R. Brown. W. C. Chewett.)

60 KING STREET EAST, TORONTO,

TRANSACTS a general Banking Business, Buys and Sells New York and Sterling Exchange, Gold, Silver, U. S. Bonds and Uncurrent Money, receives Deposits subject to Cheque at sight, makes Collections and Discounts Commercial Paper.

Orders by Mail or Telegraph promptly executed at most favourable current quotations.

☞ Address letters,   "BROWN'S BANK,
36-y   *Toronto.*"

Honore Plamondon,

CUSTOM House Broker, Forwarder, and General Agent, Quebec. Office—Custom House Building.   17-1y

Sylvester, Bro. & Hickman,

COMMERCIAL Brokers and Vessel Agents. Office—No. 1 Ontario Chambers, [Corner Front and Church Sts.] Toronto.   2-6m

Candee & Co.,

BANKERS AND BROKERS, dealers in Gold and Silver Coin, Government Securities, &c., Corner Main and Exchange Streets. Buffalo, N. Y.   21-1v

H. N. Smith & Co.,

2 EAST SENECA STREET, BUFFALO, N. Y., (correspondent Smith, Gould, Martin & Co., 11 Broad Street, N.Y.,) Stock, Money and Exchange Brokers. Advances made on securities.   21-1y

Hurd, Leigh & Co.,

IMPORTERS AND DECORATORS OF FRENCH CHINA.

Hotels and families supplied with any pattern or crest desired.

Common goods always on hand.   72 Yonge Street, oronto, Ontario.   28y

Mercantile.

Teas! Teas!! Teas!!!

FRESH ARRIVALS

NEW CROP TEAS,

WINES, AND GENERAL GROCERIES,

Special Inducements given to

PROMPT PAYING PURCHASERS.

All Goods sold at very Lowest Montreal Prices!

W. & R. GRIFFITH,

ONTARIO CHAMBERS,
Corner of Front and Church Streets,
                TORONTO
6-1y   ONTARIO

TEAS.   Reford & Dillon   TEAS.

HAVE just received ex. steamships "St. David and Nestorian:"

1000 hlf. chests new season TEAS!
   Comprising Twankays, Young Hysons, Imperials, Gunpowders, colored and uncolored Japans, Congous, Souchongs, and Pekoes.
500 hlf. bxs. new Valentia Raisins (selected fruit).
500 bags cleaned Arracan and Rangoon Rice.
500 brls. choice Currants.

—ALSO IN STORE:—

250 hhds. bright Barbadoes and Cuba Sugars.
250 brls. Portland, Standard, Golden & Amber Syrups.
100 bags Rio, Jamaica, Lagnayra, and Java Coffees.
250 bxs. 10s Tobacco, "Queen's Own" and "Prince of Wales'" brands.

WITH A GENERAL AND

WELL SELECTED STOCK OF GROCERIES;

All of which they offer to the Trade low.

12 & 14 WELLINGTON STREET, TORONTO.
                            7-1y

Robert H. Gray,

Manufacturer of Hoop Skirts

AND

CRINOLINE STEEL,

IMPORTER OF

HABERDASHERY, TRIMMINGS

AND

GENERAL FANCY GOODS,

43, YONGE STREET, TORONTO, ONT.   6-1y

John Boyd & Co.,

WHOLESALE GROCERS AND COMMISSION MERCHANTS,

61 AND 63 FRONT STREET TORONTO.

NOW in store, direct from the European and West India Markets, a large assortment of General Groceries, comprising

Teas, Sugars, Coffees, Wines and Liquors,

AND

GENERAL GROCERIES.

Ship Chandlery, Canvas, Manilla and Tarred Rope, Oakum, Tar, Flags, &c., &c.,

DIRECT FROM THE MANUFACTURERS.

OHN BOYD.   ALEX. M. MONRO.   C. W. BUNTING.

Toronto, Oct. 1st, 1868.   7-1y

Mercantile.

UNRIVALLED!

THE BRITISH AMERICAN COMMERCIAL C

Consolidated with the

Bryant, Stratton and Odell Business

AND TELEGRAPHIC INSTITUTI

STANDS Pre-eminent and Unrivalled. It is th and MOST EFFICIENT. It employs the large Teachers, among whom are the two BEST PEI CANADA.

The TUITION FEE is the same as in other In having a similar object.

The PRICE OF BOARD is the same as in ot dian Cities.

In an EDUCATIONAL point of view, there i Institution in the country that has equal advan facilities.

YOUNG MEN intending to qualify themselve ness, will find it to their advantage to send for or call at the College Rooms, corner of King an streets.

Scholarships good in Montreal and throughout States.

            ODELL & TR
October 2.   Principals and Prop

The Mercantile Agency,

FOR THE

PROMOTION AND PROTECTION OF T

Established in 1841.

DUN, WIMAN & Co.

Montreal, Toronto and Halifax.

REFERENCE Book, containing names and Business Men in the Dominion, publish annually.

The St. Lawrence Glass Compan

ARE now manufacturing and have for sale,

COAL OIL LAMPS,
      various styles and sizes.

LAMP CHIMNEYS,
      of extra quality for ordinary Bur for the 'Comet' and 'Sun' Burners.

SETS OF

TABLE GLASSWARE, HYACINTH GLASSES,
   STEAM GUAGE TUBES, GLASS RODS, or any other article made to order, in White Glass.

KEROSENE BURNERS, COLLARS and SOCK be kept on hand.

DRUGGIST'S FLINT GLASSWARE, and PHILOSOPHICAL INSTRUMENTS, made to order.

OFFICE—388 ST. PAUL STREET, MONTI
           A. McK. COCHR
8-1y

Canadian Express Company,

GENERAL EXPRESS FORWARDERS, CUSTO BROKERS,

AND

SHIPPING AGENTS.

GOODS and VALUABLES forwarded by al Passenger Trains.

Reduced rates for all large consignments.
Reduced rates on Poultry, Butter, and other p principal markets in Canada and the United Sta
All perishable articles guaranteed against frost, without extra charge, nature of goods a to be stipulated in receipt at time of shipment.
Consignments for Lower Provinces taken t at low rates, and from thence by Steamer or required, securing quick dispatch.
A Weekly Express is made up for Europe, goods should be sent forward in time to reach t Friday each week.
Unsurpassed facilities as shipping agents in L Reduced rates on large Consignments from t at Portland.
For particulars, inquire at any of the princip Consignments solicited.

            G. CHEENY
16-3t   Superi

Insurance.

BEAVER
Mutual Insurance Association.

HEAD OFFICE—20 TORONTO STREET,
TORONTO.

INSURES LIVE STOCK against death from any cause. The only Canadian Company having authority to do this class of business.

R. L. DENISON,
President.
W. T. O'REILLY,
Secretary.   8-1y-25

HOME DISTRICT
Mutual Fire Insurance Company.

Office—North-West Cor. Yonge & Adelaide Streets,
TORONTO.—(UP STAIRS.)

INSURES Dwelling Houses, Stores, Warehouses, Merchandise, Furniture, &c.

PRESIDENT—The Hon. J. McMURRICH.
VICE-PRESIDENT—JOHN BURNS, Esq.
JOHN RAINS, Secretary.
AGENTS:
DAVID WRIGHT, Esq., Hamilton; FRANCIS STEVENS, Esq., Barrie; Messrs. GIBBS & BRO., Oshawa.   8-1y

THE PRINCE EDWARD COUNTY
Mutual Fire Insurance Company.

HEAD OFFICE—PICTON, ONTARIO.
President, L. B. STINSON; Vice-President, W. A. RICHARDS.
Directors : H. A. McFaul, James Cavan, James Johnson, N. S. DeMill, William Delong.—Treasurer, David Barker Secretary, John Twigg ; Solicitor, R. J. Fitzgerald.

THIS Company is established upon strictly Mutual principles, insuring farming and isolated property, (not hazardous,) in *Townships only*, and offers great advantages to insurers, at low rates *for five years*, without the expense of a renewal.
Picton, June 15, 1868.   9-1y

Hartford Fire Insurance Company.
HARTFORD, CONN.

Cash Capital and Assets over Two Million Dollars.

$2,026,220.29.

CHARTERED 1810.

THIS old and reliable Company, having an established business in Canada of more than thirty years standing, has complied with the provisions of the new Insurance Act, and made a special deposit of

$100,000

with the Government for the security of policy-holders, and will continue to grant policies upon the same favorable terms as heretofore.
Specially low rates on first-class dwellings and farm property for a term of one or more years.
Losses as heretofore promptly and equitably adjusted.
H. J. MORSE & CO., AGENTS.
Toronto, Ont.

ROBERT WOOD, GENERAL AGENT FOR CANADA]
50-6m

THE AGRICULTURAL
Mutual Assurance Association of Canada.

HEAD OFFICE .... LONDON, ONT.

A purely Farmers' Company. Licensed by the Government of Canada.

Capital, 1st January, 1868 .... $220,121 25
Cash and Cash Items, over.................. $65,000 0
No. of Policies in force.................... 28,769

THIS Company insures nothing more dangerous than Farm property. Its rates are as low as any well-established Company in the Dominion, and lower than those of a great many. It is largely patronised, and continues to grow in public favor.
For Insurance, apply to any of the Agents, or address the Secretary, London, Ontario.
London, 3rd Nov., 1868.   12-1y

Insurance.

The Gore District Mutual Fire Insurance Company

GRANTS INSURANCES on all description of Property against Loss or Damage by FIRE. It is the only Mutual Fire Insurance Company which assesses its Policies yearly from their respective dates ; and the average yearly cost of insurance in it, for the past three and a half years, has been nearly

TWENTY CENTS IN THE DOLLAR

less than what it would have been in an ordinary Proprietary Company.
THOS. M. SIMONS,
Secretary & Treasurer.
ROBT. McLEAN,
Inspector of Agencies.
Galt, 25th Nov., 1868.   15-1y

Geo. Girdlestone,

FIRE, Life, Marine, Accident, and Stock Insurance Agent
Very best Companies represented.
Windsor, Ont. June, 1868

The Standard Life Assurance Company,
Established 1825.
WITH WHICH IS NOW UNITED
THE COLONIAL LIFE ASSURANCE COMPANY.

Head Office for Canada:
MONTREAL—STANDARD COMPANY'S BUILDINGS,
No. 47 GREAT ST. JAMES STREET.
Manager—W. M. RAMSAY.   *Inspector*—RICH'D BULL.
THIS Company having deposited the sum of ONE HUNDRED AND FIFTY THOUSAND DOLLARS with the Receiver-General, in conformity with the Insurance Act passed last Session, Assurances will continue to be carried out at moderate rates and on all the different systems in practice.
AGENT FOR TORONTO—HENRY PELLATT,
KING STREET.
AGENT FOR HAMILTON—JAMES BANCROFT.
6-6mos.

Fire and Marine Assurance.

THE BRITISH AMERICA
ASSURANCE COMPANY.
HEAD OFFICE:
CORNER OF CHURCH AND COURT STREETS.
TORONTO:

BOARD OF DIRECTION :
Hon. G. W. Allan, M.L.C.,   A. Joseph, Esq.,
George J. Boyd, Esq.,   Peter Paterson, Esq.,
Hon. W. Cayley,   G. P. Ridout, Esq.,
Richard S. Cassels, Esq.,   E. H. Rutherford,Esq.,
Thomas C. Street, Esq.
Governor:
GEORGE PERCIVAL RIDOUT, Esq.
Deputy Governor:
PETER PATERSON, Esq.
Fire Inspector: Marine Inspector:
E. ROBY O'BRIEN.   CAPT. R. COURNEEN.
Insurances granted on all descriptions of property against loss and damage by fire and the perils of inland navigation.
Agencies established in the principal cities, towns, and ports of shipment throughout the Province.
THOS. WM. BIRCHALL,
Managing Director.
22-1y

Queen Fire and Life Insurance Company,
OF LIVERPOOL AND LONDON,
ACCEPTS ALL ORDINARY FIRE RISKS
on the most favorable terms.

LIFE RISKS
Will be taken on terms that will compare favorably with other Companies.

CAPITAL, - - - £2,000,000 Stg.

CHIEF OFFICES—Queen's Buildings, Liverpool, and Gracechurch Street London.
CANADA BRANCH OFFICE—Exchange Buildings, Montreal. Resident Secretary and General Agent,
A. MACKENZIE FORBES,
13 St. Sacrament St., Merchants' Exchange, Montreal.
WM. ROWLAND, Agent, Toronto.   1-1y

Insurance.

The Waterloo County Mutual Fire Insurance Company.

HEAD OFFICE : WATERLOO, ONTARIO.

ESTABLISHED 1863.

THE business of the Company is divided into separate and distinct branches, the
VILLAGE, FARM, AND MANUFACTU[
Each Branch paying its own losses and its just prop of the managing expenses of the Company.
C. M. TAYLOR, Sec.   M. SPRINGER, M.M.P.,
J. HUGHES, Inspector.

Ætna Fire and Marine Insurance Compa
Dublin.

AT a Meeting of the Shareholders of this Co held at Dublin, on the 13th ult., it was agre the business of the "ÆTNA" should be transferred "UNITED PORTS AND GENERAL INSURANCE COM In accordance with this agreement, the business wil after be carried on by the latter Company, which a and guarantees all the risks and liabilities of the "
The Directors have resolved to continue the Ca BRANCH, and arrangements for resuming FIRE a RINE business are rapidly approaching completion.
T. W. GRIFFIT
16   MANA

The Commercial Union Assura
Company,
19 & 20 CORNHILL, LONDON, ENGLAND.
Capital, £2,500,000 Stg.—Invested over $2,000,0

FIRE DEPARTMENT—Insurance granted on scriptions of property at reasonable rates.
LIFE DEPARTMENT.—The success of this has been unprecedented—*NINETY PER CENT.* miums now in hand. First year's premiums wer $100,000. Economy of management guaranteed security. Moderate rates.
OFFICE—385 & 387 ST PAUL STREET, MONTRE
MORLAND, WATSON & C
General Agents for C
FRED. COLE, Secretary.
Inspector of Agencies—T. C. LIVINGSTON,
W. M. WESTMACOTT, Agent at Tor
16-1y

Lancashire Insurance Compa
CAPITAL, - - - - - - - £2,000,000 S

FIRE RISKS
Taken at reasonable rates of premium, a
ALL LOSSES SETTLED PROMPTLY,
By the undersigned, without reference elsew
S. C. DUNCAN-CLARK & CO.,
General Agents for Ontar
N. W. Corner of King & Church St
25-1y   TORONTO.

Ætna Fire & Marine Insurance Compa
INCORPORATED 1819.   CHARTER PERPETUAL
CASH CAPITAL, - - - $3,
LOSSES PAID IN 50 YEARS, 23,500,000

JULY, 1868.
ASSETS.
(At Market Value.)
Cash in hand and in Bank $84
Real Estate   20
Mortgage Bonds.   20
Bank Stock 1,27
United States, State and City Stock, and other Public Securities 2,84
Total $5,03
LIABILITIES.
Claims not Due, and Unadjusted $4
Amount required by Mass. and New York for Re-Insurance.......................... 1,46
THOS. R. WOOD,
50-6   Agent for To

PUBLISHED AT THE OFFICE OF THE MON
TIMES, No. 60 CHURCH STREET.
PRINTED AT THE DAILY TELEGRAPH PRINTING I
BAY STREET, CORNER OF KING.]

THE CANADIAN
MONETARY TIMES
AND
INSURANCE CHRONICLE.
VOTED TO FINANCE, COMMERCE, INSURANCE, BANKS, RAILWAYS, NAVIGATION, MINES, INVESTMENT, PUBLIC COMPANIES, AND JOINT STOCK ENTERPRISE.

| I—NO. 23. | TORONTO, THURSDAY, JANUARY 21, 1869. | { SUBSCRIPTION, 82 YEAR. |

Mercantile.

Gundry and Langley,
ECTS AND CIVIL ENGINEERS, Building Sur-
and Valuators. Office corner of King and Jordan
'oronto.
AS GUNDRY.   HENRY LANGLEY.

J. B. Boustead,
ION and Commission Merchant.   Hops bought
old on Commission.   82 Front St., Toronto.

John Boyd & Co.,
ESALE Grocers and Commission Merchants,
nt St., Toronto.

Childs & Hamilton,
ACTURERS and Wholesale Dealers in Boots
Saces, No. 7 Wellington Street East, Toronto.
                                          28

L. Coffee & Co.,
E and Commission Merchants, No. 2 Manning's
, Front St., Toronto, Ont. Advances made on
nts of Produce.

J. & A. Clark,
E Commission Merchants, Wellington Street
Toronto, Ont

D Crawford & Co.,
ACTURERS of Soaps, Candles, etc., and dealers
stroleum, Lard and Lubricating Oils, Palace St
nt.

John Fisken & Co.,
OIL and Commission Merchants, Yonge St,
nto, Ont.

W. & R. Griffith,
ERS of Teas, Wines, etc   Ontario Chambers,
burch and Front Sts . Toronto.

H. Nerlich & Co.,
ERS of French, German, English and American
loods, Cigars, and Leaf Tobaccos, No. 2 Adelaide
est, Toronto.   15

Hurd, Leigh & Co.,
8 and Enamellers of China and Earthenware,
onge St., Toronto, Ont. [see advt.]

Lyman & McNab,
ESALE Hardware Merchants, Toronto, Ontario.

W. D. Matthews & Co.
E Commission Merchants, Old Corn Exchange,
ont St. East, Toronto Ont.

R. C. Hamilton & Co.
EE Commission Merchants, 19 Lower Water
Halifax, Nova Scotia.

Parson Bros.,
EUM Refiners, and Wholesale dealers in Lamps,
neys, etc   Warerooms 51 Front St. Refinery cor.
Don Sts., Toronto.

C. P. Reid & Co.,
ERS and Dealers in Wines, Liquors, Cigars and
Tobacco, Wellington Street, Toronto.   26.

W. Rowland & Co.,
E BROKERS and General Commission Mer-
Advances made on Consignments.   Corner
of Front Streets, Toronto.

Roford & Dillon,
ERS of Groceries, Wellington Street, Toronto,
to.

Sessions, Turner & Co.,
ACTURERS, Importers and Wholesale Dealer
loots and Shoes, Leather Findings, etc., 8 Wel-
West, Toronto, Ont

Meetings.

THE CANADA COMPANY.

The half-yearly meeting of the shareholders of
this company was held at their offices, 1, East India
Avenue, London, England, on the 31st Dec.

The report was to the following effect :—

The directors propose to recommend a division
out of the assets in hand of 1l. a share, free of income
tax, as dividend for the half-year ending the 10th
of January next. They propose also to divide a
further sum of 10s. a share, as a third instalment
towards the repayment of the paid-up capital of
the company. The funds in hand in London,
according to the finance statement, are 18,585l.,
and the liabilities 1,211l. leaving a balance of
17,374l. The proportion applicable to repayment
of capital is 6,884l., and the proportion applicable
to dividend 10,490l. The balance at Bank of
British North America is 1,503l. in currency, and
the liabilities 6,115l. In addition to the above
liabilities, there is a sum of 18,749l. currency at
the credit of Settlers' Savings Bank account, which
has been deposited with the company by their
lessees to meet the rent and purchase-money of the
lands occupied by them, but which may be withdrawn at the option of the depositors, subject to
the deduction of all arrears of rent and taxes
due to the company. There was also circulated
a comparative statement of the lands disposed of
and moneys received in Canada from 1st January
to 27th November, 1868, which showed that the
lands sold and leased amounted to 43,146 acres,
against 52,561 in the same period of 1867. The
receipts in the same period amounted to 56,644l.,
against 68,847l. in 1867, showing a decrease of
12,203l.

Mr. Ransford was then elected to a seat at the
Board in place of Mr. Wilson, deceased.

The Chairman said there was a falling off in the
business as compared with 1867, but when the
figures were analysed, and the main causes of it
considered, he thought they would concur with
the board that there was nothing to discourage
them. The circumstances especially causing the
reduction in their receipts arose through the smaller
amount of conversions falling due during the year
than in the preceding one. Besides which, they
had sold less acreage, and they could not expect
year by year to keep up the maximum amount of
sales. There was a small decrease in the average price realized of about 1s. 4d. an acre. He
found that 18 per cent. of these sales in 1868 represented sales of land which in 1854 were valued
at 2s. to 10s. per acre. He might state that these
lots have been sold from 7s. 6d. to 30s. instead of
from 2s. to 10s. an acre, which was a satisfactory
evidence that they were not altogether falling behind. He would now move the declaration of a
dividend of 20s. per-share on 8,915 shares, clear
of income tax.

The resolution was carried nem con.

The Chairman had to announce that the directors proposed to divide out of moneys received
from lands in reserve to meet capital a sum of 10s.
per share, which would be paid at the same time
as the dividend—viz., on the 11th prox. Since
the closing of their account they had received considerable remittances from their commissioners,
amounting to 3,500l.

Mr. Ransford had resided some years in Canada,
and was acquainted with the Huron tract and the
country generally. The knowledge he had acquired he would be happy to give to the use of the
company, so as to further their interests. The
chairman had made some remarks about salt, and
he could fully bear out all he had said. [The hon.
gentleman here handed to the Secretary a very
beautiful sample of the salt obtainable in the
country. It was remarkable white and sparkling,
very dry, and seemed to be very pure.] There
were as many salt springs as they liked to dig for.
The country about Goderich would be the Cheshire
of America, and would be able to supply the whole
West. It was the purest salt in the world, and
contained no chloride of calcium. The sample
was perfectly dry, although it had been in this
country two months. The value of salt in Canada was five times as much as in this country, it
being about 50s. a ton.

The proceedings then terminated.

ERIE AND NIAGARA RAILWAY.

A meeting of the rate-payers of the county of
Norfolk, was held in Simcoe, on Jan. 2nd, for the
purpose of discussing the proper course to pursue
with reference to granting the right of way through
the county to the Erie and Niagara Railway Co.
The meeting was attended by a considerable number of citizens. After it had been formally called
to order by the Warden, the following resolutions
were put and carried :—

"That railroad communication would be of
immense advantage to this county, inasmuch as
it would enhance the value of real estate; would
make a better market for all kinds of produce at
all seasons of the year, more especially during the
period navigation is closed; and would tend to
the more rapid settlement of its wild lands, as it
would greatly facilitate the ingress and egress of
parties looking for lands whereon to settle. That
in view of the great advantages this county would
derive from railway communication, this meeting
pledges itself to use every effort to secure this
most desirable boon. That the people of this
County were pleased that the efforts to secure
a charter for the construction of a railroad through
the tier of counties skirting the north shore of
Lake Erie were successful; and that so soon
as the parties controlling the charter, are in a
position to proceed with the construction of this
great work, it will be the interest and duty of the
people of Norfolk to use every means to secure its
speedy completion. That having learned that the
municipalities, through which the contemplated
road is to run, will be required to give the right
of way, this meeting respectfully recommends
that the County Council should purchase the same
through the county of Norfolk, and give it to the
company, upon a good and sufficient guarantee
being given that the road will be constructed, or
the right of way revert to the County."

PORT ROWAN SHIP-CANAL Co.—The annual
meeting of the shareholders took place at Port
Rowan, on the 18th of January. The five directors
elected were, Messrs. E. Deedes, H. J. Klinnaster,
John Charlton, W. H. Stevenson, and A. Bur-
rowes. Mr. Deedes was re-elected President; and

Mr. Chauncey Pennett, Secretary, Treasurer, and Superintendent. The Simcoe *Reformer* says the company is flourishing; stock above par; and a dividend of ten per cent., declared for last year. The directors contemplate to deepen the outlet during the ensuing season.

COBOURG, PETERBOROUGH AND MARMORA RAILWAY.—The annual meeting of the Stockholders of the Cobourg, Peterborough and Marmora Railway and Mining Company was held at the Company's Offices, Cobourg, on Monday, 4th instant. John Bell, Esq., Q. C., in the chair.

After the transaction of certain business in connection with the contract with Mr. McDougall for the carrying of lumber, the following gentlemen were elected Directors for the ensuing year : Messrs. Thos. S. Blair, and J. H. Schoenberger, Pittsburg, G. K. Schoenberger, Cincinnati, Isaac Potts, Rochester, J. Huntsman, Dayton, Ohio, John Bell, Belleville, and J. H. Dumble, A. Fraser, E. P., and Col. W. P. Chambliss, Cobourg.

A resolution was adopted at a wooden railway meeting held recently in St. Eustache, Quebec, pledging aid to the extension of the proposed road to Ottawa, by the North Shore. *La Minerve* asserts that there are eighteen hundred square miles of standing timber, well adapted for fire wood, in the neighborhood of St. Jerome, another proposed terminus of the wooden railway scheme now before the public.

Insurance.

FIRE RECORD.—Port Hope, Jan. 15.—The old frame distillery buildings on Cavan street, owned by Mr. Monson, were destroyed by fire ; also a small frame building adjoining the distillery premises. The latter was occupied by Patrick Curran, while the former was unoccupied. The fire originated in the distillery building, and rapidly communicated to the other building.

GARAFRAXA Township, Ont., Dec. 31.—A barn, the property of Mr. Turnbull, on the 5th concession, was burned to the ground. The barn was filled with hay and cattle; no insurance.

AWMAR Jan.—The Court House at this place was totally destroyed, and the County Gaol partially. The cost of the building is put at $35,000, and there was an insurance of $12,000 in the Royal. There is no fire engine in the place, so that the only opposition offered to the flames was water poured on by hand. Cause unknown.

London, Ont., Jan. 16.—A fire occurred here this evening at six o'clock, by which White's Hotel, North street, was almost totally destroyed. Most of the effects were saved. The loss will be about $1,200 on building and contents; insured in the Western, the building for $1,400 and $400 on contents.

New Aberdeen, Ont., Dec. 28.—A house on the farm of John Linton was burned, and nothing saved from the flames except a few articles. The house occupied by Mr. Linton himself would also have been burned, had not a few of the neighbory arrived in time and worked manfully; thus preventing further damage.

Peel Township, Ont., Dec. 28.—The barn of Mr. Matthew Nay, 3rd concession of Peel, was totally destroyed by fire, with its contents, comprising almost all his crop of last season, and several implements. The horses and harness were saved. Loss estimated at $800 ; insured for $400 in the Waterloo Mutual.

Montmorenci, Jan. 11.—The match factory of Howard & Fitch was entirely destroyed. Loss $15,000 ; insured in the British America for $3,000. The fire originated from the stovepipe, which ignited a partition.

Halifax, Jan. 11.—A fire broke out in a wooden building on Star street, north of Temperance Hall, owned by Murdoch Lindsay, and occupied by him as a work-shop. The fire, which originated from a defective stovepipe, was soon extinguished.

Brantford, Jan. 20.—At an early hour this morning a fire broke out in a brick store on Colborne street, owned and occupied by W. Lines, grocer. The fire is supposed to have originated up stairs, which was occupied by J. D. Kirchner, as a cigar manufactory. The building is entirely destroyed. The stores adjoining were on fire several times, but by the great exertions of the firemen they were saved. W. Lines' loss not known: insured for $3,000 on building and stock. J. D. Kirchner's loss about $1,200; insured for $700. Cause of fire not known.

—Between 400 and 500 deaths took place during the past year in Montreal from small pox.

—The National Life Insurance Company of the United States has deposited $50,000 with the Government. Mr. Douglas, Jr., of Montreal, is the agent.

LAW OF LIFE INSURANCE.—A. P. Gould, of Nashua, N. H., had a policy on his life—$1,400— "for the benefit of his wife and children." But he left a will depriving his daughter of all interest in the policy. The daughter sued the executors, and the Court has decided in her favor, holding that a life insurance policy cannot be changed by a will.

ÆTNA LIVE STOCK INSURANCE COMPANY, OF HARTFORD.—This Company has determined to discontinue its agencies and withdraw from the business. The causes that have led to this step are simply the unprofitable nature of the business, and the shock to public confidence given by the failure of the *Hartford Live Stock Company* last August. The Ætna commenced business in September, 1857, and four months after the close of its first year, its statistics reveal so unpromising an experience as to discourage from further effort.

LIFE INSURANCE.—A case of interest to life insurers has recently been decided by the Superior Court of New York. A life insurance company in Maine in September, 1866, issued a policy for $10,000 upon the life of a Mr. Warner of this city, who represented, at the time of his examination by the medical officer of the company that he had no regular physician. Warner died in February, 1867, when it became known that he had availed himself of the services of one doctor for himself and family for several years, receiving prescriptions from him the month before his application for life insurance, and also after the policy had been issued. Under these circumstances the insurance company refused to pay the claim of Mr. Warner's heirs; and upon the trial of the case before the late Justice Robertson, the position of the defendants was sustained. The matter was then taken on appeal by the plaintiffs to the General Term of the Superior Court, and the decision of the court below was affirmed.—*N. Y. Times.*

LEGISLATURE OF ONTARIO.

ONTARIO MUTUAL INSURANCE COMPANY.— On January 11th the House went into committee on the Bill to grant certain powers to the Ontario Farmer's Mutual Insurance Company.

Hon. Mr. McMurrich urged that the Company should be restricted to doing business strictly on the Mutual principle. Dr. McGill said that several Bills, having the clause now objected to, were allowed to pass last session. Hon. Mr. McMurrich said he had opposed these Bills last year, both in the Private Bills committee and in the House. Dr. McGill—If he did, it was clear he did not succeed in convincing the judgment of the majority of this House. The very language of the statutes of last session was copied in this Bill. This Company found that, unless they were allowed to receive premiums entirely in cash as well as partly in cash and partly in bills, they could not compete on fair terms with other companies. If this clause were struck out, the Bill

would be of no use. Hon. Mr. McMurrich the principle was a wrong one, and a stand should be taken against it, and as well begin with Bill. Instead of expunging the clause, he would be satisfied if it were amended, by providing the man who paid a cash premium should give his note for double its amount. Dr. McGill said this proposition was altogether unreasonable. No one, after insuring on the cash principle, would consent to give his note in addition. Springer supported the Bill, which, he said, retained the same powers as were given to a Waterloo Company last year. He thought there was nothing wrong in the principle, and the companies which carried on business on it, were prosperous as any others. Mr. Ferrier supported Mr. McMurrich's view. Mr. Rykert urged on the attention of the Attorney General the desirableness of having a General Act, under which all the companies should be Incorporated, and which should define the limits of their powers. He did not think that insuring on the cash system in Insurance Companies was a sound principle. Atty.-Gen. Macdonald said the proper way to regulate these matters was by a General Act. But the t... was, that after a General Act passed, members would be introducing private legislation asking special powers for particular companies. It was willing this Bill should pass, but hoped that next session they would commence a clean slate and carry out a different system. Mr. Blake was unable to concur in the proposition of the Attorney General. He thought the principle of the Bill was entirely objectionable, and was opposed to repeating, with reference to this Bill, the mistake of last session. Hon. Mr. Cameron said he had not understood the Attorney-General to say that the principle of this Bill was wrong; he had merely said that exceptional legislation. He (Mr. Cameron) supported the Bill, because thought one company should not enjoy privileges which were denied to another, and because experience had not shown that the principle unsafe or unsound. Atty.-Gen. Macdonald those who objected to the principle, should see that bad consequences had resulted from it. Mr. McMurrich—prevention is better than cure. Mr. Rykert said, if there was any force in the Provincial Secretary's argument, this Bill should be a general one, granting to all Mutual Insurance Companies, the powers given last session to the Waterloo Company. Mr. McMurrich's amendment to expunge the clause was negatived by 33 to 24.

The Bill was reported, and ordered to be a third time to-morrow.

HARTFORD STOCKS.

—The McNab Iron Company, composed J. P. Mansfield of Detroit, Axel Dearborn at B. Nicholls, both of Boston, of H. Hills of Alton, J. W. Ward of Ottawa, are applying for incorporation. The nominal capital is $50 divided into $1 shares. The amount subscribed $30,000. The place where the operations of company are to be carried on are in the township of MacNab, in the county of Renfrew, and township of ... in the district of Algoma.

—There are some peat beds at Wawanosh the Goderich people are thinking about a tramway to the place, a distance of six miles.

—The Kincardine Salt Company have commenced the manufacture of salt at their well twenty-four kettles. They expect to turn about twenty-five barrels per day.

Financial.

TREAL MONEY MARKET.

rom our own Correspondent).

Montreal, Jan. 19, 1869.

still plentiful; the Banks supply all vants at 7 per cent. for good paper; but a small amount is offering and t of a desirable quality, as the rates so out of proportion to those demand- nks. There is still a large amount eking investment, and the difficulty increases instead of diminishes. Good e very scarce. Stocks of all descrip- ry high, in fact so much so, that the n them only leaves a small return. spring our monied men must find annel for investment, but what direc- ake it is impossible to say. A fair been done in Stocks, the tendency of vards. Bank of Montreal have been 9½ and are now held for 140. Con- s of Ontario at 99¼ to 99½, but hold- lemanding a shade higher. Merchants d their late depression and now sell ½ to 107¾, but holders are now asking s Cartier wanted at 107. Toronto no ¼ would readily be paid. The Gore llen to 42 and dull at that. City sales at 101 to 101½. Other Bank In Mining Consols there is a fair but holders are asking $3.20. Tel- some request at 133, but that is below holders. No City Railroad shares on Corporation 6 per cent. bonds worth Not much doing in other stocks. Ster- e steady 9⅜ to 9⅝ for Bank.

ONTO STOCK MARKET.

rted by Pellatt & Osler, Brokers.)

a large business done in stocks and ek, and in most cases at advanced rket closing firm with a good de- ly all kinds of securities.

—Montreal is much inquired for, ose there were no sellers under 140; were at 139. The last sale of 102, but there has been no stock in veral weeks. Ontario sold at 100½, , there being sellers and buyers to- Toronto is nominal at 118; there transactions for weeks; buyers would umerous sales of Royal Canadian ng the week at prices ranging from re is none now offering under the Commerce has been in good demand sales to-day (the 19th) at 102½. Gore occurred at 39 and 39½; there 39. Merchants' has advanced since ock now offering under 107½ to 108. ers of Quebec at 98 and sellers at k 111 for Molson's, with buyers at offered at 101. Nationale could be 3. There are buyers of Jacques and sellers at 108. Sales of Union 03; there are now buyers at 102½ 103½. Other banks nominal as

Both currency and sterling Canada tinue scarce. Dominion stock has 105 to 105½; there are now buyers at the latter rate. Toronto would en to pay 6½ per cent. interest. A ebentures have changed hands to cent. interest.

ity Gas is still asked for; no sellers. f British-America Assurance oc- to 54, ex dividend. Canada Per- ng Society has been largely dealt week at 122, 122½, 123 and 123½, uyers but no sellers at the latter able sales of Western Canada oc- curred at 114 and 114½; there are buyers now at 115, but no sellers. Freehold is much inquired for; sales were made at 106, 106½, 107 and 107½, and closes firm at the latter rate. There are buyers of Montreal Telegraph at 133; no sellers under 136. Canada Landed Credit has been asked for during the week at 72. Several good mortgages have been sold to pay 8 per cent. interest. Money is freely offered on good paper.

BANK OF ENGLAND.

	Jan. 1, 1869.	Jan. 3, 1868.
Bank rate of discount	3 per cent.	2 per cent.
Bank reserve	£9,931,228	£12,819,673
Bank stock of bullion	18,445,858	22,061,728
Price of Consols	92⅞ x d	92⅛ x d

The demand for money has been very heavy this week, although not more so than is customary just before the end of the year. The rates of discount have, however, rather stiffened, the best three months paper not being taken below 3 per cent.; we may now, however, look for an increased supply of capital, and probably a slight reduction in its value. On the Stock Exchange some pressure for money has been experienced, and for advances on British Government securities as much as 4 per cent was paid.

The bank return this week exhibits an increase of £154,237 in the stock of bullion. There is, it will be noted, a very considerable addition to the other securities, owing to the increased discount demand experienced by the bank.

CHANGES.—Mr. J. S. Meredith, for some time teller of the Commercial Bank in Berlin, and latterly in the same position in the Merchant's Bank, is about to leave Berlin, having been promoted to Ingersoll with an increase of salary.

COUNTERFEIT.—Yesterday we were shown a counterfeit $4 note on the Niagara District Bank. The counterfeit may be easily detected by a careful examination of the Vignette on the left hand corner, which is a portrait of the Hon. Mr. Merritt, being most wretchedly executed. The rest of the note is passable. We understand there are a considerable number in circulation.—*Spectator* 13th.

—The Bank of Montreal has closed its agencies at Whitby and St. Catherines. In the former place its deposits have been handed over to the Ontario Bank, and in the latter to the Bank of Commerce.

Railway News.

GREAT WESTERN RAILWAY.—Traffic for week ending January 1, 1869.

Passengers	$23,230 08
Freight and live stock	46,912 81
Mails and sundries	4,027 92
	$74,170 81
Corresponding Week of '68	63,888 89
Increase	$10,281 92

PORT WHITBY AND PORT PERRY RAILWAY.—The Ontario Legislature went into committee on the bill to amend the charter of this Co. on the 11th. Mr. Paxton said the Co. had now shown their ability to build a road from Whitby to Port Perry. The bonuses had been granted, and the contracts let, and the contractors were going on with the work. Last year he supported the Toronto and Nipissing, the Grey and Bruce, and the Erie and Niagara Bills, believing the Legislature was to support free trade in railways, even in cases where a projected railway crossed an existing one. On the same principle he claimed support for this Bill. The company asked powers to extend their line from Port Perry to Beaverton, with a branch to Uxbridge. It was urged against the Bill, that this extension to Beaverton would hinder the progress of the Toronto and Nipissing. He thought the Toronto and Nipissing must be a scheme weak in the extreme, if it was to be hindered by this little scheme from Whitby.

Hon. Mr. Cameron, did not the promoters of this Bill go into the Township of Brock and do all in their power to prevent the people of that township from supporting the Toronto and Nipissing.

Mr. Paxton said this Bill did not compel the township of Brock to support the Whitby extension. The Toronto and Nipissing must be a weak scheme, if it could not succeed without a bonus from Brock. In reply to another question, Mr. Paxton said the township of Reach had promised $12,000 to this extension. He moved an additional clause, authorising the extension to Beaverton, and a branch to Uxbridge.

Hon. Mr. Cameron said the Company's Bill of last session, authorised them to build a road, 17 miles in length, connecting Lakes Scugog and Ontario. The object of this Bill was not to provide railway facilities for the section of country through which this extension was sought, but to injure the Toronto and Nipissing, which had already received a charter for opening up that section. That this was the object, was manifest from the fact, that the township of Brock had been urged to the utmost by the promoters of this undertaking to oppose the Toronto and Nipissing. What evidence was there that the parties who had undertaken to construct the 17 miles to Port Perry, would be able to construct another 50 miles. On the contrary, was it not likely that this extension would ruin the Port Whitby and Port Perry railway as a paying undertaking. The City of Toronto did not oppose this from any sectional motive, but the question was, whether it would be desirable that that small section of country should be traversed by three railways, when already there were charters for two railways, which would give it ample facilities, the Toronto and Nipissing, and the Lindsay extension to Beaverton.

Mr. Paxton said the extension to Beaverton would be—not 50 miles in length, but 28 miles.

Dr. McGill could not see how the passage of this bill would prevent the building of the Toronto and Nipissing road. The undertaking was a good one. It opened up the most direct route from the southern to the northern section of that district; and the company seeking this extension gave a good earnest in what they had done for what they would do. The fact was, that by this line the farmers would not only be enabled to get their freight cheaper to the front, but would get it to Whitby, from whence it could be conveyed to the large markets at a much lower rate than if forwarded to Toronto.

Mr. Cumberland would vote for the measure, because he was a convert to the doctrine laid down so emphatically by the Secretary last session, that the people ought to be left free to place railroads where they liked. He (Cumberland) saw that it was useless to attempt to check this railway legislation. He hoped the hasty railway legislation of that House would not lead to any disastrous results; but his position as a railway man led him to warn the House to be more careful as to what they did in this respect.

Mr. Paxton's motion, to restore the second clause, which had been struck out in the Railway Committee, was carried. The fourth clause, which had been struck out in the Committee, was also restored, so as to stand as follows:—

"4. All the clauses and provisions contained in the said Act incorporating the said Port Whitby and Port Perry Railway Company, and the several powers and authorities conferred upon such Company by such Act, and all subsequent Acts relating thereto, and the several clauses of the "Railway Act," mentioned and referred to in said Act, shall apply to the extended powers conferred hereby. And the extension hereby authorized shall be commenced within two years, and completed within five years after the passing of this

Act, or else the charter of the said extension shall be forfeited."

The Committee then rose and reported the Bill, with amendments. Amendments concurred in, and Bill ordered for a third reading.

COSTING AND PETERBOROUGH RAILWAY.—Mr. Blake moved the second reading of the Bill to remove doubts as to the rights of the bondholders to the surplus funds paid, or to be paid, into the Court of Chancery.

Mr. Fraser objected to the Bill as unfair towards the Company. Some years ago, when the affairs of the Company came before Parliament, an arrangement was made by which this railway was sold for $100,000. Out of this sum it was agreed that the bondholders should receive $70,000, and that the balance, $30,000, should be paid over to the parties claiming for unpaid rights of way depot grounds, &c. These parties had at present their claims in the Court of Chancery, and when they were to be approved of by the Master, were to be paid. If the $30,000 were insufficient, the Company were still liable for the excess. As a matter of fact $10,000 remained in the Court of Chancery, and the Railway Company believe that this unappropriated money should revert to them, as they placed it there. He might further remark that the Company were engaged for some time in securing some of the claims against the line, and had actually paid out of other funds belonging to the Company, the sum of $3,000 in the purchase of claims against the Company. The effect of the bill, if passed, would be, not only would they receive no benefit from the money in Court, but they would not be repaid even the sum lately expended. Under these circumstances he would, seconded by Mr. Coyne, move that the Bill be read a second time that day six months.

Hon. Mr. Cameron argued that the Company had no right to the balance in Court, but that the bondholders, who were the losing parties, ought to have the benefit of it.

Mr. Pardee said the whole question turned on what was the arrangement. If it were true that $30,000 had been appropriated for the right of way, and it were bought for less, it appeared to him that the balance should go to the bondholders. But if the arrangement were as stated by the member for Northumberland—that in case the right of way cost more than $30,000, that the excess would have to be paid by the purchasers of the Road—then it appeared to him to be clearly according to the principles of law and equity, that whatever difference the purchasers made, should go into their own pockets, and no into those of the bondholders.

Hon. Mr. Cameron enquired of the member for South Bruce if he was right in understanding that the Court of Chancery, which had the matter in charge was not of opinion that the bondholders were entitled to the surplus; but that under the provisions of the law they could not so determine it.

Mr. Blake said he had no cognizance of what had taken place in the Court of Chancery. He never heard what opinion was expressed there.

Mr. McMurrich thought the parties here applying for redress should have gone to the Court of Chancery.

After some further debate,

Mr. Blake moved that the debate be adjourned in order to satisfy himself whether or not the matter was before the Court of Chancery.

The motion for adjourning the debate was then put and carried.

ROYAL INSURANCE.—This Company has issued a neat little almanack for 1869. It contains the annual report of the Company and the usual data. An immense edition has been printed and the copies distributed with a liberal hand throughout the country.

The Canadian Monetary Times.

THURSDAY, JANUARY 21, 1869.

RAILWAYS AND RAILWAY LEGISLATION.

Our neighbours across the lines think us Canadians anything but a fast people. They picture to themselves a very cold, undefined region to the North of freedom and civilization, away beyond the sound of the bugle-horn of liberty, with unenterprising, drowsy, cold-benumbed inhabitants and call that Canada. Such occurs when there is nothing to be gained by ascertaining the true character of the country thus described. But, when occasion requires, as in the case of an agitation for reciprocity in trade, there are not a few among them who exercise themselves wonderfully to prove that we are a shrewd, scheming, devil-may-care set whose sole desire is to get the better of the United States and build up our country at the expense of our virtuous neighbours; that our progress is amazing and due entirely to the advantages we obtain by superior diplomacy and sharpness.

Without laying claim to the term fast, we are not inclined to submit to the reproach of slowness. At any rate, if we were slow, we are beginning to move along at an increased pace. If progress in the construction of railways is to be considered a test, we have a good record to show and are likely from present indications, to earn a few compliments for praiseworthy intentions. We have in the Dominion, 2388 miles of railway made up as follows:—Grand Trunk 1377, Great Western 251½ London and Port Stanley 24½, Welland 25, Northern 97, Port Hope, Lindsay and Beaverton 56, Cobourg, Peterborough and Marmora 22, Brockville and Ottawa 86, St. Lawrence and Ottawa 54, Carillon and Grenville 13, Stanstead, S. and Ch. 44, St. Lawrence and Industry 12, New Brunswick and Canada 107, European and North American 108, Nova Scotia, 145. Among these we

do not include railways at present in progress of construction, of which there are several. According to these figures the mileage divided thus: Ontario (616 x 616) 1,278; bec, (69 x 515) 584; New Brunswick and Nova Scotia 145.

When the Intercolonial railway is there will be direct communication between Windsor, Sarnia, Goderich or Collingwood the four points on our Western frontier, St. John and Halifax on the Atlantic. A railway of the same gauge throughout whole of Canada, affording access to the navigation, and at all seasons with St. Halifax and Portland, is not to be sneer. The railroad between Port Huron and troit is likely to be conformed to the dian gauge, and it is possible that all the same gauge will soon be constructed Michigan to Chicago, so that, when the colonial is opened, cars loaded in Chica Detroit can pass without transhipment sides of ocean vessels at Montreal, Qu Portland, St. John or Halifax.

But our great arteries of Commerce w dis-ended by many feeders. From all of the Dominion we catch the sounds of labour. New Brunswick is pushing on its sions to the United States, boundaries. Scotia proposes to add 70 miles to its The Province of Quebec is not asleep proposes to extend the Massawippi ra and the Stanstead and Shefford railw construct a railway through Missisqu wooden railway from Quebec to Gosf wooden railway through Arthabaska Drummond, a wooden railway along t Francis, a wooden railway from Montr St. Jerome, a railway to the upper St. rice, and a narrow gauge road betwe St. Lawrence and the Kennebec.

Nor is the Province of Ontario either in the number or in the chara its railway projects. At the last session Ontario Legislature no less than eigh were passed relating to railways. The ing companies were incorporated—th llington, Grey and Bruce, the Erie and ara extension, the Grey and Simcoe, th Whitby and Port Perry, the Toront and Bruce and the Toronto and Nip and power was granted to the Cobou terborough and Marmora Company to their line to a point on the Chemong to and the Grey and Simcoe to exten to Walkerton. There are at present the Ontario Legislature five companie ing incorporation:—The Peterborou Haliburton, to construct a woden or ir way from Peterborough to a point bey town right of Haliburton; the Kings Frontenac, to construct a wooden

y from Kingston to the vicinity of
lton Lake in the Township of Lough-
gh, with power to extend into the Town-
f Alden or Oso ; the Norfolk, to con-
a railway from Simcoe, Port Dover, or
Ryerse on Lake Erie, to Caledonia in
nland or to Brantford or Paris ; the
e and Muskoka, to construct a railway
ome point on Lake Couchiong to Lake
oka ; the Presque-Isle and Belmont, to
uct a railway from Presque-Isle Har-
thence through Brighton, Norham,
worth, Meyersburgh and Campbell, in
umberland, and the Townships of Bel-
and Marmora, to the Township of Lake
stings,

Ontario Legislature has before it, other
s, pertaining to railways. The Toronto
ipissing Company seek to have legal-
e by-laws passed and to be passed, and
entures issued or to be issued under
y-laws, granting aid to their undertak-
d to amend their charter by allowing
ipalities granting a bonus of not less
150,000 to the Company, the right to
a director ; and by allowing the con-
on of a branch from Brook to Lindsay.
oronto, Grey and Bruce, besides asking
legalization of by-laws as in the for-
se, and the appointment of a director by
iunicipality that grants a bonus of no
an $250,000, prays the enactment of
lowing clauses :

the following proviso be added to the
clause of 31 Vic. c. 40 : provided al-
hat nothing in the said clause contain-
l prevent the application of any bonus
y the City of Toronto, or Township or
, or Village of Mount Forest, or by
inicipality between any of those points,
a to the mileage of the said railway
n those points.

Company may build any part of their
ilway to the West or North-west of the
iip of Arthur, or the Village of Mount
by sections, but no bonus granted by
nicipality to the West or North-west
Township of Arthur or the Village of
Forest, shall be applied to any other
than that for which such bonuses are

Corporation of Port Hope apply for
io enable them to transfer, by way of
to the Port Hope, Lindsay and Bea-
Railway Company, Port Hope Har-
erling Bonds, to the extent of $33,000,
purpose of extending the line from
p to Beaverton. Certain monies hav-
n paid into the Court of Chancery by
ourg and Peterborough Railway Com-
nder 29 Vic., cap. 79, certain bond-
of that Company have applied for an
olding their claims to the surplus mo-
gainst the Cobourg, Peterborough and
ra Railway and Mining Company.
l provides that the surplus of moneys

paid into the Court of Chancery under 29 Vic.
over and above the sum required to pay all
claims for unpaid rights of way, station and
depot grounds, as well as the further payment
directed to be made by the said act for the
like purpose, together with all interest thereon, shall be distributed by the Court among
the bondholders, in addition to, and in like
manner, as the sums formerly ordered to be
distributed among those bondholders. There
is also an act to amend and consolidate the
various acts relating to the Cobourg P. & M.
Railway & Mining Co.

The London and Port Stanley Railway
Company has, it appears, got into trouble,
and applies now, for leave to sell the railway,
the purchase-money, upon sale, to be paid
into the Court of Chancery for distribution
among the creditors according to priority.—
The Port Whitby and Port Perry Railway
Company ask to have their charter amended,
by striking out the 23 section of 31 Vic. c.
42 after the words "provided always" and
substituting the words "The said bonds, debentures and mortgages not to exceed in
amount the paid up stock of the Company,
together with the municipal or other bonuses
expended upon such Railway ;" and to obtain
for the Company power to extend their
Railway to a point on Lake Simcoe, near Beaverton, and to build a branch into the village
of Uxbridge.

THE HURON AND ONTARIO SHIP CANAL.

It seems to us that the promoters of this
scheme have taken a very injudicious course
in selecting one member of the Ontario
Government as an object of attack, by way
of revenge for the action of the Government.
Such proceeding has, very naturally evoked
opposition and we have at once two parties,
the one promoting the objects of the Company, and the other assailing the whole
scheme, as well as its supporters, with fact and
argument which they successful rebuttal. The
petition which not a few merchants and prominent men signed, received the signatures of
many who never troubled themselves to examine the scheme until this partizan warfare
broke out, and consequently, we find some of
those who numbered themselves among the
supporters of the Company, now its active
antagonists. Hence, we think, a blunder has
been committed and the promoters of the
scheme have only themselves to thank for it.
Mr. Chisholm's statements raise a distinct
issue. The Canal Company's pamphlet claims
that the proposed Canal would save, in the
carrying of grain from Chicago to New York,
a distance of 460 miles. Mr. Chisholm gives
figures to show that only 240 miles would be

saved. Mr. T. C. Keefer, in his report on
the Lake Scugog route, places the shortening
of distance at 250 miles.

The question of probable revenue is also
discussed, the conclusions arrived at being
unfavourable to the project. Were a vessel
to pass each way through the Canal, every
hour. night and day for seven months, carrying 3,276,000 tons, at 80 cents per ton, there
would be a loss of $779,200. But it is assert-
ed on good authority, that at the toll of 80
cents, not one vessel or steamboat would
pass through. A toll of 80 cents a ton on
grain is two cents and four mills per bushel
of wheat. The rate from Chicago to Toronto,
last December, was only one cent and one
mill per bushel. The Northern Railway
which runs the whole length of the proposed
Canal, carries at the rate of one cent and five
mills per bushel. Under such circumstances
the Canal would not be very profitable. If
the toll were reduced to 20 cents a ton, the
tonnage passed through being the same as in
the former case, the annual loss to the Company on their investment would be $2,744,-
800.

The Company claims that cargoes of 1000
or 1200 tons might be sent through the canal,
without transhipment, from Chicago to Liverpool. Mr. Laidlaw steps forward and shows
that no vessel drawing over nine feet of water,
equivalent to a lading of 300 tons, can come
up the St. Lawrence, and that there is no
harbour on Lake Ontario, except Kingston,
and no shipping port on the upper lakes
which a vessel drawing over eleven feet can
enter.

Mr. Kingsford, C.E., in his useful book
on the Canadian canals, considers that "as a
solitary project, were the canal constructed,
not one vessel more would pass by the St.
Lawrence than goes by it to-day ;" And further, "all the advantages sought would be
attained by the enlargement of the Welland
Canal, with the addition of having only
twenty-eight miles against one hundred of
canal by Georgian Bay. The St. Clair Flats
may be marked by objectionable features,
but they are capable of improvement, to be
obtained by increased depth." Mr. Worts,
the President of the Toronto Board of Trade,
who is the largest importer of corn, and
thoroughly experienced in shipping matters
gives evidence to the same effect.

To enlarge the St. Lawrence Canals would
cost about $12,000,000. Before Europe could
expect to profit much by a reduction caused
by the Canal, the St. Lawrence Canals would
therefore have to be enlarged. Chicago and
Oswego might possibly be benefited ; but
until the American navigation laws are
relaxed, Canadian vessels would derive little
advantage from the construction of the Canal,

as in their present state we are debarred the privilege of carrying grain from one American port to another.

The general commercial interests of Canada, it seems, would not be served to any appreciable extent by the construction of the Canal, at least, until the St. Lawrence Canals are deepened and the American navigation laws repealed. But would Toronto benefit by the work? It is true, a large amount of money would be spent within a hundred miles of the city; but it is contended with great force, that the Canal would cut off the trade on which the city depends. Vessels would clear from New Market, Barrie, &c., for Oswego and Montreal, and would load back for these places instead of loading at Toronto. What would become, therefore, of our great lumber and wheat trade?

With such facts staring one in the face, to say nothing of the practicability or impracticability of the work, the many engineering difficulties to be encountered at the ridges, or the supply of water, people very naturally look upon the scheme as chimerical, and justly feel hesitation in granting 10,000,000 of the public domain to aid it.

The popular view of the subject is that the land asked is of no value to us, and, if by granting it by way of bonus, we can get English and American capitalists to spend $40,000,000 among us, it is their look out whether the work will pay. But as Mr. Worts put it, in his masterly address to the Board of Trade, there is a question of commercial morality involved. Are our merchants justified in assisting to induce foreign capitalists to sink so much money in a work that would be useless and unprofitable? We have no right to impose on our fellow men, to take advantage of their ignorance, and to damage the good name of our country. Canada has suffered, rightfully or wrongfully, from the failure of the Grand Trunk as an investment. Suppose the $40,000,000 were sunk in the canal without the slightest prospect of a return, would not Canada again suffer? If capitalists will throw away their money we cannot help it, but we can, at least, refrain from tempting them into a great loss by indorsing a scheme which facts and figures show to be so utterly delusive as the one under consideration.

ETNA INSURANCE CO. OF DUBLIN.

It appears that the Sheriff of the county of Carleton, under four executions, amounting to $4,500, offered for sale, at Ottawa, the securities deposited by the Etna Insurance Company of Dublin with the Minister of Finance. When the Etna commenced to do business in Canada the Insurance Act of 1860

was in force, and, in accordance with its requirements, invested $10,000 in Canadian five per cents. An Ottawa paper states that the executions were sent to the Sheriff of Carleton from Toronto and Goderich, for the purpose of having these securities seized, and that "the seizure was made," and the securities duly put up for sale. The Ottawa Times says, "The bidders, however, were few, the company's agent having sent a verbal intimation "that he had lodged a written protest against "the surrender of the securities with the "Minister of Finance. The sale was consequently postponed until the 23rd inst., at "the same hour, noon, when, if the executors "are not previously satisfied, or proceedings "stayed, the securities will be peremptorily "sold to the highest bidder." We can easily understand that doubts exist as to the completeness of the Sheriff's title. The Act speaks of the deposit as a security liable to be forfeited to Her Majesty, on the breach by the Company, or its Agent, of any of the conditions of the Act, and only liable to be distributed among claimants in a certain event. It is provided that the Minister of Finance shall not issue his warrant permitting the withdrawal of the deposit or investment "until fifteen months after the day on which "the Company may have given notice that "they have ceased to carry on business in "this province." In case of the insolvency of a Company, the sum deposited "shall be applied pro rata towards the payment of all "claims duly authenticated against such Company, alike, as to losses, and premiums or "risks unexpired, or on policies issued in "this province." The evidence of insolvency is the failure to pay losses insured against, within this province, for ninety days after being due. The distribution may be made by order in Chancery, in Ontario. The contention, it appears, is that the deposit was for the benefit of all the creditors of the company. It would, certainly, seem that such a construction of the statute is both fair and reasonable.

Some one telegraphed to the New York journals the astounding information, that the total amount of deposits by Insurance Companies in Canada is $33,682,400.

FIRE IN OTTAWA.—Just as we go to press we learn by telegraph that Desbarat's block, in Ottawa, was consumed by fire last night. Insurance on Desbarat's stock, Home of New Haven $8000 ; Ætna $8000 ; Hartford of Hartford $8000 ; London Assurance Corporation $8000 ; Provincial $8000 on building. Queen's Printer's Block —Lancashire $8000 ; Queen $4000 ; Royal $8000 ; Provincial, $5,000, and $4,000 in the same company for the benefit of the Government. On Mrs. Trotter's furniture, $3,000 in Etna of Dublin.

Mr. Graham, of the Carleton Hotel, has a [ ] in the Imperial for $1,000. Total insu[ ] $75,000. Loss variously stated at $140,[ ] $200,000.

Communications.

THE UNITED PORTS AND GENERAL CO. AND THE ETNA OF DUBLIN

Editor of the Canadian Monetary Times.

DEAR SIR,—As several paragraphs have r[ ]ly appeared in the MONETARY TIMES, resp[ ]the Etna Insurance Company and the tran[ ]its business to the United Ports and General [ ]rance Company, will you oblige me by ins[ ]in the columns of your widely read journal following extract from a power of attorney, by the Directors of the latter Company, date of December 24th, 1863, authorizing [ ]settle all claims arising under Etna policies Oct. 30th, 1868, viz.:—

"To adjust, settle, and allow, upon such as the said attorney may think fit, all qu[ ]and claims of every description under any p[ ]issued in the name of the Etna Insurance Com which may have arisen since the 30th day of 1868, or which may hereafter arise in resp[ ]policies so issued, and to pay all claims a since the said 30th October, and allowed b said attorney under such Etna policies."

Yours respectfully,
T. W. GRIFFITH
Montreal, Jan. 16, 1869. *Mana[*

Mining.

NOVA SCOTIA GOLD FIELDS.

(From our own Correspondent)

HALIFAX, Jan. 12, 1[ ]

The progress of the several established panies and proclaimed districts is tolerabl indicated by the subjoined mill and bulli turns. Investments in gold stocks have wholly ceased, though there has been enqu shares in the Mt. Uniacke Co. of Uniack Wellington Co. of Sherbrooke, both contr[ ]Boston. The sale of the late Shaffer ab[ ]properties at Oldham, to parties in New wick is authentically stated.

SHERBROOKE.—The low yield from the [ ]mill, in the absence of any explanation panying the returns, must be explained by t[ ]position that this was an experimental test. Mr. Newell Snow is expected i[ ]to-night with about 500 ounces, the pr[ ]the Wellington, Hayden and Derby, and [ ]ston mines.

WINE HARBOR.—The *Eureka* mine is e[ ]to send up about 70 ounces as the result fortnight's crushing. Messrs. J. DeW. and E G., Leukie, are in Halifax, and r[ ]tenders for the new mill of sixty stamps they propose having erected on their e[ ]property in this district.

WAVERLEY.—Professor H. Y. Hind's g[ ]plan, sections and reports are nearly com and are of great interest. They cannot revive attention to this long neglected dis[ ]

TANGIER.—Mr. J. M. Forrest, the ma[ ]the Strawberry Hill mine, reports the d[ ]of a new lode that has given a large retu surface tests.

UNPROCLAIMED DISTRICTS.—Notwith[ ]the severity of the weather several pro parties have been in the field, and retur[ ]just in time for the holidays. The sub[ ]their report is thus given:

MASQUODABOIT (JENNINGS)—appears [ ]become of importance, very reliable au[ ]stating that more gold is visible there in quartz than in that of any other district. of soil, wetness and want of a good road, e present drawbacks to its popularity.

TEEN-MILE STREAM is considered so import- about three thousand areas have been taken der leases and prospecting licences—that a nment Surveyor has been sent down to lay and two mills are in course of erection. l also has been commenced, partly at Gov- nt, and partly at the miners' expense.

VER DAM—The surface boulders are re- bly rich, but the exploring party returned it having succeeded in discovering any lodes.

GOLD RETURNS.

following is an abstract of the mill-owners' s for the month of December, received up 12th inst., at the office of the Chief Com- ner. Oldham, Uniacke, and Renfrew Mills not returned, but those districts are repre- in the appended bullion report:

	Quartz Crushed. tons.	cwt.	Gold Yield. oz.	dwt.	gr.
Sherbrooke.					
ion	320	0	129	9	0
e	168	0	72	8	0
gton	207	14	232	16	12
ian	100	0	18	8	18
o	50	5	1	0	0
	8	10	3	5	0
rston	200	0	41	10	0
orth	194	16	22	15	0
Wine Harbor.					
ia	56	12	32	14	11
as	78	0	24	1	9
	—	—	7	19	7
do	202	0	49	5	6
Waverley.					
Major	111	0	39	11	14
and N.S	146	0	52	2	0
Indian Path.					
clow	27	0	5	13	22
Ecum Secum.					
tic	44	0	10	19	4
Tangier.					
	37	16	24	8	0
Montague.					
's	62	10	108	3	0
Recapitulation.					
ooke	1,249	0	521	12	6
Harbor	336	12	114	0	9
ley	257	0	91	13	14
Path	27	0	5	13	22
Secum	44	0	10	19	4
	37	16	24	8	0
gue	62	10	108	3	0
	2,013	18	876	10	7

following quantities of bar gold have been d in Halifax between the 17th December, and the 12th January, 1869:

dr. R. E. Fraser, assayer—

pany.	District.	oz.	dwt.	gr.
niacke	Uniacke,	85	17	7
St. Lawrence	do.	5	3	3
orth	Sherbrooke.	22	13	0
	do. }	8	9	0
on & Sherbrooke	do. }			
ion		160	4	5
er	Waverley,	7	6	22
	Muquodoboit,	5	13	1
	Oldham,	61	13	11
rrie	do.	7	16	0
	Wine Harbor,	34	2	22
d	Renfrew,	4	6	2
lessrs. Huse & Lowell, bankers—				
niacke	Uniacke	150	0	11
	Renfrew,	231	17	0
rd	do.	16	13	6
	do.	7	10	0
ial	do.	46	14	4
bine	Sherbrooke,	17	7	20
and N. S.	Waverley,	44	14	0
Total		869	1	18
lue		$17,380		

ed by Mr. Fraser.

Commercial.

Montreal Correspondence.

(From our own Correspondent.)

Montreal, Jan. 19. 1869.

I have to report exceeding dulness in all branches of trade, merchants, generally, being busy in making up their books and squaring up last year's operations. So far no new transactions have been gone into, and everything is conducted on purely retail principles. This is generally the case till towards the end of February, when the country trade usually brightens up, stocks running low about that time.

GROCERIES.—The market has been exceedingly quiet; some few lines of tea have changed hands, chiefly of Japans and Young Hysons. Twankays are enquired for, but all good qualities are scarce. Sugars have rather advanced, and are in good demand. Stocks here are not heavy, and the refinery prices are very stiff. Salt remains firm at 95c. for coarse and fine. Chemicals of all sorts are dull, the stocks being ample. Wines and liquors are very quiet, but not being pressed on the market, prices are maintained. Other staples are dull, with only a retail business doing.

PRODUCE.—Our receipts since the 1st January, have been heavy, in excess of our requirements, consequently prices are dull and the tendency of the market is downwards; some lots of extra strong bakers' sold at $5.00 to $5.05; but the latter is an exceptional rate; the range is—Extra, $5.25 to $5.40; Fancy, $5.00 to $5.05; Supers No. 1, $4.85 to $4.90; ditto No. 2, $4.40 to $4.50; even at these rates, buyers are very reluctant to enter the Market; the late rise in England has had comparatively but little effect here. In grain of all sorts, the business is so light that prices are purely nominal, I may quote U.C. Spring Wheat at $1.17 to $1.18; Red Winter, $1.16; Chicago No. 2, $1.10 to $1.12; Peas, 92c to 94c per 60 lbs; Corn, western mixed, 87½ to 90c per 60 lbs.; Oats are worth 45c to 46c per 32 lbs, for round lots; Barley, $1.20 to $1.25 for ordinary samples.

PROVISIONS.—The receipts of butter are considerable, but prices remain firm. Pork still rules high, and mess sells at $25 50 to $25 75. Other grades in proportion. Dressed hogs command full rates, say $9 to $9 50, for good to choice lots.—No particular change in other articles.

Toronto Market.

GRAIN.—*Wheat.*—Receipts 7,400 bush. and 8,360 bush. for the previous week. The demand for Spring continues light and there is not much offering. Good samples are worth $1.03 $1.04, and several cars sold at these figures. There is a limited demand for fall at $1.10 to $1.12; receipts are light and very little offered; the brightest samples of white are scarce and might bring an advance on these figures. *Barley.*—Receipts 1,300 bush. and 1,950 bush. last week. There is a small demand from brewers for car loads at $1.25 to $1.28 and a fair amount offering. *Oats.*—Receipts 6,700 bush. and 4,800 bush. last week. The market is rather dull at 52c. on track, a little higher was paid during the week. *Peas.*—Receipts very light and there is little doing; car loads are nominally worth our quotations. *Rye.*—Selling on the street at 70c. to 75c.

FLOUR.—Receipts 3,350 bbls. and 1,228 bbls. last week. No. 1 Superfine is dull at $4.50 to $4.55 for ordinary brands; Spring extra is worth $4.65. Sales of these two grades foot up over 1,000 bbls. in all at from $4.55 to $4.65. Extra is worth $5 to $5.25. Nothing doing in other grades.

PROVISIONS.—*Dressed Hogs.*—The market is firm and steady at our quotations with a considerable amount of business doing. Prices have ranged from $8 for very light weight to $9.25 for heavy and $9.50 for extra heavy. In other provisions little doing.

PETROLEUM.—A steady trade is doing at our quotations which remain unchanged.

DRY GOODS.—There has been no movement in trade worthy of notice since the commencement of the year. The imports of the leading articles of dry goods, at the port of Toronto, for three years were as follows:

	1866.	1867.	1868.
Woollens	$1,485,779	$1,459,404	$1,073,081
Cottons	1,3 0,000	1,307,246	979,414
Silks, satins, velvets	308,415	2 1,367	277,585
Linens	1 9,59	173 100	185,883
Hats, caps, Bonnets	46,042	54,383	63,234

GROCERIES.—There were very few changes in prices for a month past; any that have occurred are carefully noted in our price list. The imports of the articles named at the port of Toronto for 1868 were:

Sugar, yellow Muscovado	lbs.	3,213,407	$413,713
Cane juice	"	47,820	879
Confectionery	"	14,054	2,174
Coffee, green	"	226,211	26,429
Starch	"	3,805	495
Tea, green and Japan	"	662,006	273,9.9
Tea, black	"	119,264	43,742
Tobacco, manufactured	"	25,608	7,779
Mace and Nutmegs	"	19,970	5,690
Dried Fruits & Nuts			48,028

The following were the importations of liquors at the port of Toronto for the year ending 31st December, 1868:

	1865.	1866.	1867.	1868.
Whiskey, gals	4,6.2	3,313	6,387	15,367
Gin, gals	2,715	3,757	4,907	8,850
Rum, gals	2,030	2,126	9,574	7,857
Brandy, gals	6 714	15,027	13,703	18,987
Ales, beer and porter, gals	6,707	66	594	....
" " "	4,445	4,445	7,700	13,804
Wine in wood, gals	15,795	13,540	25,359	33,211

FREIGHTS.—Rates by Grand Trunk Railway:—Flour to all stations from Belleville to Lynn, inclusive, 35c., grain per 100 lbs. 18c.; flour to Brockville and Cornwall, inclusive, 45c., grain 22c.; flour to Montreal 50c., grain 25c.; flour to all stations between Island Pond and Portland, inclusive, 85c., grain 45c.; flour to Boston $1.15 US currency; flour to Halifax $1,06, grain 53c.; flour to St. John 95c.; boxed meats and butter to Liverpool per gross ton 82s 6d.; lard or butter in tinnets 87s. 6d; pork 11s. per tierce; flour 5s 6d. per bbl.; grain 12s. 0d. per 480 pounds. Rates by Great Western Railway—Flour, Toronto to Suspension Bridge 25c. gold; thence to New York 70c U. S. currency per bbl.; to Boston 90c. gold. Rates from Toronto to Liverpool, London and Glasgow are—Beef, bacon, pork, hams, lard and tallow, in lots of one car load and upwards, $1.52 gold, per 100 lbs.; grain in bags of 5 car loads and upwards, 96c., do.; flour $1.62 per bbl., do.

The Sugar Trade of 1868.

The sugar trade of late years has not been a very profitable one to anybody, and we cannot say that there has been much improvement during 1868. It is true that the British and foreign West Indian crops have been large, but, at the outside, they do not produce more than a third of the known production of sugar, and, under the present imperfect conditions of manufacture, the current rates have not been very remunerative. The home trade have not had greater reason to think well of 1868, for the year opened with falling prices, which were followed in the spring by a speculative rise—to be succeeded, as was to be expected, by a continued gradual fall in prices, which has been spread over no less than seven months, and nothing can be more unsatisfactory than such a state of things to those who have to hold stocks. Nor have diminished earnings rateably been followed by an increased return, for the consumption for the first time in many years has fallen off considerably—thus showing that the crisis of 1866 has at last affected consumption by stopping speculative enterprise, and this cause, coupled with the high price of bread in the earlier part of the year, and the continued dearness of meat and butter, are, no doubt, sufficient to account for the disappointing decrease in the use of sugar. One satisfactory point, however, is that the custom of "cutting in sugar," that is, of the retailers selling it at a loss or a little profit, appears to be rapidly diminishing, as the necessity becomes more apparent for obtaining a fair rate of profit on everything sold, instead of making some article, like tea, a kind of scapegoat to bear the sins of others.

The statistical position of sugar at the beginning of 1868 was a strong one, but the margin for the refiners' profit was insufficient, while their stocks of manufactured goods were large. The result was that the refiners were completely out of the market, and a fall in raw sugar naturally followed, and during January, and up to the middle of February, amounted to no less than 3s. per cwt. took place, to be followed in March by renewed depression, when the new West India sugars began to arrive. The statistical position of affairs, however, continued strong, and an opinion began to be entertained that the produce markets would be the scene of a revival from the effects of the panic, and that sugar would be one of the first articles most affected, as the stocks were small, while prices were low. It appeared also that the stocks in the United States were exhausted, so that the early shipments from the West Indies would be diverted from Europe. Owing to the small turnout of the beet crop it was evident also that the continental refiners would not send much of their produce here. Although the promise of the European West Indian crops was very good, these considerations, aided by news of a terrific hurricane in Mauritius, and of great damage to the crop, led to a rise during April and the first half of May of 3s. 6d. per cwt. In the meantime the void in the United States stocks had been pretty well filled, and supplies from the large crops began to pour in here, while the grocers persisted in a curious hand-to-mouth policy which completely baffled the efforts of speculators. A fall then commenced, followed by a depression and a continuous decline in prices which has lasted to the present time. This has only been relieved by fears in the autumn of injury to the beet crops by drought and by rumors of the damage to be done to the next Cuban crop by the rising in the island, and by the not improbable emancipation of the slaves. The catalogue of successive falls continued through nearly seven months would be wearisome, and it is sufficient to say that the general raw sugar market closed 6d to 1s. lower than at the end of 1867. Fine grocery sugars which, however, are too rarely to be had to affect prices, and which are therefore not included in ordinary market reports, are fully 1s. dearer. Refiners' moist sugars are on the average 2s. cheaper, but the absence of foreign competition, owing to the smallness of the present and last beet crops has enabled them to maintain the price of their stoved sugars, at the same point as at the end of 1867. The same cause has also kept up the price of crushed.

With regard to the prospects of the market, the principal element of uncertainty is the condition of Cuba, which still remains very unsettled. At present we are not disposed to attach importance to the insurrection in the island, but should it reach larger proportions, the out-turn of sugar would no doubt be reduced. The possible decrease, however, we regard as too problematical to affect prices, at present, in a commodity affected by so many causes. The beet crops will again show a decrease, or only a slight increase, while the news from the British West Indies and Mauritius is not very good at present. So far, therefore, probabilities are somewhat in favor of prices; but, on the other hand, the consumption not only here, but in all the principal markets, taking them together, shows a considerable decrease, and no immediate prospect of a revival, while the stocks, already in excess, will shortly be reinforced by the new West Indian crops; there will, in all probability, be a considerable increase in the produce of Louisiana, which indeed will, it is said, be double that of last year, although

not nearly up to the average yield before the civil war. Should Cuba settle down, an even larger crop than the last (which yielded an excess of no less than 150,000 tons) is looked for, while while we do not place much reliance on the fragmentary crop reports which come from the West Indies, and prefer to wait for actual results. The refiners also are not likely to be heavy buyers; and, on the whole, it seems to us that the immediate prospect of the price of raw sugar is downwards. No one, however, can pretend to foretell for any lengthened period the course of a market dependent entirely on the weather in fifty different countries, and on the very uncertain issue of the troubles in Cuba.

There has been no very marked advance in sugar machinery during the past year, and "Diffusion" and Mr. Fryer's Concretor are still the principal subjects of discussion among planters. The late controversy as to the desirability of cultivating the beet in England for sugar purposes, and its practical result in Mr. Duncan's experimental factory at Lavenham, as well as the successful introduction of its cultivation into the United States—the only stronghold of the cane left, besides England—together with the gradual progress of the sugar industry on the Continent, are surely sufficient to induce the closest attention to possible improvements on the part of cane growers. The wonderful results of central factories in the French West Indies, and the great dividends paid by them, contrasted with the abject and almost retrogressive position of our Islands, are at last, we trust, attracting greater attention among our colonists. The very important question of improving the cane by selection has been taken up in earnest in Mauritius, where the plant appears to be exhausted, and in the West Indies the question of adopting the Salangore cane is also being discussed. What can be done by care in cultivation in manufacture is shown by the recent complete transformation of Guadeloupe; and on a lesser scale by our own colony of Demerara, where the yield has been raised from one to two tons per acre, while its sugar, from being the by-word of our market, has assumed the first place in it. The large proportion of raw white crystals, equal to the refiners' now made in the French Islands, raises the question whether the easy further step of putting up moulds and making loaf sugar cannot be carried out. Already in France loaf sugar is made direct from the beet at a less cost than raw sugar under the old-process, and the question has at length arisen whether sugar refiners are not as unnecessary as a fifth wheel to a coach, and whether, in the course of time, they will not disappear. This, however, will not, we trust, become a practical question for many years, as the refining trade has been anything but a brilliant one of late.

The refiners, generally, have been dissatisfied with the result of their labors during the past year, and, although the position of the loaf sugar makers is no doubt much better than it was a year ago, the pieces makers have still considerable cause for complaint. The London refining trade trade is certainly not a flourishing branch of industry at present, while rumors of difficulties among the Clyde refiners, in the course of the year, have shown that their apparently wonderful prosperity did not extend to the whole trade. In fact, in these days of competition, sugar refining is no longer a Sleepy Hollow where things can jog easily along, but, on the contrary, it has become a trade which only keen men of business can make pay. It is to be regretted, therefore, that so little improvement in the processes of the London refiners is to be reported, and that they still persist in their obsolete mode of manufacture, and in refusing to meet the wants of the time. As this is the case, however, it is by no means surprising that the proportion of the sugar trade done by London continues to decrease.

Those who lean upon a delusive support like the graduated sugar duties start from an unsafe position, and one which every day that passes

renders more precarious. The Drawback Convention, by which the refiners of England, France Holland and Belgium, finding their hold on trade slipping from them, entered into a solemn league and covenant to protect and stand by each other, has proved a deceptive protection, although the weak places in its armor have again been tinkered up, it is none the less unsafe factory to those concerned, and is worthless as a defensive weapon. We have not patience to detail the incomprehensible negotiations at the Hague, which, however, were carried on in a way quite characteristic of our Government's management of the sugar duties, and consisted chiefly in leaving the Dutch in full possession of the bounty on the import of Java sugar, leaving touched the French bounty on French Colonial sugar, the differential duties on foreign bottoms the protection of 1s. per cwt. against English sugar, and evasion of the spirit of the convention which bound the French to adopt graduated duties. Such elaborate trifling is almost contemptible, and it becomes clearer every day that an antiquated diplomatic cobwebs cannot bind sugar trade, and that either a uniform duty better still, no duty at all, is the only solution of the sugar question. The latter solution has great weight given to it by Mr. Bright's breakfast table policy, which, as regards sugar not only practicable, but eminently desirable not only advancing free trade in general, but releasing one of the most important articles food from the trammels which, as we have recently shown, probably treble its price.—*Produce Markets Review.*

Petroleum.

We condense the following statistics of this important branch of trade from the annual review published in the New York *Commercial Shipping List:*

Total exports from the United States for the years:

N. Y...galls.	52,803,202	33,834,133	34,501
Boston	2,410,114	2,264,121	1,591
Philadel'a....	40,505,620	29,437,429	28,811
Baltimore....	2,587,707	1,515,454	2,488
Portland......	705,107	900	11
New Bedford	......	......	3(
Cleveland....	270,000	......	......

Total galls...99,281,750	65,052,029	67,43(
Equal to bbls			
of 40 galls..	2,482,044	1,676,300	1,68:

Of the exports from New York in 1868, 6, 180 gallons were crude, 40,347,922 gallons refined, 231,345 gallons lubricating, 5,526,920 gallons naphtha, and 72,765 residuum.

Of the exports from New York in 1867, 2,570,000 gallons were crude, 29,950,000 refined and 1,364,000 gallons naphtha.

Of the exports from Philadelphia in 2,672,055 gallons were crude, 35,449,070 gallons refined, 594,270 gallons lubricating, 3,20(gallons naphtha, and 52,920 gallons residuum total 41,974,985 gallons, allowing 45 gallons the barrel.

Of the exports from Boston, 2,041,746 gallons were refined, 27,966 gallons lubricating, 340,402 gallons naphtha. Of the exports Baltimore, 177,390 gallons were crude, 1,50(gallons refined, 847,980 gallons lubricating 55,980 gallons naphtha.

Ports to which the Exports from New and Philadelphia were shipped in 1868:

	From New York.	From Philad
	Gallons.	Gal
Liverpool 1,291,200	1,15
London 947,311	72
Bristol 184,070	5
Falmouth..................... 98,210	29
Cork, &c......................2,272,584	3,86

re 2,025,411 1,911,225
settles 3,269,600 1,914,696
en, &c .... 149,450 ....
kirk 369,501 266,582
ieux 184,600 127,186
ites .... 78,539 ....
werp 7,082,177 8,436,077
men 8,578,026 6,513,496
burg 2,458,557 2,828,901
erdam 1,695,235 3,722,467
stadt 1,523,387 605,559
ona .... 150,028 ....
tlin, &c 2,537,085 869,213
zig 384,571 250,860
iz and Malaga .... 380,531 ....
agona .... 518,250 ....
celona 470,929 185,843
raltar, &c 4,289,017 1,998,852
rto .... 251,704 ....
ides, &c 1,082,209 183,930
os, &c 2,229,928 2,195,976
ste 900,161 610,258
rna .... 388,873 ....
xandria, Egypt ... 223,000 ....
stantinople ...... 603,012 ....
enhagen 118,492 111,081
on and Seville ... 417,210 ....
ua .... 199,163 ....
na and E. I ...... 190,360 ....
tralia .... 959,959 ....
ney, N. S. W ..... 294,520 ....
sil .... 804,396 ....
dico .... 165,573 ....
a .... 288,955 ....
entine Republic .. 169,200 ....
platine Republic . 91,000 ....
li .... 168,000 ....
.... 233,000 ....
tish West Indies . 236,805 ....
uon West Indies .. 77,260 ....
tral America, &c.. 125,076 ....
ock 158,792
tock 70,517
linore 74,247
ckholm 86,020
nice 168,512
bon 43,194 142,530
ier ports 242,760 963,046

The production of crude has probably averaged
000 bbls. per day the past year, or about the
ne as in 1867, although the present yield is
lered to be not over £,500 barrels per day.
e stock held on the Allegheny River from Oil
y to Tidioute, January 1st, is 264,805 bbls. of
gallons each, against 584, 600 same time in
17. Shipments from January 1 to December
1868 shipments of crude and refined of 45
lons to the bbl., by all routes, and the total
piments of crude for the same time are:

New York, bbls 877,251
Cleveland, bbls 814,882
Boston, bbls 106,811
Philadelphia, bbls 224,479
Portland, bbls 32,648
Pittsburgh, bbls 1,121,387
other points 221,677

Total bbls 3,399,145
ference between the crude and refined
hipped bbls 100,670

al shipments of crude of bbls. of 45
gallons each 3,508,815
al production from January 1 to Dec,
, 1888 (11 months), bbls 3,413,891
erage per day, bbls 10,190

A later date, at hand after the above was
tten, makes the total production from Janu-
1 to December 31, 1868, 3,715,741 bbls. of
gallons, and the total shipments of crude,
27,063 bbls. of 45 gallons each.
The total capacity of iron tankage in the
ion mentioned is 1,140,039 bbls., of which
1534 are empty, of these latter, 244,410 in
City and vicinity; and 126,792 in Tidioute.

STATEMENT OF BANKS

ACTING UNDER CHARTER, FOR THE MONTH ENDING 31st DECEMBER, 1868, ACCORDING TO RETURNS FURNISHED BY THE BANKS TO THE AUDITOR OF PUBLIC ACCOUNTS.

NAME OF BANK	CAPITAL — Capital authorized by Act	Capital paid up	LIABILITIES — Promissory Notes in circulation not bearing Interest	Balances due to other Banks	Cash Deposits not bearing Interest	Cash Deposits bearing Interest	TOTAL LIABILITIES	ASSETS — Coin, Bullion, Provincial Notes	Landed or other Property of the Bank	Government Securities	Promissory Notes and Bills of other Banks	Balances due from other Banks	Notes and Bills Discounted	Other Debts due to the Bank not included under foregoing heads	TOTAL ASSETS
ONTARIO AND QUEBEC.															
Montreal	6,000,000	6,000,000													
Quebec	3,000,000	3,000,000													
City	1,000,000	1,000,000													
Gore															
British North America															
Banque du Peuple															
Niagara District															
Molsons															
Toronto															
Ontario															
Eastern Townships															
Banque Nationale															
Banque Jacques Cartier															
Mechanics'															
Royal Canadian															
Union B'k Lower Canada															
Merchants'															
Bank of Commerce															
NOVA SCOTIA.															
Bank of Yarmouth															
People's															
Union Bank															
Bank of Nova Scotia															
NEW BRUNSWICK.															
Bank of New Brunswick															
Commercial Bank															
St. Stephen's Bank															
People's Bank															
Totals															

A BANK WANTED.—The St. John's *Morning News* of the 12th says :—

"The extent of the shaving operations in notes and sterling exchange, done outside the Banks is sufficient evidence of the necessity for the establishment of another Bank in our City. The operations in this line were never larger or more lucrative than at present, but the element on which we would lay most stress is that the business seems to be a comparatively safe one. It is nothing unusual to see good paper, the foundation of which is all 'leather,' being hawked around various offices in town, for discount, and ultimately, as the best that can be done with it, subjected to a shave of 12 or 15 per cent. With proper Banking facilities this ought not to be ; and we are surprised that the commercial community submit quietly to such usury."

The remedy lies in the hands of our merchants —let them represent to some first-class Canadian Banks the field open here for their enterprise, and we are assured the shavers and curb-stone bookers will speedily find their occupation gone.

To Mercantile Men.

THE NEW POCKET REFERENCE BOOK OF THE MERCANTILE AGENCY revised to Christmas, and containing 35,000 names of Traders in the Dominion, is now out of press, and ready for delivery.

Subscribers having Travellers out, or about leaving, should avail themselves of this indispensable volume.

DUN, WIMAN & CO.,
Exchange Buildings, Toronto.
Canadian Offices—Montreal and Halifax.
January 19.　　　　　　　　　　　23-tf

Beaver Mutual Fire Insurance Association.

THE annual meeting of the members of the above Association will be held at the office, 20 Toronto Street, Toronto, on TUESDAY, the 9th day of FEBRUARY next, at 12 o'clock, noon, for reception of Report of Board of Directors, election of Directors to fill vacancies, and transaction of other business.

The attendance of all members is particularly requested.
By order,
22　　　　　　W. T O'REILLY, Secretary.

Oil Refiners' Association of Canada.

THE above Association hereby give notice that an Office has been opened

AT LONDON, ONTARIO,
FOR THE SALE OF ALL
THE REFINED PETROLEUM OIL
Made by the Association, at the following Rates and Terms., viz :

IN LOTS OF ONE TO FOUR CAR LOADS, INCLUSIVE, AT 35 CENTS PER GALLON.
IN LOTS OF FIVE CAR LOADS AND UPWARDS, AT 32 CENTS PER GALLON.

Terms—Cash, free on board at London.

All Oil sold to be received at the place of shipment by the purchaser ; and in the event of his failing to appoint a person to inspect and receive the oil, it must be understood that it will in all cases be subject to the Inspector's appointed by the Association ; and, after shipment is made, no drawbacks on account of quality, quantity, packages, or otherwise, will be allowed.

All orders to be addressed to the Secretary, and all remittances to be made to the Treasurer.
SAMUEL PETERS, President.
WM. DUFFIELD, Vice-President.
L. C. LEONARD, Secretary.
CHARLES HUNT, Treasurer.
London, Ont., Jan. 6, 1868.　　　　23-tf

Hurd, Leigh & Co.,
IMPORTERS AND DECORATORS OF FRENCH CHINA.

Hotels and families supplied with any pattern or crest desired.

Common goods always on hand. 72 Yonge Street, Toronto, Ontario.　　　　　　26y

---

Brown Brothers,
ACCOUNT-BOOK MANUFACTURERS,
Stationers, Book-Binders, Etc.,
66 and 68 King Street East, Toronto, Ont.

ACCOUNT Books for Banks, Insurance Companies Merchants, etc., made to order of the best materials and for style, durability and cheapness unsurpassed.

A large stock of Account-Books and General Stationery constantly on hand.
September 1, 1868.　　　　　　3-1y

KERSHAW & EDWARDS,
IMPROVED PATENT
NON-CONDUCTING AND VAPORIZING
FIRE AND BURGLAR-PROOF SAFES.
139 & 141
ST. FRANÇOIS XAVIER STREET,
MONTREAL.

AGENTS :
A. K. BOOMER, TORONTO.
J. W. MURTON, HAMILTON.
A. G. SMYTH, LONDON, ONT.　　51 6m

John Ross & Co.,
QUEBEC.
T. & F. ROSS & CO.,
GENERAL WHOLESALE GROCERS,
PRODUCE AND COMMISSION MERCHANTS,
361 Commissioner Street,
MONTREAL.　　　　6

The Albion Hotel,
MONTREAL,

ONE of the oldest established houses in the City is again under the personal management of
Mr. DECKER,

Who, to accommodate his rapidly increasing business, is adding Eighty more Rooms to the house, making the Largest Establishments in Canada.
June, 1868.　　　　　　　42-6ms

W. McLaren & Co.,
WHOLESALE
BOOT AND SHOE MANUFACTURERS
18 ST. MAURICE STREET,
MONTREAL.
June, 1868.　　　　　　48-1

Lyman & McNab,
Importers of, and Wholesale Dealers in,
HEAVY AND SHELF HARDWARE
King Street,
TORONTO, ONTARIO.

THE QUEEN'S HOTEL.
THOMAS DICK, Proprietor,
FRONT STREET,　　　　TORONTO, ON

Montreal House, Montreal, Canada.

TO MONETARY MEN—Merchants, Insurance Agents Lawyers, Bankers, Railway and Steamboat Travellers Mining Agents, Directors and Stockholders of Public Companies, and other persons visiting Montreal for business or pleasure, are here by most respectfully informed that the undersigned prepares to furnish the best hotel accommodation at the most reasonable charges. It is our study to provide every comfort and accommodation to all our guests, especially for gentlemen engaged as above. those who have been accustomed to patronize other first class hotels, we only ask a trial; we have the same accommodation and our table is furnished with every delicacy of the season.
Nov. 22, 1867.　　　　H. DUCLOS.

Commercial House,
(LATE HUFFMAN HOUSE)
PETERBOROUGH, ONTARIO.
GEORGE CRONN　　　　PROPRIETOR

large addition lately made, including Twenty End Rooms
Dec. 10, 1866.

Mercantile.

Teas! Teas!! Teas!!!

FRESH ARRIVALS

NEW CROP TEAS,

WINES, AND GENERAL GROCERIES,

Special Inducements given to

PROMPT PAYING PURCHASERS.

All Goods sold at very Lowest Montreal Prices!

W. & R. GRIFFITH,

ONTARIO CHAMBERS,
Corner of Front and Church Streets,
TORONTO
ONTARIO

1y

TEAS. Reford & Dillon TEAS.

HAVE just received ex. steamships "*St. David* and *Nestorian*:"

1000 hlf. chests new season TEAS!
Comprising Twankays, Young Hysons, Imperials, Gunpowders, colored and uncolored Japans, Congous, Souchongs, and Pekoes.
500 hlf. bxs. new Valentia Raisins (selected fruit).
500 bags cleaned Arracan and Rangoon Rice.
500 brls. choice Currants.

ALSO IN STORE:—

250 hhds. bright Barbadoes and Cuba Sugars.
250 brls. Portland, Standard, Golden & Amber Syrups.
100 bags Rio, Jamaica, Laguayra, and Java Coffees.
250 bxs. 10s Tobacco, "Queen's Own" and "Prince of Wales'" brands.

WITH A GENERAL AND

WELL SELECTED STOCK OF GROCERIES;

All of which they offer to the Trade low.

12 & 14 WELLINGTON STREET, TORONTO.

7-1y

Robert H. Gray,

Manufacturer of Hoop Skirts

AND

CRINOLINE STEEL,

IMPORTER OF

HABERDASHERY, TRIMMINGS

AND

GENERAL FANCY GOODS,

43, YONGE STREET, TORONTO, ONT. 6-1y

John Boyd & Co.,

WHOLESALE GROCERS AND COMMISSION MERCHANTS,

61 AND 63 FRONT STREET

TORONTO.

NOW in store, direct from the European and West India Markets, a large assortment of General Groceries, comprising

Teas, Sugars, Coffees, Wines and Liquors,

AND

GENERAL GROCERIES.

Ship Chandlery, Canvas, Manilla and Tarred Rope, Oakum, Tar, Flags, &c., &c.,

DIRECT FROM THE MANUFACTURERS.

JOHN BOYD. ALEX. M. MONRO. C. W. BUNTING.

Toronto, Oct. 1st, 1868. 7-1y

TORONTO PRICES CURRENT.—JANUARY 21, 1869.

Name of Article.	Wholesale Rates.	
Boots and Shoes.	$ c.	$ c.
Mens' Thick Boots	2 20	2 50
" Kip	2 50	3 25
" Calf	3 00	3 70
" Congress Gaiters	2 00	2 50
" Kip Cobourgs	1 15	1 45
Boys' Thick Boots	1 60	1 80
Youths' "	1 35	1 50
Women's Batts	95	1 30
" Congress Gaiters	1 15	1 45
Misses' Batts	0 75	1 00
" Congress Gaiters	1 00	1 30
Girls' Batts	0 60	0 85
" Congress Gaiters	0 80	1 10
Children's C. T. Cacks	0 50	0 65
" Gaiters	0 65	0 90
Drugs.		
Aloes Cape	0 12½	0 16
Alum	0 02½	0 03
Borax	0 00	0 00
Camphor, refined	0 65	0 70
Castor Oil	0 18	0 28
Caustic Soda	0 04½	0 05
Cochineal	0 90	1 00
Cream Tartar	0 25	0 30
Epsom Salts	0 03	0 04
Extract Logwood	0 09	0 11
Gum Arabic, sorts	0 30	0 35
Indigo, Madras	0 75	1 00
Licorice	0 14	0 45
Madder	0 16	0 18
Nutgalls	0 00	0 00
Opium	6 70	7 00
Oxalic Acid	0 28	0 35
Potash, Bi-tart	0 25	0 28
" Bichromate	0 15	0 20
Potass Iodide	3 80	4 50
Senna	0 12½	0 60
Soda Ash	0 03	0 04
Soda Bicarb	4 50	5 50
Tartaric Acid	0 37½	0 45
Verdigris	0 35	0 40
Vitriol, Blue	0 09	0 10
Groceries.		
Coffees:		
Java, ℔ lb.	0 27@0	24
Laguayra,	0 17	0 18
Rio	0 15	0 17
Fish:		
Herrings, Lab. split	5 75	6 50
" round	4 00	4 75
" scaled	0 35	0 40
Mackerel, small kitts	1 00	0 00
Loch. Her. wh'e firks	2 50	2 75
" half "	1 25	1 50
White Fish & Trout	3 50	3 75
Salmon, saltwater	14 00	15 00
Dry Cod, ℔112 lbs.	5 00	5 25
Fruit:		
Raisins, Layers	2 00	2 10
" M. R.	1 90	2 10
" Valentias new	0 6½	0 07
Currants, new	0 07	00 07½
" old	0 04½	0 04½
Figs	0 14	0 00
Molasses:		
Clayed, ℔ gal.	0 00	0 35
Syrups, Standard	0 49	0 50
" Golden	0 56	0 57½
Rice:		
Arracan	4 50	4 75
Spices:		
Cassia, whole, ℔ lb.	0 00	0 45
Cloves	0 11	0 12
Nutmegs	0 45	0 55
Ginger, ground	0 20	0 25
" Jamaica, root	0 20	0 25
Pepper, black	0 09½	0 10
Pimento	0 08	0 09
Sugars:		
Port Rico, ℔ lb.	0 08½	0 08½
Cuba "	0 08½	0 08½
Barbadoes (bright)	0 08½	0 09
Dry Crushed, at 60d.	——	0 11½
Canada Sugar Refine'y, yellow No. 2, 60ds.	0 00	0 09½
Yellow, No. 2½	0 09½	0 00
" No. 3	0 09½	0 00
Crushed X	0 00	0 10½
" A	0 11½	0 11½
Ground	0 11½	0 11½
Dry Crushed	0 11½	0 11½
Extra Ground	0 12½	0 12½
Teas:		
Japan com'n to good	0 40	0 55
" Fine to choicest	0 55	0 65
Colored, com. to fine	0 60	0 75
Congou & Souch'ng	0 42	0 75
Oolong, good to fine	0 50	0 65
Y. Hyson, com to gd.	0 45	0 55
Medium to choice	0 65	0 80
Extra choice	0 85	0 95
Gunpowd're. to med.	0 55	0 70
" med. to fine	0 70	0 85

Name of Article.	Wholesale Rate.	
Groceries—*Contin'd*	$ c.	$ c.
" fine to fins't	0 85	0 95
Hyson	0 45	0 80
Imperial	0 42	0 80
Tobacco, Manufact'd:		
Can Leaf, ℔ lb 5s & 10s.	0 26	0 30
Western Leaf, com.	0 25	0 26
" Good	0 27	0 32
" Fine	0 32	0 35
" Bright fine	0 40	0 50
" " choice	0 60	0 75
Hardware.		
Tin (net cash prices)		
Block, ℔ lb.	0 25	0 26
Grain	0 25	0 26
Copper:		
Pig	0 23	0 24
Sheet	0 30	0 33
Cut Nails:		
Assorted ¼ Shingles, ℔ 100 lb.	2 90	3 00
Shingle alone do	3 15	3 25
Lathe and 5 dy.	3 30	3 40
Galvanized Iron:		
Assorted sizes	0 08	0 09
Best No. 24	0 09	0 00
" 26	0 08	0 08½
" 28	0 09	0 09½
Horse Nails:		
Guest's or Griffin's assorted sizes	0 00	0 00
For W. ass'd. sizes	0 18	0 19
Patent Hammer'd do	0 17	0 18
Iron (at 4 months):		
Pig—Gartsherrie No1	24 00	25 00
Other brands. No 1	22 00	24 00
" No 2	0 00	0 00
Bar—Scotch, ℔100 lb.	2 25	2 50
Refined	3 00	3 25
Swedes	5 00	5 50
Hoops—Coopers	3 00	3 25
Band	3 00	3 25
Boiler Plates	3 25	3 50
Canada Plates	4 00	4 25
Union Jack	0 00	0 00
Pontypool	4 00	4 25
Swansea	3 90	4 00
Lead (at 4 months):		
Bar, ℔ 100 lbs.	0 07	0 07½
Sheet "	0 08	0 09
Shot	0 07½	0 07½
Iron Wire (net cash):		
No. 6, ℔ bundle	2 70	2 80
" 9, "	3 10	3 20
" 12, "	3 40	3 50
" 16, "	4 30	4 40
Powder:		
Blasting, Canada	3 50	0 00
FF "	4 25	4 50
FFF "	4 75	5 00
Blasting, English	4 00	5 00
FF loose	5 00	6 00
FFF "	6 00	6 50
Pressed Spikes (4 mos):		
Regular sizes 100	4 00	4 25
Extra "	4 50	5 00
Tin Plates (net cash):		
IC Coke	7 50	8 00
IC Charcoal	8 25	8 50
IX "	10 25	10 75
IXX "	12 25	0 00
DC "	7 25	9 00
DX "	9 50	0 00
Hides & Skins. ℔ lb		
Green rough	0 06	0 00
Green, salt'd & insp'd	0 00	0 07
Cured	0 08	0 08½
Calfskins, green	0 00	0 1[illegible]
Calfskins, cured	0 00	0 12
" dry	0 18	0 20
Sheepskins,	1 00	1 25
" country	0 60	0 80
Hops.		
Inferior, ℔ lb.	0 05	0 07
Medium	0 07	0 09
Good	0 09	0 12
Fancy	0 09	0 00
Leather, @ (4 mos.) In lots of less than 50 sides, 10 ℔ cent higher.		
Spanish Sole, 1st qual. heavy, weights ℔ lb.	0 00	0 23
Do. 1st qual middle do.	0 22	0 23
Do. No. 2, all weights	0 20	0 21
Slaughter heavy	0 25	0 26
Do. light	0 50	0 00
Harness, best	0 32	0 34
" No. 2	0 30	0 33
Upper heavy	0 44	0 38
" light	0 36	0 40

Name of Article.	Wholesale Rates.	
Leather—*Contin'd.*	$ c.	$ c.
Kip Skins, Patna	0 30	0 40
French	0 70	0 90
English	0 65	0 80
Hemlock Calf (30 to 35 lbs.) per doz.	0 75	0 85
Do. light	0 45	0 50
French Calf	0 98	1 15
Grain & Satn Cll ℔ doz.	0 00	0 00
Splits, large ℔ lb.	0 30	0 33
" small	0 20	0 30
Enamelled Cow ℔ foot	0 17	0 18
Patent	0 20	0 21
Pebble Grain	0 17	0 18½
Buff	0 17	0 18
Oils.		
Cod	0 60	0 62½
Lard, extra	0 00	1 25
" No. 1	0 00	1 15
" Woollen	0 00	1 05
Lubricating, patent	0 00	0 00
" Mott's economic	0 50	0 00
Linseed, raw	0 77½	0 85
" boiled	0 82½	0 90
Machinery	0 00	0 00
Olive, 2nd, ℔ gal.	1 45	1 60
" salad	2 00	2 30
" salad, in bots. qt. ℔ case	3 60	3 75
Sesame salad, ℔ gal.	1 60	1 75
Seal, pale	0 70	0 75
Spirits Turpentine	0 65	0 70
Varnish	0 00	0 00
Whale	0 75	0 80
Paints, &c.		
White Lead, genuine in Oil, ℔ 25lbs.	0 00	2 50
Do. No. 1 "	0 00	2 25
" 2 "	0 00	2 00
" 3 "	0 00	1 75
White Zinc, genuine	3 00	3 50
White Lead, dry	0 06	0 09
Red Lead	0 07½	0 08
Venetian Red, Eng'h	0 02½	0 03½
Yellow Ochre, Fren'h	0 02½	0 03
Whiting	0 90	1 25
Petroleum. (Refined ℔ gal.)		
Water white, car l'd	—	—
" small lots	0 37	0 38
Straw, by car load	0 33	0 34
" small lots	0 35	0 36
Amber, by car load	0 00	0 00
" small lots	0 00	0 00
Benzine	0 49	0 00
Produce.		
Grain:		
Wheat, Spring, 60 lb.	1 02	1 05
" Fall 60 "	1 10	1 14
Barley 48 "	1 25	1 28
Peas 60 "	0 85	0 87
Oats 34 "	0 51	0 52
Rye 56 "	0 70	0 75
Seeds:		
Clover, choice 60 "	—	—
" com'n 68 "	—	—
Timothy, cho'e 4 "	—	—
" inf. to good 48 "	—	—
Flax 56 "	—	—
Flour (per brl.):		
Superior extra	0 00	0 00
Extra superfine,	5 00	5 20
Fancy superfine	4 70	4 90
Superfine No 1	4 50	4 55
" No. 2	0 00	0 00
Oatmeal, (per brl.)	6 00	6 25
Provisions.		
Butter, dairy tub ℔ lb.	0 21	0 22
" store packed	0 20	0 21
Cheese, new	0 11	0 11½
Pork, mess, per brl.	23 00	23 50
" prime mess	0 00	0 00
" prime	0 00	0 00
Bacon, rough	0 8½	0 09
" Cumberl'd cut	0 10	0 10½
" smoked	0 00	0 00
Hams, in salt	0 11	0 11½
" sug. cur. & canv'd	0 10	0 11½
Shoulders, in salt	0 12	0 13
Lard, in kegs	0 13	0 14
Eggs, packed	0 18	0 20
Beef Hams	0 00	0 13
Tallow	0 00	0 00
Hogs dressed, heavy	9 00	9 50
" medium	8 50	9 00
" light	8 00	8 50
Salt, &c.		
American brls.	1 50	152
Liverpool coarse	1 25	1 30
Plaster	1 05	1 10
Water Lime	1 50	0 00

Soap & Candles.	$ c.	$ c.
D. Crawford & Co.'s ..		
Imperial.........	0 07½	0 08
" Golden Bar	0 07	0 07½
" Silver Bar........	0 07	0 07½
Crown	0 05	0 05½
No. 1	0 03½	0 04
Candles	0 00	0 11½
Wines, Liquors, &c.		
Ale:		
English, per doz	2 60	2 65
Guinness Dub Portr..	2 35	2 40
Spirits:		
Pure Jamaica Rum...	1 80	2 25
De Kuyper's H Gin..	1 55	1 65
Booth's Old Tom.....	1 90	2 00
Gin:		
Green, cases.........	4 00	4 25
Booth's Old Tom, c...	6 00	6 25
Wines:		
Port, common	1 00	1 25
" fine old	2 00	4 00
Sherry, common	1 00	1 50
" medium	1 70	1 80
"old pale or golden..	2 50	4 00

Brandy:	$ c.	$ c.
Hennessy's, per gal..	2 0	2 50
Martell's " ..	2 30	2 50
J. Robin & Co.'s " ..	2 25	2 35
Otard, Dupuy & Cos..	2 25	2 35
Brandy, cases.........	8 50	9 00
Brandy, com. per c...	4 00	4 50
Whiskey:		
Common 36 u. p......	0 62½	0 65
Old Rye	0 85	0 87½
Malt	0 85	0 87½
Toddy	0 85	0 87½
Scotch, per gal......	1 90	2 10
Irish—Kinnahan's c...	7 00	7 50
" Dunnville's Belf't..	6 00	6 25
Wool.		
Fleece, lb....	0 28	0 35
Pulled "...........	0 22	0 25
Furs.		
Bear...............	3 00	10 00
Beaver............	1 00	1 25
Coon	0 20	0 40
Fisher............	4 00	6 00
Martin............	1 40	1 60
Mink..............	4 00	4 25
Otter.............	5 75	6 00
Spring Rats	0 15	0 17
Fox	1 20	1 25

INSURANCE COMPANIES.

ENGLISH.—*Quotations on the London Market.*

No. of Shares	Last Dividend.	Name of Company.	Shares par val £	Amount paid.	Last Sale.
20,0 0		Briton Medical and General Life...	10	....	1⅝
50,000	7½	Commer'l Union, Fire, Life and Mar.	50	5	5½
24,000	8	City of Glasgow	25	2¼	5⅝
5,000	9¼	Edinburgh Life	100	15	31½
400,000	5—½ yr	European Life and Guarantee......	2½	11s6	5s
100,000	10	Etna Fire and Marine..............	10	1½	0
20,000	5	Guardian	100	50	51½
24,000	12	Imperial Fire....................	500	50	0
7,500	9½	Imperial Life	100	10	15½
100,000	10	Lancashire Fire and Life..........	20	2	2⅜
10,000	11	Life Association of Scotland.......	40	7¼	25
35,832	45s. p. sh	London Assurance Corporation ..	25	12½	49
10,000	5	London and Lancashire Life	10	1	10s
87,504	40	Liverp'l & London & Globe F. & L.	20	2	6 15-16ths
20,000	5	National Union Life	5	1	0
20,000	12½	Northern Fire and Life	100	5	11½
40,000	12 '68, bo 5s.	North British and Mercantile	50	6¼	19¾
40,000	50	Ocean Marine	25	5	19¾
2,500	£5 12s.	Provident Life..................	100	10	0
....	£4½ p. s.	Phœnix	....	....	148
200,000	2½—h.yr.	Queen Fire and Life	10	1	17s
100,000	3s. bo.4s	Royal Insurance.................	20	3	6
20,000	10	Scottish Provincial Fire and Life ..	50	2½	5
10,000	25	Standard Life	50	12	65½
4,000	5	Star Life	25	1¼	—
		CANADIAN.			℘ c.
8,000	4	British America Fire and Marine ..	$50	$25	53 54xd
....	4	Canada Life	..	....	.....
4000	12	Montreal Assurance	£50	£5	135
10,000	3	Provincial Fire and Marine........	60	11	.....
....	....	Quebec Fire	40	32½	23½
....	8	" Marine....................	100	40	90
10,000	5 7 mo's.	Western Assurance...............	40	9	.....

RAILWAYS.	Sha's	Paid	Montr	London.
Atlantic and St. Lawrence..................	£100	All.	....	58 60
Buffalo and Lake Huron	20½	"	....	3 3½
Do. do Preference	10	"	....	5½ 6½
Buff., Brantt. & Goderich, 6℘c., 1872-3-4....	100	"	....	65 69
Champlain and St. Lawrence	....	....	10	....
Do. do Pref. 10 ℘ ct..........	...	....	73	....
Grand Trunk	100	"	15 16	15¾ 16
Do. Eq.G. M. Bds. 1 ch. 6℘c..........	100	"	...	84 86
Do. First Preference, 5 ℘ c	100	"	....	50 51
Do. Deferred, 3 ℘ ct..................	100	"	....	....
Do. Second Pref. Bonds, 5℘c...........	100	"	....	39½ 40½
Do. do Deferred, 3 ℘ ct.............	100	"	...	....
Do. Third Pref. Stock, 4 ℘ct...........	100	"	...	26½ 27½
Do. do. Deferred, 3 ℘ ct..............	100	"	...	...
Do. Fourth Pref. Stock, 3½c	100	"	....	17¾ 18¼
Do. do. Deferred, 3 ℘ ct..............	100	"	....	...
Great Western	20½	"	13 14	14½ 14¾
Do. New	20½	18	....	....
Do. 6 ℘ c. Bds, due 1873-76............	100	All.	....	99 101
5 ℘c Bds. due 1877-78...................	100	"	....	93 94
Marine Railway, Halifax, $250, all.	$250	"	....	....
Northern of Canada, 6 ℘c. 1st Pref. Bds....	100	"	...	80 83

EXCHANGE.	Halifax.	Montr'l.	Quebec.	Toronto.
Bank on London, 60 days				
Sight or 75 days date............	12½	9⅜ 9⅝	9½ 9¾	9⅞
Private do.	11½ 12	8 9	9 9½	8¾ to 9
Private, with documents....	....	....	....	....
Bank on New York...............	....	25½ 26	25 25½	73¾
Private do.	....	26 26½	25½ 26	....
Gold Drafts do.	....	½ dis. to p.	par ½ dis.	par ¼ dis.
Silver	....	4 4½	....	4 to 6

STOCK AND BOND REPORT.

The dates of our quotations are as follows:—Toronto, Jan. 19; Montreal, Jan. 18; Quebec Jan. 18; London, Dec. 31.

NAME.	Shares.	Paid up.	Divid'd last 6 Months	Dividend Day.	CLOSING PRICES. Toronto.	Montre'l	Que
BANKS.			℘ ct.				
British North America	$250	All.	3	July and Jan.	101½ 102	....	100
Jacques Cartier........	50	"	4	1 June, 1 Dec.	107 108	107½ 108	107
Montreal	200	"	5	"	139 140	120½	139
Nationale........	50	"	4	1 Nov. 1 May.	105 106	100	106½
New Brunswick	100	"	......	......	....	...	..
Nova Scotia	200	28	7&b$3½	Mar. and Sept.	....	....	..
Du Peuple....	50	"	4	1 Mar., 1 Sept.	108½ 109	108½	108
Toronto	100	"	4	1 Jan., 1 July.	118 120	119	117
Bank of Yarmouth.........	....	....	......	......	....	....	..
Canadian Bank of Com'e......	50	95	......	......	102 102½	101 102	101
City Bank Montreal	80	All.	4	1 June, 1 Dec.	100½ 101	100¾ 101½	100½
Commer'l Bank (St. John)....	100	"	℘ ct.	......	....	....	..
Eastern Townships' Bank....	50	"	4	1 July, 1 Jan..	...	97½ 100	96
Gore	40	...	none.	1 Jan., 1 July.	39 40	40 45	40
Halifax Banking Company....	....	....	......	......	....	....	..
Mechanics' Bank	50	70	4	1 Nov., 1 May.	95 96	94 96	94
Merchants' Bank of Canada....	100	70	4	1 Jan., 1 July.	107 107½	107 107½	108
Merchants' Bank (Halifax)....	....	....	.....	.....	....	....	..
Molson's Bank..........	50	All.	4	1 Apr., 1 Oct.	110 111	110 111	109
Niagara District Bank...	100	70	3½	1 Jan., 1 July	....	....	..
Ontario Bank.............	40	All.	4	1 June, 1 Dec.	100 100½	99¼ 99½	99
People's Bank (Fred'kton)....	100	"	.....	......	....	....	.
People's Bank (Halifax)	20	"	7 12 m	......	....	....	..
Quebec Bank	100	"	3½	1 June, 1 Dec.	98 99	....	99½
Royal Canadian Bank	50	50	4	1 Jan., 1 July.	84 85	85	84
St. Stephens Bank	100	All	.....	......	....	....	..
Union Bank	100	70	4	1 Jan., 1 July.	103 103½	102 103½	103½
Union Bank (Halifax)........	100	40	7 12mo	Feb. and Aug.	....	....	..
MISCELLANEOUS.							
British America Land.......	250	44	2½	......	....	....	..
British Colonial S. S. Co......	250	32½	2½	......	...	....	..
Canada Company	32½	All.	5	......	....	....	..
Canada Landed Credit Co.....	50	$20	3½	......	72 72½	....	..
Canada Per. B'ldg Society....	50	All.	5	......	123 123½	....	..
Canada Mining Company.....	4	90	......	......	....	....	..
Do. Inl'd Steam Nav. Co....	100	All.	20 12 m	......	....	106 107½	106
Do. Glass Company.........	100	"	12½ "	......	....	...	..
Canad'n Loan & Investm't....	25	2½	7	......	....	....	..
Canada Agency	10	½	......	......	....	....	..
Colonial Securities Co.......	...	...	......	......	....	....	..
Freehold Building Society....	100	All.	4	......	106 107	....	..
Halifax Steamboat Co........	100	"	5	......	....	....	..
Halifax Gas Company.........	....	....	......	......	....	....	..
Hamilton Gas Company......	....	....	......	......	....	....	..
Huron Copper Bay Co........	4	12	20	......	....	25 40cps	..
Lake Huron S. and C.........	5	102	......	......	....	...	..
Montreal Mining Consols.....	20	$15	......	......	....	3.00 3.20	.
Do. Telegraph Co....	40	All.	5	......	134 136	133 136	132
Do. Elevating Co....	00	"	15 12m	......	....	100 102½	..
Do. City Gas Co.........	40	"	4	15 Mar. 15 Sep.	....	137 139	135
Do. City Pass. R. Co.....	50	"	5	......	....	110 111	bks
Nova Scotia Telegraph	20	"	.....	......	....	....	..
Quebec and L. S.	8	24	......	......	....	....	25
Quebec Gas Co..............	200	All.	4	1 Mar., 1 Sep.	....	...	119
Quebec Street R. R..........	50	25	8	.....	....	....	96
Richelieu Navigation Co.....	100	All.	7 p.a.	1 Jan., 1 July.	....	115 116	115
St. Lawrence Tow Boat Co....	100	"	......	3 Feb.	...	...	40
Tor'to Consumers' Gas Co....	50	"	2 3 m.	1 My Au Mar Fe	107 108	....	105½
Trust & Loan Co. of U. C.....	20	5	3	......	....	....	..
West'n Canada Bldg Soc'y....	50	All.	5	......	115 116	....	..

SECURITIES.	London.	Montreal	Quebec	Tor
Canadian Gov't Deb. 6 ℘ ct. stg..............	...	104	102½ 103	103
Do. do. 6 do due Ja. & Jul. 1877-84........	106½ 107½	....	....	..
Do. do. 6 do. Feb. & Aug...	105 107	....	...	..
Do. do. 6 do. Mch, & Sep.........	104 106	..	...	..
Do. do. 5 ℘ ct. cur., 1883	95 96	94	92½ 93	93
Do. do. 5 do. stg., 1885	94 96	94	92 93½	93
Do. do. 7 do. cur.,..................	....	....	....	..
Dominion 6 p. c. 1878 cy.....	....	104½ 105½	104 104½	104½
Hamilton Corporation......	.. ..	....	....	...
Montreal Harbor, 8 ℘ ct. d. 1869.............	..	....	....	...
Do. do. 7 do. 1870..........	...	....	....	...
Do. do. 6½ do. 1875..........	...	101 102	....	...
Do. do. 6½ do. 1873..............	...	...	....	...
Do. Corporation, 6 ℘ c. 1891	....	94½ 95	95½ 95¾	95
Do. 7 p. c. stock.....................	....	107½ 110	106½ 107½	107½
Do. Water Works, 6 ℘ c, stg. 1878........	...	....	....	94
Do. do. 6 do. cy. do.	...	95½ 96½	....	94
New Brunswick, 6 ℘ ct., Jan. and July	104 106	....	....	..
Nova Scotia, 6 ℘ ct., 1875..................	104 106	....	....	..
Ottawa City 6 ℘ c. d. 1880	....	....	....	..
Quebec-Harbour, 6 ℘ c. d. 1883.	....	....	60	..
Do. do. 7 do. do.	....	....	65 70	...
Do. do. 8 do. 1886............	...	....	80 85	...
Do. City, 7 ℘ c. d. 5 years	....	....	95 96	...
Do. do. 7 do. 9 do.	....	....	91 92	..
Do. do. 7 do. 2 do.	....	....	98 98½	...
Do. Water Works, 7 ℘ ct., 4 years	....	....	96 97	..
Do. do. 6 do. 2 do.	....	....	94 95	..
Toronto Corporation	....	....	...	..

ONTARIO PEAT CO.

PROSPECTUS OF THE ONTARIO PEAT COMPANY

LIMITED LIABILITY. - - - - - - HEAD OFFICE—TORONTO.

To be Organized under the Act 27 and 28 Victoria, Chapter 23, and the Amendments thereto.

THE property of the company forms a portion of the well-known "Cranberry Marsh," in the Townships of Humberstone and Wainfleet, County Welland, and Province of Ontario, traversed by the Welland Canal, as well as by its "Feeder," which is also navigable ; and is composed of the following lots, viz. :—

	Acres.
Humberstone—South halves of 28, 30, 32 and 33. Concession IV	400
Wainfleet—South halves of 6 and 7, Concession IV	200
" Whole of 10, Concession II, an i the whole of 10 and 11, Concession III	600
" Parts of 8 and 9, Concessions IV. and V., about	200
Total	1400

A main ditch six feet deep has been made by the Coun.y through the whole of this Marsh for surface drainage, at an expenditure of $50,000 ; at this ditch runs along a portion of every one of the above lots, except two which abut upon the feeder of the Welland Canal.

The several lots above enumerated were the first chosen from the Marsh, having been selected for their great value as Peat Deposits. The remaining Peat lands have been obtained by the Anglo-American Peat Company, which has been operating most successfully during the past season upon a lot adjoining one of the Company's lots. A most satisfactory report has been obtained from Frederick Holmes. Esq., the County Engineer—gentleman who has had large experience in these peat lands, having not only surveyed and laid off the whole lots for the County, but has also been employed as superintendant in the ditching operations which have been undertaken and carried out through the whole extent of the Marsh. H estimate of the quantity of Peat contained in the Company's lands is placed at three millions of tons, at the very least ; and this estimate is fully borne out by the eminent firm of Messrs. Macdougall and Skae, Civil Engineers, Toronto, who were specially despatched to make a personal examination the property, and whose report is subjoined.

Peat can be laid down on the banks of the canal at the cost of from $1 to $1.25 per ton, and can from thence be forwarded by water to market in a directions, at small cost, and without transhipment ; to say nothing of the facilities and advantages afforded by no less than five railways, one of which the "Buffalo and Lake Huron," passes within twenty chains of the property. In addition to these advantages, the fact may be noticed, that abo thirty vessels pass through the canal every day during the season of navigation, the steamers requiring fuel for their own use, and the sailing vessel seeking cargoes, and requiring ballast westward to Chicago and other points.

The demand for this fuel for private consumption will be very great when its superior qualities become more widely known. Already railways at steamers are beginning to use it instead of wood and coal, with the most satisfactory results, experience having proved that one ton of peat is equal about one and one-third cords of the best hard wood. With a view to the full and proper development of this property, it is proposed to organize t Company with a capital of $120,000, in 2,400 shares of $50 each; $50,000 of this sum to be retained by the Directors for working capital, the balance be applied to the purchase of the real estate. It is also proposed that 5 per cent shall be paid at the time of subscription, and the balance in calls 10 per cent at such times as the Directors may name, but not oftener than once in every three months, from 1st of January, 1869.

The affairs of the Company will be managed by a Board of five Directors, the first set to be provisional, and, as soon as the charter is obtained a the Company organized, the permanent Directors to be chosen by the Shareholders, and to be elected annually.

The principal office of the Company to be in the City of Toronto. The property has been conveyed to Peleg Howland, Esquire, who will hold t same in trust until the Company is organized

PROVISIONAL DIRECTORS.

HENRY S. HOWLAND, Esquire, Toronto.   JOHN FISKEN, Esquire, Toronto.   LARRATT W. SMITH, Esquire, Toronto.
ALFRED TODD, Esquire, Ottawa.   EDWARD A. C. PEW, Esquire, Welland.

Further information can be obtained at the office of C. J. Campbell, Esquire, Banker, 92 King Street East, Toronto, who will act as Provisio Treasurer, and will also receive subscriptions for Stock.

CHAMBERS, 17 TORONTO STREET, TORONTO, JANUARY 11, 1869.

To the Directors of the Ontario Peat Company,—

GENTLEMEN,—We have the honor to lay before you the following report, on the Peat Beds in the Great Cranberry Marsh, situated in the Cou of Welland. The swamp, or to call it by a more proper name, moor, for it is more like the moors of Scotland than the swamps of this country, intersected by a large drain, which at present carries off a considerable quantity of water; and from its juxta position, to the lots owned by your comp could be made available for drainage purposes. The moor rises gradually from its northern limit in concession 4, to its summit, at the south end concession 3, about four feet on two and a half miles, where it is about eight feet above the level of Lake Erie; while, on the north, from the end of moor to the Welland River, distant about a mile and a half, there is a fall of sixteen feet. Following the course of the water through the vari drains, the result arrived at is, that the moor is higher than the surrounding country, which is under cultivation.

The peat on this marsh, brought up by the boring rods, as well as that lying on the sides of the drains, thrown up when they were made, show good quality of a dark black color, in every lot. There is a layer of red peat in some of the lots of the Township of Humberstone; but generally peat was of the dark colour above mentioned. The surface of the marsh, or moor, has been burnt once or twice, so that there is not much moss or up and connections could be formed, at a small cost, to the several outlets that surround this tract of land ; and the surface being regular, no difficu would be encountered in laying tramroads.

In making the borings for this report, the valuable assistance of the County Engineer, Mr. Frederick Holmes, was obtained, as he had superinten the making of the drains, and had laid out several of the lots some years ago, and since that time had been intimately acquainted with the moor. depths arrived at give an average of six to eight feet of peat over all the lots in the 3rd and 4th concessions, while in the lot of the 2nd conces of the Township of Weinfleet, the peat is very deep, averaging 'bout 15 feet, and it is said to go even deeper. There are 200 acres in this lot.

The regularity of the upper surface of this large tract of land, both peat and arable, being combined with the result of the borings taken, tend conclusion that the bottom of the peat bed must also be regular, as there are no hills or mounds of any size or consequence in the vicinity.

The Anglo-American Peat Fuel Company have been at work during last summer on a portion of this marsh, opposite to some of the lots owned your Company. They find the loss, by weight and shrinkage to be 75 per cent. ; or to make one ton of peat fuel, four tons of peat are required. T is less than that of a similar project in the Lower Province, where the shrinkage is 85 per cent.

From the data and experience of the Anglo-American Company, taking the loss by weight and shrinkage at 75 per cent., with an average of f six to eight feet over all the lots, but that in the 5th Concession of Wainfleet, which is taken at sixteen feet, we find the property of your Compa situated in the marsh, to be capable of producing over 3,000,000 tons of fuel.

A fuller report, by us, lies in the hands of Mr. C. J. Campbell, Banker, King Street, Toronto, to which also we beg to call your attention.

We have the honor to be, gentlemen,
Your obedient servants,
MACDOUGALL & SKAE.
CIVIL ENGINE

3—

THE CANADIAN
MONETARY TIMES
AND
INSURANCE CHRONICLE.
DEVOTED TO FINANCE, COMMERCE, INSURANCE, BANKS, RAILWAYS, NAVIGATION, MINES, INVESTMENT,
PUBLIC COMPANIES, AND JOINT STOCK ENTERPRISE.

II—NO. 24.   TORONTO, THURSDAY, JANUARY 28, 1869.   { SUBSCRIPTION $2 A YEAR.

Mercantile.

Gundry and Langley.
TECTS AND CIVIL ENGINEERS, Building Sur-
s and Valuators. Office corner of King and Jordan
Toronto.
LAS GUNDRY.   HENRY LANGLEY.

J. B. Boustead.
SIO V and Commission Merchant. Hops bought
sold on Commission. 82 Front St., Toronto.

John Boyd & Co.
ESALE Grocers and Commission Merchants,
ont St., Toronto.

Childs & Hamilton.
FACTURERS, and Wholesale Dealers in Boots
Shoes, No. 7, Wellington Street East, Toronto,
28

L. Coffee & Co.
GE and Commission Merchants, No. 2 Manning's
k, Front St., Toronto, Ont. Advances made on
ents of Produce.

J. & A. Clark,
ICE Commission Merchants, Wellington Street
, Toronto, Ont.

D Crawford & Co.,
FACTURERS of Soaps, Candles, etc., and dealers
'etroleum, Lard and Lubricating Oils, Palace St.,
Ont.

k McNab.
Merchants, Toronto, Ontario.

W. D. Matthews & Co.
E Commission Merchants, Old Corn Exchange,
at St. East, Toronto Ont.

R. C. Hamilton & Co.
E Commission Merchants, 119 Lower Water
alifax, Nova Scotia.

Parson Bros.,
EUM Refiners, and Wholesale dealers in Lamps,
ays, etc. Warerooms 51 Front St. Refinery cor.
Don sts., Toronto.

      rs and
      28.

W. Rowland & Co.,
OKERS and General Commission Mer-
ances made on Consignments. Corner
ai streets, Toronto.

Reford & Dillon,
of Groceries, Wellington Street, Toronto.

Sessions, Turner & Cooper,
ACTURERS, Importers and Wholesale Dealer
and Shoes, Leather Findings, etc., 8 Wel-
West, Toronto, Ont

Mining.

NOVA SCOTIA GOLD FIELDS.

(From our own Correspondent.)

HALIFAX, Jan. 19, 1869.

The general returns for December are coming in
but slowly, and the subjoined three are all that
have been at present received at head quarters
from the several deputy commissioners.

	Sherbrooke.	Wine Isaac's Harbor.	Isaac's Harbor.
	s. s.	s. s.	s. s.
Total Gold yield...	522 2 6	114 0 9	5 0 0
Aver. per 2000 lbs.	0 8 8	0 6 4	— —
Maximum	1 2 17	0 14 16	— —
Alluvial Gold	— — —	— — —	5 0 0
	tons. cwt.	tons. cwt.	tons. cwt.
Quartz raised.......	1250 0	353 7	137 0
Quartz crushed....	1249 5	353 7	— 0
Day's work.......	5000	2562	1100
No. Mines worked.	23	5	5
No. of Mills	10	4	2

It will be seen that the amount of alluvial gold
from Isaac's Harbor, is quite insignificant, and
fully justified the cautions contained in the late
Mining Gazette. The existence of alluvial gold
was indicated by Mr. Campbell in his Reports to
the Government in 1861 and 1863, and proved by
subsequent workings in 1863-4; but it is not so
abundant as to warrant any unusual interest, still
less the excitement sought to be awakened by the
designing and unprincipled parties who spread the
report that an expert washer could easily earn an
ounce a day. The true average from one property
is under 80 cents, and from another about $1.20
per day, to the man, which is not even laborer's
wages. The yield might be increased with sluices,
but the results of the past five months tells of
much cry and little wool.

WAVERLEY.—Professor Hind's geological plans
and sections are finally completed, which pass to-day
into the hands of the lithographer. It is to be
hoped that other districts will receive the benefit
of careful professional examination, which, if it
result in no other good, helps to awaken discussion
and draw attention to the district reported upon.

UNIACKE.—The returns for December are not
all received. Investors, however, will be glad to
hear that the Montreal Gold Mining Association
again figures among the productive holders, Mr.
Robertson, the new manager (late of the Richardson mine, Madoc,) having brought up last week 44
ounces, the produce of 90 tons of quartz, raised
from a depth of 75 feet. As soon as the other
shafts are pumped dry, the works on this property
will be vigorously prosecuted, which, it is hoped,
will be an example to the owners of the neighbouring adjoining claims. In the absence of the deputy's
report, the following statistics from the managers'
sworn returns, for the quarter ending 30th Sept.
last, may not be without interest.

The Mount Uniacke Co., with 4,074 days labour,
raised 490 tons of quartz, and produced 345 ozs.
6 dwts. gold. The West Lake Co. produced 13½
ozs. 9 dwts. from 530 tons, raised by 2,207 days

labour. The Queen Co. obtained 239 ozs. 9 dwts.
from 512½ tons and 4,297 days labour. The Central Co., from 2¾ tons, obtained 35 ozs. 3 dwts.
with 38½ days labour. The lode, worked by the
Queen Co. are so wide, compared with that of the
Central Co., that the yield is but little less remunerative. There has been much dispute about
the belt of lodes, south of the Union Co. claims,
not bearing gold in appreciable quantity, for
which reason several bands of parallel lodes,(many
of considerable width) below the designated property, and extending into block seven, were, until
last fall, entirely neglected. The refutation of
this theory has now been given by practical results. 7 tons of surface quartz, from the so-called
La Mothe areas, having just passed through the
mill to yield a little bar of 5 ozs. 2 dwts. Solid
arguments of this kind outweigh fanciful theories
and ignorant prejudice. This, however, is not the
first crushing from these lodes, as the claims to
the east were sunk upon to the depth of 35 feet,
and from 38 tons, crushed last winter, under very
unfavourable circumstances, produced an average
of 9 dwts. Still further south, as far as 1,500 feet
from the boundary of blocks two and seven, gold
has been obtained by hand mortaring the surface
quartz, so that if the district continues in favour,
there is yet a large area in that direction worthy
the attention of explorers.

AN OPINION FROM NOVA SCOTIA.

"A MINER," writing recently to the *Acadian
Recorder,* tried to make it appear that the granting
of charters favored the establishment of bubble
mining companies, although an official act of incorporation has as little influence upon the respec-
ability of promoters as Tenterden Church Steeple had
in the creation of Goodwin Sands. The writer
cited two instances of public extortion,—in the
formation of the Hoggy-Suckle and Bumble-Bee
Companies of Bulliontown, Nova Scotia,—from an
exposure contained in the Canadian *Monetary
Times.*

The promoters of one of these companies pocketed eighty thousand dollars for an area that cost
them (*palm-grease excepted*) about two thousand
five hundred dollars!

By a singular coincidence, the *Recorder* has been
selected for a notice of the Woodland Gold-mining
Company, of Goldenville, originally the Woodbine Company, which by a still more singular coincidence, through synonymy of title and locality,
was assumed to be the subject of a "A Miner's"
animadversion.

An average of five ounces per ton is claimed as
the result of the last crushing; but as the amount
of ore is not stated in the *Recorder's* notice, the
omission is here remedied, and the actual average
given of previous millings:—

Tons Quartz.	Yield Gold.	Av. per Ton.
	oz. dwt. gr.	oz. dwt. gr.
69½	7 12 2	2 5
9¼	4 6 0	9 —
5¼	1 0 22	3 19
3	16 13 6	5 11 2
87½	29 12 6	0 7 2

This property would have to maintain a continuous yield of five ounces to the ton on two thousand tons of ore before it can pay dividends, on

account of the high price for which it sold ; and the present comparison is not made in disparagement, but merely to acquaint shareholders in Nova Scotia gold properties from making invidious distinctions between districts, or expecting a uniformly high yield from the most favorably represented, best managed, or even most dearly-purchased mine.—*Halifax Reporter.*

MARMORA IRON MINES.—The Company working these mines have contracted to get out 60,000 tons of ore in 1869, and 100,000 tons in 1870. The company owns 23,000 acres of land, and 150 men are kept at work. The ore is loaded on cars at the mine, is then run to the river, where it is dumped on the decks of scows, which are towed by steamers to Harwood, again loaded on the cars, and dumped into the holds of schooners at the Cobourg harbor. The whole cost of mining, railway carriage, lake freight, and American duty, we understand, is a little under $4 per ton, while the price ranges from $5.50 to $8 per ton in gold. The market is at Pittsburgh.

Insurance.

FIRE RECORD.—Hamilton, Jan. 23.—A fire occurred in Reid's cabinet manufactory, King-st. West. The building was quickly gutted. The fire was confined to the building in which it originated.

Hamilton, Jan. 21.—The sheepskin tannery of Messrs. Humphrey and Newberry, east end of the city, took fire, and the building being a very old frame one, and all as dry as tinder, was speedily consumed. 7000 lbs. of wool, about 1000 manufactured sheepskins, with tools, machinery, &c., were destroyed. Loss on stock estimated at $7,000 ; insurance $2,000. The loss of Mr. Wm. P. Moore, the owner of the building, is covered by insurance. An exchange says : The firemen were promptly on hand and did their duty, but the hose proved wretchedly inefficient ; and it is surely made plain enough at last that the hundreds of thousands which the water-works cost must not be left useless for putting out fire for the want of a small amount spent on hose. It is like letting the horse and rider perish for want of a nail in the shoe. The water is there, enough to drown out, in a very short time, any fire within its reach ; but there must be good hose, and plenty of it, to turn the water on with. A fire also broke out at half-past four this morning, at L. D. Sawyer & Co's Agricultural Implement Works, to the east of the city, and outside the limits of water supply from the works. It commenced in the blacksmith's shop, and some thousand of dollars worth of patterns and parts of machines were destroyed. Loss covered by insurance in the Ætna and Hartford Companies. The stone walls are not injured, and the burnt portion of the works will be renewed without loss of time. The firemen did good service, and to their exertions it is due that the Canada Felt Hat works, immediately adjoining were saved. But for the fact that the shingles of the roof were laid in mortar, this building would have gone, too.

This afternoon a fire broke out in the bellows factory of Mr. James Dallyn, down James-street, between Murray and Concession-streets. The firemen were promptly on hand, and the fire was quickly subdued, though here, as at the tannery, the inefficient condition of the hose was much against their efforts.

Watson's Corners, North Lanark, Ont., Jan. 15.—A fire broke out in the general store of William Horn, by which he suffered to the extent of $2,500. The Perth *Courier* learns that not a dollar's worth of anything was saved—the contents being consumed together. There was no insurance on the goods or the building. No clue as to the origin of the fire can yet be arrived at.

St. Vincent, Grey Co., Ont. Jany. 16.—A barn

belonging to Jas. Grier, on a lot near Griersville, rented by Mr. Byers, was burnt to the ground, together with about 300 bushels of wheat, some pease, hay, straw, &c., and a few hogs. The building is said to be insured for $600 by the owner, and the contents for $200 by the tenant.

Township of Stamford, Ont., Jany. 15.—L. S. Lundy had two stacks of good hay, of about 30 tons each, set fire to by some miscreant. No insurance.

Percy, Ont., Jany. 13 & 15.—A correspondent of the Trenton *Courier* informs that journal of two fires which took place in Percy, on the 13th and 15th inst. The first was the total destruction of Massy's saw-mill, near Warkworth ; and the second that of Hay's residence, at Oak Hills. There was no insurance on either buildings, and the loss in each case is said to be heavy.

Odessa, Ont., Jany. 20.—The barn, sheds and stables of Mr. K. Booth, containing a large quantity of grain, hay, straw, &c., were totally consumed. Two valuable cows were burnt in their stalls. Loss estimated at $1000. No insurance. The fire is said to have been caused by straw igniting from a lighted candle used by one of the farm hands in the stable.

Riviere du Loup, January 21.—Marchand's Hotel, at this place, was burned down. Three of Marchand's children, and Mr. Wallis, civil engineer, of Quebec, perished in the fire. Mr. Johnson escaped, though somewhat injured. Everything is lost, including the office. By this fire the Intercolonial Railway Office at Riviere du Loup, with all the plans, is destroyed. They will be replaced at once. No insurance.

Seaforth, Jany. 21.—A fire broke out in the stables attached to Cardene's bakery, which consumed the stable, two horses, one cow, a quantity of hay, and one light wagon. No particulars as to insurance.

St. Catherines, Jany. 19.—A fire was discovered in the large stable in rear of Vanderlip's Hotel. By tearing the burning portion away, with a few buckets of water placed the barn out of danger. Cause unknown.

St. Catherines, January 16.—House of Mr. D. Bessy, near village of Homer, had the roof burnt off.

Caledon, East, January 15.—Barn of Henry Smith, and contents, together with a valuable mare and colt. Loss $500 ; insurance $300.

Bronte, Jan. 17.—A second ineffectual attempt was made to fire the store of E. C. Thompson & Co. The fire had been kindled on the outside of the building, opposite a small opening in the cellar, intended for a water-pipe. Close to this hole, on the inside, was a quantity of oil, which fortunately did not ignite. The Milton *Champion* says Mr. W. Thompson, one of the firm, had a narrow escape from being suffocated by smoke. Nothing but the hard work and good will of the Brontonians saved the building and its contents from total ruin. Goods are somewhat damaged by smoke. Damage about covered by insurance—some $300 or $400.

Kingston, January 21st.—An explosion took place in one of the stores of Mr. Overend's building, occupied by a glass blower, shattering the windows and throwing down the partitions. This and the adjoining shop of Mr. Ireland, engraver, were consumed ; nothing saved. The fire spread to the adjoining property : White's store is completely gutted ; Meyer's and Cannon's partly so ; but Hewitt's is not injured. None of the tenants had any insurance whatever ; Branigan's was insured for $2,000 on the buildings, which will about cover his loss. Overend has $1,400 insurance on his building (stone) but Ireland had none on his stock, materials, or household effects. The Glass Blower loses his whole stock also. Cause of explosion unknown.

Beverly, Ont. Jan. 17.—The two-story frame dwelling of William Henry, near Westover's Corner's took fire from a defective stove-pipe, and was entirely consumed, together with a large portion

of the furniture and effects of the family, addition to other property that fell a prey to flames was $1,500 in bank bills. Mr. Henry an insurance of $1,500 in the Gore District tual. The loss is estimated at about $3,000.

St. Catherines, Jan. 27.—The Welland H stables and E. McCarty's house; the forme sured for $400 and the latter for $600.

Toronto, Jan. 27.—Jackson's Hotel on road; was valued at $2,000.

APPOINTMENTS.—Mr. William Brooks, many years connected with the Northern In ance Company, has been appointed assis manager to the Progress Insurance Comp We learn that Mr. William Beaman has appointed assistant secretary of the Briton Me and General Life Assurance Association, an the Brittania Fire Association. Mr. Beaman filled the office of chief clerk to the Britor several years past.—*Insurance Record.*

ENGLISH OFFICES.—We find in the *Post M sine Almanac* the following list of companies have transferred their business in 1868 :— cable Mutual to United Ports ; British Mutu Providential ; Etna to United Ports ; Ge Provident to Etna ; International to Herc London and Northern to National Widows' F National Union to Great Britain ; Uncondit to British Alliance. The same authority gi list of companies which have been founded in the past year, including a number of " epher companies,"—Alexandra, Britannia, British perial, Commercial Indemnity, Economic General Accident, Life Insurance Union, I pool, London and General Accident, Mac Monarch, and United Ports.

— It appears from an official memorandum the whole of the shares lately offered to the p by the Britannia Fire Association having taken up, they have now commenced busine conjunction with the Briton Medical and Ge Life Association.

—A new Company, styled the *General Ac and Guarantee Co.*, has been started in Eng C. Harding, Manager.

MODE OF VALUING ASSURANCE

The Annual Premium of each existing Assu is to be taken, not however the Annual Pre payable for the Assurance according to the of the original contract, and which is in fa actual Premium which is paid continually, b higher premium which would be chargeable under the supposition that it now was to be for the first time, and therefore at the which the life upon which it is is to be mad advanced.

This done, then the amount of the origin real Premium is to be subtracted from the a of the supposed higher Premium as abov the remainder is to be put down. The p value of such remainder is now to be found Society's Annuity Tables, treating it as an A payable during the life from the age at whi life the Assurance is made has now arrived date of the valuation ; and whatever may amount of the value of this Annuity, such amount of the value of the Assurance a time.

Assume that an Assurance for £1,000 wa out on the 1st of June, 1856, upon a life a The Annual Premium for this Assurance is £ and that will be the amount ever payable and no more.

Five years have passed away, and 1st 1861, has arrived, which is the time fir valuation of Assurances and distribution c plus Capital. Now in valuing the Assu above on 1st June, 1861, the Annual Prem be paid for it was considered to be the Premium payable at the age 29, which is £ 0d. Substracting £19 10s, 0d. from £22 1

inder of £3 is left. Finding now the pre-
lue of an annuity of £3 per annum, paya-
ing a life aged 29, such was the present
of the Assurance as above on 1st June,

n, the same Assurance being valued on 1st
866, the Annual Premium to be paid for it
isidered to be that payable at the age 34,
is £25 15s. 0d. Substracting £19 10s. 0d.
25 15s. 0d. the remainder left is £6 5s. 0d.
esent value of an annuity of £6 5s. 0d.
during a life aged 34 was therefore the
f the Assurance as above on the 1st June,

n, when the same Assurance is to be valued
June, 1871, if then on foot, the Annual
m to be paid for it will be considered to be
the age 39, which is £30 1s. 8d. Substract-
) 10, 0d. from £30 1s. 8d. the remainder
l be £10 11s. 8d. The present value of an
y of £10 11s. 8d. payable during a life
will therefore be the present value of the
nce as above on 1st June, 1871.
again, when the same Assurance is to be
on the 1st June, 1866, if then on foot, the
Premium to be paid for it will be consi-
o be that of the age 44, which is £35. Sub-
g £19 10s. 0d. from £35, the remainder
l be £15 10s 0d. The present value of an
y of £15 10s. 0d. payable during a life
will therefore be the present value of the
nce as above on 1st June, 1876.
now, passing over twenty-five years during
the value of the Assurance will be continu-
reasing year by year, in valuing it on the
June, 1901, if still on foot, the Annual
m to be paid for it will be considered to be
the age 69, which is £108 18s. 4d. Sub-
g £19 10s. 0d. from £108 18s. 4d. the
der left will be £89 8s. 4d. The premium
of an Annuity of £89 8s. 4d., payable
a life aged 69, will therefore be the present
of the Assurance as above on 1st June,

when every Assurance on foot at the time
ation has been valued according to in-
given above, and the values of all of them
up, the total will be the amount of capital
to be in the possession of the Society,
e held in reserve to meet its liabilities;
tever capital in excess of such amount
found in the possession of the Society will
plus Capital."—*Post Magazine.*

TORONTO STOCK MARKET.

(Reported by Pellatt & Osler, Brokers.)

was an average business done this week,
ks generally close firm and in good de-

Stock.—Montreal sold during the week
) to 140, the market closing with buyers
Ontario has been freely dealt in at 100
¼; closing with sellers at the latter rate.
rs of Toronto; buyers at high rates. There
rs of Royal Canadian at 85 for stock all
onsiderable sales of Commerce occurred
and 102½; there are sellers now at the
te. Buyers offer 39 for Gore; very little
et. Merchants' has advanced to 108½, at
ate there are buyers, but no sellers. For
98 would be paid; sellers ask 100; no
Sellers ask 110¼ for Molson's, with buyers
Sales of City occurred at 100½, at which
stock is still procureable. Buyers offer
Du Peuple; no sellers. Nationale would
at 106, and Jacques Cartier at 107; none
There are buyers of Union at 103, and
at 103½. Nothing to report in other

tures.—No Canada bonds of any kind of-
Sales of Dominion stock were made at 105, 105¼ and 105½. Toronto are much enquired for; none in market. A few small lots County have been placed at par.

Sundries.—No transactions in City Gas for some weeks. For a round amount of Canada Permanent Building Society 124 would be paid; last sale at 123½. Western Canada Building Society has advanced 3 ℔ cent. since our last; considerable sales have taken place at 117 to 118. Sales of Freehold Building Society were made at 106½, 107 and 107¼; there are some buyers but no sellers at the latter rate. There are buyers of Montreal Telegraph at 134, and sellers at 135.—Canada Landed Credit is asked for at 72; little offering. A few good mortgages were placed at 8 ℔ cent. There is a fair supply of money on good security.

THE LONDON MONEY MARKET, 1868, 1869.

The financial course of the past year, as was the case with that of its predecessor, has precisely realized the anticipations expressed at its commencement. A fair harvest and the avoidance of war were the only conditions requisite to insure a steady continuance of low terms of discount, and an uninterrupted though slow recovery in trade. For the year now commencing the prospect is equally or rather more satisfactory. Every month that places us further from the disastrous recollections of 1866 increases the healthy power of the nation for the development of its natural commercial vigor.

It is true that the recent rise in the bank rate from 2 to 3 per cent., in consequence of the heedless welcome given to foreign and colonial loans, has thrown, for the moment, a damper over Stock Exchange speculation. But this has been salutary. There is a total absence of danger of any persistent run of folly. The public may be tempted by adroit manipulation to go on up to a certain point; but so fresh is their sense of past penalties that the moment the slightest check happens they fall back scared, as if another general convulsion were at hand. In the present instance, the simultaneous occurrence of the contemptible Greek complication has been sufficient to cause a fall in the nominal value of all convertible property equal to that which might ordinarily occur from any severe political or commercial disturbance.

Hence it would seem that, instead of any further immediate increase in the value of money. Several of the foreign and colonial returns of the past year remain to be paid up, but the introduction of new ones being in some degree stopped, the demands thus occasioned can well be met by the surplus income always flowing into the country in the shape of dividends on the securities already existing. Looking at the sums standing in Indian railways, Australian and Canadian Government guarantees, United States bonds and foreign loans generally, these payments are now of extraordinary magnitude, and make a yearly total, in addition to the regular profits of the national trade, such as to necessitate a constant outlet through fresh loans and ventures.

Estimating the consol and railway dividends now falling due, together with the foreign dividends and sinking funds to be remitted hither, it may be calculated that a sum of at least twelve or fifteen million sterling will find its way into the hands of the investing public within the next few weeks, and the portion of this to be received from distant sources will certainly be ample to provide for the outgoings for recent commitments.

Still, so long as the rate for money in the London market is below its normal point of 3½ or 4 per cent., the tendency must be always toward an advance, and consequently every check like that now in operation is certain to be succeeded by a reaction. A momentary renewal of ease will instantly be taken advantage of by new contractors and operators, soon to be checked by a fresh fright, again to be followed by a further series of recoveries and checks until the supply of capital shall have been reduced so as to cause its employment at home to yield an average return. The tendency to a rapid restoration of our rate of discount from any extreme point, such as two per cent., on the one hand or ten per cent. on the other, is singularly stimulated both by the diffusion of telegraphic communication and the general increase of intercourse among the various financial centres of the world. As regards America, for instance, the system of borrowing money on United States securities in London, Paris, Frankfort and other European cities, whenever the difference between their rates and those of New York is sufficient to present an inducement, is every day coming into more extended operation, and cannot fail to have an important influence in equalizing the current terms at all the Exchanges. For the next few years, therefore, the prevalence of fair average rates may, in the absence of exceptional influences, be safely relied upon.

Meanwhile, as regards the intrinsic values of fixed properties, there is a silent and inevitable process still going on, which attracts but little attention from year to year, but is more powerful in its effect than any other. The increased production of the precious metals is in undisturbed operation, and although by some circumstances its influence is gradually lessened, there are others by which it is augmented. On the one hand, in proportion as the stock of gold has been added to during the last twenty years, the power of any given amount to produce an effect upon it is diminished, since, supposing the total supply in the world to be only 200,000,000, an addition of 200,000,000 would reduce its value 50 per cent., whereas after this had occurred a further addition of 200,000,000 would cause a reduction of only 25 per cent.; but, on the other, hand there is the fact that new sources of supply are being constantly discovered, including, if the accounts from the Far West may to any extent be trusted, deposits of silver of an apparently inexhaustible character, while at the same time the progress of science is constantly simplifying the methods of extraction. The circumstance that the absorption in India, which for a period had some considerable effect in retarding the changes in question, is now less active, is also to be taken into account, as well as the constant economizing of the circulation of the leading commercial countries by the resort to processes which save the passage of coin.

As regards incitements to adventure and trading enterprise, the new year is likely to offer enough for the most ardent minds. The completion of the Pacific Railroad which is to be accomplished by July next, and which, through an extent of over 1,000 miles, will bring new regions into the full tide of civilization, and at the same time, perhaps, revolutionize many of the existing relations of the Eastern and Western hemispheres, cannot fail to present openings such as will be the commencement of changes that must materially influence the destinies of future generations. Perhaps among its minor and transitory consequences will be the furnishing of the materials that during the next few years will have to be cultivated in preparation for the panic to fall due in 1876.—*London Times.*

BANKING BALANCE-SHEETS.

As the half-yearly meetings are now being held, it may be useful to call attention to some points connected with banking balance-sheets, although it appears to be generally understood that the Board of Trade will bring forward a measure, at the earliest convenient opportunity, to enforce uniformity. The form of balance-sheet is therefore of the most importance, and we think shareholders would act wisely in throwing out some suggestions, as to the propriety of separating the drawing accounts from the deposit accounts. They should also inquire what amount of bad debts have been written off during the half-year, and what have been created during the half-year, and how much is the total now outstanding under the head of bad debts. Then the amount of overdue bills should on no account be concealed, as has been clearly established in the examinations at the Mansion House, during the past week, into the case of Overend, Gurney & Co., limited. The amount of loans on which the interest is in arrear should also be clearly stated, and it might be prudent to ask what amount is owing by directors for loans and bills discounted, as managers have often very little power of ascertaining the worth of the security offered by members of the Board when they decline to answer questions. The amount lent on shares in companies is a very important subject for inquiry, and when money has been advanced on a company's own shares, it is obvious that it is a diminution of capital rather than a loan. Auditors should be able to certify that the balance-sheets which have been placed before them, and they should also have the advances so classified that they can easily separate the loans on goods and warrants, the loans on land and houses, and the loans on stock or shares in various companies. The present opportunity should not be lost of endeavoring to place before the Board of Trade all information likely to secure the most accurate details.—*Investors' Guardian*

CANADIAN GOVERNMENT SECURITIES.—The following table exhibits the fluctuations in Canada 5's & 6's for 1868:—

		5 per cents. Jan. & July.	6 per cents. Jan. & July.
January	10......	86	99½
January	24......	93	99
July	7......	86	99½
July	22......	87	100
March	7......	87	100
March	21......	87	100½
April	4......	87	100½
April	18......	87½	102½
May	2......	89¼	103½
May	16......	92	104
May	30......	93½	105½
June	13......	94	107
June	27......	94½	107¼
July	11......	91	103
July	25......	92	104
August	8......	92	104
August	22......	92	104
September	5......	91	104
September	19......	92	105
October	3......	92	105
October	17......	92	106
October	31......	93¼	107¼
November	7......	93	108
November	21......	94	108¼
December	5......	95	108
December	19......	94½	107½

SAVINGS BANKS.

Mr. Keyes, in his report to the N. Y. Legislature, says:—If a savings bank were subject to no contingencies in its business, if it were possible to protect every institution from any probable loss, no surplus would be required. But this we have shown and know to be impractible. The profoundest wisdom, the most pretending sagacity the most consumate financial skill, is vain to place any one of these institutions upon a basis of absolute exemption from loss. These qualities with strict integrity and conscientious care, may greatly diminish the chances of misfortune, but cannot eliminate them altogether. It must needs be that, sooner or later, slight and heavy losses will come. A bank of issue in which savings deposits are kept may fail, a claim for insurance may be successfully resisted, skilful buglars may get access to the cash, investments must sometimes be made at a premium that only return par on the day of redemption, or securities must sometimes be converted at a discount to meet unexpected emergencies. In these and many other ways which we need not enumerate, savings banks are exposed to perils, which all cannot be so fortunate as to escape. We can only guard agains needless exposure to these perils, and provide a means whereby the severity of the misfortune, when it comes, shall be greatly mitigated; means that will enable the institution to sustain its losses without impairing its ability to meet in full the demands of every depositor. But this can only be done by the accumulation of a surplus of assets over all liabilities for the purpose of meeting such contingencies. In no other way can perfect security against loss be secured to the depositor. In this way it can be assured; and yet, strangely enough, the provisions of the statutes in regard to this surplus, upon which the security of the depositor so greatly depends, are only permissive. If anything connected with the management of savings banks should be obligatory this should be. If anything the discretion of trustees should be controlled by law, this, upon which so much depends, should surely be thus controlled.

On the question of the rate of interest to be paid to depositors, in connection with the formation of a surplus fund Mr. Keyes says,—

No savings bank should be permitted to declare more than five per cent. dividends until it has accumulated a surplus of at least five per cent. of its assets.

With regard to savings banks to be organised hereafter, such a provision is practicable, and would have the salutary effcot of checking the mania for organising such institutions in localities already sufficiently accommodated. To make such a requirement of savings banks already organised, might lead to consequences not only perilous to their own integrity, but embarrassing in kindred institutions. Concerning these, it will be better to leave them at liberty to declare such dividends as they can, from actual earnings, after paying necessary expenses, and putting aside one-half per cent. per annum to account.

STERLING EXCHANGE.—The course of sterling exchange for three years is shown by the following figures, which represent the bank selling rates in Toronto, on the 1st and 15th of each month:—

		1866.	1867.	1868.
January	1...	9⅜ to 9⅝	9⅜ to 9⅝	10½ to —
"	15...	9⅛ " 9½	9⅜ " 9⅝	10¼ " 10½
February	1...	8 " —	9¼ " 9½	10¼ " —
"	15...	8¼ " —	9 " 9½	10¼ " —
March	1...	9¼ " —	9 " 9¼	10¼ " —
"	15...	9 " —	9½ " 9¾	10¼ " —
April	1...	8 " 8¾	9¼ " 9½	10 " —
"	15...	8 " 8½	9½ " 9¾	10¼ " —
May	1...	9 " 9¼	9⅝ " 9⅞	10½ " —
"	15...	10 " 10½	9⅝ " 9⅞	10¼ " —
June	2...	10 " 10¼	10¼ " 10⅜	10½ " —
"	15...	10¼ " 10⅜	10¼ " 10½	10½ " —
July	2...	9 " 9½	10⅜ " 10⅝	10½ " —
"	15...	9 " —	10¼ " 10⅜	10½ " 10⅝
August	1...	9 " —	10 " 10⅜	10¼ " —
"	15...	8¼ " —	10 " 10¼	10¼ " —
Sept.	1...	7 " 7½	10 " 9½	10 " —
"	15...	7½ " 7⅞	10 " —	9¼ " —
Oct.	1...	8½ " 9	9⅜ " 9⅝	9¼ " —
"	15...	9¾ " —	9⅜ " 9⅝	9¾ " —
Nov.	1...	10 " —	9⅝ " 9⅞	10¼ " —
"	15...	9⅜ " —	9½ " 9⅝	9½ " —
Dec.	1...	10 " —	9¾ " 9¾	9½ " 9¼
"	15...	10 " 10⅜	10¼ " 9¾	9¾ " —

—The name of Mr. Buchanan, of the late agency of the Bank of Montreal, at St. Catherines, is mentioned in connection with a vacant managership at Brantford. Much sympathy is expressed for him on account of the robbery of his agency.

—The Lightning *Express* says there is no better point in the great North-West peninsula for banking agencies, than Elora, and calls loudly for more banking accommodation than is afforded by a country Agency of the Bank of Montreal.

INDEBTEDNESS OF BELLEVILLE.

The Mayor of Belleville in addressing Council on Monday last made the following sta ment:

The present indebtedness of the town in form of outstanding debentures is about $54,0 which is made up as follows, viz:

A debenture overdue, bearing 8 per cent. interest........................	$ 5,(
Debentures to Trust and Loan Company, overdue, 8 per cent. interest............	14,(
Debentures issued in 1865, bearing 6 per cent interest..........................	16,(
Against which there is a county debenture in the sinking fund for $1,600 with interest for two years, leaving a balance in round numbers that will be due in less than five years of............	14,(
Balance due the Receiver General bearing 5 per cent. interest, and which will be paid off in about eight years by the yearly payment of $1,600..............	9,(
Debentures issued last year bearing 7½ per cent. interest, and due in twenty years..	12,(
Making the total of........................	$54,(

$19,000 being now over due, and $14,000 fa ing due in less than five years.

THE MONTREAL TELEGRAPH COMPANY ha recently made some sweeping reductions in th Tariff of Charges, applicable throughout the wh of the Dominion. In many instances the redi tion is equal to making the new Tariff less th one half the old rate on lengthy messages. T press rate from St. John to Montreal or Ottawa now but half what it was a fortnight ago, and presume that Halifax and other Maritime Cit share in these advantages. The Company, we lieve, will be gainers by this liberal policy, and important public result—the speedy and ch exchange of commercial, political and other n between the principal cities of the Dominion—v be brought about through the Company's inst mentality.

LAND GRANTS.

Congress up to March last, had granted in to various Western and Southern States over 000,000 acres lands for railroad purposes. It given beside over 17,000,000 acres to canals similar improvements. The Pacific Railroad branches have received 124,000,000 acres, an to this is added the even numbered sections al those routes, which the Secretary of the Inte decided to be closed for settlement, it will ap that nearly one-third of the entire public don has been made over to the control of rail companies. "The quantity of lands conveye these grants," says the Commissioner of the G eral Land Office, "is of empire extent, exceed in the aggregate, by more than 5,000,000 of ac the entire areas of the six New England Sta added to the surface of New York, New Jer Pensylvania, Ohio, Delaware, Maryland and ginia." He says the grants to the Pacific rail lines alone "are within about a fourth of b twice the united area of England, Scotland, W Ireland, Guernsey, Jersey, the Isle of Man, the Islands of the British seas, and within than a tenth of being equal to the French em proper."

In 1860 and 1861 the Government sold 234 acres of Delaware lands to the Leavenworth, nee and Western road. In 1866 it sold 92 acres of Delaware lands to the Missouri river and in 1859 it disposed of 278,200 acres to 36 purchasers. Among them were the follow The Hon. Hugh McCulloch, 7,014 acres; Fuller and McDonald, 39,058 acres; John Manus, 142,915 acres; Robert R. Stevens, 5

als. In 1865, Senator Pomeroy being then President and one of the principal owners of the Atison and Pike's Peat Railroad Company, a treaty as carried through the Senate by which this road trehased 123,832 acres of as rich lands as there e in Kansas. The above facts and figures were ought to the notice of the House by Mr. Julian, hairman of the Committee of Public Lands, in arch last, and Mr. Clarke, of Kansas, has given rect testimony upon most of the points involved the attempted Osage and the completed Cherokee swindles. These things are in the past.—It hundreds of similar schemes, quite as extensre, are now before Congress, and the lobby enged in pushing them is larger and more influential than ever before.—*U. S. Railway and ising Journal.*

THE CITIZENS' INSURANCE COMPANY
(OF CANADA.)

THORIZED CAPITAL......................$2,000,000
BSCRIBED CAPITAL...................... 1,000,000

DIRECTORS:

EDWIN ATWATER,   -   -   PRESIDENT.

HUGH ALLAN,   C. J. RHYDGES,
GEORGE STEPHEN,   HENRY LYMAN,
ADOLPHE ROY,   N. B. CORSE.

Life and Guarantee Department.
ce..............No. 71 Great St. James Street, Montreal.

HIS Company—formed by the association of nearly 100 of the wealthiest citizens of Montreal—is now prel to grant policies of LIFE ASSURANCE and Bonds FIDELITY GUARANTEE.
Application to be made to the office in Montreal or ough any of the Company's Agents.
                    EDWARD RAWLINGS, Manager.
he FIRE BRANCH of this Company is at No. 19 ce d'Armes. Applications to be made to GEORGE H. 11, Manager.   22-1-y

The Canadian Monetary Times.

THURSDAY, JANUARY 28, 1869.

ONTARIO PEAT COMPANY.

The production of peat fuel is likely to be me an important branch of industry in Cana. Wood has become so scarce that the sidents in our cities find it a very prominent item in their household expenses, and e farmers in many parts of the country are ginning to feel the effects of that wholesale struction of the forest which has goneon for ars, without a thought being bestowed on e future. The price of cordwood has goneon as high that dealers have found it profitle to bring supplies to Toronto from the ate of Michigan. The coal dealers have tle pity for the community, and by forming rings" and "corners," have run up the ice of coal to a very high figure.
The scarcity of wood and the high price of al have, we are glad to say, turned public tention to the production of peat, and stimated enterprises such as that taken in hand the Ontario Peat Company. The prosctus of this Company, which will be found another page, is worthy of a careful perusal. 1e ton of peat has been found by experisnt to be equal to about one and one-third rds of hard wood, and if the peat can be

laid down on the banks of the Welland Canal at $1 to $1.25 a ton, we have no doubt that we shall soon be freed from the clutches of a monopoly in fuel. The Company has 1400 acres, part of the well known Cranberry Marsh, in Welland, capable of producing, according to the estimate of the engineers, over 3,000,000 tons of peat. We are assured that some of the Welland peat which sold in Hamilton at $4 a ton, has given the greatest satisfaction. With such a margin for profit, as this affords, the stock of the Company should be readily floated, and, with judicious management, could not fail to prove a paying investment.

PROTECTION AND UNEQUAL TAXATION.

According to Mr. Commissioner Well's report, the price of groceries and provisions in the United States, in 1867, as compared with 1860–61, is 88 per cent; of domestic dry goods, 86½ per cent; of fuel, 57 per cent; of house rent, 65 per cent; and in the large cities the latter has increased from 90 to 100 per cent. In the first half of 1868, the average increase of all the elements which constitute the food, clothing, and shelter of a family, has been 79 per cent as compared with 1860–61. The rise of wages for 1867 has been only 50 per cent for unskilled mechanical labour. From a comparison of the expenses of labouring men in the manufacturing establishments, it appears that in 1860–61 the weekly wages were $6.04, and the expenditures $5.52, leaving a saving of 62 cents a week; in 1867–68 the wages were $9.54, and the expenses for the same articles, $9.54, showing the unskilled workman, this year, to be $27 worse off than before. If flour be taken as a standard, the average increase of price from 1860 to 1868 is 90 per cent, while the average increase of wages is 58 per cent; so that in this item the workman is worse off by at least 20 per cent than he was before the war.
The person whose annual income and expenditure before the war were $1,000—say the country clergyman, or city clerk, or teacher—finds now that his expenses for precisely the same objects are $1,790. If his salary had been raised to the gold standard—say $1,500—he is still some $400 behind annually, or so much poorer. Even in gold, his income is worth $440 less annually. Each individual with fixed income has 79 per cent less to spend. His dollar is only worth a fraction of what it was. If he has the same income in gold, his dollar will now buy 44 per cent less. If he is a labourer, earning before the war ten dollars a week in gold, and consuming it all, he now receives but $15.80, while his necessary expenses are 90 per cent greater.

The effect of the protective tariff is seen in the unnatural growth of manufactories of various kinds, and the reduced production of staples, such as breadstuffs and farm products. The capitalist is growing richer, and the labouring classes are becoming poorer. Yet with all the nursing which has been lavished on the manufacturing interests, Mr. Wells confesses that " the United States finds itself in the anomalous position of a great nation, favored in many respects as no other nation upon which the sun shines, unable to exchange its products on terms of equality with the products of any other country ; the marked exception being always its product or supplies of the precious metals." This condition of things is attributed to an irredeemable paper currency, unequal and heavy taxation, and a limited supply of skilled labour in some departments of industry.

THE GOVERNMENT AND THE TELEGRAPH.

Mr. Washburn, a member of the American Congress, is advocating the passage of a bill to annex the telegraphs of the United States to the Post Office Department. The tariff provided is one cent per word for telegrams, with an additional charge of three cents for postage and two cents for delivery, with a reduction to the press of fifty per cent. According to the New York *Times*, this rate would increase the average cost of news to the press of the United States more than three hundred per cent, and would compel the newspapers to pay an extra tax of a million dollars a year for the privileges they now enjoy. It is a very suggestive fact that, in one year, 14,725,181 telegrams furnished to the press by the Western Union Telegraph Company cost only $521,509, which quantity of news is greater than the entire telegraphic correspondence of all continental Europe, for which the paternal governments therein charge and receive $11,597,632 a year. The following table will show the contrast between the European system of State control, and the American system of private management :—

Statement showing the average cost of telegrams in Continental Europe and the average cost of press telegrams in the United States, with total amount of each per annum :

Total number of messages transmitted in Continental Europe for the year 1866...... 12,902,588	Total number of messages furnished to the newspapers of the U. States for 1866........ 14,725,181
Gross receipts for the above $11,597,632 71	Gross receipts for the above...... $521,509
Average cost of telegrams in Continental Europe........81 cents.	Average cost of press telegrams in the U. States 3½ cents.

The statistics of telegraphs constructed and operated under governmental control, as compared with those under private management, are as follows :—

Name of Country.	No. of Messages Sent.	Population.	Proportion of Offices to Population
Under Government Control.			
Austria......	861	2,0 .7,472	39,411,309	1 to 46,311
Belgium......	356	1,188,005	4,984,451	1 to 14,000
Bavaria......	..		4,341,556	
Denmark......	89	208,150	2,468,713	1 to 27,000
France.......	1,208	2,507,472	38,302,025	1 to 31,000
Italy........	549	1,760,880	25,928,717	1 to 49,000
Norway......	75	200,375	1,433,488	1 to 19,000
Prussia......	533	1,904,003	1,739,913	1 to 33,000
Russia.......	338	838,853	68,224,832	1 to 221,0 0
Swi zerland..	252	668,916	2,514,494	1 to 10,000
Spain........	142	533,375	16,302,625	1 to 109,000
Totals....4,347	12,484,311		
Under Private Control.			
Great Britain and Ireland..2,151	5,781,189	29,501,009	1 to 13,714
Dominion of Canada......	382	573,319	3,976,224	1 to 10,400
U. States....4,126	12,386,852	31,148,047	1 to 7,549
Totals......6,659	18,741,360		

The New York journal to which we have referred puts the case in a striking light when it thus compares the systems :—" In Continental Europe, where the telegraphs were built and are operated by Government, there are but 4,347 offices for a population of over 250,000,000; while in Great Britain, the United States, and the Dominion of Canada, where telegraphy has been left to private enterprise and has been untrammeled by governmental interference, by monopoly or restriction, there are 6,559 offices to a population of 64,000,000. While the number of telegrams transmitted in Continental Europe was only 12,485,311 in one year, there were sent in the three countries where telegraphy is free from governmental intermeddling and repression, 18,741,360. While the average cost of telegrams in Europe was 81¾ cents, in the three countries where the people were let alone and suffered to manage the business themselves, it averaged only 51 cents."

Communications.

CLASSIFICATION OF VESSELS.

To the Editor of the Monetary Times.

Toronto, 27th Jany., 1869.

Sir,—As the season is again at hand when the Inspectors of the various local Insurance Companies, composing our Canadian Association of Lake Underwriters, will depart on their annual tour o. inspection, will you permit me, through your co lumns, to offer one or two remarks.

During the past season of navigation complaint; were made by sundry shippers, and vessel owners, concerning what they termed the defective inspection of vessels; and no doubt their complaint, were, in several cases, not without sufficient ground. It was alleged that their vessels, with their outfit. were duly overhauled in the Spring, and classed a: standard, by which classification they were allowe to carry grain cargos on any, and all, our inlan lake waters between Chicago and Quebec. I several cases, on the approach of the equinoctia gales and the cold and boisterous weather of th fall season, they were informed, on applying fo insurance, that grain cargoes could not be con veyed by such and such vessels as their sails an standing and running rigging were not in a cou dition to encounter the gales prevalent at thi season of the year.

If a vessel at the commencement of the season classes standard, she ought, it is contended, to retain that classification until the close, unless she has, in the interval, sustained damage which has not been made good. If the vessel, or any portion of her outfit is, on inspection, found to be in a defective condition, let those defects be pointed out to the owner, with injunctions to have them remedied before the approach of heavy weather, under penalty of having the class of his vessel lowered. But to allow her to run through the whole of the fine season, and then in the height of the carrying trade, when, as is often the case, vessels are scarce and their owners, perhaps, anxious to make up for a bad Summer's business, to start these objections is, I think it will be conceded, a manifest injustice to all parties.

Truly yours,

INSURANCE.

Railway News.

GREAT WESTERN RAILWAY.—Traffic for week ending January 8, 1869.

Passengers	$23,713 68
Freight and live stock.....	48,598 79
Mails and sundries...........	3,519 13
	$75,831 60
Corresponding Week of '68.	63,327 88
Increase.............	$12,503 72

NORTHERN RAILWAY.—Traffic receipts for week ending 16th January, 1869.

Passengers	$2,330 79
Freight..................	5,416 47
Mails and Sundries	254 02
Total Receipts for week......	$8,001 28
Coresponding week, 1887,..	7,881 94
Increase.............	$119 34

RAILWAY TRAFFIC.—The Official Gazette for the 23d gives the following Railway Traffic Returns for the years ending 31st December, 1867 and 1868 :—

ROAD	1867.	1868.
Great Western..............	$3,725,169	$3,710,221
Grand Trunk...............	6,506,966	6,906,923
London & Port Stanley...	42,759	38,027
Welland..................	68,615	77,482
Northern.................	562,893	550,621
Port Hope & Beaverton...	232,476	235,904
Cobourg, Peterboro and Marmora.................	21,073	15,341
Brockville & Ottawa......	135,824	173,373
St. Lawrence & Ottawa...	105,410	117,471
New Brunswick & Canada	79,781	103,348
European & North American.............. ..	162,661	175,456
Nova Scotia...............	232,778	279,941

STEEL RAILS.—Advices from Essen state that he low rates current for Bessemer steel rails in hat district have excited the most bitter complaints on the part of Prussian industrials. Thus, at an adjudication for the Lower Silesian (Markisch and Berlin) Railway, Herr Krupp, of Essen, undertook to supply Bessemer cast steel rails at £15 6s. 6d. per ton. The manufacture of steel is attracting more and more attention among Prussian industrials. Thus, it is announced that he New Scotland Company is about to occupy tself with the production of cast steel. This society has for some time produced with success puddled steel rails.

THE CENTRAL PACIFIC RAILROAD.—Trains on the Central Pacific Railroad are running on schedule time to Carlin, in the northeast corner of Nevada, 600 miles distant. Track-layers are at Humboldt Canon, 25 miles further east.— No interruption has occurred from snow so far, though 22 miles of snow-sheds at the summit of the Sierras working satisfactorily. The commercial business of the Central for December exceeded $340,000. Out at the end of the Central Pacific Railroad track they have a complete blacksmith shop permanently fixed on a wagon. It is moved along about three times a day to keep pace with the workmen. One team is detailed regularly to move the blacksmith shop.

RAILWAY ACCOMMODATION AT GUELPH.—The Guelph Town Council have adopted a report of their railway committee, stating that they had sent a deputation to wait on Mr. Swinyard, Manager of the G. W. Railway, to ascertain from him on what terms he could be induced to move the Western Station to a central part of the town; that they found him prepared to do so, provided the right of way was secured the road on the north side of the G. T. R. to the Market Square, and ground for the Station granted somewhere in the vicinity of the Market Square. They also recommend a communication to be sent to Mr. Brydges for the purpose of ascertaining what action he will take in the matter, and that immediate action be taken to complete an arrangement between the town and the two companies for the centralization of the Stations.

Law Report.

INSURANCE—CONDITION TERMINATING RISK —A condition endorsed on an insurance policy provided that if, for any cause the company should so elect, it should be optional with them to terminate the insurance, upon notice given to the insured or his representatives of their intention so to do, in which case the company should refund a ratable proportion of the premium. I was contended that the notice contemplated by the condition was a notice giving to the plaintiff a reasonable time to afford him an opportunity o effecting a new insurance previous to the termination of the defendant's policy. The Court considered that by acceding to that interpretation they would be adding a term to the condition somewhat inconsistent with its object and intention—viz., the right to put an end to the risk any time.

Held—That the notice should precede the termination of the insurance, but that they might be contemporaneous, and that the company could terminate the risk by giving notice that they do so, and refunding the unearned premium.—*Ca v. Lancashire Ins. Co.*, 27 Q. B., 453.

INSURANCE—ARSON—LEAVING PREMISES U OCCUPIED.—In an action on a fire policy, defendants gave such evidence to show that the house had been burned by one K——, by the plaintiff procurement, as would well have warranted a fin ing for defendants. K——, however had been indicted for the arson, and acquitted. The ju having found for the plaintiff, the Court refus to interfere.

The policy provided that in case of any alteration or addition, &c., or change in the nature the occupation, or in any other manner whatever, by which the degree of risk was increase and a consequent additional premium would required, the insurance would be void in defau of notice and allowance thereof. Defendant alleged, as a breach of this condition, that t premises which, when insured, were occupied the plaintiff's tenant, became vacant and unoccupied without defendants' knowledge or conse whereby the risk was increased and an additio premium would have been required ; and that plaintiff did not give notice of this change, was it allowed by defendants.

Held—That the plea was bad, for the m ceasing to occupy was not within the conditi In delivering judgment, the Chief Justice said We are not prepared to hold that the clause in policy is to be so construed that if the assu leaves home for a week, locking up his house, a fire takes place during that time, his polic by avoided. A "change in the nature of occupation" does not, we think, point at a temporary cessor of the occupation, but ır to an application of the premises insured purpose different from that described in the cation. If the underwriters desire to guard selves against loss on unoccupied build- or to make continued residence a condition ident to the right of recovery, in the case of lding described as a dwelling-house occupied tenant, we think they must use express lan- e to meet the case.

is Court, in Hobson v. The Western District al Fire Insurance Company (6 U. C. R 536), r a plea setting out a provision that where was a change of occupation the policy should proved by the company, and averring that the tiff, though the occupier when the insurance effected, was not so at the time of the fire, that A. B. was, and that fact was not com- icated to defendants, held " that ; a mere ge of occupant, without other alteration in manner or purpose of occupation," was not in the provision.

. Boulton urged that, at all events, this ob- m would lie under the words "or in any other ıer whatsoever." It seems to us, however, as the alleged avoidance of the policy is to be the ceasing of the fact of occupation, if such ceasing do not properly fall within egal meaning of the condition, the general a cannot help them.

any event, we think the whole condition in the words "by which the degree of risk ırğased, and a consequent additional premium d be required," and that it must be left to ury to say if the risk be increased, otherwise rould have to construe the clause as a war- r that no change should take place whether isk be thereby increased or not ; or, in the ing illustration of the late Chief Baron Pol- if premises in which fireworks were made here was a provison that no alteration should ade without notice, but afterwards the pre- ı were converted into an ice-house, would vitiate the policy ?—Stokes v. Cox, (I H. & N.

the late decision of the Common Pleas in v. Liverpool and London Insurance Com- (I H. & N. 533), on a condition almost ical in its language with this, shows that alterations generally are not prohib.ted, but such as did increase the risk, and as no in- e of risk was found, the defendants must fail ıat part of their rule." The facts there were ronger against the plaintiff than here, as an tor was put in without notice after effecting policy, and the underwriter's agent who ef- l the insurance swore that a higher rate of ance would be required for a building in h such an elevator might be placed, accord- o the company's tariff.

refer to Stoke v. Cox, in error, (1 H. & N. to Baxendale v. Harvey (4 H. & N. 455), h shew the strictness with which these con- ns are construed, and that the question of ase of risk is to be submitted to the jury. In uter case Martin B. says, " Stokes v. Cox is ithority that, if the insurers wish to make it dition precedent to the validity of the policy there shall be no alteration in the circum- es, whether the risk is increased or not, they do so in distinct terms."—Gould v. British Ass. Co., 27 Q.B., 480.

Commercial.

Toronto Market.

ıY Goods.—Business has been very quiet the opening of the year. This is, of course, ral at this season, but the absence of snow, the consequent delay in getting grain and r farm produce to market, has restricted the of country merchants, and rather disap- ted the anticipations of those in the trade.

This, however, may only be temporary, as the present mild, dry, weather, cannot be expected to last. In fact, during the last few days, snow has fallen in some localities, and business is becoming more active. The total imports of Dry Goods at the port of New York for the past year amounted to $80,905,834, against $88,582,411 for the pre- vious year, and $126 222,853 for 1866—a de- crease of above $46,000,000 on 1866, and $8,000,- 000 on the imports of 1867. The decrease was principally on woollen goods, while on silk there was an increase.

GRAIN.—Wheat—Receipts by cars 17,000 bush. and 7, 400 bush last week. The market is very quiet ; receipts at the different railway stations have been light owing to the want of sleighing. There is a small demand for Spring at $1.03, and sales of cars occurred during the week at $1.03 to $1.04. There is a slow demand for prime samples of Fall; common and inferior dull of sale; the very finest samples of white are held for an advance on our quotations. Barley—Receipts 1,950 bush. and 1,300 bush. last week; the brewers are taking all that offers at $1.28 to $1.30 on the track, and $1.30 to $1.32 delivered. Peas—Receipts con- tinue very small, and the market is nominal as quoted. Oats—Receipts 6,800 bush. and 6,700 last week. The market is quiet and steady at 53c. to 53c., with some business doing at these prices. Rye—Nominal. Seeds—There is a small speculative demand for Timothy at $2 to $2.50, and $2.75 for No. 1; Clover, $6.25 to $6.50; flax, $1.70 to $2.

FLOUR.—Receipts 2,500 bbls., and 3,350 bbls. last week. The market is dull at quotations; demand light and little doing. Two or three lots sold at $4.55, which is about the value of good brands of No. 1 superfine. A lot of Spring Wheat extra sold at $4.65. Extra, nominal as quoted. Nothing doing in other grades.

PROVISIONS.—Dressed Hogs.—The market is active at quotations; car loads of heavy averaging 240 lbs. sell at $9.50 to $9.80. Pork—Mess firm and higher as quoted; Prime Mess held at $22; and English prime mess at $20. Bacon—Sales Canadian cut occurred at 9½c. to 9½c.; Cumber- land cut 10½c. to 10½c. Butter—Quiet and un- changed. Eggs—Dull at 16c.

FREIGHTS.—Rates by Grand Trunk Railway:— Flour to all stations from Belleville to Lynn, in- clusive, 35c.; grain per 100 lbs. 18c. ; flour to Brockville and Cornwall, inclusive, 43c. grain 22c. flour to Montreal 50c. grain 25c. ; flour to all stations between Island Pond and Portland, in- clusive, 85c. grain 43c. ; flour to Boston $1.15 U.S. currency ; flour to Halifax $1.05, grain 60c; flour to St. John 95c. Boxed Meats to Liverpool per gross ton 82s. 6d.; lard or butter in tinnets 87s. 6d. ; Pork 11s. per tierce ; flour 5s. 6d. per barrel ; grain 12s. per 480 pounds. Rates by Great Western Railway—Flour, Toronto to Sus- pension Bridge 25c. gold ; thence to New York, 76c. U.S. currency per bbl. ; to Boston 86c.— Rates from Toronto to Liverpool, London and Glasgow are—Beef, Bacon, Pork, Hams, Lard and Tallow, in lots of one car load and upwards, $1.52, gold, per 100 lbs. Grain, in bags of 5 car loads and upwards, 96c., do. Flour, $1.62 per bbl. do.

Produce in New York.

The following were the stocks in store in New- York at the dates mentioned :

	Jan. 18.	Jan. 11.	Jan. 20.
	1869.	1869.	1868.
Wheat......bu	3,152,461	3,524,172	1,548,361
Corn.......	1,472,266	1,508,233	1,461,721
Oats.......	2,734,854	2,864,854	2,318,725
Barley......	294,265	336,000	143,696
Rye........	246,553	263,260	189,380
Peas.......	62,425	64,645	3,320
Malt.......	65,000	54,740	43,816
Total......	8,025,354	8,315,405	5,711,875

—The agency of the Royal Canadian Bank at Ottawa has been closed.

Produce in Montreal.

The following is a statement of flour and grain in store and in hands of millers:

	Jan. 15,	Jan. 1,	Jan. 15,
	1869.	1869.	1868.
Wheat, bu....	118,847	136,097	116,254
Corn, bu.	41,000	50,000	72,860
Pease, bu.....	2,100	100	4,450
Oats, bu......	71,708	75,290	10,700
Barley, bu....	14,320	17,120	400
Flour, bbls...	69,724	64,457	70,042
Rye flour, bbls.	....	1	......
Oatmeal, bbls.	500	550	195
Cornmeal, bbls.	300	300	100

St. John Market.

BREADSTUFFS—Jan. 12.—Dullness continues in the flour trade, and prices are a trifle lower. Demand is light, and arrivals keep the stock without diminution. We quote superfine at $5.90, and choice brands 10 to 20c. higher. The competition to effect sales causes much irregular- ity in prices, and it is difficult for our quotations to show the exact state of the market. Dealers say they are not getting the cost of their goods. It is pretty certain that the whole trade in bread- stuffs is in an unsatisfactory condition, nearly all markets being overstocked, and flour selling at a loss. Cornmeal $4.50.

The following is a statement of the quantity of flour and cornmeal imported into St. ohn in the year 1868, during which period there were also imported six cargoes of corn, contain'ng 43,347 bushels:

CANADIAN FLOUR VIA PORTLAND.

January	5,522
February	9,175
March	7,782
April	18,709
May	13,970
June	23,047
July	5,600
August	6,430
September	7,229
October	39,771
November	25,305
December	10,161
	167,651
By railway, about	10,000
Total Canadian	177,651
American flour	38,050
Total flour (barrels)	215,701
Cornmeal (including 3,815 bags reduced to barrels)	32,275

Halifax Market.

BREADSTUFFS.—Jan. 19.—We note no quotable change during the past week, the absence of any speculative feeling continues, buyers still holding off with a view to lower prices.

The stocks at Picton and the vicinity are still large, thus preventing any outlet in that direction, and greatly restricting demand for home consump- tion. Our receipts are fully equal to demand. We quote:—

White Wheat extra (fall) $7 25 to $7 50. Fancy $6 60 to $6 75. Bakers' Strong, $6 40 to $6 50. Supers $6 25. No. 2 $5 to $5 50. Middlings $4 75 to $5. Pollard's $4 25 to $4 50. Rye $5 to $5 25. Oatmeal $7 75. Cornmeal, K. D., $4 50. F. G. $4 25. White Beans $3 25 to $3 50.

WEST INDIA PRODUCE.—Sugar and Molasses continue unchanged. Stock of latter, principal y Cienfuegos, and not suitable for r tailing. A mixed lot of Trinidad off·ring at 30c. Deale s anticipate early arrival of new crop, till then no transactions of any moment are likely to be made. Rum is decidedly lower, several cargoes are hourly expected. We quote: Sugar, V. P. 9 c. Port , Rico 8½ to 8½c. Cuba 7½ to 7c. Mela ses Cien. fuegos 35 to 36c. Trinidad 0 to 33c. Ru.i — Demerara—(in bond) at 60c. Coffee— amai a— 13 to 15c. St. Domingo 10 to 12c.

FISH AND OIL.—Considerable activity prevails in these markets, several round lots having changed hands at full rates. Cod Oil has been taken at 58c. cask. Stock light.

EXCHANGE—Bank Drafts on London, 60 days, 12½ per c. Montreal, sight, 3½ per c. New York Gold 3 per c. Currency 23 per c. disct. St. John, N. B. 3 per c.

English Barley Market.

There is no doubt that high prices have had the effect of bringing supplies more rapidly forward than usual, and hence it can only be concluded that as our crop is a small one, a rapid and early exhaustion of it will take place. Unless, therefore, it can be proved that the deficiency of the home growth will be compensated by an augmented yield abroad, there can be no prospect of any abatement in price. Hot, dry weather seems to have been as prejudicial to the crop of barley abroad as it has been in this country. France, however, forms an exception, for from that country we have received liberal supplies of excellent malting produce. Had it not been for the importations of barley from France, the prices of barley must have risen to a point which would have necessitated a decided advance in the price of beer. The crop in Germany seems to have turned out poorly, for as yet we have received very moderate supplies. But the fact is, that notwithstanding the high quotation current in this market, there is no profit on shipments from the Baltic ports, and consequently sufficient evidence is given of the shortness of the crop. From the United States there is no prospect of obtaining supplies.—*Morgan's Trade Journal.*

The Sugar Crop.

The New-York *Shipping & Commercial List*, in presenting its annual statement of the Sugar trade of the United States for 1868, says:

"The figures exhibit briefly the trade of the country in this food article. It will be seen that the receipts of Foreign into the United States, exclusive of the States and Territories on the Pacific, for the year ending Dec. 31, 1868, were 470, 975, tons, against receipts in 1867 of 355,801 tons; in 1866 of 493,497 tons; in 1865, 362,243 tons; in 1864. 214,099 tons; in 1863, 243,138 tons; in 1862, 247,015 tons; in 1861, 242,908 tons; in 1860, 341,532 tons, while the consumption of Foreign in 1868, was 446,033 tons, against a consumption in 1867 of 37?,068 tons; in 1866, 383, 178 tons; in 1865, 34 ,809 tons; in 1864, 192, 660 tons; in 1863, 2?1,308 tons; in 1862, 241,411 tons; in 1861, 241,4?0 tons, and in 1860, 296,950 tons, and that the total consumption of Foreign and Domestic Cane Sugar in 1868 may be placed at 469,533 tons, against a total consumption in 1867 of 400,568 tons; in 1866, 391,678 tons; in 1865, 350,809 tons; in 1864, 120,660 tons; in 1863, 284,308 tons; in 1862, 432,411 tons; in 1861, 363,819 tons, and in 1860, 416,281 tons, being an increase in the consumption of Foreign in 1868, as compared with that of 1867, of 68,465 tons, or over 18 ℔ cent., and an increase in consumption of Foreign and Domestic of 68,965 tons, or about 17¼ ℔ cent.

The manufacture of Sugar from Molasses continues to be prosecuted with great vigour, the sale of Molasses for this purpose during the past year, and the yield of Sugar, being larger than we have ever before recorded; owing, however, to the inferior quality of the crop of last year's Molasses, the Sugar product has not been as great ℔ hhd. as in former years by at least 10 ℔ cent., so that while our estimates point to a consumption in the United States of nearly one-third more Molasses—say about 160,000 hhds., against a consumption of 120,000 hhds. in 1867, the Sugar produced therefrom has only been, say 72,000,000 pounds, or in round numbers 32,000 tons, against a yield of 26,-700 tons in 1867. The Sugar also was not of as good a quality as usual, and finding a less ready sale during much of the year, the stock left over at its close is larger than is generally the case at the end of the year.

The crop of Louisana, now about made, is estimated at 100,000 hhds. The season has been usually favourable, so much so, that at one time strong hopes were entertained that the yield would reach 125,000 hhds., but the weather has been recently less propitious, and the estimates have been reduced to the first mentioned figures.

The planting interest of that State is much more hopeful, the crop has steadily advanced from a little over 10,000 hhds. in 1863-4, to about 100, 000 hhds. the present rolling, with much cane reserved for next season's planting, and already, with a favourable year, a crop of 250,000 hhds. for the coming season is talked of as not an improbable event.

Advices from the principal West India points, indicate a full supply. Cuba last year turned out a crop nearly, or quite, one-fourth larger than was ever before made upon the island, and, as it is from that quarter we receive the bulk of our supplies, the greatest interest attaches to the events now transpiring there. The insurrection has already interfered to some extent with grinding operations on the south side of the island, but it remains to be developed how far these injurious effects may be extended, and consequently our markets generally are in a waiting attitude. The prospect, until recently, was, that the yield the present season would fully equal, if it did not exceed that of last year, and the course of prices will depend very much upon the ability of the Spanish Government to suppress speedily, or prevent the spreading of, what has become rather a formidable rebellion.

Great difficulty surrounds the collection of statistics relative to the crop of maple sugar, much the larger part being consumed upon the farm; with our rather imperfect data, we make the last years' crop about 23,000 tons.

These estimates for the consumption of raw in our States and Territories on the Pacific, the past year, are in the neighborhood of 18,000 or 19,000 tons; a very considerable increase in these figures is looked for the present year, as, owing to the present unexpected short supplies and low prices for the refined article, the refineries of San Francisco were idle during a portion of the past year; besides which, one or more of the establishments have recently considerably enlarged their works, with the intention of prosecuting the work with renewed.

The cultivation of the beet root for sugar is yet entirely in its infacy, and the quantity of sugar made from it here, as well as the results of the sorgo culture, as far as sugar-making is concerned, are so inconsiderable that we make none other than this passing note of them.

Having thus reviewed the several points of interest, the consumption of the various descriptions throughout the country may be stated as follows:

	Tons.
Cane Sugar consumed in the United States on the Atlantic	469,533
In the States and Territories on the Pacific	18,500
On Sugar made from Molasses	32,000
On Maple Sugar	23,000
Total	543,033
Against a total consumption of all kinds in 1867, of	467,268
Increase	75,765

Or about 16¼ per cent.

The production of Sugar throughout the world, including the Beet Sugar of Europe, and the Palm and Date Sugar of the Indies, for the year 1867, is estimated at 2,299,600 tons, of which Cuba produced nearly one-third; and the consumption for the same year, 2,007,700; of this Great Britain and her colonies consumed about 680,000 tons, and the United States 467,300 tons: the two nationalities consuming nearly one-third of the world's supply.

Exports of Petroleum from the United States from January 1 to January 9.

	1869.	1868.
From New York......galls.	595,254	1,766,84
Boston	101,681	44,36
Philadelphia	293,078	730,35
Baltimore	6,000	3,58
Portland	....	6,80
New Bedford	....	....
Cleveland	....	....
Total Ex. from the U. States	1,194,187	2,551,96
Same time 1867		1,570,09
Same time 1866		2,012,82

Wheat in California.

An exchange says: "California produced las year, over all requirements for domestic consum tion, 8,000,000 centals of wheat for export, neat 3,000,000 more than in the previous year. Sh has exported to Great Britain 1,600,000 centals to New York and other Atlantic ports, 1,000,00 and to other countries, 4,000,000, leaving a su plus of 4,400,000 centals on hand. It would r quire, it is said, 220 ships of 1,000 each, to car away the remaining surplus of California whea alone. The *Commercial Herald*, from which w condense the foregoing, adds that the end of 18 has been nearly reached, and that but six mont remain before the next harvest year will be up us, with a larger breadth of land sown to whe than has ever been cultivated in California wit that grain. Although the rainy season has bee unusually backward, indications are greatly i favor of our chances for an average amount rain. There is no ground upon which to predi a dry or unusual winter, and the probability very great that our next harvest year will give a surplus of 10,000,000 centals for export. will require 500 ships of 1,000 tons each to car away the prospective export crop of next yea There are now thousands of acres sown to whe that is well up, and is in every way thrifty ar promising.

American vs. Canadian Flour.

Alex. S. Macrae's Liverpool Weekly Produ Statement says: Why should American sell as rule at much less money than Canadian? Simp because the former rarely finds its way direct fro the miller to the British consumer—is perha months knocking about in the stores of Uni States seaports, and consequently, cannot comp in excellency of condition with the Canadian. The very freshness of the barrel seems "finis to the flour, and the Canadian brand with legit care and special significance as to address, so th wherever that quality finds favor, that miller advertised by it to his very home. Thus par cular brands get called for, and every miller p sesses within himself the means of founding European reputation, of more value than even American one, with the power of pitting the o against the other. Western brands ought not be selling at 24s. to 26s. 6d. (7½ to 8 dollar while Canadian commands 27s. to 29s. (8¼ to dollars) per barrel, but such is the fact, the latt saving besides five to ten per cent in expenses, a direct alliance with British consumers.

BARLEY.

One of the most extraordinary features of th season is the rush of barley from Great Britain the United States! It appears that American d tillers, more especially those of Chicago, ha suddenly discovered the superiority of our grow and we are shipping, from the 1st of December the 23d some 120,000 bushels, against not a sin bushel last year! If any evidence was wanted the constant necessity of Americans and Engli to try and reciprocate produce, it is here succe fully afforded. The value of British barley malting purposes is 6s. to 6s. 6d. per bushel 60 lbs.

)WARDSBURGH STARCH COMPANY.—At the al meeting of the shareholders of this Com-, held on the 19th inst., the following gentle-were elected Directors for the present year:—hanly, Esq., M.P., Peter Redpath, John Mc-1211, W. T. Benson, Warden King, John Fair-1, Henry J. Tiffin, Esqrs. And at a meeting 1e Directors, held on the 20th instant, Mr. ly was re-elected President, and Mr. Redpath -President.

Toronto Mutual Fire Insurance Company.

E ANNUAL MEETING of the members of the above ompany will be held at the office, 29 Toronto Street ato, on

TUESDAY, 23RD FEBRUARY NEXT,

WELVE o'clock, noon, for the reception of the Report e Board of Directors, election of Directors to fill acies, and transaction of important business. The dance of members is particularly requested.

By order,
H. HANCOCK, Secretary.

To Mercantile Men.

E NEW POCKET REFERENCE BOOK OF THE ERCANTILE AGENCY revised to Christmas, and ining 35,000 names of Traders in the Dominion, is out of press, and ready for delivery.

scribers having Travellers out, or about leaving, d avail themselves of this indispensable volume.

DUN, WIMAN & CO.,
Exchange Buildings, Toronto.
anadian Offices—Montreal and Halifax.
uary 10. 28-tf

aver Mutual Fire Insurance Association.

E annual meeting of the members of the above Asso-iation will be held at the office, 29 Toronto Street, nto, on TUESDAY, the 9th day of FEBRUARY, at 12 o'clock, noon, for reception of Report of Board irectors, election of Directors to fill vacancies, and saction of other business.

e attendance of all members is particularly requested.
By order,
W. T O'REILLY, Secretary.

Oil Refiners' Association of Canada.

E above Association hereby give notice that an Office has been opened,

AT LONDON, ONTARIO,

FOR THE SALE OF ALL

E REFINED PETROLEUM OIL
de by the Association, at the following Rates and a, viz.:

OTS OF ONE TO YOUR CAR LOADS, INCLUSIVE, AT 35 CENTS PER GALLON.

DS OF FIVE CAR LOADS AND UPWARDS AT 33 CENTS PER GALLON.

r Terms—Cash, free on board at London.

l Oil sold to be received at the place of shipment by urchaser; and in the event of his failing to appoint son to inspect and receive the oil, it must be under-i that it will in all cases be subject to the Inspector's inted by the Association; and, after shipment, is no drawbacks on account of quality, quantity, age, or otherwise, will be allowed.

orders to be addressed to the Secretary, and all stances to be made to the Treasurer.

SAMUEL PETERS, President.
WM. DUFFIELD, Vice-President.
L. C. LEONARD, Secretary.
CHARLES HUNT, Treasurer.
on, Ont., Jan. 5, 1869. 23-tf

Hurd, Leigh & Co.,
IMPORTERS AND DECORATORS OF FRENCH CHINA.

s and families supplied with any pattern of crest desired.

sumen goods always on hand. 72 Yonge Street, to, Ontario. 24y

Mercantile.

TORONTO PRICES CURRENT.—JANUARY 28, 1869.

Name of Article.	Wholesale Rates.		Name of Article.	Wholesale Rate.		Name of Article.	Who. Ra
Boots and Shoes.	$ c.	$ c.	**Groceries**—*Contin'd*	$ c.	$ c.	**Leather**—*Contin'd.*	$ c.
Mens' Thick Boots ...	2 50	2 50	" fine to fins't..	0 85	0 95	Kip Skins, Patna	0 50
" Kip.........	2 50	3 25	Hyson	0 45	0 80	French	0 70
" Calf	3 00	3 70	Imperial	0 42	0 80	English	0 65
" Congress Gaiters..	2 50	2 50	Tobacco, *Manufac'd:*			Hemlock Calf (20 to	
" Kip Cobourgs...	1 25	1 45	Can Leaf, ℔ 5s & 10s.	0 26	30	35 lbs.) per doz....	0
Boys' Thick Boots...	1 00	1 80	Western Leaf, com..	0 25	26	Do. light	0
Youths'	1 25	1 50	" Good ...	0 27	32	French Calf	0
Women's Balts	95	1 30	" Fine	0 32	35	Grain & Satin Cit'ℓ doz..	0
" Congress Gaiters..	1 25	1 45	" Bright fine..	0 40	0 50	Splits, large ℔ ℔......	0
Misses' Balts.......	0 75	1 00	" 'choice..	0 60	0 75	" small	0
" Congress Gaiters..	1 00	1 30				Enamelled Cow ℔ foot..	0
Girls' Balts	0 60	0 85	**Hardware.**			Pebble Grain	0
" Congress Gaiters..	0 80	1 10	*Tin* (assorted prices)			Buff	0 72
Children's C. T. Cacks..	0 50	0 65	Block, ℔ ℔........	0 25	0 26		
" Gaiters ...	0 55	0 90	Grain.........	0 25	0 26	**Oils.**	
			Copper:			Cod	0 50
Drugs.			Pig.............	0 23	0 24	Lard, extra	0 00
Aloes Cape.........	0 12½	0 16	Sheet..........	0 30	0 33	" No. 1	0 00
Alum............	0 09¾	0 03	*Cut Nails:*			" Woollen	0 00
Borax	0 00	0 00	Assorted ¼ Shingles,			Lubricating, patent...	0 00
Camphor, refined......	0 65	0 70	℔ 100 ℔....	2 90	3 00	" Matt's economic	0 80
Castor Oil.........	0 18	0 28	Shingle alone do	3 15	3 25	Linseed, raw........	0 77½
Caustic Soda	0 04½	0 05	Lathe and 5 dy......	3 30	3 40	" boiled.......	0 82½
Cochineal........	0 90	1 0	*Galvanized Iron:*			Machinery	0 00
Cream Tartar	0 25	0 30	Assorted sizes	0 08	0 00	Olive, 2nd, ℔ gal....	1 45
Epsom Salts	0 03	0 04	Best No. 24	0 09	0 00	" salad	2 00
Extract Logwood.....	0 00	0 11	" 26	0 08	0 08½	" salad, in bots.	
Gum Arabic, sorts....	0 30	0 35	" 28........	0 09	0 09½	" qt. ℔ case ...	3 50
Indigo, Madras .,..	0 75	1 00	*Horse Nails:*			Sesame seed, ℔ gal...	1 50
Licorice	0 14	0 45	Guest's or Griffin's			Seal, pale	0 70
Madder..........	0 16	0 18	assorted sizes......	0 00	0 00	Spirits Turpentine....	0 85
Nutgalls	0 00	0 00	For W. ass'd sizes....	0 18	0 19	Varnish	0 00
Opium..........	0 70	7 00	Patent Hammer'd do..	0 17	0 18	Whale..........	0 75
Oxalic Acid.......	0 28	0 35	*Iron* (at 4 months):				
Potash, Bi-tart,.....	0 35	0 28	Pig—*Chartsierrie* No1.	24 00	25 00	**Paints, &c.**	
" Bichromate ..	0 15	0 20	Other brands. No.1..	22 00	24 00	White Lead, genuine	
Potass Iodide	3 50	4 00	" No.2..	0 00	0 00	in Oil, ℔ 25lbs....	0 00
Senna	0 12½	0 00	Bar—Scotch, ℔ 100 ℔.	2 25	2 50	Do. No. 1 " ...	0 00
Soda Ash	0 03	0 04	Refined	3 00	3 25	" 2 " ...	0 00
S da Bicarb	4 50	5 50	Swedes	5 00	5 50	" 3 " ...	0 00
Tartaric Acid.......	0 37½	0 45	Hoops—Coopers......	3 00	3 25	White Zinc, genuine..	0 00
Verdigris	0 35	0 40	Band	3 00	3 25	White Lead, dry.....	0 04
Vitriol, Blue.......	0 09	0 10	Boiler Plates......	3 25	3 50	Red Lead	0 07½
Groceries.			Canada Plates......	4 00	4 25	Venetian Red, Eng'h..	0 02½
Coffees:			Union Jack	0 00	0 00	Yellow Ochre, Fren'h..	0 02½
Java, ℔ ℔s........	0 22@0 24		Pontypool	4 00	4 25	Whiting	0 90
Laguayra,.......	0 17	0 18	Swansea	3 50	4 00		
Rio............	0 15	0 17	*Lead* (at 4 months):			**Petroleum.**	
Fish:			Bar, ℔ 100 ℔s......	0 07	0 07½	(Refined ℔ gal.)	
Herrings, Lab. split..	5 75	6 50	Sheet "	0 08	0 09	Water white, car'l'd...	
" round....	4 00	4 75	Shot...........	0 07½	0 07½	" small lots....	0 37
" scaled.....	0 35	0 40	*Iron Wire* (net cash):			Straw, by car load	0 33
Mackerel, small extra..	1 00	0 00	No. 6, ℔ bundle....	2 70	2 80	" small lots....	0 35
Loch. Her. wic'e brks..	3 50	3 75	" 9, "	3 10	3 20	Amber, by car load ...	0 08
" half " ..	1 25	1 50	" 12, "	3 40	3 50	" small lots ...	0 00
White Fish & Trout...	3 50	3 75	" 16, "	4 30	4 40	Benzine	0 40
Salmon, saltwater...	14 00	15 00	*Powder:*				
Dry Cod, ℔ 112 lbs...	5 00	5 25	Blasting, Canada....	3 50	0 00	**Produce.**	
Fruit:			FF "	4 25	0 00	*Grain:*	
Raisins, Layers ,...	2 60	2 10	FFF "	4 75	5 00	Wheat, Spring, 60 ℔..	1 02
" M R	1 90	2 10	Blasting, English	4 0	5 00	" Fall "	1 10
" Valentias new..	0 6½	0 07	FF " house..	5 50	6 00	Barley.. 48 " ...	1 25
Currants, new	0 07	00 07½	FFF "	6 00	6 50	Peas..... 6½ " ..	0 58
" old......	0 04½	0 04½	*Pressed Spikes* (4 mos):.			Oats .... 34 " ..	0 52
Figs	0 14	0 00	Regular sizes 100....	4 00	4 25	Rye ..... 56 " ..	0 72
Molasses:			Extra "	4 50	5 00	*Seeds:*	
Clayed, ℔ gal.......	0 00	0 35	*Tin Plates* (net cash):			Clover, choice 60 " ..	6 50
Syrups, Standard ...	0 49	0 50	IC Coke "	7 50	8 50	" com'n 6¼ "	6 29
" Golden	0 56	0 57½	IC Charcoal........	8 25	8 50	Timothy, cho'e 4 " ..	3 00
Rice:			IX "	10 25	10 75	" inf. to good 48 "	2 00
Arracan	4 50	4 75	IXX "	12 25	0 0	Flax...... 56 " ..	1 70
Spices:			DC "	7 25	9 00	*Flour* (per brl.):	
Cassia, whole, ℔ ℔....	0 00	0 45	DX "	9 50	0 00	Superior extra.......	0 00
Cloves	0 11	0 12				Extra superfine,.....	5 40
Nutmegs.........	0 45	0 55	**Hides & Skins.℔℔**			Fancy superfine	4 70
Ginger, gr und	0 20	0 25	Green rough	0 05	0 00	superfine No 1	4 55
" Jamaica, root..	0 00	0 05	Green, salt'd & insp'd..	0 00	0 07	" No. 2....	0 00
Pepper, black.......	0 09½	0 10	Cured	0 0¼	0 08	*Oatmeal,* (per brl.)..	6 00
Pim ento	0 08	0 09	Calfskins, green......	0 00	0 1		
Sugars:			Calfskins, cured......	0 00	0 12	**Provisions**	
Port Rico, ℔ ℔......	0 08½	0 08½	" dry......	0 16	0 20	Butter, dairy tub ℔lb..	0 21
Cuba "	0 08½	0 09½	Sheepskins,........	1 00	1 25	" store packed...	0 30
Barbadoes (bright)...	0 08½	0 09	" country....	0 60	0 80	Cheese, new	0 11
Dry Crushed, at 60 d..	0	0 11½				Pork, mess, per brl....	00 00
Canada Sugar Refine'y,			**Hops**			" prime mess....	0 00
yellow No. 2, 60 ds..	0 00	0 00½	Inferior, ℔ ℔.......	0 05	0 07	" prime	0 0
" No. 1,...	0 09½	0 00	Medium ,.......	0 07	0 00	Bacon, rough	0 0
" No. 3....	0 05½	0 00	Good	0 00	0 12	" Cumberl'd cut..	0 1
Crushed X ...,..	0 00	0 10½	Fancy	0 00	0 00	" smoked	0 0
" A	0 11½	0 1				Hams, in salt........	0 1
Ground.........	0 11½	0 11½	**Leather,** ℔℔ (4 mos.)			" sug.,cur &canv'd..	0 1
Dry Crushed	0 11½	0 11½	In lots of less than			Shoulders, in salt	0 1
Extra Ground.......	0 12½	0 12½	50 sides, 10 ℔ cent			Lard, in kegs	0 1
Teas:			higher.			Eggs, packed	0 1
Japan com'n to good..	0 40	0 55	Spanish Sole. Lst qual..			Beef Hams	0 0
" Fine to choicest..	0 55	0 65	heavy, weights ℔ ℔..	0 00	0 23	Tallow	0 6
Colored, com. to fine..	0 60	0 75	Do.1st qual middle do..	0 22	0 23	Hogs dressed, heavy..	8 0
Congou & Souch'ng...	0 42	0 75	Do. No. 2, all weights..	0 20	0 21	" medium....	0 0
Oolong, g od to fine..	0 50	0 65	Slaughter heavy	0 25	0 00	" light.......	8 0
Y. Hyson, com to gd..	0 45	0 55	Do. light........	0 30	0 20		
Medium to choice ...	0 60	0 80	Harness, best	0 32	0 34	**Salt, &c.**	
Extra choice " ...	0 85	0 95	" No. 2	0 30	0 33	American bris......	1 5
unpow'd r c. to med,..	0 55	0 70	" light.......	0 44	0 34	Liverpool coarse	1 0
" med. to fne,	0 79	0 55	Upper heavy	0 36	0 40	Plaster	1 0
			" light..	0 36	0 40	Water Lime........	1 5

andles.		
& Co.'s	$ c.	$ c.
al.	0 07½	0 08
Bar	0 07	0 07½
Bar.	0 07	0 07½
	0 05	0 05½
	0 03½	0 03¾
	0 00	0 11½
Liquors,		
r doz.	2 60	2 65
Dub Portr.	2 35	2 40
ica Rum.	1 89	2 25
's H. Gin.	1 55	1 65
d Tom.	1 90	2 00
es.	4 00	4 25
d Tom, c.	6 00	6 25
non.	1 00	1 25
ld	2 00	4 00
nmon	1 00	1 50
um	1 70	1 80
or golden.	2 50	4 00

Brandy:	$ c.	$ c.
Hennessy's, per gal.	2 30	2 50
Martell's "	2 30	2 50
J. Robin & Co.'s "	2 25	2 35
Otard, Dupuy & Cos.	2 25	2 3
Brandy, cases	8 50	9 0
Brandy, com. per c.	4 00	4 50
Whiskey:		
Common 36 u. p.	0 62½	0 65
Old Rye	0 85	0 87½
Malt	0 85	0 87½
Toddy	0 85	0 87½
Scotch, per gal.	1 90	2 10
Irish—Kinnahan's c.	7 00	7 50
" Dunnville's Belf't.	6 00	6 25
Wool.		
Fleece, lb.	0 28	0 35
Pulled "	0 22	0 25
Furs.		
Bear.	3 00	10 00
Beaver.	1 00	1 25
Coon	0 20	0 40
Fisher.	4 00	6 00
Martin.	1 40	1 60
Mink.	4 00	4 25
Otter.	5 75	6 00
Spring Rats	0 15	0 17
Fox.	1 20	1 25

NSURANCE COMPANIES.

ENGLISH.—*Quotations on the London Market.*

st Dividend.	Name of Company.	Shares parval £	Amount paid.	Last Sale.
	Briton Medical and General Life	10	....	1½
7½	Commer'l Union, Fire, Life and Mar.	50	5	5¾
8	City of Glasgow	25	2½	5¾
9½	Edinburgh Life	100	15	31½
—½ yr	European Life and Guarantee	2½	11s6	5s
10	Etna Fire and Marine	10	1½	0
5	Guardian	100	50	51
12	Imperial Fire	500	50	0
9½	Imperial Life	100	10	15½
10	Lancashire Fire and Life	20	2	2¾
11	Life Association of Scotland	40	7½	25
s. p. sh	London Assurance Corporation	25	12½	49
5	London and Lancashire Life	10	1	19s
40	Liverp'l & London & Globe F. & L.	20	2	6 15-16ths
5	National Union Life	5	1	0
12½	Northern Fire and Life	100	5	11½
12 ,bo 5s.	North British and Mercantile	50	6½	19¾
50	Ocean Marine	25	5	19¾
5 12s.	Provident Life	100	10	0
½ p. s.	Phœnix	....	....	148
—h. yr.	Queen Fire and Life	10	1	17s
bo. 4s	Royal Insurance	20	3	6
10	Scottish Provincial Fire and Life	50	2½	5
25	Standard Life	50	12	65½
5	Star Life	25	1½	—
	CANADIAN.			₩ c.
4	British America Fire and Marine	$50	$25	53 54xd
4	Canada Life	....	....	.....
12	Montreal Assurance	£50	£5	135
3	Provincial Fire and Marine	60	11	.....
......	Quebec Fire	40	32½	25½
8	" Marine	100	40	25 26
7 mo's.	Western Assurance	40	9	.....

RAILWAYS.	Sha's	Paid	Montr	London.
d St. Lawrence	£100	All.	....	58 60
Lake Huron	20½	"	....	3 3½
do Preference	10	"	....	5½ 6½
tl. & Goderich, 6 ₩c., 1872-3-4	100	"	....	65 69
and St. Lawrence	....	....	10	....
do Pref. 10 ₩ ct.	....	....	73	....
nk	100	"	15 16	15¾ 16
Eq. G. M. Bds. 1 ch. 6 ₩c.	100	"	....	84 86
First Preference, 5 ₩ c	100	"	....	50 51
Deferred, 3 ₩ ct.	100	"	....	....
Second Pref. Bonds, 5 ₩c.	100	"	....	39½ 40½
do Deferred, 3 ₩ ct.	100	"	....	....
Third Pref. Stock, 4 ₩ct.	100	"	....	26½ 27½
do. Deferred, 3 ₩ ct.	100	"	....	....
Fourth Pref. Stock, 3 ₩c.	100	"	....	17½ 18½
do. Deferred, 3 ₩ ct.	100	"	....	....
ern	20½	"	13 14	14½ 14¾
New	20½	18	....	....
6 ₩ c. Bds, due 1873-76.	100	All.	....	99 101
5½ ₩c Bds. due 1877-78.	100	"	....	93 94
lway, Halifax, $250, all.	$250	"	....	....
f Canada, 6 ₩c. 1st Pref. Bds.	100	"	....	80 83

CHANGE.	Halifax.	Montr'l.	Quebec.	Toronto.
London, 60 days				
75 days date	12½	9½ 9¾	9½ 9¾	9¾
o.	11½ 12	8 9	8¾ 9	.. to 9¾
th documents	....	7½ 8	....	....
ew York	....	25½ 26	25 25½	74
do.	....	26 26½	25½ 26	....
do.	....	½ dis. to p.	par ½ dis.	par ½ dis.
	....	4 4½	....	4 to 6

STOCK AND BOND REPORT.

The dates of our quotations are as follows:—Toronto, Jan. 26; Montreal, Jan. 25; Quebec, Jan. 25; London, Jan. 9.

NAME.	Shares.	Paid up.	Divid'd last 6 Months	Dividend Day.	CLOSING PRICES. Toronto.	Montre'l	Quebe
BANKS.			₩ ct.				
British North America	$250	All.	3	July and Jan.	101½ 102	....	103½ 104
Jacques Cartier	50	"	4	1 June, 1 Dec.	107 108	107 108	107 107½
Montreal	200	"	5	"	139 140	138½ 139	138 139
Nationale	50	"	4	1 Nov. 1 May.	106 106½	105 106	106½ 107
New Brunswick	100	"	......	......	....	....	....
Nova Scotia	200	28	7 & b $3½	Mar. and Sept.	....	....	....
Du Peuple	50	"	4	1 Mar., 1 Sept.	108½ 109	108½ 109½	109 109½
Toronto	100	"	4	1 Jan., 1 July.	118 120	119 120	119 120
Bank of Yarmouth	....	....	......	......	....	....	....
Canadian Bank of Com'e	50	95	......	......	102 102½	100½ 102	101 102
City Bank Montreal	80	All.	4	1 June, 1 Dec.	100½ 101	101 102	100½ 101½
Commer'l Bank (St. John)	100	"	₩ ct.	......	....	....	....
Eastern Townships' Bank	50	"	4	1 July, 1 Jan.	....	97½ 99	96½ 97½
Gore	40	...	none.	1 Jan., 1 July.	39 40	40 45	40 45
Halifax Banking Company	....	....	......	......	....	....	....
Mechanics' Bank	50	70	4	1 Nov., 1 May.	95 96	94 96	94 95
Merchants' Bank of Canada	100	70	4	1 Jan., 1 July.	108 108½	109 110	108 108½
Merchants' Bank (Halifax)	....	....	......	......	....	....	....
Molson's Bank	50	All.	4	1 Apr., 1 Oct.	110 110½	110 110½	110 111
Niagara District Bank	100	70	3½	1 Jan., 1 July.	....	....	....
Ontario Bank	40	All.	4	1 June, 1 Dec.	100 100½	99½ 99¾	99 99½
People's Bank (Fred'kton)	100	"	......	......	....	....	....
People's Bank (Halifax)	20	"	7 12 m	......	....	....	....
Quebec Bank	100	"	3½	1 June, 1 Dec.	98 100	....	99½ 100
Royal Canadian Bank	50	50	4	1 Jan., 1 July.	85 85½	85	85 86
St. Stephens Bank	100	All	.....	......	....	....	....
Union Bank	100	70	4	1 Jan., 1 July.	103 103½	103 103½	103½ 104½
Union Bank (Halifax)	100	40	7 12 mo	Feb. and Aug.	....	....	....
MISCELLANEOUS.							
British America Land	250	44	2½	......			
British Colonial S. S. Co	250	32½	2½	......	....	....	....
Canada Company	32½	All.	£1 10s.	......	....	....	....
Canada Landed Credit Co	50	$20	3½	......	....	....	....
Canada Per. B'ldg Society	50	All.	5	......	72 72½	....	....
Canada Mining Company	4	90	......	......	123 123½	....	....
Do. Inl'd Steam Nav. Co.	100	All.	20 12 m	......	....	....	....
Do. Glass Company	100	"	12½ "	......	....	105 107	106 107
Canad'n Loan & Investm't	25	2½	7	......	....	....	....
Canada Agency	10	½	......	......	....	....	....
Colonial Securities Co	....	....	......	......	....	....	....
Freehold Building Society	100	All.	4	......	107½ 108	....	....
Halifax Steamboat Co	100	"	5	......	....	....	....
Halifax Gas Company	....	....	......	......	....	....	....
Hamilton Gas Company	....	....	......	......	....	....	....
Huron Copper Bay Co	4	12	20	......	....	....	....
Lake Huron S. and C.	5	102	......	......	....	25 40cps	....
Montreal Mining Consols	20	$15	......	......	....	....	....
Do. Telegraph Co.	40	All.	5	......	....	.00 3.10	....
Do. Elevating Co.	00	"	15 12 m	......	134 136	133 135	134½ 136
Do. City Gas Co.	40	"	4	15 Mar. 15 Sep.	....	100 102½	....
Do. City Pass. R. Co.	50	"	5	......	....	135 137	136 137
Nova Scotia Telegraph	20	"	....	......	....	110½ 112	110½ 111
Quebec and L. S.	8	$4	......	......	....	....	....
Quebec Gas Co.	200	All.	4	1 Mar., 1 Sep.	....	....	25 cts
Quebec Street R. R.	50	25	8	......	....	....	119 120
Richelieu Navigation Co.	100	All.	7 p.a.	1 Jan., 1 July.	....	....	90 91
St. Lawrence Tow Boat Co.	100	"	......	3 Feb.	....	116½ 117½	116 117
Tor'to Consumers' Gas Co.	50	"	2 3 m.	1 My Au Mar Fe	107 108	....	35 40
Trust & Loan Co. of U. C.	20	5	3	......	....	....	107 108
West'n Canada Bldg Soc'y	50	All.	5	......	117 118	....	....

SECURITIES.	London.	Montreal	Quebec.	Toronto.
Canadian Gov't Deb. 6 ₩ ct. stg.	....	103½ 104½	102½ 103	103 106
Do. do. 6 do due Ja. & Jul. 1877-84	106½ 107½	....	....	....
Do. do. 6 do. Feb. & Aug.	105 107	....	....	....
Do. do. 6 do. Mch. & Sep.	104 106	....	....	....
Do. do. 5 ₩ ct. cur., 1883	95 96	94 95	93 93½	93 94
Do. do. 5 do. stg., 1885	94 96	94½ 95½	93 93½	93 93½
Do. do. 7 do. cur.,	....	....	....	....
Dominion 6 p. c. 1878 cy.	....	104½ 105½	104½ 105	105 105½
Hamilton Corporation	....	....	....	....
Montreal Harbor, 8 ₩ ct. d. 1869	..	....	....	....
Do. do. 7 do. 1870	....	....	....	....
Do. do. 6½ do. 1883	....	100 101	....	....
Do. do. 6½ do. 1873	....	....	....	....
Do. Corporation, 6 ₩ c. 1891	....	95 96	94½ 95½	95 96
Do. 7 p. c. stock	....	107½ 110	106½ 107½	109 110
Do. Water Works, 6 ₩ c. stg. 1878	....	....	....	95 96
Do. do. 6 do. cy. do.	....	95½ 96½	....	95 96
New Brunswick, 6 ₩ ct., Jan. and July	104 106	....	....	....
Nova Scotia, 6 ₩ ct., 1875	104 106	....	....	....
Ottawa City 6 ₩ c. d. 1880	....	92½ 83½	....	....
Quebec Harbour, 6 ₩ c. d, 1883	....	....	60	....
Do. do. 7 do. do.	....	....	65 70	....
Do. do. 8 do. 1886	....	....	80 85	....
Do. City, 7 ₩ c. d. 4½ years	....	....	96 97	....
Do. do. 7 do. 9 do.	....	....	91 92	....
Do. do. 7 do. 2 do.	....	....	93 93½	....
Do. Water Works, 7 ₩ ct., 4 years	....	....	97 97½	....
Do. do. 6 do. 2 do.	....	....	94 95	....
Toronto Corporation	87½ 92½	....	...	....

Financial.

Pellatt & Osler.

STOCK AND EXCHANGE BROKERS, Accountants, Agents for the Standard Life Assurance Company.

OFFICE—86 *King Street East, four Doors West of Church Street, Toronto.*

HENRY PELLATT,   EDMUND B. OSLER,
1y   *Notary Public.*   *Official Assignee.*

Philip Browne & Co.,
BANKERS AND STOCK BROKERS.
DEALERS IN

STERLING EXCHANGE—U S. Currency, Silver and Bonds—Bank Stocks, Debentures, Mortgages, &c. Drafts on New York issued, in Gold and Currency. Prompt attention given to collections. Advances made on Securities.

No. 67 YONGE STREET, TORONTO

JAMES BROWNE.   PHILIP BROWNE, *Notary Public.*
y

James C. Small.
BANKER AND BROKER,
No. 34 KING STREET EAST, TORONTO.

Sterling Exchange, American Currency, Silver, and Bonds, Bank Stocks, Debentures and other Securities, bought and sold. Deposits received. Collections promptly made. Drafts on New York in Gold and Currency issued.

Western Canada Permanent Building and Savings Society.

OFFICE—No 70 CHURCH STREET, TORONTO.

SAVINGS BANK BRANCH,

DEPOSITS RECEIVED DAILY. INTEREST PAID HALF-YEARLY.

ADVANCES
Are made on the security of Real Estate, repayable on the most favourable terms, by a Sinking Fund.
WALTER S. LEE,
36-1y   *Secy & Treas.*

The Canadian Land and Emigration Company
Offers for sale on Conditions of Settlement,
GOOD FARM LANDS
In the County of Peterboro, Ontario,

In the well settled Township of Dysart, where there are Grist and Saw Mills, Stores. &c., at
ONE-AND-A-HALF DOLLARS AN ACRE.

In the adjoining Townships of Guilford, Dudley, Harburn, Harcourt and Bruton, connected with Dysart and the Village of Haliburton by the Peterson Road, at ONE DOLLAR an Acre.
For further particulars apply to
CHAS. JAS BLOMFIELD,
Manager, C. L. and E Co.,
Toronto Bank Buildings, Toronto
Or to   ALEX. NIVEN, P.L.S.
Agent C. L. & E. Co., Haliburton

Canada Permanent Building and Savings Society.

Paid up Capital	$1,000,000
Assets	1,700,000
Annual Income	400,000

Directors:—JOSEPH D. RIDOUT, *President.*
PETER PATERSON, *Vice-President.*
J. G. Worts, Edward Hooper, S. Nordheimer, W. C. Chewett, E. H. Rutherford, Joseph Robinson
Bankers:—Bank of Toronto; Bank of Montreal; Royal Canadian Bank.

OFFICE—*Masonic Hall, Toronto Street, Toronto.*

Money Received on Deposit bearing five and six per cent. interest.

Accounts made on City and Country Property in the Provin of Ontario.

J. HERBERT MASON
36-y   *Sec'y & Treas*

Insurance.

J. T. & W. Pennock.

FIRE and Life Insurance Agents, Parliamentary and Departmental Agents, Mining Agents, and Exchange Brokers.

Ottawa, Dec. 21st, 1867.   10-1y

North British and Mercantile Insurance Company.

Established 1809.

HEAD OFFICE, - - CANADA - - MONTREAL,

TORONTO BRANCH:

LOCAL OFFICES, Nos. 4 & 6 WELLINGTON STREET,
Fire Department, ... R. N. GOOCH,
Agent.
Life Department, ... H. L. HIME,
29-1y   *Agent.*

Phœnix Fire Assurance Company.
LOMBARD ST. AND CHARING CROSS,
LONDON, ENG.

Insurances effected in all parts of the World
Claims paid
WITH PROMPTITUDE and LIBERALITY.
MOFFATT, MURRAY & BEATTIE,
Agents for Toronto,
36 Yonge Street.
28 1y.

INTERESTING TO LIFE AGENTS.

AGENT'S
MONETARY LIFE
AND
VALUATION TABLES,
WITH VALUABLE EXPLANATIONS.

A New Work by D. PARKS FACKLER, Esq.,
CONSULTING ACTUARY.

THIS is an interesting and valuable work. Every Life Agent should have a copy.

For sale at the office of the MONETARY TIMES, No. 60 Church street.

GRISWOLD'S
Handbook of the Adjustment of Fire Losses.

The most complete Manual of Adjustment ever published. Handsomely gotten up in blue cloth.

For sale at the office of THE MONETARY TIMES, No. 60 Church street.
Toronto, Jan. 7, 1869.   21-tf

Star Life Assurance Society,
(OF ENGLAND.)

ESTABLISHED 1843.

Capital £100,000 Stg .....Guarantee Fund £800,000 Stg.

Claims paid £541,000 Stg...Profits divided £240,000 Stg.

ONE HUNDRED THOUSAND DOLLARS
Deposited for the SECURITY OF CANADIAN POLICY HOLDERS.
Moderate rates of premium—Sound management—Ninety per cent of profits divided amongst policy holders.
J. GREGORY,
General Agent, B. N. A.

CANADA BRANCH OFFICE,
17–6m.   78 King St. East, Toronto.

Insurance.

Canada Life Assurance Company

CAPITAL AND CASH ASS
OVER $2,000,000.

SUMS ASSURED
$5,000,000.

A COMPARISON of the rates of this Comp others cannot fail to demonstrate the adva the low premiums, which, by the higher returns investments, it is enabled to offer.

IF PREFERRED, ASSURERS NEED ONLY
PAY ONE-HALF OF EACH YEAR'S PREMI CASH,

during the whole term of policies on the 10 paym or for seven years on the whole life plan.

For the unpaid portion of premiums,
"NOTES" ARE NOT REQUIRED BY THIS CO

so that assurers are not liable to be called upon ment of these, nor for assessments upon them, case of Mutual Companies. Every facility and advantage which can be aff offered by this Company.

A. G. RAMSAY, Man
E. BRADBURNE, Ag
3m11   Toronto

The Liverpool and London and Gl Insurance Company

INVESTED FUNDS:
FIFTEEN MILLIONS OF DOLLA

DAILY INCOME OF THE COMPANY:
TWELVE THOUSAND DOL.

LIFE INSURANCE,
WITH AND WITHOUT PROFITS.

FIRE INSURANCE
On every description of Property, at Lowest Rem Rates.
JAMES FRASER, A
5 King S
Toronto, 1868.

Briton Medical an General Association,
with which is united the
BRITANNIA LIFE ASSURANCE COM

Capital and Invested Funds............£750,00

ANNUAL INCOME, £220,000 St
Yearly increasing at the rate of £25,000 St

THE important and peculiar feature origin duced by this Company, in applying the Bonuses, so as to make Policies payable during li any higher rate of premiums being charged, 1 the success of the BRITON MEDICAL AND GEN almost unparalleled in the history of Life Assur Policies on the Profit Scale become payable during of the Assured, thus rendering a Policy a g means of subsistence in old age, as well as a prot family, and a more valuable security to credit event of early death; and effectually meeting urged objection, that persons do not themselv benefit of their own prudence and forethought.

No extra charge made to members of Volun for services within the British Provinces.
TORONTO AGENCY, 5 KING ST. WEST.
oct17—9-1yt   JAMES FRASER

The Victoria Mutua
FIRE INSURANCE COMPANY OF CA

Insures only Non-Hazardous Property, at
BUSINESS STRICTLY MUTU

GEORGE D. MILLS, *President.*
W. D. BOOKER, *Secretary.*

HEAD OFFICE .... HAMILTO
aug 15-1yr

Insurance.

BEAVER
Mutual Insurance Association.

HEAD OFFICE—20 TORONTO STREET,
TORONTO.

INSURES LIVE STOCK against death from any cause. The only Canadian Company having authority to do this class of business.

R. L. DENISON,
President.

W. T. O'REILLY,
Secretary.   8-1y-25

HOME DISTRICT
Mutual Fire Insurance Company.

Office—North-West Cor. Yonge & Adelaide Streets,
TORONTO.—(UP STAIRS.)

INSURES Dwelling Houses, Stores, Warehouses, Merchandise, Furniture, &c.

PRESIDENT—The Hon. J. McMURRICH.
VICE-PRESIDENT—JOHN BURNS, Esq.
JOHN RAINS, Secretary.
AGENTS:
DAVID WRIGHT, Esq., Hamilton; FRANCIS STEVENS, Esq., Barrie; Messrs. GIBBS & BRO., Oshawa.   8-1y

---

THE PRINCE EDWARD COUNTY
Mutual Fire Insurance Company.

HEAD OFFICE,—PICTON, ONTARIO.
President, L. B. STINSON; Vice-President, W. A. RICHARDS.
Directors: H. A. McFaul, James Cavan, James Johnson, N. S. DeMill, William Delong.—Treasurer, David Barker
Secretary, John Twigg; Solicitor, R. J. Fitzgerald.

THIS Company is established upon strictly Mutual principles, insuring farming and isolated property, (not hazardous,) in Townships only, and offers great advantages to insurers, at low rates for five years, without the expense of a renewal.
Pictou, June 15, 1868.   9-1y

Hartford Fire Insurance Company.
HARTFORD, CONN.

Cash Capital and Assets over Two Million Dollars.

$2,026,220.29.

CHARTERED 1810.

THIS old and reliable Company, having an established business in Canada of more than thirty years standing, has complied with the provisions of the new Insurance Act, and made a special deposit of

$100,000

with the Government for the security of policy-holders, and will continue to grant policies upon the same favorable terms as heretofore.

Specially low rates on first-class dwellings and farm property for a term of one or more years.

Losses as heretofore promptly and equitably adjusted.

H. J. MORSE & Co., AGENTS.
Toronto, Ont.

RODERT WOOD, GENERAL AGENT FOR CANADA]
50-6m

THE AGRICULTURAL
Mutual Assurance Association of Canada.

HEAD OFFICE .... LONDON, ONT.

A purely Farmers' Company. Licensed by the Government of Canada.

Capital, 1st January, 1868 .... $220,121 25
Cash and Cash Items, over $65,000 0
No. of Policies in force 28,769

THIS Company insures nothing more dangerous than Farm property. Its rates are as low as any well-established Company in the Dominion, and lower than those of a great many. It is largely patronised, and continues to grow in public favor.
For Insurance, apply to any of the Agents or address the Secretary, London, Ontario.
London, 2nd Nov., 1868.   13-1y

Insurance.

The Gore District Mutual Fire Insurance Company

GRANTS INSURANCES on all description of Property against Loss or Damage by FIRE. It is the only Mutual Fire Insurance Company which assesses its Policies yearly from their respective dates; and the average yearly cost of insurance in it, for the past three and a half years, has been nearly

TWENTY CENTS IN THE DOLLAR

less than what it would have been in an ordinary Proprietary Company.

THOS. M. SIMONS,
Secretary & Treasurer.
ROBT. McLEAN,
Inspector of Agencies.
Galt, 25th Nov., 1868.   15-1y

Geo. Girdlestone,
FIRE, Life, Marine, Accident, and Stock Insurance Agent

Very best Companies represented.
Windsor, Ont. June, 1868

The Standard Life Assurance Company,
Established 1825.
WITH WHICH IS NOW UNITED
THE COLONIAL LIFE ASSURANCE COMPANY.

Head Office for Canada:
MONTREAL—STANDARD COMPANY'S BUILDINGS,
No. 47 GREAT ST. JAMES STREET.
Manager—W. M. RAMSAY.   *Inspector*—RICH'D BULL.

THIS Company having deposited the sum of ONE HUNDRED and FIFTY THOUSAND DOLLARS with the Receiver-General, in conformity with the Insurance Act passed last Session, Assurances will continue to be carried out at moderate rates and on all the different systems in practice.

AGENT FOR TORONTO—HENRY PELLATT,
KING STREET.

AGENT FOR HAMILTON—JAMES BANCROFT.
6-6mos.

Fire and Marine Assurance.

THE BRITISH AMERICA
ASSURANCE COMPANY.
HEAD OFFICE:
CORNER OF CHURCH AND COURT STREETS.
TORONTO.

BOARD OF DIRECTION:
Hon G. W. Allan, M.L.C.,   A. Joseph, Esq.,
George J. Boyd, Esq.,   Peter Paterson, Esq.,
Hon. W. Cayley,   G. P. Ridout, Esq.,
Richard S. Cassels, Esq.,   E H. Rutherford, Esq.,
Thomas C. Street, Esq.,

Governor:
GEORGE PERCIVAL RIDOUT, ESQ.
Deputy Governor:
PETER PATERSON, ESQ.

Fire Inspector: Marine Inspector:
E. ROBY O'BRIEN.   CAPT. R. COURNEEN.

Insurances granted on all descriptions of property against loss and damage by fire and the perils of inland navigation.

Agencies established in the principal cities, towns, and ports of shipment throughout the Province.

THOS. WM BIRCHALL,
Managing Director.
23-1y

Queen Fire and Life Insurance Company,
OF LIVERPOOL AND LONDON,

ACCEPTS ALL ORDINARY FIRE RISKS
on the most favorable terms.

LIFE RISKS

Will be taken on terms that will compare favorably with other Companies.

CAPITAL,   -   -   -   £2,000,000 Stg.

CHIEF OFFICES—Queen's Buildings, Liverpool, and Gracechurch Street London.
CANADA BRANCH OFFICE—Exchange Buildings, Montreal, Resident Secretary and General Agent,
A. MACKENZIE FORBES.
13 St. Sacrament St., Merchants' Exchange, Montreal.
WM. ROWLAND, Agent, Toronto.   1-1y

Insurance.

The Waterloo County Mutual Fire I
Company.

HEAD OFFICE : WATERLOO, ONTARIO

ESTABLISHED 1863.

THE business of the Company is divided separate and distinct branches, the
VILLAGE, FARM, AND MANUFA(
Each Branch paying its own losses and its just of the managing expenses of the Company.
C. M. TAYLOR, Sec.   M. SPRINGER, M.M.
J. HUGHES, Inspector.

Etna Fire and Marine Insurance Co
Dublin.

AT a Meeting of the Shareholders of this held at Dublin, on the 13th ult., it was the business of the "ETNA" should be transfe "UNITED PORTS AND GENERAL INSURANCE In accordance with this agreement, the busines after be carried on by the latter Company, whic and guarantees all the risks and liabilities of th
The Directors have resolved to continue the BRANCH, and arrangements for resuming FIR RINE business are rapidly approaching comple
T. W. GRIF
15   M

The Commercial Union Assu
Company,
19 & 20 CORNHILL, LONDON, ENGLAN
Capital, £2,500,000 Stg.—Invested over £2,0

FIRE DEPARTMENT.—Insurance granted scriptions of property at reasonable rates.
LIFE DEPARTMENT.—The success of t has been unprecedented—NINETY PER CEN miums now in hand. First year's premiums $100,000. Economy of management guaranteed security. Moderate rates.

OFFICE—385 & 387 ST. PAUL STREET, MOT
MORLAND, WATSON
General Agents f

FRED. COLE, Secretary.
Inspector of Agencies—T. C. LIVINGST
. W. M. WESTMACOTT, Agent at
16-1y

Lancashire Insurance Com

CAPITAL, - - - - - - - - £2,000,

FIRE RISKS
Taken at reasonable rates of premium
ALL LOSSES SETTLED PROMPT
By the undersigned, without reference
S. C. DUNCAN-CLARK & C
General Agents for On
N. W. Corner of King & Churc
25-1y   TORONTO,

Etna Fire & Marine Insurance Co

INCORPORATED 1819.   CHARTER PERPET

CASH CAPITAL, ...

LOSSES PAID IN 50 YEARS, 23,500,

JULY, 1868.
ASSETS.
(At Market Value.)
Cash in hand and in Bank ....
Real Estate ....
Mortgage Bonds ....
Bank Stock ....
United States, State and City Stock, and other
Public Securities ....

     Total .... $

LIABILITIES.
Claims not Due, and Unadjusted ....
Amount required by Mass. and New York
for Re-insurance ....
THOS. R. WO
50-6   Agent fo

PUBLISHED AT THE OFFICE OF THE TIMES, No. 60 CHURCH STREE PRINTED AT THE DAILY TELEGRAPH PRINTI BAY STREET, CORNER OF KING.

THE CANADIAN
ONETARY TIMES AND INSURANCE CHRONICLE.

HE Publishers have pleasure in announcing that the success of this JOURNAL has been such as to stimulate their efforts to render it still more valuable to the classes directly and indirectly interested in the subjects with which it deals. As the only Journal in the minion which gives particular attention to INSURANCE, it has enlisted the hearty support of Insurance Companies; and while, on one hand, it contends for the rights of such Companies, it equally recognizes the rights of the public.

The subject of BANKING has become of such importance, as well by reason of past legislation as by reason of anticipated changes in law respecting circulation, that it is the duty and interest of our business men to make themselves acquainted with the principles which sound Banking rests, and to prevent any action on the part of the Legislature likely to injure the community by lessening usefulness of our banks. The discussion of this subject in the columns of this JOURNAL has called forth expressions of satisfaction m our most astute financiers, and has done much to give us the position we now occupy in the estimation of the public.

As MINING is in its infancy in this country, a journal devoted solely to the subject could not hope to thrive; but by giving full ormation regarding Mining operations, and by the employment of reliable correspondents, we have done good service to an important erest, and secured recognition from a class which, otherwise, could not have been reached.

Our purely COMMERCIAL DEPARTMENT has not been neglected, and each week's summary, while concise and pithy, has answered the le ends as a more diffuse elaboration could do, and conveyed to country dealers a complete synopsis of the changes in the Toronto and ntreal Markets.

This combination of interests which the circumstances of the country render necessary, has been of the greatest advantage to each eret by diffusing information among all classes; but, in order to do justice to all, we have been compelled to employ a large staff of ters, and to expend a considerable amount in securing trustworthy correspondents.

While we are thankful to those who have encouraged us thus far, we are anxious to extend still further the usefulness of this Journal, i we call on all who consider that the enterprise is worthy of support, to lend us their assistance in making the MONETARY TIMES a ional organ.

On our part we promise impartiality, efficiency, and the best efforts of the ablest writers that can be secured in the Dominion. On part of our clients, we expect a cordial support and active exertion to widen our sphere of usefulness. In helping us, they help mselves.

Every Merchant, Banker, Capitalist, Insurance Agent, and Broker, can aid us, and we hope that we are not asking too much, in iciting their assistance.

We shall be happy to receive at any time articles on subjects within our jurisdiction, which, if used, will be liberally paid for.

Subscription Price..$2 per Annum.

A reasonable discount will be made to Banks, Insurance Companies, &c., which subscribe for their Agencies.
SEND FOR A SPECIMEN COPY.
N.B.—Every subscriber to THE MONETARY TIMES will receive THE REAL ESTATE JOURNAL without further charge.

THE REAL ESTATE JOURNAL.

The objects of this Journal are as follows :—

(1.) To supply to those interested in real estate such information as is of special interest relating to sales or transfers of real pro- rty in the principal cities, and throughout Ontario, construction of public works, and building improvements of every kind, increase or crease of municipal expenditure, debt and taxation, and, in short, whatever tends to influence the real estate market.

(2.) Leading articles will be furnished by competent writers on questions relating to conveyancing, the rise and fall of property, land ants, emigration, and other subjects coming within the legitimate scope of the Journal.

(3.) Lists of lands and houses for sale in every city, town and village of the Province, will appear in its columns, giving buyers the st possible opportunities for selecting desirable properties of any class, and in any locality; and, at the same time, affording sellers a iable and certain medium for reaching intending purchasers.

(4.) By a circulation extending into every corner of Canada, the announcements of advertisers will be brought to the notice of an mense constituency of readers. A special feature in this connection is, that the Journal will be placed and kept on fyle at all the prin- al hotels, reading rooms, and other public places in Ontario, and in Montreal. By these means it is confidently believed that every as in the community will be reached.

THE REAL ESTATE JOURNAL is printed fortnightly, on good white paper, in quarto form, and is equal in size and appearance to anything the kind published on this continent.

Advertising, per line of nonpareil, each insertion, 5 cents. A small discount will be allowed on yearly contracts, for large spaces.
Address, "THE REAL ESTATE JOURNAL," Toronto, Ontario. Cheques should be made payable to J. M. TROUT, who will o issue all receipts for money.

OFFICE, No. 60 CHURCH STREET,
TORONTO, ONTARIO.

ONTARIO PEAT CO.

PROSPECTUS OF THE ONTARIO PEAT COMPAN

LIMITED LIABILITY. · · · · · · · HEAD OFFICE—TORONTO.

To be Organized under the Act 27 and 28 Victoria, Chapter 23, and the Amendments thereto.

THE property of the company forms a portion of the well-known "Cranberry Marsh," in the Townships of Humberstone and Wainfleet, Cou Welland, and Province of Ontario, traversed by the Welland Canal, as well as by its "Feeder," which is also navigable ; and is composed c following lots, viz. :—

		Acres.
Humberstone—South halves of 28, 30, 32 and 33, Concession IV		400
Wainfleet—South halves of 6 and 7, Concession IV		200
" Whole of 10, Concession II, and the whole of 10 and 11, Concession III		600
" Parts of 8 and 9, Concessions IV. and V., about		200
Total		1400

A main ditch six feet deep has been made by the County through the whole of this Marsh for surface drainage, at an expenditure of $50,000 this ditch runs along a portion of every one of the above lots, except two which abut upon the feeder of the Welland Canal.

The several lots above enumerated were the first chosen from the Marsh, having been selected for their great value as Peat Deposits. remaining Peat lands have been obtained by the Anglo-American Peat Company, which has been operating most successfully during the past upon a lot adjoining one of the Company's lots. A most satisfactory report has been obtained from Frederick Holmes, Esq., the County Engin gentleman who has had large experience in these peat lands, having not only surveyed and laid off the Marsh into lots for the County, but has als employed as superintendent in the ditching operations which have been undertaken and carried out through the whole extent of the Marsh. estimate of the quantity of Peat contained in the Company's lands is placed at three millions of tons, at the very least ; and this estimate is fully out by the eminent firm of Messrs. Macdougall and Skae, Civil Engineers, Toronto, who were specially despatched to make a personal examinat the property, and whose report is subjoined.

Peat can be laid down on the banks of the canal at the cost of from $1 to $1.25 per ton, and can from thence be forwarded by water to market directions, at small cost, and without transhipment ; to say nothing of the facilities and advantages afforded by no less than five railways, one of w the "Buffalo and Lake Huron," passes within twenty chains of the property. In addition to these advantages, the fact may be noticed, that thirty vessels pass through the canal every day during the season of navigation, the steamers requiring fuel for their own use, and the sailing v seeking cargoes, and requiring ballast westward to Chicago and other points.

The demand for this fuel for private consumption will be very great when its superior qualities become more widely known. Already railway steamers are beginning to use it instead of wood and coal, with the most satisfactory results, experience having proved that one ton of peat is eq about one and one-third cords of the best hard wood. With a view to the full and proper developement of this property, it is proposed to organi Company with a capital of $120,000, in 2,400 shares of $50 each ; $50,000 of this sum to be retained by the Directors for working capital, the bala be applied to the purchase of the real estate. It is also proposed that 5 per cent shall be paid at the time of subscription, and the balance in c 10 per cent at such times as the Directors may name, but not oftener than once in every three months, from 1st of January, 1869.

The affairs of the Company will be managed by a Board of five Directors, the first set to be provisional, and, as soon as the charter is obtaine the Company organized, the permanent Directors to be chosen by the Shareholders, and to be elected annually.

The principal office of the Company to be in the City of Toronto. The property has been conveyed to Peleg Howland, Esquire, who will ho same in trust until the Company is organized.

PROVISIONAL DIRECTORS.

HENRY S. HOWLAND, Esquire, Toronto.   JOHN FISKEN, Esquire, Toronto.   LARRATT W. SMITH, Esquire, Toronto.
ALFRED TODD, Esquire, Ottawa.   EDWARD A. C. PEW, Esquire, Welland.

Further information can be obtained at the office of C. J. Campbell, Esquire, Banker, 92 King Street East, Toronto, who will act as Provi Treasurer, and will also receive subscriptions for Stock.

CHAMBERS, 17 TORONTO STREET, TORONTO, JANUARY 11, 186!

To the Directors of the Ontario Peat Company,—

GENTLEMEN,—We have the honor to lay before you the following report, on the Peat Beds in the Great Cranberry Marsh, situated in the C of Welland. The swamp, or to call it by a more proper name, moor, for it is more like the moors of Scotland than the swamps of this count intersected by a large drain, which at present carries off a considerable quantity of water ; and from its juxta position, to the lots owned by your co could be made available for drainage purposes. The moor rises gradually from its northern limit in concession 4, to its summit, at the south c concession 3, about four feet on two and a half miles, where it is about eight feet above the level of Lake Erie ; while, on the north, from the end moor to the Welland River, distant about a mile and a half, there is a fall of sixteen feet. Following the course of the water through the v drains, the result arrived at is, that the moor is higher than the surrounding country, which is under cultivation.

The peat on this marsh, brought up by the boring rods, as well as that lying on the sides of the drains, thrown up when they were made, sh good quality of a dark black color, in every lot. There is a layer of red peat in some of the lots of the Township of Humberstone ; but general peat was of the dark colour above mentioned. The surface of the marsh, or moor, has been burnt once or twice, so that there is not much moss or growth, nor are there many trees alive ; and on the lots owned by your company this is more marked. The lots are conveniently placed for wo and connections could be formed, at a small cost, to the several outlets that surround this tract of land ; and the surface being regular, no dil would be encountered in laying tramroads.

In making the borings for this report, the valuable assistance of the County Engineer, Mr. Frederick Holmes, was obtained, as he had superin the making of the drains, and had laid out several of the lots some years ago, and since that time had been intimately acquainted with the moor. depths arrived at give an average of six to eight feet of peat over all the lots in the 3rd and 4th concessions, while in the lot of the 2nd conc of the Township of Wainfleet, the peat is very deep, averaging about 15 feet, and it is said to go even deeper. There are 200 acres in this lot.

The regularity of the upper surface of this large tract of land, both peat and arable, being combined with the result of the borings taken, le conclusion that the bottom of the peat bed must also be regular, as there are no hills or mounds of any size or consequence in the vicinity.

The Anglo-American Peat Fuel Company have been at work during last summer on a portion of this marsh, opposite to some of the lots ow your Company. They find the loss, by weight and shrinkage to be 75 per cent. ; or to make one ton of peat fuel, four tons of peat are required. is less than that of a similar project in the Lower Province, where the shrinkage is 85 per cent.

From the data and experience of the Anglo-American Company, taking the loss by weight and shrinkage at 75 per cent., with an average o six to eight feet over all the lots, but that in the 5th Concession of Wainfleet, which is taken at sixteen feet, we find the property of your Con situated in the marsh, to be capable of producing over 3,000,000 tons of fuel.

A fuller report, by us, lies in the hands of Mr. C. J. Campbell, Banker, King Street, Toronto, to which also we beg to call your attention.
We have the honour to be, gentlemen,
Your obedient servants,
MACDOUGALL & SKAE,
CIVIL ENGI

3-

THE CANADIAN
[ONETARY TIMES

AND
INSURANCE CHRONICLE.

IED TO FINANCE, COMMERCE, INSURANCE, BANKS, RAILWAYS, NAVIGATION, MINES, INVESTMENT,
PUBLIC COMPANIES, AND JOINT STOCK ENTERPRISE.

NO. 25.   TORONTO, THURSDAY, FEBRUARY 4, 1869.   { SUBSCRIPTION. $2 YEAR.

Mercantile.

Meetings.

WESTERN CANADA PERMANENT BUILD-ING AND SAVINGS SOCIETY.

The annual meeting of this Society was held in
their offices, Church street, Toronto, on the 3rd
February, the President, Hon. G. W. Allan, in
the chair.

The following were among the gentlemen pre-
sent:—Hon. G. W. Allan, Hon: D. L. Macpher-
son, C. S. Gzowski, Esq., A. W. Lauder, M.P.P.,
John Wallis, M.P.P., John Worthington, J. E.
Smith, Judge Gowan, of Barrie, Wm. Gooderham,
sen., John Platt, R. N. Gooch, A. G. Lee, H.
Thompson, -- Henderson, of Galt & Henderson,
Thomas Whittaker, A. J. Menet, R. James,
Henry Pellatt, A. B. Lee, Dr. Ogden, Walter S.
Lee, Com. Gen. Weir, &c., &c.

The Secretary being called upon, read the minutes of the last annual meeting, which were confirmed.

The President, the Hon. G. W. Allan, rose and
said that, before calling upon the Secretary to
read the annual report, he would first, as had
been customary on similar occasions, offer a few
brief remarks in reference to the present condition
and future prospects of the Society. His duty,
he was happy to say, was rendered a very pleasant and easy one by the prosperous conditions of
the Society's affairs, which enabled the directors
to come before the shareholders to-day with a
statement showing a large increase in all branches
of the Society's business, and a correspondingly
large increase in their profits. On reference to
the report of last year, they would observe that
the paid-up stock at that time amounted to $121,-
190 78; this year, the paid-up stock amounts to
$232,761. Last year, the loans on mortgage, at
their present value, represented $295,500; this
year, the loans on mortgage amount to $407,500.
The deposits and interest were last year $134,-
563 41; this year we show an amount of $181,105.
The surplus profits last year were $4,449 83; this
year they have increased to $6,243. But what he
particularly desired to call the attention of the
shareholders to was the large increase in the Reserve Fund. At the last annual meeting the
directors gave it as their opinion that the accumulation of a large Reserve Fund, offered the best
guarantee to the shareholders for a permanent
rate of dividend, and they recommend to their
successors to keep the augmentation of this fund
uniformly in view. This recommendation, it will
be seen, has been fully carried out. Last year the
Reserve Fund, as it appeared in their statement,
amounted to $4,600; to. this was carried, as re-
commended in the report, a further sum out of
the surplus profits, of $5,400, making the total
of $10,000. This year the fund stands in our
statement at $10,000, but to it has since been
carried $5,000 out of the surplus profits, and $4,-
424 bonus on the new stock lately issued, making
the total amount of the credit of the Reserve
Fund, $19,424—nearly double that of last year.
It afforded him (the President) great pleasure to
be able to state these facts to the shareholders,
because he really looked upon the Reserve Fund
as the sheet anchor of institutions of this kind.
Under the most careful management, losses must
sometimes occur, and a combination of circum-

stances, such as depression in trade, stringency in
the money market, or bad harvests, might for a
time interfere with the profits of the Society's
business; but with a large reserve fund, such
temporary interruptions to the prosperity of the
Society would not be felt by the shareholders;
and at all events, in that fund they possessed the
best guarantee against loss or serious inconveniences from any such contingencies. He might
further mention that this fund was carefully invested in first-class debentures, which could be
readily turned into cash, if necessary at any time
to do so.

Since the last annual meeting, in fact within
the last six weeks, the directors had, as the shareholders are aware, thought it advisable to authorize a fresh issue of new stock to the amount of
$50,000. This was issued to the shareholders
pro rata, in proportion to their stock, as directed
by the Act, and $45,000 was taken up by the
shareholders entitled to it within the prescribed
period; the remaining $5,000, which had not been
allotted or taken up, consequent upon some few
of the shareholders not holding sufficient stock to
entitle them to new shares, and a few who were
entitled, such as widows and some small holders,
not finding it convenient to avail themselves of
their privilege, was, by order of the Board, put
upon the market, and immediately sold at 18 per
cent. premium.

The Directors were induced to make this new
issue of stock for two reasons:

1. Because opportunities for profitable investment in the shape of satisfactory loans continued
to present themselves, showing that additional
capital could be safely and profitably employed;
and

2. Because the business of the Deposit and
Savings' Bank Branch had so largely increased,
that they were constantly close up to the line
to which the Directors were allowed to go in proportion to the amount of paid up stock, and repeatedly during the past twelve months they had
not only been obliged to decline receiving deposits
from new depositors; but had also been compelled
to refuse fresh deposits from old customers.
Looking therefore at these facts, the Directors believing that the time had come when the capital of
the Society might, with advantage to the shareholders, be further increased, and they accordingly
authorized, the issue of the new stock, which had
now all been taken up.

In reference to the Auditor's report, he would
state that the Directors were most anxious that
the audit should be no mere form, but that all
the Society's books, accounts, and securities
should be subjected to the most searching and
rigid scrutiny. This, he had no hesitation in saying, had been most faithfully done; and not only
had the accounts and vouchers been verified in
the usual way, but each security had been carefully examined and its present value proved by
actual computation. The appointment of Auditors was a matter which was entirely in the hands
of the shareholders ; but it would be seen, when
the resolution referring to the Auditors came, before them, that the Board had ventured a suggestion that three Auditors instead of two should be
appointed for the future. The object of this was
that there should be a change each year, one
of the gentlemen, as was the practice in some

other societies, going out in rotation, so that there was less danger of their getting into a set form or merely formal manner of performing the work, but would come to it with a fresh eye, as it were, and so discharge their duty thoroughly and satisfactorily.

Before concluding, he would desire to state the satisfaction which the directors felt at the manner in which the officers of the Society had continued to discharge their duty. In their Secretary, Mr. Lee, they had a most zealous and efficient officer, whose heart was thoroughly in his work ; and his assistant, Mr. Williamson, had also proved himself most painstaking and conscientious.

He did not think it necessary to detain them any further, but would conclude with expressing the hope that the Society would continue to be, as it has hitherto been, a profitable medium for the investment of capital, and a safe depository for the savings of the industrious.

The Secretary then read the Annual Report, as follows:—

SIXTH ANNUAL REPORT

Of the Directors of the Western Canada Permanent Building and Savings Society.

In laying before the Shareholders the usual Annual Statement of the Society's affairs, your Directors have the pleasure of again reporting that a safe, profitable, and increasing business has been done during the past year.

Applications for Loans of a thoroughly satisfactory character, having kept the capital of the Company actively employed, and the Deposit Account having also very largely increased, (this branch of the Society's business alone, shewing an increase of twenty-five per cent. over the preceding twelvemonth,) the Directors resolved upon a further augmentation of the Society's capital, by an issue of New Shares, to the amount of $50,-000, in December last, at a premium of eighteen per cent.

These Shares, as directed by the Act, were first offered to the existing Shareholders in the proportion of one to every five Shares of Stock, and 902 shares amounting to $45,100 were taken up by the Shareholders, who availed themselves of the privilege within the prescribed period of thirty days; the remaining $4,900, which had not been allotted or taken up, (holders of less than five shares not being entitled to new stock,) were placed on the market by order of the Board, and were all immediately disposed of, at a premium of eighteen per cent.

The total premiums received upon the new Stock amounting to $4,424 have been carried to the credit of the Reserve Fund.

This fund it is proposed further to increase, by carrying to its credit an amount of $5,000 out of the surplus profits, which will remain after paying the two half-yearly dividends, at the rate of ten per cent. per annum.

The Directors believe that in keeping steadily in view the augmentation of this Fund, which will now amount to $19,424, they are best promoting the interests, both of the Shareholders and Depositors of the Society.

Since the last Annual Meeting, the Directors have had to deplore the death of one of their Colleagues, Jeremiah Carty, Esquire, Vice-President of the Society.

The vacancy occasioned at the Board by that gentleman's decease, was, in accordance with the Rules of the Society, filled up by the Directors, by the election of John Wallis, Esquire, M.P.P., to the Directorship for the remainder of the year ; and John Worthington, Esquire, one of the members of the Board, was unanimously elected Vice-President.

The books, accounts, mortgages, and other assets of the Society, have been carefully examined by the Auditors, whose Report is herewith appended.

It affords the Directors great pleasure to state,

that the Secretary and other officers of the Society, continue to discharge their duties with zeal and efficiency.

G. W. ALLAN—*President.*
WALTER S. LEE—*Secretary & Treasurer.*

Abstract of Liabilities and Assets of the Western Canada Permanent Building and Savings Society, 31st December, 1868.

LIABILITIES.

Stock paid up............................	$232,791 34
Deposits and Interest....................	181,105 66
Dividends unpaid........................	220 55
Sundry Accounts........................	427 82
Reserve Fund...........................	10,000 00
Dividend No. 11, for half-year ending Dec. 31, 1868...................	11,525 67
Balance.................................	6,243 92
	$442,314 96

ASSETS.

Loans on Mortgage, (present value) ..	$407,500 00
do. Stock..........................	9,638 62
Debentures and Interest................	15,676 00
Office Furniture........................	417 50
do Premises...........................	3,275 50
Sundry Accounts.......................	693 04
Cash in Bank............$5,078 76	
do. Office............ 135 54	5,214 30
	$442,314 96

By Balance brought down, being surplus profits after paying two half-yearly Dividends of 5 per cent. each. $6,243 92
Audited and Approved, 28th January, 1869.

G. A. BARBER, WM. WILLIAMSON.

STATEMENT OF RECEIPTS AND DISBURSEMENTS.

RECEIPTS.

Stock.................................	$ 50,395 95
Deposits..............................	172,376 46
Re-payments on Loans................	72,840 36
Mortgages discharged................	45,752 10
Fines.................................	1,356 03
Interest...............................	3,080 44
Debentures sold.......................	17,994 00
Office Expenses.......................	206 96
Bonus on Stock........................	2,000 00
Re-payment of Disbursements on account of Mortgagors.............	2,777 06
Commercial Bank Drafts paid with Interest.........................	2,746 22
Cash in Bank and Office, 31st Dec.'67	5,850 53
	$377,382 13

DISBURSEMENTS.

Loans on Mortgage....................	$168,778 67
do. Stock......................	23,916 20
Deposits returned.....................	135,227 21
Stock do........................	11 64
Dividends.............................	18,290 61
Interest...............................	519 69
Debentures bought....................	16,185 30
Office Expenses, Salaries, &c.........	3,076 53
Insurance returned to Mortgagors.....	1,323 00
Office Furniture.......................	7 85
Disbursements on acct. of Mortgagors	3,136 13
Directors Compensation................	795 00
Cash in Bank and Office, 31st Dec.'68	5,214 30
	$377,382 13

Audited and Approved, 28th January, 1869.

G. A. BARBER, WM. WILLIAMSON.

AUDITORS' REPORT.

To the Shareholders of the Western Canada Permanent Building and Savings Society.

GENTLEMEN,—We have respectfully to report the completion of our Audit of the Society's Books and Transactions for the year ending Dec. 31st, 1868; and we submit herewith, duly verified abstract Statements of Receipts and Expenditure, as well as of Assets and Liabilities, at that period.

We are gratified in being enabled to again gratulate the Shareholders on the steadily continued progress of the business of the Society will be apparent when the Financial State for 1868 are compared with those for 1867.

Not only has the Deposit Account largely increased, but the Mortgage Securities, which at December 31st, 1867, were 515 in number, representing a total value of $295,500, at the present date amount to 712 in number, at an aggregate value of $500,—facts which speak for themselves.

The security has been audited by the Books; and has been carefully examined and verified, and their present value has been proved by actual examination.

Respectfully submitted,

G. A. BARBER, WM. WILLIAMSON, *Auditors.*

Judge Gowan moved, seconded by R. James Esq., "That the thanks of the shareholders are due and are hereby tendered to the President and Directors, for their services during the past year, and that the sum of eight hundred dollars be paid to the President, and that the sum of $4 for each Board meeting be paid to each of the Directors for their attendance at such meetings during the year."

Judge Gowan said, that in moving the resolution, he would avail himself of the opportunity to say a few words in approval of the way in which the Society was managed. He had only a slight interest in it, but some of his friends were largely interested. In the report laid before the meeting trinsic evidence was to be seen of the excellent way in which the Society was managed. This was of course chiefly due to the President and Secretary. While the shareholders were legally and morally responsible, and civilly and criminally responsible, yet the President and Secretary were, especially, to be held responsible for the conduct of the Society's business. He had every confidence in his friend Mr. Allan, he saw from this, and previous reports, how he was superintending the business of the Society with ability and success. He thought it a judicious and highly proper that the President should give a statement in connection with the report. He had been done, for there were often inaccuracies in detail that it was scarcely necessary to notice in the report, but which were interesting to shareholders. It was a remarkable achievement for any financial society to double its reserve in a year. The actions of the Board were deserving of all praise. He did not know how they could put into the resolution were placed there, but he had any option in the matter, he would not have altered the figures he would have inserted. He thought $800 a miserable pittance to pay the President. They required men of undoubted integrity and character to manage their affairs ; they must not be disposed to do well, but they must know how to do well. If he would be allowed liberty, he would place at least $1,000 in the resolution, instead of $800.

Hon. Mr. Allan objected to filling in the sum of $1,000. He said the directors had taken the responsibility of inserting the sum of $800 in the resolution, and would regret any alteration made.

Mr. R. James then seconded the resolution which was carried.

Hon. Mr. Allan returned thanks on behalf himself and his colleagues at the Board.

Moved by Mr. Henry Thompson, seconded by Arthur B. Lee, Esq., "That the thanks of the shareholders are due to the Auditors for their careful scrutiny of the Society's transactions, the sum of $50 each be paid them for their services. Carried.

Moved by R. James, Esq., seconded by Worthington, Esq., "That the poll opened for the election of directors, and be closed at 3 o'clock, and that Arthur, O. Lee, and Henry Pellatt be scrutineers, and that the result of the vote be handed

nd that the sum of $4 each be paid
rs for their services. Carried.

Dr. Ogden, seconded by Charl-s
., that Messrs. Wm. Williamson, G.
nd S. Spreull be the Auditors for the
out of whom the Directors shall se-
ake the audit. Carried.

ing gentlemen were elected Directors
t year:

W. Allan, John Worthington, Hon.
hereon, Wm. Gooderham, Francis
es E. Smith, and Samuel Platt.
quent meeting of the Board of Di-
Geo. W. Allan was re-elected Presi-
hn Worthington, Esq., Vice Presi-

NTO BOARD OF TRADE.

l Meeting of the Toronto Board of
ld in the Lecture Room of the Me-
tute, on the 29th of January. After
oceedings, the Secretary read the
ual Report :

l of the Board of Trade respectfully
ual report of the proceedings which
l their attention during the year just
r which may, generally, be charac-
absence of any business apart from
routine. One of the first and most
uties which the Council were called
rm, was the appointment of official
the adjoining counties. This duty
performed without some difficulty,
the claims of contending parties for
he Council felt the responsibility of
ersons personally unknown to them,
er -embarrassment of appointing too
assignees in certain localities. In
d these difficulties, the Council se-
parties who were recommended by
iumber of business men and others
the matter of insolvency, as the
securing the most competent persons
rtant office. At an early period of
was determined by the Corn Ex-
e an Inspector of Grain appointed ;
ir recommendation, the Council ap-
ames Rough, flour inspector, to that
ratifying to be able to record that
the last year has turned out a fair
cially of spring and midge proof
ie chief cereals exported from Onta-
i districts a partial failure occurred
ual dryness of the season, but in
s the crop was above an average.
rheat gradually declined from $1 60
st, to $1 03 at its close. The circum-
rose from 90c in the early part of
$1 50 at its close. The circum-
roarser grains having borne a much
han usual in proportion to the value
nduced the farmers to withhold the
om the market in the hope of rea-
rices in the spring. This hoarding
produced a general stagnation and
f business at a season when it is
active. Notwithstanding this
s acknowledged that business is in
improved condition and money con-
undant than usual.

ent of the banks for 1868 shows an
eir deposits within 12 months of
en millions of dollars, a fact signifi-
creasing industry of the country,
imulating wealth in a greater ratio
previous period of its history. A
the Council was formed for the pur-
sing the questions of banking and
bmitted by a Committee of the
mons for the consideration of the
interested. The subject being of
and many of the questions being
irly addressed to bankers, the com-
id leaving the whole matter to be

------

dealt with by the latter, they being better acquainted with the working of the present system
and the remedies required to bring it into harmony with the advanced position of the Dominion
and the increasing requirements of its trade.

The silver question, which has occasioned so
much correspondence with the various Boards of
Trade in the Province, has been satisfactorily settled as far as Toronto is concerned, the merchants
and traders having agreed in July last to place a
discount of ten per cent on all small silver, and to
continue the four per cent. discount on all large
silver. This agreement has been faithfully observed by the public at large, and the consequence
is that little or no inconvenience is now felt in
adopting the Provincial currency as a standard of
value in retail transactions. It is to be regretted,
however, that the operation of the system is confined almost exclusively to Toronto. The towns
and villages having to contend with rivals for
business on all sides, their competition has maintained the nominal rate of the American silver
coinage, thus entailing a continual loss to the
country storekeepers.

At the instance of a committee of the Legislature, amendments to the Insolvent Act were suggested and transmitted to the seat of Government.
A deputation was also appointed and sent to Ottawa to present to the Minister of Finance the
views of the Council in reference to a modification
of the tariff on certain articles of general consumption. The action of the Council on these
subjects was nearly similar to that of other
Boards of Trade, and resulted favorably. In the
report of the Council of last year, the subject of
constructing narrow-gauge railways running
northeast and northwest from the city of Toronto
was favorably noticed. Since then the public
mind has become satisfied of their ability to perform the necessary service required for the speedy
conveyance of freight and passengers. The
Council have heard the testimony of able engineers personally acquainted with the construction and working of similar roads in various
countries. The 3 ft. 6 in. gauge recommends itself, especially to a new country like Canada, for
the low rate for which it can be built and worked
as compared with the broad-gauge heretofore used.
The promoters of these enterprises have at great
personal labor, and against a strong combination
of antagonists, procured favorable charters from
the Legislature of Ontario, and are now completing arrangements for carrying into effect the
powers conferred on them by the Acts. It is satisfactory to note that these railways have met
with the most liberal support from the taxpayers
of this city—a bonus of $400,000 having been all
but unanimously granted to aid in their construction; and, in addition, a generous support has
been received from the municipalities through
and near which the railways will pass, showing
clearly the country, as well as the city, is alive to
the important benefits which these railways will
confer in lessening the distance to market; and
chespening transport on all the merchantable productions of the country.

Great efforts were made to induce the Board to
petition the Legislature for a grant of land to aid
the construction of the Huron and Ontario Ship
Canal. The Council had the subject under discussion, and adopted a report in favor of granting
the land by the Government. A memorial was
prepared for submission to the Board, with a view
of obtaining a fuller expression of opinion on so
important a question; two meetings of the Board
were held, both of which were largely attended by
the members, when the question was fully and
ably discussed, a d the action of the Council reversed by an almost overwhelming majority. The
following resolution was carried:

Resolved, That neither the commercial, shipping, nor agricultural interests of the Dominion
of Canada, or the Province of Ontario, require the
Huron and Ontario Ship Canal, and that the report of the Council be not adopted.

During the past year several international commercial conventions were held in different cities of
the United States, with the object of harmoniz-
ing the laws and customs of comtnerce, and extending its operations by means of additional
railways and canals, without reference to geographical boundaries. In the promotion of this
laudable object your Council fully sympathize as
the extension of trade in a country so closely
connected with ours must exercise a favorable
influence on our mutual relations, and under
proper appreciation, be a means of stimulating us
us to develop the latent resources of our mines
and forests. In this connection it is to be regretted that the endeavor to organize an Intercolonial Board of Trade should have
failed to meet with success, as an aggregation of
the various Boards would have brought together
a number of able minds, for the discussion and
consideration of questions of general interest to
the commerce of the Dominion, and could not
fail to contribute to a better understanding on
many points now at issue with the Maritime
Provinces. The Council would urge to their successors that the subject should not be lost sight
of, as much good may be accomplished by holding meetings similar to those being held in the
United States, with the broad and lucid views of
which your Council heartily concur.

Your Council observe with pleasure a strong
desire on the part of a number of the most intelligent merchants of the United States for a renewal
of the Reciprocity Treaty, which for ten years
existed between the United States and this country, and for the attainment of which the Board of
Trade labored assiduously for a number of years.
It may not, therefore, be considered out of place
to make a brief allusion to the subject in this
report. Under the operation of that treaty the
trade and commerce of both countries was greatly
extended and materially benefitted, and a renewal
of its provisions would be in accordance with the
commercial spirit of the age. It is gratifying to
record the fact, however, that the loss anticipated
to our trade from the abrogation of this treaty has
been but slightly felt, new markets have been
found and opened for our surplus products in the
Lower Provinces, the West Indies and South
America. A direct trade has thus sprung up
with countries heretofore supplied almost exclusively by the United States ; our altered position
necessitated a search for new channels for exports, and our merchants have proved equal to
the emergency by shipping their manufactures
with advantage to the ports of the Mediterranean
and the Levant. It is a favorite idea with some
writers in the United States that the establishment of a Zollverein such as exists between Prussia and the German States would be the right
thing for Canada to adopt, the advocates of such
a system forget that the disparity of our tariffs
would form an insurmountable barrier to such
a proposition at present.

The Council observe with satisfaction the efforts
that are being made by the Dominion Government to secure a short and easily accessible route
to the Red River settlement within our own territory, which will be the means of opening for
emigration a boundless extent of country,
stretching from Lake Superior on the East, to the
foot of the Rocky Mountains on the West, and
containing millions of acres of the most fertile
land, capable of sustaining an immense population. According to reliable information, the
trade between St. Paul and the Red River now
amounts to four millions of dollars yearly, the
greater part of which may be secured to Canada
by opening the new route of 450 miles (shortening
the distance to Fort Garry via Fort William 150
miles) mostly by water communication, as against
600 miles of land transport via St. Paul, and at a
reduction of cost of $50 per ton, an advantage
sufficient to divert the trade of that district from
the United States to Canada.

A committee of the Council was formed some
time since for the purpose of suggesting amend-

ments to the Act incorporating the Board, but no report was presented on the subject. It is now nearly a quarter of a century since the Board was incorporated; during this period many changes have taken place in the trade of the country, which call for corresponding alterations in the constitution of the Board. Your Council would respectfully suggest to their successors in office that the Legislature of Canada should be petitioned to amend their charter so that it may harmonize more fully with the advanced state of commerce at the present time.

The great increase in the wholesale and manufacturing business in Toronto that has taken place within the last two years, has had a corresponding effect in increasing rents and the value of real estate. While this improvement may be attributed in some measure to the city having become the seat of Government of Ontario, which has been the means of giving a permanent increase to the population, and making it an attraction to a large number of transient visitors, the chief cause of this prosperity may be found in the circumstance that our wholesale dealers are able to compete successfully with those of other cities; this has attracted a large number of buyers to Toronto, who find it to their interest to purchase their goods in the nearest and most convenient market.

The proposed construction of the narrow-gauge railways has also favorably influenced the value of property, as they are calculated to open new avenues of trade for our enterprising citizens, and to give employment to a large class of artizans and laborers.

All of which is respectfully submitted.

JAMES G. WORTS, President.
CHAS. ROBERTSON, Secretary.

The following office-bearers were elected for the ensuing year, by acclamation :—

President, Mr. J. G. Worts ; Vice-president, Mr. Elliott ; Secretary, Mr. Charles Robertson, Treasurer, Mr. J. Turner.

Council—A. R. McMaster, T. C. Chisholm, J. Gordon, A. M. Smith, R. Wilkes, C. Robertson, H. S. Howland, G. Laidlaw, J. C. Fitch, Hon. J. McMurrich, Noah Barnhart, W. C. McDonnell, F. Coate, W. D. Mathews, J. D. Merrick, James Adamson, H. S. Howland, James Young, J. C. Griffith, J. C. Fitch, C. W. Bunting, J. C. Campbell, W. J. Shaw, and Charles Parsons.

Harbour Commissioners.—Messrs. J. G. Worts and J. Harris.

Hospital Trustee—Mr. H. S. Howland.

Insurance.

FIRE RECORD.—Toronto, January 29.—A fire broke out in the basement of Hamlin & Co.'s confectionery store, 119 Yonge street. The flames were soon extinguished by the fire engines. Hamlin & Co.'s stock, which was insured in the Home and Hartford for $1,200, was considerably damaged by the heat and water, but the building, which is the property of Mr. Burns, of Richmond street, and is insured for $1,700 in the London Insurance Co., did not sustain any material injury. Origin unknown, but supposed to have been accidental.

St. Mary's, January 24.—The cheese factory, owned by Mr. Mayhew, of this place, and located in East Nissouri, was destroyed by fire. The factory was valued at $2,000, and was insured. The fire is believed to be the work of an incendiary, for fire had not been in the building for two months or more.

Garafraxa, January 29.—Barn of John Kirtleton, 13th concession, was totally destroyed by fire. It contained 120 bushels of wheat, and a number of farming implements. There was only a small insurance on the property.

Mount Brydges, January 24.—The steam saw-mill belonging to Mr. Jeremiah Loudon was entirely destroyed. The loss is said to amount to $4,000, supposed to be the work of an incendiary.

In consequence of the insufficient supply of water for fire purposes, in Ottawa, the Royal Insurance Company decided to discontinue its agency there.

Granby, Eastern Townships, Jan. 23.—A fire broke out in the carpenter shop of Mr. Harvey, which was consumed with its contents. The fire communicated with the dwelling house of John Bradford, which was destroyed and with the store of James A. Downs, which was considerably damaged, as was also the goods in being removed. The loss of Messrs. Bradford and Downs supposed to be about $1,200 is covered by insurance in Mutual.

Clinton, Jan. 25th.—The House of Humphrey Snell was consumed. An exchange says : The fire made such rapid progress that the inmates had barely time to escape. Loss not less than $800. There was an insurance of $200 on building and furniture.

Pain Court, Township of Dover, Ont., July 17.—Some evil-disposed person placed fire in a chest containing $800 worth of church vestments in the Roman Catholic Church at Pain Court township of Dover. The inhabitants of the village immediately held a meeting and resolved to offer a reward for the incendiary.

Carleton, N. B., Jan.—A fire broke out in the house of Mr Carpenter, Guilford street, and partially destroyed it.

Quebec, Jan. 29.—A fire broke out in the Tobacco Manufactory, Queen street, St. Roch's, belonging to John Lemeurier, Esq. The damage was principally confined to a room about 10 feet square. Nevertheless damage was effected to the amount of $1,000. The stock and fixtures were insured to the amount of $4,000.

Montreal, January 30.—The driving-house of Molson's Brewery, St. Mary street, was discovered to be on fire. The alarm was quickly given, and the fire brigade were soon at the scene. Two powerful streams of water were poured in upon the fire, and the supply being abundant, the flames were soon got under and extinguished, before much damage was done. The fire appears to have originated from the igniting of some shavings and kindling-wood, left carelessly about the boiler furnace for heating or drying purposes. Happily, the fire was confined to the room where it originated; if it had burned through into the flat above, the entire building might have been destroyed.

Owen Sound, Jan. 22.—House of Mr. Henry Sayers, 10th concession of Sydenham, was consumed by fire. He lost all his furniture and clothing; no insurance.

Milltown, Ont., Jan. 26.—The dwelling house and carriage shop belonging to Mr. George S. Doxsee, in Milltown, township of Tyendinaga, was wholly destroyed by fire. The fire was accidental; no insurance.

St. John, N.B., Jan. 25.—The Lawrence Hotel, Prince William street, was discovered to be on fire. The fire was extinguished in less than half an hour, but not before the building was considerably injured, the floors being torn up and the house deluged with water. There was some insurance, but not sufficient to cover the damage.

Orillia, Jan. 22.—The residence, with nearly the whole of its contents, of Mr. William Walters, was totally consumed. The origin of the fire is not known, but is supposed to have caught from the chimney. The loss is stated to be about $600 or $700.

Quebec, Jan. —. A fire broke out in a hay-loft of a stable in rear of Mr. Garneau, saddler, St. George street, St. John's suburb. The Fire Brigade were soon on the spot and were successful in extinguishing it before considerable damage was done. It is suspected to be the work of an incendiary.

Edmonton, Ont., July 25.—The residence of R. Quin, was entirely consumed by fire. It is supposed that the fire caught through some defective stove-pipe in the upper story. The most of the household effects were saved.

Burgess, Ont., Jan. 23.—The dwelling house occupied by Michael Stanley, Reeve of [Du]caught fire by means of a defective stove pipe was burned to the ground. The furniture household utensils were all saved, but the [?] was a total loss. Over a hundred bushels of the corn, barrels of pork, which we the cellar, were also destroyed. Loss will amount to over $500.

AGRICULTURAL MUTUAL.—A London says that this Company holds nearly $1,000 cies, of which over 11,526 were issued during past year, being an increase over any pre cash balance on hand is stated at $49,000, includes $12,000 converted into Dominion a The directors at a late meeting determined investing $13,000 more in Dominion stock. figures unfold a flattering tale.

MONTREAL FIRE MARSHALS.—The follo is an interesting list of cases in which suit brought by the Fire Marshals against Bertram for not signing their certificates [?] vestigation: Bourdon & Co., Pratt's buil $40.50, 2d December; Frechette building, street, 31st December, $20.75, damage, $3; vechio & Co., St. Paul street, 17th Decen $20.75; carpenter's shop, St. Joseph street, Years day, $20.50, damage about $5; stab rear of Waverley Terrace, 4th December, 8 examining warehouse, 8th December, $37; Shepherd, Beaver Hall, 13th December, $2 Louis Richard, Sanguinet street, 16th Decen $20.50.

FIRES IN ST. JOHN DURING 1868.—The Engineer of the fire department reports to local papers as follows: From the 1st Jan 1868, to 1st January, 1869, there were eight four fires and alarms in this city, an incre forty-six over those of 1867. The aggregat of property by these fires was about $14 like causes in the previous year. About $1 of the loss during last year was sustained a fires, one on the 15th of January, 1868, a old water-works building, and the other on t of April at Brown & Hanna's livery stables.

THE LATE FIRE AT OTTAWA.

Our own correspondent furnishes us wit following particulars relating to thisfire:— The fire which consumed Desbarats' bl supposed to have arisen from the depositi hot ashes near a wooden staircase in rear buildings. Had the division walls run the roof, the fire would not, probably, have ed beyond the first house attacked. It possible to state the exact amount of loss the debris is removed. When it is remov engine, boiler and machinery will be exa and the damage ascertained. The whole presses, type, tools, &c., were destroyed as the stock of paper, books, &c., with the ex of about $200 worth. The cost of the lo was $46,000. The insurances upon it are lows: Royal, $8,000; Lancashire, $8,000; $4,000; Provincial, $5,000. Total, $25,00 The cost of the presses, &c., was $40,000. insurances upon them are: Ætna, $4,000; of New Haven, $4,000; London Assurance, $ Hartford, $4,000; Provincial, $4,000. $20,000.

The stock cost $40,300. The last name panies are on it to the extent of $3,000 Total, $15,000.

The boiler, engine, &c., office furnitu $5,100. The insurances on them are: $1,000; Home, $1,000; London Assurance, Hartford, $1,000; Provincial, $1,000. $5,000.

The Government loss on printed matte tween $7,000 and $8,000, covered by a po the Provincial for $4,000.

Mrs. Trotter's loss is $5,400; insured

Dublin for $3,000. ; Mrs. McGuire had ance. Messrs. McKenzie & Childs' loss of ready made clothing is $1,200 ; in the Home for $2,000. A frame hotel on site side of the street, and rear premises sumed. The building is insured in the er $1,400; loss, total. The furniture is in the Imperial for $1,000; loss, $800. s no insurance on the offices of the Royal l Bank and Ottawa and Prescott Railway.

Canadian Monetary Times.

URSDAY, FEBRUARY 4, 1869.

VESTERN CANADA BUILDING SOCIETY.

ort of the proceedings of the Annual of this Society, which will be found her columns, shows that a profitable has been done during the past year. t of $192,694.87 was loaned on mort d stock, and $172,376 was received of deposit. The mortgage securities, ere last year 515 in number, repre $295,500, now number 712, and an e value of 407,500. New shares to unt of $50,000 were issued last De Some of them were sold at a premium een per cent. After paying two divi f five per cent, the reserve fund rhised to $19,424, by the addition 24 premium received on the new d $5,000 surplus profits. It is not ndered at, therefore, that expressions ratulation were exchanged. The of the society have earned the confi ! the shareholders, and, judging by ease in deposits, that of the public . The President, with much grace, . to accept increased remuneration. e seen that John Worthington, Esq., ted unanimously to the office of Vice it, and S. Platt, Esq., placed on the Thorough business men, such as e of great service to an institution of d. The Board is not one merely in ut a really serviceable staff of shrewd o appreciate their responsibilities, and make time to fulfil their duty to those who elect them. Testimony is again borne to the efficiency and zeal with which Mr. W. S. Lee discharges the duties of Secretary.

MR. HATCH WEEPING AT THE GRAVE OF RECIPROCITY.

Mr. Israel Hatch has favored the world with another report on the defunct treaty of reciprocity between the United States and Canada. It is a desultory document, taking a partial and prejudiced view of the facts, and leading to loose, unreasoned, and un tenable conclusions. The leading idea of its author is, that a true reciprocity treaty "would include all the productions of labour on both sides, or at least provide for a fair and equal exchange of them." A free ex change of all the products of labour does not necessarily mean the same thing as "a fair and equal exchange of them;" because, if they were subject to equal duties, Mr. Hatch might choose to consider that a free and equal exchange. But it is one thing to exchange raw products free of duty, and quite another thing to provide for any reciprocal exchange of manufactures. In the latter case, a common duty would have to be agreed upon, if duty there were at all. If there were no duty, insuperable difficulties would present themselves on both sides. The Ame ricans are under legal obligations to treat other countries besides Canada on the best terms they extend to the most favoured na tions. How would they get over this diffi culty, short of the impossible abolition of all customs duties ? And for Canada, we could not dispense with this source of revenue, nor could we enact a discriminating tariff against the nation which we call Mother Country, and to which we look for protection. It would be impossible, in the present state of things, to agree upon a common duty. The United States could not accept a low or moderate tariff, and about the last thing Ca nada would think of would be to adopt theirs. If there is to be no new reciprocity treaty till we can agree to include manufactures, there will be none at all.

We do not undervalue the advantages of a reciprocal free exchange of the raw products of the two countries. But the very circum stances of their being mutual is a reason why we shall never be tempted to purchase them at any figure much above their natural price. That price is the equivalent which reciprocity implies. We gave a little more in 1854, and we might be tempted to do so again, but we now know, from the best of all tests, that we can live and thrive without any such treaty at all. We believe both countries would benefit by having one ; but we are not going to purchase it at a price disproportioned to the advantages. The circumstance of the American Government procuring a new re report on the subject, implies dissatisfaction with the existing trade relations. That feeling is well founded, but the Americans brought about the present position of the matter, in a fit of spleen ; and time and re flection may have given them occasion to relent. But, if we may judge from Mr. Hatch's report, they have not yet come to that state of mind in which a treaty accepta ble to Canada is likely to originate.

Mr. Hatch probably exerted more effective influence than any other single individual in the crusade that led to the breaking up of the old treaty, and he is not likely to make any suggestions for the formation of a new one that Canada could possibly accept. He is bound hand and foot to the canal interests of the State of New York. That is the source whence all his inspiration on the reciprocity question has, from first to last, been drawn. He recommends Congress to Grant a money aid to the Erie Canal, and Canada to yield "to the destiny unalterably fixed by geo graphy, climate and boundaries," and cease to cherish an ambition to profit by the trade of the Western States. He is grieved to see us throw our money away on canals and rail roads, when we ought to be contented with the Erie Canal. But before he addressed this advice to Canadians, Mr. Hatch might have offered it to the great and rapidly in creasing Western States. It will, we fancy, be more than he can do, to convince them that they ought to be satisfied with the Erie ditch, and not seek to utilize the magnificent highway afforded by the great St. Lawrence.

Mr. Hatch is not easy to please. He makes it a sort of crime in us Canadians that we can build ships for half what they cost in the States ; that we possess boundless forests of untaxed timber ; that we can build railroads at comparatively little cost, and that when built they are untaxed, and offer too great facilities for transportation. We, on the contrary, see in these things so many reasons why we should not submit to the destiny our monitor would prepare for us. While Mr. Hatch weeps over the grave of the reci procity treaty of 1854, he should remember that he but bewails his own victim ; and we think he is not destined to see a resurrection in the form which constitutes his divine ideal of one-sided trading advantages and canal monopoly.

BOARD OF TRADE.

We print elsewhere the annual report of the Toronto Board of Trade. It gives an elaborate statement of the general features of the trade of Toronto during the past year, and deserves a careful perusal.

THE OTTAWA FIRE.

The heavy loss which the Provincial sustained by the late fire in Ottawa affords additional evidence of the correctness of our remarks respecting the management of this Company. For a Company, comparatively small, to accumulate risks to the extent of $17,000, on a printing office and its contents, is little less than tempting destruction. That sum represents their gross receipts from fire premiums for, probably, two months, and its loss is very suggestive of embarrassment, straitened circumstances, a further call on subscribed stock, besides disagreeable comments on the part of directors and stockholders. We believe the Company will be able to pay the claim, but, at the same time, we cannot help thinking that another such disaster would not be successfully encountered. It seems that some of our Insurance Company managers have yet to learn that there are other maxims in Insurance besides "trust to luck." We strongly advise the Directors of the Provincial to overhaul the policies of the Company, and send their inspector throughout the country with unlimited powers of canciliation. To carry on management such as the above indicates can have but one issue.

The exodus of Insurance Companies from Ottawa will bring the good people of that city to their senses. The cry there is water, water, everywhere, but not a drop to extinguish a fire.

INSPECTION OF VESSELS.

A correspondent last week called attention to some irregularities in the present system of inspection, which are worthy of the attention of lake underwriters. He states a case in which an owner of vessel property suffered loss by the standard of his vessel being lowered during the season of navigation. If the quality and outfit of the vessel remained the same as when last inspected, the case was one of undoubted hardship, not to say positive injustice. If our information is correct these cases are not of unfrequent occurrence. The difficulty arises from a system of inspection which is defective and unwise.

The Inspectors are thoroughly competent, but they are not disinterested. Acting as officers of the Association of Lake Underwriters, they are at the same time—all of them—salaried officers of the different Insurance Companies composing that Association. The present method is this. The marine inspectors of several different companies make a tour of inspection each year, in February or March, occupying about one month of their time. To facilitate the completion of the duty, the territory—Ontario and Quebec—is divided among them, Toronto being made the starting point. These officers fix the standard of all new vessels, and examine into the condition of all others preparatory to the business of the incoming season, and report to the Association. Many of these reports are not correct or reliable. Vessels are often reported as rebuilt, when it is only rails and decks that are made new, instead of a thorough rebuild, which can only be done by placing the vessel in dry dock. Then these Inspectors often differ in opinion as to what constitutes a standard vessel, or one fit to carry grain. In consequence of this, some companies have been insuring vessels as standard, which other companies would not take, on the ground that they did not come up to the mark. This could scarcely be otherwise. The inspector is interested in getting the insurance of the vessel, and is therefore inclined to be friendly to the builder that patronizes him. Take a new vessel which a strict and impartial inspector would make A E for instance, it would be an easy matter, if a handsome risk were offered to a particular company to which the inspector is attached, to make the vessel A 1. The difference is but slight and only few commercial men could detect it; still it would be most important to the owner. The same evil exists in the case of vessels fitting out for a season's business. It is, therefore, important not merely to ship owners, but also to shippers, to have a radical change brought about.

As it is, grain is often carried in inferior vessels which would not be allowed to take it if they had their deserts, but would be compelled to resort to the lumber or coal trade. The owners of first-class vessels would then reap the full advantage of keeping their vessels in thorough repair.

A strict and impartial method of inspection is required and must be had. An independent Inspector, paid by the Association, is wanted, whose reports would be examined and revised by the Association, and be regarded as final by all its members. It would be the duty of this Inspector to force all doubtful vessels upon the "Gridiron" for a thorough examination, where their grade could be satisfactorily ascertained. The sooner this step is taken by the Association the better for all concerned.

Mining.

MADOC GOLD DISTRICT.

(From our own Correspondent).

BELLEVILLE, Feb. 1st, 1869.

The annual statements of some of the mining companies of this district have been published, but for the most part contain little matter for comment. The only one which shows a "clean bill of health" is the "Grand Trunk Employees' Gold-mining Company," whose stock is stated at $100,000, paid up $100,000, liabilities nothing.

The Merchants' Union Gold Mining Co., held and adjourned meeting on Thursday last, at which it was resolved to raise $4,000 by voluntary assessment, one half of which is appropriated to clear off the outstanding liabilities; the other moiety to be employed in developing the mine, and in the purchase of additional machinery to increase the efficiency of their mill. The sum of $2,350 was subscribed for before the close of the meeting.

Work is still progressing under favorable indications at the Richardson mine. A few days ago the miners struck a cross vein of quartzite, from the bottom part of which were obtained specim shewing visible gold in promising quantity, acco panied by the carbonaceous mineral which form so prominent a feature at the first opening of t shaft. The work of reduction is being carried slowly, as the supply of ore from the mine, is lir ted, owing to the small number of men employ As the clearing up will be deferred until a su cient quantity shall have been crushed to mak satisfactory return, no definite information c yet be had; but Mr. Dunstan reports that af three tons had been put through, he tried t mercury and obtained four ounces of strair amalgam, which ought to contain from 1½ to oz. of gold.

The County Council of the County of Hastin at their last session, held Jan. 26th and 27 passed a By-Law, granting an annual sum of $ towards the establishment of a professorship Mines, Mineralogy and Agricultural Chemistry the Alexandra University, (late Albert Colleg of Hastings and Belleville, and have nomina Mr. James T. Bell, of Belleville, as the f occupant of the chair.

Financial.

TORONTO STOCK MARKET.

(Reported by Pellatt & Osler, Brokers.)

There has been more freedom in the market t week than for some time past, there being buy and sellers in most cases at quotations. In G ernment Securities there have been large trans tions and at advanced rates.

Bank Stock.—Montreal declined to 138 in beginning of the week, but is now firm and in mand at 138½ with no sellers under 139. Buy offer 103 for British but none in the market Ontario has been freely dealt in at 100, 100¼, 100½, and closed in fair demand. The high pr offered for Toronto have attracted sellers limited extent. Sales of Royal Canadian made at 85 to 85½; there are now buyers limited extent at 86. Commerce sold at 102½ is still offered at this rate. Gore is in active mand at 40, sellers ask 45. Merchants has in good demand during the week at advanced r last sales were at 109½. Buyers offer 99 for bec: none in market. City is 2 per cent high no sellers under 103. Buyers offer 109 for Peuple; no sellers. Nationale is asked for at none offering. Jacques Cartier could be place 108; no sellers. There are no sellers of Uni buyers offer 103 to 103½. Other banks nomi

Debentures.—There were large sales of ster five per cents at 95½ to 96, and of Dominion S at 105½. Very few Toronto offering; they readily taken at 6¾ for cash. No sales of Cou to report; they continue very scarce and in g demand.

Sundries.—No sales of City Gas; would be paid. No important transactions oc red in Canada Permanent Building Society; would be paid; small sales of Western Ca occurred at 118½, which price would readily paid; Freehold is 2 per cent higher, the last were at 109½. Montreal Telegraph is offere 134½; no buyers over 134. There is a lin demand for Canada Landed Credit at 75. A good mortgages have been offering during the at 8 per cent. Money is plentiful on good pa

BANK OF ENGLAND.

	Jan. 16, 1869.	Jan. 17, 1
Bank rate of discount	3 per cent.	2 per c
Bank reserve..........	£9,482,964	£12,761
Bank stock of bullion	18,608,324	22,016
Price of Consols.....	92½ x d	92¾ x

The money market has again exhibited gr ease, and the supply of capital being in exce the demand, the rates of discount are rather lo ıss paper of short date has been taken at ½ per cent., and six months India bills at ıt. On the Stock Exchange, advances on Government securities were made at 1 to cent.; but yesterday the rate was ¾ to 1 per gher. The Bank return shows a decrease 902 in the reserve, and of £38,963 in the bullion. The other items of the account e usual heavy variations, consequent on ernment payments.

EBT OF THE LATE PROVINCE OF CANADA.

nteresting correspondence between the r. Rose, Minister of Finance, and Hon. od, the Treasurer of Ontario respecting ıc debt, has been laid before the Legislature. e reduces the points of importance which lispute between the Dominion of Canada Province of Ontario to five:

ould debts due by the Grand Trunk, ıat Western and the Northern Rail- o in diminution of the debt of On- ıl Quebec at their par value? He con- ıat these debts are to be considered the property of the Dominion according to ing of the Confederation Act and the the compact, as Nova Scotia and New ck put in a railway asset of $11,000,000. ıod contends that though these railway ay be the property of the Dominion, they r taken in reduction of the public debt of Province of Canada; that the acquisition lower province railways, to be run under ıent control, will be an additional burden Dominion exchequer, and Ontario will be pon to contribute by its taxes the larger the sum necessary to run these railways as the Intercolonial; and that the sacri- ıtario will have to make will be quite t without giving up $4,359,272 of good. Mr. Rose replies that evidence will be ing to establish the understanding of the f the Union Act.

uld the amount due by the Bank of anada be taken at its face by the Do- s a banker's balance and deducted from incial debt ? Mr. Wood contends that ınkers' balance to be assumed at its nom- ıe, and that the Dominion alone has ı make it worth its face, which if it re- m doing, Ontario and Quebec will be the Mr. Rose considers that a "bankers' means cash available to the Dominion in hands at the time of the Union, and not debts. In December, 1863, the bank its inability to pay in cash the million lf it owed the Government. That debt agreed to liquidate by half yearly instal- ! $50,000 with interest at three per cent. the bank obtained an extension of time iting $883,300 of Grank Trunk postal collateral security. Further negotiations e which prevent the debt being viewed ht of an available bankers' balance to be by the Dominion as cash. Up to this Dominion could not have collected it, some doubt as to whether the whole of ı must not be realized before coercive can be effectually taken by the Govern- d it is not the interest of Government or hat the arbitrary process of a writ of with its attendant cost and sacrifice, e substituted for the course taken. the Dominion "will continue to make ort to make this a good debt." Mr. ws attention to the distinction in the ction of the B. N. Act between a ' balance" and "cash." He says that e claim was admittedly good—assets —writ of extent issuable—the Dominion ent int rvened and assumed the claim, ıs legislation (31 Vic. c. 17) without the f the Government of Ontario, dealt with

it in such a way as to deprive itself of all the ad- vantages which it had. It does not, therefore, rest with the Dominion to say that it is now doubtful and not to be taken at par by way of reduction.

3. Whether all investments by the late Prov- ince of Canada out of Trust moneys, and on ac- count of Trust funds, should be retained by the Dominion at their face, and the Trust funds be a liability of the Dominion to their full value?—Mr. Rose considers that Mr. Wood admits that the Trust securities should go with the funds and be deducted from the amount which the Dominion has to pay on account of these funds.

4. Whether the whole of what is termed in- direct debt incurred on account of, or as security for various institutions, should be put on the same footing and deducted absolutely from the gross liability? This debt includes the Common School, Upper Canada Grammar School, Upper Canada Building, and Lower Canada Education funds.— Mr. Wood says the law makes it obligatory upon each institution or concern on whose behalf the advances were made through debentures by the late Province, to provide for the payment of the interest and debt of these debentures, and as such institutions and funds ($150 400 debt excepted) will without reduction come to Ontario and Quebec, there is no conflict. Mr. Rose considers that whatever claims may in future be put for- ward as regards the capital of these funds, cannot in the meantime affect the amount of the debt, its apportionment or interest.

5. Whether the Dominion should pay five per cent., semi-annually, on the amount at the credit of the Common School, Upper Canada Grammar School Fund, Lower Canada Superior Education Fund and the Normal School Fund and should settle it at present ?—Mr. Rose proposes to pay five per cent., the same rate of interest on the debt composed of these funds as is charged on the excess of debt beyond the sixty-two and a half millions which is created partly by these funds. In all transactions between the Dominion and the Provinces five per cent. is the rate fixed. Mr. Wood says the Government of Ontario has no authority to deal with these funds as proposed. Ontario might, perhaps, prefer to invest these funds at six per cent. instead (not getting the principal) of receiving five per cent. in perpetuity. As these funds are for public purposes, Ontario may sweep them away altogether.

In conclusion, Mr. Wood suggests that a plan be adopted by which differences might be settled. Mr. Rose does not believe anything like arbitration to be necessary, but considers that negotiation will afford a just solution of any differences.

CHARGE OF FRAUD.—A very unpleasant diffi- culty has occurred at Kingston in connection with the Royal Canadian Bank agency there. Mr. George E. Small, late Manager of the Bank, and Mr. Isaac Barnes, teller, were arraigned be- fore the Police Magistrate, charg-d with a con- spiracy between the two to defraud the bank by cashing a bill of exchange for £1,000 stg., drawn by the wife of Mr. Small on a Mr. Gardyne, of England, which bill was not accepted. It is also charged that Mr. Small's cheque for $100 was cashed by the same clerk, in disregard of his in- structions, while there were no funds to Mr. Small's credit.

INSOLVENTS.—The following list of insolvents appear in the *Official Gazette* of last week :. George Fletcher Rice, Portage du Fort ; Lindsay Pillar, Williamsburg ; David Vrooman, Mount Brydges ; James F. Kidner, Montreal ; Donald MacDonald, Orangeville ; Horatio Nelson Jones, Quebec; Charles Risner. Portage du Fort ; Theodore Brown, Hillier ; Jas. Flynn, Orangeville ; Elie Migneron, St. Adele ; Cox & Stevenson, Montreal ; Samuel Stewart, Albion ; Joseph Hilair Prineau, St. Jean ; Chrysottonie ; Joseph May, Montreal ; Carlos D. Meigs, St. Thomas, Depierreville ; Geo. W. Creighton Kingston.

Railway News.

NORTHERN RAILWAY.—Traffic receipts for week ending 23rd January, 1869.

Passengers	$2,339 54
Freight and live stock	4,537 27
Mails and sundries	260 30
	$7,137 11
Corresponding Week of '68	9,267 15
Decrease	$2,130 02

GREAT WESTERN RAILWAY.—Traffic for week ending January 8, 1869.

Passengers	$22,077 35
Freight	58,455 90
Mails and Sundries	3,561 03
Total Receipts for week	$84,094 28
Coresponding week, 1887	63,882 66
Increase	$30,211 62

RAILWAY FROM TORONTO TO ST. PAUL.

Mr. Rankin suggests the construction of a line from Toronto to a point on the River St. Mary, in Algoma. He says :

There are several lines of railway now in course of construction through the State of Minnesota, which will terminate at or near the head of Lake Superior. They will all be completed before it would be possible to build the one I propose. These roads will throw an enormous amount of traffic upon the lake, which must pass down the River St. Mary on its way to the east, while the whole of that traffic might be intercepted at or near the Sault St. Mary, and brought down by rail through Ontario, via Toronto, to its destina- tion on whatever point on the seaboard. The distance from Sault St. Mary to Toronto is less than to Detroit, while to Buffalo it is about the same.

A railway bridge, offering no obstruction to navigation, can be built over the main channel to Sugar Island and thence over the shallow stream which separates that island from the mainland of Northern Michigan. This connection with St. Paul can be established by a line hundreds of miles shorter than by any other practical route, passing too, from one extreme point to the other, through a country favorable to agricultural pur- suits. On its way to St. Paul, the proposed line would intersect the railway from Green Bay to Marquette, now in operation, and thereby serve the interests, and secure the traffic, to and from the great Atlantic cities, of the numerous and im- portant towns, and mining settlements, along the south, or American shores of Lake Superior, while the line to St. Paul would be the germ of a great northern international route, via Fort Aber- crombie, to Fort Garry, and thence all the way through British territory to the Pacific.

Such a line as this would pay, "from the start," as the Union Pacific does now, before it is finished ; while a road to Red River, by the north of Lake Superior could not pay at first. When the time for building that road has arrived, however, it will be found a great advantage to have a road east- ward from the Sault in full operation.

It may be urged that a road to the River St. Mary would receive no way traffic, passing as it would, the greater part of the distance through an unsettled country, but it must be borne in mind, that wild as that country now is, *it is fit for settle- ment*, and only requires to be made accessible to insure its being rapidly filled up, so that while the work is progressing the settlement of the country will go on, and the foundation of a way business be established ; though irrespective of way business, the through traffic that would find its way by this route, as surely as water finds its level, would be more than sufficient to make the enterprise highly remunerative. I would suggest, that from Toronto, the line should skirt the Eastern shores of Lake Simcoe, thence proceeding in a direction west of north to French River, crossing which its course would be westward to the River St. Mary.

[We give the above for what it is worth. The proposition to build a bridge over the main channel to Sugar Island—from half a mile to a mile in width, according to the charts—would be a formidable undertaking to begin with.—Ed. C. M. T

Pro Rata Freight.—A bill has been introduced into the Illinois Legislature to compel the railroads in that State to charge a uniform rate for the transportation of freight in proportion to the distance it shall be carried, and providing that any railroad that charges more than the *pro rata* shall pay the owner of the freight five times the amount wrongfully collected. This is not a novel proposition, but it *is* an unreasonable one.

Commercial.

Toronto Market.

Business for the month of January was dull owing to the unseasonable weather. For the want of sleighing produce was brought forward very slowly, and sales, both by wholesale and retail merchants, were entirely below anticipations.—Within a week or ten days, however, the winter movement has commenced in good earnest, and grain is pouring in at a brisk rate at all the different receiving points. This has improved the tone of business, but the effect on prices has been most unfavorable. The decline which has occurred must represent considerable loss to a number of firms.

Grain—*Wheat.*—Receipts by cars 42,800 bush. and 17,000 bush. last week. The market for Spring is dull, and 3 to 4 cents lower. Sales occurred during the week at $1.02 to 1.03, and to-day, the (3rd Feb.) a few cars sold at $1.00, the market closing with sellers of round lots at that price, without buyers. Fall is 5 cents lower and closed dull; a lot of 2,000 bushels, of a good sample, changed hands to-day at $1.05, and buyers are holding off even at the reduced quotations expecting fall to go to $1.00, and spring to 90. The decline is owing to the heavy receipts and the existence of only a small demand. The stock of wheat in store here is about 90,000. *Barley.*—Receipts light; the market is steady at $1.30 to $1.35 for car loads delivered, some sales occurring within the range of these quotations. The latter figure was refused for one or two round lots f.o.b. *Peas*—Receipts very small, and no business doing.—*Oats*—Receipts 13,200 bushels and 6,800 last week. There is only a quiet demand, and the market is a little easier. Sales of cars were made at 53c. *Seeds*—Timothy nominal at $2.00 to $2.50. Clover very unsteady; there is some speculative enquiry, and a little business doing; we quote, $6.25 to $6.50; flax $1.60 to $2.00, according to quality.

Flour.—Receipts 2,200 brls., and 2,500 brls. last week. Flour, as well as all breadstuffs, is dull, and tending lower; there are few buyers, and in the present state of the market holders are not disposed to offer. The stock here is about 10,000 brls. There are sellers of No. 1 superfine at $4.50, and some demand at that price. Other grades are not quotable. Sales of No. 1 during the week were, 500 brls. at $4.53, on cars at Weston; 100 brls. at $4.55, the same place; 200 brls. at $4.35, at Norval; 200 brls., sold as fancy, brought $4.70 at Norval.

Provisions.—*Dressed Hogs*—The market is firm and again higher; receipts have been liberal and a good business done at quotations. *Mess Pork.*—Firm and higher. *Lard.*—In light stock and firm at at 16c. *Butter.*—Quiet and unchanged.

Freights.—Rates by Grand Trunk Railway:—Flour to all stations from Belleville to Lynn, inclusive, 35c., grain per 100 lbs. 18c.; flour to Brockville and Cornwall, inclusive, 43c. grain 22c. flour to Montreal 50c. grain 25c.; flour to all stations between Island Pond and Portland, inclusive, 85c. grain 43c.; flour to Boston 90c., gold, grain 45c.; flour to Halifax $1.05, grain 53c; flour to St. John 95c. Boxed Meats to Liverpool per gross ton 82s. 6d.; lard or butter in tinnets 87s. 6d.; Pork 11s. per tierce; flour 5s. 6d. per barrel; grain 12s. per 480 pounds. Rates by Great Western Railway—Flour, Toronto to Suspension Bridge 25c. gold; thence to New York, 76c. U.S. currency per bbl.; to Boston 86c.—Rates from Toronto to Liverpool, London and Glasgow are—Beef, Bacon, Pork, Hams, Lard and Tallow, in lots of one car load and upwards, $1.52, gold, per 100 lbs. Grain, in bags of 5 car loads and upwards, 96c., do. Flour, $1.62 per bbl. do.

St. John Market.

Breadstuffs.—Jan. 27.—Receipts continue large for the time of year, several schooners having arrived with cargoes from Portland during the week. The demand for flour is exceedingly small, and that is only for small retail lots. It is impossible to place large lots at any price. The markets in Western Canada are again quoted dull, with a downward tendency, which, with large receipts, has weakened our markets, and prices are lower. We quote: No. 1 superfine $5.60; choice brands and strong bakers, $5.75 to $5.80. Cornmeal is easier; we quote $4.40.

Prices of Cotton.

A Tabular Statement, showing the price of Middling Upland Cotton each week for the years 1868 and 1867, in the Liverpool Cotton Market, will be found interesting and useful for reference:

		1868.	1867.			1868.	1867.
January	9	7⅛	14⅛	July	9	14¼	11⅛
"	16	7½	14¾	"	16	11¼	10¼
"	23	7¾	14⅜	"	23	10⅞	10¼
"	30	7⅞	14⅜	"	30	9⅞	10¼
Febr'y	6	7 15-16	14⅛	August	6	9⅝	10¼
"	13	8⅝	14	"	13	10	10⅞
"	20	10⅛	13¾	"	20	10¼	10⅞
"	27	9⅝	13⅝	"	27	11	10⅛
Nov.	5	9¾	13¼	Sept.	3	10⅞	10
"	12	10⅛	13⅝	"	10	10¼	9½
"	19	10⅛	13¾	"	17	10⅛	9⅜
"	26	10⅛	13⅛	"	24	10	8¾
April	2	11¾	12½	October	1	10¼	8¼
"	9	11⅞	12	"	8	10¾	8½
"	16	12¼	11⅝	"	15	10⅝	8¾
"	23	12⅜	10½	"	22	10½	8¾
"	30	12⅝	11½	"	29	11	8¾
May	7	12⅝	11	Nov.	5	11⅛	8⅜
"	14	12	13⅝	"	12	10⅞	8¼
"	21	11½	11	"	19	10½	8¼
"	28	11¼	11½	"	26	11⅜	7⅞
June	4	11¼	11⅞	Dec.	3	11¼	7⅝
"	11	11	11⅜	"	10	10⅛	7⅜
"	18	11¼	11¼	"	17	10⅜	7⅜
"	25	11¼	11	"	24	10¼	7⅛
July	2	10⅞	10½	"	31	10⅜	7¼

Halifax Market.

Breadstuffs—Jan. 26.—We have to report a continued dullness in all descriptions of Breadstuffs during the past week. The demand, which is entirely for Supers, is still small, and only for the better description of Western. We quote:—White Wheat, Extra (Fall) $7.25 to 7.50; Fancy, $6.50 to 6.75; Bakers' Strong, $6.40 to 6.50; Supers, $7.25; No. 2, $5.00 to 5.25; Middlings, $4.50 to 4.75; Pollard's $4.25 to 4.50. Rye, $5.00 to 5.25. Oatmeal, $7.75. Cornmeal, K. D., 34.50; F. G., $4.25. White Beans, $3.25 to 3.50.

Provisions.—Pork exhibits a rather firmer feeling, without buyers; stocks are quite equal to present demand. Beef dull, without change. Butter, Lard and Cheese inactive at former quotations. We quote:—Pork (Mess), $22.50 to 23.00; Prime Mess, $18,00; Prime, $13.50 to 16.00; Bacon Rolls, 13c to 14c; Cut, 12½c; H 14c to 15c. Beef (Mess) $10.00 to 12.06; P $8.00 to $9.00. Lard, 14c. Butter, 23c to Cheese, 14c.

West India Produce.—There have bee transactions since our last in Molasses and Su Quotations, which are nominal, are unchar Several cargoes of Rum have arrived the week, one lot of which realized 55c at auc the balance, which was withdrawn, is now at 60c. Coffee dull and unchanged. We qu Sugar V. P., 9¼c; Porto Rico, 8¼c to 8½c; 7¾c to 8c. Rum, Demerara (in bond), 60c. fee, Jamaica, 13c to 15c; St. Domingo, 10c to

Fish and Oil.—Continue active at full r Large Shore Codfish in request; also Round ring. Cod Oil moves off quickly. Stock now quite reduced. Seal nominal. We quo Codfish (Large Shore), $4.25 to 4.50; Small, $ Mackerel, No. 1 L., $16.50; No. 2 L., $14. 44.50; No. 3 L., $8, to 8.50. Oil—Pale 75c; Straw, 75c; Brown, 45c; Cod, 50c to Dog, 35o to 40c. Kerosene—American, Canadian, 40c to 45c.

Exchange.—Bank drafts on London, 60 12½ per cent; Montreal Sight, 3¼ per cent; York Gold, 3 per cent; St. John, N.B., 3 per

Petroleum Trade of Pittsburgh.

The petroleum trade of Pittsburgh approxin thirteen millions annually. Sixty-eight refine some of them monster establishments, are tinually in operation. The visitor who exp these establishments will find that the gr portion of them possess iron tankage for 100 barrels. Ten thousand barrel tanks are as mon as barrows. A tank with capacity thirty thousand barrels, and a surface enough for a skating park, is, however, s thing seldom seen outside of Pittsburgh. Du the past year, 727,628 barrels of refined oil shipped to Philadelphia alone. At present t are forty-eight refineries in operation, mor less of the time. These refineries have a bility to turn out 37,000 barrels per week o fined oil, requiring about 55,000 barrels of c This, at forty-two gallons to the barrel, w amount to 80,898,000 gallons refined per or within 1,600,000 gallons of the entire am of refined sent abroad the past year. As these refineries have the capacity to turn 1,934,000 barrels per year. The capital inv in these refineries, independent of the imm capital all the time locked up in oil, is estin at $7,500,000. The amount invested in the w and in barrels, tanks, boats and other prop necessary for the prosecution of the busi would swell the aggregate capital to over 000,000.

Exports of Petroleum from the United S from Jan. 1 to Jan. 24.

	1869.	18
From New York......gals.	2,411,177	3,111
Boston	179,049	8
Philadelphia.........	1,464,649	1,57
Baltimore	3,600	81
Portland	.. ..	(
Total Export from U. S...	5,063,465	4,86
Same time 1867............		2,93
Some time 1866............		3,15

Safes.

The safe of the Royal Canadian Bank in barats' Building in Ottawa was found in ruins with its contents not much damaged. of Desbarats' safes was found with its con entirely consumed.

Shipping of Yarmouth, N. S.

The Yarmouth *Herald* publishes a list of shipping belonging to the county of Yarm at the beginning of the year. It will be seen the whole number of vessels is 263, and thei gregate tonnage 81,896. Although the nu of vessels is four less than last year, there increase of tonnage to the extent of 3,306 The losses amounted to nine vessels and

Mercantile.

TORONTO PRICES CURRENT.—FEBRUARY 4, 1869.

Name of Article.	Wholesale Rates.		Name of Article.	Wholesale Rate.		Name of Article.	
Boots and Shoes.	$ c.	$ c.	**Groceries**—*Contin'd*	$ c.	$ c.	**Leather**—*Contin'd.*	
Mens' Thick Boots	2 20	2 50	" fine to fins't..	0 85	0 05	Kip Skins, P'tna	0
" Kip	2 50	3 25	Hyson	0 45	0 80	French	0
" Calf	3 00	3 70	Imperial	0 42	0 80	English	0
" Congress Gaiters	2 00	2 50	*Tobacco, Manufact'd:*			Hemlock Calf (30 to	
" Kip Cobourgs	1 15	1 45	Can Leaf, ⅌ ℔ 5s & 10s	0 26	0 30	35 ℔s.) per doz..	0
Boys' Thick Boots	1 60	1 80	Western Leaf, com..	0 25	0 26	Do. light	0
Youths' "	1 35	1 50	" Good	0 27	0 32	French Calf	0
Women's Batts	1 00	1 20	" Fine	0 32	0 35	Grain & Satn Cif ⅌ doz..	0
" Congress Gaiters..	1 15	1 45	" Bright fine..	0 40	0 50	Splits, large ⅌ ℔..	0
Misses' Batts	0 75	1 10	" choice..	0 00	0 75	" small	0
" Congress Gaiters..	1 00	1 20				Enamelled Cow ⅌ foot..	0
Girls' Batts	0 60	0 85	**Hardware.**			Patent	0
" Congress Gaiters..	0 80	1 10	Tin (net cash prices)			Pebble Grain	0
Children's C. T. Cacks..	0 50	0 65	Block, 25 ℔	0 25	0 26	Buff	0
" Gaiters	0 65	0 90	Grain	0 25	0 25		
Drugs.			Copper:			**Oils.**	
Aloes Cape	0 12½	0 16	Pig	0 23	0 24	Cod	0
Alum	0 02½	0 03	Sheet	0 30	0 33	Lard, extra	0
Borax	0 10	0 40	*Cut Nails:*			" No. 1	0
Camphor, refined	0 65	0 70	Assorted ¼ Shingles,			Woollen	0
Castor Oil	0 18	0 28	⅌ 100 ℔...	2 90	3 00	Lubricating, patent..	0
Caustic Soda	0 04½	0 08	Shingle sizes do	3 15	3 25	" Mott's economic	0
Cochineal	0 90	1 0	Lattie and 4 dy	3 20	3 40	Linseed, raw	1
Cream Tartar	0 25	0 80	*Galvanized Iron:*			" boiled..	0
Epsom Salts	0 03	0 04	Assorted sizes	0 08	0 09	Machinery	0
Extract Logwood	0 09	0 11	Best No. 24	0 09	0 00	Olive, 2nd, ⅌ gal..	1
Gum Arabic, sorts	0 30	0 35	" 26	0 09	0 00	" salad	3
Indigo, Madras	0 75	1 00	" 28	0 09	0 03½	" salad, in bots.	0
Licorice	0 14	0 45	*Horse Nails:*			qt. ⅌ case..	3
Madder	0 16	0 18	Guest's or Griffin's			Sesame salad, ⅌ gal..	
Nutgalls	0 00	0 00	assorted sizes..	0 00	0 00	Seal, pale	0
Opium	6 70	7 00	For W. ass'd sizes..	0 18	0 19	Spirits Turpentine	0
Oxalic Acid	0 28	0 35	Patent Hammer'd do..	0 17	0 18	Varnish	0
Potash, Bi-Bart..	0 25	0 33	*Iron (4 months):*			Whale	0
" Bichromate..	0 15	0 20	Pig—Gartsherre No1..	24 00	25 00	**Paints, &c.**	
Potass Iodide	3 80	4 50	Other brands. No 1..	22 00	24 00	White Lead, genuine	
Senna	0 12½	0 60	" " No. 2..	0 00	0 00	in Oil, ⅌ 25℔s..	0
Soda Ash	0 03	0 04	Bar—Scotch, ⅌ 100 ℔..	2 25	2 50	Do. No. 1	0
S. da Bicarb	4 50	5 50	Refined	3 00	3 25	" 2	0
Tartaric Acid	0 37½	0 45	Swedes	5 00	5 50	" 3	0
Vertigris	0 35	0 40	Hoops—Coopers	3 00	3 25	White Zinc, genuine.	3
Vitriol, Blue	0 00	0 10	Band	3 00	3 25	White Lead, dry	0
Groceries.			Boiler Plates	3 25	3 50	Red Lead	0
Coffees:			Canada Plates	3 75	4 00	Venetian Red, Eng'h..	0
Java, ⅌ ℔	0 27@0 24		Union Jack	0 00	0 00	Yellow Ochre, Fren'h..	0
Laguayra	0 17	0 18	Pontypool	3 25	4 00	Whiting	0
Rio	0 15	0 17	Swansea	3 90	4 00		
Fish:			*Lead (at 4 months):*			**Petroleum.**	
Herrings, Lab. split..	5 75	6 50	Bar, ⅌ 100 ℔s..	0 03½	0 07	(Refined ⅌ gal.)	
" round	4 00	4 75	Sheet "	0 03½	0 07	Water white, car'l'd..	0
" scaled	0 85	0 40	Shot "	0 07½	0 07½	" small lots..	0
Mackerel, small kitts..	1 00	0 00	*Iron Wire (net cash):*			Straw, by car load	0
Loch. Her. wh'd bks..	2 50	2 75	No. 6, ⅌ bundle..	2 70	2 80	" small lots	0
" half	1 25	1 50	" 9	3 10	3 20	Amber, by car load..	0
White Fish & Trout..	3 50	3 75	" 10,	3 40	3 60	" small lots	0
Salmon, saltwater	14 00	15 00	" 12,	4 30	4 40	Benzine	0
Dry Cod, ⅌ 112 ℔s..	5 00	5 25	*Powder:*			**Produce.**	
Fruits:			Blasting, Canada	3 50	0 00	*Grain:*	
Raisins, Layers	2 00	2 10	FF "	4 25	4 50	Wheat, Spring, 60 ℔..	1
" M. R	1 90	2 10	FFF "	4 75	5 00	" Fall 60 "..	1
" Valentias new	0 6½	0 07	Blasting, English "	4 0	5 00	Barley 48 "..	1
Currants, new	0 07	0 07½	FF loose	5 00	6 00	Peas 60 "..	0
" old	0 04½	0 04½	FFF "	6 00	6 50	Oats 34 "..	0
Figs	0 14	0 00	*Pressed Spikes (4 mos):*			Rye 56 "..	0
Molasses:			Regular sizes 100	4 00	4 25	*Seeds:*	
Clayed, ⅌ gal	0 00	0 35	Extra	4 50	5 00	Clover, choice 60 "..	6
Syrups, Standard	0 45	0 60	*Tin Plates (net cash):*			" com'n 60 "..	
" Golden	0 56	0 57½	IC Coke	5 50	8 50	Timothy, cho'e 48 "..	2
Rice:			IC Charcoal	8 25	8 50	" inf. to good 48 "..	2
Arracan	4 50	4 75	IX "	10 25	10 75	Flax 56 "..	1
Spices:			IXX "	14 25	0 00	*Flour (per bri.):*	
Cassia, whole, ⅌ ℔...	0 00	0 45	DC "	7 25	9 00	Superior extra	4
Cloves	0 11	0 12	DX "	9 50	0 00	Extra superfine	4
Nutmegs	0 45	0 55				Fancy superfine	4
Ginger, gr'nd	0 20	0 25	**Hides & Skins. ⅌ ℔**			Superfine No 1	4
" Jamaica, root..	0 09½	0 10	Green rough	0 06	0 00	" No. 2	0
Pepper, black	0 08	0 09	Green, salt'd & insp'd..	0 07	0 00	Oatmeal, (per brl.)..	0
Pimento	0 08	0 09	Cured	0 04	0 08½	**Provisions**	
Sugars:			Calfskins, green	0 00	0 1s	Butter, dairy tub ⅌ ℔..	0
Port Rico, ⅌ ℔	0 08½	0 08½	Calfskins, cured	0 00	0 12	" store packed...	0
Cuba	0 08½	0 08½	" dry	0 16	0 20	Cheese, new	0
Barbadoes (bright)..	0 08½	0 09	Sheepskins	1 00	1 25	Pork, mess, per bri..	0
Dry Crushed, at 60 d..	—	0 11½	" country	0 60	0 80	" prime mess..	0
Canada Sugar Refine'y,						" prime	0
yellow No. 2, 60 ds..	0 00	0 00½	**Hops.**			Bacon, rough	0
Yellow, No. 2½	0 09½	0 00	Inferior, ⅌ ℔	0 05	0 07	" Cumber'd cut...	0
" No. 3	0 09½	0 00	Medium	0 07	0 00	" smoked	0
Crushed X	0 00	0 10½	Good	0 09	0 12	Hams, in salt	0
" A	0 11½	0 11½	Fancy	0 00	0 00	" sug. cur & canv'sd	0
Ground	0 11½	0 11½				Lard, in kegs	0
Dry Crushed	0 11½	0 11½	**Leather, @ (4 mos.)**			Eggs, packed	0
Extra Ground	0 12½	0 12½	In lots of less than,			Beef Hams	0
Teas:			50 sides, 10 ⅌ cent			Tallow	0
Japan com'n to good..	0 40	0 55	higher.			Hogs dressed, heavy..	10
" fine to choicest..	0 55	0 65	Spanish Sole, 1st qual..	0 00	0 28	" medium..	
Colored, com. to fine..	0 60	0 70	heavy, weights ⅌ ℔..	0 00	0 28	" light...	
Congou & Souch'ng..	0 42	0 75	Do. 1st qual middle do..	0 00	0 27		
Oolong, good to fine..	0 50	0 65	Do. No. 2, all weights..	0 26	0 31	**Salt, &c.**	
Y. Hyson, com to gd..	0 45	0 55	Slaughter heavy	0 25	0 26	American bris	0
Medium to choice	0 65	0 60	Do. light	0 82	0 24	Liverpool coarse	0
Extra choice	0 85	0 95	Harness, best	0 30	0 33	Plaster	0
unpowd'rs. to med...	0 55	0 70	" No. 2	0 44	0 34	Water Lime	0
" med. to fine ..	0 70	0 85	Upper heavy	0 36	0 40		
			" light				

..ndles.		
..& Co.'s ..	$ c.	$ c.
....	0 07½	0 08
..ar	0 07	0 07½
..r........	0 07	0 07½
....	0 05	0 05½
....	0 03½	0 03½
....	0 00	0 11½
..quors,		
..doz.......	2 60	2 65
..b Portr..	2 35	2 40
..a Rum...	1 80	2 25
..H. Gin..	1 55	1 65
..Tom.....	1 90	2 00
....	4 00	4 25
..Tom, c...	6 00	6 25
..n.......	1 00	1 25
....	2 00	4 00
..non.....	1 00	1 50
..a	1 70	1 80
..golden..	2 50	4 00

Brandy:	$ c.	$ c
Hennessy's, per gal..	2 30	2 50
Martell's " ..	2 30	2 50
J. Robin & Co.'s " ..	2 25	2 35
Otard, Dupuy & Cos..	2 25	2 35
Brandy, cases.........	8 50	9 00
Brandy, com. per c...	4 00	4 50
Whiskey:		
Common 36 u. p......	0 62½	0 65
Old Rye	0 85	0 87½
Malt	0 85	0 87½
Toddy	0 85	0 87½
Scotch, per gal........	1 90	2 10
Irish—Kinnahan's c...	7 00	7 50
" Dunnville's Belf't..	6 00	6 25
Wool.		
Fleece, lb.............	0 28	0 35
Pulled "............	0 22	0 25
Furs.		
Bear.................	8 00	10 00
Beaver..............	1 00	1 25
Coon	0 20	0 40
Fisher..............	4 00	6 00
Martin..............	1 40	1 60
Mink................	4 00	4 25
Otter...............	5 75	6 00
Spring Rats.........	0 15	0 17
Fox.	1 20	1 25

..NSURANCE COMPANIES.

ENGLISH.—*Quotations on the London Market.*

Di-..nd.	Name of Company.	Shares parval £	Amount paid.	Last Sale.
	Briton Medical and General Life...	10	....	1¾
7½	Commer'l Union, Fire, Life and Mar.	50	5	5¾
3	City of Glasgow	25	2½	5⅝
0½	Edinburgh Life	100	15	31¾
½ yr	European Life and Guarantee......	2½	11s6	5s
)	Etna Fire and Marine.............	10	1½	0
5	Guardian	100	50	51
2	Imperial Fire....................	500	50	0
9½	Imperial Life	100	10	15½
)	Lancashire Fire and Life..........	20	2	2⅝
l	Life Association of Scotland.......	40	7½	25
). sh	London Assurance Corporation ..	25	12½	49
5	London and Lancashire Life	10	1	10s
)	Liverp'l & London & Globe F. & L.	20	2	6 15-16ths
5	National Union-Life	5	1	0
7½	Northern Fire and Life	100	5	11½
}	North British and Mercantile	50	6¼	19¾
	Ocean Marine	25	5	19¾
ls.	Provident Life..................	100	10	0
. s.	Phœnix.........................	....	....	148
yr.	Queen Fire and Life	10	1	17s
.4s	Royal Insurance.................	20	3	6
	Scottish Provincial Fire and Life ..	50	2½	5
	Standard Life	50	12	65½
	Star Life	25	1¼	—
	CANADIAN.			℘ c.
	British America Fire and Marine ..	$50	$25	53 54xd
	Canada Life	...	....	.....
	Montreal Assurance	£50	£5	135
	Provincial Fire and Marine........	60	11	.....
...	Quebec Fire	40	32½	25½
	" Marine....................	100	40	25 26
's.	Western Assurance...............	40	9	.....

RAILWAYS.	Sha's	Paid	Montr	London.
.. Lawrence....................	£100	All.	....	58 60
..ce Huron	20½	"	....	3 3½
do Preference	10	"	....	5½ 6½
Goderich, 6℘c.,1872-3-4....	100	"	....	65 69
St. Lawrence	....	....	10	....
do Pref. 10 ℘ ct....	....	....	73	....
....	100	"	15 16	15¾ 16
..q.G. M. Bds. 1 ch. 6℘c..........	100	"	....	84 86
First Preference, 5 ℘ c	100	"	....	50 51
Deferred, 3 ℘ ct..	100	"	....	....
Second Pref. Bonds, 5℘c..........	100	"	....	39½ 40½
do Deferred, 3 ℘ c...........	100	"	...	....
Third Pref. Stock, 4 ℘ct..........	100	"	....	26½ 27½
do. Deferred, 3 ℘ ct....	100	"	...	....
Fourth Pref. Stock, 3℘c...........	100	"	....	17¾ 18¼
do. Deferred, 3 ℘ ct...........	100	"	....	...
....	20½	"	13 14	14¼ 14¾
New	20½	18	....	....
6 ℘ c. Bds, due 1873-76...........	100	All.	....	99 101
5½℘c Bds. due 1877-78...	100	"	....	93 94
..y. Halifax, $250, all......	$250	"	....	....
..anada, 6℘c. 1st Pref. Bds..........	100	"	.. .	80 83

..NGE.	Halifax.	Montr'l.	Quebec.	Toronto.
..lon, 60 days......				
..ys date..........	12½	9½ 9¾	9½ 9¾	10
....	11½ 12	8 9	8¾ 9¼	9 9½
..ocuments........	....	7½ 8	....	....
..York............	....	25½ 26	25 25½	74¼
....	....	26 26½	25½ 26	....
....	....	½ dis. to p.	par ½ dis.	par ¼ dis.
....	....	4 4½	....	4 to 6

STOCK AND BOND REPORT.

The dates of our quotations are as follows:—Toronto, Feb. 2; Montreal, Feb. 2; Quebec, Feb. 1; London, Jan. 9.

NAME.	Shares.	Paid up.	Divid'd last 6 Months	Dividend Day.	CLOSING PRICES. Toronto.	Montre'l	Quebec.
BANKS.			℘ ct.				
British North America	$250	All.	3	July and Jan.	102 103	103	103 103½
Jacques Cartier.............	50	"	4	1 June, 1 Dec.	107 108	107½ 108	107 107½
Montreal	200	"	5	"	138½ 139½	138½ 139½	138 138½
Nationale..................	50	"	4	1 Nov. 1 May.	106 106½	106	106½ 107
New Brunswick	100	"	....	......	....	...	....
Nova Scotia	200	28	7&b$3½	Mar. and Sept.	....	....	....
Du Peuple......	50	"	4	1 Mar., 1 Sept.	109 110	109	109 110
Toronto	100	"	4	1 Jan., 1 July.	120 121	120	119 120
Bank of Yarmouth...........	....	....	......	......	....	....	....
Canadian Bank of Com'e......	50	95	......	......	102 102½	102 103	101 102
City Bank Montreal	80	All.	4	1 June, 1 Dec.	102 103	102 102½	102½ 102½
Commer'l Bank (St. John)....	100	"	℘ ct.	.....	....	...	....
Eastern Townships' Bank.....	50	"	4	1 July, 1 Jan..	....	98 99½	97½ 98½
Gore	40	...	none.	1 Jan., 1 July.	40 42	40 45	40 45
Halifax Banking Company....	...	....	......	.....	...	....	....
Mechanics' Bank...........	50	70	4	1 Nov., 1 May.	95 96	94 96	94 95
Merchants' Bank of Canada....	100	70	4	1 Jan., 1 July.	109 109½	109½ 109½	109¾ 110½
Merchants' Bank (Halifax)....	....	....	.....	.....	....	....	...
Molson's Bank......	50	All.	4	1 Apr., 1 Oct.	110 110½	110 110½	110 111
Niagara District Bank...	100	70	3½	1 Jan., 1 July.	...	....	....
Ontario Bank...............	40	All.	4	1 June, 1 Dec.	100 100½	99½ 100	99½ 100
People's Bank (Fred'kton)....	100	"	......	......	....	....	. ..
People's Bank (Halifax)	20	"	7 12 m	......	....	...	....
Quebec Bank	100	"	3½	1 June, 1 Dec.	99 100	....	99½ 99¾
Royal Canadian Bank	50	50	4	1 Jan., 1 July.	85½ 86	86 87	85 87
St. Stephens Bank	100	All	.....	......	....	..	....
Union Bank	100	70	4	1 Jan., 1 July.	103 103½	102 103	103½ 104½
Union Bank (Halifax)........	100	40	7 12mo	Feb. and Aug.	....	....	. . .
MISCELLANEOUS.							
British America Land........	250	44	2½	......	....	....	....
British Colonial S. S. Co......	250	32½	2½	......	...	....	....
Canada Company	32½	All.	£1 10s.	......	....	....	....
Canada Landed Credit Co......	50	$20	3½	......	72½ 75	....	....
Canada Per. B'ldg Society....	50	All.	5	......	123½ 124	....	....
Canada Mining Company.....	4	90	......	......	....	....	....
Do. Inl'd Steam Nav. Co.....	100	All.	20 12 m	......	....	104 105	105 106
Do. Glass Company.........	100	"	12½ "	......	....	...	....
Canad'n Loan & Investm't....	25	2½	7	......	....	...	....
Canada Agency	10	½	......	......	....	....	....
Colonial Securities Co.........	...	....	......	......	....	....	....
Freehold Building Society....	100	All.	4	......	109 109½	....	....
Halifax Steamboat Co........	100	"	5	......	....	....	....
Halifax Gas Company........	....	....	......	......	....	....	....
Hamilton Gas Company......	....	....	......	......	....	...	....
Huron Copper Bay Co........	4	12	20	......	....	25 40cps	....
Lake Huron S. and C..........	5	102	......	......	....	...	....
Montreal Mining Consols.....	20	$15	......	......	....	3.00 3.10	...
Do. Telegraph Co...	40	All.	5	......	134 136	133 135	135 136
Do. Elevating Co...	00	"	15 12 m	......	....	100 102½	....
Do. City Gas Co.........	40	"	4	15 Mar. 15 Sep.	....	137½ 138	136 137
Do. City Pass. R.. Co.....	50	"	5	......	....	110½ 111½	110½ 111
Nova Scotia Telegraph	20	"	....	.....	....	....	....
Quebec and L. S.	8	$4	......	......	.. ..	....	25 cts
Quebec Gas Co...............	200	All.	4	1 Mar., 1 Sep.	....	...	119 120
Quebec Street R. R...........	50	25	8	......	....	.....	90 91
Richelieu Navigation Co......	100	All.	7 p.a.	1 Jan., 1 July.	....	116 118	116 117
St. Lawrence Tow Boat Co.....	100	"	......	3 Feb.	...	...	35 40
Tor'to Consumers' Gas Co.....	50	"	2 3 m.	1 My Au Mar Fe	107 108	...	107 108
Trust & Loan Co. of U. C.....	20	5	3	......	....	....	.. .
West'n Canada Bldg Soc'y....	50	All.	5	......	117 118	....	....

SECURITIES.	London.	Montreal.	Quebec.	Toronto.
Canadian Gov't Deb. 6 ℘ ct. stg..................	...	105	102½ 103	104 106
Do. do. 6 do due Ja. & Jul. 1877-84..........	106½ 107½	....	....	....
Do. do. 6 do. Feb. & Aug..........	105 107	....	.. .	....
Do. do. 6 do. Mch. & Sep..........	104 106	.. .	...	... .
Do. do. 5 ℘ ct. cur., 1883	95 96	95	93 93½	94½ 95
Do. do. 5 do. stg., 1885	94 96	94½ 95½	93 93½	95 95½
Do. do. 7 do. cur.,......................	....	....	......	....
Dominion 6 p. c. 1878 cy.....	....	105	104½ 105½	105 105½
Hamilton Corporation.....	....	....	.....	....
Montreal Harbor, 8 ℘ ct. d. 1869..................	..	....	......	....
Do. do. 7 do. 1870...................	....	....	......	....
Do. do. 6½ do. 1883...................	....	100 101	......	....
Do. do. 6½ do. 1873...................	....	....	......	....
Do. Corporation, 6 ℘ c. 1891	....	95 96	94½ 95½	95 96
Do. 7 p. c. stock..............................	....	108	110 110½	107½ 108½
Do. Water Works, 6 ℘ c. stg. 1878.......... ..	....	....	......	95 96
Do. do. 6 do. cy. do.	....	95½ 96½	......	95 96
New Brunswick, 6 ℘ ct., Jan. and July	104 106	....	......	....
Nova Scotia, 6 ℘ ct., 1875........................	104 106	....	......	....
Ottawa City 6 ℘ c. d. 1880	....	92½ 83½	......	...
Quebec Harbour, 6 ℘ c. d. 1883.	....	....	60	....
Do. do. 7 do. do........................	....	....	65 70	....
Do. do. 8 do. 1886.....................	....	....	80 85	....
Do. City, 7 ℘ c. d. 4½ years....	....	....	96 97	....
Do. do. 7 do. 9 do.	....	....	91 92	....
Do. do. 7 do. 2 do.	....	....	98 98½	....
Do. Water Works, 7 ℘ ct., 4 years	....	....	97 97½	....
Do. do. 6 do. 2 do.	....	....	94 95	....
Toronto Corporation	87½ 92½	....	....	....

Insurance.

BEAVER
Mutual Insurance Association.

HEAD OFFICE—20 TORONTO STREET,
TORONTO.

INSURES LIVE STOCK against death from any cause. The only Canadian Company having authority to do this class of business.

R. L. DENISON,
President.
W. T. O'REILLY,
Secretary.   8-1y-25

HOME DISTRICT
Mutual Fire Insurance Company.

Office—North-West Cor. Yonge & Adelaide Streets,
TORONTO.—(UP STAIRS.)

INSURES Dwelling Houses, Stores, Warehouses, Merchandise, Furniture, &c.

PRESIDENT—The Hon. J. McMURRICH.
VICE-PRESIDENT—JOHN BURNS, Esq.
JOHN RAINS, Secretary.
AGENTS:
DAVID WRIGHT, Esq., Hamilton; FRANCIS STEVENS, Esq., Barrie; Messrs. GIBBS & BRO., Oshawa.   8-1y

---

THE PRINCE EDWARD COUNTY
Mutual Fire Insurance Company.

HEAD OFFICE,—PICTON, ONTARIO.
President, L. B. STINSON; Vice-President, W. A. RICHARDS.

Directors: H. A. McFaul, James Cavan, James Johnson, N. S. DeMill, William Delong.—Treasurer, David Barker Secretary, John Twigg; Solicitor, R. J. Fitzgerald.

THIS Company is established upon strictly Mutual principles, insuring farming and isolated property, (not hazardous,) in Townships only, and offers great advantages to insurers, at low rates for five years, without the expense of a renewal.
Picton, June 15, 1868.   9-1y

Hartford Fire Insurance Company.
HARTFORD, CONN.

Cash Capital and Assets over Two Million Dollars.

$2,026,220.29.

CHARTERED 1810.

THIS old and reliable Company, having an established business in Canada of more than thirty years standing, has complied with the provisions of the new Insurance Act, and made a special deposit of

$100,000

with the Government for the security of policy-holders, and will continue to grant policies upon the same favorable terms as heretofore.

Specially low rates on first-class dwellings and farm property for a term of one or more years.

Losses as heretofore promptly and equitably adjusted.
H. J. MORSE & Co., AGENTS.
Toronto, Ont.

ROBERT WOOD, GENERAL AGENT FOR CANADA]
50-6m

THE AGRICULTURAL
Mutual Assurance Association of Canada.

HEAD OFFICE . . . . LONDON, ONT.

A purely Farmers' Company. Licensed by the Government of Canada.

Capital, 1st January, 1868 . . . . $220,121 2
Cash and Cash Items, over $45,000 0
No. of Policies in force 28,700

THIS Company insures nothing more dangerous than Farm property. Its rates are as low as any well-established Company in the Dominion, and lower than those of a great many. It is largely patronised, and continues to grow in public favor.
For Insurance, apply to any of the Agents or address the Secretary, London, Ontario.
London, 2nd Nov., 1868.   13-1y

The Gore District Mutual Fire Insurance Company

GRANTS INSURANCES on all description of Property against Loss or Damage by FIRE. It is the only Mutual Fire Insurance Company which assesses its Policies yearly from their respective dates; and the average yearly cost of insurance in it, for the past three and a half years, has been nearly

TWENTY CENTS IN THE DOLLAR

less than what it would have been in an ordinary Proprietary Company.
THOS. M. SIMONS,
Secretary & Treasurer.
ROBT. McLEAN,
Inspector of Agencies.
Galt, 25th Nov., 1868.   15-1y

Geo. Girdlestone,

FIRE, Life, Marine, Accident, and Stock Insurance Agent

Very best Companies represented.
Windsor, Ont. June, 1868

The Standard Life Assurance Company,
Established 1825.
WITH WHICH IS NOW UNITED
THE COLONIAL LIFE ASSURANCE COMPANY.

Head Office for Canada:
MONTREAL—STANDARD COMPANY'S BUILDINGS,
No. 47 GREAT ST. JAMES STREET.
Manager—W. M. RAMSAY.   Inspector—RICH'D BULL.

THIS Company having deposited the sum of ONE HUNDRED AND FIFTY THOUSAND DOLLARS with the Receiver-General, in conformity with the Insurance Act passed last Session, Assurances will continue to be carried out at moderate rates and on all the different systems in practice.

AGENT FOR TORONTO—HENRY PELLATT,
King Street.

AGENT FOR HAMILTON—JAMES BANCROFT.
6-6mos.

Fire and Marine Assurance.

THE BRITISH AMERICA
ASSURANCE COMPANY.
HEAD OFFICE:
CORNER OF CHURCH AND COURT STREETS.
TORONTO.

BOARD OF DIRECTION:
Hon G. W. Allan, M.L.C.,   A. Joseph, Esq.,
George J Boyd, Esq,   Peter Paterson, Esq.,
Hon W. Cayley,   G. P. Ridout, Esq.,
Richard S. Cassels, Esq.,   E H. Rutherford, Esq.,
          Thomas C. Street, Esq.,
Governor:
GEORGE PERCIVAL RIDOUT, Esq.
Deputy Governor:
PETER PATERSON, Esq.
Fire Inspector: Marine Inspector:
E ROBY O'BRIEN.   CAPT. R. COURNEEN.

Insurances granted on all descriptions of property against loss and damage by fire and the perils of inland navigation.

Agencies established in the principal cities, towns, and ports of shipment throughout the Province.
THOS. WM BIRCHALL,
23-1y   Managing Director.

Queen Fire and Life Insurance Company,
OF LIVERPOOL AND LONDON,

ACCEPTS ALL ORDINARY FIRE RISKS
on the most favorable terms.

LIFE RISKS

Will be taken on terms that will compare favorably with other Companies.

CAPITAL,   -   -   -   £2,000,000 Stg.

CHIEF OFFICES—Queen's Buildings, Liverpool, and Gracechurch Street London.
CANADA BRANCH OFFICE—Exchange Buildings, Montreal.
Resident Secretary and General Agent,

A. MACKENZIE FORBES,
13 St. Sacrament St., Merchants' Exchange, Montreal.
WM. ROWLAND, Agent, Toronto.   1-1y

The Waterloo County Mutual Fire In Company.

HEAD OFFICE: WATERLOO, ONTARIO

ESTABLISHED 1863.

THE business of the Company is divided separate and distinct branches, the
VILLAGE, FARM, AND MANUFAC

Each Branch paying its own losses and its just of the managing expenses of the Company.
C. M. TAYLOR, Sec.   M. SPRINGER, M.M.
J. HUGHES, Inspector.

Etna Fire and Marine Insurance Con Dublin.

AT a Meeting of the Shareholders of this held at Dublin, on the 13th ult., it was a the business of the "ETNA" should be transfer "UNITED PORTS AND GENERAL INSURANCE In accordance with this agreement, the business after be carried on by the latter Company, which and guarantees all the risks and liabilities of the The Directors have resolved to continue the BRANCH, and arrangements for resuming FIRE RINE business are rapidly approaching complet
16   T. W. GRIF
M

The Commercial Union Assu Company,
19 & 20 CORNHILL, LONDON, ENGLAND
Capital, £2,500,000 Stg—Invested over £2,0

FIRE DEPARTMENT—Insurance granted scriptions of property at reasonable rates.

LIFE DEPARTMENT—The success of th has been unprecedented—NINETY PER CEN miums now in hand. First year's premiums $100,000. Economy of management guaranteed security. Moderate rates.
OFFICE—385 & 387 ST PAUL STREET, MON
MORLAND, WATSON, General Agents f
FRED. COLE, Secretary.
Inspector of Agencies—T. C. LIVINGST
W. M. WESTMACOTT, Agent at
16-1y

Lancashire Insurance Com

CAPITAL, - - - - - - - - £2,000,0

FIRE RISKS
Taken at reasonable rates of premium
ALL LOSSES SETTLED PROMPT
By the undersigned, without reference e
S. C. DUNCAN-CLARK & C
General Agents for On
N. W. Corner of King & Churc
25-1y   TORONTO.

Etna Fire & Marine Insurance Co

INCORPORATED 1819.   CHARTER PERPET

CASH CAPITAL,   -   -   -

LOSSES PAID IN 50 YEARS, 23,500,

JULY, 1868.
(At Market Value.)
ASSETS.
Cash in hand and in Bank . . . .
Real Estate . . . .
Mortgage Bonds . . . .
Bank Stock . . . .
United States, State and City Stock, and other
   Public Securities . . . .

Total . . . . $

LIABILITIES.
Claims not Due, and Unadjusted . . . .
Amount required by Mass. and New York
   for Re-Insurance . . . .
THOS. R. WO
50-6   Agent fo

PUBLISHED AT THE OFFICE OF THE TIMES, No. 60 CHURCH STREE
PRINTED AT THE DAILY TELEGRAPH PRINTI
BAY STREET, CORNER OF KING.

THE CANADIAN

MONETARY TIMES AND INSURANCE CHRONICLE.

THE Publishers have pleasure in announcing that the success of this JOURNAL has been such as to stimulate their efforts to render it still more valuable to the classes directly and indirectly interested in the subjects with which it deals. As the only Journal in the minion which gives particular attention to INSURANCE, it has enlisted the hearty support of Insurance Companies; and while, on one hand, it contends for the rights of such Companies, it equally recognizes the rights of the public.

The subject of BANKING has become of such importance, as well by reason of past legislation as by reason of anticipated changes in law respecting circulation, that it is the duty and interest of our business men to make themselves acquainted with the principles which sound Banking rests, and to prevent any action on the part of the Legislature likely to injure the community by lessening usefulness of our banks. The discussion of this subject in the columns of this JOURNAL has called forth expressions of satisfaction m our most astute financiers, and has done much to give us the position we now occupy in the estimation of the public.

As MINING is in its infancy in this country, a journal devoted solely to the subject could not hope to thrive; but by giving full ormation regarding Mining operations, and by the employment of reliable correspondents, we have done good service to an important erest, and secured recognition from a class which, otherwise, could not have been reached.

Our purely COMMERCIAL DEPARTMENT has not been neglected, and each week's summary, while concise and pithy, has answered the ie ends as a more diffuse elaboration could do, and conveyed to country dealers a complete synopsis of the changes in the Toronto and ntreal Markets.

This combination of interests which the circumstances of the country render necessary, has been of the greatest advantage to each erest by diffusing information among all classes; but, in order to do justice to all, we have been compelled to employ a large staff of ters, and to expend a considerable amount in securing trustworthy correspondents.

While we are thankful to those who have encouraged us thus far, we are anxious to extend still further the usefulness of this Journal, l we call on all who consider that the enterprise is worthy of support, to lend us their assistance in making the MONETARY TIMES a ional organ.

On our part we promise impartiality, efficiency, and the best efforts of the ablest writers that can be secured in the Dominion. On part of our clients, we expect a cordial support and active exertion to widen our sphere of usefulness. In helping us, they help nselves.

Every Merchant, Banker, Capitalist, Insurance Agent, and Broker, can aid us, and we hope that we are not asking too much, in iciting their assistance.

We shall be happy to receive at any time articles on subjects within our jurisdiction, which, if used, will be liberally paid for.

Subscription Price..$2 per Annum.

A reasonable discount will be made to Banks, Insurance Companies, &c., which subscribe for their Agencies.
SEND FOR A SPECIMEN COPY.
N.B.—Every subscriber to THE MONETARY TIMES will receive THE REAL ESTATE JOURNAL without further charge.

THE REAL ESTATE JOURNAL.

The objects of this Journal are as follows :—

(1.) To supply to those interested in real estate such information as is of special interest relating to sales or transfers of real pro-ty in the principal cities, and throughout Ontario, construction of public works, and building improvements of every kind, increase or rease of municipal expenditure, debt and taxation, and, in short, whatever tends to influence the real estate market.

(2.) Leading articles will be furnished by competent writers on questions relating to conveyancing, the rise and fall of property, land its, emigration, and other subjects coming within the legitimate scope of the Journal.

(3.) Lists of lands and houses for sale in every city, town and village of the Province, will appear in its columns, giving buyers the possible opportunities for selecting desirable properties of any class, and in any locality ; and, at the same time, affording sellers a ble and certain medium for reaching intending purchasers.

(4.) By a circulation extending into every corner of Canada, the announcements of advertisers will be brought to the notice of an ense constituency of readers. A special feature in this connection is, that the Journal will be placed and kept on fyle at all the prin-l hotels, reading rooms, and other public places in Ontario, and in Montreal. By these means it is confidently believed that every s in the community will be reached.

HE REAL ESTATE JOURNAL is printed fortnightly, on good white paper, in quarto form, and is equal in size and appearance to anything ie kind published on this continent.

Advertising, per line of nonpareil, each insertion, 5 cents. A small discount will be allowed on yearly contracts, for large spaces. Address, "THE REAL ESTATE JOURNAL," Toronto, Ontario. Cheques should be made payable to J. M. TROUT, who will issue all receipts for money.

OFFICE, No. 60 CHURCH STREET,
TORONTO, ONTARIO.

PROSPECTUS OF THE

ONTARIO PEAT COMP'Y

LIMITED LIABILITY. - - - - - - **HEAD OFFICE—TORONTO.**

To be Organized under the Act 27 and 28 Victoria, Chapter 23, and the Amendments thereto.

THE property of the company forms a portion of the well-known "Cranberry Marsh," in the Townships of Humberstone and Wainfleet, Cou Welland, and Province of Ontario, traversed by the Welland Canal, as well as by its "Feeder," which is also navigable ; and is composed following lots, viz. :—

	Acres.
Humberstone—South halves of 28, 30, 82 and 33. Concession IV	400
Wainfleet—South halves of 6 and 7, Concession IV	200
" Whole of 10, Concession II, and the whole of 10 and 11, Concession III	600
" Parts of 8 and 9, Concessions IV. and V., about	200
Total	1400

A main ditch six feet deep has been made by the County through the whole of this Marsh for surface drainage, at an expenditure of $50,000 this ditch runs along a portion of every one of the above lots, except two which abut upon the feeder of the Welland Canal.

The several lots above enumerated were the first chosen from the Marsh, having been selected for their great value as Peat Deposits. remaining Peat lands have been obtained by the Anglo-American Peat Company, which has been operating most successfully during the past upon a lot adjoining one of the Company's lots. A most satisfactory report has been obtained from Frederick Holmes, Esq., the County Engin gentleman who has had large experience in these peat lands, having not only surveyed and laid off the Marsh into lots for the County, but has als employed as superintendent in the ditching operations which have been undertaken and carried out through the whole extent of the Marsh. estimate of the quantity of Peat contained in the Company's lands is placed at three millions of tons, at the very least ; and this estimate is fully out by the eminent firm of Messrs. Macdougall and Skae, Civil Engineers, Toronto, who were specially despatched to make a personal examinat the property, and whose report is subjoined.

Peat can be laid down on the banks of the canal at the cost of from $1 to $1.25 per ton, and can from thence be forwarded by water to market directions, at small cost, and without transhipment ; to say nothing of the facilities and advantages afforded by no less than five railways, one of the "Buffalo and Lake Huron," passes within twenty chains of the property. In addition to these advantages, the fact may be noticed, that thirty vessels pass through the canal every day during the season of navigation, the steamers requiring fuel for their own use, and the sailing seeking cargoes, and requiring ballast westward to Chicago and other points.

The demand for this fuel for private consumption will be very great when its superior qualities become more widely known. Already railwa steamers are beginning to use it instead of wood and coal, with the most satisfactory results, experience having proved that one ton of peat is e about one and one-third cords of the best hard wood. With a view to the full and proper development of this property, it is proposed to organ Company with a capital of $120,000, in 2,400 shares of $50 each ; $50,000 of this sum to be retained by the Directors for working capital, the bala be applied to the purchase of the real estate. It is also proposed that 25 per cent shall be paid at the time of subscription, and the balance in c 10 per cent at such times as the Directors may name, but not oftener than once in every three months, from 1st of January, 1869.

The affairs of the Company will be managed by a Board of five Directors, the first set to be provisional, and, as soon as the charter is obtaine the Company organized, the permanent Directors to be chosen by the Shareholders, and to be elected annually.

The principal office of the Company to be in the City of Toronto. The property has been conveyed to Peleg Howland, Esquire, who will h same in trust until the Company is organized

PROVISIONAL DIRECTORS.

HENRY S. HOWLAND, Esquire, Toronto.   JOHN FISKEN, Esquire, Toronto.   LARRATT W. SMITH, Esquire, Toronto.
ALFRED TODD, Esquire, Ottawa.   EDWARD A. C. PEW, Esquire, Welland.
Further information can be obtained at the office of

C. J. CAMPBELL, Esq., Banker, 92 King Street East, Toront
Who will act as Provisional Treasurer, and will also receive subscriptions for

CHAMBERS, 17 TORONTO STREET, TORONTO, JANUARY 11, 186

To the Directors of the Ontario Peat Company,—

GENTLEMEN,—We have the honor to lay before you the following report, on the Peat Beds in the Great Cranberry Marsh, situated in the of Welland. The swamp, or to call it by a more proper name, moor, for it is more like the moors of Scotland than the swamp to this coun could be made available for drainage purposes. The moor rises gradually from its northern limit in concession 4, to its summit, at the south concession 3, about four feet on two and a half miles, where it is about eight feet above the level of Lake Erie ; while, on the north, from the end moor to the Welland River, distant about a mile and a half, there is a fall of sixteen feet. Following the course of the water through the drains, the result arrived at is, that the moor is higher than the surrounding country, which is under cultivation.

The peat on this marsh, brought up by the boring rods, as well as that lying on the sides of the drains, thrown up when they were made, good quality of a dark black color, in every lot. There is a layer of red peat in some of the lots of the Township of Humberstone; but genera peat was of the dark colour above mentioned. The surface of the marsh, or moor, has been burnt once or twice, so that there is not much moss o growth, nor are there many trees alive ; and on the lots owned by your company this is more marked. The lots are conveniently placed for w and connections could be formed, at a small cost, to the several outlets that surround this tract of land ; and the surface being regular, no di would be encountered in laying tramroads.

In making the borings for this report, the valuable assistance of the County Engineer, Mr. Frederick Holmes, was obtained, as he had experi the making of the drains, and had laid out several of the lots some years ago, and since that time had been intimately acquainted with the moo depths arrived at give an average of six to eight feet of peat over all the lots in the 3rd and 4th concessions, while in the lot of the 2nd con of the Township of Wainfleet, the peat is very deep, averaging about 15 feet, and it is said to go even deeper. There are 200 acres in this lot.

The regularity of the upper surface of this large tract of land, both peat and arable, being combined with the result of the borings taken, t conclusion that the bottom of the peat bed must also be regular, as there are no hills or mounds of any size or consequence in the vicinity.

The Anglo-American Peat Fuel Company have been at work during last summer on a portion of this marsh, opposite to some of the lots ow your Company. They find the loss, by weight and shrinkage to be 75 per cent. ; or to make one ton of peat fuel, four tons of peat are required is less than that of a similar project in the Lower Province, where the shrinkage is 85 per cent.

From the data and experience of the Anglo-American Company, taking the loss by weight and shrinkage at 75 per cent., with an average six to eight feet over all the lots, but that in the 5th Concession of Wainfleet, which is taken at sixteen feet, we find the property of your Co situated in the marsh, to be capable of producing over 3,000,000 tons of fuel.

A fuller report, by us, lies in the hands of Mr. C. J. Campbell, Banker, King Street, Toronto, to which also we beg to call your attention.

We have the honour to be, gentlemen, your obedient servants,

MACDOUGALL & SKAE.
CIVIL Eye

THE CANADIAN

[ONETARY TIMES

AND

INSURANCE CHRONICLE.

'TED TO FINANCE, COMMERCE, INSURANCE, BANKS, RAILWAYS, NAVIGATION, MINES, INVESTMENT, PUBLIC COMPANIES, AND JOINT STOCK ENTERPRISE.

—NO. 26.   TORONTO, THURSDAY, FEBRUARY 11, 1869.   { SUBSCRIPTION 82 YEAR.

Mercantile.

Meetings.

CANADA PERMANENT BUILDING AND SAVINGS SOCIETY.

The fourteenth annual meeting of the Canada Permanent Building and Savings Society was held at the Society's offices, Masonic Hall, Toronto, on Wednesday, Feb. 10th.

The President, Joseph D. Ridout, Esq., upon taking the chair, said that he had only to repeat what it had been his pleasant duty to say upon every preceding occasion of the kind—that the affairs of the Society were in a very flourishing condition. Hitherto, in referring to the Society, he had refrained from speaking strongly about the great success which had attended it, because he was unwilling unduly to emphasize a state of things which might possibly appear less favorable at some subsequent period ; but now that the So. ciety had been working for fourteen years, with continually increasing prosperity and credit; that a good dividend had been distributed each half-year ; that a reserve fund had been created, which pretty nearly assured their ability to do so through all time to come ; that the Society had been placed at the very highest point in public estima. tion, and that, altogether, more had been accom:: plished than any experienced and reasonable per. son would have ventured to predict, he felt war. ranted in speaking of it in the strongest terms which he could find, not only and merely as a success, but as a great, brilliant, and triumphant success. He considered it proper to add in ac. knowledgment to those who have been mainly in. strumental in achieving this success ; that it was the result of extreme care, good judgment, great labour, fidelity and solicitude on the part of the directors, the executive, the solicitor, and every member of the staff in every department of the institution. Some seasonable modifications in the practice of business, to meet the varying condi. tion and circumstances of the country generally, had been made, under the recommendation of their always watchful and active Secretary and Treasurer, by which the Society had been popu. larized throughout the length and breadth of the Province.

In performing his duty of introducing the gen. tlemen present to the business of the day upon such occasions, he considered a few comprehensive observations would be sufficient for him to address to them (the shareholders), as the whole story of the Society's position had been particularly nar. rated in its several reports; and he would, there. fore, submit the Directors report for the year, and hesitated not to say that a more interesting or satisfactory one had never been read before any society which had ever been established in the Province.

CANADA PERMANENT BUILDING AND SAVINGS SOCIETY.

REPORT OF THE DIRECTORS FOR 1868.

Following the recognised usage of this and other corporate institutions, in presenting to the shareholders the audited statements of the trans. actions of the past year, and of the present posi. tion of the institution, the Directors desire to re. fer briefly to the more prominent facts developed by the business of the year. This task is, on the present occasion, made a very agreeable one by the circumstance that not only have the expecta. tions which the previous history of the society warranted, been fulfilled, but that all the most gratifying features of the preceding year's report have been remarkably improved upon.

The Directors note with satisfaction the gener. ally prosperous condition of the agricultural inter. ests of the Province, as indicated by the enhanced value of farming land, the greater frequency of loans being required to assist in purchasing, and in making improvements thereon, and in the general punctuality with which their annual in. stalments of principal and interest have been paid by this class of borrowers. And in this connec. tion it may be observed, as a matter for congratu. lation, that with an aggregate of more than three thousand loans now upon the Society's books, so few cases have occurred during the year in which the aid of the Society's solicitor has been required to enforce compliance with obligations on the part of mortgagors, thus affording the best evi. dence of the care exercised in the past in making investments, and of the desire of the Society's customers to maintain their credit with the insti. tution.

The cash receipts for the year closely approach one million of dollars. The whole of this large sum was readily disposed of in fulfilling applica. tions for loans, and in meeting current require. ments. The demand for the Society's funds upon ample securities has been most active, and during the past few months has taxed to 'the utmost the ordinary resources of the Society to supply. The number of loans made was 824, amounting to $592,000, as compared with 585, amounting to $481,000 in the previous year.

The capital of the Society is now nearly all paid up, and before another annual meeting the whole of the remaining accumulating shares will have matured, thus placing all the shares of investing members upon the same footing.

After providing for the payment of the half-yearly dividend of five per cent. each upon the capital stock, and for an enlargement of the con. tingent fund proportioned to the increased amount of the Society's securities, the profits made have allowed of the allotment of eleven per cent. per annum to the accumulating shares, and of an ad. dition of one per cent. upon the capital stock. to the reserve fund, which now amounts to the im. portant sum of $100,264. The policy of setting aside a portion of the realised profits for the pur. pose of establishing a well guarded reserve fund, which this Society several years ago adopted, has received general and unqualified approval, as is shown in the unprecedented price that is paid for its stock when offered for sale.

As in the preceding year, the Savings Bank branch exhibits an increase of one-third upon the whole amount previously held, and the num. ber of accounts open with depositors has increased f.om 965 to 1,055.

In conclusion, the Directors have only to ex. press the hope that the high degree of prosperity which has hitherto distinguished this institution may characterise its future progress.

All which is respectfully submitted,

       JOSEPH D. RIDOUT,
           President.
J. HERBERT MASON,
   Secretary and Treasurer.

FINANCIAL STATEMENT.

RECEIPTS.

Balance 1st January, 1868............$	57,030	29
Instalments on mortgages............	510,675	27
Instalments on investing shares.....	22,934	18
Deposits..................................	361,021	15
Principal and interest on special investments........................	48,693	05
	$1,000,353	94

EXPENDITURE.

Advances secured by mortgages upon real estate	560,143	89
Advances secured by mortgages upon Society's stock	33,190	00
Deposits repaid and interest.........	248,953	72
Shares purchased and cancelled......	4,362	47
Shares paid off at maturity..........	7,650	00
Accumulated profits on matured shares	22,733	96
Dividends on capital stock...........	76,394	96
Vote of general meeting to the President..............................	1,600	00
Vote of general meeting to the Directors............................	780	00
Incidental expenses—including rent, taxes, salaries, printing, stationery, advertising, etc............	11,644	46
Agency and travelling expenses......	2,242	59
Disbursements on account of mortgages............................	16,657	21
Office furniture........................	218	75
Legal expenses.........................	29	43
Balance................................	13,842	50
	$1,000,353	94

General Abstract of Assets and Liabilities.

GENERAL LIABILITIES.

Deposits and interest thereon........	$565,187	37
Sundry accounts........................	1,970	12

LIABILITIES TO MEMBERS.

Capital stock.............$879,550 00		
Accumulating stock... 137,543 00		
Matured shares. 1,200 00		
	1,018,293	00
Payments in advance and interest thereon....	54,597	05
Permanent stock reserve...............	100,264	93
Contingent fund	50,000	00
Dividends unclaimed...................	1,676	64
Seventeenth dividend declared......	42,959	32
Profit and loss—being equal to 11 per cent. per annum, compounded half-yearly on the accumulating stock	31,275	28
	$1,866,223	52

ASSETS.

Mortgages upon real estate..........$1,813,169 00		
Mortgages upon Society's stock...... 23,621 79		
Special investments, debentures, etc. 6,449 00		
Unpaid instalments on investing shares 3,490 57		
Office fixtures and furniture......... 650 00		
Cash on hand............ $393 08		
Cash in Bank of Toronto. 7,217 66		
Cash in Bank of Montreal 3,979 05		
Cash in Royal Canadian Bank...... .... 2,252 71		
	13,842	50
	$1,866,223	52

J. HERBERT MASON,
Secretary and Treasurer.

We, the undersigned, have respectfully to report the completion of our audit for the year ending 31st December, 1868, and have much pleasure in certifying to the correctness of the above statement. We cannot close our report without congratulating the stockholders on the satisfactory manner in which the duties of the office are carried on by your energetic Secretary and Treasurer and the other officers in the establishment.

W. B. PHIPPS, HENRY PELLATT,
Auditors.

Toronto, Feb. 8, 1869.

The four retiring Directors, Messrs. Joseph D. Ridout, Peter Paterson, Samuel Nordheimer, and Joseph Robinson were unanimously re-elected.

PORT HOPE, LINDSAY AND BEAVERTON RAILROAD BOARD.—At the annual meeting of the bond and stockholders of the Port Hope, Lindsay and Beaverton Railroad, held on the 19th inst., the following gentlemen were elected officers for the current year: President, Henry Covert, Esq.; Vice Presidents, William Cluxton; Solicitors, John Sidney Smith, Lewis Moffatt, D'Arcy Boulton; General Superintendent, A. T. Williams; Secretary and Treasurer, Joseph Gray.

The following resolutions were unanimously passed at the meeting: Moved by H. Covert, seconded by D'Arcy E. Boulton—Resolved, That the stockholders have heard with great satisfaction the report of A. T. Williams, Esq., General Superintendent, and they feel it would not be doing justice to that excellent officer, and the others associated with him in the management of the road and its affairs, if they did not acknowledge by resolution their gratitude for the efforts put forth, and the eminently satisfactory results which have followed. The stockholders also take this opportunity of conveying to the Secretary their grateful acknowledgements for the manner in which he has discharged the duties appertaining to his office, and for the clear and satisfactory manner in which the accounts and statements have always been submitted.

Moved by D. E. Boulton, seconded by the Hon. Sidney Smith—Resolved, That the thanks of this meeting be conveyed to the Auditor, John Smart, Esq., for his clear and satisfactory report.

COBOURG GAS WORKS.—At the annual meeting of shareholders on Monday evening last, the following gentlemen were elected directors for the ensuing year: A. Fraser, Esq., M.P.P., Dr. Beatty, A. Hewson, Esq., W. H. Weller, Esq., and W. H. Floyd, Esq.

Insurance.

INSURANCE MATTERS IN NEW YORK.

(From our own Correspondent.)

NEW YORK, February 4th, 1868.

To the Editor of the Monetary Times.

The present month—indeed the past fortnight —has been remarkable for the mildest weather remembered in this city by the "oldest inhabitant." This fact is, under the present social and business status, a most merciful dispensation. It cannot be denied that the present season is one of real suffering among the poor of this city. While the number of them increases from obvious causes, their source of life—viz., labor, diminishes. A larger number of the mechanic and laboring classes are out of employment, and, with many others, wages are at starvation prices. This fact explains the strikes among printers, bricklayers, tailors, and other trades, now disturbing the cities industries. It also explains, in part, the extraordinary flood of crime which has come upon us. The feeling of law-abiding citizens has been roused to the highest pitch, and even the suggestion of a vigilance committee, openly and repeatedly made. The two extremes of society seem for the nonce to have met on a common criminal platform; and Wall street swindlers are as unblushing, if not as dangerous to life, as the side street burglars. The press deplores the low moral tone prevailing insecurity to person and property, and the efficiency of the police ; but it is not easy to find a remedy. This is not a cheerful picture of the metropolis, but it is too true, nevertheless.

The present financial aspect is decidedly "Governments maintain themselves, and the demand, even improves. R. R. Stocks are active ; money is active for speculative purposes, but the general commercial condition is one of exceeding dullness. The sensation of the hour is the expulsion of Erie from the stock board. The stock has sunk so low that it can only be had on the curb-stone—a great corporation ruined by stock gambling.

Upon the usually quiet surface of the insurance world we scarcely discern a ruffle—yet the current is sometimes strong. The reports of life companies are not due at the Insurance department until first March, and any speculation as to the probable character of them would be less. The writer has interrogated officers of all prominent life companies, and they have rally assured him that their companies' returns for the year would shew an improvement over... We can only hope that such will prove to be the case ; but the writer is apprehensive that much of the new business, especially among new companies, will be found to have cost more than it is worth.

In the competition which grows out of the claims of the "mutual" "mixed" and "stock" companies, those which believe they have fairly liberal charters not only trumpet them but, in various ways, seek to disparage their rivals. Some time since Mr. Joseph B. Ecclesine, editor of the Underwriter, conceived the commendable idea of publishing a chart which should give a comparative view of the principle features in the charter of each company. The stockholders, of the Knickerbocker, were represented as entitled to ten per cent. of the profits, besides an interest dividend on the capital. Such a statement could company no good, just now, when the new plan is, undoubtedly, in most favor with the public. President Lyman, of the Knickerbocker made haste to deny the correctness of Mr. Ecclesine's chart in the Post—a long controversy followed, the result being that Mr. Ecclesine just been arrested on complaint of the Knickerbocker for libel—gave the usual bail—and on the trial we shall, doubtless, have some sharp talk designed to shew up, or clear, the merits of one or that "plan."

One of our most respectable literary weeklies, the Nation—not long since showed its ignorance of life insurance by declaring that the expenses of all the life companies were rapidly destroying the reserve. More recently another of these, the Round Table—devoted a slurring column to the abuse of the offices generally ; while the New York Herald has insinuated, during the past week, its doubts as to the ability of our life companies to pay claims due in the future. This record of undeniable good done by the system so far, and the confidence reposed in it by more than half a million insurants, must remain, for its present, conclusive vindication.

This year Superintendent Barnes has closed his rule with the press—none of its representatives being admitted to his department ; but the annual return of the fire offices, or a considerable number of them, are all in, abstract will be mailed, simultaneously, to the different press. It will, probably, be got about first. There are, even at this late day, several which have not made returns—of course body, including, particularly, stockholder insurance brokers, are anxious to see the system. Of the dividend returns for January, a dozen New York offices have shewn an improvement over corresponding months in January. Yet while annual statements to the Insurance department will generally be satisfactory, for unaccountable reason the insurance stock much depressed. Whether it be owing rket, or the fact that knowing ones prefer f till official statements can be examined, ient saith not.

the prevailing dissensions in the insu- p, and which have just been renewed iderable spirit, is the question of the id demerits, of the New York State Re- item, and the *demerits* of the co-operative fe insurance, so-called. A pamflet, of le ability, has recently appeared against try System, and has been widely circu- he "' plan" was originally devised by Morgan, of the North American life.— ledly a combative, as well as able officer :, and will not be likely to let the pam- unnoticed. The law provides that any iny, where the insured desires it, may lepoait, with the superintendent, a cash ual to the present net value of the po- the superintendent issues a handsomely certificate to that effect. It is contended ir companies that have adopted the prac- uing registered policies, that because the ident is made the custodian or trustee of *es'* reserve that, therefore, the *policy* is y State endorsement, while *per contra* nts insist that the law is no security *for* ; that for it, as such, or its payment, 3 security, whatever. The security is h reserve as may have been deposited, over to the company only ; and this, isk has been finally adjusted, or upon er of its officers or receivers.

i of articles, some of an actuarial and others of a general character, which ared in the Insurance *Monitor*, during vo months, discussing and dissecting the ve system of life insurance, have re- n published in pamphlet form, under es of the regular life companies. But this scheme, is like hitting a man when vn. It is substantially dead. Of the anies organized in this city, the first— attan co-operative, is the only one that business," even to a limited extent.— peciousness and utter impracticability of e, considered on any actuarial basis, was e manifest by the insurance and daily ie getters up of these affairs have only operate among the mechanic and labor- t, but have not succeeded in damaging ily. If the business classes did not see ug on its merits, the inconsequential of the "promoters" would be a sufficient that the thing was a delusion and a

aful event of the past week, in insurance s the death, in this city, of T. Jones, jr. nd for nearly sixteen years proprietor urance *Monitor*, the first strictly and r insurance journal, of note, established ited States. When the *Monitor* was i insurance laws of this State were in an shape, and there was the largest liberty g companies, with mere paper capitals. after, however, the law of 1853, which innual returns, was passed, and order merge from chaos. Of the present 98 fire offices, 56 then ; and of the 44 life , now organized or represented in this r 15 then existed.

:coRD.—Scarboro Township, Ont., Jan. barns, stables and outbuildings, with consisting of grain, hay, implements, several sheep, the property of William 'ere totally consumed by fire. The the fire is unknown, and The loss is esti- il,600. The buildings were insured to t of $600.

Village, Ont., Feb. 1.—The workshop ws, carpenter, adjoining the dwelling c fire at the roof, owing to a stovepipe ied through it, and in an incredibly the building containing Matthews'

tools, turning lathe, etc., was consumed. The dwelling house caught fire from the burning shop, but the neighbors assembled and by their prompt exertions rescued most of the furniture, together with the doors and windows of the house. Burford, Ont., Jan. 29.—A fire broke out in the barn and shed of J. W, Grove's hotel in Bur- ford Village. The barn and sheds were con- sumed; in the barn was a lot of hay, corn, oats, etc., which were also burned. The stable was full of horses, but owing to the presence of mind of those present they were all saved except two; a few pigs and a dog also perished. The origin of the fire is yet unknown, but it is supposed that it caught fire from a pipe which was being smoked by some of the party, who went to the barn to get their horses ready to go home. The furniture in the house suffered some damage by removal, on which there is no insurance. The house and barn are insured in the Niagara District Mutual In- surance Company for $600; total loss, barn, horses, pigs, etc., about $700.

Millbrook, Ont., Jan. 29.—A fire broke out in the residence of Alfred Henderson. The inmates barely escaped; they lost most of their clothing, all of their provisions, and had their furniture badly damaged. No particulars as to insurance.

Douglass, Ont., Feb. 2.—Boot and shoe shop of Alex. Todd and stock of boots and shoes, leather, etc.; loss $2,000; insured for $1,000.

Windsor, Feb. 4.—A fire broke out in a frame house on Mercer street, owned by Mrs. Thomas, ahd was burned to the ground. It was unoccu- pied at the time, and was the work of an incen- diary; insured for $400.

Ramsay Township, Ont., Feb. 3.—The dwelling house of Peter Lake, farmer, on the Sixth conces- sion, was totally destroyed by fire, with a portion of the contents. No insurance.

St. Catherines, Feb. 6.—A tank of oil at H. F. Leavenworth's oil refinery suddenly caught fire and burnt the oil in it, consisting of several barrels, and a shed in which the tank was situated. The refinery itself was in considerable danger, but the men working at the new bridge at lock No. 2 rushed up in time to save it by throwing mud on the flames.

Kitley Township, Ont., Feb. 4.—Premises of John Forgie, Kitley; loss estimated at $1,800. The fire originated from a lantern which had been carelessly left hanging in the cow house. There is no insurance.

Dundas, Feb. 6.—Residence of Jas. Coleman, known as Ogilvie Terrace; most of the furniture was saved in a damaged condition. Mr. Cole- man's loss is covered by insurance to the amount of $10,000. as follows: $5,000 in the Canada Farmers' Mutual, of Hamilton; $6,000 in two policies in the Waterloo County Mutual; of this $1,000 was on the stables, which were not de- stroyed. The loss above insurance is estimated at from $12,000 to $15,000. The fire is supposed to have originated from some defect in the furnace.

Listowel, Ont., Feb. 1.—The workshop of Rob- inson & Jackson was destroyed by fire. Loss $1,000; insured for $500. The origin of the fire is unknown.

Egremont Township, County Grey, Jan. —.— Barn of James Taylor; loss $500; no insurance; cause incendiarism.

Pakenham, Ont., Feb. 3.—Carpenter shop of John Riddell, with contents; insured in the Pro- vincial for a small amount.

Bowmanville, Feb. 1.—House of Mrs. E. Clif- ford and contents, on Clinton street, totally de- stroyed. No particulars.

St. Catherines, Jan. 29.—A St. Catherines paper says that a house was set on fire by mice in that town. After the fire had been extinguished, a scrutiny showed that some mice had build sev- eral nests close to the stovepipe, and that the straw and other combustible material of which these nests were constructed had ignited, and that from these the woodwork had caught fire.

Elizabethtown Township, Jan. 28.—A barn and

contents, belonging to Mr. Burns were totally destroyed; insured in the Agricultural Mutual; cause unknown.

Montreal, Feb. 9.—The establishment of Mr. Kennedy, a saloon-keeper in Notre Dame street, was gutted on Sunday night. The loss was about $1,200. He was fully insured.

CHANGES.—Capt. Frank Jackman has been ap- pointed to the Marine Inspectorship of the Mon- treal Assurance Company, vice Capt. Taylor who assumes a local position in connection with the Toronto Branch.

Mr. W. H. Miller has been appointed Toronto agent of the Northern Assurance Company, in the place of —— Manning, resigned.

— The British America and the Western of Canada have paid to the Minister of Finance their second instalments under the Insurance Act.

— The Royal, Lancashire, and London and Lancashire agencies have been withdrawn from Ottawa.

—Mr. Thos. Hood and Mr. Whitlaw have plunged into a newspaper squabble in the Guelph papers, over the affairs of the Township of Guelph Mutual Insurance Company. It is charged that that fruitful source of fires, over-insurance, is practised in a number of instances. Query—How often is over-insurance effected, when it is *known* that in case of loss the company would not have to pay anything like the full amount of the policy ?

THE CRIME OF FALSE PRETENCE IN LIFE INSURANCE.

Is it not time to arrest the further progress of false pretence in life insurance ?

Does not the existing competition for business threaten seriously to involve some, not to say many, of the life companies, in errors of practice, as to expense and expectation, from which, there will be, there can be, neither reform nor recovery ?

Are any of the companies indulging too large expectations in respect of their future business.

Are any of the companies making promises which they will not, in the future, be able to fulfil ?

If life insurance is an exact science, if its theo- ries of practice are based upon the knowledge of certain immutable principles, and if a scientific application of those principles determines exactly what can be done for the heirs of a man who deposits during his life time. certain amounts of money, at stated intervals, any resort to false pre- tence in getting that man to deposit his money is unnecessary and inexcusable. More than that, it is deliberate and cruel fraud. If any company, knowing, as it may, exactly what it can, or cannot, afford to undertake, promises more than the legiti- mate and possible benefits of a life insurance, then it is guilty of an offence little short of rank and violent robbery. If it perverts, or exaggerates, or misrepresents the real function and object of a life insurance policy, then—we may as well con- fess it—the effect of the transaction is to make life insurance a means of selfish and personal emolument, or advancement, the material of speculation being the "sacred funds of the widows and orphans."

It may not be well to call hard names, but we cannot close our eyes to the imminent peril which now threatens the practice of life insurance in this country, on account of five years of unchecked and appalling falsehood on the subject of life in- surance dividends. The seed has been faithfully sowed. In due time will come the harvest, and the profits of that harvest will be hundreds of thousands of dollars paid on policies, thrown up in disgust and anger by disappointed and deceived policyholders. It is possible that the true reason why agents have been permitted, in many cases encouraged, to get business through the medium of false pretences, is found in the confiscation of the moneys previously borrowed on lapsed policies! One company reports having distributed in a period of twenty years six hundred and forty thousand dollars of forfeited policies; or, in other words, having confiscated six hundred and forty thousand dollars on forfeited dividends.

Another, and by far the commonest, as well as the most wicked species of false pretence, which is bringing the business into disrepute, is the shameless practice of impressing the public with the idea that a premium note serves, in some mysterious way, to relieve the assured of half the cost of his insurance. We know a great many conscientious agents who habitually explain, in every case, the precise function, as they understand it, of the premium note; but the number of these is very small, when compared with those who, either willfully, thoughtlessly, or ignorantly, cause it to be believed, in the great majority of cases, that a man can buy a given amount of insurance on the premium note plan at half the price the same amount of insurance would cost on the all cash plan. Nor is this all. The fact is almost universally kept in the back ground that every premium note becomes, immediately on its payment, a part of the company's assets and as such must yield interest annually, which is certain to become a considerable item in the course of a few years when the policyholder begins to pay interest on the total amount of two, three, or four premium notes. The policyholder learns then that the premium, which he supposed, at the outset, was fixed and unalterable, has become materially increased. If the dissatisfaction consequent to the discovery results in a determination to surrender his policy, he learns, then, what also is contrary to what was his original understanding, that the non-forfeiture provision is available only to the extent that he has paid cash. In some cases the much vaunted paid-up policy, afforded by the non-forfeiture provision, is made subject to the outstanding notes which the policyholder has given, upon which interest must be paid annually in advance. In other cases, paid-up policies are issued for an insurance equal to the amount of cash which the policyholder has paid. Other companies more liberal in their dealings, comply strictly, from necessity or choice, with the provisions of the Massachusetts non-forfeiture law, which is a vast improvement upon the practice formerly pursued, but, nevertheless, still very much short of the demands of exact justice. In every case, however, the expectations of policyholders in regard to dividends, to premium notes, and to the forfeiture of their policies, are rarely realized. Whether this is the fault of the public, or whether it is the fault of companies, or whether it is the fault of agents, the prospects of a diminished patronage of the life companies generally demands that the fault shall be corrected. If the public estimation of the advantages of life insurance has suffered from false pretences, a competition ten times as vigorous as the existing competition will not serve to repair the damages thereof. It is only the correction of abuses, the conformity of practice to principles of strict justice, and an honorable and prompt compliance with the terms of a contract as expressed that a misapprehension or evasion of its provisions shall be impossible, that can arrest this departure from the ranks. Therefore we cry halt, Messrs. Officers, Managers, Directors, Agents, and Solicitors; put your terms clearly before the public; write explicit contracts; and, thus, overthrow the discredit, disrepute, demoralization, and disaster, which, under the banner of False Pretence, threaten to mar the ruin of a majority of all the life companies.—*Condensed from Chicago Spectator.*

THE CANADA LIFE.—This company is determined not to be driven out of the field by adversaries, either American or British. The conflict between the many Life Companies now doing business in Canada is decidedly irrepressible, and, as it sways to and fro, some pretty hard knocks are given and taken. Mr. Ramsay! has come in for his share, as well as the rest, but holds his own with praiseworthy persistency. He gives the following comparative statement of assets for each $100 assured:—

	Assets for each $100 Assured.	
Travelers...........	$2.94	
Atlantic Mutual...	6.19	More than 1-16th is in Notes.
Equitable...........	6.21	
Phoenix Mutual...	7.65	Nearly one-half is in Notes.
Ætna Life..........	8.20	More than one-half is in Notes
Connecticut Mutual	11.52	Nearly one-half is in Notes.
Union Mutual......	11.61	Nearly one-half is in Notes.
New York Life.....	13.19	One-sixth is in Notes.
Average of above..	8.44	More than a-third is in Notes.
" Canada Life	18.70	

To show that the rates for assurance in the Canada Life are lower than in the various American offices transacting business in Canada, Mr. Ramsay gives the following table of rates, by 10 annual instalments for assurances of $1000, with profits in each of the Companies named:—

Age.	CANADA.	Ætna.	Atlantic Mutual.	Connecticut Mutual.	Equitable of New York.
25	$36 20	$44 73	$45 24	$45 82	$42 56
26	37 20	45 68	46 16	46 76	43 37
27	38 30	46 62	47 12	47 73	44 22
28	39 50	47 57	48 12	48 73	45 10
29	40 50	48 59	49 14	49 77	46 02
30	41 40	49 07	50 22	50 84	46 97
31	42 30	50 44	51 32	51 95	47 98
32	43 12	51 49	52 44	53 10	49 02
33	44 30	52 36	53 60	54 28	50 10
34	45 40	53 56	54 82	55 51	51 22
35	46 70	54 82	56 08	56 78	52 40
36	48 00	55 96	57 33	58 10	53 63
37	49 40	57 96	58 72	59 47	54 91
38	50 80	59 19	60 12	60 88	56 24
39	52 30	60 80	61 56	62 36	57 63
40	53 70	61 68	63 10	63 90	59 00
41	55 10	63 00	64 70	65 50	60 60
42	56 40	64 99	66 35	67 17	62 19
43	57 70	66 43	68 10	68 90	63 84
44	59 00	68 11	69 90	70 73	65 57
45	60 40	69 40	71 80	72 70	67 37
46	62 00	71 04	73 75	74 76	69 36
47	63 60	73 42	75 80	76 70	71 25
48	63 40	75 44	77 00	78 96	73 32
49	67 00	77 77	80 05	81 00	75 49
50	70 00	80 43	82 31	83 35	77 77
51	70 70	82 23	84 65	85 70	80 14
52	73 60	84 23	87 05	88 15	82 63
53	78 70	86 50	89 52	90 68	85 32
54	81 90	89 17	92 15	93 30	87 94
55	85 50	92 24	94 85	96 05	90 79

TABLE OF RATES CONTINUED.

Age.	CANADA.	New York Life.	Phœnix Mutual.	Travellers	Union Mutual.
25	$36 20	$42 42	$46 58	$41 95	$45 85
26	37 20	43 29	47 84	42 82	46 90
27	38 30	44 19	48 87	43 71	48 05
28	39 50	45 11	50 07	44 62	49 15
29	40 50	46 08	51 01	45 55	50 23
30	41 40	47 06	51 70	46 51	51 20
31	42 30	48 05	53 68	48 48	53 10
32	43 90	49 16	54 05	49 30	54 20
33	44 30	50 26	54 05	49 30	54 20
34	45 40	51 40	55 61	50 55	55 30
35	46 70	52 50	57 38	51 02	56 55
36	48 00	53 80	58 04	52 72	57 85
37	49 40	55 00	59 20	53 86	59 15
38	50 80	56 30	60 23	55 02	60 65
39	52 30	57 74	61 04	56 21	61 05
40	53 70	59 16	62 08	57 44	63 35
41	55 10	60 66	64 40	58 71	64 65
42	56 40	62 21	65 84	60 02	65 90
43	57 70	63 84	67 20	61 38	67 10
44	59 00	65 56	68 96	62 78	68 25
45	60 40	67 32	70 95	64 23	69 60
46	62 00	69 16	72 84	65 74	71 00
47	63 40	71 00	74 64	67 31	72 45
48	63 40	73 21	76 68	68 92	74 05
49	67 60	75 42	78 96	70 50	75 90
50	70 60	77 73	81 12	72 31	77 95
51	70 70	80 12	83 66	74 08	80 30
52	73 60	82 60	85 88	75 91	82 70
53	78 70	85 18	87 73	77 81	85 30
54	81 90	87 85	90 77	79 78	88 05
55	85 50	90 70	93 85	81 83	91 05

Financial.

STATEMENT of the Revenue and Expend the Dominion of Canada for the mont 31st January, 1869:

Customs...........................	$368,
Excise.............................	259,
Post Office........................	56,
Bill Stamps.......................	11,
Public Works, including Railways..	20,
Miscellaneous.....................	55,
Total..........................	**$792,**
Expenditure.......................	$2,016,

STATEMENT OF THE BANKS OF ONT AND QUEBEC FOR 1868.

		Total Assets.	Other Debts.	Discount and Loans.	Due from other Banks.	Other Bank Notes.	Government Securities.	Property.	Specie and Provincial Notes.
	January	$75,907,209 34	$2,430,388 81	$51,175,592 48	$2,653,660 72	$1,907,255 62	$5,414,753 08	$1,596,005 80	$9,770,572 83
	February	75,850,162 63	2,567,707 68	51,905,950 66	2,860,729 52	1,732,110 33	5,099,873 42	1,590,397 21	9,414,413 71
	March	72,736,522 61	4,064,337 53	47,539,293 22	2,783,092 60	1,753,545 90	6,872,144 70	1,601,239 23	8,112,864 37
A	April	71,690,486 46	4,014,903 71	47,067,582 33	2,383,752 01	1,841,708 06	6,506,813 00	1,603,643 24	7,461,839 33
S	May	71,362,455 59	3,844,821 04	46,700,009 91	2,780,759 74	1,841,172 81	6,142,573 04	1,605,189 79	8,287,162 66
S	June	72,461,243 71	3,968,935 12	48,155,431 89	2,651,772 87	1,850,175 89	6,317,130 84	1,510,572 18	9,110,497 42
E	July	71,413,903 90	3,731,238 33	47,042,141 65	2,882,135 83	1,852,883 15	6,327,104 30	1,635,090 25	7,384,197 32
T		72,217,662 71	3,624,429 23	49,291,528 00	3,654,292 66	1,809,296 04	5,987,196 39	1,634,360 23	9,430,406 42
S		75,986,528 24	3,625,505 00						

	Circulation.	Banks.	bearing Interest.	Interest.	Liabilities.
January......	$8,718,928 00	$2,926,524 68	$12,975,045 53	$15,746,143 20	$40,366,641 41
February.....	8,603,233 00	2,572,189 03	13,531,814 37	16,352,618 92	40,496,140 21
March........	8,225,959 00	2,502,978 72	13,450,890 82	15,766,582 17	39,946,410 21
April	7,607,754 00	2,277,331 43	13,125,962 58	15,934,535 52	38,945,583 43
May	7,294,409 00	2,032,992 17	13,608,977 31	16,110,815 22	39,047,295 70
June.........	8,312,386 00	2,771,925 12	13,938,447 01	14,765,879 94	39,788,638 07
July....	6,956,497 00	2,260,800 57	13,775,772 09	16,715,836 47	39,709,005 23
August.......	7,356,861 00	1,649,655 30	13,309,438 40	17,849,454 50	40,165,349 20
September...	9,360,957 00	1,525,631 00	13,445,029 00	19,531,831 00	43,763,449 17
October	10,490,502 00	1,010,610 30	13,780,724 26	20,426,037 63	45,707,874 19
November...	9,986,771 00	1,821,856 17	14,535,018 03	22,013,878 88	50,357,523 58
December ...	9,538,243 00	1,232,894 95	15,039,803 57	21,412,884 58	48,123,516 10

ORONTO STOCK MARKET.

ported by Pellatt & Osler, Brokers.)

ness of the week has been large; a good r securities still continues, and prices ses have advanced.

tock—Montreal has been firm and in nd during the week, with very little st sales were at 139¾. British has been)4; sellers now ask 105. There were of Ontario at 100¼ and 100½; at the were buyers at 100 and sellers at 100½. rices offered for Toronto have induced come forward; considerable sales were 1½ and 122, and a small sale at 123; losed with sellers at 122½. There is a and for Royal Canadian; buyers offer ittle offering. Sales of Commerce oc- 02¾, which was the asking rate at the yers have advanced their offers for , but there are few sellers under 45. remain steady at 109 to 109½; there are the latter rate. No Quebec in the yers would give par. For Molson's 110 there are no sellers. There were sales 02¼ and 102½, closing in fair demand. of Du Peuple; buyers at 109. For 06½ is offered. There is a fair demand Cartier at 107½; no sellers under 108½. nion occurred at 103½. Other banks

es—Canada are in active demand. ives have been sold at 95½, Currency 6, and Dominion stock at 105½; there terling six per cents in market. To- ery scarce; no transactions. County rce and much enquired for.

—Canada Permanent Building Society demand; sales were made at 124, 124½, and 125. Some sales of Western Canada Building Society occurred at 118½ and 119; there are now buyers at the latter rate. Buyers offer 109½ for Freehold; there were sellers at 110½. Montreal Telegraph is held at 134, with buyers at 132½. Small sales of Landed Credit occurred at 75, but buyers generally offer only 73. British-America Assurance is held at 55½, with no buyers over 54½. Moatgages are readily negotiable at 8 per cent. Money is easy on first class paper.

The Canadian Monetary Times.

THURSDAY, FEBRUARY 11, 1869.

CANADA PERMANENT BUILDING SOCIETY.

The prosperous business done by the Canada Permanent Building and Savings Society, the largest institution of the kind in the Dominion, with its $1,039,050 of capital, and $567,187 of deposits, shows how well it adapts itself to the wants of the country and how highly valued are the advantages it offers to borrowers. Some years ago a great deal of prejudice existed against Building Societies on account of the exorbitant rates charged and the heavy fines exacted from borrowers. This prejudice has subsided, for we find well organized Building Societies, such as the Canada, are able to keep out their funds notwithstanding the competition that exists in supplying the demand for money. That they are able to find investments for their capital and deposits and pay handsome dividends without any losses of consequence, must be taken as evidence of their being well suited to the wants of the country. The Canada Permanent, under the skilful management of the Secretary, Mr. J. Herbert Mason, who may be regarded as our highest authority in Building Society matters, has progressed with rapid strides until its pro portions have attained those of a Bank. Last year its cash receipts were almost a million of dollars. In 1867, they were $800,000. The mortgage asset has increased from $1,543,000 to $1,818,000. Notwithstanding the opening of the Post Office Savings' Bank, the deposits exceeded by $140,000 those of the previous year. The directors tell us that "the demand for the Society's funds has been most active and during the past few months has taxed to the utmost the ordinary resources of the Society." After paying the usual half yearly dividends of five per cent. upon the capital stock, provision was made for the enlargement of the Contingent Fund to $50,000, for the allotment of 11 per cent. to the accumulating shares, and the increase of the Reserve Fund to $100,264. One feature in the report possesses peculiar interest for the general public and that is the acknowledged punctuality with which borrowers have paid up principal and interest. It shows that the country is in a healthy condition when such a statement is made by a Society whose operations extend in all directions throughout the Province.

SELF INSURANCE.

This journal has more than once pointed out the defects of the forfeiture plan of life insurance still adhered to by many companies. A man, in nine cases out of ten, is the best judge of his own interests. It must often happen that it would be much more advantageous to discontinue the payment of future premiums on a policy, than to go on paying till death, as where those for whose benefit the insurance was effected have died, or where the insured suffers pecuniary losses, and is consequently disabled from keeping up the policy. Again, in these days of emigration, men are frequently obliged to take up their residence permanently in another country, not included in the limits prescribed in the policy. In such cases to compel the keeping up of the policy, or in default the forfeiture of all interest in it, is a great hardship. The dread of this no doubt operates very disadvantageously in preventing life insurance growing more rapidly than it does even now.

In view of these things it is matter for congratulation that there has recently been introduced, in England, a system which promises to remedy such defects. The author of the scheme is Dr. Farr, well known for his English life tables. Its general features are that the insured has the privilege, on deposit of the policy at any time after payment of even only one premium, of drawing out, either as a loan or as a surrender-policy, nearly one half of the total premiums paid. On the back of the policy when given there is endorsed a table shewing the surrender value, and a table has also been prepared by Dr. Farr and published, shewing what will be the value of any policy after each premium is paid. The policy, therefore, becomes to all intents and purposes a negotiable instrument for its current value. If an insurer is overtaken by reverses, after his policy has been many years in existence, he can on depositing it get the endorsed surrender value in cash or a paid up policy for the amount. Again, where it is stipulated that the insured shall not go beyond certain geographical limits, in ordinary cases the breach of this would cause a forfeiture of the policy ; under the new system the policy would stand for its surrender value, which could be got by the insured at any time, or by his representatives after his death. In a former number of this journal, vol. i, p. 202 (Jan. 30, 1858), we recommended the adoption of a plan almost exactly similar to that now described, viz: the payment of a certain sum or the giving a paid up policy, in the event of an insured wishing to discontinue the policy ; the only difference being that we there contended that the choice out of the two methods indicated should be given to the company and not to the insured, for the reason there given, " in order to prevent the insured from purposely neglecting to pay his premiums, with a view of getting his policy cancelled." Upon consideration, however, we incline to think that it may be preferable to give the option to the assured for the reason mentioned at the beginning of this article, that, as a general rule, a man is the best judge of his own interests. The new system is very advantageously embodied in policies payable on attaining a certain age, or at death if that take place sooner. It is this combination which peculiarly merits the appellation of self-insurance, uniting as it does the advantages of life insurance with those of a savings' bank, in which to accumulate a sufficiency to keep one in old age, when work becomes difficult or distasteful. The plan has now been tried for a year by a company in England, with a success so marked as to promise to open a new era in life insurance. In this country the non-forfeiture plan has been adopted more generally than in England, nevertheless the new system appears to combine so many advantages as to make it well worth a trial here, and we shall watch with interest the result of any experiments which companies may make in regard to it.

HURON AND ONTARIO SHIP CANAL.

Though it be to a great extent true that the present, as it has been said to be, is the age of political economy, yet it is unfortunately equally true that there is among many, including those from whom we should expect better things, so much loose and chaotic thinking upon the subject, that it can scarcely be said that the science as now taught by its great masters is understood by more than a small minority. One of the irrational dogmas which, in common with many others equally absurd, Adam Smith found in universal acceptance in his time, and which he and his immediate successors succeeded in destroying, was that known as " The Mercantile System." The idea of which that phrase was the expression, was that wealth consisted only of money (gold, silver, etc.); that the only way in which a country could become wealthy was by hoarding up within it, as much of that commodity as its people could lay their hands upon, and that the departure of it was a sure sign of impoverishment and impending ruin. Had Adam Smith done nothing more than destroy this superstition he would have deserved the thanks of posterity to the end of time. It is well worthy of notice, however, that though this idea got its death blow about a century ago it still infects the popular ideas upon many subjects, lurking unsuspected beneath some fallacy as the root from which it springs ; the nonsense which newspapers are even yet continually writing about the "balance of trade" may be adduced as evidence of this.

Another of these fallacies is that which seems to be held by the promoters of the scheme we are considering, viz., that money brought into a country and expended in public works, etc., increases the wealth of that country to the extent of the amount so brought in, and is a permanent addition to its capital. Listen to the Corypheus of the scheme. In a letter which appeared in the *Leader* of the 11th ult., he says : "The construction of the Huron and Ontario Ship Canal, enlarging and utilizing the St. Lawrence Canals, bringing ocean ships into our lakes, and a *cash capital* from abroad, free from taxation and interest, of *forty millions of dollars*—more than the whole banking capital of the Dominion." The italics are Mr. Capreol's. The idea apparently possessed by him and wished to be instilled into others evidently is, that the money proposed to be spent, will, every dollar of it, become part of the circulating capital of the Province, in the same way as is the capital of the banks. This idea is an absurd delusion, the mercantile system being the source whence it gets its vitality. Capital is divided into two classes—circulating and fixed. Capital which is consumed in the act of producing an object of wealth (or an utility, to use the technical phrase) is circulating ; capital which is not so consumed, but is capable of being used many times over, or for an indefinite period (that is, till it is worn out) is fixed. To the former class belongs the money(or, more accurate the things which that money will represe with which it is proposed to build the car To the latter will belong the canal itself, constructed. In the act of construction capital required will be converted from former class into the latter. Let us see l this will be so. It is said that it will ($40,000,000 to construct the canal ; W does this mean ! Simply that it will requ that amount in food, clothing, tools, &c. the laborers and others engaged during 5 years in the construction of the work. the end of that time £40,000,000 of fc clothing, tools, &c. will have been consur or destroyed, never to be replaced—tha the capital of $40,000,000 will be gone; tl will be that amount less of capital in world. Let us turn to the great authorit; this subject, and see if our view is sustain Mr. Mill says, in relation to the analog case of capital spent in making land n productive,.

"The land thus increased in productive bears a value in the market proportionat the increase ; and hence it is usual to cons the capital which was invested or sun: making the improvement, as still existin the increased value of the land. There i be no mistake, however. The capital, all other capital, has been consumed. It consumed in maintaining the labourers executed the improvement, and in the and tear of the tools by which they wer sis'ed." Again : "That part of the ca of a cotton spinner which he pays away work-people, once so paid exists no long his capital, or as a cotton spinner's cap such portion of it as the workmen cons no longer exists as capital at all : even if save any part, it may now be more pro regarded as a fresh capital, the result second act of accumulation."

And this leads us to a limitation of we above put in the rough. It is true cordance with the last quoted words th: whole $40,000,000 will be consumed pital, and that we get the canal in its We shall also, however, get something viz. :—whatever is saved out of the $4C 000 by those to whom it is paid. Th proportion of it will be paid to labo who, as a rule, save little or nothing. main savings will probably be made, usual in such cases, by contractors, jo hangers on, &c. And to the extent to these persons save, to that extent will be possibly a permanent addition to th tal of the Province. It is of the utmo portance to the material well-being o Province that our business men should correct ideas upon these subjects. A glance back into an episode of our fin history will shew this sufficiently. Abo years 1853-4-5-6 a large amount of mon expended in the Western District of Canada, in the construction of railroa and Port Stanley, the Grand Trunk, the Great Western branch to Sarnia, one of the capital necessary was raised at. The far larger part, however, rom other parts of the Province and road. The inhabitants of London s this place not because what we have fers to it alone, but because it was e) indulging in a delusion similar to er which the advocates of the canal labouring, imagined that this expen-money was to increase the value of to trade in all its branches. Upon rth of this expectation they launched the wildest speculations in land, in , in merchandize, &c., expecting promised Eldorado came, all would well, and everybody would come out tune in his pocket. Though waited patience, however, the promised er came; then one began to fail, her, until a crisis came on, over-thousands in disaster and ruin, and quite an exodus to the States. In nly now that that part of Canada covering from the shock which its affairs then underwent. Here is a sson of the danger of indulging in ld ideas as to what the spending of going to effect, which the advocates eme we are considering would do idy and profit by.

Communications.

WAR TO THE KNIFE.

r of the Monetary Times,

TORONTO, Feb. 7, 1869.

iber of Insurance Companies doing the city of Toronto is not small, and of their agents, solicitors, &c., is large. onies are English, American, and Ca-iach is seemingly anxious to do as much business as possible—for it is found to a. While I do not quarrel with them up a healthy competition, I do object ner in which the work of securing risks at. I do not intend, in this letter, to elaborate report of their proceedings, be allowed to give a general idea of what able, by the recital of a few particu-the death of Mr. Chaffey, the agencies a and Hartford, both of which were a, were divided, and given to different Then there was a struggle for the ith he had controlled, and I leave it is conducted to justify their mode of It certainly brought no credit on those it.

our insurance agents are unscrupulous deed; they do not hesitate to resort e most dishonorable to undermine each ct, judging by the character each gives the whole business is conducted by a dodgers. They stand on the corner ts, planning mischief, and retailing ich they preface with—"It is said." la say." Each professes the most mi-ntance with every other body's affairs, te falsehoods with their usual accoun-

paniment—strict injunction to secresy. When tired of abusing each other, individually, they attack the different companies.

Then as to the matter of rates. The English Companies charge the Ætna, Hartford, and Home with taking risks much below tariff rates; and the Canadian Companies charge both the English (especially the Commercial Union and the Lancashire) and American, with that crime. The Provincial says the Western is ruining business by accepting such low rates, and the Western has charged the British America with allowing an agent not only to go about, abusing the Western, but taking risks below the tariff. I believe the tariff has become a non-entity, and that there is a general scramble for business at any price.

There is much "dog-eat-dog" going on. For instance: A goes to B with a risk; B declines to pay a commission, but is willing to accept the risk. A declines the terms; B therefore hurries off to the individual whose property has to be covered, and behind A's back issues a policy and saves the commission. I do not wish to take up too much of your space this week, but I hope to continue my plain unvarnished tale.

Yours, &c.,

AGENT.

Railway News.

GREAT WESTERN RAILWAY.—Traffic for week ending January 22, 1869.

Passengers......................	$22,258 34
Freight......................	58,826 54
Mails and Sundries..........	1,978 28
Total Receipts for week......	$83,063 16
Corresponding week 1887...	65,596 63
Increase............	$17,466 63

TORONTO, GREY AND BRUCE RAILWAY.—For the first section of the railway from Toronto to Luther, $470,000 in bonuses are required, of which Toronto has already voted $250,000, Albion $40,000, Caladan $45,000, Orageville $18,000, and Amaranth $30,000, making a total of $383,000, or $90,000 less than the amount absolutely needed. The municipalities from which it is proposed to raise these $90,000 are, Vaughan $10,-000, Mono $50,000, East Garafraxa, $20,000, and Melancthon $10,000.

THE NOVA SCOTIA DIFFICULTY.

The Finance Minister's report to the Privy Council summarises the objections raised by Messrs. Howe and McLellan to the Union Act and the decision of the Dominion Government thereon. The first stage in the negotiations was an enquiry by the Finance Minister, which resulted in the following acknowledgments:

1. That the principle on which the debts were arranged by the Union Act operates with some unfairness to Nova Scotia.

2. That in the division of the property, local assets and revenues, or because the assets possessed by her were not of a character to be available, Nova Scotia is less favorably situated than the other Provinces in respect of local revenues.

3. That the increase of customs presses more directly on Nova Scotia than the other Provinces, but this apparent increase and the consequent pressure, it is believed, will be mitigated every year, as goods which she formerly imported from abroad, and which were chargeable with duty, are produced in other portions of the Dominion, and will now be available to her for consumption, free of duty.

4. That she must have raised about $400,000 annually, by way of additional taxation, if she had remained out of the Union.

5. That the amount raised by the Dominion from revenue from customs and otherwise is about

adequate, if the results of last year continue in future the same, to meet all the current expenditure the Dominion is called on to make on her account, but less by $100,563, if Nova Scotia is to be charged a per capita contribution to the cost of the civil government and legislation of the Dominion.

6. That the local sources of revenue at present possessed by Nova Scotia are inadequate to carry on the services devolving on the Province.

This report, having been submitted to Mr. Howe, he and Mr. McLelan raised certain objections in the interest of Nova Scotia, which objections were made the object of discussion. The result is that the following is the basis of an Act to be submitted to Parliament next session:

1. That the debt of Nova Scotia, on entering the Union, be placed at $9,186,756; and that that Province be relieved from any charge of interest, unless her debt exceed that sum.

2. That for ten years, from the 1st July, 1867, an annual subsidy of $82,698 be paid to that Province.

The committee further report their concurrence in the recommendation of the Finance Minister that Nova Scotia be debited, after the completion of the Province building, with interest on the cost of that building, until it shall have been placed at the disposal of the Dominion.

HURON AND ONTARIO CANAL.

The Quebec Gazette deals with this project in the following style. Speaking of the late meeting in the St. Lawrence Hall, it says :—

They have of late fomented a constant turmoil among the ignorant masses, whom they marshal with torches, and for any thing we know, with trumpet blare and war-like drum, in procession, to—we shall not say intimidate but—impress the Local Legislature and Government with the danger of refusing the compacters of that wonderful scrotchet, the Toronto and Georgian Bay Canal, the modest little sop of ten millions of acres, being, we believe, about one-fifth of all that are left to the Crown in Ontario. It has been demonstrated again and again that the project is the most perfectly Utopian conception that ever proceeded from the brain of a sane man, and yet the wire pullers of the scheme persist to scold, rant and threaten all sorts of calamities to the Government if they refuse to give the ten millions. The $40,000,000 which Mr. Capreol, the inventor and promoter of the enterprise promises to get from eminent capitalists in London and Philadelphia, have no better basis than reports of verbal conversations and vague assertions on the part of some persons to whom the impressible president and factotum submitted his gorgeous prospectuses, all of course couleur de rose.

Commercial.

Toronto Market.

BOOTS AND SHOES.—Prices are steady; little trade doing.

LEATHER.—Business is very dull, and prices are steady as quoted. Hides are a se dull; prices are slightly advanced.

FURS.—There is a quiet trade doing at quotations.

GRAIN.— Wheat —Receipts, 46,799 bushels, against 42,800 bushels last week. The market is dull, and declining under continued large receipts and a slack demand. Spring is dull, and offering at 96c to 98c, with no buyers over 95c; some sales occurred in the early part of the week at 98c; sales, 7 cars at 99c, 10,000, bush. March delivery at 95c. in store. Fall is offering at $1, and several cars of a good sample sold at that price. Barley—Receipts, 2,590 bush., and 900 bush. last week. The market is firm at $1.30 to 1.32; holders are confident of higher prices. Sales, 2,000 bush., at $1.30½ at Hamilton, 1 car at $1.30 on track, 2,000 bush. at $1.30½ at Paris.

Peas—Receipts trifling ; market nominal at quotations. *Oats*—Receipts 5,000 bushs., and 13,200 bushs. last week. There is not much demand ; car loads are worth 51 to 52c. *Seeds*—The market has been quiet this week ; prices unchanged at $2 to $2.50 for timothy ; $6.25 to $6.75 for clover, and $1.60 to $2 for flax.

FLOUR.—Receipts 3,575 bbls., and 2,200 bbls. last week. Flour is dull and tending downwards in sympathy with the wheat market. No 1 superfine is now offering freely at $4.40 without buyers ; $4.30 could probably be obtained for good brands. Other grades nominal. *Cornmeal*—Little doing at $3.50 to $3.75.

PROVISIONS.—*Dressed Hogs*—The market was easier for a few days past, closing quiet as quoted; prices range from $9 to $10.12½ ; a car load, averaging 173 lbs., sold yesterday at $9. *Pork*—Mess is held at $26; some business was done at $25.50. *Cut Meats*—Quiet and firm as quoted. *Butter*—Nominal; 22c is about the outside that would be paid for shipping lots, 23 to 24c has been obtained for small parcels at retail.

FREIGHTS.—Rates by Grand Trunk Railway:—Flour to all stations from Belleville to Lynn, inclusive, 35c., grain per 100 lbs. 18c. ; flour to Brockville and Cornwall, inclusive, 43c. grain 22c. flour to Montreal 50c. grain 25c. ; flour to all stations between Island Pond and Portland, inclusive, 85c. grain 43c. ; flour to Boston 90c., gold, grain 45c.; flour to Halifax $1.05, grain 53c; flour to St. John 95c. Boxed Meats to Liverpool per gross ton 82s. 6d. ; lard or butter in tinnets 87s. 6d. ; Pork 11s. per tierce ; flour 5s. 6d. per barrel ; grain 12s. per 480 pounds. Rates by Great Western Railway—Flour, Toronto to Suspension Bridge 25c. gold ; thence to New York, 92c. U. S. currency per bbl. ; to Boston $1.02. Grain to Bridge 13c., gold; thence to New York 47c, U. S. currency; to Boston 51c. Grain, Toronto to Detroit, 18c. ber 100 lbs; flour 35c per bbl.

Demerara Sugar Market.

The following is from Sandbach, Parker & Co.'s Circular, dated Georgetown, January 7, 1869 :—

SUGARS.—Transactions have been on a small scale, the depressed state of the American market deterring shippers, and as the prospects of the English market are much better than they have been for some months past, Planters prefer shipping to the United Kingdom on their own account, to accepting the offers made to fill American orders. We quote the prices asked for the different grades of Sugar, but the sales have been very small. We regret exceedingly to see this check on the demand from the United States, as the trade has been assuming proportions of late that promised an outlet for our productions but little inferior to England. Our shipments in 1866 were 7,240 hhds.; in 1867, 13,116 hhds.; whilst in 1868 they have reached 82,614, all Vacuum Pan sugar. The total shipments have been in 1865, 86,110 hhds.; in 1866, 91,580 hhd.; in 1867, 82,039 hhds., and in 1868, 89,654.

MOLASSES.—The demand has been very slack, and planters prefer making the article into rum, to accepting the rates now current. The shipments have been in 1866, 15,180 puns.; in 1867, 24,028 puns., and in 1868, 25,221 puns.

SUGARS.—Very few transactions ; the bulk of the crop going to the United Kingdom. The shipments in 1866 were 30,968 puns.; in 1867, 25,824 puns., and in 1868, 24,680 puns,

Transactions have taken place during the fortnight at the following rates :

SUGARS (package included) sold by 100 lbs. Dutch, 10 per cent. tare.

Muscavadoes, equal at No. 8		
Dutch Standard $3.80 ⅌ 100 lbs.		
No. 10 do. $4.00	In hhds.	
" 12 do. $4.25	of about	
Vacuum Pan No. 12 do. $5.40	1800 lbs.	each.
" " 14 do. 5.60		
" " 16 do. 5.80 to 6.00		
" " 17 do. 6.00 to 6.10		
" " 18 do. 6.10 to 6.25		

MOLASSES (package included, sold by Imperial gallon.)

Muscovado, from 18 @ 23 cents, as to color and density	In puns of 100 gals.	
Vacuum Pan from 20 @ 30 cents, as to color and density		
RUM (colored, package included, sold by Imperial gal. from 35 per cent, @ 38 overproof 44 @ 48 cents. From 38 per cent. @ 44 overproof, 50 @ 54 cents.	Ditto.	

Stock of Teas in Montreal.

In the statement of the stock of Teas in the hands of importers on the 1st instant, which we published yesterday, there was a typographical error. The quantity of Souchong and Congou showed 3,201 half-chests in place of 320. The statement is repeated with the correction:—

1ST JANUARY, 1865.

	½-chts.	lbs. ea.	lbs.
Hysons	349	50	17,450
Young Hysons	10,547	55	580,085
Gunpowders	957	65	62,205
Imperial	1,408	60	84,480
Hyson Skin	83	45	3,735
Twankay	417	50	20,850
Hyson Twankay	291	50	14,550
Uncolored Japan	4,751	40	130,040
Colored Japan	570	45	25,650
	19,377		999,145
			lbs.
Souchong & Congou	3,201	40	128,040
Oolong	1,08½	35	38,080
Or'ge & Hyson Pekoe	10	35	350
	4,299		166,470

1ST JANUARY, 1868.

			lbs.
Hysons	1,360	50	68,000
Young Hysons	14,013	55	772,365
Gunpowder	2,016	65	131,040
Imperial	3,034	60	182,040
Hyson Skin	237	45	10,665
Twankay	564	50	28,200
Hyson Twankay	911	50	45,550
Uncolored Japan	17,402	40	696,080
Colored Japan	863	45	38,835
	40,430		1,972,775
Souchong & Congor.	5,438	40	217,520
Oolong	1,117	35	39,095
Or'ge & Hyson Pekoe	370	35	12,950
—*Herald.*	6,925		269,565

Halifax Market.

BREADSTUFFS—Feb. 2.—Our markets for Flour, for the past week, have been characterized by a light demand, with receipts largely in excess. Holders evince considerable anxiety to sell, and lower figures have been accepted. Buyers continue to look for lower prices, in which they are borne out by past experience, which proves that our markets do not sympathise with advances abroad when stocks are large here, holders preferring to sell even at old rates. We quote White Wheat Extra (Fall) $7.25 to $7.50; Fancy, $6.60 to 6.85 ; Bakers' Strong, $6.40 to 6.50 ; Supers, $6.00 to $6.10; No. 2 (dull), $5.00 to 5.25 ; Middlings, $4.50 to 4.75.

WEST INDIA PRODUCE—Continues firm, at former quotations, with light stock. Sugars are in request for Montreal. The first cargo of new Cienfuegos Molasses was offered at auction last week, and realized 35c to 36c, for about 50 Puns. Rum is still held at 60c, though 58c would probably be accepted for large purchases. Coffees dull, without change. We quote Sugar, V. P., 9½c; Porto Rico, 8½c to 9½c; Cuba, 8c to 8½c; Barbadoes, 7½c. Molasses — Cienfuegos, 35c to 36c; Trinidad, 30c to 33c. Rum (in bond), Demerara, 60c. Coffee—Jamaica, 13c to 15c; St. Domingo, 10c. to 12c.

Montreal Correspondence.

(From our own Correspondent).

Montreal, Feb. 10, 18¢

During last week we experienced one of most severe snow-storms that we have had several years. Our streets are piled with drifts Communication with the West was interrupted, and the country roads are very heavy, so that business has been at a standstill, and our local store-keepers being well supplied, all parties have more or less rested on their oars. We have had some failures in the dry goods trade. The prospect is not very bright that branch of business at present ; the trade has been rather overdone, and the weeding out had in the summer amongst the grocery men, is likely to be repeated in the dry goods trade this winter. Over-trading is the cause of all commercial disasters ; but this is an evil which cures itself every few years.

The only relief to the present dullness has been the visit of Sir John Young, who was cordially received. The fall of the roof of St. Patrick's Hall has also caused considerable excitement Fortunately, only few were injured, and none seriously.

GROCERIES.—The market during the week has been very dull. Sugars and Teas are firm, command full rates, especially for desirable grades of the latter. Molasses also are still. Very little doing in other goods, but the prices of all staples are firm.

IRON AND HARDWARE.—There is very little report, and no changes in prices except Tin Plates, which have advanced fully 50c per box. This caused by a rise in England.

PRODUCE.—Notwithstanding the recent snowstorm, the market for Flour has been amply supplied, and prices during the week have rather declined. It is difficult to say what the rates are, as for the most part the quotations are purely nominal. Total receipts from 1st January to 3rd instant, 44,135 barrels, against 34,109 barrels same period last year, showing an increase of 10,025 barrels, whilst the shipments show a decrease of 2,901, being in 1869, 16,190 barrels against 19,081 barrels in 1868. Grain of all sorts remains very dull, and there is no change in prices. Stocks generally are accumulating, but buyers are not pressing sales.

PROVISIONS.— It was generally thought that the recent delays in the trains would have kept the price of cattle, but such has not been the case, as we had an ample supply on hand. The rules exceedingly high, first-class heavy dressed Hogs having sold as high as $11, a price quite unprecedented. Barrelled Pork rules high in proportion, but at the price of hogs, no packing going on. The market for Butter is dull, prices are unchanged.

Brandy.

The following were the shipments of Brandy from Charente to the United Kingdom, for 3 years ending 30th June, 1864 to 1868, by the following firms. Casks commuted to puncheons

	1864.		1865
	puns.	cases.	puns.
Jas. Hennessy & Co	10,196½	73,552	7,375½
Martel & Co	8,935	37,267	6,443
Otard, Dupuy & Co	2,132	14,593	1,430
Denis Mounie & Co	674½	12,105	363

	1866.		1867.		1868
	puns.	cases.	puns.	cases.	puns.
J.Hens'y&Co	9819½	166491	12509	195623	16649½
Martel & Co	7905	89188	10190	117026	9153
Otard, D'p'y& Co	2936	20886	2401½	26546	3263
D. Mounie & Co	878	28476	512	29879	502½

Tea Movement.

A telegram from Hong Kong, Dated 15 December, gives the exports of Tea from China Japan up to that time as 125,000,000 lbs. is an increase of 31,000,000 lbs, on the exports about the same date in 1867, which amounted 94,000,000 lbs. against 91,557,800 lbs. in 1...

Mercantile.

TORONTO PRICES CURRENT.—FEBRUARY 11, 1869.

Name of Article.	Wholesale Rates.		Name of Article.	Wholesale Rates.		Name of Article.	Whol Rat	
Boots and Shoes.	$ c.	$ c.	**Groceries—Contin'd**	$ c.	$ c.	**Leather—Contin'd.**	$ c.	
Mens' Thick Boots	2 20	2 50	" fine to finn't..	0 85	0 95	Kip Skins, India	0 40	
" Kip	2 50	3 00	Hyson	0 45	0 80	French	0 70	
" Calf	3 00	3 70	Imperial	0 42	0 80	English	0 65	
" Congress Gaiters..	2 00	2 50	Tobacco, Manufac'd :			Hemlock Calf (30 to		
" Kip Cobourgs...	1 15	1 45	Can Leaf, ℔ 5s & 10s..	0 26	0 30	35 lbs.) per doz...	0 75	
Boys' Thick Boots...	1 70	1 80	Western Leaf, com..	0 25	0 29	Do. light	0 45	
Youths'	1 40	1 50	" Good	0 27	0 32	French Calf	1 05	
Women's Balls	95	1 20	" Fine	0 32	0 55	Grain & Sets Cif ℔ doz..	0 55	
" Congress Gaiters..	1 15	1 40	" Bright fine..	0 40	0 50	Splits, large ℔ lb.....	0 50	
Misses' Balls	0 75	1 00	" choice..	0 60	0 75	" small	0 50	
" Congress Gaiters..	1 00	1 20				Enamelled Cow ℔ foot..	0 20	
Girls' Balls	0 65	0 85	**Hardware.**			Patent	0 29	
" Congress Gaiters..	0 80	1 10	Tin (wt cash prices)			Pebble Grain	0 17	
Children's C. T. Conks..	0 50	0 65	Block, ℔ lb........	0 25	0 26	Buff	0 17	
" Gaiters	0 65	0 90	Grain	0 25	0 26			
Drugs.			Copper :—			**Oils.**		
Aloes Cape	0 12½	0 15	Pig	0 23	0 24	Cod	0 00	
Alum	0 07½	0 03	Sheet	0 20	0 33	Lard, extra	0 00	1 00
Borax	0 40	0 60	Cut Nails :			" No. 1	0 00	
Camphor, refined	0 65	0 70	Assorted ⅞ Shingles,			" Woollen	0 00	
Castor Oil	0 16¼	0 20	℔ 100 ℔.........	2 90	3 00	Lubricating, patent...	0 40	
Caustic Soda	0 04½	0 05	Single alone do	3 15	3 25	" Mott's economic	0 90	
Cochineal	0 50	1 00	Lathe and 5 dy....	3 20	3 40	Linseed, raw	0 76	
Cream Tartar	0 40	0 45	Galvanized Iron :			" boiled	0 81	
Epsom Salts	0 03	0 04	Assorted sizes	0 08	0 09	Machinery	0 00	
Extract Logwood	0 11	0 12	Best No. 24	0 00	0 00	Olive, common, ℔ gal..	1 00	
Gum Arabic, sorts	0 30	0 35	" 26	0 00	0 08½	" salad	1 05	
Indigo, Madras	0 70	1 00	" 28	0 00	0 09½	" saint, in bots		
Liquorice	0 14	0 45	Horse Nails :			qt. ℔ case...	3 00	
Madder	0 00	0 18	Ghust's or Griffin's			Sesame saint, ℔ gal...	1 00	
Galls	0 32	0 37	assorted sizes....	0 00	0 00	Seal, pale	0 72	
Opium	12 00	13 50	For W. and S. sizes....	0 18	0 19	Spirits Turpentine...	0 22½	
Oxalic Acid	0 25	0 35	Patent Hammer'd do..	0 17	0 18	Varnish	0 60	
Potash, Bi-tart..	0 55	0 90	Iron (at 4 months):			Whale	0 60	
" Bichromate..	0 15	0 20	Pig—Gartsherrie No 1..	24 00	26 00	**Paints, &c.**		
Potass Iodide	3 90	4 50	Other brands. No 1..	28 00	26 00	White Lead, genuine		
Senna	0 12½	0 60	" No 2..	0 00	0 00	in Oil, ℔ 25lbs...	0 00	
Soda Ash	0 02½	0 04	Bar—Scotch, ℔ 100 lb...	1 25	3 50	Do. No. 1 "	0 00	
S da Bicarb	4 50	5 00	Refined	3 00	3 25	" 2 "	0 00	
Tartaric Acid	0 40	0 45	Swedes	5 00	5 50	White Zinc, genuine..	1 40	
Vermilion	0 23	0 40	Hoops—Coopers	3 50	3 25	White Lead, dry	0 05½	
Vitriol, blue	0 08	0 10	" Band	3 00	3 25	Red Lead	0 07½	
Groceries.			Boiler Plates	3 25	3 50	Venetian Red, Eng'h.	0 02½	
Coffees :			Canada Plates	3 75	4 00	Yellow Ochre, Fren'h..	0 02½	
Java, ℔ lb	0 2½ 00	0 24	Union Jack	0 00	0 00	Whiting	0 8½	
Laguayra	0 17	0 18	Pontypool	3 25	4 00			
Rio	0 15	0 17	Swansea	3 90	4 00	**Petroleum.**		
Fish :			Lead (at 4 months):			(Refined ℔ gal.)		
Herrings, Lab. split..	5 75	6 50	Bar, ℔ 100 lbs..	0 04½	0 07	Water white, car'd...	0 27	
" round	4 60	5 00	Sheet	0 06	0 00	" small lots...	0 38	
" scaled	0 35	0 40	Shot	0 07½	0 07½	Straw, by car load...	0 35	
Mackerel, small kitts..	1 00	0 00	Iron Wire (net cash):			" small lots	0 35	
Lodi. Her. wh'sticks..	2 50	2 75	No. 6, ℔ bundle...	2 70	2 80	Amber, by car load...	0 00	
" half	1 25	1 50	" 9	3 30	3 50	" small lots	0 00	
White Fish & Trout...	3 50	3 75	" 12	3 40	3 50	Benzine	0 40	
Salmon, saltwater....	14 00	15 00	" 13	4 30	4 40			
Dry Cod, ℔ 112 lbs...	5 00	5 25	*Powder :*			**Produce.**		
Fruit :			Blasting, Canada...	3 50	0 00	*Grain :*		
Raisins, Layers	2 00	2 10	FF	4 25	4 50	Wheat, Spring, 60 ℔..	0 95	
" M R	1 90	2 10	FFF	4 75	5 00	" Fall	1 03	
" Valentias new	0 06½	0 07	Blasting, English	4 10	5 00	Barley	1 39	
Currants, new	0 07	0 07½	FF " loose.	5 60	6 00	Peas	0 85	
" old	0 04½	0 04½	FFF "	6 00	6 50	Oats	0 50	
Figs	0 14	0 00	Pressed Spikes (4 mos):.			Rye	0 79	
Molasses :			Regular sizes 100...	4 00	4 25	*Seeds :*		
Clayed, ℔ gal	0 00	0 35	Extra	4 50	5 00	Clover, choice 60 "..	5 50	
Syrups, Standard	0 49	0 60	*Tin Plates (net cash):*			" medium 6s..	6 25	
" Golden	0 56	0 07½	IC Coke	7 50	8 00	Timothy, cho's 4 "...	2 25	
Rice :			IC Charcoal	8 25	8 50	" inf to good 4s "	2 00	
Arracan	4 50	4 75	IX "	12 25	0 00	Flax	1 60	
Spices :			IXX "	12 25	0 00	*Flour (per brl.):*		
Cassia, whole, ℔ lb..	0 00	0 45	DC "	7 25	9 00	Superior extra	4 75	
Cloves	0 11	0 12	DX "	0 50	0 00	Extra superfine	4 59	
Nutmegs	0 45	0 55				Fancy superfine	4 25	
Ginger, ground	0 20	0 22	**Hides & Skins ℔ lb**			Superfine No 1		
" Jamaica, root..	0 20	0 25	Green rough	0 06	0 06½	" No. 2		
Pepper, black	0 09½	0 10	Grun, salt'd & insp'd..	0 07	0 07½	*Oatmeal, (per brl.)..*	6 00	
Pimento	0 08	0 09	Cure d	0 07½	0 03	**Provisions**		
Sugars :			Calfskins, green	0 00	0 14	Butter, dairy tub ℔ lb..	0 21	
Port Rico, ℔ lb	0 08½	0 08½	Calfskins, cured	0 00	0 12	" store packed..	0 12	
Cuba	0 08½	0 08½	" dry	0 13	0 20	Cheese, new	0 12	
Barbadoes (bright)..	0 08½	0 09	Sheepskins	1 00	1 40	Pork, mess, per brl..	25 00	
Dry Crushed, at 60d..	—	0 11½	" country	0 90	0 00	" prime mess...		
Canada Sugar Refine'y,						Bacon, rough	0 9½	
" No. 2, 60ds..	0 06	0 06½	**Hops**			" Cumberl'd cut..	0 11	
Yellow, No. 2½	0 09½	0 00	Inferior, ℔ lb	0 05	0 07	" smoked	0 00	
" No. 3..	0 09½	0 00	Medium	0 09	0 12	Hams, in salt	0 12	
Crushed X	0 00	0 10½	Good	0 00	0 00	" smg.cur & canv'd.		
" A	0 11½	0 11½	Fancy	0 00	0 00	Shoulders, in salt ...		
Ground	0 11½	0 11½				Lard, in kegs	0 16	
Dry Crushed	0 11½	0 11½	**Leather, ℔ (4 mos.)**			Eggs, packed	0 16	
Extra Ground	0 11½	0 12½	In lots of less than			Beef hams	0 00	
Teas :			50 sides, 10 ℔ cent			Tallow	0 06	
Japan com'n to good..	0 40	0 55	higher.			Hogs dressed, heavy..	0 75	
" Fine to choicest..	0 55	0 90	Spanish Sole, 1st qual..			" medium..	8 50	
Colored, com. to fine..	0 60	0 75	heavy, weights ℔ lb..	0 00	0 23	" light	9 00	
Congou & Souch'ng..	0 42	0 75	No. 2, all qual middle do..	0 21	0 23			
Colony, good to fine..	0 50	0 75	Do. No 2, all weights..	0 22	0 24	**Salt, &c.**		
Y. Hyson, com to gd..	0 45	0 60	Slaughter heavy	0 27	0 29	American brls	1 50	
Medium to choice ...	0 65	0 90	Do. light	0 25	0 00	Liverpool coarse	1 25	
Extra choice	0 95	0 95	Harness, best	0 32	0 34	Plaster	1 65	
" unpowd'r c. to med..	0 85	0 70	" No. 2	0 30	0 33	Water Lime	1 50	
" med. to fine	0 70	0 85	Upper heavy	0 33	0 38			
			" light	0 40	0 42			

Candles.	$ c.	$ c.
l & Co.'s ..		
al.........	0 07½	0 08
Bar	0 07	0 07½
Bar.........	0 07	0 07½
....	0 05	0 05½
....	0 03½	0 03¾
....	0 00	0 11½
Liquors,		
r doz......	2 00	2 65
ub Portr..	2 35	2 40
ica Rum...	1 80	2 25
's H. Gin..	1 55	1 63
l Tom.....	1 90	2 00
s.........	4 00	4 25
l Tom, c...	6 00	6 25
ion	1 00	1 25
ld	2 00	4 00
mmon	1 00	1 50
im	1 70	1 80
orgolden..	2 50	4 00

Brandy:	$ c.	$ c.
Hennessy's, per gal..	2 30	2 50
Martell's " ..	2 30	2 50
J. Robin & Co.'s " ..	2 25	2 35
Otard, Dupuy & Cos..	2 25	2 35
Brandy, cases........	8 50	9 00
Brandy, com. per c...	4 00	4 50
Whiskey:		
Common 36 u. p......	0 62½	0 65
Old Rye	0 8	0 87½
Malt	0 8	0 87½
Toddy	0 8	0 87½
Scotch, per gal.......	1 9	2 10
Irish—Kinnahan's c...	7 0	7 50
" Dunnville's Belf't..	6 00	6 25
Wool.		
Fleece, lb..........	0 23	0 35
Pulled "	0 22	0 25
Furs.		
Bear...............	8 00	10 00
Beaver, ₩ lb.........	1 00	1 25
Coon	0 20	0 40
Fisher.............	4 00	6 00
Martin.............	1 40	1 60
Mink...............	3 25	4 00
Otter..............	5 75	6 00
Spring Rats	0 15	0 17
Fox................	1 20	1 25

INSURANCE COMPANIES.

ENGLISH.—*Quotations on the London Market.*

Last Dividend.	Name of Company.	Shares par val £	Amount paid.	Last Sale.
	Briton Medical and General Life ...	10	....	1⅝
7½	Commer'l Union, Fire, Life and Mar.	50	5	5¾
8	City of Glasgow	25	2½	4⅝
9½	Edinburgh Life	100	15	32
—½ yr	European Life and Guarantee......	2½	11s6	4s. 9d.
10	Etna Fire and Marine............	10	1½	—
5	Guardian	100	50	51½
12	Imperial Fire..................	500	50	339
9½	Imperial Life	100	10	16⅞
10	Lancashire Fire and Life..........	20	2	2 15-16ths
11	Life Association of Scotland.......	40	7½	25
.p. sh	London Assurance Corporation ..	25	12½	49
5	London and Lancashire Life	10	1	19s
40	Liverp'l & London & Globe F. & L.	20	2	6⅞
5	National Union Life	5	1	par
12½	Northern Fire and Life	100	5	11⅝
12 bo 5s.	North British and Mercantile	50	6¼	19½
50	Ocean Marine	25	5	20
12s.	Provident Life..................	100	10	37
½ p. s.	Phœnix......................	....	....	145x
-h.yr.	Queen Fire and Life	10	1	18s
bo.4s	Royal Insurance..................	20	3	6
10	Scottish Provincial Fire and Life ..	50	2½	5¼
25	Standard Life	50	12	66
5	Star Life	25	1¼	—
	CANADIAN.			₩ c.
4	British America Fire and Marine ..	$50	$25	54 55xd
4	Canada Life	...	....	.....
12	Montreal Assurance	£50	£5	135
8	Provincial Fire and Marine........	60	11	.....
.....	Quebec Fire	40	32½	25½
8	" Marine..................	100	40	75 80
mo's.	Western Assurance..............	40	9	.....

RAILWAYS.	Sha's	Paid	Montr	London
St. Lawrence........................	£100	All.	....	60 61
Lake Huron	20½	"	....	3 3½
do Preference	10	"	....	5½ 6½
& Goderich, 6₩c., 1872-3-4....	100	"	....	66 69
nd St. Lawrence	....	....	10	....
do Pref. 10 ₩ ct....	....	....	73	....
k	100	"	15 16	16 16½
Eq.G. M. Bds. 1 ch. 6₩c..........	100	"	....	85 87
First Preference, 5 ₩ c	100	"	....	54½ 55½
Deferred, 3 ₩ ct..	100	"	....	....
Second Pref. Bonds, 5₩c..........	100	"	....	40½ 41½
do Deferred, 3 ₩ ct...........	100	"	...	....
Third Pref. Stock, 4₩ct...........	100	"	...	28 30
do. Deferred, 3 ₩ ct......	100	"	....	....
Fourth Pref. Stock, 3₩c...........	100	"	....	18¼ 18¾
do. Deferred, 3 ₩ ct...........	100	"	....	...
rn	20½	"	13 14	15⅜ 15⅝
New	20½	18	....	....
6 ₩ c. Bds, due 1873-76..........	100	All.	....	100 102
5½₩c Bds. due 1877-78..........	100	"	....	93½ 94½
way, Halifax, $250, all......	$250	"	....	....
Canada, 6₩c. 1st Pref. Bds..........	100	"	.. .	81 83

HANGE.	Halifax.	Montr'l.	Quebec.	Toronto.
omlon, 60 days......				
days date	12½	9⅝ 9⅞	9¼ 9⅝	9¾
. ...	11½ 12	8 9	8¾ 9½	8¾
documents...........	....	7½ 8	....	....
York...............	....	25½ 26	25 25½	74½
do.	....	26 26½	25½ 26	....
do.	....	½ dis. to p.	par ½ dis.	par ¼ dis.
....	....	4 4½	....	4 to 6

STOCK AND BOND REPORT.

The dates of our quotations are as follows:—Toronto, Feb. 9; Montreal, Feb. 8; Quebec, Feb. 18; London, Jan. 21.

NAME.	Shares.	Paid up.	Divid'd last 6 Months	Dividend Day.	CLOSING PRICES. Toronto.	Montre'l	Quebec.
BANKS.			₩ ct.				
British North America	$250	All.	3	July and Jan.	104 105	104 105	103½ 104
Jacques Cartier.............	50	"	4	1 June, 1 Dec.	107 108	108	107 107½
Montreal	200	"	5	"	139½ 140	139½ 140	138½ 139½
Nationale..................	50	"	4	1 Nov. 1 May.	106 106½	106 106½	106½ 107
New Brunswick	100	"	......	......	....	...	....
Nova Scotia	200	28	7&b$3½	Mar. and Sept.	....	....	....
Du Peuple...................	50	"	4	1 Mar., 1 Sept.	109 110	109¾	109 110
Toronto	100	"	4	1 Jan., 1 July.	121½ 122½	121½ 123	120 121
Bank of Yarmouth...........	....	....	......	......	....	....	....
Canadian Bank of Com'e......	50	95	......	......	102½ 102¾	102 103	101 102
City Bank Montreal	80	All.	4	1 June, 1 Dec.	102 103	102 103½	102½ 103
Commer'l Bank (St. John)....	100	"	₩ ct.	......	....	....	....
Eastern Townships' Bank.....	50	"	4	1 July, 1 Jan..	....	98½ 99½	98 99
Gore	40	...	none.	1 Jan., 1 July.	42 45	40 45	40 45
Halifax Banking Company....	...	....	......	......	...	....	....
Mechanics' Bank.............	50	70	4	1 Nov., 1 May.	95 96	94 96	94 95
Merchants' Bank of Canada....	100	70	4	1 Jan., 1 July.	109 109½	109 109½	109¾ 110¼
Merchants' Bank (Halifax)....	....	....	......	......	....	....	....
Molson's Bank...............	50	All.	4	1 Apr., 1 Oct.	110 110½	110 110½	110 111
Niagara District Bank...	100	70	3½	1 Jan., 1 July.	...	....	....
Ontario Bank................	40	All.	4	1 June, 1 Dec.	100 100½	99 100	99¾ 100¼
People's Bank (Fred'kton)....	100	"	......	......	....	....	..
People's Bank (Halifax)	20	"	7 12 m	......	....	...	....
Quebec Bank	100	"	3½	1 June, 1 Dec.	99½ 100	99 100	99¾ 100
Royal Canadian Bank	50	50	4	1 Jan., 1 July.	87½ 88	86 87	85 87
St. Stephens Bank	100	All	......	......	....	..	....
Union Bank	100	70	4	1 Jan., 1 July.	103 103½	102 103	103¾ 104½
Union Bank (Halifax)........	100	40	7 12mo	Feb. and Aug.	....	....	...
MISCELLANEOUS.							
British America Land........	250	44	2½	......	....	....	....
British Colonial S. S. Co......	250	32½	2½	......	....	....	....
Canada Company	32½	All.	£1 10s.	......	...	....	....
Canada Landed Credit Co.....	50	$20	3½	......	72½ 75	....	....
Canada Per. B'ldg Society....	50	All.	5	......	124½ 125	....	....
Canada Mining Company......	4	90	......	......	....	....	....
Do. Inl'd Steam Nav. Co.....	100	All.	20 12 m	......	....	105 107	105 106
Do. Glass Company.........	100	"	12½ "	......	....	...	....
Canad'n Loan & Investm't....	25	2½	7	......	....	....	....
Canada Agency	10	½	......	......	....	....	....
Colonial Securities Co........	...	....	......	......	....	....	....
Freehold Building Society....	100	All.	4	......	109 109½	....	....
Halifax Steamboat Co.........	100	"	5	......	....	....	....
Halifax Gas Company.........	....	....	......	......	....	....	....
Hamilton Gas Company.......	....	....	......	......	....	...	....
Huron Copper Bay Co.........	4	12	20	......	....	....	....
Lake Huron S. and C..........	5	102	......	......	....	25 35cps	....
Montreal Mining Consols.....	20	$15	......	......	....	3.00 3.25	....
Do. Telegraph Co...	40	All.	5	......	132½ 133½	132½ 134	133 134½
Do. Elevating Co...	00	"	15 12 m	......	....	100 102½	....
Do. City Gas Co.........	40	"	4	15 Mar. 15 Sep.	....	135 137	136 137
Do. City Pass. R. Co.....	50	"	5	......	....	110 111	110½ 111
Nova Scotia Telegraph	20	"	....	......	....	....	....
Quebec and L. S.	8	84	......	......	....	....	25 cts
Quebec Gas Co...............	200	All.	4	1 Mar., 1 Sep.	....	....	119 120
Quebec Street R. R	50	25	8	......	....	...	90 91
Richelieu Navigation Co......	100	All.	7 p.a.	1 Jan., 1 July.	....	116 119	117 117½
St. Lawrence Tow Boat Co.....	100	"	......	3 Feb.	....	...	35 40
Tor'to Consumers' Gas Co.....	50	"	2 3 m.	1 My Au Mar Fe	107 108	...	107 108
Trust & Loan Co. of U. C.....	20	5	3	......	....	....	...
West'n Canada Bldg Soc'y....	50	All.	5	......	118½ 119	....	....

SECURITIES.	London.	Montreal	Quebec.	Toronto.
Canadian Gov't Deb. 6 ₩ ct. stg..............	....	105 105½	102½ 103	104 106
Do. do. 6 do due Ja. & Jul. 1877-84........	104 105	....	....	....
Do. do. 6 do. Feb. & Aug........	105 107	....	.. .	....
Do. do. 6 do. Mch. & Sep........	104 106	.. .	...	.. .
Do. do. 5 ₩ ct. cur., 1883	93½ 94½	94 95½	93 93½	94½ 95
Do. do. 5 do. stg., 1885	94 95	96 96½	93 93½	95 95½
Do. do. 7 do. cur.,....................	....	....	......	....
Dominion 6 p. c. 1878 cy.....	....	104½ 105	105 105½	105 105½
Hamilton Corporation.....	. ..	....	... ..	....
Montreal Harbor, 8 ₩ ct. d. 1869..............	..	....	......	....
Do. do. 7 do. 1870..............	....	....	......	....
Do. do. 6½ do. 1883..............	....	102½ 103	......	....
Do. do. 6½ do. 1873..............	....	....	......	....
Do. Corporation, 6 ₩ c. 1891	....	95 96	94½ 95½	95 96
Do. 7 p. c. stock............................	....	107 110	108½ 109½	107½ 108½
Do. Water Works, 6 ₩ c. stg. 1878..........	....	....	......	95 96
Do. do. 6 do. cy. do.	....	95½ 96½	......	95 96
New Brunswick, 6 ₩ ct., Jan. and July	101 103	....	......	....
Nova Scotia, 6 ₩ ct., 1875.....................	101 103	...	......	....
Ottawa City 6 ₩ c. d. 1880	....	92½ 93½	......	...
Quebec Harbour, 6 ₩ c. d. 1883.	....	....	60	....
Do. do. 7 do. do....................	....	....	65 70	....
Do. do. 8 do. 1886....................	...	....	80 85	....
Do. City, 7 ₩ c. d. 4½ years....	....	....	96½ 97	....
Do. do. 7 do. 9 do.	....	....	91 92	....
Do. do. 7 do. 2 do.	....	....	93 93½	....
Do. Water Works, 7 ₩ ct., 4 years..........	....	....	97 97½	....
Do. do. 6 do. 2 do.	....	....	94 95	....
Toronto Corporation	....	....	...	....

Insurance.

BEAVER
Mutual Insurance Association.

HEAD OFFICE—29 TORONTO STREET,
TORONTO.

INSURES LIVE STOCK against death from any cause. The only Canadian Company having authority to do this class of business.

R. L. DENISON,
President.
W. T. O'REILLY,
Secretary.   8-1y-25

HOME DISTRICT
Mutual Fire Insurance Company.

Office—North-West Cor. Yonge & Adelaide Streets, TORONTO.—(UP STAIRS.)

INSURES Dwelling Houses, Stores, Warehouses, Merchandise, Furniture, &c.

PRESIDENT—The Hon. J. McMURRICH.
VICE-PRESIDENT—JOHN BURNS, Esq.
JOHN RAINS, Secretary.
AGENTS:
DAVID WRIGHT, Esq., Hamilton; FRANCIS STEVENS, Esq., Barrie; Messrs. GIBBS & BRO., Oshawa.   8-1y

THE PRINCE EDWARD COUNTY
Mutual Fire Insurance Company

HEAD OFFICE,—PICTON, ONTARIO.
President, L. B. STINSON; Vice-President, W. A. RICHARDS.
Directors : H. A. McFAUL, James Cavan, James Johnson, N. S. DeMill, William Delong.—Treasurer, David Barker Secretary, John Twigg; Solicitor, B. J. Fitzgerald.

THIS Company is established upon strictly Mutual principles, insuring farming and isolated property, (not hazardous,) in Townships only, and offers great advantages to insurers, at low rates for five years, without the expense of a renewal.
Pictou, June 15, 1868.   9-1y

Hartford Fire Insurance Company.

HARTFORD, CONN.

Cash Capital and Assets over Two Million Dollars.

$2,026,220.29.

CHARTERED 1810.

THIS old and reliable Company, having an established business in Canada of more than thirty years standing, has complied with the provisions of the new Insurance Act, and made a special deposit of

$100,000

with the Government for the security of policy-holders, and will continue to grant policies upon the same favorable terms as heretofore.

Specially low rates on first-class dwellings and farm property for a term of one or more years.
Losses as heretofore promptly and equitably adjusted.
H. J. MORSE & CO., AGENTS.
Toronto, Ont.

ROBERT WOOD, GENERAL AGENT FOR CANADA;
50-6m

THE AGRICULTURAL
Mutual Assurance Association of Canada.

HEAD OFFICE.....................LONDON, ONT.

A purely Farmers' Company. Licensed by the Government of Canada.

Capital, 1st January, 1868.....................$220,121 2
Cash and Cash Items, over.....................$65,000 0
No. of Policies in force.....................28,760

THIS Company insures nothing more dangerous than Farm property. Its rates are as low as any well-established Company in the Dominion, and lower than those of a great many. It is largely patronised, and continues to grow in public favor.
For Insurance, apply to any of the Agents or address the Secretary, London, Ontario.
London, 2nd Nov., 1868.   13-1y.

Insurance.

The Gore District Mutual Fire Insurance Company

GRANTS INSURANCES on all description of Property against Loss or Damage by FIRE. It is the only Mutual Fire Insurance Company which assesses its Policies yearly from their respective dates ; and the average yearly cost of insurance in it, for the past three and a half years, has been nearly
TWENTY CENTS IN THE DOLLAR
less than it would have been in an ordinary Proprietary Company.
THOS. M. SIMONS,
Secretary & Treasurer.
ROBT. McLEAN,
Inspector of Agencies.
Galt, 26th Nov., 1868.   15-1y

Geo. Girdlestone,

FIRE, Life, Marine, Accident, and Stock Insurance Agent
Very best Companies represented.
Windsor, Ont. June, 1868

The Standard Life Assurance Company,
Established 1825.
WITH WHICH IS NOW UNITED
THE COLONIAL LIFE ASSURANCE COMPANY.

Head Office for Canada :
MONTREAL—STANDARD COMPANY'S BUILDINGS, No. 47 GREAT ST. JAMES STREET.
Manager—W. M. RAMSAY.   Inspector—RICH'D BULL.

THIS Company having deposited the sum of ONE HUNDRED AND FIFTY THOUSAND DOLLARS with the Receiver-General, in conformity with the Insurance Act passed last Session, Assurances will continue to be carried out at moderate rates and on all the different systems in practice.
AGENT FOR TORONTO—HENRY PELLATT,
KING STREET.
AGENT FOR HAMILTON—JAMES BANCROFT.
6-6mos.

Fire and Marine Assurance.

THE BRITISH AMERICA
ASSURANCE COMPANY.
HEAD OFFICE :
CORNER OF CHURCH AND COURT STREETS.
TORONTO.

BOARD OF DIRECTION :
Hon G. W. Allan, M L C ,   A. Joseph, Esq ,
George J. Boyd, Esq ,   Peter Paterson, Esq.,
Hon. W. Cayley,   G P. Ridout, Esq.,
Richard S. Cassels, Esq.,   E H. Rutherford, Esq.,
          Thomas C. Street, Esq.
Governor:
GEORGE PERCIVAL RIDOUT, Esq.
Deputy Governor:
PETER PATERSON, Esq.
Fire Inspector: Marine Inspector:
E. ROBY O'BRIEN.   CAPT. R. COURNEEN.
Insurances granted on all descriptions of property against loss and damage by fire and the perils of inland navigation.
Agencies established in the principal cities, towns, and ports of shipment throughout the Province.
THOS. WM. BIRCHALL,
Managing Director.
23-1y

Queen Fire and Life Insurance Company,
OF LIVERPOOL AND LONDON,
ACCEPTS ALL ORDINARY FIRE RISKS
on the most favorable terms.

LIFE RISKS
Will b taken on terms that will compare favorably with other Companies.

CAPITAL, - - - £2,000,000 Stg.

CHIEF OFFICES—Queen's Buildings, Liverpool, and Gracechurch Street London.
CANADA BRANCH OFFICE—Exchange Buildings, Montreal.
Resident Secretary and General Agent,
A. MACKENZIE FORBES,
13 St. Sacrament St., Merchants' Exchange, Montreal.
WM. ROWLAND, Agent, Toronto.   1-1y

Insurance.

The Waterloo County Mutual Fire Insurance Company.

HEAD OFFICE : WATERLOO, ONTARIO.

ESTABLISHED 1863.

THE business of the Company is divided in separate and distinct branches, the
VILLAGE, FARM, AND MANUFACT
Each Branch paying its own losses and its just proportion of the managing expenses of the Company.
C. M. TAYLOR, Sen.   M. SPRINGER, M.M.P.,
J. HUGHES, Inspector.

Etna Fire and Marine Insurance Company
Dublin.

AT a Meeting of the Shareholders of this Company held at Dublin, on the 13th ult., it was agreed the business of the "ETNA" should be transferred "UNITED PORTS AND GENERAL INSURANCE CO." In accordance with this agreement, the business will after be carried on by the latter Company, which assumed and guarantees all the risks and liabilities of the "
The Directors have resolved to continue the CA BRANCH, and arrangements for resuming FIRE a rine business are rapidly approaching completion
16   T. W. GRIFFITH
MAN

The Commercial Union Assurance Company,
19 & 20 CORNHILL, LONDON, ENGLAND.
Capital, £2,500,000 Stg.—Invested over $2,000,0

FIRE DEPARTMENT.—Insurance granted on scriptions of property at reasonable rates.
LIFE DEPARTMENT.—The success of this has been unprecedented—NINETY PER CENT. miums now in hand. First year's premiums we $100,000. Economy of management guaranteed security. Moderate rates.
OFFICE—385 & 387 ST PAUL STREET, MONTR
MORLAND, WATSON & C
General Agents for
FRED. COLE, Secretary.
Inspector of Agencies—T. C. LIVINGSTON,
W. M. WESTMACOTT, Agent at To
16-1y

Lancashire Insurance Compa
CAPITAL, - - - - - £2,000,000

FIRE RISKS
Taken at reasonable rates of premium, s
ALL LOSSES SETTLED PROMPTLY
By the undersigned, without reference elsev
S. C. DUNCAN-CLARK & CO.,
General Agents for Onta
N. W. Corner of King & Church S
25-1y   TORONTO.

Etna Fire & Marine Insurance Comp
INCORPORATED 1819.   CHARTER PERPETUA

CASH CAPITAL, - - - - - - $

LOSSES PAID IN 50 YEARS, 23,500,00

JULY, 1868.
ASSETS.
(At Market Value.)
Cash in hand and in Bank.....................$5
Real Estate.....................2
Mortgage Bonds.....................9
Bank Stock.....................1,2
United States, State and City Stock, and other Public Securities.....................2,0
          Total.....................$5,0

LIABILITIES.
Claims not Due, and Unadjusted.....................$4
Amount required by Mass. and New York for Re-insurance.....................1,4
THOS. R. WOOD,
50-6   Agent for To

PUBLISHED AT THE OFFICE OF THE MO
TIMES, No. 60 CHURCH STREET.
PRINTED AT THE DAILY TELEGRAPH PRINTING
BAY STREET, CORNER OF KING.

THE CANADIAN

MONETARY TIMES AND INSURANCE CHRONICLE.

THE Publishers have pleasure in announcing that the success of this JOURNAL has been such as to stimulate their efforts to render it still more valuable to the classes directly and indirectly interested in the subjects with which it deals. As the only Journal in the Dominion which gives particular attention to INSURANCE, it has enlisted the hearty support of Insurance Companies; and while, on the one hand, it contends for the rights of such Companies, it equally recognizes the rights of the public.

The subject of BANKING has become of such importance, as well by reason of past legislation as by reason of anticipated changes in the law respecting circulation, that it is the duty and interest of our business men to make themselves acquainted with the principles on which sound Banking rests, and to prevent any action on the part of the Legislature likely to injure the community by lessening the usefulness of our banks. The discussion of this subject in the columns of this JOURNAL has called forth expressions of satisfaction from our most astute financiers, and has done much to give us the position we now occupy in the estimation of the public.

As MINING is in its infancy in this country, a journal devoted solely to the subject could not hope to thrive; but by giving full information regarding Mining operations, and by the employment of reliable correspondents, we have done good service to an important interest, and secured recognition from a class which, otherwise, could not have been reached.

Our purely COMMERCIAL DEPARTMENT has not been neglected, and each week's summary, while concise and pithy, has answered the same ends as a more diffuse elaboration could do, and conveyed to country dealers a complete synopsis of the changes in the Toronto and Montreal Markets.

This combination of interests which the circumstances of the country render necessary, has been of the greatest advantage to each interest by diffusing information among all classes.; but, in order to do justice to all, we have been compelled to employ a large staff of writers, and to expend a considerable amount in securing trustworthy correspondents.

While we are thankful to those who have encouraged us thus far, we are anxious to extend still further the usefulness of this Journal, and we call on all who consider that the enterprise is worthy of support, to lend us their assistance in making the MONETARY TIMES a national organ.

On our part we promise impartiality, efficiency, and the best efforts of the ablest writers that can be secured in the Dominion. On the part of our clients, we expect a cordial support and active exertion to widen our sphere of usefulness. In helping us, they help themselves.

Every Merchant, Banker, Capitalist, Insurance Agent, and Broker, can aid us, and we hope that we are not asking too much, in soliciting their assistance.

We shall be happy to receive at any time articles on subjects within our jurisdiction, which, if used, will be liberally paid for.

Subscription Price...$2 per Annum.

A reasonable discount will be made to Banks, Insurance Companies, &c., which subscribe for their Agencies.
SEND FOR A SPECIMEN COPY.
N.B.—Every subscriber to THE MONETARY TIMES will receive THE REAL ESTATE JOURNAL without further charge.

THE REAL ESTATE JOURNAL.

The objects of this Journal are as follows :—

(1.) To supply to those interested in real estate such information as is of special interest relating to sales or transfers of real property in the principal cities, and throughout Ontario, construction of public works, and building improvements of every kind, increase or decrease of municipal expenditure, debt and taxation, and, in short, whatever tends to influence the real estate market.

(2.) Leading articles will be furnished by competent writers on questions relating to conveyancing, the rise and fall of property, land grants, emigration, and other subjects coming within the legitimate scope of the Journal.

(3.) Lists of lands and houses for sale in every city, town and village of the Province, will appear in its columns, giving buyers the best possible opportunities for selecting desirable properties of any class, and in any locality ; and, at the same time, affording sellers a reliable and certain medium for reaching intending purchasers.

(4.) By a circulation extending into every corner of Canada, the announcements of advertisers will be brought to the notice of an immense constituency of readers. A special feature in this connection is, that the Journal will be placed and kept on fyle at all the principal hotels, reading rooms, and other public places in Ontario, and in Montreal. By these means it is confidently believed that every man in the community will be reached.

THE REAL ESTATE JOURNAL is printed fortnightly, on good white paper, in quarto form, and is equal in size and appearance to anything the kind published on this continent.

Advertising, per line of nonpareil, each insertion, 5 cents. A small discount will be allowed on yearly contracts, for large spaces.
Address, "THE REAL ESTATE JOURNAL," Toronto, Ontario. Cheques should be made payable to J. M. TROUT, who will also issue all receipts for money.

OFFICE, No. 60 CHURCH STREET,
TORONTO, ONTARIO.

PROSPECTUS OF THE

ONTARIO PEAT COMP'Y

LIMITED LIABILITY. · · · · · · · HEAD OFFICE—TORONTO.

To be Organized under the Act 27 and 28 Victoria, Chapter 23, and the Amendments thereto.

THE property of the company forms a portion of the well-known "Cranberry Marsh," in the Townships of Humberstone and Wainfleet, County Welland, and Province of Ontario, traversed by the Welland Canal, as well as by its "Feeder," which is also navigable; and is composed of following lots, viz.:—

	Acres.
Humberstone—South halves of 28, 30, 32 and 33. Concession IV.	400
Wainfleet—South halves of 6 and 7, Concession IV.	200
" Whole of 10, Concession II, and the whole of 10 and 11, Concession III.	600
" Parts of 8 and 9, Concessions IV. and V., about.	200
Total	1400

A main ditch six feet deep has been made by the County through the whole of this Marsh for surface drainage, at an expenditure of $50,000; this ditch runs along a portion of every one of the above lots, except two which abut upon the feeder of the Welland Canal.

The several lots above enumerated were the first chosen from the Marsh, having been selected for their great value as Peat Deposits, remaining Peat lands have been obtained by the Anglo-American Peat Company, which has been operating most successfully during the last sea upon a lot adjoining one of the Company's lots. A most satisfactory report has been obtained from Frederick Holmes, Esq., the County Engineer gentleman who has had large experience in these peat lands, having not only surveyed and laid off the Marsh into lots for the County, but has also been employed as superintendent in the ditching operations which have been undertaken and carried out through the whole extent of the Marsh. estimate of the quantity of Peat contained in the Company's lands is placed at three millions of tons, at the very least; and this estimate is full, bo out by the eminent firm of Messrs. Macdougall and Skae, Civil Engineers, Toronto, who were specially despatched to make a personal examination the property, and whose report is subjoined.

Peat can be laid down on the banks of the canal at the cost of from $1 to $1.25 per ton, and can from thence be forwarded by water to market in directions, at small cost, and without transhipment; to say nothing of the facilities and advantages afforded by no less than five railways, one of whi the "Buffalo and Lake Huron," passes within twenty chains of the property. In addition to these advantages, the fact may be noticed, that ab thirty vessels pass through the canal every day during the season of navigation, the steamers requiring fuel for their own use, and the sailing vess seeking cargoes, and requiring ballast westward to Chicago and other points.

The demand for this fuel for private consumption will be very great when its superior qualities become more widely known. Already railways a steamers are beginning to use it instead of wood and coal, with the most satisfactory results, experience having proved that one ton of peat is equal about one and one-third cords of the best hard wood. With a view to the full and proper developement of this property, it is proposed to organize Company with a capital of $120,000, in 2,400 shares of $50 each; $50,000 of this sum to be retained by the Directors for working capital, the balance be applied to the purchase of the real estate. It is also proposed that 25 per cent shall be paid at the time of subscription, and the balance in calls 10 per cent at such times as the Directors may name, but not oftener than once in every three months, from 1st of January, 1869.

The affairs of the Company will be managed by a Board of five Directors, the first set to be provisional, and, as soon as the charter is obtained a the Company organized, the permanent Directors to be chosen by the Shareholders, and to be elected annually.

The principal office of the Company to be in the City of Toronto. The property has been conveyed to Peleg Howland, Esquire, who will hold t ame in trust until the Company is organized

PROVISIONAL DIRECTORS.

Henry S. Howland, Esquire, Toronto.	John Fisken, Esquire, Toronto.	Larratt W. Smith, Esquire, Toronto.
Alfred Todd, Esquire, Ottawa.		Edward A. C. Pew, Esquire, Welland.

Further information can be obtained at the office of

C. J. CAMPBELL, Esq., Banker, 92 King Street East, Toronto,
Who will act as Provisional Treasurer, and will also receive subscriptions for Stoc

---

CHAMBERS, 17 TORONTO STREET, TORONTO, JANUARY 11, 1869.

To the Directors of the Ontario Peat Company,—

GENTLEMEN,—We have the honor to lay before you the following report, on the Peat Beds in the Great Cranberry Marsh, situated in the Coun of Welland. The swamp, or to call it by a more proper name, moor, for it is more like the moors of Scotland than the swamps of this country, intersected by a large drain, which at present carries off a considerable quantity of water; and from its juxta position, to the lots owned by your compa could be made available for drainage purposes. The moor rises gradually from its northern limit in concession 4, to its summit, at the south end concession 3, about four feet on two and a half miles, where it is about eight feet above the level of Lake Erie; while, on the north, from the end of t moor to the Welland River, distant about a mile and a half, there is a fall of sixteen feet. Following the course of the water through the vario drains, the result arrived at is, that the moor is higher than the surrounding country, which is under cultivation.

The peat on this marsh, brought up by the boring rods, as well as that lying on the sides of the drains, thrown up when they were made, shows good quality of a dark black color, in every lot. There is a layer of red peat in some of the lots of the Township of Humberstone; but generally t peat was of the dark colour above mentioned. The surface of the marsh, or moor, has been burnt once or twice, so that there is not much moss or upp growth; nor are there many trees alive; and on the lots owned by your company this is more marked. The lots are conveniently placed for workin and connections could be formed, at a small cost, to the several outlets that surround this tract of land; and the surface being regular, no difficul would be encountered in laying tramroads.

In making the borings for this report, the valuable assistance of the County Engineer, Mr. Frederick Holmes, was obtained, as he had superintend the making of the drains, and had laid out several of the lots some years ago, and since that time had been intimately acquainted with the moor. T depths arrived at give an average of six to eight feet of peat over all the lots in the 3rd and 4th concessions, while in the lot of the 2nd concessi of the Township of Wainfleet, the peat is very deep, averaging about 15 feet, and it is said to go even deeper. There are 200 acres in this lot.

The regularity of the upper surface of this large tract of land, both peat and arable, being combined with the result of the borings taken, tend t conclusion that the bottom of the peat bed must also be regular, as there are no hills or mounds of any size or consequence in the vicinity.

The Anglo-American Peat Fuel Company have been at work during last summer on a portion of this marsh, opposite to some of the lots owned your Company. They find the loss, by weight and shrinkage to be 75 per cent.; or to make one ton of peat fuel, four tons of peat are required. Tl is less than that of a similar project in the Lower Province, where the shrinkage is 85 per cent.

From the data and experience of the Anglo-American Company, taking the loss by weight and shrinkage at 75 per cent., with an average of fr six to eight feet over all the lots, but that in the 5th Concession of Wainfleet, which is taken at sixteen feet, we find the property of your Compan situated in the marsh, to be capable of producing over 3,000,000 tons of fuel.

A fuller report, by us, lies in the hands of Mr. C. J. Campbell, Banker, King Street, Toronto, to which also we beg to call your attention.

We have the honour to be, gentlemen, your obedient servants,

MACDOUGALL & SKAE,
CIVIL ENGINEERS

THE CANADIAN

IONETARY TIMES

AND

INSURANCE CHRONICLE.

OTED TO FINANCE, COMMERCE, INSURANCE, BANKS, RAILWAYS, NAVIGATION, MINES, INVESTMENT,
PUBLIC COMPANIES, AND JOINT STOCK ENTERPRISE.

—NO. 27. TORONTO, THURSDAY, FEBRUARY 18, 1869. { SUBSCRIPTION $2 YEAR.

Mercantile.

Gundry and Langley,
CTS AND CIVIL ENGINEERS, Building Sur
and Valuators. Office corner of King and Jordan
ronto.
1 GUNDRY. HENRY LANGLEY.

J. B. Boustead.
N and Commission Merchant. Hops bought
ld on Commission. 82 Front St., Toronto.

John Boyd & Co.
SALE Grocers and Commission Merchants,
1 St., Toronto.

Childs & Hamilton.
CTURERS and Wholesale Dealers in Boots
hoes, No. 7 Wellington Street East, Toronto.
28

L. Coffee & Co.
and Commission Merchants, No. 2 Manning's
Front St., Toronto, Ont. Advances made on
ts of Produce.

Honore Plamondon,
House Broker, Forwarder, and General Agent,
Office—Custom House Building. 17-17

Sylvester, Bro. & Hickman,
CIAL Brokers and Vessel Agents. Office—No.
rio Chambers, [Corner Front and Church Sts.,
2-6m

John Fisken & Co.
L and Commission Merchants, Yonge St.,
o, Ont.

W. & R. Griffith.
RS of Teas, Wines, etc. Ontario Chambers,
rch and Front Sts , Toronto.

H. Nerlich & Co.,
RS of French, German, English and American
ods, Cigars, and Leaf Tobaccos, No. 2 Adelaide
t, Toronto. 15

Hurd, Leigh & Co.
and Enamellers of China and Earthenware,
ge St., Toronto, Ont. [See advt.]

Lyman & McNab.
ALE Hardware Merchants, Toronto, Ontario.

W. D. Matthews & Co.
Commission Merchants, Old Corn Exchange,
1 St. East, Toronto Ont.

R. C. Hamilton & Co.
Commission Merchants, 119 Lower Water
Man, Nova Scotia.

Parson Bros.,
UM Refiners, and Wholesale dealers in Lamps,
ys, etc. Waterooms 51 Front St. Refinery cor.
in Sts., Toronto.

C. P. Reid & Co.,
IS and Dealers in Wines, Liquors, Cigars and
acco, Wellington Street, Toronto. 23

W. Rowland & Co.,
BROKERS and General Commission Mer-
Advances made on Consignments. Corner
Front Streets, Toronto.

Reford & Dillon.
S of Groceries, Wellington Street, Toronto,

Iessions, Turner & Cooper.
CTURERS, Importers and Wholesale Dealer
s and Shoes, Leather Findings, etc., 8 Wel-
'st, Toronto, Ont

Meetings.

NORTHERN RAILWAY.

The annual meeting of the Northern Railway
Co. took place on the 10th inst., in the Company's
offices, Brock street, Toronto.

Mr. F. W. Cumberland read the annual report
of the Canadian Directors as follows :

To the Proprietors of the Northern Railway of Canada.

TORONTO, 10th February, 1869.

The Canadian Directors have the honour to present their Report for the year ending 31st Dec.,
1868, with accompanying Statements of Account,
Auditors' Reports, and Departmental Returns :—

1. The gross Traffic receipts of the year have
amounted to $550,070 24 (£113,023 2s. 7d. stg.,)
as in comparison with $561,370.24(£115,350 0s 11d
stg.) in 1867 ; showing a decrease of $11300.01
($2,321 18s 4d stg.) On examination of the earn-
ings arising from the respective sources of traffic,
it will be seen that this decrease is more than accounted for in the one item of "square timber,"
in which the decline is due to gradual exhaustion
of the supply.

For this decline, the Directors have been prepared for some years, confidently anticipating,
however, than any special loss of this character
would be succeeded and compensated by the
growth of other and more permanent classes of
traffic of higher value. In confirmation of this
view, it is satisfactory to find that the Passenger
traffic has, during the past year, yielded an advance of $9,095.60, or in comparison with 1866,
the important increase of $22,945.90. Again,
whilst the transport of square timber has fallen
from 2,713,266 cubic feet in 1867, to 1,616.561
feet in 1868, showing a reduction of no less than
1,096,705 feet, that reduction has been compensated for by an advance in the article of sawn
lumber (a much better and more remunerative
freight) from 44,790,000 feet in 1867 to 54,954,-
000 feet in 1868, or an increase of 10,164,000 feet,
in an item of trade which is in continuous and
rapid extension, and of permanent character.

Due to an exceptional condition of the grain
market arising from the low local prices and the
abundant harvests abroad, the traffic in grain and
flour has been subject to unusual fluctuations ; but
as the area under cultivation in the districts tribu-
butary to the line is ever increasing, this class of
traffic cannot be subject to any continuous decline.
On the whole, it is very satisfactory to observe,
that notwithstanding these heavy, although but
temporary, fluctuations in the staples; the gross
earnings of the Railway have not been sensibly
affected, excepting in so far as that they have been
realized from a higher class of traffic.

2. The ordinary working expenses of the year
have amounted to $335,894.31 (£69,019 7s. 7d.
stg.) as against $332,861.20 (£68,396 2s. 9d. stg.)
in 1867; giving a rate on the gross traffic receipts
of 61.06 per cent. in 1868 as in comparison with
59.29 per cent. in 1867, being a difference of 1.77
per cent. in favour of the previous year. This
rise is directly traceable to two or three special
items of expenditure, due either to exceptional
causes or to deliberate policy. Thus, the cost of
fuel wood has risen from $2.26 per cord in 1867 to

$2.90 in 1868, resulting chiefly from undue com-
petition, and a breach of contract. Again, twice
during the year the line has suffered severely by
fires from the forest, and although the Company
was well insured upon its buildings, the damages
to permanent way and the destruction of fuel wood
were somewhat extensive. Unusual liberality,
too, has been exercised in the past year in repair
of permanent way, the expenditure upon this item
alone, in new rails and ballast, having exceeded
that of 1867 by $6,842, 1,103½ tons of new iron
and 27,347 yards of ballast, having been put into
the track during the season. In the item of Fire
Insurance, which is one rather of prudence than
actual working necessity, the Directors have adopted the policy of ample protection; and the charges
for this service have accordingly risen from $4,-
318.37 in 1867 to $7,827.20 in 1868, the latter
sum including not only largely increased fire policies, but also the insurance against casualty and
death of all employes engaged in hazardous duties;
a provision towards which the employes themselves contribute, and which it is believed attaches
great value and stability to the Company's service.
In view of these items the Directors are enabled to
state that the ordinary outlay in wages, materials,
and supplies, as set forth in the respective appendices, has been so far reduced as to admit of these
special provisions without any sensible increase in
the aggregate expenditure, which, for all services
on Revenue Account, has amounted to $391,559.29
(£80,519 0s. 8d. stg.) in 1868, as against $422,-
422.75 (£86,803 6s. stg.) in 1867, being a decrease
of $30,562.46 (£6,284 5s. stg).

3. During the year new and additional equipment in works, rolling stock, &c., has been provided for, to the amount of $55,964.98 (£11,499
13s. 1d. stg.) Amongst the items of this expenditure may be named the addition of nearly two
miles of new sidings to stations and mills, the new
stations at Allandale, and Bramley, two new locomotive engines, seven new freight-cars, and other
works and outfit, as detailed in appendices K to
N, inclusive. To these services of extension, so
essential to the active and economical handling of
the traffic, the Directors continue to devote anxious consideration, taking care, however, so to distribute the burthen as not to overtax the revenues
of any one year.

4. The current Interest Dividends on the 1st
and 2nd Preference Bonds have been duly provided for and paid, and a balance carried forward to
1869 of $33,657.80 (£6,915 19s. 9d. stg.) to the
credit of Interest Dividend Account.

5. The line has been worked during the past
year with singular and complete immunity from
accident or casualty to traffic, due in great part,
if may be reasonably claimed, to the substantial
condition of its works, and to the efficiency of its
staff, in all departments.

6. In their report of last year, the Directors adverted to the necessity of making extended provision for the further development of the traffic of
the district, and they expressed their intention of
seeking legislative sanction to such changes and
readjustment of the capital as would warrant the
Company in undertaking the necessary works.
They have now to report that during the last session of the Dominion Parliament an Act was passed
empowering the Company to make a limited addition of £50,000 sterling to its capital for certain

specific purposes, such new capital to rank for interest and security next after the existing second preference bonds. The preliminary conditions imposed by that Act having been complied with, it is now in legal operation, and the Directors have accordingly made all necessary preparations for executing such works as are primarily essential. It is contemplated to construct during the current year a new grain elevator at Toronto, having a storage capacity of 275,000 bushels, and an elevating and shipping power of 20,000 bushels per hour. The elevator wharf will be constructed in 15 feet water, will be 490 feet long, by a width of 70 feet, solid, and will be capable of storing three million feet lumber for shipment, and of accommodating seven vessels alongside for lumber and four for grain, to load simultaneously. The cost of these works, complete with approaches and tracks, is estimated at $140,000. The Directors trust to be able in the following year (1870) to erect works of a like class, but of smaller capacity, at Collingwood. With these works, together with the future appropriation of the present elevator wharves at Toronto and Collingwood to the storage and shipment of ordinary freight, the Company will be in a position to command and work an extended traffic with great economy and despatch, assuming of course that the locomotive and rolling stock equipment shall continue to receive gradual extensions, such as have been added from time to time during the past few years.

7. During the past year the Directors have actively promoted the construction of the Rama Canal and Portage, a work of much necessity and importance, as establishing cheap and efficient connections between the territory of the Black River and Lakes Saint John, Couchiching and Simcoe, and bringing those districts into direct relation to this railway and the city of Toronto; and they are now happy to report that, by the enterprise of a separate corporation, the works are already far advanced toward completion, and will be ready for public use early in the spring.

8. Authority was granted during the last session of the Legislature of Ontario for the construction of a canal uniting Lakes Muskoka and Rousseau, and for the establishment of a tramway to unite the traffic of those lakes with Lake Simcoe and (by this line) with the city of Toronto. To the success of these enterprises the Directors will contribute whatever influence and assistance they can command.

9. The lumbering interests of the North Shore of the Georgian Bay are in course of very rapid and extensive development, several large establishments having been started there during the past year, whose aggregate production is estimated at from thirty to thirty-five millions of feet per annum. Much of this production will necessarily seek Western markets, but it may, nevertheless be expected to contribute a considerable increase to the future traffic of the line, what, if this development be fairly watched, it may be made to yield a new element to the trade of this city.

10. The wise liberality of the Legislature in relation to the free grants of agricultural lands, and to mining interests, gives reasonable hope that immigration and settlement will be greatly promoted, and a new impetus given to mining enterprise. These influences cannot fail to result beneficially to this railway, especially under such a liberal policy in its management as shall assist in every effort towards the development of the Upper Lake Districts. It is with regret, therefore, that the directors observe that the steam vessel service of the Georgian Bay and of Lake Superior continues in an unstable and unorganized condition, very prejudicial to the growth of trade and to the commercial interests of Toronto. Fully prepared to contribute to the improvement and permanency of this important service, by close traffic connections of liberal character, the directors necessarily await some such combined action with the postal service as shall secure an organized system of steam communications of the extent and character which

the growing importance of the North West Territory and public interest would seem to suggest.

(Signed)   FRED. CUMBERLAND,
                        Managing Director.

                JOHN BEVERLY ROBINSON,
                        President.

On motion of the President, seconded by Mr. G. H. Wyatt, the report was adopted.

Ald. Bell moved that W. Gamble and J. Brown be re-appointed Auditors.— Carried.

Ald. Baxter, seconded by D. Crawford, moved that F. C. Capreol and E. M. Carruthers be appointed scrutineers for the ballot for election of directors.—Carried.

Some discussion then arose in reference to a reduction of the passenger rates and the rates for freight.

Mr. Cumberland said, that if he knew it to be advantageous he would instantly reduce the fares. But the danger was that they might make a mistake in that direction. He quite concurred in the general principle referred to, that, where possible, a reduction of fares should be made—although such reductions were not always attended with a beneficial effect, as in the case of the Post Office, the reductions in which had not resulted in the way expected by the public. If they could increase the travel in such a ratio as to compensate for the decrease of fare, then it would be the policy of the Company at once to lessen their rates. The matter had been a frequent subject of discussion at the Board, and one of almost continuous thought with himself. For himself, he was inclined to think it would be well to make an experiment of that character. If they had a large urban population, they could deal with the subject with courage. But, their rural population could not be drawn out, except once or twice a-year. Those interested in commercial pursuits alone would take advantage of it. As for the periods in which the other class were likely to be drawn, they could be provided for by public excursions. It had occurred to him that possibly they might, during the summer months, try the experiment of reducing the cost of return tickets. His idea was that this should be done without touching the existing tariff, or, in other words, that return tickets should be available for a return and a-half. This experiment, he thought, ought first to be tried with reference to Toronto. Return tickets to and from Toronto might, perhaps, be reduced in order to see how the main traffic of the line, that is, to and from Toronto, would be affected. Then, if desirable, the principle might be extended to other stations. At present, the freight tariff was as low as that on any other line, and indeed, as low as it could be; and for the ordinary course of freight business, it was at present so low that it would not be wise to make any further reduction. His own idea and that of the Directors generally, was to reduce the fares as low as possible and as rapidly as possible; and if trade increased in future, as might be expected, it was quite possible such reductions might with safety be made.

The meeting then adjourned until 1 o'clock, in order to allow of a ballot for the Directors.

SPECIAL MEETING.

Immediately after the above meeting, a special general meeting of the Company was held for the purpose of authorizing an issue of Third Preference Bonds under the provisions of the Northern Railway Act of 1868.

Mr. Cumberland said that this meeting had been made special in order to comply with the terms of the Northern Railway Act of 1868, passed last session. The object of that Act, as briefly stated in the annual report, was to enable the Company to proceed with such works of extension as were particularly necessary to serve the traffic of the district. During past years they had been making considerable additions to all the equipments, but found they could not do so with the rapidity with which

trade demanded. They, therefore, found themselves in this position, that they had either neglect the interest of the district of Toronto the counties of York and Simcoe, or else they to seek means to enable them to make essen additions. Among primary objects, they had felt the necessity of a good elevator at Toronto The present one was old, inconvenient and coat and the time was not far distant when it we cease to be safe. Therefore, they desired to up a good structure, of greatly increased capaci so that hereafter the whole produce of the com might find a point at which ample storage sho be given during the winter at a cheap rate. W the present building they could not secure che ness ; for the elevator was so inconvenient as give rise to an unnecessary large amount of lai ling and labour. For this reason the Comp could not come down to the ordinary aver charges of such services. But the building ab to be constructed would be one of the finest on continent for its class, and in it they would be a to handle the grain at a minimum cost. But Company did not look altogether to their own nefit. They were not avaricious—and hence difference in cost between the present rates those when the new building was up they we give to the trade. All that the Company desi was to make a legitimate profit ; and that he lieved they had already amply demonstrated. the proposed arrangement the value of the er would be increased, and also the profits of shipper. He would announce that a prelimi conditional contract had been entered into for construction of the Elevator for $150,000. plans were at present in the engineer's room could be examined by the meeting. The work in the hands of their old friend, Mr. Reekie, had undertaken the contract. This would, doubtedly, be of great advantage to the Comp for anything Mr. Reekie undertook would be done. The credit of the Company financially w be aided rather than injured by any operation the kind with which he was connected. Alre the Company had commenced the purchase of terial ; within 10 days a crib would be commen and in two or three months another, and a c table wharf would be seen arising out of the lour—attesting not only the increase of Company's trade, but also the general prospe of the city.

Mr. D. Crawford, seconded by Mr. Most, moved that the Directors be authorised to i under the provisions of the Northern Railway of 1868, third preference bonds, class A, to extent of £50,000 sterling, for the purpose templated by the said Act.—Carried.

The Scrutineers reported the election of the lowing Directors for the ensuing year :—Hon R. Robinson, F. W. Cumberland, Lewis Mol D. Crawford ; and John A. Chowne, H. Whe and H. M. Jackson, of England.

A vote of thanks was then passed to the D tors, on motion of Mr. G. H Wyatt, for very full and satisfactory report.

Mr. F. C. Capreol seconded the resolution.

Mr. Cumberland explained that Mr. Reekie ing undertaken the construction of the elev had resigned his seat at the Board. His colle regretted very much parting with him, and h that as soon as he was free to rejoin them would again have the pleasure of welcoming to the Board. The meeting then adjourned.

—At the annual general meeting of the Cam Engine and Machinery Company of Kingston, in Montreal, the following named gentlemen elected as Directors for the ensuing year, vi Henry Yates, Esq., of Brantford ; Messrs. G Stephen, R. J. Reekie and E. T. Taylor, of treal ; and Robert Cassels, Esq., of Quebec. a meeting of the new Board, held immedi after, Henry Yates, Esq., was unanimous elected President.

DA LANDED CREDIT COMP'Y.

nual Meeting of this Company was held
o on the 11th February. The President
d to the chair. The following Report
by the Secretary:—

rectors present to you the report of the
operations for the year 1868.

ore placing under your notice the figures
ncipal items of accounts, the Directors
mselves of the earliest opportunity to con-
you on the continued satisfactory posi-
ur affairs.

ring of Debentures in Canada and the
money on deposit as measures which
been in practical working for nearly
s, and as will be seen by the following
rve, with the amount received on capital
sulted in a considerable increase of busi-

	1866.	1867.	1868.
ock	$122,884	124,422	204,458
s	115,448	129,834	155,814
	27,427	36,073	56,942
	251,600	302,400	408,550
Estates			
ged	890,230	631,030	1,261,697

fuse in the Capital Stock account is the
the three calls made during the year;
very well responded to, and the amount
ed, with the amounts received on De-
it Deposit accounts, have enabled us to
ir Loans by upwards of $100,000.

ctors will follow in this account the
dopted in their preceding reports, under
l heads of Loans, Annuities, Debentures,
tnd Profits and Loss.

MORTGAGE LOANS.

gage loans effected in 1868
n amount $137,500
gage loans effected since the
ation of the Company by 31st
1868, have been in amount, 539,450
m there has been paid into
inking Fund, and received
ticipated repayments 130,900

balance due to the Company,
Dec., 1868 .... $408,550
t due 31st December, 1867, 302,400

n increase in the year of $106,150
ars ago, when our progress was so much
y the influence of the Civil War in the
Directors deemed it necessary, as a
measure, to increase the profits by low-
ats of interest allowed on payments into
g Fund ; but now, in more prosperous
y have gone back to the old law, which
per centum on such payments. This
ffect on all mortgages effected from the
ne; and the term will, of course, be
rd the old term of 23 years.

ANNUITIES.

ties payable to 31st Dec.,
amounted to $45,757 61
ount the Company has re-
.... 43,185 73

balance to receive of $2,571 88
of $2,571.88, we find has been reduced
past month to $1,930.58.

DEBENTURES.

unt of debentures issued during the
was $35,150.

mount of debentures in cir-
n on 31st December, 1868,
vas $155,814 76
 .... 129,334 74

ncrease of $26,480 02
y low rate of money which ruled in

England, during the whole of 1868 enabled the
Directors to effect a renewal of nearly all the debentures falling due there during the year, and for
longer terms than the original debentures were
issued.

But the aggregate amount of debentures held
there has not increased.

DEPOSITS.

The amount of sums deposited during
the year 1868 has been $78,621 85
The balance on 31st Dec., 1868, less
interest, was 53,222 00
Of which there was deposited at 5 per
cent 3,635 00
And at 6 per cent 49,587 00
                                  $53,222 00

PROFIT AND LOSS.

The balance of the Profit and Loss account for
the year 1868, after paying current expenses and
allowing for the usual deductions, is $3,405.39, to
be dealt with by this meeting.

The Directors recommend that a dividend of 3½
percent. for the half year be paid, which will absorb $6,300 leaving a balance of $2,105.89, to be
carried forward to the credit of the next account.

The duty of inspection which has always existed in certain parts of our administrative work, we
have during the past year extended to all our
operations, and we doubt not it will be attended
with the very best results.

The Directors regret that it should be their duty
to bring under your notice the default of certain
shareholders in payment of the calls made so far
back as 1865 and 1866. Every reasonable indulgence has been extended to them, and we recommend both for the interest of the Company generally, and in justice to those shareholders who
paid so promptly, that the declaration of forfeiture
made by the Board on the 28th of October, 1868,
be now confirmed.

The President then offered some some remarks
explanatory of the Report. He mentioned that
the amount of mortgage loans effected during the
the year, $137,500, was composed of 283 applica-
tion of which 202 were granted and 81 declined.
The balance due the Company under the head of
annuities was, on the 31st Dec., $2,571.88, and
this sum had been reduced, during the past month
to $1,930.58. During the year, $35,100 of debentures had been issued nearly all of which had been
sold in Canada. After paying the dividend
$2,105.39 would remain to the credit of next
year's accounts. He confidently expected such an
increase of loans as would enable the company to
pay 3 per cent. dividends in future. After referring to the appointment of an inspector and the
cancellation of unpaid shares, he resumed his seat.

Judge Gowan, after making some remarks complimentary to the Society and the Directors, said
that a good deal was remarked outside as to the
progress made, and these points he would like to
bring before the Board. He had endeavored to
understand something of the principle on which
the Company acted, and any one who did so must
know that it was established on the soundest,
safest and most reliable principles, giving equal
justice to the borrower and the lender. On the
principles on which it was based, the returns
would always be within a certain limit. The
present position of the Company was, he believed,
due partly to the low rate of interest, and partly
to the length of time over which the loans extended. But he desired to call attention to the
fact that notwithstanding the great inducements
held out by the Company its stock held a low position in the money market. This was difficult
to account for. And he would be happy to be
informed how it was that a Company occupying
an excellent financial position, so far as the basis
on which it was founded was concerned, and being
entitled to every confidence as to its management, had not succeeded better. Its stock stood
at 25 to 27 per cent. discount even now. As to

the character of the Company's investments, looking at the long period for repayment, extending
over twenty-three or twenty-five years, it was obvious, he need hardly say, that first class security
alone should be taken, both as regarded the title
and value of the property. The investigations
regarding title by the Company's Solicitor were,
he had every reason to believe, satisfactorily conducted. He had heard complaints that the Solicitor had been too severe in scrutinising titles,
but these very complaints were, to his mind, the
highest praise which could be given that officer.
Hence he was sorry to see that the Company had
set a gentleman to work to see whether the Solicitors fees could be cut down or not. As to the
valuation of property, the amount advanced being
gradually repaid, the valuation had, undoubtedly
to be placed at such a figure as to prevent the
possibility of loss in the future. But in fixing
such an amount it should be remembered that
this was a new country. In the old country,
where similar institutions were in existence, very
little change took place in the value of property.
For ages past, property there might be said to
have continued worth a certain figure; so that the
valuation of property was almost reduced to a
certainty. But here, as a rule, property went on
increasing in value; and, therefore, it might be
a question here as to whether a larger margin
might not be allowed in value. Such, of course
would, he believed, be in the interest of the borrower and of the Company. In this connection,
also, he would say that to complete the design of
the institution, the borrower should really take
the debentures. But as he was afraid that it was
scarcely possible in the present condition of the
country to expect men to take such current funds
for the current coin of the realm. Unless extraordinary inducements were thrown out to borrowers to accept these debentures as cash, they could
not be put to take that which, to a certain extent,
was held at a discount. He did not look for
anything of the kind for years to come. Not still
he mentioned the matter as something which had
been spoken about. He would mention also that
he thought the directory excessively large. A
feeling that this was the case was very wide-
spread. His own experience of large directories
was that it was very often more difficult to get a
quorum with them than with a smaller number;
and hence he would strongly recommend the
Board to consider whether it would not be wise to
apply to Parliament to reduce the number of
Directors. It also occurred to him that frequent
meetings of the whole body were to a certain extent unnecessary. Monthly meetings of the
directory ought to be sufficient. If three times
in a week some one or more of the Board assisted
the President to declare on all applications for
loans—leaving in reserve to the general body
any question thought proper, he thought it would
be a great improvement and facilitate the working
of the institution. Another matter which might
very properly be dealt with, was the very absurd practice of appealing to the general meeting
to say whether or not a dividend should be declared. To ask the shareholders to decide that
point was really asking them to go it blind.
They were obliged to trust in the gentlemen having charge of the institution in the matter of
dividends. Under the Act of Parliament he knew
the matter had to be left to the general meeting,
but it was a mere matter of form, and the sooner
it was done away with the better. One branch
of the business struck him as requiring the most
careful management, in order to guard against
loss. He referred to the deposit branch. They
were authorised to receive $1 and upwards to
$1,000 or $20,000—in fact to take unlimited
amount. He could not understand how without
much peril unlimited deposits could be taken subject to call, or even one, two or three months
notice. He did not profess to know much of the
subject, but it struck him that the greatest care
was required at every step, from the moment the
money was received and deposit recipt granted

until the final stage. He would like to know if deposit receipts were signed when they were given.

The President—Yes, by one officer of the Company, and countersigned by the Cashier.

Judge Gowan thought that every such document should bear on it not merely the signature of some subordinate officer, but of some member of the directory,—say the President. On the whole the report to him, on the face of it, appeared satisfactory. But there were one or two inquiries which he would like to make. On the 31st December about 5½ per cent. of the annuities were unpaid. Since then that number had been reduced to about 2½ per cent. What proportion of these unpaid annuities were over a year due?

The Secretary replied that scarcely any were over a year due. They were chiefly for annuities due in November and December; and the amount was, undoubtedly, under $500.

Judge Gowan said he was going to inquire in what way the Company proposed to deal with irregularities of this kind, but as they did not amount to anything considerable, he would not press the point. As to the payments into the sinking fund, it occurred to him that 6 per cent. would scarcely allow much margin for management and for the necessary examination of titles in effecting loans. The next point to which he would direct attention was one suggested to him from more than one quarter, viz., as to whether the officers of the Company had given security; and if so, where that security was lodged.

The President—They have given security; it is lodged with me.

Judge Gowan would not press to know the amount, but as an indication of his opinion of what it ought to be, would state that some twenty persons held office in this county—clerks and bailiffs of Division Courts. They were required to give security for the faithful performance of their duty and the duly paying over of the public money coming into their hands. Their salaries ranged from $200 to $600 or $700, and the monies passing through the hands of each varied from $1,000 to $8,000 or $9,000 a year. Their securities ranged from $1,000 to $6,000 or $7,000; and they found no difficulty in giving such securities as in the interest of the public it had been thought necessary to require. He had further to state—and though it might appear ungracious of him to do so, yet, as the matter had been spoken of by outsiders, it might as well find utterance through him as any one else—he had to state that there was a very strong feeling that the staff employed for the management of the business was entirely too large. More work was done with a much smaller staff in any other institution in the town. He mentioned this as a proper subject for consideration by the directory. With the former large number of shareholders, he was aware that the correspondence was heavy; but, with the number greatly reduced of late, and the calls pretty well paid up, the labor of the office had been considerably reduced, and it appeared to him that now was the time to consider whether the staff could not be reduced. From the report, he observed that there had been no new sale of debentures in England, and that subject, he thought, ought to engage the attention of the directory. If maintaining their connection with England, for the sake of their debentures, involved a large expenditure, he would be disposed to discontinue it. But if, as he believed, it merely required a percentage to the broker, perhaps it need not be discontinued. With regard to the forfeitures, while he would not like to be severe on those not paying up, still, those who had paid up ought to be considered. Besides, the security of the debenture-holders was partly on that unpaid stock, and nothing ought to be allowed to weaken that security. All the security contemplated by the law the debenture-holders should receive. He thought that, under all the circumstances, the Directors would not be justified in longer withholding the action now invoked from the meeting.

Directors should not occupy the position of Dean Swift's grand juryman, who,

"Out of his great bounty,
Built a bridge at the expense of the county."

The President replied. He thanked Judge Gowan for his favorable opinion of the Board of Directors, and went on to notice the queries of that gentleman. The principles on which the Company had been formed—that of lending on mortgage sums at a low rate of interest, and for long periods—would, in fact, account for the present value of the stock, as compared with other institutions. That was one of the reasons why the proprietors of the Company could not expect the same return as other institutions.

Judge Gowan—I spoke of the value of the stock—not of the return.

The President was aware of that; but still the value of the stock was always measured by the return. But less than a year ago, their stock had been sold at 42, now it was 75; and that, in six or eight months' time, was not a bad advance. With regard to the Solicitor's charges, the Board were happy to have the testimony of one so competent to judge as to the Solicitor's services. They knew and fully appreciated these services, but the value of them entered into the element of the loan. Other companies were reducing the fees allowed to valuators and solicitors, and in order that the Canada Landed Credit Company should occupy a fair position, the Directors felt bound to follow the general example. With regard to the amount of advances on property, that was settled by the Act, which sets forth that no advance shall be made unless the Company is first mortgagee, and that when made, the advance shall be only for half the cash value. As to the length of time to which the mortgage extended, it would be seen that very few took the long term. Since the commencement of the Company, the amount loaned on mortgage had been $539,450, whereas the amount due now was only $408,550, showing the amount paid up to be $130,900. As to the reduction of the quorum in the directory, it had occasionally appeared that a smaller number would be quite sufficient, and the suggestion of the Judge on that point deserved attention. With regard to deposits, he was happy to say that the greatest care was exercised. At the weekly meetings, a statement of the amount received was placed before the members of the Board present, and no time was lost in lending it out to the best advantage. If at any time the amount coming in should increase too rapidly, then orders were given to refuse further sums unless at a reduced rate of interest. Every care, he thought, was used to shield the interests of the Company in this respect.

Judge Gowan—There was a public announcement by the Company that sums under a certain amount, and deposited for a certain time, should draw so much interest, and that, on a regular given scale, interest would be allowed. If the Company held out that statement to the public and depositors in general, and failed to carry out their promises, would it not be a breach of faith?

The President—That order is good only till another is made.

Judge Gowan—Then the public will, of course, understand that according to the conditions of the market and the exigencies of the Company, so will the rate of interest be.

The President next noticed the large staff of the Company, and explained that the peculiar character of the Company's operations required more work than in ordinary offices of like description. The accounts were tolerably intricate, and so much was this felt to be the case that, with the view of obtaining the best system on which to continue the business, and probably lighten the labor, the Board had appointed an accountant, who had been acting as inspector, to examine the accounts, and see whether, in his judgment, a less intricate system might not be adopted. He had been in the office only a short time. But presently the Board hoped to be able to in-

itiate a system requiring less labor, and there enable them to reduce the present staff. W[ith] regard to the sale of debentures in England, expense had been incurred there beyond adv[er]tising. But that was a very serious item. T[hey] found that two or three months' advertising some of the leading papers costs about £250 s[o] This being the case, the Directors of late h[esi]tated to incur so large a liability for an uncert[ain] return. But he thought the time had now co[me] when it might be for the benefit of the Comp[any] to incur that expense or something like it. Fr[om] present appearances, money was so low there t[hat] people might readily be induced to take the [de]bentures of the Company. Within a week t[hey] had been advised of £600 worth of debent[ures] having been sold in that market at 5 per cent.

Hon. Wm. McMaster then addressed the me[et]ing giving his views as to the points elicited [in] the discussion.

Hon. G. W. Allan also spoke in referen[ce to] various matters—commenting on the progr[ess] and position of the Company. The Report w[as] then adopted.

It was then moved by Mr. John Beard, seco[nd]ed by Mr. C. E. Chadwick, and resolved,—"T[hat] the cordial thanks of this meeting be given to [the] President and Board of Directors for their p[ru]dent and safe management of the Compan[y's] affairs."

The President returned thanks.

Mr. Arthur McDonald, seconded by Mr. J[.] Osborne, moved that, due notice having be[en] given to all the shareholders of third call [of] per share being made on the 19th April, 18[66] and also that the notice having been given to [the] said shareholders of the fourth call of $2 [per] share, 14th March, 1866 ; and certain of the sa[id] shareholders having neglected to pay the amou[nt] of calls which have since been made upon the respect of the said shares, and such shares hav[e] been declared by the directors forfeited, this g[en]eral meeting of the Company hereby confirms s[aid] forfeiture, and order the said shares so forfeit[ed] be sold or otherwise disposed of.—Carried.

Moved by Mr. C. Tilley, seconded by Hon[.] A. Burnham, and resolved—That W. Williams and C. Robertson be appointed Auditors for [the] ensuing year, and that their remuneration be [for] each.

Moved by his Honor Judge Gowan, seconded [by] Mr. H. Mortimer, and resolved—That, when the Act of Incorporation of the Company requ[ires] the election of twelve Directors, and whereas [it is] considered expedient to reduce the number of Board to eight members—Resolved, that the B[oard] be authorized, should they see fit, to submit to [the] next half-yearly meeting of the Shareho[lders] amendments to the said Act, with the view [of] making such reduction in number of the Bo[ard] and such other amendments as they may cons[ider] desirable.

Mr. H. Mortimer in seconding the resolu[tion] explained that the advance in the Company's st[ock] was more apparent than real. The advance f[rom] 45 to 75 was almost wholly owing to the payme[nt] of calls that had been made, so that the st[ock] really stood now, relatively to the amount pai[d], nearly the same point as at the beginning of [the] year.

A letter was then read from the Hon. Ge[orge] Brown resigning his position as a Director.

Moved by Judge Gowan, seconded by Mr. Sheriff Smith, and resolved, that the thanks of [this] meeting be given to the Chairman for his ab[le] impartial conduct in the chair, and for his u[n]tiring zeal and attention to the general interest[s of] the Company.

The following gentlemen were subsequently d[e]clared elected Directors for 1869:—

Hon. G. W. Allan, C. S. Gzowski, [] W. McMaster, Samuel Spreull, L. W. Sm[ith,] Judge Gowan, John McDonald.

The meeting then adjourned.

F RICHELIEU COMPANY—The annual general
ng of the shareholders of this Company was
in Montreal pursuant to notice. After read-
he report of the Directors and Auditors the
ing Board of Directors was elected for the
nt year:—Messrs. John Pratt, Wm. Mc-
hton, Z. Benoit, David Torrance, Adolphe
Theodore Hart, Henry Starnes, Thomas
hill and J. E. Lincennes.
mediately after the meeting the new Board
rectors held a meeting, and elected the fol-
g officers:—President, John Pratt; Vice-
lent, Wm. McNaughton; General Agent, J.
mere; Secretary-Treasurer, J. N. Beaudry;
ant Secretary, A. Desforges.

ANT INSURANCE COMPANY.—At the annual
ng of the County of Brant Farmers' Mutual
nce Company, held in Paris, on Wednesday
he following officers were elected for the
1869:—President, H. Capron, Esq.; Secre-
James Maxwell, Esq; Directors, Messrs.
Nell, Horace Capron, D. Anderson, Wm.
a, Wm. Moyle, Wm. Turnbull, John Ten-
nd M. Freeman.

Insurance.

E RECORD.—Abercorn, County Brome, Q.—
of Messrs. Holmes Bros., with contents; loss
insurance $3,000.
rborough, Feb. 10.—Shop of McWilliams,
re builder; no insurance; cause unknown.
aship of Hope, Ont.—Barn of A. T. H.
ms, M.P.P., and occupied by Thos. Wilson;
ed to be the work of an incendiary; no
nce.
ick Township, Ont., Feb. 6.—The grist and
ill owned by Wm. Murray, near Mildmay,
township of Carrick, was totally destroyed
; the large water wheel being the only thing
Insurance $1000.
mpton, Feb. 12.—A fire broke out here, by
of which the British Arms hotel, with ad-
exhibition hall and stables, and the resi-
and tailoring establishment of Mr. Crozier,
lestroyed. The fire originated from some
wn cause in the hay loft over the stable,
were a number of valuable horses in the
but such was the rapidity with which the
spread, that notwithstanding all that could
e to extricate them, three of the animals
d.. All the buildings were of wood, except
tel, which was a three story brick. Fortu-
the night was very calm, else the fire would
een much more extensive, as the firemen
mbarrassed from want of water. Loss about
. Mr. T. Graham, owner of the hotel, was
l for $2,800 in the Provincial and Commer-
ion Insurance Companies, and Mr. J. H.
h, the occupant, for $1,000 in the Provin-
The furniture in the hotel was mostly saved.
gines were brought to the scene, but owing
bursting of the hose were rendered useless.
rich Township, Ont.—House of Robert
on, and contents; owing to the temporary
e of the mother, an infant child was con-
in the house.
eton, N. B. Feb. 3.—House of Mr. Joseph
in Queen Square. The fire broke out in
f, and had gained such headway before it
scovered, that in less than an hour it was
consumed. A portion of the furniture was
Mr. Wiley was insured for $800.

ts IN NEW YORK.—The Fire Marshal, in
ort of the losses by fire during the month
uary, values the destroyed property at
11, upon which the insurance amounted to
,190. The number of conflagrations was
that the average losses amount to little
han $2,000 per fire. In referring to the
of disaster we find that one-tenth are at-
ble to defective flues, three to children
; with matches, five from the explosion of
le oil, and three from incendiarism.—Is-
t Journal.

GRISWOLD'S ADJUSTMENT OF FIRE LOSSES.—
One reason why we have not printed the numerous
commendations of this valuable work, is, because
we had not room for them all, and hardly knew
where to begin a selection. We do not, however,
hesitate to insert the following well deserved
tributes to its merits:

Hon. William Barnes, in a letter to the author,
says: "It is evidently a work of great merit and
practical use. In the legal profession, it is said
that each lawyer owes some contribution to its
improvement and usefulness. You have paid
your debt to the underwriting fraternity, in this
well digested and aptly arranged volume."

H. S. Durand, the eminent adjuster for the
Home Insurance Company, says: "I have read
the 'Griswold on Adjustments,' and think is a
very clear and practical work on the subject.
Fifteen or twenty years ago I would have given
$100 for such a book. Every agent should have
it and read it carefully, and it would not hurt
many so-called Adjusters to study it well."—
Monitor.

There is a rumour to the effect that the
Guardian, which has made the requisite deposit,
will confine its operations to Montreal.

MARINE INSURANCE IN ENGLAND.

Marine Insurance was practiced in England before it came into vogue in the northern portion of
the continent of Europe; and even Antwerp,
then in the meridian of its commercial eminence,
derived it from English merchants. In 1560,
Guicciardini states that the traders of England
and the Netherlands have fallen into a way of
insuring their merchandise at sea by a joint contribution; and we may, perhaps, assume with
safety that about this period the practice became
tolerably general in the commercial world of
Europe.

By 1601, the amount of Marine Underwriting
done on the London Exchange had become so
considerable, that an Act of Parliament was in
that year passed for the establishment of a Court
of Policies, to decide disputes arising out of those
documents. For reasons which we need not now
recount, this tribunal did not meet with success,
and, although it was subsequently reorganized
upon an improved basis in the reign of Charles II.
it still failed of its object, and soon expired,
never to be revived again.

Insurance was originally carried on in England,
in Venice, and in maritime ports on the continent generally, by individual Underwriters. At
first, their headquarters in London were on 'om-
bard street, but afterwards, for their own convenience and that of the insured, they assembled
at a certain coffee-house, which was opened in a
yard off that street about the middle of the
seventeenth century. In 1710 they transferred
their place of meeting to another coffee-house,
opened by a person named Lloyd, in Abchurch
lane—and it is from this Lloyd that the body of
English Marine Underwriters have since acquired
that corporate name by which they are now known
throughout the civilized world.

In 1720, the first two Insurance Companies—
The London Assurance and the Royal Exchange
Assurance—were incorporated. They owed their
existence to the necessities of George I.; and the
consideration on which they obtained their
charters was the promise, eventually only half fulfilled, to pay His Majesty the sum of £600,000.
Established in the year of the South Sea mania,
the stock of these two Companies soon rose to an
extravagant premium, but, when the financial
bubble burst, it fell more rapidly than it had risen,
and from that circumstance, and an accumulation
of disasters at sea, they were, for a time, involved
in very serious difficulties. Eventually, however,
these were surmounted, and for more than a hundred years these companies succeeded in maintaining their exclusive privileges as the only Insurance
Companies sanctioned or permitted by law. It
required more than fourteen years' agitation to

convince Parliament of the impolicy of continuing
this monopoly.

In 1810 the New Insurance Company was
formed, with an authorized capital of £5,000,000
sterling, and Parliament was appealed to to remove the restrictions which prevented its commencing business. After a long and elaborate inquiry into the subject, a Committee of the House
of Commons reported that the exclusive privileges
of the two great Companies should be repealed,
and that encouragement should be given to other
associations for the promotion of Marine Insurance.
The influence of the monopolists so protracted the
contest that it was not until 1824 that Marine Insurance was thrown open, like Fire and Life Insurance, to joint-stock enterprise and energy.
To those unacquainted with English commercial
history, the folly of Parliament in so long maintaining these restrictions may occasion some surprise. But this is in keeping with the tenor of
their entire legislation down to a very recent
period. Every trade, industry and mercantile
enterprise has had in turn to struggle for life
against the obstinacy of rulers who are not even
yet disabused of the idea that they know better
than traders what is best for trade.

From 1824, the number of English Marine
Insurance Companies has steadily increased with
the augmenting business offered them by expanding trade. Liverpool and Glasgow have long
possessed Underwriters' rooms, and transacted a
large amount of business. Yet the enormous export and import trade of Lancashire did not lead,
until recently, to the establishment of any independent Marine Insurance Companies, either
there or at Manchester. Lately, two or three
offices have been opened there, and that thriving
city, Bristol, has also attempted to attract Marine
Insurance business to itself. Yet in all these
places the business of insurance seems to exist as
an exotic, having its true habitat in the metropolis of the Empire. There are in London, at the
present time, upwards of twenty proprietary
Marine Insurance Companies, besides several
Mutual Associations, which extend their operations, in a smaller degree to the protection of
freights and profits. The aggregate number of
members and subscribers to Lloyd's is somewhat
above 1,500, of whom 400 are Underwriting members.—Chicago Chronicle.

Railway News.

GREAT WESTERN RAILWAY.—Traffic for week
ending January 29, 1869:—

Passengers	$21,156 48
Freight	54,154 46
Mails and Sundries	1,569 10
Total Receipts for week	$76,880 04
Corresponding week, 1887	59,620 44
Increase	$17,259 60

NORTHERN RAILWAY.—Traffic receipts for week
ending 6th February, 1869.

Passengers	$2,222 93
Freight and live stock	7,619 71
Mails and sundries	259 08
	$10,101 72
Corresponding Week of '68	7,134 84
Decrease	$2,966 88

ATLANTIC AND ST. LAWRENCE RAILROAD.—
The Railway Commissioners of Maine have recently reported the condition of the Atlantic and
St. Lawrence leased to the Grand Trunk. They
say the road has been worn out and not enough
pains have been taken to repair it. In October
an application was made to the Courts and an injunction issued requiring the Company to lessen
the speed of its trains and forward repairs. Between that time and November 500 tons of new
rails were laid upon the Maine portion, but the
road still demands further repairs.

The Canadian Monetary Times.

THURSDAY, FEBRUARY 18, 1869.

NEEDED LEGISLATION IN SHIPPING MATTERS.

Some time ago we pointed out the great loss sustained by shipowners, and the peril occasioned to life from the absence of due provision in the laws of the Dominion for the regulation of matters connected with shipping. Among other matters, we explained the necessity for an examination into the qualifications of lake captains, and the granting of certificates of capability; for a proper investigation of circumstances attendant upon the loss or damage of vessels on the lakes ; for the signing of articles by seamen ; and generally for such statutory enactments as would change a state of affairs, on all hands regarded as mischievous and productive of great pecuniary loss. In the last official returns respecting Canadian shipping, the tonnage of Ontario was set down at 66,959, and its value $2,787,800 ; that of Quebec at 155,-690, and its value, $4,633,945. An interest so large and of such importance is certainly deserving of attention from our legislators. In the year 1868, there were 1272 disasters on the lakes, involving the loss of an immense amount of property and a fearful sacrifice of life. In one season, 1865, the direct and ascertained losses reached $400,000.

It is of importance, therefore, to ascertain, if possible, if this waste of property cannot be stopped, and whether means cannot be taken to prevent its annual recurrence. Of course the elements cannot be controlled by Act of Parliament, nor can accidents be prevented by Committees of inquiry. But when we come to think how many of these marine disasters are attributable to want of skill on the part of navigators, and, in only too many instances, to gross carelessness, we can imagine the reformation that is needed and can be effected.

Vessels are often run ashore intentionally, and no investigation ensues. The insurance money is obtained and the "accident," is allowed to pass unimproved. If masters were compelled to pass an examination before property and life would be placed in their care, or would be subjected to suspension or deprivation by a competent tribunal, we should have fewer cases in which the most ordinary precautions to guard against danger are neglected and consequently fewer losses.

As the law is at present, a seaman may leave his vessel at the very moment he is wanted; if the vessel be stranded he may discharge himself and refuse to work except at extravagant wages. There is no power to detain a foreign vessel in Canadian ports until she gives security for damage that she may have done. A great many other points might be gone over, all leading to the same conclusion, but it is not necessary to give them in detail, the absurdity of our present position in these matters being only too apparent.

In the Province of Quebec, the Imperial Shipping Act of 1854, can be pleaded so far as its provisions are applicable, but in Ontario, the same thing cannot be done. What we need is the machinery provided by that Act for carrying out its objects. It is the duty of the Government as it is the direct interest of our shipowners and marine insurance companies to have proper legislative remedies applied to the evils pointed out. All that is required to secure them is united and energetic action. Certainly, a Dominion claiming to be the fourth maritime power in the world should not occupy the absurd position in respect to shipping laws that we find ourselves in, more especially when we find our neighbors across the lines so well off in this particular. Our Boards of Trade had better give this subject their careful consideration.

CANADA LANDED CREDIT COMPANY.

The speech made by Judge Gowan at the annual meeting of this Company, which, by the way, was specially reported for this Journal, reflects credit on his manliness and on his honesty. As a stockholder, he thought it expedient to examine into charges passed from mouth to mouth respecting the management of the Company's affairs, and did not hesitate to come out boldly at a proper time and place and ask to be satisfied respecting them. The system of smothering dissatisfaction leads to no good and it is always best where doubts are entertained, or evils suspected, to let inquiry have full play. The stock of the Company was at a considerable discount, reasons were given for this by

brokers when the stock came to be sold as one interested in the prosperity of the Company, Judge Gowan naturally asked self and just as naturally asked the why such was the case.

From what we know of the Comp[any] are inclined to think that its trouble[s] arisen from errors in management. Board has been too large. The [Canada] Permanent Building Society, the [largest] society in the country has a Board of [nine] and the Western Canada Building S[ociety] one of the youngest and yet one [of the] most prosperous societies, has a B[oard of] seven members. Surely the Canada [Landed] Credit Company could do with less th[an nine]teen. The meeting did right in deci[ding to] reduce the number. In such instituti[ons the] work is done or should be done by th[e Pres]ident and the Secretary, and too [large a] Board is only an impediment to busine[ss. We] fancy the Board has been so large th[at busi]ness and errors passed unnoticed. [When a] moneyed institution is mismanaged [people are] always disposed to blame the Secre[tary or the] Manager in the first place and the B[oard in] the second, the former for doing wro[ng and] the latter for permitting it to be done. [The] history of the Canada Landed Credi[t Com]pany is characterized by not a few bl[unders.] It has an excellent charter and [should] have been just as successful as our m[ost suc]cessful Companies. But it was a gr[eat mis]take to rely on England for its mone[y. The] expense incurred in advertising the [last] advertisement cost £250 stg.), the [money] brokers, the expenses of the secreta[ries over] there, made up a considerable sum [and the] purchase of exchange to pay interest [in Eng]land is an item also not to be overlook[ed. It] has the effect of increasing the first co[st of] the price paid for the money that is [sent] out in Canada was rendered dear, a[nd we] can imagine how small a margin was [left for] profit. The result is that expenses [eat] up profits and place the Company in [a disad]vantageous position in competing wit[h those] institutions which obtain money at l[ower rates] and manage their affairs with more e[conomy.]

These considerations have impresse[d them]selves on the Board of Directors, an[d there] seems to be a determination to inau[gurate a] new era in the Company's history. [A good] beginning has been made, and we h[ave rea]son to expect a more flourishing [state of] affairs. The Board is made up of h[onest] and able men, and the Company is th[oroughly] sound. It requires but a little c[areful] judgment to regain public confiden[ce and] for awakening those concerned to a [sense of] what reforms are needed, the stoc[kholders] are greatly indebted to the efforts o[f Judge] Gowan.

BEET ROOT SUGAR.

previous number we gave some stat-
to the cost of producing Beet Root
and the returns that would be realized

ow refer to the best mode of raising
t, and the different methods by which
iverted into sugar.

vell known that beets will grow in any
the temperate zone, and the primary
q is the best kind of soil to employ,
ould be a light rich loam, inclining to
her than sand. Care should be taken
application of manure, lest the juice
lered, impure and the proportion of
senting matter be increased. The
iety of beets is the white Silesian, as
ips the greatest amount of saccharine
they should not be forced as the
size yield most sweet juice. Our
will well understand the best mode
ting and harvesting the crop. Roots
kept in shallow ditches dug in sandy
t there is danger of their passing into
crystalline variety. In Germany,
ts are usually stored in large cellars
he factory. The leaf stalks and roots
oved as soon as the plant is gathered.
he roots are to be used, the bruised,
and mouldy parts are to be cut away
juice may be injured; the bulbs are
in a large revolving drum, formed of
r bars of wood partly immersed in
his gets them clear of sand and dirt.
h for the preparation of beet roots
tory to the process of manufacture,
e now give:

contain some 9 to 10 parts of sugar.
t process in obtaining which, is to
up the beets so as to destroy the
parts; the pulp thus obtained is sub-
o powerful presses in order to extract
charine matter. By means of sul-
cid or chalk the juice is then cleared;
at it is forced through canvas bags,
ich a time that no residuum or im-
are left; when this process of filtera-
completed, the next proceeding is
evaporation, which is performed by
he juice in large chaldrons. When
uid has obtained a certain thickness
ulpuric acid is added, until there is a
kalic reaction. However, the em-
t of sulphuric acid must be with
test caution, as it tends to prevent
r crystalising. The next process is
the boiling juice through flannels,
e non-saccharine parts are then
ed in large pans. The result is a
up of good taste. This syrup has
be filtered through charcoal, after

which it is mixed with chalk water, to which
is added the white of eggs; after this the
syrup becomes somewhat alkalie, when it is
steamed off in copper pans, carefully skim-
ming off all impurities. After about an hour
and a half boiling the syrup is tested by
taking out a small quantity in a spoon and
blowing upon it; should it break rapidly
into bubbles, it is put into forms, previously
damped; it has then to be stirred to prevent
crystallisation, and the forms are kept in a
warm room for some time in order to let the
molasses drain. This completes the process
of making raw sugar. The process of refining is identically the same as that employed in our own refineries.

We give a new process for which a patent
has recently been taken out in Austria. The
following is a literal translation from a German
scientific paper :—"A revolution is confidently announced in the manufacture of
sugar from cane and beet-root. The extended
diffusion process of a large beet sugar manufactory in Austria, dispenses with nearly the
whole expenses of grinding, crushing and
pressing, and claims to yield more and purer
sugar. The cane or root is finely sliced by
machinery, adapted with care to avoid crushing the cellular structure, and thus liberating
the albumen and other elements, which usually mingle impurities in the product. The
material is then repeatedly soaked in water at
a certain temperature until the saccharine
juice is approximately washed out, when the
solid remainder (if roots) is in a wholesome
condition for feeding to animals. A battery
of six or eight vats is arranged in a circular
series, connected by stop-cock pipes, and
filled with the sliced material, and watered in
due proportions. After standing a certain
time, the liquid in the first vat is drawn off
into the second and replaced with pure water;
after another interval, the second is emptied
into the third and re-filled again from the
first, and so on, until from the last vat is
drawn an infusion eight times enriched
and nearly equal to the juice of the
plant. Pure water is put in its place,
which goes then to the first vat (by this time
replenished with fresh material) and thus the
circuit of operation is made continuous, each
vat in turn discharging the concentrated
juice and receiving pure water, but each in
turn replenished after eight infusions with
fresh material."

The manufacturer who invented this process uses up two hundred tons of beets every
twenty-four hours, only employing fifteen
men, who could just as well manage twice
the quantity. By this process the expensive
machinery for crushing and pulping is done
away with. The mode in treating the juice
is the same as before narrated.

INTERCOLONIAL RAILWAY.

On the 8th instant, the Railway Commissioners opened the tenders for the four sections of the Intercolonial Railroad. Two
hundred and forty-seven tenders were received. For the first section the amounts
varied from $175,000, or at the rate of
$8,700 per mile to $700,000 or $35,000 per
mile. For the second section, the lowest
tender was for the sum of $299,000 or $14,-
950 per mile to $820,000 or $41,000 per mile.
The lowest tender for the third section was
$288,000 or $12,000 per mile and the highest
$792,000 or $33,500 per mile. For the fourth
section, the lowest tender was $297,000 or
$11,000 per mile, and the highest $918,000 or
$34,000 per mile. The successful contractors
were, first section, H. H. Horsey & Co.,
of Ottawa; second section, G. & J. Worthington, of Quebec; third section, Elliott,
Grant & Whitehead, of Brantford; fourth
section, G. & J. Worthington, of Quebec.
It appears to be admitted on all hands that
the work will be done at a very low figure,
if the successful contractors abide by their
tenders. The manner in which the whole
business has been managed, shows that the
prophesied "huge job" has not as yet shewn
its head.

— We understand that the deposit by the
Ætna of Dublin is held by the Government
as forfeit, the Company having failed to comply with the provisions of the Insurance Act.
The securities held by way of deposit are
lying in England. When the Government is
in a position to sell the securities, the proceeds will be handed to the Court of Chancery for distribution among the creditors.
Under the present Act, the securities could
be sold at once as they would be held in the
name of the Receiver-General in trust.

Owing to the delay of eastern mails we are
without our usual advices of the Quebec stock
and money market.

FROM THE WEST TO THE SEABOARD.—Dr.
Barrett, of Upper Canada College, proposes that
some point on James' Bay, say Moose Fort, be
made a seaport for the Province of Ontario. The
route between Michipicoten on Lake Superior and
Moose Fort might be rendered practicable by
the improvement of their natural water courses—
a canal of three miles would connect the Michipicoten and Moose rivers. The distance from the
mouth of the Clyde to Moose Fort is 3,150 miles,
and from Moose Fort to Michipicoten 220; total
3,370 miles. The distance from the Clyde to
Quebec is about 2,500; and from Quebec to
Michipicoten 1,100; total 3,600 miles.
The Hudson Bay is free from storms. The
route mentioned would afford facilities for the
transport of the mineral products of the region
about Lakes Superior and Huron to the smelting
works of England; for the shipment of the cereals
of Western Prairies and the Red River territory;
and give Ontario a means of communication with
the seaboard wholly through British territory.

Communications.

HURON AND ONTARIO SHIP CANAL.

To the Editor of the Monetary Times.

Sir,—In an article in your last issue you slightly misapprehend the meanings I intended to convey in a published letter which you quote. The argument founded on that quotation, therefore, takes a different line from what it must have followed, but for the misapprehension. What I intended to convey was this : that the construction of the Canal would involve an outlay of forty millions of dollars ; and that the amount is larger than the whole banking capital of the Dominion. But I never intended to assume, as you seem to conceive, that this was the same thing as adding so much to the banking capital of the country. The capital, as you rightly state, in what you consider the correction of an error, into which I must plead that I did not fall, would be spent on the construction of the Canal ; and there is no difference in your view and mine, when you state that we should get, besides the Canal, for the money whatever is saved out of the forty millions by those to whom it is paid.

What I was anxious to enforce was the vast amount of labor the forty millions would set in motion, enabling laborers to make corresponding purchases, on which all, with whom they dealt, would make profits, in which view, I am glad to find, you so fully agree.

But while I do not wish to lose sight of this point, I have always placed infinitely more stress upon the benefits which the Canal would confer, alike as a source of productive investment, as a means of cheapening freights from the great West of the United States, as well as the greater and more distant Northwest of our own Dominion.

In the hope that this explanation will find insertion in your next issue,

I am, yours obdt.,
FRED. C. CAPREOL.
Toronto, Feb. 17, 1869.

BANK MANAGERS AND INSURANCE COMPANIES.

To the Editor of the Monetary Times.

Sir,—I trust it will not be considered out of place if I venture through your columns to offer a few remarks upon what I consider to be a most unjust exaction, which is practised upon insurance companies throughout our city, the discountenancing and suppression of which I think demands the attention of insurers generally.

For some time there has been, as I conceive, a just complaint that prevailing rates are inadequate to the risks borne; excessive competition, combined with the too prevalent practice by many of pitting one company against another, have from year to year tended so to reduce rates, that as some of our oldest local insurance authorities aver, it is extremely difficult to prosecute the business with even ordinary hopes of success; yet with all the cutting and competition with which we have to contend, and when rates have, as it is fancied, been reduced to the lowest possible figure compatible with safety, we are expected upon being tendered our premiums to make a still further reduction, by conferring a douceur of 10 per cent, by way of brokerage or commission.

Against those following the business of professional brokers I have nothing to say; they have a living to make; they probably induce many to insure who otherwise would not trouble themselves about the matter, and if they can by any means control a portion of the business, they have an unquestionable right to do so. Against merchants, bank agents and managers, however, who so far lower the dignity of their position and standing, as to indulge in the system of peculation on the profits of insurance companies, I earnestly protest. The extent to which this species of re-

spectable blackmail is levied in Toronto will scarcely be credited, excepting by those who suffer from its imposition; but I have it on the best authority, and indeed my own experience justifies the assertion, that during the past year a gentleman in comparatively high standing, as agent or manager of one of our banking institutions, actually doubled, perhaps trebled his salary by commissions received from insurance companies on business, which, from his position, he had in his control. The premiums on policies which had been running for years in certain offices, have been sent at time of renewal less 10 per cent., and if the deduction has been remonstrated against, the companies concerned have been coolly informed that if they don't choose to renew the policy on these terms the risk will be removed.

The modus operandi appears to be as follows: Messrs. A. B. & Co., who keep a respectable account at the bank, if not requiring favors of a more substantial character, are, as is usual with merchants, occasionally in want of a bill of exchange on London or New York, in which case it is courteously intimated by the obliging Manager—in which intimation is possibly included the saving of an eighth or quarter per cent. on the exchange operation—that the placing of their policies of assurance in his hands will be considered a favor. Do Messrs. C. D. & Co. stand in need of a little help to tide over a difficulty! Again the obliging Manager steps forward, but in this case it is made a sine qua non that all policies of assurance be deposited with the bank, ostensibly for the purpose of seeing that they be properly kept up, in reality to help the manager to feather his nest by means, that not dishonest, are, to say the least dishonorable. I would, if necessary, point to individual cases where the entire insurance business of large firms is controlled in the manner I have described. How far this is sanctioned by the principals of these institutions on the part of their subordinates remains to be seen. I think, however, there are one or two very suggestive as well very objectionable features about such a course of procedure deserving their consideration.

I fear, Mr. Editor, that I am trespassing on your valuable space by the length of my communication as, however, it is a matter of some interest, I must ask your indulgence.

Truly yours,
INSURER.
Toronto, 16th Feb., 1869.

THE EXPORT OF CANADIAN PETROLEUM.

Editor of the Canadian Monetary Times.

Sir,—In a former number of your valuable paper I showed the profit which would result from the exportation of Canadian petroleum, and those calculations were based upon what was then the price of refined oil in England, but the present state of the market is far more favorable to the exporter, as the prices have since advanced nearly 33 per cent. The quotations in Liverpool and London during the month of September last averaged 1s. 6d. per gallon for standard white, now the same article is quoted firm at 1s. 11¼d. At the former figure it was demonstrated that a profit of $5 a barrel might be made by the exporter, provided he obtained the oil from his own wells and refined it himself, but now while the increased price a clean profit of $8.50 per barrel might be made under the same circumstances.

The whole cost of producing the oil, refining it and laying it down in Liverpool, after allowing for all reasonable contingencies, need not exceed $7 a barrel, and at the present price, its value there would be $15.50. Such heavy profits are shown in this business that there is little doubt, during the present year, the export of Canadian oil will assume considerable importance; indeed, it is wonderful that so profitable a source of commerce should so long have been neglected and left entirely in the hands of the Americans. Although

the results of the shipments last fall have been made public, there is no doubt the shipments were highly successful when properly managed.

From the want of statistics in our own country we are compelled to draw our inferences from oil trade of the States. The total export from United States for 1868 was nearly 99 millions gallons, against 67 millions in 1867, an increase of more than 47 per cent. The home consumption of the United States is much larger, when compared with the extent of their oil territory, than the consumption of Canada as compared with oil districts. Hence there is not relatively much need for export from the United States from Canada, for their own population of new 40 millions does of itself support a very large trade in oil, whereas the 4 millions of people Canada are soon supplied and the market glutted.

The Americans, however, have been the first to establish the export trade of petroleum, which during the past year has so greatly increased, which has now assumed such large proportion while the export of oil from Canada is hardly worth mentioning. The location of our oil well is much more favorable for export purposes than is any of the American oil districts. Petrolia, chief producing territory, is only 18 miles distant by rail from Sarnia, whence oil can be shipped direct to Europe without breaking bulk. We are with us a great deal lower, and the produce and refining of oil could be effected much cheaper here than in the States. All the natural vantages are in our favour; the oil is there, means of transportation is easy, nothing is wanting but the application of energy and capital, nevertheless, our neighbours carry off the profit, and in Europe a Canadian exporter of oil is almost unknown.

It is to be hoped, then, that our oil men will longer remain inactive, but will energetically take this matter in hand, and thereby benefit the country and reap the large profits which so await them.

Yours, &c.,
PETROLI
Nova Scotia, February 15, 1869.

Mining.

NOVA SCOTIA GOLD FIELDS.

(From our own Correspondent.)

HALIFAX, Feb. 3, 186

Compared with last year the season is extremely dull. In actual mining there is but little progress, and speculation in stocks and land is comparatively at a stand still. The establishment of a Mining Exchange is again on the tapis, and project is this time likely to be carried out, as Haligonians are all interested in keeping up the excitement in regard to their gold mines. Here too, are still entertained of bringing in Br capital soon, and another month or so prove upon what basis those hopes are founded. There is yet a large field for profitable investment in Nova Scotia, but the stock jobbing operations of last year by which undeveloped mining territory—in some cases dear at the price of wilderness land—was traded off to the public five hundred to five thousand dollars per acre, cannot be repeated even in England. The properties for which negotiations have been opened are the Westlake, Imperial, Queen, and Brunswick blocks at Uniacke, and the Caledonia at Oldham. Overtures are said to have been made, also, for the acquisition of the Mount Uniacke Compa at Uniacke, but as two-thirds of the stock ed in Boston, and the property is the most y producing one in the district, the trans- t present doubtful.

Mines Department returns for the last of 1868 are complete with the exception se from Lawrencetown; but allowing 200 the probable quantity produced in that from 1st October to the end of December, 0 tons as the amount of quartz raised, we he following results for the year 1868 for ole Province:

ACT OF RETURNS FROM JANUARY 1 TO DECEMBER 31, 1868.

ct.	Total Gold Yield. oz.	dwt.	gr.	Quartz Crushed. tons.	cwt.	Aver. Daily No. of Miners.	
oke	7,070	0	5	9,880	4	190	10-12
...	3,373	14	9	5,094	5	126	11-12
...	3,247	3	17	3,874	15	89	5-12
y	2,387	8	22	6,372	0	118	6-12
arbor	1,232	14	5	2,938	11	74	3-12
gier	921	8	9	725	5	37	6-12
...	779	0	4	1,011	13	25	8-12
's Harb'r	673	2	17	596	5	46	8-12
ie	584	14	22	350	0	24	10-12
ncetown	419	8	17	395	0	29	4-12
oclaimed	44	4	15	136	0	15	8-12
...	20,733	0	22	32,273	18	779	6-12

ncludes 15 dwts. alluvial gold.
ncludes 18 ozs. alluvial gold.
ncludes 15 dwts. 12 grs. alluvial gold.
ncludes 3 ozs. 9 dwt. 4 grs. alluvial gold.

nany respects these results resemble the 364. The total gold yield is 6,000 ozs. less n 1867, and 5,000 ozs. less than the two ng years, 1866 and 1865. The average proportion per man is 26 ozs. 11 dwts. 23 r $531.95 specie. The average per ton n) 14 dwts. 9 grs. or 12 dwts. 20 grs. per lonial. Sherbrooke produced at the rate of s. 0·7 grains per British ton, and $741 per Uniacke averaged 18 dwts. 19·5 grains, 26.30 per man. Tangier appears to have the highest proportional yield for the t of ore reduced and labor employed; but turns were obtained so late that even the tions now submitted will extend this letter limits, and, perhaps prevent its despatch is morning's mail. The reasons for the falling off, and other interesting references, e deferred then until next week.

following notes refer to present progress:

ACKE.—The works of the *Queen Company* been closed, pending negotiations with h speculators. The *Uniacke Company* have over three ozs. of specimens from a new truck in the cross-cut. The *Montreal ny* are making satisfactory progress.

VERLEY.—All work here at present is car- by tribute. During the last fortnight of y three tributers earned $80, which speaks r the quality of the ore.

FREW.—The mill of the *Colonial Company* een started. The *Ophir Company* is re- ed in the bullion report.

QUODOBOIS.—Two mills are being erected district, one of five stamps for Barnett & d one of ten stamps for Mr. Buckner.

OVERIES.—A discovery is reported from rne, but the precise locality is not yet . It is very certain that the Western dis- his year will receive some attention from rs.

BULLION REPORT.

rs. Huse & Lowell, bankers, received the ing amount of bar gold between 11th and nuary:

	District.	ozs.	dwts.	grs.
gton	Sherbrooke	181	19	0
rston	Sherbrooke	56	11	10
& Sherbrooke	Sherbrooke	27	11	12
& Nova Scotia	Waverley	36	16	7
	Renfrew	118	19	0
do	Wine Harbor	27	2	9
e Co.	Uniacke	135	19	6
l		584	18	20

THE GALWAY LEAD MINE.

To the Editor of the Monetary Times.

DEAR SIR,—It may be interesting to some of your readers, to know something of the operations and prospects of this Mine, and with the view of giving some information on the subject, I send you the following:—

The Capital Stock of the Company, amounts to $20,000; about half of which is paid up. The balance will be called in as required to furnish smelting works, &c.

The Directors have declared a dividend at the rate of thirty per cent. per annum, on the paid up capital for the six months the Company has been in operation.

It is especially interesting to know that this dividend is the proceeds of sales of Ore obtained in sinking the shaft, and only a portion of which is sold. This is the first mine in Ontario to declare a dividend fairly earned, and is I believe the largest ever declared by any Mining Company in the Dominion, at least, that I have seen any account of.

The Company own fifty acres of land surrounding the Mine, through which several veins run other than that now working, some of which have been pronounced by competent judges quite as good as that. The work is kept going day and night, and is under the management of a competent miner from "Cumberland," England, who brings to his work thirty years experience.

The shaft is down ninety-five feet, is 10 x 6 feet, covered by a substantial building, having all the necessary arrangements to enable the men to work to advantage and with comfort.

The Company intend to erect smelting works in the Spring, and make some other necessary improvements. From the favourable situation of this Mine, being on the Bobcaygeon Road, and only distant from navigation at Bobcaygeon, ten miles; it is but reasonable to expect good results, and that the enterprising men who have shewn so much energy and spirit in pushing it to its present position, will be amply rewarded for their outlay and perseverance.

For a particular and scientific description of the Mine, &c., I refer you to a report made by Professor Chapman last September, a copy of which I send herewith.

Hoping I have not trespassed too much on your space.

I am Sir, &c.,

PETERBORO.

Peterboro, Feb. 15, 1869.

SUSSEX (N. B.) MANGANESE MINE.—This property has been taken possession of by the Sheriff of King's at the suit of the Treasurer of the Company owning it, for moneys due him. There have been ten men at work in the mine all winter, and these are still employed. The Company have spent about $60,000 on their property, and the mine is now in fine condition. It is not probable that there will be any interruption of operations at present, or that the Company's interests will be more than temporarily affected.

GALWAY MINING COMPANY.—This company being free from debt, and having sold a portion of their ore, have declared a dividend at the rate of 30 per cent. per annum on the capital paid in. This shows that notwithstanding the numerous failures of gold mining in Madoc, we have other mines in Canada that will pay. There is every reason to look for large results from this enterprise, if the Directors continue to manage it as economically as they have done.—*Peterborough Review.*

— Henry Brethour, Deputy Reeve of Brock Township, has been appointed Trustee of the Township bonuses, on behalf of the Municipalities of York, Ontario and Victoria, as provided by the Act of incorporation of the Toronto and Nipissing Railway Company.

Financial.

BANKS OF ONTARIA AND QUEBEC.

LIABILITIES.

	Circulation.	Due other Banks.	Deposits.	Total Liabilities.
Average 1868	8,537,000	2,017,000	30,608,000	42,162,000
" 1867	9,078,000	2,334,000	28,953,000	40,365,000
" 1866	11,253,000	1,123,000	27,659,000	40,350,000
" 1865	9,925,000	1,706,000	26,051,000	37,682,000
" 1864	9,576,000	1,554,000	23,687,000	34,817,000
" 1863	9,783,000	1,185,000	21,200,000	32,177,000

ASSETS.

	Specie and Pr'l Notes.	Property.	Governm't Securities.	Other B'k Notes.	Due from other B'ks.	Discount and Loans.	Total Assets.
Average 1868	$8,956,000	1,614,000	5,918,000	1,909,000	4,444,000	48,809,000	75,166,000
" 1867	7,838,000	1,542,100	6,416,000	1,736,000	4,055,000	49,636,000	73,584,000
" 1866	6,481,000	2,688,000	6,810,000	1,594,000	6,123,000	44,391,000	71,289,000
" 1865	6,500,000	2,906,000	6,826,000	1,361,000	3,349,000	44,132,000	68,631,000
" 1864	5,044,000	2,540,000	5,840,000	1,290,000	2,005,000	45,746,000	65,688,000
" 1863	6,217,000	2,047,000	4,957,000	1,321,000	1,924,000	43,306,000	62,534,000

TORONTO STOCK MARKET.

(Reported by Pellatt & Osler, Brokers.)

A good business was done in stocks during the past week.

Bank Stock—Quotations have remained steady, with the exception of Royal Canadian, which has advanced about 3 per cent. There were small sales of Montreal at 139 and 139½; a limited amount is now offered at the latter rate. No British in market; the last sales were at 104. Ontario has been freely dealt in during the week at 100½, 100¼ and 100; there were sellers at par at the close. Large sales of Toronto were made at 122, 121½ and 121; these high prices have brought numerous sellers into market, and buyers have reduced their offers to 121. Royal Canadian is 3 per cent. higher; there were sales in the early part of the week at 87½ and 88, and to-day (the 16th) arge sales took place at 90¼ and 91, and a small sale occurred at 91¼. Commerce sold at 102½, 102¾ and 103; there are now buyers to a limited extent at 103 and sellers at 103¼. Gore has declined, with buyers at 40 and sellers at 42. There are buyers of Merchants' at 108¼ and sellers at 108¾; very little in market. Quebec could be placed at 99½; nothing doing. Molson's is in good demand at 110½ and 111; sellers ask 111½. City is wanted at 102¾ to 103, a small sale occurred at the latter rate. Buyers offer 109½ for Du Peuple, without sellers. No transactions in Nationale for some time past; buyers would give 106½. Jacques Cartier is held at 109, with buyers at 108½. Union could be placed at 103, but there are no sellers. Other banks nominal.

Debentures—Canada sterling 5 and 6 per cents. are offering at our quotations. Dominion stock is in great demand at 105½. Toronto are eagerly sought for at rates to pay about 6⅞ per cent. interest. No County in market; they would be readily taken at par.

Sundries—Limited sales of Canada Permanent Building Society were made at 124½ and .125; there are buyers at the latter rate, but very little offering. Western Canada Building Society sold at 119 to 119½, and is in active demand at these quotations, but the supply is very limited. Several transactions occurred in Freehold Building Society at 109½, which rate is freely offered. There are buyers of City Gas at 107¼ and 108; none in market. British-America Assurance is heavy at .54½ to 55. Buyers would give 133 for Montreal Telegraph, but sellers ask 134. There are buyers of Canada Landed Credit at 74, with sellers at 75. Mortgages have been in good demand, with few offering. There is a fair demand for money.

Commercial.

Montreal Correspondence.

(From our own Correspondent.)

Montreal, Feb. 14, 1869.

The weather during the week has been very variable. Never within the memory of the "oldest inhabitant" has so much snow fallen as during this winter. In many of our streets it has been four to five feet deep, and some of the principal streets are blockaded by the snow sleighs of the contractors employed in removing it. Business is almost at a standstill.

We have had one large failure in the produce trade, Buck, Robertson & Co. They were about the largest dealers in cheese and butter. Mr. Robertson does not live here, and Mr. Buck has left town for parts unknown. What the liabilities are we have not yet ascertained. Joseph May, in the dry goods trade, has also gone down. There are one or two smaller failures. There are rumours, of course, of other firms, but such reports are very injurious, and often so seriously hurt the credit of a firm as, in some instances to bring it down, when it might otherwise have floated over. John Rhynas, doing a considerable business with the lower ports, and agent for the Portland Kerosene Oil Works, has also failed. These two last failures have not been so much from bad debts as from the impossibility of making sales so as to get in either money or bills to enable them to take up their acceptances.

For the proceedings of the past week I have very little to record. Our flour market is very dull, with a downward tendency. Stock on hand to-day 90,500 brls. against 67,500 same date last year. Prices are nominal. No transactions in any description of grain. Provisions share the same fate with the exception of mess pork, which is saleable, but firmly held rather above the ideas of buyers. Groceries are dull with the exception of raw sugars. Owing to the disturbances in Cuba, especially in the sugar districts, a speculative feeling has sprung up, and the market is firm with an upward tendency.

Toronto Market.

GROCERIES—*Sugar*—The market has been much excited for a week past. Influenced by the news of an insurrection in Cuba holders of sugar have rapidly advanced their prices, and with a good speculative demand, large sales were made in all the principal markets. So sharp has been the upward movement that in a single day refinery sugars rose 50 cents; and since the beginning of the week about 75c. to $1.25 per 100 pounds on Muscovadoes.—Starting at 8¼c. they have risen to 9¼ and 9¾c. in lots. On white sugars the advance amounted to $1.50 to $2 per 100 lbs. The refiners in Montreal have bought largely; in fact the business done in the various markets is quite unprecedented; as is also the rise in prices which

led to it. Sales and resales of refined sugar in Toronto are estimated for the week at 3,000 bbls., within the range of prices quoted. The market is now more steady at our quotations. Buyers for some of our houses are now in Cuba. If they were so fortunate as to secure stocks before the rise the profits will be something handsome.

Teas—There is a good business doing in teas at steady prices. There is a general opinion that the new crop teas received are inferior in quality to last season's. The market is firm and demand good for grades between 40 and 50c and between 55 and 65c particularly for greens. Fine grades of uncolored Japan are in good demand. Good values in Twankays at 42 to 46c are of ready sale.

Syrups—Have advanced from 5 to 7c per gallon in sympathy with sugar. *Molasses*—The market has not sympathized with the sugar market to any noticeable extent; prices are steady. The feeling is firm, but the large stocks of low grade syrups held in the American markets prevents any advance for the present. *Fruit*—We note an active business in the New York market for almonds, which is owing to the state of the weather in France and Spain bringing the crop forward prematurely, and rendering it almost certain to be destroyed by the frosts which must ensue. *Tobacco*—Is firm and unchanged. *Coffees*—Are also firm. *Rice*—Is inquired for, and prices favor buyers.

GRAIN.—*Wheat.*—Receipts 40,492 bush., and 46,799 bush. last week. There is a limited demand for spring at 98c., and car loads are now selling at that price. There is a firmer feeling than existed at the date of our last report. Sales reported were four cars at 98c. in store, 7,500 bush. at $1 in store. Fall is very dull, under large receipts and a light demand. The general quality offering is rather inferior; there are no buyers over $1 for good samples; sales 5,000 bush. at $1 in store. The stock of wheat in the Toronto warehouses on the 15th inst., was 95,554 bush. fall, and 87,173 bush. of spring, against 49,703 bush. of fall, and 37,849 bush. spring, on the 30th January. *Barley*—Receipts trifling; the market is firm at quotations; no sales. Stock in store on the 15th inst. 66,375 bushs., and 70,853 on the 30th January. *Peas*—Receipts 298 bushs.,

and 250 bushs. last week. The demand is also and prices are steady. Stock in store, Feb. 24,138 bushs., and 39,166 bushs. on the 30th January. *Oats*—Receipts by cars 1,200 bushs., and 5,0 bushs. last week. Stocks have increased from 1,400 bushs. on the 30th ult., to 34,606 bushs. on the 15th inst.; this has weakened the market. *Rye* Not much offering; it is worth about 70c. *Seeds* There is a better demand for clover; there a buyers of lots at $6.50 to $6.75, and sellers $6.75 to $7; timothy, $2 to $2.50 is offer while holders ask $2.50 to $2.75. *Flax*—$1.

FLOUR.—Receipts 2,248 bbls., and 3,575 bbls. last week. There are orders in the market No. 1 superfine at $4.25, and some business has been done up the line of the Grank Trunk (from whence freight to points eastward is the same from Toronto), at $4.30; holders ask $4.30. Other grades nominal as quoted; 100 bbls. fancy sold $4.50 on cars.

PROVISIONS.—*Dressed Hogs*—The market is du and a decline of $1 to $1.12½ on the quotatio of last week has occurred. *Pork*—Mess is fir at $26½ to $27, and is nominal. *Hams*—A l of 500 in salt sold at 12c.; smoked sell at 14c. 14½c. in wholesale lots. *Shoulders*—Held at 10 to 10½c. *Cheese*—Is firm and is worth 13½c. 14c. in lots. *Lard*—Held firmly at 17c.; sto light and in few hands. *Butter*—Really choi dairy would bring 25c. to 26c. and is scarce; or nary neglected, and in heavy stock. *Eggs*— good many packed are offering at 15c. to 17 market very dull. *Tallow*—Selling at quotatio

PETROLEUM.—Trade is quiet, and prices of r fined are very steady at our quotations; the dema is limited to requirements for immediate co sumption.

Galway Mining Company.

NOTICE is hereby given that a Dividend at the Rate Thirty per cent. per annum, for the half year endi 18th January, 1869, has been declared on the Capital p in at that date and that the same is payable at the office the Company at Peterborough, on and after MONDA the FIFTEENTH of FEBRUARY, 1869.

By order of the Directors,
JOHN BURNHAM,
Sec. & Treas
Peterborough, Feb. 11, 1869.   6t.-F

Mercantile.

TORONTO PRICES CURRENT.—FEBRUARY 18, 1869.

Name of Article.	Wholesale Rates.	
Boots and Shoes.	$ c.	$ c.
Mens' Thick Boots	2 20	2 50
" Kip	2 50	3 00
" Calf	3 00	3 70
" Congress Gaiters	2 00	2 50
" Kip Cobourgs	1 15	1 45
Boys' Thick Boots	1 70	1 80
Youths' "	1 40	1 50
Women's Batts	95	1 30
" Congress Gaiters	1 15	1 45
Misses' Batts	0 75	1 00
" Congress Gaiters	1 00	1 30
Girls' Batts	0 65	0 85
" Congress Gaiters	0 80	1 10
Children's C. T. Cacks	0 50	0 65
" Gaiters	0 65	0 90
Drugs.		
Aloes Cape	0 12½	0 16
Alum	0 02½	0 03
Borax	0 00	0 00
Camphor, refined	0 65	0 70
Castor Oil	0 16½	0 28
Caustic Soda	0 04½	0 05
Cochineal	0 90	1 00
Cream Tartar	0 40	0 45
Epsom Salts	0 03	0 04
Extract Logwood	0 11	0 12
Gum Arabic, sorts	0 30	0 35
Indigo, Madras	0 90	1 00
Licorice	0 14	0 45
Madder	0 00	0 18
Galls	0 32	0 37
Opium	12 00	13 50
Oxalic Acid	0 26	0 35
Potash, Bi-tart	0 25	0 28
" Bichromate	0 15	0 20
Potass Iodide	3 90	4 50
Senna	0 12½	0 60
Soda Ash	0 02½	0 04
Soda Bicarb	4 50	5 00
Tartaric Acid	0 40	0 45
Verdigris	0 35	0 40
Vitriol, Blue	0 08	0 10
Groceries.		
Coffees:		
Java, ₩ lb.	0 22@	0 24
Laguayra,	0 17	0 18
Rio	0 15	0 17
Fish:		
Herrings, Lab. split	5 75	6 50
" round	4 00	4 75
" scaled	0 35	0 40
Mackerel, small kitts	1 00	0 00
Loch. Her. wh'e firks	2 50	2 75
" half "	1 25	1 50
White Fish & Trout	0 00	0 00
Salmon, saltwater	14 00	15 00
Dry Cod, ₩ 112 lbs	5 00	5 25
Fruit:		
Raisins, Layers	2 00	2 10
" M R	1 90	2 00
" Valentias new	0 6¾	0 7½
Currants, new	0 5½	0 06½
" old	0 04	0 04½
Figs	0 14	0 00
Molasses:		
Clayed, ₩ gal.	0 00	0 35
Syrups, Standard	0 56	0 00
" Golden	0 60	0 00
Rice:		
Arracan	4 50	4 75
Spices:		
Cassia, whole, ₩ lb.	0 00	0 45
Cloves	0 11	0 12
Nutmegs	0 45	0 55
Ginger, ground	0 20	0 25
" Jamaica, root	0 20	0 25
Pepper, black	0 09½	0 10
Pimento	0 08	0 09
Sugars:		
Port Rico, ₩ lb.	0 10¾	0 11
Cuba "	0 10¼	0 11
Barbadoes (bright)	0 10½	0 11
	—	00 0
Canada Sugar Refine'y, yellow No. 2, 60 ds.	0 10¼	0 10½
Yellow, No. 2½	0 10¾	0 10¾
No. 3	0 11	0 11½
Crushed X	0 12	0 12¼
" A	0 12¼	0 12½
Ground	0 13	0 13¼
Dry Crushed	0 13	0 13¼
Extra Ground	0 13¾	0 14
Teas:		
Japan com'n to good	0 40	0 55
" Fine to choicest	0 55	0 65
Colored, com. to fine	0 60	0 75
Congou & Souch'ng	0 42	0 75
Oolong, good to fine	0 50	0 65
Y. Hyson, com to gd	0 45	0 55
Medium to choice	0 65	0 80
Extra choice	0 85	0 95
Gunpowd'r c. to med	0 55	0 70
" med. to fine	0 70	0 85

Name of Article.	Wholesale Rate.	
Groceries—*Contin'd*	$ c.	$ c.
" fine to fins't	0 85	0 95
Hyson	0 45	0 80
Imperial	0 42	0 80
Tobacco, Manufact'd:		
Can Leaf, ₩ lb 5s & 10s.	0 26	0 30
Western Leaf, com	0 25	0 26
" Good	0 27	0 32
" Fine	0 32	0 35
" Bright fine	0 40	0 50
" " choice	0 60	0 75
Hardware.		
Tin (net cash prices)		
Block, ₩ lb.	0 25	0 26
Grain	0 25	0 26
Copper:		
Pig	0 23	0 24
Sheet	0 30	0 33
Cut Nails:		
Assorted ¼ Shingles, ₩ 100 lb.	2 90	3 00
Shingle alone do	3 15	3 25
Lathe and 5 dy	3 30	3 40
Galvanized Iron:		
Assorted sizes	0 08	0 09
Best No. 24	0 09	0 00
" 26	0 08	0 08½
" 28	0 09	0 09½
Horse Nails:		
Guest's or Griffin's assorted sizes	0 00	0 00
For W. ass'd sizes	0 18	0 19
Patent Hammer'd do	0 17	0 18
Iron (at 4 months):		
Pig—Gartsherrie No1	24 00	25 00
Other brands. No 1	22 00	24 00
" No 2	0 00	0 00
Bar—Scotch, ₩ 100 lb	2 25	2 50
Refined	3 00	3 25
Swedes	5 00	5 50
Hoops—Coopers	3 00	3 25
Band	3 00	3 25
Boiler Plates	3 25	3 50
Canada Plates	3 75	4 00
Union Jack	0 00	0 00
Pontypool	3 25	4 00
Swansea	3 90	4 00
Lead (at 4 months):		
Bar, ₩ 100 lbs	0 06½	0 07
Sheet "	0 08	0 09
Shot	0 07½	0 07¾
Iron Wire (net cash):		
No. 6, ₩ bundle	2 70	2 80
" 9, "	3 10	3 20
" 12, "	3 40	3 50
" 16, "	4 30	4 40
Powder:		
Blasting, Canada	3 50	0 00
FF "	4 25	4 50
FFF "	4 75	5 00
Blasting, English	4 00	5 00
FF loose	5 00	6 00
FFF "	6 00	6 50
Pressed Spikes (4 mos):		
Regular sizes 100	4 00	4 25
Extra "	4 50	5 00
Tin Plates (net cash):		
IC Coke	7 50	8 50
IC Charcoal	8 25	8 50
IX "	10 25	10 75
IXX "	12 25	0 00
DC "	7 25	9 00
DX "	9 50	0 00
Hides & Skins, ₩ lb		
Green rough	0 06	0 06½
Green, salt'd & insp'd	0 07	0 07½
Cured	0 07½	0 08½
Calfskins, green	0 00	0 10
Calfskins, cured	0 00	0 12
" dry	0 18	0 20
Sheepskins,	1 00	1 40
" country	0 60	0 80
Hops.		
Inferior, ₩ lb	0 05	0 07
Medium	0 07	0 09
Good	0 09	0 12
Fancy	0 00	0 00
Leather, @ (4 mos.) In lots of less than 50 sides, 10 ₩ cent higher.		
Spanish Sole, 1st qual. heavy, weights ₩ lb	0 00	0 23
Do. 1st qual middle do	0 22	0 23
Do. No. 2, all weights	0 23	0 24
Slaughter heavy	0 27	0 29
Do. light	0 50	0 00
Harness, best	0 32	0 34
" No. 2	0 30	0 33
Upper heavy	0 36	0 38
" light	0 40	0 42

Name of Article.	Wholesale Rates.
Leather—*Contin'd.*	$ c.
Kip Skins, Patna	0 46
French	0 70
English	0 65
Hemlock Calf (30 to 35 lbs.) per doz	0 75
Do. light	0 45
French Calf	1 05
Grain & Satn Clt ₩ doz	0 00
Splits, large ₩ lb	0 30
" small	0 20
Enamelled Cow ₩ foot	0 20
Patent	0 20
Pebble Grain	0 17
Buff	0 17
Oils.	
Cod	0 00
Lard, extra	0 60
" No. 1	0 00
" Woollen	0 00
Lubricating, patent	0 00
" Mott's economic	0 50
Linseed, raw	0 76
" boiled	0 81
Machinery	0 00
Olive, common, ₩ gal.	1 00
" salad	1 05
" salad, in bots. qt. ₩ case	3 60
Sesame salad, ₩ gal.	1 60
Seal, pale	0 75
Spirits Turpentine	0 52½
Varnish	0 00
Whale.	0 00
Paints, &c.	
White Lead, genuine in Oil, ₩ 25 lbs.	0 00
Do. No. 1 "	0 00
" 2 "	0 00
" 3 "	0 00
White Zinc, genuine	3 [illegible]
White Lead, dry	0 05
Red Lead	0 07
Venetian Red, Eng'h	0 02
Yellow Ochre, Fren'h	0 02
Whiting	0 85
Petroleum. (Refined ₩ gal.)	
Water white, car l'd	—
" small lots	0 37
Straw, by car load	0 33
" small lots	0 35
Amber, by car load	0 00
" small lots	0 00
Benzine	0 00
Produce.	
Grain:	
Wheat, Spring, 60 lb	0 98
" Fall 60 "	0 90
Barley 48 "	1 30
Peas 60 "	0 8
Oats 34 "	0 5
Rye 56 "	0 7
Seeds:	
Clover, choice 60 "	6 7
" com'n 68 "	6 5
Timothy, cho's 4 "	2 2
" inf. to good 48 "	2 0
Flax 56 "	1 6
Flour (per brl.):	
Superior extra	4 9
Extra superfine,	4 6
Fancy superfine	4 4
Superfine No 1	4 2
" No. 2	
Oatmeal, (per brl.)	
Provisions	
Butter, dairy tub ₩ lb	
" store packed	
Cheese, new	
Pork, mess, per brl	2
" prime mess	
" prime	
Bacon, rough	
" Cumberl'd cut	
" smoked	
Hams, in salt	
" sug. cur. & canv'd	
Shoulders, in salt	0
Lard, in kegs	0
Eggs, packed	0
Beef Hams	0
Tallow	0
Hogs dressed, heavy	8
" medium	8
" light	7
Salt, &c.	
American brls	1
Liverpool coarse	1
Plaster	1
Water Lime	1

p & Candles.	$ c.	$ c.
awford & Co.'s ..		
mperial.........	0 07½	0 08
olden Bar	0 07	0 07½
ilver Bar........	0 07	0 07½
n	0 05	0 05½
1	0 03½	0 03¾
es	0 00	0 11½
nes, Liquors, &c.		
ish, per doz......	2 60	2 65
ness Dub Portr..	2 35	2 40
s:		
Jamaica Rum...	1 80	2 25
uyper's H. Gin..	1 55	1 65
h's Old Tom.....	1 90	2 00
n, cases.........	4 00	4 25
h's Old Tom, c. ..	6 00	6 25
s:		
, common	1 00	1 25
fine old	2 00	4 00
ry, common	1 00	1 50
medium........	1 70	1 80
d pale or golden..	2 50	4 00

Brandy:	$ c.	$ c
Hennessy's, per gal..	2 30	2 50
Martell's " ..	2 30	2 50
J. Robin & Co.'s " ..	2 25	2 35
Otard, Dupuy & Cos..	2 25	2 35
Brandy, cases........	8 50	9 00
Brandy, com. per c...	4 00	4 50
Whiskey:		
Common 36 u. p.......	0 62½	0 65
Old Rye	0 85	0 87½
Malt	0 85	0 87½
Toddy	0 85	0 87½
Scotch, per gal........	1 90	2 10
Irish—Kinnahan's c...	7 00	7 50
" Dunnville's Belf't..	6 00	6 25
Wool.		
Fleece, lb.............	0 28	0 35
Pulled "	0 22	0 25
Furs.		
Bear..................	3 00	10 00
Beaver, ℔	1 00	1 25
Coon	0 20	0 40
Fisher..................	4 00	6 00
Martin..................	1 40	1 60
Mink....................	3 25	4 00
Otter....................	5 75	6 00
Spring Rats	0 15	0 17
Fox......................	1 20	1 25

INSURANCE COMPANIES.

ENGLISH.—*Quotations on the London Market.*

[of. ...es.]	Last Dividend.	Name of Company.	Shares par val £	Amount paid.	Last Sale.
00		Briton Medical and General Life ...	10	....	2
00	7½	Commer'l Union, Fire, Life and Mar.	50	5	6
00	8	City of Glasgow	25	2½	5¼
00	9½	Edinburgh Life	100	15	33
00	5—½ yr	European Life and Guarantee......	2½	11s6	4s. 9d.
00	10	Etna Fire and Marine	10	1½	—
00	5	Guardian	100	50	52
00	12	Imperial Fire............	500	50	350
00	9½	Imperial Life............	100	10	16¼
00	10	Lancashire Fire and Life,.........	20	2	3¾
00	11	Life Association of Scotland.......	40	7½	25
62	45s. p. sh	London Assurance Corporation ..	25	12½	49
00	5	London and Lancashire Life	10	1	19s
04	40	Liverp'l & London & Globe F. & L.	20	2	6¼
00	5	National Union Life	5	1	1
00	12½	Northern Fire and Life	100	5	11⅜ x d.
0	12 '68, bo 5s.	North British and Mercantile	50	6¼	19¾
00	50	Ocean Marine	25	5	20
00	£5 12s.	Provident Life............	100	10	37
...	£4½ p. s.	Phoenix	....	....	145
00	2½—h.yr.	Queen Fire and Life	10	1	18s
00	3s. bo.4s	Royal Insurance............	20	3	6¼
00	10	Scottish Provincial Fire and Life ..	50	2½	5¼
00	25	Standard Life	50	12	66
00	5	Star Life	25	1½	—
		CANADIAN.			℘ c.
00	4	British America Fire and Marine ..	$50	$25	54 55xd
...	4	Canada Life	...	....	.....
00	12	Montreal Assurance	£50	£5	135
00	8	Provincial Fire and Marine........	60	11	.....
...	....	Quebec Fire	40	32½	25½
...	8	" Marine............	100	40	75 80
00	5 7 mo's.	Western Assurance............	40	9	......

RAILWAYS.	Sha's	Paid	Montr	London
tic and St. Lawrence............	£100	All.	....	60 62
lo and Lake Huron	20½	"	....	3 3½
do Preference	10	"	....	5½ 6½
Brantf. & Goderich, 6℘c.,1872-3-4....	100	"	....	66 69
plain and St. Lawrence	....	....	10	....
do Pref. 10 ℘ ct.	....	....	78	....
Trunk	100	"	15 16	16 16½
Eq. G. M. Bds. 1 ch. 6℘c.	100	"	....	85 87
First Preference, 5 ℘ c	100	"	....	54½ 55½
Deferred, 3 ℘ ct.	100	"	....	....
Second Pref. Bonds, 5℘c.	100	"	....	40½ 41½
do Deferred, 3 ℘ ct.	100	"	....	....
Third Pref. Stock, 4 ℘ct.	100	"	....	28 30
do. Deferred, 3 ℘ ct.	100	"	....	....
Fourth Pref. Stock, 3℘c.	100	"	....	18½ 18¾
do. Deferred, 3 ℘ ct.	100	"	....	....
Western	20½	"	13 14	15½ 15¾
New	20½	18	....	....
6 ℘ c. Bds, due 1873-76.	100	All.	....	100 102
5½ ℘c Bds. due 1877-78.	100	"	....	94 95
e Railway, Halifax, $250, all.	$250	"	....	....
ern, of Canada, 6℘c. 1st Pref. Bds.	100	"	....	81 83

EXCHANGE.	Halifax.	Montr'l.	Quebec.	Toronto.
on London, 60 days......				
t or 75 days date	12½	9½ 9½	9½ 9¾	9½
te do.	11½ 12	8 9	8¾ 9¼	8¾
te, with documents............	....	7½ 8	....	....
on New York,............	....	25½ 26	25 25½	74½
te do.	....	26½ 27	25½ 26	....
Drafts do.	....	½ dis. to p.	par ½ dis.	par ¼ dis.
....	....	8½ 8¾	....	4 to 5

STOCK AND BOND REPORT.

The dates of our quotations are as follows:—Toronto, Feb. 16; Montreal, Feb. 12; Quebec, Feb. 18; London, Jan. 28.

NAME.	Shares.	Paid up.	Divid'd last 6 Months	Dividend Day.	CLOSING PRICES. Toronto.	Montre'l	Quebec.
BANKS.			℘ ct.				
British North America	$250	All.	3	July and Jan.	104 105	104 105	103½ 104
Jacques Cartier..............	50	"	4	1 June, 1 Dec.	108½ 109	108 109	107 107½
Montreal	200	"	5		139 139½	139½ 139½	138½ 139½
Nationale..............	50	"	4	1 Nov. 1 May.	106 106½	106½	106½ 107
New Brunswick	100	"	......	......	....	...	...
Nova Scotia	200	28	7&b$3½	Mar. and Sept.	....	....	....
Du Peuple..............	50	"	4	1 Mar., 1 Sept.	109½ 110	109½ 110	109 110
Toronto	100	"	4	1 Jan., 1 July.	121 122	121 122	120 121
Bank of Yarmouth..............	....	....	......	......	....	....	....
Canadian Bank of Com'e..........	50	95	......	......	102½ 103	102½ 103	101 102
City Bank Montreal	80	All.	4	1 June, 1 Dec.	102½ 103	102½ 103	102½ 103
Commer'l Bank (St. John).....	100	"	℘ ct.		....	....	....
Eastern Townships' Bank.....	50	"	4	1 July, 1 Jan..	....	98½ 99½	98 99
Gore	40	...	none.	1 Jan., 1 July.	40 41	40 45	40 45
Halifax Banking Company......	....	....	......	......	....	....	....
Mechanics' Bank	50	70	4	1 Nov., 1 May.	95 96	94 96	94 95
Merchants' Bank of Canada....	100	70	4	1 Jan., 1 July.	108½ 109	108 108½	109¾ 110½
Merchants' Bank (Halifax)......	....	....	......	......	....	....	....
Molson's Bank..............	50	All.	4	1 Apr., 1 Oct.	110 111½	110½ 112	110 111
Niagara District Bank..........	100	70	3½	1 Jan., 1 July.	....	....	....
Ontario Bank..............	40	All.	4	1 June, 1 Dec.	99½ 100	99 99½	99¾ 100½
People's Bank (Fred'kton)......	100	"		......	....	....	....
People's Bank (Halifax)........	20	"	7 12 m	......	....	....	....
Quebec Bank	100	"	3½	1 June, 1 Dec.	99½ 100	99½ 100	99¾ 100
Royal Canadian Bank	50	50	4	1 Jan., 1 July.	90 91	88 90	85 87
St. Stephens Bank	100	All	.....	......	....	....	....
Union Bank	100	70	4	1 Jan., 1 July.	103 103½	103½	103¾ 104½
Union Bank (Halifax)..........	100	40	7 12 mo	Feb. and Aug.	....	....	....
MISCELLANEOUS.							
British America Land..........	250	44	2½	......	....	....	....
British Colonial S. S. Co........	250	32½	2½	......	....	....	....
Canada Company	32½	All.	£1 10s.	......	....	....	....
Canada Landed Credit Co.......	50	$20	3½	......	73 75	....	....
Canada Per. B'ldg Society.......	50	All.	5	......	124½ 125	....	....
Canada Mining Company........	4	90	......	......	....	....	....
Do. Inl'd Steam Nav. Co.......	100	All.	20 12 m	......	....	105 107	105 106
Do. Glass Company............	100	"	12½ "	......	....	....	....
Canad'n Loan & Investm't......	25	2½	7	......	....	....	....
Canada Agency	10	½	......	......	....	....	....
Colonial Securities Co..........	....	....	......	......	....	....	....
Freehold Building Society......	100	All.	4	......	109 109½	....	....
Halifax Steamboat Co..........	100	"	5	......	....	....	....
Halifax Gas Company..........	....	....	......	......	....	....	....
Hamilton Gas Company..........	....	....	......	......	....	....	....
Huron Copper Bay Co..........	4	12	20	......	....	25 35cps	....
Lake Huron S. and C............	5	102	......	......	....	....	....
Montreal Mining Consols........	20	$15	......	......	....	3.00 3.25	....
Do. Telegraph Co............	40	All.	5	......	132½ 133½	132½ 134	133 134½
Do. Elevating Co............	00	"	15 12 m	......	....	100 102½	....
Do. City Gas Co............	40	"	4	15 Mar. 15 Sep.	....	137½ 140	136 137
Do. City Pass. R. Co........	50	"	5	......	....	111 112	110½ 111
Nova Scotia Telegraph	20	"	....	......	....	....	....
Quebec and L. S.	8	$4	......	......	....	....	25 cts.
Quebec Gas Co..............	200	All.	4	1 Mar., 1 Sep.	....	...	110 120
Quebec Street R. R..............	50	25	8	......	....	....	90 91
Richelieu Navigation Co........	100	All.	7 p.a.	1 Jan., 1 July.	....	110 112½	117 117½
St. Lawrence Tow Boat Co......	100	"	......	3 Feb.	....	...	35 40
Tor'to Consumers' Gas Co.......	50	"	2 3 m.	1 My Au MarFe	107 108	...	107 108
Trust & Loan Co. of U. C........	20	5	3	......	....	....	....
West'n Canada Bldg Soc'y......	50	All.	5	......	118½ 119	....	....

SECURITIES.	London.	Montreal.	Quebec.	Toronto.
Canadian Gov't Deb. 6 ℘ ct. stg............	....	103½	102½ 103	104 105
Do. do. 6 do due Ja. & Jul. 1877-84......	104½ 105½	....	....	....
Do. do. 6 do. Feb. & Aug.......	105 107	....	....	....
Do. do. 6 do. Mch. & Sep.......	105 107	....	....	....
Do. do. 5 ℘ ct. cur., 1883	94½ 95½	93 95	93 93½	94½ 95
Do. do. 5 do. stg., 1885	93 95	93 95	93 93½	94½ 95
Do. do. 7 do. cur.,............	....	....	....	....
Dominion 6 p. c. 1878 cy............	....	105 105½	105 105½	105 105½
Hamilton Corporation............	....	....	....	....
Montreal Harbor, 8 ℘ ct. d. 1869............	..	....	......	....
Do. do. 7 do. 1870............	....	....	......	....
Do. do. 6½ do. 1883............	....	102½ 103	......	....
Do. do. 6½ do. 1878............	....	....	......	....
Do. Corporation, 6 ℘ c. 1891	....	95 96	94½ 95½	95 96
Do. 7 p. c. stock............	....	107 110	108½ 109½	109 110
Do. Water Works, 6 ℘ c. stg. 1878............	....	....	......	95 96
Do. do. 6 do. cy. do.	....	95½ 96½	......	95 96
New Brunswick, 6 ℘ ct., Jan. and July	102 104	....	......	....
Nova Scotia, 6 ℘ ct., 1875............	102½ 103½	....	......	....
Ottawa City 6 ℘ c. d. 1880	....	92½ 93½	......	...
Quebec Harbour, 6 ℘ c. d. 1883............	....	....	60	....
Do. do. 7 do. do............	....	....	65 70	....
Do. do. 8 do. 1886............	....	....	80 85	....
Do. City, 7 ℘ c. d. 4½ years............	....	....	96½ 97	....
Do. do. 7 do. 9 do............	....	....	91 92	....
Do. do. 7 do. 2 do............	....	....	98 98½	....
Do. Water Works, 7 ℘ ct., 4 years............	....	....	97 97½	....
Do. do. 6 do. 2 do.	....	....	94 96	....
Toronto Corporation	....	87½ 92½	...	....

Insurance.

BEAVER
Mutual Insurance Association.

HEAD OFFICE—20 TORONTO STREET, TORONTO.

INSURES LIVE STOCK against death from any cause. The only Canadian Company having authority to do this class of business.

R. L. DENISON,
President.
T. O'REILLY,
Secretary. 8-1y-25

HOME DISTRICT
Mutual Fire Insurance Company.

Offices—North-West Cor. Yonge & Adelaide Streets, TORONTO.—(UP STAIRS.)

INSURES Dwelling Houses, Stores, Warehouses, Merchandise, Furniture, &c.

PRESIDENT—The Hon. J. McMURRICH.
VICE-PRESIDENT—JOHN BURNS, Esq.
JOHN RAINS, Secretary.
AGENTS:
DAVID WRIGHT, Esq., Hamilton; FRANCIS STEVENS, Esq., Barrie; Messrs. GIBBS & BRO., Oshawa. 8-1y

THE PRINCE EDWARD COUNTY
Mutual Fire Insurance Company.

HEAD OFFICE,—PICTON, ONTARIO.
President, H. B. STINSON; Vice-President, W. A. RICHARDS.
Directors : H. A. McFaul, James Cavan, James Johnson, A. DeMill, William Delong.—Treasurer, David Barker Clary, John Twigg ; Solicitor, R. J. Fitzgerald.

THIS Company is established upon strictly Mutual principles, insuring farming and isolated property, (not dangerous,) in Townships only, and offers great advantages to insurers, at low rates for five years, without the expense of renewal.

Picton, June 15, 1868. 9-1y

THE AGRICULTURAL
Mutual Assurance Association of Canada.

HEAD OFFICE.............................LONDON, ONT.

Purely Farmers' Company. Licensed by the Government of Canada.

Capital, 1st January, 1868............... $220,121 2
Land and Cash Items, over................. $46,000 0
No. of Policies in force...................28,7d

THIS Company insures nothing more dangerous than Farm property. Its rates are as low as any well-managed Company in the Dominion, and lower than those of a great many. It is largely patronized, and continues to grow in public favor.
For Insurance, apply to any of the Agents or address Secretary, London, Ontario.
London, 3nd Nov., 1864. 12-1y

Briton Medical and General Life
Association,
with which is united the
BRITANNIA LIFE ASSURANCE COMPANY.

Capital and Invested Funds........£750,000 Sterling.

ANNUAL INCOME, £220,000 STG. :
Yearly increasing at the rate of £25,000 Sterling.

THE important and peculiar feature originally introduced by this Company, in applying the periodical use, so as to make Policies payable during life, without a higher rate of premiums being charged, has caused a success of the BRITON MEDICAL AND GENERAL to be wholly unparalleled in the history of Life Assurance. Life Policies on the Profit Scale become payable during the lifetime of the Assured, thus rendering a Policy of Assurance a means of subsistence in old age, as well as a protection for a family, and a more valuable security to creditors in the event of early death ; and effectually meeting the often made objection, that persons do not themselves reap the benefit of their own prudence and forethought.

An extra charge made to members of Volunteer Corps for services within the British Provinces.
2 TORONTO AGENCY, 5 KING ST. WEST.
117—9-1yr JAMES FRASER, Agent.

Insurance.

The Gore District Mutual Fire Insurance Company

GRANTS INSURANCES on all description of Property against Loss or Damage by FIRE. It is the only Mutual Fire Insurance Company which assesses its Policies yearly from their respective dates ; and the average yearly cost of insurance in it, for the past three and a half years, has been nearly

TWENTY CENTS IN THE DOLLAR

less than what it would have been in an ordinary Proprietary Company.
THOS. M. SIMONS,
Secretary & Treasurer.
ROBT. McLEAN,
Inspector of Agencies.
Galt, 25th Nov., 1868. 15-1y

Geo. Girdlestone,

FIRE, Life, Marine, Accident, and Stock Insurance Agent

Very best Companies represented.
Windsor, Ont. June, 1868 15-1y

The Standard Life Assurance Company.
Established 1825.
WITH WHICH IS NOW UNITED
THE COLONIAL LIFE ASSURANCE COMPANY.

Head Office for Canada :
MONTREAL—STANDARD COMPANY'S BUILDINGS,
No. 47 GREAT ST. JAMES STREET.
Manager—W. M. RAMSAY. Inspector—RICH'D BULL.

THIS Company having deposited the sum of ONE HUNDRED AND FIFTY THOUSAND DOLLARS with the Receiver-General, in conformity with the Insurance Act passed last Session, Assurances will continue to be carried out at moderate rates and on all the different systems in practice.

AGENT FOR TORONTO—HENRY PELLATT,
KING STREET.

AGENT FOR HAMILTON—JAMES BANCROFT.
6-6mos.

Fire and Marine Assurance.

THE BRITISH AMERICA
ASSURANCE COMPANY.
HEAD OFFICE,
CORNER OF CHURCH AND COURT STREETS,
TORONTO.
BOARD OF DIRECTION :
Hon G. W. Allan, M L C.,   A. Joseph, Esq.,
George J. Boyd, Esq.,   Peter Paterson, Esq.,
Hon. W. Cayley,   G. P. Ridout, Esq.,
Richard S. Cassels, Esq.,   E. H. Rutherford, Esq.,
        Thomas C. Street, Esq.
—Governor :—
GEORGE PERCIVAL RIDOUT, Esq.
Deputy Governors :
PETER PATERSON, Esq.
Fire Inspector: Marine Inspector:
E ROBY O'BRIEN.   CAPT. R. COURNEEN.
Insurances granted on all descriptions of property against loss and damage by fire and the perils of inland navigation.
Agencies established in the principal cities, towns, and ports of shipment throughout the Provinces.
23-1y   THOS. WM. BIRCHALL,
Managing Director.

Queen Fire and Life Insurance Company,
OF LIVERPOOL AND LONDON,
ACCEPTS ALL ORDINARY FIRE RISKS
on the most favorable terms.
LIFE RISKS
Will be taken on terms that will compare favorably with other Companies.
CAPITAL, . . . £2,000,000 Stg.
CHIEF OFFICES.—Queen's Buildings, Liverpool, and Gracechurch Street London.
CANADA BRANCH OFFICE.—Exchange Buildings, Montreal.
Resident Secretary and General Agent,
A. MACKENZIE FORBES,
13 St. Sacrament St., Merchants' Exchange, Montreal.
WM. ROWLAND, Agent, Toronto. 1-1y

Insurance.

The Waterloo County Mutual Fire Insurance Company.

HEAD OFFICE : WATERLOO, ONTARIO.

ESTABLISHED 1863.

THE business of the Company is divided into three separate and distinct branches, the
VILLAGE, FARM, AND MANUFACTURES.
Each Branch paying its own losses and its just proportion of the managing expenses of the Company.
C. M. TAYLOR, Sec.   M. SPRINGER, M.M.P., Pres.
J. HUGHES, Inspector. 15-1y

Etna Fire and Marine Insurance Company of Dublin.

AT a Meeting of the Shareholders of this Company, held at Dublin, on the 18th ult., it was agreed that the business of the "Etna" should be transferred to the "UNITED PORTS AND GENERAL INSURANCE COMPANY." In accordance with this agreement, the business will hereafter be carried on by the latter Company, which assumes and guarantees all the risks and liabilities of the "Etna."
The Directors have resolved to continue the CANADIAN BRANCH, and arrangements for resuming FIRE and MARINE business are rapidly approaching completion.
T. W. GRIFFITH,
16 Manager.

Lancashire Insurance Company.

CAPITAL, ... £2,000,000 Sterling.

FIRE RISKS Taken at reasonable rates of premium, and ALL LOSSES SETTLED PROMPTLY.

By the undersigned, without reference elsewhere.
S. C. DUNCAN-CLARK & CO.,
General Agents for Ontario,
25-1y   B. W. Corner of King & Church Streets
TORONTO.

Canada Life Assurance Company

CAPITAL AND CASH ASSETS
OVER $3,000,000.
SUMS ASSURED
$9,000,000.

A COMPARISON of the rates of this Company with others cannot fail to demonstrate the advantage of the low premiums, which, by the higher returns from its investments, it is enabled to offer.

IF PREFERRED, ASSURERS NEED ONLY
PAY ONE-HALF OF EACH YEAR'S PREMIUM IN CASH
during the whole term of policies on the life-payment plan, or for seven years on the whole life plan.
For the unpaid portion of premiums,
"NOTES" ARE NOT REQUIRED BY THIS COMPANY, so that assurers are not liable to be called upon for payment of these, nor for assessments upon them, as in the case of Mutual Companies.
Every facility and advantage which can be afforded is offered by this Company.
A. G. RAMSAY, Manager.
E. BRADBURNE, Agent,
3 11   Toronto Street.

The Victoria Mutual
FIRE INSURANCE COMPANY OF CANADA.
Insures only Non-Hazardous Property, at Low Rates.
BUSINESS STRICTLY MUTUAL.
GEORGE H. MILLS, President.
W. D. BOOKER, Secretary.
HEAD OFFICE : HAMILTON, ONTARIO
aug 15-1yr

PUBLISHED AT THE OFFICE OF THE MONETARY TIMES, No: 60 CHURCH STREET.
PRINTED AT THE DAILY TELEGRAPH PRINTING HOUSE, BAY STREET, CORNER OF KING.

THE CANADIAN

MONETARY TIMES AND INSURANCE CHRONICLE

THE Publishers have pleasure in announcing that the success of this JOURNAL has been such as to stimulate their efforts to rend it still more valuable to the classes directly and indirectly interested in the subjects with which it deals. As the only Journal in t Dominion which gives particular attention to INSURANCE, it has enlisted the hearty support of Insurance Companies ; and while, the one hand, it contends for the rights of such Companies, it equally recognizes the rights of the public.

The subject of BANKING has become of such importance, as well by reason of past legislation as by reason of anticipated changes the law respecting circulation, that it is the duty and interest of our business men to make themselves acquainted with the princip on which sound Banking rests, and to prevent any action on the part of the Legislature likely to injure the community by lesseni the usefulness of our banks. The discussion of this subject in the columns of this JOURNAL has called forth expressions of satisfacti from our most astute financiers, and has done much to give us the position we now occupy in the estimation of the public.

As MINING is in its infancy in this country, a journal devoted solely to the subject could not hope to thrive; but by giving f information regarding Mining operations, and by the employment of reliable correspondents, we have done good service to an importa interest, and secured recognition from a class which, otherwise, could not have been reached.

Our purely COMMERCIAL DEPARTMENT has not been neglected, and each week's summary, while concise and pithy, has answered t same ends as a more diffuse elaboration could do, and conveyed to country dealers a complete synopsis of the changes in the Toronto a Montreal Markets.

This combination of interests which the circumstances of the country render necessary, has been of the greatest advantage to es interest by diffusing information among all classes ; but, in order to do justice to all, we have been compelled to employ a large staff writers, and to expend a considerable amount in securing trustworthy correspondents.

While we are thankful to those who have encouraged us thus far, we are anxious to extend still further the usefulness of this Journ and we call on all who consider that the enterprise is worthy of support, to lend us their assistance in making the MONETARY TIMES national organ.

On our part we promise impartiality, efficiency, and the best efforts of the ablest writers that can be secured in the Dominion. (the part of our clients, we expect a cordial support and active exertion to widen our sphere of usefulness. In helping us, they he themselves.

Every Merchant, Banker, Capitalist, Insurance Agent, and Broker, can aid us, and we hope that we are not asking too much, soliciting their assistance.

We shall be happy to receive at any time articles on subjects within our jurisdiction, which, if used, will be liberally paid for.

Subscription Price.. ....**$2 per Annum.**

A reasonable discount will be made to Banks, Insurance Companies, &c., which subscribe for their Agencies.

SEND FOR A SPECIMEN COPY.

N.B.—Every subscriber to THE MONETARY TIMES will receive THE REAL ESTATE JOURNAL without further charge.

THE REAL ESTATE JOURNAL.

The objects of this Journal are as follows :—

(1.) To supply to those interested in real estate such information as is of special interest relating to sales or transfers of real p perty in the principal cities, and throughout Ontario, construction of public works, and building improvements of every kind, increase decrease of municipal expenditure, debt and taxation, and, in short, whatever tends to influence the real estate market.

(2.) Leading articles will be furnished by competent writers on questions relating to conveyancing, the rise and fall of property, la grants, emigration, and other subjects coming within the legitimate scope of the Journal.

(3.) Lists of lands and houses for sale in every city, town and village of the Province, will appear in its columns, givi g buyers best possible opportunities for selecting desirable properties of any class, and in any locality ; and, at the same time, affording sellen reliable and certain medium for reaching intending purchasers.

(4.) By a circulation extending into every corner of Canada, the announcements of advertisers will be brought to the notice of immense constituency of readers. A special feature in this connection is, that the Journal will be placed and kept on fyle at all the pi cipal hotels, reading rooms, and other public places in Ontario, and in Montreal. By these means it is confidently believed that ev class in the community will be reached.

THE REAL ESTATE JOURNAL is printed fortnightly, on good white paper, in quarto form, and is equal in size and appearance to anyth of the kind published on this continent.

Advertising, per line of nonpareil, each insertion, 5 cents. A small discount will be allowed on yearly contracts, for large spaces.

Address, "THE REAL ESTATE JOURNAL," Toronto, Ontario. Cheques should be made payable to J. M. TROUT, who i also issue all receipts for money.

OFFICE, No. 60 CHURCH STREET,

TORONTO, ONTARIO.

THE CANADIAN
MONETARY TIMES
AND
INSURANCE CHRONICLE.

DEVOTED TO FINANCE, COMMERCE, INSURANCE, BANKS, RAILWAYS, NAVIGATION, MINES, INVESTMENT, PUBLIC COMPANIES, AND JOINT STOCK ENTERPRISE.

II—NO. 28. | TORONTO, THURSDAY, FEBRUARY 25, 1869. | SUBSCRIPTION $3 YEAR.

Mercantile.

Meetings.

CANADA FARMERS' MUTUAL INSURANCE COMPANY.

At the annual meeting of the members of "The Canada Farmers' Insurance Company," holden Thursday, 4th February, 1869,

Thomas Stock, Esq., was called to the chair, and after setting forth the objects of the meeting, viz :—the reception of the report, and the election of two Directors to serve in the place of William Macklem and John Weir, Esqs., whose term of service had expired, but who were eligible for re-election,—he called upon the Secretary to read the

Seventeenth Annual Report.

The Directors, in presenting their Seventeenth Annual Report, have pleasure in being able to state that, notwithstanding the keen competition they now meet with from other companies of a similar nature, they still continue to hold their own, the number of policies issued having slightly exceeded that of the previous year.

Amount of Business done.—The accounts were closed on the 31st December, 1868, up to which time 5,144 policies had been issued, covering $4,056,986.00. The total amount then at risk was $10,776,010, represented by 14,069 policies, averaging $769.22 to each policy.

Losses.—The number of claims notified during the year have been 74, involving the amount of $20,824.55 ; of these, 64, amounting to $19,638.05, have been paid : 4, amounting to $922, were refused ; while the remaining 6 ($264.50) were, at the close of the year, under investigation, 5 of which have have since been settled. Of these 74 claims, 31 were in sums not exceeding one hundred dollars each.

There has been no action instituted against the Company for the past two years. In connection with this subject, the directors point with justifiable pride to the fact that in the seventeen years of the Company's existence, during which time it has issued 44,946 policies, but 5 suits have been brought against the Company for the recovery of claims.

Auditors' Report.

To the President and Directors of the Canada Farmers' Mutual Insurance Company :—Gentlemen,—We, the undersigned Auditors, have the honor to report that we have carefully examined the books and accounts of your Secretary and Treasurer, for the year ending on the 31st December, 1868, and have much pleasure in certifying to their correctness.

We submit herewith the following statements prepared by your Secretary, viz :—Receipts and Disbursements, Assets and Liabilities, Details of Expenses, Agency Account and General Balances— all of which we have examined, and find that they agree with the books and vouchers. Respectfully submitted.

DAVID WRIGHT, J. J MASON, Auditors.

Receipts and Disbursements.

RECEIPTS.
Balance on hand January 1st, 1868...	$1,744 25
Assessment dues on Nos. 5, 6 and 7...	1,134 82
On account of Notes for Cash Premium	29,484 40
" Premiums paid in Cash..	4,077 15
" Division Court Suits.....	1,197 72
" Interest......	963 12
" Bills Suspense	
Account, ... $208 93	
Less refunded.. 75 45	133 48
" Law Costs refunded......	253 24
	$38,688 10

DISBURSEMENTS.
Balance due on last year's claims...	$1,553 55
On account of claims in 1868....	19,638 05
	21,191 30
On account of investigation thereof...	774 10
" Expenses, Salaries, Directors' Fees, &c...	5,282 50
" Assessment Expenses on Collection	44 71
" Paid to Agents......	1,779 26
" Law Costs.........	249 44
" Prepaid Policies	96 67
" Premiums refunded...	96 20
Cash deposited at Interest. $35,000 00	
" in Mont'l B'nk 3,865 17	
" in Silver and Post. Stamps... 358 72	
	9,228 89
	$38,688 16

Assets and Liabilities.

ASSETS.
Cash in Bank at interest...$15,000 00	
Cash in Bank not bearing interest 3,865 17	
Cash in Silver and Postage Stamps.......... 358 72	
Cash in Notes at short dates 14,139 39	$33,363 28
Real Estate	1,348 92
Furniture	170 67
Premium Notes..........	9,847 75
Assessment Dues No.	101 05
Bills in Suit..........	5,069 46
Due by Agents.........	721 20
	$50,631 33

LIABILITIES.
Claims under investigation......	$269 25
Notes Reserved	57 74
Board attendance	272 57
Fire Inspector	157 65
Agents	2,620 60
Suspense Account..........	199 48
Bill Stamps due to Agents.....	40 05
Balance	47 003 93
	$50,631 33

At the first session of the Dominion Parliament, the Directors obtained power to alter the name of the Company, abbreviating it to "The Canada Farmers' Mutual Insurance Company ;" also, power to enable the Board to increase the limit of a single risk from $2,000 to $4,000, and power to re-insure with other companies. The Directors have taken advantage of the privilege conferred on them by the amendment to their Act of Incorporation to very materially increase the amount of insurance on first-class risks, the result of which has been to raise the average risk on each policy, which stood last year at $685.00, to $769.22.

Rates.—The rates on first and second class brick dwelling houses were reduced early last year to 50 cts. and 70 cts. respectively per $100. The rate on isolated wooden buildings and contents was reduced to one per cent for a three year's risk, no premium note being required, so that a member knows exactly what he has to pay, and incurs no further liability. The premium note being abolished, and there being consequently no further security to members than that afforded by the rates imposed, prudence requires that those rates should be maintained sufficiently high not only to provide for the ordinary annual average loss, but likewise for the contingency of increased losses in casual years, a contingency which past experience—particularly that of the unusually heavy losses sustained by more than one company in the years 1864 and 1865, reaching in the case of this Company in the year 1865 to nearly double the ordinary average—has shown will most certainly arise. The Directors are satisfied that the rates now imposed will, with prudent management and a careful selection of risks on the part of their Agents, be sufficient to accomplish both these ends.

Much pressure has been brought to bear on the Directors to induce them to make a still further reduction in the rates, the argument being that other companies did so, and have so far succeeded in meeting their losses. This may be true, but it must be borne in mind that, while a company is doing a large business at the low rate of 75 cents on the $100, the cash accumulating from the premiums being paid in advance, in anticipation of losses that will occur only in the future, will enable it to pay all present claims with ease, it by no means follows, should the business of such a company fall off, that it would be sufficient ultimately to pay all the losses in full. In view of these facts, your Directors are not prepared at present to advise a further reduction, deeming it better, for the interests of the members, as well as for their own credit, to maintain such rates as will provide undoubted protection to the insured, feeling convinced that such a course will tend to still further secure that confidence in the stability of the Company which the public have ever entertained, and which it is the earnest desire of the Directors to perpetuate.

THOS. STOCK, Chairman.
RICHARD P. STREET, Sec. & Treas.

The report, after some conversation, was, on motion of Thos. Bain, Esq., seconded by Archd. Stewart, Esq., adopted.

Messrs. John Weir and William Macklem were re-appointed as Directors, and Messrs. S. S. Peck, Warden of the County of Peterboro', and William Sexton, M.P.P. for South Wentworth, and Barth. Bull, Reeve of York, were nominated as Honorary Directors.

Several of the agents suggested that, from the very high reputation of the Company, if the Directors could see their way to making a further reduction of the rates, the business would be very largely increased.

The President, as well as R. Christie, M.P.P., who is a member of the Board, and the Secretary, all stated that the matter had, during the past year, as stated in the report, occupied their attention, but feeling the responsibility to preserve undoubted safety under the most exceptional circumstances as the first object in view, they felt it was not wise to try experiments with their past experience showed at least to be open to question.

Votes of thanks were passed to the Directors, Secretary, Inspector, and Agents, after which the meeting adjourned.

At a meeting of the Directors, held immediately after the annual meeting, Thos. Stock, Esq., was re-elected President, and William Macklem, Esq., Vice-President.

ONTARIO MUTUAL INSURANCE CO.

The first annual meeting of the policy holders in the Ontario Mutual Fire Insurance Company was held in the company's rooms, Richmond Street, London. Ald. S. McBride, President, occupied the chair. The Secretary, James Johnston, Esq., read the annual report and submitted the financial statement as follows:

Annual Report.

Your Directors, in presenting their first report, beg to congratulate the membership at large upon the great and flattering success which has attended the organization of the company. Its promotion was instigated by a local necessity, and time has shown that the necessity was generally extended. The fact that the special class of risks which are patronized by us having mostly provided the dividends which accrue to insurance companies who accept mixed risks, has made our efforts to reduce their cost appreciated. Your Directors, in striking the tariff of rates, deemed it advisable that it should be based upon an average of the rates of respectable and paying companies. And while a premium note is taken for the full amount, it in no wise follows that the whole will be collected. All that is required is a sufficiency for working expenses and losses; the the unpaid balance, if any, is pocketed by the member, inasmuch as he does not pay it. Insurance being effected for a period of three years, the expenses in annually issuing policies are reduced at least one half. Steps, under the General Insurance Act, were taken in March, 1867, for organization, and in September following the first batch of policies were issued. In this, as well as in any new undertaking, there have been prejudices to overcome and difficulties to surmount, yet still those assist in the end to make the success greater. Zeal, in an honest purpose, is only made the more determined by opposition. Your Board now feel that the path for their successors is favorably opened.

During the time the company has been in existence, there have been received 1,059 applications for insurance, 33 of which were rejected; 17 have been cancelled, mostly on account of alienation of property, leaving the number in force 1,009, with an average risk of $514.

The expenses for the first year, compared with the business done, may appear large. They are, however, inseparable from a commencement in business; and should rather be spread over two years—as, for instance, in the case of furniture, books, &c., necessary for starting, which will probably serve for the next year. Even in this we compare favorably with other companies.

Your Directors have unanimously declined receiving any pay for their past services.

Your Directors regret that several letters and policies have miscarried. Every care is taken by the office in posting, yet they go astray. Several duplicate, as well as triplicate policies have been mailed.

Your Directors hoped that they would pass the first year without levying an assessment, but, unfortunately, a large loss occurred which could not be met in any other way. This call made it rather severe on the older members of the company; but still a further hope is expressed, based on months of exemption from losses, that no further assessment will be made on the same notes.

The losses have been six in number, and to the extent of $2030.50; of these four have been paid, and appear in the account, amounting to $2020.50; the remainder are only awaiting the vouchers to be settled.

The cash statement and capital account are annexed, and have been duly audited.

Under the general act your directors retire, but

are eligible for re-election. Several Com[ ] have applied to and received from the Legis[ ] a special Act, amending this clause, as w[ ] others, so that two or three Directors only annually, leaving (should they not be re-el[ ] a sufficiency to induct the incomers into their duties and responsibilities. We have deferre[ ] action in the matter this year, preferri[ ] agitate the question in proper quarters for it bodiment in the general Act. All of wh[ ] respectfully submitted.

(Signed) SAMUEL McBRIDE, Presi[ ]
JAS. JOHNSON, Secretary

Capital Account.

ASSETS.

Amount available on Premium Notes	$10,5
Due from Agents (mostly secured by due bills)	8
Due on Assessment	6
Cash in Bank of Commerce	$336 37
Cash and stamps in Secretary's hands	104 49
Office furniture, etc	
	$12,5

LIABILITIES.

Losses	$
Printing, etc	1
Law expenses	
Auditors	
Salaries	8
	$11.

Examined and compared with the book[ ] vouchers, and found correct,
WM. McBRIDE, } Audit[ ]
T. R. WESTCOTT, }

No. of policies issued during the year
Less cancelled policies

No. remaining in force
Amount covered by insurance ... $519,5
Average amount of each policy 5

LOSSES.

Philip Cole	
C. Gerhard	
Jno. Going	
J. D. Dalton	2,0
	$2,0

Cash Account.

RECEIPTS.

From Agents, in cash premiums	$1,6
From Assessment	1,8
	$3,

DISBURSEMENTS.

Losses	$2,0
Salaries, on account	4
Printing and Advertising	
Stationery	
Postages	4
Discount	
Office Furniture	
Rent, $75; Taxes, $20 74	
Fuel, Light, Cleaning, etc	
Incidentals (small sums)	
	$3,0
Cash in Bank of Commerce	$336 37
Cash in Secretary's hands, including stamps	104 49
	$3,

Examined and compared with the boo[ ] vouchers and found correct.
WM. McBRIDE, } Audi[ ]
T. R. WESTCOTT, }

30th Jan. 1869.

r, James Reid moved a resolution, seconded lr. Wm. Pope, that the report of the Directors, iad, be received and adopted. The resolution carried unanimously.

ie members then proceeded to elect a new d of Directors, Messrs. A. S. Emery and John donald acting as scrutineers.

ie vote being taken, the retiring Board Messrs. lcBride, T. Wilson, S. Peters, John Macbeth, Srown, Edward Harris, Chas. F. Goodhue, ffim Starr, R. S. Murray, were declared re-ied unanimously.

. C. Macdonald, Esq., addressed the meeting i short time, making a few suggestions for the itance of the Board in their future operations, moved that a vote of thanks be tendered to Board for their services during the past year. motion was seconded by Mr. Williams, and iimously carried.

ie chairman, on behalf of himself and his orkers responded appropriately and briefly, ly commending the invaluable services of James Johnston, their energetic secretary.

ie thanks of the meeting, on motion of Mr. i, seconded by Mr. Emery, were unanimously ered to Mr. Johnston. That gentleman re-l in a very neat acknowledgment.

ie Board re-elected Alderman Samuel McBride, ident, and Capt. Thompson Wilson, Vice ident for the ensuing year. The meeting then irned.

ST. JOHN BUILDING SOCIETY.

i adjourned meeting of this Building Society held Feb. 9th. A balance sheet of liabili-and assets of the Society in a condensed form, a summary of the transactions during the year, was read by the Secretary, in which he rated the present position with that of 1st iary, 1868 :

DECEMBER 31, 1868.

Dr.

lepositors.	$53,990 11	
tock—Cash	60,369 07	
ccumulating Interest	71,027 91	
undries	515 32	
	$185,963 51	

Cr.

dvances to members, covered by 4 mortgages	$172,087 03	
ontingent account	6,026 20	
undries	850 28	
	$185,863 51	

ie operations of the Society are based on ½ shares, viz : 591 monthly investing shares, paid up shares, and 547½ advanced shares ; whole representing a subscribed capital of ,750.

ie 547½ advanced shares (to whom $200 on share have been advanced) are debited with nterest for a period of ten years (the time for h the loans are usually made), and are cover-r mortgage security same as the amount ad-ed.

ie monthly repayment from the 547½ shares advanced, amount to $1,555.10.

e deposit branch of the Society's business s the increasing confidence which the public in the institution ; the amount now held on ait is $53,980.11, against $41,726.84 on 1st ary last year. Six per cent ;n_eres_ per an-is paid on the 1st January and 1st July in year. On the 1st January, 1868, the opera-of the Society were based on 1,111 shares, senting a subscribed capital of $220,200 ; the ase of subscribed capital is $40,550. The ase of advances during the year under review n $140,352.31 on 1st January, 1868, to $179,-3 on 1st January, 1869, or $38,734.72. This des principal and interest for the time for i the advances are made.

The members' monthly investments during the year, including borrowers' repayments, have averaged $2,049.98—being monthly increase of $394.45 over the previous year.

ANGLO-AMERICAN PEAT COMPANY.

The first annual general meeting of stockholders of the Company, was held at the Company's office, No. 388 St. Paul street, in Montreal, on the 16th January, 1869, pursuant to law, and convened by special notice, duly published, ten days previous to said meeting.

Mr. Barton being called upon to take the chair, and Mr. A. McK. Cochrane to act as Secretary.

The Chairman stated that the charter, incorpo-rating the Company under the general Act of Li-mited Liability (Act 27-28 Victoria, cap. 23), had been issued, and that the preliminary steps had been duly complied with according to law. The charter was laid on the table for examination.

The Secretary submitted statements of what had been done thus far by the Provisional Board, finan-cial statement, working account, and statement of expenditure on land, and permanent construc-tion account.

Mr. Edgar proceeded to give some history of the undertaking ; he stated that some four years ago, he learned that there was valuable peat land near the Welland Canal, and after examining it, he, with some other parties, had purchased first one lot of a hundred acres, and then another lot, and so on as they could obtain it. Before purchasing largely, he had visited a number of peat beds in the United States, both East and West ; made himself acquainted with the quality of the mate-rial produced, and became satisfied that there was no finer article in existence than was found in the County of Welland ; nor could a peat bed be dis-covered in a more convenient location, being mid-way between the two great lakes, and close to the canal, it was easy to lay the peat down in the markets of all the cities and towns surrounding those lakes. It was also within half a mile of the Welland Railway, which connected with the Grand Trunk and Great Western Railroads. It was deemed advisable to secure the whole of the land, or nearly so, from which peat could be profitably taken, and this Company was therefore projected and the land purchased. The next thing to be done was to get a proper machine at work to test the estimate that had been made as to the cost of production. For this purpose he examined various machines in actual operation, but found only one that he considered suitable, namely, that used by Mr. Smith, of Troy, who had a large peat bog, something like that of Welland, and had spent large sums of money in testing ,varjous ma-chines.

From all the machines, with some addition of his own invention, he had made a good machine, but had some further improvements to make, and between Mr. Smith and himself, a better machine had been constructed for the Anglo-American Peat Company, than had ever before been used.

Last summer, while the machine was being got ready, they had built a railway from the Welland Canal well into the property, a mile and a half in length ; then the works had to be put up, and the season was pretty well advanced before they were ready to begin manufacturing. It was found from experiments there, as well as in other peat beds, that while the weather was warm the peat could be nicely dried and ready for shipment in two weeks' time; but in the fall a good article could not be produced, especially in frosty weather.— After getting to work, they found they could pro-duce peat and deliver it on the banks of the canal for one dollar and forty-five cents a ton ; and they could sell it readily at $3 50 a ton ; though to make very large sales they might have to reduce their price to $3 a ton. The results of actual work thus far had been far in excess of what had been anticipated. They had been examining Mr. Hodges' machine, and were satisfied that, with

some improvements which his (Mr. Edgar's) ex-perience during the past season suggested, one or two of these machines would prove of great value. Mr. Walter Shanley had given it as his opinion that the company's peat bed was better suited for the Hodges' machine than any they had in Lower Canada, and that the material was better, being a pure moss peat.

Mr. Edgar said he thought they could make the ordinary peat for domestic purposes best with the kind of machine they already had ; but the Hod-ges' machine would make a better article for use of railways, steamboats, and engines. He was fully satisfied from the experience of the year that they would be able to manufacture peat much cheaper than they had originally estimated.

Value of machinery, buildings, &c.—permanent construction account.

Buildings—Engine House, Work Shops, Boarding House, Stables, &c	$4,500
Railway and Wharf, and Tramways	3,000
Machinery—2 Engines, and 2 Boilers, Dredge, Scow, 2 Peat Machines, Cars, Crates, &c	9,000
Horse and Cart, Tools, Trucks, Black-smiths' Tools, &c	600
Materials on hand—Nails, Lumber, &c	1,400
Total	$18,500
Paid on account of Land	$117,000

Working Account.

Result of eight days work with one machine, "Smith's" Dry Fuel, 154 tons; cost of production $222.37,—equal to $1.44½ per ton.

Two machines, now complete and in working order, will make in season of 100 days, at same rate, 3,850 tons; cost at same rate, $5,559.25, which, if sold at $3 a ton, $11,550,—showing a profit of $5,990.75, with machinery we have now in operation.

One Hodges' machine to be put in by 1st of May next, will cost all complete, with permanent right to use it, about $10,000.

It will make 8,000 tons Dry Peat in the season, at a less cost than the other machines; but say, at same rate, 8,000 tons will cost $11,551.74, which, if sold at $3 a ton, $24,000,—showing a profit of $12,448.26.

The foregoing estimates for the result of next season's work are low, as by late improvements the small machines now on hand can be made to work up to 25 tons or more in ten hours, instead of about 20 tons as in the calculations.

The peat is also calculated as if sold at three dollars a ton, which is fifty cents less than it will probably bring. The same material is now being sold in Montreal at $5 to $5.50 a ton, though de-livered from boat last summer at $4 to $4.25.

On motion of Mr. Henry Starnes, seconded by Mr. Edwards, it was

Resolved,—That the transactions of the Provi-sional Directors are hereby confirmed and adopted, and all sums paid to them, or to the Provisional Treasurer, are hereby acknowledged as if paid after the incorporation and organization of the Company, and the thanks of the shareholders are tendered to the Provisional Directors for their services.

Moved by Mr. Barton, seconded by Mr. Major, that the present meeting sustain in all respects the by-laws, as set forth in the charter constituting the Company, and which are embodied in the book of records of the company. These are the ordi-nary regulations and by-laws prescribed by the law of limited liability.

On motion of Mr. Foster, seconded by Mr. Thomson, it was

Resolved,—That the election of Directors be now proceeded with by ballot according to law. Mr. Dillon and Mr. Egginton were appointed scruti-neers.

The ballot having been taken up, the scrutineers retired, and in a short time returned with their Report, stating that Messrs. R. Reford, H. Starnes, A. M. Foster, J. E. Major, of Montreal; R. Milroy, Wm. Edgar, F. M. Wilson, of Hamilton, were duly elected Directors for the ensuing year.

On motion of Mr. Kent, seconded by Mr. Starnes, it was

Resolved,—The Directors are hereby authorized and empowered to accept and take from the proprietors of the land on which the works of the Company are carried on, being the lands now held in trust for this Company by Messrs. David Edgar and W. J. McAllister of Hamilton, (being 3,050 acres in the Townships of Wainfleet and Humberstone, in the County of Welland,) the said lands as they stood at the commencement of the Company's works, according to the prospectus issued. Carried unanimously.

Mr. William Edgar was elected President; Mr. Robert Reford, Vice-President; Mr. A. McK. Cochrane, Secretary Treasurer; and Messrs. John Dillon and J. U. Barton, Auditors.

After a vote of thanks to the Chairman and Secretary the meeting was closed.

St. Lawrence Tow Boat Company.—At a general meeting of the shareholders of the St. Lawrence Tow Boat Company, held in Quebec, the following gentlemen were elected Directors for the ensuing year :—Hon. T. McGreevy, A. Joseph, Esq., S. J. Shaw, Esq., D. C. Thomson, Esq., L. Parent, Esq., John Roche, Esq., A. H. Murphy, Esq.; H. J. Chaloner, Esq., and Julien Chabot, Esq. And at a subsequent meeting of the Directors, the Hon. T. McGreevy was re-elected President, and A. Joseph, Esq., was elected Vice-President.

Insurance.

Fire Record.—Kingston, Feb. 17.—A fire broke out in the stables of Jno. Robb, carter, on the corner of George Street west, two cows were consumed in the stables. The fire extended to the dwelling house of Mr. Dodds, a workman in the foundry of the Canadian Engine and Machinery Company, which immediately adjoined the stable on George Street. His furniture was all rescued in advance of the flames, but the building fell an easy prey. Mr. Robb was insured for $200, and Mr. Dodds for $300, which will not cover the losses. The fire is believed to have been accidental.

Springfield, Kings County, N. B.—Two barns, with their contents, belonging to Allen Price, were destroyed by fire on the 8th. Loss $1,200 A large wooden house on the City Road, belonging to Mr. Lawler, also caught fire. The flames were extinguished without the assistance of the engines. As the house was unoccupied, it is supposed to have been set on fire.

Melrose, Feb. —.—The Congregational Church at this place was burned down. Loss $20,000; insured for $10,000.

Guelph, Feb. .—A serious explosion occurred in Clark's refinery, by which three men were injured. No damage to the building.

Winding Up.—It will be remembered that the Hercules Insurance Company (life) recently took over the business of the International of London. Some circumstances attending the transfer gave dissatisfaction to the shareholders of the former company. One circumstance complained of was that somebody got £15,000 for promoting, or according to the arrangement. In consequence of the feeling existing, some seven petitions were filed in Chancery, praying that the Hercules be wound up. A meeting of shareholders was called to consider what should be done. The proceedings lasted from two o'clock until nearly eight, and eventually, on the recommendation of the company's solicitor, Mr. Merriman, but contrary to the urgent advice of the manager, Mr. Shrubb,

who stated that the company was perfectly solvent and had a profitable fire and life business, and contrary to the advice of other independent shareholders, who wished that a call should be at once made to pay the pressing liabilities of the company, it was eventually resolved that the company should be liquidated—Mr. Shrubb, however, to have the power of selling the fire and life business to other companies, subject to the approval of the liquidators.

—Notices are given in the *Gazette* that application will be made to the Dominion Parliament, next session, for a charter to establish the Imperial Bank of Canada; also for acts to incorporate the "Dominion Life Insurance and Guarantee Association," and the "Dominion Fire and Marine Insurance Company;" also for an Act to incorporate the Niagara and Erie Canal Company, with power to construct a ship-canal from the Niagara River at or near Fort George, to the Welland Canal, immediately above Lock No. 25, in or near the village of Thorold, and to extend the same to the upper Niagara, at or near Chippewa.

—The Quebec Marine Insurance Company have declared a dividend of 7 per cent., payable on the 22nd inst.

Railway News.

Great Western Railway.—Traffic for week ending February 5, 1869.

Passengers	$20,514 39
Freight	50,899 96
Mails and Sundries	1,915 85
Total Receipts for week	$73,330 20
Corresponding week, 1887...	67,107 65
Increase	$6,222 55

—A meeting of the Montreal and Champlain Railway Company was adjourned to May 1st:

—It is stated that Mr. Brydges recently visited Lennoxville, Q., to arrange for the connection of the Massawippi Valley Railway with the Grand Trunk. A third rail is proposed from Lennoxville to Sherbrooke. The Concord Railroad Company have offered to transport the rails for the M. V. R. R. over their line free of charge. On the part of the Grand Trunk, Mr. Brydges offers to bring rails from Quebec at a nominal charge.

—The preliminary survey of the section of the proposed "Central Railway," between Ottawa and Vaudreuil, on the Grand Trunk, is now on foot, but, so far, is merely undertaken with the object of securing a proximate estimate of the cost of the road.

—At the first meeting of the new Council for East Garafraxa, a petition was presented, asking a bonus of $20,000 to the Toronto, Grey and Bruce Railway. The Council "could not see" any return for the money, and accordingly they passed a resolution, stating that they considered it inexpedient to take any action in the matter.

—The Prince Edward Island papers are discussing the advantages of a railway from Charlottetown to Georgetown. It is held that as Georgetown harbour remains open to navigation a month longer than any other in the Island, the benefits derived from this railway connection would more than compensate for the cost. Produce that is now held during the winter and very often deteriorates in value before spring, could by this means be run by rail to Georgetown, and shipped from that place after Charlottetown and Summerside have been closed by ice. The cost of the road is, however, a serious consideration.

A Bad Prospect for Montreal.—The efforts now being made by Portland to secure more direct railway communication with the Western States by aiding a projected railway to Rutland through to connect with the New York Central and

another to Swanton, Vt., there to connect the Vermont and Canada and the Ogdensburg railway, trouble Montrealers. When these r are built, the Atlantic and St. Lawrence have formidable competitors for the trade w now uses the Grand Trunk. They see that dace from the West coming through Mon must travel a few more miles than via Ogdens and Swanton or Buffalo and Rutland. *Gazette* says that one of three things must be by the Montreal interests:

1. To compete with water-borne traffi Caughnawaga against Ogdensburg. Will Grand Trunk Railway Company and t new company agree in this ? Will the fe consent so to manage the road from Caughna through traffic over its main line ? Will Lanolle Valley people, now in strict league the Ogdensburg Company, become parties to an arrangement ? 2. The people of Mon may join the Grand Trunk Railway in putt third track on the road to St. Johns, and lay an air line thence to Island Pond via Newpo making the distances pretty even and the chi of successful competition much greater. O If the Grand Trunk Railway is indisponent or able to do anything, Montrealers may hel Foster to push on the line via Chambly and j ham, and thence to tap the new line by an en independent route, either directly at She or through the Passaumsic via Newport an Johnsbury. To us it seems that the time sitting still is past. If the capitalists of Mon had built the Portland line over the best r this danger would not now have arisen. instead of putting money into wharves at Mo Island and a Rouse's point extension, they run out one branch from St. Johns to Swa over the route now occupied by the Vermont tral, and another to Newport, to connect wi Passumpsic, the remedy would have beer much easier to-day. But we have steadily persistently scorned to take the direct route place. We go to Three Rivers, Quebec and land via Richmond ; we go to Ottawa via cott, we go to Waterloo via Granby; we soon to go to Montreal via Lennoxville !

Muskoka Railway.—At Orillia, a few ago, the following were elected officers o Simcoe and Muskoka Railway:—Isaac May, ident; A. P. Cockburn, M.P.P., Vice Pres Arthur Robinson, C. E., Chief Engineer; R. Grant, Secretary and Treasurer; S. Rob Solicitor. The stock books were opened and siderable amount subscribed. The matter terminus at the south end is left an open qu

INTERESTING STATISTICS OF AMER RAILROAD IRON.

Subjoined is an extract of the thoughtf instructive report of Henry McAllister, Jr retary of the "American Iron and Steel A tion," made to the Annual Meeting he Thursday, February 18 :

Total number of miles of railroad (including 2nd track sidings, &c.)	52,500
Total increase for 10 years, ending Dec. 31, 1868	16,536
Total increase for last five years...	9,448
Average annual increase for the last ten years	1,654
Average number of miles in use for 10 years ending Dec. 31, 1868...	43,123
Iron required in laying 43,153 miles averaged at 90 tons per mile, 3,781,070 tons, which at 6½ per cent for average annual wear gives iron required for renewal of track	250,948
Iron required for last ten years for renewal of track	2,599,490
Iron required for last ten years for new track, 16,536 miles, averaged at 96 tons per mile	1,587,450

.d consumption of railroad iron
r last ten years........ ....4,186,936 tons
rails imported for 10 years end-
g June 30, 1868..................1,015,685 "
itity of rails manufactured in
e U. S. during the last 10 yrs. 3,171,251 "
'age quantity of rails imported
r annum for the last 10 years. 101,568 "
'ge domestic production per
nnu for last ten years.......... 317,125 "
l average annual consumption
r last 10 years..................... 418,693 "
iut 62 per cent of the consump-
on of rails is required for re-
wals and 38 per cent for new
uck.)
ortation of rails for years end-
g June 30, 1888................ 228,277 "
uction of American mills for
ur ending Dec. 31, 1868...... 506,714 "
ase of importations on average
ten years............................ 125,709 "
ase of domestic production on
erage of ten years............... 189,589 "
increase of consumption in
68 upon annual average of last
t years...... .... 316,298 "
seems to be the impression, particularly
g those whose observations do not extend
1d our great trunk lines, that the per centage
ls worn out each year is much greater than
given above ; but this cannot be the case un-
ll the estimates that have been made of the
oer of miles of railroad in the country have
greatly exaggerated. It must be remember-
nt, whilst many of the rails on main lines
our great railroad centres are worn out in a
: year, there are thousands of miles of track
e Southern States and in the thinly settled
ons of other sections that last over twenty

England the actual waste of iron rails by
ing, oxidation, and loss is said to amount to
0 tons a year, whilst about 250,000 tons re-
to be taken up and re-rolled. As the num-
f miles of road there, including a second
and sidings, may be safely put down at
0, it follows that the average wear and tear
ack amounts to 10.36 per cent per annum.
In [that country, where the destruction of
ls so much greater than here, we are told
n some lines of light traffic, rails frequently
0 years, while on lines near London, which
ider constant and heavy work, many miles
ack require relaying in less than twelve
ha.—U. S. Railway Journal.

  * In all cases tons of 2,000 pounds.

The creditors of the Peterboro Petroleum
'e requested to send in their claims before
i 1st.

'he Canadian Navigation Company have de-
l a dividend of 7 per cent, and re-elected
directors.

The Canadian Monetary Times.

THURSDAY, FEBRUARY 25, 1869.

ANGLO-AMERICAN PEAT COMPANY.

The proceedings at the annual meeting o
this Company will, we doubt not, be read
with interest, for we are all anxious to learn
what are the prospects of being able to obtain
cheap fuel. The Company seem to have gone
to work in earnest. A railway a mile and a
half long has been built by them from the
Welland Canal to their property, and a peat
machine of improved character was constructed specially for their operations. Their
experience thus far is that they can produce
peat and deliver it on the banks of the Canal
for $1.45 a ton which can be sold at $3.50 a
ton, the same material being sold in Montreal at $5 to $5.50. We need scarcely say
that we wish these peat producers every success, and we doubt not, through the zeal and
energy of the Secretary, Mr. A. Mc. K. Cochrane, that 'the stockholders will find their
profits handsome.

CANADA FARMERS' MUTUAL.

The amount of business done by this Company in 1867 exceeded that of any previous
year, and the report for 1868 shows that the
Company has held its ground notwithstanding the increased competition with which
it has to contend. The following exhibits
at a glance the substance of the business for
the year just closed :

Premium earnings...................$37,828 56
Less agents' fees...................... 3,846 25
                                      _____
                                        $33,982 31
Losses paid...........$19,902 55
Expense of investi-
  gation...............   743 20
                     _____
                      $20,645 75
Current expenses... 5,573 78— 26,219 53
                                      _____
Balance.................................. 7,762 78

The premium note system was done away
with last year and rates were reduced. The
Directors very properly decline to advise a
further reduction until a reser.,e is accumulated. The special privileges allowed to this
Company under their amended charter give
them a great advantage, which the judicious
management of Mr. Street will not fail to
improve fully.

ONTARIO MUTUAL.

We give elsewhere the first annual report
of the Ontario Mutual Fire Insurance Company, the head office of which is at London,
Ontario. The members of this infant association are to be congratulated on the success

which has attended the efforts of those on
whom its management devolves. In little
more than a year the Company has issued
1,026 policies, all on non-hazardous risks,
and generally spread over the country. The
average risk is small, only $514, a good
feature in a Mutual Company. The expenses of management are light, while the
assets apparently available shew ample security to the insured for payment of losses.

NORTHERN RAILWAY.

The traffic receipts of this railway indicate
in their rise or fall, the increase or diminution of certain branches of Toronto trade.
The gross traffic receipts for the year 1868,
$550,070, were less by $11,300 than those of
the year previous, the falling off being accounted for by the decline in the supply of
square timber. On the other hand, the passenger traffic and the article of sawed lumber
have been the sources of increased receipts.
The working expenses give a rate of 61.06
per cent. for 1868, about 1.77 per cent. higher
than in 1867. This increase is attributable
to the high price of fuel wood, and two disasters which involved injury to the permanent
way, as well as the destruction of a considerable
amount of property. Great credit is due to
Mr. Cumberland for his admirable management of this line of railway and his unceasing
efforts to extend its usefulness and increase
its efficiency. It is contemplated to construct
a new elevator and wharf at Toronto, at a cost
of $140,000, and one of large capacity at
Collingwood. With the Rama and Muskoka
Canals constructed, the lumbering interest of
the north shore of the Georgian Bay developed
and the free grant region settled and cultivated, the Northern Railway traffic will undoubtedly be largely increased, so that the
prospects may be regarded as the best. These
matters are known to and appreciated by the
Directors of the Company, and their efforts
seem turned to a prudent preparation for the
the good time coming and the hastening of
its approach, by contributing influence and
assistance to such enterprises as are likely to
secure it.

EXTRACT OF HEMLOCK BARK.

Heretofore we have set forth in these
columns the advantages likely to accrue to
Canada from an energetic development of her
material products, dwelling with particular
emphasis on the production of peat and the
manufacture of sugar from beet root and
describing succintly the various processes of
manufacture. We propose, now, to consider
another branch of industry which might be
pursued with benefit to the country. The
hemlock is a native of Canada and if a cheap

mode of extracting from its bark a tannic acid superior to the agencies now used in tanning is available, we may naturally urge its utilization.

Tanners employ different ingredients, all more or less efficacious, in converting the raw hide into leather. We will enumerate the leading ones, viz.—the bark of the larch, oak, cork-tree, birch, willow, mimosa, valonia, myrabolanis, and divi-divi. The question now arises, can the extract of hemlock bark be made so cheap as to come into competition with the above enumerated articles, nearly all of which have to be imported at considerable cost. We will try to solve the question. We quote from Powell & Sing's Liverpool Circular the prices, and also the amount of tannic acid contained in the different articles used by tanners :

	Per cent of Tannic.	Price per Ton.
English Oak	10 to 20	£ 7
Valonia	30 to 35	18
Divi-divi	28 to 29	13
Myrabolanis	18 to 20	17
Mimosa	15	11
Cork-tree	8 to 10	9
Sunrack (Sicily)	12 to 20	21
Cutch (Bombay)	40 to 45	24

We can place on the European market 400 pounds of extract of hemlock bark of the first quality, which will contain about 360 per cent of tannic acid, for £4 sterling. One ton prepared oak bark, at 10 per cent, yields only 224 of tannic acid, and at 20 per cent, 448 of tannic extract. The mean of this will be 360, or 24 degrees less than is contained n 400 pounds hemlock acid. For oak bark, the price is £7 to £8 10, unground and unleached. These figures apparently show that it only requires enterprise, capital and ability to secure for the sale of the hemlock extract a market superior to any attainable for most other products used in tanning.

The method at present generally used for extracting the tannic acid from hemlock is as follows : The bark is ground when dry, and by the necessary friction it becomes so heated as to give out a large amount of hydrogen, thus rendering it less soluble, and consequently requiring a great amount of heat to eliminate the tannic from the pulverized mass. This is done by submitting it to heated baths or leaches, and afterwards inspissated or vacuum pans, which to a greater or lesser extent decomposes the tannic acid, but heightens the color of the extract, a property very objectionable to the tanner. The amount of heat thus produced also causes the resin and other residuum to become so incorporated with the extract as to produce fermentation, which seriously damages its quality for both tanner and dyer.

Various methods have been patented, each of them having for its object the elimination and the condensing of the extract in the cheapest and best manner. Among the many, we notice a process patented by Mr. Wm. Maynard, of Montreal, in which the patentee sets forth or claims—1st. The absence of dry heat in disintegrating the fibre, since he crushes instead of grinding, as is done by other methods ; this saves the extra expense of storing in order to dry the bark. 2nd. The fibre being so thoroughly pulverized, the extract is given out without the expense of leaching, being merely filtered from the organic and gummy matter or residuum. 3rd. Evaporation is produced by a method altogether novel, and doing away with explosive or boiling heat, and by means of mechanical appliances in conjunction with chemical action, all foreign particles tending to fermentation are thoroughly separated. Besides this being a cheaper method of obtaining the tannic, there is a great[saving in manual labor, the process not requiring more than half the number of hands usually employed by other manufacturers.

Of the value of the different patents, tanners must judge for themselves ; but the subject generally is one of considerable importance, and may open up a large new branch of local manufacture, if taken up with skill and energy.

The failure of Messrs. W. R. Brown, & Co., brokers, is attributable to heavy losses on gold speculations in New York. They have been holding a large quantity of gold since September, at heavy margins, in expectation of a rise. It is said that they had to sell $200,000 and realized a loss on the whole transaction of at least $50,000. Keeping up the margins was a heavy drain on themselves and their backers. Speculation in Erie Stocks finished them. Their largest creditor is the Royal Canadian Bank, but it is said that it holds sufficient securities to protect itself.— Deposits to the extent of six or seven thousand dollars are gone. It is not probable that anything will be realized by creditors not directly secured.

According to the Public Accounts of the Province of Quebec submitted to the Quebec Legislature, the total receipts for eighteen months ending 31st December were, $2,612,514 51, and the expenditure, $1,794,297 23, leaving a balance of $618,216 92.

BANKERS' MAGAZINE.

The February number contains articles on the National Currency—Paper Money and its Evils— Wells' Report on the Financial Policy of the Government—besides the usual quantity of interesting and useful information.

—The Quebec Gas Co. has declared a dividend of four per cent, for the half year. Transfer books will be closed until the 1st March.

Correspondence.

CANADA LANDED CREDIT COMPANY

Editor of the Canadian Monetary Times.

SIR,—I was very glad to find in the last number of your paper a full report of the proceedings of the annual meeting of the Canada Landed Credit Company. The reports in the daily papers gave me but a poor opinion of those present at the meeting, but when I came to read your account of what had occurred, I did my co-shareholders justice. But it seems to me that a fuller report than that presented by the Board of Directors to the meeting should have been forthcoming. I have searched through it in vain for an account of the working expenses of the institution. Other companies, panics and societies do not hesitate to give their publicity to their affairs, and it is hard to see why it is to be gained by the exceptional position of the Canada Landed Credit Company. I know to my cost that such management does positive harm, for I am met with all sorts of questions when I try to sell my stock. I know further, that the cancellation and forfeiture of shares have been going on for some time past in a wholesale manner. For all that appears, the present dividend is the most of the past have been paid out of the proceeds of these forfeitures. I hope that the new Directors will see that a full investigation is had, and so that our stock will improve. Enclosed you find my card.

Yours, etc.,
ONE INTERESTED

Toronto, Feb. 22, 1869.

CLASSIFICATION OF VESSELS.

To the Editor of the Monetary Times.

Your correspondent who wrote respecting disposition and classification of vessels is speaking of the opinion that one Inspector can class a vessel. He is mistaken. In 1865, one can do so ; in 1866 it required two ; but in 1867 inspector should be employed, as Inspector is likely to be friendly to those builders who patronize them. The thirty-five years experience of Lloyd's and the thirteen at Buffalo proves that the "independent inspector" is quite as friendly to builders who "appreciate his friendship," as the company inspector to the builders who "patronize" him. He says the report of the independent inspector should be revised by the association. "association" means company inspectors; the influence of the builders and owners will at once be felt; the independent inspector will simply be an assistant to the company inspectors. If "association" does not mean company inspectors then they are not to revise the report then the opinions in the various offices as to which vessel standard and which are not, will probably be absurdly conflicting; and the number of (complained of by your correspondent) in which the same vessels are classed differently in different offices will be greatly increased. A fact must not be overlooked that there are vessels belonging to Ontario, that the Inspectors of Ontario Companies know or ought to know about them all, and no approach to unanimity can be expected unless these inspectors are consulted to their class. Would not the employment of a surveyor (overlooked and paid fairly by owners, merchants and underwriters,) for classing and altering class of old vessels be fairer for all parties?

Another grievance complained of is, the owner of vessel property has suffered loss through standard of his vessel having been lowered during the sailing season. Such alterations we inevitable under any system. If sails blow or a vessel springs a-leak she loses class till sails are replaced or the vessel repaired. Of course it is not known that a vessel is water rotten till a storm demonstrates the fact

, season is half over. Is there any injustice classing her down? Would it not be grossly just to publish a vessel as fit to carry ain, when the grain would be destroyed if t on board ?. It is as much the business of owners know the state of their vessels as it is that of underwriters, and, if a vessel has been classed high, her owner has no cause of complaint en she is put right.

When the underwriters think it advantageous go to the expense of an assistant inspector they l, doubtless, employ one. It is probable that every $5 they lose from errors in the register, y lose $100 from overloading and carelessness masters.

The custom has been for the inspectors to travel nd in March, not so much for the purpose of veying, as for seeing what repairs the vessels undergoing, and examining those as to whose dition they are in doubt.

Yours, &c.

OBSERVER.

Toronto, Feb. 23, 1869.

MERCANTILE AGENCIES.

the Editor of the Monetary Times.

IR,—I have heard the question debated whether cantile Agencies are a benefit or otherwise to trading community. Some affirm that they e the merchant rely less on his own judgment, ; they help to expand credit, &c., but my own ion is that the tendency is on the whole for l. Still, I think, I see what is a glaring inice in their management. Most of your readers aware of the method used in procuring the atings." The objection I see is that the merit rated has no opportunity of judging of the ectness of his character and means as set forth heir books, unless he is a member of the ination and even then it is questionable if he d, with a good grace, get the *minutiæ* on ch they base their judgment. The plan, I k, that should be adopted is this: Let the ncies mail every merchant and tradesman a ement of his character, &c., as entered by n. If it is incorrect, the injured party can claim the right to show wherein it is wrong. uld it be urged that the Agencies by this se would leave themselves open to action for , let them be protected by legislative enactt. By the present system, many men are ring unknown to themselves, through the dental errors of the Mercantile reporters; and otless the insertion of malicious mis-statements t unknown to the offices in Canada any more in the United States. I could give instances, quired, of great injustice having been done, ced from my own mercantile experience. An ement, such as I have above suggested would ve the strongest objections to these organiza. Commending the matter to the attention ourself and of your readers.

I am, &c., D. T.

ronto, Feb. 23, 1869.

SOLVENTS GAZETTED.—Theophile Rolland, Rhynas, J. W. Butler, W. Horigan, Victor iault, Dame Celina, Charpentier Theophile, ion, and Buck, Robertson & Co., all Mon-; D. C. Morrison, Almonte, Henry McNelly, nship of King; Alexander Quimette, West ham; Benjamin Smith, Ancaster; Todman iminston, of Wellington, County of Prince ard; Richard H. Collier, Seaforth; Victor ins Parish of Guilliaume; D. Upton, Samuel ow, Artemesia; Alexander Cuthbert, Cobourg; iam Mantel Shaw, Georgetown; Eusebe lx, Ste. Genevieve François Leduc Lange, ien; Robert Thacker, Woodstock; Edwin ummer, Toronto; Matthew Roger, London.

Financial.

MONTREAL MONEY MARKET.

(From Our Own Correspondent.)

Montreal, Feb. 23, 1869.

There is still plenty of money, and a difficulty in finding good and profitable investments, first class paper being readily taken up by the Banks at the minimum rate of discount, say 7 per cent. 2nd and 3rd class paper 8 to 9 per cent., but in this class the Banks are cautious in their discounts. Very little is offering on the street and only such as the Banks declined, the rates ranges from 12 to 16 according to the names. Money can be obtaind on first-class documentary security at 6½ per cent. The stock and share market continues dull owing to holder being indifferent, and buyers being unwilling to pay the extreme rates; the supply of capital seeking investment is large, the high prices demanded being the chief obstruction to a large business being done. Bank of Montreal has sold from 139¼ to 139½. Holders now asking higher rates. City has rather receded and is worth 102¾ to 103—sellers now asking 104¼. Merchants' 108 to 108½. Toronto 120 to 122½. Molsons' are in favor at 111 to 111¼—not much change in other Banks. In stocks, sales of telegraph 132½ to 133 with some enquiry. City Gas Co, asked for at 142—sellers demanded 145. Mining Consols have sold moderately at $3 12½. Not much doing in other shares.

TORONTO STOCK MARKET.

Business for the past week has been pretty active and prices in most cases well maintained. There have been large transactions in township Debentures at high rates and in Government Bonds at a slight decline on the last week's prices.

Bank Stock.—A few small sales of Montreal was made at 139¾. There are buyers of British at 104, but none in the market. Ontario declined in the beginning of the week to 99, but has since slightly revived there being buyers to-day at 99½ and no sellers under par. Small sales of Toronto occurred at 121, sellers generally asking 122 but buyers will not advance over 121. Royal Canadian has been dealt in during the week at 90, and 91, buyers now offer 90, sellers ask 90½ to 91. There were large sales of Commerce at 103, sellers now ask 103½. Sales of Gore were made at 40, 40½ and 41, no buyers now over 40. Merchants declined during the week to 107, but closed stronger with no sellers under 108½. There are buyers of Quebec at 99, but no sellers. Molson's sold at 111¼ to 112, closing with no sellers under 112½. Buyers offer 103 for City, but sellers want 103¾. There are buyers of National at 106½. Jacques Cartier could be placed at 108½, but sellers want 109. For Mechanics 95 would be paid, no sales. Buyers offer 103½ for Union, but sellers ask 104. Nothing doing in other banks.

Debentures.—Sterling Canada sixes have been largely dealt in at 103¼, 103, and 102½; five per cents. offer at 94½. Dominion Stock has been sold at 105½. Toronto are much enquired for, but none offering. County would be readily taken at par.

Sundries.—Canada Permanent Building Society have been dealt in at 125, and for small lots 125½ has been paid; Western Canada sold at 119½ to 120; there are buyers at the latter rate but no sellers under 121; Freehold has advanced to 110, but there is very little offering. City Gas is scarce with numerous buyers. Several sales of British America Assurance occured at 55 to 55½, it is still procurable at the latter rate. Montreal Telegraph sold at 133½, there are now buyers but no sellers at that rate. Large sales of Canada Landed Credit were made at 75, but holders want higher rates. Some large mortgages are offering at 8 per cent. There is more demand for money.

ALTERED NOTES.—A one dollar note of the Royal Canadian Bank has been changed to a ten very cleverly. The altered bills are thus described:—The word *one*, wherever it occurs, is erased, and *ten* put in its place, both on the back and the face of the bill. There are two large figures *one* on the face of the bill in *green* color. But this green is the common green ink, not the patent color—and these figures have evidently been erased by means of acids, and the figures *ten* substituted, painted in green ink. Had the original figures been printed in the patent green, they could not have been erased. Another test by which the genuine *tens* of this bank may be known from altered *ones* is that the former have a vignette of the Queen on the left hand face of the bills.

GOLD CONTRACTS IN THE STATES.—The Supreme Court of the United States has decided that a contract stipulating payment in gold coin is valid in law and can be enforced. The case before the Court was one in which the contract had been made prior to the Legal-Tender Act, and the issue of greenbacks. The decision, however, is interpreted as in no way depending on the date of the contract, and it is inferred from the reasoning of the Judges that they would enforce contracts to pay gold goin, even if made since the Legal-Tender Act was passed.

INTEREST REMITTANCE.—The City Chamberlain yesterday remitted to the Bank of London, where payable, the interest on the city debt to the amount of £5,500 sterling. It would not be due until next April.—*Hamilton Times.*

—Another investment in Dominion stock, to the amount of $750,000, has been made by the Ontario Government. This, taken with the amount previously invested, gives us over one million and a half dollars so invested, and brings us 6 per cent, or about $90,000 in the shape of interest.

—By the failure of the Commercial Bank, the north shore of New Brunswick has been deprived of all banking accommodation. A large and influential meeting was held at Miramichi, and a deputation appointed to visit the Upper Provinces, and confer with the banks here as to the opening of branches.

Commercial.

Montreal Correspondence.

(From our own Correspondent).

Montreal, Feb. 23, 1869.

Since my last, we have had a succession of snow storms, and if before our country roads were pretty well blocked up, they are now almost impassable, so that all business communication with the country districts may be said to be for the time suspended. The amount of snow on the level ground in the country averages over six feet, and in town it is fully more than one foot deeper than has ever been known. Our streets are consequently in a wretched state, the centre of the street being in most instances four to six feet above the pavement. A large number of carters are employed in carting away the snow, thus adding to the confusion which prevails.

As regards business, I can only report it as perfectly stagnant; no transactions beyond mere retail, the general feeling is of a decidedly gloomy cast.

GROCERIES.—Stocks of the chief staples are light, and holders therefore are firm. *Teas* are quiet; small sales, chiefly of uncolored Japans at 46c. to 56c. *Sugars* and *Molasses* are very unsettled, owing to the disturbances in Cuba; the feeling is that prices must rise higher, especially as the insurgents seem to be fairly in the Cienfuegos district, the great sugar-growing part of the island. With an estimated short crop in Brazil, Mauritius and some of the West India Islands, in all probability a high range of prices will be maintained;

several hundred hhds. of raw have changed hands at 8½c. to 9½c., passing chiefly into the refiners' hands. Molasses have participated in the advance in sugars, and several hundred hhds. of different sorts have changed hands at high rates. *Fish*—A large business has been done in herrings at full rates, say $5.50 to $5.65 for No. 1 split. Not much doing in other sorts. *Petroleum* in good demand, 37½c. by the car load, stocks are light. Nothing to notice in other articles.

PRODUCE.—Buyers will not operate in flour at present rates, and holders are equally averse to submit to any decline; our stocks are large, some 14,000 brls. over last year, and no demand for shipment. The late decline has caused a suspension of all operations to arrive, and both buyers and sellers have abandoned the market. I give the latest quotations, but must state that they are nominal; Extra, $5.25 to $5.40; Fancy,$4.95 to $5; strong Supers, $4.70 to $4.75; Supers No. 2, $4.35; Fine, $4.10 to $4.15. Grain of all sorts at nominal prices. U. C. Spring wheat, $1.12 to $1.14; Peas, 80c. to 92c.; Oats dull and easier, 46c. to 47c. per car load; Barley, $1.20 to $1.25 for ordinary.

PROVISIONS.—Dressed hogs have declined, but what is the cause I cannot see, they range from $8.75 to $10.50 over the market; Butter remains firm but nominal, at 23c to 24c. for choice dairy. Nothing doing in other articles.

DRY GOODS.—The spring assortments are arriving, but I expect the imports will be light. Nothing will be done till the middle of next month. Prospects for the spring trade are not bad.

HARDWARE.—I have to report a very quiet market, few orders from the country coming in and the town trade is very quiet.

Toronto Market.

DRY GOODS.—Since the 1st of January the amount of business done has been below the anticipations entertained of it. Some houses report good sales of Cottons and Tweeds, these goods being somewhat low in stock with country merchants. Spring goods are now arriving, and will be opened out about the 1st of March, though it is not anticipated that the Spring trade will open for some weeks yet. Owing to the backward state of the winter trade, the spring business is expected to begin late, and to amount to a fair average. Importers are operating cautiously. They all depend largely on sorting up as the season progresses. This they are now able to do with great facility. The same competition between rival routes which gives us through rates of freight from Liverpool to Toronto as low as those to Montreal, gives us also an advantage in time; that is to say, goods are laid down in Toronto from Liverpool as quickly (and often quicker) as they are brought to Montreal, because the competition extends not merely to rates of freight, but embraces the element of time as well, which is often quite as important as low rates of freight. The different Woollen factories in the country are running steadily, and are constantly making improvements in the quality and style of their goods. As bearing on this point, we find the following in a late number of *Morgan's Trade Journal*, in the annual report of the Huddersfield market: "Canadian buyers visiting this neighborhood have been very cautious in their purchases, and have not bought as many goods as usual. The low class of goods they have abandoned; they are making large quantities them-selves. What they want from us is a better and firmer class."

BOOTS AND SHOES.—Orders are coming in pretty freely. Now that the sleighing has improved, it is expected that remittances from the the country will also increase.

GROCERIES.—Trade has been moderately active. —*Sugar*—The market continues firm, and prices are ½c higher. The New York "Shipping List" of Feb. 20th has the following on the state of the market: "The continued alarming accounts from Cuba of the rapid progress of the revolution into the principal sugar-growing districts, if not now overspreading the whole island, more and more interrupting railroad and other communication with the interior, and of course preventing the due course of shipments *to*, and by consequence *from*, the ports of delivery, together with advices of rains and cholera—the unsettled state of the slave population—continual skirmishes with the insurgents in every direction—the almost total suspension of trade, and all the waste and destruction to property incidental to internal strife —give promise of a much greater reduction of the crop than was estimated in the early part of the season, which, without these drawbacks, was 20 to 25 per cent below the crop of last year. These occurrences sufficiently account for the late excited state of the Sugar market, and the considerable advance in prices noticed by us, now going on for more than a month past, the worst point being about the 10th December. The excitement consequent upon this state of things has continued unabated since our last, the most serious advices having come to hand since Tuesday. Refiners, having a larger margin for their products than for a long time past, buy freely even at the constantly advancing prices demanded from day to day—we might say from hour to hour. Speculation is also busy to secure probable profits, and the Trade, so far as the small stock suitable for their use will allow, are also ready purchasers. Holders continue to offer their rapidly diminishing stocks very sparingly, or refuse to name prices at all. A large portion of the stock here is new crop, mostly offered on arrival; that of old is small and rapidly diminishing. The stocks in New York at the dates mentioned were:

	Sugar.		Molado.
	Hhds.	Brls. Bags.	Hhds.
Stock, Feb. 19, 1869.....	9,700	4,000 1,967	500
" 19, 1868.....	3,034	3,826 500	100
" 19, 1867.....20,889	35,278 117,731	100
" 19, 1866.....19,172	36,311 96,601	33
" 19, 1865.....10,200	23,600 89,372	26

Molasses—The market is again firmer; in New York, prices are 2c to 5c higher, owing to the Cuban advices above noted. *Fruit*—Upwards of 25,000 boxes raisins changed hands in New York, the market closing firm at $3.20 for Layers in trade lots.

GRAIN.—*Wheat.*—Receipts 26,000 bush., and 36,492 bush. last week. Spring is dull and nominal; there is a good deal offering and not much demand. Good samples of Fall are scarce, and in demand at about $1, one or two cars sold at higher price; a choice lot is held out of market at a higher figure; smutty samples are plenty, but can't be sold. *Barley.*—Receipts 2,000 bush., and 450 bush. last week; the market is quiet and steady at quotations. *Oats.*—Receipts 600 bush. and 1,200 bush. last week; car loads are worth 51 to 52c. on the track. *Peas.*—Receipts 350 bush. and 290 bush. last week; offering at 80 to 85c. with buyers at 75c. *Rye*—Nominal, at 70c. *Corn.*— Market glutted; lots are offering with a limited demand at 60 to 63c. retail lots, 65c. *Seeds*—Are quiet; Timothy is offering freely in car loads; lots are worth about $2 to $2.50; holders ask $2.75 for small parcels of No. 1. Clover is quiet and unchanged, at $6.50 to $6.75, which are the prices paid by dealers. *Flax*—is higher, at $2 to $2.50.

FLOUR.—Receipts 2,389 brls., and 2,248 brls. last week. No. 1 Superfine is held at $4.15 to $4.20, with buyers at $4; 100 brls. sold at $4.20. Fancy nominal, at $4.25. For a lot of extra $4.60 was bid; no sales. *Bag Flour* held at $3.90, with buyers at $3.80.

PROVISION.—*Dressed Hogs*—The season is pretty well over, and there is very little doing. *Pork*— Mess is held at $26.50 to $27.50, no sales reported; Extra Prime is worth $20 to $21. *Butter*—

really choice continues to be inquired for, f local use, at 25c to 26c, but it is scarce; ordina lots are worth about 19c to 21c, with not mu doing. *Oatmeals*—Are steady and nominal quotations. *Cheese*—There is a good local dema at quotations. *Lard*—Quiet and firm at 16. to 17c.

HIDES.—Prices are steady, and the supply equal to the demand. Our quotations are th buying rates in this market.

FREIGHTS.—Rates by Grand Trunk Railway: Flour to all stations from Belleville to Lynn, i clusive, 35c., grain per 100 lbs. 18c.; flour Brockville and Cornwall, inclusive, 43c. grain 2 flour to Montreal 50c. grain 25c.; flour to r clusive, 85c. grain 43c.; flour to Boston 96 gold, grain 45c.; flour to Halifax $1.10, grain 55 flour to St. John $1.02. Boxed Meats to Liverpo per gross ton 80s.; lard or butter in tinne 85s.; Pork 11s. per tierce; flour 5s. 6d. p barrel; grain 12s. per 480 pounds. Rates t Great Western Railway—Flour, Toronto to Su pension Bridge 25c. gold; thence to New Yo 62c. U. S. currency per bbl.; to Boston $1.0 Grain to Bridge 13c., gold; thence to New Yo 47c, U. S. currency; to Boston 51c. Grain, T ronto to Detroit, 15c. per 100 lbs; flour 3 per bbl.

English Tea Trade in 1868.

The tea market during the last year has be subject to severe fluctuations. It opened und the influence of extended deliveries and of decrea ing stocks, so much so that, viewing the statisti of the previous four years, it appeared that co sumption had for the time outstripped productio This led to active speculation, raising the price common classes fully 4d. per lb. from the low point. The large advance, however, checked t clearances, and although the old stock was reduc to sixty-four millions, still, as the reduction w not so great as expected by some, a retrogra movement set in, resulting in a fall as sudden a almost as extended as the previous advance h been, stimulated also by the news of the enorm and hurried shipments of the season 1868-9, a eventuating in losses on the bulk of the import large or larger than ever experienced.

But worse even than the market being flood by arrivals has been the results of inferior qual to which we have often before had cause to adve Of the Foo-chow teas, what with the mixture old leaf and the amount of dust, it may be fa said that there are scarcely any really fine parc though chop after chop has been bought as su and this remark applies to fancy teas as well a Congou. Of the teas from the north, we speak more favorably; the Oonfaas have been markably fine, the Ningchows good; but e here the Monings and Oopacks, though fine make, have been mixed with inferior leaf, so a increase the quantity, and are altogether defici in richness and flavour.

If it is to be admitted that the altered relati of trade in China will in future necessitate overwhelming supply during the early mont the position at home must also be realized—th with the increasing rapidity of communicat and freeness of transit, the necessity of any a moderate stock is a thing of the past—that la exports from China will inevitably depress pri at home for a time at least, and that, therefo if the trade hereafter is to be a remunerative o there must be a radical change in the mode of b ing, in the rates paid, and the quality purchas The present system holds out a premium to Chinese to make bad tea, and has been the fer source of ruinous loss.

Indian teas continue to show great improvem in manufacture, and we have reason to hope t before long the bulk of the import will be te really high class character. They have fluctu with China teas, and at one time prices had rec considerably even for Pekoes; but the better gra have since recovered, and all high conditio lities of the new crop have met a ready sale at prices.

'he imports of tea into the United Kingdom e been 153,000,000 lbs, against 124,750,000 in 1867; the deliveries for home consumption, ,250,000 lbs, against 111,000,000 in 1867; o, for exportation, 35,500,000 lbs, against 32,- ,000 lbs in 1867; the stock remaining on the t of December was 88,500,000 lbs, against 77,- ,000 lbs in 1867.

	IMPORTS 1868.	1867.
ea........lbs	39000	17500
gou........	107882000	88411000
er........	23000	25000
ited Caper........	4315000	3766500
chong........	145500	18000
g Yong and Oolong........	2376000	1805000
chong and Campoi........	4620500	3698000
k-leaf Pekoe and Hng. Muy........	425500	242500
wery Pekoe........	188000	135500
nge Pekoe........	120500	9000
nge Pekoe, scented........	6450500	4865000
nkay........	346500	552500
ion Skin........	32000	18500
ion........	1274000	1094500
ing Hyson........	5431000	5114000
erial........	1011000	1519000
powder........	5911000	4325000
ts........	218500	387000
am........	8002500	7112000
an........	1194500	528000
t........	—	—
Total, London........	15068000	123622000
" Liverpool........	4080245	4915426
Black (London)........	134588500	110082500
Green "	10091500	13539500

xports of Petrolem from the United States.

FROM JANUARY 1 TO FEBRUARY 13.

m New York........galls.	6,000,967	5,518,646
Boston........	342,325	322,223
Philadelphia........	2,738,416	2,794,472
Baltimore........	60,361	83,250
Portland........	....	6,800
New Bedford........	....	....
Cleveland........	....	....
al Export from the U. States..	9,142,169	8,825,390
ie time 1867........		4,522,794
ie time 1866........		7,646,581

Stocks of Petroleum.

The following is the stock of Petroleum the United States: On January 1st, 1869, there re 780,000 barrels of crude or its equivalent, inst 1,000,000 barrels at the same time in 38, showing a reduction during the year of a le over 200,000 barrels. The foregoing applies oil produced in Pennsylvania, and does not lude a stock of about 50,000 on hand in West ginia and Ohio on January 1, 1868, and one of ut 10,000 or 15,000 barrels in the same States the 1st inst. The annexed table shows the ck on hand on the 1st days of January, 1868-9:

	1869. Bbls.	1868. Bbls.
New York........	75,233	91,000
Pittsburg........	225,000	100,000
Philadelphia........	60,793	111,304
Cleveland........	100,000	46,000
Boston and Baltimore........	20,000	20,000
Erie, Corry and Baltimore..	5,000	25,000
Oil Regions........	264,805	554,600
railroads & Alleghany River	30,000	50,000
Total........	780,831	997,904

Ve estimate that the stocks of Refined in the ited States and in and afloat for Europe, Janu- 1st, 1869, compares as follows:

	Bbls.
the United States, Jan. 1st, 1868.....	664,270
and afloat for Europe, Jan. 1st, 1869.	607,911
Total........	1,273,181
the United States, Jan. 1st, 1869.....	520,588
and afloat for Europe, Jan. 1st, 1868.	439,668
Total........	960,256
Decrease on Jan; 1st, 1869........	312,925

llowing 27,000 barrels of Refined for the decrease in the stock in Western Virginia and Ohio, the total decrease in the United States and Europe was about 340,000 barrels, or a crude equivalent of about 450,000 barrels.

Lake and Canal Freights, 1868.

The following will show the average rate of lake freights on wheat and corn from Chicago to Buffalo, and Chicago to Oswego; and canal freights from Oswego to New York, and Buffalo to New York, for the navigation season of 1868:

	Wheat. 60 lbs. bu. c.	m.	f.	Corn. 56 lbs. bu. c.	m.	f.
Average Freight.						
Lake, Chicago to Buffalo ...	7	1	4	6	1	5
Canal, Buffalo to New York..	15	6	5	13	0	1
Total, Chicago to N.Y...	22	7	9	19	1	6
Average Freight.						
Lake, Chicago to Oswego....	11	6	5	10	5	8
Canal, Oswego to New York.	11	2	2	9	6	7
Total, Chicago to N. Y..	22	8	7	20	2	5

The rate to New York per ton of 2,000 lbs. based on the price of wheat by way of Buffalo at 22.7.9 cents per 60 lbs. is $7.59.6 per ton.

Annual Cotton Trade Report.

The past year opened with animation, but the demand was so freely supplied that it was not until the middle of January that any material advance in prices was noticeable. Middling Orleans was then 8d per lb, and fair Dhollera 6d. The trade was then supplying themselves freely, and the stock in this port ran down by the middle of February to 260,000 bales, and middling Orleans went to $10\frac{5}{8}$d per lb. This advance, however, was too rapid, and a reaction took place, reducing prices $\frac{3}{4}$d per lb. The first week in March found us again advancing, and the market was extremely active, a very large business being done "to arrive." The 27th of April brought us to the maximum figures of the year; middling Orleans was worth $13\frac{1}{2}$d and $13\frac{1}{4}$d to arrive. This, however, proved too high for Manchester, and prices began to decline steadily, and continued doing so until the beginning of August, when middling Orleans touched $9\frac{3}{4}$d. That figure was the signal for a revival, and $1\frac{1}{4}$d per lb was soon gained. The last three months of the year have found the demand steady, prices fluctuating occasionally between $10\frac{1}{2}$d and 11d for middling American, the close of the year showing prices $3\frac{1}{2}$d. per lb higher than the opening.

Having thus briefly sketched the course of the cotton market during the past twelve months, we will venture an opinion as to the future. There seems to be a pretty general belief among business men that the position of commercial affairs is on the eve of improvement. The opening price of cotton is unquestionably high, but the consumption of the world has so far outrun the supply of the raw material that we can see but little prospect of a low range of prices for some months to come. The receipts at the American ports have been on too small a scale hitherto to warrant the proper estimate for $2\frac{3}{4}$ millions. But it must be borne in mind that almost every available pound of Cotton found its way to this country last year, and that the increased consumption of the United States will prevent a similar occurrence this season. It is, therefore, not at all probable that we shall receive more, if as much, from America as last year. A continued prospect of a high range of prices would naturally induce more cotton to this country than would otherwise be the case from other cotton growing countries, and a fine planting season in the United States, with a prospect of a large crop next year, will probably prevent such an advance as that reached in April last. The accounts from India are generally satisfactory; the quality of the new cotton is good, but it is feared that the Oomrawuttee and Broath districts may be a little short. Egypt will give us rather more than last year; and Brazil, whose production is rapidly increasing, considerably more, possibly 150,000 bales in excess of last crop.

The short-time movement in Manchester of late so much threatened has made but little progress. There is an evident disposition to place orders, and many manufacturers are under orders for delivery, which has the effect of keeping quotations steady; at the same time the stocks of manufactured goods are unprecedentedly low, though the Eastern markets are well supplied. *Morgans' Trade Journal.*

The Diffusion Process in Sugar Making.

On the 22nd ult, 2,651 bags of sugar produced by the new "diffusion" process of M. Jules Robert at the Aska Sugar Works (Madras Presidency) were sold in Mincing-lane for account of Messrs. Baring, Brothers & Co. This lot is a part of last season's produce of the Aska Works, and is the first considerable shipment of "diffusion sugar" that has been sold in the European market. The "diffusion' sugar is produced from cane without the application of the sugar mill. The cane is cut into thin ribands, or slices, and the saccharine contents of its cells are extracted by bringing the slices into contact with water at an elevated temperature. The water extracts only the soluble substances contained in the juice of the plant, while most of the impurities (which in the ordinary process pass into the juice, and must be subsequently removed at great expense) are left in the unbroken cells of the cane and do not contaminate the juice. By the diffusion process, it is said, the extraction can be carried so far that 95 per cent. of all the sugar contained in the cane is passed into the clarifier, while the best roller mills at present in use do not extract more than 75 per cent. of the sugar contained in the cane, and the average of West Indian practice is an extraction of less than 60 per cent. From this it would appear that the diffusion process, besides improving the quality of the raw sugar, is capable of yielding about 50 per cent. more sugar from a given quantity of cane than the sugar mills yield at present, and the invention is therefore attracting general attention in the trade.

—During the year 1868, seventy-two vessels of 40,144 tons were built in Nova Scotia and New Brunswick under the inspection of the French Lloyds, and ten vessels, of 6,685 tons, were repaired under direction of the agency during the same period.

Galway Mining Company.

NOTICE is hereby given that a Dividend at the Rate of Thirty per cent. per annum, for the half year ending 18th January, 1869, has been declared on the Capital paid in at that date and that the same is payable at the office of the Company at Peterborough, on and after MONDAY the FIFTEENTH of FEBRUARY, 1869.

By order of the Directors,
JOHN BURNHAM,
Sec. & Treas.

Peterborough, Feb. 11, 1869. 6t.-F.18.

Montreal House, Montreal, Canada.

TO MONETARY MEN.—Merchants, Insurance Agents Lawyers, Bankers, Railway and Steamboat Travellers, Mining Agents, Directors and Stockholders of Public Companies, and other persons visiting Montreal for business or pleasure, are here by most respectfully informed that the undersigned proposes to furnish the best hotel accommodation at the most reasonable charges. It is our study to provide every comfort and accommodation to all our guests, especially for gentlemen engaged as above. To those who have been accustomed to patronize other first-class hotels, we only ask a trial; we have the same accommodation and our table is furnished with every delicacy of the season.

H. DUCLOS.

Nov. 22, 1867. 15-1y

Commercial House,

(LATE HUFFMAN HOUSE)

PETERBOROUGH, ONTARIO.

GEORGE CRONN : : : : : : PROPRIETOR.

Large addition lately made, including Twenty Bed Rooms
Dec. 10, 1868. 17-1L

STATEMENT OF BANKS

ACTING UNDER CHARTER, FOR THE MONTH ENDING 31st JANUARY, 1869, ACCORDING TO RETURNS FURNISHED BY THE BANKS TO THE AUDITOR OF PUBLIC ACCOUNTS.

Mercantile.

TORONTO PRICES CURRENT.—FEBRUARY 25, 1869.

Name of Article.	Wholesale Rates.		Name of Article.	Wholesale Rate.		Name of Article.	Wholesale Rates.	
	$ c.	$ c.	**Groceries**—*Contin'd*	$ c.	$ c.	**Leather**—*Contin'd.*	$ c.	$ c.
Boots and Shoes.			Gunpowd'r c. to med..	0 55	0 70	Kip Skins, Patna	0 46	0 65
Mens' Thick Boots ...	2 20	2 50	" med. to fine.	0 70	0 80	French	0 70	0 0
" Kip.............	2 50	3 00	" fine to finr't..	0 85	0 95	English	0 65	0 8
" Calf	3 00	3 70	Hyson...............	0 45	0 80	Hemlock Calf (30 to		
" Congress Gaiters..	2 00	2 50	Imperial............	0 42	0 80	35 lbs.) per doz....	0 75	0 8
Boys' Thick Boots.....	1 15	1 45	*Tobacco, Manufac'd:*			Do. light	0 45	0 5
Youths'	1 70	1 80	Can Leaf, ✠ lb.5s & 10s.	0 26	0 30	French Calf..........	1 45	1 6
Women's Baits	1 40	1 50	Western Leaf, com...	0 25	0 26	Grain & Satn Ch'ld doz..	0 60	0 6
"	0 95	1 30	" Good......	0 27	0 32	Splits, large ✠ lb......	0 30	0 7
" Balmoral.........	1 20	1 50	" Fine......	0 32	0 35	" small......	0 29	0 3
" Congress Gaiters..	1 15	1 45	" Bright fine...	0 40	0 50	Enamelled Cow'y foot..	0 20	0 2
Misses' Baits.........	0 75	1 00	" choice..	0 60	0 75	Patent	0 30	0 2
" Balmoral.........	1 10	1 20				Pebble Grain	0 17	0 1
" Congress Gaiters..	1 00	1 30	**Hardware.**			Buff	0 17	0 1
Girls' Baits	0 65	0 85	*Tin* (*per cask prices*)					
" Balmoral.........	0 90	1 05	Block, ✠ lb........	0 25	0 26	**Oils.**		
" Congress Gaiters..	0 80	1 10	Grain..............	0 25	0 26	Cod	0 00	0 7
Children's C. T. Cacks...	0 50	0 65	*Copper:*			Lard, extra	0 00	0 0
" Gaiters	0 65	0 90	Pig	0 23	0 24	" No. 1	0 00	0 0
			Sheet..............	0 30	0 33	" Woolen.......	0 00	0 0
Drugs.			*Cut Nails:*			Lubricating, patent.....	0 00	0 0
Aloes Cape...........	0 12½	0 16	Assorted ¼ Shingles,			" Mott's economic	0 50	0 0
Alum................	0 02½	0 03	✠ 100 lb..........	2 90	3 00	Linseed, raw.......	0 76	0 8
Borax...............	0 00	0 00	Shingle alone do	3 15	3 25	" boiled......	0 81	0 8
Camphor, refined......	0 65	0 70	Lathe and 5 dy......	3 30	3 40	Machinery	0 00	0 0
Castor Oil...........	0 16½	0 28	*Galvanized Iron:*			Olive, common, ✠ gal..	1 00	1 0
Caustic Soda........	0 04½	0 05	Assorted sizes......	0 08	0 09	" salad......	? 1 95	2 3
Cochineal............	0 90	1 00	Best No. 24........	0 09	0 09½	" salad, in bots.		
Cream Tartar........	0 40	0 45	" 26.........	0 09	0 09½	qt. ✠ case...	3 60	2 7
Epsom Salts.........	0 03	0 04	" 28.........	0 09	0 09½	Sesame salad, ✠ gal...	1 09	1 7
Extract Logwood.....	0 11	0 13	*Horse Nails:*			Seal, pale........	0 75	0 8
Gum Arabic, sorts.....	0 30	0 35	Gnod's or Griffin's			Spirits Turpentine....	0 52½	0 6
Indigo, Madras.......	0 90	1 00	assorted sizes......	0 00	0 00	Varnish	0 60	0 0
Licorice	0 14	0 48	For W. ass'd sizes....	0 18	0 19	Whale..........	0 00	0 0
Madder..............	0 00	0 18	Patent Hammer'd do..	0 17	0 18			
Galls	0 32	0 37	*Iron* (at 4 months):			**Paints, &c.**		
Opium...............	12 00	13 50	Pig—Gartsherrie No1..	24 00	25 00	White Lead, genuine		
Oxalic Acid.........	0 20	0 25	Other brands. No.1	22 00	24 00	in Oil, ✠ 25 lbs......	0 00	2 3
Potash, Bi-tart......	0 25	0 28	" No.2..	0 00	0 00	Do. No. 1 "	0 00	2 1
" Bichromate..	0 15	0 20	Bar—Scotch, ✠100 lb..	2 25	2 50	" 2 "	0 00	1 9
Potass Iodide	3 90	4 50	Refined	3 00	3 25	" 3 "	0 00	1 6
Senna	0 12½	0 60	Swedes	5 00	5 50	White Zinc, genuine..	3 00	3 5
Soda Ash	0 02½	0 04	Hoops—Coopers......	3 00	3 25	White Lead, dry......	6 00½	0 0
Soda Bicarb	4 50	5 00	Band	3 00	3 25	Red Lead..........	0 07½	0 0
Tartaric Acid........	0 40	0 45	Boiler Plates.......	3 25	3 50	Venetian Red, Eng'h..	0 02½	0 0
Verdigris	0 35	0 40	Canada Plates......	3 75	4 00	Yellow Ochre, Fren'h..	0 02½	0 0
Vitriol, Blue.......	0 08	0 10	Union Jack	0 00	0 00	Whiting	0 85	1 2
Groceries.			Pontypool	2 25	4 00			
Coffees:			Swansea	3 00	4 00	**Petroleum.**		
Java, ✠ lb.	0 22@0 24		*Lead* (at 4 months):			(Refined ✠ gal.)		
Laguayra............	0 17	0 18	Bar, ✠ 100 lbs......	0 06½	0 07	Water white, car'l'd..		0 3
Rio............	0 15	0 17	Sheet	0 06	0 07	" small lots..	0 37	0 3
Fish:			Shot	0 00	0 07½	Straw, by car load....	0 32	0 3
Herrings, Lab. split...	5 75	6 50	*Iron Wire* (net cash):			" small lots...	0 35	0 3
" round...	0 00	0 00	No. 6, ✠ bundle.....	2 70	2 80	Amber, by car load...	0 00	0 0
" scaled...	0 35	0 40	" 9 "	3 10	3 20	" small lots...	0 00	0 0
Mackerel, small kitts..	1 00	0 00	" 12, "	3 40	3 60	Benzine	0 00	0 0
Loch. Her. wk'y 8rks..	8 50	2 75	" 15, "	4 30	4 40			
" half "	1 25	1 50				**Produce.**		
White Fish & Trout...	0 00	0 00	*Powder:*			*Grain:*		
Salmon, saltwater....	14 00	15 00	Blasting, Canada....	3 50	0 00	Wheat, Spring, 60 lb...	0 95	0 9
Dry Cod, ✠112 lbs....	5 00	5 25	FF "	4 25	4 50	" Fall "	0 99	1 0
Fruit:			FFF "	4 75	5 00	Barley... 48 "	1 30	1 3
Raisins, Layers	2 00	2 10	Blasting, English ...	4 00	5 00	Peas........ 60 "	0 75	0 8
" M. R.	1 00	2 00	FF loose..	5 00	6 00	Oats........ 34 "	0 51	0 5
" Valentias new..	0 6½	0 7½	FFF "	6 00	6 50	Rye .... 56 "	0 70	0 7
Currants, new......	0 5½	0 06½	*Pressed Spikes* (4 mos):			*Seeds:*		
" old......	0 6	0 04½	Regular sizes 100...	4 00	4 50	Clover, choice 60 " ..	6 50	6 7
Figs	0 14	0 00	Extra	4 50	5 00	" good 48 " ..	6 25	6 5
Molasses:			*Tin Plates* (net cash):			Timothy, cho's 4 " ..	3 00	3 7
Clayed, ✠ gal........	0 00	0 35	IC Coke	7 50	8 00	" inf. to good 48 "	2 25	2 8
Syrups, Standard ...	0 60	0 00	IC Charcoal.......	8 25	8 50	Flax .... 56 "	2 00	2 2
" Golden	0 62	0 65	IX "	10 25	10 75	*Flour* (per brl.):		
Rice:			IXX "	12 25	0 00	Superior extra.....	4 90	5 0
Arracan	4 25	4 50	DC "	7 25	9 00	Extra superfine,....	4 60	4 8
Spices:			DX "	9 50	0 00	Fancy superfine	4 25	4 5
Cassia, whole, ✠ lb....	0 00	0 45				Superfine No 1.....	4 00	4 1
Cloves	0 11	0 12	**Hides & Skins, ✠lb**			No. 2.....		
Nutmegs	0 45	0 55	Green rough	0 06½	0 07½	Oatmeal, (per brl.)...	5 00	5 0
Ginger, gr'nd........	0 20	0 25	Green, salt'd & insp'd...	0 07½	0 08			
" Jamaica, root..	0 20	0 25	Cured	0 00	0 00	**Provisions.**		
Pepper, black........	0 09½	0 10	Calfskins, green ...	0 00	0 11	Butter, dairy tub ✠ lb..	0 33	0 0
Pimento	0 08	0 09	Calfskins, cured ...	0 00	0 12	" store packed...	0 19	0 2
Sugars:			" dry	0 18	0 20	Cheese, new	0 13	0 1
Port Rico, ✠ lb.......	0 10½	0 11	Sheepskins, ...	1 00	1 40	Pork, mess, per brl...	26 00	27 0
Cuba	0 10½	0 11	" country ..	1 00	1 40	" prime mess....		
Barbadoes (bright)....	0 10½	0 11				" prime	0 00	0 0
Canada Sugar Refine'y,			**Hops.**			" Cumberl'l cut...	0 11	0 1
yellow No. 2, 60 ds...	0 10½	0 11	Inferior, ✠ lb.......	0 05	0 07	" smoked	0 00	0 0
Yellow, No. 2½	0 11	0 11½	Medium............	0 07	0 09	Hams, in salt	0 12	0 1
No. 3.	0 11½	0 11½	Good	0 00	0 12	" smoked....	0 10	0 1
Crushed X	0 13	0 13½	Fancy	9 00	0 09	" sug.cur & smo'd.	0 16	0 1
" A	0 13	0 13½				Shoulders, in salt	0 00	0 0
Ground............	0 13½	0 14	**Leather,** @ (4 mos.)			Lard, in kegs.......	0 14	0 1
Dry Crushed	0 14½	0 14½	In lots of less than			Eggs, packed	0 16	0 1
Extra Ground........	0 15½	0 15½	Side, 30 ✠ cent			Beef Hams	0 00	0 0
Teas:			higher.			Tallow	0 8	0 0
Japan com'n to good ..	0 48	0 58	Spanish Sole, 1st qual'y			Hogs dressed, heavy..	8 50	9 0
" fine to choicest..	0 60	0 65	heavy, weights ✠ lb..	0 22	0 23	" medium....	8 00	8 5
Colored, com. to fine..	0 48	0 75	Do.1st qual middle do..	0 21	0 22	" light......	7 50	8 0
Congou & Souch'ng...	0 45	0 75	Do. No. 2, light weights	0 20	0 21			
Oolong, good to fine...	0 60	0 85	Slaughter heavy	0 00	0 00	**Salt, &c.**		
Y. Hyson, com to gd...	0 45	0 55	Do. light, ...	0 00	0 00	American brls......	1 50	1 5
Medium to choice	0 65	0 80	Harness, best	0 32	0 34	Liverpool coarse	1 25	1 1
Extra choice	0 85	0 95	" No. 2.......	0 30	0 33	Plaster	1 65	0 1
			Upper heavy........	0 36	0 38	Beef Lime	1 50	0 0
			"	0 40	0 42	Water Lime	1 50	0 0

ap & Candles.	$ c.	$ c.
Crawford & Co.'s ..		
Imperial.........	0 07½	0 08
Golden Bar	0 07	0 07½
Silver Bar........	0 07	0 07½
wn	0 05	0 05½
o. 1	0 03½	0 03¾
dles	0 00	0 11½
ines, Liquors, &c.		
glish, per doz......	2 60	2 65
inness Dub Portr..	2 35	2 40
rits:		
re Jamaica Rum...	1 80	2 25
Kuyper's H. Gin..	1 55	1 63
oth's Old Tom.....	1 90	2 00
:		
een, cases.........	4 00	4 25
oth's Old Tom, c...	6 00	6 25
ses:		
rt, common	1 00	1 25
fine old	2 00	4 00
erry, common	1 00	1 50
medium........	1 70	1 80
old pale or golden..	2 50	4 00

Brandy:	$ c.	$ c.
Hennessy's, per gal..	2 30	2 50
Martell's " ..	2 30	2 50
J. Robin & Co.'s " ..	2 25	2 35
Otard, Dupuy & Cos..	2 25	2 35
Brandy, cases........	8 50	9 00
Brandy, com. per c...	4 00	4 50
Whiskey:		
Common 36 u. p......	0 62½	0 65
Old Rye	0 85	0 87½
Malt	0 85	0 87½
Toddy	0 85	0 87½
Scotch, per gal.......	1 90	2 10
Irish—Kinnahan's c...	7 00	7 50
" Dunnville's Belf't..	6 00	6 25
Wool.		
Fleece, lb............	0 28	0 35
Pulled "...........	0 22	0 25
Furs.		
Bear.................	8 00	10 00
Beaver, ₩ lb..........	1 00	1 25
Coon	0 20	0 40
Fisher...............	4 00	6 00
Martin...............	1 40	1 60
Mink.................	3 25	4 00
Otter................	5 75	6 00
Spring Rats..........	0 15	0 17
Fox..................	1 20	1 25

INSURANCE COMPANIES.

ENGLISH.—*Quotations on the London Market.*

No. of Shares.	Last Dividend.	Name of Company.	Shares par val £	Amount paid.	Last Sale.
0,000		Briton Medical and General Life ...	10	....	2
0,000	7½	Commer'l Union, Fire, Life and Mar.	50	5	6
4,000	8	City of Glasgow	25	2½	5½
5,000	9½	Edinburgh Life	100	15	33
0,000	5—½ yr	European Life and Guarantee......	2½	11s6	4s. 9d.
0,000	10	Etna Fire and Marine............	10	1½	—
0,000	5	Guardian	100	50	52
4,000	12	Imperial Fire..................	500	50	350
7,500	9½	Imperial Life	100	10	16½
0,000	10	Lancashire Fire and Life.........	20	2	3¾
0,000	11	Life Association of Scotland......	40	7½	25
5,862	45s. p. sh	London Assurance Corporation ..	25	12½	49
0,000	5	London and Lancashire Life	10	1	19s
7,504	40	Liverp'l & London & Globe F. & L.	20	2	6¾
0,000	5	National Union Life	5	1	1
0,000	12½	Northern Fire and Life	100	5	11⅜ x d
,000	12 '63, bo 5s.	North British and Mercantile	50	6¼	19¾
0,000	50	Ocean Marine	25	5	20
2,500	£5 12s.	Provident Life..................	100	10	37
.....	£4½ p. s.	Phœnix.........................	....	....	145
0,000	2½—h. yr.	Queen Fire and Life	10	1	18s
0,000	3s. bo. 4s	Royal Insurance.................	20	3	6½
0,000	10	Scottish Provincial Fire and Life ..	50	2½	5¼
0,000	25	Standard Life	50	12	66
4,000	5	Star Life	25	1¼	—
		CANADIAN.			₩ c.
8,000	4	British America Fire and Marine ..	$50	$25	54 55xd
......	4	Canada Life	...	....	.....
4000	12	Montreal Assurance	£50	£5	135
0,000	3	Provincial Fire and Marine........	60	11	.....
.....	....	Quebec Fire	40	32½	25½
.....	8	" Marine..................	100	40	75 80
0,000	5 7 mo's.	Western Assurance...............	40	9	.....

RAILWAYS.	Sha's	Paid	Montr	London
antic and St. Lawrence....................	£100	All.	....	60 62
ffalo and Lake Huron	20½	"	....	3 3½
Do. do Preference	10	"	....	5½ 6½
ff., Brantf. & Goderich, 6₩c., 1872-3-4.....	100	"	....	66 69
amplain and St. Lawrence	....	....	10	....
Do. do Pref. 10 ₩ ct....	....	....	73	....
and Trunk	100	"	15 16	16 16½
Do. Eq.G. M. Bds. 1 ch. 6₩c..........	100	"	....	85 87
Do. First Preference, 5 ₩ c	100	"	....	54½ 55½
Do. Deferred, 3 ₩ ct..................	100	"	....	....
Do. Second Pref. Bonds, 5₩c..........	100	"	....	40½ 41½
Do. do Deferred, 3 ₩ ct..........	100	"	....	....
Do. Third Pref. Stock, 4₩ct..........	100	"	....	28 30
Do. do. Deferred, 3 ₩ ct..........	100	"	....	....
Do. Fourth Pref. Stock, 3₩c..........	100	"	....	18¼ 18¾
Do. do. Deferred, 3 ₩ ct..........	100	"	....	....
eat Western	20½	"	13 14	15½ 15¾
Do. New	20½	18	....	....
Do. 6 ₩ c. Bds, due 1873-76..........	100	All.	....	100 102
5½₩c Bds. due 1877-78..........	100	"	....	94 95
rine Railway, Halifax, $250, all.........	$250	"	....	....
rthern, of Canada, 6₩c. 1st Pref. Bds.......	100	"	....	81 83

EXCHANGE.	Halifax.	Montr'l.	Quebec.	Toronto.
nk on London, 60 days.......				
ight or 75 days date..........	12¼	9½ 9¾	9½ 9¾	9¾
vate do.	11½ 12	8 9	8¾ 9¼	8¾
vate, with documents..........	....	7½ 8	....	....
nk on New York..............	....	25½ 26	25 25½	74½
vate do.	....	26½ 27	25½ 26	....
ld Drafts do.	....	½ dis. to p.	par ½ dis.	par ¼ dis.
ver	....	3½ 3¾	....	4 to 5

STOCK AND BOND REPORT.

The dates of our quotations are as follows:—Toronto, Feb. 23; Montreal, Feb. 12; Quebec, Feb. 18; London, Jan. 28.

NAME.	Shares.	Paid up.	Divid'd last 6 Months	Dividend Day.	Closing Prices: Toronto.	Montre'l	Quebec.
BANKS.			₩ ct.				
British North America	$250	All.	3	July and Jan.	104 105	104 105	103½ 104
Jacques Cartier..............	50	"	4	1 June, 1 Dec.	108½ 109	108 109	107 107½
Montreal	200	"	5	"	139½ 139¾	139½ 139¾	138½ 139½
Nationale.....................	50	"	4	1 Nov. 1 May.	106½ 107	106½	106½ 107
New Brunswick	100	"	......	......	....	....	....
Nova Scotia	200	28	7&b$3¼	Mar. and Sept.	....	....	....
Du Peuple.....................	50	"	4	1 Mar., 1 Sept.	Bks closd	109¾ 110	109 110
Toronto	100	"	4	1 Jan., 1 July.	121 122	121 122	120 121
Bank of Yarmouth.............	....	....	......	......	....	....	....
Canadian Bank of Com'e......	50	95	......	......	102¾ 103	102½ 103	101 102
City Bank Montreal	80	All.	4	1 June, 1 Dec.	102½ 103	102½ 103	102½ 103
Commer'l Bank (St. John)....	100	"	₩ ct.	......	....	....	....
Eastern Townships' Bank.....	50	"	4	1 July, 1 Jan..	....	98½ 99½	98 99
Gore	40	...	none.	1 Jan., 1 July.	40 41	40 45	40 45
Halifax Banking Company.....	...	....	......	......	....	....	....
Mechanics' Bank.............	50	70	4	1 Nov., 1 May.	95 96	94 96	94 95
Merchants' Bank of Canada....	100	70	4	1 Jan., 1 July.	108 108½	108 108½	109¾ 110¼
Merchants' Bank (Halifax)....	....	....	......	......	....	....	....
Molson's Bank................	50	All.	4	1 Apr., 1 Oct.	112 112½	110½ 112	110 111
Niagara District Bank........	100	70	3½	1 Jan., 1 July.	....	....	....
Ontario Bank..................	40	All.	4	1 June, 1 Dec.	99 100	99 99½	99¾ 100½
People's Bank (Fred'kton)....	100	"	......	......	....	....	....
People's Bank (Halifax)	20	"	7 12 m	......	....	....	....
Quebec Bank	100	"	3½	1 June, 1 Dec.	99½ 100	99½ 100	99¾ 100
Royal Canadian Bank	50	50	4	1 Jan., 1 July.	90 91	88 90	85 87
St. Stephens Bank	100	All	.....	......	....	....	....
Union Bank	100	70	4	1 Jan., 1 July.	103 103½	103½	103¾ 104¼
Union Bank (Halifax).........	100	40	7 12 mo	Feb. and Aug.	....	....	....
MISCELLANEOUS.							
British America Land.........	250	44	2½	......			
British Colonial S. S. Co......	250	32½	2½	......	....	....	....
Canada Company	32½	All.	£1 10s.	......	...	....	....
Canada Landed Credit Co.....	50	$20	3½	......	74½ 75	....	....
Canada Per. B'ldg Society....	50	All.	5	......	124½ 125	....	....
Canada Mining Company.....	4	90	......	......	....	....	....
Do. Inl'd Steam Nav. Co....	100	All.	20 12 m	......	....	105 107	105 106
Do. Glass Company.........	100	"	12½ "	......	....	...	....
Canad'n Loan & Investm't....	25	2½	7	......	....	....	....
Canada Agency	10	¼	......	......	....	....	....
Colonial Securities Co........	...	....	......	......	....	....	....
Freehold Building Society....	100	All.	4	......	109½ 110	....	....
Halifax Steamboat Co........	100	"	5	......	....	....	....
Halifax Gas Company.......	....	....	......	......	....	....	....
Hamilton Gas Company......	....	....	......	......	....	....	....
Huron Copper Bay Co........	4	12	20	......	....	25 35cps	....
Lake Huron S. and C.........	5	102	......	......	....	....	....
Montreal Mining Consols......	20	$15	......	......	....	3.00 3.25	....
Do. Telegraph Co....	40	All.	5	......	133½ 134	132½ 134	133 134½
Do. Elevating Co....	00	"	15 12 m	......	....	100 102½	....
Do. City Gas Co.......	40	"	4	15 Mar. 15 Sep.	....	137½ 140	136 137
Do. City Pass. R. Co....	50	"	5	......	....	111 112	110½ 111
Nova Scotia Telegraph	20	"	....	......	....	....	....
Quebec and L. S.	8	$4	......	......	....	....	25 cts.
Quebec Gas Co..............	200	All.	4	1 Mar., 1 Sep.	....	...	119 120
Quebec Street R. R..........	50	25	8	......	....	....	90 91
Richelieu Navigation Co......	100	All.	7 p.a.	1 Jan., 1 July.	....	110 112½	117 117½
St. Lawrence Tow Boat Co....	100	"	......	3 Feb.	....	...	35 40
Tor'to Consumers' Gas Co....	50	"	2 3 m.	1 My Au Mar Fe	107 108	...	107 108
Trust & Loan Co. of U. C.....	20	5	3	......	....	....	....
West'n Canada Bldg Soc'y....	50	All.	5	......	120 120½	....	....

SECURITIES.	London.	Montreal.	Quebec.	Toronto.
Canadian Gov't Deb. 6 ₩ ct. stg..................	....	103½	102½ 103	102½ 103½
Do. do. 6 do due Ja. & Jul. 1877-84.........	104½ 105½	....	....	....
Do. do. 6 do. Feb. & Aug..........	105 107	....	....	....
Do. do. 6 do. Mch. & Sep..........	105 107	....	....	....
Do. do. 5 ₩ ct. cur., 1883	94½ 95½	98 95	98 98½	93 94
Do. do. 5 do. stg., 1885	93 95	93 95	93 93½	94 94½
Do. do. 7 do. cur., ...	....	....	......	....
Dominion 6 p. c. 1878 cy......................	....	105 105½	105 105½	105 105½
Hamilton Corporation..........................	....	....	......	....
Montreal Harbor, 8 ₩ ct. d. 1869................	..	....	......	....
Do. do. 7 do. 1870................	....	....	......	....
Do. do. 6½ do. 1883................	....	102½ 103	......	....
Do. do. 6½ do. 1873................	....	....	......	....
Do. Corporation, 6 ₩ c. 1891	....	95 96	94½ 95½	95 96
Do. 7 p. c. stock............................	....	107 110	108½ 109½	109 110
Do. Water Works, 6 ₩ c. stg. 1878..........	....	....	......	95 96
Do. do. 6 do. cy. do.	....	95½ 96½	......	95 96
New Brunswick, 6 ₩ ct., Jan. and July..........	102 104	....	......	....
Nova Scotia, 6 ₩ ct., 1875.....................	102½ 103½	....	......	....
Ottawa City 6 ₩ c. d. 1880	....	92½ 93½	......	....
Quebec Harbour, 6 ₩ c. d. 1883.................	....	....	60	....
Do. do. 7 do. do..................	....	....	65 70	....
Do. do 8 do. 1886..................	....	....	80 85	....
Do. City, 7 ₩ c. d. 4½ years.................	....	....	96½ 97	....
Do. do. 7 do. 9 do.	....	....	91 92	....
Do. do. 7 do. 2 do.	....	....	98 98½	....
Do. Water Works, 7 ₩ ct., 4 years............	....	....	97 97½	....
Do. do. 6 do. 2 do.	....	....	94 95	....
Toronto Corporation	....	87½ 92½	....	....

Insurance.

BEAVER
Mutual Insurance Association.

HEAD OFFICE—20 TORONTO STREET,
TORONTO.

INSURES LIVE STOCK against death from any cause. The only Canadian Company having authority to do this line of business.

R. L. DENISON,
President.

T. O'REILLY,
Secretary.   8-1y-25

HOME DISTRICT
Mutual Fire Insurance Company.

Office—North-West Cor. Yonge & Adelaide Streets,
TORONTO.—(Up Stairs.)

INSURES Dwelling Houses, Stores, Warehouses, Merchandise, Furniture, &c.

PRESIDENT—The Hon. J. McMURRICH.
VICE-PRESIDENT—JOHN BURNS, Esq.
JOHN RAINS, Secretary.

AGENTS:
DAVID WRIGHT, Esq., Hamilton; FRANCIS STEVENS, Esq., Barrie; Messrs. GIBBS & BRO.; Oshawa.   8-1y

THE PRINCE EDWARD COUNTY
Mutual Fire Insurance Company.

HEAD OFFICE,—PICTON, ONTARIO.
President, L. B. STINSON; Vice-President, W. A. RICHARDS.
Directors; H. A. McFaul, James Cavan, James Johnson, S. DeMill, William Delong.—Treasurer, David Barker Secretary, John Twigg; Solicitor, R. J. Fitzgerald;

THIS Company is established upon strictly Mutual principles, insuring farming and isolated property, (not hazardous,) in Townships only, and offers great advantages to insurers, at low rates for five years, without the expense of a renewal.
Picton, June 15, 1868.   9-1y

THE AGRICULTURAL
Mutual Assurance Association of Canada.

HEAD OFFICE .... LONDON, ONT.

A purely Farmers' Company. Licensed by the Government of Canada.

Capital, 1st January, 1869 .... $230,193 82
Cash and Cash Items, over $86,000 00
No. of Policies in force 80,892 00

THIS Company Insures nothing more dangerous than Farm property. Its rates are as low as any well-established Company in the Dominion, and lower than those of a great many. It is largely patronised, and continues to grow in public favor.
For Insurance, apply to any of the Agents or address the Secretary, London, Ontario.
London, 2nd Nov., 1866.   12-1y

Briton Medical and General Life
Association,

with which is united the

BRITANNIA LIFE ASSURANCE COMPANY.

Capital and Invested Funds ....£750,000 Sterling.

ANNUAL INCOME, £220,000 STG. :
Yearly increasing at the rate of £25,000 Sterling.

THE important and peculiar feature originally introduced by this Company, in applying the periodical bonuses, so as to make Policies payable during life, without any higher rate of premiums being charged, has caused the success of the BRITON MEDICAL AND GENERAL to be most unparalleled in the history of Life Assurance. Life Policies on the Profit Scale become payable during the Lifetime of the Assured, thus rendering a Policy of Assurances a means of subsistence in old age, as well as a protection for a family, and a more valuable security to creditors in the event of early death; and effectually meeting the often urged objection, that persons do not themselves reap the benefit of their own prudence and forethought.
No extra charge made to members of Volunteer Corps for services within the British Provinces.

TORONTO AGENCY, 5 KING ST. WEST.
oct 17—9-1yr   JAMES FRASER, Agent.

Insurance.

The Gore District Mutual Fire Insurance
Company

GRANTS INSURANCES on all description of Property against Loss or Damage by FIRE. It is the only Mutual Fire Insurance Company which assesses its Policies yearly from their respective dates; and the average yearly cost of insurance in it, for the past three and a half years, has been nearly

TWENTY CENTS IN THE DOLLAR

less than what it would have been in an ordinary Proprietary Company.

THOS. M. SIMONS,
Secretary & Treasurer.
ROBT. McLEAN,
Inspector of Agencies.
Galt, 25th Nov., 1868.   15-1y

Geo. Girdlestone,

FIRE, Life, Marine, Accident, and Stock Insurance Agent
Very best Companies represented.
Windsor, Ont. June, 1868

The Standard Life Assurance Company,
Established 1825.
WITH WHICH IS NOW UNITED
THE COLONIAL LIFE ASSURANCE COMPANY.

Head Office for Canada:
MONTREAL—STANDARD COMPANY'S BUILDINGS,
No. 47 GREAT ST. JAMES STREET.
Manager—W. M. RAMSAY.   Inspector—RICH'D BULL.

THIS Company having deposited the sum of ONE HUNDRED AND FIFTY THOUSAND DOLLARS with the Receiver-General, in conformity with the Insurance Act passed last Session, Assurances will continue to be carried out at moderate rates and on all the different systems in practice.

AGENT FOR TORONTO—HENRY PELLATT,
KING STREET.

AGENT FOR HAMILTON—JAMES BANCROFT.
6-6mos:

Fire and Marine Assurance.

THE BRITISH AMERICA
ASSURANCE COMPANY.
HEAD OFFICE :
CORNER OF CHURCH AND COURT STREETS.
TORONTO.

BOARD OF DIRECTION :

Hon G. W. Allan, M L C.,	A. Joseph, Esq.,
George J. Boyd, Esq ,	Peter Paterson, Esq.,
Hon. W. Cayley,	G. P . Ridout, Esq.,
Richard S. Cassels, Esq.,	E H . Rutherford, Esq.,
	Thomas C. Street, Esq.

Governor:
GEORGE PERCIVAL RIDOUT, Esq.
Deputy Governor:
PETER PATERSON, Esq.
Fire Inspector: Marine Inspector:
E. ROBY O'BRIEN.   CAPT. R. COURNEEN.

Insurances granted on all descriptions of property against loss and damage by fire and the perils of inland navigation.
Agencies established in the principal cities, towns, and ports of shipment throughout the Province.

THOS. WM. BIRCHALL,
28-1y   Managing Director.

Queen Fire and Life Insurance Company,
OF LIVERPOOL AND LONDON,

ACCEPTS ALL ORDINARY FIRE RISKS
on the most favorable terms.

LIFE RISKS

Will be taken on terms that will compare favorably with other Companies.

CAPITAL, - - - £2,000,000 Stg.

CHIEF OFFICES—Queen's Buildings, Liverpool, and Gracechurch Street London.
CANADA BRANCH OFFICE—Exchange Buildings, Montreal.
Resident Secretary and General Agent,
A. MACKENZIE FORBES,
13 St. Sacrament St., Merchants' Exchange, Montreal.
WM. ROWLAND, Agent, Toronto.   1-1y

Insurance.

The Waterloo County Mutual Fire Insurance
Company.

HEAD OFFICE : WATERLOO, ONTARIO.

ESTABLISHED 1863.

THE business of the Company is divided into three separate and distinct branches, the
VILLAGE, FARM, AND MANUFACTURES.
Each Branch paying its own losses and its just proportion of the managing expenses of the Company.
C. M. TAYLOR, Sec.   M. SPRINGER, M.M.P., Pres.
J. HUGHES, Inspector.   15-yr

Etna Fire and Marine Insurance Company of
Dublin,

AT a Meeting of the Shareholders of this Company, held at Dublin, on the 13th ult., it was agreed that the business of the "ETNA" should be transferred to the "UNITED PORTS AND GENERAL INSURANCE COMPANY." In accordance with this agreement, the business will hereafter be carried on by the latter Company, which assumes and guarantees all the risks and liabilities of the "ETNA."
The Directors have resolved to continue the CANADIAN BRANCH, and arrangements for resuming the Fire and Marine business are rapidly approaching completion.
T. W. GRIFFITH,
16   MANAGER.

Lancashire Insurance Company.

CAPITAL, - - - - - - - £2,000,000 Sterling

FIRE RISKS
Taken at reasonable rates of premium, and
ALL LOSSES SETTLED PROMPTLY,
By the undersigned, without reference elsewhere.
S. C. DUNCAN-CLARK & CO.,
General Agents for Ontario,
N. W. Corner of King & Church Streets,
25-1y   TORONTO.

Canada Life Assurance Company.

CAPITAL AND CASH ASSETS
OVER $2,000,000.

SUMS ASSURED
$5,000,000.

A COMPARISON of the rates of this Company with others cannot fail to demonstrate the advantage of the low premiums, which, by the higher returns from its investment, it is enabled to offer.

IF PREFERRED, ASSURERS NEED ONLY

PAY ONE-HALF OF EACH YEAR'S PREMIUM IN CASH,

during the whole term of policies on the 10 payment plan, or for seven years on the whole life plan.

For the unpaid portion of premiums,

"NOTES" ARE NOT REQUIRED BY THIS COMPANY,

so that assurers are not liable to be called upon for payment of these, nor for assessments upon them, as in the case of Mutual Companies.
Every facility and advantage which can be afforded are offered by this Company.

A. G. RAMSAY, Manager.
E. BRADBURNE, Agent,
3 11   Toronto Street.

The Victoria Mutual
FIRE INSURANCE COMPANY OF CANADA.

Insures only Non-Hazardous Property, at Low Rates.

BUSINESS STRICTLY MUTUAL.

GEORGE H. MILLS, President.
W. D. BOOKER, Secretary.
HEAD OFFICE. ....HAMILTON, ONTARIO.
aug 15-1yr

PUBLISHED AT THE OFFICE OF THE MONETARY
TIMES, No. 60 CHURCH STREET.
PRINTED AT THE DAILY TELEGRAPH PRINTING HOUSE,
BAY STREET, CORNER OF KING.

THE CANADIAN

MONETARY TIMES AND INSURANCE CHRONICLE

THE Publishers have pleasure in announcing that the success of this JOURNAL has been such as to stimulate their efforts to rend it still more valuable to the classes directly and indirectly interested in the subjects with which it deals. As the only Journal in th Dominion which gives particular attention to INSURANCE, it has enlisted the hearty support of Insurance Companies; and while, the one hand, it contends for the rights of such Companies, it equally recognizes the rights of the public.

The subject of BANKING has become of such importance, as well by reason of past legislation as by reason of anticipated changes the law respecting circulation, that it is the duty and interest of our business men to make themselves acquainted with the principl on which sound Banking rests, and to prevent any action on the part of the Legislature likely to injure the community by lessenin the usefulness of our banks. The discussion of this subject in the columns of this JOURNAL has called forth expressions of satisfactic from our most astute financiers, and has done much to give us the position we now occupy in the estimation of the public.

As MINING is in its infancy in this country, a journal devoted solely to the subject could not hope to thrive; but by giving ft information regarding Mining operations, and by the employment of reliable correspondents, we have done good service to an importa interest, and secured recognition from a class which, otherwise, could not have been reached.

Our purely COMMERCIAL DEPARTMENT has not been neglected, and each week's summary, while concise and pithy, has answered tl same ends as a more diffuse elaboration could do, and conveyed to country dealers a complete synopsis of the changes in the Toronto a Montreal Markets.

This combination of interests which the circumstances of the country render necessary, has been of the greatest advantage to ea interest by diffusing information among all classes; but, in order to do justice to all, we have been compelled to employ a large staff writers, and to expend a considerable amount in securing trustworthy correspondents.

While we are thankful to those who have encouraged us thus far, we are anxious to extend still further the usefulness of this Journ and we call on all who consider that the enterprise is worthy of support, to lend us their assistance in making the MONETARY TIMES national organ.

On our part we promise impartiality, efficiency, and the best efforts of the ablest writers that can be secured in the Dominion. C the part of our clients, we expect a cordial support and active exertion to widen our sphere of usefulness. In helping us, they he themselves.

Every Merchant, Banker, Capitalist, Insurance Agent, and Broker, can aid us, and we hope that we are not asking too much, soliciting their assistance.

We shall be happy to receive at any time articles on subjects within our jurisdiction, which, if used, will be liberally paid for.

Subscription Price ....**$2 per Annum.**

A reasonable discount will be made to Banks, Insurance Companies, &c., which subscribe for their Agencies.

SEND FOR A SPECIMEN COPY.

N.B.—Every subscriber to THE MONETARY TIMES will receive THE REAL ESTATE JOURNAL without further charge.

THE REAL ESTATE JOURNAL.

The objects of this Journal are as follows :—

(1.) To supply to those interested in real estate such information as is of special interest relating to sales or transfers of real pr perty in the principal cities, and throughout Ontario, construction of public works, and building improvements of every kind, increase decrease of municipal expenditure, debt and taxation, and, in short, whatever tends to influence the real estate market.

(2.) Leading articles will be furnished by competent writers on questions relating to conveyancing, the rise and fall of property, la grants, emigration, and other subjects coming within the legitimate scope of the Journal.

(3.) Lists of lands and houses for sale in every city, town and village of the Province, will appear in its columns, giving buyers tl best possible opportunities for selecting desirable properties of any class, and in any locality ; and, at the same time, affording sellers reliable and certain medium for reaching intending purchasers.

(4.) By a circulation extending into every corner of Canada, the announcements of advertisers will be brought to the notice of immense constituency of renders. A special feature in this connection is, that the Journal will be placed and kept on fyle at all the pri cipal hotels, reading rooms, and other public places in Ontario, and in Montreal. By these means it is confidently believed that eve class in the community will be reached.

THE REAL ESTATE JOURNAL is printed fortnightly, on good white paper, in quarto form, and is equal in size and appearance to anythii of the kind published on this continent.

Advertising, per line of nonpareil, each insertion, 5 cents. A small discount will be allowed on yearly contracts, for large spaces. Address, "THE REAL ESTATE JOURNAL," Toronto, Ontario. Cheques should be made payable to J. M. TROUT, who v also issue all receipts for money.

OFFICE, No. 60 CHURCH STREET,

TORONTO, ONTARIO.

THE CANADIAN
ΙΟΝΕΤΑRY TIMES
AND
INSURANCE CHRONICLE.

OTED TO FINANCE, COMMERCE, INSURANCE, BANKS, RAILWAYS, NAVIGATION, MINES, INVESTMENT, PUBLIC COMPANIES, AND JOINT STOCK ENTERPRISE.

—NO. 29.   TORONTO, THURSDAY, MARCH 4, 1869.   { SUBSCRIPTION.

Mercantile.

Meetings.

AGRICULTURAL MUTUAL ASSURANCE ASSOCIATION OF CANADA.

At a general meeting of the members of the Association, held for the election of Directors and for such other business as might be brought before it, in London, Ont., on 17th February, 1869, the President, Crowell Willson, Esq., M. P., was called to the chair, when the ninth annual report was presented. It is as follows :

To the Members of the Agricultural Mutual Assurance Association of Canada :

In presenting to you the ninth annual report of the Company, the Directors have to treat of a year (1868) in which the losses somewhat exceeded the average rate, partly owing to the dry weather that prevailed through a long period of the summer, when burnings were more than usually frequent from fires running over the country. Every Farmers' Insurance Company suffered in the same way; almost every one, if the information that has been received be correct, in a greater degree than our Company.

Losses.—The number reported for last year was 130 ; 122 of these were admitted as claims, and paid without unnecessary delay ; their amount, $51,148.78 ; 3 have not been regarded as valid claims ; the Directors require further light in respect to them. If they can only see that these claims ought to be paid it will afford every one of the Board very great pleasure in doing it. Four claims that arose previously were paid last year, amounting to $1,244.25. A claim was presented a few weeks ago resulting from a fire that occurred in 1867, during the assured's absence in the States. The Directors have as yet come to no decision regarding it ; but it will be attended to without delay. (This claim has since been paid in full, the Directors being satisfied it was an honest claim. The claimant, W. H. McDowell, had, however, forfeited every shadow of legal right.)

Policies.—11,526 were issued on applications received during the year. Of these 8,571 were on the cash system, and 2,955 on the premium note one. Of the aggregate 217 did not come into force till this year, while 164 issued in 1867 did not begin to run till last year. During the year 9,343 either lapsed or were cancelled. On the 1st of January, 1868, there were in force 28,764; on the first of the current year, 30,892, showing an increase of 2,128. The average amount of those in force it will be seen is $758.51.

Continued Preference of Cash System.—It is shewn that the cash system still commands the preference. Whether this will continue in so marked a manner when it becomes more generally known that the pre-payment theretofore required on the premium note system was last year decided to be dispensed with, may be questioned. Members, or those desirous of becoming so, may take their choice. Only farm property, however, is insured on the premium note system.

Capital.—Appended will be found a full financial statement. The Directors flatter themselves they may fairly congratulate you on the exhibit there made. It must not be supposed, however, that the cash and stock on hand is all *earned* premium ; it is available, and will be used to meet the current losses that may, and in fact

must be looked for. At the same time it ought to be borne in mind that the rates of this Company have been as low as those of any well established company, and much lower than of a great many; yet your Directors have so managed matters that no other "Fire Mutual" in the country can present anything like so favorable a financial aspect. This is the only one that, having complied with the Dominion Insurance Act, has been licensed by that Government. The Directors last year paid into the Receiver General $12,000 pursuant to that Act, and last week—subsequently to the completion of the appended exhibit—$13,000 more—$25,000 in all. It bears 6 per cent. interest, producing $1,500 a year. The Directors doubt not you will approve of their course in the premises. The sum of $65,000 would more than reinsure all outstanding risks at the ratio of your losses hitherto. We have in cash and Dominion stock $48,652.92, besides other available assets to the extent of $181,540.90, less by a few hundred dollars as stated—as to which, as well as for details generally, see appendix. Members may rest quite satisfied of the Company's ability to pay, if they unfortunately get burned out.

Incendiarism—Proposed Remedy.—It has been stated that numerous losses occurred during the dry term last summer. Unfortunately, there were other prominent causes of loss in operation. The demon of incendiarism still stalks abroad on his fiendish course. By referring to the table of losses, several such cases will be seen. No less than eleven fires are supposed to have so originated; while of those for which no probable cause has been assigned—43 in number—some may reasonably enough be attributed to the same source. The Directors do all they can to bring such offenders to justice—they offer a standing reward of $200 for such information as will convict. But they are of opinion the Legislature could apply, at any rate, a partial remedy for the fearful evil. In the report for 1864 it was stated : "It is to be regretted there does not exist some thorough mode of investigating into the origin and circumstances of suspicious fires throughout the country. A coroner's inquest is a cumbrous affair, and the head of it, for the most part, more qualified to deal with matters of life and death, than with ferreting out the intricacies of evidence so as to convict of incendiarism. A fire inspector in each county, selected for adaptation to the work, and clothed with ample powers, would probably prove a more effective check to those diabolical acts. It is to be hoped, not in the interests of Insurance companies alone, but for the sake of the country at large, and of public morality, that the Legislature may before long see fit to apply some correction to the great and growing evil." The Royal Insurance Company of England, one of the most important in the world, the following year took up the same idea. They recommended a similar course to the British Legislature. Towards the close of the last Parliament a committee was appointed to whom the matter was referred. Mr. Thos. B. Horsfall, one of the representatives for Liverpool, was a member; they brought in a report, recommending among other things, that "judicial enquiry should be made into fires, with power to examine witnesses on oath.

Your Board think if suitable persons were appointed at convenient centres throughout the country, endued with inquisitorial powers to investigate suspicious fires when duly called on, a great good would be done. An innocent man would be glad of an opportunity of removing suspicion from himself—and as for the guilty, the intention is not, of course, to study their comfort. The very existence of such an ordeal would tend to deter. There would be fewer burnings—rates would be lower, and not only that, but there would be less litigation in proportion before the Courts. Honest claimants, with somewhat doubtful surroundings (for such things do occur), might oft-times be able to secure a prompt payment of their rights, for it would not be profitable for an insurance company to brave the decision, if against it, of an able, competent inquisitor of high standing, pronounced after a full judicial examination. Protection would be afforded to companies and individuals alike. Nor would the plan necessarily involve any drain on the public exchequer.

Cases of malicious incendiarism are more particularly referred to above. It seems to the Directors, as well as to our efficient inspector, Mr. Niles, that there has been a diminution in speculative burnings.

Other causes of Fire.—Fires have also arisen from other causes, which might be well avoided. Only the other day notice was received of a loss, in which the claimant states. I can suppose no other cause than soot in the pipes." More than likely such was the case; eleven of the paid for losses in the appended list arose from stove pipes, and nineteen from dirty defective chimneys, setting fire to roofs or other parts of the buildings. Another prolific source of fires is children playing with matches. A very little care might have prevented most of the losses occurring under these heads.

Two-thirds Clause—Is a modification wanted?—It has been a rule of the Company to insure up to two thirds only of buildings and their contents, requiring each member to bear at least one-third the risk of the property insured. This seemed to be approved of by the great bulk of the members. Of late, however, very many have become dissatisfied with it, desiring that they should no longer be required to risk a third of the "ordinary contents". In view of this feeling, the Directors have resolved to submit the question to-day to your decision, to which, whatever it is, effect will be given. It will be put to the vote by-and-bye.

Improvement in paying up.—The Board willingly bear testimony to the fact that the members generally are paying up their dues much better than formerly. The Directors will use no coercive means hastily—but at the same time they have a duty to perform, which they will not neglect. They trust to have but little trouble on this score.

Retiring Directors.—There now go out in rotation—Messrs. Biddulph, Eccles, and Dunlop; they are eligible for re-election.

CROWELL WILLSON, President.
D. C. MACDONALD, Secretary.

The Report being read, it was moved by James Johnson, Esquire, Sunnyside, seconded by John Kearns, Esq., Deputy Reeve of London Township, that the Directors' report be received and adopted. Carried unanimously.

A few remarks were made by the Rev. J. H. Robinson, Geo. G. Magee, W. R. Vining, Esquires, and others, touching the conditions of the policies, the two former gentlemen contending they were too stringent. Explanations were then given, after which it was put to the meeting, whether it is advisable to alter the conditions of Insurance so that the full amount of loss on "ordinary contents" of buildings be paid, not exceeding the amount insured? which was decided in the affirmative.

Captain O'Malley, Andrew Ell's and Alexander McKenzie, Esquires, were appointed scrutineers, when the election for three Directors was proceeded with. After a ballot was taken, the scrutineers reported that Samuel Eccles, Hamilton Dunlop and Richard Biddulph had been re-elected.

A vote of thanks was then passed to the Chairman, and the meeting adjourned.

At a meeting of the Board held subsequently, C. Wilson, Esq., M.P., was re-elected President, and W. R. Vining, Esq., Vice-President, for the ensuing year; and the Board passed a by-law giving effect to the vote of the annual meeting, as to the insurance on the "ordinary contents" of buildings, to take effect as regards all losses from the first of this year.

CAPITAL ACCOUNT.

Amount available of Premium Notes...........		$138,831 17
Due by Agents, mostly secured by due bills from members of the Company...........		18,753 70
Dominion Stock...........	$12,000 00	
Cash in B'k Commerce..	30,015 61	
" Merchants' B'k.	6,292 23	
" Secretary's hand,		
(Postage Stamps)......	345 08	
		48,652 92
Due on old assessments in course of collection.		13,260 15
Due on No. 7, assessments, now payable...		6,195 88
Real Estate, Office Furniture, &c...........		4,500 00
		$230,193 82
Liabilities estimated at	$1,200 00	

No. of Policies in force 1st January, 1868......		28,764
No. of Policies issued previously but come in force during the year.		164
No. of Policies issued in 1868, Cash System...	8,571	
No. of Policies issued in 1868, Premium Note System	2,955	
	11,526	
Of these not yet in force.	217	
		11,309
		40,237
Less lapsed and cancelled Policies		9,345
Remaining in force......		30,892
Amount covered by Insurance...........	$23,428,945 00	
Average amount of each Policy...........	758 41	

Cash Account.

RECEIPTS.   Dr.

Balance from last Report............		$31,478 54
Received from Agents.........	$47,188 49	
Less fees and commissions allowed	7,707 88	
		39,480 66
Received on assessments...........		20,725 67
" Interest on Deposits		1,189 11
		$92,873 92

DISBURSEMENTS.   Cr.

Losses...........		$32,593 03
Bank Agency paying Losses		49 34
Salaries.		
Secretary and Clerks	$4,254 00	
" balance from 1867	1,393 15	
General Agency, Inspection, &c., including General Agent's Salary and Travelling Expenses...........	1,672 02	
Auditors...........	200 00	
Directors	792 90	
		8,312 07

Law Expenses		
Postages on Reports...........	288 25	
" Policies	289 67	
" Assessment No. 7	189 00	
Agents' Postages	151 15	
General Postages	542 81	
Discount on Stamps sold...	36 04	
		1,
Stationery		
Printing and Advertising		
Fuel and Light...........		
Repairs to Office and Premises, Furniture, Cleaning, &c.		
Taxes, $44 16; Insurance, $20 25...........		
Unearned Premium on Cancelled Policies		
Printing Reports		
Gratuities—Wm. Knox, $25; Ellen Renwick, $10		
Copies of Government License		
Incidentals (small sums)...........		
		$44,

Dominion Stock $12,000 00		
Cash in Bank of Commerce. 30,015 61		
" Merchants' Bank... 6,292 23		
" Secretary's hand,		
(Postage Stamps) 345 08		
		$92,

Examined and compared with Books Vouchers, and found correct.

A. G. SMITH, } Aud
J. HAMILTON, }

HURON AND ERIE SAVINGS AND SOCIETY.

The following is the fifth annual report Society:

The Directors of the Huron and Erie and Loan Society have much pleasure in ting their annual report of the affairs Society; and in doing so can only reiterate statements in former annual reports, "t Society is in a most prosperous condition. amount advanced on mortgages during year was $142,080.79, which is largely in of any former year's investments, and in s the accepted applications in the Solicitor at the end of the year amounted to $ The Directors continue to exercise the care in the selection of their investment they have, by the appointment of a travel spector—whose especial duty it is to property mortgaged to the Society—est what they hope will be a thorough chee Society's valuators.

The Directors need only refer to the fo comparative statement of the increase Society, as a proof of its growing pop both amongst the borrowing communi those seeking investment for their money.

	Stock.	Savings Branch Deposits.	
Dec. 31, 1864..$ 36,862 24		$7,986 79	
Dec. 31, 1865... 122,632 18		24,771 88	1
Dec. 31, 1866.. 150,880 47		50,795 36	2
Dec. 31, 1867.. 210,482 48		80,222 04	3
Dec. 31, 1868.. 292,455 79		91,425 15	3

The profits of the Society for the year ar to $55,348. Out of this two half-yearly di on stock, of 4½ per cent. each, have been d the interest on Savings Bank deposits working expenses of the Society have be and the sum of $1,833.82 carried to the co and reserve funds. These now amount 833.92, and being invested at the same the other funds of the Society, are, of that a source of profit to the Society. The I invite attention to the accompanying statement. All of which is respectfully sub

E. W. HYMAN, Pres
CHAS. MURRAY, Sec. and Treas.

for year ending December 31, 1868.
Cash Account.

RECEIPTS.

m 1867........................	$22,374 55
: pen loans....................	71,152 88
m bank, etc...................	1,956 25
arrears........................	1,464 53
ing stock.....................	23,773 05
stock..........................	65,850 00
anch deposits.................	93,860 53
	$285,431 79

DISBURSEMENTS.

n mortgages...................	$142,086 79
anch deposits repaid..........	96,648 72
deposits repaid...............	4,381 74
ng stock withdrawn............	11,369 67
stock withdrawn...............	2,112 97
mortgage payments in ad-	
....	148 59
r year........................	3,949 29
n Permanent stock.............	16,215 56
r—excess of payments..........	1,292 23
1869..........................	7,226 23
	$285,431 79

Statement of Books.

nd interest...................	$587,168 38
....	322 70
debentures and interest......	4,075 00
ure...........................	240 00
i on hand and in bank........	7,226 23
tty ledger....................	262 72
	$599,295 03
loans.........................	$194,580 17

Savings Branch and in-

....	91,425 15
ng stock and interest........	78,205 75
stock.........................	214,250 00
und...........................	833 92
l.............................	20,000 00
	$599,295 03

Assets and Liabilities.

ASSETS.

f mortgages...................	$392,588 22
....	322 70
debentures and interest......	4,075 00
are...........................	240 00
y ledger......................	262 72
....	7,226 23
	$404,714 86

LIABILITIES.

Savings Bank and in-

....	$ 91,425 15
g stock and interest.........	78,205 79
stock.........................	214,250 00
und...........................	833 92
....	20,000 00
	$404,714 86

Profit and Loss Account.

avings Branch deposits.......	$ 4,394 59
accumulating stock...........	5,811 35
permanent stock..............	16,215 56
mt............................	3,949 29
balance of loss	143 20
und...........................	833 92
l.............................	4,000 00
	$35,348 00
est account..................	$ 1,798 54
rears.........................	1,464 53
nortgages.....................	32,084 93
	$35,348 00

on mortgages amounted to $629 52, been written off thus : $486 23 to a and set aside at December 31, 1867, to profit and loss account as above. these losses was on mortgages taken nnion Permanent Building Society, h an allowance was made by that

---

QUEBEC MARINE AND FIRE INSURANCE COMPANY.—The annual general meeting of the above Company was held on Monday, at its office, in Quebec, when the report and statements for the year were read and adopted, and the following gentlemen elected Directors :—Messrs. W. Withall, A. Joseph, Ed. Burstall, Jas. G. Ross, J. Gaudry, J. B. Renaud, M. G. Mountain, D. C. Thomson and Thomas Becket.

—At the general meeting of the Directors of the St. Lawrence Navigation Company, held on the 24th instant, the Hon. Louis Renaud, Messrs. C. L. Rodier, L. Haineault, H. Coote, J. Bte. Auger, A. Rimmer, A. Shannon, M. McKenzie, and M. Cuvilier, were elected Directors for the ensuing year. The new Board met the same afternoon, and elected the following officers for the next year ;— Hon Louis Renaud, President ; C. L. Rodier, Vice-President ; F. A. Trudel, Secretary ; J. Bte. Auger, General Manager ; and John McMartin, Agent.

—At the general annual meeting of the Saint John Mutual Insurance Company, held at their office in Wiggins building, Princess street, on Monday, February 1, 1869, the following gentlemen were elected for the current year, viz: John Smith, President; C. H. Estabrooks, W. K. Reynolds, James Harris, Robert J. Leonard, Directors; A. Ballentine, Barrister and Solicitor, and J. Woodward; Secretary. A dividend of forty-five per cent was declared on the business of 1867.

—A meeting has been called at Laurent, Jacques Cartier Co., Province of Quebec, for the 29th Feb., to organize a mutual fire insurance company.

Insurance.

FIRE RECORD.—Ottawa, Feb. 27.—A fire broke out in the rear of a saloon occupied by John Cahill, just opposite the Russell House, caused, it is supposed, by some defect in the chimney. Cahill lost all his furniture and stock of liquors, with the exception of some bar fixtures. His loss is but partially covered by an insurance of $1,000 in the Imperial. The building adjoining, occupied by Robertson & Lawrence, merchant tailors, was also destroyed. They had a large stock of cloths and ready-made clothing on hand, principally saved. Insured for $1,000 in the British America; will more than cover the damage sustained. The upper flat of the same building was occupied by Mrs. Greenwood as a boarding-house. A portion of the furniture saved. No insurance. Owing to the exertions of the hook and ladder company, the great quantity of snow on the roofs, and the arrival after a long time of a few barrels of water, the fire was checked at the west building, owned by Messrs. Durie & Son, and occupied by them as a book-store. The roof of the building was partially burned ; $1,200 insurance in the British America on building. The stock saved; the insurance on stock, $2,000 in Western and Home. The flat above the book-store was occupied by Mr. Peckett, dentist; loss not large; insured for $500 in the Western of Canada. The buildings totally destroyed were owned by Alderman James, and insured in the Liverpool and London for $2,000. They were wooden buildings and old. Total loss estimated at over $10,000. Mr. Orme is insured in the North British and Mercantile; loss very slight.

February 21.—Mr. Charles Mathews, lot 21, first concession, south of the Egremont road, had his dwelling house and furniture totally destroyed by fire. Loss of house and furniture, $1,000; insured in the Agricultural Mutual— building $300 and furniture $150. The fire is supposed to have occurred by a defect in the chimney.

Brock Township, Ont., Feb. 22.—The barn, stables, sheds and other buildings of a farmer named Quin, near to Vroomanton, Brock, were consumed, including everything in and around

---

the barn, grain, hay, straw stacks, etc. We have failed to learn particulars.

Fredericton, N. B., Feb. 16.—The billiard room and bowling alley belonging to F. W. Miles, was discovered to be on fire. The new steam fire-engine was on the spot soon after the alarm was given, and speedily extinguished the flames, but not before considerable damage had been done to both building and furniture, which, however, were partly insured.

Normanby Township, Ont., Feb. —.—Barn of Robert Hopkins, with contents, comprising a quantity of hay, wheat and other farm produce, was totally consumed by fire on Thursday night last. The origin of the fire is unknown. No insurance.

King Township, Feb. 22.—The dwelling house and woodshed of Abram Carley, on lot No. 7, in the 6th concession, was burned with contents. The family had barely time to escape with their lives. The house was insured for $400; loss about $1,000. The origin of the fire is supposed to be accidental.

Strathroy, Feb. 30.—The dwelling house of Wm. Matthews, lot 21, 2d concession, Adelaide, was destroyed by fire supposed to have originated in the chimney. Mr. Matthews and his family had barely time to escape, and saved very little of their effects.

Belleville, Feb. —.—A fire broke out in the building formerly used as a malthouse, adjoining the "Tiger" Brewery, Bridge street, but lately occupied as a storehouse, grinding mill and stables. The building burned contained a large quantity of hops, oats, hay, etc., valued at about $900, the greater part of which was destroyed. L. J. Williams, the owner, we understand, is insured in the Western for $600. The building was owned by F. McAnnany, and was insured in the Provincial. The origin of the fire is a mystery, as no fire had been used in the building for a year past.

Sarnia, Feb. 24.—The dwelling house of Mrs. Gilbert, situated on the River road, between Corunna and Moore, was destroyed by fire. The fire originated, it is said, from a defective chimney. Furniture partly saved. The building is said to be insured for $200, but this will fall far short of covering the loss.

Digby, N. S., Mar. 1.—A telegram says,[that six houses were destroyed by fire; no insurance.

Roxton, Pond, Prov. of Quebec, July 11.— Kimpton's store and contents were totally destroyed. The stock was fully insured in the Home, of New Haven.

PHŒNIX OF LONDON.—The following shows the results of the business of the Phœnix Insurance Co. of London, in Canada, for the year ended 30th November, 1868 :—Premiums received $84,562.15 ; number of policies issued, 1,069 ; amount of same, $4,159,188.00 ; amount at risk, $9,202,098.00 ; number of policies that have become claims, 41 ; amount of same, $358,375.00 ; losses, $37,988.49 ; losses in suspense and waiting further proof, $1,500.00 ; losses, the payment of which is resisted, none ; premiums earned, $84,562.15.

WRECKS OF AMERICAN VESSELS FROM 1858 TO 1868.

Year.	No.	Value.
1858..........................	355	$8,897,665
1859 (nine months)...........	300	8,389,271
1860 (eleven months).........	405	12,011,080
1861..........................	558	17,367,100
1862..........................	452	12,765,060
1863..........................	452	20,521,800
1864..........................	495	20,446,850
1865..........................	502	33,794,300
1866..........................	471	31,056,100
1867..........................	536	21,742,200
1868 (nine months)...........	257	11,698,500
Total, 10 years 5 mo's..4,883		$198,702,876

Railway News.

GREAT WESTERN RAILWAY.—Traffic for week ending February 12, 1869.

Passengers	$20,720 87
Freight	47,799 29
Mails and Sundries	2,525 88
Total Receipts for week......	$71,046 04
Corresponding week, 1867...	59,122 43
Increase	$11,923 61

NORTHERN RAILWAY.—Traffic receipts for week ending February 21st, 1869.

Passengers	$2,028 06
Freight and live stock......	6,850 26
Mails and sundries.........	246 51
	$9,124 83
Corresponding Week of '68.	5,928 22
Increase...........	$3,196 61

ANOTHER INTERNATIONAL BRIDGE.

A report by a Committee of the Buffalo City Council on the subject of a new International Bridge between Buffalo and Fort Erie has been published. The following letter, from Mr. Brydges, explains what he is prepared to do in the matter :—

"I hold the control of the bridge charters of both sides of the river, and control the majority of the stock held by the corporations existing—one chartered by the Legislature of the State of New York, and the other by the Parliament of Canada. The amount of stock subscribed for under both charters is $1,300,000, viz., $1,000,000 upon the American side and $300,000 upon the Canadian side.

"My object, and that of the Canadian railway companies which I represent, is to get the Bridge constructed at the earliest possible date ; so that the American railway companies on the one side, and the Canadian railways, on the other, and the city of Buffalo, may obtain the advantage of the communication which the Bridge will afford.

"The construction of the Bridge being assured, I am prepared, so far as my control of the charters is concerned, to place such control in the hands of those who will bring about the arrangements necessary for the construction of the work.

"I, therefore, as President of the Bridge Company, now state to you that so soon as the City of Buffalo has, in accordance with the powers which it now possesses, undertaken to guarantee interest upon $1,350,000 of bonds, which sum will be sufficient to secure the completion of the Bridge, I shall be prepared at once to transfer, upon the execution of the necessary deeds, the sum of $700,000 of the stock of the Bridge Company, which will be sufficient to give the control of the Bridge Company to the parties holding those shares.

"I will take care that, before making this transfer, a resolution is passed by the Bridge Company which will prevent the creation of any new shares beyond the $1,300,000 now in existence.

"The right of issuing any further shares will therefore rest, if it is hereafter desired, with those who hold the majority of stock."

The Committee of the Council reply as follows: The Committee feel assured that Mr. Brydges is not only desirous, but has full authority, to carry out the measures which he proposes, and that upon the City agreeing that in case the said stock is transfered, and the other stipulations contained in Mr. Brydge's communication complied with, that the control of the stock will be transferred to citizens of Buffalo, and his propositions will be fully carried out.

And your Committee are equally confident that no difficulty will be encountered in finding citizens of Buffalo of sufficient character and ability to take the transfer of the stock upon the conditions proposed by Mr. Brydges, and pay the advance thereon.

* * * * * * * * *

The proposition of the Grand Trunk Railway to pay $50,000 annually for the use of the Bridge of itself, provides for nearly two-thirds of such interest, and the compensation received from the other great lines of railway, including in fact all the completed lines from the East to the Great West, together with the tolls received from the use of the Bridge by the general public, will not only secure the city from loss, but render the work remunerative to those who shall complete the same.

Financial.

TORONTO STOCK MARKET.

(Reported by Pellatt & Osler, Brokers.)

Business was rather more active during the past week, and prices are in most instances without change.

Bank Stock.—There were sales of Bank of Montreal at 139½; holders now ask 140. Ontario is much firmer this week; there are no sellers under par. Buyers offer 121 for Toronto; very little is offered. Royal Canadian has declined 1 per cent.; the last sales were at 89. There were large transactions in Commerce at 103; holders now ask 103½. Gore is inquired for at 41; nothing doing. Merchants' has advanced, and transactions have occurred at 109. Buyers offer 99 for Quebec, but there are no sellers. Molson's is inquired for at 112. Sales of City occurred at 103 and 103¼, but the demand is small. Du Peuple sold at 106, ex-dividend. Nationale is nominal at 106½; there are no sellers. Jacques Cartier is asked for at 108½. Mechanics' is inquired for at 95, and there are buyers of Union at 104; no sales. Other banks nominal.

Debentures.—Canada sterling six per cents sold at 103, and five per cents are offered at 94½. No Dominion Stock in market. Toronto are enquired for but not offered. No County offering. There were large sales of Township debentures at rates to pay 6¾ per cent.

Sundries.—Sales of British America Assurance at 55½, at which rate it is still offering. Canada Permanent Building Society sold at 125 to 125½, with little offering ; sales of Western Canada occurred at 120 and 120½ ; sellers now asking 121; no Freehold offering; there are buyers at 110. Montreal Telegraph sold at 133½. There were several transactions in Canada Landed Credit at 73½, ex dividend. Several mortgages have been placed during the week at 8 per cent. Money is in rather more demand.

MONTREAL STOCK MARKET.

MONTREAL, March 1, 1869.

In stocks this week there has been little doing. Montreal closes at 140, with prospects of higher prices ; City 103; Molson's 112 to 113; Ontario about par; Bank of Toronto 121 to 122; Merchants' Bank 108½ to 109 ; Royal Canadian 89 and 89½ ; Bank of Commerce 103.

In bonds there have been some transactions at our quotations. There is little doing in exchange which is quoted at about 9 per cent. premium. Gold drafts on New York are worth par and a small premium owing to the decline in sterling. Silver keeps steady at 3½ discount notwithstanding the immense export demand. The principal feature in our market has been the decline of gold in New York, through which it is rumoured one of our heaviest capitalists has lost heavily. Several small dabblers also find themselves slightly crippled.

A NEW BANK.—It is proposed to orga soon as possible, the Exchange Bank of Ya of Nova Scotia, for which a charter was (two years ago. The proposed capital is $: divided into 2,000 shares of $100 each. books are now open, and it is intended tc operation by 1st August, 1869.

NOVA SCOTIA GOLD FIELDS

HALIFAX, N. S.. Feb. 18,

The present lull in gold mining affairs felt by speculators than by the older est companies whose mill returns for Januar below as far as received at the Chief (sioner's Office) prove the presence of the for metal in quantity sufficient to well r intelligent and economical search for it from the several districts there are nor returns from Uniacke are not in, but th from the Mount Uniacke Company con existence of two lodes of aggregate width in their cross-cut which yield an aver dwts., and can be mined and reduced f Prospecting parties are to work on the M lot, and other small properties on the san The Prince of Wales Company, the Cent pany, the Montreal Association, and th Uniacke Company, however, are the onl producers.

Prospectors are busy, too, at Musqu Beaver Dam, and Fifteen Mile Stream.

Mill Returns.

Mill.	Quartz Crushed. tons.	cwt.	G oz.
SHERBROOKE.			
Glencoe	209	19	39
Palmerston	479	0	54
Wellington	224	0	185
Chicago	50	0	2
Meridian	48	0	5
Dominion	400	0	163
TANGIER.			
Gladstone	9	0	2
MONTAGUE.			
Montague .... (R. G. Leckie & Co.)	63	6	98
WINE HARBOR.			
Orient	16	0	0
Eldorado	63	10	14
Victoria	120	0	0
Machias	66	15	28
WAVERLEY.			
Boston & N. S.........	125	0	78
INDIAN PATH.			
Waddelow	10	0	6

Recapitulation.

District.	tons.	cwt.	oz.
Sherbrooke	1,410	19	451
Tangier	9	0	[illegible]
Montague...............	63	6	9
Wine Harbor	266	5	4
Waverley...	125	0	7
Indian Path	10	0	
Total...............	1,884	10	

Average per ton, 7 dwts. 6 grs

BULLION RECEIPTS.

The following returns of bar gold received by Messrs. Huse & Lowell, Halifax, since the 1st inst.

Mine.	District.	oz.
Woodbine,	Sherbrooke..................	3
Not stated,	"	
Palmerston,	"	7
Wellington,	"	17
Mount Unicke,	Unicke............ ..	11
Not stated,	Renfrew.................. ..	
Boston & N. S.,	Waverley	2
		43

BY A. HEATHERINGTON.

District and Person.		Gold Product.			Average.				Miners.			Maximum per 2,240 lbs.	Quartz.		Mills at the End of the Year.			Mines worked. Average No.	Remarks.
		Total.	From Quartz.	Alluvial.	per 2240 lbs.	Per Miner.			Aggregate No.	Daily No.	Two years.		Raised.	Crushed.	Steam	Water	Total.		
						Annual Weight.	Annual Value.												

(Table data — detailed numeric columns by district: Isaac's Harbor, Wine Harbor, Sherbrooke, Tangier, Montague, Waverley, Oldham, Renfrew, Uniacke, Lawrencetown, Unclassified, For the whole Province as per seven Returns, Estimated, Stolen or not reported, Grand Total 1860 to 1868.)

a. The average of thirteen tons, Colonial.

b. The average of one and a half tons.

c. By ton Colonial is meant the ton of 2,000 by ton British, that of 2,240 lbs.

d. The quantity stolen and not reported is estimated variously from 15 to 30 per cent, therefore the quantity sent here is unsafely within bounds.

Sherbrooke.

The ounce is valued at $20, or £4, 2s. 6d. average for Australia.

Equal to 365,407 tons, 18 cwt, 1 3 qrs, Colonial; or 147,085 tons, 12 cwt, 4 lbs British.

The Canadian Monetary Times.

THURSDAY, MARCH 4, 1869.

THE GODERICH SALT MEN AND THEIR BACKERS.

We once heard a person, experienced in the ways of the world, propose to wager that he could practically demonstrate the thoughtless alacrity with which large numbers of persons will sign any petition presented to them, by getting a formidable array of signatures to a petition to hang the Governor General, without trial or benefit of clergy. And it must be confessed that even this exaggerated way of stating the fact was not without its germ of truth. Nor are the excusably or inexcusably ignorant the only offenders in this respect. A notable example is before us. During the last session, sixty-four members of the Legislature of Ontario petitioned the Ottawa Parliament to impose a duty on salt, in the interest of the Goderich salt men. The prominence given to the question in this and other ways forces its consideration upon us.

A duty on salt has always been an odious duty, because the article is a prime necessary of life, with which civilized men find it impossible to dispense. It would almost be easier to do without bread than salt. The Scottish peasant finds no difficulty in subsisting mainly on oatmeal. Sugar and tea may be dispensed with in extreme cases; but salt is required to season or preserve an endless variety of articles of food. It is not too

much to say that among the chief articles of food consumed by the majority of the population of this Dominion, a prominent place must be assigned to fish and pork, both of which owe their preservation to salt.

It may safely be laid down as a maxim that the prime necessaries of existence—that which forms the indispensable aliment, or any adjunct to that aliment, of the poorest portion of the great mass of the population—should be free from taxation. It was in obedience to this principle that the corn duty, which was justly stigmatized as an odious bread-tax, was repealed by Sir Robert Peel. In levying taxes, it is the duty of the Government to avoid striking at the great sources of the people's existence. Very recently the Parliament at Ottawa committed the error of putting a duty on foreign flour. This tax was in effect, though not in form, a discrimination against American flour. The object was to compel the Nova Scotians to eat Canadian flour, at an enhanced cost, which they could not afford to pay. The circumstance of the fishermen of that Province passing through a cruel famine, almost immediately after this unwise and unjust duty was put on, showed in a striking manner the inhumanity of that piece of protectionist legislation which attainted the people in the very source of their existence. We need not add that this temporary bread-tax, after bringing discredit on all concerned, was repealed on the first opportunity.

Are we now to shift the burthen which we removed from one shoulder of the Nova Scotia fishermen to the other? Having repealed the duty on their flour, are we to lay it on the salt that preserves their fish? Both articles of food are equally necessary to their existence; and we might just as well have left the tax on their bread as turn round, after taking it off, and put it on their fish. The proposed tax on imported salt is advocated on grounds which are altogether indefensible. We are told that the new salt men have some sort of a claim to be defended against the competition of American salt. The advocates of the duty tell us that they do not desire to go beyond this. They do not even wish to tax English salt. They ask simply and solely that a duty be placed on American salt; and we are not sure but they would agree to confine it to the dreaded Syracuse product. This demand shows an extraordinary unacquaintance with the fundamental laws by which the action of the Ottawa Parliament is limited and controlled. It is not within the competence of that Parliament to levy a discriminating duty, even in favor of English productions. The Governor General's instructions always contain a special prohibition against the enactment of such a

duty. Thus the way to a realization object of the salt duty agitators is [eff]barred.

There are other parts of the subject these petitioners do not appear to have to better advantage. They mistak[e] might be the natural effects of com[petition] for remote, unusual and abnormal They tell us, as if it were somethin[g] ordinary. It is the result of an ordin[ary] cause that Syracuse salt is sold in Canada when it comes into com[petition] with the Goderich product than wh[ich] competition is withdrawn. What natural? But even if there is something mo[re] does not alter the case, in favor of [peti]tioners. It is quite possible that th[e Syra]cuse salt interest may make a special retain a footing in this market. The[re] we believe, two separate companies; gaged in the manufacture and the the distribution of the Syracuse sal[t] mercantile company agrees to take salt the manufacturing company p[ay] at a price agreed upon. In case of e[xcess of] production, which may easily occu[r] would be great difficulty in disposin[g of] surplus; and it requires no stretch imagination to conceive that Canad[a] enjoy its full share of the benefit cheapened article. Salt is a thing o[f which] the consumption has fixed limits, w[hich] not admit of artificial extension. Th[e] limit once overstepped in produc[tion] price inevitably comes down. But always an advantage to the c[onsumer] The Goderich men may or may [not] jeopardized their capital. We h[ave] their attempts to develop and utilize source of wealth to the country are [worthy] of every legitimate aid.

But is aid of any kind required in the successful development of the salt territory? The following is an [estimate] of the cost of manufacturing 100 b[arrels of] salt at Goderich, obtained from . . . facturer there:

16 cords wood at $2	
Labor	
100 barrels (empty) at 30c.	
Cartage to wharf or railroad	
Oil and sundries	
Total	

Or 83 cents per barrel. America[n salt is] sold in Goderich at $1.30, so that t[here is a] margin for interest on investment a[nd profit] of 43 cents per barrel, or nearl[y 50 per] cent. Such a margin ought to be sat[isfactory.]

The arguments adduced in favo[r of a re]taliatory tariff come half a centur[y too late] to find favor where economical [principles] have been carefully studied, with the honest application of correct p[rinciples]

rguments, if they mean anything, return to that never ending war of hich, leading to the marshaling of rmies, has so often drenched the :h blood and blighted the best hopes .n progress. Sir Robert Peel deter- c apply the true principle, long)y the economists, that it was the l the interest of England to do right, e other nations to their own choice. uestion raised by this salt interest :educed to a very simple form : Are :alt consumers to be taxed for the)enefit of the Goderich salt raisers?)untry to pay so much the more for :hat these few individuals may put s in their pockets ? Why cannot we, 'ominion, produce salt that will suc- compete with Syracuse salt? We great advantage of untaxed labor and means of subsistence ; of proximity to and consequent reduced cost of car- ! a first-rate if not an altogether su- rticle. Everything is in our favor. en, can we not compete? It is too expect any one to believe that the :salt men will always continue to favor their salt at a price that does not e cost of production, and if they did :rofit would be on our side. There ason to despair. If our salt works 'ully, prudently and economically l, there is no reason to fear for their success ; and that success will be all > certain and enduring that it rests nd foundation.

AGRICULTURAL MUTUAL.

gricultural Mutual Assurance Asso- ı, we believe, the leading Company ss in the Province of Ontario. It has ts amounting to $48,652 92, and pre- tes liable to assessment $138,831 17; income, (less commissions) for the was $61,395.38, and its expenditure Policies to the number of 11,526 ued, 8,571 on the cash and 2,955 on nium note system. The Directors h evident pride to their $25,000 in- ; in Dominion Stock, under the In- Act, and we see for the first time in of a Canadian Insurance Company, ste of the amount required to re- standing risks. Although we are :o think the sum mentioned, $65,000, astimate, we hope other Companies w the example of the Agricultural .nd, at least, recognize the existence lity which they have hitherto at- to ignore. There are other matters :cellent report which suggest com- :h as the need of official investiga-

tion, in cases of fire and the abrogation of the two-thirds rule; but the crowded state of our columns compels us to defer further remarks. The financial condition of the Company, and its success in business, exhibit great care in underwriting and general good management.

NOVA SCOTIA GOLD MINING.

Our readers will not fail to observe the valuable information respecting gold mining in Nova Scotia furnished by our Halifax correspondent. The official returns of the various mining districts, compiled specially for this journal, by A. Heatherington, Esq., late editor of the *Mining Gazette*, will be found useful by those interested in that region. — These returns, by the way, we publish in ad- vance of every other journal in the Domi- nion. The Nova Scotia mining interest has become so large that we deemed it advisable to secure the services of a competent corres- pondent to chronicle operations in Nova Scotia, and we think that our readers will agree that success has crowned our efforts. A great deal of money here sought investment in that gold region. At the last Session of the Legislature of that Province about thirty companies were incorporated. Various loca- lities have furnished money for these enter- prizes. There are Montreal, Kingston, Co- burg, Toronto, Hamilton, Chicago, Hartford, Boston and New York Companies, all en- gaged in gold mining. Toronto, alone, is the head-quarters of five or six chartered, or about to be, chartered, companies. So that a considerable number of persons had a direct interest in being fully informed as to what is going on down there. We hope to number all these companies, and their stockholders, among our list of subscribers.

REPORT OF THE SECRETARY OF THE BOSTON BOARD OF TRADE FOR 1868.

We are indebted to a friend for a copy of the very interesting report of the Secretary of the Boston Board of Trade, Hamilton H. Hill, Esq. He discusses very fully the various subjects affecting the trade and pros- perity of Boston ;—railway communication, harbour improvements, finance, the shipping interest, &c. The repeal of the Reciprocity Treaty was initiated by a Boston man, and under the influence of temporary hostility to Britain and British Colonists. The feeling has passed away, but the measures adopted and their consequences remain ; and it will take many years of agitation and of intelligent enterprise before Boston will be able to re- gain the customers against whom she closed her warehouses. It is possible that she may never again occupy the position she once

held as the emporium for the trade of the Maritime Provinces of the Dominion ; for New York, like Aaron's rod, seems to have the faculty of swallowing up its lesser rivals, and in trade, as well as in every-day life, the scriptural aphorism is singularly true—" To him that hath shall be given." The Boston Board of Trade is fortunate in having so able a Secretary. Mr. Hill refers to the Na- tional Board of Trade, whose first report is before us. Our neighbors have set us a good example by combining the various Chambers of Commerce into a National Board. Mr. Hill, under the head of "Steam Commu- nication with Europe," says :—

"We believe that the rule holds good, that vessels will always go wherever there is likely to be an accumulation of freight. New York has been made the port of desti- nation for ten or twelve foreign steamship lines, because it is known that there will al- ways be more or less business there for them. Portland and Baltimore have been able to draw similar lines to themselves, because the policy of the Grand Trunk and Baltimore and Ohio Railroads has been able to make it possible for their merchants to engage in the export trade. The Cunard Company de- spatches a steamer once a week (which will hereafter carry a mail), from Liverpool to Boston, sending it to New York for its re- turn cargo ; and there can be little doubt that this line will return from here to Liver- pool direct, as soon as the freight shall be forthcoming."

IS IT TRUE?

Rumour has been whispering for some time that Vanderbilt has become the purchaser of the old plans of the Southern Railway at $120,000 or $130,000. Is this true? It has been further stated that he has made an offer—some $15,000 more—for the new charter for this line granted by the Legisla- ture of Ontario, but that he did not succeed in this particular, the holders believing there was more money in it. There seems to be little doubt that Mr. Vanderbilt has attempted to obtain control over this project. What is the object? Is it to build the road, or to kill it off?

There is still some doubt about the precise extent of the loss recently sustained by the Bank of Montreal in New York. It is certain, however, that in one instance the loss was $60,000, and it arose in this way. The bank makes advances on Government securi- ties, and one person with whom it had done business for a great number of years, coming in one day and gave a cheque for $60,000 and took up his securities. The cheque was not marked good, and next morning when the cash was asked for it, the drawer was found to be bankrupt. Whether there were any other losses than this is still a matter of doubt and conjecture which ought to be removed by an authorized statement, for the uncertainty gives a wide latitude to the imagination, and probably causes exaggerated reports to obtain some credence.

The Ottawa Government promises a Banking Bill that will be satisfactory both to the banks and Parliament. We doubt it, and still more that it will be satisfactory to the people; if, as generally believed, its main feature should make Government notes the unique currency of the country—thus threatening the future advent of an irredeemable currency, of which the value would constantly fluctuate from day to day.

—THE Municipal Council of Hastings has granted a sum of money to establish a chair of mineralogy and agricultural chemistry in Albert College, at Bellville, and we are glad to learn that Mr. James T. Bell has been appointed its first occupant.

—The *Globe* states that the tenders for Canada Landed Credit forfeited stock came up to the market rate. The actual rate was about 43 on the amount paid up on each share, instead of 73, the market rate.

PROVINCIAL INSURANCE COMPANY.—The Manager and Assistant Manager of this Company are at loggerheads. The latter having preferred charges of mismanagement and incompetency against the former, the Board of Directors appointed a committee to inquire into the matter. Evidence was taken on both sides and the decision arrived at was to advise the belligerents to settle their little differences and attend to their work. It is stated that the Board, or some of its members, have expressed a willingness to give the Manager a pension of $1,200 a year if he will retire. This proposition has not, however, been accepted. However advantageous it might prove, its legality is very questionable. The salary is $2,400, and a bonus of 2½ per cent. on profits, making the position of Manager of the Provincial Insurance Company worth at least $3,200 a year. This Company is certainly liberal to its Manager.

Communications.

LIFE INSURANCE.

To the Editor of the Monetary Times.

SIR,—In your issue of the 11th February is an article upon "The Crime of False Pretence in Life Insurance," taken from a Western journal, and immediately following it another, which furnishes a striking illustration of the first. A statement of figures is there given, attributed to Mr. Ramsay, of the Canada Life Insurance Company, to the effect that eight American life companies doing business here possess assets averaging only $8.44 for each $100 assured, while the Canada has $18.70 for every $100 assured.

I had previously seen a circular to the above effect, over the name of a newly-appointed agent of the Canada, and had attributed its publication and use in canvassing to his ignorance of the business; but when it appears in your journal as coming from Mr. Ramsay, it assumes quite a different character. That gentleman cannot but know that the statement, correct enough in its proper place, is to the last degree deceptive and false when placed before the public as a means of influencing business. * * *

The general public do not know, but every well-informed insurance agent must, that the soundness and strength of an insurance company cannot be determined by any comparison of its assets with the face of its policies, irrespective of the age and terms of those policies. A company having $10,000,000 assured on the ten-year endowment plan, and only $5,000,000 on the whole life plan, must show an amount of assets for each $100 very different from another company having the same amount insured, but on the whole life plan exclusively. Suppose cash policy to have paid two premiums: the first company would then have to possess $12 of assets for each $100 assured, but the second company would be a much stronger one if it had only $3 for each $100 assured.

Another illustration, more applicable to the case. Suppose two life companies, each about twenty years in business. One of them may have assured pretty much the same amount from year to year from the first, thus making comparatively slow progress in increasing its business. From assuring an average of say $200,000 per annum during the first five years, it may have grown to an average of $400,000 during the last five years. The other company, from an annual average of $500,000, now averages say $40,000,000. It is manifest that the new and the old business on the books of the two companies respectively bear a very different relation to each other. No. 1 company will probably have received, and be required to account for, an average of ten premiums on each policy, while No. 2 will probably have received, on the average, only four or five. The policy-holders of No. 1 would be insecure with anything short of from $20 to $25 for each $100 assured, while those of No. 2 would be quite safe with from $6 to $8.

As an instance of slow growth, and necessarily large assets ($17) for each $100 insured, take the "State," of Worcester, Mass., which has spent twenty-two years in getting $5,138,711 on its books; and as an instance of more energetic management, take the "Knickerbocker," of New York, which has consumed but fourteen years in assuring $44,270,805, and whose assets for each $100 assured are only about $6.50. And yet, unless the Massachusetts Commissioner greatly misleads the public, the "Knickerbocker's" assets are, proportionately to its liability, far greater than the "State's," being $114.22, while the "State's" assets figure at $107.75.

If I correctly understand the design of Mr. Ramsay's figures, he would have his agents and the public believe that in all the above cases each company ought to possess about the same amount of assets for each $100 assured; that the companies possessing the largest ratios are the best and safest, and that others should be avoided!

A word as to notes. Every one will admit that a note is a better security than a book account. How particularly Mr. Ramsay informs the public that "more than one-tenth" of a certain company's assets are in notes; and how blank is the space opposite his own company's name, though it has a large amount loaned in the same manner, but devoid of the security and accuracy afforded by a premium note. It is singular how few people with beams in their eyes can so clearly discover motes in the eyes of their neighbors.

No figures can be presented to the public giving a single view of the respective companies, that will afford a perfectly accurate test of their good standing. The table presented on page 88 of the last Massachusetts Report, however, furnishes the best index procurable. All of the eight companies whose names Mr. Ramsay uses so freely, submit their affairs annually to an official valuation by the Massachusetts Insurance Commissioner, and the result is obtainable at a trifling cost. The table above alluded to shows the nett assets and the nett liabilities, and gives the ratios of the one to the other for each company during 1865, 1866, and 1867. If the Canada Life would submit its accounts, in like manner, to an official annual valuation, the public could get a better idea of its standing than by the ridiculous exhibition it makes of "assets for each $100 insured." What is the proportion of its present assets to present liabilities? The last report of the Canada only showed its liabilities, as valued by some private individual employed by the company, they stood four years ago!

The following table is from page 88 of the Massachusetts Report, and shows the standing, exclusive of capital stock, of the eight American companies referred to, on the 1st of January 1868:—

Companies.	Ratio of Assets for each $ of present liability.		
	1865.	1866.	18..
Ætna	$118 86	$120 97	$12.
Atlantic	......	129 64	9.
Connecticut	144 30	145 03	14.
Equitable	100 98	114 22	10.
New York	125 28	129 65	11.
Phœnix	117 38	120 27	12.
Travellers	......	149 86	12.
Union	124 44	121 67	12.

The Atlantic, being a new company, appears little below par in the above comparison; but possesses a large guarantee capital, making ratio, with capital, $169.58. The ratios of some of the other companies would be affected also by including their capital stock, but a really solvent company can always retire its capital unimpaired. The Connecticut, the Phœnix, and Union appear to better advantage than they would had they made dividends earlier than four years from the date of their policies, as all the others have done. The main point, however, is, by an independent governmental investigation all are shown to have large balances on the right side of the ledger. Can Mr. Ramsay furnish figures corresponding to the above for the any other years?

As to low rates, of which a special point is made, all insurance men know that when a company lowers its rates, it correspondingly lessens its security, and renders its ultimate solvency more or less doubtful. To adopt rates also per cent lower than either the oldest and strongest or the youngest and most reckless of English American companies presume to venture upon, left to the Canada alone! It would be fairly titled to the glory were its capital adequate to the risk; but where institutions with millions surplus funds and wide experience stand back, it is to be regretted that any ordinary set of capitalists should make Canada the exclusive field for which to try so hazardous an experiment.

I enclose my card, Mr. Editor, and remain
Truly yours,
Montreal, Feb. 27, 1869.

REDUCED RATES AND OVER INSURANCE

Editor of the Canadian Monetary Times.

DEAR SIR.—An "Agent" in one of your recent numbers complains that some Companies cutting down fire rates and that the tariff dead letter. I am glad to say it is, for it was of errors, and was only valuable as to price construction and locality of buildings. No to rates; I am convinced that it is not always highest rate that pays a company the best a clear view displayed by an Agent in the sale of risks, is much more important; first, by taining the character and standing of the owning or occupying the property; next, the carefully explaining to the person that he is only insure two-thirds of the actual value being his own insurer for the other one-third am aware that this is often not done, as I frequently been told "such a company will pay any amount I will give them." The reply very simple one, "they may take your premium but would not pay you more than your two-thirds of the value." For instance, i...

lue of a property is $4,000, no company y more than $2,667. I am satisfied that e precautions were taken, many fires might ded. I could mention several fires in this itain the last twelve months, where the y was largely over insured. Insurance is, like every other mercantile transaction, e based upon careful and prudential prin- and I am sure my commercial friends will s out in saying that it is not by the ap- high rate of profits upon any business tion, but the uniform care with which the iers are selected that success depends, and e most successful business men are those ontent with a moderate profit, will only ealings with reliable parties, and not with ho do not care whether they fail or not, or rice they pay for goods; so with insurance, doing an unprofitable trade will often let perty burn if he sees it to his advantage, res little for the rate he pays. A serious ck to placing insurance upon a legitimate : is the anxiety of some companies to obtain pon any terms and the employment of per- ot connected with the office to canvass. of those men never expect to get more than rst commission, and consequently care little e character of risk taken.

I remain, dear sir, yours truly,
INSURANCE.
NTO, Feb. 27, 1869.

Commercial.

Montreal Correspondence.

(From our own Correspondent).

Montreal, March 1, 1869.

ite to you a day in advance of my usual : the mails are so uncertain, the train from ity which. left on Saturday morning not arrived, and the English mail from Port- hich arrived there on Friday is not expected me time to-morrow. From this you can e the state of blockade we are in; the r roads are impassable. This state of isola- as caused a dullness in every branch of and as there seems no prospect of an im- ient for some days to come, we must look i to continued dullness. There is some town of getting up a new branch of Com- viz., shipping ice to the East and West The idea is very feasible. At Longueil ce warehouses could be erected at slight s site of the old Grand Trunk sheds could cheap, and the wharf could be put in repair iderate rate; the water is deep enough to ssels of moderate tonnage, such as would ired for the trade, and the ice is on this ly requiring cutting and warehousing. The n then arises why should not Canada be compete in this business with Boston, has to draw her supplies from inland lakes which are over 70 miles distant.

OCK.—I have to report an exceedingly narket and prices purely nominal. Not- nding the stoppage of trains the supply is fully ample for our own local wants, the European markets are dull, and it is a own fact that should a favorable turn take t them, there is plenty of stuff ready for at at the leading exporting ports. The y naturally is to a feeling of quietness. idity of telegraphic reports between this nt and the Old World has had the effect ing the markets of America and Europe on is, and operators know their chances almost ively as between this and your city. ovisions there has been a falling off in the pork, and dressed hogs would not bring 0.25 for heavy weights. I cannot account decline as the stocks in the country are vy and prices in the West are firm. Cattle ot sold briskly as the butchers are fairly

supplied. For butter a fair inquiry has recently sprung up; for the States and extra qualities have been picked up at full rates, the stock here is light. Lard is very active and scarce.

GROCERIES.—The only movement of conse- quence in the market is in Sugars and Molasses; a steady advance has occurred in raw and refined Sugars and also in Molasses. Cuba Sugar is held at 10½c, Barbadoes 10½c., Porto Rico 10¾ to 11c., and holders are not anxious sellers, at these rates. For Molasses, Centrifugal have reached 32½ to 35c. Clayed 35 to 37½c. The market closes firm at ex- treme rates. Tobacco, Montreal manufactured, is in good demand, and our manufactories are fully employed. Teas and other staples are very quiet.

IRON AND HARDWARE.—Business is dull, owing chiefly to the blocking up of the country roads. There is no change in prices, with the exception of Tin Plates, which have advanced fully 50c. per box; this is owing to the rise in England.

Toronto Market.

There is little change in the state of the market since last week. A fair business is being done in Groceries at steady prices. In Dry Goods, Boots and Shoes, etc., preparations are being made for the spring trade.

PETROLEUM.—We are glad to learn that there is some inquiry from Germany for Canadian oil. It is expected that a considerable export trade with Europe will ensue.

GRAIN.—Wheat — Receipts by cars, 14,940 bush., and 26,000 bush. last week. The market continues dull. Spring is steady, holders asking 96c to 97c ; very little offering, and no late sales. Fall is dull, and offering at 98c to $1.00, but there is little demand ; a few cars sold during the week at 98c to $1.00. Barley—Receipts, 624 bush., and 2,000 bush. last week. There are a number of small lots offering at $1.31 to $1.33, and on the street the latter p.ice was paid. Pease—Receipts light ; on the street, 80c to 83c is paid, and these figures are asked for car-loads, but the demand is slack, and the general quality inferior ; no sales. Oats—Receipts 2,600 bush., and 600 bush. last week. The market is dull ; car-loads are offering at 50c to 51c, with little enquiry. Seeds—Timothy is quiet at $2.25 to $2.50 ; Clover is selling in small lots at $6.85 to $7.10 for good to prime seed ; Flax $2. White Beans—A considerable business has been done in car-loads within a recent period ; they are now worth $1.75 to $2.15 per bushel.

FLOUR.—Receipts, 2,200 barrels, and 2,389 last week. Some business was done in No. 1 Superfine at $4.00 to $4;10, the market closing with sellers at $4.10, and buyers of round lots at $4.00. Sales : 100 barrels at $4.10 in store ; 100 barrels at same price, free of winter storage ; 200 barrels at $4.05 in store ; 200 barrels at $4.00 at a point west ; and 100 barrels at $4.00 free in cars. Extra—Very little doing ; a lot of 500 bar- rels reported sold on p.t., supposed to be about $4.50. Nothing doing in other grades. Oat- meal—There are buyers of 100 barrel lots at $5.60; no sellers.

FREIGHTS.—Rates by Grand Trunk Railway:— Flour to all stations from Belleville to Lynn, in- clusive, 35c., grain per 100 lbs. 18c ; flour to Brockville and Cornwall, inclusive, 43c. grain 22c. flour to Montreal 50c. grain 25c. ; flour to all stations between Island Pond and Portland, in- clusive, 85c. grain 43c. ; flour to Boston 90c. gold, grain 45c.; flour to Halifax $1.10, grain 55c; flour to St. John $1.02. Boxed Meats to Liverpool per gross ton 80s. ; lard or butter in tinnets 85s. ; Pork 11s. per tierce ; flour 5s. 6d. per barrel ; grain 12s. per 480 pounds. Rates by Great Western Railway—Flour, Toronto to Sus- pension Bridge 25c. gold ; thence to New York, 92c. U. S. currency per bbl. ; to Boston $1.02. Grain to Bridge 18c., gold; thence to New York 47c, U. S. currency; to Boston 51c. Grain, To- ronto to Detroit, 18c. ber 100 lbs; flour 35c per bbl.

Trade of Montreal.

The following is a summary of the import and export trade of Montreal in 1868:

Total value of imports to Dec. 31,
1868 .... $22,919,197
Total value of imports to Dec. 31,
1867 28,378,117

Decrease $5,458,920

This decrease is caused more by the falling off in the value than any decrease in the quantities. The same holds good of the customs' duties, which were :

1864..........$3,963,992 1867.........$4,318,875
1865.......... 3,378,686 1868.......... 3,540,604
1866............ 4,646,783

Showing a falling off of nearly one million dollars in the face of these shew a considerable increase.

In the export trade the Custom House returns in the face of these shew a considerable increase, being :

Exports 1st Jan. to 31st Dec., 1868...$10,898,554
Exports 1st Jan. to 31st Dec., 1867... 15,444,745

Increase $1,453,809

But this excess disappears when we deduct the great increase in the amount of silver exported, which was in

1868 .... $2,339,260
1867 91,767

Increase $2,247,493

Deducting this specie from. the whole exporta- tion of 1868, we have a falling off in merchandise of $793,684. The chief falling off is in wheat, which is $650,000. There is also a falling off in the exportation of barley, oats and peas, and a further cause is to be found in the depreciated value of flour and oatmeal, to the extent of nearly $1,500,000. On the other hand there has been a considerable increase in minerals, live stock and manufactures :

1868—Minerals $239,988
1867—Minerals 95,686

Increase $144,301
1868—Fish $84,085
1867—Fish 15,831

Increase $68,254
1868—Horses, butter, pork, etc....... $4,218,518
1867—Horses, butter, pork, etc....... 2,858,830

Increase $1,269,688
1868—Manufactures $756,273
1867—Manufactures 499,405

Increase $256,868

The Petroleum Trade.

The Titusville Herald, in its review of the oil business for the month of January, says, touching

The Production.—"The mild weather that pre- vailed during nearly the whole of the period under review, allowing the whole to be worked almost as in the summer season, and the finding of seve- ral moderately productive wells, have had the effect of slightly enlarging the production. The average daily yield for the month was 10,192 barrels of 43 gallons each, an increase of about 450 barrels per day from the average for December. But very little addition was made to the product by the starting up of old or abandoned wells or small producing capacities, and from torpedoing and other means of resuscitating wells, the in- crease was on the whole comparatively inconsider- able. Near the confluence of Lower Cherry Run with Oil Creek, on Charley run, near Oil City, on Bull Run and in the Pleasantville district, eight wells were struck, the yields of which ranged from 50 to 125 barrels per day. Other wells, with less important producing capacities, were found in different parts of the region. From the last named district the shipments to Titusville, Pithole and Miller by two pipe transportation lines and to Titusville by teams during the month, reached an aggregate of 76,000 barrels, but as the stock at the wells was reduced 9,000 barrels, the total product for the month was 67,000 barrels—an average for 31 days of 2,161 barrels. The production of Church Run and the wells in the immediate vicinity by the receipts by pipe line and teams at Titusville, and the difference in stocks, reached an average of 500 barrels per day for the month.

"The following table shows the total production for January, and the average per day :

Total shipment of crude for January of barrels,		
of 43 galls each......................brls.	292,965	
Add to reduce to brls. of 43 gals. each...... "	13,626	
		306,591
Total shipment of brls. of 43 galls. each....... "		
Stock on hand, January 1st........brls. 364,865		
Stock on hand, February 1st........ " 274,167		
		9,362
Total production during January ....brls.	315,953	
Average per day for 31 days ....brls.	10,192	

"The Development and the Territory.—The development has not been attended by the finding of new deposits of petroleum, nor have any large producing wells been struck, but yet it is considered satisfactory, as a large proportion of the wells completed produce in paying quantities, and very valuable additions have been made to the territory on the outskirts of the districts that were producing at and previous to the publication of our last report. The total number of wells completed during the month was about 53, of which 35 were located in Pleasantville District, one at Tidioute, and of the remaining 17 most were located along Oil Creek, at Shamburg and near Oil City—only three having been completed along the River of Reno. Of the 53 wells completed, fully 42 and possibly more, from all appearances, proved pecuniarily successful. The most important feature connected with the development, is the large decrease in the number of wells being drilled. The total number on February 1st was 341, against 373 on the 1st of the previous month —decrease of 32. This decrease was caused principally by a large number of wells being completed, as 21 new wells were commenced during the month. The territory in the vicinity of Church Run, which was scarcely thought of for a year previous to January 1st, is again attracting attention, and several farms in its vicinity have been secured and leases have been given on them. In all other productive parts of the region the demand for territory is good, but this is particularly the case in regard to certain tracts at the northern and southern termini of the Pleasantville District, on Lower Cherry Run, on Charley Run, and at Parker's Landing on the Allegheny River. At the latter place we learn that operations have been commenced on ten leases, and six or seven wells are being drilled. The largest yield from one well is 25 barrels per day. This district is about fifty miles south of Titusville."

Halifax Market.

BREADSTUFFS.—Feb. 16—We have to report a continued dullness in Flours for the past week.— The demand which is entirely for the better description of supers is a small local one and quotations are purely nominal, lower prices having been accepted. We quote white wheat extra (fall) $7.25 ; fancy $6.50 to $6.60 ; bakers' strong $6.30 to $6.40 ; super. $5.90 to $6.00 ; No. 2 $5.00 to $5.50 ; middlings $4.25 to $4.50 ; Pollard's $4.25 to $4.35. Rye $5.00. Oatmeal $7.50 to $7.60. Cornmeal K. D. $4.25 to $4.40 ; F. G. $4.10 to $4.25.

PROVISIONS.—Pork is held at higher figures without enquiry. At auction yesterday P. E. I. realized $21.00 to $18.00 cash, for mess and prime respectively ; the lots were rather indifferent.

WEST INDIA PRODUCE.—Sugars are in request at higher rates with small receipts. Molasses inactive at former quotations. Rum tends downwards, 55c. has been accepted for round lots of

Demerara. Coffee continues dull. Sugar V. P. 9¾c. ; Porto Rico 8¼ to 8¾c ; Cuba 8¼c ; Barbadoes 8¼s ; Coffee—Jamaica 13 to 15c ; St. Domingo 10 to 12c.

FISH AND OIL.—Are still active and improved. We quote :—Codfish (large shore) $4.50 to $5.00 ; small $3.60 to $3.70 ; Mackarel No. 1 (L.) $18.00 ; No. 2 (L.) $15.00 ; No. 3 $11.00. Herring, shore (split) $4.50 ; round $3.25 to $3.50.

Driving Away Commerce.

How excessive taxation results in the reverse of that contemplated is being realized in England. The establishment of lines of steamers between Havre and the United States has had the effect of depriving sailing vessels, which carry American products to France, of return cargoes; and the custom has been to cross the Channel to a British port, chiefly Newport and Cardiff, for return cargoes, generally of railroad iron and coal. It has been found, however, that the expense of shipping these cargoes owing to the heavy British port charges, pilotage, light dues, brokerage, &c., is so onerous as, added to the expense at the French port of discharge, to eat up the profit on the return freight. To remedy this, one or two British companies at Havre are procuring from England cargoes of iron for transhipment to vessels wanting freight to the States. Two steamers lately arrived at Havre with cargoes of rails for the American ships "Halcyon" and "Lady Blessington," both bound to New Orleans, and others were expected to follow shortly. If the undertaking succeeds—and there is a good prospect for it—Havre will become the depot for British goods destined for American and other ports, and vessels that hitherto resorted to the United Kingdom for return freights will procure them at Havre instead. This new phase in the British carrying trade is not at all relished by the business people at the places so seriously affected, and they loudly denounce a suicidal policy, which induces British subjects to assist in extending the trade of foreign ports at the expense of their own—a policy which British shipowners have so long and loudly complained of. If produce can be taken from England to Havre, and then transhipped to a foreign port on better terms for the ship than when shipped in England, it shows that the maritime laws of the latter country are behind the age, and the fact contains a warning which British lawmakers will do well not to neglect, if they desire the prosperity of such an important industry.

INTERCOLONIAL RAILWAY.

THE Commissioners appointed to construct the Intercolonial Railway give notice that they are now prepared to receive TENDERS for THREE FURTHER SECTIONS of the line.

Section No. 5 will be in the Province of Quebec and will extend from forty miles East of Rivière du Loup, at the end of Contract No. 2, to the Sixty-sixth Mile Post, near Rimouski, a distance of about Twenty-six miles.

Section No. 6 will be in the Province of New Brunswick, and will extend from the Easterly end of Contract No. 3, opposite Dalhousie to the West side of the Main Post Road near the 46th Mile Post, Easterly from Jacquet River, about Twenty-one miles.

Section No. 7 will be in the Province of Nova Scotia and will extend from the Southerly end of Contract No. 4, near River Phillip, to Station Fifty at Folly Lake, about Twenty-four miles.

Plans and profiles with specifications and plans of contract will be exhibited at the office of the Board of Works, Toronto, and at the offices of the Commissioners at Ottawa, Rimouski, Dalhousie, St. John, and Halifax, on and after the FIFTH day of March, 1869, and SEALED TENDERS addressed to the Commissioners of the Intercolonial Railway, and marked "Tender," will be received at their office in Ottawa up to SEVEN o'clock, p. m., on the TWENTY-NINTH day of MARCH, 1869.

A. WALSH,
ED. B CHANDLER,
C. J. BRYDGES,
W. F. COFFIN,
Commissioners.

Intercolonial Railway Office,
Ottawa, 11th February, 1869.

Philip Browne & Co.,
BANKERS AND STOCK BROKERS.
DEALERS IN
STERLING EXCHANGE—U.S. Currency, Silver and
Bonds—Bank Stocks, Debentures, Mortgages, &c.
...ts on New York issued, in Gold and Currency.
...mpt attention given to collections. Advances made
securities.
No. 67 Yonge Street, Toronto
...RS Browne.   Philip Browne, Notary Public.

**Canada Permanent Building and Savings
Society.**
Paid up Capital $1,000,000
Assets 1,700,000
...nnual Income 400,000

Directors:—Joseph D. Ridout, President.
Peter Paterson, Vice-President.
...G. Worts, Edward Hooper, S. Nordheimer, W. C.
Chewett, E. H. Rutherford, Joseph Robinson.
...kers:—Bank of Toronto; Bank of Montreal; Royal
Canadian Bank.
OFFICE—Masonic Hall, Toronto Street, Toronto.
...ne, Received on Deposit bearing five and six per
cent. interest.
...ances made on City and Country Property in the Provin
of Ontario.
J. HERBERT MASON,
Sec'y & Treas

Pellatt & Osler,
STOCK AND EXCHANGE BROKERS, Accountants,
Agents for the Standard Life Assurance Company.
OFFICE—86 King Street East, four Doors West of
Church Street, Toronto.
HENRY PELLATT,   EDMUND B. OSLER,
...y, Notary Public.   Official Assignee.

The St. Lawrence Glass Company
ARE now manufacturing and have for sale,

COAL OIL LAMPS,
various styles and sizes.
LAMP CHIMNEYS,
of extra quality for ordinary Burners also,
for the 'Comet' and 'Sun' Burners.
SETS OF
TABLE GLASSWARE, HYACINTH GLASSES,
STEAM GUAGE TUBES, GLASS RODS, &c.,
any other article made to order, in White or Color
Glass.
KEROSENE BURNERS, COLLARS and SOCKETS, will
be kept on hand.
DRUGGISTS' FLINT GLASSWARE, and
PHILOSOPHICAL INSTRUMENTS,
made to order.
OFFICE—388 ST. PAUL STREET, MONTREAL.
A. McK. COCHRANE,
Secretary.

Candee & Co.,
BANKERS AND BROKERS, dealers in Gold and Silver
Coin, Government Securities, &c., Corner Main and
...hange Streets Buffalo, Y. N.   21-1v.

W. McLaren & Co.,
WHOLESALE
BOOT AND SHOE MANUFACTURERS,
18 St. Maurice Street,
MONTREAL.
...ne, 1868.   42-1y

Lyman & McNab,
Importers of, and Wholesale Dealers in,
HEAVY AND SHELF HARDWARE,
King Street,
TORONTO, ONTARIO.

THE QUEEN'S HOTEL.

THOMAS DICK, Proprietor.
...ONT STREET,   -   -   -   TORONTO, ONT
3-1y

STATEMENT OF BANKS

ACTING UNDER CHARTER, FOR THE MONTH ENDING 31st JANUARY, 1869, ACCORDING TO RETURNS FURNISHED BY THE BANKS TO THE AUDITOR OF PUBLIC ACCOUNTS.

NAME OF BANK	CAPITAL Capital authorized by Act	Capital paid up	LIABILITIES Promissory Notes in circulation not bearing interest	Balances due to other Banks	Cash Deposits not bearing interest	Cash Deposits bearing interest	TOTAL LIABILITIES	ASSETS Coin, Bullion, Provincial Notes	Landed or other Property of the Bank	Government Securities	Promissory Notes, and Bills of other Banks	Balances due from other Banks	Notes and Bills Discounted	Other Debts due to the Bank not included under foregoing heads	TOTAL ASSETS
ONTARIO AND QUEBEC															
Montreal															
Quebec															
City															
Gore															
British North America															
Banque du Peuple															
Niagara District															
Molson's															
Toronto															
Ontario															
Eastern Townships															
Banque Nationale															
Banque Jacques Cartier															
Merchants'															
Royal Canadian															
Union St. Low. Canada															
Mechanics'															
Bank of Commerce															
NOVA SCOTIA															
Bank of Yarmouth															
Merchants' Bank															
People's Bank															
Union Bank															
Bank of Nova Scotia															
NEW BRUNSWICK															
Bank of New Brunswick															
Commercial Bank															
St. Stephen's Bank															
People's Bank															
Totals															

Mercantile.

TORONTO PRICES CURRENT.—MARCH 4, 1869.

Name of Article	Wholesale Rates	
Boots and Shoes.	$ c.	$ c.
Mens' Thick Boots	2 50	2 50
" Kip	2 50	3 00
" Calf	3 00	3 70
" Congress Gaiters	2 00	2 50
" Kip Cobourgs	1 15	1 45
Boys' Thick Boots	1 70	1 95
Youths' "	1 40	1 50
Women's Butts	0 95	1 30
" Balmoral	1 20	1 50
" Congress Gaiters	1 15	1 45
Misses' Butts	0 75	1 00
" Balmoral	1 10	1 20
" Congress Gaiters	1 00	1 30
Girls' Butts	0 65	0 85
" Balmoral	0 90	1 05
" Congress Gaiters	0 80	1 10
Children's C. T. Cnxks	0 60	0 65
" Gaiters	0 65	0 90
Drugs.		
Aloes Cape	0 12½	0 18
Alum	0 02½	0 03
Borax	0 00	0 00
Camphor, refined	0 65	0 70
Castor Oil	0 16½	0 28
Caustic Soda	0 04½	0 05
Cochineal	0 90	1 00
Cream Tartar	0 40	0 45
Epsom Salts	0 03	0 04
Extract Logwood	0 11	0 12
Gum Arabic, sorts	0 30	0 35
Indigo, Madras	0 90	1 00
Licorice	0 14	0 45
Madder	0 00	0 18
Galls	0 32	0 37
Opium	12 00	13 50
Oxalic Acid	0 25	0 35
Potash, Bi-tart	0 25	0 28
" Bichromate	0 15	0 20
Potass Iodide	3 90	4 50
Senna	0 12½	0 00
Soda Ash	0 02½	0 04
Soda Bicarb	4 50	5 00
Tartaric Acid	0 40	0 45
Verdigris	0 35	0 40
Vitriol, Blue	0 08	0 10
Groceries.		
Coffees:		
Java, ℔ lb	0 22½	0 24
Laguayra	0 17	0 18
Rio	0 15	0 17
Fish:		
Herrings, Lab. split	5 75	6 50
" round	0 00	0 00
" scaled	0 35	0 40
Mackerel, small kitts	1 00	0 00
Loch. Her. wh'e'firks	2 50	2 75
" half	1 25	1 50
White Fish & Trout	0 00	0 00
Salmon, saltwater	14 00	15 00
Dry Cod, ℔ 112 ℔s	5 00	5 25
Fruit:		
Raisins, Layers	2 60	2 10
" M. R.	1 90	2 00
" Valentiasnew	0 07	0 7½
Currants, new	0 5½	0 06
	0 04	0 04½
Figs	0 14	0 00
Molasses:		
Clayed, ℔ gal	0 00	0 35
Syrups, Standard	0 60	0 00
" Golden	0 62	0 65
Rice:		
Arracan	4 25	4 50
Spices:		
Cassia, whole, ℔ ℔	0 00	0 45
Cloves	0 11	0 12
Nutmegs	0 45	0 55
Ginger, ground	0 20	0 25
" Jamaica, root	0 29	0 25
Pepper, black	0 08	0 09
Pimento	0 08	0 09
Sugars:		
Port Rico, ℔ lb	0 10½	0 11
Cuba	0 10½	0 11
Barbadoes (bright)	0 10½	0 11
Canada Sugar Refine'y,		
Yellow No. 2, 60 ds	0 10½	0 11
Yellow, No. 2½	0 11	0 11½
No. 3	0 11½	0 11½
Crushed X	0 13	0 13½
A	0 13	0 13½
Ground	0 13½	0 14
Dry Crushed	0 14½	0 14½
Extra Ground	0 15½	0 15½
Teas:		
Japan com'n to good	0 48	0 55
" Fine to choicest	0 00	0 00
Colored, com. to fine	0 60	0 75
Congou & Souch'ng	0 42	0 75
Oolong, good to fine	0 00	0 65
Y. Hyson, com to gd	0 45	0 55
Medium to choice	0 65	0 80
Extra choice	0 85	0 9

Name of Article	Wholesale Rate	
Groceries—Continued.	$ c.	$ c.
Gunpowd'r c. to med	0 55	0 70
" med. to fine	0 70	0 85
" fine to fin'st	0 85	0 95
Hyson	0 45	0 80
Imperial	0 42	0 80
Tobacco, Nransfuet'd:		
Can Leaf, ℔ ℔. &s 10s	0 26	0 30
Western Leaf, com	0 25	0 30
" Good	0 27	0 32
" Fine	0 3½	0 35
" Bright fine	0 40	0 50
" choice	0 60	0 75
Hardware.		
Tin (net cash prices)		
Block, ℔ ℔	0 25	0 26
Grain	0 25	0 26
Copper:		
Pig	0 23	0 24
Sheet	0 30	0 33
Cut Nails:		
Assorted ½ Shingles,		
" 100 ℔	2 90	3 00
Shingle alone do	3 15	3 25
Lathe and 5 dy	3 30	3 40
Galvanized Iron:		
Assorted sizes	0 08	0 09
Best No. 24	0 00	0 00
" 26	0 08	0 08½
" 28	0 09	0 09½
Horse Nails:		
Guest's or Griffin's		
assorted sizes	0 00	0 00
For W. ass'd sizes	0 18	0 19
Patent Hammer'd do	0 17	0 18
Iron (at 4 months):		
Pig—Gartsherrie No1	24 00	25 00
Other brands No1	22 00	24 00
" No2	0 00	0 00
Bar—Scotch, ℔ 100 ℔	2 25	2 60
Refined	3 00	3 25
Swedes	5 00	5 50
Hoops—Coopers	3 00	3 25
Band	3 00	3 25
Boiler Plates	3 25	3 60
Canada Plates	3 75	4 00
Union dack	0 00	0 00
Pontypool	3 25	4 00
Swansea	3 90	4 00
Lead (at 4 months):		
Bar, ℔ 100 ℔s	0 06½	0 07
Sheet "	0 08	0 09
Shot	0 07½	0 07½
Iron Wire (net cash):		
No. 6, ℔ bundle	2 70	2 80
" 9, "	3 10	3 20
" 12, "	3 40	3 50
" 16, "	4 30	4 40
Powder:		
Blasting, Canada	2 50	0 00
FF "	5 25	4 50
FFF "	4 75	5 00
Blasting, English	4 00	5 00
FF loose	5 00	6 00
FFF "	5 00	6 50
Pressed Spikes (4 mos):		
Regular sizes 100	4 00	4 25
Extra	4 50	5 00
Tin Plates (net cash):		
IC Coke	7 50	8 50
IC Charcoal	8 25	3 50
IX	12 25	13 75
IXX "	12 25	0 00
DC "	7 25	9 40
DX "	9 50	0 00
Hides & Skins, ℔ lb.		
Green rough	0 06½	0 07½
Green, salt'd & insp'd	0 07½	0 08
Cured	0 00	0 00
Calfskins, green	0 00	0 10
Calfskins, cured	0 00	0 12
" dry	0 18	0 20
Sheepskins	1 00	1 40
" country	1 00	1 40
Hops.		
Inferior, ℔ ℔	0 05	0 07
Medium, "	0 07	0 09
Good "	0 09	0 12
Fancy "	0 00	0 00
Leathers @ (4 mos.)		
In lots of less than		
50 sides, 10 ℔ cent		
higher.		
Spanish Sole, 1st qual'y		
heavy, weights ℔ ℔	0 22	0 23
Do.1st qual middle do	0 21	0 22
Do. No. 2, light weights	0 20	0 21
Slaughter heavy	0 26	0 27
Do. light	0 00	0 00
Harness, ℔ ℔	0 32	0 34
" No. 2	0 30	0 33
Upper heavy	0 36	0 38
" light	0 40	0 42

Name of Article	Wholes Rates	
Leather—Contin'd.	$ c.	$
Kip Skins, Patna	0 46	0
French	0 70	0
English	0 65	0
Hemlock Calf (30 to		
35 ℔s.) per doz	0 75	0
Do. light	0 45	0
French Calf	1 05	1
Grain & Satn Ch'b'doz	0 00	0
Splits, large ℔ ℔	0 30	0
" small	0 20	0
Enamelled Cow ℔ foot	0 20	0
Patent	0 20	0
Pebble Grain	0 17	0
Buff	0 17	0
Oils.		
Cod	0 00	0
Lard, extra	0 60	0
" No. 1	0 00	0
" Woollen	0 00	0
Lubricating, patent	0 00	0
" Mott's economist	0 5o	0
Linseed, raw	0 74	0
" boiled	0 81	0
Machinery	0 00	0
Olive, common, ℔ gal	1 00	1
" salad	1 50	2
" salad, in bots.		
qt. ℔ case	3 60	3
Sesame salad, ℔ gal	1 60	1
Seal, pale	0 75	0
Spirits Turpentine	0 58½	0
Varnish	0 00	0
Whale	0 00	0
Paints, &c.		
White Lead, genuine		
in Oil, ℔ 25℔s	0 00	2
Do. No. 1	0 00	2
" 2	0 00	1
" 3	0 00	0
White Zinc, genuine	3 60	3
White Lead, dry	0 05½	0
Red Lead	0 07½	0
Venetian Red, Eng'h	0 02½	0
Yellow Ochre, Fren'h	0 02½	0
Whiting	0 85	1
Petroleum.		
(Refined ℔ gal.)		
Water white, car'd	0 00	0
" small lots	0 37	0
Straw, by car load	0 33	0
" small lots	0 35	0
Amber, by car load	0 00	0
" small lots	0 00	0
Benzine	0 00	0
Produce.		
Grain:		
Wheat, Spring, 60 ℔	0 95	0
" Fall 60 "	0 99	1
Barley 48 "	1 30	1
Peas 60 "	0 75	0
Oats 34 "	0 51	0
Rye 56 "	0 70	0
Seeds:		
Clover, choice 60 "	6 50	6
com'n 08 "	6 25	6
Timothy, cho's 4 "	2 50	2
" inf. to good 48 "	2 24	2
Flax 56 "	2 60	2
Flour (per brl.):		
Superior extra	4 00	5
Extra superfine	4 60	4
Fancy superfine	4 25	4
Superfine No. 1	4 00	4
No. 2	5 90	6
Oatmeal, (per brl.)	5 90	6
Provisions		
Butter, dairy tub ℔ ℔	0 23	0
" store packed	0 19	0
Cheese, new	0 13	0
Pork, mess, per brl	26 00	27
" prime mess		
" prime		
Bacon, rough	0 19	0
" Cumberl'd cut	0 11	0
" smoked	0 00	0
Hams, in salt	0 12	0
" aug.cur &canv'd		
Shoulders, in salt	0 10	0
Lard, in kegs	0 16	0
Eggs, packed	0 16	0
Beef Hams	0 00	0
Tallow	0 00	0
Hogs dressed, heavy	8 50	9
" medium	8 00	8
" light	7 50	8
Salt, &c.		
American bris	1 5o	1
Liverpool coarse	1 25	1
Plaster	1 05	1
Water Lime	1 50	0

& Candles.

	$ c. $ c	Brandy:	$ c. $ c
wford & Co.'s ..		Hennessy's, per gal..	2 30 3 50
iperial.	0 07½ 0 08	Martell's	2 30 2 50
olden Bar	0 07 0 07½	J. Robin & Co.'s "	2 25 2 35
lver Bar	0 07 0 07½	Otard, Dupuy & Cos.	2 25 2 35
.	0 05 0 05½	Brandy, cases.	3 50 9 00
..	0 08½ 0 08½	Brandy, com. per c.	4 00 4 50
..	0 09 0 11½	Whiskey:	

STOCK AND BOND REPORT.

The dates of our quotations are as follows:—Toronto, March 3 ; Montreal, March 1 ; Quebec, March 1 ; London, Jan. 28.

(table content illegible)

INSURANCE COMPANIES.

ENGLISH.—Quotations on the London Market.

RAILWAYS.

EXCHANGE.

THE CANADIAN
MONETARY TIMES
AND
INSURANCE CHRONICLE.
DEVOTED TO FINANCE, COMMERCE, INSURANCE, BANKS, RAILWAYS, NAVIGATION, MINES, INVESTMENT,
PUBLIC COMPANIES, AND JOINT STOCK ENTERPRISE.

L. II—NO. 30.   TORONTO, THURSDAY, MARCH 11, 1869.   { SUBSCRIPTIONS $2 YEAR.

Mercantile.

Meetings.

BEAVER MUTUAL FIRE INSURANCE ASSOCIATION.

The annual general meeting of the members of this Association was held at the office, 20 Toronto street, on Tuesday, February 9, 1869. The chair was taken by R. L. Denison, Esq., and after the usual routine business, the annual report of the Board of Directors was read by the Secretary, as follows:

Annual Report.

The Board of Directors have much pleasure in laying before the members their usual annual statement of the affairs of this Association, for the year ending November 30, 1868, of which the following is a condensed summary:

Cash receipts	$30,959 74
Cash payments	$32,673 59
No. of policies issued during year	6,283
Am't of property covered thereby	$3,931,030 00
Number of policies expired and cancelled	3,561 00
Total number of policies in force November 30, 1868	13,579 00
Total amount of property covered thereby	$9,559,710 00
Number of policies on premium note system	8,175 00
Number of policies on cash system	5,404 00
Average amount covered by each policy	$704 00
Amount of premium notes at same date liable to assessment	$91,681 10
Fire claims (settled and unsettled) during year	$14,918 17

For further details reference may be made to the Treasurer's accounts and Inspector's report, both appended hereto.

The above figures show a gain of 2,183 policies over the number reported last year, with an increase in premium notes of $11,496 62, which facts, taken together, are of great value, as indicating a healthy business, and proving the continued popularity of the Association.

That the receipts from premiums have not increased in a like degree, is due to a reduction in first payments on premium notes, which your Board ordered last spring, their object being to encourage the premium note system, and thus check the too rapid increase of cash policies. They look upon the cash system, when not confined within narrow limits, as defective in principle and unsafe in practice. While some other Mutual Companies seem to be running the cash system altogether, your Board have taken a different course; and they recommend their successors to give a trial, in preference, to the "cash mutual" system, now common in the neighboring States, under which the applicant for insurance pays down a sum sufficient to cover costs of insurance, and to leave also a margin for profits, which profits are either repaid him at the end of the term or credited on his renewal premium when the insurance is continued.

It will be seen that owing to the long summer drought our losses were heavy in July and August, to which must be added a large number of additional claims reported since the close of the financial year, and not included in the present report.

Your Board, much to their regret, have found it necessary in consequence to call in a special assessment of one-sixth of all premium notes for policies in force 1st January, 1869, in order to provide in due course for payment of our indebtedness. It is hoped that the current year may prove more auspicious in respect to losses by fire.

A further draft upon last year's income has arisen from the circumstance that we have paid all agents' commissions in full, instead of deferring part payment until another year, as has been the general practice with Mutual Companies. Your Board consider it better to charge all liabilities in the accounts of the year to which they belong.

In obedience to the vote of last annual meeting your Board requested the President to subscribe for one hundred shares of $40 each, in the guarantee stock of the Toronto Mutual Fire Insurance Company, on which the sum of $3,000 has been paid as called for. This investment forms a set-off to the amount received on our own guarantee stock, and provides for the interest payable thereon.

Notwithstanding so many unusual calls upon our funds, the net assets of the Association show a marked improvement as compared with last year, and a balance of no less than $58,000, which forms a reserve fund abundantly sufficient to satisfy the most critical judgment, as to the responsibility and permanency of this Association.

Your Board have under discussion the very important question of an union between this Association and the Company above named—the Toronto Mutual Insurance Company—which devotes itself to the insurance of town and village property chiefly, and they understand that the Board of Directors of that body are ready to meet us thereon. It is proposed to carry on the business of the two offices under one Board, each continuing to exist as a separate branch; and that all accounts, assets and liabilities shall be kept distinct as at present. The chief end to be gained will be economy, which such union will assuredly facilitate; the saving in advertising, printing, stationery, Directors' fees, etc., cannot but be considerable; and financially we may expect to gain strength enough to place us above all ordinary trials, and out of danger of injury from fair business competition. The two companies united would possess not less than $160,000 of premium note capital, and ought to occupy a high position among the Insurance Companies of the Dominion.

Your Board take this occasion to call attention to the case of certain parties, who have put in claims for payment of losses by fire, although they had neglected to give the notice required by law of the existence of encumbrances on their property, created either before or after the date of their application for insurance. Your Board being unwilling to enforce the law too rigidly, have laid it down as a rule in cases where no fraud was apparently intended, to allow one-half of such claim rather than reject them altogether. This liberality has been misunderstood in some localities, parties holding that either the whole claim or none at all ought to be paid. Your Board would suggest, therefore, that in future such claims be paid in exact proportion to the insurable interest of the policy holder in the property insured. That is to say, if the property proves to be encumbered to one-half its value without notice to the Association, then the insured shall receive one-half his claim. If mortgaged to its whole value, he shall receive none at all, and so on; and that if necessary an arbitration be held on the spot to ascertain the true insurable interest of the insured in the property destroyed. A case of this class, which arose in the neighborhood of Barrie, was tried at the Assizes there last year. The plaintiff, who was non-suited on a legal point, had accumulated mortgages on his farm to more than its full value, and even his cattle, grain, etc., were overburthened with chattel mortgages. The property was destroyed by fire under suspicious circumstances, no doubt by an incendiary. Your Board refused payment on several grounds, but mainly because no notice had been given of the excessive encumbrance; because the man had really parted with his interest in the property, both building and stock; and because he had obtained his policy by deceit, after having had a former policy in this Association, on the same property, cancelled for not giving notice of encumbrance and other reasons. It may be well to mention that this is only the third suit brought against this Association since it begun to insure farm property seven years ago, a pretty good proof that the Directors have been influenced by no litigious spirit in settling fire claims.

As a step in the direction of economy, it is recommended that the number of Directors be reduced to 12 instead of 15 as at present. Five directors retire by rotation, namely, Messrs. Blake, Chadwick, Campbell, Collins and Sutherland. One of these, David Campbell, Esq., of Almonte, has recently been removed by death; the others are of course eligible for re-election. Should the number be reduced as above proposed, there will be but two vacancies to be filled, as also one occasioned by the appointment of W. Henderson, Esq., a member of this Board, to the office of Fire Inspector, thus making three vacancies in all. It will be your duty also to appoint suitable persons as Honorary Directors.

All which is respectfully submitted.

R. L. DENISON,
President.

S. THOMPSON,
Managing Director.

February 8, 1869.

The Treasurer's statements, Auditors' report, and Fire Inspector's report were also read.

The Chairman moved the adoption of the report, which, after some discussion, was carried.

A resolution was then carried, giving the Board of Directors full power to carry out an union of this Association with the Toronto Mutual Fire Insurance Company, and to prepare a petition to Parliament, and a Bill to carry out the same.

It was ordered that 14,000 copies of the report be printed for the use of members and other policy holders.

Messrs. Blake, Chadwick and Collins were re-elected Directors.

Messrs. Holland and Pellatt were re-appointed as Auditors, and the following gentlemen were elected Honorary Directors of the Association: W. H. Berry, March; Thomas Bowles, Reeve, Chinguacousy; Hon. George Bryson, M. L. C., Pontiac; James Dryden, Whitby; William Edwards, Clarence; T. Higginson, West Hawkesbury; H. S. Howland, York; Thomas McConkey, M. P., Barrie; J. McDermott, Reeve of Wallace; Hon. J. Simpson, Senator, Bowmanville; Alfred O. Stephens, Tecumseh.

After votes of thanks to the President and other officers, the meeting separated.

The Board of Directors held a meeting immediately afterwards, when Charles E. Chadwick, Esq., of Ingersoll, was elected President, and David Thurston, Esq., of Toronto, Vice-President of the Association.

Statement of Receipts and Expenditure for the year ending November 30, 1868.

RECEIPTS.

To balance of cash in hand and in bank		$5,177 56
Cash received—		
Premium notes and assessments	$20,010 62	
Cash premiums	7,709 92	
Live stock	357 66	
Arrears	370 35	
		28,448 55
Reinsurances		45 45
Bills payable		2,465 74
		$38,137 30

EXPENDITURE.

Guarantee fund, instalments repaid		$200 00
Fire claims		13,114 62
Deposits repaid		756 29
Toronto M. F. Ins. Co. guarantee stock		3,000 00
Bills receivable		1,197 89
Returned Premiums		104 91
Expenses—		
Travelling expenses	$759 16	
Auditing accounts	100 00	
Rent and taxes	205 00	
Postage	577 57	
Petty expenses	161 79	
Advertising, printing and stationery	350 47	
Writing policies, etc.	173 19	
Legal and detective expenses	268 95	
		2,596 13
Reinsurances		768 25
Commissions to agents		5,601 40
Salaries		4,300 73
Directors' fees		402 23
Interest		451 51
Interest on guarantee stock		170 50
Cash in hand and in bank		463 71
		$33,137 30

Examined and found correct.
T. J. THOMPSON,
Treasurer.

HENRY PELLATT,	}
GEO. B. HOLLAND,	} Auditors.
Toronto, Feb. 9, 1867.

Statement of Assets and Liabilities, Nov. 30, 1868.

ASSETS.

Cash in hand and in bank		$463 71
Premium notes liable to assessment	$91,681 10	
Less assessments collected	22,792 78	
		68,888 32
Short date notes taken for cash premiums		2,127 89
Arrears on expired policies, estimated at		750 00
Office furniture		228 50
Bills receivable		1,197 89
Toronto Mutual Fire Insurance Co. guarantee stock		3,000 00
Sundries		227 14
		$76,883 45

LIABILITIES.

Payments in guarantee fund		$2,085 79
Bills payable, including fire claims settled but not due		15,626 35
Fire claims since settled		1,427 14
Current interest on guarantee stock		191 19
Directors' fees and travelling expenses		720 10
Deposits on interest		171 00
Printing		293 93
Salaries		363 29
Agents' balances due		118 62
All other liabilities, including premium notes given for reinsurance		2,754 66
		$23,952 06
Balance of Assets over Liabilities		52,931 39
		$76,883 45

LA BANQUE DU PEUPLE.

Pursuant to notice the Annual General of the Stockholders of this Institution w the 1st day of March, 1869, at three o'cloc at their Banking House, Great St. Jame Montreal.

The meeting having been organized by pointment of John Crawford, Esq., as Ch and A. A. Trottier, Esq., as Secretary.

The Chairman called the meeting to ord which A. M. Delisle, Esq., one of the A read the following report of the Auditors past year :—

GENTLEMEN,—

After having given our most careful a to the affairs of the Bank, by the examin its books, papers and securities, we have t to report that the result of our labours ha that they have been managed with the care and regularity.

The various assets, such as debentures, ment bonds, cash on hand, and, in a wor thing comprising the assets of the Bank, l received our careful attention, and the w found to correspond with the books in wh are represented.

We would observe that, if on the o the transactions of the Institution ha comparatively restricted during the past y therefore, not so remunerative as they mi atily have been, yet, on the other hand, be gratifying to the Shareholders to kno owing to the good management and pru the Board of Directors, it has suffered since the last Annual Meeting, of the 2nd 1868.

We beg to embody a Statement of the the Bank, as exhibited on the 27th Febru viz :—

ASSETS.

Amount of discounted notes and other debts due to the Bank, the balance due by other Banks excepted	$1,96
Amount of mortgages, hypothèques, and judgments	6
Amount of real estate	5
Amount of balances due by other banks or bankers	3
Amount of specie in silver and gold	13
Amount of Provincial notes	3
Amount of bank bills and cheques of chartered banks of this Province	3
Amount of Government securities	10
	$2,44

LIABILITIES.

Amount of stock paid up	$1,60
Amount of bank notes in circulation	8
Amount of deposits not bearing interest	30
Amount of deposits bearing interest	24
Amount of net profits on hand this day, all expenses deducted	20
Amount of balances due to other banks or bankers	
	$2,44

In examining this statement you will remark, that notwithstanding a financi which for a long period, has more or les in commercial matters, the want of cont public credit, and particularly owing (we state) to the protection afforded to dish ders by the bankruptcy laws of 1864 a the bank is found to be in such a prospe dition as can hardly fail to increase the c of the stockholders and the public gener

The decision which has consequently rived at by the Board of Directors to dec annual dividend of 4 p. c. for the last meets with our unqualified sanction.

nk, that we should fail in our duty if
it avail ourselves of this opportunity to
the resignation of Benjamin H. LeMoine,
r late cashier so well known for his finan-
ies and prudence; but we are happy to
t, although relieved of the more respon-
onerous duties of cashier, that gentle-
continues to give the institution the
his long experience by exercising a gene-
ntendence over its management.

lance sheet above quoted, gives the
of real estate" held by the Bank at
1; but it is but fair to mention that this
at it originally cost, whereas at the pre-
, owing to the increase in value of landed
is not exaggerating to set its intrinsic
$100,000, beyond its cost, and which
perly be added to the rest or profit and
int.

ve, therefore, great satisfaction in con-
g the Stockholders on the uninterrupted
of the Bank, and much pleasure in
ur thanks to Mr. Trottier, the Cashier,
fficers of the Bank generally, for the
id extended to us in the performance of
t.

A. M. DELISLE,
JOHN OGILVIE.

hich the following resolutions were pro-
unanimously carried.

motion of Jacques Grenier, Esq., se-
Ephrem Hudon, Esq.:—
d,—That the Report of the Auditors for
ear, as well as the statement of the affairs
uk, be received and adopted.

n motion of C. J. Coursol, Esq., second-
Dubord, Esq.:—
d,—That the Report of the Auditors and
ent of the affairs of the Bank, just sub-
e very satisfactory; and this meeting
much pleasure that the affairs of the
tinue prosperous; and would express its
in the Directors of the Bank for their
gement.

motion of A. M. Delisle, Esq., second-
is Boyer, Esq.:—
e Shareholders of this Bank consider it
to offer to Benjamin H. Lemoine, Esq.,
cashier, their warmest acknowledgments
e and efficient management of the affairs
nk, whilst committed to his care, and
h that circumstances should have com-
t to offer his resignation; but they are
learn that, although this respected gen-
ceased to be its first officer, he never-
tinues to give the institution the bene-
eneral supervision.

wford made a suggestion, recommending
ansfer Book be opened for inspection,
list of the Stockholders be published

motion of T. M. Thomson, Esq., se-
John Ogilvie, Esq.:—
t,—That a vote of thanks be given to
ford, Esq., for his able conduct in the

A. TROTTIER,
Secretary.

AN MUTUAL AND STOCK COMPANIES.—
agent of one of the American Mutuals
Stratford paper as follows: "My at-
s been called to an incorrect statement,
e National Life Insurance Co., regarding
of Mutual Companies. The National
grant a policy for $1,000 for a premium
and that the Mutual Companies will
a policy for $783.48 for that sum.
are the facts? The largest Life Com-
e world, the C. M., nearly twenty-four
and the National has existed only since
will give a policy to a person aged
rs for $2,000 gold for a premium of
d require no note.

Insurance.

INSURANCE MATTERS IN NEW YORK.

(From Our Own Correspondent.)

NEW YORK, March 7, 1869.

With the advent of spring and the more joyous
aspects of external nature, we felicitate ourselves
upon the steadily improving condition of our
political and financial situation. The gold premium has been steadily receding, money is easy
for all legitimate purposes, the quotations for national bonds have been rapidly advancing on both
sides of the Atlantic. Congress has passed several
assuring measures such as the national credit,
coin, contract, certified check, and national bank
Bills, by which the movements of trade will be,
to a certain extent, exempted from the spasmodic
disturbances of speculation; the inaugural of General Grant everywhere inspires universal confidence
and his Cabinet appointments argue an honest
and wise administration of the Departments. All
the conditions of a good business for the spring
and summer are present, and our trading classes
are confidently expecting a good time coming.

The underwriting fraternity of this city are well
satisfied not only with the business of 1868, but
more especially with the remarkable exemption
from fires, thus far in 1869. Although we have
as yet only unofficial statements of the operations
for 1868 they are sufficiently accurate for purposes
of comparison.

Year.	No. Co'y's.	Premiums Received.	Losses.	Expenses.	Net Surplus.
1868	104	$20,261,081	$10,059,502	$7,062,415	$7,824,286
1867	106	24,006,469	14,313,481	6,384,901	6,728,253

Amount of risks unsettled in 1867.........$2,508,426,421
" " 1868.........2,504,199,562

Deducting the excess of expenses in 1868 over
1867 from the difference in the losses of the two
years, and we readily find where the increase of
net surplus has come from. The fire dividends
to stockholders for 1868 were $2,752,101, and for
1867 $2,232,354. Twenty-one companies passed
their dividends in 1867 and only ten in 1868.

The Massachusetts Insurance Department has
just issued advance sheets, showing the general
condition of the stock, fire, marine, mutual and
fire-marine companies in that Commonwealth for
the year ending January 1, 1869. Of the thirteen
companies represented in this city twelve report,
and they are all credited with respectable balances;
total surplus $2,655,412; average $211,284, after
charging 50 per cent. reinsurance, and 100 per
cent. on all unearned marine premiums. This
surplus represents only $3,250,000 capital, being
over 60 per cent. on capital. The Boston companies have always pursued a highly conservative
course, and are usually stronger than New York
offices—the reserve being held to a satisfactory
point despite the clamor of stockholders.

We continue to multiply our life companies
—the Hercules, has organized, with William
B. Lambert, formerly an agent of the Equitable Life, as President. The original Hercules was a thorough-going character, if we
are to credit the mythological accounts of
him. He performed his seven labors with wonderful vigor and success. The Hercules Life, of
New York, will require both strength, patience
and perseverance before it lands on the safe side
of Jordan. The Empire Life, and Commonwealth
Life, were announced two or three weeks ago.
They are officered by former employees of the
Continental Life. But the important question concerning the future of these companies is where
is the business to build upon? The number of
New York Life Companies has doubled within
five years and now amounts to 33, besides 22

of other States reporting to this department,
not to speak of the balance of 65 company's
now reporting, making the total in the United
States 120 companies. The enormous waste connected with the too rapid multiplication of life
companies is shown not only in the extravagant
ratio of expenses to premium receipts, but in the
ratio of lapsed, surrender and not taken policies.
The business is inflated and demoralized, and the
insuring community disgusted. Five months experience, to Jan. 1, 1869, of the National Life
Insurance Company of the United States, capital
$1,000,000, is an illustration of the existing in-
tense competition and cost of getting business.
"Cash premiums," $174,201, cost, $146,125, so far
as reported. But the premiums recived included
$33,628 still in hands of agents, so that the actual
expenditures exceeded the receipts by nearly
$10,000!! Our Legislature has before it several
bills of a general character affecting life insurance,
but the law most needed is one that shall hereafter
require every new life company to have at least
$500,000 deposited with the Superintendent. This
would probably cool off a number of ardent people
who combine to raise $100,000, for the purpose of
making snug berths for themselves and their
friends. The United States Casualty, organized
in 1866, and reorganized in May, 1868, as a life
and casualty company, has finally become an exclusively life company, to be known as the Anchor
Life. Mr. E. C. Fisher, a very energetic and
capable officer, continues as heretofore President
of the Company, which now confidently hopes to
get into a prosperous business, rapidly. They have
about 500 policies to start with.

There are several bills before the Legislature
which are designed to make material changes in
the character of our life companies. Of these the
new Forfeiture Bill reported in the Senate, has
attracted much attention. It is substantially like
the act passed by the Massachusetts Legislature in
1861, and provides that a policy shall not become
void for non-payment of premium till the sum
already paid has been exhausted in temporary
insurance; or in other words, till the policy has no
longer any value, and that nothing shall be forfeited, but the right to reinstate the policy. A large
committee of the New York actuaries has been
before the Senate, to ask certain modifications of
the bill as reported; and, in accordance with their
wishes, a new bill is to be introduced. The Massachusetts act is indisputably equitable, and has
been found of easy application. Several New York
offices have already adopted it, but there promises to
a law to enforce it upon all companies.

Heretofore, New York life offices have been restricted to this State, and within a circuit of fifty
miles around, as the geographical limit for investing surplus. As the rate of interest in several
Western States is much higher than in New York,
the Eastern offices, which have not been so restricted, have enjoyed a decided advantage over
our companies. It is now proposed, by a bill before the New York Legislature, to place our companies on an equal footing with others in this
respect.

The annual statements of the life companies
doing business in this State are probably all at the
N. Y. Department by this time, and the Superintendent, with his army of clerks, busy with the
great labor of his forthcoming report—the valuation of some 450,000 policies. But the doctors
will not agree, as the two departments of Massachusetts and New York have a different assumption of mortality and interest. Besides, the companies will not agree with the doctors. For
instance, the National Life of the United States
assumes 6 per cent. interest in its valuation, while
the departments will allow severally 4 and 4½.
The new form of return will enable the superintendent to present in contrast, what he calls
"realized" and "unrealized" assets, and it will be
noted when the returns appear, that the deferred
and unpaid premiums, premium notes, and premium loans, are generally, and largely in excess
of the cash, real estate, mortgages, stocks, bonds,

and call loans. The column "expenses of management" will make some of the old companies that can do business for 12 to 16 per cent. smile, as they will see many instances in which young offices have spent nearly the whole of their premium receipts for their business. Among this class of companies 30 to 40 per cent. commissions is below the average, and it is evident to the merest tyro in life assurance, that nothing but failure awaits such extravagance.

In a former letter, I referred briefly to the suit of the Knickerbocker Life Insurance Company vs. J. B. Eccleshie, of the New York Underwriter. Mr. E. was arrested for an alleged libel on the company, but on an argument of a motion to vacate the order of arrest, Judge Freedman held that the matter was not libelous of itself and released the defendant. A further motion by the defendant, requiring the company to amend its complaint, by alleging the specific cases in which persons had refused to insure or been deterred from insuring in the company, by reason of the publication of the alleged libelous matter was also granted by Judge Freedman. So that the Knickerbocker's complaint, does not thus far appear to have found much favor with the courts. This suit has attracted a good deal of attention among insurance people, and the final task required of the company, i.e. prove before a jury, specifically, instances of damage, to its business will necessarily be a very difficult one.

The meeting of the Executive Committee of the the National Board of Fire Underwriters, recently held in this city with closed doors, was neither harmonious nor satisfactory in its final conclusions. Two questions particularly agitated the Committee—the rating of dwellings by the National Board, and the interesting rebate question. With respect to the dwellings, it was finally agreed that where a local board declined to rate the dwellings in its locality, the rate should be left free for the companies to write as they pleased. This was a defeat of the high pretensions of certain members, who quite dogmatically insisted that all such ratings should be by the National Board. The Committee of Conference, to whom was referred the questions of rebate and brokerage, at the late convention of out-town companies held in this city, made an informal statement, for information, that they would report to the National Board, at its spring meeting, a recommendation for the adoption of flat or net rates, leaving parties getting insurance to pay brokers if they employed them, and relieving the companies from all rebate, brokerage and commission on direct risks. Unless the National Board can meet the difficulties connected with this rebate question, it will soon become disintegrated. The New York city companies, which do no agency business, are allowed the unequal privilege of allowing a rebate to customers in lieu of commissions, while out-town companies are deprived of this privilege. But the greatest difficulty is in this annoyance and loss occasioned to respectable agents over the country, adhering to Board rates, by agencies of strong companies not in the Board, which advertise to take the same class of risks for one-sixth to one-eighth less. It is hard for an agent to stand by uncomplainingly and see his business carried away by these guerrillas. The National Board has already accomplished much good in the cause of sound underwriting, and it is to be hoped that the several agencies can be so far protected as to secure the cheerful adhesion of their companies to the Board.

New York capital is largely represented in the insurance business of Missouri, and therefore our underwriters have just heard with marked satisfaction of the passage, after a protracted and bitter struggle, of an excellent general law for that State, to be administered by a department. It requires all stock fire and life companies to put up a guarantee deposit of $100,000, and make specific annual statements after the forms provided in New York. This act will rid Missouri of some fifty "wild cats," and clear up the at-

mosphere, so that the business classes can see the inside of any company, home or foreign, soliciting confidence and business. Thus the good work goes bravely on. The area in which bogus companies can operate is, happily, being rapidly restricted.

Now that they have reached a third story, the new building of the New York Life and Equitable Life Insurance Companies are the notable objects on Broadway. The New York Life's building will be ready for occupation in about a year, and will cost, with lot, about $1,500,000. Numerous applications for rooms have already been made, and the company expect to have their own apartments at a nominal rent. I have not been able to learn the cost of the Equitable building and lot. The building is granite, and a most solid and beautiful structure, and cannot cost less, probably, than the New York Life's structure. These buildings, and the corporations that own them, are doubtless destined to stand for generations, and long after their founders shall all have become companions with the insensible clod—continue the beneficent work to which they are devoted. M. A. C.

FIRE RECORD.—Collingwood, March 5.—Mrs. Cooke's tavern, on the road to Meaford, six or seven miles from this place, was totally consumed with contents; the inmates had barely time to escape; loss $1,200 to $1,500. No insurance; the fire caught from a defect in the chimney.

Osprey Township, Co. Grey, Ont., March —. The barn and outbuildings of John Hutchinson, with contents, were consumed. No insurance. The fire was caused, as is supposed, from a spark from a lighted pipe.

St. Catherines, March 5.—Barn of Mr. Hagan; no particulars.

London, March 6.—S. Stewart's brick cottage on Maitland street, occupied by Mrs. Chisholm, caught fire, it is thought, from the hall stove. The flames were extinguished, but the house and furniture were damaged to the extent of $500.

Tavistock, Ont., Feb. 28.—The store and premises of Mr. Moore, were consumed. Mr. M. had just received a large stock of goods, and his loss is therefore heavy.

Mount Forest, March 4.—The premises occupied by Mr. Colclough, druggist, together with the telegraph office and Examiner printing office, were totally consumed by fire. The fire commenced in the rooms above the telegraph office, and is supposed to have originated from a defect in the chimney. Insurance on Mr. Colclough's stock, $2,000, and on the Examiner office, $500.

Peel Township, Ont. Feb. 25.—The barn of Terence Hanlen, lot 2, con 3, Peel, was totally destroyed by fire. The whole of his grain, hay, and farming implements in the building were consumed.

Brockville, Ont., March 4.—The dwelling of Robert Ferguson took fire; the flames were soon put out; the premises and furniture sustained considerable damage.

Stratford, Feb. 28.—The cooper shop of Mr. Needham was entirely destroyed by fire, with its contents. The Council, satisfied that it was the work of an incendiary, offered a reward of $200 for his conviction.

Thorold, March 2.—A disastrous fire broke out in the grocery store of Mr. John Cloy, and the flames quickly communicated to the stores of Mr. Leonard and Mr. Hart, all of which, with most of their contents, were totally destroyed. During the progress of the fire, great consternation was created amongst the crowd, by the explosion of a quantity of gunpowder, kept for sale in Mr. Cloy's establishment. Fortunately, nobody was seriously injured. Mr. Cloy was insured for $8,000 in the British America ; Mr. Leonard for $2,200 ; Mr. Hart was also fully insured. The total loss is estimated at $20,000, and the amount of insurance on goods and buildings about $14,000. The origin of the fire is unknown.

SUPERINTENDENT BARNES AND THE LIFE COMPANIES.—There can be no doubt that the the condition of several life companies in New York demand a prompt and searching investigation on the part of Mr. Barnes. There can be no doubt that the official report of officers to the department are "cooked," and fail to show the real condition of many of the companies. The unrest is easily dressed, and named real ; the fictitious is easily reported in a guise that will not necessarily excite suspicion. That these things have been done, everybody believes. That some of the companies are reckless is well known. That four and one half per cent reserve cannot be hand after paying losses, and the extraordinary expenses incurred, is manifest. The public welfare demands a thorough investigation. The reckless companies should be punished. Mr. Barnes should let the companies know that he is superintendent, and that the duties of the office will be performed. There must be retrenchment, or there will be ruin.—Chicago Spectator.

—Mr. Chisholm, of the North British and Mercantile Insurance Company, Edinburgh, and who holds the diploma of the Faculty of Actuaries in Scotland, has been appointed Actuarial Assistant in the Imperial Life Assurance Company, London.

—The Chicago Spectator objects to the attempted introduction into American Life Assurance of the tontine principle, as unwise and dangerous. It considers such schemes dangerous, because they eventually strain the resources of a Company, and tempt it for the sake of maintaining its past position to encroach on the future, while at the same time it conceals both the fact and the results.

—Mr. Barnes is preparing to make a valuation of the business of all the Life Companies doing business in New York.

TONTINE DIVIDEND SYSTEM.

Tontine annuities, which were first made attractive by Lorenzo Tonti about the middle of the seventeenth century, have become exceedingly popular throughout Europe, and in some parts of South America. A tontine is quite the reverse of life assurance, it being, in fact, a combination of persons who contribute to a common fund ; that as years roll on, and the numbers surviving diminish, the income is, of course, constantly increasing to those who live, until the last member of a class enjoy most extraordinary advantages from the system. In 1689 the last survivor of the tontine in France, a widow, just before her death, enjoyed an income equivalent to $20,000 of our money, for her original subscription of about $80. So popular has this system been in Europe, that many governments have used it for the purpose of raising money for national support. There are many persons so situated that they can little for leaving money for those that come after them (who, they may consider, have little no claim upon them), and prefer to enjoy while living a large annual income, which, combined with entire safety, their money could not produce in the shape of interest in any other way. So are those who invest in tontine. Life insurance has already been observed, is quite the reverse of the tontine principle ; and the arguments which cause persons to invest in securities of this character appeal to a higher and more unselfish motive than those which influence the investment in tontines. The popular apprehension of the minds of many persons who are asked to insure their lives, but who have not given life assurance much study, is that, in case of a long life the investment may prove a bad one ; but a careful investigation will prove that this objection is not well founded. We have before us a published one of the leading mutual companies, issued more than twenty-five years ago, taken out originally for $5,000, on which, when the policy became a death claim, more than $10,000 was paid, the excess over the original amount of the policy being

receive the face of their policies, respectively, and no more. Persons discontinuing their policies during the non-dividend period, lose all they have paid.

This plan will admit of a number of variations : For instance (1), the division of profits may begin at the end of the arbitrary period of ten, fifteen, or twenty years ; or (2) a separate class of policies may be issued, upon the surrender of which paid-up policies will be given for the value thereof, in case the same are allowed to lapse by non-payment of premium before the dividend begins.

Financial.

MONTREAL MONEY MARKET.

(From our own Correspondent).

Montreal, 9th March, 1869.

The money market continues easy, though there is rather more demand for payment of duties. The remittances have, however, been better lately—fully equal to the general receipts at this period ; notwithstanding the long list of insolvents weekly reported. Bank rates are unchanged; good bills are readily taken at 7 per cent. Not much doing in the street ; the few bills offering not being of a desirable quality. As has been the case for the last few weeks there continues a good demand for stocks and shares, and favourite securities are firmly held. The highest rate of the Bank of Montreal is 141, but few sales at that price. Considerable transactions in City at 103 @ 103½. British, sellers 104½ ; buyers 104. Peoples in favour at 107, now held for 108½. Molson's have risen, and sales have been made at 118. Merchants dull at 105 to 108½. Not much doing in other Banks. Miscellaneous stocks and shares quiet, but the market is firm.

TORONTO STOCK MARKET.

(Reported by Pellatt & Osler, Brokers.)

There has been a fair amount of business done in stocks and bonds during the week, and prices are without much change.

Bank Stock.—Montreal has been sold to a limited extent at 140½; there are new buyers at that rate and sellers at 141. British has been offered at 105½, but there are no buyers over 104. There were small transactions in Ontario at par. Sales of Toronto have taken place at 121, at which rate there are still buyers. Royal Canadian was sold at 88 during the week, but declined to 85, at which rate there have been small sales. Commerce is offering in small lots at 103; very little demand. There are sellers of Gore at 41; no buyers over 40. Merchants' has been inquired for during the week at 108½; there are sellers now at 109. Buyers offer 99½ for Quebec, with sellers at par. Molson's is in fair demand at 113, at which rate there were sales. Sellers ask 103½ for City, with buyers at 103. For Du Peuple 107 is asked; some sales were made at that rate. No Nationale in market; buyers would give 100½. Jacques Cartier is in demand at 109, with no sellers under 109½. No sellers of Union; buyers offer 104½. In other banks nothing doing.

Debentures.—Dominion stock is in good demand at 105½; nothing doing in Canada's. Toronto are in good demand to pay 6½ per cent.; none in market. Some first-class County have been placed at par.

Sundries.—City Gas has been sold at 108, and there are still buyers at that figure. Considerable sales of British-America Assurance took place at 55½, and there are still buyers at that rate. Transactions in Canada Permanent Building Society occurred at 125 to 126; stock is now offered at 126. Sales of Western Canada Building Society were made at 121; little offering. Freehold is in good demand at 110 to 110½. Notwithstanding the large amount of forfeited Canada Landed

Credit shares offered, they have advanced over 2 per cent. in the week. Several large mortgages were placed at rates to pay 8 per cent. There is an average demand for money.

BROWN'S FAILURE.

On Friday an examination of W. C. Chewett took place before the Judge of the County Court, under the Insolvent Act. The Royal Canadian Bank, the Merchants' Bank, the City Bank and Philip Brown & Co. were represented. Mr. Chewett testified that he was engaged in the publishing business, but sold out in April, 1867 ; entered into partnership with W. R. Brown, 2d Feby., 1868, but put no capital into the concern ; dont know whether Brown had any capital in it ; Brown stated he had between $10,000 and $20,000 in it ; no statement was made out ; Brown had real estate worth $40 to $50,000 ; the mistake was not converting his currency into gold day by day ; large amounts were accumulated, and when gold went up loss was certain ; Brown's business was simply speculation in gold ; gave Brown the guarantee to the City Bank without knowing how he stood ; gave a guarantee to the Royal Canadian ; the City's guarantee was broken, and the debt due it was $50,000, but the bank subsequently made terms with Brown relative to its payment ; the debt now due is the balance ; half of Brown's property was settled on his wife prior to opening the account with the Royal Canadian ; this property was mortgaged to the Royal Canadian in December last ; I put no money into the concern; I had transactions with Brown before entering into partnership ; lent him money ; I had a claim on Chewett & Co. for $15,000, but assigned it to my mother in April, 1867 ; I built a house which cost me $25,000, and deeded it to my wife in Dec. 1867 ; assigned a mortgage on the Rossin House for $2,600 to my wife at same time ; at the time of these conveyances was not a partner with Brown and had no idea of becoming such ; I anticipated the making of a will ; the conveyances, through neglect of my lawyer, were not registered till July 1868 ; my surplus, after making these settlements, was $14,000 stock in the Canada Permanent Building Society ; $1,000 in Bank of Toronto ; $3,000 Rossin House ; $400 Yorkville and Vaughan Plank Road ; $600 Western Assurance ; cash due $2,000—gross total $30,000 ; my indirect liabilities amounted to $15,000, and direct to $10,000 ; I sold stock in the Canada Permanent to pay $7,500 to the City Bank in January last, as it was a debt before the settlement, and I wished to make the settlements secure ; did not think I was insolvent ; the firm could not at the time pay its debts in full ; the Royal Bank fully understood our position as to the gold margin. (The President denied this) ; kept my private account at the Bank of Toronto ; on 4th Feby., 1869, I owed it $10,000 ; gave a mortgage to Mr. Worts on Granville street property for $7,500, which amount he paid over to the Bank ; cannot say why the mortgage was not made direct to the Bank ; transfered to Mr. Copp the 100 Western Assurance shares to secure him in a $1,000 note ; still hold $600 stock in the Rossin House, a debt of $925, shares in Yorkville Road, worth $40, and an interest in land in Bloor street worth $100 ; the City Bank holds a cheque of W. R. Brown & Co. for $8,000, but has security for it ; have no further interest in my father's will ; my brother lost everything in the Commercial Bank and I assigned him my interest in the estate without consideration ; previous to my marriage there was no agreement relative to a settlement ; my wife's relatives have frequently spoken to me about it ; have heard Mr. Brown is in New York ; have not heard from him since we stopped payment.

—Molson's bank has declared a semi-annual dividend of four per cent, payable on 1st April. Transfer books closed from the 16th to the 31st March.

The Canadian Monetary Times.

THURSDAY, MARCH 11, 1869.

THE BANK CHARTER QUESTION—ITS EXTERNAL SURROUNDINGS.

The Bank charters expire in 1870. The question of their renewal and the terms and conditions on which it shall be done, cannot well be postponed till next year. It will be desirable to dispose of the question next session of Parliament, which cannot now commence before April, and is likely to drag on through the greater part of the summer. There will be an opportunity of applying some general principle to the constitution of all the banks in the Dominion, and it is pretty certain to be embraced. The reasons in favor of a general law, or at least of the application of some general principles, to all the banks, are obvious. It is right to take advantage of the lessons of experience to strengthen weak points, to eliminate what has proved to be vicious, and to preserve what has stood the test of time.

There are numberless points over which men might differ in arranging a new scheme of banking or giving a new lease to an old one. But, in this instance, there will be one great dividing line, on either side of which contending parties will array themselves. The question of questions will be whether the Government is to be allowed to take from the banks the power of issuing notes and to fill the void by an issue of Dominion notes. The intentions of Mr. Rose and his colleagues have not been fully declared. The question

is apparently in its incipient stages. A committee of enquiry was appointed last session, at the instance of the Government, and had scarcely entered on its task when the proro-gation took place. But committees of en-quiry are not always intended to elicit the whole truth and nothing else. When the Government has a design, not very easy of execution, a committee is often selected as the best means of covering it: the conclusion of its enquiries is pretty certain to be in ac-cordance with the secret predetermination of the Executive. Something of this kind is expected in the present case. Nobody doubts that the Government at Ottawa has made up its mind to use all its influence to displace the existing bank circulation by Dominion notes. This is universally regarded as a foregone conclusion; and there is no reason why the question should not be discussed on that basis.

The exterior circumstances under which the change is proposed must, first of all, be taken into account. Unfortunately the issue of Government notes did not originate in the consideration of what would be best for the country; how the soundest currency could be provided ; how the bill-holder could best be protected, and the convertibility of the paper circulation be most certainly maintained. The Government was not in a position to consider these questions. It was in the po-sition of a man who is too hungry to philoso-phize ; it could think only of its own pressing and imperious wants. It was reeling under a heavy load of floating debt, of which it was desirous to rid itself, even temporarily ; and it catched at the suggestion to put its pressing obligations into a shape that would admit of their being used as currency. The Provincial note had its birth in this way. It was the child of poverty ; it had Debt for its father and Necessity for its mother.

And while this is true of the first-born, it will be doubly true of the rest of the progeny, if more there are to be. The class of jour-nals whose business it is to supply the public with political information announced, as long ago as last summer, that Government had obtained leave from the guardians of the Intercolonial Railway loan to apply to a purpose, different from that for which it was borrowed, the portion that had come to hand. It was alleged that the money was used to pay off that balance of the floating debt which the issue of Provincial notes to the Bank of Montreal had been insufficient to cover. And we have never seen any direct and absolute denial of the statement. The silence seems to carry a tacit consent.

On the supposition that this fund was tem-porarily turned from its purpose, the en-quiry arises, how is it to be restored ? There

is no hope of its coming out of the re[venue] for that would imply a surplus, whic[h never] entered into the calculations of the [Minister] of Finance. And borrowing for suc[h a pur]pose, in the ordinary direct way of [selling] securities on the market, is out of th[e ques]tion. The deposits paid by insuran[ce com]panies and the small savings of the [working] classes, which have gone into the Gove[rnment] Savings' Banks, amount to but an in[signifi]cant sum compared with what was o[riginally] on the Intercolonial Railway loan, [and was] supposed to have been temporarily [diverted] from its destination. Appearances fa[vor the] suggestion that the seizing of the ban[k circu]lation is looked to as a means of resto[ring to] its rightful destination, the Inter[colonial] Railway loan.

Here again we find the necessities [of the] Ottawa Government usurping the [place of] the consideration of what is the best [way to] place the currency on a sound basis. [It is] manifest that there could be no co[nsidera]tion of anything but how to sup[ply the] pressing wants of the Dominion Tr[easury.] If a Government currency is to gro[w out of] considerations of this kind, and if th[e mode] in which it is to be embodied are to [be] the unique currency of the country[, it is] evident that we are in the greatest [danger,] and it would be no difficult task to e[stablish] how near a Banking law, originating [in such] motives, and framed on such pri[nciples,] would bring us to that form of nation[al bank]ruptcy which is implied in a gov[ernment] paper currency, originally issued [with a] promise of redemption in specie on [demand] but for which specie cannot be thus o[btained.] Two years would be the utmost st[retch of] time that could be expected to ela[pse before] the commencement of the system[atic] collapse and the era of an irredeemab[le] currency. No event short of a war i[nva]sion, famine, or an earthquake, wou[ld be so] great a calamity as the bringing a[bout of] such a state of things.

The danger that the replacing of th[e bank] note currency, by an issue of Gov[ernment] paper, would lead to an irredeem[able cur]rency, lies in the circumstance that th[e money] power, and the political power, wou[ld be in] the same hands. The issuer would o[nly have] to desire a release from the oblig[ation to] convert the notes into specie on dem[and, and] it could be done by the exertion of [the poli]tical power of the government. A[nd here] lies one of the great differences betw[een bank] notes and Government notes. The l[atter are] simple trading corporations, with ne[ither the] power to release themselves from th[e obliga]tion of paying their notes in specie. [A sus]pension involves their credit, their [fate,] their very existence. They have th[e] rest to make every possible exertion tain specie payments. The Government on the other hand, would have the st temptation to dispense with that on ; and as their object, in usurping er circulation, has been from the first ly temporary necessities, we are justioncluding that they would again yield ences which they have, in the past, nd are now, unable to withstand. 1ere be no self-delusion on the sub- Government issue of notes to disie existing bank note circulation, in the not distant future, an irree currency, whatever professions made to the contrary, and whatever ns of law may be made that would form a gaurantee against that danger. would come by degrees ; its march a by stealthy steps ; but the result e inevitable, and it would come on first pressing financial emergency of ernment.

THE BEAVER MUTUAL.

usiness of this Company, for the past ws a gain of 2,183 policies, and an in-! premium notes of $11,496 over the rious. The Company holds premium able to assessment, amounting to $91, s cash receipts were $30,959, and ure $32,673 ; the losses by fire were The Directors are strongly in favor emium note system, and consider the tem a departure from true mutual s. The cash mutual system, now n the States, is recommended as one f adoption. The union of this Comith the Toronto Mutual, is received out as likely to promote efficiency iomy and financial strength. The stained by fire during the Summer vere heavy, and the Inspector, very draws attention to the number of h arise from defective chimnies. it on this score has been made, again 3, by all our Insurance Companies, wonder is that so much carelessness ng timber into brick work is allowed us. The Directors make very senarks respecting the concealment of nces on property insured. The mode l is an admirable one, and if the Diave the necessary courage to carry it will earn the gratitude of the comt large by adhering to it. Cases y frequently in which fires are diceable to this fearful source of cri-The Barrie case referred to was ct of comment in this journal at the me of the political newspapers, in country, attacked this Company for

its defending the suit. It turns out just as we expected that the defence was based on a true sense of what is due to the honestly disposed portion of the community. The plaintiff had mortgaged his property, without notice to the Company, and when a fire occurred, under such circumstances, the Company decided to stand on their rights. The Legislature has thought fit to protect the members of Mutual Companies by a rigorous enactment on the subject of concealing incumbrances, and we do not think that Directors are justified in virtually abrogating it by paying claims in full which are tainted with suspicion. We are disposed to give this Company great credit for the stand they have taken in the matter, as well as for the spirit of economy displayed, and we see no reason to doubt that its progress will be steady under its present efficient management.

INTERNATIONAL LIFE INSURANCE COMPANY OF LONDON.

There are quite a number of Canadians interested in this Company, and from what we learn from our English exchanges respecting its position, we judge it is about time for them to take measures to protect themselves. The purchase of the business of the International by the Hercules appears to have been a piece of cool and magnificent impudence. Although the financial state of the Hercules, at its last annual meeting, did not warrant the declaration of a dividend, yet, within a few months thereafter, it became the purchaser of a Company of thirty years standing, with, according to the *Post Magazine,* "its attached liabilities and a tainted character." The presumptuous purchaser is now undergoing that truth-evolving process styled liquidation. It came out in Court that the International lost one-fourth of its capital between 1862 and 1865. This state of affairs had led to negotiations for the transfer of its business. The Hercules was the favoured Company which was sought out to shoulder the burden. This Company had a paid-up capital of only £53,688, and after receiving £150,000 from the International possessed invested funds slightly in excess of $150,000. Those who negotiated or promoted the transfer seem to have made a good thing of it. The Directors of the International paid £150,000 to the Directors of the Hercules in consideration of the latter taking upon themselves the liabilities of the former. One gentleman, Mr. Sheridan, was paid £8,000 ; £15,000 was to be paid to the Secretary of the International for compensation for his loss of office. This nice little arrangement, however, was not communicated to the shareholders. The journal above quoted says :

"The worst part of the story remains to be told. It is so positively stated in the report that £150,000 was the sum paid over to the *Hercules* Company, that we must conclude the money was actually received by the directors and brought under their control and disposition. We know, however, from the best authority that, within the last fortnight, a cheque for £200 was returned unpaid on presentation at their bankers. The circumstance, possibly, admits of satisfactory explanation, and it is to be hoped that it does but at present the matter wears an ugly look."

It appears further that the shareholders of the International are not satisfied with these arrangements on their behalf, and are taking steps to have the contract rescinded. The Hercules, as well as the International, is in liquidation, so that the pair are well matched. The latest intelligence is given in the following paragraph from the *Post Magazine :*

"These two Companies having become involved in heavy Chancery proceedings by which the assets of the Companies would become materially reduced, to the great injury of the share and policyholders, an arrangement is in progress by which the threatened litigation will be prevented, or be much reduced ; and the difficult questions of equities and cross equities which have arisen will be solved. As a part of the arrangement the Life Policies of both Companies will pass to the Prudential, if the funds in hand and securities to be provided are sufficient to cover the responsibilities associated with so large a transaction, and the terms of the transfer be such as to obtain the sanction of the Court of Chancery."

We are glad to say that we are seldom called upon to chronicle such a disgraceful transaction in life insurance as that above set out; but the fact that such things do occur shews how necessary it is for those interested in insurance companies to make themselves acquainted with their standing and by timely precautions guard against loss.

THE FAILURE OF BROWN & Co.

The examination of Mr. Chewett, of the firm of W. R. Brown & Co., brokers, has revealed a state of facts in connexion with that firm's affairs little creditable to that gentleman. It appears that, five years ago Mr. Chewett gave a guarantee to the City Bank for the indebtedness of Mr. Brown, which amounted to $50,000. In 1867 he sold out his interest in the firm of Chewett & Co., but the name of the firm continued unaltered, and no notice was given that his interest had ceased. He then settled on his wife his house, which cost $25,000, and a mortgage for $26,000 on the Rossin House ; and in February, 1868, being possessed, in his own name, of almost nothing, became a partner with Mr. Brown, without even asking for a statement of Mr. Brown's financial position. The fact is that at the time of Mr. Chewett's becoming such partner, the concern was insolvent. Although Mr. Chewett had disposed of his property, the public were not aware of it, and as he had the reputation of being the possessor of ample means, and certainly had the reputation of an honourable man, his name in the partnership gave it a position which it otherwise could not have commanded. We do not know whether persons were induced to deposit with a "banking house" whose business was, as Mr. Chewett confesses, merely speculation in gold, by reason of their confidence in Mr. Chewett, but we can easily understand the influence of his name in connection with it. The circumstances tell strongly against Mr. Chewett.—He first parted with all his property, and then became a partner with a man whose financial position he must have known to be unsound. At the least he did not think it worth his while to ask for a statement of his affairs. Whatever may be said of the legality of the settlements there cannot be two opinions as to the morality of Mr. Chewett's conduct.

THE Directors of the Gore Bank have decided to close the remaining branches of the bank, and confine operations to Hamilton, under the management of Mr Read.

Communications.

OVER-INSURANCE.

Editor of the Canadian Monetary Times.

SIR,—In a communication over the signature "Insurance," in your issue of last week is a clause which, as it is calculated to mislead those not conversant with matters of which the writer professes to treat, deserves a passing notice. Your correspondent says, in speaking of the insurable value of buildings: "It ought to be explained to the insured that 'he can only insure two-thirds of the actual value, he being his own insurer for the other one-third. I am aware this is often not done as I have frequently been told, 'such a Company will take any amount I will give them.' The reply is a very simple one, they may take your premium but would not pay you more than your loss or two-thirds of the value. For instance if the cash value of a property is $4,000 no company will pay more than $2,667.

I am surprised at any one professing a knowledge of insurance matters advancing such an absurd statement. If my building is worth $4,000, and the company insuring is so injudicious as to cover the whole amount—a circumstance which through the ignorance or avarice of agents I am sorry to say often occurs—I have only, in the event of the total destruction of my building, to prove that it was actually worth that amount, and I recover in full. In support of what I aver, I will only for the present cite one authority, which I have no doubt will be considered sufficient. Angell on Fire Insurance, sec. 249, page 307 says, "The difference between the mode of adjustment and satisfaction, in the contract of Marine and that of Fire Insurance in the event of loss (as has been stated by a very learned judge, whose attention through a long course of judicial duty has often been directed to both branches of insurance law) is distant and obvious. The following is his language: 'In fire policies the assured recovers the whole loss if within the amount insured, with-out regard to the proportions between the amount insured and the value of the property at risk.'"

Your correspondent must, I fancy, have got some confused idea about the average clause in Marine Insurance and mixed it up with a condition of that nature embodied in some English fire policies, but which, however suitable to some of the various branches of business in England, certainly, unless in very exceptional cases (and then by special agreement) finds no favour in Canada.

Truly yours,
INSURER.

Toronto, March 10, 1869.

Mining.

MADOC GOLD DISTRICT.

(From our own Correspondent.)

BELLEVILLE, March 8th, 1869.

Very little progress has been made in mining operations for several weeks past; and such strict secresy has been observed in almost every quarter where work has been done, that I shall be obliged in some cases, however unwillingly, to give you current reports instead of authentic intelligence.

The Richardson Company affect no reserve as to their doings; but from various causes they have not done much work of late. Mr. Dunstan, their manager, came down last week, bringing with him a "brick" of gold of the value of $260, the produce of about 50 tons of rock, or about $5.25 per ton.

The Merchants' Union Company lately sent 3 tons of their vein-stone to be reduced at the Caldwell (Severn) Mill. The total result was gold to the value of $2; but if, as is reported, the mill is in a bad state of repair, this crushing may not be a true index of the value of their ore; indeed, both from inspection and experiment, I am inclined to think more favorably of their lode.

The mill in question (Severn's) has been running night and day for some weeks upon quartz from the Fiegel mine, with very satisfactory results. The mill-owners have not let anything be known as to the actual amount realized, but $20 per ton is freely mentioned. The supply of ore from this source is, however, cut off, as Mr. Feigel intends to put up machinery to reduce his ore on his own account. This I give merely as a current report.

The proprietors of the Barry mine, in the Township of Elzevir, have been running their new machinery experimentally, with, it is said, "splendid results." As the shareholders have got their disputes settled, they will shortly commence to work commercially—also a common report.

The Toronto and Whitby Company's mill at Bannockburn is now complete, and in working order; but I have not heard whether or not any crushing has been done there.

The machinery for Mallorytown is well advanced. The boiler and other essential parts have been sent down, and the remainder of the apparatus is being got ready as quickly as possible.

A company of gentlemen from Cincinnati are about to commence working a deposit of grey crystalline limestone, banded with plumbago, at Eagle Hill, in the Township of Deubigh, which has given good results by small assays.

Some of the principal mining men in the Town of Belleville, contemplate erecting a test mill to make assays of rock of 100 lbs. each, on the pan system of amalgamation, under the management of Prof. Bell, of Albert College. When ready to go into operation, it will be advertised in the MONETARY TIMES.

—The Elgin Mining Company's well at Port Stanley is over 400 feet deep, but no sign.
—Bank of New Brunswick stock was recently sold at 47½ premium.

Law Report.

GUARANTEE POLICY—FRAUD.

The Bank of Toronto having taken process in the Superior Court, Montreal, against the pean Assurance Society, upon a guarantee p issued to secure the Bank to the extent of $1 against "such loss as might be occasioned t said Bank by the want of integrity, defau irregularities" of Alexander Munro, the ma at Montreal, judgment was given, substan as follows :—

The precise charges set forth in the decla and upon which the plaintiffs seek to recov whole amount named in the policy may be : as follows :—That Munro, without any auth in direct violation of his instructions, and trary to every rule followed by banking ir tions in this country fraudulently allowed th of Nichols and Robinson, brokers of this (overdraw their current account in the B Montreal from the 1st of March, 1865 to the May of the same year.

The balance of which overdrafts on th mentioned day being $28,160.29 cy. ; that overdrafts were allowed without security, various devices were made use of each mor conceal such overdrafts and that they were trived and carried out in collusion with N and Robinson, who subsequently became vent ; that a judgment had been obtained a the latter by the Bank for the amount, could not be recovered, and that Munr absconded and had left nothing wherewith t the debt.

The Defendants met this action by the g issue, and ly two special pleas which raise stantially three points—namely :—

1st. That the overdrafts were allowed by : in the exercise of the discretion appertain him as Manager at Montreal, and in the tr tion of the ordinary business of the Bank.

2nd. That they were allowed openly an out fraud, and passed regularly through th of the bank of Montreal for months bef 1st March, 1865, as was well known to the tiffs ; and 3d, that although large overdanf constantly allowed by Munro, and regula tered in the books of the bank, which acc to the proposals for the policy were und stant supervision by the head office, the pl had never notified the defendants of the and that by withholding such notice, the had become void under the 4th condition stated, if, in point of fact, the allowing ov as in the present case could give rise to a the clause adverted to is as follows :— (subject to a discretionary power exercis certain cases by the Directors in Canada e ting the forfeiture) a policy of guarantee l void as to future claims, upon its bein known to the directors of the said societ nada by the employers that the party honesty is guaranteed has committed or any act which gives the right to make : under the policy ; and that the employ bound immediately upon discovering, or notice of the commission or omission of a act, to forward a written intimation of th and so far as circumstances will permit of ticulars attending the commission or o thereof to the directors ; and that by wilfu knowingly omitting or neglecting so to two months after such discovery or not policy becomes absolutely void, both as to and future claims thereunder.

These questions appear to me susceptibl following definite and condensed arrangem 1st. Was the allowing of the overdrafts security, a default or irregularity within th ing of the policy, apart from any fraud o sion ? 2nd. If not, was there any fraud o sion between Munro and the firm of Nich Robinson in respect of these advances ?

ground a claim arose, had the character s acts in regard to these overdrafts be- wn to the Bank more than two months to the notice by them given to the de- í

eeding to adjudicate upon the main—the ssues raised by the parties in this case, I advert to the rules of the Bank, and to e with respect to over-drafts. This is a ssential—of paramount importance, and, has received the careful consideration of . Now, as a matter of fact, admitting bt, there was no rule of the Bank, pro- alled, prohibiting over-drafts previous urrences under review, although such a identally referred to by one of the wit- having been since made; and there seems oubt from the evidence adduced, that s were frequently permitted. Mr. Worts, President, does not deny that an agent donally so accommodate a good customer, ccount of his firm in Toronto seems to frequently overdrawn. It was attempt- v a distinction in this respect between s of the Cashier and the highest officers ged the Bank at Toronto, and those of ho managed it at Montreal. But Mr. nself says, that "the functions of the , Manager and Agent are similar as re- he management of the local institution uch such officer is appointed;" and this appears to be justified by the character functions, and the plaintiff's description s powers in their proposal for insurance. eal over-drafts were permitted by Munro ersous besides Nichols and Robinson; made evident in many of the reports by him to the Board at Toronto. He lso to have allowed them at Peterboro', ugh he was found fault with on that oc- t was evidently very leniently censured; vithstanding his having allowed them, iffs, in their guarantee proposal, declare as been in their employ for several years, given them satisfaction. Afterwards r-drafts were found when his accounts ected in December, 1864. Mr. Dallas, ger who succeeded him, seems to have hem, to a certain extent; and Mr. Arnold, t-keeper, declares "that although it was e general practice in the Bank to allow afts, it was not unusual and it was always el that the agent or manager had the o allow them or not, as he might think "and he says he was perfectly justified under his orders in passing the cheques, done so for the large and small amounts Dallas' instructions since Munro's dis- And there is strong confirmation of this e found in the fact, that this Mr. Arnold, id all the over-drafts allowed to Nichols ason, Sidey, Crawford and others, was ssed by the Bank, nor so far as appears ce, was even censured for having done so, he was perfectly cognizant of all the cir- es of the over-drafts, including the ab- ecurity. markable, if not incredible, that the 12 he deposit ledger which have been pro- ewing the enormous transactions of Ni- obinson, from 1st November, 1864, to s of May, would have exhibited column nn, composed chiefly of debit balances— not most of which are overdrafts, if s not recognized by every official in the aving this species of discretionary power. tempt is made to distinguish between rafts complained of, and the numerous iibited in the record, on the ground of unt or of the security taken for them.— llacy of this pretension is plain. The is the same, so far as this case is con- hether the overdrafts be small or great. fts are permitted or tolerated at all, the them is in the discretion of him who m. To permit too large an overdraft,

then, becomes an imprudent or injudicious act, not an irregular one. The same argument applies to the distinction as to security. The taking of security seems to have been far from an invariable rule, apart from Nichols & Robinson's case; and this is also plainly referable to the discretion of the manager. If he could, without censure, ad- vance fifty dollars without security, the advance of fifty thousand is within his functions, and it might easily be conceived that the loan of fifty dollars to one man without security might be more certain to be productive of loss to the Bank than the loan of fifty thousand to another, and, in this case, the immense transactions of Nichols & Ro- binson with the Bank reduce the amount of over- drafts to comparative insignificance. I am, there- fore, of opinion that the allowance of overdrafts was not in itself an irregularity within the mean- ing of the policy.

But if the facilities given to Nichols & Robinson originated in any fraudulent or collusive design, the case would undoubtedly fall within the terms of the policy ; and this point is of the gravest importance.

The fraudulent collusion alleged materially rests upon the assertion that Munro and Nichols and Robinson carried on joint operations in stocks and gold, and that Munro afforded them facilities by way of over-drafts to assist in these joint specula- tions, to float over the margins which required to be put up for them, and the others of his own in New York; his object being to share the profits, and in some cases of transactions to receive com- missions for the aid he was giving, and that he fraudulently contrived to conceal these over-drafts from his employers by conniving at fictitious balances being made up at the end of the month. These are serious charges, and, if substantiated, would, in the absence of every other obstacle, sustain the plaintiff's action.

After going over the evidence the learned judge considered that there was no evidence against the defendants on this point. He said further: I con- sider the ruin of Nichols & Robinson and their inability to meet their engagement at the bank sufficiently accounted for by the terrible monetary crisis through which this and the neighboring country was at this moment passing. A catas- trophe which swept away from them $150,000 in one month might well have deranged the calcula- tions of a bank manager to a greater extent than that suffered by the plaintiffs, and the fact that the firm had such a capital to lose, and that any less misfortunes would have left them competent to fill all their engagements, may not be without significance in the consideration of the conduct of Munro.

I am unable, therefore, to find the evidence of fraudulent collusion involved in the second branch of inquiry; and as to the third very little remains to be said.

If the fact of allowing over-drafts in itself give rise to the right to make a claim under the policy, then I would be of the opinion that the policy was void by a breach of the fourth condition. But as I hold that allowing over-drafts per se with- out a positive ney, a peremptory rule and prac- tice of the Bank against it, does not constitute a default or irregularity within the meaning of the policy, my decision in regard to the breach of the fourth clause becomes unnecessary; and also holding as I do, that no fraud or collusion in respect to these over-drafts is established or has been proved by legal and sufficient testimony to have been perpetrated by Munro. I am under the necessity of dismissing plaintiff's action.

~~~~~~~~~~~~~~~~~~~~~~~

BANKERS' MAGAZINE.—The March number con- tains an Essay on Banking and the Currency, The Currency system of United States and Europe. The London Money Market of 1866, &c.

—The New City Gas Co., of Montreal, has de- clared a semi-annual dividend of four per cent., payable after the 15th. Transfer books closed to the 15th.

Railway News.

NORTHERN RAILWAY.—Traffic receipts for week ending February 27th, 1869.

Passengers	$2,092 19
Freight and live stock	4,799 32
Mails and sundries	762 77
	$7,654 28
Corresponding Week of '68	2,447 67
Increase	$5,206 61

GREAT WESTERN RAILWAY.—Traffic for week ending February 19, 1869.

Passengers	$20,263 34
Freight	45,147 13
Mails and Sundries	2,167 72
Total Receipts for week	$67,578 19
Coresponding week, 1868	67,302 79
Increase	$275 40

INTERCOLONIAL RAILWAY.—Messrs. H. H. Horsey & Co., who tendered for No. 1 section of the Intercolonial at $8,750 per mile, having dis- covered an error of one million cubic feet in adding up the quantity of earth excavation, withdrew their tender, and the Commissioners unwilling to litigate the matter, have given the contract to G. & J Worthington, of Quebec, the next lowest on the list. The tender of the latter was $9,485 per mile. The contract obtained by the Messrs. Wor- thington for No. 4 section is allowed to be assign- ed to Elliott, Grant & Whitehead.

WOODEN RAILWAYS IN QUEBEC. — The Rail- way Committee of the Quebec Assembly adopted the following resolution :—" That the charter for the Sherbrooke and Eastern Townships Railway from Sherbrooke via Dudswell and Weedon, and thence on the most feasible route and grade to connect with the Levis and Kennebec Railway, be granted, and that the charter of the Saint Francis Valley Railway from Lennoxville to De- courtenay place in Bury, thence to or near Bishop's Landing, and thence to Lake St. Fran- cis, and thence to Kennebec road, be granted." The charter of the former road to be for a wooden railway, with the right hereafter to substitute iron ; and the charter of the latter to be for an iron railway, with the right hereafter to substi- tute wooden rails. In both charters the right to compromise, and amalgamate both companies into one company ; or to arrange upon connections for the common use of both roads for track, in case the two companies are kept up.

REVENUE AND EXPENDITURE.—The following is a statement of the Revenue and Expenditure of the Dominion of Canada for the month ended 28th February, 1869 :

Customs	$409,790 95
Excise	206,281 61
Post Office	47,360 73
Bill Stamp Duty	11,976 93
Public Works including Railways	44,835 73
Miscellaneous	536,276 36
Total	$1,256,522 31
Expenditure	$638,728 43

—Counterfeit $4 bills on the Gore Bank are in circulation in Galt.

—The Welland County Council has decided not to purchase right of way through that county for the proposed Erie and Niagara Extension Railroad Company.

—The Hamilton Gas Company, has declared a half-yearly dividend of 3½ per cent.

—A despatch from Montreal states that coun- terfeit bills on the Bank of Montreal are in circu- lation in that city.

—Mr. John Henderson of the Gore Bank has obtained a position in the Bank of Toronto.

Commercial.

Montreal Correspondence.

(From our own Correspondent.)

Montreal, March 1, 1869.

The weather has been bright and cold, with so far no appearance of spring. You may fancy the state of our streets when I mention that several of our leading photographers were busy taking views of the miniature snow mountains in them, to commemorate the remarkable winter we have had.— Business continues very dull, but rather improved, and hopes are already entertained of a fair and safe business in the spring. It is to be hoped that the insane competition in all branches of trade will this year be modified ; our merchants have been so severely bitten for the last three or four years that I expect a more cautious policy will prevail. The large grocers have suffered, especially ; but all branches have sustained severe losses as well be seen by the long lists of insolvents weekly published. Our present bankrupt law does not give satisfaction, and, I have no doubt, some very considerable alterations in it will be proposed next session. The present system of official assignees is strongly commented on. The agitation is, either do away with them altogether, or appoint more and of a higher and more efficient class. At present such is the pressure of business that all new cases are pigeon-holed, and, like Chancery suits, in England, a glorious uncertainty rules as to whether the estates will ever be wound-up.

THE PRODUCE MARKET is exceedingly dull, the state of the roads having seriously interfered with all business. In Flour, prices are nominally unchanged. Total receipts from 1st January to 3rd March, 1869, 69,058 brls. against 52,569 brls. last year. Total shipments for same period, 1869, 34,961 brls. against, 1868, 26,612 brls. Stocks in hands of Millers, 1st inst., 88,473 brls. against 64,400 in 1868. No sales of grain on the spot, and only very small ones of U. C. spring wheat to arrive. Receipts of wheat 1st January to 3rd March, 1869, 22,750 bus, against 13,329 bus. in 1868.

PROVISIONS.—Pork is rather firmer for barrelled, but dressed hogs have declined fully $1 per 100 lb. Butter firm, and there is only a moderate demand for good to choice, as high as 25c. having been paid ; stocks are light; little doing in other articles.

GROCERIES.—There has been but little animation generally. Sugars have followed the New York market; no animation and prices unchanged. Teas more active, and several sales have been made at good rates. Dried fruits have rather advanced, but little doing. Molasses, the recent high prices have checked sales. Very little doing in other articles. I give the imports of the leading articles from 1st January to 1st March:—

	1868.		1869.	
	Quant.	Value.	Quantity.	Value.
Coffee......lbs.	3,436	$ 081	lbs. 640,176	$17,065
Fruit............	....	2,570	....	14,141
Brandy.....gals	132	....	165	....
Gin	2,400	....	67	....
Rum	103	....	1,615	....
Molasses........	200,370	5,377	451,920	5,251
Sugars........lbs	321,656	42,869	lbs.1,707,037	82,619
Teas, green....	167,080	40,087	490,146	181,174
„ " black......	40,869	13,706	73,994	20,305

DRY GOODS.—It is expected that this business will open earlier than usual, large quantities of goods are arriving by each steamer. I give you the imports, 1st January to 1st March, of leading articles:—

	1868.	1869.
Woollens...........	$333,687	305,256
Cottons...........	508,125	525,090
Silks, &c...........	54,450	33,762
	$901,262	$864,108

I give you a statement, furnished by Messrs. Robertson, Steven & Co., shewing the imports from 1850 to 1867 into Montreal, Toronto, Quebec, and also the total into all Canada:—

*	Montreal.	Toronto.	Hamilton.	Quebec.	All other Ports.	Total Imports.
	$	$	$	$	$	$
1850	290,4088	1441208	802612	588310	876000	6713748
1	3075070	1327688	1015832	840572	1357910	8295080
2	4151000	1342988	1154048	825012	762002	8340043
3	6920704	2706188	1753063	1588940	1192802	13242076
4	5698793	2878540	2023570	2035050	1431834	14940484
5	3161730	2325786	1354065	657068	1309730	9056073
6	6856612	2928877	1303075	813056	1557880	13175203
7	6091174	2912009	1541000	960084	1390250	12128511
8	4008643	1073082	620044	875780	815400	7296901
1860	6307578	1716084	928806	985785	1079471	10885564
1	6984085	1842086	1214441	1180498	1471570	13451145
2	6904484	2205020	1250750	1267704	1461120	15056297
3	5866184	1799700	1140778	1289700	1664841	11163222
4	6364002	1935160	908762	1234410	969575	11541100
5	4907148	1195382	506928	851340	847405	12057010
6	8091806	2067478	890417	1551523	1506471	13515007
7	11793517	3515455	1693585	1541510	1496032	19574803
7	12317860	3905501	1773050	1410750	2003901	21395761

Toronto Market.

Trade has been much interrupted by snow during the past fortnight ; complaints of this are heard from all quarters. Mail communication has been so uncertain that no dependence whatever could be placed in it. This applies more particularly to the district east of Toronto. The Quebec mails have only reached us in a spasmodic kind of way, several days accumulations usually coming together.

GROCERIES.—Sugars—Are steady ; a decline of 1c. in New York has been counter-balanced by a fall in the gold premium so that prices here are not altered from last week's quotations. Teas— There is a little better demand for teas, but the market is pretty bare of some grades owing to shipments ex the S. S. St. Andrew, Moravian, North American, Prussian and St. George being delayed on the eastern section of the Grand Trunk by snow. So soon as these goods arrive the assortment will be complete. These steamers brought out a large quantity of dry goods, hardware, &c., as well as groceries.

BOOTS AND SHOES.—Orders are coming in steadily, but owing to the state of blockade the country is now in, there is less doing this week ; prices are unchanged.

GRAIN.—Wheat.—Receipts 6,800 bush., and 14,640 bush. last week ; the market for spring is dull, with only a moderate supply offering ; there are buyers of good samples at 95c. Sales of car loads were made some days since, at 96c to 98c free on cars. Fall is dull and nominal at quotations; there is a good deal offering. The stock in store on the 8th inst., was 127,715 fall; and 98,450 bush. spring, against 85,200 fall and 111,500 spring on 16th March, 1868. Barley.—Receipts, 1,750 bush., and 640 bush., last week. The market is very dull and the demand slack, with a good deal offering ; lots are held at about $1 30. Stock in store on the 8th, 57,000 bush. ; against 70,800 on the 30th Jan., and 1,400 on 16th March, 1868. Oats.—Receipts, 2,533 bush., and 2,600 bush., last week ; car loads are offering at 50c. on the track and there is very little demand. Stock in store on the 8th, 25,200 bush., on the 30th Jan., 1869, 11,400 bush., and on the 16th March, 1868, 32,100 bush. Peas.—Receipts about 1,000 bush., and 560 bush., last week. Peas are offering at 78c. but are unsaleable ; prices are nominally lower, as quoted. Stock in store on the 8th, 30,000 bush., on the 30th January, 1869, 29,050 bush., and on 16th March, '68, 21,660 bush. Rye. —No lots moving, on the street 70c to 75c is paid for sleigh loads. Seeds.—There is a good demand for Timothy, at $2 to $2 75 for lots ; the supply is moderate. Clover, is wanted at $7 to $7 10 ; for lots of No. 1 seed. Flax—$2 to $2 50.

FLOUR.—Receipts 6,800 bbls., and 2,400 bbls. last week. There is very little demand, and we quote No. 1 superfine at $4 to $4 05 ; two or three lots of 100 bbls. sold at $4 05 in store. A lot of 500 bbls. fancy sold at $4 25 at Malton, there is not much demand, extra is worth our quotations. 100 brls. extra sold at $4,55 on cars, and 100 bbls.

at $4 50. No Superior in market. Bag flour is held at $3 90, but could not be sold over $3 80. Oatmeal—is offered freely at $5 75 with no buyer over $5 50, no sales to report. Cornmeal—unchanged. Stock of flour in store on the 8th inst., 22,560 bbls., on the 30th Jan., 1869, 9,700 bbls. and on 16th March, 1868, 12,900 bbls.

PROVISIONS.—Butter.—Stocks are small, nearly all available lots being placed for the New York market ; we note sales of 400 packages, selected 24¼c. ; ordinary is neglected ; the market closes quiet for all qualities. Pork.—There are buyers of Mess at $25 50 to $26, holders asking $26; stocks reduced by retail sales at some advance on old quotations. Bacon.—The stock is ample and held in few hands at 11½c with 11c offered. Cheese.—there is a good local demand, but the supplies are light and there is no wholesale movement. Eggs—very dull, fresh packed 19 to 20c limed are a slow sale at 15 to 16c.

PETROLEUM.—Trade is quiet, and prices of refined are very steady at our quotations ; the demand is limited to requirements for immediate consumption.

LEATHER.—A number of job lots of sole were placed with the city trade at prices within the range of quotations ; other articles quiet.

FREIGHTS.—Rates by Grand Trunk Railway: Flour to all stations from Belleville to Lynn, inclusive, 35c., grain per 100 lbs. 18c. ; flour Brockville and Cornwall, inclusive, 43c. grain 22c. flour to Montreal 50c. grain 25c. ; flour to all stations between Island Pond and Portland, inclusive, 85c. grain 43c. ; flour to Boston 90c. gold, grain 53c. ; flour to Halifax $1.10, grain 55c. flour to St. John $1 02. Boxed Meats to Liverpool per gross ton 89s. ; lard or butter in time 85s. ; Pork 11s. per tierce ; flour 5s. 6d. per barrel ; grain 12s. per 480 pounds. Rates by Great Western Railway—Flour, Toronto to Suspension Bridge 25c. gold ; thence to New York 92c. U. S. currency per bbl. ; to Boston $1.00. Grain to Bridge 18c., gold ; thence to New York 47c. U. S. currency; to Boston 51c. Grain, Toronto to Detroit, 18c. ber 100 lbs; flour 33c. per bbl.

Halifax Market.

BREADSTUFFS.—Feb. 23.—Our market for this week shews a considerable decline, and still tends downwards. The absence of speculative demand continues, and receipts largely in excess. White wheat extra (fall) $6.75 to $7.00 ; fancy $6.25 to $6.35 ; bakers' strong $6.10 to $6.25 ; super $5.75 to $5.90 ; No. 2 $5.00 ; middlings $4 25 to $4.50 ; Pollard's $4.00 to $4.25 ; rye $4.75 to $5.00 ; cornmeal N. D. $1.15 to $4.25 ; F. G. $4.00 to $4.10 ; oatmeal $7.00 (dull).

PROVISIONS.—The demand for Pork is still small, and receipts light. Beef continues dull and unchanged. Butter more active at 24c. to 25c. for good dairy, 22c. to 23c. for shipping tubs. Lard active, sales have been effected at 17c for American. Cheese is firmer without enquiry. Pork, Prince Edward Island mess, $23. to $24; prime mess $18.50 ; prime $13 to $16 beef (mess) $10 to $12 ; prime $7.50 to $8.00 butter 23c. to 26c. ; lard 19c. to 20c. ; cheese 14c to 14½c.

WEST INDIA PRODUCE.—Considerable excitement prevails in Sugars and Molasses. Several cargoes of the latter have changed hands here, and to arrive, at 35c. to 36c. (in bond) being an advance of 5c. to 6c. ¶ gallon on last week's sales. Higher prices are anticipated, and holders refuse to sell at present. Sugars at Auction on Saturday last realized 8½c. to 9c. for V. P. and Barbadoes, respectively. Rum is still inactive and unchanged. Coffee dull. We quote — Sugar V.P. 8½c; Porto Rico, 9½ to 9½c; Cuba 9c. to 9½c Barbadoes 8c. ; molasses, Cienfuegos 40c. to 42c Trinidad 38c. to 40c.; rum (in bond) Demerara 55c. to 58c. ; coffee, (Jamaica) 13c. to 15c. ; St. Domingo, 10c. to 13c.

Mercantile.

Teas! Teas!! Teas!!!

FRESH ARRIVALS

NEW CROP TEAS,

WINES, AND GENERAL GROCERIES,

Special Inducements given to

PROMPT PAYING PURCHASERS.

All Goods sold at very Lowest Montreal Prices!

W. & R. GRIFFITH,

ONTARIO CHAMBERS

Corner of Front and Church Streets,

TORONTO,

6-1y ONTARIO

TEAS. Reford & Dillon **TEAS.**

HAVE just received ex. steamships "*St. David* and *Nestorian*:"

1000 hlf. chests new season TEAS!
Comprising Twankays, Young Hysons, Imperials, Gunpowders, colored and uncolored Japans, Congous, Souchongs, and Pekoes.
500 hlf. bxs. new Valentia Raisins (selected fruit).
500 bags cleaned Arracan and Rangoon Rice.
500 brls. choice Currants.

—ALSO IN STORE:—

250 hhds. bright Barbadoes and Cuba Sugars.
250 brls. Portland, Standard, Golden & Amber Syrups.
100 bags Rio, Jamaica, Laguayra, and Java Coffees.
250 bxs. 10s Tobacco, "Queen's Own" and "Prince of Wales'" brands.

WITH A GENERAL AND

WELL SELECTED STOCK OF GROCERIES;

All of which they offer to the Trade low.

12 & 14 WELLINGTON STREET, TORONTO.

7-1y

Robert H. Gray,

Manufacturer of Hoop Skirts

AND

CRINOLINE STEEL,

IMPORTER OF

HABERDASHERY, TRIMMINGS

AND

GENERAL FANCY GOODS,

43, YONGE STREET, TORONTO, ONT. 6-1y

John Boyd & Co.,

WHOLESALE GROCERS AND COMMISSION MERCHANTS,

61 AND 63 FRONT STREET

TORONTO.

NOW in store, direct from the European and West India Markets, a large assortment of General Groceries, comprising

Teas, Sugars, Coffees, Wines and Liquors,

AND

GENERAL GROCERIES.

Ship Chandlery, Canvas, Manilla and Tarred Rope' Oakum, Tar, Flags, &c., &c.,

DIRECT FROM THE MANUFACTURERS.

JOHN BOYD. ALEX. M. MONRO. C. W. BUNTING

Toronto, Oct. 1st, 1868. 7-1y

TORONTO PRICES CURRENT.—MARCH 11, 1869.

Name of Article.	Wholesale Rates.	
Boots and Shoes.	$ c.	$ c.
Mens' Thick Boots ...	2 20	2 50
" Kip....	2 50	3 00
" Calf	3 00	3 70
" Congress Gaiters..	2 00	2 50
" Kip Cobourgs....	1 15	1 45
Boys' Thick Boots.....	1 70	1 80
Youths' "	1 40	1 50
Women's Batts	0 95	1 30
" Balmoral.........	1 20	1 50
" Congress Gaiters..	1 15	1 45
Misses' Batts.	0 75	1 00
" Balmoral	1 10	1 20
" Congress Gaiters..	1 00	1 30
Girls' Batts	0 65	0 85
" Balmoral..........	0 90	1 05
" Congress Gaiters..	0 80	1 10
Children's C. T. Cacks..	0 50	0 65
" Gaiters	0 65	0 90
Drugs.		
Aloes Cape.......	0 12½	0 16
Alum................	0 02½	0 03
Borax	0 00	0 00
Camphor, refined......	0 65	0 70
Castor Oil............	0 16½	0 28
Caustic Soda..........	0 04½	0 05
Cochineal............	0 90	1 00
Cream Tartar	0 40	0 45
Epsom Salts	0 03	0 04
Extract Logwood......	0 11	0 12
Gum Arabic, sorts.....	0 30	0 35
Indigo, Madras........	0 90	1 00
Licorice	0 14	0 45
Madder	0 00	0 18
Galls	0 32	0 37
Opium................	12 00	13 50
Oxalic Acid...........	0 26	0 35
Potash, Bi-tart........	0 25	0 28
" Bichromate....	0 15	0 20
Potass Iodide	3 90	4 50
Senna	0 12½	0 60
Soda Ash	0 02½	0 04
Soda Bicarb	4 50	5 00
Tartaric Acid.........	0 40	0 45
Verdigris	0 35	0 40
Vitriol, Blue..........	0 08	0 10
Groceries.		
Coffees:		
Java, ⅌ lb..........	0 22@0 24	
Laguayra, ...	0 17	0 18
Rio.................	0 15	0 17
Fish:		
Herrings, Lab. split..	5 75	6 50
" round......	0 00	0 00
" scaled......	0 35	0 40
Mackerel, small kitts..	1 00	0 00
Loch. Her. wh'e firks..	2 50	2 75
" half " ..	1 25	1 50
White Fish & Trout...	None.	
Salmon, saltwater....	14 00	15 00
Dry Cod, ⅌112 lbs....	5 00	5 25
Fruit:		
Raisins, Layers	2 00	2 10
" M. R..........	1 90	2 00
" Valentias new..	0 6¾	0 7½
Currants, new........	0 5½	0 06½
" old........	0 04	0 04½
Figs	0 14	0 00
Molasses:		
Clayed, ⅌ gal.........	0 00	0 35
Syrups, Standard	0 60	0 00
" Golden	0 00	0 65
Rice:		
Arracan	4 25	4 50
Spices:		
Cassia, whole, ⅌ lb...	0 00	0 45
Cloves	0 11	0 12
Nutmegs	0 45	0 55
Ginger, ground	0 20	0 25
" Jamaica, root..	0 20	0 25
Pepper, black........	0 09½	0 10
Pimento	0 08	0 09
Sugars:		
Port Rico, ⅌ lb.......	0 10¾	0 11
Cuba "	0 10¼	0 11
Barbadoes (bright)...	0 10½	0 11
Canada Sugar Refine'y, yellow No. 2, 60 ds..	0 10¾	0 11
Yellow, No. 2½.......	0 11	0 11¼
No. 3........	0 11½	0 11½
Crushed X	0 13	0 13¼
" A	0 13	0 13¼
Ground..............	0 13½	0 14
Dry Crushed	0 14½	0 14½
Extra Ground.........	0 15½	0 15½
Teas:		
Japan com'n to good..	0 48	0 55
" Fine to choicest..	0 50	0 65
Colored, com. to fine..	0 60	0 75
Congou & Souch'ng...	0 42	0 75
Oolong, good to fine..	0 50	0 65
Y. Hyson, com to gd..	0 45	0 55
Medium to choice	0 65	0 80
Extra choice	0 85	0 95

Name of Article.	Wholesale Rate.	
Groceries—*Contin'd*	$ c.	$ c.
Gunpowd'r c. to med..	0 55	0 70
" med. to fine.	0 70	0 85
" fine to fins't..	0 85	0 95
Hyson	0 45	0 80
Imperial	0 42	0 80
Tobacco, Manufact'd:		
Can Leaf, ⅌ lb 5s & 10s.	26	0 30
Western Leaf, com..	25	0 26
" Good.......	27	0 32
" Fine.......	32	0 35
" Bright fine..	0 40	0 0
" " choice..	0 60	0 65
Hardware.		
Tin (net cash prices)		
Block, ⅌ lb.........	0 25	0 26
Grain...............	0 25	0 26
Copper:		
Pig	0 23	0 24
Sheet................	0 30	0 33
Cut Nails:		
Assorted ¼ Shingles, ⅌ 100 lb..........	2 90	3 00
Shingle alone do	3 15	3 25
Lathe and 5 dy.......	3 30	3 40
Galvanized Iron:		
Assorted sizes........	0 08	0 09
Best No. 24..........	0 09	0 00
" 26..........	0 08	0 08½
" 28..........	0 09	0 09½
Horse Nails:		
Guest's or Griffin's assorted sizes......	0 00	0 00
For W. ass'd sizes...	0 18	0 19
Patent Hammer'd do..	0 17	0 18
Iron (at 4 months):		
Pig—Cartsherrie No1..	24 00	25 00
Other brands. No1..	22 00	24 00
" No2..	0 00	0 00
Bar—Scotch, ⅌100 lb..	2 25	2 50
Refined	3 00	3 25
Swedes	5 00	5 50
Hoops—Coopers.......	3 00	3 25
Band	3 00	3 25
Boiler Plates.........	3 25	3 50
Canada Plates........	3 75	4 00
Union Jack	0 00	0 00
Pontypool...........	3 25	4 00
Swansea	3 90	4 00
Lead (at 4 months):		
Bar, ⅌ 100 lbs... ...	0 06½	0 07
Sheet "	0 08	0 09
Shot.................	0 07½	0 07¾
Iron Wire (net cash):		
No. 6, ⅌ bundle....	2 70	2 80
" 9, "	3 10	3 20
" 12, "	3 40	3 50
" 16, "	4 30	4 40
Powder:		
Blasting, Canada....	3 50	0 00
FF " ...	4 25	4 50
FFF " ...	4 75	5 00
Blasting, English ...	4 00	5 00
FF loose..	5 00	6 00
FFF " ..	6 00	6 50
Pressed Spikes (4 mos):..		
Regular sizes 100.....	4 00	4 25
Extra " ..	4 50	5 00
Tin Plates (net cash):		
IC Coke	7 50	8 50
IC Charcoal.........	8 25	8 50
IX "	10 25	10 75
IXX "	12 25	0 00
DC "	7 25	9 00
DX "	9 50	0 00
Hides & Skins, ⅌lb		
Green rough	0 06½	0 07
Green, salt'd & insp'd..	0 07½	0 08
Cured	0 00	0 00
Calfskins, green.......	0 00	0 10
Calfskins, cured.......	0 00	0 12
" dry.........	0 18	0 20
Sheepskins, ...	1 00	1 40
" country......	1 00	1 40
Hops.		
Inferior, ⅌ lb...... ...	0 05	0 07
Medium...	0 07	0 09
Good	0 09	0 12
Fancy	0 00	0 00
Leather, @ (4 mos.) In lots of less than 50 sides, 10 ⅌ cent higher.		
Spanish Sole, 1st qual'y heavy, weights ⅌ lb..	0 21½	0 22
Do. 1st qual middle do..	0 22½	0 00
Do. No. 2, light weights	0 00	0 21
Slaughter heavy	0 26	0 27
Do. light............	0 00	0 00
Harness, best	0 28	0 30
" No. 2........	0 34	0 36
Upper heavy..........	0 38	0 40
" light.......	0 40	0 42

Name of Article.	W[illegible]
Leather—*Contin'd.*	$
Kip Skins, Patna	0
French	0
English	0
Hemlock Calf (30 to 35 lbs.) per doz....	0
Do. light	0
French Calf, ...	1
Grain & Satn Clt ⅌ doz..	0
Splits, large ⅌ lb......	0
" small	0
Enamelled Cow ⅌ foot..	0
Patent	0
Pebble Grain	0
Buff...	0
Oils.	
Cod	0
Lard, extra	0
" No. 1	0
" Woollen	0
Lubricating, patent...	0
" Mott's economic	0
Linseed, raw..........	0
" boiled..... ..	0
Machinery............	0
Olive, common, ⅌ gal..	1
" salad	1
" salad, in bots. qt. ⅌ case....	3
Sesame salad, ⅌ gal...	1
Seal, pale...	0
Spirits Turpentine....	0
Varnish	0
Whale.	0
Paints, &c.	
White Lead, genuine in Oil, ⅌ 25 lbs......	0
Do. No. 1 "	0
" 2 "	0
" 3 "	0
White Zinc, genuine..	3
White Lead, dry.......	0
Red Lead.............	0
Venetian Red, Eng'h..	0
Yellow Ochre, Fren'h..	0
Whiting	0
Petroleum. (Refined ⅌ gal.)	
Water white, car l'd..	
" small lots....	0
Straw, by car load....	0
" small lots....	0
Amber, by car load..	0
" small lots	0
Benzine	0
Produce.	
Grain:	
Wheat, Spring, 60 lb..	0
" Fall 60 "..	0
Barley........ 48 "..	1
Peas... ...... 60 "..	0
Oats..... .... 34 "..	0
Rye .... 56 "..	0
Seeds:	
Clover, choice 60 "..	7
" com'n 68 "..	6
Timothy, cho'e 4 "..	2
" inf. to good 48 "..	2
Flax .... 56 "..	2
Flour (per brl.):	
Superior extra.......	0
Extra superfine,......	4
Fancy superfine.......	4
Superfine No 1......	4
" No. 2......	
Oatmeal, (per brl.)....	
Provisions	
Butter, dairy tub ⅌lb..	
" store packed...	
Cheese, new	
Pork, mess, per brl....	25
" prime mess......	
" prime	
Bacon, rough	
" Cumberl'd cut...	
" smoked	
Hams, in salt.........	
" sug. cur. & canv'd..	
Shoulders, in salt	0
Lard, in kegs.........	0
Eggs, packed	0
Beef Hams	0
Tallow	0
Hogs dressed, heavy..	9
" medium.....	8
" light.... ...	8
Salt, &c.	
American brls.........	1
Liverpool coarse	1
Plaster	1
Water Lime	1

Candles, Liquors, etc.

'andles.	$ c.	$ c.
& Co.'s ..	0 07¼	0 08
il........	0 07¼	0 07¼
Bar	0 07	0 07¼
lar	0 05	0 05¼
....	0 08¼	0 08¼
....	0 09	0 11¾

Liquors,

r doz...	2 60	2 65
)ub Fort'..	2 35	2 40
lca Rum...	1 80	2 25
's H. Gin..	1 55	1 65
d Tom...	1 90	2 00
es........	4 00	4 25
2 Tons, c...	6 00	6 25
nou.....	1 00	1 25
old	2 90	4 00
mmon...	1 00	1 50
un.......	1 70	1 80
or golden..	2 50	4 00

Brandy:

	$ c.	$ c.
Hennessy's, per gal...	2 30	2 50
Martell's "	2 30	2 50
J. Robin & Co.'s " ..	2 25	2 35
Otard, Dupuy & Cos..	2 25	2 35
Brandy, cases.....	8 50	9 00
Brandy, com. per c ...	4 00	4·50

Whiskey:

Common 36 u. p.....	0 63¼	0 65
Old Rye	0 85	0 87¼
Malt	0 85	0 87¼
Toddy	0 85	0 87¼
Scotch, per gal...	1 90	2 10
Irish—Kinnahan's c...	7 00	7 50
" Dunnville's Belf't..	6 00	6 25

Wool.

Fleece, lb..........	0 28	0 35
Pulled "	0 22	0 25

Furs.

Bear.............	3 00	10 00
Beaver, ℔ ℔.......	1 00	1 25
Coon	0 20	0 40
Fisher............	4 00	6 00
Martin............	1 40	1 60
Mink.............	3 25	4 00
Otter.............	5 75	6 00
Spring Rats.......	0 15	0 17
Fox..............	1 00	1 25

INSURANCE COMPANIES.

ENGLISH.—*Quotations on the London Market.*

ast Di-idend.	Name of Company.	Shares	Paid up Amount paid.	Last Sale.
7¼	Briton Medical and General Life ...	10		2¼
8	Commer'l Union, Fire, Life and Mar.	55	5	6¼
9½	City of Glasgow ...	25	2¼	5¼
6	Edinburgh Life	100	18	35
...Tr	European Life and Guarantee ...	2¼	11s6d	4s. 9d.
10	Etna Fire and Marine.........	10	1½	
5	Guardian	100	50	52
12	Imperial Fire.........	500	50	350
9½	Imperial Life	100	10	10⅜
10	Lancashire Fire and Life....	20	2	3⅜
11	Life Association of Scotland.....	40	7½	25
.a. p. sh.	London Assurance Corporation...	25	12½	49
8	London and Lancashire Life	10	1	18¾
40	Liverp'l & London & Globe F. & L.	20	2	6⅛
5	National Union Life .·.....	5	1	
13½	Northern Fire and Life	100	5	11½ x d
8, No ¼s.)	North British and Mercantile	50	6¼	20¼
50	Ocean Marine	25	5	19¼
15 10s.	Provident Life	100	10	67
4¼ p. s.	Phoenix......................	...	...	145
...L. yr.	Queen Fire and Life	100	15	
t. bc. 5s	Royal Insurance	20	3	6¼
10	Scottish Provincial Fire and Life ..	50	2½	5¼
25	Standard Life	50	12	66
5	Star Life	25	1½	—

CANADIAN.

			℔ c.	
4	British America Fire and Marine ..	$50	$25	55 55½
4	Canada Life	...	...	...
12	Montreal Assurance	$50	25	135
3	Provincial Fire and Marine.......	60	11	...
...	Quebec Fire	40	33½	36¼
...	" Marine............	100	40	75 80
7, mo's.	Western Assurance	40	9	...

RAILWAYS.

	Sha's	Paid	Montr	London
d St. Lawrence...............	£100	All.	61	62
l Lake Huron	20½	"	5½	6½
do Preferences ...	10	"	5½	6½
tf. &Goderich, 6%c.,1873-3-4...	100	"	66	69
1 and St. Lawrence	...	...	10	11
do Pref. 10 ℔ ct........	50	85	...	...
nk	100	"	16⅝16½	15½ 16½
Eq. G. M. Bds. 1 ch. 6%c........	100	"	...	86 87
First Preference, 5 ℔ c	100	"	...	55 55½
Deferred, 3 ℔ ct.......	100	"	...	...
Second Pref. Bonds, 5%c........	100	"	40	41
do Deferred, 3 ℔ ct.......	100	"	...	...
Third Pref. Stock, 4%ct......	100	"	28	30
do. Deferred, 3 ℔ ct........	100	"	...	...
Fourth Pref. Stock, 3%c......	100	"	17½ 18½
do. Deferred, 3 ℔ ct.......	100	"	...	...
lern	20¼	"	13 14	15¼ 15½
New	100	All.	...	...
6 ℔ c. Bds, due 1878-78.....	100	"	100 102
5½ ℔c Bds, due 1877-78.......	$250	all.	94 95
lway, Halifax, $250, all.....	$250	"	...	...
of Canada, 6%c. 1st Pref. Bds........	100	"	81 83

CHANGE.

	Halifax.	Montr'l.	Quebec.	Toronto.
London, 60 days.......	12⅜	9	9½	9½
75 days date	11½ 12	8 8½	8¼ 8½	9¼
.o. documents.........	...	7⅞ 8½	...	...
sw York......	24 24½	24 24½	...	77¼
do.	24¼ 25	...	...	...
s do.	par to ½ p.	par ⅜ dis.	par ½ dis.	...
	3 5½		3½ to 4½

STOCK AND BOND REPORT.

The dates of our quotations are as follows :—Toronto, March 3; Montreal, March 7; Quebec, March 1; London, Jan. 28.

NAME.	Shares.	Paid up.	Divid'd last 6 Months	Dividend Day.	Toronto.	Montre'l	Quebec.
BANKS.				℔ ct.			
British North America.......	$250	All.	3	July and Jan.	104	105½	104½ 105	108½104½
Jacques Cartier.......	50	"	3	1 June, 1 Dec.	109	109½	108½109½	108 109
Montreal..........	200	"	4		140½	141	140½ 141	139½139½
Nationale..........	50	"	4	1 Nov. 1 May.	100½	107	107 108	107¼108
New Brunswick	100	"			...	...	...	...
Nova Scotia	200	25	7&b68¼	Mar. and Sept.	...	...	...	...
Du Peuple.........	50	"	4	1 Mar., 1 Sept.	107	108	107 108	Bks cls'd
Toronto...........	100	"	4	1 Jan., 1 July.	121	122	121 122	121 122
Bank of Yarmouth......	...	...	...		...	...	...	...
Canadian Bank of Com'e...	50	95			108	108½	108½108½	102 108
City Bank Montreal.......	80	All.	4	1 June, 1 Dec.	108	108½	108 108½	108 108½
Commer'l Bank (St. John)..	100	"	℔ ct.		...	...	...	...
Eastern Townships' Bank..	50	"	4	1 July, 1 Jan..	...	...	98 99½	98 99
Gore	40	"	none.	1 Jan., 1 July.	43	41	41 45	42 45
Halifax Banking Company.....	...	...	...		...	...	...	...
Mechanics' Bank.......	50	70	4	1 Nov., 1 May.	95	96	95 96	95 96
Merchants' Bank of Canada...	100	70	4	1 Jan., 1 July.	108½	108½	108½ 109	108 108½
Merchants' Bank (Halifax)...	...	...	...		...	...	...	...
Molson's Bank	50	All.	4	1 Apr., 1 Oct.	113½	114	112 114	112 112½
Niagara District Bank.....	100	70	3¼	1 Jan., 1 July.	...	...	...	...
Ontario Bank	40	All.	4	1 June, 1 Dec.	100	100½	99½ 100	99 100
People's Bank (Fred'kton)...	100	"	...		...	...	...	...
People's Bank (Halifax)....	20	"	7 12 m		...	...	...	...
Quebec Bank	100	"	2	1 June, 1 Dec.	90	100	100 100½	99½ 100½
Royal Canadian Bank	50	50	4	1 Jan., 1 July.	85	86	86 87½	90
St. Stephens Bank	100	All.	...		...	...	...	...
Union Bank	100	70	4	1 Jan., 1 July	104	104½	104½ 105	104 105
Union Bank (Halifax).....	100	40	7 12mo	Feb. and Aug.	...	...	...	...
MISCELLANEOUS.								
British America Land.......	250	44	2¼		...	...	...	...
British Colonial S. S. Co.....	250	22½	2¼		...	...	50 60	
Canada Company	33½	All.	£1 10s.		...	...	...	...
Canada. Landed Credit Co.....	50	$20	3¼		...	...	74½ 75	
Canada Per. B'ldg Society...	50	All.	5		...	...	155½ 156	
Canada Mining Company ...	4	90	...		...	...	...	...
Do. Tal'd Steam Nav. Co....	100	27	7 "		...	...	100 100½	98 99
Do. Glass Company......	100	17	12½ "		...	...	40 65	
Canad'n Loan & Investm't..	25	2½	...		...	...	...	...
Canada Agency	10	¼	...		...	...	...	...
Colonial Securities Co.......	...	...	...		...	...	...	...
Freehold Building Society..	100	All.	4		...	...	110 110½	
Halifax Steamboat Co.......	100	"	5		...	...	...	...
Halifax Gas Company......	...	...	...		...	...	...	...
Hamilton Gas Company ...	...	...	...		...	...	...	...
Huron Copper Bay Co......	4	12	90		...	...	32½ 45	
Lake Huron S. and Co.......	20	6	...		...	...	...	...
Montreal Mining Consols....	20	$15	...		...	...	3.15 8.25	
Do. Telegraph Co.....	40	All.	5		138½	134	132½133½	132 134
Do. Elevating Co.....	40	"	15 12m		...	...	100 101	
Do. City Gas Co......	40	"	4	15 Mar. 15 Sep.	...	...	Bks cls'd	142 143
Do. City Pass. R., Co....	50	"	5		...	...	112 112½	111 112
Quebec and L. S.	8	$4	...		...	...	...	...
Quebec Gas Co	200	All.	4	1 Mar., 1 Sep.	...	...	Bks cls'd	
Quebec Street R. R.........	60	25	3		...	...	90 91	
Richelieu Navigation Co....	100	All.	10 p.a.	1 Jan., 1 July.	...	...	108 109	108 109
St. Lawrence Glass Company.	100	"	...		...	...	80 85	
St. Lawrence Tow Boat Co....	100	All.	...	3 Feb.	...	...	...	35 45
Tor'to Consumers' Gas Co....	50	"	4	1 My A. 1 MarFe	107	108	...	107 100
Trust & Loan Co. of U. C....	20	5	3		...	...	...	...
West'n Canada Bldg Soc'y....	50	All.	5		120½	121	...	...

SECURITIES.

	London.	Montreal.	Quebec.	Toronto.
Canadian Gov't Deb. 6 ℔ ct. stg..........	...	...	...	...
Do. do. 6 do due Ja.& Jul. 1877-84....	104½ 105½	102 108½	108 108½	109½ 108
Do. do. 6 do Feb. & Aug.....	108 105	108 109	108 109	...
Do. do. 6 do Mch. & Sep.....	106 108	...	...	...
Do. do. 5 ℔ ct. cur., 1883	94 96	94 96	94 94½	92½ 95
Do. do. 5 do. aug.,1885	96¼ 96½	94 94½	94 94½	92½ 94½
Do. do. 7 do. cur.,..........	...	...	...	...
Dominion 6 p. c. 1878 cy......	...	105 105½	108½105½	105 105½
Hamilton Corporation........	...	...	...	...
Montreal Harbor, 3 ℔ ct. d. 1860....	...	...	...	...
Do. do. 7 do. 1879.....	...	102 108	...	...
Do. do. 7 do. 1883.....	...	...	...	...
Do. do. 6 do. 1882.....	...	...	...	...
Do. Corporation, 6 ℔ c. 1891...	...	96 96½	96½ 96	96 96½
Do. 7 p. c. stock.....	...	108 109	108 109	109 110
Do. Water Works, 6 ℔ c. stg. 1878.....	...	...	...	95 96
Do. do. 6 do. cy. do......	...	96½ 97	...	96 96
New Brunswick, 6 ℔ ct., Jan. and July......	104 105	...	...	...
Nova Scotia, 6 ℔ ct., 1875.......	104 105	...	...	...
Ottawa City 6 ℔ c. d. 1880.....	...	93½ 95½	...	...
Quebec Harbour, 6 ℔ c. d. 1883........	...	...	80	...
Do. do. 7 do. do......	...	...	85 70	...
Do. do. 6 do. 1885......	...	...	80 85	...
Do. City, 7 ℔ c. d. 4½ years......	...	...	96½ 97	...
Do. do. 7 do. 9 do......	...	...	91 92	...
Do. do. 7 do. 3 do......	...	...	98 98½	...
Do. Water Works, 7 ℔ ct., 4 years	...	...	97 97½	...
Do. do. 6 do. 2 do......	...	...	94 95	...
Toronto Corporation........	...	90 92½	...	...

Insurance.

BEAVER
Mutual Insurance Association.

HEAD OFFICE—20 TORONTO STREET,
TORONTO.

INSURES LIVE STOCK against death from any cause. The only Canadian Company having authority to do this class of business.

R. L. DENISON,
President.

W. T. O'REILLY,
Secretary.			8-1y-25

HOME DISTRICT
Mutual Fire Insurance Company.

Office—North-West Cor. Yonge & Adelaide Streets,
TORONTO.—(UP STAIRS.)

INSURES Dwelling Houses, Stores, Warehouses, Merchandise, Furniture, &c.

PRESIDENT—The Hon. J. McMURRICH.
VICE-PRESIDENT—JOHN BURNS, Esq.
JOHN RAINS, Secretary.
AGENTS:
DAVID WRIGHT, Esq., Hamilton; FRANCIS STEVENS, Esq., Barrie; Messrs. GIBBS & BRO., Oshawa.		8-1y

---

THE PRINCE EDWARD COUNTY
Mutual Fire Insurance Company.

HEAD OFFICE,—PICTON, ONTARIO.
President, L. B. STINSON; Vice-President, W. A. RICHARDS.
Directors : H. A. McFaul, James Cavan, James Johnson, N. S. DeMill, William Delong.—Treasurer, David Barker Secretary, John Twigg ; Solicitor, R. J. Fitzgerald.

THIS Company is established upon strictly Mutual principles, insuring farming and isolated property, (not hazardous,) in Townships only, and offers great advantages to insurers, at low rates for five years, without the expense of a renewal.
Picton, June 15, 1868.			9-1y

THE AGRICULTURAL
Mutual Assurance Association of Canada.

HEAD OFFICE.........................LONDON, ONT.

A purely Farmers' Company. Licensed by the Government of Canada.

Capital, 1st January, 1869...................$250,103 82
Cash and Cash Items, over..................$96,000 00
No. of Policies in force........................30,892 00

THIS Company insures nothing more dangerous than Farm property. Its rates are as low as any well-established Company in the Dominion, and lower than those of a great many. It is largely patronised, and continues to grow in public favor.
For Insurance, apply to any of the Agents or address the Secretary, London, Ontario.
London, 2nd Nov., 1868.			12-1y.

Briton Medical and General Life
Association,
with which is united the
BRITANNIA LIFE ASSURANCE COMPANY.

Capital and Invested Funds.............£750,000 Sterling.

ANNUAL INCOME, £220,000 STG. :
Yearly increasing at the rate of £25,000 Sterling.

THE important and peculiar feature originally introduced by this Company, in applying the periodical Bonuses, so as to make Policies payable during life, without any higher rate of premiums being charged, has caused the success of the BRITON MEDICAL AND GENERAL to be almost unparalleled in the history of Life Assurance. Life Policies on the Profit Scale become payable during the lifetime of the Assured, thus rendering a Policy of Assurance a means of subsistence in old age, as well as a protection for a family, and a more valuable security to creditors in the event of early death ; and effectually meeting the often urged objection, that persons do not themselves reap the benefit of their own prudence and forethought.

No extra charge made to members of Volunteer Corps for services within the British Provinces.
☞ TORONTO AGENCY, 5 KING ST. WEST.
oct 17—9-1yr			JAMES FRASER, Agent.

Insurance.

The Gore District Mutual Fire Insurance
Company

GRANTS INSURANCES on all description of Property against Loss or Damage by FIRE. It is the only Mutual Fire Insurance Company which assesses its Policies yearly from their respective dates ; and the average yearly cost of insurance in it, for the past three and a half years, has been nearly

TWENTY CENTS IN THE DOLLAR

less than what it would have been in an ordinary Proprietary Company.
THOS. M. SIMONS,
Secretary & Treasurer.
ROBT. McLEAN,
Inspector of Agencies.
Galt, 26th Nov., 1868.			15-1y

Geo. Girdlestone,
Agent
FIRE, Life, Marine, Accident, and Stock Insurance
Very best Companies represented.
Windsor, Ont. June, 1868

The Standard Life Assurance Company,
Established 1825.
WITH WHICH IS NOW UNITED
THE COLONIAL LIFE ASSURANCE COMPANY.

Head Office for Canada :
MONTREAL—STANDARD COMPANY'S BUILDINGS,
No. 47 GREAT ST. JAMES STREET.
Manager—W. M. RAMSAY.		Inspector—RICH'D BULL.

THIS Company having deposited the sum of ONE HUNDRED AND FIFTY THOUSAND DOLLARS with the Receiver General, in conformity with the Insurance Act passed last Session, Assurances will continue to be carried out at moderate rates and on all the different systems in practice.

AGENT FOR TORONTO—HENRY PELLATT,
KING STREET.

AGENT FOR HAMILTON—JAMES BANCROFT.
6-6mos.

Fire and Marine Assurance.
THE BRITISH AMERICA
ASSURANCE COMPANY.
HEAD OFFICE :
CORNER OF CHURCH AND COURT STREETS,
TORONTO.

BOARD OF DIRECTION :
Hon G. W. Allan, M.L.C.,	A. Joseph, Esq.,
George J. Boyd, Esq ,	Peter Paterson, Esq.,
Hon. W. Cayley,	G. P. Ridout, Esq.,
Richard S. Cassels, Esq.,	E H. Rutherford, Esq ,
Thomas C. Street, Esq.

Governor:
GEORGE PERCIVAL RIDOUT, Esq.
Deputy Governor:
PETER PATERSON, Esq.

Fire Inspector:		Marine Inspector:
E. ROBY O'BRIEN.		CAPT. R. COURNEEN.

Insurances granted on all descriptions of property against loss and damage by fire and the perils of inland navigation.
Agencies established in the principal cities, towns, and ports of shipment throughout the Province.
THOS. WM. BIRCHALL,
23-1y			Managing Director.

Queen Fire and Life Insurance Company,
OF LIVERPOOL AND LONDON,

ACCEPTS ALL ORDINARY FIRE RISKS
on the most favorable terms.

LIFE RISKS

Will be taken on terms that will compare favorably with other Companies.

CAPITAL, - - - £2,000,000 Stg.

CHIEF OFFICES—Queen's Buildings, Liverpool, and Gracechurch Street London.
CANADA BRANCH OFFICE—Exchange Buildings, Montreal.
Resident Secretary and General Agent,
A. MACKENZIE FORBES,
13 St. Sacrament St., Merchants' Exchange, Montreal.
WM. ROWLAND, Agent, Toronto.			1-1y

Insurance.

The Waterloo County Mutual Fire Insu
Company.

HEAD OFFICE : WATERLOO, ONTARIO.

ESTABLISHED 1863.

THE business of the Company is divided int separate and distinct branches, the

VILLAGE, FARM, AND MANUFACTU

Each Branch paying its own losses and its just pro of the managing expenses of the Company.
C. M. TAYLOR, Son.		M. SPRINGER, M.M.P ,
J. HUGHES, Inspector.

Ætna Fire and Marine Insurance Compa
Dublin.

AT a Meeting of the Shareholders of this Co held at Dublin, on the 13th inst., it was agre the business of the " ÆTNA" should be transferred "UNITED PORTS AND GENERAL INSURANCE CON In accordance with this agreement, the business wi after be carried on by the latter Company, which a and guarantees all the risks and liabilities of the ".
The Directors have resolved to continue the CA BRANCH, and arrangements for resuming FIRE a RINE business are rapidly approaching completion
16			T. W. GRIFFIT
MAN

Lancashire Insurance Compa

CAPITAL, - - - - - £2,000,000 S

FIRE RISKS
Taken at reasonable rates of premium, a
ALL LOSSES SETTLED PROMPTLY,
By the undersigned, without reference elsew
S. C. DUNCAN-CLARK & CO.,
General Agents for Ontar
25-1y		N. W. Corner of King & Church St
TORONTO.

DIVISION OF PROFITS NEXT X.

ASSURANCES
EFFECTED BEFORE 30TH APRIL NEXI
IN THE
CANADA LIFE ASSURANCE COMF
OBTAIN A YEAR'S ADDITIONAL PROFI
OVER LATER ENTRANTS,
And the great success of the Company warrants rectors in recommending this very importa advantage to assurers.

SUMS ASSURED.............................£
AMOUNT OF CAPITAL AND FUNDS.........
ANNUAL INCOME................................

Assets (excluding capital) for each $100 of L about $150.
The income from interest upon investments alone sufficient to meet claims by death.
A. G. RAMSAY, Man
E. BRADBURNE, Ag
3 11			Toronto

The Victoria Mutual
FIRE INSURANCE COMPANY OF CAN

Insures only Non-Hazardous Property, at Lo

BUSINESS STRICTLY MUTUA

GEORGE H. MILLS, President.
W. D. BOOKER, Secretary.
HEAD OFFICE ....HAMILTON.
aug 15-1yr -

PUBLISHED AT THE OFFICE OF THE MO. TIMES, No. 60 CHURCH STREET.
PRINTED AT THE DAILY TELEGRAPH PUBLISHING BAY STREET, CORNER OF KING.

THE CANADIAN
IONETARY TIMES
AND
INSURANCE CHRONICLE.

OTED TO FINANCE, COMMERCE, INSURANCE, BANKS, RAILWAYS, NAVIGATION, MINES, INVESTMENT,
PUBLIC COMPANIES, AND JOINT STOCK ENTERPRISE.

—NO. 31. TORONTO, THURSDAY, MARCH 18, 1869. { SUBSCRIPTION: $3 YEAR.

Mercantile.

Meetings.

TORONTO MUTUAL FIRE INSURANCE COMPANY.

The second annual meeting of this Company
was held at the office, 20 Toronto street, on Tuesday, February 23, 1869. The chair was taken by
R. L. Denison, Esq. After the usual routine
business, the Secretary read the report of the
Board of Directors, as follows:

Report.

In submitting the usual annual statement of
the affairs of the Company, the Board of Directors
are glad to congratulate the members upon the
satisfactory result of last year's operations.

The following summary will show, that since
the 31st December, 1867, up to the end of the
year, the business has been more than doubled;
and it is believed that our position at the present
time will compare favorably with that of any
other Mutual Company doing the like class of
insurance.

Household Branch.

Applications to Dec. 31st, 1867	516	
Less cancelled in 1868	8	
		508
Applications to Dec. 31st, 1868	852	
		1360

Amount Insured to Dec.		
31st, 1867	$300,285	
Less cancelled in 1868..	3,900	
		$296,385 00
Amount insured to Dec 31st, 1868..	506,722 00	
		$803,107 00

Premium Notes to Dec'r		
31st, 1867	$9,452 53	
Less cancelled in 1868..	165 25	
		$9,287 28
Premium Notes to Dec. 31st, 1868..	14,495 30	
		$23,782 58

Mercantile Branch;

Applications to Dec. 31st, 1867	354	
Less cancelled in 1868	21	
		333
Applications to Dec. 31st, 1868	529	
		862

Amount Insured to Ded.		
31st, 1867	$282,682	
Less cancelled in 1868..	19,350	
		$263,332 00
Amount insured to Dec. 31st, 1868	381,336 00	
		$644,668 00

Premium Notes to Dec.		
31st, 1867	$18,446 24	
Less cancelled in 1868	1,189 68	
		$17,256 56
Premiums to Dec. 31st, 1868.....	26,035 79	
		$43,842 35

Total Policies in both Branches		2,222
" Amount Insured		$1,447,775 00
" Amount of Premium Notes		$67,124 93

The average amount insured per policy is—
Household Branch, $591—Mercantile Branch,
$749. The cash receipts for the year were $14,-
692.13—Disbursements, $14,015.95. Fire claims,
Household Branch, $2,022.81—Mercantile Branch
$6,688.63. The number of policies expired or
cancelled during the year was—Household Branch
33—Mercantile Branch, 100.

Your Board might easily have done a two-fold
larger business, had they followed the example of
other Mutual Companies in taking heavy risks, or

risks on property specially hazardous." · However
legitimate such business may be in the abstract,
your Board have felt it to be the wiser course to
defer accepting it until the Company should be
older, and better able to incur the hazard. It
will, of course, be for their successors to decide
whether this policy of exclusion shall be relaxed,
and to what extent.

Your Board have, by way of further precaution,
re-insured with another company all risks exceeding $1,500 in amount; and have besides, em-
ployed a competent Inspector, whose sole duty it
is to examine and report upon every existing risk
in turn, and whose services are kept in constant
requisition for that purpose. Could any further
precaution in the selection of risks have been
taken, your Board would certainly have done so.

Up to the end of last year, it was found impracticable to carry out the promise held out in
your prospectus, by assessing all members of each
Branch in exact proportion to the losses and expenses in that Branch ; and in consequence, an
assessment of 2-9ths of all premium notes in force,
was directed to be made temporarily. Now, however, the books of the Company are carefully made
up with a view to a complete system of assessment
on that principle ; and every member will be credited in his next year's assessment with the surplus (if any) he may have been charged on his
former assessment. This, it is hoped, will be entirely satisfactory in every case, especially as no
such difficulty can possibly occur hereafter.

It may be perhaps too soon to ascertain accurately, what proportion the rates of insurance in
the two branches bear to each other ; but from
present appearances they are very evenly balanced,
which would tend to prove, that no change in our
tariff rates is likely to be called for, by way of
doing equal justice to all members in proportion to
the hazard of their respective risks.

Your Board have had under consideration, a
resolution passed at the recent annual meeting of
the Beaver Mutual Fire Ins. Association, of which
a copy has been officially communicated to them,
authorizing the Board of Directors of that body to
make arrangements for its union with this Company. In the desirability of such a union your
Board entirely concur, and recommend immediate
action on your part to carry it into effect. The
reason assigned at the meeting held in December,
1867, for the formation of a distinct company,
viz: that farmers would not insure in a company
taking town or village risks, has been removed in
a great degree by the introduction on a large scale
of the cash system into farm insurance, under
which system it matters nothing to the insured
what classes of risks may be taken together. Besides, there are several companies now in existence
doing a mixed farm and village business, and
they find that the prejudice above notice 1 is
dying out, more particularly as it is now seen
that the better class of town and village risks can
be insured quite as cheaply as farm property,

By the special Act of last session of the Ontario Legislature, passed 4th March last, secs. 4 and 5, three only of your Directors retire on this occasion, viz: Messrs. Fleming, McCord and Howland, whose places it will be your duty to fill up, by re-election or otherwise, as you may determine by ballot, according to the statute.

R. L. DENISON, President.
S. THOMPSON, Managing Director.

Toronto, Feb. 23, 1869.

The Treasurer's statements of receipts and expenditures, and of assets and liabilities, were also read:

Statement of Assets and Liabilities for the year ending December 31st, 1868.

ASSETS.

To Cash on hand and in Agents' hands. $1,098 30
" Premium Notes liable to Assessment, Household Branch............$23,782 53
" Less 1st Payments and Assessments.............. 3,900 63
                                    ———— 19,881 90

" Premium Notes liable to Assessment, Mercantile Branch 43,342 35
" Less 1st Payments and Assessments.............. 6,763 44
                                    ———— 36,578 91
" Office Furniture...................... 98 15
                                    ————
                                    $57,657 29

LIABILITIES.

By Receipts on Guarantee stock $4,934 13
" Bills Payable................... 1,823 16
" Bills Payable for fire claims settled, but not matured 904 30
" Fire Claims, since settled . 2,986 66
" Claims in dispute............ 750 00
" Printing..................... 46 28
" Salaries..................... 367 02
" Legal Expenses.............. 162 22
" Premium Notes given for Re-insurance, liable to Assessment, Household Branch.............. 114 40
" Premium Notes given for Re-insurance, liable to Assessment, Mercantile Branch..... . ... 8,867 31
" Interest on Guarantee Stock...................... 188 40
                                    ———— $21,649 47
Balance of assets over liabilities. 36,007 82
                                    ————
                                    $57,657 29

Statement of Receipts and Expenditure for the year ending 31st December, 1868.

RECEIPTS.

Cash on hand January 1st, 1868.. ..... $ 422 02
" 1st Payments on Prem. Notes, Household Br.$1,601 61
" 1st Payments on Prem. Notes, Mercantile Br. 2,727 25
                                    ———— 4,328 86
" Assessments on Mercantile Branch........ 1,687 26
" Assessments on Household Branch... .... 1,005 12
                                    ———— 2,692 38
" Premiums on Re-insurances, H. B. 2,229 42
" Premiums on Re-insurances, M. B. 310 29
" Premiums on Cash Policies, Household Br... 208 25
" Premiums on Cash Policies, Mercantile Br.... 570 75
                                    ———— 779 00
" Insurance, Carpenters' Risks...... 13 03
" Guarantee Stock................... 3,898 90
" Re-insurance Claim............... 415 30
" Charges........................ 20 25
                                    ————
                                    $15,109 57

EXPENDITURE.

Fire Claims, Household Dr..$ 722 83
Do.   Mercantile Br.. 3,766 83
                                    ———— $ 4,489 66
Printing and Advertising, 1867 & 1868. 614 09
Bill Stamps and Postages................ 171 46
Paeliamentary Expenses................ 165 43
Legal Expenses...................... 213 59
Petty Expenses...................... 44 74
Travelling Expenses.................. 595 85
Rent and Taxes...................... 130 57
Writing Policies..................... 179 80
Commission to Agents................. 2,567 72
Office Furniture..................... 35 00
Directors' Fees..................... 292 33
Salaries........................... 2,909 93
Interest on Guarantee Stock and Bills Payable..................... 58 21
First Payments and Assessments on Policies Re-insured.............. 1,205 50
Returned Premiums on Declined and Cancelled Policies, M. B 436 97
Returned Premiums on Declined and Cancelled Policies, H. B.......... 69 43
Auditing Accounts................... 30 00
Cash on hand January 1st, 1869......... 40 82
Cash in Agents' hands 1,057 48
                                    ————
                                    $15,109 57

Audited this 27th February, 1869,
JOHN MAUGHAN,   H. HANCOCK,
    Auditor.   Sec. and Treasurer.

The chairman then moved the adoption of the report, which was carried unanimously.

Dr. Riddel then moved, seconded by Mr. Fleming: "That the Board of Directors be authorized to take steps for carrying out the union of this Company with the Beaver Mutual Fire Ins. Association, and to prepare a petition to Parliament, and also a bill to give effect thereto." Carried.

On motion of Mr. J. W. Hancock, seconded by Mr. Gregory, it was resolved, "That 2,500 copies of the annual report be printed for the use of policy holders."

On motion of Mr. Paterson, seconded by Mr. Rowsell, Mr. John Maughan was appointed Auditor for the current year.

The ballot for the election of three Directors in the place of those retiring, was then proceeded with, and the scrutineers reported that the choice of the meeting had fallen on Messrs. C. E. Chadwick, A. Barker and Joseph Gregory.

After the usual vote of thanks to the President and Directors, and to the officers of the Company, the meeting broke up.

At a meeting of the Board of Directors, held subsequently, Charles E. Chadwick, Esq., was elected President, and D. Thurston, Esq., Vice President for the current year.

UNION PERMANENT BUILDING AND SAVINGS SOCIETY.

The annual general meeting of the stockholders of this Society was held at the Society's office, on the afternoon of Monday, the 15th instant. A statement of the affairs of the Society was submitted, together with the Auditors' report thereon. From these it was shown that the Society has made decided progress during the past year, there being a considerable increase both in the amount of paid-up stock and the amount of deposits. Two half-yearly dividends had been paid to the stockholders at the rate of 10 per cent. per annum, and a sum added to the permanent rest.

It was agreed that a new issue of shares be made to the extent of $25,000, at a premium of 6 per cent.; and resolved that the paid-up stock be capitalized as soon as the necessary arrangements can be completed for that purpose.

A ballot being then taken, the following gentlemen were re-elected Directors for the ensuing year, viz.:
MR. FRANCIS RICHARDSON,
MR. ARTHUR LEPPER,
MR. THOMAS HENNING,
MR. ISAAC C. GILMOR,
MR. J. C. FITCH,
MR. A. HENDERSON,
MR. GEORGE GOULDING.

PESQU' ISLE AND BELMONT RAILWAY.—A meeting of the Provisional Directors of the Isle and Belmont Railway, held at Campbe on Monday, the 8th March, the following gentlemen were elected officers, viz:—
John Eyre, Esq., M.P.P. President.
J. M. Ferris, Esq., Vice President.
John E. Proctor, Esq., Treasurer.
M. K. Lockwood, Esq., Secretary.

The liveliest interest was manifested, to operations commenced as soon as possible.

Insurance.

FIRE RECORD.—Lucknow, Ont., February John Grundy's waggon shop and content surance on the latter $300, none on the bui which were valued at $400.

Napanee, March 16.—A fire occurred at nce on Monday night, about half-past ten o by which a frame building on Dundas stre belonging to Messrs. Webster & Boyes, ca nakers, was consumed. Part of the b was occupied by them as a store-room for un ed work, a large quantity of which, being in the garret, was burned. They were insu the British American Insurance Company— stock $100, and on the building $200—whi not cover their loss. The upper story was pied by the Misses Wales as a dwelling an liner shop. They lost nearly all their cl jewellery, $70 in cash, and only escaped i nights clothes. Insured for $200 on goods.

Howes occupied the ground floor as a g Her goods and effects were nearly all saved.

Kings, N.S., March 7.—A dwelling hous contents, owned by Mr. Goddard, of South I Kings County (between Penobsquis and D in Albert County), was almost wholly des by fire. How the fire originated is unkno

Caledonia, March 12.—House of Robt. kin, with most of the contents. Loss on co $150; loss on building, $600. No insuran

Thorold, March 13.—The Thorold carried on by Messrs. Broden & Boot formerly in the possession of Mr. William b was destroyed by fire. We have not been obtain accurate information as to the ex the loss; but it could not have been very g the establishment was not extensive.

Bosworth, Ont., Feby. 23.—Store of A the stock was insured in the Waterloo Mu $1,200, but the furniture and building wer sured. The building was owned by Mr. B and is a total loss.

Seaforth, March 11.—Mr. Trainer's Tuckersmith, was destroyed; the buildin stone.

Goderich, March 11.—A Goderich pap that the shed attached to the house o Mr. Finley, teller in the Bank of Montre enveloped in flames, Mr. Finlay had tim move his family and most of his furniture of the fire unknown. His loss we have no but that of the house is about $800.

Dereham, Ont., March 7.—House of C on 2nd Con., with contents was destro insurance.

Toronto, March.—An old farm house Cruickshank farm, and an adjacent shed, a stable. The latter contained two hors were destroyed, said to be insured ; th thought to be incendiary.

ierines, March 15.—The Thorold Pot-
ed and occupied by Mr. Baker, in the
atskirts of the village, was destroyed by
urday night last. The amount of loss
ot learned, but understand it is fully
y insurance.
evi, 2 Feby.—A dwelling and store were
on through the explosion of a coal oil
he owner had a narrow escape. The loss
3,000. The buildings were uninsured.
lle, March 6.—A fire originated in the
of the drug store of Mr. Fulford, under
circumstances. The fire was extin-
ith a loss of about $100. We are in-
at Fulford has since left for parts un-

, March 8.—A fire broke out in the attic
Skinner's drug store, and damage to the
of the store to the extent of $500 re-
nsured in the Western Assurance Co. for
Fire is supposed to have resulted from

, March 3.—The roof and upper story
lding owned by Patrick Smith was da-
fire to the extent of about $600 ; in-
he Western for $2,000.
, March 12.—The frame store of Nicholson caught fire. The contents of the
the effects on the first flat were dama-
ere was no insurance on the building; but
ch America had $1,500 on stock, which
of packages, &c., done up in business-like
consisting mostly of saw dust, blocks of
We were shown a sample of "Flavoring"
selected from their stock. It was beau-
belled, and bore the name of a leading
uggists in Montreal, but, when opened,
to contain a neat block of pine wood.
value of their stock world, it is thought,
o $40. At an examination of Beeson, at
wa Police Court, charged with setting
ises on fire, he made a statement admit-
guilt.
ch, March 11.—Another destructive fire
here last night, in a frame block on the
of the Market Square, owned by Dr.
ll, and occupied by G. N. Davis, dealer
. etc.; Mrs. Wilson, milliner; Thomas
shoemaker, and Mrs. Mack, restaurant
which is supposed to have originated
rdy's shop, broke out about midnight,
first it was evident that no part of the
could be saved, and the citizens directed
rts to the salvation of the adjoining brick
occupied by F. Jordan, druggist, and J.
ry goods merchant, and to the removal
from the different shops in the burning
Mrs. Mack saved most of her goods, but
amaged; she was partially insured.
ved but a small portion of his stock; in-
$400. Mrs. Wilson lost nearly all her
household goods; partially insured. G.
' stock and furniture were very badly
in removal; loss unknown; insured for
F. Jordan's building was saved through
ordinary exertions of the citizens and the
wind; but the stock was very much de-
y removal; loss not known. As is gen-
e case, our fire engines could not be
into action, owing to their being frozen
me other trivial cause. The buildings
ured. Had the wind and weather been
some, some eight or ten other stores, and
the Bank of Montreal, would have fallen
the devouring element.
al, March .—A fire occurred in the
over Clendenen's hardware store, in
et, by which the stock of the latter was
bly damaged.
ncial Union.—The directors of the
ial Union Assurance Company have re-
recommend at the meeting on the 9th of
t., with a bonus of 2s. 6d. per share, free
e tax, being at the rate of 7½ per cent.
m.

Dismissed. — Mr. Drury has been dismissed
from his place as Assistant Manager of the Provincial Insurance Company, with a douceur of
three months' pay in advance.
Liverpool, London and Globe.—The avail-
able total at the end of the year's business is stated
by the directors of this company at £211,237 17s.
11d., from which it is determined to take £117,-
525 12s. for distribution among the proprietors.
This will yield a dividends for the year of 30 per
cent, free from income tax.
Marine Losses.—The losses for February include 22 vessels—all American or foreign vessels
insured at New York. Total value of the property
burned, lost and missing estimated at $900,000.

	Vessels.	Value.
Total losses for January...	36	$1,817,500
Total losses for Feby......	22	900,000
Total for two months...	58	$2,717,500
Same period in 1868....	75	$4,137,700
" " 1867....	130	6,028,500
" " 1866...	151	8,911,500

PUBLICATION OF SURRENDER VALUES.

The late recommendation by D. Parks Fackler
of a system of endorsing the surrender value on a
policy, appears to have met the favorable concurrence of some of the life companies, and will
probably be adopted, mutatis mutandis, by most
of them—half-note companies, it may be, excepted. This improvement—for anything having
a tendency. to make clear the precise financial
relationship existing between the companies and
their members, should. be viewed in the light of
an improvement—is of no pecuniary advantage to
any one, as it merely sets forth the exact value of
the policy at the end of each year, the next annual
premium being due. The insured may at any
time inform himself as to the cash value of his
contract and the legal obligations which the company have assumed; or, if he should desire it, the
endorsement will enable him to hypothecate his
policy at any bank; or, more correctly speaking,
it may be used as a collateral security of loans.
As it is now, the surrender value of a policy is
somewhat mythical, as no one outside of the
company can tell exactly what it is, and the company generally exercise arbitrary rules in its estimation. The exact value of a policy is the amount
of its reserve, but it is obvious that this amount
is not paid. Policies lapsed or surrendered, work
an injury to any company, notwithstanding it
appears to be a source of congratulation that the
offices have profited by them, for the ultimate loss
to the company is obvious, as the surrendered
policies are generally on the best lives, and the
source of profit is incontinently stopped. But so
long as the company holds an amount over and
above the expense, and other cost of insurance,
it is but justice to return it to the party from
whom it was received; and, as every reputable
office feels morally bound to return, when desired,
the estimated value of the policy, either in cash
or its equivalent, there can be no satisfactory objection to making known to the insured the
amount to be expected in the event of a surrender,
for the simple reason, if no other, that it may be
made transferable to its fullest extent, and that
any uncertainty as to its negotiable value may be
removed.
Just so far, however, as it encourages the surrender of policies, it is mischievous; and it were
better for the company to keep the insured uninformed as to the cash value of his contract, if such
information tends to lessen the duration of it—a
result more likely to occur among good lives than
bad ones, and, as a sequence, the return loss to
the company would be greater.
The probable return would be about four-fifths
of the reserve, deducting the obligations of the
insured; provided, the second annual payment had
been paid, for we doubt the practicability, or, at

any rate, the expediency, of paying any consideration at an earlier period. The return values attaching to policies issued by a mutual company,
should be estimated in connection with the loss
which accrues indirectly to other members, and
also the expense which was incurred in procuring
the risk; but the equity of deducting the cost of
replacing the risk might be questioned on the
ground of injustice, for the insured has already
paid the cost of it once. But it is argued that,
as an appreciable advantage accrues to other
members by the introduction of a new one, it is
to their benefit to lessen the actual expense of the
newly insured member by a contribution, which
will eventually return to them; and, for this
reason, if he should retire before they have been
fully indemnified, it is but right that he should
pay the cost of filling the vacancy. Upon this
basis the St. Louis Mutual Life proposes to estimate all surrender values; that is, to deduct from
the reserve the per centage on the premium, which
the company would have to pay to replace the
risk.
If this system is to prevail to any extent, and
the auguries are that it will, a noticeable difference will arise from the valuations on the Ac
tuaries at four per cent. and the Americans at four
and a half, which will have a tendency to militate
valuations should be sufficiently wide to enable
agents to draw disparaging conclusions. This
new feature has been adopted by the Brooklyn,
of New York; atlas, of St. Louis; and, we believe,
by the National Life, of Washington. The Hon.
Elizur Wright speaks most favorably of it, and
recommends it as a plan that will show to the
policy-holder why such large sums of money
must be held in reserve to meet future liabilities.—
Western Insurance Review.

Insolvents.—Zophar Locke, Goderich; Ulhric
Jean Francoeur, Sorel; George Brown, Goderich;
William John Percy, Kingston; Lewis Houck,
Whitby; Jno. Glassford, Barrie; Edwin B. Turner,
Montreal; George M. Labaye, Compton Centre;
Wm. Moss, Montreal; Duncan Campbell, Eldon;
Henry J. Lawton. Montreal; R. A. & R. H.
Jennison, Ravenshoe; Godfrey Gingras, Quebec;
Alex. & Donald McDonnell, Cornwall; Wm. Hill,
Cornwall; Thomas Grory Owen Sound; J. H.
Brown, Brampton; Porlier & Porlier, St. John's;
Irving & Hogg, Paisley; Marie Simard, Montreal;
William Ennis, Montreal; James Hiscott, St.
Catherines; R. H. Hudgin, Guelph; Andrew
Morris, Montreal; John E. Fitzgerald, Fenelon
Falls; Robert Scanes & Thos. Allan, Montreal; L.
Lavoie, Quebec; Walter Brown & W. C. Chewett,
Toronto; John Jacob Marshall, Ingersoll; David
Henderson, London; Richard Pidgeon, Napanee;
John Clements, Berthier; John M. Bowen,
Napanee; Thomas McWilliams, Brougham; Geo.
Church, Chatham; William Little & John Wilson,
Guelph; Andrew Warner, Guelph; Alexander
McKelvy, Chatham; Ninian Holmes, Chatham;
John Creighton, Prescott; James Spratt Wilde,
Napanee; Arthur & John Stickle, Waterford;
Anaclette Bissonnette, Henryville.
Writs of attachment have been issued against
Eli Spencer, James Armstrong & Alex. Soutter,
and William Trent, Toronto; William Howe,
Guelph; James Dallyn Hamilton, Wm. Truman,
and Thos. Daville, Hamilton.

The wharf and dock property at Niagara have
been again taken possession of by the Bank of
Montreal, by a decision of the courts and are to
be leased to Captain Milloy.

The Town Treasurer of Collingwood has been
directed to deposit the whole of the funds of the
town in the Bank of Commerce, Toronto, provided the usual interest be allowed.

F. W. Cumberland, Esq., Manager of the Northern Railway, has gone to Cuba for the benefit
of his health.

THE CANADIAN MONETARY TIMES AND INSURANCE CHRONICLE *is printed every Thursday evening and distributed to Subscribers on the following morning.*

Publishing office, No. 60 Church-street, 3 doors north of Court-street.

Subscription price—$2 per annum.

Casual advertisements will be charged at the rate of ten cents per line, each insertion.

Address all letters to "THE MONETARY TIMES." *Cheques, money orders, &c., should be made payable to* J. M. TROUT, *Business Manager, who alone is authorized to issue receipts for money.*

All Subscribers to THE MONETARY TIMES *will receive* THE REAL ESTATE JOURNAL *without further charge.*

The Canadian Monetary Times.

THURSDAY, MARCH 18, 1869.

THE BANK CHARTER QUESTION — THE PARAMOUNT NECESSITY OF CONVERTIBILITY.

ARTICLE II.

The wisdom of man has not invented and never can invent, a system of banking that shall be so absolutely perfect as to be free from the consequences of human weakness and human error. To look after absolute perfection, would only be to chase a will-o'-the-wisp with the usual result of being landed in a quagmire. The best scheme of banking that can be devised will be insufficient to guard against occasional losses and disasters. To reduce these evils to the minimum is all that it is possible to accomplish. Occasions will sometimes occur when the temptation to forget these inevitable facts is strong ; when, neglecting the possible, we shall be in danger of arriving at the impossible. Of this nature is the desire, which now has partial possession of the public mind, to see provided some absolute security for bill-holders. Nothing is more natural than such a desire. The whole community are virtually, if not legally, obliged to take bank notes, and few things are more desirable than that some positive material security should be given for their redemption. But here there is much more to be lost than gained by attempting too much. If banks are required to deposit with some third party, as security for their note circulation, a value equal to the whole amount of their notes, they will, by that fact, be deprived of the means of maintaining their convertibility. The first great essential of a sound and uniform currency will be gone. Ultimate security, or what is supposed to be such, will have been purchased at the frightful cost of present convertibility.

The necessity of providing for the redemption of the paper currency, whatever form it may assume, in specie on demand, is so paramount, and so well understood, that we do not expect to see it now denied. Whatever scheme of currency and banking may be presented to the Dominion Parliament, we may be sure that it will set out with the pretence of providing for the convertibility of the paper circulation. Any other course would, at the present time, be fatal to it. But there is great danger that, while professing to secure this great essential, it will, by its nature, render the continued maintenance of convertibility impossible. What will be necessary to see to will be that the scheme be such as not to be incompatible with continuous convertibility, but shall contain all reasonable guarantees for its maintainance. More professions on this point must go for nothing.— Even Law, whose "system" ran into the wildest and most extravagant excesses, set out with the declaration, in which he was joined by the Regent, that a banker who issued notes beyond his means of redemption, deserved death. But the moment Law's bank was made a Royal Institution, it began to do what was incompatible with continued redemption. The issues were at once increased from sixty to a thousand millions of livres. Law soon began to think, and the general insanity favored the idea, that paper could take the place of coin. Notes were issued on the deposit of shares. A run for specie gave birth to a decree declaring the notes to be worth five per cent more than coin. All transactions which would bring more than a hundred francs were compulsorily obli[ged] be effected in notes. But no sooner ha[d] chants taken the notes than they flew [to the] bank to have them cashed. At la[st] notes were made a legal tender. A f[or]reduction in the value of gold and [silver] was decreed.

Here, it will be seen, the notes we[re] no means made a legal tender, at first. [Step] by step the downward progress to bank[ruptcy] and ruin went. The lesson is not with[out] uses to us. It teaches us to watch na[rrowly] and strenuously to guard against th[e] steps towards the rejection of the co[nverti-] bility of the note circulation. Alread[y] government notes have been put to [uses] for which they are, by their nature, un[fit]. Certain amounts of them have been for[ced on] the banks to be held in lieu of specie. [That] is, in plain terms, a substitution of cre[dit for] capital, and it is the first step on the r[oad to] ruin. It is the first blow to converti[bility.] In other respects we have gone as fa[r as law] took Law some time to go. We ma[de] Government note a legal tender, at th[e start,] but that does not qualify it to take th[e place] of specie. Confessedly there is only [a small] amount of specie at the back of it—onl[y what] is necessary to meet casual demands.

The main question which Parliame[nt] have to decide is so broad that we n[eed not] waste time on nice distinctions, which [at] times enter into the discussion of econ[omic] questions elsewhere. We need not dal[ly with] the doubt whether a convertible cu[rrency] can ever sink below the value of th[e coin] into which it is exchangeable at the [will of] the holder. It will be safe to assume [that] depreciation can never be greater th[an the] fractional percentage chargeable, in t[erms] of exchange, to cover the cost of its c[arriage] from the point where it is found in [rela-] tion to the designated place of rede[mption.] This is seldom more than a quarter [of one] per cent.; and if the issuers were un[wisely] debarred from issuing at one poin[t notes] payable at another, for the purpose [of ob-] structing convertibility, even this [loss] would hardly ever be payable. Ind[eed the] cases in which it has to be paid now [are] rare. Not one man out of a thousa[nd, who] receives notes, requires to have the[m con-] verted into gold. In receiving a b[ank note] which can be exchanged for gold, at [the op-] tion of the receiver, every one kno[ws what] he is getting. It is not a thing t[o which] one value is attached to-day and an[other to-] morrow, and a third next week. It [is part] of the stability of the gold on wh[ich it is] based. If a man agrees to pay or to [receive a] three months, six months, or a year [at any] given sum of money, he knows [exactly] what he has to count on. This an element of strict justice and absecurity into all transactions in money plays a part. No one can get antage over another; no one suffers at ads of another. There is the same e for all.

an irredeemable paper currency, all reversed. No one knows what the y will be worth from one day to another. Under the greenback system of the States we have seen gold touch three l per cent.—that is it took three l dollars in Government paper currency buy one hundred dollars in gold—have seen it halting at every point that figure and about thirty per remium. Imagine the chronic condition daily and hourly injustice of such a, the uncertainty, the disappointment l robberies, frauds and misery of is necessarily the parent. In France that a much worse state of things lted from inconvertible paper money; re was a time when a man with fifty of assignats in his pockets could purchase the most meagre breakfast; tree thousand dollars would not to buy a load of firewood, and a would be swallowed up in providing family dinner.

not be necessary to say more to prove mate security would be purchased too t the price of present and continuous bility. And all provisions for ulticurity are more or less delusive. this is not what the note holder wants; he wants this, but he also onvertibility. Now, and in the future suppose the ultimate redemption ote secured by a deposit somewhere rnment securities. A bank breaks, necessary to realize on the securities at becomes of the bona fide note n the meantime? Do they, as a rait the process of winding up? Is it power to do so? Before these s are answered it is necessary to in whose hands the bulk of k or government note currency is be found. It is well known that in rity of large transactions, such notes rcely any share. Payment is made les; and all the money that passes goes to adjust the bankers' balances. tes are mainly paid out for labour mall trading operations. It thus that the great bulk of the bank culation is to be found in the laborers, mechanics, and others of or classes of the community. They t wait till the securities of a bank or ent were realized to get the proceeds tes they held, at the time of failure.

Their circumstances would compel them to sell at the moment of the greatest depreciation : they could not hold on a week, many of them not three days; and they would have to submit to whatever shave a moment of panic might enable speculative purchasers to extort. So that even if the notes were ultimately redeemed, the benefit would accrue, not to the bona fide holder, but to the speculative purchaser.

This is another reason, if more were wanted, why present and continuous convertibility should not be jeopardized, by embarrassing precautions for ultimate realization. No scheme which endangers or makes practically impossible the convertibility of the bank note should receive the sanction of Parliament, no matter how plausible soever may be the pretexts with which it is ushered into being.

THE INSOLVENT'S JUBILEE.

According to the good old common law of England, it was the duty of a debtor to pay his debts, and that duty was enforced by giving creditors a remedy, either against the person or the effects of the debtor. The bankrupt was considered in the light of a criminal, and Sir Edward Coke tells us that the name, as well as the wickedness, of bankrupts, are fetched from foreign nations. The old Romans had little pity for a man who failed to pay his debts, and allowed creditors to cut up their debtor's body, and then share the pieces. This not very pleasant way of paying old debts must have had a wholesome effect on all parties disposed to extravagance. Modern legislation has, however, raised the debtor from the level of the criminal; not only so, but the trouble now-a-days is to restrain legislators from investing the debtor with a sanctity which repels the touch of the profane creditor. A debtor, with the Insolvent Act in one hand, and the scalps of his creditors in the other, is a sight which, thanks to our humanity in legislation, is not rare or surprising. Every issue of the Canada Gazette teems with notices of application for relief under that Act, which instead of exciting surprise, naturally suggest the enquiry why everybody does not follow suit; the creditors being in the minority, a year of one-sided jubilee would be the consequence if that course were taken.

That the Insolvency Act has had a fair trial, none will deny. What is the experience of the country? We doubt if there is a man from Sarnia to Quebec who has had the opportunity of witnessing its operation and its effects who will pronounce it a success in aught but in affording to dishonesty the most ample facilities for carrying out its designs. Liberal principles lie at its base, the intentions of its promoters were good,

the objects aimed at were proper, but it is now admitted on all hands that it is the bane of the honest, and a most fruitful source of public demoralization. From every part of the country a cry has gone up which Parliament cannot and should not disregard. Boards of Trade and Bank Directors in their corporate, and merchants and public men in their individual, capacity, have expressed their opinions on the subject with an unanimity as singular as it is impressive. The banker finds his trust and confidence met by stratagems and threats; the wholesale merchant's calculations are thrown out of gear by twists and turns which ordinary, or even extraordinary, precautions cannot guard against; and the retail dealer is subjected to a species of competition which honesty cannot cope with. The old saying, "his word is as good as his bond" is dying, or has died, out. The successful insolvent of two campaigns is a hero in his way; the unsuccessful insolvent is called a fool, or too conscientious a person for this world. To pay one's debts with nothing indicates a higher order of business ability than to hand over assets for division among grasping creditors; while to fail for a large amount is a much surer passport to future eminence than to go down under a miserable petty sum of two or three figures. Far be it from us to say that honest men do not fail in business, or that a discharge is in every case a badge of disgrace. Honest men have their misfortunes as well as others, but honest men rarely need to chaffer and fight with creditors in this era of grace. The trouble is that the Insolvent Act takes in the chaff with the wheat, and the former seems to come out the sooner, while the latter is ground the more to make up for many cases will occur to any one who chooses to count over the insolvents of his acquaintance, in which the emancipated debtor develops, like Jonah's gourd, from a sapless root into a veritable green bay tree? It would require a Hogarth to picture in fulness of detail the Before and After of Insolvency. But we all know how frequently the poor and much persecuted debtor, who has given up everything to a merciless set of cormorant creditors, as soon as his discharge is made out, springs at a bound into his old seat, and enjoys the luxuries of this life with quite as much appreciation, and has them to enjoy, in quantities quite as large, as his humdrum acquaintances who have not been subjected to the disagreeable (for the time) necessity of going through the form of satisfying debts. The fact is, it is quite unfashionable to pay debts, and while an Insolvent Act is in force, it is a useless piece of extravagance. We would suggest that it might be well under the circumstances to strike out the words "to pay" in promissory notes, and substitute for them the words "to satisfy;" then those coming from an old-fashioned, honest region would not be so liable to be misled as they are now.

We admit that an Insolvency Act of some kind is a necessity under ordinary circumstances, but if it can be shewn that its good results bear but an infinitesimal proportion to its evil ones, it will not require much argument to make us doubt the expediency of having one at all. It is a principle of legislation that public interests must not be prejudiced even to cover cases of individual hardship. We cannot afford as a people to set a premium upon fraud. Let us see how the Insolvency Act may be and is made to work. A, an honest trader, has been in business, in say a village, for a number of years and has earned a character for integrity. B starts a rival establishment in the same village, and forthwith reduces prices to compel custom. He has no invested character—capital, and very little of any other kind; his goods were obtained on credit and they must be sold. He sells at "alarming sacrifices," for if the worst come to the worst, he has a haven of rest in the nearest Insolvency Court. His competition has the effect of bringing his name into the *Gazette*, but it has also the effect of ruining A.'s trade. The one comes from under the *débris*, hale and hearty, with more money in his pocket than he had before, while the other has lost everything ; the one is ready to repeat the operation elsewhere, whilst the other with more conscience and shame than "energy and tact," ponders over how hard it is to be honest.

But we cannot, in justice, lay all the blame on the Insolvent Act. Who backed up Nichols and Robinson's gambling in gold, W.R. Brown & Co's gambling in gold, Connor's, Taylor's and Scott's gambling in barley ?— Banks. Who support mere speculators without capital while drawing a tight rein on the careful ones who do a legitimate business ? Banks. Who over insure stocks of goods and allow themselves to be led into insuring empty boxes, bottles and suppositious articles ? Insurance Companies. Who give credit, indiscriminately, to every applicant, force goods on would-be honest dealers, and cry out most lustily when their sins come home to roost ? Merchants. It is all very well to condemn the Insolvency Act ; but with all its faults, with all its facilities to fraud, with all its perjuries, it is not the only, nor yet the greatest, cause of what we are pleased to term the demoralization in trade. While we seek to amend it—to remedy one set of evils—we must not overlook others quite as apparent, and quite as injurious, if we are in earnest in the endeavor to bring about a more creditable state of affairs.

OVERINSURANCE—FRAUD.

Facts which have reached us respecting several fires, of recent occurrence, involving serious destruction of property, and entailing consequent severe loss on several insurance companies, both local and foreign, justify us in saying that if a profitable result is to be expected from the prosecution of fire insurance in Canada, a closer surveillance must be exercised by companies over the actions of their agents.

There is every reason to believe that, at least three of these fires, were not the result of accident, but the work of incendiaries, who have sought, in the destruction of their property, relief from pecuniary embarrassment or insolvency. Experience has taught us that a depreciation of merchandize and manufactures, or a depression of business, combined with a too active competition between agents—leaving little or nothing at the risk of the insured, and indeed, not unfrequently, insuring in excess of the actual value of property—tends to open the door of temptation to overinsurance and subsequent fraud.

We are not ignorant of the difficulties with which an agent has to cope in his endeavours to satisfy himself, and do justice to his principals, in obtaining information on which their interest and safety materially depend. Enquiries which he would, perhaps, be anxious to make respecting the nature and condition of the property to be insured, the mode of keeping accounts, and other matters of vital importance are, we know, often regarded by the applicant as unnecessarily inquisitive, and resented accordingly. So that to secure business the agent is often tempted to forego his duty in relation to these particulars, and the result is, too frequently, as we have stated.

In one of the cases to which we have adverted there existed, at the time of the disaster, insurances to the extent of about seven-ninths of the invoiced value of the stock, one half of which, it is alleged, would not, had it been sold, have realized half cost, from the fact of its being by age, and consequent deterioration, rendered almost unsaleable. In another case where the premises were, as admitted, purposely fired, there was an insurance of $1,500 on stock which, on investigation, proved not worth $50.

We do not pretend to assert that an agent can, in all cases, make himself as thoroughly acquainted with the value and condition of every stock which is offered for insurance, as is desirable ; or that he is supposed to know that nicely done-up parcels, representing quors, patent medicines, and the like, nothing but blocks of wood, papered labelled in imitation of the genuine artic or that chests, half-chests and caddies, s posed to contain the finest flavored and cl cest teas, are filled with saw-dust ; but do know that an agent, especially if a re ent, ought, before assuming risks, part larly if on stock, to use all laudable lawful means to satisfy himself as to the ral character and business capabilities of applicant ; to obtain, if possible, at least approximate idea of the amount of busi done, additional existing assurances, and ot particulars, as directed by his code of structions, and which are essential to the terest and prosperity of the company.

THE TORONTO MUTUAL.

This Company claims to have gained a sition in two years which will compare fa ably with that of other mutual companic the longest standing. It possesses prem notes to the amount of $67,124 93, issues no cash policies for periods longer t one year. The Company's exhibit is as lows : Policies in force, 2,222 ; propert; sured, $1,447,775 ; cash receipts for year, $14,692 13 ; disbursements, f 015 95 ; losses, $3,711 54 ; total liabili $21,649 47, of which $14,103 84 consi paid-up guarantee stock and reinsur premium notes, leaving its total cash lia ties on 1st January at $7,545 63, inclu unsettled fire claims to the same date.

Its business is conducted on the mutual principle, of charging every me yearly with his exact share of all losse expenses up to the day of assessment has adopted the correct course of inspe all risks systematically by its own trave inspector, instead of trusting solely t information, often deceptive, furnishe agents ; and seems to have taken precau to secure a safe and respectable busi without venturing upon heavy risks, or of a specially hazardous character. It v be well for all institutions of the kind t the same prudence and caution in the agement of their affairs ; in which cas doubt they might stand much better wit public than some of them do at present is not a little discreditable that a larger of our insurances are not undertaki companies domiciled within our own bor and that so much money is allowed sent out of the country in the shape c insurance premiums.

The rival railway companies, the We ton, Grey and Bruce, and the Toronto, and Bruce, have been taking legal a respecting each others Acts. Mr. Hil Cameron, Q. C., is of opinion that th visional directors of the Toronto and .

ilway have exceeded their powers in bonds to municipalities to build their a particular direction. Mr. Matthew n, Q. C., and Mr. Harrison, Q. C., r, however, that such bonds would be if the Company, after its organiza- cepted the bonuses on the faith of onds. The Company, furthermore, isk that the by-laws in aid of the road finally ratified until the companies en fully organized.

ie other hand, Mr. Hillyard Cameron nion that by-laws conditioned on the out of money, the location of route ions, etc., are legal, and that buyers ntures issued under those by-laws iold them subject to the conditions y-laws, neither principal nor interest llectable from the municipalities on n the performance of the conditions. his catches the Wellington, Grey and Company is in the value of the de- s they have already secured under nal by-laws. Such debentures are, Cameron points out, valueless as ble securities.

MR. W. R. BROWN.

V. R. Brown is, by his own account, injured individual. He has written from New York which contains an return if his creditors will guarantee m arrest. He considers that Mr. , the cashier of the City Bank, was "extortion" in compelling him to his over-draft account of from $40, 60,000. We believe we are correct g that his account was kept open the wish of Mr. Workman, the Pre- Mr. Brown to the contrary, notwith- g. Mr. Graham's "annoyances" led own to make an arrangement with the anadian. Mr. Brown's indignation 'treachery" of the Royal is rather s, and his bombast about the business house" proves nothing but the spe- character of what he did. Mr. says he knew nothing of the state R. Brown & Co. when he became a of the firm; Mr. Brown asserts that not aware, until some time after, that ewott had made the settlements upon e. Previous to "my unfortunate s" entering the firm, Mr. Brown's n gold gambling had reached $55,000, 21st June last, when he went to New ie had to sell his plate and some arti- furniture, to procure the means to go So that W. R. Brown & Co., while insolvent, had the audacity and dis- to accept money on deposit. He his creditors to "cease their malice secution, and unite against one common enemy." The advice is pleasant, considering the source whence it comes, and if taken we incline to the opinion that Mr. Brown will be the "enemy" selected.

Mr. Wm. Smith, late manager of the Gore Bank at Woodstock, has been appointed Accountant in the Bank of Commerce, Toronto, in the place of Mr. Sampson who goes to Woodstock as manager of that branch of the Bank of Commerce.

Northern Assurance.—This Company was established in 1836, and has a capital of £2,000,000 sterling. Its accumulated funds amount to £850,000: in 1867 the fire premiums footed up to £160,000, and the losses to less than 50 per cent of that sum. Its affairs seem to be conducted with care and prudence, and it is understood to be a thoroughly sound office. It is both a fire and a life company, but only fire business is done here, and none but the better class of risks is accepted.

Communications.

THE BEAVER MUTUAL.

To the Editor of the Monetary Times.

Sir,—I perceive that under the above heading, in your issue of the 11th inst., you say, in referring to the case of Findlay vs. Beaver Mutual, tried at the last Barrie Assizes: "It turns out just as we expected, that the defence was based on a true sense of what is due to the honestly disposed portion of the community. The plaintiff had mortgaged his property without notice to the Company, and when a fire occurred under such circumstances, the Company decided to stand on their rights." You surely, sir, could not have carefully perused my letter to the daily *Globe* of the 19th October last, the statements (all of them susceptible of proof) in which have never been denied by the Company, or by their solicitor, to whose letter in the *Globe* a few days previously, mine was a reply.

I ask you, sir, if after reading both the letters above alluded to, and which embrace all that the public know of the matter, you can reiterate the remarks I have quoted. No doubt you have made these remarks upon the strength of the Company's annual report, published in the same issue; but what does this report (so far as this case is concerned) amount to, when my letter to the *Globe* is left unanswered?

In justice to my client, (the plaintiff), I ask your insertion of these few lines. Yours, etc.

J. A. Ardagh.

Barrie, March 15, 1869.

Financial.

TORONTO STOCK MARKET.

(Reported by Pellatt & Osler, Brokers.)

The market has been very dull during the past week, particularly in bank stocks, many of which close slightly weaker.

Bank Stock.—Montreal has been freely dealt in at 140½ and 140¾, and closed firm and in demand at 141. There are buyers of British at 104½, and no sellers under 105½. Ontario has been sold to a limited extent at 100 to 100½, to-day (the 16th) there is an enquiry for the stock at par. Small amounts of Toronto are offering at 121, but buyers will not give over 120½. Nothing doing in Royal Canadian; offering at 80. Commerce is offering in limited amounts at 103; no demand. There are sellers of Gore at 41, but no buyers. Sales of Merchants' have taken place at 108¼, 108½ and 108¾, there are no sellers now under 109. There are buyers of Quebec at par, and no sellers. Molson's is in active demand at 113½, sellers holding for 114. Sales of City were made at 103 and 103½, there are now buyers at the latter rate and sellers at 104. No Du Peuple in market; buyers would give 107½. The same price would be paid for Nationale; none offering. Jacques Cartier could be placed at 109. For Union 104½ would be paid; none in market. Other banks nominal as quoted.

Debentures.—Canada are slightly lower; fives are offering at 94½, sixes are in little demand at 102 to 103. Dominion stock is in demand at 105½. Toronto are very scarce and could be readily placed to pay 6¾ per cent. Long dated County are readily saleable at par.

Sundries.—City Gas has been sold at 108 and 108½, there are still buyers at 108. British America Assurance is enquired for at 55½, no sellers under 56½. Large sales of Canada Permanent Building Society were made at 126. Small transactions in Western Canada B. S. occurred at 121, at which rate it is still procurable. Freehold B. S. has been freely dealt in at 110 and 110¾, there are still buyers at 110½. Canada Landed Credit has further advanced with sales at 77 and 78. Mortgages have been more freely offered than for some time past. Money is in good demand.

Stock Sale in Halifax.—At Mr. W. M. Gray's stock sale on the 9th, by J. D. Nash, the following prices were realized: 50 shares People's Bank, $28.50; 16 Union Bank, $56.25; 2 Bank of Nova Scotia, £70 5s. 0d; 15 Halifax Fire Insurance Co, £10 11s. 3d.; 3 Bank of British North America, £70 3s. 9d.; 3 $109 City Water Debentures, $105.

—The St. John *Globe* says that at an adjourned meeting of the stockholders of the Commercial Bank, the Directors submitted a satisfactory statement, showing that since November last, the liabilities of the institution had been reduced virtually 50 per cent.

Railway News.

Northern Railway.—Traffic receipts for week ending February 6th, 1869.

Passengers....................	$2,178 59
Freight and live stock......	5,163 48
Mails and sundries.........	190 94
	$7,533 01
Corresponding Week of '68.	5,985 05
Increase............	$1,547 96

Great Western Railway.—Traffic for week ending February 26, 1869.

Passengers	$21,349 93
Freight........................	31,555 20
Mails and Sundries	1,138 75
Total Receipts for week......	$54,043 88
Coresponding week, 1868...	51,632 09
Increase	$2,411 79

Mississquoi Railroad.—On the 3rd instant, the Directors of the Mississquoi Railroad held a meeting at Newport, Vermont, for the election of officers, at which the Hon. Lucius Robinson, of Newport, was elected President; Col. O. N. Elkins, North Troy, Treasurer, and Mr. Allen, Attorney at Law, of Newport, Secretary; the choice in each case being unanimous. This road commences at Newport, Vermont, in connection with the Passumpsic Railroad, and is to connect with the South Eastern Counties Junction Railroad at the Province line at Potton. Operations on the railway have commenced.—*Montreal Herald.*

Law Report.

AN INSURANCE POLICY DECISION.—The Supreme Court of Illinois has recently rendered a decision of considerable importance to insurance interests, concerning the power of insurance companies to vitiate policies. The case involved was that of a butcher, (or rather the keeper of a meat shop), who kept a keg of saltpetre in his shop, notwithstanding that the terms written in his policy of insurance declared that the keeping of saltpetre should vitiate it. It also appeared that on one occasion he sold a quantity of saltpetre to a customer. The proof showed that it was customary for dealers in meat to use saltpetre in small quantities in their business. The court held that such customary use of the article implied a knowledge of the fact on the part of the underwriter ; and that the mere fact of use, or of keeping for use, in a reasonable quantity, would not vitiate the policy. But a keg of saltpetre was, under the proofs, more than a reasonable quantity, and the fact of selling to a customer made the butcher a dealer in the article to such an extent as clearly to render the policy void under its terms.

SALE OF STOCK—DIVIDENDS ACCRUED.

In a case of Currie vs. White, in the Supreme Court of New York (March 4), it appeared that the defendant sold to the plaintiffs, by a contract dated February 18th, 1867, 1,000 shares of Hudson River Railroad stock at 128, the purchaser to pay interest on the purchase money, and the vendor to deliver, at his option, at any time during the year 1867. While this contract was pending, and in April, 1867, the capital stock was doubled, by the issue of new shares, each stockholder receiving a number of new shares equal to the number of old shares held at the time of the increase, on the payment of fifty per cent in cash. The whole of the new stock was taken by the stockholders on these terms. Dividends were also declared and paid in cash, as follows : On the 15th of April, 1867, four per cent. on the old stock, and on the 15th of October, 1867, four per cent. on the stock as increased, on both the old and new.

On the 18th of December, 1867, the vendor gave notice that he would perform his contract, and tendered the first 1,000 shares, and demanded the contract price—128 and interest. The purchasers offered to take the stock and pay this price, and also demanded the second 1,000 shares of the new issue, and the cash dividend. The vendor refused to comply with these demands, or to deliver the first 1,000 shares.

The plaintiffs, the purchasers, then sued to recover damages for the non-delivery of the first 1,000 shares mentioned in the contract, claiming the difference between the contract price, 128, and the highest price, 149, which the stock had reached before the trial ; and also claiming the value of the second 1,000 shares, the new issue, less the price, 50, at which the same had been issued, and also the dividends.

The purchasers claimed these on the ground that they paid interest on the purchase money from the date of the contract, and were, therefore, entitled to the dividends and advantages accruing to the stock while it remained in the owner's hands awaiting delivery.

The Court, at special term, Jones, J., decided against these claims of the plaintiffs, and held that the contract was executory, operating as an agreement to sell, to be carried into effect on a future day ; that the dividends declared and the additional stock issued became the property of the owner of the stock at the time they were declared and issued ; that the owner did not, by such a contract, deprive himself of any profit which might accrue from the property, or of any advantages which might arise from its possession or use during the time he held it under his option to deliver ; and that such profits or advantages

did not pass to the purchaser in the absence of an express contract that they should pass.

He also held that the measure of damage which the purchaser could recover on a breach of contract by the vendor was the market value of the stock on the day of the breach, and not the higher value which the stock might reach before the trial ; that the market value on the day of breach was not equal to the contract price and interest, and that therefore the purchaser suffered no actual damage.

The plaintiffs appealed from all this decision to the General Term, and argued that the agreement to pay interest on the purchase money, from the date of the contract, controlled its interpretation.

That the contract contemplated that there was something existing to be bought and sold ; that 1,000 shares of the stock, as it existed at the date of the contract before the increase, was the existing thing sold ; that the vendor must deliver, with the stock, all the dividends and accretions which he has received pending the contract ; and that his contract was not satisfied by the delivery of 1,000 shares of the stock after the increase.

That the agreement to pay interest bound the purchaser to keep the purchase money at all times in readiness to answer the vendor's demand for it, and also to pay interest on it ; and that the vendor must be held to the reciprocal obligation of performing as at the date of the contract, and of delivering the stock as it then existed, with all the increments ; that the purchaser's rights attached to the stock as it existed at the date of the contract ; and that although the contract on its face bound the purchaser to pay the interest, and did not bind the vendor to deliver the dividends and accretions, such an obligation, though not expressed, could be implied as a correlative and reciprocal obligation.

That the vendor in this case, having received the dividends and increased stock, must deliver the same. The plaintiff's counsel cited many cases showing that where the purchaser had paid interest he was entitled to the increase, where that increase had accrued to the property in the shape of dividends, rents, additions to insurance policies, and to estates by the dropping of lives ; and that it was inequitable that one party should receive interest, and also the profits and increase from the possession of the estate.

That the thing sold was the stock as it stood before the increase of the capital ; that the new stock was issued one-half for cash and one-half as bonds ; that to allow the defendant to perform his contract by the delivery of 1,000 shares of the stock, after such an increase, would be like allowing a man who sold 1,000 gallons of specific wine to mix that wine with 1,000 gallons composed one-half of the same wine and one-half water, and then to deliver 1,000 gallons of this 2,000 gallons of compound in performance of his sale ; or to allow a man to sell stock before it was watered, and then to perform his contract by a delivery of watered shares.

They also claimed that the defendant had broken the contract, and that the plaintiffs were entitled to recover the highest market value of the stock, after the breach and before the trial, as the just measure of damages.

FAILURES IN MONTREAL.—A despatch dated March 15 says Smyth & Edminston, large boot and shoe manufacturers in McGill street, stopped payment to-day ; liabilities stated at $103,000. One of the partners in the firm of C. Derwin & Co., brokers, left the city on Saturday, and his whereabouts cannot be discovered. It seems to be a fact that this old house has also suspended, and it is stated that Mr. Derwin has taken $8,000 with him. Extent of liabilities not ascertained. Mr. Derwin's partner, Mr. Gault, is still here.

— The Propeller, Georginna was sold at Montreal, a few days since, to Mr. W. M. H. Irish, for $8,500.

MONTREAL CIVIC AFFAIRS.

At the installation of the Mayor of Montreal W. Workman, Esq., the following statement was made by him respecting the city affairs :

The financial statements, which in a few days will be laid before you, will exhibit the affairs of the city in a most prosperous condition. Notwithstanding that the city of Montreal, in comparison to other cities on the continent, is very lightly taxed, our revenue is ample for all purposes, and without any increased burthens upon the citizens, is annually increasing.

In the year 1866 it was............................ $621,
In the year 1867 it was............................ 705,
And the year just closed, 1868, it has
risen to... 812,

Our floating casual indebtedness to banks and other sources has been paid off ; and had it been for the very large amount we have, from operation of the expropriation law, been compelled to deposit in Court for expropriation purposes, our cash account would exhibit a large balance on hand for employment, if we thought fit, in the redemption of our immatured bonds.

Whilst, upon the one hand, the actual revenue of the city exhibits these pleasing features, our consolidated liabilities and fixed assets of the Corporation, exhibit results which are not less gratifying. Although the present bonded or consolidated debt of the city is put down, in round numbers, at five million of dollars ($5,000,000), it is strictly speaking, not more than one million, cause we have in fixed property and actual bona fide assets, the safe representative of four millions, yielding a corresponding revenue, so that in reality our taxation has only to provide for the interest on one million. That these gratifying results are properly appreciated in the financial world is fully demonstrated by the present price of our city obligations, as compared with other securities and with former years, in our money market — our seven per cent Consols having reached a premium of ten per cent.

It is to be hoped that the doubts and anxieties which have so long pervaded the Council, and city generally, upon the question of the water supply, have found a solution, and will soon entirely disappear under the successful application of steam power, and an auxiliary pumping force. The present temporary derangement of this by consequent upon some defect, not in the engine but between the engine house and supply basin or settling pond, though certainly very inconvenient at this season, ought not to discourage anmuch as such "contretemps," or mishaps almost inseparable from new enterprises of magnitude. All intelligent, impartial judgment will discern that a defect or derangement in supply pipe which brings the water to be pumped would easily derange breast wheel, turbine wheel, steam, or any other power, and should, therefore not be chargeable as an inherent defect against any of these modes of pumping. I entertain doubts myself that in a few days the defect will be repaired, and the steam engine be again permitted to proceed with its work, fill the reservoir and supply the city as before. Let us earnestly hope that during the coming year our progress to good results and further improvements in important service may be equally successful, and that for a long a permanent and abundant supply of water, at all seasons of the year, may be secured to the city.

Our fire force and fire alarm system are equally creditable to the city. In true efficiency and prompt action in extinguishing fires, they perhaps, unrivalled on this continent ; and such perfect discipline and working as the exhibit, it is difficult to see, under a proper administration of this most important part of water, how any extensive conflagration could again afflict our city. Everything in relation to the administration of these most important departments reflects credit upon all connected with them.

rithstanding the increased vigilance of the
y police, the public health of the city is
from satisfactory. The death rate last
1e to within a fraction of 40 per 1,030, or
1ry 25 ; that of Boston averaging 1 in 44,
e island of Montreal, outside the city,
The average weekly death rate of chil-
1t year, in winter, was 64 per 1,000 ; in
and autumn, 90 per 1,000 ; summer, 146
·00, which rose in one week to 209 per
against one winter week of 44 per 1,000.
esults show how much in this important
1ent is yet to be done. Our Health Com-
should have power to prohibit the erection
1ings upon low or swampy ground, without
1rainage ; and our inspector of buildings
1e empowered to prevent the construction
building, intended either for factory or
1, without proper regard to ventiiiation
and through. All wooden drains should
1 up and replaced with good vitrified clay
5ewers and drains should be ventilated at
1ghest point, and trapped and flushed in
1eather, and every means taken to prevent
1le from saturating the soil in their yards
1rts with slops and filthy water.
1eviously shown, our city is rich in means
1he necessary discipline and requirements
perfect efficiency in every department.
1enue for the year just closed exceeds by
1undred thousand dollars that of the pre-
1ear ;—it is $812,300. The chief items of
ture during the past year are as follows :

l.................................$138,429
r ....$74,994 } 135,471
Permanent Works... 60,477
.... 24,811
.... 13,634
h....................................... 5,818
l...........................!........ 74,088
der's Court....................... 10,312
                              _____
                              $407,563

Commercial.

Toronto Market.

css continues generally quiet; in the re-
1artment there are loud complaints of dull-
1·or several days the produce trade has
a state of panic. Prices of wheat, barley
1 have undergone a serious decline as our
1ns show, greatly augmenting the losses
1ly incurred from the late steady down-
1nlency in prices. Confidence has been
by the sudden disappearance of Mr. W.
or, a dealer who for the past season occu-
1rominent place, principally as a dealer in
1which he bought and sold to a very large
He has always been regarded as a reck-
1ator, and this quality brought him to the
bankruptcy before. It is quite impossible
1ain the extent of his assets or liabilities,
1as carried his books off with him. The
Bank is supposed to be a considerable
1ther banks are no doubt short to some
and one individual loses some $4,000.
was raised on fraudulent warehouse re-
1ssued by a party named Scott, who had
1n of Church-street wharf. Mr. Scott has
1t the country. Since this escapade all
1paper has been closely scrutinized by the
1nd a good many refusals have been given.
1urns.—There was a decided improvement
1css as compared with last week. Teas—
1better demand and some lines are moving
1reely for both city and country trade.
1—are easier, all grades of yellow refined
be purchased on the basis of 10½c. for
stocks of raw are uncommonly light, and
1few brands, and in consequence, the mar-
1m. Syrups—are firm, not having sympa-
1ith the decline in sugar, owing to scarcity.
1—are firm, with a prospect of an advance
0 per cent., consequent upon a rise in the

price of leaf in the Southwestern States. Fish.—
With the approaching end of the Lenten season
the demand has fallen off, and the market is pretty
well cleared out. Fruit—nominal.
[GRAIN.—Wheat—Receipts 4,900 bush., and
6,800 last week. The market is in an unsettled
and panicky state, in consequence of the failure
and flight of a prominent operator and a warehouseman, who had issued to him fraudulent
warehouse receipts. Produce paper is scanned
by the banks with unusual care, and money, so
far as produce operators are concerned, is tight.
Spring wheat is dull and nominal, no car loads
offering and no demand; on the street 80 to 85c.
is paid for sleigh loads. Fall nominal at 85 to
90c.; none offering. There are no buyers of either
spring or fall, and in the present state of the
market holders think it useless to offer. Barley—
Receipts 900 bushs., and 1,750 bushs. last week.
The market is unsettled and sales are difficult to
make except in small lots; it is nominally worth
$1.15 to $1.25; four cars sold at $1.20 free of
charges, and one car at $1.25. Peas—Receipts
500 bushs., and 1,000 bushs. last week. Car loads
are offering at 70c., without buyers; on the street
65 to 73c. was paid. Oats—Receipts 1,200 bushs.,
and 2,533 bushs. last week. Oats are selling at
49 to 50c. on track, but there is no demand.
Rye—Selling on the street at 65c. Seeds—
Timothy is quiet, at $1.75 to $2.25 for common,
and $2.50 to $2.75 for No. 1. There is a fair demand for clover at $6.50 to $7. Flax is worth
$1.75 to $2, and tares the same price.
FLOUR.—Receipts 1,475 bbls., and 6,800. bbls.
last week. No. 1 superfine is dull and offering at
$4 in store, with a limited demand at about that
price; a lot of 800 bbls. sold at $4 in store. In
other grades there is nothing doing.
PROVISIONS.—Butter—No. 1 lots are a ready
sale at 20 to 23c.; common and inferior lots are
not saleable. Pork—Mess is offering at $25.75 to
$26, not much demand; some business was done
at $25.50 to $25.75. Cutmeats—Unchanged.
Dressed Hogs—Are in good demand, but are scarce.
Eggs—Packed are selling at 15c.
FREIGHTS.—Rates by Grand Trunk Railway:—
Flour to all stations from Belleville to Lynn, inclusive, 35c., grain per 100 lbs. 18c. ; flour to
Brockville and Cornwall, inclusive, 45c. grain 22c.
flour to Montreal 50c. grain 25c. ; flour to all
stations between Island Pond and Portland, inclusive, 85c. grain 43c. ; flour to Boston 90c.,
gold, grain 45c.; flour to Halifax $1.10, grain 55c;
flour to St. John $1 02. Boxed Meats to Liverpool
per gross ton. 80s. ; lard or butter in tinnets
85s. ; Pork 11s. per tierce ; flour 5s. 6d. per
barrel ; grain 12s. per 480 pounds. Rates by
Great Western Railway—Flour, Toronto to Suspension Bridge 25c. gold ; thence to New York
92c. U. S. currency per bbl. ; to Boston $1.02.
Grain to Bridge 18c., gold; thence to New York
47c, U. S. currency; to Boston 51c. Grain, Toronto to Detroit, 18c. ber 100 lbs; flour 35c
per bbl.

Salt Production in the United States.

The Chicago Republican has the following interesting accounts, embracing statistics of the salt
product of the Saginaw Valley and the Onondaga
Springs. It is peculiarly satisfactory to notice
the marked improvement in the business of manufacturing salt in the Saginaw Valley. Our saline
waters are an inexhaustible resource; the product
they afford take away none of the natural wealth
of the country, while their development has had
the effect to render valuable for staves and heading many varieties of timber of but little worth
before, and the immense quantities of fuel consumed in the kettle boiling process in particular,
has caused the clearing of thousands of acres of
land, which is thus being brought rapidly into
profitable use for agricultural purposes.
From 1864 to 1866 there was a falling off in the
saline product, the number of barrels manufactured in 1866 being 58,359 less than the number
manufactured in 1865, even, and 121,076 less than

the number manufactured in 1864. In 1867
there was an increase of 66,734 barrels over the
product of the previous year, and last year, 1868,
the product exceeded that of any former year,
26,617 barrels, being the excess over the product
of 1864, up to this time the leading year in the
salt business.
The following summary of the manufacture of
salt since the business was inaugurated is given:

	Barrels.
1800	4,000
1861	125,000
1862	243,000
1863	466,356
1864	529,073
1865	477,200
1866	407,997
1867	474,721
1868	555,690

Nine years ago the first barrel of salt was made
in the Saginaw Valley.
The Saginaw and Bay Salt Company, which
has handled four-fifths of the salt shipped from
the Saginaw Valley during the past year has
shipped and sold 382,385 barrels, of which 41,860
barrels were home sales. Chicago received and
consumed the largest amount, and Cleveland and
Toledo next. The company have agents at every
port of any consequence on the lakes, and also at
inland cities. The amount delivered to the association during the season is as follows:

	Barrels.
First District (Bay county)................	158,141
Second District (part of Carrollton)........	57,900
Third District (Rochester Works to Buf-	
falo Salt Company's Works)............	74,507
Fourth District (all works south of above	139,194
Bought by Company......................	17,141
Total...............................;	392,335

Production and Stock of Petroleum.

From the monthly petroleum report of the
Titusville Herald we take the following table
which shows the production during February, the
average per day, the production previously reported in 1869, and the average per day since Jan.1st:

Total shipment of Crude for February of	
bbls., of 45 gallons each bbl.......	252,415
Add to reduce to bbls. of 43 galls. each,	
bbls.................................	11,740
Total shipment of bbls. of 43 galls. each,	
bbls.................................	264,155
Stock on hand Feb. 1st, bbls 274,167	
Stock on hand March 1st bbls...282,450	
Add increase on March 1st, bbls.........	8,283
Total production during February, bbls.	272,438
Average per day for 28 days, bbls..9,765	
Production previously reported, bbls......	315,953
Total product since January 1st, bbls....	588,391
Average per day for 59 days, bbls..9,973	

On the 1st of March there were 334 wells being
drilled, seven less than on the first of February.

Exports of Petroleum.

Exports from New York from Jan. 1,
galls................................... 7,746,040
Exports from New York same time last
year, galls.............................. 7,575,024
The following is the quantity exported from
other ports, Jan. 1 to March 6:

	1869.	1868.
From Boston.........galls.	536,439	418,200
Philadelphia..........	3,454,032	3,568,935
Baltimore............	73,054	205,155
Portland.............		6,800
Cleveland............		
Total................	4,061,125	4,199,200
Total exports from the U.S.	12,115,233	11,835,963
Same time in 1867........		7,025,889
Same time in 1866........		9,762,291

Halifax Market.

BREADSTUFFS.—We have to report a more active demand for Flour during the past week.—Stocks at Outports are now somewhat reduced, and orders come forward more freely. Purchases are made only for immediate use, as lower prices are looked for. Our Stocks are still large, with less liberal receipts. We quote white wheat extra (fall) $6.75 to $7.00; fancy $6.25; bakers' strong $5.90 to $6.00; supers. $5.70 to $5.75; No. 2 $5.50; middlings $4.25 to $4.35; Pollard's $4.00 to $4.15; rye $4.75 to $5; cornmeal K.D. $4.15; F.G. $4.00 to $4.10; oatmeal $7.00 to $7.25.

WEST INDIA PRODUCE.—The market is still excited, and several offers for cargoes to arrive, have been refused, holders views differ largely from buyers, and sales for home consumption have been very limited. A cargo of molasses was offered at Auction last week, and 36½c. (in bond) offered for a parcel, but the lot was withdrawn, and has since been shipped. Higher prices are looked for. Sugars continue firm, with light stocks. Rum is somewhat firmer. The imports for the week are 50 puns. molasses; 69 puns. rum; 20 bbls. sugar; 4 bags coffee. Exports 160 hhds. 205 bbls sugar; 5 puns. molasses; 80 bags coffee; 11 bags cocoa. We quote:—sugar V.P. 9½c. to 10c.; Porto Rico 8½c. to 9½c.; Cuba 8c. to 9½c.; Barbadoes 9c.; molasses, Cienfuegos 40c. to 42c.; Trinidad 38 to 40.; rum (in bond) Demerara 58c.; coffee—Jamaica 13c. to 15c.; St. Domingo 10 to 13c.

EXCHANGE.—Bank drafts London 60 days at 13 ⅌ cent.; Montreal sight 4 ⅌ cent; New York gold ¼ ⅌ cent.; currency 20 ⅌ cent. disct.; St. John, N.B. 3 ⅌ cent. premium.—*R. C. Hamilton & Co's. Circular, March 3.*

Shallow Harbors.

A petition addressed to the Dominion Minister of Public Works is being signed by lake captains and others, and sets forth "that in consequence of the large class of vessels now navigating the lakes, and the low state of the water, the depths of the harbors of Port Colborne and Port Dalhousie are not sufficient, and in consequence vessels cannot pass these harbors drawing their full capacity; and in many instances vessels entering Port Colborne harbor have gone ashore, and vessels and cargoes have proved a total loss; and in some instances vessels have been detained from one to two days waiting to be lightened into the harbor; large vessels have also been frequently detained at Port Dalhousie in consequence of having to lighten out of the harbor at a heavy expense. For this reason many of the larger class of vessels are diverted, whereas, if the dimensions of these harbors are increased they could return to it.

"We, therefore, pray that you will cause them to be increased in depth, also their dimensions extended, as much damage is occasioned and delays frequently ensue in consequence of their being filled with vessels during adverse winds.

"And we beg respectfully to suggest that no expenditure be made towards the construction of a harbor of refuge upon Lake Erie until these harbors are completed to their utmost capacity, as the vessels trading upon the lakes have much greater interest in having these harbors increased than in the expenditure of money in providing harbors of refuge, as Long Point, on Lake Erie, now furnishes a harbor of refuge from various winds.

"Your petitioners would also pray that you employ a double set of lock masters, or a sufficient number of men, independent of the vessels' crews, to work Port Dalhousie lock and lock No. 2; also Port Colborne and Allanburgh locks, as vessels' crews are actually required at all those points in getting vessels in readiness to pass through the canal. And," etc.

Syracuse Salt Manufacture in 1868.

The total amount of salt inspected at Syracuse during the year 1868 was 8,666,616 bushels of fifty-six pounds each. Of this 2,027,490 bushels

were made by solar evaporation, and 6,639,126 bushels by artificial heat. The amount manufactured in 1867 was 7,595,565 bushels; increase this year over last, 1,071,051 bushels. The State collected revenue duties, 1c. per bushel, $85,666.36, and penalties, $164.89. Total revenue, $86,830.76. The expenses of pumping water and cost of the inspection was $45,586.70, leaving a net revenue to the State of $37,244.06. The aggregate production of salt at Syracuse for the ten years ending with 1868 has been 73,869,715 bushels, an average of 7,386,971 bushels annually.

Trade in Sugar Shooks.

The shipments of sugar shooks from St. John to the West India Islands in the years named were:—

In 1865-6	481,416
1866-7	766,554
1867-8	813,821
1868-9	882,378

Before New Brunswick entered into the manufacture and exportation of shooks, Maine enjoyed a monopoly of the business. Since then, while our exports have been increasing, those of Portland, Me., have been falling off. Thus in the season, extending from October, 1867, to June, 1868, Portland shipped to Cuba as follows: Havana, 172,692; Matanzas, 348,231; Cardenas, 130,445; total, 651,368. In the season extending from October, 1868, to February 18, 1869, as follows: Havana, 74,877; Matanzas, 170,000; Cardenas, 60,594; total, 310,977.

The Suez Canal.

From St. Petersburg to Ceylon, the centre of the India trade, via the Suez Canal, the distance is 8,600 miles; from London to Ceylon, 7,360; from Marseilles, 5,500; from Constantinople, 4,700; from Ceylon to Canton, 3,000 miles; total from London to Canton, via Suez, 10,300. London to Canton via the Pacific Railroad, 13,500; London to Canton via Good Hope, 16,100; Canton to San Francisco, 7,000 miles; San Francisco to New York, 3,500; New York to London, 3,000; New York to Canton via the Pacific Railroad, 10,500; New York to Canton via Suez, 11,500; New York to Canton via Panama, the same, 11,500; New York to Canton via Good Hope, 16,400, via Cape Horn, 21,700. The Suez Canal, says a contributor to the Washington *Chronicle*, will not only be the shortest and cheapest route from all parts of Europe to the Indies and China, but it will be the cheapest route from our Atlantic ports for the same trade. The average distance from Europe to the Indies and China via Suez will not be half as great as the distance via the Pacific Railroad, with 3,000 miles of transportation by rail, with two reshipments, the cost of land carriage alone being being more than three times the entire cost via the Suez Canal, with no reshipments. Our Western States will be supplied with Eastern goods, teas, coffees, silks, etc., by direct trade through San Francisco. New York and other Eastern cities will merely supply the immediate Atlantic States, and an immense domestic trade will be lost. To make up for this change and loss of trade through the completion of the Suez Canal and Pacific Railroad, it becomes of paramount importance that the Atlantic and Gulf States should make immediate efforts to construct a canal across the Isthmus of Panama. The distance from New York to Canton by this route is the same as by the Suez Canal, but it would be far preferable for sailing vessels on account of the dangers of the Mediterranean and Red Seas.

Commercial House.
(LATE HUFFMAN HOUSE)

PETERBOROUGH, ONTARIO.

GEORGE CROSS : : : : : : PROPRIETOR.

Large addition lately made, including Twenty Bed Rooms.

Dec. 10, 1868.   17-1L

Mercantile.

TORONTO PRICES CURRENT.—MARCH 18, 1869.

Name of Article.	Wholesale Rates.		Name of Article.	Wholesale Rate.		Name of Article.	Wholesale Rates.	
Boots and Shoes.	$ c.	$ c.	**Groceries**—*Contin'd*	$ c.	$ c.	**Leather**—*Contin'd.*	$ c.	$ c.
Mens' Thick Boots	2 20	2 50	Gunpowd'r c. to med ..	0 55	0 70	Kip Skins, Patna	0 35	0 50
" Kip.............	2 50	3 00	" med. to fine.	0 70	0 85	French	0 70	0 90
" Calf	3 00	3 70	" fine to fin's'.	0 85	0 95	English	0 65	0 80
" Congress Gaiters..	3 00	3 50	Hyson	0 45	0 80	Hemlock Calf (30 to		
" Kip Cobourgs	1 15	1 45	Imperial	0 42	0 80	35 lbs.) per doz ..	0 50	0 60
Boys' Thick Boots......	1 70	1 80	Tobacco, Mons'fed'd:			Do. light	0 45	0 50
Youths' "	1 40	1 50	Can Leaf, ℔ 5s & 10s.	0 26	0 30	French Calf........	1 05	1 25
Women's Batts	0 95	1 30	Western Leaf, com...	0 25	0 26	Grain & Satn Cit'd'ds.	0 00	0 00
" Balmoral	1 20	1 50	" Good	0 27	0 32	Splits, large ℔ ℔...	0 30	0 33
" Congress Gaiters..	1 15	1 45	" Fine ...	0 32	0 35	" small.....	0 26	0 30
Misses' Batts........	0 75	1 00	" Bright fine..	0 42	0 50	Enamelled Cow ℔ foot..	0 20	0 21
" Balmoral	1 10	1 20	" choice.	0 00	0 75	Patent	0 20	0 21
" Congress Gaiters..	1 00	1 30	**Hardware.**			Pebble Grain	0 17	0 18
Girls' Batts	0 65	0 85	Tea (net cash prices)			Buff	0 17	0 18
" Balmoral	0 10	1 05	Block, ℔ ℔	0 25	0 26	**Oils.**		
" Congress Gaiters..	0 80	1 10	Grain............	0 25	0 26	Cod	0 65	0 70
Children's C. T. Cneks...	0 50	0 65	Copper :			Lard, extra	0 00	0 00
" Gaiters	0 50	0 90	Pig	0 22	0 24	" No. 1	0 00	0 00
Drugs.			Sheet.............	0 30	0 33	" Woollen	0 00	0 00
Aloes Cape...........	0 12	0 16	Cut Nails :			Lubricating, patent...	0 00	0 00
Alum...............	0 02½	0 03	Assorted ¼ Shingles,			" Mott's economis	0 00	0 00
Borax	0 00	0 00	℔ 100 ℔....	2 90	3 00	Linseed, raw	0 78	0 82
Camphor, refined......	0 65	0 70	Shingle alone do	3 15	3 25	" boiled......	0 81	0 57
Castor Oil...........	0 19½	0 24	Lathe and 3 dy....	3 30	3 40	Machinery	0 00	0 00
Caustic Soda..........	0 04½	0 05	Undenatured Iron :			Olive, common, ℔ gal..	1 00	1 00
Cochineal.............	0 00	1 00	" salad	1 95	2 30	" salad, in bots.		
Cream Tartar	0 40	0 45	Assorted sizes......	0 08	0 00	qt. ℔ case...	3 60	3 75
Epsom Salts	0 05	0 04	Best No. 24........	0 08	0 00	Sesame salad, ℔ gal...	1 60	1 75
Extract Logwood......	0 11	0 13	" 50......	0 08	0 08¼	Seal, pale...........	0 75	0 85
Gum Arabic, sorts.....	0 30	0 35	" 58..	0 09	0 00¼	Spirits Turpentine....	0 52½	0 00
Indigo, Madras	0 90	1 00	Horse Nails :			Varnish	0 00	0 00
Licorice	0 14	0 45	Guest's or Griffin's			Whale. ·.·...	0 00	0 90
Madder	0 00	0 18	assorted sizes.......	0 00	0 00	**Paints, &c.**		
Galls	0 33	0 37	For W. sas'd sizes..	0 18	0 19	White Lead, genuine		
Opium...............	12 00	13 50	Patent Hammer'd do..	0 17	0 18	in Oil, ℔ 25 ℔s......	0 00	2 85
Oxalic Acid...........	0 26	0 35	Iron (at 4 months):			Do. No. 1 "	0 00	2 10
Potash, Bi-tart.......	0 25	0 28	Pig—Gartsherrie No1..	24 00	25 00	" 2 "	0 00	1 90
" Bichromate..	0 15	0 20	Other brands. No 1..	23 00	24 00	" 3 "	0 00	1 65
Potass Iodide	3 90	4 50	" No 2..	22 00	23 00	White Zinc, genuine..	3 50	3 50
Senna	0 13½	0 60	Bar—Scotch, ℔100 ℔..	2 25	2 50	White Lead, dry	0 03¼	0 03
Soda Ash	0 03½	0 04	Refined	2 60	3 25	Red Lead...........	0 07¼	0 04
Soda Bicarb	4 50	5 00	Swedes	5 00	5 00	Venetian Red, Engh...	0 02¾	0 02¼
Tartaric Acid.........	0 40	0 45	Hoops—Coopers.....	5 00	3 25	Yellow Ochre, Fren'h..	0 02¾	0 03½
Verdigris	0 33	0 40	Band	3 00	3 25	Whiting............	0 85	1 25
Vitriol, Blue..........	0 08	0 10	Boiler Plates........	3 25	3 50	**Petroleum**		
Groceries.			Canada Plates........	3 75	4 00	(Refined ℔ gal.)		
Coffees:			Union Jack	0 00	0 00	Water white, car'l'd..		0 36
Java, ℔ lb...........	0 22@0 24		Pontypool	3 25	4 00	" small lots..	0 37	0 38
Laguayra, ...	0 17	0 18	Swansea	3 90	4 00	Straw, by car load...	0 00	0 00
Rio	0 16	0 17	Lead (at 4 months):			" small lots...	0 00	0 00
Fish:			Bar, ℔ 100 lbs.......	0 03½	0 07	Amber, by car load....	0 00	0 00
Herrings, Lab. split...	5 75	6 50	Sheet "	0 0s	0 00	" small lots...	0 00	0 00
" round...	0 00	0 00	Shot	0 07½	0 07½	Benzine	0 00	0 00
" scaled......	0 35	0 40	Iron Wire (net cash):			*Grain:*		
Mackerel, small kitts..	1 00	0 00	No. 6, ℔ bundle....	2 70	2 80	Wheat, Spring, 60 lb..	0 0	0 90
Loch. Her. wh's Erks..	3 50	3 75	" 9, "	3 10	3 20	" Fall 60 "	0 5	0 90
" half "	1 25	1 50	" 12, "	3 40	3 50	Barley .... 48 "	1 5	1 25
White Fish & Front...	None.		" 15, "	4 20	4 40	Peas.......... 60 "	0 65	0 70
Salmon, saltwater....	14 00	15 00	*Powder:*			Oats.......... 34 "	0 49	0 50
Dry Cod, ℔ 112 ℔s.....	5 00	5 25	Blasting, Canada....	3 50	0 00	Rye.......... 56 "	0 65	0 70
Fruit:			FF "	4 25	4 50	*Seeds:*		
Raisins, Layers	2 00	2 10	FFF "	4 75	5 00	Clover, choice 60 "	6 75	7 00
" M R	1 90	2 00	Blasting, English ...	4 0	5 00	" com'n 68 "	6 50	6 75
" Valentias new..	0 6½	0 7¼	FF "	5 00	0 00	Timothy, cho'e 4 "	3 50	3 75
Currants, new........	0 05	0 06½	FFF locuc..	6 00	6 50	" inf. to good 48 "	1 75	3 25
" old........	0 04	0 04¾	Pressed Spikes (4 mos):.			Flax .... 56 "	1 15	1 25
Figs	0 14	0 00	Regular sizes 100....	4 00	4 25	*Flour (per brl.):*		
Molasses:			Extra "	4 50	5 00	Superior extra........	0 00	0 00
Clayed, ℔ gal........	0 00	0 85	Tin Plates (net cash):			Extra superfine,......	4 35	4 50
Syrups, Standard ...	0 00	0 00	IC Coke	7 50	8 50	Fancy superfine	4 10	4 40
" Golden ...	0 00	0 08	IC Charcoal	8 25	8 50	Superfine No 1	4 00	
Rice:			IX "	10 25	10 75	" No. 2		
Arracan	4 2	4 50	IXX "	12 25	0 00	Oatmeal, (per brl.)....	5 40	5 50
Spices:			DC "	7 25	9 00	**Provisions**		
Cassia, whole, ℔ ℔....	0 00	0 45	DX "	9 50	0 00	Butter, dairy tub ℔ lb..	0 20	0 23
Cloves	0 11	0 13	**Hides & Skins, ℔ lb**			" store packed....	0 18	0 19
Nutmegs	0 45	0 55	Green rough	0 05¾	0 07	Cheese, new	0 13	0 14
Ginger, ground	0 20	0 25	Green, salt'd & insp'd.	0 07½	0 08	Pork, mess, per brl...	25 50	26 00
" Jamaica, root...	0 20	0 75	Cured	0 00	0 00	" prime mess....		
Pepper, black........	0 00	0 19	Calfskins, green.......	0 00	0 10	" prime.......	0 00	0 00
Pimento	0 08	0 00	Calfskins, cured.......	0 00	0 14	Bacon, rough	0 10	0 10½
Sugars:			" dry.......	0 14	0 00	Cumberl'n cut...	0 11	0 11½
Port Rico, ℔ lb.......	0 10½	0 11	Sheepskins, ...	1 00	1 40	" smoked.......	0 00	0 00
Cuba	0 10	0 10½	" country..	1 00	1 40	Hams, in salt........	0 13	0 12½
Barbadoes (bright)...	0 10	0 11	*Hops.*			" sug.cur'd sm'd''.		
Canada Sugar Refine'y,			Inferior, ℔ ℔.......	0 05	0 07	Shoulders, in salt	0 10	0 10½
Yellow No. 2, 60 ds...	0 11	0 11½	Medium	0 07	0 09	Lard, in kegs	0 16	0 17½
Yellow, No. 2¾......	0 11	0 11½	Good	0 09	0 12	Eggs, packed	0 13	0 20
" No. 3......	0 11½	0 11½	Fancy	0 00	0 00	Tallow	0 08	0 8½
Crushed X	0 13	0 13½	*Leather.* ℔ (4 mos.)			Hogs dressed, heavy..	0 00	0 8½
" A	0 13	0 13½	In lots of less than			" medium..	8 75	9 00
Ground..............	0 00	0 75	50 sides, 10 ℔' cnt			" light....	8 50	8 75
Dry Crushed	0 14½	0 14½	higher.					
Extra Ground	0 15½	0 15½	Spanish Sole, 1st qual'y			**Salt, &c.**		
Teas :			heavy, weights ℔ ℔..	0 21½	0 22	American bris........	1 50	1 52
Japan com'n to good..	0 48	0 55	Do.1st qual middle do..	0 23½	0 00	Liverpool coarse	1 15	1 70
" Fine to choicest..	0 60	0 65	Do. No. 2, light weights	0 00	0 21	Goderich		1 00
Colored, com. to fine..	0 40	0 75	Slaughter heavy ...	0 26	0 27	Plaster	1 05	1 10
Congou & Souch'ng...	0 42	0 75	Do. light........	0 00	0 00	Water Lime	1 50	0 00
Oolong, good to fine...	0 80	0 00	Harness, best	0 28	0 30			
Y. Hyson, com to gd..	0 45	0 55	" No. 2	0 34	0 20			
Medium to choice	0 65	0 80	Upper heavy........	0 33	0 40			
Extra choice	0 85	0 95	" light........	0 00	0 42			

Soap & Candles.	$ c.	$ c.
D. Crawford & Co.'s ..		
Imperial.........	0 07½	0 08
" Golden Bar	0 07	0 07½
" Silver Bar........	0 07	0 07½
Crown	0 05	0 05½
No. 1	0 03½	0 03
Candles	0 00	0 11½
Wines, Liquors, &c.		
Ale:		
English, per doz......	2 00	2 65
Guinness Dub Portr..	2 35	2 40
Spirits:		
Pure Jamaica Rum...	1 80	2 25
De Kuyper's H. Gin..	1 55	1 65
Booth's Old Tom.....	1 90	2 00
Gin:		
Green, cases.........	4 00	4 25
Booth's Old Tom, c...	6 00	6 25
Wines:		
Port, common	1 00	1 25
" fine old	2 00	4 00
Sherry, common	1 00	1 50
" medium	1 70	1 80
"old pale or golden..	2 50	4 00

Brandy:	$ c.	$ c.
Hennessy's, per gal..	2 30	2 50
Martell's " ..	2 30	2 50
J. Robin & Co.'s " ..	2 25	2 35
Otard, Dupuy & Cos..	2 25	2 35
Brandy, cases........	8 50	9 00
Brandy, com. per c...	4 00	4 50
Whiskey:		
Common 36 u. p......	0 62½	0 65
Old Rye	0 85	0 87½
Malt	0 85	0 87½
Toddy	0 85	0 87½
Scotch, per gal........	1 90	2 10
Irish—Kinnahan's c...	7 00	7 50
" Dunnville's Belf't..	6 00	6 25
Wool.		
Fleece, lb.............	0 28	0 35
Pulled ".............	0 22	0 25
Furs.		
Bear.......	3 00	10 00
Beaver, ℔ lb....	1 00	1 25
Coon	0 20	0 40
Fisher...............	4 00	6 00
Martin....	1 40	1 60
Mink.................	3 25	4 00
Otter.................	5 75	6 00
Spring Rats..........	0 15	0 17
Fox.	1 20	1 25

INSURANCE COMPANIES.

ENGLISH.—*Quotations on the London Market.*

No. of Shares.	Last Dividend.	Name of Company.	Shares par val £	Amount paid.	Last Sale.
20,000		Briton Medical and General Life ...	10	....	2
50,000	7½	Commer'l Union, Fire, Life and Mar.	50	5	6½
24,000	8	City of Glasgow	25	2½	5½
5,000	9½	Edinburgh Life	100	15	33
400,000	5—½ yr	European Life and Guarantee......	2½	11s6	4s. 3d.
100,000	10	Etna Fire and Marine.............	10	1½	—
20,000	5	Guardian	100	50	51¼
24,000	12	Imperial Fire.....................	500	50	350
7,500	9½	Imperial Life	100	10	16½
100,000	10	Lancashire Fire and Life..........	20	2	2¾
10,000	11	Life Association of Scotland.......	40	7½	25
35,862	45s. p. sh	London Assurance Corporation ..	25	12½	49
10,000	5	London and Lancashire Life	10	1	—
87,504	40	Liverp'l & London & Globe F. & L.	20	2	7 1-16
20,000	5	National Union Life	5	1	1
20,000	12½	Northern Fire and Life	100	5	12
40,000	12 '68, bo 5s.	North British and Mercantile	50	6¼	21
40,000	50	Ocean Marine	25	5	18½
2,500	£5 12s.	Provident Life.....................	100	10	35
....	£4½ p. s.	Phœnix............................	....	....	145
200,000	2½—h.yr.	Queen Fire and Life	10	1	1
100,000	3s. bo. 4s	Royal Insurance....................	20	3	6½
20,000	10	Scottish Provincial Fire and Life ..	50	2½	5¼
10,000	25	Standard Life	50	12	66½
4,000	5	Star Life	25	1¼	—
		CANADIAN.			℔ c.
8,000	4	British America Fire and Marine ..	$50	$25	55 55½
....	4	Canada Life	...	....	.....
4000	12	Montreal Assurance	£50	£5	135
10,000	3	Provincial Fire and Marine........	60	11	.....
....	....	Quebec Fire	40	32½	20½
....	7	" Marine.....................	100	40	80 90
10,000	5 7 mo's.	Western Assurance................	40	9	.....

RAILWAYS.	Sha's	Paid	Montr	London
Atlantic and St. Lawrence........................	£100	All.	....	61 62
Buffalo and Lake Huron	20½	"	....	3 3½
Do. do Preference	10	"	....	5½ 6½
Buff., Brantf. & Goderich, 6℔c.,1872-3-4....	100	"	....	66 69
Champlain and St. Lawrence	....	....	10 11	....
Do. do Pref. 10 ℔ ct...	....	....	80 85	....
Grand Trunk	100	"	15½16½	15¾ 16½
Do. Eq.G. M. Bds. 1 ch. 6℔c............	100	"	....	86 87
Do. First Preference, 5 ℔ c	100	"	....	55 55½
Do. Deferred, 3 ℔ ct..	100	"	....	....
Do. Second Pref. Bonds, 5℔c..........	100	"	....	40 41
Do. do Deferred, 3 ℔ ct...........	100	"	...	....
Do. Third Pref. Stock, 4℔ct...........	100	"	...	28 30
Do. do. Deferred, 3 ℔ ct......	100	"	...	....
Do. Fourth Pref. Stock, 3℔c	100	"	....	17¾ 18½
Do. do. Deferred, 3 ℔ ct............	100	"	....	...
Great Western	20½	"	13 14	15½ 15¾
Do. New	20½	18	....	....
Do. 6 ℔ c. Bds, due 1873-76...........	100	All.	....	100 102
5 ℔c Bds. due 1877-78....	100	"	....	94 95
Marine Railway, Halifax, $250, all......	$250	"	....	....
Northern, of Canada, 6℔c. 1st Pref. Bds...........	100	"	.. .	81 83

EXCHANGE.	Halifax.	Montr'l.	Quebec.	Toronto.
Bank on London, 60 days......				
Sight or 75 days date	12½	9 9½	9¼ 9½	9½
Private do.	11½ 12	8 8½	8¼ 8¾	8½
Private, with documents.........	....	7½ 8½	....	....
Bank on New York................	....	23 23½	23½ 24	23½
Private do.	....	23½ 24	23½ 24	....
Gold Drafts do.	....	par to ½ p.	par ⅛ dis.	par ¼ dis.
Silver	....	3 3½	....	3½ to 4½

STOCK AND BOND REPORT.

The dates of our quotations are as follows:—Toronto, March 16; Montreal, March 13; Que March 13; London, Jan. 28.

NAME.	Shares.	Paid up.	Divid'd last 6 Months	Dividend Day.	CLOSING PRICES Toronto.	Montre'l	Qu
BANKS.			℔ ct.				
British North America	$250	All.	3	July and Jan.	104 105½	105 105½	104
Jacques Cartier.........	50	"	4	1 June, 1 Dec.	109 109½	109 109½	108
Montreal	200	"	5	"	140½ 141	140½ 141	139
Nationale...................	50	"	4	1 Nov. 1 May.	107½ 108	108 108½	108
New Brunswick	100	"	....	......	....	...	.
Nova Scotia	200	28	7&b33½	Mar. and Sept.	....	....	.
Du Peuple......	50	"	4	1 Mar., 1 Sept.	107 108	108 108	107
Toronto	100	"	4	1 Jan., 1 July.	120 120½	120½ 122	121
Bank of Yarmouth............	....	....	......	......	....	....	.
Canadian Bank of Com'e......	50	95	......	......	102½ 103	102 103½	102
City Bank Montreal	80	All.	4	1 June, 1 Dec.	103 103½	103½103¾	103
Commer'l Bank (St. John)....	100	"	℔ ct.	. ...	...	...	.
Eastern Townships' Bank.....	50	"	4	1 July, 1 Jan..	....	98 99½	9½
Gore	40	...	none.	1 Jan., 1 July.	40 41	41 45	42
Halifax Banking Company....	.	....	......	. ....	....	....	.
Mechanics' Bank.............	50	70	4	1 Nov., 1 May.	96 97	95 96	95
Merchants' Bank of Canada....	100	70	4	1 Jan., 1 July.	108½ 109	108¾109½	109
Merchants' Bank (Halifax)....	....	....	.....	.....	....	...	.
Molson's Bank......	50	All.	4	1 Apr., 1 Oct.	113½ 114	113¾114	113
Niagara District Bank...	100	70	3½	1 Jan., 1 July.	....	....	.
Ontario Bank.................	40	All.	4	1 June, 1 Dec.	100 100¼	99½ 100	99½
People's Bank (Fred'kton)....	100	"	......	......	....	....	.
People's Bank (Halifax)	20	"	7 12 m	......	....	...	.
Quebec Bank	100	"	3½	1 June, 1 Dec.	100 101	100 100½	100
Royal Canadian Bank	50	50	4	1 Jan., 1 July.	80 80½	80 85	.
St. Stephens Bank	100	All	.....	......	....	...	
Union Bank	100	70	4	1 Jan., 1 July.	104 104½	104½ 105	104
Union Bank (Halifax)........	100	40	7 12mo	Feb. and Aug.	....	....	.
MISCELLANEOUS.							
British America Land........	250	44	2½	......	....	....	.
British Colonial S. S. Co......	250	32½	2½	......	...	50 60	.
Canada Company	32½	All.	£1 10s.	......	....	....	.
Canada Landed Credit Co.....	50	$20	3½	......	75 77	....	.
Canada Per. B'ldg Society....	50	All.	5	......	125½ 126	....	.
Canada Mining Company.....	4	90	....	... ..	....	....	.
Do. Inl'd Steam Nav. Co....	100	All.	7	......	....	100 101	.
Do. Glass Company.........	100	"	12½ "	......	....	40 55	.
Canad'n Loan & Investm't....	25	2½	7	. ....	....	....	.
Canada Agency	10	¼	......	......	....	....	.
Colonial Securities Co........	...	....	.....	.....	....	....	.
Freehold Building Society....	100	All.	4	......	110 110½	....	.
Halifax Steamboat Co........	100	"	5	......	....	....	.
Halifax Gas Company........	....	....	......	. .. .	....	...	.
Hamilton Gas Company......	....	....	.....	. ..	....	....	.
Huron Copper Bay Co........	4	12	20	. ....	....	32½ 40	.
Lake Huron S. and C.........	5	102	......	......	....	...	.
Montreal Mining Consols.....	20	$15	......	. ....	....	3.10 3.20	
Do. Telegraph Co...	40	All.	5	.....	133½ 134	132½133½	133
Do. Elevating Co...	00	"	15 12 m	......	....	100 102½	.
Do. City Gas Co.........	40	"	4	15 Mar. 15 Sep.	....	Bks clsd	Bk
Do. City Pass. R,. Co....	50	"	4	......	....	111½112½	111
Quebec and L. S.	8	$4	......	... .	....	....	
Quebec Gas Co...............	200	All.	4	1 Mar., 1 Sep.	....	...	11
Quebec Street R. R..........	50	25	3	......	....	....	9
Richelieu Navigation Co.....	100	All.	10 p.a.	1 Jan., 1 July.	....	108 109	10
St. Lawrence Glass Company.	100	"	....	......	....	80 85	
St. Lawrence Tow Boat Co....	100	"	......	3 Feb.	...	...	3
Tor'to Consumers' Gas Co....	50	"	4	1 My Au Mar Fe	107½108	...	10
Trust & Loan Co. of U. C.....	20	5	3	......	....	....	
West'n Canada Bldg Soc'y....	50	All.	5	......	120½ 121	....	

SECURITIES.	London.	Montreal	Quebec.	
Canadian Gov't Deb. 6 ℔ ct. stg..................	...	102 103½	103 103½	102
Do. do. 6 do due Ja. & Jul. 1877-84........	104½ 105½	....	....	.
Do. do. 6 do. Feb. & Aug........	103 105	....	... .	..
Do. do. 6 do. Mch. & Sep........	105 108	.. .	...	.
Do. do. 5 ℔ ct. cur., 1883	94 96	93 95	92½ 95	95
Do. do. 5 do. stg., 1885	95½ 96½	93 94½	92½ 94½	95
Do. do. 7 do. cur.,...................	....	....	......	..
Dominion 6 p. c. 1878 cy.....	....	105 106	105½105½	105
Hamilton Corporation.....	. ..	....	... ..	..
Montreal Harbor, 8 ℔ ct. d. 1869..................	..	....	......	..
Do. do. 7 do. 1870....	...	....	......	..
Do. do. 6½ do. 1883........	....	102 103	......	..
Do. do. 6½ do. 1873..................	....	....	......	..
Do. Corporation, 6 ℔ c. 1891	....	96 9½	96 96½	95
Do. 7 p. c. stock	....	108½109	110 110½	109
Do. Water Works, 6 ℔ c. stg. 1878........ ..	....	....	......	95
Do. do. 6 do. cy. do.	....	96½ 97	......	95
New Brunswick, 6 ℔ ct., Jan. and July	104 105	....	.. ...	..
Nova Scotia, 6 ℔ ct., 1875.......................	104 105	...	......	..
Ottawa City 6 ℔ c. d. 1880	....	92½ 93½	......	.
Quebec Harbour, 6 ℔ c. d. 1883.	....	....	60	..
Do. do. 7 do. do................	....	....	65 70	..
Do. do 8 do. 1886................	...	....	80 85	..
Do. City, 7 ℔ c. d. 1½ years....	....	....	97½ 98	..
Do. do. 7 do. 9 do.	....	....	91 92	..
Do. do. 7 do. 5 do.	....	....	94½ 95	..
Do. Water Works, 7 ℔ ct., 4 years	....	....	97 97½	..
Do. do. 6 do. 2 do.	....	....	94½ 95	..
Toronto Corporation	....	90 92½	...	.

Insurance.

BEAVER
uul Insurance Association.

HEAD OFFICE—20 TORONTO STREET,
TORONTO.

ES LIVE STOCK against death from any cause.
only Canadian Company having authority to do this
business.

R. L. DENISON,
President.

VREILLY,
Secretary.   -8-1y-25

HOME DISTRICT
al Fire Insurance Company.

-North-West Cor. Yonge & Adelaide Streets,
TORONTO.—(Up Stairs.)

ES Dwelling Houses, Stores, Warehouses, Mer-
lise, Furniture, &c.

PRESIDENT—The Hon. J. McMURRICH.
VICE-PRESIDENT—JOHN BURNS, Esq.
JOHN RAINS, Secretary.
AGENTS:
VRIGHT, Esq., Hamilton; FRANCIS STEVENS, Esq.,
Barrie; Messrs. GIBBS & BRO., Oshawa.   8-1y

THE PRINCE EDWARD COUNTY
ial Fire Insurance Company.

HEAD OFFICE,—PICTON, ONTARIO.
J, L. B. STINSON; Vice-President, W. A. RICHARDS.
er H. A. McFaul, James Cavan, James Johnson,
Mill, William Delong.—Treasurer, David Barker
, John Twigg ; Solicitor, R. J. Fitzgerald.

Company is established upon strictly Mutual prin-
es, insuring farming and isolated property, (not
as,) in Township only, and offers great advantages
ers, at low rates for five years, without the expense
ewal.
., June 15, 1868.   9-1y

THE AGRICULTURAL
ual Assurance Association of Canada.

FFICE .... LONDON, ONT.

y Farmers' Company. Licensed by the Government of Canada.

1st January, 1869 .... $250,193 82
d Cash Items, over $86,000 00
'olicies in force 30,292 09

Company insures nothing more dangerous than
m property. Its rates are as low as any well-es-
d Company in the Dominion, and lower than those
at many. It is largely patronised, and continues
in public favor.
surance, apply to any of the Agents or address
etary, London, Ontario.
m, 2nd Nov., 1868.   12-1y

ton Medical and General Life
Association,

with which is united the

TANNIA LIFE ASSURANCE COMPANY.

and Invested Funds............£750,000 Sterling.

ANNUAL INCOME, £220,000 STG, :
rly increasing at the rate of £25,000 Sterling.

important and peculiar feature originally intro-
d by this Company, in applying the periodical
s, so as to make Policies payable during life, without
ther rate of premiums being charged, has caused
cess of the BAITON MEDICAL AND GENERAL to be
unparalleled in the history of Life Assurance. Life
on the Profit Seals become payable during the lifetime
Assured, thus rendering a Policy of Assurance a
f subsistence in old age, as well as a protection for o
and a more valuable security to creditors in the
if early death ; and effectually meeting the often
bjection, that persons do not themselves reap the
of their own prudence and forethought.
xtra charge made to members of Volunteer Corps
ices within the British Provinces.
'ORONTO AGENCY, 5 KING ST. WEST.
'—9-1yr   JAMES FRASER, Agent.

Insurance.

The Gore District Mutual Fire Insurance
Company

GRANTS INSURANCES on all description of Property
against Loss or Damage by FIRE. It is the only Mutual Fire Insurance Company which assesses its Policies
yearly from their respective dates ; and the average yearly
cost of insurance in it, for the past three and a half years,
has been nearly

TWENTY CENTS IN THE DOLLAR
less than what it would have been in an ordinary Pro-
prietary Company.
THOS. M. SIMONS,
Secretary & Treasurer.
ROBT. McLEAN,
Inspector of Agencies.
-Galt, 25th Nov., 1868.   15-1y

Geo. Girdlestone,

FIRE, Life, Marine, Accident, and Stock Insurance
Agent
Very best Companies represented.
Windsor, Ont. June, 1868

The Standard Life Assurance Company,
Established 1825.
WITH WHICH IS NOW UNITED
THE COLONIAL LIFE ASSURANCE COMPANY.

Head Office for Canada :
MONTREAL—STANDARD COMPANY'S BUILDINGS,
No. 47 GREAT ST. JAMES STREET.
Manager—W. M. RAMSAY.   Inspector—RICH'D BULL.

THIS Company having deposited the sum of ONE HUN-
DRED AND FIFTY THOUSAND DOLLARS with the Receiver-
General, in conformity with the Insurance Act passed last
Session, Assurances will continue to be carried out at
moderate rates and on all the different systems in practice.

AGENT FOR TORONTO—HENRY PELLATT,
KING STREET.

AGENT FOR HAMILTON—JAMES DANCROFT.
6-6mos.

Fire and Marine Assurance.

THE BRITISH AMERICA
ASSURANCE COMPANY.
HEAD OFFICE :
CORNER OF CHURCH AND COURT STREETS,
TORONTO.

BOARD OF DIRECTION :
Hon G. W. Allan, M L C.,   A. Joseph, Esq.,
George J. Boyd, Esq ,   Peter Paterson, Esq.,
Hon. W. Cayley,   G. P. Ridout, Esq.,
Richard S. Cassels, Esq.,   E H. Rutherford, Esq ,
Thomas O. Street, Esq.

Governor:
GEORGE PERCIVAL RIDOUT, Esq.
Deputy Governor:
PETER PATERSON, Esq,

Fire Inspector: Marine Inspector:
E ROBY O'BRIEN.   CAPT. R. COURNEEN.

Insurances granted on all descriptions of property
against loss and damage by fire and the perils of inland
navigation.
Agencies established in the principal cities, towns, and
ports of shipment throughout the Province.
THOS. WM. BIRCHALL,
23-1y   Managing Director.

Queen Fire and Life Insurance Company,
OF LIVERPOOL AND LONDON,

ACCEPTS ALL ORDINARY FIRE RISKS
on the most favorable terms.

LIFE RISKS
Will be taken on terms that will compare favorably with
other Companies.

CAPITAL, - - - - £2,000,000 Stg.

CHIEF OFFICES—Queen's Buildings, Liverpool, and
Gracechurch Street London.
CANADA BRANCH OFFICE—Exchange Buildings, Montreal.
Resident Secretary and General Agent,

A. MACKENZIE FORBES,
13 St. Sacrament St., Merchants' Exchange, Montreal.
WM. ROWLAND, Agent, Toronto.   1-1y

Insurance.

The Waterloo County Mutual Fire Insurance
Company.

HEAD OFFICE : WATERLOO, ONTARIO.

ESTABLISHED 1863.

THE business of the Company is divided into three
separate and distinct branches, the

VILLAGE, FARM, AND MANUFACTURES.

Each Branch paying its own losses and its just proportion
of the managing expenses of the Company.
C. M. TAYLOR, Sec.   M. SPRINGER, M.M.P., Pres.
J. HUGHES, Inspector.   16-yr

Ætna Fire and Marine Insurance Company of
Dublin,

AT a Meeting of the Shareholders of this Company,
held at Dublin, on the 19th ult., it was agreed that
the business of the "ETNA" should be transferred to the
"UNITED FORTS AND GENERAL INSURANCE COMPANY,"
In accordance with this agreement, the business will here-
after be carried on by the latter Company, which assumes
and guarantees all the risks and liabilities of the "ETNA."
The Directors have resolved to continue the CANADIAN
BRANCH, and arrangements for resuming FIRE and MA-
RINE business are rapidly approaching completion.

T. W. GRIFFITH,
16   MANAGER.

Lancashire Insurance Company,
CAPITAL, - - - - - - - - £3,000,000 Sterling

FIRE RISKS
Taken at reasonable rates of premium, and
ALL LOSSES SETTLED PROMPTLY,
By the undersigned, without reference elsewhere.

S.C. DUNCAN-CLARK & CO.,
General Agents for Ontario,
N. W. Corner of King & Church Streets,
25-1y   TORONTO.

DIVISION OF PROFITS NEXT YEAR.

ASSURANCES
EFFECTED BEFORE 30TH APRIL NEXT,
IN THE

Canada Life Assurance Company,
OBTAIN A YEAR'S ADDITIONAL PROFITS
OVER LATER ENTRANTS,

And the great success of the Company warrants the Directors in recommending this very important
advantage to assurers.

SUMS ASSURED $5,300,000
AMOUNT OF CAPITAL AND FUNDS........ 1,000,000
ANNUAL INCOME......................... 900,000

Assets (exclusive of uncalled capital) for each $100 of
liabilities, about $150,.
The income from interest upon investments is now
alone sufficient to meet claims by death.

A. G. RAMSAY, Manager.
E. BRADBURNE, Agent.
Feb. 1.   1y   Toronto Street.

The Victoria Mutual
FIRE INSURANCE COMPANY OF CANADA.

Insures only Non-Hazardous Property, at Low Rates.

BUSINESS STRICTLY MUTUAL.

GEORGE H. MILLS, President.
W. D. BOOKER, Secretary.
HEAD OFFICE ....HAMILTON, ONTARIO.
aug 15-1yr

PUBLISHED AT THE OFFICE OF THE MONETARY
TIMES, No. 60 CHURCH STREET.
PRINTED AT THE DAILY TELEGRAPH PUBLISHING HOUSE,
BAY STREET, CORNER OF KING.

THE NORTHERN FIRE INSURANCE COMPANY

1836. ESTABLISHED 1836.

CHIEF OFFICES:

1 MOORGATE STREET, LONDON.   3 KING STREET, ABERDEEN

GENERAL AGENTS FOR CANADA:

TAYLOR BROTHERS, MONTREAL.

CAPITAL:

TWO MILLION POUNDS STERLIN

ACCUMULATED FUNDS...EIGHT HUNDRED AND FIFTY THOUSAND POUNDS STERLING

ANNUAL REVENUE FROM FIRE PREMIUMS.............. .....ONE HUNDRED AND SIXTY THOUSAND POUNDS STERLING.

Insurances against LOSS by Fire effected on the most favorable terms. Losses paid without reference to the Board in London.

W. H. MILLER, Agent for TORONTO

Office—Corner CHURCH AND COLBORNE STREETS.

THE CANADIAN

IONETARY TIMES

AND

INSURANCE CHRONICLE.

)TED TO FINANCE, COMMERCE, INSURANCE, BANKS, RAILWAYS, NAVIGATION, MINES, INVESTMENT,
PUBLIC COMPANIES, AND JOINT STOCK ENTERPRISE.

—NO. 32.	TORONTO, THURSDAY, MARCH 25, 1869.	{ SUBSCRIPTION: $2 YEAR.

Mercantile.

Gundry and Langley,
CTS AND CIVIL ENGINEERS, Building Sur-
nd Valuators. Office corner of King and Jordan
:onto.
GUNDRY.   HENRY LANGLEY.

J. B. Boustead.
)N and Commission Merchant. Hops bought
d on Commission. 82 Front St., Toronto.

John Boyd & Co,
ALE Grocers and Commission Merchants,
. St.. Toronto.

Childs & Hamilton.
CTURERS and Wholesale Dealers in Boots
hoes, No. 7 Wellington Street East, Toronto,
                                          28

L. Coffee & Co.
l and Commission Merchants, No. 2 Manning's
Front St., Toronto, Ont. Advances made on
ts of Produce.

Honore Plamondon,
House Broker, Forwarder, and General Agent.
. Office—Custom House Building.   17-1y

Sylvester, Bro. & Hickman,
.CIAL Brokers and Vessel Agents. Office—No.
rio Chambers, [Corner Front and Church Sts.,
                                          2-6m

John Fisken & Co.
L and Commission Merchants, Yonge St,
o, Ont.

W. & R. Griffith.
RS of Teas, Wines, etc. Ontario Chambers,
rch and Front Sts , Toronto.

H. Nerlich & Co.,
RS of French, German, English and American
ods, Cigars, and Leaf Tobaccos, No. 2 Adelaide
t, Toronto.   15

Hurd, Leigh & Co.
l and Enamellers of China and Earthenware,
ge St., Toronto, Ont. [See advt.]

Lyman & McNab.
ALE Hardware Merchants, Toronto, Ontario.

W. D. Matthews & Co.
f Commission Merchants, Old Corn Exchange,
at 84. East, Toronto Ont.

R. C. Hamilton & Co.
f Commission Merchants, 119 Lower Water
alifax, Nova Scotia.

Parson Bros.,
jUM Refiners, and Wholesale dealers in Lamps,
eys, etc. Waterooms 51 Front St. Refinery cor.
)on Sts., Toronto.

C. P. Reid & Co.
RS and Dealers in Wines, Liquors, Cigars and
bacco, Wellington Street, Toronto.   28.

W. Rowland & Co.,
f BROKERS and General Commission Mer-
Advances made on Consignments. Corner
. Front Streets, Toronto.

Beford & Dillon.
RS of Groceries, Wellington Street, Toronto,

Sessions, Turner & Cooper.
ACTURERS, Importers and Wholesale Dealers
ots and Shoes, Leather Findings, etc., 8 Wel-
West, Toronto, Ont

Meetings.

NORTH BRITISH AND MERCANTILE INSURANCE COMPANY.

The fifty-ninth annual meeting of this Company was held at Edinburgh, on the 1st March, 1869. The Directors submitted the following Statement of the transactions of the Company during the year 1868 :

Fire Business.

Last year the Directors reported that the premiums received during the year 1867, after deducting re-insurances,
Amounted to the sum of...........£333,984 18 9
During the year
1868 the pre'ms
received were....£491,288 19 11
Deducting pre'ms
paid to other-Of-
fices for re-insu-
rances........... 75,744 14 9
                 _____
The net Premiums received are.... 415,544 5 2

Exhibiting an increase of........... £81,559 6 5
The continued increase which has been thus manifested is satisfactory, as showing the progressive character of the business.   The Directors have, as usual, set aside one-third of the fire premiums received during the past year, amounting to £138,514 15s 1d, to meet any losses which may arise on the unexpired fire policies of 1868. The losses by fire during the year 1868 have amounted to £222,792 14s.

Life Business.

There have been issued during the year 908 policies, assuring £738,582, and the new premiums amount to £23,574 0s 3d. The deaths which occurred during the year were 185 in number, under 206 policies ; and the sums which have become payable on account of these amount, with bonus additions, to the sum of £135,640 1s 6 1. In the Annuity Department there have been issued 41 bonds, securing annuities to the amount of £1,569 4s 10d yearly, for which the Company have received the sum of £17,263 7s 9d. During the year 36 annuities have fallen in, relieving the company of an annual payment of £1,305 13s 4d.
The Directors recommend that a dividend of £13 per cent or 15s per share, with a bonus of 5s per share—making together 20s per share, or £16 per cent on the paid-up capital stock of the Company—be declared payable on the 15th March current, free of income tax. After paying this dividend and bonus, the result of the business for the year has been to add £44,452 14s 7d to the reserved fund.
There is submitted to the meeting the balance sheet of the Company's books, showing that the amount of the reserve fund, after paying the above dividend and bonus, will be £297,153,10s 10d, exclusive of the premium reserve of £138,514 15s 1d, amounting together to £435,668 5s 11d. At 31st December, 1866, these funds, after payment of the dividend then declared, amounted to £290,861 1s, so that during the last two years there has been an increase of £144,807 4s 11d. The assets of the Company now amount to £2,838,

118 18s 11d, and the annual revenue from all sources is £301,801 12s 9d.
In consequence of the death of Mr. Laurence Davidson, the Law Agent of the Company in Scotland, that office became vacant, and has been filled up by the appointment of Mr. John Brown Innes. W.S., who had for many years been a Director of the Company. By the acceptance of this appointment Mr. Innes vacated his seat as a Director, and Mr. Alexander Howe, W.S., of the firm of Messrs. Lindsay, Howe & Co., W.S., was elected an interim Director in his place.
The Directors retiring this year from the Edinburgh Board are : James Campbell Tait, Esq., David Baird Wauchope, Esq., Frederick Pitman, Esq., who retire by rotation, and Alexander Howe, Esq., lately elected ; and from the London Board : Edward Cohen Esq., Pascoe du pre Grenfell, Esq., Adolphus Klockmann, Esq. They are all recommended for re-election. Mr. Alexander H. Campbell, of the London Board, having resigned in consequence of his being now resident in Bombay, the Directors recommend the election of Richard Brandt, Esq., merchant, in his room.
The following Extraordinary Directors retire by rotation : John Cookson, Esq., of Meldon Park ; the Right Hon. Viscount Melville ; and the Right Hon. Sir James Fergusson, Bart., of Kilkerran ;— and they are all recommended for re-election.
The Directors have to acknowledge the valuable services of the various local boards and agents of the Company. They tender them their best thanks, and earnestly request renewed and continued exertions in endeavoring still further to extend the Company's business in all departments.

CANADIAN LAND AND EMIGRATION COMPANY.

The fifteenth annual meeting of the shareholders of this company was held at the London Tavern, London, on the 3rd inst.
The Chairman, in moving the adoption of the report referred to the reconstruction of the Board, and the completion of such arrangements as would have the effect of giving more harmony to their deliberations. The directors, as you are aware, have shelved for some time the question of remuneration except such as should be voted to them at the annual meeting of the company. Now with regard to Canada. The Toronto board ceased to exist on the last day of last year, at the general wish of by far the greater part of the shareholders, and we believe that the time has come when its services are no longer required. We are at a great distance from the scene of the operations of the company, and it is important that we should have a gentleman there as manager in whom we could place thorough reliance, but upon whom there should be a check. Mr. Blomfield had been appointed—a man in whom, from all accounts, and from our experience of him for three years, we can place an implicit confidence; and we are agreed that within certainly defined limits he should have the fullest liberty to act for us to the best of his ability. Up to this time he was hampered by the Toronto board, to whom he acted as secretary, on the one hand, and on the other by fear of misrepresentations sent home. I believe and hope, now that he is solely appointed, he will be able to conduct the affairs of the company to a prosperous

conclusion. (Hear, hear.) I do not think I need now go into the questions to which we proposed to turn our attention. I may say that the arrangement of the board, as at present constituted, has occupied a great share of our time during the last few months, and has practically left little time to do anything else than agree as to the principles on which we are now to proceed, and it will now devolve upon us, if this meeting re-elects this board, to go on to carry them out to the best of our ability. There are several questions to which we intend to give our earnest attention—the sale of land, the making of roads, and the aiding of emigrants—and these are the ones to which we look for profitable return upon our investment. Gentlemen, these are all the remarks with which I need detain you. I move, then, the adoption of this report, having fully placed before you the state of the company, and I shall be glad to answer any questions which may be put either upon the report or the speech I have just made. I beg to move the adoption of the report.

The Rev. Mr. Tucker did not see any mention in the report as to an agency either at Cobourg or Port Hope. There was an agency at Toronto, but he thought they should have some agency at Port Hope or Cobourg, because their settlers were compelled to go there; but he only wished to call the directors' attention to the matter. It would give confidence to the shareholders if they saw that anything of that sort was entered into by the board. (Hear, hear). He thought it would be of advantage to the company to give away to bona fide settlers certain portions of land, say 100 acres, for they had now to compete with Government, who gave away gifts of land to the extent of 100 acres to any one who proved themselves to be a bona fide settler. And unless they did so, how could they expect men to take land from them? He would counsel the board to take the question into consideration, and to try it at least for two or three years. He wished to say nothing more, only to reserve to himself the right of proposing a director at the proper time.

Mr. Montgomerie (director) said—With regard to free grants of land by the Government, the company had made a remonstrance with them, not to ask them to give this up, but to say that it was scarcely fair to the company, considering the terms on which they had taken their lands. The Government recognized the justness of the complaint, and expressed themselves ready to discuss the question with the company. But it was already a fact that we had given several free grants of land upon the roads through their lands where it was necessary to keep them open for traffic. The land was given upon the condition that the settlers kept the roads free from underbrush. So that there was considerable difference between their free lands and those of the Government; for by the means of their free lands they kept open the roads upon their estates, which the Government did not undertake to do. And so great was this benefit, that all persons who had any money to buy land preferred to buy the land of the company rather than take the free lands of the Government. With regard to forfeitures, he thought that the directors could scarcely be blamed for pressing upon these persons to pay; they had abstained from doing so as long as they could with justice to the other shareholders. As to the proposition which had been made, that they should accept the money which had been paid on the part of the whole as sufficient to pay up some of the shares, they had consulted their solicitor, and were of opinion that it could not be done. Still, the notice of "intention of forfeiture" was very different from the forfeiture itself, and would only bring before the defaulting shareholders their responsibility, and might be accompanied by a statement that if such shareholders paid the calls due, with interest and legal expenses, that such shares would revert to the shareholders. This would meet entirely the difficulty suggested by Mr. Tucker.

Mr. Tucker—Do I understand that Government will compensate us?

Mr. Montgomerie—No.

Mr. Tucker—I think, considering our agreement, that the Government are bound to compensate us for our loss. I do not think we should do any harm by bringing these facts before Government.

A shareholder asked if the directors had any fresh news from Canada.

The Chairman—Yes, we have sold [more acres of land than ever before, and in leasing we have done a great deal. We have leased 1,800 acres during the past year, while during the whole previous course of the company the leasings amount to only 7,500 acres; which I consider a very encouraging return. They are at ten cents per annum. The Chairman further remarked, in reference to the questions which had been asked, that the directors already had under consideration the question of establishing an agency at either Port Hope or Cobourg. With respect to the grants of land by the Government, he considered they had a moral claim upon the Government in consequence of the different position it placed the company's land in.

Mr. Gurney said that he intended, on the morrow, paying a visit to two members of the Canadian Government, who are at present staying in London, with respect to the question.

In answer to a shareholder, Mr. Gurney said they had not alluded in the report to the question of tramways, because they had not yet decided upon any steps in connection therewith. They should be happy if any shareholder who was acquainted with the question would come forward and give them any advice he could.

After some further discussion the meeting separated.

Insurance.

FIRE RECORD.--Stratford, March 13.—A fire caught in the cast end of Battershall's block; the buildings were saved with the aid of a small hand engine, but were damaged to the extent of about $500, which is said to be covered by insurance.

Stayner, March 18.—A telegram says the flour and grist mill at Warrington, one mile from Stayner, owned by Mr. Dewe, and occupied by J. Barclay, was totally destroyed by fire; cause not known. There was not much flour or grain in at the time. The contents were insured; but it is not known if there was any insurance on the building.

Barrie, March 12.—The dwelling house and store of Geo. Ford, Market square, was destroyed. There was a good supply of water, so that the fire was prevented from spreading.

St. Catherines, March.—The livery stable of Mr. Gordon, and contents, were consumed. Insurance, $2,000; loss stated at $3,000 to $4,000. The fire is thought to have been the work of an incendiary. The Stephenson House had a narrow escape.

Goderich, March 11.—Two stables belonging to William Campbell and Mr. Doyle, respectively, were entirely consumed. In Mr. Doyle's stable there was a span of horses, and it was with some difficulty that the animals were rescued. The stable was worth $300, $100 of which was covered by insurance. Mr. Campbell's was an old one. It is thought that the fire originated from ashes deposited in the latter.

Digby, N. S., Feb. 27.—A destructive fire occurred here, seriously injuring or totally destroying half a dozen houses. The fire appeared to have broken out in R. B. Stark's premises. The other sufferers are Messrs. R. P. Payson (two houses), Churchill & Taylor, Richard Thorn, and Ebenezer Beaman. We believe there was no insurance.

Bow Park, Ont., March 12.—The house on the farm of Hon. Geo. Brown, at this place, was burned with contents; insured for $2,000 in the Hartford and $2,000 in the Etna.

Garden Island, March 12.—A house occupi[ed] by Mr. Johnson was gutted. The fire was pr[e]vented from spreading.

Belleville, March 20.—A small unoccupi[ed] brick cottage, owned by the estate of the la[te] Edmund Murney, was destroyed.

St. John, March.—James Nelson's Intern[a]tional Hotel, at Shutenacadie, was complete[ly] destroyed by fire on Sunday last, with all t[he] barns and outhouses. Nothing but a few artic[les] of furniture were saved. The property, valued [at] $12,000, was only insured for $800, leaving M[r.] Nelson a heavy loser.

—"An Adjuster" sends us the following re[liable] able account of a number of recent fires:—

Clearville, County Kent, March 2.—Laycoo[k] Hotel was burnt down. The building was i[n]sured in the Western of Canada for $500, a[nd] valued at $800; loss total. The contents we[re] insured in the Provincial Insurance Company [for] $900; loss about $400.

Goderich has become notorious within the l[ast] few days for fires. The first occurred on the 7[th] inst.; it was a private dwelling, owned by M[r.] Haftel, and occupied by Mr. Findley of t[he] Bank of Montreal. It was entirely consume[d;] cause said to be carelessness. It was valued [at] $1,000, and insured in the Western for $700; [loss] total.

The next fire was in three frame buildi[ngs] owned by Dr. McDougall, and occupied as milliner shop, shoe shop, and tin and store sh[op.] The buildings were insured in the Western a[nd] British-America for $1,000, and valued at $1,5[00;] loss total. At the same time Mr. McMinch'[s] restaurant was totally consumed. The buildi[ngs] and contents were said to be insured in the Co[m]mercial Union for $800, which is a total l[oss.] The stock of boots and shoes was insured in [the] Western for $400; loss $300. The millin[ery] stock was insured in the Liverpool and Lon[don] and Globe for $400; loss $300. The tin s[hop] was insured in the Western for $1,500; [loss] $1,350.

On the 11th inst., 2 stables, owned by B.D[ewe] and W. Campbell, worth $300. Insured for $[?] in Western.—Total loss. Cause of fire said to [be] by piling up ashes against buildings.

On the 14th inst., 3 frame buildings, owned [by] H. Horton, occupied by J. Johnson, as dry go[ods] and groceries ; Martin, saddler and harness sh[op,] and Horton, as liquor and grocery. The bu[ild]ings were valued at $2,000, and insured in Phœn[ix] of London, for $1,500.—Total loss. Johnst[on's] stock was insured in Western for $2,000 ; dam[age] to the extent of $950. Martin's stock was [in]sured in Provincial for $600 ; damaged to the tent of $400. Horton's stock was insured in C[om]mercial Union and Provincial for $3,000.—T[otal] loss. Besides the above, Gardiner & Co's. ha[rd]ware stock was removed and sustained dama[ge] to the extent of $300. Insured in Phœnix, C[om]mercial Union and Provincial. Cassidy, b[oots] and shoes, were also removed, and damaged ab[out] $100; fully insured in Phœnix. The cause of last fire is looked upon with some suspicion ; s[ome] suspect foul play ; others again think it was cau[sed] by ashes having been put on the top of the out[side] stairs.

APPOINTMENT.—Mr. Dixon, for some y[ears] accountant to the Provincial Insurance Comp[any] has been promoted to the post of Assistant M[an]ager. Mr. Dixon has been a faithful officer, his promotion is a just recognition of the [faithful service.] Mr. Donaldson, late with W. R. Brown a[s ?] has been appointed Accountant.

—Notice is given that application will be m[ade] to Parliament to incorporate "The Domi[nion] Life Insurance and Guarantee Association," [and] "The Dominion Fire and Marine Insur[ance] Company."

NECTICUT MUTUAL.—The officers of the
ecticut Mutual Life Ins. Co., after a diligent
horough examination of the different plans
tted for their new building to be erected in
ord, have adopted that furnished by James
tterson, Esq. The building will be consi-
ed of light Concord or Rhode Island granite,
with rich columns, in each story, of po-
Scotch granite, with a relief of Quincy
e, and will be altogether one of the most
ficent structures in New England. In front,
Main street side, over the entrance, two
al figures in marble, representing "Insur-
and "Plenty," will be placed, between
is the State coat of arms, and the insignia
Company, wrought in polished granite. It
per to have figures representing "Insurance"
Plenty," since the following figures from the
any's official statement Jan. 1, 1869, repre-
"plenty" of "Insurance :"

es issued	11,960
....	$22,669,079.29
e from premiums	7,161,304.11
e from interest	1,584,905.48
income for the year	8,746,209.59
paid	1,221,335.00
ends paid	928,284.00
losses paid to date	8,089,883.00
dividends paid to date	5,197,258.00
Chronicle.	

URANCE RATES ADVANCED.—For the pur-
f placing the business of underwriting on
aks in San Francisco on a paying basis, the
, Union, Fireman's Fund, Occidental, Home,
al and People's of the local Companies; and
Eastern Companies the Ætna, of Hartford;
hoenix, of Hartford; Home, of New York;
attan, of New York; and the Phœnix, of
lyn ; and of the European Companies the
ool and London and Globe, Hamburg-
n, North British, Imperial and Northern,
agreed on an advanced tariff of rates as fol-
—On first and second class brick, 70 cents ;
ird class brick, $1 on the $100; on ware-
, 75 cents; on detached dwellings, 75 cents.
dvance will be from 15 to 50 per cent., tho
st advance being on second class brick,
0 to 70 cents, and the largest on detached
ngs, from 50 to 75 cents on the $100.—San
isco Real Estate Circular.

RBOURS OF REFUGE.—A meeting was lately
n Walsingham, to consider the expediency
ing before Parliament the advantages which
w cut at the S. W. entrance of Long Point
osesses, as a site for a Harbour of Refuge
ke Erie. The following resolutions were
d:—

t the increasing commerce of the lakes im-
voly demands the construction of a commodi-
arbour of Refuge at some convenient point
north shore of Lake Erie, for the safety of
nd property—the want of such a harbour
the cause, annually, of a fearful sacrifice of

t while the Ports of Burwell, Stanley, and
ondeau may have some claims for the estab-
ent of a Harbour of Refuge, yet the want of
at those points, and their being, as is parti-
y the case with Port Stanley and the Ron-
out of the track of vessels navigating the
is sufficient argument why those points
l not be selected.

t in the opinion of this meeting, the new
Long Point affords the best site for a Har-
f Refuge, on the north shore of Lake Erie,
e following reasons:—1st. Its location is
the harbour is most needed, and is where
marine disasters occur—lying, as it does, in
te of the lake. Long Point, running south
nd the main shore south-west, land-lo-ked.
s on their voyage are frequently driven by
avy south-west winds on the north shore,
nd it impossible to work off, or in attempt-
do so, become stranded on Long Point.

2nd. It is easily entered, nature having formed a
channel running nearly south-west, through the
Point of sufficient width for vessels to beat out,
with from twelve to fifteen feet water, and a commodious basin inside Long Point Bay, free from
any sea, and with good anchorage.

SAVING PROPERTY AT FIRES.—To a person who
can "keep his head" during the progress of a fire,
the different methods adopted by different people
in the saving of property is something wonderful
to behold. One man has a penchant for smashing
windows and nothing else. With a piece of board
he will demolish a common window in short order
and his complacency when the fragments are saved
is intense. His forte is shop windows—the more
costly they are the better. It may be useless,
worse than useless as it speedily admits fire, but
crash he sends a battering ram through the cost-
liest plates thus enabling those working these to
cut their hands to pieces. Another will pitch valuable furniture, such as sofas, centre-tables, glassware, mirrors, &c., from the upper window to the
street. His work is to throw the stuff out, on the
crowd devolves the task of saving the pieces.—
Still another destroys all that he carries out. Salt
bags are thrown into sugar barrels, pepper is hur-
led into tea caddies, grindstones are thrown upon
piles of delf, butter is heaped on coal oil barrels,
matches are stored in the most convenient puddle.
We are speaking of facts, and we feel assured that
a large per centage of what is saved at fires would
be better completely destroyed. And all this for
want of a little systematic common-sense.—Goderich Signal.

A NEW FIRE LADDER.

The Chicago Chronicle describes a new fire
ladder thus:—The Truck consists of a frame in
two parts, and runs upon four wheels. To the
hinder part of the truck is attached the main
ladder, upon which a slide ladder works, being
raised by means of a winch at the foot. Each of
these ladders is 30 feet in length, and a socket
ladder at the top 16 feet in length. The pipe for
the hose is affixed to the side of the sliding ladder,
and is projected with it. From the top of each
ladder extends a guy wire rope, the other end of
which is fastened to a windlass on the frame. By
means of this contrivance the ladder is given any
degree of elevation required, and sustained in that
position in the same manner as a builder's derrick.
When the machine is housed or running, the
ladders are very nearly horizontal, and arrangements are made for carrying other ladders under
them. When about to be used, a pin is withdrawn which connects the two parts of the frame;
and the ladder, with the hinder part turning on
the axle of the hind wheels, comes to the ground
at an angle of 45°, and thus may be wheeled into
any position by two men, and raised to any
height, having the ground for its base, instead of
working from a platform as do others, which have
also to choose an even spot for their operations.
The ladder may be easily worked by two men, and
elevated to its full height within three minutes.
Among the advantages of this truck and ladder
over the machines in ordinary use, is its compact-
ness. It occupies less space in the engine-house,
and in running its extreme length, horses included,
is only 22 feet, which permits it to be turned with
facility in any street in the city. It does not require a tiller to the hind wheels, and while it
carries a ladder that can be elevated to a height
of 66 feet, it is self-supporting. The pipes
affixed to the sides of the slide-ladder have a screw
top and bottom, to which the hose and branch
pipe may be readily attached so that two streams
of water can be thrown into any window from an
elevation of from 25 to 70 feet, without carrying
therewith a current of air to feed the fire, as is
done by the present method. A stream of water
thrown 20 or 30 feet from the ground, conveys
with itself five or six times its own bulk of atmo-

sphere, and, consequently, more damage is often
done by water than by fire. This improvement
also enables an engine to cast a stream of water
to double the height it could otherwise attain, and
the stream can be dirccted either from the bottom
of the ladder or from the top. Weavell's machine,
the one used in London, is especially adapted to
effect the rescue of persons from burning premises,
while the Brooklyn invention is not only adapted
to this purpose, but is far more effective in
extinguishing fires, as it enables the firemen to
reach the seat of the fire, even at the loftiest ele-
vations, and beat it out with the force of the
water. In the hands of the Fire Department,
it would prove an invaluable adjunct to their
efficiency.

HARTFORD COMPANIES.

The Courant gives the following synopsis of the
standing of the Hartford offices, Jan. 1, 1869, re-
insurance at 50 per cent. of unexpired risks:—

Name of Company.	Capital.	Assets.	Liabilities including Re-Insurance	Net Value.	Net Value per Cent
Phœnix	$600,000	$1,467,835	$1,283,100	$284,686	130.10
Connect'l.	200,000	342,837	284,109	58,672	120.33
Hartford	1,00,000	3,247,210	3,043,481	203,728	120.37
Ætna	3,000,000	5,150,932	4,715,841	435,091	114.50

—The Yarmouth (N. S.) Herald says : "We
understand that the capitalists of this town are
about to establish a Life Insurance Association."

Railway News.

GREAT WESTERN RAILWAY.—Traffic for week
ending March 5, 1869.

Passengers	$22,744 47
Freight	39,715 80
Mails and Sundries	3,007 61
Total Receipts for week	$65,467 88
Coresponding week, 1868	53,299 12
Increase	$12,168 76

NORTHERN RAILWAY.—Traffic receipts for week
ending March 13th, 1869.

Passengers	$2,233 47
Freight and live stock	5,190 97
Mails and sundries	524 46
	$7,948 90
Corresponding Week of '68	6,160 18
Increase	$1,788 72

WOODEN RAILWAYS IN QUEBEC.—Mr. Dunkin
has announced his policy with respect to wooden
railways. The Gosford and Quebec, the Drummond and Arthabaska, Northern Railway of Mon.
treal and Levis and Kenebec, are to have each 3
per cent. on the cost, provided it does not exceed
$5,000 per mile; and the Sherbrooke and Lennox-
ville lines are to share the 3 per cent. between
them if both are built, or if only one or an amalgamation is effected, the subsidy to go to the line
built. The roads must have 15 miles in operation
by the 1st September, 1872.

—At the annual meeting of the Sidney (N. B.)
Boot and Shoe Company, held recently, a dividend
of four per cent. per annum, or twenty per cent.
on the twenty months the company has been in
operation, was declared.

—The Toronto Assessors have demanded from
the Building Societies, and other companies, lists
of their stockholders. Legal advice is being taken
on the subject.

—Notice is given that a charter will be sought
for "The Imperial Bank of Canada" at the next
session of Parliament.

THE CANADIAN MONETARY TIMES AND INSURANCE CHRONICLE *is printed every Thursday evening and distributed to Subscribers on the following morning.*

Publishing office, No. 60 Church-street, 3 doors north of Court-street.

Subscription price:—

Canada $2.00 per annum.

England, stg. 10s. per annum.

United States (U.S.Cy.) $3.00 per annum.

Casual advertisements will be charged at the rate of ten cents per line, each insertion.

*Address all letters to "*THE MONETARY TIMES.*"*

Cheques, money orders, &c. should be made payable to J. M. TROUT, *Business Manager, who alone is authorized to issue receipts for money.*

☞ *All Canadian Subscribers to* THE MONETARY TIMES *will receive* THE REAL ESTATE JOURNAL *without further charge.*

The Canadian Monetary Times.

THURSDAY, MARCH 25, 1869.

THE BANK CHARTER QUESTION.

SCHEMES INCOMPATIBLE WITH CONVERTIBILITY.

III.

When a government takes security for the entire issue of bank notes, and insists that the security shall consist of its own evidences of debt, as under the National Bank system of the United States, the banks are in effect obliged to make a loan of a large part of their capital to the government. When this loan is made a condition of continuing the business of banking, it partakes of the nature of a forced loan. Capital is displaced—it changes hands—through the instrumentality of credit, and this capital is not kept by the government to be made available for emergencies in which the banks may be placed. It is dissipated; perhaps it is thrown into the open gulf of an already created debt. The United States National Bank system is non-specie paying, and while it lasts, redemption is admittedly impossible. The capital necessary for the redemption of the notes has been handed over to the government; and its restoration is the only road to a resumption of specie payments. This capital cannot at the same time be made to serve two different purposes. The banks in loaning it to the government—for that is the true way to describe the operation—put it out of their power to use it again, on a specie basis, for any other purpose whatever. The paper currency which the government issues to the banks is not based on the capital which the banks have transferred; but on the evidence of government debt for which it has been exchanged. Credit is substituted for capital, and that portion of the capital of the banks comprised in the advance to say nothing of the impossibility of maintaining specie payments, is made to share the fluctuations and partake of the hazards of the government credit.

The limits within which a bank can safely make loans to a government are very restricted. It may occasionally make loans at short dates, to anticipate a revenue which is sure to come in; provided the amount advanced does not exceed the revenue that will have accrued when the advance becomes repayable. And this is the full extent to which it can, as a rule, safely go. There are plenty of instances to show that when this limit is not observed, disaster will follow. In the latter part of the last century, the Bank of England made advances to the government, in amounts so large, and for periods so long, that a suspension of specie payments had to be resorted to. The Bank of France pursued a like course, under the old government, with a like result. The Bank of Stockholm, founded in 1657, flourished as long as it confined itself to what was then its legitimate business—borrowing at one rate and lending to the public at another—but when it changed its policy, after becoming a bank of circulation, and made loans to the government and the aristocracy, it paid the usual penalty of being obliged to suspend specie payments. Its ruin was so complete that it finally paid its creditors but twenty-six per cent. of their claims.

The loans exacted from banks by governments, under the guise of exercising a paternal care for the interests of note-holders, are in the worst of all forms. They are perpetual. There is no date fixed for their repayment; and it is not intended that they should ever be repaid so long as the banks remain solvent. And even when the banks fail, the capital which they had loaned to the government is not forthcoming. In its place have been substituted government evidences of debt. These "securities," as they are called, must be thrown on the market, and sold for what they will bring. Their market value will depend entirely upon the state of the government credit at the moment; and in the case of this country, it might easily happen that they would not be saleable at all. A foreign war, with England for one of the combatants, or even a small Fenian raid, would give such a shock to Canadian credit that government securities would not be saleable at all.

A bank lending money to a government to cover deficiencies from ordinary expenditure or to meet demands arising out of any unproductive expenditure, has nearly the same effect as would be produced by lending to a spendthrift. Capital is displaced through the agency of credit, and it is devoted to non-productive purposes. Somebody else deprived of the opportunity of borrowing it does not go where it could be employed to the best advantage, and the nation is thereby poorer for the operation. When it is used to cover a deficiency between the ordinary revenue and the ordinary expenditure, there is something wrong. The equilibrium ought to have been maintained between the revenue and the expenditure, in one of two ways, either the expenditure ought to have been reduced or the revenue increased. But when a state of things does arise that renders a loan indispensable, it ought to be contracted in the open market, and not by borrowing from banks, whose means are destined to totally different purposes. In that case, it will often be an advantage to borrow abroad; for then the capital required to conduct commerce and business of the country is not trenched upon.

Greenbacks, if we may generalize a term now sufficiently understood, differ from assignats, in having for their basis evidence of government debt, which bears an annual interest; while the assignat was receivable in payment of purchases of public domain. The assignat, in general terms, entitled the holder to its value in public lands; the greenback is based on an obligation which confers on the holder the right to receive annually a portion of the public revenue, in the shape of interest. This obligation is a mortgage on the future; and it is obvious that these claims to a share of the revenue may be increased to an amount beyond the capacity of the revenue to meet them. As a substitute for capital, in banking, it is a miserable expedient.

The structure of the national system is strictly logical: the only result which it can be productive of is paper money—paper redeemable in specie—and accordingly it dispenses with specie, for that purpose. banks being deprived of the greater portion of their capital, and the government having put it to a purpose in no way connected with banking, there remains nothing but to substitute paper specie; to drive specie from the channels of rculation, and leave only a trace of it, in the mlts of the banks. It is idle to talk of nvertibility, in connection with anything pied from the national bank system of the nited States.

A closer inspection of the organization of e national banking associations will remove y possible doubt that could exist on this int. The last annual report of the comp-oller of the currency, published on the 7th)cember, 1868, presents us with a general ew of these banks, and their internal opera-in, to the 30th September previous. A tional bank before going into operation, is juired to deposit with the government, lited States bonds to secure the ultimate lemption of its note circulation. For every e hundred dollars so deposited, it receives, return, legal tender notes to the amount ninety dollars. In other words, the bonds posited exceed in amount ten per cent. of a notes it receives for circulation. On this sia, the banks commence. This proportion y, in time, become somewhat disturbed by umber of the banks going into liquidation, luntary or forced. At the date to which . Halburd's report comes down, the aggre-e paid up capital of the national banks a four hundred and twenty-six millions, a hundred and eighty-nine dollars ($426,189,111), 1 the bonds on deposit amounted to three ndred and forty-two millions, nineteen)usand, nine hundred and fifty dollars 42,019,950). In other words, the national ıks, all taken together, had loaned to the ernment, in this form, about four-fifths all their capital. In return, they had got al tender notes, to be used as currency, to amount of three hundred and nine mil-ıs, nine hundred and fifteen thousand, one ıdred and sixty-six dollars ($309,915,166). e actual circulation was, however, reduced, the process of liquidation, some ten mil-as below the amount of notes originally ued; bringing it down to two hundred 1 ninety-nine millions, eight hundred and thousand, five hundred and sixty-five lars ($299,806,565.) It is evident that se proportions are altogether incompatible h a specie b̶asis; and that would have m a sufficient reason, if there had been no er, why no attempt was made to introduce o the system the element of convertibility.

The question is not whether, speaking in ind numbers, a reserve of gold equal to >-fifth of the capital of a bank is sufficient maintain the convertibility of a note cir-ation equal to the remaining four-fifths ; if that proportion were sufficient, in any e, it could only be when the bank was at l liberty to make the best use of its re-

sources ; and that condition is wanting when it is obliged to commence by a loan of four-fifths of the whole amount of its capital to the government. It is quite useless, in this discussion, to point to instances where, the the conditions being wholly different, con-vertibility has been maintained on a mini-mum reserve of gold. It is true, the govern-ment gives the bank, in return for its loan, legal tender notes in the proportion of one hundred to one hundred and ten ; and these notes having a forced circulation every where within the country, may serve its purposes so long as holders cannot demand gold for them ; but if there should be one place—the counter of the bank—where specie could be demanded for them, the whole conditions would be so changed that the colossal ma-chinery of the national banks would come to to a stand-still. It is the circumstance of the notes having a forced circulation that in-vests them with effective utility for the pur-poses of the banker. Deprive them of their character of a legal tender, at the counter of the bank, by making them exchangeable into gold, and it would be found that converti-bility could be effected only through liquida-tion, in which case the loan to the govern-ment would be returned by a sale of the bonds deposited.

THE QUESTION OF SAFETY.

IV.

If the national banking system of the United States is not a safe one, it has con-fessedly nothing whatever to recommend it. It has led to speculation on a gigantic scale ; speculation which partakes of all the worst features of gambling, and is a great source of danger, both morally and financially, and by it the public mind is being debauched. The comptroller shows the nature of the loans made and the speculations encouraged, in the city of New York, by the National Banks. The total amount of their loans is one hundred and sixty-three millions five hundred thousand dollars ($163,500,000). Of the whole amount, only nine-sixteenths, or rather more than half, goes to discount busi-ness paper; the rest is used for gambling spec-ulations in gold and stocks. The comptroller is led, by official data, to the conclusion that "nearly one-half of the available resources of the National Banks, in the City of New York, are used in the operations of the stock and gold exchange ; that they are loaned upon the security of stocks which are bought and sold largely on speculation, and which are manipulated by cliques and combinations, according as the bulls or bears are, for the moment, in the ascendancy."

The loans on call, of which the proceeds are used for speculation, appear to absorb the

entire amount of the deposits. If there is not direct and positive proof of this, there is the remarkable coincidence that, on a given day —the day to which the official report of the comptroller comes down—the deposits held by the New York banks amounted to sixty-eight millions five hundred and twenty-nine thousand four hundred and seventeen dollars, (68,529,417) and the call loans to sixty-eight millions five hundred thousand dollars, ($68,-500,000). It is true these loans are made on the security of bonds of one kind or another ; but that does not justify the reckless extent to which they are carried. Let the reader try to conceive what would happen in a panic that should greatly reduce the market value of all these securities, and render many of them altogether unsaleable. And even this is not all. Besides the direct loan of seventy millions for gold and stock gambling opera-tions, the banks create a fictitious daily credit of from one hundred and ten to one hundred and twenty millions, by means of cheques certified to be good, when the drawers have no cash deposits to meet them. Some of the banks, we are told, deprecate the practice, and look with anxiety at the final issue ; but they are all involved in the dan-ger. The failure of one or more institutions, through reckless management, would endan-ger the whole. The comptroller traces the incentive to this mad speculation to that fea-ture of the system which relieves the banks from the obligation of providing for the pay-ment of their notes in specie, on demand. It is quite certain that the dangerous expansion of credit which fosters and sustains this spe-culation would be impossible if the paper is-sued by the banks were liable to be returned on them for specie. The necessity of being obliged to meet the demand for specie, in exchange for notes, is a great and salutary regulator of the currency. It has a constant tendency to keep discounts within the limits of actual transactions ; for notes issued in excess of that limit, and for mere purposes of accommodation and speculation, return to the issuer almost immediately. They are not absorbed by the employment of labur, or in any other way carried into the circulation. It thus happens that specie-paying banks have very little power to inflate the currency be-yond the legitimate demands of business. And, practically, when under no artifical restriction, and no monopoly is encouraged, they have almost as little power to con-tract it beyond that limit. If one bank fails to issue up to the maximum point at which a convertible paper currency can be maintained, another steps in and fills the vacancy. But where the check which con-vertibility imposes is wanting, excesses of all kinds receive the utmost license.

We must conclude, then, that the National

Bank system of the United States is not, take it all in all, a safe system. By its encouragement of speculation, it puts at hazard and induces individual operators to stake, at the gambling boards of the stock and gold exchange, enormous amounts, of much of which neither the banks nor the speculators are really in possession. The enormous amount represented by falsely certified cheques is wholly fictitious. But it creates a real liability, and places everybody's capital in jeopardy. When a national bank fails, the public seldom escape loss, even in the quietest times. Take an instance : "The affairs of the National Bank of Newton," the comptroller reports, "have been finally closed. The government claims were paid in full, and a dividend of forty per cent paid to the general creditors ;" on which latter, it follows, a loss of sixty per cent must have fallen. If the circulation be secured—a great consideration in itself, we admit—there is created a more than corresponding insecurity in other directions ; and the system, taken as a whole, could hardly be defended on the ground of safety, the only advantage that any one pretends to claim for it. On a view of the whole system, it is impossible not to condemn it.

For immunity from loss, by the failure of banks, the public are more dependent upon good management and integrity, in bank parlours, than the deposit of stocks with a third party. Capital may be lost, under almost any conditions. It may be lost by bankers who issue no notes, as in the case of Overend, Gurney & Co. It may be lost, where only specie is made use of, as was the case before banks of circulation came into existence. It may be lost by banks of issue, under legal obligations to redeem their notes in specie, on demand; and it may be lost where paper money—that is inconvertible paper—is alone used. The National Bank system affords the public no immunity from loss. All it aims at is to protect one class of creditors—the note-holders—a class primarily entitled to consideration, all will admit—but, by its encouragement of speculation, it. opens the door to serious losses, in other directions. On the 1st Oct. last, fourteen National Banks had been placed in the hands of receivers. This step was not taken till they failed to redeem their note circulation themselves. Of these banks the affairs of only one had been wound-up, with a final loss of sixty per cent. of the claims of general creditors. Any firm or body corporate, that deals largely on credit, will make losses. This is foreseen, and taken into account, in calculations of profit. There is, perhaps, no reason why persons who loan capital should lose more than persons who loan—by selling on credit—goods. But this

depends on good management. If a bank discounts doubtful paper, it is pretty certain to suffer loss. When the paper discounted is that of solvent persons, it is full security for the note circulation : it is security to the bank and ought to be to the public. That portion of a bank's note circulation, which is in excess of its specie reserve, has for its basis the commercial paper in exchange for which it is given, and the general credit and capital of the bank. With ordinary prudence, these should be sufficient ; or, if any deposit of securities be insisted on, it should be such an amount as would not interfere with the free action of the bank, and prevent it making the best use of its means. When a bank outruns its credit and resources, it pays the penalty in temporary discredit, if it does not suffer more severely.

There are two ways in which the affairs of a bank may be brought into embarrassment : either the loss or locking up of a considerable part of its capital, and either cause may be carried so far as to be fatal. A bank note is an obligation which matures the moment it is issued; and this is the reason why banks cannot safely make loans at long dates. As the bank note is payable at the shortest of all dates, the commercial paper for which it is exchanged cannot safely be at long dates. Whenever this fact is lost sight of, and the means of a bank become locked up, its efficiency is destroyed. The great error of the old system of bank management in this country, now happily passed away, was to imitate the Scotch system of cash credits, or what amounted to the same thing, frequent renewals, on the strength of endorsations. But a practice which had answered well in Scotland proved disastrous here. The Bank of Upper Canada made loans to persons because they were known or supposed to possess some property. But the property often consisted of land on which no labor had been expended, and which was consequently cursed with the sterility of unproductiveness, for which there was no demand by cultivators, because land was largely in excess of capital and labor. In Scotland the name of a landed proprietor on the back of a bill for a thousand pounds implied no risk to the bank. In Canada it led to great losses—losses which however fell on the shareholders rather than on the public. This proves a fault of management, rather than a defect of system. The tendency to throw out everything but bona fide commercial paper, marks a great improvement in modern banking. All unsecured accounts—as notes without endorsers, and over-drafts—should be ruled out. They are inconsistent with good management, which after all is about the best security of the public against loss.

directors are. not honorable men, for tand high in the community ; but we at they do themselves gross wrong in ng their names to be made use of to : up a corporation whose sole strength ir names ; and they do the public in professing to insure against fire the financial state of the company is extreme embarrassment. This alle- is not made on hearsay. Last week s announced in this paper that Mr. y, the Assistant Manager, had been sed, with a gift of three months' salary ·ance. This strange sort of dismissal lly prompted inquiry into the circum- s attending it, and we find that Mr. y laid formal charges before the Board ectors respecting the Manager's incom- ·y, and drew their attention to the ity that existed for some provision t immediate suspension. It appears Mr. Drewry's statement that the Pro- l Insurance Company has, at the pre- ime, outstanding losses to the amount ·ty-nine thousand three hundred and ·y eight dollars ($39,378). It has a age on its building for $8,000, and it le for $15,000 on its issue of debentures urities to the Church Society. It will to make a second deposit of $17,000 he Government in a few months. Its are all in pawn. The position is just

Dr.

ı and Claims............	$39,378
age.....................	8,000
itures to Church Soc.	15,000
. Fund, at 50 per cent	75,000
ity to Stockholders...	79,000
	——————
	—$216,378

Cr.

....	$1,000
it with Government..	16,666
	——————
	—$17,666
·eficit	$198,712

at, if the company were now to go ·quidation, the sum of $119,712 would to be called up. There are some e notes held by the Halifax agency, s they may yet be swallowed up by ı, we do not ·feel justified. in tak- hem into account. It may be said there. is the subscribed capital of ?60 to fall back upon ; but we know the work of forfeiture has gone on ·me time, and has diminished sadly alue of that intangible and mythical The condition of this company is le ; it seems to be going from bad ·orse. As a home institution whose ·ects at one time seemed good, even in ·rrassment, we were disposed to view ·ritably, but we should fail in our duty ·s public if we concealed the present of its affairs. The dismissal of Mr.

Drewry is so suspicious that we can attribute it to no other cause than to a desire to cloak what his unselfish zeal has laid bare. Unless the Directors put the Company on a different footing, we shall· be compelled to conclude that they are ready to sacrifice their well- won reputation as men and citizens for the sake of drawing their weekly stipends. They seem to imagine that there is some magic in the· words "subscribed capital." If the words have substance in them, why in the name of all that is reasonable, do they not call the capital in and pay .off the $40,000 of claims standing unpaid ! Why. heap up law costs in staving off claims by letting themselves be sued ? why haunt banks for petty discounts? why mortgage their office ? If the Insolvent Act applied to corporations they would have been .wound up long ago. It affords us little satisfaction to write these comments, but while home enterprises have their claims upon us, the interests of confiding policy-holders have to be regarded, and we are determined that the community shall not be deceived by a silence on ·our part, which would make us partners in the deception.

THE NORTH BRITISH AND MERCANTILE :— The report of this Company shows a state of affairs that will prove very satisfactory to policy- holders as well as stockholders. The net pre- miums for the year were £415,544, being an increase of £81,559 over those of the year previous. A dividend of fifteen shillings and a bonus of five shillings per share, free of income tax, is certainly something to be proud of. At the end of ·the year, the Reserve Fund and Premium reserve amounted to £290,861. The annual revenue from all sources is about four millions of dollars, and the assets of the Com- pany amount to.about twelve millions. We have no hesitation in expressing our opinion that this is one of the soundest of the British Companies doing business in this country.

MINERALOGY OF NOVA SCOTIA. By HENRY HOW, D.C.L., Professor of Chemistry and Natural History, King's College, Windsor Nova Scotia. Published by Charles Annand, Hali- fax, N. S., 1869. An official report. The above work is the most useful compendium on the mineral resources of the sister Province, which has yet appeared, and one which does honor to its author's research and industry. It is to be hoped that the Dominion Government· will authorize its translation into French and German, and that a few thousand copies will be sent to the forthcoming International Exhibition at Vienna, Austria, where its circulation would be of great benefit. All foreign consuls and emigration agents should also be provided with copies, if it is really wished to show that Nova Scotia, with its stern climate, is still a country where capital and labor may be advantageously employed. Further reference to the work will be made in a future number.

Communications.

COMMISSIONS TO BANK MANAGERS.

Editor of the Canadian Monetary Times.

SIR,—With· your permission, I shall supple- ment with a few remarks the observations which I took occasion to make in your issue of the 18th ult., respecting what I conceived to be a just cause of grievance on the part of insurance com- panies, concerning an unwarrantable interference. with their business by bank managers and others throughout the towns and cities of the Province. I am led to believe that there is, on the part of át least one or two of our local companies, a dis- position to resist in future the ten per cent ·exac- tion ·referred to. It is also intimated that. the representatives of American companies doing business in the city are, by direction of their prin- cipals, urging its abolition.

I regret, however, that whilst there are many ready in denouncing the practice, there are those, who, inasmuch as they have hitherto been enabled by this means to control a larger amount of busi ness than what would otherwise probably have fallen to their share, defend it; alleging that for years past the ten per cent. has been allowed, and that to discontinue it now would seriously in- terfere with their arrangements. Others plead the force of example. "If we refuse to allow it business will be driven from our doors," and they are therefore induced to yield compliance with a demand, which under other circumstances they would not for a moment listen to.

It is to be deplored that any considerations of a selfish nature should be permitted to interfere with our general interests as insfrers ; but un- questionably the course now being pursued by many, in their eagerness for business at any rates, will be found fraught with evil results to them- selves and to others. If those who are now prac- tising this system of extortion upon insurance companies find that they can do so with impunity, may we not suppose that they will ere long ex- tend their operations to other portions of the com- munity? The next step may be that the ware- house in which is stored the grain and other pro- duce upon which the bank ·may have advances, will be named, and the vessels provided for its transportation, in order that they may levy a tax on the warehouseman and the shipper.

In glancing over the pages of an American In- surance Journal recently, I was surprised at the statement, that of all the American Companies engaged in fire assurance in the British Province.ı during the past twenty-five years it was believed that scarcely one could, to-day, show a balance on the credit side of their Canadian account. And what has been the experience of English Companies during the same period? I believe that facts will bear me out in the assertion, that during the past 15 or 18 years nearly a dozen, after encountering a succession of reverses felt that here was no profitable field for their operations and withdrew from the country.

If this, then, is the experience of the past are we justified, with the prevailing excessive com- petition, in allowing our reduced rates to be still further whittled down by a few individuals who are backed up in such unscrupulous acts by their principals, who with a pompous air, hesitate not to say that these are perquisites which all their subordinates are allowed.

In conclusion, I have only to say that I hope a determined stand will be made to resist and pnt down this practice, and that it will shortly be . looked upon as abuse of the past.

Truly yours, INSURER.

Toronto, March 24, 1869.

Mining.

NOVA SCOTIA GOLD FIELDS.

(From Our Own Correspondent.)

HALIFAX, N. S., March 16, 1869.

The "Chase" on her last trip came in at nine o'clock on Friday evening and left the following day at daybreak, and thus the present budget will be of more than ordinary length, but it is hoped, for all that, of not less interest. The heavy snow-falls within the past fortnight have interrupted mail communication, and the reports of the Deputy Commissioners, usually to hand by the 16th of the month, are still wanting. However, between the bullion receipts and the notes on the districts it will be seen that gold mining here has still some claims to be regarded as a progressive and profitable industry :

SHERBROOKE.—The *Palmerston, Dominion* and *Metropolitan* mines are flooded and works temporarily suspended. The *Wellington* speaks largely for itself through the bullion report, to which also the *Wentworth* and *Woodbine* contribute a moderate quota. At Cochrane's Hill, on the extreme limits of the district, about twelve miles west of Goldenville, a new mine is being opened. The shaft is already forty feet down, and exposes a gold bearing lode averaging eighteen inches in width. The proprietors intend erecting a mill, which will give them the privilege of ten acres free of rent and royalty.

WINE HARBOR.—Three serious accidents have occurred since the beginning of the year ; one poor fellow getting injured through the premature explosion of a blast, a second through coming in contact with some machinery, and a third, recently, the engineer of the steam drill, through falling down the air shaft, forty-five feet deep. Each one is maimed for life, and the wonder is that no more accidents happen where so little care and forethought is shown. But little progress is reported from this district. A property forming the southeast of the district as originally laid off, and embracing the lodes worked by the Provincial and Eldorado companies is being stocked in New Brunswick for $500,000. The property belongs to Messrs. R. G. Leckie and J. DeWolfe Spurr, and is now styled the *Napier*, significant of the unapproachable as well as irreproachable character which its enterprising proprietors intend to acquire for it. The capital stock is divided into 50,000 shares of $10 each, and is to be paid for by 25,000 shares at 2 per share ; 12,500 shares at $2 a share are to be disposed of for working capital, and the remaining 12,500 shares will be reserved as treasury stock, to be disposed of as circumstances may require. Work has already commenced, and the company has temporarily rented the *Eureka* mill.

TANGIER.—The Strawberry Hill Company have made no returns since last October, but have been repairing their mill and lying fallow. They began work a few weeks ago, and the manager is daily expected in town with a bar of about 300 ounces, as evidence of his reactivity and the company's healthful awakening.

UNIACKE.—Productive workings are confined to the mines of the Montreal Association, the Mount Uniacke Company, and Mr. La Mothe. From the latter, Mr. Touquoy reports that he has about ten tons ready for reduction, that the lode he is drifting on increases from four to twelve inches, the greatest width being towards the eastern boundary. He estimates an average of one ounce per ton from the quantity raised, as the quality of the ore improves in depth. The cost of raising will be about $8 per ton.

WAVERLEY.—Work confined to tribute. It is expected that the circulation of Professor Hind's report will have the effect of reviving interest in this district, and its issue from press is impatiently looked for.

MUSQUODOBOIT (JENNINGS').—About 800 areas are now held under license and 100 under lease. Mr. Burkner, when in town last week, brought with him a specimen of quartz from his southern lode. The rock weighed sixteen ounces, and was estimated by Mr. R. G. Fraser to contain one and a half ounces of gold. This lode has proved to be gold-bearing for a distance of 1,500 feet, and to a depth of 45 feet. One drawback of the central and southern part of this district is the depth of soil and quantity of water. In one place the bed rock had not been struck at 78 feet depth, and the other shafts were making water so fast that a steam pump will be required to keep them dry. The anticlinal passes immediately north of the Burnett property, and the recurrence of the rich lodes now opened to the south is anticipated to be met with in the first seven ranges of areas north of the "free" claim. In fact, the prospecting party working for Mr. Longmaid report the discovery of two gold-bearing lodes already on these ranges. The depth of soil there is only from four to six feet, and further east, in block one, the rock is bare, but the quartz veins have not been tested in that direction. As the first started mill of eight stamps confers, in a new district, the privilege of ten areas free of rent and royalty, there was much competition between Messrs. Burnett & Co. and Mr. Burkner for the rapid completion of their mills, and the former company, it is alleged, induced the carrier of Mr. Burkner to delay the delivery of some machinery for two days. Still Mr. Burkner set his mill to work at six o'clock on the morning of the 8th inst., but unfortunately after a short time the boiler burst. The Burnetts started theirs later in the day, and as it has been continuously running, they now claim the benefit of the ten free areas. The dispute will probably be settled by awarding five areas to each claimant, and the Chief Commissioner of Mines and the Provincial Deputy left yesterday for Musquodoboit to take evidence on the spot, and thus be in a position to make a fair award. The Surveyor, Mr. Murphy, returned last week.

FIFTEEN-MILE STREAM.—Some activity is reported here and very excellent prospects. A new company, the Havilah, has gone into operation, and being controlled by practical miners, there is reason to suppose that something more tangible than mere "prospects" has induced their location in this district.

GOLD RIVER.—This is the next district on the list for an official survey, systematic explorations for gold in quartz and alluvium being intended in the spring. Dr. How's report on the "Mineralogy of Nova Scotia," a most interesting work, just published by order of the local Government, speaks of this district as containing numerous quartz veins, and of an assay made at New York from one of the lodes being worked in 1866 by a company which has since failed, yielding 3 ozs. 17 dwts. gold, and 12 ozs. silver, to the ton of ore. More recent assays by Mr. J. Longmaid gave 4 ozs. 0 dwt. 19 grs. and 2 ozs. 11 dwts. 11 grs., while actual millings of several hundred weight of surface stuff from other lodes yielded 6 dwts. 1 grs and 4 dwts. 18 grs per ton. These results justify some confidence in the district, and the expenditure both of research and capital to more thoroughly test its capabilities.

THE OVENS.—The properties formerly owned by Alderman McCulloch and Mr. D. S. Macdonald have been purchased by Canadian capitalists and will be explored this summer. The expensive furnace erected by another company for reducing ore on a large scale with the aid of Stevens' flux got out of order, and no results were made known.

DISCOVERIES. — Experimental crushings of quartz from Cranberry Head and the Cross Pot, in Yarmouth county, have been of sufficiently satisfactory nature to induce some of the monied men of Yarmouth to form a mining company, which will be in operation early in the spring. These localities were specially referred to by Mr. Henry Poole, the Special Geological Commissioner for the Nova Scotia Government, who reports upon the western districts in 1862.

New discoveries are also reported at Scrag Lake and Preston.

BULLION RECEIPTS.

The following quantities of bar gold have been received in Halifax since last report:—

By Mr. R. C. Fraser, Assayer.

DISTRICT.	M.NE.	oz.	dwt.
L. Burkner's......Waverley......	17	11	
" ....Musquodoboit	10	15	
Central ....Uniacke......	10	13	
Mount Uniacke...... "	45	0	
McLeod.......... "	2	6	
Toldn & Canning..Oldham	92	1	
Wentworth ... ...Sherbrooke...	19	2	

By Messrs. Huse and Lowell, Bankers.

		oz.	dwt.
Ophir ....Renfrew......127	10		
Hartford .... "	6	1	
R. G. Leckie....Montague ...	97	3	
Boston and N. S...Waverly.........	21	7	
Mulgrave.........Isaac's Harbor 69	17		

By Mr. R. G. Fraser, Assayer.

		oz.	dwt.
Woodbine.........Sherbrooke... 12	2		

By Messrs Huse & Lowell, Bankers.

		oz.	dwt.
Ophir ....Renfrew....217	10		
Colonial .... " 29	17		
North American.......Waverley.... 31	14		
Boston and N. S..... " 40	9		
Meridian..........Sherbrooke... 14	2		
Wentworth ...... " 26	18		
Not stated......... " 16	1		
Wellington .... " 244	2		
Montreal ....Uniacke 58	0		
Eldorado .. ..Wine Harbor. 13	12		

RECAPITULATION.

	oz.	dwt.	grs.
Sherbrooke.........	332	10	4
Wine Harbor.........	13	12	8
Renfrew.........	380	19	12
Waverley.........	111	3	15
Isaac's Harbor.........	69	17	8
Uniacke.........	116	0	7
Oldham.........	92	1	7
Musquodoboit	10	15	2
Montague.........	97	3	22
	1,224	3	13

Financial.

TORONTO STOCK MARKET.

(Reported by Pellatt & Osler, Brokers.)

The commercial failures of late have tended to depress all bank stocks, and large amounts have accordingly been thrown on the market. The market, however, closed rather firmer.

Bank Stock.—Montreal continues in fair demand at 141½, closing firm at the latter rate. Sales of British were made at 105; buyers at 104½. Ontario sold at 100, closing with buyers at 99½, and no sellers under par. Transactions in Toronto occurred at 121 and 121½, with little offering. No demand for Royal Canadian; closing heavy at 80. Small sales of Commerce occurred at 102½, 103 and 103½; it is still procurable at latter rate. There are buyers of Gore at 41; little offering. Merchants' has declined during the week to 107¾, closing rather heavy at this rate. Quebec is enquired for at par; little doing. Transactions advanced to 104, but fell to 102½ to 103, closed heavy. Sales of Du Peuple were made at 108, and there is still a fair demand at 107. Nationale is asked for at 107¼. Jacques Cartier continues in good demand at 109¼. Buyers of 96 for Mechanics'; no sellers under 98. Ontario banks nominal.

Debentures.—Canada sterling five per cents. closing at 94½; no six per cents. doing. Dominion stock in market. There is a good demand for Toronto—none offering. Large sales of Corporation were made during the week at par.

dries.—City Gas sold at 108; little offering. a Permanent Building Society is enquired 126; and sales were made at 125½ to 126. rn Canada B.S. sold at 121; little in market. old is inquired for at 110¼; sales occurred at 110½. British-America Assurance is in demand at 55½ to 56. Sales of Canada d Credit were made at 75, 76 and 77; it is nand at the latter rate. Mortgages are offering to pay 8 per cent., and in some s high as 9 per cent. has been paid. Money er tight, and first-class paper is offering at ates.

VENUE AND EXPENDITURE OF CANADA.

following is a statement of the Revenue xpenditure of the Dominion of Canada for onth, and eight months ending the 28th of ary, 1869:—

ue—Customs	$409,791
Excise	206,282
Post Office	47,360
Bill Stamp Duty	11,977
Public Works, including Railways	44,836
Miscellaneous	536,276
ue for February, 1869	$1,256,522
" July, 1868	1,375,720
" August	1,377,933
" September	1,846,361
" October	1,545,857
" November	1,214,155
" December	1,002,610
" January, 1869	792,764
Total for 8 months	$10,411,922
diture for July 1868	$1,801,622
" " August	964,298
" " September	2,294,409
" " October	1,560,063
" " November	877,448
" " December	956,577
" " January, 1869	2,016,483
" " February	638,728
Total	$11,109,623

BANK OF ENGLAND.

	March 6, 1869.	March 5, 1868.
rate of discount	3 per cent.	2 per cent.
reserve	£9,454,907	£12,542,812
stock of bullion	18,021,457	21,130,192
f Consols	92⅞	93

money market continues tolerably active, mand being increased this week by the lling due on Thursday; there is, however, table change in the rates of discount. The charge is 3 per cent. at the bank, as well as open market, but from the state of the accounts (as shown in this weeks return) y expect that an upward movement cannot delayed.

WIN & Co.'s FAILURE.—The Montreal l says of this affair: Among the rumors e that Mr. Dorwin had taken with him the f $80,000. This we hear on reliable au- is not the case. The most which the partner may have carried off does not ex- 10,000, and it is probable the amount is $7,000. The exact position of the estate t yet been exactly ascertained. The lia- are about $250,000, $150,000 of which are t, being notes discounted and in the hands banks here, chiefly the Molson's and Peo- ome of the others also holding a portion . Very little, if any, loss is expected to ained by the banks who hold their paper, curity in most cases being satisfactory to nks interested. Of the $100,000 direct ies, about the half is due in Boston and New York, $10,000 to the Union Bank for gold drafts sold that institution, which of course will not be honored on presentation, but no doubt would have been secured had the mails been running regularly. The two ladies who are reported to have had on deposit $4,000 each, had only $2,000 each, and that of $4,000 by another of our citizens is exaggerated, being less than $400. Several leading houses in the city who were in the habit of leaving silver in special deposit, will suffer in sums ranging from $1,500 to $2,500. The other liabilities are scattered and vary in amount. The available assets are very small, being chiefly in promissory notes to the extent of about $5,000, and cash $2,000, all the real estate consisting of vacant lots in Griffintown, and the residence in Drummond street, having been secured to Mrs. Dorwin. These properties are, we understand, estimated as being worth about $30,000, but the residence is mortgaged to the extent of $3,000. It is rumored that Mrs. Dorwin has consented to place these properties at the disposal of the creditors, but of this we are not certain. Many reasons have been assigned for the failure; but the more immediate cause of the stoppage was the withdrawal by several persons of large amounts on deposit.

DOMINION NOTES.—The following is a statement of the Dominion Notes in circulation 3rd of March, 1869, and of the specie held against them under the Dominion Note Act:

Dominion Notes in circulation—		
Payable at Montreal	$2,759,807	
Payable at Toronto *	938,193	
Payable at Halifax †	336,000	
		$4,034,000
Specie held—		
At Montreal	450,000	
At Toronto	400,000	
At Halifax	67,200	
		$917,200
Debentures held by Receiver General under the Dominion Note Act		$3,000,000

* Including $, marked St. John.

† The Nova Scotia dollar not being equal in value to that of the other Provinces, the notes issued at Halifax are worth their face value in Nova Scotia only. They are stamped "Payable at Halifax," and are numbered in black ink. None but $5 notes are yet in circulation.

Law Report.

WAREHOUSE RECEIPTS.—M. & Co, being indebted to the plaintiffs on certain overdue notes, it was agreed that plaintiffs should discount a further note for them, with the proceeds of which, it was understood, the overdue paper should be retired; that M. & Co. should hand over to plaintiffs certain warehouse receipts for wool, stored in their warehouse, as collateral security. This note was accordingly, on the 23rd January, 1868, discounted by plaintiffs, and the old notes duly retired, an agreement being signed by M. & Co. at the time of the discount, reciting that they had indorsed over the receipts as collateral security for the note, &c., &c. The receipts, nearly all in the same form, were as follows: "*Warehouse Receipt*—Received in store in our warehouse, at . . . from sundry parties, 17,900 pounds batting, to be delivered pursuant to an order of the Bank of British North America, to be indorsed hereon. The said batting is separate from, &c., &c." Neither M. & Co. nor the Bank indorsed the receipts. *Held*, that they were not warehouse receipts under the statutes, and that the Bank could not, therefore, claim the property covered by them. Per Hagarty, C.J., that the transaction of the 23rd January was not in substance, though in form, a present advance to M. & Co., but merely a mode adopted of paying off an already existing debt.—*Bank of British North America* v. *Clarkson, Assignee of Miller.*

Commercial.

Toronto Market.

Trade is in a rather unsatisfactory state. A feeling of distrust and uncertainty seems quite general, and business-men are mostly moving with great caution. Within the last day or two signs of an improvement are not wanting, but whether a permanent change for the better is likely to set in, depends on so many contingencies that it cannot be relied on. The dullness of the winter trade—the fall in wheat and flour—the import trade overdone—are all circumstances which are pointed to as possible causes of still further trouble in the commercial world. The position is a delicate one. If it be tided over without further casualties among traders, their escape will have to depend upon the exercise of caution and prudence and that degree of leniency on the part of creditors, which is always requisite in cases of the kind. The country, as a whole, is in a sound state, and any mishaps that may result must spring from an undue expansion of credit in the trade in imported goods, or the disappointment of the anticipations of over-hopeful speculators. A check, such as is now being imposed, was required, and we shall welcome it if it do not cost us too dearly.

DRY GOODS.—Goods have arrived freely, and are now pretty well opened out, but buyers are not expected before the 1st April.

GROCERIES.—Prices have ruled steady since our last, and the trade has been without any marked activity. *Teas*—Have arrived freely, and a good many have been moved. In our English market reports, we notice a good enquiry for Congou, for Canada, is reported, in anticipation of the spring trade, but transactions have been on a limited scale. *Sugars*—Are quiet at quotations, which have not changed from last week. *Pepper*—Has advanced rapidly; a rise of 100 per cent. is reported in prices in the English market.

HARDWARE.—Prices are steady, except those of Tin, which are rapidly advancing, owing, it is said, to diminished production.

LEATHER.—A fair business has been done with the city and country trade at our quotations, which are purely wholesale.

HIDES.—Have been pretty lively; the market is rather unsettled, and cured are higher. Sheepskins have also advanced.

PETROLEUM.—The combination is still master of the situation, but how long it will hold together is now a matter of some uncertainty. Meantime, prices are steady, as quoted.

GRAIN.—*Wheat*—Receipts 7,140 bushs., and 4,900 bushs. last week. There is a fair enquiry for spring at current prices, and sales reported are: 20,000 bushs. at Meaford at 87½c., f.o.b.; 10,000 bushs. at Toronto at 92½c., f.o.b.; 10,000 bushs. at Kingston at 97½c., f.o.b. at the opening of navigation. At the close there were buyers of car loads at 90c., holders asking 95c.; some sales of cars at 90c. There are no buyers of round lots of fall, and little is offered; our quotations are purely nominal. No midge proof offering. *Barley*—Receipts 900 bushs., and 900 bushs. last week. Barley is held at $1.20 to $1.27, with buyers a. $1.10 to $1.20; no sales. *Peas*—Receipts light; market dull at 65 to 72c.; no sales reported. *Oats*—Receipts 1,200 bushs., and 1,200 bushs. last week. The market is steady and firm at 49 to 50c. on the track; very little offering; sales of cars are reported at these prices. *Rye*—Nominal at 65 to 70c. *Seeds*—There is a moderate demand for clover at $6 to $6.50. Timothy is in good demand at $2.25 to $2.85 for fair to choice, with some sales at our outside quotations.

FLOUR.—Receipts 1,300 bbls., and 1,475 bbls. last week; No. 1 superfine has met with a fair demand, but is sparingly offered. Sales reported are: 800 bbls. at $4, in store; 1,200 bbls. at $4, f.o.b.; 100 bbls. at $4, in store; and 500 bbls. at $4, free of charges. In other grades there is nothing doing.

PROVISIONS.—*Butter*—No. 1 dairy is scarce

and in good demand at from 24 to 26c.; store-packed is almost unsaleable, holders would gladly accept 20c. *Pork*—Mess is very scarce, and held in few hands at $26; no sales reported. *Dressed Hogs*—A small lot sold at $9.20, which is an outside price; market bare. *Bacon*—Is in light supply and held at 12c.; additional receipts will be to hand in a few days. *Eggs*—Are readily saleable to-day at 24c.; but as soon as the Easter demand is over they may be expected to drop to 10c.

FREIGHTS.—Rates by Grand Trunk Railway:—Flour to all stations from Belleville to Lynn, inclusive, 35c., grain per 100 lbs. 18c. ; flour to Brockville and Cornwall, inclusive, 43c. grain 22c. flour to Montreal 50c. grain 25c. ; flour to all stations between Island Pond and Portland, inclusive, 85c. grain 43c. ; flour to Boston 90c.. gold, grain 45c.; flour to Halifax 98c., grain —c; flour to St. John 98c. Boxed Meats to Liverpool per gross ton 82s. 6d.; lard or butter in tinnets 87s. 6d.; Pork 11s. per tierce; flour 5s. 6d. per barrel ; grain 12s. per 480 pounds. Rates by Great Western Railway—Flour, Toronto to Suspension Bridge 25c. gold ; thence to New York 92c. U. S. currency per bbl. ; to Boston $1.02. Grain to Bridge 13c., gold; thence to New York 46c, U. S. currency; to Boston 51c. Grain, Toronto to Detroit, 18c. ber 100 lbs; flour 35c per bbl.

Imports, Production, and Consumption of Sugar and Molasses in 1868.

	1867	1868
	Tons.	Tons.
FRANCE—Imports	178,712	225,287
" Production	236,901	237,682
" Total	415,625	462,969
ZOLLVEREIN—Imports	4,950	8,977
" Production	190,056	180,615
" Total	204,606	189,592
Other countries	1,057,263	1,253,410
Total imports of Cane Sugar in Europe and the United States, and Production of Beetroot in France and Zollverein	1,677,492	1,905,072
Add Stock at end of 1867	...	298,607
		2,204,579
Deduct Stock at end of 1868	413,488	...
And imports at Italian Ports, mostly transhipments	58,531	472,119
Total deliveries of Sugar in the principal markets of Europe and America during 1868		1,732,460

To this total of 1,732,460 tons has to be added the consumption of Beet Sugar in Austria, Russia, Holland, Sweden and Norway, Belgium, &c., or any (less exports to France and England) 200,000 tons. We have also to add the consumption of the Pacific States of the American Union 18,500 tons; the deliveries, including the total exports in the minor Atlantic ports of the United States, 138,000 tons ; the consumption of Maple Sugar in Canada and the United States, 30,000 tons; the deliveries of Molasses in the United States, 80,-000 tons. Adding the consumption of Molasses in England, and the difference between the official exports and consumption of Raw Sugar in the United Kingdom, and in the return of imports 26,000 tons, also, adding 70,000 tons for the consumption of Spain, Portugal, Gibraltar, Malta, and the consumption of English treacle in the German Union with other minor matters—we arrive at a total consumption of Sugar in Europe and North America, during 1868, of 2,294,960 tons. Adding 70,000 tons for the non-producing British Colonies, and temperate South America, we have a total consumption for Europe, the United States, the non-producing British Colonies, and temperate South America, of 2,394,960 tons of Sugar. From this amount we must deduct the exports of Beet Sugar from France and Germany to other places given in the table, or say 40,000 tons, which reduces the consumption of Europe and North America during 1868 to 2,354,000 tons. We made a similar estimate in a different form,

where we estimated the Sugar deliveries of 1867 at 2,060,000 tons. Adding 100,000 tons to the American consumption for Molasses and the Pacific States, which we did not then include, we arrive at a total of 2,160,000 tons, or an apparent increase in the total deliveries of 194,960 tons. This, however, is not really an increase, but is due simply to taking the actual deliveries from the great Sugar markets, both for consumption and for export, and to not estimating the consumption of each country separately—in fact, in taking more accurate returns than estimates, which latter were before the only means possible for getting at the statistics. The total deliveries appear, as far as we can gather, to have really increased about 100,-000 tons, or, say four per cent. over 1867.

As a complete check upon the above, we have compiled the following table, showing as far as possible the actual deliveries of Sugar in the consuming countries — excluding Italy, Turkey, Greece, Mediterranean ports, and Switzerland, where the sugar is nearly all transhipped, and deducting 28,000 tons from France, and 12,000 tons for North Germany, for exports of Raw to other countries in the table. The difference of 4,000 tons in such a large total shows the close approximation of our figures to the actual state of the case. It must be recollected that we take Molasses at its full weight, and include it in all cases, so far as we can ascertain :

Deliveries of Sugar for Consumption and Export during 1868.

	Tons.
Great Britain	635,000
United States	598,000
North Germany	145,000
France	408,000
Holland	148,000
	1,933,000
Russia and Poland	100,000
Austria	95,000
Spain and Portugal	67,000
Belgium	40,000
British Colonies	65,000
Norway, Sweden, and Denmark	20,000
	387,000
	2,320,000
River Plate, &c	30,000
Total	2,350,000

It is greatly to be regretted that no statistics are available to show the consumption in the great producing districts of India, China, Japan, the Eastern Archipelago, the Sandwich and other Pacific islands, Mauritius, Reunion, Brazil, Mexico, and the British and Foreign West Indies. But in the meantime, the above statistics are of very great interest, and afford a firm basis for judging of the course of markets. Our returns show the approximate Sugar consumption of 313,000,000 souls, and the average per head is thus 16.8 lbs. per annum. The net official British consumption during 1868 was 611,151 tons, or taking our population at 31,000,000, 44·14 per head. At this rate —a very moderate one—the consumption of 313,-000,000 souls would be 6,150,000 tons, or at the Victorian rate of 92 lbs. per head, 12,800,000 tons. English Sugar duties are excessive and oppressive—how much more so they are in other countries we have shown previously. The abolition of the Sugar duties over the civilized world would develope a trade only second to that in Corn, it would revolutionize agriculture in Europe, restore tropical colonies to more than their former prosperity; give employment to thousands of ships and millions of laborers, and cause a development in commerce only second to the withdrawal of protection on Corn.—*London Produce Markets Review.*

Lyman & McNab,

Importers of, and Wholesale Dealers in,

HEAVY AND SHELF HARDWARE,

KING STREET,

TORONTO, ONTARIO.

Mercantile.

eas! Teas!! Teas!!!

FRESH ARRIVALS

NEW CROP TEAS,

, AND GENERAL GROCERIES,

Special Inducements given to

)MPT PAYING PURCHASERS.

sold at very Lowest Montreal Prices!

W. & R. GRIFFITH,

o CHAMBERS
ront and Church Streets,
TORONTO
ONTARIO

Reford & Dillon, **TEAS.**

ist received ex. steamships *"St. David"* and *an:"*

chests new season TEAS!
nprising Twankays, Young Hysons, Imperials, Gunpowders, colored and uncolored Japans, Congous, Souchongs, and Pekoes.
bxs. new Valentia Raisins (selected fruit).
; cleaned Arracan and Rangoon Rice.
. choice Currants.

—ALSO IN STORE:—

s. bright Barbadoes and Cuba Sugars.
. Portland, Standard, Golden & Amber Syrups.
s Rio. Jamaica, Laguayra, and Java Coffees.
10s Tobacco, "Queen's Own" and "Prince of les'" brands.

WITH A GENERAL AND

ELECTED STOCK OF GROCERIES;

l of which they offer to the Trade low.

14 WELLINGTON STREET, TORONTO.

7-1y

Robert H. Gray,

facturer of Hoop Skirts

AND

CRINOLINE STEEL,

IMPORTER OF

RDASHERY, TRIMMINGS

AND

ENERAL FANCY GOODS,

48, YONGE STREET, TORONTO, ONT. 6-1y

John Boyd & Co.,

SALE GROCERS AND COMMISSION MERCHANTS,

[D 63 FRONT STREET

TORONTO.

tore, direct from the European and West India ts, a large assortment of General Groceries,

ugars, Coffees, Wines and Liquors,

AND

GENERAL GROCERIES.

ndlery, Canvas, Manilla and Tarred Rope, Oakum, Tar, Flags, &c., &c.,

'T FROM THE MANUFACTURERS.

ALEX. M. MONRO. C. W. BUNTING

Oct. 1st, 1868. 7-1y

TORONTO PRICES CURRENT.—MARCH 25, 1869.

Name of Article.	Wholesale Rates. $ c.	$ c.
Boots and Shoes.		
Mens' Thick Boots	2 20	2 50
" Kip	2 50	3 00
" Calf	3 00	3 70
" Congress Gaiters	2 00	2 50
" Kip Cobourgs	1 15	1 45
Boys' Thick Boots	1 70	1 80
Youths' "	1 40	1 50
Women's Batts	0 95	1 30
" Balmoral	1 20	1 50
" Congress Gaiters	1 15	1 45
Misses' Batts	0 75	1 00
" Balmoral	1 10	1 20
" Congress Gaiters	1 00	1 30
Girls' Batts	0 65	0 85
" Balmoral	0 90	1 05
" Congress Gaiters	0 80	1 10
Children's C. T. Cacks	0 50	0 65
" Gaiters	0 65	0 90
Drugs.		
Aloes Cape	0 12½	0 16
Alum	0 02½	0 03
Borax	0 00	0 00
Camphor, refined	0 65	0 70
Castor Oil	0 16½	0 28
Caustic Soda	0 04½	0 05
Cochineal	0 90	1 00
Cream Tartar	0 40	0 45
Epsom Salts	0 03	0 04
Extract Logwood	0 11	0 12
Gum Arabic, sorts	0 30	0 35
Indigo, Madras	0 90	1 00
Licorice	0 14	0 45
Madder	0 00	0 18
Galls	0 32	0 37
Opium	12 00	13 50
Oxalic Acid	0 26	0 35
Potash, Bi-tart	0 25	0 28
" Bichromate	0 15	0 20
Potass Iodide	3 90	4 50
Senna	0 12½	0 60
Soda Ash	0 02½	0 04
Soda Bicarb	4 50	5 00
Tartaric Acid	0 40	0 45
Verdigris	0 35	0 40
Vitriol, Blue	0 08	0 10
Groceries.		
Coffees:		
Java, ℔ lb.	0 22@0 24	
Laguayra,	0 17	0 18
Rio	0 15	0 17
Fish:		
Herrings, Lab. split	5 75	6 50
" round	0 00	0 00
" scaled	0 35	0 40
Mackerel, small kitts	1 00	0 00
Loch. Her. wh'e firks	2 50	2 75
" half "	1 25	1 50
White Fish & Trout	None.	
Salmon, saltwater	14 00	15 00
Dry Cod, ℔ 112 lbs.	5 00	5 25
Fruit:		
Raisins, Layers	2 00	2 10
" M R.	1 90	2 00
" Valentias new	0 6¾	0 7½
Currants, new	0 5½	0 06½
" old	0 04	0 04½
Figs	0 14	0 00
Molasses:		
Clayed, ℔ gal.	0 00	0 35
Syrups, Standard	0 60	0 00
" Golden	0 00	0 65
Rice:		
Arracan	4 25	4 50
Spices:		
Cassia, whole, ℔ lb.	0 00	0 45
Cloves	0 11	0 12
Nutmegs	0 50	0 55
Ginger, ground	0 20	0 25
" Jamaica, root	0 20	0 25
Pepper, black	0 12½	0 00
Pimento	0 08	0 09
Sugars:		
Port Rico, ℔ lb.	0 10¾	0 00
Cuba "	0 10½	0 00
Barbadoes (bright)	0 10½	0 00
Canada Sugar Refine'y, yellow No. 2, 60ds.	0 10½	0 11
Yellow, No. 2½	0 10¾	0 11¼
No. 3	0 11	0 11½
Crushed X	0 13	0 13¼
" A	0 13	0 13¼
Ground	0 13¾	0 14
Dry Crushed	0 14¼	0 14½
Extra Ground	0 15¼	0 15½
Teas:		
Japan com'n to good	0 48	0 55
" Fine to choicest	0 50	0 65
Colored, com. to fine	0 60	0 75
Congou & Souch'ng	0 42	0 75
Oolong, good to fine	0 50	0 65
Y. Hyson, com to gd	0 45	0 55
Medium to choice	0 65	0 80
Extra choice	0 85	0 95

Name of Article.	Wholesale Rate. $ c.	$ c.
Groceries—*Contin'd*		
Gunpowd'r c. to med	0 55	0 70
" med. to fine.	0 70	0 85
" fine to fins't	0 85	0 95
Hyson	0 45	0 80
Imperial	0 42	0 80
Tobacco, Manufact'd:		
Can Leaf, ℔ lb 5s & 10s.	0 26	0 30
Western Leaf, com	0 25	0 26
" Good	0 27	0 32
" Fine	0 32	0 35
" Bright fine	0 40	0 50
" " choice	0 60	0 75
Hardware.		
Tin (net cash prices)		
Block, ℔ lb	0 28	0 00
Grain	0 30	0 00
Copper:		
Pig	0 23	0 24
Sheet	0 30	0 33
Cut Nails:		
Assorted ¼ Shingles, ℔ 100 lb.	2 90	3 00
Shingle alone do	3 15	3 25
Lathe and 5 dy	3 30	3 40
Galvanized Iron:		
Assorted sizes	0 08	0 09
Best No. 24	0 09	0 00
" 26	0 08	0 08¼
" 28	0 09	0 09½
Horse Nails:		
Guest's or Griffin's assorted sizes	0 00	0 00
For W. ass'd sizes	0 18	0 19
Patent Hammer'd do	0 17	0 18
Iron (at 4 months):		
Pig—Gartsherrie No1	24 00	25 00
Other brands. No1	22 00	24 00
" No2	0 00	0 00
Bar—Scotch, ℔ 100 lb	2 25	2 50
Refined	3 00	3 25
Swedes	5 00	5 50
Hoops—Coopers	3 00	3 25
Band	3 00	3 25
Boiler Plates	3 25	3 50
Canada Plates	3 75	4 00
Union Jack	0 00	0 00
Pontypool	3 25	4 00
Swansea	3 90	4 00
Lead (at 4 months):		
Bar, ℔ 100 lbs.	0 06½	0 07
Sheet "	0 08	0 09
Shot	0 07½	0 07½
Iron Wire (net cash):		
No. 6, ℔ bundle	2 70	2 80
" 9, "	3 10	3 20
" 12, "	3 40	3 50
" 16, "	4 30	4 40
Powder:		
Blasting, Canada	3 50	0 00
FF "	4 25	4 50
FFF "	4 75	5 00
Blasting, English	4 00	5 00
FF loose	5 00	6 00
FFF "	6 00	6 50
Pressed Spikes (4 mos):		
Regular sizes 100	4 00	4 25
Extra "	4 50	5 00
Tin Plates (net cash):		
IC Coke	7 50	8 50
IC Charcoal	8 50	9 00
IX "	10 50	11 00
IXX "	13 50	14 00
DC "	8 00	8 50
DX "	9 50	0 00
Hides & Skins, ℔ lb		
Green rough	0 06½	0 07
Green, salt'd & insp'd	0 08½	0 09
Cured	0 00	0 00
Calfskins, green	0 00	0 10
Calfskins, cured	0 00	0 12½
" dry	0 18	0 20
Sheepskins,	1 50	1 70
" country	1 00	1 40
Hops.		
Inferior, ℔ lb	0 05	0 07
Medium	0 07	0 09
Good	0 09	0 12
Fancy	0 00	0 00
Leather, @ (4 mos.) In lots of less than 50 sides, 10 ℔ cnt higher.		
Spanish Sole, 1st qual'y heavy, weights ℔ lb	0 21½	0 22
Do. 1st qual middle do	0 22½	0 00
Do. No. 2, light weights	0 22½	0 00
Slaughter heavy	0 26	0 27
Do. light	0 00	0 00
Harness, best	0 28	0 30
" No. 2	0 00	0 00
Upper heavy	0 32	0 35
" light	0 36	0 38

Name of Article.	Wholesale Rates. $ c.	$ c.
Leather—*Contin'd.*		
Kip Skins, Patna	0 30	0 35
French	0 70	0 90
English	0 65	0 80
Hemlock Calf (30 to 35 lbs.) per doz.	0 50	0 00
Do. light	0 45	0 50
French Calf	1 03	1 06
Grain & Satn Clt ℔ doz	0 00	0 00
Splits, large ℔ lb	0 30	0 38
" small	0 23	0 28
Enamelled Cow ℔ foot	0 20	0 21
Patent	0 20	0 21
Pebble Grain	0 15	0 17
Buff	0 14	0 16
Oils.		
Cod	0 65	0 70
Lard, extra	0 00	0 00
" No. 1	0 00	0 00
" Woollen	0 00	0 00
Lubricating, patent	0 00	0 00
" Mott's economic	0 50	0 00
Linseed, raw	0 76	0 82
" boiled,	0 81	0 87
Machinery	0 00	0 00
Olive, common, ℔ gal.	1 00	1 60
" salad	1 95	2 30
" salad, in bots. qt. ℔ case	3 60	3 75
Sesame salad, ℔ gal.	1 60	1 75
Seal, pale	0 75	0 85
Spirits Turpentine	0 52½	0 60
Varnish	0 00	0 00
Whale.	0 00	0 90
Paints, &c.		
White Lead, genuine in Oil, ℔ 25lbs.	0 00	2 35
Do. No. 1 "	0 00	2 10
" 2 "	0 00	1 90
" 3 "	0 00	1 65
White Zinc, genuine	3 00	3 50
White Lead, dry	0 05½	0 09
Red Lead	0 07½	0 08
Venetian Red, Eng'h	0 02½	0 03½
Yellow Ochre, Fren'h	0 02¾	0 03
Whiting	0 85	1 25
Petroleum. (Refined ℔ gal.)		
Water white, car l'd	—	0 36
" small lots	0 37	0 38
Straw, by car load	0 00	0 00
" small lots	0 00	0 36
Amber, by car load	0 00	0 00
" small lots	0 00	0 00
Benzine	0 00	0 00
Produce.		
Grain:		
Wheat, Spring, 60 lb	0 90	0 95
" Fall 60 "	0 95	1 00
Barley 48 "	1 15	1 25
Peas 60 "	0 65	0 72
Oats 34 "	0 49	0 50
Rye 56 "	0 65	0 70
Seeds:		
Clover, choice 60 "	6 25	6 50
" com'n 68 "	6 00	6 25
Timothy, cho'e 4 "	2 60	2 85
" inf. to good 48 "	2 25	2 50
Flax 56 "	2 15	2 25
Flour (per brl.):		
Superior extra	0 00	0 00
Extra superfine,	4 25	4 30
Fancy superfine	4 10	4 20
Superfine No 1	4 00	—
" No. 2	—	—
Oatmeal, (per brl.)	0 40	5 50
Provisions		
Butter, dairy tub ℔ lb	0 20	0 23
" store packed	0 18	0 19
Cheese, new	0 13	0 14
Pork, mess, per brl.	25 50	26 00
" prime mess	—	—
" prime	—	—
Bacon, rough	0 10	0 10½
" Cumberl'd cut	0 11½	0 12
" smoked	0 00	0 00
Hams, in salt	0 12	0 12½
" sug. cur. & canv'd	—	—
Shoulders, in salt	0 10	0 10½
Lard, in kegs	0 15	0 17
Eggs, packed	0 22	0 24
Beef Hams	0 00	0 13
Tallow	0 08	0 8½
Hogs dressed, heavy	9 00	9 20
" medium	8 75	9 00
" light	8 50	8 75
Salt, &c.		
American brls.	1 50	1 52
Liverpool coarse	1 15	1 25
Goderich	0 00	1 60
Plaster	1 05	1 10
Water Lime	1 50	0 00

Soap & Candles.

	$ c.	$ c.
D. Crawford & Co.'s ..	8 c.	8 c.
Imperial....	0 07½	0 08
" Golden Bar ...	0 07	0 07½
" Silver Bar......	0 07	0 07½
Crown......	0 05	0 05½
No. 1	0 03½	0 03½
Candles	0 09	0 11½

Wines, Liquors, &c.

Ale:		
English, per doz......	2 00	2 65
Guinness Dub Portr..	2 35	2 40
Spirits:		
Pure Jamaica Rum...	1 80	2 25
De Kuyper's H. Gin..	1 55	1 65
Booth's Old Tom, c...	1 90	2 00
Gin:		
Green, cases.........	4 00	4 25
Booth's Old Tom, c...	6 00	6 25
Wines:		
Port, common	1 00	1 25
" fine old	2 00	4 00
Sherry, common	1 00	1 50
" medium	1 70	1 80
"old pale or golden..	2 50	4 00

Brandy:

	$ c.	$ c.
Hennessy's, per gal..	2 30	2 50
Martell's " "	2 30	2 50
J. Robin & Co.'s "	2 25	2 34
Otard, Dupuy & Cos...	2 25	2 25
Bramly, cases........	8 50	9 00
Brandy, com. per c...	4 00	4 50
Whisky:		
Common 36 u. p......	0 62½	0 65
Old Rye	0 85	0 87½
Malt	0 85	0 87½
Toddy	0 85	0 87½
Scotch, per gal	1 90	2 10
Irish—Kinnahan's c..	7 00	7 50
" Dunnville's Belf't..	0 00	0 25

Wool.

Fleece, lb............	0 23	0 25
Pulled "	0 22	0 23

Furs.

Boar,..............	3 00	10 00
Beaver, ₱ lb........	1 00	1 25
Coon	0 20	0 40
Fisher	4 00	6 00
Martin.............	1 40	1 60
Mink	3 25	4 00
Otter...........	3 75	6 00
Spring Rats	0 15	0 17
Fox...............	1 20	1 25

INSURANCE COMPANIES.

ENGLISH.—*Quotations on the London Market.*

No. of Shares.	Last Dividend.	Name of Company.	Shares paid up	Amount paid.	Last Sale.
20,000		Briton Medical and General Life ...	10	...	2
50,000	7½	Commer'l Union, Fire, Life and Mar.	50	5	6½
24,000	8	City of Glasgow	25	2½	4
5,000	9½	Edinburgh Life	100	15	23
400,000	5—3 yr	European Life and Guarantee.....	3½	11s6	4s. 3d.
100,000	10	Etna Fire and Marine..........	10	1½	...
20,000	5	Guardian	100	50'	51½
24,000	12	Imperial Fire............	500	50	250
7,500	9½	Imperial Life	100	10	16½
100,000	10	Lancashire Fire and Life........	20	2	4
10,000	11	Life Association of Scotland.....	40	7½	25
33,862	15s. p.sh	London Assurance Corporation ..	25	12½	40
10,000	5	London and Lancashire Life	10	1	...
87,504	40	Liverp'l & London & Globe F. & L.	20	2	7 1-16
20,000	5	National Union Life	5	1	1
20,000	12½	Northern Fire and Life	100	5	12
40,000 { '63,50 5s.		North British and Mercantile	50	6½	21
40,000	50	Ocean Marine	25	5	18½
2,500	25 12s.	Provident Life	100	10	35
	£44 p. s.	Phœnix...................			145
200,000	2½—¼ yr.	Queen Fire and Life	10	1	1
190,000	3s. 50.4s	Royal Insurance............	20	3	6½
20,000	10	Scottish Provincial Fire and Life ..	50	2½	6½
10,000	20	Standard Life	50	12	66½
4,000	5	Star Life	25	1½	...

CANADIAN.

					₱ c.
8,000	4	British America Fire and Marine..	$50	$25	55½ 56
...	4	Canada Life	...	...	...
4000	12	Montreal Assurance	£50	£5	135
10,000	3	Provincial Fire and Marine	60	11	...
		Quebec Fire	40	33½	36½
	7	" Marine......	100	40	80 90
10,000	5 7 mo's.	Western Assurance.........	40	9	...

RAILWAYS.

	Sha's	Paid	Montr	London
Atlantic and St. Lawrence...........	£100	All.	....	61 63
Buffalo and Lake Huron	20½	"	....	3 3½
Do. Preference ...	10	"	....	5½ 6½
Buff., Brantf. & Goderich, 6⅌c.,1872-3-4...	100	"	....	66 69
Champlain and St. Lawrence	...	"	10 11	....
Do. Pref. 10 ⅌ ct.	...	"	90 95	....
Grand Trunk	100	"	15½16½	15½ 16
Do. Eq. Q. M. Bds. 1 ch. 6⅌c........	100	"	....	87 89
Do. First Preference, 5 ⅌c	100	"	....	£4 85
Do. Deferred, 3 ⅌ ct.	100	"	....	....
Do. Second Pref. Bonds, 5⅌c........	100	"	....	39½ 40½
Do. do. Deferred, 3 ⅌ ct.	100	"	....	....
Do. Third Pref. Stock, 4⅌ct	100	"	....	28 30
Do. do. Deferred, 3 ⅌ ct.......	100	"	....	....
Do. Fourth Pref. Stock, 3⅌c	100	"	....	....
Do. do. Deferred, 3 ⅌ ct.......	100	"	....	....
Great Western	20½	All.	13 14	15 15½
Do. New	20½	18	....	....
Do. 6 ⅌ c. Bds, due 1878-76.......	100	All.	....	100 102
Do. 5½⅌c. Bds. due 1877-78.....	100	"	....	94 95
Marine Railway, Halifax, $250, all.....	$250	"	....	....
Northern, of Canada, 6⅌c. 1st Pref. Bds.	100	"	....	82 83

EXCHANGE.

	Halifax.	Montr'l.	Quebec.	Toronto.
Bank on London, 60 days.........	12½	8½	9½ 9½	8½
Sight or 75 days date	20½	9 8½	9½ 9½	...
Private, with documents.........	11½	12	8 8½	6½ 8½	7½ 8
Bank on New York............			7½ 8½	....
Private do.	....		22½ 24	23½
Gold Drafts do.	....		24 24½	24½
Silver	....	par to 3 p.	par ½ dis.	par ½ dis.
		3 3½	....	3½ to 4½

STOCK AND BOND REPORT.

The dates of our quotations are as follows:—Toronto, March 24; Montreal, March 29; March 13; London, March 1.

NAME.	Shares	Paid up.	Divid'd last 6 Months	Dividend Day.	CLOSING PR	
					Toronto.	Montrel
BANKS.			₱ ct.			
British North America	$250	All	8	July and Jan.	104 105½	105 105
Jacques Cartier...........	50	"	4	1 June, 1 Dec.	109 109½	109 110
Montreal	200	"	5		141 141½	141½142
Nationale	50	"	4	1 Nov. 1 May.	107½ 108	108 108
New Brunswick	100	"	...		....	....
Nova Scotia............	200	$8	7&15&3½	Mar. and Sept.	....	....
Du Peuple............	50	"	4	1 Mar., 1 Sept.	107 108	107½108
Toronto	100	"	4	1 Jan., 1 July.	120 120½	120 12
Bank of Yarmouth......					....	....
Canadian Bank of Com'c..	50	95			102½ 103	102 103
City Bank Montreal ...	80	All.	4	1 June, 1 Dec.	102½ 103	102½ 10
Commer'l Bank (St. John)..	100	"	3½ ct.		....	....
Eastern Townships' Bank..	50	"	4	1 July, 1 Jan.	....	98 99½
Gore	40	"	none.	1 Jan., 1 July.	40 41	41 43
Halifax Banking Company...					....	....
Mechanics' Bank........	50	70	4	1 Nov., 1 May.	90 97	96½ 98
Merchants' Bank of Canada..	100	70	4	1 Jan., 1 July.	107 108	107 107
Merchants' Bank (Halifax)..					....	....
Molson's Bank.........	50	All.	4	1 Apr., 1 Oct.	Bks.cls'd	Bks.cls
Niagara District Bank...	100	70	3½	1 Jan., 1 July.	....	....
Ontario Bank..........	40	All.	4	1 June, 1 Dec.	100 100½	99½ 100
People's Bank (Fred'kton)..	100	"	...		....	....
People's Bank (Halifax)...	20	"	7 12 m		....	....
Quebec Bank	100	"	3½	1 June, 1 Dec.	100 100½	100 100½
Royal Canadian Bank ...	50	50	4	1 Jan., 1 July.	75 86	73½ 77
St. Stephens Bank	100	All			....	....
Union Bank	100	70	4	1 Jan., 1 July.	104 104½	104½ 10
Union Bank (Halifax)...	100	40	7 12 mo	Feb. and Aug.	....	....
MISCELLANEOUS.						
British America Land......	250	44	2½		....	....
British Colonial S. S. Co.....	250	32½	2½		....	50 60
Canada Company	32½	All.	£1 10s.		....	....
Canada Landed Credit Co.....	50	$20	3½		75 77	....
Canada Per. B'ld'g Society...	50	All.	5		125½ 126	....
Canada Mining Company....	4	90	...		....	....
Do. Int'l Steam Nav. Co.....	100	All.	7		....	100 100½
Do. Glass Company	100	"	12½ "		....	40 45
Canad'n Loan & Investm't...	25	5½	7		....	....
Canada Agency	50	10	...		....	....
Colonial Securities Co.....	...				....	....
Freehold Building Society...	100	All.	4		110 110½	....
Halifax Steamboat Co......	100	"	5		....	....
Halifax Gas Company.....					....	....
Hamilton Gas Company.....					....	....
Huron Copper Bay Co......	4	12	20		....	32½ 45
Lake Huron S. and C.....	5	102			....	....
Montreal Mining Consols....	20	$15	...		....	3.15 3.20
Do. Telegraph Co.......	40	All.	5		133 133½	132½13
Do. Elevating Co.....	40	"	15 12 m		....	100 102
Do. City Gas Co.....	40	"	4	15 Mar. 15 Sep.	....	125 130
Do. City Pass. R'y. Co....	50	"	4		....	110 111
Quebec and L. S.	3	$84	...		....	....
Quebec Gas Co	200	All.	4	1 Mar., 1 Sep.	....	....
Quebec Street R. R.....	50	35	3		....	....
Richelieu Navigation Co...	100	All.	10 p.a.	1 Jan., 1 July.	....	107½ 10
St. Lawrence Glass Company..	100	"	...		....	80 85
St. Lawrence Tow Boat Co....	100	"	4		....	....
Tor'to Consumers' Gas Co....	50	"	4	1 My au MarFe	107½108	....
Trust & Loan Co. of U. C....	20	5	3		....	....
West'n Canada Bldg Soc'y....	50	All.	5		120½ 121	....

SECURITIES.	London.	Montreal.	Quebec.
Canadian Gov't Deb. 6 ⅌ ct. stg........	....	102 103½	103 103½
Do. do. 6 do due Ja. & Jul. 1877-84...	104½ 105½	....	....
Do. do. 6 do. Feb. & Aug........	103 105	....	....
Do. do. 6 do. 6th & Sep........	102 104	....	....
Do. do. 5 ⅌ ct. cur., 1883	93½ 94½	92½ 95	92½ 95
Do. do. 5 do. stg.,1885.......	93 94	92½ 94½	94½ 94½
Do. do. 7 do. cur..........	....	....	....
Dominion 6 p. c. 1878 cy........	....	Bks. cls'd	105½105½
Hamilton Corporation.......	....	....	....
Montreal Harbour, 8 ⅌ ct. d. 1869.....	....	....	....
Do. do. 7 do. 1870.......	....	102 102½	....
Do. do. 6½ do. 1883.......	....	....	....
Do. do. 6 do. 1873.......	....	....	....
Do. Corporation, 6 ⅌ c. 1801......	....	96 96½	96 96½
Do. 7 p. c. stock.........	....	108 110	109 110½
Do. Water Works, 6 ⅌ ct. stg. 1878......	....	....	....
Do. do. 6 do. cy. do.......	....	96½ 97	....
New Brunswick, 6 ⅌ ct., Jan. and July...	103 104	....	....
Nova Scotia, 6 ⅌ ct., 1875........	103 104	....	....
Ottawa City 6 ⅌ c. d. 1880........	....	92½ 93½	....
Quebec Harbour, 6 ⅌ c. d. 1883........	....	....	....
Do. do. 8 do. 1869........	....	....	65 70
Do. do. 6 do. 1886........	....	....	80 85
Do. City, 7 ⅌ c.d. 1½ years.....	....	....	97½ 98
Do. do. 7 do. do........	....	....	91 92
Do. do. 6 do. cy........	....	....	94½ 95
Do. Water Works, 7 ⅌ ct., 4 years...	....	....	97 97½
Do. do. 6 do. 2 do........	....	....	94½ 95
Toronto Corporation........	....	90 92½	....

Insurance.

BEAVER
Mutual Insurance Association.

HEAD OFFICE—20 TORONTO STREET,
TORONTO.

INSURES LIVE STOCK against death from any cause.
The only Canadian Company having authority to do this class of business.

R. L. DENISON,
President.
O'REILLY,
Secretary.   8-1y-25

HOME DISTRICT
Mutual Fire Insurance Company.

—North-West Cor. Yonge & Adelaide Streets,
TORONTO.—(UP STAIRS.)

INSURES Dwelling Houses, Stores, Warehouses, Merchandise, Furniture, &c.

PRESIDENT—The Hon. J. McMURRICH.
VICE-PRESIDENT—JOHN BURNS, Esq.
JOHN RAINS, Secretary.
AGENTS:
WRIGHT, Esq., Hamilton; FRANCIS STEVENS, Esq., Barrie; Messrs. GIBBS & BRO., Oshawa.   8-1y

THE PRINCE EDWARD COUNTY
Mutual Fire Insurance Company.

HEAD OFFICE,—PICTON, ONTARIO.
President, L. B. STINSON; Vice-President, W. A. RICHARDS.
Directors; H. A. McPaul, James Cavan, James Johnson, John McMill, William Delong.—Treasurer, David Barker Henry, John Twigg; Solicitor, R. J. Fitzgerald.

This Company is established upon strictly Mutual principles, insuring farming and isolated property, (not stores,) in Townships only, and offers great advantages to insurers, at low rates for five years, without the expense of renewal.
Picton, June 15, 1868.   9-1y

THE AGRICULTURAL
Mutual Assurance Association of Canada.

OFFICE ....LONDON, ONT.

The only Farmers' Company. Licensed by the Government of Canada.

1st January, 1860	$250,103 32
Cash Items, over	$86,000 00
Policies in force	30,892 00

This Company insures nothing more dangerous than farm property. Its rates are as low as any well-conducted Company in the Dominion, and lower than those that want many. It is largely patronized, and continues to grow in public favor.
For insurance, apply to any of the Agents or address Secretary, London, Ontario.
London, 2nd Nov., 1868.   12-1y

Hamilton Medical and General Life
Association,
with which is united the
BRITANNIA LIFE ASSURANCE COMPANY.

Paid and Invested Funds...........£750,000 Sterling.

ANNUAL INCOME, £220,000 STG. :
nearly increasing at the rate of £25,000 Sterling.

An important and peculiar feature originally introduced by this Company, in applying the periodical bonuses, so as to make Policies payable during life, without higher rate of premiums being charged, has caused success of the BRITON MEDICAL AND GENERAL to be unparalleled in the history of Life Assurance. Life based on the Profit Scale become payable during the lifetime of the assured, thus rendering a Policy of Assurance a means of subsistence in old age, as well as a protection for a family, and a more valuable security to creditors in the event of early death; and effectually meeting the often objection, that persons do not themselves reap the benefit of their own prudence and forethought.
Extra charge made to members of Volunteer Corps and persons within the British Provinces.
TORONTO AGENCY, 5 KING ST. WEST.
17—0-1yr   JAMES FRASER, Agent.

Insurance.

The Gore District Mutual Fire Insurance
Company

GRANTS INSURANCES on all description of Property against Loss or Damage by FIRE. It is the only Mutual Fire Insurance Company which assesses its Policies yearly from their respective dates; and the average yearly cost of insurance in it, for the past three and a half years, has been nearly
TWENTY CENTS IN THE DOLLAR
less than what it would have been in an ordinary Proprietary Company.
THOS. M. SIMONS,
Secretary & Treasurer.
ROBT. McLEAN,
Inspector of Agencies.
Galt, 26th Nov., 1868.   15-1y

Geo. Girdlestone,

FIRE, Life, Marine, Accident, and Stock Insurance Agent
Very best Companies represented.
Windsor, Ont. June, 1868

The Standard Life Assurance Company,
Established 1825.
WITH WHICH IS NOW UNITED
THE COLONIAL LIFE ASSURANCE COMPANY.

Head Office for Canada :
MONTREAL—STANDARD COMPANY'S BUILDINGS,
No. 47 GREAT ST. JAMES STREET.
Manager—W. M. RAMSAY.   Inspector—RICH'D BULL.

THIS Company having deposited the sum of ONE HUNDRED AND FIFTY THOUSAND DOLLARS with the Receiver General, in conformity with the Insurance Act passed last Session, Assurances will continue to be carried out at moderate rates and on all the different systems in practice.
AGENT FOR TORONTO—HENRY PELLATT,
KING STREET.
AGENT FOR HAMILTON—JAMES BANCROFT.
6-6mos.

Fire and Marine Assurance.

THE BRITISH AMERICA
ASSURANCE COMPANY.
HEAD OFFICE:
CORNER OF CHURCH AND COURT STREETS.
TORONTO.

BOARD OF DIRECTION :
Hon G. W. Allan, M L C,	A. Joseph, Esq.,
George J. Boyd, Esq ,	Peter Paterson, Esq.,
Hon. W. Cayley,	G. F. Ridout, Esq.,
Richard S. Cassels, Esq.,	R. H. Rutherford, Esq ,
Thomas C. Street, Esq.	

Governor:
GEORGE PERCIVAL RIDOUT, Esq.
Deputy Governor:
PETER PATERSON, Esq.
Fire Inspector: Marine Inspector:
E. RODY O'BRIEN,   CAPT. R. COURNEEN.
Insurances granted on all descriptions of property against loss and damage by fire and the perils of inland navigation.
Agencies established in the principal cities, towns, and ports of shipment throughout the Province.
THOS. WM. BIRCHALL,
23-1y   Managing Director.

Queen Fire and Life Insurance Company,
OF LIVERPOOL AND LONDON,
ACCEPTS ALL ORDINARY FIRE RISKS
on the most favorable terms.
LIFE RISKS
Will be taken on terms that will compare favorably with other Companies.
CAPITAL,   -   -   £2,000,000 Stg.
CHIEF OFFICES—Queen's Buildings, Liverpool, and Gracechurch Street London.
CANADA BRANCH OFFICE—Exchange Buildings, Montreal.
Resident Secretary and General Agent,
A. MACKENZIE FORBES,
13 St. Sacrament St., Merchants' Exchange, Montreal.
WM. ROWLAND, Agent, Toronto.   1-1y

Insurance.

The Waterloo County Mutual Fire Insurance
Company.

HEAD OFFICE : WATERLOO, ONTARIO.
ESTABLISHED 1863.

THE business of the Company is divided into three separate and distinct branches, the
VILLAGE, FARM, AND MANUFACTURES.

Each Branch paying its own losses and its just proportion of the managing expenses of the Company.
C. M. TAYLOR, Sec.   M. SPRINGER, M.M.P., Pres.
J. HUGHES, Inspector.   15-yr

Etna Fire and Marine Insurance Company of
Dublin.

AT a Meeting of the Shareholders of this Company, held at Dublin, on the 19th ult., it was agreed that the business of the "ETNA" should be transferred to the "UNITED PORTS AND GENERAL INSURANCE COMPANY." In accordance with this agreement, the business will hereafter be carried on by the latter Company, which assumes and guarantees all the risks and liabilities of the "ETNA." The Directors have resolved to continue the CANADIAN BRANCH, and arrangements for resuming FIRE and MARINE business are rapidly approaching completion.
T. W. GRIFFITH,
16   Manager.

Lancashire Insurance Company.

CAPITAL, - - - - - - - £2,000,000 Sterling

FIRE RISKS
Taken at reasonable rates of premium, and
ALL LOSSES SETTLED PROMPTLY,
By the undersigned, without reference elsewhere.
S. C. DUNCAN-CLARK & CO.,
General Agents for Ontario,
25-1y   N. W. Corner of King & Church Streets,
TORONTO.

DIVISION OF PROFITS NEXT YEAR.

ASSURANCES
EFFECTED BEFORE 30TH APRIL NEXT,
IN THE
Canada Life Assurance Company,
OBTAIN A YEAR'S ADDITIONAL PROFITS
OVER LATER ENTRANTS,
And the great success of the Company warrants the Directors in recommending this very important advantage to assurers.

SUMS ASSURED	$6,300,000
AMOUNT OF CAPITAL AND FUNDS	1,000,000
ANNUAL INCOME	200,000

Assets (exclusive of uncalled capital) for each $100 of liabilities, about $150.
The income from interest upon investments is now alone sufficient to meet claims by death.
A. G. RAMSAY, Manager.
E. BRADBURNE, Agent,
Feb. 1.   1y   Toronto Street.

The Victoria Mutual
FIRE INSURANCE COMPANY OF CANADA.
Insures only Non-Hazardous Property, at Low Rates.
BUSINESS STRICTLY MUTUAL.
GEORGE H. MILLS, President.
W. D. BOOKER, Secretary.
HEAD OFFICE ....HAMILTON, ONTARIO.
aug 15-1yr

PUBLISHED AT THE OFFICE OF THE MONETARY TIMES, No. 60 CHURCH STREET.
PRINTED AT THE DAILY TELEGRAPH PUBLISHING HOUSE, BAY STREET, CORNER OF KING.

THE NORTHERN FIRE ASSURANCE COMPANY

1836. ESTABLISHED 1836.

CHIEF OFFICES:

1 MOORGATE STREET, LONDON.   3 KING STREET, ABERDEEN

GENERAL AGENTS FOR CANADA:

TAYLOR BROTHERS, MONTREAL

CAPITAL:

TWO MILLION POUNDS STERLIN

ACCUMULATED FUNDS.......................................EIGHT HUNDRED AND FIFTY THOUSAND POUNDS STERLING
ANNUAL REVENUE FROM FIRE PREMIUMS............ ....ONE HUNDRED AND SIXTY THOUSAND POUNDS STERLING.

Insurances against LOSS by Fire effected on the most favorable terms. Losses paid without reference to the Board in London.

W. H. MILLER, Agent for TORONTO

Office—Corner CHURCH AND COLBORNE STREETS.

MINERAL LANDS OF NOVA SCOTIA.
A. Hetherington,
MINE AGENT.

OFFICE:—SOMERSET HOUSE,
Mail Address:—P O Box 266.
HALIFAX, N. S.

A GUIDE TO THE GOLD FIELDS OF NOVA SCOTIA, published by Mr. H., and procurable at most Booksellers, will be found extremely useful to Tourists, Miners, and Investors.

TORONTO SAVINGS BANK.
72 CHURCH STREET.

DEPOSITS received, from Twenty Cents upwards; invested in Government and other first class securities.
Interest allowed at 5 and 6 per cent.

BANKS OF DEPOSIT:
Ontario Bank and Canadian Bank of Commerce.
W. J. MACDONELL,
30-1y   MANAGER.

TO BUILDING SOCIETIES,
INSURANCE COMPANIES, AND PERSONS HAVING TRANSACTIONS WITH THEM.—TO CAPITALISTS, AND ALL CONCERNED IN THE SALE OR EXCHANGE OF SECURITIES:—

For Calculations as to the Surrender Value of Life or Endowment Insurance Policies by any Tables of Mortality, and at any rate of interest.
The interest earned on buying, selling, or exchanging Stocks, Debentures, Mortgages, &c., above or below par value.
The buying or selling value of Annuities for Life or terms of years.
The valuations of Building Societies' Mortgages, or any similar obligations, &c., &c., &c.
Address
ARTHUR HARVEY, F.S.S., &c.,
OTTAWA.
MINIMUM FEE, $5.00

TORONTO SAFE WORKS.

J. & J. Taylor
MANUFACTURERS OF
Fire and Burglar Proof
SAFES,
BANK LOCKS, VAULTS, DOORS, &c., &c.

AGENTS:
JAS. HUTTON & Co.............. MONTREAL.
H. S. SCOTT & Co.............. QUEBEC.
ALEX. WORKMAN & Co........ OTTAWA.
RICE LEWIS & SON .... TORONTO.
D. FALCONER.................. HALIFAX, N.S.

Manufactory & Sale Rooms, 198 & 200 Palace Street.
30-1y

Canada Permanent Building and Savings Society.

Paid up Capital $1,000,000
Assets 1,700,000
Annual Income 400,000

Directors:—JOSEPH D. RIDOUT, President.
PETER PATERSON, Vice-President.
J. G. Worts, Edward Hooper, S. Nordheimer, W. C. Chewett, E. H. Rutherford, Joseph Robinson.
Bankers:—Bank of Toronto; Bank of Montreal; Royal Canadian Bank.
OFFICE—Masonic Hall, Toronto Street, Toronto.

Money Received on Deposit bearing five and six per cent. interest.

Advances made on City and Country Property in the Provin of Ontario.
J. HERBERT MASON
30-y   Sec'y & Treas.

W. McLaren & Co.,
WHOLESALE
BOOT AND SHOE MANUFACTUR
18 ST. MAURICE STREET,
June, 1868.   MONTREAL.

W. PATERSON & Co.,
BANKERS AND BROKE
Insurance, Passage, and General Ag
NORTH-WEST COR. KING AND CHURCH STREE
TORONTO.

BUY AND SELL, AT BEST RATES,
NEW YORK STERLING EXCHANGE,
UNCURRENT FUNDS, STOCKS,
GOLD, SILVER, &
COMMERCIAL PAPER DISCOUNTED.
DEPOSITS RECEIVED, SUBJECT TO DE
Money Advanced on Good Securiti
AGENTS,
LONDON AND LANCASHIRE LIFE ASSURA
20-1y

Philip Browne & Co.,
BANKERS AND STOCK BROKE
DEALERS IN
STERLING EXCHANGE—U. S. Currency, Sil Bonds—Bank Stocks, Debentures, Mortgag Drafts on New York issued, in Gold and C Prompt attention given to collections. Advanc on Securities.
No. 67 YONGE STREET, TORONTO
JAMES BROWNE.   PHILIP BROWNE, Notari
y

THE CANADIAN
￼ONETARY TIMES
AND
INSURANCE CHRONICLE.

￼OTED TO FINANCE, COMMERCE, INSURANCE, BANKS, RAILWAYS, NAVIGATION, MINES, INVESTMENT,
PUBLIC COMPANIES, AND JOINT STOCK ENTERPRISE.

I—NO. 33.   TORONTO, THURSDAY, APRIL 1, 1869.   { SUBSCRIPTION: $3 YEAR.

Mercantile.

Gundry and Langley,
￼ECTS AND CIVIL ENGINEERS, Building Sur-
, and Valuators. Office corner of King and Jordan
'oronto.
AS GUNDRY.   HENRY LANGLEY.

J. B. Boustead.
￼O￼ and Commission Merchant. Hops bought
￼old on Commission. 82 Front St., Toronto.

John Boyd & Co.
￼SALE Grocers and Commission Merchants,
nt St., Toronto.

Childs & Hamilton.
ACTURERS and Wholesale Dealers in Boots
Shoes, No. 7 Wellington Street East, Toronto.
     23

L. Coffee & Co.
￼E and Commission Merchants, No. 2 Manning's
, Front St., Toronto, Ont. Advances made on
nts of Produce.

Honore Plamondon,
f House Broker, Forwarder, and General Agent.
ec. Office—Custom House Building.   17-1y

Sylvester, Bro. & Hickman,
RCIAL Brokers and Vessel Agents. Office—No.
ario Chambers, [Corner Front and Church Sts.,
     3-0m

John Fisken & Co.
￼OIL and Commission Merchants, Yonge St.,
￼nto, Ont.

W. & R. Griffith.
ERS of Teas, Wines, etc. Ontario Chambers,
hurch and Front Sts., Toronto.

H. Nerlich & Co.,
ERS of French, German, English and American
Goods, Cigars, and Leaf Tobaccos, No. 2 Adelaide
est, Toronto.   15

Hurd, Leigh & Co.
￼S and ￼Enamellers of China and Earthenware,
￼age St., Toronto, Ont. [see advt.]

Lyman & McNab.
￼SALE Hardware Merchants, Toronto, Ontario.

W. D. Matthews & Co.
￼E Commission Merchants, ￼Old Corn Exchange,
￼ont St. East, Toronto Ont.

R. C. Hamilton & Co.
￼E Commission Merchants, 119 Lower Water
￼alifax, Nova Scotia.

Parson Bros.,
￼EUM Refiners, and Wholesale dealers in Lamps,
￼neys, etc. Warerooms 51 Front St. Refinery cor.
￼Don Sts., Toronto.

C. P. Reid & Co.
ERS and Dealers in Wines, Liquors, Cigars and
Tobacco, Wellington Street, Toronto.   73-

W. Rowland & Co.,
￼E BROKERS and General Commission Mer-
￼Advances made on Consignments. Corner
￼ ￼nd Streets, Toronto.

Beford & Dillon.
ERS of Groceries, Wellington Street, Toronto,
io.

Sessions, Turner & Cooper.
ACTURERS, Importers and Wholesale Dealer
oots and Shoes, Leather Findings, etc., 8 Wel-
West, Toronto, Ont

CANADIAN AFFAIRS IN LONDON.

(From a Correspondent.)

LONDON, March 11, 1869.

Perhaps some of your readers may not have
heard of a new society recently founded here, and
entitled the Colonial Society. Its design is to
afford facilities for the discussion of all topics of a
non-political character, which relate either to the
internal concerns of the British dependencies or
to their position as sections of the Empire. It is
obvious that such an institution will prove useful
in diffusing useful information on Colonial subjects, and thereby exercising a beneficial influence
over Imperial policy and legislation. Lord Bury
is the President. Among the Vice-Presidents are
the Duke of Buckingham, the Earl of Carnarvon,
Lord Lytton, and the Right Hon. Edward Cardwell. The Council is composed of men whose
practical experience of colonial affairs is very
great. Suffice it, however, to mention but one
name, that of the Right Hon. Sir John
Young, Bart., G.C.B. A few months only have
elapsed since the formation of the society, and it
is already in a flourishing state. The best proof
of its importance was furnished last night when
the leading English and Colonial statesmen assembled together at the society's inaugural dinner.
The report of speeches you will find in the
newspapers. There are some things, however,
not fully reported which I may here repeat. The
Hon. Reverdy Johnson made a speech, which contained some expressions that jarred on the ears of
the company. After stating that the United
States had not renounced their idea of acquiring
fresh territory, he observed that the Stars and
Stripes might wave hereafter over some of her
Majesty's Colonies. This of course was supposed
to intimate that the wild dreams of certain
American writers might be realized, and the
Dominion of Canada be absorbed into the Great
Republic. This part of his speech was not permitted, however, to pass unrebuked. Earl
Granville ridiculed the notion in a pointed yet brief
manner, while Sir George Cartier repelled it with
a vigor which gave evident gratification to the
audience. Indeed, if Mr. Reverdy Johnson was
sincere in his belief, and if he purposely chose the
opportunity in order to give expression to his
opinion, he certainly counted without his host.
Another topic of special interest to you was referred to by several speakers. This also was a
question of ceding territory; but, instead of the
United States being the prospective gainer by
the transaction this time it is the Dominion of
Canada which would be aggrandized. I need
hardly add that I allude to the Hudson's Bay
Company's territory. On the preceding evening
Lord Granville intimated in the House of Lords
that he has now made up his mind and offered a
final proposal to the Company, on the one hand,
and to the representatives of your Government on
the other. In his speech last night he made
special mention of this. It was likewise briefly
noticed by Sir Stafford Northcote, the present
Governor of the Hudson's Bay Company, and by
your Minister of Public Works, the Hon. W.
McDougall. Of course Sir Stafford could not say
much, as he must consult not only his colleagues,
but also take the opinion of the shareholders before closing with the Colonial Secretary's pro-

posal. The Hon. W. McDougall, in like manner,
was precluded, both by his official position and
the occasion itself, from entering into detail; but
he took advantage of the opportunity of returning
thanks for the "New Dominion and the Colonies
in the West," to enlarge on the necessity for a
speedy settlement of the matters in dispute, so
that the great territory of the North-West might
be at once opened up and peopled. Whatever
may be the success of the representatives of your
Government now in this country in accomplishing
their mission, there can be no doubt that their
presence at the banquet of the Colonial Society,
and their speeches on that occasion, will hereafter
prove of no small advantage to the Dominion.
During the past few weeks, the words "Hudson's
Bay Company" have frequently appeared in the
newspapers, and have more than once been uttered
in Parliament. I think the public here is slowly
awakening and becoming impressed with the magnitude of the issues at stake. It is quite certain
that the shareholders and the servants of the
company are apprehensive as to the result. Some
very strong language has been used respecting the
greed of the Canadians. Indeed, the chief difficulty of your Ministers now here must be to reduce the terms on which the final settlement is to
be made. Not a few of the shareholders seriously
maintain that they ought to receive five millions
sterling for the relinquishment of their territorial
claims. The misfortune is that they have been
dazzled by the statements put forth by the company, and believe the charter to be impregnable.
It may be that this belief will be shaken by some
statements about to be made public for the first
time, which, I understand, will appear in an
article entitled "The Hudson's Bay Company,"
in the next number of the *North British Review.*
I feel certain that the day of reckoning is at hand
for the company. Should the present negotiations
be broken off, the matter will assuredly be discussed in Parliament.

A cloud, that has hung over the commercial
horizon for a few days is now dispelled. War between France and Prussia is adjourned to a
more convenient opportunity. The Belgium railway dispute is to be referred to arbitration;
but the conviction is general that the contest is
simply postponed, and is still certain to occur.
In consequence of this, an uneasy feeling prevails
to the detriment of commerce. There is much
speculation on the Stock Exchange, but little
solid business. The supply of foreign loans shows
no signs of falling off. Russia is again a borrower;
Turkey requires a trifle of two millions sterling,
and is ready to pay 12 per cent for the accommodation; while Spain is about to ask for another
twenty millions. The colony of Victoria has just
obtained upwards of two millions wherewith to
extend her railway system. As a result of these
demands the value of money is increasing and an
early rise in the bank rate of discount is inevitable. Meantime trade is dull, and confidence in
joint-stock enterprise at a low ebb.

A bill has been introduced by a private member into the House of Commons with a view to
regulate the working of life assurance companies.
It is high time that something were done to
remedy the existing abuses. Not long ago a
witness in a court of justice, when under cross-
examination, was compelled to admit that his

occupation had been the foundation of assurance companies, and that he made a treble profit, for he obtained something as their founder, a salary as manager, and a per centage when they were in liquidation. According to a statement I have met with, it would appear that during the past twenty-five years, 355 assurance companies have been founded, that of these 328 have ceased to exist. Last year 30 were projected and 17 became bankrupt. It is now proposed to exercise a supervision over the accounts, making it compulsory on every company which issues life policies to make a yearly return to a Government office of its income and expenditure; to furnish the balance sheet for the past year and a statement of the new business transacted, and to supply an actuarial report every 10 years. The penalty for non-compliance with the law is to be a fine of £20 for every day's delay. Even should this bill fail to pass, there must be legislation on the subject before long, because the present state of things is too scandalous to last.

Insurance.

FIRE RECORD.—Seneca, March —,—.The residence of John Anderson took fire and was totally consumed. The family saved nothing of the contents, and only escaped in their night clothes.

Beachville, March 19.—The foundry and machine shop of R. Whitelaw, was totally consumed by fire. The loss of the workman were in the neighborhood of $5,000. No information as to insurance.

Dover East, Ont., March 22.—The Big Point Inn, kept by F. Martin, was burnt to the ground with all its contents. The loss is considerable, as there was no insurance. The fire originated from a defective stove pipe.

Guelph, March 20.—A shanty occupied by a switchman was consumed. It was the property of the Grand Trunk Company.

Davenport, March.—House occupied by Rev. E. T. Bromfield and most of the contents; we are informed there was no insurance.

A correspondent sends us the following account of recent fire losses in Nova Scotia:—Feb. 24, 6 buildings burnt at Digby, viz.: Small store, where fire originated, owned and occupied by B. Stack; loss on store, total value $160, insured in the Royal for $150; loss on stock, partial; $269 also insured in the Royal. Store owned by Mr. Conwell, total loss, insured in Royal for $400, full value. Stock of E. Payson insured in Royal removed without loss. Two stores owned by Estate John Hammond, valued at $500 and $600, total loss; insured for $400 each in Liverpool and London and Globe; one unoccupied, the other occupied by Churchill & Taylor, who saved their stock. Store owned and occupied by R. Thorn; store total loss, no insurance; stock saved. Store owned and occupied by D. Beman; total loss; no insurance; stock saved.

Feb. 26.—Adam McKay's framed boiler shop at Dartmouth, Halifax; total loss, $1000 on building in Royal, $1200 on stock in Liverpool & London and Globe. Owner losses heavily.

Feb. 26.—Barn in suburbs of Halifax, owned by P. Forristall, uninsured.

March 8.—Dwelling at Dartmouth, Halifax, owned and occupied by John Jones; total loss; value $600; insured for $400 in Ætna of Hartford.

March 11.—The "C. B. News" says on Thursday morning last, between the hours of five and six o'clock, a fire broke out in the dwelling house of Mr. Samuel E. Peters, at Cow Bay, which was entirely consumed; as also the Store adjoining, owned by Mr. Peters, and occupied by Messrs O. B. Spencer & Co., as a General Store. Both buildings and the stock of merchandise destroyed were partially insured in the " London and Liverpool and Globe Insurance" office. Some of the goods were saved in a damaged condition.

Port Dalhousie, March 26.—An unoccupied house of G. W. Reid; it is thought to be the work of an incendiary.

Warrington.—We were informed that the mill lately burned at this place was not insured; we now learn that there was a policy for $2,000 in the Provincial.

UNIFORMITY IN THE WORDING OF POLICIES.— We have to thank Messrs. Taylor Brothers, of Montreal, for the following extract from the minutes of a meeting of London offices, held in London, on the 6th February, and would commend it to the notice of fire underwriters :

Resolved,—That, in order to prevent, in future, complications and delays, vexatious alike to claimants and the offices, such as have heretofore arisen in the settlement of losses from want of uniformity in the wording of all policies designed to cover one and the same risk, all the offices do simultaneously instruct their agents abroad that in all cases of joint assurance with other companies, uniformity of wording is essential for the convenience and security of the insured, as well as the offices.

That, in order to secure this important object, every agent be directed, before issuing a policy to cover any risk on which there is reason to believe that other insurances have been or are being effected, to point out to the proposers the importance of such uniformity, and arrange with them a form of wording to be used in all policies covering the same risk ; and that the same precautions be strictly observed on any alteration being made, by endorsement or otherwise, in a policy.

LANCASHIRE.—At the meeting of the Lancashire Insurance Company at Manchester on March 9th, it was stated that the income from fire premiums was £112,579; from life premiums, £39,527 and from interest, £16,635; and that the fire losses paid during the year amounted to £45,350 and the life claims to £15,978. A dividend of 10 per cent. was declared, and the reserve funds were reported to be £199,330 in the life department and £62,350 in the fire branch.

UNITED PORTS AND GENERAL INSURANCE COMPANY.—Arrangements have now been finally completed for the acquisition by this company of the business, good will, and connections of the Bristol Marine Insurance Company, Limited, a local Company which was started in 1864; and which has been very successful in accumulating a large and sound marine business. A branch office has been opened at Bristol for the west of England, and will, doubtless, secure a good share of business, more especially as a large number of shares have been placed there by the arrangements between the Companies.—*Post Magazine.*

INSURANCE REBATE.—This question still troubles the managers of our fire insurance companies. The meeting of the 17th inst. adjourned without having advanced on the subject of discussion. The report was referred back to the committee, and that a similar document might not reappear, the committee was enlarged by the addition of five other members, the committee now numbering ten. We learn that the committee now report that net rates of insurance should be adopted and adhered to, and that all rebate, brokerage, commission or other return of premium to the insured or others should be abandoned; that a fine should be the punishment of a breach of faith in these conditions, and that a deposit of $1,000 should be made by each company as a security for the fine imposed. We much doubt if these suggestions will meet with sufficient support to enable the Board to sustain them, and we greatly doubt if such a change in the method of transacting business would be altogether one of prudence. Even if all existing New York companies could be induced to enter this rather precarious citadel, new companies might appear upon the principle of commissions, and be sustained by a very powerful body of those whom we may term,

under the circumstances, the disfranchised, and then the Board would be reduced to capitulati —*N. Y. Insurance Journal.*

NEW LIFE ASSURANCE BILL IN ENGLAND In the House of Commons on the 3d March, the motion of Mr. S. Cave, leave was given bring in a Bill to amend the law relating to assurance. Mr. Cave said that it proposed extend to life assurance associations similar visions to those enacted by Parliament last y with reference to railway companies, for the p lication of fuller and more uniform accounts. was introduced in no spirit of hostility to as ance companies, by whom it was generally proved, and he believed he did not go too fa saying it would have the support of her Majes Government. He reserved a full explanatio the provisions of the Bill for the second readin *Post Magazine.*

LIFE INSURANCE.—The sum insured upon policies in Great Britain is estimated at four h dred million pounds, upon which permit amounting to twenty million pounds are annu paid. This is half the amount of the natic debt, which is eight hundred million pounds, the insurance premiums nearly reach the am interest paid upon the debt, which is twenty million pounds.

LIVERPOOL AND LONDON AND GLOBE.—At annual meeting, on the 26th Feby., the Ann Report of the Company for 1868, was read. F it we take the following extract:

"The capital in the hands of the proprie was the same as last year, £391,752, and of 1 £146,742 was held by trustees, as considered for Globe 6 per cent. annuities. The fire] mium of the year had increased to £867,374 1d., and the amount paid in losses was £509, 18s. 1d.; 1,123 life policies were issued, insu £639,780; 167 proposals were declined for the —of £118,300; 129 proposals were accepted, but yet completed, for £131,200. The new ann premiums were £23,403 5s. 8d.; and the renev £242,338 2s. 9d.; giving as the premium inco of the year a total of £265,641 8s. 5d. The cla under policies, including the bonuses on suc belonged to that class, were £193,573 6s. 5d.; bonds for annuities were issued for £3,971 1 74 annuities had fallen in, amounting to £3, 4s. 9d.; the annuities now payable being £56, 15s. 15d. The reserve for this department now £2,081,204 4s. 2d. In terms of the ag ment under which the business of the Globe O was taken over, a valuation had been made of liabilities under their life policies, with the re of which there was every reason to be cont As the profit on the business for the quinquen period, ending with the 31st December last, sum of £85,957 16s. 5d. had been carried to credit of the profit and loss account. The res surplus fund remained at £971,409 12s. 10d. the credit of the profit and loss account was sum of £211,237 17s. 11d., arrived at after mak further liberal provisions for possible contingen From it the Directors had determined to take sum of £117,525 12s. for distribution amongst proprietors, which yielded a dividend for the of 30 per cent., free of income tax, on the am of their respective holdings. The balance at credit of account would then be £93,712 5s. 1 The funds of the Company thus consisted capital, £391,752; life reserve, £2,081,204 4s. reserve fund, £971,409 12s. 10d.; undivided pr £93,712 5s. 11d.—total £3,538,073 2s. 1. being an increase upon last year of £137,072 1d. After the report was read,

The Chairman, in moving its adoption, denced by the important increase in amount of the fire premiums, the aggregat which far exceeded the receipts of any sin company in the world. In attaining that]

however, there had been no relaxation of :rtious policy which had hitherto been pur-:y the directors. It would be hazardous at t to venture any opinion as to the pros-of the present year; at the same time he remark that the year opened very favor-and encouraged the anticipation of a good.

It would no doubt be perceived that the tage of loss on fire premiums had exceeded :io of last year; and it was to be regretted :ome steps had not been taken by the :ment for the establishment of, some board :stigation, with a view to trace the origin :. Until some such step was taken he feared :ould not be able to reduce the average of :in connection with their fire business. The :rs, although satisfied with the favorable attained, had investigated, and would con-:o investigate, each description of business, .view to improve still further the general

With regard to the life business of the :ny, the progress made might also be con-. to be satisfactory, as the new premiums :l an increase over those of the preceding :nd the accumulated funds of that branch :ceeded the large sum of two millions.

NSFER OF INTEREST IN LIFE POLICIES.—:llowing clause was added to Mr. Carter's Committee of the Quebec Legislature :—:rithstanding, and without prejudice to arti-, 82 and 25, 91, of the Civil Code, any per-:ne life is insured, may by notarial or other :nent in writing, and without any induce-:n the policy, assign and transfer as collate-:rity for money or otherwise, any portion interest in the said policy not less than one thereof. Such transfer, when duly served :he insurer or his agent, shall be binding on :d insurer, if at the time of the service, the shall have been produced, and he or his :hall have been allowed, if he thinks fit, to :an entry thereon of such transfer ; and :on, whether such entry shall have been; :r not, the transferee shall have the same :gainst the insurer as he might have had if :nsfer had been made upon the policy, and :e the holder thereof."

ISNOMER.—We notice frequent allusions in :vertisements and year books of American :surance Companies to their "non-forfeita-:licies. The phrase, so far as the non-for-of a policy *for any cause* (assuring absnd :rment of annual premiums) is a misnomer :ied to American policies. In every stage :e of a policy it is forfeitable for fraud in the :l application, whenever that fraud is dis-:l. Policies, are, also, always forfeitable in the violation of any one of the several :itions" named in the body of the policy, suicide, traveling without special permis-:yond specified limits, &c. Therefore, in :an practice, a non-forfeitable policy is a :er.

Prudential, a wealthy London life office, a income of $1,075,000, has recently re-:to issue policies that shall be "unforfeita-:conditional and unchangeable," for fraud, :rment of premiums, or any other cause. :rpose is to make a policy of insurance an :s negotiable mercantile security, good for :in the hands of every bona fide holder for :ible consideration. Besides every policy :ressly state what sum can at any time be :wn on the discontinuance of it.:

:ssured will thus always have the option of :ig either an ascertained fixed sum payable :ase, or, in case of need, of withdrawing a :amount, according to the duration of the :such amounts being set forth on every :and rendering unnecessary any future :e to the company on these points, as is the :h ordinary assurances. Creditors, bankers, :sts and others, who are in. the habit of :advances collaterally secured by life poli-:ll find this form of policy a convenience,

as they can at any time learn, by mere inspection the exact value, either immediate or reversionary. Every policy issued on this plan will be without any conditions as to voyaging, foreign residence or other usual limitations. By this freedom from restrictions of all kinds, the policies will become at once positively valuable as actual securities. The number of premiums is strictly defined. The longest term provided for is twenty-five years, and the shortest five years, as shown by the tables Thus, bankers, creditors, and others, holding policies of this class as security, may always know the utmost amount they may be called upon to advance so as to maintain the full benefit of the assurances. The Prudential's policies being un-forfeitable and unconditional, they will be unchal-lengeable on any ground whatever. They may therefore be aptly termed absolute security poli-cies.—*Insurance Monitor*.

—The Directors of the Reliance Mutual have appointed Mr. Hugh Gibson, late of the Stand-ard, resident secretary of that company in Glas-gow.

ASSOCIATION OF CANADIAN LAKE UNDERWRITERS.

A meeting of this Association was held on the 24th inst., to take into consideration certain mat-ters relating to the practical working of certain clauses of the Insurance Act of last Session.

Correspondence was read from the Marine De-partment, Ottawa, in reference to the petition for an amendment of the existing law for the regula-tion of inland navigation.

A number of questions were raised respecting the clause affecting Marine Insurance Companies. It was considered desirable that some steps should be taken to determine whether a Marine Company allowed by law to transact Ocean, but not Inland Marine Insurance, can legally insure a vessel from Toronto to Liverpool, or even from Toronto to Halifax; also whether it is Ocean or Inland Marine Insurance from Montreal to Quebec. Instances were given in which the provisions of the act had been deliberately violated by agents who have canvassed for and obtained risks for foreign com-panies, not having any deposit in Canada, and received the premiums on this side of the lakes. It was considered, that the fact of the policies being issued on the other side, does not protect such agents from the guilt of violating the law, but makes them liable to the penalty mentioned in clause 13, which says : "Any person who shall deliver any policies of insurance, or collect any premiums, or transact any business of Insurance *** shall be liable to a penalty of one thousand dollars."

The companies composing the Association de-cided, for the present, not to prosecute parties so violating the law, but merely noted the cases of which they possess uncontrovertible proof, until the whole matter is fully investigated, when pro-ceedings will be taken against all who continue to disregard the law, and to render themselves liable to the penalty it imposes.

THE NEW YORK STATE FIRE INSURANCE COMPANIES.

From the official returns of the Fire Insurance business of this State we have the following statistics up to December 31, 1868:

Chartered capital paid up............	$28,911,232
Total assets...........................	49,704,334
Net cash premiums	22,774,624
Total income	26,039,098
Total losses in 1868, as reported...	12,948,257
Disbursements in :1868...............	22,602,423
Expenses of management:.........	6,486,544
Liabilities	11,818,174
Surplus over reinsurance and capital	9,249,722
Gross amount of fire risks written...	2,534,683,704
Total cash dividends declared. ...	2,740,586
National and State Taxes...	1,257,679

By the tables of the New York Insurance De-partment, from 1859 to the present time, we find for nine consecutive years the following result:

Year.	Capital.	Dividends.	Per cent.
1859........	$20,007,000	$2,851,722	14.25
1860........	20,482,860	2,469,090	12.05
1861........	20,282,860	2,111,788	10.41
1862........	20,432,860	2,043,898	10.00
1863........	23,632,860	2,024,742	8.56
1864..	28,807,070	2,483,370	8.62
1865........	31,557,010	2,621,284	8.30
1866........	30,649,660	2,073,375	6.76
1867........	28,561,232	2,416,354	8.46
Total...$224,413,412		$21,095,628	9.40

—showing a decrease in per centage of average dividends from 14.25 per cent. in 1859, to 6.76 per cent. in 1866, the year of the organization of the Board, and 8.46 per cent. for 1867, the first year of its efficient working, and a general average for the entire nine years of only 9.40 per cent.

We also find that the per centage of losses on net premiums have increased from 42.57 per cent. in 1859 to 76.08 per cent. in 1866, as will be seen from the following table:

Year.	Premium.	Losses.	Per cent.
1859........	$6,299,688	$2,681,986	42.57
1860........	7,261,595	3,984,441	54.87
1861........	6,827,736	3,771,189	55.23
1862........	7,742,190	4,679,823	60.44
1863........	10,181,030	4,189,673	41.15
1864........	15,618,603	8,737,600	55.94
1865........	17,052,086	12,046,793	71.38
1866........	20,786,847	15,812,751	76.08
1867........	22,071,638	14,423,122	65.33
Total...$113,841,418		$69,826,880	61.33

DAMAGES BY REMOVAL.

An " Adjuster," writing to the *Insurance Moni-tor* on this subject, says :

First. As against loss by fire, the underwriter is sole insurer, but for the damages by removal, the owner of the property is co-insurer. It is precisely as if one insurance company insured against loss and damage by fire and damage by removal, and another company insured the same property against damages by removal only. Or it is the same as when one company insured on flour and pork, and another company insured on pork only. The former pays the loss on the flour first, and the balance of its policy contributes with the other policy for the loss on the pork. This rule, I believe, is uniformly conceded and adopted, and it is fully sustained by the Supreme Court of Missouri in case of Augelrodt & Barth *vs.* Delaware Insurance Company. This case was decided in 1862, and seems so conclusive on the point that it has not since been questioned. Bearing in mind that as against damages by re-moval, the owner stands co-insurer, precisely as though he were another insurance company, " Tother side " must be careful about " inverting the order of adjuster's calculation," lest he "hoist by his own petard." Suppose A insures $5,000 against loss and damage by fire and damages by removal, and B insures $5,000 on the same stock against damages by removal only. Value of the stock $10,000. A loss happens by burning, say $4,000, and damages by removal $3,000. Now apply "Totherside's" rule. 1st. A contribut-ing on $5,000, one half $5,000 to the damages by removal. $3,000, one half $1,500, would leave but $3,500 to pay the loss of $4,000 by the burn-ing. But let us look again at the original exam-ple stated, and which is the subject under criti-cism. Here Underwriters had a risk against fire of $5,000, on $10,000 worth of goods. A fire happens, by which $3,000 of the goods are con-sumed; this loss falling wholly on Underwriter. What interest did Underwriter have in the goods saved ? Or how much would his loss have been increased had the whole stock been burned ? Manifestly he had but $2,000 in trust in balance of the stock, whether saved or lost, while the owner had $5,000. There was in fact but $2,000 insurance on the goods saved, except by the owner. The fire itself has settled this. It had first absorbed $3,000 of the policy. Suppose it had all been absorbed by the goods consumed, there certainly would have been nothing left to contribute to the damages by removal. I fail to see the difference in principle, whether the whole or any part of the policy was absorbed by the burning, as only the balance contributes with owner (the co-insurer) on the damages to goods removed, and if there is no balance, the owner, of course, has to stand the whole of the latter damage.

Now, there is no principle of justice in one insurer claiming contribution from his co-insurer, to the prejudice of the assured, unless the contract has some stipulation which renders such result inevitable. But when the contract is silent, it is to be otherwise construed; for two reasons. First, by a well-known rule of law, contracts are to be construed most severely against the parties making them. And, second, the assured has paid for the indemnity for himself, and not for one of the co-insurers. These principles have the same application where the owner of the property stands as co-insurer, as in cases where he is fully covered. But this risk of damages by removal is made by the contract a separate and distinct subject from that of the risk of burning, and is provided for accordingly in the most distinct and explicit manner. The risk of burning is primary, and that of damages by removal is secondary. The primary duty under the policy is, first to be performed, and then the secondary, to the extent of any further indemnity afforded by the policy. In some cases the policy may be wholly absorbed by the first, and in other cases it may be untouched by the first risk and wholly absorbed by the second, but in no case can any claim be sustained beyond the sum underwritten in a fire policy. From a somewhat extended experience and observation, I have come to the conclusion that it would be about as well for underwriters, in the long run, to let the *insured public* settle the rules of adjustment of fire losses, provided they would uniformly live up to them and agree to be satisfied.

Railway News.

Northern Railway.—Traffic receipts for week ending March 20th, 1869.

Passengers	$2,404 37
Freight and live stock	4,920 95
Mails and sundries	212 66
	$7,607 97
Corresponding Week of '68	6,418 74
Increase	$1,189 23

Northern Railway.—Traffic receipts for week ending March 27, 1869:—

Passengers	$2,547 40
Freight	5,554 02
Mails and sundries	190 30
Total receipts for week	$8,291 72
Corresponding week 1868	8,252 15
Increase	$39 57

Great Western Railway.—Traffic for week ending March 12, 1869.

Passengers	$22,257 09
Freight	35,212 46
Mails and Sundries	2,418 67
Total Receipts for week	$59,888 22
Corresponding week, 1868	55,676 15
Increase	$4,212 07

Detroit and Milwaukee Railroad.—The report for the year ending 31st December, 1868, show that the g oss traffic and rents for the year were $1,718,093.72, being $43,244.42 less than those of 1867. The working expenses, taxes and insurance were $1,013,636.06, being $21,116.96 greater than those of 1867. The net revenue is $704,457.66, being $69,395.26 greater than that of 1866, and $64,331.33 less than that of 1867. This has been applied to the interest on the bonded debt existing prior to 1866, $368,685 80 ; in part towards interest on bonds of June 30, 1866, $53,550 ; to sundry discounts and exchanges, $5,670.27 ; to new works and rolling stock, $33,-899 32 ; to rebuilding on account of the fire in April, 1866, $1,571.52 ; to new cars on same account, $93.08 ; to payment for baggage and merchandise consumed in that fire, $20,573,15 : to old debts of the Detroit and Milwaukee Railway Company, for supplies, $3,588.71 ; to redemption of bonds issued to the Commercial Bank of Canada, 30th June, 1866, $100,000 ; and on account of dividend of dividend to Great Western Railway Company of Canada, on preference shares, $73,-325 ; the whole, exclusive of interest and dividend, amounting to $311,725.78 ; and after deducting the amount received for insurance on the steamer *Milwaukee*, less paid for losses of through freight and baggage, being net $36,717.96, to $175,007.82. The balance to credit of net revenue, 31st December, 1867, was $75,210.84, and the balance to credit of that account 31st December, 1868, is $103,429.61.

Mining.

NOVA SCOTIA GOLD FIELDS.

(From Our Own Correspondent.)

HALIFAX, N. S., March 22, 1869.
There is but little progress to report. Messrs. Huse & Lovell omitted a bar of 109 ozs. received from the Uniacke Company's mine in last statement. The Strawberry Hill Company, of Tangier, have sent up a bar of 272 ozs. From Sherbrooke a new lode is reported on the property of the Canada Company. From Wine Harbor a slight falling off for February, through lack of water for the mills, the flumes having frozen. A serious discrepancy occurred in my report published in THE MONETARY TIMES of 4th March, under mill returns for Wine Harbor, having obtained them by deputy, while completing the octennial table for the mail. The mistakes are as follows, and in assuming the blame and apologising for them a repetition of anything of the kind is promised to be guarded against:

	tons.	cwt.	oz.	dwt.	gr.
For Orient Mill	16	0	0	1	7
Read	0	16	0	4	7
For Victoria Mill	120	0	0	10	11
Read	120	10	45	6	11
For total, Wine Harbor	266	5	45	11	6
Read	251	1	88	10	6

In the table for 1860 to 1868, the fraction under "daily average number of miners" should have read "twelfths" instead of "two years."

To future communications will be added, in turn, a descriptive as well as statistical review of each district, so that the current volume of the MONETARY TIMES will present a complete record of the most interesting data from the mining region.

Remarkable Mountain of Salt.—In the Pahranagat District, in the southeastern part of the State of Nevada—distant from Austin, estimated at 180 miles—is a remarkable mountain of salt, about 70 miles—south of the mines. It is reported to be about five miles in length and 600 feet in height. The body of salt is of unknown depth. It is chemically pure and crystalline, and does not deliquesce on exposure to the atmosphere. Like rock, it requires blasting from the mines, whence it is taken in large blocks, and is transpa-

rent as glass. This would afford an abund supply to the world, could it be cheaply mined transported ; but it now stands in the wilderne an object for the admiration of the curious a the inspection of the scientific. It is believe that there is but one other place on the globe wh it exits in such a state of purity in workable qu tities, and that is at Cracow, Poland. This but another evidence of the state of purity, which the force of nature has left her deposits this interesting portion of the continent.

OTTAWA BOARD OF TRADE.

In the report of this Board for 1868, the follo ing paragraph in reference to the banking syst and other matters are of interest :—

"The Committee on banking are of the opin that the present Canadian system of Banking based upon sound principles and has worked su successfully in developing the resources, and c rying out the business of the country, and th would deplore any legislation that would cur the privileges of the Banks as they exist at p sent. The Committee think that they are t called upon to enter more fully into the questi as they are happy to find that the Government determined to submit the whole question to a P liamentary Committee, and they trust the res will be to establish on a permanent footing, present system which so largely enjoys the co dence of the community.

The Committee beg to report that in view of fact the Parliamentary Committee is now sitt on the insolvent laws, and that the Governm have taken steps to elicit the opinions of the Boa of Trade, and others having practical experie of the working of the law, do not deem it nec sary to offer any suggestions, but would expre hope that the result of the deliberations of par ment will be the enactment of a more perfect satisfactory law.

The "Act to facilitate the winding up of In vent Companies" was brought under the notic the Council, when it was resolved that the foll ing amendments were necessary, viz., in sub-tion 1 of clause 5, after the words Company in first line "against lands" be added ; and in a section 2 of same the words "provided that w any Company shall be able to appropriate 10 cent over its working expenses towards paym of interest and sinking fund on its debt—or w ever a sufficient sum is realized to pay legal in est on its debts, and its plant and property s sufficient security to the creditors shall be exe from the operations of the provision of sub-see 3 of clause 4."

Insolvents.—The following appeared in Gazette of the 24th :—

Charles Banting, Tecumseth ; Wm. Hill, C wall ; Ammon Powell, Fenelon Township ; V Torrence, jr. Guelph ; William Steward, Toro George French, Harriston ; Henry Penford, P John A. Robinson, Milton ; Joseph Bentl Belleville ; Wellby McAlister, Brantford ; Da Ias Gonek, Guelph ; Thomas McCormick, Ba C. McGrory, jr. Prescott ; Alexander Smith, P hill ; George Rankin, Windsor ; Thomas Dun Walkerton ; Aaron Reynolds, Woodstock ; field Dorwin and R. Gault, Montreal ; J. C. W. Bond, Walkerton ; Samuel McNeil, Corn George Humphries, Ottawa ; William Camp Goderich ; James Armstrong, Toronto ; Frea Warrick, Toronto ; Patley Ayre, Lindsay ; T Levallee, jr. Quebec ; Forest, Brothers, Que Damien Hernult, Montreal ; Thomas Addie, burg ; John Ford, Prescott ; William Smith, bert Edminston and Hugh Mathewson, Moat James Mitchell, Petrolia ; David Richards, Fly ton ; Angus Sutherland, Montreal ; Geo. Mu Tilsonburg; Peddie and Bayley, Woodstock; C Warner, Napanee ; Rueben Hurlbut, Whitby McKinnon and Charles Augustus Clark, Bellev F. X. Lapage, Quebec; Alphonso De Celles, John.

E CANADIAN MONETARY TIMES AND INSU-
E CHRONICLE is printed every Thursday even-
nd distributed to Subscribers on the following
ing.

blishing office, No. 60 Church-street, 3 doors
of Court-street.

scription price—

anada $2.00 per annum.

England, stg. 10s. per annum.

nited States (U.S.Cy.) $3.00 per annum.

nual advertisements will be charged at the rate
. cents per line, each insertion.

dress all letters to "THE MONETARY TIMES."

ques, money orders, &c. should be made pay-
) J. M. TROUT, Business Manager, who alone
horized to issue receipts for money.

All Canadian Subscribers to THE MONETARY
s will receive THE REAL ESTATE JOURNAL
ut further charge.

e Canadian Monetary Times.

THURSDAY, APRIL 1, 1869.

E BANK CHARTER QUESTION.

ARRASSMENT DURING THE TRANSITION
PERIOD.

V.

every country there is a certain relation
en the business to be done and the
nt of money necessary to do it with.
that amount ought to be, experience
can determine. For if we could arrive
transactions of a community in which
y plays a part—which is impossible—it
l form no guide to the amount of money
ed, since so much depends upon the
ty of circulation, and the number of
.ctions which any given number of pieces
tal money or bank bills may be used to
mmate. But where there is a mixed
.cy, of specie and bank notes, and where
is no great variation in the aggregate
.t at a given season of the year, it is
. assume that that amount represents
nal condition of the currency. The
.tion of the various banks in the Domi-

nion, at the end of January last, may be
taken as the average circulation. At that
period there had been neither speculation on
the one hand, nor on the other depression—
nothing to give undue inflation or enforced
contraction to the currency.

In view of the impending legislation for
the renewal of the bank charters, and
on the subject of the currency, the bank
returns made up to the 31st January may be
studied to advantage. They may be presented under three different aspects : we may
take the entire return, or we may take the
returns for the Banks of Ontario proper by
themselves, or we may take the latter with
an addition of two banks, which, though they
are not Ontario banks, are, nevertheless,
doing considerable business in this Province:
the Bank of British North America and the
Merchants Bank.

The enquiry will be more exhaustive, and
present the question in a fuller light, if we
view the returns in these various aspects ;
and we shall do so for the purpose of showing what would be the effect on the circulation of a compulsory extension of the Provincial notes, so as to supersede the existing
circulation of bank notes, or by the adoption
in this country, substantially, of the national
banking system of the United States. In
either case the banks would have to make an
advance to the government, which would
really be in the nature of a forced loan, of
an amount of capital equivalent to their
future circulation. It is obvious that so
long as the requirement of specie payment
was kept up, so radical a change in the constitution of our banks would press heavily
on their resources, and greatly curtail their
general usefulness. . In what way, and to
what possible extent, this could be done, we
now propose to consider, taking the bank returns for our guide.

At present the banks are required to hold
a limited amount of government securities.
In either of the alternative schemes above
named they would be required to deposit
with the government, securities to the full
amount of their circulation. Let us see what
the difference would be between the amount
of securities they now hold and what they
would then be required to deposit. The circulation of the banks on the 31st January
was $9,720,253, and they held government
securities to the amount of $3,352,016. To
enable them to maintain their present circulation they would have to extend their purchase of securities by $7,340,282. Those
securities would have to be purchased with
go d, bills of exchange, or something else
equivalent in value to gold. But it is obvious that the banks could not bear so great
a strain on their resources as this enforced
loan, wrapt up in another and less odious

name, would demand. They would not find
it convenient to buy between seven and eight
millions of additional government securities,
and they would have to content themselves
with a much less amount. As the amount
of the securities they deposited would, with
those they already possess, be the measure
of their future circulation, it is evident that
an unnatural contraction of the currency
would take place, from which the business
of the country would seriously suffer.

From this general view let us descend to
the Provincial aspect of the question. By
far the largest part of the circulation of the
Dominion is to be found in Ontario. The
Ontario banks alone circulate over five millions of notes (5,018,607). These banks hold
among them $692,639 in government securi-
ties. The difference between their circulation
and the securities they hold is therefore $4,-
325,968. That is the amount they would,
under either of the schemes in question, have
to advance to the government for the privilege of maintaining a circulation equal to
that which they now sustain. Their present
investment in government securities is but
slightly over the requirement of ten per cent.
of their paid-up capital ; while under either
of the alternative schemes we are discussing
they would be obliged to loan to the government considerably over four-sixths of their
entire capital. Whatever amount they fell
short of that point would be deducted from
their future circulation. It would probably
not be too much to say that such a requirement would reduce their circulation by one-
half: a circulation which rests on a specie
basis, and in which the notes are maintained
at par with gold for which they can any day
be exchanged.

There are no means of arriving precisely
at the circulation, in Ontario, of the Merchants' Bank, and the Bank of British North
America, but it is considerable, and this Province would suffer through them, as well as
our own local banks, if the changes in question were made.

The contraction of currency thus artificially superinduced, would, by an inevitable
law, produce a fall in prices. Every producer would get less for the results of his
labor ; industry would be discouraged and
production would suffer a diminution. There
being less to sell, and lower prices for what
was sold, foreign bills of exchange—unless
importations were correspondingly · diminished—would be scarce and dear ; thus while
we got less for our produce we should have to
buy imported articles at a dearer rate. The
country would lose at both ends by the unnatural contraction of the currency operating
through a forced loan which would have been
made under false pretences.

FOREIGN MARINE COMPANIES.

The Underwriters Association has raised the question whether foreign marine insurance companies, which have not made a deposit under the Act, have the right to accept premiums here and issue policies from the other side of the lines, or to evade the law by doing inland marine business under the name of ocean marine. The Act says: "Except companies transacting in Canada "ocean marine insurance business exclusively, it shall not be lawful for any "insurance company to issue any policy of "insurance, or take any risk or receive any "premium, or transact any business of in-"surance in Canada, etc., without first "obtaining a license from the Minister of "Finance." It is provided that this license shall issue on a certain deposit being made, in the case of an inland marine company not less than fifty thousand dollars, or proper securities. Any person who delivers any policy of insurance, or collects any premium, or transacts any business of insurance on behalf of a company which has not complied with the law is liable to a penalty of one thousand dollars for each offense, or in default of payment to imprisonment for three months.

The wording of the Act is certainly extensive enough to embrace cases such as those complained of by the Underwriters' Association, and it is the duty of the proper authorities at Ottawa to take prompt measures to save marine companies that have made a deposit from the unfair competition of companies that have not done so. It is little to the credit of respectable foreign marine companies that they allow themselves to be drawn through the mire of evasion and trickery for the sake of the premiums they get here, and we scarcely think that the head offices are aware of the dishonor thus brought upon companies otherwise unimpeachable. Large and wealthy companies should be above the meanness of stealing business in this manner.

THE MONEY MARKET.

A marked change is observable in the condition of our local money market within the past fortnight. The demand for money has greatly increased, absorbing a large portion of the surplus seeking investment. Building Societies, and companies whose business is chiefly with the country districts, now find ready borrowers for all the cash they have at their command. The demand in this way has been larger than for some years past. Some farmers are, we understand, so foolish as to borrow money in preference to selling their live stock and the produce of their farms at the present reduced prices. The rate on mortgages in the open market is firmer, and in many cases from one-half to one per cent. advance on the ruling rate for a long time past (8 per cent) has been readily conceded on good mortgages. This change is no doubt, to a very great extent, the result of the adoption of a more conservative policy by wholesale merchants. Confidence has been somewhat shaken, resulting in an inclination rather to reduce credits than to increase sales, and the consequent pressure brought on country merchants for payment, has caused them to borrow or to compel their creditors to do so, in order to pay their accounts.

Western Assurance Company.—We have seen a statement of the business of this Company for the half year, ending the 31st December, 1868. During that period the premium receipts amounted to $145,617; and the total expenditure including losses, reassurances, and an estimate of the claims under adjustment at the end of the year, footed up to $111,021, leaving a balance in favor of the Company of $34,596. The net assets at the end of the year were $186,059 exclusive of unpaid capital, and these figures have been, as appears from the Company's books, considerably increased within the three months of the present year. $50,000 have been deposited with the Government in compliance with the provisions of the Insurance Act. The premium receipts are now at the rate of $300,000 per annum. We are glad to state on the authority of the management, that the Company's shares have appeared once more in the market; transfers at 50 occurred some time since, and we learn that there are now buyers at an advance on that quotation.

North British and Mercantile.—In alluding to the annual report of this Company last week, some inaccuracies and misplacement of figures occurred. These would be readily detected on reference to the Report itself, but to prevent misapprehension we desire to make a few corrections. We desired to direct attention to the fact that an increase of £81,559 had occurred in the net fire premiums over last year, and the gross fire premiums for 1868 amounted to no less a sum than £491,288 19s. 11d. The losses by fire were £222,792 14s., or a little over 45 per cent. of the gross premiums in the fire department. Out of last year's fire premiums £134,515 were reserved to meet losses on unexpired fire policies of that year.

In the Life Department 908 new policies were issued, assuring £738,582 and producing in new premiums £23,574. The Company's assets now amount to fully fourteen millions of dollars, and the annual revenue from all sources is nearly four millions of dollars.

—Dr. Guy R. Phelps, President of the Connecticut Mutual Life Insurance Company, died at his residence, in the city of Hartford, on Thursday, March 18.

Financial.

TORONTO STOCK MARKET.

(Reported by Pellatt & Osler, Brokers.)

The Easter Holidays have interfered to some extent with the business of the week. There has been very little change in quotations and stocks generally closed firm.

Bank Stock.—Montreal has again advanced with sales at 143 and 143¼; there are no sellers now under 144. There are buyers of British at 104¾ and sellers at 105½. Very little doing in Ontario; there are sellers at par and buyers at 99¼. Buyers would give 120 for Toronto, but there are no sellers under 121½. Holders ask 80 for Royal Canadian but buyers will not advance over 78. Small sales of Commerce were made at 103, at which rate it is still procurable. Sales of Gore took place at 41. There were sales of Merchants in the beginning of the week at 107, but it has since advanced, there are no sellers now under 108. Buyers offer 100¼ for Quebec, no sellers. Small sales of City occurred at 102½ to 102¾, sellers now ask 103. Du Peuple is held at 108½ with buyers at 107½. For Jacques Cartier 109 would be paid but holders ask 109¼. Buyers offer 97 for Mechanics. Sellers want 105½ for Union with buyers at 104¾. In other banks nothing to report.

Debentures.—Canada currency and sterling six per cents and Dominion stock are in great demand at quotations; five per cents are offering at 94½. No Toronto in market, they could be readily placed to pay 6¾c. interest. County have been sold to some extent during the week.

Sundries.—Buyers offer 108 for City Gas, little offering. There are buyers of British America Assurance at 55 and sellers at 56. Sales of Canada Permanent Building Society were made at 126 at which rate it is still procurable. Western Canada Permanent Building Society is offered at 121½ with buyers at 121. There is but little Freehold Building Society in market, buyers offer 110¼. Montreal Telegraph nominal as quoted. There are buyers of Canada Landed Credit at 77; very little in market. Mortgages have been freely dealt in at 8, 8½ and in some cases 9 per cent. Money is in demand, and advanced rates are paid.

QUEBEC CITY FINANCES.

The citizens of the ancient capital appear to be somewhat disturbed at the prospect of having to pay a special income tax. Since 1859, the City debt has been increasing without a proportionate increase of revenue. During the next eight years $2,325,194 of debentures have to be provided for; of these $809,021 mature in 1870. It is stated that the arrears of assessment and special tax uncollected on the 31st December, 1868, amounted to $255,116 55, and it is also alleged that within the last twelve months a small amount of the city debentures could not find a purchaser unless at a sacrifice of about ten per cent., although yielding seven per cent. interest, and having only five years to run. Such a state of affairs naturally begets anxiety on the part of those who expect to bear a share in relieving the city from the burden of debt which it has taken on its shoulders. Some advocate the appointment of three Commissioners whose duty it shall be to take the place of the City Council in the administration of civic affairs. The justification for such a move is proved in the following summary:—

"The imminent danger of civic bankruptcy the reckless disregard and contempt of all legislative enactments shown for years by the Council their utter incapacity or persistent and ruinous neglect to collect the revenue of the city; their continually recurring applications to Parliament for additional powers of taxation; the evidences of gross departmental mismanagement, which are periodically coming to light; and, finally, the absolute necessity of confiding the management ntrol of civic affairs, for a few years, to the ded attention of men not only of integrity, financial ability, prudence and experience.

THE NATIONAL BANK SYSTEM WORKS. first National Bank of Rockford, Illinois, rted in June, 1864. Its capital stock was 0, owned almost entirely by two parties. ckford *Register*, says : Early in 1865, Mr. resigned the cashiership in consequence of bility to reconcile his ideas of sound bank- h those of the principal owner. George W. n succeeded Mr. Griggs, and continued to der up to the time of his sudden disap- 2e. The bank was, some time after the in the cashiership, visited by J. H. Dun- f Chicago, National Bank Examiner for trict, who found such a condition as in his nt to justify the Government in winding and he so reported to Mr. Clark. Comp- of the Currency. No action was taken by nptroller, and he and his successor, Mr. d, were afterwards frequently notified by nham that the bank was in an unsound on, and should be wound up. Secretary ooh was also in possession of the same in- on, but no action was taken by the officials the concern. Mr. Dunham finally re- his office on account of the neglect of the ment to act upon his recommendation.— the last few months the bank has been l as in an unsafe condition, but as in for- es the recommendations of the examiner sregarded, and the bank allowed to con- On Monday evening of last week the cashier city, ostensibly for the purpose of visiting , to raise funds for the bank, and the next doors were closed. S. B. Scott, of Mil- , examiner, took possession immediately, nd the entire assets in the vault footed up an dollars in postal currency ! Everything l been abstracted. It is difficult to ascer- . liabilities of the bank, but it is believed ey will scarcely fall below $100,000.

BNATIONAL COINAGE.—A bill was intro- nto Congress last summer to establish an ional metrical system of coinage, which mitted by the Secretary of the Treasury to Elliot, for examination. This gentleman. reported favorably upon it, and it may y shortly become law :—"The bill pro- First, That the future gold coinage of the States shall weigh one and two-thirds s to the dollar, and shall be nine-tenths hat is, each dollar shall contain one and a umes of pure gold, and the remainder alloy. Second, Such coins shall be legal in payments after a specified future date, 003 of this new coinage shall be the legal nt of $1,000 of the old coinage of the States. Third, That they shall have their in grammes and fineness stamped upon Fourth, That silver half-dollars and smaller oins shall, in future coinage, consist of l silver, nine-tenths fine, and weigh twenty mmes to each dollar of value ; and shall ir weight and fineness stamped upon them; ll be legal tender for payment of all sums eeding ten dollars." Were this act in ope- the following gold coins would be equiva- each other.—viz., three German Union twenty American dollars, one hundred francs, four English sovereigns.

e St. John *Telegraph*, says of the finances Brunswick : It appears then that, throw- of the accounts the items of income and ture properly belonging to the previous ar or years, and also eliminating from them i both sides not belonging to the regular ial income and expenditure, such as Rail- nstruction and Railway subsidies, &c., per Provincial Revenue for the year ....$442,341 nding Expenditure.................. 412,055 ....$30,286

Law Report.

MORTGAGE INTEREST.

A mortgagor's interest is in the property, so long as his right of redemption continues. Even after he has sold the property subject to the mort- gage, he will still retain an insurable interest, as he is still liable to the mortgagee for any injury that may occur to the mortgaged estate, and thus diminish its value as security. When a mort- gagor insures in his own right, and assigns the policy to the mortgagee as security, or makes the policy payable in case of loss to the mortgagee, then the underwriter is subrogated to the mort- gagee's securities.

The assignment of a part of a mortgage debt secured by insurance, will not void the policy as to the balance.

In answer to a question in the application as to incumbrance upon the property, the amount as then existing was stated. An additional mort- gage was subsequently executed, and an existing policy assigned as collateral security therefor, held : that the execution of the latter mortgage, without notice to the company, did not avoid the policy.

The sale of mortgaged property by a master of chancery, under a foreclosure, terminates the in- terest of the mortgagor, though no deed has yet been executed.

A mortgagor's insurable interest is not affected by the fact that the mortgage exceeds the value of the property.

A mortgagor, whose equity of redemption has been seized on execution, may recover the entire value of the building, not exceeding the sum in- sured.

THE MORTGAGEE.

The mortgagee's interest is in the debt secured by the policy. He must possess an equitable in- terest when the insurance is effected and when the loss occurs. If a mortgagee insures with his own funds, for his own exclusive benefit, the in- surance money paid on the loss is not in discharge of the mortgage ; but, he if insures at the request of, and for the benefit of the mortgagor as well as himself, the money paid is in discharge of the indebtedness.

When the interest of a mortgagee is insured by himself, the underwriters, in case of loss, on pay- ing the mortgage debt, are entitled to subroga- tion of the securities.

The holder of a mortgage for the purchase money may insure for his whole interest ; and is not bound to look to the land for its value ; the underwriters being entitled to subrogation on payment of the loss under the policy.

A policy of insurance, assigned as collateral security for the payment of a mortgaged debt, is subject to all the express stipulations of the policy ; and is liable to be avoided in the hands of the assignee by any subsequent breach of the conditions of the policy by the assignor, though the assignment may have been duly assented to by the insurers.

A lien upon property creates no lien upon any policy held by others upon such property ; hence the mortgagee has no claims upon a policy of the mortgagor upon the mortgaged property, nor can the mortgagee insure the property of the mort- gagor.

The purchase of property already subject to mortgage for debt, exceeding its value, has no in- surable interest therein, unless he has assumed the payment of the debt.

Whether the interest of a mortgagee in property as security for a debt, is insured generally or specifically, he can recover only to the extent of that interest.

Notwithstanding the form of the contract, a mortgagee insures—not the ultimate safety of the whole property—but only so much thereof as may be enough to satisfy his mortgage. It is not the

specific property that is insured, but its capacity to pay the debt.

The insurance of an exclusively mortgage in- terest is not upon the property, but is simply a guaranty of the payment of the debt, in case of loss of the security by fire. In this case the underwriter becomes subrogated to the security.

If a policy of insurance against fire be assigned to a mortgagee, with consent of the insurers, the assignee can recover, in case of loss, only where the assignor could have done so, had no assign- ment been made. Such assignment does not change the policy into one of indemnity to the assignee ; the interest of the mortgor is alone covered by it.

If the owner of an insured mortgage interest part with any of his securities, or if a portion of the mortgage claim to be paid before loss, the underwriter is only liable for the amount remain- ing unpaid. But if the insured parts with a por- tion of his securities, or receives a part of the claim after suit is commenced against the under- writer, it does not affect the case.

When the mortgagor effected insurance in his own name, and assigned the policy to mortgagee with consent of the underwriter, and the latter recovered from the company more than enough to pay his debt : held, that as to the balance, he was trustee for the mortgagor.

It is not competent for the underwriter, in order to diminish or defeat recovery by the in- sured, to show that the mortgaged premises, not- withstanding the loss, are still ample security for the debt.

CONDITION REQUIRING PARTICULAR ACCOUNT OF LOSS.—One of the conditions of the policy in this case required the insured within thirty days after loss "to deliver in a particular account of such loss or damage, signed by their own hand and verified by their oath or affirmation, and by their books of account or other proper vouchers." The plaintiff sent in his affidavit, stating in gen- eral terms the value of the different kinds of goods destroyed, but without in any way mentioning his loss on the buildings insured, the mere statement as to them being that they had been totally de- stroyed, and without verifying his deposition by account books or other proper vouchers. *Held*, the following Greaves vs. Niagara District Mutual Insurance Company, 25 U. C. 127, clearly, no compliance with the condition, and a non-suit was therefore ordered to be entered.—*Carter* v. *Niagara District Mut. Ins. Co.*

DIFFERENT SUBJECTS OF INSURANCE AT SEPA- RATE AMOUNTS ; CONSTRUCTION OF POLICY.—A policy insuring several different subject of insu- rance at separate amounts, and containing a pro- vision that "the Company shall be liable to pay the insured two-thirds of all such loss or damage by fire as shall happen to the property, amount- ing to no more in the whole than the aggregate of the amounts insured, and to no more on any of the different properties than two-thirds of the actual cash value of each at the time of the loss, and not exceeding on each the sum it is insured for," is to be treated as a separate insurance upon each subject of insurance, and therefore the Com- pany is liable only for two-thirds of the loss on each subject, notwithstanding that on some of the subjects the loss is less than the amount for which those subjects are insured and notwith- standing that the whole loss is less than the ag- gregate amount insured.—*King* v. *the Prince Ed- ward County Mutual Ins. Co.*

FITZGERALD VS. GORE DISTRICT MUTUAL INSURANCE COMPANY.—At the Hamilton As- sizes this action was brought on trial.— Plaintiffs, in 1865, insured property in Guelph in the above Company to the amount of $1,000. Plaintiff afterwards mortgaged the property to a party named Newton for the amount of $1,000, to whom he transfered the po- licy—notifying the Insurance Company of the same. The property was afterwards accidentally destroyed by fire, and defendants claim that assessments made by them were unpaid and in arrears, and that after the transfer of the policy, defendants had nothing to do with plaintiff ; plaintiff set up that a by-law had been adopted by the Company, extending the time of levying assessments, but that it had never been enforced, and he was unaware that they were levied monthly.

After the examination of two witnesses for the plaintiff and one for defendants, His Lordship ordered a nonsuit, with leave to enter a verdict for $1,000 if it was proved by law, he was entitled to recover.

Commercial.

Toronto Market.

The prevailing feeling in business circles is still one of dullness, though we think there are signs of an improvement. There is still a lack of confidence, which tends greatly to restrict business. Money is also closer under an increased demand. We are not disposed at all to take a gloomy view of the incoming season's business. The present stringency is largely due to the detention of produce by the farmers, which should have been exchanged for money, and which would ere this have passed into the hands of the country merchants and thence to the wholesale trade. But as this produce is still in the country it has yet to come out, and when it moves a healthy reaction will ensue. This must come at some time within the next three months at the farthest. We are inclined to think that though present appearances are not flattering, the spring trade will at least compare favorably with the winter trade, and probably exceed the anticipations now generally formed of it.

GROCERIES.—A good business has been done in sugars and teas at steady prices. Other articles quiet.

HARDWARE.—Tin keeps firm and our quotations are fully maintained. As a sign of progress we may mention that Messrs. Lyman & McNab, one of our best firms, have removed from their old premises on King street to a new and most eligible business site on Front street. The steady expansion of the business of this house required better facilities, and these are amply secured at the new establishment.

GRAIN.—Wheat—Receipts for the week, 1,460 bushels, and 7,140 last week. There is a better feeling in the market, though the amount of business done was very moderate. Spring is firmer ; there is a good enquiry for May delivery at 95c, and at 90c to 92c on the spot ; holders are asking 95c to 97c for cargo lots ; no sales reported. Fall is held at about $1.05 f.o.b., but is dull ; there is some enquiry, and probably good samples could be placed at $1.00. Barley—Receipts, 500 bush., and 900 bush. last week. Barley is dull, and offering at $1.20 to $1.25, without buyers. Peas —Receipts, 500 bush., and —— bush. last week. There is a considerable amount offering, and cars are selling at 70c to 75c, but there is not much demand. Oats—Receipts light. They are in good demand at 50c on the track. Rye—Selling on the street at 60c to 65c. Seeds—Clover is dull ; holders ask $6.25 to $6.50, with buyers of small lots at $5.75 to $6. Timothy is in fair demand at $2 to $2.50 ; held at $2.25 to $2.75. Flax, $2 to $2.25.

FLOUR—Receipts 1,026 brls., and 1,300 brls. last week. The market is firmer, owing to advices of an improvement in England ; No. 1 Superfine is held at $4.10 to $4.15, with buyers at $4 to $4.05; no sales reported. Fancy, nominal. Extra has been taken pretty freely for export at $4.40 to $4.50; the market closing nominal at these prices. Sales—1,000 brls. Extra, at $4.40 f.o.b. cars at Malton; 500 brls. at $4.47 f.o.b. cars here, and 500 brls. at $4.50 f.o.b. cars here.

PROVISIONS.—Butter—Is a little easier under good receipts, a small lot choice tub sold at 24½c.

and another lot at 25c. ; ordinary neglected. Dressed Hogs—Receipts light, a small business done at quotations. Pork—Mess in light stock, not much demand, it is worth $26 in lots. Bacon—Stocks have run low, retail lots selling at quotations. Hams—A lot of good smoked sold at 13½c. Cheese—Firm and in light supply. Eggs—Are still high but must soon drop.

FREIGHTS.—Rates by Grand Trunk Railway:— Flour to all stations from Belleville to Lynn, inclusive, 35c., grain per 100 lbs. 18c. ; flour to Brockville and Cornwall, inclusive, 43c. grain 22c. flour to Montreal 50c. grain 25c. ; flour to all stations between Island Pond and Portland, inclusive, 85c. grain 43c. ; flour to Boston 90c., gold, grain 45c.; flour to Halifax 98c., grain —c; flour to St. John 98c. Boxed Meats to Liverpool per gross ton 32s. 6d.; lard or butter in tinnets 37s. 6d.; Pork 11s. per tierce; flour 4s. 6d. per barrel ; grain 12s. per 480 pounds. Rates by Great Western Railway—Flour, Toronto to Suspension Bridge 25c. gold ; thence to New York, 92c. U. S. currency per bbl. ; to Boston $1.02. Grain to Bridge 13c., gold; thence to New York 46c, U. S. currency; to Boston 51c. Grain, Toronto to Detroit, 18c. per 100 lbs; flour 35c per bbl.

Demerara Sugar Market.

The following is from Sandbach, Parker & Co.'s Market Report, dated Georgetown, 23rd Feb., 1869 :—

We have had an active fortnight for business. Imports have been in excess, and prices have, in most instances, favored buyers. The transactions have been on a large scale, and our markets have presented more animation than for some time past. The arrivals consist of five vessels from United Kingdom, ten from United States, thirteen from British Provinces, and fifteen from neighbouring Colonies.

SUGARS.—An active demand, and but little offering, has forced up prices. Many vessels are detained for want of Sugars, and we confidently look forward to higher rates being paid. Vacuum Pans of the best grades are scarce, and when offered for sale the competition is very keen. Muscovado values have also advanced, but the offerings for the fortnight have not exceeded 100 hhds., and for these outside quotations have not been given.

MOLASSES.—The inquiry is active, and both Vacuum Pan and Muscovado are sought after at the extreme limits of anything like good quality.

RUM—Has been weaker with us, and about 100 puns. have been reported sold from 46c to 48c.

SUGARS (package included) sold by 100 lbs. Dutch, 10 per cent. tare.

Muscavadoes, equal to No. 8)		In hhds.
Dutch Standard 4½c 1¢ 100 lbs.		of about
No. 10 do. $4.25 "		1800 lbs. each.
" 12 do. $4.75 "		
Vacuum Pan No. 12 do. $5.50		
" " 14 do. 5.75		
" " 16 do. 6.00		
" " 17 do. 6.20		
" " 18 do. 6.40		

MOLASSES (package included, sold by Imperial gallon.)

Muscovado, from 23 @ 26 cents, as to color and density	In puns
Vacuum Pan from 27 @ 32 cents, as to color and density	of 100 gals.
RUM (colored, package included, sold by Imperial gal. from 35 per cent, @ 38 overproof 40 @ 45 cents. From 38 per cent. @ 40 overproof, 45 @ 50 cents.	Ditto.

Halifax Market.

BREADSTUFFS.—March 23.—We have to report a concession of 5c. to 10c. per barrel on last week's quotations. The demand for Supers. continues, holders offering at $5.65, accepting $5.60. The demand for White Wheat, Extra and Fancy, has been very limited, buyers rejecting them even at a reduced rate. Oatmeal continues without

any demand, and large stocks. Corn Meal declined still further, lots having changed hands at $4 for K. D. White Beans, at Auction week, realized $2 per 60 lbs. for good new.

White Wheat Extra (Fall) $6.50 to $6 Fancy $6.10 to $6.25. Bakers' Strong $5.7 $5.90. Supers. $5.60 to $5.65. No. 2, $5 to $5.75. Middlings $1.25 to $4.50. Rye $4 $3.90. Oatmeal $7.00.

PROVISIONS.—We notice no change in P declined still further as regards to P transactions are very limited, dealers looking ward to more liberal receipts from Outport opening of navigation. Beef is still dull and changed. Butter more active at advanced r Lard in request. Cheese inactive, stocks lig

WEST INDIA PRODUCE.—We note the sal several cargoes of Molasses at 42c. to 42½ for C fuegos, being about 4c. advance on former s There still exists a diversity of opinion as to sent prices, and dealers are unwilling to ope largely, and hold off for lower figures. Sugar unchanged, receipts particularly of Cuba cont very light. Rum unchanged, without tran tions. Coffee inactive.

EXCHANGE.—Bank Drafts London at 60 at 13 per cent. Montreal sight 4 per cent. York Gold 4 per cent. Currency 19 per cent. St. John, N. B., 3 per cent. prem.—R. C. Ho ton & Co's. Circular.

The Sugar Duties.

The following order in Council is passed; d the 25th inst., on recommendation of the Min of Customs : From and after this date there be allowed for tare on sugar imported in heads, 12 per cent., and in tierces 14 per cen the gross weight of each; and on barrels an al ance of 26 pounds each; on bags in which sug imported an average tare shall be allowed, t ascertained by weighing one bag out of every If in any case objection is taken to the a scale of allowances for tare, then the actual according to the original invoice may be allo subject, however, to such examination, eith actual weighing or appraisement, as may thought necessary by the Collector of the to prove that the actual weight of the packa not less than that stated in such invoice.

Pork Packing for 1868-9.

The Cincinnati Price Current publishes its plate figures of the packing of the season closed, which compares with its figures for past two seasons, as follows:—

States.	1868-9.	1847-8.	Hogs cut up.
Ohio 544,561	562,955	55	
Illinois 806,633	1,068,495	1,07	
Indiana......... 326,638	321,588	32	
Iowa...........126,835	182,944	17	
Wisconsin 207 1-2	207 1-6	164,958	16
Missouri 361,067	333,111	32	
Kentucky......183,426	157,880	15	

Totals 2,477,264   2,792,032   2,7 Or 325,668 less than last season; and 304,1 than the season before.

The average weight and average yield per hog, compare for two years, as follows:

	Av. weight per hog.		Av. yield	
	1868-9.	1867-8.	1868-9.	
Ohio 224 1-2	204 1-2	24 5-8	2	
Illinois 202 4.5	205 5-8	23 5-7	2	
Indiana.....205 1-4	202 3-8	23 5-8	2	
Kentucky...207 1-2	207 1-6	24 1-2	2	
Missouri ...206 1-2	198 7-9	23 3-8	2	
Iowa 201 1-2	196 1-4	22	2	
Wisconsin..211	189 3-4	24	1	

The general average according to the Price rent is 206¾ lbs. and 24½ lbs. lard, against 20 211 lbs. last season, and 235 1-7 and 29½ lb previous season.

Taking the average given above as a basi virtual decrease from last season in the nu of hogs packed is given as 244,901 hogs c of the season of 1867-8, and the actual in the yield of lard—other than head and 4,781 lbs.

otal number of hogs packed in the West, of the last twenty years, is given by the errent as follows:—

No. Hogs.	Year.	No. Hogs
....1,652,290	1859-60	2,355,832
....1,432,867	1860-61	1,156,302
....1,182,846	1861-62	2,803,636
....2,201,110	1862-63	 3,069,526
....2,534,779	1863-64	3,261,100
....2,124,404	1864-65	2,422,775
....2,489,592	1865-66	1,705,955
....1,818,498	1866-67	2,781,450
....2,219,787	1867-68	2,792,032
....2,465,552	1868-69	2,477,264

The Salt Mines of Cracow.

d, as every one knows; was formerly an in-nt sovereignty, existing from an early date. int its ancient territory is divided between Prussia and Austria. The city of Cracow, residence of its kings, now belongs to the wer, though the products of the celebrated es of the region are shared with the two in certain proportions stipulated by the f partition. These salt mines, the most d in the world, are situated about eight m the city of Cracow, having their mouth ipal entrance in the pleasant village of ta, which lies on the slope of a wooded i is very picturesque. The superintend-he mines reside here, and their dwellings, with the government offices and large ues for salt, occupy a pretty eminence, conspicuous from a distance. A great ople from various countries visit these re-e excavations, and are well rewarded for ouble. Every year for many centuries hav-al to their depth and extent, these mines of immense and almost inconceivable mag-In order to visit them the traveller must a permit from the government, which is one, the proper officer being on the spot. ning or square shaft, through which the is made is covered by a building or office ; the visitor is dressed in a long, coarse, ouse, to protect his clothing while under

A door is opened, and he goes down by receded by boys who carry lamps, only to te darkness more visible. Or, if he is so l, he can descend by the windlass and ropes ed in the centre of the shaft. More fre-visitors descend by the stairways and come ne ropes. No salt is seen for a depth of an two hundred feet ; then the veins be-ppear in a bed of clay and limestone.—st further down the stairs terminate, and is everywhere ; nothing but salt ; over-ider foot, on every side are dark grey masses salt, whose points and surfaces sparkle in p light. Galleries now branch off in all us. Lights twinkle, and groups of laborers hacking the floors or removing in wheel-blocks that have already been cut out.—on through one of these galleries, a chapel el, which is only the first and oldest of partments thus designated, differing only nd decorations. It is called the Chapel of hony, and is supported by columns of salt quarrying the solid rock. It has an altar, statutes of saints large as life, and all of t. The air in this part of the mines, near ace, is much more moist than that of the ixcavations, so that the process of dissolv-s on slowly, and in consequence some of atutes of salt are gradually losing their The head of one is nearly gone, the limbs her, while deep furrows are observable in laces upon their bodies, making them pre-ery grotesque appearance when lighted up ibition. The smoke of the torches and added to the dampness of the air, blackens ace of all objects not recently cut, so that atutes might be mistaken for black mar-

ble. Onward and downward goes the visitor, through halls, chambers, tunnels innumerable.—Stairs descend lower and lower, and similar apart-ments reappear, till he loses all sense of distance or direction ; blindly following his conductors, who point out, from time to time, localities or ob-jects of peculiar interest, where all is surpassingly wonderful. Everything is solid salt, except where some insecure roof is supported by huge timbers ; or a wooden-bridge is thrown over some vast chasm from which thousands of tons of salt have been quarried and removed. The air grows drier and purer the deeper you go ; the points and faces of the rock more crystalline and brilliant. One enormous hall, out of which has been cut a mil-lion hundred weight of salt, has the appearance of a theatre. It is over one hundred feet high, and the blocks, taken out in regular layers, represent the seats for the spectators. In another spacious vault stand two obelisks of salt, which commemo-rate the visit of the Emperor Francis I. and his Empress. Further on you come to a lake more than twenty feet deep, intensely salt, of course, which is crossed in a heavy square boat. In this you are paddled through a tunnel which connects two immense halls. While in the middle of the tunnel the walls behind you and before you are brilliantly lighted up, and a gun is discharged which, with its echoes and reverberations, almost deafens you. Both air and water tremble visibly under the strange and frightful concussion, and you are only too thankful to reach the end of your voyage and stand once more on solid salt. Francis Joseph's ballroom is another of the wonders of this subterranean world. It is an immense apartment, both in height and extent, and on some festive occasions is used for dancing. It is lighted by six chandeliers, which resemble cut glass, but are in reality of crystalline rock salt. Statues of Vulcan and Neptune, sculptured from salt, also adorn this hall, which, when well illuminated, exhibit a marvellous splendour, the light being reflected from innumerable brilliant points and angles of the glittering rock.—Down, down, down, hundreds of feet further, through labarinths of shafts, galleries, and cham-bers, crooked passages, vaulted archways, and openings which have no name and seemingly no end. Groups of miners, naked to the hips, are everywhere busy with the implements of their labours ; pick, mallet, and wedge are employed incessantly in blocking out and separating the solid mass. Their manner of work is the same simple process in our centuries ago, perhaps by the remotest ancestors of these very same men, in these very mines, for they are immensely old. The blocks are marked out on the surface of the rock by grooves. One side is then deepened to the required thickness, and wedges being inserted under the block, it is soon slit off. It is then divided into pieces of a hundred pounds each, and in this shape is ready for sale. It is removed in carts or barrows to the shaft, where it is hoisted up, stage after stage, to the sur-face. Horses and mules are employed, and it is said that some of these animals are born and raised in the mines. The number of laborers con-stantly at work is from one to two thousand. They all live outside the excavations at the pres-ent day, although traditions exist of times when the families of some of the miners had their abodes in these fearful depths, and where children were born and reared to the occupation of their parents, seldom or never visiting the outside world. The thing is neither impossible nor incredible, as the air in the lowest part of the mine is considered more salubrious than in their upper regions. But the practice was long ago discontinued, if it ever existed to any extent. The miners, who are fine, muscular, and healthy looking men, are divided into gangs for work, and relieve each other every six hours. A gang will quarry in that time about one thousand hundred-weight. The temperature is very even all the year round, and the preserva-tive power of the air is such that wood never de-cays, but retains its qualities for centuries.

People with pulmonary affections are said to have been much benefited by inhaling freely the at-mosphere of the mines. When and how this wonderful deposit of salt was originally discovered is unknown. It was worked in the twelfth cen-tury, and how much earlier none can tell. Some traditions are held by the ignorant and supersti-tious. peasants of the country, which ascribe the discovery to miraculous or supernatural agency. Others say that a certain Queen of Poland, on visiting the spot, commanded her subjects to dig there, assuring them that there was a most pre-cious treasure beneath them. After a while a crystal of salt was found, which, as an earnest of the abundance afterwards discovered, this princess had set in a ring, as a royal gem, and wore to the day of her death. The extent of the deposit has not yet been fully ascertained. It commences, as we have before stated, about two hundred feet below the surface, and has a solid depth of nearly seven hundred feet, and rests on a bed of compact limestone, such as forms the peaks of the Car-pathian mountains, which it seems to follow. It has already been explored to the continuous length of two miles and a half ; and it is esti-mated that the aggregate length of all the in-numerable excavations of these mines amount to more than four hundred miles !

Cost of Transportation.

The actual cost of ocean transportation averages two mills per ton per mile. That of the lakes and Hudson River averages (and that of the lakes and St. Lawrence would average, if canals for ocean vessels were built) 2¼ mills per ton per mile.—The Erie Canal, owing to its great length and the number of locks, averages five mills per ton per mile. Ordinary railway transportation has here-tofore averaged from 12½ to 15 mills per ton per mile. But by the introduction of the Bessemer steel rail, which is expected to wear from twenty to forty years, the cost of railway freights is re-duced to 7¼ mills per ton per mile. The new Ods-hauser process of making iron by which the cost of manufacture will be diminished a third or half and its quality improved, will still further reduce the cost of railway transportation.

The Wine Trade.

The following relates to the Bordeaux vintage of 1868 :—Our merchants here do not seem to repent having paid such high prices for the wines of the vintage of 1868. The remnants of lots partly disposed of have been taken up lately at full rates. The last sale was of the balance of Duluc, a fourth-class wine, at 3,000 francs per ton (£30 per hogshead), to which add some 35 per cent. to cover charges, &c., before it can be fit for shipment. Some opinion of the quality of the 1868's is possible now, on tasting the deliveries made by the proprietors recently, and so far the impression is very favorable.

Exports of Petroleum from the United States from Jan. 1 to March 15.

	1869.	1868.
From New York......galls.	8,648,575	9,027,786
Boston	560,900	484,417
Philadelphia..........	3,458,034	3,568,985
Baltimore	78,654	285,821

Total Export from the U. States..	12,746,161	13,366,459
Same time, 1867,..		7,982,092
Same time, 1866 ...		10,2938440

Petroleum Shipments.

We are permitted to make the following extract from a private letter from Mr. B. Shaw, dated Liverpool, February 24th, written to Charles Man-ning, of this city: I am glad to say that I found the staunch little bark (the Wirralite) at Gibraltar, as tight as a bottle. I started her off, and she arrived here in eleven days, and on now discharg-ing cargo we found only four barrels of 'naptha empty (total leakage) out of 1,572 barrels of oil and naptha. This speaks favourably for direct shipment, when made in well-fastened strong vessels.—*Cleveland Herald.*

Silk Culture.

The production of silk is becoming an important industry in California. The climate seems peculiarly favorable; from three to five crops of cocoons are raised in one season. It is said that the worms are less liable to disease and produce a remarkably fine and tough fibre which, unlike that of Europe, will not fray after it is made into cloth. Those in the trade last season represent that a profit as high as $2,800 per acre of mulberry trees was realized—a most flattering result. The silk industry is rapidly extending. Los Angeles county is expected to raise twenty millions of cocoons in 1869.

Exports of Prince Edward Island.

Exports for the last two years :

	1868.	1867.
Oats ....bus.	1,467,053	1,453,615
Barley	56,681	53,478
Potatoes.................	543,593	441,483
Turnips.................	41,949	64,775

Tonnage of the New York Canals.

The following will show the total tonnage of the New York canals from 1855 to 1868 inclusive, as compared with coal tonnage of the canals for the same period :

Years.	Total tonnage. Tons 2,000 ℔s.	Coal tonnage. Tons 2,000 ℔s.	Five years' aggregate.
1850..........	3,076,617	80,127	
1851..........	3,582,733	112,277	
1852..........	3,863,441	145,296	
1853..........	4,247,852	225,507	
1854..........	4,165,862	275,662	
			838,869
1855..........	4,022,017	290,775	
1856..........	4,116,082	368,348	
1857..........	3,344,061	384,729	
1858..........	3,665,192	335,176	
1859..........	3,781,684	432,075	
			1,811,103
1860..........	4,650,214	490,405	
1861..........	4,507,635	542,150	
1862..........	5,598,783	636,720	
1863..........	5,557,602	732,557	
1864..........	4,852,941	655,063	
			3,056,985
1865..........	4,729,654	720,683	
1866..........	5,775,220	1,136,613	
1867..........	6,688,325	1,282,594	
1868..........	6,442,225	1,611,699	
			4,751,589

—Application will be made by Hon. J. Young, Montreal, for an Act to revise and amend the Act to incorporate the Canadian and British Telegraph Company, 22 Vic., cap. 161.

—A new bank is to be established at Liverpool, Nova Scotia.

STATEMENT OF BANKS

ACTING UNDER CHARTER, FOR THE MONTH ENDING 28th FEBRUARY, 1869, ACCORDING TO RETURNS FURNISHED BY THE BANKS TO THE AUDITOR OF PUBLIC ACCOUNTS.

NAME OF BANK	CAPITAL — Capital authorized by Act	Capital paid up	LIABILITIES — Promissory Notes in circulation not bearing Interest	Balances due to other Banks	Cash Deposits not bearing Interest	Cash Deposits bearing Interest	TOTAL LIABILITIES	ASSETS — Coin, Bullion and Provincial Notes	Landed or other Property of the Bank	Government Securities	Promissory Notes or Bills of other Banks	Balances due from other Banks	Notes and Bills Discounted	Other Debts due the Bank not included under Foregoing heads	TOTAL ASSETS
ONTARIO AND QUEBEC															
Montreal															
Quebec															
City															
Gore															
British North America															
Banque du Peuple															
Niagara District															
Molsons															
Toronto															
Ontario															
Eastern Townships															
Banque Nationale															
Banque Jacques Cartier															
Merchants'															
Royal Canadian															
Union B'k Lower Canada															
Mechanics'															
Bank of Commerce															
NOVA SCOTIA															
Bank of Yarmouth															
Merchants' Bank															
People's Bank															
Union Bank															
Bank of Nova Scotia															
NEW BRUNSWICK															
Bank of New Brunswick															
Commercial Bank															
St. Stephen's Bank															
People's Bank															
Totals															

Mercantile.

TORONTO PRICES CURRENT.—APRIL 1, 1869.

Name of Article.	Wholesale Rates.		Name of Article.	Wholesale Rate.		Name of Article.
Boots and Shoes.	$ c.	$ c.	**Groceries**—*Contin'd*	$ c.	$ c.	**Leather**—*Contin'd*
Mens' Thick Boots	2 20	2 50	Gunpowd'r c. to mod.	0 55	0 70	Kip, Skins, Patna
" Kip	2 50	2 60	" mod. to fine.	0 70	0 85	French
" Calf	3 00	3 70	" fine to finest	0 85	0 95	English
" Congress Gaiters	2 00	2 50	Hyson	0 45	0 80	Hemlock Calf (30 to
" Kip Cobourgs	1 75	1 45	Imperial	0 42	0 80	35 lbs.) per doz.
Boys' Thick Boots	1 70	1 80	*Tobacco, Manufac'd:*			Do. light
Youths'	1 40	1 50	Can Leaf, ℔ lb 5s & 10s.	0 26	0 30	French Calf
Women's Batts	0 95	1 30	Western Leaf, com..	0 25	0 26	Grain & Satn Cl'h doz.
" Balmoral	1 20	1 50	" Good	0 27	0 32	Splits, large ℔ lb
" Congress Gaiters..	1 15	1 45	" Fine	0 32	0 35	" small
Misses' Batts	0 75	1 00	" Bright fine	0 40	0 60	Enamelled Cow ℔ foot.
" Balmoral	1 10	1 20	" choice.	0 60	0 75	Patent
" Congress Gaiters..	1 15	1 45	**Hardware.**			Pebble Grain
Girls' Batts	0 65	0 85	Tin (network prices)			Buff
" Balmoral	0 10	1 05	Block, ℔ lb	0 28	0 00	**Oils.**
" Congress Gaiters..	0 89	1 10	Grain	0 30	0 00	Cod
Children's C. T. Cacks.	0 50	0 65	*Copper:*			Lard, extra
" Gaiters	0 65	0 90	Pig	0 23	0 24	" No. 1
Drugs.			Sheet	0 30	0 33	" Woollen
Aloes Cape	0 12½	0 16	*Cut Nails:*			Lubricating, patent..
Alum	0 02½	0 03	Assorted ¼ Shingles,			" Mott's economic
Borax	0 60	0 60	℔ 100 ℔.	2 90	3 00	Linseed, raw
Camphor, refined	0 65	0 70	Shingle alone do	3 15	3 25	" boiled
Castor Oil	0 16½	0 28	Lathe and 5 dy	3 30	3 40	Olive, common, ℔ gal.
Caustic Soda	0 04½	0 05	*Galvanized Iron:*			" salad
Cochineal	0 90	1 00	Assorted sizes	0 08	0 09	" salad, in kegs
Cream Tartar	0 40	0 45	Best No. 24	0 00	0 00	" qt. ℔ case
Epsom Salts	0 03	0 04	" 26	0 08	0 08½	Sesame salad, ℔ gal.
Extract Logwood	0 11	0 12	" 28	0 09	0 09½	Seal, pale
Gum Arabic, sorts	0 30	0 35	*Horse Nails:*			Spirits Turpentine
Indigo, Madras	0 90	1 00	Gnest's or Griffin's			Varnish
Liquorice	0 14	0 45	assorted sizes	0 00	0 00	Whale
Madder	0 00	0 18	For W. and't sizes	0 18	0 19	**Paints, &c.**
Galls	0 32	0 37	Patent Hammer'd do	0 17	0 18	White Lead, genuine
Opium	12 00	13 50	*Iron (at 4 months):*			in Oil, ℔ 25 lbs.
Oxalic Acid	0 26	0 35	Pig—Gartsherrie No1.	24 00	25 00	Do. No. 1
Potash, Bi-tart	0 24	0 28	Other brands. No 1	22 00	24 00	" 2
" bichromate	0 15	0 20	No 2.	0 00	0 00	" 3
Potass Iodide	3 90	4 50	Bar—Scotch, ℔ 100 ℔.	2 25	2 50	White Zinc, genuine
Senna	0 12	0 00	Refined	3 00	3 25	White Lead, dry
Soda Ash	0 02½	0 0½	Swedes	5 00	5 50	Red Lead
S da Bicarb	4 50	5 00	Hoops—Coopers	3 00	3 25	Venetian Red, Eng'h
Tartaric Acid	0 40	0 45	Band	3 60	3 25	Yellow Ochre, Fren'h
Verdigris	0 35	0 40	Canada Plates	3 75	4 00	Whiting
Vitriol, Blue	0 08	0 10	Union Jack	0 00	0 00	**Petroleum.**
Groceries.			Pontypool	3 25	4 00	(Refined ℔ gal.)
Coffees:			Swansea	3 90	4 00	Water white, car'd..
Java, ℔ lb	0 22½@0 24		*Lead (at 4 months):*			" small lots..
Laguayra,	0 17	0 18	Bar, (at 100 lbs	0 06½	0 07	Straw, by car load
Rio	0 15	0 17	Sheet	0 07½	0 07½	" small lots..
Fish:			Shot	0 07½	0 07½	Amber, by car load..
Herrings, Lab. split..	5 75	6 50	*Iron Wire (net cash):*			" small lots..
" round	0 00	0 00	No. 6, ℔ bundle	2 70	2 80	**Produce.**
" scaled	0 35	0 40	" 9	3 10	3 20	*Grain:*
Mackerel, small kitts..	1 00	0 00	" 12	3 40	3 50	Wheat, Spring, 60 lb
Loch. Her. wk'd brks..	2 50	2 75	" 16	4 30	4 40	" Fall 60
" half	1 25	1 50	*Powder:*			Barley 48
White Fish & Trout..	None.		Blasting, Canada	3 50	0 00	Peas 61
Salmon, saltwater	14 00	15 00	FF	4 25	4 50	Oats 34
Dry Cod, ℔ 112 lbs..	5 00	5 25	FFF	4 75	5 00	Rye 56
Fruit:			Blasting, English	4 ½ 0	5 00	*Seeds:*
Raisins, Layers	2 00	2 10	FF loose..	5 00	6 00	Clover, choice 60
" M R	1 90	2 00	FFF	6 00	6 50	" com'n do
" Valentias new..	0 6½	0 7½	Premed Spikes (4 mos):			Timothy, cho'e 4
Currants, new	0 5½	0 6½	Regular sizes 100	4 00	4 25	" inf. to good 48
" old	0 04	0 0½	Extra	4 50	5 00	Flax 56
Figs	0 14	0 00	*Tea Plates (net cash):*			*Flour:* (℔ per brl.)
Molasses:			IC Coke	7 50	8 50	Superior extra
Clayed, ℔ gal	0 00	0 35	IC Charcoal	4 50	9 00	Extra superfine,
Syrups, Standard	0 60	0 00	IX	10 50	11 00	Fancysuperfine
" Gohlen	0 00	0 65	IXX	13 50	14 0.	Superfine No 1..
Rice:			DC	8 00	8 50	
Arracan	4 25	4 50	DX	℔ 50	0 00	*Oatmeal:* (℔ r brl.)..
Spices:			*Hides & Skins:* ℔ lb			**Provisions.**
Cassia, whole, ℔ lb..	0 00	0 45	Green rough	0 06½	0 07	Butter, dairy tub r'lls,
Cloves	0 11	0 12	Green, salt'd & insp'd.	0 06½	0 0½	" store, packed.
Nutmegs	0 80	0 65	Cured	0 00	0 00	Cheese, new
Ginger, gr'und	0 20	0 25	Curdskins, green	0 40	0 1	Pork, mess, ℔ brl..
" Jamaica, root.	0 20	0 26	Calfskins, cured	0 0	0 14½	" prime mess..
Pepper, black	0 12½	0 00	dry	0 18	0 0	Bacon, rough
Pimento	0 00	0 00	Sheepskins,	1 50	1 70	" Cumberl'd cut..
Sugars:			" country	1 00	1 40	" smoked
Port Rico, ℔ lb	0 10½	0 02	*Hogs.*			Hams, in salt
Cuba	0 10½	0 00	Inferior, ℔ lb	0 05	0 07	" smoked
Barbadoes (Porto)..	0 10½	0 00	Medium	0 07	0 00	Shoulders, in salt
Canada Sugar Refine'y,			Good	0 0½	0 12	Lard, in kegs
Yellow No. 2, 60 ds..	0 10½	0 11	Fancy	0 00	0 00	Eggs, packed
Yellow, No. 2½	0 10½	0 11½	*Leather,* ℔ (4 mos.)			Beef mess
No. 3	0 11	0 11½	In less of least amt			Tallow
Crushed X	0 13	0 13½	50 sides, 10 ℔ cent			Hogs dressed, heavy,
A	0 13	0 13½	higher			" medium..
Ground	0 13½	0 14	Spanish Sole, 1st qual'y			" light
Dry Crushed	0 14	0 14½	heavy, weights ℔ ℔..	0 21½	0 22	**Salt, &c.**
Extra Ground	0 14	0 14½	Do 1st qual middle do.	0 22	0 0	American bris.
Teas:			Do No 2, light weights	0 22½	0 00	Liverpool coarse
Japan com'n to good..	0 43	0 55	Slaugh'r heavy	0 26	0 27	Goderich
" Fine to choicest..	0 50	0 65	" do light	0 00	0 00	Plaster
Colored, com. to	0 60	0 75	Harness, best	0 28	0 30	Water Lime
Congou & Souch'ng..	0 42	0 75	" No. 2	0 00	0 00	
Oolong, good to fine..	0 50	0 65	Upper heavy	0 32	0 35	
Y. Hyson, com to gd..	0 45	0 55	" light	0 36	0 38	
Medium to choice	0 65	0 80				
Extra choice	0 55	0 95				

…ndles.			*Brandy:*	$ c.	$ c.
			Hennessy's, per gal..	2 20	2 50
…& Co.'s ..	$ c.	$ c.	Martell's " ..	2 30	2 50
………	0 07½	0 08	J. Robin & Co.'s " ..	2 25	2 35
…ar ……	0 07	0 07½	Otard, Dupuy & Cos..	2 25	2 35
…r………	0 07	0 07½	Brandy, cases………	8 50	9 00
………	0 05	0 05½	Brandy, com. per c...	4 00	4 50
………	0 08½	0 03½	*Whiskey:*		
………	0 00	0 11½	Common 36 u. p……	0 62½	0 65
…quors,			Old Rye ………	0 85	0 87½
			Malt ………	0 85	0 87½
			Toddy ………	0 85	0 87½
…doz……	2 60	2 65	Scotch, per gal…….	1 90	2 10
…b Portr..	2 35	2 40	Irish—Kinnahan's c...	7 00	7 50
			" Dunnville's Belf't..	6 00	6 25
…a Rum...	1 80	2 25	**Wool.**		
…H. Gin..	1 55	1 63	Fleece, lb………	0 28	0 35
…Tom……	1 90	2 00	Pulled "………	0 22	0 25
			Furs.		
………	4 00	4 25	Bear………	3 00	10 00
…Tom, c...	6 00	6 25	Beaver, ℘ lb………	1 00	1 25
			Coon ………	0 20	0 40
			Fisher………	4 00	6 00
…n ………	1 00	1 25	Martin………	1 40	1 60
………	2 00	4 00	Mink………	3 25	4 00
…nou……	1 00	1 50	Otter………	5 75	6 00
…a ………	1 70	1 80	Spring Rats ………	0 15	0 17
…golden..	2 50	4 00	Fox………	1 20	1 25

…NSURANCE COMPANIES.

ENGLISH.—*Quotations on the London Market.*

…Di-…nd.	Name of Company.	Shares par val £	Amount paid.	Last Sale.
	Briton Medical and General Life …	10	….	2
7½	Commer'l Union, Fire, Life and Mar.	50	5	6½
8	City of Glasgow ……	25	2½	5½
9½	Edinburgh Life ………	100	15	33
½ yr	European Life and Guarantee……	2½	11s6	4s. 3d.
…0	Etna Fire and Marine………	10	1½	—
5	Guardian ………	100	50	51¼
2	Imperial Fire………	500	50	350
9½	Imperial Life ………	100	10	16¾
0	Lancashire Fire and Life………	20	2	2¾
1	Life Association of Scotland………	40	7½	25
…p. sh	London Assurance Corporation ..	25	12½	49
5	London and Lancashire Life ……	10	1	—
0	Liverp'l & London & Globe F. & L.	20	2	7 1-16
5	National Union Life ………	5	1	1
2½	Northern Fire and Life ………	100	5	12
2 …o …s.	North British and Mercantile ……	50	6¼	21
…0	Ocean Marine ………	25	5	18½
12s.	Provident Life………	100	10	35
…p. s.	Phœnix………	….	….	145
…yr.	Queen Fire and Life ………	10	1	1
…o.4s	Royal Insurance………	20	3	6½
…0	Scottish Provincial Fire and Life ..	50	2½	5½
…5	Standard Life ………	50	12	66½
5	Star Life ………	25	1¼	—
	CANADIAN.			℘ c.
4	British America Fire and Marine ..	$50	$25	55½ 56
4	Canada Life ………	…	….	…..
…2	Montreal Assurance ………	£50	£5	135
8	Provincial Fire and Marine………	60	11	…..
…..	Quebec Fire ………	40	32½	26¼
7	" Marine………	100	40	85 90
…no's.	Western Assurance………	40	9	…..

RAILWAYS.	Sha's	Paid	Montr	London
…St. Lawrence………	£100	All.	….	61 63
…ake Huron ………	20½	"	….	3 3½
do Preference ………	10	"	….	5½ 6½
…& Goderich, 6℘c., 1872-3-4………	100	"	….	66 69
…d St. Lawrence ………	….	….	10 11	….
do Pref. 10 ℘ ct………	….	….	8· 85	….
…t………	100	"	15½ 16½	15½ 16
Eq. G. M. Bds. 1 ch. 6℘c………	100	"	….	87 89
First Preference, 5 ℘ c ………	100	"	….	53 54
Deferred, 3 ℘ ct………	100	"	….	….
Second Pref. Bonds, 5℘c………	100	"	….	39½ 40½
do Deferred, 3 ℘ ct………	100	"	….	….
Third Pref. Stock, 4℘ct………	100	"	….	28 30
do. Deferred, 3 ℘ ct………	100	"	….	….
Fourth Pref. Stock, 3℘c………	100	"	….	17½ 18½
do. Deferred, 3 ℘ ct………	100	"	….	….
…n………	20½	"	13 14	14½ 15½
New ………	20½	18	….	….
6 ℘ c. Bds, due 1873-76………	100	All.	….	100 102
5 ℘c Bds. due 1877-78………	100	"	….	94 95
…ay, Halifax, $250, all………	$250	"	….	….
…Canada, 6℘c. 1st Pref. Bds………	100	"	…	82 83

…HANGE.	Halifax.	Montr'l.	Quebec.	Toronto.
…ndon, 60 days……				
…days date ………	12½	8½ 8¾	9½ 9¾	8¾
………	11½ 12	7½ 8½	8⅝ 8⅞	8
…documents………	….	7½ 8½	….	….
…York………	….	23½ 24	23½ 24	23½
…do. ………	….	24 24½	24 24½	….
…do. ………	….	par to ½ p.	par ½ dis.	par ½ dis.
………	….	3 3½	….	3½ to 4½

STOCK AND BOND REPORT.

The dates of our quotations are as follows:—Toronto, March 30; Montreal, March 26; Quebec, March 23; London, March 11.

NAME.	Shares.	Paid up.	Divid'd last 6 Months	Dividend Day.	CLOSING PRICES. Toronto.	Montre'l	Quebec.
BANKS.			℘ ct.				
British North America ………	$250	All.	3	July and Jan.	104 105½	104¾ 105¼	104½ 105¼
Jacques Cartier………	50	"	4	1 June, 1 Dec.	109 109½	108½ 109½	108 109
Montreal ………	200	"	5	"	143 144	143 144	141 142
Nationale………	50	"	4	1 Nov. 1 May.	107½ 108	108 108½	108 108½
New Brunswick ………	100	"	……	……	….	…	…
Nova Scotia ………	200	28	7&b$3½	Mar. and Sept.	….	….	….
Du Peuple………	50	"	4	1 Mar., 1 Sept.	107 108	107½ 108½	107 108
Toronto ………	100	"	4	1 Jan., 1 July.	121 121½	119 121	120 121
Bank of Yarmouth………	….	….	……	……	….	….	….
Canadian Bank of Com'e………	50	95	……	……	102½ 103	102 103	103 103½
City Bank Montreal ………	80	All.	4	1 June, 1 Dec.	102½ 103	103 103½	103½ 104
Commer'l Bank (St. John)….	100	"	℘ ct.	……	…	….	….
Eastern Townships' Bank…..	50	"	4	1 July, 1 Jan..	….	99 100	98 99
Gore ………	40	…	none.	1 Jan., 1 July.	40 41	40 42½	40 42
Halifax Banking Company….	…	….	……	……	…	….	…
Mechanics' Bank………	50	70	4	1 Nov., 1 May.	97½ 98	97 98	95 96
Merchants' Bank of Canada….	100	70	4	1 Jan., 1 July.	107 108	107½ 108	107½ 108½
Merchants' Bank (Halifax)….	….	….	…..	…..	….	….	….
Molson's Bank………	50	All.	4	1 Apr., 1 Oct.	Bks. cls'd	Bks. clsd	Bks cl'sd
Niagara District Bank………	100	70	3½	1 Jan., 1 July.	….	….	….
Ontario Bank………	40	All.	4	1 June, 1 Dec.	100 100½	99½ 100	99½ 100
People's Bank (Fred'kton)….	100	"	……	……	….	….	…
People's Bank (Halifax) …..	20	"	7 12 m	……	….	…	….
Quebec Bank ………	100	"	3½	1 June, 1 Dec.	100 101	100 100½	100 101
Royal Canadian Bank ………	50	50	4	1 Jan., 1 July.	75 80	72½ 82½	80 81
St. Stephens Bank ………	100	All.	…..	……	….	…	…
Union Bank ………	100	70	4	1 Jan., 1 July.	104½ 105½	104¾ 105¼	105 106
Union Bank (Halifax)………	100	40	7 12 mo	Feb. and Aug.	….	….	…
MISCELLANEOUS.							
British America Land………	250	44	2½	……	….	….	….
British Colonial S. S. Co……	250	32½	2½	……	…	50 60	….
Canada Company ………	32½	All.	£1 10s.	……	….	….	….
Canada Landed Credit Co…..	50	$20	3½	……	75 77	….	….
Canada Per. B'ldg Society….	50	All.	5	……	125½ 126	….	….
Canada Mining Company…..	4	90	……	……	….	….	….
Do. Inl'd Steam Nav. Co…..	100	All.	7	……	….	100 101	….
Do. Glass Company………	100	"	12½ "	……	….	40 55	….
Canad'n Loan & Investm't….	25	2½	7	……	….	….	….
Canada Agency ………	10	¼	……	……	….	….	….
Colonial Securities Co………	….	….	……	……	….	….	….
Freehold Building Society….	100	All.	4	……	110 110½	….	….
Halifax Steamboat Co………	100	"	5	……	….	….	….
Halifax Gas Company………	….	….	……	……	….	….	….
Hamilton Gas Company………	….	….	……	……	….	….	….
Huron Copper Bay Co………	4	12	20	……	….	32½ 45	….
Lake Huron S. and C………	5	102	……	……	….	…	….
Montreal Mining Consols…..	20	$15	……	……	….	3.15 3.25	…
Do. Telegraph Co………	40	All.	5	……	133 133½	132½ 133½	133 134
Do. Elevating Co………	00	"	15 12 m	……	….	100 102½	….
Do. City Gas Co………	40	"	4	15 Mar. 15 Sep.	….	132 134	134 135
Do. City Pass. R. Co………	50	"	4	……	….	102½ 107½	112 113
Quebec and L. S. ………	8	34	……	……	….	….	….
Quebec Gas Co………	200	All.	4	1 Mar., 1 Sep.	….	…	118 119
Quebec Street R. R ………	50	25	3	……	….	….	90 91
Richelieu Navigation Co…….	100	All.	10 p.a.	1 Jan., 1 July.	….	107½ 108½	108 108½
St. Lawrence Glass Company.	100	"	….	……	….	80 85	…
St. Lawrence Tow Boat Co…..	100	"	……	3 Feb.	…	…	35 40
Tor'to Consumers' Gas Co…..	50	"	4	1 My Au Mar Fe	107½ 108	…	107 108
Trust & Loan Co. of U. C…..	20	5	3	……	….	….	…
West'n Canada Bldg Soc'y….	50	All.	5	……	121 121½	….	….

SECURITIES.	London.	Montreal.	Quebec.	Toronto.
Canadian Gov't Deb. 6 ℘ ct. stg………	….	102 103½	103 103½	102½ 103
Do. do. 6 do due Ja. & Jul. 1877-84………	104½ 105½	….	….	….
Do. do. 6 do. Feb. & Aug………	103 105	….	…	….
Do. do. 6 do. Mch. & Sep………	102 104	….	….	….
Do. do. 5 ℘ ct. cur., 1883 ………	92 94	92 94½	94 94½	93 94
Do. do. 5 do. stg., 1885 ………	92 94	92 94½	93½ 94½	93 94½
Do. do. 7 do. cur.,………	….	….	……	….
Dominion 6 p. c. 1878 cy………	….	105½ 106	105½ 106	105½ 106
Hamilton Corporation………	….	….	…..	….
Montreal Harbor, 8 ℘ ct. d. 1869………	..	….	……	….
Do. do. 7 do. 1870………	….	….	……	….
Do. do. 6½ do. 1883………	….	102 103	……	….
Do. do. 6½ do. 1873………	….	….	……	….
Do. Corporation, 6 ℘ c. 1891 ………	….	96 97	95½ 96	96 96½
Do. 7 p. c. stock………	….	108 110	108 109	109 110
Do. Water Works, 6 ℘ c. stg. 1878………	….	….	……	96 96½
Do. do. 6 do. cy. do. ………	….	96½ 97	……	96 96½
New Brunswick, 6 ℘ ct., Jan. and July ………	103 104	….	……	….
Nova Scotia, 6 ℘ ct., 1875………	102 104	…	……	….
Ottawa City 6 ℘ c. d. 1880 ………	….	92½ 93½	……	…
Quebec Harbour, 6 ℘ c. d. 1883. ………	….	….	60	….
Do. do. 7 do. do………	….	….	65 70	….
Do. do 8 do. 1886………	…	….	80 85	….
Do. City, 7 ℘ c. d. 1½ years………	….	….	98 98½	….
Do. do. 7 do. 9 do. ………	….	….	91 92	….
Do. do. 7 do. 5 do. ………	….	….	94 95	….
Do. Water Works, 7 ℘ ct., 4 years………	….	….	97 97½	….
Do. do. 6 do. 2 do. ………	….	….	94 95	….
Toronto Corporation ………	….	90 92½	…	….

THE CANADIAN

IONETARY TIMES

AND

INSURANCE CHRONICLE.

OTED TO FINANCE, COMMERCE, INSURANCE, BANKS, RAILWAYS, NAVIGATION, MINES, INVESTMENT, PUBLIC COMPANIES, AND JOINT STOCK ENTERPRISE.

—NO. 34.   TORONTO, THURSDAY, APRIL 8, 1869.   { SUBSCRIPTION $3 YEAR.

Mercantile.

Gundry and Langley,
CTS AND CIVIL ENGINEERS, Building Sur- nd Valuators. Office corner of King and Jordan routo.
GUNDRY.   HENRY LANGLEY.

J. B. Boustead.
)N and Commission Merchant. Hops bought ld on Commission. 82 Front St., Toronto.

John Boyd & Co.,
IALE Grocers and Commission Merchants, : St., Toronto.

Childs & Hamilton.
CTURERS and Wholesale Dealers in Boots hoes, No. 7 Wellington Street East, Toronto.
28

L. Coffee & Co.
: and Commission Merchants, No. 2 Manning's Front St., Toronto, Ont. Advances made on ts of Produce.

Honore Plamondon,
House Broker, Forwarder, and General Agent, . Office—Custom House Building.   17-1y

Sylvester, Bro. & Hickman,
CIAL Brokers and Vessel Agents. Office—No. cio Chambers, [Corner Front and Church, 8t.,.
2-gm

John Fisken & Co.
IL and Commission Merchants, Yonge St., o, Ont.

W. & H. Griffith.
8S of Teas, Wines, etc. Ontario Chambers, rch and Front Sts., Toronto.

H. Nerlich & Co.,
8S of French, German, English and American ods, Cigars, and Leaf Tobaccos, No. 2 Adelaide t, Toronto.   15

Candee & Co.,
3 AND BROKERS, dealers in Gold and Silver iovernment Securities, &c., Corner Main and treets, Buffalo, Y. N.   21-1v

Lyman & McNab.
ALE Hardware Merchants, Toronto, Ontario.

W. D. Matthews & Co.
: Commission Merchants, Old Corn Exchange, :t St. East, Toronto Ont.

R. C. Hamilton & Co.
: Commission Merchants, 119 Lower Water lifax, Nova Scotia.

Parson Bros.,
UM Refiners, and Wholesale dealers in Lamps, ys, etc. Warerooms 51 Front St. Refinery cor. on Sts., Toronto.

C. P. Reid & Co.
8S and Dealers in Wines, Liquors, Cigars and bacco, Wellington Street, Toronto.   98.

W. Rowland & Co.,
BROKERS and General Commission Mer- Advances made on Consignments. Corner Front Streets, Toronto.

Reford & Dillon.
1S of Groceries, Wellington Street, Toronto.

Sessions, Turner & Cooper.
CTURERS, Importers and Wholesale Dealer ts and Shoes, Leather Findings, etc., 8 Wel- last, Toronto, Ont

Meetings.

THE LANCASHIRE INSURANCE COMPANY.

The annual general meeting of the proprietors of this company was held at their offices, Exchange-street, London ; Mr. John Todd, the chairman of the Board of directors, presiding.

Mr. George Stewart, the general manager of the company, read the following report of the direc-tors :—

"The directors have much pleasure in meeting the proprietors, and in reporting the result of the business of the Company, during the year 1868.

"ACCOUNTS AND BALANCE SHEET.—Accom-panying the present report will be found, as in former years, detailed accounts of the fire and life business and the general balance sheet of the company.

"FIRE BUSINESS.—The fire premiums received during the year 1868 amounted to £112,579. The sums paid during the year for re-insuring the surplus risks of the company amounted to £21,307, and for claims for loss and damage by fire to £45,350. After payment of all claims, expenses of management and reinsurances, and making due provision for claims unadjusted at 31st December, 1868, there was a clear profit of £21,813 8s. 1d. on the fire business of the year, which sum has been carried to the credit of the proprietors' fund.

"LIFE BUSINESS.—The income of this depart-ment during the year amounted to £46,636. The claims from 41 deaths amounted to £15,978, and after providing for these, and the various other sums detailed in the balance sheet, the sum of £18,359 18s. 6d., has been added to the life reserve fund, which has thereby been increased from £150,970 19s. 8d. to £169,330 18s. 2d.

"FUNDS AND INVESTMENTS.—The satisfactory nature of the investments may be seen by a refer-ence to the balance sheet of the company. The amount of interest realized on these investments during the year was £16,635 1s. 6d.

"PROPRIETORS' AND RESERVE FUNDS.—The income of the proprietors' and reserve funds for the year amounted to £30,289 4s. 5d., out of which the directors have already declared a divi-dend of ten per cent. per annum, which absorbed the sum of £14,614, leaving a surplus of £15,675 4s. 5d. of which £10,023 2s. 8d. has been appro-priated to the Birmingham purchase, and £5,652 1s. 9. has been added to the reserve fund. The paid up capital amounts as formerly to £146,140. The ordinary reserve fund has been increased from £40,598 11s. 4d. to £46,350 13s. 1d., and the amount reserved towards the Birmingham office purchase has been increased from $8,000 to £16,000.

"The directors retiring are Messrs. Clegg, Har-greaves, Kay, Pilkington, Smith ; and Wood (deceased), of whom Messrs. Clegg, Hargreaves, Kay and Smith, being eligible, are recommended for re-election, and John Pender, Esq., merchant, Manchester, is recommended for election."

The Chairman said : The report just read, and which has been in your hands some days, is so plain and explicit that it leaves me very little to add by way of explanation, and I am sure only a very few words are needed to secure its adoption. The year 1868, all things considered, has been the

most successful year in the history of this company. Our income is larger, our total profits larger, and our reserve funds are larger, than we have ever previously reported. In proof of this, let me call your attention very briefly to the figures contained in the printed balance sheet. And first as to the income. You will find it therein stated that the income during 1868 was as follows :—

Fire premiums	£112,579
Life do	39,527
Interest on investments	16,635

Making a total of............£168,741

Now, our income from these three sources during the previous year amounted to £157,172, so that the year's increase exceeds 1867 by £11,500 ; secondly, as to the profits, the year 1867 was con-sidered by us to be a successful one ; but that year's profits have been exceeded by the year 1868 :—

The fire profits for 1868 amount to	£21,813
The life surplus fund	18,359

Together............£40,172

Whereas the fire profits and life surplus for the previous year, 1867, amounted to £37,756. Lastly, the reserve funds, at the close of these two years are :—

	1867.	1868.
Life department	£150,970	£169,330
Fire department	48,698	62,350
	£199,668	£231,689

Thus showing an increase in one year of no less than £32,012, a fact I leave to speak for itself. There is only one other remark I wish to make, and it is this, that there has been a profit in every one of our branch offices during the past year. I think this is a satisfactory feature, and proves that the careful management of the company is extended over the whole range of its operations; and now, gentlemen, I move that the report now read be approved and adopted.

Mr. Darbyshire said it was with great pleasure that he rose to second the adoption of the report, which he was sure would meet with the approval of all the proprietors. He especially would refer to the addition made to the reserve fund, believ-ing it was much better and safer to act upon the principle of adding to the reserve than to increase the dividend. He remembered in the first years of the existence of the company there was a strong desire to add to dividend; but the course of the directors had always been to keep the capital in-tact from the commencement, and the consequence had been that the capital had gone on gradually increasing, and the position of the company was improving in the confidence of the public. In Liverpool they stood as high as any office there. The seven other offices that took up the ground before themselves, and naturally people were dis-inclined to change. There was no question, as to insurances generally, there was not much profit on premiums, sufficient care being taken to keep them as low as was possible; but the foreign busi-ness, so far as he had had the opportunity of judging, he found was excellently and profitably managed. Everything that was done was sub-mitted to the Manchester directors, and he was proud of the gentlemen who constituted that board; they were all business men, who like himself had fought their way in the world. He was, therefore, truly happy in being able to state that in all the departments of the company, as the worthy chairman had stated, everything had been conducted in the most satisfactory manner. (Hear, hear.) As he should not probably have the opportunity of speaking again, he would remark of the officials that he was convinced that there was not another office in Manchester, London or Liverpool so well arranged; and he congratulated the meeting on this fact, as well as on the ability and efficiency of their manager, as an augury of success for the future. (Hear, hear.)

Mr. Thomas Stolterfoht, of Liverpool, supported the resolution, and said that next to getting hold of business the consideration of the company should be directed as to how they should take care of their money---to guard against losses either by fire or life or unfortunate investments. He thought this was an occasion on which they might congratulate most warmly those gentlemen who had devoted their attention to the investments of the company, and to their excellent manager for the manner in which he conducted the business of the concern. They all knew how many private persons had lost a large amount, even with the knowledge they possessed, and many companies had been crippled through some unfortunate omission. This was not the case with this company, and he attributed much of it to the care exercised in every department. (Hear, hear.)

The resolution was then passed.

The Chairman then moved, "That Messrs. Clegg, Hargeaves, Kay and Smith be re-elected directors, and that Mr. John Pender be elected a director of the company."

Mr. Thomas Broadbent seconded the resolution, which was passed.

The next resolution was the re-appointment of Mr. Adam Murray and Mr. James Halliday as auditors of the company.

The resolution was moved by the Chairman, and seconded by Mr. Shelmerdine, and passed.

Mr. Nicholas Heald moved :---"That the thanks of the shareholders are due and are hereby tendered to the directors of the Company, and to the members of the local boards of directors in Liverpool and Glasgow, for their valuable services." Mr. Heald said : I think myself highly honored by having this resolution entrusted to my hands. Some of the older shareholders, and many of the directors present, who sat at the board with me, will remember I was at issue with them respecting the fair apportionment of the general charges to the life department. I am not going to renew that controversy here; for the balance sheets lately presented give no cause for cavil, the proportion of general expenses to life being about one-fifth, and of fire four-fifths, and to that no one can or ought to object. (Applause.) Before taking leave of the life business, I cannot help remarking on the rapid accumulation of its reserve. In 1863, it was £34,700 ; in the next two years, 1864 and 1865, it rose to £155,300, being an average addition of £10,500 per annum ; the two following years, 1866 and 1867, we find it at £151,000, or an average added of £17,500 per annum ; and this last year, 1868, it is £169,300, being an addition of £18,350, the largest yet made. Fire premiums at the same time have run up from £37,000 to £113,500, and that branch has now a reserve fund of nearly £49,000, a sum nearly equal to the annual premium of five years ago. These facts speak volumes for the directors, and I can have no hesitation in saying that they have earned and deserve our heartfelt thanks. (Applause.) One word before I sit down. I congratulate the board and the shareholders at the total avoidance of annuity business by this company. I think it stands almost alone in what I believe is an unprofitable and onerous branch of business. (Applause.)

Mr. T. Fielden seconded the resolution, which was passed unanimously.

The Chairman briefly responded, and on vacating the chair a cordial vote of thanks was passed to him personally, and the proceedings terminated.

BRITON MEDICAL AND GENERAL LIFE ASSOCIATION.

The fifteenth annual meeting of this company was held in London (Eng.,) on the 18th March, 1869. The following is the

FIFTEENTH ANNUAL REPORT.

The Directors of the Briton Medical and General Life Association have much pleasure in reporting to the shareholders and policyholders the transactions of the Association for the year ending December 31st, 1868.

New Business.—The Directors have received 3,242 proposals for assuring the sum of £972,166 18s. 9d. Of these 171 for £76,430 have been declined ; 599 for £194,985 14s. 9d. were not completed from various other causes. The remaining number have been carried into effect, and 2,472 policies issued assuring £703,451 4s., and producing in annual premiums the sum of £25,277 8s. Four annuities have been granted, for which £1,150 has been paid to the Association.

The Association having now completed its fifteenth year, it will be interesting to trace its progress since its formation by the following tabulated returns, which exhibit the new business transacted during these three quinquennial periods :—

Quinquennial period ending	No. of Proposals	Amount Proposed	No. of Policies Issued.	Amount Assured.
1858	4,807	1,023,140 0 0	3,318	654,140 0 0
1863	13,244	2,779,646 0 0	9,746	2,947,383 0 0
1868	17,460	4,261,303 5 0	13,609	3,752,967 4 8
Total...	35,512	8,064,100 5 0	26,703	6,444,490 4 8
Annual Premiums, 1858				£21,347 16 5
" 1863				68,207 19 10
" 1868				122,557 17 6
Total				£207,113 13 9

General Income.—The net premium income has increased to the sum of.................£216,704 1 7
The interest on investments and other items of receipt yield...... 21,276 18 1

Making a total income of........£237,980 19 8

Claims.—The claims have been 335 in number of lives and 379 in policies, amounting, less reassurance, to the sum of £127,886 12s. 1d. This sum includes all claims which were admitted, but not due, at the close of the year.

Balance of income.—After deducting all claims, surrenders, expenses, charges of management, and other out-goings, the balance of the year's income is £68,026 9s. 4d., which sum has been duly carried to the capital account. The assets of the Association at the close of the year amounted to £667,493 8s. 5d.

Accounts and Audit.—The accounts of the Association, from which the foregoing figures are taken, have been carefully audited by the four appointed auditors who have reported to the board as follows:—

To the Directors of the Briton Medical and General Life Association—Gentlemen: We have carefully examined the various books, accounts and vouchers of the Association, and find them correct and satisfactory. We have also inspected the whole of the securities, which we also find to be in perfect order. The excellent system of quarterly audits has been maintained, by which we have been enabled to exercise perfect supervision over the extensive transactions of the Association. It is again our pleasing duty to bear testimony to the very efficient manner in which the books are kept, and noting with satisfaction the continued increase in the affairs of the Association. Henry Alcock, John Brown, William Brooks, C. R. Rowland, auditors.

Dividend.—The Directors recommend that dividend of £8 per cent. per annum on the paid up capital of the Association, free of income tax, be declared.

Bonus.—During the year the consulting actuary, Mr. Arthur Scratchley, completed his investigation into the affairs of the Association, and the Directors in accordance with his recommendation distributed the sum of £87,247 17s. 6d. among the shareholders and policyholders, in accordance with the terms of the deed of constitution. In connection with this subject the Directors would here draw especial attention to the fact that the next bonus valuation will take place at the end of the year 1872, and that all policies effected prior to the 31st December, 1868, will be entitled to participate in the same.

Branches and Agencies.—The Directors are happy to be able to report continued efficient and hearty co-operation in the working of the various branches and agencies. The arrangements by which the affairs of the Association in Scotland were placed under the supervision of influential and energetic local board continues to work satisfactorily.

Directors and Auditors.—Four of the Directors viz., Mr. Chapman, Mr. Coventry and Mr. Oliver retire from the Direction, but, being eligible offer themselves for the honor of re-election. The auditors also retire and offer themselves re-election.

Conclusion.—The Directors, in conclusion, would draw attention to the successful establishment during the past year, of the Brittannia Fire Association, under the auspices of the Briton. The Company, to work in active co-operation with the Life, will tend much to the advantage and growth of both institutions. From using the same Offices, in London and elsewhere, and employing certain members of the staff and other business elements in common, the expenses of each institution must be materially lessened, and a corresponding benefit accrue. The large field of operations necessarily occupied by a successful Fire Office, will also augment the facilities of extending the business of the Briton. On all these grounds the Directors believe they are justified in augur ing a new source of prosperity to the Life Office from the establishment of the Britannia Association. It is scarcely necessary to remark that the two funds and constitution of each office are quite separate and distinct.

The Directors have again the pleasure to acknowledge the large measure of support they have received from the members of the Medical Profession, and they beg respectfully to repeat their appeal to the shareholders and policy-holders of the Briton Association not only for a continuance of their confidence, but also that they should extend that confidence to the two companies. By order of the Board, FRANCIS WEBB, Chairman, W. TYLER SMITH, Deputy Chairman ; JOHN MESSENT, Actuary and Secretary.

London, 18th March, 1869.

The Chairman said he had great pleasure in rising to move the adoption of the report. The first thing that would probably strike them was the fact that the new business was a trifle less than it was in the preceding year. The falling off, however, was very small, the new premiums of the year amounting to £25,277, which was £189 less than the sum reported last year. The number of policies issued had been less than that of the preceding year. Though this might seem a trifle discouraging, yet there was the counterbalancing fact that the policies were of a higher class, the average amount being £284, against average of £257 in 1867. The general income of the year was £237,980, and after allowing for the claims and expenses of every kind they carried £68,000, which was a fraction over 29 per cent of their receipts. The claims had been upon 335 policies ; and though they amounted to £14,0...

n in the preceding year, they had not ex-
.e expected amount, and if they carried
comparison, they would find that. the
1867 were £27,000 less than they were in
.c claims last year happened to have fallen
larger policies, the average being £350,
:he average of the new policies was £284.
tgages upon freehold and leasehold pro-
v now amounted to £225,000 ; and when
.ed to that the amount invested upon
.d other loans incident to an insurance
, amounting to £177,538, £104;058 fund-
lties, and a few other investments, the
.unt was brought up to £667,493. (Hear,
Jpon this large sum they have received
.ar an income of £21,000 as interest. The
.it referred to was the dividend. If the
lers did not get more than 8 per cent, it
ly because the Directors thought it wise
.ulate their profits rather than divide too
amount. The result of the bonus inves-
had been made known. It must be a
.sfaction to them to find that he could
.nd so large a sum as £87,000 for distri-
of which about £70;000 went to the
.ders ; and it was an additional satisfac-
now that the result showed the office to
.ound and healthy position. (Cheers.)
I not detain them longer, but he thought
.l be wrong in sitting down without al-
. the institution of the Britannia Fire As-
. This was a subject that had been
.em for many years, and at last the board
.animous in acceding to the wishes of
.ands, shareholders and policyholders, to
.that company. The result, so far as
.gone, proved that they were fully justi-
.is belief that the institution of the Bri-
.'ould be most useful in promoting the
.of the Briton Life. (Hear, hear.) They
.t remove their life policies from one office
.er without a sacrifice, but that was not
.with regard to fire policies. These were
. renewed every year, and as they ex-
. had no doubt that many who were in-
.the Briton would transfer their fire poli-
.he Britannia, as many persons preferred
.their life and fire policies in one office.
.ese men he need not tell them that both
.uld be assisted in regard to expenditure ;
.jh it was quite true that nothing could
.distinct than the two companies were as
.capital funds and liabilities, still there
.ain items of expenditure in common, in
.1e Briton would for a time help the
. s, and where the Britannia would come
.'elieve the expenses of the Briton to a
.ent. (Hear, hear.)
. Tyler Smith (Deputy-Chairman) second-
.iotion. He would refer to the remark-
.mer in which the first 15,000 shares in
.annia Fire Association were subscribed
.the course of a few days this number was
.for and allotted. (Hear, hear.) Of
.e reason why they had no difficulty in
.: of the shares was the position the
.the Briton held in the money world.
.nal shares were at the present time pay-
.lr cent, and there could be no doubt that
.er five years this would be largely in-

liver had great pleasure in moving that
thanks of the meeting be given to Mr.
cratchley for the efficient services he had
to the association during the past year.
. heard much about the prosperity of the
.nd for that success they owed a great
.oss gentlemen who had been called in
.ieir opinions upon different matters, and
the rest—perhaps pre-eminently so—
l had the advice and assistance of the
.n whose name he had just introduced to
.heir bonus reports for the year would
the merits and ability of Mr. Scratchley.
.ear.) No small amount of actuarial
.je and skill was necessary to present such

a report as that ; and he need hardly say that Mr.
Scratchley occupied the very highest position as
an actuary, and it was their happiness to have
had the benefit of his advice for so many years.
(Cheers.) He hoped they would continue to have
his services, and that under his guidance the association would continue to progress. (Cheers.)
Dr. Carmichael, of Edinburgh, in seconding
the motion, remarked that Mr. Scratchley's name
was thoroughly well known in the actuarial world,
and he believed that the bonus report which he
had presented would add to his reputation.
The resolution having been agreed to, Mr.
Scratchley, in returning thanks, said that this
time last year he felt it his duty to speak diffi-
dently of the prospects of the result of his valuation, and to utter words of caution ; but he could
now tell them unhesitatingly that the bonus allotted had been fully and fairly earned. (Hear,
hear.) The investigation involved 38,000 calculations, but he was greatly assisted in his labors
by the returns which Mr. Messent furnished him
with, and in which there was not a single error.
(Hear, hear.) He had left a large and ample reserve for future liabilities ; and if the same careful management was continued for another five
years, he hoped to have to make the same pleasant tale at the close of the next valuation.
The thanks of the meeting were tendered to
Mr. Messent, the Actuary and Secretary of the
company, who made a suitable reply.
A cordial vote of thanks was then given to the
Chairman, and the proceedings terminated.

Insurance.

FIRE RECORD.—Omemee, March 31.—The new
steam saw mill of Wm. Cottingham, and the old
mill formerly used as a saw mill but lately converted into a shingle mill. The entire premises
were entirely destroyed. The value of the property is estimated at about $5,000. A local paper
says there was no insurance on the buildings.
Chesterville, Ont., March 31.—Hilliers grist;
saw and shingle mills, and Messrs. Ault and
Edgerton's carding mill were totally destroyed.
The mills were the property of J. P. Crysler, and
were insured in the Western for $2,500 ; the
loss will exceed that amount by seven or eight
thousand dollars.
Niagara Township, Ont., March.—Dwelling
house of Robert Thompson and contents; nothing
saved, no particulars as to insurance.
Eden Mills, Ont., March 26.—The wagon shop
of Ralph Richardson, was partially destroyed ; a
cow and a horse perished in the flames. The fire
was caused by a barrel of ashes which took fire.
Esquesing Township, Halton Co., Ont., March
27.—The barns, stables and sheds of Francis Kent,
containing a quantity of wheat and other grain,
hay, etc., were totally destroyed. No insurance.
The origin of the fire is supposed to be incendiarism.
Balmoral, Ont., March 31.—The store occupied
by F. Butler, was consumed with contents. The
fire spread to the store of G. B. Lundy, the shoe-
shop and house of Mr. Dougherty and the house
of J. Reid. The three first mentioned parties will
it is said lose heavily. .
On River Severn, April 7.—Christie's saw mills
were destroyed by fire. Insured in the Ætna of
Hartford for $3,000 ; North British and Mercan-
tile, $3,000. Property valued at $25,000.
Toronto, April 3.—.A fire broke out in Brown's
bookbindery on King street, but was extinguished.
The loss on stock was from $3,000 to $4,000;
tha insurances were as follows : Royal, $3,000;
British-America, $4,000; Imperial, $4,000; Lancashire, $2,000; Liverpool and London, $2,000;
Queen Insurance, $2,000; Commercial Union,
$2,000; Western, $2,300; total, $21,300. The
Ætna had had a risk on the building of about
$2,000. Loss $500 to $600.
Toronto, Feb. 26.—We have some particulars
as to the fire in Shack's tobacco factory. The

building was owned by Captain Strachan. —Loss
on building $384. Insured in Ætna. The Queen
had a policy of $4,000 on machinery ; damage
about $400. No stock on the premises.
RESIGNATION.—Mr. John Turnbull, Fire Inspector of the Provincial Insurance Company has
resigned. Mr. Turnbull was a most efficient
and reliable inspector, and his resignation will be
a serious blow to the company.
APPOINTMENT.—We understand that Mr. James
Grant, late Secretary to the Life Association of
Scotland, Montreal, and previously resident
secretary at the Dublin office of the Edinburgh
Life, has received from the directors of the Reliance
Mutual the appointment of resident secretary at
the Canadian branch of the Reliance in Montreal.
—Post Magazine.
INTERNATIONAL LIFE OF LONDON.—A bill has
been filed in the United States Supreme Court,
praying that it will employ its authority to enforce
the winding up of the American business of the International Insurance Company of London, and
empower the Superintendent of the Insurance Department of New York to appropriate the funds
belonging to this company, in his possession, to
the benefit of its policy-holders in this country.
The deposit made with Mr. Barnes and its accumulations are sufficient to reinsure in sound and reliable American life institutions all this company's
risks in the United States, and all who hold its
policies should therefore present their claims to
our Superintendent. We are convinced that every
policy holder is equally entitled to reinsurance from
this fund, no matter in what State of the Union
he may reside.—Insurance Times.
THE NEW FEATURE.—" Absolute security, not
forfeitable, unconditional, and unchallengeable,"
are the striking terms which herald the introduction of the latest new feature in life insurance
practice. The company which thus, at a single
bound, overleaps the barriers which prudence has
always interposed in the way of fraudulent
claims, breaks ground vigorously for the life insurance policy of the future. We would not have
been so greatly surprised if the innovation had
first obtained in some of the twenty or thirty
American companies which, groping about for
some new and unheard of device for forcing business, had accidentally hit upon this most dangerous of all the heresies. But its introduction in
England, where even annual distributions of surplus are almost unknown, warns us that not in
this country alone are the old maxims and the
old theories in danger.—Chicago Spectator.
CONSERVATISM IN INSURANCE.—Conservatism
is observed in the management of a few of our
American life insurance companies. It is a kind
of conservatism, too, which is strangely distant
from the headlong, impetuous, and irresistible
manner in which the most of our companies are
hurried forward to the brilliant fruition of a wonderful and vigorous growth. But for genuine
illustrations of proverbially and persistently conservative management we shall have to go across
the water. In England, for instance, an agent
would be considered insane who should ask a
a commission of more than ten per cent. Then,
again, it seems to be, very generally, a matter of
supreme indifference whether the amount of new
business is small or large. But there is one
reason why the managers of English life insurance
companies are entitled to the highest commendations, and that is their obstinate and characteristic opposition to extravagant expenditures for
getting business. Said the chairman of the annual meeting of a prominent London company, a
few weeks ago : "Where a large commission is
given to agents, it must materially interfere with
the profits of any society. A small new business
of five thousand pounds a year, that enables
large bonus additions to be made to the policies
is preferable to a very large new business that
yields much smaller bonuses. The medical examinations are so strict, and the board are so
careful not to waste their money in wild compe-

tition, costly advertisements, and so forth, that their business, though small, is very sound and choice." How earnestly we wish that such sentiments prevailed in the United States.—*Chicago Spectator.*

—A fire inquest was held the village of Douglas, Ont., in reference to the burning of the store of Alexander Todd, who is going through the Insolvent Court. The inquest was held at the instance of the Gore District Mutual Insurance Company but nothing of consequence was elicited.

TORONTO FIRE DEPARTMENT.

The annual report of Mr. Ashfield, the Chief Engineer of the Fire Brigade, for 1868, states that "the Fire Department was called out to fires 79 times; there were 56 fires and 26 false alarms. The total loss on buildings destroyed or damaged was $25,382, and the insurance on these $86,100. The total loss on merchandize, furniture, etc., was $20,596, and the insurance $122,-800. The amount of losses not covered by insurance included in the foregoing was, on buildings, $3,713; on merchandize, etc., $2,810. The Engineer observes that the amounts paid by the insurance companies on the above losses were in several instances far more than the real amount of loss. There were 28 brick buildings damaged; none destroyed; 47 frame buildings were damaged, and 62 destroyed. The causes of fires were: Cause not known or satisfactorily accounted for, 16; incendiary, 9; from lighted gas, 6; careless about stoves, etc., 5; chimnies on fire, 4; boiling over of chemicals, pitch, etc., 4; tobacco smoking, 3; hot ashes placed in or near wood, 2; lighted candles, 1; defective flue, 1; children playing with lucifer matches, 1; explosion of heavy metal casting, 1; fire crackers thrown into yard, 1; burning out bees' nests, 1; total, 56.

The Engineer complains of the water supply and says there has been no improvement since the date of his last annual report. He objects to the shutting off of the water on Tuesdays and Fridays, as when it is off should a fire occur considerable delay must ensue before a supply could be obtained for the engines. He mentions an instance where this occurred in December last, and a delay of eleven minutes was incurred. A large amount of property was in consequence destroyed. In August last a large amount of property on Adelaide street was destroyed through an insufficient supply of water at a hydrant belonging to the Water Company. Mr. Ashfield thinks the present annual charge of $4,524 excessive for the supply of water; the amount required annually is three quarters of a million gallons, but if a million gallons were used the cost would then be $4.50 for every 1,000 gallons, which it is said other consumers get for twenty cents.

A large portion of the city deriving no advantage whatever from the Water Works, the City Councils of former years, made appropriations for the construction of water tanks in various parts of the city far distant from any supply of water for extinguishing fire. There are now sixteen of these tanks each of which will contain about 14,000 gallons, and will afford a good supply of water to a steam engine, doing ordinary fire work, for about one hour and a half. Several of these tanks were in use for extinguishing fires during the past year—and in every instance afforded a sufficient supply for the purpose.

Mr. Ashfield then refers to the location of these tanks, and says:—

For the protection of the valuable buildings and the vast amount of property on Front street, and the south of it, and as far north as to King street, in case of accident to the Water Works; it is again respectfully recommended that a small Tank with feeder—similar to that on Bay street, be placed on each of the principal streets leading to the Bay, and as near to Front street as possible. These Tanks would always be ready with an unlimited supply of water, and with the Steam Fire Engines, would be a means of protection to property within a distance of one-fourth of a mile from each. Three of these Tanks, one on Yonge street, one on Church street, and one on the street East or West of the City Hall, are most urgently required, and could all be completed for about one thousand dollars.

The apparatus of the fire department consists of 3 Steam Fire Engines; 2 Large Hose Carts, and one small one; 1 Hook and Ladder Truck with Ladders, Hooks and Axes; 2,350 feet of good Rubber Hose; 800 feet of middling Rubber Hose; 600 feet of indifferent Rubber Hose; 2 waggons for hauling fuel, &c. &c.

The Fire Department consists of one Chief Engineer and one Assistant Engineer, two engineers and two firemen of steam engines, one caretaker of hose, &c., and one Fire Company of thirty four men, including one buglar, in all forty-one men, exclusive of supernumeraries. The Fire Company is told off into three sections of eleven to each—ten men and a foreman. Sections Nos. 1 and 2 are branch and hose men, section No. 3 are hook and ladder men, and to each section are appointed three supernumerary members.

The total expenses of the fire department in 1868 were $12,547.37. In reference to a better system of fire alarm, the Engineer says:—The Automatic Telegraph Fire Alarm, respecting which a communication from Messrs. Gamewell & Co. was recently laid before the Council, is deserving of the best and most serious consideration as soon as possible. It is probable that with that system of fire alarm in operation, the two steam engines at present in ordinary use would be more effective for the protection of property in parts of the city distant from the engine stations, than four engines would be without it. With the telegraph in operation, several of the expenses connected with the alarm bells at present in use, could be dispensed with.

Financial.

TORONTO STOCK MARKET.

(Reported by Pellatt & Osler, Brokers.)

A fair business was done during the week. Building Society stock, debentures and mortgages have been freely dealt in.

Bank Stock.—The business done in the shares of the various banks was, with one or two exceptions, very limited. Montreal sold at 144, 144½ and 145; the market closed with sellers at 145½ and buyers at 145. Sales of British were made at 105, at which rate there are buyers. No sellers of Toronto under 122, and buyers at 121. Royal Canadian has been largely dealt in; there were sales in the early part of the week at 75 and 76; buyers have now advanced to 77½, but there is very little stock on the market under 80. Small sales of Commerce were made at at 102¼ and 102½; there is some inquiry for the stock at the former rate. Gore is offered at 41 without buyers. Merchants' has sold at 107½ and 108, but declined slightly, closing with no buyers over 107¼. Quebec is firm and in demand at 101½, with no sellers under 102. There are buyers and sellers of Molson's at 109 and 110 respectively. City closed rather heavy at 102½ and 102¾. Du Peuple is in fair demand at 108; little in market. Buyers offer 107½ for Nationale; none offering. Small sales of Jacques Cartier occurred at 109 and 109½; it is offered at the latter price.

Debentures.—Government securities are in good demand; Canada currency and sterling six per cents are asked for at 103; five per cents are nominal at 93 and 94½. Dominion stock has been sold at 106½, and Dominion bonds at 105½. There have been no Toronto debentures on the market for some time; they would be readily taken to pay 6¾ per cent. County have been sold to some extent at 99 to 100. There is a slight tendency to lower rates.

Sundries.—Canada Permanent Building Societ has been freely dealt in at 125¼ to 126; there a still buyers at the latter rate. Sales of Westeı Canada Building Society were made at 120½, 120 121 and 121¼. Freehold B. S. sold at 110½ an 111; there are now buyers at 111. Buyers off 132½ for Montreal Telegraph, with sellers at 133 Small sales of Canada Landed Credit occurred 78 and 79; sellers generally ask 80. City Gas enquired for at 108 and 108½, at which latter ra there have been small sales. British-Ameri Assurance is asked for at 55; there are sellers to limited extent at 56. Mortgages have been free offered at 8 and 8½ per cent on first class farm aı city property. Money continues in demand advanced rates.

TORONTO CITY FINANCES.

At a meeting of the City Council on Mond last the Chamberlain submitted a statement shov ing the receipts and expenditures of the Corpor tion of Toronto for 1868.

The total amount of revenue received for tl year, including the sum of $51,553.66, which w in bank and on hand, on the first of Jan., 186 was, $803,921.41. The amount of payments f the year was $692,208.84, which, with cash bank and on hand, 31st December, viz: $111,7 57, amounts to $803,921.41.

Statement of the floating liabilities and asse of the Corporation of the City of Toron for the financial year ending 31st Decembe 1868:

LIABILITIES.—Due to sundry special accoun being balances at credit of said accounts 31st De 1868: Debentures due and not presented for pa ment, $14,567.50; sinking fund accounts, $17 678.88; police reserve fund, $667.73; private drai account, $429.01; common school account, $5,9 00; grammar school account, $827.00; City Reg try Office building, $5,000.00; public walks a gardens fund, $234.48; local improvement sewe $25.78; western market fund, $3,413.62; str watering accounts, $594.22. Total—$210,362.

Due to the following accounts being balan at credit of said accounts required to meet o standing claims: Discount on debentures und posed of, $8,922.00; interest on debentures d 1st January, 1869, $15,521.66; Municipal sa ries, $3,094.53; gas supply, $5,386.04; wa supply, $2,358.48; Board of Health, $159.8 advertising, $12.46; consolidation city by-la $1,672.50; street repairs, $1,477.15; special m adamizing, $12,414.00; printing, $471.58; s tionery, 1,012.38; water tanks, $277.66; electi expenses, $231.15; charitable grants, $1,757. County York rent of Court-house, $700.00.— tal, $55,469.00. Due to Bank of Toronto notes under discount not yet matured, $111,00 00.—Total liabilities on account of year, 18 $376,831.00.

ASSETS.—Due from following sources: Deb tures to be negotiated on account of Sinking Fu $58,290.03; rentals due, $13,500; market f $2,625.67; maintenance of county prisone $550.80; Province of Ontario on account of g expenditure, $2,500; bills receivable, $262. taxes of 1868 uncollected, $225,108.25, less p bable losses and arrearages, $28,108.45—$196,0 public buildings account, amount over expen ture in 1868, $365.97; gaol and industrial fa amount over expenditure in 1868, $427.50.

Cash on hand and in bank 31st. Dec. 186 Bank of Toronto, general account, $39,233. Bank of Toronto, Sinking Fund account, $69, 93; Bosanquet, Salt & Co., Sinking Fund accou $62.80; Bosanquet, Salt & Co. general accou $2,380.55; on hand, as per cash book, $930.8 Total, $111.712.57. Total amount of ass $386,241.19. Surplus assets over liabilities, $ 539.92.

The statement of the financial results of year showing a surplus of $10,534.06, cannot to be satisfactory to the Council. This sur

incipally from a large amount of arrears
axes of the year 1867 having been received,
arger amount received for commutation of
ates than what was estimated, together
eral Esplanade awards having been paid

ount of debenture debt on
st Dec. 1867, was...........$2,114.853 44
do. .1868, " 2,065,594 22
                                    _____
                                    $49,259 22
ng that the debt has been reduced during
year by the sum of $49,259.22. This
reduction of the debt must be a source of
ion to the citizens, and there is no doubt
he present prosperous state of the city a
ble reduction can be made during the
year.
mount at the credit of the sinking fund
1st December, was $168,678.88, the par-
of which are as follows :—Debentures held
in on account of the fund, $58,156.70 ;
Bank at Toronto, 31st December, $69,-
amounts in process of collection, $51,-
-Total $178,678.87. The latter amount
ed in the assessment rate of 1868, a large
on of which had been realized since the
December, and is now lodged in the Bank
to. The amount at the credit of the
Bank at this date—5th April—is $112,-

ry important that the whole of this fund, a
ible portion of which is yielding only four
interest, should be immediately applied
yment of the debentures for which the
instituted. These debentures might be
d at a discount and the amount thus legi-
invested would be a saving to the Corpo-
about three per cent per annum. The
hich would be thus effected would be
,000 annually.

MENT of the revenue and expenditure of
inion of Canada for the month ended 31st
869 :
........................$630,592 24
.... 265,764 83
e........................ 15,584 04
p Duty........................ 8,095 34
orks, including Railways... 43,773 85
eous... .... 28,847 20
                                    _____
)tal........................$992,657 50

ure........................$546,019 79

lE.—The numbers and amounts of the
len about a year ago from the Western
elegraph Company are: No. 17, $600;
600; No. 187, $500; No. 188, $500; No.
); No. 208, $500; No. 842, $500. Pay-
he bonds has been stopped. The robbers
o have been traced to Canada.

THE CANADIAN MONETARY TIMES AND INSU-
RANCE CHRONICLE *is printed every Thursday evening and distributed to Subscribers on the following
morning.*

*Publishing office, No. 60 Church-street, 3 doors
north of Court-street.*

Subscription price—
    Canada $2.00 *per annum.*
    England, stg. 10s. *per annum.*
    United States (U.S.Cy.) $3.00 *per annum.*
*Casual advertisements will be charged at the rate
of ten cents per line, each insertion.*
Address all letters to " THE MONETARY TIMES."
*Cheques, money orders, &c. should be made pay-
able to* J. M. TROUT, *Business Manager, who alone
is authorized to issue receipts for money.*

All Canadian Subscribers to THE MONETARY
TIMES *will receive* THE REAL ESTATE JOURNAL
without further charge.

The Canadian Monetary Times.

THURSDAY, APRIL 8, 1869.

THE BANK CHARTER QUESTION.

AN INCONVERTIBLE CURRENCY.

V.

At the outset of this discussion we asserted,
on what we think will be admitted to be
tenable grounds, that an extension of the
Provincial note system that should displace
the existing bank notes, or the substantial
adoption of the National Bank law of the
United States, would prove the inevitable
precursor of a suspension of cash payments.
Adhering to this idea we proceed to examine
some of the consequences that would result
from so disastrous a monetary revolution.

Most objects of desire and commerce
possess properties of which it is necessary to
ascertain definitely the extent or value.
When a web of cloth is sold its superfices has
to be ascertained, and we have a determinate
measure which we can apply to it and thereby ascertain its length, width and extent.
The measure by which this is done is a thing
of unvarying value, a foot, or an ell, or
a metre, or a yard, is not longer or shorter
at one time than another ; it neither contracts nor expands, and it is this quality of
being always of the same determinable length
that gives it its value as a common measure.
If a chest of tea has to be sold the operation
is a different one ; here we must be guided by
weight, and that weight consists of a certain
positive and unchanging quantity. It is
never more or less at one time than another,
but is always the same. Besides superfices
and weight, either of which may without the
other, attach to exchangeable commodities,
all objects of commerce have ano..her property —value—which requires an instrument
by which it can be measured. That instru-

ment is money. All civilized nations for
reasons which they have regarded as sufficient, have unanimously agreed in making
one or both of the precious metals, gold and
silver, a common measure of all other values.
Not that a pound of silver or an ounce of
gold will at all times, and in all places,
measure or exchange for an equal quantity of
flour, cloth, iron, or any other commodity ;
but either of them would be a perfect measure
as nearly as possible, of all kinds of commodities at the same time and place. The
variation here indicated does not take place
in the measure of value, but in the value
itself. Gold and silver have not always
been absolutely unchangeable in value, but
any deviation they may have undergone in
this respect has extended over so great a
length of time that it has produced no practical inconvenience. This quality of being
but little liable to variation in value is perhaps the strongest of all those which have
combined to compel the general assent of
mankind to their adoption as a measure
of value. They have other qualities
which have had a share in recommending
them. They have cost much labor to produce them ; they are useful in the arts and
are nearly indestructible. You may submit
them to fire, bury them in the earth, let
them lie for ages in the water, subject
them to acids that would destroy ball metal,
and they will neither be diminished in quantity nor deteriorated in quality. Compared
with almost anything else that could be
adopted as a measure of value, they are
free from cumbrousness, being compact and
easily handled.

All experience shows that with our present
knowledge, and in the existing state of human
society, a wise selection was made when, by
common consent, the precious metals were
converted into an instrument for measuring
the value of all other commodities. There
have been times of crisis, of peril, of danger
to national existence, of mad and visionary
speculation, when nations have attempted to
supersede the precious metals by the substitution of printed bits of paper, promising to
pay on demand, what the issuers notoriously
did not possess. The result has always been
disastrous. Of the governments which have
so issued their promises, there is not one,
Simondi tells us, " which has not sacrificed
" to the wants of the moment the security
" of the future, and the justice which it
" owed to its own subjects ; not one which
" has not multiplied its paper to three, often
" ten, and even twenty times the nominal
" value of its specie." In 1805, Spain had
in circulation under the name of *vales*—
reales, one hundred and twenty millions of
paper dollars, which were at a discount of 58
per cent ; and afterwards, the discount rose as

high as 88 per cent. The States of Sardinia, of Naples, and of the Pope, also made a like abuse of paper money, of which the value was reduced to nothing, and was cancelled by the force of revolution. "The circulating " capital of France," according to Sismondi, " was twice almost entirely destroyed by " paper money ; the first time by Law's Bank, " and the second time by assignats. Dur- " ing the depreciation of paper, no one sold " without being obliged to replace his goods " at a higher figure, so that every exchange " was a loss, and the results of the accumu- " lated labor of preceding ages being gradu- " ally subjected to like sales, were in the end " destroyed." * * *. " At the second epoch, " anything that was susceptible of being sold, " however by its nature unlikely to become " an object of commerce was exported. Shops " of every kind were emptied of their goods ; " the book stores even underwent the same " process, and old furniture was in its turn " shipped off to foreign countries. Commerce " had acquired a false activity. The nation " seemed to be selling heavily, but it received " for its pay only paper which had no value, " and in the end it found that it had exchanged " all its material wealth for 45,579,000,000 of " francs in assignats, which at the moment " of their suppression, on the 7th of Sept., " 1796, were worth only three sous, six " deniers to the one hundred francs."

These lessons of history ought to be a sufficient warning not to set up a system of banking and currency which will bring about like calamities. If the govern- ment of this country were to insist on com- pelling the banks to advance to it the great bulk of their capital, no matter what might be the pretext under which the law was framed, there could be but one result. The banks would, in that case, become much more liable to failure than at present, and the catastrophe would not be unattended with individual, almost amounting to public, suffering. The bill-holders might possibly be secured but the depositors would suffer. The notes might, or might not, be guar- anteed by the government. If they were, the operation might take this shape. The government, we will suppose, wants to raise money outside of the revenue, to add a few millions to the public debt. This can only be done by borrowing. The question is what is the best way of doing it ? by going into the open market or by a forced loan from the banks. In the former case the government would know precisely at what rate it was borrowing, and what it would have to pay. In the latter case, it would be groping in the dark, and might have to repay twice as much as it borrowed. That might occur in this way, the faith of the Dominion being pledged to the redemption

of the notes, if the securities deposited by the banks became depreciated in value, the government, that is, the people, would have to pay the difference. It is quite conceivable that something might occur to reduce the selling price of Dominion debentures to fifty per cent. of their face value. In that case new securities would have to be issued and sold at a time when the public credit could least bear an additional pressure upon it. Every successive sale would bring down the value. On the other hand, if the notes were not guaranteed by the government and the securities on which they were based, under- went a great depreciation, how would the note-holders be paid more than a fraction of their claims ? Certainly not out of the fund destined for the redemption of the notes. In the first case the general public would lose ; those very bill-holders for whose benefit the scheme would have been ostensibly adopted would be the victims.

The downward course, once entered upon, would be rapid. If the Government itself, issued or authorized others to issue paper of this description, it could not refuse to receive it in payment of public dues. Thus while it was nominally receiving one dollar revenue it would really be only receiving fifty cents. Further expansions of credit would follow, and the paper would at last become only of mere nominal value. That is the course and the history of nearly every such transaction, and we need not flatter ourselves that any exceptional immunity will be accorded in our case.

Let no one say that these predictions are founded on false fears. We have already de- clared, by legislative enactment, the Provin- cial note to be equivalent in value to gold. Everybody to whom it is offered is obliged to accept it. It is true specie can, under the law, be demanded for these notes, but the operation is little better than a farce when they can be re-issued as specie the next mo- ment. *

When paper money begins to depreciate the usual course is for the Legislature to step in and declare it equivalent to gold. In France Law's bank notes were declared, by Gover- mental authority, worth five per cent. more than specie, and the public was ordered to take them on those terms.

In England, during the long suspension of specie payments, which commenced near the close of the last century, a law was enacted declaring Bank of England notes equivalent in value to gold,‡ and annex- ing a penalty to the offence of offering or taking them for less. So gross an interfer-

‡ Tout papier duut les course is forcé doit être con- sidéré comme un papier-monnaie, encore qu'il soit acquitté à bureau ouvert car ce paiement est sans doute illusoire des l'instant qu'on s'est vu obligé de forcer ac- ceptation du papier et de la déclarer par la loi équivalent à l'argent.—Sismondi.

ence with existing contracts has only name to describe it, and that is robbery.

Let us be guided by the experience of past to avoid the wide-spread calami which an irredeemable paper currency wc inflict on the country.

DOMINION TELEGRAPH COMPA

The stockholders of this company are il ease. A few days since a number of th resident at London, held a meeting and solved to pay no calls on their stock u more satisfactory information was receive to the precise character of the scheme ; people of Owen Sound seem also interes in the solution of a few knotty points, clamor for more light ; the Quebec peo out of a prying curiosity, we suppose, se representative directly to headquarters facts and figures, and this after the issu a lengthy certificate signed by the Presic and all those influential directors who h the scheme in hand, as to the soundne the undertaking. However if the des information is at last obtained we hop will be given to the public ; surely Quebec subscribers will not hide their li under a bushel. Meantime, in the abs of such intelligence respecting the arra ments of the Company as ought, under circumstances, to be given to the public, to all the shareholders especially, we ha few facts to submit, which at least poin moral.

The Directors admit the existence o contract binding on the Company to Mr. Reeves, the promoter, floater, tractor and principal stockholder, the sur $250 a mile for some two thousand mile double wire. Making a note of this le state another fact : A telegraph line o similar character is about to be constru running from Ottawa to Quebec. Thi called "The People's Line." Quite rece the contract for building the section o Ottawa to Montreal was let—the line t turned over to the Company by the 1s August next—at the rate of 876 per without the wires. These the Company to furnish, and will cost from $40 to $44 mile for a double wire. Taking this this line :

Contract price, building, per mile	.....
Wire (double)	.....
Instruments, batteries, etc., average	.....
Cables	.....
Advertising and sundries	.....
Total cost, per mile	.....

No one who knows anything practicall the subject will deny that we have ma liberal allowance for expenses and con gencies. At this rate then the two thou of line which the Dominion Company se- to build would cost $300,000. But Mr. Reeves as contractor and $250 per is the rate, the two thousand miles will 500,000—leaving the modest balance of)00 as Mr. Reeves' profit after paying l expenses !

re than this, we believe that when the ; are admitted to the secret history of liberations of Mr. Reeves and *his* di- s, it will appear that the contract was ally at the rate of $400 per mile of e wire and that on the urgent represen- s of the directors—in consequence of the ures made by the press—Mr. Reeves, out generosity of his heart, made the com- a present of $150 per mile on his con- or $300,000 on the whole job. This reduction being made, the contract gned and concluded with the directors iow exists.

ll this there is a practical question for hareholders to consider. We have that Mr. Reeves must make a clear if he carries out the contract, of)00; what then will the company have resent this large sum, or to earn a div- on it ? This is the point to be invest- . The subscribers will act wisely to the contribution of another cent to mpany's exchequer, till this all impor- it matter is cleared up—till something than vague general statements are ed such as those with which the officers company have endeavored to conciliate who believe themselves to have been ed by false representations to subscribe e stock.

rill not do for the backers and tooters company to raise the cry of "grasping joly" as an answer to those who are nined to know the truth respecting his has been the watchword of these men from the start, and has done duty vhere. Monopolies are always bad e would not, if we could, offer an apol- r them; but it is just possible that the olders of the Dominion Company may to the conclusion before they are much that there are still greater evils in the than even such a monopoly as now ds the telegraphing business of Canada.

RITON LIFE ASSOCIATION.

devote a good deal of space to the il Report, and the proceedings had at nnual meeting of this Association. The sults of the year's business were: a div- to the proprietors at the rate of 8 per and a balance of profit, after paying penses and charges, of over $340,000. nnual premium income has risen to $1,000,000 and the interest on invest-

ments to over $100,000. The new business of the past year is represented by 2,472 poli- cies, assuring over seven hundred thousand pounds sterling and producing in annual pre- miums over twenty-five thousand pounds. A careful valuation of the company's policies was made by Mr. Arthur Scratchley, aided by the actuary and secretary of the company, Mr. John Messent, upon whose report a bonus was declared to the shareholders and policyholders of over $430,000—the latter receiving all but 10 per cent of this sum.

The meeting seems to have been a most agreeable one, and with the existing state of affairs it would be difficult to find fault. Arrived at the close of the fifteenth year of the Company's existence, the directors very properly give us the history of its progress during that period. This is done in a neat but comprehensive table in the report. Every effort seems to be put forth in the direction of thoroughness, economy and general good management, and we think the exhibit made at the close of 1868 is the best possible proof that the control of the Com- pany's affairs has fallen into good hands.

REFINING PETROLEUM—A GREAT DISCOVERY.

For years past the petroleum trade of Ca- nada has been in a stagnant condition. The demand has been strictly limited to the re- quirements for home consumption, so that a little over-production always resulted in glutted markets, a fall in prices, and losses to the well-owners and refiners. The offensive odor that Canadian refined oil exhales has condemned it in European markets, and branded it as unfit for use. All the numerous attempts to remove this odor have hitherto proved fruitless, but we now have the true satisfaction of informing the public that this seemingly insuperable obstacle *has been en- tirely overcome.*

So thoroughly has this been accomplished that a number of the most experienced refin- ers in this Province have organized a company in order to unite their capital, energy, and business capacity in the establishment of an export trade in this most valuable product. Already works are in operation in the city of Hamilton where the process of deodorization is being carried on. The refinery of Messrs. J. M. Williams & Co. is being used tempo- rarily for the purpose. When the manufact- uring establishment which the company are erecting at Hamilton shall be completed, it will have a refining capacity equal to one-half of the united capacity of all the refineries in the Province, or from 2,000 to 3,000 barrels per week. The latest and most useful ma- chinery will be used, reducing the cost of manufacturing to the minimum.

It is proposed to distil the oil at Petrolia, and convey it to Hamilton in tank cars, where it will be "treated" and shipped by the narrow gauge on the Great Western Railway to the seaboard at Boston or New York. A still is being erected at Petrolia of 2,800 bris. capacity—probably the largest still ever built, the largest in Pensylvania being about 1,200 barrels. A great portion of the oil for ex- portation will be put in tin cans of 5 gallons each, which will be shipped in wooden cases, two in each case. This is the most approved package for shipment to the European coun- tries, the oil being in a suitable shape for re- tailing without change of package. It will, besides, be shipped in barrels in the usual way.

"The Ontario Carbon Oil Comp'y of Ham- ilton" consists of the following well-known gentlemen, the mention of whose names is in itself a guarantee of the entire success of the enterprise, and that whatever capital may be necessary to the vigorous prosecution of the business will be forthcoming :

Messrs. Parson, Brothers, Toronto.
Messrs. Duffield, Brothers, London.
Messrs. J. M. Williams and James Cumming, Hamilton.
Judge Higgins, Chicago.

These gentlemen have already purchased about 40,000 barrels of crude oil, which is a proof of their full confidence in the success of what they have undertaken. The matter is not, however, a mere experiment, the com- pany having already turned out some 2,000 barrels of the finest oil ever offered in the market, not excepting the best Pennsylvanian. Such, at least, is the opinion of the most com- petent judges. A lot of 500 barrels is being shipped this week from London to the Bos- ton market, where it has been sold to ar- rive, at a price equal to that obtained for the very highest grade of American oil. Another lot of 500 barrels, made by this process, was shipped to Halifax, where it is selling readily, and is spoken of in the highest terms in con- trast with American oil.

Oil prepared by this process is found to have a specific gravity of 44 degrees, while Pensylvania stands at 46°; the fire test by the American standard is 130°, and the Pensylva- nia, by the same standard, is 112°, so that both in point of burning qualities and safety, it must take the precedence over American oil. In the new mode of manufacture such a saving is effected in the cost of refining that the very best oil can be produced at as low a rate as the commonest grades now manufac- tured. It is also affirmed of the new product that the pleasant aromatic odor it possesses in the first place becomes (quite contrary to the usual experience) more pleasant the longer the oil is kept. The peculiar chemical process by which all this is brought about is, of course, a secret, the value of which may be inferred from the above facts; and the profit likely to arise from it to those directly interested we do not attempt to estimate. It is sufficient for the general public to know that the home market will be supplied and a large export trade also opened up in Canadian Petroleum—a trade which will permanently relieve this suffering industry, and confer an inestimable benefit on the whole country.

THE LANCASHIRE INSURANCE COMPANY.

The annual report of this office for 1868 shows an increase in every department of the business. The fire premiums amounted to £112,579, and the net profit made after paying losses, re-insurances, &c., was over £21,813. In the Life department the income was £46,636, from which were deducted £15,978 for 41 death claims, and some smaller sums, leaving a profit of £18,359 18s. 6d., which was added to the life reserve fund, increasing it from £150,971 last year to £169,331.

The rapid accretion of the life reserve was pointed out by one of the speakers—in 1863 it was £94,700; in 1865 it was £155,300—an average addition of £10,500 per annum—in 1865 and 1867 it stood at £151,000—an average addition of £17,500 per annum—and in 1868 it was swelled to $169,330, showing an addition in the year of £18,350, being the largest addition yet made. The fire premiums in the same time run up from £57,000 to £113,500, and the reserve in this branch is nearly £49,000. A dividend of 10 per cent. was declared on the year's business.

The remarkable statement was made by the chairman that every one of the branch offices made a profit during the year. No better proof could be given that a careful supervision is exercised. The Ontario agents Messrs. S. C. D.—Clark & Co.—have fully maintained the character of the company for good management, having a very satisfactory account to render of the Toronto and Hamilton business—the only points where agencies are located in Ontario.

We understand the Montreal Assurance Company have determined to resume ocean business, and are prepared to take risks to and from ports of Great Britain.

—The township of Scott has voted a bonus of $10,000 to the Toronto and Nipissing Railway. The total amount voted in aid of this road is $399,000. Two townships more are expected to vote bonuses in aid of the road bringing the total up to $426,000.

LONDON CORRESPONDENCE.

(From a correspondent.)

London, 18th March, 1869.

On the Stock Exchange there has been much excitement during the past week, with regard to the Hudson's Bay Company's shares. A few days ago buyers were numerous and prices advanced. Rumours were circulated that the terms of settlement proposed by Earl Granville would prove highly satisfactory to the Company. This was gratifying, and those who purchased shares at par, that is £20, cannot dispose of them except at from 6 to 7 per cent discount. The rise in the price was nearly £1, and the expectation was that a greater rise would take place. These hopes were blasted yesterday, on the announcement of the arrangement offered to the Company on the one hand and to Canada on the other. The nature of that proposition will doubtless have been transmitted to you by telegraph. Instead, then, of recapitulating the proffered terms, let me state for the information of your readers, the relation they bear to the anticipations formed here by those having a pecuniary stake in the Company. Two shareholders have taken leading parts in the discussion, as to terms, and have been authorized to represent many of their brethren in misfortune. According to one of them, £5,000,000 sterling is the amount which the Company ought to receive for the cession of its territorial rights. If these terms cannot be got then it is proposed to employ the Company's funds in colonization. No less than 130 shareholders are stated to have pledged themselves to insist upon carrying out this programme. Another shareholder is more reasonable. He maintains that as the territorial rights from 1863 have represented one-half of the assets, a sum equivalent to this is the minimum at which those rights ought to be sold. This amount is £1,073,192. I do not err, I think, in stating that the latter proposition is the one which finds general favor among the shareholders. The belief is current among them that the least they ought to receive is £1,000,000. Moreover, they have resolved to make large claims in the shape of territory. Under these circumstances, as you may well suppose, the announcement that the price fixed by Earl Granville was £300,000 only, gave general dissatisfaction. The shares were at once offered for sale and declined in value. At the meeting on the 24th of this month, the answer of the shareholders will be formally given. That it will be adverse is not improbable. If so, the delegates from your Government will have to return home empty-handed. Yet they will not have labored in vain. At present the feeling is gaining ground that Canada is acting both prudently and graciously in this matter. It may seem to you quite natural that such should be the opinion of the majority. But it must be remembered that in this country, and more particularly in this city, the social and political influence of the Hudson's Bay Company have heretofore sufficed to prepossess the public mind in its own favor. Among the shareholders are men of high position and great power. Of course they do what they can to further their own interests. It is no light task to run counter to these men and come off victorious. I think, however, that the efforts of Sir George Cartier and the Hon. W. McDougall to gain their point have been remarkably successful. The best proof of this is furnished by the newspapers. In the most influential and widely circulated journals there have appeared articles of a kind which the Company cannot relish, and with which Canadians ought to be pleased. I hope that the shareholders will listen to reason. As earnestly do I hope that in the event of the Company taking the prudent course, that Canada will manifest no reluctance to accept the solution of the problem.

The first general meeting of the Colonial Society was held last Monday, when Lord Bury, the

president, delivered the inaugural address. a short report of the proceedings has yet appea The address was very able and produced a r favorable impression. Perhaps too much we was attributed by Lord Bury to Mr. Gold Smith. Many persons are disposed to con the opinions of that skilful tutor as the basi Imperial policy. This is contrary to fact. N of our distinguished statesmen agree with Smith. At the meeting of the Colonial Soci the Right Hon. Chichester Fortescue, repudi the notion that any government would approv the dismemberment of the empire in opposi to the wishes of the colonists. As an estee member of the existing government he o speak on this head with good effect. At the meeting of the Society a paper will be read b Australian colonist on the question which been raised by Mr. Smith. It will then be what views are entertained by enlightened here as to the relationship which ought to o between the Mother Country and her dependen At this moment, the subject of emigratio coming before the public under various for Societies have been formed to aid those desi to proceed and settle in some county w wages are high and labor scarce. Some of Australian Colonies are making strenuous effor turn the tide of emigration to their shores. A meeting, chiefly composed of workingmen. last week, the advantages of settling in Aust were enlarged on by several speakers. Ind the object of the meeting was to put forth claims of Australia as a land of promise to industrious. Among the notables who rece an invitation to the meeting was your Minist Public Works. Being allowed to address assembly, he urged the claims of Canada · vigor and success. The picture he presented more attractive to the majority than that w the representatives of Australia held up for t admiration. Had it not been for the accide circumstance of the Hon. W. McDougall b at present in this country, this meeting w have heard nothing in favor of Canada. Ea the Australian Colonies has a representative commissioned to speak in its behalf when occ requires.

The money market continues stagnant. vestors still hesitate to embark their savin new undertakings. The only exception ap to be that of Companies for laying subm telegraphs. Two of these are now competin public patronage, both being designed to co India and our other Eastern possessions England. In the case of one, however, a experiment will be tried. The cable is much lighter, and consequently much less than those at the bottom of the Atlantic. S this proves successful, a great impetus wi given to submarine telegraphy. From L shire there are bad news. A strike is impe among the cotton workers. The dullness of has compelled the masters to reduce the ra wages ten per cent., and this is resisted b operatives. Altogether, the prospect is a gl one.

Commercial.

Toronto Market.

At this comparatively early period vessels begun to move and navigation is fairly Some two or three vessels loaded with grain cleared for Oswego, and one or two arrivals a port are reported. Among the clearances the Paragon and New Dominion with white w freight at 3c. U. S. currency; the Tranche tague also with wheat, freight 4c. U. S. curr The steamer Norseman has commenced run from Port Hope to Rochester with passenger freight; the schooners Garabaldi and John St son have left that port with wheat for Osw Charters have been made from Chicago to B at 10c. for wheat, 9½c. for corn, and 7½c. for

spect for vessels is, upon the whole, con-
fair.
has somewhat improved during the week;
re a number of country buyers in town,
siness for the season is only just com-
g.
ERIES.—*Sugars*—The New York market
⅜ to ¼c. lower on raw sugars, and ½ to ¾c.
ied than it was a week ago. *Teas*—A
trade is doing; some common kinds are
dearer without much quotable change.
r articles there is little to report.
s.—The market is dull, and there is very
emand for trimmed and inspected; our
ons show a reduction on the figures of last

HER.—A fair business was done with the
le at quotations.
N—*Wheat*—Receipts 2,342 bush., and
ast week. There has been some demand
ng during the week, and sales of 10,000
t 90c. at Kincardine, and some cars at
c. are reported; and there are also reports
amounting to 20,000 bush. at $1 in ships'
e on cars; the market closes dull and un-
with no buyers at these figures, and hold-
ningly anxious to sell. Fall is dull at
ns; no demand and no sales; midge proof
nal. The stock of Wheat in Toronto on
31st was—Spring, 105,100 bus.; Fall,
bus. *Barley*—Receipts light; the market
in sympathy with New York, where there
rge receipts from Germany, and sales at
$2.12; in our market small lots are selling
5 to $1.20; stock on 31st March 30,500
Peas—Receipts trifling; they are held at
good samples in car loads, and are worth
5c., but there is little demand; stock 31st
35,100 bush. *Oats*—Receipts 1,800 bushs.
200 bushs. last week. The market is firm
her at 53c., and 55c. has been paid for
on the Northern Railway; stock 31st
21,900 bushs. *Rye*—Nominal at 60c.
s worth from 60 to 62c. in car loads.
Timothy seed is offering freely, and some
No. 1 were made at $2.60 to $2.65; we
he market at $2.25 to $2.60. Clover is
l held at $6.25 to $6.50, but no buyers at
side quotation. Flax seed $2.
R.—Receipts 2,342 bbls. and 1,300 bbls.
k. There is some demand for small lots
5 to $4.10, holders asking higher prices;
0 bbls. at $4.05 in store; 500 bbls at $4.05
wood; 100 bbls. at $4.10 free in cars, and
at $4 in store. Extra is held at $4.50.
rades not quotable. Bag flour may be
at $3.80 to $3.90. The stock of flour in
31st March was 25,800 bbls. *Oatmeal*—
at $5.50 to $5.60; the demand is very

ISIONS.—*Butter*—Prime is scarce, and
bring 24 to 26c.; anything under this
is not wanted. *Mess Pork*—Car loads are
nly at $26, and a sale occurred at that
Lard—Is dull; a lot of 60 pkgs. sold at
Eggs—Are rapidly declining; offering at
c. and buyers at 15c.; they will soon be
10 to 11c. *Bacon*—Cumberland scarce
d at 12c., ordinary at 11½c. *Dressed*
None selling.
OLEUM.—The price for car loads of white
d to 33½c., which is the only quality now
n lots; there is a quiet demand.
HTS.—Rates by Grand Trunk Railway:—
all stations from Belleville to Lynn, in-
35c., grain per 100 lbs. 18c.; flour to
lle and Cornwall, inclusive, 43c. grain 22c.
Montreal 50c. grain 25c.; flour to all
between Island Pond and Portland, in-
85c. grain 43c.; flour to Boston 90c.,
ain 45c.; flour to Halifax 98c., grain —c;
St. John 98c. Boxed Meats to Liverpool
s ton 82s. 6d.; lard or butter in tinnets
; Pork 11s. per tierce; flour 5s. 6d. per
grain 12s. per 480 pounds. Rates by
estern Railway—Flour, Toronto to Sus-

pension Bridge 25c. gold; thence to New York, 92c. U. S. currency per bbl.; to Boston $1.02. Grain to Bridge 13c., gold; thence to New York 46c, U. S. currency; to Boston 51c. Grain, Toonto to Detroit, 18c. ber 100 lbs; flour 35c per bbl.

Halifax Market.

BREADSTUFFS.—We note no quotable change in flours during the past week. Supers continue in request, while other grades are entirely neglected. Oatmeal is still without buyers, with stocks increasing from local supply. Cornmeal is without change at former quotations. White wheat extra, fall, $6.50 to $6.60; fancy, $6.10 to $6.25; bakers' strong, $5.75 to $5.90; supers, $5.60 to $5.65; No. 2, $4.50 to $4.75; middlings, $4.25 to $4.50. Rye, $4.75. Cornmeal K. D., $4 to $4.10; F. G. $3.80 to $3.90. Oatmeal, $7. White beans, $2.80 to $3.

PROVISIONS.—Pork continues without change at former quotations. Beef dull and unchanged. Pork, $18. Beef, mess, $10 to $12. Lard, 16c. Cheese, 15c.

WEST INDIA PRODUCE.—The demand for sugars and molasses has somewhat abated, sellers being supplied to a certain extent, are now waiting the opening of the spring trade before making any further transactions. Our receipts of both the above are considerably short, as compared with those of the same period last year. Holders are willing to take the risk of the markets, while buyers act cautiously in expectation of lower figures. Sugar V. P., 10½ to 11c.; Porto Rico, 9¼ to 9½c.; Barbadoes, 9c. Molasses---Cienfuegos, 44 to 45c.; Trinidad, 41 to 42c. Rum, in bond, Demerara, 58 to 60c. Coffee, Jamaica, 13 to 15c.; St. Domingo, 11 to 13c.

FISH AND OIL.—Our markets for fish exhibit no change. Stock continues light, with small receipts. Cod oil has somewhat improved; we notice a sale at 59 net, best, for a small lot. Other descriptions unchanged.

EXCHANGE.---Bank drafts, London, 60 days, at 13 per cent.; Montreal sight, 4 per cent.; New York sight, gold, 4 per cent.; Currency, 20 per cent. discount; St. John, N.B., 3 per cent. prem. —*R. C. Hamilton & Co.'s Circular.*

Havana Sugar Market.

HAVANA, March 24, 1869.—The *Weekly Report* says: The increase of shipments observable from this port to all ports from 1st January to date, as compared with the corresponding period in former years, is large. The cause of this increase we need not state as any one may easily trace it to the actual lamentable condition of the island, which induces planters to hurry up to market as fast as it can be manufactured, and buyers excited by the high prices paid abroad, to send out of the island all they can produce as fast it can be shipped. This explains the heavy receipts from the interior this year, which in quiet times would have led to the belief that an unprecedented large crop was being produced. The contrary, as is already known will prove to be the case, and the extent of the decrease at this date would not be exaggerated if placed at 30 per cent. comparing with last year's production. Receipts, exports and stock of boxes at Havana and Matanzas have been as follows:

Year.	Rec'd this week.	Total export Week.	Total export Since Jan. 1.	Stocks, boxes.
1869........	60,930	57,846	404,537	207,869
1868........	82,451	50,902	359,928	266,684
1867........	77,650	37,464	303,424	321,542

New Line of Steamships.

A Montreal paper says that the British Colonial Company have determined to cease running their line between London and Montreal, and that a new line will probably be put on that route. Messrs Temperly, Carter and Darke who were formerly the agents for the British Colonial Company, will despatch the Dacia on the 22nd inst. for this port, and will follow during the season. Mr. David Shaw will, we believe, represent the new line here.

The Next Cotton Crop.

The *Financial Chronicle* estimates the next crop as follows:

New Orleans........................	850,000
Mobile........................	366,000
Charleston........................	250,000
Savannah........................	500,000
Texas........................	175,000
North Carolina........................	38,000
Virginia........................	166,000
Tennessee, &c........................	450,000
Consumed in the South........................	95,000
Making the total crop below..........	2,890,000

Unusually favorable circumstances would add something to the above; but these figures show that all who are looking for a yield the coming season of about 4,000,000 bales and upwards (and there are many such) are doomed to a very severe disappointment; while on the other hand, those who say that the freedmen cannot pick over 2,250,000 bales, are equally in error. The above statement is given simply as furnishing an indication of the present *capabilities* of the country.

Breadstuffs.

The receipts of flour and grain at Chicago, Milwaukee, Toledo, Detroit and Cleveland from January 1 to March 27 were:

	1869.	1868.	1867.	1866.
Flour, bbls.......	1,321,309	684,931	747,492	570,602
Wheat, bush.....	4,993,277	2,198,873	2,123,585	5,513,232
Corn, bush.......	6,562,050	6,305,275	2,776,714	1,668,026
Oats, bush.......	2,094,024	1,439,594	1,095,894	1,287,735
Barley, bush,....	318,725	316,854	350,568	168,224
Rye, bush........	374,932	134,480	214,150	175,912
Total grain, bush..	14,433,014	10,895,076	6,260,911	5,813,149

The stocks of wheat in store at Chicago and Milwaukee in 1867, 1868 and 1869, were near upon the following figures at a late date:

	1867.	1866.	1869.
Chicago, bush....	541,300	1,055,500	1,558,900
Milwaukee, bush..	656,400	1,114,000	1,673,000
Total..........	1,197,700	2,169,500	3,231,900

New Lake Tonnage.

The following additions to the existing lake tonnage will be made this season:

	No.	Tons.
Steamers....................	5	1,300
Propellers....................	8	5,380
Barques....................	5	3,400
Schooners....................	25	5,315
Scows....................	5	385
Barges, including steam..........	9	3,775
Tugs....................	18	1,100
	75	20,655
Vessels lost last season............	105	20,441
	20	5,786

NEW INSOLVENTS.---The following names of new insolvents appear in the last Canada *Gazette*: John Irving and W. W. Hogg, Toronto; Joseph Duhamel, Montreal; W. J. Biggar, Napanee; J. C. and W. Bond, Owen Sound; R. W. Rossiter, do; Arthur Haines, St Catharines; Stephen S. Skinner, Stamford; James Russell, Nottawasaga; Francis Kebble, London; Thomas G. Harrold, Oakville; Robert Gamble, Barrie; James Dayllyn, Hamilton; Reuben Lawrence, Ottawa; Thomas McWilliams, Pembroke; S. Gunsalus, Belleville; Peter Patterson, Hamilton; G. L. Perry, Montreal; Thomas Tuer, Toronto; Henry Gauntley, Berlin; A. Souter and W. Trent, Toronto; A. McDougall, London; J. Brock, do. A writ of attachment has been issued against H. Stewart and Alexander T. Watson, by the Sheriff of the County of Perth.

—Messrs. B. & W. Rosamond, of Almonte, have their new large mill ready for operations; from 140 to 150 hands will be employed.

—Work is about to be resumed on the St. Clair Flats Canal with five dredges and the accompanying scows and other apparatus.

LIST OF INSURANCE COMPANIES LICENSED TO DO BUSINESS IN CANADA

Under the Act respecting Insurance Companies (31 Vic. Cap. 48), published in accordance with the twenty-third section thereof.

NAME OF THE COMPANY.	General Agent, Manager or Secretary.	Amount of Deposit.	For whose Security deposited.	Description of Insurance business for which licensed.
1. The British America Assurance Company of Toronto.	T. W. Birchall, Managing Director, Toronto.	$400,000, cash.	....	Fire & Inland Marine.
2. The Canada Life Assurance Company of Hamilton.	A. G. Ramsay, Manager, Hamilton.	$17,600, cash.	....	Life.
3. The Agricultural Mut'l Ass'n Ass'n of Canada, London, Ont.	D. C. Macdonald, Secretary, London.	$25,600, cash.	....	Fire.
4. The Home Insurance Company of Newhaven, Connecticut.	J. T. & W. Pennock, General Agents, Ottawa.	$72,500, U. S. bonds.	Canadian policy holders.	Fire & Inland Marine.
5. The North British and Mercantile Assurance Company.	Macdougall & Davidson, Gen'l Agents, Montreal.	$150,253, viz: $50,000 cash, and $100,253 Canada 5 p.c. consols...	Canadian policy holders.	Fire & Life.
6. The Western Assurance Company of Toronto.	Bern. Haldan, Secretary, Toronto.	$50,000 cash.	....	Fire & Inland Marine.
7. The Liverpool and London and Globe Insurance Company.	G. F. C. Smith, Esq., Resident Secretary, Montreal.	$150,693, viz: $60,000 cash, $62,293, Canada 5's, & $28,400 Canada 6's	Canadian policy holders.	Fire and Life.
8. The Royal Insurance Company.	H. L. Routh, General Agent, Montreal.	$150,515, viz: $96,982 cash, and $53,533 Canada 5's.	Canadian policy holders.	Fire and Life.
9. The Ætna Insurance Company.	Robt. Wood, General Agent, Montreal.	$50,444, viz: $1,534 cash, and $48,510 bank stocks.	Canadian policy holders.	Fire & Inland Marine.
10. The Reliance Mutual Life Assurance Society, London, Eng.	T. W. Griffith, Manager, Montreal.	$1,500 cash.	Canadian policy holders.	Life.
11. The Imperial Insurance Company, London, England.	Rintoul, Bros., General Agents, Montreal.	$107,073, viz: $54,993 British 3 per cents, $1,400 Canada 6 per cents, $48,667 Canada 5 p. cents, and $2,013 cash.	Canadian policy holders.	Fire.
12. The Hartford Insurance Company of Hartford, Connecticut.	Robt. Wood, General Agent, Montreal	$130,000 U. S. 5-20 bonds.	Canadian policy holders.	Fire.
13. The Northern Assurance Company of London and Aberdeen.	Taylor Bros., General Agents, Montreal.	$100,000, viz: $83,833 cash, $12,167 Canada 5's, and $2,000 Canada 6's.	Canadian policy holders.	Fire.
14. The Phœnix Mutual Life Assurance Co. of Hartford, Conn.	A. R. Bethune, General Agent, Montreal.	$70,000 U.S. 5-20 bonds.	Policy holders generally.	Life.
15. The Connecticut Mutual Life Insur. Co. of Hartford, Conn.	Robt. Wood, General Agent, Montreal.	$140,000 U.S. 5-20 bonds.	Policy holders generally.	Life.
16. The Lancashire Insurance Company.	William Hobbs, General Agent, Montreal.	$90,172, viz., $1,505 cash, and $48,667 Canada 5's.	Canadian policy holders.	Fire.
17. The Phœnix Fire Insurance Company of London, England.	Gillespie, Moffatt & Co., General Agents, Montreal.	$100,297, viz., $80,171 cash, and $20,126 Canada 6's.	Canadian policy holders.	Fire.
18. The Commercial Union Assurance Company of London, Eng.	Morland, Watson & Co., General Agents, Montreal.	$150,956, viz: $100,343 cash, and $50,613 Canada 5's.	Canadian policy holders.	Fire and Life.
19. The Travellers Insurance Company of Hartford, Connecticut.	T. E. Foster, General Agent, Montreal.	$140,000 U.S. 5-20 bonds.	Policy holders generally.	Life and Accident.
20. The Ætna Life Insurance Company of Hartford, Connecticut.	S. Pedlar & Co., General Agents, Montreal.	$140,000 U.S. 5-20 bonds.	Policy holders generally.	Life.
21. The Provincial Insurance Company of Canada.	Jas. Sydney Crocker, Manager, Toronto.	$16,666 cash.	Canadian policy holders.	Fire & Inland Marine.
22. The Life Association of Scotland.	Peter Wardlaw, Chief Agent, Montreal.	$150,000 cash.	Canadian policy holders.	Life.
23. The Standard Life Assurance Company.	W. M. Ramsay, Manager, Montreal.	$150,000 cash.	Canadian policy holders.	Life.
24. The Queen Fire and Life Insurance Company.	A. McK. Forbes, General Agent, Montreal.	$102,600, viz: $51,666 cash, and $51,100 Canada 5's.	Canadian policy holders.	Fire and Life.
25. The Edinburgh Life Insurance Company.	David Higgins, Secretary, Toronto.	$150,515 cash.	Canadian policy holders.	Life.
26. The London Assurance Corporation.	Romeo H. Stephens, Gen. Agent, Montreal.	Provisional deposit of consols	....	Fire.
27. The Scottish Provincial Assurance Company.	A. Davidson Parker, Gen. Agent, Montreal.	$102,123, viz.: $51,500 cash, and $50,446 Canada 6's.	Canadian policy holders.	Fire and Life.
28. The London and Lancashire Life Assurance Company.	Ticonas Simpson, Gen. Agent, Montreal.	$61,457 cash.	Canadian policy holders.	Life.
29. The New York Life Insurance Company.	Walter Burke, General Agent, Montreal.	$75,000 U.S. 5-20 bonds.	Policy holders generally.	Life.
30. The Atlantic Mutual Life Insurance Co'y of Albany, N. Y.	H. C. Allen, General Agent, Brantford.	$50,000 U.S. 10-40 bonds.	Policy holders generally.	Life.
31. The Equitable Life Insurance Society of the U. States, N.Y.		$75,458, viz: $70,000 U.S. 5-20 bonds, and $458 cash.	Policy holders generally.	Life.
32. The Briton Medical & Gen'l Life Association, London, Eng.	(Not yet appointed.)	$100,343 cash.	Canadian policy holders.	Life.
33. The Union Mutual Life Insurance Company of Maine.	R. K. Corwin, Gen. Agent, St. John, N.B.	$100,000 U.S. 6's of 1881.	Policy holders generally.	Life.
34. The Guardian Fire and Life Assurance Office, London, Eng.	(Not yet appointed.)	$100,343 cash.	Canadian policy holders.	Fire.
35. The Star Life Assurance Society of England.	Joseph Gregory, General Agent, Toronto.	$100,343 cash.	Canadian policy holders.	Life.
36. The National Life Insurance Co. of the U. States of America.	Wm. Douglas, Jr., Gen. Agent, Montreal.	$50,665 cash.	Canadian policy holders.	Life.
37. The Quebec Fire Assurance Company.	A. D. Bivvin, Secretary, Quebec.	$33,666.	Canadian policy holders.	Fire.

Mercantile.

TORONTO PRICES CURRENT.—APRIL 8, 1869.

Name of Article.	Wholesale Rates.		Name of Article.	Wholesale Rate.		Name of Article.	Wholesale Rates.	
Boots and Shoes.	$ c.	$ c.	**Groceries—***Contin'd*	$ c.	$ c.	**Leather—***Contin'd.*	$ c.	$
Mens' Thick Boots ...	2 20	2 50	Gunpowd'r c, to med .	0 55	0 70	Kip Skins, Patna	0 30	0
" Kip	2 50	3 00	" med. to fine.	0 70	0 85	French	0 70	0
" Calf	2 90	3 70	" fine to fins't.	0 85	0 95	English	0 65	0
" Congress Gaiters ..	2 00	2 50	Hyson	0 45	0 80	Hemlock Calf (30 to		
" Kip Cobourgs....	1 15	1 45	Imperial	0 42	0 90	35 lbs.) per doz...	0 50	0
Boys' Thick Boots	1 70	1 80	*Tobacco, Manufact'd:*			Do. light	0 45	0
Youths'	1 40	1 50	Can Leaf, ₩ lb.&s&10s.	0 20	0 30	French Calf.......	1 03	1
Woman's Balts	0 95	1 30	Western Leaf, com ...	0 25	0 26	Grain & Sats Clt'b'der..	0 00	0
" Balmoral......	1 20	1 50	" Good	0 27	0 32	Splits, large ₩ lb......	0 20	0
" Congress Gaiters..	1 15	1 45	" Fine	0 32	0 35	" small	0 25	0
Misses' Balts	0 75	1 00	" Bright fine..	0 40	0 50	Enamelled Cow ₩ foot..	0 20	0
" Balmoral	1 10	1 30	" choice...	0 00	0 75	Patent	0 20	0
" Congress Gaiters..	1 00	1 20				Pebble Grain	0 15	0
Girls' Balts	0 65	0 85	**Hardware.**			Buff	0 14	0
" Balmoral	0 90	1 05	*Tin (not cash prices)*					
" Congress Gaiters..	0 80	1 10	Block, ₩ lb........	0 28	0 00	**Oils.**		
Children's C T. Cacks..	0 50	0 65	Grain.............	0 30	0 00	Cod	0 65	0
" Gaiters.........	0 65	0 90	*Copper:*			Lard, extra	0 00	0
Drugs			Pig	0 23	0 24	" No. 1	0 00	0
Aloes Cape........	0 12½	0 16	Sheet............	0 30	0 33	" Woollen	0 00	0
Alum.............	0 02½	0 03	*Cut Nails:*			Lubricating, patent...	0 00	0
Borax	0 06	0 00	Assorted ½ Shingles,			Mott's economic	0 50	0
Camphor, refined....	0 65	0 70	₩ 100 lb........	2 90	3 00	Linseed, raw	0 76	0
Castor Oil.........	0 10½	0 28	Shingle alone do ..	3 15	3 20	" boiled.....	0 81	0
Caustic Soda.......	0 04½	0 05	Lathe and 5 dy ..	3 30	3 40	Machinery	0 00	0
Cream Tartar......	0 40	0 45	*Galvanized Iron.*			Olive, common, ₩ gal.	1 00	1
Epsom Salts	0 03	0 04	Assorted sizes.....	0 08	0 00	" salad	1 95	1
Extract Logwood....	0 11	0 12	Best No. 24........	0 00	0 00	" saind, in bots.		
Gum Arabic, sorts...	0 20	0 25	" 26........	0 00	0 00	qt. ₩ case ..	3 69	3
Indigo, Madras.....	0 90	1 00	" 28........	0 00	0 00½	Sesame salad, ₩ gal..	1 60	1
Licorice	0 14	0 45	*Horse Nails:*			Seal, pale	0 75	0
Madder...........	0 00	0 18	Gnest's or Griffin's			Sperm Turpentine...	0 22½	0
Galls	0 32	0 37	assorted sizes.....	0 00	0 00	Varnish	0 00	0
Opium...........	10 00	13 50	For ₩ aneil sizes..	0 18	0 19	Whale............	0 00	0
Oxalic Acid........	0 20	0 25	Patent Hammer'd do .	0 17	0 18			
Potash, Bi-tart.....	0 25	0 28	*Iron (at 4 months):*			**Paints, &c.**		
" Bichromate...	0 15	0 20	Pig—Gartsherrie No 1.	24 00	25 00	White Lead, genuine		
Potass Iodide	3 00	4 50	Other brands. No 1..	23 00	24 00	in Oil, ₩ 25 lbs...	0 00	0
Senna	0 12½	0 50	" No. 2..	0 00	0 00	Do. No. 1 " ...	0 00	0
Soda Ash	0 02½	0 04	Bar—Scotch, ₩ 100 lb..	2 25	2 50	" 2 " ...	0 00	0
Soda Bicarb	4 50	5 00	Refined	3 00	3 25	" 3 " ...	0 00	0
Tartaric Acid.......	0 40	0 45	Swedes	5 00	5 50	White Zinc, genuine.	3 60	3
Verdigris	0 35	0 40	Hoops—Coopers....	3 00	3 25	White Lead, dry.....	0 65½	0
Vitriol, Blue.......	0 08	0 10	Band	3 00	3 25	Red Lead..........	0 07½	0
Groceries			Boiler Plates	3 25	3 50	Venetian Red, Eng'h .	0 02½	0
Coffees:			Canada Plates......	3 75	4 00	Yellow Ochre, Fish'h..	0 02½	0
Java, ₩ lb........	0 22	0 24	Union Jack	0 00	0 00	Whiting	0 85	1
Laguayra,........	0 17	0 18	Pontypool	3 50	4 00			
Rio..............	0 15	0 17	Swansea	3 90	4 00	**Petroleum.**		
Fish:			*Lead (at 4 months):*			*(Refined ₩ gal.)*		
Herrings, Lab. split..	5 75	6 50	Bar, ₩ 100 lbs.....	0 06½	0 07	Water white, car'd ...	—	0
" round......	0 00	0 00	Sheet............	0 00	0 00	small lots...	0 37	0
" scaled......	0 85	0 40	Shot.............	0 07½	0 07¾	Straw, by car load..	0 00	0
Mackerel, small kitts..	1 00	0 00	*Iron Wire (net cash):*			small lots...	0 00	0
Loch. Her. wh'efirks..	3 50	3 75	No. 6, ₩ bundle ..	2 70	2 80	Amber, by car load..	0 00	0
" half	1 85	1 95	" 9 " ..	3 40	3 50	small lots...	0 00	0
White Fish & Trout...	None.		" 10, " ..	3 40	3 50	Benzine	0 00	0
Salmon, saltwater....	14 00	15 00	" 12, " ..	4 30	4 40	**Produce.**		
Dry Cod, ₩ 112 lbs....	5 00	5 25	*Powder:*			*Grain:*		
Fruit:			Blasting, Canada...	3 50	0 00	Wheat, Spring, 60 lb..	0 92	0
Raisins, Layers	2 00	2 10	FF "	4 25	4 50	" Fall 60 " ..	1 00	1
" M R.......	1 90	2 00	FFF "	4 75	5 00	Barley .... 48 " ..	1 15	1
" Valentias new	0 6½	0 7½	Blasting, English ..	4 00	5 00	Peas....... 60 " ..	0 75	0
Currants, new.......	0 5½	0 00½	FF loose..	5 00	5 40	Oats....... 34 " ..	0 52	0
" old.......	0 04	0 04½	FFF "	6 00	6 50	Rye .... 56 " ..	0 00	0
Figs	0 14	0 00	*Pressed Spikes (4 mos):*			*Seeds:*		
Molasses:			Regular sizes 100....	4 00	4 25	Clover, choice 60 " ..	6 25	6
Clayed, ₩ gal.......	0 00	0 35	Extra	4 50	5 00	" com'n 65 " ..	6 00	6
Syrups, Standard ...	0 00	0 00	*Tin Plates (net cash):*			Timothy, cho'e " ..	2 00	2
" Golden ...	0 00	0 65	IC Coke	7 50	8 50	" inf. to good 48 " ..	0 00	0
Rice:			IC Charcoal.......	8 50	9 00	Flax .... 56 " ..	2 00	2
Arracan	4 25	4 50	IX "	10 50	11 00	*Flour (per brl.):*		
Spices:			IXX "	13 50	14 00	Superior extra......	0 00	0
Cassia, whole, ₩ lb...	0 00	0 45	DC "	8 00	8 60	Extra superfine......	4 40	4
Cloves	0 11	0 12	DX "	9 50	0 00	Fancy superfine	0 00	0
Nutmegs	0 80	0 85				Superfine No. 1......	4 63	4
Ginger, ground	0 20	0 25	**Hides & Skins, ₩ lb**			" No. 2......		
" Jamaica, root..	0 30	0 35	Green rough	0 00	0 06½	Oatmeal, (per brl.)...	5 40	5
Pepper, black......	0 12½	0 00	Green, salt'd & insp'd..	0 00	0 0⅛	**Provisions**		
Pimento	0 08	0 09	Cured	0 00	0 0⅛	Butter, dairy tub ₩ lb..	0 23	0
Sugars:			Calfskins, green	0 00	0 1⅛	store packed...	0 15	0
Port Rico, ₩ lb......	0 10½	0 00	Calfskins, cured.....	0 13	0 20	Cheese, new	0 12½	0
Cuba	0 10½	0 00	Sheepskins, ...	1 40	1 50	Pork, mess, per brl....	25 50	26
Barbadoes (bright)..	0 10½	0 00	country.....	1 00	1 40	" prime mess...		
Canada Sugar Refine'y,			**Hops.**			" prime		
yellow No. 2, 60 ds..	0 10½	0 11	Inferior, ₩ lb........	0 05	0 07	Bacon, rough	0 11	0
Yellow, No. 2½......	0 10⅞	0 11½	Medium...........	0 07	0 09	" Cumberled cut..	0 12	0
" No. 3.......	0 11	0 11½	Good	0 09	0 12	" smoked	0 00	0
Crushed A	0 13	0 13½	Fancy	0 00	0 00	Hams, in salt	0 13	0
AA	0 13	0 13¼				" smoked......	0 13½	0
Ground...........	0 13	0 14	**Leather,** (₩ 4 mos.)			" canvased...	0 15	0
Dry Crushed.......	0 14½	0 14½	In lots of less than			Shoulders, in salt	0 15	0
Extra Ground......	0 15½	0 15½	½ doz. sides, ₩ ℔			Lard, in kegs	0 14	0
Teas:			Spanish Sole, 1st qual'y			Eggs, packed	0 15	0
Japan com'n to good..	0 48	0 55	heavy, weights ₩ ℔..	0 21½	0 22	Beef Hams	0 00	0
" Fine to choicest..	0 50	0 65	Do. 1st qual middle do..	0 23	0 00	Tallow	0 06	0
Colored, com. to fine..	0 60	0 72	Do. No. 2, light weights	0 22	0 00	Hogs dressed, heavy,..	0 00	0
Congou & Souch'ng..	0 43	0 75	Slaughter heavy ...	0 00	0 00	medium...	0 00	0
Oolong, good to fine..	0 50	0 65	Do. light	0 00	0 00	**Salt, &c.**		
Y. Hyson, com to gd..	0 47½	0 65	Harness, best	0 35	0 37	American hrls.	1 50	1
Medium to choice ...	0 65	0 80	" No. 2	0 32	0 35	Liverpool coarse	0 00	1
Extra choice	0 85	0 95	Upper heavy,......	0 35	0 36	Goderich	0 00	1
			" light......	0 35	0 36	Plaster	1 05	1
						Water Lime	1 50	0

andles.	$ c.	$ c.
& Co.'s ..	$ c.	$ c.
l.........	0 07½	0 08
Bar	0 07	0 07½
ar........	0 07	0 07½
....	0 05	0 05½
....	0 03½	0 03¾
....	0 00	0 11½
Liquors,		
r doz......	2 60	2 65
ub Portr..	2 35	2 40
ca Rum...	1 80	2 25
's H. Gin..	1 55	1 65
l Tom.....	1 90	2 00
s.........	4 00	4 25
l Tom, c...	6 00	6 25
ion	1 00	1 25
ld	2 00	4 00
nmon	1 00	1 50
m.........	1 70	1 80
or golden..	2 50	4 00

Brandy:	$ c.	$ c.
Hennessy's, per gal..	2 30	2 50
Martell's " ..	2 30	2 50
J. Robin & Co.'s " ..	2 25	2 35
Otard, Dupuy & Cos..	2 25	2 35
Brandy, cases........	8 50	9 00
Brandy, com. per c...	4 00	4 50
Whiskey:		
Common 36 u. p......	0 62½	0 65
Old Rye	0 85	0 87½
Malt	0 85	0 87½
Toddy	0 85	0 87½
Scotch, per gal.......	1 90	2 10
Irish—Kinnahan's c...	7 00	7 50
" Dunnville's Belf't..	6 00	6·25
Wool.		
Fleece, lb............	0 28	0 35
Pulled "............	0 22	0 25
Furs.		
Bear................	8 00	10 00
Beaver, ⅌ lb..........	1 00	1 25
Coon	0 20	0 40
Fisher..............	4 00	6 00
Martin..............	1 40	1 60
Mink................	3 25	4 00
Otter...............	5 75	6 00
Spring Rats..........	0 15	0 17
Fox.................	1 20	1 25

NSURANCE COMPANIES.

ENGLISH.—*Quotations on the London Market.*

st Dividend.	Name of Company.	Shares par val £	Amount paid.	Last Sale.
	Briton Medical and General Life ...	10	....	2
7½	Commer'l Union, Fire, Life and Mar.	50	5	6½
8	City of Glasgow	25	2½	5½
9½	Edinburgh Life	100	15	33
—½ yr	European Life and Guarantee......	2½	11s6	4s. 3d.
10	Etna Fire and Marine............	10	1½	—
5	Guardian	100	50	51½
12	Imperial Fire..................	500	50	350
9½	Imperial Life	100	10	16½
10	Lancashire Fire and Life.........	20	2	2½
11	Life Association of Scotland.......	40	7½	25
s.p. sh	London Assurance Corporation ..	25	12½	49
5	London and Lancashire Life	10	1	—
40	Liverp'l & London & Globe F. & L.	20	2	7 1-16
5	National Union Life	5	1	1
12½	Northern Fire and Life	100	5	12
12 },bo 5s.	North British and Mercantile	50	6¼	21
50	Ocean Marine	25	5	18½
5 12s.	Provident Life..................	100	10	35
½ p. s.	Phœnix.......................	....	....	145
—h. yr.	Queen Fire and Life	10	1	1
. bo. 4s	Royal Insurance................	20	3	6½
10	Scottish Provincial Fire and Life ..	50	2½	5½
25	Standard Life	50	12	65½
5	Star Life	25	1½	—
	CANADIAN.			⅌ c.
4	British America Fire and Marine ..	$50	$25	55½ 56
4	Canada Life	...	....	.....
12	Montreal Assurance	£50	£5	135
3	Provincial Fire and Marine........	60	11	.....
....	Quebec Fire	40	32½	£25 26
7	" Marine..................	100	40	85 90
mo's.	Western Assurance...............	40	9	.....

RAILWAYS.	Sha's	Paid	Montr	London
d St. Lawrence....................	£100	All.	....	59 61
Lake Huron	20½	"	....	3 3½
do Preference	10	"	....	5½ 6½
tt. & Goderich, 6⅌c.,1872-3-4....	100	"	....	66 69
and St. Lawrence	....	....	10 11	....
do Pref. 10 ⅌ ct.............	....	....	80 85	....
nk	100	"	16½ 16½	15½ 15¾
Eq. G. M. Bds. 1 ch. 6⅌c..........	100	"	....	87 89
First Preference, 5 ⅌ c	100	"	....	50 53
Deferred, 3 ⅌ ct..	100	"	....	....
Second Pref. Bonds, 5⅌c..........	100	"	....	37 40
do Deferred, 3 ⅌ ct..........	100	"	...	....
Third Pref. Stock, 4⅌ct...........	100	"	....	28 30
do. Deferred, 3 ⅌ ct..........	100	"	....	....
Fourth Pref. Stock, 3⅌c..........	100	"	....	17 18
do. Deferred, 3 ⅌ ct...........	100	"	....	....
ern	20½	"	13 14	14½ 14¾
New	20½	18	----	....
6 ⅌ c. Bds, due 1873-76...........	100	All.	....	100 102
5½ ⅌ c Bds. due 1877-78...........	100	"	....	94 95
lway, Halifax, $250, all......	$250	"	....	....
f Canada, 6⅌c. 1st Pref. Bds.........	100	"	.. .	32 34

CHANGE.	Halifax.	Montr'l.	Quebec.	Toronto.
London, 60 days......				
75 days date	12½	8½ 8¾	9 9¼	8½
o.	11½ 12	7 8	8 8¼	7½
h documents..........	....	7 8	....	....
w York..............	....	23½ 24	23½ 24	23½
do.	....	24 24½	24 24½	....
do.	....	par to ½ p.	par ½ dis.	par ½ dis.
....	....	3 3½	....	3½ to 4½

STOCK AND BOND REPORT.

The dates of our quotations are as follows:—Toronto, April 6; Montreal, April 5; Quebec, April 5; London, March 18.

NAME.	Shares.	Paid up.	Divid'd last 6 Months	Dividend Day.	CLOSING PRICES. Toronto.	Montre'l	Quebec.
BANKS.			⅌ ct.				
British North America	$250	All.	3	July and Jan.	104½ 105½	104½ 105½	104½ 105½
Jacques Cartier...............	50	"	4	1 June, 1 Dec.	109 109½	109 109½	109 109½
Montreal	200	"	5	"	145 145½	144¾ 145¼	145½ 146
Nationale......................	50	"	4	1 Nov. 1 May.	107½ 108½	108 108½	108½ 109
New Brunswick	100	"	....	....	....	...	....
Nova Scotia	200	28	7&b$3½	Mar. and Sept.	....	....	....
Du Peuple......	50	"	4	1 Mar., 1 Sept.	107½ 108½	108 108½	108 108½
Toronto	100	"	4	1 Jan., 1 July.	121 122	120 122	120 121
Bank of Yarmouth............	....	....	......	......	....	....	....
Canadian Bank of Com'e......	50	95	......	......	102½ 103	102 103½	102 102½
City Bank Montreal	80	All.	4	1 June, 1 Dec.	102½ 103½	101½ 102½	102 102½
Commer'l Bank (St. John)....	100	"	⅌ ct.	......	....	...	....
Eastern Townships' Bank.....	50	"	4	1 July, 1 Jan..	.....	99 100½	99 100
Gore	40	....	none.	1 Jan., 1 July.	40 41	40 41	40 42
Halifax Banking Company....	...	....	......	......	...	....	....
Mechanics' Bank............	50	70	4	1 Nov., 1 May.	97½ 98½	97 98	97 98
Merchants'Bank of Canada....	100	70	4	1 Jan., 1 July.	107 108	107 107½	107 107½
Merchants' Bank (Halifax)....	....	....	.....	......	....	.. ..	....
Molson's Bank...............	50	All.	4	1 Apr., 1 Oct.	109 110	109 110	108 109
Niagara District Bank...	100	70	3½	1 Jan., 1 July.	....	....	....
Ontario Bank...............	40	All.	4	1 June, 1 Dec.	100 100½	99¾ 100½	99¾ 100½
People's Bank (Fred'kton)....	100	"	....	......	....	....	. ..
People's Bank (Halifax)	20	"	7 12 m	......	....	...	....
Quebec Bank	100	"	3½	1 June, 1 Dec.	101 102	101 102	100½ 101
Royal Canadian Bank	50	50	4	1 Jan., 1 July.	77 80	72½ 82½	80 85
St. Stephens Bank	100	All.	.....	......	....	..	...
Union Bank	100	70	4	1 Jan., 1 July.	104½ 105½	104¾ 105½	105½ 106
Union Bank (Halifax)........	100	40	7 12 mo	Feb. and Aug.	....	....	.. .
MISCELLANEOUS.							
British America Land........	250	44	2½	......	....	....	....
British Colonial S. S. Co......	250	32½	2½	......	...	50 60	....
Canada Company	32½	All.	£1 10s.	......	....	----	....
Canada Landed Credit Co.....	50	$20	3½	......	77 80	----	....
Canada Per. B'ldg Society....	50	All.	5	......	125½ 126	....	....
Canada Mining Company.....	4	90	......	......	....	....	....
Do. Inl'd Steam Nav. Co.....	100	All.	7	......	----	100 101	....
Do. Glass Company.........	100	"	12½ "	......	....	40 55	....
Canad'n Loan & Investm't....	25	2½	7	......	....	....	----
Canada Agency	10	½	......	......	....	....	----
Colonial Securities Co........	...	....	......	.....	....	....	....
Freehold Building Society....	100	All.	4	......	110½ 111	----	....
Halifax Steamboat Co........	100	"	5	------	....	....	....
Halifax Gas Company........	....	----	------	......	....	....	....
Hamilton Gas Company......	----	----	-----	......	....	....	....
Huron Copper Bay Co........	4	12	20	......	....	32½ 45	....
Lake Huron S. and C.........	5	102	......	......	....	....	....
Montreal Mining Consols......	20	$15	......	......	....	3.15 3.25	...
Do. Telegraph Co...	40	All.	5	......	133 133½	133 134	132 133
Do. Elevating Co...	00	"	15 12 m	......	....	100 102½	----
Do. City Gas Co.........	40	"	4	15 Mar. 15 Sep.	....	132 135	133 134
Do. City Pass. R,. Co.....	50	"	4	......	....	105 106	102 107
Quebec and L. S.	8	$4	......	......	....	....	....
Quebec Gas Co...............	200	All.	4	1 Mar., 1 Sep.	....	...	118 119
Quebec Street R. R	50	25	3	......	....	....	90 91
Richelieu Navigation Co......	100	All.	10 p.a.	1 Jan., 1 July.	....	108 108½	107 107½
St. Lawrence Glass Company.	100	"	....	......	....	80 85	.. ..
St. Lawrence Tow Boat Co....	100	"	......	3 Feb.	....	...	35 40
Tor'to Consumers' Gas Co.....	50	"	4	1 My Au MarFe	107½ 108	...	108 109
Trust & Loan Co. of U. C.....	20	5	8	......	....	....	.. .
West'n Canada Bldg Soc'y....	50	All.	5	......	121 121½	....	----

SECURITIES.	London.	Montreal.	Quebec.	Toronto.
Canadian Gov't Deb. 6 ⅌ ct. stg..............	....	103 104	103 103½	103 104
Do. do. 6 do due Ja. & Jul. 1877-84..........	104½ 105½	....	....	....
Do. do. 6 do. Feb. & Aug..........	102 104	....	....	....
Do. do. 6 do. Mch. & Sep..........	102 104	...	...	....
Do. do. 5 ⅌ ct. cur., 1883	92 94	92½ 95	93 94	93 94
Do. do. 5 do. stg., 1885	92 94	92½ 94½	93½ 94½	93 94½
Do. do. 7 do. cur.,....................	....	....	......	----
Dominion 6 p. c. 1878 cy.....	....	106 106½	105½ 106	106 106½
Hamilton Corporation....	....	....	......	....
Montreal Harbor, 8 ⅌ ct. d. 1869..................	..	....	......	....
Do. do. 7 do. 1870..................	....	....	......	....
Do. do. 6½ do. 1883..................	....	102 103	......	....
Do. do. 6½ do. 1873..................	....	....	......	....
Do. Corporation, 6 ⅌ c. 1891	....	96 97	95½ 96	96 97
Do. 7 p. c. stock.........................	....	108 110	108 109	109 110
Do. Water Works, 6 ⅌ c. stg. 1878........	....	....	......	96½ 97
Do. do. 6 do. cy. do.	....	96½ 97	......	96 97
New Brunswick, 6 ⅌ ct., Jan. and July	103 104	....	......	....
Nova Scotia, 6 ⅌ ct., 1875..................	102 104	...	......	....
Ottawa City 6 ⅌ c. d. 1880	....	95 96	......	....
Quebec Harbour, 6 ⅌ c. d. 1883..................	....	....	60	....
Do. do. 7 do. do..................	....	....	65 70	....
Do. do 8 do. 1886..................	....	....	80 85	....
Do. City, 7 ⅌ c. d. 1½ years..................	....	....	98 98½	....
Do. do. 7 do. 8 do.	....	....	91 92	....
Do. do. 7 do. 5 do.	....	....	94 95	....
Do. Water Works, 7 ⅌ ct., 4 years	....	....	97 97½	....
Do. do. 6 do. 2 do.	....	....	94 95	....
Toronto Corporation	....	90 92½	...	....

Insurance.

Briton Medical and General Life Association,

with which is united the

BRITANNIA LIFE ASSURANCE COMPANY.

Capital and Invested Funds............£750,000 Sterling.

ANNUAL INCOME, £220,000 STG. :

Yearly increasing at the rate of £25,000 Sterling.

THE important and peculiar feature originally introduced by this Company, in applying the periodical Bonuses, so as to make Policies payable during life, without any higher rate of premiums being charged, has caused the success of the BRITON MEDICAL AND GENERAL to be almost unparalleled in the history of Life Assurance. *Life Policies on the Profit Scale become payable during the lifetime of the Assured, thus rendering a Policy of Assurance a means of subsistence in old age, as well as a protection for a family,* and a more valuable security to creditors in the event of early death; and effectually meeting the often urged objection, that persons do not themselves reap the benefit of their own prudence and forethought.

No extra charge made to members of Volunteer Corps for services within the British Provinces.

☞ TORONTO AGENCY, 5 KING ST. WEST.

Oct 17—9-1yr   JAMES FRASER, *Agent.*

BEAVER
Mutual Insurance Association.

HEAD OFFICE—20 TORONTO STREET,
TORONTO.

INSURES LIVE STOCK against death from any cause. The only Canadian Company having authority to do this class of business.

R. L. DENISON,
President.

W. T. O'REILLY,
Secretary.   8-1y-25

HOME DISTRICT
Mutual Fire Insurance Company.

Office—North-West Cor. Yonge & Adelaide Streets,
TORONTO.—(UP STAIRS.)

INSURES Dwelling Houses, Stores, Warehouses, Merchandise, Furniture, &c.

PRESIDENT—The Hon. J. McMURRICH.
VICE-PRESIDENT—JOHN BURNS, Esq.
JOHN RAINS, Secretary.

AGENTS:
DAVID WRIGHT, Esq., Hamilton ; FRANCIS STEVENS, Esq., Barrie ; Messrs. GIBBS & BRO., Oshawa.   8-1y

THE PRINCE EDWARD COUNTY
Mutual Fire Insurance Company.

HEAD OFFICE,—PICTON, ONTARIO.

President, L. B. STINSON; *Vice-President,* W. A. RICHARDS.

Directors : H. A. McFaul, James Cavan, James Johnson, N. S. DeMill, William Delong.—*Treasurer,* David Barker *Secretary,* John Twigg; *Solicitor,* R. J. Fitzgerald.

THIS Company is established upon strictly Mutual principles, insuring farming and isolated property, (not hazardous,) in *Townships only,* and offers great advantages to insurers, at low rates for *five years,* without the expense of a renewal.

Picton, June 15, 1868.   9-1y

THE AGRICULTURAL
Mutual Assurance Association of Canada.

HEAD OFFICE............................LONDON, ONT.

A purely Farmers' Company. Licensed by the Government of Canada.

Capital, 1st January, 1869...................$230,193 82
Cash and Cash Items, over....................$86,000 00
No. of Policies in force......................30,892 00

THIS Company insures nothing more dangerous than Farm property. Its rates are as low as any well-established Company in the Dominion, and lower than those of a great many. It is largely patronised, and continues to grow in public favor.

For Insurance, apply to any of the Agents or address the Secretary, London, Ontario.

London, 2nd Nov., 1868.   12-1y.

Insurance.

The Gore District Mutual Fire Insurance Company

GRANTS INSURANCES on all description of Property against Loss or Damage by FIRE. It is the only Mutual Fire Insurance Company which assesses its Policies yearly from their respective dates ; and the average yearly cost of insurance in it, for the past three and a half years, has been nearly

TWENTY CENTS IN THE DOLLAR

less than what it would have been in an ordinary Proprietary Company.

THOS. M. SIMONS,
Secretary & Treasurer.

ROBT. McLEAN,
Inspector of Agencies.
Galt, 25th Nov., 1868.   15-1y

Geo. Girdlestone,

FIRE, Life, Marine, Accident, and Stock Insurance Agent

Very best Companies represented.

Windsor, June, 1868

London Assurance Corporation.

No. 7, ROYAL EXCHANGE, CORNHILL,
LONDON, ENGLAND.

HEAD AGENCY OFFICE:
56 ST. FRANCOIS XAVIER STREET,
MONTREAL.

$150,000 *invested in Government Securities,*
In conformity with the Act of Parliament.

FIRE DEPARTMENT:
INSURANCES against LOSS by FIRE, effected on the most favourable terms.

LIFE DEPARTMENT:
The Corporation has granted Assurances on Lives for nearly a CENTURY AND A HALF, having issued its First Policy on the 7th June, 1721.

ROMEO H. STEPHENS, AGENT FOR CANADA.
ISAAC C. GILMOR, AGENT AT TORONTO.   31-1m

Fire and Marine Assurance.

THE BRITISH AMERICA
ASSURANCE COMPANY.

HEAD OFFICE:
CORNER OF CHURCH AND COURT STREETS.
TORONTO.

BOARD OF DIRECTION :

Hon G. W. Allan, M.L.C.,   A. Joseph, Esq.,
George J. Boyd, Esq.,   Peter Paterson, Esq.,
Hon. W. Cayley,   G. P. Ridout, Esq.,
Richard S. Cassels, Esq.,   E H. Rutherford,Esq.,
Thomas C. Street, Esq.

Governor:
GEORGE PERCIVAL RIDOUT, Esq.
Deputy Governor:
PETER PATERSON, Esq.
Fire Inspector: Marine Inspector:
E. ROBY O'BRIEN.   CAPT. R. COURNEEN.

Insurances granted on all descriptions of property against loss and damage by fire and the perils of inland navigation.

Agencies established in the principal cities, towns, and ports of shipment throughout the Province.

THOS. WM. BIRCHALL,
Managing Director.
28-1y

Queen Fire and Life Insurance Company,
OF LIVERPOOL AND LONDON,

ACCEPTS ALL ORDINARY FIRE RISKS
on the most favorable terms.

LIFE RISKS

Will be taken on terms that will compare favorably with other Companies.

CAPITAL,   -   -   -   £2,000,000 Stg.

CHIEF OFFICES—Queen's Buildings, Liverpool, and Gracechurch Street London.

CANADA BRANCH OFFICE—Exchange Buildings, Montreal.
Resident Secretary and General Agent,

A. MACKENZIE FORBES,
13 St. Sacrament St., Merchants' Exchange, Montreal.

WM. ROWLAND, Agent, Toronto.   1-1y

Insurance.

The Waterloo County Mutual Fire Insurance Company.

HEAD OFFICE : WATERLOO, ONTARIO.

ESTABLISHED 1863.

THE business of the Company is divided into separate and distinct branches, the

VILLAGE, FARM, AND MANUFACTU[…]

Each Branch paying its own losses and its just prop[…] of the managing expenses of the Company.
C. M. TAYLOR, Sec.   M. SPRINGER, M.M.P., P[…]
J. HUGHES, Inspector.

Etna Fire and Marine Insurance Compa[…] Dublin.

AT a Meeting of the Shareholders of this Com[…] held at Dublin, on the 13th ult., it was agreed the business of the "Etna" should be transferred t "UNITED FORTS AND GENERAL INSURANCE COMP in accordance with this agreement, the business will after be carried on by the latter Company, which assi and guarantees all the risks and liabilities of the "E[…]

The Directors have resolved to continue the CAN[…] BRANCH, and arrangements for resuming FIRE and RINE business are rapidly approaching completion.

T. W. GRIFFITH
16   MANAG[…]

Lancashire Insurance Compan[…]

CAPITAL, - - - - - - - £2,000,000 St[…]

FIRE RISKS
Taken at reasonable rates of premium, and
ALL LOSSES SETTLED PROMPTLY,
By the undersigned, without reference elsewh[…]

S. C. DUNCAN-CLARK & CO.,
General Agents for Ontario
N. W. Corner of King & Church Stre[…]
25-1y   TORONTO.

DIVISION OF PROFITS NEXT YE[…]

ASSURANCES

EFFECTED BEFORE 30TH APRIL NEXT,

IN THE

Canada Life Assurance Comp[…]

OBTAIN A YEAR'S ADDITIONAL PROFIT

OVER LATER ENTRANTS,

And the great success of the Company warrants rectors in recommending this very important advantage to assurers.

SUMS ASSURED...........................$5,[…]
AMOUNT OF CAPITAL AND FUNDS........ 1,[…]
ANNUAL INCOME...........................

Assets (exclusive of uncalled capital) for each [liabilities, about $150. The income from interest upon investments [alone sufficient to meet claims by death.

A. G. RAMSAY, Manag[…]
E. BRADBURNE, Ages[…]
Feb. 1.   1y   Toronto S[…]

The Victoria Mutual

FIRE INSURANCE COMPANY OF CANAD[…]

Insures only Non-Hazardous Property, at Loa[…]

BUSINESS STRICTLY MUTUAL

GEORGE H. MILLS, *President.*
W. D. BOOKER, *Secretary.*

HEAD OFFICE ....HAMILTON, ON[…]

aug 15-1yr

PUBLISHED AT THE OFFICE OF THE MONE[…]
TIMES, No. 60 CHURCH STREET.
PRINTED AT THE DAILY TELEGRAPH PUBLISHING
BAY STREET, CORNER OF KING.

THE CANADIAN
[M]ONETARY TIMES
AND
INSURANCE CHRONICLE.

[DEVO]TED TO FINANCE, COMMERCE, INSURANCE, BANKS, RAILWAYS, NAVIGATION, MINES, INVESTMENT, PUBLIC COMPANIES, AND JOINT STOCK ENTERPRISE.

| [VOL.II]—NO. 35. | TORONTO, THURSDAY, APRIL 15, 1869. | { SUBSCRIPTION, { $2 YEAR. |

Mercantile.

Meetings.

TORONTO BOARD OF TRADE.

An adjourned meeting of the Board of Trade to consider the Insolvency Act was held in the Mechanics' Institute, April 12, the president, Mr. J. G. Worts in the chair. There was a large attendance of members.

Mr. Worts, in opening the meeting, explained its object, and stated that he had received a communication from Montreal in which the idea was prominent that it would be better to do away with the Insolvent Act altogether.

The Secretary read the report of the Committee as follows: The committee appointed by the Board of Trade to consider the present Bankruptcy Law with the view of suggesting any alteration they may deem advisable for the protection of mercantile interests generally, beg to submit the following report:

Your committee have carefully considered the Insolvent Act of 1864, with the amendments thereto, clause by clause, and have also had before them the amendments suggested on the subject by the Montreal Board of Trade.

Your Committee find that several of the suggestions of the Montreal Board are embodied in the existing Act; they also find that the present Act contains several important provisions for the examination of insolvents and the management of their estates, which are not sufficiently known to the public, and which they think advisable to retain.

They are of opinion, after careful consideration, that the ends desired by the commercial community will be better served by continuing the present law in its main features and adding such amendments as experience may suggest, than abrogating or suspending the same. The principal provisions recommended by the committee as desirable to introduce and incorporate with the present law are—

First. The making it impossible for an insolvent debtor to assign his estate without the consent of his creditors; and,

Secondly. The power of the creditors to appoint a custodian to take immediate possession of the insolvent's estate pending an assignment being made; and,

Thirdly. The appointment of an inspector to act conjointly with the official assignee in the management of the estate.

The other amendments suggested by your committee are upon matters of detail, the most important of which is a classification of certificates in bankruptcy. They have added one paragraph suggested by the Montreal Board of Trade in relation to fraud and concealment of property. All of which is respectfully submitted for the consideration of the Board.

A. R. McMASTER, *Chairman.*

Recommendations of the Committee of the Board of Trade.

"Amend 2nd clause of 1st paragraph as follows: The meeting of creditors to be called where the majority of the creditors reside. The Insolvent shall not have the power to make a voluntary assignment without the consent of a majority of his creditors.

2nd paragraph. The list of creditors in the notice of meeting to contain the residence of each creditor and the amount of their respective claims.

3rd paragraph. That a pro rata scale of voting at all meetings be established as follows:—One vote for each $100 claim up to $1,000, and another vote for every $1,000 additional.

That power be given the creditors at their first meeting to appoint a custodian of the Insolvent's estate who shall take immediate possession, and if necessary prepare a statement for submission to the creditors, with or without the assistance of the Insolvent, who if a party thereto, shall verify the same by oath to the best of his knowledge and belief. When the debtor fails to meet his engagements generally as they become due, three or more creditors representing claims of $1,000 or upwards may demand a statement of his affairs to be furnished within ten days, the accuracy of which statement they shall be empowered to test by personal inspection of the debtor's books, &c. When an Insolvent has assigned his estate, the creditors shall have the power to appoint an inspector who shall be remunerated for his services at the discretion of the creditors out of the estate, whose duty shall be to advise with the assignee as to the disposition of the estate, audit his accounts, and keep the creditors informed from time to time of its position, &c. That goods in *transitu* be protected from being taken as part of the Insolvent's estate until placed in his store or actual possession. Before an Assignee is finally discharged from his duties and liabilities, he shall mail notices to each creditor, informing him of his intention, to ask for a discharge in regard to A. B.'s estate; and if his discharge is not objected to by the inspector of the estate, he may obtain the same at the discretion of the Judge. That the Judge shall not be empowered to give a bankrupt a discharge without the consent of the inspector on behalf of the creditors. That there be three classes of certificates of discharge, under which the Insolvent shall rank according to the determination of the Court. Certificates of the 1st class shall be given in cases where the conduct of the Insolvent as a trader, or otherwise, is not impugned under any of the conditions specified in the rules for the 2nd and 3rd classes. That any debtor who has lived extravagantly, or has been reckless in endorsing or in becoming security for others, or who has incurred debts without a reasonable expectation of paying them, shall only receive a second class certificate. Any debtor who, by acts of intemperance, gambling, fraud, or reckless waste of property, or who is unable to produce proper accounts of his business, shall be ranked in the third class; and his discharge shall be suspended for a period of five years. No insolvent shall be discharged whose estate shall realize less than 50 cents on the dollar unless by consent of a majority of his creditors, representing two-thirds of the amount of his indebtedness. All post-nuptial settlements to be void if made within two years of insolvency, unless registered at the time they are made, and unless the bankrupt can prove he had a sufficient surplus when the settlement was executed. That the Insolvent be considered guilty of a misdemeanor, and liable, on conviction, to imprisonment, if he shall not, upon examination, fully and truly discover, to the best of his knowledge and belief, all his property real and personal;

and how, and to whom, and for what consideration, and when he disposed of, assigned or transferred any part thereof, except such part as has been really and *bona fide* disposed of in the way of his trade and business, or laid out in the ordinary expenses of his family ; or shall not deliver up to the assignee all such part thereof as is in his possession, custody or power, except such portion as may be exempted ; and, also, all books, papers and writings in his possession, custody or power, relating to his property or affairs." A discussion ensued, in which a number of members joined. The consideration of the report was finally adjourned for a week.

MONTREAL CITY AND DISTRICT SAVINGS BANK. —The annual meeting was held in Montreal on the 6th February. The institution has been in operation twenty-three years. The Directors state that the net profits of the year were $20,781.62, out of which $6,035 was distributed to the poor making $56,575 in all given to the poor. During the year, $2,975,000 were received from depositors at the counter, and $2,720,000 were paid out to depositors, and besides the sum of $50,270.76 as interest. This large amount of business, transacted with a daily average number of over two hundred persons at the counter, has forced upon the Directors the necessity of making preparations to obtain a larger and more commodious building for the transaction of business; and a lot on the corner of St. John and Great St. James streets has been secured, with a frontage on those two streets of one hundred and twenty feet.

Statement of the affairs of the Montreal City and District Savings Bank, the 31st Dec., 1868 :

DR.

To amount due Depositors	$1,861,574 55
To amount due to minors and others on the property of the Bank	5,337 04
To amount due to sundry persons not depositors	36,247 48
To amount of Reserve Fund, after paying all expenses and making the Annual Donation to Charitable Societies	148,222 61
Total	$2,051,382 58

CR.

By City of Montreal, Provincial and Champlain and St. Lawrence Railroad first Mortgage Bonds	$457,696 00
By Bank Stocks, viz., La Banque du Peuple, City Bank, Bank of Montreal, Ontario and Merchants' Banks	110,796 92
By Loans on short dates, with the collateral security of Bank Stocks and Bonds, such as required by law	709,834 92
By Property occupied by the Bank, and office furniture	25,227 45
By amount due on sale of portion of the above	2,453 32
By deposits on call and interest in Banks of the city	745,373 97
Total	$2,051,382 58

E. J. BARBEAU, *Actuary.*

The election of officers was then proceeded with, when the following gentlemen were declared unanimously elected :—

As Managing Directors for the term of office required by law—Messrs. Dealisle, Workman and Larocque. As Auditors for the ensuing year—Messrs. W. Bristow and C. T. Palsgrave. As Honorary Directors—Messrs. W. H. Hingston and Maurice Laframboise.

At a meeting of the Managing Directors, held subsequently, the Hon. Henry Starnes was elected President, and the Hon. L. H. Holton, Vice-President, for the current year.

MONTREAL PERMANENT BUILDING SOCIETY.— The eleventh annual meeting was held in Montreal, on the 6th inst. The annual report states that the demand for money during the year has been sufficient to absorb the payments as received.

The Permanent Stock is	$184,750 00
The Running Stock is	3,730 81
Total paid up	$188,480 81

The loans made during the year were 70 in number, and in amount $85,929 95 ; making a total since organization of $738,704 00, of which there has been paid $461,451 07; leaving a balance of $247,342 93. Two half-yearly dividends of four per cent. have been paid to holders of Permanent stock. The same rates have been added to the Running Shareholders' accounts, to each of whom a statement has been sent. A sum of $4,665 07 has been added to the Rest, which now is $19,578 90. The following gentlemen retire, but are eligible for re-election :—G. H. Frothingham, R. Esdaile, A. W. Ogilvie, and Charles Alexander.

HENRY THOMAS, President.

The Report was submitted and adopted, and the retiring Directors and the Auditors were re-elected.

QUEBEC PROVIDENT AND SAVING'S BANK.— The twenty-second annual meeting of this Institution was held in Quebec, on the 20th March ; J. Greaves Clapham, occupied the chair, and Mr. G. Veasey, acted as Secretary. The Report says,—In submitting their twenty-second Annual Report and accompanying cash statement, the Trustees have again great pleasure in announcing the satisfactory position of the Bank. In consequence thereof, they have voted the sum of $2,500 to the following charitable institutions : Jeffery Hale hospital, $1,000 ; St. Bridget's asylum, $500 ; Finlay asylum, $500 ; Ladies' Protestant home, $500. Total—$2,500. The deposits during the year have amounted to $343,631 40, and the drafts to $342,630.66, leaving a balance due depositors of $548,445.04, while 339 new accounts have been opened during the twelve months. The following gentlemen were elected directors for the ensuing year :—Messrs. C. Wurtele, J. S. Fry, W. Hossack, D. McGie, H. S. Scott, J. Musson, Weston Hunt, T. Norris, M. G. Mountain, L. Massue, M. Stevenson, W. Walker, A. F. A. Knight.

A general meeting of the stockholders of the Erskine Slate Company was held at Waterloo, E. S. on the 23rd ult., at which meeting A. B. Parmalee, John Erskine, H. L. Robinson, James Irwin, and John Williams, were elected Directors of the Company; and on the 22nd instant, at a meeting of Directors, the following officers were appointed for the ensuing year:—A. B. Parmelee, President, W. G. Parmelee, Treasurer; J. F. Leonard, Secretary; and John Erskine, Managing Director.

Insurance.

FIRE RECORD.—Stratford, April 4.—A fire originated in a building on the market square, owned by John Sayer and occupied by H. Hammond as a grocery; the flames spread to Thomas Stoney's saddlers shop, Mrs. Patterson's shop, H. Gibson's confectionery store and the *Herald* office. A local paper says:—Very little of Mr. Stoney's stock was saved, and he is a heavy loser by the fire. The principal portion of Mr. Hammond's and Mrs. Patterson's goods were removed." Mr. Sayers had no insurance on his building, his loss will be about $900 or $1,000. Mr. Stoney is a loser to the extent of about $2,000. No insurance. Mrs. Patterson had no insurance on her stock, but the principal part was saved. The goods of Mrs. H. Gibson, W. Down and D. Davis were much damaged by removal. The printing material of the *Herald* was subjected to a hasty removal; much of the type was scattered on the

street, and cases thrown into "pi." The stationery was much damaged, and the building is gutted. Mr. Lobb's loss will be between $700, $800, which is partially covered by insurance in the Waterloo Mutual. There was a large representation of both fire companies on the ground and to their endeavors, in which they were assisted by the citizens, is due the saving of principal business part of the town from the stroying element.

Durham, Ont., April 7.—Mrs. Burt's dwelling was destroyed; the fire caught from stove-pipe.

Adelaide, Township, Ont., March 30.—House of T.omas Harris, on 3nd con., including tents. Loss $400; no insurance. The fire originated in the kitchen.

Lindsay, Ont., April 9.—House of Alex. and out buildings ; said to be insured for $1,000.

Hamilton, April 7.—A fire broke out in cellar of E. & G. Magill's hardware store; was extinguished; damage, chiefly by water, $1000; insurance on stock, $45,000, in different companies, of which the Commercial U had $15,000 ; damage to building trifling. The fire is supposed to have been caused by the explosion of a lighted lamp in the cellar.

Wyoming, April 12.—A destructive fire occurred here early on Sunday morning, resulting in total destruction of George Taylor's oil refining establishment, together with about 350 barrels refined oil, and 700 barrels of crude. The fire was first discovered about half-past three, and then confined to the still houses, which left but hopes of saving the other parts of the works, when a pipe in the side of an elevated crude oil came out, which caused the oil to flow in a jet directly into the fire. The flames then ran spread over all parts of the establishment. Loss estimated at $10,000.

Thorold, April 12.—An unoccupied house owned by James Taggart, was burned last night being nine and ten o'clock. Fully insured.

Waterdown, April 12.—The Methodist Connexion Church here was burned down yesterday morning about nine o'clock. The fire is supposed to have originated from stove-pipes. No insurance.

Brooklin, April 10.—A telegram says: Fire were discovered this morning at 7.30 o'clock issuing from the steam planing mill and box factory here, belonging to Nelson Thomas. The building contained about 1,000 hee hives, fixtures and in course of construction; also a quant planed lumber and machinery, all of which consumed. Loss about two thousand five hundred dollars. The fire originated from a stove.

Clifton, April 12.—A telegram says: at 2.30 on Sunday morning a fire was discovered in rear of Roslin's barn, which spread rapidly to the adjoining buildings, destroying Roslin's hotel, being heim's and Bull's taverns, also, Mulhein's stables. Three valuable horses, the property of Mr. Davis, were burnt in the fire. All the buildings were insured. Loss about $8,000.

GALT FIRE BRIGADE.—The annual report of the Galt Fire Brigade, states that it was only called out twice during the year, and both fires extinguished without their assistance and with very little damage. The different companies number 112 men against 108 last year. The expenditure for the year was $581.22, principally in clothing for new clothing for the men.

FIRE LOSSES IN THE U. STATES.—The aggregate losses by fire for the three months of January, February and March, 1869, throughout the United States (not including those under twenty thousand dollars) are considerably less than in the corresponding months of 1868, although the losses of March in the current year exceed those of March, 1868, by nearly half a million of dollars. Taking, however, the three months' total, we find that the losses of the past three months of the present year and of January, February and March of 1868, the result is as much as three millions

:d and seventy-five thousand dollars in
19, a circumstance of the greatest satis-
'he following table will exhibit the
more concisely:

	1868.	1869.
January	$5,494,000	$2,294,000
February	4,399,000	2,637,000
March	2,405,000	2,892,000
	$12,298,000	$8,823,000

W ENGLISH ASSURANCE BILL.

wing is a copy of the bill introduced
'e, into the House of Commons on the
We give it as published in the *Insur-*

it is desirable to provide for the secur-
y holders in life insurance companies
g publicity of such companies accounts:
acted by the Queen's most Excellent
y and with the advice and consent of
spiritual and Temporal, and Commons,
ent parliament assembled, and by the
f the same, as follows :
after the passing of this act every com-
g Life policies within the United King-
within sixty days from the first of Jan-
h year, deposit returns with the Regis-
st Stock Companies, in the forms set
Schedules attached to this act, showing,
acome and expenditure of the company
: year :
ulance sheet of the company for the past
t year.
ew business transactions of the company
t year.
every assurance company issuing life
thin the United Kingdom shall be re-
ave an actuarial report prepared once
n years, or at such shorter intervals as
rovided by the deed of settlement or
association of the company for an act-
stigation into its condition, and that
io often as such actuarial investigation
place a return, showing,—
instructions on which the actuarial
'epared :
table of mortality on which the valuation

rate of interest assumed : and
amount of margin of premium income
r future expenses and profits ; together
ified copy of the actuarial report itself,
iosited with the Registrar of Joint Stock
within twenty-one days after the said
have been submitted to the directors
any.
an amalgamation shall take place be-
companies or when the business of one
all be transferred to another company,
ed company or the purchasing company
in ten days from the date of the com-
he amalgamation or transfer, respect-
it with the Registrar of Joint Stock
certified copies of statements of the
liabilities of the companies concerned
algamation or transfer, together with
copy of the agreement or deed under
a amalgamation or transfer is effected,
d copies of the actuarial or other re-
which such agreement or deed is found-
at the agreement or deed of amalgama-
sfer shall be accompanied by a statu-
stion, made by the principal manager
arman of the board for the time being,
payment made or to be made to any
tsoever on account of the said amalga-
ransfer is therein fully set forth, and
r payments beyond those set forth have
or are to be made either in money,
onds, or other valuable securities
the knowledge of any parties to the

4. Any refusal or neglect to comply with the
requirements of this act shall be a misdemeanor,
and shall subject the directors, manager, and
secretary of the defaulting company to a penalty
of twenty pounds sterling for every day beyond
the several dates herein-before fixed during which
the requirements of this act shall not be complied
with ; and it shall be the duty of the Registrar of
Joint Stock Companies to sue for such penalties,
and to pay them into Her Majesty's Treasury.
5. This act may be cited as The Life Assurance
Act, 1869.

SCHEDULE (A.)
Account of the Receipts and Expenditure of the—
Life Office from 1st Jan. 186—to 31st Dec. 186—.
186—Dec. 31st. £ s. d.
Amount of funds.........Dec. 31st. 186—
Gross amount of new annual
premiums...............
Single premiums.................
Renewal premiums...............
£
Consideration for annuities............
Claims on re-insurance................
Commission on re-assurances...........
Surrender of re-assurances...........
Fines for extension of time............
Interest on Investments..............
Other receipts (accounts to be specified)..
£
186—Dec. 31st. £ s. d.
Claims............................
Surrenders........................
Re-assurances.....................
Annuities.........................
Gross amount commissions...........
Expenses of management............
Bad debts.........................
Other payments (accounts to be specified)
Balance.......... ....
£

(SCHEDULE B.)
Balance Sheet of the——Life Office on 31st of De-
cember, 186—".
LIABILITIES.
£ s. d. £ s. d.
Claims due.....................
&c. &c.....................
Sundry accounts............ ....
(Specify principal ones)........

Balance—
Proprietor's fund (if any)......£
Assurance fund...................
Annuity fund....................
Surplus reserve fund (if any)...

ASSETS. £ s. d.
Freehold properties (if any).....
Leasehold " " .....
Mortgages—
On freehold and leasehold....£
On policies . ...
On reversions..................
Investments (specify all prin-
cipal accounts) :—
Government securities.........£
Colonial "
Railway "
&c. &c.
Loans upon personal security...
Miscellaneous sums due :—......
Agents' balances, all considered
good, and owing less than six
months...................
Agents' balances (owing more
than six months...........
Premiums due "
Interest "
&c. &c....................

Cash—
On deposit...................£
On current account with bank-
ers, &c. &c...................
£

SCHEDULE (C.)
New Transactions of the——Life Office in the
year 186—.

Description of Transactions.	No. of Policies.	Sums Assured.	Annual Premium.
ASSURANCES.			
1. With participation.			
For the whole term of life...................			
Do. (Premium by a limited number of payments.)...........			
Other assurances....			
Assurances with profits.			
2. Without participation			
For the whole term of life..................			
Do. (Premium by a limited number of payments.............			
Endowment assurances.			
Joint lives..........			
Other Assurances......			
Assurances without pro-fits...................			
Total assurances.......			
Deduct re-assurances...			
Net amount of assu-rances..................			

	Number granted.	Annuity per annum.	Consideration paid.
ANNUITIES.			
Present.........			
Deferred.........			

PEAT.—The *Canadian Monetary Times* of February 25th, tells us with respect to the Anglo
American Peat Company, that the Company seem
to have gone to work in earnest. "A railway a
mile and a half long has been built by them from
the Welland Canal to their property, and a peat
machine of improved character was constructed
specially for their operations. Their experience
thus far is that they can produce peat and deliver
it on the banks of the canal for $1.45 a ton, which
can be sold at $3.50 a ton, the same material being
sold in Montreal at $5 to $5.50."
Peat must look sharp and be economical, or it
will be beaten by coal, when the Intercolonial
railway is made. Nova Scotia produces the finest
coal, and in large quantities ; upon a line not overcrowded with traffic, it will go long distances at a
profit. It has never yet been proved how far coal
can be carried by railways under favourable circumstances. It depends upon the quantity that
can be conveyed in one train at from 12 to 15 miles
an hour. If a train of cars could take 400 tons
leisurely, and without interruption, the coal could
be carried at a charge of ¼d. a mile a ton, and
leave a profit of about 50 per cent. The train
mile receipt would be 8s. 4d., which is a full
amount and would admit of half being netted as
profit. At a charge of only ¼d. per ton per mile
coal would travel nearly 1,000 miles, and coming
on the Grand Trunk railway at both its ends it
might be found at all its stations.—*Herepath's*
Journal.

--Mr. James Goodwin has been elected President of the Connecticut Mutual Life Insurance
Company.

—Messrs. Lawson & Bros., of Hamilton, submitted a statement of their affairs at a meeting in
this city, showing assets amounting to $39,500 and
liabilities of $48,609 ; deficit $9,109.

THE CANADIAN MONETARY TIMES AND INSURANCE CHRONICLE *is printed every Thursday evening and distributed to Subscribers on the following morning.*

Publishing office, No. 60 Church-street, 3 doors north of Court-street.

Subscription price—

Canada $2.00 per annum.
England, stg. 10s. per annum.
United States (U.S. Cy.) $3.00 per annum.

Casual advertisements will be charged at the rate of ten cents per line, each insertion.

Address all letters to "THE MONETARY TIMES."

Cheques, money orders, &c. should be made payable to J. M. TROUT, Business Manager, who alone is authorized to issue receipts for money.

☞ *All Canadian Subscribers to* THE MONETARY TIMES *will receive* THE REAL ESTATE JOURNAL *without further charge.*

The Canadian Monetary Times.

THURSDAY, APRIL 15, 1869.

THE BANK CHARTER QUESTION.

THE PROVINCIAL NOTES.

VII.

By the issue of Government notes, to which the law gives a forced circulation, we have already entered on a career which has been full of disaster in many countries both in the old world and the new. The Provincial note is a legal tender for the payment of all debts; and though it is nominally redeemable in specie it does not differ in this respect from the paper issued by so many Governments, the value of which sunk in time to a mere nominal figure. France, Spain, Austria, Russia, Sardinia, Naples and the States of the Church have all in their time gone through a like experience. We are only following in their footsteps, when we should have been warned by their example so fatal and so full of instructive lessons. We have in truth commenced with greater boldness than many of these nations displayed at the outset; for we began by declaring the Provincial note to be of equal value with gold, and no matter how much it may become depreciated by excessive issues, or some other cause of Government discredit, it will still be a legal tender for the payment of all debts.

It was at one time the design of the Government to supersede the bank note circulation entirely by Provincial notes. One thing was wanting to enable this arrangement to be carried out, and that was the consent of the banks; a consent which to their everlasting credit be it said was, with one solitary exception, withheld. If the Government had succeeded in this essay it is probable, almost certain, that cash payments would have ceased ere now. There is no example, we venture to say, of cash payments being long preserved on the strength of a specie reserve so low as that required for the Provincial notes —one-fifth of the amount in circulation. It must always be difficult to determine what minimum of specie will, at all times, be sufficient to meet the demands of convertibility. Something must depend on the credit of the issuer, which is not, and cannot, especially in the case of a Government, be always the same. There have been periods when the Bank of England and the Bank of France required for the maintenance of convertibility about half as much gold as they had issued notes. The banks of New York were, at one time, obliged to suspend specie payments with a reserve of bullion in their vaults equal to half their note circulation. But it may be supposed that there is some magic in the credit of a Government which will exempt it from the laws to which individuals and corporations are liable. It has often proved true that the credit of a Government has, at the first commencement of issues of paper money, had the fatal effect of causing these promises to circulate far above their real value. But the period of over-confidence once passed, corresponding depression and discredit follow; and all experience shows that a decline in the credit of Government paper money is more rapid than that of any other depreciated paper. All who take such paper in its declining stage suffer a loss on the depreciation. There is, perhaps, no way in which a community can be so effectually robbed without being fully conscious of the extent to which it is suffering.

Whatever scheme be proposed this Session it is not probable that the Provincial notes will be suppressed. They are much more likely to be made to perform the functions which greenbacks now perform in the United States. Nothing would be easier than the transition from the Provincial note, with an enforced circulation, payable in specie, to the Provincial note performing all the functions of a legal tender, and not convertible specie. It is already pretty well under that the Government scheme of currency to be proposed to Parliament will be cordance with the recommendations o King's circular—a modification of the Na banking system of the United States. will be held out to lure the banks into resisting acceptance of this scheme. probable that one, or perhaps two of will fall in with this fatal plan, but it is hoped that the majority will hold out against it. We are aware that a susp of specie payments—for that is what it —may be made to present an attracti pearance in the eyes of certain banker is calculated that during the long susp of specie payments in England, the B England saved £300,000 a-year in inter bullion which it would otherwise have obliged to hold. And the holding of amount of interest-paying securities without its attractions to the banker, ally if he does not stop to consider tha exchanging a large part of his capital mere promises of the Government. Sir Robert Peel's Act was passed it was that a necessity existed to curtail, by la amount of Government securities whi Bank of England might hold. In Sept 1839, the bullion in the vaults of the was below £3,000,000, while it held se to the amount of nearly £26,000,00 Robert Peel's Act provided that notes not be issued against securities to a amount than £14,000,000.

Here is the bait that will be offered banks. They will be told that by ma advance to the Government of a large their capital they will be able to perf double operation of drawing interest securities purchased, and of making on the notes which they can issue t This may doubtless be done if we ar sort to a suspension of cash payme not otherwise.

Two contrivances have been res for preventing the Provincial notes c for redemption. These notes were, divided into two classes, one of which able at Montreal, and the other at latterly, however, a third class h issued, payable at Halifax. From the notes payable at Montreal were i Toronto, those payable at Toron issued at Montreal. The object of th device was very plain. It costs a qu one per cent. to transport notes f city to the other, and the mode o the Provincial notes is equivalent to ciating them to that extent.

The other contrivance is to lock u siderable amount of Provincial Not anks, under pretence of taking or the adjustment of accruing between the Banks. Some of the d in this way as much as $150,000 ial notes. There is some analogy his practice and that by which h Banks effect a settlement of Each of the Scotch Banks holds purpose a certain amount of Ex- lls. These bills bear upon them of their belonging to the Edin- hange, and they are used only for ment of balances. The Exchequer s as widely as possible from the note. It is not a legal tender, ly pass from hand to hand volun- he Provincial notes kept for the of balances, are placed where they presented for redemption in specie. hows an inclination to do every- ble to exempt these notes from all ordinary and extraordinary, of ity, and is far from being a cheer- stic of the future.

IAL INSURANCE COMPANY.

1861, Mr. Cassels was appointed the Bank of Upper Canada, and tely commenced a thorough inves- its affairs," and prepared a report as intended to satisfy the public the perfect solvency of the Bank." directors congratulated the share- on the improved condition of the i were satisfied " in having been lare a dividend of three per cent. f year ;" as notwithstanding bad were sure " they had maintained nd firm position." In 1863 the gain assured the shareholders that ition of the Bank was steadily im- nd Mr. J. H. Cameron moved a "for the information of absent rs," which expressed " satisfaction fairs of the institution." In 1864 d " with perfect truthfulness and hat this Bank is now in a sounder, nd more satisfactory position than our years." Fifteen months after rords were given to the public the ended. Thereupon, to cap the absurdity, a statement of affairs ted by the Board which showed a $1,488,862. At the last meeting terested in its affairs it was admit- trustees that if the Government e payment of its debt from the nly would every penny of assets be ut it would be necessary to fall back ble liability. It is possible then s to be deceived, and to deceive and it is equally possible to rear lus-fabric on a quicksand.

The Manager of the Provincial has published an advertisement in the Toronto papers which has attached to it the signatures of the Di- rectors. This advertisement is in the form of a letter, and is intended to be a reply to our remarks on the position of the Company. The Directors are made to say that they feel it due to the public to state " the correct finan- cial position of the Company, and to express their confidence in its complete ability to meet all engagements with every claimant and policy-holder, whether present or pros- pective." This is fair enough, but the Direc- tors of the Bank of Upper Canada were just as amiable, just as respectable, and just as trust-worthy as the Directors of the Provin- cial, and, unfortunately, their assurances and expressions of opinion were just as strong as those contained in the Provincial's advertise- ment. The Directors of the Bank of Upper Canada had a large stake in the institution over which they presided, which is more than can be said of some of the Directors whose names appear in this advertisement. Messrs. Howland, McMaster, Campbell, and Fulton, by an extraordinary coincidence, are the happy possessors of just twenty shares a piece of the Provincial Stock. The coincidence, we say, is extraordinary, for we happen to know one prominent citizen to whom just twenty shares were offered, as a gift, if he would allow his name to be numbered among the Provincial's Directors. Taking it for granted, however, that these twenties were paid for, each of these four gentlemen would have $220 invested in a concern out of which he draws, in fees, about $250 per annum, be- sides a share of the three per cent. dividend. There are pickings also : for instance, one Di- rector got fifty dollars for settling a loss lately, and another Director got forty dollars for negotiating the mortgage which now encum- bers the Company's head-quarters. There are waifs, also, such as per centages on business secured through the zeal of Directors, just as an Agent would get his commission. So that the Directors have every inducement to keep the machine running, and restrain inquisi- tiveness. The Manager very naturally de- sires to be even with his Directors, and draws a commission of two-and-a-half per cent. in addition to his salary. Of course it is his interest to make the profits appear as large as possible, as the better the exhibit, the higher his pay. This commission yielded him last year $800, over and above his $2,400 salary. The reason he got so much was because his statement shewed last year a net profit of $35,549. Just think of an institution which paid a spasmodic dividend of three per cent, giving its Manager two-and-a-half per cent. on the net profits of the year, in addition to a salary of $2,400, and distributing among its

Directors between two and three thousand dollars ! The worst of it is that this costly Manager is notoriously unfit for his position, and holds it only by trickery ; and we say it with regret, but we say it emphatically, since the truth must be told, by equivocation. Were Mr. Crocker a young man we should be com- pelled, in the public interest, to bring him face to face with a record which would bring the blush of shame to any honest counten- ance ; but we extend to him a charity, and a consideration, which his language respecting this JOURNAL at various times and places, has fairly disentitled him to receive. If his Directors are satisfied with him, well and good. On them be the responsibility. We do not say that the gentlemen constituting the Board of Directors are not honest upright men, but we do say that in a matter in which the public have such a deep interest, they exhibit, either culpable ignorance, or amazing carelessness. And now for our reasons.

In our article on the Provincial Insurance Company to which so much objection has been taken by the Directors, we did not pre- tend to give the exact position of the Com- pany, for we had not the means of doing so. What we did endeavor to do was to give a general idea of its standing. We asserted that there were losses unpaid, to the extent of about $40,000 clamoring for payment. Is that correct? The Directors say, "at this moment, there not only is no adjusted loss overdue and unpaid, but there is no unad- justed loss in respect of which there is not sufficient ground for delaying the settlement for further proofs or disputing the claims altogether." We have heard of a man who on giving his note for a debt, exclaimed with refreshing joyousness, "Thank heaven, that debt's paid!" There are a number of suits pending against the Provincial. The Des- barats loss was settled by drafts at thirty and sixty days, instead of by cheque as was so triumphantly asserted in the newspapers, and if we are not misinformed the first draft had to be met by discounts raised on the faith of the Company's Halifax agency notes. The Company's accepted drafts are only negotiable at a ruinous discount. In one case, an accepted draft for $800 at thirty days was offered for discount in Toronto to parties who should know the Company's affairs, and the only offer made for the draft was at the rate of thirty per cent. discount. Another draft of $363 at thirty days was offered to the Company itself for $300 cash and declined, and every effort to part with it at this shave failed to find a purchaser.

The Directors are of opinion, that they have a surplus of $87,356; we are of opinion that as matters now stand there is a deficit of $94,047. The difference between us is not slight. In order to make up the surplus, the

Manager first casts out of the debtor side of the account an item of $75,000 which we set down as a provision for re-insurance, but which the Manager calls "a mythical liability," and then ignores the $89,738 of paid up capital. Were we right in charging the Company with a sum such as would re-insure the business in case of stoppage? The Manager of the Provincial is an actuary, at least in name, and should be disposed to yield to actuarial authority on a matter of this kind. He calls a re-insurance fund "a mythical liability." Mr. Barnes is Superintendent of the Insurance Department of the State of New York, and by the laws of the State is empowered to withdraw the license of any Insurance Company whose position is not sound. All the Fire Insurance Companies doing business in New York have to charge themselves, as a liability, with the amount required to re-insure all outstanding risks at an average of 50 per cent. of unexpired premiums. In one of his Annual Reports, Mr. Barnes states: "The question of what amount "should be charged as a liability to a Marine "Company as a re-insurance fund for out- "standing risks, is very important in stating "the condition of such a Company. In "accordance with the recommendation of "the Board of Underwriters, and the "opinion of the soundest and most expe- "rienced marine underwriters, the reinsur- "ance reserve has been fixed at 100 per cent. "of the full amount of premiums received on "unexpired risks or policies. All the Marine "Companies are now charged with this "amount, and also the Fire Companies em- "ployed in marine insurance, on their marine "and inland risks."

The Insurance laws of the State of Massachussetts are explicit on this point—"in "making up their annual statement they "(the directors) shall be required to charge "the company only such portions of the cash "or notes received on policies which are un- "expired or would be requisite to reinsure "all outstanding risks." That is, the amount requisite to reinsure all outstanding risks is to be considered just as much a liability as the unpaid losses and charged as such. According to the manager of the Provincial Insurance Company of Canada all this is wrong; the experts across the lines have compelled their 164 fire and marine insurance companies to charge themselves with "a mythical liability," and actually have the audacity to restrain by statutory enactment, the declaration of dividends until that "mythical liability" is first deducted from the Cr. side of the account! Still worse if the financial condition of a company will not admit the deduction of that "mythical liability," the Superintendent walks into the defaulters' office, stops business, and levies contributions on the stockholders until the "mythical liabil-

ity" takes shape and substance. Verily, Jonothan is a simpleton! In this matter we are simple enough to coincide with Jonothan; so supported on either side by Superintendents Barnes and Sandford, we take the liberty of replacing an item for reinsurance among the liabilities of the Provincial. We have English precedents also. For instance, the Lancashire has a fire reserve of £49,000; the North British set aside one third of the fire premiums, £138,514, of the past year, as a reserve, but the point is so clear that it is idle to enlarge upon it.

The Manager has made the Directors say some very absurd things, but the most absurd of all perhaps is this "a reinsurance fund of $75,000 is double the sum that would be necessary." According to their own statement the premium income is $200,000, of which $100,366 (which was the sum of marine premiums last year) may be taken as on marine policies and $100,000 as on fire policies. According to the American practice, 50 per cent. of fire premiums and 100 per cent. of marine premiums are taken to constitute a reinsurance fund. To say that $37,- 500 would reinsure the Provincial, its premium income being as above stated, is such absurd nonsense, that we wonder at the stupidity which could have even suggested such a thing, and the crass ignorance which could have endorsed it.

We fearlessly assert that no respectable Insurance Company would assume its outstanding risks at the same rates at which they have been taken. This Company has got the very refuse of the insurance business of this Province, and the increase of its business is due to the fact that the English and American Companies have withdrawn their agencies from country towns or ceased to take any but first class risks.

The Manager seems to think that we should have taken the current income for the year as an asset. Perhaps we should, but we might just as well have gone ahead a little further and taken the income from premiums for five or ten years yet to come and used it in the same way. A reductio ad absurdum would be to add $70,000, the "net profits" of 1867 and 1868, to the $200,000 current income of 1869 and ask the Com'y to show the money. The Manager points triumphantly to the fact that no portion of the $470,760 subscribed capital has been forfeited. According to the Company's statement of June, 1867, the subscribed capital was $533,940, of which $97,889 was called in. The statement of June, 1868, shews the subscribed capital at $470,760, of which $89,738 was called in. So that between 1867 and 1868 stock to the amount of $63,180 was forfeited. If the work of forfeiture ceased then, it was because calls were not pressed.

It is claimed that the following are the Company's assets:

Balance in Bank and Agent's hands,	848,427
Investments	5,250
Real and personal property	22,366
Good debts	5,247
Bills receivable	48,927
Calls in process of payment	2,903
	$133,068

Taking this as correct, the Company's account with itself would stand—

Dr.—Losses	$39,378
Mortgage on office	8,000
Debentures to Church Society	15,000
Re-insurance fund	75,000
Paid up Capital	89,738
	227,116
Cr.	$133,068
Deficit	894,047

Were this Company doing business in the States, it would lose its license until the impaired capital should be made good. I ever, let us pass to its position as regards the public.

One is struck by the quaint book-keeping terms which characterize the Manager's statement. He is careful to club the balance in bank and agent's hands together. Does the word balance mean cash? If so, how much in the bank? About the 27th of March last the bank account was overdrawn. Last year the balance at agencies was $35,665, so little progress has been made in getting the money in. Though that amount was out in agents' hands the petty sum of $8,000 was raised by mortgaging the Comp'ys office, which we suppose pays interest at the rate of ten per cent. If the Manager would acknowledge that $48,427 means bad debts made through agents, we could understand why a mortgage was necessary, but even then we should be anxious about the net profit of $35,000. He speaks afterwards of "good debts $5,247." As a matter of curiosity, we should like to have seen the Company's accountant ferret out the details of this item. The investment referred to are we suppose a Brantford debenture, and Detroit and Milwaukee bonds. Our old friends, "bills receivable," are again doing duty for $48,927 63. Last year they represented $47,499 28. We fancy of these that were available have been in vulgar phrase, "shoved up the spout," or are in the way of discounts or as collaterals.

The next in order is "calls in process of payment." What is a call in process of payment? Two years ago the Company went to make a call on the stock. Last year nothing was credited to calls so we take it for granted that the calls were not then in process of payment. If it takes two years or these calls to win recognition in the balance sheet under the equivocal title mentioned, how many years will it require to comess of payment ? We commend to nts this new description of asset. re "sundry debtors $40,013," who to such advantage in the last state- Surely the manager must have for- is valuable asset. Under these cus- rcumstances, we are compelled to balances, the investments, the calls, egard as worthless, for immediate bility, the bills receivable The ac- uld therefore stand : .

..........................$39,378	
....	8,000
res	15,000
nce Fund	75,000
	$137,378

Cr.

)	$1,000
....	16,666
personal prop'ty	22,308
ots	5,247
	45,228
oficit...............	$92,150

re again and again called the atten- ne Directors to the wrong they do es and their policy holders in allow- Company to drag out a miserable nouth existence when there is every int to place it on a sound footing. is worthless, its credit at the Bank it is looked upon as a pauper by all it with insurance matters, and is is such. If the subscribed capital, , is a good asset why is it not called id of raising money at ten per cent.' ages and debentures. Why borrow at ten per cent. while $48,000 is o lie in the hands of agents? Why law costs in litigation to gain time 000, the "net profit" of two years Why be dependent on banks for pay the current expenses ? When nt is compelled to resort to such ex- he is set down as one going to ruin. ne public will be satisfied with such is, an independent investigation made; and with such skilled accoun- Mr. J. H. Mason, Mr. W. T. Mason, les Robertson and Mr. Lee, whose sould possibly be secured, we do hy the present uncertainty should ted to continue.

important economical question is n the competition now existing be- s of railway and water communica- th sides of these lakes. The great roads running between Chicago and , in their keen rivalry for the im- de passing between these cities both r and winter, have reduced rates to oint that freight is now carried al- heaply as by water. The water grain from Chicago to Buffalo last

season averaged as follows: wheat, 14 cents per 100 lbs ; corn, 19 8-10 cents per 100 lbs ; oats, 15 cents per 100 lbs. Canal rates from Buffalo are estimated at 23 4-10 cents per 100 lbs ; making a total average rate from Chicago to New York, via lakes and canal, including 3 cents for insurance, warehouse commissions and transfer at Buffalo, of 40 cents per 100 lbs., or $8.00 per ton. It has been suggested in the interest of the railways that the dif- ferent kinds of freight might be arranged into classes paying $7, $8 and $9 per ton during the season of navigation, and $9, $10 and $11 per ton in winter, making an average of $8 in summer, and of $9 per ton through- out the year.

A writer in a western paper, demonstrated by an analysis of the inward and outward trade of Chicago, that it could all be handled by a railway with a double track for freight trains, and another for passenger trains. In fact this writer goes so far as to say that the capacity of such a road would be equal to five times the volume of that trade. Trains would be run at a low rate of speed, say six or eight miles per hour, and with the double track could run within fifteen or twenty minutes of each other. The capacity of such a road would be equal to five canals in this latitude, as the speed of the train is three times that of the canal movement during navigation, and the railway would have five months of winter traffic in its favor.

Even with the present intermixing, and of- ten necessary conflict, of freight and passenger traffic, these American roads have carried at rates almost as low as those charged by water. If this can be accomplished under existing circumstances, it is not too much to expect that when the great improvements and the increased economy of which railway transpor- tation is undoubtedly susceptible, are realized, freight will be carried quite as cheaply as by our present mixed system of inland naviga- tion. The idea is most important one, as it points the direction that our proposed pub- lic improvements should take for opening up the country, and extending facilities for easy ingress and egress to the newer and more un- settled districts.

—Sir Edward Watkin retired from the Pre- sidency of the Grand Trunk on the 23rd of March, and Messrs. Blake and Young retired from the Direction on the same day. Messrs. Grosvenor, Hodgkinson, Gillespie and Gra- ham Menzies succeeded these gentlemen on the Board.

—We learn by telegraph that the steamer "Calumet" was burned last night at Portage du Fort. The boat was insured for about $9,000 in the British America and the Western Insurance Companies. She was the property of the Union Forwarding Company. Value, $14,000.

LONDON CORRESPONDENCE.

(From Our Own Correspondent.)

London, March 25, 1869.

Yesterday the shareholders of the Hudson's Bay Company assembled to consider the terms of settlement proposed by Earl Granville. As might have been expected the meeting was by no means favorable to an acceptance of these terms. Many shareholders think that they have been badly treated. Their grievance is a two-fold ene. In their opinion, Canada ought to buy them out on their own terms; failing this, the directors of the Company should give effect to the policy enun- ciated in 1863, and hitherto shirked. They con- sider that the re-constitution of the Company in 1863, and the increase of the capital to the extent of a million and a half sterling, were sanctioned and supported subject to the application of the fresh funds to the colonization of the North West. Having been disappointed in this matter, their next hope was that what the directors had failed to accomplish the Government of Canada would undertake, and that prior to commencing operations, the Canadian Government would satisfy the Company's claims. Believing as they do, that a million sterling is the smallest sum which could be accepted, they naturally regard Lord Gran- ville's proposal to compensate them with a cash payment of three hundred thousand pounds as little better than a mockery. One of them told the meeting that his first impression was that the whole affair was a hoax. Although Sir Stafford Northcote, the Governor, Sir Curtis Lampson, the Deputy Governor and their colleagues were unanimous in recommending acquiescence in the proposal, yet the majority were in favor of ad- journing the decision, in the expectation that something might yet occur to turn the current into a more propitous course. It is not impossible that the end will be a reference of the question to the Judicial Committee of the Privy Council. Nearly all the shareholders believe in the validity of the charter; hence, they have no fear that it can be successfully impugned. They argue that, if a confident tribunal pronounced the charter to be a binding document and if its powers proved to be as comprehensive as has been supposed, the position of the Company would be strengthened and that it might then conclude whatever arrange- ment it chose with Canada. On the other hand, there are persons whose impartiality cannot be questioned and whose capacity for pronouncing a valid judgment is acknowledged, who maintain that the charter is legally worth nothing, more than the parchment on which it is engrossed. For my own part, I hold that the Judicial Com- mittee of the Privy Council would pronounce a decision adverse to the Company's title. Yet it is desirable that this dispute should be settled, if possible, without recourse being had to arbitration or litigation. It is now twenty-three years since the Company first made a formal claim for compensa- tion by the United States for the loss incurred owing to having to abandon its settlements in Oregon. I think the present case would be de- termined more rapidly. Still, there might be delay of a year or two. During this time the completion of Confederation by the incorporation of British Columbia into the Dominion would be postponed. The shareholders assemble again a fortnight hence, when the question will be put to the vote. I hope that the result will be the ap- proval of the proposed arrangements.

The continuous rise in the value of shares in the Electric Telegraph Companies is attracting public notice. A year ago these shares rose nearly as rapidly. As soon as it became known that the Government meant to purchase the lines of tele- graph throughout the country, the price of the shares increased enormously. This was due to the speculators having inferred that the bargain about to be made would have been most advan- tageous to the companies. Had the Administra- tion of Mr. Disraeli continued in office their notions would probably have been verified to the letter. The present Government, however, is not inclined to squander public money, and is resolved that the telegraph companies shall not be over-paid. In consequence of this, the shares are receding from the high point which they touched.

Attempts are constantly being made to persuade the investing portion of the public to embark in new undertakings. The most successful of these have been the companies formed to lay submarine telegraphs; yet, even as regards such companies enthusiasm has not been excited. A new enterprise has just been announced which it is thought may be considered as the type of a sound investment. This is a company formed to purchase a freehold property at Trowville, a fashionable watering place in Normandy. The peculiarity is that there is no share capital. Mortgage debentures bearing interest at the rate of 7 per cent. are offered to the extent of £400,000. Now, a "mortgage debenture" may sound better than a share, yet the difference in name does not make any difference in fact. It is said that should this venture be patronized by the public, that many offers of a similar kind will be brought forward.

Since the introduction of a Bill into the House of Commons relating to life assurance, the subject has been canvassed in several journals. Statements are made which, if true, ought to prove beneficial as warnings. In one newspaper it is said, for instance, that some sixty or seventy millions sterling of the present aggregate of sums insured on lives in the United Kingdom are not worth more than sixpence in the pound. A correspondent who made inquries as to the status of one assurance company which had attracted his attention, discovered that the directors were either gentlemen's servants or clerks who had given the addresses of their masters and employers as their own. The company's bankers when applied to professed ignorance of the company's existence. The auditor, whose name appeared in the prospectus, could not be heard of. Yet this company must have done a flourishing business, if there were a foundation for its boast that it had ten thousand policies in existence. The indignation which these discoveries arouses, is generally expended in calling for legal protection and supervision; that some legislation ought to take place is very probable, but for the most part the public has the remedy in its own hands. An Act of Parliament would not hinder the credulous from purchasing quack medicines, nor would an Act prevent those willing to be deceived from trusting in the promises of bubble companies. It is most desirable that all assurance companies should make yearly returns of their affairs. But this is the only piece of legislation on this head for which there is a proved necessity.

Financial.

TORONTO STOCK MARKET.

(Reported by Pellatt & Osler, Brokers.)

There has been a large business done during the week in debentures and mortgages.

Bank Stock.--Bank stocks are very little enquired for and close, in most cases slightly lower. Montreal was sold in the beginning of the week at 145 and 145½; the market closed with sellers at 144½ and buyers at 144. Buyers offer 105 for British, none in market. There are sellers of Ontario at par and buyers at 99¾. Toronto is offered at 122 with no buyers over 121, little in market. Royal Canadian was again active and sales were made at 77½, 78 and 79 and closed with buyers at 78 and sellers at 78½. Small sales of Commerce occurred at 102½ and 102¾; there are sellers now at 102½ but no buyers over 102. No buyers of Gore; it is a little lower. Merchants sold at 107¼ and 107½, holders now ask 107¾. Buyers offer 101 for Quebec with sellers at 102. Molson's has declined one per cent closing dull at 107½ to 108½. Sellers would accept 102 for City but buyers offer only 101½. There were sales of Du Peuple at 108, which price would still be paid. Sales of Jacques Cartier were made at 109 and 109½; there are still buyers at the latter rate. Mechanics sold at 97½ which price would still be be paid. There are buyers and sellers of Union at 105 and 106 respectively.

Debentures.—There were small sales of Canada Debentures during the week. Dominion Stock and Bonds are in demand at 106½ and 105 respectively. No Toronto have been offered for some time past. There were considerable sales of first class County debentures at very high rates.

Sundries.—There are buyers of City Gas at 107½, none in market. Canada Permanent Building Society sold at 125½ to 126, very little in market. Western Canada Building Society is offered to a limited extent at 121½, buyers will not give over 121. Freehold Building Society is in good demand at 111, and buyers would probably advance ½ per cent. Sales of Montreal Telegraph were made at 133½; there are buyers now at 133 and sellers at 134. Canada Landed Credit is enquired for at 78, there are sellers at 80. British America Assurance is enquired for at 55, sellers at 56. Several mortgages have been placed at 8 per cent and in many cases as high as 10 per cent has been paid. Money is much wanted and the banks are scarcely able to meet the demand.

POST OFFICE SAVINGS BANK.—The statement for the month of March shows that the amount in the hands of the Receiver General on the 31st, $676,383 40 against $628,384 82 on 28th February. Amount received from depositors in March, $85,875, interest in closed accounts $283 26; withdrawn cheques in March, $38,659 68. Of the total deposits, $384,146 bears interest at 4 per cent., and $285,800 at 5 per cent.

—The Montreal papers state that Mr. Weir's scheme for the exportation of $2,000,000 of American silver from Canada has failed, the principal cause of such failure being the neglect or refusal of the subscribers to "the guarantee fund," to pay up their subscriptions—involving serious loss to Mr. Weir on the large amounts already shipped. It is also stated that in consequence of the failure of several houses in Montreal, Mr. Weir has been compelled to make an assignment for the benefit of his creditors. It is added that his liabilities are small and almost wholly limited to a few friends. Since the collapse of the scheme, silver has declined considerably as our quotations elsewhere show.

—The report of the Bank of British North America for the year 1868 gives the net profit at £70,304 14s. 9d. which will allow the payment of a dividend at the rate of 6 per cent. per annum, and a bonus of 1 per cent.

—The annual report of the British American Land Company, recommends a dividend of 1*l.* per share, which will absorb 6,000*l.* and leave 442*l.* to be carried forward.

INSOLVENTS—Ottawa, April 13. The following insolvents are gazetted:—Ronald McDonald, Ailsa Craig; Duncan McNaughton, Lindsay; A. & E. Amos, Montreal; Thomas and Henry Lindop, St. Thomas; James Bradshaw, Hamilton; Joseph Manning, Bond Head; Wm. Elliott, Wilberford; C. A. Ward, Sherbrooke; Harry Joslin, Toronto; Wm. Weir, Montreal; Jay Ketchum, Toronto; Charles Pegnem, Montreal; Henry Trent, Newmarket; R. S. Aikman, Norwich; John Turner, Blairton; Wm. Mallish, Bradford; Wm. Dunn, Hamilton; Mrs. T. C. Scott (wife of Charles Wilson), Montreal; Thomas Isaac, Ottawa; Francis Kettle, London; John Curry, Walkerton; Ira Fulford Walkerton; R. Wright, London; McMillen & Carsen, Montreal; Aaron Reynolds, Woodstock; Geo. Humphries, Ottawa.

Railway News.

RAILWAY TRAFFIC RETURNS
FOR THE MONTH OF FEBRUARY, 1869.

NAMES OF THE RAILWAYS.	Passengers.	Mails and Sundries.	Freight.	Total 1869.	Total 1868.	Miles in Operation, 1869.	Miles in Operation, 1868.
	$	$	$	$	$		
Great Western Railway	82848	7748	173402	263998	241164	351	351
Grand Trunk Railway	107838	22000	282536	412374	397819	1377	1377
London and Port Stanley Railway*	......	......	......	......	......	......	......
Welland Railway	758	297	947	2002	2179	25	25
Northern Railway	8765	1513	27758	38036	23118	97	97
Port Hope, Lindsay, and Beaverton Railway, and Peterborough Branch	2233	247	4829	7309	5023	56	56
Cobourg, Peterborough and Marmora Railway†	......	......	......	......	......	......	......
Brockville and Ottawa Railway	1874	60	4770	6704	6094	86	86
St. Lawrence and Ottawa Railway	3053	527	2437	6017	7756	54	54
Carillon and Grenville Railway†	......	......	......	......	......	......	......
Stanstead, Shefford & Chambly Rail'y*	......	......	......	......	......	......	......
St. Lawrence and Industry Railway†	......	......	......	......	......	......	......
New Brunswick and Canada Railway	614	......	2223	2837	3927	116	116
European & North American Railway	9759	598	6304	9701	8581	108	108
Eastern Extension Railway	221	81	272	673	......	43	......
[illegible]	[illegible]	178	7608	14694	11964	145	145

†Road closed. *No returns.

JOHN LANGTON,
Aud

Audit Office,
Ottawa, April 9, 1869.

GREAT WESTERN RAILWAY.—Traffic for ending March 26, 1869.

Passengers	$26,281 7
Freight	57,264 1
Mails and Sundries	2,008 0
Total Receipts for week	$85,
Coresponding week, 1868	78,
Increase	$6,933 5

NORTHERN RAILWAY.—Traffic receipts fo ending April 3th, 1869.

Passengers	$2,966 6
Freight and live stock	4,672 6
Mails and sundries	632 4
	$8271
Corresponding Week of '68	270
Increase	$4433 5

NORTHERN RAILWAY.—Traffic receipts for ending March 27, 1869:—

Passengers	$2,547 4
Freight	5,554 0
Mails and sundries	190 8
Total receipts for week	$8,29
Corresponding week 1868	8,25
Increase	$39

EUROPEAN AND NORTH AMERICAN RAI —The receipts of the E. & N. A. Railw

1869, and March, 1868, compare as fol-

gers	$4,120	$3,776
t	7,592	6,791
and Sundries	648	504

il	$12,360	$10,871

crease of $1,489 over March, 1868. The chiefly in freight.

Commercial.

Toronto Market.

is no improvement in the state of trade it week. The impending legislation on ting system is the cause of a good deal of nty among financial and mercantile men is to keep business quiet. Every day new s arise which go to illustrate the neces change in the bankrupt law or in the modes of doing business. There is a great omplaint of tardiness on the part of coun hants in paying off their debts. It is serted that they are as a class, more ready han to pay for what they get.

Foods.—The returns at the port of Mon the first quarters of the present and last

	1868.	1869.
ns	$ 806,795	$ 617,898
s	1,085,378	1,046,206
and velvets	159,209	137,485
goods	90,730	71,378
	81,051	32,215
s	2,568	1,241
caps & bonnets	134,470	140,664
y	33,819	62,133

	$2,391,650	$2,109,020

ares.—In this branch the week has been y quiet and payments are very slow ; changed. The imports of leading articles real for the last quarter were—

	1868.	1869.
green	$194,973	$369,339
black	29,914	36,198
os, manufactured	9,764	4,209
	6,179	5,275
ses	9,941	16,428

	$250,776	$431,449

AND SHOES.—The leading houses report at steady prices.

t.—Wheat—Receipts 4,280 bushs. and shs. last week. Spring is dull and about ower on the quotations of last week. The ecline in the British markets has sensi ted this market. Spring is now worth c. f.o.b ; a lot was offered for May deliv e latter price. Sales of 1 car at 94c. on t. Fall, in the absence of any demand ; there were no transactions; it is held at .05 and freely offered at the latter quota lidge Proof is worth about the same prices g ; one car sold at 96c. f. o. b. Barley— 500 bush. and 340 bush. last week. The s dull and nominal, nothing doing except street; there is very little offering and re now small. For a cargo which was 1.20 was asked ; choice for seed would out that figure. Peas—Receipts trifling; ket is dull at quotations; round lots are 80c., no sales. Oats—Receipts 3,600 ad 1,800 bush. last week. The market easier in consequence of good receipts ; s are worth about 52c. on the track, with ns; sales were made early in the week at l later at 52c. Rye—is offered in car 65c., and no sales reported. Corn—sales ar loads are reported at 65c. and one or at 64½. Seeds—Timothy is dull as 2 cars sold on p.t. ; good samples are .25 to $2.40, inferior is dull and almost e. Clover is offering at $5.75 to $6.25.

Flax seed, $2. A large business has been done with farmers during the week.

FLOUR.—Receipts 4,280 bbls., and 3,242 bbls. last week. No. 1 Superfine is in demand at $4.10 and favorite brands a few cents more ; 200 bbls. Whitchurch, spring wheat extra sold at 4,25 f.o.b. 500 bbls. choice No. 1 sold at $4,12½, and 500 more at the same price. Two lots of .100 bbls. each sold at $4.10 on the cars. Fancy is in some demand, a lot of 800 bbls. sold during the week at $4.25, in store. Extra is offering at $4.50 to 4.60, and a lot of 100 bbls., good brand, sold at $4.50 ; also, 1,000 bbls. on private terms. No Superior in market ; the millers have ceased to manufacture it some time ago. Oatmeal—Good ordinary 100 bbls., lots are worth $5.50 ; very choice for retail purposes is worth $5.75. Corn meal selling slowly at $3.50 in lots.

STOCKS.—in store in Toronto on the 12th April were : Flour, 26,012 bbls. ; do. April 1st, 25,800 bbls.; fall wheat, April 12, 66,400 bushs.; do. April 1st, 124,400; Spring wheat, April 12, 97,412 bushs.; do. April 1st, 105,100 bushs. Oats, April 12, 18,400 bushs.; do. April 1st, 21,900 bushs. Barley, April 12, 11,415 bushs., do. April 1st, 30,500 bushs. Peas, April 12, 30,600 bushs.; do. April 1st, 35,100 bushs.

PROVISIONS.—The market is uncommonly dull; as there is nothing doing our quotations are purely nominal. Stocks of most every article are down to 12½c. No. 1 dairy butter is worth our quota tions, but anything inferior cannot be placed.

FREIGHTS.—Though the season is open there is very little doing ; one or two vessels who started out have discharged their hands in the absence of freight. Vessels are offering to Toledo at 5c., and to Oswego at 3c., U. S. Currency, on grain. Fright steamers are contracting for flour to Hali fax at 75c. The Grand Trunk have reduced the rates to Halifax to 90c., to St. John 85c., to Mon treal 30c. Freights by the Great Western Rail way, to all points, unchanged.

MONEY AND EXCHANGE.—Money is in good demand and works close. Bank lending rate 7 per cent; street rate 10 to 12 per cent. Sterling—Bank Exchange selling rate for 60 day bills, 8½; buying rate, ½ to 1 less. Gold drafts on New York par ¼ premium. Silver cought and sold by the brokers at 3½ to 4½ per cent. discount.

Halifax Market.

BREADSTUFFS. April 6.—Supers. for the week continue active, with a growing demand for No. 2, and fine flours. We note the arrival of several vessels from outports, and there is now every pros pect of an early Spring trade, and continued de mand. Several round lots of 1,000 bbls. changed hands last week at $5.50 to $5.60 for supers. and are now held at higher prices, and we feel that any permanent advance abroad will meet with sym pathy here, and increase the disposition to specu late. Our stocks are quite reduced, and demand is in excess of receipts. Corn and oatmeal are without quotable change, and inactive. Rye flour is without enquiry. White beans dull and lower.

WEST INDIA PRODUCE.—At auction yesterday Cienfuegos Molasses realized 36½c. (in bond) for several small parcels. A cargo of Sugar was of fered at 10c. and 9½c. refused. It will probably go to Montreal.

FISH AND OIL.—Fish continues in request at quotations. Oil in sympathy with foreign mark ets, is somewhat easier. Stocks are too light to make it an object to press sales, and the market is without tone.

EXCHANGE.—Bank drafts London at 60 days at 13 per cent. Montreal sight 4 per cent. New

York gold 4 per cent. Currency 20 per cent. dis count. St. John, N. B. 3 per cent. premium.— R. C. Hamilton's Circular.

Petroleum.

The Titusville Herald gives the following table, showing the production of petroleum during March, the average per day, the production pre viously reported in 1869, and the average per day since January 1st last year, and the average per day for the same time :

Total shipment of crude for March of brls of 45 gallons each, brls. 245,241
Add to reduce to brls of 43 gals each, brls 11,406

Total shipment of brls of 43 gallons each, brls ....256,647.
Stock on hand March 1, brls. 282,450
Stock on hand April 1, brls. 329,324

Add increase on April 1, brls. 46,874

Total production during March, brls 303,521
Average per day for 31 days, brls... 9,791
Production previously reported, brls 588,391

Total product since January 1, brls 891,912
Average per day for 90 days, brls... 9,910
Total product same time last year... 834,760
Average per day same time last year 9,280
The following table shows the number of new wells drilling at the date named:

November 17, 1867	255
January 7, 1868	182
April 7, 1868	193
July 7, 1868	299
October 7, 1868	370
January 1, 1869	373
February 1, 1869	341
March 1, 1869	134
April 1, 1869	292

The following were the shipments from January 1 to April 1, 1869, and the crude equivalent:

To New York, brls.	512,571
To Cleveland, brls.	245,756
To Boston, brls.	30,176
To Philadelphia, brls.	25,474
To Pittsburgh, brls.	152,040
To Portland, brls.	9,350
To other points	65,545

Total brls 771,912
Difference between crude and refined ship ped, brls 18,989

Shipment of crude equivalent, brls......790,901

Lake Tonnage.

The Detroit Post publishes a very elaborate and valuable comparative statement of the merchant marine now on the lakes, compared with the same at different periods, from which we extract the following table :

	No.	Tons.	Value.
American steamers	75	76,524	$1,670,000
American propellers	153	82,330	2,527,000
American tugs	205	16,506	1,396,000
American sail vessels	1,376	355,562	10,977,000
American barges	30	9,202	209,000
Total American	1,839	540,814	$18,579,000
Canadian steamers	56	18,572	$1,176,000
Canadian propellers	19	7,563	498,000
Canadian tugs	62	12,162	314,000
Canadian sail vessels	266	52,943	1,753,000
Canadian barges	27	8,800	123,000
Total Canadian	430	99,079	$4,054,000
Am. and Can. steamers	131	95,196	$2,846,000
Am. and Can. propellers	172	89,898	5,025,000
Am. and Can. tugs	267	28,668	5,11-,000
Am. and Can. sail vessels	1,642	408,525	12,710,000
Am. and Can. barges	57	19,071	342,000
Total Am. and Can. craft	2,269	636,903	$25,033,000
Total, 1867	2,388	615,761	$30,316,810
Total, 1860	1,166	547,587	17,062,900
Total, 1861	1,545	383,807	15,100,300
Total, 1856	1,197	319,523	12,418,000

*About 70,000 of tonnage, worth $1,000,000, are now in process of construction, which are not included above.

—A large meeting of the inhabitants of Petrolia was held on the 2nd instant, to consider the deficiency of railway accommodation, and to submit a report of their grievances to the Manager of the Great Western. The correspondent of the *Free Press* says the certain traffic for the coming year is much larger than usual. The Crude Oil Association have already contracted for delivering over 112,000 barrels of oil for shipment outside the Dominion of Canada, and it will require at least 50,000 barrels in addition to supply the home consumption, all of which must be shipped from this point. The producing and handling of this amount of oil will add no little to the necessities of convenient railway facilities.

NOTICE

IS hereby given that the Liquidators of the Western Insurance Company, Limited, will apply to the Minister of Finance for his warrant authorizing the withdrawal of the deposit made by said Company with the Minister of Finance, as required by statute of the late Province of Canada, chapter 83 of 22nd Victoria, the said Company having ceased to do business in Canada.

CARTON & HATTON,
35 Attorneys for Liquidators.

THE TORONTO AND NIPISSING RAILWAY COMPANY.

Total Length to Lake Nipissing, about 200 Miles.

FIRST SECTION FROM TORONTO TO COBOCONK, 85 MILES;

With a Branch of 18 miles from the Main Line to the Town of Lindsay.

Total Capital, $3,000,000.

Capital for the First Section (Main Line) **$1,275,000.**

BONUSES already Voted by Municipalities for the First Section of the Main Line, $399,000.

AS FOLLOWS:—

City of Toronto, $150,000; Scarboro', $10,000; Markham, $30,000; Uxbridge, $50,000; Scott, $10,000; Brock, $50,000; Eldon, $44,000; Bexley, $15,000; Luxton, Digby and Longford, $25,000; Somerville, $15,000.

BONUSES yet to be obtained, including those for the Lindsay Branch, $155,000.

First issue of stock in $100 shares, $400,000.

Upon which will be Issued Bonds for $476,000.

Upon $126,000 of which a Guarantee from the Government of Ontario will be applied for, as equitable assistance for the construction of the Railway through and into Crown Lands on the route of the First Section.

PRESIDENT—John Crawford, Esq., M.P.

VICE-PRESIDENT—J. E. Smith, Esq., Collector of Customs.

DIRECTORS:

Hon. M. C. Caméron, Provincial Secretary; Hon. David Reesor, Senator; W. F. McMaster, Esq., Captain Taylor, Wm. Gooderham, Jun., Esq., H S. Howland, Esq., Vice-Pres. Bank of Commerce; G. Laidlaw, Esq., H. P. Crosby, Esq., M.P.P., Joseph Gould, Esq., Thomas Wilson, Esq., John Gordon, Esq., A. M. Smith, Esq., T. C. Chisholm, Esq., D. McRae, Esq., Reeve Eldon; Edward Wheeler, Esq., Ex-Reeve Whitehurch; John Leys, Esq., Solicitor; R. W. Elliot, Esq., Ald. F. H. Medcalf, A. P. Cockburn, Esq., M.P.P., J. C. Fitch, Esq., Jas. E. Ellis, Esq., Ald. Dickey, John Shedden, Esq., J. D. Merrick, Esq., Dr. Wright.

TRUSTEES OF BONUSES GRANTED BY MUNICIPALITIES.—Hon. Geo. W. Allan, Senator—Government Trustee; Hon. M. C. Cameron, Provincial Secretary—Company's Trustee; Henry Brethour, Esq., Deputy Reeve of Brock—Municipalities' Trustee.

COUNSEL—Hon. M. C. Cameron, Provincial Secretary.
SOLICITOR—John Leys, Esq.
CONSULTING ENGINEERS—Sir Charles Fox & Sons.
BANKERS—Bank of Toronto.
BROKERS—Blaikie & Alexander, Pellatt & Osler.
SECRETARY—Charles Robertson, Esq.

OFFICES—46 FRONT STREET, TORONTO.

PROSPECTUS.

The Provisional Directors of the Toronto and Nipissing Railway Company, finding that the further progress in the building of Broad Gauge Railways in Canada, with English capital, was no longer financially practicable or expedient for lines of Railway projected for local traffic, and having become cognizant of the successful working for a number of years of Railways built on the three feet six gauge, in the Kingdoms of Norway and Sweden, in the colonies of Queensland and New Zealand, and also in India, and that these Railways were capable of accommodating a traffic of about a million or a million and a half of tons of goods per annum, and of carrying passengers at a speed of twenty-five to thirty miles an hour, and seeing that the average speed of passenger trains, including stoppages, in Canada does not exceed twenty miles an hour, and that the total traffic of the Northern Railway (which offers a fair illustration of the traffic to be obtained by the Toronto and Nipissing Railway) did not exceed 196,000 tons and 140,000 passengers, have therefore resolved to construct the Toronto and Nipissing Railway on the three feet six gauge, in the most economical and efficient manner consistent with a total cost of $15,000 per mile.

The Directors have also noted Capt. Tyler's report on the Festiniog Railway, two feet gauge, in Merionethshire, Wales, the freight and passenger traffic of which approximates closely to that of the Northern Railway, and, with the exception of the lumber traffic, largely exceeds that carried on the Lindsay and Port Hope, or on the London and Port Stanley Railway.

With a view to a just apportionment of the risks incidental to capital invested in Railway enterprise in Canada, it was resolved to ask the municipalities most to be benefitted by the construction of the Railway, for *one-third of the total cost of the Railway, viz.*, $5,000 *per mile, by way of bonus* or gift. This proportion of the cost has *already been voted* for the main line, excepting less than $50,000, yet obtainable, in debentures bearing six per cent., payable in 20 years—securities which are unexceptionable, and will sell here at or near par.

Of the remaining two-thirds of the capital, it is proposed now to offer here $400,000 to be subscribed in stock. If that or a larger amount is not subscribed, bonds will be issued for the balance of about $6,000 per mile. Thus local capital to the extent of about two-thirds of the cost of the Railway, will be security to the holders of the bonds of this Company.

The interest-bearing capital will thus be $10,000 per mile.

The Directors do not propose to extend the line beyond Coboconk, towards Lake Nipissing, unless subsidized by the Government of this Province with land or money sufficient to guarantee the Company from the loss of any private capital to be invested in the sections of the line beyond Coboconk.

Nevertheless, the Company feel assured that the first section being successfully completed, the remaining sections will immediately receive aid from the Government to the extent necessary to secure the construction of the line to the ultimate terminus at Lake Nipissing—thus ensuring to the proprietors of the first section the practically unlimited timber traffic, as well as the general business of an immense new territory of twenty thousand square miles.

The terminus of the first section being located on the Gull River, with access to all its tributaries, and to the Burnt River, insures for this Railway a timber and lumber traffic certain to exceed in duration of supply and quantity the timber and lumber traffic of the Northern Railway, and which will undoubtedly equal or exceed that of the Lindsay and Port Hope Railway, which amounted to nearly one hundred millions of feet in the year 1868.

The sawn lumber traffic of the Northern Railway of Canada in 1868, amounted only to about fifty-five (55) million feet, and the square timber traffic to one million six hundred thousand cubic feet.

IN 1861.

The local traffic of the Northern Railway of Canada amounted to..		120,000 tons
Through..........................		25,000 "
Passengers..........................		100,618 "
Local Receipts..........................	$262,507	
Through..........................	48,432	$410,939
Running Expenses..........................		68 per cent.
Excess of earnings over running expenses on local traffic..........	115,982	
Do. on through traffic..........	15,498	
Local earnings equal to 8½ per cent on a cost of $15,000 per mile; or 12½ on $10,000 per mile.		

1864.

Local Traffic..........................		180,700 tons
Through Traffic..........................		8,344 "
Passengers..........................		104,349
Local Receipts..........................	$452,382	
Through "	14,884	$467,266
Running Expenses..........................		52 per cent.
Excess of earnings over running expenses on local traffic..........	217,143	
Do. on through traffic..........	7,144	
Local earnings equal to 16 2-5 per cent on a cost of $15,000 a mile; or 23 1-10 per cent on $10,000 per mile.		

1868.

Local and through traffic..........		194,583 tons
Passengers..........................		138,965 "
Local Receipts..........................	$537,380	
Through "	12,690	$550,070
Running expenses..........................		61 per cent.
Excess of earnings over running expenses on local traffic..........	209,578	
Do. on through traffic..........	4,949	
Or equal to 14⅞ per cent on $15,000 a mile (local earnings); or 22½ per cent on $10,000 per mile.		

1861—Running expenses per cent, 68; local tonnage, 120,000 through tonnage, 25,000; total tons, 145,000; passengers, 106,618; local receipts, gross, $362,507; through receipts, gross, $48,432; total receipts, gross, $410,939; local receipts, nett, $115,982; through receipts, nett, $15,498; dividend on $15,000 a mile, local, 8 1-3; dividend on $15,000 a mile, through, 1 1-10.

1864—Running expenses per cent, 52; local tonnage 180,700; through tonnage, 8,340; total tons, 189,040; passengers, 104,340; local receipts, gross, $452,382; through receipts, gross, $14, 834; total receipts, gross, $467,266; local receipts, nett, $217,143; through receipts, nett, $7,144; dividend on $15,000 a mile, local, 15 2-5; dividend on $15,000 a mile, through, 1-2.

1863—Running expenses per cent, 61; total tons, 194,588; passengers, 138,965; local receipts, gross, $537,380; through receipts, gross, $12,690; total receipts, gross, $550,070; local receipts, nett, $209,578; through receipts, nett, $4,949; dividend on $15,000 a mile, local, 14 7-8; dividend on $15,000 a mile, through, 1-3.

Total tons, 528,620; passengers, 349,029; local receipts, gross, $1,352,269; through receipts, gross, $76,006; total receipts, gross, $1,428,275; local receipts, nett, $542,702; through receipts, nett, $27,501; dividend on $15,000 a mile, local, 12 5-6; dividend on $15,000 a mile, through, 2-3.

AVERAGE.—Total tons, 176,200; passengers, 116,643; local receipts, gross, $450,756; through receipts, gross, $25,335; total receipts, gross $476,091; local receipts, nett, $180,901; through receipts, nett, $9,197; dividend on $15,000 a mile, local, 12 5-6; dividend on $15,000 a mile, through, 2-3.

From the above data it will be seen that the Northern Railway carried an average for those three years of 176,200 tons of freight, and 116,643 passengers; the average gross receipts being $450,756, while the nett receipts from local traffic were $180,901, equal to an annual dividend of 12 5-6 per cent on a cost of $15,000 per mile; or 19 1-4 on $10,000 per mile.

It is remarkable and of consequence to intending subscribers for stock of the T. & N. R., that the nett receipts for through traffic for the same years only averaged $9,19[illegible] per annum, equal to a dividend of ⅔ of one per cent. on cost of $15,000 per mile. This fact clearly proves the value of local as against through traffic.

The Grain Traffic tributary to the Toronto and Nipissing Railway undoubtedly will not fall below 900,000 bushels and probably will largely exceed that quantity. The Passenger Traffic is anticipated to average 100,000 per annum.

The country through which the first section of the Toronto and Nipissing Railway will pass, is more populous, wealthy and extensive than that tributary to the Northern Railway—being one of the oldest and finest settled districts in the Province of Ontario. Various unsuccessful efforts have previously been made to accommodate this district with railways.

The most moderate estimate of the gross receipts from the traffic in timber, lumber, cereals, passengers, etc., to be carried over the T. & N. R. place the amount at an average of $400,000 to $500,000 per annum, for the first eight or ten years, when the traffic must necessarily increase to a much larger amount.

The traffic to create this revenue will be derived from the following items, and in about the proportions set forth:

Pine, or sawn lumber, for the first eight years, 80,000,000 ft. at $2 per 1,000 ft..........	$160,000
Square timber, 1,250,000..........................	37,500
Cereals, 900,000 bushels, at 5c. per bush......	45,000
General goods, 15,000 tons, at an average of $3 40 per ton..........................	51,000
Mails and Express..........................	15,000
Cordwood, 25,000 cords at $1 50 per cord.....	37,500
Passengers, 100,000..........................	100,000
	$446,000

Allowing 60 per cent. for running expenses, the net earnings amount to $178,400—equal to a dividend of 14 per cent. on a cost of $15,000 per mile: and on the actual cost to the Company of $10,000 per mile, the dividend from such nett earnings would be 21 per cent.

The Provisional Directors invest their own means on their faith in the correctness of these estimates.

The terminus at Coboconk, on the Gull River, will connect the Railway with a vast stretch of Inland Navigation upon which steamers now trade, and which, with comparatively inexpensive improvements already partly undertaken by the government, will give these boats access to the Railway, and will afford almost inexhaustible supplies of pine and hard wood.

By the Act of Incorporation, the Company is specially bound to carry cordwood, and to afford every necessary facility for so doing at the specified rate of 3 cents per cord per mile for dry wood, for all distances under 50 miles and 2½ cts. per cord per mile for all distances over 50 miles—a rate which has been found satisfactory, by the test of actual experience on the Government Railways in New Brunswick.

This condition will enhance the cost of fuel to the Company; but the increased traffic and prosperity consequent upon this trade it is fully believed will more than compensate for the extra cost of fuel.

The numerous association of gentlemen who have promoted and borne the preliminary expenses of this enterprise, and who desire to see it carried out in good faith on sound commercial principles, *are resolved*, in so far as their influence is equal to the task, to have this railway controlled by the most respectable capitalists of this city and the country on the route of the railway, who may take stock in it; to convert their own securities and pay cash to contractors, and not to surrender control of the railway to contractors or bondholders; to let the contracts in

r calculated to ensure the healthiest competition:
sr words, to have value for the money from the
g of the first sod to the laying of the last rail.
ountry on the route of the first section of the rail-
s generally level, although in two townships it is
1 er rolling, yet the soil being loamy in these excep-
and there being almost no bridges; the superficial
nation had and the flexibility of the gauge ensures a
um of cuttings and fillings—while timber for bridges
es, and lumber for buildings and fences, can be had
least cost possible in Canada.
y other consideration in the first instance will be
iinated to the construction of a first-class permanent
he best of timber bridges; deep and good ballasting
a weigh 40 lbs. to the yard, and to, be selected of
st quality.
ngements are in progress which will secure to the
any free right of way, through the city, and egress,
ired, for a few miles out of the city, on the line of
and Trunk, by means of a third rail; and the dispo-
of the proprietors and other circumstance along the
s so favorable that the whole right of way will be
ed for an amount not exceeding $20,000.
ion grounds and dockage will be had in this city
free or for a nominal rental.
the desire of the Provisional Directors to have their
Engineer appointed with the concurrence, and sub-
the approval of the Company's Consulting Engi-
Sir Charles Fox & Sons, who will be held responsible
excellence of the works, economy of construction,
a success here of the system of narrow gauge railways
ch they have large experience elsewhere, and with
tistion of which in this country they are honorably
ied.
hese premises the Provisional Directors appeal for
subscriptions to the citizens of Toronto, to the
palities and to the business men and proprietors
along the route of the railway, and to capitalists
ere, believing that the most cautious and prudent
irs will find the stock of the Toronto and Nipissing
y worthy of their attention.
stock books will be opened at the Company's offices
Street, on the 12th April, at 10 o'clock a.m.; mean-
orms of application for shares can be had on appli-
from the secretary and from the reeves and clerks
several municipalities on the route of the railway,
on Messrs. Blaikie & Alexander, Toronto, and
& Osler.
   CASEY S. WOOD, Esq., Lindsay.
   JOSEPH GOULD, Esq., Uxbridge.
   McDOUGALD & DAVIDSON, Montreal.
   ALEXANDER FRASER, Esq., Québec.
nber of the firm of Charles Fox & Son will be here
, and immediately on his arrival operations will be
nced.

Pellatt & Osler.

K AND EXCHANGE BROKERS, Accountants,
nts for the Standard Life Assurance Company.
  *ICE—86 King Street East, four Doors West of
Church Street, Toronto.*

Y PELLATT,   EDMUND B. OSLER,
Notary Public.   *Official Assignee.*

The Queen's Hotel.

THOMAS DICK, Proprietor.

' STREET, - - - - *TORONTO, ON?*
                       3-1y

Commercial House.
(LATE HUFFMAN HOUSE.)
PETERBOROUGH, ONTARIO.

'GE CRONN : : : : : : : :PROPRIETOR
ddition lately made, including Twenty Bed Rooms.
10, 1868.   17-1L

The St. Lawrence Glass Company
now manufacturing and have for sale,

'OAL OIL LAMPS,
    various styles and sizes.
AMP CHIMNEYS,
    of extra quality for ordinary Burners also
    for the 'Comet' and 'Sun' Burners.
    SETS OF
GLASSWARE, HYACINTH GLASSES,
'TEAM GUAGE TUBES, GLASS RODS, &c.,
other article made to order, in White or Colored
             Glass.
ENE BURNERS, COLLARS and SOCKETS, will
        be kept on hand.
'ISTS' FLINT GLASSWARE, and
  PHILOSOPHICAL INSTRUMENTS,
         made to order.
'ICE—388 ST. PAUL STREET, MONTREAL.
         A. McK, COCHRANE.
                Secretary.

John Morison,
IMPORTER OF
GROCERIES, WINES, AND LIQUORS,

. 38 AND 40 WELLINGTON STREET,

TORONTO.   33-1y

Geo. Girdlestone,
FIRE, Life, Marine, Accident, and Stock Insurance
   Agent
    Very best Companies represented.
Windsor, Ont. June, 1868

REMOVAL.

Lyman & McNab

Have removed to their

NEW WAREHOUSE,
No. 5 FRONT STREET,

OPPOSITE AMERICAN HOTEL.

Toronto, March 30.   33-4t

R. T. Muir,
125 GRANVILLE STREET, Halifax, Nova Scotia, sells
   every article of Stationery requisite for the Office
of a Miner, Manager, or Engineer.
  Books and Forms ruled and printed to order.
                33-31Dec.69.

H. G. Fraser,
91 GRANVILLE STREET, Halifax, Nova Scotia, Gold
  Broker and Assayer, Crucibles, Retorts, Patent
Amalgam and Smelting Necessaries for sale.
. 21 Dec., 1869.   33.

Lyman & McNab,
Importers of, and Wholesale Dealers in,
HEAVY AND SHELF HARDWARE,
KING STREET,
TORONTO, ONTARIO.

Philip Browne & Co.,
BANKERS AND STOCK BROKERS.
DEALERS IN
STERLING EXCHANGE—U, S, Currency, Silver and
  Bonds—Bank Stocks, Debentures, Mortgages, &c,
Drafts on New York issued, in Gold and Currency.
Prompt attention given to collections. Advances made
on Securities.
     No. 67 YONGE STREET, TORONTO
JAMES BROWNE.   PHILIP BROWNE, Notary Public
y

James C. Small,
BANKER AND BROKER,
No. 34 KING STREET EAST, TORONTO.

Sterling Exchange, American Currency, Silver, and
Bonds, Bank Stocks, Debentures and other Securities
bought and sold.
  Deposits received. Collections promptly made. Drafts
on New York in Gold and Currency issued.

Campbell & Cassels,
C. J. CAMPBELL,] 92 King Street, East, [W. G. CASSELS.
             TORONTO,
BANKERS AND BROKERS,
STERLING EXCHANGE,
     AMERICAN CURRENCY,
        BONDS AND STOCKS,
               GOLD, SILVER,
          AND
  CANADIAN STOCKS AND SECURITIES,
      BOUGHT AND SOLD.

ORDERS EXECUTED PROMPTLY ON BEST TERMS.
29-1y

W. PATERSON & Co.,
BANKERS AND BROKERS,
Insurance, Passage, and General Agents,
NORTH-WEST COR. KING AND CHURCH STREETS,
           TORONTO.
BUY AND SELL, AT BEST RATES,
NEW YORK AND STERLING EXCHANGE,
      UNCURRENT FUNDS, STOCKS,
            GOLD, SILVER, &c., &c.
    COMMERCIAL PAPER DISCOUNTED.
DEPOSITS RECEIVED, SUBJECT TO DEMAND.
Money Advanced on Good Securities.
       AGENTS FOR THE
LONDON AND LANCASHIRE LIFE ASSURANCE CO.
 29-1y

TORONTO SAVINGS BANK.
72 CHURCH STREET.

DEPOSITS received, from Twenty Cents upwards; in
   vested in Government and other first class securities.
   Interest allowed at 5 and 6 per cent.
       BANKS OF DEPOSIT:
  Ontario Bank and Canadian Bank of Commerce.
           W. J. MACDONELL,
301y   MANAGER.

TO BUILDING SOCIETIES,
INSURANCE COMPANIES, AND PERSONS HAVING
 TRANSACTIONS WITH THEM.—TO CAPITAL-
 ISTS, AND ALL CONCERNED IN THE SALE OR
 EXCHANGE OF SECURITIES :—

For Calculations as to the Surrender Value of Life or
Endowment Insurance Policies by any Tables of Mortality,
and at any rate of Interest.
  The interest earned on buying, selling, or exchanging
Stocks, Debentures, Mortgages, &c., above or below par
value.
  The buying or selling Value of Annuities for Life or
terms of years.
  The valuations of Building Societies' Mortgages, or any
similar obligations, &c., &c., &c.
    Address
      ARTHUR HARVEY, F.S.S., &c.,
                      OTTAWA.
MINIMUM FEE, $5.00

TORONTO SAFE WORKS.

J. & J. Taylor
MANUFACTURERS OF
Fire and Burglar Proof
SAFES,
BANK LOCKS, VAULTS, DOORS, &c., &c.

AGENTS :
JAS. HUTTON & Co............. MONTREAL.
H. S. SCOTT & Co............. QUEBEC.
ALEX. WORKMAN & Co......... OTTAWA.
RICE LEWIS & SON .... TORONTO.
D. FALCONER................. HALIFAX, N.S.

Manufactory & Sale Rooms, 198 & 200 Palace Street.
30-1y

Canada Permanent Building and Savings
Society.

Paid up Capital $1,000,000
Assets 1,700,000
Annual Income   400,000

Directors:—JOSEPH D. RIDOUT, President.
       PETER PATERSON, Vice-President.
J. G. Worts, Edward Hooper, S. Nordheimer, W. C.
  Chewett, E. H. Rutherford, Joseph Robinson.
Bankers:—Bank of Toronto; Bank of Montreal; Royal
       Canadian Bank.
  OFFICE—Masonic Hall, Toronto Street, Toronto.
MONE Received on Deposit bearing five and six per
        cent. interest.
Advances made on City and Country Property in the Province
         of Ontario.
            J. HERBERT MASON,
35-y   Sec'y & Treas

H. N. Smith & Co.,
2, EAST SENECA STREET, BUFFALO, N. Y., (correspondent Smith, Gould, Martin & Co., 11 Broad Street,
N.Y.,) Stock, Money and Exchange Brokers. Advances
made on securities.   21-2y

Mercantile.

TORONTO PRICES CURRENT.—APRIL 8, 1869.

Name of Article.	Wholesale Rates.	
Boots and Shoes.	$ c.	$ c.
Mens' Thick Boots ...	2 20	2 50
" Kip....	2 50	3 00
" Calf	3 20	3 70
" Congress Gaiters..	1 65	2 50
" Kip Cobourgs....	1 15	1 45
Boys' Thick Boots.....	1 70	1 80
Youths' "	1 40	1 50
Women's Batts	0 95	1 30
" Balmoral.........	1 20	1 50
" Congress Gaiters..	0 90	1 50
Misses' Batts.	0 75	1 00
" Balmoral	0 87	1 20
" Congress Gaiters..	1 00	1 30
Girls' Batts	0 65	0 85
" Balmoral.........	0 90	1 05
" Congress Gaiters..	0 75	1 10
Children's C. T. Cacks..	0 50	0 65
" Gaiters..........	0 65	0 90
Drugs.		
Aloes Cape........	0 12½	0 16
Alum.............	0 02½	0 03
Borax	0 00	0 00
Camphor, refined......	0 65	0 70
Castor Oil.........	0 16½	0 28
Caustic Soda.........	0 04½	0 05
Cochineal...........	0 90	1 00
Cream Tartar	0 40	0 45
Epsom Salts	0 03	0 04
Extract Logwood......	0 11	0 12
Gum Arabic, sorts.....	0 30	0 35
Indigo, Madras.......	0 90	1 00
Licorice	0 14	0 45
Madder..............	0 00	0 18
Galls	0 32	0 37
Opium...............	12 00	13 50
Oxalic Acid..........	0 26	0 35
Potash, Bi-tart.......	0 25	0 28
" Bichromate....	0 15	0 20
Potass Iodide	3 90	4 50
Senna	0 12½	0 60
Soda Ash	0 02½	0 04
Soda Bicarb	4 50	5 00
Tartaric Acid.........	0 40	0 45
Verdigris	0 35	0 40
Vitriol, Blue.........	0 08	0 10
Groceries.		
Coffees:		
Java, ℔ lb..........	0 22@	0 24
Laguayra, ...	0 17	0 18
Rio..............	0 15	0 17
Fish:		
Herrings, Lab. split..	5 75	6 50
" round......	0 00	0 00
" scaled......	0 35	0 40
Mackerel, small kitts..	1 00	0 00
Loch. Her. wh'e firks..	2 50	2 75
" half " ..	1 25	1 50
White Fish & Trout...	None.	
Salmon, saltwater....	14 00	15 00
Dry Cod, ℔112 lbs....	5 00	5 25
Fruit:		
Raisins, Layers	2 00	2 10
" M R.........	1 90	2 00
" Valentias new..	0 6½	0 7½
Currants, new........	0 5½	0 06½
" old.........	0 04	0 04½
Figs...............	0 14	0 00
Molasses:		
Clayed, ℔ gal........	0 00	0 35
Syrups, Standard	0 60	0 00
" Golden	0 00	0 65
Rice:		
Arracan	4 25	4 50
Spices:		
Cassia, whole, ℔ lb...	0 00	0 45
Cloves	0 11	0 12
Nutmegs	0 50	0 55
Ginger, ground	0 20	0 25
" Jamaica, root..	0 20	0 25
Pepper, black........	0 12½	0 00
Pimento............	0 08	0 09
Sugars:		
Port Rico, ℔ lb.......	0 10¾	0 00
Cuba "	0 10¼	0 00
Barbadoes (bright)...	0 10¼	0 00
Canada Sugar Refine'y, yellow No. 2, 60ds..	0 10½	0 11
Yellow, No. 2½.	0 10¾	0 11½
No. 3........	0 11	0 11½
Crushed X	0 13	0 13¼
" A	0 13	0 13¼
Ground.............	0 13¾	0 14
Dry Crushed	0 14½	0 14½
Extra Ground........	0 15¼	0 15½
Teas:		
Japan com'n to good..	0 48	0 55
" Fine to choicest..	0 50	0 65
Colored, com. to fine..	0 60	0 75
Congou & Souch'ng...	0 42	0 75
Oolong, good to fine..	0 50	0 65
Y. Hyson, com to gd..	0 47½	0 55
Medium to choice	0 65	0 80
Extra choice	0 85	0 95

Name of Article.	Wholesale Rate.	
Groceries—*Contin'd*	$ c.	$ c.
Gunpowd'r c. to med..	0 55	70
" med. to fine.	0 70	85
" fine to fins't..	0 85	95
Hyson	0 45	0 80
Imperial	0 42	0 80
Tobacco, Manufact'd:		
Can Leaf, ℔ lb 5s & 10s.	0 26	0 30
Western Leaf, com..	0 25	0 26
" Good	0 27	0 32
" Fine	0 32	0 35
" Bright fine..	0 40	0 50
" " choice..	0 60	0 75
Hardware.		
Tin (net cash prices)		
Block, ℔ lb	0 28	0 00
Grain.............	0 30	0 00
Copper:		
Pig	0 23	0 24
Sheet.............	0 30	0 33
Cut Nails:		
Assorted ¼ Shingles, ℔ 100 lb........	2 90	3 00
Shingle alone do	3 15	3 25
Lathe and 5 dy.......	3 30	3 40
Galvanized Iron:		
Assorted sizes.......	0 08	0 09
Best No. 24.........	0 09	0 00
" 26.........	0 08	0 08½
" 28.........	0 09	0 09½
Horse Nails:		
Guest's or Griffin's assorted sizes......	0 00	0 00
For W. ass'd sizes...	0 18	0 19
Patent Hammer'd do..	0 17	0 18
Iron (at 4 months):		
Pig—Gartsherrie No1..	24 00	25 00
Other brands. No1..	22 00	24 00
" No2..	0 00	0 00
Bar—Scotch, ℔100 lb..	2 25	2 50
Refined	3 00	3 25
Swedes	5 00	5 50
Hoops—Coopers......	3 00	3 25
Band	3 00	3 25
Boiler Plates........	3 25	3 50
Canada Plates.......	3 75	4 00
Union Jack	0 00	0 00
Pontypool..........	3 25	4 00
Swansea	3 90	4 00
Lead (at 4 months):		
Bar, ℔ 100 lbs.....	0 06½	0 07
Sheet "	0 08	0 09
Shot..............	0 07½	0 07½
Iron Wire (net cash):		
No. 6, ℔ bundle....	2 70	2 80
" 9, "	3 10	3 20
" 12, "	3 40	3 50
" 16, "	4 30	4 40
Powder:		
Blasting, Canada....	3 50	0 00
FF " ...	4 25	4 50
FFF " ...	4 75	5 00
Blasting, English ...	4 00	5 00
FF loose..	5 00	0 00
FFF " ..	6 00	6 50
Pressed Spikes (4 mos):..		
Regular sizes 100.....	4 00	4 25
Extra " ..	4 50	5 00
Tin Plates (net cash):		
IC Coke	7 50	8 50
IC Charcoal.........	8 50	9 00
IX "	10 50	11 00
IXX "	13 50	14 00
DC "	8 00	8 50
DX "	9 50	0 00
Hides & Skins, ℔ lb		
Green rough	0 00	0 06
Green, salt'd & insp'd..	0 08	0 08½
Cured	0 00	0 00
Calfskins, green.......	0 00	0 10
Calfskins, cured.......	0 00	0 12½
" dry.........	0 18	0 20
Sheepskins, ...	1 40	1 50
" country......	1 00	1 40
Hops.		
Inferior, ℔ lb........	0 05	0 07
Medium........	0 07	0 09
Good	0 09	0 12
Fancy	0 00	0 00
Leather, @ (4 mos.) In lots of less than 50 sides, 10 ℔ cent higher.		
Spanish Sole, 1st qual'y heavy, weights ℔ lb..	0 21½	0 22
Do. 1st qual middle do..	0 23	0 00
Do. No. 2, light weights	0 23	0 00
Slaughter heavy	0 00	0 24
Do. light........	0 00	0 00
Harness, best	0 25	0 27
" No. 2	0 00	0 00
Upper heavy..........	0 32	0 35
" light........	0 35	0 36

Name of Article.	Wholesale Rate.	
Leather—*Contin'd.*	$ c.	$
Kip Skins, Patna	0 30	
French	0 70	
English	0 65	
Hemlock Calf (30 to 35 lbs.) per doz....	0 60	
Do. light	0 45	
French Calf.	1 03	1
Grain & Satn Clt ℔ doz..	0 00	
Splits, large ℔ lb......	0 30	
" small	0 23	
Enamelled Cow ℔ foot..	0 20	
Patent	0 20	
Pebble Grain	0 15	
Buff..	0 14	
Oils.		
Cod	0 65	0
Lard, extra	0 00	0
" No.	0 00	0
" Woollen........	0 00	0
Lubricating, patent...	0 00	0
" Mott's economic	0 50	0
Linseed, raw.........	0 76	0
" boiled..... ..	0 81	
Machinery	0 00	0
Olive, common, ℔ gal..	1 00	1
" salad	1 95	2
" salad, in bots. qt. ℔ case....	3 60	2
Sesame salad, ℔ gal...	1 60	1
Seal, pale	0 75	0
Spirits Turpentine....	0 52½	0
Varnish	0 00	0
Whale.	0 00	0
Paints, &c.		
White Lead, genuine in Oil, ℔ 25lbs.....	0 00	2
Do. No. 1 "	0 00	2
" 2 "	0 00	1
" 3 "	0 00	1
White Zinc, genuine..	3 00	3
White Lead, dry......	0 05½	
Red Lead...........	0 07½	0
Venetian Red, Eng'h..	0 02½	0
Yellow Ochre, Fren'h..	0 02½	0
Whiting	0 85	1
Petroleum. (Refined ℔ gal.)		
Water white, car l'd..	—	
" small lots....	0 37	
Straw, by car load....	0 00	
" small lots....	0 00	
Amber, by car load..	0 00	
" small lots	0 00	
Benzine	0 00	
Produce.		
Grain:		
Wheat, Spring, 60 lb..	0 93	
" Fall 60 "..	1 00	
Barley........ 48 "..	1 11	
Peas...... 60 "..	0 70	
Oats..... .... 34 "..	0 52	
Rye .... 56 "..	0 60	
Seeds:		
Clover, choice 60 "..	5 75	
" com'n 68 "..	6 00	
Timothy, cho'e 4 "..	2 00	
" inf. to good 48 "..	2 00	
Flax .... 56 "..	2 00	
Flour (per brl.):		
Superior extra.......	0 00	
Extra superfine,......	4 45	
Fancy superfine	4 20	
Superfine No 1......	4 10	
" No. 2......	—	
Oatmeal, (per brl.)....	5 50	
Provisions		
Butter, dairy tub ℔ lb..	0 23	
" store packed...	0 15	
Cheese, new	0 12½	
Pork, mess, per brl....	25 50	2
" prime mess......	—	
" prime..........	—	
Bacon, rough	0 11	
" Cumberl'd cut...	0 12	
" smoked	0 00	
Hams, in salt.........	0 12	
" smoked........	0 13½	
Shoulders, in salt	0 10	
Lard, in kegs........	0 15	
Eggs, packed	0 15	
Beef Hams	0 00	
Tallow	0 08	
Hogs dressed, heavy..	0 00	
" medium....	0 00	
" light.... ..	0 00	
Salt, &c.		
American brls.........	1 50	
Liverpool coarse	1 15	
Goderich	0 00	
Plaster.............	1 05	
Water Lime	1 50	

& Candles.

	$ c.	$ c.
ford & Co.'s ..		
perial.........	0 07½	0 08
den Bar	0 07	0 07½
er Bar........	0 07	0 07½
....	0 05	0 05½
....	0 03½	0 03¾
....	0 00	0 11½

s, Liquors, &c.

, per doz......	2 60	2 65
ss Dub Portr..	2 35	2 40
maica Rum...	1 80	2 25
per's H. Gin..	1 55	1 65
Old Tom.....	1 90	2 00
cases.........	4 00	4 25
Old Tom, c...	6 00	6 25
ommon	1 00	1 25
ne old	2 00	4 00
common	1 00	1 50
edium	1 70	1 80
ale or golden ..	2 50	4 00

	$ c.	$ c.
Brandy:		
Hennessy's, per gal..	2 30	2 50
Martell's " ..	2 30	2 50
J. Robin & Co.'s " ..	2 25	2 35
Otard, Dupuy & Cos..	2 25	2 35
Brandy, cases.........	8 50	9 00
Brandy, com. per c...	4 00	4 50
Whiskey:		
Common 36 u. p.......	0 62½	0 65
Old Rye	0 85	0 87½
Malt	0 85	0 87½
Toddy	0 85	0 87½
Scotch, per gal........	1 90	2 10
Irish—Kinnahan's c...	7 00	7 50
" Dunnville's Belf't..	6 00	6 25
Wool.		
Fleece, lb.............	0 28	0 35
Pulled ".............	0 22	0 25
Furs.		
Bear..................	8 00	10 00
Beaver, ⅌ lb..........	1 00	1 25
Coon	0 20	0 40
Fisher.................	4 00	6 00
Martin.................	1 40	1 60
Mink...................	3 25	4 00
Otter..................	5 75	6 00
Spring Rats	0 15	0 17
Fox....................	1 20	1 25

INSURANCE COMPANIES.

ENGLISH.—*Quotations on the London Market.*

Last Dividend.	Name of Company.	Shares par val £	Amount paid.	Last Sale.
	Briton Medical and General Life ...	10	....	2½
7½	Commer'l Union, Fire, Life and Mar.	50	5	5⅝xd
8	City of Glasgow	25	2½	5½
9½	Edinburgh Life	100	15	33
5—½ yr	European Life and Guarantee......	2½	11s6	4s. 6d.
10	Etna Fire and Marine..............	10	1½	—
5	Guardian	100	50	51¼
12	Imperial Fire......................	500	50	350
9½	Imperial Life	100	10	17
10	Lancashire Fire and Life..........	20	2	2⅞
11	Life Association of Scotland.......	40	7½	25
45s. p. sh	London Assurance Corporation ..	25	12½	49
5	London and Lancashire Life	10	1	—
40	Liverp'l & London & Globe F. & L.	20	2	7 1-16
5	National Union Life	5	1	1
12½	Northern Fire and Life	100	5	12 1-16
12 '68, bo 5s.	North British and Mercantile	50	6¼	19½xd
50	Ocean Marine	25	5	17
£5 12s.	Provident Life.....................	100	10	35
£4½ p. s.	Phœnix...........................	....	....	145
2½—h. yr.	Queen Fire and Life	10	1	1
3s. bo. 4s	Royal Insurance...................	20	3	6⅝
10	Scottish Provincial Fire and Life ..	50	2½	5 3-8
25	Standard Life	50	12	66½
5	Star Life	25	1¼	—
	CANADIAN.			⅌ c.
4	British America Fire and Marine ..	$50	$25	55½ 56
4	Canada Life	...	....	.....
12	Montreal Assurance	£50	£5	135
8	Provincial Fire and Marine........	60	11	.....
....	Quebec Fire	40	32½	£25 26
7	" Marine..................	100	40	85 90
4 6 mo's.	Western Assurance................	40	9	.....

RAILWAYS.	Sha's	Paid	Montr	London
and St. Lawrence..................	£100	All.	....	59 61
and Lake Huron	20½	"	....	3 3½
do Preference	10	"	....	5½ 6½
antt. & Goderich, 6⅌c., 1872-3-4..........	100	"	....	66 69
in and St. Lawrence	....	....	10 11	....
do Pref. 10 ⅌ ct..........	....	....	80 82½	....
runk	100	"	15 16	15½ 15¾
Eq. G. M. Bds. 1 ch. 6⅌c...........	100	"	....	87 89
First Preference, 5 ⅌ c	100	"	....	50 53
Deferred, 3 ⅌ ct..................	100	"	....	....
Second Pref. Bonds, 5⅌c...........	100	"	....	37 40
do Deferred, 3 ⅌ ct...........	100	"	....	....
Third Pref. Stock, 4⅌ct...........	100	"	....	28 30
do. Deferred, 3 ⅌ ct..........	100	"	....	....
Fourth Pref. Stock, 3⅌c...........	100	"	....	17 18
do. Deferred, 3 ⅌ ct..........	100	"	....	....
estern	20½	"	14 15	14½ 14¾
New	20½	18	....	....
6 ⅌ c. Bds, due 1873-76...........	100	All.	....	100 102
5½⅌c Bds. due 1877-78...........	100	"	....	94 95
Railway, Halifax, $250, all............	$250	"	....	....
n. of Canada, 6⅌c. 1st Pref. Bds..........	100	"	....	82 84

EXCHANGE.	Halifax.	Montr'l.	Quebec.	Toronto.
n London, 60 days......				
r 75 days date	12½	8 8½	9 9¼	8½
do.	11½ 12	7 8	8 8¼	7½
with documents.........	....	7 8	....	....
New York..............	....	24 24½	23½ 24	24½
do.	....	24½ 25	24 24½	....
afts do.	....	par to ½ p.	par ½ dis.	par ¼ dis.
....	....	4½ 5	....	3½ to 4½

STOCK AND BOND REPORT.

The dates of our quotations are as follows;—Toronto, April 13; Montreal, April 12; Quebec, April 5; London, March 18.

NAME.	Shares.	Paid up.	Divid'd last 6 Months	Dividend Day.	CLOSING PRICES. Toronto.	Montre'l	Quebec
BANKS.			⅌ ct.				
British North America	$250	All.	3	July and Jan.	105 105½	105 105½	104½ 105½
Jacques Cartier..............	50	"	4	1 June, 1 Dec.	109 109½	100 110	109 109½
Montreal	200	"	5	"	144 145	144½ 145	145½ 146
Nationale....................	50	"	4	1 Nov. 1 May.	108 109	108½ 109	108½ 109
New Brunswick	100	"	......	......	....	...	....
Nova Scotia	200	28	7&b$3½	Mar. and Sept.	....	....	....
Du Peuple...................	50	"	4	1 Mar., 1 Sept.	108 108½	108 108½	108 108½
Toronto	100	"	4	1 Jan., 1 July.	121 122	121 122	120 121
Bank of Yarmouth.............	....	....	......	......	....	....	....
Canadian Bank of Com'e.......	50	95	......	......	102 102½	102 103½	102 102½
City Bank Montreal	80	All.	4	1 June, 1 Dec.	102 102½	101¾ 102¼	102 102¼
Commer'l Bank (St. John)....	100	"	⅌ ct.	......	....	...	....
Eastern Townships' Bank.....	50	"	4	1 July, 1 Jan..	....	99 100½	99 100
Gore	40	....	none.	1 Jan., 1 July.	39 40	40 42	40 42
Halifax Banking Company.....	...	....	......	......	...	....	....
Mechanics' Bank.............	50	70	4	1 Nov., 1 May.	97½ 98½	97½ 99	97 98
Merchants' Bank of Canada....	100	70	4	1 Jan., 1 July.	107 107½	107¼ 107¾	107 107½
Merchants' Bank (Halifax)....	....	....	......	......	....	....	....
Molson's Bank................	50	All.	4	1 Apr., 1 Oct.	108 108½	107½ 108½	108 109
Niagara District Bank........	100	70	3½	1 Jan., 1 July.	...	....	....
Ontario Bank.................	40	All.	4	1 June, 1 Dec.	100 100¼	99¾ 100¼	99¾ 100¼
People's Bank (Fred'kton)....	100	"	......	......	....	....	....
People's Bank (Halifax)	20	"	7 12 m	......	....	...	....
Quebec Bank	100	"	3½	1 June, 1 Dec.	101 102	101 102	100½ 101
Royal Canadian Bank	50	50	4	1 Jan., 1 July.	78 79	77 78	80 85
St. Stephen's Bank	100	All.	.....	......	....	..	....
Union Bank	100	70	4	1 Jan., 1 July.	104½ 105½	105 105½	105½ 106
Union Bank (Halifax)........	100	40	7 12 mo	Feb. and Aug.	....	....	...
MISCELLANEOUS.							
British America Land........	250	44	2½	......	....	....	....
British Colonial S. S. Co......	250	32½	2½	......	...	50 60	....
Canada Company	32½	All.	£1 10s.	......	....	....	....
Canada Landed Credit Co.....	50	$20	3½	......	78 80	....	....
Canada Per. B'ldg Society....	50	All.	5	......	125½ 126	....	....
Canada Mining Company.....	4	90	......	......	....	....	....
Do. Inl'd Steam Nav. Co.....	100	All.	7	......	....	100½ 101	....
Do. Glass Company.........	100	"	12½ "	......	....	40 55	....
Canad'n Loan & Investm't....	25	2½	7	......	....	....	....
Canada Agency	10	¼	......	......	....	....	....
Colonial Securities Co........	...	....	......	......	....	....	....
Freehold Building Society....	100	All.	4	......	110½ 111	....	....
Halifax Steamboat Co.........	100	"	5	......	....	....	....
Halifax Gas Company........	...	....	......	......	....	....	....
Hamilton Gas Company.......	....	....	......	......	....	....	....
Huron Copper Bay Co........	4	12	20	......	....	82½ 45	....
Lake Huron S. and C.........	5	102	......	......	....	....	....
Montreal Mining Consols......	20	$15	......	......	....	3.15 3.25	....
Do. Telegraph Co........	40	All.	5	......	133½ 134	133½ 134	132 133
Do. Elevating Co.........	00	"	15 12 m	......	....	100 102½	....
Do. City Gas Co...........	40	"	4	15 Mar. 15 Sep.	....	134½ 135	133 134
Do. City Pass. R,. Co......	50	"	4	......	....	105 106	102 107
Quebec and L. S.	8	$4	......	......	....	....	....
Quebec Gas Co...............	200	All.	4	1 Mar., 1 Sep.	....	...	118 119
Quebec Street R. R..........	50	25	3	......	....	....	90 91
Richelieu Navigation Co......	100	All.	10 p.a.	1 Jan., 1 July.	....	108½ 108¾	107 107½
St. Lawrence Glass Company.	100	"	....	......	....	80 85	....
St. Lawrence Tow Boat Co.....	100	"	......	3 Feb.	...	...	35 40
Tor'to Consumers' Gas Co.....	50	"	4	1 My Au MarFe	107½ 108	...	108 109
Trust & Loan Co. of U. C.....	20	5	3	......	....	....	....
West'n Canada Bldg Soc'y....	50	All.	5	......	121 121½	....	....

SECURITIES.	London.	Montreal.	Quebec.	Toronto.
Canadian Gov't Deb. 6 ⅌ ct. stg..................	....	103 104	103 103½	103 104
Do. do. 6 do due Ja. & Jul. 1877-84........	104½ 105½	....	....	....
Do. do. 6 do. Feb. & Aug........	102 104	....	....	....
Do. do. 6 do. Mch. & Sep........	102 104	....	...	....
Do. do. 5 ⅌ ct. cur., 1883	92 94	92½ 95	93 94	93 94½
Do. do. 5 do. stg., 1885	92 94	92½ 94½	93½ 94½	93 94½
Do. do. 7 do. cur.,....................	....	....	......	....
Dominion 6 p. c. 1878 cy..........................	....	106½ 107	105½ 106	106 107
Hamilton Corporation............................	....	....	......	....
Montreal Harbor, 8 ⅌ ct. d. 1869..................	..	....	......	....
Do. do. 7 do. 1870..................	....	....	......	....
Do. do. 6½ do. 1883..................	....	102 103	......	....
Do. do. 6½ do. 1873..................	....	....	......	....
Do. Corporation, 6 ⅌ c. 1891	....	96 97	95½ 96	96 97
Do. 7 p. c. stock............................	....	108 110	108 109	109 110
Do. Water Works, 6 ⅌ c. stg. 1878............	....	....	......	96½ 97
Do. do. 6 do. cy. do.	....	96½ 97	......	96 97
New Brunswick, 6 ⅌ ct., Jan. and July	103 104	....	......	....
Nova Scotia, 6 ⅌ ct., 1875.........................	102 104	...	......	....
Ottawa City 6 ⅌ c. d. 1880	....	95 96	......	...
Quebec Harbour, 6 ⅌ c. d. 1883......................	....	....	60	....
Do. do. 7 do. do......................	....	....	65 70	....
Do. do 8 do. 1886......................	....	....	80 85	....
Do. City, 7 ⅌ c. d. 1½ years.....................	....	....	93 93½	....
Do. do. 7 do. 8 do.	....	....	91 92	....
Do. do. 7 do. 5 do.	....	....	94 95	....
Do. Water Works, 7 ⅌ ct., 4 years	....	....	97 97½	....
Do. do. 6 do. 2 do.	....	....	94 95	....
Toronto Corporation	....	90 92½	....	....

THE CANADIAN
[ONETARY TIMES
AND
INSURANCE CHRONICLE.

TED TO FINANCE, COMMERCE, INSURANCE, BANKS, RAILWAYS, NAVIGATION, MINES, INVESTMENT,
PUBLIC COMPANIES, AND JOINT STOCK ENTERPRISE.

-NO. 36.   TORONTO, THURSDAY, APRIL 22, 1869.   SUBSCRIPTION $2 A YEAR.

Mercantile.

Meetings.

GRAND TRUNK RAILWAY.

The directors of this company state in their
report that the gross receipts upon the whole undertaking, including the Buffalo and Champlain
lines, had been for the half-year ending the 31st
December, 1868, 756,163l. The working expenses,
exclusive of renewals (being at the rate of 59.44
per cent. against 63.50 of the corresponding half
of last year) 449,487l; the renewals and improvements of the permanent way and works in the
half year debited to revenue were 126,772l,
making together 576,259l, leaving an available
net balance of 179,904l. Deducting the loss on
American currency, 43,318l, left 136,586l, against
125,705l in the corresponding half of 1867. To
the 136,586l was added 3,835l, net revenue from
the preceding half-year, making a total balance of
145,421l. From this was deducted 16,171l for
postal and military revenue due to the postal
bondholders, leaving 129,250l. From this was
deducted 17,362l for interest; 73,231l for rents
of Atlantic and St. Lawrence line, Detroit line,
Champlain and Buffalo lines; and 10,779l for
equipment bond interest, leaving a balance of 27,-
877l. Comparing the results of the half year's
working with the corresponding period of 1867,
there was an increase in the gross revenue of 51,-
784l, equal to 7.35 per cent, with an increase in
the working expenses, exclusive of renewals and
improvements, of only 2,181l on the increased
traffic carried. But for the fact that there had
been charged in the half year 5,400l for insurances
on the company's property, the working expenses
would have been less than in the same period of
1867, notwithstanding the increase of traffic of
nearly 52,000l. This amount for insurance represented the half year's premium on a policy which
came into force last July for $4,300,000 not only
for the company's buildings, but also for the wooden
bridges on the railway, the stocks of cordwood
and lumber at the different stations, and also
freight in the warehouses and in transit. The late
serious losses by fires at Toronto and Sarnia led to
this insurance being effected, and although the
full value of the company's property in buildings,
&c., was of course not embraced in this policy,
still it was believed to be sufficient to meet all
ordinary risks. The renewals in the half year
amounted to 126,772l, against 85,819l, for the
corresponding period of 1867. In this sum was
included a charge of 22,747l for improvements in
the renewal of the permanent way and works, an
item which in 1867 amounted to 17,351l, and which
was then charged to capital. The weight of the
rails had been increased from 62lb to 75lb per
yard. The number of miles of railway relaid with
new iron in the half year was 88½, and the number of new ties put in was 491,993l. The large
outlay that had been made for renewals had, of
course, resulted in a very much improved condition of the line, as was shown by the reduction in
the cost of the maintenance of the road, amounting in the half year to 6,880l. The directors regretted that the rails sent out from this country in
1867, purchased from the best makers, were not
giving satisfaction. The directors took every precaution to secure the best rails which could be
made, and exacted guarantees from the makers

which they were putting in force. The small
quantity of steel rails sent out in 1865, although
placed on a part of the line where the traffic was
very heavy, showed no signs of giving way. The
average receipt per passenger was 6s. 9½d. against
6s. 9¾d. in 1867, and the average receipt per ton
of freight was 16s. 8⅓d. against 15s. 10⅜d. in the
corresponding period of last year. The loss on
American currency was 43,318l. against 39,384l,
in the corresponding half of 1867. Gold fluctuated during the half year from 149½ on the 6th of
August to 132¼ on the 6th of November. Since
then its premium value had further declined. The
indirect loss from increased prices of labour and
materials was in the half year 60,000l. The directors believed they were justified in saying that
but for the loss, direct and indirect, through the
war in the States, the company would have
been in a position to pay cash dividends on the
first and second preference bonds and stocks at
least, and probably on the third preference stock,
also, since 1863. The total amount charged
against revenue for renewals between 1862 and
December, 1868, amounted to 907,809l.; the loss
on American currency amounted to 413,521l. A
table shows that the total profit on working the
company's lines in the past 1861 amounted to 142,-
492l. ; in the year 1862 to 155,674l. ; in the year
1863 to 288,414l. ; in the year 1864 to 271,074l. ;
in the year 1865 to 221,377l. ; in the year 1866
to 364,999l. ; in the year 1867 to 218,231l. ; and
in the year 1868 to 297,894l. In their last report
the directors called attention to the fact that certain bonds, issued by the city of Portland in aid
of the construction of the Atlantic and St. Lawrence Railroad, amounting in the aggregate to $1,-
500,000, and, covered by a first mortgage on the
undertaking, would begin to fall due in Dec. last,
and that the whole amount would mature between
that period and January, 1871, and that the sinking funds created for the redemption of these
bonds would not provide for the payment of more
than half the amount. The Grand Trunk Company, under the terms of the lease of the Atlantic
and St. Lawrence line, was bound to provide for
the payment of these bonds at maturity, either
by means of the sinking funds or otherwise. The
Board having no available funds with which to
meet the half of the bonds not covered by the
sinking fund, had to approach the authorities of
the city of Portland with the view of obtaining
an extension of time, and the directors were happy
to be able to state that an agreement had been
concluded with the city of Portland, under which
the city undertook to issue new bonds for the balance of the original issue, which would not be
taken up by the moneys accumulated and to accumulate in the sinking fund before 1871. After
the transaction of the ordinary business, the
meeting would be made special to consider a proposed new agreement with the Buffalo and Lake
Huron Railway Company, the object being to
settle past differences and to lease the line in perpetuity instead of for 21 years, the original term.
Also to substitute a fixed half-yearly payment, instead of at present a fluctuating amount in proportion to the net receipts of the two undertakings. Contracts for the construction of portions
of the Intercolonial Railway had been entered into
by the Canadian Government, and the works
would be commenced as soon as the snow left the

ground. The four sections were together 91 miles in length. Tenders had also been invited for three more, together 71 miles in length. It would be seen that 162 miles would be let by the end of this month, and tenders for the whole of the remaining sections would, it was expected, be immediately advertised, as it was intended to have the entire length of the railway opened for traffic not later than 1872. The work would therefore be pushed on with the utmost vigor.

BRITISH AMERICAN LAND COMPANY.—The annual general meeting of this company was held recently in London. The report was taken as read.

The Chairman said that their commissioner from Canada was present, and had made recently a very careful survey of the property. The sales last year had been at an average of 6s. 4d. per acre as against 18s. 2d. the average of the year before, but this was accounted for by the sale of a large tract which was not arable land, but only of value for the timber on it. This had been bought at half a dollar an acre and sold at a dollar. There had been much less of cancelled sales than in former years. The timber accounts were not satisfactory, as there was now no demand for the article. He looked forward for improvement and for a renewal of the Reciprocity Treaty with the United States. He concluded by moving the adoption of the report, which being seconded by Mr. A. Gillespie, deputy-governor, was carried unanimously.

The proposed dividend of £1 per share, payable on and after the 16th March, was then declared. Mr. H. W. Heneker, from Sherbrooke, the Canada commissioner, gave the proprietors a detailed and highly interesting account of the condition and character of their property, both the town of Sherbrooke and their landed estates.—*Investors' Guardian.*

Mining.

NOVA SCOTIA GOLD FIELDS.

(From our own Correspondent.)

HALIFAX, April 6, 1869.

The project of establishing a Stock Exchange in Halifax has been temporarily abandoned, and the interest, here and abroad, in the gold mines is becoming confined to a very limited circle. Yet an industry producing at the rate of seven shillings sterling per day to all engaged in it; which has been the means of creating prosperous settlements where before all was waste or wilderness; which has produced over three million dollars from the barren soil, and which already has yielded a quarter of a million dollars revenue to the Province, should be worth sustaining and expanding. The managers of the properties which have contributed so much to the reputation of the country promise better returns for 1869 than any preceding year has given; and with prosperity must come confidence. There will be very little speculation this year, but when investments are made they are likely to be made more discriminatingly than heretofore. The following is the summary of news from the outlying districts:

TANGIER.—The Strawberry Hill Company crushed 125 tons of quartz in March, and obtained 225 oz. 10 dwt. of gold from the same. The mine is looking well. The new lode discovered in January, and now called the "Hill" lode, is of good promise. The manager, Mr. Forrest, reports: "We crush about twelve inches of quartz

and slate, and thus far have taken out one ounce to the ton. The Forrest lode averages 3 oz., the Dunbrack 16 dwt., and the Wallace 12 dwt. Messrs. Esty & Barton still continue working on a small scale with very good success. I look forward to stirring times this summer." At Moose-land some men are at work on the property of Messrs. Fletcher & Neilson.

UNIACKE.—The Mount Uniacke Co.'s yield for March will be about 100 oz. The Montreal Co.'s shaft has lately produced some rich specimens, which the manager has forwarded to the company's office at Montreal. The works have been slightly interrupted by water. The Queen and Central Companies are working on a small scale. The quartz from the LaMothe areas yielded 19 dwt. to the ton—within 1 dwt. also of the previously given estimate.

OLDHAM.—The Shaffer lot, now owned by Messrs. Tobin & Cunning, of this city, continues to make satisfactory returns, though the last crushing of an ounce to the ton was under former averages. This district, however, is reviving in favor.

ISAAC'S HARBOR.—Mr. Balcam is fitting up appliances for testing the alluvium, and the results are looked forward to with interest. The weather will not be favorable for extended operations until May.

WINE HARBOR.—The tunnel in the Eldorado property was completed within ten feet. The engineer, Mr. Holman, has quite recovered from the effects of his fall, and although much shaken, is not maimed or injured, as previously reported. The Provincial Co. are working with a small force. An interesting fact concerning this mine, ascertained by the writer during a recent visit, is, that from a space of 300 feet in length by 160 feet in depth, $300,000 (three hundred thousand dollars) worth of gold was obtained. The Globe Co. produced, during March, 48 oz. 1 dwt. 4 gr. from 190½ tons. This is a small but steadily yielding property, the returns for December, January and March being 36¼, 45½ and 48 ounces respectively. It contains two belts of lodes—the Wiscasset, 9 ft. 3 in., and MacKenzie, 11 ft. wide. The Napier is being laid out with a view to permanent and systematic mining. Three shaft houses are nearly completed, and the shafts so located as to facilitate thorough underground exploration of the whole property. Through the same are supposed to extend no less than eight belts of lodes, from five to eighteen feet in width—namely, the Middle, Mitchell, Washington, Great Western, Wiscasett, MacKenzie, Caledonia, and South belts, besides numerous separate lodes, varying from five to fourteen inches in width, which have been partially worked by the MacIntosh and Stadacona Companies.

It is expected that the properties eastward of the Napier, and the Temple property, will be opened up during the summer. The Eureka Co. had eight men employed, on contract work, stopping. In cross-cutting south from their eastern shaft, they came across a rich lode two and a half inches wide, and look for several more in work progresses in that direction. The mill is well finished, but was not in operation; and the statement that it had been rented by the Napier Co., although coming from a usually well-informed source, was found to be premature.

SHERBROOKE.—The ice on the St. Mary's is beginning to give way, and was already dangerous to cross on Monday last. The projected harbor at Jeggogin is not in much favor with the people of Goldenville, and it is still uncertain whether a steamer will be placed on that route this year. The Palmerston and Dominion mines were still stopped with water. The Metropolitan is yet working. Some very rich ore was being raised from the Wellington, and a small but rich lode had just been discovered on the New York and Sherbrooke Co.'s areas. The Meridian and Delta and Crescent are reported to be looking favorably. The Woodbine was in successful operation. The

new lode on the Canada showed many sights, some excellent quartz was coming out of Wentworth shaft. On the whole, prospects very encouraging, and unless appearances are ceptive, the gold yield for this month will above the average. The quartz from Cochra Hill had not all reached the crusher, and several tons have been reduced (at Goldenville) found to be remunerative, it is not likely that owners of the mine will erect a mill of their own. The roads between Sherbrooke and New Glas are in bad condition, and the journey now oc pies about sixteen hours—an average of less t four miles an hour.

RENFREW.—The manager of the Ophir min Mr. Prince, brought to town last week a be 248 oz., and spoke encouragingly of the fu prospects of the mine.

WAVERLEY.—Professor Hind's Report is being distributed, and may be the means of dir ing fresh attention to the district. The Bo and Nova Scotia Co. sent up 32 oz. before the o of the month. A few men are working on trib and Mr. Burkner has let a contract to sink t 60 feet on a newly discovered promising lode.

MONTAGUE.—The progress in this field is quite hopeful. The properties of Messrs. Le & Co., Angus McQuarrie and Temple, are un development, and from the latter some rich sp mens were obtained last week.

MUSQUODOBOIT.—The Burnett property has been bought by Mr. Hyde, contractor, for ten thou dollars. The dispute with reference to the two areas has not been settled. Mr. Burkner wa town last week with further rich specimens, the surveyor, who had special business to call again to the district, returned yesterday and ported increasing richness of the Burkner m lode. Another disinterested and reliable inf ant stated that he saw a piece of the lode br off, weighing about two hundred pounds, and taining at a low estimate one hundred dollars w of visible gold. Notwithstanding all this the no excitement, and but few additional areas been leased in consequence of these results. typographical (perhaps clerical) error occurs report published under this head in the MONE TIMES of 29th March; for "seventy-eight" "twenty-eight" feet depth of soil, and for "f five" read twenty-five" feet present depth of s There are now twenty-six gold-bearing lodes o ed, and one has been tasted at various points i course for two thousand feet, and everyw showed gold.

FIFTEEN-MILE-STREAM.—Some rich specir from the Nonpareil property were seen by writer last week, at the office of Mr. J. W. J son, New Glasgow. The Pioneer mill (of 15 sta belonging to this company will ensure the on ten free areas. The Halifax Mill (of 10 stan belonging to Messrs. Chipman and Lockhart, is in successful operation. The Government ha ceived over three thousand dollars in rents licenses fees from this district, but has faile return to make a traversible road.

OVENS.—The price paid for the McCulloch perty was six thousand dollars. The adjoi McDonald property, bought by Mr. McCull and offered to the same buyers, is still an hargain, the sale having been communicate the writer by anticipation only. A steamer be put on the western route early in May, and give tourists and investors an opportunity of v ing the long neglected western districts.

GOLD RIVER.—The systematic explorations templated by the Gold River Exploration Co., other companies, are to be undertaken early month.

YARMOUTH.—No results from this new l but some miners from Sherbrooke, who have v ed the mine, report a probability of extended extended operations.

ERRATA.—The average per ton of 2,249 lbs 1862 to 1868 should read 18 dwt. 20 gr., instea

10 gr. in the table published in issue of
o fourth.

NOVA SCOTIA GOLD FIELDS.

Statistical Summary.

1866 to 1868.

	(a) The ore valued at $20.	(b) Counting 312 working days to the year.	(c) The returns for Uniacke begin only with Oct., 1866.	These districts have not been continuously worked during the whole period.

(table of figures)

HALIFAX, N.S., April 12, 1869.

lowing returns show the actual progress
in the leading districts, excepting
Lawrencetown, Montague, and Isaac's
rom which the monthly statements are
ag:

SERIAL RESULT FOR MARCH, 1869.

	Sherbrooke.		Wine Harbor.
...ed	91		.....
New...cked	13		6
...r	3,120	–	3,153
...ised ...... tons	1,080		306 8-20
...ushed ...... tons	1,079 8-20		306 8-20

	oz. dwt. gr.	oz. dwt. gr
Average gold yield p. ton	8 22	4 11
Total "	482 11 18	68 8 14
Maximum " "	6 9 13	00 11 6
Mills	10	5
" steam	9	4
" water	1	1

Mill Returns for March, 1869.

TANGIER.

	Quartz Crushed.	Gold Yield.
	tons cwt.	oz. dwt. gr.
Strawberry Hill 125 00		255 10 0
Barton 49 00		37 7 0

RENFREW.

Hartford 50 00		29 17 0
Colonial 87 00		47 15 9
Ophir 541 00		268 5 0
Thomas 7 00		2 18 0

WAVERLEY.

Lake Major 23 16		10 15 0
Rockland 89 00		31 3 3
Boston & Nova Scotia...212 00		96 12 0

WINE HARBOR.

Globe 164 00		43 17 10
Mill 26 10		4 3 18
Provincial 56 00		3 11 15
Eldorado .... 59 .10		16 11 7
Orient........................ 00 8		00 4 12

SHERBROOKE.

Cobourg 14 10		1 1 0
N. Y. and Sherbrooke... 2 4		.14 5 0
N. Snow................Old copper plates.		6 15 0
Dominion Mill—sundry owners 461 10		162 5 4
Hayden & Derby 6 00		1 17 0
Palmerston 190 27		28 1 0
Woodbine................... 14 00		3 11 17
Caledonia 27 00		5 7 6
Hart 00 14		0 5 15
Wentworth...............153 10.		21 3 0
Wellington 210 00		238 0 0

Recapitulation.

	tons. cwt.	oz. dwt. gr.
Sherbrooke...........1079 8	482 11 18
Wine Harbor.... 306 8	68 8 14
Waverley.... 324 16	138 10 3
Renfrew.... 685 00	343 15 9
Tangier.... 174 00	292 17 0
	2567 12	1326 2 20

REVIEW OF MINING FOR PRECIOUS METALS IN CALIFORNIA IN 1868.

The weather in 1868 was favorable to mining. The supply of water was considerably above the average, and there was no extraordinary frost or flood to interrupt work in either the quartz or gravel mines.

In quartz there was little change. The mines which occupied a leading position in 1867 have it still, notwithstanding some variations. No great mine has fallen, nor has any new one risen. The Eureka, at Grass Valley, extracted about 18,000 tons of ore, and paid $280,000 of dividends last year, or an average of $23,500 per month. The Amador Mine, in fourteen months ending on the first of December last, worked 28,311 tons, and extracted $617,437, an average of $21.80 per ton. The dividends were $340,400, about $24,000 per month, or $12.62 per ton. The North Star, at Grass Valley, has produced $176,000 in the last six months, and $60,000 have lately been expended in extensive and important improvements; so that, according to report, the mine is now in a better condition than ever to pay regular monthly dividends. The gross production of the Empire Mine is is estimated at $240,000 for 1868. The Banner, at Nevada, produced $200,000 gross for the year. It turned out $44,000 in the last sixty days, but that was exceptional. The yield per ton is about $18, and the current monthly expenses about $9,000. The Sierra Buttes turned out $215,000

gross, an average of $14.50 per ton, and paid $138,000 dividends, an average of about $9.35 per ton. The Keystone Mine, Amador County, yielded $188,588.15 for the calendar year, the average per ton being about $16. The Quail Hill Mine, as worked during the early part of the year with stamps, did not pay expenses, though the tailings were rich in the assays; so a Howland's rotary crusher, which bears some resemblance to a big coffee mill, was set up, and four tons were run through it daily, and then worked in two Wheeler pans. The result was that $35 were saved to the ton, and the tailings left from the old workings paid from $10 to $25, the latter sum having been obtained from the tailings nearest the mill. This experiment was tried for four months, and the success being considered certain, the mill is to be remodelled, and the work resumed next spring. The Whiskey Diggings Mill, in Placer County, which was at work on a similar deposit, has been idle for a long time, and we have no information from it. Whether the success at Qail Hill will lead to a trial of the same machinery there is unknown to us.

The Mariposa estate is in the hands of Mark Brumagin, J. A. Stewart, and J. J. McEwen, Trustees, who are now preparing to work the Josephine Mine. The dam across the Merced River is completed, and the mill will soon commence reducing by the Lungren and Ryerson process on a larger scale than ever before. The miners are now taking out ore from the Josephine, and rumour says that it will yield at least $25 per ton, and that the amount in sight equally as good is considerable. The Bear Valley Mill, which was burned down in the summer, will not be rebuilt, having been in an unfavourable situation. A very rich lode, known as the Petticoat, near Mokelumne Hill, and several in Sierra County, have been opened, but their production has not been large as yet. Two quartz mills have been erected in the Soledad District, 30 miles from Los Angelo, and the reports from them are favourable.

In placer mining there has been a steady decline. The Chinese, who did most of the shallow mining a few years since, have been employed on the railroads in such numbers that the rivers and ravines have been neglected, but next summer many of them will get back to their old haunts. Several good hydraulic claims have been worked out, and others have been beset by difficulties of drainage, so that consolidation has been necessary. The Blue Gravel Mine, at Smartsville, still maintains its pre-eminence among the placer mines of the State. Its gross yield last year was about $200,000, of which probably 55 per cent. was net. A few days since, a blast of 15 tons of powder, the largest ever used for gold mining in this State, was let off in the Blue Point claim, at Sucker Flat, to loosen the gravel for hydraulic washing. Several large tail sluices were commenced last summer, but none of them have been finished.

The trial near Cisco of the Hagan furnace for roasting ore by burning water was one of the notable events of the year. A small woodfire is kindled in the fireplace under the ore, and as soon as it burns well, steam is turned on through pipes which pass over the fire, and the doors are closed as tightly as possible, so as to exclude all draft, and thus compel the fire to take the oxygen from the steam while the hydrogen burns and serves as fuel. Those who have witnessed the trials declare this new process a certain success, and a large furnace is now being built at Angels. The expense of roasting the ore of the Enterprise Mine near Cisco was reported at $1.50 per ton, the largest pieces of ore being of the size of a goose egg. The Giant Powder has been introduced in mining with a decided saving. On account of its greater explosive power, a smaller drill hole is sufficient; one man can hold and strike the drill at the same time, and the drifts may be much smaller than where large drills are used. In the New Almaden Mine it was found that to cut a drift with common powder cost $65 per yard, and with Giant Powder $45.45—a saving of $19.55, or 29 per cent.

But in all cases where a one-man drift would serve the purpose, the saving by using Giant Powder would be nearly if not quite 50 per cent.

A new and valuable process of chlorination for silver ores containing base metals has been patented by Kustel and Hoffman, of this city. The ore is crushed to pass through a number three screen, and is then roasted for two hours with not more than two per cent of salt, after which it is subjected to the ordinary gold chlorination process, and then leached with a solution of hypo-sulphate of soda to dissolve and carry away the silver, which is precipitated by sulphide of sodium. Those familiar with the customary methods of reducing argentiferous ores containing large proportions of base metals will perceive that this a simple and cheap mode of reduction. It will not cost more than $12 per ton.

In the beginning of the year the Supreme Court rendered a decision that the exemption of mines from taxation was unconstitutional, and it was supposed that there would be an addition of $10,000,000 or more to the tax of the State in consequence; but so far we have not heard that any assessments on mines have been made save in Sierra County, where the Butte Mine was valued at $300,000 on the tax roll! It may be that the assessments have been made in the other counties, but that they are not considered of sufficient interest for publication. It is scarcely probable that the assessors would undertake to reverse the judgment of the Supreme Court.—*Exchange.*

Insurance.

FIRE RECORD.—Port Rowan, April 16.—John Winch, merchant, near Laughton, 12th concession, Walsingham, was burned out yesterday—store and dwelling house. Loss about three thousand dollars.

St. John, N.B., April.—Frost's drug store sustained considerable damage; insured for $1,500; cause unknown.

Mitchell, April 19.—A large and destructive fire on Sunday morning about 3 o'clock broke out in McQuade's grocery, rapidly spreading east and west, destroying George Barnet's grocery and liquor store; George Ritz's furniture and stove warehouse, Stephen's building; Porter's dry goods store and Town Clerk's office; Sinclair's hardware store and part of the large brick building owned by E. Millar, of Hilbert, and occupied by Peterson & Huston. All parties were partially insured, excepting Mr. Millar, his policy having expired a few days previous. Mr. Barnet's loss is estimated at about $2,000; Porter's, $2,000; McQuaid's, $600; the others not heard from yet. All the Corporation property was saved. Property covered by policies—$13,642. Nothing saved.

Port Colborne, April 20.—Lightning struck the barns and sheds of Samuel Springer, third concession, Humberstone township, burning them, and their contents of grain and hay. Loss about $1,200. Insured for $600 in the Agricultural Mutual, of London. The cheese house of Josse Steele was also struck, and the end of the building knocked out. The barn of Owen Kinseley was struck, but no damage done.

Mitchell, April 19.—The barn owned by Mr. Frank Oliver, of Hibert, was struck by lightning last night and totally destroyed, together with all the farming implements and two horses. Loss—$1,000. No insurance.

Belleville, April 16.—A frame building occupied by three families, adjoining Wallace's grist-mill, was consumed; no insurance on building; furniture mostly saved.

St. Louis Suburbs, Quebec, April 13.—The stables and dwelling of M. Leady, carter and D. Fitzpatrick; Leady's insurance was $200; Fitzpatrick's, $100.

Quebec, April 13.—A house belonging to E. Michon, of Quebec, was destroyed by fire in Charlesbourg; insurance $250.

North Merrickville, Ont., April 10.—An occupied frame house, owned by Charles Holden, was totally destroyed; no particulars.

Dawn Mills, Ont., April 13.—Store of W. A. Ward; no insurance; the goods were mostly removed.

Wellington Square, April 15.—A fire took place near Wellington Square Station, on the farm of John Waldie, merchant, this afternoon, at half-past one. The barns and sheds adjoining were destroyed. There were four sheep and four lambs, a fanning mill and other farming utensils, besides some eight or ten bushels of corn and a small quantity of hay and straw consumed by the fire. There was some difficulty in saving the stable and driving shed. It is not known how the fire originated. His man states that there was no one in the barn since morning. Mr. Waldie being in Montreal, I cannot ascertain whether his loss is covered by insurance or not. Loss about $800.

Financial.

TORONTO STOCK MARKET.

(Reported by Pellatt & Osler, Brokers.)

The business of the week has been unimportant, and with the exception of Building Society stocks and County debentures, the supply has in nearly all cases exceeded the demand.

Bank Stock.—Limited sales of Montreal were made at 144½ and 144¾, there are buyers at the latter rate. Small sales of British American were made at 105½, at which rate there are buyers. Ontario sold at par, sellers generally ask 100½. There are buyers of Toronto at 120 and sellers at 121. Small sales of Royal Canadian were made during the week at 78, 78½ and 79, very little offering under 80. Several sales of Commerce took place at 102¼, at which rate it is still procurable. There are sellers of Gore at 39 and no buyers. Merchants sold at 107½ and 107¾, there are buyers and sellers at these rates. Sales of Quebec were made at 101½, buyers would now give 102. Molson's closed dull at 107½ to 108. Considerable sales of City were at 101¾; there are buyers now at 101½, and sellers at 102. Buyers offer 108½ for Du Peuple, none in Market. For Nationale 108 would be paid, none offering. There are buyers of Jacques Cartier at 109½, and sellers at 110. Buyers offer 105½ for Union, with sellers at 106.

Debentures.—Dominion stock is wanted; little doing in Canada bonds. Toronto would be readily taken at rates to pay 6¾ per cent interest; none in market for weeks past. Large sales of first class county have been made at high rates.

Sundries.—Small sales of City Gas were made at 107 to 107½; limited amounts are still procurable at the latter rate. Very little doing in Building Society stock; Canada Permanent is offered at 126 with buyers at 125½: Small lots Western Canada are obtainable at 121. Freehold is in demand at 112. Montreal Telegraph is wanted at 133½, sellers ask 134. For Canada Landed Credit 79 would be paid, none in market. Money is scarce and in active demand.

FINANCES OF NIAGARA.—The Auditors' Report of the town of Niagara has been published. During last year, the revenue from all sources, including a balance of $884:11 on hand from 1867, amounted to $7,038:11, and the expenditure to $5,993:70, leaving on hand on 1st January, 1869, $1,044:31. The expenditure for common school purposes amounted to $1,784,00¼. Only $1,797.08 was collected in 1868 as taxes. The liabilities of the town are stated to be $59,018.55, and the assets $95,079:40 as follows:—Taxes in arrear, $2,896:09; rents due, $639; stock in and due from plank road, $4,240; mortgage on Erie and Niagara Railroad, $45,000; interest due on said mortgage, $7,500; court house and other buildings and four acres of land, $25,000; brick school house, $4,000; fire engines, hooks and ladders, and hay sca $1,000; R. N. Hotel stock $8,000; cash on ha $1,044. total, $95,079:40.—*St Catherines Journ*

BANK OF ENGLAND.

Week ended, April 3.—The Bank return sents some important changes this week, the st of bullion having diminished to the extent £462,202, whilst the reserve has decreased as m as £1,137,302.

The following are the particulars as compa with the preceding week:—

Rest	£3,689,5
Decrease	5,8
Public Deposits	7,891,0
Increase	384,0
Other Deposits	17,479,2
Increase	445,8

On the other side of the account:—

Government Securities	£14,999,0.
Increase	1,000,0
Other Securities	20,130,8
Increase	1,006,3
Notes unemployed	7,862,2
Decrease	1,119,8

The amount of notes in circulation is £23,6 525, being an increase of £675,100,

Railway

GREAT WESTERN RAILWAY.—Traffic for ending April 2, 1869.

Passengers	$26,535 83
Freight	57,367 96
Mails and Sundries	1,877 75
Total Receipts for week	$85,801 54
Coresponding week, 1868	90,539 49
Decrease	$4,735 95

NORTHERN RAILWAY.—Traffic receipts for ending April 10th, 1869.

Passengers	$3,303 87
Freight and live stock	5,456 00
Mails and sundries	192 01
	$8,951 88
Corresponding Week of '68.	11,549 39
Increase	$2,597 51

THE SOUTHERN RAILWAY.—At a late rai meeting in Detroit, Mr. W. A. Thompson present, and set forth the present prospects, n sities and conditions of this line, which is t he thought, the great thoroughfare through ada in the route to and from the seab It was a line with no curvatures to speak of; grades were very light, and the material for ing and preparing the road bed of the best k the road could be cheaply built, and could be at a much less cost than the heavy gradient the Great Western Road, reducing the freight materially between the East and the West. asked that Detroit would show herself favo to this project, if only to the extent of expre the desire to see the road built, for he though would induce the Michigan Central Road to its favor and assistance to the project. It w road which the Central would certainly requ the proposed roads South and West of here built, to carry away the produce brought here. gave a history of the organization, and assure committee that the road would certainly be structed sooner or later.

HUDSON BAY COMPANY.—It is announced the £300,000 for the purchase of this terr from the Hudson Bay Company is to be r under Imperial guarantee. We presume it pretty well understood that the amount n would be accepted.

Canadian Monetary Times.

THURSDAY, APRIL 22, 1869.

BANK CHARTER QUESTION.

MENT PAPER AND GOVERNMENT CREDIT.

VIII.

issue of state notes, intended to circu-
currency, is generally the last despe-
ancial resource of a government. The
.ce of such paper is proof of embarrass-
of deranged finances, is redolent of
ncies: it is the worst form of a floating
hich it is impossible to wipe out, and
t, if not impracticable, to fund. In-
f representing the results of labour, it
gap of inordinate, and, almost always,
uctive consumption. The issuer, un-
ank, possesses no capital as a guaran-
the redemption of the paper; the
re not issued in exchange for commer-
ls, which, drawn by solvent persons,
hemselves be sufficient to redeem them
But, it will be said, the government
resource of taxation, and the whole
y of the country is pledged for the

payment of its debts. Such terms as these,
though in constant use, are really without
meaning. The issue of the notes was proof
that the resource of present taxation had been
exhausted; and as there is no way in which
the property of the nation can be made to
answer for the debts of the state, except
through taxation, it is evident that the payment of the notes must be postponed until
additional taxes, which it is now impossible
to levy, can be raised. As for selling the
whole property of the nation, or any portion
of it, to satisfy the demands of public creditors, the operation is manifestly impossible.
If all the property of the nation were offered
for sale, there could be no buyers; and if the
property of particular individuals were arbitrarily selected for sacrifice, a feeling of common danger would prevent any one from purchasing. We have the proof in an applied
test, in at least one municipal corporation of
Ontario.

If the state notes be issued to a bank, instead of being issued to the general public,
the obligation to redeem them is the same;
and if a reserve of specie, equal to one-fifth
of the amount, be held for their redemption,
it follows that no provision is made for the
remaining four-fifths. We say no provision,
because, as we have seen, there is no capital
in the transaction, and the maker of the notes
parted with them to fill the void of a contracted debt, and not in exchange for commercial paper representing valuable commodities, which, in due time, would suffice to
cancel the notes. The bank will not part
with them without an equivalent; but that
is its own affair, and will not enable the government to provide a guarantee for the redemption of the notes.

The conjunction of the credit of a bank
and a government has before now given rise
to the worst delusions of over-confidence. The
case of Laws' Bank may be cited in proof;
there the original shares went up to many hundred times the figure at which they were originally issued. But the recoil, when it comes,
corresponds in depression to the original out-
burst of enthusiasm, and the effects of the
catastrophe are universally felt. All legislative attempts to arrest the downward course
are always ineffectual for that purpose, and
often accelerate the descent. The consideration that a government cannot be sued like
an individual without its consent, or be made
amenable to laws which oblige individuals
and corporations to pay their debts, is, at this
stage, felt with its utmost force.

Sometimes the credit of the government
takes another shape, and is largely substituted for the capital of the bank. This com-
plexity is traceable in the National Bank
system of the United States, with a modified
but dangerous copy of which, there is reason

to believe, the country is now threatened.
The notes issued under such circumstances
must partake of the nature of their origin.
Credit, like a great many other things, is excellent when used in moderation and with
discretion; but it presents nothing but danger when pushed to excess. The substituting of government indebtedness for the capital of a bank is an inevitable cause of discredit. Whenever the credit of the paper
circulation depends upon the government, its
will follow the latter in all its varying fortunes. When, from any cause whatever, the
credit of the government sinks, the paper
will fall along with it, to the general derangement and confusion of all private and business transactions in the country. Such
paper is, of all possible kinds, most ill adapted for the purposes of currency.

ELASTICITY A REQUISITE OF CURRENCY.

IX.

In every country the amount of currency
fluctuates at different periods to accommodate itself to the volume of transactions in
which its instrumentality is requisite. In
England, the periodical payment of the interest on the public debt causes a temporary
expansion of the currency, which is, however,
short-lived. In Ireland, the currency reaches
its lowest point just before harvest, and attains its greatest volume in January. In
Scotland, the two great periods of expansion
are in May and November, when the interest
on mortgages and annuities is chiefly payable. It is in evidence before a committee
of the House of Commons, that these fluctuations are in the proportion of three to
seven : that the minimum circulation is three
and the maximum circulation seven millions
sterling. In other words, that it requires a
currency of seven millions to maintain a circulation which, for the whole year, averages only three millions. Coming to our
own country, we find that the circulation
reaches its lowest point in July or August—
just before the grain crops begin to come to
market—and that it attains its highest point
in October, when the bulk of the harvest is
passing from the producers to the consumers.
Between these two periods in 1865, the expansion was, in round numbers, six millions;
in 1866, four millions; in 1867, two millions;
and in 1868, three and a quarter millions.
These facts show the necessity of the currency being sufficiently elastic to meet the
varying demands of commerce. That element is not to be found in government notes,
and almost as little need it be looked for in
any system copied from the National Banks of
the United States. Government notes admit
of a fatal expansion, though of scarcely any
contraction through redemption. National
Bank notes, on the contrary, have a pre-

scribed maximum which cannot be over-stepped, no matter what are the necessities of commerce. It would be a mistake to suppose that ten millions of bank notes would imply a uniform circulation of that amount. At no time could the banks get on without a reserve, of greater or less amount, of notes in their vaults, so that to issue a given amount of notes would not ensure a circulation of that amount.

If experience has proved anything, it is that all special restrictions applied to the limits of a bank currency are false in principle and fatal in practice. Whenever, any undue pressure comes in England, the restrictions imposed by Sir Robert Peel's Act have to be arbitrarily and illegally removed. It would be unspeakable folly to adopt in this country a principle that has worked so badly elsewhere.

TORONTO AND NIPISSING RAILWAY.

The indefatigable and zealous promoters of this railway have launched their scheme fairly before the public, with an array of facts and figures which must carry conviction to the most cautious and the most calculating minds. While the citizens of Toronto, and the farming population, whose interests this railway will especially serve, have a direct and personal concern in its success, the people of the Province of Ontario, as beneficiaries, more or less affected, cannot remain indifferent to its prospects. Though the country through which the first section of the road will pass is wealthy, extensive and populous, but hitherto destitute of railway facilities, the region beyond, which awaits tapping, is one boundless in undeveloped resources, and at present, "the forest primeval" there holds sway. We have railways which carry immigrants through the country; we want a few more that will carry immigrants into it. Railways are the best colonizers, and certainly have not been found bad emigration agents. Hence it is that we await the completion of this Nipissing railway with a real interest. It will bring to Toronto the trade of a large region of country, but it will also open up to colonization lands hitherto valueless and useless.

As regards the first eighty-five miles of road, with the Lindsay branch of eighteen miles, the capital is placed at $1,275,000. Bonuses to the amount of $399,000 have been already voted by various Municipalities, and $155,000 is expected. Stock to the amount of $400,000 in $100 Shares is now on the market, and it is for investors to judge from the statistics furnished in the Company's prospectus, whether or not the inducements to subscribe are sufficiently tempting. So far as our opinion goes, we think they are, and

we shall be surprised if local capital, to the required amount, cannot be easily procured. The local traffic of the Northern Railway for three years shows an average earned dividend on $15,000 per mile, of 12 5-6 per cent. The estimate of gross receipts of traffic in timber, lumber, cereals, passengers, &c. likely to be carried on the Toronto and Nipissing railway is $446,000 per annum, for the first eight or ten years, and allowing 60 per cent. for running expenses, the net earnings would be $179,400, or 14 per cent. on a cost of $15,-000 per mile. As the actual cost of the road to the Company will be $10,000 per mile (the bonuses covering $5,000 per mile) the dividend from such net earnings would be 21 per cent. After making a liberal allowance for contingencies the margin afforded is still large.

As a line of railway, such as the proposed Toronto and Nipissing will be, cannot fail to promote the growth of the section through which it will pass, as well as benefit the province by the opening up of new territory, now part of the public domain, the Government will see the justice of coming to the Company's assistance and ensuring the completion of the whole project. The steady increase in the receipts of the Northern shows how a railway which serves a new territory can build up a business for itself. The road has been chiefly dependent on freight for its revenue, and the expansion of that revenue from $240,044 in 1859 to $591,370 in 1867, shows how rapidly traffic extends. The traffic of the Toronto and Nipissing will be of the same elastic character; and as the country is opened up and peopled, the effect will be felt in a large increase in receipts.

PROPOSED LEGISLATION.

The Government have announced that they propose to introduce during the present session of the Dominion Parliament, measures respecting bankruptcy and insolvency, and patents and discoveries. In the Governor's speech it is stated, "The charters of several banks are drawing to a close, and the important subjects of banking and currency will be brought under your notice. In considering these questions, which so deeply affect not only the important interests of commerce but the daily transactions of life, I feel assured that you will endeavour to adopt the greatest measure of safety to the public, without curtailing the facilities requisite for the encouragement and extension of trade." The general impression is that the Government proposes to substitute for our present system of banking, a modified form of the United States National Bank System.

—The receipts at the P. E. Island Treasury, for the past year, are stated to have been £83,391; the expenditure £92,400, shewing an excess of expenditure over revenue of £9,006.

may be impolicy, but there is no injustice in
g duty on sea going vessels for the purpose
ilding and maintaining light-houses and
as. Nor can foreigners allege that they are
ited in this respect, for they are on a footing
fect equality with English subjects. They
t reasonably expect more than this. In like
ir, American tobacco and whiskey are taxed
same rate as tobacco imported from Brazil
illa, and as spirits imported from France.
ards whiskey, the home producer is subject
competition of the foreign importer. As re-
tobacco. the foreigner has the advantage of
iopoly, inasmuch as the law forbids the
i of tobacco in the United Kingdom. If
ie has a reason for complaining about free-
f trade being violated, in this case it is the
i agriculturist and not the American planter.
oteworthy that the upholders of protection
rays shocked at what they conceive to be a
ird, of free-trade doctrines on the part of
h statesmen. They forget that these doc-
would be none the less admirable if repu-
ly all the writers and by rulers in this
y. So far from being the model country of
iders, England is still a land of anomalies,
political economists view with dislike.
i affirming that as a commercial policy free-
s the only true one, and in acting on this
i with undeniable pertinacity; at no little
s, England may claim to lead the van of a
ient destined some day to make the circuit
globe.

meeting of the Hudson's Bay shareholders,
was appointed for the 7th, is postponed till
i inst. At present the feeling among them
ise to the acceptance of Earl Granville's
al. On reflection, they consider the amount
paid by Canada wholly disproportionate to
n which they may have to pay hereafter in
o the Canadian government. Should they
ie in this temper, the question will be subto the Judicial Committee of the Privy
l. This will be anything but a gain to
i, even should the decision be in her favor.
e award be made nothing can be done, and
ompany will continue to hold its own.
hile, the question of settling the North
n boundary would not be simplified. A
if a year or two is to be deprecated for
i of sound policy. It is to be hoped then
ie shareholders will, take the advice ten-
by the directors, and close at once with
iranville's offer. Seventeen hundred dis-
ted shareholders are not, however, easily
ith and induced to follow the course chalked
them by their well wishers.

newspapers are still filled with complaints
he way in which many Life Assurance Cos.
t their affairs. Now that Parliament has
mbled, a discussion on the subject may be
for at no distant date. One company has
y issued a lot of rules designed to afford
ximum of security and convenience to the
holders. It is a Manchester company, and
d the British Imperial Insurance Corpora-
Its rules provide for the whole of the net
ms being invested in consols in the names
:rustees whom the policy holders may elect.
; a periodical audit on Dr. Farr's system.
time the policy holders may draw in whole
part to the extent of 70 per cent. of the
ms paid.

LISH BANKRUPTS.—There were 9,195 cases
kruptcy in England and Wales last year.
total number, 817 adjudications were on
ition of the creditors, 6,679 on the petition
btor, 1,152 by registrars at the prisons, 532
tions in-forma pauperis, and 15 on judg-
lebtor summonses. The gross produce
l from bankrupt estates was £832,639 11s.
.h creditors' assignees realized £542,309 3s.
al the official assignees, £309,730 2s. 1d.

STATEMENT OF BANKS

ACTING UNDER CHARTER, FOR THE MONTH ENDING 31st MARCH, 1869, ACCORDING TO RETURNS FURNISHED BY THE BANKS TO THE AUDITOR OF PUBLIC ACCOUNTS.

NAME OF BANK	CAPITAL		LIABILITIES						ASSETS							
	Capital authorized by Act	Capital paid up	Promissory Notes in circulation not bearing Interest	Balances due to other Banks	Cash Deposits bearing Interest	Cash Deposits not bearing Interest	Cash Deposits bearing Interest	TOTAL LIABILITIES	Coin, Bullion, and Provincial Notes	Landed or other Property of the Bank	Government Securities	Promissory Notes, or Bills of other Banks	Balances due from other Banks	Notes and Bills Discounted	Other Debts due the Bank not included under foregoing heads	TOTAL ASSETS
ONTARIO AND QUEBEC																
Montreal																
Quebec																
City																
Gore																
Banque Nord Amérique																
Banque du Peuple																
Niagara District																
Molson's																
Toronto																
Ontario																
Eastern Townships																
Banque Nationale																
Banque Jacques Cartier																
Merchants																
Royal Canadian																
Union Bk Low. Canada																
Mechanics																
Bank of Commerce																
NOVA SCOTIA																
Bank of Yarmouth																
Merchants' Bank																
People's Bank																
Union Bank																
Bank of Nova Scotia																
NEW BRUNSWICK																
Bank of New Brunswick																
Commercial Bank																
St. Stephen's Bank																
People's Bank																
Totals																

Commercial.

Toronto Market.

There were a good number of buyers in town during the past week, but business drags owing to a generally cautious feeling among both buyers and sellers of imported goods. The warm showers have removed the frost from the ground, so that ploughing and seeding have commenced. The winter wheat looks uncommonly beautiful—a circumstance which will have a favorable effect on general business.

GRAIN.—*Wheat*—Receipts 3,540 bush., and 4,280 bush. last week. Spring is dull dull and nominal at 95c. to 96c. f.o.b.; there are no buyers. Sales, a cargo lot of 10,000 bush. at 95c., f.o.b. at Whitby, and 400 bushels here, May delivery, at 95c. f.o.b. bagged. Fall is exceedingly dull, there is no enquiry whatever; holders ask $1.00 to $1.05; no sales. *Barley*—Receipts 500 bush., and 350 bush. last week; the stock is very small, and there is no demand; what little comes in by waggons sells at $1.10 for seed. A lot of 3,000 bush. sold at $1.10 f.o.b. bagged. Grand Trunk barely is unsaleable. *Peas*—Receipts very light; market quiet; holders ask 75c. to 78c. for good samples, with buyers at 70c. to 75c. *Oats*—Receipts 1,800 bush., and 3,600 bush. last week. Car loads are selling at our quotations on the railway track. *Rye*—Selling on the street market at 60c. *Corn*—Quiet at quotations; two cars No. 1 sold at 65c., and one car at 63½c, at Brampton; one car 64c. *Seeds*—Timothy is a little better; prices range from $2.40 to 2.70. Clover, though the stock is not heavy, the near approach of the close of the season makes buyers disposed to realize; prices are therefore a little down at $5.75 to $5.90. Flax $1.65 to $2.00.

FLOUR.—Receipts 3,350 bbls., 4,280 bbls., last week. The tendency of the market has been toward lower prices; while at the close holders of No. 1 superfine asked $4.10, and buyers would give about $4.05 for good brands. Sales 700 bbls. at $4.05 f.o.b., and 600 bbls. at $4.10 at Weston. A lot of 900 bbls. choice sold for May delivery at $4.15 for shipment east, the advance on current market rates being more than compensated by the reduced rates of freight at which the steamers are now contracting for the lower ports. On Tuesday a lot of inspected Spring Extra offered on Change at $4.10 without finding a buyer. Fancy is steady, 200 bbls. sold at $4.20 on cars at Georgetown, and 100 bbls. at $4.25 here, which is an outside figure. Extra is held at $4.50 without sales; there is no demand except at a considerable reduction on that figure. No Superior in market. *Oatmeal*—Ordinary brands are worth $5.40 to 5.50, and choice $5.50 to $5.65 for retailing purposes. *Cornmeal*—Unchanged.

PROVISIONS.—*Butter*—The market is unsettled; fine dairy sells at 22c. to 23c. in a retail way; ordinary unsaleable. *Eggs*—are worth 12½ to 13½ in quantity. *Mess Pork*—dull at $25.75 to $26.00 in small lots. *Bacon*—There is a fair jobbing demand at 12c. to 12½c. for Cumberland, and 11c. to 11½c. for ordinary. *Hams*—are held firmly, but there is not much demand. *Lard*—dull, and selling in retail lots at 16½c. to 17c. *Cheese*—scarce, fine qualities are fully 1c. higher; a lot of 60 cheeses sold at 14¾c.

PETROLEUM.—There is only a very moderate business doing at unchanged prices.

HIDES AND SKINS.—The market is weak and prices are lower as quoted.

FREIGHTS.—Though the season is open there is very little doing with vessels. They are offering to Toledo at 5c., and to Oswego at 3c., U. S. Currency, on grain. Frright steamers are contracting for flour to Halifax at 75c. The Grand Trunk have issued their summer tariff: Flour, Toronto to Kingston 25c., grain 13c., to Prescott 30c., grain 15c., to Montreal 35c., grain 18c., d tto St. John 85c., to Halifax to 90c. Freights by the Great Western Railway, to all points, unchanged.

Halifax Market.

BREADSTUFFS.—April 13.—Our markets for Supers for the past week evince no change. The demand for No. 2's still increases. White Wheats continue dull, sales of small parcels only being effected at low prices for better description of city trade. There is some enquiry for Oatmeal, but demand continues limited, and stocks are still large. Cornmeal inactive at former quotations. Rye dull and unchanged. White Beans in limited request at quotations.

White Wheat Extra (Fall) $6.25 to $6.50. Fancy $5.90 ao $6.00. Supers $5.60 to $5.65. No. 2, $4.75 to $5.00. Middlings $4.50 to $4.75. Cornmeal K.D. $4.10 to $4.15. F. G. $3.80 to $4. Oatmeal $7 to $7.25. White Beans $2.50 to $3.

WEST INDIA PRODUCE.—Molasses is very dull, and price, somewhat easier. Sugars continue in light receipt and firm. Rum dull and unchanged. Coffee offered freely without buyers, low prices would be accepted for round lots. We quote:—Sugar, V. P. 10½c. to 11c. Porto Rico 9½c. to 9¾c. Barbadoes 9c. to 9½c. (nominal). Molasses—Cienfuegos 41c. to 42c. Trinidad 40c. to 41c. Rum 58c. to 60c. for Demerara.

OIL.—(Pale Seal) 75c.; Straw 65c.; Brown 45c.; Cod 55c.; Dog 45c. Kerosene—Am. 48c. to 50c. Canada 36c. to 38c.

THE TORONTO, GREY AND BRUCE RAILWAY COMPANY.

TOTAL LENGTH, ABOUT 200 MILES. INCLUDING BRANCHES TO KINCARDINE AND OWEN SOUND.

Length of First Section, from Toronto to the Garafraxa Road, about 70 Miles.

TOTAL CAPITAL, $3,000,000.

CAPITAL REQUIRED FOR THE FIRST SECTION, $1,050,000.

Bonuses already Voted by Municipalities for the First Section of the Main Line, $425,000.

As follows:—City of Toronto, $250,000; Albion, $40,000; Caledon, $45,000; Mono, $45,000; Orangeville, $15,000; Amaranth, $30,000.

Bonuses yet to be obtained for the first section, $77,000.

Bonuses required and obtainable to extend First Section, from Arthur to Mount Forest, $138,000.

First issue of Stock in $100 shares, $325,000.

Upon which bonds will be issued for $300,000.

The arrangements for the extension to Mount Forest, now in progress, when completed, will involve the further issue of Stock and Bonds to the extent of $125,000.

PRESIDENT—John Gordon, Esq.
VICE-PRESIDENT—A. R. McMaster, Esq.

DIRECTORS:

Hon. M. C. Cameron, Provincial Secretary; Hon. John McMurrich, M.P.P.; S.B. Harman, Esq., Mayor of Toronto; Noah Barnhart, Esq.; H. S. Howland, Esq., Vice-Pres. Bank of Commerce; James Michie, Esq. (Fulton, Michie & Co); John Crawford, Esq., M. P.; William Elliot, Esq. (of Messrs. Lyman, Elliot & Co.): Thos. Swinarton, Esq., M.P.P.; R. A. Harrison, Esq., Barrister, M.P.; J. E. Smith, Esq., Collector of Customs, Toronto; D Sinclair, Esq. M.P.P., North Bruce; John Turner, Esq. (of Messrs. Sessions, Turner & Co.) George Laidlaw, Esq; Thos. Scott, Esq., M.P.P.; Robert Paterson, Esq.; Thos. Lailey, Esq.; T. C. Chisholm, Esq.; Frank Smith, Esq.; C. J. Campbell, Esq.; Adam Crooks, Esq., Q.C.; John Worthington, Esq.

TRUSTEES OF BONUSES—Hon. John McMurrich, Company's Trustee; A. W. Lauder, M.P.P., Government Trustee; Lewis Moffat, Esq., Municipalities' Trustee.

COUNSEL—Hon. John Hillyard Cameron.
SOLICITOR—W. H. Beatty, Esq.
CONSULTING ENGINEERS—Sir Charles Fox & Sons.
BANKERS—Bank of Toronto, Bank of Commerce.
BROKERS—Campbell & Cassels, Blaikie & Alexander.
SECRETARY—W. Sutherland Taylor.

TEMPORARY OFFICES,—46 FRONT STREET, TORONTO.

PROSPECTUS.

The Provisional Directors of the Toronto, Grey and Bruce Railway Company, finding that further progress in the building of Broad Gauge Railways in Canada, with English Capital, was no longer financially practicable or expedient for lines of Railway projected for local traffic, and having become cognizant of the successful working for a number of years of Railways built on the three feet six gauge in the Kingdoms of Norway and Sweden, in the Colonies of Queensland, in India, and elsewhere, and that these Railways were capable of accommodating a traffic of about a million, or a million and a half of tons of g[oods] per annum, and of carrying passengers at a speed [of] twenty-five to thirty miles an hour, and that the t[otal] traffic of the Northern Railway of Canada has not exce[ed]ed 195,000 tons, and 140,000 passengers per annum, h[ave] therefore resolved to construct the Toronto, Grey [and] Bruce Railway on the three feet six inch gauge, in [the] most economical and efficient manner, at a total cost [of] $15,000 per mile.

The Directors have also noted Capt Taylor's (now V[ice] President Grand Trunk Railway) report on the Festi[niog] Railway, two feet gauge, in Merionethshire, Wales, [the] freight and passenger traffic of which approximates clo[se] to that of the Northern Railway of Canada, and, with [the] exception of the lumber traffic, largely exceeds that carr[ied] on the Lindsay and Port Hope, or on the London [and] Port Stanley Railways.

With a view to the just apportionment of the risks [in]cidental to capital invested in railway enterprise in [Ca]nada, it was also resolved to ask the municipalities m[ost] to be benefitted by the construction of the Railways, [to give] one-third of the total cost by way of bonus or gift. T[his] proportion of the cost has already been voted for the f[irst] section (excepting small sums yet obtainable), in deb[en]tures bearing six per cent interest, payable in 20 year[s]; securities which are unexceptionable, and will sell a[t or] near par.

Of the remaining capital, it is proposed now to o[ffer] $325,000 to be subscribed in stock. If that or a lar[ger] amount is not so subscribed, bonds will be issued for [the] balance of about $300,000.

Local capital to the extent of *more than* two-thirds of [the] cost of the railway will be security to holders of the bo[nds] of this Company.

The interest and dividend bearing capital will not [ex]ceed $9,000 per mile.

The Directors, although anxious, and having autho[rity] under their charter to make the village of Mount Fo[rest] the terminus of the first section, are unwillingly constr[ain]ed to select an eligible point, nearer, on the Garafr[axa] Road, in the Township of Arthur.

This decision may be altered, and Mount Forest m[ade] the terminus of the first section, by the Municipali[ties] concerned voting the amounts of bonuses, as required [by] the Company.

In either case the capital derivable from bonusses w[ill] be about the same per mile.

Arrangements to complete the remaining sections of [the] Railway through the counties of Bruce and Grey, will [be] prosecuted with unremitting vigour, as soon as the f[irst] section is fairly under construction.

The Garafraxa Road, the great highway from Ow[en] Sound, through the counties of Grey and Wellington [to] Guelph; and the other great highway, the Elora and S[au]geen Road, from Southampton, through the counties [of] Bruce and Wellington, ultimately uniting with the Ga[ra]fraxa Road, *passes within from 5 to 8 miles of the propo[sed] terminus of the first section* of the Railway, to connect w[ith] which a gravel road will be built; while the Toronto [and] Sydenham gravelled road, from Chatsworth, intersect[ing] the Durham and Collingwood road, reaches to within tw[elve] or fifteen miles of the Orangeville station, and when co[m]pleted, together with the others, assures to the Toron[to,] Grey and Bruce Railway the traffic of the whole heart [of] the North-western peninsula.

The bulk of the products of the great counties of Br[uce] and West Grey is shipped by water, on account of [the] distance from the Grand Trunk Railway, only a part be[ing] moved in the autumn, the principal portion being m[ar]keted and stored, during winter, at the ports on the sho[res] of Lake Huron and the Georgian Bay. At four of th[ese] points there are now stored a quarter of a million bush[els,] while the aggregate at all the points amounts to ab[out] 500,000 bushels.

The loss of interest on the capital thus invested, to[ge]ther with the proportionately lower prices paid for prod[uce] during winter in these remote districts, are serious dra[w]backs to their prosperity.

The distance deprives producers of the facilities affor[ded] by the *Grand Trunk Railway, and the Montreal Steams[hip] line* for moving, in winter, produce to markets, as well [as] of the very great advantage of Railway communication [with] the flourishing city of Toronto, (the best distributing p[oint] either in winter or summer,) and now the capital [of] Ontario.

The total area between the Grand Trunk and the North[ern] Railway of Canada is 6,800 *square miles*, of the *richest a[nd]* most fertile land in Canada. The Toronto, Grey and Br[uce] Railway will intersect this district, about mid-way betw[een] the two other Railways, and when completed will con[fer] immense benefits on the people in that district, while i[t is] quite evident that the general business *which will [be] brought to the city of Toronto* (exclusive of through traf[fic]) will equal that brought to it by all the other Railways.

The Toronto, Grey and Bruce Railway will obtain a mu[ch] larger passenger, grain, cattle, and first-class goods tra[ffic] than the Northern Railway; while the sawn pine, wh[ich] *must be imported* to supply the absence of that build[ing] material, and the export of square hardwood timber, su[ch as] oak, elm, cherry, &c., staves, bark, fencing, and cordwo[od] (fuel), will afford a very large and remunerative busin[ess] to the Toronto, Grey and Bruce Railway.

The Freestone and other stone used for building mate[rial] in Toronto are now imported from Cleveland or Kingst[on.] On the route of the T. G. & B. R. there are, near Oran[ge]ville, extensive quarries of the very best soft and h[ard] brown and white freestone, which will be in great requ[est] for export and general city building purposes. The [ad]vantages to the Railway and this city, of these quarries [are] not yet generally appreciated.

The subjoined tables of the traffic of the Northern R[ailway] serve to illustrate the local business of a railway long, through an average country in Canada.

IN 1861.

al Traffic of the Northern ay of Canada amounted to	120,090 tons.	
rs	25,000 "	
celpls	100,618 "	
	$808,507	$410,939
..celpls	48,482	68 per cent.
expenses.....................		
of earnings over running ...		
ses on local traffic........	$115,982	
Through Traffic.............	15,468	
rnings equal to 5½ per cent. on a of $815,000 per mile. Or 12½ on $10,- ar mile.		

1864.

affic...........................	182,000 tons.	
Traffic........................	8,844 "	
rs	104,545 "	
ceipts	$453,332	
	14,884	$467,963
expenses.....................		52 per cent.
f earnings over running ses on local Traffic.......	217,148	
hrough Traffic..............	7,144	
rnings equal to 12 2-3 per cent. on . of $15,000 a mile. Or 23 1-10 per on $10,000 per mile.		

1868.

d Through Traffic.........	194,586 tons.	
rs	138,065 "	
ceipts	$537,380	
	12,690	Total $550,070
expenses.....................		61 per cent.
f earnings over running ses on local Traffic......	$209,578	
Through Traffic	4,949	
to 14½ per cent. on $15,000 a mile earnings). Or 22½ per cent. on 10 per mile.		

Running expenses per cent. 68; local tonnage, 120,- ough tonnage, 26,000; total tons, 145,000; passen- ,618; local receipts, gross, $362,507; through re- ross, $48,432; total receipts, gross, $410,939; local nett, $115,982; through receipts, nett, $15,408; dividend on $15,000 a mile, local, 8 1-3; dividend on $15,- le, through, 1 1-10.

Running expenses per cent. 52; local tonnage, through tonnage, 8,346; total tons, 189,046; pas- 104,545; local receipts, gross, $453,332; through gross, $14,884; total receipts, gross, $467,266; cipts, nett, $217,148; through receipts, nett, $7,- idend on $15,000 a mile, local, 12 2-5; dividend on a mile, through ½.

Running expenses per cent. 61; total tons, 194,- sengers 138,065; local receipts, gross, $537,380; receipts, gross, $12,690; total receipts, gross, local receipts, nett, $209,578; through receipts, 949; dividend on $15,000 a mile, local, 14½; divi- $15,000 a mile, through ½.

ons, $26,629; passengers, 349,929; local receipts, ,362,500; through receipts, gross, $75,006; total gross, $1,428,975; local receipts, nett, $542,703; receipts, nett, $27,591; dividend on $15,000 a mile, 5-6; dividend on $15,000 a mile, through, 8. —Total tons, 176,209; passengers, 116,643; local gross, $450,756; through receipts, gross, $25,335; cipts, gross, $476,091; local receipts, nett, 180,901; receipts, nett $9,197; dividend on $15,000 a mile, 5-6, dividend on $15,000 a mile, through 8. the above data it will be seen that the Northern carried an average for those three years of 176,209 reight; and 116,643 passengers; the average gross being $450,756, while the nett receipts from local are $180,901, equal to an annual dividend of 12 5-6 . on a cost of $15,000 per mile.

nmarkable and of consequence to intending sub- for stock of the T. G. & B. R., that the net re- r through traffic for the same years only averaged er annum, equal to a dividend of ⅓ of one per cent t of $15,000 per mile. This fact clearly proves the local as against through traffic.

ain, cattle, pork, goods and passenger traffic tri- o the first section of the Toronto, Grey and Bruce will equal, if not exceed, for the same length of local traffic of any other railway in Canada. llowing estimate of traffic from the first section oronto, Grey and Bruce Railway, is based upon ons on the returns made by the Municipalities, intimate acquaintance with their trade and re-

ngers, 140,000................	$145,000	
a, 2,000,000 bushels.........	100,000	
50,000 barrels................	15,000	
al goods, 50,000 tons........	150,000	
: timber, 1,000,000 cubic feet	30,000	
, lumber, bark, posts, &c.....	10,000	
'ood, 20,000 cords............	25,000	
and express...................	20,000	
Total........................	$490,000	

ing 60 per cent for running expenses, the nett earn- ild amount to $196,000—equal to a dividend of 13 on a cost of $15,000 per mile. ing reasonable margin for increased cost or less he moderate estimate of which will be undisputed,) nain the strongest reasons for anticipating a divi- 13 per cent per annum.

By the Act of Incorporation, the Company is specially bound to carry cordwood, and to afford every necessary facility for so doing at the specified rate of 3 cents per cord per mile for dry wood, for all distances under 50 miles, and 2½ cents per cord per mile for all distances over 50 miles—a rate which has been found satisfactory, by test of actual experience, on the Government Railways of New Brunswick.

This condition will enhance the cost of fuel to the Com- pany, but the increased traffic and prosperity consequent upon this trade, it is fully believed, will more than com- pensate for the extra cost of fuel.

The gentlemen who have promoted and borne the pre- liminary expenses of this enterprise, and who desire to see it carried out in good faith on sound commercial principles, are resolved, in so far as their influence is equal to the task, to have this railway controlled by the most respect- able capitalists of this city and the country on the route of the railway, who may take stock in it; to convert their own securities, and pay cash to contractors, and not to surrender control of the railway to contractors or bond- holders; to let the contracts in a manner to ensure the healthiest competition. In other words, to have value for the money from the turning of the first sod to the laying of the last rail.

The country on the route of the first section, with the exception of a short distance in Caledon, is one of the easiest for railway construction in Canada, especially the 22 or 25 miles from Orangeville to the Garafraxa Road.

In the Township of Caledon—the country is hilly and rolling. This portion of the route was carefully and com- pletely surveyed and cross-sectioned under the auspices and by the direction of Mr. J. E. Boyd, M.I.C.E., and Engineer for the Government of New Brunswick, before the Company obtained their charter, and, as anticipated, no real difficulties were encountered; the highest grade, with moderate cuttings, being 65 feet to the mile. Mr. Charles Douglas Fox examined, for the Company, the figures and plans of the profile, and, together with Mr. Boyd, gave their written opinion that the cost of this portion, per mile, for earth-works, would not exceed $15,000. There are no rock cuttings.

Ballast, ties, timber for bridges, and lumber for fences,

---

are convenient and available at the lowest cost in Canada, along the whole route of the first section.

Every other consideration, in the first instance, will be subordinated to the construction of a first-class permanent way; the best of timber bridges; deep and good ballasting. Rails to weigh 40 lbs. to the yard, and to be selected of the best quality.

Arrangements are in progress which will secure to the Company free right of way through the city, and egress, if desired, for a few miles out of the city, on the line of the Grand Trunk, by means of a third rail; and the disposi- tion of the proprietors, and other circumstances along the line are so favorable, that the whole right of way will be obtained for an amount not exceeding $25,000.

Station grounds and dockage will be had in this city, either free, or for a nominal rental.

It is the desire of the Provisional Directors to have their Chief Engineer appointed, with the concurrence and sub- ject to the approval of the Company's Consulting Engineers, Sir Charles Fox & Sons, who will be held responsible for the excellence of the works, economy of construction, and the success here of the system of narrow guage railways, of which they have had large experience elsewhere, and with the initiation of which in this country they are honor- ably identified.

On these premises the Provisional Directors appeal for stock subscriptions to the citizens of Toronto, to the mu- nicipalities, and to the business men and proprietors of land along the route of the railway, and to capitalists else- where, believing that the most cautious and prudent in- vestors will find the stock of the Toronto, Grey and Bruce Railway worthy of their attention.

The stock books will be opened at the Company's offices, Front street, on the 21st April, at 10 o'clock, a.m. Forms of application for shares can be had on application to the secretary, and from the reeves and clerks of the several municipalities on the route of the railway, and from Messrs. Campbell & Cassels, and from Messrs. Blaikie & Alexander, Toronto, and from McDougall & Davidson, Montreal.

In conjunction with the Toronto and Nipissing Railway Company, it is agreed that a member of the firm of Sir Charles Fox & Sons, Consulting Engineers, will be invited here immediately by telegraph, when active operations will be commenced.

Royal Fire & Life Insurance Company
OF LIVERPOOL AND LONDON.

CAPITAL, TWO MILLION STERLING,
WITH LARGE RESERVE FUNDS.

ANNUAL INCOME, - - - - - - - - £800,000 STG.

FIRE BRANCH.

Very moderate rates of Premium. Prompt and liberal settlement of losses. Loss and damage by explosion of gas made good. No charge for policies or transfers.

LIFE BRANCH.

The following are amongst the important advantages offered by this Company: Perfect security to assurers. Moderate rates of premium. Large participation of profits—the benuses being amongst the largest hitherto declared by any office, and divided every five years. EXEMPTION OF ASSURED FROM LIABILITY OF PARTNERSHIP. Claims settled promptly on proof of death. Liberal allowance for surrendered policies. Forfeiture of policy cannot take place from unintentional misstatement. No charge for policies or assignments. Medi- cal fees paid by the Company. Tables and forms of application, with all other information, can be obtained on appli- cation to

FRANCIS H. HEWARD,
MANAGER TORONTO BRANCH.

GEORGE OLIVER, Inspector.

W. B. NICOL, M.D., Medical Examiner.

TORONTO, April 19, 1869.   36-44

EDINBURGH LIFE ASSURANCE COMPANY.
FOUNDED 1823.

AMOUNT OF ACCUMULATED AND INVESTED FUNDS—OVER ONE MILLION STERLING.
HEAD OFFICE—EDINBURGH.

PRESIDENT—The Rt. Hon. the Earl of Haddington. MANAGER—D. Maclagan, Esq. SECRETARY—Alex. H. Whytt, Esq.
CANADIAN OFFICE ESTABLISHED 1857.   WELLINGTON STREET, TORONTO.
CANADIAN BOARD—Hon. John Hillyard Cameron, M.P., Chairman. J. W. Gamble, Esq., L. Moffatt, Esq., Hon.
J. B. Robinson, C. J. Campbell, Esq. David Higgins, Secretary.

THE Edinburgh Life Assurance Company offer to the public the advantages of a Canadian as well as a British Com- pany. They have invested a large amount of money on securities in this country, and the Toronto Local Board have full power, by an Imperial Statute, to take risks, make investments, and settle claims in Canada, without refe- rence to the Head Office, Edinburgh. Some of the old Policies in the Company, which became claims during the past year, were settled by payment of amounts double of those originally insured, in consequence of the large bonuses that accrued on the Policies.

Every information that intending assurers may require can be obtained at the Company's Office in Toronto, or at any of the Agencies which have been established in the principal towns in Canada.

J. HILLYARD CAMERON, CHAIRMAN.   (36-1y)   DAVID HIGGINS, SECRETARY.

IN THE MATTER OF THE COMPANIES' ACTS, 1862 AND 1867,

AND OF

The International Life Assurance Society.

THE creditors of the above named Society are required, on or before the 31st day of May, 1869, to send their names and addresses, and the particulars of their debts or claims, and the names and addresses of their Solicitors, if any, to Frederick Maynard and Edmund Shepyard Symes, the Official Liquidators of the said Society, at the office of the said Official Liquidators, situate at No. 205 Gresham House, Old Broad Street, in the City of London.

Dated the 11th day of March, 1869.

JOHN TUCKER,
28 St. Swithin's Lane, London,
Solicitor for the said Official Liquidators.

April 12, 1869.   33-1t.

NOTICE

IS hereby given that the Liquidators of the Western Insurance Company, Limited, will apply to the Minister of Finance for his warrant authorizing the withdrawal of the deposit made by said Company with the Minister of Finance, as required by statute of the late Province of Canada, chapter 83 of 22nd Victoria, the said Company having ceased to do business in Canada.

CARTER & HATTON,
35   Attorneys for Liquidators.

THE TORONTO AND NIPISSING
RAILWAY COMPANY.

Total Length to Lake Nipissing, about 220 Miles.

FIRST SECTION FROM TORONTO TO COBOCONK,
85 MILES ;

With a Branch of 18 miles from the Main Line to the Town of Lindsay.

Total Capital, $3,000,000.

Capital for the First Section (Main Line) $1,275,000.

BONUSES already Voted by Municipalities for the First Section of the Main Line, $395,000.

AS FOLLOWS:—

City of Toronto, $150,000; Scarboro', $10,000; Markham, $70,000; Uxbridge, $50,000; Scott, $10,000; Brock, $50,000; Eldon, $44,000; Bexley, $15,000; Laxton, Digby and Longford, $25,000; Somerville, $15,000.

BONUSES yet to be obtained, including those for the Lindsay Branch, $155,000.

First issue of stock in $100 shares, $400,000.

Upon which will be Issued Bonds for $470,000.

Upon $120,000 of which a Guarantee from the Government of Ontario will be applied for, as equitable assistance for the construction of the Railway through and into Crown Lands on the route of the First Section.

PRESIDENT—John Crawford, Esq., M.P.

VICE-PRESIDENT—J. E. Smith, Esq., Collector of Customs.

DIRECTORS :

Hon. M. C. Cameron, Provincial Secretary ; Hon. David Reesor, Senator ; W. F. McMaster, Esq., Captain Taylor, Wm. Gooderham, Jun., Esq., H. S. Howland, Esq., Vice-Pres. Bank of Commerce ; G. Laidlaw, Esq., H. P. Crosby, Esq., M.P.P., Joseph Gould, Esq., Thomas Wilson, Esq., John Gordon, Esq., A. M. Smith, Esq., T. C. Chisholm, Esq., D. McRae, Esq., Reeve Eldon ; Edward Wheeler, Esq., Ex.-Reeve Whitchurch ; John Leys, Esq., Solicitor; R. W. Elliot, Esq., Ald.-F. H. Medcalf, A. P. Cockburn, Esq., M.P.P., J. C. Fitch, Esq., Jas. E. Ellis, Esq., Ald. Dickey, John Shedden, Esq., J. D. Merrick, Esq., Dr. Wright.

TRUSTEES OF BONUSES GRANTED BY MUNICIPALITIES.—Hon. Geo. W. Allan, Senator—Government Trustee ; Hon. M. C. Cameron, Provincial Secretary—Company's Trustee; Henry Brethour, Esq., Deputy Reeve of Brock—Municipalities' Trustee.

COUNSEL—Hon. M. C. Cameron, Provincial Secretary.
SOLICITOR—John Leys, Esq.
CONSULTING ENGINEERS—Sir Charles Fox & Sons.
BANKERS—Bank of Toronto.
BROKERS—Blaikie & Alexander, Pellatt & Osler.
SECRETARY—Charles Robertson, Esq.

OFFICES—40 FRONT STREET, TORONTO.

PROSPECTUS.

The Provisional Directors of the Toronto and Nipissing Railway Company, finding that the further progress in the building of Broad Gauge Railways in Canada, with English capital, was no longer financially practicable or expedient for lines of Railway projected for local traffic, and having become cognizant of the successful working for a number of years of Railways built on the three feet six gauge, in

the Kingdoms of Norway and Sweden, in the colonies of Queensland and New Zealand, and also in India, and that these Railways were capable of accommodating a traffic of about a million to a million and a half of tons of goods per annum, and of carrying passengers at a speed of twenty-five to thirty miles an hour, and seeing that the average speed of passenger trains, including stoppages, in Canada does not exceed twenty miles an hour, and that the total traffic of the Northern Railway (which affords fair illustration of the traffic to be obtained by the Toronto and Nipissing Railway) did not exceed 195,000 tons and 140,000 passengers, have therefore resolved to construct the Toronto and Nipissing Railway on the three feet six gauge, in the most economical and efficient manner consistent with a total cost of $15,000 per mile.

The Directors have also noted Capt. Tyler's report on the Festiniog Railway, two feet gauge, in Merionethshire, Wales, the freight and passenger traffic of which approximates closely to that of the Northern Railway, and, with the exception of the bus.es traffic, largely exceeds that carried on the Lindsay and Port Hope, or on the London and Port Stanley Railway.

With a view to an apportionment of the risks incidental to capital invested in Railway enterprise in Canada, it was resolved to ask the municipalities must be be smelted by the construction of the Railway, for one-third of the total cost of the Railway, viz., $5,000 per mile, by way of loans or gift. This proportion of the cost has already been asked for the main line, excepting less than $50,000, yet obtainable, in debentures bearing six per cent, payable in 20 years—securities which are unexceptionable, and will sell here at or near par.

Of the remaining two-thirds of the capital, it is proposed now to offer here $400,000 to be invested in stock. If that on a larger amount is not subscribed, bonds will be issued for the balance of about $6,000 per mile. Thus local capital to the extent of about two-thirds of the cost of the Railway, will be security to the holders of the bonds of this Company.

The interest-bearing capital will thus be $10,000 per mile.

The Directors do not propose to extend the line beyond Coboconk, towards Lake Nipissing, unless authorized by the Government of this Province until there is any traffic sufficient to guarantee the Company from the loss of any private capital to be invested in the sections of the line beyond Coboconk.

Nevertheless, the Company feel assured that the first section being successfully completed, the remaining sections will immediately receive aid from the Government to the extent necessary to secure the construction of the line to the ultimate terminus at Lake Nipissing—thus ensuring to the population of the first section the practically unlimited timber traffic, as well as the general business of an immense new territory of twenty thousand square miles.

The terminus of the first section being located on the Gull River, with access to all its tributaries, and to the Burnt River, insures for this Railway a timber and lumber traffic certain to exceed in duration of supply and quantity the timber and lumber traffic of the Northern Railway, and which will undoubtedly equal or exceed that of the Lindsay and Port Hope Railway, which amounted to nearly one hundred millions of feet in the year 1868.

The sawn lumber traffic of the Northern Railway of Canada in 1868, amounted only to about fifty-five (55) million feet, and the square timber traffic to one million six hundred thousand cubic feet.

IN 1861.

The local traffic of the Northern Railway of Canada amounted to..

Through ....   120,000 tons
Passengers   25,000   "
Local Receipts ....$362,597   100,618   "
Through 48,432 $410,929
Running Expenses ....   68 per cent.
Excess of earnings over running expenses on local traffic 115,982
Do. on through traffic 15,498
Local earnings equal to $8 per cent on a cost of $15,000 per mile ; or 14½ on $10,000 per mile.

1864.

Local Traffic.....................   180,700 tons
Through Traffic...................   8,344   "
Passengers   104,349
Local Receipts $462,832
Through 14,884 $467,503
Running Expenses ....   52 per cent.
Excess of earnings over running expenses on local traffic.......... 217,143
Do. on through traffic............ 7,144
Local earnings equal to 1o 2·5 per cent on a cost of $15,000 a mile ; or 28 1·10 per cent on $10,000 per mile.

1868.

Local and through traffic.....   104,553 tons
Passengers   138,905   "
Local Receipts ....(?637,350)
Through ".................. 13,990 $650,670
Running expenses............   81 per cent.
Excess of earnings over running expenses on local traffic............ 209,573
Do. on through traffic 4,949
Or equal to 14½ per cent on $15,000 a mile (local earnings) ; or 22½ per cent on $10,000 per mile.

1861—Running expenses per cent, 68 ; local tonnage, 120,000 through tonnage, 25,000 ; total tons, 145,000 ;

passengers, 100,613; local receipts, gross, $362,597; through receipts, gross, $48,432; total receipts, gross, $410,929; local receipts, nett, $115,962; through receipts, nett, $432; division 1 on $15,000 a mile, local, 8 1·3 ; dividend $15,000 a mile, through, 1 1·10.

1864—Running expenses per cent, 52 ; local tons 180,700 ; through tonnage, 8,344 ; total tons, 189,044; passengers, 104,349; local receipts, gross, $462,832 ; through receipts, gross, $14,884 ; total receipts, gross, $467,503 local receipts, nett, $217,143 ; through receipts, nett, 344 ; dividend on $15,000 a mile, local, 15 2·5 ; dividend $15,000 a mile, through, 1·2.

1868—Running expenses per cent, 81 ; total tons, 104,553 ; passengers, 138,905 ; local receipts, gross, $637,350 ; through receipts, gross, $12,990 ; total receipts, nett, $650,670 ; local receipts, nett, $209,573 ; through receipts, nett, $4,949 ; dividend on $15,000 a mile, local, 14 7·8 ; viidend on $15,000 a mile, through, 1·3.

Total tens, 528,627; passengers, 340,922 ; local receipts gross, $1,562,203 ; through receipts, gross, $76,006 ; total receipts, gross, $1,628,275 ; local receipts, nett, $442,733 through receipts, nett, $27,591 ; dividend on $15,000 mile, local, 12 5·6 ; dividend on $15,000 a mile, through, average.

AVERAGE.—Total tons, 176,209 ; passengers, 116,8 local receipts, gross, $450,765 ; through receipts, gr $25,335 ; total receipts, gross $476,091 ; local receipts, nett, $30,591 ; through receipts, nett, $9,197 ; divid on $15,000 a mile, local, 12 5·6; dividend on $15,000 a mile through, 2·3.

From the above data it will be seen that the North Railway carried an average for these three years of 1 200 tons of freight, and 116,643 passengers ; the average gross receipts being $450,765, while the nett receipts for local traffic were $188,501, equal to an annual dividend 12 5·6 per cent on a cost of $15,000 per mile ; or 19 1·4 $10,000 per mile.

It is remarkable and of consequence to intending stockholders for stock of the T. & N. R., that the nett receipts for through traffic for the same years only averaged $9,197 per annum, equal to a dividend of ½ of one per cent, or cost of $15,000 per mile. This fact clearly proves the value of local as against through traffic.

The Gain Traffic tributary to the Toronto and Nipissing Railway undoubtedly will not fall below 300,000 both and probably will largely exceed that quantity. The Passenger Traffic is anticipated to average 100,000 per annum.

The country through which the first section of the Toronto and Nipissing railway will pass, is more populous wealthy and extensive than that tributary to the Northern Railway—being one of the oldest and finest settled districts in the Province of Ontario. Various improvements have previously been made to accommodate this class with railways.

The most moderate estimate of the gross receipts from the traffic in timber, lumber, cereals, passengers, &c., be carried over the T. & N. R. places the amount at an average of $400,000 to $450,000 per annum, for the first eight ten years, when the traffic must necessarily increase by much larger amount.

The traffic to create this revenue will be derived from following items, and in about the proportions set forth :

Flue, or sawn lumber, for the first eight years,
80,000,000 ft. at $2 per 1,000 ft..................$160,000
Square timber, 1,250,000.....................   37,500
Cereals, 900,000 bushels, at 5c. per bush.....   45,000
General goods, 15,000 tons, at an average of
$8 40 per ton...................................   51,000
Mails and Express.............................   15,000
Cordwood, 25,000 cords at $1 50 per cord...   37,500
Passengers, 100,000..........................   100,000
                                                     —————
                                                    $446,000

Allowing 60 per cent for running expenses, the earnings amount to $178,400—equal to a dividend of 14 cent on a cost of $15,000 per mile ; and on the actual to the Company of $10,000 per mile, the dividend from such nett earnings would be 21 per cent.

The Provisional Directors invest their own means their faith in the correctness of these estimates.

The terminus at Coboconk, on the Gull River, will meet the Railway with a vast stretch of Inland Navigation upon which steamers now trade, and which, with only a lively inexpensive improvements already partly undertaken by the government, will give these boats access the Railway, and will afford almost inexhaustible supply of pine and hard wood.

By the Act of Incorporation, the Company is expressly bound to carry cordwood, and to afford every means facility for so doing at the specified rate of 3 cents cost per mile for dry wood, for all distances under 50 miles and 2½ cts. per cord per mile for all distances over 50 miles—a rate which has been found satisfactory, by the test actual experience on the Government Railways in New Brunswick.

This condition will enhance the cost of fuel to the Company ; but the increased traffic and prosperity consequent upon this trade it is fully believed will more than compensate for the extra cost of fuel.

The numerous association of gentlemen who have joined and form the preliminary expenses of this enterprise, and who desire to see it carried out in good faith sound commercial principles, are resolved in so far their influence is equal to the task, to have this railway controlled by the most respectable capitalists of this country, and the country on the route of the railway, who may take stock in it ; to convert their own securities and pay to contractors, and not to surrender control of the railway to contractors or bondholders ; to let the contracts to

Mercantile.

John Boyd & Co.,

HAVE now in store, ex steamships "Peruvian," "North American," "Moravian," &c., their usual spring stock of

NEW SEASON TEAS,

COMPRISING

YOUNG HYSONS,
GUNPOWDERS,
IMPERIALS,
COLORED and UNCOLORED JAPANS,
CONGOUS,
SOUCHONGS,
TWANKEYS,
and PEKOES.

ALSO,

Ex "MORO CASTLE," "EAGLE," & "ELLA MARIA,',

Direct from Havana,

BOXES BRIGHT CENTRIFUGAL SUGAR.

61 AND 63 FRONT STREET
TORONTO.

Toronto, April 14th, 1869. 7-1y

Teas! Teas!! Teas!!!

FRESH ARRIVALS

NEW CROP TEAS,

WINES, AND GENERAL GROCERIES,

Special Inducements given to

PROMPT PAYING PURCHASERS.

All Goods sold at very Lowest Montreal Prices!

W. & R. GRIFFITH,

ONTARIO CHAMBERS
Corner of Front and Church Streets,
TORONTO
-1y ONTARIO

NEW CROP TEAS!

1,000 Half Chests

NEW CROP TEAS!

THE SUBSCRIBERS are now receiving a large and well selected Stock of NEW CROP TEAS, (to which they beg to call the attention of the Trade,) comprising,—

YOUNG HYSONS AND HYSONS,
HYSON TWANKAYS,
TWANKAYS,
IMPERIALS,
GUNPOWDERS,
SOUCHONGS,
CONGOUS,
COLOURED JAPANS,
NATURAL LEAF JAPANS,
OOLONGS.

REFORD & DILLON.

12 & 14 WELLINGTON STREET, TORONTO.
7-1y

Robert H. Gray,

Manufacturer of Hoop Skirts

AND

CRINOLINE STEEL,

IMPORTER OF

HABERDASHERY, TRIMMINGS

AND

GENERAL FANCY GOODS,

43, YONGE STREET, TORONTO, ONT. 6-1y

TORONTO PRICES CURRENT.—APRIL 22, 1869.

Name of Article.	Wholesale Rates.	
Boots and Shoes.	$ c.	$ c.
Mens' Thick Boots	2 20	2 50
" Kip	2 50	3 00
" Calf	3 20	3 70
" Congress Gaiters	1 65	2 50
" Kip Cobourgs	1 15	1 45
Boys' Thick Boots	1 70	1 80
Youths' "	1 40	1 50
Women's Batts	0 95	1 20
" Balmoral	1 20	1 50
" Congress Gaiters	0 90	1 50
Misses' Batts	0 75	1 00
" Balmoral	0 87	1 20
" Congress Gaiters	1 00	1 30
Girls' Batts	0 65	0 85
" Balmoral	0 90	1 05
" Congress Gaiters	0 75	1 10
Children's C. T. Cacks	0 50	0 65
" Gaiters	0 65	0 90
Drugs.		
Aloes Cape	0 12½	0 16
Alum	0 02½	0 03
Borax	0 00	0 00
Camphor, refined	0 65	0 70
Castor Oil	0 16½	0 28
Caustic Soda	0 04½	0 05
Cochineal	0 90	1 00
Cream Tartar	0 40	0 45
Epsom Salts	0 03	0 04
Extract Logwood	0 11	0 12
Gum Arabic, sorts	0 30	0 35
Indigo, Madras	0 90	1 00
Licorice	0 14	0 45
Madder	0 00	0 18
Galls	0 32	0 37
Opium	12 00	13 50
Oxalic Acid	0 26	0 35
Potash, Bi-tart	0 25	0 28
" Bichromate	0 15	0 20
Potass Iodide	3 90	4 50
Senna	0 12½	0 60
Soda Ash	0 02½	0 04
Soda Bicarb	4 50	5 00
Tartaric Acid	0 40	0 45
Verdigris	0 35	0 40
Vitriol, Blue	0 08	0 10
Groceries.		
Coffees:		
Java, ℔ lb.	0 22@0 24	
Laguayra,	0 17	0 18
Rio	0 15	0 17
Fish:		
Herrings, Lab. split	5 75	6 50
" round	0 00	0 00
" scaled	0 35	0 40
Mackerel, small kitts	1 00	0 00
Loch. Her. wh'e firks	2 50	2 75
" half "	1 25	1 50
White Fish & Trout	None.	
Salmon, saltwater	14 00	15 00
Dry Cod, ℔112 lbs	5 00	5 25
Fruit:		
Raisins, Layers	2 00	2 10
" M R	1 90	2 00
" Valentias new	0 6¾	0 7½
Currants, new	0 5½	0 06½
" old	0 04	0 04½
Figs	0 14	0 00
Molasses:		
Clayed, ℔ gal	0 00	0 35
Syrups, Standard	0 60	0 00
" Golden	0 00	0 65
Rice:		
Arracan	4 25	4 50
Spices:		
Cassia, whole, ℔ lb	0 00	0 45
Cloves	0 11	0 12
Nutmegs	0 50	0 55
Ginger, ground	0 20	0 25
" Jamaica, root	0 20	0 25
Pepper, black	0 12½	0 00
Pimento	0 08	0 09
Sugars:		
Port Rico, ℔ lb	0 10¾	0 00
Cuba "	0 10½	0 00
Barbadoes (bright)	0 10½	0 00
Canada Sugar Refine'y, yellow No. 2, 60ds	0 10½	0 10¾
Yellow, No. 2½	0 10¾	0 11
No. 3	0 11	0 11¼
Crushed X	0 13	0 13½
" A	0 13	0 13¼
Ground	0 13¾	0 14
Dry Crushed	0 14½	0 14½
Extra Ground	0 15¼	0 15½
Teas:		
Japan com'n to good	0 48	0 55
" Fine to choicest	0 50	0 65
Colored, com. to fine	0 60	0 75
Congou & Souch'ng	0 42	0 75
Oolong, good to fine	0 50	0 65
Y. Hyson, com to gd	0 47½	0 55
Medium to choice	0 65	0 80
Extra choice	0 85	0 95

Name of Article.	Wholesale Rate.	
Groceries—*Contin'd*	$ c.	$ c.
Gunpowd'r c. to med	0 55	0 70
" med. to fine	0 70	0 85
" fine to fins't	0 85	0 95
Hyson	0 45	0 80
Imperial	0 42	0 80
Tobacco, Manufact'd:		
Can Leaf, ℔ lb 5s & 10s	0 26	0 30
Western Leaf, com	0 25	0 26
" Good	0 27	0 32
" Fine	0 32	0 35
" Bright fine	0 40	0 50
" " choice	0 60	0 75
Hardware.		
Tin (net cash prices)		
Block, ℔ lb	0 28	0 00
Grain	0 30	0 00
Copper:		
Pig	0 23	0 24
Sheet	0 30	0 33
Cut Nails:		
Assorted ¼ Shingles, ℔ 100 lb	2 90	3 00
Shingle alone do	3 15	3 25
Lathe and 5 dy	3 30	3 40
Galvanized Iron:		
Assorted sizes	0 08	0 09
Best No. 24	0 09	0 00
" 26	0 08	0 08½
" 28	0 09	0 09½
Horse Nails:		
Guest's or Griffin's assorted sizes	0 00	0 00
For W. ass'd sizes	0 18	0 19
Patent Hammer'd do	0 17	0 18
Iron (at 4 months):		
Pig—Gartsherrie No1	24 00	25 00
Other brands. No 1	22 00	24 00
" No 2	0 00	0 00
Bar—Scotch, ℔100 lb	2 25	2 50
Refined	3 00	3 25
Swedes	5 00	5 50
Hoops—Coopers	3 00	3 25
Band	3 00	3 25
Boiler Plates	3 25	3 50
Canada Plates	3 75	4 00
Union Jack	0 00	0 00
Pontypool	3 25	4 00
Swansea	3 90	4 00
Lead (at 4 months):		
Bar, ℔ 100 lbs	0 06½	0 07
Sheet "	0 08	0 09
Shot	0 07½	0 07¾
Iron Wire (net cash):		
No. 6, ℔ bundle	2 70	2 80
" 9, "	3 10	3 20
" 12, "	3 40	3 50
" 16, "	4 30	4 40
Powder:		
Blasting, Canada	3 50	0 00
FF "	4 25	4 50
FFF "	4 75	5 00
Blasting, English	4 00	5 00
FF loose	5 00	6 00
FFF "	6 00	6 50
Pressed Spikes (4 mos):		
Regular sizes 100	4 00	4 25
Extra "	4 50	5 00
Tin Plates (net cash):		
IC Coke	7 50	8 50
IC Charcoal	8 50	9 00
IX "	10 50	11 00
IXX "	13 50	14 00
DC "	8 00	8 50
DX "	9 50	0 00
Hides & Skins, ℔ lb		
Green rough	0 00	0 06
Green, salt'd & insp'd	0 07½	0 07¾
Cured	0 00	0 00
Calfskins, green	0 00	0 11
Calfskins, cured	0 00	0 12½
" dry	0 18	0 20
Sheepskins,	1 40	1 75
" country	1 00	1 40
Hops.		
Inferior, ℔ lb	0 05	0 07
Medium	0 07	0 09
Good	0 09	0 12
Fancy	0 00	0 00
Leather, @ (4 mos.) In lots of less than 50 sides, 10 ℔ cent higher.		
Spanish Sole, 1st qual'y heavy, weights ℔ lb	0 21½	0 22
Do. 1st qual middle do	0 23	0 00
Do. No. 2, light weights	0 22	0 00
Slaughter heavy	0 00	0 24
Do. light	0 00	0 00
Harness, best	0 25	0 27
" No. 2	0 00	0 00
Upper heavy	0 32	0 35
" light	0 35	0 36

Name of Article.	Wholesale Rates.	
Leather—*Contin'd.*	$ c.	$
Kip Skins, Patna	0 30	0
French	0 70	0
English	0 65	0
Hemlock Calf (30 to 35 lbs.) per doz	0 50	0
Do. light	0 45	0
French Calf	1 03	1
Grain & Satn Clt ℔ doz	0 00	0
Splits, large ℔ lb	0 30	0
" small	0 23	0
Enamelled Cow ℔ foot	0 20	0
Patent	0 20	0
Pebble Grain	0 15	0
Buff	0 14	0
Oils.		
Cod	0 65	0
Lard, extra	0 60	0
" No. 1	0 00	0
" Woollen	0 00	0
Lubricating, patent	0 00	0
" Mott's economic	0 30	0
Linseed, raw	0 76	0
" boiled	0 81	0
Machinery	0 00	0
Olive, common, ℔ gal	1 00	1
" salad	1 05	2
" salad, in bots. qt. ℔ case	3 60	3
Sesame salad, ℔ gal	1 60	1
Seal, pale	0 75	0
Spirits Turpentine	0 52½	0
Varnish	0 00	0
Whale	0 00	0
Paints, &c.		
White Lead, genuine in Oil, ℔ 25 lbs	0 00	2
Do. No. 1 "	0 00	2
" 2 "	0 00	1
" 3 "	0 00	1
White Zinc, genuine	3 00	3
White Lead, dry	0 05½	0
Red Lead	0 07½	0
Venetian Red, Eng'h	0 02½	0
Yellow Ochre, Fren'h	0 02½	0
Whiting	0 85	1
Petroleum. (Refined ℔ gal.)		
Water white, car l'd	—	0
" small lots	0 30	0
Straw, by car load	0 00	0
" small lots	0 00	0
Amber, by car load	0 00	0
" small lots	0 00	0
Benzine	0 00	0
Produce.		
Grain:		
Wheat, Spring, 60 lb	0 93	0
" Fall 60 "	0 98	1
Barley 48 "	1 05	1
Peas 60 "	0 70	0
Oats 34 "	0 52	0
Rye 56 "	0 60	0
Seeds:		
Clover, choice 60 "	5 80	5
" com'n 68 "	6 70	5
Timothy, cho'e 4 "	2 60	2
" inf. to good 48 "	2 30	2
Flax 56 "	1 75	2
Flour (per brl.):		
Superior extra	0 00	0
Extra superfine	4 40	4
Fancy superfine	4 20	4
Superfine No 1	4 00	4
" No. 2	—	—
Oatmeal, (per brl.)	5 50	5
Provisions		
Butter, dairy tub ℔ lb	0 22	0
" store packed	0 15	0
Cheese, new	0 14½	0
Pork, mess, per brl	25 50	26
" prime mess	—	—
" prime	—	—
Bacon, rough	0 11	0
" Cumberl'd cut	0 12	0
" smoked	0 00	0
Hams, in salt	0 12½	0
" smoked	0 14	0
Shoulders, in salt	0 00	0
Lard, in kegs	0 16½	0
Eggs, packed	0 12½	0
Beef Hams	0 00	0
Tallow	0 08	0
Hogs dressed, heavy	0 00	0
" medium	0 00	0
" light	0 00	0
Salt, &c.		
American brls	1 50	1
Liverpool coarse	0 00	0
Goderich	0 00	1
Plaster, grey	0 00	0
Water Lime	1 50	0

Candles.	$ c.	$ c.
rd & Co.'s ..		
rial.........	0 07½	0 08
n Bar	0 07	0 07½
Bar........	0 07	0 07½
....	0 05	0 05½
....	0 03½	0 03¾
....	0 00	0 11½
Liquors, &c.		
per doz......	2 60	2 65
Dub Portr..	2 35	2 40
nica Rum...	1 80	2 25
er's H. Gin..	1 55	1 63
Old Tom.....	1 90	2 00
ases.........	4 00	4 25
Old Tom, c...	6 00	6 25
mmon.......	1 00	1 25
old	2 00	4 00
ommon	1 00	1 50
lium........	1 70	1 80
e or golden..	2 50	4 00

	$ c.	$ c
Brandy:		
Hennessy's, per gal..	2 30	2 50
Martell's " ..	2 30	2 50
J. Robin & Co.'s " ..	2 25	2 35
Otard, Dupuy & Cos..	2 25	2 35
Brandy, cases........	8 50	9 00
Brandy, com. per c...	4 00	4 50
Whiskey:		
Common 36 u. p......	0 62½	0 65
Old Rye	0 85	0 87½
Malt	0 85	0 87½
Toddy	0 85	0 87½
Scotch, per gal.......	1 90	2 10
Irish—Kinnahan's c...	7 00	7 50
" Dunnville's Belf't..	6 00	6 25
Wool.		
Fleece, lb............	0 28	0 35
Pulled "	0 22	0 25
Furs.		
Bear................	3 00	10 00
Beaver, ℔ lb.........	1 00	1 25
Coon	0 20	0 40
Fisher..............	4 00	6 00
Martin..............	1 40	1 60
Mink................	3 25	4 00
Otter...............	5 75	6 00
Spring Rats..........	0 15	0 17
Fox.................	1 20	1 25

INSURANCE COMPANIES.

ENGLISH.—*Quotations on the London Market.*

Last Dividend.	Name of Company.	Shares par val £	Amount paid.	Last Sale.
	Briton Medical and General Life...	10	....	2½
7½	Commer'l Union, Fire, Life and Mar.	50	5	5¾xd
8	City of Glasgow	25	2½	5½
9½	Edinburgh Life	100	15	33
5—½ yr	European Life and Guarantee......	2½	11s6	4s. 6d.
10	Etna Fire and Marine........	10	1½	—
5	Guardian	100	50	51½
12	Imperial Fire........	500	50	350
9½	Imperial Life	100	10	17
10	Lancashire Fire and Life........	20	2	2⅝
11	Life Association of Scotland.......	40	7½	25
5s. p. sh	London Assurance Corporation ..	25	12½	49
5	London and Lancashire Life	10	1	—
40	Liverp'l & London & Globe F. & L.	20	2	7 1-16
5	National Union Life	5	1	1
12½	Northern Fire and Life	100	5	12 1-16
12 / 38, bo / 5s.	North British and Mercantile	50	6¼	19½xd
50	Ocean Marine	25	5	17
£5 12s.	Provident Life........	100	10	35
4½ p. s.	Phœnix........	....	....	145
½—h. yr.	Queen Fire and Life	10	1	1
s. bo. 4s	Royal Insurance........	20	3	6⅝
10	Scottish Provincial Fire and Life ..	50	2½	5 3-8
25	Standard Life	50	12	66½
5	Star Life	25	1¼	—
	CANADIAN.			℘ c.
4	British America Fire and Marine ..	$50	$25	55½ 56
4	Canada Life	....	....	.....
12	Montreal Assurance	£50	£5	135
8	Provincial Fire and Marine........	60	11	.....
....	Quebec Fire	40	32½	£26
7	" Marine........	100	40	85 90
6 mo's.	Western Assurance........	40	9	.....

RAILWAYS.	Sha's	Paid	Montr	London
nd St. Lawrence........	£100	All.	....	58 60
d Lake Huron	20½	"	....	3⅝ 3½
do Preference	10	"	....	5 6¼
ntf. & Goderich, 6℘c.,1872-3-4........	100	"	....	66 69
n and St. Lawrence	....	....	10 11	....
do Pref. 10 ℘ ct........	....	....	80 82½	....
ank	100	"	15 16	15 15½
Eq. G. M. Bds. 1 ch. 6℘c........	100	"	....	87 89
First Preference, 5 ℘ c........	100	"	....	51 53
Deferred, 3 ℘ ct........	100	"	....	....
Second Pref. Bonds, 5℘c........	100	"	....	37 40
do Deferred, 3 ℘ ct........	100	"	...	....
Third Pref. Stock, 4℘ct........	100	"	....	28 30
do. Deferred, 3 ℘ ct........	100	"	....	....
Fourth Pref. Stock, 3℘c........	100	"	....	17 18
do. Deferred, 3 ℘ ct........	100	"	....	....
tern	20½	"	14 15	14⅝ 15½
New	20½	18	----	....
6 ℘ c. Bds, due 1873-76........	100	All.	....	100 102
5½ ℘c Bds. due 1877-78........	100	"	....	94 95
ilway, Halifax, $250, all........	$250	"	....	....
of Canada, 6℘c. 1st Pref. Bds........	100	"	.. .	32 34

EXCHANGE.	Halifax.	Montr'l.	Quebec.	Toronto.
London, 60 days........				
75 days date........	12½	8 8¼	9 9¼	8½
do.	11½ 12	7 8	8 8¼	8⅛
ith documents........	....	7 8	....	....
New York........	....	24 24½	23½ 24	24½
do.	....	24½ 25	24 24½	....
s do.	....	par to ½ p.	par ⅛ dis.	par ¼ dis.
....	....	4½ 5	....	3½ to 4½

STOCK AND BOND REPORT.

The dates of our quotations are as follows:—Toronto, April 20; Montreal, April 19; Quebec, April 19; London, April 1.

NAME.	Shares.	Paid up.	Divid'd last 6 Months	Dividend Day.	CLOSING PRICES. Toronto.	Montre'l	Quebec.
BANKS.			℘ ct.				
British North America	$250	All.	3	July and Jan.	105 105½	105 105½	105 106
Jacques Cartier........	50	"	4	1 June, 1 Dec.	109 109½	108½ 109½	109 110
Montreal	200	"	5	"	144 145	145⅛ 145½	144 145
Nationale........	50	"	4	1 Nov. 1 May.	108 109	bks cls'd	bks cls'd
New Brunswick	100	"	......	......	....	...	....
Nova Scotia	200	28	7&b$3½	Mar. and Sept.	....	....	....
Du Peuple........	50	"	4	1 Mar., 1 Sept.	108 109	107½ 108½	108 108½
Toronto	100	"	4	1 Jan., 1 July.	120 120½	121 122	121 122
Bank of Yarmouth........	....	....	......	......	....	....	....
Canadian Bank of Com'e........	50	95	......	......	102 102½	102 103	102 102½
City Bank Montreal	80	All.	4	1 June, 1 Dec.	101½ 102	101½ 102¼	101½ 102
Commer'l Bank (St. John)........	100	"	℘ ct.	......	....	...	....
Eastern Townships' Bank........	50	"	4	1 July, 1 Jan..	....	99½ 100	99½ 100
Gore	40	...	none.	1 Jan., 1 July.	38 39	39 40	40 41
Halifax Banking Company........	....	....	......	......	....	....	....
Mechanics' Bank........	50	70	4	1 Nov., 1 May.	97½ 98½	Bks cls'd	97 98
Merchants' Bank of Canada........	100	70	4	1 Jan., 1 July.	107 107½	107½ 107¾	107½ 107¾
Merchants' Bank (Halifax)........	....	....	.....	......	....	....	....
Molson's Bank........	50	All.	4	1 Apr., 1 Oct.	108 108½	107½ 108½	107 108
Niagara District Bank........	100	70	3½	1 Jan., 1 July.	....	....	....
Ontario Bank........	40	All.	4	1 June, 1 Dec.	100 100½	99¾ 100¼	99¾ 100¼
People's Bank (Fred'kton)........	100	"	......	......	....	....	....
People's Bank (Halifax)	20	"	7 12 m	......	....	...	....
Quebec Bank	100	"	3½	1 June, 1 Dec.	101 102	101½ 102	101 101½
Royal Canadian Bank	50	50	4	1 Jan., 1 July.	78 79	75 80	78 80
St. Stephens Bank	100	All.	.....	......	....	..	....
Union Bank	100	70	4	1 Jan., 1 July.	105 106	105½ 106	106 106½
Union Bank (Halifax)........	100	40	7 12 mo	Feb. and Aug.	....	....	.. .
MISCELLANEOUS.							
British America Land........	250	44	2½	......	....	....	....
British Colonial S. S. Co........	250	32½	2½	......	...	50 60	...
Canada Company	32½	All.	£1 10s.	......	....	----	....
Canada Landed Credit Co........	50	$20	3½	......	78 80	----	....
Canada Per. B'ldg Society........	50	All.	5	......	125½ 126	....	....
Canada Mining Company........	4	90	......	......	....	....	....
Do. Inl'd Steam Nav. Co........	100	All.	7	......	----	100½ 101	....
Do. Glass Company........	100	"	12½ "	......	....	40 55	....
Canad'n Loan & Investm't........	25	2½	7	......	....	....	----
Canada Agency	10	¼	......	......	....	....	----
Colonial Securities Co........	....	....	......	......	....	....	....
Freehold Building Society........	100	All.	4	......	111½ 112	----	....
Halifax Steamboat Co........	100	"	5	......	....	....	....
Halifax Gas Company........	....	----	------	......	....	....	....
Hamilton Gas Company........	----	----	-----	......	....	....	....
Huron Copper Bay Co........	4	12	20	......	....	32½ 45	....
Lake Huron S. and C........	5	102	......	......	....	....	....
Montreal Mining Consols........	20	$15	......	......	....	3.15 3.25	...
Do. Telegraph Co........	40	All.	5	......	133½ 134	133½ 134	133½ 134
Do. Elevating Co........	00	"	15 12 m	......	....	100 102½	----
Do. City Gas Co........	40	"	4	15 Mar. 15 Sep.	....	134 135	134 135
Do. City Pass. R,. Co........	50	"	4	......	....	105½ 106	105 106
Quebec and L. S.	8	$4	......	......	....	....	....
Quebec Gas Co........	200	All.	4	1 Mar., 1 Sep.	....	...	118 119
Quebec Street R. R	50	25	3	......	....	....	90 91
Richelieu Navigation Co........	100	All.	10 p.a.	1 Jan., 1 July.	....	108¼ 108¾	108¼ 108¾
St. Lawrence Glass Company.	100	"	.....	......	....	80 85	....
St. Lawrence Tow Boat Co........	100	"	......	3 Feb.	....	...	30 35
Tor'to Consumers' Gas Co........	50	"	4	1 My Au Mar Fe	107 107½	...	107 108
Trust & Loan Co. of U. C........	20	5	3	......	....	....	.. .
West'n Canada Bldg Soc'y........	50	All.	5	......	120 121	....	----

SECURITIES.	London.	Montreal.	Quebec.	Toronto.
Canadian Gov't Deb. 6 ℘ ct. stg........	....	103 104	102½ 103	102½ 104
Do. do. 6 do due Ja. & Jul. 1877-84........	104½ 105½	....	....	....
Do. do. 6 do. Feb. & Aug........	102 104	....	....	....
Do. do. 6 do. Mch. & Sep........	102 104	....	....	....
Do. do. 5 ℘ ct. cur., 1883	92½ 93½	92½ 95	93½ 94	93 94½
Do. do. 5 do. stg., 1885	92 94	92½ 94½	93½ 94½	93 94½
Do. do. 7 do. cur.,........	....	....	......	....
Dominion 6 p. c. 1878 cy........	....	106 107	105½ 106	106½ 107
Hamilton Corporation........	....	....	......	....
Montreal Harbor, 8 ℘ ct. d. 1869........	..	....	......	....
Do. do. 7 do. 1870........	....	....	......	....
Do. do. 6½ do. 1883........	....	102 103	......	102 103
Do. do. 6½ do. 1873........	....	....	......	....
Do. Corporation, 6 ℘ c. 1891	....	96 97	96 96½	96 97
Do. 7 p. c. stock........	....	108 110	108 109	109 110
Do. - Water Works, 6 ℘ c. stg. 1878........	....	....	......	96½ 97
Do. do. 6 do. cy. do.	....	96½ 97	......	96 97
New Brunswick, 6 ℘ ct., Jan. and July	102½ 103½	....	......	....
Nova Scotia, 6 ℘ ct., 1875........	102 104	...	......	....
Ottawa City 6 ℘ c. d. 1880	....	95 96	......	....
Quebec Harbour, 6 ℘ c. d. 1883........	....	....	60	....
Do. do. 7 do. do........	....	....	65 70	....
Do. do 8 do. 1886........	...	....	80 85	....
Do. City, 7 ℘ c. d. 1½ years........	....	....	98 98½	....
Do. do. 7 do. 8 do.	....	....	91 92	....
Do. do. 7 do. 3 do.	....	....	94 95	....
Do. Water Works, 7 ℘ ct., 4 years	....	....	97 97½	....
Do. do. 6 do. 2 do.	....	....	94 95	....
Toronto Corporation	....	90 92½	....	....

THE CANADIAN
MONETARY TIMES
AND
INSURANCE CHRONICLE.
VOTED TO FINANCE, COMMERCE, INSURANCE, BANKS, RAILWAYS, NAVIGATION, MINES, INVESTMENT, PUBLIC COMPANIES, AND JOINT STOCK ENTERPRISE.

| II—NO. 37. | TORONTO, THURSDAY, APRIL 29, 1869 | SUBSCRIPTION $2 A YEAR. |

Mercantile.

Insurance.

INSURANCE MATTERS IN NEW YORK.

(From our own Correspondent.)

NEW YORK, April 26th, 1869.

The deliberations of the National Board of Fire Underwriters, held in this city on Wednesday, Thursday and Friday, of the past week, were distinguished not only for ability in debate, and a harmonious and urbane spirit, but for final and decisive action on several subjects that had long agitated the profession, and in regard to which, no practical action had been deemed possible. If, as thus far done, a large majority of the respectable companies shall continue to sustain the Board, its resolves will gradually assume the character and weight of decrees, and companies will be unwilling to incur the odium of defection from, or opposition to, the deliberations of a body that can never have any motive for action which shall not, in its deliberate judgment, be for the best good of the profession at large.

The real practical work of the session was in the discussion and final adoption of a series of resolutions, submitted by Mr. E. W. Crowell, Chairman of the Committee on Local Boards, Rates, and Commissions, and Resident Director here, of the Imperial of London. The debate on the 'vexed question of brokerage, rebate and commissions showed, that a large majority of the Board were of the opinion that the business pays too high a rate, not only as compared with other kinds of business, but that the rate is entirely out of proportion to the profits of insurance capital. After a protracted and animated discussion, the basis of calculating commissions was changed from gross to net, by the adoption of the following resolution:—

" *Whereas* The present mode of calculating commissions (whereby a stated percentage is allowed upon premiums received, regardless of agency expenses) is a serious error, and one demanding immediate reform, be it

Resolved, That from and after May 1, 1869, all companies connected with the National Board of Fire Underwriters hereby pledge themselves that the rate of commissions which they allow to agents shall be calculated only upon the net premiums due after deducting taxes, licenses, advertising, and all other agency expenses, except in cases where only ten per cent. commission is paid."

Henceforth, agents will be paid on the amount of benefit conferred on the companies. There are some six thousand agents representing American companies. They are not always conscientiously considerate of their companies' interests. They get their gross earnings in, and don't care for the year's results. In too many instances excessive commissions is a temptation for over-insurance, to which agents are parties. They allow States and cities to pile discriminating taxation upon the companies, when their united opposition would doubtless do much towards preventing it. With the net idea before them, they will doubtless be more careful and energetic. The remaining resolutions adopted, with amendments, were as follows :

" *Whereas,* There appears to be a misunderstanding among many companies as to their duties

as members of the National Board of Fire Underwriters, and, as it is essential to the welfare of the organization that there should be plain and explicit rules applying to all ; therefore, be it

" *Resolved,* That wherever local Boards exist, it is the duty of all companies, members of the National Board, to instruct their agents to join the same ; and where no Board exists, it is their duty, when called upon, to instruct their agents to co-operate with other agents in effecting such organization ; and where existing local Boards decline to admit representatives of outside companies, that such companies organize Boards for themselves, and establish correspondence with the National Board.

" *Resolved,* That it is the first essential to membership in this Board that tariff rates should be maintained, and no company is justified under any circumstances in taking a risk, or in allowing one to be taken by an agent, at less than tariff figures.

" *Resolved,* That from and after this date, the Chicago compact shall be a rule of this Board, and all companies members thereof shall be governed by its provisions and penalties.

" *Resolved,* that it is inconsistent with the interests of this Board that any company be recognized as a member thereof that declines to cancel or collect full rates on every policy written under the tariff figures ; or that allows an agent to remain out of a local Board where one exists in his locality ; or or that allows him to retain commissions not belonging to this Board for which he violates the tariff.

" *Resolved,* That it is incumbent upon the Chairman of the Committee on Local Boards, Rates and Commissions to report, either to the Executive Committee or the National Board, the names of such companies, members of this Board, that decline to comply with the above rules and regulations, with the circumstances connected therewith, and upon due conviction the Executive Committee or the National Board, as the case may be, shall expel such company, and notice with the cause for such action shall be sent to every company belonging to this Board."

It will be seen from the tenor of these resolutions that the machinery of local Boards, accepting and enforcing the rates established by the National Board, through its Rating Committees, is deemed of vital importance.

Much of the Convention's time (part of the second and all of the third day) was consumed in the consideration of some plan to increase its power and inefficiency. Its means of action have been, as experience since its organization in July, 1866, shows, too much diffused. It meets annually, and its large Executive Committee quarterly. But the action of the Executive Committee is not deemed final, and not sufficiently respected by companies that, while finding it a matter of character to belong to the Board, yet act in bad faith towards it, by winking at the irregularities of their agents. Besides, the difficulties and complaints constantly springing up in every section of the country between agents and local Boards, with respect to rates, have not been treated summarily enough.

The radical idea of the Convention for a remedy was embodied in a report by the Committee on Local Boards and Rates: An Executive Manager, with a sufficient salary to command the exclusive services of a competent person; a number of salaried assistants; and an Advisory Board, to whom such Manager should report monthly. Several other plans were suggested, looking to the division of the country into districts, the affairs of each district to be supervised by a section of a large committee to reside in that district. But the longer the debate was continued the more evident it became that the Convention would not reach a conclusion without extending its session. An informal vote had shown that the report of the Committee on Local Boards, as modified by Mr. Howard of Hartford (amendment accepted by Committee) was in greatest favor, viz.—that the Executive Committee appoint an Executive Manager, as aforesaid, and an Advisory Board, from its own members, and the requisite number of paid assistants. A resolution, that all the plans be referred to the Executive Committee, with powers to devise and put in action a suitable plan without necessary delay, was finally adopted. It is understood that the work will be consummated at an early day. This Manager and Advisory Committee will supersede the Committee on Local Boards, Rates and Commissions—a committee, by the way, which has done an enormous amount of hard and important service in organizing boards and rating hundreds of localities.

The Dominion, not being a part of His Majesty Uncle Sam's Empire, will not feel so lively an interest in the question of discriminating taxation as the people on this side. Congress taxes the companies 1½ per cent on *gross* premiums, and 5 per cent on dividends, and the States pile on from 2 to 5 per cent more. The total averages about 6 per cent of the whole expenses of managing the business. Besides, in many States, companies are compelled, as in Canada, to purchase local bonds, or make other form of deposit. It is the very decided conviction of several eminent jurists that when this question of inter-State taxation is reached in the United States Superior Court, the State practice of discriminating legislation will be declared unconstitutional and void.

The Committee on Taxation reported to the National Board that they had resolved to aid a test case, Paul vs. Commonwealth of Virginia, put on the U. S. Supreme Court Calendar, Dec., 1868, for the amount of $15,000 towards costs of suit. Virginia will not issue a license to any fire insurance company, not incorporated by its laws, unless the company shall first purchase Virginia bonds to an amount varying from $35,000 to $50,000, according to their capital. Your correspondent has examined the brief of the points upon which the suit of Paul was taken up, and he feels confident that the Supreme Court will finally break down all these state barriers. If states may erect barriers to internal commerce with impunity, how is the great inland commerce of the country to be carried on, when the Pacific Railroad is opened to the Golden Gate?

The reports of the several Special Committees, submitted to the Convention on the opening day, embody a vast array of statistics, and show how wide the field, varied the interests, and numerous the dangers, over which fire insurance operates. The revelations made by the committee on the storage, sale, &c., of petroleum, ought to lead to some remedial measures which shall secure a material reduction in the number of destructive accidents and fires, almost daily reported from this source. There is a general want of adequate municipal regulations for storage, and handling, and in the subjection of kerosene to a due test of its specific gravity. It is almost impossible to get a pure article of kerosene. In 715 tests made by our Boards of Health and Fire Commissioners, the average vaporizing test was only 80, and the average burning test, which should be 110° Fahrenheit, was only 92! In the manufacture of kerosene, the conscientious refiner runs all the dangerous oil into the benzine tank; but as this dangerous article must be sold at a lower price than burning oil, most of these refiners collect as little benzine, and

as much kerosene as possible. Specific gravity is not a reliable test of inflammability, but the fire test is. Its general application, under ordinance, to all oils before sold, would remedy the evil. The committee recommended a set of precautionary rules for loading vessels, &c., at petroleum yards and depots, and submitted a form of ordinance for general adoption by cities and towns. If its general acceptance can be enforced through the influence of the National Board, a great boon will have been conferred upon the Union, and the Dominion as well.

A large amount of important labor was accomplished by the Executive Committee during the year ending with the Board's session. Some 75 local Boards were organized, making 475 in all, nearly all of which are working harmoniously. The rooms of this committee now contain 1,824 different tariffs, of which 390 were made during the past year. Hundreds of extra and special hazards have also been surveyed and rated: 37,095 printed documents have been distributed, and 7,000 letters answered, so that it will be seen that the sub-machinery of the National Board is quite extensive.

Doubtless the readers of the MONETARY TIMES, are as much interested in the growing evil of incendiarism as the folks on this side; Canada, like the mother country, and every other nation has its share of said experience, and grievous loss from this crime, and the enquiry how it can be checked, if not entirely suppressed, is of paramount importance, everywhere. The convictions of late, have been more numerous than heretofore, but the frequency of the crime is not perceptibly diminished. It has been satisfactorily determined by investigation among American companies, that 32 per ct. of their losses is attributable to this crime. The loss is not a loss to the insurance companies merely, but to the community at large, it is so much property value wiped out of existence. Moreover as the companies recognize incendiarism as occasioning one third of their losses, the premiums are by that amount greater than they would be, if the evil could be suppressed. The Executive Committee have resolved to *follow* up every case with persistent energetic aid to the authorities, and intimidation will ultimately to a large extent, follow *habitual* conviction. The form of an act was submitted to the National Board, and laid over until its next session (when it is believed public sentiment will be ready for it) to be urged upon the several states for adoption, providing that in a loss under a policy, the insured shall not in any case recover more than ⅔ of the amount of the loss as proved. Such a law, with more stringent regulations and precautions, in regard to the chief cause of incendiarism, *over insurance*, would no doubt do much towards putting an end to this great evil, and disgrace to modern civilization.

M. A. C.

FIRE RECORD.—Bethany, Ont., April 17.—The store of W. M. Graham, Postmaster, was totally destroyed, with all its contents. The building was insured, but a quantity of newly arrived goods will add to the loss of Mr. Graham.

Stanley Township, Ont., April 17.—The barn and shed and contents of Wm. Curry, 8th con., were burned. The origin of the fire was the dropping of a live coal from the proprietor's own pipe.

Nissouri West Township, Ont., April 17.—The stable of John Switzer caught fire, it is supposed, from a spark from the chimney of the house, and, with contents, was burned to the ground. No insurance.

Ottawa, April 23.—A fire took place this morning on Rideau street, destroying two frame buildings and out-buildings — one occupied by Mr. Amos Rowe, auctioneer, and owned by Mr. Matthew Stephenson; the other owned by Walker, grocer, and owned by Robinson & Beatty, Montreal. Insurance — Rowe, $1,000 each in the

Home, Ætna, and Imperial; M. Stevenson, $1 in the Hartford; Whelan, $1,000 in the West of Canada, and $3,000 in the British Amer, Robinson & Beatty in the Montreal. The insurances will more than cover the losses. The stocks were all removed in a damaged condition.

Murray Township, Ont., April 14.—The barn and sheds of John McColl, of the 8th con., a fire, and burned to the ground with all their tents. A span of horses, 3 hogs, 6 tons of 100 bushels of wheat, 80 bushels of oats, bushels of peas, a lumber waggon, a buggy, a fanning mill were consumed. There was light insurance on the barn. The loss is estimated at about $1,000. The fire is supposed be the work of an incendiary.

Whitby Township, April 16.—The barn stable of Henry Graham, lot 6, on the 7th con., with 5 fat hogs, 120 bushels wheat, 40 bushels oats, a quantity of peas and barley, 7 tons of 2 bushels clover seed, 100 bushels turnips, quite an assortment of farming implements. The loss amount to something in the neighborhood of $1,000, about $200 of which is covered by insurance. Cause, smoking.

Blenheim, Ont., April 18.—Mr. Morris's post office, store and contents were burned to the ground. Nothing saved. It is thought the fire originated from the match-box. Quite a number of letters and stamps were destroyed. The loss will amount to $6,000. Insured for $2,000 in the Niagara District Mutual.

Fullarton Township, Ont., April 19.—The barn of Jabez Parsons, on lot 1, concession 11, took fire and before any attempt could be made to extinguish it, the building with its contents were totally consumed. There were 6 horses 5 cows, a number of sheep, a quantity of grain, &c., in the barn the time, but the only thing saved was one of the horses, which was so severely burnt and otherwise injured that it was deemed advisable, as an act of mercy to the poor brute to shoot it next day. The loss is estimated at between $800 and $1,000. No insurance. The origin of the fire is not known, but the supposition is lightning.

Grand Narrows, C. B., April 4.—The Cape Breton *News* says that the forge of Allan McNeil, Grand Narrows, with all its contents, including new work, was destroyed by fire.

East Flamboro' Township, Ont., April 17.—A fire broke out in the kitchen of the house occupied by John Brown, on the farm of Alexander Brown near Aldershott, East Flamboro', which quickly consumed. The building, and a good deal of the furniture, together with money, surgical instruments and photograph apparatus, was destroyed. No insurance on the furniture.

London Township, Ont., April 18.—During the severe thunder-storm, a barn belonging to Hobbs, on lot No. 3, 14th concession, London, was struck by lightning, and burnt to the ground. It contained a large quantity of straw and agricultural implements, and two complete tool chests, besides doors and sashes intended for his new house, all of which were consumed. Loss about $5,000. No insurance.

Bayfield, County Huron, Ont., April 16.—A storehouse owned by Mr. Rankin, was burnt down. There was in the building $1,200 worth of peas belonging to the Royal Canadian Bank, which the insurance had run out, and 1 bushels of wheat belonging to Mr. Walker, Windsor. The building was insured for $600. As no fire had been used in the building, it is feared it was the act of an incendiary.

St. John, N. B., April 10.—A fire broke out at Messrs. Knox & Thompson's workshop, in rear of their warerooms on Germain Street. The engine were quickly on the ground, and the flames subdued, but not before the principal portion of tools, patterns, and other valuable property was found in a cabinet maker's shop, were destroyed. The place was insured. It is stated that the

no fire in the room from half-past five
ıd the impression is that the shop must
set on fire.

ı, Ont., April.—Scoble's mill, in Stanley
, was burned to the ground ; the loss is
ʒ1,000. No insurance.

l, Ont., April 13.—The *Advocate* gives
tional particulars respecting the recent
fire at this place :—"As yet it is a mys-
the fire originated, but it started in the
occupied by McQuade. The two build-
as stores, at the east end, were owned
Awty, insured for 1,000 ; George Ritz's
ırniture was insured for. $400 ; the gro-
iquors of George Barrett were insured
There were three shops in the next
which were owned by R. B. Stephens
Porter, and insured jointly in the sum
; one was occupied by McQuade, whose
insured for $400 ; the next was unoccu-
ynde having moved out of it a few days
. The next was occupied as a dry goods
ry store by James Porter, the village
whose goods there was an insurance of
ıis gentlemen lost very heavily, some-
$2,000 over and above his insurance.
l, of Fullarton, owned the next building,
r $700. It was occupied by O. Sinclair,
vare store, whose stock was insured for
The next was a brick building, owned by
Miller, of Hibbert, damaged about $300.
nce. Peterson & Hueston were the oc-
general merchants; stock saved, but in
ımaged state. Insured for $2,000. In
ilding were four families, all of whom
r furniture, but in a damaged condition.
ıı to those losses, there were several
lings and a large quantity of fire-wood
"

Ætna Live Stock Insurance Company,
:d, which stopped some time since, offers
mise with Canadian claimants at 50 per
he amount of such claims—a very good
n of the wisdom of exacting a deposit
gn insurance companies.

Financial.

ORONTO STOCK MARKET.

(eported by Pellatt & Osler, Brokers.)

s has been very inactive for the past
vernment and County Bonds continue
avorite investment.

ocks.—Sales of Montreal were made at
45½ during the week, but closed in de-
46, and no sellers under 147. Buyers
e 105 for British America, with little
Small Sales of Ontario were made at
offering under 100½. Toronto is offer-
with no buyers over 120. Some sales
anadian were made at 79, sellers gene-
g 80. Commerce sold at 102 and 102½,
offering at that rate. Transactions in
ported at 38½ and 39, closing heavy at
rate. Sales of Merchants' were made
ıd there is little demand. Quebec has
to 102½, with little in market. Sales
's were made at 108½ and 109. For
euple 108 would be paid ; little doing.
ırtier is wanted at 109 ; none offering
No Union in market ; 105 and 105½
aid. Transfer books of Nationale and
closed. City nominal.

es.—No Canada of any kind offering.
Stock is still in demand at 107. To-
nal ; none offering. First-class County
at very high rates.

.—Small sales of City Gas were made
hich rate is still offered. There were
s in British America Assurance at 55½
ales of Canada Permanent Building So-
made at 125½ and 126 ; there are buyers at the former and sellers at the latter rate. Small lots of Western Canada B. S. are offering at 121 ; transactions unimportant. Large sales of Freehold B. S. were made at 112½, which rate would still be paid. Seventy-nine would be paid for Canada Landed Credit ; none on the market. Several mortgages have been placed during the week to pay from 8 to 10 per cent. Money continues scarce, and high rates are paid on first-class paper.

BANKING AND CURRENCY.—The Commons Committee on Banking is composed of the following :—Sir John A. Macdonald, Messrs. Rose, J. S. Macdonald, Wood, Mackenzie, Gibbs, Blake, Sir G. E. Cartier, Galt, Holton, Chauveau, Dunkin, Tilley, Smith, D. A. Macdonald and Campbell.

A STATEMENT *of the engagements which the Dominion has to meet at an early date.—Approximate.*

Amount of Loan due to the Province of Ontario		$ 500,000
Amount payable to do. on 29th Sept., on account of subsidy		300,000
Amount for redemption of 7 per cent. debentures, due 1st. September		887,000
Amount of loans per Bank of Montreal, due on 30th September	$1,000,000	
Amount do. 31st December	1,500,000	
		2,500,000
Amount payable on account of Nova Scotia and New Brunswick, on account of works		700,000
Amount balances due to financial agents in London		973,333
Total		$5,860,333

Finance Department, Ottawa,
August, 27th, 1868.

A STATEMENT *of the amount deposited on account of the Intercolonial Loan, together with other balances available to the Government.—Approximate.*

Deposit on account Intercolonial Loan	$2,000,000
Balances in Banks in Canada	1,200,000
Instalments on account—	
Intercolonial Loan payable in October	2,500,000
Bank balance on account of silver	500,000
Total	$6,200,000

Finance Department, Ottawa,
August 27th, 1868.

BANK OF UPPER CANADA.—In the House of Commons, on Friday, the 23d,

Mr. Mackenzie moved for copies of all correspondence between the Government and the Trustees appointed, under Cap. 17, 31st Vic., on the Corporation of the Bank of Upper Canada, and copies of all Orders in Council or other documents connected therewith. He explained that when the Bill of last session passed the House there was a general demand that there should be an enquiry into the winding up of the affairs of the institution. He was satisfied that the trust reposed in the Trustees had not been exercised with the accuracy and despatch that should have been used. He did not desire to enter upon a discussion of the matter. He merely gave his reasons for asking for the documents to such an extent as the Government see fit to bring down. It was a matter which required considerable discussion ; but he would cheerfully hold to the decision of the Government.

Mr. Rose thought that he (Mr. Mackenzie) was right in asking for these papers, as the Bank of Upper Canada was an institution of public interest.

Mr. Street was sure the trustees were exercising their rights by all possible means to convert the property to the interest of the shareholders, and all interested in the winding up of the estate.

Mr. Mackenzie did not question the honesty of the trustees ; but he thought there was not the proper expedition used.

—A general meeting of the creditors of W. R. Brown & Co., was held on the 27th. Their liabilities are stated at $115,640, of which $25,000 was secured by mortgage; $7,500 are immediately available. The assignee stated that the estate shows about five cents in the dollar. The Royal Canadian Bank has fyled a bill for the forclosure of a mortgage held by the Bank, but the assignee has fyled an answer to that bill. Efforts are being made to get hold of Brown's property in the States. A bill has also been fyled to set aside the settlement made on Mrs. Chewett.

Railway News.

GREAT WESTERN RAILWAY.—Traffic for week ending April 9, 1869.

Passengers	$31,074 08
Freight	57,283 86
Mails and Sundries	2,173 54
Total Receipts for week	$90,531 48
Coresponding week, 1868	88,042 17
Increase	$2,489 20

NORTHERN RAILWAY.—Traffic receipts for week ending April 17th, 1869.

Passengers	$2,711 05
Freight and live stock	8,423 78
Mails and sundries	260 20
	$11,395 03
Corresponding Week of '68	11,303 60
Increase	$91 43

FARES BY THE PACIFIC RAILWAY.—First-class passage by rail from New York to Chicago, a distance of 960 miles, costs 2½ cents a mile. At the same rate a first class passage from New York to San Francisco would cost about $82.50 in greenbacks. The present charges on the Pacific Railroad are at the rate of 5 cents per mile on the Union, and 10 cents per mile, gold, on the Central. At these figures, and reducing the charges to gold rates, calculating 75 cents on the dollar, we get the following approximate estimates of the cost of a first class through ticket :

	Miles.	*Fare.*
New York to Chicago	900	$18.75
Chicago to Omaha	496	17.53
Omaha to Salt Lake	1,070	40.13
Salt Lake to San Francisco	775	77.50
Total	3,299	$153.91

In the statement of distances, six miles should be added for ferriage from Oakland to San Francisco, making a total of 3,305 miles. We have assumed that the Union and Central Pacific will meet at the head of Salt Lake, 775 miles east of the Bay of San Francisco. For this distance, not quite one-fourth of the entire distance to New York, the charge on the Central Pacific is a little over that for the remaining three-fourths of the journey. The company has given a promise, which its interests will require it to keep, materially to reduce its rates of fare in July next ; when, we may presume, they will not exceed the rate charged on the Union Pacific, and between Chicago and Omaha, and which we have placed at five cents in currency. This would reduce the charge on the Central to $38.75 gold, and the cost of a through trip to $115.16.

COAL MINES.—We regret to learn that the fire in the Foord Pit, Albion Mines, is likely to prove a more serious affair than was one time anticipated. On Wednesday evening last, several explosions occurred, since which time we have not learned any further particulars.—*Eastern Chronicle*, 3rd *April.*

THE CANADIAN MONETARY TIMES AND INSU-
RANCE CHRONICLE *is printed every Thursday evening and distributed to Subscribers on the following
morning.*

*Publishing office, No. 60 Church-street, 3 doors
north of Court-street.*

Subscription price—

Canada $2.00 per annum.

England, stg. 10s. per annum.

United States (U.S.Cy.) $3.00 per annum.

*Casual advertisements will be charged at the rate
of ten cents per line, each insertion.*

*Address all letters to "*THE MONETARY TIMES.*"
*Cheques, money orders, &c. should be pay-
able to J. M. TROUT, Business Manager, who alone
is authorized to issue receipts for money.*

All Canadian Subscribers to THE MONETARY
TIMES *will receive* THE REAL ESTATE JOURNAL
without further charge.

The Canadian Monetary Times.

THURSDAY, APRIL 29, 1869.

MR. KING AND THE NEW BANKING SCHEME.

As it is well known that Mr. King, the manager of the Bank of Montreal, is, if not the prime mover, at least the active and energetic promoter of the proposed new system of banking with which we are threatened, it may be instructive to endeavour to discover the motives which prompted his now line of action. His Provincial note venture fully equalled his expectations, as he took care to have the manipulation of the legal tenders himself, and the Bank of Montreal, of course, profited enormously by it. The country was robbed, the other banks were threatened and the Bank of Montreal reaped all the benefit. Mr. King is too able a manager either to sug-gest or support any change which would bring disadvantage to his institution, so we may take it for granted that no banking scheme would number him among its supporters, if it were likely to deprive the Bank of Montreal

of its vantage ground or of its immense profits. Last year that bank added no less than $250,090 to its rest. At the Annual Meeting Mr. King said "the Committee of the Legis-lature *might* introduce a different banking system and I think it of very great conse-quence that our rest be increased so that we may be able to meet any phase of the ques-tion". This statement was made so long ago as June last. Mr. King must have had, therefore, a pretty fair idea of what was coming, and it is now generally understood, that he has had a hand in framing or revising the proposed Government measure.

The Bank of Montreal is a wealthy institu-tion. It has to work with

Capital paid up....................	$6,000,000
Circulation............................	238,000
Deposits..............................	14,015,000
Total	$20,302,000

Its money is thus invested,—

Coin, Provincial and other bank notes.................................	$3,775,200
Government securities.............	92,400
In hands of foreign bankers.......	5,494,600
Bills discounted, real estate and other debts in Canada............	13,235,800
Total	$22,598,000

This shows a surplus of $2,295,000, or over 38 per cent. above its whole capital.

All the other banks have the following amount to work with :—

Capital paid up	$24,788,300
Circulation.............................	9,617,000
Deposits..............................	22,961,200
Total......................	$57,367,000

Their money is thus invested,—

Coin, Provincial and other bank notes.................................	$7,936,200
Government securities...............	3,025,800
In hands of foreign banks, bills discounted, real estate, and other debts in Canada............	47,417,000
Total......................	$59,226,900

The proportion which these investments bear to the capital, and other funds placed in their hands, to work with, may be thus stated :

	B'k of Montreal.		Other B'ks.	
Coin and notes, ...	18½ p. c.		14 p. c.	
Government securities...	½ "		5⅛ "	
Investments with foreign banks...................	2 "		1½ "	
Investments in Canada..	65½ "		82½ "	

In giving these figures, we would again re-mind our readers of what has already been shewn in these columns, that they are no criterion of the relative strength of the Bank of Montreal and the other banks, because the Bank of Montreal, as financial agent of the Government, is at any moment liable to be called on to redeem a very large propor-tion of the Provincial notes in the hands of the other banks, and in circulation.

We presuppose that the proposed scheme of banking is, substantially, that the whole

of the banks shall deposit the amount of circulation with the Government, and, in sideration thereof, that the banks sha allowed six per cent. interest on that am by the Government, and that the Gov ment shall redeem the debentures at pr held by the banks, and guarantee the circulation of the country; the banks, present, redeeming their circulation and d sits, in specie, on demand. Under this sch if adopted, the banks would have to over to the Bank of Montreal, as fina agent of the Government, an amount to their circulation, or say $9,617,500. W is this sum to be obtained ? According t best authorities the banks would still ha hold one-fifth of their deposits availabl actual specie, unless they followed the e ple of the Bank of Montreal, and called own notes or "Provincial notes," speci that they could only spare out of their sent cash about $3,300,000. Then they the Government debentures, $3,025,800, the balances with foreign banks, $847, These three items make a total of $7,172, But between this sum, and the amou circulation as above stated, ($9,617,500) t is a difference of $2,444,700, which w have to be raised in some way, and the way would be by reducing discounts. So at the first start off the already contr discounts would have to be reduced, at by about two millions and a-half of do This is putting the matter in its most derate light. A bank could not leave without a considerable sum in its vault general use ; so that the margin, so hel each bank, would, in the aggregate, amou a great deal which would necessarily r discounts still further. Then, if they de with Government, the full amount of meximum circulation, the evil would b creased immensely. What does our com cial community think of a prospect so sant ? The point is simple and clear, the figures given show, in a slight degr portion of the immediate effects. The b will have to pay nine and a-half millions, having only seven millions to pay it must needs make up the balance by cout ing discounts to the extent of the differ What say our merchants ? What say all new railway companies, and those abou launch out into new enterprizes ? The York *Financial Chronicle*, speaking of experience of the New York merchants u the National Bank system, says: "A sp cause of embarrassment to business has arisen from the abnormal condition of currency system, resulting in frequent sp in the money market, and rendering it in sible for merchants to get needful accom dation from the banks ; this difficulty ha been but little less felt in the country a

in the city, where for several weeks
n impossible to get the best paper
d at less than 10 to 12 per cent."
bable effect of the proposed scheme
Bank of Montreal would be some-
the following:—As financial agent
vernment it would receive from the
ks $9,617,500, less the amount of
nt debentures, $3,025,800, which
ual $6,591,700. This is the sum
ld be placed in its hands, on account
vernment, and its working capital
thereby increased from $20,303,000
,700.
e the Government might, and pro-
ld withdraw a portion of this amount
ank's hands, but that very with-
uld be for payment of public works,
e Intercolonial Railway, &c., which
re the bank a circulation equal to
it so withdrawn. In other words,
working fund would not be de-
all by such withdrawal, for as the
nt balance would decrease, the cir-
ould increase, and Mr. King would
th himself, as financial agent, the
f such increased circulation, and
per cent. interest upon it. A very
ortion of this $6,591,700 would
main in the bank's hands for some
ly rate, for various purposes, allowing the present legal tenders, as
a specie reserve, to be held against
d be a new guarantee fund neces-
eet demands by banks when their
became reduced. Mr. King, we
have the use of it for a consider-
for good or evil.
ther banks would have to curtail
unts, to meet the demand for a
nt deposit of such a large sum as
ns and a half of dollars, the effect
felt in the increased stringency
ey market. Mr. King being the
f this two millions- and a half,
enabled to extend his operations
r banks contracted theirs. Who is
rofit by this? the very cream of
nt accounts would leave the other
, of course, the Bank of Montreal
them for the taking.
pect that the Bank of Montreal's
money, in the hands of foreign
es not include gold loans in New
our suspicion is correct, why does
hold five and a half millions in
it one and a half per cent. when he
much per day in New York for it?
e purpose of reducing the Govern-
ice here, to the minimum, by paying
entures, with Intercolonial railway
explained by the Finance Minister
nd then coercing the Government
unds are all exhausted and money

is required for the actual construction of that
railway. Suppose the Government should
find that no more funds could be got from an.
additional issue of legal tenders, or, at least;
not enough to meet current demands, what
new concession might not Mr. King ask.
Suppose he bought up the legal tenders, and
made a run upon himself, as the financial
agent of the Government. The Government
would have to suspend specie payments, or
give Mr. King any rate he liked to ask for a
loan or for exchange.

Who is Mr. King, and what is the Bank of
Montreal that they should be allowed to
take the Dominion of Canada by the throat?
Note the position of the Bank of Montreal
and that of the other banks, as regards the
actual facilities they at present afford the mercantile community. The Bank of Montreal
gives in the shape of advances, in Canada,
about 65½ of its available funds, and sends
27 per cent. out of the country. The other
banks give 82¾ of their available funds, in
advances, in Canada, and keep a reserve of
only 1½ per cent. abroad. Would Mr. King
give the needful additional accommodation
which the other banks would be compelled to
withdraw? He might take that course. Much
would depend on the state of affairs in Canada; very much would depend on the state
of the gold market in New York. With six
and a half millions to invest, he might place
it in foreign banks, and he might place it in
discounts in Canada. The power would be in
Mr. King's own hands, and his movements up
to the present lead to the belief that he
would not hesitate to exhibit it.

TORONTO, GREY AND BRUCE RAIL-WAY.

After the experience that the people of this
country have had in the expenditure of money
on railway projects, and with the knowledge
of what is thought abroad of Canadian railway investments, it appears, at the first sight,
little short of temerity on the part of the
promoters of these two new undertakings—
the Toronto, Grey and Bruce, and Toronto
and Nipissing Railways—to ask from the citizens of Toronto and the inhabitants of the
surrounding country no less a sum than two
or three millions of dollars, for railway purposes. The subscribers to the stock of the
Grand Trunk have not yet received a farthing
of dividend on their investment. The original stockholders of the Northern Railway
have not realized any return for their money;
and so with other roads. Under these circumstances, it is surprising that such a remarkable degree of confidence should be
shewn in the success of these narrow guage
railways, as is apparent from the readiness

with which leading business men subscribe
for the stock. After a careful examination
of the facts and statements presented, we.
give it as our firm belief, that the shares of
the Toronto, Grey and Bruce Railway will
prove a paying investment; and this belief. is
much strengthened by the circumstance that
the control of the whole enterprise will be
vested in a Board of the most respectable of
our city merchants, the value of whose property and business depends largely on the
success of the enterprise.

The Grand Trunk Railway and its subsidi-
ary lines cost $74,683 per mile; the Great
Western cost $70,340 per mile; the Northern
cost $56,411 per mile; the London and Port
Stanley cost $43,035 per mile; the Ottawa.
and Prescott cost $37,204 per mile; the Port
Hope and Lindsay cost $35,285 per mile; the
Welland $64,914 per mile, and the Brockville
and Ottawa $30,601 per mile.

The directors of the Toronto, Grey and
Bruce,—basing their statement on the report
of their engineers, who examined the most
difficult section on the route,—assure us that
their road can be constructed on the three.
feet-six-inch. gauge for $15,000 per mile.
This is one-half the sum expended on the
cheapest railway in the above list, or about
one-fifth the cost per mile of the Grand
Trunk.

But will a road so cheaply constructed accommodate the local traffic? Will it serve
the district and the stockholders as well, or
nearly as well, as a road of greater cost and
greater capacity? The directors meet this
point by citing the case of a Welsh two-feet
railway which accommodates a freight and
passenger traffic closely approximating to that
of the Northern. It is scarcely possible to
doubt that three-foot-six railways have, in
other countries, carried more freight and
passengers than are likely to fall into the
way of the Toronto, Grey and Bruce Railway
for a quarter of a century to come.

The capacity of this road for carrying the
requisite traffic being conceded, it is worth
worth while to enquire, Will that traffic be
forthcoming? The directors very properly
appeal to the experience of the Northern
Railway to prove that it will. The country
through which this road will pass is not less
fertile nor less productive of traffic, in the
aggregate, than that traversed by the Northern. True, there will not be the heavy export movement of lumber and timber, but
this, it is believed, will be more than compensated for by a greater supply of cereals,
cattle, and general farm produce. The gross
receipts are, therefore, estimated at $490,000,
or nearly $48,000 less than the local receipts
of the Northern last year. The working expenses are put at 60 per cent, leaving $196,-

000 as the net earnings available for the payment of interest, dividends, &c.

Let us now see how the account stands. There are already bonuses pledged to the amount of $425,000. The directors say that there are $77,000 yet to come by way of bonus. But let us suppose that they get half that amount, or in round numbers, $40,-000, then we have—

Capital required for first section $1,050,000
Less bonuses obtained.....$425,000
 " " expected..... 40,000
                                        —————— $465,000

Leaving to be raised $585,000

or, say $600,000. One-half of this sum, $300,000, it is proposed to raise by subscription, and the rest by a mortgage bearing interest at, say, eight per cent. It is clear that the owners of the $300,000 of stock would be the proprietors of the entire undertaking, and after paying the interest on 300,000 per annum, or $24,000 (interest at 8 per cent), would be entitled to divide the remainder of the net earnings as a dividend among themselves. Taking the estimate of the company's engineers, these net earnings would be $196,000, or after paying interest, $172,000, which would give something handsome in the way of a dividend. But supposing the cost of construction is underrated and the traffic overrated, there would still be an *ample margin* of profit. The work is in good hands, and is not likely to be saddled with fat contracts or burdened with expensive appointments. It will be supervised by the men who have put their money into it, and who have the deepest interest in its success. If the company's engineers can give us a road of the quality of construction and adequacy of equipment promised, and at the cost stated, the conclusion follows irresistibly that the stock of this road must prove one of the most profitable investments ever offered to the public of this country.

PAMPHLET ON BANKING AND CURRENCY.—Mr. Jack, Cashier of the Peoples Bank, of Halifax has published, in pamphlet form, his very able letters to the local press on the subject of Banking and Currency. After disposing of Senator Wilmott's wild proposition to substitute a government irredeemable currency, for the bank note circulation, he shows how the present banking system has assisted the development of the Provinces, and whatever loss has been occasioned by one or two bank failures has been amply compensated for in the general benefit resulting from the operations of the banks. In Nova Scotia there never has been a bank failure. With reference to the notes issued by the government of Nova Scotia he says, "it has often been difficult to obtain specie for them, as they are not at all redeemable in specie, and holders have sometimes found trouble in paying their debts with them." On the subject of loss, he asserts "that there have been fewer losses

to the holders of bank notes in these colonies than in any other country which possesses a similar bank note circulation, or one based on government securities." His advice to the government is to let the present system alone. The pamphlet thoughout is full of information, and the argument is well sustained.

INTERCOLONIAL RAILWAY.—There were 82 tenders for section No. 5, varying from $361,574 or $13,907 per mile to $1,014,000 or $39,000 per mile. The successful tenderer is Edward Haycock, of Ottawa, at the first named amount. For section 6 there were 85, ranging from $241,500 or $11,500 per mile to $674,560 or $27,359. The contract was awarded to Jacques Jobin, of Levis. For section 7 there were 82 tenders, from $358,-248 or $11,927 to $1,008,000 or $42,000 per mile. The contract was awarned to H. J. Sutton & Co., at $413,995 or $17,248 per mile.

Mining.

MADOC GOLD DISTRICT.

(From Our Own Correspondent.)

BELLEVILLE, April 26th, 1869.

As spring is now advancing, some of your readers are no doubt desirous of hearing what is being done, or likely to be done, in this district. Very little is being done just now, and the prospect of what is going to be done is rather gloomy at present. Of all the quartz-mills which have been put up in the Madoc region, eight in number, not one is running at this time ; and it is likely that some of them will not resume working at their present location.

The Richardson Company have stopped working, chiefly on account of the inefficient manner in which their shaft, &c., was originally laid out, rendering it impossible to get out the ore from the mine without incurring a much greater cost than the produce will repay. It is not likely that work will be resumed before the Sheriff's sale comes off, when the future ownership of the property will be determined.

The Severn mill is undergoing repairs, some of the gearing, &c., being badly damaged. The mill at the Barry Mine, in Elziver, is laid in ; the announcement of the settlement of disputes among the shareholders being premature, as a law-suit is pending among them. The Merchant's Union Company have not yet determined what course to adopt as to the contemplated alterations in their mill, and are consequently doing nothing either in mining or milling. Mr. Berry's operations in Addington County are also suspended, although the construction of his apparatus is said to be excellent, and its operation quite satisfactory. He has evidently been misled as to the quantity of free or amalgamable gold contained in the rock of his mineral veins. The Anglo-Saxon mill is in the same state as when last reported on. The Eldorado mill has been removed to Marmora township, and will shortly be employed in crushing ore from some of the veins discovered in that township last fall. The mill at Bannockburn, belonging to the Toronto and Whitby Mining Company, after running a few days, and having some of the shoes of the muller broken, has been stopped. The damaged parts have been sent into Belleville for repair. The Company at Mallorytown, county of Leeds, have got their machinery completed, and I expect to hear of their shortly going into operation.

The reduction works of Messrs. Jones & Robbins, lot 23 in the 12th concession of Hungerford, have been, idle all winter. It will be recollect-

ed that some of the "matt" from these wo (which were built for operating with the Steph flux) was sent by the proprietors to Swans Wales, for reduction ; but the report received ing unfavorable, it is uncertain whether they resume operations or not. It turns out, as I ticipated, that their ore is too poor to be profit reduced by smelting with this or any other flu its native or unconcentrated state. This int seems to be the case with most of the ores of region. Free gold—that is, gold in its meta state, uncombined with sulphuretted matter— not exist in our rocks in sufficient quantity give returns by mill-amalgamation, except i few localities ; though both fire-assay and hu analysis prove that the sulphides of some of veins contain gold, either pure or alloyed v silver and other metals, in paying quantities, occasionally are very rich. These precious met however, are so combined with the pyrites t they cannot be taken up by quicksilver ; and proportion of the sulphides to the bulk of rock as it comes from the mine is so small a preclude profitable smelting or roasting ; so t the only prospect of remunerative mining is submitting the ores to the process of dry crush and concentration, before desulphurization final reduction.

But to attain this end (remuneration) in highest degree, the miner must avail himsel the improvements lately introduced into t several branches of his pursuit. Crushers v revolving discs ; concentrators on the principle the one described and figured in the *Amer. Journal of Mining* of Feb. 20th, 1869. Roast furnaces in which the concentrated ore is desul urized by dropping through flame, and is receiv into water. All these pieces of apparatus do t work cheaply, rapidly and effectually ; and one, after being submitted to their action may treated for the collection of the gold, &c., eit by amalgamation, by smelting, or by chlorinati which last process is being introduced with g success into the mining operations of the Pa States.

Communications.

LONDON CORRESPONDENCE.

To the Editor of the Monetary Times.

LONDON, April 8, 186

The agitation for a reform of life assurance c panies increases daily. All the leading newspap contain articles or letters from correspondents on subject. Both the critiques and the complaints very bitter. In one case the ludicrous is blen with imposture. This is the company to wh I referred a few weeks ago without mention names. Since then the Secretary has had to year and give evidence in a court of Justice. revelations then made took many persons aba They are not, however, by any means startlin those whose knowledge of what goes on beh the scenes is in excess of that of the general pub This company is named the "National and Pro cial Union Assurance and Loan Society." It formed on the 23rd of last month, with a cap of £10,000, in shares of £1 each. The direc were men living in the most expensive and a trocratic quarter of the metropolis. On clos inquiry it was found that although these direc did live at the addresses given, yet they li there as servants, and not as householders. deed, they were butlers in respectable and weal families. The company's articles of associa are couched in high-flown terms. It is tl said that the operations of the company are to be confined to London, and that "it is inte ed to establish in many of the large towns of Empire local boards of directors, who will ad the resources of the Society by developing business of the institution, and giving confid to a large circle of policyholders. By this m ciety's influence will develop an amount of ls which a purely London board could accomplish." While we laugh at this affect of the butlers to mystify the public, let it forgotten that their masters have set them imple. Even companies managed by those m confidence is reposed, do not escape adriticism, and probably deserve it. As an .e of this, let me cite the statement made correspondent in the *Daily News* of this g. Referring to the Prudential Assurance, that the difficulty is to ascertain when a ry is justified in boasting, as that one does, great success it has achieved, adding that, ag to the report for last year, "its total tee fund is £241,301·12s. 6d., and that its u's premium?" Meantime, Mr. Cave's bill d a second time last night in the House of nns. There is a probability of its being 2d in committee so as to become a useful ctical measure.

re quitting this subject, let me furnish a ures which have recently been compiled gard to the companies designed to extend vantages of life assurance to the poorer The expenses of management in these les is enormous. In one case, where the eceipts were £94,000, the outlay for man-t was £36,000. In another it was dis-that £6,000 more were paid away in cer-ars than the receipts! This is the more ensured if it be true, as has been stated, me of the oldest and best companies in r cent. in management. Unfortunately, r, the poor are the easy victims of swin-for they believe the promises made, and risk without counting the cost. Yet the well-to-do cannot be absolved from a reck-r as gross as that of the working man who his life in an insolvent company. Ac-to a statement published in the *Pall Mall* last night, the income of the gaming f Germany amount to about half a million g, while the total staked in the course of a seventeen millions! If to this could be he sums risked in betting at horse-racing, peculative" tendencies of the age would an illustration which would startle the s in progress.

only recognized gambling here in England llock Exchange. At present there is little a doing there. That section of the pub-ch delights in speculation still keeps aloof le scene of its losses. The demand for the Bank of England still continues, not-nding the advance last week of the rate of t from 3 to 4 per cent. It is believed that of the American eagles have been shut-from the cellars of the Bank. At one time said that there was a larger stock of Ame-ld coin in the Bullion Office of the Bank and than in the United States. Patriotic ans will now rejoice at the thought that ld has returned home. It is to be hoped will remain there, and become before long rency of the country. However, the trade rrency of England being established on a asis, the flow of gold to America does not the accumulation of as much bullion in ars of the Bank as can be desired. And nd the Continent furnish supplies which ll up the temporary gap. Against the) worth taken away for exportation must £150,000 which have arrived during the

pplication has just been made to the in-public on behalf of three companies form-the purposes of gold mining and quartz

crushing. Two of these companies will conduct their operations in Australia ; the third will develop the gold fields of New Zealand. The capital of the two Australian companies exceeds half a million sterling. It is noteworthy that the gold mining companies are seldom formed here with a view to conduct operations in Australia. There is capital enough there for the purpose. Besides, the Australians are too shrewd to allow a good thing to slip through their fingers. Out of the many companies projected here when gold was first discovered in Australia, but one survives. This is the "Port Philip and Colonial Gold Mining Company." It has proved a success. The shares are at nearly 100 per cent. premium. Yet the success of companies formed on the spot has been far greater. Hence there is a reluctance to embark capital in schemes which are not supported in the Colony. It was the same, I should think, in Nova Scotia. The mines which yield returns there are in the hands of persons well acquainted with the locality. A company which was formed here for the purpose of working a Nova Scotian gold mine became popular for a time ; its shares were quoted at a large premium, but its shareholders are not to be envied. The company is now wound up, I suppose ; at all events, its name has disappeared from the share list. The most successful gold mining companies, having their headquarters in London, are those which carry on operations in Brazil. Some of them have proved most remunerative. In the case of one not many years old, the shares on which 14s. are paid cannot be purchased under £5. The shareholders receive yearly a sum equivalent to their capital in the shape of dividends. It is hardly necessary to add that this company is an exception.

PROVINCIAL INSURANCE COMPANY.

To the Editor of the Monetary Times.

TORONTO, April 28, 1869.

SIR,—Accept the thanks of a large insurer for the plain and masterly manner you have exposed the standing of the Provincial Insurance Company. I trust you will do the same with every suspicious corporation that the public depend upon for security. It cannot be too strongly urged on the attention of the insurer that security is the first disideratum in all insurance transactions, and that his object is not attained unless the event or contingency against which he wishes to guard is provided for from the moment he has paid his premium, under all possible circumstances. It is, therefore, manifest that the capital of an insurance company should be sufficiently large to meet all possible demands, with a proportionate reserve fund, and that its amount should be distinctly stated, or shown how invested, in order that its entire sufficiency to meet all claims may plainly appear. By the Provincial Company's own showing, they are far from being in the desired position as security to the insurance public.

Yours truly,

A CONSTANT READER AND A LARGE INSURER.

—Notices of application from the Erie and Niagara Extension Railway Company and Erie and Niagara Railway Company to the next Dominion Parliament for powers authorizing both or either of these railway companies to construct and operate for a railway or other purposes a bridge over or a tunnel under Niagara River, or near Fort Erie, in the County of Welland, to co-operate in construction and management with any similar corporate powers existing within the State of New York, or to be created by the Congress of the United States; said bridge to have 250 feet span, to rise above high-water mark 20 feet, to be of stone or iron piers, or wrought iron or steel superstructure, and to have a draw of 270 feet for vessels.

THE NEW ENGLISH BANKRUPTCY BILL.

Another attempt is about being made to establish such an equilibrium of opinion as will be equally acceptable to the creditor, the debtor and the public. The task will tax all the energies of the many legislators upon whose shoulders and by whose strength it will be supported. The proposal is to make a clean sweep in the beginning, by turning adrift the highest officials to the lowest and poorest hangers-on, superanuating some, and leaving the touting many to burrow as they can into the new warren. The basis of the new plan proposed is ostensibly for the benefit of the creditors, to whom great concessions are to be made, in the way of prevention rather than of cure; a rather doubtful case, which calls upon the creditors, after losing their money, to lose their time also. The first thing proposed is, when a man is made a bankrupt by his creditors, or when he suffers judgment to go by default, he should be adjudged bankrupt, and then his creditors would be called together to determine upon the right of different creditors to vote ; this is to be done under the supervision of the Court, there being then three courses open to them. They might accept a composition and there end the affair, the bankruptcy terminating ; they may agree to a deed of arrangement, proceed to elect a trustee from among themselves or other acceptable person, deciding upon his remuneration, whose duties would be to receive proof of debts and determine on them, subject to an appeal to the Court, realise assets, declare dividends, and have power to wind up the estates. As an additional security, an inspector (so termed) may be appointed to watch over the trustee, the accounts to be audited by the accountant in bankruptcy, the whole under the supervision of the Judge, who will also have the power to appoint a receiver, on the application of the creditors, having also the power to supersede the bankruptcy. The third course is, under justifiable circumstances, to bring the debtor into a criminal court. The object of the bankruptcy being for the benefit of the creditors, not for the bankrupt, the latter will not be permitted to make a bankrupt of himself, which provision was accorded to him when imprisonment for debt was exacted. It is also proposed to hold the bankrupt in after-acquired property for six years, unless he has before that time paid a certain amount of dividend, say 10s. in the pound ; the property only to be liable on the order of the Court. As a matter of course the creditors can release him from these responsibilities. Acts coming under the denomination of fraud, fraudulent concealment, obtaining goods while in a state of hopeless insolvency, &c., to be tried before the judges of the land, the laws on these heads being made more stringent. It is also proposed that all post-nuptial settlements made by a bankrupt, if between two years of the bankruptcy, unless he can prove that he was solvent at the time, shall be absolutely void.

The commencement of the programme reads well, so far as concerns the real interests of the creditors themselves, it being left to them to take the wisest course, and compromise, or get what they can from the estates and effects of the bankrupts ; and in ordinary cases it is all that the creditor can reasonably require : but, in failures to a large amount, the creditors have before them nearly all the machinery, and all the evils and inconveniences, of the present system—fees, receivers appointed by the court to assist, accountants who know so well how to take the cream from the milk ; fees of court, and the chance of being called upon to appear as prosecutor or witness at the Old Bailey, or any other criminal court. It is true, Commissioners of Bankruptcy vanish, but a well-paid Judge is to supply their place. Another onerous thing is, that when a man, being called upon to pay a debt, does not come into court, he should be made a bankrupt. This negatives at once the decaration that no man shall make himself a bankrupt, a friend being substituted for himself, a friend not difficult to find on such occasions. Again, fraudulent motives shown are to be taken as proofs of guilt, not adduced by the creditor in accordance with the laws of the land, but to be disproved by the the debtor arraigned as a criminal. Again, he is called upon to furnish proof of his solvency when he made a post-nuptial settlement. The most honorable man, failing under circumstances over which he had no control, might be subjected to this ordeal, being called upon at short notice, and the means taken from him to furnish proofs involving expenses far beyond his means. In this free country, no man has a right to be called upon to indirectly criminate himself by failing to prove a negative.

The Scotch system of bankruptcy is acknowledged on all hands to work well. While securthe relics of the property of the defaulter from waste, or being legally frittered away, it effectually guards against the many open and barefaced frauds so much and so justly complained of as taking place in the Bankruptcy Court of Eng-England; and also against the rapacity of the *attachés* and parasites that find a living in the wreck, leaving little or nothing for the creditors. The bill may, with an immensity of tinkering, be made a good one, but moulded as it will be under a multitude of clauses, it will never be acceptable to the mercantile and trading classes if a loophole is left for the great defaulter to escape, while the trumpery scape-goat is sacrificed at the altar of public opinion. It is of no use saving the cheese-paring while the mice are actively devouring the interior. It is no satisfaction to the creditor to be called upon all trifling occasions to confront a petty larceny rogue at the bar of a criminal court. Devise means to prevent a crime, rather than frame modes for punishing it. Simplify the law, but do not encourage those who imagine they can speculate in giving credit on the strength of its stringent powers. It would be better to cling to imprisonment for debt than subject the innocent of intention with the guilty to the crucial test of an Old Bailey prosecution on questionable or debatable ground. Make the strictest inquisition into their affairs and the cause of default, but do it free from passion or prejudice; and avoid law whenever it may be avoided. As so much is said in praise of the Scotch system, why not give it a fair trial, with such additional clauses only as are imperatively required for this country.—*Investors' Guardian.*

DOMINION TELEGRAPH COMPANY.

(From the Northern Gazette.)

The readers of the *Gazette* have had their attention drawn to the above Company at various times, and certain features presented which appear anything but complimentary to the management. Extensive criticism on the part of the press and individuals has only served to reveal more glaringly the inception and consummation of immense jobs, the culminating one being in the letting of a contract for building two thousand miles of line at a price just double the full value of the work.

That the Dominion Telegraph Company was a speculation of outside adventurers we well know; but that a body of Canadian merchants could be found to wink at gross irregularities, we hesitated to believe, until recent investigations proved the fact. It is certainly a new order of things in our unassuming country, to find the Dominion directors knowingly sanctioning the absorption of $250,000 of the capital stock of the Company, despising the slow process of earning profits before using them, and avoiding, altogether, the commercial risks incidental to a new enterprise. Yet, such is indubitably the case, and the lucky individual who is the medium of all this magnanimity is an unobtrusive young man, by the name of Seela Reeve, whose daily round of duties involves nothing more onerous than a regular appearance at the well-stocked tables of the Rossin House, and a certain stately presence occasionally in the parlors of that famous hostelry. It is a fact for the confiding shareholders to take note of, that $250,000 of the capital stock is yet to be cfilhed from their pockets and absolutely mortgaged to above happy-go-lucky Seela, without a return to the value of a cent being asked for or required. Really, in this age of magnificent charities, we have heard of nothing equal to it, so completely does it stagger our limited comprehension.

Now, as to particulars. Some time since the stockholders at London held a meeting, and resolved to pay no further calls on their stock until more satisfactory information was vouchsafed. Hamilton, Owen Sound and Quebec have followed suit; as yet we have heard nothing to mitigate the case against the Directory. It is admitted a contract, *binding on the Company*, to pay Mr. Reeve, the promoter, contractor, and principal stockholder, the sum of $250 a mile, for two thousand miles of double wire. It is well known that such a line can be built for $150 per mile, which netts a profit of $250,000 on the contract! It is further well understood that the contract with Reeve was originally $400 per mile, and which was modified only by the storm created by the press against the concern and its backers. The directors were a party to both contracts, and the conclusion is almost resistible that Reeve was not the sole participator in the grand spoils.

Such is the present status of the great Dominion Telegraph Company, the Directors of which have already enjoyed one or two public feasts, and given out to the public charming accounts of the progress made. We cannot fancy the stockholders can be further gulled.

DOMINION TELEGRAPH COMPANY.—The Quebec shareholders of this company held a meeting last week, and after hearing the report of Mr. Owen Murphy, who was deputed to Toronto to get a statement of the company's affairs, resolved that, "The gentlemen who have lent their names as Directors to the Dominion Telegraph Company are highly censurable for not attaching more moral importance to the obligation incurred by them as Directors." And further, "That the information furnished by Mr. Murphy, proves it to be unsound in its inception and in all its management, and that the meeting by this resolution binds itself to resist the payment of any calls made upon such stockholders, the expense of the defence to be borne *pro rata* to their stock." This was amended by adding the words "until such time as a satisfactory account is given." Resolutions of thanks to Mr. E. Wiman and the Montreal *Trade Review* for exposing the affairs of the company and to Mr. Murphy for the valuable services rendered the shareholders by his visit to Toronto.

The above are strong resolutions. Coming, as they do, from a number of gentlemen, members of the Company, who could have no hostility to the project; and this, too, after hearing the circumstances of its organization and management fully explained by one who penetrated to the bottom of it; they must have great weight with the public.

Commercial.

Mr. E. Wiman, of the firm of Dun, Wiman & Co., proprietors of the Mercantile Agency, has supplied a daily city contemporary with some facts and suggestions respecting the present unsatisfactory condition of trade. He says, "a general feeling of apprehension and perceptible want of confidence prevails. Failures are frequent, and disastrous losses loom up at every turn; and, what is worse than all, a very low grade of mercantile morality is painfully prevalent." The primary cause of this we consider to be increased importations of goods. In illustration of this point he gives the following from the Trade Returns Canada.

Imports into Canada (East and West) of kinds of goods from the year 1852 to 1867, clusive:—

	Imports of Dry Goods.	Total Imports.
1852	8,240,640	20,286,494
1853	13,203,076	31,981,436
1854	14,660,684	40,529,322
1855	9,509,773	36,086,169
1856	13,173,288	43,584,387
1857	12,123,511	30,430,596
1858	7,398,904	29,077,858
1859	10,825,564	33,535,912
1860	12,451,125	34,412,431
1861	13,156,397	39,750,161
1862	11,163,239	45,980,939
1863	11,481,107	41,312,204
1864 half year	7,987,919	21,406,712
1864-65	13,546,997	39,851,991
1865-66	19,874,852	48,607,038
1866-67	21,486,754	52,633,676

By a glance at these figures will be seen a v remarkable increase from 1852 to 1856, resulti doubtless, in largely augmenting the crisis of year following. But the increase from 1861 1867 is also very great, especially in dry goods from thirteen to twenty-one millions. The en mous rate, however, of increase will be best se in estimating the per centage as compared with growth of the population.

	1861	1867	Per centage Increas
Population	2,507,675	3,091,000	23¼
Imports of Dry Goods	$13,156,397	$21,486,564	63¼
Total Imports	$39,750,161	$52,633,670	32¼

The population in 1867 is estimated at t annual rate of increase as actually took place ten years previous to the last census, and can be far out of the way.

In addition to the dry goods imported there now four-and-a-half or five millions of dollars m nufactured at home, against about one million 1861; so that adding the home manufactured the imported we have twenty-five millions of d lars of dry goods thrown on the market in 1867 against fourteen millions in 1861—an increase eleven millions of dollars.

This is an increase of at the rate of 78⅝ per ce as against an increase in population of certai not exceeding 25 per cent. In other words, h the quantity of goods thrown upon the mark kept pace only with the increase in population, should have only seventeen and-a-half millio instead of twenty-five millions. In round figu we have been putting dry goods into the count at the rate of $8, in 1867, for each man, wom and child; whereas in 1861 the quantity for ea inhabitant was only $5.60. [There are one or t considerations that have an important bearing the question here raised which Mr. Wiman h not stated. The normal demand for dry goo from consumers has increased much faster than t increase of population. This arises from the i crease of wealth, and hence of purchasing pow giving rise to a desire for more expensive and st lish goods; so that Canadian factory made, a imported cloths, yarns, blankets, &c., have be largely substituted for the coarse woolly hom made articles of which every well-to-do farmer f merly produced, at least, enough for his own requirements. Besides, no account is taken of large quantity of goods annually exported—a gre portion smuggled—since the United States ha raised their import duties to the present hi point. In Secretary Well's last report, he stat if our memory be not at fault, that some fourte millions were annually lost to the revenue this way. So that, in our opinion, Mr. Wima figures put the case a little too strong.—ED. M. T.]

e is then given-showing the relative im-
the principal ports of Ontario, compiled
Andrew Robertson, which has already ap-
a these columns.

iman, very properly, censures the present
lard of credit, and the disposition among
sons, and others, to rush into mercantile
which they are wholly unfit. In conse-
of over-importations, excessive stocks,
essure to sell, merchants encourage these
run accounts with them, foster and nurse
y these accounts on. If the market were
ly supplied with goods, accounts of this
r would never have been undertaken. In
at the present moment, there are three
here there ought to be only two. In illus-
f this Mr. Wiman starts with Chatham.
here are fifty-two stores. He says it is
hat there are more stores in Chatham in
sorted stocks of dry goods are to be found
the whole city of Detroit. Take Gode-
another instance, where may be found
ven dry-goods and grocery stores ; Strat-
St. Mary's 20; Seaforth, a place without
ance eight years ago, 20 ; Brantford, 58 ;
, 25 ; Woodstock, 37 ; St. Catharines, 52.
east of Toronto, we find in Port Hope, 29
ll of more or less importance ; Belleville,
as far east as Renfrew, a town which long
hed its growth, there are now 14 stores.
s needless to mention further instances,
erhaps such towns as Paisley, in which
e 12 stores; Lucknow, 9; Owen Sound,
order to show that in towns, new and old,
allways and off them, the same state of
xists.

nsolvent Law, Mr. Wiman thinks, is not
e of the present state of things, but only
effect of aggravating the complaint. To
what extent the Insolvent Law has been
f, the following statement is given :

t Sept. to Dec. 31st, 1864	487
1865	481
1866	792
1867	772
1868	650
t Jan. to March 31st, 1869	200

al number of insolvents 3,832
s includes traders and non-traders, and
lo' in the earlier years of the law, availed
es of its provisions to get rid of old em-
ents, it is difficult to form an idea from
number of merchants that have failed.

iman then refers to the ease with which
ises are made, as the most alarming fea-
he whole case. If one-third of the retail
to get off without paying one-half their
othing will prevent the other two-thirds
ing the same. With the trade over-
as at present, it is impossible that all
ake an honest living out of a trade that
better done by half the number. Some
; suffer from the ruinous competition, the
u prices, the profitless exchange of goods
money or poor outstandings. Who is
e the sufferer ? It is clear that he who
f his debts at 10s. in the pound has much
of the bargain. While the wholesale
t suffers a direct loss, the honest, capable
A retailer is equally a loser. Take a small
which there are six stores. Two of them
e at five to ten shillings—in other words,
stock and assets at less than half price,
completely can they defy competition
ir solvent and very probably more honest
irs. Is it possible that the four remaining
can live and pay twenty shillings in the
The thing is impossible ; and thus like
playing with a row of bricks on end—
. and the whole lot will fall.

iman then goes on to elaborate this idea,
ludes by making some suggestions in ac-
with the foregoing, which are well worthy.
tion of every one in trade. Importations

of dry goods should, in the first place, be cut
down fifty per cent. ; the present system of granting compositions should be stopped, at once; the
Bankrupt Law should be so amended as to aid the
wholesale merchant in reforming the present ini-
quitous practices; the term of credit should be
shortened, and the system of renewals be done
away with. There are already signs of a better
state of things in the reduced importations of dry
goods within the past year, and in a strong feeling
among merchants in favor of the much needed
changes pointed out.

Toronto Market.

Merchants are acting with great caution in every
branch of the importing trade. They are not
opening new accounts, and are generally very careful about extending old ones. The spring fleet is
now daily arriving at Quebec with the usual stock
of groceries, heavy hardware, crockery, &c. ; those
goods will be to hand shortly.

FLOUR.—Receipts, 2,014 barrels, and 3,350
barrels last week. The market for Superfine is
dull ; the offerings are in excess of the demand ;
sales of one or two 100-barrel lots at $4.05 f. o. b.
Spring Extra has met with some demand ; a lot
of 100 barrels sold at $4.15 on cars. Fancy,
nominal at quotations. Extra held at $4.40 to
$4 50 ; no sales. No Superfine in market.

GRAIN.—Wheat—Receipts, 1,000 bush., and
3,540 last week. The market for Superfine is
state of the English market, there is almost no
demand for Wheat, and only a small business was
done. Spring is dull, and offering at 95c to 96c,
with some small sales at 93c to 94c. Two cars
sold at 94c on Northern cars, and 5,000 bush. at
Whitby on p.t. Fall is held at $1.00 to $1.05,
but it is impossible to say what figures could be
realized for a round lot, as there are no buyers.
Barley—Receipts very small ; market inactive
and few sales. Sale 200 bush. choice White at
$1.04 in store here. Peas—Receipts trifling ;
market steady and unchanged from last week ;
holders ask 80c, and there is some demand for
car loads at four quotations. Oats—Receipts, 500
bush., and 1,300 bush. last week. The market
has ruled firm, but closed with an easier feeling
at 52½c ; sales 500 bush at 52½c delivered in the
city, and two or three cars at 53c on track. Rye—
Nominal at 60c on the street. Seeds—Timothy
is firm, and has advanced, buyers offering $2.40
to $2.55, and sellers asking $2.75. The season
is now about over, and it is doubtful if our quotations will be maintained more than two or three
days. Clover is lower, and difficult to place ;
round lots could be had at $5.25 to $5.60. Flax
$2.00 to $2.25.

SHIPMENTS. — The following vessels cleared
from this port with Barley since the opening of
navigation : Schr. Paragon, with 11,100 bush. ;
the Oddfellow, with 3,000 bush. ; the Wanderer,
with 4,804 bush., all for Oswego—total, 18,904
bush. The Sea Gull cleared with 8,000 bush.
Malt for Chicago. The following vessels cleared
for Oswego with Wheat : The D. M. Foster, with
16,373 bush. ; the Eureka, with 8,757 bush. ; the
Sea Gull, with 12,600 bush. ; the New Dominion,
with 1,000 bush. ; and the Tranchemontagne, with
8,613 bush.—total, 57,343 bush.

HIDES AND LEATHER.—Hides.—The market is
very dull, and weak, at quotations, and a decline
to 5½c. is looked for. Leather—is quiet at unchanged quotations.

PETROLEUM.—The Combination has ceased,
and in consequence prices are unsettled. Our
quotations are nominal ; some decline in prices
is expected.

FREIGHTS.—The following are the Grand Trunk
Railway Company's summer rates from Toronto to
the undermentioned stations, which came into
force on the 10th inst. :—Flour to all stations from
Bellville to Lynn, inclusive, 25c ; grain per 100 lbs.
13c ; flour to Brockville and Cornwall, inclusive,
30c ; grain 15c ; flour to Montreal, 35c ; grain 18c ;

flour to all stations between Island Pond and Portland, inclusive, 75c ; grain 38c ; flour to Boston,
80c gold ; grain 40c ; flour to Halifax, 90c ; flour
to St. John, 85c.

Halifax Market.

BREADSTUFFS.—April 20—We have to report
a continued demand for Supers during the past
week. The enquiry for No. 2's has fallen off, and
is likely to be restricted while Supers are low.
White Wheat Flours continue dull (nominal).
Oatmeal is offered freely, with small sales, with
considerable local receipts. Cornmeal, in sympathy with U. S. market, has declined, and is
dull and nominal. We quote :. White Wheat Extra (Fall), $6.25 to $6.50 ; Fancy, $5.90 to $6.00;
Supers, $5.50 to $5.60 ; No. 2, $4.75 to $5.00 ;
Middlings, $4.50 to $4.75. Cornmeal, K. D.,
$4.00 to $4 05 ; F. G. $3.80. Oatmeal, $6.50 to
$7.00. White Beans, $2.50 to $3.00.

WEST INDIA PRODUCE.—Sugar and Molasses
continue without quotable change, and few transactions. Rum unchanged ; Coffee active at quotations. We quote: Sugar, V.P., 10½c to 11c ;
Porto Rico, 9½c to 9½c ; Barbadoes, 9c to 9½c
(nominal). Molasses, Cienfuegos, 41c. to 42c ;
Trinidad, 40c to 41c. Rum, 58c to 60c for Demerara, in bond. Coffee, Jamaica, 12c, nominal.

EXCHANGE.—Bank Drafts, London, at 60 days,
at 13 per cent ; Montreal sight at 4 per cent ; New
York Gold, 4 per cent ; Currency, 21 per cent
discount ; St. John, N.B., 3 per cent pranium.

Trade of Guelph.

The report of the Guelph Board of Trade gives
the following :—Goods entered at Guelph, for the
twelve months, ending 31st March, $250,015;
duty, $269,12; value of exports entered, $279,813.
The flour and grain exported, amounted to 130,000
barrels, and 240,000 bushels. Cattle shipped by
the G. T. R. R. and G. W. R. R. 8,553, valued at
$427,050 ; Sheep do. 4,000, valued at $16,000;
Sheep Skins bought 17,000 lbs., $289,000 ; Wool,
133,000 lbs., $87,240; Hogs bought, 17,000, $289,-
000; Packed Hogs 6,500; Butter, 7,000 lbs. The
average quantities of grain grown in the County
of Wellington were:—Fall Wheat 20 bushels, to
the acre; Spring 15; Peas 10; Oats 15; Barley 30.

Cotton.

The following is a statement showing the stocks
of cotton in Liverpool and London, including the
supplies of American and Indian produce ascertained to be afloat to those ports :

	1868.	1869.
Stock in Liverpool......Bales	356,550	318,960
" London......	54,809	77,850
American cotton afloat.........	227,000	152,000
Indian "	204,121	302,854
Total......................	842.480	851,664

Tea.

A telegram from Hong-Kong, dated Feb. 8th,
gives the total exports from China and Japan since
the commencement of the season at 135,000,-
000 lbs.

THE TORONTO, GREY AND BRUCE
RAILWAY COMPANY.

TOTAL LENGTH, ABOUT 200 MILES. INCLUDING
BRANCHES TO KINCARDINE AND OWEN
SOUND.

Length of First Section, from Toronto to the
Garafraxa Road, about 70 Miles.

TOTAL CAPITAL, $3,000,000.

CAPITAL REQUIRED FOR THE FIRST SECTION,
$1,050,000.

Bonuses already Voted by Municipalities for the First
Section of the Main Line, $425,000.

As follows:—City of Toronto, $250,000 ; Albion, $40,000 ;
Caledon, $45,000 ; Mono, $45,000 ; Orangeville, $15,000 ;
Amaranth, $30,000.

Bonuses yet to be obtained for the first section, $77,000.
Bonuses required and obtainable to extend First Sec-
tion, from Arthur to Mount Forest, $138,000.
First issue of Stock in $100 shares, $325,000.
Upon which bonds will be issued for $360,000.
The arrangements for the extension to Mount Forest,
now in progress, when completed, will involve the further
issue of Stock and Bonds to the extent of $125,000.

PRESIDENT—John Gordon, Esq.
VICE-PRESIDENT—A. R. McMaster, Esq.

DIRECTORS:
Hon. M. C. Cameron, Provincial Secretary ; Hon. John
McMurrich, M.P.P. ; S. B. Harman, Esq., Mayor of Toronto;
Noah Barnhart, Esq. ; H. S. Howland, Esq., Vice-Pres.
Bank of Commerce; James Michie, Esq. (Fulton, Michie
& Co); John Crawford, Esq., M. P.; William Elliot,
Esq. (of Messrs. Lyman, Elliot & Co.) ; Thos. Swinarton,
Esq. M.P.P. ; R. A. Harrison, Esq., Barrister, M.P.; J. E.
Smith, Esq., Collector of Customs, Toronto ; D Sinclair,
Esq. M.P.P., North Bruce ; John Turner, Esq (of Messrs.
Sessions, Turner & Co.); George Laidlaw, Esq ; Thos. Scott,
Esq., M.P.P. ; Robert Paterson, Esq. ; Thos. Lailey, Esq. ;
T. C. Chisholm, Esq. ; Frank Smith, Esq. ; C. J. Campbell,
Esq.; Adam Crooks, Esq., Q.C.; John Worthington, Esq.
TRUSTEES OF BONUSES—Hon. John McMurrich, Com-
pany's Trustee ; A. W. Lauder, M.P.P., Government Trus-
tee ; Lewis Moffat, Esq., Municipalities' Trustee.
COUNSEL—Hon. John Hillyard Cameron.
SOLICITOR—W. H. Beatty, Esq.
CONSULTING ENGINEERS—Sir Charles Fox & Sons.
BANKERS—Bank of Toronto, Bank of Commerce.
BROKERS—Campbell & Cassels, Blaikie & Alexander.
SECRETARY—W. Sutherland Taylor.

TEMPORARY OFFICES, — 46 FRONT STREET,
TORONTO.

PROSPECTUS.

The Provisional Directors of the Toronto, Grey and
Bruce Railway Company, finding that further progress in
the building of Broad Gauge Railways in Canada, with
English Capital, was no longer financially practicable or
expedient for lines of Railway projected for local traffic,
and having become cognizant of the successful working
for a number of years of Railways built on the three feet
six gauge in the Kingdoms of Norway and Sweden, in the
Colonies of Queensland, in India, and elsewhere, and that
these Railways were capable of accommodating a traffic of

serve to illustrate the local business of a railway
long, through an average country in Canada.

IN 1861.

l Traffic of the Northern
ay of Canada amounted to .... 120,000 tons.
re .... 25,000 "
ceipts .... 100,613 "
.... $302,507
expenses 48,432 $410,930
f earnings over running .... 68 per cent.
ass on local traffic...... $115,982
hrough Traffic 15,493
nings equal to 5½ per cent. on a
f $15,000 per mile. Or 12½ on $10,-
r mile.

1864.

uffic.................... 130,000 tons.
Traffic.................. 8,344 "
re .... 104,346 "
ceipts $452,382
.... 14,884 $467,266
expenses................ 52 per cent.
f earnings over running
ass on local Traffic...... 217,143
hrough Traffic 7,144
nings equal to 15 2-5 per cent. on
of $15,000 a mile. Or 23 1-10 per
on $10,000 per mile.

1868.

1 Through Traffic.......... 194,583 tons.
re .... 136,965 "
ceipts $537,350
.... 12,090 Total $550,079
expenses .... 61 per cent.
f earnings over running
ass on Local Traffic...... $209,578
hrough Traffic 4,949
to 14½ per cent. on $15,000 a mile
earnings). Or 22½ per cent. on
0 per mile.

Running expenses per cent. 68 ; local tonnage, 120,-
ough tonnage, 25,000; total tons, 145,000 ; passen-
,618 ; local receipts, gross, $362,507 ; through re-
ross, $48,432 ; total receipts, gross, $410,930 : local
nett, $115,982 ; through receipts, nett, $15,406 ;
on $15,000 a mile, local, 8 1-3 ; dividend on $15,-
le, through, 1 1-10.
Running expenses per cent. 52 ; local tonnage,
through tonnage, 8,346 ; total tons, 130,346 ; pas-
104,346 ; local receipts, gross $452,382 ; through
gross, $14,884 ; total receipts, gross, $467,266 ;
ipts, nett, $217,143 ; through receipts, nett, $7,-
dend on $15,000 a mile, local, 15 2-5 ; dividend on
mile, through ½.
Running expenses per cent. 61 ; total tons, 194,-
passengers 136,965.; local receipts, gross, $587,350 ;
receipts, gross, $12,690 ; total receipts, gross,
ons, $38,029 ; passengers, $49,929 : local receipts,
,362,369 ; through receipts, gross, $75,000 ; total
gross, $1,428,278 ; local receipts, nett, $542,708 ;
receipts, nett, $27,591 ; dividend on $15,000 a mile,
5-6 ; dividend on $12,000 a mile, through, ½.
as—Total tons, 176,209 ; passengers, 116,643 : local
gross, $450,756 : through receipts, gross, $25,385 ;
ipts, gross, $476,091 ; local receipts, nett, 180,901 ;
receipts, nett $6,197 ; dividend on $15,000 a mile,
5-6, dividend on $15,000 a mile, through ½.
he above data it will be seen that the Northern
carried an average for those three years of 176,209
eight ; and 116,643 passengers ; the average gross
eing $450,756, while the nett receipts from local
re $180,901, equal to an annual dividend of 12 5-6
on a cost of $15,000 per mile.
markable and of consequence to intending sub-
for stock of the T. G. & B. R.,'that the net re-
through traffic for the same years only averaged
r annum, equal to a dividend of ½ of one per cent
of $15,000 per mile. This fact clearly proves the
ocal as against through traffic.
in, cattle, pork, goods and passenger traffic tri-
the first section of the Toronto, Grey and Bruce
will equal, if not exceed, for the same length of
local traffic of any other railway in Canada.
lowing estimate of traffic from the first section
ronto, Grey and Bruce Railway, is based upon
ns on the returns made by the Municipalities,
ntimate acquaintance with their trade and re-

pers, 140,000........................$145,000
2,000,000 bushels.................... 100,000
50,000 barrels.......................... 15,000
l goods, 50,000 tons 150,000
timber, 1,000,000 cubic feet 80,000
lumber, bark, posts, &c.............. 10,000
ood, 20,000 cords 25,000
nd express 20,000
'otal................................$490,000
q 60 per cent for running expenses, the net earn-
equal to $196,000—equal to a dividend of 18
n a cost of $15,000 per mile.
g reasonable margin for increased cost or less
e moderate estimate of which will be undisputed,)
ain the *strongest reasons* for anticipating a divi-
0 per cent per annum.

By the Act of Incorporation, the Company is specially
bound to carry cordwood, and to afford every necessary
facility for so doing at the specified rate of 3 cents per
cord per mile for dry wood, for all distances under 50
miles, and 2½ cents per cord per mile for all distances over
50 miles—a rate which has been found satisfactory, by test
of actual experience, on the Government Railways of New
Brunswick.

This condition will enhance the cost of fuel to the Company, but the increased traffic and prosperity consequent
upon this trade, it is fully believed, will more than compensate for the extra cost of fuel.

The gentlemen who have promoted and borne the preliminary expenses of this enterprise, and who desire to see
it carried out in good faith on sound commercial principles,
are resolved, in so far as their influence is equal to the
task, to have this railway controlled by the most respectable capitalists of this city and the country on the route
of the railway, who may take stock in it; to convert their
own securities, and pay cash to contractors, and not to
surrender control of the railway to contractors or bondholders ; to let the contracts in a manner to ensure the
healthiest competition. In other words, to *have value for
the money from the turning of the first sod to the laying of
the last rail.*

The country on the route of the first section, with the
exception of a short distance in Caledon, is one of the
easiest for railway construction in Canada, especially the
22 or 23 miles from Orangeville to the Garafraxa Road.

In the Township of Caledon—the country is hilly and
rolling. This portion of the route was carefully and completely surveyed and cross-sectioned under the auspices
and by the direction of Mr. J. E. Boyd, M.I.C.E., and
Engineer for the Government of New Brunswick, before
the Company obtained their charter, and, as anticipated,
no real difficulties were encountered ; the highest grade,
with moderate cuttings, being 55 feet to the mile. Mr.
Charles Douglas Fox examined, for the Company, the figures
and the profile, and, together with Mr. Boyd, gave their
written opinion that the cost of this portion, per mile for
earth-works, would not exceed $15,000. There are no rock
cuttings.

Ballast, ties, timber for bridges, and lumber for fences,

are convenient and available at the lowest cost in Canada,
along the whole route of the first section.

Every other consideration, in the first instance, will be
subordinated to the construction of a first-class permanent
way; the best of timber bridges ; deep and good ballasting.
Rails to weigh 40 lbs. to the yard, and to be selected of the
best quality.

Arrangements are in progress which will secure to the
Company free right of way through the city, and egress, if
desired, for a few miles out of the city, on the line of the
Grand Trunk, by means of a third rail ; and the disposition of the proprietors, and other circumstances along the
line are so favorable, that the whole right of way will be
obtained for an amount not exceeding $22,000.

Station grounds and dockage will be had in this city,
either free, or for a nominal rental.

It is the desire of the Provisional Directors to have their
Chief Engineer appointed, with the concurrence, and subject to the approval of the Company's Consulting Engineers,
Sir Charles Fox & Sons, who will be held responsible for
the excellence of the works, economy of construction, and
the success here of the system of narrow gauge railways,
of which they have had large experience elsewhere, and
with the initiation of which in this country they are honorably identified.

On these premises the Provisional Directors appeal for
stock subscriptions to the citizens of Toronto, to the municipalities, and to the business men and proprietors of
land along the route of the railway, and to capitalists elsewhere, believing that the most cautious and prudent investors will find the stock of the Toronto, Grey and Bruce
Railway worthy of their attention.

The stock books will be opened at the Company's offices,
Front street, on the 21st April, at 10 o'clock, a.m. Forms
of application for shares can be had on application to the
secretary, and from the reeves and clerks of the several
municipalities on the route of the railway, and from Messrs.
Campbell & Cassels, and from Messrs. Blaikie & Alexander,
Toronto, and from McDougall & Davidson, Montreal.

In conjunction with the Toronto and Nipissing Railway
Company, it is agreed that a member of the firm of Sir
Charles Fox & Sons, Consulting Engineers, will be invited
here immediately by telegraph, when active operations will
be commenced.

EDINBURGH LIFE ASSURANCE COMPANY.

FOUNDED 1823.

AMOUNT OF ACCUMULATED AND INVESTED FUNDS—OVER ONE MILLION STERLING.

HEAD OFFICE—EDINBURGH.

PRESIDENT—The Rt. Hon. the Earl of Haddington. MANAGER—D. Maclagan, Esq. SECRETARY—Alex. H. Whytt, Esq.

CANADIAN OFFICE ESTABLISHED 1857.   WELLINGTON STREET, TORONTO.

CANADIAN BOARD—Hon. John Hillyard Cameron, M.P., Chairman. J. W. Gamble, Esq., L. Moffatt, Esq., Hon.
J. B. Robinson, C. J. Campbell, Esq. David Higgins, Secretary.

THE Edinburgh Life Assurance Company offer to the public the advantages of a Canadian as well as a British Company. They have invested a large amount of money on securities in this country, and the Toronto Local Board
have full power, by an Imperial Statute, to take risks, make investments, and settle claims in Canada, without reference to the Head Office, Edinburgh. Some of this old Policies in the Company, which became claims during the past
year, were settled by payment of amounts double of those originally insured, in consequence of the large bonuses that
accrued on the Policies.

Every information that intending assurers may require can be obtained at the Company's Office in Toronto, or at
any of the Agencies which have been established in the principal towns in Canada.

J. HILLYARD CAMERON, CHAIRMAN.   (36-1y)   DAVID HIGGINS, SECRETARY.

Royal Fire & Life Insurance Company
OF LIVERPOOL AND LONDON.

CAPITAL, TWO MILLION STERLING,
WITH LARGE RESERVE FUNDS.

ANNUAL INCOME, - - - - - - - - £800,000 STG.

FIRE BRANCH.

Very moderate rates of Premium. Prompt and liberal settlement of losses. Loss and damage by explosion of
gas made good. No charge for policies or transfers.

LIFE BRANCH.

The following are amongst the important advantages offered by this Company :
Perfect security to assurers. Moderate rates of premium. Large participation of profits—the bonuses being
amongst the largest hitherto declared by any office, and divided every five years. EXEMPTION OF ASSURED FROM
LIABILITY OF PARTNERSHIP. Claims settled promptly on proof of death. Liberal allowance for surrendered policies.
Forfeiture of policy cannot take place from unintentional mis-statement. No charge for policies or assignments. Medical fees paid by the Company. Tables and forms of application, with all other information, can be obtained on application to

FRANCIS H. HEWARD,

MANAGER TORONTO BRANCH.

GEORGE OLIVER, Inspector.

W. B. NICOL, M.D., Medical Examiner.

TORONTO, April 19, 1869.   95-4t

TORONTO PRICES CURRENT.—APRIL 29, 1869.

Name of Article.	Wholesale Rates.	
Boots and Shoes.	$ c.	$ c.
Mens' Thick Boots	2 20	2 50
" Kip	2 50	3 00
" Calf	3 20	3 70
" Congress Gaiters	1 65	2 50
" Kip Cobourgs	1 15	1 45
Boys' Thick Boots	1 70	1 80
Youths' "	1 40	1 50
Women's Batts	0 95	1 30
" Balmoral	1 20	1 50
" Congress Gaiters	0 90	1 50
Misses' Batts	0 75	1 00
" Balmoral	0 87	1 20
" Congress Gaiters	1 00	1 30
Girls' Batts	0 65	0 85
" Balmoral	0 90	1 05
" Congress Gaiters	0 75	1 10
Children's C. T. Cacks	0 50	0 65
" Gaiters	0 65	0 90
Drugs.		
Aloes Cape	0 12½	0 16
Alum	0 02½	0 03
Borax	0 00	0 00
Camphor, refined	0 65	0 70
Castor Oil	0 16½	0 28
Caustic Soda	0 04½	0 05
Cochineal	0 90	1 00
Cream Tartar	0 40	0 45
Epsom Salts	0 03	0 04
Extract Logwood	0 11	0 12
Gum Arabic, sorts	0 30	0 35
Indigo, Madras	0 90	1 00
Licorice	0 14	0 45
Madder	0 00	0 18
Galls	0 32	0 37
Opium	12 00	13 50
Oxalic Acid	0 26	0 35
Potash, Bi-tart	0 25	0 28
" Bichromate	0 15	0 20
Potass Iodide	3 90	4 50
Senna	0 12½	0 00
Soda Ash	0 02½	0 04
Soda Bicarb	4 50	5 00
Tartaric Acid	0 40	0 45
Verdigris	0 35	0 40
Vitriol, Blue	0 08	0 10
Groceries.		
Coffees:		
Java, ₩ lb	0 22@	0 24
Laguayra	0 17	0 18
Rio	0 15	0 17
Fish:		
Herrings, Lab. split	5 75	6 50
" round	0 00	0 00
" scaled	0 35	0 40
Mackerel, small kitts	1 00	0 00
Loch. Her. wh'e firks	2 50	2 75
" half "	1 25	1 50
White Fish & Trout	None.	
Salmon, saltwater	14 00	15 00
Dry Cod, ₩ 112 lbs	5 00	5 25
Fruit:		
Raisins, Layers	2 00	2 10
" M R	1 90	2 00
" Valentias new	0 6¾	0 7¼
Currants, new	0 5½	0 06½
" old	0 04	0 04½
Figs	0 14	0 00
Molasses:		
Clayed, ₩ gal	0 00	0 35
Syrups, Standard	0 60	0 00
" Golden	0 00	0 65
Rice:		
Arracan	4 25	4 50
Spices:		
Cassia, whole, ₩ lb	0 00	0 45
Cloves	0 11	0 12
Nutmegs	0 50	0 55
Ginger, ground	0 20	0 25
" Jamaica, root	0 20	0 25
Pepper, black	0 12½	0 00
Pimento	0 08	0 09
Sugars:		
Port Rico, ₩ lb	0 10¾	0 00
Cuba "	0 10½	0 00
Barbadoes (bright)	0 10½	0 00
Canada Sugar Refine'y, yellow No. 2, 60ds	0 10½	0 10¾
Yellow, No. 2½	0 10¾	0 11
No. 3	0 11	0 11¼
Crushed X	0 13	0 13½
" A	0 13	0 13¼
Ground	0 13¾	0 14
Dry Crushed	0 14¼	0 14½
Extra Ground	0 15¼	0 15½
Teas:		
Japan com'n to good	0 48	0 55
" Fine to choicest	0 50	0 65
Colored, com. to fine	0 60	0 75
Congou & Souch'ng	0 42	0 75
Oolong, good to fine	0 50	0 65
Y. Hyson, com to gd	0 47½	0 55
Medium to choice	0 65	0 80
Extra choice	0 85	0 95

Name of Article.	Wholesale Rate.	
Groceries—*Contin'd*	$ c.	$ c.
Gunpowd'r c. to med	0 55	0 70
" med. to fine	0 70	0 85
" fine to fins't	0 85	0 95
Hyson	0 45	0 80
Imperial	0 42	0 80
Tobacco, Manufact'd:		
Can Leaf, ₩ lb 5s & 10s	0 26	0 30
Western Leaf, com	0 25	0 26
" Good	0 27	0 32
" Fine	0 32	0 35
" Bright fine	0 40	0 50
" " choice	0 60	0 75
Hardware.		
Tin (net cash prices)		
Block, ₩ lb	0 28	0 00
Grain	0 30	0 00
Copper:		
Pig	0 23	0 24
Sheet	0 30	0 33
Cut Nails:		
Assorted ¼, Shingles, ₩ 100 lb	2 90	3 00
Shingle alone do	3 15	3 25
Lathe and 5 dy	3 30	3 40
Galvanized Iron:		
Assorted sizes	0 08	0 09
Best No. 24	0 09	0 00
" 26	0 08	0 08
" 28	0 09	0 09½
Horse Nails:		
Guest's or Griffin's assorted sizes	0 00	0 00
For W. ass'd sizes	0 18	0 19
Patent Hammer'd do	0 17	0 18
Iron (at 4 months):		
Pig—Gartsherrie No1	24 00	25 00
Other brands. No1	22 00	24 00
" No2	0 00	0 00
Bar—Scotch, ₩ 100 lb	2 25	2 50
Refined	3 00	3 25
Swedes	5 00	5 50
Hoops—Coopers	3 00	3 25
Band	3 00	3 25
Boiler Plates	3 25	3 50
Canada Plates	3 75	4 00
Union Jack	0 00	0 00
Pontypool	3 25	4 00
Swansea	3 90	4 00
Lead (at 4 months):		
Bar, ₩ 100 lbs	0 06½	0 07
Sheet "	0 08	0 09
Shot	0 07½	0 07¾
Iron Wire (net cash):		
No. 6, ₩ bundle	2 70	2 80
" 9, "	3 10	3 20
" 12, "	3 40	3 50
" 16, "	4 30	4 40
Powder:		
Blasting, Canada	3 50	0 00
FF "	4 25	4 50
FFF "	4 75	5 00
Blasting, English	4 00	5 00
FF loose	5 00	6 00
FFF "	6 00	6 50
Pressed Spikes (4 mos):		
Regular sizes 100	4 00	4 25
Extra "	4 50	5 00
Tin Plates (net cash):		
IC Coke	7 50	8 50
IC Charcoal	8 50	9 00
IX "	10 50	11 00
IXX "	13 50	14 00
DC "	8 00	8 50
DX "	9 50	0 00
Hides & Skins, ₩ lb		
Green rough	0 00	0 06
Green, salt'd & insp'd	0 07½	0 07¾
Cured	0 00	0 00
Calfskins, green	0 00	0 11
Calfskins, cured	0 00	0 12½
" dry	0 18	0 20
Sheepskins	1 40	1 75
" country	1 00	1 40
Hops.		
Inferior, ₩ lb	0 05	0 07
Medium	0 07	0 09
Good	0 09	0 12
Fancy	0 00	0 00
Leather, @ (4 mos.) In lots of less than 50 sides, 10 ₩ cent higher.		
Spanish Sole, 1st qual'y heavy, weights ₩ lb	0 21½	0
Do. 1st qual middle do	0 23	0
Do. No. 2, light weights	0 22	0 23
Slaughter heavy	0 00	0 [illegible]
Do. light	0 00	0 00
Harness, best	0 25	0 27
" No. 2	0 00	0 00
Upper heavy	0 32	0 35
" light	0 35	0 36

Name of Article.	Wholesale Rates.	
Leather—*Contin'd.*	$ c.	$ c.
Kip Skins, Patna	0 30	0
French	0 70	0
English	0 65	0
Hemlock Calf (30 to 35 lbs.) per doz	0 50	0
Do. light	0 45	0
French Calf	1 03	1
Grain & Satn Clt ₩ doz	0 00	0
Splits, large ₩ lb	0 30	0
" small	0 23	0
Enamelled Cow ₩ foot	0 20	0
Patent	0 20	0
Pebble Grain	0 15	0
Buff	0 14	0
Oils.		
Cod	0 65	0 7
Lard, extra	0 00	0 0
" No. 1	0 00	0 0
" Woollen	0 00	0 0
Lubricating, patent	0 00	0 0
" Mott's economic	0 30	0 0
Linseed, raw	0 76	0 8
" boiled	0 81	0 8
Machinery	0 00	0 0
Olive, common, ₩ gal	1 00	1 6
" salad	1 95	2 3
" salad, in bots. qt. ₩ case	3 60	3 7
Sesame salad, ₩ gal	1 60	1 7
Seal, pale	0 75	0 8
Spirits Turpentine	0 52½	0 6
Varnish	0 00	0 0
Whale	0 00	0 9
Paints, &c.		
White Lead, genuine in Oil, ₩ 25 lbs	0 00	2 3
Do. No. 1 "	0 00	2 1
" 2 "	0 00	1 9
" 3 "	0 00	1 6
White Zinc, genuine	3 10	3 5
White Lead, dry	0 05½	0 0
Red Lead	0 07½	0 0
Venetian Red, Eng'h	0 02½	0 0
Yellow Ochre, Fren'h	0 02¾	0 0
Whiting	0 85	1 2
Petroleum. (Refined ₩ gal.)		
Water white, car l'd	—	0 -
" small lots	0 30	0 3
Straw, by car load	0 00	0 0
" small lots	0 00	0 0
Amber, by car load	0 00	0 0
" small lots	0 00	0 0
Benzine	0 00	0 0
Produce.		
Grain:		
Wheat, Spring, 60 lb	0 93	0 9
" Fall 60 "	0 98	1 0
Barley 48 "	1 00	1 0
Peas 60 "	0 70	0 7
Oats 34 "	0 52	0 5
Rye 56 "	0 60	0 0
Seeds:		
Clover, choice 60 "	5 50	5
" com'n 68 "	5 25	5
Timothy, cho'e 4 "	2 60	2 7
" inf. to good 48 "	2 40	2 6
Flax 56 "	2 00	2 2
Flour (per brl.):		
Superior extra	0 00	0 0
Extra superfine	4 40	4 5
Fancy superfine	4 20	4 2
Superfine No 1	4 00	4 1
" No. 2	—	
Oatmeal, (per brl.)	5 50	
Provisions		
Butter, dairy tub ₩ lb	0 22	
" store packed	0 15	
Cheese, new	0 14½	
Pork, mess, per brl	25 50	2
" prime mess	—	
" prime	—	
Bacon, rough	0 11	0 1
" Cumberl'd cut	0 12	0 1
" smoked	0 00	0 1
Hams, in salt	0 12½	0 1
" smoked	0 14	0 1
Shoulders, in salt	0 00	0 0
Lard, in kegs	0 16½	0 1
Eggs, packed	0 12½	0 1
Beef Hams	0 00	0 1
Tallow	0 08	0 8
Hogs dressed, heavy	0 00	0 0
" medium	0 00	0 0
" light	0 00	0 0
Salt, &c.		
American brls	1 50	1 5
Liverpool coarse	0 00	0 0
Goderich	0 00	1 6
Plaster, grey	0 00	0 9
Water Lime	1 50	0 0

& Candles.	$ c.	$ c.
rford & Co.'s ..		
perial.........	0 07½	0 08
lden Bar	0 07	0 07½
yer Bar........	0 07	0 07½
....	0 05	0 05½
....	0 03½	0 03¾
....	0 00	0 11½
s, Liquors, &c.		
ı, per doz......	2 60	2 65
ss Dub Portr..	2 35	2 40
amaica Rum...	1 80	2 2
yper's H. Gin..	1 55	1 6
s Old Tom.....	1 90	2 05
cases.........	4 00	4 25
s Old Tom, c...	6 00	6 25
ommon	1 00	1 25
ne old	2 00	4 00
, common	1 00	1 50
iedium........	1 70	1 80
pale or golden..	2 50	4 00

Brandy:	$ c.	$ c.
Hennessy's, per gal..	2 30	2 50
Martell's " ..	2 30	2 50
J. Robin & Co.'s " ..	2 25	2 35
Otard, Dupuy & Cos..	2 25	2 35
Brandy, cases........	8 50	9 00
Brandy, com. per c...	4 00	4 50
Whiskey:		
Common 36 u. p......	0 62½	0 65
Old Rye	0 85	0 87½
Malt	0 85	0 87½
Toddy	0 85	0 87½
Scotch, per gal........	1 90	2 10
Irish—Kinnahan's c...	7 00	7 50
" Dunnville's Belf't..	6 00	6 25
Wool.		
Fleece, lb.............	0 28	0 35
Pulled ".............	0 22	0 25
Furs.		
Bear..................	8 00	10 00
Beaver, ℘ lb...........	1 00	1 25
Coon	0 20	0 40
Fisher................	4 00	6 00
Martin................	1 40	1 60
Mink..................	3 25	4 00
Otter.................	5 75	6 00
Spring Rats	0 15	0 17
Fox..................	1 20	1 25

INSURANCE COMPANIES.

ENGLISH.—*Quotations on the London Market.*

Last Dividend.	Name of Company.	Shares par val £	Amount paid.	Last Sale.
	Briton Medical and General Life ...	10	....	2½
7½	Commer'l Union, Fire, Life and Mar.	50	5	5½xd
8	City of Glasgow	25	2½	5½
9½	Edinburgh Life	100	15	33
5—½ yr	European Life and Guarantee......	2½	11s6	4s. 6d.
10	Etna Fire and Marine............	10	1½	—
5	Guardian	100	50	51½
12	Imperial Fire...................	500	50	350
9½	Imperial Life	100	10	17
10	Lancashire Fire and Life........	20	2	2⅜
11	Life Association of Scotland.....	40	7½	25
45s. p. sh	London Assurance Corporation ..	25	12½	49
5	London and Lancashire Life	10	1	—
40	Liverp'l & London & Globe F. & L.	20	2	7 1-16
5	National Union Life	5	1	1
12½	Northern Fire and Life	100	5	12 1-16
12 '68, bo 5s.	North British and Mercantile	50	6¼	19½xd
50	Ocean Marine	25	5	17
£5 12s.	Provident Life..................	100	10	35
£4½ p. s.	Phœnix..........................	....	....	145
2½—h. yr.	Queen Fire and Life	10	1	1
3s. bo. 4s	Royal Insurance.................	20	3	6⅝
10	Scottish Provincial Fire and Life ..	50	2½	5 3-8
25	Standard Life	50	12	66½
5	Star Life	25	1¼	—
	CANADIAN.			℘ c.
4	British America Fire and Marine ..	$50	$25	55½ 56
4	Canada Life	...	.....	.....
12	Montreal Assurance	£50	£5	135
3	Provincial Fire and Marine........	60	11	.....
....	Quebec Fire	40	32½	£25½
7	" Marine..................	100	40	85 90
4 6 mo's.	Western Assurance................	40	9	.....

RAILWAYS.	Sha's	Paid	Montr	London
and St. Lawrence.....................	£100	All.	....	57 59
nd Lake Huron	20½	"	....	2½ 3½
do Preference	10	"	....	5 6
antf. & Goderich, 6℘c., 1872-3-4........	100	"	....	66 69
in and St. Lawrence	....	....	10 11	....
do Pref. 10 ℘ ct...............	....	....	80 82½	....
runk	100	"	14 15	14½ 15¼
Eq. G. M. Bds. 1 ch. 6℘c..........	100	"	....	85 87
First Preference, 5 ℘ c............	100	"	....	49 50
Deferred, 3 ℘ ct..................	100	"	....	....
Second Pref. Bonds, 5℘c...........	100	"	....	37 39
do Deferred, 3 ℘ ct............	100	"	...	....
Third Pref. Stock, 4℘ct............	100	"	....	27 29
do. Deferred, 3 ℘ ct............	100	"	....	....
Fourth Pref. Stock, 3℘c............	100	"	....	16½ 17½
do. Deferred, 3 ℘ ct............	100	"	....	....
estern..................................	20½	"	14 15	14¼ 14¾
New	20½	18	....	....
6 ℘ c. Bds, due 1873-76............	100	All.	....	100 102
5½ ℘c Bds. due 1877-78............	100	"	....	94 95
Railway, Halifax, $250, all............	$250	"	....	....
, of Canada, 6℘c. 1st Pref. Bds........	100	"	....	92 93

EXCHANGE.	Halifax.	Montr'l.	Quebec.	Toronto.
London, 60 days......				
r 75 days date..........	12½	8⅞ 9½	8 9¼	8⅞
do.	11½ 12	7 8	7½ 7¾	8
with documents...........	....	7 7½	....	....
New York.................	....	24½ 25	23 24	24¾
do.	....	25 25½	24 24½	....
fts do.	....	par to ½ p.	par ⅛ dis.	par ¼ dis.
....	....	4½ 5	....	3½ to 4½

STOCK AND BOND REPORT.

The dates of our quotations are as follows:—Toronto, April 27; Montreal, April 27; Quebec, April 26; London, April 18.

NAME.	Shares.	Paid up.	Divid'd last 6 Months	Dividend Day.	CLOSING PRICES. Toronto.	Montre'l	Quebec.
BANKS.			℘ ct.				
British North America	$250	All.	3	July and Jan.	105 105½	104¾ 105½	105 106
Jacques Cartier..............	50	"	4	1 June, 1 Dec.	109 110	109 110	109 110
Montreal	200	"	5	"	146 147	148 149	146¼ 146¾
Nationale....................	50	"	4	1 Nov. 1 May.	bks cls'd	bks cls'd	bks cls'd
New Brunswick	100	"	......	......	....	...	....
Nova Scotia	200	28	7&b$3½	Mar. and Sept.	....	....	....
Du Peuple....................	50	"	4	1 Mar., 1 Sept.	108 108	108 108½	107½ 108
Toronto	100	"	4	1 Jan., 1 July.	120 120½	120½ 122	121 121½
Bank of Yarmouth.............	....	....	......	......	....		
Canadian Bank of Com'e.......	50	95	......	......	102 102½	101¼ 103	102 102½
City Bank Montreal	80	All.	4	1 June, 1 Dec.	101½ 102	101 101¾	101 101½
Commer'l Bank (St. John).....	100	"	℘ ct.	.....	....	...	....
Eastern Townships' Bank......	50	"	4	1 July, 1 Jan..	....	99 101	99½ 100½
Gore	40	....	none.	1 Jan., 1 July.	37 38	37½ 39	38 39
Halifax Banking Company......	....	....	......	.....	....	....	....
Mechanics' Bank..............	50	70	4	1 Nov., 1 May.	bks cls'd	Bks cls'd	bks cls'd
Merchants' Bank of Canada....	100	70	4	1 Jan., 1 July.	107 107½	107 107½	107½ 108
Merchants' Bank (Halifax)....	....	....	......	......	....	....	
Molson's Bank................	50	All.	4	1 Apr., 1 Oct.	108½ 109	108½ 109	108 109
Niagara District Bank........	100	70	3½	1 Jan., 1 July.	...	....	....
Ontario Bank.................	40	All.	4	1 June, 1 Dec.	100 100½	100¼ 100¾	100¼ 100¾
People's Bank (Fred'kton)....	100	"	......	......	....	....	....
People's Bank (Halifax)	20	"	7 12 m	......	....	....	....
Quebec Bank	100	"	3½	1 June, 1 Dec.	101 102	100½ 102	102 102½
Royal Canadian Bank	50	50	4	1 Jan., 1 July.	78½ 79½	77½ 80	78 80
St. Stephens Bank	100	All.	.....	.....	....	....	....
Union Bank	100	70	4	1 Jan., 1 July.	105 106	105½ 106	106 106½
Union Bank (Halifax).........	100	40	7 12 mo	Feb. and Aug.	....	....	....
MISCELLANEOUS.							
British America Land.........	250	44	2½	......	....	....	....
British Colonial S. S. Co....	250	32½	2½	......	...	50 60	....
Canada Company	32½	All.	£1 10s.	......	....	....	....
Canada Landed Credit Co......	50	$20	3½	......	78 80	....	....
Canada Per. B'ldg Society....	50	All.	5	......	125½ 126	....	....
Canada Mining Company........	4	90	......	......	....	....	....
Do. Inl'd Steam Nav. Co.....	100	All.	7	......	....	100½ 101	....
Do. Glass Company.........	100	"	12½ "	......	....	40 55	....
Canad'n Loan & Investm't.....	25	2½	7	......	....	....	....
Canada Agency	10	¼	......	......	....	....	....
Colonial Securities Co.......	...	....	......	.....	....	....	....
Freehold Building Society....	100	All.	4	......	112 112½	....	....
Halifax Steamboat Co.........	100	"	5	......	....	....	....
Halifax Gas Company..........	....	....	......	......	....	....	....
Hamilton Gas Company.........	....	....	.....	.....	....	....	....
Huron Copper Bay Co..........	4	12	20	.....	....	30 45	....
Lake Huron S. and C..........	5	102	......	.....	....	....	....
Montreal Mining Consols......	20	$15	......	......	....	3.15 3.25	...
Do. Telegraph Co..........	40	All.	5	......	133½ 134	133 133½	133½ 134
Do. Elevating Co..........	00	"	15 12 m	......	....	100 102½	....
Do. City Gas Co...........	40	"	4	15 Mar. 15 Sep.	....	133 135	134 135
Do. City Pass. R,. Co.....	50	"	4	......	....	105½ 106	105 106
Quebec and L. S.	8	$4	......	......	....	....	....
Quebec Gas Co................	200	All.	4	1 Mar., 1 Sep.	....	...	118 119
Quebec Street R. R...........	50	25	3	......	....	....	90 91
Richelieu Navigation Co......	100	All.	10 p.a.	1 Jan., 1 July.	....	108 108½	108 108½
St. Lawrence Glass Company.	100	"	....	......	....	80 85	....
St. Lawrence Tow Boat Co.....	100	"	......	3 Feb.	....	...	30 35
Tor'to Consumers' Gas Co.....	50	"	4	1 My Au MarFe	107 107½	...	107 107½
Trust & Loan Co. of U. C.....	20	5	3	......	....	....	.. .
West'n Canada Bldg Soc'y.....	50	All.	5	......	120½ 121	....	....

SECURITIES.	London.	Montreal.	Quebec.	Toronto.
Canadian Gov't Deb. 6 ℘ ct. stg..................	....	103 104	101 102	102½ 104
Do. do. 6 do due Ja. & Jul. 1877-84.......	104½ 105½	....	....	....
Do. do. 6 do. Feb. & Aug........	102 104	....	....	....
Do. do. 6 do. Mch. & Sep........	102 104	.. .	...	....
Do. do. 5 ℘ ct. cur., 1883	92½ 93½	92½ 95	93½ 94	93 94½
Do. do. 5 do. stg., 1885	92 94	92½ 94½	93½ 94½	93 94½
Do. do. 7 do. cur., ...	....	....	......	....
Dominion 6 p. c. 1878 cy.........................	....	107 108	105½ 106	106½ 107
Hamilton Corporation............................	....	....	......	....
Montreal Harbor, 8 ℘ ct. d. 1869................	..	....	......	....
Do. do. 7 do. 1870..................	....	....	......	....
Do. do. 6½ do. 1883..................	....	102 103	......	02 103
Do. do. 6½ do. 1873..................	....	....	......	....
Do, Corporation, 6 ℘ c. 1891................	....	96 96½	96 96½	96 96½
Do. 7 p. c. stock............................	....	108½ 110	108 109	109 110
Do. Water Works, 6 ℘ c. stg. 1878............	....	....	......	96 96½
Do. do. 6 do. cy. do.	....	96½ 97	......	96 97
New Brunswick, 6 ℘ ct., Jan. and July	103 104	....	......	....
Nova Scotia, 6 ℘ ct., 1875......................	102 104	...	......	....
Ottawa City 6 ℘ c. d. 1880	....	95 97	......	....
Quebec Harbour, 6 ℘ c. d. 1883..................	....	....	60	....
Do. do. 7 do. do.......................	....	....	65 70	....
Do. do 8 do. 1886.......................	....	....	80 85	....
Do. City, 7 ℘ c. d. 1½ years................	....	....	98 98½	....
Do. do. 7 do. 8 do.	....	....	91 92	....
Do. do. 7 do. 4 do.	....	....	94 95	....
Do. Water Works, 7 ℘ ct., 3 years	....	....	97 97½	....
Do. do. 6 do. 1½ do.	....	....	94 95	....
Toronto Corporation	....	90 92½	...	....

Insurance.

Briton Medical and General Life Association,

with which is united the

BRITANNIA LIFE ASSURANCE COMPANY.

Capital and Invested Funds...........£750,000 Sterling.

ANNUAL INCOME, £220,000 STG. :
Yearly increasing at the rate of £25,000 Sterling.

THE important and peculiar feature originally introduced by this Company, in applying the periodical Bonuses, so as to make Policies payable during life, without any higher rate of premiums being charged, has caused the success of the BRITON MEDICAL AND GENERAL to be almost unparalleled in the history of Life Assurance. *Life Policies on the Profit Scale become payable during the lifetime of the Assured, thus rendering a Policy of Assurance a means of subsistence in old age, as well as a protection for a family,* and a more valuable security to creditors in the event of early death ; and effectually meeting the often urged objection, that persons do not themselves reap the benefit of their own prudence and forethought.

No extra charge made to members of Volunteer Corps for services within the British Provinces.

☞ TORONTO AGENCY, 5 KING ST. WEST.

Oct 17—9-1yr   JAMES FRASER, *Agent.*

BEAVER
Mutual Insurance Association.

HEAD OFFICE—20 TORONTO STREET,
TORONTO.

INSURES LIVE STOCK against death from any cause. The only Canadian Company having authority to do this class of business.

R. L. DENISON,
President.
W, T. O'REILLY,
Secretary.   8-1y-25

HOME DISTRICT
Mutual Fire Insurance Company.

Office—North-West Cor. Yonge & Adelaide Streets,
TORONTO.—(UP STAIRS.)

INSURES Dwelling Houses, Stores, Warehouses, Merchandise, Furniture, &c.

PRESIDENT—The Hon. J. McMURRICH.
VICE-PRESIDENT—JOHN BURNS, Esq.
JOHN RAINS, Secretary.

AGENTS:
DAVID WRIGHT, Esq., Hamilton ; FRANCIS STEVENS, Esq., Barrie : Messrs. GIBBS & BRO., Oshawa.   8-1y

THE PRINCE EDWARD COUNTY
Mutual Fire Insurance Company.

HEAD OFFICE,—PICTON, ONTARIO.
President, L. B. STINSON ; *Vice-President,* W. A. RICHARDS.
Directors ; H. A. McPAUL, James Cavan, James Johnson, N. S. DeMill, William Delong.—*Secretary.* John Twigg ; *Treasurer,* David Barker; *Solicitor,* R. J. Fitzgerald.

THIS Company is established upon strictly Mutual principles, insuring farming and isolated property, (not hazardous,) in *Townships only,* and offers great advantages to insurers, at low rates *for five years,* without the expense of a renewal.
Picton, June 15, 1868.   9-1y

THE AGRICULTURAL
Mutual Assurance Association of Canada.

HEAD OFFICE ....LONDON, ONT

A purely Farmers' Company. Licensed by the Government of Canada.

Capital, 1st January, 1803.................. $280,108 82
Cash and Cash Items, over.................. $86,000 00
No. of Policies in force.................. 30,802 00

THIS Company insures nothing more dangerous than Farm property. Its rates are as low as any well-established Company in the Dominion, and lower than those of a great many. It is largely patronised, and continues to grow in public favor.
For Insurance, apply to any of the Agents or address the Secretary, London, Ontario.
London, 2nd Nov., 1808.   12-1y.

Insurance.

The Gore District Mutual Fire Insurance Company

GRANTS INSURANCES on all description of Property against Loss or Damage by FIRE. It is the only Mutual Fire Insurance Company which assesses its Policies yearly from their respective dates ; and the average yearly cost of insurance in it, for the past three and a half years, has been nearly

TWENTY CENTS IN THE DOLLAR
less than what it would have been in an ordinary Proprietary Company.

THOS. M. SIMONS,
Secretary & Treasurer.
ROBT. McLEAN,
Inspector of Agencies.
Galt, 25th Nov., 1808.   15-1y

Western Assurance Company,

INCORPORATED 1851.

CAPITAL, ... $400.000.

FIRE AND MARINE.

HEAD OFFICE.................TORONTO, ONTARIO.

DIRECTORS.
Hon. JNO. McMURRICH, President.
CHARLES MAGRATH, Vice-President.
A. M. SMITH, Esq.   JOHN FISKEN, Esq.
ROBERT BEATY, Esq.   ALEX. MANNING, Esq.
JAMES MICHIE, Esq.   N. BARNHART, Esq.
R. J. DALLAS, Esq.
B. HALDAN, Secretary.
J. MAUGHAN, JR., Assistant Secretary.
WM. BLIGHT, Fire Inspector.
CAPT. G. T. DOUGLAS, Marine Inspector.
JAMES PRINGLE, General Agent.

Insurances effected at the lowest current rates on Buildings, Merchandize, and other property, against loss or damage by fire.
On Hull, Cargo and Freight against the perils of Inland Navigation.
On Cargo Risks with the Maritime Provinces by sail or steam.
On Cargoes by steamers to and from British Ports.

WESTERN ASSURANCE COMPANY'S OFFICE, }
TORONTO, 1st April, 1869   }   23-1y

Fire and Marine Assurance.

THE BRITISH AMERICA
ASSURANCE COMPANY.
HEAD OFFICE :
CORNER OF CHURCH AND COURT STREETS.
TORONTO.

BOARD OF DIRECTION :
Hon G. W. Allan, M L.C.,   A. Joseph, Esq.,
George J. Boyd, Esq.,   Peter Paterson, Esq.,
Hon. W. Cayley,   O. P. Ridout, Esq.,
Richard S. Cassels, Esq.,   E H. Rutherford, Esq.,
Thomas C. Street, Esq.
Governor:
GEORGE PERCIVAL RIDOUT, Esq.
Deputy Governor:
PETER PATERSON, Esq.
Fire Inspector: Marine Inspector:
E. ROBY O'BRIEN.   CAPT. R. COURNEEN.
Insurances granted on all descriptions of property against loss and damage by fire and the perils of inland navigation.
Agencies established in the principal cities, towns, and ports of shipment throughout the Province.
THOS. WM. BIRCHALL,
Managing Director.
23-1y

Queen Fire and Life Insurance Company,
OF LIVERPOOL AND LONDON,
ACCEPTS ALL ORDINARY FIRE RISKS
on the most favorable terms.

LIFE RISKS
Will be taken on terms that will compare favorably with other Companies.

CAPITAL,   -   -   -   £2,000,000 Stg.

CHIEF OFFICES—Queen's Buildings, Liverpool, and Gracechurch Street London.
CANADA BRANCH OFFICE—Exchange Buildings, Montreal.
Resident Secretary and General Agent,
A. MACKENZIE FORBES,
13 St. Sacrament St., Merchants' Exchange, Montreal.
WM. ROWLAND, Agent, Toronto.   1-1y

The Waterloo County Mutual Fire Insur Company.

HEAD OFFICE : WATERLOO, ONTARIO.

ESTABLISHED 1863.

THE business of the Company is divided into separate and distinct branches, the

VILLAGE, FARM, AND MANUFACTU

Each Branch paying its own losses and its just prop of the managing expenses of the Company.
C. M. TAYLOR, Sec.   M. SPRINGER, M.M.P., P
J. HUGHES, Inspector.

Etna Fire and Marine Insurance Compa Dublin,

AT a Meeting of the Shareholders of this Com held at Dublin, on the 13th ult., it was agree the business of the "ETNA" should be transferred "UNITED PORTS AND GENERAL INSURANCE COM In accordance with this agreement, the business will after be carried on by the latter Company, which as and guarantees all the risks and liabilities of the "E
The Directors have resolved to continue the CAN BRANCH, and arrangements for resuming FIRE an RINE business are rapidly approaching completion.
T. W. GRIFFITH
16   MANA

Lancashire Insurance Compa

CAPITAL, - - - - - - - £2,000,000 S

FIRE RISKS
Taken at reasonable rates of premium, an
ALL LOSSES SETTLED PROMPTLY,
By the undersigned, without reference elsew

S. C. DUNCAN-CLARK & CO.,
General Agents for Ontario
25-1y   N. W. Corner of King & Church Stre
TORONTO.

DIVISION OF PROFITS NEXT Y

ASSURANCES

EFFECTED BEFORE 30TH APRIL NEXT,

IN THE

Canada Life Assurance Comp:

OBTAIN A YEAR'S ADDITIONAL PROFIT:

OVER LATER ENTRANTS,

And the great success of the Company warrants t rectors in recommending this very important advantage to assurers.

SUMS ASSURED..........................$5,3
AMOUNT OF CAPITAL AND FUNDS........ 1,9
ANNUAL INCOME.......................... 2

Assets (exclusive of uncalled capital) for each $ liabilities, about $150.
The income from interest upon investments is alone sufficient to meet claims by death.
A. G. RAMSAY, Manage
E. BRADBURNE, Agent
Feb. 1.   1y   Toronto Str

The Victoria Mutual
FIRE INSURANCE COMPANY OF CANAD.

Insures only Non-Hazardous Property, at Low .

BUSINESS STRICTLY MUTUAL.

GEORGE H. MILLS, President.
W. D. BOOKER, Secretary.
HEAD OFFICE ....HAMILTON, ONT
Aug 15-1yr

PUBLISHED AT THE OFFICE OF THE MONE
TIMES, No. 60 CHURCH STREET.
PRINTED AT THE DAILY TELEGRAPH PUBLISHING B
BAY STREET, CORNER OF KING.

THE CANADIAN

MONETARY TIMES

AND

INSURANCE CHRONICLE.

'OTED TO FINANCE, COMMERCE, INSURANCE, BANKS, RAILWAYS, NAVIGATION, MINES, INVESTMENT, PUBLIC COMPANIES, AND JOINT STOCK ENTERPRISE.

[—NO. 38. TORONTO, THURSDAY, MAY 6, 1869. SUBSCRIPTION $2 A YEAR.

Mercantile.

Gundry and Langley,

ECTS AND CIVIL ENGINEERS, Building Sur- and Valuators. Office corner of King and Jordan oronto.

S GUNDRY. HENRY LANGLEY.

J. B. Boustead.

ON and Commission Merchant. Hops bought old on Commission. 82 Front St., Toronto.

John Boyd & Co.

SALE Grocers and Commission Merchants, at St., Toronto.

Childs & Hamilton.

ACTURERS and Wholesale Dealers in Boots Shoes, No. 7 Wellington Street East, Toronto, 28

L. Coffee & Co.

E and Commission Merchants, No. 2 Manning's Front St., Toronto, Ont. Advances made on nts of Produce.

Honore Plamondon,

House Broker, Forwarder, and General Agent, c. Office—Custom House Building. 17-1y

Sylvester, Bro. & Hickman,

RCIAL Brokers and Vessel Agents. Office—No. ario, Chambers, [Corner Front and Church Sts., 2-6m

John Fisken & Co.

OIL and Commission Merchants, Yonge St., to, Ont.

W. & R. Griffith.

ERS of Teas, Wines, etc. Ontario Chambers, urch and Front Sts., Toronto.

H. Nerlich & Co.,

ERS of French, German, English and American oods, Cigars, and Leaf Tobaccos, No. 2 Adelaide st, Toronto. 15

Candee & Co.,

S AND BROKERS, dealers in Gold and Silver Government Securities, &c., Corner Main and Streets, Buffalo, Y. N. 21-1y

Lyman & McNab.

SALE Hardware Merchants, Toronto, Ontario.

W. D. Matthews & Co.

E Commission Merchants, Old Corn Exchange, nt St. East, Toronto Ont.

R. C. Hamilton & Co.

E Commission Merchants, 119 Lower Water Halifax, Nova Scotia.

Parson Bros.,

EUM Refiners, and Wholesale dealers in Lamps, neys, etc. Warerooms 51 Front St. Refinery cor. Don Sts., Toronto.

C. P. Reid & Co.

RS and Dealers in Wines, Liquors, Cigars and obacco, Wellington Street, Toronto. 28.

W. Rowland & Co.,

E BROKERS and General Commission Mer- Advances made on Consignments. Corner Front Streets, Toronto.

Reford & Dillon.

RS of Groceries, Wellington Street, Toronto, .

Sessions, Turner & Cooper.

ACTURERS, Importers and Wholesale Dealer ots and Shoes, Leather Findings, etc., 8 Wel- West, Toronto, Ont

Insurance.

INSURANCE CONVENTION.

In accordance with a circular issued some time ago, a convention of the representatives of Mutual Insurance Companies was held in Hamilton, on 28th April. The companies represented, and their representatives, were as follows :—Beaver Mutual, Toronto, S. Thompson and C. E. Chadwick ; Toronto Mutual, Toronto, S. Thompson and C. E. Chadwick ; Ontario Farmers' Mutual, Whitby, L. Fairbanks and J. B. Bickell ; Agricultural Association, London, Wm. Niles, W. R. Vining, and D. C. McDonald ; Niagara Mutual, St. Catharines, Thos. H. Graydon ; Wellington Mutual, Guelph, Charles Davidson ; Waterloo Mutual, Waterloo, Moses Springer and C. M. Taylor ; Ontario Mutual, London, James Johnston ; Canada Farmers' Mutual, Hamilton, R. P. Street and Thos. Stock ; Hamilton Mutual, Hamilton, N. Hammond and W. G. Crawford ; Gore District Mutual, Galt, Thomas M. Simons and Robert McLean.

Mr. C. E. Chadwick, of Ingersoll, was called to the chair, and Mr. Robert McLean, of Galt, was appointed Secretary. The circular calling the convention having been read, a discussion arose as to the best mode of proceeding, when the following resolution was carried :

Moved by Mr. Thompson, seconded by Mr. Simons, That Messrs. Charles Davidson, Moses Springer, D.C. McDonald, R. P. Street, Thos. H. Graydon, the mover and seconder, be a committee to draft an amended bill for submission to the Legislature, to consolidate the laws having reference to mutual insurance, and to report to an adjourned meeting, at which all the Mutual Fire Insurance Companies in the Province of Ontario shall have the opportunity of being represented.

Moved by J. B. Bickell, seconded by C. M. Taylor, That the foregoing Committee be requested to send a copy of the proposed act, as adopted by them, to each Mutual Insurance Company in the Province of Ontario, at least six weeks before the next meeting of the representatives of the different insurance companies, to enable the Board of Directors of each company to pass their judgment thereon.

Moved by C. M. Taylor, seconded by Mr. Bickell, That Messrs. R. P. Street, W. R. Vining, C. E. Chadwick, the mover and seconder, be a committee to report on the propriety of adopting a uniform tariff of rates in connection with the question of re-assurance for purely farm Mutuals.

Moved by Mr. Simons, seconded by Mr. Graydon, That Messrs. Moses Springer, S. Thompson, Chas. Davidson, the mover and seconder, be a committee to consider the question of re-insurance, in connection with a uniform tariff of rates in mixed companies.

The Convention adjourned till 3 o'clock, p.m., to enable the foregoing committees to report.

The Convention met as per adjournment, when the committee appointed to report in regard to purely Farmer's Mutuals, presented the following report, which, on the motion of Mr. Street, seconded by Mr. Graydon, was received :

The committee appointed to consider a uniform tariff of rates with a view to the question of re-insurance, beg leave to report : Your Committee recommend that the Mutual Farm Insurance Companies should agree to adopt the following scale of rates :—Premium note system, 1st class isolated dwellings, 1 ; 2nd class isolated dwellings, $1\frac{1}{4}$; 3rd barns, outbuildings and stables, $1\frac{1}{2}$; with a uniform cash payment of one-sixth of the premium note.

And on the cash system :—A payment of six tenths of what the premium note would amount to.

And in scale of distances :—That 80 feet shall be considered isolation ; that under 80 feet and over 60, the rates shall be, on 1st, 2nd and 3rd class—$1\frac{1}{4}$, $1\frac{1}{2}$, and $1\frac{3}{4}$, respectively ; under 60 and over 40 feet, $1\frac{1}{2}$, $1\frac{3}{4}$, and 2. That your Committee recommend the adoption of the above rates as a basis upon which to effect re-insurance with other companies. All of which is respectfully submitted. RICHARD P. STREET, Chairman.

On motion being made, the representatives of mixed Companies were added to the above Committee, and a resolution passed appointing the next meeting of the Convention to be held in Hamilton. Resolutions were passed expressing the opinion that the insurance of more than two-thirds of the actual cash value of either buildings or contents is opposed to the interests of Mutual Insurance Companies ; that unity of action in the matter of offering a liberal reward by Mutual Insurance Companies, for the conviction of incendiaries, is highly desirable, and that this subject be specially referred to at the next meeting of the Convention. That a multiple of four of the tariff of the Associated Proprietary Companies, form the basis of the Premium Note System for a three-years' insurance of Mutual Companies doing business. This rule to apply to all risks except isolated private dwellings and farm properties ; that one-fifth of the premium note rate be the cash premium for re-insurance for one year.

That a multiple of four of the lowest rates of Proprietary Companies be the premium note rate on isolated private dwellings, and that isolation for first-class buildings be 66 feet; second-class 80 feet; and third-class 120 feet; and further, that one-fourth of the premium note rate be the cash premium for one year's insurance. That each Mutual Fire Insurance Company do supply each other with copies of policies, applications, and instructions to agents, when so requested, with a view to the assimilation of the conditions of insurance. The Convention meet again at the call of the chairman.—Condensed from *Hamilton Times.*

FIRE RECORD.—Bowmanville, April 30.—A fire broke out this morning in the brick block occupied by the Royal Canadian Bank, McCullough & Co., dry goods, and Joseph Jeffery, tailor. By the exertions of the fire company and citizens, the fire was confined to the part of the building where it was first discovered. The principal sufferer is Mr Jeffery, who has lost all the furniture in the third story. The building is badly injured. McCullough & Co's goods were slightly injured by removal.

Brantford, April 30.—Mr. Ott's tannery was destroyed by fire last night. The Loss amounts to about $2,000 ; insured for $1,500. Cause of fire unknown.

Blenheim, Ont., April 18.—Mr. Morris' premises, and Mr. Osborne's Cabinet Shop, and principle contents were destroyed by fire, loss $600, insured for $300. Joseph McMichael lived above Osborne's Shop, and lost a considerable quantity of furniture.

Halifax, April 16.—Fire broke out in a building on Salter Street, south end of Granville Street, belonging to the Eason estate, and occupied by Dennis Carroll, as a forage barn. The building, with a large quantity hay, was almost wholly destroyed.

Southold, County Elgin, Ont., April 16.—A fire in the premises of John McLay, destroyed the dwelling house and the greater part of its contents ; but a trifling portion of the furniture being saved owing to the rapid progress of the flames, and the absence of almost any assistance, The house and barns were insured, but the principal weight of the insurance was on the barns.

Thorold, April 25.—Birbeck's House sustained some injury and the furniture was destroyed though the fire was soon extinguished ; covered by insurance.

Aylmer, Ont., April, 24.—The Times says, that a fire at the village of Hall destroyed the Wright homestead, no insurance ; cause unknown.

Georgetown, Ont., April 25.—House of one Johnston, entirely consumed ; furniture saved, the fire is attributed to a defective stove-pipe.

Toronto, April 25.—The "Gloucester House," on Yonge Street, was gutted ; most of the furniture was saved ; insured in the Western for $2000 Beckett's stables also on Yonge Street, were consumed with four horses and a quantity of hay.

Chatham, Ont., April 30.—Great Western Railway freight house, with several car loads of produce. Robert Lowe and George Stringer are the principal losers. The loss is stated by Mr. Swinyard, manager of the Railway, at $9,000 and fully insured. The fire is thought to be the work of an incendiary and one arrest was made.

Rothesay, Ont., April.—Store and dwelling of of Mr. Stull. There was an insurance of $400 in the Waterloo Mutual. The stock was estimated at $2,500, on which there was an insurance of $1,500 in the Provincial.

A Correspondent in Halifax sends us the following list of fires in Nova Scotia :—

Halifax, N. S., April 16th.—Barn, owned by estate late John Eason, Salter Street, Halifax ; total loss ; insured with the Acadia (local) Company, for $400.

Cornwallis, N. S., April 17th.—Dwelling house at Cornwallis, King's County, owned by Henry Lovett, and occupied by him. Partial loss of $400 ; Insured for $1,200 with the "Ætna" of Hartford.

Riversdale, N. S., April 20th.—Spool Factory, at Riversdale, Pictou County ; in operation for two months only. Building and machinery total loss ; Insured for $10,000 with the "Liverpool and London, and Globe." which, however, will not cover the loss estimated by the proprietors.

Halifax, N. S., April 24th.—Union Engine Company's Hall, Grand Parade, Halifax ; partial loss of $400. Insured with the Liverpool and London and Globe Insurance Company.

Greenwood, May 3.—House of Ira B. Carpenter, on lot 3, 3rd concession, Pickering ; the house, and nearly all the furniture were burned.

Greenwood, May 4.—The steam planing mill and sash factory at Whitevale, was totally destroyed by fire. The building was owned by T. P. White, reeve of Pickering, and occupied by Gilchrist & Co., who lost all their new and valuable machinery. The fire is supposed to have originated by a spark from the engine. Loss estimated to be $5,000 ; no insurance.

St. Catherines May 3.—The barns and stables of the "Pickwick House" with three horses and a cow were burnt; one, a valuable animal, the property of Mr. John McCurrie. Several carriages, sleighs, and harness were also destroyed. This fire is supposed to be the work of an incendiary.

Kincardine, May 4.—The barn of Mrs. McPherson, tavernkeeper, at Amberly, containing six

tons of hay, a quantity of oats and wheat, two cows, a number of farming implements, and about a hundred dollars worth of fruit trees, was totally destroyed by fire yesterday evening ; loss about five hundred dollars ; no insurance ; supposed to have taken fire from the pipe of an intoxicated man, who had been smoking on the premises.

TORONTO FIRE LIMITS.—The limits within which rough-casted frame shanties may be erected with shingles laid in mortar, are as follows :—Commencing at the junction of Yonge and Queen streets, and running in a line 120 feet north of the north side of the latter street (so as to include outbuildings) to East William street ; thence south to Adelaide street, and so on, including those intervening blocks, back to Yonge street. The limits are also extended up Teranley street to Edward street, and thence to Yonge street, including those blocks also.

—Mr. William Henderson has been appointed Inspector of the Provincial Insurance Company, vice Turnbull, resigned.

—Mr. Daniel L. Sills has been dismissed from the Ontario agency of the Connecticut Mutual Life of Hartford.

ARSON AS A RESULT OF FIRE INSURANCE MISMANAGEMENT.

Fire-Marshal Brackett the other day expressed in a public Court an opinion which all familiar with the methods of acquiring fire insurance business will indorse. Referring to a case of alleged arson, he complained — the reporters tell us—"about the careless manner in which policies are granted at the instance of insurance agents," contending that "their general manner of transacting business is simply paying a premium on arson, and multiplying this heinous crime more rapidly then justice can overtake it."

The statement, strong as it is, does not admit of doubt. The excessive competition in fire insurance has developed a recklessness which at once demoralizes the community and imperils the solvency of the companies concerned. The rule seems to be to get business at any cost—to get it, in fact, with little regard for the conditions that are essential not only to its profitableness, but to its safety. Risks are taken which no prudent company should assume, and in a manner which seems designed to encourage fraud. There is little scrutiny into the value of the property to be insured, and still less into the character of its professed owners. No systematic supervision is exercised after insurance, to hold in check the plans of schemers, and exact compliance with the conditions on which the policies are based. The consequence is that knaves are enabled to obtain insurances for amounts greatly exceeding the worth of the property, and thus to render arson more profitable than trade.

The almost absolute impunity with which the crime is perpetrated doubtless contributes much to its spread. The first duty of a company upon which a claim is made is to investigate the circumstances in which it originates—to ascertain that the precautionary requirements of the policy have been fulfilled, that the property alleged to have been destroyed was actually there to the amount claimed, and that the cause of the fire was beyond the control of the claimant. If careful inquiry reveal the fact of falsehood or fraud in any of these respects, the company is equally bound to withhold payment, and, where willful destruction is apparent or even probable, to prosecute the supposed offender. A firm regard for these twin "duties" is incumbent upon companies, as well with a view to the protection of their own interests as from a proper regard for the welfare of the community.

Competition pushed to an extreme has, however, produced quite a different method of dealing with claims. Instead of being carefully investigated, they are promptly paid. The companies are eager only for business, and to acquire if they boast that they never dispute the claims of the insured,

ɔefore leaving off for the day, a last shot
;ht out a piece of quartz weighing twenty-six
s, twelve ounces of which were pure gold,
vas at seven feet from the sufface. Tenders
ut for sinking on the Toronto Co's. shaft.
ɪSQUODOBOIT.—Mr. Hyde has now one hun-
men at work, including all who are at the
and engaged on the tramway, which he is
g built. The results from his mill have not
ɔired. Mr. Burkner brought up about 50
s as the first yield from his mill, and the lode
. he is working has widened out to five and
feet, and still shows much shotty gold on
ce. The average yield from last crushing of
ıd a half feet of vein stuff was fifteen penny-
ts per ton.
.L MINES.—We regret to learn that the fire
Foord Pit, Albion Mines, is likely to prove
serious affair than was one time anticipated.
ednesday evening last, several explosions
ed, since which time we have not learned
urther particulars.—*Eastern Chronicle*, 3rd

hé fibrous mineral, asbestos, has often been
ı of as a substitute for rags, but as the sup-
asbestos was uncertain, no practical use has
made of the knowledge. The Montreal
l believes there are several deposits of asbes-
Canada, particularly in the eastern town-
and these will, no doubt receive attention
demond for their mineral increases. A
of asbestos, which has a long fibre, and
eqaal to the Italian, exists on the property
Slate Company at Melbourne, and is being
l by parties in New York.

Financial.

TORONTO STOCK MARKET.

(Reported by Pellatt & Osler, Brokers.)

h the exception of Bank of Montreal, which
vanced 6 per cent., stocks generally close
, and in some cases show a considerable de-

k Stock.—Montreal has advanced, owing to
laration of a 6 per cent. dividend, and there
v buyers at 152, and no sellers. No sales
ish. Ontario firm at 101½. Toronto has
d since our last report, the latest sales being
½. Royal Canadian.—In consequence of
circulars issued in reference to this Bank
ɔck rapidly declined, but there are now
at over 60. Commerce is rather heavy at
vith buyers at 102. Gore has again de-
sales having taken place at 36½. Transac-
Merchants' occurred at 107 and 107½, clo-
avy at the latter rate. Quebec continues
demand at 102 to 102½. Sales of Molson's
ɔrted at 109, which rate is still procureable.
City were made at 101 to 102, but the
eclined to 101½, with no buyers over par.
ple is in fair demand at 108; little offer-
he latest sales of Jacques Cartier were at
ttle offering. Mechanics—Very little of-
buyers and sellers a part. Other banks
l.
ıtures.—No Canada five or six per cents. in
ket. Dominion stock has been sold at
holders now demanding 108½ to 109. To-
ɔnds having ten years to run offering at
pay a little over 6¾ per cent. No County
; they would command high rates.
ries.—There are limited sales of City Gas
o 107½. There are buyers of British Ame-
ssurance at 56. Small sales of Canada
ent Building Society were made at 125½,
h rate there are buyers. Western Canada
offered at 121, with buyers to a limited
t 120½. Freehold B. S. sold at 112½, at
ate there are buyers. Holders ask 134 for
l Telegraph, with no buyers over 133.
ges have been freely placed to pay 8 to 10
. Money tight; commercial paper com-
high rates.

THE ROYAL CANADIAN BANK.

Some correspondence has taken place with reference to the affairs of this bank. Hon. Donald McDonald, in a circular issued by him from Ottawa, alleges that the advances by the Bank to Brown and Chewett were characterized by recklessness; that he was ignorant of the transactions, though a member of the Board; that the original agreement with Brown was entered into by A. M. Smith, on his own responsibility, without consulting the Board, and even without reporting it, and that the final loan of money to be used in gold speculation was, in the same manner, granted by Mr. Smith, on his individual authority; that the Board has been kept uninformed of all important business despite Mr. McDonald's repeated protests, and the President has assumed absolute authority; that the system has worked badly, as shown by the losses at Agencies; that the influence of Mr. Smith caused the Cobourg agent, Mr. Wallace, [whose appointment he, Mr. McDonald remonstrated against] to be reinstated, after suspension by the Cashier, and thereby caused the total loss of the amounts the Agent had improvidently advanced; that when the accounts of the Seaforth Agency, under Mr. Russell, (whose dismissal he, Mr. McDonald, proposed) became unsatisfactory, Mr. Smith interfered to give time to Mr. Russell to close his accounts, which extension enabled him to go on with the irregularities which led to his absconding; that the losses of the Kingston Agency occurred on credits of which the Board had not been informed; that Agents were allowed, on their own responsibility, to make advances to persons of doubtful credit, and to engage in transactions which proper supervision would have rendered impossible; that the Bank itself has made advances, without exacting adequate security, the President alone being the judge; that the monthly returns to Government, which are prepared under the direction of the President, have been so manipulated as to conceal losses and debts known to be bad have been included among available assets. He concludes that although the position of the Bank is such as to enable it to meet all obligations, to keep the public safe, to provide amply for all claims, yet the Shareholders have need to act promptly to protect their interests.

Mr. A. M. Smith, in reply, asserts that Mr. McDonald was advised and knew of Browne's transactions and arrangements with the Bank, as well as of other transactions of which he claims to be ignorant, and this can be attested on oath by an officer of the Bank; that the books showing the daily discounts, and past due bills, were at all times open to inspection of the Board, and lay on the table at the weekly meetings; that Mr. McDonald never remonstrated, as he alleges, against the appointment of Mr. Wallace; that Mr. W's. suspension was at Mr. Smith's instance, and his dismissal would have followed had it not been for the fear of jeapordizing large amounts; that the general management and correspondence with the Agencies was conducted by the Cashier, and seldom came under Mr. Smith's notice; that the statements and insinuations respecting Mr. Smith's connection with the Seaforth Agency, and his action at the Board with reference thereto are pure fabrications; that Mr. Smith had no more connection with the affairs of the Kingston Agency than Mr. McDonald had; that, as is well known, Mr. McDonald is anxious to occupy the position of President, and the first cause of his discontent was that he was not elected last July, on which occasion he received his own vote only. Mr. Smith says:

"It is no doubt known to many of the stockholders, but perhaps not to all, that Mr. McDonald is at times engaged in speculations not only hazardous, but which require manipulating in a rather questionable way, as the following fact will show: he applied on the 29th January last, to the President and Cashier for a loan of one hundred thousand dollars (*say nearly one-tenth*) of the paid up capital of the Bank, saying, however, that he wished it kept from the knowledge of Mr. Smith; and actually proposed to another member of the Board to assist him in holding a meeting with the President, to be called specially for the purpose of granting the loan of the above sum with the cognizance of the other members of the Board. When they refused, he made a formal application in writing for that amount, which came before the Board at it next sitting, at which there were present the President, Mr. McDonald, and another besides himself, four in all; he there pressed the loan, and I was forced to have recourse to a clause in the by-laws, which prohibits the discount of a note, if objected to by one member of the Board present; he, Mr McD. insisting all the time that the clause in the by-laws, refering to the discount of a note, did not apply to a foreign credit, which was what he wanted. When this *ruse* failed him, a special meeting of the Board, called for the purpose, finally disposed of the matter by unanimously refusing the credit, which he wanted for the purpose of investing in one of the most dangerous enterprises in the United States which has already ruined some four or five contractors. Let Mr. McDonald contradict the above if he dare—let him show the stockholders that he could have met the loss had his contract failed, and then convince them that I would have been justified in permitting the investment of the funds of the Bank in such a mad speculation in a foreign country. Since then it has come to my knowledge that this Mr. McDonald has been endeavouring to intimidate the President, Cashier and other members of the Board, by threats of sending a circular to the stockholders, unless they would comply with an improper demand, which he said in presence of the Board, that unless he got what he wanted, he would issue the circular when he went to Ottawa, as he could then save the postage by franking them."

As regards the Brown affair, Mr. Smith says; "It is true that during the absence of the Cashier from the city, I authorized a credit not to exceed $25,000 to Mr. Brown, after satisfying myself by an examination of his books, and a special report obtained from the Commercial Agency, of his standing and responsibility for that amount; which arrangement continued for more than a year with satisfaction and profit to the Bank. Finding then that Mr. Brown was endeavoring to overstep his understood limits, I suspended the arrangement until he gave Mr. Chewett's note for $25,000, which fully covered his indebtedness at the time; and he having thus placed the account in a position which was considered safe and satisfactory, I never again interfered with it while President. By a reference to a report of Mr. Chewett's examination in bankruptcy, you will see that the gold transactions referred to by by Mr. McDonald, which resulted so disastronsly to that firm, were not engaged in till after I had ceased to be President."

The following Directors, Messrs. Metcalfe, Barber, Harman, Manning, Crombie and Smith, have also replied jointly to Mr. McDonald. They allege that a short time since he made a proposal to the Board, which they felt bound unanimously to decline, and from that time a change was observed in Mr. McDonald's conduct; that he next endeavored, "under threat of issuing a circular of some kind, such as he has issued, to gain a personal advantage, coupled with a promise that if his offer was accepted his lips would be sealed;" that the endeavor was not successful, and hence the circular; that the appointment of Mr. Wallace was not made against Mr. McDonald's remonstrance, as he was not present at the meeting at which Mr. Wallace was appointed, nor at any of the ten preceding meetings, and he did not enter his protest against the appointment; that Mr. McDonald did not propose the dismissal of Mr. Russell, and what was done was done by the unanimous vote of the Board; that the Cashier was the first to direct attention to the irregularities at the Kingston agency; that the Board was not divided, with a majority against the measures of the late President, and there was no such division ; that it is not correct that the returns to Government have been so manipulated as to conceal losses ; that these returns have been prepared by the proper officers of the Bank, and are correct ; that full inquiry is courted by the Directors into all matters connected with the management of the Bank.

STATEMENT of the Dominion Notes in circulation, Wednesday, the 7th day of April, 1869, and of the Specie held against them at Montreal, Toronto and Halifax, according to the returns of the Commissioners under the Dominion Note Act :—

Dominion Notes in circulation—

Payable at Montreal	$2,597,037
Payable at Toronto*	947,963
Payable at Halifax †	340,000
	$3,885,000

Specie held—

At Montreal	450,000
At Toronto	400,000
At Halifax	68,000
	$918,000

Debentures held by the Receiver General under the Dominion Note Act...$3,000,000

* Including $190,000, marked St. John.

† The Nova Scotia dollar not being equal in value to that of the other Provinces, the notes issued at Halifax are worth their face value in Nova Scotia only. They are stamped "Payable at Halifax," and are numbered in black ink. None but $5 notes are yet in circulation.

BANKER'S ALMANAC.—The second edition of "The Merchants' and Bankers' Almanac," for 1868, has been issued, continuing the history of 850 insurance companies and their officers ; also a list of 1,650 National Banks ; 300 State Banks ; 1,400 Private Bankers in the United States ; Banks and Bankers in Canada ; 1,200 Bankers and Brokers in New York City, including names of members of the New York Stock Exchange, the Open Board of Brokers, the Gold Board and the Mining Board, Annual Reports of 1868 on Banks, Coinage, aal Ninety Staple Articles ; Capital, Circulation and Profits of each Bank in New York City. List of Banks and Bankers in England, Scotland, Ireland, Europe, &c.; Deposits in each. Summary view of the Annual Production of Gold and Silver throughout the world. The monthly prices for forty years at New York of the following sixteen articles : Bar Iron, Steel Iron, Pig Iron, Pig Copper, Anthracite Coal, Coffee, Cotton, Wool, Wheat, Rye, Corn, Oats, Hops, Molasses, Sugar, Pork. The Grain products (quantity, acreage and value) of every State in the Union—Corn, Wheat, Rye, Oats, Barley, Buckwheat, Potatoes, Hay and Tobacco—Years 1856, 1866. Also the monthly prices of Ninety Staple Articles at New York—1868. The daily price of Gold at New York, 1862 to 1868. Alphabetical List of 2,000 Cashiers; and Engravings of New Bank Buildings.

STOCK SALE AT HALIFAX. — At W. Myers Gray's stock sale, April 23, the following prices were realized : Five shares in the Bank of British North America, £70 ; 8 do. £70 2s. 6d ; twenty-five shares in the People's Bank, $27.75 ; 1 share in the Halifax library, $11 ; 20 shares Bank of Nova Scotia, £66 15s. ; 1 share Salt Company, 39 cents ; 2 shares Union Marine Insurance Company, £21.

—Counterfeit $5 notes of the Bank of New Brunswick are in circulation.

—A St. John paper says : The Merchants' Bank is about to establish a branch in Chatham, and Mr. King, Manager of the Bank of Montreal, is pretty sure to establish a branch of his bank at Newcastle.

ST. JOHN BUILDING SOCIETY.—A balance sheet of liabilities and assets of the Society are as follows :

Dr.	DECEMBER 31, 1868.	
To depositors		$53,900 11
To stock, cash		60,369 97
To accumulating interest		71,027 91
Sundries		575 52
		$185,903 51

Cr.		
By advances to members, secured by 204 mortgages		$179,087 03
By contingent account		6,026 20
By sundries		850 28
		$185,963 51

The operations of the Society are based on 1,303¾ shares, viz : 591 monthly investing, and 165¼ paid up shares, and 547½ advanced shares, the whole representing a subscribed capital of $260,750. The amount now held on deposit is $53,990, against $41,726 on 1st January last year.

—A special meeting of the stockholders of La Banque Jacques Cartier is called for the 14th June, to take into consideration a proposition to dismiss the President, the Hon. J. L. Beaudry, on account of neglect to fulfil his duties, having neglected to attend the meetings of the bank since the 19th Dec., 1868.

Railway News.

GREAT WESTERN RAILWAY.—Traffic for week ending April 16, 1869.

Passengers	$29,935 27
Freight	53,667 10
Mails and Sundries	2,246 07
Total Receipts for week	$85,848 44
Coresponding week, 1868	82,191 64
Increase	$3,656 80

NORTHERN RAILWAY.—Traffic receipts for week ending April 24th, 1869.

Passengers	$2,194 33
Freight and live stock	8,713 77
Mails and sundries	388 04
	$11,296 14
Corresponding Week of '68.	11,281 23
Decrease	$985 09

Law Report.

IN CHANCERY.—In re. Etna Insurance Co. of Dublin.—Mr. T. H. Spencer presented a petition on behalf of the creditors of the company, praying that the Government may be ordered to pay into Court the moneys shown to have been deposited with them by the company under the statute 24 Vic., chap. 33, and that said moneys be distributed among the creditors of the company. S. H. Strong Q. C., and J. Bain for the Minister of Justice, showed that the money has been forfeited to the Government under the statute, and contend that the creditors are not entitled to the benefit of the deposit. They also contend that the Court has no jurisdiction to make such an order. Stands for petitioner to show more clearly the existence of such a fund, and the condition in which it now stands. V. C. Sprague expressing a doubt whether he could under any circumstance make the order sought for as against the Government.

MARKLE vs. NIAGARA DISTRICT MUTUAL INSURANCE CO.—This action, which was tried at the Lincoln Assizes, was brought by Mr. W. Markle, of Listowel, to recover $800 dollars, the amount of an insurance policy on his tavern in Listowel, which was destroyed by fire in October, 1867. The claim was resisted on the plea that when the insurance was effected there was a mortgage on

the property of $500, which the plaintiff failed notify the Company of. Verdict for plaintiff $800, and $56 interest.

RUSS vs. CLINTON MUTUAL INSURANCE COMPANY.—This was an action at the present Toronto Assizes, on a policy of insurance effected with Mutual Fire Insurance Company, at Clinton, brought to recover the sum of $900, being amount of the plaintiff's claim for loss in consequence of the premises insured being destroyed by fire on the 20th of March 1868. Defendants I plea denied the making of the policy ; Second fraud ; Third, that at the time of effecting the surance, the premises were mortgaged to one W. Ketchen ; Fourth, that after effecting insurance, plaintiff mortgaged the property ; Fi a plea in bar denying the plaintiff's interest in property insured. Defendants abandoned t first and second pleas, and went to the jury the others. Verdict for the plaintiff, $940 56

—At the St. Catharines Assizes the case of Niagara Falls Suspension Bridge Company Gardener, came up on the 5th inst. This was action brought to test the question whether Suspension Bridge at Clifton is real estate or ; sonal property, and whether it can be assesse ordinary property in the corporate limits. Ju Price, of Welland, has already given two decisi on the subject ; but it is contended that his decisions are not final. No jury was called in case, and Mr. J. H. Cameron said it was opinion that the new law would lead to differ yet. For instance, when his Lordship was Ju and and jury, he should like to know the rem if the jury was misdirected. A verdict of $10 entered for the plaintiff, with leave to defend to enter a non-suit, or a verdict for defendant

INSOLVENTS.—Wm. Waterson, Henry Graham John Simon, John Courtenay, John Cameron, Bruce, Jacob Silverstone, Theodore Lanc Wm. A. Curry, Montreal; William Lawra Charles Coburn Jerome, London; J. & D. Wi ton, Ward McCullum, [Chatham; Arthur Hai John Secord, St. Catharines; S. C. Seagel, Hi Converse, Owen Sound; John Braidwood, W stock; George Boisenault, Quebec; Elizabeth P Newmarket; Richard Flynn, Shakespeare; R Duncan, West Zorra; Wm. Stapleton, Paris; V H. Henry Crotty, Ingersoll; X. Boles, Elder Wm. Reid Stayner, Geo. Watson, Bolton Vill Alex. Kirkbridge, Goderich; James Ferrier, lington Wilson, Guelph; Ed. McGreery, Presc Rob't Findlay, G. G. Buck, Lindsay; P. Am De Licard, Princeville; Edmund Longley, W loo; James Cunningham, Mitchell; Fenner Buckingham; Robert Gamble, Thornton.

AMERICAN CUSTOM HOUSE FEES.—The Un States Treasury Department has recently pro gated the following as the fees to be charged sels by the Custom House Officers during present season :

1. That when a vessel enters light from same or another district, she pays a fee of 25 c for an official certificate to the master's oat making report, under 16th paragraph of the

2. That when a vessel enters with a cargo a port or place in the same district, she pays a of 25 cents for a permit to land or deliver go under the 14th paragraph of the act.

3. That when a vessel clears, with or wit cargo, for a port or place in the same district, pays a fee of 25 cents for a clearance and Collec certificate, under the 16th paragraph of the ac

4. That when a vessel clears light to ano district, she pays the same fees that she wou laden, under the 7th paragraph of the act.

5. That vessels trading on Lake Michigan, clusively, laden exclusively with American ducts, pay the same fees on entry and cleara as other vessels.

6. That Collectors are authorized to charg fee of 25 cents for certifying triplicate manife goods transported in bond from eastern to wes ports (or vice versa) through Canada.

z CANADIAN MONETARY TIMES AND INSU-
: CHRONICLE *is printed every Thursday even-
id distributed to Subscribers on the following
ng.*

*lishing office, No. 60 Church-street, 3 doors
of Court-street.*

scription price—

'anada $2.00 per annum.

ingland, stg. 10s. per annum.

'nited States (U.S.Cy.) $3.00 per annum.

*ual advertisements will be charged at the rate
cents per line, each insertion.*

iress all letters to "THE MONETARY TIMES."

*ques, money orders, &c. should be made pay-
> J. M. TROUT, Business Manager, who alone
'horized to issue receipts for money.*

*All Canadian Subscribers to THE MONETARY
: will receive THE REAL ESTATE JOURNAL
it further charge.*

e Canadian Monetary Times.

THURSDAY, MAY 6, 1869.

HE ROYAL CANADIAN BANK.

> evil of placing a mere speculator on a
l of Bank Directors was never more fully
ated than in the case of the Hon. Do-
McDonald, whose "private and confi-
l" circulars to the stockholders of the
. Canadian Bank have provoked rejoin-
iqually "private and confidential" from
. M. Smith, the late President, and
the Directors themselves. By some
i these "private and confidential" cir-
have found their way into the news-
s, and the public have been regaled with
perusal. Mr. McDonald is a Senator,
vailing himself of his privileges as such,
ie country to the expense of circulating
rcularized grievances. We deem this
;e-saving operation of Mr. McDonald's
y of notice, in connection with his
pt to win the sympathy and assistance
fellow shareholders in the Royal Cana-
by his seemingly patriotic effort to ren-

der them a service. The record of a public
benefactor should be stainless, if he wish to
command attention and gratitude : so this
simple evasion of postage is sufficient to throw
doubt on Mr. McDonald's sincerity. But
when we find that his alleged facts sink into
airy nothings before contradiction and dis-
proof, we begin to doubt his honesty. When
we find still further, that this would-be reformer of abuses threatened his fellow directors with dreadful revelations, in case
they refused to grant him what the directors
call "a personal advantage," and promised
that "his lips would be sealed" if his proposals were acquiesced in, we cannot help concluding that this Senator is the compeer of
the sender of threatening letters, and that
his words are wholly unworthy of credence.
A step further brings us face to face with a
piece of impudence so brazen and cool, that
we are lost in amazement at the audacity of
the man who could have perpetrated it. According to Mr. A. M. Smith, a gentleman
whose veracity none would dare to question,
the Hon. Donald McDonald applied to the
President and Cashier of the Royal Canadian
Bank, on 29th January last, for a loan of
nearly one-tenth of the paid up capital of the
bank. Verily, Senator McDonald is a nice
man to have on a bank Board! If Mr. Smith's
statement is true, it is high time that an extraordinary meeting of shareholders were
held, and such proceedings taken as would
ensure Mr. McDonald's expulsion from the
Board. Even supposing that Mr. McDonald
were not a director, not a speculator, and
were good for any amount, we all know that
large loans have been the ruin of such of
our banks as have failed, and that the managers of our banks must and should avoid
them. Mr. McDonald quarrels with the bank
management, but he would have had the directors do what every bank manager, aye,
every bank clerk here, knows to be the worst
possible thing for a bank with limited means.
He condemns Mr. Smith for assisting Mr.
Brown in his gold speculations in New York,
yet he would have forced the bank to lend
himself a large amount, to enable him to
engage in dangerous enterprises in the States !

The shareholders of the Royal Canadian
have, of course, by this time been placed in
possession of the charges and the replies. If
there is one lesson more important than another to be learned from their perusal, it is that
the election of a man such as Mr. McDonald
would appear, from the evidence, to be,—one
whose speculations are incessant, leading to a
constant demand for large sums of money—
one who is always tempted to make use of his
position to his own advantage pecuniarily—
one whose associations are with either the
needy or the speculator—is fraught with the

greatest danger to their interests. If they
believe that the statements of Mr. Smith and
the directors are correct, it is a duty they owe
to themselves, to the other banks, and to the
public, to free the Board of his presence.
Such an one must shake confidence in the
management, for if one director could obtain by way of loan, one-tenth of the bank's
capital, what reason would there be against
assuming that the other directors could
not secure the remaining nine-tenths. A
Board of Bank Directors should be individually and collectively above suspicion, and
when one is found recreant to his trust, a
public example should be made of him. Now
or never. If what Mr. Smith and the Directors say is true, Mr. McDonald is not fit
to be trusted on the Board; on the other
hand, if Mr. McDonald's assertions are true,
the whole management should be changed.
It has come to this that a choice must be
made or public confidence will be lost to the
institution. We are glad, for the sake of the
Royal Canadian, that the worst is now known,
and it will be for the Shareholders, by prompt
action, to convince the public that a Director
cannot remain as their trustee and act the
part which Mr. Senator McDonald has been
so directly charged with.

THE CANADIAN CANALS.

I.

We see by the journals, that proceedings
have been taken in Parliament, with regard
to the Ottawa navigation scheme. It may
briefly be stated that those who are interested in this project, or we may say who advocate its necessity, have petitioned the Dominion Government for aid. An issue is therefore raised, and we are very glad of it. It is
in every way desirable that such should be
the case ; and there can now be no means of
evading the decision, whether the St. Lawrence is to be the line of communication or
not; and whether the St. Lawrence route
shall be developed to its full capacity.

No one could blame us if we assumed the
standing point of arguing from local considerations. We could say—look to the results
of Confederation. In Eastern Canada a line
of railway is placed under contract, to cost a
very large sum of money,—we will not be
precise, but some millions of dollars—the
creation of which is not demanded by a solitary commercial necessity. Even the political uses are not self-apparent ; for, from all
we can learn, in summer, the travel incident
to parliament will, in Nova Scotia, turn to
Halifax, and pass by boat to Portland or Boston, and thence follow the nearest railway
route to Ottawa. While, in New Brunswick,
the movement will turn to St. John, or by the
Maine railway connections with the Grand

Trunk. In winter, it is somewhat hard to say what will be the fate of the northern portion of the line. If it be subjected to such management, and to such results as marked the Grand Trunk last winter, the inference is that it will experience the fate of the Riviere du Loup and the Three Rivers branch. After a couple of months of winter, it will become impassable, and the snow will rest upon it in peace. While this extraordinary expenditure is the great feature to the east of the Dominion, we have the Ottawa route, hanging over central and north-western Canada. Ontario might well enquire, what counterbalancing benefit was to be extended to her population. We might here diverge from the main question, and inquire from what population the Dominion revenue is principally raised, and leave the sister Province of Quebec to tell us what sum the inhabitants of that part of the Dominion contribute. We would then be in a position to claim some equivalent, some equipoise, some sectional expenditure, by which the interests of Western Canada should be advanced. We say that with justice and with propriety this line of argument could be taken. It is not, however, our intention to follow it. We will examine the scheme of this Ottawa Canal, purely on its merits, and on the results promised, we were nearly writing threatened, because once upon a time, there was much vigor shewn in its advocacy.

The Ottawa has an ill name for experiments and blunders. One of the great arguments for placing the seat of government there, used to be, the admirable fortifications which could be placed on Citadel Hill, the site of the present parliament buildings, to defend the city from—the river, a stream unapproachable, except through the Rideau Canal, and through the narrow canals to the east. It is here that that gigantic blunder, the Rideau Canal, was perpetrated. An expense incurred by the Imperial Government, it is true, but which never gained the most shadowy result, except dissatisfaction. It is supposed to have cost five millions of dollars. But even its narrow limit was made unavailable by the extraordinary proceeding of building three locks on the Grenville Canal, 106 ft. x 19 ft.—while the remaining locks would a limit a boat passing through 127 ft. by 32 ft., drawing 5 feet of water. It is here that the Ottawa members sold their support for the commencement of the memorable Chats Canal, given out as a political job, at prices wholly below the value, and which still stands a monument of executive folly, unfinished and useless. Indeed, that it is unfinished is a mark of wisdom, for it would have been valueless; that it is useless, is proved by this Ottawa scheme, which is again claiming the

privilege to swallow up about twenty-five million of dollars.

We do not wish to write flippantly on this subject, for its importance cannot be over-rated. It has always been the case with Canada, that the country has been without a canal policy. Our system, such as it is, is an adaptation of isolated efforts of men who saw a good operation, and so advocated a certain improvement. Thus the necessity of the Lachine Canal was seen a few years after the Conquest, and the design was fostered by the Imperial Government, which, with the persistent kindness which has marked the course of the Mother Country to this Province contributed to its construction. The Cornwall Canal may be considered a more legitimate operation; for it was the work of the Upper Canada Legislature, under commissioners who performed their work in a careful manner. It is true the engineering work of this canal is as bad as it can be, but that was not the fault of the non-professional men. It was not possible to force Lower Canada to construct the Beauharnois Canal; and it was not until the Union that that indispensable link in the navigation was made. In the extreme west, the Welland Canal was seized by a knot of men, and the result of their mismanagement, and their desire to enrich themselves, has cost the country a serious sum. Even off the main route, we have the several projects dictated by private ends, more than by public advantage. There is what is known as the Trent Navigation; and we have at our own door the Georgian Bay Canal. The proprietors of this scheme are also applicants for aid. Possibly they may urge that it would be a just counterpoise to subsidise that scheme, and the Ottawa route together; and that then, justice would be observed, and the various populations equally benefitted.

For our part we do not approach the subject in any local spirit. We wish simply to examine the results which are claimed for the route, and we set entirely out of sight everything else. We will even cease to inquire if anything better can be done. We will take the project as we find it, and we will accept the arguments offered by its advocates. What there is to be gained by spending twenty millions or so by improving the Ottawa navigation? We presume that we need not consider the question of settlement west of Pembroke. It must, indeed, be an enthusiast, who at such a cost wishes to place a few settlers around Lake Nipissing, or send some northern stragglers to Lake Temiscomingue. Some few statistics of the progress of settlement on the eastern shores of Georgian Bay, by the county of Simcoe, will furnish data of what we may expect. We have then

but one ground of advocacy—commerc necessity; a quicker transit for produ between Chicago and Montreal. Nothi seems easier than to establish this argumer "Look" exclaims the advocate, "See inste "of going south by Lake Huron and passi "through the unpleasant navigation of La "St. Clair, and so by Lake Erie and the W "land Canal to Lake Ontario and the ¡ "Lawrence, we at once come to the south "the Manitoulin Islands, enter the Frer "River to Lake Nipissing, and taking ! "Mattawan we go directly by the Otta "to the Lake Saint Louis, at the foot of ¡ "Beauharnois Canal. We positively a¡ "368 miles." "Wonderful!" says the ¡ tener. At least one or two generals have ¡ so; men, too, who have the reputation of be good soldiers, and not without sense. ¡ what are these 368 miles really worth in ti¡ and in controlling the course of trade? I argued that the trip between Chicago ¡ Montreal can be made in 44 hours ¡ time than by the St. Lawrence, and t freights will be reduced in value 37 cen ton. Here is the result, the cost of whi says Mr. Walter Shanly, who examined route, will be twenty-five millions of doll an expense which takes us only to the cit; Ottawa. That is totally independent of improvement of the Ottawa, itself and Grenville and Carillon Canals to Lake S¡ Louis. How does the matter now stand ? is conceded that the route by the St. Lawre to Montreal—the most inland Canadian ¡ bor for sea-going vessels—in comparison ¡ that by the Erie Canal to New York, i¡ every way pre-eminent; that the chea¡ and slowest by the St. Lawrence is in e¡ way superior to that by the Erie Canal the Hudson. The difficulty is not in get to Montreal. The difficulty is at Montr For when you bring produce thither you ¡ no vessels to carry it away to Europe or ¡ where. That is, the vessels are regulatec the imports. So long as these are light, t¡ will be a scarcity of vessels to carry ¡ large cargoes. Therefore, however much reduce the cost of river navigation, the q¡ tion is untouched—we will not say unre died, for literally nothing is done to ¡ upon it. The comparison may be rou¡ made that between any given point at West, and Montreal and New York, the¡ a difference in time of ten days in favor of former, at half the cost. What need th¡ there for any Ottawa Canal, even on data which those who battle for it preten advance in its favor? But are we sure this very advantage is gained? Does saving of 368 miles of distance represe saving of time. The Ottawa route is ¡ Georgian Bay; a canal route in which

83 feet above Lake Huron, and de-76 feet to the basin at Ottawa city, ience the descent to Lake St. Louis is 0 to 120 feet. In the St. Lawrence m water; and, with the exception of lland Canal, and possibly the Lachine the river is kept. It is a route tra-daily, and the distance is passed iwn time. On the other hand the equired to pass the proposed parallel .on, is a matter of estimate; all that ed for it is 44 hours. It is quite pos-may not be 4 hours; and yet for this asked to spend twenty-five millions of

SUPERIOR AND RED RIVER ILWAY AND NAVIGATION COMPANY.

seting of influential merchants and took place on Saturday last, in , to receive the report of the Com-ippointed to prepare a prospectus for ipany. The Committee recommended itruction of a railway from Fort Wil-Rainy Lake, a distance of about 156 t a cost of $4,000,000, a canal with is at Fort Francis, at a cost of $2,00-d the purchase of two steamers for .ake and the Lake of the Woods, at . From the Lake of the Woods to .rry, about 95 miles of railway, costing 2,000,000, would be the second sec-The capital required would be, there-out $6,500,000, and if Government rant 8,000,000 acres of land in alter-tions and guarantee the bonds of the .y to the extent of $2,500,000, the would be a success, and Fort Garry >e placed within 40 hours travel of illiam on Lake Superior.

ng by the names of those who have upon the work, we have every con-that strong pressure could be brought upon the Government for the re-ssistance, and if there is the slightest n the part of the authorities to assist ing for Canada the trade of the vast ver Territory, such assistance could efused. Unless something be done, it immediately too, we shall have . vain the $1,500,000 which the Hud-y Company are to get for their sup-ghts. The States, with their Pacific have got the start of us, and we w to make up for lost time. Our in-t may be made to pay at once, and ier our statesmen take the matter in e better for us all. If the Dominion nent will not recognize the obligation-ote the interests of the West, it will duty of the Province of Ontario to rward single-handed, and apply its

surplus to an undertaking, which will pay this Province, at least, far better than an in-vestment in Dominion stock.

MEETING OF BANKERS. — On the 1st inst., a meeting of the representatives of various banks took place at Ottawa. Mr. Jack, of Halifax, rep-resented the banks of Nova Scotia, and Mr. Lewin, of St. John, those of New Brunswick. The other representatives were as follows: Mr. Hague, Bank of Toronto; Mr. Stephenson, Que-bec; Mr. Dunn, Union; Mr. Sache, Molson's; Mr. McMaster, Bank of Toronto; Messrs. Met-calfe and Woodside, Royal Canadian; Mr. Ben-son, Niagara District; Mr. Simpson, Ontario. Communications were received from the City and Merchants' Banks, endorsing proposed action by the meeting. Messrs. Lewin, Hague, Stevenson, Gibbs and Simpson were appointed a committee to wait on the Finance Minister in reference to his banking policy.

—We understand that Mr. Heatherington, of Halifax, has decided to resume the publication of his Mining Gazette. His connection with this journal as correspondent has, therefore, ceased. It is scarcely necessary to assure our readers that we will still continue to supply them with reliable mining intelligence from the different points of interest. Meantime, we hope that the people of Nova Scotia will show their appreciation of so useful a paper as the Gazette in a more substan-tial manner than they seem to have done hitherto.

THE NEW YORK TIMES.—To Canadians, who desire a New York journal of the first rank, we can recommend the Times, for its ability and its im-partiality. Weekly Times, $2 per annum.; Daily, $12. Address, H. J. Raymond & Co., New York.

QUEBEC LEGISLATURE—The following are some of the acts which passed at the late session of the Legislature of the Province of Quebec;—To incor-porate the St. Maurice lumber and land company; the Sherbrooke, Eastern Townships and Kennebec railway company; the St. Francis Valley and Ken-nebec railway company; to reduce the capital stock of the St. Francis mining and smelting company of the township of Cleveland, Province of Quebec; to incorporate the Montreal Northern colonization railway company; the Maganacippi River Im-provement company; respecting the St. Lawrence Warehouse, Dock, and Wharfage company; to in-corporate the Missisquoi Junction Railway Com-pany; to amend the act incorporating the South Eastern countries Junction Railway company; to incorporate the Richelieu, Drummond and Artha-baska counties railway company; to incorpo-rate the St. Francis and Yamaska Rivers Im-provement and deepening company; to amend the act to incorporate the Chambly and Hydraulic and manufacturing company; to amend the act 29th Victoria, chapter 17, relating to life assurance; further to amend the acts relating to the Stanstead, Shefford and Chambly railroad company; to repeal the act to incorporate the Canada Marine Insur-ance Company; to amend act 31 Vic., chapter 32, respecting the Fire Marshals for the cities of Mon-treal and Quebec, and to change their name of office to that of Fire Commissioner; to incorporate the Levis and Kennebec Railway company; to amend the Joint Stock companies general clauses act; to amend the Joint Stock companies in-corporation act; to incorporate the Quebec and Gosford Railway company.

Commercial.

Toronto Market.

The spring trade is now pretty well advanced, or should be, but the amount of business done falls short of what was expected. GROCERIES.—The only change, worthy of notice, is in sugars, which are down ¼ a cent. They have been gradually falling in New York, and the ten-dency is still downwards. We give the following particulars respecting the current crop in the Greek Islands: Total crop 1868, 57,500 tons; total crop, 1867, 65,000 tons. LIQUORS.—The usual trade has been doing at our quotations. The following is from the London Wine Trade Review:— "The political disturbances in Spain have in-terfered considerably with the even tenor of the Sherry trade, tending greatly to retard the proper execution of business. At Xerez the state of af-fairs has been most alarming. The rioters came into collision with the soldiery, resulting in the defeat of the former with considerable loss. Con-sidering the lamentable state of affairs, business has been satisfactorily forwarded, and it is now hoped that a better position will supervene. The consumption in Great Britain has been well main-tained, and as a great portion of the last vintage is hardly fit for shipment, prices will probably continue firm. Notwithstanding the supposed downfall of Port, advices from Oporto state that a very satisfactory business is being transacted, especially in the 1867's, which are expected to develope well, and consequently command a con-siderable amount of attention. A tolerable quan-tity of 1868 have changed hands; the fine wines of this vintage are expected to develope extraor-dinary quality, and in the lower descriptions there will probably be selected a fair average of good serviceable wines.

PETROLEUM.—The Hamilton Carbon Oil Co. are refining about 1,000 brls. per week, by the new process, and about that quantity is being shipped each week to Boston and New York, where it brings the price of the best American. The Com-pany are, at present, refining at Hamilton, but they expect their works at Hamilton to be in operation in a few days. We hear of a sale of about 2½,000 brls. crude, in tank at Petrolia, at the rate of $1.55 per barrel. This was a nice little cash trans-action of $32,000. Messrs. Parsons, Bros. are the sellers.

GRAIN.—Wheat-Receipts 1.445 bush. and 1,000 bush last week. Spring has met with a fair demand at 94 to 95c. and sales of lots amounting to about 24,-000 bushs. in all were made at these quotations; the market closed steady. Fall is dull and nominal with holders asking $1.00 to $1.05; no demand and no sales reported. Barley.—Receipts trifling; the market is nominal at quotations; sale of 800 bushs., at $1.05, bagged: the only business doing is in small lots for seed. Oats—Receipts 2,400 bushs. and 500 bushs. last week; The market is firm and higher, with sales of car loads at 54 to 55c. Peas—Receipts very light; market quiet; no lots selling; quotations unchanged. Rye—nominal, as quoted. Corn—is worth about 60c.; sales, 1 car at 60c. on track; 4 cars at 60c. f.o.c. Seeds—Timothy closes firm and higher, at $2.50 to $2.75; Clover, $5.50 to $5.75. Stocks—The stock of grain in store in Toronto on the 3rd May were; Fall wheat 57,952 bushs., do April 12th, 66,400 bushs.; Spring wheat, May 3rd, 75,083, do April 12th, 97,512 bushs.; Oats, May 3rd, 10,603 bushs., do 12th April, 18,400; Barley, May 3rd, 4,200 bushs., do April 12th, 11,415 bushs; Peas, May 3rd, 24,603 bushs., do April 12th, 36,600 bushs. FLOUR.—Receipts 1,777 bbls. and 2,014 bbls. last week. No. 1 Superfine has met with a fair demand and sales of 1,000 bbls. are reported, at $4.05, holders asking $4.10 and higher; about 1,000 bbls., in all, of spring wheat extra, sold during the week at $4.15. Fancy is also in fair demand; 300 bbls. sold at $4.25 free of storage. Extra is nominal at $4.50, no sales during the week. Superior Extra, none offering. Stock of flour in store on 3rd May, 22,056., and the 12th April 26,012 bbls. The first cargo of flour for the season has cleared for Halifax. *Oatmeal*—is in a good deal better demand ; small lots selling at $5.75 to $6. *Cornmeal*—is also in good demand, and is selling in small lots at $3.75 to $4.

PROVISIONS.—Stocks of provisions in this market are very light, being only sufficient for the requirements of local consumption. *Butter*—is a drug, no demand except in retail. *Eggs*—have been received more freely and are worth 12c. Other articles nominal as quoted.

FREIGHTS.—The following are the Grand Trunk Railway Company's summer rates from Toronto to the undermentioned stations, which came into force on the 19th inst. :—Flour to all stations from Belleville to Lynn, inclusive 25c. ; grain per 100 lbs. 13c. ; flour to Brockville and Cornwall, inclusive, 30c.; grain, ,15c.; flour to Montreal, 35c. ; grain, 18c. ; flour to all stations between Island Pond and Portland, inclusive, 75c. grain 38c. ; flour to Boston, 80c. gold ; grain 40c. ; flour to Halifax, 90c. ; flour to St. John, 85c. Freights by the Great Western Railway, to all points, unchanged.

Demerara Sugar Market.

The following is from Sandbach, Parker & Co's. market report, dated, Georgetown, Demerara, 23rd March, 1869 :

SUGARS.—We have had a very active market, and prices have advanced fully twenty per cent. Immediately after the arrival of last mai', buyers entered into keen competition, and sales were made as high as $7 90 for Vacuum Pan, the next ten days prices reduced a little, and, $7 60 to $7 70, was the ruling quotation ; since the arrival of the present mail, there is not so much disposition to operate, and the views of buyers are not in accordance with those of sellers : the transactions at public sale yesterday and to-day have been limited, our quotations are however, framed on the mean between the two parties, and are rates which we expect to see obtained during the week ; the demand for Muscovadoes was quite as good as for Vacuum Pan, the quantity offering was however small.

MOLASSES.—For really good samples, there has been an active demand, and the extreme prices of 38½ for Vacuum Pan and 32½ for Muscovado have been realized ; for the lower grades the enquiry has been dull, and we have the same remark to make regarding the present state of this market as of Sugar.

RUM.—Very little doing, holders prefer shipping to accepting the rates offered here ; we have not heard of a single transaction of consequence

SUGARS (package included) sold by 100 lbs. Dutch, 10 per cent. tare.

Muscovadoes, equal to No. 8 ⎫
Dutch Standard $4.50 ⅌ 100 lbs.
  No. 10 do. $5.00   "
  " 12 do. $5.50   " ⎬ In hhds.
Vacuum Pan No. 12 do. $6.00 ⎫ of about
  "   " 14 do. 6.50 ⎬ 1800 lbs. each.
  "   " 16 do. 6.75
  "   " 17 do. 7.00
  "   " 18 do. 7.50 ⎭

MOLASSES (package included, sold by Imperial gallon.)—

Muscovado, from 26 @ 30 cents, as ⎫ In puns
to color and density   ⎬ of
Vacuum Pan from 27 @ 35 cents, as ⎭ 100 gals.
to color and density

RUM (colored, package included, sold ⎫
by Imperial gal. from 35 per cent, @ 38 ⎬ Ditto.
overproof 40 cents.   ⎭
From 38 per cent. @ 40 overproof, 45 ⎱
cents.

Halifax Market.

BREADSTUFFS.—Our markets for supers. continue active at quotations. The demand for No. 2 is reviving. Rye flour continues unsought for. White fall wheatsdull at nominal price, with large stocks. Cornmeal active at quotations. Oatmeal dull and lower, with large stocks.

WEST INDIA PRODUCE.—Sugar continues active at full rates, with light receipts. Molasses dull and nominal, holders and buyers continue apart, and transactions are small. Rum inactive at former quotations. Coffee inactive and nominal.

Sugar V. P. 10½c to 11c. ; Porto Rico 9½ to 9⅞c; Cienfuegos ——— ; Barbadoes 9c. to 9½c. (nominal); Molasses (P. R.) ——— ; Cienfuegos 41c. to 42c. : Trinidad 40c. to 41c. ; Rum 58c. to 60c. for Demerara (in bond) ; Coffee—Jamaica 12c. (nominal).

EXCHANGE.—Bank drafts London at 60 days at 13 per cent. ; Montreal sight 4 per cent. : New York gold 4 per cent. ; currency 21 per cent. discount ; St. John, N.B. 3½ per cent. premium.

Petroleum Regulations.

The Commissioner of Inland Revenue has issued a departmental notice, based on an order in Council dated 23rd April, allowing petroleum in process of manufacture to be removed under removal bonds. To reduce the fire test from 115° to 100° Faht. for petroleum intended solely for exportation. To dispense in part, or in whole, with the payment of the fee for testing petroleum. To dispense with the branding or marking the same, if deemed necessary.

His Excellency in Council has also been pleased to authorise the following regulations respecting the removal and exportation of petroleum :—1st—Petroleum may be removed, in bond, from the place where it has been distilled to any other licensed refinery for the purpose of deodorizing it, or otherwise completing its manufacture in bond, without payment of duty. 2nd—When petroleum in process of manufacture is removed in bulk—that is to say, in tank cars, or other vessels containing large quantities—and when the removal is made under removal bonds, the inspection fee of twenty cents per package is only to be collected on each tank or other package. 3rd—Petroleum, refined for exportation, may be inspected and branded ; or it may be exported without inspection or branding, at the option of the exporter, and if exported without inspection or branding, the inspection fee is not to be collected, but the refiner shall nevertheless, make a full return of his operations, and give a true account of the quantities refined by him in the same manner as if the products of his refinery were going into consumption. An allowance for waste occasioned by the process of deodorization, not exceeding 7 per cent., may be deducted from the quantity specified in the removal bonds, provided that such waste is proven to the satisfaction of the Collector of the Inland Revenue, and provided also that no part of the residuum composing the waste occasioned shall go into consumption for any purpose whatever.

SUGAR RAISING.—Within a few years past several European countries have directed considerable attention to the manufacture of sugar from beet roots. Last year 220,000 tons were made in France; 165,000 in Germany ; 97,500 in Russia ; 92,500 in Austria ; 82,500 in Belgium ; 15,000 in Poland and Sweden, and 7,500 tons in Holland. Some English capitalists are making extensive arrangements for the manufacture of beet root sugar, while the French government is doing all in its power to stimulate it. Many assert that beet sugar is clearer than cane sugar, and because of this and other reasons, is preferable to the latter.

—The following notice appears in the Canada *Gazette:*—Notice is hereby given that application will be made to the Parliament of Canada, at its next Session, for an Act to incorporate Freeman Tupper, Thomas R. Pattillo, James F. Forbes. John H. Mulhall, John G. Morton, John D. McClearn, Lewis Sponagle, Stephen C. Tupper, James S. Sponagle, J. N. Freeman, Thomas Day, Joseph James, all of Liverpool, Queen's County, Nova Scotia, and others, under the name of "The Bank of Liverpool."

— The Anglo-American Peat Company launched a double-decked scow, called the *Nellie C* at Edgarville, Welland County, the other day She is to be employed in the service of the Company, and will have a peat machine on board.

—Notices of application from the Erie & Niagara Extension Railway Company and Niagara Railway Company to the next Dominion Parliament for powers authorizing both either of these railway companies to construct : operate for a railway or other purposes a bridge over or a tunnel under Niagara River, or Fort Erie, in the County of Welland, to operate in construction and management any similar corporate powers existing within State of New York, or to be erected by the Congress of the United States; said bridge to b 250 feet span, to rise above high-water mark feet, to be of stone or iron piers, or wrought i or steel superstructure, and to have a draw of feet for vessels.

TORONTO AND NIPISSING RAILWAY COMPANY.

ength to Lake Nipissing, about 200 Miles.

SECTION FROM TORONTO TO COBOCONK, 85 MILES ;

ranch of 18 miles from the Main Line to the Town of Lindsay.

'otal Capital, $8,000,000.

for the First Section (Main Line) **$1,275,000.**

S already Voted by Municipalities for the rst Section of the Main Line; $399,000.

AS FOLLOWS :—

Coronto, $150,000 ; Scarboro', $10,000 ; Markham, 00 ; Uxbridge, $50,000 ; Scott, $10,000 ; Brock, 00 ; Eldon, $44,000 ; Bexley, $15,000 ; Luxton, y and Longford, $25,000 ; Somerville, $15,000.

es yet to be obtained, including those for the Branch, $155,000.

ssue of stock in $100 shares, $400,000.

which will be Issued Bonds for $476,000.

$126,000 of which a Guarantee from the Govern- Ontario will be applied for, as equitable assistance nstruction of the Railway through and into Crown the route of the First Section.

ENT—John Crawford, Esq., M.P.

RESIDENT—J. E. Smith, Esq., Collector of Cus-

DIRECTORS :

M. C. Cameron, Provincial Secretary ; Hon. David Senator ; W. F. McMaster, Esq., Captain Taylor, derham, Jun., Esq., H. S. Howland, Esq., Vice- nk of Commerce ; G. Laidlaw, Esq., H. P. Crosby, P.P., Joseph Gould, Esq., Thomas Wilson, Esq., rdon, Esq., A. M. Smith, Esq., T. C. Chisholm, McRae, Esq., Reeve Eldon; Edward Wheeler, Esq., Whitchurch ; John Leys, Esq., Solicitor ; R. W. sq., Ald. F. H. Medcalf, A. P. Cockburn, Esq., J. C. Fitch, Esq., Jas. E. Ellis, Esq., Ald. Dickey, dden, Esq., J. D. Merrick, Esq., Dr. Wright.

ES OF BONUSES GRANTED BY MUNICIPALITIES.— D. W. Allan, Senator—Government Trustee ; Hon. meron, Provincial Secretary—Company's Trustee; ethour, Esq., Deputy Reeve of Brock—Municipal- istee.

SL—Hon. M. C. Cameron, Provincial Secretary.

TOR—John Leys, Esq.

LTING ENGINEERS—Sir Charles Fox & Sons.

RS—Bank of Toronto.

RS—Blaikie & Alexander, Pellatt & Osler.

TARY—Charles Robertson, Dsq.

FICES—46 FRONT STREET, TORONTO.

PROSPECTUS.

ovisional Directors of the Toronto and Nipissing Company, finding that the further progress in the of Broad Gauge Railways in Canada, with English was no longer financially practicable or expedient of Railway projected for local traffic, and having ognizant of the successful working for a number of Railways built on the three feet six gauge, in the Kingdoms of Norway and Sweden, in the colonies of Queensland and New Zealand, and also in India, and that these Railways were capable of accommodating a traffic of about a million or a million and a half of tons of goods per annum, and of carrying passengers at a speed of twenty-five to thirty miles an hour, and seeing that the average speed of passenger trains, including stoppages, in Canada does not exceed twenty miles an hour, and that the total traffic of the Northern Railway (which offers a fair illustration of the traffic to be obtained by the Toronto and Nipissing Railway) did not exceed 195,000 tons and 140,000 passengers, have therefore resolved to construct the Toronto and Nipissing Railway on the three feet six gauge, in the most economical and efficient manner consistent with a total cost of $15,000 per mile.

The Directors have also noted Capt. Tyler's report on the Festiniog Railway, two feet gauge, in Merionethshire, Wales, the freight and passenger traffic of which approximates closely to that of the Northern Railway, and, with the exception of the lumber traffic, largely exceeds that carried on the Lindsay and Port Hope, or on the London and Port Stanley Railway.

With a view to a just apportionment of the risks incidental to capital invested in Railway enterprise in Canada, it was resolved to ask the municipalities most to be benefitted by the construction of the Railway, for *one-third of the total cost of the Railway, viz.*, $5,000 *per mile, by way of bonus* or gift. This proportion of the cost has *already been voted* for the main line, excepting less than $50,000, yet obtainable, in debentures bearing six per cent., payable in 20 years—securities which are unexceptionable, and will sell here at or near par.

Of the remaining two-thirds of the capital, it is proposed now to offer here $400,000 to be subscribed in stock. If that or a larger amount is not subscribed, bonds will be issued for the balance of about $6,000 per mile. Thus local capital to the extent of about two-thirds of the cost of the Railway, will be security to the holders of the bonds of this Company.

The interest-bearing capital will thus be $10,000 per mile.

The Directors do not propose to extend the line beyond Coboconk, towards Lake Nipissing, unless subsidized by the Government of this Province with land or money sufficient to guarantee the Company from the loss of any private capital to be invested in the sections of the line beyond Coboconk.

Nevertheless, the Company feel assured that the first section being successfully completed, the remaining sections will immediately receive aid from the Government to the extent necessary to secure the construction of the line to the ultimate terminus at Lake Nipissing—thus ensuring to the proprietors of the first section the practically unlimited timber traffic, as well as the general business of an immense new territory of twenty thousand square miles.

The terminus of the first section being located on the Gull River, with access to all its tributaries, and to the Burnt River, insures for this Railway a timber and lumber traffic certain to exceed in duration of supply and quantity the timber and lumber traffic of the Northern Railway, and which will undoubtedly equal or exceed that of the Lindsay and Port Hope Railway, which amounted to nearly one hundred millions of feet in the year 1868.

The sawn lumber traffic of the Northern Railway of Canada in 1868, amounted only to about fifty-five (55) million feet, and the square timber traffic to one million six hundred thousand cubic feet.

IN 1861.

The local traffic of the Northern Railway of Canada amounted to..		120,000 tons
Through....................................		25.000 "
Passengers..................................		100,618 "
Local Receipts..............................	$362,507	
Through.....................................	48,432	$410,939
Running Expenses............................		68 per cent.
Excess of earnings over running expenses on local traffic	115,982	
Do. on through traffic..............	15,498	

Local earnings equal to 8½ per cent on a cost of $15,000 per mile ; or 12½ on $10,000 per mile.

1864.

Local Traffic...............................		180,700 tons
Through Traffic.............................		8,344 "
Passengers..................................		104,340
Local Receipts..............................	$452,332	
Through "	14,884	$467,266
Running Expenses............................		52 per cent.
Excess of earnings over running expenses on local traffic..............	217,143	
Do. on through traffic..............	7,144	

Local earnings equal to 16 2-5 per cent on a cost of $15,000 a mile ; or 23 1-10 per cent on $10,000 per mile.

1868.

Local and through traffic..................		194,583 tons
Passengers..................................		138,965 "
Local Receipts..............................	$537,380	
Through "	12,690	$550,070
Running expenses............................		61 per cent.
Excess of earnings over running expenses on local traffic..............	209,578	
Do. on through traffic	4,949	

Or equal to 14½ per cent on $15,000 a mile (local earnings) ; or 22½ per cent on $10,000 per mile.

1861—Running expenses per cent, 68 ; local tonnage, 120,000 through tonnage, 25,000 ; total tons, 145,000 ; passengers, 100,618 ; local receipts, gross, $362,507 ; through receipts, gross, $48,432 ; total receipts, gross, $410,939 ; local receipts, nett, $115,982 ; through receipts, nett, $15,498 ; dividend on $15,000 a mile, local, 8 1-8 ; dividend on $15,000 a mile, through, 1-1-10.

1864—Running expenses per cent, 52 ; local tonnage, 180,700 ; through tonnage, 8,346 ; total tons, 189,046 ; passengers, 104,346 ; local receipts, gross, $452,382 ; through receipts, gross, $14, 884 ; total receipts, gross, $467,266 ; local receipts, nett, $217,143 ; through receipts, nett, $7,144 ; dividend on $15,000 a mile, local, 15 2-5 ; dividend on $15,000 a mile, through, 1-2.

1868—Running expenses per cent, 61 ; total tons, 194,588 ; passengers, 188,965 ; local receipts, gross, $537,380 ; through receipts, gross, $12,890 ; total receipts, gross, $550,070 ; local receipts, nett, $209,578 ; through receipts, nett, $4,949 ; dividend on $15,000 a mile, local, 14 7-8 ; dividend on $15,000 a mile, through, 1-3.

Total tons, 528,629 ; passengers, 349,929 ; local receipts, gross, $1,352,269 ; through receipts, gross, $76,006 ; total receipts, gross, $1,428,275 ; local receipts, nett, $542,703 ; through receipts, nett, $27,591 ; dividend on $15,000 a mile, local, 12 5-6 ; dividend on $15,000 a mile, through, 2-3.

AVERAGE.—Total tons, 176,209 ; passengers, 116,643 ; local receipts, gross, $450,756 ; through receipts, gross, $25,335 ; total receipts, gross $476,091 ; local receipts, nett, $180,901 ; through receipts, nett, $9,197 ; dividend on $15,000 a mile, local, 12 5-6; dividend on $15,000 a mile, through, 2-3.

From the above data it will be seen that the Northern Railway carried an average for those three years of 176,209 tons of freight, and 116,643 passengers ; the average gross receipts being $450,756, while the nett receipts from local traffic were $180,901, equal to an annual dividend of 12 5-6 per cent on a cost of $15,000 per mile ; or 19 1-4 on $10,000 per mile.

It is remarkable and of consequence to intending subscribers for stock of the T. & N. R., that the nett receipts for through traffic for the same years only averaged $9,197 per annum, equal to a dividend of ⅔ of one per cent. on a cost of $15,000 per mile. This fact clearly proves the value of local as against through traffic.

The Grain Traffic tributary to the Toronto and Nipissing Railway undoubtedly will not fall below 900,000 bushels, and probably will largely exceed that quantity. The Passenger Traffic is anticipated to average 100,000 per annum.

The country through which the first section of the Toronto and Nipissing Railway will pass, is more populous, wealthy and extensive than that tributary to the Northern Railway—being one of the oldest and finest settled districts in the Province of Ontario. Various unsuccessful efforts have previously been made to accommodate this district with railways.

The most moderate estimate of the gross receipts from the traffic in timber, lumber, cereals, passengers, etc., to be carried over the T. & N. R. place the amount at an average of $400,000 to $500,000 per annum, for the first eight or ten years, when the traffic must necessarily increase to a much larger amount.

The traffic to create this revenue will be derived from the following items, and in about the proportions set forth :

Pine, or sawn lumber, for the first eight years, 80,000,000 ft. at $2 per 1,000 ft..............	$160,000
Square timber, 1,250,000....................	37,500
Cereals, 900,000 bushels, at 5c. per bush......	45,000
General goods, 15,000 tons, at an average of $3 40 per ton..............................	51,000
Mails and Express...........................	15,000
Cordwood, 25,000 cords at $1 50 per cord.....	37,500
Passengers, 100,000.........................	100,000
	$446,000

Allowing 60 per cent. for running expenses, the nett earnings amount to $178,400—equal to a dividend of 14 per cent. on a cost of $15,000 per mile : and on the actual cost to the Company of $10,000 per mile, the dividend from such nett earnings would be 21 per cent.

The Provisional Directors invest their own means on their faith in the correctness of these estimates.

The terminus at Coboconk, on the Gull River, will connect the Railway with a vast stretch of Inland Navigation upon which steamers now trade, and which, with comparatively inexpensive improvements already partly undertaken by the government, will give these boats access to the Railway, and will afford almost inexhaustible supplies of pine and hard wood.

By the Act of Incorporation, the Company is specially bound to carry cordwood, and to afford every necessary facility for so doing at the specified rate of 3 cents per cord per mile for dry wood, for all distances under 50 miles, and 2½ cts. per cord per mile for all distances over 50 miles —a rate which has been found satisfactory, by the test of actual experience on the Government Railways in New Brunswick.

This condition will enhance the cost of fuel to the Company; but the increased traffic and prosperity consequent upon this trade it is fully believed will more than compensate for the extra cost of fuel.

The numerous association of gentlemen who have promoted and borne the preliminary expenses of this enterprise, and who desire to see it carried out in good faith on sound commercial principles, *are resolved*, in so far as their influence is equal to the task, to have this railway controlled by the most respectable capitalists of this city and the country on the route of the railway, who may take stock in it; to convert their own securities and pay cash to contractors, and not to surrender control of the railway to contractors or bondholders; to let the contracts in a manner calculated to ensure the healthiest competition: in other words, to have value for the money from the turning of the first sod to the laying of the last rail.

The country on the route of the first section of the railway is generally level, although in two townships it is broken or rolling, yet the soil being loamy in these exceptions, and there being almost no bridges; the superficial examination had and the flexibility of the gauge ensures a minimum of cuttings and fillings—while timber for bridges and ties, and lumber for buildings and fences, can be had at the least cost possible in Canada.

Every other consideration in the first instance will be subordinated to the construction of a first-class permanent way, the best of timber bridges; deep and good ballasting Rails to weigh 40 lbs. to the yard, and to be selected of the best quality.

Arrangements are in progress which will secure to the Company free right of way, through the city, and egress, if desired, for a few miles out of the city, on the line of the Grand Trunk, by means of a third rail; and the disposition of the proprietors and other circumstance along the line are so favorable that the whole right of way will be obtained for an amount not exceeding $20,000.

Station grounds and dockage will be had in this city either free or for a nominal rental.

It is the desire of the Provisional Directors to have their Chief Engineer appointed with the concurrence, and subject to the approval of the Company's Consulting Engineers, Sir Charles Fox & Sons, who will be held responsible for the excellence of the works, economy of construction, and the success here of the system of narrow gauge railways of which they have large experience elsewhere, and with the initiation of which in this country they are honorably identified.

On these premises the Provisional Directors appeal for stock subscriptions to the citizens of Toronto, to the municipalities and to the business men and proprietors of land along the route of the railway, and to capitalists elsewhere, believing that the most cautious and prudent investors will find the stock of the Toronto and Nipissing Railway worthy of their attention.

The stock books will be opened at the Company's offices Front Street, on the 12th April, at 10 o'clock a.m.; meanwhile forms of application for shares can be had on application from the secretary and from the reeves and clerks of the several municipalities on the route of the railway, and from Messrs. Blaikie & Alexander, Toronto, and Pellatt & Osler.

CASEY S. WOOD, Esq., Lindsay.
JOSEPH GOULD, Esq., Uxbridge.
McDOUGALD & DAVIDSON, Montreal.
ALEXANDER FRASER, Esq., Quebec.

A member of the firm of Charles Fox & Son will be here shortly, and immediately on his arrival operations will be commenced.

TORONTO SAFE WORKS.

J. & J. Taylor

MANUFACTURERS OF

Fire and Burglar Proof

SAFES,

BANK LOCKS, VAULTS, DOORS, &c., &c.

AGENTS:

JAS. HUTTON & Co. .... MONTREAL.
H. S. SCOTT & Co. .... QUEBEC.
ALEX. WORKMAN & Co. .... OTTAWA.
RICE LEWIS & SON .... TORONTO.
D. FALCONER .... HALIFAX, N.S.

Manufactory & Sale Rooms, 198 & 200 *Palace Street.*

30-1y

Canada Permanent Building and Savings Society.

Paid up Capital $1,000,000
Assets 1,700,000
Annual Income 400,000

Directors:—JOSEPH D. RIDOUT, *President.*
PETER PATERSON, *Vice-President.*
J. G. Worts, Edward Hooper, S. Nordheimer, W. C. Chewett, E. H. Rutherford, Joseph Robinson.
Bankers:—Bank of Toronto; Bank of Montreal; Royal Canadian Bank.

OFFICE—*Masonic Hall, 1oronto Street, Toronto.*

Mone, Received on Deposit bearing five and six per cent. interest.

Advances made on City and Country Property in the Province of Ontario.

J. HERBERT MASON,
Sec'y & Treas

36-y

H. N. Sm̈ith & Co.,

2, EAST SENECA STREET, BUFFALO, N. Y., (correspondent Smith, Gould, Martin & Co., 11 Broad Street, N.Y.,) Stock, Money and Exchange Brokers. Advances made on securities. 21-1y

R. G. Fraser,

91 GRANVILLE STREET, Halifax, Nova Scotia, Gold Broker and Assayer, Crucibles, Retorts, Patent Amalgam and Smelting Necessaries for sale.
31 Dec., 1860. 33.

John Morison,

IMPORTER OF

GROCERIES, WINES, AND LIQUORS,

88 AND 40 WELLINGTON STREET,

TORONTO. 33-1y

Philip Browne & Co.,

BANKERS AND STOCK BROKERS.

DEALERS IN

STERLING EXCHANGE—U. S. Currency, Silver and Bonds—Bank Stocks, Debentures, Mortgages, &c. Drafts on New York issued, in Gold and Currency. Prompt attention given to collections. Advances made on Securities.

No. 67 YONGE STREET, TORONTO

JAMES BROWNE. PHILIP BROWNE, *Notary Public*
y

THE TORONTO, GREY AND BRUCE RAILWAY COMPANY.

TOTAL LENGTH, ABOUT 200 MILES. INCLUDING BRANCHES TO KINCARDINE AND OWEN SOUND.

Length of First Section, from Toronto to the Garafraxa Road, about 70 Miles.

TOTAL CAPITAL, $3,000,000.

CAPITAL REQUIRED FOR THE FIRST SECTION, $1,050,000.

Bonuses already Voted by Municipalities for the First Section of the Main Line, $425,000.

As follows:—City of Toronto, $250,000; Albion, $40,000; Caledon, $45,000; Mono, $45,000; Orangeville, $15,000; Amaranth, $30,000.

Bonuses yet to be obtained for the first section, $77,000.

Bonuses required and obtainable to extend First Section, from Arthur to Mount Forest, $138,000.

First issue of Stock in $100 shares, $325,000.

Upon which bonds will be issued for $300,000.

The arrangements for the extension to Mount Forest, now in progress, when completed, will involve the further issue of Stock and Bonds to the extent of $125,000.

PRESIDENT—John Gordon, Esq.
VICE-PRESIDENT—A. R. McMaster, Esq.

DIRECTORS:

Hon. M. C. Cameron, Provincial Secretary; Hon. John McMurrich, M.P.P.; S.B. Harman, Esq., Mayor of Toronto; Noah Barnhart, Esq.; H. S. Howland, Esq., Vice-Pres. Bank of Commerce; James Michie, Esq. (Fulton, Mich & Co.); John Crawford, Esq., M. P.; William Elliot, Esq. (of Messrs. Lyman, Elliot & Co.); Thos. Swinarton, Esq., M.P.P.; R. A. Harrison, Esq., Barrister, M.P.; J. E. Smith, Esq., Collector of Customs, Toronto; D. Sinclair, Esq. M.P.P., North Bruce; John Turner, Esq. (of Messrs. Sessions, Turner & Co.) George Laidlaw, Esq; Thos. Scott, Esq., M.P.P.; Robert Paterson, Esq.; Thos. Lailey, Esq.; T. C. Chisholm, Esq.; Frank Smith, Esq.; C. J. Campbell, Esq.; Adam Crooks, Esq., Q.C.; John Worthington, Esq.

TRUSTEES OF BONUSES—Hon. John McMurrich, Company's Trustee; A. W. Lauder, M.P.P., Government Trustee; Lewis Moffat, Esq., Municipalities' Trustee.

COUNSEL—Hon. John Hillyard Cameron.
SOLICITOR—W. H. Beatty, Esq.
CONSULTING ENGINEERS—Sir Charles Fox & Sons.
BANKERS—Bank of Toronto, Bank of Commerce.
BROKERS—Campbell & Cassels, Blaikie & Alexander.
SECRETARY—W. Sutherland Taylor.

TEMPORARY OFFICES,—46 FRONT STREET, TORONTO.

PROSPECTUS.

The Provisional Directors of the Toronto, Grey and Bruce Railway Company, finding that further progress in the building of Broad Gauge Railways in Canada, with English Capital, was no longer financially practicable or expedient for lines of Railway projected for local traffic, and having become cognizant of the successful working for a number of years of Railways built on the three feet six gauge in the Kingdoms of Norway and Sweden, in the Colonies of Queensland, in India, and elsewhere, and that these Railways were capable of accommodating a traffic of about a million, or a million and a half of tons of g
per annum, and of carrying passengers at a spe
twenty-five to thirty miles an hour, and that the
traffic of the Northern Railway of Canada has not exc
ed 195,000 tons, and 140,000 passengers per annum,
therefore resolved to construct the Toronto, Grey
Bruce Railway on the three feet six inch gauge, in
most economical and efficient manner, at a total cos
$15,000 per mile.

The Directors have also noted Capt. Tayler's (now
President Grand Trunk Railway) report on the Festi
Railway, two feet gauge, in Merionethshire, Wales
freight and passenger traffic of which approximates cl
to that of the Northern Railway of Canada, and, wit
exception of the lumber traffic, largely exceeds that ca
on the Lindsay and Port Hope, or on the London
Port Stanley Railways.

With a view to the just apportionment of the risk
cidental to capital invested in railway enterprise in
nada, it was also resolved to ask the municipalities
to be benefitted by the construction of the Railways
one-third of the total cost by way of bonus or gift.
proportion of the cost has already been voted for the
section (excepting small sums yet obtainable), in de
tures bearing six per cent interest, payable in 20 yea
securities which are unexceptionable, and will sell a
near par.

Of the remaining capital, it is proposed now to
$325,000 to be subscribed in stock. If that or a l
amount is not so subscribed, bonds will be issued fo
balance of about $300,000.

Local capital to the extent of *more than* two-thirds o
cost of the railway will be security to holders of the b
of this Company.

The interest and dividend bearing capital will no
ceed $9,000 per mile.

The Directors, although anxious, and having auth
under their charter to make the village of Mount F
the terminus of the first section, are unwillingly const
ed to select an eligible point, nearer, on the Gara
Road, in the Township of Arthur.

This decision may be altered, and Mount Forest
the terminus of the first section, by the Municipa
concerned voting the amounts of bonuses, as require
the Company.

In either case the capital derivable from bonusses
be about the same per mile.

Arrangements to complete the remaining sections o
Railway through the counties of Bruce and Grey, wi
prosecuted with unremitting vigour, as soon as the
section is fairly under construction.

The Garafraxa Road, the great highway from
Sound, through the counties of Grey and Wellingt
Guelph; and the other great highway, the Elora and
geen Road, from Southampton, through the counti
Bruce and Wellington, ultimately uniting with the
fraxa Road, *passes within from 5 to 8 miles of the pro
terminus of the first section* of the Railway, to connect
which a gravel road will be built; while the Toronto
Sydenham gravelled road, from Chatsworth, interse
the Durham and Collingwood road, reaches to within t
or fifteen miles of the Orangeville station, and when
pleted, together with the others, assures to the Tor
Grey and Bruce Railway the traffic of the whole hea
the North-western peninsula.

The bulk of the products of the great counties of
and West Grey is shipped by water, on account o
distance from the Grand Trunk Railway, only a part
moved in the autumn, the principal portion being
keted and stored, during winter, at the ports on the s
of Lake Huron and the Georgian Bay. At four of
points there are now stored a quarter of a million bu
while the aggregate at all the points amounts to
500,000 bushels.

The loss of interest on the capital thus invested,
ther with the proportionately lower prices paid for pr
during winter in these remote districts, are serious
backs to their prosperity.

The distance deprives producers of the facilities aff
by the *Grand Trunk Railway, and the Montreal Stea
line* for moving, in winter, produce to markets, as w
of the very great advantage of Railway communicati
the flourishing city of Toronto, (the best distributing
either in winter or summer,) and now the capi
Ontario.

The total area between the Grand Trunk and the Nor
Railway of Canada is 6,800 square miles, of the riches
most fertile land in Canada. The Toronto, Grey and
Railway will intersect this district, about mid-way be
the two other Railways, and when completed will c
immense benefits on the people in that district, whil
quite evident that the general business *which*
brought to the city of Toronto (exclusive of through t
will equal that brought to it by all the other Railway

The Toronto, Grey and Bruce Railway will obtain a
larger passenger, grain, cattle, and first-class goods
than the Northern Railway; while the sawn pine,
must be imported to supply the absence of that bu
material, and the export of square hardwood timber,
oak, elm, cherry, &c., staves, bark, fencing, and cord
(fuel), will afford a very large and remunerative bu
to the Toronto, Grey and Bruce Railway.

The Freestone and other stone used for building ma
in Toronto are now imported from Cleveland or King
On the route of the T. G. & B. R. there are, near O
ville, extensive quarries of the very best soft and
brown and white freestone, which will be in great re
for export and general city building purposes. Th
vantages to the Railway and this city, of these quarri
not yet generally appreciated.

The subjoined tables of the traffic of the Northern

» to illustrate the local business of a railway , through an average country in Canada.

IN 1861.

affic of the Northern
f Canada amounted to .... 120,000 tons.
.... 25,000 "
.... 100,618 "
ts... $862,507
.... 48,432 $410,939
enses... 68 per cent
urnings over running
on local traffic............ -$115,983
igh Traffic................. 15,498
ge equal to 8½ per cent. on a
5,000 per mile. Or 11½ on $10,-
ile.

1864.

.... 130,000 tons.
ffic.. 8,344 "
.... 104,946 "
ds.. $452,882
.... 14,884 $467,206
enses... 52 per cent.
urnings over running
on Local Traffic........... $17,143
ugh Traffic................. 7,144
ge equal to 18 8-6 per cent. on
$15,000 a mile. Or 28 1-10 per
,10,000 per mile.

1868.

rough Traffic................ 104,882 tons.
.... 138,965 "
ds.. $597,380
.... 12,690 Total $550,070
enses... 61 per cent
urnings over running
on Local Traffic........... $209,578
ugh Traffic................. 4,049
nings... Or 22½ per cent. on
r mile.

ning expenses per cent. 68 ; local tonnage, 130,-
a tonnage, 25,000 ; total tons, 145,000 ; passen-
; local receipts, gross, $862,507 ; through re-
, $48,482 ; total receipts, gross, $410,939 ; local
ts, $115,983 ; through receipts, nett, $15,498 ;
$15,000 a mile, local, $ 1-3 ; dividend on $15,-
through, 1 1-10.

ning expenses per cent. 52 ; local tonnage, 8,346 ; total tons, 189,046 ; pas-
846 ; local receipts, gross, $452,882 ; through
ss, $14,884 ; total receipts, gross, $467,206 ;
s, nett, $217,143 ; through receipts, nett, $7,-
d on $15,000 a mile, local, 15 2-5 ; dividend on
le, through ⅓.

ning expenses per cent. 61 ; local tons, 104,-
gers 138,965 ; local receipts, gross, $597,380 ;
eipts, gross, $12,690 ; total receipts, gross,
cal receipts, nett, $209,578 ; through receipts,
: dividend on $15,000 a mile, local, 14⅓ ; divi-
000 a mile, through ⅓.
, 528,929 ; passengers, 549,929 ; local receipts,
,369 ; through receipts, gross, $75,606 ; total
ss, $1,428,275 ; local receipts, nett, $542,790 ;
ipts, nett, $27,591 ; dividend on $15,000 a mile,
, dividend on $15,000 a mile, through ⅜
-Total tons, 176,209 ; passengers, 116,643 ; local
es, $450,756 ; through receipts, gross, $25,335 ;
s, gross, $476,091 ; local receipts, nett, 180,901 ;
ipts, nett $30,197 ; dividend on $15,000 a mile,
, dividend on $15,000 a mile, through ⅓.
above data it will be seen that the Northern
ied an average for those three years of 176,209
nt ; and 116,643 passengers ; the average gross
g $450,756, while the nett receipts from local
180,901, equal to an annual dividend of 12 5-6
a cost of $15,000 per mile.
rable and of consequence to intending sub-
stock of the T. G & B R., that the net re-
rough traffic for the same years only averaged
num, equal to a dividend of ⅓ of one per cent
$15,000 per mile. This fact clearly proves the
l as against through traffic.
cattle, pork, goods and passenger traffic tri-
e first section of the Toronto, Grey and Bruce
equal, if not exceed, for the same length of
l traffic of any other railway in Canada.
ing estimate of traffic from the first section
to, Grey and Bruce Railway, is based upon
on the returns made by the Municipalities,
mate acquaintance with their trade and re-

, 140,000............................ $145,000
300,000 bushels.................... 100,000
00 barrels......................... 15,000
ods, 50,000 tons................... 150,000
ber, 1,000,000 cubic feet.......... 80,000
nber, bark, posts, &c.............. 20,000
20,000 cords....................... 25,000
expense............................ 50,000

1.................................. $400,000
0 per cent for running expenses, the net earn-
mount to $196,000—equal to a dividend of 18
. cost of $15,000 per mile.
'easonable margin for increased cost or less
oderate estimate of which will be undisputed,)
the strongest reasons for anticipating a divi-
r cent per annum.

By the Act of Incorporation, the Company is specially bound to carry cordwood, and to afford every necessary facility for so doing at the specified rate of 3 cents per cord per mile for dry wood, for all distances under 50 miles, and 2½ cents per cord per mile for all distances over 50 miles—a rate which has been found satisfactory, by test of actual experience, on the Government Railways of New Brunswick.

This condition will enhance the cost of fuel to the Company, but the increased traffic and prosperity consequent upon this trade, it is fully believed, will more than compensate for the extra cost of fuel.

The gentlemen who have promoted and borne the preliminary expenses of this enterprise, and who desire to see it carried out in good faith on sound commercial principles, are resolved, in so far as their influence is equal to the task, to have this railway controlled by the most respectable capitalists of this city and the country on the route of the railway, who may take stock in it ; to convert their own securities, and pay cash to contractors, and not to surrender control of the railway to contractors or bond-holders ; to let the contracts in a manner to ensure the healthiest competition. In other words, to have value for the money from the turning of the first sod to the laying of the last rail.

The country on the route of the first section, with the exception of a short distance in Caledon, is one of the easiest for railway construction in Canada, especially the 22 or 25 miles from Orangeville to the Garafraxa Road.

In the Township of Caledon—the country is hilly and rolling. This portion of the route was carefully and completely surveyed and cross-sectioned under the auspices and by the direction of Mr. J. E. Boyd, M.I.C.E., and Engineer for the Government of New Brunswick, before the Company obtained their charter, and, as anticipated, no real difficulties were encountered ; the highest grade, with moderate cuttings, being 65 feet to the mile. Mr. Charles Douglas Fox examined, for the Company, the figures and the profile, and, together with Mr. Boyd, gave their written opinion that the cost of this portion, per mile for earth-works, would not exceed $15,000. There are no rock cuttings.

Ballast, ties, timber for bridges, and lumber for fences,

are convenient and available at the lowest cost in Canada, along the whole route of the first section.

Every other consideration, in the first instance, will be subordinated to the construction of a first-class permanent way ; the best of timber bridges ; deep and good ballasting. Rails to weigh 40 lbs. to the yard, and to be selected of the best quality.

Arrangements are in progress which will secure to the Company free right of way through the city, and egress, if desired, for a few miles out of the city, on the line of the Grand Trunk, by means of a third rail ; and the disposition of the proprietors, and other circumstances along the line are so favorable, that the whole right of way will be obtained for an amount not exceeding $22,000.

Station grounds and dockage will be had in this city, either free, or for a nominal rental.

It is the desire of the Provisional Directors to have their Chief Engineer appointed, with the concurrence, and subject to the approval of the Company's Consulting Engineers, Sir Charles Fox & Sons, who will be held responsible for the excellence of the works, economy of construction, and the success here of the system of narrow gauge railways, of which they have had large experience elsewhere, and with the initiation of which in this country they are honourably identified.

On these premises the Provisional Directors appeal for stock subscriptions to the citizens of Toronto, to the municipalities, and to the business men and proprietors of land along the route of the railway, and to capitalists elsewhere, believing that the most cautious and prudent investors will find the stock of the Toronto, Grey and Bruce Railway worthy of their attention.

The stock books will be opened at the Company's offices, Front street, on the 21st April, at 10 o'clock, a.m. Forms of application for shares can be had on application to the secretary, and from the reeves and clerks of the several municipalities on the route of the railway ; and from Messrs. Campbell & Cassels, and from Messrs. Binkie & Alexander, Toronto, and from McDougall & Davidson, Montreal.

In conjunction with the Toronto and Nipissing Railway Company, it is agreed that a member of the firm of Sir Charles Fox & Sons, Consulting Engineers, will be invited here immediately by telegraph, when active operations will be commenced.

EDINBURGH LIFE ASSURANCE COMPANY.

FOUNDED 1823.

AMOUNT OF ACCUMULATED AND INVESTED FUNDS—OVER ONE MILLION STERLING.

HEAD OFFICE—EDINBURGH.

PRESIDENT—The Rt. Hon. the Earl of Haddington. MANAGER—D. Maclagan, Esq. SECRETARY—Alex. H. Whytt, Esq

CANADIAN OFFICE ESTABLISHED 1857. WELLINGTON STREET, TORONTO.

CANADIAN BOARD—Hon. John Hillyard Cameron, M.P., Chairman. J. W. Gamble, Esq., L. Moffatt, Esq., Hon. J. B. Robinson, C. J. Campbell, Esq. David Higgins, Secretary.

THE Edinburgh Life Assurance Company offer to the public the advantages of a Canadian as well as a British Company. They have invested a large amount of money on securities in this country, and the Toronto Local Board refer to the Head Office, Edinburgh. Some of the old Policies in this Company, which became claims during the past year, were settled by payment of amounts double of those originally insured, in consequence of the large bonuses that accrued on the Policies.

Every information that intending Assurers may require can be obtained at the Company's Office in Toronto, or at any of the Agencies which have been established in the principal towns in Canada.

J. HILLYARD CAMERON, CHAIRMAN. (33-1y) DAVID HIGGINS, SECRETARY.

Royal Fire & Life Insurance Company

OF LIVERPOOL AND LONDON.

CAPITAL, TWO MILLION STERLING,

WITH LARGE RESERVE FUNDS.

ANNUAL INCOME, - - - - - - - - - £800,000 STG.

FIRE BRANCH.

Very moderate rates of Premium. Prompt and liberal settlement of losses. Loss and damage by explosion of gas made good. No charge for policies or transfers.

LIFE BRANCH.

The following are amongst the important advantages offered by this Company :
Perfect security to assurers. Moderate rates of premium. Large participation of profits—the bonuses being amongst the largest hitherto declared by any office, and divided every five years. EXEMPTION OF ASSURED FROM LIABILITY OF PARTNERSHIP. Claims settled promptly on proof of death. Liberal allowance for surrendered policies. Forfeiture of policy cannot take place from unintentional misstatement. No charge for policies or assignments. Medical fees paid by the Company. Tables and forms of application, with all other information, can be obtained on application to

FRANCIS H. HEWARD,

MANAGER TORONTO BRANCH.

GEORGE OLIVER, Inspector.

W. B. NICOL, M.D., Medical Examiner.

TORONTO, April 19, 1869.

36-4t

Mercantile.

TORONTO PRICES CURRENT.—MAY 6, 1869.

Name of Article.	Wholesale Rates.		Name of Article.	Wholesale Rates.		Name of Article.	Wholesale Rates.	
	$ c.	$ c.		$ c.	$ c.		$ c.	$ c.
Boots and Shoes.			**Groceries—**Contin'd			**Leather—**Contin'd.		
Mens' Thick Boots	2 20	2 50	Gunpowd're, to med	0 55	0 70	Kip skins, Patna	0 2	
" Kip	2 50	3 00	" med. to fine	0 70	0 85	French	0 7	
" Calf	3 30	3 70	" fine to fine't	0 85	0 95	English	0 6	
" Congress Gaiters	1 65	1 90	Hyson	0 45	0 80	Hemlock Calf (30 to 35 lbs.) per doz	0 5	
" Kip Cobourgs	1 15	1 45	Imperial	0 42	0 80	Do. light	0 4	
Boys' Thick Boots	1 70	1 80	Tobacco, Manufac'd:			French Calf	1 6	
Youths'	1 40	1 50	Can Leaf, ℔ lb & 10s.	0 26	0 30	Grain & Satn Cl'rdoz	0 0	
Women's Batts	0 95	1 30	Western Leaf, com	0 25	0 26	Splits, large ℔ lb	0 2	
" Balmoral	1 20	1 50	" Good	0 27	0 32	" small	0 3	
" Congress Gaiters	0 90	1 50	" Fine	0 33	0 35	Enamelled Cow ℔ foot	0 2	
Misses' Batts	0 75	1 00	" Bright fine	0 40	0 50	Patent	0 2	
" Balmoral	0 87	1 20	" choice	0 60	0 75	Pebble Grain	0 1	
" Congress Gaiters	1 00	1 30				Buff	0 1	
Girls' Batts	0 65	0 85	**Hardware.**					
" Balmoral	0 00	1 05	*Tin (net cash prices)*			**Oils.**		
" Congress Gaiters	0 75	1 10	Block, ℔ lb	0 23	0 00	Cod	0 6	
Children's C. T. Cncks	0 50	0 65	Grain	0 30	0 00	Lard, extra	0 0	
" Gaiters	0 65	0 90	*Copper:*			" No. 1	0 0	
			Pig	0 23	0 24	" Woollen	0 0	
Drugs.			Sheet	0 30	0 33	Lubricating, patent	0 3	
Aloes Cape	0 12½	0 16	*Cut Nails:*			" Mott's economist	0 8	
Alum	0 02½	0 03	Assorted ½ Shingles,			Linseed, raw	0 7	
Borax	0 00	0 00	℔ 100 lb	2 00	3 00	" boiled	0 8	
Camphor, refined	0 65	0 70	Shingle alone do	2 15	3 25	Machinery	0 0	
Castor Oil	0 10½	0 23	Lathe and 5 dy	3 30	3 40	Olive, common, ℔ gal	1 0	
Caustic Soda	0 04½	0 05	*Galvanized Iron:*			" salad	1 9	
Cochineal	0 00	1 00	Assorted sizes	0 08	0 00	" salad, in bots		
Cream Tartar	0 40	0 45	Best No. 24	0 09	0 00	" qt ℔ case	3 6	
Epsom Salts	0 03	0 04	" 26	0 08	0 08½	Sesame salad, ℔ gal	1 6	
Extract Logwood	0 11	0 12	" 28	0 09	0 00½	Seal, pale	0 7	
Gum Arabic, sorts	0 30	0 35	*Horse Nails:*			Spirits Turpentine	0 0	
Indigo, Madras	0 00	1 00	Ghest's or Griffin's			Varnish	0 0	
Licorice	0 14	0 45	assorted sizes	0 00	0 00	Whale	0 0	
Madder	0 00	0 18	For W. nav'd sizes	0 18	0 19			
Oatmeal	0 32	0 37	Patent Hammer'd do	0 17	0 18	**Paints, &c.**		
Opium	14 00	15 00	*Iron (at 4 months):*			White Lead, genuine		
Oxalic Acid	0 20	0 25	Pig—Gartsherrie No1	24 00	25 00	in Oil, ℔ 25 lb	0 0	
Potash, Bi-tart,	0 20	0 25	Other brands. No1	22 00	24 00	Do. No. 1	0 0	
" Bichromate	0 15	0 30	" No2	0 00	0 00	" 2	0 0	
Potass Iodide	3 00	4 00	Bar—Scotch, ℔100 lb	2 25	2 50	" 3	0 0	
Senna	0 12½	0 60	Refined	3 00	3 25	White Zinc, genuine	3 0	
Soda Ash	0 02½	0 04	Sweden	5 00	5 50	White Lead, dry	0 0	
Soda Bicarb	4 50	5 00	Hoops—Coopers	3 00	3 25	Red Lead	0 0	
Tartaric Acid	0 40	0 45	" Band	3 00	3 25	Venetian Red, Eng'h	0 0	
Verdigris	0 35	0 40	Boiler Plates	3 25	3 50	Yellow Ochre, Fren'h	0 0	
Vitriol, Blue	0 08	0 10	Canada Plates	3 75	4 00	Whiting	0 0	
			Union Jack	0 00	0 00			
Groceries.			Pontypool	3 25	4 00	**Petroleum**		
Coffees:			Swansea	3 00	4 00	(Refined ℔ gal.)		
Java, ℔ lb	0 22	0 24	*Lead (at 4 months):*			Water white, car'd		
Laguayra	0 17	0 18	Bar, ℔ 100 lbs	0 06½	0 07	" small lots	0	
Rio	0 15	0 17	Sheet	0 08	0 00	Straw, by car load	0	
Fish:			Shot	0 07½	0 07¾	" small lots	0	
Herrings, Lab. split	5 75	6 00	*Iron Wire (net cash)*			Amber, by car load	0	
" round	0 00	0 00	No. 6, ℔ bundle	2 70	2 80	" small lots	0	
" scaled	0 35	0 40	" 9	3 30	3 35	Benzine	0	
Mackerel, small kitts	1 00	0 00	" 12	3 40	3 50			
Loch. Her. wh's firks	3 50	3 75	" half	4 30	4 40	**Produce**		
" half	1 25	1 50	*Powder:*			*Grain:*		
White Fish & Trout	None.		Blasting, Canada	3 50	0 00	Wheat, Spring, 60 lb	0	
Salmon, saltwater	14 00	15 00	FF	4 25	4 50	" Fall 60 "	0	
Dry Cod, ℔112 lbs	5 00	5 25	FFF	4 75	5 00	Barley 48 "	1	
Fruit:			Blasting, English	4 00	5 00	Peas 60 "	0	
Raisins, Layers	2 00	2 10	FF loose	4 50	5 00	Oats 34 "	0	
" M. R	1 00	2 00	FFF	6 00	6 50	Rye 56 "	0	
" Valentias new	0 06½	0 07½	*Pressed Spikes (4 mos):*			*Seeds:*		
Currants, new	0 05½	0 06½	Regular sizes 100	4 00	4 35	Clover, choice 60 "	5	
" old	0 04	0 04½	Extra	4 50	5 00	" com'n 60 "	5	
Figs	0 14	0 00	*Tin Plates (net cash):*			Timothy, cho'e 4 "	2	
Molasses:			IC Coke	7 50	8 50	" 1st to good 48 "	2	
Clayed, ℔ gal	0 00	0 35	IC Charcoal	8 50	9 00	Flax 56 "	2	
Syrups, Standard	0 60	0 00	IX "	10 50	11 00	*Flour (per brl.):*		
" Golden	0 00	0 65	IXX "	13 50	14 00	Superior extra	0	
Rice:			DC "	8 00	8 50	Extra superfine	4	
Arracan	4 25	4 50	DX "	9 50	0 00	Fancysuperfine	4	
Spices:						Superfine No. 1	4	
Cassia, whole, ℔ lb	0 00	0 45	**Hides & Skins, ℔ lb**			" No. 2		
Cloves	0 11	0 12	Green rough	0 00	0 06	*Oatmeal,* (per brl.)		
Nutmegs	0 60	0 85	Green, salt'd & insp'd	0 07½	0 07½	**Provisions**		
Ginger, ground	0 20	0 25	Cured	0 09	0 00	Butter, dairy tub ℔ lb		
" Jamaica, root	0 20	0 55	Calfskins, green	0 00	0 11	" store packed		
Pepper, black	0 12½	0 00	Calfskins, cured	0 00	0 12½	Cheese, new		
Pimento	0 08	0 09	" dry	0 18	0 20	Pork, mess, per brl	2	
Sugars:			Sheepskins,	1 40	1 75	" prime mess		
Port Rico, ℔ lb	0 10½	0 00	" country	1 00	1 40	" prime		
Cuba	0 09	0 00	**Wools.**			Bacon, rough	0	
Barbadoes (bright)	0 10	0 00	Inferior, ℔ lb	0 05	0 07	" Cumberl'd cut	0	
Canada Sugar Refine'y,			Medium	0 07	0 00	" smoked	0	
yellow No. 3, 60 ds	0 10	0 10½	Good	0 00	0 12	Hams, in salt	0	
Yellow, No. 2½	0 10	0 10½	Fancy	0 00	0 00	" smoked	0	
" No. 3	0 10½	0 10½				Shoulders, in salt	0	
Crushed X	0 12½	0 12½	**Leather,** ℔ (4 mos.)			Lard, in kegs	0	
" A	0 12½	0 12½	In lots of less than			Eggs, packed	0	
Ground	0 13½	0 13½	50 sides, 10 ℔ cnt			Beef Hams	0	
Dry Crushed	0 13½	0 14	higher.			Tallow	0	
Extra Ground	0 14½	0 15	Spanish Sole, 1st qual'y			Hogs dressed, heavy	0	
Teas:			heavy, weights ℔ lb	0 21½	0 32	" medium	0	
Japan com'n to good	0 45	0 55	Do.1st qual middle do	0 22	0 00	" light	0	
" Fine to choicest	0 50	0 65	Do. No. 2, light weights	0 22	0 00	**Salt, &c.**		
Colored, com. to fine	0 50	0 75	Slaughter heavy	0 00	0 00	American bris	1	
Congou & Souch'ng	0 42	0 75	Do. light	0 00	0 00	Liverpool coarse	0	
Oolong, good to fine	0 50	0 65	Harness, best	0 35	0 37	Goderich	0	
Y. Hyson, com to gd	0 47½	0 55	" No. 2	0 00	0 00	Plaster, grey	0	
Medium to choice	0 65	0 90	Upper heavy	0 32	0 33	Water Lime	1	
Extra choice	0 85	0 95	" light	0 35	0 36			

ındles.		
& Co.'s ..	c.	$ c.
....	07½	0 08
ıar	07	0 07½
ır........	07	0 07½
....	05	0 05½
....	$ 03½	0 03½
....	0 00	0 11½
ıquors,		
doz......	2 60	2 6
ıb Portr..	2 35	2 45
a Rum...	1.80	2 25
H. Gin..	1 55	1 65
Tom.....	1 90	2 00
ı.........	4 00	4 25
Tom, c...	6 00	6 25
ɔn	1 00	1 25
l	2 00	4 00
mon	1 00	1 50
n........	1 70	1 80
golden..	2 50	4 00

	$ c.	$ c.
Brandy:		
Hennessy's, per gal..	2 30	2 0
Martell's " ..	2 30	2 0
J. Robin & Co.'s " ..	2 25	2 5
Otard, Dupuy & Cos..	2 25	2 5
Brandy, cases........	8 50	9 0
Brandy, com. per c...	4 00	4 50
Whiskey:		
Common 36 u. p......	0 62½	0 65
Old Rye	0 85	0 87½
Malt	0 85	0 7½
Toddy	0 85	0 7½
Scotch, per gal.......	1 90	2 10
Irish—Kinnahan's c...	7 00	7 50
" Dunnville's Belf't..	6 00	6 25
Wool.		
Fleece, lb............	0 28	0 35
Pulled "............	0 22	0 25
Furs.		
Bear.................	3 00	10 00
Beaver, ⅌ lb..........	1 00	1 25
Coon	0 20	0 40
Fisher...............	4 00	6 00
Martin...............	1 40	1 60
Mink.................	3 25	4 00
Otter................	5 75	6 00
Spring Rats	0 15	0 17
Fox.	1 20	1 25

NSURANCE COMPANIES.

ENGLISH.—*Quotations on the London Market.*

t Dividend.	Name of Company.	Shares parval £	Amount paid.	Last Sale.
	Briton Medical and General Life....	10	....	2½
7½	Commer'l Union, Fire, Life and Mar.	50	5	5½xd
8	City of Glasgow	25	2½	5½
9½	Edinburgh Life	100	15	33
½ yr	European Life and Guarantee......	2½	11s6	4s. 6d.
0	Etna Fire and Marine............	10	1½	—
5	Guardian	100	50	51½
2	Imperial Fire..................	500	50	350
0½	Imperial Life	100	10	17
0	Lancashire Fire and Life.........	20	2	2⅝
1	Life Association of Scotland.......	40	7½	25
p. sh	London Assurance Corporation ..	25	12½	49
5	London and Lancashire Life	10	1	—
0	Liverp'l & London & Globe F. & L.	20	2	7 1-16
5	National Union Life	5	1	1
2½	Northern Fire and Life	100	5	12 1-16
2 ɔo s.	North British and Mercantile	50	6¼	19½xd
0	Ocean Marine	25	5	17
12s.	Provident Life..............	100	10	35
p. s.	Phœnix....................	....	....	145
ı.yr.	Queen Fire and Life	10	1	1
ɔo.4s	Royal Insurance..............	20	3	6⅝
0	Scottish Provincial Fire and Life ..	50	2½	5 3-8
5	Standard Life	50	12	66½
5	Star Life	25	1¼	—
	CANADIAN.			⅌ c.
4	British America Fire and Marine ..	$50	$25	55½ 56
4	Canada Life	...	....	.....
2	Montreal Assurance	£50	£5	135
8	Provincial Fire and Marine........	60	11	.....
....	Quebec Fire	40	32½	25½ 26
7	" Marine..................	100	40	85 90
ɪo's.	Western Assurance.............	40	9	.....

RAILWAYS.	Sha's	Paid	Montr	London
St. Lawrence.....................	£100	All.	....	57 59
ake Huron	20½	"	....	2¾ 3½
do Preference	10	"	....	5 6
& Goderich, 6⅌c., 1872-3-4..........	100	"	....	66 60
d St. Lawrence	....	....	10 11	....
do Pref. 10 ⅌ ct..............	....	....	80 82½	....
....	100	"	14 15	14¾ 15¼
Eq. G. M. Bds. 1 ch. 6⅌c............	100	"	....	85 87
First Preference, 5 ⅌ c	100	"	....	49 50
Deferred, 3 ⅌ ct..................	100	"	....	....
Second Pref. Bonds, 5⅌c............	100	"	....	37 39
do Deferred, 3 ⅌ ct..............	100	"	....	....
Third Pref. Stock, 4⅌ct............	100	"	...	27 29
do. Deferred, 3 ⅌ ct.............	100	"	...	....
Fourth Pref. Stock, 3⅌c............	100	"	....	16½ 17½
do. Deferred, 3 ⅌ ct..............	100	"	....	....
n	20½	"	14 15	14¼ 14¾
New	20½	18	....	....
6 ⅌ c. Bds, due 1873-76..........	100	All.	....	100 102
5½ ⅌c Bds. due 1877-78............	100	"	....	94 95
ay, Halifax, $250, all..........	$250	"	....	....
anada, 6⅌c. 1st Pref. Bds..........	100	"	.. .	92 93

ANGE.	Halifax.	Montr'l.	Quebec.	Toronto.
ndon, 60 days......				
days date	12½	9¼ 9½	9 9¼	9¼
....	11½ 12	8 9	8 8½	8¾
documents...........	....	7 7½	....	....
York................	....	25½ 26	23 24	26
o.	....	26 26½	24 24½	....
o.	....	par to ½ p.	par ½ dis.	par ½ dis.
....	....	4 4½	....	3½ to 4½

STOCK AND BOND REPORT.

The dates of our quotations are as follows:—Toronto, May 4: Montreal, May 3; Quebec, May 3; London, April 18.

NAME.	Shares.	Paid up.	Divid'd last 6 Months	Dividend Day.	CLOSING PRICES. Toronto.	Montre'l	Quebec.
BANKS.			⅌ ct.				
British North America	$250	All.	3	July and Jan.	105 105½	105 105½	104 105
Jacques Cartier.............	50	"	4	1 June, 1 Dec.	109 110	109 110	109 110
Montreal	200	"	6	"	152 154	155 156	152 153
Nationale..................	50	"	4	1 Nov. 1 May.	108 108½	105 106	105 106
New Brunswick	100	"	......	......	....	...	....
Nova Scotia	200	28	7&b$3½	Mar. and Sept.	....	....	....
Du Peuple..................	50	"	4	1 Mar., 1 Sept.	118 119	108 108½	108 109
Toronto	100	"	4	1 Jan., 1 July.	118 119	118½ 119½	119 120
Bank of Yarmouth...........	....	....	......	......	....	....	....
Canadian Bank of Com'e......	50	95	......	......	102 102½	101½ 102½	101 102
City Bank Montreal	80	All.	4	1 June, 1 Dec.	101 101½	101 102	100 100½
Commer'l Bank (St. John)....	100	"	⅌ ct.	.....	...	...	....
Eastern Townships' Bank.....	50	"	4	1 July, 1 Jan..	....	99 101	99½ 100½
Gore	40	...	none.	1 Jan., 1 July.	36 37	35 36½	36 37
Halifax Banking Company....	...	....	......	......	...	...	....
Mechanics' Bank............	50	70	4	1 Nov., 1 May.	94 95	94 95	92 93
Merchants' Bank of Canada....	100	70	4	1 Jan., 1 July.	107 107½	107 107½	107 107½
Merchants' Bank (Halifax)....	....	....	......	.....	....	....	....
Molson's Bank..............	50	All.	4	1 Apr., 1 Oct.	108½ 109	108½ 109	108 109
Niagara District Bank.......	100	70	3½	1 Jan., 1 July.	....	....	....
Ontario Bank...............	40	All.	4	1 June, 1 Dec.	100 100½	100 101	100½ 101
People's Bank (Fred'kton)....	100	"	......	......	....	....	. ..
People's Bank (Halifax)......	20	"	7 12 m	......	....	...	....
Quebec Bank	100	"	3½	1 June, 1 Dec.	101 102	100½ 102½	103 103½
Royal Canadian Bank	50	50	4	1 Jan., 1 July.	55 60	70 75	74 75
St. Stephens Bank	100	All.	.....	......	....	..	...
Union Bank	100	70	4	1 Jan., 1 July.	105 106	105½ 106	107 108
Union Bank (Halifax)........	100	40	7 12 mo	Feb. and Aug.	....	....	. .
MISCELLANEOUS.							
British America Land........	250	44	2½	......	....	....	....
British Colonial S. S. Co......	250	32½	2½	......	...	50 60	....
Canada Company	32½	All.	£1 10s.	......	....	....	....
Canada Landed Credit Co.....	50	$20	3½	......	78 80	....	....
Canada Per. B'ldg Society....	50	All.	5	......	125 125½	....	....
Canada Mining Company......	4	90	......	......	....	....	....
Do. Inl'd Steam Nav. Co....	100	All.	7	......	....	....	....
Do. Glass Company.........	100	"	12½ "	......	....	100 101	....
Canad'n Loan & Investm't....	25	2½	7	......	....	40 55	....
Canada Agency	10	¼	......	......	....	....	....
Colonial Securities Co.......	...	....	......	......	....	....	....
Freehold Building Society....	100	All.	4	......	112 112½	....	....
Halifax Steamboat Co........	100	"	5	......	....	....	....
Halifax Gas Company........	....	....	......	......	....	...	....
Hamilton Gas Company.......	....	....	.....	......	....	...	....
Huron Copper Bay Co........	4	12	20	......	....	30 45	....
Lake Huron S. and C.........	5	102	......	......	....	....	....
Montreal Mining Consols......	20	$15	......	......	....	3.15 3.25	...
Do. Telegraph Co........	40	All.	5	......	133½ 134	133 134	133 133½
Do. Elevating Co........	00	"	15 12 m	......	....	100 102½	....
Do. City Gas Co.........	40	"	4	15 Mar. 15 Sep.	....	133 135	134 135
Do. City Pass. R. Co.....	50	"	4	......	....	105½ 106	106 107
Quebec and L. S.	8	$4	......	......	....	....	....
Quebec Gas Co..............	200	All.	4	1 Mar., 1 Sep.	....	...	118 119
Quebec Street R. R..........	50	25	3	......	....	....	90 91
Richelieu Navigation Co......	100	All.	10 p.a.	1 Jan., 1 July.	....	108½ 109½	108 108½
St. Lawrence Glass Company.	100	"	....	......	....	80 85	.. ..
St. Lawrence Tow Boat Co.....	100	"	......	3 Feb.	...	...	30 35
Tor'to Consumers' Gas Co.....	50	"	4	1 My Au MarFe	107 107½	...	104 105
Trust & Loan Co. of U. C.....	20	5	3	......	....	....	.. .
West'n Canada Bldg Soc'y....	50	All.	5	......	120 120½	....	....

SECURITIES.	London.	Montreal.	Quebec.	Toronto.
Canadian Gov't Deb. 6 ⅌ ct. stg................	....	103 104	101 101½	103 104.
Do. do. 6 do due Ja. & Jul. 1877-84........	104½ 105½	....	....	....
Do. do. 6 do. Feb. & Aug........	102 104	....	.. .	....
Do. do. 6 do. Mch. & Sep........	102 104	....	...	....
Do. do. 5 ⅌ ct. cur., 1883	92½ 93½	92½ 95	93½ 94	93 94½
Do. do. 5 do. stg., 1885	92 94	92½ 94½	93½ 94½	93 94½
Do. do. 7 do. cur.,......................	....	....	......	....
Dominion 6 p. c. 1878 cy.......................	....	107 109	107½ 108½	108 108½
Hamilton Corporation...........................	. ..	....	... ..	....
Montreal Harbor, 8 ⅌ ct. d. 1869................	..	....	......	....
Do. do. 7 do. 1870...................	...	....	......	....
Do. do. 6½ do. 1883...................	....	102 103	......	102 103
Do. do. 6½ do. 1873...................	....	....	......	....
Do. Corporation, 6 ⅌ c. 1891...............	....	96 96½	96 96½	96 96½
Do. 7 p. c. stock..............................	....	108½ 110	109 110	108 110
Do. Water Works, 6 ⅌ c. stg. 1878............	....	....	......	96 96½
Do. do. 6 do. cy. do.	....	96½ 97	......	96 97
New Brunswick, 6 ⅌ ct., Jan. and July	103 104	....	......	....
Nova Scotia, 6 ⅌ ct., 1875......................	102 104	...	......	....
Ottawa City 6 ⅌ c. d. 1880	....	95 97	......	...
Quebec Harbour, 6 ⅌ c. d. 1883..................	....	....	60	....
Do. do. 7 do. do.....................	....	....	65 70	....
Do. do 8 do. 1886.....................	...	....	80 85	....
Do. City, 7 ⅌ c. d. 1½ years..................	....	....	98 98½	....
Do. do. 7 do. 3 do.	....	....	91 92	....
Do. do. 7 do. 4 do.	....	....	94 95	....
Do. Water Works, 7 ⅌ ct., 3 years..............	....	....	97 97½	....
Do. do. 6 do. 1½ do.	....	....	94 95	....
Toronto Corporation	....	90 92½	...	....

Insurance.

Briton Medical and General Life Association,

with which is united the

BRITANNIA LIFE ASSURANCE COMPANY.

Capital and Invested Funds............£750,000 *Sterling.*

ANNUAL INCOME, £220,000 STG. :
Yearly increasing at the rate of £25,000 Sterling.

THE important and peculiar feature originally introduced by this Company, in applying the periodical
Bonuses, so as to make Policies payable during life, without
any higher rate of premiums being charged, has caused
the success of the BRITON MEDICAL AND GENERAL to be
almost unparalleled in the history of Life Assurance. *Life
Policies on the Profit Scale become payable during the lifetime
of the Assured, thus rendering a Policy of Assurance a
means of subsistence in old age, as well as a protection for a
family, and a more valuable security to creditors in the
event of early death; and effectually meeting the often
urged objection, that persons do not themselves reap the
benefit of their own prudence and forethought.*

No extra charge made to members of Volunteer Corps
for services within the British Provinces.

☞ TORONTO AGENCY, 5 KING ST. WEST.

Oct 17—9-1yr JAMES FRASER, Agent.

BEAVER
Mutual Insurance Association,

HEAD OFFICE—20 TORONTO STREET,
TORONTO.

INSURES LIVE STOCK against death from any cause.
The only Canadian Company having authority to do this
class of business.

E. C. CHADWICK,
President.
W. T. O'REILLY,
Secretary. 8 1y-25

HOME DISTRICT
Mutual Fire Insurance Company.

Office—North-West Cor. Yonge & Adelaide Streets,
TORONTO.—(UP STAIRS.)

INSURES Dwelling Houses, Stores, Warehouses, Merchandise, Furniture, &c.

PRESIDENT—The Hon. J. McMURRICH.
VICE-PRESIDENT—JOHN BURNS, Esq.
JOHN RAINS, Secretary.

AGENTS:
DAVID WRIGHT, Esq., Hamilton; FRANCIS STEVENS, Esq.,
Barrie; Messrs. GIBBS & BRO., Oshawa. 8–1y

THE PRINCE EDWARD COUNTY
Mutual Fire Insurance Company.

HEAD OFFICE,—PICTON, ONTARIO.
President, L. B. STINSON; *Vice-President*, W. A. RICHARDS.
Directors : H. A. McFaul, James Cavan, James Johnson,
S. S. DeMill, William Delong.—*Secretary*, John Twigg;
Treasurer, David Barker; *Solicitor*, R. J. Fitzgerald.

THIS Company is established upon strictly Mutual principles, insuring farming and isolated property, (not
hazardous,) in *Townships only*, and offers great advantages
to insurers, at low rates for *five years*, without the expense
of a renewal.
Picton, June 1½, 1868. 9-1y

THE AGRICULTURAL
Mutual Assurance Association of Canada.

HEAD OFFICE.............................LONDON, ONT

A purely Farmers' Company. Licensed by the Government of Canada.

Capital, 1st January, 1860...................$250,193 82
Cash and Cash Items, over...................$86,000 00
No. of Policies in force...................30,892 00

THIS Company insures nothing more dangerous than
Farm property. Its rates are as low as any well-established Company in the Dominion, and lower than those
of a great many. It is largely patronised, and continues
to grow in public favor.
For Insurance, apply to any of the Agents or address
the Secretary, London, Ontario.
London, 2nd Nov., 1868. 12-1y.

Insurance.

The Gore District Mutual Fire Insurance Company

GRANTS INSURANCES on all description of Property
against Loss or Damage by FIRE. It is the only Mutual Fire Insurance Company which assesses its Policies
yearly from their respective dates ; and the average yearly
cost of insurance in it, for the past three and a half years,
has been nearly

TWENTY CENTS IN THE DOLLAR
less than what it would have been in an ordinary Pro-
prietary Company.
THOS. M. SIMONS,
Secretary & Treasurer.
ROBT. McLEAN,
Inspector of Agencies.
Galt, 25th Nov., 1868. 15-1y

Western Assurance Company,

INCORPORATED 1851.

CAPITAL, ... $490.

FIRE AND MARINE.

HEAD OFFICE.................TORONTO, ONTARIO

DIRECTORS.
Hon. JNO. McMURRICH, President.
  CHARLES MAGRATH, Vice-President.
A. M. SMITH, Esq. | JOHN FISKEN, Esq.
ROBERT BEATY, Esq. | ALEX. MANNING, Esq.
JAMES MICHIE, Esq. | N. BARNHART, Esq.
  R. J. DALLAS, Esq.
B. HALDAN, Secretary.
J. MAUGHAN, JR., Assistant Secretary.
WM. BLIGHT, Fire Inspector.
CAPT. G. T. DOUGLAS, Marine Inspector.
JAMES PRINGLE, General Agent.

Insurances effected at the lowest current rates on
Buildings, Merchandise, and other property, against loss
or damage by fire.
On Hull, Cargo and Freight against the perils of Inland
Navigation.
On Cargo Risks with the Maritime Provinces by sail or
steam.
On Cargoes by steamers to and from British Ports.
WESTERN ASSURANCE COMPANY'S OFFICE, }
  TORONTO, 1st April, 1869. } 33-1y

Fire and Marine Assurance.

THE BRITISH AMERICA
ASSURANCE COMPANY.
HEAD OFFICE:
CORNER OF CHURCH AND COURT STREETS,
TORONTO.

BOARD OF DIRECTION :
Hon G. W. Allan, M.L.C., A. Joseph, Esq .,
George J. Boyd, Esq ., Peter Paterson, Esq.,
Hon. W. Cayley, G. P. Ridout, Esq.,
Richard S. Cassels, Esq., E H.Rutherford,Esq ,
  Thomas C. Street, Esq.
Governor :
GEORGE PERCIVAL RIDOUT, Esq.
Deputy Governor:
PETER PATERSON, Esq.
Fire Inspector: Marine Inspector:
E ROBY O'BRIEN. CAPT. R. COURNEEN.
Insurances granted on all descriptions of property
against loss and damage by fire and the perils of inland
navigation.
Agencies established in the principal cities, towns, and
ports of shipment throughout the Province.
THOS. WM. BIRCHALL,
23-1y Managing Director.

Queen Fire and Life Insurance Company,
OF LIVERPOOL AND LONDON,
ACCEPTS ALL ORDINARY FIRE RISKS
on the most favorable terms.

LIFE RISKS
Will be taken on terms that will compare favorably with
other Companies.

CAPITAL, • • • £2,000,000 Stg.

CHIEF OFFICES—Queen's Buildings, Liverpool, and
Gracechurch Street London.
CANADA BRANCH OFFICE—Exchange Buildings, Montreal.
Resident Secretary and General Agent,
A. MACKENZIE FORBES,
13 St. Sacrament St., Merchants' Exchange, Montreal.
WM. ROWLAND, Agent, Toronto. 1-1y

Insurance.

The Waterloo County Mutual Fire Insu Company.

HEAD OFFICE : WATERLOO, ONTARIO.

ESTABLISHED 1863.

THE business of the Company is divided int
separate and distinct branches, the

VILLAGE, FARM, AND MANUFACTU

Each Branch paying its own losses and its just pro
of the managing expenses of the Company.
C. M. TAYLOR, Sec. M. SPRINGER, M.M.P.,
J. HUGHES, Inspector.

Ætna Fire and Marine Insurance Compa Dublin.

AT a Meeting of the Shareholders of this Co
held at Dublin, on the 13th ult., it was agree
the business of the "ETNA" should be transferred
"UNITED PORTS AND GENERAL INSURANCE COM
In accordance with this agreement, the business wi
after be carried on by the latter Company, which a
and guarantees all the risks and liabilities of the "E
The Directors have resolved to continue the CAN
BRANCH, and arrangements for resuming FIRE an
RINE business are rapidly approaching completion.
T. W. GRIFFIT
16 MANA

Lancashire Insurance Compa
CAPITAL, - - - - - - - - - £2,000,000 S

FIRE RISKS
Taken at reasonable rates of premium, an
ALL LOSSES SETTLED PROMPTLY,
By the undersigned, without reference elsewi
S. C. DUNCAN-CLARK & CO.,
General Agents for Ontari
N. W. Corner of King & Church Str
25-1y TORONTO.

DIVISION OF PROFITS NEXT Y

ASSURANCES

EFFECTED BEFORE 30TH APRIL NEXT,

IN THE

Canada Life Assurance Comp

OBTAIN A YEAR'S ADDITIONAL PROFI

OVER LATER ENTRANTS,

And the great success of the Company warrants
rectors in recommending this very importan
advantage to assurers.

SUMS ASSURED $5,
AMOUNT OF CAPITAL AND FUNDS........ 1,
ANNUAL INCOME............................

Assets (exclusive of uncalled capital) for each
liabilities, about $150.
The income from interest upon investments
alone sufficient to meet claims by death.
A. G. RAMSAY, Manag
E. BRADBURNE, Age
Feb. 1. 1y Toronto S

The Victoria Mutual
FIRE INSURANCE COMPANY OF CANA

Insures only Non-Hazardous Property, at Low

BUSINESS STRICTLY MUTUAL.

GEORGE H. MILLS, President.
W. D. BOOKER, Secretary.

HEAD OFFICE . . . . HAMILTON, O
aug 15-1yr

PUBLISHED AT THE OFFICE OF THE MON
TIMES, No. 60 CHURCH STREET.
PRINTED AT THE DAILY TELEGRAPH PUBL ISHING
BAY STREET, CORNER OF KING

THE CANADIAN
MONETARY TIMES
AND
INSURANCE CHRONICLE.

VOTED TO FINANCE, COMMERCE, INSURANCE, BANKS, RAILWAYS, NAVIGATION, MINES, INVESTMENT,
PUBLIC COMPANIES, AND JOINT STOCK ENTERPRISE.

| I—NO. 39. | TORONTO, THURSDAY, MAY 13, 1869. | SUBSCRIPTION $2 A YEAR. |

Mercantile.

Meetings.

BANK OF UPPER CANADA.

The half-yearly meeting was held on the 5th
inst. The minutes of the November semi-annual
meeting were then read, and subsequently the following balance sheet :—

LIABILITIES.

Bank Notes in circulation............	$103,558 00
Due to Depositors on all accounts...	105,386 50
" on Trustees certificates	226,317 91
" Glyn & Co.....................	126,085 44
" Government.................	1,122,639 10
Total liabilities.............	1,683,986 94
Balance at credit of Profit and Loss account.............................	461,455 60
	$2,145,442 54

ASSETS.

Specie and balances with banks......	$18,739 35	
Mortgages and securities new............$78,953 81		
Mortgages in course of completion........... 59,853 44		
	129,807 25	
Mortgages, old account...............	54,437 83	
Real Estate............................	928,963 51	
Railway Stocks, Debentures, &c....	11,251 67	
Bills, Judgments, &c..................	1,002,242 93	
Total assets.................	$2,145,442 54	

MEM:—The above does not include interest,
which has not been added either to the Assets or
Liabilities.

The Assets are held in the Balance Sheet at the
same valuations at which they were handed over
by the Bank of Upper Canada to the Trustees.

Mr. McCord, from what he gathered from the
correspondence with the Government—and that
contained more satisfactory information respecting
the facts of the whole matter than he had yet
seen published in any other form—it appeared to
him that the amount due to the Government was
$1,122,639, and to depositors $460,000 more ;
making in all $1,482,659. In paying this off, it
is calculated there will be a deficiency of from
$500,000 to $600,000.

The Chairman—This is a rough estimate. We
cannot calculate within $100,000 or $200,000 as
yet, but we do not consider that it will be less
than $500,000. It may, however, be more; there
is not much prospect of it being less.

Mr. McCord had thought over the whole matter,
and, after doing so, had determined to submit a
proposition which would be, he imagined, satisfactory to all concerned. He submitted his idea
in writing, as follows, placing it in the form of a
series of resolutions :—The stockholders present
consider that it is desirable, in the interest of all
parties concerned, that the affairs of the Bank
should be immediately wound up ; and that a
special meeting of all the stockholders be called
together with that object, on the first Monday of
October next, to consider the following propositions : 1st. That the bill-holders and depositors
be paid in full. 2nd. That the balance, after
paying expenses, be equally divided between the
Government and such stockholders, widows and

orphans, and others, who have lost their all by
the failure of the Bank.

This meeting also desires to make the following
recommendations to the trustees :—They are of
opinion that all the real estate should be marked
at a very low upset price, and offered immediately
to public competition by auction. That the
trustees receive from every one indebted to the
Bank, for property sold since the failure of the
Bank, as well as for all the property which may
hereafter be sold, the notes of the Bank at 75
cents on the dollar, at least. That the trustees
revise the present expenses of the trust, with the
view of cutting them down to the lowest figure
possible. The stockholders are also of the opinion
that a less expensive means of winding up the
affairs of the Bank, by the appointment of a
liquidator, might be adopted.

In introducing these resolutions Mr. McCord
pointed out the necessity of winding up affairs as
speedily as possible ; the expenses were large ; in
England very large banking institutions were
wound up by one person, and if a liquidator were
appointed here the expense would be reduced at
least one-half. Mr. Mead asked for the trustee's
reply to the Finance Minister, but the chairman
considered it inadvisable to give it publicity.

Mr. Hime offered an amendment, which, although agreeing in some respects, would, he
thought, meet the views of the meeting better.
He did not wish to see the lands sold by auction,
but thought it would be far better to try and reduce
the expenses by having only one man as liquidator
under the supervision of the Government. The
Government then would be more likely to deal
favourably with them. He moved in amendment.
"Whereas it appears that the Government are making enquiries with a view to enforcing their claim
against the shareholders of the Bank of Upper
Canada, and that from the relation which the assets bear to the liabilities such enforcement would
not only absorb the available assets, but would also
render a call upon the shareholders necessary.
And whereas a large number of the shareholders
are foreigners, minors, trustees, and persons residing in foreign countries, from whom nothing could
be collected, and all the shareholders have already
lost so much by the institution that further calls
must produce great distress."

"Resolved, that it is expedient to reduce the
expenses of winding up (now over $14,000 per an-
num), to the minimum, and that such action be
taken either by appeal to Government or otherwise,
as will do away with the allowance of $4,000 per
annum, now paid to the three trustees, and place
the winding up under the control of one competent
manager, who shall, under the supervision and inspection of the proper department of Government,
bring to an end, with as great expedition as the
interests of all concerned will allow, the process of
liquidation."

In answer, after some further discussion, the
motion and amendment were allowed to stand over,
and the meeting adjourned.

The Finance Minister in his communication to
the trustees says:—It becomes necessary to consider what course ought to be taken in the public
interest. The undersigned is of opinion that com
munication should be had with the shareholders,
and that they should be afforded the option either
of paying off the Government and taking the assets into their hands ; or of making payment to the

Government of a sum of money to be relieved of their liability, allowing the estate to be realized under the present Trust, or otherwise, as the Government may see fit; or, thirdly, of suggesting any other course, either as respects the present method of liquidation, or touching the ultimate payment of the debt to the Government. Unless the Government bring the property of the Bank to sale under a writ of extent, and thus anticipate the time which the Trustees are of opinion will be occupied in realizing the estate, five years will elapse before the creditors can enforce by law any contribution from the shareholders under the double liability clause. It is impossible to anticipate what changes in the personnel of the shareholders may take place before that time, whereby their capacity to make good their respective contributions might be affected. Delay increases probability that the loss will ultimately be borne less equally than if an adjustment now took place and that the sources to which the Government might look for payment, will every year be of less worth.

The course which the Government may deem it its duty in the public interests to adopt, whether to await the gradual realization of the assets, or to enforce its remedy at once, will doubtless be influenced by the action of the shareholders, and the proposals they may make to the Government after due consideration of the actual situation and when apprised that the Government deems it fitting that a definite arrangement should now take place.

In conclusion the undersigned would observe that until the shareholders have had an opportunity of electing either to pay off the Government, or to make an offer on some terms to make good the anticipated deficiency, or of suggesting some anticipated deficiency, or of suggesting some other course of action from that now followed, it would be premature to consider whether any and what means might be taken to deal with the other creditors, or to prosecute the liquidation of the estate by less expensive means than those now adopted.

BANKERS' MEETING.

At a meeting of Representatives of Banks of the Dominion of Canada, held at Ottawa on the first of May, the following were present: The Hon. Mr. Simpson, Mr. Starnes, representing the Ontario Bank; Hon. Mr. McMaster, Bank of Commerce; Hon. Mr. McDonald, Mr. Metcalfe, M. P., Mr. Woodside, Royal Canadian Bank; Hon. Mr. Burnham, Mr. Hague, Bank of Toronto; Hon. Mr. Benson, Niagara District Bank; Mr. Stevenson, Quebec Bank; Mr. Sache, Molsons' Bank; Mr. Lewin, Bank of New Brunswick; Mr. Jack, all the Halifax banks and the Commercial Bank of Windsor.

It was moved, seconded and Resolved:
That Mr. Lewin, of the Bank of New Brunswick take the chair; and that Mr. Jack be the secretary.

Mr. Hague, as convener of the meeting stated its objects, and read a letter from the cashier of the Merchants' Bank, Montreal, regretting the inability of the President or himself to be present at the meeting, and expressing their hope that the preservation of the Bank circulation in Canada may be one of its results.

He also read the resolutions adopted by the banks of Halifax, and certain banks in the Provinces of Quebec and Ontario (copies of which are hereto appended)—

Whereupon it was moved by Mr. Simpson, seconded by Mr. Stevenson, and resolved,
That this meeting concur generally in the sentiments expressed in the resolutions adopted at meetings of the Bankers of Halifax and of Montreal, Quebec and the Province of Ontario, and is of the opinion that it is desirable by all proper means to secure the continuance of the bank note circulation of the Dominion as it at present exists.

A further resolution was moved by Hon. Mr. Simpson, seconded by Mr. Medcalf, M.P., to the effect—
That safety to creditors of banks may be fully attained without sacrificing those resources, on which the business of the country depends and without endangering a gold basis by introducing into the charters of the Banks provisions as to the double liability of shareholders, the impairment of capital, reserves, rents, etc. This resolution was carried.

Moved by Hon. Mr. Simpson, seconded by Mr. Sache,
That a deputation, consisting of the five following gentlemen, wait on the Finance Minister, and lay before him the views of the meeting and report to a future meeting at the call of the Chairman: The Chairman; the Secretary; Hon. Mr. Simpson, (or Mr. Gibbs, M.P., in his absence); Mr. Stevenson; Mr. Hague.

The Meeting then adjourned.

Resolutions adopted by the Halifax Banks.

HALIFAX, N.S., April 17, 1869.

1. That the banking system in existence in Nova Scotia has been in successful operation for more than thirty years, and has been largely instrumental in aiding the development of the resources of this province and building up its trade and commerce. That there has never been the failure of any bank, nor any suspension of specie payments. That bank notes have always been on a par with gold and convertible into gold on demand, and note holders have never sustained any loss by them. That the public are satisfied with the system, and neither ask nor desire any change.

2. That the loanable capital, together with the loanable funds derived from the bank note circulation and the substitution of that of the government, would seriously interfere with and lessen the resources of the banks, cause discounts to be reduced nearly if not quite one fourth, and thereby cripple trade and commerce.

3. That the introduction of such a radical change as the withdrawal of the Bank note circulation and the substitution of that of the Government would seriously interfere with and lessen the resources of the Banks, cause discount to be reduced nearly, if not quite, one-fourth and thereby cripple trade and commerce.

4. That the national banking system of the United States, having taken its rise under a suspension of specie payments, is not applicable to the state of the Province. If adopted, the banks will be compelled to loan to the government about one-half of the amount now advanced for mercantile purposes which would almost, if not entirely prostrate and ruin the business of the province.

5. That the adoption of either plan would permanently reduce the resources available for banking purposes. By giving time for withdrawal of the circulation, or the purchase of bonds, this might prevent sudden distress and mitigate the stringency of the money market, but there would be nevertheless a certain gradual reduction of discount which would soon tell most injuriously on trade. Under the circumstances to increase the capital stock, would not make up the deficiency; for the monies available for this purpose are already held by the banks in the shape of deposits, and to take from the deposits and add to the capital stock could not possibly improve the financial position.

6. That if it is thought desirable to give increased security to note holders, this could be done without deranging the present arrangement by making the notes, in case of failure, a first lien on the assets of the bank, and payable as soon as sufficient funds might be collected. There are reasons why note holders should be protected, but none why depositors should be, and this plan would perfectly secure the former without inflicting any injury on business, or diminishing in any way the funds available for banking purposes.

7. That in our opinion the present system, whereby the circulating medium is furnished by the banks, is the best adapted to the circumstances of the country, as it increases the banking funds employed in the encouragement of trade and manufactures, which in a new country are always required; and we would strongly deprecate any change in the law which would have the effect of overthrowing the present note circulation of the banks, or curtailing their capital by a compulsory loan to the government, by their legislature to invest a portion of it in government debentures, which are of variable value, and could not be converted into gold during financial panic or pressure in time to prevent suspension of specie payments or greater loss.

Resolutions adopted by the Ontario and Quebec Banks.

At a meeting of Bankers held in the Merchants' Bank of Canada, on the 17th day of April, 1869.

It was moved by Mr. Jackson Rae, seconded Mr. William Sache, and carried:
Whereas, the existing system of banking in Canada has been found subservient in a high degree to its commercial interests has been tested by a long experience, has proved itself to be well adapted to the requirements of an agricultural community and has resulted in a high degree of security and stability:

Resolved.—That in any renewal of the charters of banks it is important for the best interests of the public that no change of a fundamental character be made in the system and particularly that the note circulation be preserved.

2nd. That the adoption of a system of the same character as the national banking system of the United States, or founded on the same principle of imposing a rigid limit to the total circulation to be covered by government securities would be highly detrimental to the public interest, causing a large withdrawal of capital now engaged in furthering its commercial enterprises, consequent scarcity of money, high rates of interest with greater loss to the lender and general finance distress.

3rd. That a system of note issues made directly by the government would have the same injurious effect upon the commercial and financial affairs of the country, and would in addition have an inevitable tendency to depreciation with all disastrous consequences to every class of community.

4th. That holding these views we deem it of importance that they be urged upon the attention of the legislature during the present session in every practicable mode.

Insurance.

FIRE RECORD.—St. Catherines, May 7.—House of P. Donohoe, Niagara-street; loss stated at $ to $500, and insurance at $200.

Carleton, N.B.—Workshop of Levi Long, adjoining grocery and liquor store of Mrs. O'Leary. The buildings were owned by H. Tooney; insurance $800.

St. Catherines, May 3.—A fire broke out in Murray House stables. The stables were consumed and with them most of their contents. Insured in Hartford for $250. A tavern just below the stables, belonging to J. C. Rykert, Esq., and occupied by Mr. Burtch, was badly damaged in its roof and sides.

Brantford, May 7.—A large flax mill was consumed by fire this morning at one o'clock, near Brantford. It has been unused for some time. Loss about $5000; fully insured. It is supposed to have been the work of an incendiary. The building was owned by Kerr, Brown & Co., Hamilton, and rented to Mr. Elliott, of Galt.

Peterboro, May 6.—Sutherland's store-house, Ashburnham, and the adjoining dwelling house, grocery and outbuildings, were all destroyed by fire, and the flames soon spread to two neighboring tenements one occupied by Mr. Thomas Coe, butcher, which was entirely consumed; the other Mr. George Brown, plasterer; uninsured. Mr. Sutherland's loss on grain is about $2,000; insured in the Royal for $1,500; Imperial $1,000. Mr. Wood's loss on buildings is covered by insurance in the Western to the extent $1,000 or $1,250

Catherines, May 6.—Workshop occupied by
Orr as a paint s1op; an adjoining wooden
ng occupied by a man named Matthew's was
down. The buildings destroyed were
by Daniel McGuire, and were insured in
artford of Connecticut, for $500. Orr had
ck of paints, oils, &c. insured in the same
any for $600.

t Zorra Township, May 3.—Barn of Wm.
with contents, he is a heavy loser.

Oxford Co., Ont., May 2.—Dwelling house
in Clark; insured for $1,000. Furniture
y saved.

obell, May 11.—Last night the barn belong-
George Moodie, of Logan, was burnt,
er with a quantity of grain and implements.
800. No insurance. A warrant was issued
this morning against Moodie's brother-in-
r lucendiarism.

treel, May.—The store of Wm. Hagan, on
wrence, Main street, caught fire from the
ion of a coal oil lamp. Mr. Hagan's loss
heavy, it is said, although he is insured.
rorkshop of Mr. Kieltier, cabinet-maker—
stables of Mr. Marchand, in St. Charles
nee street.

point, Ont., May 10.—The dwelling house
Francis Van de Bogart, about one mile
of Napanee, was burned this morning.
to have been insured. Cause of fire
wn.

rFORFEITURE.—The new Insurance law of
an contains the following provision relative
non-forfeiture of Life Insurance Policies:
licy of Insurance on life, issued after this
all take effect, by any Company organized
the laws of this State, shall be forfeited or
void by the non-payment of any premium
, after the first, any further than as follows:
t value of the Policy when the premium be-
due and is not paid, shall be ascertained ac-
g to the "American Experience Table" rate
tality, with interest at four and a half per
per annum. Three-fourths of such net
hall be considered a net single premium of
ole Life Insurance, and the amount it will
shall be determined according to the age of
ty at the time when the unpaid premium
due, and the assumption aforesaid in re-
interest and rate of mortality; but if no
tion be made to the Company for such
Policy within one year after default shall
en made in payment, then all liability in
t of the Company on the Policy on which
ty is in default, shall cease.

.UABLE INSURANCE STATISTICS.

he recent meeting of the U. S. Board of
nderwriters the Executive Committee re-
the following:—

en years from 1859 to 1868 inclusive, give
hat aggregate, for the decade, capital $379,-
; dividends $39,503,643; average percent-
19; but the average earnings of capital
en 9 per cent., leaving the average results
usiness so shown as 1.39 per annum. But
is is not the whole truth, for in that time
323 of actual capital have been absolutely
should be deducted from the dividends,
only $32,735,020 as the actual net result.
r, the increase in actual profits during
iod is $6,160,072, which should be added
duction for loss of capital, and this shows
rage annual percentage to be 10.23, of
was from other sources than premiums,
the net earnings of the business as such
3, a figure utterly insignificant in view of
ire of the business and the risks assumed.
ar tables of figures for ten years, aggregate
wa: premiums received, $213,857,860;
id, $126,456,476; percentage, 59.26.
h statistics indicate losses at 55 per cent.
ums; German figures show 57½ per cent.;

Russian; 58.26. The New York companies doing
fire, inland and marine business, from 1848 to
1866, inclusive, show 66.32 of losses to premiums,
while the strictly mutual State companies show
61.40. The companies reporting to Massachusetts, from 1859 to 1866, inclusive, show 60.18,
while the grand totals brought out by Mr. Barnes
new blank, show of premiums received since organization by the companies, $347,088,679; against
losses paid of $207,330,534; or a grand average
of 59.73; a strong confirmation of a more uniform
certain law of average than is generally admitted.
We may therefore assume 60 per cent. as the average percentage of losses to premiums, and be sustained by the inexorable logic of official sworn
facts.

Similar tables give aggregates for the year of
premiums, including inland, $247,997,692; ex-
penses, $74,014,794; percentage, 29.84. English
companies average about 31. French and German
companies about 30. We therefore assume 30 per
cent. in round numbers as the average expenses
of conducting the business. Adding losses and
expenses together, we find only one-tenth for profit, loss of capital, sweeping conflagrations and
epidemic periods. How far this can be trifled
with by ignorance and credulity, the public must
judge for themselves. To the intelligent and honest underwriter these figures are full of meaning
and admonition.

To us, as practical underwriters, it is of vital
importance to know the absolute relation between losses and risks assumed. With this in
view, tables have been prepared embracing nine
years from 1860 to 1868, inclusive, whose aggregates are these: fire risks written, $25,348,253,481;
fire premiums received, $198,944,401; fire losses
paid, $118,425,228; percentage of losses to pre-
miums, 59.42; percentage of fire losses to fire
risks written, .4671; amount of fire risks written
to $1, of losses, $214 04; average rate of premiums
on fire risks .2848. In 1860 we paid for losses,
4 323-1000 mills per cent. on risks written; In
1868, 4798-1000 mills per cent., and during the
entire nine years, an average of 4 671-1000 mills
per cent. The average of 1868 is therefore in
excess of that for the whole period, yet happily
far below that of 1867, and very far below that of
1866, thus showing the advance that has been
made, and indicating the causes which have operated favorably to this reduced average as compared
with those years; towards which the labors of this
Board have so largely contributed.

In 1860 we could write $231 27 for every dollar
of loss; in 1868, $208 40; while the average for
the nine years was, $214 04; yet our ability to
write during the past year was far greater than in
1867, and greatly in excess of 1866, when the
lower average is reached. It is apparent, therefore, that no essential reduction of rates can be
entertained with safety to ourselves and the insured until our ability to write shall equal the
general average, or at least of the period named.
The average rate of premiums in 1860 was
.7336; in 1868, .9342; with an average rate for
the nine years of .7848; the maximum being in
1867, while the minimum loss for the last four
years was in 1868. The past year witnessed a
reduction of 143-1000 of a mill per cent. in the
rate of premiums, and of 662-1000 of a mill per
cent. in the average losses. There may seem to
be unimportant infinitesimals, but when we consider that the margin of profits is less than one-
tenth of the premium, and that over twenty-five
thousand million dollars were underwritten during
the time under review, we shall more fully appreciate the necessity of having these infinitesimals
on the RIGHT SIDE of our calculations.

Of the many evils that have grown up in the
business of fire underwriting, none has been more
prolific of loss than "over insurance." This evil
has become so conspicuous as to alarm the public,
and call from the public press most severe and
deserved criticism. At least one-third of the
losses on personal property are on property largely
over-insured. The pernicious "privilege" for

other insurance, without notice, makes it impossible to retain an interest on the part of the
insured in the preservation of his property. It
not only permits, but it induces over insurance,
and is a direct temptation to fraud and arson.
How wantonly an old landmark of the business
has been removed, the increase of fraud during
the past few years bears convincing testimony.
This practice of over insurance must be corrected
by our own efforts, or it will soon assume such
proportions as to demand the interference of
the law. The matter has already caused much
discussion, but the evil is as yet unremoved.
Although no extensive conflagrations have occurred since we last met, the loss records will bear
testimony that the torch of the incendiary has
not been idle, but the numerous convictions for
that crime furnish gratifying evidence that this
nefarious trade has not been plied with the usual
impunity of former years.
Statistics gathered in detail from the companies,
indicate that about 32 per cent of losses are the
result of design on the part of the insured, or the
direct act of the incendiary. Records kept in the
city of New York for 13½ years show that of
4,387 fires, 1,283 were incendiary, and that of
$23,679,005 losses paid, $7,909,002 were incendiary, being nearly 33½ per cent. Even as a
pecuniary question, the arrest and conviction of
incendiaries will be found a good investment; but
there is a higher point from which to view these
obligations—that of duty to the State and the
people. This duty requires of us rigid investigation and due presentment, with a constant and
er ergetic care of cases, until conviction is followed
by punishment.

Railway News.

NORTHERN RAILWAY.—Traffic receipts for week
ending May 1st, 1869.

Passengers	$2,922 31
Freight and live stock	12,187 52
Mails and sundries	1,688 60
	$16,798 43
Corresponding Week of '68.	14,674 79
Increase	$2,123 64

GREAT WESTERN RAILWAY.—Traffic for week
ending April 23, 1869.

Passengers	$27,904 60
Freight	55,973 30
Mails and Sundries	2,060 56
Total Receipts for week	$85,938 46
Corresponding week, 1868..	80,756 53
Increase	$5,181 93

THE EUROPEAN AND NORTH AMERICAN RAIL-
WAY traffic receipts for the month of April of the
present year, as compared with those of April of
1868, are as follows:—

	April, 1869.	April, 1868.
Passengers	$5,082 66	$4,213 85
Freight	6,733 19	5,736 33
Mails and Sundries	613 61	484 71
Totals	$12,879 46	$10,484 89

STATEMENT of the Revenue and Expenditure of
the Dominion of Canada for the month ended 30th
April, 1869.

Customs	$822,784 07
Excise	240,572 94
Post Office	82,523 66
Public Works, including Railways..	37,696 35
Bill Stamp Duty	11,168 24
Miscellaneous	48,308 24
Total	$1,243,003 50
Expenditure	$756,706 46

THE CANADIAN MONETARY TIMES AND INSURANCE CHRONICLE *is printed every Thursday evening and distributed to Subscribers on the following morning.*

Publishing office, No. 60 Church-street, 3 doors north of Court-street.

Subscription price—

Canada $2.00 per annum.

England, stg. 10s. per annum.

United States (U.S. Cy.) $3.00 per annum.

Casual advertisements will be charged at the rate of ten cents per line, each insertion.

Address all letters to "THE MONETARY TIMES."

Cheques, money orders, &c. should be made payable to J. M. TROUT, *Business Manager, who alone is authorized to issue receipts for money.*

All Canadian Subscribers to THE MONETARY TIMES *will receive* THE REAL ESTATE JOURNAL *without further charge.*

The Canadian Monetary Times.

THURSDAY, MAY 13, 1869.

THE BANK OF UPPER CANADA.

On the 18th of September, 1866, this Bank suspended, and, on the 12th November, following, assigned to certain trustees. An Act of Parliament (31 Vic. c. 17) was obtained confirming that assignment, and creating a new body corporate under the name of "The Trustees of the Bank of Upper Canada." The Act provided for the nomination and appointment of three trustees to carry out the deed of assignment, one to represent the shareholders, and the other two, "the interests of the creditors of the said bank." One was elected by the shareholders, and two were appointed by the government. The Act further provided that the trustees should meet at least once in every two weeks and be entitled to receive for their own remuneration the sum of four thousand dollars per annum, to be divided among them.

The present state of affairs appears to be this: The Bank owes the Government, exclusive of interest, $1,122,639, and is liable to others,

exclusive of Glyn & Co., who hold security, for about $460,000; the assets will be insufficient to meet what is owed by about $600,000; and the assets "cannot be realized in a shorter period than five years." The subscribed capital of the Bank was originally about $3,100,000 divided into shares of $50 each; but it has since been reduced, and is now only $1,930,000, divided into shares of $30 each, and held by upwards of 1,000 persons. Estimating the deficiency at $600,000, a contribution of about $9.33 per share would be required.

The shareholders are classified under the following heads:—

Executors, guardians, minors........$129,360
Trustees.............................. 337,500
Municipalities........................ 12,800
Females living abroad................. 585,165
Residents in Canada, not known to Trustees............................. 172,220
Residents in Canada, believed to be bad.................................. 139,900
Residents in Canada (including females), believed to be good........ 562,890

The cost of winding up is $14,000 per annum. Of this amount, $4,000 are divided among the Trustees and $4,000 go to the Solicitor. $350 are paid out by way of "travelling expenses." A secretary receives $2,000, the manager of the land department $1,200, a clerk $600 and a messenger $200.

What naturally strikes one in reading over this list is the formidable character of the defunct institution, with its three Trustees, its Solicitor, its Secretary, its clerks, and its messenger; its estimated deficiency of $600,000 and its $14,000 per annum working expenses. Why has the largest Building Society in the country, with a million of dollars of cash receipts in one year, does not pay out in working expenses more than $16,300 per annum! Its President and seven Directors received, last year, just $2,380, while the three Trustees of an institution in liquidation drew $4,000 as "remuneration." These three gentlemen receive $1,333.33⅓ a-piece. If they met twice a month, and were paid by the sitting, at the rate of $4,000 per annum, each sitting would have yielded them about $56, each; if they met once a week, about $26 a sitting, for each. Now, from $3 to $5 a meeting is considered good pay for the Directors of even the most flourishing Corporations; so that the unfortunate shareholders of the Bank of Upper Canada have the exquisite pleasure of witnessing the accumulation of liability, and paying for the sight the highest possible price. These three Trustees are excellent men, and we cannot blame them for drawing the pay secured to to them by the Act. But in the name of all that is reasonable, what occasion is there for three Trustees at all? why should they be

paid such an extravagant sum? They are responsible, except for loss attendant [] ficient neglect, misconduct or default, eac his own acts; while in the case of Dire of Corporations, generally, there is a amount of responsibility. They are h respectable men, but they do not bring t task of winding up any unusual or ext dinary qualifications. It is no disparage of their abilities to say that they could have executed their trust without the a ance of those who knew something abou affairs of the Bank, and we venture th sertion that even now, if left to their devices, they would make sad work. fact is they are useless luxuries. If Trustees must be retained, and paid $4, year, the three gentlemen now in poss are, we suppose, just as capable and as any who could be named. But what ness man can look with approbation o paraphernalia with which that decayed is surrounded! What shareholder can with equanimity an extravagant expen which is widening his liability slowl surely! No wonder dissatisfaction i played at semi-annual meetings. The wonder is that there is so little irritation ifested, so little indignation expressed reference to the proceedings at the late ing it will be seen that the absurd posit affairs is fully recognized. Mr. M pointed out how expeditiously and cl Corporations are wound up in England. Hime's resolution hit the nail on the It affords the only sensible solution Bank problem that has as yet been offe the consideration of the shareholders away with the Trustees altogether, or a two of them, place some competent m charge, as liquidator, with such assists the way of clerks as may be necessar have the accounts audited, and the pr ings supervised by an officer of the F Department. Hon. Mr. Ross in his c nication to the Trustees asked for sugg respecting the liquidation. No more s suggestion has been made than the fered by Mr. Hime, and it would be w all concerned if it were given due con tion. Under the present method of liqu the concern is eating itself up.

Since the above was written we hav informed that the Trustees have dism clerk, and have given the messenger no leave. Such laudable economy is wo recognition, but we are disposed to thi they are beginning at the wrong end grievous items in their accounts are to the Trustees and $4,000 to the So The Solicitor will certainly not accept a ship while he can feast on such a ri case.

BANKING AND CURRENCY.

unanimity with which the bankers of Scotia, New Brunswick, Quebec and io have expressed themselves against rogation of the system of banking un- iich this country has so long prospered, hich has been found so well adapted to uliar circumstances, should cause those ting a change to hesitate. It is neither nor statesmanlike to run full tilt t experience. When men who have the subject of banking a special study we had the best opportunities of judg- the requirements of the country, are ided in their condemnation of the pro- government scheme, common sense indnce politicians to give heed to opi- having all the weight of authority. The at present in force is fundamentally st for Canada. Of course it is not so as to be above amendment. Machinery be devised for the enforcement of the liability of shareholders, and provision for summary liquidation. No banker or could object to having the note cir- n made a first lien on the assets, thus ing its prompt redemption an absolute ty. In case of impairment of capital, it be made imperative to have the de- y called up at once. Stringent rules be framed to prevent the declaration of ads unless an adequate reserve were n hand. But to secure such advisable ments, it is not necessary to sweep he whole system. The banks are now g a renewal of their charters, and such ons could be incorporated in their new

it must not be supposed that the pro- scheme is opposed by bankers only. umber of petitions which have been ted to Parliament, signed by the most ent merchants of our cities and towns, that our mercantile community is d. There is good reason for such a . The U. S. Comptroller of the Cur- n his report for 1867, said :

paper currency furnished exclusively government * * * possesses no inher- alities which adapt it to the wants of * * There is no relation between the of supply and the business of the r. It is an iron currency in its utter l that elasticity so essential in a circu- medium. This has been abundantly by the experience of the last five years. has the legal-tender currency been rforming the equable and harmonious as of money, in its relation to trade lustry, that it has been the great dis- element. By it all relatives values een unsettled, trade interrupted

and industry disorganized. * * *. * * Nothing has been permanent. Violent fluc- tuations have characterized the market for every commodity, and speculation has usurp- ed the place of regular and legitimate traffic." The last number but one of the New York *Financial Chronicle* contains the following significant statement :—"A special cause of embarrassment to business has also arisen from the abnormal condition of our currency system, resulting in frequent spasms in the money market, and rendering it impossible for merchants to get needful accommodation from the banks." So that merchants are interested in this matter, and merchants will be the first to suffer from the introduction of the proposed system. The present is, of all times, the most inopportune for effecting a change of system. Should times grow harder, and the banks curtail their discounts by the large amount necessary to carry on business under a system in which all circula- tion must be covered by a deposit of govern- ment bonds, no one can help feeling that a period of embarrassment is before us, as a community, more trying, more provocative of ruin and distress, than any crisis through which this country has ever passed. Ontario has the greatest interest in this matter, and it will not be well for the Government of the Dominion to gall the shoulders of a Province which has; and will have, to bear an unequal share of our national burdens. It is folly to kill the goose that lays the golden eggs. But while it is possible to beget grievances in Ontario which may lead many to despair of Confederation, it is equally possible to add fuel to the flame of repeal in Nova Scotia. That Province has enjoyed its present bank- ing system for thirty years without the fail- ure of a single bank. All the bankers of Nova Scotia have protested in the most ear- nest manner against change ; and it certainly is not politic, in the present state of affairs there, to alienate men who wield such in- fluence as these bankers do.

It is not a question of party politics. Those most opposed to the Government scheme are supporters of the Government. The bankers' Ottawa meeting was attended by such men as Messrs. Simpson, Benson, McMaster and Gibbs, all in the Government ranks ; and we understand that among the opponents of a fundamental change will be found Hon. D. L. McPherson, Hon. G. W. Allan, and Messrs. Hillyard Cameron, Cart- wright, Beaty, Harrison, and many others equally well disposed towards the Coalition. So that both inside the House and out of it the Government will find itself opposed by its warmest supporters ; and we may rest as- sured that it will receive but little aid from its political enemies.

THE INSOLVENCY ACT.

Some petitions have been presented to the Legislature praying the repeal of the Insol- vency Act altogether, and some praying its amendment. The Government measure con- solidating the law on the subject and extend- ing its operation to the various provinces of the Dominion, has been introduced. It is an improvement upon the old law, but we hope that, in its passage through the House, it will receive such amendments as will meet the wishes of the mercantile community. It deprives the debtor of power to choose an as- signee, and makes the first step an assignment to one called the Interim Assignee, whose duty it will be to take possession, at once, of the debtor's property, and call a meeting of creditors. The Interim Assignee must be an Official Assignee of the county in which the debtor resides, or the Official Assignee of the nearest county. This prompt change of pos- session, of course, is intended to prevent that dissipation of effects which has too frequently characterised the period between the assign- ment and the first meeting of creditors. The creditors may continue the Interim Assignee or appoint an Assignee in his stead. When it is sought to compel liquidation, any one or more claimants may proceed in the manner that two or more could do under the old law. An additional ground for compelling assign- ment is where a trader sells or conveys the whole or the main part of his stock or assets, without the consent of his creditors and with- out satisfying their claims. At the first meeting of creditors, or afterwards, they may appoint Inspectors, from among themselves, whose services shall be gratuitous, and who shall superintend and direct the Assignee. Between meetings the Inspectors act for the creditors, but their directions are subject to revision by the subsequent meeting. Very full powers are given the Assignee to sell realty and personalty, to the best advantage. The remuneration of the Assignee shall be fixed by the creditors ; if not fixed an amount may be allowed, not exceeding five per cent of the cash receipts, subject to appeal on the ground of excess or inadequacy. The As- signee's accounts are to be ready in one month after his appointment, and statements are to be furnished by him every three months. No lien is created by a *fi. fa.*, if before payment to plaintiff under it, an assignment is made or the estate is put in liquidation. Preferential sales or transfers of real as well as personal property are presumed fraudulent and void, whether to a creditor or otherwise. A deed of composition and discharge may be made in consideration of cash or credit, secured or not, and the discharge contained in it may be absolute or conditional upon the payments being made. Where a discharge is contested, if the evidence shows extravagance, recklessness in over-trading, or negligence in keeping books, continuing to trade unduly after the debtor believed himself insolvent, incurring debts without a reasonable expectation of paying them, the judge may order a suspension of the discharge for five years. This suspension may be also directed at the instance of a majority of the creditors, or the discharge may be made second-class. A very proper provision is made for the examination of the wife of the debtor touching the retention or concealment of his effects, and the Assignee is empowered to receive and open the insolvent's letters. Subpœnas to compel the attendance of witnesses may issue to any part of the Dominion. A discharge under a foreign bankrupt or insolvent law will be no defence to any action instituted in the Dominion for the recovery of a debt contracted within it. Very stringent provisions are introduced respecting the removing of property, not fully discovering it, not denouncing false claims, omitting property from the schedule, withholding books, falsifying books, stating fictitious losses, disposing of goods not paid for, and a three years imprisonment may be the penalty for such offences.

This bill is certainly an advance in the right direction, and the sooner it is passed the better, so as to secure the application of some of its wholesome provisions to parties who are now seeking discharges.

THE JACQUES CARTIER BANK.

The President of this bank has followed the example of the Vice-President of the Royal Canadian. This almost simultaneous outbreak has something extraordinary about it. At a time when all banks and their officer should pull together we find a President in the east and a Vice-President in the west pricked into unwonted activity. Mr. Beaudry is the twin of Mr. McDonald. For several years past a sum of a thousand dollars has been voted to the President for his services, but in December last nothing was voted to him, though two thousand dollars were voted for distribution among the Directors. On the 14th April last, the President went to the Directors meeting and charged the cashier with allowing a firm in which his (the Cashier's) brother was a partner to overdraw their account. The Directors took the matter up and afterwards on the 15th April, addressed the Cashier as follows :

Sir,—The undersigned Directors of the Jacques Cartier Bank, feel obliged by these presents to express our lively regret at the excessively disagreeable scene which took place at our meeting. We also beg you to believe that we repudiate in the most energetic manner, the conduct of the President towards you. We consider that conduct was altogether improper and insulting not only to you in whom we have always had unlimited confidence which we know to be deserved, but to ourselves ; and we seize this occasion to censure in the most

distinct manner, the conduct of the President in our regard, since the general meeting of shareholders of the Bank held on the 17th December last. And. Lapierre, R. Trudeau, L. J. Béliveau, P. M. Galarneau, V. Hudson, C. S. Rodier, Louis Boyer.

This was followed by the adoption of the following resolution by the Board :

Proposed by Mr. Victor Hudson, seconded by Chas. S. Rodier,

In as much as the Honorable Jean Louis Beaudry one of the Directors of the Jacques Cartier Bank and President of the said Bank, has been guilty of grave neglect toward this institution by failing in his duties as such Director and President, and has failed to be present at the meetings of the Directors of the said Bank from the 19th December last, when he was unanimously elected to the charge of President, until the 10th April instant, inclusively, the meetings of Directors having taken place twice a week during that period, that it is resolved that it is now the duty of the Directors of the said Bank to request the said Jean Louis Beaudry to resign his said charges of Director and President, and that the Cashier of this Bank shall transmit to him, without delay, a copy of the present resolution.

The President replied to this declining to acquiesce in the demand because he was elected a director by the shareholders.

REPORT ON THE WAVERLY GOLD DISTRICT, with maps and sections; by Henry Youle Hind, M.A., F. R. G. S. Charles Annand, Halifax, N. S.

We should have acknowledged the receipt of this work from the author some time since. It is an extensive report made under instructions from the Commissioner of Public Works and Mines, and contains, besides all the details of interest relating to the particular district in question, a good many valuable suggestions of a general character on gold mining in Nova Scotia, which should be read by everyone in that Province who is directly interested in mining operations.

—The Canada Life Assurance Co., has increased its deposit with the government to $50,000.

—The last rail of the Pacific Railway was laid on the 10th inst., near Ogden, Utah Territory, by the President of the Central Pacific Company.

LONDON CORRESPONDENCE.

(From a Correspondent).

LONDON, April 22, 1869.

The discussion as to the merits of Mr. Lowe's Budget has taken an unusually wide range. Not only have the House of Commons and the press of England debated and commented on its provisions; but the press of foreign countries has also given special attention to it. Two journals, the one being a great commercial authority in Germany, the other numbering among its contributors the most eminent political economists of France, have recently passed judgment on Mr. Lowe as a financier. By the *Hamburgher Borsen Halle* it is said that the Budget teaches a lesson to Europe, inasmuch as it provides for paying all the expenses of the Abyssinian Expedition without having to resort to a loan, yet provides also for the remission of several millions of taxation. It is added that other nations may well envy this state of things. The *Journal des Debats*, on the other hand, finds nothing to praise in the scheme propounded by our Chancellor of the Exchequer.

With the fondness of Frenchmen for claiming the merit of originating everything, the writer, M. Loen, lays claim for France the merit of teaching Mr. Lowe a lesson by which he has profited. In has done nothing more, it is said, than copy the plan which the late M. Fould adopted when he was finance minister of France. As the subject has attracted so much notice, is so important itself, and may be misunderstood by those of your readers who peruse the European Journals, a few words of explanation cannot be considered out of place. Now, the Budget of Mr. Lowe has more relation to the financial arrangement of all other country than it has to the financial arrangement which may be proposed by the responsible keeper of the Moon. In order to meet a deficit the late M. Fould resorted to the expedient of altering the day on which the interest was paid to the national creditor. By this means, he was enabled to show that within a particular twelve months the expenditure would not exceed the revenue. What Mr. Lowe proposes is that certain taxes which heretofore have been paid a year after date, shall be paid immediately after they are levied. It has been the custom to give a year's credit to many English tax-payers. This arrangement has not been extended to Scotland and there no change will be made. Of course it seems hard when a butcher who has never called for payment till a year has elapsed, suddenly tells his customers that they must pay ready money. In like manner, some tax-payers will object to the introduction of prompt payment. Still, there can be no doubt that the State will be in every way the gainer by the introduction of a practice which is based of common sense. But the hardship is not so great as it appears to be. For, while a year's assessment taxes are to be called for at once on the first next January, no taxes of the same class are to be paid during the preceding nine months. This differs from the scheme of M. Fould. All that he desired was to stave off the evil day on which a loan would have to be contracted in order to fill up the inevitable deficit. But the difference is greater still. M. Fould, and other French Ministers of Finance, have never concerned themselves about the repeal of taxes. This is Mr. Lowe's chief aim. If he subjects a few persons to an apparent hardship, he confers on the country a substantial boon. One of the taxes so far to be repealed; an oppressive tax on locomotives is to be repealed also, while prudence is no longer to pay dues to the State where houses or goods are insured against fire. There are not wanting objectors to this or that item; but the general feeling is in favor of the Budget as a whole. It as a whole that it must either be approved or rejected. Of its rejection there is no danger.

If the German paper to which I have referred had thought only of the interests of some German companies, it would not have written so eulogistically of the Budget. That provision which gives the greatest satisfaction, the repeal of the duty on fire insurance, will interfere with the business of some German Insurance companies. These companies have done a good deal of business here. The rates they could offer were of course much more favourable to insurers than were the rates of companies in England. Indeed the competition was unfairly conducted. After this, however, there will be an end soon to Juc fire will doubtless become as general here as it is in Germany. There, hardly a house is uninsured. Here, it is the exception, for the houses or furniture of the poorer classes to be secured against risk. It is not that the workman grudges the few shillings of premium which he has to pay yearly, but that he grudges the proportion of which constitutes the tax. Experience in this matter ought to prove useful to those who advocate the substitution of direct and indirect taxation. There is no doubt about direct taxation being the simplest, fairest and most remunerative method of raising the national revenue. B lifficulty lies in convincing persons of this, :her in putting the theory into practice. As as the population of any country becomes to its own interest it will approve of the sition of direct taxes. But then, notwith- ing the saying that every man is the best : of his own interest, much education is red to teach a body of men to submit cheer- to do that which will benefit them collect- and individually.

ere is still a marked perplexity in the public as to what should be done to guard the rs of policies of assurance from being de- d and robbed. A great disinclination is fested towards measures designed to take if the public by regulating the proceedings e insurance companies. It is argued that nterference of the Government will foster d of preventing swindling, inasmuch as the companies will be careful to comply out- ly with the rules while disregarding them in tials. Perhaps the most certain remedy will und in the plan about to be adopted with d to policies for small sums to be issued by Government. This is an extension of the nment Savings Bank arrangement, from great results are anticipated. As it is the r classes who now suffer the most, and for this method of assuring is framed, the most complained of must be materially d.

e most notable circumstance connected with Ioney Market is the continued demand for ecurities of the United States. The 5-20 s have become a favorite investment both and on the Continent. It is estimated that ,000,000 of United States securities are now in Europe. This is but a guess, the truth be less startling. Nevertheless, it is a fact, d dispute that the amount of these securi- n European hands is enormous. Since the ical assurance was given that the 5-20 bonds l be paid in gold their popularity has in- d. They have the two-fold advantage of ng to the public a safe and a remunerative tment. Certainly they are much better buying than are the bonds of Russia, that ally of America. Doubts are now cast on afety of Russian securities. The feeling Russia will always pay her debts in full s strong than it was. It was held that se that power regularly paid the interest on ebt during the Crimean campaign, therefore 'ould never prove a defaulter. The logic of s not unassailable. It was the interest of a at that time to be scrupulous in meeting bligations. That the policy of honesty s to be successful is evinced by this, that then she has been able to borrow £100,000,- 'om us. I do not think that she will get more.

(From a Correspondent.)

LONDON, 29th April, 1869.

a contribution to the elucidation of the k Charter Question," which you have dis- l in a series of leading articles, let me y some details concerning the methods of ng in operation throughout the United lom. It is one of the many anomalies which se philosopher that England, Scotland and d should not have a uniform system of ng, and that even the system prevailing in n should differ from that of England gener- It is true that Sir Robert Peel legislated ich of these countries, so that all are sub- ally governed by the same principles of ce, yet differences in practice are none the ary marked and significant. For example, English landowner wishes an advance from nker, he deposits his title deeds as security. entleman who possesses no land and is not iness wishes an advance, he may get it on ng over securities, such as railway or other , or government stock. But in Scotland it sible to get an advance without depositing

title deeds or producing securities. It is enough if the borrower gets sureties who will vouch for him. Thus the Scotch method conduces to the developement of credit in its personal sense. The danger is that the absence of a material guarantee increases the risk run by the banker. But then this risk is not so great as it appears. For Scotland being a small country, the whole population is less than that of London, the knowledge of individuals affairs is more complete there then it could be in a larger and more populous country. This fact is often lost sight of when comparing the Scotch banking system with that of England or of other countries. At present there is a controversy in progress here, regarding the limits within which bankers ought to confine their operations. It would appear that some of the Australian banks have engaged in dealings in wool. It is asked if this is legitimate business? There is no reason why a banker should not trade in all kinds of commodities. Indeed, some merchants habitually act as bankers. But then it ought to be understood by the share- holders that when a bank departs from the line generally followed, and ceasing to take charge of the money of its customers exclusively, competes with these customers in any department of busi- ness, that the risks are increased. In a company formed for the purpose of combining mercantile operations with banking transactions, the share- holders know what they may expect. But they are misled when the company which was formed to deal with money is converted into a trading concern. The deception is nearly as complete and improper where a bank or the State attempts, under the guise of increasing the currency, to fabricate money. Your remarks on this head are alike just and indisputable. But the fallacies you expose are by no means powerless for evil. They are not without influence here. Attempts are frequently made to alter the English banking system, on the ground that it is antiquated and unsuited for the wants of the age. It is supposed that the restrictions imposed on the issue of bank notes are artificial barriers to the acquisition of wealth. No doubt if there were more paper money there would be more speculation, and this would be considered by the unreflecting as a revival of trade. But this would in reality be as little evidence of prosperity as the huge bulk of a dropsical patient is a proof of fat. Your Dominion notes may, for a time and within a limited area, be equal to gold, not by legislative enactment only, but in actual fact. Your number of these notes must be small. Some of the notes of the Bank of England are issued on the security of national credit, that is they re- present a portion of the country's debt. No one doubts that these can be redeemed. As for those issued in excess of this amount, they are covered by bullion deposited while they are in circulation. When this bullion is withdrawn from the bank cellars these notes are cancelled. Hence it is that not only is every one in England ready to take a note for five pounds, with as much confidence as he would take the like amount in sovereigns, but these notes are held to be equivalent to bullion in every quarter of the globe under the name of England is known. If the case were reversed and the issue of notes entirely based on the deposit of government securities, then it would be impossible for the foreigner to tell whether the Bank of England notes represented the whole or only the half of the sum marked on its face. If again the old system were in force here, as it now is in France, and the notes being payable in gold on demand were issued at the discretion of the bank directors, then, when a panic came, the bank would be compelled to suspend payment, or else sacrifice enormous sums in order to purchase bullion wherewith to ride over the crisis. It is a significant commentary on the two systems that whereas a Bank of England note is readily taken in France at par, a French note cannot be cashed here save at a money-changers. The weakest point in our system is due to the manner in which

it has been worked. More than once the opera- tion of the Act of 1844 has been suspended, and notes issued without their places being supplied by bullion. It is true that the relief thereby caused was beneficial to many persons. Firms on the brink of insolvency were enabled to get their bills discounted. But it would have been better had those who brought about the crisis through over trading andrash speculation, suffered the consequences of their folly. The State is not bound to foster gamblers in merchandise any more than it is justified in encouraging gambling in money. An unlimited issue of paper money is simply an incentive to speculation and a dis- couragement to prudence.

However sound the banking system of this country may be, it cannot be said that English capitalists always display good sense when invest- ing their savings. The readiness with which they lend money to foreign governments is astounding. A calculation has been made to the effect that the amount of English capital invested in foreign stocks is £400,000,000, on which the annual interest received, when interest is paid, amounts to £20,000,000. The temptation offered is a high rate of interest. It is doubtful, how- ever, whether the same sum invested in the funds would not, on the whole, prove more remunerative, whether it would not be wiser to be certain of receiving three per cent. than hopeful about receiving more. Before long many will probably regret their credulity. There are tokens that the borrowings of Russia, Turkey, and Spain are becoming exhausted. Now, when these countries can no longer borrow, they must repudiate their obligations. This admits of no dispute. Given a permanent deficit, bankruptcy or repudiation is a mere question of time. Spain has just offered 10½ per cent. return to subscribers to a new loan, and has had great difficulty in getting money on these onerous terms. Russia will soon have to bid as high for the money she requires. In a few weeks Turkey will beg for £16,000,000, wherewith to accomplish a grand financial reform; in other words pay off the arrears of the obligations she has incurred and cannot meet. When an end is put to these things, the ground will be cleared for those who can offer a fair percentage in return for the surplus capital of those who desire that interest should be punctually paid, while the principal is secure.

Among the emigrants who have recently sailed from this country to America, a band of sixteen merit attention. They are members of a "Mutual Colonization and Co-operative Emigration Land Company," formed here about six months ago, by some working men. The Society numbers 800, the majority of whom are skilled artisans. A large tract of land has been bought by the Com- pany, for a merely nominal price, in Nebraska. The expenses of each emigrant are defrayed out of the common fund. As the Company is registered under the Friendly Societies Act, due provision is made against differences of opinion among indivi- duals, the whole being subject to a code of rules having a legal sanction. If the reports sent home by the first sixteen are favorable, others will follow. The movement has this in its favor, that it gives to each man the advantage of combined capital, while it preserves the independence of each. The drawback of eleemosynary aid to emi- grants is that the man who has once been the recipient of pecuniary help is apt, when things go ill with him, to look to others for further assist- ance. It is a pity that the working men did not make a happier choice. There are better places on the American Continent than Nebraska. However, the experiment is none the less worthy of notice. Should it succeed, there will be many repetitions of it on a larger scale, and under more favorable circumstances.

—In referring to the Eureka mine, in our Min- ing Review last week, the words "best crushing" were put for "last crushing," making an import- ant difference in the sense.

Financial.

TORONTO STOCK MARKET.

(Reported by Pellatt & Osler, Brokers.)

The stock market has been very inactive during the past week, and with one or two exceptions the business done has been unimportant.

Bank Stock.—Montreal has further advanced, sales having been made during the week from 152 to 156, there are no sellers now under 157. Buyers offer 104¼ for British, with sellers at 105½. Sales of Ontario were made during the week at 100¼, 100½ and 101; there are now sellers at the latter rate. There are small amounts of Toronto offering at 118½. Royal Canadian shows a marked improvement on last week's quotations; buyers rapidly advanced rates and sales were made at 75; there were buyers at the close at 70 and sellers at 75. Commerce is in demand at 102½ at which rate there have been sales. Small sales of Merchant's were made at 107 and 107¼, none now on market under 107¾. Buyers offer 103¼ for Quebec, no sellers. Molson's has been sold at 108 to 108½, little in market. City declined in the begining of the week but has since advanced, closing with buyers at 102. Du Peuple sold at 108 and 108½. No Nationale offering, there are buyers at 104 ex dividend. For Jacques Cartier 109½ would be paid, sellers asking 110. Mechanics' could be placed at 93½ with sellers at 94. Union has been sold at 106½ and 106¾. Other banks nominal.

Debentures.—Canada are heavy at quotations. Dominion Stock and Bonds are in demand at 107 to 108. Toronto would be content to pay 7 per cent., very little in market. Not much demand for County.

Sundries.—City Gas is offered at 107½. Small sales of Canada Permanent Building Society were made at 125, 125½ and 126, and of Western Canada B. S. at 120½ to 121, small amounts of this stock still procurable at the latter rate; Freehold closed firmer at 112½, with sales at 112 to 112½. Buyers offer 134 for Montreal Telegraph and sellers ask 134½. Mortgages have been largely dealt in, first class can be readily placed at 8 per cent. Money is in demand and higher rates are paid.

THE BRITISH COINAGE.

The weight of gold is expressed in this country in ounces troy and decimal parts of an ounce, and the metal is always taken to be of standard fineness (11 gold and 1 alloy) unless otherwise described. The degree of fineness of gold, as ascertained by assay, is expressed decimally, fine pure gold being taken as unity, or 1·000. Thus gold of British standard is said to be 0·9166th fine, of French standard 0·900 fine. Another method of expressing fineness is still in pretty general use, founded on an ideal pound, "the carat pound," which is divided into 24 parts, called carats. When the gold is entirely fine, it is said to be gold of 24 carats. British standard gold contains two carats of alloy, and is said, therefore, to be gold of 22 carats. Jewellery gold may be of 22, 18, 15, 12, or 9 carats fine. The legal weight of the sovereign is 0·2568 ounce of standard gold, or 123·274 grains. The weight came from one pound of standard gold, 5,760 grains being coined into 44½ guineas. Sovereigns are legal tender to any amount, provided that the weight of each does not fall below 122·5 grains, or in the case of a half-sovereign, 61·125 grains; these are the "least current" weights of the coins. One pound troy of standard silver is coined into 66 shillings, of which the metal is worth from 60s. to 62s., according to the market price of silver. The standard fineness of silver is 0·925, three alloy in 40. The fineness of the French standard silver is 0·900 in the five-franc piece, but an inferior alloy of 0·835 is used for the lower denominations. The single five-france piece, composed of the latter alloy, is still made to weigh five grains, the weight originally chosen for the franc, as the unit of the monetary scale when the fineness of the coin was 0·900. It has now become a token, like the British shilling, of which the nominal value exceeds the metallic value. The material of our copper coinage is now a bronze mixture, composed in 100 parts by weight of 95 copper, four tin, and one zinc, the same as in the copper coinage of France. The penny is coined at the rate of 48 pence in one pound avoirdupois, of 7,000 grains, or 453·59 grains; the half-penny at 80 in the pound avoirdupois, and the farthing at 160. British silver coins are a legal tender in payments to the amount of 40s. only; copper pence to the amount of 1s.; half-pence and farthings to the amount of 6d.—*Produce Markets Review.*

A SINGULAR SCHEME—TRAFFIC IN SHARES.—Mr. S. Finney, manager of the English Joint Stock Bank, which suspended in 1866, was arrested and brought before the Lord Mayor of London. Some interesting facts were brought to light on that occasion. This Bank had £100,000 paid up capital. The promoters received £6000 between them. The directors were to receive, by the articles of association, £3,000 a year for the management of the business, which they were to divide among themselves; and whenever the company should declare a dividend exceeding £6 per cent., and below £8 per cent., they were to receive an additional £1,000, and a further sum of £1,000 for every £2 per cent. of the dividend above 8 per cent. The prisoner had been the general manager from the first, at a salary of £1,200, which was to be raised to £1,500, in the event of the dividend reaching 6 per cent. As might have been expected from such an arrangement a fraudulent dividend was soon declared. During the trial of Mr. Finney, the Lord Mayor said: "It has been laid down as the law of this country, by the highest authority, that if the directors of a company trafficked in its shares, even for the purpose of maintaining its credit, that was a fraud."

Mining.

GOLD MINING IN QUEBEC.

The following extracts from reports of the gold mining inspector of the Province of Quebec for the 18 months ended 31st December, 1869, will be found of interest.

4th January, 1868. At Jersey Point, near the Strafford stream, a Mr. Maynard, of Boston, United States, had a number of men employed in June and July, 1867, in cutting a tunnel so as to traverse several of the quartz veins, which at this spot intersect his property. This tunnel is about six feet wide, 150 feet long and seven feet high, and well timbered and secured. Portions of the quartz taken from some of these veins, have been assayed by Professor Hayes, of Boston, and are said to have yielded from $11 to $19 to the ton. Professor Hind examined this property in August last, and has published a Report speaking in very favorable terms of it. On the Famine River a number of men prospected during a portion of the summer, and have located claims which they intend to work early in the spring, and anticipate rich results therefrom. On the Gilbert River, mining was carried on more actively during the latter half of the past year than at any previous period, and the work was more effectively and scientifically prosecuted. A great number of shafts have been sunk, and are being worked on this river, on lots 14, 15, 16, 17, 18 and 19, in the De Lery Concession of the Seigniory Rigaud Vaudreuil, and some of them have richly rewarded the labor employed. One of these shafts, known as McRae's shaft, on lot 15, sunk in the latter part of July, and worked by about ten men, yielded by the 1st October, being about 60 days labor 334, ounces of gold, or $6,000, making an average of $10 per day, per man. Since October, a lar quantity of pay dirt has been hoisted from this sh preparatory to its being washed, in spring, a it is expected will prove as rich as that which h already been washed. On lots 7 and 8 in this co cession, a Mr. Lockwood, representing an Engli company, has a number of men employed making preparations for carrying on mining ope tions on a large scale in the spring. On t Riviere des Plantes, in this Seigniory, a Mr. Na of New York, had a number of men employed prospecting for alluvial gold, but the results so have not proved sufficiently encouraging to justi him in continuing further operations for the p sent. Professor Hind was engaged for three four months during the summer, in making a ge logical survey of certain portions of this Seignio at the instance of the De Lery Gold Mining Co pany, and his report, though not yet published, I am told, very favorable and encouraging. Mo sieur Michael was engaged for about three mont during the summer, on behalf of a Mining Co pany, in prospecting a portion of the Parish St. Joseph, adjoining this Seigniory. His Rep has not yet been published, but I am led to belie the results of his preliminary operations, so fa have not been very encouraging. The De Le Gold Mining Company had parties of men employ during the summer, prospecting in various p tions of the Seigniory, preparatory to laying o mining claims. This Company is now maki arrangements for letting out large mining lots claims to companies and capitalists with a view an extensive development, during the ensui year, of the rich alluvial deposits which the Se niory, undoubtedly contains; and it is also maki arrangements for the development of some of t auriferous quartz veins by which the Seigniory reticulated. It is therefore confidently anti pated that both alluvial and quartz mining will carried on in the Seigniory on an extensive sc during the ensuing year. This Company's mill in excellent order, works admirably, and h tested surface specimens of the quartz veins whi have been uncapped in the Seigniory, with suffi ently encouraging indications to justify the ho that some of these veins will prove to be ric About 100 men have been daily employed, on average, throughout the year, either actually mi ing or engaged in preliminary mining labor. is impossible for me to give exact returns of t amount of gold taken out during the year, mining was almost exclusively confined to t Seigniory Rigaud Vaudreuil, and was carried by persons who, up to the month of July la were not acting under the De Lery Company, a from whom I could not exact license fees, or e force statements upon oath as to the amount gold taken out, as the Gold Mining Act giving this power in all other parts of the Gold Mini Division, does not extend to this Seigniory. July last an agreement was made by the Recipr city Mining Company, under which these perso were mining with the De Lery Company, wherel the right to the gold in the Seigniory was admi ted to belong to the latter Company, in virtue Letters Patent, and a per centage on all go taken out was agreed to be paid to the De Le Company, whereby, in virtue of the memorandu of agreement between this Company and t Government of the 11th May, 1866, all tho persons so mining became liable to the payme of license fees, and since that period the retur of gold taken out by them are probably mo accurate.

From the most reliable date I can obtain, estimate the amount of gold taken out of t Division during the year, to be, in round figur $31,000 of which about $9,000 were taken out the first half of the year, and about $22,000 in t latter half. Of this amount about $30,000 we taken out of lots 15, 16, 17, 18 and 19 in t De Lery Concession of the Seigniory Riga Vaudreuil, and the remaining $1,000, from Jers Point, the Strafford Stream, Famine Branch, a the Des Plantes Rivers.

ed 164 Private Lands Gold Licences and l Licences during the year, amounting to of $272.

April, 1868.—Alluvial mining was actively on, during the quarter ending the 31st 1868, on lots 14, 15, 16 and 17 in the De ncession of the Seigniory Rigaud Vaud-Owing to the mild weather and heavy vhich took place towards the latter end of and the consequent excessive flow of water of the shafts, mining was discontinued and will not be resumed until after the haws—probably about the end of the pre-nth of April. Mining was confined during rter principally to hoisting the pay-dirt he shafts and placing it on the surface for er convenience of sluicing in the spring, the costly and inefficient method of wash-he shafts by rockers—necessary in winter, great measure avoided, claim holders who means to work their shafts did not wash ad those who washed, did so merely to ufficient gold to pay their laborers. The of these washings have been in most cases tory and encouraging, and in some in-rich and highly remunerative. In a shaft lot 15, the owners only washed for about four hours once, and sometimes, twice, a y means of a common rocker at the bottom shaft, and even by this expensive incon-and imperfect mode of washing; they d from 7 to 13 ounces of gold each washing. ld of gold obtained from this shaft alone the quarter is 200 oz. 8 dwts. 12 grs. otal yield from all the various shafts is as :—

	oz.	dwt.	grs.
iuary,	64	1	4
bruary	181	16	8
irch,	57	3	11

ng a total for the quarter of 303 oz. 0 dwt.

An immense quantity of wash dirt has isted from the various shafts, which will ied as soon as the spring thaws permit, is expected to be about the later end of rom which a large yield of gold and rich are confidently anticipated. About 150 ve been employed in mining, and in pre-y mining labor, such as felling and draw-ber for timbering the shafts, making sluice &c. Preparations are in progress for g on the mining operations on an extensive uring the present year. A Mr. Nash, and merican gentlemen associated with him, lessees of large mining claims from the r Gold Mining Company, and the owners of the best paying shafts that are worked e making preparation for extending their ne upon an enlarged scale. A Mr. Lock-representing an English company has a large mining claim from the De Lery ining Company, and intends to work the on an extensive basis. Capt. Smith, of rk, has erected a steam pump on his shaft iew to facilitate and expedite his mining ind supersede the necessity of manual emptying and keeping the water out of t. A number of experienced miners in-the spring to prospect along the banks of River, in the township of Watford, and ults are expected from their skill and ex- in mining.

was done during the quarter, in quartz

mens of quartz were collected from some mcaupped veins in the Seigniory and for-to New York for assay, but with what have not yet learnt.

npany has been been formed, composed of gentlemen, who intend to import a port-urastra." for the purpose of testing the quartz veins which have been opened in the y. The De Lery Gold Mining Company, ormed, will give a new impetus to both nd alluvial mining enterprise in the Seig-

niory, by the favorable terms which, I believe, it has determined to adopt with regard to capitalists and miners for the development of the rich auri-ferious deposits which the Seigniory undoubtedly contains. I issued 111 licenses during the quarter.

1st July.—Alluvial mining has steadily pro-gressed in this division during the quarter ending on the 30th June.

In the Seigniory of Rigaud Vaudreuil several additional shafts have been sunk on lots 10, 12, 13, 14, 15, 16 and 17 in the De Lery Conces-sion, and on lot 8 in the St. Charles Concession. In most of these new shafts the bed-rock or bottom has not yet been reached, owing to excess of water. To obviate this difficulty steam-pumps have been imported from England and the United States, four of which are now in the course of erection, by means of which it is expected the shafts will be speedily emptied, and the bed-rock reached. An English Company called the Canada and North West Land and Mining Company, is carrying on extensive mining operations in this Seigniory, and has sunk several of the new shafts above adverted to. The De Lery Gold Mining Company has recently let large mining claims in different locali-ties, on the 1st Range N. W. of the Seigniory, which are to be prospected and worked during the present season. The amount of gold obtained during the quarter, is 452 oz 12 dwts. 7 grains. The mint value of this gold varies from $17.80 to $18.05 per ounce ; thus making in round figures the sum of $8,100. A number of experienced miners, taking advantage of the recent dry weather have gone off prospecting in Forsyth, Shenely, Liniere, and other places in the Division, and hopes are entertained that they will succeed in finding rich locations.

I have issued 293 licenses during the quarter, amounting to $293.

14th October.—Alluvial mining was not so profitable during the quarter ending on the 30th September, as during the preceding quarter. A number of the shafts adverted to in my last report particularly those on lots 12, 13 and 14 in the De Lery Concession of the Seigniory Rigaud Vaud-retil were abandoned, some owing to excess of water, and there by no means on the spot to combat against it, others owing to their compara-tively barren appearance. The weather, too, during the quarter, was unfavorable to mining operations,—the long continued drought rendered sluicing, and even rocking almost impossible, that when the rain did set in, during the month just ended, there was too much of it to enable the miners to reach the bottom of most of the shafts then opened, without expensive appliances which were not then at hand. On lots, 15, 16 and 17, mining was carried on more vigorously and profit-ably, though in some instances the results obtained although comparatively good, fell short of the outlay, owing to the heavy expenses and costly appliances used. The North West Land and Mining Company has an engine in operation on lot 15, connected with a pump, for bailing the water out of the shaft, which was imported from England at the cost of $6,000. There are also two smaller engines and pumps in operation on other shafts. The amount of gold taken out during the quarters 236 oz. 17 dwts. 12 grs. In quartz mining, operations have been more actively and extensively carried on during the quarter, than at any previous period. Several companies are at work getting out quartz, from different veins in the Seigniory, and are having it carted to the mill of the De Lery Company to be crushed and tested. This mill has been in full operation for some weeks past, under the superin-tendence of a mining engineer employed by the De Lery Company, and the results are looked forward to with confident assurance of good success. Speci-mens of all these veins have been treated theoreti-cally, and yielded rich results—in one case amounting to the rate of $133 to the ton, while all have shown traces of gold.

I issued 303 licenses during the quarter, amount-ing to $303.

9th January, 1869.—Alluvial mining was carried on in the Seigniory Rigaud Vaudreuil, on lots 14, 15, 16, 17, 18 and 19 during quarter ending on the 31st December, 1869, with comparatively good results, although mining was carried on less actively than during the preceeding quarter, owing to the great depth of some of the shafts, which, in some cases, are from 60 to 75 feet be-neath the surface, thereby necessitating expensive machinery, consisting of steam engines with pumps attached thereto, for the purpose of hoisting the water and pay-dirt therefrom. Some of these shafts barely paid expenses, while others yielded rich results.

In other parts of the Seigniory, at the St. George and Jersey Point. a considerable amount of prospecting was carried on with variable re-sults. The amount of gold taken out during the quarter is 324 oz. 16 dwts. 22 grs. In quartz mining a good deal of work was done, and a con-siderable quantity of ore extracted from several of the veins in the Seigniory. A few tons of ore from some of these veins were passed through the De Lery Company's Crushing Mill and gave more or less good traces of gold. This mill has been temporarily closed.

I issued 154 private licenses, and two monthly mill licenses up to the 21st December.

PROXIES.

Nothing but abuses arise, as a general thing, from the use of proxies. This does not necessarily follow, but, as we say, generally. Proxies are for the most part obtained for selfish, and often for vile purposes, and the worst species of tyranny, and the foulest prostitution of authority are the result of their misuse. The bold robberies, and high-handed swindling practiced in Wall street are accomplished by proxies. The rich villains whose names appear daily in the daily papers, have amassed their wealth by the most gigantic species of fraud wrought by the abuse of proxies. Stock-holders have been robbed, scoundrels enriched, and the public sense outraged by the adroit man-ipulations of proxies. They are the means of per-petuating wrong, if wrong exists, and the means of developing wrong, if bad men are so disposed. Any set of officers can make themselves a self-per-petuating oligarchy, by voting themselves in through the use of proxies. There is no limit to the abuse, provided proxies can be secured; and it is a most shameful state of things that they can be secured, usually by the mere asking, and always for pay. One man can often clandestinely secure proxies enough to carry in his own person the determination of offices for an entire corporation. He can come in, and to the astonishment of all honest persons, eject the ruling powers, constitute himself chief, and put his own hangers on in the subordinate places. This has been done often, and attempts of this sort are not unknown in life insurance annals. Some dissatisfied official may aspire to the Presidency, and reach it, too, by the vile use of proxies. Influential agents, with vast territories under control, may secure proxies enough to revolutionize any of our city companies. Power is attained in this way, and almost always in order to be abused, There is nothing more scandalous in the management of corporations than this system of proxies, which is now so common. It is an allurement to evil doing, and offers a premium on the practice of dishonesty and fraud. It is of itself a revolutionary system. It carries rebellion in its face, as the flint carries fire.

Many an unworthy line of officers have made themselves secure for life in lucrative positions, because of the self-perpetuating principle inherent in proxies. Shrewd men can easily retain their places, because proxies are always easily obtained. And so long as the system is current and liable to be used by any one, officers can never feel secure against the machinations of evil-disposed persons, unless they are armed with the same sort of wea-pon as is employed by their adversaries. Hence it is that nearly every election of officers of our life companies, and very likely, too, of many other corporations, is a farce, having no significance. There is not the slightest evidence that an officer is the choice of the body he represents, in the fact that he has been unanimously elected. All that follows is that the proxies have been secured in advance, used successfully, and that, fit or unfit, the incumbent will hold the position till some one picks up more proxies than he.

One reason why directors are in general inefficient, is due to the servility they manifest toward tht chief officers, who have the power to make or unmake them at pleasure. A director gets his ideas from his president. He espouses the side which will be popular with the reigning powers. He has no will of his own ; he has no preferences till he is told to have them. He is called upon nominally for consultation, but really for his nod and assent to some proposition from the chief directory. The excuse given for this state of things on the part of directors is, that the officers know best what is best for the company, and it would be arrogance to make suggestions, and especially so to urge them. If that is so, why have any directors at all? If their office is merely nominal, why not abolish the sham, and make the ruling oligarchs irresponsible?

The law concerning proxies is one of the worst on the statute book. It gives legality to villany, licenses fraud, creates an irresponsible and self-perpetuating oligarchy, and has no redeeming feature whatever. It opens the highway to all sorts of evil, deprives elections of their significance or utility, and tends to weaken the public morals and the public faith. In no aspect is it useful or necessary. It is the tool of villains, the strong tower of designing and unscrupulous men, and should be obliterated from the books forthwith. The New York law on this subject is especially obnoxious, as there is no limit to the time that a proxy may continue. Therefore thousands of votes are cast, often determining elections, that were secured six or even twenty years ago, while the parties are unconscious that their franchise is used and abused, and have even forgotten that their proxy was ever intrusted to another.—*Insurance Times.*

Commercial.

While admitting the general inadvisability of exceptional legislation, there is at least, one article which now comes in free of duty, into the Dominion, that ought, under the circumstances, to pay its fair share of the revenue. We refer to hops. Hop growing which promised so favorably two years ago, is now in a sadly depressed condition, in fact, there is no market for hops in this country, except in a retail way. As the matter now stands a really choice article can be sold, but if anything less than number one they are simply "dead stock." Growers are quite digusted, as a rule. Hops are peculiarly liable to the attacks of insects, to the drought, to damage in curing, &c., and the experience this year and last, that, when placed in the market, they cannot be sold.

Why is this ? In the first place the demands of the market are limited ; we can consume only so much and no more, whatever the price may be. When the season sets in the brewers always hold off, and will not buy except at *their* prices. If holders are firm importations of American and Belgian hops soon make their appearance, duty free, and replace the home-grown, which must then be exported if sold at all. But this cannot be done. Our hops can not be exported so as to take the place in other markets of those imported as above. The fact of importations into this country, proves that our market is better than New

York ; and hence how is it possible for our hops to pay the American duty and compete in the New York market ? the thing is impossible.

The free-trade objection that we get hops cheaper on that account, might apply if hops were a necessity instead of a luxury. There is no good reason why we should pay a premium on beer-drinking.

As Mr. Rose said in his Budget Speech, " we " cannot go on this way for ever, the time may " come soon when we shall have a national policy " of our own, and that national policy will be " shaped solely by those considerations which " affect our own resources."

A duty on hops need not be deferred till the development of a "national policy." They are in every sense a proper subject for taxation ; not one class or interest in the country that it is desirable to encourage would suffer by the change ; a growing industry would thrive under the stimulus of fair play, and the revenue of the Dominion would be increased.

Toronto Market.

The weather of the past week has been favorable for business, which is, if any change, slightly improved.

GROCERIES.—There was a little more doing this week, prices unchanged.

BOOTS AND SHOES.—Manufacturers continue busy ; prices keep firm and steady.

LEATHER.—There is a fair trade doing at our quotations, which are for strictly wholesale lots.

HIDES—are very dull ; green have declined to 5½c ; cured almost unsaleable at present.

PETROLEUM.—Trade is very flat at our quotations.

PRODUCE—*Wheat*—Receipts 21,680 bush. and 15,462 bush. last week. There is a little better demand for spring, and prices have improved somewhat ; the market closed with buyers at 96c. to 97c. ; about 3,000 to 4,000 bush. in all changed hands at 95c. to 96c. Fall is dull and offering at 98c. ; no sales of consequence. Midge proof—some sales reported at 97c. f.o.b. *Barley*—No receipts ; market dull, street buyers pay 55c. to 90c. *Oats*—Receipts 12,000 bush. against 500 bush. last week ; the market advanced to 58c. and fell off closing at 55c. ; sales of car loads were made at quotations. *Peas*—No receipts ; market dull and nominal. *Corn*—Sales at 60c. by the carload. *Seeds*—Timothy scarce and advanced in price. Clover quiet, $5.25 to $5.75 ; fresh $2 to $2.25.

FLOUR.—Receipts 1,550 brls. and 1,000 brls. last week. Superfine has met with a considerable demand ; from 1,000 to 2,000 have changed hands at $4.05 to $4.10, the market closing with round lots offering at $4.05 without buyers. This is no doubt owing to the warm weather which has now commenced. Fancy—one or two lots sold at $4.20, and sales of choice were made at $4.25. Extra held at $4.50, without sales. *Oatmeal*—The best qualities are worth $5.50 to $5.75 for retail purposes. *Cornmeal*—Selling at $3.50.

PROVISIONS.—Business is limited to the local demand. *Oatmeals.*—In consequence of the smallness of stocks of cutmeats our quotations are of retail character. *Butter*—is very dull ; no lots moving. *Eggs*—Packers would not pay over 11½c to 12c. *Cheese.*—Scarce and selling for local use at quotations.

FREIGHTS.—The following charters have been made within the last four days :—Schr. Antelope, from Meaford to Kingston, 10,000 bush. spring wheat at 8c. ; schr. Trade Wind, from Hamilton to Kingston, 10,000 bush. spring wheat at 2½c. ; schr. Ocean Wave, from Toronto to Kingston, 6,000 bush. wheat at 2c. ; a schooner left here for Owen Sound to take a cargo of wheat to Montreal at 11½c. ; schr. J. G. Beard is now being loaded with wheat for Montreal ; rate 11½c.

The Coming Harvest.

The scarcity of breadstuffs and consequent high prices which have remunerated agricultural labor and enterprise for the past six years, have stimu-

lated the culture of wheat not only in this coun but generally throughout the opposite contin If favorable weather lends its aid to the effor the cultivator, there is reason to believe that coming wheat harvest will prove heavy bey any previous yield. At home the breadth land prepared this year are greatly enlarged, on the Pacific and Atlantic sides. Abroad, R is extending her fields into immense areas, an make them practically available, so that t products may be brought cheaply to market, is projecting railroads with a most liberal po into her best grain sections. France and Pri are equally active, as well as Germany and P land. Indeed, it would seem that the proba ties of a general war throughout Europe stirred the nations to these extensive preparati Should peace remain unbroken, plenty m pervade the earth ; otherwise, with all the dences to which we have alluded, of a munifi Providence, want and destitution may stalk the fairest lands of the globe.—*St. Louis Jour of Commerce.*

Receipts of Grain.

The following will show the comparative ceipts of flour and grain at the ports of Milwa Chicago, Toledo, Detroit and Cleveland, January 1 to May 1, for 1862 and 1869 :—

		1869.	1868.
Flour	bbls	1,789,375	1,102,43
Wheat	bu	6,156,480	3,648,01
Corn		8,922,627	9,238,5
Oats		2,680,320	2,204,4
Barley		365,937	360,09
Rye		432,525	160,41

INSOLVENTS.—The following insolvents been gazetted during the week ending the April : Michael Dolan, William Kennedy, Richardson Borradaile, Ottawa City ; J. M. J & Co., Montreal ; Austin & Werrett. Sim What & McLean, London ; John Reynolds, I ley township ; Joshua Doty, Alymer vill Ontario ; Abram Lewis, Chatham ; Thorn Richardson, Owen Sound ; Salem Ruth, New village ; Lawrence Cohen, Montreal ; A. D. C eron, Hamilton ; Dame Genevieve, Arniot, cheres ; J. & C. Chagnon, Dellarose, Verche Lawson Bros., Hamilton ; Donald Park, Hib township ; Andrew Park, do., John Fergu Sunnidale ; L. Elliot, Belleville ; L. W. And Colborne ; W. G. Strong, Colborne ; Ro Young, Toronto ; Dame Charlotte K. O'Gra Lennoxville ; Pierre Bourdreaux, North H Bernard Graham, Toronto ; M. L. Vance, Ba ton ; Thomas Gray, Toronto ; John Hack Ingersoll ; E. C. Lee, Chatham ; Lewis Hor Whitby ; A. F. Martin, Whitby ; O. C. Buchar Guelph.

The following is a list of the new insolve Chas. Wilson, Montreal ; Robert Jamieson, O' Sound ; J. Barber, Port Perry ; D. Tier Smith's Falls ; Thomas Lusigman, St. Ou Dougald McEwen, Lanark ; B. B. Lecom Labre du Fabvre ; W. Greenfield and Rol Moir, Blanshard ; John White, St. Mar Napoleon ; Jacques and Hector Lamontag Montreal ; Westman, Toronto ; P O'Br Belleville ; Donald McKenzie late of Franci Goderich township ; Thos. Benet, St. Generic Alex. C. Brown, Port Stanley ; R. H. Huds Hamilton ; Clement Patenande, Montreal ; Bradley, Thorold ; Benj. Stode, Peterboro ; L rence Losie, Stayner ; Sidney Smith, Cowansv David Rynal, West Flamboro ; Webster Lum County, Frelighsburgh ; W. Houchier, Notta saga ; A. Paul, London ; John Guernsey, d H. W. Jack, Toronto ; J. Gibbs, Lindsay ; W Hunter, Napanee ; T. Flynn, do. ; Schnide Co., Carillon.

Writs of attachment are issued against McS non, Woodstock, and Edward R. Lee, Chatha

:SSEMER STEEL RAILS.—The *Iron and Coal les Review* refers to an important change about our in,one branch of the iron business, from termination of the Bessemer patents. The ipal part of these patents expire next year, but Bessemer, it is said, has patented so many of ppliances, blowing engines, valves, and, com-ions, that he will have claims for royalties for al years after the lapse of the patents which bsolutely essential to the process with which ame is identified. It is understood, however, after conferring with his leading licensees, he ignified his willingness to reduce his royalties their present high rate of £2 per ton on every-; (except steel rails, for which a rebate of 20s. in of finished rails is allowed), to a charge of 1. per ton. This, it is added, will practically o the price of ordinary Bessemer steel £2 per and rails about 30s. per ton, so that the man-urers of iron rails have before them the pros-of seeing steel rails in the market at £9 per in the course of another year or so. "The in between iron and steel rails will then be all that it is easy to see that a great impetus e given to the steel rail trade, and should no lty be experienced in obtaining the neces-supplies of pig-iron suitable for conversion Bessemer steel, it is hard to say how far the opment of cheap steel will be carried.

ORONTO SAFE WORKS.

J. & J. Taylor

MANUFACTURERS OF

ire and Burglar Proof

SAFES,

i LOCKS, VAULTS, DOORS, &c., &c.

AGENTS:

S. HUTTON & Co.	MONTREAL.
S. SCOTT & Co.	QUEBEC.
EX. WORKMAN & Co.	OTTAWA.
ICE LEWIS & SON	TORONTO.
FALCONER	HALIFAX, N.S.

factory & Sale Rooms, 198 & 200 *Palace Street.*

ada Permanent Building and Savings Society.

d up Capital	$1,000,000
ets	1,700,000
ual Income	400,000

Directors:—JOSEPH D. RIDOUT, *President.*
PETER PATERSON, *Vice-President.*
Worts, Edward Hooper, S. Nordheimer, W. C. Chewett, E. H. Rutherford, Joseph Robinson.
rs—Bank of Toronto; Bank of Montreal; Royal Canadian Bank.
ICE—*Masonic Hall, Toronto Street, Toronto.*
Received on Deposit bearing five and six per cent. interest.
ces made on City and Country Property in the Province of Ontario.
J. HERBERT MASON,
Sec'y & Treas

John Morison,

IMPORTER OF

CERIES, WINES, AND LIQUORS,

38 AND 40 WELLINGTON STREET,

TORONTO.   33-1y

Philip Browne & Co.,

NKERS AND STOCK BROKERS.

DEALERS IN

LING EXCHANGE—U. S. Currency, Silver and nds—Bank Stocks, Debentures, Mortgages, &c. on New York issued, in Gold and Currency. t attention given to collections. Advances made urities.
No. 67 YONGE STREET, TORONTO
BROWNE.   PHILIP BROWNE, *Notary Public*

"The Whitby Gazette,"

A WEEKLY POLITICAL NEWSPAPER,

PUBLISHED

EVERY THURSDAY MORNING,

IN WHITBY, COUNTY OF ONTARIO.

Having a large circulation, it is one of the best adver-tising mediums in the country.
Wholesale Houses will find this a valuable medium for having their announcements reach retail dealers.
GEO. H. HAM,
39-1y   Editor and Proprietor.

Quebec Bank.

NOTICE.

NOTICE is hereby given that a Dividend of 3½ per cent. upon the Capital Stock of this institution has been declared for the current half year, and that the same will be payable at the Banking House, in this city, on and after the FIRST DAY OF JUNE NEXT.
The Transfer Books will be closed from the 15th to the 13th May next, both days inclusive.
The Annual Meeting of Shareholders will be held at the Bank on MONDAY, the SEVENTH day of JUNE next, at ELEVEN o'clock A.M.
By order of the Board,
J. STEVENSON, Cashier.
Quebec, April 28, 1869.   38-td

H. N. Smith & Co.,

2, EAST SENECA STREET, BUFFALO, N. Y., (corres-pondent Smith, Gould, Martin & Co., 11 Broad Street, N.Y.,) Stock, Money and Exchange Brokers. Advances made on securities.   21-y1

EDINBURGH LIFE ASSURANCE COMPANY.

FOUNDED 1823.

AMOUNT OF ACCUMULATED AND INVESTED FUNDS—OVER ONE MILLION STERLING.

HEAD OFFICE—EDINBURGH.

PRESIDENT—The Rt. Hon. the Earl of Haddington. MANAGER—D. Maclagan, Esq. SECRETARY—Alex. H. Whytt, Esq.
CANADIAN OFFICE ESTABLISHED 1857,   WELLINGTON STREET, TORONTO.
CANADIAN BOARD—Hon. John Hillyard Cameron, M.P., Chairman. J. W. Gamble, Esq., L. Moffatt, Esq., Hon. J. B. Robinson, C. J. Campbell, Esq. David Higgins, Secretary.

THE Edinburgh Life Assurance Company offer to the public the advantages of a Canadian as well as a British Com-pany. They have invested a large amount of money on securities in this country, and the Toronto Local Board have full power, by an Imperial Statute, to take risks, make investments, and settle claims in Canada, without refe-rence to the Head Office, Edinburgh. Some of the old Policies in the Company, which became claims during the past year, were settled by payment of amounts double of those originally insured, in consequence of the large bonuses that accrued on the Policies.
Every information that intending assurers may require can be obtained at the Company's Office in Toronto, or at any of the Agencies which have been established in the principal towns in Canada.

J. HILLYARD CAMERON, CHAIRMAN.   (36-1y)   DAVID HIGGINS, SECRETARY

Royal Fire & Life Insurance Company

OF LIVERPOOL AND LONDON.

CAPITAL, TWO MILLION STERLING,

WITH LARGE RESERVE FUNDS.

ANNUAL INCOME, - - - - - - - - £800,000 STG.

FIRE BRANCH:

Very moderate rates of Premium. Prompt and liberal settlement of losses. Loss and damage by explosion o gas made good. No charge for policies or transfers.

LIFE BRANCH.

The following are amongst the important advantages offered by this Company:
Perfect security to assurers. Moderate rates of premium. Large participation of profits—the bonuses being amongst the largest hitherto declared by any office, and divided every five years. EXEMPTION OF ASSURED FROM LIABILITY OF PARTNERSHIP. Claims settled promptly on proof of death. Liberal allowance for surrendered policies. Forfeiture of policy cannot take place from unintentional misstatement. Medical fees paid by the Company. Tables and forms of application, with all other information, can be obtained on appli-cation to

FRANCIS H. HEWARD,

MANAGER TORONTO BRANCH.

GEORGE OLIVER, Inspector.

W. B. NICOL, M.D., Medical Examiner.

TORONTO, April 19, 1869.   36-4

Mercantile.

John Boyd & Co.,

HAVE now in store, ex steamships "Peruvian," "North American," "Moravian," &c., their usual spring stock of

NEW SEASON TEAS,

COMPRISING

YOUNG HYSONS,
GUNPOWDERS,
IMPERIALS,
COLORED and UNCOLORED JAPANS,
CONGOUS,
SOUCHONGS,
TWANKEYS,
and PEKOES.

ALSO,

Ex "MORO CASTLE," "EAGLE," & "ELLA MARIA,"

Direct from Havana,

BOXES BRIGHT CENTRIFUGAL SUGAR.

61 AND 63 FRONT STREET
TORONTO.

Toronto, April 14th, 1869. 7-1y

Teas! Teas!! Teas!!!

FRESH ARRIVALS

NEW CROP TEAS,

WINES, AND GENERAL GROCERIES,

Special Inducements given to

PROMPT PAYING PURCHASERS.

All Goods sold at very Lowest Montreal Prices!

W. & R. GRIFFITH,

ONTARIO CHAMBERS
Corner of Front and Church Streets,
TORONTO
-1y ONTARIO

N E W C R O P T E A S !

1,000 Half Chests

N E W C R O P T E A S !

THE SUBSCRIBERS are now receiving a large and well selected Stock of NEW CROP TEAS, (to which they beg to call the attention of the Trade,) comprising,—

YOUNG HYSONS AND HYSONS,
HYSON TWANKAYS,
TWANKAYS,
IMPERIALS,
GUNPOWDERS,
SOUCHONGS,
CONGOUS,
COLOURED JAPANS,
NATURAL LEAF JAPANS,
OOLONGS.

REFORD & DILLON.

12 & 14 WELLINGTON STREET, TORONTO.
7-1y

Robert H. Gray,

Manufacturer of Hoop Skirts

AND

CRINOLINE STEEL,

IMPORTER OF

HABERDASHERY, TRIMMINGS

AND

GENERAL FANCY GOODS,

43, YONGE STREET, TORONTO, ONT. 6-1y

TORONTO PRICES CURRENT.—MAY 13, 1869.

Name of Article.	Wholesale Rates.	
Boots and Shoes.	$ c.	$ c.
Mens' Thick Boots	2 20	2 50
" Kip	2 25	3 00
" Calf	3 20	3 70
" Congress Gaiters	1 65	2 50
" Kip Cobourgs	1 20	1 40
Boys' Thick Boots	1 70	1 80
Youths' "	1 40	1 60
Women's Batts	0 95	1 30
" Balmoral	1 20	1 50
" Congress Gaiters	0 90	1 50
Misses' Batts	0 75	1 00
" Balmoral	1 00	1 20
" Congress Gaiters	1 00	1 30
Girls' Batts	0 65	0 85
" Balmoral	0 90	1 05
" Congress Gaiters	0 75	1 10
Children's C. T. Cacks	0 50	0 65
" Gaiters	0 65	0 90
Drugs.		
Aloes Cape	0 12½	0 16
Alum	0 02½	0 03
Borax	0 00	0 00
Camphor, refined	0 65	0 70
Castor Oil	0 10½	0 28
Caustic Soda	0 04½	0 05
Cochineal	0 90	1 00
Cream Tartar	0 40	0 45
Epsom Salts	0 03	0 04
Extract Logwood	0 11	0 12
Gum Arabic, sorts	0 30	0 35
Indigo, Madras	0 90	1 00
Licorice	0 14	0 45
Madder	0 00	0 18
Galls	0 32	0 37
Opium	12 00	13 50
Oxalic Acid	0 26	0 35
Potash, Bi-tart	0 25	0 28
" Bichromate	0 15	0 20
Potass Iodide	3 90	4 50
Senna	0 12½	0 60
Soda Ash	0 02½	0 04
Soda Bicarb	4 50	5 00
Tartaric Acid	0 40	0 45
Verdigris	0 35	0 40
Vitriol, Blue	0 08	0 10
Groceries.		
Coffees:		
Java, ℔ lb.	0 22@	0 23
Laguayra,	0 17	0 18
Rio	0 15	0 17
Fish:		
Herrings, Lab. split	0 00	0 00
" round	0 00	0 00
" scaled	0 35	0 40
Mackerel, small kitts	1 00	0 00
Loch. Her. wh'e firks	2 50	2 75
" half "	1 25	1 50
White Fish & Trout	None.	
Salmon, saltwater	14 00	15 00
Dry Cod, ℔ 112 lbs.	4 75	5 25
Fruit:		
Raisins, Layers	2 00	2 10
" M. R.	1 90	2 00
" Valentias new	0 6¾	0 7
Currants, new	0 4¾	0 05
" old	0 04	0 04½
Figs	0 11	0 12½
Molasses:		
Clayed, ℔ gal.	0 00	0 35
Syrups, Standard	0 56	0 58
" Golden	0 00	0 62
Rice:		
Arracan	4 25	4 40
Spices:		
Cassia, whole, ℔ lb.	0 00	0 45
Cloves	0 11	0 12
Nutmegs	0 50	0 55
Ginger, ground	0 20	0 25
" Jamaica, root	0 20	0 25
Pepper, black	0 12½	0 00
Pimento	0 08	0 09
Sugars:		
Port Rico, ℔ lb.	0 9¾	0 10
Cuba "	0 9¼	0 10
Barbadoes (bright)	0 9⅝	0 10
Canada Sugar Refine'y, yellow No. 2, 60ds.	0 9¾	0 10
Yellow, No. 2½	0 10¼	0 10½
No. 3	0 10¾	0 10½
Crushed X	0 11¾	0 12
" A	0 12	0 12½
Ground	0 12¾	0 13
Dry Crushed	0 12¾	0 13
Extra Ground	0 13½	0 14
Teas:		
Japan com'n to good	0 48	0 55
" Fine to choicest	0 50	0 65
Colored, com. to fine	0 60	0 75
Congou & Souch'ng	0 42	0 75
Oolong, good to fine	0 50	0 65
Y. Hyson, com to gd.	0 47½	0 55
Medium to choice	0 65	0 80
Extra choice	0 85	0 95

Name of Article.	Wholesale Rate.	
Groceries—*Contin'd*	$ c.	$ c.
Gunpowd'r c. to med.	0 55	0 70
" med. to fine.	0 70	0 85
" fine to fins't.	0 85	0 95
Hyson	0 45	0 80
Imperial	0 42	0 80
Tobacco, Manufact'd:		
Can Leaf, ℔ lb 5s & 10s.	0 26	0 30
Western Leaf, com.	0 25	0 26
" Good	0 27	0 32
" Fine	0 32	0 35
" Bright fine	0 40	0 50
" " choice	0 60	0 75
Hardware.		
Tin (net cash prices)		
Block, ℔ lb.	0 28	0 00
Grain	0 30	0 00
Copper:		
Pig	0 23	0 24
Sheet	0 30	0 33
Cut Nails:		
Assorted ¼ Shingles, ℔ 100 lb.	2 90	3 00
Shingle alone do	3 15	3 25
Lathe and 5 dy	3 30	3 40
Galvanized Iron:		
Assorted sizes	0 08	0 09
Best No. 24	0 09	0 00
" 26	0 08	0 08½
" 28	0 00	0 09½
Horse Nails:		
Guest's or Griffin's assorted sizes	0 00	0 00
For W. ass'd sizes	0 18	0 19
Patent Hammer'd do	0 17	0 18
Iron (at 4 months):		
Pig—Gartsherrie No1	24 00	25 00
Other brands. No1	22 00	24 00
" No2	0 00	0 00
Bar—Scotch, ℔ 100 lb.	2 25	2 50
Refined	3 00	3 25
Swedes	5 00	5 50
Hoops—Coopers	3 00	3 25
Band	3 00	3 25
Boiler Plates	3 25	3 50
Canada Plates	3 75	4 00
Union Jack	0 00	0 00
Pontypool	3 25	4 00
Swansea	3 90	4 00
Lead (at 4 months):		
Bar, ℔ 100 lbs.	0 06½	0 07
Sheet "	0 08	0 09
Shot	0 07½	0 07½
Iron Wire (net cash):		
No. 6, ℔ bundle	2 70	2 80
" 9, "	3 10	3 20
" 12, "	3 40	3 50
" 16, "	4 30	4 40
Powder:		
Blasting, Canada	3 50	0 00
FF "	4 25	4 50
FFF "	4 75	5 00
Blasting, English	4 00	5 00
FF loose	5 00	6 00
FFF "	6 00	6 50
Pressed Spikes (4 mos):		
Regular sizes 100	4 00	4 25
Extra "	4 50	5 00
Tin Plates (net cash):		
IC Coke	7 50	8 50
IC Charcoal	8 50	9 00
IX "	10 50	11 00
IXX "	13 50	14 00
DC "	8 00	8 50
DX "	9 50	0 00
Hides & Skins, ℔ lb		
Green rough	0 00	0 05½
Green, salt'd & insp'd	0 06½	0 07
Cured	0 00	0 00
Calfskins, green	0 00	0 11
Calfskins, cured	0 00	0 12½
" dry	0 18	0 20
Sheepskins,	1 40	1 75
" country	1 00	1 40
Hops.		
Inferior, ℔ lb.	0 00	0 00
Medium	0 00	0 00
Good	0 00	0 00
Fancy	0 00	0 00
Leather, @ (4 mos.) In lots of less than 50 sides, 10 ℔ cent higher.		
Spanish Sole, 1st qual'y heavy, weights ℔ lb.	0 21½	0 22
Do. 1st qual middle do.	0 23	0 00
Do. No. 2, light weights	0 22	0 00
Slaughter heavy	0 00	0 24
Do. light	0 00	0 00
Harness, best	0 25	0 27
" No. 2	0 00	0 00
Upper heavy	0 32	0 35
" light	0 35	0 36

Name of Article.	Wholesale Rat[e]
Leather—*Contin'd.*	$ c.
Kip Skins, Patna	0 30
French	0 70
English	0 65
Hemlock Calf (30 to 35 lbs.) per doz.	0 50
Do. light	0 45
French Calf,	1 03
Grain & Satn Clf ℔ doz.	0 00
Splits, large ℔ lb.	0 30
" small	0 23
Enamelled Cow ℔ foot	0 20
Patent	0 20
Pebble Grain	0 15
Buff	0 14
Oils.	
Cod	0 65
Lard, extra	0 00
" No. 1	0 00
" Woollen	0 00
Lubricating, patent	0 00
" Mott's economic	0 30
Linseed, raw	0 76
" boiled	0 81
Machinery	0 00
Olive, common, ℔ gal.	1 00
" salad	1 95
" salad, in bots. qt. ℔ case	3 60
Sesame salad, ℔ gal.	1 60
Seal, pale	0 75
Spirits Turpentine	0 52½
Varnish	0 00
Whale.	0 00
Paints, &c.	
White Lead, genuine in Oil, ℔ 25 lbs.	0 00
Do. No. 1 "	0 00
" 2 "	0 00
" 3 "	0 00
White Zinc, genuine	3 00
White Lead, dry	0 05½
Red Lead	0 07½
Venetian Red, Eng'h	0 02½
Yellow Ochre, Fren'h	0 02½
Whiting	0 85
Petroleum. (Refined ℔ gal.)	
Water white, car l'd	—
" small lots	0 00
Straw, by car load	0 00
" small lots	0 00
Amber, by car load	0 00
" small lots	0 00
Benzine	0 00
Produce.	
Grain;	
Wheat, Spring, 60 lb.	0 95
" Fall 60 "	0 98
Barley 48 "	0 90
Peas 60 "	0 70
Oats 34 "	0 54
Rye 56 "	0 60
Seeds:	
Clover, choice 60 "	5 50
" com'n 68 "	5 25
Timothy, cho'e 4 "	2 75
" inf. to good 48 "	2 60
Flax 56 "	2 00
Flour (per brl.):	
Superior extra	0 00
Extra superfine,	4 40
Fancy superfine	4 20
Superfine No 1	4 00
" No. 2	—
Oatmeal, (per brl.)	5 50
Provisions	
Butter, dairy tub ℔ lb.	0 20
" store packed	0 13
Cheese, new	0 14½
Pork, mess, per brl.	25 50
" prime mess	—
" prime	—
Bacon, rough	0 11
" Cumberl'd cut	0 12
" smoked	0 00
Hams, in salt	0 12½
" smoked	0 14
Shoulders, in salt	0 00
Lard, in kegs	0 16½
Eggs, packed	0 11½
Beef Hams	0 00
Tallow	0 08
Hogs dressed, heavy	0 00
" medium	0 00
" light	0 00
Salt, &c.	
American brls.	1 50
Liverpool coarse	0 00
Goderich	0 00
Plaster	0 90
Water Lime	1 50

Candles.	$ c.	$ c.
d & Co.'s ..		
ial........	0 07½	0 08
Bar	0 07	0 07½
Bar........	0 07	0 07½
....	0 05	0 05½
....	0 08½	0 08¾
....	0 00	0 11

Liquors,
s.

er doz. qrts.	2 60	2 65
Dub Portr..	2 35	2 40
iica Rum...	1 80	2 25
r's H. Gin..	1 55	1 65
ld Tom.....	1 90	2 00
ses........	4 00	4 25
ld Tom, c...	6 00	6 25
mon	1 00	1 25
old	2 00	4 00
mmon	1 00	1 50
ium........	1 70	1 80
or golden..	2 50	4 00

Brandy:	$ c.	$ c.
Hennessy's, per gal..	2 30	2 50
Martell's " ..	2 30	2 50
J. Robin & Co.'s " ..	2 25	2 35
Otard, Dupuy & Cos..	2 25	2 35
Brandy, cases........	8 50	9 00
Brandy, com. per c...	4 00	4 50
Whiskey:		
Common 36 u. p......	0 58	0 60
Old Rye	0 77½	0 80
Malt	0 77½	0 80
Toddy	0 77½	0 80
Scotch, per gal........	1 90	2 10
Irish—Kinnahan's c...	7 00	7 50
" Dunnville's Belf't..	6 00	6 25
Wool.		
Fleece, lb............	0 28	0 35
Pulled "............	0 22	0 25
Furs.		
Bear..................	3 00	10 00
Beaver, ℘ lb...........	1 00	1 25
Coon	0 20	0 40
Fisher................	4 00	6 00
Martin................	1 40	1 60
Mink..................	3 25	4 00
Otter.................	5 75	6 00
Spring Rats	0 15	0 17
Fox...................	1 20	1 25

INSURANCE COMPANIES.

ENGLISH.—*Quotations on the London Market.*

ast Dividend.	Name of Company.	Shares parval £	Amount paid.	Last Sale.
	Briton Medical and General Life...	10	....	2½
7½	Commer'l Union, Fire, Life and Mar.	50	5	5⅜xd
8	City of Glasgow	25	2½	5½
9½	Edinburgh Life	100	15	33
5—½ yr	European Life and Guarantee......	2½	11s6	4s. 6d.
10	Etna Fire and Marine............	10	1½	—
5	Guardian	100	50	51½
12	Imperial Fire..................	500	50	350
9½	Imperial Life	100	10	17
10	Lancashire Fire and Life.........	20	2	2⅜
11	Life Association of Scotland.......	40	7½	25
5s. p. sh	London Assurance Corporation ..	25	12½	49
5	London and Lancashire Life	10	1	—
40	Liverp'l & London & Globe F. & L.	20	2	7 1-16
5	National Union Life	5	1	1
12½	Northern Fire and Life	100	5	12 1-16
12 } 3, bo } 5s. }	North British and Mercantile	50	6¼	19½xd
50	Ocean Marine	25	5	17
25 12s.	Provident Life.................	100	10	35
4½ p. s.	Phœnix........................	....	....	145
½—h. yr.	Queen Fire and Life	10	1	1
s. bo. 4s	Royal Insurance................	20	3	6⅝
10	Scottish Provincial Fire and Life ..	50	2½	5 3-8
25	Standard Life	50	12	66½
5	Star Life	25	1¼	—
	CANADIAN.			℘ c.
4	British America Fire and Marine ..	$50	$25	55½ 56
4	Canada Life	....	....	.....
12	Montreal Assurance	£50	£5	135
8	Provincial Fire and Marine.......	60	11	.....
....	Quebec Fire	40	32½	25½ 26
7	" Marine................	100	40	85 90
6 mo's.	Western Assurance..............	40	9	.....

RAILWAYS.	Sha's	Paid	Montr	London
ad St. Lawrence..................	£100	All.	....	57 59
l Lake Huron	20½	"	....	2½ 3½
do Preference	10	"	....	5 6
tt. & Goderich, 6℘c., 1872-3-4....	100	"	....	66 69
and St. Lawrence	....	....	10 11	....
do Pref. 10 ℘ ct....	....	....	80 82½	....
nk	100	"	14 15	14½ 15¼
Eq.G. M. Bds. 1 ch. 6℘c..........	100	"	....	85 87
First Preference, 5 ℘ c	100	"	....	40 50
Deferred, 3 ℘ ct..	100	"	....	....
Second Pref. Bonds, 5℘c..........	100	"	....	37 39
do Deferred, 3 ℘ ct..........	100	"	....	....
Third Pref. Stock, 4℘ct...........	100	"	...	27 29
do. Deferred, 3 ℘ ct.....	100	"	...	....
Fourth Pref. Stock, 3℘c...........	100	"	....	16½ 17½
do. Deferred, 3 ℘ ct...........	100	"	....	...
tern	20½	"	14 15	14½ 14¾
New	20½	18	....	....
6 ℘ c. Bds, due 1873-76..........	100	All.	....	100 102
5½ ℘c Bds. due 1877-78...	100	"	....	94 95
ilway, Halifax, $250, all......	$250	"	....	....
f Canada, 6 ℘c. 1st Pref. Bds.........	100	"	.. .	92 93

CHANGE.	Halifax.	Montr'l.	Quebec.	Toronto.
London, 60 days......				
75 days date	12½	9½ 9¾	9 9¼	9¼
lo.	11½ 12	8 9	8 8½	8½
ith documents.........	....	7 7½	....	....
ew York.............	....	26½ 27	26 26½	26¾
do.	....	27 27½	26½ 27	....
s do.	....	par to ½ p.	par ⅛ dis.	par ¼ dis.
....	....	4 4½	....	3½ to 4½

STOCK AND BOND REPORT.

The dates of our quotations are as follows:—Toronto, May 11; Montreal, May 10; Quebec, May 10; London, April 18.

NAME.	Shares.	Paid up.	Divid'd last 6 Months	Dividend Day.	CLOSING PRICES. Toronto.	Montre'l	Quebec.
BANKS.			℘ ct.				
British North America	$250	All.	3	July and Jan.	105 105½	105 105½	105 105½
Jacques Cartier..............	50	"	4	1 June, 1 Dec.	109 110	109 110	109 110
Montreal	200	"	6	"	155 157	155½ 156	155 156
Nationale....................	50	"	4	1 Nov. 1 May.	104½ x d	105 106	105 106
New Brunswick	100	"	......	......	....	...	....
Nova Scotia	200	28	7&b$3½	Mar. and Sept.	....	....	....
Du Peuple....................	50	"	4	1 Mar., 1 Sept.	108 108½	108 108½	108 108½
Toronto	100	"	4	1 Jan., 1 July.	118 118½	118 119	117½ 118
Bank of Yarmouth.............	....	....	......	......	....	....	....
Canadian Bank of Com'e......	50	95	......	......	102 102½	102 102½	102 102½
City Bank Montreal	80	All.	4	1 June, 1 Dec.	101 101½	101½ 102	101 101½
Commer'l Bank (St. John)....	100	"	℘ ct.	......	...	...	....
Eastern Townships' Bank.....	50	"	4	1 July, 1 Jan..	....	99 101	99½ 100½
Gore	40	...	none.	1 Jan., 1 July.	35 36	35 38	37 38
Halifax Banking Company....	..	....	......	......	....	....	....
Mechanics' Bank..............	50	70	4	1 Nov., 1 May.	93 94	93 94	93 94
Merchants' Bank of Canada....	100	70	4	1 Jan., 1 July.	107 107½	107½ 108½	107½ 108
Merchants' Bank (Halifax)....	....	....	.....	.....	....	....	....
Molson's Bank................	50	All.	4	1 Apr., 1 Oct.	108½ 109	108 109	108 109
Niagara District Bank...	100	70	3½	1 Jan., 1 July.	...	....	....
Ontario Bank.................	40	All.	4	1 June, 1 Dec.	100½ 101	100½ 101	100½ 101½
People's Bank (Fred'kton)....	100	"	......	......	....	....	.. ..
People's Bank (Halifax)	20	"	7 12 m	......	....	...	....
Quebec Bank	100	"	3½	1 June, 1 Dec.	102½ 104	102 104	103½ 104
Royal Canadian Bank	50	50	4	1 Jan., 1 July.	70 75	70 75	70 75
St. Stephens Bank	100	All.	.....	......	....	...	....
Union Bank	100	70	4	1 Jan., 1 July.	106 106½	106 106½	106¾ 107½
Union Bank (Halifax)........	100	40	7 12 mo	Feb. and Aug.	....	....	. .
MISCELLANEOUS.							
British America Land........	250	44	2½	......	....	....	....
British Colonial S. S. Co......	250	32½	2½	......	...	50 60	...
Canada Company	32½	All.	£1 10s.	......	....	....	....
Canada Landed Credit Co.....	50	$20	3½	......	78 80	....	....
Canada Per. B'ldg Society....	50	All.	5	......	125 125½	....	....
Canada Mining Company.....	4	90	......	......	....	....	....
Do. Inl'd Steam Nav. Co.....	100	All.	7	......	....	....	....
Do. Glass Company.........	100	"	12½ "	......	....	100 102½	....
Canad'n Loan & Investm't.....	25	2½	7	......	....	40 60	....
Canada Agency	10	¼	......	......	....	....	....
Colonial Securities Co........	...	....	......	.....	....	....	....
Freehold Building Society....	100	All.	4	......	112 112½	....	....
Halifax Steamboat Co........	100	"	5	......	....	....	....
Halifax Gas Company........	....	....	......	...	....	....	....
Hamilton Gas Company.......	....	....	.....	......	....	....	....
Huron Copper Bay Co........	4	12	20	......	....	30 45	....
Lake Huron S. and C.........	5	102	......	......	....	....	....
Montreal Mining Consols.....	20	$15	......	......	....	3.20 3.30	...
Do. Telegraph Co...	40	All.	5	......	133½ 134	134 134½	133½ 134
Do. Elevating Co...	00	"	15 12 m	......	....	100 105	....
Do. City Gas Co.........	40	"	4	15 Mar. 15 Sep.	....	134 136	134 135
Do. City Pass. R,. Co.....	50	"	4	......	....	107 109	107 108
Quebec and L. S.	8	$4	......	......	....	....	....
Quebec Gas Co...............	200	All.	4	1 Mar., 1 Sep.	....	...	118 119
Quebec Street R. R..........	50	25	3	......	....	....	90 91
Richelieu Navigation Co......	100	All.	10 p.a.	1 Jan., 1 July.	....	110½ 112½	109½ 110
St. Lawrence Glass Company.	100	"	....	......	....	80 85	.. ..
St. Lawrence Tow Boat Co....	100	"	......	3 Feb.	...	...	80 85
Tor'to Consumers' Gas Co....	50	"	4	1 My Au Mar Fe	107 107½	...	104 105
Trust & Loan Co. of U. C.....	20	5	3	......	....	....	..
West'n Canada Bldg Soc'y....	50	All.	5	......	120 120½	....	....

SECURITIES.	London.	Montreal	Quebec.	Toronto.
Canadian Gov't Deb. 6 ℘ ct. stg.....................	....	103 104	101 101½	103 103½
Do. do. 6 do due Ja. & Jul. 1877-84........	104½ 105½	....	....	....
Do. do. 6 do. Feb. & Aug.........	102 104	....	.. .	....
Do. do. 6 do. Mch. & Sep.........	102 104	.. .	...	.. .
Do. do. 5 ℘ ct. cur., 1883	92½ 93½	91 93	93½ 94	93 94½
Do. do. 5 do. stg., 1885	92 94	91 93	93½ 94½	93 94½
Do. do. 7 do. cur.,....................	....	....	......	....
Dominion 6 p. c. 1878 cy.....	....	107½ 108½	1 08 108½	107½ 108
Hamilton Corporation....	. ..	....	... ..	....
Montreal Harbor, 8 ℘ ct. d. 1869..................	..	....	......	....
Do. do. 7 do. 1870....	...	....	......	....
Do. do. 6½ do. 1883.........	....	102 103	......	102 103
Do do. 6½ do. 1873.....................	....	....	......	
Do. Corporation, 6 ℘ c. 1891	....	96 96½	96 96½	96 96½
Do. 7 p. c. stock...	....	108½ 110	108½ 109½	109 110
Do. Water Works, 6 ℘ c. stg. 1878......... ..	....	....	......	96 96½
Do. do. 6 do. cy. do.	....	96½ 97	......	96 97
New Brunswick, 6 ℘ ct., Jan. and July	103 104	....	. ...	....
Nova Scotia, 6 ℘ ct., 1875..........................	102 104	...	......	...
Ottawa City 6 ℘ c. d. 1880	....	95 97	......	...
Quebec Harbour, 6 ℘ c. d. 1883....................	....	....	60	....
Do. do. 7 do. do....................	.....	....	65 70	....
Do. do 8 do. 1886.................	...	....	80 85	....
Do. City, 7 ℘ c. d. 1½ years....	....	....	98 98½	....
Do. do. 7 do. 8 do.	....	....	91 92	....
Do. do. 7 do. 4 do.	....	....	94 95	....
Do. Water Works, 7 ℘ ct., 3 years..............	....	....	97 97½	....
Do. do. 6 do. 1½ do.	....	....	94 95	....
Toronto Corporation	....	92 94	..	....

Insurance.

Briton Medical and General Life Association,

with which is united the

BRITANNIA LIFE ASSURANCE COMPANY.

Capital and Invested Funds.............£750,000 Sterling.

ANNUAL INCOME, £220,000 STG. :

Yearly increasing at the rate of £25,000 Sterling.

THE important and peculiar feature originally introduced by this Company, in applying the periodical Bonuses, so as to make Policies payable during life, without any higher rate of premiums being charged, has caused the success of the BRITON MEDICAL AND GENERAL to be almost unparalleled in the history of Life Assurance. *Life Policies on the Profit Scale become payable during the lifetime of the Assured, thus rendering a Policy of Assurance a means of subsistence in old age, as well as a protection for a family,* and a more valuable security to enrollers in the event of early death; and effectually meeting the often urged objection, that persons do not themselves reap the benefit of their own prudence and forethought.

No extra charge made to members of Volunteer Corps for services within the British Provinces.

☞ TORONTO AGENCY, 5 KING ST. WEST.

Oct 17—9-1yr   JAMES FRASER, Agent.

BEAVER
Mutual Insurance Association.

HEAD OFFICE—20 TORONTO STREET,
TORONTO.

INSURES LIVE STOCK against death from any cause. The only Canadian Company having authority to do this class of business.

E. C. CHADWICK,
President.

W. T. O'REILLY,
Secretary.   8-1y-26

HOME DISTRICT
Mutual Fire Insurance Company.

Office—North-West Cor. Yonge & Adelaide Streets,
TORONTO.—(UP STAIRS.)

INSURES Dwelling Houses, Stores, Warehouses, Merchandise, Furniture, &c.

PRESIDENT—The Hon. J. McMURRICH.
VICE-PRESIDENT—JOHN BURNS, Esq.
JOHN RAINS, Secretary.

AGENTS:

DAVID WRIGHT, Esq., Hamilton; FRANCIS STEVENS, Esq., Barrie; Messrs. GIBBS & BRO., Oshawa.   8-1y

---

THE PRINCE EDWARD COUNTY
Mutual Fire Insurance Company.

HEAD OFFICE,—PICTON, ONTARIO.

President, L. B. STINSON; *Vice-President,* W. A. RICHARDS. *Directors :* H. A. McPaul, James Cavan, James Johnson, N. S. DeMill, William Delong.—*Secretary,* John Twigg; *Treasurer,* David Barker; *Solicitor,* R. J. Fitzgerald.

THIS Company is established upon strictly Mutual principles, insuring farming and isolated property, (not hazardous,) in *Township only,* and offers great advantages to insurers, at low rates for *five years,* without the expense of a renewal.

Picton, June 15, 1868.   9-1y

THE AGRICULTURAL
Mutual Assurance Association of Canada.

HEAD OFFICE............................LONDON, ONT

A purely Farmers' Company. Licensed by the Government of Canada.

Capital, 1st January, 1869....................$230,193 82
Cash and Cash Items, over..................$80,000 00
No. of Policies in force....................36,892 00

THIS Company insures nothing more dangerous than Farm property. Its rates are as low as any well-established Company in the Dominion, and lower than those of a great many. It is largely patronised, and continues to grow in public favor.

For Insurance, apply to any of the Agents or address the Secretary, London, Ontario.

London, 2nd Nov., 1868.   12-1y

Insurance.

The Gore District Mutual Fire Insurance Company

GRANTS INSURANCES on all description of Property against Loss or Damage by FIRE. It is the only Mutual Fire Insurance Company which assesses its Policies yearly from their respective dates; and the average yearly cost of insurance in it, for the past three and a half years, has been nearly

TWENTY CENTS IN THE DOLLAR

less than what it would have been in an ordinary Proprietary Company.

THOS. M. SIMONS,
Secretary & Treasurer.

ROBT. McLEAN,
Inspector of Agencies.
Galt, 26th Nov., 1868.   15-1y

Western Assurance Company,

INCORPORATED 1851.

CAPITAL, ... $400,000.

FIRE AND MARINE.

HEAD OFFICE................ TORONTO, ONTARIO.

DIRECTORS.

Hon. JNO. McMURRICH, President.
     CHARLES MAGRATH, Vice-President.
A. M. SMITH, Esq.,   JOHN PISKEN, Esq.,
ROBERT BEATY, Esq.,   ALEX. MANNING, Esq.,
JAMES MICHIE, Esq.,   N. BARNHART, Esq.,
     J. J. DALLAS, Esq.
     B. HALDAN, Secretary.
     J. MAUGHAN, JR., Assistant Secretary.
     WM. BLIGHT, Fire Inspector.
     CAPT. G. T. DOUGLAS, Marine Inspector.
     JAMES PRINGLE, General Agent.

Insurances effected at the lowest current rates on Buildings, Merchandise, and other property, against loss or damage by fire.
On Hull, Cargo and Freight against the perils of Inland Navigation.
On Cargo Risks with the Maritime Provinces by sail or steam.
On Cargoes by steamers to and from British Ports.

WESTERN ASSURANCE COMPANY'S OFFICE, }
TORONTO, 1st April, 1869. }   23-1y

Fire and Marine Assurance.

THE BRITISH AMERICA
ASSURANCE COMPANY.

HEAD OFFICE:
CORNER OF CHURCH AND COURT STREETS,
TORONTO.

BOARD OF DIRECTION :

Hon. G. W. Allan, M.L.C.,   A. Joseph, Esq.,
George J. Boyd, Esq.,   Peter Paterson, Esq.,
Hon. W. Cayley,   G. P. Ridout, Esq.,
Richard S. Cassels, Esq.,   E. H. Rutherford, Esq.,
     Thomas C. Street, Esq.

Governor:
GEORGE PERCIVAL RIDOUT, Esq.
Deputy Governor
PETER PATERSON, Esq.
Fire Inspector!   Marine Inspector:
E. BODY O'BRIEN.   CAPT. R. COURNEEN.

Insurances granted on all descriptions of property against loss and damage by fire and the perils of inland navigation.
Agencies established in the principal cities, towns, and ports of shipment throughout the Province.

THOS. WM. BIRCHALL,
Managing Director.

23-1y

Queen Fire and Life Insurance Company,

OF LIVERPOOL AND LONDON,

ACCEPTS ALL ORDINARY FIRE RISKS
on the most favorable terms.

LIFE RISKS

Will be taken on terms that will compare favorably with other Companies.

CAPITAL, ... £2,000,000 Stg.

CHIEF OFFICES—Queen's Buildings, Liverpool, and Gracechurch Street London.
CANADA BRANCH OFFICE—Exchange Buildings, Montreal.
Resident Secretary and General Agent,
A. MACKENZIE FORBES.
13 St. Sacrament St., Merchants' Exchange, Montreal.
WM. ROWLAND, Agent, Toronto.   1-1y

Insurance.

The Waterloo County Mutual Fire Insurance Company.

HEAD OFFICE : WATERLOO, ONTARIO.

ESTABLISHED 1863.

THE business of the Company is divided into the separate and distinct branches, the

VILLAGE, FARM, AND MANUFACTURI

Each Branch paying its own losses and its just property of the managing expenses of the Company.
C. M. TAYLOR, Sec.   M. SPRINGER, M.M.P., Pres
   J. HUGHES, Inspector.   1o

Ætna Fire and Marine Insurance Company Dublin.

AT a Meeting of the Shareholders of this Company held at Dublin, on the 12th ult., it was agreed t the business of the "ETNA" should be transferred to "UNITED PORTS AND GENERAL INSURANCE COMPAN In accordance with this agreement, the business will be after be carried on by the latter Company, which assum and guarantees all the risks and liabilities of the "Et
The Directors have resolved to continue the CANAD BRANCH, and arrangements for resuming Fire and A RINE business are rapidly approaching completion.

16   T. W. GRIFFITH,
     MANAGER

Lancashire Insurance Company.

CAPITAL, · · · · · · · · · · £2,000,000 Sterli

FIRE RISKS

Taken at reasonable rates of premium, and

ALL LOSSES SETTLED PROMPTLY,

By the undersigned, without reference elsewhere.

S. C. DUNCAN-CLARK & CO.,
General Agents for Ontario,
N. W. Corner of King & Church Streets
TORONTO.

25-1y

DIVISION OF PROFITS NEXT YEAI

ASSURANCES

EFFECTED BEFORE 30TH APRIL NEXT,

IN THE

Canada Life Assurance Compan

OBTAIN A YEAR'S ADDITIONAL PROFITS

OVER LATER ENTRANTS,

And the great success of the Company warrants the f rectors in recommending this very important advantage to assurers.

SUMS ASSURED..................................$5,300,0
AMOUNT OF CAPITAL AND FUNDS.... 1,900,0
ANNUAL INCOME............................... 200,0

Assets (exclusive of uncalled capital) for each $100 liabilities, about $150.
The Income from interest upon investments is n alone sufficient to meet claims by death.

A. G. RAMSAY, Manager.
E. BRADBURNE, Agent
Feb. 1.   1y   Toronto Street

The Victoria Mutual

FIRE INSURANCE COMPANY OF CANADA.

Insures only Non-Hazardous Property, at Low Rate.

BUSINESS STRICTLY MUTUAL.

GEORGE H. MILLS, President.
W. D. BOOKER, Secretary.

HEAD OFFICE . . . . .HAMILTON, ONTARI

aug 15-1yr

PUBLISHED AT THE OFFICE OF THE MONETAR TIMES, No. 60 CHURCH STREET.
PRINTED AT THE DAILY TELEGRAPH PUBLISHING HOUS
BAY STREET, CORNER OF KING!

THE CANADIAN

?ONETARY TIMES

AND

INSURANCE CHRONICLE.

?OTED TO FINANCE, COMMERCE, INSURANCE, BANKS, RAILWAYS, NAVIGATION, MINES, INVESTMENT, PUBLIC COMPANIES, AND JOINT STOCK ENTERPRISE.

?II—NO. 40. TORONTO, THURSDAY, MAY 20, 1869. SUBSCRIPTION $2 A YEAR.

Mercantile.

Gundry and Langley,

?TECTS AND CIVIL ENGINEERS, Building Sur- ?s and Valuators. Office corner of King and Jordan Toronto.

?AS GUNDRY. HENRY LANGLEY.

J. B. Boustead.

?SION and Commission Merchant. Hops bought sold on Commission. 82 Front St., Toronto.

John Boyd & Co.

?ESALE Grocers and Commission Merchants, ?ont St., Toronto.

Childs & Hamilton.

?FACTURERS and Wholesale Dealers in Boots Shoes, No. 7 Wellington Street East, Toronto, 28

L. Coffee & Co.

?CE and Commission Merchants, No. 2 Manning's ?k, Front St., Toronto, Ont. Advances made on ?ents of Produce.

Honore Plamondon,

?M House Broker, Forwarder, and General Agent, ?ec. Office—Custom House Building. 17-1y

Sylvester, Bro. & Hickman,

?ERCIAL Brokers and Vessel Agents. Office—No. ?tario Chambers, [Corner Front and Church Sts., 2-6m

John Fisken & Co.

?OIL and Commission Merchants, Yonge St., ?nto, Ont.

W. & R. Griffith.

?ERS of Teas, Wines, etc. Ontario Chambers, ?hurch and Front Sts., Toronto.

H. Nerlich & Co.,

?ERS of French, German, English and American ?Goods, Cigars, and Leaf Tobaccos, No. 2 Adelaide ?est, Toronto. 15

Candee & Co.,

?RS AND BROKERS, dealers in Gold and Silver Government Securities, &c., Corner Main and Streets, Buffalo, Y. N. 21-1v

Lyman & McNab.

?ESALE Hardware Merchants, Toronto, Ontario.

W. D. Matthews & Co.

?CE Commission Merchants, Old Corn Exchange, ?ont St. East, Toronto Ont.

R. C. Hamilton & Co.

?CE Commission Merchants, 119 Lower Water ?Halifax, Nova Scotia.

Parson Bros.,

?EUM Refiners, and Wholesale dealers in Lamps, ?neys, etc. Warerooms 51 Front St. Refinery cor. Don Sts., Toronto.

C. P. Reid & Co.

?ERS and Dealers in Wines, Liquors, Cigars and ?Tobacco, Wellington Street, Toronto. 28.

W. Rowland & Co.,

?E BROKERS and General Commission Mer- Advances made on Consignments. Corner ? Front Streets, Toronto.

Reford & Dillon.

?ERS of Groceries, Wellington Street, Toronto, ?o.

Sessions, Turner & Cooper.

?ACTURERS, Importers and Wholesale Dealer ?oots and Shoes, Leather Findings, etc., 8 Wel- West, Toronto, Ont

Meetings.

GREAT WESTERN RAILWAY.

Report of the Directors.

The receipts on capital account remained unchanged, the total amount received being £5,260,-829, as in last report. The aggregate expenditure to January 31, 1869, amounted to $5,388,103, leaving a balance of £127,274 at the debit of capital account. The outlay on capital account during the half year, after deducting sales of surplus lands, has been £5,509. This expenditure is specified in the engineer's report, and includes the proportion of the cost of forming an embankment behind the abutments of St. George's bridge, near Paris, the cost of building four wooden culverts under the railway embankment near Prairie siding to provide increased waterway; the final proportion of the cost of building in stone the bridge over the Twenty-mile creek at Jordan; of extending sidings at the Suspension Bridge, London, Copetown, and Lynden, and laying down a third rail in sidings at Beamsville, Komoka, and London; the balance of the payment on account of the new freight house at Detroit; and the building of a windmill pump and water tank at Belle River. The receipts and expenditure on revenue account were as follows:

Gross receipts		£423,312
Working expenses, including renewals		209,752
		£213,560
From which there is to be deducted—		
Interest on bonds, loan, &c.	£52,536	
Loss on conversion of American funds	70,362	
Loss on working Erie & Niagara Railway	1,453	
Detroit fire claims	1,158	
Amount set aside for renewal of ferry steamers	3,000	
		£128,509
		£85,051
Add surplus from last half-year		1,129
Proportion of half-year's dividend on Detroit and Milwaukee preference shares		5,311
Profit on working Galt and Guelph Railway		211
Available for dividend		£91,702

From this amount the Directors recommend a dividend at the rate of 5 per cent per annum, payable in London on May 12, free of income-tax, which will absorb £89,124, and leave a surplus of £2,578 to be carried to the credit of the next half-year. The renewal fund for the ferry steamers now amounts, with interest, to £10,303. The amount charged for Detroit fire claims is caused by writing off as a bad debt the entire claims in suit against certain insurance companies, although a portion may hereafter be collected. The loss on conversion of American currency for the half-year amounts to £70,362, as compared with £66,-612 for the corresponding half-year in 1868. The average rate of conversions made during the half-year was $138\frac{1}{2}$, the average price of gold for the same period having been $140\frac{1}{2}$. The unconverted American funds in hand and outstanding traffic payable in that currency at January 31, 1869, show a decrease of $18,838.20, compared with the amount at the end of last half-year. The following table exhibits the receipts and expenses for seven corresponding half-years:

RECEIPTS.

Half-year ending	Passengers, mails, and sundries. £	Ereight, and live stock. £	Rents. £	Total. £
Jan 31, 1863	122,627	186,099	579	309,305
" 1864	129,684	171,329	621	301,634
" 1865	154,125	157,854	730	312,730
" 1866	205,131	181,071	837	387,039
" 1867	168,986	161,254	1.273	331,518
" 1868	186,537	213,476	800	400,813
" 1869	183,703	238,764	846	418,312

EXPENSES.

	Including renewals. £	Per cent. of gross receipts.
Jan. 31, 1863	172,563	55.79
" 1864	171,336	56.80
" 1865	168,577	53.91
" 1866	170,008	48.93
" 1887	166,632	50.26
" 1868	193,667	48.31
" 1869	209,752	49.55

The total traffic receipts show an increase of £22,-453, as compared with the corresponding half-year. This increase arises as follows:

Increase in local passenger traffic		£6,455
Increase in through freight and live stock		26,659
		£33,114
Decrease in through passenger traffic	£570	
" emigrant	907	
" express freight and sundries	7,722	
" local freight and live stock	1,351	
		10,661
Total increase		£22,453

The low tariff of rates and fares referred to in the last half-yearly report arising from the competition of other lines, has continued; hence the percentage of working expenses is somewhat higher than at the corresponding period of 1868; but, notwithstanding this, the percentage of working expenses compares favorably with the average of the six preceding corresponding half-years, as will be seen by the above table. The cost of ordinary working expenses per train mile in the last and four previous corresponding half-years was—

Jan. 31, 1865	5s. $1\frac{1}{4}$d.	sterling.
" 1866	4s. $6\frac{3}{4}$d.	"
" 1867	4s. $7\frac{1}{4}$d.	"
" 1868	4s. $5\frac{3}{4}$d.	"
" 1869	4s. $3\frac{3}{4}$d.	"

The usual detailed report of the engineer and mechanical superintendent are appended, and there is also a special certificate from each of these officers, in the form prescribed for English railways. The mechanical superintendent's report mentions that a new passenger engine has been completed during the past half year, and set to work, the cost being defrayed out of revenue. On the 22nd of January last a special meeting of shareholders was held in London, to consider a definite communication from the Government of the Dominion of Canada, for the settlement of the Provincial advance and arrears of interest on the following basis, viz.: that the principal sum of £573,688 should be repaid by four equal annual instalments commencing from 1st January, 1870, and that for the arrears of interest, a sum should be fixed, equivalent to placing the Government, as regards interest, on about an equal footing with the shareholders of the Company, since the Company ceased in 1860 to make the half-yearly interest payments to the Government. The Proprietors concurred with the Directors that such a settlement would be desirable. In consequence thereof the Honorable William McMaster, Chairman of the Executive Committee, with the officers of the Company in Canada, after several conferences at Ottawa, with the Minister of Finance and the Auditor General, came to a final adjustment of figures, and agreed that the principal sum (representing the Government advance,) with the accrued interest up to the 1st January, 1869, less money due from Government for mail and military transport service, should be commuted for a total sum of £668,815, payable by annual instalments, the liquidated balance, year by year to bear interest at the rate of 4 per cent. per annum, instead of 6 per cent. as at present. The remission of interest which has been already charged against revenue, together with the further advantage resulting from the diminished rate of interest on the unpaid balance, amount in the aggregate to upwards of £180,000. The first stipulation of the Government was the payment in Canada of £100,000 on the 10th February, and this has been complied with. It is expected that the Government will bring the terms of this settlement under the notice of the Legislature, which meets on the 16th April, by message from the Governor-General, on which resolutions of the House of Commons will have to be passed, and a bill introduced to carry them into effect. It is hoped that intelligence of the Parliamentary confirmation of these terms will be received previous to the general meeting, in which event the meeting will be made special, to ratify the same, and to submit a plan for raising the necessary funds. The Proprietors are aware that in 1864, and again in 1868, a deputation from the English board visited Canada, and upon both occasions rendered most essential services to the Company. To the mission in 1868 must be mainly attributed the settlement now happily arrived at with the Canadian Government. The actual expenses incurred on these occasions have been paid by the Company. The board, however, trust that the Proprietors will readily acquiesce with them in thinking that important services of this nature call for some special recognition, and they ask permission to appropriate for this purpose the sum of 1,500 guineas, which will provide an acknowledgment for the two gentlemen who formed the deputation. The Directors are glad to announce that a Canadian Company are about to construct an extension of the Galt and Guelph branch northwards, across the fertile agricultural country beyond Guelph, a district hitherto without railway communication. This line is called the Wellington, Grey and Bruce railway, and it is intended ultimately to be extended to the shores of Lake Huron. The Great Western Company have agreed to supply rolling stock, and work the first section of 16 miles, when completed as far as the town of Fergus, at 70 per cent. of the gross earnings. Further, it is agreed that an account shall be kept of the railway traffic exchanged between the Great Western railway and the new line, and that 20 per cent. of this traffic shall be set aside annually and appropriated to redeem the capital cost of the line, so that in the course of years the branch will gradually become a part of the Great Western system. The Directors have the satisfaction of stating that the net revenue of the Detroit and Milwaukee Company for the half-year ended 31st December, 1868, has, as was anticipated in the last report, permitted of a payment on account of arrears of dividend on the $2,095,000 preference shares of that Company (being the securities representing the loan of £250,000 with accrued interest) at the rate of 7 per cent. per annum, amounting to $73,325, which, after deducting United States internal revenue tax and cost of conversion, has produced in gold £10,622. The Directors, as will be seen by the net revenue account No. 3, have placed one-half of this amount to the credit of revenue, and the remaining portion has been applied in part liquidation of the old Detroit and Milwaukee Interest account standing in the balance-sheet, which latter is now reduced to £9,957. The receipts and expenditures

of the Detroit and Milwaukee railroad for the year ending 31st Dec., 1868, have been satisfactory, and show the following results:—Gross earnings, £363,033 ; working expenses, £208,281 ; net, £144,752. The Detroit and Milwaukee Company is progressing very satisfactorily, and the receipts show an increase over the corresponding period up to March 25th of £8,204, or upwards of 15 per cent.

On behalf of the board of Directors,
THOMAS DAKIN, President.
London, April 14, 1869.

COMMERCIAL BANK OF N. B.—An adjourned meeting of the Stockholders was held early in the present month. The President submitted a statement showing a reduction of the circulation from $261,400, on the 23rd Nov. last, to $30,582, on the 30th April, 1869, and of the discounts from $262,932 to $57,644. The total liabilities were reduced from $630,988 to $293,052, and the assets from $765,671 to $427,765. It was agreed that the President should be paid at the rate of £500 per annum since the Bank closed. A motion to proceed to the election of Directors for the ensuing year, was opposed by Mr. Kerr and others as illegal but was carried. The following gentlemen were elected Directors for the ensuing year :—Hon. A. McL. Seely, Wm. Parks, James Vernon, Robert Reed, J. V. Troop. And at a subsequent meeting of the Directors, the Hon. A. McL. Seely was chosen President.

Financial.

TORONTO STOCK MARKET.

(Reported by Pellatt & Osler, Brokers.)

The stock market is quiet, and little change has taken place in prices during the week.

Bank Stock.—Sales of Montreal were made at 159 to 160½. There are buyers of British at 105, sellers asking 105½. Sales of Ontario were made at 101. Little Toronto offering; small sales were made at 118½. Royal Canadian opened at 75, but closed lower, with sales at 68 to 70. No Commerce offering under 103 to 103½; buyers offer 102½. There are buyers of Gore at 35; sellers asking 36½. Sales of Merchants were made at 107, 107¼ and 107½; buyers now offer 108. No Quebec offering; it would bring 103. Molson's sold at 108 and 108½. Transactions in City occurred at 101½ and 102, closing with sellers at the latter rate. Buyers offer 106 for Nationale; little offering. Sales of Jacques Cartier were made at 109½ and 110, closing with buyers at the latter rate. Mechanics sold at 93. Other banks nominal.

Debentures.—Dominion stock is offered at 108½. There is a large lot of Toronto debentures on market at present, offering to pay about 7 per cent. interest. County are not so much enquired for; buyers hold off.

Sundries—City Gas is offered at 107½; no buyers. Little Canada Permanent Building Society in market; no sales. A small amount of Western Canada D. S. is offered at 121. The Freehold has declared a 5 per cent. dividend, causing the stock to advance 2 or 3 per cent. Sales of Montreal Telegraph were made at 134½; no sellers now under 135. Sellers ask 79 for Canada Landed Credit; little in market. Several mortgages have been placed, during the week, to pay 8 per cent. Money continues in good demand, and high rates were paid on Commercial paper.

RATE OF INTEREST.

Mr. Rose has laid before the House a series of six short resolutions relating to the rate of interest, which, if passed, will be embodied in a bill to be enacted by Parliament. They provide that six per cent per annum shall continue to be the legal rate of interest in all cases where by the agreement of

the parties or by law, interest is payable at the rate has been fixed by the parties in writing the law; that any rate of interest not exceeding eight per cent per annum may be paid in advance or otherwise, and being paid may be retained; may be stipulated in writing, and may be received or being paid may be retained ; that if any higher rate than eight per cent. per annum is received latel, such rate shall be ipso facto reduced to per cent. per annum, as a penalty, and that only shall be recoverable, and if any higher interest and usury shall be repealed; that the existing provisions shall apply to any loan, or contract for the loan or forbearance of money, made or entered after the day of next ; that these resolutions shall not apply to any person or body corporate which by any existing law or by the law of any charter or act of incorporation, may lawfully stipulate for and receive a higher rate of interest than eight per cent.

DOMINION ACCOUNTS.—The following is an analysis of the receipts and expenditure of the Dominion during the first year of existence :—The gross receipts of the Dominion on account of the Province of Canada—the several Provinces. $16,830,060
Less loans 2,994,600

Ordinary Revenue of Dominion.. $13,835,460

Gross Expenditure of the Dominion $13,704,170
Less Redemption 337,650

Balance $13,366,490
Whereof, on account of Public Works chargeable to Capital 587,780

Balance.. .... $12,778,700

Subsidies, Ontario and Quebec... $2,156,120
Add one year's interest on Trust Funds 177,160

Deduct interest on debt $2,333,280
Less interest on excess of debt (say $11,000,000) 535,000

Payable annually............................ $1,783,280
Actually paid 1,588,780

Excess payable beyond actual payments $194,500
Ordinary expenditure of the Dominion 12,973,210

Surplus $862,240

Total $13,834,460

THE BUDGET.

The speech of the Minister of Finance, in moving the House into Committee of ways and means, furnishes the following particulars :—On reference to the estimates laid before the House in March, 1868, the receipts were estimated in round numbers at $14,696,000. This was the gross sum the Dominion was expected to receive. Eliminating from these receipts what was found upon subsequent examination to belong to the Provinces, the receipts on the Dominion account proper were found to be $13,835,000 and a further sum, ascertained to belong to the Provinces of $556,000, making together the total receipts of $14,381,000, against an estimated receipt of $14,696,000 showing an over estimate for the year of $315,000. This discrepancy would be accounted for by the fact that in April, May and June the customs fell short $345,000 and miscel-328,000. With reference to the-ascer-penditure for the same year, it would be the estimate submitted to the House, in , was $14,321,000, and the ascertained regarded the Dominion proper, was $12,-the expenditure on account of the Pro-ith which they have been charged, was making a total of $13,235,790 of ex-. This fell short of the estimate $775,-desired to place them into possession of l result brought down to a Dominion ring out on both sides the receipts and found to belong to the various provin-ving this out of account, he found that 'ear's revenue of the Dominion proper 35,460 and the expenditure $12,973,211, n apparent surplus of $862,259 ; but it an apparent surplus, the House must t to be an actual surplus, for during the of Confederation those various services ild in ordinary years have gone to swell s of 1867-8 were not so chargeable that ine of the services of the preceeding year account the first year of our existence, ime of the services properly ascertain-t year were postponed until 1868-9. ditor estimates that amount at $300,000 l leave as the actual surplus for 1867-8, f $862,259 ; but he the Finance Minis-iclined to reduce the amount $500,000 ; 'ery effort has been made to act with artiality, and fairness, yet possibly their m Ontario and Quebec might take ex-soms of the items. Taking this sum of rom the $862,259, the apparent surplus, rplus of the first year of Confederation luced to a little over $360,000.

t came to the current year 1868-9, of months had already elapsed. He de-ll the attention of the House to the made in March, 1868, of the probable d expenditure for the current year. At there were three great sources of reve-ms, Excise and Miscellaneous. Only se sources exist now ; Miscellaneous iced to very small dimensions ; from therefore, the estimated receipts were Customs was set down at $9,000,000. result, judging from the Customs re-ie past ten months, will be a deficiency . million. The Excise was estimated at , but it would probably not be so much 800,000. The Miscellaneous was esti-2,500,000, whereas the yield be $3,716,-ing an excess of $216,000. The result ms shew that while the Revenue was imated at $15,114,000, the real revenue by the experience of the past ten ild be about $13,750,000, which will ug off in receipts of about $1,364,000. l next refer to the operations of the . The gross receipts of the year were '; deduct from this loans for redemp-} $12,124,381, will leave as ordinary 4,743,656. The gross expenditure for e period was $22,409,151 ; from this mptions of public debt and investments it of arrears, amounting in all to $8,-ring as ordinary expenditure $12,470,-leaves a balance in favor of the year's f $274,032. (Hear, Hear.) In stating l he had concealed nothing, there had tponement of payments. rnment knew that the revenue was und that they were asked to submit an the probable expenditure for the e months. With care and accuracy 'ed it at $4,733,195. He then reverted l financial position as affected by the f last session. When he addressed st session, there was a considerable , to the Bank of Montreal and the igland ; there was also a million of it bonds maturing ; in addition, pay-iount of the Provinces of New Bruns-

wick and Nova Scotia for public works. To meet these payments, and sponge out the National Debt required a very great strain at the outset upon the resources of the Dominion.

The Savings Banks, though, in operation for so short a time, had been evidently productive of great good ; there were 213 banks with 6,079 de-positors the majority of whom were minors and married men. The Deposits amounted to $676,-883. The total amount received an account of the Intercolonial loan was $10,283,003 ; of this government invested $270,000 at 6 per cent. in the Sinking Fund, thus reducing our debt by. so much. They had paid off the old Imperial loan for building canals, bearing 4 per cent. interest $671,000, they had paid off the loan from Baring's and Glyn's bearing 5 per cent. interest $983,000. Next they paid off the Bank of Montreal $2,500,-000 together with $500,000, due to the Ontario Government, and besides had redeemed the 7 per cent. debentures issued two years ago, to the amount of $873,000. Of the balance of the Inter-colonial loan, there was in the Bank of Montreal $1,500,000, and the remainder $2,900,000 was in the Agents hands in London.

For recouping the loan when required, they had $270,000 of Sinking Fund, $2,900,000 in hands of London Agents, $749,000 of India Bonds, $3,254,000 of Great Western Railway debts, re-ceipts from insurance companies for two years $1,-500,000, deposit in Bank of Montreal at 4 per cent. $1,500,000, the Savings Bank deposits, a credit of £500,000 with the Bank of Montreal and £250,000 with Baring's and Glyn's—total an excess of $974,000 over and above the amount of the Intercolonial loan.

As regards the condition of the country, he con-sidered it good. Whatever of embarrassment ex-isted was owing to over-trading. He took as In-dications of the soundness of the country the facts that the deposits in the banks had increased from $8,300,000 in 1858 to $26,700,000 in 1868 ; that the deposits in the savings banks-in Ontario and Quebec had increased from $2,900,000 in 1866 to $3,234,000 in 1868 ; and the building society de-posits from $555,000 to $919,000, besides the deposits in the post office savings banks, amount-ing to $670,000. The savings bank deposits in New Brunswick and Nova Scotia had also in-creased, so that during the last three years the total deposits in the banks and savings banks had increased from $32,600,000 to $37,500,000. The railway traffic also showed an increase from $4,620 per mile in 1866 to $4,800 in 1867, and $5,020 per mile in 1868. In 1866 there was an increase of bankers' capital of $1,618,000, in 1867 of $1,799,000, and in 1868 of $2,838,000. He al-luded also to the progress. made by the principal cities in the Dominion, and said that the muni-cipal returns from twenty counties of Ontario showed for the year 1868, as compared with 1867, an increase in assessed value of real estate of $1,716,000 ; of cattle, $385,00, ; of sheep, $156,-000 ; and of horses, $458,000. In some of these counties there was a decrease under certain heads to the amount of $242,000, but altogether there was an increase in those twenty counties of $2,480,000. If the same increase were preserved for the other counties there would be an increase in one year in the value of assessed property for the whole of Ontario -of $3,588,000. In view of such facts as these he thought he was warranted in asserting that though some interests might be languishing, the country was substantially in a sound condition. He referred also, in this con-nection, to the great rise in the value of our secu-rities in England, and then adverted to the spe-cial circumstances which had produced the over-importations of some years back, especially to the great demand from the United States to fill the vacuum caused there by the war. From these causes our total imports had visen from $37,800,-000 in 1864-65 to $52,600,000 in 1866-67. The imports of dry goods in the same period increased from $13,500,000 to $21,500,000. In the latter part of 1867-68 the imports began to fall off,

principally in cottons, woollens and linens. The decrease in the percentage of duties this year was not less than 25½ per cent. on woollens, 16¾ on cottons, and 2¾ per cent. on linens. In millinery there was an increase, however of. 12 per cent., and there was an increase-in the article of liquors in much the same proportion. On the first nine months of the fiscal year, 1868-69, as compared with the corresponding period of 1867-68, there was a decrease in customs duties of $450,000 or 9 per cent in the old Province of Ontario ; of $161,000 or 15 per cent. in New Brunswick ; and of $321,000 or 37 per cent. in Nova Scotia. The total falling off in the Dominion was $870,000 or 13 per cent. He proceeded to show on what grounds he had based his estimates for the com-ing year, 1869-70. In the first place he had ascertained the amount of goods in bond, which was $3,100,000, in April, 1869, against $2,906,000 in April, 1868. The duty on the goods now in bond would be $1,021,000. The next inquiry was as to the amount of goods in the hands of merchants. Seven returns said the stocks were about the same this year as last ; six said the stocks were larger ; ten, and these from the more important points, said the stocks were consider-ably smaller. The next inquiry was as to the prospects of importation. Returns from eleven localities said the importation of the coming year would probably be in excess of those of the past year ; seven said they would be cer-tainly equal ; six said they would be about equal ; and five said they would be less. He thought that already there were symptoms, that trade was reviving. He did not expect the same excess of importation as had characterized some previous years, but already there were signs of a revival. The customs duties of the first four months of this year showed an increase of 2½ per cent. over the corresponding months of last year. The month of April showed an increase of nearly 9 per cent. over 1868. From these facts he drew the inference that the recent falling off in imports was not due to any inherent, deep-rooted, deep-seated distress in the country, but was merely owing to an over importation of certain articles. He did not attach so much importance as some did to the Reciprocity Treaty. During the last year of its existence the export to the United States was $21,-340,000, and in 1868 $20,061,000, or a little over five per cent. In a lumber there was an increase of 44 per cent. ; in animals a decrease of 46 per cent ; in grain and flour there had been a falling off, and in other articles a decrease of $300,000. In 1866-7 there was sent from Canada to Nova Scotia and New Brunswick 408,000 barrels of flour. In 1868 there was an aggregate of 443,000 or an excess of 33 per cent. The increase in coal sent up was 17 per cent.

The gross estimate for the coming year was $17,-659,000 ; from customs $8,600,000; excise $3,300,-000. In 1868 he might mention the consumption was $3,886,000; then as regards malt the estimated consumption last year was 27,000,000 lbs. Next year he estimated that the consumption will be 28,000,000 lbs. The tobacco estimate taking into account the large stocks on hand in the Maritime Provinces and the imperfect machinery yet in ex-istence for the collecting of the duty, amounted to $515,000. This he had no doubt would be very sensibly and largely increased. From petroleum last year, the receipts were $99,000, and this year they were estimated at $120,000. These three items constituted the $3,300,000. The third item of revenue which includes the revenue from Public Works, Post Office, Stamps, &c., he estimated at $2,665,000. The revenue, therefore, at a mode-rate estimate would be $14,565,000 against an ex-penditure of $14,319,000, leaving a very small but he believed a very certain balance on the right side of the account of- $246,132. In regard to the item in the estimates of $336,000 for the Sinking Fund, he mentioned that he charged that item against the income for the year, because we had really and honestly to provide for it; that Sinking Fund as provided for was in hand, we have brought it in advance, and having more money in hand than we know what to do with, he thought it would not be amiss to anticipate the Sinking Fund knowing that next year we would have to provide for it, but he thought it but right this sum should be put in as an estimate for the year. Yet being on hand of course it augmented our cash balance at the close of the year.

THE CANADIAN MONETARY TIMES AND INSURANCE CHRONICLE is printed every Thursday evening and distributed to Subscribers on the following morning.

Publishing office, No. 60 Church-street, 3 doors north of Court-street.

Subscription price—

Canada $2.00 per annum.

England, stg. 10s. per annum.

United States (U.S.Cy.) $3.00 per annum.

Casual advertisements will be charged at the rate of ten cents per line, each insertion.

Address all letters to "THE MONETARY TIMES."

Cheques, money orders, &c. should be made payable to J. M. TROUT, Business Manager, who alone is authorized to issue receipts for money.

☞ All Canadian Subscribers to THE MONETARY TIMES will receive THE REAL ESTATE JOURNAL without further charge.

The Canadian Monetary Times.

THURSDAY, MAY 20, 1869.

USURY.*

The time was when to receive interest upon money, no matter at how trifling a rate, was held to be an offence against the law of nature and the law of God. For upwards of 1500 years this was the universally accredited doctrine throughout Europe. It was a sin to borrow money at interest; it was a far greater to lend it. The fathers of the Church, its Popes and Councils, its theologians, and its law, as embodied in the Canon, were unanimous in denouncing this thing as a species of robbery, as a crime which like murder, &c. was palpably contrary to the law of nature.

*This word is used throughout the article as meaning the receiving of any interest whatever.

It was condemned by 17 Popes, and 28 Councils of the Church. Money-lenders were subject to legal penalties, were put to the torture and were held up to public odium as infamous persons. In the year 1179, the third Lateran Council, convened by Pope Alexander III., decreed that money-lenders, unless they repented of their crime, should not be admitted to the altar, nor be absolved at the hour of death, nor receive Christian burial. Any one who denied that the receiving of interest on money was a sin was denounced as a vile heretic, the proper expiation of whose offence was to be burnt alive, a sentence which was executed upon more than one poor wretch, who was afflicted in this way by the malady of thought. In some countries the property of money-lenders was subject, after their death, to confiscation by the crown. This arrangement was eminently satisfactory, for, as an acute writer remarks, it enabled the government to obtain a loan from a money-lender, while he was living, and to rob his children when he was dead. The Act of 3 Henry VII. c. 6 (1486) provided that "all brokers of such bargains shall be set on the pillory, put to open shame, be half a-year imprisoned and pay £20." Traces of the same feeling are to be found in comparatively recent times. Thus, in the preamble to the Act of 5 & 6 Edward VI. c. 20, (1552) it is recited that the charging of interest is a vice most odious and detestable, and contrary to the word of God. Again in sec. 5 of 13 Eliz. c. 8 (1570) we find these words, "And forasmuch as all usury, being forbidden by the law of God, is sin and detestable." The Act of 21 James I. c. 17, (1623) while allowing as a commercial necessity the taking of interest at the rate fixed by it, was careful to add as a proviso (sec. 6) " That no words in this law contained shall be construed or expounded to allow the practice of usury in point of religion and conscience." Even so late as 1745 Pope Benedict XIV. (in many respects a great and enlightened man) issued an encyclical letter, in which the doctrine of the Church was authoritatively laid down, that the taking of interest on money is always a sin, and that its amount being small, or exacted from rich men only, or to further commercial undertakings, does not alter its character in the least. The superstition which we have above sketched has now happily almost disappeared, being found to any great extent only in Russia, where, according to Storch, a well known political economist of that country, some sects of dissenters from the national Church, still hold that it is sinful to lend money at interest. This happy change is due to the influence partly of the reformation, and partly of the works of speculative writers on the subject, principally political economists. But though the original feelin[g] thus almost extinct, there is ample evide[nce] that some relics of it still linger in our mi[dst] We need go no further than our legisla[ture] has taken a new form, which objects, no[w to] the receiving of any interest, but to the re[?]ceiving of what is considered too much.

Since the almost total abolition in Can[ada] of the usury laws, about ten years ago, Parliament, annually, has had inflicted u[pon] it, bills to re-enact such a law with mor[e or] less stringency. This session the flood co[mes] stronger than ever. Not less than thi[rty] members have introduced such bills. [One] proposes to limit the rate of interest to e[ight] per cent., the penalty for infringement t[o be] the forfeiture of all interest if sued for wi[thin] one year. Another proposes to limit [the] rate to seven per cent. If more is recei[ved] the contract to be void ; all interest and half the principal to be recoverable on[e] by any one ; one half the amount recov[ered] to go to the informer, the other half to [the] schools. The third bill makes the limit e[ight] per cent., the penalty being forfeitur[e of] treble the value of the subject of the contract ; one-half to go to any one who [shall] sue as informer, the other half to the [re]ceiver General. This last is substant[ially] the same as the old Act of 51 Geo. III., which was abolished in 1859, except th[at] that act the limit was six per cent. If [this] had been a prospect that these bills, like [those] in former years, would be consigne[d to] merited oblivion, we should not have th[ought] it worth while to notice the subject. [How]ever, as there is an evident determinati[on on] the part of a considerable section of the com[mu]mons to force through the House a b[ill of] some kind on the subject, and as the p[res]sure has become so strong as to induc[e the] Government to give way, and itself to [intro]duce a bill, we deem it our duty to pr[otest] in the strongest manner, against the [course] tated wrong. When the greater part o[f the] world is steadily advancing towards p[erfect] freedom in all matters of trade and com[]merce between both men and nations ; [when] even countries so backward on these su[bjects] as Austria and Spain are joining in the gene[]ral movement ; it would be no other t[han a] great misfortune that Canada, which [has so] often set an enlightened example to [other] nations, should now betake herself t[o this] crab-like motion of going backwards. [We] do not wish to question the motives of [those] who introduce such measures ; dou[btless] they mean well. Their mistake is [made] through want of sufficient knowledge o[f the] operation of such laws, they do not [see] that it is impossible to put a stop, by [penal] penalties, to things of the kind ; tha[t] how strongly such enactments may ged about with precautions, they are systematically evaded, and that their n practice, has been found to be al-, make the evil worse, by raising, in-f lowering the rate of interest. It n truly said that well-intentioned ig-ι has inflicted more evil on the world y other thing whatever.

particular mischiefs which usury laws ι has been pointed out and discussed erous writers during the last 300 years. he first by whom it was partially recog-as the great Reformer Calvin. He it .o first pointed out the absurdity of e's dictum that "all money is sterile ιre," and consistently he maintained rfulness of taking interest. He lowed by Salmasius (the celebrated ιt of Milton), who, about the year rrote some works attacking the old ι. Then came Locke, who, in 1691, 'Considerations on 'the lowering of ," showed that interest depends on ιnd demand, and that all attempts to it would be pernicious and abortive. t important work on the subject was ιhe great French economist, Turgot, ιury," published in 1769—just one ι years ago. In it the modern doo-laid down so fully and clearly as to 't little to be added since. Hume ιm Smith (1776), though somewhat with the old errors, were, on the trongly inclined to the modern and ral view. The coup de grâce was re-however, for Bentham, whose mas-Letters on the Usury Laws," pub-ι 1787, gave the death-blow to the ι, and added the finishing touch to ιct theory. Since then the policy of ng by law the rate of interest has ιeived the support of a single writer ote, while all the great writers, such Mill, Buckle, McCulloch and Lecky, ε with Bentham and his predeces-the same side. It usually takes at ιundred years for new truths, after 'e been thoroughly understood and y the speculative thinker, to per-wn to the level of ordinary politi-ιs, therefore, nearly that time has ιince Bentham gave the finishing the theory of the subject, we may ιdulge the hope that the present ι nearly the last which will be made ιountry; that it is no more than flash of the candle expiring in its With a view of hastening its total ιment, we give a few of the results y be gathered from the works of the ιmed. We begin by pointing out 'e of interest. . It is composed of ιents:

1. The price paid for the use of the money. This depends upon the laws of supply and demand, as affected by the profit on produc-tion. In countries where the natural pro-ductive power is small, interest will be lower (other things being equal) than in those where the productive power is great.

2. The interest (or price) of . insurance. This is to insure the lender against the risk which he runs of losing the whole or a part of his principal. As in other species of insu-rance the greater the risk, the greater will be the premium required to meet it. A money-lender, of course, charges more where the debt is not well secured. The better the security the lower will be the rate.

3. The business of money-lending is, even now, though far less intensely than for-merly, the subject of some popular odium. To repay a person adopting the business for this disagreeable adjunct to it, a rate of profit (or interest) is charged higher than could be obtained by investing money in ways not subject to a similar social stigma. Men can-not be expected to undergo humiliation of this kind for nothing. Formerly, when the feeling referred to was so strong that hardly any but Jews could be induced to become "money - lending dogs," as the common phrase went, it had an immense effect in raising the rate of interest. Now, when the feeling is comparatively very feeble, it ope-rates very slightly. So long, however, as any stigma exists, so long will an extra rate be charged as compensation. So much, then, as to the nature of interest. The foregoing analysis will be sufficient of itself to indicate to many the impolicy of tying down to a fixed limit a thing affected by such varying circumstances.

THE GOVERNMENT BANKING SCHEME.

The Government scheme which it is pro-posed to substitute for our present system of banking is now before the country. It is substantially the National Bank system of the United States on a quasi specie basis. The difficulty is to discover why a change of system is necessary. The Finance Minister asserts that the Government are not in pres-sing want of money, and he admits that con-servative and cautious management has on the whole distinguished the operations of the Banks. It is not denied that the present system has proved itself well adapted to the circumstances of the country, and that there have been fewer losses to the holders of bank notes in Canada than in any other country which possesses a similar bank-note circula-tion, or even one based on Government secu-rities, while it is contended by those most familiar with the working of the system that

the new scheme will, if adopted, affect disas-trously the interests of the country, and, in all probability lead to an irredeemable cur-rency. So that, at the outset, it is a fit sub-ject of inquiry why it is deemed advisable to jeopardize immediate and continuous conver-tibility for the certainty of ultimate redemp-tion; to substitute a non-elastic currency for one which has proved itself so well suited to the wants of trade; to attach a Dead-Weight to all our banking institutions and lessen by so much their available resources. The onus probandi is clearly on those who would effect a change which almost all our bankers con-demnas fraught with injurious consequences, and our merchants protest against as uncalled for, and nicely calculated to tell on their in-terests not only now when their circumstances are embarrassed, but in the future as well.

The Government scheme has some good features. No one has asserted that our pre-sent system could not be improved. These good features to which we refer might be easily grafted on that system, and there would be no dissentient voice. All our bankers are willing to see proper provision made for the security of note-holders, and, have, themselves, suggested most of the re-strictions which the Finance Minister has so dexterously twined around his scheme to secure a forced loan.

The great objection to a currency system nailed to government securities is its want of elasticity. In every country the amount of currency fluctuates at different periods to accommodate itself to the volume of transac-tions to which its instrumentality is requisite. In England it was stated that these fluctua-tions are in the proportion of three to one. In other words, it requires a currency of seven millions to maintain a circulation which, for the whole year, averages only three millions. In Canada, circulation attains the highest point in the month of October. In the Province of Ontario an elastic currency is an absolute necessity, and any system not characterized by that great element is likely to prove ruinous. It would be a mistake to suppose that twelve millions of bank notes would imply an uniform cir-culation of that amount. At no time could the banks get on without a reserve of greater or less amount of notes in their vaults, so that to issue a given amount of notes would not ensure a circulation of that amount. The amount of securities deposited would then, with those the banks already possess, be the measure of the future circulation. Herein lies the great fault of the Finance Minister's scheme. By way of glossing it over he says it would pay the banks to keep an extra six or seven millions and the twenty per cent. gold reserve lying in their vaults until required in the autumn! Ontario, as the chief producing province of the Dominion, will be the real sufferer.

It has already been shown in these columns that, if securities have to be purchased by the banks, an unnatural contraction of the currency will take place. If five millions be taken as the circulation of the Ontario banks, and the Government securities they now hold be subtracted, they would have to advance to the government, for the privilege of maintaining a circulation equal to that which they now enjoy, a little less than four millions and a half. The contraction thus induced would, by an inevitable law, cause a fall in prices. Every producer would get less for the results of his labor, and while getting less for our produce, we should have to buy imported articles at a dearer rate. The country would thus lose at both ends.

The present system can be easily amended so as to give the note holder security which is nearly perfect. Take the case of one bank, say, for example, the Bank of Commerce. According to the returns for March, that bank held coin, etc., $1,059,306, and government securities, $104,385, while its circulation was $1,149,844. Under the new scheme it might reduce its gold to $229,968, and would increase its government securities to $1,149,844. Or take all the banks. They held $9,924,769 coin, etc., and $3,118,206 government securities, against $9,905,410 of circulation. Under the new scheme they could reduce their gold to $1,931,082, while they would increase their government securities to $9,905,410. This is a singular feature; it lessens the amount of gold necessary to be held, and increases the amount of government securities. Before Sir Robert Peel's act was passed, it was found that a necessity existed to curtail by law the amount of government securities which the Bank of England may hold. In September, 1839, the bullion in its vaults was below £3,000,000, while it held securities to the amount of nearly £26,000,000. Sir Robert Peel's act provided that notes should not be issued against securities to a greater amount than £14,000,000. Our Finance Minister wishes to reverse this process.

It cannot be said that this substitution of Government promises to pay for gold is an additional safeguard to the currency. The substitution of Government indebtedness for the capital of a bank is an inevitable cause of discredit. The loans forced under the guise of protecting note holders are perpetual. When the banks fail they are not forthcoming. The securities must be thrown on the market and sold for what they will bring. Their market value will depend entirely upon the state of the Government credit at the moment, and in the case of this country it might easily happen that they would not be saleable at all. A foreign war, with England one of the combatants, or a Fenian raid, would give a shock to Canadian credit that Government securities would scarcely be saleable.

But the proposed scheme will not necessarily save the bona fide note-holders from loss. When a bank suspends, its legal tenders cease to be such. If it is necessary to realize the securities, what becomes of the note holders in the meantime? Would they, as a body, await the process of winding up? The great bulk of circulation is to be found in the hands of laborers, mechanics, and others of the poorer classes of the community. Their circumstances would compel them to sell at the moment of the greatest depression, and they would have to submit to whatever shave a moment of panic might enable speculative purchasers to extort. So that even the certainty of ultimate redemption will not prevent loss to individuals. On this Mr. McCulloch says, "The taking of security for notes is not of itself capable of placing the currency on a proper footing. It would not prevent the stoppage of banks and the serious loss that might result to the holders of notes from their not being negotiable except at a discount, during the period required to realize the securities on which they have been issued."

The conjunction of Government credit and bank credit and the withdrawal of so much gold, may lead as it has often hitherto done in other countries to a suspension of specie payments. In the last century the Bank of England made such large advances to Government, that a suspension of specie payments had to be resorted to. The Bank of France did the same with a like result. The Banks of the United States did so virtually, but the result was anticipated by making the currency irredeemable. The descent to inconvertibility is easy. We have already learned the first lesson. Our Provincial notes were made a legal tender and forced on the banks to be held in lieu of specie. Difficulties were thrown in the way of their redemption by issuing in Toronto notes payable at Montreal and vice versâ. It costs a fourth of one per cent to transport notes from one city to another. Such a contrivance shows how irresistible the inclination is to exempt these notes from all demands of convertibility when occasion arises. The same plan is offered as a bait to the banks. Under the new scheme they would be at liberty to issue in Halifax or Fort Garry legal tenders redeemable in gold only at their head office, wherever it might be.

A specie reserve of twenty per cent. is seemingly relied upon as the great preservative of convertibility. There have been periods when the Bank of England and the Bank of France required for the maintenance of convertibility about half as much gold as they had issued notes. The banks of New York were at one time obliged to suspend specie payment with a reserve of bullion to their vaults equal to half their note circulation. At present, as we have shown, our banks hold nearly one hundred per cent. their circulation in gold and legal tender, and we may rest assured that they do not hold it unnecessarily.

The Finance Minister takes it for granted that the increase of deposits will go on at a rapid rate. It must be remembered, however, that the new scheme lessens somewhat the security of the depositor by making the circulation a first mortgage. Why there should be a distinction between the deposit on call and the deposit bearing interest, in the matter of specie reserve, we fail to see. A specie reserve of one-seventh is to be held against deposits at call, while the other deposits are left to take care of themselves. It has never before been pretended that it is any part of the duty of Government to inquire into the security given by the borrower to the lenders of money any more than into the security given by the borrowers to the lenders of anything else. This is a matter as to which individuals are fully competent to judge for themselves, and there not nor can be any reason why a lender or depositor of gold, silver or notes should be protected more than a lender or depositor of wood or coal. If A trusts a sum of money in the hands of B, it is the affair of the parties, and of none else. The fact it is a deposit at interest, which should be protected if any protection be given for the deposit on call is generally the consideration, either direct or indirect, for a line of discount and may be withdrawn at once in time of danger, while the deposit at interest draws a more nominal rate of interest, and must be for its time before it can be withdrawn.

Why is the proportion one-seventh fixed the reserve against deposits at call? It was considered sufficient to keep one-fifth specie against the Provincial note circulation.

The new scheme, therefore, does not furnish that absolute security which is claimed for it: it is unsuited to the circumstances this country by reason of the absence of the element of elasticity; it is calculated to injure the country, by curtailing discounts, by narrowing the resources of the banks, in rendering bank stocks a less desirable investment than at present, and in reducing the deposits at interest, by transferring from the banks the government a large amount of money which will, in all likelihood, be dissipated, endangering the convertibility of the bank note, and by paving the way for that one to any community, an irredeemable paper currency.

RJURY IN INSURANCE CASES.

; week we published an extract from the
of the New York Board of Fire Un-
ters, which furnished some statistics of
tling character.   Thirty-two per cent.
ies are the result of design on the part
insured or the direct act of the incen-

Seven millions nine hundred and
housand dollars were paid for losses
in the city of New York during the
½ years, by the incendiary ! The returns
he Insurance Companies lately laid be-
e Dominion Parliament indicate losses
-5th per cent. of the premiums.   How
of the losses were the result of design
unable to say, but it may be assumed
.e per centage in Canada fully equals
New York ; in fact some place it much

However that may be, there is not
ghtest doubt that our Insurance Com-
suffer greatly from the crime of in-
-ism.   We have noticed by the law
that some of our judges lean strongly
Insurance Companies in the allowance
ral pleas, by way of defence, to actions
cies.   Of course some Companies may
heir privileges, and bring discredit on
allows, but there is no reason why all
suffer for the misconduct of one, or
criminal should gain advantage by
aided in his attempt to secure the
f his crime.   If arson and incendiar-
to be put down, the only way of doing
an union between the honest portion
community and the Insurance Com-

Juries must be taught to feel that
ce against Companies in favor of
ts is the shield in only too many cases
criminal.   Insurance Companies must
e to track out the incendiary, and by
tion secure his conviction.   The law
so amended as to narrow the circle
which the criminal can move with
y.

ve is being made in the direction last
d, and it is likely we shall have a
n in our criminal, law which will
a company to prosecute for perjury
proper case can be made out.

after case has come up in which there
ubt that premises have been fired in-
ully, but evidence sufficient to convict
be brought forward ; whereas facts
shown sufficient to sustain an indict-
r perjury in respect of the declarations

The Act now before the Senate re-
: offences has been amended in Com-
o as to embrace the following excel-
vision :—

affirmation, affidavit, or declaration
by any Fire, Life, or Marine Insu-
ompany, authorised by law to do bu-
a Canada, in regard to any loss of

property or life insured or assured therein,
may be taken before any Commissioner authorised by any of her Majesty's Superior
Courts to take affidavits, any Justice of the
Peace, or before any Notary Public, for any
Province in the Dominion, and any such officer as is hereby required to take such affirmation, affidavit or declaration. Any person
knowingly, wilfully and corruptly making
any affirmation, affidavit or declaration required by any Fire, Life, or Marine Insurance
Company authorised by law to do business in
Canada, claiming to be entitled to any Insurance money in respect of any loss of property
or life insured or assured therein, or on behalf of any person making such claim containing any false statement of fact, matter,
or thing, in regard to such loss of property,
or life, shall be guilty of wilful and corrupt
perjury, and shall be liable to be imprisoned
in the Penitentiary for any term not exceeding fourteen years, and not less than two
years, or to be imprisoned in any other gaol
or place of confinement for any term less than
two years, and to pay such fine as the Court
may award.

Insurance Companies will see the propriety
of framing the conditions on their policies so
as to utilize this enactment.

IMITATING THE CURRENCY.

An objectionable practice obtains to some extent
among patent medicine dealers and others, of getting up an imitation of a bank bill, and circulating
it as an advertising dodge. We are not aware
of any cases of swindling in this connection here;
but in the American cities, there are numerous
instances in which the ignorant and unwary have
been entrapped into taking these imitations for
money. For instance, a party of soldiers purchased
fifty dollars worth of wine with a "Mustang Lini-
ment" note ; a New Mexican sold a horse for forty
dollars, receiving the "greenback" of a commercial house in payment, and did not discover his
error till too late.

We contend that this is not a legitimate way of
advertising, and ought to be discouraged.

GALWAY MINING COMPANY.—We understand
that this company is pushing on vigorously
with three relays of men at work night and day.
A specimen of galena, of great purity, has been
sent to the office of this journal for exhibition,
and we shall have great pleasure in submitting it
to the inspection of those interested. Plans of
new buildings, smelting works, &c., are being prepared as the great success thus far achieved has
given heart to the enterprise. A quantity of
ore was sold to American buyers at the mouth of
the shaft, at satisfactory prices; besides that a
ready market can be had at Montreal for all the
ore that can be raised. We hope to be able to
send one of our correspondents to the scene of
operations ere long, as the development of that
mining region is a matter of importance to the
country at large.

ONTARIO PEAT COMPANY.—Some changes have
been made in the arrangements of this Company,
and we are assured that the undertaking will be

prosecuted vigorously.   Nearly $20,000 of the
stock has been subscribed, $44,000 has been taken
in part payment of the land, and $36,000 will
now be placed on the market, and a canvass for
subscriptions made.   It is intended to commence
operations very soon; we shall watch the progress
of the enterprise with much interest.

Insurance Agents in the cities, towns and villages, of the Dominion, would oblige us by furnishing, at our expense, the particulars of fires, in
their respective localities, either by mail or telegraph.   It is difficult to get strictly reliable
information of this kind, so that agents and
adjusters would confer upon us a favor—which we
would be happy to recognize in a substantial way
—and also do their own and other companies an
important service, by complying with this request.

—The steamer Grecian struck on Split Rock,
in the Cedar Rapids, St. Lawrence River, on
Tuesday ; it is feared she will prove a total loss.
A telegram says "her bottom is out." Valued at
$50,000, insured for $40,000, in the British America for $5,000, also in the Home, the Ætna of
Hartford, and Security for amounts which we
have not ascertained.

The Insurance Companies' Returns have been
laid before Parliament; the totals are as follows :—

	Premiums.	Losses.
Fire	2,000,000	1,085,000
Life	1,000,000	258,000
Marine	290,000	82,000

Communications.

LIFE INSURANCE.

Editor of the Canadian Monetary Times.

Life insurance, as one of the easiest and most
legitimate modes of providing for a family or old
age, is now happily receiving the attention of the
thoughtful and prudent. To meet this demand,
offices are every day springing into existence :
many holding out inducements which the most
moderate study of the subject must convince any
any one who reflects upon it, that they cannot
carry out. Unfortunately, the great majority of
insurers take it for granted that all companies are
equally good, relying upon the agents' statements.
Now, entering into such a compact, which, in the
great majority of instances, continues through
life, is as important a step as entering into business ; and any one, in this case, would require
carefully to consider the advantages or disadvantages of it before committing himself to such an
undertaking.   I shall therefore, with your permission, briefly call the attention of your readers
to the principles which I think should govern the
choice of a company. One of the most important
is the conditions contained in the policy as to
its restrictions and privileges. Most of the English companies doing business in Canada are based
upon the same conditions, the difference being
that, in one or two, claims are paid in one month
after death, instead of three, and that all policy-
holders derive equal advantages from the time of
entrance, instead of the older policy-holders taking the larger share of the bonuses. The American companies' policies, as a rule, contain conditions which place the insured entirely at the
mercy of the company, besides this most important consideration, that in case of trouble between
England and the United States, their policies
would be valueless, as it is not to be supposed

that any company would allow the insured to take up arms against his country, and which he could not do without their permission, as the clause in the policy expressly provides that they cannot do so. I think that, in order to avoid any difficulty in the future, all intending insurers should insist upon seeing a copy of a policy before signing an application. Another important difference is, that the deposits made by the American companies are applicable to the whole of the policy-holders, both in America and Canada, and not, as in the case of the English companies, for Canadian policy-holders only. The next consideration is the balance sheet, showing the expenses, mode of investment, &c. The rule which, in my opinion, ought to govern a company, is to impose no restrictions but what are essential, and to carry out their contract with the utmost liberality, bearing in mind that it is with those for whose benefit the insurance was taken out that they will have to arrange. Let a person reflect what a comfort it will be to him to feel that those he is bound by every tie to protect, and prevent their being left to the cold charity of the world, are provided for, and the small pecuniary sacrifice it has cost him to do so, and he will never regret having undertaken such a charge. But in order that he may have such a feeling, he must have the utmost confidence in the company he selects.

Yours, &c.,

INSURANCE.

Toronto, May 8, 1869.

Insurance.

FIRE RECORD.—Dundas, May 12.—John Leslie's brick store, occupied by A. D. Callen, druggist, was consumed, with most of the contents; also some adjoining property. A local paper says: Mr. Lesslie estimates his loss on buildings, furniture, &c., at nearly $8,000, on which he has an insurance of $4,000—$2,000 in the Victoria Mutual, of Hamilton, and $2,000 in the Home District Mutual. Mr. Callen estimates his stock to have been between $4,000 and $5,000, on which he has an insurance of $3,000—$1,700 in the Western, of Canada, and $1,300 in the Commercial Union. The Engine House, which was the property of the town was worth, probably $300; no insurance.

Esau Township, Ont., May.—Outbuildings of Robert Latimer, with contents, were destroyed; loss estimated at $1,500; no insurance; cause—a coal from Latimer's pipe.

Brooklin, May 11.—Daniel Hallilay's barn, stables and sheds, were consumed, with contents. The fire originated from a burning chimney at the house. Loss about $1,500; partly covered by insurance.

Bridgewater, Ont., May 11.—Five buildings were consumed; said to be without insurance.

Carleton, N. B., May.—House of T. Witchenhahi; insured for $1,200.

Breslau, Ont., May 9.—Barn of Jacob Clemens, with contents; loss estimated at $1,200; the fire originated from a heap of rubbish which a hired man had, contrary to orders, lighted.

Quebec, May.—House of Smith, butcher, was entirely destroyed.

Lott Inisy, May.—J. B. Lazier's laying kiln, with contents; loss estimated at $1,600.

Trafalgar Township, Ont., May 8.—Barn and outbuildings of A. Mitchell; caused by a heap of rubbish in the yard taking fire in some way.

Esquesing Township, Ont., May 11.—Saw-mill and shingle factory of James Morrison; loss stated at $1,600; without insurance.

Flamboro Township, Ont., May 11.—William Mortens's frame building, near Flamboro Village, took fire from sparks from the chimney, and with adjoining house of A. Raymond, was consumed; contents mostly saved; loss stated at $1,000.

Waterdown, Ont., May 11.—House and barn of Richard Attridge, and barn of William Attridge,

in East Flamboro; and 500 coils wool were consumed. A local paper states the insurance on R. Attridge's barn at $800.

Loisley, Ont., May 11.—Store of W. C. Bruce, and hotel of Robert Mitchell. The last named insured in the Toronto Mutual for $800 on buildings; most of the furniture saved; barn said to be insured for $1,000 on building, and $2,000 on stock.

Sarnia, May 11.—Dr. Shoebotham's stable and barn. Loss stated at $1,000.

Cardiffton, Ont., May 11.—Fairman's hotel, and a number of houses and barns; Fairman's loss is stated at $3,000, and the total loss at $7,000, part of which is said to be covered by insurance.

—We regret to learn from the Ottawa papers of the death of Mr. Donough O'Brien, for some years assistant secretary of the Provincial Insurance Company, a position he filled most creditably until he was compelled to resign on account of failing health.

Railway News.

GREAT WESTERN RAILWAY.—Traffic for week ending April 23, 1869.

Passengers	$27,964 60
Freight	55,073 80
Mails and Sundries	2,000 56
Total Receipts for week	$85,038 46
Corresponding week, 1868	80,756 53
Increase	$5,181 93

NORTHERN RAILWAY.—Traffic receipts for week ending May 8, 1869:—

Passengers	$2,572 17
Freight	11,360 61
Mails and sundries	204 36
Total receipts for week	$14,137 14
Corresponding week 1868	13,243 82
Increase	$893 32

THE GOVERNMENT BANKING SYSTEM.

Hon. Mr. Rose, in bringing forward his resolutions, said that three systems were now in force in the Provinces. In Nova Scotia the bank charters provide that the banks' liabilities shall not exceed three times the amount of their capital, and there is no special restriction with reference to circulation, nor provision for keeping specie on hand. In New Brunswick there is a provision that the total liabilities of the bank shall not exceed twice the amount of their capital. In Ontario and Quebec the general provision exists that circulation shall not exceed the amount of capital stock plus the specie kept in vault and the government securities held. Many of the banks are now asking the renewal of their charters, and the enlargement of their operations, consequent on Confederation, calls for great consideration. He would admit that most prudent, conservative, and cautious management had, on the whole, distinguished the operations of the various Provinces. But without further restrictions than exist in the present charters, it was possible for a bank to begin its operations, lend money to the public, and make the public its first creditor, without having any capital actually paid in. Such a thing as this was quite possible under the present provisions governing bank charters; for if a certain number of persons subscribed the amount of stock required to start a bank, such an institution could commence operations and issue its notes; those notes would be discounted, and its circulation would be placed in the hands of the public, although the bank had no real capital except the notes of the individuals starting it. It was possible so to insure the power given under the present banking charters as to produce the result

It was possible to start such a bank and to circulate its notes, though it need have no specie behind its circulation to protect the public. He had to ask the calm and deliberate attention of the House to those weak points of the existing system, and to the question whether they were to be perpetuated in the future or not. And that was another difficulty. Not only might there be a circulation out without any capital actually behind it, but even after the capital had been paid in, there might be a circulation kept up to the amount permitted by the charter, after the whole capital had been entirely annihilated, and the public had nothing whatever to look to; for there was no provision requiring an amount of specie to be kept in the vaults in order to represent the circulation.

After referring to the various bank failures, continued: There were at this moment in the Dominion about forty chartered banks, with capitals varying from $60,000 up to $6,000,000. One bank had a capital of $120,000, with an average circulation of $151,000, and specie to the amount of only $21,000. Another, with a capital of $200,000, had a circulation of $205,000, and had $29,000 in specie to meet the circulation. A third, with a capital of $72,000, had a circulation of $154,000, and only $32,000 of specie. Now although the past management of our banks might have been conducted without resulting in any general or overwhelming calamity to the country, circumstances were very different now from what they had been when the business of the various banks was restricted by the isolated condition of the Provinces in which they were situated. Now the means of communication between all parts of the Dominion were becoming rapidly improved, and the notes of any of our banks might circulate from British Columbia on the one side to Halifax on the other. This consideration, that the operation of the various banks would now extend to the whole of British North America, made it all the more incumbent on Parliament to consider whether the system on which they had hitherto been conducted was a safe one to be continued under these altered circumstances. We are about engaging, very shortly, in large and extensive public works. The temptation to over-circulate would soon be very great, and it was therefore, of essential importance that the circulating medium should be placed on a sound basis. The Government had no special object of its own to obtain in this matter. They were not urged by any pressing wants, but they were actuated solely by a single-minded desire to place the banking institutions of the country on the soundest and most wholesome basis that could be reached. He admitted that they could not deal with existing interests or existing institutions rashly or inconsiderately. The average circulation of the banks of Ontario and Quebec was about $12,000,000. The highest circulation ever reached was in October, 1868—$15,120,000. The capital of these banks at this time was $30,000,000, and they had deposits to the amount of $11,600,000, so that the had ever reached, $45,000,000 of available cash, above the highest point of circulation the circulation represented only one-fifth of the capital which the banks had at their disposal. The Government proposed to allow the banks to continue as they were without any change whatever in their condition, or any further restriction upon their operations until July, 1871, that being the time when their charters expire. The limitation as to time in their charters was, that they should continue till 1st July, 1870, and thence to the end of the next session of Parliament. They therefore, proposed that until the 1st July, 1871, banks should be left in possession of their existing charters, but that after that time they should gradually reduce their circulation by 20 per cent a year, until the circulation should be ultimately entirely based on government securities. Thus for the year ending July, 1872, the banks should be allowed to circulate 80 per cent. of the highest m, that, namely, of October, 1868 ; that ext year they should replace 20 per ceut. their circulation by Government securi- :il in July, 1876, the whole circulation e based on government securities. The n consequence of the gradual and almost atible contraction of the circulation, would lt as injurious to the banks, and would ive them in any sensible degree of the heretofore enjoyed for carrying on the ial operations of the country. It was that this measure would needlessly cur- acilities which the banks now possess for on the business of the country. Well, that in seven years from now the whole on of the country was based upon govern- urities. The average circulation, he had as $12,000,000 ; the average amount of ey held last year was $8,900,000 ; they $3,000,000 of government securities, the ther being about $12,000,000. It was that in return for government securities rnment would return to the banks circu- otos on much the same principle as the bank currency of the United States. s would be of uniform appearance, bear- heir face that they were secured by de- Dominion securities only. They would to be issued by the particular bank to ey were delivered, and would be signed icer of the bank.

lbbe asked whether, as the Bank circula- displaced, it would be compulsory on ;the replace it at once in Government circu-

Mr. Rose—Certainly not. If any Banks confine themselves to carrying on the business of banking, they might do so proposed that the Banks should keep a serve of 20 per cent. of their circulation, a specie reserve equal to one-seventh of ut of deposits at call not bearing interest. sits on call represented the commercial from day to day, and the Government ght it necessary to make a difference in ect between these and the deposits bearing which must be regarded simply as invest- t to which the depositor must assume he same risk as he had with reference to investment. The amount of specie and ent securities which would ultimately be as the reserve for Government notes, and th of the deposits on call, would, on nt basis of circulation and deposits, be 000. Against this, as he had said, the d specie and Government securities, in the amount of about $12,000,000,—leav- made up in cash, during the next seven 900,000. This was but a little over 5½ per annum spread over seven years on the irculation, and rather less than one and r cent. per annum on the average dis- nd would any one tell him that this gra- almost imperceptible contraction was iously to cramp the operations of the

lr. Holton enquired whether the banks at liberty to purchase these securities in market, or whether there would be pre- certain class of securities to be furnished vernment.

lr. Rose said they might purchase the in the open market. He proceeded to the calculation would stand. Instead of rculation, the highest circulation, $15,- as taken, bringing out the result that nce to be made by the banks in 7 years $3,320,000, or 7 9-10 per cent per an- he next seven years on the highest circu- 2½ per cent per annum for the same time ghest discounts. In these calculations included the circulation of Dominion : it was proposed that these should be withdrawn and the present Government isue should be withdrawn. If the specie erve for these Dominion notes, $925,000

was deducted, the amount to be made up would be reduced to $7,400,000, which was a small fraction of over 7 per cent per annum on the highest cir- culation, and a small fraction over 2 per cent per annum on the highest discounts. Mr. Rose pro- ceeded to apply the same mode of calculation to the case of five Ontario banks,—the Bank of To- ronto, Merchants' Bank, Ontario Bank, Royal Canadian Bank and the Bank of Commerce, bring- ing out the result that the difference to be made up by these banks would be $3,717,000, being seven and seven-tenths per cent. per annum for seven years, on their highest circulation, $8,883,- 000, and not quite 3 per cent. per annum for the same time on their highest discounts, $17,771,000. These figures, he contended, proved that this scheme, by its gradual operation, would not cramp the facilities which the banks had to give to their customers and the public. Moreover, he had in these calculations put the matter on most unfavor- sible footing, by assuming that there would be no increase of banking capital and of deposits. But that was not a result to be anticipated. There were at present before the House a number of ap- plications for new Banking Incorporations and for an increase of capital to existing institutions. He might mention, also, that from March, 1862, to March, 1869, while the aggregate circulation of banks had only increased six per cent, their capi- tal had increased 9 per cent and their deposits 90 per cent. It was reasonable to suppose, with the prospects before us, that the increase of capital deposits would go on at a rapid ratio. He then answered the objection that the banks would not be able to afford the additional facilities required dur- ing the three months of the year for moving the crops. He said this would require about $6,000,- 000 which bore a comparatively small proportion to $30,000,000 of deposits and $15,000,000 of capital, and contended that it would pay the banks to keep that amount on hand for autumn, use, as they would be getting the interest for it.

In answer to Mr. Lawson,

Hon. Mr. Rose said that the Dominion notes would be redeemed by each bank issuing them at its head office.

In reply to Mr. Young,

Hon. Mr. Rose said that each bank must redeem its notes at the capital city of the Province where the headquarters of the bank were, the redemption being in fact exactly the same as at present.

Mr. Gibbs asked if bills payable in Halifax were held by a party in Toronto, who wanted to get gold for them, would not the holder either have to pay the rate of exchange or express them there ?

Hon. Mr. Rose—The notes held were legal ten- ders anywhere in the Dominion. Of course, if a merchant, having in his possession that which was as good as gold, chose to send to Halifax for the specie, he must incur the expense of sending it there, but there was no motive in his doing so.

Hon. Mr. Dorion asked whether it was the in- tention of the Government to prevent any of the bank charters from being prolonged.

Hon. Mr. Rose said that all applications for prolongations of charters would go to the Commit- tee on Banking and Commerce, and remain there until the sense of the House was taken with refe- rence to the measure.

Hon. Mr. Wood asked what was to be done in the case of the Bank of British North America, the charter which was placed on a different footing from that of other banks.

Hon. Mr. Rose was under the impression that all the charters expired at the same time, June 1870.

Mr. Lawson said this was not the case. Part of their circulation was under the Free Banking Act.

Hon. Mr. Holton—In the case of these banks, too, the double liability is not in their charter; it would be well if the Finance Minister would ex- plain whether the Government meant the double liability to continue in any case.

Hon. Mr. Rose—The Government proposal is to

continue the charters as they are for a period of ten years—the organization not being touched in any instance.

Sir John A. Macdonald explained that it was the desire of the Government to get an expression of opinion from Parliament this session on the resolutions.

Hon. J. H. Cameron objected to the measure being presented this session. A little, but only a little, of its details had leaked out and become known in the country; and, in his opinion, a more extended time than that day week was required for the discussion of these resolutions in the coun- try. The Government proposition was one which it was said placed a great deal more power, and a great deal more money, in the hands of the Go- vernment than was desirable. Besides the Govern- ment scheme assumed that the banking system of the country was so entirely defective as not to be relied on—an assumption which would be repudi- ated by many commercial men. In coming down with a measure of such great importance, the Government ought to have given stronger reasons for the proposed change than they had done. It was so important a measure, dealing with the whole banking capital of the country, that hon. gentlemen had a right to claim that full opportu- nity should be given the public at large for ex- pressing an opinion on it. One thing was clear, even at this stage, that, so far from asking for such a measure, petitions from all parts of the country had poured in against it.

Commercial.

Toronto Market.

There was no improvement in the general trade of the city during the week, and there is still a good deal of depression, and great caution is ex- ercised in every department. This could not be otherwise under present circumstances. A cer- tain result of the pending change in the banking system of the country will be that of cur- tailing discounts and advances for a short time at least. This will bear with unusual severity on very many wholesale men at the present time, owing to the difficulty of getting in their debts from the country. Apprehension of this acts as a powerful check upon business.

PRODUCE.—Large stocks of breadstuffs in all the principal markets, and most favorable reports of the growing crops from every quarter, has caused a further fall in prices, amounting to 10 or 15 cents per barrel on Flour. The near ap- proach of the warm season tends somewhat in the same direction, though our flour being generally very sound is not exposed to much damage from that cause. Wheat.—Receipts, 26,467 bushels and 29,000 bush. for the corresponding week last year. Stock in store on the 15th 106,750 bush.; sales of spring at 96c., closing at 94c. ; fall sold at 98c. but closed lower. Barley.—No receipts, stock in store on the 15th, 4,500 bush.; market lower ; 2,100 bush. sold at 80c. Oats.—Receipts 4,200 bush. and 2,400 bush. for the corresponding week of last year; stock in store on the 15th, 9,600 bush.; demand active and sales at 55 to 56c. for carloads. Peas.— No receipts ; stock on the 15th, 23,000 bush. ; carlots nominal at 70 to 72c. Corn.—Sales of cars were made at 60c. Seeds.— Timothy dearer and higher, $3 to $3.25.

FLOUR—Receipts, 1,750 brls, and 1,800 brls for the corresponding week of last year ; stock in store on the 15th, 18,631 brls ; market dull and lower ; 1,000 brls No. 1 sold at $4.05, but the market closed with sellers at $4. Spring Wheat —Extra sold at $4.15 ; fancy sold at $4.25 ; there occurred early in the week, since when the mar- ket has been nominal, with a downward tendency. Oatmeal—Small lots of choice $5.75 to $6. Corn- meal—Selling, in small lots, at $3.75 to $4.

PROVISIONS—New crop butter is beginning to arrive, but the market for all grades is dull at quotations. Eggs have met with a good demand at 14c. Cutmeats—Nothing doing in a wholesale way.

GROCERIES—Raw sugars are easier. Teas unchanged.

HIDES—Dull and lower as quoted.

LEATHER—All curried stock is rather easier ; sole keeps firm.

HARDWARE—The enquiry for haying and harvest tools has commenced, which gives a little more activity.

FREIGHTS—Rates of Vessels—3c to Oswego, U. S. C'y, and 2c gold to Kingston ; grain to Montreal, by steamer, 6½c to 7c ; flour, 20c to 25c ; lumber to Oswego, $1.50, greenbacks, per M feet.

The following are the Grand Trunk Railway Company's summer rates from Toronto to the undermentioned stations, which came into force on the 19th ult. :—Flour to all Stations from Belleville to Lynn, inclusive, 25c ; grain, per 100 lbs, 13c ; flour to Prescott, 30c ; grain, 15c ; flour to all stations between Island Pond and Portland, inclusive, 75c ; grain, 38c ; flour to Boston, 80c, gold ; grain, 40c ; flour to Halifax, 90c ; flour to St. John, 85c.

Halifax Market.

BREADSTUFFS—May 11—We quote no change in flours during the past week. Supers continue in active request, at quotations with reduced stocks. Extras dull and nominal, stocks large. Fancy in moderate request at quotations. No. 2 has met with some demand for better description only. Oatmeal offers freely, with only a small local demand.

WHITE WHEAT EXTRA (FALL)—$6.00 to $6.25 ; Fancy $5.60 to $5.70 ; Bakers' Strong $5.50 to $5.60 ; Superfine $5.40 ; No. 2, $4.75 to $5.00. Cornmeal (K. D.) $3.80, F. G. $3.60 to $3.70. Oatmeal $6.50 to $6.75. Rye Flour, $5.85. White Beans $2.50 to $3.00. Round Peas $4.50 ; Split $6.00 to $7.00 per lb.

WEST INDIA PRODUCE.—Molasses and Sugars dull, with only a limited demand. Holders evince considerable anxiety to effect sales, and quotations may be considered nominal. Rum inactive at quotations. Coffee more active ; rates improved. We quote Sugar (V. P.) 10 to 11c. ; Porto Rico, 10½c. ; Cuba — ; Barbadoes, 9½ to 9¾. Molasses, Cienfuegos, 41 ; Demerara, 38 to 40c. Rum 58 to 60c. (in bond). Coffee (Jamaica), 15 to 16c. nominal ; St. Domingo, 12 to 13c.

Exports of Petroleum from the United States, from January 1 to May 11.

	1869.	1868.
From New York,....gals.	18,537,692	14,545,780
Boston	1,013,105	872,594
Philadelphia	6,510,591	9,057,391
Baltimore	469,149	652,517
Portland		19,072
Total export from the U. States	26,530,537	25,147,354
Same time 1867		18,467,852
Same time 1866		16,776,436

Cotton.

Annexed is a statement showing the stocks of cotton in Liverpool and London, and also the stocks of America and Indian produce ascertained to be afloat to those ports :

	1868.	1869.
Stock in Liverpool,..... bales	526,230	351,540
" London	45,520	77,922
American cotton afloat	139,000	182,000
Indian "	255,067	384,658
Total	965,817	1,006,120

Imports and Exports.

The Exports and Imports throughout the Dominion, for the year ending the 30th of June, 1868, were as follows:—

	Total Exports.	Total Imports.
Ontario and Quebec	$47,499,876	$57,805,013
Nova Scotia	5,441,285	9,131,236
New Brunswick	4,626,727	6,523,395
Grand Total	$57,567,888	$73,459,644

STATEMENT OF BANKS

ACTING UNDER CHARTER, FOR THE MONTH ENDING 30TH APRIL, 1869, ACCORDING TO RETURNS FURNISHED BY THE BANKS TO THE AUDITOR OF PUBLIC ACCOUNTS.

EDINBURGH LIFE ASSURANCE COMPANY.

FOUNDED 1823.

THE ONTARIO PEAT COMPANY.

CAPITAL, ... $120,000.

Mercantile.

TORONTO PRICES CURRENT.—MAY 20, 1869.

Name of Article.	Wholesale Rates.		Name of Article.	Wholesale Rate.		Name of Article.	Wholes. Rates
	$ c.	$ c.	**Groceries**—*Contin'd*	$ c.	c.	**Leather**—*Contin'd.*	$ c. $
Boots and Shoes.			Gunpowd'r c. to med ..	55	70	Kip Skins, Patna	0 30 0
Mens' Thick Boots	2 20	2 50	" med. to fine.	70	85	French	0 70 0
" Kip............	2 25	3 00	" fine to fin's't..	85	95	English	0 65 0
" Calf	3 20	3 70	Hyson	0 45	0 80	Hemlock Calf (30 to	
" Congress Gaiters..	1 65	2 50	Imperial	0 42	0 80	35 lbs.) per doz...	0 50 0
" Kip Coloueg's....	1 20	1 40	*Tobacco, Monuf'act'd:*			Do. light	0 45 0
Boys' Thick Boots	1 70	1 80	Can Leaf, ℔ b. 5s & 10s.	0 26	0 30	French Calf........	1 02 1
Youths' "	1 40	1 50	Western Leaf, com ..	0 25	0 26	Grain & Satn Ch'd doz.	0 00 0
Women's Batts	0 95	1 80	" Good	0 27	0 32	Splits, large ℔ b.....	0 30 0
" Balmoral	1 20	1 50	" Fine	0 33	0 35	" small	0 23 0
" Congress Gaiters.	0 90	1 50	" Bright fine...	0 40	0 50	Enamelled Cow ℔ foot.	0 20 0
Misses' Batts	0 75	1 00	" choice..	0 60	0 75	Patent	0 20 0
" Balmoral	1 00	1 30	**Hardware.**			Pebbld Grain	0 15 0
" Congress Gaiters.	1 00	1 30	*Tin (net cash prices)*			Buff	0 14 0
Girls' Batts	0 65	0 85	Block, ℔ b.	0 28	0 00	**Oils.**	
" Balmoral	0 90	1 05	Grain	0 30	0 00	Cod	0 65 0
" Congress Gaiters.	0 75	1 10	*Copper:*			Lard, extra	0 00 0
Children's C. T. Cacks..	0 50	0 65	Pig	0 23	0 24	" No. 1	0 00 0
" Gaiters ..	0 55	0 90	Sheet...........	0 30	0 23	" Woollen	0 00 0
Drugs.			*Cut Nails:*			Lubricating, patent..	0 00 0
Aloes Cape.	0 12½	0 16	Assorted ½ Shingles,			" Mott's economic	0 30 0
Alum................	0 02½	0 03	℔ 100 ℔	2 90	3 00	Linseed, raw........	0 75 0
Borax	0 00	0 00	Shingle alone do ..	3 15	3 25	" boiled.......	0 81 0
Camphor, refined......	0 65	0 70	Lathe and 4 dy......	3 30	3 40	Machinery	0 00 0
Castor Oil...........	0 16½	0 18	*Galvanized Iron:*			Olive, common, ℔ gal..	1 00 1
Caustic Soda........	0 04½	0 05	Assorted sizes......	0 08	0 00	" salad	1 95 2
Cochineal...........	0 90	1 00	Best No. 24........	0 00	0 00	" salad, in bots.	
Cream Tartar	0 40	0 45	" 26.......	0 08	0 08½	" qt. ℔ case....	3 60 3
Epsom Salts	0 03	0 04	" 28.......	0 09	0 00½	Sesame salad, ℔ gal...	1 00 1
Extract Logwood......	0 11	0 12	*Horse Nails:*			Seal, pale..........	0 75 0
Gum Arabic, sorts	0 30	0 35	Guest's or Griffin's			Spirits Turpentine ...	0 62½ 0
Indigo, Madras	0 90	1 00	assorted sizes......	0 00	0 00	Varnish	0 00 0
Licorice	0 14	0 45	For W. ass'd sizes...	0 18	0 19	Whale..............	0 00 0
Madder.............	0 00	0 18	Patent Hammer'd do..	0 17	0 18	**Paints, &c.**	
Galls	0 32	0 37	*Iron (at a month):*			White Lead, genuine	
Opium	12 00	13 50	Pig—Gartsherrie No1..	24 00	25 00	in Oil, ℔ 25 lbs.....	0 00 2
Oxalic Acid........	0 08	0 35	Other brands. No1..	22 00	24 00	Do. No. 1 "	0 00 2
Potash, Bi-tart......	0 25	0 28	" No2..	0 00	0 00	" 2 "	0 00 1
" Bichromate..	0 15	0 20	Bar—Scotch, ℔ 100 ℔..	3 00	3 25	" 3 "	0 00 1
Potass Iodide	3 90	4 50	Refined............	3 50	3 75	White Zinc, genuine..	3 00 3
Senna	0 12½	0 60	Swedes	5 00	5 50	White Lead, dry.....	0 05½ 0
Soda Ash	0 02½	0 04	Hoops—Coopers......	3 25	3 50	Red Lead	0 07½ 0
Soda Bicarb	4 50	5 00	" Band	3 00	3 25	Venetian Red, Eng'h..	0 02½ 0
Tartaric Acid	0 40	0 45	Boiler Plates.......	3 25	3 50	Yellow Ochre, Fren'h..	0 02½ 0
Verdigris	0 35	0 40	Canada Plates.......	3 75	4 00	Whiting	0 80 1
Vitriol, Blue........	0 08	0 10	Union Jack	0 00	0 00	**Petroleum.**	
Groceries.			Pontypool..........	3 25	0 00	(Refined ℔ gal.)	
Coffee:			Swansea	3 90	4 00	Water white, car'l d..	— 0
Java, ℔ lb.	0 22	0 23	*Lead (at a month):*			" small lots..	0 00 0
Laguayra, "	0 17	0 18	Bar, ℔ 100 ℔s......	0 06½	0 07	Straw, by car load...	0 00 0
Rio	0 16	0 17	Sheet "	0 08	0 00	" small lots...	0 00 0
Fish:			Shot...............	0 07½	0 07½	Amber, by car load..	0 00 0
Herrings, Lab. split...	0 00	0 00	*Iron Wire (net cash):*			" small lots...	0 00 0
" round.....	0 00	0 00	No. 6, ℔ bundle.....	2 70	2 80	Benzine	0 00 0
" scaled.....	0 35	0 40	" 9, "	3 10	3 20	**Produce.**	
Mackerel, small kitts...	1 00	0 00	" 12, "	3 40	3 50	*Grain:*	
Loch. Her. wh'd brks..	2 50	2 75	" 16, "	4 30	4 40	Wheat, Spring, 60 ℔..	0 95 0
" half "	1 25	1 50	*Powder:*			" Fall 60 " ..	0 98 1
White Fish & Trout...	None.		Blasting, Canada ...	3 50	0 00	Barley .... 48 " ..	0 90 1
Salmon, saltwater....	14 00	15 00	FF "	4 25	4 50	Peas.......... 60 " ..	0 70 0
Dry Cod, ℔ 112 lbs...	4 75	5 25	FFF "	4 75	5 00	Oats .... 34 " ..	0 54 0
Fruit:			Blasting, English ...	4 00	5 00	Rye .... 56 " ..	0 60 0
Raisins, Layers	2 00	2 10	FF " loose..	5 50	6 00	*Seeds:*	
" M. R.	1 90	2 00	FFF "	6 00	6 50	Clover, choice 60 " ..	5 50 5
" Valentias new..	0 00	0 7	*Pressed Spikes (4 mos):.*			" com'n 68 " ..	5 25 5
Currants, new	0 4½	0 0½	Regular sizes 100..	4 00	4 25	Timothy, cho's 4 " ..	2 75 3
" old.......	0 04	0 04½	Extra "	4 50	5 00	" inf. to good 48 " ..	2 50 2
Figs	0 11	0 12½	*Tin Plates (net cash):*			Flax .... 56 " ..	2 00 2
Molasses:			IC Coke	7 50	8 00	*Flour (per brl.):*	
Clayed, ℔ gal........	0 00	0 35	IC Charcoal........	8 60	9 00	Superior extra......	0 00 4
Syrups, Standard	0 56	0 78	IX "	10 00	11 00	Extra superfine,.....	4 40 4
" Golden	0 60	0 62	IXX "	13 50	14 00	Fancy superfine	4 20 4
Rice:			DC "	8 00	8 50	Superfine No 1.......	4 00 4
Arracan	4 25	4 40	DX "	9 50	0 00	" No. 2..	
Spices:			**Hides & Skins, ℔ ℔.**			Oatmeal, (per brl.)...	5 50 5
Cassia, whole, ℔ ℔. ..	0 00	0 45	Green rough	0 00	0 05½	**Provisions.**	
Cloves	0 11	0 12	Green, salt'd & Insp'd..	0 06½	0 07	Butter, dairy tub ℔ lb.	0 20 0
Nutmegs	0 50	0 55	Cured	0 00	0 00	" store packed.	0 13 0
Ginger, ground	0 20	0 25	Calfskins, green.....	0 00	0 11	Cheese, new	0 14½ 0
" Jamaica, root..	0 20	0 25	Calfskins, cured.....	0 09	0 16½	Pork, mess, per brl...	25 50 26
Pepper, black........	0 12½	0 00	" dry......	0 14	0 00	" prime mess...	
Pimetta	0 08	0 09	Sheepskins,........	1 40	1 75	" prime.......	
Sugars:			" country...	1 00	1 40	Bacon, rough	0 11 0
Port Rico, ℔ lb.......	0 9½	0 10	**Hops.**			" Cumberl'd cut..	0 12 0
Cuba	0 9½	0 10	Inferior, ℔ ℔........	0 00	0 00	" smoked	0 00 0
Barbadoes (bright)...	0 9½	0 10	Medium	0 00	0 00	Hams, in salt	0 12½ 0
Canada Sugar Refne'y,			Good	0 00	0 00	" smoked	0 14 0
yellow No. 2, 60 da..	0 9½	0 10	Fancy	0 00	0 00	Shoulders, in salt ...	0 00 0
Yellow, No. 2½	0 10	0 10½				Lard, in kegs	0 16½ 0
" No. 3......	0 10½	0 10½	**Leather.** ℔ (4 mos.)			Eggs, packed	0 11½ "
Crushed A	0 11½	0 12	In lots of less than			Beef Hams	0 00 0
" AA	0 12	0 12½	50 sides, 10 ℔ cent.			Tallow	0 08 0
Ground	0 12½	0 13	higher.			Hogs dressed, heavy..	0 00 0
Dry Crushed	0 12½	0 13	Spanish Sole, 1st qual'y			" medium..	0 00 0
Extra Ground........	0 13½	0 14	heavy, weights ℔ b..	0 21½	0 22	**Salt, &c.**	
Teas:			Du 1st qual middle do..	0 23	0 00	American brls.......	1 50 1
Japan com'n to good ..	0 48	0 55	No. 2, light weights..	0 22	0 00	Liverpool coarse	0 00 0
" Fine to choicest..	0 50	0 65	Slaughter heavy	0 00	0 24	Goderich...........	0 00 1
Colored, com. to fine..	0 60	0 75	Do. light	0 00	0 00	Plaster	0 90 0
Congou & Souch'ng..	0 45	0 75	Harness, best	0 27	0 00	Water Lime	1 50 0
Oolong, good to fine..	0 50	0 65	" No. 2.......	0 00	0 00		
Y. Hyson, com to gd..	0 47½	0 65	Upper heavy........	0 32	0 35		
Medium to choice ...	0 65	0 80	" light.......	0 35	0 36		
Extra choice	0 85	0 95					

Candles.	$ c.	$ c.
rd & Co.'s ..	$ c.	$ c.
rial........	0 07½	0 08
n Bar	0 07	0 07½
Bar.......	0 07	0 07½
....	0 05	0 05½
....	0 03½	0 03½
....	0 00	0 11
Liquors, &c.		
per doz. qrts.	2 60	2 65
Dub Portr..	2 35	2 40
aica Rum...	1 80	2 25
er's H. Gin..	1 55	1 65
Old Tom.....	1 90	2 00
ases.........	4 00	4 25
Old Tom, c...	6 00	6 25
mmon	1 00	1 25
old	2 00	4 00
common	1 00	1 50
dium........	1 70	1 80
le or golden..	2 50	4 00

	$ c.	$ c
Brandy:		
Hennessy's, per gal..	2 30	2 50
Martell's " ..	2 30	2 50
J. Robin & Co.'s " ..	2 25	2 35
Otard, Dupuy & Cos..	2 25	2 35
Brandy, cases........	8 50	9 00
Brandy, com. per c...	4 00	4 50
Whiskey:		
Common 36 u. p......	0 58	0 60
Old Rye	0 77½	0 80
Malt	0 77½	0 80
Toddy	0 77½	0 80
Scotch, per gal.......	1 90	2 10
Irish—Kinnahan's c...	7 00	7 50
" Dunnville's Belf't..	6 00	6 25
Wool.		
Fleece, lb............	0 28	0 35
Pulled "............	0 22	0 25
Furs.		
Bear........	0 00	0 00
Beaver, ℘ lb........	0 00	0 00
Coon	0 00	0 00
Fisher.............	0 00	0 00
Martin....	0 00	0 0)
Mink..............	0 00	0 00
Otter..............	0 00	0 00
Spring Rats	0 00	0 00
Fox.	0 00	0 00

INSURANCE COMPANIES.

ENGLISH.—*Quotations on the London Market.*

Last Dividend.	Name of Company.	Shares par val £	Amount paid.	Last Sale.
	Briton Medical and General Life ...	10	....	2½
7½	Commer'l Union, Fire, Life and Mar.	50	5	5¾
8	City of Glasgow	25	2½	5¼
9½	Edinburgh Life	100	15	33
5—½ yr	European Life and Guarantee......	2½	11s6	4s. 6d.
10	Etna Fire and Marine............	10	1½	—
5	Guardian	100	50	51½
12	Imperial Fire..................	500	50	352
9½	Imperial Life	100	10	17½
10	Lancashire Fire and Life.........	20	2	2⅜
11	Life Association of Scotland......	40	7½	25
45s. p. sh	London Assurance Corporation ..	25	12½	48 x d
5	London and Lancashire Life	10	1	—
40	Liverp'l & London & Globe F. & L.	20	2	7¾
5	National Union Life	5	1	1
12½	Northern Fire and Life	100	5	12⅝
12 '68, bo 5s.	North British and Mercantile	50	6¼	19½
50	Ocean Marine	25	5	17¾
£5 12s.	Provident Life..................	100	10	35
£4½ p. s.	Phœnix.......................	....	....	145
2½—h. yr.	Queen Fire and Life	10	1	1
3s. bo. 4s	Royal Insurance................	20	3	6¾
10	Scottish Provincial Fire and Life ..	50	2½	5 3-8
25	Standard Life	50	12	66½
5	Star Life	25	1¼	—
	CANADIAN.			℘ c.
4	British America Fire and Marine ..	$50	$25	55½ 56
4	Canada Life	...	....	.....
12	Montreal Assurance	£50	£5	135
3	Provincial Fire and Marine........	60	11	.....
....	Quebec Fire	40	32½	25½ 26
7	" Marine..................	100	40	85 90
6 mo's.	Western Assurance..............	40	9	.....

RAILWAYS.	Sha's	Paid	Montr	London
and St. Lawrence......................	£100	All.	....	56
nd Lake Huron	20½	"	....	2⅜ 3½
do Preference	10	"	....	5 6
ntf. & Goderich, 6℘c., 1872-3-4....	100	"	....	66 69
n and St. Lawrence	....	....	10 11	....
do Pref. 10 ℘ ct..............	....	....	80 85	....
unk	100	"	14 15	14½ 14¾
Eq. G. M. Bds. 1 ch. 6℘c.............	100	"	....	89
First Preference, 5 ℘ c	100	"	....	47
Deferred, 3 ℘ ct..	100	"	....	....
Second Pref. Bonds, 5℘c...........	100	"	....	37
do Deferred, 3 ℘ ct............	100	"	....	....
Third Pref. Stock, 4℘ct...........	100	"	....	28½
do. Deferred, 3 ℘ ct..............	100	"	....	....
Fourth Pref. Stock, 3℘c...........	100	"	....	16
do. Deferred, 3 ℘ ct............	100	"	....	....
stern	20½	"	14 15	15 15½
New	20½	18	....	....
6 ℘ c. Bds, due 1873-76...........	100	All.	....	100½ 102
5½ ℘c Bds. due 1877-78....	100	"	....	95
ilway, Halifax, $250, all......	$250	"	....	....
of Canada, 6 ℘c. 1st Pref. Bds..........	100	"	.. .	82 83

XCHANGE.	Halifax.	Montr'l.	Quebec.	Toronto.
London, 60 days......				
75 days date	12½ 13	9¾ 9¼	8¾ 9¾	9¼
do.	11½ 12	8 9	8¾ 8¾	8½
ith documents...........	....	7 7½	....	....
New York...............	....	28 29	28 28½	28½
do.	....	29 29½	28½ 29	....
s do.	....	par	par ⅛ dis.	par ¼ dis.
....	....	4½ 5	....	3½ to 4½

STOCK AND BOND REPORT.

The dates of our quotations are as follows:—Toronto, May 18; Montreal, May 17; Quebec, May 17; London, May 8.

NAME.	Shares.	Paid up.	Divid'd last 6 Months	Dividend Day.	Closing Prices: Toronto.	Closing Prices: Montre'l	Closing Prices: Quebec.
BANKS.			℘ ct.				
British North America	$250	All.	3	July and Jan.	105 105½	105 105½	105 105½
Jacques Cartier.............	50	"	4	1 June, 1 Dec.	109 110	bks. clsd	bks. clsd
Montreal	200	"	6	"	156 156½	bks. clsd	bks. clsd
Nationale..................	50	"	4	1 Nov. 1 May.	105 106	106 107	106 106½
New Brunswick	100	"	......	......	....	....	....
Nova Scotia	200	28	7&b$3½	Mar. and Sept.	....	....	....
Du Peuple......	50	"	4	1 Mar., 1 Sept.	108 108½	107½ 108½	108 108½
Toronto	100	"	4	1 Jan., 1 July.	118 118½	118 119	117½ 118½
Bank of Yarmouth.........	....	....	......	......	....	....	....
Canadian Bank of Com'e......	50	95	......	......	102½ 103	102¼ 102½	102 102½
City Bank Montreal	80	All.	4	1 June, 1 Dec.	101½ 102	bks. clsd	bks. clsd
Commer'l Bank (St. John)....	100	"	℘ ct.	......	....	....	....
Eastern Townships' Bank....	50	"	4	1 July, 1 Jan..	....	99 101	99½ 100½
Gore	40	...	none.	1 Jan., 1 July.	35 36½	35 37	35 36
Halifax Banking Company....	....	....	......	......	....	....	....
Mechanics' Bank............	50	70	4	1 Nov., 1 May.	93 93½	93 93½	92 93
Merchants' Bank of Canada....	100	70	4	1 Jan., 1 July.	107½ 108	108 108½	108 108½
Merchants' Bank (Halifax)....	....	....	......	......	....	....	....
Molson's Bank...............	50	All.	4	1 Apr., 1 Oct.	108 108½	107½ 108½	108 109
Niagara District Bank........	100	70	3½	1 Jan., 1 July.	....	....	....
Ontario Bank...............	40	All.	4	1 June, 1 Dec.	100½ 101	bks. clsd	bks. clsd
People's Bank (Fred'kton)....	100	"	......	......	....	....	....
People's Bank (Halifax)	20	"	7 12 m	......	....	....	....
Quebec Bank	100	"	3½	1 June, 1 Dec.	102½ 104	bks. clsd	bks. clsd
Royal Canadian Bank	50	60	4	1 Jan., 1 July.	68 70	65 70	70 71
St. Stephens Bank	100	All.	.....	......	....	....	....
Union Bank	100	70	4	1 Jan., 1 July.	106 106½	106 106½	106¾ 107½
Union Bank (Halifax)........	100	40	7 12 mo	Feb. and Aug.	....	....	..
MISCELLANEOUS.							
British America Land........	250	44	2½	......	....	....	....
British Colonial S. S. Co......	250	32½	2½	......	...	....	...
Canada Company	32½	All.	£1 10s.	......	....	....	....
Canada Landed Credit Co.....	50	$20	3½	......	78 80	....	....
Canada Per. B'ldg Society....	50	All.	5	......	125½ 126	....	....
Canada Mining Company.....	4	90	......	......	....	....	....
Do. Inl'd Steam Nav. Co....	100	All.	7	......	....	103 105	....
Do. Glass Company.........	100	"	12½ "	......	....	40 60	....
Canad'n Loan & Investm't....	25	2½	7	......	....	....	....
Canada Agency	10	½	......	......	....	....	....
Colonial Securities Co........	...	....	......	......	....	....	....
Freehold Building Society....	100	All.	4	......	112½ 114	....	....
Halifax Steamboat Co........	100	"	5	......	....	....	....
Halifax Gas Company........	....	....	......	......	....	....	....
Hamilton Gas Company......	....	....	......	......	....	....	....
Huron Copper Bay Co........	4	12	20	......	....	30 45	....
Lake Huron S. and C.........	5	102	......	......	....	....	....
Montreal Mining Consols......	20	$15	......	......	....	3.25 3.45	...
Do. Telegraph Co...	40	All.	5	......	134 134½	134 135	134 135
Do. Elevating Co...	00	"	15 12 m	......	....	102½ 105	....
Do. City Gas Co.........	40	"	4	15 Mar. 15 Sep.	....	135 136	134 135
Do. City Pass. R. Co.....	50	"	4	......	....	108 109	108 109
Quebec and L. S.	8	$4	......	......	....	....	....
Quebec Gas Co..............	200	All.	4	1 Mar., 1 Sep.	....	...	118 119
Quebec Street R. R	50	25	3	......	....	....	90 91
Richelieu Navigation Co......	100	All.	10 p.a.	1 Jan., 1 July.	....	114 116	112 114
St. Lawrence Glass Company.	100	"	....	......	....	80 85	....
St. Lawrence Tow Boat Co.....	100	"	......	3 Feb.	....	...	30 35
Tor'to Consumers' Gas Co.....	50	"	4	1 My Au Mar Fe	107 107½	...	105 106
Trust & Loan Co. of U. C.....	20	5	3	......	....	....	....
West'n Canada Bldg Soc'y....	50	All.	5	......	120½ 121	....	....

SECURITIES.	London.	Montreal.	Quebec.	Toronto.
Canadian Gov't Deb. 6 ℘ ct. stg..................	....	102 103	101 101½	102 103
Do. do. 6 do due Ja. & Jul. 1877-84........	104½ 105½	....	....	....
Do. do. 6 do. Feb. & Aug..........	102 104	....	...	....
Do. do. 6 do. Mch. & Sep..........	102 104	....	...	....
Do. do. 5 ℘ ct. cur., 1883	93¾ 94½	91 92½	92 93	93 94½
Do. do. 5 do. stg., 1885	93½ 94	91 92½	92½ 93	93 94½
Do. do. 7 do. cur., ...	....	....	......	....
Dominion 6 p. c. 1878 cy..........................	....	107½ 108½	107½ 108½	107½ 108
Hamilton Corporation..............................	....	....	......	....
Montreal Harbor, 8 ℘ ct. d. 1869.....................	..	....	......	....
Do. do. 7 do. 1870....................	....	....	......	....
Do. do. 6½ do. 1883....................	....	102 103	......	102 103
Do do. 6½ do. 1873....................	....	....	......	....
Do. Corporation, 6 ℘ c. 1891	....	96 96½	96½ 97	96 96½
Do. 7 p. c. stock..............................	....	108½ 110	109 110	109 110
Do. Water Works, 6 ℘ c. stg. 1878..............	....	96½ 97	......	96 96½
Do. do. 6 do. cy. do.	....	....	......	96 97
New Brunswick, 6 ℘ ct., Jan. and July	104 104½	....	......	....
Nova Scotia, 6 ℘ ct., 1875..........................	103 104	...	......	....
Ottawa City 6 ℘ c. d. 1880	....	95 97	......	....
Quebec Harbour, 6 ℘ c. d. 1883.....................	....	....	60	....
Do. do. 7 do. do........................	....	....	65 70	....
Do. do 8 do. 1886......................	...	....	80 85	....
Do. City, 7 ℘ c. d. 1½ years......................	....	....	98 98½	....
Do. do. 7 do. 3 do.	....	....	91 92	....
Do. do. 7 do. 4 do.	....	....	94 95	....
Do. Water Works, 7 ℘ ct., 3 years	....	....	97 97½	....
Do. do. 6 do. 1½ do.	....	....	94 95	....
Toronto Corporation	....	92 94	....	....

Insurance.

Briton Medical and General Life Association,

with which is united the

BRITANNIA LIFE ASSURANCE COMPANY.

Capital and Invested Funds............£750,000 Sterling.

ANNUAL INCOME, £220,000 STG. :

Yearly increasing at the rate of £25,000 Sterling.

THE important and peculiar feature originally introduced by this Company, in applying the periodical Bonuses, so as to make Policies payable during life, without any higher rate of premiums being charged, has caused the success of the BRITON MEDICAL AND GENERAL to be almost unparalleled in the history of Life Assurance. *Like Policies on the Profit Scale become payable during the lifetime of the Assured, thus rendering a Policy of Assurance a means of subsistence in old age, as well as a protection for a family,* and a more valuable security to creditors in the event of early death; and effectually meeting the often urged objection, that persons do not themselves reap the benefit of their own prudence and forethought.

No extra charge made to members of Volunteer Corps for services within the British Provinces.

☞ TORONTO AGENCY, 5 KING ST. WEST.

Oct 17—9-1yr   JAMES FRASER, *Agent.*

BEAVER
Mutual Insurance Association,

HEAD OFFICE.—20 TORONTO STREET, TORONTO.

INSURES LIVE STOCK against death from any cause. The only Canadian Company having authority to do this class of business.

E. C. CHADWICK, President.

W. T. O'REILLY, Secretary.   8-1y-25

HOME DISTRICT
Mutual Fire Insurance Company.

Office.—North-West Cor. Yonge & Adelaide Streets, TORONTO.—(UP STAIRS.)

INSURES Dwelling Houses, Stores, Warehouses, Merchandise, Furniture, &c.

PRESIDENT—The Hon. J. McMURRICH.
VICE-PRESIDENT—JOHN BURNS, Esq.
            JOHN RAINS, Secretary.

AGENTS:
DAVID WRIGHT, Esq., Hamilton; FRANCIS STEVENS, Esq., Barrie; Messrs. GIBBS & BRO., Oshawa.   3-1y

THE PRINCE EDWARD COUNTY
Mutual Fire Insurance Company

HEAD OFFICE.—PICTON, ONTARIO.
President, L. B. STINSON; Vice-President, W. A. RICHARDS.
Directors: A. McFaul, James Cavan, James Johnson, N. S. DeMill, William Delong.—Secretary. John Twigg; Treasurer, David Barker; Solicitor, R. J. Fitzgerald.

THIS Company is established upon strictly Mutual principles, insuring farming and isolated property, (not hazardous,) in Townships only, and offers great advantages to insurers, at low rates for five years, without the expense of a renewal.
Picton, June 15, 1868.   9-1y

THE AGRICULTURAL
Mutual Assurance Association of Canada.

HEAD OFFICE........................LONDON, ONT

A purely Farmers' Company. Licensed by the Government of Canada.

Capital, 1st January, 1869.....	$230,103 82
Cash and Cash Items, over.....	$36,000 00
No. of Policies in force.......	30,592 00

THIS Company insures nothing more dangerous than Farm property. Its rates are as low as any well-established Company in the Dominion, and lower than those of a great many. It is largely patronised, and continues to grow in Public favor.
For Insurance, apply to any of the Agents or address the Secretary, London, Ontario.
London, 2nd Nov., 1868.   12-1y.

Insurance.

The Gore District Mutual Fire Insurance Company

GRANTS INSURANCES on all description of Property against Loss or Damage by FIRE. It is the only Mutual Fire Insurance Company which assesses its Policies yearly from their respective dates; and the average yearly cost of insurance in it, for the past three and a half years, has been nearly

TWENTY CENTS IN THE DOLLAR

less than what it would have been in an ordinary Proprietary Company.

THOS. M. SIMONS, Secretary & Treasurer.

ROBT. McLEAN, Inspector of Agencies.
Galt, 25th Nov., 1868.   15-1y

Western Assurance Company,

INCORPORATED 1851.

CAPITAL, ... $400,000.

FIRE AND MARINE.

HEAD OFFICE.................TORONTO, ONTARIO.

DIRECTORS.
Hon. JNO. McMURRICH. President.
            CHARLES MAGRATH, Vice-President.
A. M. SMITH, Esq.   JOHN FISKEN, Esq.
ROBERT BEATY, Esq.   ALEX. MANNING, Esq.
JAMES MICHIE, Esq.   N. BARNHART, Esq.
            R. J. DALLAS, Esq.
B. HALDAN, Secretary.
J. MAUGHAN, JR., Assistant Secretary.
WM. BLIGHT, Fire Inspector.
CAPT. G. T. DOUGLAS, Marine Inspector.
JAMES PRINGLE, General Agent.

Insurances effected at the lowest current rates on Buildings, Merchandize, and other property, against loss or damage by fire.
On Hull, Cargo and Freight against the perils of Inland Navigation.
On Cargo Risks with the Maritime Provinces by sail or steam.
On Cargoes by steamers to and from British Ports.
WESTERN ASSURANCE COMPANY'S OFFICE, }
TORONTO, 1st April, 1869.   }   33-1y

Fire and Marine Assurance.

THE BRITISH AMERICA
ASSURANCE COMPANY.
HEAD OFFICE:
CORNER OF CHURCH AND COURT STREETS.
TORONTO.

BOARD OF DIRECTION :
Hon G. W. Allan, M L C.,   A. Joseph, Esq.,
George J. Boyd, Esq.,   Peter Paterson, Esq.,
Hon. W. Cayley,   G. P. Ridout, Esq.,
Richard S. Cassels, Esq.,   E. H. Rutherford, Esq,
            Thomas C. Street, Esq.

Governor:
GEORGE PERCIVAL RIDOUT, Esq.
Deputy Governor:
PETER PATERSON, Esq.
Fire Inspector: Marine Inspector:
E. ROBY O'BRIEN.   CAPT. R. COURNEEN.

Insurances granted on all descriptions of property against loss and damage by fire and the perils of inland navigation.
Agencies established in the principal cities, towns, and ports of shipment throughout the Province.
THOS. WM. BIRCHALL,
28-1y   *Managing Director.*

Queen Fire and Life Insurance Company,
OF LIVERPOOL AND LONDON,
ACCEPTS ALL ORDINARY FIRE RISKS
on the most favorable terms.

LIFE RISKS

Will be taken on terms that will compare favorably with other Companies.

CAPITAL,   -   -   -   £2,000,000 Stg.

CHIEF OFFICE—Queen's Buildings, Liverpool, and Gracechurch Street London.
CANADA BRANCH OFFICE—Exchange Buildings, Montreal.
Resident Secretary and General Agent,
A. MACKENZIE FORBES.
13 St. Sacrament St., Merchants' Exchange, Montreal.
WM. ROWLAND, Agent, Toronto.   1-1y

Insurance

The Waterloo County Mutual Fire Insur Company.

HEAD OFFICE : WATERLOO, ONTARIO.

ESTABLISHED 1863.

THE business of the Company is divided into separate and distinct branches, the
VILLAGE, FARM, AND MANUFACTU
Each Branch paying its own losses and its just prop of the managing expenses of the Company.
C. M. TAYLOR, Sec.   M. SPRINGER, M.M.P., P
            J. HUGHES, Inspector.

Etna Fire and Marine Insurance Compa Dublin.

AT a Meeting of the Shareholders of this Com held at Dublin, on the 13th ult., it was agreed the business of the "ETNA" should be transferred t UNITED FIRE AND GENERAL INSURANCE COMP In accordance with this agreement, the business will after be carried on by the latter Company, which ass and guarantee all the risks and liabilities of the "E
The Directors have resolved to continue the CANA BRANCH, and arrangements for resuming FIRE and MINE business are rapidly approaching completion.
16   T. W. GRIFFITH
                                MANAG

Lancashire Insurance Compan

CAPITAL, - - - - - - - - £2,000,000 Ste

FIRE RISKS
Taken at reasonable rates of premium, and
ALL LOSSES SETTLED PROMPTLY,
By the undersigned, without reference elsewhe
            S. C. DUNCAN-CLARK & CO.,
            General Agents for Ontario,
            N. W. Corner of King & Church Stre
25-1y   TORONTO.

DIVISION OF PROFITS NEXT YE₄

ASSURANCES

EFFECTED BEFORE 30TH APRIL NEXT,

. IN THE .

Canada Life Assurance Compa

OBTAIN A YEAR'S ADDITIONAL PROFITS

OVER LATER ENTRANTS,

And the great success of the Company warrants the rectors in recommending this very important advantage to assurers.

SUMS ASSURED	$5,30(
AMOUNT OF CAPITAL AND FUNDS......	1,90(
ANNUAL INCOME..................	20(

Assets (exclusive of uncalled capital) for each $10 liabilities, about $150.
The income from interest upon investments is alone sufficient to meet claims by death.
            A. G. RAMSAY, Manager.
            E. BRADBURNE, Agent
Feb. 1!   1y   Toronto Stree

The Victoria Mutual
FIRE INSURANCE COMPANY OF CANADA.

Insures only Non-Hazardous Property, at Low Ra

BUSINESS STRICTLY MUTUAL.

GEORGE H. MILLS, *President.*
W. D. BOOKER, *Secretary.*

HEAD OFFICE ....HAMILTON, ONTAR
aug 15-1yr

PUBLISHED AT THE OFFICE OF THE MONETA TIMES, No. 60 CHURCH STREET.
PRINTED AT THE DAILY TELEGRAPH PUBLISHING HOU BAY STREET, CORNER OF KING.

THE CANADIAN

ΛONETARY TIMES

AND

INSURANCE CHRONICLE.

:VOTED TO FINANCE, COMMERCE, INSURANCE, BANKS, RAILWAYS, NAVIGATION, MINES, INVESTMENT, PUBLIC COMPANIES, AND JOINT STOCK ENTERPRISE.

II—NO. 41.   TORONTO, THURSDAY, MAY 27, 1869.   SUBSCRIPTION $2 A YEAR.

Mercantile.

Meetings.

COMMERCIAL UNION ASSURANCE CO.

The annual general meeting of the company was held on Tuesday, the 9th March, 1869. The report and accounts for the year were submitted :—

The Directors of the Commercial Union Assurance Company have the satisfaction to report to their shareholders that the improvement exhibited in 1867 has been maintained during the past year.

The revision of the risks in the Fire branch alluded to in the last report has been continued, and it is satisfactory to the Directors that the reduction of premium income, thereby entailed has been compensated by new premiums on risks of a better character. The balance in hand is in excess of that carried down last year, while the losses outstanding amount to £8,000 as against £11,000 on 31st December, 1867.

With respect to the Life branch the Directors have to state that since their last report the Actuary's valuation has been completed, and that in accordance therewith the sum of £41,000 has been distributed out of profits for the period ending 31st December, 1867. One-fifth of this amount, or £8,200, belonged to shareholders, and was transferred to their account ; the balance £32,-800 belonged to the policy holders and was equivalent on an average to a reversionary addition of over £2 2s per cent. per annum on the sums assured.

The business for the year 1868 was as follows:— 508 policies were effected, assuring £306,670, and yielding £10,186 in new premiums. The claims were 14, amounting to £18,532, of which £5,080 was re-assured.   Of the net claims £5,100 had accrued in 1867, as stated in the last report, whereas only 6 for £2,150 were outstanding on the 31st December last. The Directors have to notice the maturing of endowment assurance policies for £30,000, which closes some large and profitable transactions.   The charges connected with the valuation and distribution of the bonus are included in the expenses of management.

The business of the Marine branch continues steadily to progress. Notwithstanding the general depression in trade, the premium income has been maintained. The outstanding liabilities on 31st December, 1868, were considerably less than at the end of 1867, while the balance had increased by upwards of £30,000.

The Directors recommend the distribution of a dividend at the rate of 5 per cent. and a bonus of 2s 6d per share, free of income tax, being 7¼ per cent. on the paid up capital of the company.

The Directors have to record, with deep regret, the loss of three of their esteemed colleagues, Mr. D. Hart, and Mr. J. Humphery, by death, and of Mr. J. K. Welch by retirement.

The Directors [have elected to seats at the Board Mr. Alfred Giles and Mr. Alexander Robertson, whose influence will, they believe, largely promote the interests of the company. Resolutions confirmatory of their election, will be submitted to the general meeting.

In accordance with the provisions of the deed of settlement, the following Directors retire by rotation, viz., Messrs. Coleman, Griffiths, Hanson, Harris and Leaf, who offer themselves for re-election.

The Auditors, Messrs. Milnes, Tate and Porter offer themselves for re-election.

By order of the Board.

ALEX. SUTHERLAND, *Secretary.*

Life Account.

From 1st January to 31st December, 1868.

Dr.		£	s.	d.
To Liabilities under Assurance, Annuity, and Endowment Policies, as per Actuary's Valuation		129,694	0	0
" Surplus in Cash, exclusive of Interest accrued, and other outstanding Assets		39,929	8	7
Being Balance from 1869	£159,623	8	7	
" Premiums new £10,186 16	4			
" re-newals	48,211 2 1			
		58,397	18	5
" Interest		6,654	17	10
" Consideration for Annuity		452	5	0
" Fines for Extension of Time		39	2	5
		£235,157	12	3

Cr.		£	s.	d.
By Claims with Bonus additions £16,532 2 0				
Less received under Reassurances 5,080 0 0				
		11,452	2	0
" Shareholders' Proportion of Profits		8,200	0	0
" Bonuses paid in Cash		6,082	7	7
" Endowment Assurance Policies matured		30,000	0	0
" Re-assurances		7,697	7	9
" Annuities		782	17	0
" Surrenders		1,741	9	2
" Commu. less received on reassurances		1,975	12	3
" Bad Debts by Agents		9	13	0
" Expenses of Management		4,777	18	8
" Balance		162,488	4	10
		£235,157	12	3

All investments on account of life fund are made in the names of the Life Trustees.

General Account.

From 1st January to 31st December, 1868.

Dr.		£	s.	d.
To Balance of Fire Account		31,721	15	2
" do. Marine Account		232,155	8	1
" Interest		10,149	0	11
" Transfer Fees		89	17	6
" Shareholders' proportion of Profits of Life Department £8,200 0 0				
Less Bonus paid 6,250 0 0				
		1,950	0	0
		£276,016	1	8

Cr.		£	s.	d.
By Remuneration to Directors and Auditors		4,710	0	0
" Salaries—				
Head Office......£2,673 9 5				
Branches....... 2,544 13 10		6,218	3	3
By Rent and Taxes—				
Head Office...... 3,690 15 3				
Branch Offices. 1,148 10 1		4,838	11	4
By Freehold Offices, Cornhill—				
Amount written off this Account		1,695	2	1
By Advertising, Printing, and Stationery...... 1,672 12 5				
" Travelling Postages and Parcels ·673 12 2				
" Law Expense... 130 5 7				
" Local Boards, and Agents expenses........... 3,828 3 1				
" Messengers, Servants, and Miscellaneous...... 832 9 6		7,101	2	9
By Balance....................		252,453	2	3
		£276,016	1	8

The Chairman John Bonstead, Esq., then made the following statement in moving the adoption of the Report :—

On the occasion of our last meeting, we had reason to congratulate ourselves upon the improved prospects of the company. I think it is again a matter of congratulation that a like measure of prosperity has characterized our transactions in the past year. Our increased premiums indicate that our place in the confidence of the public has been maintained, and our increased balances show that the business we have secured has been of a remunerative character. The accounts of our several departments are in the usual form, and call for little remark. In the Fire Account the premiums of 1868 show an increase of about £3,000 over those of 1867. The average percentage of loss is rather higher, but still below the estimated average. Some sections of the business have resulted most favourably ; others, though in no case entailing a loss, have not yielded an equal profit. As in the first, we think we recognize the consequence of that careful elimination of hazardous risks referred to in the report, so we believe that the application of the same principles to other sections of business will tend to establish more uniform results in all, and a lower percentage of loss than has yet been attained in the transactions of the Fire branch. [Hear, hear.] It will be satisfactory to you to know that the premiums received since the 1st January, have sufficed to meet the claims of £8,000 outstanding at that date, and all losses that have occurred since. In the Life Department our report refers to two subjects of the greatest interest in connection with that branch, viz., the appropriation of the first bonus declared, and the progress of the business during 1868. The allocation of the bonus, and the various methods of distribution were so fully explained last year that it only remains for me to state that the satisfaction which it was expected the policy holders would feel at the addition made to their policies has been fully realized. If our shareholders and our policy holders will bear in mind that the Life Reserve of the office is proportionately larger than that of most other Assurance Companies, and its bonus amongst the largest ever declared, and will do their best to impress this point upon their connections, their is no doubt that a large increase of business would result to us during the present year (Hear, hear.) On reference to the business of 1868, it will be seen that the policies affected were 508 in number, as compared with 439 of the previous year, and the total sum assured was £290,- 760 in 1867. The new premiums are slightly less

owing to the average of the lives assured being less, but the amount of business is actually greater. The claims which have arisen in the year have again been very small, for out of the £16,000 paid, re-assurances gave us £5,000, and a further sum of £3,000 which accrued during 1867, was deducted from the assets before the bonus was declared, so that the claims accrued and paid during 1868 amounted to only £8,000. To this should be added £2,000 outstanding on 31st December last, making a total for the year of £8,000. The importance and value of this circumstance will be best appreciated when I state that the claims expected and provided for (mind, I say provided for,) at the valuation were £20,000 ; in other words, we made a provision of £12,000 in excess of the amount that we have been called upon to pay. (Hear, hear.) There has been an additional source of profit in the falling in of the largest annuity granted by the office. The annuity was for £150, and the sum of £3,284 was reserved in respect to it at the valuation in the beginning of the year. The changes of management show an increase over preceding years ; but, as mentioned in the report, the increase is owing chiefly to the expenses in connection with the valuation and bonus. There is one other feature deserving notice, and that is, the direct business effected at the Head Office, where the character of the company is best known, and where the advantages it offers can be best tested, is greater than the total amount received from all the branches and all the agencies. To those but little acquainted with the company, this circumstance should give the assurance that if they strive to know us better, they will not know us worse. (Cheers.) The events of the past year, otherwise so favorable, have been clouded by the deaths of our esteemed colleagues Mr. David Hart and Mr. Humphery. Their long connection with the company, and their watchful care of its interests, render the circumstances of their removal from amongst us peculiarly sad to the directors, who have been associated with them from the first promotion of the company. (Hear, hear.) The directors have elected Mr. Giles, who will be recognised among us at our annual general meetings as one of our largest shareholders, and who has at all times shown himself to be well versed in our accounts, and to possess a thorough knowledge of our proceedings. In Mr. Alexander Robertson we have a Director of the National Provincial Bank of England, whose experience in that capacity, and whose great influence must contribute to the interests of our company. (Cheers.) The only other subject to which I need advert, is in connection with the dividend and bonus, which we ask you to confirm at the rate together of 7½ per cent. Our recommendation of the dividend is based upon the fact that after providing the £18,750, that it will absorb, and making ample provision for our liabilities on the Fire and Marine accounts, (I purposely except the Life account, as all the liabilities in connection therewith are provided for by special funds in the names of separate trustees), I say that after making ample provision for Fire and Marine liabilities, there will still remain a very large reserve. The circumstance that the balance is much in excess of our liabilities, may possibly have originated a whisper that has reached us that some of our shareholders looked for a higher dividend than the 7½ per cent. we propose to recommend for your confirmation. There are one or two reasons, however, that should induce us to a certain self restraint in this matter. We do not feel justified in appropriating towards dividend or bonus any portion of the sums that have come into our hands in respect to liabilities we have undertaken, so long as those liabilities are undischarged. When those liabilities have run off, then, and not till then, will a certain proportion of the sums which remain in our hands become properly available for distribution. Again we must remember that credit abroad is the very breath of existence to an Assurance company, and that upon the maintenance of this credit must depend the extension of our business, and the

opportunity of increasing our dividends in future. No directorate, however influential, proprietary, however wealthy, can ever influ the insuring world in a degree equal to ties that a company possesses large and adequate reserves. (Cheers.) Names and reputations nothing compared with balances in h (Cheers.)

The comments of the shareholders upon report and accounts were chiefly of a congratula character, and it is not necessary therefore record them.

In the evening, says an exchange, Directors—not the Company—gave a dinner which several bankers and men of high comme standing were invited, and among the guests Sir G. E. Cartier, Bart., and the Hon. Wm. Dougall, C. B., who sat on the right and lef the Chairman. Among the toasts, that of "I perity to the Colonies" was proposed by Mr. L worthy, one of the Directors, who remarked most men of property in England had a direc terest in the colonies, and he might venture to that every other gentleman in the room der from them a large portion of his income. Ad ing especially in Canada, he considered that ng the model dependency of England, who view das to its population, system of educa loyalty to the mother country, or lightne taxation.

Sir George E. Cartier responded to the t and observed that the prosperity of the n country was implied in that of the colonies. I ever important Canada was to England at the sent time, it was destined to become of much importance in the future, as Canadians had d mined to extend their territory from the Atl to the Pacific, and to assume in America the tion, without the despotism, of Russia in Eu He insisted upon the loyalty of Canada, and s that should a disagreement arise between Eng and the United States, the Canadians were prepared to fight the battles of England Canadian territory. He concluded with the that the success which the 'Commercial Union achieved in England might be equalled by success in Canada.

The Hon Wm. MacDougall proposed "I perity to the Commercial Union Assurance C pany," and said that, having the pleasure to k the Company's representative in Canada, he beli the Branch there could not help progressing v it continued so ably directed. Alluding to distress which the scheme of Assurance tend mitigate, he spoke at length upon the subje emigration as a powerful means of lessening pe and misery, and directed attention to the fru territory of Hudson's Bay, which, if it were pos ed by Canada, only awaited labourers to be one of the most fertile regions in the world.

MONTREAL AND CHAMPLAIN RAILW

The following is the report of the director the year ended 31st Dec., 1868 :—

The accounts for the year 1868, which are pended to this report, show that the propo of net revenue due to this company, under agreement with the Grand Trunk Company, amounted to the sum of £98,663.56. The am accruing under the lease, for the year 1866, $72,013.02, showing an improvement during year 1868 of $18,050.47. The amount earne 1868, is very nearly sufficient to meet the int on bonds, and pay the dividend on ten per preferred stock. The large extent of rene rendered necessary upon the amalgamated l has rendered the amount of net profit below would otherwise have been the case. The acc have been examined by the joint committee provided for by the agreement—and they r that they are satisfied that justice has been both to the line and rolling stock during the twelve months, within the meaning of the t of an amalgamation of the two companies.

and rolling stock are now in excellent
u, a very large amount having been ex-
uring the last two years upon the bridge
.le, the abutments of which were falling
The amount at the credit of the Sinking
now $28,541.87.
(Signed) JAMES FERRIER, President.

Capital Account at Dec. 31st, 1868.
DR.

Property	$2,384,376	19
Stores, Stock	33,111	22
of Capital Account	200	92
	$2,417,688	33

CR.

ated Stock	$1,130,275	00
l Stock	404,600	00
rtgage Bonds	80,300	00
ated Loan $882,813 33		
o in hand for		
Retirement of		
g. Bonds 80,300 00		
	802,513	33
	$2,417,578	33

Revenue Account, 1868.
DR.
at debit of Revenue, Dec.

67	$21,669	88
Account	597	79
al Expenses	789	61
on Bonds	50,574	40
l Stock Dividends	40,460	00
on Sinking Fund	1,615	57
	$115,657	25

CR.

count	$90,663	56
at debit of Revenue	24,993	69
	$115,657	25

eneral Balances at Dec. 31st, 1868.
DR.
ce at debit of Revenue $24,993 69
Assets.

lidated Bonds, available ...	39,966	68
ge Irving	1,000	00
n, Mills, Currie & Co	18,825	24
	$84,725	61

CR.
ce of Capital Account $200 92
Liabilities.

(over draft)	. 163	70
rred Stock Dividends unpaid	10,115	00
st on Bonds	24,354	31
red Stock Sinking Fund ...	28,541	87
payable	10,000	00
y & Rutherford	3,897	05
Guy	1,100	00
Trunk Railway	6,942	76
	$84,725	61

led and found correct.
T. MORLAND, W. SACHE, Auditors.
flot was taken for the election of Direc-
ie current year, and the following gentle-
found to have been elected: Hon. James
l. J. Brydges, W. E. Phillips, Hugh Al-
am Molson, E. H. King, Johnston Thom-
ard M. Hopkins, Gilbert Scott. The
uditors (Messrs. Thomas Morland and
Sache) were unanimously re-elected. At
ent meeting of the newly appointed Di-
le Hon. James Ferrier was elected Presi-
liam Molson, Esq., Vice-President, and
ickson, Esq., Secretary of the Company
rrent year.

AND GOSFORD RAILWAY.—The first
f the newly elected Board took place
, when H. G. Joly, Esq., was elected
and Henry Fry, Esq., Vice-President.

Insurance.

FIRE RECORD.—Mitchell, Ont., May 19.—A
fire broke out in the large flour mill owned by
Francis Holland, totally destroying the building
and contents. Loss $9,000 ; insured for $3,850
in the Liverpool and London and Globe, and
$5,000 in the Ætna of Hartford. The Western
had $1,000 on the contents. Cause unknown.

Whitby, May 19. —The driving house and barn
owned by Wm. Blair, was burnt to the ground.
It contained two horses. Insured in the Beaver
Mutual Co.

Meaford, May 16.—Foundry of D. Sinclair ; he
estimates his loss at $5,000·; insured in the Gore
District and Provincial.

Peterborough, May 17.—House of A. W. Kempt
destroyed by fire ; covered by insurance.

Wawanosh, Co. Huron, March 12.—The barn
of James Deacon, 10th con., caught fire from some
stumps, and was totally consumed ; lost a very
valuable span of horses, a fanning mill, part of a
threshing machine, and some hay. No insurance.

Euphrasia Township, Co. Grey, May 14.—The
house of William Wilson, 10th con., was destroyed.
No insurance.

Sarawak Township, Ont., May 12.—Barn and
stable, with contents, of Wm. Garvie; loss $800 ;
insured for $220.

St. Catharines, May 20.—A building connected
Mr. Ollie's machine shop; loss stated at $1,000;
without insurance.

Bothwell, May 24 —A telegram says:—Another
very destructive fire took place here to-day, level-
ling with the ground the American House, Lebu's
Livery Stable, Mr. Brady's dwelling-house, the
New England Dining-room, the Pepper Well
Office, the Great Western Buildings, comprising
Station House, Freight House, Baggage Room,
Tank House, and Western Wood Shed. In the
latter were two engines which were also destroyed.
The cause of the fire is as yet unknown ; but supposed to be the work of an incendiary, from the
fact of its having originated in the roof of the
American House, which was unoccupied at the
time. Great credit is due to those present, in
the manner in which they exerted themselves.
The loss is estimated at between $15,000 and $20,-
000. Few Insurances.

Toronto, May.—House of Unwin & Kirkpatrick, Seaton street; loss about $3,000 on
building and contents; insured in Toronto Mutual
for $1,000.

Whitby, May.—Barn of Daniel Holliday, reported last week, was insured in the Beaver
Mutual for $400.

In response to our invitation to insurance agents
to send information, we have the following batch
of fires from an obliging agent:—

Thomas Campbell, lot 11, 7th con. Hope; barn
burned; loss $800 ; insurance had expired in the
Agricultural Mutual. Campbell thought insurance a humbug; suppose it to be set on fire by parties stealing grain.

Richard Morton, lot 15, 5th con. Hope; barn
and stable burned. Insured in Agricultural Mutual for $230. · Cause either smoking or children
playing with matches; (total) $500, or about.

Mrs. Rowland, lot 25, 1st con. Manvers; barn
burned. Insured in either Beaver Mutual, or
Canada Farmers, for $150; cause unknown.

Francis Early, of Orono (Clarke township), had
barn in Manvers barned. I hear it was insured.

INSURANCE IN PRINCE EDWARD ISLAND.—In
the Annual Report of the Charlottetown Mutual
Fire Insurance Company it is stated that all
foreign insurance offices have withdrawn except
one, and it seemed doubtful if that office would
remain after some pending claims have been settled. The Directors state that the Company has
been in operation twenty years. After the great
fire which occurred in July, 1866, burning down
nearly one-fourth of the business part of Charlottetown, this company has only been obliged to levy
one per cent. and had the company not have re-

turned a bonus of one half year's premium to
policy holders a short time previous, it would not
have been obliged to levy even the one per cent.
and it must be borne in mind that many of the
old policy holders are insured at half per cent.

—One Walsh recently sued the Waterloo Mutual Insurance Co. on a policy covering a barn on
his premises. The company resisted payment.
The case came on at the Woodstock assizes some
time since, and a verdict was rendered for the defendants. Walsh's criminality in connection with
the burning was proved beyond a doubt. So
strong was the evidence, that the Judge ordered
the arrest of Walsh when the trial was over. The
company deserves credit for having, at the risk of
becoming unpopular, defeated the swindle attempted by this knave.

LIVE STOCK INSURANCE COMPANIES.

The last of these companies has disappeared
from its field of operations, and as its light went
out an impression went abroad that there exists no
sound basis on which to establish such a class of
risks. But the disasters of these companies were
chiefly attributable to their own incaution, by
which the worthless cattle of a band of knaves
were admitted to protection, and the ample funds
provided for better purposes were squandered in
remunerating unscrupulous policy holders for the
loss of animals, more than half of which had been
assisted in their passage to the grave.

The pioneer company, the Hartford Live Stock
Insurance Company—was chartered by the Legislature of Connecticut, in May, 1866, with a capital
of five hundred thousand dollars, of which one
hundred thousand dollars were deposited with the
State Treasurer. At the start premiums flowed in
plentifully, and the stockholders were highly delighted at the apparent success in this hitherto
unexplored field of commerce. In the following
January the assets of the company were reported
to be $178,939, out of which ten per cent. divi-
dend was paid to the stockholders.

The success of this company gave birth to a
rival, and in May, 1867, the Ætna Live Stock Insurance Company appeared upon the field with a
paid up capital of one hundred and fifty thousand
dollars, and both companies seemed in a flourishing condition, the stock of the older company
being quoted at fifty and of the younger at ten
dollars premium.

In the spring of 1868 a new board of officers took
charge of the Hartford Company, when a very
bad state of affairs was disclosed, the directors
having neglected to report nearly eighty thousand
dollars sustained in losses, while the books were
encumbered with a large volume of bad risks.

The new direction attempted to secure the company from its impending ruin ; but the agents
were hopelessly demoralized and the losses too
frequent, so that in July, 1868, about three months
after the retirement of the old directors, the company succumbed to its fate, the losses exceeded the
paid up capital by forty thousand dollars.

Admonished by the collapse of its rival, the
Ætna advanced its rates thirty-three and a third
per cent., and as it had a surplus of sixty thousand dollars as the result of a years business, and
had been managed with more caution and ability
it was hoped that it might weather the storm.
But confidence had been shaken. Those policy-
holders who had met with no losses objected to
the increased rates, and business declined, so that
in January in 1869 the directors decided that the
losses on the policies already issued made the
future too doubtful to warrant a continuance of
the experiment, and the agents were directed to
issue no more policies nor write more renewals.
The Hartford was in existence a year and ten
months and lost four hundred and ten thousand dollars. The Ætna closed its business after
sixteen months practice and lost one hundred and
twenty thousand dollars.

The original tariff of rates of the two companies

were about the same. On farming and private horses from four to twelve years old, five per cent.; from twelve to sixteen, six per cent.; on store and express horses, five and a half per cent.; from twelve to sixteen, six and a half per cent.; truck and dray horses in cities, seven per cent.; car horses, eight per cent.; colts, stallions, and brood mares, six per cent.; trotting horses, six to ten per cent.; oxen and cows, five per cent. Agents were directed to insure but two-thirds of the real value, and to refer all risks for over eight hundred dollars on any one animal to the home office. The insurance risk was against death only, but a theft risk would be granted for an addition of two and one quarter and two and three quarters per cent. Inland transportation risks were taken at one half to three per cent.

Risks on canal horses, street car horses, sheep and racehorse stock were soon rejected. Upon the failure of the Hartford the Ætna advanced its rates to six or seven per cent. on private horses, eight or nine per cent. on horses used for business purposes, and six or seven per cent. on horned cattle.

The Ætna made a manful struggle to sustain its life; but it fell a prey to its agents, some of whom were but sorry judges of a horse, and accepted the opinion of others on its value, and thus often insured a decaying animal for treble its worth; whilst those officers who knew something more of there living risks than their confreres, were deficient in integrity, which was no less calamitous to the company. Thus experience teaches us that unless these great defects can be surmounted, it is impossible for a company taking a wide range of country as its area of business to conduct a live stock company to a profitable purpose.

It is to be regretted that the protective principle of insurance can not be made to extend to live stock because of the w nt of co-operation on the part of the agents; but the severe lesson experienced by two companies of this character, one of which at least seems to have been well managed, is not likely to go forgotten amongst those anxious for such protection. In England several have succeeded, one particularly, which confines its operations to the live stock of the county of Norfolk, stood through the calamitous period of the rinderpest without being reduced to either bankruptcy or dissolution, and perhaps in this country if the risks were confined to a small district and full inquiries made into each case before a policy is granted, great benefit might arise to the insurers without ending in the ruin of the adventurers.—*Insurance Journal.*

Financial.

TORONTO STOCK MARKET.

(Reported by Pellatt & Osler, Brokers.)

The market has been inactive for the past week, partly on account of so many of the transfer books being closed for dividends payable on the 1st of next month.

Bank stock.—150 is offered for Montreal ex dividend, without sales. There were small sales of British at 105½, it is now offered at 106. For Ontario 97½ ex dividend is offered, without transactions. There are buyers of Toronto at 118½, no stock on the market. The Royal Canadian suspended specie payment on the 21st inst.; various prices are named for the stock, from 10 to 40 per cent, but we believe no sales have been made. There were sales of Commerce at 102½ to 103, closing firm and in demand. Buyers offer 35 for Gore, with sellers at 36. Merchants' has advanced closing with buyers at 109 and sellers at 109½. City is offered at par ex-dividend. There are buyers of Du Peuple at 108 and of Nationale at 106, no sales of either. Mechanics' could be placed at 93½, but sellers ask 94. Buyers would give 106½ for Union, none in market. Nothing doing in other banks.

Debentures.—Canada sterling six per cents sold during the week at 106, and Dominion stock at 108½. Toronto are offering at rates to pay about 7 per cent to purchasers. Little demand for County.

Sundries.—City Gas is offered at 107 without demand. Small lots Canada Permanent Building Society are offered at 126, with buyers at 125½; some sales of Western Canada were made at 120½ and 121; 112 exdividend is offered for Freehold. There are sellers of Montreal Telegraph at 135½ and buyers at 134½. Canada Landed Credit, nominal. Several large mortgages are offering to pay 8 per cent. Money continues close and high rates are paid on first-class mercantile paper.

ROYAL CANADIAN BANK.

This Bank closed its doors on Friday morning the 21st inst. The first intimation that the general public had of the position of affairs was communicated by the following notice, posted on the windows of the banking house:

Royal Canadian Bank.—This Bank has, for the present, suspended specie payment. By order of the Board, T. Woodside, Cashier. Toronto, May 21, 1869." During the day the directors issued the following circular:—

To the public.

The Directors of the Royal Canadian Bank regret that the action of the Hon. Donald McDonald, in issuing a circular to the shareholders, has had the effect of shaking public confidence in its stability, and causing a large withdrawal of deposits.

The assistance of a number of other banks having been sought, but declined, no other alternative was left to the Board than to suspend specie payment for the present.

The Directors would urge upon bill-holders and depositors not to be alarmed, as there is not the slightest danger of loss to them, and many hopes are entertained that within a short time the business of the Bank will be resumed.

They may further state that, having the assets carefully estimated, and all known losses deducted, there is still a surplus over the paid-up capital intact. A statement of the affairs of the Bank will be prepared and published as speedily as posible. By order of the Board,

T. Woodside, Cashier.

The following statement of the affairs of the Bank for the month ending May 15th, has also been issued:

CAPITAL	
Capital authorized by Act	$2,000,000 00
Capital paid up	1,103,728 34
LIABILITIES.	
Promissory Notes in circulation not bearing interest	887,916 00
Balances due to other Banks	38,731 01
Cash deposits not bearing interest	370,113 78
Cash deposits bearing interest	633,671 57
Total liabilities	$1,930,432 36
ASSETS.	
Coin, Bullion and Provincial Notes	185,629 81
Government Securities	128,911 10
Promissory Notes or Bills of other Banks	68,737 98
Balances due from othe. Banks	273,467 83
Notes and Bills discounted	2,643,590 02
Other debts due to the Bank not included under the foregoing heads	83,817 58
Total assets	$3,384,154 33

PROFITS OF BANKING.—Twenty-four of the Philadelphia banks have declared their semi-yearly dividends. One of the banks—the Fourth National—which usually divides its profits at this period, having met with serious misfortunes which swallowed up a greater portion of its capital, wisely abstained from any attempt to make a

division of profits. Taking the dividends for the year, it must be confessed that bank stock pays well. The Kensington bank has divided twenty five per cent. in the last year; the Southwark bank twenty per cent.; the Northern Liberti bank twenty per cent.; the Philadelphia ban fifteen per cent.; the Mechanics' bank sixteen p cent.; the Germantown National fifteen per cent the Western fifteen per cent.; the Corn Exchange fourteen per cent. Eight and a half per cent. of the banks pay ten and twelve per cent. The dividends are clear of taxes, and they show th our banking institutions, with one exception, a carefully conducted. They furnish constant a satisfactory profits to the owners.—*Philadelph Commercial List.*

Railway News.

GREAT WESTERN RAILWAY.—Traffic for we ending May 7, 1869.	
Passengers	$28,396 96
Freight	47,268 70
Mails and Sundries	2,252 12
Total Receipts for week	$77,857 78
Coresponding week, 1868	76,732 48
Increase	$1,125 30

NORTHERN RAILWAY.—Traffic receipts for we ending May 15, 1869:—	
Passengers	$2,468 70
Freight	14,196 14
Mails and sundries	389 24
Total receipts for week	$17,054 08
Corresponding week 1868	14,813 55
Increase	$2,240 53

MINING LANDS.—The following appears in Nova Scotia *Royal Gazette.*

CROWN LAND OFFICE, April 23th, '69. Mining Leases on Crown Lands, in the Count of Charlotte and Victoria, wi.l be offered for s by Public Auction, at this Office, at noon, Tuesday the 25th day of May next, agreeab y the following conditions:

Upset price, $20 per lot.

1st.—Every Mining Lease to be exempted fr Royalty for five years from its date.

2nd.—That the right of Mining within a Tr of one Square Mile, for the term of twenty years, be put up at a fixed rent of twenty-five ce per Children on Coal, and five per cent. on value of all other Minerals raised, to be p id in each year after the fifth, to the Receiver Ge ral, or an agent to be appointed by the Govern

3rd.—That the upset preference price for e Lot be twenty dollars.

4th.—That the preference money be paid, the ground selected within one hour after the t of sale, after which other lots will be offered required, in like manner.

5th.—That the Lease contain a clause of rene or that the Government may resume and take improvements at a valuation to be made by A trators mutually chosen by the Surveyor Gen for the time being, and by the Lessee or his signs.

6th.—That if the Lessee shall not actually r Coal or other Mineral, to the value of four l dred dollars, from his ground within any one (the first five years excepted) during the cont ance of his Lease, the same shall become forfei

W. P. FLEWELLING, *Sur. Ge*

SUFFOLK MINE.—Last week Gen. Adams s in Boston, 10,000 tons of low grade copper f this mine at $22.50 per ton. This ore, which formerly been considered of very little value now used for manufacturing sulphuric aci *Sherbrooke Gazette.*

'ANADIAN MONETARY TIMES AND INSU-
BRONICLE *is printed every Thursday even-
listributed to Subscribers on the following

.ing office, No. 60 Church-street, 3 doors
Court-street.

.iption price—
.ida $2.00 per annum.
.and, stg. 10s. per annum.
.ed States (U.S.Cy.) $3.00 per annum.
. advertisements will be charged at the rate
.ts per line, each insertion.
. all letters to " THE MONETARY TIMES."
.s, money orders, &c. should be made pay-
M. TROUT, Business Manager, who alone
.izal to issue receipts for money.
.Canadian Subscribers to THE MONETARY
.ill receive THE REAL ESTATE JOURNAL
.urther charge.

Canadian Monetary Times.

THURSDAY, MAY 27, 1869.

HE CANADIAN CANALS.

II.

.riter upon the Canadian Canals can-
.ighly estimate the importance and
of the subject. Possibly there is no
.ch of practical economy which has
.ring on the well-being of the Pro-
d certainly there is no one less under-
:ndeed, as a rule, the subject is lost
by Canadian journalism, and there
.ircumstances to give it adventitious
It is only when some special claim
:o public support, that the least at-
i aroused ; and then the influence
.ealthful. The two schemes, the
.iavigation and the Georgian Bay
e cases in point. In both instances
.e earnest hearty advocates, and as
.rts were continued, so proselytes
.ed. There are very few men who
the appeal to thoir interest put in
.inguage. "Here is this scheme,sure
.t has this and that support, and is of

"great national benefit—look at the statistics
"—count up the results," and a formidable
sheet of paper appears with tabulated statements of elaborate calculation, proving certain profit. "You see," continues the speaker,
"here it is. All this money has to be spent ;
"there is plenty for every body ; throw your
"influence in with ours, and participate in
" these certain benefits." Who can blame a
struggling man, one not well informed on the
subject, who sees the project sustained by
many most estimable persons, and who is
possibly himself taken with the one-sided
view advanced—who can blame him, we say,
if he joins in the common cry and swells the
chorus ? The difficulty lies in allowing canal
schemes of this character to be taken up by
private parties. It is precisely in this situation that the Government should intervene,
for a Canadian Canal is not, and by no circumstance can be, looked upon as a private
isolated effort. To our mind the difficulty
in the Province has been that each canal has
been more or less regarded as an individual
project. Private influences have been allowed
to direct and fashion in part that which should
have been considered as a portion of the
whole. The navigation of the St. Lawrence
is a unity, in short, and anything at all dis-
cordant with the requirements which ought
to govern that unity, is self-evidently objectionable. Thus the Georgian Bay Canal is
quite independent of the St. Lawrence Navigation. As the Welland Canal is at present
constituted, that is if the limit be maintained,
it would have had one use only. At present
a propeller by the Welland can carry 4,400
bbls. of flour. The proposed locks on the
Georgian Bay Canal, with but moderately
increased expenses, would admit a cargo of at
least seven thousand barrels, cheapening of
course its freight. But such a vessel must
discharge at Oswego, because she could not
pass through the St. Lawrence Canals, which
have but nine feet depth of water. Therefore
the .only result which could have accrued,
would have been an increase of the trade
between Chicago and Oswego, thus giving
Buffalo the go-by. Consequently the scheme
has found opponents in the latter place, and
supporters in the former cities. . To the St.
Lawrence itself the canal, if completed, could
bring no commerce. It is indeed in its bearing anti-Canadian, and would rather carry
the trade from the country. Not that there
are now special inducements to take exports
down the St. Lawrence. We mean, that if
New York and Montreal offered equal inducements to the shippers of grain to Europe,
the Georgian Bay Canal would be more to
the interest of New York. As to the time
taken in passing through the canal, and the
time taken through the open water of the
river, the following figures to us seem

unanswerable. It is urged that a propeller
taking the open water will have to pass over
400 miles of additional distance, which with
a propeller at nine miles the hour may be assumed at 44 hours, and adding for the passage through the Welland Canal 15 hours, we
have a total of 59 hours. Against this there
is the Georgian Bay Canal, itself 100 miles.
in length; locking up 475 feet, and locking
down 130 feet. · As a first-class passenger
steamer in the Beauharnois Canal, 11½ miles
in length. with 9 locks and a lift of 82½ feet,
takes six hours to pass through it, so the
Georgian Bay Canal would exact from 60 to
70 hours, at the fastest rate of speed, and
without the least contretemps. If this reasoning be correct, and we conceive it to be un-
impugnable, there can be no saving of time.
The gain is simply in the ability to bring
larger vessels into the trade, which could
not get out of Lake Ontario ; and this result
is to be effected at a cost of from twenty to
thirty millions of dollars. So incomplete is
the project, that one of its earliest and ablest
supporters, Mr. Tully, saw the weakness of
it, and declared that the improvement was
only contemplated in connection with the
important work of deepening the St. Lawrence Canals. The. answer to this view is.
very plain—Why not then begin with the
deepening and enlargement of the St. Lawrence Canals ?

Enough surely has been said to show that
a scheme of such a character is no portion of
the St. Lawrence navigation proper, and as
such it ought summarily to be dismissed
from consideration ; in any case until that
navigation be brought to its extreme development. It is the recognition of such a principle as we are now striving to establish ; a
principle we fear only imperfectly understood.
A commercial contest is now being waged. As
in the old days when the French held Canada,
the positive fighting arose, whether the trade
with the Indians should have its passage by
the waters of the Hudson or by the St.
Lawrence ; whether it should follow the
debouchure of the lakes, or whether it should
turn by the southern streams to the Mohawk
and thence to the Hudson. These early wars
in the settlement of Canada were in reality
wars of trade, and it was purely to control
its course that Fort Duquesne on the Ohio
was constructed, to destroy which Braddock
advanced so futilely—to be defeated by a
handful of men. It was the recollection of
these struggles which nerved the State of
New York, then not over rich, and thinly
populated to the extraordinary effort of the
Erie Canal with its several branches. The
policy of this State has been a canal policy,
and it has richly earned its reward. The
policy of Canada, or rather the want of
policy of this country is to neglect the na

tural advantages which its geographical position offers. When the history of the last twenty years is soberly written, one of the most extraordinary features will be this systematic and unchallenged neglect. One could conceive that politicians even on the score of selfishness would have greedily clutched a subject promising honor and reward to its advocate. But the contrary is the case. Year after year passes, session after session is overloaden with verbose but ill considered legislation, and not a word is said in favor of the canals. Or at best, some experiment is tried such as removing the tolls, throwing into the pocket of the forwarder the rightful due of the State. Is it that politicians cannot understand the subject? Is it that there are no means of studying it? The labor of more than one writer has placed the subject sufficiently clear; but their reward has been to see their work utterly unacknowledged and repudiated by successive governments, who love not literature or thought in any form. The matter is a puzzle. Politicians of most countries have one end in view—their own success. Now and then some great mind endowed above his fellows breaks the ranks, and some few intellects are distinguished by honest and unselfish patriotism. But looking to the list of the public men for the last quarter of a century, with the exception of the Hon. John Young, of Montreal, no single name occurs to our mind, of those who have battled for the great water communications of the country. To-day are we any better? In the preliminary discussions with regard to Confederation, the Canals were entirely lost sight of; and it is a fact that ought never to be forgotten. The 69th Resolution is as follows:

"The communications with the North-Western Territory, *and the improvements required for the development of the trade of the great West* with the seaboard, are regarded by the conference as subjects of the highest importance to the Federated Provinces, and shall be prosecuted at the earliest possible period that the state of the finances will permit."

There is a great deal of magniloquence in all this, and it would have been better to have dealt with the subject in a simple and more natural way. If the words mean anything they are a distinct and positive pledge that the Canals shall not be neglected. The North West Territory is acquired—what now about the "communications" with it? What about the "improvements for the development of the trade of the great West?"

—The Toronto and Nipissing Railway project is making satisfactory progress; a large share of the stock of the Toronto, Grey and Bruce is already taken.

USURY.

Taking up the subject where we left it last week, we now proceed to point out the modes in which usury laws operate to raise the rate of interest. These are principally three:

1. Many capitalists who invest in loans are unwilling to run the risk of evading the law, and finding that they can use their capital more profitably in other ways, withdraw it from the loan market. The supply decreases; the demand remains the same. Every one knows that, with regard to other commodities, the inevitable consequence is that the price will rise. So will it be with regard to money, which has no peculiar or occult virtue to protect it against the operation of the laws of supply and demand.

2. The capitalists who are left in the field being those who are willing to break the law, are inevitably the less scrupulous and conscientious class of the class. What the worst of this kind are we need not characterize; they are too well known. As a rule, their demands are limited only by the necessities of those whose misfortune it is to fall in their hands. So far from being satisfied with two per cent. per month (the rate which so sorely grieves our legislators), they will exact ten or twenty if they can get it. The more conscientious class of lenders being driven from the field by the operation of the law, the pressure of their competion is removed, and the others have no check upon their avarice. So that not only is the rate of interest still further raised in this way, but borrowers are consigned to the tender mercies of the hardest of the lending class—the Shylocks who, in default of payment, will exact their full pound of flesh without remorse.

3. Borrowers burthened with a tender conscience will not take advantage of the law, but, as a point of honor, will, rather than break their plighted word, pay to the uttermost whatever they promise. Those who do take advantage of such laws are the less delicately conscientious; who are not particular about violating their contracts, no matter how solemnly these may have been entered into. They will agree to pay any interest that may be asked, but when the time comes, will pay only what the law compels. A money-lender who knows his business will generally arrange matters so that this shall be whatever has been agreed upon. The ingenuity of the class has never, in the past, been at a loss to find means to do this, and there is no reason to suppose that there would be any greater difficulty in the future. It will frequently happen, however, that the law will be able to be taken advantage of, and the amount limited be all that is re-

coverable. This, in the most liberal of three bills now before the Commons, is principal only, the borrower getting the of the money for nothing. By the Government resolutions, it is six per cent. interest besides. How will this operate? Le suppose that the natural rate of interest ten per cent., and that the law is taken vantage of in one-half the cases, in the o half the borrower paying, either of his accord or from compulsion, the rate ag upon. All borrowers must, at the time loan. be treated alike, and charged a sufficiently high to obtain the natural on the average. By the supposition, one will pay only six per cent.—the rate prop by the Government. To make up the ficiency. it is obvious that fourteen per c must be got out of the other half. the law, in attempting to lower the rate ten to six, will increase it from ten to f teen. This would be the rise in theory. practice, however, it would be much great for, in so uncertain a case, the lender w take care to charge a rate sufficient to c all contingencies, so that any error woul in his own favor. This uncertainty w cause the rate to go as high, probably twenty from this cause alone. The sult would then be that half the borro would pay six and the other half two making an average of thirteen in pla ten, which it would be without the And what is especially to be noticed is, the extra rate will be paid by the borro class.

It is clear, then, that the effect of t laws is to raise interest in favor of the class of lenders, and at the expense o best class of borrowers. Illustrations of effect are not wanting. Thus Storch Russian economist, points out that the Empress Catherine passed a law h the object of lowering interest from si cent. to five, it had the effect of raising seven. Similarly, when Louis XV. of F passed an edict to reduce the rate from to four, he caused it to rise to six. Pro the country where interest is lowest is land, where the usury laws have. been ished for fifteen years past, and where is perhaps more freedom of borrowin, lending than in any other country. usual rate at the Bank of England is t three per cent. Perhaps, however, the striking illustration is afforded by the rience of our own country. In 1858, before the abolition of the usury laws, the limit fixed by law was six per cent actual rate on first-class mortgage se was from twenty-five to thirty per This is a notorious fact, well known to lawyer and capitalist in the habit of d mortgages at that time. The repeal of law caused an immediate fall in the rate, in the next two years went down to per cent., and has been steadily declining ever since, until now it is about or eight per cent., the lowest, we believe reached in the Province. This obvious difference is almost altogether due to the repeal of the law, and in particular to the large additional capital which an thrown into the loan market in conce. In a country like ours, where is comparatively scarce, any restriction its circulation will inevitably give far more disastrous consequences than ntrips where it is comparatively ul.

absurdity of fixing a limit to a thing fluctuating as the rate of interest, is shewn by the extremely wide variation which have taken place in it at different and places. In ancient Athens, by the Solon (B.C. 594). the rate of interest restricted. It varied from about ten it. to sixty. The average was about m, which it was in the time of Demosthenes.

Twelve per cent. was always con a low rate. At Rome, by the laws Twelve Tables (B.C. 453), the rate ed at twelve. Far higher rates, however, were paid in practice, and the law was observed that it became obsolete, and than one hundred years had to be re l. In 347 B.C., the limit was reduced and a few years afterwards the re any interest whatever was prohibited w which was, of course, completely naught. By Justinian, the taking of was again legalised up to four per In the Middle Ages, in spite of legal es, of spiritual censure, and of popular m, usury was everywhere practised, a consequence of the restrictions , at extremely high rates. In English Common Law, supplemented by statutes, prohibited the taking of any This was first legalised, as one of sequences of the Reformation, by the Henry VIII., c. 9 (1541), which fixed t at ten per cent. This Act was re und the receipt of interest again made by 5 and 6 Ed. VI., c. 20 (1552.) a years' experience of this Act was Accordingly it was, in its turn, and the Act of Henry revived, the ag again fixed at ten per cent. This e by 13 Elizabeth, c. 8 (1570.) The to this Act is instructive. Speaking he Act of Edward VI., it says :— said latter Act hath not done so good as was hoped it should, but the said vice of usury, and specially of sale of wares and shifts of in-

"terest, hath much more exceedingly abound-"ed, to the utter undoing of many gentle-"men, merchants, occupiers, and others, and "to the importable hurt of the Common-"wealth." By 21 James I., c. 17 (1623), the rate was lowered from ten per cent. to eight. During the Commonwealth it was reduced to six, which was confirmed by 12 Charles II., c. 13 (1660.) In Scotland, in like manner, before the Reformation, no interest was allowed. After that event, and in 1587, the restriction was removed, and the rate fixed at ten per cent. In 1633 it was reduced to eight, and in 1661 to six. After the union of the two kingdoms, the Act 12 Anne, c. 16, fixed the rate at five. No alteration was made in the law till Wm. IV., when it was somewhat relaxed ; and finally, in 1854, by 17 and 18 Vic., c. 90, the usury laws were totally abolished. The natural fluctuation of interest is also shown by the Bank of England rates. Within the last few years they have varied from less than two per cent. to upwards of ten. The average rate, however, has been considerably less than before the Act of abolition. It seems, therefore, that, in the old country at least, it is at last recognized, even by politicians, that the true and only way by which to reduce the rate of interest to its lowest point, is to leave capital and borrowers and lenders to the free and unrestricted operation of the natural laws which govern them.

Another mischief, which is to be charged against usury laws, being of a very serious character, must not fail to be noticed. We refer to their effect in retarding the development and industrial progress of a country. The main element of progress in a new country is the opening of new branches of industry and of new channels of trade. These, because new, and therefore untried and unknown, are necessarily more hazardous than the old and well-tried ones. Now, capitalists will not lend their money for the purpose of investment in enterprises of extra hazard without an inducement in the shape of extra interest, which, being prevented by law, the consequence is that new branches of industry languish for want of the necessary support. We have not the slightest doubt that to our former usury laws is to be attributed much of the want of energy and enterprise with which we have been so often twitted by our American neighbors. If there is no such connection as this, it is certainly a very remarkable coincidence that the rapid development of such hazardous enterprises as those connected with petroleum, salt, and mining for gold and other minerals, should follow so closely on the heels of the repeal of our usury laws. Again, look at other countries, where the religious prejudice against

usury still exists. In Mohammedan nations this prejudice is still as strong as ever, their religion absolutely forbidding the receiving of any interest. In Roman Catholic countries the same feeling still has some vitality, and though not so strong as formerly, yet is much stronger than in Protestant countries. Compare, then, the industrial and commercial torpor of such countries as Turkey (the sick man), Spain, and Italy, with the life and activity of England and the United States. We have seen what, during the Middle Ages, was the popular doctrine in regard to interest. There is no need to shew further, how, during that long night, and while the doctrine reigned supreme, the whole frame of industry, trade and commerce shrivelled up and withered beneath the curse of its blighting influence, and was paralysed into a stillness as of death. From facts such as these we may form some notion of the evil in these respects which usury laws occasion.

Another charge which we have to bring against these laws, is that they are an infringement upon the rights of property, being an attempt to dictate the terms upon which a man shall deal with his own.

In short, in whatever aspect usury laws are regarded, they are seen to be productive of mischief, and mischief only. They belong to the same class with those which were frequently passed in times gone by, to regulate wages and the price of food. The same evils and the same inherent absurdity belong to both.

As we said before, we are unwilling to impugn the motives of those who are moving in this matter ; but the facts and arguments which we have given are so indisputable, that it is impossible to do other than ascribe to these men, one of two things, either that they are grossly ignorant of all that has been written on the subject about which they propose to legislate, or that, for reasons best known to themselves, they wish to raise the rate of interest throughout the country. We hope that there is, in the Dominion, sufficient intelligence and public spirit to prevent the intended wrong.

THE ROYAL CANADIAN BANK.

On the 21st this bank suspended specie payments. We were aware prior to last week's issue of this journal that such a step was contemplated, but as negotiations were in progress which might have prevented it, we did not feel justified in contributing in any way to such an undesirable result. A glance at the returns for the last two months was sufficient to show that the process of depletion was going on steadily. Between the 1st March and 15th May, the reduction was as follows :—

Circulation	£625,150
Debts to Banks	3,703
Deposits on call	256,876
Deposits on interest	320,898

Total...................... $1,215,627

So that from the 1st March up to the time of suspension, no less than a million and a quarter of gold was paid out. That it was possible for the bank to sustain such extreme pressure for so great a length of time, certainly speaks well for it.

The question naturally arises—what caused this sudden strain upon the resources of the Royal Canadian? We have no hesitation in saying that it is directly traceable to a want of confidence in the management. There were those on the Board whose names were a source of weakness rather than of strength. They were objectionable to many. Whether they deserved this or not we do not pretend to say, but it must be admitted that antecedents have a great influence on public opinion when men are placed in positions of trust. However, the fact is there, that the Board did not command confidence, and that in time of trouble, the want of it proved disastrous. But there is another consideration. There has been all along a seeming lack of harmony among those who controlled the institution. Internal quarrels and disputes arose, and the bank interests were insensibly sacrificed to the petty vanity of those who should have known better than attempt to display it in such a sensitive quarter. This objectionable feature culminated in the circulars of Mr. Macdonald, the Vice-President, who chose the worst possible time to avenge himself of his colleagues, for his insinuations and statements gave the finishing stroke to the hesitating confidence which kept the institution afloat. A depositor or note-holder does not stop to argue out the merits of such discussions; he merely says to himself, there is doubt, and though everything may be right, self preservation is the first law of nature. Who can wonder that suspension should have been the result of all this. Had Mr. Macdonald himself acted in an honest manner, and from pure motives, and, first exhausted all legitimate means of putting a a stop to abuses before coming before the public, we should not find fault. But as the contrary fully appears, we cannot do other than condemn as inexcusable his conduct throughout. Under the circumstances, we are disposed to think that suspension is the best thing that could have happened the institution, for it will bring all parties to their senses. Directors will now understand that public confidence is not to be trifled with, and shareholders will have fully illustrated the

necessity of exercising judiciously their power of choice.

While we are thus disposed to lay blame on the management we can find no excuse for the course of conduct pursued by the Bank of Montreal to this Western institution. The ruin of a bank means wide-spread individual loss and general commercial disaster. It throws business out of gear and affects too many to render such an occurrence a matter of joke. When one bank in Canada attempts to destroy a rival it seeks to bring about a national calamity, and we should hesitate to say that the Bank of Montreal, the financial agent of the Government, did deliberately contemplate such a thing were it not that the facts scarcely admit of any other explanation.

Notwithstanding that many evidences of, to say the least, want of friendship towards kindred institutions have been given by the Bank of Montreal, we are far from believing that it caused the suspension of the Royal Canadian, or that it has the power which some political journals seem to consider it possesses. It is quite a mistake to suppose' that it is responsible for the Royal's troubles, and it is just as well to have that mistake corrected. It acted in an unfriendly spirit, no doubt, but that line of conduct should not be twisted into an exhibition of a power which in reality it has not, and, even if it had, it dare not wield.

It is, of course, a question—what is best to be done under the circumstances? From what we know of the bank's state, we incline to the opinion that every effort should be put forth to cause a resumption. The discounts do not represent very large advances, but, on the contrary, are, we believe, distributed over a large surface; so that we may take it for granted, that the percentage of good paper would be found in excess of the ordinary estimate. But as this would depend on the result of a rigid investigation, we leave it for the present. In the event of resumption, a change in the Board must be made; and, we understand, all the directors are ready to resign. Under the charter, such a wholesale resignation would let in men who are more objectionable than the present occupants, so that it will be necessary to wait until the annual meeting in July, before a change can be made.

The fact that the notes of the Royal are taken at par by traders in Toronto, is a striking commentary on the character of our present banking system, which speaks for itself, and, instead of injuring the prospects or defeating the attempt now being made to substitute Government indebtedness for gold, will convince our legislators that we may be worse off than we are at present.

NATIONAL LIFE INSURANCE COMPANY OF UNITED STATES.—This company, chartered year by Congress, having deposited $50,665 with the Receiver General for the security of Canadian policy-holders, has commenced business in this country. It is a stock company, with paid-up capital of one million of dollars; from its connection with the well-known banking house of Messrs. Jay Cooke & Co., is popularly known as "Jay Cooke's Company." The business is done upon the "non-participating" cash plan," there being no distribution of profits and the premiums being all payable in c The rates charged are, therefore, low. In case of "return premium" policies, not only amount insured in the first instance, but also the premiums paid are returned at the maturity of the policy. The policies are non-forfeitable This company has met with a good deal of position in various quarters, chiefly on the ground that it is a stock company; but it has made rapid progress. By a statement we have seen appears that for the nine months the company has been in business, up to the end of April 4,791 policies were issued, amounting to $ 653,500, on which the premiums were $562,831 Agents are being appointed in the various c and towns, and every effort will no doubt be made to push the company's business in Dominion.

COMMERCIAL UNION ASSURANCE.—We have at this late date the annual report and the proceedings had at the annual meeting, which be found interesting. The business of this western company is making satisfactory progress.

LONDON CORRESPONDENCE.

(From a Correspondent).
LONDON, 8th May, 18(

Commercial men regard the immediate future with unconcealed apprehension. The state of continent is not satisfactory. Prussia and France have not yet agreed to give an indisputable test of their love for peace by disbanding soldiers diminishing the outlay for munitions of war. Italy the deficit has become chronic. Spain not yet completed her revolution, and is in meantime hard put to it in order to meet necessary expenses. The Turks are about to borrow money wherewith to discharge their pecuniary obligations and Russia has tried, but in vain, to persuade capitalists of England to advance additional funds for the purpose of constructing railways which never pay in a commercial sense, but which prove serviceable for the transport of troops. An outbreak of war would readily shake the fabric of European commerce. It is hoped rather believed that the beginning of hostilities is more contingency. Men flatter themselves the longer the fatal hour is postponed the less certain does its arrival become. Before the lapse of many months, the question of peace or war may be definitely answered. The armed truce i costly to last. This consideration is not one which has suddenly received attention from speculators. They have been calculating the chances of a continental war for some time back. But they not take into account the possibility of hostilities breaking out in other quarters of the globe. A war between the United Kingdom and the United States would break out is a notion which but one person in the thousand has regarded as more than a horrid but an idle vision. However great change has taken place in the views of ere on this score. It is perceived that not fluential persons in the United States are ag to the prejudices of the poorer or less i class, and that, if this course be perⁿ, 'the issue cannot be doubtful. If it itention of President Grant to pick a quarⁿ this country, in the hope that he may nd absorb Canada, he has sadly miscalcu-is opportunity. Such speeches as those d by Mr. Sumner and Mr. Chandler have ffect their authors may not have foreseen. uster and open threats have never yet per-Englishmen to follow in an appointed path, these means prove effectual now. Coming, speeches do, after the contemptuous rejec-a treaty in which English ministers went tmost verge of concession, they have ope-insults to the national honour. I should regret if the kindred or rival nations were clared foes, were it but for a day. How-the worst must come, the chances will be that nation which is the wanton and pur-aggressor. In a war of conquest, or in a which this country should act as the ally ign power, success might be imperilled by of opinion among the people. But let the be called upon to vindicate its outraged and to defend any portion of its violated the unanimity of sentiment would aur-a world as well as tend to render victory.

not know that in the highest and best-in-quarters a feeling of uneasiness prevails, I not have treated the question of war be-his country and America as one of any This much, I may say, without fear of it proving me a false prophet, and that is, s of our Government will be firm and should the new American ambassador areasonable demands. Indeed, Mr. Mot-find that the responsible advisers of the an say "No" with as great coolness and as the President of the United States It is probable that as this is now at Washington, the proposals of Mr. Mot-be neither startling nor inadmissible. This inion, but it is an opinion which does not with the money market. The desire to get nited States securities is as great as this as it was a few weeks ago to obtain pos-of them. The investors as well as the ors have taken fright. If the chances of e being broken were to increase, the con-f the foreign holders of these bonds would mined. What will hasten the re-action, flow of the bonds to European markets, e thousands to return whence they came, crease in the value of money. In a few e Bank rate of discount will be raised nat is from 4½ to 5 per cent. As a conse-he business of the Joint Stock Banks will he dividends paid by them will increase, attractions of the 5-20 bonds be materially ed in the eyes alike of the bold speculator prudent investor.

s foreseen by many persons here, the terms a the Hudson's Bay Company surrenders vereign rights are considered objectionable ction of the Canadian press. The worst Earl Granville's proposal is that relating reservations of land. In the published adence between the Canadian Ministers Colonial Office; exception is taken by this part of the scheme. I read in your ers that bad though it may be to pay such £300,000, it is infinitely worse to give pany one-twentieth part the future town-the Fertile Belt, and that a large payment w for the whole would be economy in the Now, if this view were to prevail in it might find acceptance here also. I have nade for s'ating that some of the largest lers would not object to taking a sum of istead of retaining an interest in the land. culty would be to persuade them to accept ble sum. Yet I cannot think the obsta-

cles to an arrangement are so great now as they were before Earl Granville drew up his ultimatum. At any rate, the matter might be discussed at the time when the details of the arrangement are finally settled. Of course, the offer of money must come from Canada. What should be done by those who desire the Northwestern Territory and Rupert's Land to form part of the Dominion, unburdened by conditions, is to consider the price they would pay for this. It is certainly for the advantage of the Dominion that the Company should be bought off now, because, unless that be done, the result will be envenomed and dangerous strife in the future.

The cost of messages by the Atlantic Cable is again reduced, being £2 for 100 words. A few months hence the French Cable will, probably, be in operation. It is proposed, I see, to lay a third. Now, it may interest as well as instruct many persons to learn that the reductions in the price have not proved as remunerative as was expected. When the highest price was charged, the number of messages was few; but then, the expenses were proportionately small. Each additional message requires a larger staff of messengers and others; besides, when a message has to be repeated, in order to a correct a mistake, there is a waste of time and labor which seriously affects the profits. As far as the public is concerned, their cannot be too many cables and too low rates charged. It is not always the case that what benefits the public is an unmixed blessing to shareholders.

Commercial.

The event of the week in business circles was the suspension of the Royal Canadian Bank, which closed its doors on Friday morning, the 21st inst. The occurrence caused some commotion, but the business public generally were not unprepared for the event, a knowledge of the difficulties of the bank's situation being pretty generally diffused. Had the suspension occurred in the height of the produce season it would have been much more severely felt, as the bank had a very considerable run of produce business. Owing to the dullness of the market just now, there is very little produce paper stirring, the dealers have adopted a conservative policy and do not care to do much business till prices settle to the bottom and the trade assumes a more satisfactory shape. The dullness of the winter and spring in other branches of trade has led to a general curtailment of obligations in that quarter, also, so that the present moment finds the business houses of Toronto in a favorable position to meet a shock of this kind. The bills sold to some extent on morning of the suspension at from 50 to 75 per cent, but soon went to 80 and 90 and even 95 per cent (some retail shops taking them at par for goods); no doubt the general belief that little loss will be suffered by either bill-holders or depositors together with some hope that the bank may resume, has had much to do with mitigating the evil consequences of the disaster.

The failure of M'. Wm. Hughes, of Brampton, a day or two previous to the bank suspension just noticed, involved several wholesale firms here in losses ranging from $1,000 to $3,000. He did a general store business and operated in grain to a considerable extent; liabilities stated by him at $59,000 and assets at $78,000. He has proposed a compromise with his creditors at 50c. on the dollar.

The wool season is just opening, but the late advance in gold operates against business, so that

buyers do not offer more than 26c. for washed fleece. Unless the gold premium declines from the present quotations we shall have a much duller season than was otherwise anticipated.

Toronto Market.

Under so many depressing influences trade could not be otherwise than dull, and no improvement of consequence need be looked for till the fall business sets in.

LEATHER.—The demand for leather has fallen off and the market is dull.

HIDES.—Prices have taken a decided tumble involving holders in considerable losses, and prices are likely to go still lower.

PRODUCE.—The tendency of the market is decidedly downward both in flour and wheat. The stock of wheat in the principal American markets is much larger than last year. Chicago and Milwaukee had on the 15th 1,757,000 bush. against 883,000 last year, and 308,000 the previous year. New York had 914,700 bush. against 813,699, and 731,330 in 1868 and 1867, respectively. These increased supplies, and the continued reports of a fine harvest in prospect, fully justify the steady fall in prices. Fall wheat one year ago sold at $1.80 it is now worth $1 ; spring sold at $1.60 and now at 95c. ; superfine flour was worth $6.90 and may be quoted now at $3.90. Wheat—Receipts, for the week, 18,839 bush. ; 26,467 bush. last week and 4,100 bush. for the corresponding week last year. Spring is dull, only a small demand at 95c. Fall nominal, no buyers, holders ask $1 to $1.05. Barley—No receipts, little stock and nothing doing ; it is nominally lower at 75 to 80c., the decline is partly owing to the advance in gold. Peas—Receipts trifling, nominal at 65 to 70c. Oats—Receipts 1,200 bush., and 4,200 bush. last week. The market is easier at 54 to 55c. owing to a better supply. Corn—There were sales of carloads at 60c.

FLOUR.—Receipts 750 bbls. ; 1,750 bbls. last week and 700 bbls. for the corresponding week of last year. There is not much flour offering, and there is no demand except for local use ; spring wheat flour may be quoted nominal at $4.00 to $4.05, the latter being for spring wheat extra. In the other grades there is nothing doing to establish prices. Meal—Quiet at unchanged quotations.

PROVISIONS.—Butter—New butter is coming in more freely, but as the demand will be no demand for export for a good while yet, the market is dull ; no demand for lots, holders ask 14 to 15c. for packages and large rolls ; small rolls for retail purposes are worth 15 to 17c. Eggs—Are in better supply and sell at 13c. Cheese.—Nominal, the late wholesale transaction was at 15c. Pork.—Is in light stock and very few hands ; mess by the carload is held at $26 ; in small lots, $26.50 Bacon.—tough is moving off more freely at 12c. ; Cumberland sells at 12½c. Ham.—Smoked are selling in a small way at 14c.for smoked and 16c. for smoked and covered.

FREIGHTS.—the rates by vessels are unchanged ; to Oswego, 3c U. S. Currency; to Kingston, 2c gold ; to Montreal via steamer, 7 to 8c. ; flour to Montreal by steamer, 20 to 25c. Lumber to Oswego, $1.50 U. S. Currency. The steamer Her Majesty will shortly leave for Halifax, her cargo is already contracted for.

The following are the Grand Trunk Railway Company's summer rates from Toronto to the undermentioned stations, which came into force on the 19th ult. :—Flour to all Stations from Belle-velle to Lynn, inclusive 25c ; grain, per 100 lbs., 13c. ; flour to Prescott, 30c ; grain 15c ; flour to all stations between Island Pond and Portland, inclusive, 75c ; grain, 38c ; flour to Boston, 80c, gold ; grain 40c ; flour to Halifax, 90c ; flour to St. John, 85c.

Halifax Market.

BREADSTUFFS—May 18—The demand for Supers for the past week has been quite equal to supply. Stocks continue light, but prices have again receded about 10 cts. Extras continue unchanged, forced sales only being effected, in limited amount, at nominal prices. Fancy meets with limited request, at quotations. No. 2 dull and unchanged. Rye Flour, without enquiry, K. D. Cornmeal in request. Stock light. Oatmeal is coming forward freely, and stocks are now largely in excess of last year's, with a very limited consumption, comparatively.

We quote White Wheat Extra.—$5.75 to 6.00; Fancy $6.50. Supf. $5.30 to 5.40 ; No. 2, $4.50 to 4.75. Cornmeal $3.80 to 3.90; Oatmeal (N.S.), $6.00 ; Canada $6.50; (dull). Rye Flour $4.76; White Beans $2.50;

FISH AND OIL.—We note no quotable change in above, there being no transactions to report. Large catches of superior Codfish are reported from Western Shore, which may influence prices slightly though the requirements of Boston and the want of stock here are likely to give tone to the market.

EXCHANGE.—Bank Drafts London at 60 days at 13 ⅛c. Montreal sight 4 ⅛c. New York Gold 4 ⅛c. Currency 24 ⅞c. disct. S. John, N.B. 3½ ⅞ c. prem.

Demerara Sugar Market.

The following is from Sandbach, Parker, & Co's. Market Report, dated, Georgetown, Demerara, 23rd April, 1869.

SUGAR.—The decline advised in our last was arrested by the American advices received by that Mail, and prices have been firm with an upward tendency since ; the drought is now telling severely on the yield, and the quantity of Sugar coming forward for sale is so small, that the ten vessels loading for the U. States will find great difficulty in getting cargoes ; the competition amongst buyers to secure any lots offering is so keen that prices have been forced beyond what latest quotations from America would warrant, and must result in a loss to shippers. These remarks refer more particularly to Vacuum Pan, the demand for Muscovado is not so animated.

MOLASSES—Has advanced considerably, and the demand for both Vacuum and Muscovado is very brisk.

RUM—Very little doing, holders prefer shipping to accepting rates offered here ; we have not heard of a single transaction of consequence. Transactions have taken place during the fortnight at the following rates :—

SUGARS (package included) sold by 100 lbs. Dutch. 10 per cent. tare.

Muscovadoes, equal to No. 8) Dutch Standard $4.00 ℗ 100 lbs.

No. 10 do. $4.50
"   "   12 do. $5.25   }   In hhds.
Vacuum Pan No. 12 do. $6.50   }   of about
"   "   14 do.   6.75   }   1800 lbs. each.
"   "   16 do.   7.25
"   "   17 do.   7.40
"   "   18 do.   7.70

MOLASSES (package included, sold by Imperial gallon.)—

Muscovado, from 22 @ 29 cents, as)   In puns to color and density   }   of
Vacuum Pan from 25 @ 38 cents, as}   100 gals. to color and density

RUM (colored, package included, sold) by Imperial gal. from 25 per cent, @ 38 }   Ditto. overproof 40 cents.
From 38 per cent. @ 40 overproof, 45 } cents.

Cotton Bales.

The following is an extract from a circular of the Manchester Board of Trade:—We have never known a period when there was such irregularity in the weight of American bales, as is now apparent. We find the variation per bale to be from 1¼ cwt to 4½ cwt in the same lot, and the average weight of bales is decidedly lighter than last year. And not only so, but there never was a time, in our opinion, when American cotton was so dishonestly packed and so abominably ginned. The very same condemnation of quality applies to Brazilian. Egyptian cotton, in weight of bales, ranges from 3 cwt to 6 cwt, and the mere report of the number

of bales would be utterly fallacious as regards the quantity. It is of vital importance to the trade that the weight should be declared.

Sugar Movement.

The Havana *Weekly Report* says of the sugar movement. The receipts at the warehouses from 1st January to date amount to 879,486 bxs, against 959,380 bxs during the same period in 1868 ; the exports up to date from Havana and Mantazas exceed those of last year by 48,079 bxs ; and the stocks at both ports to-day amount to 359,382 bxs, a decrease of 126,571 bxs when compared with those at same date last year.

INSOLVENTS:—Andrew Crawford, Montreal, Lactance E. Lamarche, Montreal; Jos. Dolan, Port age Du Fort ; Samuel Clark, Logan ; Jno. Held, Berlin ; John Raine, Brampton ; Mary Neagle, Arthur ; Andrew Woodcock, Toronto ; Harris, Scarff & Co., Owen Sound ; J. S. Ratherson, Almonte ; David Ross, Treswater ; C. Ives. Ancott; Edward Bingham, Bradford ; C. Turner, Brantford ; Donald J. O'Brien, L'Orignal; Charles Jones Mills, London; R. Malcolm, Kincardine ; S. Smith, Guelph; Michael J. Doherty, Montreal ; J. D. H. Fenner, Buckingham ; William How, Toronto ; Adam Oliver Buchanan, Guelph.

Imperial Fire Insurance Company
OF LONDON.

No. 1 OLD BROAD STREET, AND 16 PALL MALL.

ESTABLISHED 1803.

Canada General Agency,

RINTOUL BROS.,
            24 St. Sacrament Street.

JAMES E. SMITH, Agent,
Toronto, Corner Church and Colborne Streets.

Mercantile.

TORONTO PRICES CURRENT.—MAY 27, 1869.

Name of Article.	Wholesale Rates.	
	$ c.	$ c.
Boots and Shoes.		
Men's Thick Boots	2 05	2 50
" Kip	2 25	2 60
" Calf	3 00	3 70
" Congress Gaiters.	1 05	2 50
" Kip Cobourgs..	1 30	1 40
Boys' Thick Boots	1 70	1 80
Youths'	1 40	1 50
Women's Batts	0 95	1 30
" Balmoral	1 20	1 50
" Congress Gaiters..	0 90	1 50
Misses' Batts.	0 75	1 00
" Balmoral	1 00	1 20
" Congress Gaiters.	1 00	1 30
Girls' Batts	0 65	0 85
" Balmoral	0 10	1 05
" Congress Gaiters	0 75	1 10
Children's C. T. Cacks..	0 50	0 65
" Gaiters	0 55	0 90
Drugs.		
Aloes Cape.	0 12½	0 16
Alum,	0 02½	0 03
Borax,	0 10	0 00
Camphor, refined	0 65	0 70
Castor Oil,	0 16½	0 28
Caustic Soda,	0 04½	0 05
Cochineal,	0 90	1 00
Cream Tartar	0 40	0 45
Epsom Salts	0 03	0 04
Extract Logwood	0 11	0 12
Gum Arabic, sorts.	0 30	0 35
Indigo, Madras,	1 00	1 00
Licorice	0 14	0 45
Madder	0 00	0 16
Galls	0 32	0 37
Opium	12 00	13 50
Oxalic Acid	0 26	0 25
Potash, Bi-tart.	0 25	0 28
" bichromate,	0 15	0 20
Potass Iodide	3 90	4 50
Senna	0 12½	0 50
Soda Ash	0 03½	0 04
Soda Bicarb	0 60	5 00
Tartaric Acid,	0 40	0 45
Verdigris	0 35	0 40
Vitriol, Blue	0 08	0 10
Groceries.		
Coffees—		
Java, ᵽ lb.	0 22@0 23	
Laguayra,	0 17	0 18
Rio,	0 15	0 17
Fish:		
Herrings, Lab. split..	0 00	0 00
" pickled...	0 00	0 00
" scaled...	0 35	0 40
Mackerel, small kitts..	1 00	0 00
Loch Her. wh'e fir'ks..	2 50	2 75
" half	1 25	1 50
White Fish & Trout...	0 00	0 00
Salmon, saltwater....	14 00	15 00
Dry Cod, ᵽ112 fts....	4 75	5 25
Fruit:		
Raisins, Layers	2 00	2 10
" M. R	1 90	2 00
" Valentias new...	0 08½	0 7
Currants, new.	0 04½	0 04½
" old...	0 04	0 04½
Figs	0 11	0 13½
Molasses:		
Clayed, ᵽ gal.	0 00	0 35
Syrups, Standard	0 56	0 78
Golden	0 00	0 02
Rice:		
Arracan	4 25	4 40
Spices:		
Cassia, whole, ᵽ fb...	0 00	0 45
Cloves	0 10	0 12
Nutmegs	0 60	0 53
Ginger, gm und	0 20	0 25
" Jamaica, root..	0 30	0 23
Pepper, black.......	0 12½	0 00
Pimento	0 08	0 09
Sugars:		
Port Rico, ᵽ fb.....	0 0½	0 10
Cuba	0 0½	0 10
Barbadoes (bright)...	0 0½	0 10
Canada Sugar Refine'y, yellow No. 2, 60 ds	0 9½	0 10
Yellow, No. 2½	0 10½	0 10½
No. 3.	0 10½	0 10½
Crushed X	0 11	0 12½
" A	0 12	0 12½
Ground,	0 12½	0 13
Dry Crushed	0 12½	0 13
Extra Ground...	0 13½	0 14
Teas:		
Japan com'n to good..	0 48	0 55
" Fine to choicest..	0 50	0 65
Coloured, com. to me..	0 60	0 75
Congou & Souchong...	0 42	0 75
Goomg'g d t' b ne...	0 50	0 65
Y. Hyson, com to gd..	0 47½	0 55
Medium to choice	0 65	0 80
Extra choice	0 85	0 95

Name of Article.	Wholesale Rate.	
	$ c.	$ c.
Groceries—Contin'd.		
Gunpow'd'r c. to med..	0 55	0 70
" med. to fine.	0 70	0 85
" fine to fin's't..	0 85	0 65
Hyson	0 45	0 80
Imperial	0 42	0 80
Tobacco, Manufact'd :		
Can Leaf, ᵽ fb.5s&10s..	0 25	0 30
Western Leaf, com...	0 25	0 26
" Good...	0 27	0 32
" Fine..	0 32	0 35
" Bright fine..	0 40	0 50
" choice..	0 60	0 75
Hardware.		
Tin (net cash prices)		
Block, ᵽ fb...	0 28	0 00
Grain...	0 30	0 00
Copper:		
Pig	0 23	0 24
Sheet...	0 30	0 33
Cut Nails:		
Assorted ¼ Shingles, ᵽ 100 fb...	2 90	3 00
Shingle alone do	3 15	3 25
Lathe and 5 dy...	3 30	3 40
Galvanized Iron:		
Assorted sizes...	0 08	0 00
Best No. 24	0 09	0 00
" 26...	0 09	0 08
" 28..	0 09	0 09½
Horse Nails:		
Gnest's or Griffin's assorted sizes...	0 00	0 00
For W. an'd sizes...	0 18	0 19
Patent Hammer'd do..	0 17	0 18
Iron (at 4 months):		
Pig—Gartsherrie No1..	24 00	25 00
Other brands. No1...	22 00	24 00
No 2..	0 00	0 00
Bar—Scotch, ᵽ100 fb..	2 25	2 50
Refined...	3 00	3 25
Sweder...	5 00	5 50
Hoops—Coopers...	3 00	3 25
Band	3 00	3 25
Boiler Plates...	3 25	3 50
Canada Plates...	3 75	4 00
Union Jack	0 00	0 00
Pontypool...	3 25	4 00
Swansea	3 90	4 00
Lead (at 4 months):		
Bar, ᵽ 100 fbs...	0 06½	0 07
Sheet "	0 06	0 09
Shot...	0 07½	0 07½
Iron Wire (net cash):		
No. 0, ᵽ bundle...	2 70	2 80
" 6, "	3 30	3 40
" 12, "	3 40	3 50
" 16, "	4 30	4 40
Powder:		
Blasting, Canada....	3 50	0 00
FF "	4 25	4 50
FFF "	4 75	5 00
Blasting, English	4 10	5 00
FF loose..	5 00	6 00
FFF "	0 00	6 50
Pressed Spikes (4 mos):..		
Regular sizes 1sQ..	4 00	4 25
Extra...	4 50	5 00
Tin Plates (net cash):		
IC Coke	7 50	8 50
IC Charcoal...	8 50	9 00
IX "	10 50	14 u·
IXX "	13 50	14 u·
DO "	9 50	0 00
Hides & Skins, ᵽ fb.		
Green rough	0 00	0 05
Green, sal'd & linp'd..	0 06½	0 07
Cured	0 00	0 00
Calfskins, green	0 00	0 14
Calfskins, cured...	0 00	0 15
" dry...	0 14	0 0u
Sheepskins,	1 20	1 60
" country...	1 00	1 4u
Hogs		
Inferior, ᵽ fb......	0 00	0 00
Medium	0 00	0 00
Good	0 00	0 00
Fancy	0 00	0 00
Leather: ᵽ (4 mos.)		
In b'ds of least 1 and 50 sides, 10 ᵽ cent higher.		
Spanish Sole, 1st qual'y heavy, weights ᵽ	0 21	0 22
Do 1st qual middle do..	0 22	23
Do. No. 2, light weight..	0 00	0 00
Slaughter heavy	0 00	0 24
light	0 00	0 00
Harness, best	0 30	0 33
No. 2	0 30	0 33
Upper heavy	0 30	0 33
light...	0 33	0 34

Name of Article.	Wholesale Rates.	
	$ c.	$ c.
Leather—Contin'd.		
Kip Skins, Patna	0 80	00
French	0 70	0u
English	0 65	0u
Hemlock Calf (30 to 35 lbs.) per doz...	0 50	0u
Do. light	0 45	0u
French Calf	1 03	15
Grain & Satn Cl'f p'doz..	0 00	0u
Splits, large ᵽ fb...	0 30	0u
" small	0 21	0u
Enamelled Cow ᵽ foot..	0 20	0u
Patent "	0 20	0u
Pebble Grain	0 15	0u
Buff	0 14	0u
Oils.		
Cod	0 65	0u
Lard, extra	0 00	0u
" No. 1	0 00	0u
" Woollen	0 00	0u
Lubricating, patent...	0 00	0u
" Mott's standard	0 3u	0u
Linseed, raw	0 76	0u
" boiled...	0 81	0u
Machinery	0 00	0u
Olive, common, ᵽ gal.	1 00	1u
" salad	1 95	3u
" salad, in bots. qt. ᵽ case...	2 60	3u
Sesame salad, ᵽ gal...	1 50	1u
Seal, pale	0 75	0u
Spirits Turpentine...	0 62½	0u
Varnish	0 0u	0u
Whale	0 00	0u
Paints, &c.		
White Lead, genuine in Oil, ᵽ 25fts...	0 00	00
Do. No. 1 "	0 00	2u
" 2 "	0 00	1u
" 3 "	0 00	00
White Zinc, genuine..	3 00	3u
White Lead, dry...	0 165	0u
Red Lead	0 07	0u
Venetian Red, Eng'h ..	0 00	0u
Yellow Ochre, Fren'h..	0 02½	0u
Whiting	0 85	1u
Petroleum.		
(Refined ᵽ gal.)		
Water white, car'l'd...	—	—
" small lots...	0 00	0u
Straw, by car load	0 00	0u
" small lots...	0 00	0u
Amber, by car load...	0 00	0u
" small lots...	0 00	0u
Benzine	0 00	0u
Produce.		
Grain:		
Wheat, Spring, 60 fb..	0 95	0u
" Fall 60 " ..	0 98	1u
Barley	0 75	0
Peas	0 68	6u
Oats	0 54	0u
Rye	0 55	0u
Seeds:		
Clover, choice ᵽ	5 00	5u
" com'n 60 "	5 25	5u
Timothy, choice ᵽ	2 75	3u
" inf. to good 48 "	2 00	2u
Flax	2 25	0u
Flour (per brl.):		
Superior extra...	0 00	0u
Extra superfine	4 40	4u
Fancy superfine	4 10	0u
Superfine No 1...	3 90	4u
No. 2...		
Oatmeal, (per brl.)..	5 50	0u
Provisions		
Butter, dairy tub ᵽ fb..	0 15	0u
store packed...	0 11	0u
Cheese, new	0 14	0u
Pork, mess, per brl...	25 00	0u
" prime mess...		
" prime ...		
Bacon, rough	0 11½	0u
" Cumberl'd cut..	0 12	0u
" smoked	0 00	0u
Hams, in salt	0 13	0u
" smoked	0 14	0u
Shoulders, in salt	0 00	0u
Lard, in kegs	0 16½	0u
Eggs, packed	0 12½	0u
Beef hams	0 00	0u
Tallow	0 00	0u
Hogs, dressed, heavy...	0 00	0u
" light...	0 00	0u
Salt, &c.		
American brls.	1 50	1u
Liverpool coarse	0 00	1u
Goderich	0 00	1u
Plaster	0 9½	0u
Water Lime	1 50	0u

Candles.	$ c.	$ c.
l & Co.'s ..		
ul........	0 07½	0 08
Bar	0 07	0 07½
Bar........	0 07	0 07½
....	0 05	0 05½
....	0 03½	0 03½
....	0 00	0 11
Liquors,		
r doz. qrts.	2 60	2 65
Dub Portr..	2 35	2 40
ica Rum...	1 80	2 25
's H. Gin..	1 55	1 65
l Tom.....	1 90	2 00
es.........	4 00	4 25
l Tom, c...	6 00	6 25
non.......	1 00	1 25
ld	2 00	4 00
mmon	1 00	1 50
am	1 70	1 80
or golden..	2 50	4 00

Brandy:	$ c	$ c
Hennessy's, per gal..	2 30	2 50
Martell's " ..	2 30	2 50
J. Robin & Co.'s " ..	2 25	2 35
Otard, Dupuy & Cos..	2 25	2 35
Brandy, cases........	8 50	9 00
Brandy, com. per c...	4 00	4 50
Whiskey:		
Common 36 u. p......	0 58	0 60
Old Rye	0 77½	0 80
Malt	0 77½	0 80
Toddy	0 77½	0 80
Scotch, per gal......	1 90	2 10
Irish—Kinnahan's c...	7 00	7 50
" Dunnville's Belf't..	6 00	6 25
Wool.		
Fleece, lb...........	0 26	0 27
Pulled "............	0 00	0 00
Furs.		
Bear................	0 00	0 00
Beaver, ℘ lb........	0 00	0 00
Coon	0 00	0 00
Fisher..............	0 00	0 00
Martin..............	0 00	0 00
Mink................	0 00	0 00
Otter...............	0 00	0 00
Spring Rats	0 00	0 00
Fox	0 00	0 00

NSURANCE COMPANIES.

ENGLISH.—*Quotations on the London Market.*

st Dividend.	Name of Company.	Shares par val £	Amount paid.	Last Sale.
	Briton Medical and General Life...	10	....	2½
7½	Commer'l Union, Fire, Life and Mar.	50	5	5½
8	City of Glasgow	25	2½	5½
9½	Edinburgh Life	100	15	33
—½ yr	European Life and Guarantee......	2½	11s6	4s. 6d.
10	Etna Fire and Marine............	10	1½	—
5	Guardian	100	50	51½
12	Imperial Fire...................	500	50	352
9½	Imperial Life	100	10	17½
10	Lancashire Fire and Life........	20	2	2¾
11	Life Association of Scotland.....	40	7½	25
s. p. sh	London Assurance Corporation ..	25	12½	48 x d
5	London and Lancashire Life	10	1	—
40	Liverp'l & London & Globe F. & L.	20	2	7¾
5	National Union Life	5	1	1
12½	Northern Fire and Life	100	5	12¾
12 ,bo 5s.	North British and Mercantile	50	6½	19½
50	Ocean Marine	25	5	17¾
5 12s.	Provident Life..................	100	10	35
½ p. s.	Phœnix	....	....	145
—h.yr.	Queen Fire and Life	10	1	1
bo.4s	Royal Insurance..................	20	3	6¾
10	Scottish Provincial Fire and Life ..	50	2½	5 3-8
25	Standard Life	50	12	66½
5	Star Life	25	1½	—
	CANADIAN.			℘ c.
4	British America Fire and Marine ..	$50	$25	55½ 56
4	Canada Life	..	....	.....
12	Montreal Assurance	£50	£5	135
3	Provincial Fire and Marine........	60	11	.....
......	Quebec Fire	40	32½	25 25½
7	" Marine..................	100	40	85 90
mo's.	Western Assurance................	40	9	.....

RAILWAYS.	Sha's	Paid	Montr	London
d St. Lawrence........................	£100	All.	....	56
Lake Huron	20½	"	....	2¾ 3½
do Preference	10	"	....	5 6
t. & Goderich, 6 ℘c., 1872-3-4..........	100	"	....	60 69
and St. Lawrence	....	....	10 11	....
do Pref. 10 ℘ ct..............	...	....	80 85	....
nk	100	"	14 15	14½ 14¾
Eq.G. M. Bds. 1 ch. 6 ℘c..........	100	"	...	89
First Preference, 5 ℘ c	100	"	....	47
Deferred, 3 ℘ ct..................	100	"	....	....
Second Pref. Bonds, 5 ℘c..........	100	"	....	37
do Deferred, 3 ℘ ct............	100	"	...	....
Third Pref. Stock, 4 ℘ct..........	100	"	...	28½
do. Deferred, 3 ℘ ct............	100	"	...	....
Fourth Pref. Stock, 3 ℘c..........	100	"	....	16
do. Deferred, 3 ℘ ct...........	100	"		...
ern	20½	"	13 14	15 15¼
New	20½	18	....	....
6 ℘ c. Bds, due 1873-76........	100	All.	....	100½ 102
5 ℘c Bds. due 1877-78..........	100	"	....	95
lway, Halifax, $250, all.	$25	"	....	....
Canada, 6 ℘c. 1st Pref. Bds...........	100	"	.. .	82 83

CHANGE.	Halifax.	Montr'l.	Quebec.	Toronto.
London, 60 days.....				
75 days date...........	12½ 13	9¼ 9⅝	9⅜ 9½	9¾
o.	11½ 12	8 9	8⅝ 9	8½
h documents....	....	7 7½	....	....
w York.............	....	30 30¼	28 28½	2∂
do.	....	30½ 31	28½ 29	....
do.	....	par	par ⅛ dis.	par ¼ dis.
....	....	4½ 5	....	3½ to 4½

STOCK AND BOND REPORT.

The dates of our quotations are as follows:—Toronto, May 25; Montreal, May 24; Quebec, May 24; London, May 8.

NAME.	Shares.	Paid up.	Divid'd last 6 Months	Dividend Day.	CLOSING PRICES. Toronto.	Montre'l	Quebec.
BANKS.			℘ ct.				
British North America	$250	All.	3	July and Jan.	105 105½	105 106	105 105½
Jacques Cartier..............	50	"	4	1 June, 1 Dec.	bks. clsd	bks. clsd	bks. clsd
Montreal	200	"	6	"	bks. clsd	40 x d.	bks. clsd
Nationale.....................	50	"	4	1 Nov. 1 May.	105 106	106 107	106½ 107
New Brunswick	100	"	......	......	....	...	....
Nova Scotia	200	28	7&b$3½	Mar. and Sept.	....	....	....
Du Peuple.....................	50	"	4	1 Mar., 1 Sept.	108 108½	107½ 108	108 108½
Toronto	100	"	4	1 Jan., 1 July.	118 118½	118 119	117½ 118½
Bank of Yarmouth..............	....	....	......	......	....	....	....
Canadian Bank of Com'e........	50	95	......	......	102½ 103	102 103	102 102½
City Bank Montreal	80	All.	4	1 June, 1 Dec.	bks. clsd	98 x d.	bks. clsd
Commer'l Bank (St. John)......	100	"	℘ ct.	......	...	...	....
Eastern Townships' Bank.......	50	"	4	1 July, 1 Jan..	...	99 101	99½ 100½
Gore	40	...	none.	1 Jan., 1 July.	35 36	35 37	34 35
Halifax Banking Company.......	....	....	......	......	....	....	....
Mechanics' Bank...............	50	70	4	1 Nov., 1 May.	93½ 94	93 94	92 93
Merchants' Bank of Canada.....	100	70	4	1 Jan., 1 July.	109 109½	108 108½	109½ 1108
Merchants' Bank (Halifax).....	....	....	......	......	....	....	....
Molson's Bank.................	50	All.	4	1 Apr., 1 Oct.	107½ 108	109½ 109¾	107½ 10
Niagara District Bank.........	100	70	3½	1 Jan., 1 July.	...	....	....
Ontario Bank..................	40	All.	4	1 June, 1 Dec.	bks. clsd	98 x d.	bks. clsd
People's Bank (Fred'kton).....	100	"	......	......	....	....	.. .
People's Bank (Halifax).......	20	"	7 12 m	......	....	....	....
Quebec Bank	100	"	3½	1 June, 1 Dec.	bks. clsd	bks. clsd	bks. clsd
Royal Canadian Bank	50	60	4	1 Jan., 1 July.			
St. Stephens Bank	100	All.	.....	......	....	..	...
Union Bank	100	70	4	1 Jan., 1 July.	106 106½	106½ 107	107 108
Union Bank (Halifax)..........	100	40	7 12mo	Feb. and Aug.	....	....	.. .
MISCELLANEOUS.							
British America Land..........	250	44	2½	......	....	....	....
British Colonial S. S. Co.....	250	32½	2½	......	...	....	....
Canada Company	32½	All.	£1 10s.	......	....	....	....
Canada Landed Credit Co.......	50	$20	3½	......	78 80	....	....
Canada Per. B'ldg Society.....	50	All.	5	......	125½ 126	....	....
Canada Mining Company.........	4	90	......	......	....	....	....
Do. Inl'd Steam Nav. Co.......	100	All.	7	......	....	100 102½	....
Do. Glass Company.............	100	"	12½ "	......	....	40 60	....
Canad'n Loan & Investm't......	25	2½	7	......	....	....	....
Canada Agency	10	½	......	......	....	....	....
Colonial Securities Co........	...	....	......	......	....	....	....
Freehold Building Society.....	100	All.	4	......	bks. clsd	....	....
Halifax Steamboat Co..........	100	"	5	......	....	....	....
Halifax Gas Company...........	....	....	......	......	....	...	....
Hamilton Gas Company..........	....	....	......	......	....	....	....
Huron Copper Bay Co...........	4	12	20	......	....	30 45	....
Lake Huron S. and C...........	5	102	......	......	....	...	....
Montreal Mining Consols.......	20	$15	......	......	....	$.25 3.35	...
Do. Telegraph Co..........	40	All.	5	......	134½ 135	134½ 135½	134 135
Do. Elevating Co..........	00	"	15 12 m	......	....	102½ 105	...
Do. City Gas Co...........	40	"	4	15 Mar. 15 Sep.	....	135 136	134 135
Do. City Pass. R. Co......	50	"	4	......	....	108 109	108 109
Quebec and L. S.	8	$4	......	......	....	....	....
Quebec Gas Co.................	200	All.	4	1 Mar., 1 Sep.	....	...	118 119
Quebec Street R. R............	50	25	3	......	....	....	9.. 91
Richelieu Navigation Co.......	100	All.	10 p.a.	1 Jan., 1 July.	....	115 116	115½ 116½
St. Lawrence Glass Company ...	100	"	...	......	....	80 85	..
St. Lawrence Tow Boat Co......	100	"	......	3 Feb.	...	...	30 35
Tor'to Consumers' Gas Co......	50	"	4	1 My Au MarFe	107 107½	...	106 107
Trust & Loan Co. of U. C......	20	5	3	......	....	....	.. .
West'n Canada Bldg Soc'y......	50	All.	5	......	120½ 121	....	....

SECURITIES.	London.	Montreal	Quebec.	Toronto.
Canadian Gov't Deb. 6 ℘ ct. stg..................	...	102 103	101½ 102	102½ 104
Do. do. 6 do due Ja. & Jul. 1877-84........	104½ 105½	....	....	.. ..
Do. do. 6 do. Feb. & Aug...........	102 104	....	.. .	....
Do. do. 6 do. Mch. & Sep...........	102 104	.. .	...	.. .
Do. do. 5 ℘ ct. cur., 1883	93¾ 94½	92 93	92 93	91½ 93½
Do. do. 5 do. stg., 1885	93½ 94	91 92½	92½ 93	91½ 93½
Do. do. 7 do. cur.,.......................	....	....	......	...
Dominion 6 p. c. 1878 cy.........................	....	107½ 108½	108 108½	108 108½
Hamilton Corporation.............................	.. ..	....	... ..	....
Montreal Harbor, 8 ℘ ct. d. 1869.................	..	....	......	....
Do. do. 7 do. 1870........................	....	....	......	....
Do. do. 6½ do. 1883........................	....	102 103	......	102 103
Do do. 6½ do. 1873........................	....	...	......	
Do. Corporation, 6 ℘ c. 1891.....................	....	96 96½	96½ 97	96 96½
Do. 7 p. c. stock................................	....	1..8½ 110	109 110	109 110
Do. Water Works, 6 ℘ c. stg. 1878...............	....	96½ 97	......	9.. 96½
Do. do. 6 do. cy. do.	....	....	......	96 97
New Brunswick, 6 ℘ ct., Jan. and July	104 104½	....	.. ...	....
Nova Scotia, 6 ℘ ct., 1875........................	103 104	...	......	....
Ottawa City 6 ℘ c. d. 1880	....	95 97	......	...
Quebec Harbour, 6 ℘ c. d. 1883....................	....	....	60	....
Do. do. 7 do. do.	....	....	65 70	....
Do. do 8 do. 1886..........................	...	....	80 85	....
Do. City, 7 ℘ c. d. 1½ years......................	....	....	98 98½	....
Do. do. 7 do. 3 do.	....	....	91 92	....
Do. do. 7 do. 4 do.	....	....	94 95	....
Do. Water Works, 7 ℘ ct., 3 years.................	....	....	97 97½	....
Do. do. 6 do. 1½ do.	....	....	94 95	....
Toronto Corporation	....	92 94	...	....

Insurance.

Briton Medical and General Life Association,

with which is united the

BRITANNIA LIFE ASSURANCE COMPANY.

Capital and Invested Funds............£750,000 Sterling.

ANNUAL INCOME, £220,000 STG. :

Yearly increasing at the rate of £25,000 Sterling.

THE important and peculiar feature originally introduced by this Company, in applying the periodical Bonuses, so as to make Policies payable during life, without any higher rate of premiums being charged, has caused the success of the BRITON MEDICAL AND GENERAL to be almost unparalleled in the history of Life Assurance. *Life Policies on the Profit Scale become payable during the lifetime of the Assured, thus rendering a Policy of Assurance a means of subsistence in old age, as well as a protection for a family*, and a more valuable security to creditors in the event of early death ; and effectually meeting the often urged objection, that persons do not themselves reap the benefit of their own prudence and forethought.

No extra charge made to members of Volunteer Corps for services within the British Provinces.

☞ TORONTO AGENCY, 5 KING ST. WEST.

Oct 17—9-1yr　　　　JAMES FRASER, *Agent.*

BEAVER
Mutual Insurance Association.

HEAD OFFICE—20 TORONTO STREET,
TORONTO.

INSURES LIVE STOCK against death from any cause. The only Canadian Company having authority to do this class of business.

E. C. CHADWICK,
President.

W. T. O'REILLY,
Secretary.　　　　　　　　　8-1y-25

HOME DISTRICT
Mutual Fire Insurance Company.

Office.—North-West Cor. Yonge & Adelaide Streets,
TORONTO.—(UP STAIRS.)

INSURES Dwelling Houses, Stores, Warehouses, Merchandise, Furniture, &c.

PRESIDENT—The Hon. J. McMURRICH.
VICE-PRESIDENT—JOHN BURNS, Esq.
JOHN RAINS, Secretary.

AGENTS:
DAVID WRIGHT, Esq., Hamilton; FRANCIS STEVENS, Esq., Barrie : Messrs. GIBBS & BRO., Oshawa.　　8-1y

THE PRINCE EDWARD COUNTY
Mutual Fire Insurance Company.

HEAD OFFICE.—PICTON, ONTARIO.

President, L. B. STINSON; *Vice-President*, W. A. RICHARDS. *Directors :* H. A. McFaul, James Cavan, James Johnson, N. S. DeMill, William Delong.—*Secretary*, John Twigg ; *Treasurer*, David Barker; *Solicitor*, R. J. Fitzgerald.

THIS Company is established upon strictly Mutual principles, insuring farming and isolated property, (not hazardous,) in *Townships only*, and offers great advantages to insurers, at low rates for *five years*, without the expense of a renewal.

Picton, June 15, 1868.　　　　　　　　9-1y

THE AGRICULTURAL
Mutual Assurance Association of Canada.

HEAD OFFICE ....LONDON, ONT

A purely Farmers' Company. Licensed by the Government of Canada.

Capital, 1st January, 1869.................... $230,192 82
Cash and Cash Items, over..................... $86,000 00
No. of Policies in force....................... 30,804 00

THIS Company insures nothing more dangerous than Farm property. Its rates are as low as any well-established Company in the Dominion, and lower than those of a great many. It is largely patronised, and continues to grow in public favor.

For Insurance, apply to any of the Agents or address the Secretary, London, Ontario.
London, 2nd Nov., 1868.　　　　　　　12-1y.

Insurance.

The Gore District Mutual Fire Insurance Company

GRANTS INSURANCES on all description of Property against Loss or Damage by FIRE. It is the only Mutual Fire Insurance Company which assesses its Policies yearly from their respective dates ; and the average yearly cost of insurance in it, for the past three and a half years, has been nearly

TWENTY CENTS IN THE DOLLAR less than what it would have been in an ordinary Proprietary Company.

THOS. M. SIMONS,
Secretary & Treasurer.

ROBT. McLEAN,
Inspector of Agencies.
Galt, 25th Nov., 1868.　　　　　　　13-1y

Western Assurance Company,

INCORPORATED 1851.

CAPITAL, ... $400,000.

FIRE AND MARINE.

HEAD OFFICE.................TORONTO, ONTARIO

DIRECTORS.
Hon. JNO. McMURRICH, President.
　　　　　CHARLES MAGRATH, Vice-President.
A. M. SMITH, Esq.　　　　JOHN F ISKEN, Esq.
ROBERT BEATY, Esq.　　ALEX. MANNING, Esq.
JAMES MICHIE, Esq.　　N. BARNHART, Esq.
　　　　　R. J. DALLAS, Esq.
　　B MALDAN, Secretary.
　　J. MAUGHAN, JR., Assistant Secretary.
　　WM. BLIGHT, Fire Inspector.
　　CAPT. G. T. DOUGLAS, Marine Inspector.
　　JAMES PRINGLE, General Agent.

Insurances effected at the lowest current rates on Buildings, Merchandise, and other property, against loss or damage by fire.

On Hull, Cargo and Freight against the perils of Inland Navigation.

On Cargo Risks with the Maritime Provinces by sail or steam

On Cargoes by steamers to and from British Ports.
WESTERN ASSURANCE COMPANY'S OFFICE, ⎫
　　TORONTO, 1st April, 1869.　　　⎬　33-1y
　　　　　　　　　　　　　　⎭

Fire and Marine Assurance.

THE BRITISH AMERICA
ASSURANCE COMPANY.
HEAD OFFICE:
CORNER OF CHURCH AND COURT STREETS,
TORONTO.

BOARD OF DIRECTION :
Hon G. W. Allan, M L C,　　A. Joseph, Esq.,
George J Boyd, Esq ,　　Peter Paterson, Esq.,
Hon W. Cayley,　　　　G. P. Ridout, Esq.,
Richard S. Cassels, Esq.,　E H. Rutherford, Esq ,
　　　　　Thomas C. Street, Esq.

Governor:
GEORGE PERCIVAL RIDOUT, Esq.
Deputy Governor:
PETER PATERSON, Esq.
Fire Inspector:　　　　Marine Inspector:
E ROBY O'BRIEN.　　　CAPT. R. COURNEEN.

Insurances granted on all descriptions of property against loss and damage by fire and the perils of inland navigation.

Agencies established in the principal cities, towns, and ports of shipment throughout the Province.

THOS. WM BIRCHALL,
23-1y　　　　　　　　*Managing Director.*

Queen Fire and Life Insurance Company,
OF LIVERPOOL AND LONDON,
ACCEPTS ALL ORDINARY FIRE RISKS
on the most favorable terms.

LIFE RISKS
Will be taken on terms that will compare favorably with other Companies.

CAPITAL,　•　•　•　£2,000,000 Stg.

CHIEF OFFICE—Queen's Buildings, Liverpool, and Gracechurch Street London.
CANADA BRANCH OFFICE—Exchange Buildings, Montreal.
Resident Secretary and General Agent,
A. MACKENZIE FORBES,
13 St. Sacrament St., Merchants' Exchange, Montreal.
WM. ROWLAND, Agent, Toronto.　　　1-1y

Insurance.

The Waterloo County Mutual Fire Insu Company.

HEAD OFFICE : WATERLOO, ONTARIO.

ESTABLISHED 1863.

THE business of the Company is divided into separate and distinct branches, the

VILLAGE, FARM, AND MANUFACTU

Each Branch paying its own losses and its just prop of the managing expenses of the Company.
C. M. TAYLOR, Sec.　　M. SPRINGER, M.M.P., P
　　　　　J. HUGHES, Inspector.

Ætna Fire and Marine Insurance Compai
Dublin.

AT a Meeting of the Shareholders of this Com held at Dublin, on the 13th ult., it was agreed the business of the "ETNA" should be transferred t "UNITED FORTS AND GENERAL INSURANCE COMP in accordance with this agreement, the business will after be carried on by the latter Company, which Ass and guarantees all the risks and liabilities of the "E The Direct rs have resolved to continue the CAN BRANCH, and arrangements for resuming FIRE an MINE business are rapidly approaching completion.

16　　　　　　　　T. W. GRIFFITI
　　　　　　　　　　　　　　　MANAG

Lancashire Insurance Compan

CAPITAL, - - - - - - - - - £2,000,000 St

FIRE RISKS
Taken at reasonable rates of premium, and
ALL LOSSES SETTLED PROMPTLY,
By the undersigned, either at reference elsewa

S. C. DUNCAN-CLARK & CO.,
General Agents for Ontario,
N. W. Corner of King & Church Stre
25-1y　　　　　　　TORONTO.

Canada Life Assurance Compa

SPECIALLY LICENSED BY THE GOVERNME
OF CANADA.

ESTABLISHED 1847.

CAPITAL.....A MILLION DOLL/

DEPOSIT WITH GOVERNMENT, $50,000.

The success of the Company may be judged of b fact that during the financial year to the 30th April, the gross number of

NEW POLICIES
ISSUED WAS
8 9 2 !
FOR ASSURANCES OF
$1,357,134,
WITH
ANNUAL PREMIUMS OF
$49,783.73.

Rates lower that those of British or Foreign Offi e every advantage offered which safety and liberali afford.

A. G. RAMSAY, Manage
E. BRADBURNE, Agent
May 25.　1y　　　　　　　Toronto Str

The Victoria Mutual
FIRE INSURANCE COMPANY OF CANAD.

Insures only *Non-Hazardous Property, at Low*

BUSINESS STRICTLY MUTUAL.

GEORGE H. MILLS, President.
W. D. BOOKER, Secretary.

HEAD OFFICE . . . . .HAMILTON, ON
aug 15-1yr

PUBLISHED AT THE OFFICE OF THE MONE
TIMES, No. 60 CHURCH STREET.
PRINTED AT THE DAILY TELEGRAPH PUBLISHING H
BAY STREET, CORNER OF KING.

THE CANADIAN

IONETARY TIMES

AND

INSURANCE CHRONICLE.

)TED TO FINANCE, COMMERCE, INSURANCE, BANKS, RAILWAYS, NAVIGATION, MINES, INVESTMENT,
PUBLIC COMPANIES, AND JOINT STOCK ENTERPRISE.

—NO. 42. TORONTO, THURSDAY, JUNE 3, 1869. SUBSCRIPTION $2 A YEAR.

Mercantile.

Financial.

DEBATE ON THE BANKING SCHEME.

The banking resolutions were brought up in
the House of Commons, in Committee, on Tuesday night, the 1st June, for discussion.

Mr. Holton rose and argued at length in favor
of delay. He charged the Minister of Finance
with having gone beyond the limits of prudence
in referring to the insecurity afforded to the country by the present banking system. He defended
the present banking system at some length, and
concluded by moving an amendment to the resolutions, postponing the further consideration of
the subject till the next session.

Mr. McKenzie seconded the amendment. He
believed the policy of the Finance Minister would
be disastrous to the commerce of the country, and
especially of Ontario. There was, in his opinion,
nothing whatever to recommend the changes proposed. The press displayed an unanimous hostility to the measure such as had never before
been seen in reference to any measure, great or
small, which had ever been proposed in Parliament. Petitions from almost the entire commercial community, from one end of the country to
the other, had poured in to Parliament against the
measure, and not a single petition, to his knowledge, had been presented in its favor. He believed the disasters experienced by the banks in
the past few years were the direct result of government interference with the banking institutions of the country. By next session the people
would be able to pronounce an opinion upon the
scheme, and if it was a good one, the Government
would profit by the delay. If carried into effect,
the scheme would bring about one of the most
disastrous periods ever experienced in the history
of the country.

Mr. Cartwright followed. He regarded the
amendment as dictated by partizan feeling; and
as it was designed as as a vote of censure on the
Government, it could not be accepted by the supporters of the Government. The question had
not been sprung on the House, and the plan was
not unalterable, like the laws of the Medes and
Persians. On the contrary, the Finance Minister
had invited members to favour him with their
views and opinions on the subject. He then proceeded to state his objections to the scheme. Before doing so, he wished to know the determination of the Government as to whether the banks
would be allowed to purchase the securities in
the open market, or direct from the Government;
and also what was the penalty if a bank fell short
in its reserve.

Mr. Rose replied that these matters of detail
could be settled afterwards.

Mr. Cartwright continued. He approved of a
a uniform system of currency, but if we had to
pay for that uniformity by the shattering and
convulsing of the whole monetary system of the
larger portion of the Dominion, and the destruction of the elasticity of the currency, we
would pay too dearly for it. There was great
danger that these results would be experienced.
The result of this scheme would be the universal
cessation of the power of issuing notes on credit.
He had made some calculations, showing the extent to which the Upper Canadian Banks would be

affected by this measure. On the 31st March,
1869, the capital of the four principal banks then
existing in Ontario, the Bank of Toronto, Ontario
Bank, Royal Canadian Bank, and Bank of Commerce, amounted, as nearly as might be, to $5,000,-
000. Their circulation at that time was about
$4,000,000. Their resources of all kinds in cash,
Government securities, notes and Bank balances
was $4,400,000. Their total liabilities amounted to
$12,250,000. Now the House would observe that
their reserves, to the extent of $4,400,000, were
held against the circulation of 4½ millions,
but against the total liabilities of 12½ millions;
and it would be absurd to say that in order to
protect their circulation they could safely denude
themselves of all those reserves and disregard the
risks they might run from the withdrawal of deposits. On the other hand, to shew how little the
withdrawal of circulation would affect the Lower
Canada Banks, he stated that at the same date the
Bank of Montreal, against a total liability of 14½
millions, held cash assets, including bank balances,
of nearly 10 millions, and had no circulation at all
to protect. From the calculations he had made,
it appeared that so far from two or three millions
additional being all that was required to be provided by the Ontario Banks to cover their liabilities
in the event of these resolutions being passed,
some eight or nine millions would be required, in
order to place the Banks in the same relative
position of strength in which they stood to-day.
It was well to remember that if the silver currency
were removed a large increase of bank circulation
would be required. If Ontario continued to prosper all the natural increase of banking capital on
which the Finance Minister relied to fill up the
gap caused by this measure would be more than
required for the growing business of the country.
The measure would necessarily affect Ontario. In
Nova Scotia the lowest bank note was $20, so
that the bank circulation could not there be extensively diffused among the people. Losses had
been suffered to the extent of, perhaps, $400,000
in all, by the suspension of banks in Ontario, but
the people of that Province had made no complaints as to the inadequacy of the security. The
scheme would destroy all the elasticity which our
currency at present possessed. Under it the
banks, for every $100 of notes would have to pay
$120 of money or money's worth. The Finance
Minister was about to create a gold currency, the
only distinction between which and an absolute
gold currency was the convenience there would
be in having our current coin in paper instead of
gold, which was troublesome to carry. It might
be better to use gold altogether, but this system
would shift the danger from circulation to deposits. Mr. Cartwright continued at length reviewing the scheme in an able speech, for even a
summary of which we have not space. He concluded by asking time for the consideration of the
measure in all its bearings and effects.

Hon. Mr. Tilley spoke in support of the resolutions. He referred to the petitions which he
said had only 3,723 signatures, and said that in
his own Province there was not a change in the
law against which they could not get 3,000 signatures in a few days. He contended that its
uniform currency was most desirable, and this
was admitted. The stockholders of the banks
would be placed in a better position than now.
He then referred to the present position of bank-

ing operations in Ontario and Quebec. The banking capital of those Provinces was $30,000,000; the average of gold held by the banks was $9,000,000; the average of Government securities was $6,000,000 at 5 and 6 per cent. interest, together $15,000,000. The banks would still have $15,000,000 of their capital left. The result of the present arrangement is to give the stockholders of Ontario and Quebec $2,460,000, but the new arrangement proposed by the Finance Minister would give them $2,570,000, a gain of $110,000. If the Government securities were issued at 6, instead of 5 per cent., the comparison would be still more favorable. Then as to the accommodation to be given to the public ; at present the aggregate stock was $30,000,000 gold and Government securities $15,000,000, leaving $15,000,000 stock and $15,000,000 paper, on which the banks could give accommodation under the present law. Under the proposal of the Minister of Finance there would be $30,000,000 of capital, $41,000,000 of gold, and $15,000,000 of stock, leaving $11,000,000 of stock for discount and $15,000,000 of paper, or in all $26,000,000. This made a difference of $4,000,000 only under the operation of the resolution. He did not think the banks would suffer materially from the change.

Mr. Rose defended the scheme and argued the necessity of proceeding with it. The signatures to the petitions had been obtained by the banks and bank clerks. He referred warmly to the opposition of the banks to the government. We had, he said, three different systems of banking, in operation, and members preferred that in their own respective Provinces. . In reply to Mr. Cartwright he said that at the time of the failure of the Bank of Upper Canada, it had $800,000 circulation, and only $39,000 reserve, and the Commercial Bank, at the time of its failure, had a circulation of about $1,100,000. He denied that the failure of the Bank was caused by the distrust of depositors, and took the case of the Royal Canadian Bank as an illustration. In January its circulation was $1,534,000. In April it had fallen to $993,000, and when it closed its doors the circulation had decreased to $800,000. The St. John Commercial Bank had, when it failed, a circulation of $300,000 and only a reserve of $41,000. These failures were most serious disasters to the commercial prosperity of the country. He would call attention to the importance reserves have to circulation, as showing the tendency of the present system of diminishing the amount of deposit. In 1865, the lowest per centage of reserve was 16, the highest 43; in 1866, the lowest 14 per cent, the highest 29 ; in 1867, the lowest 14, the highest 22 ; in 1868, the lowest 13, the highest 26 per cent—showing a continual diminution of reserves in proportion to circulation. He contended that the change would not give the Government any new political power, and replied at length to the objections raised by previous speakers.

Hon. Mr. Galt opposed the resolutions ; he pointed out that in various respects Mr. Rose's scheme was not so useful or safe as a direct Government issue of notes and was more expensive. Banks would fail just the same, because they could not by legislation prevent bad management. The principal objection to the scheme was the want of elasticity. He pointed out the injurious effect that would be produced on the trade of Ontario, and urged that delay be granted.

Hon. J. H. Cameron moved an amendment to the amendment as follows : "That this House recognizes the great importance of having a uniform system of currency, but inasmuch as immediate uniformity cannot be obtained, it is expedient that the several Bank charters about to expire be extended to such a period as Parliament shall determine."

Mr. Morris seconded this amendment and supported it in a short speech.

Mr. Gibbs opposed the resolutions. The House then adjourned.

ASSIMILATION OF THE CURRENCY.

Mr. Savary brought up this matter in the House of Commons, on the 4th May. Hon. Mr. Rose, in reply, stated the reasons why the Government had felt it to be their duty not to issue any proclamation in accordance with the authority given them by the Act of last Session. At the time the legislation of last session was sought, there was a Bill before the American Congress, which its introducer, Senator Sherman, believed would become law during that session, and which would have had the effect of carrying out the recommendation of the Paris Conference, adopted some months ago in favour of an international assimilation of currency based on the 25 franc piece; and the American five dollar piece the English sovereign being made equal to it. The European Continental Governments had generally given their assent to this project, and our Act of last session authorized this Government also to adopt it, so soon as it should be adopted by the American Government. But since that time an entirely new phase had come over the question, in consequence of the researches by an English Royal Commission which was named about the time this House was last sitting. The enquiries made by that Commission had brought so many important facts under the notice of the European and American Governments, that the state of public opinion had undergone very considerable change with reference to the whole question ; in so much so that the American Congress had deferred legislation on the subject, and a new commission had been appointed by the French, and he believed, other Continental Governments, to ascertain whether the statements made by the English Commissioners were or were not founded on fact and logical in their recommendation. The recommendation of the English Commissioners went for a good way in harmony with those of the Paris Conference. They agreed that some one coin should be taken as the standard of a currency which should be uniform among the commercial nations of the world. They agreed that the coin should be gold and not silver, and they agreed that it should be nine-tenths fine, instead of being of the fineness of the English sovereign, which contained only 1-12th alloy. But in the course of their inquiries they had discovered an important fact which materially affected the calculation on which the recommendation of the Paris Conference had been based—that in France there had been a double standard, one of gold and one of silver ; there was a large amount of this silver currency in circulation, bearing a higher proportion in value to gold than it ought to do with gold nine-tenths fine—that a silver franc, for example, was worth a good deal more than one-fifth of a gold five franc piece. This important fact having been disclosed by the English Commissioners, the French Government had caused inquiries to be made with regard to it, and if the fact was found to be as alleged, the whole question would assume a different phase. The English Commissioners, while going with the Paris Conference in the first three steps he had mentioned, recommended as the standard for the proposed international currency the English sovereign instead of the French twenty-five franc piece, as the most convenient for the world at large ; and they showed strong reasons indeed for this conclusion at which they had arrived. In the first place, they said the English sovereign had never varied in value from the well known gold value of a pound sterling, by which most of the coin in the world had been regulated. The adoption of any other standard they considered would cause a great deal of inconvenience all the world over. Another reason for adopting the sovereign was, that if the twenty-five franc piece were adopted as the basis, France and the United States would have to call in all their silver coin in order to assimilate it to the gold standard. And these reasons were fortified by another consideration. The English Government had never charged seignorage for gold left at the Mint, but for so many ounces in gold

returned, after so many days, their equivalent coin ; whereas France and the United States and other countries, did charge seignorage for verting bar gold into current coin. The consequence would be that the many millions of now in circulation, which would require to be coined, would be all brought to England for purpose, as the coining would there be done nothing. The commissioners also recommended that any change should be carried out by means a convention or treaty, into which the various nations should enter, and suggested a number matters, such as the remitting of coin which lost by sweating or use, as to which there may internal arrangements. He understood the was now the impression, both in France and United States, that the recommendation of English Commissioners had much merit in the they should not wholly be accepted, and the English Sovereign adopted as the standard. This would cause very little inconvenience to these countries for the pound sterling had been practically standard throughout the world up to the time the French Revolution, and in the United States during the suspension of specie payments, it of little consequence what particular coin taken as the standard, whereas the investigations of the Commissioners had shown that the world large would be more inconvenienced by change from the English sovereign than the United States by a change from their five-dollar piece France by assimilating her 25 franc piece to sovereign. Under these circumstances he thought we should submit a little longer to the inconvenience arising from the difference of currency these Provinces. He hoped we should soon Newfoundland into the Confederation. Newfoundland also had a different standard of money differing both from Nova Scotia and the rest of the Dominion. In Newfoundland, the sovereign he believed, was worth $4.80, while in Nova Scotia it was worth $5, and here, $4.86⅔. Hudson's Bay Territory, again, which we have soon to incorporate into the Union, had at fourth standard ; and Prince Edward Island which we hoped by and bye to bring into the had another peculiar to itself. He observed the report of the Commissioners that the Government, and he believed another reason which was mentioned in the Report, had adopted the same course as we had done, and passed permissive Bill.

TORONTO STOCK MARKET.

(Reported by Pellatt & Osler, Brokers.)

Business continues still inactive in stocks bonds ; transactions that have taken place been at high rates.

Bank Stock.—Sales of Montreal have taken place at 150 and 150½ ex-dividend ; there buyers at the former rate. Buyers offer 10. British ; none in market. Ontario is offered 97½ ex-dividend, a small sale reported at 97. Toronto in market, enquired for at 118. There are buyers of Royal Canadian at 30, but no se Commerce is firm and in demand at 103 ; sellers under 104. Gore is offering freely at buyers will not advance on 35. Small sale Merchants' were made at 109 which rate is off Nothing doing in Quebec. There are buyers Molson's at 108 and sellers at 108½. No sale City. For Du Peuple 109 would be paid ; in market. There are buyers of Nationale a Small sales of Mechanics' at 93½. Jacques Canominal at 105 ex-dividend. Union has advanced to 107 and is in demand at that rate.

Debentures.—Sales of Dominion Stock made at 108 and 108¼, there are now buyers 107⅜ ; five and six per cents. are enquired Toronto are offering at rates to pay 7 per interest. County are offering to pay 100 and not in much demand.

Sundries.—City Gas was pressed for sale beginning of the week at 105, there are

at that rate. No sellers of British America nce under 60 ; nothing doing. There were if Canada Permanent Building Society at .nd 126, still procurable at the latter rate. n Canada Building Society sold at 120½ :1 ; a small lot on market at latter rate. id Building Society is in demand, sales have .ade at 113 ex-dividend. There are buyers .treal Telegraph at 135 and sellers at 135¼. if Landed Credit were made at 78 and .re are buyers at 79½ and no sellers under ne or two large mortgages were offered at ent. ; $1,000 and $2,000 mortgages are in l. Money is in demand and on the street advance on bank rate is paid.

BANKING SCHEME—ACTION OF THE TO-BOARD OF TRADE.—A meeting of the was held on Monday, the 29th of May, mee G. Worts in the chair ; there was attendance of members. A draft of a i to Parliament was read by the Secretary, stance of which is as follows :—That the iers, while admitting that some of the reso-on banking and currency are worthy of n, in so far they tend to the promotion, of id security in banking operations, are y of opinion that the change which would uced in the Canadian Banking system, by posed abolition of the existing note circu-and the substitution in its place of a cir-i founded upon government debentures, ve seriously detrimental to the Province of , inasmuch as it would deprive the banks power of expansion which, exercised under :onditions and limitations, is calculated so lly to advance, and has hitherto advanced nall measure the well-being and progress Province ; that the security of the note would be sufficiently gained by inserting ns in bank charters, making the notes in s the first lien upon the assets, of a bank, the affairs of a suspended bank under the on of a public officer, with instructions to te notes from the first available funds in nd enforcing the principle of double liabil-sspect of stockholders. That any further protection of the note-holder would be ous ; that the principle of discriminating different classes of depositors in the man-down in Resolution 10 is unsound, and rove unjust and injurious in practice ; that tioners deem it highly impolitic, in the of any pecuniary pressure upon the Gov-, to place so large a portion of the capital untry in the hands of any Administration ; petitioners highly approve of that portion roposed plan, which would effect the with-of the Provincial notes from circulation, assured that the issue of such notes is a the direction of an irredeemable currency, es an undue advantage in the hands of ernment bank, for the time being, over anking institutions—both which results imental to the interests of the country.

; SALE IN HALIFAX.—At the sale of ; the Merchant's Exchange Reading Room' Nash, for W. M. Gray, the following sposed of :—10 shares People's Bank at 40 do. at $27 ; 18 do. Union do. at $55 ; lank of Nova Scotia at £69 ; 4 do. Half Insurance Company at £10 5s. ; 12 shares Fire Insurance Company at £10 3s 9d. ; 7 Insurance Company at £19 5s. ; several .cadia Fire Insurance Company at $51.

OF NATIONAL BANKS WHICH HAVE RE-THEIR PRIVILEGES.—The following is a he National Banks which have resigned .vileges as designated depositories since of April last, and have withdrawn their s: New York County National Bank of rk; the Second, Third, Fifth, Tenth and l Park Banks of New York; the First of N.Y.; the Blackstone and Third Nation-

al Bank of Boston; the First and Union National Banks of Chicago, Ill.; Ridgely National Bank of Springfield, Ill.; National Bank of Germantown and Philadelphia, Notional Bank of Philadelphia, and the First National Bank of Williamsport, Pa.

P. O. SAVINGS BANKS.—In answer to an inquiry on this subject in the Senate, Hon. Mr. Campbell replied :—"That already the Post Office Savings Banks have been extended to the Maritime Provinces. It was the wish of the Government to make these Savings Banks as general throughout the Dominion as possible. However, as the expense of management had already cost about two per cent., it was necessary to proceed with caution."

—The bills for increasing the capital stock of the Bank of Commerce, and of the Bank of New Brunswick have been passed by the House of Commons and also have received the second reading in the Senate.

Insurance.

FIRE RECORD.—Montreal, May 26.—A brick building on George street was set on fire; damage $300. Also the workshop of a shoemaker, corner Magill and Lemoine streets, damage slight.

Aylesford, N. B., May 14.—House of W. J. Kirkpatrick was totally destroyed; loss partly covered by insurance.

St. John, N. B., May.—An unfinished house was struck by lightning and damaged to the extent of $500.

Niagara Township, Ont., May 24.—House of Jos. Stevens was destroyed; the fire caught from the chimney; no insurance.

Plattsville, May 27.—Kerr, Brown & McKenzie's shingle factory was destroyed by fire. Loss stated at $1,500; partially insured.

RATES OF INSURANCE IN CHICAGO.—A Chicago paper says—The Board of Underwriters of this city have passed a resolution permitting all its members to fix their own rates of premiums to be charged, without reference to the uniform rates which they had heretofore endeavored to sustain in their board organization. As the leading idea in the formation of a board of Underwriters was to secure uniform and also higher rates than they could while competing with each other by cutting down rates, the adoption of this resolution was equivalent to a dissolution of the Board. The result has been that, during the last week, rates of insurance on buildings and their contents, in the business part of the city, have fallen nearly fifty per cent. in many cases, and in some cases even more. This, however, only applies to buildings in the business parts of the city, as these were the only risks on which the Board of Underwriters attempted to establish uniform rates for all the companies. Rates for insurance on dwellings in all parts of the city have always been open to competition, and therefore remain unaffected by the action of the Board.

FOREIGN LIVES.—The following is an extract from a circular issued by a prominent American Company to its agents and solicitors:—"Our experience has demonstrated that residents in this country of foreign birth, and especially those emigrating in middle life, are not equally good risks as native-born citizens; and that, of those, the Irish are decidedly the poorest, and the Germans the next. It is believed that of the above two classes who now embrace life insurance, the number is so large as to materially disturb the average rate of mortality expected from selected lives, and to materially increase the cost of insurance. We therefore request that agents will not make any special efforts to solicit applications from among those classes, and that they will use discretion and care in selecting cases from those classes to be sent to this office."

ENDOWMENT POLICY.—This form of policy embraces the principles of both Life Insurance and the Savings Bank. By it a party protects his family or others whom he wished to benefit ; and upon attaing a specific age, reaps for his own use the advantage of the savings he had made in earlier years, thus, in addition to providing for contingencies on the pathway of life, returning him the principal and a fair interest on the investment. The payments upon these policies may be made to cease in ten years, or to continue during the term of the policy. Endowment policies, after the payment of two entire years' premiums, are non-forfeitable in most of the companies, for such a proportion of the original sum as the number of annual premiums paid bears to the total number required by the Policy.—Monitor.

A NEW TABLE OF MORTALITY.

The Institute of Actuaries, of England, have been engaged for three or four years past in collecting and tabulating the mortality experience of some twenty English and Scotch Life Insurance Companies, part of which experience extends over nearly a quarter of a century. Great care was taken in the elimination of duplicate policies on the same life, and the large number of entrants and the great length of time, forming the basis of these calculations, gives extraordinary value and authority to the result.

The following table, from the London Insurance Gazette, exhibits that result :

	Entered.	Years of life exposed.	Died.	Discontinued.	Exist'g at end of 1868.
Healthy lives, male....	130,243	1,283,034	20,521	25,024	74,698
Do. female....	16,604	161,417	8,332	5,507	7,782
Both	146,847	1,444,451	23,856	40,531	82,460
Diseased lives, male & female.	11,146	101,695	2,456	3,305	5,325
Lives exposed to extra risk from climate or occupation, male and female....	2,483	16,503	409	1,480	544
Total	160,426	1,562,649	26,721	45,376	88,329

The Institute have further pursued their investigations with a view of determining, so far as possible, the value of medical selection. This may be traced in varying measures according to the age at entry, appearing to continue longest in the middle periods of life ; but for all practical purposes, seems to cease entirely after five years. The first year of insurance shows a remarkably low rate of mortality, averaging at all the ages only 46 deaths among 10,000 entrants.

The comparative rate of mortality among female lives shows an excess at all ages below 45. beginning at the age of twenty, with an excess of nearly 70 per cent., and descending gradually until the age of 45 is reached, when it is nearly equal. From that time onward it improves to the end of the table, being at the close some twenty per cent. better than the mortality among male lives. The average excess of mortality among females is about 20 per cent.

The mean duration of insurance, including those living, December 31, 1868, was 9.12 years. Out of the entrants, the proportion who died had been 16.2 per cent., discontinued, 27.6 per cent., living and keeping up their policies, December 31, 1863, 56.2 per cent. The result of these elaborate researches into the experience of Life Insurance Companies, is to give us a new table of mortality, more accurative and authoritive than any we have ever had. Under the age of fifty-five, this table differs very little from that in most general use in this country, and is considerably below the Carlisle. It exhibits a more perfectly graduated scale of mortality than any table extant, and until the experience of our American Companies shall have been extended over a sufficient length of time, and been recorded and tabulated with sufficient care to rival this work, our own Actuaries will continue to be indebted to the Institute for the most valuable data accessible for the purposes of their calculations.—*The Chronicle.*

THE CANADIAN MONETARY TIMES AND INSURANCE CHRONICLE *is printed every Thursday evening and distributed to Subscribers on the following morning.*

Publishing office, No. 60 Church-street, 3 doors north of Court-street.

Subscription price—
　　Canada $2.00 *per annum.*
　　England, stg. 10s. *per annum.*
　　United States (U.S. Cy.) $3.00 *per annum.*

Casual advertisements will be charged at the rate of ten cents per line, each insertion.

Address all letters to "THE MONETARY TIMES."

Cheques, money orders, &c. should be made payable to J. M. TROUT, *Business Manager, who alone is authorized to issue receipts for money.*

☞ *All Canadian Subscribers to* THE MONETARY TIMES *will receive* THE REAL ESTATE JOURNAL *without further charge.*

The Canadian Monetary Times.

THURSDAY, JUNE 3, 1869.

THE CANADIAN CANALS.

NO. III.

The arrival at Montreal of the splendid propeller, "Her Majesty," from Toronto, with a cargo equal to 4,000 barrels of flour, and its increase there to 6,300 barrels, is a very suggestive fact. Her destination was Halifax, but the necessity of floating through the present canal navigation of the St. Lawrence, had imposed a limit on the cargo with which she started on her trip. Ten barrels of flour are held to be a ton of freight; therefore if the canals permitted such a vessel to load to her full capacity, one third more freight would be carried at the same cost of carrying it, and, accordingly, the normal rate of freight would be one third cheaper, even with such a vessel as "Her Majesty." Starting easterly from Toronto, to proceed to the salt

water, there are two systems of navigation, the St. Lawrence Canals and the river below Montreal. As the Allan steamers now lie at the Montreal wharves, it needs but mention of the fact to establish the extent of the latter. To be precise, however, it may be described as a 20 foot navigation. There has been some unpleasant correspondence on this subject, and doubt has been thrown upon the fact. But after examination of the charts, and what has been advanced on both sides, we deliberately say that there is a 20 foot channel east of Montreal, although it may not be sufficiently marked off by beacons and lighthouses. West of Montreal the limit is established by the canals, viz., the lock of 45 feet wide, with a depth of 9 feet, and a length of 200 feet. Such is the condition between Montreal and Lake Ontario, extending up to St. Catharines, on the Welland Canal. Here the navigation is again changed, to be governed by the Welland Canal, where the lock is 150 ft. by 26 ft. 6 in., but with 10 ft. water on the sills, until Lake Erie is reached. Therefore the navigation of the St. Lawrence is composed of four systems.

1. From the ocean passing Quebec to Montreal: a 20-foot navigation admitting the noble Allan boats of 3,000 tons.

2. The St. Lawrence Canals extending through Lake Ontario to St. Catharines, admitting such vessels as the propeller "Her Majesty." She is 180 long and has 30 feet breadth of beam. In the St. Lawrence Canals she can carry 4,400 barrels of flour only; as has been shown when freed from these restrictions, she increased her cargo one-third.

3. The Welland Canal propeller is a type of this class. She is principally engaged in the Oswego trade, that is, passing from Chicago to Oswego, discharging at the foot of the Oswego Canal into barges, which ascend to Syracuse to take the Erie Canal. There is also a class of vessels which descend the St. Lawrence, but as the depth of the Welland is 10 feet and the St. Lawrence but 9, this class of vessel carries 1,100 barrels of flour, less than she could otherwise do, and from want of draft and general build, such vessels are not fitted for the salt water.

4. The Lake Erie steamers are representative boats of the fourth class. Affected only by the depth of the St. Clair flats, they are magnificent steamships travelling between Buffalo and Chicago, regardless of the storms which sweep these waters.

With a little effort it ought not to be difficult to understand the imperfection of the St. Lawrence navigation, while at the same time, any one who opens the map must see that it is the river which should be the channel of communication for the great west to the ocean. Further, it must be plain to

every one, that the whole system is und[er] the control of Canada, and without effort · the part of the Dominion, the navigation w[ill] continue to be, as it is to-day, ineffective a[nd] incomplete. It has been said that power[ful] influences prevail in Montreal against a extension or amendment of the route a policy hurtful to that City, and it is in th[e] City that opposition would be looked t when the improvement is claimed. We sh[all] not stop to consider if the accusation be tr[ue] or if true, that results unfavorable to Montr[eal] will accrue. The latter, possibly, will be c[on]sidered in its place. Suppose, for our purp[ose] to say now, that we consider that the ben[efit] to Montreal would be incalculable, for i geographical position of that City is, of cour[se] greatly in its favor. But as such opini[ons] are supposed to prevail, we are not surpri[sed] to read in the Montreal journals that "H[er] Majesty" has little business west of th[e] City. The *Montreal Herald*, which is g[en]erally written· in a fair and thoughtful spi[rit] and nevertheless the very blue-blood of c[om]mercial orthodoxy for Montreal, thus allu[des] to the departure of this propeller: "F[rom] "what we know of canal navigation, we h[ave] "no doubt after the first trip, her owner[s will] "find it greatly to his advantage to run "steamer from *here* instead of Toronto, [as] "have no doubt she would be crowded w[ith] "both freight and passengers every tr[ip.]

The italics are not ours. If we ventur[e to] paraphrase this very suggestive sentenc[e it] may read thus, "What is the use of goin[g to] "Toronto? You only lose time useles[sly.] "Whatever you carry, 'canal navigation' "allow you but two-thirds of your ca[rgo.] "You must take your remaining third h[ere.] "And, accordingly, it is better, not "make two bites of a cherry. Receive [your] "three-thirds here—your whole here; M[ontreal] "treal is the natural harbor of ocean-g[oing] "vessels. It is *here*—we will follow the "phasis of our extract—it is *here* that tr[ans]"shipment has been made and must [be] "made."

These facts enable us to establish a l[ine] on which the Canal question really ca[n be] argued. Even so far as Canada is concer[ned] without any reference to the great Stat[es of] the American Union bordering on the la[kes] it may take a short time or it may ta[ke a] long time to educate public opinion on subject. But one day that public opi[nion] will be formed, to be uttered in every co[unty] west of the Province line, and to be a of the political faith of every public ma[n in] Ontario, that the Canal question must re[ceive] its solution. It is the fashion, still in n[any] quarters, to treat any comment on the [sub]ject as visionary, as mere Utopean i[deas] which "practical" men cannot entertain

f the duties of this periodical, to keep the subject before the We belive, possibly, the wish is e thought, that the hour is 'hen the demand of Western ossess a sufficient outlet to the longer be met by jaunty jokes, nisters of finance will cease in- oostpone it by threats of finan- id protestations of national , so far as Canada is concerned, i capable of fair and just con- ut what can be said when it is he whole immense district of ch clusters round the lakes is ! The Erie Canal is now the i by the produce of the West. isly insufficient. On the other ve "Her Majesty" going to ely if a vessel can go to Halifax al, she can go to Boston and to From Montreal to Halifax the omething short of 1,200 miles, ge is shortened by taking the . From Halifax to Boston the nly 450 miles, and from Boston the trip is made in a few hours. ropeller could steer direct from o Nantucket, and there is but a erence of time between the two ies. There is nothing visionary ing fanciful. For "Her Ma- ig 10 feet 6 inches now virtually ip. How much better could it vith vessels drawing a greater ilt specially for the trade? f the case appears to us to meet of the necessity of the Caugh- l, a water communication pro- effected between the waters of nce and Lake Champlain. We this work with such useless, we in no offensive spirit, such pre- emes as the two projects of the l navigation, and the Toronto Bay Canal. As we have ad- we venture to think we have oth are merely parallel lines to s, and their construction would ng. If completed and in oper- y result would be that vessels fferent route come to the same hey can now reach, the advo- chemes say, in less time. Ex- nd mariners, and men who all e been engaged in the business se. Our own opinion we un- ronounce, that no time would Ve look upon the schemes as and placing our confidence in of the community, we are cor- ultimate rejection. We, how- o see the question, without forward and argued and sup-

ported with vigor, so that it may be settled; for the public attention is dissipated by contradictory projects to utter bewilderment. Therefore we hope to see that zeal which is idly and to ill purpose employed, ultimately turned on more healthy projects. We look forward to the date of the improvement of the St. Lawrence, the one great saving policy of Canada. The Caughnawaga Canal is no visionary scheme. Indeed it has much to be commended, and it cannot be summarily dismissed. Our argument, however, for the moment, with regard to it is that the time has not come for its construction. Possibly it is only a work of time. But we counsel those who advocate it to join in the effort of first completing the St. Lawrence navigation. Let this improvement take precedence of all others. Let it remain without complication and without the trammel of any inter-depen- dent project. We have shown that from Quebec to Chicago, there are four distinct classes of navigable waters, that is to say, reaches of navigation controlled by distinct circumstances, so that a representative vessel is peculiar to each as a type of maximum tonnage passing on its waters. As it is ex- travagance to consider that we can ever attain the 20-feet of navigation from Montreal to Quebec, we may at once cease to discuss it. We have, therefore, in the distance between Chicago and Montreal harbor, three distinct navigations. What is required is to bring these three varied systems into one system. This is the first point to be gained. We need a unity of navigation for the St. Lawrence. It is on this proposition—a proposition which when understood, will be acknowledged to be plain and simple, it is on this policy we wish to rally support, and we trace more than one reason in the necessity of laying down this principle. In the first place it is the key note, the very centre stone of our argument for an improved navigation. It will show not only what is needed, but what is not needed; it will establish the true policy of the country and point where we may look for its real resources. It will sug- gest fields of industry and the wise employ- ment of capital. These are not exaggerations. The advocates of the policy indicated are con- tent, however, for a time to incur the ridicule of the jaunty politician, who finds in the theme many a subject of vapid joke, and on the other hand, to bear unmoved, the sneers of those respectable imbecilities who affect to frown down a new project as simply an im- practicable theory. We are all sustained by the hope that the time will come when the complete development of the St. Lawrence navigation will be a political dogma; when the struggle at the hustings will be, who shall be the loudest profess it. It is this thought which leads us to persevere, for we are on the

side of common sense and ought to work out an enlarged, wise, national policy—not of littleness, bickering and one-sidedness—but one raising our own land to wealth and pros- perity, and extending to our neighbors the like advantages; a policy cheering and bene- fitting them, which likewise will enrich our- selves.

INSOLVENCY.

As the principle of a law for the relie of insolvents has been sustained in the House of Commons, and as the measure now before that body amends in many particulars the law that heretofore prevailed respecting insolvency, it is manifestly advisable to make it as perfect as possible. In many respects the old law has been found defective, and in some of its features the proposed act is objection- able. The liberty to make voluntary assign- ments has undoubtedly been abused. It is proposed to make the first step in insolvency, an assignment to an Interim assignee, who shall prepare a statement of affairs for the creditors, at a meeting to be held not less than three weeks from the date of the assign- ment. At the meeting the creditors may ap- point another assignee, who shall supersede the Interim assignee. The power of the In- terim assignee is very limited, while his duties cover the most laborious part of the work. If the stock assigned to him is perishable, it must lie there until he has completed his examination of the insolvent's affairs, and procured a meeting of creditors. Though promptness in extinguishing rent or saving bailiff's fees, be of the utmost importance to the creditors, nothing can be done. Cases have occurred in which, the only hope of creditors receiving anything lay in an imme- diate sale. If it is possible to avoid this dead- lock, and attain the same object to be gained by the immediate appointment of a custodian satisfactory to creditors, it is well to search out a method. An assignee, satisfactory to one or more of the principal unsecured credi- tors, would in almost every case prove accept- able to the other creditors; admitting this, we naturally conclude that a voluntary assign- ment should be made at the outset to one named or approved of by such principal un- secured creditor or creditors, giving him the same powers as are possessed by a permanent assignee. Delay, expense, and loss might thereby be saved, and increased facilities would be afforded for bringing the estate into liquidation. If the Interim assignee is to be retained, he certainly should not be required to do work which the assignee when appoint- ed will be required to do over again. In wind- ing up small estates, this duplication of work would be a serious matter. Clearly the duty of the Interim assignee should be limited to taking charge of the estate, calling a meeting of creditors, and selling perishable goods.

Where notice of contestation is given, the creditor should not be at liberty to withdraw except on cause shewn ; for it has occasionally happened, that compromises are made which are very suspicious. In the absence of a contestant, as where his debt is garnished, his objection should nevertheless be inquired into and decided upon. In the case of secured claims, it should be imperative on the creditors relying on such to furnish the assignee with full particulars of his securities. As it is now, he merely ignores the proceedings, resting content with the weapon he holds.

Privileged and secured creditors should be disqualified from voting, as it is manifestly unjust that they should have equal rights with those who are interested in doing the best for all concerned. A creditor who tenders for purchase of the insolvent's estate, or part of it, should not be allowed to decide upon the acceptance or rejection of his offer.

It is sometimes found that agreements exist between the insolvent and debtors to take out indebtedness in trade. If it is just to landlords to interfere with their rights, under leases, it is certainly no less just and proper that such agreements as these indicated should be voided, so far as receiving payment in trade is concerned.

The power of the assignee is too limited. It might be extended, so as to give additional powers to seize property, after the manner of sheriffs, and in such case, the provisions of the Interpleader Act might be made to apply. It would be well, also, to reduce the number of official assignees in each county. A reduction in number would give each one such employment as would enable him to employ a staff such as justice to the business demands.

The assignee should be empowered to compound for debts due to, and to sign composition deeds on behalf of the insolvent, and when authorized, by power of attorney, to execute the insolvent's composition deed on behalf of such creditors as wish it. There is no provision for the absence of the assignee. The delay necessitated by his absence might be avoided if there were a power of appointing a deputy. In the event of a dividend being declared on claims based on promissory notes, where the insolvent is indirectly liable, there is no power in the assignee to sue the parties directly liable. There is no provision for commuting dower in the case of a sale of land. Were such commutation to be made, upon the basis of the amount realized by the sale of the property subject to dower, it would be a reasonable way of selling to the best advantage, without injustice to anybody. Assignees are required to keep duplicates of and file every original document. This is of no practical value, and only adds to the expense.

There is no provision for the assignee's right of appeal when he is dissatisfied with his allowance. One creditor, by buying up claims, may hold the assignee at his mercy. It has been held that an assignee cannot obtain a discharge if no dividend has been paid. This is certainly unreasonable, and should be provided for. There is difference in the power over the sale of leases and that of stock. Now many a time a stock can be sold for the sake of the lease, and if the assignee could sell the one on the same terms as the other, and at the same time, the insolvent's estate would undoubtedly be the gainer.

There is also a difficulty where one partner absconds and the other wishes to make voluntary assignment. In the case of concealment or absconding there is great delay. The method of bringing the estate into liquidation is not expeditious. Perhaps it would, in such case, be better for the judge to call a meeting of creditors at once.

In all the particulars mentioned, there is such apparent reason for amendment in the law that we do not think it necessary to do more than summarize. As the Insolvent Act is being amended, it only requires a little trouble to obviate the necessity for future tinkering.

EXPORTATION OF AMERICAN SILVER.

The public were made aware, a few days ago, by a return laid before Parliament, that the Government, through the Bank of Montreal, had exported about one million dollars of American silver coin in February and March last. The history of the operation—very properly kept quiet till completed—throws light upon this question, which, if simple in theory, is beset with many difficulties in practice. In consequence, no doubt, of the state of the market, the sale of bonds to the full amount of the silver purchased was not completed ; but we have the opinion of Mr. Angus that the entire operation would have resulted in giving the Government the loan —for such it really was—at a rate not to exceed 6½ per cent. About two-thirds of the silver was exported to Liverpool and London, and the balance to New York ; several lots were disposed of in the latter city at from 4¾ to 5 per cent. The transaction seems to have been well managed throughout.

Although a million dollars were exported in this way, and a large quantity also under the exploded Weir scheme, the effect on the market was comparatively slight. This proves either that there is a much larger quantity of American (and British) silver in the market than was supposed, or that the existing duty, meant for the collection of the revenue, are valueless for the purpose of preventing its importation. We

believe the quantity in circulation has been very generally under-estimated. These coin are to be found in the remotest districts of the country ; they are distributed through all the ramifications of capital and industry ; and as there is no central point to which they can be returned for conversion at par as a bank note, or used in payment of indebtedness, current funds are so used, and these coins are retained outside in circulation. Hence the attempt to export the surplus silver of the Dominion is a Herculean task, and cannot be made successful by any fitful attempts, to say the least. Whether it can be accomplished at all by the use of reasonable measures, so long as monetary affairs in the States remain as at present, is yet to be proven ; for ourselves, we are decidedly skeptical on the point. To get it out is one thing, but to keep it out is quite another affair. An export movement is directly calculated to defeat itself, and the nearer apparent success is reached, the more difficult the task becomes. So soon as enough is exported to appreciate the coins to par, the inducement to bring them in becomes too powerful to be successfully resisted. The strictest surveillance on the part of customs officials could not prevent a stream of illicit importation large enough to nullify any export scheme.

It is pretty well understood that the flood of American silver in Canada is directly traceable to the system of irredeemable paper currency in vogue in the United States. Silver coins having disappeared from the channels of circulation, have become useful only for shipment abroad, and for the few other purposes to which specie is now applied. But for all these purposes gold is better medium, and hence silver is at a discount, as compared with gold, ranging from four to six or seven per cent., according to circumstances. To buy it at this discount and pay it out in Canada at par, affords a clear percentage of profit as large as the discount itself, less expenses. The discount here now rules much the same as in New York, and is to a great extent governed by the rate in that city. There is, therefore, no special inducement to ship either way at present.

While the obstacles to immediate relief, by means of exportation, seem insuperable there is no reason why the Government should not avail itself of the opportunity to exchange bonds for this specie on favorable terms. If profitable export operations may be carried on for the account of the Government, the people will have no reason to complain : rather the contrary. But to attempt the riddance of the country of this silver, at an expense to the country, is clearly unwise

uld not be entirely successful, and while sulted in a loss to the whole people, d greatly benefit a few speculators. aether there are not other means of relief n the scope of legislation that might be ssfully adopted, is worthy of diligent iry.

TUAL FIRE INSURANCE COMPANIES.

der the Act respecting these companies Stat. U.C., cap. 52), when forty or more as, duly qualified, have bound them- to effect insurance amounting together rty thousand dollars, they may become y corporate. Each member before he es his policy, deposits a promissory note, le to the Company or its proper officer, e premium, and pays a certain part of ash towards working expenses. At the ition of the term of insurance, the note, deducting all losses and expenses, oc- g during the term, is given up, as member is bound to pay his proportion losses and expenses accruing during the uance of his policy. The company may premiums in cash for insurance for not longer than one year. The cash um paid at the time of insurance is not f the annual assessment (31 Vic., c. 32). policies are issued and premiums in cash ed, for periods of one year, the persons ing are not liable to further charge or ment. In case payment or note given ah premiums or assessments upon a am or deposit note be not made within days after it is due, the policy be- void, but the company may waive the ure, and even though no waiver took the party in default still remains liable amount in arrear (29 Vic., c. 37).

ase of loss, the Directors fix the pro- n to be paid by each member on the al amount of his deposit note. When ole of the deposit notes are insufficient the loss, the sufferer receives not only ortionate dividend on the amount of but also a sum to be raised by an assess- f members, not exceeding one per cent. amount each has insured.

ompany may, for the speedy and cer- ayment of losses, raise a guarantee not to exceed $500,000, which shall le for all losses, debts and expenses; much as two-thirds of the premium belonging to the company may be d as a security to the subscribers of uarantee capital (27, 28 Vic., cap. 38). rve fund may be formed of all moneys d at the end of each year after pay- of ordinary expenses and losses, such to be applied to pay off the guarantee or such liabilities as cannot be pro-

vided for out of the ordinary receipts (31 Vic., c. 32, sec. 6). Debentures, promissory notes, bills or drafts may be issued for losses, so long as the amount outstanding does not exceed one-fourth part of the amount then unpaid on the deposit or premium notes held; and the members may be assessed for such sums as may be necessary to meet them. Any member, upon payment of the whole of his deposit note and surrendering his policy before any subsequent loss or expense occurs, is discharged from the company.

Various special acts have been passed by the Legislature, giving to particular companies powers beyond those conferred by the general Act, and modifying its general clauses. For instance, the Toronto Mutual, by 31 Vic., cap. 52, is empowered to issue policies and collect premiums in cash for a term of one year, on which the insured are not liable for any further charge or assessment, and are not held as members of the company in any respect. The Oxford Farmers' may (31 Vic. c. 54) issue cash policies for insurance for terms of one or more years, not exceeding five, with the like exemption from liability. The Waterloo Mutual (31 Vic., c. 55) issue cash policies for terms of two or more years, with like exemption. The Gore District may issue cash policies for one year, in the same manner.

The Canada Farmers' Mutual have abolished the premium note system and the members have no security other than is afforded by the rates imposed. The last report of the Agricultural Mutual speaks of the preference shown for the cash system.

It appears, therefore, that the various mutual companies have been gradually leaving the premium note system. There is no doubt that there is on the part of the insured a preference for the cash system and its exemption from liability and in order to compete successfully for business, the Mutuals have been compelled to depart from the true mutual principle. But this breaking loose from premium notes deprives the insured of that security for payment which he naturally looks for. In the absence of a guarantee capital, there is no security at all but the honesty and good management of the Directors. It may be said that they confine their business to narrow circles, but the contrary is becoming the case, and we find Mutuals branching out in all directions and competing successfully with Stock companies. We know the note system may have abuses attached to it, such as in one case we have heard of, where the agent taking risks gets $2 a policy and the company gets nothing until an assessment is made. But that is no sufficient answer. Where the note system prevails there is a show of security, at the least, but in the cash

system there may be neither shadow nor substance. Under such circumstances, we conclude that some remedy should be applied to a state of affairs manifestly wrong. It is questionable what steps should be taken to bring about a proper settlement of the matter, but it is not impossible that any move would be in the direction of a deposit, with Government, of a portion of the cash premiums until a certain amount is reached. However the subject is open for discussion and we shall be glad to give publicity to the views of those who are disposed to make suggestions.

THE ASSESSMENT ACT.

The Assessment Act of 1869 has given rise to more indignation, has caused more trouble, and has proved itself more unjust than any act ever passed having the same object. The exemptions are, property belonging to the Crown, places of worship, public educational institutions, public roads, municipal property, poor houses, hospitals, mechanics' institutes, etc., personal property of governors, imperial military or naval pay, salaries, pensions, etc., income of a farmer derived from his farm, personal property secured by mortgage or provincial or municipal debentures, bank stock, railroad stock, property owned out of the Province, personal property equal to debts owed on account of such property except debts secured by mortgage upon real estate, or unpaid on account of purchase money, personalty under $100, income under $400, ministers salaries, rental of real estate, household effects and salaries of officials of government departments. The real and personal property are required to be estimated at their actual cash value as they would be appraised in payment of a just debt from a solvent debtor. As regards the assessment of personalty, the act reads as follows :

"No person deriving an income exceeding $400 per annum from any trade, calling, office, profession, or other source whatsoever, not declared exempt by this act, shall be assessed for a less sum, as the amount of his net personal property, than the amount of such income during the year then last past, in excess of the said sum of $400, but no deduction shall be made from the gross amount of such income by reason of any indebtedness, save such as shall equal the annual interest thereof; and such last year's income, in excess of the said sum of $400, shall be held to be his net personal property, unless he has other personal property liable to assessment, in which case such excess and other personal property shall be added together and constitute his personal property liable to assessment."

Clause 36 applies to companies:

"The personal property of an incorporated company shall not be assessed against the corporation, but each shareholder shall be assessed for the value of the stock or shares held by him as part of his personal property, unless such stock is exempted by this act ;

provided always, that in companies investing their moans in gas-works. water-works, plank and gravel roads, manufactories, hotels, railway and tram roads, harbours, or other works requiring the investment of the whole or principal part of the stock in real estate already assessed, for the purpose of carrying on such business, the shareholders shall only be assessed on the income derived from such investment."

According to an estimate made in the city clerk's office, the total exemptions in Toronto amount to about six millions of dollars. While the land owner is exempt from taxation on the income he derives from rental, the merchant is taxed first on his stock or capital and then on the supposed income he derives from selling it. The holder of say, building society stock, purchased to yield eight per cent. is forced to pay one and a half per cent tax. The holder of stock, such as that of the Provincial Insurance is assessed not on the dividend it yields but on the amount of the shares held, so that one may be compelled to pay taxes on what is not only absolutely worthless, but which would be got rid of if any one would accept it as a gift. The uneveness of assessment is also apparent, as the dishonest can easily "declare" themselves through all the provisions, while the honest are unable to move. The fact is, the whole system, at least in cities, needs revision, and if anything like justice is to be done, we must have commissioners appointed so that something like uniformity shall be brought about. For the present we confine ourselves to a notice of the evils so generally complained of.

SCOTTISH PROVINCIAL ASSURANCE COMPANY.—The annual report of this Company shows that 988 policies were issued during the past year, assuring the sum of $1,800,000, on which the new annual premiums were about fifty-five thousand dollars. The death claims, including bonuses, were £54,774. The Company's business shows a steady and safe increase, derived solely through the exertions of the agents, and without those wholesale purchases of other offices, which often sow the seeds of ruin in otherwise sound Companies. Its affairs are conducted in a prudent, non-speculative way, resulting in that stability and ultimate success which Scottish Assurance Companies may fairly lay claim to. We are glad to be able to add, with all confidence, that the affairs of the Canadian Branch are in excellent hands.

PROVINCIAL INSURANCE COMPANY.—We understand that the Manager of this Company will shortly leave for Halifax to try and arrange matters with the Company's Agent there, who declines to pay over any of the premium notes in his hands until the Company is off the risks he has secured for them. The different agents throughout the country who are in arrears have been notified to pay up or prepare for legal proceedings. It is said that a fresh call will be made on the stock at the next annual meeting.

NOVA SCOTIA GOLD FIELDS.

(Advance Reports to the N. S. Mining Gazette.)

HALIFAX, N. S., May 11, 1869.

MONTAGUE.—A bar of 24 oz. received to-day from the mine of Messrs. Leckie & Gay, of which property the manager reports favorably.

UNIACKE.—The crushings from the two newly discovered lodes on the Montreal Co.'s property resulted as follows : 120 tons from the fourteen feet lode, gave an average of 4 dwts. ; the 10 inch lode, 10 dwts. The Uniacke Co., are still working with a fair profit. The Central Company sent no quarts to the mill last week. The Queen Company are working in a small way. The Union Company and the Toronto Company have each let one shaft on contract ; the former on a two feet lode, the latter on two lodes of an aggregate of 10 inches, opened by Mr. Burkner.

MUSQUODOBOIT.—The Hyde property is still employing about fifty men. The Burkner property forty. Results from both continue good ; the lodes still showing gold in horizontal as well as vertical extent. Mr. Burkner has discovered a new live feet lode as rich as the one before struck. He has thus ten feet of good ore ; one hundred tons of which are now ready for the mill.

INDIAN PATH.—A telegram from Mr. Waddelow reports the discovery of a rich vein on the Waddelow & McDonald claims and has created some stir in Lunenberg and vicinity.

GOLD RIVER.—The foreman and two miners in the employ of the Gold River Exploration Co., directed by Mr. A. Michel, were to have left on Monday, but have been detained by a heavy storm. Mr. Samuel Kelly has been deputed by the Government to re-survey the district, and he will leave on Thursday.

ECUM SECUM.—Discoveries have been reported on the claims of the Atlantic Co., but failed to cause any excitement.

Before the Legislative Assembly Charters of Incorporation have been applied for by the following Gold Mining Companies :—

Name.	Where Operating.	Where Owned.
Cobourg.	Sherbrooke.	Cobourg, Ont.
Cochran's Hill.	Melrose, N.S.	Sherbrooke, N. S.
Toronto & Uniacke.	Uniacke.	Toronto, Ont.

Halifax, May 21, 1869.

The following crushings have been reported to the Mining Gazette Office for the month of April. Renfrew and Uniacke districts having yet to be added :

Mine.	District.	Qrtz. Crushed. tons. cwt		Gold Yield. oz. dwts grs
Sundry.....Oldham	98...	10...	32...	2... 6
Do. .....Isaac's Harbor 10...	10...	12...	19...	9
Eureka........Wine Harbor. 13...	0...	19...	2...	0
Provincial.... do.	...59...	14...	9...	12...12
Eldorado.... do.	...94...	0...	21...	15... 0
Sundry.—Waverley.. 117...	18...	37...	19...	5
Wellington.Sherbrooke.. 175...	0...172...	8...	0
Do.	do.	...75...	0...	93... 0... 0
Sundry....	do.	...147...	14...	69... 17... 3
Bendigo....	do.	...40...	0...	2 .. 3..12
Burkner...Musq'doboit. 100...	0...	48...	0...	0

SHERBROOKE.—The Wellington Company paid a dividend of $10,000 on the 1st May, and expect to be in a position to pay $15,000 more on the 1st August, if present yield is maintained. The Caledonia, Woodbine, and Crescent mines are temporarily idle. A new manager, Mr. Corson, has assumed charge of the Wentworth, and Mr. Twist, of the Chicago.

WAVERLEY.—An attempt was made to break into Mr. Burkner's mill last week, but fortunately the lessee had cleaned up the night before, so that the would-be thieves got nothing for their pains. Mr. Burkner obtained an average of 16 dwts. from his last crushing.

WINE HARBOR.—The Eureka mill started and gives satisfaction. Improvement reported from

the Provincial, and steady progress on the Napoleon works.

MUSQUODOBOIT.—Here, too, Mr. Burkner is in luck, two lodes having run together, and now give him eighteen feet of quartz, which at last trial yielded an average of 7 dwts. per ton, or nearly fifty per cent. above cost.

ECUM SECUM.—Activity reported by the Atlantic Company, but no results. The management of this Company's Works now devolves upon Mr. Edward Capel.

GOLD RIVER.—Mr. Samuel Kelly has been deputed to make an official survey of this field. A foreman of the Gold River Exploration Company, with a couple of men commenced operations last week.

Reports from other district not to hand this week.

Railway News.

GREAT WESTERN RAILWAY.—Traffic for week ending May 14, 1869.

Passengers	$29,291 23
Freight......................	40,594 64
Mails and Sundries........	3,002 46
Total Receipts for week......	$72,888 33
Corresponding week, 1868...	70,151 72
Increase	$2,736 61

NORTHERN RAILWAY.—Traffic receipts for w' ending May 22nd, 1869.

Passengers..................	$2,940 78
Freight and live stock......	12,220 35
Mails and sundries..........	286 28
	$15,447 41
Corresponding Week of '68	14,823 31
Increase	$624 10

—The township of Weedon, eastern township, says the Sherbrooke Gazette, has taken $25,000 stock of the Sherbrooke and Kennebec (wood) Railway company.

Commercial.

An Order in Council has been issued exempting coal from the payment of canal tolls upward through the canals. This is a concession to Nova Scotia coal interest, which is but just right under the circumstances. This important industry is in a languishing state, owing chiefly to the prohibitory duty imposed on imports to the United States. We hope, therefore, to Nova Scotia coal generally used throughout the Province. The quality is about as good as that of Cumberland coals, so that if a trade were fairly opened up there is every reason to believe it would be successful. We happen to know that the concession now made is due to the exertions of R. G. Haliburton, of Halifax, who has persistently urged upon the Government the wisdom of the course now adopted.

The bills of the Royal Canadian Bank are selling at 95 to 96, being slightly lower.

A meeting of the London Board of Trade held on the 31st May, when strong resolutions were passed in opposition to the proposed bank scheme, and recommending the postponement action on the subject till next session.

We learn that Mr. Thos. Haworth, of the firm of Haworth & Co., hardware merchants, received his discharge from the Judge of the solvent Court and has resumed business on Yonge Street, in this City, as a general commission merchant for the sale of hardware and general goods. Mr. Haworth is well known to the trade, having done business for many years in Toronto. There is no doubt but orders entrusted to him will be executed with care and dispatch.

e Lybster cotton mills, the property of Messrs. on & McKay, of this City, and situated on 'elland Canal at Thorold, have been as good pped on account, it is said, of the dullness e dry goods trade. Only a few hands will ployed till trade revives.

Toronto Market.

ere is a rather better feeling in trade this but the amount of business doing is small. eneral policy is to open no new accounts and l only to first class men. oduce.—The market is rather better and lerable sales were made. *Wheat*—Receipts 0 bushels, and 1,080 bush. in the same of last year. Stock in store on the 31st 14,800 bush. against 133,000 bush. on the May. Sales of spring 4,000 bush. at 95½c. and other lots amounting to 10,000 bush. to 96. About 14,000 bush. fall sold at $1 ,000 bush. midgs proof at 90 f.o.b. There free shipments of wheat and other grain g the week. *Oats*—No receipts—Stock in on the 31st 10,600 bush. against 14,500 on the 3rd May. The market is steady at to 54c. in car loads. *Peas*—No receipts— : in store on the 31st 12,500 and 24,200 on the 3rd May. Some sales at 73 to 73½. y.—No receipts—Stock 800 bush. and 4,200 on the 3rd May. There were some sales of in the neighborhood of 80c., the market g firm at that figure. *Corn* is held at 60c. loads. our.—Receipts 1,510 brls. against 630 brls. eek. Stock in store on the 31st 12,912 brls. 2.900 brls. on the 3rd May. The market uled firmer and more active and is from 5c. c. higher on the week. Sales of several and barrels in all were made at $3.90 to early in the week and latterly at $4 to $4.05, narket closing steady at the latter quotations. y is also firmer and has recovered to $4.20 4 25, a lot of 1,000 brls. of a choice brand at the latter price. Extra is worth about with little doing. Superior, none. *Oat*—A lot of 100 brls. sold at $5.50 on track; lots of choice for retail sell at $5.75 to $6. *meal*—Unchanged at $3.75 to $4. ovisions.—*Butter*—There is no demand and ng doing in a wholesale way. This season is vorable that a large crop is expected and rs are therefore holding off in expectation of g at low prices. *Pork.*—Nominal as quo- *Bacon.*—A lot of 2,000 lbs. sugar cured sold 5c.; stock light. *Lard.*—In light stock, nal. *Eggs.*—Firm and steady at 12 to 12½c. a good supply. DES.—The market continues very dull; prices kely to decline still further. 1NS AND WOOL—Calf skins are a cent down; skins are unchanged. Wool is steady at 28 c. LT.—American is 15c. lower as quoted; Goder- unchanged. RDWARK.—Trade is slightly improved. *Tin* a and higher. EIGHTS.—Rates by vessels to Oswego remain American Currency. Flour to Montreal by er 20c.; grain 6c. Lumber to Oswego $1.50 t, American Currency. e following are the Grand Trunk Railway any's summer rates from Toronto to the un- ntioned stations, which came into force on 9th ult. :—Flour to all Stations from Belle- te Lynn, inclusive 25c.; grain, per 100 lbs. flour to Prescott, 30c; grain 15c; flour to ations between Union Pond and Portland, in- 'e, 75c.; grain, 38c; flour to Boston, 80c, ; grain 40c; flour to Halifax, 90c; flour to hin, 85c.

'r. Frank Drummond has been appointed ger of the People's Telegraph Company, said to be a first-class operator. fr. Thomas Drewry has been appointed agent of the London and Lancashire Life ance Company.

Mercantile.

TORONTO PRICES CURRENT.—JUNE 3, 1869.

Name of Article.	Wholesale Rates.		Name of Article.	Wholesale Rate.		Name of Article.	Who. Rat.	
Boots and Shoes.	$ c.	$ c.	**Groceries**—*Contin'd*	$ c.	$	**Leather**—*Contin'd*	$ c.	
Mens' Thick Boots	2 05	2 50	Gunpow'r'c. to med ...	0 55	0	Kip Skins, Patna	0 30	
" Kip............	2 25	3 00	" medl. to fine.	0 70	0	French	0 70	
" Calf............	3 20	3 70	" fine to fins't.	0 85	0	English	0 65	
" Congress Gaiters...	1 65	2 50	Hyson	0 45	0	Hemlock Calf (30 to		
" Kip Cobourgs.....	1 20	1 40	Imperial...........	0 42	0 80	35 lbs.) per doz...	0 50	
Boys' Thick Boots	1 70	1 80	*Tobacco, Manufact'd:*			Do. light	0 45	
Youths'	1 40	1 50	Can Leaf, ℔ 5s & 10s.	0 26	0 30	French Calf.	1 05	
Women's Balts	0 95	1 30	Western Leaf, com...	0 25	0 26	Grain & Satn Cif℔doz	0 00	
" Balmoral........	1 20	1 50	" Good	0 27	0 32	Splits, large ℔ ℔...	0 20	
" Congress Gaiters..	0 90	1 50	" Fine	0 32	0 35	" small	0 23	
Misses' Balts	0 75	1 00	" Bright fine..	0 40	0 50	Enamelled Cow ℔foot.	0 20	
" Balmoral........	1 00	1 30	" choice..	0 60	0 75	Patent	0 20	
" Congress Gaiters..	1 00	1 30	**Hardware.**			Pebble Grain	0 15	
Girls' Balts	0 65	0 85	*Tin (net cash prices)*			Buff	0 14	
" Balmoral.........	0 90	1 25	Block, ℔ ℔........	0 35	0 00	**Oils.**		
" Congress Gaiters..	0 75	1 10	Grain............	0 30	0 00	Cod	0 65	
Children's C. T. Cncks..	0 50	0 65	*Copper:*			Lard, extra	0 00	
" Gaiters	0 65	0 00	Pig...............	0 23	0 24	" No. 1	0 00	
Drugs.			Sheet.............	0 30	0 33	" Woollen	0 00	
Aloes Cape.........	0 12½	0 16	*Cut Nails:*			Lubricating, patent...	0 00	
Alum	0 02½	0 03	Assorted ¼ Shingles,			" Mott's economic	0 20	
Borax	0 06	0 00	℔ 100 ℔........	2 95	3 00	Linseed, raw	0 76	
Camphor, refined....	0 65	0 70	Shingle alone do ...	3 15	3 25	" boiled.......	0 81	
Castor Oil.........	0 16½	0 28	Lathe and 5 dy.....	3 30	3 40	Machinery.........	0 00	
Caustic Soda.......	0 04½	0 05	*Galvanised Iron:*			Olive, common, ℔gal.	1 00	
Cochineal.........	0 90	1 00	Assorted sizes.....	0 08	0 09	" salad, in lots.	1 95	
Cream Tartar	0 40	0 45	Best No. 24........	0 07½	0 08	" salad, ℔ case..	3 60	
Epsom Salts	0 03	0 04	" 26........	0 08	0 09	Sesame salad, ℔ gal..	1 80	
Extract Logwood....	0 11	0 12	" 28........	0 09	0 00½	Seal, pale.........	0 75	
Gum Arabic, sorts....	0 20	0 25	*Horse Nails:*			Spirits Turpentine...	0 28½	
Indigo, Madras.....	0 90	1 00	Guest's or Griffin's			Varnish	0 60	
Licorice	0 14	0 45	assorted sizes...	0 00	0 00	Whale.............	0 00	
Madder	0 00	0 18	For W. ass'd sizes..	0 18	0 19	**Paints, &c.**		
Galls	0 32	0 37	Patent Hammer'd do..	0 17	0 18	White Lead, genuine		
Opium	13 00	13 50	*Iron (at 4 months):*			in Oil, ℔ 25lbs.....	0 00	
Oxalic Acid........	0 30	0 35	Pig—Gartsherrie No1..	24 00	25 00	Do. No. 1 "	0 00	
Potash, Bi-tart.....	0 25	0 28	Other brands. No1..	22 00	24 00	" 2 "	0 00	
" Bichromate...	0 15	0 20	No 2..	0 00	0 00	" 3 "	0 00	
Potass Iodide	3 00	4 50	Bar—Scotch, ℔ 100 ℔..	2 25	2 50	White Zinc, genuine..	3 00	
Senna	0 12½	0 60	Refined..........	3 00	3 25	White Lead, dry......	0 05½	
Soda Ash..........	0 02½	0 04	Swedes	5 00	5 50	Red Lead..........	0 07¼	
Soda Bicarb	4 50	5 00	Hoops—Coopers.....	3 00	3 25	Venetian Red, Eng'h.	0 02½	
Tartaric Acid.......	0 40	0 45	Band	3 00	3 25	Yellow Ochre, Frch'h..	0 02½	
Verdigris	0 35	0 40	Boiler Plates......	3 25	3 50	Whiting	0 55	
Vitriol, Blue.......	0 08	0 19	Canada Plates......	3 75	4 00	**Petroleum.**		
Groceries.			Union Jack	0 00	0 00	(Refined ℔ gal.)		
Coffees:			Pontypool........	3 25	4 00	Water white, car'd ..		
Java, ℔ ℔........	0 22½0	0 23	Swansea	3 90	4 00	" small lots ..	0 00	
Laguayra, ...	0 17	0 18	*Lead (at 4 months):*			" small lots...	0 00	
Rio...........	0 15	0 17	Bar, ℔ 100 ℔s.....	0 06½0	07	Straw, by car load....	0 00	
Fish:			Sheet "	0 06	0 00	" small lots...	0 00	
Herrings, Lab. split..	0 00	0 00	Shot............	0 07½	0 07¾	Amber, by car load.	0 00	
" round......	0 00	0 00	*Iron Wire (net cash):*			" small lots ...	0 00	
" scaled......	0 33	0 35	No. 6, ℔ bundle....	2 70	2 80	Benzine	0 00	
Mackerel,small kitts..	1 00	0 00	" 7........	3 10	3 20	**Produce**		
Loch Her. wh'e kits..	2 50	1 75	" 12........	3 40	3 50	*Grain:*		
" half "	1 25	1 50	" 16........	4 30	4 40	Wheat, Spring, 60 ℔..	0 95	
White Fish & Trout ..	0 00	0 00	*Powder:*			" Fall " 60 "	0 98	
Salmon, saltwater....	14 00	15 00	Blasting, Canada....	3 50	0 00	Barley........ 48 "	0 80	
Dry Cod, ℔112 lbs ...	4 50	5 00	FF	4 25	4 50	Peas........ 60 "	0 45	
Fruit:			FFF	4 75	5 00	Oats........ 34 "	0 52	
Raisins, Layers	1 90	2 00	Blasting, English ..	4 00	5 00	Rye .... 56 "	0 55	
" M. R.......	1 90	2 00	FF loose..	5 00	6 00	*Seeds:*		
" Valentianew..	0 6	0 6½	FFF	6 00	6 50	Clover, choice 60 "	5 50	
Currants, new.......	0 4½	0 04	*Pressed Spikes (4 mos):*			" com'n 60 "	5 25	
" old......	0 3½	0 04	Regular sizes 100...	4 00	4 25	Timothy, cho's 4 "	2 75	
Figs	0 11	0 12	Extra	4 50	5 00	" inf. to good 48 "	2 50	
Molasses:			*Tin Plates (net cash):*			Flax .... 56 "	2 55	
Clayed, ℔ gal.......	0 00	0 35	IC Coke	7 50	8 50	*Flour (per brl.):*		
Syrups, Standard ...	0 55	0 76	IC Charcoal......	8 50	9 00	Superior extra.....	0 00	
" Golden ...	0 50	0 60	IX "	10 50	11 00	Extra superfine.....	4 35	
Rice:			IXX "	13 50	14 00	Fancy superfine.....	4 20	
Arracan	4 00	4 25	DC "	8 00	8 50	Superfine No 1.....	4 00	
Spices:			DX "	9 50	0 00	" No. 2...		
Cassia, whole, ℔ ℔...	0 00	0 45	**Hides & Skins, ℔℔**			Oatmeal, (per brl.)...	5 50	
Cloves	0 11	0 12	Green rough	0 00	0 05	**Provisions**		
Nutmegs	0 50	0 55	Green, salt'd & insp'd..	0 06	0 06½	Butter, dairy tub ℔℔b..	0 13	
Ginger, ground	0 18	0 23	Cured	0 00	0 00	" store packed..	0 11	
" Jamaica, root..	0 20	0 25	Calfskins, green....	0 00	0 10	Cheese, new	0 14½	
Pepper, black......	0 10½	0 11	Calfskins, cured....	0 00	0 12½	Pork, mess, per brl...	25 50	
Pimento	0 08	0 09	" dry....	0 18	0 20	" prime mess...		
Sugars:			Sheepskins, ...	1 20	1 60	" prime		
Port Rico, ℔ ℔.....	0 9½	0 10	" country..	1 00	1 40	Bacon, rough	0 12	
Cuba "	0 9	0 9½	**Hops.**			" Cumberl'd cut...	0 13	
Barbadoes (bright)..	0 9½	0 34½	Inferior, ℔ ℔........	0 00	0 00	" smoked	0 00	
Canada Sugar Refine'y,			Medium...........	0 00	0 00	Hams, in salt.......	0 14	
yellow No. 2, 60 ds..	0 9½	0 9½	Good	0 00	0 00	" smoked.......	0 14	
Yellow, No. 2......	0 10	0 10½	Fancy	0 00	0 00	Shoulders, in salt	0 00	
No. 3......	0 10	0 10¼				Lard, in kegs.......	0 13	
Crushed X	0 11½	0 11¾	**Leather.** ℔ (4 mos.)			Eggs, packed	0 11½	
A	0 11½	0 12	In lots of less than			Beef Hams	0 00	
Ground...........	0 12½	0 12¾	50 sides, 10 ℔ cnt			Tallow	0 08	
Dry Crushed	0 12½	0 12¾	higher.			Hogs dressed, heavy..	0 00	
Extra Ground......	0 13½	0 13¾	Spanish Sole, 1st qual'y			" medium....	0 00	
Teas:			heavy, weights ℔℔..	0 21	0 22	**Salt, &c.**		
Japan, com'n to good..	0 48	0 50	Do 1st qual middle do..	0 22	0 23	American hds.......	1 35	
" Fine to choicest..	0 55	0 00	Do. No. 2, light weights	0 20	0 00	Liverpool coarse	0 00	
Colored, com. to fine..	0 60	0 70	Slaughter heavy ...	0 00	0 24	Goderich	0 00	
Congou & Souch'ng..	0 42	0 75	" light ...	0 00	0 00	Plaster	1 00	
Oolong, good to fine..	0 50	0 65	Harness, best	0 15	0 27	Water Lime	1 50	
Y. Hyson, com to gd..	0 47½	0 55	" No. 2......	0 00	0 00			
Medium to choice	0 65	0 80	Upper heavy.......	0 30	0 32			
Extra choice	0 85	0 95	" light......	0 33	0 34			

andles.		
& Co.'s ..	$ c.	$ c.
l.........	0 07½	0 08
Bar	0 07	0 07½
ar........	0 07	0 07½
....	0 05	0 05½
....	0 03½	0 03¾
....	0 00	0 11
iquors,		
doz. qrts.	2 60	2 65
ib Portr..	2 35	2 40
a Rum...	1 80	2 25
H. Gin..	1 55	1 65
Tom....	1 90	2 00
....	4 00	4 25
Tom, c...	6 00	6 25
on	1 00	1 25
l	2 00	4 00
mon	1 00	1 50
n........	1 70	1 80
golden..	2 50	4 00

Brandy:	$ c.	$ c.
Hennessy's, per gal..	2 30	2 50
Martell's " ..	2 30	2 50
J. Robin & Co.'s " ..	2 25	2 35
Otard, Dupuy & Cos..	2 25	2 35
Brandy, cases........	8 50	9 00
Brandy, com. per c...	4 00	4 50
Whiskey:		
Common 36 u.p......	0 58	0 60
Old Rye	0 77½	0 80
Malt	0 77½	0 80
Toddy	0 77½	0 80
Scotch, per gal.......	1 90	2 10
Irish—Kinnahan's c...	7 00	7 50
" Dunnville's Belf't..	6 00	6 25
Wool.		
Fleece, lb............	0 26	0 27
Pulled "............	0 00	0 00
Furs.		
Bear................	0 00	0 00
Beaver, ℘ lb.........	0 00	0 00
Coon	0 00	0 00
Fisher..............	0 00	0 00
Martin..............	0 00	0 00
Mink................	0 00	0 00
Otter...............	0 00	0 00
Spring Rats..........	0 00	0 00
Fox.................	0 00	0 00

NSURANCE COMPANIES.

ENGLISH.—*Quotations on the London Market.*

Di-vidend.	Name of Company.	Shares par val £	Amount paid.	Last Sale.
	Briton Medical and General Life ...	10	....	2½
7½	Commer'l Union, Fire, Life and Mar.	50	5	5¾
8	City of Glasgow	25	2½	5½
9½	Edinburgh Life	100	15	33
½ yr	European Life and Guarantee......	2½	11s6	4s. 6d.
0	Etna Fire and Marine............	10	1½	—
5	Guardian	100	50	51½
2	Imperial Fire..................	500	50	352
9½	Imperial Life	100	10	17½
0	Lancashire Fire and Life.........	20	2	2⅜
1	Life Association of Scotland.......	40	7½	25
p. sh	London Assurance Corporation ..	25	12½	48 x d
5	London and Lancashire Life	10	1	—
0	Liverp'l & London & Globe F. & L.	20	2	7⅜
5	National Union Life	5	1	1
2½	Northern Fire and Life	100	5	12⅝
2 o s.	North British and Mercantile	50	6½	19½
0	Ocean Marine	25	5	17¾
12s.	Provident Life...................	100	10	35
p. s.	Phœnix..........................	....	....	145
.yr.	Queen Fire and Life	10	1	1
o.4s	Royal Insurance..................	20	3	6¾
0	Scottish Provincial Fire and Life ..	50	2½	5 3-8
5	Standard Life	50	12	66½
5	Star Life	25	1½	—
	CANADIAN.			℘ c.
4	British America Fire and Marine ..	$50	$25	58 60
4	Canada Life	...	....	.....
2	Montreal Assurance	£50	£5	135
3	Provincial Fire and Marine........	60	11	.....
....	Quebec Fire	40	32½	£25 26
7	" Marine..................	100	40	85 90
o's.	Western Assurance...............	40	9	.....

RAILWAYS.	Sha's	Paid	Montr	London
St. Lawrence........................	£100	All.	....	56
ake Huron	20½	"	....	2⅞ 3¼
do Preference	10	"	....	5 6
& Goderich, 6℘c., 1872-3-4...........	100	"	....	66 69
d St. Lawrence	....	....	10 11	....
do Pref. 10 ℘ ct....	....	....	80 85	....
....	100	"	13 14	14½ 14¾
Eq. G. M. Bds. 1 ch. 6℘c............	100	"	....	89
First Preference, 5 ℘ c	100	"	....	47
Deferred, 3 ℘ ct..	100	"	....	....
Second Pref. Bonds, 5℘c.............	100	"	....	37
do Deferred, 3 ℘ ct..............	100	"	....	....
Third Pref. Stock, 4℘ct............	100	"	....	28½
do. Deferred, 3 ℘ ct......	100	"	....	....
Fourth Pref. Stock, 3℘c............	100	"	....	16
do. Deferred, 3 ℘ ct............	100	"	....	....
n	20½	"	13 14	15 15½
New	20½	18	....	....
6 ℘ c. Bds, due 1873-76............	100	All.	....	100½ 102
5½ ℘c Bds. due 1877-78............	100	"	....	95
ay, Halifax, $250, all.......	$250	"	....	....
anada, 6 ℘c. 1st Pref. Bds..........	100	"	....	82 83

ANGE.	Halifax.	Montr'l.	Quebec.	Toronto.
ndon, 60 days......				
days date	12½ 13	9 9½	9½ 9¾	9½
....	11½ 12	8 8½	8½ 8¾	9
documents...........	....	7½ 8½	....	....
York................	....	27 27½	27 27½	27¾
. ...	....	27½ 28	27½ 28	....
. ...	....	par	par ⅝ dis.	par ½ dis.
....	....	4½ 5	....	3½ to 4½

STOCK AND BOND REPORT.

The dates of our quotations are as follows:—Toronto, June 1; Montreal, May 31; Quebec, May 29; London, May 3.

NAME.	Shares.	Paid up.	Divid'd last 6 Months	Dividend Day.	CLOSING PRICES. Toronto.	Montre'l	Quebec.
BANKS.			℘ ct.				
British North America	$250	All.	3	July and Jan.	105½ 106	105½ 106	105 105½
Jacques Cartier.............	50	"	4	1 June, 1 Dec.	106 108	106 107	bks. clsd
Montreal	200	"	6	"	150 151	150½ 151½	bks. clsd
Nationale..................	50	"	4	1 Nov. 1 May.	106 108	106 107	106½ 107
New Brunswick	100	"	......	......	....	...	....
Nova Scotia	200	—	7&b$3½	Mar. and Sept.	....	....	....
Du Peuple..................	50	"	4	1 Mar., 1 Sept.	108½ 109	108½ 109	108 108½
Toronto	100	"	4	1 Jan., 1 July.	118 118½	118 119	117½ 118
Bank of Yarmouth............	....	....	......	......	....	....	....
Canadian Bank of Com'e......	50	All.	......	......	103 103½	102 104	102 102½
City Bank Montreal	80	"	4	1 June, 1 Dec.	99xd	98 99	bks. clsd
Commer'l Bank (St. John)....	100	"	℘ ct.	......	....	....	....
Eastern Townships' Bank.....	50	"	4	1 July, 1 Jan..	....	100 101	99½ 100½
Gore	40	...	none.	1 Jan., 1 July.	35 35½	34 35	34 35
Halifax Banking Company.....	...	....	......	......	....	....	....
Mechanics' Bank.............	50	All.	4	1 Nov., 1 May.	93½ 94	93 94	93 94
Merchants' Bank of Canada....	100	"	5	1 Jan., 1 July.	109 109½	110 111	109 109½
Merchants' Bank (Halifax)....	....	....	.....	......	....	....	....
Molson's Bank...............	50	All.	4	1 Apr., 1 Oct.	108 108½	108 108½	108 108½
Niagara District Bank.., ...	100	70	3½	1 Jan., 1 July.	....	....	....
Ontario Bank................	40	All.	4	1 June, 1 Dec.	97½xd	96 97	bks. clsd
People's Bank (Fred'kton)....	100	"	......	......	....	....	.. ..
People's Bank (Halifax)	20	"	7 12 m	......	....	...	....
Quebec Bank	100	"	3½	1 June, 1 Dec.	100 100½	99 100	bks. clsd
Royal Canadian Bank	50	60	4	1 Jan., 1 July.	30 50	40 50	30 35
St. Stephens Bank	100	All.	.....	......	....	..	....
Union Bank	100	"	4	1 Jan., 1 July.	106½ 107	106½ 107	107½ 108½
Union Bank (Halifax)........	100	....	7 12mo	Feb. and Aug.	....	....	. .
MISCELLANEOUS.							
British America Land........	250	44	......	......	....	....	....
British Colonial S. S. Co.....	250	32½	......	......	...	....	....
Canada Company	32½	All.	......	......	....	....	....
Canada Landed Credit Co.....	50	$50	3½	......	79 80	....	....
Canada Per. B'ldg Society....	50	All.	5	......	125½ 126	....	....
Canada Mining Company.....	4	90	......	......	....	....	....
Do. Inl'd Steam Nav. Co....	100	All.	15 12m	......	....	99 100½	....
Do. Glass Company.........	100	"	None.	......	....	40 60	....
Canad'n Loan & Investm't....	25	2½	......	......	....	....	....
Canada Agency	10	¼	......	......	....	....	....
Colonial Securities Co........	...	....	......	.....	....	....	....
Freehold Building Society....	100	All.	5	......	113½xd	....	....
Halifax Steamboat Co........	100	"	......	......	....	....	....
Halifax Gas Company........	....	....	......	.. ..	....	...	....
Hamilton Gas Company......	....	....	.....	. ....	....	....	....
Huron Copper Bay Co........	4	12	20	. ....	....	30 45	....
Lake Huron S. and C.........	5	102	......	......	....	...	....
Montreal Mining Consols.....	20	$15	......	......	....	3.25 3.40	...
Do. Telegraph Co...	40	All.	5	......	135 135½	135 135½	134½ 135½
Do. Elevating Co...	00	"	5½	......	....	102 107½	....
Do. City Gas Co.........	40	"	4	15 Mar. 15 Sep.	....	135 136	134 135
Do. City Pass. R., Co....	50	"	2	......	....	109 112	109 110
Quebec and L. S.	8	$4	......	......	....	...	....
Quebec Gas Co..............	200	All.	4	1 Mar., 1 Sep.	....	...	119 120
Quebec Street R. R	50	25	3	......	....	....	90 91
Richelieu Navigation Co.....	100	All.	7-12m	1 Jan., 1 July.	....	117½ 120	118 119
St. Lawrence Glass Company.	100	"	....	......	....	80 85	. ..
St. Lawrence Tow Boat Co....	100	"	......	3 Feb.	....	...	30 35
Tor'to Consumers' Gas Co....	50	"	⅜ m	1 My Au MarFe	105 106	...	105 106
Trust & Loan Co. of U. C....	20	5	3	......	....	....	.. .
West'n Canada Bldg Soc'y....	50	All.	5	......	120½ 121	....	....

SECURITIES.	London.	Montreal.	Quebec.	Toronto.
Canadian Gov't Deb. 6 ℘ ct. stg..................	....	102 104	102½ 103	103½ 105
Do. do. 6 do due Ja. & Jul. 1877-84.........	104½ 105½	....	....	....
Do. do. 6 do. Feb. & Aug.........	102 104	....	.. .	....
Do. do. 6 do. Mch. & Sep...........	102 104	.. .	...	.. .
Do. do. 5 ℘ ct. cur., 1883	93¾ 94½	90 91	90 91	91 92
Do. do. 5 do. stg., 1885	93½ 94	91 93	90 92	91½ 92
Do. do. 7 do. cur.,....................	....	....	......	....
Dominion 6 p. c. 1878 cy....	....	107½ 109	108 108½	108 108½
Hamilton Corporation....	. ..	....	......	....
Montreal Harbor, 8 ℘ ct. d. 1869..................	..	....	......	....
Do. do. 7 do. 1870.....................	...	....	......	....
Do. do. 6½ do. 1883.....................	....	102 103	......	102 103
Do do. 6½ do. 1873.....................	....	....	......	
Do. Corporation, 6 ℘ c. 1891	....	96 96½	96½ 97	96 96½
Do. 7 p. c. stock...	....	108½ 110	109 110	109 110
Do. Water Works, 6 ℘ c. stg. 1878...........	....	96½ 97½	......	96 96½
Do. do. 6 do. cy. do.	....	....	......	96 97
New Brunswick, 6 ℘ ct., Jan. and July	104 104½	....	. ...	....
Nova Scotia, 6 ℘ ct., 1875........................	103 104	...	......	...
Ottawa City 6 ℘ c. d. 1880	....	95 97	......	...
Quebec Harbour, 6 ℘ c. d. 1883....................	....	....	60	....
Do.. do. 7 do. do.......................	....	....	65 70	....
Do. do 8 do. 1886.......................	...	....	80 85	....
Do. City, 7 ℘ c. d. 1½ years....	....	....	98 98½	....
Do. do. 7 do. 8 do.	....	....	91 92	....
Do. do. 7 do. 4 do.	....	....	94 95	....
Do. Water Works, 7 ℘ ct., 3 years............	....	....	97 97½	....
Do. do. 6 do. 1½ do.	....	....	94 95	....
Toronto Corporation	....	92 94	...	....

Insurance.

on Medical and General Life Association,

with which is united the

'ANNIA LIFE ASSURANCE COMPANY.

ond *Invested Funds*............£750,000 *Sterling.*

ANNUAL INCOME, £220,000 STG. :

ly increasing at the rate of £25,000 Sterling.

important and peculiar feature originally intro-
1 by this Company, in applying the periodical
so as to make Policies payable during life, without
wer rate of premiums being charged, has caused
ess of the BRITON MEDICAL AND GENERAL to be
nparalleled in the history of Life Assurance. *Life
in the Profit Scale become payable during the lifetime
asured, thus rendering a Policy of Assurance a
subsistence in old age, as well as a protection for a
nd a more valuable security, to creditors in the
early death; and effectually meeting the often
jection, that persons do not themselves reap the
f their own prudence and forethought.*

tra charge made to members of Volunteer Corps
ees within the British Provinces.

RONTO AGENCY, 5 KING ST. WEST.

—9-1yr   JAMES FRASER, Agent.

BEAVER

t1l Insurance Association.

HEAD OFFICE—20 TORONTO STREET,
TORONTO.

ES LIVE STOCK against death from any cause.
n y Canadian Company having authority to do this
business.

E. C. CHADWICK,
President.
'REILLY,
Secretary.   8-1y-25

HOME DISTRICT

1l Fire Insurance Company.

North-West Cor. Yonge & Adelaide Streets,
TORONTO.—(UP STAIRS.)

ES Dwelling Houses, Stores, Warehouses, Mer-
ise, Furniture, &c.

PRESIDENT—The Hon. J. MCMURRICH.
/ICE-PRESIDENT—JOHN BURNS, Esq.
JOHN RAINS, Secretary.

AGENTS:

'RIGHT, Esq., Hamilton; FRANCIS STEVENS, Esq.,
Barrie; Messrs. GIBBS & BRO., Oshawa.   8-1y

THE PRINCE EDWARD COUNTY

al Fire Insurance Company.

HEAD OFFICE,—PICTON, ONTARIO.
, L. B. STINSON; *Vice-President*, W. A. RICHARDS.
rs : H. A. McFaul, James Cavan, James Johnson,
Mill, William Delong.—*Secretary*, John Twigg ;
, David Barker; *Solicitor*, R. J. Fitzgerald.

ompany is established upon strictly Mutual prin-
s, insuring farming and isolated property, (not
s,) in *Townships only*, and offers great advantages
's, at low rates for *five years*, without the expense
ral.

June 15, 1868.   9-1y

THE AGRICULTURAL

1al Assurance Association of Canada.

FICE ....LONDON, ONT

Farmers' Company. Licensed by the Government of Canada.

it January, 1869 ....$230,193 82
Cash Items, over..................$86,000 00
licies in force....................30,892 00

ompany insures nothing more dangerous than
property. Its rates are as low as any well-es-
Company in the Dominion, and lower than those
; many. It is largely patronised, and continues
a public favor.
surance, apply to any of the Agents er address
tary, London, Ontario.

, 2nd Nov., 1868.   12-1y.

Insurance.

The Gore District Mutual Fire Insurance Company

GRANTS INSURANCES on all description of Property
"ainst Loss or Damage by FIRE. It is the only Mutual Fire Insurance Company which assesses its Policies
yearly from their respective dates ; and the average yearly
cost of insurance in it, for the past three and a half years,
has been 'nearly

TWENTY CENTS IN THE DOLLAR

less than what it would have been in an ordinary Proprietary Company.

THOS. M. SIMONS,
Secretary & Treasurer.
ROBT. McLEAN,
Inspector of Agencies.
Galt, 25th Nov., 1868.   15-1y

Western Assurance Company,

INCORPORATED 1851.

CAPITAL, ... $400,000.

FIRE AND MARINE.

HEAD OFFICE .... TORONTO, ONTARIO.

DIRECTORS.

Hon. JNO. McMURRICH, President.
CHARLES MAGRATH, Vice-President.
A. M. SMITH, Esq,   JOHN F ISKEN, Esq.
ROBERT BEATY, Esq.   ALEX. MANNING, Esq.
JAMES MICHIE, Esq.   N. BARNHART, Esq.
                R. J. DALLAS, Esq.
                B. HALDAN, Secretary.
        J. MAUGHAN, JR., Assistant Secretary.
            WM. BLIGHT, Fire Inspector.
    CAPT. G. T. DOUGLAS, Marine Inspector.
        JAMES PRINGLE, General Agent.

Insurances effected at the lowest current rates on
Buildings, Merchandize, and other property, against loss
or damage by fire.
On Hull, Cargo and Freight against the perils of Inland
Navigation.
On Cargo Risks with the Maritime Provinces by sail or
steam.
On Cargoes by steamers to and from British Ports.
WESTERN ASSURANCE COMPANY'S OFFICE, }
TORONTO, 1st April, 1869.   }   33-1y

Fire and Marine Assurance.

THE BRITISH AMERICA
ASSURANCE COMPANY.

HEAD OFFICE :
CORNER OF CHURCH AND COURT STREETS,
TORONTO.

BOARD OF DIRECTION :

Hon. G. W. Allan, M.L.C.,   A. Joseph, Esq.,
George J. Boyd, Esq.,   Peter Paterson, Esq.,
Hon. W. Cayley,   G. P. Ridout, Esq.,
Richard S. Cassels, Esq.,   E H. Rutherford, Esq.,
        Thomas C. Street, Esq.
                ' Governor:
        GEORGE PERCIVAL RIDOUT, ESQ.
                Deputy Governor:
                PETER PATERSON, Esq.
Fire Inspector: Marine Inspector:
E. ROSY O'BRIEN.   CAPT. R. COURNEEN.

Insurances granted on all descriptions of property
against loss and damage by fire and the perils of inland
navigation.
Agencies established in the principal cities, towns, and
ports of shipment throughout the Province.

THOS. WM. BIRCHALL,
22-1y   *Managing Director.*

Queen Fire and Life Insurance Company,
OF LIVERPOOL AND LONDON,
ACCEPTS ALL ORDINARY FIRE RISKS
on the most favorable terms.

LIFE RISKS

Will be taken on terms that will compare favorably with
other Companies.

CAPITAL, - - - £2,000,000 Stg.

CHIEF OFFICES—Queen's Buildings, Liverpool, and
Gracechurch Street London.
CANADA BRANCH OFFICE—Exchange Buildings, Montreal.
Resident Secretary and General Agent,
                A. MACKENZIE FORBES,
13 St. Sacrament St., Merchants' Exchange, Montreal.
WM. ROWLAND, Agent, Toronto.   1-1y

Insurance.

The Waterloo County Mutual Fire Insurance Company.

HEAD OFFICE : WATERLOO, ONTARIO.

ESTABLISHED 1863.

THE business of the Company is divided into three
separate and distinct branches, the

VILLAGE, FARM, AND MANUFACTURES.

Each Branch paying its own losses and its just proportion
of the managing expenses of the Company.
C. M. TAYLOR, Sec.   M. SPRINGER, M.M.P., Pres.
        J. HUGHES, Inspector.   15-yr

Etna Fire and Marine Insurance Company of Dublin.

AT a Meeting of the Shareholders of this Company,
held at Dublin, on the 13th ult., it was agreed that
the business of the "ETNA" should be transferred to the
"UNITED PORTS AND GENERAL INSURANCE COMPANY."
In accordance with this agreement, the business will here-
after be carried on by the latter Company, which assumes
and guarantees all the risks and liabilities of the "ETNA."
The Directors have resolved to continue the CANADIAN
BRANCH, and arrangements for resuming FIRE and MA-
RINE business are rapidly approaching completion.

T. W. GRIFFITH,
16   MANAGER.

Lancashire Insurance Company.

CAPITAL, - - - - - - - £2,000,000 Sterling

FIRE RISKS

Taken at reasonable rates of premium, and
ALL LOSSES SETTLED PROMPTLY,
By the undersigned, without reference elsewhere.

S. O. DUNCAN-CLARK & CO.,
General Agents for Ontario,
N. W. Corner of King & Church Streets,
25-1y   TORONTO.

Canada Life Assurance Company.

SPECIALLY LICENSED BY THE GOVERNMENT
OF CANADA.

ESTABLISHED 1847.

CAPITAL...... ....A MILLION DOLLARS.

DEPOSIT WITH GOVERNMENT; $50,000.

The success of the Company may be judged of by the
fact that during the financial year to the 30th April, 1869,
the gross number of

NEW POLICIES

ISSUED WAS

8 9 2!

FOR ASSURANCES OF
$1,357,734,

WITH

ANNUAL PREMIUMS OF
$49,783.73.

Rates lower than those of British or Foreign Offices, and
every advantage offered which safety and liberality can
afford.

A. G. RAMSAY, Manager.
E. BRADBURNE, Agent,
May 25.   1y   Toronto Street.

The Victoria Mutual
FIRE INSURANCE COMPANY OF CANADA.

Insures only Non-Hazardous Property, at Low Rates.

BUSINESS STRICTLY MUTUAL.

GEORGE H. MILLS, President.
W. D. BOOKER, Secretary.

HEAD OFFICE .... HAMILTON, ONTARIO.

aug 15-1yr

PUBLISHED AT THE OFFICE OF THE MONETARY
TIMES, No. 60 CHURCH STREET.
PRINTED AT THE DAILY TELEGRAPH PUBLISHING HOUSE,
BAY STREET, CORNER OF KING!

THE SCOTTISH PROVINCIAL
ASSURANCE COMPANY.

ESTABLISHED IN 1825.   INCORPORATED BY SPECIAL ACT OF PARLIAMENT.

ANNUAL MEETING.

THE FORTY-THIRD ORDINARY ANNUAL MEETING OF THIS COMPANY was held within the Company's Office, Aberdeen, on FRID the 16th APRIL, 1869.

ALEXANDER STRONACH, Esq., of Drumallan, Chairman of the Ordinary Directors, in the chair.

The Advertisement calling the meeting having been read, there were submitted—

1.—The Balance-sheet for the past year, with detailed States relative thereto, duly certified as correct, in terms of the Act of Incorporation, by Chairman and Manager, and also by the Auditor.

2.—Report by the Directors, which on the motion of the Chairman, was cordially and unanimously approved of and adopted.

The following particulars, derived from the Balance Sheet and States before mentioned, show the result of the operations of the Company for the past ye

LIFE DEPARTMENT.

Amount Proposed for Life Assurance during the year, contained in 1,201 Proposals	£456,775 0 0
Amount of Proposals accepted, and for which 988 Policies were issued	363,871 0 0
New Annual Premiums thereon	11,314 10 1
Claims by Death, including Bonuses on Participation Policies	54,774 8 3
Sum Assured under Current Life Policies	3,700,000 0 0
Life Revenue	125,889 7 0
ACCUMULATED FUND	£641,100 10 8

Statement showing the progress of the Company's Business, as exhibited by a comparison of its operations during the Five Years terminating 31st Janu last, with the Five Years immediately preceding.

Years inclusive.	Amount proposed for Life Assurance.	Amount of New Policies issued.	No. of		New Annual Premiums.	Total Revenue in each Period.
			New Proposals.	Policies issued.		
1860 to 1864	£2,108,324	£1,699,807	5131	4253	£51,188 16 5	£490,145 14 8
1865 to 1869	2,418,282	1,998,871	5698	4821	60,574 11 10	747,902 2 6

NOTE.—These results have been achieved through the Company's own connections, and without the aid of amalgamation with other Offices.

CANADA.

HEAD OFFICE......................125 St. James Street ....MONTREA

AGENT FOR CANADA,

A. DAVIDSON PARKER.

AGENT FOR TORONTO, ... G. L. MADDISON.

Agent for Hamilton—J. D. PRINGLE.   Agent for Kingston—J. V. NOEL.   Agent for London—G. M. GUNN.

The *London Scotsman* says of Scottish Companies:—

"We have on several occasions directed attention to the highly creditable manner in which the Insurance principle is carried out by Scot Associations. Scotland has been happily free from Insurance Company failures, and there is not an unsound Company in the Country. The in shrewdness of the national character has not afforded much inducement to mere adventurers and speculators. A great deal of the success obtained the Scottish Associations is, we believe, due to the fact that those who give the sanction of their names to them, feel that by so doing, they take u themselves the responsibility of seeing that the affairs of the Company are properly conducted. Directors in fact are not considered mere necessary honorary appendages to a Company, but the machinery of management. We have been led to these observations by a perusal of the report of Scottish Provincial Assurance Company. We do not refer to it as the leading example of its kind, but as a fair type of the Scottish Assurance Corp ations, it was established in the "granite city" rather more than Forty years since, and it has extended its influence widely. The progress of business will bear successful comparison with any of the other Companies in the Country."

Referring to the "SCOTTISH PROVINCIAL" we observe in the *Post Magazine* and *Insurance Monitor* of London, of a late date, the following rema with reference to the enormous Reserve Fund acquired by the Company:—

"Suppose that the Scottish Provincial were to decline all new business and were to rely upon the present accumulated fund and future premi accumulations, for meeting the Company's obligations, it will be seen that the fund alone, at the last years rate of claims, would cover the whole of th for very nearly fifteen years to come: while in the interval a fund of much larger amount would be created out of the resulting premiums from unexpired policies, with considerably diminished claims to be provided for. Our readers can determine for themselves what are the prospects o Company whose annual premiums with interest therefrom, produce a surplus income of £78,000 acquired during the past year, to be added to an exist fund of upwards of Six Hundred Thousand Pounds Sterling.

THE CANADIAN
MONETARY TIMES
AND
INSURANCE CHRONICLE.

:VOTED TO FINANCE, COMMERCE, INSURANCE, BANKS, RAILWAYS, NAVIGATION, MINES, INVESTMENT, PUBLIC COMPANIES, AND JOINT STOCK ENTERPRISE.

| II—NO. 43. | TORONTO, THURSDAY, JUNE 10, 1869. | SUBSCRIPTION $2 A YEAR. |

Mercantile.

Meetings.

RELIANCE MUTUAL LIFE ASSURANCE SOCIETY.

The annual meeting of the members of this Society (office for the Dominion in Montreal, James Grant Esq., Resident Secretary,) was held on April 27th, at the Society's office, London, England, Mr. W. W. Duffield, chairman of the board, presiding.

Mr. Edward Butler, the secretary, read the advertisement convening the meeting, together with the Directors' report, the report of the actuary(Mr. Samuel Brown), and the statement of accounts for the past year.

The Chairman, in moving the adoption of the report and accounts, said he had very great pleasure in meeting the members upon this occasion. In reference to the report the first thing which struck them was that, in the distribution of the bonus on the last occasion, the amount proved to be of a greater cash value than at any former period. Of course this was very gratifying to those who participated in the distribution, but the Directors hoped that, upon some future occasion, they would have the opportunity of putting that paragraph in far stronger language. As the report told them, nearly all the members who had previously applied their bonus to the temporary reduction of their premiums had adopted the recommendation of the Directors, and accepted the system of a permanent reduction of their annual payments. With regard to the new premiums of the past year, which, of course, represented the new business of the Society, he would call attention to the fact that this year they had only received in new premiums the sum of £7,711, whereas last year they had received £7,894. This would appear at first sight to show rather a retrograde movement, though to a small extent,—still when he told them that last year they received in single premiums the sum of £369, and the single premiums this year represented a sum of £63 only; and if they deducted these sums from the respective amount of premiums received this year and last year, they would find that the balance was really in favor of this year. (Hear, hear.) He thought he might fairly call their attention to the depressed state of trade, because there was no doubt that whenever the general business of the country was depressed—and this was proved by the statistics of all the old insurance offices—there was a gradual falling off in the number of assurances effected, and the moment the general trade and commerce of the country revived they would find a great increase in their new assurance premiums. (Hear, hear.) He, therefore, thought that taking that fact into consideration, they might fairly congratulate themselves that they had been able during the past year to increase the new business of their office. There was another fact which he thought he ought to call attention to. On the last occasion that they met in that room, he was unfortunately compelled to state that the claims by death had exceeded the estimate of their actuary—that, although the three years with which the bonus period ended, showed an amount of mortality something under the actuary's calculations, still during the year 1867 their death claims were above the average; and

exceeded the estimated amount. If they looked to the report they would find that the amount of claims by death paid during the last year was less by over £3,000 upon a sum of £24,000, which was the actuary's estimate of the year's mortality—therefore, that whatever other disadvantages they might labor under they had saved something like £3,000 during the last year on our actuary's estimate of the amount required to meet the claims by death.. (Hear, hear.) Mr. Samuel Brown had made an elaborate report with regard to the affairs of the Society, and he (the chairman) thought that as they had increased their accumulation fund something like £20,000 during the past year, and that the cash estimate of the liabilities was £225,-434, and that they had assets to meet them amounting to £236,703, they might be well satisfied with the position of the office. They found a surplus of something like £11,000 in their assets over all the liabilities which the actuary calculated the present policies in the office laid them under. (Hear, hear.) There was also another fact to which Mr. Brown—than whom a more careful and able actuary did not exist in London—called attention in his report. He said that, in making this valuation, he had taken as his basis the Equitable Experience Table of 3½ per cent., as published by Mr. Griffith Davies. Now, he believed he was correct in saying that this was not the table taken by all the insurance offices, neither was it the table most favorable to the appearance of an office. It was strictly in favor of the policyholders, and not in favor of the office, and any person knowing that their liabilities were calculated upon this principle might be thoroughly well satisfied that the actuary had not painted their Society in brighter colors than it deserved; but, on the contrary, it was to a certain extent rather an unfavorable calculation so far as the office was concerned. (Hear, hear.) There was another fact worthy of notice, and that was that the whole of the bonus reserves were allotted last year, and, in addition, Mr. Brown told them that he had reserved the full loading of the future premiums. This plan was not always adopted by assurance offices; it was not the custom to reserve the full loading of the future premiums in one year, but a portion was appropriated every year for the purpose of showing the surplus between the assets of the Society; and, therefore, they might be thoroughly satisfied that in the actuarial calculations here made, Mr. Brown had put the most unfavorable construction on the Society's position, and they might fairly consider that the real position of the Society was better than it was represented to be in the actuary's report. (Cheers.) He did not say this by way of finding fault with what that gentleman had done, but he mentioned it as showing the extreme caution and care with which he valued the affairs of a Society of this kind, and how far they might rely upon the valuation placed before them. There was one other point; during the past year the Directors thought it advisable to avail themselves of an opportunity which offered itself of purchasing the lease of their premises—the unexpired lease of over 40 years; at such a price as would pay them a clear 5 per cent. upon the money expended. (Hear, hear.) This had enabled the Directors to lay out a considerable sum for the purpose of making the office that which it was necessary to make it, in order to meet the increasing business of the Society, and he entertained no doubt that they would approve of what the Directors had done. They had also made some change in the officers of the Society; they had endeavored to extend their operations in various parts of England, Scotland and Ireland, and also in Canada, and while upon this ground he might mention that some gentlemen had intimated that the expenses of the Society upon this portion of their operations had been rather larger than in previous years. That was perfectly true, but shareholders must look upon that expenditure not as the expenditure of the one year, but as an expenditure to be spread over a series of years, and to come back in the shape of a considerable amount of new business. They had not incurred that expense in places where they did not think they would get a remunerative business in return, and it was the firm belief of the Directors, and also of the officers of the Society, in whose judgment they placed the utmost reliance, that the result of this expenditure would be a considerable accession of new business to the Society. (Hear, hear.) Speaking of the expenditure they had made in the office proper, he might mention that the Directors had thought it right to give to their secretary (Mr. Butler) some assistance in the shape of an assistant secretary. Mr. Skirving had been appointed in order that every department of the office might be well overlooked, and the business would, they were sure, continue to improve under their able management. (Hear, hear.) They had appointed Mr. James Grant as their resident secretary in Canada, a gentleman in whose favor they received testimonials of a most satisfactory character. He resided in Canada for a considerable number of years, and acted there for one of the first offices in Scotland, and they received from that office a testimonial with regard to that gentleman which induced them without hesitating for one moment to place him in Canada, as their Secretary, and they sincerely believed, from all they had heard of him and from the amount of assurance business he did in Canada, while acting for the office to which he had referred, that he would be able to increase the business of the Society in that part of the world to a very great extent. The chairman concluded by moving the adoption of the report and accounts.

The Rev. Mr. Whittington seconded the motion.

Some discussion followed on a suggestion of Mr. Pulling, as to whether it would not be advantageous to the Society if a fire branch could be added to its business, but it was stated by the chairman and by the solicitor that a fire business could not be carried on under the existing deed of settlement, which provided only for a life business.

The report was adopted nem. con.

The retiring Directors and auditors were then re-elected, and a cordial vote of thanks having been voted to the chairman, directors, and the various officers of the Society, the proceedings terminated.

STANDARD LIFE ASSURANCE COMPANY.

The annual meeting of this company was held in Edinburgh on the 19th April, 1869, George Moir, Esq., in the chair. The annual report and the balance sheet having been submitted the chairman then addressed the meeting as follows:

The progress of the company during the past year has been so fully brought before you in the report of the Directors, that little remains for me to say in addressing you from the chair; but it may, perhaps, tend to a fuller appreciation of the results communicated, if I place them before you in a somewhat less formal shape than they are given in the report.

The first point which claims your attention is the large amount of new business offered to the Company during the year 1868, being larger than in the previous year—which was one of marked increase—and of such an amount as to bear ample testimony, not only to the favorable position

which the company occupies in the public estimation, but to its wide-spread and influential connection. Neither the amount or the number of assurances accepted quite reaches the sum of 1867 although the amount and number proposed exceed its results: but the Directors consider themselves quite entitled to claim credit for the exercise of a wise discretion in entering into a smaller number of contracts out of a larger number of proposals; indeed, the "Selection of Lives," which is the point involved, is one of the most important parts of the Directorial Duties, requiring constant watchfulness and attention.

But while making this explanatory statement, I would claim for the year 1868 a special advantage over the year 1867 its first-class general progress, although its actual progress may have been very similar; for it is a noteworthy fact, that, while within a few weeks of the closing of the year's business the year 1868 was in advance upwards of £100,000 in new assurances over the same period in 1867, the progress made in these few remaining weeks was so much interfered with by the general elections, that the anticipated large increase, of which the Directors had just hope, was not realized at the close of the year, although the large and satisfactory results now reported were reached.

Next in importance to the selection of lives is the investment of the Company's funds, and unrelaxed attention is paid to that department of management. The rule of the Board is to invest chiefly on the security of real estate, as the most reliable mode of safely employing the funds which, in the course of the business, it is their duty to accumulate and protect, and it will be observed that the company have upwards of two-thirds of their funds invested in first-class mortgages and landed securities. The other securities and investments held are also unexceptionable, although not coming under the class of "mortgages." Some are first-class debentures and stocks guaranteed by the government of India; others consist of government securities; and loans to the Company's policyholders within the value of their policies; while a considerable amount consists of the remaining investments of those companies whose business has been transferred to the Standard, and which, being of a more general character than those we are in the practice of selecting in connection with our larger opportunity of investment, cannot be so easily branched under precise heads. The obligations of other companies; investments in connection with the Colonial branch; current balances due by banks, agents and others; and "miscellaneous property," make up the total. The Directors are satisfied that the investments held are of the first-class, a point which will be more fully brought out next year, when a committee, specially appointed, will report on each separate transaction, with a view to the investigation of 1870.

The company continue to receive a fair and remunerative rate of interest on their investments. It is not possible to secure a larger rate without seeking less eligible transactions for the investment of the funds, which the Directors are not prepared to do; and, pursuing that course, they will consider themselves fortunate if they can continue to realize an average return of 4½ to 4½ per cent on the large sums for the investment of which they have to make provision. Such a return will, it is scarcely necessary to add, prove highly remunerative, and yield a considerable margin of profit.

The quinquennial periods which separate our investigations and divisions of profits succeed each other with what seems to be increasing rapidity, for the company's transactions are now so extensive, that, no sooner has one period been closed and reported on, than the attention of the Directors is called to the preparation of another investigation. Already the manager and his assistants have, for twelve months, been engaged in the preliminary arrangements and calculations for the periodical investigation of 1870. These investigations have become a truly gigantic work,

and the more so, as the Directors, acting on advice of their manager, are not content to investigate the Company's position by the test of a set of observations only, but, watching closely their own experience and that of other companies as well as the Registrar-General's observations to the value of life among the population generally, they do not hesitate, acting on the wide discretion which the company's constitution affords to use every precaution, by the employment of new and improved data, to keep the institution in the soundest position. The Manager expects that all Assurance companies will derive very great advantage from an enquiry now in progress into the mortality experienced by the Scotch offices, by a separate inquiry instituted into the results shown by these offices in combination with a number of the English companies. The report on both sets of observations will shortly be published, and the Directors will not fail to avail themselves of the results.

The bill as to Assurance Companies' accounts which has been introduced into Parliament this session is an important one, as, if passed into law it will enable the public to see the progress and position of the different offices by the registration of accounts in a set form. Your Manager has acted on the committee of managers for the revision of the bill, and anticipates confidently its adoption will be a service to the cause of Assurance. The balance-sheets and schedules required are highly important; and whether measure becomes an Act or not, the Directors propose to adopt these forms, as adjusted by committee, for the better exemplification of business in future years.

On previous occasions, when you have done me the honor to call me to this chair, I have deprecated upon the means employed by the Directors to extend the business, but I do not now find room for any observations under that head, as, in our advanced position in which we now stand have very nearly, I think, exhausted our power of extension. We must now endeavor to consolidate our connection, and to render our source of supply as far as possible continuous. No doubt we require to be alive to the Company's interests and alert in maintaining its high character; but I think we act wisely in laying out for current not plans for increased extension, but plans for the permanency of the institution, doing the work which we have taken in hand conscientiously and prudently, while we afford as much benefit as possible to those who confide in us.

The Report was unanimously adopted.

FREEHOLD PERMANENT BUILDING AND SAVINGS SOCIETY.

In presenting the tenth annual report of Society's affairs—full particulars of which herewith annexed—the Directors have the satisfaction of informing the shareholders that business of the Society has been steadily increasing, the loans on mortgage being $85,445 in excess of those during the previous year. There been a considerable increase in re-payments well as deposits, and all the funds of the Society are now profitably employed.

The profits of the year after deducting all penses, amount to $43,739.90, out of which half-yearly dividends have been declared, amounting together to $36,054.24. $7,524.13 has added to the reserve fund, which is now $40 and the remaining $161.53 is at the credit of tingent account.

The position of the Society being so favourable the Directors having resumed their former practice of paying a ten per cent dividend, which reduced for a time in order to accumulate a reserve of ten per cent on the entire capital. This having been accomplished, in connection with the that the securities held by the Society are of undoubted character, the Directors apprehend

paying in future the rate of dividend d.

observed that besides carefully exam-
ie mortgages and other securities, the
ave certified to their intrinsic value.
nance of these duties by competent
, in the opinion of the Directors, hard-
stimated, when it is considered that
ition of a Building Society can only
ed by a proper valuation of its securi-

the Directors pleasure to state that
ry and other officers of the Society
discharge their respective duties to the
action of the Board.
ich is respectfully submitted. WM.
, President: CHARLES ROBERTSON.

*f Receipts and Disbursements of the
Permanent Building and Savings
r the year ending 30th April, 1869.*

RECEIPTS.

r Stock	$ 164 00
s on Mortgages	130,539 44
s on Collaterals	29,482 32
eived	158,123 93
Sundries	10,599 27
r Fines	546 22
r Sundries	24,828 34
ik, 30th April 1868	34,637 43
	$388,920 95

DISBURSEMENTS.

n Mortgages	$189,413 83
i Collaterals	25,345 72
s Returned	115,577 40
paid	674 04
ds paid	31,833 82
s paid	4,595 27
s, Salaries and Rent	5,917 95
Bank, 30th April, 1869	15,562 92
	$388,920 95

f Liabilities and Assets, April 30, 1869.

LIABILITIES.

ed Stock	$400,705 67
s and Interest thereon	182,335 87
ds unpaid	618 02
d No.19, payable 1st June,	
	20,028 20
Fund, 30th April, 1868	32,475 87
added to Reserve Fund,	
April, 1869	7,524 13
to Contingent Fund	161 53
	$643,849 29

ASSETS.

'alue of Mortgages	$554,562 00
i Collaterals and Interest	68,148 50
tate	5,084 52
urniture	382 35
Arrear	109 00
Bank, 30th April, 1869	15,562 92
	$643,849 29

nt Fund brought down	$161 53

nnual General Meeting of the Share-
l on Wednesday, 2nd June, the follow-
n were elected directors for the current
y:—Hon. Wm. McMaster, James
l., Alexander Murray, Esq., James
, A. T. Fulton, Esq., Henry S. Howland,
J. McDonell, Esq., and at a sub-
ting of the Directors, the Hon. Wm.
ras re-elected President, and James
, Vice-President, Charles Robertson

' REPORT—1869. *To the President
s of the Freehold Permanent Building
s Society:* GENTLEMEN,—We certify
examined and compared the Books,
id Vouchers, and have found them

correct, and in accordance with annexed Balance
Sheet. We have also checked the valuations of
the said Securities, and are pleased to observe the
improved position of the Society, with a large
reserve, enabling the return to an increased dividend. Respectfully your obedient servants,
SAMUEL SPREULL, WM. WILLIAMSON, Auditors.

WELLINGTON, GREY & BRUCE RAILWAY.

The third annual meeting of the shareholders
of this Company was held at Hamilton, some days
ago; Mr. Adam Brown, President, in the chair.

The Secretary read the report of the Directors
for the past year. The report adverts to the visit
of Alderman Dakin, Mr. Falconer and Mr. Brack-
stone Baker, and states that since that visit active
negotiations have been going on and that arrangements are completed, by which the Great Western
Railway Company agree to supply rolling stock
and work and maintain the road constructed for
70 per. cent. of the gross earnings, and further,
that 20 per cent. of all the traffic interchanged
between the two companies shall be set aside
annually to redeem the bonds of the Company at
par. The contract for the first section of the
line, from Guelph to Fergus, has been let to Mr.
Donald Robertson, of Queenston. The contract
for the iron rails for the same section was
awarded to Mr. John Proctor, of Hamilton.
The first shipment is at sea and will shortly
arrive. The Directors express their confidence
that the line will be opened for traffic on or before
the 1st January, 1870. So soon as the equitable
bonuses are granted by the County of Bruce the
Directors promise an extension of the line through
that County. Satisfactory arrangements have been
made for the right of way; the shareholders are
also reminded that the Township of Normandy
granted a bonus of $50,000 in aid of the project
since the last annual meeting. A vacancy on the
Board caused by the death of the late Dr. Parker,
has been filled up by the appointment of A.
Sproat, M.P., for North Bruce. The total expenditure of the Company for the first two years
foot up to $18,378. The report concludes with
a reference to the opening up of the North-West
Territory, and the belief is expressed that the
Wellington, Grey and Bruce Railway will have a
portion of the increased travel and traffic which
must result.

The report of the Company's engineer, Mr.
George Lowe Reid, is subjoined. He states that
rails and fastenings have been purchased in England, amounting to 1,700 tons, all in course of
shipment and that the first cargo of 400 tons will
shortly be at hand. The contractors are now at
work clearing the line of standing timber, getting
out ties and timber for bridges and culverts, and
grading the road bed under the supervision of Mr.
Ridout, who has been steadily engaged since the
snow left the ground, in getting out the slope
stakes and determining the positions and levels
of all the bridges and culverts. This preliminary engineering work is now completed, and everything has been done to place the contractors in
a position for the vigorous prosecution of their
work.

The Director's report was adopted, and the
shareholders then proceeded to the election of the
Board of Directors for the ensuing year. The re-
tiring Board was unanimously re-elected as mem-
bers of the new Board: Adam Brown, President;
George D. Ferguson, Vice-President; Donald Mc-
Innes, J. M. Fraser, A. Sproat; A. T. Wood,
William McGiverin, James Turner, John Brown,
John Ferrie, and James Wilson.

At a subsequent meeting of the Directors, Mr.
Adam Brown was elected President, and Mr. Geo.
D. Ferguson, of Fergus, Vice-President.

—A ponderous peat machine for the Anglo-
American Peat Company, costing $10,000, has
been landed at the Welland peat beds by the
steamer Acadia,—*St. Catharines Times.*

Insurance.

FIRE RECORD.—Quebec, June 4.—The extensive stables attached to the residence of G. H.
Simard, M.P., at St. Fevis, were burned down.
Property including valuable horses, carriages, &c.,
to the amount of $6,000 was destroyed. No insu-
rance. Origin of the fire unknown.

Ashfield Township, Ont., May 25.—Barn and
stable of Jas. McKnight were consumed. A quantity of grain, lumber, fanning mill, &c., were also
lost. Loss about $800. Fully insured in the
Agricultural Mutual. The fire originated from
some burning brush.

Acton, June 7.—A telegram says:—a fire last
night consumed five houses and some outbuildings,
also one span of horses. The principal losers are:
Thos. Ebbage, dwelling house and grocery; loss
about $800. James Bell, span of horses, value
about $250. Chas. Weiger, tea shop; loss about
$200. Mrs. Fearnley, household furniture, &c.;
loss not yet known. No insurance on any of the
property. The cause of the fire is not known.

St. John, N. B., May 26.—House of Thomas
Murray, Sussex, was totally destroyed, with the
household furniture, &c. No insurance. Loss
about $2,000.

East Gwillimbury, Township Ont., May 27.—
Dwelling house of Edward Provost, Harrold Road,
was consumed by fire. No particulars.

Quebec, June 1.—A barn belonging to one Trudel, of Beaufort parish, was burnt to the ground.
It was struck by lightning during a thunder-
storm.

Pickering Township, Ont., May 25.—Head's
Mill, near Duffin's Creek, was consumed; cause
unknown.

St. Catharines, June.—The grocery store of F.
Clifford, St. Paul Street, caught fire in the cellar,
and was clearly the work of an incendiary. The
stock, though run down low, was insured in the
Western for $2,500. At the instance of Mr. Peter
McCallum, Clifford was placed under arrest.

Toronto, June 8.—A fire broke out in the auction rooms of J. H. Dickson, at No. 12, Yonge
Street; Dickson's stock was insured in the Royal
for $1,000, and Lancashire, $1,000; loss, partial.
The confectionery store occupied by Weissinger,
but lately sold by the Sheriff to Haberhouse, was
insured for $1,000 in the Lancashire; partial loss.
The Ætna of Hartford had a policy of $470 on
the furniture; loss about $195. The building is
owned by David Burns, and is insured in the
Lancashire for $4,000; loss $800 to $1,000;
cause unknown.

Hamilton, June 8.—A fire broke out in Magill's
hardware store, King street, the premises were
gutted, and the flames spread to the adjoining
store eastward and injured the top story. The
goods of Mr. Adams, plumber, and Huton &
Wood, tailors, were damaged by removal. Magill's
loss, from $60,000 to $70,000; insured for $45,000
in the following companies:—Commercial Union,
$15,000; Western, $4,000; British America, $4,-
000; Hartford, $6,000; Ætna of Hartford, $6,000;
Home, $3,000; Victoria Mutual (old branch),
$1,000. The building was owned by Stinson's
Bank, and was insured for a comparatively small
amount—$1,200 in the Hartford, and $1,000 in
the Lancashire. Building adjoining on the east,
owned by J. Stinson—Damage to roof and upper
stories, over $2,000, insured; J. A. Chadwick,
occupant, damage to whose stock of merchandise by water, about $1,000; Huton & Wood,
tailors, stock damaged by removal, covered by
$1,600 insurance in the Royal; J. Adams, same
building, plumber, loss $1,000 insured for $200,
building damaged about $5,000.

Richmond, Quebec, May 27.—Scott's Hotel was
burned down; supposed to be the work of an
incendiary.

Napanee, June 1.—A fire broke out in a small
building and soon enveloped the large frame building of Briggs & Waddell, occupied by various
parties. Wells' new building was damaged to the
extent of $1,000; insured for $500. Mr. Allan,

chief constable, lost 'about $500 in furniture ; no insurance. Burgess, baker and confectioner, lost $200 ; no insurance. Mr. Fralick, general grocer, $500 ; no insurance. Mrs. Bell, $100. Mr. Brigg's loss $1,200, insured in British America for $800.

THE CITIZENS' INSURANCE COMPANY
(OF CANADA.)

Authorized Capital..............................$2,000,000
Subscribed Capital.............................. 1,000,000

HEAD OFFICE—MONTREAL.

DIRECTORS·

HUGH ALLAN,	- - - PRESIDENT.
C. J. BRYDGES,	EDWIN ATWATER,
GEORGE STEPHEN,	HENRY LYMAN,
ADOLPHE ROY,	N. B. CORSE.

Life and Guarantee Department.

THIS Company—formed by the association of nearly 100 of the wealthiest citizens of Montreal—is prepared to transact every description of LIFE ASSURANCE ; also, to grant Bonds of FIDELITY GUARANTEE, for Employees holding positions of trust.
Applications can be made through any of the Company's Agents, or direct to
EDWARD RAWLINGS, Manager.
Agent for Toronto: Agent for Hamilton :
W. T. MASON. R. BENNER.

THE CANADIAN MONETARY TIMES AND INSURANCE CHRONICLE *is printed every Thursday evening and distributed to Subscribers on the following morning.*

Publishing office, No. 60 Church-street, 3 doors north of Court-street.

Subscription price—
Canada $2.00 per annum.
England, stg. 10s. per annum.
United States (U. S. Cy.) $3.00 per annum.
Casual advertisements will be charged at the rate of ten cents per line, each insertion.
Address all letters to "THE MONETARY TIMES."
Cheques, money orders, &c. should be made payable to J. M. TROUT, *Business Manager, who alone is authorized to issue receipts for money.*
All Canadian Subscribers to THE MONETARY TIMES *will receive* THE REAL ESTATE JOURNAL *without further charge.*

The Canadian Monetary Times.

THURSDAY, JUNE 10, 1869.

A NEW CANAL PROJECT.

It is proposed to construct what is called a ship canal from the town of Niagara to the Welland Canal, above lock No. 25 in the village of Thorold, and to continue the work to the upper Niagara River to Chippawa, and a bill has been laid before Parliament by Mr. Angus Morrison having that as its supposed object. The lock named is 350 feet long, 70 wide, and 10 deep, and the very dimensions prove that the term "ship-canal" is unwarranted. The cost of the work is estimated at $5,300,000, which is much below the probable cost, if undertaken, and the period assigned for the completion of the undertaking, namely, two and a half years, is too limited in point of time. The whole

project seems to have in view the advantage of Oswego ; it would certainly be inimical to the St. Lawrence. The enlargement of the Welland itself is a matter of expense, not of difficulty, and in no way should it be allowed to be thwarted by a rival scheme. Were Mr. Morrison's canal in operation, the whole Oswego trade, and the large river craft for which it is designed, would pass through it to Oswego without in any way benefitting any portion of Canada. It is simply a Georgian Bay scheme in another place with even more objectionable features. It is not in this way that the imperfections of the St. Lawrence are to be removed. Indeed, this very canal would at once subtract a certain portion of the dues payable to the public revenue and could in no way advance the great policy of the Dominion, which is briefly,—Unity in the navigation of the St. Lawrence developed to the greatest possible extent. On the contrary it would turn traffic away from Canada. The route is objectionable. The ground is suitable between Niagara and Thorold, but thence to Chippawa and against the strong current of the Niagara river, the line has little in it to recommend it. Indeed, it was in this direction that the Welland Canal was originally marked out, but it was abandoned, because it did not answer expectations.

The fact cannot be overlooked, that a very large sum is necessary to complete the project. We have had some experience in schemes of this nature in the Province. The Grand Trunk, which was to have been built with stipulated aid, before its completion, became a debtor to the Province to the extent of nine millions of dollars. The Welland Canal itself is a case in point. It was begun by a private company with an empty exchequer, and a knot of incapable men obtained control of the work to retain it all their lives. Every one knows, or should know, what was the cost to the community.

On many grounds, therefore, is Mr. Morrison's project objectionable, but as far as the Government is concerned we fail to see how they can allow the transfer from public to private control of that which it is, essentially, the perogative and duty of the Central Government to direct. The resolutions on which Confederation is based recognize the obligation to improve the St. Lawrence, and if there is the slightest inclination to act on that obligation, the Legislature will scarcely see the expediency of such legislation as that asked by Mr. Morrison, or deem it a duty to encourage a project hostile to Canadian interests, and of service only to the Oswego trade and those who operate in it. The mercantile interests of Eastern Canada and of Montreal are equally concerned with those of Toronto and Central Canada, and we can-

not be expected to make our welfare subservient to that of Oswego. We contend th the interests of Montreal are identical w those of Western Canada in the improveme of the St. Lawrence navigation, and we pect that our representatives in Parliame object is one of hostility, shall be permitt to stand between us and the attainment an object which it is the proclaimed policy the Dominion to secure.

THE ROYAL CANADIAN BANK.

It has been decided to subject the aff of this Bank to a searching investigati Two well known and reliable men in e locality where an agency exists will be as to go over the business of the agency, report to a Central Committee. This C tral Committee will consist of the Mayo Toronto, John Crawford, M.P., and J Gordon, President of the Toronto, Gre Bruce Railway Company. Should Gordon, who is in every respect well quali for the task, feel unable to give the necess time, it is not improbable that Mr. McGiv of Hamilton, will be asked to take his pl The application to Parliament for powe amalgamate, is to provide against future tingencies, but the feeling is universal am the Bank shareholders that resumption is only possible but advisable. A reduc of about $350,000 has been made in Bank's liabilities to the public since the i tution suspended. The following is statement up to the 5th June :

LIABILITIES.

Circulation............................	$709,966
Balances to other Banks	26,556
Deposits	711,120
	$1,447,643

ASSETS.

Coin, &c..............................	$146,625
Property.............................	16,119
Government Securities.............	123,911
Notes of other Banks...............	37,175
Bank Balances......................	96,269
Notes discounted	2,422,307
	$2,847,408

THE NARROW GAUGE RAILWA

Remarkable progress has been made i taining subscriptions to the stock of roads. For the Toronto and Nipissing $160,000 has been subscribed—more th requisite to enable the company to com its regular organization. It is inte to receive still further amounts, as the stock is taken, the less money will have borrowed. For the Toronto, Grey and B stock, to more than $200,000 is sect and without doubt the entire amount a for—$300,000—will shortly be absorbed.

ient state of the money market, it was pected that the public would have such readiness to invest in these enter- and the fact that they have done so ch promptness, must be taken as an on that they are regarded with favor of capital.

INSURANCE RETURNS.

evote a good deal of space to the pub- of the insurance returns laid before ent, a portion of which only we are make room for this week. On page l be found detailed returns of the iness done by the different stock com- On page 683 we give the total Fire s done by all the companies, and also l Life business, to which our readers ase refer.

.NCE MUTUAL LIFE ASSURANCE CO.— port by the Directors shows a steady increase in the business of this Company. pears very clearly in the following from ion *Post Magazine*: In 1866 the new assur- :ounted to £221,675; in 1867 to £222,945; to £223,257. In the last two of the three e difference was only £312; as nearly as the amount of a single transaction, ac- to the average of the policies issued. The miums are of like uniformity, £7,894 in l £7,611 in 1868. In the former year, as d by the chairman at the meeting, one as issued for a single and final premium , and in 1868 one policy for a like single l premium of £63. Making these deduc- e results will be £7,525 and £7,548:— e of only £23 in the receipts of so many is of pounds spread over the long period e months—the difference, small as it is, i favor of the past year's new business. sement is very remarkable; and serves to it the agencies of the office are in a com- te of organization, and that the engage- 16 entered into with persons belonging to i classes in society; so far as the fact can ained from the average amount assured ch policy.

mes Grant, formerly of the Life Association land, in Montreal, and for some time Secretary of the Edinburgh Life in Dublin, i appointed to the management of the i branch.

.ARD LIFE ASSURANCE COMPANY.—A if the Chairman's speech at the annual must impress every one who comprehends ion and magnitude of the Standard's busi- h the conviction that that gentleman has preciation of the proper course to pursue terests both of the shareholders and policy- f the company. When a Life Assurance ion has attained such results as an annual of about three and a half millions of dol- l an accumulated fund of twenty mil-

lions, the great aim and study of the manage- ment should be, not to extend, but to fortify; not to strive after new business, but to conserve and protect that already secured. The Directors show that such is their policy in rejecting nearly four hundred proposals for assurance, during the year, and declaring that they have exhausted their plans of extension, and also by their deter- mination to invest their funds only in the very safest and most non-speculative way, though the average return is moderate. About two-thirds of the Company's funds are invested in mortgages producing 4½ to 4½ per cent. Reference is made by the chairman to the bill introduced into the English Parliament, which has been revised by a meeting of the managers of the different life com- panies; and he expresses the determination of the company to make out their statements ac- cording to the form of accounts provided for by the bill whether it becomes law or not. This is wise. The more publicity that is given to the affairs of all sound companies the more confidence will the public repose in them; such, at least, is our belief. In these days people prefer to rely upon facts and figures rather than upon the un- supported statements of Directors and managers. We need scarcely remind the readers of THE MON- ETARY TIMES that the Standard has $150,000 cash deposited with the Receiver-General for the security of Canadian policy holders, and that it stands in the very front rank of English Life As- surance Companies.

FREEHOLD BUILDING SOCIETY.—The report for the past year shows that the loans on mortgage were $85,445 in excess of the previous year, and that there has been a considerable increase in re- payments and also in deposits. The profits of the year amount to $43,739.90 out of which $36,054 has been paid by way of dividend. The reserve fund has been increased by $7,524 and it now amounts to $40,000. In consequence of the pro- gress thus shown and the accretion of the Society's reserve to the sum named; the directors have thought it well to resume the payment of 5 per cent. half-yearly dividends. The whole dividend for the past year was at the rate of 9 per cent. The retiring directors were re-elected.

NEW YORK CORRESPONDENCE.

NEW YORK, June 5, 1869.

To the Editor of the Monetary Times.

The appearance of the annual report of either the New York or Massachusetts Department, is always an "interesting event," and creates a good deal of interest and some flutter in our insurance circles. We have before us, just received, Part I (Fire and Marine Insurance) of the Massachusetts Report on the business of 1868. This Department has been administered with such conspicuous ability for many years that its tabular deductions form the experience of the business, always carry great weight with the underwriting profession throughout the country. With much of their Report's details, the readers of the *Monetary Times* could have no possible interest, but there is still much of general interest, and lessons to be learned from it, affecting the business equally in the Dominion and the States.

The law of Massachusetts requiring annual re-

ports from joint stock companies dates back to 1837, and the report of the Secretary of the Com- monwealth for that year was the first report of the kind, in this or any other country. And *mutatis mutandis*, of 48 stock companies covered by that report only 11 survived to put in an ap- pearance for the year 1868. But it was not until 1852 that all companies of every description, in and out of the State, were brought under legal supervision. In 1854 began the career of the In- surance Commissioners and in 1855 a Department was erected.

While the growth of the Massachusetts' com- panies has been considerable during all this period, the noticeable fact is, that the best of the Boston companies, such is the characteristic timidity of Massachusetts' capitalists, still persist in doing a local business, consequently, and naturally the business of the New York and other offices has increased ten-fold from 1853 to 1868, and amounted for the latter year to $250,000,000 of property insured, and the figures show that this large busi- ness was done with a very handsome profit to these companies. So much for New York enter- prise, which knows "no pent up Utica." The outside companies netted over $1,000,000 premiums for 1868. Commissioner Sanford does not seem to like this, but admits that the only remedy is for the Massachusetts' companies to make reprisals, get out of their well worn ruts, and "go in and win."

Commissioner Sanford does not believe in the recent "hue and cry" about the unprofitableness of the insurance business. He has lately been demonstrating the very small margin of profit which the business yielded, but at the same time most of them have been adding a very liberal margin to their surplus. Certainly the condition of the Boston companies is strong and comfortable enough.

Any attempt to analyse the numerous elaborate tables in this report would be impracticable and of little interest to your readers. In 29 Massa- chusetts stock companies, the average ratio of loss to premiums received was 38.1 and the ratio of loss to risks written .368—ratio of expenses to premium received, 20.28 and to gross income 16.84. No less than 90 companies of other States, are represented in the Old Bay State. Average ratio of loss to premiums received 49.18; of loss to risks written 52.50; of expenses to premiums received 24.97; and of expenses to gross income 22.38. It will be seen that the home averages are much the lowest.

On the whole it is gratifying to record the fact, that the year 1868 has been attended with some degree of relief in the amount of property destroyed as well as with increased strength and profit to the companies. The Massachusetts Joint Stock Companies declared nearly 13 per cent. to stock- holders and carried nearly 20 per cent. to surplus account. The companies of other States have done well, but not equally well. They declared 9½ per cent. and carried 5 per cent. to surplus account. The per centage of fire loss was 49 per cent. of the cash premiums and has been about 60 per cent. average for 11 years. But it appears, when the subject is considered in the light of the cost to the insured the result is not so satisfactory. The Joint Stock Companies of Massachusetts and other States, in 1868, paid 51 cents of loss on each $100 of fire risks written, against about 48 cents average for 10 years, and charged $1.06 premium, against an average of from 75 to 80. The rates are therefore increasing, but the losses are not diminishing. The business has been done at below the supposed average in England and in this coun- try 30 per cent., viz.: for 25 per cent.

The National Board of Fire Underwriters, of whose last annual session in this City I furnished you an account in a former letter, has now become such a power among the companies, that Commis- sioner Sanford does not deem it impertinent or beneath the dignity of an official document to dis- cuss and sharply censure its action. He seems to think that the machine has thus far been run mainly for the purpose of securing an advance in rates, instead of doing the one thing needful, viz.: endeavouring to procure a reduction in the annual amount of loss. The present admitted evils of the system are:—hasty adjustment of losses—hasty payment of the same—over insurance—and the granting of unlimited privileges for other insurance. Yet it is charged that the Board took no practical action with reference to a reform of these evils; and with reference to a determination of the question,—what is an an adequate rate?—the Board is charged with further dereliction in not having, after admitting the necessity of a bureau of statistics, taken some practical action for the establishment of one.

The Commissioner's parting kick is, that the only thing that will reconcile the public to the continuance of present control of the Board over the price of insurance, or that will make its existence desirable in any aspect affecting the public good, is that it address itself to the immediate reform of acknowledged evils in the practice of the Companies, and reduce the rates of insurance by preventing the fearful amount of fraud and loss these pernicious practices entail upon the public. But if the Commissioner had been present at the last annual session of the Board as your correspondent was, he would have seen how many conflicting sections there were among the members present and how reluctant many companies are to submit to any general action which may be supposed to affect their local interests. The Board is but a congress of the companies. It has no original, chartered or delegated powers. Its leading minds are willing to take advanced measures and to cover the ground fully. But it can advance only with and express the current sentiment of the companies. Let the companies give it in some form original jurisdiction, agree to be unanimously bound by its action, and all causes of complaint on the score of inadequate and inefficient action will be removed.

The general aspect of insurance business in this city, is at present one of repose. All branches of trade are dull, and we are approaching the heated term when matters will be worse. There is little to be spoken of outside routine office affairs, except that the fire losses for the past two months have been unusually heavy. The largest agency company in this city reports its losses for May as fully double what they were for the corresponding month of 1868.

M. A. C.

Financial.

TORONTO STOCK MARKET.

(Reported by Pellatt & Osler, Brokers.)

There was a marked improvement in business this week; Bank and Building Society stocks have been largely dealt in, and in one or two cases at a considerable advance.

Bank Stock.—Montreal shows a large advance on last week's quotations, sales have taken place since the opening of the books at 151 to 157, the stock is firm at the latter rate. There are buyers of British at 106, very little in the market. A large amount of Ontario has been thrown on the market since the opening of the books and the price is somewhat lower. Toronto has advanced over 2 per cent. buyers to-day offer 120 but there are no sellers. A small sale of Royal Canadian took place at 40, very little offered at quoted rates. Some small sales of Commerce took place at 103½, there are buyers at that rate but little on the market. There are buyers of Gore at 35 and sellers at 36½. Merchants has advanced 2 per cent., buyers to-day offer 111½. There are buyers of Quebec at par, but no sellers. Sales of Molson's are reported at 108½ and 109, sellers at the latter rate. Buyers offer 97½ for City, no sellers under 98½. Sellers ask 109 for Du Peuple, with buyers at 108½. Nationale is nominal at 107 to 108. There are buyers and sellers of Jacques Cartier at 105½ and 106 respectively. Union is asked for at 107 to 107½, none in the market. Mechanics' nominal.

Debentures.—Dominion Stock sold at 108; Sterling six per cents are asked for at 103, sellers want 104; fives are offered at 91. Large sales both of Sterling and Currency Toronto bonds have taken place at rates to yield about 7 per cent. interest. A few County are on market at ¼ per cent. premium, buyers offer par.

Sundries.—Large sales of Canada Permanent Building Society have taken place at 125½ and 126, closed firm at the latter rate. Western Canada Building Society has been freely dealt in at 121 and 121½. Freehold Building Society sold at 113, 113½ and 114, buyers freely offer the latter rate, but holders ask for an advance. Nothing doing in Montreal Telegraph Company, last sales 134½ to 135. Large sales of Canada Landed Credit Company were made at 79 to 79½, there are buyers at the former rate. Buyers offer 56 for British America Assurance, sellers at 60. Mortgages are asked for to pay 8 per cent.

REVENUE AND EXPENDITURE.—Statement of Revenue and expenditure of the Dominion for the month ending 31st May, 1868:—

Customs	$940,294 37
Excise	229,700 41
Post-Office	89,690 32
Public Works, including Railways	72,784 38
Bill Stamp Duty	10,970 25
Miscellaneous	69,017 01
Total	$1,412,456 74
Expenditure	$604,722 27

QUEBEC PROVIDENT AND SAVINGS' BANK.—QUARTERLY ABSTRACT.—Balance at the credit of Depositors on the 1st March, 1869, $548,445 04. Received from Depositors from 1st March, to 31st May inclusive, $81,313 17. Withdrawn during the same period, $96,238 60. Decrease in the last quarter, $14,935 43. Due to depositors this day, $533,219 61.—GEO. VEASEY, Cashier.

TRUST AND LOAN COMPANY.—The report to be presented on the 31st May, shows an available balance, including £3,235 brought forward from September last, of £18,122, and recommends a dividend at the rate of 8 per cent. per annum, less income tax; and that £4,499 be carried to the reserve fund, leaving 3,623 to be carried forward. The reserve fund, after charging it with £2,272 for losses on realisation of securities in default, will now be £70,618.

BANK OF ENGLAND.—The return for the week ending 19th May, shows the following changes compared with those of the previous week:—

A decrease of Public Deposits of	£292,804
An increase of Other Deposits of	748,606
No change in Government Securities	
An increase of Rest of	12,549
A decrease of other Securities of	735,061
An increase of Bullion of	245,551
Ad increase of Notes unemployed	584,595
Total amount of Notes in circulation	23,337,285
Ditto of Bullion and Gold and Silver Coin	16,808,940
Bank minimum rate of Discount since May 6th, 1869	4½ per ct.

The bank has increased sufficiently to justify the Directors in abstaing from further advancing the rate of discount. There is a moderate accession to the bullion, causing the stock to approximate to £17,000,000, and a still larger addition to the reserve, which now stands at not much less than eight millions and a-half. If the present rate of progress be maintained a few weeks longer anticipations of rising discounts may be dismissed. *Herepath's Journal.*

—The Bank of Commerce has opened a branch at Simcoe.

—It is reported that the Scottish Amicable Life Assurance Company will shortly make a deposit in this country.

Railway News.

GREAT WESTERN RAILWAY.—Traffic for week ending May 21, 1869.

Passengers	$28,145 35
Freight	42,855 83
Mails and Sundries	2,320 08
Total Receipts for week	$73,321 26
Coresponding week, 1868	70,130 23
Increase	$3,191 03

NORTHERN RAILWAY.—Traffic receipts for week ending May 29th, 1869.

Passengers	$33,27 44
Freight and live stock	12,626 97
Mails and sundries	2,515 43
	$18,469 84
Corresponding Week of '68.	17,116 28
Increase	$1,353 66

KINGSTON AND FRONTENAC RAILWAY COMPANY.—A provisional Company with the above name has been formed in Kingston, and a prospectus was, some time since, issued. The capital stock is placed at $100,000 in 1,000 shares of $100 each. The Provisional Directors are: R. J. Cartwright, John Caruthers, Hon. A. Campbell, John Paton and O. S. Strange, M.D. It is proposed to run a wooden road from twenty to fifty miles into the back country from Kingston. The Board think it can be done for $4,000 per mile or less.

RAILWAY TRAFFIC RETURNS.

FOR THE MONTH OF APRIL, 1869.

NAMES OF THE RAILWAYS.	Passengers.	Mails and Sundries.	Freight.	Total 1869.	Total 1868.	Miles in Operation, 1869.	Miles in Operation, 1868.
	$	$	$	$	$		
Great Western Railway	142367	10570	275669	428606	420955	351½	351½
Grand Trunk Railway	132372	19000	280153	431525	441883	1377	1377
London and Port Stanley Railway§	1031	93	1032	2156	2242	24½	24½
Welland Railway	1075	860	854	2789	2932	25	25
Northern Railway	11176	1472	27266	39914	47839	97	97
Port Hope, Lindsay, and Beaverton Railway, and Peterborough Branch	3618	247	8262	12127	13265	56	56
Cobourg, Peterborough and Marmora Railway*	......	......	....	......	......	....	....
Brockville and Ottawa Railway	4426	1081	9144	14651	9618	86	86
St. Lawrence and Ottawa Railway	5766	720	7538	14024	11222	54	54
Carillon and Grenville Railway*	......	......	......	......	......	....	....
Stanstead, Shefford & Chambly Rail'y*	......	......	......	......	......	....	....
St. Lawrence and Industry Railway*	......	......	......	......	......	....	....
New Brunswick and Canada Railway	1427	......	9408	10835	9371	116	107
European & North American Railway	5033	613	6733	12379	10434	108	108
Eastern Extension Railway	346	80	199	625	......	23	....
Nova Scotia Railway	9058	190	11181	20329	18522	145	145
Total	$317605	34826	637439	989960	987973	2463	2491

§Three weeks. *No returns.

MARINE LOSSES.—The steamer "Dove" was sunk by colliding with the propellor "May Flower," in the St. Clair river; no lives were lost; it is stated that there was no insurance.

Picton, June 4.—The schooner "Lady Moulton" went down in 250 feet of water near Picton; she was insured for $1,200 or $1,500 in the Provincial.

1868. FIRE BUSINESS IN CANADA.—STOCK COMPANIES.

COMPANY.	1 Premiums of the Year.	2 No. of Policies (new)	3 Amount of Policies, (new)	4 Amount at Risk December 31st, 1868	5 No. losses during the year.	6 Amount of Losses Paid.	Losses in Suspense.	Losses Resisted.
ritish America	$121,162 00	3,033	$5,808,849 00	$10,287,751 00	152	$55,493 67	$643 30	$3,200 00
he.Home	68,144 76			3,676,539 00		75,279 86	11,097 00	6,000 00
orth British and Mercantile	129,715 82	4,756	11,049,077 00		154	82,212 38	None	None
/estern	146,061 56	3,861	4,928,084 00	9,703,776 00	111	77,297 74	1,180 00	800 00
he Liverpool & London & Globe								
oyal	237,810 32	11,535	29,487,665 00	26,284,880 00	204	94,229 25	6,355 70	5,150 00
tna	87,000 00					78,858 00		
mperial	57,600 94	2,353	7,150,368 00	5,879,384 00	37	19,384 34	483 57	3,400 00
artford	53,687 43					41,277 84	700 00	None
orthern	11,838 78	647	2,899,981 00	1,815,365 00	6	269 73		
ancashire	49,835 52	1,545	3,646,784 66	5,804,498 65	55	39,350 70	1,150 20	1,900 00
hœnix	84,562 15	1,069	4,159,188 00	9,202,098 00	41	37,988 49	1,500 00	
ommercial Union	71,067 57	2,631	5,502,574 00	6,973,450 00	60	42,581 71	6,850 00	5,650 00
rovincial	98,966 66	2,940	2,732,175 00	5,806,583 00	108	37,209 85	10,836 75	4,384 16
he Queen								
ondon Assurance	52,234 74	1,154	4,236,228 00	6,500,000 00	39	16,464 06	None	None
cottish Provincial	10,000 00	232	852,580 00	1,190,625 00	3	1,203 62	2,901 57	None
he Guardian								
hé Quebec Fire								
	$1,279,688 25	35,156	$82,453,403 66	$92,724,949 66	970	$699,101 24	$43,678 11	$30,484 16

FIRE BUSINESS IN CANADA.—MUTUAL COMPANIES.

gricultural Mutual	$67,914 16	11,526	$8,890,928 00	$23,428,945 00	(a) 50	$82,393 03	None	$1,000 00

Estimate. To the above should be added, to show the whole extent of Fire business in Canada:—1. Estimated figures for Companies which have not reported their losses separate from Life, and for the Quebec Fire Insurance Company not yet included above. Also for the blanks in the returns of the Home, The North British, The and the Hartford Insurance Companies.

| | $475,000 00 | 10,200 | $24,500,000 00 | $51,500,000 00 | 545 | $254,000 00 | $16,500 00 | $16,000 00 |

stimated figures for the Mutual Insurance Companies registered, but not licensed.

| | $150,000 00 | 18,000 | $9,500,000 00 | $35,000,000 00 | 150 | $80,000 00 | $20,000 00 | $10,000 00 |

ada, ss,	Premiums paid during the year ... $1,972,602 41 Number of New and Renewed Policies ... 69,882 Amount of New Policies of the year ... $124,884,331 66 Total amount at Risk 31st December ... 202,653,894 66	No. of Losses of the year ... 1,715 Amount of Losses paid in the year ... $1,065,494 27 Losses in Suspense ... 80,178 11 Losses Resisted ... 57,484 16

368. LIFE BUSINESS IN CANADA. 1868.

COMPANY.	Premiums of the year in Canada.	No. policies issued in the year.	Amount of Policies issued during the year.	Amount of Policies in force, 31st Dec., 1868.	No. Policies become claims.	Amount of Policies become claims.	Claims paid in 1868.	Claims in suspense Dec. 31, 1868.	Claims Resisted.
nada Life									
orth British and Mercantile	$35,866 87	37	$81,223 31	$1,250,000 00	5	$14,920 51	$14,920 51		
verpool and London and Globe									
oyal	34,462 96	27	58,217 42	1,165,837 52	3	7,300 00	7,300 00		
lliance Mutual									
œnix Mutual	25,499 69	246	569,925 00	780,600 00	1	4,000 00			
nnecticut Mutual	51,155 27	444	1,211,650 00	1,750,000 00	1	3,000 00	3,000 00	None.	
mmercial Union	21,610 51	147	320,470 00	740,210 77	2	1,460 00	1,000 00	$580 00	
avelers (Life Branch)	2,323 60	81	130,700 00	130,700 00					
tna Life	165,080 00	1,008	2,654,280 00	4,066,990 00	8	29,600 00	29,600 00		
fe Association	116,795 59	231	443,450 13	3,606,563 73	13	34,389 25	22,659 23	11,680 02	
indard	112,562 80	292	527,552 00	4,236,915 19	8	16,921 92	6,450 16	9,471 76	
e Queen									
e Edinburgh Life									
ottish Provincial	72,000 00	217	370,000 00	1,703,000 00	10	28,810 66	26,864 00	1,946 66	
ndon and Lancashire	13,026 62	159	342,450 00	501,365 00	4	6,500 00	6,000 00	500 00	
w York Life	9,944 47	103	301,600 00	302,600 00					
lantic Mutual	4,619 64	140	215,000 00	400,000 00					
uitable	1,299 88	23	98,200 00	141,500 00					
e Briton									
e Union Mutual									
e Star									
e National									
	$666,247 90	3,155	$7,254,667 86	$20,776,282 21	60	$145,882 34	$117,823 90	$24,128 44	

he above should be added, to show the whole extent of Life Insurance business in Canada, the estimated figures for the Liverpool and London and Globe and the Queen e Companies, which have not separated their Life from their Fire business; also for the "Canada Life Insurance Company," the "Edinburgh Life Insurance Company," e Life Insurance Company," and the "Union Mutual Insurance Company," of Maine, whose returns have not been received.

| | $300,000 00 | 850 | $1,370,000 00 | $8,750,000 00 | 50 | $102,000 00 | $102,000 00 | | |

as the it Life ss in 1861.	Premiums paid during the year ... $666,247 90 No. of new and renewed Policies ... 4,005 Amount of new Policies of the year ... 8,624,667 86 Total amount of Policies ... 29,526,282 21 No. of Policies become claims during the year ... 110	Amount of Policies become claims during the year, $247,882 34 Claims paid, during the year ... 219,823 90 Claims in suspense ... 24,128 44 Claims resisted ... None.

STATEMENT made by Insurance Companies, to 31st December, 1868, in terms of the Act 31st Vic., cap. 48, submitted in accordance with the 14th Section of the said Act.

FIRE INSURANCE COMPANIES (STOCK). THESE MARKED * ALSO TRANSACT LIFE OR INLAND MARINE INSURANCE BUSINESS IN CANADA.

No.	NAME OF THE COMPANY	The British America Assurance Com'y.*	The Home Ins. Com'y of New Haven, Ct.*	The Provincial Insurance Co., of Canada.*	The Western Assurance Comp'y of Toronto.*	The Ætna Ins. Company of Hartford, Ct.*	The Hartford Ins. Co., of Hartford, Ct.	The North's F. L. Ins. Co., Lon don & Aberdeen
	Statements called for from all the Companies.	$ cts.	$ cts.	$ cts.	$ cts.	$ cts.	$ cts.	$ cts.
1	1. Total premiums received during the year in Canada	121,162 00	68,144 76	98,900 66	146,001 56	87,000 00	53,657 43	11,838 78
2	2. Number of Policies, new, including renewals, issued during the year in Canada	3,033 00		2,940 00	3,361 00			547 00
3	3. Amount of the said Policies	5,803,849 00		2,732,175 00	4,038,084 00			2,809,061 00
4	4. Amount at risk on all Policies in force in Canada	10,287,751 00	3,676,519 00	5,806,583 00	9,703,776 00			1,815,385 00
5	5. Number of Policies in which losses have occurred during the year in Canada	152		108	111			6
6	6. Amount of Losses in Canada paid during the year	55,492 67	75,379 86	37,299 85	77,297 74	78,858 00	41,277 84	259 73
7	7. Amount of losses in Canada in suspense	613 30	11,007 00	19,836 75	1,100 00		700 00	
8	8. Amount of losses in Canada resisted	(c) 3,200 00	(a) 6,900 00	(f) 4,384 16	800 00		None.	
9	7. Amount of premium earned during the year in Canada, being (where no exact calculation is made by the Company) the unearned premiums of the previous year, and 40 per cent. of the premium receipts of the current year.	(h) 120,937 96	(c) 59,386 51	90,220 91	(f) 146,340 02			3,657 22
10	3. Amount of premiums unearned, viz., 40 per cent. of the year's receipts (where no exact calculation is made by the Com'y)	(h) 42,406 70	(c) 44,119 47	24,741 66	49,721 54		21,474 97	3,181 55
	Additional Statements by sundry Companies. (Form D.)							
11	Assets of the Company	278,802 03	1,622,074 39	82,030 00	214,729 08	5,150,931 71	2,247,209 72	4,503,363 00
12	Liabilities of the Company, excluding liabilities (see No. 8, above) on current risks	29,333 00	65,653 32	51,251 17	6,676 62		129,612 89	
13	Amount of Total policies in force	10,287,751 00	96,187,137 00	5,806,583 00	9,703,776 00	280,563 28		
14	Amount of Capital Stock	400,000 00	3,000,000 00	479,760 00	400,000 00	3,000,000 00	1,000,000 00	(2)10,000,000 00
15	Amount paid thereon	200,000 00	1,000,000 00	89,733 00	81,124 00		1,000,000 00	
	Deposits in Canadian Securities, viz:					3,000,000 00		
16	1. Dominion Stock	50,000 00		18,666 00	50,000 00	1,834 00		
17	2. Canada 5 per cents.							
18	3. Canada 6 per cents.							
19	4. Canada Bank Shares							
	Other Canadian Investments—							
20	4) Government Securities owned, not deposited	52,115 00		4,000 00	16,000 00	48,510 00	25,850 00	
21	5. Municipal Debentures	129,084 82						
22	6. Mortgages on Real Estate	13,599 77		22,308 00	29,106 17			
23	7. Real Estate owned in Canada	35,972 75		47,543 31	16,000 00			
24	Cash in Bank and in hand in Canada		72,500 00		23,835 02		130,000 00	
25	Deposit if in United States Securities	121,168 00		98,905 66	146,001 56	2,852,974 40	1,824,135 92	1,300,000 00
26	Total prem's received by the Comp'y in the year, in all countries	3,033 00		2,940 00	8,361 00			
27	Number of policies new or renewals, issued by the Company in the year in all countries	5,308,849 00		2,732,175 00	4,038,084 00			
28	Amount of the above policies	55,492 67		37,399 00	77,297 74		847,880 25	
	Amount of the year's losses, viz.:							
29	(a) Losses paid (all countries)	None.		None.	None.			
30	(b) Losses due and unpaid	9,057 03	27,872 32	5,770 00	29,106 17	30,112 21		
31	(c) Losses adjusted and not due	643 30	40,769 00	5,060 75	16,000 00	290,143 77	94,334 85	
32	(d) Losses in suspense, awaiting further proof	(f) 3,200 00		4,384 16	800 00	None.	35,406 50	
33	(e) Losses resisted	15,683 57				300 00		
34	All other claims against the Company	(h) 120,937 96						
35	Amount of premiums earned during year (see above explanations)	(h) 42,406 70						
36	Amount of the premiums earned during the year (see above)							
	Additional Statements by sundry Companies where deposits are less than $100,000 (Form C.)	These Statements are not called for from this Company.	68,144 76, 17,036 19, 70,379 86	These Statements are not called for from this Company.	These Statem'nts are not called for from the Company.	87,000 00, 21,750 00, 75,858 00, None., say 2,000 00	These statements are not called for from this Company.	These statements are not asked for from this Company.
37	Amounts of premiums received during the year in Canada							
38	Less—25 per cent							
39	Less—also the amount of losses paid							
40	Balance, to be deposited in conformity with Sec. 6 of said Act		2,100 00					
41	Interest, to be deposited		2,500 00			44 00		
42	Actually deposited against the two preceding items							

No.	NAME OF THE COMPANY	The Lancashire Insurance Company.	The Phœnix Ins. Co. of England.*	The Commercial Union Insurance Co.*	The North Brit. and Mercantile In. Co.*	The Royal Insurance Company.*	The Imperial Insurance Company.*	The London Assurance Corporation.	The Scottish Provincial Assurance Comp'y.*
	Statements called for from all the Cos. Continued.	$ cts.	$ cts.	$ cts.	$ cts.	$ cts.	$ cts.	$ cts.	$ cts.
1	1. Total premiums received during the year in Canada	40,835 52	84,562 15	71,067 57	129,715 82	237,810 32	57,600 00	52,234 74	(p) 10,000 00
2	2. Number of Policies, new, including renewals, issued during the year in Canada	1,545 00	1,060 00	2,531 00	4,756	11,535	2,353	1,154	232
3	3. Amount of the said Policies	3,946,734 00	4,159,158 00	5,802,574 00	11,049,077 00	20,847,665 00	7,150,308 00	4,236,228 00	852,550 00
4	3. Am't at risk on all Policies in force in Canada	5,804,498 00	9,202,008 00	6,573,450 00		20,284,880 00	5,879,384 00	(d) 6,530,000 00	1,190,025 00
5	3. Number of Policies in which losses have occurred during the year in Canada	53	41	60	154	204	27	39	3
6	6. Amount of losses in Canada paid during the year	39,550 70	37,088 49	42,581 71	82,219 38	94,229 25	19,384 34	16,464 06	1,203 67
7	7. Amount of losses in Canada in suspense	1,130 30	1,600 00	0,850 00	None.	(f) 16,355 79	483 57		2,901 35
8	Amount of losses in Canada resisted	(c) 1,900 00	None.	3,050 00	None.	(g) 6,150 00	(i) 3,400 00		
9	7. Amount of premiums earned during the year in Canada, being (where no exact calculation is made by the Company) the unearned premiums of the previous year, and 40 per cent. of the premium receipts of the current year	(a) 46,216 09	69,140 50	(d) 76,000 00	112,214 11	(n) 215,821 04	(r) 55,847 05	(m) 51,340 65	7,600 00
10	3. Amount of premiums unearned, viz., 40 per cent. of the year's receipts (where no exact calculation is made by the Company)	18,618 02	33,824 86	28,427 03	51,936 25	102,289 28	21,753 89	20,804 09	4,000

§ These amounts are given as they stood May 1st, 1869. (a) Infraction and non-compliance with the terms of the Policy. (b) Also $1,434,541, Inland Marine risks. (c) Amounts calculated in detail. (d) Estimate. (e) Cause-fraud. (f) Since paid. (g) Resisted for want of just proof. (h) Unearned premiums taken at 35 per cent. (i) Resisted on account of non-existence at the time of fire of the goods insured. (k) Liability unlimited. (l) $50,000 added for unearned premiums from previous year. (m) $20,000 added for unearned premiums from previous year. (n) 0.001 added for unearned premiums from previous year. (o) $15,000 added for unearned premiums from previous year. (r) Business confined to first-class risks in Montreal City al one.

NOTE.—The Liverpool and London and Globe Company does not separate its Fire and Life business claiming that the Act does not require it. The Queen do. The business of the Guardian in Fire and Life only commenced in the current year. The Quebec Fire makes no return. The Companies named in the lower table on this page are not required give the details of their business mentioned in Forms B and C of the upper table.

Commercial.

New York Chamber of Commerce passed a tion at a meeting on the 3rd, endorsing the of the Committee of Ways and Means in mending the President to renew negotiations Great Britain, for the purpose of bringing a renewal of the Reciprocity Treaty, and ng to citizens of the United States the free- f the St. Lawrence and of the inshore fish- f British North America. Gen. Wallbridge a lengthy speech; and stated the questions m the United States and the Provinces as— an interchange of the natural products of th on such reciprocal terms as may be agreed Second, an assimilation of excise duties f patent and copyright laws. Third, free and navigation of the river St. Lawrence llargement of its canals. Fourth, freedom i inshore fisheries of the coast of British ca. Fifth, the regulation of transit trade. seléss to discuss, these propositions, as they not be even taken into serious consideration e Government or people of this country, on their face, one-sided and unfair.

first shipment of lead from the Frontenac nines was forwarded to Montreal recently Carruthers & Co., and consigned to the Can; ud Company...

receipts of flour and grain at the five West- als ports, since August, 1867, and 1868,

	1868.	1867.
, bbls	4,766,900	3,637,000
h, bush	32,933,100	30,400,300
bush	24,728,600	25,826,200
y, bush	17,140,900	14,561,200
	2,634,600	2,756,900

schooner Magdala was chartered on the 8th to carry 10,000 bush. malt to Chicago, the rs being Messrs. Aldwell & Co., of this city. t the second shipment made by this firm ar. The freight was 5c. U. S. currency.

al Canadian Bank Bills now sell at 95c.

Rose has announced in the House of Com- hat he proposes to take steps to protect the d hop growing interests in this country.

stocks of the following articles in Halifax, i 1st June, were :—Rum—446 puns., 18 Sugar—1,736 hhds., 205 tres., 826 brls. , Molasses—3,951 puns., 535 tres., 585 brls. eople of Picton held a meeting the other out the silver question. Mr. Striker, occupied the chair, and Mr. Twigg acted as ry, a committee was struck to draw up a n to the Legislature, asking that "Silver ie a legal tender in payment of customs at its intrinsic value, in order that it may be i out of the country, or in some other way to remove what is felt to be so great an We do not know what the ideas of this g may have been about the intrinsic value r coin ; their remedy is, we fear, no remedy

Toronto Market.

e for the past week shows no indication of ement whatever, in fact their seem s to be sater dullness. The weather has kept cool bundant showers of rain ; the season is lly late.

UGE.—The slight improvement noted last as, as we anticipated, been entirely lost, t market has again became dull and trade it. Wheat.—Receipts for the week 35,240 Stock in store on the 7th, 89,450 bush. f 2,000 bush. spring, sold at 96c. f.o.b. and ush at 95c.; one or two cars sold at 94 to car of midge proof sold at 95. Fall nomi- he tendency of the market is downward. Receipts 1,200 bush ; stock in store on the

7th, 35,000 bush., the market has declined to 50c for carloads on the track. Barley.—Is out of market ; there are buyers at 80 to 85c. Peas.— No receipts; stock on the 7th, 12,744 bush.; mar- ket unsettled, and nominal at 65c. Corn.—Sellers at 60c. by the car load. Rye.—On the street market is worth 56c. Flour.—Receipts 1,000 bbls. and 1,440 bbls. last week; stock in store on the 7th 10,995 bbls. The market closed dull and 5 to 10c. lower. A lot of 200 bbls. sold at $4.00. Fancy sold $4.25 and extra at the same price, f.o.b. Oatmeal.— Small lots sell for retail at $5.75 to $6. Cornmeal. Remains unchanged at $3.75 to $4. Bran.—Car lots are worth $14 per ton.

Provisions.—Business has dwindled down to almost nothing except a small trade with retailers. Butter—Is nominal. Eggs—Were firmer but have since declined and closed at 12 to 12½c. There is nothing doing in cheese except in small lots of old at 15 to 16c. Bacon—Sells at 12 to 13c. Hams —Smoked 12½ to 13½c. Salt.—Goderich has also been reduced 15c. and sells freely at the reduc- tion.

Hardware.—There is some demand for har- vest tools. Bar iron is also quoted firmer.

Groceries.—A fair trade reported by some houses but there is no disposition to extend busi- ness just at present. Prices are unchanged.

Wool.—The new crop is now coming forward and sells at 32c.

Petroleum.—The market is dull at 22 to 25c. Benzole is in good demand.

Freights.—Rates remain unchanged ; grain to Oswego, by vessel, 3c. U. S. Currency. Grain to Montreal 8c.; flour 20c. Lumber to Oswego $1.50 per M. U. S. Currency.

Mercantile.

TORONTO PRICES CURRENT.—JUNE 10, 1869.

Name of Article.	Wholesale Rates.		Name of Article.	Wholesale Rate.		Name of Article.	Whole Rate
	$ c.	$ c.	**Groceries**—*Contin'd*	$ c.	$ c.	**Leather**—*Contin'd.*	$ c.
Boots and Shoes.			Gunpowd'r c. to med ..	0 55	0 70	Kip Skins, Patna ...	0 30
Mens' Thick Boots ...	2 66	2 50	" med. to fine.	0 70	0 55	French	0 76
" Kip..........	2 25	3 60	" fine to fin't..	0 85	0 95	English	0 65
" Calf	3 99	3 70	Hyson	0 45	0 80	Hemlock Calf (30 to 35 lbs.) per doz...	0 50
" Congress Gaiters..	1 65	2 50	Imperial	0 42	0 80	Do. light	0 45
" Kip Cobourgs ...	1 20	1 40	Tobacco, Manufac'd:			French Calf..........	1 03
Boys' Thick Boots ...	1 70	1 80	Can Leaf, ℔.&&10s.	0 25	0 30	Grain & Satn Ch'ld or.	0 09
Youths'	1 40	1 50	Western Leaf, com.	0 25	0 26	Splits, large ℔ ℔..	0 30
Women's Batts	0 95	1 30	" Good	0 27	0 32	" small	0 23
" Balmoral	1 20	1 50	" Fine	0 32	0 35	Enamelled Cow ℔ foot..	0 20
" Congress Gaiters.	0 90	1 50	" Bright fine..	0 40	0 50	Patent	0 20
Misses' Batts......	0 75	1 00	" choice..	0 09	0 75	Pebble Grain	0 15
" Balmoral	1 00	1 20	**Hardware.**			Buff	0 14
" Congress Gaiters.	1 00	1 50	*Tin (net cash prices)*			**Oils.**	
Girls' Batts	0 65	0 85	Block, ℔ ℔......	0 35	0 00	Cod	0 65
" Balmoral......	0 90	1 05	Grain............	0 30	0 00	Lard, extra	0 60
" Congress Gaiters..	0 75	1 10	*Copper:*			" No. 1	0 00
Children's C.T. Cacks..	0 50	0 65	Pig	0 23	0 24	" Woollen	0 00
" Gaiters	0 65	0 90	Grain............	0 30	0 33	Lubricating, patent...	0 00
Drugs			*Cut Nails:*			Mott's economist	0 80
Aloes Cape.........	0 12½	0 16	Assorted ¼ Shingles,			Linseed, raw........	0 79
Alum..............	0 02½	0 03	℔ 100 ℔...	2 95	3 00	" boiled.....	0 81
Borax	0 02	0 00	Shingle alone do	3 15	3 25	Machinery	0 00
Camphor, refined....	0 65	0 70	Lathe and 5 dy	3 30	3 40	Olive, common, ℔ gal..	1 00
Castor Oil.........	0 16½	0 28	*Galvanized Iron:*			" salad	1 95
Caustic Soda.......	0 04½	0 05	Assorted sizes.....	0 08	0 00	" salad, in bots.	
Cochineal	0 90	1 00	Best No. 24........	0 07½	0 00	" qt. ℔ case...	3 60
Cream Tartar	0 40	0 45	" 26........	0 08	0 09½	Sesame salad, ℔ gal..	1 60
Epsom Salts	0 03	0 04	" 28........	0 09	0 09½	Seal, pale........	0 75
Extract Logwood....	0 11	0 12	*Horse Nails:*			Spirits Turpentine..	0 62½
Gum Arabic, sorts..	0 30	0 35	Guest's or Griffin's			Varnish	0 00
Indigo, Madras	0 90	1 00	assorted sizes..	0 00	0 00	Whale............	0 00
Licorice	0 14	0 45	For ℔, ass'd sizes...	0 18	0 19	**Paints, &c.**	
Madder	0 00	0 18	Patent Hammer'd do..	0 17	0 18	White Lead, genuine	
Galls	0 32	0 37	*Iron (at 4 months):*			in Oil, ℔ 25lbs....	0 00
Opium	12 00	13 60	Pig—Cartsherrie No1..	24 00	25 00	Do. No. 1	0 00
Oxalic Acid........	0 26	0 35	Other brands. No 1..	22 00	24 00	" 2	0 00
Potash, Bi-tart,...	0 25	0 26	No 2.	0 00	0 00	" 3	0 00
" Bichromate...	0 15	0 20	Bar—Scotch, ℔100 ℔..	2 25	2 50	White Zinc, genuine..	3 05
Potass Iodide	3 99	4 60	Refined...........	2 35	3 60	White Lead, dry....	0 05
Senna	0 12½	0 00	Swedes	5 00	5 50	Red Lead..........	0 07½
Soda Ash	0 02½	0 04	Hoops—Coopers....	3 00	3 25	Venetian Red, Eng'h..	0 02½
Soda Bicarb	4 50	5 00	Banit	3 00	3 25	Yellow Ochre, Fres'h..	0 02½
Tartaric Acid......	0 40	0 45	*Boiler Plates*	3 25	3 50	Whiting	0 85
Verdigris	0 35	0 40	Canada Plates......	3 75	4 00	**Petroleum**	
Vitriol, Blue......	0 08	0 10	Union Jack	0 00	0 00	*(Refined ℔ gal.)*	
Groceries.			Pontypool	3 25	4 00	Water white, car'l'd..	
Coffees:			Swansea	3 99	4 00	in small lots..	0 00
Java, ℔ ℔..........	0 22	0 23	*Lead (at 4 months):*			Straw, by car load....	0 00
Laguayra, ...	0 17	0 18	Bar, ℔ 100 ℔s.....	0 03½	0 07	small lots....	0 00
Rio...............	0 15	0 17	Sheet "	0 08	0 09	Amber, by car load..	0 00
Fish:			Shot.............	0 07½	0 07½	small lots....	0 00
Herrings, Lab. split..	0 00	0 00	*Iron Wire (net cash):*			Benzine	0 00
" round...	0 00	0 00	No. 6, ℔ bundle..	2 70	2 80	**Produce.**	
" scaled...	0 33	0 35	" 9, " ..	3 10	3 20	*Grain:*	
Mackerel, small kitts..	1 00	0 00	" 10, " ..	3 40	3 60	Wheat, Spring, 60 ℔..	0 98
Lock. Her. ℔'chks...	2 50	2 75	" 11, " ..	4 30	4 40	" Fall 60 " ..	0 95
" half "	1 25	1 50	*Powder:*			Barley .... 48 " ..	0 80
White Fish & Trout...	None.		Blasting, Canada...	3 50	0 00	Peas.......... 60 " ..	0 65
Salmon, saltwater..	14 00	15 00	FF "	4 25	4 50	Oats.......... 34 " ..	0 52
Dry Cod, ℔ 112 ℔s..	4 50	5 00	FFF "	4 75	5 00	Rye .... 56 " ..	0 55
Fruit:			Blasting, English ..	4 00	5 00	*Seeds:*	
Raisins, Layers ...	1 90	2 00	FF loose..	5 00	5 50	Clover, choice 60 "...	5 50
" M. R......	1 00	2 00	FFF "	6 00	6 50	" com'n 60 "...	5 25
" Valentias new..	0 6	0 6½	*Pressed Spikes (4 mos):..*			Timothy, cho'e 4 "...	2 75
Currants, new......	0 4½	0 05	Regular sizes 100...	4 00	4 25	" inf. to good 48 "...	2 60
" old......	0 3½	0 04	Extra	4 50	5 00	Flax .... 56 " ..	2 25
Figs	0 11	0 12	*Tin Plates (net cash):*			*Flour (per brl.):*	
Molasses:			IC Coke	7 50	8 50	Superior extra.......	0 00
Clayed, ℔ gal	0 00	0 35	IC Charcoal.......	8 50	0 00	Extra superfine,.....	4 35
Syrups, Standard ...	0 55	0 75	IX "	10 50	11 00	Fancy superfine......	4 20
" Golden ...	0 50	0 60	IXX "	13 50	14 00	Superfine No 1......	4 00
Rice:			DC "	8 00	9 50	" No. 2..	
Arracan	4 00	4 25	DX "	9 50	0 00	Oatmeal, (per brl.)..	5 50
Spices:			**Hides & Skins,℔.**			**Provisions**	
Cassia, whole, ℔ ℔..	0 00	0 45	Green rough	0 00	0 05	Butter, dairy tub ℔ ℔..	0 13
Cloves	0 11	0 12	Green, salt'd & insp'd..	0 06	0 00	" store packed..	0 11
Nutmegs	0 50	0 55	Cured	0 00	0 00	Cheese, new	0 14½
Ginger, ground	0 18	0 23	Calfskins, green	0 00	0 10	Pork, mess, per brl...	23 50
" Jamaica, root..	0 20	0 25	Calfskins, cured.....	0 00	0 12½	" prime mess.....	
Pepper, black......	0 10½	0 11	" dry.....	0 18	0 20	" prime.........	0 00
Pimento	0 08	0 09	Sheepskins, ...	1 20	1 60	Bacon, rough	0 12
Sugars:			" country....	1 00	1 40	" Cumberl'd cut..	0 13
Port Rico, ℔ lb.....	0 9½	0 10	**Hops.**			" smoked	0 00
Cuba	0 9	0 9½	Inferior, ℔ ℔......	0 00	0 00	Hams, in salt.......	0 12½
Barbadoes (bright)..	0 9½	0 9¾	Medium............	0 00	0 00	" smoked.......	0 14
Canada Sugar Refine'y,			Good	0 00	0 00	Lard, in kegs.......	0 00
yellow No. 2, 56 ds..	0 9½	0 9¾	Fancy	0 00	0 00	Eggs, packed.......	0 12½
Yellow, No. 2½......	0 0½	0 0½	**Leather,** ℔ (4 mos.)			Beef Hams	0 00
" No. 3	0 10	0 10½	In lots of less than			Tallow	0 00
Crushed X	0 11	0 11½	50 sides, 10 ℔ cnt			Hogs dressed, heavy..	0 00
" A...........	0 11½	0 12	higher.			" medium..	0 00
Ground............	0 12½	0 12½	Spanish Sole, 1st qual'y			" light ..	0 09
Dry Crushed	0 12½	0 12½	heavy, weights ℔ ℔..	0 11	0 22	**Salt, &c.**	
Extra Ground......	0 13½	0 13½	Do. 1st qual middle do..	0 21	0 23	American bris.......	1 35
Teas:			Do. No. 2, light weights	0 20	0 00	Liverpool coarse	0 00
Japan com'n to good..	0 48	0 50	Slaughter heavy ..	0 00	0 00	Goderich	0 00
" Fine to choicest..	0 55	0 60	Do. light	0 00	0 00	Plaster	1 00
Colored, com. to fine..	0 60	0 70	Harness, best	0 25	0 27	Water Lime	1 80
Congou & Souch'ng ..	0 42	0 75	" No. 2..	0 00	0 00		
Oolong, good to fine...	0 50	0 65	Upper heavy	0 30	0 32		
Y. Hyson, com to gd..	0 47½	0 55	" light..	0 33	0 34		
Medium to choice ...	0 65	0 80					
Extra choice	0 85	0 95					

Candles.	$ c.	$ c.
rd & Co.'s ..		
rial.........	0 07½	0 08
n Bar	0 07	0 07½
Bar.......	0 07	0 07½
....	0 05	0 05½
....	0 03½	0 03½
....	0 00	0 11
Liquors,		
c.		
per doz. qrts.	2 60	2 65
Dub Portr..	2 35	2 40
aica Rum...	1 80	2 25
r's H. Gin..	1 55	1 65
ld Tom.....	1 90	2 00
ses.........	4 00	4 25
ld Tom, c. >.	6 00	6 25
mon.......	1 00	1 25
old........	2 00	4 00
ommon.....	1 00	1 50
ium........	1 70	1 80
e or golden..	2 50	4 00

Brandy:	$ c.	$ c.
Hennessy's, per gal..	2 3	2 50
Martell's " ..	2 3	2 50
J. Robin & Co.'s " ..	2 2	2 35
Otard, Dupuy & Cos..	2 2	2 35
Brandy, cases........	8 50	9 00
Brandy, com. per c...	4 00	4 50
Whiskey:		
Common 36 u. p......	0 58	0 60
Old Rye	0 77½	0 80
Malt	0 77½	0 80
Toddy	0 77½	0 80
Scotch, per gal.......	1 90	2 10
Irish—Kinnahan's c...	7 00	7 50
" Dunnville's Belf't..	6 00	6 25
Wool.		
Fleece, lb............	0 26	0 27
Pulled "............	0 00	0 00
Furs.		
Bear.................	0 00	0 00
Beaver, ℘ lb..........	0 00	0 00
Coon	0 00	0 00
Fisher...............	0 00	0 00
Martin..............	0 00	0 00
Mink................	0 00	0 00
Otter................	0 00	0 00
Spring Rats..........	0 00	0 00
Fox..................	0 00	0 00

INSURANCE COMPANIES.

ENGLISH.—*Quotations on the London Market.*

ast Dividend.	Name of Company.	Shares par val £	Amount paid.	Last Sale.
	Briton Medical and General Life...	10	....	2½
7½	Commer'l Union, Fire, Life and Mar.	50	5	5¼
8	City of Glasgow	25	2½	5¾
9½	Edinburgh Life	100	15	33
5—½ yr	European Life and Guarantee......	2½	11s6	4s. 6d.
10	Etna Fire and Marine............	10	1½	—
5	Guardian	100	50	51½
12	Imperial Fire..................	500	50	352
9½	Imperial Life	100	10	17½
10	Lancashire Fire and Life........	20	2	2¾
11	Life Association of Scotland.....	40	7½	25
5s. p. sh	London Assurance Corporation ..	25	12½	48 x d
5	London and Lancashire Life	10	1	—
40	Liverp'l & London & Globe F. & L.	20	2	7¾
5	National Union Life	5	1	1
12½	Northern Fire and Life	100	5	12⅝
12 } 8, bo } 5s. }	North British and Mercantile	50	6¼	19¼
50	Ocean Marine	25	5	17¾
25 12s.	Provident Life..................	100	10	85
4½ p. s.	Phœnix........................	....	....	145
½—h.yr.	Queen Fire and Life	10	1	1
. bo. 4s	Royal Insurance................	20	3	6¾
10	Scottish Provincial Fire and Life ..	50	2½	5 3-8
25	Standard Life	50	12	66½
5	Star Life	25	1¼	—
	CANADIAN.			℘ c.
4	British America Fire and Marine ..	$50	$25	56 60
4	Canada Life	...	....	.....
12	Montreal Assurance	£50	£5	135
3	Provincial Fire and Marine........	60	11	.....
....	Quebec Fire	40	32½	£25 25½
7	" Marine....................	100	40	85 90
3 mo's.	Western Assurance..............	40	9	.....

RAILWAYS.	Sha's	Paid	Montr	London
d St. Lawrence..................	£100	All.	....	56
Lake Huron	20½	"	....	2½ 3½
do Preference	10	"	....	5 6
f. & Goderich, 6℘c., 1872-3-4........	100	"	....	66 69
and St. Lawrence	....	....	10 12	....
do Pref. 10 ℘ ct..............	....	....	80 85	....
k	100	"	15 17	14½ 14¾
Eq. G. M. Bds. 1 ch. 6℘c..........	100	"	....	89
First Preference, 5 ℘ c..........	100	"	....	47
Deferred, 3 ℘ ct................	100	"	....	....
Second Pref. Bonds, 5℘c..........	100	"	....	37
do Deferred, 3 ℘ ct..........	100	"	....	....
Third Pref. Stock, 4℘ct..........	100	"	....	28½
do. Deferred, 3 ℘ ct..........	100	"	....	....
Fourth Pref. Stock, 3℘c..........	100	"	....	16
do.. Deferred, 3 ℘ ct...........	100	"	....	....
ern	20½	"	13 15	15 15½
New	20½	18	....	....
6 ℘ c. Bds, due 1873-76..........	100	All.	....	100½ 102
5½ ℘c Bds. due 1877-78..........	100	"	....	95
way, Halifax, $250, all...........	$250	"	....	....
Canada, 6 ℘c. 1st Pref. Bds........	100	"	.. .	82 83

HANGE.	Halifax.	Montr'l.	Quebec.	Toronto.
ondon, 60 days......				
5 days date............	12½ 13	9 9½	9½ 9¾	9¾
....	11½ 12	8½ 8¾	8 8½	9¼
n documents........	....	7½ 8¼	....	....
w York..............	....	27 27½	27 27½	27½
do.	....	27½ 28	27½ 28	....
do.	....	par	par ⅛ dis.	par ¼ dis.
....	....	4½ 5	....	3½ to 4½

STOCK AND BOND REPORT.

The dates of our quotations are as follows:—Toronto, June 8; Montreal, June 7; Quebec, June 5; London, May 3.

NAME.	Shares.	Paid up.	Divid'd last 6 Months	Dividend Day.	CLOSING PRICES. Toronto.	Montre'l	Quebec.
BANKS.			℘ ct.				
British North America........	$250	All.	3	July and Jan.	105½ 106	106 106½	105 105½
Jacques Cartier..............	50	"	4	1 June, 1 Dec.	105½ 106	105½ 106	105 106
Montreal	200	"	6	"	156½ 157½	158 160	155 156
Nationale..................	50	"	4	1 Nov. 1 May.	107 107½	106 107	107 107½
New Brunswick	100	"	......	......	....	....	....
Nova Scotia	200	—	7&b$3½	Mar. and Sept.	....	....	....
Du Peuple..................	50	"	4	1 Mar., 1 Sept.	108½ 109	108½ 109	108 108½
Toronto	100	"	4	1 Jan., 1 July.	119½ 120	119 121	118 119
Bank of Yarmouth...........	....	....	......	......	....	....	....
Canadian Bank of Com'e......	50	All.	......	......	103½ 104	102 103	102 102½
City Bank Montreal	80	"	4	1 June, 1 Dec.	97½ 98	98 98½	97½ 98
Commer'l Bank (St. John)....	100	"	℘ ct.	......	....	....	....
Eastern Townships' Bank.....	50	"	4	1 July, 1 Jan.	....	100 100½	99½ 100½
Gore	40	....	none.	1 Jan., 1 July.	35 35½	34 35	34 35
Halifax Banking Company....	....	....	......	......	....	....	....
Mechanics' Bank............	50	All.	4	1 Nov., 1 May.	92½ 93½	92½ 93½	92 93
Merchants' Bank of Canada....	100	"	5	1 Jan., 1 July.	111 112	111½ 112	111 112
Merchants' Bank (Halifax)....	....	....	......	......	....	....	....
Molson's Bank..............	50	All.	4	1 Apr., 1 Oct.	108½ 109	108½ 109	108 108½
Niagara District Bank........	100	70	3½	1 Jan., 1 July.	....	....	....
Ontario Bank...............	40	All.	4	1 June, 1 Dec.	94 95	94 95	95 96
People's Bank (Fred'kton)....	100	"	......	......	....	....	....
People's Bank (Halifax)......	20	"	7 12 m	......	....	....	....
Quebec Bank	100	"	3½	1 June, 1 Dec.	100 100½	100	99½ 100
Royal Canadian Bank	50	60	4	1 Jan., 1 July.	40 50	35 50	40 45
St. Stephens Bank	100	All.	.....	......	....	....	....
Union Bank	100	"	4	1 Jan., 1 July.	106½ 107	106 107	107½ 108½
Union Bank (Halifax)........	100	....	7 12 mo	Feb. and Aug.	....	....	...
MISCELLANEOUS.							
British America Land........	250	44	......	......	....	....	....
British Colonial S. S. Co......	250	32½	......	......	....	....	....
Canada Company	32½	All.	......	......	....	....	....
Canada Landed Credit Co.....	50	$50	3½	......	79 80	....	....
Canada Per. B'ldg Society....	50	All.	5	......	125½ 126	....	....
Canada Mining Company......	4	90	......	......	....	....	....
Do. Inl'd Steam Nav. Co....	100	All.	15 12 m	......	....	95 98	97 99
Do. Glass Company.........	100	"	None.	......	....	35 45	....
Canad'n Loan & Investm't....	25	2½	......	......	....	....	....
Canada Agency	10	½	......	......	....	....	....
Colonial Securities Co........	...	....	......	......	....	....	....
Freehold Building Society....	100	All.	5	......	113½ 114	....	....
Halifax Steamboat Co.........	100	"	......	......	....	....	....
Halifax Gas Company........	....	....	......	......	....	....	....
Hamilton Gas Company.......	....	....	......	......	....	....	....
Huron Copper Bay Co........	4	12	20	......	....	30 40	....
Lake Huron S. and C.........	5	102	......	......	....	....	....
Montreal Mining Consols......	20	$15	......	......	....	3.10 3.20	...
Do. Telegraph Co..........	40	All.	5	......	135 135½	134½ 135½	135½ 136½
Do. Elevating Co..........	00	"	5½	......	....	101 105	....
Do. City Gas Co...........	40	"	4	15 Mar. 15 Sep.	....	135 137	136 137
Do. City Pass. R'y. Co.....	50	"	2	......	....	110 112	109 111
Quebec and L. S.	8	$4	......	......	....	...	....
Quebec Gas Co..............	200	All.	4	1 Mar., 1 Sep.	....	...	120 121
Quebec Street R. R..........	50	25	3	......	....	....	90 91
Richelieu Navigation Co......	100	All.	7-12m	1 Jan., 1 July.	....	118 122	118 119
St. Lawrence Glass Company.	100	"	....	......	....	80 85	....
St. Lawrence Tow Boat Co....	100	"	......	3 Feb.	....	...	30 35
Tor'to Consumers' Gas Co.....	50	"	⅜ m	1 My Au Mar Fe	105 106	...	105 106
Trust & Loan Co. of U. C.....	20	5	3	......	....	....	.. .
West'n Canada Bldg Soc'y....	50	All.	5	......	120½ 121	....	....

SECURITIES.	London.	Montreal.	Quebec.	Toronto.
Canadian Gov't Deb. 6 ℘ ct. stg..............	....	103½ 104	102 103	102½ 104½
Do. do. 6 do due Ja. & Jul. 1877-84......	104½ 105½	....	....	....
Do. do. 6 do. Feb. & Aug........	102 104	....	....	....
Do. do. 6 do. Mch. & Sep........	102 104	.. .	...	.. .
Do. do. 5 ℘ ct. cur., 1883	93¾ 94½	91 92	90 91	91 92
Do. do. 5 do. stg., 1885	93½ 94	89 91	90 92	91 91½
Do. do. 7 do. cur., ...	....	....	......	....
Dominion 6 p. c. 1878 cy..................	....	107½ 108	108 108½	108 108½
Hamilton Corporation......................	....	....	......	....
Montreal Harbor, 8 ℘ ct. d. 1869.............	..	....	......	....
Do. do. 7 do. 1870....................	....	....	......	....
Do. do. 6½ do. 1883....................	....	102 103	......	102 103
Do do. 6½ do. 1873....................	....	....	......	....
Do. Corporation, 6 ℘ c. 1891...............	....	96 96½	96½ 97	96 96½
Do. 7 p. c. stock.........................	....	109 110	109 110	109 110
Do. Water Works, 6 ℘ c. stg. 1878...........	....	96½ 97½	......	95 96½
Do. do. 6 do. cy. do.	....	....	......	96 97
New Brunswick, 6 ℘ ct., Jan. and July	104 104½	....	......	....
Nova Scotia, 6 ℘ ct., 1875....................	103 104	....	......	....
Ottawa City 6 ℘ c. d. 1880....................	....	95 97	......	....
Quebec Harbour, 6 ℘ c. d. 1883...............	....	....	60	....
Do. do. 7 do. do.......................	....	....	65 70	....
Do. do 8 do. 1886....................	....	....	80 85	....
Do. City, 7 ℘ c. d. 1½ years................	....	....	98 98½	....
Do. do. 7 do. 3 do.	....	....	91 92	....
Do. do. 7 do. 4 do.	....	....	94 95	....
Do. Water Works, 7 ℘ ct., 3 years............	....	....	97 97½	....
Do. do. 6 do. 1½ do.	....	....	94 95	....
Toronto Corporation	....	94 95	....	....

Insurance.

Medical and General Life Association,

with which is united the

ÆTNA LIFE ASSURANCE COMPANY.

Invested Funds........... £750,000 Sterling.

ANNUAL INCOME, £220,000 Stg. :

increasing at the rate of £25,000 Sterling.

portant and peculiar feature originally intro-
by this Company, in applying the periodical
o as to make Policies payable during life, without
r rate of premiums being charged, has caused
es of the BRITON MEDICAL AND GENERAL to be
paralleled in the history of Life Assurance. Life
the Profit Scale become payable during the lifetime
ured, thus rendering a Policy of Assurance a
abstinence in old age, as well as a protection for a
a more valuable security. to creditors in the
early death ; and effectually meeting the often
ction, that persons do not themselves reap the
their own prudence and forethought.

a charge made to members of Volunteer Corps
s within the British Provinces.

ONTO AGENCY, 5 KING ST. WEST.

9-1yr   JAMES FRASER, Agent.

BEAVER
Insurance Association,

HEAD OFFICE—20 TORONTO STREET,

TORONTO.

LIVE STOCK against death from any cause.
ly Canadian Company having authority to do this
usiness.

          E. C. CHADWICK, President.
REILLY, Secretary.   8-1y-25

HOME DISTRICT
Fire Insurance Company.

North-West Cor. Yonge & Adelaide Streets,
TORONTO.—(UP STAIRS.)

Dwelling Houses, Stores, Warehouses, Mer-
ie, Furniture, &c.
RESIDENT—The Hon. J. McMURRICH.
CE-PRESIDENT—JOHN BURNS, Esq.
          .JOHN RAINS, Secretary.
          AGENTS:
JOHT, Esq ; Hamilton : FRANCIS STEVENS, Esq
arrie ; Messrs. GIBBS & BRO., Oshawa.   8-1y

THE PRINCE EDWARD COUNTY
Fire Insurance Company

HEAD OFFICE,—PICTON, ONTARIO.
L. B. STIMSON; Vice-President, W. A. RICHARDS.
: H. A McFaul, James Cavan; James Johnson,
ill, William Delong.—Secretary. John Twigg ;
David Barker; Solicitor, R. J. Fitzgerald.

mpany is established upon strictly Mutual prin-
insuring farming and isolated property, (not
) in Townships only, and offers great advantages
at low rates for five years, without the expense
al.

June 15, 1868.   9-1y

Fire and Marine Assurance.

THE BRITISH AMERICA
SURANCE COMPANY.
HEAD OFFICE:
R. OF CHURCH AND COURT STREETS.
TORONTO.
BOARD OF DIRECTION :
. Allan, M L C.,   A. Joseph, Esq ,
loyd, Esq ,   Peter Paterson, Esq ,
yley, ..   G. P. Ridout, Esq.,
Cassels, Esq.,   E H.Rutherford,Esq ,
Thomas C. Street,Esq.
          Governor:
GEORGE PERCIVAL RIDOUT, Esq.
     Deputy Governor:
     PETER PATERSON, Esq.
nspector: Marine Inspector:
O'BRIEN.   CAPT. R. COURNEEN.
es granted on all descriptions of property
s and damage by fire and the perils of inland

established in the principal cities, towns, and
pment throughout the Province.
          THOS. WM. BIRCHALL,
               Managing Director.

Insurance.

Reliance Mutual Life Assurance Society
OF LONDON, ENGLAND. Established 1840.

Head Office for the Dominion of Canada :
131 ST. JAMES STREET, MONTREAL.
DIRECTORS—Walter Shanly, Esq., M.P.; Duncan Mac
donald, Esq.; George Winks, Esq., W. H. Hingston, Esq.,
M.D., L.R.C.S.
RESIDENT SECRETARY—James Grant.
Parties intending to assure their lives, are invited to
peruse the Society's prospectus, which embraces several
entirely new and interesting features in Life Assurance.
Copies can be had on application at the Head Office, or at
any of the Agencies.
          JAS. GRANT, Resident Secretary.
Agents wanted in unrepresented districts.   43-1y

The Gore District Mutual Fire Insurance Company

GRANTS INSURANCES on all description of Property
against Loss or Damage by FIRE. It is the only Mutual Fire Insurance Company which assesses its Policies
yearly from their respective dates ; and the average yearly
cost of insurance in it, for the past three and a half years,
has been nearly TWENTY CENTS IN THE DOLLAR
less than what it would have been in an ordinary Proprietary Company.
          THOS. M. SIMONS, Secretary & Treasurer.
ROBT. McLEAN, Inspector of Agencies.
Galt, 25th Nov., 1868.   15-1y

Canada Life Assurance Company.

SPECIALLY LICENSED BY THE GOVERNMENT
OF CANADA.

ESTABLISHED 1847.

CAPITAL..... .....A MILLION DOLLARS.

DEPOSIT WITH GOVERNMENT, $50,000.

The success of the Company may be Judged of by the
fact that during the financial year to the 30th April, 1869,
the gross number of

NEW POLICIES
ISSUED WAS

892!

FOR ASSURANCES OF
$1,257,734,
WITH
ANNUAL PREMIUMS OF
$49,783.73.

Rates lower that those of British or Foreign Offices, and
every advantage offered which safety and liberality can
afford.

          A. G. RAMSAY, Manager.
          E. BRADBURNE, Agent,
May 25.   1y   Toronto Street.

Queen Fire and Life Insurance Company,
OF LIVERPOOL AND LONDON,
ACCEPTS ALL ORDINARY FIRE RISKS
on the most favorable terms.

LIFE RISKS
Will be taken on terms that will compare favorably with
other Companies,
CAPITAL, - - - £2,000,000 Stg
CANADA BRANCH OFFICE—Exchange Buildings, Montreal.
Resident Secretary and General Agent,
          A. MACKENZIE FORBES,
     13 St. Sacrament St., Merchants' Exchange, Montreal.
WM. ROWLAND, Agent, Toronto.   1-1y

THE AGRICULTURAL
Mutual Assurance Association of Canada.

HEAD OFFICE........................LONDON, ONT.
A purely Farmers' Company. Licensed by the Govern-
ment of Canada.
Capital,1st January, 1869............ $230,193 82
Cash and Cash Items, over............ $80,000 00
No. of Policies in force................ 30,892 00

THIS Company insures nothing more dangerous than
Farm property. Its rates are as low as any well-established Company in the Dominion, and lower than those
of a great many. It is largely patronised and continues
to grow in public favor.
For Insurance, apply to any of the Agents or address
the Secretary, London, Ontario.
London, 2nd Nov., 1868.   12-1y

Insurance.

The Waterloo County Mutual Fire Insurance Company.

HEAD OFFICE : WATERLOO, ONTARIO.
ESTABLISHED, 1863.

THE business of the Company is divided into three
separate and distinct branches, the

VILLAGE, FARM, AND MANUFACTURES.

Each Branch paying its own losses and its just proportion
of the managing expenses of the Company.
C. M. TAYLOR, Sec.   M. SPRINGER, M.M.P., Pres.
          J. HUGHES, Inspector.   15-yr

Lancashire Insurance Company.

CAPITAL,- - - - - - - - £2,000,000 Sterling

FIRE RISKS

Taken at reasonable rates of premium, and
ALL LOSSES SETTLED PROMPTLY,
By the undersigned, without reference elsewhere.
          S. C. DUNCAN-CLARK & CO.,
          General Agents for Ontario,
25-1y   N. W. Cor. of King & Church Sts., TORONTO.

Western Assurance Company,

INCORPORATED 1851.

CAPITAL, ... $400,000.

FIRE AND MARINE.

HEAD OFFICE................TORONTO, ONTARIO.

DIRECTORS:
Hon. JNO. McMURRICH, President.
          CHARLES MAGRATH, Vice-President.
A. M. SMITH, Esq.   JOHN FISKEN, Esq.
ROBERT BEATY, Esq.   ALEX. MANNING, Esq.
JAMES MICHIE, Esq.   N. BARNHART, Esq.
          B. J. DALLAS, Esq.
          B. HALDAN, Secretary.
          J. MAUGHAN, Jr., Assistant Secretary.
          WM. BLIGHT, Fire Inspector.
          CAPT. G. T. DOUGLAS, Marine Inspector.
          JAMES PRINGLE, General Agent.

Insurances effected at the lowest current rates on
Buildings, Merchandize, and other property, against loss
or damage by fire.
On Hull, Cargo and Freight against the perils of Inland
Navigation.
On Cargo Risks with the Maritime Provinces by sail or
steam.
On Cargoes by steamers to and from British Ports.
WESTERN ASSURANCE COMPANY'S OFFICE, }
     TORONTO, 1st April, 1869.   }   33-1y

The Victoria Mutual

FIRE INSURANCE COMPANY OF CANADA.

Insures only Non-Hazardous Property, at Low Rates.

BUSINESS STRICTLY MUTUAL.

          GEORGE H. MILLS, President,
          W. D. BOOKER, Secretary.

HEAD OFFICE ....HAMILTON, ONTARIO
aug 15-1yr

Star Life Assurance Society,
(OF ENGLAND.)

ESTABLISHED 1843.

Capital £100,000 Stg..... Guarantee Fund £800,000 Stg.
Claims paid £541,000 Stg...Profits divided £240,000 Stg.

ONE HUNDRED THOUSAND DOLLARS

Deposited for the Security of CANADIAN POLICY HOLDERS
Moderate rates of premium—Sound management—Ninety
per cent of profits divided amongst policy holders.

          J. GREGORY,
          General Agent, B. N. A.
          CANADA BRANCH OFFICE,
17-6m.   78 King St. East, Toronto.

PUBLISHED AT THE OFFICE OF THE MONETARY
TIMES, No. 60 CHURCH STREET.
PRINTED AT THE DAILY TELEGRAPH PUBLISHING HOUSE,
BAY STREET, CORNER OF KING.

THE STANDARD
LIFE ASSURANCE COMPANY

ESTABLISHED 1825. CONSTITUTED BY SPECIAL ACTS OF PARLIAMENT.

ANNUAL REPORT, 1869.

THE FORTY-THIRD ANNUAL GENERAL MEETING of the STANDARD LIFE ASSURANCE COMPANY was held at Edinburgh on M day, the 19th of April, 1869.

GEORGE MOIR, Esq., Advocate, in the Chair.

The Manager submitted to the Meeting a Report by the Directors as to the progress of the business. He also submitted—

The Annual Report on the Books and Accounts by the Auditor of the Company, certifying that he had found the whole Accounts accurately stated a properly vouched.

Balance Sheet of the Company's affairs, certified by the Auditor and three of the Directors, in accordance with the Acts of Parliament constituting Company.

The following results were communicated in the Report:—

Amount proposed for Assurance during the year 1868 (2198 Proposals)	£1,385,562 19 6
Amount of Assurances accepted during the year 1868 (1802 Policies)	£1,104,264 19 6
Annual Premiums on new Policies	£36,404 12 6
Claims by death during the year, exclusive of Bonus Additions	£315,070 15 6
Annual Revenue at 15th November, 1868	£703,450 19 8
Accumulated Fund invested in Mortgages, Government Securities, Land, &c.	£4,095,589 16 2

STATEMENT SHOWING THE INVESTMENT OF THE FUNDS
AT 15TH NOVEMBER, 1868.

Mortgages and other Landed Securities	£2,687,308 17 3
Government Securities	64,548 19 0
Loans on the Company's Policies within their Surrender Value	205,552 12 9
Various Investments, including the obligations of other Companies	355,179 8 7
Stocks and Debentures	280,475 6 7
Bank Balances, Agents' Balances, and Premiums upon which Days of Grace are current	273,906 9 9
Invested abroad in connection with Colonial business	84,459 1 5
Life Annuities and Reversions purchased	35,694 16 10
Miscellaneous Property	108,464 4 0
	£4,095,589 16 2

(See address of the Chairman in another part of this paper.)

HEAD OFFICE, CANADA.

STANDARD COMPANY'S BUILDINGS, MONTREAL, 47 GREAT ST. JAMES STRE

DIRECTORS IN MONTREAL:

B. H. LEMOINE, Esq., Banker. | ANDREW ROBERTSON, Esq., Merchant.
H. COTTE, Esq., Banker.   GEORGE STEPHEN, Esq., Merchant.

RICHARD BULL, Inspector of Agencies.

WM. RAMSAY, Manager.

AGENT FOR TORONTO, ... HENRY PELLATT.

Agent for Hamilton—JAMES BANCROFT.   Agent for Kingston—C. F. GILDERSLEEVE.   Agent for London—CHAS. MURRAY.

THE CANADIAN
IONETARY TIMES
AND
INSURANCE CHRONICLE.
)TED TO FINANCE, COMMERCE, INSURANCE, BANKS, RAILWAYS, NAVIGATION, MINES, INVESTMENT, PUBLIC COMPANIES, AND JOINT STOCK ENTERPRISE.

| —NO. 44. | TORONTO, THURSDAY, JUNE 17, 1869. | SUBSCRIPTION $2 A YEAR. |

Mercantile.

Meetings.

VICTORIA MUTUAL FIRE INSURANCE COMPANY.

The sixth annual meeting of this Company was held at their office, corner James and Main streets, on Monday, 7th June.   The meeting was called to order by Mr. George H. Mills, President, and the following Annual Report was read by the Secretary, Mr. W. D. Booker:

Report.

In submitting the usual Annual Report the Board of Directors congratulate the members of the "Victoria" on the continued increase of the business of the Company, and the satisfactory nature of the past year's operations.   The financial arrangements are such that payments for loss may be made at once, after necessary proofs are furnished.   Every claim against the Company during the year has been settled, as soon as its correctness was shown; and the total of assessments ordered has been less in proportion to the amount at risk than in any previous year.

The number of policies now in force in the "General Branch" (covering non-hazardous property only) is.   6,363
Insuring the sum of. $4,389,561
And in the Hamilton Branch. . . .   218
Insuring the sum of.   187,324
Making a total of.   6,581
Insuring the sum of.   4,576,855

Last year.   4,789
Insuring the sum of.   3,419,721

Showing an increase in No. of
Policies   1,792
And in amount insured of. $1,157,164

The premium notes in hand after deducting all payments and assessments, amount to $76,817.13, making, with other securities a balance over and above all liabilities of $118,571.28, as available assets for the payment of future losses; 169 of the largest risks have been partially re-insured with other Companies to the extent of $124,085, making the average risk of the Company $671.92 in the "General Branch," and $813.41 in the "Hamilton Branch."

Two matters of importance, materially affecting the interests of the Company, have been decided by the Board during the past year; the one, regulating the annual collection of assessments; the other, the establishment of a Branch for the insurance of property in the City of Hamilton.

Hitherto the books have been made up to the 31st May of each year, and all assessments ordered for that year, made payable on 1st October following.   This system, however, has been found objectionable, inasmuch as in most cases it became necessary to make four collections upon a three years' policy; the first for part of a year, from date of policy to 31st May following; the second and third for full years; and the fourth, from 1st June to the end of the term of insurance; the last payment in some cases occurring many months after the policy had expired.   To obviate this,

and still to retain the strictly mutual character of the Company, it was decided that the assessments, to cover the losses of each year, should be made payable annually from the date of each policy, or as soon thereafter as notice, with particulars of the several amounts due, could be forwarded to members; but for existing policies, where collections have already been made for portions of a year (ending 31st May), the next notice would be deferred until one year from the end of the policy year already partially paid.   Your Directors are convinced that this change will evidently prove satisfactory to all concerned.

The propriety of establishing a Branch Company to meet the requirements of property holders within the protection of the City Hydrants, having been frequently pressed upon the notice of your Board, after full consideration, it was determined (in January last) to establish such a Branch, subject to the following conditions: "That a scale of risks should be prepared for each department. That direct, separate and distinct accounts should be kept.   That members should only be liable for claims against the department in which they are insured, and not the one for the other.   That all necessary expenses incurred in the conducting and management of such departments should be assessed and divided between each, in proportion to the amounts insured in each.   And that the business in all respects should be managed in like manner, and by the same officers as the 'General Branch.'"

The result has been that during the past four months 218 policies, covering property to the extent of $187,324, have been issued, and no loss has occurred.

The question of Cash Receipts in lieu of the Premium Note System, has occupied the attention of your Board; and the decision of your previous Board, in favor of the continuance of the latter system, has been confirmed.   It is believed that the inconvenience of making a small annual remittance to cover the losses incurred during the year, is incomparably less than the danger attendant upon a business where all the assets of the Company are in hand, without a reserve fund to fall back upon in case of a succession of extraordinary losses.   It is quite evident that a Company without any capital beyond its current receipts must either collect a larger sum than is required to cover the ordinary average of losses; or use the moneys received on new business to meet unusual losses; and thus weaken, if not totally destroy its ability to pay the ordinary average of claims arising from loss on property, for which such moneys were received.   In relation to this important subject your Board would, in conclusion, call attention to an article in a recent number of the *Canadian Monetary Times and Insurance Chronicle*, as conveying a plain and full expression of their views: "The breaking loose from Premium Notes," (says this paper) "deprives the insured of that security for payment which he naturally looks for.   In the absence of a Guarantee Capital, there is no security at all but the honesty and good management of the Directors. * * * In the Cash System there may be neither shadow nor substance.   Under such circumstances (the writer concludes that) some remedy should be applied to a state of affairs manifestly wrong." The Mutual system, as understood and strictly adhered to by your Board, is perfectly safe, and pliable enough to meet every exigency. In years of light loss the annual collections will be small; and when heavier losses occur the existing business will bear the whole, without sacrificing the interests of any member, and without affecting new insurances as every policy must pay its own way, leaving the future to provide only for its own liabilities. Under these circumstances your Board could not advise any change in the system heretofore approved.

In moving the adoption of the Report, Mr. Mills gave a history of the establishment and growth of the Company since its formation, which showed the progress of the Company to have been steady and most satisfactory.

Mr. R. N. Law, as a policy-holder, had great pleasure in seconding the adoption of the Report. The success could not be otherwise than satisfactory, and reflected most creditably not only on the Board of Directors but on the executive of the Company as well. The motion was carried unanimously.

On motion of Mr. A. T. Wood, seconded by Mr. Stephen King, the President was requested to prepare a synopsis of his very interesting remarks for publication with the annual Report.

Mr. Cahill and Mr. R. N. Law were appointed as scrutineers, and reported the unanimous re-election of the old Board. They are: G. H. Mills, L. Lewis. Alexander Brown, Jas. Calder, P. Carroll James Cummings, J. H. Fisher, A. Gibbons, Thomas Lottridge, Geo. Murison. Thos. McIlwraith Joseph Ryual. S. B. Wylie and A. T. Wood.

Messrs. R. N. Law and J. J. Mason were appointed Auditors.

The meeting than adjourned and the new Board was constituted by the re-election of Mr. Geo. H. Mills, as president, and Mr. Levi Lewis, as Vice President.

BANK OF MONTREAL.—The annual meeting was held at Montreal on the 7th; Senator Ryan in the chair. It appears from the Directors' report that the balance at the credit of profit and loss account on the 30th April, 1868, amounted to $71,749, and that the profits for the year ending 30th April, 1869, were, after excluding bad doubtful debts, and deducting charges of management, $1,120,979.88, making with the above the sum of $1,192,728.88. From this sum has been taken one five per cent. dividend amounting to $300,000, a six per cent dividend amounting to $360,000; and $500,000 has been added to the Rest, and the balance of $42,728.83 carried forward. The rest now amounts to $290,000. The profits of the past year are stated to have exceeded those of any previous year. A general statement of the banks position was subjoined.

Mr. Crawford moved, seconded by Mr. Esdaile: That the Transfer Books be opened to the inspection of shareholders within bank hours. In support of the motion he said, that unless this motion were granted he could not see how any director could expect the confidence of the shareholders. There were many reasons indeed why the transfer books should be open; and having brought this forward at other meetings of banks and companies it had been there conceded that it was a right which shareholders ought to claim. He did not doubt that the directors now present would do so too, after the question had been before them. The presidents of the City and of the People's Bank, and Mr. Allan, President of the Telegraph Company, had all conceded the principle. He asked whether, if directors of means were to give place to men of straw, it would not have this effect on the value of stock. If disastrous news came, was that a fact which should belong to the directors alone, or whether the shareholders should not be able to sell out before the price was precipitated by 10 or 15 per cent.

Mr. Thos. Cramp moved, seconded by Mr. H. Lyman: That the question of opening the transfer books of the bank for the inspection of the shareholders be referred to the directors for their con-

sideration. The amendment was put and carried unanimously.

The following gentlemen were elected Directors: T. B. Anderson, T. E. Campbell, G. W. Campbell, M.D., E. M. Hopkins, J. G. Mackenzie, Peter Redpath, Hon. Thomas Ryan, Henry Thomas, David Torrance.

PORT HOPE GAS COMPANY.—The annual meeting was held on the 15th inst.; the following Directors were elected:—J. Helm, Wm. Craig, sen., Robert Eerlandson, and C. Brent. The following is the eleventh annual report of the Directors: The Directors of the Port Hope Gaslight Company beg to report that the past year has been a successful one; and in carrying out the policy adopted some time ago, to pay off the Bonds of the Company, they are happy to state, that at the present time but three of them remain unpaid, amounting to twelve hundred dollars, and they hope that in the course of a few months these also will be paid off, leaving the Company entirely free from debt, and allowing the profits to be paid in dividends to the Shareholders.

During the past year, the net amount received for gas, after paying all the expenses of manufacture and management, including two hundred dollars for new retorts, is about nineteen hundred dollars.

In addition to paying off two of the Bonds, there has been expended during the past year four hundred and twenty seven dollars for extensions.

For a fuller statement of the Finances of the Company, we would refer you to the Financial Report of the Manager.

Your Directors would respectfully submit that it is desirable that no further extensions be made, until not only the Bonds be paid off, but five per cent. be paid as a dividend on the Capital Stock of the Company. After that, all the proceeds with propriety may be expended on such extensions as would yield a reasonable return in revenue.

All the works are in good order, and in consequence of the increased consumption of gas, and the prospect of the Bonds being speedily paid off, your Directors are of the opinion that the Company is in a better position than ever before. All of which is respectfully submitted.

WILLIAM CRAIG, President.

Insurance.

FIRE RECORD.—Brockville, June 12.—A telegram states the loss on Messrs. Borst, Holliday & Co.'s old distillery at $50,000, and fully insured. The following are a portion of the insurances on the building:—London Assurance Corporation, $2,500; North British and Mercantile, 2,500; Lancashire, 1,500.- Total, $6,500. The machinery and fixtures were insured for the following amounts:—London, $2,500; Royal, $5,000; North British, etc., $3,000; Queen, $5,000; Lancashire, $5,000; Provincial, $2,500.—Total, $25,500. The stock was also covered to the same amount.

Magog, Eastern Townships, June 8.—The store owned by J. Webster and occupied by Webster & Willey, was burned with nearly all the contents. There has been no fire in the building for some weeks, and how it took, is a mystery. Loss in goods estimated at $3,000, and building $500 or $600. Insured on goods for $2,000 and on building $300 in Sherbrooke Mutual.

Barton Township, Ont., June 12.—Barn of Rev. G. A. Bell, was destroyed. The horses and carriages were got out and most of the things were saved. Loss about $400, insured for $100 in the Victoria Mutual.

Quebec, June 6.—Church of the Sisters of Charity caught fire from a suspended lamp. Loss about $10,000. Insured in the Quebec Fire Insurance Co., for $20,000.

Bronte, Ont., June 9.—House of Mr. Tolmie, with most of the furniture; said to be insured for $500.

—A new company is starting business in the State of New York—to be called the Merchants and Farmers' Life—which will receive its premiums weekly, on what is called, in England, the industrial plan, not heretofore tried on this continent.

AMALGAMATION OF INSURANCE COMPANIES.—The act for the union of the Beaver Mutual and the Toronto Mutual Insurance Companies provides that the name of the united companies shall be "The Beaver and Toronto Mutual Fire Assurance Company." The Board of Management of the Beaver Mutual become the Board of the united company, the Board of the other company ceasing to exist. The united company may take up the guaranteed stock of the two companies and may issue new stock therefor. The business may be divided into three branches, the Farm Branch, the Household Branch, and the Mercantile Branch.

ARSON.—Some interesting disclosures have been made in reference to the Clifford Fire at St. Catharines. Clifford's wife has informed against father-in-law and his daughter, charging them as accessories to the arson. She explained the whole infamous plot, stating that it had been planned sometime previously, and that the Cliffords, father and son, had arranged the combustible material in the manner in which they were found. The information states that Mrs. Clifford herself applied the torch. Owen Clifford and daughter were immediately arrested.

INSURANCE STOCKS IN HARTFORD.—The following are the latest quotations of Insurance stock in Hartford:—

Fire Insurance Companies.	Bid.	Asked.
Ætna	193	
Hartford	214	
Connecticut	135	
Phœnix	217	
Charter Oak, par $50	50	

Life Insurance Stocks.		
Ætna	210	
Travelers', (Accident)	100	
Hartford Life & Ann.	75	
Conn. General	97	

ACT RESPECTING INVESTIGATIONS INTO SHIPWRECKS, &c.

The Hon. Mr. Mitchell's Bill is substantially as follows:

1. Whenever any ship is lost, abandoned, materially damaged on or near the coast of Canada, or any island or place adjacent thereto, whenever any ship causes loss or material damage to any other ship on or near such coasts, island or place; whenever by reason of any casualty pening to or on board of any ship on or near such coasts, island or place, loss of life ensues; whenever any such loss, abandonment, damage or casualty happens elsewhere, and any complaint or witnesses thereof arrive or are found at any port in Canada; the principal officer of Customs residing at or near the place where such loss, abandonment, damage or casualty occurred, if the loss occurred on or near the coasts of Canada, or island or place adjacent thereto, but if elsewhere at or near the place where such witnesses as aforesaid arrive, or are found, or can be conveniently examined, or any other person appointed for purpose by the Minister of Marine and Fisheries, may make enquiry respecting such loss, abandonment, damage or casualty.

2. Such officer or person as aforesaid shall have the following powers: He may go on board such ship, and may inspect the same or any part thereof, or of any of the machinery, boats, equipment, or articles on board thereof, the boarding or inspection of which app are to him to be requisite the purposes of the enquiry he is required to; not unnecessarily detaining any such ship proceeding on any voyage. He may enter

pect any such premises, the entry and inspec- n of which appears to him to be requisite for ; purpose of the enquiry he is to make. He y, by summons under his hand, require the -ndance of all such persons as he thinks fit to l before him and examine for such purpose, l may require answers or returns to any in- iries he thinks fit to make. He may require d enforce the production of all books, papers or cuments which he considers important for such rpose. He may administer oaths, or may, in 1 of requiring or administering an oath, require ry person examined by him to make and sub- ibe a solemn affirmation or declaration of the th of the statement made by him in his exam- tion.

Jpon the conclusion of such enquiry the officer person who made the same shall send to the uister of Marine and Fisheries a full statement the case, and of his opinion thereon, and such ervations, if any, as he may think fit.

f it appears to the Governor, either upon or hout such preliminary inquiry as aforesaid, or any case of a charge of misconduct or incapacity ught by any person against any master or mate any ship, that a formal investigation is requi- , the Governor may appoint any competent són or persons to be a court or tribunal for the pose of such investigation. Such tribunal ll have the power of summoning before them persons, and of requiring them to give evi- ce on oath, orally or in writing (or on solemn rmation, if they be parties entitled to affirm in il matters), and to produce such documents things as such court or tribunal may deem uisite to the full investigation of the matters which they are appointed to examine; and h court or tribunal shall have the same power nforce the attendance of witnesses and to com- them to give evidence, as is vested in any rt of Law in civil cases; and any wilfully false ement made by any such witness on oath or mn affirmation, shall be a misdemeanor pun- ible in the same manner as wilful and corrupt jury; but no such witness shall be compelled nswer any question by his answer to which he ht render himself liable to a criminal prosecu- ; and the proceedings of such court shall be milated as far as possible to those of ordinary rts of Justice, with the like publicity.

nd whereas it is enacted by Section 242 of . Act, 17 and 18 V., c. 104 intituled, "An to amend and consolidate the Acts relating to chant Shipping," that the Board of Trade may end or cancel the certificate (whether of com ncy or service) of any master or mate of the chant Service, in certain cases, one of which , set forth in sub-section five of the said sec- is as follows,—"If upon any investigation e by any court or tribunal authorised or here- to be authorised by the legislative authority ny British possession, to make inquiry into ges of incompetency or misconduct on the of masters or mates of ships, or as to ship- ks or other casualties affecting ships, a report de by such court or tribunal to the effect he has been guilty of any gross act of mis- uct, drunkenness or tyranny, or that the loss andonment of, or serious damage to any ship, ss of life, has been caused by his wrongful r default, and such report is confirmed by overnor or person administering the govern- of such possession;" and whereas it is further ect enacted by Section 23 of Imp. Act 75 and , c. 63, that the power of cancelling or sus- ing the certificate of a master or mate con- l by the above cited 242nd section on the Board ade, shall in future vest in and be exercised e court or tribunal by which the case is tigated or tried: Be it hereby further enacted such court or tribunal authorised to be nted by this Act, shall be held to be in all ts a court or tribunal under the hereinbe- ited sub-section of the Imperial Act.

on the conclusion of such investigation, the al shall send to the Governor a full report upon the case, together with the evidence, and their judgment thereon, and such observations it any, as the court or tribunal may think fit to make, and shall state in open court the decision to which they have come with respect to any recommendation to cancel or suspend any certificate, or to cancelling or suspending any certificate.

Any such court or tribunal may, if they think proper, require any master or mate possessing a certificate of competency or service, whose conduct is called in question, or appears to them to be likely to be called in question in the course of any investigation before them, to deliver such certificate to them, and they shall hold the certificate so delivered until the conclusion of the investigation, and shall then either return the same to such master or mate, or, if their report is to the effect that they have cancelled or suspended a certificate, or is such as to enable the Board of Trade to cancel or suspend such certificate, shall forward the same to the Governor; and if any master or mate fails so to deliver his certificate when so required, he shall incur a penalty not exceeding *two hundred dollars*.

The Governor in Council may from time to time by warrant, order and direct that any expenses incurred, or to be incurred under the provisions of this Act be defrayed out of any moneys appropriated by Parliament for that purpose, or for the purpose of defraying unforeseen expenses.

Nothing in this Act contained shall be taken to affect in any way the jurisdiction of any Vice Admiralty Court in Canada, however the same may be acquired.

Financial.

TORONTO STOCK MARKET.

(Reported by Pellatt & Osler, Brokers.)

Business has been rather more active this week, especially in mortgages and Building Society stocks, the latter in particular being a favorite investment.

Bank Stock.—There are sellers of Montreal at 161½, 161, 160 and 159½, and there are buyers at the latter rate. No British in market. There were considerable sales of Ontario during the week at 94½, 95 and 95½; there are buyers at the latter rate. A large sale of Toronto took place at 122, and there are still buyers at that rate, transfer books closed. Buyers offer 45 for Royal Canadian, holders not disposed to sell at that rate. Small sales of Commerce were made at 104; little offering; transfer books closed. Gore is enquired for at 35, but no sellers under 36½. There were sales of Merchants at 111, 111½ and 112; still procurable at the latter rate. Par is offered for Quebec, none in market. Molson's sold at 108½, sellers now asking 109. Transactions in City occurred at 97¾ to 98, no sellers now under 99. Buyers offer 108 for Du Peuple, with sellers at 108½. Nationale is wanted at 107. For Jacques Cartier 105½ is offered, sellers asking an advance of one per cent. There were sales of Mechanics at 92 and 92½, it is still offering at that rate. No Union offering, 107 would be paid.

Debentures.—Canada sterling six per cents are offering at 104½. Sterling fives at 91, and Dominion stock at 108. There were large sales of Toronto at rates to pay 7 per cent interest. Some first class County are offering at high rates, but purchasers are unwilling to advance.

Sundries.—There are buyers of City Gas at 106½, little doing. Several sales of Canada Permanent Building Society were made at 125½ and 126, closing firm and in demand at the latter rate. Large sales of Western Canada were made at 121 and 121½; closed firm at the latter rate. Freehold Building Society has advanced since our last report to 115, at which rate there were buyers, but no sellers. Montreal Telegraph sold at 134½ and 135½, sellers now asking 136. British America Assurance nominal at quotations. Little doing in Canada Landed Credit. Mortgages are more numerous than usual, several large ones have been placed at 8 per cent.

Stock Sale in Halifax.—At W. M. Gray's stock sale on the 4th June, by J. D. Nash, the following prices were realized: 10 shares, Union Bank, $54,50; 50 Peoples Bank, $26.75; 2 Bank of Nova Scotia, £68 5s.; shares in Bank B. N. A., £68; Casco Bay Copper Mining Co., 62½c.; 8 Union Marine Insurance; 12 do. £19 3s. 9d.; 2 Temperance Hall, £3 2s. 6d.

—At a meeting of the Board of Directors of the Bank of North America, held in New York city, on June 5th, Mr. Henry A. Kent was elected Vice-President of the Bank, in place of Mr. Charles M. Connolly, deceased.

—Mr. J. L. Beaudry, the President of the Jacques Cartier Bank, has resigned, and his resignation has been accepted.

—The annual meeting of the St. Catharines and Welland Gaslight Company is called for the 13th July.

Railway News.

Great Western Railway.—Traffic for week ending May 28, 1869.

Passengers	$31,349 13
Freight	36,799 27
Mails and Sundries	2,442 36
Total Receipts for week	$70,590 76
Coresponding week, 1868	63,978 34
Increase	$6,612 42

Northern Railway.—Traffic receipts for week ending June 5th, 1869.

Passengers	$3,461 87
Freight and live stock	14,492 81
Mails and sundries	679 04
	$18,633 72
Corresponding Week of '68	15,187 63
Increase	$3,446 09

European and North American Railway.—The Traffic Receipts on the Railway for the month of May, 1869, compared with the corresponding month last year are as follows:—

	1869.	1868.
Passengers	$7,029 71	$5,830 82
Freight	9,539 51	8,504 72
Mails and Sundries	621 51	411 00
Totals	$17,190 73	$14,746 55
Increase	2,444 17	

—The Sherbrooke, Eastern Townships & Kennebec Railway Company was organized by the election of J. G. Robertson, Esq., President; R. D. Morkill, Esq., Vice-President. The Directors named in the charter are, Messrs. Galt, Brydges, Robertson, G. F. Bowen, Borlase, Morkill, Evans, Addie, Brodeur, and H. Camirand. The Secretary is not yet appointed.

—The first sod of section five of the Intercolonial Railway was turned at Kamouski, on the 24th May, with great ceremony.

The Municipal Council of the township of Stoke has passed a By-Law authorizing the Mayor to subscribe for $25,000 stock in the Sherbrooke, E. Townships and Kennebec Railway. The meeting to obtain the sanction of the ratepayers is to be held on the 12th July next.

— We learn that 300 men, divided into 7 gangs, are engaged on the 24 mile section of the Intercolonial Railway between Campbellton and Eel River—Messrs Grant and Elliott's section. On the 24 mile section of J. Jobin & Co., extending from Eel River to near Jacquet River, 100 are employed. The former are chiefly Irish just from Newfoundland, and the latter principally French Canadians.

THE CANADIAN MONETARY TIMES AND INSURANCE CHRONICLE *is printed every Thursday evening and distributed to Subscribers on the following morning.*

Publishing office, No. 60 Church-street, 3 doors north of Court-street.

Subscription price—
Canada $2.00 *per annum.*
England, stg. 10s. *per annum.*
United States (U.S.Cy.) $3.00 *per annum.*
Casual advertisements will be charged at the rate of ten cents per line, each insertion.
*Address all letters to "*THE MONETARY TIMES.*"*
Cheques, money orders, &c. should be made payable to J. M. TROUT; *Business Manager, who alone is authorized to issue receipts for money.*
☞ *All Canadian Subscribers to* THE MONETARY TIMES *will receive* THE REAL ESTATE JOURNAL *without further charge.*

The Canadian Monetary Times.

THURSDAY, JUNE 17, 1869.

THE CANADIAN CANALS.

NO. IV.

Hitherto the functions of the Canadian Canals have been but imperfectly argued, because much of the result to be attained has been a matter of theory. Indeed the basis of argument has been incomplete, from the confined character of our knowledge. Within the last few days the want has been supplied; and in place of venturing on conclusions from what is unknown and untried, we have the solid hypothesis of what has been effected. We have facts to guide us. Between Chicago and Montreal the route is known, for it has long been established. The limit of vessels navigating this distance, both as regards burden and time, is admitted beyond dispute. Thus, the question of what can be effected in this limit is not even raised. At the moment, however, we propose to pass Montreal, we meet contradictory opinions. While experienced mariners of the lake and river navigation have argued that vessels should pass from Chicago to the Atlantic; that with the navigation developed to its maximum, a class of vessels would come into use fitted satisfactorily to serve the trade; the contrary view has been urged—and it is especially in favor in Montreal—that ocean going vessels are unfitted for river navigation. And the formula thus roughly couched, is confidently adduced as a sound reason why the depth of the Canals should remain unaltered. Consequently all improvements of locks is conceived in the direction of width and length, so as to admit of large river going vessels which are to discharge their cargo at the Montreal wharves, or to transfer it to one of the Allan steamers. It can easily be seen how the argument, if such it can be called, becomes interminable, and that assertion on either side is the great weapon of controversy according to the temper of the disputant. These days are now passed away for ever. We have the known experience of the propeller "Her Majesty," which returned from Halifax to Montreal harbor the last day of May.

We are now able to prove every anticipated result, and that which until now has been supposition, becomes positive. Accordingly we may say that a propeller on lake Erie in front of Buffalo harbor, is much nearer to New York in time and that its cargo, can be delivered at less cost, if the vessel continue its route by the Saint Lawrence, and pass by the gulf to Halifax and so to New York, than if it proceeded to Buffalo to one of the basins of the Erie Canal and transferred its cargo to barges, navigating that canal, and so follow its line to Albany, to be towed up to New York by the steam tugs of the Hudson. The time necessary for the trip may be set down at 13 days.

Proceeding to wharf and transfer of cargo, 1 day
Passage through the Erie Canal, ... 11 "
Proceeding to New York, ... 1 "
                                                               ——
                                                               13 "

Such may be taken as the average result established in practice. Equally, we have now the opposite condition satisfied, and the proof has been made by the last trip of "Her Majesty." The distances are as follows:—

From Montreal to Quebec,   180 miles.
    "   Quebec to Pictou,   500   "
    "   Pictou to Halifax,   210   "
                                          ——
Total from Montreal to Halifax, 890   "

This distance was easily made by "Her Majesty" in six days, and such is the time counted upon and estimated as the basis, on which the arrangement of her trips is determined. She loads in Montreal with sufficient coals to carry her to Pictou, a voyage of four days—680 miles. Here she remains some 20 hours, and receives an additional supply to carry her to Halifax and back. Thence she takes one day to proceed to Halifax. On her return, this vessel again loads up at Pictou with coal, and if her cargo is entirely of coal, for it is here that the mines are situate, and coal is sold at $2 a ton, she retains enough to carry her back there. This place, indeed, is the coal depôt, and will ever be so on this route, and the importance of the fact is great. Vessels leaving for England, if ever such pass by the St. Lawrence, from Chicago, would take in a supply at some station on the Gulf laid down by tenders from Pictou. Why not make such vessels the means of supplying the wants of Gaspé? There, such a depôt could be economically established, and the circumstance of calling with regularity would ensure a moderate degree of freight, and give a great impetus to the district. But, for vessels going from the West to Boston or New York, Pictou lies directly on the route, and furnishes at once a magazine, where fuel not only can be cheaply bought, but where it can be more cheaply obtained than elsewhere. Accordingly, so far as fuel is considered, it would be the starting point, whence the propeller would base its supply, taking in sufficient to proceed to New York, and return; or, on the other hand, sufficient to proceed to Toronto or Chicago, and return, as the case might be. Consequently, on the examination of this view, we at once get rid of all thought of fuel, simply stating that it can be more readily and economically obtained than on any other route.

It is proved that a vessel can reach Halifax from Montreal in six days, and it follows that a vessel going to Halifax can go any where else.

From Halifax to Boston, the distance is about 380 miles, which can be made in less than two days.

From Halifax to New York, by Cape Sable and passing within Long Island, the distance is about 625 miles, and it can be made in about three days.

Thus we have the trip from Montreal to Boston, including loading with fuel at Pictou, determined to be a matter of eight days.

The same trip from Montreal to Halifax, and thence to New York, will not exceed 9 days.

To each of these periods must be added the time necessary to descend from the foot of Lake Erie to Montreal, a matter of 6 hours; that is, passing through all the Canals is equal to 2½ days.

Consequently, while we have a cargo of wheat transhipped at Buffalo, passing by the Erie Canal to New York, taking 13 days to arrive there.

We have by the St. Lawrence route the same result, much more economically effected—that is, of course, arguing on the base that the canals be deepened, and the navigation made a unity—in the space of 11¼ days, and with a different class of propeller, engaged to meet the altered navigation, the saving of many hours would, doubtless, be effected.

From Chicago to Montreal and back, the round trip is now made on an average in 18 days. From Chicago to Montreal, the descent, however, has taken even so short a period as 8 days. We may accordingly, with propriety, count on 8 days as a fair average; therefore, cargo from Chicago would be delivered in New York in 17 days. Incident to the route is the cheapness of fuel as we have pointed out. In point of navigation there are no difficulties in the gulf or sea-board, specially to be considered. Generally it is well lighted. But there is one marked deficiency in this defect, to which we earnestly call the attention of the Executive. A light is needed in Northumberland Straits on the east coast of New Brunswick on Cape Tormentine, and if steps are not taken to supply this defect, we fear that some day a great disaster will notify the world of a necessity. We ask those who are in authority to place the map before them, and consider what we are writing. They there in note that vessels going to the north-west are liable to run on the bad shore, the north shoals of Bay Verte. The call for this light ill, we venture to say, be clearly seen, and with this addition there is nothing, we have been given to understand, to be desired.

In the foregoing few lines we have to our minds a convincing proof of the extent of commerce to which the St. Lawrence may aspire. As plainly as a truth can be set forth, it is evident that it is an outlet for the West preferable to any other, and that it opens out opportunities of trade not yet attempted. It is held back simply by the reason of an insufficient navigation. However, opinions may differ as to the extent, it is admitted, that the present navigation can be greatly improved. It is not asserted, at least anywhere that we have seen, that it is capable of further improvement. Then if the present limit can be extended, the question is, how and how much it can be increased? Some special cases are named of what are held to be permanent obstructions, which cannot be overcome, except at fabulous expense, such as the entrance at Lachine to the canal, the entrance to the upper lock at the Beauharnois Canal from Lake St. Francis, a spot at the Galops' Rapids, and some other questionable shoal by one of the Williamsburgh Canals. But all these difficulties disappear when they are faced. For instance,

at Lachine, if it be found that the bottom cannot be removed the construction of a lock, with a prolongation of the basin wall to it, will certainly be sufficient enough. But these special criticisms are beside the question. The point to be kept in view is, what is the maximum depth which can be attained in the St. Lawrence, between Chicago and Montreal harbor; how can it be attained and what will it cost. If we have this query satisfactorily answered, we have the opposite side very clearly before us. Given the satisfactory condition of the navigation of the great river, a unity, a known and acknowledged route; we have as a consequence, that it will immediately receive the whole commerce of the great West, and yet the politicians of the hour have not a thought on the subject. We hope soon to see what impetus public opinion will give to this inexplicable indifference.

THE ETNA OF DUBLIN.

We pointed out when the stock deposit of this company with government was seized by the Sheriff of Carleton, that it was within the power of government to prevent the judgment creditor obtaining an undue preference over the other creditors, under the forfeiture clause of the old insurance act. Subsequently, the Finance Minister with the object of securing the interests of all the policy holders declared the deposit forfeit. The deposit consisted of $10,000 consolidated Stock of the Province of Canada, and stood in the name of Baring & Glyn and of one of the Directors of the Etna. After instructions were given for the sale of the stock, it was found that the Director had become an insolvent, and it was necessary to get a decree in Chancery to compel him to join Baring & Glyn in the sale, hence the delay.

It seems that the Finance Minister has determined not to proceed with his resolutions respecting Banking and Currency. It would have been the height of folly to legislate directly in the teeth of the firmly expressed wishes of the Province of Ontario, on a matter of such vital importance to its commercial interests, and we commend the discretion of the government in accepting the advice of its friends and bowing to public opinion. The resolutions referred to provoked almost unanimous opposition on the part of the largest and wealthiest Province of the Dominion. The opposition was not the result of party. Some of the best friends of the government were loudest in their condemnation of what all the business men of Ontario, and the bankers of Quebec, St. John and Halifax, considered a scheme fraught with the most injurious consequences. Our Boards of Trade petitioned against it; our most prominent

merchants petitioned against it; and our banks, with a few interested exceptions, also recorded their protest. Such unanimity of sentiment produced its natural effect. The Finance Minister, doubtless, saw clearly that he could not hope to carry a measure which was so determinedly opposed, and submitted with the best grace to necessity. The greater number of bank charters expire in June, 1870, and some four or five in January, 1870. The government proposition is to extend those requiring extension, until the end of next session of Parliament, and then deal with all on the same footing. Meantime, it would be well for all parties to consider whether the time has not arrived for the repeal of the Dominion Note Act, as it has, according to law, fulfilled its alleged mission. It should now be dispensed with.

VICTORIA MUTUAL INSURANCE COMPANY.— The annual report of this Company shows that the number of policies now in force is 6,581, covering risks to the amount of $4,576,885, an increase in policies over last year of 1,792, and in the amount of risks, $1,157,164. In the beginning of the previous year arrangements were made for the establishment of a branch for the insurance, at low rates, of property lying within the water limits of the city of Hamilton. This move so far has been attended with success, inasmuch as not a single loss has occurred in the Hamilton branch, with 218 policies out, covering property to a value of $187,824.

The Directors enter at length into a discussion of Premium Notes versus Cash Receipts and express their determination to adhere to the notes instead of cutting loose from the mutual system and taking cash only. This latter method of doing business is tolerably safe in good hands, but is liable to great abuse. When it is adopted some other form of security ought to be substituted for the Notes. We are not by any means in love with premium notes, but as they seem to be the kind of security contemplated by the Legislature they ought to be retained, or a guarantee to the public given in some other shape.

The Victoria is, without doubt, making steady progress and increasing in public confidence.

REPORT OF THE CHIEF COMMISSIONER OF MINES FOR NOVA SCOTIA.—We have been favored with a copy of the official report for the 15 months ended 31st December, 1868. The Commissioner's statement is very full, and will be welcomed by all interested in the Nova Scotia mines. The principal facts respecting gold mining, embraced in the report, have been in the hands of the readers of THE MONETARY TIMES for some weeks. We, however, append a brief summary: In the 15 months, some 40,000 tons of quartz was crushed, yielding 28,342 ounces of gold, which, at $18.50 per oz., shows a value of $505,327—or $12.50 to the ton of quartz. About 800 men and 40 to 45 crushers, on an average, were employed. The average yield per man for the last 12 months was about $490.34. Of coal, the total quantity raised and sold for the year ended Dec. 31, '68, was 453,617 tons—of which all except about 40,000 tons was "round." Of the total, 117,624 tons went into home consumption, 102,761 tons were exported to neighboring Colonies, and 233,178 tons shipped to other countries, principally to the States. 2,630 men and boys were employed in the coal mines, and 60 engines of 2,382 horse power.

THE LIABILITY OF DIRECTORS.

In a previous article on the rights and liabilities of Directors we referred at length to the case of Turquand vs. Marshall, then recently decided by the Master of the Rolls. We chose that case, not only as being the most recent decision, but because in the arguments and judgment almost every leading case on the subject had been cited and commented on. It will be seen from the report which we abstract below, both of the case and the judgment, that on appeal to the Lord Chancellor, the rules of law which were enunciated by Lord Romily in his judgment, have been affirmed to their fullest extent, but the Lord Chancellor decided against the form of the application, and limited the time and mode within and by which shareholders can recover against negligent or fraudulent Directors.

This was an appeal from a decree of the Master of the Rolls. The suit was instituted by Mr. W. Turquand, the official liquidator of the Herefordshire Banking Company, and it sought to render certain of the directors liable for various acts and defaults in the management of the company's affairs. The acts complained of commenced in 1846, from which time down to the termination of the business of the company, it was alleged, the directors annually presented to the shareholders false reports of the progress and proceedings of the company, and false balance-sheets, and recommended the declaration of dividends upon repeated false statements that profits had been earned; that they had failed to dissolve the company under the 108th clause of the deed of settlement; the whole of the surplus fund and one-fourth of the paid-up capital having, to the knowledge of the directors, been lost in 1846; and that one of the directors was improperly allowed to overdraw his account without the sanction of any resolution of the board. It was held in the court below that the directors were liable for all loss occasioned by continuing the business of the bank after the surplus fund and one-fourth of the capital had been lost; that in the absence of the shareholders who had received the dividends, and who therefore could not be compelled to refund them, the directors could not be compelled to repay the dividends paid out of the capital; that they were liable for loss occasioned by the allowing the directors to overdraw their accounts; but that they could not, in this suit, be fixed with liability for issuing false reports or balance sheets, the damage thereby done being caused to the shareholders individually and not to the company in its corporate character.

The Lord Chancellor said that, after looking carefully through the evidence, he entirely concurred with the opinion of the Master of the Rolls, that the managing directors were aware of the inaccuracy of the accounts, and that the other directors, who might not have examined the books, must be taken to be liable to all the consequences. The case alleged, however, was simply that the directors gave a favorable aspect to matters which they ought not to have done, but not that they obtained any advantage by so doing. This might or might not have injured any particular share-

holder, and would require investigation into each particular case, but the extent of the injury was a matter which that court could never satisfactorily ascertain. It could not be the subject of a suit of this nature in which the court had only to consider whether the directors, in their character of directors, or quasi trustees, had committed breaches of trust against the shareholders which had injured the whole body alike. With regard to the non-stoppage of the company after the exhaustion of the surplus fund and one-fourth of the capital, the proceedings of the shareholders, in agreeing to receive dividends, fixed them with a knowledge of the fact. He had no difficulty in treating the directors as trustees in respect to the assets subjected to their charge, and with regard to those assets they must account. Under all the circumstances, his lordship thought the suit was not one in which it was possible for that court to give relief; but he would mark his opinion of the conduct of the directors by dismissing the bill and the appeal without costs.

MADOC GOLD DISTRICT.

(From our own Correspondent.)

BELLEVILLE, June 14th, 1869.

After a long interval of dormancy, interspersed with fleeting periods of spasmodic excitement, a few symptoms of returning activity are beginning to appear in the mining region of Hastings. It may be expected that whatever is done hereafter will be upon a surer and sounder footing than the rash and ill-considered enterprises which have resulted so unfortunately for their promoters. Many of those undertakings were based upon nothing more substantial than the ipse dixits of a few pretenders to practical skill or scientific knowledge, whose ability was unequal to the tasks they set themselves to perform; or whose honesty was like that of the celebrated Dr. Dousterswivel, in Sir Walter Scott's admirable tale of "The Antiquary," a tale which all who intend to go into mining should read before selecting their assayer or their operator. Another obstacle to the substantial development of the really valuable mineral deposits which exist in this district, arises from the multiplicity of cross titles and conflicting claims that encumber almost every lot or portion of a lot of land which promises to afford remuneration to the miner. These encumbrances have, for the most part, originated in the cupidity of speculators, and the simplicity of the farmers, mostly ignorant men, who granted long leases for hypothetical considerations, or made time bargains, *allowing the leases to draw their own agreements*, and when the periods had elapsed for which they considered themselves bound, made new agreements with other persons, who when they attempt to develop what they consider they are the indisputed owners of, find themselves entrapped into law suits, from which they can only be released by the tedious and expensive process of the Chancery Court. To such an extent has this practice prevailed, that I myself know several instances where responsible persons have been for some time, and still are ready to invest capital to a large amount, if they could be assured that the title of the property they propose to purchase is sound, and that they are not likely to be involved in legal proceedings. One of the best mines in the district, the ore of which has stood the test of repeated assays, yielding gold, silver and copper, to the amount of $300 to $500 per ton severral parties, is claimed by no less than four several parties, and is besides now in Chancery. If our Legislature is too timid or too supine to deal with these pseudo claims, by enacting that all time-bargains for mining rights which shall have lapsed, or which shall hereof er lapse, by reason of non-fulfilment of their respective conditions, shall become void and of none effect from the passing of such Act, or from the termination of the period over which they extend respectively, notwithstanding any omission or in-

formality in the instruments by which they are evidenced and sustained; it would surely be better for the holders of such documents to agree among themselves to sell the property in dispute, join in the conveyance to the purchasers, and divide the proceeds in a rateable proportion. If this course could be pursued in a few instances, several good mines might be brought into profitable operation before the close of the year.

The Merchants' Union Company, finding the machinery purchased by them from Mr. Daniels too small, and otherwise unsuited for the reduction of their ore, have advertised the mill for sale, intending to apply the proceeds to a more searching investigation into the worth of their mine. The vein looks well, and has given some fair and some inferior assays, but will require the working of a few tons to determine its real value; for which purpose the present time affords a favorable opportunity, as none of the mills are running upon their own ores.

It is pleasant to turn from the contemplation of these disasters and disappointments to an example of a more cheering tendency. The Mallorytown Company have got their mill (10 stamps) into working order, and have made two crushings. The first of 20 tons, 16 tons of surface rock, and 4 tons from the body of the vein, produced 8 ounces of gold of good standard. The second, four day's work with nine stamps running (I have not learned the exact quantity of ore crushed, but suppose from 25 to 30 tons) yielded 13 ounces; which fully bears out the assays on the faith of which the enterprise was undertaken.

I fully believe that, with similar good management, equal success may be had in this region; as a gentleman on whose judgment and veracity I can rely, informed me lately that he had visited some of the veins discovered last summer in the Township of Marmora, th t he crushed and panned out some of the rock, and washed over some of the super-incumbent soil, and saw many gold than he had seen before in all his mining experience—and he was one of our earliest and most active prospectors. He also reports favorably on some of the veins in the vicinity of Bannockburn, Township of Madoc.

[We understand that the preliminary assays of the Mallorytown mine were made by Prof. Bell, of Albert College, Belleville.—Ed.]

WHAT BECOMES OF THE PRECIOUS METALS.

The product of the precious metals throughout the world in 1858 (estimate of the Commissioner from California to the Paris Exposition) was $156,-600,000 gold and $37,000,000 silver, or a total of $193,000,000. Of this total, $61,000,000 is credited to the United States, and $90,000,000 to Australia, the remaining $72,000,000 being apportioned to Europe, Asia, Africa, South America, Mexico, Russia and Siberia. According to the same authority, the aggregate for 1867 was $184,-500,000, of which $130,650,000 was gold and $53,820,000 silver. Of this, the United States is credited with $7,000,000, viz: $56,000,000 in gold and $16,000,000 in silver. Thus while the product of the precious metals in the United States increased $11,000,000 in 14 years, according to this authority, the yield of Australia, the next largest producer, fell off about $29,000,000, and nearly all other foreign sources show more or less decrease. It is not probable that the limit of production of gold and silver in the United States will be reached during the present generation. The mines of California, Nevada, Washington, Idaho, Montana, Arizona, New Mexico, Colorado and Utah, are the strongholds of innumerable millions of precious metals, and to adopt the metaphor of the Executive in his inaugural, the Pacific and lateral railroads constitute the key that is being forged to release this treasure.

The answer to the question that is often propounded, as to what becomes of all the gold and is found in recent statistics, showing that is drawn from Europe and America the en aggregate of $850,000,000 in 1½ years. rain to the east has been going on from a "whereof the memory of man runneth not contrary," and the curious feature of it is, er returns. That the absorption of the nds of millions of gold and silver by this il maelstrom has been a leading cause of the sions to which the money markets of the (and, especially that of England,) have subjected, during the last half century, there seem to reason to doubt. The necessity of ng this drain of the precious metals from stern world has long been felt, but all efforts ve been made to this end have been withisfactory results. But a breach has at length ade in the barriers to freer commercial inse with China and Japan, and it is possible probable, that American and European rith those countries will ere long be so enand extended as to bring about a greater ation of the exchanges, and thus greatly if not put a stop to the specie current to t.

following statistics of the export of silver ngland to India, China, and the Straits, interest in this connection :

	India.	China.	Straits.	Total.
	£6,490,810	£2,830,663	£909,987	£10,091,460
	5,971,681	1,995,909	295,470	8,263,021
	5,098,691	231,833	924,576	6,254,004
	2,736,762	560,026	299,270	3,595,058
	2,409,580	203,198	52,850	2,665,628
	370,231	265,766	6,915	642,912
	1,000,633	474,445	160,068	1,635,643
late) . 248,800		85,211	nil.	484,011

ill be seen that there has been a marked in the drain from England, but this is pparent than real, and arises from the fact a route to the east has been changed from sinsular and Oriental to the California and steam line, the exports of silver from San so to the east being nearly in the same tion as the decrease indicated by the foreigures. Thus the exports of treasure from ancisco to England fell from $34,436,428 in o $6,312,979 in 1868, while, from the same China, they increased from $2,660,754 in o $9,081,504 in 1867, though last year l] to $6,193,995.

e competition for the trade of the Orient. ited States, has the advantage in steam nication ; in addition to which, the Pacific d will contribute greatly in bringing the ith China to and across the American conand in enlarging her commerce. In fact, untry occupies the most favorable position way, for reaching and distributing the of China, and for controlling its foreign

PROFITS OF LEAD MINING.—The Leeds' Circular thus reviews lead mining in the Kingdom:—" We have to report a considerenewal of activity in the lead mining disf the United Kingdom, due partly to the ed prospects of trade, which are slowly but sending up the prices of this metal, and to the greatly improved prospects of mining ise in almost all the lead mining districts. wall, West Chiverton, paid last year £24,000 lends; close upon cent. per cent., upon the capital. In the Isle of Man, Great Laxey . £30,000 profit; being at the rate of 50 t. per annum on the nominal capital. In Miners paid $27,000 for the year ; being ate of 60 per cent. per annum on the paid tal. The Lisburne Mines, as usual, dividend nt per cent.; and hosts of other important ues, such as the Snailback, Maes-y-Safn, Mary Ann, Herodsfoot, Wheal Trelawny, fin, Cwmystwith, Wheal Mining Company of Ireue mines of the London Lead Company, , East Darren, Mr. Beaumont's mines, ie score or so of others, have given to their te owners profits averaging on the whole

about 60 per cent. on the invested capital. The new mines also are in all directions turning out rich. The Van mine and the Plynlimmon mine in Wales—Which have only come into existence quite recently, and are owned by private companies —are turning out magnificent successes; the former paying, it is said, between 200 and 300 per cent. profit on the capital expended. Indeed, in every direction lead mining is asserting its traditional character of being at once the most profitable and least uncertain of any branch of British industry; which is scarcely to be wondered at when we consider that England yields from a few mountain districts annually between one and a half and two millions, in ultimate value, of lead and argentiferous lead, at a cost comparatively trifling, as lead mines are rarely very deep or very expensive to work.

THE IRON ORE.—The shipment of the Marmora Iron Ore has now commenced in earnest, about 4,000 tons having already been cleared from Cobourg. Mr. Munson has already delivered to the Company about thirty of the dumping cars which he has been building, and expects to be able to deliver the remainder of the fifty, the number contracted for, during the ensuing week. The ore is now coming forward as fast as it can be shipped.

—A valuable deposit of coal has just been discovered on the side of the Norton Mountain, near Oneskeag station, on the European and North American Railway. The seam was laid bare by a land slide from the side of the hill. Arrangements are making to commence work at once.

Law Report.

SUBSEQUENT INSURANCE WITHOUT NOTICE.— In a case of Obermeyer vs. the Globe Mutual Insurance Co., before the Supreme Court of Missouri, it appeared that the assured having been notified that one of his policies would be cancelled at a certain time, procured another insurance of an equal amount, intending to comply literally with the terms of his contract. But it turned out that the policy was not cancelled until about a month after the last insurance had been effected, thus making an over insurance for a period terminating more than two months before the loss. It was held that this was not such a violation of the conditions as to discharge the defendants. In giving judgment the Court said:—

The general doctrine that a previous or subsequent insurance without notice, in a policy requiring such notice, and with a clause of forfeiture like that of the defendant, discharges the obligation of the company that insures, is well settled and universally recognized. That this should be the effect of the concealment is not only a part of the contract, and obligatory upon that ground, but the forfeiture is reasonable and just. The contract can never know the full extent of his risk unless he knows everything that bears upon that risk.

But there are some apparent, though not real, exceptions to this doctrine. The contract is to be enforced according to its spirit - not its letter merely. Thus it is also well settled, though perhaps not with the same unanimity, that if the second policy, against which the contract stipulates, is itself a void one, or one that cannot be enforced, it shall not avoid the first, notwithstanding the clause of forfeiture. The construction given such covenants fully accords with their object to take away from the assured any motive to destroy his property, or to be lax in saving it.

The Supreme Court of Illinois, in N. E. F. and M. Insurance Co., vs. Shettler, 38 Ill., 166, have applied the principle to another state of facts. The plaintiff in error had insured the defendant, with a proviso in regard to other insurance similar to the one under consideration. During the year the person insured, by the written consent of

plaintiff's agent, moved his store, building and goods upon another building in town. Before and after he so moved, he had three other policies upon the property, of which the plaintiff had no notice. The Court held that the policy was not forfeited, for the reason that the removal of the store rendered the other policies worthless, and, though there had been an over-insurance during part of the life of the plaintiff's (?) policy, yet, when the loss occurred it was the only subsisting one, and therefore valid.

Upon the effect of over insurance, the Supreme Court of Pennsylvania uses this language : " The over-insurance was attempted to be surmounted by the alleged invalidity of the subsequent policies. We think the Court adopted the proper distinction—if they were void at the time of the loss, they constitute no obstacle ; but if avoidable only by reason of some breach of condition enabling the insurers to avoid them, but which they had waived, the over-insurance undoubtedly existed." Mitchell vs. Mutual Ins. Co., supra.

These last two cases expressly require, one by statement and the other directly, that the policies relied upon to avoid the one containing the covenant of forfeiture, should exist and be in force at the time of the loss ; and upon an examination of the numerous authorities upon the general subject, I do not find one to contradict them. In the great body of the cases, the over insurance existed when the loss occurred, and the question could not be raised.

Analogous to the forfeitures for over-insurance, are those that arise from selling the property. Such sale ends the insurance, both because the insurable interest is parted with and because it is contrary to the usual terms of the policy. And yet a sale, in the ordinary sense of the word, has not that effect. The syllabus of Trumbull v. The Portage C. M. I. Co., 12 Ohio, 305, states the recognized doctrine : " When the assured has contracted to convey the assured premises at a future day, upon payment of the purchase money, and between the date of the contract and the day of payment the premises are destroyed by fire, this is not such an alienation as would defeat the policy ; that the plaintiffs had an insurable interest and the legal title, and an equitable title in the purchase money or the whole value of the premises, and, being in possession, they might recover upon the policy." In Kane vs. Maine M. F. Ins. Co., 3 Fairfield (Maine) 44, upon a policy expressly stipulating against sale, when, during the existence of a policy, a merchant held the goods and leased the store, both of which were insured, and in about six months, and before the fire, took back both the store and the unsold goods, it was held that the policy was not forfeited. So, in Powers vs. Ocean Ins. Co., 19 La., 28, the Supreme Court of Louisiana held that if in an ed property were sold, and, upon non-payment of the purchase money, were taken back, and afterwards burned, the policy was good, notwithstanding the stipulation for forfeiture, and that " there was a suspension of the risk, but the risk revived as soon as the property reverted back to the plaintiff."

Thus it is seen that the rigid rules of the English Courts, in relation to express warranties, are not applied to stipulations for notices of subsequent insurances, or to subsequent sales. They are construed, to be enforced, like other contracts, according to their true spirit.

There is an obvious distinction between a concealment or false statement of facts existing at the commencement of the risk and a neglect of duty in regard to a matter occurring afterwards. In the one case the policy never takes effect—the risk is never assured—while in the other it is only interrupted. I cannot find that it has ever been held that a temporary non-compliance with an express warranty, of itself works a forfeiture, unless it is simultaneous with the commencement of the risk. It must have been in view of this distinction that courts have held, as before quoted, that the operation of a policy might be suspended and the risk re-attached, which could hardly be true if it never began to run, though in N. E. F. M. Ins. Co. vs. Schetler it does not appear that it attached until after the removal of the store.

TRANSFER OF POLICIES.—This suit was on a policy of insurance, issued to Margaret Mann, covering a stock of millinery goods in store. The plaintiff avers that before the expiration of the policy the defendant consented, in writing, to the transfer of the policy by Margaret Mann to him. It appeared, further, that Mrs. Mann had removed her entire stock, and that the plaintiff put in a new stock of the same description of goods. The Supreme Court of Missouri, was of opinion, upon principle that the only identity of the subject of the insurance contemplated by a time policy upon a stock of goods in a store is that that it should be a stock of the same kind of goods owned by the insured in that store; that the removal of one stock by the insured, and replacing it by another of the same kind does not change the subject of insurance within the meaning of the policy; and that where defendant consented to the assignment to the plaintiff in this case, it must be taken to have consented to his stock of millinery and fancy goods in that store being covered by the policy in the same manner and to the same extent as a like stock of goods would have been covered if there had been no assignment. Under such a policy the change of goods is expected, and even the entire change, as in the present case, is not a material circumstance for the defendant to know.

—A case of Allingham vs. The Liverpool and London and Globe Insurance Company in which it was sought to recover $800 on a mill, was lately tried in St. John, N. B., and decided in favor of the defendants. The grounds of defense were found and false swearing.

Commercial.

As will be seen by a report elsewhere, the Corn Exchange Association have adopted a memorial to the Dominion Parliament, asking for the imposition of a duty on flour. We do not see that the advocates of this change in our tariff make out any better case than can easily be made out for other interests; and were the Government to grant the prayer of the petition, it would find itself committed to a protective policy which would have to be extended to a large number of articles. Our commercial position is, at present, somewhat anomalous, and the whole question is worthy of a careful review at this stage.

Delegates have been appointed by the shareholders of the Royal Canadian Bank, in several of the country towns, to attend a meeting to be held in this city on the 25th instant, as specified by an advertisement in another column.

The crops are generally reported as making good progress. The weather has, however, been too wet and cold. By the way, there are accounts of damage by grubs in some places, but we believe their devastations have, so far, been limited.

The Insolvency Bill finally passed the House of Commons on Tuesday, having received several amendments at the third reading.

The annual meeting of the Toronto and Nipissing Railway is called for the 20th of July, as advertised elsewhere, for the election of officers. The subscriptions on the stock books now amount to $174,200.

Toronto Market.

There is no improvement in the tone of business whatever. A wholesale merchant remarked to our reporter, in this way; "There are so many shaking the bankrupt law in our face that we scarcely dare to do business at all, and we positively refuse to sell to any body, until we have satisfied ourselves by enquiry as to his antecedents, his financial

standing, and indeed until we know all about him; it is only throwing away our goods to sell the man in any other way just now. Some look for an improvement in the fall, but we are not so sure about that." We give this as an instance of the tone in which the present position of trade is discussed every day. For ourselves, we do not take so gloomy a view of the situation. Credits have been granted so recklessly in the past, that the reaction is severe and sorely trying. We feel confident that the fall business will happily disappoint very many.

GROCERIES.—Prices remain very steady; sugars are easier at quotations.

PRODUCE.— Wheat.— Receipts 16,000 bush.; stock in store on the 14th, 75,060 bush. The market is dull and tends downward under advices of a decline in England, and continued favorable reports of the crops from all quarters. Spring is nominal, at 92c. and fall at 95c. f.o.b. Oats.— Receipts 1,800 bush., stock on the 14th, 17,133 bush.; market dull with sales of 1,000 bush. at 50c., and two cars at 51c on Northern Railway track. Barley.—No receipts nor stocks: good car lots would bring 85 to 90c. Peas.—No receipts, stock on the 14th, 12,764 bush.; 2 cars sold at 86c f.o.b. Corn.—Sellers at 60c. by the carload.

FLOUR.—Receipts 1,100 brls. and 1,120 last week. Stock in store on the 14th 5,587 brls. No. 1 Superfine is weak at $4, several lots sold at that price; 800 brls. of Spring wheat extra brought $4.10 f.o.b. and 100 brls. sold at $4.05 in store; a lot of choice fancy, of a particular brand, sold at Malton for $4.30. Nothing doing in other grades. Meal unchanged.

PROVISIONS.—There is really nothing doing in a wholesale way. Butter, in the absence of demand is flat and nominal. Eggs.—There is a fair supply and some business doing at quotations. Cutmeats, nominal.

WOOL.—There is an active demand for wool and the receipts were pretty good: good fleece now brings 38c. readily, being an advance of 3c. on the quotations of last week.

HIDES AND SKINS.—The market is very dull without any decline in prices.

FREIGHTS.—There is very little doing with vessels and rates are unchanged.

The following are the Grand Trunk Railway Company's summer rates from Toronto to the undermentioned stations, which came into force on the 19th ult. :—Flour to all Stations from Belleville to Lynn, inclusive 25c ; grain, per 100 lbs., 13c ; flour to Prescott, 30c ; grain 15c ; flour to all stations between Island Pond and Portland, inclusive, 75c ; grain, 38c: flour to Boston, 80c, gold ; grain 40c ; flour to Halifax, 90c ; flour to St. John, 85c.

Protective Duties.

A petition was laid before the Corn Exchange Association of this city, on Tuesday, which sets forth that the free admission into Canada of the raw and manufactured agricultural products of the United States, is a material injury to the agricultural and milling interests of the Dominion, for which no corresponding advantage is given by the United States ; and that whenever the American markets are overstocked, our markets become at once, over-crowded with their surplus, and the trade is deranged, and we are made to suffer from all the evils that a fluctuating currency imposes on the people of the States ; that the free admission of American products into this country, while the States have levied a duty on our products going into that country, is a sufficient proof of our desire for free commercial relations ; that in the face of this action, the American Government give us no reason to expect a renewal of the treaty, and that therefore the producing and manufacturing interests of this country ought to be protected, at least, until reciprocal relations with the United States are renewed on equable terms.

A motion for the adoption of the memorial was moved by Mr. Jas. Brown, Jr., and seconded by Mr. W. H. Howland; both of these gentlemen supported the motion with a speech.

Mr. Jas. G. Worts, moved an amendment seconded by Mr. Rolph, which was lost; another amendment was also moved which shared the same fate, and the memorial was adopted.

Demerara Sugar Market.

The following is from Sandbach, Parker & Co. Market Report, dated Georgetown, Demerara, 8 May, 1869:—

SUGAR.—Very little has been offered for sale during the past fortnight. In many districts the want of water for navigation purposes, has been the retarding cause why so little produce has been made, in others, the Canes owing to the drought are so backward. The planters prefer giving them the benefit of the coming wet season to cutting it at present ; all lots have been readily taken up at full rates, and a larger business would have been done if Sugar had been more plentiful for the first four months of this year the shipments to America were double that when the war during the same time last season ; from now until October Sugars will be very scarce, and although in this Colony we have not suffered the same extent from the absence of rain, some of the Islands, yet we estimate that will be fully twenty-five thousand hogsheads short of last year's total.

MOLASSES.—There has been an active demand and full prices realized for all good samples offered. Muscovadoes of the higher grades have realized better prices than Vacuum Pan owing to the competition for the British Provinces, the inhabitants of these localities preferring Muscovado to Vacuum Pan.

RUM.—Very little doing, holders prefer shipping to accepting the rates offered here, we have not heard of a single transaction of consequence.

SUGARS (package included) sold by 100 lb. Dutch, 10 per cent. tare.

Muscovadoes, equal to No. 8			
Dutch Standard $4.00 ℣ 100 lbs.			
No. 10 do. $4.50			In hhds.
" 12 do. $5.25			of about
Vacuum Pan No. 12 do. $6.50			1800 lbs. each
" " 14 do. 7.00			
" " 16 do. 7.40			
" " 17 do. 7.60			
" " 18 do. 7.80			

MOLASSES (package included, sold by Imperial gallon.)—

Muscovado, from 22 @ 36 cents, as to color and density		In pur of
Vacuum Pan from 25 @ 38 cents, as to color and density		100 gal
RUM (colored, package included, sold) by Imperial gal. from 35 per cent, @ 38 overproof 40 cents.		Ditto
From 38 per cent. @ 40 overproof, 45 cents.		

Halifax Market.

BREADSTUFFS.—June 8.—We note no change in Flours during the past week. The receipts by G. T. have been light, and stocks are considerably reduced, awaiting the arrival of the Gulf Boats. Supers continue in good demand at quotation. No. 2 are active (at high rates comparatively) without stocks. Fancy in request at quotation. Strong Bakers is much sought with light stocks. Imports from January 1st to June 8th, 1868 and 1869 :—

	Bbls. Flour.	Bbls. Cornmeal
1860	68,878	13,650
1868	77,006	25,401

WEST INDIA PRODUCE.—Sugar and Molasses. Transactions continue dull with feeling in favor of buyers. Transactions continue in retail way, and though no great concession has been made the tendency continues downward. Rum is in good demand with light stocks.

EXCHANGE.—Bank Drafts, London, 60 days 12½ per cent. Montreal sight 3½ per cent. St. John, N. B. 3 per cent. premium.—R. C. Hamilton & Co.'s Circular.

LIFE INSURANCE COMPANIES.

ATEMENTS made by Insurance Companies in terms of the Act, 31 Vic., cap. 48, submitted in accordance with the Fourteenth Section of said Act.

NAME OF COMPANY	The Phœnix Mutual Life Ins. Society.	The Connecticut Mutual Life Insurance Company.	The Ætna Life Ins. Co., of Hartford, Conn	The Standard Life Insurance Company.	The London & Lancashire Life Ass. Co.	The New York Life Insurance Company.	The Atlantic Mutual Life Ins. Co., of Albany, N. Y. (d)	The Equitable Life Insurance Soc'y, U.S.A,
Statements called for from all the Companies.	$ cts.	$ cts	$ cts.	$ cts.	$ cts.	$ cts.	$ cts.	$ cts.
otal Premiums received during the year in Canada..	25,499 60	51,155 27	168,060 00	112,562 30	13,026 62	9,944 47	4,619 64	1,209 88
um er of Policies issued do .. do .. do ..	246 00	444 00	1,008	292	159	108	140	32
mount of Policies issued do .. do .. do ..	569,2 5 00	1,211,650 00	2,684,280 00	827,652 00	242,450 00	301,600 00	215,000 00	98,200 00
mount at risk on all Policies in force in Canada....	780,500 00	1,750,000 00	4,066,990 00	4,236,915 19	501,965 00	302,600 00	400,000 00	141,500 00
umber of Policies became claims during the year in Canada		3	8	4	None.	None.	None.	None.
mount of Policies do .. do .. do	4,000 00	3,000 00	29,000 00	15,921 92	6,500 00	None.	None.	None.
mount paid on claims during the year in Canada...	....	3,000 00	29,800 00	6,450 16	6,000 00	None.	None.	None.
do of claims in suspense in Canada	....	None.	None.	(b) 9,471 76	500 00	None.	None.	None.
do do , in Canada resisted............	....	None.	None.	None.	None.	None.	None.	None.
Additional Statements made by Sundry Companies. (Form B.)								
ts of the Company......	3,664,060 00	22,669,079 29	10,462,581 75	19,931,871 51	....	11,000,822 60	878,414 02	7,721,077 02
tities of the Company......	2,381,860 00	....	7,756,532 27	(e)	....	9,811,540 43	245,841 00	7,009,889 00
unt of Capital Stock of the Company......	100,000 00	....	150,000 00	....	481,150 00	None.	110,000 00	100 000 00
unt paid thereon......	16,000 00	....	....	....	48,115 00	....	110,000 00	100,000 00
s above assets consist in part of deposits under bot								
b. Dominion Stock......	....	....	....	....	....	....	....	....
t. Canada 5 per cents	....	....	....	....	....	....	....	....
l. .. 6 per cents	....	....	....	....	....	....	....	....
t. "c Bank Shares......	....	....	....	....	....	....	....	....
r Canadian Investments, viz.:								
. Government Securities owned, not deposited....	....	....	....	....	....	....	....	....
. Municipal Debentures......	....	....	....	....	....	....	....	....
. Mortgages on Real Estate......	....	....	....	....	....	....	....	....
. Real Estate owned in Canada......	....	....	....	....	....	....	....	....
h Bank and in hand in Canada......	....	....	....	....	....	....	....	....
l Premiums received by the Company during the year in all Countries......	1,745,173 35	7,161,304 11	5,388,944 23	....	150,380 90	5,912,136 07	....	4,479,196 61
iber of Policies issued by the Company during the year in all Countries......	8,279	11,950 00	13,337	1,802	576	9,105	....	11,986
unt of Policies issued by the Company during the year in all Countries......	22,535,549 00	....	36,891,486 00	5,374,050 75	1,230,750 00	30,765,947 67	....	51,891,825 00
her of Policies become Claims during the year in all Countries......	87	....	....	....	13	....	....	....
unt of Policies become Claims during the year in all Countries......	166,980 66	1,221,886 00	855,084 22	1,523,844 44	29,280 00	741,043 22	....	766,189 23
mses of Management, Agency, &c., &c......	342,898 43	....	196,454 54	....	46,140 05	735,190 48	....	344,247 73
tional Statements made by Sundry Companies whose Deposits are less than $100,000. (Form C.)								
tal of Premiums rec'd during the year in Canada...	25,499 59	....	....	....	13,026 62	9,944 47	4,619 64	1,299 88
ess 25 per cent......	6,374 90	....	....	....	3,256 65	2,695 12	1,154 91	324 97
ess also the amount of losses paid......	4,000 00	....	....	....	6,000 00	....	....	....
nce to be deposited in conformity with Sec. 6.....	15,124 77	....	....	....	3,769 97	7,258 35	3,464 73	974 91
unt to be deposited do do do	2,100 00	....	....	....	2,085 00	2,250 00	1,250 00	2,250 00
ally deposited against the two preceding items....	50,000 00	....	....	....	11,315 28	10,000 00	10,000 00	2,512 00

NAME OF COMPANY	The North British and Mercantile Insurance Comp'y.	The Royal Insurance Company.	The Commercial Union Insurance Comp'y	The Travellers' Insurance Company of Hartford, Conn.	The Life Association of Scotland.	The Scottish Provincial Insurance Company.
atements called for from all the Companies.—(Continued.)	$ cts.	$ cts.	$ cts.	$ cts.	$ cts.	$ cts.
tal Premiums received during the year in Canada........	35,896 87	34,462 96	21,610 51	(c) 2,323 50	116,795 59	(d) 72,000 00
umber of Policies issued do do do	87	27	147	81	331	217
nount of Policies issued do do do	81,223 31	58,217 42	320,470 00	130,700 00	448,450 13	370,000 00
nount of Risk on all Policies in force in Canada	1,250,000 00	1,168,887 52	740,510 77	130,700 00	5,606,503 72	1,708,000 00
umber of Policies became Claims during the year in Canada	5	3	3	None.	18	10
nount	14,920 51	7,300 00	1,400 00	None.	84,860 25	25,510 65
nount paid in Claims during the year in Canada......	14,920 51	7,800 00	1,000 00	None.	22,089 23	25,864 00
nount of Claims in Suspense in Canada.	None.	None.	580 00	None.	(a) 11,680 02	1,954 65
nount of Claims, in Canada, resisted................	None.	None.	None.	None.	None.	None.
tional Statements made by Sundry Companies. (Form A.) (Continued.)						
s of the Company......	These statements	These statements	These statements	1,050,805 24	These statements	These statements
ilities of the Company......	not called for from	not called for from	not called for from	51,647 82	not called for from	not called for from
nt of Capital Stock of the Company......	this Company.	this Company.	this Company.	500,000 00	this Company.	this Company.
nt paid thereon......				500,000 00		

) Since Paid. (b) Not yet due. (c) Revenue of this Company, $3,423,467.55 ; total insurance in force, $78,539,915.68. (d) Business confined to Quebec ntario. These statements are voluntarily made, not being required from this Company by the Act.

ote.—The Canada Life Assurance Company claims that the law gives it till the 1st August to make its returns. The Liverpool and London and Globe and also the Queen t appear to have their fire and life business, and therefore appear in a separate table. The Reliance states that Canadian business only commenced in 1869. The Edinburgh Life ot sent in a statement. The Briton Medical and General does not report any Canadian business. The returns of the Union Mutual Insurance Company of Maine have been d. The returns of the Star Life have not yet been received from England. The National Life Insurance Company of the United States commenced business in Canada in 1869.

INLAND MARINE INS. COMPANIES.

STATEMENTS *made by Insurance Companies in terms of 31 Vic., c. 48, submitted in accordance with the 14th section of said Act.*

No.	NAME OF COMPANY	The British America Assurance Co. of Toronto.	The Home Ins. Company of Newhaven, Conn.	The Western Ass. Co. of Toronto.	The Ætna Ins. Co. of Hartford.	The Provincial Insurance Company.
	Statements called for from all the Companies.					
1	Total premiums received during the year in Canada	$46,184 10	Has done no marine business in Canada in 1868.	$52,029 35	$9,142 06	$100,366 16
2	No. of policies, new, including renewals, issued during year in Canada	1,583		1,926	(d) 200	2,033
3	Amount of said policies	3,890,597 00		2,463,302 00	(d) 500,000 00	3,023,053 00
4	Greatest amount at risk on all policies in force in Canada at one time	(?)		(?)	....	(?)
5	No. of policies on which losses have occurred during year in Canada	....	....	....	....	....
6	Amount of losses in Canada, paid during the year	14,621 49	....	15,381 06	5,885 85	46,967 59
	Do. due and unpaid	None.	....	None.	None.	None.
	Do. adjusted and not due	6,714 26	....	None.	85 45	396 00
	Do. in suspense, and waiting further proof	2,000 00	....	1,257 50	1,000 00	7,950 70
	Do. resisted	(a) 5,000 00	....	None.	None.	11,534 00
7	Amount of premiums earned during the year in Canada, being those received on policies which have expired during the year	45,913 23	....	(b) 51,717 85	9,142 06	(c) 99,773 94
8	Amount of premiums unearned, being those received on policies which have not yet expired	2,332 92	....	3,311 50	None.	10,587 22
9	Date to which statement made	Dec. 31, 1868.	....	Dec. 31, 1868.	Dec. 31, 1868.	June 30, 1868.

(a) Cause—fraud. (b) ...,000 added for unearned premiums of the previous year. (c) $10,000 added for unearned premiums of previous year. (d) Estimate.

SUMMARY.—		
Inland Marine premiums received	$307,721 67	
Number of policies about	5,042	
Amount of do.	9,877,853 00	—Cargo policies probably covering 5-6ths of this amount.
Losses paid	82,855 90	
Losses awaiting payment	36,267 91	

COMPANIES *which have not separated their Fire and Life Insurance Business.*

—	The Liverpool and London and Globe Insurance Co.	The Queen Insurance Company.
	$ c.	$ c.
Premiums receiv'd in Canada	308,755 71	105,875 56
No. of Policies issued	5,345	2,903 00
Amount of do.	11,998,672 00	5,802,690 00
Amount at risk in Canada	24,014,782 00	17,472,637 00
Number of Policies become claims in Canada during the year	325	76
Amount paid of do. do.	207,412 48	35,163 01
" in suspense	14,007 87	2,489 96
" resisted	(a) 15,641 00	(a) 586 00

(a) Cause—fraud.

W. G. & B. RAILWAY.—Active operations appear to have been commenced at last on this road. Mr. Lackey, takes a contract for the grading and fencing of two miles. Mr. Reynolds has a like contract on part of the line near Guelph, the remainder of the line has been let in small contracts to parties in Fergus, Hamilton, Drayton, and Elora. The grading on the road must be completed in four months, and it is expected that the locomotives will be running in Fergus by January next. It is asserted that Messrs. Robertson and Worthington have the contract for the construction of the road to the county line of Bruce.—*Mount Forest Examiner.*

WESTERN CANADA

Permanent Building and Savings Society.

DIVIDEND NO. 12.

NOTICE is hereby given, that a Dividend of Five per cent. on the Capital Stock of this Institution has been declared for the half-year ending 29th inst. and that the same will be payable at the Office of the Society, No. 70 Church Street, on and after THURSDAY, the EIGHTH day of JULY next.

The Transfer Books will be closed from the 20th to the 30th June, inclusive.

By order of the Board.

WALTER S. LEE,
Secretary and Treasurer.

Toronto, June 15, 1869.

Insurance Clerk Wanted.

A YOUNG OR MIDDLE-AGED MAN, practically acquainted with the details and routine of Insurance business, particularly marine. Satisfactory testimonials as to character and qualifications will be required. Address "Insurance Company," Box No. 790, Post Office, Toronto. 41-3t

The European Mail for North America,

WITH WHICH IS INCORPORATED

"WILMER & SMITH'S EUROPEAN TIMES,"

(Established in 1843.)

A Full and Complete Summary of

HOME AND FOREIGN NEWS.

Published Weekly for despatch by the Mail Steamer.

THE EUROPEAN MAIL.

FOR North America, with which is incorporated 'Wilmer & Smith's European Times,' is published in the interest of the mercantile and general community.

In each issue is to be found all the reliable information commercial and general, that can in any way prove of value to our subscribers. The greatest possible care has been, and will continue to be, taken by the Proprietors to obtain, regardless of expense, a faithful record of all market transactions in which our friends are more particularly concerned, up to within three hours of the closing of the Mail.

We furnish our readers with quotations of articles staple not generally noted in ordinary lists, of which the following is an example :—

Articles.	Prices per ton.	Cash discount.
CANADA PLATES		
Staffordshire (in L'pool) f.o.b.	£18 18 6	2½ per ct.
Glamorgan " "	19 15 0	"
GALVANIZED IRON—		
Corrugated Shts., 20 gauge fob.	17 0 0	"

The latest shipping intelligence, comprising arrivals, departures, sailings, and loadings, alphabetically arranged, is laid before our subscribers; and the tabular form adopted in the current number will be adhered to throughout—every casualty being regularly noted, and the state of the freight market duly advised.

Agricultural, Legal, and Medical news, of interest is given in detail.

We publish a list of Military and Naval Stations, and all changes are promptly noted.

The proprietors of the EUROPEAN MAIL urge the great advantages of this Journal, and trust for the friendly co-operation of all who think it of importance that the Old and New World should be more closely associated by these reciprocal ties resulting from a mutual furtherance of their material interests.

The subscription is 52s. or $13 (gold) per annum, payable in advance.

Sole Agent for Toronto,

A. S. IRVING.

Canada Permanent Building and Savings Society.

EIGHTEENTH HALF-YEARLY DIVIDEND.

NOTICE is hereby given that a Dividend of Five per cent. on the Capital Stock of this Institution has been declared for the half-year ending 30th instant, and the same will be payable at the Office of the Society on and after THURSDAY, the EIGHTH day of July next.

The Transfer Books will be closed from the 20th to the 30th June, inclusive.

By order of the Board.

J. HERBERT MASON,
Secretary and Treasurer.

Toronto, June 10th, 1869. 44-td

Office of the Toronto and Nipissing Railway Company.

A GENERAL MEETING of the subscribers to the Capital Stock of the Toronto and Nipissing Railway Company, will be held at the office of the said Company, No. 46 Front street in the said City of Toronto, on TUESDAY, the 20th day of JULY next, at twelve o'clock noon, for the purpose of electing Directors and organizing the said Company.

By order. CHAS. ROBERTSON,
Secretary.

Toronto, June 16.

NOTICE.

Royal Canadian Bank.

A MEETING of Delegates appointed at the different Agencies of this Bank, for a conference with the Directors as to the present position of its affairs, is hereby called for FRIDAY, 25th inst, at noon, at the Head-Office in Toronto, for the purpose of said conference.

By order of the Board.

T. WOODSIDE, *Cashier.*

Toronto, June 16, 1869.

The Canadian Bank of Commerce.

DIVIDEND No. 4.

NOTICE is hereby given that a Dividend of Four per cent. upon the paid-up capital stock of this institution has been declared for the current half year, and that the same will be payable at the Bank and its Branches on and after FRIDAY, the second day of JULY next.

The Transfer Books will be closed from the 16th to the 30th days of June next, both days inclusive.

The Annual General Meeting of the Stockholders will be held at the Banking House in this city, on MONDAY, the fifth day of JULY next. Chair to be taken at twelve o'clock, noon, precisely.

By order of the Board.

R. J. DALLAS, Cashier.

Toronto, May 22nd, 1869 42-td

Bank of Toronto.

DIVIDEND No. 26.

NOTICE is hereby given that a Dividend of Four per cent. for the current half-year, being at the rate of Eight per cent. on the paid up capital of this Bank, has this day been declared, and that the same will be payable at the Bank or its branches on and after

FRIDAY, the 2ND DAY OF JULY NEXT.

The transfer books will be closed from the fifteenth to the thirtieth of June, both days inclusive.

The Annual Meeting of the Shareholders will be held at the Bank on Wednesday, the twenty-first day of July next. The chair to be taken at noon.

By order of the Board.

G. HAGUE, Cashier.

Toronto, May 16th, 1869. 41-td

Royal Canadian Bank.

ALL shareholders in this Bank who are in arrears in their instalments are required to pay the same at the Head Office, or any of its agencies, within Thirty days from this date, otherwise such proceedings will be taken against all defaulters as the Board may deem most advisable. It is hoped that all will pay up promptly, in order that the Bank may resume at an early day.

By order of the Board.

T. WOODSIDE.
Cashier.

Toronto, 29th May, 1869.

Niagara District Bank.

DIVIDEND No. 31.

NOTICE is hereby given, that a DIVIDEND OF FOUR PER CENT. on the paid up capital stock of this Institution, has this day been declared for the current half-year; and that the same will be payable at the Bank on and after THURSDAY, the first day of July next.

The Transfer Books will be closed from the 20th to the 30th of June, both days inclusive.

By order of the Board,

C. M. ARNOLD, Cashier.

Mercantile.

TORONTO PRICES CURRENT.—JUNE 17, 1869.

Name of Article.	Wholesale Rates.		Name of Article.	Wholesale Rate.		Name of Article.	Wholesale Rates.	
	$ c.	$ c.	*Groceries—Contin'd*	$ c.	$ c.	**Leather—**Contin'd.	$ c.	$ c.
Boots and Shoes.			Gunpowd'r c. to med..	0 55	0 70	Kip Skins, Patna	0 30	0 35
Mans' Thick Boots ...	2 65	2 50	" melt. to fine.	0 70	0 85	French	0 30	0 60
" Kip	2 25	3 00	" fine to fine't..	0 85	0 95	English	0 65	0 80
" Calf	3 90	3 70	Hyson	0 45	0 80	Hemlock Calf (30 to		
" Congress Gaiters..	1 65	2 50	Imperial	0 42	0 50	35 lbs.) per doz...	0 50	0 60
" Kip Cobourgs....	1 20	1 40	Tobacco, Manufac'd:			Do. light	0 45	0 50
Boys' Thick Boots....	1 70	1 80	Con 100 size	0 26	0 30	French Calf,	1 05	1 05
Youths' "	1 40	1 50	Western Leaf, com..	0 25	0 28	Grain & Satn Cl'd doz	0 00	0 55
Women's Batts	0 95	1 30	" Good	0 97	0 3¼	Splits, large ℔ lb...	0 30	0 38
" Balmoral ...	1 20	1 50	" Fine	0 33	0 35	" small	0 28	0 38
" Congress Gaiters..	0 90	1 50	" Bright fine..	0 40	0 80	Enamelled Cow ℔ foot..	0 20	0 21
Misses' Batts.	0 75	1 00	" choice..	0 60	0 75	Patent	0 30	0 33
" Balmoral ...	1 00	1 20	**Hardware.**			Pebble Grain	0 15	0 17
" Congress Gaiters..	1 00	1 30	Tin (net cash prices)			Buff	0 14	0 16
Girls' Batts.	0 65	0 85	Block, ℔ lb........	0 35	0 00	**Oils.**		
" Balmoral ...	0 10	1 05	Grain............	0 30	0 00	Cod	0 65	0 70
" Congress Gaiters..	0 75	1 10	Copper:—			Lard, extra	0 00	0 00
Children's C.T. Cacks..	0 00	0 65	Pig............	0 22	0 24	" No. 1	0 00	0 00
" Gaiters	0 55	0 00	Grain............	0 30	0 33	" Woollen	0 00	0 00
Drugs.			Cut Nails:—			Lubricating, patent..	0 00	0 00
Aloes Cape..........	0 12½	0 15	Assorted ¼ Shingles,			" Mott's economic	0 80	0 00
Alum	0 02½	0 03	℔ 100 ℔.......	2 95	3 00	Linseed, raw	0 70	0 82
Borax	0 05	0 00	Shingle alone do ..	3 15	3 25	" boiled.....	0 81	0 87
Camphor, refined.....	0 65	0 70	Lathe and 1 dy	3 90	3 40	Machinery	0 00	0 00
Castor Oil..........	0 16½	0 28	*Galvanized Iron:—*			Olive, common, ℔ gal.	1 00	1 00
Caustic Soda........	0 04¼	0 05	Assorted sizes.....	0 08	0 09	" salad	1 95	2 30
Cochineal...........	0 90	1 00	Best No. 24.......	0 07¼	0 00	" salad, in bots.		
Cream Tartar	0 30	0 35	" 26.......	0 08	0 08½	qt. ℔ case ..	3 60	3 75
Epsom Salts	0 02	0 04	" 28.......	0 09	0 09½	Sesame salad, ℔ gal. .	1 60	1 75
Extract Logwood.....	0 11	0 12	*Horse Nails:—*			Seal, pale	0 75	0 85
Gum Arabic, sorts....	0 30	0 35	Gnests or Griffin's			Spirits Turpentine..	0 23½	0 00
Indigo, Madras......	0 90	1 00	assorted sizes....	0 00	0 00	Varnish	0 00	0 00
Licorice	0 14	0 15	For W. ass'd sizes..	0 18	0 19	Whale.	0 00	0 00
Madder	0 00	0 16	Patent Hammer'd do..	0 17	0 18	**Paints, &c.**		
Galls	0 82	0 87	*Iron (at 4 months):*			White Lead, genuine		
Opium	12 00	13 50	Pig—Gartsherrie No1.	24 00	25 00	in Oil, ℔ 25lbs....	0 00	2 35
Oxalic Acid.........	0 26	0 28	Other brands. No1..	23 00	24 00	Do. No. 1	0 00	3 10
Potash, Bi-tart......	0 25	0 28	" No.2..	0 00	0 00	" 2	0 00	1 90
" Bichromate...	0 15	0 20	" No.3..	0 00	0 00	" 3	0 00	1 65
Potass Iodide	3 90	4 30	Bar—Scotch, ℔100 ℔.	2 45	2 50	White Zinc, genuine..	3 40	3 50
Senna	0 12½	0 60	Refined...........	3 00	3 25	White Lead, dry.....	0 05½	0 09
Soda Ash	0 02½	0 04	Swedes	3 90	3 40	Red Lead	0 07½	0 08
S da Bicarb	0 00	0 00	Hoops—Coopers....	3 00	3 25	Venetian Red, Eng'h.	0 02½	0 02¾
Tartaric Acid........	0 40	0 45	Band	3 00	3 25	Yellow Ochre, Fren'h.	0 02½	0 03
Verdigris	0 35	0 40	Boiler Plates	3 25	3 50	Whiting	0 85	1 25
Vitriol, Blue........	0 08	0 10	Canada Plates.....	3 75	4 00	**Petroleum**		
Groceries.			Union Jack	0 00	0 00	(Refined ℔ gal.)		
Coffees:			Pontypool	3 25	4 00	Water white, car'd ..		0 25
Java, ℔ lb..........	0 27@0 33		Swansea	3 90	4 00	" small lots..	0 00	0 37
Laguayra, ...	0 17	0 18	*Lead (at 4 months):*			Straw, by car load...	0 00	0 00
Rio	0 15	0 17	Bar, ℔ 100 ℔s.....	0 06½0 07		" small lots..	0 00	0 00
Fish:			Sheet "	0 08	0 09	Amber, by car load..	0 00	0 00
Herrings, Lab. split...	0 00	0 00	Shot "	0 07½	0 07¾	" small lots..	0 00	0 00
" round.....	0 00	0 00	*Iron Wire (net cash):*			Benzine	0 00	0 00
" scaled.....	0 35	0 53	No. 6, ℔ bundle.....	2 70	2 80	**Produce**		
Mackerel, small kitts..	0 00	0 00	" 9.......	3 40	3 50	*Grain;*		
Louh. Her. wh's firks..	2 50	2 75	" 12, "	3 60	3 60	Wheat, Spring, 60 ℔..	0 92	0 93
" half " ...	1 25	1 50	" 13, "	3 90	4 40	" Fall 60 " ..	0 94	0 96
White Fish & Trout....	0 00	0 00	*Powder:*			Barley	0 43	0 45
Salmon, saltwater....	14 00	15 00	Blasting, Canada....	3 50	0 00	Peas........ 60 " ..	0 65	0 70
Dry Cod, ℔ 112 ℔s...	4 50	5 00	FF "	4 25	4 50	Oats........ 34 " ..	0 50	0 51
Fruit:			FFF "	4 75	5 00	Rye .... 56 " ..	0 65	0 60
Raisins, Layers	1 00	2 00	Blasting, English	4 00	5 00	*Seeds:*		
" M B	1 90	2 00	FF loose..	5 00	6 00	Clover, choice 60 " ..	0 00	0 00
" Valentias new..	0 0	0 0½	FFF "	6 00	0 50	" com'n 68 " ..	0 00	0 00
Currants, new	0 4½	0 0½	*Pressed Spikes (4 mos):..*			Timothy, cho'e 4 " ..	0 00	0 00
" old........	0 4½	0 04	Regular sizes 1½0....	4 00	4 25	" inf. to good 48 "	0 00	0 00
Figs	0 11	0 12	Extra	5 00	0 50	Flax	0 00	0 00
Molasses:			*Tin Plates (net cash):*			*Flour (per brl.):*		
Clayed, ℔ gal.......	0 00	0 35	IC Coke	7 50	8 00	Superfine extra......	0 00	0 00
Syrups, Standard	0 55	0 76	IC Charcoal........	8 50	9 00	Extra superfine....	4 25	4 50
" Golden	0 50	0 60	IX "	10 50	11 00	Fancy superfine	4 15	4 20
Rice :			XX "	13 50	14 00	Superfine No 1	3 95	4 00
Arracan	0 03	0 04	IXX "	13 50	14 00	" No. 2....		
Patna	0 00	0 04	DC "	9 00	9 50	Oatmeal, (per brl.)..	5 50	5 75
Spices:			DX "	9 50	9 00	**Provisions**		
Cassia, whole, ℔ lb...	0 00	0 45	**Hides & Skins, ℔lb**			Butter, dairy tub ℔ lb.	0 12	0 13
Cloves	0 11	0 12	Green rough	0 00	0 05	" store packed..	0 10	0 12
Nutmegs	0 50	0 55	Green, and'd & insp'd..	0 06	0 04½	Cheese, new	0 14½	0 15
Ginger, gr und	0 18	0 23	Cured	0 00	0 0¾	Pork, mess, per brl...	25 00	26 50
" Jamaica, root..	0 00	0 00	Calfskins, green	0 00	0 00	" prime mess,...		
Pepper, black.......	0 10½	0 11	Calfskins, cured.....	0 00	0 1¼	" prime	0 00	0 00
Pimento	0 08	0 09	" dry.....	0 18	0 2½	Bacon, rough	0 12	0 12½
Sugars:			Sheepskins, ...	1 20	1 60	" Cumberl'd cut..	0 13	0 14
Port Rico, ℔ lb.......	0 9½	0 10	"	1 00	1 60	" smoked	0 00	0 13
Cuba "	0 9	0 9½	**Hops.**			Hams, in salt.......	0 12½	0 13½
Barbadoes (bright)...	0 9½	0 9½	Inferior, ℔ lb.......	0 00	0 00	" smoked	0 14	0 14½
Canada Sugar Refine'y,			Medium	0 00	0 00	Shoulders, in salt	0 00	0 11
yellow No. 3, 60 ds...	0 9½	0 9½	Good	0 00	0 00	Lard, in kegs	0 12	0 12½
Yellow, No. 2½.......	0 10	0 0½	Fancy	0 00	0 00	Eggs, packed.......	0 11	0 12
" No. 3.......	0 10	0 10½	**Leather,** ℔ lb. (4 mos.)			Tallow, rough	0 00	0 00
Crushed X.	0 12	0 12½	Sole, weights ℔ ℔...			" refined	0 08	0 8½
" A	0 11½	0 11¾	In lots of less than			Hogs dressed, heavy..	0 00	0 00
Ground.	0 12½	0 12¾	50 sides, 10 ℔ per			" medium..	0 00	0 00
Dry Crushed	0 12	0 12½	higher.			**Salt, &c.**		
Extra Ground.	0 13	0 13½	Spanish Sole, 1st qual'y			American brls.	1 35	1 37
Teas:			heavy, weights ℔ ℔..	0 21	0 22	Liverpool coarse	0 00	0 00
Japan cm'n to good..	0 43	0 50	Do.1st qual middle do..	0 21	0 23	Goderich, ...	1 00	0 00
" Fine to choicest..	0 55	0 90	Do. No. 2, light weight	0 20	0 00	Plaster	1 00	0 00
Colored, com. to fine..	0 60	0 65	" No. 2, light ℔ ℔	0 19	0 00	Water Lime	1 50	0 00
Congou & Souch'ng...	0 42	0 75	Slaughter heavy	0 00	0 00			
Oolong, g ed to fine..	0 50	0 55	Do. light...........	0 00	0 00			
Y. Hyson, com to gd..	0 47½	0 55	Harness, best	0 35	0 37			
Medium to choice	0 65	0 80	" No. 2	0 00	0 00			
Extra choice	0 85	0 95	Upper heavy	0 30	0 32			
			" light.	0 33	0 34			

Soap & Candles.	$ c.	$ c.
D. Crawford & Co.'s ..		
Imperial.........	0 07½	0 08
" Golden Bar	0 07	0 07½
" Silver Bar........	0 07	0 07½
Crown	0 05	0 05½
No. 1	0 03½	0 03½
Candles	0 00	0 11
Wines, Liquors, &c.		
Ale:		
English, per doz. qrts.	2 60	2 65
Guinness Dub Portr..	2 35	2 40
Spirits:		
Pure Jamaica Rum...	1 80	2 25
De Kuyper's H. Gin..	1 55	1 65
Booth's Old Tom.....	1 90	2 00
Gin:		
Green, cases.........	4 00	4 25
Booth's Old Tom, c...	6 00	6 25
Wines:		
Port, common	1 00	1 25
" fine old	2 00	4 00
Sherry, common	1 00	1 50
" medium	1 70	1 80
"old pale or golden..	2 50	4 00

Brandy:	$ c.	$ c.
Hennessy's, per gal..	2 30	2 50
Martell's " ..	2 30	2 50
J. Robin & Co.'s " ..	2 25	2 35
Otard, Dupuy & Cos..	2 25	2 35
Brandy, cases........	8 50	9 00
Brandy, com. per c...	4 00	4 50
Whiskey:		
Common 36 u. p......	0 58	0 60
Old Rye	0 77½	0 80
Malt	0 77½	0 80
Toddy	0 77½	0 80
Scotch, per gal........	1 90	2 10
Irish—Kinnahan's c...	7 00	7 50
" Dunnville's Belf't..	6 00	6 25
Wool.		
Fleece, lb............	0 36	0 37
Pulled "............	0 00	0 00
Furs.		
Bear..................	0 00	0 00
Beaver, ℘ lb..........	0 00	0 00
Coon	0 00	0 00
Fisher................	0 00	0 00
Martin................	0 00	0 00
Mink..................	0 00	0 00
Otter.................	0 00	0 00
Spring Rats	0 00	0 00
Fox...................	0 00	0 00

INSURANCE COMPANIES.

ENGLISH.—*Quotations on the London Market.*

No. of Shares.	Last Dividend.	Name of Company.	Shares par val £	Amount paid.	Last Sale.
20,000		Briton Medical and General Life...	10	....	2½
50,000	7½	Commer'l Union, Fire, Life and Mar.	50	5	5¼
24,000	8	City of Glasgow	25	2½	5¼
5,000	9½	Edinburgh Life	100	15	33
400,000	5—½ yr	European Life and Guarantee......	2½	11s6	4s. 6d.
100,000	10	Etna Fire and Marine.............	10	1½	—
20,000	5	Guardian	100	50	51½
24,000	12	Imperial Fire....................	500	50	35½
7,500	9½	Imperial Life	100	10	17½
100,000	10	Lancashire Fire and Life..........	20	2	2⅝
10,000	11	Life Association of Scotland.......	40	7½	25
35,862	45s. p. sh	London Assurance Corporation ..	25	12½	48 x d
10,000	5	London and Lancashire Life	10	1	—
87,504	40	Liverp'l & London & Globe F. & L.	20	2	7¾
20,000	5	National Union Life	5	1	1
20,000	12½	Northern Fire and Life	100	5	12⅝
40,000	12 '68, bo 5s.	North British and Mercantile	50	6¼	19¼
40,000	50	Ocean Marine	25	5	17¾
2,500	£5 12s.	Provident Life....................	100	10	35
....	£4½ p. s.	Phœnix	....	....	145
200,000	2½—h. yr.	Queen Fire and Life	10	1	1
100,000	3s. bo. 4s	Royal Insurance..................	20	3	6⅜
20,000	10	Scottish Provincial Fire and Life ..	50	2½	5 3-8
10,000	25	Standard Life	50	12	66½
4,000	5	Star Life	25	1¼	—
		CANADIAN.			℘ c.
8,000	4	British America Fire and Marine ..	$50	$25	56 60
....	4	Canada Life	...	....	.....
4000	12	Montreal Assurance	£50	£5	135
10,000	8	Provincial Fire and Marine........	60	11	.....
....	....	Quebec Fire	40	32½	£23 24
....	7	" Marine.....................	100	40	85 90
10,000	4 6 mo's.	Western Assurance................	40	9	.....

RAILWAYS.	Sha's	Paid	Montr.	London
Atlantic and St. Lawrence........................	£100	All.	....	56
Buffalo and Lake Huron	20½	"	....	2¾ 3¼
Do. do Preference	10	"	....	5 6
Buff., Brantf. & Goderich, 6℘c., 1872-3-4....	100	"	....	66 69
Champlain and St. Lawrence	....	....	10 11	....
Do. do Pref. 10 ℘ ct....	....	....	80 85	....
Grand Trunk	100	"	13 14	14½ 14¾
Do. Eq.G. M. Bds. 1 ch. 6℘c............	100	"	....	89
Do. First Preference, 5 ℘ c	100	"	....	47
Do. Deferred, 3 ℘ ct..	100	"	....	....
Do. Second Pref. Bonds, 5℘c............	100	"	....	37
Do. do Deferred, 3 ℘ ct............	100	"	....	....
Do. Third Pref. Stock, 4℘ct...........	100	"	....	28½
Do. do. Deferred, 3 ℘ ct............	100	"	....	....
Do. Fourth Pref. Stock, 3℘c............	100	"	....	16
Do. do. Deferred, 3 ℘ ct............	100	"	....	....
Great Western	20½	"	13 14	15 15½
Do. New	20½	18	....	....
Do. 6 ℘ c. Bds, due 1873-76............	100	All.	....	100½ 102
5½ ℘c Bds. due 1877-78............	100	"	....	95
Marine Railway, Halifax, $250, all......	$250	"	....	....
Northern of Canada, 6 ℘c. 1st Pref. Bds...........	100	"	.. .	82 83

EXCHANGE.	Halifax.	Montr'l.	Quebec.	Toronto.
Bank on London, 60 days......				
Sight or 75 days date	12½ 13	9¼ 9½	9½ 9¾	9¾
Private do.	11½ 12	8½ 8¾	8¼ 8½	9
Private, with documents..........	....	7½ 8½	....	....
Bank on New York................	....	27¾ 28	27 27½	27½
Private do.	....	28 28½	27½ 28	....
Gold Drafts do.	....	par	par ¼ dis.	par ¼ dis.
Silver	....	4¾ 4¾	....	4 to 5

STOCK AND BOND REPORT.

The dates of our quotations are as follows:—Toronto, June 15; Montreal, June 14; Qu[ebec] June 12; London, May 3.

NAME.	Shares.	Paid up.	Divid'd last 6 Months	Dividend Day.	CLOSING PRIC[ES] Toronto.	Montre'l
BANKS.			℘ ct.			
British North America	$250	All.	3	July and Jan.	Bks closed	Bks cl'd
Jacques Cartier..............	50	"	4	1 June, 1 Dec.	105½ 106	106 107
Montreal	200	"	6	"	159½ 160	159 159½
Nationale....................	50	"	4	1 Nov. 1 May.	107 107½	106½ 107
New Brunswick	100	"	......	......	....	....
Nova Scotia	200	—	7&b$3½	Mar. and Sept.	....	....
Du Peuple......	50	"	4	1 Mar., 1 Sept.	108 108½	108 108½
Toronto	100	"	4	1 Jan., 1 July.	121½ 122	Bks cl'd
Bank of Yarmouth............	....	....	......	......	....	....
Canadian Bank of Com'e......	50	All.	......	......	Bks closed	Bks cl'd
City Bank Montreal	80	"	4	1 June, 1 Dec.	97½ 98	98 98½
Commer'l Bank (St. John)....	100	"	℘ ct.	......	....	....
Eastern Townships' Bank.....	50	"	4	1 July, 1 Jan..	....	100 100½
Gore	40	....	none.	1 Jan., 1 July.	35½ 36	37 38
Halifax Banking Company....	...	....	......	......	....	....
Mechanics' Bank.............	50	All.	4	1 Nov., 1 May.	91½ 92½	92 93
Merchants' Bank of Canada....	100	"	5	1 Jan., 1 July.	Bks closed	Bks cl'd
Merchants' Bank (Halifax)....	....	....	......	......	....	....
Molson's Bank......	50	All.	4	1 Apr., 1 Oct.	108½ 109	108½ 109
Niagara District Bank........	100	70	3½	1 Jan., 1 July.	....	....
Ontario Bank................	40	All.	4	1 June, 1 Dec.	95 95½	95 95½
People's Bank (Fred'kton)....	100	"	......	......	....	....
People's Bank (Halifax)......	20	"	7 12 m	......	....	....
Quebec Bank	100	"	3½	1 June, 1 Dec.	100 100½	100 101
Royal Canadian Bank	50	60	4	1 Jan., 1 July.	45 50	40 50
St. Stephens Bank	100	All.	.....	......	....	....
Union Bank	100	"	4	1 Jan., 1 July.	Bks closed	Bks cl'd
Union Bank (Halifax)........	100	....	7 12 mo	Feb. and Aug.	....	....
MISCELLANEOUS.						
British America Land........	250	44	......	......	....	....
British Colonial S. S. Co......	250	32½	......	......	...	....
Canada Company	32½	All.	......	......	....	....
Canada Landed Credit Co.....	50	$50	3½	......	79 80	....
Canada Per. B'ldg Society....	50	All.	5	......	125½ 126	....
Canada Mining Company.....	4	90	......	......	....	....
Do. Inl'd Steam Nav. Co.....	100	All.	15 12 m	......	....	97 99
Do. Glass Company.........	100	"	None.	......	....	40 60
Canad'n Loan & Investm't....	25	2½	......	......	....	....
Canada Agency	10	½	......	......	....	....
Colonial Securities Co........	...	....	......	......	....	....
Freehold Building Society....	100	All.	5	......	114½ 115	....
Halifax Steamboat Co.........	100	"	......	......	....	....
Halifax Gas Company.........	....	....	......	......	....	...
Hamilton Gas Company......	....	....	......	......	....	....
Huron Copper Bay Co........	4	12	20	......	....	30 45
Lake Huron S. and C.........	5	102	......	......	....	....
Montreal Mining Consols.....	20	$15	......	......	....	2.95 3.15
Do. Telegraph Co...	40	All.	5	......	135 135½	136 137
Do. Elevating Co...	00	"	5½	......	....	105 107½
Do. City Gas Co.........	40	"	4	15 Mar. 15 Sep.	....	135 136
Do. City Pass. R,. Co.....	50	"	2	......	....	110 112
Quebec and L. S.	8	$4	......	......	....	...
Quebec Gas Co..............	200	All.	4	1 Mar., 1 Sep.	....	...
Quebec Street R. R..........	50	25	3	......	....	....
Richelieu Navigation Co......	100	All.	7-12m	1 Jan., 1 July.	....	119 120
St. Lawrence Glass Company.	100	"	....	......	....	80 85
St. Lawrence Tow Boat Co.....	100	"	......	3 Feb.	....	...
Tor'to Consumers' Gas Co.....	50	"	⅝ m	1 My Au MarFe	106½ 107½	...
Trust & Loan Co. of U. C.....	20	5	3	......	....	....
West'n Canada Bldg Soc'y....	50	All.	5	......	121 121½	....

SECURITIES.	London.	Montreal.	Quebec.	To[ronto]
Canadian Gov't Deb. 6 ℘ ct. stg...................	....	103½ 104	102 103	10
Do. do. 6 do due Ja. & Jul. 1877-84........	104½ 105½	....	....	
Do. do. 6 do. Feb. & Aug........	102 104	....	....	
Do. do. 6 do. Mch. & Sep........	102 104	....	...	
Do. do. 5 ℘ ct. cur., 1883	93¾ 94½	92½ 93	90 91	91
Do. do. 5 do. stg., 1885	93½ 94	90 91	90 90½	90
Do. do. 7 do. cur.,......................	....	....	......	
Dominion 6 p. c. 1878 cy.....	....	107½ 108	106 108½	10
Hamilton Corporation....	....	....	......	
Montreal Harbor, 8 ℘ ct. d. 1869.....................	..	....	......	
Do. do. 7 do. 1870......................	...	....	......	
Do. do. 6½ do. 1883......................	....	102 103	......	10
Do do. 6½ do. 1873......................	....	....	......	
Do. Corporation, 6 ℘ c. 1891	....	96 96½	96½ 97	9
Do. 7 p. c. stock...	....	108½ 110	109 110	10
Do. Water Works, 6 ℘ c. stg. 1878..........	....	96½ 97½	......	9
Do. do. 6 do. cy. do.	....	....	......	9
New Brunswick, 6 ℘ ct., Jan. and July	104 104½	....	......	
Nova Scotia, 6 ℘ ct., 1875..........................	103 104	...	......	
Ottawa City 6 ℘ c. d. 1880	....	95 97	......	
Quebec Harbour, 6 ℘ c. d. 1883.	....	....	60	
Do. do. 7 do. do........................	....	....	65 70	
Do. do 8 do. 1886.....................	...	....	80 85	
Do. City, 7 ℘ c. d. 1½ years.....................	....	....	98 98½	
Do. do. 7 do. 8 do.	....	....	91 92	
Do. do. 7 do. 4 do.	....	....	94 95	
Do. Water Works, 7 ℘ ct., 3 years..............	....	....	97 97½	
Do. do. 6 do. 1½ do.	....	....	94 95	
Toronto Corporation	....	94 95	...	

Insurance.

ntreal-Assurance-Company
(MARINE).
INCORPORATED 1840.

CAPITAL,........................... $800,000
NVESTED FUNDS (approximately).. 400,000
HEAD OFFICE........MONTREAL.
ANCH OFFICE—82 *Wellington Street, Toronto.*
Consulting Inspector......CAPT. A. TAYLOR.
Marine Inspector.........CAPT. F. JACKMAN.
Local Secretary and Agent......R. N. GOOCH.
nd Navigation, also Ocean Risks (to and from Ports of
rest Britain) covered at moderate rates.   84-6ms

ada Farmers' Mutual Insurance Company.

HEAD OFFICE, HAMILTON, ONTARIO.
SURE only Farm Property, Country Churches, School
Houses, and isolated Private Houses. Has been
rateen years in operation.
THOMAS STOCK, President.
HARD P. STREET, Secretary and Treasurer.   26

Geo. Girdlestone,

RE, Life, Marine, Accident, and Stock Insurance
Agent, Windsor, Ont.
Very best Companies represented.

Phoenix Fire Assurance Company

LOMBARD ST. AND CHARING CROSS,
LONDON, ENG.
nsurances effected in all parts of the World;
Claims paid
WITH PROMPTITUDE and LIBERALITY.
MOFFATT, MURRAY & BEATTIE,
Agents for Toronto,
y.   36 Yonge Street.

Insurance.

THE CONNECTICUT MUTUAL
LIFE INSURANCE COMPANY,
HARTFORD, CONNECTICUT.

WOODBRIDGE S. OLMSTEAD, SECRETARY,   JAMES GOODWIN, PRESIDENT,
EDWIN W. BRYANT, ACTUARY,   ZEPHANIAH PRESTON, VICE PRESIDENT.
LUCIAN S. WILCOX, MEDICAL EXAMINER.

Organized in 1846.   Charter Perpetual.

The Largest Mutual Life Insurance Company.   Numbering Over 75,000 Members.

BEING A PURELY MUTUAL COMPANY ITS ASSETS BELONG EXCLUSIVELY TO ITS MEMBERS.
ASSETS, $21,000,000.—Acquired by prudent and economical management of twenty-two years, without the aid of
a single dollar of original capital.
SURPLUS ASSETS, $6,301,967—All profits divided among the members. Each policy holder is a member. There are
no stockholders.
ITS DIVIDENDS—Have averaged over 50 per cent. annually. Total amount of dividends paid the members since its
organization, $4,307,142.
ITS SUCCESS UNPARALLELED—It has arrived at the extraordinary condition where the income from annual interest
alone is more than sufficient to pay all the losses. Total amount of losses paid by the Company, $6,868,628.
ITS RESPONSIBILITY—For every $100 of liabilities it has $154 of assets.

LAST YEAR'S PROSPEROUS BUSINESS.

Amount insured fiscal year, 1867 ......$45,647,191 00 | Income received fiscal year, 1867........$7,530,886 19
During its last fiscal year this Company paid to its living members, and to the families of deceased members,
nearly $2,000,000, and at the same time added more than four millions to its accumulated capital.
The whole record of this Company has been one of prudent management and prosperous advancement. Among the
older and leading Life Insurance Companies its average ratio of expenses to income has, through its entire history, been
the lowest of any.
ITS LIBERALITY—It accommodates the insured by giving credit for part premium, and grants insurance to meet
all the contingencies and wants to which Life Insurance is applicable.
It issues policies on a single life from $100 to $25,000.
MEDICAL REFEREES—J. WIDMER ROLPH, M.D.; H. H. WRIGHT, M.D.

OFFICE - - - - - No. 90 King Street East, Toronto.
J. D. FEE, AGENT, TORONTO.
Toronto, December 24, 1868.   DANIEL L. SILLS, GENERAL MANAGER FOR CANADA.   12-1y

LIFE ASSOCIATION OF SCOTLAND.

Invested Funds Upwards of £1,000,000 Sterling.

THIS Institution differs from other Life Offices, in that the BONUSES FROM PROFITS
are applied on a special system for the Policy-holder's personal benefit and enjoy-
it during his own lifetime, with the option of large bonus additions to the sum
ured. The Policy-holder thus obtains a large reduction of present outlay, or a
vision for old age of a most important amount in one cash payment, or a life
uity, without any expense or outlay whatever beyond the ordinary Assurance
mium for the Sum Assured, which remains intact for Policy-holders' heirs, or
r purposes.

CANADA—MONTREAL—PLACE D'ARMES.

DIRECTORS:
DAVID TORRANCE, Esq., (D. Torrance & Co.)
GEORGE MOFFATT, (Gillespie, Moffatt & Co.)
ALEXANDER MORRIS, Esq., M.P., Barrister, Perth.
Sir G. E. CARTIER, M.P., Minister of Militia.
PETER REDPATH, Esq., (J. Redpath & Son.)
J. H. R. MOLSON, Esq., (J. H. R. Molson & Bros.)
Solicitors—Messrs. TORRANCE & MORRIS.
Medical Officer—R. PALMER HOWARD, Esq., M.D.
Secretary—P. WARDLAW.
Inspector of Agencies—JAMES B. M. CHIPMAN.
TORONTO OFFICE—No. 32 WELLINGTON STREET EAST.
R. N. GOOCH, Agent.

THE LIVERPOOL AND LONDON AND GLOBE
INSURANCE COMPANY.

Capital, Surplus and Reserved Funds ....$17,005,028.
Life Reserve Fund............................. $9,865,100.
Daily Cash Receipts .... $20,000.

Directors in Canada:
T. B. ANDERSON, Esq., Chairman (President Bank of Montreal).
HENRY STARNES, Esq., Deputy Chairman (Manager Ontario Bank).
E. H. KING, Esq., (General Manager Bank of Montreal).
HENRY CHAPMAN, Esq., Merchant.
THOS. CRAMP, Esq., Merchant.

FIRE INSURANCE Risks taken at moderate rates, and every description of Life
Assurance effected, according to the Company's published Tables, which afford
various convenient modes (applicable alike to business men and heads of families) of
securing this desirable protection.

JAMES FRASER, Esq., Agent,   THOMAS BRIGGS, Esq, Agent
5 King street West, Toronto.   Kingston.
F. A. BALL, Esq., Inspector of Agencies, Fire Branch.
T. W. MEDLEY, Esq., Inspector of Agencies, Life Branch.
G. F. C. SMITH,
23 1y   Chief Agent for the Dominion,
Montreal

COMMERCIAL UNION ASSURANCE COMP'Y.

CHIEF OFFICES—19 and 20 Cornhill, London, England, and 385 and 387 St. Paul Street, Montreal.

RLAND, WATSON & CO., General Agents for Canada.   FRED. COLE, Secretary.

CAPITAL..£2,500,000 STERLING.

LIFE DEPARTMENT

The LIFE FUNDS are entirely separate, and are invested in the names of special Trustees.
ECONOMY OF MANAGEMENT guaranteed by a clause in the Deed of Association.
80 PER CENT. of PROFITS divided among participating Policy-holders.
Bonus declared to 1867 averaged £2 2s. per cent., equalling a cash return of about every THIRD year's Premium.

FIRE DEPARTMENT

Assurances granted on Dwelling-houses and their contents, as well as on General Mercantile Property, Manufactories, &c.

Agents in the principal Cities, Towns and Villages in Canada.
W. M. WESTMACOTT, Agent for Toronto.

Insurance.

Briton Medical and General Life Association,

with which is united the
BRITANNIA LIFE ASSURANCE COMPANY.

Capital and Invested Funds............£750,000 Sterling.

ANNUAL INCOME, £220,000 STG. :
Yearly increasing at the rate of £25,000 Sterling.

THE important and peculiar feature originally introduced by this Company, in applying the periodical
Bonuses, so as to make Policies payable during life, without
any higher rate of premium being charged, has caused
the success of the BRITON MEDICAL AND GENERAL to be
almost unparalleled in the history of Life Assurance. *Life
Policies in the Profit Scale become payable during the lifetime
of the Assured, thus rendering a Policy of Assurance a
means of subsistence in old age, as well as a protection for a
family,* and a more valuable security to creditors in the
event of early death; and effectually meeting the often
urged objection, that persons do not themselves reap the
benefit of their own prudence and forethought.

No extra charge made to members of Volunteer Corps
for services within the British Provinces.
☞ TORONTO AGENCY, 5 KING ST. WEST.

Oct 17—9-1yr   JAMES FRASER, Agent.

BEAVER
Mutual Insurance Association.

HEAD OFFICE—29 TORONTO STREET,
TORONTO.

INSURES LIVE STOCK against death from any cause.
The only Canadian Company having authority to do this
class of business.
E. C. CHADWICK, President.
W. T. O'REILLY, Secretary.   8-1y-25

HOME DISTRICT
Mutual Fire Insurance Company.

Office—North-West Cor. Yonge & Adelaide Streets,
TORONTO.—(UP STAIRS.)

INSURES Dwelling Houses, Stores, Warehouses, Mer-
chandise, Furniture, &c.
PRESIDENT—The Hon. J. McMURRICH.
VICE-PRESIDENT—JOHN BURNS, Esq.
JOHN RAINS, Secretary.
AGENTS:
DAVID WRIGHT, Esq., Hamilton; FRANCIS STEVENS, Esq.,
Barrie; Messrs. GIBBS & BRO., Oshawa.   8-1y

THE PRINCE EDWARD COUNTY
Mutual Fire Insurance Company

HEAD OFFICE.—PICTON, ONTARIO.
President, L. B. STINSON; Vice-President, W. A. RICHARDS.
Directors: H. A. McPaul, James Cavan, James Johnson,
N. S. DeMill, William Delong.—Secretary, John Twigg;
Treasurer, David Barker; Solicitor, R. J. Fitzgerald.

THIS Company is established upon strictly Mutual principles, insuring farming and isolated property, (not
hazardous,) in Townships only, and offers great advantages
to insurers, at low rates for five years, without the expense
of a renewal.
Picton, June 15, 1868.   9-1y

Fire and Marine Assurance.
THE BRITISH AMERICA
ASSURANCE COMPANY.
HEAD OFFICE:
CORNER OF CHURCH AND COURT STREETS.
TORONTO.

BOARD OF DIRECTION :
Hon G. W. Allan, M L C.,   A. Joseph, Esq ,
George J Boyd, Esq ,   Peter Paterson, Esq.,
Hon W. Cayley,   G. P. Ridout, Esq.,
Richard S. Cassels, Esq.,   E H. Rutherford, Esq ,
Thomas C. Street, Esq.
Governor:
GEORGE PERCIVAL RIDOUT, Esq.
Deputy Governor:
PETER PATERSON, Esq.
Fire Inspector: Marine Inspector:
E. ROUS O'BRIEN.   CAPT. R. COURNEEN.

Insurances granted on all descriptions of property
against loss and damage by fire and the perils of inland
navigation.
Agencies established in the principal cities, towns, and
ports of shipment throughout the Province.
THOS. WM. BIRCHALL,
23-1y   Managing Director.

Insurance.

Reliance Mutual Life Assurance Society
OF LONDON, ENGLAND. Established 1840.

Head Office for the Dominion of Canada:
131 ST. JAMES STREET, MONTREAL.
DIRECTORS—Walter Shanly, Esq., M.P.; Duncan Mac-
donald, Esq.; George Winks, Esq., W. H. Hingston, Esq.,
M.D., L.R.C.S.
RESIDENT SECRETARY —James Grant.

Parties intending to assure their lives, are invited to
peruse the Society's prospectus, which embraces several
entirely new and interesting features in Life Assurance.
Copies can be had on application at the Head Office, or at
any of the Agencies.
JAS. GRANT, Resident Secretary.
Agents wanted in unrepresented districts.   43-1y

The Gore District Mutual Fire Insurance Company

GRANTS INSURANCES on all description of Property
against Loss or Damage by FIRE. It is the only Mutual Fire Insurance Company which assesses its Policies
yearly from their respective dates ; and the average yearly
cost of insurance in it, for the past three and a half years,
has been nearly TWENTY CENTS IN THE DOLLAR
less than what it would have been in an ordinary Proprietary Company.
THOS. M. SIMONS, Secretary & Treasurer.
ROBT. McLEAN, Inspector of Agencies.
Galt, 25th Nov., 1868.   15-1y

Canada Life Assurance Company.
SPECIALLY LICENSED BY THE GOVERNMENT
OF CANADA.

ESTABLISHED 1847.

CAPITAL.... .... A MILLION DOLLARS.

DEPOSIT WITH GOVERNMENT, $50,000.

The success of the Company may be judged of by the
fact that during the financial year to the 30th April, 1869,
the gross number of

NEW POLICIES
ISSUED WAS
8 9 2 1
FOR ASSURANCES OF
$1,257,734,
WITH
ANNUAL PREMIUMS OF
$49,783.73.
Rates lower that those of British or Foreign Offices, and
every advantage offered which safety and liberality can
afford.
A. G. RAMSAY, Manager.
E. BRADBURNE, Agent.
May 25.   1y   Toronto Street.

Queen Fire and Life Insurance Company,
OF LIVERPOOL AND LONDON,
ACCEPTS ALL ORDINARY FIRE RISKS
on the most favorable terms.

LIFE RISKS
Will be taken on terms that will compare favorably with
other Companies.
CAPITAL,   -   -   £2,000,000 Stg.
CANADA BRANCH OFFICE—Exchange Buildings, Montreal.
Resident Secretary and General Agent,
A. MACKENZIE FORBES,
13 St. Sacrament St., Merchants' Exchange, Montreal.
WM. ROWLAND, Agent, Toronto.   1-1y

THE AGRICULTURAL
Mutual Assurance Association of Canada.
HEAD OFFICE ....LONDON, ONT.
A purely Farmers' Company. Licensed by the Govern-
ment of Canada.

Capital, 1st January, 1869.....................$230,103 82
Cash and Cash Items, over...................$80,000 00
No. of Policies in force..........................39,692 00

THIS Company insures nothing more dangerous than
Farm property. Its rates are as low as any well-established Company in the Dominion, and lower than those
of a great many. It is largely patronised, and continues
to grow in public favor.
For insurance, apply to any of the Agents or address
the Secretary, London, Ontario.
London, 2nd Nov., 1865.   12-1y.

Insurance.

The Waterloo County Mutual Fire Insurance Company.

HEAD OFFICE : WATERLOO, ONTARIO.
ESTABLISHED 1863.
THE business of the Company is divided into three
separate and distinct branches, the
VILLAGE, FARM, AND MANUFACTURE
Each Branch paying its own losses and its just proportion
of the managing expenses of the Company.
C. M. TAYLOR, Sec.   M. SPRINGER, M.M.P., Pres.
J. HUGHES, Inspector.   15

Lancashire Insurance Company.
CAPITAL, - - - - - - - - £2,000,000 Sterl

FIRE RISKS
Taken at reasonable rates of premium, and
ALL LOSSES SETTLED PROMPTLY,
By the undersigned, without reference elsewhere
S. C. DUNCAN-CLARK & CO.,
General Agents for Ontario,
25-1y   N. W. Cor. of King & Church Sts., Toronto

Western Assurance Company
INCORPORATED 1851.
CAPITAL, ... $400,000.
FIRE AND MARINE.
HEAD OFFICE................ TORONTO, ONTARIO

DIRECTORS :
Hon. JNO. McMURRICH, President.
CHARLES MAGRATH, Vice-President
A. M. SMITH, Esq.   JOHN F ISKEN, Esq.
ROBERT BEATY, Esq.   ALEX. MANNING, E
JAMES MICHIE, Esq.   N. BARNHART, Esq.
B. J. DALLAS, Esq.
B. HALDAN, Secretary.
J. MAUGH'N, JR., Assistant Secretary.
WM. BLIGHT, Fire Inspector.
CAPT. G. T. DOUGLAS, Marine Inspector.
JAMES PRINGLE, General Agent.

Insurances effected at the lowest current rates
Buildings, Merchandize, and other property, against loss
or damage by fire.
On Hull, Cargo and Freight against the perils of Inla
Navigation.
On Cargo Risks with the Maritime Provinces by sail
steam
On Cargoes by steamers to and from British Ports.
WESTERN ASSURANCE COMPANY'S OFFICE, }
TORONTO, 1st April, 1869   33

The Victoria Mutual
FIRE INSURANCE COMPANY OF CANADA.
Insures only Non-Hazardous Property, at Low Rai
BUSINESS STRICTLY MUTUAL.
GEORGE H. MILLS, President.
W. D. DOOKER, Secretary.
HEAD OFFICE ....HAMILTON, ONTAR
aug 15-1yr

North British and Mercantile Insurance Company.

Established 1809.

HEAD OFFICE, - - CANADA. - - MONTREA

TORONTO BRANCH :
Local Offices, Nos. 4 & 6 WELLINGTON STREET.
Fire Department, ... R. N. GOOCH, Agent
Life Department. ....H. L. HIME, Agent.

Imperial Fire Insurance Company
OF LONDON.
No. 1 OLD BROAD STREET, AND 16 PALL MA
ESTABLISHED 1803.
Canada General Agency,
RINTOUL BROS.,
24 St. Sacrament Street.
JAMES E. SMITH, Agent,
Toronto. Corner ' hurch and Colborne Streets.

PUBLISHED AT THE OFFICE OF THE MONETA
TIMES, No. 60 CHURCH STREET.
PRINTED AT THE DAILY TI ES PUBLISHING HOU
BAY STREET, CORNER OF KING

THE CANADIAN
ΛONETARY TIMES
AND
INSURANCE CHRONICLE.
:VOTED TO FINANCE, COMMERCE, INSURANCE, BANKS, RAILWAYS, NAVIGATION, MINES, INVESTMENT,
PUBLIC COMPANIES, AND JOINT STOCK ENTERPRISE.

| II—NO. 45. | TORONTO, THURSDAY, JUNE 24, 1869. | SUBSCRIPTION $2 A YEAR. |

Mercantile.

Meetings.

ONTARIO BANK.

Proceedings of the Twelfth Annual Meeting of
the Stockholders of the Ontario Bank, held at the
Banking House, Bowmanville, on Monday, the
7th day of June, 1859.

The chair was taken by the Hon. John Simpson,
President, who read the following Twelfth Annual
Report of the Directors to the Stockholders.

The business transactions of the Bank for the
year have been large, and the profits quite equal
to the average of former years ; while the losses, so
far as ascertained, are less than usual.

The harvest of the past year was below an
average, with perhaps the single exception of
wheat. The extraordinary prices realized by our
agricultural community for all their productions
in the past, placed them in a position of comparative ease, and in many cases of affluence; the
rapid decline in the prices of breadstuffs has not
therefore seriously affected their position ; and
having but little indebtedness, they have been
able to withhold from market a large proportion
of the last year's wheat crop. The effect of this
is, that the decline has been felt mainly by the
producers, which, but for the fact already stated,
would have been borne by the produce dealer, and
would have entailed upon this class of the Bank's
customers serious if not embarrassing consequences.

The prospects of an abundant harvest are everywhere indicated ; and when the balance of last
year's crop shall be brought to market, in addition
to that now on the ground, a great impetus must
be given to those branches of trade and commerce
which are now in a somewhat languishing condition. While shrinkage in values have been going
on in most of our cereals, the timber and sawn
lumber interests—in the latter of which your
Bank is largely interested—are in a healthy and
flourishing condition ; and your Directors are
happy to be able to state that the present year
promises to be more profitable than the past.

The renewal of the Reciprocity Treaty, on a
fair and equitable basis, we trust may be effected
during the present year ; when, doubtless, this
and other important branches of Canadian industry
will be greatly stimulated.

Your Directors may, without exceeding their
legitimate sphere, refer to a few facts in connection
with our manufactures and importations. Canada
requires, and must seek, new outlets for many ac-
ticles now manufactured in the Dominion, (if our
industries are to be continued or extended.) Prominent amongst these may be placed the productions of our woolen mills, the limited demand for
which has not absorbed the supply. The importations of the past two or three years have been
largely in excess of the consuming capacity
of the country ; these over importations, and the
eagerness evinced to affect purchases therefor, have
induced a large number of persons to engage in
mercantile pursuits, many of whom were not possessed of sufficient capital, and lacked the business
training and experience so necessary in these days
of keen competition, to lead them on to success.
The general uneasiness in trade has left many with
stocks of goods on hand, for which they have been
unable from their own resources to pay; and being
pressed for remittances, has led a great number

to go into bankruptcy, as the readiest way to get
rid of their financial embarrassments. Your Directors would call the attention of importers and
wholesale dealers to the necessity of looking more
closely into the affairs of debtors, when their
estates are being disposed of, as a means of preventing fraud and over-trading. The ease with
which discharges have been obtained, has induced traders and others to avail themselves of
our bankrupt laws, who, with more energy and
economy, might have honourably met all their
engagements. It is hoped that the Bill now before Parliament will effectually check the facilities
at present so readily availed of, and deter many
from entering into pursuits for which they have
no natural or acquired ability, and in which too
many are already engaged. The result of this
general over-trading has led to the withdrawal of
a large amount of labor from agricultural pursuits,
wherein it might have been more profitably directed, for their own advantage and the general good.

All the Bank Charters expire next year, and the
question of their renewal is now engaging the
earnest attention of Parliament and the country.
If the Government scheme becomes law, the system now in existence, which has been productive
of so much benefit to the country generally and
particularly to the Province of Ontario, will be so
changed as to limit to a large extent the facilities
now afforded to the public.

A large number of the Stockholders of the Bank
having expressed the conviction that their interests, as well as those of the public, would be
better subserved by removing the Head Office to
one of the large commercial centres in Ontario or
Quebec, petitions have been presented to Parliament, and a Bill will be immediately introduced,
asking for a renewal of the present Charter, and
also authority to be given to the majority of the
Stockholders present in person or by proxy, to
determine whether such removal shall be made,
and if so, to what point; such meeting to be called
specially for that purpose.

Your Directors determined last fall to close the
Hamilton Branch. This is now being done, and
this office will be finally closed within a few weeks.
The Cashier, Managers, and other officers of the
Bank, have discharged their respective duties with
zeal and ability, and are, in our opinion, entitled
to your thanks. The profits of last year, after
the payment of all current expenses, and making
provision for interest on deposits, and discount on
U. S. funds, is........................$221,873,90
To which add balance as credit of pro-
fit and loss from last year............   25,240 82
                                         ———————
                                         $247,114 72
Which has been appropriated as follows:—
To payment of dividend,
  1st of December last...$30,000 00
To dividend payable 1st
  of June instant........ 80,000 00
To Government tax on
  circulation............ 2,697 94
To reduction on Bank
  property............... 4,000 00
To add to reserve........ 20,000 00—$186,697 94
                                     ———————
Leaving a balance at credit of profit
  and loss account..................... $60,416 73
              J. SIMPSON, President.
              JOHN J. ROBSON, Secretary.

General Statement of the affairs of the Ontario Bank, as on Monday, the 31st of May, 1869: —

ASSETS.

Gold, Silver and Provincial Notes on hand	$762,597 14
Government Securities	206,892 69
Balances due by other Banks	136,462 04
Notes and Cheques of other Banks.	96,063 07
Bank Property	154,843 14
Notes and Bills discounted	4,202,088 47
	$5,559,247 35

LIABILITIES.

Capital Stock		$2,000,000 00
Circulation		881,754 00
Deposits not on interest	$974,416 18	
do on interest	1,097,962 94	2,072,379 12
Balances due to other Banks		198,230 54
Dividends unclaimed		2,707 71
Dividend No. 24, payable 1st June		80,000 00
Reserve Fund		250,000 00
Interest and Exchange reserved		13,669 20
Profit and Loss		60,416 78
		$5,559,247 35

D. FISHER, Cashier.

Moved by T. N. Gibbs Esq, seconded by James Dryden, Esq.,—Resolved: That the report of the President and Directors, together with the General Statement of the affairs of the Bank, now submitted, be received, adopted, and printed for the information of the shareholders.

Moved by C. J. Campbell, Esq., seconded by H. A. Massey, Esq.,—Resolved: That the thanks of the Shareholders are hereby given to the President and Directors, for their efficient management of the affairs of the Bank during the past year.

Moved by Dr. McGill, seconded by A. F. Wallbridge, Esq.,—Resolved: That Messrs. Massey, Draper and Turner be Scrutineers of this election, and that they report the result to the Cashier.

Moved by Wm. McMurty, Esq., seconded by J. W. Little, Esq.,—Resolved: That the balloting now commence and that it be closed at three o'clock; but if at any time ten minutes shall have expired without a vote being tendered; the ballot may be closed by the Scrutineers.

Moved by T. N. Gibbs, Esq., seconded by J. P. Lovekin, Esq.,—Resolved: That the Chairman do now leave the chair, and that C. J. Campbell, Esq., be requested to take the same.

Moved by Dr. Gunn, seconded by Wm. Sisson, Esq.,—Resolved: That the thanks of the meeting are hereby given to the President for his efficient services in the chair.

Moved by Henry Hopkins, Esq., seconded by Daniel Betts, Esq.,—Resolved: That the thanks of the meeting be given to Mr Robson, for his services as Secretary.

The following gentlemen were elected as Directors for the current year:—Hon. J. Simpson, T. N. Gibbs, J. Dryden, J. P. Lovekin, D. A. McDonald, Hon. W. P. Howland, Wm. McMurty.

The Board of newly elected Directors reelected the Hon. J. Simpson, President, and T. N. Gibbs, Esq., M. P. Vice-President.

QUEEN INSURANCE COMPANY.

The annual general meeting of shareholders was held in Liverpool, England, on the 27th May, M. Bernard Hall, the Chairman of the Company, presiding.

The Chairman moved the adoption of the report (see last page) in a speech relating to the past and present position of the Company. Dealing, in first instance, with the life business. he announced that during the past five years it had more than doubled itself. The business of that branch for the quinquennial period ending in 1863 was, he said, £71£,00⅓, and in the five years just ended it was £1,412,466, and the life funds which stood at £29,000 in the former period, had been increased to £110,000 in the latter. The quality of the business, too, had been as satisfactory as its progress. The profits earned upon the life business in the five years had been $26,690, of which the shareholders would take one-fourth, and beyond that the policy-holders would receive a reversionary bonus of about 40 per cent. The valuations had been made upon a three per cent. basis, which was the lowest figure adopted by any life office, and it was to the difference between that and the 4½ per cent. at which the life fund had been improved that the large amount of profits was attributable. The position of the Company with regard to its life business was most satisfactory, and his colleagues and himself had no doubt that the searching investigation of their affairs under this head had attracted the large share of public confidence which was apparent in the amount of new business transacted. Passing from the life to the fire department, he regretted that he could no longer use the language of congratulation, but he considered that it was a kind of negative consolation that their misfortune had not been greater than those of many of the largest and oldest offices in the kingdom. They had made £1,000 or £2,000 by the fire business, so that it had not been a drag upon them. Their actual losses, he might mention, had been about 66 per cent. of the premiums. Directing his remarks to the question of expenditure, he expressed his gratification at the success which had attended the efforts of the Directors in the way of reduction. Their average expenditure for 1867 was 40 per cent., and for 1868 it was only 33¼ per cent., the difference representing a curtailment to the extent of about £8,000, and they intended further to reduce the expenses, if they found their desire to be consistent with the retention and development of the business. With regard to the general result of their operations, he remarked that they had a balance of £20,290, and the Directors proposed out of that to pay a dividend of 7 per cent., which would absorb £12,586; to carry to the reserve fund £4,571 (bringing that fund up to £80,000), and carry forward the sum of £3,133. He was sure the shareholders would concur in the propriety of forming a strong reserve, ensuring as it did the confidence of the public, without which they could not exist. The wish of the directors was, if possible, to create a fund which would admit of the equalisation of dividends, and enable the shareholders to look with confidence upon a steady return upon their investment. Returning to the subject of the life business, which he said was the backbone of the company, he told them that with its increase they would have a proportionate increase of profits. Life business could be conducted upon known and fixed principles, which was not the case with fire business, subject as it was to great fluctuations. However, even in the fire business, if they could only get the normal amount of losses which existed a few years ago, of something like 50 or 60 per cent., or less, they would have a very handsome profit from that source. Alluding to the London business, he said the fire losses in connection with it had been very great, but he was glad that the directors and secretary there was not blame, inasmuch as the risks undertaken were the same as those with which some of the most respectable offices in London were mixed up, and, besides, there was the gratifying fact that a great reduction had been effected in the expenditure. Dealing next with the company's investments, he began with the *Queen* Insurance Building, which cost $97,000. The net interest derived from them up to the year 1868, was 5 per cent., and that return would ultimately be increased to six per cent. The buildings in London cost £24,500, and they were yielding an interest of five per cent. They had invested in Canada £30,000, which at present prices exhibited a loss of £1,100. Their investments in the State of New York, where they were doing a good business, amounted to £33,000, the gain upon them being £2,100. The loan made in London was £20,000, against which they had securities valued at £23,000, and they had besides that a dividend from the General Estates Company of £3,000, so that they had against the £20,0 securities amounting to £26,000. They held 372 shares of the company, which cost the £10,460, or 18s. 4d. per share, the cash valu which they stood in the company's books be 29s. per share. The entire amount of real prop held by the company was £304,000, of wh £124,000 represented buildings in London, Li pool, and Southampton. There were loans u real property valued at £83,000, the loans on liamentary securities amounting to £44,000. T had £28,000 in the hands of various brokers, £38,000 in bonds and negotiable securities, wh could be realized at any moment. The average of interest on investments had been 4½ per ce while the loss under that item since the commement of the company, with an outlay of betw £3,000,000 and £5,000,000 had not been more £300. The Chairman then stigmatised with m severity what he termed the "injudicious in ference of a few intermeddlers;" and, after hav with satisfaction the proposed introduction Parliament of a Bill prepared by Mr. McLa M.P., on the subject of judicial inquiries into outbreak of fires, concluded by assuring the sh holders that the Company was in a thorou sound position, and that its prospects were exc ing hopeful in their character.

Mr. McLagan, M.P., (chairman of the Lon board) on rising to second the motion, was ceived with applause. His remarks were pri pally devoted to an explanation of the af made by his colleagues and himself to cut d the expenses. He announced, amidst cheers, the expenditure, which stood at £11,691 in 1 when the old directors seceded, had been red to £4,800, and with the able co-operation of secretary (Mr. Rumford) he hoped to lower amount by £1,000. With regard to the merca risks, he said that owing to the diligence of Swanton the superintendent of the salvage c fires in bonded warehouse were much rarer hitherto. He was glad to be able to report fav ably of the business transacted during the months of the present year. They had for premiums £200 more than at the same last and in the life business the amount had nearly quadrupled. Referring to the nece of instituting judicial inquiries into the outl of fires, he mentioned that the Home Secr had requested him to draft a Bill which it w be possible for him (Mr. Bruce) to take up Government measure. It would be introd either by himself or the Government next and it would no doubt add greatly to the see of insurance companies.

The motion was then put and agreed to.

The following directors, retiring by rota were re-elected (an amendment that Mr. Page not re-elected only finding four supporters)— C. Tunleliffe, Alfred H. Cowie, John Bing John Bethune Thomson, and Charlton R. Liverpool; John T. Pagan, London; John S Dundee; and Andrew Galbraith, Glasgow.

A cordial vote of thanks was accorded to chairman and directors, and £1,800 award them for their services.

Votes of thanks were also awarded to the tors and officers of the branches at home abroad, to the actuary and manager, the sub ager, the company's physician, and the me referees, the auditor, solicitor, and the office the chief office.

The customary compliment to the chai terminated the proceedings.

PRINCE EDWARD MUTUAL INSURA COMPANY.

The annual meeting of this company wa in Picton, Ont., on the 14th June.

On motion, Mr. G. Striker took the chai the Secretary of the company, Mr. Twigg appointed Secretary.

The chairman called upon the Presiden L. B. Stinson, to read the annual report.

m this, the fourteenth annual report, we use the following general statement, refer-se interested reader to the report itself for liers :

: policies issued last year...... 319
nt of property insured......... $287,913 00
Premium Notes......... 7,262 81
Cash Premiums......... 740 07
number of Policies in force... 1,544
amount of property insured...$1,642,423 00
ze on each Policy... .... 925 00
number of policies now in force is about excess of last year. The losses paid dur-e past year amount to $2,830 88. The Di-i report that they thought proper to refuse yment for the loss sustained by Mr. King, ghton. A suit was instituted thereon, resulted in favor of Mr. King.
Treasurer's account shows a balance on of $26.48.
general statement of the Company's affairs the total amount of assets to be $57,637.26, in excess of the total liabilities by $52,.

as moved by Mr. S. P. Niles, seconded by . Clapp, and resolved, that the annual re-s read, be adopted.

question as to the advisability of issuing s of three years as well as five years, was it up, and a motion favorable to it was ut upon being put to the meeting, was lost.

election of Directors was proceeded with. 1. John B. Solmes and John Abercrombie ppointed scrutineers, who, by their report, d the following gentlemen elected, viz :
. D. B. Stinson, W. A. Richards, James , David W. Ruttan, William Delong, H. Paul, and James Johnson.

ote of thanks was given to and suitably wledged by the chairman for his services, e meeting closed.

r the close of the general meeting, the new ors met at the Secretary's office, and ap-d L. B. Stinson, Esq., President, and Wm. g, Esq., Vice-President for the present also, committees on finance and printing ppointed, and they adjourned.

ERN TOWNSHIPS BANK.—The annual meet-s held at the bank on Monday, 7th inst., Sleeper, Esq., in the chair. The report mts the business of the past year as having rofitable. A dividend of four per cent. for at six months was declared, and $6,000 to the rese ve fund, which now amounts to 0. The directors condemn the new bank-eme of the Government, as well as the bill trict the rate of interest now before the ature. The net earnings of the bank for the ear, after providing for losses, was $43,531. apital paid in, $400,000 ; bills in circula-108,163 ; due to other banks, $7,297.79 ; ts not bearing interest, $77.818.71 ; bearing it, $81,137.05 ; profit and loss account, 0 ; balance of profit for the year, $27,023.18. sonves of the bank are : Coin and provin-tes, $62,748.42 ; bills and cheques on other $28,048.29 ; due from other banks, $51,-; Government securities, $67,833.33 ; sil-:516,343.65 ; real estate, $16,500 ;—total, 39.73. The old board of directors was re-l, viz : B. Pomroy, Charles Brooks, A. A. s, J. H. Hope, R. W. Heneker, G. K. , and H. L. Robinson. At a meeting of rectors, Major B. Pomroy was re-elected ent, and C. Brooks Vice-President.

r. W. P. Street, for nearly thirty years r of the Bank of Montreal agency at Simcoe tired from it to take a position of trust in ton. His numerous friends in the County rfolk, have presented an address to Mr.

Financial.

ROYAL CANADIAN BANK.

The following is a summary of the evidence given before the Commons Committee on Banking and Currency, on considering the Act respecting the affairs of the Royal Canadian.

Mr. Woodside.—In January, 1868, there were 30,000 shares of subscribed stock; some had been subscribed, in certain localities, upon the condi-tion that agencies should be opened there; and where this condition was not carried out, the sub-scriptions were considered as null. There was also some stock subscribed for by individuals, and not paid up; but we did not enforce the payment of calls. The amount of stock on which payments have actually been made is 27,488 shares; the amount paid on these shares up to the 5th June last; was $1,168,828.34.

The statement of assets and liabilities on 5th June embraces the whole of the liabilities. With the exception of $50,000, held by the government of Ontario, as security, $148,625.52 of coin, &c., are actually on hand. The landed property con-sists of furniture and chattels, at its agencies. The government securities h ve never been pledged. The notes and bills of other banks are all available assets. The estimate of loss on the discounts is $300,000. Between $500,000 and $600,000 is over-due paper. Very little of current paper is bad. Losses have been chiefly sustained at King-ston, Cobourg, and Seaforth, and resulted from the culpable misconduct of the agents. The notes discounted are generally of small amounts of legi-timate character, and diffused over twenty-two agencies; the largest is a lumber account of $50,-000, which is secure. We have not written off any paper. The accommodation afforded to direc-tors has never exceeded $100,000, or thereabout, at any one time. The largest amount of paper on which the names of directors appeared at any one time in the year 1866 was about $80,000, but in addition to this there was a liability on the part of a director on a Sterling Bill of Exchange for $40,000 endorsed by him, which was cashed by the bank and was subsequently paid off. Ordina-rily the amount of discounted paper done for the directors was very small, less, I think, than pre-vailed in any similar institution in the country. Some transactions in stock took place, but with-out the knowledge of the Board. It was believed to be in the interest of the shareholders to prevent the stock being forced on the market. During the year 1868, stock to the amount of $19,200 was purchased by the President, Mr. A. M. Smith, from a number of parties, and was held in the name of his brother, Mr. John Smith. From October, 1868 to February, 1869, stock to the amount of $14,700 was transferred to the name of Mr. Alexander Campbell, an employee of the bank. The stock held in these names cost respectively $16,102.87, and $11,973.61. The funds of the bank were used to pay for it. When these trans-actions came to the knowledge of the Board, they recognize them. I am not aware that any director, other than Mr. A. M. Smith (then President), and the Hon. Donald McDonald, who is now Vice-President, were engaged in these transactions.

James Metcalfe, President of the Bank.—To the best of my knowledge and belief, the state-ment of the 5th June is correct. My impression is that there will be a loss of nearly $300,000 on the paper in default, and on that respecting which there is already some doubt. Although I consider the residue of the paper held by the Bank to be good, it is of course possible that upon so large an amount outstanding there may be some further loss. I think the loss would be considerably in-creased by a forced liquidation. I do not think that any of the assets are pledged, with the excep-tion of $50,000 to the Ontario Government. I think the accounts were generally proportionate to the means of the parties, with the exception of

the Brown case. I believe that stock has been purchased to a small extent, though not directly by the Board, or with its sanction. I only know positively the particulars of one case. I refer to the purchase of stock to the extent of several thousand dollars by the Hon. Donald McDonald, when the market price was about 80. He bought it in his own name, and gave cheques on the Bank for the purchase money, stating to me and Mr. Manning, another director, that he did it to keep the stock up in the interest of the Bank. The stock subsequently advanced about 3 per cent, when he said he would keep it, but he afterwards transferred it to Mr. Campbell, the accountant, on behalf of the Bank, and, as I believe, got the money from the Bank for it. I do not think the purchases of stock by directors or others in the interest of the Bank, would amount to $15,000 during the last year. The Board had no know-ledge of the transactions. I never bought any myself for the account of the Bank, nor did I sell any. The directors had usually very small accom-modation. I never had any myself, though I was once endorser on a Bill of Exchange for about $40,000, which was brought to the Bank at my instance, for the purpose of supplying them with foreign exchange. It was not long since with-drawn from the Bank.

James Michie, Assistant Cashier.—The subscrib-ed capital is $1,500,000. Stock was taken at vari-ous agencies, and different arrangements as to pay-ment were made. About $1,168,000 has been paid up; and about $300,000 remains to be paid, of which $100,000 to $150,000 is in default. The statement given in embraces the whole of the liabilities. Of the Government securities £2,500 sterling of these are in Toronto, and the balance in the hands of the Union Bank of London, and is available, that Bank being indebted to us. This asset is unpledged. The balances due from other banks are all available. Very little of the current discounts can be considered bad. All the paper on which the names of directors appeared was about $80,000, $45,000 of which consists of indi-rect liability as endorsers for others. A very small proportion of the discounts is for accommodation of a permanent nature, as the cashier has always objected to it. A large amount of the discounts is secured by real estate, including part of the overdue paper. The collaterals have been taken on renewals. Very little of the discounts is with-out endorsers. About 3500 shares have been sub-scribed, on which no payments whatever have been made; but no stockholder has been pressed for payment who has not voluntarily paid the calls. I estimate the overdue paper as worth about 10s. in the pound. The only paper in default bearing the name of a director, is for some $800 or $600. There has been stock purchased by one of the directors for, I think, $18,000 or $19,000; the purchase money was advanced by the bank, and charged to account standing in the name of the party in trust. This transaction took place more than a year ago. I do not know under what authority the advance was made. I am not aware whether the party in question is held personally liable for the stock, or whether the bank is held responsible for it.

Hon. Donald McDonald.—I have been on the Board since July, 1865, and Vice-President since July last. With regard to the four first items, "Coin and Bullion, &c.," "Real Estate, &c.," "Government Securities," and "Notes of other Banks," I have no reason to doubt the value of these. I believe $50,000 of the securities were pledged to the Ontario Government as security for their balance, but cannot say whether they are deposited with the Government or with the Mon-treal Bank. I did not know of the transaction at the time. It was admitted to me by the directors at the Board that the aggregate of losses on dis-counts amounted to $300,000. My own estimate of this loss is larger. I should say that very few of the accounts reached 85c,000; they were gene-rally of moderate amount, though in many in-stances large or excessive in proportion to the means or resources of the individuals. I have reason to believe that the funds of the bank were used to purchase stock, from an early period, without, so far as I know, the formal sanction of the Board. Some stock appeared in the publish ed statements, as standing in the name of Mr. John Smith, Mr. A. M. Smith acting as his attorney. I was never able to discover who this John Smith was, and believed him to be a myth. I think there is some stock in the name of Mr. Campbell, the Accountant, held for the benefit of the Bank. I am under the impression that the amount of paper on which directors' names appeared exceeded 1-20 of the entire discount in 1866, though I cannot state so of my own knowledge. The total amount of discounts on 30th April, 1866, as shown by the official returns, was $628,-328, and if my information be correct, a Bill of Exchange for $40,000 was discounted about that time, on which the name of one of the directors appeared.

Statement of Stock.

Amount of stock subscribed......	30,973 shares.
Amount of stock subscribed, on which payments have been made......	27,488
	53
	$1,374,400
Amount of Stock paid..	$1,168,828.34
" still to pay...............	$205,571.66

The calls upon the above 27,488 shares have all been made and are therefore past due with the exception of about one hundred shares.

Liabilities of Directors.

On 21st May, 1869,.......	$103,021 24
On 11th June, 1869	89,216 00

Securities held against Notes under Discount.

Produce and other securities.........	$250,900 00
Real Estate..............................	121,200 00

Paper in Default.

On 30th April, 1869	$411,762 86
On 21st May, 1869................. ..	475,179 07
On 5th June, 1869.....................	578,172 84

TORONTO STOCK MARKET.

(Reported by Pellatt & Osler, Brokers.)

The business of the week has been somewhat restricted in consequence of the number of transfer books now closed, in anticipation of July dividends. Transactions that have taken place, however, have generally been at an advance on last weeks' quotations.

Bank Stock.—Montreal closed with buyers at 160; sales occurred at 159½ to 160. There are buyers of British at 106; books closed. Ontario has been in good demand at advancing rates, buyers now offer 96½ and sellers ask 97½. Sales of Toronto have taken place at 118¼, ex-dividend, buyers would advance. Royal Canadian has been freely dealt in at from 45 to 47¼, buyers now offer 48 but there is little stock in market. There are sellers of Commerce at par, ex-dividend. Gore sold during the week at 37½ and 38, there are buyers at 37½. The last sales of Merchants were at 111½ and 112. Buyers offer 99½ for Quebec with sellers at par. No Molson's in market, it could be placed at 108. There are buyers and sellers of City at 99 and 99½ respectively. Small sales of Du Peuple were made at 108 and 108½. Buyers offer 107 for Nationale. Jacques Cartier sold at 106, at which rate there are buyers. Nothing doing in Mechanics', buyers offer 91½.

Debentures.—Canada currency six per cents are offering at 105, and sterling sixes are asked for at 104½. Dominion stock is heavy at 107½. There were small sales of Toronto at rates to pay 7 and 7½ per cent. interest. There are considerable lots of County on the market at par.

Sundries.—City Gas is wanted at 107. There were small sales of British America Assurance at 56¼ and 57, it is still offering at the latter rate. The books of the Canada Permanent and Western Canada Building Societies are closed; last sales at 120 and 121½, respectively. Freehold Building Society is in demand at 115 and 115¼, none on market. There are sellers of Montreal Telegraph at 136¼ and buyers at 136. There were small sales of Landed Credit at 78 and 78½. One or two large mortgages have been placed at 8 per cent.

BANK OF UPPER CANADA.

Mr. McKenzie having inquired of the Government whether they had decided on any course relative to this Bank.

Mr. Rose replied that the Government had made up their minds that the time had arrived when less expense was necessary.

There had been notice issued by the trustees for a meeting of shareholders to take place at an early day, to see what steps could be taken. If they agree to pay up the Government, they will give up all claim to the arrangement of the bank, and if not the Government will then reduce the expenses by placing the affairs in the hands of two executive officers to wind them up.

If the legal right existed in favor of the Crown over all the assets, it is quite impossible for him, or any other member of the Government, to say he would give up that priority. All that he could say now was, that he could certainly endeavor so to do, so that the process of liquidation might be made as rapid as possible.

AN OPINION ON THE BANKING SCHEME.—The *Paisley Advocate* has from time to time devoted a good deal of attention to the banking scheme. Here is something from the last issue:—What the Canadian people want, is the National Greenback system of our neighbors, without the excrescence of the so-called National Banks; and with the added security that Canadian Bonds, bearing six per cent. gold interest, may always be obtained for the notes. This would give the notes a gold value, and prevent their depreciation beyond a trifling extent; and would leave gold to rise and fall in price like any other commodity, as it should. Mr. Rose would then be able to discard his forty or fifty resolutions and replace them by half a dozen. By adopting this simple plan, the country would not be flooded with currency notes more more than it needed. These would seldom be much under par value in relation to gold, and would always pass at their face value in Canada. The country would also be saved a few million dollars yearly in taxation—there would be plenty of money to build railroads and carry on other public enterprises— the Finance Minister would be able to meet all demands on him without borrowing from England—and the bankers, while losing their special privileges, would share in, and rejoice in the general prosperity.

THE BANKING SCHEME.—The following extract from a letter, written by a gentleman of high position in Canada, to a merchant of this city, is very complimentary to our friend, Mr. Jack, of the People's Bank: "Mr. Rose's Banking Resolutions have apparently been abandoned for the present, and is not likely they will again be brought forward in their present shape. This result has been greatly aided by the strenuous exertions of Mr. Jack, of the People's Bank of your city, whose able letters on the subject of Banking and Currency, were printed in pamphlets and distributed among the members of both branches of the Legislature. His arguments against any such radical change in our banking system, as that proposed, were very convincing, and were read with much interest and good effect. His replies to the queries propounded by the select committee on Banking and Currency, are considered here to be the ablest of any that were sent in. Your banks acted wisely in sending Mr. Jack to Ottawa to represent them, as his thorough knowledge of the subject enabled him, in his personal interviews with prominent members of both Houses, to f explain what the evil effects of the proposed sch would be, and his indefatigable exertions, w here, did much to strengthen the opposition to measure. The ability displayed by Mr. Jack his writings on this banking question, as als his letters on the assimilation of the Curre reflects credit on your Halifax bankers, and l entitled to the thanks of your mercantile trading community for the assistance he has dered in defeating a scheme, the adoption of w would be much more injurious to them tha the banks."—*Halifax Chronicle.*

BILLS PASSED.—The following bills are an those passed the House of Commons last wee To amend the Act to Incorporate the Union E of Lower Canada; to amend the Act to Inco rate the Quebec Bank--Mr. Simard; to amend charter and increase the capital stock of the N Shore Transportation Co.—Hon. Mr. Carling amend the Act Incorporating the Royal Can Bank, by extending, if necessary, the time for resumption of specie payment, and also to au rize the amalgamation of the said Bank with other Bank or Banks, and for other purposes— R. A. Harrison; to amend the Charter of the tario Bank—Hon. J. H. Cameron; to amend extend the Acts Incorporating the Bank of To to—Hon. J. H. Cameron; to amend the Ac Incorporate the British America Fire and Assurance Company—Mr. Street.

BANK CHARTERS.—A bill has been introd by Mr. Rose to extend the following bank char Quebec Bank, City Bank of Montreal, Banqu Peuple, Bank of Toronto, Commercial Ban Canada, Ontario Bank, Bank of Brantford, C dian Bank of Commerce, Royal Bank of Can Banque Nationale, Bank of Nova Scotia.

—At a meeting of the Banking Committ the House of Commons, the Gore Bank Am ment Bill was passed, giving permission fo reduction of the number of Directors to five, of the capital stock from $800,000 to $500, Permission is given to change the name of Bank to the Bank of Hamilton.

Railway News.

GREAT WESTERN RAILWAY.—Traffic for ending June 4, 1869.

Passengers	$28,917 93
Freight........................ ...	41,826 01
Mails and Sundries...........	2,781 45
Total Receipts for week......	$73,525 39
Coresponding week, 1868...	70,407 99
Increase	$3,117 40

NORTHERN RAILWAY.—Traffic receipts for ending June 17th, 1869.

Passengers......	$2,940 82
Freight and live stock......	14,445 85
Mails and sundries.........	255 38
	$17,642 05
Corresponding Week of '68.	15,424 46
Increase	$2,217 59

GRAND TRUNK.—A body of gentlemen i ested in this Company met in London, on the May, and organized themselves into a comm with power to add to their number, with object of bringing about a change in the ma ment both in England and Canada. The 8 June was appointed for a meeting to take ste accomplish that object. A circular was addr to a large number of the bond and stockho setting forth the views of this committee asking their co-operation.

—The Chatham Council lately passed a b granting $30,000 to the Southern R. R. Co., it was lost on a vote of the people.

CANADIAN MONETARY TIMES AND INSU-
CHRONICLE is printed every Thursday even-
distributed to Subscribers on the following
.

thing office, No. 60 Church-street, 3 doors
Court-street..

ription price—
ada $2.00 per annum.
gland, stg. 10s. per annum.
ited States (U. S. Cy.) $3.00 per annum.

l advertisements will be charged at the rate
nts per line, each insertion.

ess all letters to "THE MONETARY TIMES."
tes, money orders, &c. should be made pay-
. M. TROUT, Business Manager, who alone
rized to issue receipts for money.

ll Canadian Subscribers to THE MONETARY
will receive THE REAL ESTATE JOURNAL
further charge.

Canadian Monetary Times.

THURSDAY, JUNE 24, 1869.

THE CANADIAN-CANALS.

IV.

e is a phrase used by American poli-
and writers which, in one sense, has
eaning, but, on the other hand, with-
planation, is entirely without force.
t the meeting of the New York Cham-
Commerce of the 3rd June, in the
ion submitted by General Wallbridge
ort of the proceedings of the Comit-
Vays and Means of the House of Rep-
tives of the 23rd March, he sets forth
essity of securing to the citizens of
ited States "the freedom of the St.
ce." Unaccompanied by any explan-
this does not convey the meaning of
l Wallbridge and those who think
im. At this moment, the St. Law-
s practically "a free navigation."
loaded at Chicago pass through the
l Canal to Oswego. This principle
ical with a propeller proceeding from
m to Massachusetts. The difference

is simply in the length of voyage ; a voyage
not now made, because it is not profitable.
One vessel has already made the trip from
Chicago to Liverpool. So far as "free"
navigation is concerned, there is, accordingly,
nothing to be asked or granted. The point
of General Wallbridge's remarks is apparent
when he adds, "and the enlargement of the
canals to a capacity of floating vessels of
1,000 tons." We think it would simplify
matters if the public men of the Western
States and of New York would adopt a phrase
fully setting out their views, such as—The development of the St. Lawrence navigation
to the attainable maximum of depth, free to
all flags. One of the arguments urged
against increased depth will be met by the
very action we recommend. When the few
who have pressed the question have dwelt
upon this necessity as an act of justice to
Western Canada, the somewhat spacious objection has been raised, that scarcely a Canadian harbor has twelve feet of water—certainly none on Lake Erie—and that any increase of such depth must be unnecessary.
The reply is simple enough. The harbors
themselves could be improved ; indeed, it is
part of the scheme to include such work.
But the main argument must lie in the necessity for opening a sufficient channel for vessels from the West to the seaboard ;—that is
to say, the establishment of a route more
advantageous than any other, and which will
extend all the necessary inducements for
trade to leave its accustomed channel in
order to pass through it.

The Americans themselves point to the
fact that alone of the canals they control,
the Sault Ste. Marie, about a mile in length,
and the size of the locks has been considered
typical of American requirements. The
question is not worth argument. Science so
extends our operations and increases our resources, that what a few years back was in
advance of what was then known, in many
cases falls so entirely behind modern requirements as soon to become antiquated. Our
wants increase by the very facility with
which they are supplied. In no direction is
the axiom more plain than in the conveniences for locomotion. In a navigation
they are determined by the objects attainable ; and the Sault Ste. Marie locks, 350
feet long, 70 feet wide, and 10 feet deep,
were suggested by the large paddle steamers
of Lake Erie; and by freight steamers loaded
with ore from the Lake Superior mines. The
successful working of the propeller has substituted a totally different class of vessels,
the characteristic of which is length and
depth, with but moderate width of beam.
When we have satisfactorily determined what
can be effected in respect of depth, we can

at once decide what proportion the remaining characteristics must assume. We shall
then be able to name the width of the lock,
and it will be very different from that of the
one American canal.

In the speech in which General Wallbridge
addressed the New York Chamber of Commerce, he states that "Canada has officially
"offered to enlarge her canals, and give us
"their freedom." We should like to know
the form in which this proposition has been
made. He says : "In 1866, the Provincial
"Commissioners, before a Committee of the
"House of Representatives, stated their
"willingness to embark in this outlay." We
do not ourselves know any proposal of this
character freighted with the weight of Minis-
terial responsibility, and sustained by the
sanction of a Parliamentary vote. Some
negotiations have certainly been carried on
by Mr. Young, a known advocate for the development of the St. Lawrence navigation,
who proceeded to Washington in the time of
Mr. Sandfield Macdonald's Government. Mr.
Galt has also visited the United States capital
in connection with the Reciprocity Treaty.
The question is, has the Dominion Government ever made any offer to the United
States Government with regard to the canals?
and if so, what are its terms? It is certain
that nothing will satisfy the West—or, as
the General puts it, will be of "substantial
service "—unless the improvement be extended. He speaks of vessels of 1,000 tons
burden. We think that the argument should
not be limited by figures, which cumber
rather than assist. There is, within moderate effort, a certain depth attainable, to be
determined by examination. It is a safe
phrase to call it a maximum development,
and it is on this term that the advocates of
the improvement should meet. If there be
any difference of view, or divergence of
thought, it can be battled out when the detail comes up for consideration. There
seems, however, to be an error in one direction. It is assumed that the canals are large
enough for Canadian purposes. Those who
so think appear to have been led by the
opinions expressed in Montreal, where, with
a class, the western propeller is looked upon
as a tender to the Allan steamer. Western
Canada is dissatisfied with the capacity of
the canals. The argument of Wisconsin
and Illinois is the very language we use.
We desire to deal directly with the ocean.
It is true that we are not cramped in the
way of tariffs, as the Western States are.
The importer of Chicago must now break
bulk at Boston or New York. He cannot
transfer his cargo at Montreal to a lake-going
vessel, for he would increase the duty, the
cargo being valued by a Custom House regu-

lation, not at the value at the place of manufacture, but at the place of river shipment. So, independently of the duties on the true value of the goods, he would have to pay a duty on all the incidental charges added to that value. In Western Canada we are not sufferers, as the Western States are ; but, with this exception, we anticipate the realization of the same advantages they look to receive from canal development.

Are these advantages theoretical? or, to use a word which is now finding a recognized place in the academy of politics, are the complaints which are preferred merely sentimental? On the other hand, can any practical results, promising profit, be said to loom in the future as dependent on this policy? We reply : It is a matter of experience, that a cargo of wheat can be carried more rapidly and more economically from the foot of Lake Erie by the St. Lawrence, than by the Erie Canal to Boston, to New York, to the West India Islands, and to Europe. The saving in the cost of freight and the removal of the charge for brokerage tend to swell the profits of the producer, and, as such, to give an increased value to real estate. The increased annual receipts of the owners and workers of land are divided among all classes of the district by the commercial supply of the wants increased with the means of gratifying them.

We must bear in mind that the St. Lawrence is the only channel capable of improvement. The Erie Canal has reached its greatest extent of development, or at best, but little can be done to increase the tonnage of its boats. The complaint has long been its want of water. It must be remembered that the supply from Lake Erie goes no further than Port Byron, 158 miles ; at that point the level ascends, and is supplied by other sources than those of Lake Erie. Therefore the whole hope of the West turns to the Canadian Government. It is evident that if negotiation on this policy is to be a matter of diplomatic intercourse, the Government should in no way leave a link of the canals out of their control. This theory was virtually acted upon when the original Welland Canal proprietors were bought out, and that canal made the property of the Province. Indeed, this principle should be clearly laid down, and one would conceive that all applications for private control over enterprises of this character would at once be met by the Government with the assertion that all canal enterprise must remain under the superintendence of the Dominion. Without such regulations, how is it possible to enter into any treaty with the United States with regard to the St. Lawrence ? A private company holding a link of the navigation may enforce a tariff of tolls in every way objectionable, and institute a series of by-laws oppressive and in opposition to the true interests of commerce. In our judgment, the Dominion Government should lay down a broad plan for the improvement of the river, and, while carrying it out with vigor, allow no interference with it. They should not only not countenance any private scheme, but they should veto it on the principle above set forth. It is a policy necessary to effect what is due to ourselves, and certainly indispensable when we think how the contrary line of action may affect ourselves with the United States ; and it is the only one by which we can hope to carry out that which we are striving to establish—viz., "the development of the St. Lawrence navigation to "the attainable maximum of depth, free to "all flags," and, we will add here, the whole chain of canals being under the direct ownership and control of the Dominion.

THE COMMERCIAL SITUATION.

The grumbler is a kind of animal not peculiar to any country or climate; he is indigenous everywhere. His croakings have been observed to be unusually loud for a while back; and with perverse ubiquity he is met with everywhere, in city and country. The "hard times" have been the chief subject of his bemoanings of late, the wail proceeding mostly from the direction of Montreal. Many in Toronto, also, give vent in piteous tones to their grievances endured for six months past, and point with ominous finger to the indications of the future.

While it must be admitted that there is a cause for all this, yet the adverse influences to which it owes its rise have been greatly over-estimated. The cry of "hard times" began with the importing trade, and to that it is mostly confined. The country correspondents of the importing houses have sent in money very slowly; hundreds of them have sent none, but gone, instead, into bankruptcy, and the winding-up process has proved much more prolific of discharges than dividends. Losses succeeding losses have swept away profits, in some cases entrenched upon capital, and so left the aggregate result in the neighborhood of zero. Over-supplies of goods and bad debts are leading results of the six months operations. This ailment of the importing trade has proved epidemical; it has infected more or less every other branch of commerce and industry.

Having stated these facts, the gloomy part of the story is pretty well exhausted. In no other department is there any real ground of complaint. Labor is abundant. This is apparent in Toronto, at least, from the exten sive building operations that are going on in every part of the city. If the country were from any cause impoverished or panic-stricke how would it be possible to place the thou sands of emigrants, that have arrived quit recently, in good positions for earning a live lihood? Labor is not only abundant, but is well paid. An immense number of me chanics flocked to Toronto at the opening the present season, enough to build a tow kept profitably employed.

In consequence of the condition of the in porting interest, and the outcry thereat, cap talists have become cautious, some of the timid and fearful, resulting in a good deal hoarding. This, with a large demand at t same time, has kept the money market clos and slightly raised the rate paid by borrower But it will not be denied that there is as mu money in the country as a year ago. The is no diminution of the deposits in savin banks—demonstrating the prosperity of t industrial classes; the funds placed by t public in the chartered banks are untouche The greatest willingness has been shown t subscribe no less a sum than $400,000 to t two proposed railways centering here, a thi which would be impossible of accomplishme if the city was not really prosperous. To th may be added, the instructive fact, that t suspension of the Royal Canadian Bank, loc ing up or withdrawing some millions of c culating capital, has not produced a sin failure. In any other than a really healt state of business affairs, we should not ha this pleasant fact to record.

Our importers who feel so gloomy just n may as well remember, that "it is a long la which has no turning." They are passi through an ordeal, which, trying though it is: the time, will put the trade on a healthy fo ing. It will prune away the rubbish of the tail trade, and impress so deeply, the less that selling goods on credit is not necessar making money, that it will not be soon f gotten. It will tend to lessen competiti and give those who do sell goods, in futu a chance to make fair profits, and lessen t danger of losses. It will prevent their tru ing rogues and honest men alike, which I been so much the custom. It will induce diligent enquiry into the antecedents, ch acter and position of every applicant : credit. These wholesome lessons were mu needed; and we may rest content that t severely practical way in which they are bei taught, has been attended with no r disasters.

A careful survey of the whole situati leads to the conclusion that matters with are not nearly so bad as has been represent The present commercial dullness was to nt necessary, and from its nature must nly temporary. The Intercolonial Railis now giving employment to a great number of men. In a month or so contracts will a been given out and work commenced he Toronto and Nipissing Railway; labor soon be in demand for the construction he sister enterprise. The Wellington, y and Bruce Railway is also being pushed 'ard. The opening up by a railway of Great North West, is in the immediate re. With these, and perhaps other importworks to be. completed within a brief od, and with an abundant harvest in pect the country cannot fail to prosper. ry goods merchants import more than ' can sell, that is their own affair. No one le country can regret it more than themes, for the reason that they suffer most. evil carries within itself an infallible cure. m 'the statement given in another part of paper, it will appear that imports of dry ls have received a decided check; the total e entered at Montreal for the first six ths of the year being $3,285,136, against 28,277, showing a decrease of $256,859, affording the best kind of proof that the e is fully competent to take care of itself.

FICIAL INSURANCE STATEMENTS.

or confusion worse confounded commend o the Statements furnished by the Inance Companies to the Finance Minister upposed accordance with 31 Vic. c. 48. le companies have refused to make any rns; some have given partial returns; e have given such returns as only mislead, some have mixed figures in an abomile manner. Fire and Life business are bled together, and Inland and Ocean ine seem so have shared a like fate. Of se it is impossible under such circumnces to arrive at any reliable result reting the extent of business done in any Department of Insurance in Canada. ing the return of such Fire Companies as e given an intelligible statement and accept as correct, the estimated figures for such panies as have not made returns we have,

Premiums $1,972,602
Losses 1,203,156

Difference...............$ 779,446
l per centage of loss to premiums of 66 cent. In Life these figures stand,

Premiums.....................$966,247
Claims 491,834

. Difference...............,.... $474,413
. per centage of claims to premiums of 51 cent. The Marine business of four comlies gives an aggregate of,

---

Premiums ....$ 207,721
Losses 119,123

Difference................... $ 99,598
or a per centage of 57½ per cent.
But we warn our readers against accepting these conclusions as reliable. Some Canadian journals and some foreign ones, too, have published the totals as above figured up with the idea that they were giving the aggregate insurance business of Canada. An examination of the tables first given to the public in our issue of last week and the week previous, will serve to correct such a misapprehension.

The absurdity is manifest of expecting anything like intelligible statements when each company is allowed to furnish returns according to its own ideas or to withhold statements at its pleasure or to jumble up what should be distinct and clear, as interest dictates. If we are to have statements at all we should have such as would be of some value. It were far better to avoid putting companies to the trouble of preparing them, if the result is to be not only valueless, but absolutely injurious in giving false ideas respecting the extent of business done in Canada. If anything be wanting to prove the necessity that exists for the employment of an Insurance Supervisor or Commissioner, these statements supply it.

We cannot see on what principle the premiums of the Mutual Fire Companies which have not made returns are estimated at $150,000. In 1866 there were 19 local mutual companies in Ontario, whose aggregate income was $224,819.

QUEEN INSURANCE COMPANY.—The report for 1868, which we copy from the Post Magazine, shows an available balance of about one hundred thousand dollars, out of which a dividend of seven per cent. was declared to the shareholders. A sum of between four and five thousand pounds was alloted to the reserve fund, raising it to £80,000 sterling, and the balance carried forward. The life business shows good results; a large increase appears with a decreased expenditure of about forty thousand dollars on the whole business. In the fire branch the losses were heavy—reaching the high average of 66 per cent.—a large share of which occurred in London; still a small balance of profit appears in this department. In the matter of investments the Queen has been very fortunate. On a total investment, of from three to five millions of pounds, producing the average rate of 4½ per cent. interest, the losses ever since the commencement of the company, have been merely trifling. The investment of £30,000 in Canada seems to have resulted in a loss of £1, 100 at present prices of our securities, while a slightly larger sum, invested in New York State, where the company does a good business, shows a gain of £2,100

The favorable position of the Company, as shown by the report, has led to an advance in the shares to a premium; and not only retained but increased the measure of confidence reposed by the public at home and abroad, in its present soundness and future success.

ONTARIO BANK.—In the annual report of this Bank the position and prospects of trade are reviewed, and the causes of the present dullness pointed out. It is proposed to remove the Head Office to Toronto or Montreal; the former city will no doubt be selected, as there are many weighty reasons why the headquarters of the Bank should be located here. The profits of the year, after paying expenses, were $221,873; out of this, with the balance from last year, two half-yearly dividends of $80,000 each were paid, and $20,000 was added to the reserve fund, a balance of over $60,000 being carried forward. The profits were quite equal to the average of former years, while the losses were less than usual.

Insurance.

FIRE RECORD.—Brantford, June 23rd.—A fire broke ont in the furniture store of Adam Burgy, caused by the explosion or boiling over of benzine varnish, and spread rapidly. The following, as far as can be ascertained, are the sufferers:—Burgy, insured on building for $1,200 in the Gore Mutual on stock, $1,000 in the Provincial, and $500 in the Royal—nothing saved; loss about $4,000 on stock. John Welsh, shoemaker, shoe store and dwelling; no insurance; loss about $300. Enos Bunnell, grain buyer, insured on building and scales $500 in the Hartford. S. Simons' grocery, adjoining Burgy on east, got very little out; insured in the Home on stock and furniture for $1,000. John W. Downs, owner of building, insured for $1,000 in London Assurance. William Calder, grain dealer, saved most of his stock; insured in Hartford $800, and Liverpool London and Globe $400. Mr. Wilks, on building in the Hartford, $600.

The fine four-story row of brick, called Victoria buildings, was totally destroyed. Owned by the Trust and Loan Company, and insured in the Royal. It was occupied by J. Sayles, saloon keeper, who saved his furniture. J. Hunter, grocer, not much loss. J. Wilkes, insurance agent, got out his papers. Mrs. Wilkie, milliner and dressmaker, suffered a slight loss, and Robert Gorman, boot and shoe-dealer, saved the greater part of his stock; all damage fully covered by $1,200 in the Liverpool & London & Globe, and $800 in the Hartford. On the corner of Colborne and King streets, Mason & Hamilton, druggists, cleared out the bulk of their stock; insured for $2,000 in Commercial Union. The Orange Lodge, on the 3rd floor lost everything. Wesley Howell, grocer, saved a portion of his stock; insured for $2,000 on stock in the Provincial. His loss is about $3,200; the building is owned and insured by Mrs. Wallace for $2,000. A. S. Hardy, barrister, saved his dockets and valuable papers, losing his books; the loss is covered by insurance. The Brant Lodge of Free Masons and Royal Arch Chapter, did not get out a single article, being in the third floor; insured on the organ and furniture for $800 in the Western of Canada, and the Chapter for $350. Hugh Spence, grocer, dwelling over his store, lost everything, not saving even the wearing apparel of the family. Insured on stock in the Home for $1,000. Alfred Cox, watchmaker, got out a good deal of his stock. Loss covered by $400 in the Liverpool, London and Globe. Mr. Craig, grocer—portion saved; no insurance. Mrs. Nolan, milliner; insured for $300 in the Commercial

Union; will cover loss. Hon. E. B. Wood's office was cleaned out, and his valuable library only saved by hard work. No insurance. Building owned by Bank B. N. A. destroyed; insured in Royal for $2,500. The splendid building occupied by Cleghorn & Co., hardware dealers, is a total ruin. They got out a portion of their stock, damaged; insured for $3,000 in Hartford, and $6,000 in Home. Brooks & Wilkes, barristers; insured on library $250; saved a good deal of it, lost their office, furniture and papers. Mr. McKenzie & Griffin, barristers, got out their things without much loss. No insurance. The fire was stopped here; but considerable damage was done to B. G. Tisdale, adjoining, whose loss is covered by insurance. William Ryan, grocer, J. A. Aldred, tailor; Thos. Tune, confectioner; and J. B. King, hatter, occupying the four stores east of Tisdale's, all packed up and moved out. In King street, John Brooke, liquor dealer, stock was got out; he had no insurance, nor had the owner of the building, Mrs. Wallace. Two old wooden buildings, nearly opposite the Brant House, were pulled down; they were occupied by Joseph Wright, shoemaker and George Aird, butcher. Stock insured in Hartford for $250.

NATIONAL LIFE INSURANCE COMPANY OF THE U. S.—It is now about ten months since the establishment of this company, with a capital of a million dollars fully paid up, and we find that the magnitude of business that it transacted in the first nine months of its operations, is altogether unprecedented in the annals of life insurance corporations. The first three months must have been almost wholly sacrificed in preliminary arrangements, and yet at the end of three quarters of a year the company had issued 5,120 policies, insuring the immense sum of $14,537,000, on which the annual premium is $592,128.53. It is confidently expected that by the end of the company's first year(the 1st of August) that it will have issued 2,000 more policies, thus adding about $3,000.000 more to the sum insured, and $250.000 more to its annual income, an achievement which no other company in the world has ever even remotely approached in the first year of its existence.—N. Y. Insurance Journal.

A COMPARISON.—The following is an interesting comparative table on Prussian and American insurance facts, which we find copied into the Monitor, from a Prussian paper.

	All Prussia.	N. Y. State.
1866.		
Value covered by Ins.	$5,440.000,000	$3,929,000,000
Premiums paid	12,054,924	$2,982,000
Fire losses................	8,680,208	23,962,000
Pre. pr. mille of value cov'd	2.22	8.22
Loss pr mille of value cov'd	1.59	6.10
Percentage of loss to pre...	71.07	74.30
Paid up capital...........	5,381,800	19,957,008
Nominal capital...........	20,179,400	39,857,000

It will be seen that the average rate of premiums in Prussia is '22, while in New York it is '82. The losses on $5,440,000,000 of property covered were $8,630,208; and in New York, $23,-962,000, on a value of only $3,929,000,000, or about three times as great.

—The steamer Her Majesty met with an accident to her hull, at Pictou, on her down trip to Halifax from the anchor of another vessel. The damage was soon repaired, and, with the consent of the underwriters she proceeded on her voyage.

—The barque Niagara from Greenock to Montreal and Hamilton, with a cargo of iron is reported abandoned at sea. She was owned by Mr. McAllister, of Windsor, and is said to be insured in the Provincial for $5,000.

—The following is a correct list of the insurance on the ill-fated Queen of the Lakes, which was destroyed by fire at Marquette, Lake Superior: Underwriters, $8,000; Security, of New York, $3,000; Home, of New Haven, $3,500; Roger Williams, $2,500; National, of Boston, $2,000; total insurance, $20,000.

—Chatham has decided to purchase a steam fire engine.

Commercial.

—The following quantities of dry goods were imported into Montreal in the five months ending June 1st:—

	1868.	1869.
Carpets, &c....	367,493	$3,563
Cottons................	1,494,811	1,481,543
Hats, Caps, &c............	150,526	123.282
Linen....................	193,701	199,273
Parasols, &c.............	25,898	29,181
Shawls..................	2,726	3,882
Silks, Satins and Velvets..	217,280	202,243
Woollens................	1,127,701	934,310
	$3,285,136	$3,028,277

The total imports at Montreal from the 1st Jan. to the 1st June were $9,001,939, against $7,997,-984 last year, an increase of $1,003.955.

—Mr. Isaac Briggs, of Cananoque, an extensive manufacturer of steel springs has absconded to the States, having liabilities of some $200,000. Great confidence was reposed in his integrity, and this he seems to have basely betrayed by getting the endorsement of his friends on his paper, many of whom it will probably bring to ruin. He owed the Bank of British North America some $55,000.

—It is not generally known that wool-growing in South America has grown into such mammoth proportions as it really has. Even the Australian breeders have cause for alarm from this competition. It is reported on good authority that the number of sheep shorn there exceed 70,000,000. The exports of wool to Europe and this country amounted to about 230,000,000 pounds.

—The estimated tobacco crop for 1868-'69 says the St. Louis Journal of Commerce, in Kentucky, Tennessee, Missouri, Indiana and Illinois, is 120,-000 hogshead. The foreign requirements for the same year are estimated as follows: England, 25,-000 hhds; Spain, 10,000; France, 9,000; Italy, 10,000; North Germany, 15,000; Belgium, 4,500; Mediterranean. 4.000; Portugal, 1,000; other countries, 3,000—a total of 82,000. The home consumption will be about 132,000 hhds.

Toronto Market.

PRODUCE.—An advance of about 2 shillings in flour in Liverpool, has not only given a firm tone to our market, but caused a sharp upward turn in prices, the advance in flour being 40 to 50c., and in wheat 5 to 10cts. The rise is attributed to unfavorable weather in Europe; causing very serious apprehensions respecting the wheat crop. We copy elsewhere from the Mark Lane Express, an account of prospects up to a late date. Wheat.—Receipts—17,000 bush. and 16,000 bush. last week; stock in store on the 21st June, 69,900 bush. The market opened nominal at 93c. and sold up to 97¼ and is held for an advance on that quotation; cars of fall sold at $1, it is firm at that prices. The total business of the week was unusually large. Barley.—Receipts and stocks very light; a car sold at quotations, but the market is now lower and cannot be quoted reliably. Peas.—Receipts light, stock on the 21st 12,300 bush., car loads are worth 74 to 75c. there being buyers at these quotations. Oats.—Receipts light, stock on the 21st 12,700 bush.; car loads sell at 52c. and are firm at that figure. Corn.—Nominal at 80c. in car loads.

FLOUR.—Receipts 2,200 brls., and 1,100 brls. last week. Stock in store on the 21st, only 5,930 brls. The market opened quiet at $4.00 to $4.10 for No. 1 superfine, with considerable sales within the range of these quotations, but subsequently sold up to $4.40 and $4.50, closing firm. Extra sold early in the week at $4.35, but advanced to $4.60 and $4.65. Nothing doing in the other grades, but are nominally higher.

PROVISIONS.—Butter—is dull and nominal; stocks are accumulating in the country. Pork—is firmer, which has led to considerable importations. Eggs—are in fair demand for the home

trade and for export at quotations. Cheese—little doing; prices nominal.

WOOL.—The market has been fairly supplied and the demand is active at 33 to 34c.; some sales of round lots were made at the latter figure; the market closes rather dull.

HIDES.—There is a better feeling this week but no change in prices.

FREIGHTS.—The nominal rates are 3c. U. S. Currency, for grain to Oswewo; 2c. gold to Kingston, by vessels; grain to Montreal, by steamer 6c.; flour 20c., with a good deal going. The Grand Trunk rates to Liverpool are now as follows: flour, 4 shillings sterling; wheat, 8s. 9d. per quarter; boxed meats, 55s per ton.

The following are the Grand Trunk Railway Company's summer rates from Toronto to the undermentioned stations, which came into force on the 19th ult. :—Flour to all Stations from Belleville to Lynn, inclusive 25c ; grain, per 100 lbs 13c ; flour to Prescott, 30c ; grain 15c ; flour to all stations between Island Pond and Portland, inclusive, 75c ; grain, 38c; flour to Boston, 80c gold ; grain 40c ; flour to Halifax, 90c ; flour to St. John, 85c.

Halifax Market.

BREADSTUFFS.—June 15.—In consequence of the reduced state of our stocks of Supers, holders are realizing an advance of 10c. on last week's quotations. The demand continues active, and the markets are quite bare of this description. White Wheats continue in good supply. Sales are effected in small way only at low rates. Consigners would do well to consult their agents here before shipping Extras, as there is no outlet for them, the demand being merely a small local one and stocks are generally in excess. Fancy takes the place of Supers, and is in demand at quotations. Stocks of No. 2's continue light, with good demand. Cornmeal in demand at quotations. Oatmeal—Stocks are large, without inquiry, and tendency still downward. We quote White Wheat Extra $5.75; Fancy $5.50. Supf. $5.30 to $5.40. No. 2, $4.75. Imports from January 1st to June 15th, 1868 and 1869:—

	Brls. Flour.	Brls. Cornmeal
1869..............	70,562	14,880
1868..............	80.607	27,343

WEST INDIA PRODUCE.—Sugars continue inactive at nominal rates. On Tuesday, at auction, a cargo of Demerara Molasses realized 36, 35 and 33, for bbls., tierces, and hhds. (duty paid) respectively, other sales met with no bidders and the general tone of the market is unchanged. Rum is in demand, stocks light.

FISH AND OIL.—We note the arrival of a cargo of Codfish, and expect to see the new crop coming forward in a few days, and be enabled to have quotations on new transactions. Codfish are in active request for local wants. Herring in demand stocks of fat, small. Oils continue nominal, no new lots being offered; the markets are unopened. Stocks of oil are very much reduced.

EXCHANGE.—Bank drafts, London, at 60 days at 12¼ per cent. Montreal, sight, 3¼ per cent. St. John, N.B., 3 per c. prem.—R. C. Hamilton & Co.'s Circular.

Review of the British Corn Trade.

Although the aspect of the wheat varies considerably, it is generally too strong for much corn without some thoroughly dry and warm weather. Should this set in the plant would soon lose its yellow aspect, and we might expect an average yield. In some parts of France the ear begins to show itself, and more rain is greatly feared; prices, therefore, both of wheat and flour, have advanced somewhat in Paris, and still more in some other places. Belgium, Holland and many parts of Germany show the same state of things brought about it would seem, from reports of injury by frosts in Hungary. Whether they will seriously reduce the corn crop we shall be able shortly to judge; but rapeseed has certainly received damage enough to diminish the yield ioning from the past, there seems a probability the character of this season is likely to be imely variable; and, if our blooming period ld be caught by driving rains or frost, we may even worse than in 1867, from the circum- ce of the great abundance of plants. The ares, too, from want of warmth, do not pro-as well as they did, as no growth can be e at night at such a low temperature. There ough therefore, in the present, to check any of plenty, while, in the event of serious re, there is nowhere such an accumulation of ts as to make the British public independent ome supplies. California and the Western is would then be our principle granaries, but would not suffice to fill up the want incurred ne great national failure. Algeria is in full est, with fairer prospects as to quality than . The arrivals off the coast since May were ity-five cargoes, of which six were wheat, teen maize, five barley.—*Mark Lane Express,* 24.

Nova Scotia Coal.

e give the following statements of the coal d and sold in the Province during the years ng September 30, 1866, 1867, and 1868:

	1866.	1867.	1868.
berland Co.	16,449	9,819	10,470
ou County	205,780	132,609	125,034
Breton	379,124	349,649	276,754
l Tons	601,303	492,077	412,258

stern Chronicle.

Cotton.

ie following is a statement showing the stocks otton in Liverpool and London, and also the cs of American and Indian produce ascertain- o be afloat to those ports :—

	1868.	1869.
k in Liverpool, ...bales	648,820	392,130
" London	37,360	71,170
rican cotton afloat	110,000	140,000
an "	441,470	608,850
Total	1,237,650	1,212,150

inancial Chronicle.

Petroleum.

he Titusville *Herald*'s report on the Pennsyl- a region for the month ending May 31st, says: nder a large falling off in the product of the s in the other districts, and but a moderate ee of success in the development of new terri- , there was a considerable decrease in the d under review, and the daily average, as rn by the difference between the stocks at the nning and the close of the month and the ments meantime, was 10,158 barrels or about barrels less than the daily average during l, and an increase of about 375 barrels over iverage for March. The decrease in the oil icts was caused by the gradual failing of the , and by but few of the old wells having been idoed and resuscitated. ie number of wells in process of drilling ased during May, and on June 1st the total ber in all parts of the region was 345, against on the 1st May. There was a decrease in the sanville District, where about 25 wells were leted, while operations were commenced on about 8. On Cherry Tree Run there was a decrease, but in other parts of the region : was no great change. is stock of petroleum did not undergo any rtant change during May. The amount in tankage was decreased about 10,000 barrels, the stock at the wells about 6,000, while the : in wooden storage tanks in the hands of ers, dealers and pipe companies was enlarged t 16,000 barrels. The last named stock ag- ited about 22,850 barrels, and was situated llows: At Oil City 300 barrels, on the Rynd a 1,100, on Cherry Tree Run 1,800, at Petro- Centre 3,400, on the Story Farm 2,850, at r 2,100, on Bull Run 1,000, at Titusville ', and at Pithole 2,900.

Of the amount of unmerchantable oil at the wells, 3,000, barrels, which were included in the stock on May 1st, were not reported on June 1st. There is still eight to ten thousand barrels of the the above quality of oil at the wells, and about 30,000 barrels in iron tankage.

Crops in the States.

With regard to the next cotton crop, the in-creased area of cultivation, the improved imple-ments and better conditioned animals now employed by the planters, and the larger means at the disposal of the latter, leave little doubt that the aggregate attained will approach 3,000,000 bales. Along the Mississippi, from the Red River, through, and in upper Louisiana, a backward season, and protracted cold rains, of which we are having our full share at the North, somewhat darken the prospects of cotton, but it is believed that the augmented planting elsewhere will compensate for the deficiency there. Near Baton Rouge, La., the planters have already begun to scrape out their cotton, and the crops in the adjacent section are very promising. In Georgia, they are rapidly reviving, and the negro laborers, having had their fill of politics, are again heartily at work. In fine, none are likely to be disappointed excepting speculators, who have been counting upon a defi-cient yield for this year, at the South. This favorable return is accompanied by glowing accounts from the cereals in all quarters. The wheat har-vest will be particularly fine both at the South and the West, and the harvest has already com-menced in several counties in Texas. In California, the corn was 18 inches high about the 1st of June. The fruit crop in all parts of the West will be large, and of very fine quality. In New York and Ohio, the apples are thriving admirably, and in Maryland and Deleware peaches are promising. In New Jersey, the crops look well.—*N. Y. Mer-cantile Journal, June 17th.*

WESTERN CANADA

Permanent Building and Savings Society.

DIVIDEND NO. 12.

NOTICE is hereby given, that a Dividend of Five per cent. on the Capital Stock of this Institution has been declared for the half-year ending 25th inst. and that the same will be payable at the Office of the Society, No. 70 Church Street, on and after THURSDAY, the EIGHTH day of JULY next. The Transfer Books will be closed from the 20th to the 30th June, inclusive. By order of the Board. WALTER S. LEE, *Secretary and Treasurer.* Toronto, June 15, 1869.

The Canadian Bank of Commerce.

DIVIDEND No. 4.

NOTICE is hereby given that a Dividend of Four per cent. upon the paid-up capital stock of this institu-tion has been declared for the current half year, and that the same will be payable at the Bank and its Branches on and after FRIDAY, the second day of JULY next. The Transfer Books will be closed from the 16th to the 30th days of June next, both days inclusive. The Annual General Meeting of the Stockholders will be held at the Banking House in this city, on MONDAY, the fifth day of JULY next. Chair to be taken at twelve o'clock, noon, precisely. By order of the Board. R. J. DALLAS, Cashier. Toronto, May 22nd, 1869. 42-td

Bank of Toronto.

DIVIDEND No. 26.

NOTICE is hereby given that a Dividend of Four per cent. for the current half-year, being at the rate of Eight per cent. on the paid up capital of this Bank, has this day been declared, and that the same will be payable at the Bank or its branches on and after FRIDAY, the 2ND DAY OF JULY NEXT. The transfer books will be closed from the fifteenth to the thirtieth of June, both days inclusive. The Annual Meeting of the Shareholders will be held at the Bank on Wednesday, the twenty-first day of July next. The chair to be taken at noon. By order of the Board. G. HAGUE, Cashier. Toronto, May 10th, 1869. 41-td

Canada Permanent Building and Savings Society.

EIGHTEENTH HALF-YEARLY DIVIDEND.

NOTICE is hereby given that a Dividend of Five per cent. on the Capital Stock of this Institution has been declared, for the half-year ending 30th instant, and the same will be payable at the Office of the Society on and after THURSDAY, the EIGHTH day of July next. The Transfer Books will be closed from the 20th to the 30th June, inclusive. By order of the Board. J. HERBERT MASON, Secretary and Treasurer. Toronto, June 10th, 1869. 44-td

Niagara District Bank.

DIVIDEND No. 31.

NOTICE is hereby given, that a DIVIDEND OF FOUR PER CENT. on the paid up capital stock of this Institution, has this day been declared for the current half-year, and that the same will be payable at the Bank on and after THURSDAY, the first day of July next. The Transfer Books will be closed from the 20th to the 30th of June, both days inclusive. By order of the Board. C. M. ARNOLD, Cashier.

Office of the Toronto and Nipissing Railway Company.

A GENERAL MEETING of the subscribers to the Capital Stock of the Toronto and Nipissing Railway Company, will be held at the office of the said Company, No. 46 Front street in the said City of Toronto, on TUESDAY, the 20th day of JULY next, at twelve o'clock noon, for the purpose of electing Directors and organizing the said Company. By order. CHAS. ROBERTSON, *Secretary.* Toronto, June 16.

The European Mail for North America,

WITH WHICH IS INCORPORATED

"WILMER & SMITH'S EUROPEAN TIMES."

(Established in 1843.)

A Full and Complete Summary of

HOME AND FOREIGN NEWS,

Published Weekly for despatch by the Mail Steamer.

THE EUROPEAN MAIL,

FOR North America, with which is incorporated "Wil-mer & Smith's European Times," is published in the interest of the mercantile and general community. In each issue is to be found all the reliable information commercial and general, that can in any way prove of value to our subscribers. The greatest possible care has been, and will continue to be, taken by the Proprietors to obtain, regardless of expense, a faithful record of all market transactions in which our friends are more particularly concerned, up to within three hours of the closing of the Mail. We furnish our readers with quotations of articles staple not generally noted in ordinary lists, of which the follow-ing is an example :—

Articles.	Prices per ton.		Cash discount.
CANADA PLATES			
Staffordshire (in L'pool) f.o.b.	£18 18	6	2½ per ct.
Glamorgan "	19 15	0	"
GALVANIZED IRON—			
Corrugated Stats., 20 gauge f.o.b.	17 0	0	"

The latest shipping intelligence, comprising arrivals, departures, sailings, and loadings, alphabetically arranged, is laid before our subscribers; and the tabular form adopted in the current number will be adhered to through-out—every casualty being regularly noted, and the state of the freight market duly advised. Agricultural, Legal, and Medical news, of interest is given in detail. We publish a list of Military and Naval Stations, and all changes are promptly noticed. The proprietors of the EUROPEAN MAIL urge the great advantages of this Journal, and trust for the friendly co-operation of all who think it of importance that the Old and New World should be more closely associated by those reciprocities resulting from a mutual furtherance of their material interests. The subscription is 52s. or $13 (gold) per annum, pay-able in advance. Sole Agent for Toronto,

A. S. IRVING.

Mercantile.

TORONTO PRICES CURRENT.—JUNE 24, 1869.

Name of Article.	Wholesale Rates.	
Boots and Shoes.	$ c.	$ c.
Mens' Thick Boots	2 05	2 50
" Kip	2 25	3 00
" Calf	3 20	3 70
" Congress Gaiters	1 65	2 50
" Kip Cobourgs	1 20	1 40
Boys' Thick Boots	1 70	1 80
Youths' "	1 40	1 50
Women's Batts	0 95	1 30
" Balmoral	1 20	1 50
" Congress Gaiters	0 90	1 50
Misses' Batts	0 75	1 00
" Balmoral	1 00	1 20
" Congress Gaiters	1 00	1 30
Girls' Batts	0 65	0 85
" Balmoral	0 10	1 05
" Congress Gaiters	0 75	1 10
Children's C. T. Cacks	0 50	0 65
" Gaiters	0 65	0 90
Drugs.		
Aloes Cape	0 12½	0 16
Alum	0 02½	0 03
Borax	0 00	0 00
Camphor, refined	0 65	0 70
Castor Oil	0 16½	0 28
Caustic Soda	0 04½	0 05
Cochineal	0 90	1 00
Cream Tartar	0 30	0 35
Epsom Salts	0 03	0 04
Extract Logwood	0 11	0 12
Gum Arabic, sorts	0 30	0 35
Indigo, Madras	0 90	1 00
Licorice	0 14	0 15
Madder	0 00	0 16
Galls	0 32	0 37
Opium	12 00	13 50
Oxalic Acid	0 20	0 35
Potash, Bi-tart	0 25	0 28
" Bichromate	0 15	0 20
Potass Iodide	3 90	4 50
Senna	0 12½	0 00
Soda Ash	0 02½	0 04
S da Bicarb	0 00	4 00
Tartaric Acid	0 40	0 45
Verdigris	0 35	0 40
Vitriol, Blue	0 08	0 10
Groceries.		
Coffees:		
Java, ℔ lb	0 22@0 23	
Laguayra,	0 17	0 18
Rio	0 15	0 17
Fish:		
Herrings, Lab. split	0 00	0 00
" round	0 00	0 00
" scaled	0 33	0 35
Mackerel, small kitts	1 00	0 00
Loch. Her. wh'e firks	2 50	2 75
" half "	1 25	1 50
White Fish & Trout	0 00	3 50
Salmon, saltwater	14 00	15 00
Dry Cod, ℔ 112 lbs	4 50	5 00
Fruit:		
Raisins, Layers	1 90	2 00
" M R.	1 90	2 00
" Valentias new	0 6	0 6½
Currants, new	0 4½	0 06
" old	0 3½	0 04
Figs	0 11	0 12
Molasses:		
Clayed, ℔ gal	0 00	0 35
Syrups, Standard	0 55	0 76
" Golden	0 59	0 60
Rice:		
Arracan	3 60	4 00
Spices:		
Cassia, whole, ℔ lb	0 00	0 45
Cloves	0 11	0 12
Nutmegs	0 50	0 55
Ginger, ground	0 18	0 23
" Jamaica, root	0 20	0 25
Pepper, black	0 10½	0 11
Pimento	0 08	0 09
Sugars:		
Port Rico, ℔ lb	0 9¾	0 10
Cuba "	0 9	0 9½
Barbadoes (bright)	0 9½	0 34½
Canada Sugar Refine'y, yellow No. 2, 60 ds	0 9½	0 9¾
Yellow, No. 2½	0 9¾	0 9¾
No. 3	0 10	0 10½
Crushed X	0 10¾	0 11
" A	0 11½	0 11½
Ground	0 12½	0 12½
Dry Crushed	0 12	0 12½
Extra Ground	0 13	0 13½
Teas:		
Japan com'n to good	0 48	0 50
" Fine to choicest	0 55	0 60
Colored, com. to fine	0 60	0 70
Congou & Souch'ng	0 42	0 75
Oolong, good to fine	0 50	0 65
Y. Hyson, com to gd	0 47½	0 55
Medium to choice	0 65	0 80
Extra choice	0 85	0 95

Name of Article.	Wholesale Rate.	
Groceries—*Contin'd*	$ c.	$ c.
Gunpowd'r c. to med	55	0 70
" med. to fine	70	0 85
" fine to fins't	85	0 95
Hyson	0 45	0 80
Imperial	0 42	0 80
Tobacco, Manufact'd:		
Can Leaf, ℔ lb 5s & 10s	0 26	0 30
Western Leaf, com	0 25	0 26
" Good	0 27	0 32
" Fine	0 32	0 35
" Bright fine	0 40	0 50
" " choice	0 60	0 75
Hardware.		
Tin (net cash prices)		
Block, ℔ lb	0 35	0 00
Grain	0 30	0 00
Copper:		
Pig	0 23	0 24
Sheet	0 30	0 33
Cut Nails:		
Assorted ¼ Shingles, ℔ 100 lb	2 95	3 00
Shingle alone do	3 15	3 25
Lathe and 5 dy	3 30	3 40
Galvanized Iron:		
Assorted sizes	0 08	0 09
Best No. 24	0 07½	0 00
" 26	0 08	0 08
" 28	0 09	0 09½
Horse Nails:		
Guest's or Griffin's assorted sizes	0 00	0 00
For W. ass'd sizes	0 18	0 19
Patent Hammer'd do	0 17	0 18
Iron (at 4 months):		
Pig—Gartsherrie No1	24 00	25 00
Other brands. No 1	22 00	24 00
" No 2	0 00	0 00
Bar—Scotch, ℔ 100 lb	2 25	2 50
Refined	3 00	3 25
Swedes	5 00	5 50
Hoops—Coopers	3 00	3 25
Band	3 00	3 25
Boiler Plates	3 25	3 50
Canada Plates	3 75	4 00
Union Jack	0 00	0 00
Pontypool	3 25	4 00
Swansea	3 90	4 00
Lead (at 4 months):		
Bar, ℔ 100 lbs	0 06½	0 07
Sheet "	0 08	0 09
Shot	0 07½	0 07¾
Iron Wire (net cash):		
No. 6, ℔ bundle	2 70	2 80
" 9, "	3 10	3 20
" 12, "	3 40	3 50
" 16, "	4 30	4 40
Powder:		
Blasting, Canada	3 50	0 00
FF "	4 25	4 50
FFF "	4 75	5 00
Blasting, English	4 00	5 00
FF loose	5 00	6 00
FFF "	6 00	6 50
Pressed Spikes (4 mos):		
Regular sizes 100	4 00	4 25
Extra "	4 50	5 00
Tin Plates (net cash):		
IC Coke	7 50	8 50
IC Charcoal	8 50	9 00
IX "	10 50	11 00
IXX "	13 50	14 00
DC "	8 00	8 50
DX "	9 50	0 00
Hides & Skins, ℔ lb		
Green rough	0 00	0 05
Green, salt'd & insp'd	0 00	0 06½
Cured	0 00	0 00
Calfskins, green	0 00	0 10
Calfskins, cured	0 00	0 12½
" dry	0 18	0 20
Sheepskins,	1 20	1 60
" country	1 00	1 40
Hops.		
Inferior, ℔ lb	0 00	0 00
Medium	0 00	0 00
Good	0 00	0 00
Fancy	0 00	0 00
Leather, @ (4 mos.) In lots of less than 50 sides, 10 ℔ cent higher.		
Spanish Sole, 1st qual'y heavy, weights ℔ lb	0 21	0 22
Do. 1st qual middle do	0 22	0 23
Do. No. 2, light weights	0 20	0 00
Slaughter heavy	0 00	0 24
Do. light	0 00	0 00
Harness, best	0 25	0 27
" No. 2	0 00	0 00
Upper heavy	0 30	0 32
" light	0 33	0 34

Name of Article.	Wholesale Rates.	
Leather—*Contin'd.*	$ c.	$ c.
Kip Skins, Patna	0 30	0 3[illegible]
French	0 70	0 [illegible]
English	0 65	0 [illegible]
Hemlock Calf (30 to 35 lbs.) per doz	0 50	0 [illegible]
Do. light	0 45	0 5[illegible]
French Calf	1 03	1 [illegible]
Grain & Satn Clt ℔ doz	0 00	0 5[illegible]
Splits, large ℔ lb	0 30	0 3[illegible]
" small	0 23	0 2[illegible]
Enamelled Cow ℔ foot	0 20	0 2[illegible]
Patent	0 20	0 2[illegible]
Pebble Grain	0 15	0 1[illegible]
Buff	0 14	0 1[illegible]
Oils.		
Cod	0 65	0 7[illegible]
Lard, extra	0 00	0 0[illegible]
" No. 1	0 00	0 0[illegible]
" Woollen	0 00	0 0[illegible]
Lubricating, patent	0 00	0 0[illegible]
" Mott's economic	0 30	0 [illegible]
Linseed, raw	0 76	0 8[illegible]
" boiled	0 81	0 8[illegible]
Machinery	0 00	0 0[illegible]
Olive, common, ℔ gal	1 00	1 [illegible]
" salad	1 95	2 2[illegible]
" salad, in bots. qt. ℔ case	3 60	3 7[illegible]
Sesame salad, ℔ gal	1 60	1 7[illegible]
Seal, pale	0 75	0 [illegible]
Spirits Turpentine	0 52½	0 [illegible]
Varnish	0 00	0 [illegible]
Whale	0 00	0 [illegible]
Paints, &c.		
White Lead, genuine in Oil, ℔ 25 lbs	0 00	2 [illegible]
Do. No. 1 "	0 00	2 [illegible]
" 2 "	0 00	1 [illegible]
" 3 "	0 00	1 [illegible]
White Zinc, genuine	3 00	3 [illegible]
White Lead, dry	0 05½	0 [illegible]
Red Lead	0 07½	0 [illegible]
Venetian Red, Eng'h	0 02½	0 [illegible]
Yellow Ochre, Fren'h	0 02½	0 [illegible]
Whiting	0 85	1 [illegible]
Petroleum. (Refined ℔ gal.)		
Water white, car l'd	—	0 [illegible]
" small lots	0 00	0 [illegible]
Straw, by car load	0 00	0 [illegible]
" small lots	0 00	0 [illegible]
Amber, by car load	0 00	0 [illegible]
" small lots	0 00	0 [illegible]
Benzine	0 00	0 [illegible]
Produce.		
Grain:		
Wheat, Spring, 60 lb	0 97	0 [illegible]
" Fall 60 "	1 00	1 [illegible]
Barley 48 "	0 00	0 [illegible]
Peas 60 "	0 65	0 [illegible]
Oats 34 "	0 52	0 [illegible]
Rye 56 "	0 55	0 [illegible]
Seeds:		
Clover, choice 60 "	0 00	0 [illegible]
" com'n 68 "	0 00	0 [illegible]
Timothy, cho'e 4 "	0 00	0 [illegible]
" inf. to good 48 "	0 00	0 [illegible]
Flax 56 "	0 00	0 [illegible]
Flour (per brl.):		
Superior extra	0 00	0 [illegible]
Extra superfine,	4 60	4 [illegible]
Fancy superfine	4 50	4 [illegible]
Superfine No 1	4 45	4 [illegible]
" No. 2	—	—
Oatmeal, (per brl.)	5 50	5 [illegible]
Provisions		
Butter, dairy tub ℔ lb	0 12	0 [illegible]
" store packed	0 10	0 [illegible]
Cheese, new	0 14½	0 [illegible]
Pork, mess, per brl	26 50	27 [illegible]
" prime mess	—	—
" prime	—	—
Bacon, rough	0 12	0 [illegible]
" Cumberl'd cut	0 13	0 [illegible]
" smoked	0 00	0 [illegible]
Hams, in salt	0 12½	0 [illegible]
" smoked	0 14	0 [illegible]
Shoulders, in salt	0 00	0 [illegible]
Lard, in kegs	0 16½	0 [illegible]
Eggs, packed	0 11	0 [illegible]
Beef Hams	0 00	0 [illegible]
Tallow	0 08	0 [illegible]
Hogs dressed, heavy	0 00	0 [illegible]
" medium	0 00	0 [illegible]
" light	0 00	0 [illegible]
Salt, &c.		
American brls	1 35	1 [illegible]
Liverpool coarse	0 00	1 [illegible]
Goderich	0 00	1 [illegible]
Plaster	1 00	0 [illegible]
Water Lime	1 50	[illegible]

p & Candles.		
awford & Co.'s ..	$ c.	$ c.
mperial..........	0 07½	0 08
olden Bar	0 07	0 07½
ilver Bar........	0 07	0 07½
l	0 05	0 05½
l	0 03½	0 03¾
es	0 00	0 11
aes, Liquors, &c.		
ish, per doz. qrts.	2 60	2 65
ness Dub Portr..	2 35	2 40
s:		
Jamaica Rum...	1 80	2 25
uyper's H Gin..	1 55	1 63
h's Old Tom.....	1 90	2 00
a, cases.........	4 00	4 25
h's Old Tom, c...	6 00	6 25
::		
common	1 00	1 25
fine old	2 00	4 00
ry, common	1 00	1 50
medium	1 70	1 80
d pale or golden..	2 50	4 00

Brandy:	$ c.	$ c.
Hennessy's, per gal..	2 30	2 50
Martell's " ..	2 30	2 50
J. Robin & Co.'s " ..	2 25	2 35
Otard, Dupuy & Cos..	2 25	2 35
Brandy, cases........	8 50	9 00
Brandy, com. per c...	4 00	4 50
Whiskey:		
Common 36 u. p......	0 58	0 60
Old Rye	0 77½	0 80
Malt	0 77½	0 80
Toddy	0 77½	0 80
Scotch, per gal........	1 90	2 10
Irish—Kinnahan's c...	7 00	7 50
" Dunnville's Belf't..	6 00	6 25
Wool.		
Fleece, lb............	0 33	0 34
Pulled "............	0 00	0 00
Furs.		
Bear................	0 00	0 00
Beaver, ℘ lb.........	0 00	0 00
Coon	0 00	0 00
Fisher...............	0 00	0 00
Martin...............	0 00	0 00
Mink.................	0 00	0 00
Otter................	0 00	0 00
Spring Rats	0 00	0 00
Fox..................	0 00	0 00

INSURANCE COMPANIES.

ENGLISH.—*Quotations on the London Market.*

of s.	Last Dividend.	Name of Company.	Shares par val £	Amount paid.	Last Sale.
00		Briton Medical and General Life...	10	....	2½
00	7½	Commer'l Union, Fire, Life and Mar.	50	5	5¼
00	8	City of Glasgow	25	2½	4¼
00	9½	Edinburgh Life	100	15	33½
00	5—½ yr	European Life and Guarantee......	2½	11s6	4s.
00	10	Etna Fire and Marine............	10	1½	—
00	5	Guardian	100	50	53¼
00	12	Imperial Fire..................	500	50	352
0	9½	Imperial Life	100	10	17½
00	10	Lancashire Fire and Life.........	20	2	2¾
00	11	Life Association of Scotland......	40	7½	25
62	45s. p. sh	London Assurance Corporation ..	25	12½	48¾
00	5	London and Lancashire Life	10	1	—
04	40	Liverp'l & London & Globe F. & L.	20	2	7½
00	5	National Union Life	5	1	1
00	12½	Northern Fire and Life	100	5	13
)	12 '68, bo 5s.	North British and Mercantile	50	6¼	19½
00	50	Ocean Marine	25	5	17¾
0	£5 12s.	Provident Life..................	100	10	35
...	£4½ p. s.	Phœnix........................	....	....	139½ x d
00	2½—h. yr.	Queen Fire and Life	10	1	21
00	3s. bo. 4s	Royal Insurance................	20	3	6¼
00	10	Scottish Provincial Fire and Life ..	50	2½	5½
00	25	Standard Life	50	12	66 x d
00	5	Star Life	25	1¼	—
		CANADIAN.			℘ c.
00	4	British America Fire and Marine ..	$50	$25	56 57
...	4	Canada Life	...	....	.....
00	12	Montreal Assurance	£50	£5	135
00	3	Provincial Fire and Marine.......	60	11	.....
...	....	Quebec Fire	40	32½	£23 24
...	7	" Marine..................	100	40	85 90
00	4 6 mo's.	Western Assurance..............	40	9	.....

RAILWAYS.	Sha's	Paid	Montr	London
tic and St. Lawrence..............	£100	All.	....	56
o and Lake Huron	20½	"	....	2¾ 3½
do Preference	10	"	....	5 6
Brantt. & Goderich, 6℘c., 1872-3-4..........	100	"	....	66 69
plain and St. Lawrence	....	....	10 11	....
do Pref. 10 ℘ ct....	....	....	80 85	....
Trunk	100	"	13 14	13½
Eq. G. M. Bds. 1 ch. 6℘c........	100	"	....	80
First Preference, 5 ℘ c	100	"	....	44½
Deferred, 3 ℘ ct..	100	"	....	....
Second Pref. Bonds, 5℘c.........	100	"	....	37
do Deferred, 3 ℘ ct.........	100	"	....	....
Third Pref. Stock, 4℘ct.........	100	"	....	28½
do. Deferred, 3 ℘ ct.......	100	"	....	....
Fourth Pref. Stock, 3℘c.........	100	"	....	15½
do. Deferred, 3 ℘ ct.........	100	"	....	...
Western	20½	"	13 14	13½
New	20½	18	....	....
6 ℘ c. Bds, due 1873-76.........	100	All.	....	99
5½℘c Bds. due 1877-78........	100	"	....	92½
e Railway, Halifax, $250, all.....	$250	"	....	....
ern of Canada, 6 ℘c. 1st Pref. Bds..........	100	"	.. .	82 83

EXCHANGE.	Halifax.	Montr'l.	Quebec.	Toronto.
on London, 60 days......				
t or 75 days date...........	12½ 13	9¾ 9½	9½ 9¾	9¾
e do.	11½ 12	8 9	9 9¼	8¾
e, with documents..........	....	8 8½	....	....
on New York................	....	27 27½	27 27½	26¾
e do.	....	27½ 28	27½ 28	....
Drafts do.	....	par	27½ 28	par ½ dis.
....	....	4¾ 4¾	....	4 to 5

STOCK AND BOND REPORT.

The dates of our quotations are as follows:—Toronto, June 23; Montreal, June 21; Quebec, June 19; London, June 5.

NAME.	Shares.	Paid up.	Divid'd last 6 Months	Dividend Day.	CLOSING PRICES. Toronto.	Montre'l	Quebec
BANKS.			℘ ct.				
British North America	$250	All.	3	July and Jan.	Bks closed	Bks cl'd	Bks cl'd
Jacques Cartier..............	50	"	4	1 June, 1 Dec.	106 106½	106½ 107	106 107
Montreal	200	"	6	"	159½ 160	161 162	160 160½
Nationale...................	50	"	4	1 Nov. 1 May.	107 107½	106½ 107	107½ 108
New Brunswick	100	"	....	......	....	...	....
Nova Scotia.................	200	—	7&b$3½	Mar. and Sept.	....	....	....
Du Peuple..................	50	"	4	1 Mar., 1 Sept.	108 108½	108 108	108 108½
Toronto	100	"	4	1 Jan., 1 July.	Bks closed	Bks cl'd	Bks cl'd
Bank of Yarmouth...........	....	....	......	......	....	...	....
Canadian Bank of Com'e......	50	All.	......	......	Bks closed	Bks cl'd	Bks cl'd
City Bank Montreal	80	"	4	1 June, 1 Dec.	98½ 99½	99 100	98½ 99½
Commer'l Bank (St. John)....	100	"	℘ ct.	......	....	....	....
Eastern Townships' Bank.....	50	"	4	1 July, 1 Jan..	....	97½ 98	Bks cl'd
Gore	40	...	none.	1 Jan., 1 July.	37½ 38	38 40	37 40
Halifax Banking Company.....	..	....	......	......	....	....	....
Mechanics' Bank.............	50	All.	4	1 Nov., 1 May.	91½ 92½	91½ 92½	91 92
Merchants' Bank of Canada....	100	"	5	1 Jan., 1 July.	Bks closed	Bks cl'd	Bks cl'd
Merchants' Bank (Halifax)....	....	....	.....	.....	....	....	....
Molson's Bank...............	50	All.	4	1 Apr., 1 Oct.	108½ 109	108½ 109	108½ 109
Niagara District Bank...	100	70	3½	1 Jan., 1 July.	....	....	....
Ontario Bank...............	40	All.	4	1 June, 1 Dec.	96½ 97½	95½ 96½	94½ 95½
People's Bank (Fred'kton)....	100	"	......	......	....	....	....
People's Bank (Halifax)	20	"	7 12 m	......	....	....	....
Quebec Bank	100	"	3½	1 June, 1 Dec.	99½ 100	100 101	100 100½
Royal Canadian Bank	50	60	4	1 Jan., 1 July.	48 50	48 50	45 50
St. Stephens Bank	100	All.	.....	......	....	....	....
Union Bank	100	"	4	1 Jan., 1 July.	Bks closed	Bks cl'd	Bks cl'd
Union Bank (Halifax)........	100	....	7 12 mo	Feb. and Aug.	....	....	. .
MISCELLANEOUS.							
British America Land........	250	44	......	......	....	....	....
British Colonial S. S. Co.....	250	32½	......	......	...	....	...
Canada Company	32½	All.	......	......	....	....	....
Canada Landed Credit Co.....	50	$50	3½	......	78½ 79	....	....
Canada Per. B'ldg Society....	50	All.	5	......	Bks cl'd	....	....
Canada Mining Company.....	4	90	.....	......	....	....	....
Do. Inl'd Steam Nav. Co....	100	All.	15 12m	......	....	97 99	90 100
Do. Glass Company.........	100	"	None.	......	....	40 60	....
Canad'n Loan & Investm't....	25	2½	......	......	....	....	....
Canada Agency	10	¼	......	......	....	....	....
Colonial Securities Co........	...	....	.....	.....	....	....	....
Freehold Building Society.....	100	All.	5	......	115 115½	....	....
Halifax Steamboat Co........	100	"	......	......	....	....	....
Halifax Gas Company........	....	....	......	......	....	....	....
Hamilton Gas Company.......	....	....	.....	......	....	...	....
Huron Copper Bay Co........	4	12	20	......	....	30 45	....
Lake Huron S. and C.........	5	102	......	......	....	....	....
Montreal Mining Consols......	20	$15	......	......	....	3.00 3.10	....
Do. Telegraph Co........	40	All.	5	......	135½ 136	136 137	136 136½
Do. Elevating Co........	00	"	5½	......	....	105 107½	....
Do. City Gas Co.........	40	"	4	15 Mar. 15 Sep.	....	135 136	136 137
Do. City Pass. R. Co.....	50	"	2	......	....	110 112	110 112
Quebec and L. S.	8	$4	......	......	....	...	....
Quebec Gas Co..............	200	All.	4	1 Mar., 1 Sep.	....	...	120 121
Quebec Street R. R..........	50	25	3	......	....	....	90 91
Richelieu Navigation Co......	100	All.	7-12m	1 Jan., 1 July.	...	119 120	119 120
St. Lawrence Glass Company	100	"	....	......	....	80 85	.. ..
St. Lawrence Tow Boat Co....	100	"	......	3 Feb.	...	...	30 35
Tor'to Consumers' Gas Co....	50	"	½ m	1 My Au Mar Fe	106½ 107½	...	106 107
Trust & Loan Co. of U. C.....	20	5	3	......	....	....	.. ..
West'n Canada Bldg Soc'y....	50	All.	5	......	Bks clo ed	....	....

SECURITIES.	London.	Montreal	Quebec	Toronto.
Canadian Gov't Deb. 6 ℘ ct. stg..................	....	103 104	102 103	104½ 105
Do. do. 6 do due Ja. & Jul. 1877-84........	104½ 105½	....	....	....
Do. do. 6 do. Feb. & Aug........	102 104	....	....	....
Do. do. 6 do. Mch. & Sep.........	102 104	....	....	....
Do. do. 5 ℘ ct. cur., 1883	93¾ 94½	92½ 95	90 91	92 93
Do. do. 5 do. stg., 1885	93½ 94	90 92½	90 90½	91 92
Do. do. 7 do. cur.,....................	....	....	......	....
Dominion 6 p. c. 1878 cy.....	....	107½ 108	108 108½	107½ 108
Hamilton Corporation.....	....	....	......	....
Montreal Harbor, 8 ℘ ct. d. 1869..................	..	....	......	....
Do. do. 7 do. 1870....................	....	....	......	....
Do. do. 6½ do. 1883....................	....	102 103	......	102 103
Do do. 6½ do. 1873....................	....	....	......	....
Do. Corporation, 6 ℘ c. 1891	....	96 96½	96½ 97	96 96½
Do. 7 p. c. stock...	....	108½ 110	109 110	109 110
Do. Water Works, 6 ℘ c. stg. 1878............	....	96½ 97½	......	96 96½
Do. do. 6 do. cy. do.	....	....	......	96 97
New Brunswick, 6 ℘ ct., Jan. and July	104 104½	....	......	....
Nova Scotia, 6 ℘ ct., 1875........................	103 104	....	......	....
Ottawa City 6 ℘ c. d. 1880	....	95 97	......	...
Quebec Harbour, 6 ℘ c. d. 1883.	....	....	60	....
Do. do. 7 do. do......................	....	....	65 70	....
Do. do 8 do. 1886....................	....	....	80 85	....
Do. City, 7 ℘ c. d. 1½ years....	....	....	98 98½	....
Do. do. 7 do. 8 do.	....	....	91 92	....
Do. do. 7 do. 4 do.	....	....	94 95	....
Do. Water Works, 7 ℘ ct., 3 years	....	....	97 97½	....
Do. do. 6 do. 1½ do.	....	....	94 95	....
Toronto Corporation	....	94 95	....	....

EDINBURGH LIFE ASSURANCE COMPANY.
FOUNDED 1828.

AMOUNT OF ACCUMULATED AND INVESTED FUNDS—OVER ONE MILLION STERLING.

HEAD OFFICE—EDINBURGH.

PRESIDENT—The Rt. Hon. the Earl of Haddington. MANAGER—D. Maclagan, Esq. SECRETARY—Alex. H. Whytt, Esq.

CANADIAN OFFICE ESTABLISHED 1867. WELLINGTON STREET, TORONTO.

CANADIAN BOARD—Hon. John Hillyard Cameron, M.P., Chairman ; J. W. Gamble, Esq., L. Moffatt, Esq., Hon J. B. Robinson, C. J. Campbell, Esq. David Higgins, Secretary.

THE Edinburgh Life Assurance Company offer to the public the advantages of a Canadian as well as a British Company. They have invested a large amount of money on securities in this country, and the Toronto Local Board have full power, by an Imperial Statute, to take risks, make investments, and settle claims in Canada, without reference to the Head Office, Edinburgh. Some of the old Policies in the Company, which became claims during the past year, were settled by payment of amounts double of those originally insured, in consequence of the large bonuses that accrued on the Policies.

Every information that intending assurers may require can be obtained at the Company's Office in Toronto, or at any of the Agencies which have been established in the principal towns in Canada.

J. HILLYARD CAMERON, CHAIRMAN. (30-1y) DAVID HIGGINS, SECRETARY.

NATIONAL LIFE INSURANCE COMPANY
OF THE
UNITED STATES OF AMERICA.
CHARTERED BY SPECIAL ACT OF CONGRESS.

CASH CAPITAL. $1,000,000. PAID IN FULL.

CANADIAN BOARD OF REFERENCE :

Hon. LUTHER H. HOLTON, M.P. H. A. NELSON, Esq., Messrs. Nelson & Wood.
MICHAEL P. RYAN, Esq., M.P., Montreal. JACKSON RAE, Esq., Cashier Merchants' Bank.
GILMAN CHENEY, Esq., Manager Canadian Express CHAMPION BROWN, Esq., of Messrs. Brown &
Company. Childs.

SOLICITORS. MEDICAL REFEREE. BANKERS.
Messrs. PERKINS & RAMSAY. JOSEPH H. DRAKE, M.D. THE BANK OF MONTREAL.

This Company has deposited with the Canadian Government the required amount in GOLD, for benefit of Canadian Policyholders.

DOMINION OFFICE — 91 GREAT ST. JAMES STREET, MONTREAL.

CHAS. A. PUTNEY, WILLIAM DOUGLAS, Jr.,
SPECIAL AGENT. GENERAL AGENT, CANADA.

The National Charter, the large Capital, the low rates, the common-sense plan, the definite contract, the honorable and fair dealings, the non-forfeiting policies, the perfect security, the liberal terms of the policies, the Gold Deposit in Canada, render the NATIONAL LIFE ASSURANCE COMPANY of the United States of America worthy of the patronage of every business man.

1-1y C. G. FORTIER, AGENT, Toronto, Ont.

Insurance.

Briton Medical and General Life Association,
with which is united the

BRITANNIA LIFE ASSURANCE COMPANY.

Capital and Invested Funds................£780,000. Sterling.

ANNUAL INCOME, £220,000 STG. :
Yearly increasing at the rate of £25,000 Sterling.

An important and peculiar feature originally introduced by this Company, in applying the periodical uses, so as to make Policies payable during life, without higher rate of premiums being charged, has caused success of the BRITON MEDICAL AND GENERAL to be unparalleled in the history of Life Assurance. Life cies on the Profit Scale become payable during the lifetime of the Assured, thus rendering a Policy of Assurance a source of subsistence in old age, as well as a protection for a wife, and a more valuable security to creditors in the event of early death; and effectually meeting the often felt objection, that persons do not themselves reap the benefit of their own prudence and forethought.

No extra charge made to members of Volunteer Corps for services within the British Provinces.

TORONTO AGENCY, 5 KING ST. WEST.

ap17—9-1yr   JAMES FRASER, Agent.

BEAVER

Mutual Insurance Association.

HEAD OFFICE—60. TORONTO STREET,
TORONTO.

INSURES LIVE STOCK against death from any cause. The only Canadian Company having authority to do this a of business.

...............E. C. CHADWICK, President.
T. O'REILLY, Secretary.   8-1y-25

HOME DISTRICT

Mutual Fire Insurance Company.

ce—North West Cor. Yonge & Adelaide Streets,
TORONTO.—(Up Stairs.)

INSURES Dwelling Houses, Stores, Warehouses, Merchandise, Furniture, &c.

PRESIDENT—The Hon. J. McMURRICH,
VICE-PRESIDENT—JOHN BURNS, Esq.
        JOHN RAINS, Secretary.

AGENTS:
D. WRIGHT, Esq., Hamilton; FRANCIS STEVENS, Esq., Barrie; Messrs. GIBBS & BRO., Oshawa.   8-1y

THE PRINCE EDWARD COUNTY

Mutual Fire Insurance Company.

HEAD OFFICE,—PICTON, ONTARIO.

President, L. B. STINSON : Vice-President, WM. DELONG. Directors: W. A. Richards, James Johnson, James Cavan, W. Buttan, H. A. McFaul,—Secretary, John Twigg; Treasurer, David Barkel; Solicitor, M. J. Fitzgerald.

THIS Company is established upon strictly Mutual principles, insuring farming and isolated property, (not villous), in Townships only, and offers great advantages insurers, at low rates for five years, without the expense renewal.

Picton, June 17, 1869   9-1y

Fire and Marine Assurance.

THE BRITISH AMERICA
ASSURANCE COMPANY.
HEAD OFFICE:
CORNER OF CHURCH AND COURT STREETS.
TORONTO.

BOARD OF DIRECTION :
G. W. Allan, M.L.C.,   A. Joseph, Esq.,
George J. Boyd, Esq.,   Peter Paterson, Esq.,
Jas. W. Cayley,   G. P. Ridout, Esq.,
Richard S. Cassels, Esq.,   E. H. Rutherford, Esq.,
        Thomas O. Street, Esq.

Governor:
GEORGE PERCIVAL RIDOUT, Esq.
Deputy Governor:
PETER PATERSON, Esq.
Fire Inspector: Marine Inspector:
ROBT O'BRIEN.   CAPT. R. COURNEEN.

Insurances granted on all descriptions of property against loss and damage by fire and the perils of inland navigation.
Agencies established in the principal cities, towns, and places of shipment throughout the Province.
        THOS. WM. BIRCHALL,
9-1y   Managing Director.

Insurance.

Reliance Mutual Life Assurance Society
OF LONDON, ENGLAND. Established 1840.

Head Office for the Dominion of Canada:
181 ST. JAMES STREET, MONTREAL.

DIRECTORS—Walter Shanly, Esq., M.P.; Duncan Macdonald, Esq.; George Winks, Esq., W. H. Hingston, Esq., M.D., L.R.C.S.

RESIDENT SECRETARY—James Grant.

Parties intending to assure their lives, are invited to peruse the Society's prospectus, which embraces several entirely new and interesting features in Life Assurance. Copies can be had on application at the Head Office, or at any of the Agencies.

JAS. GRANT, Resident Secretary.
Agents wanted in unrepresented districts.   49-1y

The Gore District Mutual Fire Insurance Company

GRANTS INSURANCES on all descriptions of Property against Loss or Damage by FIRE. It is the only Mutual Fire Insurance Company which assesses its Policies yearly from their respective dates; and the average yearly cost of insurance in it, for the past three and a half years, has been nearly TWENTY CENTS IN THE DOLLAR less than what it would have been in an ordinary Proprietary Company.

THOS. M. SIMONS, Secretary & Treasurer.
ROBT. McLEAN, Inspector of Agencies.
Galt, 26th Nov., 1868.   15-1y

Canada Life Assurance Company.

SPECIALLY LICENSED BY THE GOVERNMENT OF CANADA.

ESTABLISHED 1847.

CAPITAL........A MILLION DOLLARS.

DEPOSIT WITH GOVERNMENT, $50,000.

The success of the Company may be judged of by the fact that during the financial year, to the 30th April, 1869, the gross number of

NEW POLICIES

ISSUED WAS

8 9 2 1

FOR ASSURANCES OF
$1,257,734,

WITH

ANNUAL PREMIUMS OF
$49,183.73.

Rates lower than those of British or Foreign Offices, and every advantage offered which safety and liberality can afford.

A. G. RAMSAY, Manager.
E. BRADBURNE, Agent,
May 26.   1y   Toronto Street.

Queen Fire and Life Insurance Company,
OF LIVERPOOL AND LONDON,
ACCEPTS ALL ORDINARY FIRE RISKS
on the most favorable terms.

LIFE RISKS
Will be taken on terms that will compare favorably with other Companies.

CAPITAL, ...£2,000,000 Stg.
CANADA BRANCH OFFICE—Exchange Buildings, Montreal.
Resident Secretary and General Agent,
A. MACKENZIE FORBES,
13 St. Sacrament St., Merchants' Exchange, Montreal.
WM. ROWLAND, Agent, Toronto.   1-1y

THE AGRICULTURAL
Mutual Assurance Association of Canada.
HEAD OFFICE.......................LONDON, ONT.
A purely Farmers' Company. Licensed by the Government of Canada.

Capital, 1st January, 1869...............................$280,183 82
Cash and Cash Items, over.........................$80,000 00
No. of Policies in force............................30,624 00

THIS Company insures nothing more dangerous than Farm property. Its rates are as low as any well-established Company in the Dominion; and lower than those of a great many. It is largely patronised, and continues to grow in public favor.

For insurance apply to any of the Agents or address the Secretary, London, Ontario.
London, 2nd Nov., 1868.   13-1y.

Insurance.

The Waterloo County Mutual Fire Insurance Company.

HEAD OFFICE: WATERLOO, ONTARIO.
ESTABLISHED 1863.

THE business of the Company is divided into three separate and distinct branches, the

VILLAGE, FARM, AND MANUFACTURES.

Each Branch paying its own losses and its just proportion of the managing expenses of the Company.
C. M. TAYLOR, Sec.   M. SPRINGER, M.M.P., Pres.
J. HUGHES, Inspector.   15-yr

Lancashire Insurance Company.
FIRE RISKS
CAPITAL,...................£2,000,000 Sterling

Taken at reasonable rates of premium, and
ALL LOSSES SETTLED PROMPTLY,
By the undersigned, without reference elsewhere.
S. C. DUNCAN-CLARK & CO.,
General Agents for Ontario,
25-1y   N. W. Cor. of King & Church Sts., Toronto.

Western Assurance Company.
INCORPORATED 1851.
CAPITAL, ... $400,000.
FIRE AND MARINE.
HEAD OFFICE.............TORONTO, ONTARIO.

DIRECTORS:
Hon. JNO. McMURRICH, President.
        CHARLES MAGRATH, Vice-President.
A. M. SMITH, Esq.   JOHN FISKEN, Esq.
ROBERT BEATY, Esq.   ALEX. MANNING, Esq.
JAMES MICHIE, Esq.   N. BARNHART, Esq.
        R. J. DALLAS, Esq.

B. HALDAN, Secretary.
J. MAUGHAN, Jr., Assistant Secretary.
WM. BLIGHT, Fire Inspector.
CAPT. G. T. DOUGLAS, Marine Inspector.
JAMES PRINGLE, General Agent.

Insurances effected at the lowest current rates on Buildings, Merchandise, and other property, against loss or damage by fire.
On Hull, Cargo and Freight against the perils of inland Navigation.
On Cargo Risks with the Maritime Provinces by sail or steam.
On Cargoes by steamers to and from British Ports.
WESTERN ASSURANCE COMPANY'S OFFICE,
TORONTO, 1st April, 1869 }   33-1y

The Victoria Mutual
FIRE INSURANCE COMPANY OF CANADA.
Insures only Non-Hazardous Property, at Low Rates.
BUSINESS STRICTLY MUTUAL.
GEORGE H. MILLS, President.
W. D. BOOKER, Secretary.
HEAD OFFICE ....HAMILTON, ONTARIO.
aug 15-1yr

North British and Mercantile Insurance Company.

Established 1809.

HEAD OFFICE, CANADA   MONTREAL,

TORONTO BRANCH:
LOCAL OFFICES, NOS. 4 & 6 WELLINGTON STREET.
Fire Department.   R. N. GOOCH, Agent.
Life Department.   H. L. HIME, Agent.

Imperial Fire Insurance Company
OF LONDON.
No. 1 OLD BROAD STREET, AND 16 PALL MALL.
ESTABLISHED 1803.
Canada General Agency,
RINTOUL BROS.,
24 St. Sacrament Street.
JAMES E. SMITH, Agent,
Toronto, Corner Church and Colborne Streets.

PUBLISHED AT THE OFFICE OF THE MONETARY TIMES, No. 60 CHURCH STREET.
PRINTED AT THE DAILY TELEGRAPH PUBLISHING HOUSE, BAY STREET, CORNER OF KING.

QUEEN INSURANCE COMPANY.

ANNUAL REPORT

AND

QUINQUENNIAL LIFE INVESTIGATION.

THE REPORT AND ACCOUNTS for the year 1868, presented to the Shareholders at the ANNUAL MEETING, on Thursday, 27th May, 186. at which BERNARD HALL, Esq., Chairman of the Company, presided, showed, in the

LIFE BRANCH,

That 565 POLICIES had been completed and issued, insuring the sum of	£235,246
Yielding in NEW PREMIUMS	6,697
That there was ADDED TO THE LIFE FUND a sum equal to 69 per cent. of the Net Premiums, viz.	25,313
Increasing that FUND from £84,840 to	110,153

The Actuary, in his Report to the Directors on the results of the last five years, remarks as follows :—

"As in the case of my investigation for the period ending in 1863, the calculations were based upon the Carlisle bills of mortality, and upon th assumption that not more 3 per cent. interest would be realized on the Life Premium accumulations. Further, all loadings were discarded, the pu Premiums only being taken into consideration ; and when extra rates had been charged, for foreign residence or any other cause, the office ages wer fixed accordingly.

"It is, I believe, mainly owing to the publicity given to the searching nature of our first investigation that, during the period under review, th new business transacted by the Company has attained its present magnitude. The amount assured was £1,412,466, as compared with £718,385 assure during our first quinquennium ; and the new Premiums were £40,400, as contrasted with £21,292, while the life fund, which at the close of the firs quinquennium stood at £29,339, had increased at the close of the second to £110,153."

IN THE
FIRE BRANCH,

That the PREMIUMS for 1868, after deducting re-insurances, amounted to.	£122,129
Being an INCREASE of	18,141

on the Net income of 1867.

A portion of the Balance at the disposal of the Shareholders was appropriated in payment of a Dividend of 7 per cent. The Fire Reserved Fund was increased to £80,000 by the addition of £4,571. And the sum of £3,133 was carried forward to next year's Accounts.

A Bonus averaging 40 per cent. of the Premiums paid was declared to holders of ordinary Participating Life Policies

THE INCOME OF THE COMANY WAS SHOWN TO BE	**£217,876**
AND THE FUNDS IN HAND	**433,464**

J. MONCRIEFF WILSON, Actuary and Manager.   THOS. W. THOMSON, Sub-Manager.
JOS. K. RUMFORD, Res. Secretary, London.

A. McKENZIE FORBES,
General Agent, Montreal.

WM. ROWLAND, Agent, Toronto.   F. B. BEDDOME, Agent, London.   McKENZIE & McKAY, Agents, Hamilton.

THE CANADIAN

MONETARY TIMES

AND

INSURANCE CHRONICLE.

:VOTED TO FINANCE, COMMERCE, INSURANCE, BANKS, RAILWAYS, NAVIGATION, MINES, INVESTMENT, PUBLIC COMPANIES, AND JOINT STOCK ENTERPRISE.

| II—NO. 46. | TORONTO, THURSDAY, JULY 1, 1869. | SUBSCRIPTION { 2 A YEAR. |

Mercantile.

J. B. Boustead.
SION and Commission Merchant. Hops bought
sold on Commission. 82 Front St., Toronto.

John Boyd & Co.
.ESALE Grocers and Commission Merchants,
unt St., Toronto.

Childs & Hamilton.
FACTURERS and Wholesale Dealers in Boots
i Shoes, No. 7 Wellington Street East, Toronto.
28

L. Coffee & Co.
'CE and Commission Merchants, No. 2 Manning's
.k, Front St., Toronto, Ont. Advances made on
ents of Produce.

Candee & Co.,
ERS AND BROKERS, dealers in Gold and Silver
, Government Securities, &c., Corner Main and
s Streets, Buffalo, Y. N.   21-1y

John Fisken & Co.
OIL' and Commission Merchants, Yonge St.,
onto, Ont.

W. & R. Griffith.
'ERS of Teas, Wines, etc. Ontario Chambers,
Church and Front Sts., Toronto.

Guudry and Langley,
TECTS AND CIVIL ENGINEERS, Building Sur-
s and Valuators. Office corner of King and Jordan
Toronto.
IAS GUNDRY.   HENRY LANGLEY.

Lyman & McNab.
ESALE Hardware Merchants, Toronto, Ontario.

W. D. Matthews & Co.
CE Commission Merchants, Old Corn Exchange,
ront St. East, Toronto Ont.

A. C. Hamilton & Co.
CE Commission Merchants, 119 Lower Water
Halifax, Nova Scotia.

H. Nerlich & Co.,
ERS of French, German, English and American
loods, Cigars, and Leaf Tobaccos, No. 2 Adelaide
est, Toronto.   15

Parson Bros.,
.EUM Refiners, and Wholesale dealers in Lamps,
neys, etc. Wareooms 51 Front St. Refinery cor.
Don sts., Toronto.

Reford & Dillon.
ERS of Groceries, Wellington Street, Toronto,
o.

C. P. Reid & Co.
ERS and Dealers in Wines, Liquors, Cigars and
'obacco, Wellington Street, Toronto.   28.

W. Rowland & Co.,
E BROKERS and General Commission Mer-
Advances made on Consignments. Corner
d Front streets, Toronto,

Sessions, Turner, & Cooper.
ACTURERS, Importers and Wholesale Dealer
ots and Shoes, Leather Findings, etc., 8 Wel-
West, Toronto, Ont

Sylvester, Bro. & Hickman,
ICIAL Brokers and Vessel Agents. Office—No.
:rio Chambers, [Corner Front and Church S s.,
24tn

Insurance.

FIRE RE-INSURANCE FUND.

The following is from advance sheets of Superintendent Barnes' report on the Insurance business
of the State of New York, for 1868:—

One of the most flexible items in Fire Insurance
statements has generally been the re-insurance
reserve. Before the organization of the Insurance
Department, many sanguine officers were accustomed entirely to ignore the future probable loss
on their existing policies as creating any kind of
liability to be recognized on the debit side of their
accounts; and the unearned premiums received,
as well as the funds applicable to the payment of
fixed and absolute debts, were coolly set down on
the credit side as surplus assets. The Comptrollers'
Insurance Reports for the years 1853, 1854, 1855,
1856 and 1857, were all made on this theory. In
1855 the Superintendent, as a special Commissioner under Comptroller James M. Cook, examined several fraudulent organizations in the City
of New York; the special reports in these cases
first introduced the practice of charging among
the liabilities the unearned premium or sum
necessary to re-insure all outstanding risks. In
the Comptroller's Insurance Report for 1855, this
liability was recognized for the first time, and was
fixed at an average of forty per cent. of the premiums received on unexpired risks. The same
rule was necessarily pursued in the Superintendent's
first annual report for the calendar year 1859.

In the Superintendent's Reports for the years
1860, 1861, 1862, 1863 and 1864, re-insurance was
carried inside (as a check) at fifty per cent. of the
premiums on unexpired risks, but was carried outside and into the column of Liabilities, at the
sum estimated therefor by the officers, which was
generally forty per cent. of unexpired premiums.
Some companies, however, especially those with
impaired capitals, estimated this liability at less
than this standard, and considerable dissatisfaction was created in consequence of allowing this
discretion to the officers, resulting, as was evident,
in several under-estimates. Under these circumstances, and an Act having been passed inhibiting
the declaration of any dividend without a reservation of at least fifty per cent. of the premiums on
unexpired risks, the standard for re-insurance was
fixed at this percentage, throwing inside for information the company's own estimate. The insurance Reports for the calendar years 1865, 1866 and
1867, were made upon this rule. The fifty per
cent. uniform standard, however, failed to give
entire satisfaction. The Executive Committee of
the National Board of Fire Underwriters, at their
Chicago meeting in October, 1868, recommended
to the Supervising insurance officers of the several
States the adoption of forty per cent. of the gross
premiums received on Fire risks during the year
as a proper Fire re-insurance reserve.

This rule operates well in many cases, but in
others it is grossly erroneous or insufficient. In
order to show its practical effect, and to compare
the re-insurance funds of the different companies,
a Table has been prepared showing the application
of the forty per cent. premium-income rule, the
company's own estimate, and the amount charged
to each company by the Department standard, as
per the statements for 1868. In revising the Fire

blank last year, it was determined, after considerable examination and consultation with insurance
officers, to fix the standard at one-half of the premiums received and receivable on Fire risks running less than one year, and at pro rula rates for
longer Fire risks, inland risks to be charged at
one-half the premium, and Marine risks at the
full amount of premiums thereon. This mode of
estimating re-insurance is considered the best yet
devised, as being the most accurate and well
adapted to the peculiar situation of any and all
companies. In addition to the percentage of the
deposit or principal returnable on perpetual fire
risks, one-half of the interest premium on sum
received or receivable thereon for the current year
is charged to the company.

PRUDENTIAL INSURANCE COMPANY.

Hon. Elizur Wright has supplied a paper to
the Insurance Times on British Life Insurance,
in which he takes the above company severely to
task. "Their advertisement," he says, "which
expatiates with much rose-color on the advantages of their new style of policy, is signed by
Henry Harben, Sec. This is the same irrepressible gentleman, and the same prudential society
which received, in 1864, a first-rate notice from
Mr. Gladstone. In that remarkable speech of
Mr. Gladstone, I find the following words in regard to the balance-sheet of this society, in addition to those quoted in my report :—'As it stands,
it presents a balance of £41,000 in favor of the
society, but it has been examined by actuaries,
and these gentlemen, proceeding upon principles
which are no more open to question than a proposition in Euclid, say, that instead of a balance of
£41,000 in favor of, there is one of £30,000
against the society. There was, it is true, a capital of £45,000 not paid up, and which, if paid
up, would undoubtedly more than liquidate this
balance ; but all I can say is, that in 1861, when
its balance-sheet was published, it did not appear
to be in contemplation to demand that it should
be paid up, and the account stands as I have
said."

"According to their highly delusive balance
sheet, the balance in favor of the society has
arisen to three times that claimed in 1861, and is
entered in this curious and peculiar phraseology:
'Surplus available for future bonus, subject to revalu-
tion of policies........... £124,515 8s. 7d.'
The cause of the queer little cloud of uncertainty
which is left hanging over this interesting item,
will be explained by and by.

"The directors' report informs us that besides
swallowing up 'a small but most respectable company,' with a premium income amounting to
£15,375 15s. 9d. per annum,' the society has
realized a premium income on its own business of
£220,978 5s. 10d. during the last year, and
has paid claims during the year amounting to
$67,181 10s. 5d., 'raising the total disbursed
under this head since the establishment of the
company to £480,986 18s. 3d.;' yet it does not
state the amount of the policies outstanding,
neither can I find that statement in the company's
advertisement or in the enthusiastic report of its
annual meeting. A company dealing principally
in ordinary whole-life policies, and receiving premiums, which, as it appears from this report,

arc, on the whole, equivalent to the Carlisle net at 3 per cent., loaded 21.77 per cent. to the amount of £220,978 per annum, would necessarily have about £7,500,000 insured, and with a pretty regular growth from 1848, reserving by Carlisle 3 per cent., should have a premium reserve of about £600,000, probably more rather than less. The whole actual fund which it claims to have is £241,361 12s. 4d. It is true that outside of the 'balance-sheet,' the directors speak of a 'Proprietors' Fund Account, amounting to £45,449 14s. 6d.,' which swells the 'assets' to £286,751 6s. 10d.; but if this fund had any existence, it must have been 'paid up' since Mr. Gladstone's speech, and it would appear on both sides of the 'balance-sheet.' This remarkable sheet, omitting the details of investment in some dozen kinds of antipodal securities, is as follows :

Assurance Fund Accounts, 31st Dec., 1869.

Dr.				
To present value of sums assured as per Actuary's valuation (at Carlisle 3 per cent.,) as on 31st Dec., 1868	£542,033	0	0
Bonus on Policies..........................	36,852	3	9
(Sundry guarantee funds, &c.)............	5,045	0	0
Surplus available for future bonus, subject to revaluation of policies................	134,515	8	7
	£686,445	12	4

Cr.				
*By present value of pure net premiums receivable as per Actuary's valuation (at Carlisle 3 per cent) as on 31st Dec., 1866.	£445,144	0	0
(By investments and cash)................	241,311	12	4
	£686,445	12	4

"Now, supposing the figures of this 'balance-sheet' all perfectly honest and correct, it could not show the condition of the company on the 31st Dec., 1868, because the valuation of the policies was for Dec. 31, 1866, two years earlier, when the premium income, according to Mr. Harben's statement, was £154,000. A very good reason why the authors of such a trick should make the 'surplus' alleged 'subject' to another valuation. But the figures cannot possibly be all honest. If Mr. Harben spoke the truth when he told the annual meeting that the premium income in 1866 was £154,000, and if the relation stated between the premiums and loading in the balance sheet and its note is at all near the truth, it follows that if the policies had all been entered for life at the age of 60, the insurance outstanding Dec. 31, 1866, must have been £2,185,000, and the net present value of it, even if we suppose it all entered that year, could not be less than £1,454,000. If it had all been entered at 40, the sum insured would have been £4,864,000, and its present value at the least £2,274,000. Or, if we suppose it all entered at 20, the sum insured was then £8,468,000, and it present value, by Carlisle 3 per cent., was at least £2,870,000. But the balance sheet debits, as by an actuary's valuation for Dec. 31, 1866, the society, with precisely £542,033 as the present value of the sums assured, with £16,852 3s. 8d. as the present value of the bonus additions. As to the actuary's calculations of the present value of the sums assured, it is pretty obvious that if Mr. Harben gave him the data of policies having a premium income of £154,000, to operate upon, the only mental faculty he could have exercised to reach his result was the will. The Carlisle 3 per cent. table is as stubborn as any other fact, and it proclaims that Mr. Harben and his actuary cannot be reconciled without either dividing the figures of the former or multiplying those of the latter by about 4. In short, and in plain Saxon, somebody has lied for the purpose of converting a huge and fatal deficit into a surplus of £124,515 8s. 7d.

"The false debit of £542,033 is offset by a credit of £445,144 as present value of the 'pure premiums.' Of course the difference £96,889 should be the net value of the policies, and it is curious to observe that this is also within two

*The pure net premiums only were valued, the present value of the loading not taken into account, is £95,567 3s., which is reserved for future bonuses and expenses.

shillings the 'present value of the loading' as given in the note to the directors balance sheet. The Society in 1866, when this marvelous valuation was made, had been running some 18 years, and, according to Mr. Harben's statement, had received during the 10 years immediately preceding, to say nothing of the previous 8 years, £606,- 297 in premiums, of which it appears that about £497,163 must have been 'pure premiums' and out of all this the valuation tells us only £96,889 needs to be on hand ! Mr. Harben says in 1869, on the strength of this valuation in 1866, "we have more than we want." The directors accordingly voted a dividend of 5 per cent to the pure water of the stock, and one of the stockholders, a Mr. Chefferell, whose name would seem to imply that he had faith in figures, argued stoutly that it should be more."

NON-FORFEITURE.

A bill before the New York Legislature providing, in imitation of the admirable example of Massachusetts, for the prevention of forfeiture of policies in any case, was finally rejected. The *Weekly Circular* says that "the money power of the companies opposed to abolishing forfeiture was too strong for the virtue of the promoters of the bill. Some report that the bill was only brought forward by parties who speculated on being bought up."

Be this as it may, the fact remains that the opposition arrayed against the bill was sufficiently strong to prevent its passage. Companies which have made hundreds of thousands by the lapsing of policies are loath to give up, and evidently will not give up, without a struggle, so fruitful a source of surplus revenue. The Mutual Life added millions to its coffers from Southern policy-holders who were cut off by the war from communication with the office or its agents, and thereby was enabled to declare immense dividends to those who were in no sense equitably entitled to them. But an opportunity for plunder and robbery on a scale of such unusual magnitude is not likely to occur again for generations, and those who, instead of insuring for the sake of insurance, invest simply for dividends, as if dividends were the end, aim, endeavor, and all in all of insurance, must henceforth lessen their expectations, or prepare for disappointment.

Except those who have given some attention to the statistics of cancellation of policies by lapsing, no persons have any conception of the large per centage of policies allowed to lapse, as shown in official records. In many cases the losses incurred by policy-holders in this way result from misfortune and consequent inability to make renewal payments, but in a general proportion of instances it is found that the applications were originally obtained through deceptive and illusory promises, or wrested from the hands of unwillingness by ceaseless importunity. In either of these cases if there is any sum remaining over and beyond the amount actually required to keep up the risk, its retention by the company is a wrong which conflicts with the tone and temper of the present age. The party insured is entitled to a full equivalent for every dollar paid in, and the Company is morally, at least, if not legally bound for this equivalent.

The State of Massachusetts enjoy the signal honor of requiring by its statute law that policies be kept in force until the premium is exhausted. The net value of a policy allowed to lapse must be used as a single premium to purchase a term assurance. Some of the New York companies, impressed with the equity of this arrangement, and also as a politic measure, have adopted a similar plan. What they lose by thus surrendering to the assured the amounts which under the old regime they would have appropriated to their own uses, they gain in the confidence and respect of the business community.

What yet remains for these progressive companies to do is to convince the public that a dividend

is an incidental or supplementary affair, and i the primary object of insurance, as might be ferred from the everlasting harping of some of t agents. When the non-forfeiture feature come be generally adopted, dividends will proportic ately diminish. but all right thinking policy-ho ers will enjoy the satisfaction which will ar from the consciousness that they are not fatteni upon the misfortunes of others.—*Baltimore Und writer.*

FIRE RECORD.—The Chaudiere, June 17. H. McCormick's grist mill was destroyed; part the machinery was saved. The building was sured for $4,000 in the Ætna. McCormic stock was insured, says a local paper, for $7,0 in Liverpool & London & Globe, and $1,500 another company. Value of property destroy estimated at $14,000.

Oakville, June 20.—The Presbyterian ma was consumed; insured in Provincial for $300.

Granby, June —The residence of Peter Bas has been destroyed by fire. Insured for $275.

Dalhousie, N. B., June.—A fire partly destr ed a house belonging to the estate of P. Hay insured for $800.

St. Catharines, June 26.—A two-storey fra building on the corner of Ontario street a Cherry Alley, occupied by several families, v destroyed by fire. · Loss about $800.

St. John, N.B., June 23.—Hon. McSeely's s mill was totally destroyed by fire; loss estima at $800,000, insured in Provincial for $300.

—The Norwegian barque *Glenter*, bound Quebec, iron laden, from Greenock, and consigr to Winn & Hallard, Montreal, has been lost Bird Rock. All hands were saved and have rived at Montreal.

THE AVERAGE CLAUSE.—The form of Aver Clause as laid down in Hine's Form Book, bei form No. 64, runs as follows:—"It is understo and agreed that claims under this policy shall o be for such proportion of the whole loss as t amount of this insurance bears to the whole va of the property insured."

A set of policies has recently been issued which the clause reads "amount of the insuran instead of "this insurance."

The value of the property is..............$200,(	
The whole insurance is......................	100,(
And the loss is..............................	10,(

The question is what would be the limit claim upon a $10,000 policy, with the aver clause reading "the insurance" instead of "t insurance." Each contract is, from one poin view, sole and separate, and if it agrees to liable for such proportion of the loss as the in ance bears to the value, it could certainly, un that reading, be made to answer for one-half any loss not exceeding the sum it insured, beca the proportion of "the insurance" is, to the v of the property just one-half ; and for a pa loss such an average clause would be practic inoperative, and the insured could collect whole claim up to the amount of $100,000, bec it is so written in the bond.

Had the average clause been written "this surance" it would have applied as Underwri always intend that clause to apply, and amount of claim would have been limited to s proportion of the whole loss as the whole v bears to the particular policy. This is a very pertant distinction and should be thoroughly derstood by all who use that clause.—*Monitor*

COMPANY LIABLE FOR ACTS OF AGENT.—' doctrine has been again affirmed in a case dec May 14, against the St. Marks Fire Insur Company. This action was brought in the C of Common Pleas, of New York, part 2, term, to recover $2,500 on a policy of insur against fire, issued to E. S. Green. The plai applied for insurance on property in Trenton, Jersey, to an insurance agent named Phillip Trenton. Phillips applied to Mr. Smith, a York agent, who procured the policy from y and transmitted it to Phillips, who de-t to plaintiff, and received from him his the amount of the premium, which was ds paid. Phillips never transmitted the o Smith, and Smith never paid the Com-ough there was some testimony tending that the Company might have charged int of the premium to Smith's account. cy contained a receipt for the amount of ium, and the Court held that the Com-ving placed it in the power of the agent r the policy to the plaintiff with such ttached, the Company became bound by he plaintiff was entitled to recover. The directed to find for the plaintiff the full claimed. It is observable that the term used instead of Broker, and it may be s decision is based upon facts dissimilar that have held the broker procuring e to be the agent of the insured and not ompany.

S BY FIRE IN THE STATES.—The losses hroughout the States for the month of ; under $20,000 in value, or upwards of 00, or upwards of $2,000,000 more than the corresponding month of 1868. Not-ding this great disparity of figures the of the fires of 1868 is still greater than uction of 1869 by $467,000, as will ap-he following statement:

	1868.	1869.
January	$5,494,000	$3,294,000
February	4,399,000	2,637,000
March	2,405,000	2,892,000
April	2,890,000	3,880,000
May	1,812,000	3,830,000
	$17,000,000	$16,533,000

he advantage received in the first three f the current year was lost in the last whilst there was a difference in January, , and March of $3,471,000, that favor-nce has been reduced to $467,000 by the sses of the last two months, which to-nount to $7,710,000.—*N. Y. Insurance*

ts.—It is a practice with the officers of npanies to ask of policy-holders their o vote elections, and to instruct the procure them when issuing policies. thus enabled to put in their own friends rs, and control the entire assets of the The power thus obtained is often A correspondent suggests as a remedy, nent by the Legislature, of a law that hould be cast by the officers to solicit emselves or through others. It would also, to have the following questions a committee of the Legislature of the f the several companies in this city: ount has been paid since the establish-his Company to the officers of the Com-heir relatives, as commissions on future , giving names, dates, and amounts ch? What proportion of the votes for were cast by officers or their friends roxies?

'T BE FOOLED TWICE.—A certain Dutch-er of a small house, had effected an In-it of eight hundred pounds, although n built for much less. The house got n, and the Dutchman then claimed the it for which it had been insured; but of the company refused to pay more ctual value—about 600 pounds. He his dissatisfaction in powerful broken nterlarding his remarks with some choice aths. "If you wish it," said the ac-e insurance company, "we will build e larger and better than the one burned e are positive it can be done for even ix hundred pounds." To this proposi-utchman objected, and was at last com-pelled to take the six hundred pounds. Some weeks after he had received the money, he was called upon by the same agent, who wanted him to take out a policy of life insurance on himself or on his wife. "If you insure your wife's life for £2,000," the agent said, "and she should die, you would have the sum to solace your heart." "You 'surance fellows ish all tiefs!" said the Dutchman. "If I insure my vife, and my vife dies, and if I goes to the office to get my two thousand pounds, do I gits all de money? No, not quite. You will say to me, "She vasn't vert two thousand pounds; she vas vert 'bout six hundred. If you don't like de six hundred pounds, ve vill give you a bigger and better vife!"

Financial.

TORONTO STOCK MARKET.

(Reported by Pellatt & Osler, Brokers.)

The business of the week has been large considering the many transfer books that are closed, and there is a good demand for nearly all securities at quoted rates.

Bank Stock.—There were small sales of Montreal at 161½ and 161¾, closing with buyers at 161½. British is quoted at 104 ex-dividend. There were large sales of Ontario at 95½, 96 96¼ and 97; stock was offering on the 29th at 96¾. Toronto has advanced, sales have been made at 120½ ex-dividend, which rate could readily be had. No sales of Royal Canadian. Commerce sold to a considerable extent at 100 and 100¼ ex-dividend, and there is a fair demand at the latter rate. Buyers have advanced their offers for Gore to 39; little in market. Merchants' has advanced with sales from 108 to 110 ex dividend; there are buyers at the latter rate. Quebec is offering in small lots at par. Buyers offer 108½ for Molsons', no late sales. There are buyers and sellers of City at 98½ and 99 respectively. Sales of Du Peuple were made at 108 which rate could still be obtained for small lots. There were sales of Jacques Cartier at 107, and the stock is in demand. Other banks nominal.

Debentures.—Dominion Stock is offered at 107½ and Canada currency six per cents at 105; no sterling bonds in market. Toronto offering to pay about 7½ per cent. interest. There were sales of County at 99½ and 100 for small lots.

Sundries.—There are buyers of City Gas at 107, none in market. British America Assurance is offering at 57 with buyers at 56. There were small sales of Canada Permanent Building Society at 120½ ex dividend, books closed. No sales of Western Canada Building Society, books closed. No Freehold Building Society in market, buyers have advanced to 116. There are buyers of Montreal Telegraph at 135½ and sellers at 136½. Considerable sales of Canada Landed Credit were made at 78, 78½ and 79, it is asked for at the latter rate. One or two large mortgages were offering at 8 per cent.

ROYAL CANADIAN BANK.

A meeting of delegates appointed at the rural agencies, and of the Toronto shareholders, was held in this city on the 25th June. The President of the Bank, Mr. Metcalfe, occupied the chair. There was a large attendance of delegates and Toronto stock holders.

The CHAIRMAN, in opening the proceedings, said the object of the meeting was that those interested in the affairs of the Bank might have certain statements laid before them, from which they might be able to judge of the condition of the concern, and to come to some conclusion as to what should be done in the future.

The Chairman then read the following report of the state of the financial position of the Bank up to the 19th of June, 1869:—

Capital authorized by Act	$2,000,000 00
" paid up	1,172,613 00
Promissory notes in circulation bearing interest	505,430 00
Balance due other Banks	33,248 94
Cash deposits not bearing interest	202,102 40
Cash deposits bearing interest	422,869 97
Total liabilities	$1,163,711 31

ASSETS.

Coin, &c.	$173,220 91
Real Estate, &c.	13,464 65
Government Securities	128,911 10
Notes on other Banks	47,453 99
Balances due from other Banks	51,939 49
Notes and Bills discounted	1,853,308 82

The Chairman then made a lengthened statement, showing the transactions of the various agencies, from which it appeared that the losses were to the following amounts:—

LOSSES.

Bowmanville	$1,000 00
Brampton	2,000 00
Chatham	1,500 00
Clinton	1,104 53
Cobourg	89,084 00
Fergus	250 00
Galt	Nil.
Goderich	1,932 00
Hamilton	4,493 00
Kingston	32,381 00
Montreal	3,930 00
Newmarket	3,119 29
Paris	14,322 00
Perth	1,497 00
Peterborough	1,160 00
Port Hope	Nil.
Port Credit	Nil.
Seaforth	58,624 00
St. Catharines	Not known.
Stratford	2,600 00
Whitby	2,851 00
Woodstock	7,000 00
Toronto	70,087 00
Ottawa	2,084 61

Total bills discounted	$41,960,598 00
Total loss	300,962 00
Total profit	704,078 00
Total Stock paid up	1,170,438 00
Expenses	236,244 00
Net Profits	467,834 00

The proceedings were very lengthy, occupying most of the afternoon, and were continued in the evening. In answer to an inquiry, the President stated that the overdue bills discounted were now $407,779. It was stated also that the liabilities are being reduced, since the suspension, at the rate of $150,000 a week. The discussion was mostly relative to the affairs of some of the agencies, especially those at Kingston, Seaforth, and Cobourg, and to a large number of personal matters of little consequence to the public. A committee was appointed, which proposed the following gentlemen as the future directors of the company: Peleg Howland, President; J. H. Dumble, J. Crombie, K. Chisholm, J. Taylor, Jos. Gould, J. McGee. The motion for the adoption of the report in favor of these gentlemen was carried by 31 yeas against 23 nays. The proceedings then terminated.

POST OFFICE SAVINGS BANKS.—The returns for May show $729.303.22 to have been in the hands of the Receiver-General on the 30th April. Amount received during May from depositors $84.831; interests paid on closed accounts $519.72; withdrawals during May $43,269.11. In hands of Receiver-General 31st May $771,389.83. The sum of $435,409.05 bears interest at 4 per cent and $333,000 at 5 per cent; bearing no interest $2,980.78

—The Bank of Commerce has opened a branch at Simcoe.

MR. SMALL'S DISMISSAL.

The following is a summary of a correspondence published by Mr. J. C. Small, late Inspector of the Royal Canadian Bank. On the 15th July, Mr. Small received this notice from the Cashier: I am instructed by the Board of Directors to notify you that your service are dispensed with from this date.

Mr. Small considered this short notice and decided to stand on his rights. The Cashier replied, admitting his right of applying to the courts for redress if he thought himself improperly used. On the 27th, Mr. Small addressed the Board as follows: Having consulted my legal advisers, Messrs. Cameron & McMichael, as to the best course to pursue to obtain redress for my summary and wrongful dismissal from the office of Inspector of the Royal Canadian Bank, by the Cashier, Mr. Woodside, under the authority of an alleged resolution of the Board of Directors, I am advised that although an action at law may lie, my covenant to the Bank, will stand in the way of the recovery of substantial damages, and that my best course will be to appeal to a special general meeting of the shareholders of Bank, called in accordance with the 9th Section of the Act of Incorporation. But before taking the necessary steps to procure that meeting, I am advised to state my case for the reconsideration of the Board —and first let me premise, I am not aware of having failed in the slightest degree in the faithful discharge of my duties to the Bank—but without being favored with any official intimation of the ground or cause for my dismissal, am informed by letters of the Cashier, without any previous notification whatever, that my services are no longer required, and so go forth to the world to seek employment with the brand of a discarded servant upon me, and the difficulty of getting employment thus greatly increased. It ought not, therefore, to be matter of wonder, if so deprived of the means of living, I endeavor to set myself right with the shareholders whose interests I have tried to protect, and to manifest that the interests of the Bank are not safe in the hands of those who will dismiss a faithful servant for the discharge of his duty. Not, as I said before, being favored with the ground of my dismissal, I can only look for it in the rumors that are current on the subject, and in the acts of duty I have performed which may have given offence to some of those who sit at the Board of Directors. First, then, as to the rumors—it is said my dismissal was owing to the fact that I had exerted myself to secure the re-election of some members of the Board, and to defeat others. The truth of this rumor I deny. I did not interfere in the election; but, if I had done so, I am advised as a shareholder, I had a perfect right to do so—that I owed no duty to the Directors personally, but was bound to obey their orders as the managing body of the Corporation, which, in all things, I believe, I did —that Directors are only annual trustees, whom to endeavor to change does not amount to treason or breach of duty to the Bank, and would not prevent the efficient discharge of my official duty.

Secondly—it is said—that I connived with the late President, Mr. Smith, to bring about the removal of the Cashier, Mr. Woodside, and to take his place. This, I most emphatically deny—it was never in the remotest degree hinted between Mr. Smith and myself that I should get the Cashier's place, and it did not enter my head. If these rumours had anything to do with the action of the Board in common fairness, and as a matter of business, I should have been informed of them and asked for an explanation then. In the discharge of my duty, has there been anything to give offence to the Directors? I can only recall two things,—my inspection of the Cashier's cash, under the direction of the President, which, if wrong, ought not to have attached any blame to me; but to the President who ordered me to make it—and secondly my report, showing among other things the amount of accommodation enjoyed by individual directors upon the security of notes without endorsers. This report was made as part of and in the discharge of my duty. If the facts stated in it were known to the directors collectively, no harm could be done thereby—if they were not known, then they ought to have been reported, because the accommodation received was in direct violation of sections 5 and 10 of the By-laws of the Bank; and under any circumstances, it was my duty in making my report upon the condition of the affairs of the Bank at the head office, and its management to report the unusual state of things I found existing.

The existence of the matters reported must have been wrong, or the report ought not to have given offence. But was it an offence against the interests of the Bank? If not, why should it have led to my dismissal? And who will boldly affirm that in making that report one thing was stated that in the interests of the shareholders, the depositors, and the public dealing with the bank ought not to have been stated? If an Inspector is not allowed to discharge his duty fearlessly, what use is he? Had his salary not better be saved to the bank? Having done my duty while in the bank faithfully, and having done nothing except this, that I can imagine, that could have given annoyance to the directors, I may fairly be pardoned for adopting it as the reason why I was dismissed; and if so, I have strong and just cause to appeal to a special general meeting of the shareholders from your unjust and harsh treatment of me. I am advised by my legal advisers above referred to, that my dismissal on this ground, and the discounts in favour of directors reported by me as well as other matters referred to in said report, was a mal-administration of the affairs of the bank —properly the subject for a call of a special general meeting—that such meeting must be called by public notice, setting forth the cause of the call and the names of the directors taking part in the mal-administration, and having no feeling of hostility against any member of the Board, and no desire to give publicity to the dealings of any of the directors other than in the way in which my duty called upon me to do; but determined that I shall not be turned upon the world as a man who had misconducted himself, with prospects blighted. I make this statement to you, in the hope that you will right the wrong done me, to some extent, by giving me a certificate under the hand of the Inspector, that I have faithfully and efficiently discharged the duties of Inspector while I was in the employ of the bank—and an additional quarter's salary—and I would request the Board, while considering this proposition, not to forget that my conduct is approved of by members of the Board pecuniarily interested in the bank as shareholders, to an amount greater than the whole stock held by those passing the resolution for my dismissal; and I wish it to be understood that I am writing nothing with the view of giving offence to any. I am merely stating my case, and basing it upon the facts, as I believe them to be in self-justification, and in advocacy of my own rights.

This receipt of the epistle not being acknowledged, Mr. S. on the 30th wrote—"I presume you do not deem the same of sufficient importance to notice; nevertheless, I take the liberty of sending you a copy of the notice which it is my intention to submit to certain of the shareholders with the view of getting their signatures thereto, and for which purpose I will leave town this afternoon."

This stirred up Mr. Metcalfe, who telegraphed--"See me in Toronto before you do anything, and I will endeavour to make things satisfactory."

Mr. S. replied– "In refrence to your telegraph to me of Saturday, on the strength of which I returned from Stratford to Toronto, I have only to say that I can make no arrangement to stay my contemplated action, except that indicated in my letter of the 27th ult, viz; that I am to receive from yourself, as President of the Bank, with the authority of the Board, a certificate that while inspector of the bank I discharged the duties of the position faithfully and efficiently, and the payment of an additional quarter's salary and the su[m] of fifty-nine dollars, to cover my legal and travelling expenses incurred in the matter."

THE SUMMERSIDE (P. E. I.) BANKS.--The[re] appears to be some difficulty between the stockholders and directors of this bank. A number [of] the stock holders have signed a call for a gener[al] meeting to be held on the 15th of June, "to i[n]vestigate all the affairs of the said Bank, in ord[er] to close and wind up all its affairs, or continue th[e] same, if found to be for the benefit of the Shar[e]holders." The President and Directors have issu[ed] a notice setting forth that whereas certain stoc[k]holders, including some of the late directors [of] the Summerside Bank, are circulating false repor[ts] prejudicial to the interests of the said Bank; a[nd] whereas the financial condition of the Bank h[as] of late improved and is now much more satisfacto[ry] than at the period of the last annual meeting and the undersigned President and Directors, co[n]vinced of the stability of said Bank, and desiro[us] of challenging the fullest enquiry into its affair[s] and into the conduct of the present Board [of] Directors, give notice of a general meeting to [be] held on the 23rd of June, "with a view of sati[s]fying all persons interested, that the repor[ts] above referred to are wholly unfounded a[nd] false."

BANK OF ENGLAND.—The return for the wee[k] ending 9th June, shows the following changes compared with those of the previous week:—

	£
An increase of Public Deposits of..........	381,93[illegible]
An increase of Other Deposits of..........	65,031
An increase in Government Securities of....	50,00[illegible]
A decrease of Rest of....................	5,97[illegible]
A decrease of other Securities of............	551,918
An increase of Bullion of	809,86[illegible]
An increase of Notes unemployed..........	1,487,030
Total amount of Notes in circulotion......	22,842,48[illegible]
Ditto of Bullion and Gold and Silver Coin..	23,630,88[illegible]
Bank minimum rate of discount since June 10, 1809..............................	4 per cen[t]

—A writer advocates in the Montreal *Gazette* t[he] adoption of a plan of banking, the counterpart [of] the Bank of England. He proposes that t[he] Bank of Montreal and the Bank of British Nor[th] America should amalgamate under the title of t[he] Bank of Canada, with a capital of twenty-fi[ve] million of dollars, three-fifths of the stock to [be] owned by private proprietors and two-fifths by t[he] government of the Dominion, the latter to be p[aid] for by the deposit of 5 per cent. debentures. T[he] bank to be the sole bank of issue for the Dominio[n], the notes to be legal tender except at the coun[ter] of the bank at the chief place of business, wh[ere] they shall be payable on demand in gold. T[he] bank to be a bank of issue and deposit, but [not] of discount except to the other chartered ban[ks] and government of the Dominion, or on depo[sit] of government securities.

—A counterfeit has appeared on the notes [of] the Government Issue. It is in the shape of a [$1] bill cleverly changed to represent a $4. The w[ord] and figure of the original amount are altered [to] the larger denomination. There are no $4 no[tes] of the Provincial currency.

—A friend who has just returned from a v[isit] to Cape Breton, informs us that the only plac[e in] the whole island where mining operations is at [all] active is Port Caledonia. The Caledonia Co[m]pany have expended between $200,000 and $3[00,]000 in the construction of a new harbor at Glace Bay, and a railway to and from their wo[rks], a distance of about four miles. The place [has] been declared a port of entry under the nam[e of] Port Caledonia. The company are doing a la[rge] business in shipping coal to the States, chiefl[y] Boston.—*Chr.*

—A St. John paper says: The prospectus [of a] company called the "New Brunswick and C[ape] Breton Gold Mining Association," is publish[ed]. The association propose to work at the Wagancook Gold District, Victoria County, N. B.

IE CANADIAN MONETARY TIMES AND INSU-
DE CHRONICLE *is printed every Thursday even-
ind distributed to Subscribers on the following
ving.*

*iblishing office, No. 60 Church-street, 3 doors
ı of Court-street.*

ibscription price—

Canada $2.00 per annum.

England, stg. 10s. per annum.

United States (U.S.Cy.) $3.00 per annum.

*usual advertisements will be charged at the rate
n cents per line, each insertion.*

*ddress all letters to "THE MONETARY TIMES."
iegues, money, orders, &c. should be made pay-
to* J. M. TROUT, *Business Manager, who alone
ithorised to issue receipts for money.*

r All Canadian Subscribers to THE MONETARY
ES *will receive* THE REAL ESTATE JOURNAL
out *further charge.*

he Canadian Monetary Times.

THURSDAY, JULY 1, 1869.

THE CANADIAN CANALS.

VI.

ie promoters of the Caughnawaga Canal
: a clear and distinct end in view, attain-
at a cost which cannot be regarded as
ssive. The scheme stands prominently
ard in connection with the St. Lawrence
gation. Its leading advocates are men
eight and character, who have carefully
ied the question, and whose opinions are
iled to respect. Up to a certain point,
: can be no difference of opinion as to
esults looked for, and possibly they are
iiently strong to exact general support
the work. That is, even the limited
fits attainable—if the phrase is not too
ig, we will add, by common consent—
ar to mark out this work as an actual
ssity. The question is, if the line is not
n somewhat in advance of what really
asible. The object of the canal is to
ect the waters of the St. Lawrence, at
Lake Champlain—itself the head waters of
a tributary of the great river, the Richelieu
which deboucîres at Sorel. The connection is now made by the Chambly Canal.
Lumber for the Albany market, from the
Ottawa, now passes to the north of the
island of Montreal, and proceeds by the St.
Lawrence to Sorel, at which point it ascends
the Richelieu river. One lock only occurs
in this navigation before the Chambly basin
is met—a beautiful sheet of water, at the
base of which, a quarter of a century ago,
stood the old fort, constructed under the
French domination. It was then in good
order, and was used as a garrison, having
been kept in repair by the Imperial Government. It passed into Provincial keeping, at
once to fall into ruin. We mention the site
to assist the memory of those of our readers
whose geography needs to be refreshed. It
is here that the Chambly Canal has been constructed to overcome the rapids which impede the navigation between this spot and St.
John's. The length is 11½ miles ; the locks
are not large—120 by 24 feet, with a depth
of 6 feet. The proposed Caughnawaga Canal
from Lake St. Louis to St. John's would
pass over ground, being the base of the tri-
angle, having its apex at Sorel. A comparison may thus be made :

	Miles.
From a point in the St. Anne's basin of the Ottawa, by the channel north of the island of Montreal, to the St. Lawrence, and by that river to Sorel......	60
By the Richelieu River to Chambly......	45½
Chamby Canal to St. John's..............	11½
	117

On the other hand—

	Miles.
From the above-named point in St. Anne's basin to the Lake St. Louis, at the point proposed as the entry to the Caughnawaga Canal, opposite entry of Lachine Canal...............................	15
Length of proposed canal...................	25½
	40½

Accordingly, by this important water connection about 78 miles of navigation would
be saved. This saving of distance would
lessen the freight of lumber destined from
the west to the New York market. In that
fact alone, therefore, an argument may be
said to lie for the necessity of the canal. It
would appear that the most feasible plan is
to commence the canal above the tier of locks
at the Beauharnois canal. The reports speak
of this work as a navigable feeder. But the
term is a misnomer, and tends to mislead, and
the sooner it is rejected the better. In round
figures, Lake St. Louis—that is the water at
the head of the Lachine canal—is about 30
feet lower than the level of Lake Champlain.
Accordingly, the proposed canal, taking its
origin in the reach of the Beauharnois canal,
and supplied by the waters of the St. Lawrence, would have its main level 37½ feet
above the water of Lake Champlain, to which
it would descend by three locks; whereas five
locks will be needed to fall to the level of
the St. Lawrence, identical, indeed, with the
sortie of the Beauharnois canal. With this
location we have the supply of the St. Lawrence as the fountain head, the canal itself
following a line of country suitable to it, a
line sufficiently direct, a connection given in
the most feasible mode both with the St.
Lawrence proper and with the Ottawa, at a
cost estimated, and we believe fairly, at
from four and a quarter to four and a half
millions of dollars. We are quite prepared
to concede the importance of this work, even
its necessity, but when we come to the consideration of the view that it ought to take
precedence of the development of the St.
Lawrence, we fear we must differ from some
with whom we should prefer to agree.

The present Chambly canal would by no
means be superseded by the proposed canal,
but it would necessarily lose a portion of the
traffic now passing through it, that of the
Ottawa. The Chambly Canal is essential to
the region of the St. Maurice, having its
outlet at Three Rivers which is yearly becoming of more importance. The misfortune
is, that it has not been well managed, and it
is one of those things in which men of astute
intellect and honest intentions are likely to
be over-reached. The limits have fallen into
too few hands, and this monopoly has worked
the usual result in impeding the progress of
the district. We trust, however, that this
will be the fact but for a time. As the Chambly Canal can receive, without delay, all
that may be sent through it, extraordinary
facilities are offered for the transport of
lumber.

Agreeing thoroughly with an anticipation
of the favorable influence the Caughnawaga
Canal would work in the lumber trade, either
from Ottawa, or by the St. Lawrence with Boston and Albany, it remains for us to consider,
this larger and more commercial side of the
question. It is urged that vessels freighted
with grain, from the Western States, will
descend the Saint Lawrence, and passing by
this canal to Lake Champlain, will connect
with the Boston Railway at Burlington.
There the transfer of cargo will take place
to supply the necessities of the Eastern States.
The return trip will be freighted with
New England manufactures. Further, it is
considered that this water communication
will be followed to Whitehall, and thence by
the canal to Albany, superseding the Erie
Canal. We must leave for a future occcasion,
the former view, i. e., the bearing of the
proposed Caughnawaga Canal, on the trade

with the Western States, and Canada, on the one side, with Boston. We will now endeavor to examine the extent of the influence to be exercised over the New York trade.

It must be remembered, in the examination of the canal question, that the end in view of the advocate of a given policy must not be lost sight of. Thus many of the advocates of the Caughnawaga Canal, cannot be brought to contemplate a direct connection between the west and the seaboard. There ever remains the transhipment at Montreal, the break in the navigation, the assumed necessity of a difference of build in vessels navigating the lakes, and vessels sailing on the ocean. We see this view plainly in the reports of the engineers who reported on the project. They name the locks at 230 feet by 36 feet by 10 feet; that is, of course, for a purely river navigation. While consistently advocating the construction of this canal, we would lay down, as a principle, that its locks should be identical with those of the Saint Lawrence Canals. To argue on the capacity suggested, is to some extent to weaken our case; still, for the moment, we are quite content to do so. The readers of these articles must have seen that the connection between Lake Erie and Albany, is by the Erie Canal, or by the Welland Canal to Oswego, by the branch Canal to Syracuse, where the Erie Canal is joined, the time of transit being 11 days. It is argued that the propeller having a new and sufficient connection to Lake Champlain, would abandon this old route. We have only to suppose such a vessel in Lake Champlain, to see how little chance there is of such a consequence. All would be plain sailing until the propeller, needing a lock 230 feet in length, came to the Whitehall Canal. This canal is 67 miles long, and unless the locks have lately been enlarged, they are 90 feet by 15 feet, with 4 feet water. Moreover, we believe, that it is impossible to enlarge this canal to any extent. It is supplied by a feeder from the upper waters of the Hudson, at Glen's Falls; and it is a question whether the supply will admit of any great additional tax. Nothing positive can be said on the subject, without examination of the capabilities at the engineer's command, but we believe that very little additional enlargement can be counted upon. But even were it otherwise, there is every reason to expect great opposition in the State of New York, to such an improvement, especially in the cities of Buffalo, Syracuse, Oswego, and we will add, even Troy, and Whitehall, and Albany, because such propellers, would sail through the entire distance without having any business to transact in these cities. There would be great disinclination to create a rival to the Erie Canal, a State work, bringing in a certain income, and which has cost upwards of $32,000,000. There is the expense of enlarging the present Canal, some ten or fifteen millions of dollars. These various reasons, each one powerful in itself,—in one case to the extent of shewing that the improvement called for is itself impossible,—all tend to establish the view that the Caughnawaga Canal would have no bearing on the New York trade; and, indeed, if that end be put prominently forward as a reason for the construction of this Canal, it may be added that no step should be taken until a satisfactory capacity of the Whitehall Canal be assured by the New York Legislature. But even if it be developed to the theoretical requirement and we have the route perfected to all that fancy can suggest, there is the St. Lawrence, itself, the waters of the river passed over by the propeller *Her Majesty*, furnishing a known result. With a developed navigation and a class of vessels, fitted to it, the propeller could proceed directly to the harbor of New York from Montreal in 9 days. The distance by the Canals and Lake Champlain may be estimated from 6 to 8 days. But we conceive that, practically, all the advantages lie on the side of the longer sea route; because there is no break of bulk, no canal dues, while a larger cargo would be taken than the more contracted vessel could carry, with perfect freedom from charge of brokerage. Moreover, the passage by Nova Scotia, would give the chance of purchasing fuel cheaply. If all this be correct, the advantages of a passage through Lake Champlain to New York, cannot be said to be in any way great.

THE ROYAL CANADIAN BANK.

The next worst thing to indifference is unwise zeal. Neither is commendable; but, perhaps, the latter produces the greater variety of ill consequences. The shareholders of the Royal Canadian are fast proving this. They are, naturally, provoked at the loss of their money. We cannot quarrel with them for displaying some irritation, and we can find excuse for their striking about wildly, hitting many heads in an endeavour to bruise the right one. But the question arises, is such conduct wise; is it calculated to restore the public confidence in their bank? For our part, we are inclined to think that recriminations and abuse are very poor substitutes for earnest work, judicious pruning and the determination to inaugurate a proper state of affairs. Hence we are bound to condemn as unwise in the extreme the recent exhibition of temper at the meeting of delegates in Toronto. Hon. Mr. McDonald allowed himself to be carried away by a desire to avenge himself of his colleagues, and we know with what applause his name was struck from the list of those nominated for the presidency the bank. This action is an indorsement the same rule to themselves, and restraine their vituperative tendencies, for the sake appearances.at least. We have no desire t take sides in the quarrel, for it is essential one of their own making, but we have a interest in its result. The existence of i important institution is at stake, and the lo of a large amount of capital is threatene If the annual meeting is to be but a repetitio of the recriminations and abuse which chara terised the meeting of the 25th, the long it is postponed the better for all concerne

It must be very gratifying to the Cashier know, that amidst so much suspicion, doul and turmoil, his integrity stands unimpeac ed. In answer to any charge of participatio in mismanagement, he may reasonably ur that he has not had a fair chance. We hav indeed, reason to believe, that most of t losses were made through not following h advice. However, as executive officer he h to bear an equal share of blame, and shou be afforded an opportunity of setting hims right with the shareholders.

Apart from these objectionable features the present crisis, there are sufficient reaso for a careful examination into the bank affairs, and a cool estimate of the bank strength.

The figures furnished by the Board of I rectors show the following :—

Total profit .... $794,573 say 60·17 p. c. of present capi
Expenses...... 236,244 " 20·19 p. c.

Net profits...... 467,634
Supposed loss.. 300,962 " 25.77 p. c.

Net profits .... $166,882 " 14·25 p. c.

The total profit has been equal to about 6 per cent. of the present capital, the expen to 20¼, the losses equal to 25¾, and the i profits, according to their own estimate losses, 14¼. The expenses were equal to ? per cent. of the gross profits, the suppo losses 42¾ per cent., and their net profits eq to 23¾ per cent. of their gross profits.

Total Liabilities (ex. stock)......$1,163,711
" Assets, as shewn............ 2,268,298

Apparent surplus.................$1,104,587
Admitted loss....................... 300,962

Available.......................... $803,625

Taking this as a basis, we find that $1,170,488 of paid up capital has an appar value of $803,625, or about 68 per cent. the losses be $600,000, instead of $300,0 the stock would have an apparent valu 49 per cent.

Of course it is impossible to tell exa how affairs stand, without such a thoro investigation at the various agencies as be free from the bias of an interested scruti The necessity for such investigation has b an ; it has been acknowledged also by the poinjment of a Committee of outsiders iose instructions are, we take for granted, satisfy themselves fully. We would have en better pleased if a banker or a profes- mal accountant were on the Committee, irhaps it is not yet too late to procure the rvices of such. If so, we know no one iose name would be more generally accept- le than Mr. Morton of the Bank of Upper nada. He has had just the experience ich is now required to guide and direct a itematic inquiry.

The proposition to fill the Board with per- is resident outside the city seem to us to rour of absurdity. Of course, the share- lders outside the city should have their resentatives at head-quarters ; but to say t the majority of the Board should be out- ers, is to show a very limited acquaintance th the management of Bank affairs. At same time, we admit that a change should made in the Board. In fact, we cannot why the present members should decline retire. The great object to be sought is restoration of public confidence, for with- t that confidence a resumption would be of avail. If a change in the Board be de- nded, it is expedient that even a sacrifice uld be made.

Various names have been mentioned in nnection with the presidency, among others t of Mr. Crawford, M. P. While we nk that Mr. Crawford would make a trust- rthy head for the institution, we find in multiplicity of engagements, as a lawyer i a politician, very serious objections to election, for upon the president and hier necessarily devolves the largest share the bank management, and a president uld not be absent for long periods. Mr. Howland also has been named. We ow of no objection that could be made to n. Mr. Gordon, of the firm of Gordon & Kay, is also spoken of. Both of these ntlemen would hold the money bags tightly d either would make a good president. wever, the selection of a president is a tter for the shareholders themselves to judicate upon But there is no occasion for tion fights. The creation of parties is to deprecated. If the shareholders divide mselves into antagonist bands, whose sole ject is to secure supremacy, the bank had ter be wound up at once. It has had to tend with the intrigues of presidents and e-presidents, the threats and dictation of derlings, private quarrels and public dis- tes, and we know the result. A new era larger disturbances and more extended varting may be entered upon, but it will uredly soon cease. Unless all unite in thering the interests of the bank, resump- n will be an act of folly.

Since the above was in type, we have been informed that Mr. Gordon has expressed his intention to refuse the Presidency, if tendered him. A strong party is working vigorously to secure the election of Messrs. P. Howland, Wm. Gooderham, Junr., and John Macdo- nald, as City Directors, the remainder of the Board being selected from the names put forward at late meeting.

OUR attention has been drawn to the fact that the Western of Canada separated their Inland from their Ocean Marine business in the official returns. The Provincial certainly did not do so, as we find in their last annual report, presented on the 8th June, 1868, the item of $100,366.16 set down as " marine premiums received during the year, ended 30th June, 1868. "

THE unfortunate policy-holders in the In- ternational Life which was swallowed up by the Prudential, will derive little comfort from the expose of the affairs of the latter com- pany given by Elizur Wright, the able In- surance Commissioner, of Massachusetts. The "non-forfeitable, unconditional and unchal- lengeable " policies of the Prudential, have had the gloss rudely rubbed off them by Mr. Wright's actarial analysis of the Company's position.

GEORGIAN BAY CANAL.

A Select Committee of the House of Commons has reported on this project. The committee was composed of the following members :—Robt. A. Harrison, West Toronto, Chairman ; Chas. Con- nell, Carleton, N.B.; Charles Tupper, Cumber- land, N.S.; J. H. Gray, St. John, N. B.; J. G. Blanchet, Levis, P.Q. ; James Beaty, East To- ronto ; James Metcalfe ; Amos Wright, West York ; G. H. Simard, Quebec Centre ; I. H. Masson, Soulanges ; Thos. D. McConkey, Simcoe; J. P. Wells, North York ; W. C. Little, South Simcoe ; George Jackson, South Grey ; Thomas R. Ferguson, Cardwell.

After recounting a number of matters with which the public are already familiar, the Com- mittee state that they have no doubt as to the ex- pediency of the proposed canal. They are satis- fied that, if constructed, it would be of immense value to the commercial and general interests of the Province of Ontario, and of the whole Do- minion of Canada. The interests of Ontario would be greatly promoted by the local expendi- ture and the development of the extensive region of unoccupied land north and west of the canal, and the interests of the Dominion would be ad- vanced by the introduction into the country of the large amount of capital, estimated at forty millions of dollars, required for its construction ; by the encouragement of emigration, and by the completeness of a most important link in the chain of through communication between the great West and the Old World. The canal, if constructed, is it would be wholly within British territory, would be a most important key to the trade of the West, and greatly conduce to the establishment and continuance of reciprocal trade between the Dominion and the United States of America. Independently of these important na- tional, commercial, and social considerations, it

is obvious to the committee that a large accession of revenue must accrue to the Dominion exchequer from the construction of this work, as out of an expenditure of forty millions of dollars, chiefly for imported labor, a large amount would flow into the public chest through the customs and excise. The testimony adduced before the com- mittee has satisfied them that the work is practi- cable in an engineering point of view, but that unless a liberal grant of land be given in aid of the company, the work, in the opinion of the commit- tee, cannot be accomplished.

The following statement of comparative dis- tances by different routes, shows the great saving that will be effected by this canal when con- structed :—

Chicago to Quebec.

Via Lake Erie, the Welland Canal and St. Lawrence	1,550	miles.
Via Huron and Ontario Ship Canal and St. Lawrence	1,180	"
Making a saving of	370	"

Chicago to New York.

Via Lake Erie and Erie Canal	1,504	miles.
Via Lake Erie and Welland Canal and Oswego	1,500	"
Via Huron and Ontario Canal and Oswego	1,225	"

Chicago to Liverpool.

Via Mississippi and New Orleans	6,000	miles.
Via Erie Canal and New York	4,000	"
Via Welland Canal and St. Lawrence	4,180	"
Via Huron and Ontario Canal and St. Lawrence	3,736	"

And it is shown, in the report of the Canal Com- pany's engineer, Mr. Sykes, that by the saving of transhipment, a cargo of 1,000 or 1,200 tons ship- ped at Chicago for Liverpool via the Huron and Ontario Canal, would, under ordinary circum- stances, reach Liverpool before a similar cargo shipped at the same time via the Buffalo and Erie Canal could reach New York.

The relations of the proposed canal to the North West Territory, and the development of that extensive and valuable portion of the Domi- nion, are also, in the opinion of the Committee, additional reasons for the undertaking of the work.

THE OTTAWA SHIP-CANAL.

In the House of Commons Mr. Wright (Ottawa) presented the first report of the select committee on the improvement of the River Ottawa.

It states that the waters comprising the pro- posed line of navigation are as follows:

Ottawa River, Montreal to Matawan	305	miles
Matawan River and Summit Ridge	46	"
Lake Nipissingue	30	"
French River	48	"
Total distance from Montreal to Lake Huron	430	"

In the year 1856, the Commissioner of Public Works obtained from the Legislature an appro- priation for the purpose of exploring and survey- ing the route, a task which they entrusted to Mr. Walter Shanly, civil engineer, who made a gen- eral exploration of the entire line of communica- tion, and actual surveys of the Mattawan River and of those portions of the Upper Ottawa where the greatest difficulties in the way of improvement are to be encountered. The appropriation having been insufficient to meet the expenses of a com- plete survey of the whole route, an order to com- plete the work was issued in May, 1857; but a further appropriation having been asked and ob- tained the following year, the survey was resumed under Mr. T. C. Clark, civil engineer.

The reports of Messrs. Shanly and Clark are on record, and the facts they establish may be summed up as follows:—

That the distance from the mouth of French

River to Montreal is 430 miles. That the saving in distance by this route, as compared with that by the Welland Canal, between Chicago and Montreal is 368 miles. That it is possible to obtain a continuous navigation throughout with a depth of water according to Mr. Shanly's report of 10 feet; and according to Mr. Clark of 12 feet. That the Bay of the French River affords safe and accessible harborage for the largest vessels navigating the Upper Lakes. That an abundant supply of water for all possible purposes can be obtained at the summit. That the total ascent and descent to be overcome by lockage is 698 feet. That the total length of canal required to improve the several obstructive portions of the route, and including the enlargement of the Lachine Canal, will not exceed 58 miles; and the highest estimate (Mr. Shanly's) for the completion of the whole scheme of navigation, providing for locks of 250 feet in length, by 50 feet in width, with 10 feet depth of water, is $24,000,000; while the lower estimate (Mr. Clark's) places the entire cost for a 12 feet navigation at not much over half that amount. It is also shown by the engineering reports referred to, that the saving in time in the round trip of a propeller between Chicago and Montreal, would be about ninety hours less than by the circuitous lake route; and that the cost of transport, not taking into account the great saving in insurance, would be less by fully 10 per cent. on the Ottawa route than on that by Lake Erie.

It is also satisfactorily established that there are no extraordinary engineering difficulties to be overcome in constructing the several canals needed as connecting links between the long stretches of deep water which form the leading feature on the entire length of the chain. At the summit dividing the upper waters of the Matawan from those of Lake Nipissingue, a cut of twenty feet depth and scarce three quarters of a mile in length, would cause the former now tributary to the Ottawa, to change their course and flow through the French River to Lake Huron.

Another feature deserving of remark is that the improvements required are made up of a number of small canals no fewer than 21 separate links in a total of 58 miles; the largest link in the chain being the Lachine canal, 8½ miles long; and while it is admitted that in some places the excavations will be of hard rock. It is also shown that there are no very deep or long cuttings and that the dams which will enter largely into the system of construction can be generally constructed without damage to the surrounding country.

Railway News.

GREAT WESTERN RAILWAY.—Traffic for week ending June 11, 1869.

Passengers	$31,497 22
Freight	39,711 93
Mails and Sundries	1,874 02
Total Receipts for week	$73,083 17
Coresponding week, 1868	60,997 57
Increase	$12,035 60

NORTHERN RAILWAY.—Traffic receipts for week ending June 19th, 1869.

Passengers	$2,961 99
Freight and live stock	14,732 22
Mails and sundries	258 00
	$17,952 21
Corresponding Week of '68.	14,736 32
Increase	$3,215 89

UNION PACIFIC.—It is reported that at the meeting of the Union Pacific Railroad Company, held at Boston recently, the balance of the first mortgage bonds of the Company, and also $10,000,000 of land-grant bonds, were taken by the stockholders. The proceeds of this sale will enable the Company to pay all their floating liabilities, build a branch toad to Denver, and fully equip the maie track with all the rolling stock needed, and have a balance in the treasury.—*U. S. R. R. Journal.*

—Mr. C. D. Fox, the engineer of the Narrow Gauge Railway Companies arrived here on the 25th June from England. The survey of the Toronto and Nipissing line has commenced.

— About forty navvies on the Frederickton branch railway struck for 5 cents advance per day increase in wages.

RAILWAY TRAFFIC RETURNS.

FOR THE MONTH OF MAY, 1869.

NAMES OF THE RAILWAYS.	Passengers.	Mails and Sundries.	Freight.	Total 1869.	Total 1868.	Miles in Operation, 1869.	Miles in Operation, 1868.
		$	$	$	$		
Great Western Railway	117183	10017	167458	294658	280008	351½	351½
Grand Trunk Railway	260449	32000	444468	736917	640824	1377	1377
London and Port Stanley Railway	1716	107	1548	3371	3642	24½	24½
Welland Railway	1236	1624	6341	9201	10793	25	25
Northern Railway	14231	5064	62501	81906	74671	97	97
Port Hope, Lindsay, and Beaverton Railway, and Peterborough Branch	3437	247	20779	24463	27273	56	56
Cobourg, Peterborough and Marmora Railway	36	......	6104	6140	3860	22	22
Brockville and Ottawa Railway	4411	101	14832	19344	16556	86	86
St. Lawrence and Ottawa Railway	7010	1078	6000	14088	10263	54	54
Carillon and Grenville Railway*	......	......	......	......	......	......	......
Stanstead, Shefford & Chambly Rail'y*	......	......	......	......	......	......	......
St. Lawrence and Industry Railway	389	......	600	989	1027	12	12
New Brunswick and Canada Railway	1718	......	10606	12324	11273	116	107
European & North American Railway	7030	621	9539	17190	14746	108	108
Eastern Extension Railway*	......	......	......	......	......	......	......
Nova Scotia Railway	10204	129	13228	23561	23118	145	145
Total $	429050	51008	764094	1244752	1125045	2474	2465

*No returns.

Law Report.

MARINE INSURANCE—NON-DISCLOSURE OF DESTINATION.—In a case of Harrower vs. Hutchinson before the Court of Q. B., in England, the following facts appeared. The plaintiffs are merchants of Glasgow, and the defendants are underwriters in Glasgow and Liverpool. The policy of insurance was effected on goods in a ship to sail at and from Buenos Ayres to a port or ports of loading in that province, and to discharge in the United Kingdom. The ship went to Buenos Ayres, and then to Laguna des Corrientes, and on her way back to Buenos Ayres she was lost. The underwriters refused to pay, as the port of Laguna des Corrientes was not within the meaning of the policy of insurance. Mr. Cohen urged for the defendants that "a port or ports of loading" did not include a port at which there was no custom house, and from which the ship could not clear for a port in Europe. It did not include an entirely new and unknown port, such as Laguna des Corrientes. The insurers had shown a want of good faith in not disclosing the name of the port, in which there would have been charged a much higher rate, as the risk had been greater. On the other hand, Mr. Baylis (with Mr. Milward, Q. C.) argued that underwriters were supposed to know geography; and if they did not know, they ought to make inquiries, as the insurers are not bound to communicate anything. The Court gave judgment in favor of the plaintiffs. It was not necessary for merchants to disclose to underwriters those things which the latter were presumed to know. In this case the underwriters undertook to insure the goods at and from a port or ports of loading in the province of Buenos Ayres, and it must be presumed that along the coast of a large province there may be ports of which the underwriters had no knowledge, as to which there may be particular risks; but, if they did not intend the full scope of the words they used, it was there duty to make inquiry as to what port the plaintiff intended to go. The underwriters not having done so, the plaintfffs were not bound to communicate anything. The judgement must therefore be for the plaintiffs.

TELEGRAPHY IN SWITZERLAND.—The reduction from 1 franc to 50 centimes, which was made at the beginning of last year, has on the whole proved a success. Without counting the 44,805 despatches relating to the telegraph service, there were 1,596,353 inland telegrams sent during 1868, against 794,666 in 1867, an increase of 801,687 despatches in favour of 1868. The number of international despatches sent in 1868 was 282,627, against 245,154 during the previous year, an increase also in favour of the former of 37,473 despatches. The receipts during 1868, as compared with those of the previous year, were as follows:

	1867. frs.	1868. frs.
Gross receipts	832,538.61	921,182.45
Expenditure	748,976.46	846,900.60
Net receipts	74,562.15	74,281.85

Although the net receipts during 1868 were 280 frs. 30c. less than those of the previous year, it cannot be attributed to the lowering of the price for telegrams, but rather to the extraordinary expenses incurred by the telegraphic administration in the laying of new lines.

—The annual meeting of the Huron Copper Bay Company will be held in Montreal on the 5th July.

—Stock of the People's Telegraph Company is quoted in the Quebec stock lists at 101 to 105.

Commercial.

The Messrs. Beard, of this city, have made such arrangements with their creditors as to enable them to resume possession of the estate. It was returned into their hands early in the present week.

Bills of the Royal Canadian Bank are much inquired for and very scarce. The principal brokers have orders for many thousands of dollars, but can only get a small supply. This is probably owing in a great measure to a general impression in the country that the bank will shortly resume.

Since the commencement of the present month there has been an extraordinary movement of wheat, &c., in the principal American markets. For the four weeks ended June 19th, the receipts at five western lake ports were 458,268 brls. of flour and 54,664,910 bush. wheat, against 230,758 brls. of flour and 1,693,937 bush. of wheat, last year; being more than three times as much wheat and nearly three times as much flour as last year. A Buffalo paper estimates the wheat movement as follows:—

	Bush.
In store at Chicago and Milwaukee 21st	1,200,000
Afloat on lakes for Buffalo & Oswego 21st	1,024,000
Afloat on canal, destined for tide water	1,800,000
In store in New York 21st	528,836
Total (not including stocks at Buffalo and Oswego)	5,552,836

total stock of tea in London, June 11, was ,942 lbs., against 76,003,365 last year; and rpool 1,146,716 lbs. this year against 1,-8 last year.

Western Tobacco Leaf, published at Cin-i, says: We are in receipt of information he various sections of the West and South rd to the present condition of the coming > crop. From some sections reports are ', while in the majority of cases, we are to say, the prospects for a good crop are

London Produce Markets' Review says of gar trade: The stocks in Europe and the States are largely in excess, and the quan-land sown for beet root in the Zollverein to have increased from 5 to 6 per cent. In : and in other countries a large increase in wings has also taken place—and Messrs. son look for an increased European pro-a of 160,000, or perhaps 125,000 tons, this , which is sufficient to fill the void which he caused should the most extreme estimate in the Cuban crop be realised.

he exports of cotton piece goods, from the l Kingdom, in the first four months of the t year, there was as compared with the cor-ding period in 1868, an increase of 1,500,-rds in those to the Hanse Towns, 4,650,000 to France, 11,400,000 yards to Italy, 3,700,-rds to Egypt, 14,480,000 yards to the United 38,000,000 yards to Brazil, 2,000,000 yards gtsay, 500,000 yards to the Argentine Cor-tion, 1,780,000 yards to Peru, 2,550,000 to China and Hong Kong, 740,000 yards to and 450,000 yards to Canada. On the hand, there is a diminution of 90,000,000 to the East Indies, of 2,400,000 yards to est Indies, of 1,800,000 yards to the Philip-lands, of 1,500,000 yards to New Granada, 50,000 yards to Mexico, of 5,900,000 yards ia and Palestine, of 10,000,000 yards to y, of 4,750,000 yards to Portugal, and of 000 yards to Holland.

i stated that the Russian Government have d to certain parties in London the conces-of the right of laying a submarine cable, monopoly for forty years, from the mouth River Amoor, in Eastern Siberia. The s to run to Japan, and thence to Shanghai, vernment undertaking to complete as far mouth of the river the land line of tele-wire, which already crosses the greater tpart eria, up to a point within 608 miles from ast. In connection with this affair it is o be proposed to make arrangements for ing the co-operation of the Telegraph Con-on and Maintenance Company.

Sales of Petroleum.

Petrolia the price of crude oil, up to the 26th ;, remained unchanged. The Wyoming Letter reports a sale of 1,500 barrels to Mr. Duncan Clark, of Toronto, for exportation crude state at $1.25 per barrel. There was ting of the Crude Oil Association on the 1st., ratifying the sale made by the com-to Mr. Berringer, of 10,000 brls. at $1.25 per We understand Mr. McMillan has just d an order from the old country for 2,000 of crude oil.

Toronto Market.

DUCE.—At the commencement of the pre-sek, the market for breadstuffs was firm tive, under the influence of less favorable from Europe respecting the crops ; but hen there has been a steady falling off, so ur closes 25c. lower, and wheat in propor-It is, indeed, rather remarkable that prices p so well in the face of the enormous re-of wheat at all the principal American s, and it is not quite certain whether the olume of this movement has yet had its set on the market. In this Province the l has been abundant, if not excessive, so

that some warm and dry weather would now be acceptable. In the present state of matters our market could not be otherwise than dull, and the week closed without any animation, prices being purely nominal, Wheat.—Receipts 16,812 bush., and 17,600 bush. last week. The market closed dull, with sellers at 97c., f.o.b., for lots of Spring. Fall is held for $1.00, but there is no demand. Oats—Are quiet at 51 to 54c. for car loads ; little doing. Peas—Nominal, at 70 to 75c. ; no tran-sactions during this week. Barley—Out of market.

FLOUR.—Receipts, 3,275 brls., and 2,200 brls. last week. No. 1 Superfine is offering at $4.25, without demand. Sales of several lots occurred during the week at $4.30. Nothing doing in other grades.

PROVISIONS.—The large receipts at the country stores has tended to depress the market still further, and no wholesale movement has yet taken place ; the indications are for continued low prices. Cheese—Nothing doing in the new crop yet, except in a small way. Oatmeals—Nominal. Pork—Mess is rather firmer at quota-tions.

HIDES—The market is very dull and unchanged. WOOD—Receipts are light for the season ; lots sell at 32¼ to 35c.

The following are the Grand Trunk Railway Company's summer rates from Toronto to the un-dermentioned stations, which came into force on the 19th ult. :—Flour to all Stations from Belle-ville to Lynn, Inclusive 25c.; grain, per 100 lbs., 13c.; flour to Prescott, 30c ; grain 15c ; flour to all stations between Island Pond and Portland, in-clusive, 75c ½-grain, 38c; flour to Boston, 80c, gold ; grain 40c ; flour to Halifax, 90c ; flour to St. John, 85c.

Exports of Petroleum from the United States from January 1 to June 22.

	1869.	1868.
From New York...galls.	27,916,772	21,656,146
Boston.....................	1,173,772	1,132,608
Philadelphia.............	10,698,428	14,574,201
Baltimore.................	579,890	855,695
Portland...................		153,131
Total Export from the		
U. States.................	40,389,782	38,671,775
Same time 1867..........		26,717,653
Same time 1866..........		23,631,440

The Cotton Trade.

Advices from the cotton crop in the Southern States continue favorable; this is the most critical period on the growing crop. The stocks of Indian and American cotton in Liverpool and London, on the 12th, and the quantities afloat for the same ports at that date were 1,198,835 bales this year, against 1,201,247 bales last year.

Petroleum.

The stocks in and afloat for the five leading markets of Europe, at the dates indicated, com-pare as follows:

	Jan. 1st.	
	bbls.	bbls.
Stock in London May 31............	18,841	10,800
Afloat for London	5,886	3,300
Stock in Bremen May 26....,..,.	48,813	85,000
Afloat for Bremen	26,725	
Stock in Antwerp May 31........	85,900	53,000
Afloat for Atwerp..............	30,000	28,000
Stock in Rotterdam May 29.......	15,062	12,500
Afloat for Rotterdam..........	4,500	14,500
Stock in Hamburg May 27........	27,373	35,000
Afloat for Hamburg............	13,615	5,000
Totals..................	276,717	253,100

The total amount in and afloat for the ports is the latest dates is, it will be seen, about 25,000 barrels greater than on January 1st. In the table the cases have been reduced to barrels of forty-five gallons each.

A bill to levy a duty on petroleum imported into the Zollverein was rejected ; it has all along been admitted free of duty.

The completion of the Lake Superior and Mis-sissippi River Road, the New York Evening Post thinks, will effect a material reduction in the price of wheat by furnishing a channel for the surplus of Minnesota, Dakota, Northwestern Wisconsin and Northeastern Iowa, to reach the market. Last year Minnesota raised a surplus of twelve million bushels of wheat. Thirty miles of the Lake Superior road are in operation; eighty miles are under contract, and the remaining 30 will be let next month. Men are at work on the 80 miles, cutting out and grubbing the track. The company has in use and under construction six locomotives and 100 freight and passenger cars. At Du Luth, the Lake Superior terminus of the road, two immense grain elevators have been con-tracted for, and a large hotel and two churches are now building by the company. Owners of propeller lines on Lake Ontario and Lake Erie are negotiating for the carriage of the grain from the elevators at Du Luth. The Danville (Pennsylvania) rolling mills are turning out large quantities of rails, spikes, &c., for the road.

—A telegram from Hong Kong, dated June 12th, gives the total exports of tea from China and Japan up to that date as 189,500,000 lbs.

Royal Canadian Bank.

THE ANNUAL GENERAL MEETING of the Share-holders of this Bank will be held at the Banking Office here, on MONDAY, the FIFTH DAY OF JULY NEXT, at NOON.

By order of the Board.

T. WOODSIDE, Cashier.

Toronto, June 23, 1869.

WESTERN CANADA Permanent Building and Savings Society.

DIVIDEND NO. 12.

NOTICE is hereby given, that a Dividend of Five per cent. on the Capital Stock of this Institution has been declared for the half-year ending 29th inst., and that the same will be payable at the Office of the Society, No. 70 Church Street, on and after THURSDAY, the EIGHTH day of JULY next.

The Transfer Books will be closed from the 20th to the 30th June, inclusive.

By order of the Board.

WALTER S. LEE, Secretary and Treasurer.

Toronto, June 15, 1869.

The Canadian Bank of Commerce.

DIVIDEND NO. 4.

NOTICE is hereby given that a Dividend of Four per cent. upon the paid-up capital stock of this institu-tion has been declared for the current half year, and that the same will be payable at the Bank and its Branches on and after FRIDAY, the second day of JULY next.

The Transfer Books will be closed from the 15th to the 30th days of June next, both days inclusive.

The Annual General Meeting of the Stockholders will be held at the Banking House in this city, on MONDAY, the 12th day of JULY next. Chair to be taken at twelve o'clock, noon, precisely.

By order of the Board.

R. J. DALLAS, Cashier.

Toronto, May 22nd, 1869.

Bank of Toronto.

DIVIDEND No. 26.

NOTICE is hereby given that a Dividend of Four per cent. for the current half-year, being at the rate of Eight per cent. on the paid up capital of this Bank, has this day been declared, and that the same will be payable at the Bank or its branches on and after

FRIDAY, the 2ND DAY OF JULY NEXT.

The transfer books will be closed from the fifteenth to the thirtieth of June, both days inclusive.

The Annual Meeting of the Shareholders will be held at the Bank on Wednesday, the twenty-first day of July next. The chair to be taken at noon.

By order of the Board.

G. HAGUE, Cashier.

Toronto, May 16th, 1869.

STATEMENT OF BANKS

ACTING UNDER CHARTER, FOR THE MONTH ENDING 31st MAY, 1869, ACCORDING TO RETURNS FURNISHED BY THE BANKS TO THE AUDITOR OF PUBLIC ACCOUNTS.

NAME OF BANK	CAPITAL authorized by Act	CAPITAL paid up	Promissory Notes in circulation not bearing interest	Balances due to other Banks	Cash Deposits not bearing Interest	Cash Deposits bearing Interest	Cash Deposits bearing Interest, rest	TOTAL LIABILITIES	Coin, Bullion, and Provincial Notes	Landed or other Property of the Bank	Government Securities	Promissory Notes, Bills of other Banks	Balances due from other Banks	Notes and Bills Discounted	Other Debts due the Bank not included under foregoing heads	TOTAL ASSETS
ONTARIO AND QUEBEC:																
Montreal	6,000,000															
Quebec																
City																
Gore																
British North America																
Banque du Peuple																
Niagara District																
Molsons																
Toronto																
Ontario																
Eastern Townships																
Banque Nationale																
Banque Jacques Cartier																
Merchants'																
Royal Canadian																
Union of Lower Canada																
Mechanics'																
Bank of Commerce																
NOVA SCOTIA:																
Bank of Yarmouth	900,000	195,400	159,100	7,121 98	12,599 62	6,965 00		177,467 60	11,891 10	7,561 12		224 00	4,433 13	538,359 95	77,844 60	327,563 95
Merchants' Bank																
People's Bank																
Union Bank	1,000,000	480,000	104,930	92,733 59	154,080 04	391,016 00		610,743 63	204,240 14	29,000 00	83,000 00	7,100 00	12,463 63	692,543 99	60,390 83	1,088,390 87
Bank of Nova Scotia																
NEW BRUNSWICK:																
Bank of New Brunswick																
Commercial Bank	500,000	300,000	36,100	72,484	68,081 99	70,537 67		246,759	13,115	4,394 90		13,050 13	50,397	288,340 29	96,905	454,258 74
St. Stephen's Bank																
People's Bank																
Totals	38,896,000	30,574,014	7,805,443	1,386,409 40	14,886,972 46	97,435,935 10		35,514,609 96	23,547,790 19	1,642,388	83,140,637 96	1,737,825 69	5,740,676 30	52,250,008 18	3,115,940 39	80,341,667 34

TORONTO PRICES CURRENT.—JULY 1, 1869.

Name of Article.	Wholesale Rates.	
Boots and Shoes.	$ c.	$ c.
Mens' Thick Boots	2 05	2 50
" Kip	2 25	3 00
" Calf	3 20	3 70
" Congress Gaiters	1 65	2 50
" Kip Cobourgs	1 20	1 40
Boys' Thick Boots	1 70	1 80
Youths' "	1 40	1 50
Women's Batts	0 95	1 30
" Balmoral	1 20	1 50
" Congress Gaiters	0 90	1 50
Misses' Batts	0 75	1 00
" Balmoral	1 00	1 20
" Congress Gaiters	1 00	1 30
Girls' Batts	0 65	0 85
" Balmoral	0 90	1 05
" Congress Gaiters	0 75	1 10
Children's C. T. Cacks	0 50	0 65
" Gaiters	0 65	0 90
Drugs.		
Aloes Cape	0 12½	0 16
Alum	0 02½	0 03
Borax	0 00	0 00
Camphor, refined	0 65	0 70
Castor Oil	0 16½	0 28
Caustic Soda	0 04½	0 05
Cochineal	0 90	1 00
Cream Tartar	0 30	0 35
Epsom Salts	0 03	0 04
Extract Logwood	0 11	0 12
Gum Arabic, sorts	0 30	0 35
Indigo, Madras	0 90	1 00
Licorice	0 14	0 15
Madder	0 00	0 16
Galls	0 32	0 37
Opium	12 00	13 50
Oxalic Acid	0 26	0 35
Potash, Bi-tart	0 25	0 28
" Bichromate	0 15	0 20
Potass Iodide	3 90	4 50
Senna	0 12½	0 60
Soda Ash	0 02½	0 04
Soda Bicarb	0 00	4 00
Tartaric Acid	0 40	0 45
Verdigris	0 35	0 40
Vitriol, Blue	0 08	0 10
Groceries.		
Coffees:		
Java, ℘ lb	0 22@	0 23
Laguayra,	0 17	0 18
Rio	0 15	0 17
Fish:		
Herrings, Lab. split	0 00	0 00
" round	0 00	0 00
" scaled	0 33	0 35
Mackerel, small kitts	1 00	0 00
Loch. Her. wh'e firks	2 50	2 75
" half "	1 25	1 50
White Fish & Trout	0 00	3 50
Salmon, saltwater	14 00	15 00
Dry Cod, ℘112 lbs	4 50	5 00
Fruit:		
Raisins, Layers	1 90	2 00
" M. R.	1 90	2 00
" Valentias new	0 6	0 6½
Currants, new	0 4¾	0 05
" old	0 3½	0 04
Figs	0 11	0 12
Molasses:		
Clayed, ℘ gal	0 00	0 35
Syrups, Standard	0 55	0 56
" Golden	0 59	0 60
Rice:		
Arracan	3 60	4 00
Spices:		
Cassia, whole, ℘ lb	0 00	0 45
Cloves	0 11	0 12
Nutmegs	0 50	0 55
Ginger, ground	0 18	0 23
" Jamaica, root	0 20	0 25
Pepper, black	0 10½	0 11
Pimento	0 08	0 09
Sugars:		
Port Rico, ℘ lb	0 9¾	0 10
Cuba "	0 9	0 9½
Barbadoes (bright)	0 9¾	0 34½
Canada Sugar Refine'y, yellow No. 2, 60ds	0 9¼	0 9¾
Yellow, No. 2½	0 9¾	0 9⅞
No. 3	0 10	0 10½
Crushed X	0 10¾	0 11
" A	0 11¼	0 11½
Ground	0 12½	0 12¾
Dry Crushed	0 12	0 12¼
Extra Ground	0 13	0 13½
Teas:		
Japan com'n to good	0 48	0 50
" Fine to choicest	0 55	0 60
Colored, com. to fine	0 60	0 70
Congou & Souch'ng	0 42	0 75
Oolong, good to fine	0 50	0 65
Y. Hyson, com to gd	0 47½	0 55
Medium to choice	0 65	0 80
Extra choice	0 85	0 95

Name of Article.	Wholesale Rate.	
Groceries—*Contin'd*	$ c.	$ c.
Gunpowd'r c. to med	0 55	0 70
" med. to fine	0 70	0 85
" fine to fins't	0 85	0 95
Hyson	0 45	0 80
Imperial	0 42	0 80
Tobacco, Manufact'd:		
Can Leaf, ℘ lb 5s & 10s	0 26	0 30
Western Leaf, com	0 25	0 26
" Good	0 27	0 32
" Fine	0 32	0 35
" Bright fine	0 40	0 50
" " choice	0 60	0 75
Hardware.		
Tin (net cash prices)		
Block, ℘ lb	0 35	0 00
Grain	0 30	0 00
Copper:		
Pig	0 23	0 24
Sheet	0 30	0 33
Cut Nails:		
Assorted ¼ Shingles, ℘ 100 lb	2 95	3 00
Shingle alone do	3 15	3 25
Lathe and 5 dy	3 30	3 40
Galvanized Iron:		
Assorted sizes	0 08	0 09
Best No. 24	0 07½	0 00
" 26	0 08	0 08½
" 28	0 09	0 09½
Horse Nails:		
Guest's or Griffin's assorted sizes	0 00	0 00
For W. ass'd sizes	0 18	0 19
Patent Hammer'd do	0 17	0 18
Iron (at 4 months):		
Pig—Gartsherrie No1	24 00	25 00
Other brands. No1	22 00	24 00
" No2	0 00	0 00
Bar—Scotch, ℘100 lb	2 25	2 50
Refined	3 00	3 25
Swedes	5 00	5 50
Hoops—Coopers	3 00	3 25
Band	3 00	3 25
Boiler Plates	3 25	3 50
Canada Plates	3 75	4 00
Union Jack	0 00	0 00
Pontypool	3 25	4 00
Swansea	3 90	4 00
Lead (at 4 months):		
Bar, ℘ 100 lbs	0 06½	0 07
Sheet "	0 08	0 09
Shot	0 07½	0 07¾
Iron Wire (net cash):		
No. 6, ℘ bundle	2 70	2 80
" 9, "	3 10	3 20
" 12, "	3 40	3 50
" 16, "	4 30	4 40
Powder:		
Blasting, Canada	3 50	0 00
FF "	4 25	4 50
FFF "	4 75	5 00
Blasting, English	4 00	5 00
FF loose	5 00	6 00
FFF "	6 00	6 50
Pressed Spikes (4 mos):		
Regular sizes 100	4 00	4 25
Extra "	4 50	5 00
Tin Plates (net cash):		
IC Coke	7 50	8 50
IC Charcoal	8 50	9 00
IX "	10 50	11 00
IXX "	13 50	14 00
DC "	8 00	8 50
DX "	9 50	0 00
Hides & Skins, ℘lb		
Green rough	0 00	0 05
Green, salt'd & insp'd	0 06	0 06½
Cured	0 00	0 00
Calfskins, green	0 00	0 10
Calfskins, cured	0 00	0 12½
" dry	0 18	0 20
Sheepskins,	1 20	1 60
" country	1 00	1 40
Hops.		
Inferior, ℘ lb	0 00	0 00
Medium	0 00	0 00
Good	0 00	0 00
Fancy	0 00	0 00
Leather, @ (4 mos.) In lots of less than 50 sides, 10 ℘ cent higher.		
Spanish Sole, 1st qual'y heavy, weights ℘ lb	0 21	0 22
Do. 1st qual middle do	0 22	0 23
Do. No. 2, light weights	0 20	0 00
Slaughter heavy	0 00	0 24
Do. light	0 00	0 00
Harness, best	0 25	0 27
" No. 2	0 00	0 00
Upper heavy	0 30	0 32
" light	0 33	0 34

Name of Article.	Wholesale Rates.	
Leather—*Contin'd.*	$ c.	$ c.
Kip Skins, Patna	0 30	0 35
French	0 70	0 90
English	0 65	0 80
Hemlock Calf (30 to 35 lbs.) per doz	0 50	0 60
Do. light	0 45	0 50
French Calf	1 03	1 06
Grain & Satn Clt ℘ doz	0 00	0 55
Splits, large ℘ lb	0 30	0 38
" small	0 23	0 28
Enamelled Cow ℘ foot	0 20	0 21
Patent	0 20	0 21
Pebble Grain	0 15	0 17
Buff	0 14	0 16
Oils.		
Cod	0 65	0 70
Lard, extra	0 00	0 00
" No. 1	0 00	0 00
" Woollen	0 00	0 00
Lubricating, patent	0 00	0 00
" Mott's economic	0 30	0 00
Linseed, raw	0 76	0 82
" boiled	0 81	0 87
Machinery	0 00	0 00
Olive, common, ℘ gal	1 00	1 60
" salad	1 95	2 30
" salad, in bots. qt. ℘ case	3 60	3 75
Sesame salad, ℘ gal	1 60	1 75
Seal, pale	0 75	0 85
Spirits Turpentine	0 52½	0 60
Varnish	0 00	0 00
Whale	0 00	0 90
Paints, &c.		
White Lead, genuine in Oil, ℘ 25lbs	0 00	2 35
Do. No. 1 "	0 00	2 10
" 2 "	0 00	1 90
" 3 "	0 00	1 65
White Zinc, genuine	3 00	3 50
White Lead, dry	0 05½	0 09
Red Lead	0 07½	0 08
Venetian Red, Eng'h	0 02½	0 03½
Yellow Ochre, Fren'h	0 02¾	0 03
Whiting	0 85	1 25
Petroleum. (Refined ℘ gal.)		
Water white, car l'd	——	0 25
" small lots	0 00	0 27
Straw, by car load	0 00	0 00
" small lots	0 00	0 00
Amber, by car load	0 00	0 00
" small lots	0 00	0 00
Benzine	0 00	0 00
Produce.		
Grain:		
Wheat, Spring, 60 lb	0 97	0 98
" Fall 60 "	1 00	1 03
Barley 48 "	0 00	0 00
Peas 60 "	0 65	0 75
Oats 34 "	0 52	0 53
Rye 56 "	0 55	0 00
Seeds:		
Clover, choice 60 "	0 00	0 00
" com'n 68 "	0 00	0 00
Timothy, cho'e 4 "	0 00	0 00
" inf. to good 48 "	0 00	0 00
Flax 56 "	0 00	0 00
Flour (per brl.):		
Superior extra	0 00	0 00
Extra superfine,	4 60	4 65
Fancy superfine	4 50	4 60
Superfine No 1	4 20	4 25
" No. 2	——	——
Oatmeal, (per brl.)	5 50	5 75
Provisions		
Butter, dairy tub ℘ lb	0 12	0 13
" store packed	0 10	0 12
Cheese, new	0 14½	0 15
Pork, mess, per brl	26 50	27 00
" prime mess	——	——
" prime	——	——
Bacon, rough	0 12	0 12½
" Cumberl'd cut	0 13	0 14
" smoked	0 00	0 13
Hams, in salt	0 12½	0 13½
" smoked	0 14	0 14½
Shoulders, in salt	0 00	0 11
Lard, in kegs	0 16½	0 17
Eggs, packed	0 11	0 12
Beef Hams	0 00	0 13
Tallow	0 08	0 8½
Hogs dressed, heavy	0 00	0 00
" medium	0 00	0 00
" light	0 00	0 00
Salt, &c.		
American brls	1 35	1 37
Liverpool coarse	0 00	1 00
Goderich	0 00	1 45
Plaster	1 00	0 00
Water Lime	1 50	0 00

Soap & Candles.	$ c.	$ c.
D. Crawford & Co.'s ..		
Imperial.........	0 07½	0 08
" Golden Bar	0 07	0 07½
" Silver Bar........	0 07	0 07½
Crown	0 05	0 05½
No. 1	0 03½	0 03¾
Candles	0 00	0 11
Wines, Liquors, &c.		
Ale:		
English, per doz. qrts.	2 60	2 65
Guinness Dub Portr..	2 35	2 40
Spirits:		
Pure Jamaica Rum...	1 80	2 25
De Kuyper's H. Gin..	1 55	1 65
Booth's Old Tom.....	1 90	2 00
Gin:		
Green, cases.........	4 00	4 25
Booth's Old Tom, c...	6 00	6 25
Wines:		
Port, common	1 00	1 25
" fine old	2 00	4 00
Sherry, common	1 00	1 50
" medium........	1 70	1 80
"old pale or golden..	2 50	4 00

Brandy:	$ c.	$ c.
Hennessy's, per gal..	2 30	2 50
Martell's " ..	2 30	2 50
J. Robin & Co.'s " ..	2 25	2 35
Otard, Dupuy & Cos..	2 25	2 35
Brandy, cases........	8 50	9 00
Brandy, com. per c...	4 00	4 50
Whiskey:		
Common 36 u. p......	0 58	0 60
Old Rye	0 77½	0 80
Malt	0 77½	0 80
Toddy	0 77½	0 80
Scotch, per gal.......	1 90	2 10
Irish—Kinnahan's c...	7 00	7 50
" Dunnville's Belf't..	6 00	6 25
Wool.		
Fleece, lb............	0 33	0 34
Pulled "............	0 00	0 00
Furs.		
Bear..................	0 00	0 00
Beaver, ℔ lb.........	0 00	0 00
Coon	0 00	0 00
Fisher................	0 00	0 00
Martin................	0 00	0 00
Mink..................	0 00	0 00
Otter.................	0 00	0 00
Spring Rats..........	0 00	0 00
Fox..................	0 00	0 00

INSURANCE COMPANIES.

ENGLISH.—*Quotations on the London Market.*

No. of Shares.	Last Dividend.	Name of Company.	Shares par val £	Amount paid.	Last Sale.
20,000		Briton Medical and General Life...	10	....	2½
50,000	7½	Commer'l Union, Fire, Life and Mar.	50	5	5½
24,000	8	City of Glasgow	25	2½	4½
5,000	9½	Edinburgh Life	100	15	33½
400,000	5—½ yr	European Life and Guarantee......	2½	11s6	4s.
100,000	10	Etna Fire and Marine............	10	1½	—
20,000	5	Guardian	100	50	53½
24,000	12	Imperial Fire...................	500	50	352
7,500	9½	Imperial Life	100	10	17½
100,000	10	Lancashire Fire and Life..........	20	2	2¾
10,000	11	Life Association of Scotland.......	40	7½	25
35,862	45s. p. sh	London Assurance Corporation ..	25	12½	48¾
10,000	5	London and Lancashire Life	10	1	—
87,504	40	Liverp'l & London & Globe F. & L.	20	2	7½
20,000	5	National Union Life	5	1	1
20,000	12½	Northern Fire and Life	100	5	13
40,000	12 '68, bo. 5s.	North British and Mercantile	50	6½	19½
40,000	50	Ocean Marine	25	5	17¾
2,500	£5 12s.	Provident Life...................	100	10	35
....	£4½ p. s.	Phœnix.........................	....	....	139½ x d
200,000	2½—h.yr.	Queen Fire and Life	10	1	21
100,000	3s. bo.4s	Royal Insurance.................	20	3	6½
20,000	10	Scottish Provincial Fire and Life ..	50	2½	5½
10,000	25	Standard Life	50	12	66 x d
4,000	5	Star Life	25	1¼	—
		CANADIAN.			℔ c.
8,000	4	British America Fire and Marine ..	$50	$25	56 57
....	4	Canada Life	...	....	.....
4000	12	Montreal Assurance	£50	£5	135
10,000	8	Provincial Fire and Marine........	60	11	.....
....	....	Quebec Fire	40	32½	£23 24
....	7	" Marine....................	100	40	85 90
10,000	4 6 mo's.	Western Assurance...............	40	0	.....

RAILWAYS.	Sha's	Paid	Montr	London
Atlantic and St. Lawrence.......................	£100	All.	....	56
Buffalo and Lake Huron	20½	"	....	2⅞ 3½
Do. do Preference	10	"	....	5 6
Buff., Brantf. & Goderich, 6℔c., 1872-3-4....	100	"	....	66 69
Champlain and St. Lawrence	....	....	10 11	....
Do. do. Pref. 10 ℔ ct..............	....	....	80 85	....
Grand Trunk	100	"	14 15	13½
Do. Eq. G. M. Bds. 1 ch. 6℔c...........	100	"	....	80
Do. First Preference, 5 ℔ c............	100	"	....	44½
Do. Deferred, 3 ℔ ct..................	100	"	....	....
Do. Second Pref. Bonds, 5℔c............	100	"	....	37
Do. do Deferred, 3 ℔ ct............	100	"	....	....
Do. Third Pref. Stock, 4℔ct............	100	"	....	28½
Do. do. Deferred, 3 ℔ ct............	100	"	....	....
Do. Fourth Pref. Stock, 3℔c............	100	"	....	15½
Do. do. Deferred, 3 ℔ ct............	100	"	....	....
Great Western	20½	"	14 15	13½
Do. New	20½	18	....	....
Do. 6 ℔ c. Bds, due 1873-76............	100	All.	....	99
5½ ℔c Bds. due 1877-78............	100	"	....	92½
Marine Railway, Halifax, $250, all................	$250	"	....	....
Northern of Canada, 6 ℔c. 1st Pref. Bds...........	100	"	....	82 83

EXCHANGE.	Halifax.	Montr'l.	Quebec.	Toronto.
Bank on London, 60 days......				
Sight or 75 days date..........	12½ 13	9¾ 9½	9¼ 9¾	10
Private do.	11½ 12	8 9	9 9¼	9
Private, with documents..........	....	8 8½	....	....
Bank on New York................	....	27 27½	27 27½	26¾
Private do.	....	27½ 28	27½ 28	....
Gold Drafts do.	....	par	....	par ½ dis.
Silver	....	4¼ 4¾	....	4 to 5

STOCK AND BOND REP

The dates of our quotations are as follows:—Toronto, June 20; M June 19; London, June 5.

NAME.	Shares.	Paid up.	Divid'd last 6 Months	Dividend Day.	Toronto.	Montre'l	Que
BANKS.			℔ ct.				
British North America	$250	All.	3½ b½pc	July and Jan.	Bks closed	103½104½	Bks
Jacques Cartier.............	50	"	4	1 June, 1 Dec.	107 107½	107 107½	107
Montreal	200	"	6	"	161 161½	160½141½	161
Nationale..................	50	"	4	1 Nov. 1 May.	107 107½	106½107	107½
New Brunswick	100	"	......	......	....	....	..
Nova Scotia	200	—	7&b$3½	Mar. and Sept.	....	....	..
Du Peuple..................	50	"	4	1 Mar., 1 Sept.	108 108½	107½108½	108
Toronto	100	"	4	1 Jan., 1 July.	Bks closed	117½118	Bks
Bank of Yarmouth............	....	....	......	......	....	....	...
Canadian Bank of Com'e......	50	All.	......	......	Bks closed	100 103	Bks
City Bank Montreal	80	"	4	1 June, 1 Dec.	98½ 99	98½ 99½	98½
Commer'l Bank (St. John)....	100	"	℔ ct.	......	....	..	...
Eastern Townships' Bank.....	50	"	4	1 July, 1 Jan..	....	98 99	Bks
Gore	40	....	none.	1 Jan., 1 July.	39 40	38½ 40	38
Halifax Banking Company....	....	....	......	......	....	...	...
Mechanics' Bank............	50	All.	4	1 Nov., 1 May.	92 92½	92 93	92
Merchants'Bank of Canada....	100	"	5	1 Jan., 1 July.	Bks closed	110 110½	Bks
Merchants' Bank (Halifax)....	....	....	......	......	....	....	..
Molson's Bank..............	50	All.	4	1 Apr., 1 Oct.	108½ 109	108½ 109	108½
Niagara District Bank........	100	70	3½	1 Jan., 1 July.	...	....	...
Ontario Bank...............	40	All.	4	1 June, 1 Dec.	96½ 96½	9:½ 96½	95½
People's Bank (Fred'kton)....	100	"	......	......	....	...	.
People's Bank (Halifax)	20	"	7 12 m	......	....	....	..
Quebec Bank	100	"	3½	1 June, 1 Dec.	99½ 100	100 101	100
Royal Canadian Bank	50	60	4	1 Jan., 1 July.	49 50	50 55	50
St. Stephens Bank	100	All.	......	......	....	....	..
Union Bank	100	"	4	1 Jan., 1 July.	Bks closed	104 105	Bks
Union Bank (Halifax)........	100	....	7 12mo	Feb. and Aug.	....	....	.
MISCELLANEOUS.							
British America Land........	250	44	......	......	....	----	...
British Colonial S. S. Co......	250	32½	......	......	...	----	...
Canada Company	32½	All.	......	......	....	----	...
Canada Landed Credit Co.....	50	$50	3½	......	78½ 79	----	...
Canada Per. B'ldg Society....	50	All.	5	......	Bks cl'd	....	...
Canada Mining Company.....	4	90	......	......	....	....	...
Do. Inl'd Steam Nav. Co.....	100	All.	15 12m	......	----	90½ 100	90
Do. Glass Company.........	100	"	None.	......	....	40 60	...
Canad'n Loan & Investm't....	25	2½	......	......	....	....	---
Canada Agency	10	¼	......	......	....	....	---
Colonial Securities Co........	....	....	......	.....	....	....	...
Freehold Building Society....	100	All.	5	......	115½ 116	----	...
Halifax Steamboat Co........	100	"	......	------	....	....	...
Halifax Gas Company........	....	----	------	.....	....	....	...
Hamilton Gas Company.......	----	----	------	......	....	....	...
Huron Copper Bay Co........	4	12	20	.....	....	30 45	...
Lake Huron S. and C.........	5	102	......	......	....	....	...
Montreal Mining Consols......	20	$15	......	......	....	2.25 3.75	..
Do. Telegraph Co......	40	All.	5	......	135½ 136	135½136½	135½1
Do. Elevating Co......	00	"	5½	......	....	105 107½	...
Do. City Gas Co.........	40	"	4	15 Mar. 15 Sep.	....	136 137	136 1
Do. City Pass. R,. Co.....	50	"	2	......	....	110 112	110 1
Quebec and L. S.	8	$4	......	......	....	...	...
Quebec Gas Co..............	200	All.	4	1 Mar., 1 Sep.	....	....	120 1
Quebec Street R. R	50	25	3	......	....	....	90
Richelieu Navigation Co......	100	All.	7-12m	1 Jan., 1 July.	....	120 125	120 1
St. Lawrence Glass Company.	100	"	....	......	....	80 85	...
St. Lawrence Tow Boat Co.....	100	"	....	3 Feb.	....	....	30
Tor'to Consumers' Gas Co.....	50	"	⅗ m	1 My Au Mar Fe	107 107½	...	106 1
Trust & Loan Co. of U. C.....	20	5	3	......	....	....	..
West'n Canada Bldg Soc'y....	50	All.	5	......	Bks closed	....	---

SECURITIES.	London.	Montreal.	Quebec.	Toront
Canadian Gov't Deb. 6 ℔ ct. stg......................	....	103 104	102 103	104½ 1
Do. do. 6 do due Ja. & Jul. 1877-84.........	104½ 105½	....	....	....
Do. do. 6 do. Feb. & Aug..........	102 104	....	....	....
Do. do. 6 do. Mch. & Sep..........	102 104	....	...	..
Do. do. 5 ℔ ct. cur., 1883	93¾ 94½	92½ 95	90 91	92 93
Do. do. 5 do. stg., 1885	93½ 94	90 92½	90 90½	91 92
Do. do. 7 do. cur.,.....................	....	....	......	....
Dominion 6 p. c. 1878 cy..........................	....	106½ 107½	107 107½	107½ 1
Hamilton Corporation..............................	....	....	......	....
Montreal Harbor, 8 ℔ ct. d. 1869...................	..	.....	......	....
Do. do. 7 do. 1870.........................	...	....	......	....
Do. do. 6½ do. 1883.........................	....	102¾ 103	......	102 1
Do do. 6½ do. 1873.........................	....	....	......	..
Do. Corporation, 6 ℔ c. 1891	....	96 96½	96½ 97	96 9
Do. 7 p. c. stock................................	....	108½110	108½ 109½	109 1
Do. Water Works, 6 ℔ c. stg. 1878.............	....	96½ 97½	......	98 9
Do. do. 6 do. cy. do.	....	....	......	96 9
New Brunswick, 6 ℔ ct., Jan. and July	104 104½	....	......	....
Nova Scotia, 6 ℔ ct., 1875..........................	103 104	....	......	....
Ottawa City 6 ℔ c. d. 1880	....	95 97	......	...
Quebec Harbour, 6 ℔ c. d. 1883......................	....	....	60	....
Do. do. 7 do. do...........................	....	....	65 70	....
Do. do 8 do. 1886..........................	....	....	80 85	....
Do. City, 7 ℔ c. d. 1½ years......................	....	....	98 98½	....
Do. do. 7 do. 8 do.	....	....	91 92	....
Do. do. 7 do. 4 do.	....	....	94 95	....
Do. Water Works, 7 ℔ ct., 3 years................	....	....	97 97½	....
Do. do. 6 do. 1½ do.	....	....	94 96	....
Toronto Corporation	....	94 95	....	....

Mercantile.

The Mercantile Agency,
FOR THE
ROMOTION AND PROTECTION OF TRADE.
Established in 1841.
DUN, WIMAN & Co.
Montreal, Toronto and Halifax.
FERENCE Book, containing names and ratings of
Business Men in the Dominion, published semi
ally. 24-1y

Brown Brothers,
COUNT-BOOK MANUFACTURERS,
Stationers, Book-Binders, Etc.,
66 and 68 King Street East, Toronto, Ont.

COUNT Books for Banks, Insurance Companies
Merchants, etc., made to order of the best materials
or style, durability and cheapness unsurpassed.
large stock of Account-Books and General Stationery
tantly on hand. 2-1y

ORONTO SAFE WORKS.

J. & J. Taylor
MANUFACTURERS OF
Fire and Burglar Proof
SAFES,
(K LOCKS, VAULTS, DOORS, &c., &c.

AGENTS:
JAS. HUTTON & Co. .... MONTREAL.
H. S. SCOTT & Co. .... QUEBEC.
ALEX. WORKMAN & Co. ...... OTTAWA.
RICE LEWIS & SON .... TORONTO.
D. FALCONER .... HALIFAX, N.S.
nufactory & Sale Rooms, 198 & 200 Palace Street.

The St. Lawrence Glass Company
IE now manufacturing and have for sale,
COAL BURNERS, various styles and sizes. LAMP
MNEYS, of extra quality for ordinary Burners; also
he 'Comet' and 'Sun' Burners.
4s of Table Glassware, Hyacinth Glasses, Steam Guage
es, Glass Rods, &c., or any other article, made to
r, in White or Colored Glass.
erosene Burners, Collars and Sockets, will be kept on
l.
ruggists' Flint Glassware and Philosophical Instru-
ts, made to order.
OFFICE—388 ST. PAUL STREET, MONTREAL.
A. McK. COCHRANE.
Secretary.

Thos. Haworth & Co.,
WHOLESALE
RDWARE & COMMISSION MERCHANTS,
52 Yonge Street,
m TORONTO.

Lyman & McNab,
Importers of, and Wholesale Dealers in,
FAVY AND SHELF HARDWARE,
KING STREET,
TORONTO, ONTARIO.

Mercantile.

John Morison,
IMPORTER OF
GROCERIES, WINES, AND LIQUORS,
38 AND 40 WELLINGTON STREET,
TORONTO. 33-1y

To Mercantile Men.

THE NEW POCKET REFERENCE BOOK OF THE
MERCANTILE AGENCY revised to Christmas, and
containing 35,000 names of Traders in the Dominion, is
now out of press, and ready for delivery.
Subscribers having Travellers out, or about leaving,
should avail themselves of this indispensable volume.
DUN, WIMAN & CO.,
Exchange Buildings, Toronto.
Canadian Offices—Montreal and Halifax.
January 19. 23-t

W. McLaren & Co.,
WHOLESALE
BOOT AND SHOE MANUFACTURERS,
18 St. MAURICE STREET,
MONTREAL.
June, 1868. 2-1y

THE ONTARIO PEAT COMPANY.

CAPITAL, ... $120,000.

THIS COMPANY is PROVISIONALLY organized as follows:—

DIRECTORS:
HENRY S. HOWLAND, Esq. ...... Toronto. | LARRATT W. SMITH, Esq., ... Toronto.
JOHN FISKEN, Esq. .... Toronto. | ALFRED TODD, Esq. .... Ottawa.
EDWARD A. C. PEW, Esq. .... Welland.

TRUSTEES OF THE LANDS:
PELEG HOWLAND, Esq. .... Toronto. | CHARLES J. CAMPBELL, Esq. .... Toronto.

TREASURERS:
CHARLES J. CAMPBELL, Esq., ... Toronto. | WALTER G. CASSELS, Esq. ...... Toronto.

BROKERS:
Messrs. CAMPBELL AND CASSELS, ... 92 King Street, Toronto.

SOLICITORS:
Messrs. SMITH and WOOD, ... Wellington Street, Toronto.

SECRETARY:
JOHN WEBSTER HANCOCK, Esq. .... 22 Toronto Street, Toronto.
The lands of the Company are 1.375 acres, in the County of Welland, of the purchase value of $55,000.
The owners of the land have taken stock to the amount of $44,000
It is proposed to reserve for future contingencies 20,000
And to put upon the market the balance of 56,000
                                                        $120,000
Nearly 20,000 of the said balance is already subscribed, and the rest is in the hands of the Brokers of the Company.
A Charter of Incorporation is being applied for, and the operations of the Company will commence very soon.
Subscription Books for the Stock not yet taken up lie at the office of Messrs. Campbell and Cassels, 92 King St., Toronto.
May 18, 1869.

Montreal House, Montreal, Canada.

TO MONETARY MEN.—Merchants, Insurance Agents
Lawyers, Bankers, Railway and Steamboat Travellers,
Mining Agents, Directors and Stockholders of Public Companies, and other persons visiting Montreal for business
or pleasure, are here by most respectfully informed that
the undersigned proposes to furnish the best hotel accommodation at the most reasonable charges. It is our study
to provide every comfort and accommodation to all our
guests, especially for gentlemen engaged as above. To
those who have been accustomed to patronize other first-
class hotels, we only ask a trial; we have the same accom
modation and our table is furnished with every delicacy
of the season.
H. DUCLOS.
Nov. 22, 1867. 15-1y

The Albion Hotel,
MONTREAL,
ONE of the oldest established houses in the City is again
under the personal management of
Mr. DECKER,
Who, to accommodate his rapidly increasing business, is
adding Eighty more Rooms to the house, making the
ALBION one of the Largest Establishments in Canada.
June, 1868. 42-6ms

Commercial House,
(LATE HUFFMAN HOUSE)
PETERBOROUGH, ONTARIO.
GEORGE CRONN : : : : : : PROPRIETOR.
Large addition lately made, including Twenty Bed Rooms.
Dec. 10, 1868. 17-1 L

ANGLO-AMERICAN PEAT COMPANY.

CAPITAL, ... $200,000,
IN 8,000 SHARES—$25 EACH.

sident—WM. EDGAR, Esq., Hamilton.   Vice-President—ROBERT REFORD, Esq. (Messrs. Reford & Dillon), Montreal.
Secretary-Treasurer—A. McK. COCHRANE, 388 St. Paul Street, Montreal.

HIS COMPANY, with machinery now in working order and in course of construction, will be able to manufacture this year FROM TEN TO TWELVE THOUSAND TONS
OF GOOD FUEL. Actual working shows—
I. That the fuel can be produced for $1.45 a ton, and with the improved machinery, at a much less cost.
II. That, for steam purposes, one ton of it is superior to one cord of wood, in the proportion of 31 to 27.
III. That, for domestic purposes, it is equal to wood or coal, and leaves very little ashes—about five per cent.
At the annual meeting of the Company in Montreal, it was decided to offer one thousand shares of Stock in Toronto. Mr. Isaac C. Gilmor has been appointed agent of the
pany in Toronto, and is authorised to receive subscriptions for the Stock.
Prospectus, Map of the Property, and further information may be obtained by addressing

A. McK. COCHRANE, Secretary-Treasurer, 388 St. Paul Street, Montreal.   ISAAC C. GILMOR, 58 Colborne Street, Toronto.
                                                                                       30-85t

EDINBURGH LIFE ASSURANCE COMPANY.

FOUNDED 1823.

AMOUNT OF ACCUMULATED AND INVESTED FUNDS—OVER ONE MILLION STERLING.

HEAD OFFICE—EDINBURGH.

PRESIDENT—The Rt. Hon. the Earl of Haddington.　MANAGER—D. Marlagan, Esq.　SECRETARY—Alex. H. Whytt, Esq.

CANADIAN OFFICE ESTABLISHED 1857.　WELLINGTON STREET, TORONTO.

CANADIAN BOARD—Hon. John Hillyard Cameron, M.P., Chairman.　J. W. Gamble, Esq., L. Moffatt, Esq., Hon J. B. Robinson, C. J. Campbell, Esq.　David Higgins, Secretary.

THE Edinburgh Life Assurance Company offer to the public the advantages of a Canadian as well as a British Company. They have invested a large amount of money on securities in this country, and the Toronto Local Board have full power, by an Imperial Statute, to take risks, make investments, and settle claims in Canada, without reference to the Head Office, Edinburgh. Some of the old Policies in the Company, which became claims during the past year, were settled by payment of amounts double of those originally insured, in consequence of the large bonuses that accrued on the Policies.

Every information that intending assurers may require can be obtained at the Company's Office in Toronto, or at any of the Agencies which have been established in the principal towns in Canada.

J. HILLYARD CAMERON, CHAIRMAN.　　(36-1y)　　　　DAVID HIGGINS, SECRETARY.

NATIONAL LIFE INSURANCE COMPANY

OF THE

UNITED STATES OF AMERICA.

CHARTERED BY SPECIAL ACT OF CONGRESS.

CASH CAPITAL.　　　　$1,000,000　　PAID IN FULL.

CANADIAN BOARD OF REFERENCE :

Hon. LUTHER H. HOLTON, M.P.　　　　H. A. NELSON, Esq., Messrs. Nelson & Wood.
MICHAEL P. RYAN, Esq., M.P., Montreal.　　JACKSON RAE, Esq., Cashier Merchants' Bank.
GILMAN CHENEY, Esq., Manager Canadian Express　CHAMPION BROWN, Esq., of Messrs. Brown & Company.　　　　　　　　　　　　　　Childs.
　　SOLICITORS.　　　　　| MEDICAL REFEREE.　　　| BANKERS.
Messrs. PERKINS & RAMSAY.　| JOSEPH H. DRAKE, M.D.　| THE BANK OF MONTREAL.
This Company has deposited with the Canadian Government the required amount in GOLD, for benefit of Canadian Policyholders.

DOMINION OFFICE— 91 GREAT ST. JAMES STREET, MONTREAL.

CHAS. A. PUTNEY,　　　　　　　　　　**WILLIAM DOUGLAS, Jr.,**

SPECIAL AGENT.　　　　　　　　　　GENERAL AGENT, CANADA.

The National Charter, the large Capital, the low rates, the common-sense plan, the definite contract, the honorable and fair dealings, the non-forfeiting policies, the perfect security, the liberal terms of the policies, the Gold Deposit in Canada, render the NATIONAL LIFE ASSURANCE COMPANY of the United States of America worthy of the patronage of every business man.

1-1y　　　　　　　　　　　C. G. FORTIER, AGENT, Toronto, Ont.

Insurance.

Briton Medical and General Life Association,
with which is united the
BRITANNIA LIFE ASSURANCE COMPANY.

Capital and Invested Funds............£750,000 Sterling.

ANNUAL INCOME, £220,000 STG. :
Yearly increasing at the rate of £25,000 Sterling.

THE important and peculiar feature originally introduced by this Company, in applying the periodical Bonuses, so as to make Policies payable during life, without any higher rate of premiums being charged, has caused the success of the BRITON MEDICAL AND GENERAL to be almost unparalleled in the history of Life Assurance. *Life Policies on this System become payable during the lifetime of the Assured, thus rendering a Policy of Assurance a means of subsistence in old age, as well as a protection for a family, and a more valuable security to creditors in the event of early death; and effectually meeting the often urged objection, that persons do not themselves reap the benefit of their own prudence and forethought.*

No extra charge made to members of Volunteer Corps for service within the British Provinces.

☞ TORONTO AGENCY, 5 KING ST. WEST.

Oct 17—9-1yr   JAMES FRASER, *Agent.*

BEAVER
Mutual Insurance Association.

HEAD OFFICE—30 TORONTO STREET,
TORONTO.

INSURES LIVE STOCK against death from any cause. The only Canadian Company having authority to do this class of business.

E. C. CHADWICK, President.
W. T. O'REILLY, Secretary.   8-1y-25

HOME DISTRICT
Mutual Fire Insurance Company.

Office—North-West Cor. Yonge & Adelaide Streets,
TORONTO.—(UP STAIRS.)

INSURES Dwelling Houses, Stores, Warehouses, Merchandise, Furniture, &c.

PRESIDENT—The Hon. J. McMURRICH.
VICE-PRESIDENT—JOHN BURNS, Esq.
JOHN RAINS, Secretary.
AGENTS:
DAVID WRIGHT, Esq., Hamilton ; FRANCIS STEVENS, Esq.,
Barrie : Messrs. GIBBS & BRO., Oshawa.   8-1y

THE PRINCE EDWARD COUNTY
Mutual Fire Insurance Company.

HEAD OFFICE,—PICTON, ONTARIO.

President, L. B. STINSON ; *Vice-President,* WM. DELONG.
Directors : W. A. Richards, James Johnson, James CaVan, D. W. Ruttan, H. A. McFaul.—*Secretary,* John Twigg ; *Treasurer,* David Barket ; *Solicitor,* R. J. Fitzgerald.

THIS Company is established upon strictly Mutual principles, insuring farming and isolated property, (not hazardous,) *in Townships only,* and offers great advantages to insurers, at low rates for *five years,* without the expense of a renewal.

Picton, June 15, 1869.   9-1y

Fire and Marine Assurance.

THE BRITISH AMERICA
A S S U R A N C E C O M P A N Y .

HEAD OFFICE :
CORNER OF CHURCH AND COURT STREETS.
TORONTO.

BOARD OF DIRECTION :

Hon G. W. Allan, M L C.,	A. Joseph, Esq.,
George J Boyd, Esq ,	Peter Paterson, Esq.,
Hon. W. Cayley,	G. P. Ridout, Esq.,
Richard S. Cassels, Esq ,	E H. Rutherford, Esq ,

Thomas C. Street, Esq.
Governor:
GEORGE PERCIVAL RIDOUT, Esq.
Deputy Governor:
PETER PATERSON, Esq.
Fire Inspector: Marine Inspector:
E. ROBT O'BRIEN.   CAPT. R. COURNEEN.

Insurances granted on all descriptions of property against loss and damage by fire and the perils of inland navigation.

Agencies established in the principal cities, towns, and ports of shipment throughout the Province.

THOS. WM. BIRCHALL,
23-1y   *Managing Director.*

Insurance.

Reliance Mutual Life Assurance Society
OF LONDON, ENGLAND. Established 1840.

Head Office for the Dominion of Canada:
131 ST. JAMES STREET, MONTREAL.

DIRECTORS—Walter Shanly, Esq., M.P.; Duncan Macdonald, Esq.; George Winks, Esq., W. H. Hingston, Esq., M.D., L.R.C.S.
RESIDENT SECRETARY —James Grant.

Parties intending to assure lives, are invited to peruse the Society's prospectus, which embraces several entirely new and interesting features in Life Assurance. Copies can be had on application at the Head Office, or at any of the Agencies.

JAS. GRANT, Resident Secretary.
Agents wanted in unrepresented districts.   43-1y

The Gore District Mutual Fire Insurance Company

GRANTS INSURANCES on all description of Property against Loss or Damage by FIRE. It is the only Mutual Fire Insurance Company which assesses its Policies yearly from their respective dates ; and the average yearly cost of insurance in it, for the past three and a half years, has been nearly TWENTY CENTS IN THE DOLLAR less than what it would have been in an ordinary Proprietary Company.

THOS. M. SIMONS, Secretary & Treasurer.
ROBT. McLEAN, Inspector of Agencies.
Galt, 25th Nov., 1868.   15-1y

Canada Life Assurance Company.

SPECIALLY LICENSED BY THE GOVERNMENT
OF CANADA.

ESTABLISHED 1847.

CAPITAL..... ....A MILLION DOLLARS.

DEPOSIT WITH GOVERNMENT, $50,000.

The success of the Company may be judged of by the fact that during the financial year to the 30th April, 1869, the gross number of

NEW POLICIES

ISSUED WAS

8 9 2 !

FOR ASSURANCES OF
$1,257,734,

WITH

ANNUAL PREMIUMS OF
$49,783.73.

Rates lower that those of British or Foreign Offices, and every advantage offered which safety and liberality can afford.

A. G. RAMSAY, Manager.
E. BRADBURNE, Agent,
May 25.   1y   Toronto Street.

Queen Fire and Life Insurance Company,
OF LIVERPOOL AND LONDON,
ACCEPTS ALL ORDINARY FIRE RISKS
on the most favorable terms.

LIFE RISKS
Will be taken on terms that will compare favorably with other Companies.

CAPITAL, . . . £2,000,000 Stg.
CANADA BRANCH OFFICE—Exchange Buildings, Montreal.
Resident Secretary and General Agent,
A. MACKENZIE FORBES,
13 St. Sacrament St., Merchants' Exchange, Montreal.
WM. ROWLAND, Agent, Toronto.   1-1y

THE AGRICULTURAL
Mutual Assurance Association of Canada.

HEAD OFFICE ....LONDON, ONT.
A purely Farmers' Company. Licensed by the Government of Canada.

Capital, 1st January, 1869.................$250,103 82
Cash and Cash Items, over................$80,000 00
No. of Policies in force.....................30,692 00

THIS Company insures nothing more dangerous than Farm property. Its rates are as low as any well-established Company in the Dominion, and lower than those of a great many. It is largely patronised, and continues to grow in public favor.

For Insurance, apply to any of the Agents or address the Secretary, London, Ontario.
London, 2nd Nov., 1868.   12-1y.

Insurance:

The Waterloo County Mutual Fire Insurance Company.

HEAD OFFICE : WATERLOO, ONTARIO.

ESTABLISHED 1863.

THE business of the Company is divided into separate and distinct branches, the

VILLAGE, FARM, AND MANUFACTURING

Each Branch paying its own losses and its just proportion of the managing expenses of the Company.
C. M. TAYLOR, Sec.   M. SPRINGER, M.M.P., President.
J. HUGHES, Inspector.

Lancashire Insurance Company
CAPITAL, - - - - - - - - - £2,000,000 Sterling.

FIRE RISKS

Taken at reasonable rates of premium, and
ALL LOSSES SETTLED PROMPTLY,
By the undersigned, without reference elsewhere.
S. C. DUNCAN-CLARK & CO.,
General Agents for Ontario,
25-1y   N. W. Cor. of King & Church Sts., Toronto.

Western Assurance Company

INCORPORATED 1851.
CAPITAL, ... $400,000.

FIRE AND MARINE.

HEAD OFFICE................. TORONTO, (ONTARIO.)

DIRECTORS.

Hon. JNO. McMURRICH, President.
CHARLES MAGRATH, Vice-President.
A. M. SMITH, Esq.   JOHN FISKEN, Esq.
ROBERT BEATY, Esq.   ALEX. MANNING,
JAMES MICHIE, Esq.   N. BARNHART, Esq.
R. J. DALLAS, Esq.
B. HALDAN, Secretary.
J. MAUGHAN, JR., Assistant Secretary.
WM. BLIGHT, Fire Inspector.
CAPT. G. T. DOUGLAS, Marine Inspector.
JAMES PRINGLE, General Agent.

Insurances effected at the lowest current rates on Buildings, Merchandize, and other property, against loss or damage by fire.
On Hull, Cargo and Freight against the perils of Inland Navigation.
On Cargo Risks with the Maritime Provinces by sail or steam.
On Cargoes by steamers to and from British Ports.

WESTERN ASSURANCE COMPANY'S OFFICE, }
TORONTO, 1st April, 1869.   }

The Victoria Mutual
FIRE INSURANCE COMPANY OF CANADA.

Insures only Non-Hazardous Property, at Low Rates.

BUSINESS STRICTLY MUTUAL.

GEORGE H. MILLS, President.
W. D. BOOKER, Secretary.

HEAD OFFICE ...., ...HAMILTON, ONTARIO.
aug 15-1yr

North British and Mercantile Insurance Company.

Established 1809.

HEAD OFFICE, - - CANADA;   - MONTREAL

TORONTO BRANCH :
Local Offices, Nos. 4 & 6 WELLINGTON STREET.
Fire Department.....................R. N. GOOCH, Agent
Life Department....................H. L. HIME, Agent,

Imperial Fire Insurance Company
OF LONDON.
No. 1 OLD BROAD STREET, AND 16 PALL MALL,
ESTABLISHED 1803.
Canada General Agents,
RINTOUL BROS.,
24 St. Sacrament Street.
JAMES E. SMITH, Agent,
Toronto, Corner Church and Colborne Streets.

PUBLISHED AT THE OFFICE OF THE MONETARY TIMES, No. 60 CHURCH STREET.
PRINTED AT THE DAILY TELEGRAPH PUBLISHING HOUSE, BAY STREET, CORNER OF KING.

THE CANADIAN
MONETARY TIMES
AND
INSURANCE CHRONICLE.

)EVOTED TO FINANCE, COMMERCE, INSURANCE, BANKS, RAILWAYS, NAVIGATION, MINES, INVESTMENT, PUBLIC COMPANIES, AND JOINT STOCK ENTERPRISE.

| ., II—NO. 47. | TORONTO, THURSDAY, JULY 8, 1869. | SUBSCRIPTION $2 A YEAR. |

Mercantile.

J. B. Boustead.
VISION and Commission Merchant. Hops bought and sold on Commission. 82 Front St., Toronto.

John Boyd & Co.
OLESALE Grocers and Commission Merchants, Front St., Toronto.

Childs & Hamilton.
NUFACTURERS and Wholesale Dealers in Boots and Shoes, No. 7 Wellington Street East, Toronto, io. 28

L. Coffee & Co.
DUCE and Commission Merchants, No. 2 Manning's dock, Front St., Toronto, Ont. Advances made on nments of Produce.

Candee & Co.,
KERS AND BROKERS, dealers in Gold and Silver in, Government Securities, &c., Corner Main and age Streets, Buffalo, Y. N. 21-1y

John Fisken & Co.
K OIL and Commission Merchants, Yonge St., oronto, Ont.

W. & R. Griffith.
RTERS of Teas, Wines, etc. Ontario Chambers, r. Church and Front Sts, Toronto.

Gundry and Langley,
HITECTS AND CIVIL ENGINEERS, Building Surveyors and Valuators. Office corner of King and Jordan s, Toronto.
TOMAS GUNDRY.   HENRY LANGLEY.

Lyman & McNab.
OLESALE Hardware Merchants, Toronto, Ontario.

W. D. Matthews & Co.
DUCE Commission Merchants, Old Corn Exchange, 5 Front St. East, Toronto Ont.

R. C. Hamilton & Co.
DUCE Commission Merchants, 119 Lower Water t., Halifax, Nova Scotia.

H. Nerlich & Co.,
RTERS of French, German, English and American cy Goods, Cigars, and Leaf Tobaccos, No. 2 Adelaide West, Toronto. 13

Parson Bros.,
ROLEUM Refiners, and Wholesale dealers in Lamps, himneys, etc. Warerooms 51 Front St. Refinery cor. and Don Sts., Toronto.

Reford & Dillon.
RTERS of Groceries, Wellington Street, Toronto, tario.

C. P. Reid & Co.
RTERS and Dealers in Wines, Liquors, Cigars and af Tobacco, Wellington Street, Toronto. 28.

W. Rowland & Co.,
)UCE BROKERS and General Commission Merta. Advances made on Consignments. Corner t and Front Streets, Toronto.

Sessions, Turner & Cooper.
IUFACTURERS, Importers and Wholesale Dealer n Boots and Shoes, Leather Findings, etc., 8 Welbt West, Toronto, Ont

Sylvester, Bro. & Hickman,
MERCIAL Brokers and Vessel Agents. Office—No. Ontario Chambers, [Corner Front and Church Sts., o. 3-6m

Meetings.

MERCHANTS' BANK OF CANADA.

The annual meeting of this Bank was held in Montreal, July 5th, Mr. Hugh Allan in the chair.

The following report of the Directors to the Shareholders of the Merchants' Bank of Canada, at the annual meeting, 5th July, 1869, was then read:

The statement of the affairs of the Bank now submitted are evidence that its progress during the year has been very satisfactory.

In the face of the numerous bankruptcies that have occurred during the past year, it must not be supposed that this Bank could have escaped scatheless. So far from this being the case, it is a fact that the Bank sustained several not inconsiderable losses, but the Directors determined at once, and without hesitation, to write off from the profits a sum that after the severest scrutiny satisfied not only themselves, but their principal officers, would meet and cover every probable shortcoming.

The Shareholders may therefore accept the assurance that so far as can be seen at present, the assets of the Bank are good value for what they represent.

Fair progress continues to be made in the realization of the assets received from the Commercial Bank. The apparent result of the arrangement of amalgamation continues to encourage the belief that the original expectation will be realized.

The statements on the table show the present position of the Bank. The rest has attained the respectable figure of $700,000, and there seems every prospect that it will continue to increase.

During the late sitting of the Legislature, several measures came before it materially affecting the interests of the Banks.

The Directors regarding the continuance of the Act relating to Insolvency as a great and nearly unmixed evil, petitioned the Legislature for its total repeal. This was not acceded to, and the act was amended, but not in the opinion of the Directors materially improved.

The Banking and Interest measures introduced had fortunately to be withdrawn, the latter being of such a retrograde character, as to excite surprise that in this age of financial knowledge, any party could be found to support it.

The Act of Incorporation establishes the Capital of the Bank at $6,000,000—of this only $4,000,000 has been offered for subscription or taken up.

The Directors now invite the Shareholders to subscribe the remaing $2,000,000, and with this view a series of resolutions will be submitted for your approval.

In conformity with the Act of Incorporation, the following Directors retire at this meeting: Messrs. Damase Mason, Andrew Allan, Adolphe Roy, and Hugh Fraser, all of whom are eligible for re-election.

The By-laws of the Bank have been remodelled and are now to be submitted for your consideration.

All of which is respectfully submitted.

HUGH ALLAN,
President.

The President then moved, and it was carried unanimously, that the report just read be approved

of and printed for circulation among the Shareholders of the Bank.

The proposed By-Laws for the government of the Bank, were then read by the President, all of which were approved and adopted by the meeting.

A series of resolutions relating to the increase of the capital of the Bank were then submitted, all of which were approved and carried by the Shareholders.

Messrs. W. B. Cumming and George Templeton were requested to act as scrutineers to receive the votes of the Shareholders.

General Statement Merchants' Bank of Canada.

LIABILITIES.

Circulation			$1,148,510 00
Deposits bearing interest		$1,928,025 33	
Deposits not bearing interest		1,267,611 18	
			3,195,636 51
Balances due to other banks and Foreign Agents			169,274 21
Dividends unclaimed.$	8,931 60		
Do. No. 3	143,334 40		
			147,266 00
			$4,660,686 72
Capital paid up			3,585,426 87
Rest			700,000 00
Contingent Funds			63,549 00
Interest Reserved			10,100 00
			$9,019,762 59

ASSETS.

Gold and Silver coin on hand		$864,871 11	
Province Notes		431,943 00	
			1,296,814 11
Notes and other Cheques of other Banks			200,840 42
Government Securities			533,606 22
			2,030,760 75
Real Estate			360,279 34
Notes discounted and other Debts not otherwise included			6,627,722 50
			$9,018,762 59

To Jackson Rae, Esq., Cashier Merchants' Bank of Montreal.

SIR:—We, the undersigned scrutineers, appointed this day by the Shareholders of the Merchants' Bank of Canada, declare the following gentlemen duly elected Directors for the ensuing year:—Damase Masson, Hugh Fraser, Andrew Allan, Adolphe Roy. Signed, W. B. Cumming; Geo. Templeton, scrutineers.

Subsequently at a meeting of the Board Mr. Hugh Allan was elected President, and Mr. Edwin Atwater, Vice-President, respectively.

ROYAL CANADIAN BANK.

The annual general meeting of the shareholders of the Royal Canadian Bank, was held in this city on the 5th July, inst., Mr. Metcalfe, President of the Bank, occupied the chair. There were present about two hundred shareholders.

The chairman in opening the meeting said that he exceedingly regretted that any display of temper had been shown by any of the delegates at the last meeting held in that room. Mutual recriminative language certainly was not, nor would be productive of any good effect. He hoped that the proceedings of this meeting would show a marked improvement in that respect over the former one. As for himself he would announce that he was not a candidate for, nor did he desire re-election. All he wanted was that the best men might be elected to take care of the interests of the shareholders for the ensuing year. The chairman then proceeded to read the following annual report:—

Fourth Annual Report of the Directors of the Royal Canadian Bank.

The Directors of the Royal Canadian Bank beg leave to present, to the shareholders, their fourth annual report.

The year just closed has been one long to be remembered in the history of the Bank. Business, notwithstanding some difficulties, commenced under favorable auspices, and at the end of the year showed very favorable results, as, as a reference to the following figures will show:—

Net profits for half year ending Dec. 20, were.............................. $89,201 72
From this was deducted the semi-annual dividend, at the rate of 8 % per annum...................... 44,416 20

And there was left to be added to reserve................................. $44,785 52
The circulation at the last annual meeting was........................$1,095,452 00
The circulation at the end of the first half of the past year as ... 1,569,611 00

Showing an increase of.............. $474,159 00
The Deposits at last annual meeting$1,398,050 60
The deposits at end of half year.... 1,684,388 00

Showing an increase of............... $286,337 40
Paid-up capital at last annual meeting was $1,071,260 00
Paid up capital at end of half year. 1,140,183 34

Showing an increase of.............. $68,923 34
The above comparison discloses for the first half-year a steady increase of business and public confidence, affording good grounds for the belief that the second half of the year's business would be equally satisfactory.

During the month of January, however, the Vice-President of the Bank made a demand for accommodation to the extent of nearly one-tenth of the paid-up capital of the Bank. This demand was unanimously refused by the rest of the Board. A series of malevolent attacks by the Vice-President upon the management of the Bank, in connection with mischievous rumors, industriously circulated by those who were interested in its downfall, caused the withdrawal of public confidence to an alarming extent, as the following figures evince:

Circulation on 31st Dec. was...$1,569,611 00
"   on 21st May was......... 902,198 00

Showing a reduction of......... *$667,413 00
Deposits on 31st Dec. were...........$1,684,388 00
"   on 21st May were...... 828,868 69

Showing a reduction of.......... $855,519 37
Specie, etc., on 31st Dec. was....$1,163,343 04
"   on 21st May was...... 126,033 09

Showing a reduction of.........$1,037,309 95
The Directors, in this emergency, applied to some of the local banks for a re-discount of commercial paper to a limited extent by each. Their application for assistance having been declined,

---

the necessity for the suspension of specie payment was, after much anxious deliberation, absolutely forced upon the Directors, and the doors were closed on the morning of the 21st day of May.

That the Directors have not since been idle in their efforts to realize the assets of the Bank and reduce its liabilities, the following table will prove :

Paid-up capital on May 21st....... $1,163,728 34
"   " June 30th 1,176,973 34
Increase in 40 days..................... 13,245 00
Total liabilities on May 21st 1,786,934 40
"   " June 30th......... 1,066,069 81
Decrease in 40 days..................... 700,864 59
Total assets on May 21st............. 3,169,100 70
"   " June 30th 2,178,218 47
Decrease in 40 days 990,882 23
The latter decrease includes $297,060, bad debts written off.

While every effort was thus being made by the Board and Cashier to enable the Bank to resume specie payments within the sixty days allowed by the charter of the Bank, they deemed it prudent to look forward to the worst possible contingency, and obtained from the Parliament of the Dominion, during the last session, an Act extending the time for the resumption of specie payment to ninety days from the date of the passing of the Act, providing also for amalgamamation with any other bank, if necessary, and for liquidation, if unavailable.

The assets of the bank, both at the head office and agencies, have been estimated as carefully as possible, within the limited time between the date of suspension and the day fixed for the annual meeting. The result has been that about $300,000 of notes have been actually written off as bad. This amount, so far as at present can be ascertained, includes all losses sustained by the bank since it went into operation on an aggregate of discounts of over forty-two millions of dollars, being about five-sevenths of one per cent. loss—a result not so disastrous by any means as has been stated by the enemies of the bank.

Considering the amount of good this bank has done in advancing the material interests of the country, the large amount of business it has transacted throughout the Province, and its present solvent state, the Directors, in resigning their trust to the shareholders, venture to hope that their successors will accept office with a determination to resume specie payments at as early a day as possible.

The Directors, as on previous occasions, bear willing testimony to the great attention of the President and Cashier to the interests of the bank during the past year.

Subjoined is the usual annual general statement of the affairs of the bank, as required by the Act of Incorporation to which the shareholders are referred for further information regarding the bank's affairs.

Statement for the year ending June 30th, 1869.

LIABILITIES.

Circulation $416,128 00
Due to other banks 22,734 53
Deposits not bearing interest........ 207,496 60
"   bearing interest 412,345 02
Unclaimed dividends 7,365 66
Accrued interest....................... 6,783 35

To shareholders..................... $1,072,853 16
Capital paid up.......$1,176,973 34
Suspense account...... 6,344 11
Interest and exchange 3,024 46
                       $1,186,341 91
Less preli-
  minary
  expense
  account .$17,620 00
Ordinary do. 1,792 13
Profit & loss 61,564 47
                       $80,976 60 $1,105,365 31

ASSETS.

Coin and Provincial notes $196,014 28
Notes and cheques of other banks.. 50,621 74
Due by other banks ... . } 39,152 47
Sterling exchange....... $52,587 21 { 13,428 74
Government debentures 128,911 10
Notes and bills discounted 1,736,619 39
Furniture, &c...... .... 13,464 65
                                    $2,178,218 47

Statement of Profits and Loss account for year ending June 30, 1869.

DR.

To amount paid President and Directors for last year.................$ 5,355 00
" 20 per cent. off preliminary expenses 4,105 02
" 30 per cent. off office furniture.... 539 22
" Dividend No. 7...................... 44,416 20
" bad and doubtful debts written off 297,247 67
                                    $351,663 12

Total amount of paper in default...$438,434 29

CR.

By balance at end of last year.........$ 6,519 23
" profits of To-
  ronto office..$70,289 55
" less working
  expenses..... 27,313 08 $42,976 47
" profits of Agencies (net)112,989 72 155,966 19
" " from suspense account......... 19,265 04
" balance of reserve.................... 108,266 40
" amount recovered on account
  Stauffer's (expenses)............ 81 80
" balance at debit of account.......... 61,564 47
                                    $351,663 15

The following is the report of the special Committee appointed to examine the paper at the Head Office:—

TORONTO, July 3, 1869.
To the President and Directors of the Royal Canadian Bank, Toronto:

GENTLEMEN:—The very limited time placed at our disposal, rendering it apparent that it would be a matter of impossibility for us to comply with the terms of the resolution of your Board, first submitted to us, viz:—"That we should make an examination into the affairs of the Royal Canadian Bank." We were disposed to decline entering upon so arduous a task, when it was suggested that we might perform a temporary service by examining and reporting upon the paper dis counted at the Head Office, in Toronto, and our duty was consequently so limited by another reso lution to that effect.

The bills and notes submitted to us for exami nation amounted to the sum of $283,722.57, and we have estimated the same as worth the sum o $228,941.37.

Of the paper valued, the whole was examine and inspected by us, with the exception of pape to the amount of $50,783.34, which, being pay able out of Toronto was, therefore, not produced to the sum of $18,250. The remaining deduction

The paper considered entirely bad, amounte were made from paper considered weak and slow a fair per centage from which we struck off fo reasons satisfactory to us.

We have not made any estimate as regard paper in suit, being of opinion that the solicitor of the Bank are better qualified than we are t form a proper judgment of their value.—(Signed Samuel B. Harman, John Crawford, William Thompson.

The reports from the different agencies wer then read by the President, amidst a good deal o interruption, which showed the results indicate in the subjoined table :

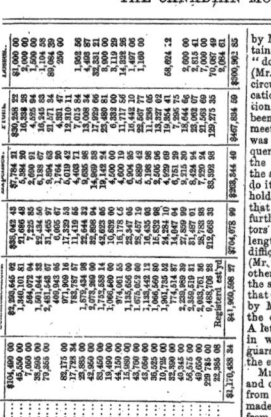

otal amount of dividend, paid, $186,527 98.

Mr. Craig stated that there were reports in circulation to the effect that quite recently some of directors had over-drawn their accounts. As he stated on the authority of Mr. A. M. ith.

Mr. Smith acknowledged having made the ement that one of the directors had got a large ance when the bank was in its death-throes; but he had over-drawn his account to the extent of $16,000. (Sensation.)

Mr. Manning admitted having got $14,000, but that the bank had as good security as any in the ... He then charged Mr. Smith with having ted a cheque to a friend of his to the amount of $50,000, who had not a dollar of interest in the k.

Mr. Smith, in reply, said that the cheque referred to was granted to Messrs. Gooderham & ts, and the cheque was paid to the hour; a ement which fully satisfied the meeting, as expressions of approval indicated.

Mr. Donald McDonald then rose and commenced, amidst hisses, the delivery of a somewhat thy address, referring to his past action in rence to the bank, and charging upon the directors, the Cashier and the President and President, the entire blame of the bank's ortunes. We cannot attempt even a summy of his speech. It contained nothing which ot already before the public, except that the ctors had refused him all access to the books documents of the bank since the 12th of May. r. J. Ham Perry reviewed the speech and the luct of Mr. McDonald during the years of his storship, and showed effectively the inconsisy between the statements put forward in the ual reports and those made in Mr. McDonald's ilars, and contended that that gentleman had ed himself to be entirely unworthy of confice.

r. Manning followed in a lengthy review of McDonald's course. He read a letter of Mr. d. Smith's, which had been partly published

by Mr. McDonald. The suppressed portion contained the statement that Mr. McDonald was a "donkey," and with this part of the letter he (Mr. Manning) fully agreed. He recounted the circumstances relating to Mr. McDonald's application for a loan of $100,000, and read a resolution of the directors to prove that the loan had been positively refused. A threat of calling a meeting of the shareholders to oust the President was then made by Mr. McDonald, and subsequently his first circular, which was printed in the United States, was issued. Before issuing the second circular, he, on being implored not to do it, as it would ruin the bank, offered to withhold it if the directors would take his stock and that of a friend of his off their hands, and stated further that his lips would be sealed. The directors refused to do this. The speaker dwelt at length on the history of the bank, recounting the difficulties which it had to contend with, and he (Mr. Manning) thought it questionable if any other bank in the Province would have stood under the same circumstances. He read letters proving that the arrangement with W. R. Brown was made by Mr. A. M. Smith, without the knowledge of the directors, to give Brown a credit of $25,000. A letter was also read from Mr. W. C. Chewett, in which that gentleman gave a "continuing guarantee" to the bank on behalf of Brown to the extent of $25,000.

Mr. Smith defended his action in the matter, and charged that the loss that resulted to the bank from this account was owing to new arrangements made by the Board subsequent to his retirement from the Presidency.

Mr. Dumble defended himself from charges made against him respecting the Cobourg agency and the account of the Marmora Company, of which he was President. He showed that the account of that company was quite safe, and that very profitable. The advances made in Cobourg, in connection with which losses were made, were without his consent or approval.

The meeting then adjourned, collecting again at 4 o'clock p.m.

Mr. Harrison, M.P., stated that the law required the new Board to be elected on that day, and he therefore moved that a ballot be opened.

Hon. J. H. Cameron advised that if any votes were cast after 12 a.m., they should be kept separate, as he doubted the legality of voting after that hour.

The scrutineers for the election of directors then to take place were, viz.:—W. B. Phipps, F. Shanley, Dr. Wright, and A. Fletcher.

The sum of $2,000 were then voted to the President, for his services during the past year.

The result of the voting was declared at half-past five, on the morning of the 6th July, to be as follows:—Hon. Jno. Crawford, 4,752; Wm. Thomson, 4,660; J. McGee, 3,061; J. Crombie, 2,736; W. Barber, 2,656; W. McGivern, 2,474; J. H. Dumble, 2,125; Alex. Manning, 1,992; W. H. Howland, 1,955; J. Trow, 1,916; T. Griffith, 1,585; T. C. Chisholm, 1,098; Dr. Patterson, 1,022; Jos. Gould, 167; W. C. McLeod, 127; J. D. Merrick, 103; J. E. Smith, 76; R. A. Harrison, 76; H. H. Meredith, 57; J. Medcalf, 41; A. M. Smith, 30; C. W. Bunting, 16.

The seven first on the list, Hon. John Crawford, barrister; Mr. William Thomson, of Thomson & Burns; hardware merchants, Toronto; Mr. McGee, lumber merchant, King Station; Mr. Crombie, Galt; Mr. Wm. Barber, manufacturer, Georgetown; Mr. Wm. McGivern, hardware merchant, Hamilton; and Mr. John H. Dumble, Cobourg were therefore re-elected.

At a subsequent meeting of the Board, Hon. Jno. Crawford was elected President and Wm. Thomson Vice-President.

TORONTO, GREY AND BRUCE R. R.—A meeting of shareholders and others was held on the evening of July 1st, to hear the report of a delegation sent to Montreal, to procure subscriptions to the

stock. The delegates reported that a number of the leading citizens had been called and some subscriptions obtained. Mr. E. H. King, General Manager of the Bank of Montreal, had subscribed $10,000. A statement of the share-list was then made by the Secretary, from which it appeared that the total subscriptions taken up amounted to $276,300; balance of subscriptions still to be raised in order to the closing of books, $23,700.

It was then stated by the Secretary, that there were $2,300 of subscriptions out, not entered in the books, which reduced the balance to $21,400. This amount was then promptly made up by the gentlemen on the spot. The notice convening the meeting for the election of directors will appear in next Saturday's Canada Gazette.

Insurance.

FIRE RECORD.—There have been very few fires in the country for some weeks past, which is owing chiefly to the unusually frequent and heavy showers of rain.

Iroquois, Ont., June.—A telegram states that the stave mill of Mr. James Armstrong was burned last night. Loss $6,000.

Hibbert Township, Ont., June 26.—Residence of Robert Gardner, Deputy Reeve of Hibbert, was entirely consumed by fire. The fire caught accidentally. No insurance. Mr. Gardner is a heavy loser.

Weston, Ont., July 4th.—J. B. Gracey's brewery was burnt down. The fire is supposed to be the work of an incendiary. Insured for $4,000 in the Western of Canada.

Toronto, July 5th.—A stable in rear of the building 460 King Street West. It was occupied by a cabman named Clark.

Port Colborne, July 3.—The captain of the propellor Prairie State reports passing a barque sunk, with her top masts out of water, between Fairport and Ashtabula, supposed to be the barque Garry-owen, of Toronto, loaded with coal from Cleveland to Toronto. It is reported that all hands were saved.

The ship Sunbeam, bound out, has gone around in Lake St. Peter.

—The California Insurance Commissioner has just issued his first annual report.

—The farmers of Sydenham Township, Grey County, are taking the preliminary steps towards the formation of a farmers Mutual Insurance Company.

—The Underwriters of New York are circulating a petition for the appointment of Superintendent Barnes as one of the representatives of the United States, in the Statistical Congress to be held at Hague, in September.

—The promoters of the National and Provincial Union Assurance Society, started some time ago in London, England, by certain footmen and butlers, an account of which was given in The Monetary Times, have come to grief, two of them, Reid and Jones, being sentenced, the former to five years penal servitude, and the latter to twelve months imprisonment.

ENGLISH INSURANCE COMPANIES IN THE U. S. —The following figures indicate the business of the Companies named in the year 1868, in the State of New York (U. S. cur'y): —

Liverpool, London and Globe, Liverpool............	$709,945 54	$427,373 96
North British and Mercantile, London, Eng....	202,108 49	79,084 44
Queen In. Co., Liverpool, Eng..	113,625 10	72,780 40
Royal In. Co., Liverpool, Eng..	96,962 92	30,671 28
Imperial In. Co., London, Eng.	87,415 79	22,679 73
Total............	$1,208,109 84	$632,589 81
Grand Total............	$4,943,966 22	$3,754,416 21

RATES OF INSURANCE.—The following are the rates charged on the different descriptions of building mentioned in the principal cities of the States:

	Brick or Stone. 1st Class.	Brick or Stone. 2nd Class.	Brick or Stone. 3rd Class.	Or frame detached 100 ft. 4th Class.
New York........	$0 85	$0 95	$1 10	.....
St. Louis	0 75	0 75	0 90	.....
Cincinnati	0 75	0 90	1 25	$1 50
Louisville	0 90	1 00	1 25	.....
Chicago..........	0 85	1 00	1 25	1 50
Cleveland.......	0 70	0 85	1 10	1 25
Boston	0 50	0 50	0 90	.....
National Board rates for cities and large towns generally	0 95	1 00	1 12½	1 50
San Francisco ..	0 70	0 80	1 00	1 12½

BOGUS INSURANCE COMPANIES.—The London *Insurance Record* says: The amalgamation of the Progress and the United Ports and General Assurance Companies is announced as having been completed, and the joint business will be henceforth conducted under the title of the latter. The subscribed capital of the united companies is £550,203, of which £127,661 is said to be paid up. We presume that before the public have time to breathe after this announcement, the other venture which comes of the same parentage will be brought into the swim; and whether the strength of the three—or rather, the four or five,—new schemes will be sufficient to make one decent company time will show. By the way, how much does a certain official net by this little piece of business?

FIRE INSURANCE DUTIES.—In the year 1867, farming Stock in the United Kingdom was insured against fire to the amount of £79,643,401; in the year 1868, to the amount of £83,768,784. There was, and is no duty or tax on these Insurances. Other property has hitherto been liable to duty on insurance against fire; but in 1865, the duty was reduced from 3s. to 1s. 6d. per £100 insured. The amount insured was at that time increasing at about £60 millions sterling a year; in the year ending the 31st of March, 1866, it increased to £1,-59,893,000, and in the next year it was £1,-183,484,000, an increase of 73 millions, or nearly 6 per cent. But this rate of increase did not continue; in the year ending the 31st March, 1868, the increase was but about 43 millions, or very little more than had become usual under the higher duty. The Inland Revenue Board stated in their last report that, so far as they could then judge, there would not be a larger amount insured in the year ending the 31st of March, 1869, which, by the present budget, will be the last complete year of fire insurance duty.

INSTITUTE OF ACTUARIES.—The London *Insurance Record*, in commenting upon an article in the *Journal of the Institute of Actuaries*, of which the Thirteenth Annual Report of the Insurance Commissioner of Massachusetts is the subject, remarks as follows: That the Americans have succeeded in striking out new ideas and methods to which we, in this country, are entire strangers, there can be no doubt at all. "These ideas and methods are not simply fantastic devices, but the product of sober reason and practical sense, and are directed not only to the developement of the Assurance principle, but also to the regulation of Assurance practice." It would probably be well for us to take a lesson or two from our American cousins, who have managed to develop Assurance to an extent unknown in any other part of the world. Probably one of the principal causes, if not the greatest of this large developement, is the compulsory publicity of the assets and liabilities of the Assurance Companies. Legislation has at last come to be regarded in England as necessary, and although it is not intended to set a Commissioner in authority over the Companies, we believe that, with the passing of a moderately strict bill, Life Assurance will take a fresh start, and become

more popular in our own country than it is at present.

The discussion of the great "bonus question" —as to the comparative merits of the "percentage" and the "contribution" methods of dividing surplus—has been carried on for a considerable time, and with great warmth in America, until one would almost imagine that the subject had been exhausted, but we think that much new light has been thrown upon it in the present article. Whatever the comparative merits of the different methods may be, we concur with the author of the article in considering that "bonuses have worked a moral mischief, by withdrawing the attention of the assured from the safety of his office, in which it should be chiefly fixed, and concentrating it on the accident of gain. We are inclined to think that nothing would purify and benefit the cause of assurance so much as a well-considered reduction of the premium. By circumscribing the area of chance, the arts of prudence and caution would succeed the contrivances of reckless ambition."

A LIFE POLICY OR A MORTGAGE.—At a recent meeting in London, Mr. Edward Butler, Secretary of the Reliance Mutual Life, made the following comparison between the result of investment in a Life Policy and in a Mortgage. We find it in our London Exchanges:—

We will take a sum of money just within a ready grasp; you can multiply it as many times as you please, but for the sake of following the argument we will say that a man agrees to invest £5 every year at 4 per cent. upon mortgage. At the end of five years he will find that his investment, with the interest and compound interest— that is, interest upon interest—will amount to £33 3. 4d. He will have paid £5 every year for five years, and at the end of the time he will find that it amounts to the sum I have stated. At the end of ten years he will find that it amounts to £60 and a few pence, within twenty years he will find that it amounts to £148 18s. 7d., and at the end of thirty years it amounts to £280 9s. 3d. Supposing that the gentleman who made the investment was at the age of thirty when he agreed to pay £5 per annum, he will have reached the age of sixty at the time when his investment amounts to £280 9s. 3d. But you must bear in mind that there are very important conditions to this result. It means that the man should be always able to invest readily both the principal and the interest he receives, and also that he shall live long enough to make the investment. Of course a man at thirty contemplates that he will live to reach the age of sixty. I think there are few who hear me, aged thirty, who are not of that opinion. Brown, Jones and Robinson, who are also thirty, may be differently situated. For instance, you may say—"Brown is rather plethoric," "Jones seems a bit consumptive," "Robinson does not sufficiently take care of himself." Therefore you will say that Brown, Jones and Robinson may not last another thirty years, although you don't contemplate that any such result will happen to yourselves. But you know, ladies and gentlemen, as well as I do, that none of us can be sure of life, and that very often in our experience we find the healthiest lives—those lives which have received unimpeachable certificates from medical men—are the lives that become claims first. Our experience frequently shows this to be the case. Now, let us just see how many lives may be calculated to last until sixty, starting, for instance, at the age of thirty, and basing our calculation on the fact that there are one thousand children born in the same year. We will take these thousand children and judge them by the standard of the Carlisle table, because that is least favorable to my observations. By the Carlisle table, it appears that at the age of thirty, there are 564 of these thousand infant lives, the rest being dead. Now, at the age of thirty-five, there are only 536 alive; so that in these five years, twenty-eight lives have fallen in. At the age of forty, there are only 503 of these lives to be found in existence; and at the age of sixty three are only 364;

so that you see this gentleman, who makes these investments of £5 a year, believing and hoping that he will live to realize the sum I have spoken of, may have his expectations put an end to by his decease. Now, there is another kind of investment to which I would call your attention, and which provides against the advent of death. We do not affect to tell you that if a man is living in the full expectation of a long life, that life assurance is the best investment he can make. It is not so; not altogether so. Let us look at the comparison. If a man assures his life at the age of thirty in a respectable office—for I will take none in particular—he pays £5; and that £5, in the event of his death, will realise £200. By our system, we have profits or bonuses added to the policy; and I have here a table which estimates the rate of bonus additions. Now, at the age of sixty, this policy, which was taken out for £200, with these bonuses, is worth £303 8s. 4d. Therefore, you see, an investment in life assurance is not an unprofitable one.

THE ENGLISH LIFE ASSURANCE BILL.

The Bill to amend the law relating to life insurance companies now before the House of Commons is a very good example of the timid and hesitating manner in which English legislation is conducted. The object of the bill is to secure the solvency of life insurance companies. Probably no one will doubt that this is a most desirable object, although there is much difference of opinion as to the best way of obtaining it. The principle of the bill apparently is to require life insurance companies to make official returns of the income, expenditure, mode of doing business, &c., which may be to some extent a guide by which the solvency of the company may be ascertained. The way in which it is proposed to carry out this idea is, however, very faulty and incomplete. The provisions do not go far enough. The companies are required to make a return every year of their income and expenditure, of their balance sheet, and of the new business transactions during the past year. Also an actual return once in every ten years showing the principles on which the business of the company is conducted. These returns are to be deposited with the registrar of Joint-stock Companies in certain forms contained in schedules to the bill. There are also special provisions for the deposit of copies of accounts, &c., with the Register of Joint-stock Companies on an amalgamation between two companies, or when the business of one company is transferred to another. A neglect or refusal to comply with the requirements of the bill is made a misdemeanour punishable by fine. The chief defects in this bill are—first, it appoints no officer to examine and check the accounts required from the companies (and without such a person the giving of accounts would be almost wholly nugatory); secondly, it makes no provision for the separation of accounts between different classes of business in those companies which are engaged in marine and other insurance business as well as in life insurance; thirdly, it is not rendered necessary that there should be any fixed amount or proportion of capital actually paid up in cash before policies are granted. These omissions are such serious defects in the bill that it may perhaps be doubted whether it is desirable that the bill should pass at all. The object of the bill is, however, so desirable, and the probability of anything approaching complete legislation on this or any other subject is so small, that it would probably be best that the bill should pass, and thus become a nucleus round which subsequent and more efficient legislation may be collected. It is something to have made a step in the right direction, however little may at first be directly achieved thereby.—*Solicitors' Journal.*

—Col. J. W. H. Rowley, of Yarmouth, has been appointed Collector of Internal Revenue at that port. He is Cashier of the Yarmouth Bank.

:HE CANADIAN MONETARY TIMES AND INSU-
NCE CHRONICLE *is printed every Thursday even-
and distributed to Subscribers on the following
rning.*

ublishing office, No. 60 *Church-street,* 3 *doors*
th of Court-street. ·

lubscription price—

Canada. $2,00 *per annum.*

England, stg. 10s. *per annum.*

United States (U. S. Cy.) $3.00 *per annum.*

lasual advertisements will be charged at the rate
ten cents per line, each insertion.

Iddress all letters to " THE MONETARY TIMES.*"*

:heques, money orders, &c. should be made pay-
: to J. M. TROUT, *Business Manager, who alone*
authorized to issue receipts for money.

☞ *All Canadian Subscribers to* THE MONETARY
:ES *will receive* THE REAL ESTATE JOURNAL
hout further charge.

;he Canadian Monetary Times.

THURSDAY, JULY 8, 1869.

AMALGAMATIONS.

t is possible for one insurance company to
llow. another ·without· bursting, unless,
haps, the devourer be actually hide-bound.·
dern experience, however, prepares us
receiving with equanimity these gas-
iomic feats. In too many cases they
e proved merely conjuring tricks, in-
led to deceive. They bring money into
'pockets of the principal performers,
leave their dupes confused and robbed.
:he case of the International and the Her-
s, it appears that a raw company of
:hroom growth bought out a company of
: 'thirty years' standing, the transaction
:g of the most disgraceful character. The
companies had no sooner completed the
ngement 'than' they were forced into
ncery, and their life policies passed over
ie Prudential. For a knowledge of this
named company's affairs, those interested
refer to the paper by Hon. Elizur

Wright, which appeared in last week's number of this journal. In these transactions,
not a few Canadians are interested to their
sorrow. We know at least two or three persons who have been paying premiums to the
International on life policies for over a quarter of a century. In the Lower Provinces
the number of policy-holders is, we believe,
considerable. The last series of amalgamations which has affected us in Canada is
the purchase of the Ætna's business by the
United Ports, and the subsequent purchase
of the United Ports by the Progress. One
policyholder can hardly tell where he is to
look for payment in case of loss, or what is
the condition of the company to which he is
trusting for indemnity. So that we have had
some experience of amalgamations, both as
regards life and fire business, and we have
no hesitation in saying that such experience
is anything but pleasant. In the case of
life assurance, a great deal of distress of
mind has been caused to policyholders. It
is a hard thing for the innocent victims of
successive swindles, who have paid out money
for a series of years, in the expectation that
they were making provision for their families,
to discover now, when past the prime of life,
that their forethought has been in vain,
that their savings have been thrown away,
and that they have built upon the sand.
Nothing could be more disheartening to the
careful and industrious man, who, appreciating the benefits of life assurance, had sought,
in good faith, to partake of them.

We know amalgamation is fashionable in
life assurance. In twenty years, two hundred transfers of business took place in England, some of the companies, parties to such
transfers, being of great age and of the
highest character. In 1868 there were eight
transfers. Much may be said in justification
of the practice, and we do not consider that
amalgamation is necessarily to be objected to.
But there is a class of men known as promoters, who start insurance companies (and
many other kinds of companies, too,) for the
express purpose of having a finger in amalgamation. Whoever loses, they win. They
draw pay for floating a company, and when
their creation is about to sink, as many of the
ephemerals do, they set their wits to work to
bring about an amalgamation, and, if successful, draw a second commission. In the
case of the Hercules and International, one
gentleman, who had influence, received
£8,000 for using it, and another, who happened to be Secretary, was paid £15,000 as
compensation for his loss of office. So that
amalgamations are not without profit to
somebody.

We do not say that the fact of one com-

pany purchasing the business of another is,
of itself, sufficient to beget suspicion ; but
we do say that certain recent amalgamations
have a suspicious look. The only safeguard
against untoward contingencies, so far as the
public is concerned, is the selection of sound
companies in which to place insurance. The
man of ordinary intelligence, who takes out
a life policy in a company of whose affairs he
is ignorant, is little better than a fool, and
deserves any misfortune that may result
from his absurd action. He need expect no
sympathy. *Caveat emptor* applies just as
clearly, whether a horse, a cow, or so much
insurance be purchased. Some imagine that
there is magic in the name company, and
go blindfold to their own destruction. Insurance companies are no exception to the
general rule, that good and bad herd together. Yet we cannot help feeling surprised,
although it is hard to be surprised at anything
now-a-days, that so many intelligent and
shrewd men are indifferent as regards the insurance companies they trust to for indemnity
in case of loss. Year after year they continue to pay premiums, and, if asked as to
the financial condition of the particular company they do business with, will unblushingly
confess their total ignorance of the subject.
We know this to be the case, and can point to
individuals who never thought of informing
themselves, as to the financial state of their
insurers, until the matter was brought home
to them, directly, by disaster. These self-
same men would not have loaned a few hundred dollars on mortgage security, without a
full examination of title being first had, and
every possible provision made against even
remote contingencies. This carelessness and
neglect in the selection of an insurer has been
the real table on which the calculations of
some companies have been framed. Swindlers have waxed fat, and incompetency has
feasted luxuriously, upon it. It is to be hoped
that the lessons, few, comparatively, though
they be, which Canadians have learned through
a bitter experience, will not be without fruit,
and that more discrimination will be exercised
in the matter of insurance, than has hitherto
prevailed among us. The soundest companies in
the world are represented here, so that there
is little excuse for accepting, and paying for
a doubtful or valueless policy of insurance,
when the best may be had. The man who
takes his policy without acquainting himself
with its conditions, acts about as sensibly as
the one who applies for insurance without
first satisfying himself that his vendor is
reasonably solvent. The insured is bound in
duty to himself, (more especially if he holds
a life policy,) not to rest content with satisfaction at the outset, but to inform himself,
from time to time, whether that solvency

continues, and whether there is a reasonable prospect of his annual expenditure in premium proving of some avail, else he may find that he has been but pouring his money into a sieve, or into the pockets of swindlers.

THE ROYAL CANADIAN BANK.

The proceedings at the annual meeting of the shareholders of the Royal Canadian Bank were an improvement upon the mere noise and abuse which prevailed at the meeting of "delegates." For the future, those connected with public institutions will see the expediency of having as little as possible to do with delegates; and, we are sure, delegates' meetings will receive small encouragement. Delegates are too apt to imagine that their delegated duty is to bicker; that their appointment is equivalent to the conferment of an illimitable right to talk. Those who undertake to set a large monetary institution to rights, and to win back public confidence, must vary the monotony of abuse, hisses and cheers, with the exhibition of a little common sense, before they can hope to attain their object.

In looking over the directors' report, we find that the first half of the year just closed showed an increase in circulation of $474,159, in deposits of $286,337, and in paid up capital of $68,923. With the second half year began the bank's troubles. The Vice-President, through motives now clearly seen to have been of a very unworthy character, attacked his colleagues, and the result was the withdrawal of public confidence from the institution. Between the 1st of January and the 21st of May, the circulation ran down $607,413, and the deposits were reduced by $835,519. A depletion of specie to the amount of $1,037,309 rendered a suspension necessary. According to the statements now furnished, it appears that the capital is impaired to the extent of only $71,608 or six per cent.

The report of the gentlemen appointed to examine into the affairs of the bank was confined for the reasons set forth, to the valuation of the paper discounted at the head office. The four agencies at which the principal losses occurred were Cobourg, $89,084; Kingston, $32,331; Seaforth, $58,624; and Paris, $14,322. These losses are so enormous in proportion to the business done at each place, as to bear on their face the true explanation of their occurrence, namely, wholesale fraud. On the other hand, the profits at Bowmanville, Peterborough, Whitby, Montreal and Toronto, stand out in bold relief.

From what came out at the meeting, we conclude that Mr. McDonald, the virtuous Vice-President, is not a fit man to be on a

bank board; that Mr. A. M. Smith, arrogated to himself a power in management which he was incompetent to use aright; that Mr. Dumble's explanation of the Marmora matter was perfectly satisfactory; that the advance to Mr. Manning, no matter how well secured, was ill-timed, and open to the gravest suspicion; that the directors made an indiscreet use of the information they acquired in the Board room; and that the astutest and most self-willed Cashier in the world could not have fought successfully against such odds as Mr. Woodside had against him. The great wonder to us is, that he has come so well out of the ordeal.

The new President, as we have said, is a gentleman in whom all have the greatest confidence. As a member of Parliamentary Committees, he proved himself to be a hard working man, conscientious and shrewd. If he will devote the necessary time and labour to his office, the best results may be anticipated. Mr. Thompson, the Vice-President, is a merchant of more than average capacity, who stands well with the community. Of the other members of the Board, nothing need be said, as they are well known. They have now before them experience dearly purchased, and if they avoid the shoals and quick-sands on which the old Board was wrecked, they may not only repair the errors of the past, but also evoke a new era of prosperity and confidence.

MERCHANTS' BANK OF CANADA.

From the annual report it appears that the directors have determined to avail themselves of the entire capital authorized by the Act of Incorporation—$6,000,000. Hitherto only $4,000,000 has been offered for subscription or taken up. The shareholders are, therefore, invited to take up the $2,000,000 yet to be subscribed, and as they will have the opportunity of getting this stock at par, they will no doubt very generally avail themselves of the privilege. A telegram from Montreal informs us that on the announcement being made public, the stock went down from 111½ to 105, in consequence of the anticipated increased supply in the market. The bank's rest has been increased to the handsome sum of $700.000. Fair progress is reported in the work of realizing the assets of the late Commercial Bank, and it is believed the original anticipations respecting the amalgamation will be realized. The business of the Bank continues to make satisfactory progress.

—It is stated, in Montreal, that Mr. Reekie has got the contract for the Toronto, Grey and Bruce Railway.

We are not sensitive on the score of infallibility, but we prefer that those who assume the responsibility of setting us right should not magnify our mistakes, if such there be, or misrepresent our language. The Toronto Leader, in referring to the affairs of the Royal Canadian Bank, assures its readers that we made "the serious mistake of deducting the $300,000 of losses from the amount of the paid up capital, and reason upon the assumption that the capital has been impaired to that extent." Unfortunately for the Leader's sagacity, we neither deducted $300,-000 of losses from the paid up capital, nor reasoned on the assumption that the capital was impaired to that amount. Our contemporary must have been groping about in the dark when it tumbled over the mistake referred to. We deducted the $300,962, admitted loss, from the difference between assets and liabilities, excluding the capital altogether, and then found that $366,863 represented the amount by which the capital was impaired. The mode by which we arrived at this result was quite correct; but we did fall into a trap. Mr. Woodside stated before the House of Commons' Committee, that no paper had been written off. In dealing with the bank balance sheet, we proceeded on the assumption that the $300,962 of losses had not been written off. It now appears that $297,247 were written off subsequently, and that, in ignorance of the fact, we duplicated the work of the directors. This new light, of course, makes the way clear to some results different from those at which we arrived.

TORONTO, GREY AND BRUCE RAILWAY.—The entire amount of subscriptions necessary to the complete organization of the company, under the charter, has now been obtained, and the meeting for the election of officers will take place as soon as practicable. Great credit is due to some of our leading citizens, for the enterprise and public spirit displayed by them in connection with the project and that of the Nipissing Road, since their inception. We hope no unnecessary delay will be made in putting both Roads under construction.

—Arrangements are nearly completed for the purchase of the telegraph companies by the English Government, and it is expected that a money bill will be introduced before long for the purpose of acquiring the business of the various undertakings. The sum needed will be about £7,000,000, of which the Electric and International Telegraph Company will claim nearly £3,000,000. Under the management of the Post Office, much greater facilities are anticipated for the transmission of messages from and to the various towns and villages of the kingdom. At the present the system with regard to the smaller towns and to the villages in particular, is very imperfect; but it is expected that in the course of a few years every town and village in which there is a Post Office, will be connected with the metropolis by wire.

Financial.

THE GOLD MARKET.

'he following table exhibits the fluctuations in l, from January 1862 to May 1869.

Date.	1862. Lowest..	1862. Highest.	1863. Lowest..	1863. Highest.
uary	par	105	134	160¾
ruary	102½	104¾	153	172¼
ch	101⅜	102¼	139	171¾
il	101½	102¼	146	159
y	102⅛	•104⅛	143½	155
e	103½	109½	140½	148⅞
y	109	120⅛	123¼	145
gust	112½	116¼	122⅛	129¾
tember	116½	124	127	143¼
ober	122	137	140⅝	156¾
vember	129	133¼	143	154
ember	130	134	147	152¾

Date.	1864. Lowest..	1864. Highest.	1865. Lowest..	1865. Highest.
uary	151½	160	197¼	234½
ruary	157⅛	161	196⅜	218¾
ch	159	169½	148⅛	201
il	166¼	187	144	160
y	168	190	128⅛	145¼
e	189	251	135¾	147⅜
y	222	285	138	146⅝
gust	231½	262	140⅛	144¼
tember	185	255	142⅝	145
ober	189	229	144	149
vember	209	260	145¼	148¾
ember	211	244	144½	148½

Date.	1866. Lowest..	1866. Highest.	1867. Lowest..	1867. Highest.
uary	136¾	144⅛	132⅛	137⅞
ruary	135⅞	140⅝	135¼	140½
ch	125	136⅛	133½	140⅝
il	125	129⅛	132⅝	142
y	125⅛	141⅛	134⅞	138⅞
e	137⅜	167¾	136⅜	138⅜
y	147	151¾	138	140⅜
gust	146½	152¼	139⅞	142⅜
tember	143¼	147⅞	141	146⅜
ober	145¼	154⅜	140⅜	145⅜
vember	137⅛	148⅜	137⅞	141¼
ember	131¼	141¾	132¾	137⅞

Date.	1868. Lowest..	1868. Highest.	1869. Lowest..	1869. Highest.
uary	133½	142¼	134	136⅛
ruary	139¾	144	130⅞	136¼
ch	137⅞	141¼	130	132⅛
il	137¾	140⅝	131¼	134⅝
y	139⅛	140⅛	134⅝	144⅞
e	139⅝	141¼	......	......
y	140⅛	145¼	......	......
gust	143¼	146	......	......
tember	141⅛	145	......	......
ober	133¾	140½	......	......
vember	132⅛	137	......	......
ember	134⅛	136¾	......	......

TORONTO STOCK MARKET.

(Reported by Pellatt & Osler, Brokers.)

We have to note considerable sales of Stocks ex dividends, and at high rates. The feeling of investors seems to be more in favor of Bank Stocks than for some time past.

Bank Stock.—There were small sales of Montreal at 161 and 161½, the market closing with sellers at 161 and buying at 160. Sellers ask 104½ ex dividend for British America. Sales of Ontario were made at 96 and 96½, closing with sellers at 96½. Toronto has been dealt in at 118½ and 120½ ex dividend and there are still buyers at the latter rate. Royal Canadian is nominal at last week's quotations; no sales since annual meeting. Commerce has been largely dealt in at 100 and 100½, and a small sale was made at 101; buyers freely offer 100⅝, but there are no sellers under 101. There are buyers of Gore at 38; none in market. Merchants advanced to 111½ ex dividend, but closed lower in consequence of the increase of the issue of stock. There were small sales of Quebec at par. Buyers offer 108½ for Molson's; none in market. There are buyers and sellers of City at 98 and 98½ respectively. Small sales of Du Peuple were made at 108. Sellers offer Nationale at 107. Nothing doing in Mechanics. Union is quoted at 104 ex dividend.

Debentures.—No transactions to report in Currency and Sterling Canada Debentures. Dominion Stock is lower, there are no buyers over 106½. Toronto are offering at rates to pay 7⅛ to 7¼ per cent. interest. County are offering at 99 to 99½.

Sundries.—Large sales of British America Assurance were made at from 56 to 57; the books are now closed for dividend due on the 10th inst. City Gas is in demand at 107 to 107½; none in market. Small sales of Canada Permanent Building Society were made at 121½ ex dividend, and it is in demand. Western Canada in demand at 116½ to 117 and a slight advance on these quotations would be paid. There were sales of Freehold at 116, 116½ and 117, in demand at the latter rate. Buyers offer 136 for Montreal Telegraph, with sellers at 137. Sales of Canada Landed Credit were made at 79 and 79½. Fair average Mortgages can be placed at from 8 to 9 per cent. interest.

—A fall in Merchants' Bank stock from 111 to 105, is in consequence of the increase of the stock from $4,000,000 to $6,000,000.

—Very well excuted counterfeit five dollars on the Bank of British North America are in circulation in St. John N.B.

—According to the report of Treasurer Boutwell, the total debt of the United States exhibits a decrease during the past month of $16,410,132.

—By the amended charter of the Bank of Commerce, the day for holding the annual meeting has been changed from the first Monday to the second Tuesday in July.

—The Directors of the Commercial Bank, N. B., having taken steps for the release of Mr. Sancton, that gentleman is now at liberty. It is understood that the bank folks were pretty well "salted" by their New York lawyers by the time proceedings against Mr. S. were stopped.—*St. John Telegraph.*

THE USURY LAWS.—The Usury Laws of several States are now being revised. New Hampshire provides that the lender may receive as high as nine per cent., by special contract, the legal rate remaining at six unless otherwise specified. The usuary bill pending in the Connecticut Legislature is substantially a copy of the Massachusetts laws, providing that six per cent. shall continue to be the legal rate where no rate is mentioned, but borrowers and lenders may agree in writing to any other. The House hesitates to interfere with the ancient usages of the State in this respect, but its hesitation will hardly affect the practice of business men.

PRICES OF SPECIE.—The following are the quotations for specie in New York:

American silver	95⅜	to	96
Mexican dollars	103¼	"	104½
English silver	475	"	480
Five francs	95	"	96
English sovereigns	486	"	488
Twenty francs	384	"	386
Thalers	70	"	70¾
Spanish doubloons	16.30	"	16.45
Mexican "	15.50	"	15.65

BANK OF ENGLAND.—The return from the Bank of England for the week ending 16th of June, gives the following results when compared with the previous week:

Rest	£3,142,205	Increase	£10,640
Public deposits.	7,139,111	Increase	189,210
Other deposits	17,455,401	Increase	286,082

On the other side of the account:

Gov. securities	£14,173,667	Increase	£25,391
Other securities	16,986,400	Decrease	344,944
Notes	10,465,500	Increase	838,265

The amount of notes in circulation is £22,577,720, being a decrease of £264,765; and the stock of bullion in both departments is £19,153,625, showing an increase of £522,742, when compared with the preceding return.

Subjoined is a comparison of the present position of the Bank of England, and the prices of Consols and French Rentes with the corresponding week of last year:

	At present.	Same week last year.
Bullion	£19,153,625	£22,571,045
Reserve	11,575,905	14,046,310
Notes in circulation	12,577,720	23,524,735
Rate of discount	4 per cent.	2 per cent.
Consols	92½	95
French Rentes	70f. 22c.	70f. 17c.

By telegram from London, dated July 1st, we learn that the regular weekly statement of the Bank of England, published yesterday, shows that the amount of bullion in vault has increased £185,000 since last week.

Railway News.

NORTHERN RAILWAY.—Traffic receipts for week ending June 26th, 1869.

Passengers	$2,513 72
Freight and live stock	14,920 45
Mails and sundries	303 44
	$17,737 61
Corresponding Week of '68.	13,771 63
Increase	$3,965 98

GREAT WESTERN RAILWAY.—Traffic for week ending June 18, 1869.

Passengers	$30,374 61
Freight	36,862 77
Mails and Sundries	2,083 67
Total Receipts for week	$69,321 05
Coresponding week, 1868	58,633 63
Increase	$10,687 42

—A large portion of the iron for the first section of the Wellington, Grey, and Bruce Railway, arrived at Quebec lately.

—A novel law-suit is to be tried in the London Division Court. Mr. J. M. Cousins bought a ticket for Stratford, marked "Good this day only." but the conductor collected his fare because he did not travel on the day so marked. The plaintiff sues for the sum of ninety cents.

—The St. Catharines Revision Court last week added $35,000 to the personal property of Mr. S. D. Woodruff, Canal Superintendent, because it was asertained he held United States bonds to the amount of $50,000.

NOTES ON PEAT—ITS MANUFACTURE AND USES AS FUEL.

In many parts of the country the process of peat-formation has been for ages, and is even now, going on. Mosses, and, to some extent, other plants usually found in low, swampy localities, grow, die, and accumulate before destructive decomposition takes place. To that incessant operation of nature are due the immense deposits of a substance which may be considered in a certain degree a rudimentary lignite, and perhaps even coal. But little attention has been paid to it in this country until within a very few years. But the abundance of wood and the comparatively low price of coal account for this fact. However, the demand for fuel, which seems to increase in a greater ratio than the usual avenues for procuring it, has, in many localities, drawn attention to the necessity of seeking a substitute or auxiliary to ordinary combustibles. Peat has been utilized for many years in Ireland, Scotland, Belgium, and other European countries, mainly for household purposes. The process of manufacture usually resorted to in such instances, was confined to merely cutting square pieces of the decuer layers and allowing them to dry upon the ground until required for use. Under such a method of treatment, peat is, except in very few cases, light and porous, burns rapidly, emits a good deal of smoke, and cannot withstand the blast of iron-furnaces, or the strong draught of locomotives. Many efforts have been made to increase its density, and thus extend the range of its usefulness. But the difficulty of overcoming the resistance of water, which constitutes from fifty to ninety per cent. of its volume in the natural state, and the cost of the different devices to which inventors have had recourse, in order to deprive the crude peat of that element, have, in numerous instances, presented great obstacles in the way of the attainment of the end in view. Of late years, several contrivances have been adopted, having for their object the cutting or grinding and moulding of peat into bricks of different sizes and forms. These have met with more or less success. In the works of the "Central Peat Fuel and Machine Company, of Connecticut," the several desiderata looked for by those who have studied the subject, seem to have been attained in a very simple and economical manner. The machinery used is free from complication, and yet accomplishes its work in a thorough and rapid manner. The peat is simply dug out of the bog by hand labor, which is considered, after all, as the cheapest in view of its adaptability to local changes and circumstances. It is thrown directly into ordinary dumping-cars, running upon tracks laid in the space already excavated. It is then hoisted by steam-power, and thrown into a large hopper leading to the machine. This consists of a horizontal cylinder, to the interior surface of which are fastened knives of different shapes. These cut, grind, and reduce to pulp the crude peat, which is then expelled by means of the rotary action of a central drum, to the periphery of which other knives and grinding projections are affixed.

The cylinder or shell is constructed of boiler plate, and is in three sections, which can be quickly and easily taken apart, and again put together. The whole interior portion of the machine can thus be readily inspected. At one end of the cylinder is a wide spout, through which the peat is expelled in the form of pulp, and from which it passes into moulds underneath. These moulds are propelled by means of an endless chain, furnished with catches. One man attends to the feeding of these moulds, which are conveyed to him from the returning car in a trough filled with water. The moulds are simply oblong boxes, with tapering sides and moveable bottoms, furnished with cross projections. They are carried away in cars, running upon wooden rails and drawn by horses, to the drying grounds, which are either an adjacent field or the surface of the bog itself. The moulds are upset upon the grass,

and the peat allowed to dry without any further attention or cost. In the process of drying, the mass breaks into pieces of different sizes and forms —the lines of separation being usually those of the indications made by cross-pieces on the bottom of the moulds. These pieces have, indeed, many of them, almost the hardness and density of bituminous or anthracite coal. The total cost of the manufacture of peat by means of this simple process is found, from actual tests, not to exceed one dollar and fifty cents per ton of peat ready for market ; the lowest wages paid to men being two dollars per day. Of course the cost of manufacture will vary with that of labor, which constitutes the largest expense attending it. The works of the above company are proportioned so as to produce one hundred tons of dry peat per day, and including steam-engine, moulds, cars, tracks, etc., cost, we are informed ten thousand dollars. Peat when thus prepared seems to be of a very uniform consistency ; constitutes a very convenient, useful, and economical fuel, either for household or manufacturing purposes, for generating steam, and for many metallurgic operations.

It burns with a far reaching flame, almost without smoke. The combustion is kept up in the form of glowing coals, the heat of which can be carried to a great degree of intensity without running the risk of covering the grate-bars with clinkers, or it may be reduced to a very low point without being extinguished. This latter property, it may be remarked in closing, renders it very useful for warming greenhouses, drying lofts, dwell ings, etc. Cooking stoves in which this fuel was used have continued in operation for a whole year without the necessity of relighting the fire.—The Engineering and Mining Journal.

INSOLVENTS.—The following insolvents are gazetted:—M. T. Rogers, Napanee; John Durham, Montreal ; William Kennedy, Ottawa ; Edward Welsh, Perth; James Delahey, Walkerton; George Wilson, Napanee ; Wm. Snellgrove, Woodstock; R. P. Street, John Peacock, Hamilton ; Anathas Cavan, H. Smeaton, C. Corcoran, Quebec; H. Stichler, Galt; T. McLean, Toronto; H. Tibbit, Ottawa ; Widmeyer and Schroder, Ayton.

—The annual meeting of the Port Burwell Harbour Co. will be held at Port Burwell on the 14th inst.

—The Patent law of last session came into force on the 1st July inst. ; also the act passed by the Ontario Legislature, last session, providing for the registration of births, marriages and deaths.

—It has been ordered that the manufacture in Canada of benzine, and other light products of petroleum, which will not stand the prescribed fire-test of 115 degrees of Fahrenheit be authorized.

Commercial.

Toronto Market.

PRODUCE.— Wheat — Receipts, 4,665 bush.; stock in store on the 5th inst., 42,799. Owing to an advance in the English market, prices here have tended upward, and though there is scarcely enough business reported to establish prices, an advance of a few cents may be quoted. Car-loads of Spring sold at 95c. to $1, and Fall at $1 to $1.02 f.o.b. Though the weather has been too wet the accounts received respecting the crops in Ontario are uniformly favorable. The certainty of a large yield of wheat over the greater portion of this continent is now established almost beyond doubt. The markets fluctuate with every change in the weather in Europe, so that the course of prices for the next month or so is as uncertain as the movements of the clouds. Oats.—Receipts, 609 bush; in store on the 5th, 5,500 bush. There are scant supplies in market but prices keep steady at 53 to 54c., with very little doing. Barley. —No receipts; market nominal. Peas.—No receipts; in store on the 5th, 5,800 bush. Lots are held at 80 to 82c., without buyers. Corn.—Two cars sold at 65c. on the track.

FLOUR.—Receipts, 3,080 brls.; in store about 5,000 bbls. The market is firm and more active and closed at an advance of 20c. on last week's prices. Several lots of No. 1 Superfine sold at from $4.30 to $4.55. A lot of 400 bbls. Extra sold at $4.45 at Weston and 100 bbls. at the same price here. Fancy, nominal. Oatmeal—Nothing doing except in small lots, at $5.75 to $6. Cornmeal.—Small lots are worth $3.50 to $3.75.

PROVISIONS —Butter.—Is arriving more freely, and is taken on speculation at 13 to 14c. There is no shipping movement of consequence, as the weather is too warm, but a small lot has been sent forward to New York, by way of experiment. The crop is generally understood to be large. Cheese —Stocks are accumulating pretty fast, holders seem more inclined to realize, but owing to the high prices paid for the May product they do not care to sell at the figures named by shippers ; it is selling in small lots at 13¼ to 14½c. Pork.—The last of the stock was cleared out to supply the gangs at work on the government road, above Lake Superior, so that there is now no stock in market; the last sales were made at our quotations. Cu ments.—There is a light stock of bacon in market rough 12½c; cumb. cut 13c; shoulders 11½c; hams canvassed, are selling more freely at 15 to 16c. and there is a fair supply in market. Eggs.—are scarce and worth our quotations. Lard.—There is but a small demand owing to the decline in butter, holders are firm and stock light, selling at 16 to 17c.

WOOL.— The market is again a little easier at 31c. Some of the leading dealers report their receipts in excess of last year.

HIDES—Dull and unchanged as quoted.

FREIGHTS.—Rates for grain to Kingston and Oswego, remain unaltered, at 2c gold, and 3 greenbacks, respectively. There is less demand than at the date of our last weekly report. Rate by steamers also remain unchanged at 20c. for flour to Montreal, and 6c for grain. The rate of grain from Kingston to Montreal is 4c and toll. There is not as much freight offering as was the case last week; but the steamers are still kept pretty busy. Rates for lumber are still $1.50 per M., greenbacks, but some parties predict a rise for coal $1.30 is paid.

The steamer Her Majesty, is expected to sail on her next trip on the 14th prox. Her cargo is already completed.

The Grand Trunk rates to Liverpool are:—Flour 4s. stg. per bbl.; wheat 8s. 6d. stg., per quarter and boxed meats 55s. per ton.

The following are the Grand Trunk Railway Company's summer rates from Toronto to the undermentioned stations, which came into force on the 19th ult. :—Flour to all Stations from Belleville to Lynn, inclusive 25c ; grain, per 100 lbs 13c ; flour to Prescott, 30c ; grain 15c ; flour to all stations between Island Pond and Portland, inclusive, 75c ; grain, 38c: flour to Boston, 80 gold ; grain 40c ; flour to Halifax, 90c ; flour to St John, 85c.

Halifax Market.

BREADSTUFFS.—June 29th.—We have to report an active speculative feeling for flour during the past week. Reports of improvement abroad, reduced stocks here, and uncertainty as to the result of injury to Her Majesty, created an exciting feeling and speculative demand. Sales at 50c for Supers. were reported; but the demand has been supplied, to a large extent by State Extra and as buyers are unwilling to operate at the advanced rates, the demand has subsided, and stocks are quite equal to requirements. Extra and Fancy are dull, at improved rates. No. 2 in request, with light stocks. We quote White Wheat Extra (fall) $6.25; Fancy, $6; Superfine @ $5.75; No 2, $5.

Imports from January 1st to June 29th, 1868 and 1869:

	Bbls. Flour.	Bbls. Cornmeal.
1869	74842	15945
1868	91227	28755

ROVISIONS.—We note no particular activity ɪis branch of trade. In pork and beef there ɪe usual local consumption; but no speculative ɪiry exists. The same remarks are applicable utter; the feeling for which is decidedly down- l. Last week 22 @ 23c. was realized for good . To-day, 19c. was accepted: the supply is cess of demand. Cut meats are in request ɪotations. Cheese in demand. Stocks light. quote: Pork—P. E. I. Mess, $24 @ $25; N. $22; Prime Mess, $20; Prime, $14 @ $16; (mess), $8 @ $10; Prime, $6; Butter, 19c.; se 16c.; Hams, $15; Lard, 16c.

EST INDIA PRODUCE.—Sugar and molasses, sual, at this season are dull. Holders are sing small lots, on the market, at nominal . Rum is in good demand, with moderate cs. Coffee, inactive at quotations. The at movement here was confined to Jamaica; r grades unchanged.

SH AND OIL.—Continue in active request, at ations.

XCHANGE.—Bank drafts, London, at 60 days, 2¼ per cent. Montreal sight, 3¼ per cent. John, N. B., 3 per cent prem.—*R. C. Hamil- & Co.'s Circular.*

The Cottons of the World.

ur esteemed fellow-citizen, Wm. F. Herring, he established house of Claghorn, Herring o., has obtained from Liverpool, the great re of the cotton trade, a collection of cotton ples of the cotton producing area of the world, itary to European wants, arranged and classi- according to Liverpool standards by Liverpool rts. This collection the owner designs to ent to the Board of Trade of Augusta to be as the standard for reference in the adjust- t of classifications in the Augusta market. It been acquired through the well-known Liver- house of Messrs. Robert Lockhart, Dempster o. Neither pains nor expense have been held to make the collection accurate in classi- ion, and to represent faithfully Liverpool es. Several months of time have been taken make the collection, and six of the leading rpool cotton brokers have each severally fur- ed the samples, determining each upon his judgment the respective classifications.

his collection comprises specimens of cotton n in the United States, South America, ca (or Algeria), Egypt, Asia Minor (Turkey, rna, &c.), the West Indies; from the valleys he Mississippi, the Nile and the Ganges; all s of the world furnishing cotton as a surplus export. Accompanying the collection is a ılar statement made by Messrs. Robert Lock- , Dempster & Co., from which we collate some s of general interest. Cotton grown in the th is denominated American cottons, and de- ed in the Liverpool market as Sea Island, nds and New Orleans, and the standard grade ch regulates their relative values, above and w it, in market is good middling for uplands New Orleans. Cotton grown in South America ives the denomination of Brazils. These cot- comprise Pernams (or cotton from Pernam-) Maranham and Maccios; and the standard ood fair.

otton grown in Egypt is described and denom- ed Egyptian; the standard grade for which is l fair.

otton grown in Asia Minor is denominated as rna (Turkey cottons, &c.—) and is described Smyrna cotton—the standard grade of which ir.

otton grown on the West India Islands is ominated and described as "West Indias," the standard grade is fair, also Tahiti, ranking our Sea Island.

otton grown in British India is denominated t, and described as Dhollerah, Saw-ginned war, known and described by these respective es. The standard grade for India cottons is

Imports of 1868.

Denomination.	bales.	av. weight of bales.
American	1,267,060	443
Brazil	636,897	155
Egyptian	188,689	500
Smyrna	12,758	380
West India	100,651	180
Surats	1,038,925	380
Madras	243,949	300
Bengal	169,198	300
Total	3,660,127	354

Of Brazilian cotton, Pernams and Maranhams are noted in the Liverpool market for good color and staple, but it is a coarser cotton than Egyptian. The staple of Maccios is generally good, but the cotton seedy and color dull; the supply of this cotton is increasing. Smyrna cottons are of fair color, and staple "pretty strong but short."

Of the various descriptions of East Indian and Surat cottons, Dhollerah is generally received as the great standard in the Liverpool market; but the saw-ginned Dhawar, grown from American seed, is fair in color and staple, and the better grades come into competition with American cotton "and are much liked;" while the "McAuthur-ginned broach" is put down as giving less waste in manufacture than any other East India cotton; and Bengal is the "poorest cotton on the Liverpool market, a good deal of which is exported to the continent of Europe."

Our readers will not fail to observe that while the average weight per bale of American cotton is 443 pounds, Surats average 380 pounds; the average weight of all bales received at Liverpool in 1868 being 354 pounds.

Our cotton merchants are examining this collection of samples with great interest. It would be of advantage if our farmers should examine them also, not, perhaps, with the same view as that which governs the merchant, but to form a correct idea of the kinds of cottons which is to compete with their labors. We submit a resume of the opinions expressed by some of our experts in the cotton line at such an examination made lately.

American Cottons.—The samples, six of each grade of American cottons, comprise Orleans and Texas and Uplands, valued and classified on the 24th of April, 1869, to wit:—Orleans—Good Middling, 12¾d.; Middling, 12½d.; Low Middling, 11⅝d. Georgia—Upland, Good Middling, 13¾d.; Middlings, 12d.; Low Middling, —. It was agreed that the classification of uplands was not fully up to the standard of the Augusta market. The sample Orleans good middling exhibited a finer staple but no stronger fibre, and was not superior to Augusta classification of the same grade of uplands in color and cleanliness. The same judgment was pronounced on the sample of middlings, while general concurrence made the low middling of the uplands superior to the same grade of Orleans.

South America Cotton.—The samples of these cottons comprised:—Pernams—Good Fair, 12⅝d.; Fair, 12⅜d. Maccio—Good Fair, 12⅝d.; Fair, 12⅜d. —valuations, as with the American cottons, being made on the 24th of April, and this holds true of the valuations of all the samples. The Pernams possess a longer staple than either Orleans or Texas cotton, but is similar in other qualities. The appearance of good fair Pernams is similar to Augusta good middling; in cleanliness, ginning, &c., no better than Georgia uplands of the grade indicated above, color hardly so bright; would be classed here middling Orleans. The grade fair is similar in appearance to Georgia low middlings, but the staple is better. The other samples of South American cottons are Maranhams. Grade, fair; value at 12½d. These cottons assimilate to Georgia middlings in ginning, color, &c., with no perceptible difference, except as to staple, which is not so good.

West India Cottons.—West India grade, good fair, value 12½d. This cotton has a superior staple; color is not good, having a yellowish tinge; looks very much like our commonest Sea Island. The staple has a fine silky feeling, and the samples were deemed equal, but not superior, to Georgia Zipporah.

The Tahiti, the samples of which were classed as fair, and valued at 30c., ranked with our best Sea Islands.

Asia Minor Cottons.—The standard grade of these cottons is fair, and they are denominated Smyrnas. The sample of this collection is classed and valued at 10¼. The staple is short and brittle, and such cotton would be classed as to appearance in the Augusta market as ordinary, but as having an inferior staple and body. Good fair of this cotton valued in Liverpool at 10¾d per pound was classed as to appearance with low middling Georgia uplands of inferior staple and body.

Egyptian Cotton.—The samples of these were: Good fair, valued at 13½d.; Fair, valued at 13d.; Good Middling, valued at 15d. The sample of good fair is not so handsome in appearance, but not equal in staple to our Moina and Zipporah, and is deficient in color, cleanliness and ginning. The good middling has the appearance of our low ordinary, but possesses a better staple.

African Cotton.—This cotton is from Algeria—sample classed as fair, and valued at 10⅜d. This cotton is coarse in staple and brown in color, having somewhat the appearance of Augusta low middling, but is shorter than this grade of uplands in staple.

India Cottons.—The highest priced sample of the India cotton is Broach, which is grown from American seed. The sample of this collection is classed "good to fine," and valued at 11⅞d This cotton could be classed in the market ordinary uplands, which it resembles very much in appearance. But the standard cotton of India is Dhollerah. The sample of this collection are as follows: Good Fair, valued at, 10½d.; Fair, do. 10⅜d.; Middling Fair, do. 9¾d. The sampless of good fair Dhollerah's are short and brittle in staple full of trash, deficient in color and badly ginned. It has the appearance of some of our damaged repacked cottons and might be classed low ordinary upland. The "fair," after the forgoing description, could only be classed as very low ordinary, while the "middling fair," is lumpy, stringy, and trashy, looking more like inferior warehouse sweepings than anything that can be found in the United States. The samples of fair Madras, valued at 9⅜d. per pound, are not so good as those of middling fair Dhollerah's, looking like very badly damaged cotton of the most inferior grade repacked. The staple is weak and brittle. Fair Bengal is represented the poorest cotton shipped to the port of Liverpool.—*Georgia Chronicle and Sentinel.*

Petroleum.

The following shows the exports of Petroleum from the United States, from January 1 to June 29:

	1869.	1868.
From New York......gals	29,064,896	22,733,445
Boston	1,192,540	1,265,060
Philadelphia	11,536,832	15,137,736
Baltimore	699,993	1,047,546
Portland	....	152,131
New Bedford	....	....
Cleveland	....	....
Total Export from U. S.	42,394,261	40,276,917
Same time 1867		27,782,570
Same time 1866		25,350,065

The Tobacco Crop of 1869.

Estimates of the crop of 1869, put down for Kentucky, 70.000 hhds.; Tennessee, 23,000; Indiana and Illinois, 19,000; Missouri, 8,000; total, 120,000. Stock in the West, 8,000; stock at the seaports, 19,000; total, 147,000.

Foreign countries take the tobacco crop in the following proportions:—England, 25,000 hhds.; North Germany, 15,000; Spain, 10,000; Italy, 10,000; France, 9,000; Belgium, 4,000; the Mediteranean ports 3,900; countries not specified 5,500; total 82,400.

The United States demand is put as follows:—

For the West, 35,000 hhds.; for the East, 15,000; total, 50,000. Add foreign demand, 82,400; total, 132,400—a total which would exceed the crop of the year by 12,400 hhds. It must be remembered, however, that the foregoing are the estimates of the trade as represented at the tobacco fair recently held at Louisville.

It is stated that the governments of Austria; France, Spain and Italy, countries where the manufacture is conducted under stringent rules, have permanent agents in the West for the purchase of tobacco.

English Sugar Duties.

It appears that the memorandum which accompanies the North German Sugar Duties Bill, to which we alluded last week, suggests that the saccharine strength of the sugar exported should be ascertained by the polariscope, and the drawback allowed accordingly. In remarking upon the proposition before the Customs' Union Parliament, Messrs. Rueb & Sons, of Rotterdam, make the following remarks on the question of graduated Sugar duties, and their argument seems to us irrefutable:—"We welcome this Bill still more for its good sense in imposing a single duty on all Raw Sugars, of whatever shade or quality, and for establishing a draw back according to intrinsic quality. This step is the more remarkable, as Cologne was the town where the four Governments made the experiments on Sugar, which resulted in the disastrous Drawback Convention. The project explains why the German delegates last year were wise enough to refuse to enter the league formed between Holland, France, Belgium, and England, to resist the progress of industry and science, and to protect laziness and imperfectly-made goods, by differential duties on each grade of Sugar. This unfortunate Convention, which yields no more revenue than a single duty would give, without any fear of giving bounties to refiners, is extremely prejudicial to the true interests of commerce and of the colonies. Let us hope that the lesson given by Germany to the delegates of the four nations, will not be lost, and that it will bring them back to rational principles. If, with the assistance of science and of industry, No. 15 is what the Cane and Beetroot naturally yield, it is evident that Nos. 10 and 6 deserve no protection. The Dutch are now suffering the consequences of their joining a false system. Java, the finest Sugar colony in the world, is affected, and White Sugar, in consequence of the Convention, actually fetches less money than brown kinds. Government, thinking of nothing but its receipts, forgets that is materially injuring the colonies. And we are tied to such a system till 1875!—*Produce Markets Review.*

Morton & Smith,

ACCOUNTANTS, REAL ESTATE AGENTS, AND VALUATORS,

48 AND 50 CHURCH STREET, TORONTO.

R. MORTON. 47-1y J. LAMOND SMITH.

NOTICE.

Office of the Toronto, Grey and Bruce Railway Company.

A GENERAL Meeting of the Subscribers to the Capital Stock of the Toronto, Grey and Bruce Railway Company will be held at the office of the said Company, No. 46 Front Street, in the City of Toronto, on TUESDAY, the 10th day of August next, at TWELVE o'clock noon, for the purpose of electing Directors and organizing the said Company.
W. SUTHERLAND TAYLOR,
Toronto, July 7, 1869. Secretary.

Montreal Telegraph Company,

NOTICE is hereby given, that a Dividend of FIVE per cent. for the half-year ending THIRTY-FIRST MAY, has been declared upon the Capital Stock of the Company, and the same will be payable at the offices of the Company, on and after FRIDAY, the NINTH JULY.
The Transfer Book will be closed from 1st to 9th JULY.
By order of the Board,
(Signed)
JAMES DAKERS,
Secretary

Insolvent Act of 1864.

PROVINCE OF ONTARIO, }
COUNTY OF YORK. }

In the County Court of the County of York.

In the matter of HENRY S. LEDYARD, an Insolvent.

THE undersigned has filed a consent by his Creditors to his discharge, and on Monday, the Thirteenth day of September next, he will apply to the Judge of the said Court for a confirmation thereof.
Dated at Toronto, this Third day of July, A.D. 1869.
46-10t. H. S. LEDYARD.

The Canadian Bank of Commerce.

DIVIDEND No. 4.

NOTICE is hereby given that a Dividend of Four per cent. upon the paid-up capital stock of this institution has been declared for the current half year, and that the same will be payable at the Bank and its Branches on and after FRIDAY, the second day of JULY next.

The Transfer Books will be closed from the 16th to the 30th days of June next, both days inclusive.

The amendment to the Charter of the Bank, recently sanctioned by Parliament, changes the day for holding the Annual General Meeting from the first Monday to the SECOND TUESDAY IN JULY.

Stockholders will therefore please note that the meeting this year will be held on Tuesday, the THIRTEENTH PROX.

Chair to be taken at Twelve o'clock, noon, precisely.
By order of the Board. R. J. DALLAS, Cashier.
Toronto, June 23rd, 1869. 42-td

British America Assurance Company.

FIFTY-FIRST DIVIDEND.

NOTICE is hereby given, that a Dividend of Four per cent on capital stock paid up, has been this day declared for the half year ending 30th ult, and that the same will be payable on and after
SATURDAY, THE TENTH DAY OF JULY INSTANT.
The Stock and Transfer Books will accordingly be closed from this date to the Eighth instant, inclusive.
By order of the Board. J. W. BIRCHALL,
Managing Director.
Brit. Amer. Assur. Office,
Toronto, 3rd July, 1869. 46-3t

Western Assurance Company.

NOTICE is hereby given, that a dividend for the half-year, ending the 30th ult., at the rate of EIGHT per cent. per annum, upon the capital paid-up stock of this Company, has been declared, and will be payable at the Company's office, on and after Friday, the 9th inst.
By order of the Board.
BERNARD HALDAN,
Secretary.
Western Assurance Co.'s Office,
Toronto, 1st July, 1869.

WESTERN CANADA

Permanent Building and Savings Society.

DIVIDEND NO. 12.

NOTICE is hereby given, that a Dividend of Five per cent. on the Capital Stock of this Institution has been declared for the half-year ending 29th inst. and that the same will be payable at the Office of the Society, No. 70 Church Street, on and after THURSDAY, the EIGHTH day of JULY next.
The Transfer Books will be closed from the 20th to the 30th June, inclusive.
By order of the Board.
WALTER S. LEE,
Secretary and Treasurer.
Toronto, June 15, 1869.

Bank of Toronto.

DIVIDEND No. 26.

NOTICE is hereby given that a Dividend of Four per cent. for the current half-year, being at the rate of Eight per cent. on the paid up capital of this Bank, has this day been declared, and that the same will be payable at the Bank or its branches on and after
FRIDAY, the 2ND DAY OF JULY NEXT.
The transfer books will be closed from the fifteenth to the thirtieth of June, both days inclusive.
The Annual Meeting of the Shareholders will be held at the Bank on Wednesday, the twenty-first day of July next. The chair to be taken at noon.
By order of the Board.
G. HAGUE, Cashier.
Toronto, May 16th, 1869. 41-td

Canada Permanent Building and Savings Society.

EIGHTEENTH HALF-YEARLY DIVIDEND.

NOTICE is hereby given that a Dividend of Five per cent. on the Capital Stock of this Institution has been declared for the half-year ending 30th instant, and the same will be payable at the Office of the Society on and after THURSDAY, the EIGHTH day of July next.
The Transfer Books will be closed from the 20th to the 30th June, inclusive.
By order of the Board.
J. HERBERT MASON,
Secretary and Treasurer
Toronto, June 10th, 1869. 44-td

Niagara District Bank.

DIVIDEND No. 31.

NOTICE is hereby given, that a DIVIDEND OF FOUR PER CENT. on the paid up capital stock of this Institution, has this day been declared for the current half-year; and that the same will be payable at the Bank on and after THURSDAY, the first day of July next.
The Transfer Books will be closed from the 20th to the 30th of June, both days inclusive.
By order of the Board,
C. M. ARNOLD, Cashier.

Office of the Toronto and Nipissing Railway Company.

A GENERAL MEETING of the subscribers to the Capital Stock of the Toronto and Nipissing Railway Company will be held at the office of the said Company, No. 46 Front street, in the said City of Toronto, on TUESDAY, the 30th day of JULY next, at twelve o'clock noon, for the purpose of electing Directors and organizing the said Company.
Toronto, June 16. CHAS. ROBERTSON,
Secretary

The European Mail for North America,

WITH WHICH IS INCORPORATED

"WILMER & SMITH'S EUROPEAN TIMES"

(Established in 1843.)

A Full and Complete Summary of

HOME AND FOREIGN NEWS

Published Weekly for despatch by the Mail Steamer

THE EUROPEAN MAIL.

FOR North America, with which is incorporated 'Wilmer & Smith's European Times,' is published in the interest of the mercantile and general community.

In each issue is to be found all the reliable information commercial and general, that can in any way prove of value to our subscribers. The greatest possible care has been and will continue to be, taken by the Proprietors to obtain regardless of expense, a faithful record of all market transactions in which our friends are more particularly concerned, up to within three hours of the closing of the Mail.

We furnish our readers with quotations of articles staple not generally noted in ordinary lists, of which the following is an example:—

Articles.		Prices per ton.		Cash discount.
CANADA PLATES				
Staffordshire (in L'pool) f.o.b.		£18 18 6		2½ per c
Glamorgan "	"	19 15 0		"
GALVANIZED IRON—				
Corrugated Shts., 20 gauge fob.		17 0 0		"

The latest shipping intelligence, comprising arrival departures, sailings, and loadings, alphabetically arranged, is laid before our subscribers; and the tabular form adopted in the current number will be adhered to throughout—every casualty being regularly noted, and the state of the freight market duly advised.

Agricultural, Legal, and Medical news, of interest given in detail.

We publish a list of Military and Naval Stations, and any changes are promptly noted.

The proprietors of the EUROPEAN MAIL urge the great advantages of this Journal, and trust for the friendly co-operation of all who think it of importance that the Old and New World should be more closely associated in those reciprocal ties resulting from a mutual furtherance of their material interests.

The subscription is 52s. or $13 (gold) per annum, payable in advance.

Sole Agent for Toronto,

A. S. IRVING.

Mercantile.

TORONTO PRICES CURRENT.—JULY 8, 1869.

Name of Article.	Wholesale Rates.		Name of Article.	Wholesale Rate.		Name of Article.	Wholesale Rates.	
Boots and Shoes.	$ c.	$ c.	**Groceries**—Contin'd	$ c.	$ c.	**Leather**—Contin'd.	$ c.	$ c.
Mens' Thick Boots ...	2 05	2 50	Gunpowd'r o. to med..	0 55	0 70	Kip Skins, Patna	0 80	0 85
" Kip	2 25	3 00	" med. to fine.	0 70	0 85	French	0 70	0 90
" Calf	3 20	3 70	" fine to fin't..	0 85	0 95	English	0 65	0 80
" Congress Gaiters..	1 65	2 50	Hyson	0 45	0 80	Hemlock Calf (30 to		
" Kip Cobourgs..	1 90	1 40	Imperial	0 42	0 80	35 lbs.) per doz...	0 50	0 60
Boys' Thick Boots ...	1 70	1 80	*Tobacco, Manufac'd:*			Do. light	0 45	0 50
Youths' " ...	1 40	1 50	Can Leaf, ℔ lb & 10s.	0 26	0 30	French Calf........	1 05	1 00
Women's Batts	0 95	1 80	Western Leaf, com ..	0 25	0 26	Grain & Satn Cl℔ doz.	0 00	0 55
" Balmoral....	1 20	1 80	" Good	0 27	0 32	Splits, large ℔ lb ...	0 80	0 38
" Congress Gaiters..	0 90	1 50	" Fine	0 32	0 35	" small	0 23	0 28
Misses' Batts	0 75	1 00	" Bright fine..	0 40	0 50	Enamelled Cow℔ foot..	0 20	0 21
" Balmoral	1 00	1 20	" choice..	0 60	0 75	Patent	0 20	0 21
" Congress Gaiters..	1 00	1 50	**Hardware.**			Pebble Grain	0 15	0 17
Girls' Batts	0 65	0 85	*Tin (net cash prices)*			Buff	0 14	0 16
" Balmoral	0 90	1 05	Block, ℔ lb.........	0 35	0 00	**Oils.**		
" Congress Gaiters..	0 75	1 10	Grain..............	0 30	0 00	Cod	0 65	0 70
Children's C.T. Cacks..	0 50	0 65	*Copper:—*			Lard, extra	0 00	0 00
" Gaiters	0 65	0 90	Pig...............	0 23	0 24	" No. 1	0 00	0 00
Drugs.			Sheet	0 30	0 33	" Woollen	0 00	0 00
Aloes Cape..........	0 12½	0 16	*Cut Nails:*			Lubricating, patent...	0 80	0 00
Alum	0 02½	0 03	Assorted ½ Shingles,			" Mott's economic	0 20	0 00
Borax	0 00	0 00	℔ 100 lb..	2 95	3 00	Linseed, raw	0 76	0 82
Camphor, refined.....	0 65	0 70	Shingle alone do	3 15	3 25	" boiled......	0 81	0 87
Castor Oil..........	0 16½	0 18	Lathe and 5 dy	3 30	3 40	Machinery.........	0 00	0 00
Caustic Soda........	0 04½	0 05	*Galvanised Iron:*			Olive, common, ℔ gal.	1 00	1 60
Cochineal...........	0 90	1 00	" Assorted sizes....	0 08	0 09	" salad	1 55	2 80
Cream Tartar	0 30	0 85	Best No. 24........	0 07½	0 00	" salad, in bots.		
Epsom Salts	0 03	0 04	" 26........	0 08	0 08½	qt. ℔ case...	3 60	3 75
Extract Logwood.....	0 11	0 12	" 28........	0 09	0 09½	Sesame salad, ℔ gal.	1 60	1 75
Gum Arabic, sorts....	0 30	0 85	*Horse Nails:*			Seal, pale.........	0 75	0 85
Indigo, Madras......	0 90	1 00	Guest's or Griffin's			Spirits Turpentine....	0 52½	0 00
Licorice	0 14	0 15	assorted sizes......	0 00	0 00	Varnish	0 00	0 00
Madder	0 00	0 16	For W. ass'd sizes..	0 12	0 19	Whale............	0 00	0 00
Galls	0 22	0 27	Patent Hammer'd do..	0 17	0 18	**Paints, &c.**		
Opium.............	12 00	13 50	*Iron (at 4 months):*			White Lead, genuine		
Oxalic Acid.........	0 26	0 35	Pig—Gartsherrie No1..	24 00	25 00	in Oil, ℔ 25lbs.	0 00	2 35
Potash, Bi-tart.......	0 25	0 28	Other brands. No1...	22 00	24 00	Do. No. 1	0 00	2 10
Bichromate........	0 15	0 20	" No.2	0 00	0 00	" 2 "	0 00	1 90
Potass Iodide	3 90	4 50	Bar—Scotch, ℔ 100 lb..	2 25	2 50	" 3 "	0 00	0 00
Senna	0 12½	0 60	Refined	3 00	3 25	White Zinc, genuine..	3 00	3 50
Soda Ash	0 02½	0 04	Swedes	4 00	4 50	White Lead, dry.....	0 06½	0 09
Soda Bicarb	0 04	4 00	Hoops—Coopers.....	3 00	3 25	Red Lead..........	0 07½	0 08
Tartaric Acid.......	0 40	0 45	Band	3 00	3 25	Venetian Red, Eng'h.	0 02½	0 03½
Verdigris	0 30	0 40	Boiler Plates	3 25	3 50	Yellow Ochre, Fren'h..	0 02½	0 03
Vitriol, Blue........	0 08	0 10	Canada Plates......	3 75	4 00	Whiting	0 85	1 25
Groceries.			Union Jack	0 00	0 00	**Petroleum.**		
Java, ℔ lb	0 22	0 23	Frottytool.........	3 25	4 00	(Refined ℔ gal.)		
Laguayra, "	0 17	0 18	Swansea	3 90	4 00	Water white, car-ld...	0 00	0 00
Rio	0 15	0 17	*Lead (at 4 months):*			" small lots ..	0 25	0 25
Fish:			Bar, ℔ 100 lb.— ...	0 06½	0 07	" car load ..	0 00	0 00
Herrings, Lab. split...	0 00	0 00	Sheet "	0 08	0 09	" small lots..	0 00	0 00
" round......	0 00	0 00	Shot, ℔	0 07½	0 07½	Amber, by car load...	0 00	0 00
" scaled......	0 33	0 35	*Iron Wire (net cash):*			" small lots...	0 00	0 00
Mackerel, small kitts..	2 00	0 00	No. 6, ℔ bundle....	2 70	2 80	Benzine............	0 00	0 00
Loch. Her. wh'd frks...	2 50	2 75	" 9, "	3 10	3 20	**Produce.**		
" half "	1 25	1 50	" 12, "	3 40	3 50	*Grain.*		
White Fish & Trout...	0 00	3 50	" 16, "	3 90	4 40	Wheat, Spring, 60 lb..	0 98	1 00
Salmon, saltwater.....	14 00	15 00	*Powder:*			" Fall "	1 00	1 03
Dry Cod, ℔ 112 lbs....	4 50	5 00	Blasting, Canada....	3 50	0 00	Barley....... 48 "	0 00	0 00
Fruit:			FF "	4 25	4 50	Peas........ 60 "	0 70	0 80
Raisins, Layers	1 90	2 00	FFF "	4 75	0 00	Oats........ 34 "	0 53	0 54
" M. R.......	1 90	2 00	Blasting, English ...	4 50	0 00	Rye......... 56 "	0 00	0 00
" Valentinesw	0 0	0 00	FF " loose..	5 00	0 00	*Seeds:—*		
Currants, new........	0 04½	0 05	FFF "	5 50	0 00	Clover, choice 60 "..	0 00	0 00
" old......	0 03½	0 04	*Pressed Spikes (4 mos):*			" com'n 68 "..	0 00	0 00
Figs	0 11	0 12	Regular sizes 100...	4 00	4 25	Timothy, cho'e 4 "..	0 00	0 00
Molasses:			Extra	4 50	5 00	" inf. to good 48 "	0 00	0 00
Clayed, ℔ gal........	0 00	0 45	*Tin Plates (net cash):*			Flax .... 56 "..	0 00	0 00
Syrups, Standard	0 55	0 76	IC Coke	7 50	8 50	*Flour* (per brl.):		
" Golden ...	0 59	0 60	IC Charcoal.......	8 00	10 00	Superior extra......	0 00	0 00
Rice:			IX "	10 50	11 00	Extra superfine......	4 60	4 60
Arracan	3 60	4 00	IXX "	13 50	14 00	Fancy superfine......	0 00	0 00
Spices:			DC "	8 50	9 00	Superfine No 1	4 45	4 55
Cassia, whole, ℔ lb....	0 40	0 45	DX "	11 00	12 00	" No. 2....		
Cloves	0 11	0 12	**Hides & Skins, ℔ lb**			*Oatmeal*, (per brl.)....	5 50	6 00
Nutmegs	0 00	0 00	Green rough	0 00	0 05	**Provisions**		
Ginger, ground	0 18	0 25	Green, salt'd & insp'd..	0 06	0 06½	Butter, dairy tub℔ lb..	0 13½	0 14½
" Jamaica, root...	0 30	0 32	Cured	0 00	0 00	" store packed..	0 12½	0 13
Pepper, black........	0 10½	0 11	Calfskins, green......	0 00	0 10	Cheese, new	0 13½	0 14½
Pimento	0 08	0 09	Calfskins, cured.....	0 18	0 00	Pork, mess, per brl...	27 00	27 50
Sugars:			" dry......	0 18	0 20	" prime mess....	0 00	0 00
Port Rico, ℔ lb.......	0 9	0 9½	Sheepskins, ...	1 20	1 60	" prime	0 00	0 00
Cuba "	0 8½	0 8½	" pelts......	0 10	0 20	Bacon, rough	0 12	0 12½
Barbadoes (bright)....	0 8½	0 8½	**Hops.**			" Cumberl'd cut...	0 13	0 00
Canada Sugar Refne'y,			Inferior, ℔ lb........	0 00	0 00	" smoked	0 00	0 00
yellow No. 2, 60ds...	0 9½	0 9½	Medium............	0 00	0 00	Hams, in salt.......	0 00	0 00
Yellow, No. 2½.......	0 10	0 10½	Good	0 00	0 00	" smoked.......	0 00	0 00
" No. 3........	0 00	0 10	Fancy	0 00	0 00	Shoulders, in salt	0 00	0 00
Crushed X	0 10½	0 11	**Leather**, @ (4 mos.)			Lard, in kegs.......	0 16½	0 17
A....	0 12½	0 12½	In lots of less than			Eggs, packed	0 13	0 15
Ground............	0 12½	0 13½	60 sides, 10 ℔ cent			Beef Hams	0 00	0 00
Dry Crushed	0 12	0 12½	discount.			Tallow............	0 08	0 8½
Extra Ground.......	0 13	0 13½	Spanish Sole, 1st qual'y			Hogs dressed, heavy..	0 00	0 00
Teas:			heavy, weights ℔ b...	0 21	0 22	" medium ...	0 00	0 00
Japan com'n to good..	0 48	0 60	Do.1st qual middle do..	0 22	0 23	" light......	0 00	0 00
" Fine to choicest..	0 55	0 60	Do. No. 2, light weights	0 20	0 00	**Salt, &c.**		
Colored, com. to fine..	0 60	0 70	Slaughter heavy	0 00	0 00	American brls........	1 35	1 37
Congou & Souch'ng...	0 42	0 75	Do. light	0 00	0 00	Liverpool coarse	0 00	1 00
Oolong, good to fine...	0 60	0 65	Harness, best	0 00	0 00	Goderich	0 00	1 45
Y. Hyson, com to gd..	0 47½	0 65	" No. 2	0 00	0 00	Plaster	1 00	0 00
Medium to choice	0 00	0 90	Upper heavy........	0 30	0 32	Water Lime	1 50	0 00
Extra choice	0 85	0 90	" light.....	0 33	0 34			

Soap & Candles.	$ c.	$ c.
D. Crawford & Co.'s ..		
Imperial.........	0 07½	0 08
" Golden Bar	0 07	0 07½
" Silver Bar........	0 07	0 07½
Crown	0 05	0 05½
No. 1	0 03½	0 03¾
Candles	0 00	0 11
Wines, Liquors, &c.		
Ale:		
English, per doz. qrts.	2 60	2 65
Guinness Dub Portr..	2 35	2 40
Spirits:		
Pure Jamaica Rum...	1 80	2 25
De Kuyper's H. Gin..	1 55	1 65
Booth's Old Tom.....	1 90	2 00
Gin:		
Green, cases.........	4 00	4 25
Booth's Old Tom, c...	6 00	6 25
Wines:		
Port, common	1 00	1 25
" fine old	2 00	4 00
Sherry, common	1 00	1 50
" medium........	1 70	1 80
"old pale or golden..	2 50	4 00

Brandy:	$ c.	$ c.
Hennessy's, per gal..	2 30	2 50
Martell's " ..	2 30	2 50
J. Robin & Co.'s " ..	2 25	2 35
Otard, Dupuy & Cos..	2 25	2 35
Brandy, cases........	8 50	9 00
Brandy, com. per c...	4 00	4 50
Whiskey:		
Common 36 u. p......	0 58	0 60
Old Rye	0 77½	0 80
Malt	0 77½	0 80
Toddy	0 77½	0 80
Scotch, per gal........	1 90	2 10
Irish—Kinnahan's c...	7 00	7 50
" Dunnville's Belf't..	6 00	6 25
Wool.		
Fleece, lb............	0 31	0 32
Pulled "............	0 00	0 00
Furs.		
Bear................	0 00	0 00
Beaver, ℘ lb..........	0 00	0 00
Coon	0 00	0 00
Fisher...............	0 00	0 00
Martin...............	0 00	0 00
Mink.................	0 00	0 00
Otter................	0 00	0 00
Spring Rats..........	0 00	0 00
Fox..................	0 00	0 00

INSURANCE COMPANIES.

ENGLISH.—*Quotations on the London Market.*

No. of Shares.	Last Dividend.	Name of Company.	Shares par val £	Amount paid.	Last Sale.
20,000		Briton Medical and General Life...	10	....	2½
50,000	7½	Commer'l Union, Fire, Life and Mar.	50	5	5½
24,000	8	City of Glasgow	25	2½	4½
5,000	9½	Edinburgh Life	100	15	33½
400,000	5—½ yr	European Life and Guarantee......	2½	11s6	4s. 0d
100,000	10	Etna Fire and Marine.............	10	1½	—
20,000	5	Guardian	100	50	53½
24,000	12	Imperial Fire....................	500	50	352
7,500	9½	Imperial Life	100	10	17½
100,000	10	Lancashire Fire and Life..........	20	2	2⅞
10,000	11	Life Association of Scotland.......	40	7½	25
35,862	45s. p. sh	London Assurance Corporation ..	25	12½	48¾
10,000	5	London and Lancashire Life	10	1	—
87,504	40	Liverp'l & London & Globe F. & L.	20	2	7½
20,000	5	National Union Life	5	1	1
20,000	12½	Northern Fire and Life	100	5	13
40,000	12 '68, bo 5s.	North British and Mercantile	50	6½	19½
40,000	50	Ocean Marine	25	5	17¾
2,500	£5 12s.	Provident Life....................	100	10	35
....	£4½ p. s.	Phœnix..........................	....	....	130½ x d
200,000	2½—h.yr.	Queen Fire and Life	10	1	21s.
100,000	3s. bo.4s	Royal Insurance..................	20	3	6½
20,000	10	Scottish Provincial Fire and Life ..	50	2½	5⅛
10,000	25	Standard Life	50	12	66 x d
4,000	5	Star Life	25	1½	—
		CANADIAN.			℘ c.
8,000	4	British America Fire and Marine ..	$50	$25	56 57
....	4	Canada Life	...	....	.....
4000	12	Montreal Assurance	£50	£5	135
10,000	3	Provincial Fire and Marine........	60	11	.....
....	....	Quebec Fire	40	32½	£23 24
....	7	" Marine..................	100	40	85 90
10,000	4 6 mo's.	Western Assurance................	40	9	.....

RAILWAYS.	Sha's	Paid	Montr	London
Atlantic and St. Lawrence.........................	£100	All.	....	56
Buffalo and Lake Huron	20½	"	....	2⅜ 3½
Do. do Preference	10	"	....	5 6
Buff., Brantf. & Goderich, 6℘c., 1872-3-4....	100	"	....	66 69
Champlain and St. Lawrence	....	....	10 11	....
Do. do Pref. 10 ℘ ct..............	....	....	80 85	....
Grand Trunk	100	"	14 14½	13½
Do. Eq.G. M. Bds. 1 ch. 6℘c..............	100	"	....	80
Do. First Preference, 5 ℘ c	100	"	....	44½
Do. Deferred, 3 ℘ ct..	100	"	....	....
Do. Second Pref. Bonds, 5℘c............	100	"	....	37
Do. do Deferred, 3 ℘ ct............	100	"	....	....
Do. Third Pref. Stock, 4℘ct.............	100	"	....	28½
Do. do. Deferred, 3 ℘ ct.......	100	"	....	....
Do. Fourth Pref. Stock, 3℘c............	100	"	....	15½
Do. do. Deferred, 3 ℘ ct...........	100	"	....	....
Great Western	20½	"	14 14½	13½
Do. New	20½	18	....	....
Do. 6 ℘ c. Bds, due 1873-76............	100	All.	....	99
5½℘c Bds. due 1877-78..............	100	"	....	92½
Marine Railway, Halifax, $250, all......	$250	"	....	....
Northern of Canada, 6 ℘c. 1st Pref. Bds..........	100	"	....	82 83

EXCHANGE.	Halifax.	Montr'l.	Quebec.	Toronto.
Bank on London, 60 days......				
Sight or 75 days date	12½ 13	9⅜ 9½	9⅜ 9½	10⅓
Private do.	11½ 12	8 9	8¾ 9	9¼
Private, with documents..........	....	8 8½	....	....
Bank on New York................	....	26½ 27	26 26½	26¾
Private do.	....	27 27½	26½ 27	....
Gold Drafts do.	....	par	par ⅛ dis.	par ¼ dis.
Silver	....	4 4½	....	4 to 5

STOCK AND BOND REPORT.

The dates of our quotations are as follows:—Toronto, July 6; Montreal, July 5; Quebec, July 3; London, June 5.

NAME.	Shares.	Paid up.	Divid'd last 6 Months	Dividend Day.	CLOSING PRICES. Toronto.	Montre'l.	Quebe[c]
BANKS.			℘ ct.				
British North America	$250	All.	3½ b½pc	July and Jan.	103 104	103½104½	104 10
Jacques Cartier.........	50	"	4	1 June, 1 Dec.	107 107½	107 108	107 10
Montreal	200	"	6	"	160½161	150½160	160½16
Nationale....................	50	"	4	1 Nov. 1 May.	106½107	107 108	107½ 1
New Brunswick	100	"	......	......	....	....	....
Nova Scotia	200	—	7&b$3½	Mar. and Sept.	....	....	....
Du Peuple.....	50	"	4	1 Mar., 1 Sept.	108 108½	108 108½	108 10
Toronto	100	"	4	1 Jan., 1 July.	120 120½	118 119	118 11
Bank of Yarmouth...........	....	....	......	......	....	....	....
Canadian Bank of Com'e......	50	All.	......	......	100½101	100 101	100 10
City Bank Montreal	80	"	4	1 June, 1 Dec.	98½ 99	98½ 99	97½ 9
Commer'l Bank (St. John)....	100	"	℘ ct.	......	....	..	....
Eastern Townships' Bank.....	50	"	4	1 July, 1 Jan..	....	98 99	97½ 9
Gore	40	...	none.	1 Jan., 1 July.	39 40	38½ 39½	38 4
Halifax Banking Company....	....	....	......	......	....	....	....
Mechanics' Bank.............	50	All.	4	1 Nov., 1 May.	92½ 95	92 94	92 9
Merchants' Bank of Canada....	100	"	5	1 Jan., 1 July.	104 105	103 105	110 11
Merchants' Bank (Halifax)....	....	....	.....	......	....	....	....
Molson's Bank...............	50	All.	4	1 Apr., 1 Oct.	108½ 109	108½ 109	108½ 1
Niagara District Bank...	100	70	3½	1 Jan., 1 July.	...	....	....
Ontario Bank................	40	All.	4	1 June, 1 Dec.	96½ 96½	95½ 96½	95 9
People's Bank (Fred'kton)....	100	"	......	......	....	...	....
People's Bank (Halifax)	20	"	7 12 m	......	....	....	....
Quebec Bank	100	"	3½	1 June, 1 Dec.	100 100½	100 100½	100½10
Royal Canadian Bank	50	60	4	1 Jan., 1 July.	49 50	50 55	50 55
St. Stephens Bank	100	All.	.....	......	....	....	....
Union Bank	100	"	4	1 Jan., 1 July.	103 104	104 105	104 10
Union Bank (Halifax)........	100	....	7 12mo	Feb. and Aug.	....	....	.. .
MISCELLANEOUS.							
British America Land........	250	44	......	......	....	....	....
British Colonial S. S. Co......	250	32½	......	......	...	....	...
Canada Company	32½	All.	......	......	....	....	....
Canada Landed Credit Co.....	50	$50	3½	......	77 78	....	....
Canada Per. B'ldg Society....	50	All.	5	......	121 122	....	....
Canada Mining Company.....	4	90	......	......	....	....	....
Do. Inl'd Steam Nav. Co.....	100	All.	15 12m	......	....	99½100½	90 1
Do. Glass Company.........	100	"	None.	......	....	40 60	....
Canad'n Loan & Investm't....	25	2½	......	......	....	....	....
Canada Agency	10	¼	......	......	....	....	....
Colonial Securities Co.........	...	....	......	......	....	....	....
Freehold Building Society....	100	All.	5	......	116½ 117	....	....
Halifax Steamboat Co........	100	"	......	......	....	....	....
Halifax Gas Company........	....	....	......	......	....	....	....
Hamilton Gas Company......	....	....	.....	......	....	....	....
Huron Copper Bay Co........	4	12	20	......	....	30 45	....
Lake Huron S. and C.........	5	102	......	......	....	....	....
Montreal Mining Consols......	20	$15	......	......	....	2.90 3.10	...
Do. Telegraph Co...	40	All.	5	......	Bks cl'd	Bks cl'd	Bks cl
Do. Elevating Co...	00	"	5½	......	....	105 107	....
Do. City Gas Co.........	40	"	4	15 Mar. 15 Sep.	....	136 137½	136 13
Do. City Pass. R,. Co....	50	"	2	......	....	110½111	110 11
Quebec and L. S.	8	$4	......	......	....	...	....
Quebec Gas Co...............	200	All.	4	1 Mar., 1 Sep.	....	...	120 12
Quebec Street R. R	50	25	3	......	....	....	90 91
Richelieu Navigation Co......	100	All.	7-12m	1 Jan., 1 July.	....	120 123	120 12
St. Lawrence Glass Company.	100	"	....	......	....	80 85	....
St. Lawrence Tow Boat Co....	100	"	......	3 Feb.	....	...	30 3
Tor'to Consumers' Gas Co.....	50	"	⅔ m	1 My Au Mar Fe	107 107½	...	106 107
Trust & Loan Co. of U. C.....	20	5	3	......	....	....	....
West'n Canada Bldg Soc'y....	50	All.	5	......	116½117	....	....

SECURITIES.	London.	Montreal.	Quebec.	Toronto.
Canadian Gov't Deb. 6 ℘ ct. stg.....................	....	103 104	102 103	104½ 105
Do. do. 6 do due Ja. & Jul. 1877-84........	104½ 105½	....	....	....
Do. do. 6 do. Feb. & Aug.........	102 104	....	....	....
Do. do. 6 do. Mch. & Sep..........	102 104	....	...	....
Do. do. 5 ℘ ct. cur., 1883	93¾ 94½	92½ 95	91 92	92 93
Do. do. 5 do. stg., 1885	93½ 94	90 92½	90 90½	91 92
Do. do. 7 do. cur.,.....................	.....	....	......	....
Dominion 6 p. c. 1878 cy.....	....	106½ 107½	107 107½	106½ 107
Hamilton Corporation.....	....	....	......	....
Montreal Harbor, 8 ℘ ct. d. 1869.....................	..	....	......	....
Do. do. 7 do. 1870......................	....	....	......	....
Do. do. 6½ do. 1883......................	....	102¾ 103	......	102 103
Do do. 6½ do. 1873......................	....	....	......	....
Do. Corporation, 6 ℘ c. 1891	....	96 96½	96½ 97	96 96½
Do. 7 p. c. stock..................................	....	108½110	108½ 109½	109 110
Do. Water Works, 6 ℘ c. stg. 1878...............	....	96½ 97½	......	98 96½
Do. do. 6 do. cy. do.	....	....	......	96 97
New Brunswick, 6 ℘ ct., Jan. and July	104 104½	....	......	....
Nova Scotia, 6 ℘ ct., 1875...........................	103 104	....	......	....
Ottawa City 6 ℘ c. d. 1880	....	95 97	......	...
Quebec Harbour, 6 ℘ c. d. 1883........................	....	....	60	....
Do. do. 7 do. do..........................	....	....	65 70	....
Do. do 8 do. 1886.........................	...	....	80 85	....
Do. City, 7 ℘ c. d. 1½ years.....................	....	....	98 98½	....
Do. do. 7 do. 8 do.	....	....	91 92	....
Do. do. 7 do. 5 do.	....	....	96 96½	....
Do. Water Works, 7 ℘ ct., 3 years	....	....	97 97½	....
Do. do. 6 do. 1½ do.	....	....	94 95	....
Toronto Corporation	....	94 95	....	....

Insurance.

Br ton Medical and General Life Association,

with which is united the

BRITANNIA LIFE ASSURANCE COMPANY.

Capital and Invested Funds............£750,000 Sterling.

ANNUAL INCOME, £220,000 STG. :

Yearly increasing at the rate of £25,000 Sterling.

THE important and peculiar feature originally introduced by this Company, in applying the periodical Bonuses, so as to make Policies payable during life, without any higher rate of premiums being charged, has caused the success of the BRITON MEDICAL AND GENERAL to be almost unparalleled in the history of Life Assurance. *Life Policies on the Profit Scale become payable during the lifetime of the Assured, thus rendering a Policy of Assurance a means of subsistence in old age, as well as a protection for a family,* and a more valuable security to creditors in the event of early death ; and effectually meeting the often urged objection, that persons do not themselves reap the benefit of their own prudence and forethought.

No extra charge made to members of Volunteer Corps for services within the British Provinces.

☞ TORONTO AGENCY, 5 KING ST. WEST.

Oct 17—9-1yr   JAMES FRASER, Agent.

BEAVER Mutual Insurance Association.

HEAD OFFICE—20 TORONTO STREET, TORONTO.

INSURES LIVE STOCK against death from any cause. The only Canadian Company having authority to do this class of business.

E. C. CHADWICK, President.

W. T. O'REILLY, Secretary.   8-1y-25

HOME DISTRICT Mutual Fire Insurance Company.

Office—North-West Cor. Yonge & Adelaide Streets, TORONTO.—(UP STAIRS.)

INSURES Dwelling Houses, Stores, Warehouses, Merchandise, Furniture, &c.

PRESIDENT—The Hon. J. McMURRICH.

VICE-PRESIDENT—JOHN BURNS, Esq.

JOHN RAINS, Secretary.

AGENTS :

DAVID WRIGHT, Esq., Hamilton ; FRANCIS STEVENS, Esq., Barrie : Messrs. GIBBS & BRO., Oshawa. 8-1y

THE PRINCE EDWARD COUNTY Mutual Fire Insurance Company.

HEAD OFFICE,—PICTON, ONTARIO.

President, L. B. STINSON ; *Vice-President,* WM. DELONG. *Directors :* W. A. Richards, James Johnson, James Cavan, D. W. Ruttan, H. A. McPaul.—*Secretary,* John Twigg ; *Treasurer,* David Barker; *Solicitor,* R. J. Fitzgerald.

THIS Company is established upon strictly Mutual principles, insuring farming and isolated property, (not hazardous,) in Townships only, and offers great advantages to insurers, at low rates for *five years,* without the expense of a renewal.

Picton, June 15, 1869.   9-1y

Fire and Marine Assurance.

THE BRITISH AMERICA ASSURANCE COMPANY.

HEAD OFFICE :

CORNER OF CHURCH AND COURT STREETS, TORONTO.

BOARD OF DIRECTION :

Hon. G. W. Allan, M L C.,	A. Joseph, Esq ,
George J Boyd, Esq ,	Peter Paterson, Esq.,
Hon. W. Cayley,	G. P. Ridout, Esq.,
Richard S. Cassels, Esq.,	E H. Rutherford, Esq.,

Thomas C. Street, Esq.

Governor:

GEORGE PERCIVAL RIDOUT, Esq.

Deputy Governor:

PETER PATERSON, Esq.,

Fire Inspector: Marine Inspector:

E. ROBY O'BRIEN.   CAPT. R. COURNEEN.

Insurances granted on all descriptions of property against loss and damage by fire and the perils of inland navigation.

Agencies established in the principal cities, towns, and ports of shipment throughout the Province.

THOS. WM. BIRCHALL,

23-1y   *Managing Director.*

Insurance.

Reliance Mutual Life Assurance Society

OF LONDON, ENGLAND. Established 1840.

Head Office for the Dominion of Canada :

131 ST. JAMES STREET, MONTREAL.

DIRECTORS—Walter Shanly, Esq., M.P.; Duncan Macdonald, Esq.; George Winks, Esq., W. II. Hingston, Esq., M.D., L.R.C.S.

RESIDENT SECRETARY—James Grant.

Parties intending to assure their lives, are invited to peruse the Society's prospectus, which embraces several entirely new and interesting features in Life Assurance. Copies can be had on application at the Head Office, or at any of the Agencies.

JAS. GRANT, Resident Secretary.

Agents wanted in unrepresented districts. 43-1y

The Gore District Mutual Fire Insurance Company

GRANTS INSURANCES on all description of Property against Loss or Damage by FIRE. It is the only Mutual Fire Insurance Company which assesses its Policies yearly from their respective dates ; and the average yearly cost of insurance in it, for the past three and a half years, has been nearly TWENTY CENTS IN THE DOLLAR less than what it would have been in an ordinary Proprietary Company.

THOS. M. SIMONS, Secretary & Treasurer.

ROBT. McLEAN, Inspector of Agencies.

Galt, 25th Nov., 1868.   15-1y

Canada Life Assurance Company.

SPECIALLY LICENSED BY THE GOVERNMENT OF CANADA.

ESTABLISHED 1847.

CAPITAL ....A MILLION DOLLARS.

DEPOSIT WITH GOVERNMENT, $50,000.

The success of the Company may be judged of by the fact that during the financial year to the 30th April, 1869, the gross number of

NEW POLICIES

ISSUED WAS

892!

FOR ASSURANCES OF

$1,957,734,

WITH

ANNUAL PREMIUMS OF

$49,783.73.

Rates lower that those of British or Foreign Offices, and every advantage offered which safety and liberality can afford.

A. G. RAMSAY, Manager.

E. BRADBURNE, Agent,

May 25. 1y   Toronto Street.

Queen Fire and Life Insurance Company,

OF LIVERPOOL AND LONDON,

ACCEPTS ALL ORDINARY FIRE RISKS

on the most favorable terms.

LIFE RISKS

Will be taken on terms that will compare favorably with other Companies.

CAPITAL, · · · · £2,000,000 Stg.

CANADA BRANCH OFFICE—Exchange Buildings, Montreal.

Resident Secretary and General Agent,

A. MACKENZIE FORBES,

13 St. Sacrament St., Merchants' Exchange, Montreal.

WM. ROWLAND, Agent, Toronto.   1-1y

THE AGRICULTURAL Mutual Assurance Association of Canada.

HEAD OFFICE ....LONDON, ONT.

A purely Farmers' Company. Licensed by the Government of Canada.

Capital, 1st *January,* 1869.....................$239,193 82
Cash and Cash Items, over....................$80,000 00
No. of Policies in force...................30,892 00

THIS Company insures nothing more dangerous than Farm property. Its rates are as low as any well-established Company in the Dominion, and lower than those of a great many. It is largely patronised, and continues to grow in public favor.

For Insurance, apply to any of the Agents or address the Secretary, London, Ontario.

London, 2nd Nov., 1868.   12-1y.

Insurance.

The Waterloo County Mutual Fire Insurance Company.

HEAD OFFICE : WATERLOO, ONTARIO.

ESTABLISHED 1863.

THE business of the Company is divided into thr separate and distinct branches, the

VILLAGE, FARM, AND MANUFACTURE

Each Branch paying its own losses and its just proporti of the managing expenses of the Company.

C. M. TAYLOR, Sec.   M. SPRINGER, M.M.P., Pres.

J. HUGHES, Inspector. 12-

Lancashire Insurance Company.

CAPITAL, - - - - - - - - - £2,000,000 Sterli

FIRE RISKS

Taken at reasonable rates of premium, and

ALL LOSSES SETTLED PROMPTLY,

By the undersigned, without reference elsewhere.

S. C. DUNCAN-CLARK & CO.,

General Agents for Ontario,

25-1y   N. W. Cor. of King & Church Sts., TORONT

Western Assurance Company,

INCORPORATED 1851.

CAPITAL, ... $400,000.

FIRE AND MARINE.

HEAD OFFICE.................TORONTO, ONTARIO

DIRECTORS.

Hon. JNO. McMURRICH, President.

	CHARLES MAGRATH, Vice-President
A. M. SMITH, Esq.	JOHN FISKEN, Esq.
ROBERT BEATY, Esq.	ALEX. MANNING, Es
JAMES MICHIE, Esq.	N. BARNHART, Esq.

R. J. DALLAS, Esq.

B. HALDAN, Secretary.

J. MAUGHAN, JR., Assistant Secretary.

WM. BLIGHT, Fire Inspector.

CAPT. G. T. DOUGLAS, Marine Inspector.

JAMES PRINGLE, General Agent.

Insurances effected at the lowest current rates o Buildings, Merchandize, and other property, against lo or damage by fire.

On Hull, Cargo and Freight against the perils of Inlar Navigation.

On Cargo Risks with the Maritime Provinces by sail steam.

On Cargoes by steamers to and from British Ports.

WESTERN ASSURANCE COMPANY'S OFFICE, }

TORONTO, 1st April, 1869.   } 23-1

The Victoria Mutual FIRE INSURANCE COMPANY OF CANADA.

Insures only Non-Hazardous Property, at Low Rate

BUSINESS STRICTLY MUTUAL.

GEORGE H. MILLS, President.

W. D. BOOKER, Secretary.

HEAD OFFICE . . . .HAMILTON, ONTARI

aug 15-1yr

North British and Mercantile Insuranc Company.

Established 1809.

HEAD OFFICE - - CANADA; - MONTRE

TORONTO BRANCH :

LOCAL OFFICES, Nos. 4 & 6 WELLINGTON STREET.

Fire Department, ...R. N. GOOCH, Agen

Life Department................H. L. HIME, Agent.

Imperial Fire Insurance Company OF LONDON.

No. 1 OLD BROAD STREET, AND 16 PALL MAL

ESTABLISHED 1803.

Canada General Agency,

RINTOUL BROS.,

24 St. Sacrament Street.

JAMES E. SMITH, Agent,

Toronto, Corner Church and Colborne Streets.

PUBLISHED AT THE OFFICE OF THE MONETAR TIMES, No. 60 CHURCH STREET.

PRINTED AT THE DAILY TELEGRAPH PUBLISHING HOUS BAY STREET, CORNER OF KING

THE CANADIAN
MONETARY TIMES
AND
INSURANCE CHRONICLE.
DEVOTED TO FINANCE, COMMERCE, INSURANCE, BANKS, RAILWAYS, NAVIGATION, MINES, INVESTMENT,
PUBLIC COMPANIES, AND JOINT STOCK ENTERPRISE.

| L. II—NO. 48. | TORONTO, THURSDAY, JULY 15, 1869. | SUBSCRIPTION $2 A YEAR. |

Meetings.

CANADIAN BANK OF COMMERCE.

Proceeding of the second annual general meet-
ing of the shareholders, held in the Banking
House, Toronto, on Tuesday, 13th July, 1869 :—
The chair was taken at noon by the Hon. William
McMaster, the President, at whose request the
Cashier read the following

Report.

The directors beg to present to the shareholders
their second annual report, and they do so in the
belief that the accompanying statement of the result of the year's business, ending 30th June, will
give general satisfaction.

The net available profits for the past
year amount to..........................$141,236 07
To which add balance at credit of
profit and loss account of last year   362 01

$141,598 08

From which have been taken—
Dividend No. 3, paid 1st
January, 1869.............$38,393 79
Dividend No. 4, paid 2nd
July inst................. 39,728 58
Transferred to " Rest " ac-
count.................... 60,000 00
$138,122 37

Leaving a balance at credit of profit
and loss account of ....$ 3,475 71

It will be seen that after paying a dividend of
eight per cent for the year, the surplus profits
amounted to $63,475 71, of which $60,000 has
been carried to the " Rest " account, making that
fund $100,000, and the remaining $3,475.71 is at
the credit of the profit and loss account.

The sound business principle of writing off annually all debts that appear bad, has been scrupulously observed. The branches have been recently inspected, the assets were thoroughly examined,
and the directors regard every item therein as
being perfectly good.

Numerous applications for the establishing of
branches in various sections of the Province were
received during the year, but none of them were
entertained except those from Woodstock and
Simcoe, where the business of the Gore Bank
was offered to the directors under circumstances
which, in their judgment, rendered its acceptance
not only expedient, but desirable, in the interests
of the bank.

The Directors, after mature consideration, came
to the conclusion that it was advisable to increase
the capital of the bank from one million to two
millions of dollars ; and acting on the discretion
given to them by the shareholders at last meeting,
they applied to Parliament for the necessary
power to make the increase. An Act for this
purpose was carried through the Legislature, and
is now on the Statute Book.

The decision to extend the capital having been
arrived at, the Directors deemed it advisable to
anticipate a portion of the proposed new stock by
the issue of provisional receipts to those who
desired to obtain it. $409,200 was taken up in
this way, and paid in full. $190,800 has been
alloted to those of the original proprietors who re-

sponded to a circular inviting them to send in
applications.

These arrangements had the effect not only of
furnishing means to meet the demands of a constantly increasing business, but also prevented
the old stock from being materially affected in
price, which is usually the case when a large
amount of new shares has to be placed on the
market.

A considerable portion of the remaining stock
could have been readily disposed of to applicants
other than the present shareholders, but in view
of the valuable business established, and the fact
that a reserve of $100,000 has accumulated in two
years, the Directors are of opinion that the $400,-
000 stock still on hand, which it may not be advisable to dispose of for some time, should be held at
a premium.

(Signed)
WM. McMASTER, President.

General Statement.

LIABILITIES.		
Capital stock paid up		$1,408,875 00
Circulation..........$1,045,236 00		
Deposits............ 2,064,650 75		
		3,109,886 75
Reserve for interest		
and exchange...... 17,229 24		
Dividends unpaid ... 334 67		
Fourth dividend,		
payable 1st July.. 39,728 58		
		57,292 49
Rest..................... 100,000 00		
Balance of profits		
carried forward.... 3,475 71		
		103,475 71
		$4,679,529 95

ASSETS.		
Specie and Provin-		
cial notes........... $972,561 78		
Notes and cheques of		
other banks........ 145,493 74		
Balance due by other		
Banks, after de-		
ducting balances		
due to other banks 37,581 74		
		1,155,577 26
Government Securities..		143,246 70
Notes and Bills discounted..........		3,329,111 24
Bank premises and furniture........		51,594 75
		$4,679,529 95

(Signed,)   R. J. DALLAS, Cashier.
Canadian Bank of Commerce,
Toronto, 30th June, 1869.

The following resolutions were then put and
carried unanimously :—

Moved by Joseph McKay, Esq., of Montreal,
seconded by Æmilius Irving, Esq., of Hamilton
—That the report of the directors now read be
adopted, and printed for distribution among the
shareholders.

Moved by T. D. McConkey, Esq., M. P., of
Barrie, seconded by D. Buchan, of Toronto—That
the by-laws made and enacted by the Board of
Directors, numbering from one to twenty-two
and which have been now read by the Cashier, be
confirmed, and that by-law No. 6, relating to the

remuneration of the directors, be applied retrospectively to the past year.

Moved by Hon. J. G. Currie, of St. Catharines, seconded by James Campbell, Esq., of Toronto—That the directors be authorised to apply to the Dominion Parliament at its next session for an extension of the charter of the bank, with such alterations as experience, the action of the other banks, and possible Government legislation on the subject of banking, may render desirable.

Moved by T. D. McConkey, Esq., and seconded by E. A. Rutherford, Esq., of Toronto—That the thanks of the meeting be tendered to the President, Vice-President and directors, for their services during the past year.

Moved by A. T. McCord, Esq., of Toronto, and seconded by W. J. McDonnell, Esq., Toronto—That the ballot-box be now opened, and remain open until 3 o'clock this day, for the receipt of ballot tickets for the election of directors and that Messrs. James Brown and Henry Pellatt do act as scrutineers—the poll to be closed, however, whenever five minutes shall have elapsed without a vote being tendered.

The following is the report of the scrutineers: We, the undersigned scrutineers, appointed at the general meeting of the shareholders of the Canadian Bank of Commerce, held this day, hereby declare the following gentlemen duly elected directors for the ensuing year:—Hon. William McMaster, Messrs. H. S. Howland, William Alexander, James Austin, William Elliot, T. Sutherland Stayner, and John Taylor. (Signed,) James Browne and Henry Pellatt, scrutineers.

At a meeting of the newly elected Board of Directors, the Hon. Wm. McMaster was elected President, and H. S. Howland, Esq., Vice-President, by a unanimous vote.

         R. J. DALLAS, *Cashier.*

WESTERN EXTENSION RAILWAY COMPANY.

The annual meeting of the stockholders of the European and North American Railway Company for extension westward, was held on the 16th June, in St. John, N.B. The report states the total length of the road, from the west bank of the river St. John at the Suspension Bridge to the State of Maine, at about 88 miles. Nearly the whole of this distance is graded and ready to receive the rails as soon as they arrive from England. The directors believe that uy the end of July, or early in August, the track will be laid so that a train can proceed from the station at Fairville to the junction of the Fredericton Branch Railway. Sleepers sufficient for laying the track on the whole line have been delivered, and 41¾ miles of double fencing has been put up. The rails for the whole length of the road have been purchased, and it is calculated that it will require about 9,000 tons. Of this quantity about 4,020 tons were received during the season of 1868, about 1,830 tons have already arrived this spring, and the balance, about 3,205 tons, are reported afloat. Two vessels loaded with iron for this company were unfortunately lost, one off the coast of Nova Scotia and the other off Cadiz. Information of these disasters was immediately telegraphed to England, and the parcels have been repeated ; so that the delay of the receipt of these cargoes is the only loss that the company will sustain. Three locomotives and fifty flat cars for ballasting and other purposes have been procured, and are kept constantly occupied in the construction of the road. Temporary bridges have been constructed, or are in course of construction, over all the large streams, and will be used only until the permanent superstructures can be brought from the United States. All bridges over 40 feet pan are to have iron superstructures. Stations buildings have been erected in a number of places. At a special meeting of the stockholders, held on the 2nd of November, 1867, the directors of the company were authorized and empowered to exe-

cute a mortgage on the road, and to procure and issue first mortgage sterling bonds, by the sale of which bonds they would procure means to complete the road. The bonds were to be like the form submitted, and an issue of about $2,000,000 was ordered. The mortgage was duly executed, and 2,055 first mortgage sterling bonds, of £200 each, amounting in all to £411,000 sterling were prepared.

On the 3rd of December, 1867, Wm. G. Case, Esq., of Columbia, Pennsylvania, U.S., was appointed the agent of this company to proceed to England and negotiate and sell these bonds. On the 6th of May following he concluded an agreement with Messrs. J. S. Morgan & Co., bankers, London, to introduce these bonds in the London Stock Market, and under this arrangement Messrs. J. S. Morgan & Co. disposed of £38,800 for the net sum of £26,431 15s. 6d., and £41,000 were subsequently sold by Mr. Case for £27,913 0s. 2d. stg. On the 12th of December last, the directors of this company sold and transferred to the International Railway Construction and Transportation Company, an association organized in the United States, £180,000 of these bonds at 71 per cent. of their par value, for which this company were to receive £40,000 stg. in cash, by monthly instalments, 5,000 tons of railroad iron, and the balance is to be paid by them in two years from the date of the same. £11,400 of these bonds have been used in procuring rolling stock, and £6,600 of them have been paid on account of station buildings on the road. Of the whole amount of bonds authorized, only £278,200 have been issued, which leaves £132,800 still under the control of the directors.

By the provisions of the Act of Assembly, 27th Vic., cap. 3, intituled, "An Act to aid in the Construction of Railways," a subsidy of $10,000 per mile is granted to assist in constructing this line of railway. The whole length of this road is about 88 miles, so that the total amount arising from this source is about $880,000. Twenty instalments, or $500,000, of this amount has been called for, which leaves a balance of $380,000 still available.

The total amount of stock subscribed for and owned by individuals principally resident in St. John is $193,750. Of this amount $116,760.55 has been collected, leaving a balance of $76,989.45 due and unpaid. The Treasurer's accounts were duly audited by the Hon. A. McSeely and James U. Thomas, Esq. ;—the Treasurer's account showing the total cash receipts of the company, up to 31st May last, to be $1,131,517.88, and the total expenditure up to the same period to be $1,130,-476.15, and also a general business sheet of the company's accounts are also submitted. All of which is respectfully submitted. — Wm. Parks, President ; A. Jardine, Wm. B. Robinson, Lewis Carvell, Directors.

THE INTERNATIONAL BRIDGE CO.

The American and Canadian International Bridge Companies each held its annual general meeting on the 5th, the former at Buffalo, the latter at Fort Erie. Beyond the election of Directors, no action was taken at either meeting, except the passage of a resolution declaring void the contract for building the bridge held by James McHenry of London, and the two companies, for two years have been repeating this annual ceremony. In both companies, the directors elected are almost entirely gentlemen in some way connected with the Grand Trunk Railway Company, so that the bridge organization is wholly controlled and possessed by that corporation.

The following are the Directors of the Canadian Bridge Company, chosen at the Fort Erie Meeting :—C. J. Brydges, Managing Director of the Grand Trunk Railway; John Bell, Solicitor of the G. T. R. Company; R. Easton, Mechanical Superintendent of the G. T. R. Company; J. Ferrier,

President of the G. T. R. Company; J. Hickson, Secretary of the G. T. R. Company; A. Walsh, M. P. Commissioner of the Intercolonial Railway; P. R. Jarvis, connected with the G. T. R. Company at Stratford, Canada; H. Yates, ditto at Kingston, Canada; E. G. Spaulding, of Buffalo.

For the American Company, the same Directors as the above were elected, with the exception of Messrs. Eaton and Yates, in whose places were chosen Adam Brown, of Hamilton, Canada ; and E. Carlton Sprague, Buffalo.

MECHANICS' BANK.—The annual meeting was held in Montreal on the 5th July. The directors submitted to the shareholders the following annual statement of affairs:—The business for the year ending 30th June, 1869, has been conducted with caution, and has proved remunerative in its results, while losses and doubtful debts are more than covered by the amounts written off. Balance at credit after last annual meeting $12,736.35; the profits of the year, after deducting bad and doubtful debts, and crediting contingent fund, are $35,-641.16; making $47,771.41; from which have been deducted—dividend 4 per cent. 1st November $11,-828.75; dividend 4 per cent. 1st May 12,752.85; working and other expenses $4,188.55; making $28,770.15; balance $19,007.26.

The system of conducting the affairs of the bank in former years has been adhered to in that which has just closed, viz :—"City Accounts," "No Branches," and "No Circulation." All transactions are made in Government Legal Tenders and the Notes of other Chartered Banks, and in view of the important changes in the Banking system of the country, which the next few years may possibly bring about, the Directors believe it it to be for the interest of the Mechanics' Bank, that for the present, at all events, there should be no departure from a mode of doing business, which so far has been attended with success.

The following gentlemen were elected to serve as Directors for the ensuing year:—Walter Shanly, M.P., C. J. Brydges, Alexander Molson, John Aitkinson, William McNaughton.

General Statement.

LIABILITIES.	
Capital stock	$311,124 58
Deposits bearing interest	154,111 59
Deposits not bearing interest	58,827 17
Dividends unclaimed	1,000 95
Balances due to other banks	707 07
Credit of Contingent Fund $4,552 92	
Balance	19,007 26
	23,530 18
	$549,301 54

ASSETS.	
Coin, bullion, and Provincial notes on hand	$45,510 38
Balances due by other banks	4,503 02
Notes and cheques of other banks	56,726 64
Bank premises	35,658 19
Notes discounted	387,963 80
Other debts due the bank not included under the foregoing heads	18,737 51
	$549,301 54

MERCHANTS' BANK.—The following resolutions were passed at the annual meeting on the 5th, and referred to in the annual report published ir these columns last week:—

1. That, with a view to carry out the intention of the Shareholders in establishing the Bank, and to keep faith with the public by realizing the representation on the notes in circulation, it is expedient to increase the subscribed capital stock to a total sum of $6,000,000.

2. For this purpose the Directors be authorized and empowered as soon as convenient to open Books of subscription, and under such regulations as they may see necessary.

3. Each shareholder as shown by the books of the Bank on the last day of the month of June

hall be entitled to subscribe at par an amount qual to one half of what he may have held, at last date, or in other words, to add fifty per cent o his stock.

4. An instalment of ten per cent on the amount f new stock thus subscribed will be payable at le time of subscription, but no further calls will e made on it unless it should seem to the Direc- rs that the interests of the Bank require it, and en only in instalments of ten per cent with at ast three months interval between the payment f each instalment.

5. No transfer in the Books of the Bank of the ew Stock will be permitted unless the whole nount of the shares desired to be transferred is reviously fully paid up, with accrued interest from te of last dividend.

6. Shareholders may at any time make such yments as may be convenient for them on ac- unt of this New Stock, provided such payments in equal instalments of ten per cent., and may y up in full from time to time such number of ares as they may desire, with interest from date last dividend.

7. Such shares on being paid up in full with terest may be transferred to the credit of the areholders in the Stock Books of the Bank and ill then carry full dividend.

8. Pro rata dividends will be paid at the regular riod on all stock partially paid up.

9. Such shares of this new stock as may not subscribed within the time and under the gulations prescribed by the Directors, may be sposed of by them as they shall see fit for the terests of the Bank.

10. The Directors will advertise in one or two wspapers the dates when the Books of subscrip- on to the new stock will be opened, and will so intimate the same to the Shareholders by nding to their address printed notices through ₤ post office.

To the first resolution Mr. Crawford moved an endment to the effect that the consideration of increase in the stock should be deferred. This as seconded by Mr. Fraser and lost on a division a large majority.

MUTUAL INSURANCE COMPANY OF NICHOL.— le annual meeting of this company was held in nottville, Ont., on the 7th June, Mr. A. W. ewwelling in the chair. The chairman having iefly explained the object of the meeting, the cretary read the following report of the Direc- :s for the past year:—Your Directors in present- g their tenth Annual Report have much pleasure stating that another year has passed without y loss having been sustained by fire—being the rd year in succession that the company has rn so fortunate. The unprecedented dry sea- 1 of 1868 very materially increased the risk of s amongst farm buildings, and many companies uring this description of property sustained vy losses, although our institution escaped. e hundred and seventy-eight policies, including ewals, have been recorded during the past year covering property to the amount of $200,160. are are 385 policies now in force, covering pro- ty to the amount of $305,720. The available mium notes amount to $7,944.76, and the lance at credit of the Company is $402.79. A rtion, however, of this balance ($85.32) is re- sented by promissory notes, &c. Of late eral mutual insurance Companies have shan- ed the premium note system and collected the ole premium in cash. It is not the province your directors to criticise the management of er companies, but they deem it their duty to rn their brother farmers that there is not so ch safety in the cash system as appears at first ht. The following extract from an editorial in Monetary Times shows very clearly the danger the system:—"It appears, therefore, that the eous mutual companies have been gradually ving the premium note system. There is no tbt that there is on the part of the insured a

preference for the cash system and its exemption from liability and in order to compete successfully for business, the Mutuals have been compelled to depart from the true mutual principle. But this breaking loose from premium notes deprives the insured of that security for payment which he naturally looks for. In the absence of a guaran- tee capital, there is no security at all but the honesty and good management of the directors. It may be said that they confine their business to narrow circles, but the contrary is becoming the case, and we find Mutuals branching out in all directions and competing successfully with Stock Companies. We know the note system may have abuses attached to it, such as in one case we have heard of, where the agent taking risks gets $2 a policy and the company gets nothing until an assessment is made. But that is no sufficient answer. Where the note system prevails there is a show of security, at the least, but in the cash system there may be neither shadow nor substance. Under such circumstances, we conclude that some remedy should be applied to state of affairs mani- festly wrong." The report was adopted and the members of the late board were all re-elected, viz. —Messrs. David Allan, Alexander Watt, William Robinson, Francis Cassidy, Alexander Burnett, J. Bonnalie and A. F. Sherratt. The board met the same evening and re-elected David Allan, Esq., president.

UNION BANK.—The annual meeting was held in Quebec on the 5th July, Charles E. Levy was called to the chair, and N. H. Bowen acted as Secretary. The directors report the result of the business of the past year as follows:—The profits after the payment of all charges and provision for losses amount to $105,445.04; to which is to be added the balance of the account of profit and loss brought from the former year $1,567.95; making $107,012.99; which has been thus appro- printed:—To two dividends of per cent. each $80,390.22; vote to President at last annual meet- ing $1,000; reserve for doubtful debts $8,000; reduction of the account for preliminary expenses $2,000; addition to reserve from profits $15,000; total $106,890.22; leaving $622.77 to be carried forward to the account of profit and loss.

The directors are glad to report that the opera- tions of the year have been attended by very little loss. Ample provision has been made for this, and a further sum of $8,000 has been reserved to meet a possible but it is hoped improbable loss on a claim, the value of which cannot now be ascer- tained.

The directors thought it well to procure during the last session of the Parliament of the Dominion an amendment of the charter of the bank affecting the election of Directors in the case of vacancies at the Board. The act is now submitted to the shareholders, and will take effect only after their approval.

The following directors were elected for the en- suing year:—Charles E. Levey, Hon. Thos. Mc- Greevey, Hon. Geo. Irvine, Colonel Rhodes, Jas. Gibb, John Sharples and Geo. H. Simard. And at a meeting of the newly elected Directors, held the same day, Messrs. Charles E. Levey and Thos. McGreevey were elected respectively President and Vice-President for the ensuing year.

CANADA COMPANY.—The ordinary general meet- ing of this Company was held in London, Eng- land, June 24. The report stated that the net profit for the half-year had been £32,932, of which £15,299 was made applicable to the repayment of capital, leaving £17,633 available for distribution, out of which the Directors recommended a divi- dend of 30s. per share, free of income tax. The chairman, in moving the adoption of the report, said that the business of the Company had fallen off during the last half-year, consequent upon the commercial depression in the colony, but from the last accounts received the Directors anticipated that in the current half-year business would again

be restored. The Directors had felt it their duty to aid the emigration movement, and had sub- scribed £100 from the Company's fund to the East-end Emigration Committee. They had also directed their agent in Canada to expend a similar sum in providing for the emigrants on their arrival. He thought the recent discovery of gold on the Company's estate might prove valuable to them.

Insurance.

FIRE RECORD.—Kincardine July 2.—A tele- gram says, the planing mill and factory and a block of three frame tenement buildings, belong- ing to Messrs. McKerricker & Evans, builders, were totally destroyed by fire. Mr. Rastall's new frame building in the course of erection was con- siderably damaged, and a large quantity of lumber destroyed. Loss about $4,000; insured for $2,500.

Carleton, N. B., July.—Fire broke out in John Hanna's three story house, opposite Clarke mill, Carleton, and it was speedily burned to the ground There was $1,000 insurance upon it.

Kentville, N. B., June 30.—A despatch says a fire broke out in a building owned by Daniel Moore, and occupied by T. L. Dodge as flour store. Store and goods entirely destroyed. No insurance. The fire spread itself to the adjoining house of Geo. E. Masters, and notwithstanding all efforts made to subdue it, the house and part of the fur- niture were consumed. No insurance. The far- thur progress of the fire was stopped by the pulling down Lockhart's blacksmith shop. The goods of W. H. Tighe & Co. were considerably damaged by hasty removal from fear of the fire spreading. A correspondent at Kentville states that the loss is about $10,000.

Woodstock, July 10.—The boiler of Clarke & Davidson's steam grist mill, at the east end of the town, exploded, damaging property to the extent of two or three thousand dollars Fireman John Eddy was badly burnt and had the back of his head cut. No lives were lost, and the doctors think the fireman will recover. The windows in the mill were nearly all smashed, and the windows in the Woodstock Hotel across the street were broken. The mill was stopped at the time. No damage was done to the chimney.

St. Catharines, July 13.—About one o'clock this morning, a fire broke out in the stable attached to Edward McCarthy's blacksmith shop. The stable and a horse in it, owned by Mr. E. Goodman, was burnt. The shop and a new dwelling in the course of erection by Mr. McCarthy, was injured by the fire. The stable was insured for thirty-five dol- lars. The fire was evidently the work of an in- cendiary, it having broken out in the manger at the horse's head.

St. John, July 10.—An obliging correspondent writing under the above date says:—In your paper of the 1st inst., the Hon. A. McL. Seely's mill is valued at $300,000 instead of $30,000. The insurance is stated to be $10,000, should be $10,- 000, viz: $12,000 in the "Liverpool, and London, and Globe," and $4,000 in the "Royal." The cause of the fire arose from the common practice, in this Province, of placing tile boilers, &c., in a wing, with a low slanting, unprotected roof. The constant heat, after some years, seems to cause some chemical change in the nature of the wood, so that a single spark will set it flames. This was seen to occur in a mill burnt about 2¼ years ago. The watchman tried to put it out, when the fire was only about the size of his hand, but the fire ran away from him. A high roof, over the boilers, protected with sheets of zinc, would, I am con- vinced, save mills from being burnt in the way I have described.

INSURANCE STOCKS IN HARTFORD.—These have somewhat advanced under the stimulus of hand- some July dividends, which have been declared as follows: The Ætna quarterly of $6 per share; the Phœnix $5 and the City $3. The Hartford and Merchants have each made a semi-annual dividend of $10 per share, and the Connecticut of

$6. The others, at this writing have not been heard from. All of the Fire Companies are understood to have done a successful business the last six months, and to have added somewhat to their surpluses, besides saving the handsome dividend just declared. The following are the latest quotations of Insurance stocks in Hartford:

Fire Insurance Companies.

	Bid.	Asked.
Æetna	217	220
Hartford	230	...
Connecticut......................	140	...
Phœnix	230	...
City	167	180
Charter Oak, par $50........	54	55
North American..............	125	130
Merchants'	220	...
Putnam	92½	95

Life Insurance Stocks.

Æetna Life	210	225
Travellers' (Accident)	103	106
Hartford Life & Ann........	75	82
Continental	128	130
Conn. General	98	99½

AMALGAMATION. — An extraordinary general meeting of the shareholders of the Progress Assurance Company was held in London on the 24th June, when the transfer of the business to the United Ports and General Insurance Company was unanimously confirmed, as was a resolution to wind up the company voluntarily under the supervision of the court.

THE PASSPORT.—This steamer, in making the down trip, passed the first rapid, and was about entering the second, when the chain attached to the rudder gave away. Control of the vessel was for a moment lost. She made a wide sweep to the right, but was brought to again by the men at the tiller, four men being always at the wheel and four at the tiller. The engines were immediately reversed, and both anchors let go. Finding that it would be impossible to repair the chain before dark, the Captain very wisely determined to remain there all night. She arrived in port next morning, 5 o'clock. ,

LONGEVITY IN MARRIAGE.—It appears that between the ages of 20 and 25, the number of deaths among bachelors is double those that occur among married men. This inequality of mortality diminishes during subsequent ages, but always remains on the side of the married men. The average age attained by married men, from the age of 20 to the end of life, is 59½ years, while that of the bachelor is only 40. In other words, a young man after the age of 20 unmarried, is likely to live 20 years longer; but married, 39½ years longer. After the age of 25, the average age reached by married men is a little over 60, while it is not quite 48 for bachelors. This curious fact shows that the chances of life vary with every age, and that the mere fact of one's having attained a certain period is an earnest of sufficient vital powers to carry us to a later age. It is an indisputable fact, that one-half the bachelors die before reaching the age of 30, while, on the contrary, an immense majority of married men live to between 60 and 80 years. Among females, the difference in the duration of life between the married and unmarried woman is not so great as among the other sex : nevertheless that difference is very largely in favor of the married. In wedlock, it is true, females are more subject to premature death than otherwise, from 15 to 30, but they find ample compensation between the ages of 35 and 45, when spinsters in their turn die in much greater numbers ; and beyond the age of 50, the advantage is constantly in favor of the married woman.—Ins. Journal.

CONDITION OF LIMITATION IN POLICIES AS TO SUITS THEREON. — The Supreme Court of the United States, in a case of Riddlesburger vs. Hartford Fire Ins. Co , has affirmed the validity of the condition in policies, "that no action against the company for the recovery of any claim upon the

policy shall be sustained, unless commenced within twelve months after the loss shall have occurred," &c. The condition is not even affected by the fact that an action which was dismissed, had been commenced within the stipulated period. A stipulation to refer all disputes to arbitration stands on a different footing, as an attempt to oust the courts of jurisdiction.

—A despatch from Plymouth, Eng., of the 6th July, says:—The ship Cavalier, Capt. Manson, of Aberdeen, which cleared from Quebec, Canada, on May 31st for London, has arrived at this port waterlogged, having been run into by a Bremen mail steamer.

—The schooner Lafayette Cook, with a cargo of lumber for Kingston, stranded in the Saginaw Bay, Mich., on the 10th July. Insured in the British America and Ætna for $6,000. Steam pumps and wrecking material have already been dispatched to her assistance.

Railway News.

NORTHERN RAILWAY.—Traffic receipts for week ending July 3, 1869.

Passengers......	$4,942 54
Freight and live stock......	13,125 18
Mails and sundries.........	2,248 39
	$20,316 11
Corresponding Week of '68.	15,916 79
Increase	$4,399 32

GREAT WESTERN RAILWAY.—Traffic for week ending June 25, 1869.

Passengers	$31,736 72
Freight...........................	33,094 22
Mails and Sundries...........	2,076 87
Total Receipts for week.....	$66,907 81
Corresponding week, 1868...	57,282 84
Increase	$9,624 97

GREAT WESTERN RAILWAY.—It is stated that the Company have received applications for the whole of the unissued portion of their new 5 per cent. stock, which is issued at 80 per cent., and which up to the year 1880 is convertible at the option of the holders into ordinary shares of the Company. The 6 per cents. of the Company, which have no such convertible rights, being at par, 5 per cents., with the option of conversion, must be worth more than 80, especially if the line prosper as it seems likely to do. This week ending June 18th, 1869, there is a very large increase in the traffic. The Great Western of Canada is a line in good condition, with a good traffic on it, and with excellent prospects, and if in a few years' time it pays 10 per cent. dividend we shall not be surprised.—Herepath's Journal.

PORT WHITBY AND PORT PERRY RAILWAY.— The Whitby Gazette furnishes us with a report of the proceedings in the Council of that town on the occasion of the introduction of a by-law to authorize the corporation to take $10,000 of stock in the railway. Mr. Draper said it might be asking too much for the town to take so much stock after granting a bonus of $50,000. But in 1857 he went on to say, the rate-payers were called upon to vote for a bonus of $300,000 for a railway which they did about unanimously. The annual interest to meet the sinking fund would amount to $22,000, and there was a larger debt hanging over Whitby at that time, than at present. Taking all matters into consideration, he thought it was his duty to lay the question before the council, and endeavour to make the first link of the road to Lake Huron, for he believed if 20 miles were built, the extension would only be a matter of time. He said that $60,000 of the private stock had been subscribed, and that $40,000 had been subscribed for by the gentlemen who proposed to build the road. The contract was let to them

conditionally, they were to pay 10 per cent., as other shareholders, and to give a line suitable to the directors. The reason the contract was given to them was that they had taken a larger amount of private stock than other contractors. Of course, there were other tenders; but the directors thought that if the contractors took stock, they would build a good road. Had the contractors, he said, a map of our county, and it would be seen that baldy would have been going on. A month was given them to raise funds, but they failed. Mr. Draper went on to say: if the town felt in '57 that it could assume the responsibility of giving $300,000 with nothing to oppose its interests, should it not be able to give a good sum, with opposition ? But the town was not asked to give more, only to take stock, and he believed it would be good stock. On the east we were cut off by Port Hope road, on the west by the Toronto narrow gauge; what was to follow but a division of the county? Take the county, long and narrow, would have to be divided, and that before many years. If half or one-third of assessed property be taken from the county, so much would be taken from the ratepayers, and every man's taxes in the county would be raised in proportion. If the road were constructed to Beaverton, the county would be bound with an iron band, and would do away with all talk of a county division. If the by-law were passed our taxes would only be slightly increased. Where a ratepayer paid $14 taxes last year, his rate would be $15 this year, and for one taxel $28 last year, the rate this year would be $30, &c., or only one dollar increase for every fourteen. He referred to the prospects of similar by-laws in Reach and West Whitby.

After some further discussion, the motion was carried.

RAILWAY IRON.—From South Wales it is stated that all the great iron masters are of opinion that prices of railway iron must advance before long, as the requirements of the United States and Russia are known to be large, and, as at the same time, there is little, if any, competition with Belgium and other continental markets. Considerable activity is evinced in the shipment of rails at the local ports of South Wales for the United States and the Southwest coast of America, and it is expected that with fine weather large quantities will be sent away. As compared with last year the increase in the shipments will be very important.—London cor. Financial Chronicle.

GRAND TRUNK TRAFFIC.—The aggregate increase (from Jan. 1st to June 5th, 1869) appears to be only £7,197, but it is really about £16,000, the period this year being 2 days less, and 2 days traffic is equal to more than £8,000. There are three weeks more to the end of the half year and if in these three weeks there be no increase (but doubtless there will be increase) the traffic account will stand well. £16,000 increase in half a year when the most severe snow storms ever known have occurred, and over a period last year remarkable for its very considerable addition in traffic receipts, must be considered good progress. The traffic this year will probably be little short of £1,500,000. A great authority in Grand Trunk matters has stated his opinion that when the line is fully stocked and fairly developed in traffic it will have a gross revenue of £50,000 a week, or upwards of £2,500,000 a year, a million a year more than it has.—Herepath.

AN AERIAL SHIP.—There is little reason to doubt that a successful attempt has been made to float an aerial engine by a mechanic of San Francisco. We are informed that "the ship rose in the air, and was propelled backward and forward, and guided in any desired direction by the steering apparatus. The engine and boiler weigh less than one hundred pounds." This is a great success, and we hope that important results may flow from it.

THE CANADIAN MONETARY TIMES AND INSU-
ANCE CHRONICLE is printed every Thursday even-
g and distributed to Subscribers on the following
orning.

Publishing office, No. 60 Church-street, 3 doors
rth of Court-street.

Subscription price—
   Canada $2.00 per annum.
   England, stg. 10s. per annum.
   United States (U.S. Cy.) $3.00 per annum.

Casual advertisements will be charged at the rate
ten cents per line, each insertion.

Address all letters to "THE MONETARY TIMES."
Cheques, money orders, &c. should be made pay-
le to J. M. TROUT, Business Manager, who alone
authorized to issue receipts for money.

All Canadian Subscribers to THE MONETARY
MES will receive THE REAL ESTATE JOURNAL
hout further charge.

The Canadian Monetary Times.

THURSDAY, JULY 15, 1869.

THE CANADIAN CANALS.

VII.

There is an additional argument advanced
favor of the Caughnawaga Canal, on the
ound that the Erie Canal presents constant
lays to the passage of freight. It is held that
vater communication by Lake Champlain
uld admit a full laden propeller to White-
ll, where the process now observed at
ffalo (to pass to Albany) would take place,
.; the transfer of cargo to barges. It is
r to say that is not impossible that a cer-
n quantity of the freight might take that
ate. As an incidental argument it is not
thout value; but to place such reasoning
the first rank, is to give the Caughnawaga
nal no higher claim than that of an experi-
nt. For it is just as possible, that on the
ite being tried, it would be found not to
swer, and hence in no way would be fol-
red.

Independently of the facilities gained for
Ottawa timber trade, the strongest reasons

for the construction of this work are said to
lie in the direction of the New England States,
which must ever be large consumers of Western cereals. There are now four routes traversed by the cargoes which supply this want,
two of which are tributary to the Erie Canal,
at Albany. The first by the Hudson River
to New York, and thence to the sea ports
convenient for its distribution, Boston standing first in the list. The second, by railway,
the freight crossing the Hudson to Greenbush,
opposite Albany, whence it follows the railway to Boston, a distance of 200 miles. The
third is found on the main railway lines at
Buffalo, the New York Central and the New
York and Erie. Both have established
western connections, and the former runs on
to the Boston railway, so that freight once
placed on the cars, is carried undisturbed to
its destination. The amount received at
Buffalo is about one-half of the whole movement of the western freight. To be more
precise, it may be said to vary from nine to
eleven twentieths. At Oswego, it ranges
from one-eighth to one-fifth, while at Montreal it is from one-eighth to one-eleventh.
The quantity passing by Buffalo is divided between the Erie Canal and these two railroads.
Owing to the imperfection of the figures
at the service of the writer, no reliable comparison can be made of the relative quantities.
According to the report of the Auditor of the
Canal Department of the State of New York,
dated March 12, 1869, the "tons arriving
at tide water by way of the Erie Canal, products of Western States and Canada," are as
follows: [p. 161.]

Products of the Forest .....   891,071 Tons.
 "   Agriculture..........1,183,816   "
Manufactures   4,354   "
                                          ─────────
           Total......................2,215,222   "

and the difference between this amount and
the total passing east from Buffalo, will give
the quantity carried by railway, whereas compared with the quantity taken by railways,
we have the following [p. 38] total movements
for 1868:—

New York Canals .... 6,442,225 Tons.
 "   Central Railway.... 1,846,509   "
Erie Railway ....,,..... 3,908,243   "
                                          ─────────
           Total................,........12,197,067*   "

that is up and down, giving a rude approximation, that half the total passes by the Canal.
The fourth connection between the Western waters and the east has been dictated by
the principle on which the Caughnawaga
Canal is advocated ; that, as a railway con-

nection, is indispensable to bring freight inland—(this peculiar side of the problem must
be borne in mind)—to New England, from
the Albany terminus of the Erie Canal,—why
not seek that connection without the geography of the canal ? Ogdensburgh, on the St.
Lawrence, furnishes exactly that point. It
is 223 miles distant by water from the Ontario
mouth of the Welland Canal, and by railway
158 miles from Burlington. This distance,
added to the railway interval, between Burlington and Boston, 248 miles, will give a
total distance of 406 miles between Ogdensburgh and Boston. It was held, and the
theory seems so perfect that it stands out as
a warning against indulgence in a priori
reasoning, that the Welland propeller, with
its 4,400 bbls. of flour, would leave Chicago
and passing through the Welland Canal in
place of depositing its cargo at Oswego, a
distance of 138 miles on Lake Ontario, could
go on to Ogdensburgh, 85 miles farther. At
Oswego the cargo actually and positively was
known to be from 11 to 15 days from Boston.
At Ogdensburgh, by every fair calculation, it
was 30 hours. The line was accordingly
built by Boston capital. The result has
totally disappointed expectations; in round
figures only five per cent. of the quantity
carried from the west having passed by this
line. It may be explained, to some extent,
by the fact that a certain portion of the grain
destined for Boston never enters lake Ontario
at all. For, conceding in any way the necessity of railway connection. it was open to
apply the principle at any point, and practically it has resulted that it has been appealed
at Buffalo itself, and grain once placed on
the railway cannot be profitably moved from
it, except under very special circumstances.

The effect of the water connection of the
St. Lawrence with Boston by Burlington,
viewed by the light of the experience of the
Ogdensburgh Railway, to our mind is not
encouraging. If we suppose a propeller at
Burlington quay, and inquire what has been
achieved, what attained, by passing the St.
Lawrence and entering Lake Champlain, the
answer can be given categorically. The
propeller is 158 miles nearer (railway distance) to Boston than it was at Ogdensburgh,
with the identical necessities of transhipment
to the railway cars, and in the expectation
of receiving back a cargo of a like character,
having traversed the distance,

From Ogdensburg to the Beau-
harnois Canal...................... 97   Miles.
Through the Beauharnois Canal
   and the Caughnawaga Canal to
   St. Johns .... 41¼   "
From St. Johns to Burlington... 75   "
                                          ─────────
           Total .... 213¼   "

The distances are mentioned as a matter of comparison, not from the belief that great weight is to be attached to them. Indeed we have too many opportunities of observing what fallacious deductions can be drawn from comparative distances. Nevertheless, they do form a portion of the whole problem, more or less minute, more or less governing the conclusions. It is in the application of a fact of this character, that the judgment and ability of men come to the surface. The danger of their misapplication is seen in such schemes as the Georgian Bay and Ottawa Canals, and not one of the least effective modes of considering them is to place them side by side. For as both cannot be essential, so on examination of the arguments by which both are sustained, it will be seen how in each case they are identical, viz: the saving of distance, blended with the patriotic assurance, that each passes through Canadian territory. As in these instances, so in every other, the real inquiry must lie in the effect produced. In this case, are we not asked to expend from four to five millions of dollars, so that a propeller may do at Burlington, that which can be done at Ogdensburg, with the addition of 158 miles of railway. It must be remembered, too, that the Ogdensburg route has drawn only one-twentieth part of the freight, when it was fairly reasoned it would bring a very large proportion of it. Fortunately the examination of this matter is not encumbered by considerations of custom houses, for both points lie within the domain of the United States. Certainly it is fair to ask that when it is assumed that great changes in the direction of trade will result from a policy, that some special reasons will be given for the assumption. We must say, with great respect to the gentlemen who advocate this Canal, that we can hardly recognize this assurance in the theory of the forwarder adhering to the water as long as he can or that this saving of distance is a warranty that a propeller carrying from 7,000 to 10,000 barrels of flour, will succeed, where a propeller carrying 4,400 barrels, with the distance additional by railway has failed. On the other hand, it is quite possible that it would practically prove so, if the whole system of the Canals were increased, so that a vessel capable of carrying the larger cargo could pass by the Welland Canal direct to Burlington. We are even prepared to assert that this proposition is not the same as that offered by the more limited cargo at present taken to Ogdensburg. Therefore, the argument is not without a certain possibility, that the ends sought by the advocates of the Caughnawaga Canal may actually be attained; but no one can pretend that they are matters of certainty, leading up to a known deducible consequence.

It seems then the fair mode of summing up the merits of the Caughnawaga Canal is to make the starting point, the enlargement and development of the St. Lawrence navigation. Certainly without such development, it may be said that no additional trade will seek Lake Champlain. The lumber which follows the present circuitous route would pass by the new canal, but the facilities extended to it, would have no appreciable influence on the quantity manufactured. If we understand the advocates of the route, they themselves demand, in conjunction with the new canal, an equal navigation throughout, and the size of the lock as named is longer and deeper than that of the St. Lawrence lock. The doctrine then may with propriety be enunciated that it is secondary to that great work, and that it not only ought not to take precedence of it, but that as a project, it should be held to be subordinate to it. The great cost of deepening the St. Lawrence, precludes the hope that the five millions necessary to construct the canal, will be at once at our command. On financial grounds, therefore, it may be advisable to defer any consideration of the undertaking until the motive for so doing no longer exists. With this proviso, it may be said that the canal would—

1. Extend very great facilities to the lumber trade.

2. That it is not impossible that Western produce would seek its waters, and cargoes be discharged at Burlington.

But on the other hand—

3. That little is to be hoped from it in opening up a communication through Lake Champlain to New York.

As it is now known practically that a vessel can reach Boston from Montreal in eight days, and New York in nine days, it is a perfectly open argument to suggest, that with a properly constructed propeller, the route through the St. Lawrence—developed, it must be understood—from Chicago to the sea-board, may prove more economical than any other. That such vessel can carry freight at the cheapest rate, and deliver it with regularity in the shortest period, at the same time finding a market, where fuel can be the most economically purchased.

If all this be determined in favor of the sea-going route, where will be the special benefit of the Caughnawaga Canal?

THE ROYAL CANADIAN.

It is announced that Mr. Yarker, of the Bank of Montreal, has been assigned the task of investigating the affairs of the Royal Canadian Bank. That gentleman is, we have no reason to doubt, fully competent to discharge the duty in a thorough and business-

like manner; but while making this acknowledgment, we must express our dissent from those who selected him. The Royal Canadian has complained, time and again, that the Bank of Montreal exhibited hostility towards it, and we cannot see, after such complaints, the expediency or wisdom of placing the fate of the institution at the mercy of an alleged persecutor. Mr. Yarker, without necessarily being biassed by his position under Mr. King, might insensibly be swayed by prejudices acquired naturally in the discharge of his duties as a Manager of the Bank of Montreal. Suppose the interest of the Bank of Montreal lay in closing up the Royal Canadian, and Mr. Yarker chose (we do not by any means say that he would do so) to give the Royal its death-blow, what is to prevent his doing it? Suppose Mr. King wished to buy out the Royal, could he not bring some pressure to bear on Mr. Yarker? We merely suppose such a state of affairs for the sake of showing the folly manifested in selecting one whose interests are bound up with the Bank of Montreal to say whether the Royal shall continue to exist or not. If Mr. Yarker report that the condition of the Royal is bad, or even throw out hints of unsoundness, what position will Mr. Crawford and the new board find themselves in? There is another side to the case. Is not the selection of an officer by the Bank of Montreal calculated to beget the suspicion in the minds of the people, that the Bank of Montreal has some mysterious, irresistible power which brings all the other bankers on their knees before it, deprecating its amnesty and asking its permission to live?

Again, suppose Mr. Yarker's report to be unfavorable to the Royal, though the Board may be bound by it, will the shareholders be satisfied that the interests of the Bank of Montreal have not prevailed. The share_ holders may refuse to recognize it as a trustworthy exhibit. If so we shall have the shareholders and the directors again at cross purposes with an additional burden to bear. The Bank of Montreal will undoubtedly accept the report of its own officer, if such report be against the soundness of the Royal.

As we have said the general opinion is that Mr. Yarker is an efficient officer, but it would have been well, both for Mr. Yarker and the Royal, to have associated with him in the investigation some other well known banker. There are Mr. Hague, Mr. Fisher, Mr. Dallas, Mr. Bethune, Mr. Moat and Mr. Morton, all gentlemen of good repute. Why not ask the assistance of one or more of these? Perhaps it is not yet too late to do so. If not, we think it will be generally conceded that such a course is likely to be more satis-tory than risking the existence of a west-banking institution on the opinion of an ser of the Bank of Montreal.

ANADIAN BANK OF COMMERCE.

'he past year's business has resulted in a profit of $141,236, out of which dividends the amount of $78,122 have been paid, sum of $60,000 added to the rest, and a unce of $3,475 was carried forward. The now amounts to $100,000. Such a state-it at the end of the second year of the k's existence, cannot fail to gratify every nd of the institution. It gives the firmest trance that the high anticipations formed its success were well grounded. For the ults achieved, the shareholders are largely sbted to Hon. Mr. McMaster, the Presi-t; who, we know, has made the welfare he bank a subject of constant solicitude, has not spared vigorous and persistent rts, indoors and out, to extend the bank's nections and prosperity. The Cashier, Mr. las, and the Directors have shown uncom-l zeal in doing what they could.

f the $1,000,000 additional capital au-ized by an amendment to the charter, tined last Session, six hundred thousand ars have been taken, and the balance is rved to be held at a premium, and to be osed of as the directors find to be ex-ient. Two new agencies were opened at its from which the Gore Bank had with-wn, whose business at these places was m up under favorable circumstances. The ring directors were re-elected, and the ting passed off with the greatest nimity.

CITIZENS' INSURANCE COMPANY.—This Com-', whose Directors are well known men of tion and influence, whose Manager is trust-hy and energetic, and whose share list embraces : of the best names in Montreal, has taken place of the European Assurance Society, in ida, and assumed the very successful busi-which Mr. Rawlings had gathered during the years of his agency. But the Citizen does confine itself to a guarantee business. It has red the field of competition with life com-es, local and foreign. It bases its claims to ic support on the character of its proprietory, low rate of mortality and the high rate of in-it in Canada. The indisputability of its des after five years, their practical non-for-re; theft facility of renewal after lapse; the nce of excessive restriction on travel; the gnition of the services of volunteers, and the ntage of commanding the security of the pany through its guarantee branch to a pro-ionate extent to the assurance, are all set . as inducements to Canadians to patronise local institution.

MADOC GOLD DISTRICT.

(From our own Correspondent.)

BELLEVILLE, July 12th, 1869.

The event of the week has been the land sales on the part of the Commissioner of Crown lands. Mr. Richards must feel very much disappointed by the result of his policy, which has realized the old Scotch proverb of "great cry and little wool."

Paying twenty-five or thirty thousand dollars for an untried mining lot is a fine thing to brag about in promiscuous conversation, or to write sensation paragraphs upon in newspapers; but when it comes to bidding such amounts as a mat-ter of business, with the assurance that the money is to be paid down in legal tender on the nail, these bold orators lapse into solemn silence. On the day of sale, the attendance was not numerous, and the bidders were but few. The chief interest centered, of course, in the famous lot "nine in the ninth " of Marmora, which was put away at one dollar per acre, the area being 100 acres. The contest for this lot lay between Mr. Cook, of To-ronto, and Mr. Morton, of Mallorytown. After a spirited competition, it was knocked down to the latter gentleman at the rated price of forty dollars and ten cents per acre, making a total of $4,010. The purchaser, however, failing to pay in the money according to the conditions of the sale, the lot was set up again on Friday, and finally knocked down to his former competitor, Mr. Cook, at the rate of twenty-six dollars per acre, or a total of $2,600, or about one-tenth of what Mr. Richards was assured could be easily obtained for the lot.

"The next lot to it," viz., No. 8 in the 9th, was sold to a Mr. Maxwell for $12.50 per acre. A few lots possessing minor attractions were also bought by Mr. Cook.

The fact is, that the action of the Government, or rather of successive Governments, in this mat-ter, as in mining matters generally, has been ill-advised, and prejudicial throughout to the in-terests both of the Province and of the miners. In the first place, regulations, restrictions and taxes, which were only suitable for rich places or alluvial diggings, were remorselessly imposed upon those who undertook to develop the poor and re-fractory rocks of Hastings. Next, a heavy license fee was imposed upon reduction works, regardless of the fact that such works were necessary for the development of the prospective riches to be de-rived in the future from as yet untested veins, and that the true policy of the ruling powers would have been to offer premiums for the intro-duction and erection of such works; and exorbi-tant taxes were collected from men who were de-riving, and who could possibly derive, no benefit whatever from their labors, until they made such substantial discoveries as might induce capitalists to enter into the business, and invest their means in its prosecution : after which, if it proved remu-nerative, it might become a legitimate subject for taxation. Had such a wise and far-sighted policy been adopted at first, I have no doubt, though the country is far from being so rich as men, in the first glitter and dazzle of anticipated wealth, were fain to imagine, but a few remunera-tive mining adventures might have been in opera-tion long enough to have returned to the ex-chequer a much larger total sum than has been exacted (including the sales of last week) from the district at the expense of a long delay, if not total extinction of its prospective prosperity. To use another proverb "they have killed the goose that laid the golden eggs." Let us hope that the eyes of the Commissioner may be opened, and that he will conceive and carry out a more liberal and a more beneficial policy hereafter, and that Government will come down to Parliament, early in the next session, with a well-digested mining law, which may undo, so far as may be, the mis-chief which has resulted from their former crude attempts at legislation, not only in this district, but throughout all the mining regions of the Pro-

vince, and which may help to foster and encourage honest and well-conducted enterprise, and at the same time sternly and strongly repress the ras-cality and deception which exercise so baneful an influence, not only on mining, but on all other commercial and industrial pursuits into which they are introduced.

Mr. Gilbert has got his mill in work upon ore from lot No. 6, in the same concession. I have not heard of his cleaning up as yet, but a gentle-man who visited the mine a few days ago told me that a fine amalgam was gathering upon the cop-per-plated shoot which conveys the ore from the stamps to the pans, which is a good sign of success.

The next subject of interest on the cards is the sale of the Richardson Mine, which is to take place on August 14th; after which we may ex-pect to arrive at something like a true estimate of the mining capabilities of this region, which, as it was without doubt enormously over-rated at first, I believe to be considerably under-rated at the present time.

THE SILVER MINES ON THE NORTH SHORE OF THUNDER BAY.

Silver was discovered on the north shore of Thunder Bay in 1867; and since that time large tracts of land have been surveyed and taken up by men of capital, and two companies are now quietly at work mining for the precious metal. The Thunder Bay Mining Company, composed of some of the heaviest capitalists of Montreal, have been working their vein for over a year. They have all the machinery necessary for mining on a large scale on the ground, and are now erecting their stamp mills. They have about one thousand tons of ore ready for crushing. It was hauled down last winter from their shaft which is two and three-quarters miles from the Bay, where they have built a fine dock, at which a vessel drawing from twelve to fifteen feet of water can land. The company seemed determined, however, to keep their business entirely secret, and all the informa-tion concerning their doings must be obtained (if obtained at all) from the miners or outside parties. I was told that they had barrelled and shipped about twenty-five tons of ore, which would yield 20 per cent of silver. I was shown a specimen of 200 pounds in weight, which would yield fully 50 per cent of pure silver; and I succeeded in obtaining a specimen of that kind myself, which I am satisfied will yield from 40 to 50 per cent of silver. Their gentlemanly superintendent, Mr. McDonald, did all in his power to make my stay pleasant and agreeable as possible; but positively refused to give me any information as to what they were doing; neither would he let me have any specimens of their rich ore, as he said it was positively forbidden by his company. Mr. Mc-Donald was manager of the silver mines in Nor-way for about twelve years, and was brought from there by the company about one year ago. He expressed himself highly pleased with the prospect of this vein.

The Shuniah Mining Company, composed of gentlemen from this side of the line, commenced to mine on their property in the summer of 1867, and had sunk a shaft sixty or seventy feet deep, from which they have taken some very fine ore. Their vein is from twenty to twenty-three feet in width; and native silver, I am told, has been found on the surface wherever the earth and moss have been removed from the back of the vein, which in most places is not more than two or three feet in depth. I made a small opening myself with an explorer's pick, and took out a small piece of ore, weighing only 3 ozs. from which I extracted 1 oz. 3 pwts, of pure silver, which I have since had made into a teaspoon.

It is a matter of surprise to me that men of capital in New York and elsewhere in the United States have not given more attention to this country instead of sending their money to the almost inaccessible regions of Nevada, Colorado, and Montana, especially since the heretofore short-sighted policy of the Canadian Government has been changed in regard to mining for the precious metals. By an act of the last Parliament of Canada, the imposition of all royalty, tax, or duty on gold and silver was repealed, and now the country is open free to all, on the payment of one dollar per acre (the Government price) for the land. It is my opinion that persons seeking investments of capital can find no more promising opening, and it only requires an inspection of the country to convince any reasoning man of the correctness of my assertions.

NEW BRUNSWICK GOLD DISCOVERIES.—A St. John paper says: the Eel River gold discoveries are likely to prove of no account. We were this morning shown a telegram from a most reliable gentleman in Woodstock who had visited the ground, and who is conversant with gold mining, sent to a friend in this city in reply to an inquiry. It was as follows:—"*Do not come up. Investigations unsatisfactory. Circumstances suspicious.*"

—At the annual meeting of the De Lery Gold Mining Company, Mr. Joseph, of Quebec, was elected president, Mr. Guacen, of New York, vice do, and Mr. Vezina, treasurer.

Financial.

TORONTO STOCK MARKET.

(Reported by Pellatt & Osler, Brokers.)

The stock market has been active during the week. Building Society stocks have especially been in large demand, and at advancing rates.

Bank Stock.—There were sales of Montreal at 159 and 160, the market closing with buyers at 159 and sellers at 159½. Small sales of British are reported at 104½, sellers now ask 104¾. Ontario has slighly declined, closing with no buyers over 95. Sales of Toronto was made during the week at 120½, sellers now hold for an advance. Large sales of Royal Canadian were made from 50 to 55, the latter price, however, was not maintained and at the close there were no buyers over 50. We have to report a steady advance in Commerce, sales have been made at 100½, 100¾, 101 and 101½, there is a good demand at the latter rate. Gore would command 39. Merchants' which sold before the meeting at 111 and 111½, suddenly declined to 103; but has since revived, with sales at 104, 104½ and 105, there are now buyers at 105½ and no sellers; the capital stock of the bank is to be increased from $4,000,000 to $6,000,000. Small sales of Quebec were made at 100½, at which rate there are still buyers. There were sales of Molson's at 109, and that price could still be paid. Some sales of City are reported at 98½, with buyers at this rate and sellers at 99. There is a demand for Du Peuple at 108 and 108½, and for Jacques Cartier at 107½. No transactions in Union, buyers would give 105. Nothing doing in Mechanics' or Nationale.

Debentures.—Canada sterling five per cents are asked for at 92, nothing doing in other issues. Toronto have been sold to pay 7 and 7½ per cent. and some short dated bonds were sold at 7¼ per cent interest. County are in fair demand at 99.

Sundries.—There were sales of British America Assurance at 53, ex-dividend. City Gas is in good demand at 107½, no stock has been offered for some time past. There were sales of Canada Permanent Building Society at 122, 122½ and 122¾, buyers freely offer the latter rate. Western Canada Building Society sold at 117½, 117¾ and 118, and is in demand at the latter rate, but very scarce. No Freehold has been offered during the week; 117½ would be paid. No transactions in Montreal Telegraph. Canada Landed Credit has been sold at 80 for stock carrying the July dividend. Mortgages are asked for to pay 8 per cent.

NEW YORK MONEY MARKET.—An excessive stringency has been the leading feature of the market for a week past; on this account borrowers were placed at the mercy of lenders, and rates ranging from ⅛ to ⅜ per cent. per day, additional to 7 per cent. per annum, have been exacted. At the close of last week, the feeling was somewhat easier. It is confidently stated, that the late stringency stands unequalled in the history of Wall street. The *Financial Chronicle* says of last week's business:—"Discount operations have been confined almost entirely to the accommodations of the commercial banks to their customers. On the street there has been no market for the best paper, at even 10 to 12 per cent. The banks have been unable to discount grain paper, with much consequent inconvenience to the west; and paper sent here in considerable amounts from Boston has been returned as unsaleable." A decline in gold from 137⅜ to 134 was in consequence of a large amount of gold being thrown on the market.

STATEMENT of the Revenue and Expenditure of the Dominion of Canada, for the month ended 30th June, 1869.

Revenue—Customs	$616,567 25
Excise	236,771 65
Post Office	222,11 75
Public Works, inluding Railways	88,124 36
Bill Stamp Duty	6,317 41
Miscellaneous	60,927 57
Total	$1,030,919 99
Expenditure	$598,437 50

BANK OF ENGLAND.—Statement for week ending Wednesday, June 23, 1869:—

ISSUE DEPARTMENT.

Notes issued	£33,412,150
Government debt	£11,015,100
Other Securities	3,984,900
Gold Coin and bullion	18,412,150
Silver bullion	
	£33,412,150

BANKING DEPARTMENT.

Proprietors' capital	£14,553,000
Rest	3,147,807
Public deposits (including Exchequer, Commissioners of National Debt, Savings Banks, and dividend Accounts)	7,498,189
Other Deposits	16,972,956
Seven day and other Bills	448,456
	£42,620,408
Government Securities (including Dead Weight Annuity)	£14,239,874
Other securities	16,465,014
Notes	10,731,710
Gold and Silver coin	1,183,810
	£42,620,408

INTERCOLONIAL RAILWAY LOAN.—Mr. Aytoun called attention to the application of the Government loan to the Canadian Intercolonial Railway, and moved a resolution, that in the opinion of the House such an application of public funds was contrary to the terms of the Dominion Act authorizing the road, and that no further guarantees should be given except in such form as will insure direct application to its construction. Messrs. Baring and Hunt opposed the resolution. Mr. Gladstone said that in his opinion no case had been presented which called for the interference of the House, and recommended the withdrawal of the resolution. The resolution was then withdrawn.

THE FALL IN MERCHANTS' BANK STOCK.—The *Montreal Herald* says:—Since the annual meeting of the "Merchants" the shares have been heavy at a decline of about 8. Numerous sales were made up till Monday at 111 to 111½, and to-day the transactions were at 103, 103¼ and 103½, buyers continuing to offer the latter rate. The sale of a large number of shares, while the books were closed, is likely to lead to trouble which may not be easily settled. Those who sold the stock in question refuse to transfer the new stock, and, in assuming this position, they are fortified by the action of the Directors, in determining that the list of shareholders entitled to the new stock, should be those registered in the books on the 15th ult. The point may be a very fine one, but it strikes us that, in equity, the purchasers should enjoy any advantage arising out of the purchase. This, we think, is only reasonable and just, because, had the condition of the bank been unsatisfactory and the stock below par, the sellers would naturally have declined the new shares, and properly too, since the stock virtually had passed out of their hand, with no reservation except the collection of the dividend. The following is one of the clauses in the resolutions passed at the annual meeting.

3. Each shareholder as shown by the Books of the Bank on the last day of the month of June, shall be entitled to subscribe at par an amount equal to one half of what he may have held at that date, or in other words to add fifty per cent to his stock.

The purchasers of stock prior to the last day of June would we infer according to the above be entitled to any advance or profit of whatever nature. We notice, however, that although at the general meeting of the shareholders this was assented to, the Directors have changed the date establishing the right of those who should rank and be entitled to subscribe for new stock. This may not alter the position of those who bought while the books were closed, but it would have been better, we think for all concerned if the change had not been made.

—A branch of the Bank of Montreal is to be established at Newcastle, N. B.

—Peterborough paper says, that D. S. Eastwood, of that place, has been promoted to the management of the Ottawa agency of the Ontario Bank.

—An investigation into the affairs of the Summerside, P. E. I., Bank has resulted in the shareholders voting confidence in the Directors and the institution.

Commercial.

Hon. John Rose has gone to Washington, bu the political papers seem to be much in doubt a to the precise object of his mission. It is supposed that the question of Reciprocity will com up in some shape during his visit there. We hav no faith in the success of any negociations for new treaty just now. The San Juan question and matters relating to the Hudson's Bay Territory are more likely to engage attention.

We are in receipt of detailed accounts of th condition of the growing crops throughout th States. In the West there are numerous complaints of "drowning out" by the late rain; corn has been materially injured from this cause. Fo the same reason, it is almost impossible to ge off the crop of grass in a condition to keep. Th report of the Agricultural Bureau says that th returns show a high average condition of wheat and indicate a good prospect of an abundant crop, if no casualties occur before harvest. The "lodging" or "laying" of the stalk is reported as somewhat serious in parts of the South and West. There is an increase of about 6 per cent. on th average under wheat. The department estimate the acreage in wheat in 1868 exceeded 18,000,000 acres; the returns of correspondents indicate an aggregate increase of more than 1,000,000 acres in California, Iowa, and Minnesota, and elsewhere. Full returns from the Pacific have not been received, but the following estimates of increase ar warranted by a careful analysis of returns:

	Acres.
Iowa	224,000
Indiana	130,000
Minnesota	145,000
Tennessee	130,000
Ohio	140,000
Missouri	96,000

considerable increase has also been made in nsylvania, Virginia, West Virginia, Michigan, other States. No increase can be shown either few York, Illinois, or Wisconsin, among the er States. A decrease is apparent in Louisiana, h Carolina, and Texas. In Illinois a small ease in winter wheat is balanced by a reduce of spring wheat acreage. Other grains are ne condition. The largest increase is in bar and in the States west of the Mississippi, icularly in California, while an enlargement of is reported in the Ohio valley, as well as elsewhere. Oats in the Ohio valley have ely been sown to the usual extent, but a ter area has been put in elsewhere in the West, Michigan, Wisconsin, Iowa, Missouri, and ssat The crop is not quite in average condi in some parts of New England, and in parts hio, Indiana, Illinois, and Minnesota, while e more Southern States the low temperature e spring months has effected a decided im ement in a crop that generally suffers in those udes by sudden and extreme elevation in tem ture at the season of heading.

Toronto Market.

ODUCE.—Our market has been irregular and ttled throughout the week past, prices fluctu g; mostly, according to the tenor of the ad respecting the growing crops. The week ed with a firm market for wheat and flour, h soon became strong, and a rapid advance wed, but during the last two or three days the ag has been quiet and the tendency, if any g downward; prices are about 5 cents higher wheat and 15 cents on flour. With us the her has been uncommonly hot, unless there change to dry, warm weather, the consequence t be rather serious. A fortnight or three s hence, will unfold a tale as to the future of s, the nature of which can now only be ied at. Wheat.—Receipts 5,340 bush. and 5 bush. last week. Stock in store on the inst., 42.740 bush. There was a fair demand sales as follows: 8 cars midge proof at $1.06 .; 2 cars of spring at $1.05 ; 14 cars at 98c. ucan; 400 bush. at $1.05. A cargo of fall on p.t., and 2 cars at $1. Oats.—Receipts light and demand good ; eastern oats sold at 524c. on the track, and western at 56 to 57c. ks very light. Peas.—No receipts, the mar s firm but nominal, holders asking 83 to 85c. ey.—No receipts or stocks, selling on the t at 60.

OUR.—Receipts 1,425 bbls. and 3,080 bbls. week; stock in store on the 12th, 4,700 bbls. st 4,799 on the 5th inst. The market ed at about $4.55 for No. 1 Superfine and need to be $4.75 and $4.80, holders asking as as $5. During the last two or three days the et has been weak and nominal and tending iward; at the close there were no buyers over 5 to $4.70 and little demand. In other grades ing doing.

OVISIONS.—Butter—has been more active, i being considerable disposition to buy on lation; there is no shipping movement yet. ss—is quiet with an easier feeling. Pork— of the market, there is some enquiry. Eggs. s scarce and under the influence of the local and, have advanced.

OOL.—The stringency of the United States ey market, acts as an efficient check on specu n and tends to keep prices down. The course e market since the opening has not been favor to profitable operating, as there has been a y movement downward since the receipts be of any consequence.

Freights.

FREIGHTS.—Rates by vessels to lake ports remain unchanged, at 3c. U. S. cy. on grain to Oswego and 2c gold to Kingston. Lumber to Oswego $1.50 per M.

The Grand Trunk rates to Liverpool are:—Flour 4s. stg. per bbl.; wheat 8s. 6d. stg., per quarter; and boxed meats 55s. per ton.

The following are the Grand Trunk Railway Company's summer rates from Toronto to the un dermentioned stations, which came into force on the 19th ult. :—Flour to all Stations from Belle velle to Lynn, inclusive 25c ; grain, per 100 lbs., 13c ; flour to Prescott, 30c ; grain 15c ; flour to all stations between Island Pond and Portland, in clusive, 75c ; grain, 38c; flour to Boston, 80c, gold ; grain 40c ; flour to Halifax, 90c ; flour to St. John, 85c.

Halifax Market.

BREADSTUFFS.—July 6th.—We have to report an inactive market for Flours, during the past week. Transactions have been based on immediate requirements—buyers expressing a want of con fidence in present prices, and are operating with great caution. Holders are not pressing the mar ket, knowing that large sales could not be effected at any reasonable reduction on quotations. About 1,500 bbls. (damaged), ex "Her Majesty," were offered at auction, and realized $4.25, upwards ; affecting the regular trade, to some extent. Fancy is in limited request, at quotations. No. 2 has been superseded, by damaged lots, and is without enquiry.

Imports from January 1st to July 6th, 1868, and 1869:

	Bbls. Flour.	Bbls. Cornmeal.
1869	78244	17945
1868	92470	3,814

PROVISIONS. — Pork and Beef continue un changed, at quotations. We note the shipment of 100 bbls. Mess pork, per S. S. "City of Wash ington," for Liverpool, last week, which is very expressive of the dullness of our market, with its present reduced stocks. Butter continues inac tive, with accumulating stocks.

WEST INDIA PRODUCE.—Molasses continues without quotable change. Holders express con fidence in present prices, on the ground that stocks are not in excess of requirements for Fall Trade. Sugars are giving way gradually; the disposition being to realize. At Auction last week, part of a lot 60 hhds. Porto Rico, realized 84c. ; being from 4 to 3c. less than market rates; but no specu lative feeling existed at the reduction. Rum is in request with fair stocks.

EXCHANGE.— Bank Drafts, London, at 60 days, 124 per cent. Montreal sight, 4 per cent. St. John, N. B., 3 per cent. prem.—R. C. Hamilton & Co.'s Circular.

Petroleum.

The following were the exports of Petroleum from the United States, from January 1st, to July 6th:—

	1869.	1868.
From New York..galls.	30,677,540	24,040,672
Boston	1,285,940	1,214,838
Philadelphia	12,234,081	15,608,639
Baltimore	751,103	1,047,546
Portland	....	177,771

Total Export from the		
United States	44,948,664	42,089 467
Same time 1877		29,509,108
Same time 1866		26,492,748

Profits of Manufacturing.

The Manufacturing Corporations of Boston do not show so profitable a business as during the previous six months, several companies passing their dividends, and others decreasing the per centage. Three companies, however, have in creased their dividends—the Androscoggin from 5 to 6 per cent., the Langdon from 8 to 10 and the Middlesex from 5 to 8. The other changes are as follows: The Appleton decreases from 10 to 8 per cent. ; the Atlantic from 4 to 3; the Chicopee from

25 to 15; the Contocook from 5 to 4; the Everett from 5 to 3; the Hill from 10 to 6; the Man chester Print Works which paid 5 per cent. in January, now passes; the Nashua decreases from 8 to 3; the Naumkeag from 10 to 5; the New market from $70 to $40; the Salisbury from 7½ to 5; the Salmon Falls from 5 to 4; and the Stark from 10 to 5. The Dwight Company has made $40,000 profit for the past six months, and $70,000 the preceding six months; but as they are making some improvements in their mills, the Directors concluded to pass the dividend at this time. The Hill Mill pays its dividend on $1,000,000, the capital being increased from $700,000. The Franklin also increased its capital on June 1st, from $600,000 to $1,000,000. The Naumkeag also pays on $1,500,000—$800,000 having been added since the 1st of January.

Vessels Built in Thirteen Years.

The Chicago Tribune publishes the following table, giving the total number of American and Canadian vessels built in each year on the lakes.

	Strs.		Props.		Tugs.		Sailing.	
	A.	C.	A.	C.	A.	C.	A.	C.
1856	4	3	24	1	9	1	137	24
1857	4	3	19	1	15	2	123	18
1858	3	1	2	..	5	..	32	5
1859	5	3	2	2	4	..	19	9
1860	1	4	3	1	9	...	15	6
1861	2	1	5	...	13	1	56	14
1862	1	..	12	...	27	...	64	7
1863	2	..	8	5	36	...	81	23
1864	7	7	9	5	29	6	39	18
1865	5	1	2	..	9	...	19	7
1866	5	..	10	1	21	2	59	15
1867	..	3	29	1	19	...	128	35
1868	..	2	12	2	33	1	52	19
	46	28	137	20	229	13	834	198

Receipts of Breadstuffs.

The receipts at the ports of Chicago, Milwaukee, Toledo, Detroit and Cleveland, from the 1st of January to the 3rd July, in the years indicated, were as follows:—

	1869.	1868.
Flour. brls	2,667,600	1,626,100
Wheat, bush	15,627,600	7,888,400
Corn	16,197,500	16,590,300
Oats	5,484,100	4,861,100
Barley	398,200	394,700
Rye	533,800	197,700
	37,241,200	29,902,200

Manchester Market.

A report by last mail says—

Prices are unchanged since Tuesday, but the tone of the market has been quieter, and pro ducers are rather more easy to deal with than they have been in the beginning of the week, although they adhere very firmly to the quotations. The upward movement, however, has been checked. On Mon day and Tuesday there was some excitement in the cotton market, which compelled spinners to put up their prices, and some were indifferent about giving quotations. When it was found that the merchants here would not support the upward movement, spinners gave over buying cotton in excess of their wants, and a quieter feel ing came over the cotton market. The general feeling, however, is that the position of cotton is inherently very strong, and that the market is liable to speculative movement any day. Conse quently producers are chary about selling a long way in advance, being apprehensive that a possi ble rise in the raw material might put them in even a worse plight than they are at present.

In the early part of the week there were rumors of failures, which gave some uneasiness, but they appear to have been only idle reports, and any effects which they have produced have passed away. The reduction of the Bank rate of interest is a favorable feature in maintaining the stability of prices, but it has had no perceptible influence here. Buyers resolutely set their faces against higher prices; and, unless better advices arrive from abroad to stimulate things here, it is probable they may desist from buying until producers hold more stocks than they do at present.

Beef Cattle from Toronto.

A St. John paper says,—Thirty three fine oxen have been brought from Toronto by Mr. P. Dean and M. Caulin of this City. Many of them were by far the finest ever seen in this market.

—The Montreal Telegraph Co. have extended their wires, and opened offices at Aylmer, Ont., Exeter, Ont., and Listowell, Ont., all of which offices are now in full operation and ready for business.

A telegram from Hong Kong, dated 26th May, gives the total exports from China and Japan up to that date as 140,000,000 lbs.

ROSSEAU AND MUSKOKA CANAL.—The Barrie *Advance* says, the work of constructing a lock to connect Lakes Rosseau and Muskoka is commenced at last. The impediment which existed to navigation will soon be overcome, and steamers and sailing craft can pass to and fro from one lake into the other without difficulty. The completion of this lock, will not only materially assist through navigation, but also greatly contribute to the general advancement and settlement of the country contiguous to Lakes Rosseau and Joseph, as well as the lands in the vicinity of the Nippissing line. The removal of this obstruction, which has hitherto caused considerable delay and inconvenience to freight *in transitu* to the different points northward, will confer a boon on the inhabitants around this chain of lakes, who kindly and properly appreciate the efforts of their representative in their behalf. Arthur Robinson, Esq., C. E., of Orillia, is appointed to take charge of the works. The canal will be about 200 feet in] length, solid rock composes the obstruction, this will have to be blasted and removed, which will occupy considerable time. However, the work will be prosecuted with vigor, and it is expected to be finished ere navigation closes.

—There is a family living near Brockville, of which seven brothers are of the following ages, respectively, 72, 71, 70, 66, 64, 63 and 58—total 464.

British America Assurance Company.

NOTICE IS HEREBY GIVEN that the Annual Court of proprietors of this Institution, at which the election of Directors for the ensuing year takes place, will be held in conformity with the Charter, at the House of Business of the Company, Church Street, city of Toronto, on MONDAY, the 2nd day of AUGUST, next.

The chair will be taken at twelve o'clock noon.

By order of the Board.

T. W. BIRCHALL,
Managing Director.

British America Assurance Office,
Toronto, 10th July, 1869.

Morton & Smith,

ACCOUNTANTS, REAL ESTATE AGENTS,

AND VALUATORS,

48 AND 50 CHURCH STREET,

TORONTO.

R. MORTON.　47-ly　J. LAMOND SMITH.

NOTICE.

Office of the Toronto, Grey and Bruce Railway Company.

A GENERAL Meeting of the Subscribers to the Capital Stock of the Toronto, Grey and Bruce Railway Company will be held at the office of the said Company, No. 46 Front Street, in the City of Toronto, on TUESDAY, the 10th day of August next, at TWELVE o'clock noon, for the purpose of electing Directors and organizing the said Company.

W. SUTHERLAND TAYLOR,
Secretary.
Toronto, July 7, 1869.

Insolvent Act of 1864.

PROVINCE OF ONTARIO. }
COUNTY OF YORK. }

In the County Court of the County of York.

In the matter of THOMAS D. LEDYARD, an Insolvent.

THE undersigned has filed a consent by his creditors to his discharge, and on Monday, the twentieth day of September next, he will apply to the Judge of the said Court for a confirmation thereof.

Dated at Toronto this fourteenth day of July, A.D. 1869.

48-101　　　　　　　　　T. D. LEDYARD.

Insolvent Act of 1864.

PROVINCE OF ONTARIO, }
COUNTY OF YORK. }

In the County Court of the County of York.

In the matter of HENRY S. LEDYARD, an Insolvent.

THE undersigned has filed a consent by his Creditors to his discharge, and on Monday, the Thirteenth day of September next, he will apply to the Judge of the said Court for a confirmation thereof.

Dated at Toronto, this Third day of July, A.D. 1869.

46-101.　　　　　　　　H. S. LEDYARD.

Montreal Telegraph Company.

NOTICE is hereby given, that a Dividend of FIVE per cent. for the half-year ending THIRTY-FIRST MAY, has been declared upon the Capital Stock of the Company, and the same will be payable at the offices of the Company, on and after FRIDAY, the NINTH JULY.

The Transfer Book will be closed from 1st to 9th JULY.

By order of the Board,

(Signed)

JAMES DAKERS,
Secretary

British America Assurance Company.

FIFTY-FIRST DIVIDEND.

NOTICE is hereby given, that a Dividend of Four per cent. on the capital stock paid up, has been this day declared for the half year ending 30th ult., and that the same will be payable on and after

SATURDAY, THE TENTH DAY OF JULY INSTANT.

The Stock and Transfer Books will accordingly be closed from this date to the Eighth instant, inclusive.

By order of the Board.

J. W. BIRCHALL,
Managing Director.

Brit. Amer. Assur. Office,
Toronto, 3rd July, 1869.　　　　46-31

Western Assurance Company.

NOTICE is hereby given, that a dividend for the half-year, ending the 30th ult., at the rate of EIGHT per cent. per annum, upon the capital paid-up stock of this Company, has been declared, and will be payable at the Company's office, on and after Friday, the 9th inst.

By order of the Board.

BERNARD HALDAN,
Secretary.

Western Assurance Co.'s Office,
Toronto, 1st July, 1869.

WESTERN CANADA

Permanent Building and Savings Society.

DIVIDEND NO. 12.

NOTICE is hereby given, that a Dividend of Five per cent. on the Capital Stock of this Institution has been declared for the half-year ending 29th inst., and that the same will be payable at the Office of the Society, No. 70 Church Street, on and after THURSDAY, the EIGHTH day of JULY next.

The Transfer Books will be closed from the 20th to the 30th June, inclusive.

By order of the Board.

WALTER S. LEE,
Secretary and Treasurer.
Toronto, June 15, 1869.

Bank of Toronto.

DIVIDEND No. 26.

NOTICE is hereby given that a Dividend of Four per cent. for the current half-year, being at the rate of Eight per cent. on the paid up capital of this Bank, has this day been declared, and that the same will be payable at the Bank on its branches on and after

FRIDAY, the 2ND DAY OF JULY NEXT.

The transfer books will be closed from the fifteenth to the thirtieth of June, both days inclusive.

The Annual Meeting of the Shareholders will be held at the Bank on Wednesday, the twenty-first day of July next.

The chair to be taken at noon.

By order of the Board.

G. HAGUE, *Cashier.*
Toronto, May 16th, 1869.　　　　41-td

Canada Permanent Building and Savings Society.

EIGHTEENTH HALF-YEARLY DIVIDEND.

NOTICE is hereby given that a Dividend of Five per cent. on the Capital Stock of this Institution has been declared for the half-year ending 30th instant, and the same will be payable at the Office of the Society on and after THURSDAY, the EIGHTH day of July next.

The Transfer Books will be closed from the 20th to the 30th June, inclusive.

By order of the Board.

J. HERBERT MASON,
Secretary and Treasurer.
Toronto, June 10th, 1869.　　　　44-td

Niagara District Bank.

DIVIDEND No. 31.

NOTICE is hereby given, that a DIVIDEND OF FOUR PER CENT. on the paid up capital stock of this Institution, has this day been declared for the current half-year; and that the same will be payable at the Bank on and after THURSDAY, the first day of July next.

The Transfer Books will be closed from the 20th to the 30th of June. both days inclusive.

By order of the Board.

C. M. ARNOLD, Cashier.

Office of the Toronto and Nipissing Railway Company.

A GENERAL MEETING of the subscribers to the Capital Stock of the Toronto and Nipissing Railway Company, will be held at the office of the said Company, No. 46 Front street in the said City of Toronto, on TUESDAY, the 20th day of JULY next, at twelve o'clock noon, for the purpose of electing Directors and organizing the said Company.

By order.　　　　CHAS. ROBERTSON,
Secretary.
Toronto, June 16.

The European Mail for North America,

WITH WHICH IS INCORPORATED

"WILMER & SMITH'S EUROPEAN TIMES.

(Established in 1843.)

A Full and Complete Summary of

HOME AND FOREIGN NEWS.

Published Weekly for despatch by the Mail Steamer.

THE EUROPEAN MAIL.

FOR North America, with which is incorporated ' Wilmer & Smith's European Times,' is published in the interest of the mercantile and general community.

In each issue is to be found all the reliable information commercial and general, that can in any way prove of value to our subscribers. The greatest possible care has been, and will continue to be, taken by the Proprietors to obtain, regardless of expense, a faithful record of all market transactions in which our friends are more particularly concerned, up to within three hours of the closing of the Mail.

We furnish our readers with quotations of articles staple not generally noted in ordinary lists, of which the following is an example :—

Articles.	Prices per ton.	Cash discount.
CANADA PLATES		
Staffordshire (in L'pool) f.o.b.	£18 18 5	2½ per ct.
Glamorgan　"	19 15 0	"
GALVANIZED IRON--		
Corrugated Shts., 20 gauge fob.	17 0 0	"

The latest shipping intelligence, comprising arrivals, departures, sailings, and loadings, alphabetically arranged, is laid before our subscribers; and the tabular form adopted in the current number will be adhered to throughout—every casualty being regularly noted, and the state of the freight market duly advised.

Agricultural, Legal, and Medical news, of interest is given in detail.

We publish a list of Military and Naval Stations, and all changes are promptly noted.

The proprietors of the EUROPEAN MAIL urge the great advantages of this Journal, and trust for the friendly co-operation of all who think it of importance that the Old and New World should be more closely associated by those reciprocal ties resulting from a mutual furtherance of their material interests.

The subscription is 52s. or $13 (gold) per annum, payable in advance.

Sole Agent for Toronto,

A. S. IRVING.

Mercantile.

TORONTO PRICES CURRENT.—JULY 15, 1869.

Name of Article.	Wholesale Rates.		Name of Article.	Wholesale Rate.		Name of Article.	Wholesale Rates.
Boots and Shoes.	$ c.	$ c.	**Groceries**—*Contin'd*	$ c.	$ c.	**Leather**—*Contin'd.*	$ c. $ c.
Mens' Thick Boots ...	2 05	2 50	Gunpowd'r c. to med..	0 55	0 70	Kip Skins, Patna	0 80 0 85
" Kip............	2 25	3 00	" med. to fine.	0 70	0 85	French	0 70 0 90
" Calf	2 20	2 70	" fine to fin'st..	0 85	0 95	English	0 65 0 80
" Congress Gaiters..	1 65	2 50	Hyson	0 45	0 80	Hemlock Calf (30 to	
" Kip Coburgs....	1 20	1 40	Imperial	0 42	0 80	35 lbs.) per doz....	0 50 0 60
Boys' Thick Boots....	1 70	1 80	*Tobacco, Manufac'd:*			Do. light	0 45 0 50
Youths' "	1 40	1 50	Can Leaf, ℔ 5s & 10s..	0 26	0 30	French Calf........	1 05 1 05
Women's Batts	0 95	1 80	Western Leaf, com....	0 25	0 26	Grain & Satin Cl'f ℔ doz.	0 00 0 55
" Balmoral	1 30	1 50	" Good	0 27	0 32	Splits, large ℔ ℔.......	0 50 0 58
" Congress Gaiters	0 90	1 50	" Fine	0 32	0 35	" small	0 23 0 28
Misses' Batts	0 75	1 00	" Bright fine..	0 40	0 50	Enamelled Cow ℔ foot..	0 20 0 21
" Balmoral	1 00	1 20	" choice..	0 60	0 75	Patent	0 20 0 21
" Congress Gaiters..	1 00	1 30	**Hardware.**			Pebble Grain	0 15 0 17
Girls' Batts	0 65	0 85	*Tins (net cash prices)*			Buff	0 14 0 16
" Balmoral	0 00	1 05	Block, ℔ ℔.......	0 35	0 00	**Oils.**	
" Congress Gaiters..	0 75	1 10	Grasp............	0 30	0 00	Cod	0 65 0 70
Children's C. T. Cacks..	0 50	0 65	*Copper:*—			Lard, extra	0 00 0 00
" Gaiters	0 00	0 00	Pig...............	0 23	0 24	" No. 1	0 00 0 00
Drugs.			Sheet.............	0 30	0 33	" Woollen	0 00 0 00
Aloes Cape.........	0 12½	0 16	*Out Nails:*			Lubricating, patent'..	0 00 0 00
Alum	0 02½	0 03	Assorted ℔ Shingles,			" Mott's economic	0 30 0 00
Borax	0 00	0 00	℔ 100 lb.......	2 95	3 00	Linseed, raw	0 75 0 83
Camphor, refined....	0 65	0 70	Shingle alone do	3 15	3 25	" boiled......	0 81 0 87
Castor Oil..........	0 16½	0 28	Lathe and 4 dy.....	3 30	3 40	Machinery.........	0 00 0 00
Caustic Soda........	0 04½	0 05	*Galvanized Iron:*			Olive, common, ℔ gal..	1 00 1 60
Cochineal...........	0 90	1 00	Assorted sizes.......	0 08	0 09	" salad	1 95 2 30
Cream Tartar	0 30	0 35	Best No. 24.........	0 07½	0 00	" salad, in bots:	
Epsom Salts	0 02	0 04	" 26.........	0 08	0 08½	qt. ℔ case..	3 50 3 75
Extract Logwood....	0 11	0 12	" 28.........	0 09	0 00½	Sesame salad, ℔ gal..	1 50 1 75
Gum Arabic, sorts....	0 30	0 35	*Horse Nails:*			Seal, pale.........	0 75 0 85
Indigo, Madras......	0 90	1 00	Griset's or Griffin's			Spirits Turpentine....	0 62½ 0 60
Liocrice............	0 14	0 15	assorted sizes......	0 18	0 19	Varnish	0 00 0 00
Madder	0 00	0 16	For W. nas'd sizes...	0 18	0 19	Whale.	0 00 0 90
Galls	0 33	0 37	Patent Hammer'd do..	0 17	0 18	**Paints, &c.**	
Opium.............	12 00	13 50	*Iron (at 4 months):*			White Lead, genuine	
Oxalic Acid........	0 26	0 35	Pig—Gartsherrie No1..	24 00	25 00	in Oil, ℔ 25 lbs.....	0 00 2 35
Potash, Bi-tart......	0 25	0 28	Other brands.	22 00	24 00	Do. No. 1	0 00 2 00
" Bichromate...	0 15	0 20	" No 2...	0 00	0 00	" 2 "	0 00 1 65
Potass Iodide	3 90	4 60	Bar—Scotch, ℔100 lb..	2 25	2 60	" 3 "	0 00 1 65
Senna	0 12½	0 60	Refined	3 00	3 25	White Zinc, genuine..	3 00 3 50
Soda Ash	0 03½	0 04	Swedes	5 00	5 50	White Lead, dry......	0 05½ 0 09
Soda Bicarb	0 00	4 00	Hoops—Coopers	3 00	3 25	Red Lead..........	0 07½ 0 08
Tartaric Acid........	0 40	0 45	Band	3 00	3 25	Venetian Red, Eng'h..	0 02½ 0 03½
Verdigris	0 35	0 40	Boiler Plates.......	3 25	3 50	Yellow Ochre, Fren'h..	0 02½ 0 03
Vitriol, Blue........	0 08	0 10	Canada Plates......	3 75	4 00	Whiting...........	0 85 1 25
Groceries.			Union Jack	0 00	0 00	**Petroleum.**	
Coffees:			"	3 35	4 00	(Refined ℔ gal.)	
Java, ℔ lb...........	0 22 @0 23		Swansea	3 90	4 00	Water white, car'l'd..	0 20 0 21
Laguayra, ...	0 17	0 18	*Lead (at 4 months):*			" small lots...	0 22 0 23
Rio	0 15	0 17	Bar, ℔ 100 lbs......	0 06½	0 07	Straw, ℔ car load...	0 00 0 00
Fish:			Sheet	0 08	0 09	" small lots....	0 00 0 00
Herrings, Lab. split..	6 00	0 00	Shot.............	0 07½	0 07½	Amber, by car load..	0 00 0 00
" round....	0 00	0 00	*Iron Wire (net cash):*			" small lots ...	0 00 0 00
" scaled.....	0 33	0 33	No. 6, ℔ bundle.....	2 70	2 50	**Produce.**	
Mackerel, small kits..	1 00	0 00	" 9, "	3 10	3 20	*Grain:*	
Loch. Her. wh'e fírks..	2 50	2 75	" 12, "	3 40	3 50	Wheat, Spring, 60 ℔..	1 00 1 05
half "	1 25	1 50	" 16, "	4 30	4 40	" Fall " ..	1 05 0 00
White Fish & Trout..	4 50	5 00	*Powder:*			Barley........ 48 "	0 00 0 00
Salmon, saltwater	14 00	15 00	Blasting, Canada....	3 50	0 00	Peas........... 60 "	0 00 0 00
Dry Cod, ℔112 lbs....	4 50	5 00	FF	4 25	4 50	Oats.......... 34 "	0 58 0 00
Fruit:			FFF	4 75	5 00	Rye .... 56 "	0 56 0 00
Raisins, Layers	1 00	2 00	Blasting, English ...	4 00	5 00	*Seeds:*	
" M. R......	1 90	1 50	FF loose.	5 00	6 00	Clover's, choice 60 "	0 00 0 00
" Valentias new ..	0 6	0 6½	FFF "	6 00	0 00	" com'n 68 " ..	0 00 0 00
Currants, new.......	0 4½	0 0½	*Pressed Spikes (4 mos):.*			Timothy, cho'e. 4 "	0 00 0 00
old....	0 0½	0 04	Regular sizes 100	4 00	4 25	" inf. to good 48 "	0 00 0 00
Figs	0 11	0 12	Extra	4 50	5 00	Flax........... 56 " ..	0 00 0 00
Molasses:			*Tin Plates (net cash):*			*Flour (per brl.).*	
Clayed, ℔ gal.	0 00	0 35	IC Coke	7 50	8 50	Superior extra......	0 00 0 00
Syrups, Standard ...	0 55	0 76	IC Charcoal........	8 50	9 00	Extra superfine.....	4 75 0 00
" Golden ..	0 59	0 60	IX	10 50	11 00	Fancy superfine.....	0 00 0 00
Rice:			IXX "	13 50	14 00	Superfine No 1	4 65 4 75
Arracan	60	4 00	DC "	8 50	8 50	" No 2..	
"			DX "	9 50	0 00	Oatmeal, (per brl.)..	5 50 6 00
Spices:			**Hides & Skins, ℔ ℔.**			**Provisions.**	
Cassia, whole, ℔ ℔...	0 00	0 45	Green rough	0 00	0 05	Butter, dairy tub ℔ ℔..	0 13½ 0 14½
Cloves	0 11	0 12	Green, salt'd & insp'd..	0 00	0 05½	" store packed	0 13½ 0 13 "
Nutmegs	0 50	0 55	Cured	0 00	0 10	Cheese, new	0 11½ 0 12½
Ginger, ground	0 18	0 23	Calfskins, green ...	0 00	0 13½	Pork, mess, per bri...	27 00 27 50 "
" Jamaica, root..	0 20	0 25	Calfskins, cured....	0 18	0 19½	" prime mess..	
Pepper, black.......	0 10½	0 11	" dry......	0 18	0 20	" prime	
Pimento	0 08	0 09	Sheepskins, ...	1 90	1 60	Bacon, rough	0 12 0 12½
Sugars:			" pelts.......	0 00	0 20	" Cumberl'd cut..	0 12 0 0½ "
Port Rico, ℔ lb.......	0 9½	0 10	**Hops.**			" smoked......	0 00 0 00
Cuba.............	0 9	0 9½	Inferior, ℔ lb........	0 00	0 00	Hams, in salt.......	0 00 0 00
Barbadoes (bright)..	0 9½	0 9½	Medium	0 00	0 00	" smoked.....	0 00 0 00
Canada Sugar Refine'y,			Good	0 00	0 00	Shoulders, in salt	0 00 0 00
Yellow, No. 2, 66 ds..	0 9	0 9½	Fancy	0 00	0 00	Lard, in kegs........	0 14½ 0 15
Yellow, No. 2½......	0 9½	0 9½	**Leather, ℔ lb.** (4 mos.)			Eggs, packed	0 13 0 14
No. 3........	0 10	0 10½	In lots of less than			Beef Hams	0 08 0 00
Ground...........	0 11	0 11½	50 sides, 10 ℔ cnt			Tallow	0 08 0 08
Dry Crushed	0 12	0 12½	higher.			Hogs dressed, heavy,.	0 00 0 00
Extra Ground......	0 13	0 13½	Spanish Sole, 1st qual'y			" medium...	0 00 0 00
Teas:			heavy, weights ℔ ℔..	0 21	0 22	" light........	0 00 0 00
Japan com'n to good..	0 48	0 50	Do. 1st qual middle do.	0 22	0 23	**Suft, &c.**	
" Fine to choicest..	0 55	0 69	Do. light weights....	0 20	0 00	American brls.......	1 55 1 87
Colored, com. to fine..	0 60	0 70	Slaughter heavy ...	0 00	0 24	Liverpool coarse.....	0 00 0 00
Congou & Souch'ng..	0 42	0 75	Do. light........	0 00	0 00	Ground	0 00 1 45
Oolong, good to fine..	0 50	0 65	Harness, best	0 15	0 27	Plaster............	1 00 0 00
Y. Hyson, com to gd..	0 70	0 55	" No. 2	0 00	0 00	Water Lime	1 50 0 00
Medium to choice ...	0 65	0 80	Upper heavy	0 30	0 32		
Extra choice	0 85	0 95	" light.......	0 33	0 34		

	$ c.	$ c.
Soap & Candles.		
D. Crawford & Co.'s ..	$ c.	$ c.
Imperial.........	0 07½	0 08
" Golden Bar	0 07	0 07½
" Silver Bar........	0 07	0 07½
Crown	0 05	0 05½
No. 1	0 03½	0 03½
Candles	0 00	0 11
Wines, Liquors, &c.		
Ale:		
English, per doz. qrts.	2 60	2 65
Guinness Dub Portr..	2 35	2 40
Spirits:		
Pure Jamaica Rum...	1 80	2 25
De Kuyper's H. Gin..	1 55	1 65
Booth's Old Tom.....	1 90	2 00
Gin:		
Green, cases.........	4 00	4 25
Booth's Old Tom, c...	6 00	6 25
Wines:		
Port, common	1 00	1 25
" fine old	2 00	4 00
Sherry, common	1 00	1 50
" medium........	1 70	1 80
" old pale or golden..	2 50	4 00

	$ c.	$ c.
Brandy:		
Hennessy's, per gal..	2 30	2 50
Martell's " ..	2 30	2 50
J. Robin & Co.'s " ..	2 25	2 35
Otard, Dupuy & Cos..	2 25	2 35
Brandy, cases........	8 50	9 00
Brandy, com. per c...	4 00	4 50
Whiskey:		
Common 36 u. p.......	0 58	0 60
Old Rye	0 77½	0 80
Malt	0 77½	0 80
Toddy	0 77½	0 80
Scotch, per gal........	1 90	2 10
Irish—Kinnahan's c...	7 00	7 50
" Dunnville's Belf't..	6 00	6 25
Wool.		
Fleece, lb.............	0 30	0 31
Pulled "............	0 00	0 00
Furs.		
Bear..................	0 00	0 00
Beaver, ⅌ lb..........	0 00	0 00
Coon	0 00	0 00
Fisher................	0 00	0 00
Martin................	0 00	0 00
Mink..................	0 00	0 00
Otter.................	0 00	0 00
Spring Rats...........	0 00	0 00
Fox...................	0 00	0 00

INSURANCE COMPANIES.

ENGLISH.—*Quotations on the London Market.*

No. of Shares.	Last Dividend.	Name of Company.	Shares parval £	Amount paid.	Last Sale.
20,000		Briton Medical and General Life ...	10	....	2½
50,000	7½	Commer'l Union, Fire, Life and Mar.	50	5	5¼
24,000	8	City of Glasgow	25	2½	4¼
5,000	9½	Edinburgh Life	100	15	33½
400,000	5—½ yr	European Life and Guarantee......	2½	11s6	4s. 0d
100,000	10	Etna Fire and Marine.............	10	1½	—
20,000	5	Guardian	100	50	53½
24,000	12	Imperial Fire....................	500	50	352
7,500	9½	Imperial Life	100	10	17½
100,000	10	Lancashire Fire and Life.........	20	2	2⅛
10,000	11	Life Association of Scotland......	40	7½	25
35,862	45s. p. sh	London Assurance Corporation ..	25	12½	48¾
10,000	5	London and Lancashire Life	10	1	—
87,504	40	Liverp'l & London & Globe F. & L.	20	2	7½
20,000	5	National Union Life	5	1	1
20,000	12½	Northern Fire and Life	100	5	13
40,000	12 '68, bo 5s.	North British and Mercantile	50	6¼	19½
40,000	50	Ocean Marine	25	5	17¾
2,500	£5 12s.	Provident Life...................	100	10	35
....	£4½ p. s.	Phœnix..........................	....	....	130½ x d
200,000	2½—h.yr.	Queen Fire and Life	10	1	21s.
100,000	3s. bo.4s	Royal Insurance..................	20	3	6¼
20,000	10	Scottish Provincial Fire and Life ..	50	2½	5½
10,000	25	Standard Life	50	12	66 x d
4,000	5	Star Life	25	1¼	—
		CANADIAN.			⅌ c.
8,000	4	British America Fire and Marine ..	$50	$25	53 54 x d
....	4	Canada Life	...	....	.....
4000	12	Montreal Assurance	£50	£5	135
10,000	3	Provincial Fire and Marine........	60	11	.....
....	....	Quebec Fire	40	32½	£22½ 23
....	7	" Marine......................	100	40	85 90
10,000	4 6 mo's.	Western Assurance................	40	9	.....

RAILWAYS.	Sha's	Paid	Montr	London
Atlantic and St. Lawrence........................	£100	All.	....	56
Buffalo and Lake Huron	20½	"	....	2⅜ 3½
Do. do Preference	10	"	....	5 6
Buff., Brantf. & Goderich, 6⅌c.,1872-3-4....	100	"	....	66 69
Champlain and St. Lawrence	....	....	10 11	....
Do. do Pref. 10 ⅌ ct............	....	....	80 85	....
Grand Trunk	100	"	14 15	13½
Do. Eq.G. M. Bds. 1 ch. 6⅌c............	100	"	....	80
Do. First Preference, 5 ⅌ c.............	100	"	....	44½
Do. Deferred, 3 ⅌ ct....................	100	"	....	....
Do. Second Pref. Bonds, 5⅌c..............	100	"	....	37
Do. do Deferred, 3 ⅌ ct.............	100	"	....	....
Do. Third Pref. Stock, 4⅌ct............	100	"	....	28½
Do. do. Deferred, 3 ⅌ ct............	100	"	....	....
Do. Fourth Pref. Stock, 3⅌c............	100	"	....	15½
Do. do. Deferred, 3 ⅌ ct..............	100	"	....	....
Great Western	20½	"	14½ 15	13½
Do. New	20½	18	....	....
Do. 6 ⅌ c. Bds, due 1873-76.............	100	All.	....	99
5½⅌c Bds. due 1877-78...............	100	"	....	92½
Marine Railway, Halifax, $250, all..............	$250	"	....	....
Northern of Canada, 6 ⅌c. 1st Pref. Bds..........	100	"	....	82 83

EXCHANGE.	Halifax.	Montr'l.	Quebec.	Toronto.
Bank on London, 60 days.......				
Sight or 75 days date	12½ 13	9⅝ 9¾	9¼ 9¾	10½
Private do.	11½ 12	8 9	8¾ 9¼	9¼
Private, with documents........	....	8 8½	....	....
Bank on New York...............	....	26 26½	26 26½	27
Private do.	....	26½ 27	26½ 27	....
Gold Drafts do.	....	⅛ dis.	par ⅛ dis.	par ¼ dis.
Silver	....	4 4½	....	4 to 5

STOCK AND BOND REPORT.

The dates of our quotations are as follows:—Toronto, July 13; Montreal, July 12; Quebec, July 10; London, June 5.

NAME.	Shares.	Paid up.	Divid'd last 6 Months	Dividend Day.	CLOSING PRICES. Toronto.	Montre'l	Quebec
BANKS.			⅌ ct.				
British North America	$250	All.	3½ b½pc	July and Jan.	104 104½	103¾ 104¾	104 10
Jacques Cartier..............	50	"	4	1 June, 1 Dec.	107 107½	107 107½	107 10
Montreal	200	"	6	"	158½ 159½	159½ 160½	159½
Nationale....................	50	"	4	1 Nov. 1 May.	107 108	107 107½	107½
New Brunswick	100	"	......	......	....	....	....
Nova Scotia	200	—	7&b$3½	Mar. and Sept.	....	....	....
Du Peuple....................	50	"	4	1 Mar., 1 Sept.	108½ 109	108½ 109	108 10
Toronto	100	"	4	1 Jan., 1 July.	120 120½	120 122½	120 1
Bank of Yarmouth.............	....	....	......	......	....	....	....
Canadian Bank of Com'e.......	50	All.	......	......	101½ 101¾	101 102	100 10
City Bank Montreal	80	"	4	1 June, 1 Dec.	98½ 99	98½ 99½	98
Commer'l Bank (St. John)....	100	"	⅌ ct.	......	....	..	....
Eastern Townships' Bank.....	50	"	4	1 July, 1 Jan..	....	98 99	98
Gore	40	....	none.	1 Jan., 1 July.	30 40	30 40	38 4
Halifax Banking Company.....	....	....	......	......	....	....	....
Mechanics' Bank..............	50	All.	4	1 Nov., 1 May.	92½ 95	92 94	92
Merchants'Bank of Canada....	100	"	5	1 Jan., 1 July.	105½ 106	105 105½	103½ 10
Merchants' Bank (Halifax)....	....	....	.....	......	....	....	....
Molson's Bank................	50	All.	4	1 Apr., 1 Oct.	100 100½	100 110	100 1
Niagara District Bank........	100	70	3½	1 Jan., 1 July.	....	....	....
Ontario Bank.................	40	All.	4	1 June, 1 Dec.	95 95½	94½ 95	94
People's Bank (Fred'kton)....	100	"	......	......	....	...	....
People's Bank (Halifax)	20	"	7 12 m	......	....	....	....
Quebec Bank	100	"	3½	1 June, 1 Dec.	100 100½	100 101	100½ 10
Royal Canadian Bank	50	60	4	1 Jan., 1 July.	40 50	45 50	50 55
St. Stephens Bank	100	All.	.....	......	....	....	....
Union Bank	100	"	4	1 Jan., 1 July.	104 105	104½ 105	105 10
Union Bank (Halifax).........	100	....	7 12 mo	Feb. and Aug.	....	....	..
MISCELLANEOUS.							
British America Land.........	250	44	......	......	....	....	....
British Colonial S. S. Co.....	250	32½	......	......	...	....	...
Canada Company	32½	All.	......	......	....	....	....
Canada Landed Credit Co......	50	$50	3½	......	77 78	....	....
Canada Per. B'ldg Society....	50	All.	5	......	122½ 122¾	....	....
Canada Mining Company........	4	90	......	......	....	....	....
Do. Inl'd Steam Nav. Co.....	100	All.	15 12 m	......	....	99½ 100½	99 1
Do. Glass Company...........	100	"	None.	......	....	40 60	....
Canad'n Loan & Investm't....	25	2½	......	......	....	....	....
Canada Agency	10	¼	......	......	....	....	....
Colonial Securities Co........	....	....	......	......	....	....	....
Freehold Building Society....	100	All.	5	......	117 117½	....	....
Halifax Steamboat Co.........	100	"	......	......	....	....	....
Halifax Gas Company.........	....	....	......	......	....	...	....
Hamilton Gas Company........	....	....	.....	......	....	....	....
Huron Copper Bay Co.........	4	12	20	......	....	30 40	....
Lake Huron S. and C..........	5	102	......	......	....	....	....
Montreal Mining Consols......	20	$15	......	......	....	3.90 3.15	...
Do. Telegraph Co..........	40	All.	5	......	132 x d	131½ 135	131 13
Do. Elevating Co..........	00	"	5½	......	....	105 107	....
Do. City Gas Co...........	40	"	4	15 Mar. 15 Sep.	....	137 140	136 13
Do. City Pass. R,. Co.....	50	"	2	......	....	110½ 111½	110 11
Quebec and L. S.	8	$4	......	......	....	...	....
Quebec Gas Co................	200	All.	4	1 Mar., 1 Sep.	....	...	120 12
Quebec Street R. R...........	50	25	3	......	....	....	Bks cl
Richelieu Navigation Co......	100	All.	7-12m	1 Jan., 1 July.	....	120 123	120 12
St. Lawrence Glass Company.	100	"	....	......	....	80 85	....
St. Lawrence Tow Boat Co.....	100	"	......	3 Feb.	....	...	30 3
Tor'to Consumers' Gas Co.....	50	"	⅝ m	1 My Au MarFe	107 107½	...	107 10
Trust & Loan Co. of U. C.....	20	5	3	......	....	....	.. .
West'n Canada Bldg Soc'y....	50	All.	5	......	117½ 118	....	....

SECURITIES.	London.	Montreal.	Quebec.	Toronto
Canadian Gov't Deb. 6 ⅌ ct. stg..................	....	103 104	102 103	104½ 10
Do. do. 6 do due Ja. & Jul. 1877-84........	104½ 105½	....	....	....
Do. do. 6 do. Feb. & Aug........	102 104	....	....	....
Do. do. 6 do. Mch. & Sep........	102 104	....	...	....
Do. do. 5 ⅌ ct. cur., 1883	93¾ 94½	92½ 95	91 92	92 93
Do. do. 5 do. stg., 1885	93½ 94	91½ 92½	90 90½	91 92½
Do. do. 7 do. cur.,........................	....	....	......	....
Dominion 6 p. c. 1878 cy.........................	....	106½ 107½	107 107½	106½ 10
Hamilton Corporation.............................	....	....	......	....
Montreal Harbor, 8 ⅌ ct. d. 1869..................	..	....	......	....
Do. do. 7 do. 1870..................	....	....	......	....
Do. do. 6½ do. 1883..................	....	102½ 107½	......	102 10
Do do. 6½ do. 1873..................	....	....	......	....
Do. Corporation, 6 ⅌ c. 1891	....	96 96½	96½ 97	96 96
Do. 7 p. c. stock..............................	....	108½ 110	108½ 109½	109 11
Do. Water Works, 6 ⅌ c. stg. 1878..............	....	96½ 97½	......	96 96
Do. do. 6 do. cy. do.	....	....	......	96 97
New Brunswick, 6 ⅌ ct., Jan. and July	104 104½	....	......	....
Nova Scotia, 6 ⅌ ct., 1875........................	103 104	...	......	....
Ottawa City 6 ⅌ c. d. 1880........................	....	95 97	......	...
Quebec Harbour, 6 ⅌ c. d. 1883....................	....	....	60	....
Do. do. 7 do. do.....................	....	....	65 70	....
Do. do 8 do. 1886..................	...	....	80 85	....
Do. City, 7 ⅌ c. d. 1½ years.....................	....	....	98 98½	....
Do. do. 7 do. 8 do.	....	....	91 92	....
Do. do. 7 do. 5 do.	....	....	96 96½	....
Do. Water Works, 7 ⅌ ct., 3 years	....	....	97 97½	....
Do. do. 6 do. 1½ do.	....	....	94 95	....
Toronto Corporation	....	92 94	...	....

Insurance.

Br ton Medical and General Life Association,

with which is united the

BRITANNIA LIFE ASSURANCE COMPANY.

Capital and Invested Funds............£750,000 Sterling.

ANNUAL INCOME, £220,000 STG. :

Yearly increasing at the rate of £25,000 Sterling.

THE important and peculiar feature originally Introduced by this Company, in applying the periodical Bonuses, so as to make Policies payable during life, without any higher rate of premiums being charged, has caused the success of the BRITON MEDICAL AND GENERAL to be almost unparalleled in the history of Life Assurance. *Life Policies on the Profit Scale become payable during the lifetime of the Assured, thus rendering a Policy of Assurance a means of subsistence in old age, as well as a protection for a family,* and a more valuable security to creditors in the event of early death ; and effectually meeting the often urged objection, that persons do not themselves reap the benefit of their own prudence and forethought.

No extra charge made to members of Volunteer Corps for services within the British Provinces.

☞ TORONTO AGENCY, 5 KING ST. WEST.

Oct 17—9-1yr   JAMES FRASER, Agent.

BEAVER

Mutual Insurance Association.

HEAD OFFICE—29 TORONTO STREET, TORONTO.

INSURES LIVE STOCK against death from any cause. The only Canadian Company having authority to do this class of business.

E. C. CHADWICK, President.

W. T. O'REILLY, Secretary.   8-1y-25

HOME DISTRICT
Mutual Fire Insurance Company.

Office—North-West Cor. Yonge & Adelaide Streets, TORONTO.—(UP STAIRS.)

INSURES Dwelling Houses, Stores, Warehouses, Merchandise, Furniture, &c.

PRESIDENT—The Hon. J. McMURRICH.
VICE-PRESIDENT—JOHN BURNS, Esq.
JOHN RAINS, Secretary.

AGENTS:

DAVID WRIGHT, Esq., Hamilton ; FRANCIS STEVENS, Esq., Barrie : Messrs. GIBBS & BRO., Oshawa.   8—1y

THE PRINCE EDWARD COUNTY
Mutual Fire Insurance Company.

HEAD OFFICE,—PICTON, ONTARIO.

President, L. B. STINSON ; *Vice-President,* WM. DELONG. *Directors :* W. A. Richards, James Johnson, James Cavan, D. W. Ruttan, H. A. McFaul.—*Secretary,* John Twigg ; *Treasurer,* David Barker; *Solicitor,* R. J. Fitzgerald.

THIS Company is established upon strictly Mutual principles, insuring farming and isolated property, (not hazardous,) in *Townships only,* and offers great advantages to insurers, at low rates for *five years,* without the expense of a renewal.

Picton, June 15, 1869.   9-1y

Fire and Marine Assurance.

THE BRITISH AMERICA

ASSURANCE COMPANY.

HEAD OFFICE :

CORNER OF CHURCH AND COURT STREETS.
TORONTO.

BOARD OF DIRECTION :

Hon. G. W. Allan, M L C.,	A. Joseph, Esq.,
George J. Boyd, Esq ,	Peter Paterson, Esq.,
Hon. W. Cayley,	G. P. Ridout, Esq.,
Richard S. Cassels, Esq.,	E H. Rutherford, Esq ,

Thomas C. Street, Esq.

Governor:

GEORGE PERCIVAL RIDOUT, Esq.

Deputy Governor : -

PETER PATERSON, Esq.

Fire Inspector: Marine Inspector:
E. ROBY O'BRIEN.   CAPT. R. COURNEEN.

Insurances granted on all descriptions of property against loss and damage by fire and the perils of inland navigation.

Agencies established in the principal cities, towns, and ports of shipment throughout the Province.

THOS. WM. BIRCHALL,

23-1y   *Managing Director.*

Insurance.

Reliance Mutual Life Assurance Society

OF LONDON, ENGLAND. Established 1840.

Head Office for the Dominion of Canada :

131 ST. JAMES STREET, MONTREAL.

DIRECTORS—Walter Shanly, Esq., M.P.; Duncan Macdonald, Esq.; George Winks, Esq., W. H. Hingston, Esq., M.D., L.R.C.S.

RESIDENT SECRETAR—James Grant.

Parties intending to assure their lives, are invited to peruse the Society's prospectus, which embraces several entirely new and interesting features in Life Assurance. Copies can be had on application at the Head Office, or at any of the Agencies.

JAS. GRANT, Resident Secretary.

Agents wanted in unrepresented districts.   43-1y

The Gore District Mutual Fire Insurance Company

GRANTS INSURANCES on all description of Property against Loss or Damage by FIRE. It is the only Mutual Fire Insurance Company which assesses its Policies yearly from their respective dates ; and the average yearly cost of insurance in it, for the past three and a half years, has been nearly TWENTY CENTS IN THE DOLLAR, less than what it would have been in an ordinary Proprietary Company.

THOS. M. SIMONS, Secretary & Treasurer.

ROBT. McLEAN, Inspector of Agencies.
Galt, 25th Nov., 1868.   15-1y

Canada Life Assurance Company.

SPECIALLY LICENSED BY THE GOVERNMENT OF CANADA.

ESTABLISHED 1847.

CAPITAL......... A MILLION DOLLARS.

DEPOSIT WITH GOVERNMENT, $50,000.

The success of the Company may be judged of by the fact that during the financial year to the 30th April, 1869, the gross number of

NEW POLICIES

ISSUED WAS

8921

FOR ASSURANCES OF

$1,257,734,

WITH

ANNUAL PREMIUMS OF

$49,783.73.

Rates lower that those of British or Foreign Offices, and every advantage offered which safety and liberality can afford.

A. G. RAMSAY, Manager.

E. BRADBURNE, Agent,
May 25.   1y   Toronto Street.

Queen Fire and Life Insurance Company,
OF LIVERPOOL AND LONDON,

ACCEPTS ALL ORDINARY FIRE RISKS

on the most favorable terms.

LIFE RISKS

Will be taken on terms that will compare favorably with other Companies.

CAPITAL,   -   -   £2,000,000 Stg.

CANADA BRANCH OFFICE—Exchange Buildings, Montreal.

Resident Secretary and General Agent,

A. MACKENZIE FORBES,

13 St. Sacrament St., Merchants' Exchange, Montreal.

WM. ROWLAND, Agent, Toronto.   1-1y

THE AGRICULTURAL
Mutual Assurance Association of Canada.

HEAD OFFICE.........................LONDON, ONT.

A purely Farmers' Company. Licensed by the Government of Canada.

Capital, 1st January, 1869..................	$230,193 82
Cash and Cash Items, do....................	$80,000 00
No. of Policies in force...................	50,892 00

THIS Company insures nothing more dangerous than a Farm property. Its rates are as low as any well-established Company in the Dominion, and lower than those of a great many. It is largely patronised, and continues to grow in public favor.

For Insurance, apply to any of the Agents or address the Secretary, London, Ontario.

London, 2nd Nov., 1868.   12-1y.

Insurance.

The Waterloo County Mutual Fire Insurance Company.

HEAD OFFICE : WATERLOO, ONTARIO.

ESTABLISHED 1863.

THE business of the Company is divided into three separate and distinct branches, the

VILLAGE, FARM, AND MANUFACTURES.

Each Branch paying its own losses and its just proportion of the managing expenses of the Company.

C. M. TAYLOR, Sec.   M. SPRINGER, M.M.P., Pres.
J. HUGHES, Inspector.   15-yr

Lancashire Insurance Company.

CAPITAL, - - - - - - - - - £2,000,000 Sterling

FIRE RISKS

Taken at reasonable rates of premium, and ALL LOSSES SETTLED PROMPTLY,

By the undersigned, without reference elsewhere.

S. C. DUNCAN-CLARK & CO.,

General Agents for Ontario,

25-1y   N. W. Cor. of King & Church Sts., TORONTO.

Western Assurance Company.

INCORPORATED 1851.

CAPITAL, ... $400,000.

FIRE AND MARINE.

HEAD OFFICE................. TORONTO, ONTARIO.

DIRECTORS.

Hon. JNO. McMURRICH, President.

	CHARLES MAGRATH, Vice-President
A. M. SMITH, Esq.	JOHN F ISKEN, Esq.
ROBERT BEATY, Esq.	ALEX. MANNING, Esq.
JAMES MICHIE, Esq.	N. BARNHART, Esq.

R. J. DALLAS, Esq.

B. HALDAN, Secretary.

J. MAUGHAN, JR., Assistant Secretary.

WM. BLIGHT, Fire Inspector.

CAPT. G. T. DOUGLAS, Marine Inspector.

JAMES PRINGLE, General Agent.

Insurances effected at the lowest current rates on Buildings, Merchandize, and other property, against loss or damage by fire.

On Hull, Cargo and Freight against the perils of Inland Navigation.

On Cargo Risks with the Maritime Provinces by sail or steam.

On Cargoes by steamers to and from British Ports.

WESTERN ASSURANCE COMPANY'S OFFICE, }
TORONTO, 1st April, 1869. }   83-1y

The Victoria Mutual
FIRE INSURANCE COMPANY OF CANADA.

Insures only Non-Hazardous Property, at Low Rates.

BUSINESS STRICTLY MUTUAL.

GEORGE H. MILLS, President.
W. D. BOOKER, Secretary.

HEAD OFFICE ....HAMILTON, ONTARIO

aug 15-1yr

North British and Mercantile Insurance Company.

Established 1809.

HEAD OFFICE, - - CANADA, - MONTREAL,

TORONTO BRANCH :

LOCAL OFFICES, Nos. 4 & 6 WELLINGTON STREET.

Fire Department, ...R. N. GOOCH, Agent.
Life Department, ...H. L. HIME, Agent.

Imperial Fire Insurance Company
OF LONDON.

No. 1 OLD BROAD STREET, AND 16 PALL MALL.

ESTABLISHED 1803.

Canada General Agency,

RINTOUL BROS.,

24 St. Sacrament Street.

JAMES E. SMITH, Agent,

Toronto, Corner Church and Colborne Streets.

PUBLISHED AT THE OFFICE OF THE MONETARY TIMES, No. 60 CHURCH STREET.
PRINTED AT THE DAILY TELEGRAPH PUBLISHING HOUSE, BAY STREET, CORNER OF KING

THE CANADIAN
MONETARY TIMES
AND
INSURANCE CHRONICLE.

DEVOTED TO FINANCE, COMMERCE, INSURANCE, BANKS, RAILWAYS, NAVIGATION, MINES, INVESTMENT, PUBLIC COMPANIES, AND JOINT STOCK ENTERPRISE.

| L. II—NO. 49. | TORONTO, THURSDAY, JULY 22, 1869. | SUBSCRIPTION $2 A YEAR. |

Mercantile.

J. B. Bonstead.
DIVISION and Commission Merchant. Hops bought and sold on Commission. 82 Front St., Toronto.

John Boyd & Co.
WHOLESALE Grocers and Commission Merchants, Front St., Toronto.

Childs & Hamilton.
MANUFACTURERS and Wholesale Dealers in Boots and Shoes, No. 7 Wellington Street East, Toronto, Ontario.   28

L. Coffee & Co.
PRODUCE and Commission Merchants, No. 2 Manning's Block, Front St., Toronto, Ont. Advances made on guments of Produce.

Candee & Co.,
BANKERS AND BROKERS, dealers in Gold and Silver coin, Government Securities, &c., Corner Main and Seneca Streets, Buffalo, Y. N.   21-1v

John Fisken & Co.
JK OIL and Commission Merchants, Yonge St., Toronto, Ont.

W. & R. Griffith.
IMPORTERS of Teas, Wines, etc. Ontario Chambers, cor. Church and Front Sts., Toronto.

Gundry and Langley,
ARCHITECTS AND CIVIL ENGINEERS, Building Surveyors and Valuators. Office corner of King and Jordan ts, Toronto.
THOMAS GUNDRY.   HENRY LANGLEY.

Lyman & McNab.
WHOLESALE Hardware Merchants, Toronto, Ontario.

W. D. Matthews & Co.
PRODUCE Commission Merchants, Old Corn Exchange, 5 Front St. East, Toronto Ont.

R. C. Hamilton & Co.
PRODUCE Commission Merchants, 119 Lower Water St., Halifax, Nova Scotia.

H. Nerlich & Co.,
IMPORTERS of French, German, English and American Fancy Goods, Cigars, and Leaf Tobaccos, No. 2 Adelaide , West, Toronto.   15

Parson Bros.,
PETROLEUM Refiners, and Wholesale dealers in Lamps, Chimneys, etc. Warerooms 51 Front St. Refinery cor. and Don Sts., Toronto.

Reford & Dillon,
IMPORTERS of Groceries, Wellington Street, Toronto, Ontario.

C. P. Reid & Co.
IMPORTERS and Dealers in Wines, Liquors, Cigars and Leaf Tobacco, Wellington Street, Toronto.   28.

W. Rowland & Co.,
PRODUCE BROKERS and General Commission Merchants. Advances made on Consignments. Corner Bath and Front Streets, Toronto.

Sessions, Turner & Cooper.
MANUFACTURERS, Importers and Wholesale Dealer in Boots and Shoes, Leather Findings, etc., 8 Wellington St West, Toronto, Ont

Sylvester, Bro. & Hickman,
COMMERCIAL Brokers and Vessel Agents. Office—No. Ontario Chambers, [Corner Front and Church Sts.,
.   3-6m

Meetings.

BANK OF TORONTO.

The Annual General Meeting of the Bank of Toronto (being the thirteenth since the commencement of business), was held in pursuance of the terms of the Charter, at the Banking House of the Institution, on 21st July. 1869.

William Gooderham, Esq., President, being called to the chair, the Cashier then, at his request, read the following report:

The Directors of the Bank of Toronto have pleasure in rendering to the Stockholders a statement of the operations of the Bank for the year just closed.

In following the example of the Joint Stock Banks of England, by placing the statement in the hands of Stockholders before the Annual Meeting, they desire to afford them such information as will enable them to form an opinion upon the position of the institution before they are called upon to take any action thereupon. This course they trust, will commend itself to the judgment of Stockholders.

The business of the Bank during the year has been well maintained in every department both at the Head Office and Branches, and although circumstances have rendered it desirable to keep larger reserves of available funds than formerly, and consequently to curtail discounts to some extent, the net result compares very satisfactorily with that of former years.

Owing to continued over-importations in the commercial centre of the Province, with its inevitable consequence of unreasonable competition in the wholesale trade, along with the temptations incident to the working of a defective insolvent law, the number of failures for some time back has been far larger than usual. Your Board, knowing the condition of affairs, have exercised more than ordinary vigilance and caution in this branch of business, and they are happy to state that the losses suffered by the Bank will be of a trifling character.

The gradual and continuous fall in the price of grain during the last few months has occasioned less of loss to parties in the trade than might have been feared under the circumstances. Farmers have held back their grain in many parts of the country, and the depreciation, to some extent, has fallen upon them. The customers of the Bank have fully appreciated the advice given them to operate with extreme caution, and the consequence is that the casualties of the year in this important branch of business have been very few and of small amount.

All losses were provided for before the closing of the books. Every bad debt was written off in full, and provision made for such as are doubtful; and to enable this necessary part of their duty to be discharged, the Directors subjected the loans and discounts of the Bank to a rigid scrutiny, and by personal conference with the Managers of Branches, satisfied themselves as to the operations of the Bank at distant points.

After making provision for losses as above stated, the net profits of the Bank, deducting expenses, interest on current and permanent deposits,

and rebate of interest on notes discounted amounted to $140,423 66
Add balance at credit of Profit and Loss account, brought forward from last year.. 5,003 91

$145,427 57

This sum was appropriated as follows:—
Government Tax on circulation...... $2,580 15
Dividend No. 25 of four per cent., paid 2nd January last............... 32,000 00
Dividend No. 26 of four per cent., payable 2nd July, instant.......... 32,000 00
Added to "Rest" 75,000 00
Balance carried forward to next year. 8.847 42

$145,427 57

The accounts, securities, and cash of the Bank, both at the Head Office and Branches, have been frequently examined by the Inspector, and found correct.

In the report of last year the expectation was held out that the securities and collaterals held to cover the contingencies of certain accounts would realize sufficient, with appropriations, to guard the Bank against loss. The Directors are happy to state that this expectation has been more than realized. Profit and loss account has been credited during the year with various sums received on account of debts which have been written off or provided for.

In pursuance of the policy indicated in the same Report, the amount of Government Securities held by the bank has been increased by the sum of £10,000 sterling, making the total amount of such securities $147,155.

In view of the approaching termination of the Charter of the Bank, your Board petitioned Parliament during its late session, for a renewal of the same with amendments. An Act was passed, which has received the Royal assent, empowering the capital stock to be increased during the next three years to any sum not less than one million or more than two millions of dollars, and also changing the time for holding the Annual Meeting from July to June. This last will take effect for the first time next year, but no action can be taken representing an increase in the Capital without the concurrence of the stockholders. By a general act the charters of several banks, and this among the number, were renewed until 30th June, 1870, and the close of the next following session of parliament.

Your Board, along with a majority of the banks of the Dominion, have petitioned against any fundamental change in the currency system of Canada, and they trust that the unanswerable reasons urged against this course will have due weight with the legislature. Your directors conceive that the maintenance, under all circumstances, of a specie basis for the currency, is a matter of fundamental importance, and as the change proposed has a tendency, in their judgment, to undermine that basis, and entails other serious disadvantages, they trust that legislation may be in the direction of amending and perfecting what already exists, rather than in that of radical and undesirable change.

The Directors, in conclusion, have pleasure in bearing testimony to the very satisfactory manner in which their respective duties have been discharged by the Cashier, Assistant Cashier, Managers, and other Officers of the Bank. The whole respectfully submitted.

(Signed,)
　　　　Wm. Gooderham, President.
Toronto, July 21st, 1869,

General Statement of Liabilities and Assets, as on 30th June, 1869.

LIABILITIES.

Notes in circulation	$724,860 00
Balances due to other banks.......	38,500 35
Deposits	1,769,305 29
Total liabilities to the public...	2,532,665 64
Capital paid up	800,000 00
Rest	300,000 00
Contingent fund.....................	40,000 00
Reserve for rebate on interest on notes discounted...............	21,822 41
Reserve for accrued interest on deposit receipts.................	15,731 19
Dividends unclaimed	264 00
Dividend No. 26, payable 2nd July	32,000 00
Balance of profit and loss carried forward to next year...........	3,847 42
	$3,746,330 66

ASSETS.

Specie and Provincial notes.........	525,264 72
Notes and cheques of other banks.	79,863 20
Balances due from other banks.....	189,900 40
Total assets immediately available	795,028 32
Government securities................	147,155 82
Notes discounted—current.........	2,655,017 80
Notes discounted—overdue	64,341 69
Other debts not before included....	41,918 22
Bank premises in Toronto............	36,000 00
Furniture	4,989 81
Bill stamps on hand..................	1,618 00
Real estate owned by the bank.....	261 00
	$3,746,330 66

Profit and Loss Account—30th June, 1869.

To Government tax on circulation...	$ 2,580 15
" Dividend No. 25, of 4 per cent., paid 2nd January, 1869	32,000 00
" Dividend No. 26, of 4 per cent., payable 2nd July, 1869	32,000 00
" Amount added to rest	75,000 00
" Balance carried forward to next year	3,847 42
	$145,427 57

By balance brought from last year...	$ 5,003 91
" Net profit for year ending 30th June, 1869, after payment of expenses, writing off bad and providing for doubtful debts, interest on current accounts and deposit receipts, and rebate of interest on bills discounted	140,423 66
	$145,427 57

(Signed)　　G. Hague, Cashier.

The foregoing having been read, it was moved by Hon. J. H. Cameron, seconded by John Wickson, Esq., and

Resolved.—That the stockholders concur in the propriety of placing the report in the hands of stockholders before the day of the annual meeting, and that the report for the last year be adopted.

Moved by Judge Gowan, seconded by J. D. Armour, Esq., and

Resolved.—That the cordial thanks of the stockholders are due and hereby tendered to the President, Vice-President, and Directors of the Bank, for the care and attention they have bestowed upon its interest during the year.

Moved by Joseph Gould, Esq., seconded by his Worship Mayor, Esq., and

Resolved, That Messrs. W. J. Macdonell, and Henry Pellatt, be appointed scrutineers of the

election about to take place, and that they report the result to the cashier.

Moved by W. J. Macdonell, Esq., seconded by Amos Bostwick Esq., and

Resolved.—That the poll commence at once and that it be kept open till one o'clock this day, except in the event of five minutes elapsing without the tender of a vote in which case it shall be closed.

Moved by Wm. Fraser, Esq., seconded by A.T. Fulton, Esq., and

Resolved,—That the thanks of this meeting be presented to the chairman for his able and impartial conduct in the chair.

Report of the Scrutineers.

Wm. Gooderham, Wm. Cawthra, Wm. Fraser, A. T. Fulton, James G. Worts, Wm. Cantley, Hon. Asa A. Burnham.

We, the undersigned Scrutineers, appointed at the annual meeting of the stockholders of the Bank of Toronto, held this day, declare the gentlemen above named unanimously elected Directors for the ensuing year.

(Signed),　　W. J. Macdonell,
　　　　　　　Henry Pellatt,
　　　　　　　　　　　Scrutineers.

The new Board met the same afternoon, when Wm. Gooderham, Esq., was unanimously elected President, and James G. Worts, Esq., Vice-President.

By order of the Board,
(Signed),　　G. Hague, Cashier.

GORE DISTRICT MUTUAL INSURANCE COMPANY.

The annual meeting of the members of the Gore District Mutual Insurance Company took place in Galt, on the 12th inst.

The President, John Davidson, Esq., took the chair, and Mr. Thos. M. Simons, the Secretary of the company, read the following:

Thirtieth Annual Report.

The following is a summary of the transactions of the Company for the year ended 31st May, 1869.

The number of policies issued was 1,290—insuring $1,005,700, and the amount of premium notes thereon was $66,796.11. The number of policies in force at the end of the year was 2,597, insuring $2,117,875, and the premium notes thereon amounted to $151,250.85. The average risk was $815.51. The amount of cash premiums received was $3,685.28. The number of claims during the year 34, amounting to $18,101.44. The Inspector's report on claims and policies in force in each class of risk contains ample information concerning them and accompanies this. The claim to which allusion was made in the report of the Directors for the year ended 31st of May, 1868, yet remains unsettled. At the last spring assizes in Hamilton, the plaintiff was again non-suited and the matter referred to the Judges in term on a point of law. After this claim shall have been finally disposed of the precise grounds upon which the Directors decided to resist it will be published, and the facts then brought out will be found fully to justify their decision.

In regard to the cost of insurance within the period embraced by this report, it has for many months been maintained at twenty per cent. less than what the cost would have been in an ordinary, Proprietary Company, and past experience warrants the assumption that this average will not be materially exceeded.

Based upon this experience, the promise is again repeated to the insurer for a period of three years, provided he will pay each year in advance twenty per cent. of his premium note that no further call shall be made upon him unless at the end of three years, it shall have been ascertained that the cost of his insurance shall have exceeded the amount paid by him, when he will be required to make up the deficiency. If, however, he shall have paid more than was required, a result which

is not unlikely—the surplus will be returned to him. Moreover one year's interest will be allowed him on each payment made in advance. An assessment of twenty per cent. on the premium notes of this Company is equivalent to a saving of twenty cents in each dollar charged by an ordinary proprietary company. The system of daily assessment inaugurated by this Company has now been fairly in operation for two years, and very great benefit has resulted from it as the following statement will prove.

The liabilities of the Company for the year ended 31st of May, 1867, amounted to $13,482, and could have been paid had the Company had no other source of revenue such as cash premiums and first payments from assessments alone by the 31st January, 1868. Between that date and the 1st of September next thereafter, the date of which under the old system, assessments would have been levied, assessments amounting to $19,796 had been received in daily instalments, of which under the old system not one cent would have been received before the 1st September. A similar result is gradually unfolding itself this year. Aided by the system of cash premiums which this Company has adopted, it is confidently anticipated that the system of daily assessment will at no very distant period enable the Company to pay claims upon it as soon as established without the aid of borrowed money. Your Directors deem that it would be out of place in their report to enter into any discussion concerning the propriety of Mutual Insurance Companies adopting the cash system, nor would they allude to the subject had it not recently been assailed. However the fact that during a series of years the cost of insurance in any well managed Mutual Fire Insurance Company will maintain a certain average, should certainly justify such a Company in offering to insure at rates which shall exceed that average and to return to the insurer a portion of the profits so realized. Cash premiums may moreover be regarded as so many assessments paid in advance but without that risk or trouble and cost in collection which is unavoidably incidental to the premium note system, or all credit systems.

That this Company has experienced considerable benefit from the system of cash premiums during the past year, it is simply necessary to say that while the premium notes are but $1,874 less than they were on the 31st May, 1868, the amount of cash premiums received was $3,685, which sum represents at least $16,000 in premium notes.

The option to insure in either the premium note or cash system is freely offered by the agents of this company, thus enabling the applicant to select that which he conceives is best suited to his own interests. It is peculiarly gratifying to your Directors to be enabled to report that, while the receipts of the company have, during the past year exceeded those of the preceding year by nearly $2,000, its expenditure has been less by over $300; and of more importance still, that the amount of the company's liabilities is less at the date of this report by $8,000 than it was twelve months ago. Nor is it a matter of small gratification to the Board to be enabled to assert that the company has now one thousand policies more in force than it had in July, 1865, and that its value of its assets has increased in like proportion Connected with this subject, the Board cannot but refer to the assistance which they have received from their agents. It were almost invidious to particularize, but the Messrs. Doyl and Mr. Hadden certainly deserve special mention.

The importance of united action on the part of mutual insurance companies has long been apparent, not only to the management of this company but to others, who have felt that their interests generally would be enhanced could an uniformity in rates, so as to facilitate reinsurance operations, one uniform statute governing all alike, and uniform rules and regulations generally be adopted. With this end in view, a convention of the managers and representatives of all the leading mutual companies in Ontario was ed in April last. It was well attended, and meters affecting mutual insurance companies s fully and ably discussed, the result being nimously in favor of an uniform tariff, uniform dlations, and one general statute ; and your ectors have to report that when the minutes he convuntion were laid before them, its proings met with cordial approval.

he election of Directors will take place to-day, previous Board retiring ; each Director is, ever, eligible for re-election.

JOHN DAVIDSON, President.
THOS. M. SIMONS, Secretary.

alt, 12th July, 1869.

n the conclusion of the report, Mr. McLean, ector, read the following statement as to the es, etc., of the company for the past year :— number of claims made against the company oss or damage by fire during the past year, ng 31st May, 1869, is 37, amounting to $22,- 16 ; last year the number of claims was 49, unting to $35,707.50. All but three of the ns of the past year have been satisfactorily sted, and such as have matured have been . Of the three claims above referred to, one y had become void for months previous to fire by the non-payment of assessment, in us of the statute. In another, the assured effected an additional insurance on his proy without the knowledge or consent of this pany, thus rendering the first policy void. third case—that of Todd & Co.—is as clear a of fraud as ever was perpetrated. One of partners acknowledged under oath that the value of the property insured had been mis-sented in the application, the value stated ich application being more than double the value of the property. No company would ustified in paying such a claim as that of l & Co. I have prepared a table showing the rent kinds of risks insured by the company ; number of each kind, the total amount in-n each class, and the average amount of risk, together with the loss sustained last on each class of risk. I also append a state-: showing the number of applications taken ich agency for the past two years, and the s at the agencies for the same time ; and r, a schedule of losses during each month of past year, the cause of fire, if known, the of the party insured, the number of the y, amount paid in each case, and the nature e risk.

en followed an analysis of the causes of fire, &c.

fore the passage of the report a general dis-on took place regarding the general expenses e Company, and amount of working expenses e Company. Mr. Strickland asked, "What entage of the receipts of the Company does it re to pay the working expenses of the Com-l" Upon investigation it was answered that ross working expenses of the Company were 6, of which sum it required about $3,000 for expenses.

e election of the Board of Directors was then eded with and resulted as follows: John David-R. S. Strong, James Crombie, Adam War-James McTague, Samuel Richardson, M.D., H. Ball, Chas. Magill, M. P., Wm. Turn-John Watson, John Quarrie, James Young, , and Hugh McColloch.

a meeting of the newly elected directors, on the 19th, John Fleming, Esq., Warden e County, was elected President and R. S. g, Esq., Vice-President.

ΓY BANK OF MONTREAL.—The annual meet-f this bank was held in Montreal on the 7th ; the President, Mr. Wm. Workman in the . Messrs. Wm. McDougall and Henry Mul-nd were appointed scrutineers to the meet-. The report states the losses of the year to been trifling.

The balance at the credit of the Reserve Fund last year was......... $134,777 17
The net profits on the business of the
year just closed, after deducting
expenses and allowances for bad
and doubtful debts, are.............. 102,062 98
                                       —————
                                       $236,840 15
Deduct two dividends of four per
cent. each paid during the year.   96,000 00
                                       —————
Balance at credit of Reserve Fund.. $140,840 15

This reserve, which is about 11½ per cent. on the capital, the Board believe to be sound and reliable.

The Directors enter at length into the consid_ration of the Bankrupt and Usury Laws, and Mr. Rose's Banking scheme. We have not space for the opinions and arguments expressed on these important subjects, or even a summary of them.

The following is an abstract from the books of the City Bank, exhibiting a general statement of the affairs of the institution, Monday, May 10th, 1869:

To Capital stock all paid up........ $1,200,000 00
" Bills in circulation............ 341,613 00
" Dividends unpaid............ · 5,536 38
" Dividend........................... 48,000 00
" Deposits not bearing interest... 606,119 56
" Deposits bearing interest....... 839,010 56
" Balances due to other banks.... 41,693 82
" Interest reserved.................. 19,000 00
" Exchange reserved................ 4,450 00
" Contingent fund 140,840 15
                                       —————
                                       $3,246,263 47
                   CR.
By Cash on hand,
Gold, Silver and
Provincial notes $365,594 48
Cheques and bills on
other banks....... 71,296 34
                    —————
                                       436,890 82
Real estate.......................... 41,470 02
Government bonds.................... 158,939 99
Balances due from other banks... 42,034 74
Balances due from foreign agencies.. 64,541 7¾
Notes and bills discounted, and
other debts not otherwise in-
cluded.............................. 2,502,386 19
                                       —————
                                       . $3,246,263 47
                           F. McCULLOCH, Cashier.

The following directors were elected for the cur-rent year :—William Workman, Joseph Tiffin, Wm. McDonald, Champion Brown, John Grant.

QUEBEC AND LAKE SUPERIOR MINING ASSO-CIATION.—The Annual General Meeting of share-holders in this Company, was held, in Quebec, on the 12th inst. The following Report was read by the Secretary :—

It is with feelings of deep regret that your Di-rectors have to report the death, since the last annual meeting, of their much esteemed colleague, the late J. B. Forsyth, Esquire, one of the first Directors of the Company, for twelve years its Vice-President, and for six its President, whose interests were so thoroughly. indentified with the Company, that he has been present at every meet-ing since its formation. His zeal for the success of the Company was not less than his unbounded faith in its resources. Your Directors trust that the Shareholders, animated by a like spirit, will cheerfully come forward and furnish the necessary funds to enable them, not only to pay the govern-ment tax of 2 cents an acre, (now past due,) but also to have their valuable property surveyed and reported upon by a practical mining Engineer next summer, as without such a data for their guidance, your directors find it impossible to induce capital-ists even to entertain the idea of purchasing. Your Directors feel the more justified in making this appeal, now that the value of their property has been so much enhanced by the discovery of

---

rich silver veins in the vicinity of their locations. Failing this, your Directors see no alternative but either to make a forced sale of the lands, or have the 26,000 acres divided among the shareholders by a tirage au sort. By this method each share-holder will get a little more than half an acre of land for each share, and it will then be·optional with him to pay the Government tax, or not, as he may deem best. After such an enormous outlay, your Directors cannot but contemplate such a winding up of the Company with regret, at th·· same time they consider it their duty to lay the matter clearly before the shareholders, leaving them to take such action therein as they may see fit.

· The following gentlemen were elected Directors for the ensuing twelve months. Messrs: E. Burstall, D. C. Thompson, G. B. Hall, P. A. Shaw, Jos. B. Forsyth, and G. Veasey.

At a meeting of the Directors held on the fol-lowing day, Mr. D. C. Thompson, was elected President, Mr. G. B. Hall, Vice-President, and Mr. Geo. Veasey, Secrétary-Treasurer, of the Company. ,

Insurance.

FIRE RECORD.—St. Vincent Township, Grey &c.—Barn of R. S. Lynn, with 1,000 bush. wheat, wagons, &c. ; loss estimated at $2,500 to $3,000 ; insured for $1,200 in a London and Mutual.

Aytown, Ont., July 7.—Shop of Mr. Leisner, and tavern, stables, shed, &c., of August Basler ; no insurance on Leisner's property ; Basler had a policy of $1,600 in some company.

Middle River, Nova Scotia, July 10.—Kerr & Son's Woolen Factory. The Eastern Chronicle says the loss will be $10,000 ;. no insurance.

—The insurance companies interested in the late McGill fire at Hamilton have delayed the payment of the amounts of the respective policies, under the strong impression· that. there is "a nigger in the fence."

—Two of the crew of the schooner ·Garry own reported lost near Cleveland, on July 1st, made affidavits before H. W. Heemans, British Consul, that the vessel was scuttled by the captain, as the vessel and cargo were insured. Underwriters are put on the guard until the Consul has closed the investigation.

—On the 14th inst., the barge Royal Oak foundered out of Port Dalhousie. She was being towed to Toronto, with the barge Enterprise, by the tug Young Lion. The cargo of the Royal Oak, valued at $600, uninsured, was lost. Both the barge and the wood belonged to Mr. Hutchinson, of Dunville.

THE INTERNATIONAL AND PRUDENTIAL·

Our readers will remember that at the beginning of last year the International Society entered into a deed of amalgamation with the Hercules Life Office, and consequent upon this, ·various Chan-cery proceedings were instituted, involving both companies in most expensive litigation. Subse-quently both companies were ordered to be wound up under the supervision of the Court of Chancery. An agreement has now been entered into with the Hercules for the transfer of the life policy and annuity liabilities to the Prudential Assurance Company, subject to certain conditions. The most important of these conditions is that, on payment of £329,685 to the Prudential, the poli-cies and annuities of the International would be undertaken by the latter company.

The difficulty of obtaining so large a sum being great, very considerable delay would necessarily arise before the transfer could be made and the security of the Prudential be given to the policy-holders and annuitants. In addition to this, complications arose between the Hercules and the International, and it was feared that very heavy law expenses would be incurred. With the view of affording immediate relief, negotiations were opened with the official liquidator of the International Life Assurance Society, which have resulted in the following agreement: "On the transfer by the International of certain securities, named, and on payment by the International, on the 20th July, 1869, of the sum of £65,937, being one-fifth of the above amount and interest, the Prudential will become bound to pay one-half of all annuities falling due since 30th January, 1869, and one-half of all claims on policies subsequent to the 30th January, 1869, with interest at 4 per cent. from the date when the payment should have been made up to payment. On each subsequent 20th July for four years, the International is to pay the Prudential another instalment of £65,937, being a further fifth of the said sum of £329,685 with interest, and on receipt of each instalment to pay or be responsible for one-eighth part more of the annuities and claims, together with interest at 4 per cent. on all arrears. All premiums and interest from 30th January, 1869, to be paid to the Prudential." The agreement has received the sanction of Vice-Chancellor Malins, who has made an order directing it to be carried out.

Immediately on receipt of the first instalment and interest, the fact will be notified to the policyholders and annuitants; and as soon as possible afterwards proper certificates, under the common seal of the Prudential, undertaking the above-mentioned liability, will be forwarded to the policyholders and annuitants. This relates to all policy-holders other than those in the United States of America, whose interests are also properly provided for. This arrangement places the policyholders and annuitants in a much more satisfactory position than might have been expected a short time since; and it is further beneficial to them, as it will save very protracted and expensive litigation, by which the interests of the creditors would have most materially suffered.

The following circular has been issued to the policyholders of the International Assurance Society:—

In the Matter of The Companies Acts 1862 *and* 1867, *and of the International Assurance Society.*

Sir,—The affairs of this society being now arranged as regards the current life policies and annuity policies, I think it desirable to give to the shareholders and policyholders such information as I can regarding what has been done for the protection of their interests, and also as to the present position of the society. The society as you are probably aware, in May of last year transferred its business, and also the whole of its assets to the Hercules insurance Company, a young office, that had not the means of carrying out its contracts, and which passed into liquidation early in the present year. Prior to the Hercules Company going into liquidation petitions had been presented to the Court of Chancery for an order to wind up the affairs of the International Society, and on the 19th of February the Court made an order for that purpose, and appointed Mr. Symes, the late chairman of the society, and myself official liquidators. Dr. Symes acted with me in that capacity for a short time, and then ceased to do so, whereupon his Honour Vice Chancellor Malins appointed me sole liquidator. I have succeeded in carrying out with the Prudential Assurance Company an arrangement for their taking over the liabilities of this society in respect of life policies and annuities and have seen a print of the circular issued by that company dated the 8th June inst., containing the particulars of the agreement entered into by me, and the same contains correct extracts from such agreement. For the information of the policyholders I may mention that the amount, £329.685 the sum at which the policy and annuity liabilities of the International had been recently valued by Messrs. Bailey and Sprague, two actuaries of great experience and reputation, and which valuation has been certified for my guidance by Mr. Robt. Tucker, the eminent actuary of the Pelican Assurance Company, and he recommended its adoption, and also stated that he considered the terms proposed by the Prudential to be more favourable to this society than were likely to be obtained from any other office affording a resonable prospect of being able to carry out their contracts. This agreement has been sanctioned by the Vice-Chancellor, and he has directed me to carry it out. This arrangement, having for its object to secure to the policyholders as much certainty with regard to their policies when they become claims as in the position of the Society's affairs it is possible to do, will, I trust, be regarded as satisfactory to all parties interested.

(Signed) FRED. MAYNARD, Official Liquidator.
London, 55 Old Broad St., E.C.

—*Insurance Record.*

A PRETTY LOT!—In 1866 the European Fire Assurance Society took over the fire business of the British Nation. In 1867 the Etna Fire (established 1866) took over the European fire business. In 1868 the Etna also took over the life business of the General Provident (established 1862), which had in 1864 taken over the business of the Confident (established 1862.)—The Etna, in 1868, becoming insolvent, was ordered to be wound up, and the fire businesses were transferred over to the United Ports and General, which had, singularly enough, just started, having agreed to take over the marine business of the Bristol Marine (established 1864) and the Amicable Mutual Life (established 1857. The amalgamation of the Progress will leave the United Ports the embodiment of no less than nine different companies. As the institution transacts fire, life, and marine business, and is unlimited, we cannot be at a loss for an opinion as to its future prospects.—*The Cosmopolitan.*

Financial.

TORONTO STOCK MARKET.

(Reported by Pellatt & Osler, Brokers.)

An average business has been done during the past week; the demand for most securities, however, exceeds the supply, and prices closed very firm.

Bank Stock.—Montreal has again advanced; sales were made at 159¾ and 160½; no sellers now under 161. Sales of British have been made at 104½, which price would still be paid. There are sellers of Ontario at 96, and buyers at 95½. Toronto is in good demand at 120½ to 121; small sales have been made at these rates, but holders generally ask an advance. Royal Canadian is asked for at 50; none in market. Commerce has been much sought after at last week's quotations, and buyers have advanced to 102; holders want a further advance. Buyers would give 39 for Gore; there are sellers at 40. Merchants' has been largely dealt in at 106 and 106½; buyers offer the latter rate, but the stock is held for an advance. There are buyers of Quebec at 100½. Sales are reported of Molsons' at 109½, at which rate there are buyes. Buyers offer 99½ for City, with sellers at par. Du Peuple nominal at 108½ to 109, and Nationale at 107 to 108. No Jacques Cartier in market; buyers would give 108½. Small sales of Mechanics' were made at 93. Union sold at 105; none now offering under 105½.

Debentures.—Sales of Dominion Stock are reported at 107, 107½, 107¾ and 108; Fives and Sixes are asked for, but none on market. Considerable sales of Sterling Toronto Bonds were made at rates to pay 7 and 7½ per cent. County are asked for at 99.

Sundries.—City Gas is much inquired for; buyers would give 107½. No sales of British America Assurance since our last; buyers would give 54. Sales of Canada Permanent Building Society were made at 122½ to 122¾; it is in demand at the latter rate. Western Canada Building Society is in demand at 118, but none on market; buyers would advance ½ per cent. Freehold Buildin Society continues to be much sought after, bu without attracting sellers. Small lots of Montrea Telegraph offer at 133. Sales of Canada Lande Credit were made during the week at 80. First class mortgages are readily taken to pay at 8 p. cent

UNITED STATES CURRENCY.

The New York *Economist*, in a recent numbe says:—It is not our purpose to hazard any theor in regard to the currency; we merely design to pr sent the facts, and leave our readers to frame the own theories. None but those familiar with th difficult nature of statistical inquiry can apreciat the great amount of labour compressed into th following table; although it will be perhaps enoug to state that the information it contains was d rived from a careful perusal of all the Treasur documents, Congressional Committee reports, an a large portion of all the statistical works publis ed in the United States since 1830. Even as it i no complete authentic data for the years 183 1832, and 1834 have been obtained.

Statistics of the Currency of the United States, i cluding Bank Notes, Greenbacks, and Specie.

Year.	Currency.	C'y per Capit
1830	$93,000,000	$7 20
1833	119,700,000	8 50
1835	183,000,000	12 40
1836	205,000,000	13 30
1837*	222,000,000	14 00
1838	203,000,000	12 50
1839	222,000,000	13 40
1840	190,000,000	11 20
1841	187,000,000	10 70
1842	143,700,000	8 00
1843	128,500,000	6 90
1844	175,000,000	9 10
1845	186,000,000	9 40
1846	202,500,000	9 90
1847	225,500,000	10 70
1848	240,000,000	11 10
1849	284,70[illegible],000	10 50
1850	285,000,000	12 20
1851	341,000,000	14 20
1852	360,000,000	14 20
1853	380,000,000	14 50
1854	418,600,000	15 80
1855	444,600,000	16 40
1856	446,200,000	16 10
1857*	474,300,000	16 70
1558	406,600,000	14 00
1859	457,800,000	15 40
1860	457,000,000	14 50
1861*	443,400,000	13 70
1862	482,500,000	21 00
1863	672,000,000	27 40
1864†	743,000,000	28 50
1865‡	754,000,000	24 90
1866	850,000,000	23 60
1867	844,000,000	22 80
1868	839,000,000	22 00
1869	832,000,000	21 20

Glancing along this table, it will be observ that the currency was an increasing one from 18 to the time of the great suspension in 1837; th then it became a decreasing one until 1843, wh it again became an increasing one until 1857, ag a decreasing one until 1861, again an increasi one until 1864, and that it is now a decreasi one. These alternate movements of the curren may, with great propriety, be termed *crescen* and *diminuendo* movements. The crescendo riods are all noted as eras of great commerc activity; the diminuendo ones are as eras of co mercial depression—thus:

Period.	Currency per capita.	Movement.	Characterist
1830–37	$7.20 to $14.00	Crescendo.	Great activi
1837–43	14.00 " 6.90	Diminuendo.	Depression.
1843–57	6.90 " 16.70	Crescendo.	Great activi
1857–61	16.70 " 13.70	Diminuendo.	Depression.
1861–64	13.70 " 28.50	Crescendo.	Great activi
1864–69	28.50 " 21.20	Diminuendo.	Shrinkage.

*Suspension. † Highest inflation during suspensio
‡ Spring panic.

Mining.

ENORMOUS COAL DEPOSITS IN TENNESSEE.—Gen'eral J. T. Wilder, of Rockwood Iron Works, been in the city for a short time. He informs that the miners in his coal mines, are now struck upon a deposit of coal, which exceeds in thickness anything ever known in the world. air course driven across the bed shows it to be r one hundred feet thick! This is more than be the thickness of anthracite coal in Pennsylvania.—*Knoxville Press & Herald.*

NEVADA.—WHITE PINE MILLING OPERATIONS. The *News* says that in a short time the milling capacity will be increased to one hundred and ity-five stamps, and will be doubled during the inner. Meanwhile, large stacks of ore are accumulating at the mine dumps. It is not unlikely district will turn out $150,000 to $200,000 a k in a few months hence, and $500,000 is proped for July, to begin with. The shipments n this source will partly meet the enlarged dend for money created by the rapid industrial elopment of California and Nevada.

GIANT POWDER.—A correspondent asks: "What a giant powder consist of, and where is it le?" It is nothing but nitro-glycerine, reduced ryness by combining it with hydrated silica. latter substance may be obtained from *water*-s by means of an acid which precipitates a tinoüs mass from it. This mass when dry is mpalpable powder, and such is found in natural oats in California, where giant powder is manatured, Mr. Nobel, who patented several exive, also posesses a patent for this one. It so manufactured in New York City, but we not at liberty to publish the manufacturer's ie without his permission.—*N. Y. Mining rnal.*

OLD AT EEL RIVER.—A gentleman who lately ted Eel River, and whose experience in mines minerals is very extensive, favored us with a at our office lately, He is a resident of Westeland and has no interest, whatever, in the River Gold Mines, or any other property e, and he has placed in our hands the following memorandum:—Accompanied by a highly ectable and intelligent gentleman, I visited al River" on Wednesday last, and examined gold formation lately discovered in that locaThe lode, where uncovered, is about four ies, and evidently gold bearing. The quartz a matrix of slate enclosed by what I would call outtain Limestone," resembling in some dethe " Whin Rock," accompanying gold bearquartz in Nova Scotia. I had a piece of quartz h was taken from the lode crushed and washshout half pound weight) and which gave fiveths of gold. I consider the prospects are sufftly encouraging to warrant a judicious expenre of capital in prospecting the property.—*St. is Telegraph.*

THE GILLAN CO.'s MILL, MADOC.—The maery of this mill, formerly known as the Gilbert urley, has, since its removal to Marmora, been erially improved,—the alterations being adoptafter consultation with Mr. J. H. Dunstan, by Gilbert, who deserves great credit for the good substantial manner in which the works have erected. The building is 30 feet by 30, with ddition of 12 by 14 feet, for the office. In main building there are three story floors, (the steps of a staircase) of 10 feet each. On the floor stands the stamps-battery, the frame of h is large enough to admit of ten stamps g erected, though only five are put in at pre; on the second floor is, first, a copper-plated lgamated *strake*, 6 feet long, which joins the ery,—and at the end of the strake is placed grinding-pan; and on the bottom-floor are the er and a copper-plated amalgamated dischargg, on leaving which, the slime passes through es and traps to the outside of the mill. Thus quartz has only to be fed into the battery, and

needs no handling a second time, as every portion of the machinery clears itself completely. It consequently requires only one man on a tour to work the whole mill, which is driven by a 30-horsepower turbine water-wheel. The cost of milling, we understand, will not exceed one dollar per ton to the Company; this mill is superior to any yet erected in the country. Three weeks ago, the mill being very nearly completed, the Company sent for Mr. Dunstan, to examine the machinery and superintend the first run. The mill was ready to run, on the 29th of June. After working thirty tons of surface soil, quartz and everything that came from the shaft, he decided to clean up; and in presence of a large number of visitors, in a short time turned out a nice bar of gold which caused much rejoicing, the results of 30 tons being $6 per ton.—*Madoc Mercury.*

LEAD.—We have been shown a specimen of lead from the Galway Mines which came down while the men were "drifting" a few days ago. It is perhaps 15 or 18 inches in diameter, flat, like a turtle somewhat, and weighs 33 lbs. It is almost wholly the genuine article, and verifies the extraordinary wealth of these regions behind us. We are glad to learn that the works will soon be advanced in greater force than heretofore. A steam engine is about to be set in motion, and with the encouragement now dropping down on the shareholders almost unsought, the Galway Lead Mines will speedily be more widely and favorably known than ever.—*Peterborough Review.*

THE EEL RIVER GOLD DISCOVERY.—In regard to this the Woodstock *Acadian* of Friday says:— "It is well that the very truth should be known. We understand that gold *has* been found in the locality named. Of the existence of extensive seams of quartz there can be no doubt. Whether this quartz contains gold in sufficient abundance to make its crushing a profitable business is the point, and it is a point which is as yet utterly undecided. But means are in operation by which the value of the quartz will be thoroughly tested. and that soon. Meanwhile it is scarcely worth while for any one to take the gold fever severely."

—The Chicore, from Lake Superior, brought down 16 packages of silver ore from the Thunder Bay Mining Co'y. valued at $20,000.

Railway News.

GREAT WESTERN RAILWAY.—Traffic for week ending July 2, 1869.

Passengers	$37,176 22
Freight	28,271 52
Mails and Sundries	2,093 72
Total Receipts for week	$67,541 46
Coresponding week, 1868	60,048 65
Increase	$7,492 81

NORTHERN RAILWAY.—Traffic receipts for week ending July 16, 1869.

Passengers	$3,269 33
Freight and live stock	12,589 43
Mails and sundries	337 55
	$16,196 31
Corresponding Week of '68	12,215 35
Increase	$3,980 96

WOODEN RAILWAYS.—The *Sherbrooke Gazette* says:—At the Stratford and Garthby meetings of the 14th inst., $7,000 worth of stock was taken in the Sherbrooke and Kenebec railway; at Lambton, on Thursday, $25,000; North Winslow, $15,000; total $47,000. The Municipalities of Aylmer, Forsyth, Shenly, and Tring having a gross population of 66,000, will be good for $60,000 at least, as these municipalities are liable to contribute money from market, and equally well accomodated by the proposed route as those who have already declared themselves by taking stock. Friday, South Wins-

low confirmed the impression made on behalf of wooden railroads versus iron. The belief is fast becoming fixed in the public mind, notwithstanding all efforts to the contrary, that in the present condition of a thinly settled country, such as that between Sherbrooke and Chaudiere river, a wooden, and not an iron road is the only financially possible solution to the problem of supplying the means of transit for these now insolated localities.

Law Report.

MARINE INSURANCE—UNSEAWORTHINESS.—In this case the court, though of opinion that defendants were entitled to a nonsuit, granted a new trial, suggesting whether, if evidence were given of defendant's knowledge of the age, build, and materials of which the vessel was built at the time of the insurance, it might not be held to modify the condition as to unseaworthiness, so as to make it subordinate to the particular vessel being assured. On the new trial, one H was called by the plaintiff, who proved that he, as agent of the defendants, accepted the risk on the vessel in question; that he had seen, but did not examine her, but judged her wholly from the registry, and insured her as B 1; that a B 1 vessel would be insured as readily as an A 1, the charge on freight being the same, and the seaworthiness would be expected to be the same, though the A 1 would not be so likely to go to pieces.

Held, that these facts did not bring the case within the principle laid down in Burgess *v.* Wickham, 3 B. & S. 669, and Clapham *v.* Langton, 34 L. J., Q. B. 40; and.therefore, that the new evidence did not alter the position of the parties, and that a nonsuit has been properly directed.— *Coons v. Ætna Ins. Co.,* 19. C. P. Rep. 239.

WAREHOUSE RECEIPTS.—When two partners, not carrying on business or warehousemen, have their partnership stock in their own cellar, a receipt given by one to the other for that stock, though in the form of a warehouse receipt, is not a warehouse receipt within the meaning of Con. Stat. of C. ch. 54.—*Ontario Bank v. Newton,* 19 C. P. Rep. 258.

FIRE INSURANCE—Cancellation of Policy.— *Declaration* on a fire policy, averring an assignment of the policy with the assent of the defendants to H. B., and that the action was brought as well on behalf of H. B. as on plaintiffs' behalf.

Plea, on equitable grounds that H. B. was never interested in the insured property, and that before the loss the policy was cancelled by an arrangement between plaintiffs and defendants by which a policy on other goods was substituted and the unearned part of the premium credited by defendants to plaintiff on account of the new policy.

Held, on demurrer a good answer in equity also a good legal defence.—*Miall v. Western Ins. Co.,* 19 C. P. Rep. 270.

TELEGRAPH ENTERPRISE.—Another great European telegraph project is on foot. A company just formed in London has purchased, with concessional rights, the following cables, namely: 1st, Denmark to England, from Sonderwig to Newbiggin, actual distance 534 miles. 2nd. Denmark to Norway, from Hirtshals to Arendal, actual distance, 60 miles. 3rd. Denmark to Russia, from Moen to Bornholm, and Bornholm to Libau, actual distance, 304 miles. 4. Norway to Scotland, from Egersund to Peterhead, actual distance, 270 miles. 5th. Sweden to Russia, from Grislehamn to Nystad, actual distance, 96 miles. Of these, the three first are already laid, and have been for some time working; the fourth is shipped on board ready for laying; and the arrangements for the fifth are in course of completion, and both the latter are to be laid at the risk and cost of the old companies. The new company undertakes the working, and will be entitled to the receipts from the first of June. The cost of purchase was $3,500,000. The ultimate intention of the company is a connection with North America by the Russian dominions.

THE CANADIAN MONETARY TIMES AND INSU-
RANCE CHRONICLE *is printed every Thursday evening and distributed to Subscribers on the following
morning.*

*Publishing office, No. 60 Church-street, 3 doors
north of Court-street.*

Subscription price.—

Canada $2.00 *per annum.*
. *England, stg.* 10s. *per annum.*
United States (U.S. Cy.) $3.00 *per annum.*
*Casual advertisements will be charged at the rate
of ten cents per line, each insertion.*

*Address all letters to "*THE MONETARY TIMES.*"
*Cheques, money orders, &c. should be made pay-
able to* J. M. TROUT, *Business Manager, who alone
is authorized to issue receipts for money.*

☞ *All Canadian Subscribers to* THE MONETARY
TIMES *will receive* THE REAL ESTATE JOURNAL
without further charge.

The Canadian Monetary Times.

THURSDAY, JULY 22, 1869.

THE INSPECTION OF TRANSFER BOOKS.

At the last meeting of the shareholders of the Bank of Montreal, a motion was made to the effect that the transfer books be opened to the inspection of shareholders within bank hours. The motion was opposed by the chairman, Mr. King and others, and finally shelved. The chief grounds of objection urged against opening the transfer books to shareholders were that it was illegal, inconvenient, not in conformity with English or Irish practice, and that shareholders might be imposed upon by fictitious sales. Mr. King considered the inconvenience depended entirely upon the number of shareholders who chose to look at the books. The double liability afforded no reason for shareholders making themselves acquainted with the details of the transfer book, as that liability is a protection to the public, and consequently on such ground the right to inspect would

be in the public, not in the shareholders. The double liability principle, as the law now stood, he considered worth very little, and if he could influence legislation he would have it abolished altogether.

In so far as the legal right is concerned, it would seem to be clear that shareholders are entitled to inspect the transfer book. One counsel to whom the case of the Bank of Montreal was presented for his opinion sustains that view and considers there is nothing in the charter or the by-laws of the bank impairing the right. The only prohibition established by the charter as to the right of inspection by a shareholder, who is not a Director, is confined to the account of a person dealing with the bank. The charter itself, therefore, may be said to recognize, in effect, the right of such shareholders to have free access to the transfer books. Mr. Abbott also considered that there would be nothing illegal in opening the transfer books, but he thought that to do, so was within the discretion of the Directors. In Smith on Banking it is laid down—that, "Fund holders and those who have an interest in the funds have a right, which the Court of Chancery will enforce, of inspecting and copying entries relating to the stock in which they are interested, and the transfers of such stock, and the bank is bound to furnish to such persons on application, a list of books containing entries relating to the stock in which they are interested."

Independently of the legal right, there are grounds of expediency which may fairly be relied upon in support of the position of those contend for a free inspection. This side of the case has been well put by Mr. Crawford in a letter to a Montreal journal. Promoters of all banking enterprises have drawn special attention to the names of subscribers as an evidence of good faith. Should confidence become impaired every prudent man would withdraw from the partnership and as it is desirable for one to know the character of those associated with him, the only means of acquiring that information is by first learning their names from the transfer book. The published annual list is regarded as a poor compromise for the book itself. The double liability furnishes a strong reason, as during monetary excitements it is well to take soundings from time to time respecting the general schemes of shareholders. Should a large order from England or elsewhere be transmitted to a bank to dispose of stock it is considered right to place it beyond the power of any one connected with the institution, either directly or indirectly, to speculate thereon. In the event of a disastrous failure or embezzlement being telegraphed to a bank, directors or managers should not be placed

in a position by which they could reduce their own stock and advise their friends to do so likewise, to the detriment of the general shareholder. Should a bonus be resolved upon, the only effectual method of providing against the forestalling of the stock by those in the secret, is the inspection of the transfer book. Should directors lose confidence in themselves or grow tired of deceiving shareholders and the public by purchasing stock, the transfer book would reveal it.

From the above summary of the arguments for and against, it will be seen that there is a show of reason on both sides. But, on the whole, we are disposed to think that the unchecked license to inspect transfer books would be attended with so much inconvenience and so little real advantage that the present system of restraint had better be retained. Were the books kept open the possessor of one share might inflict considerable injury to individuals by noising abroad dealings which are now invested with a character of privacy, and also injure a banking institution very seriously. If any particular advantage would accrue from keeping the transfer book lying open it would be enjoyed by shareholders resident at or near the Head Office, perhaps to the prejudice of non-resident shareholders. It might, furthermore, give rise to speculation, to nominal sales, and to various devices for bulling and bearing the market successfully. If the book were kept open for general inspection, there would be nothing to prevent an eager crowd of speculators in stocks from creating a daily tumult in the bank premises. As to the vantage ground held by Directors, their position necessarily secures it to them and no inspection of transfer books will deprive them of it. A list of shareholders is now published annually; perhaps the more solid objections to the present system might be met by the semi-annual publication of the share list.

BANK OF TORONTO.

The report of the Directors of this Bank is one of the most satisfactory documents of the kind ever presented to Canadian Shareholders. We say it unhesitatingly, that no better exhibit is to be found among the records of Canadian banking. After providing for losses, &c., the net profits for the year amounted to $140,423; the rest was increased by $75,000, and a balance of $3,847.42 carried forward. The rest now amounts to the large sum of $300,000, or 37½ per cent. of the capital. The statement appended to the report will be found more explicit, and much more full than such documents usually are. We notice, with great pleasure, the item "rebate of interest on notes discounted $21,·822," in its proper place among the liabilities.

s feature is somewhat novel, in Canada, it has hitherto appeared in the statements :he Scotch banks, and of the Joint Stock ks of England. The neglect to include h rebate among liabilities, always appeared us to be culpable. It will be observed, her that discounts current are distinguished n discounts overdue. This also is com-ndable.

'he prosperity of this bank has a peculiar rest for Toronto. The assistance it lends our most important branches of trade, ders its existence and welfare a matter of at importance, while the admirable charac- of its management supplies, the best wer to the self sufficient sneers of Mon-il brokers, who circulate slanders about banking skill of the west. The extensive wledge of business, and business men, sessed by the President and Vice-Presi-it, have proved of great service to this ik. Such knowledge wielded with the l of a Cashier so accomplished as Mr. gue, and so well versed in the science and of banking may be regarded as the secret the Bank's great success.

RONTO AND NIPISSING RAILWAY.

'he company which has undertaken to ld this road has at length taken shape. the 21st the election of directors took ce, with the following result : George dlaw, 1,131 votes ; W. F. McMaster, 16 ; Wm. Gooderham, Jr., 1,098 ; Joseph ald, 1,086 ; Robert Elliot, 1,060 ; T. C. aholm, 1,008 ; J. C. Fitch, 998 ; James Smith, 992 ; John Shedden, 867. The eting was harmonious, and congratulations 'e exchanged on the success which had wned the efforts of those who have so rgetically brought the project to a head. . C. J. Fox was present, and expressed iself fully satisfied, after a personal in-ction of the line of route, that the original imate of $15,000 per mile would be ample. dr. Laidlaw, although placed at the head the poll, declined to act as director. His gnation is to be regretted, but we can reciate his motives, and respect him all more for sticking to his determination. ile on the subject, we may be permitted iay a few words respecting the man whose omitable energy and perseverance, com-ed with an ability which was at first ques-i, then admitted, and is now recognized and led, were the heart and soul of the enter. ie. Few men are willing to devote them-res so thoroughly to a scheme such as s railway is, and still fewer are competent oring it to a successful issue. The tact, zeal, the perseverance displayed by him n the first, mark him out as one for whom

a place on a board of directors is no fitting reward. With all the energy of the most enterprising of Yankees, he wrote, and spoke, and worked ; with all the tenacity of a Scotchman, he held on his course, worrying enemies and hugging friends with a bear-like squeeze, until some how or other his recruits fell into line, submitted to their fate, and marched as joyfully as possible towards Lake Nipissing. At one time in the van, at an-other in the rear, but always sufficiently near to keep would-be stragglers up to the mark, Mr. Laidlaw was ever in motion—a veritable guide, philosopher and friend to his com-patriots. Such men as he, in spite of their restless, uncomfortable energy, are those who bring progress to a country, and should have such rewards as public benefactors are entitled to receive. The new Board is made up of live men, and we hope that the enthu-siasm of their inaugural proceedings will be but the herald of prompt and honorable action.

THE ROYAL CANADIAN BANK.

It is announced that Mr. Yarker, seeing the difficult position in which he was placed, by the acceptance of the appointment as ex-aminer, requested that he should be relieved of a portion of the task assigned to him, and that the directors invited Mr. Fisher, of the Ontario Bank, to co-operate with him. It is intended, we understand, that Mr. Yarker shall confine himself entirely to passing upon the paper and securities of the bank at the head office as well as at the agencies, and Mr. Fisher confine himself to the matters con-nected with internal management, such as deposits, cash, &c. This is all very well, but we cannot see the advisability of limiting Mr. Fisher's duties to the mere counting of the cash. The real work is that which Mr. Yarker has kept under his own control, and unless Mr. Fisher co-operate therein, of course, the report to be made will be that of Mr. Yarker exclusively. Mr. Fisher may tell us how much cash is on hand, but what the share-holders want to know is the value of the paper estimated by an impartial authority. This division of labour, if limited in its scope as above stated, does not meet the objections urged by us last week. The general impres-sion is, that Mr. King wishes to buy out the Royal, and such transparent pieces of humbug as this division of labor is, serve but to con-firm it. The purchase of the Commercial by the Merchants', and the rise of the latter to its present position, both in the east and west, show Mr. King that a rival of power and in-fluence is on the heels of the Bank of Mon-treal. The Merchants' is increasing its busi-ness very fast, and with its new capital taken up (which will undoubtedly be the case), the

Bank of Montreal will have to confront a rival firmly rooted in the good will of the people of Ontario. There is then good reason for supposing that, if the Royal is to go into the market, Mr. King will not be among the last to send up a tender. Mr. Yarker is his officer, and will learn exactly how it is with the Royal. Such information cannot but be of service in case of competition. Mr. King may wish the Royal to resume business ; he has expressed himself to that effect. But, like every other zealous officer, he has the interest of his own institution at heart, and will be guided in his action by the dictates of expediency.

As outsiders, having no special information respecting the motives of the Board, we view the whole matter from the stand point of the public welfare and the interests of the shareholders. But we must say that the course pursued does seem to us to be unwise. Mr. Fisher is quite competent to pass upon the bank's paper, he is implicitly trusted by his own Directors and by the public and we fail to see why he should be asked merely to count the cash. We believe it will be found that reports of an exaggerated character have been circulated to the detriment of the Royal and an impartial investigation will reveal their incorrectness. It will be furthermore found that the details of management are in more perfect order than has been supposed by some, and it will be made apparent that the necessity for suspension arose entirely from a loss of public confidence not from want of ability to withstand ordinary pressure. If all this be made manifest, resumption will be but a question of expediency. We have heard that some large depositors have agreed to stand by the institution and that the Gov-ernment balance will not be hastily with-drawn. However, that may be, there can be but one opinion relative to the nature of the investigation now being made.

The latest intelligence is to the effect that Mr. Fisher has declined to act. One can readily understand why that gentleman should be unwilling to place himself in a false posi-tion, as undoubtedly would be the case if he were to be hampered by the arrangement above referred to.

THE GORE DISTRICT MUTUAL.

The report of the Directors of this Mutual Fire Company will be found worthy of atten-tive reading. The system of "daily assess-ment" is practised by that company and, after two year's trial, the Directors claim that great benefit has resulted from it. Most, if not all, of the other Mutuals assess their policies up to a given day, say 31st December in each year. The Gore District assesses each of its policies yearly upon the day of the month in which it was issued. The result is that under the "daily assessment" system an assessment for loss may be made on the very day of advice, while under the other system the assessment can only take place sometime after the occurrence of losses. Further, in one case revenue is constantly coming in, while in the other, the bulk of revenue comes in during one or two months in the year. The working of the system is more clearly shown by the statement in the report.

There is a short reference to the discussion concerning the propriety of Mutual Companies adopting the Cash System which shows that the question is one of general interest. When the various Mutuals have expressed their opinions we shall treat the question more fully. We agree with the Directors in their estimate of the importance of united action in securing uniformity of rates and such statutory provisions as will place all companies on a common basis. At the meeting of the representatives of Mutual Companies held in Hamilton, on the 29th of April, this seemed to be generally acquiesced in.•

The Gore District is evidently making good progress. The receipts for the last year exceeded those of the year previous by $2,000, with an expenditure less by $500. The company has now in force over one thousand policies more than it had in July, 1865. It was natural, in the face of such an exhibit, that satisfaction was expressed with the manner in which the Secretary, Mr. Simons, and the Inspector, Mr. McLean, had discharged their duties. Some objection was taken to the amount of salary paid these gentlemen, but, as Mr. McGill well put it, "good men should be well paid." It is false economy to pay inadequate salaries to efficient officers. Their value is soon learned by rivals, and competent, energetic, and trustworthy men always will command their price. As regards inspectors, there seems to be an idea abroad that they are to a degree superfluities. This is quite a mistake. As a class of men they are ill-paid, considering the temptations to which they are exposed and the nature of their duties. An inspector with a stinted salary may, if possessed of an elastic conscience, make considerable additions to it in the way of perquisites, presents, &c., to say nothing of the sums of money that might be got by questionable compromises. We have heard of an inspector who levied systematically on claimants, and almost furnished a house with articles obtained as thank-offerings. We conclude, therefore, and insurance men generally will coincide with us, that a fair salary to an inspector is the best safeguard against such practices.

The President of the Gore District is an excellent business man, intelligent and fully capable of discharging the duties of his office aright. He is surrounded by a Board of practical business men. The prospects of this Company are, therefore, on all hands, of the most satisfactory character.

IT is not improbable that the British Government will sever its connection with the Bank of England. In a recent debate the Chancellor of the Exchequer announced that the Government contemplated making a new arrangement respecting the disbursement of the public funds. He spoke of the bank as "a private institution," whose sovereignty was baneful, and that it was largely maintained by means of the deposits of public money intrusted to the bank. It is objected that its management is illiberal, and that its whole policy seems to consist in embarrassing trade by making money artificially dear at the time when it should be cheap, and vice versa. It is now claimed that the time has arrived for establishing free trade in money and in banking, the same as in other departments of business. This stirring up of the "old lady" will be interesting news to those wiseacres among us who sigh for a similar institution in Canada, and would have the Bank of Montreal lifted into that position.

GRAND TRUNK RAILWAY.

Mr. Brydges has parried a good many thrusts, but in few cases with more success than in his replies to the interrogatories of Mr. Creak, who may be called the leader of the opposition to those who at present control the management of the Grand Trunk Railway. Of course Mr. Creak, or any other shareholder in the company, is justified in getting all the information respecting the property in which he has an interest, and in taking all fair means to correct errors of management, but there is a limit beyond which such endeavours cease to be productive of good results. The following is the substance of Mr. Brydges replies:

Scoville never sent me a copy of the printed letter Mr. Creak refers to, and I know nothing of its contents. Scoville's price for wheels was $15 each from November, 1861, to April 1864, when he raised it to $16, at which it remained till December, 1865, after which we took what he made from materials he had on hand or had contracted for at $15 each up to June, 1867, when we ceased buying from him. In the early part of 1864 the Three Rivers concern got into difficulties, and we could not depend upon their supply. Scoville delivered all his wheels at Toronto, we carrying those used at Montreal, a distance of 333 miles, at our own cost. The consumption of wheels at Montreal is about five sixths of the whole. The carriage of Scoville's wheels from Toronto to Montreal added for bare cost at least 50c. to his price

for each wheel. We got the first wheels from Montreal in the spring of 1865 at $17 each. Finding Scoville impracticable we agreed to buy all our wheels from the Montreal Foundry at $14.50 each, delivered where we use them. All those we take at other points besides Montreal are delivered at the places we use them at the cost of the makers, we paying only $14.50. We pay now $14.50 each wheel, which is fully $1 a wheel, less than Scoville's price, carriage included. I did refuse to make a contract with Scoville, because he declined to deliver anywhere except at his works at Toronto, which, as I have said, added $1 at least to his price, as compared with the Montreal rate.

The rise of wages in 1867 and 1863 is owing to the fact that the increase in the rate of American wages culminated or reached its highest point at the end of 1866. Wages in the States to-day are at the highest point they have ever been at in my experience of sixteen years. Our staff is not larger, but each man costs more now than he did in the first half of 1866 and previously.

The increase in fuel is owing to several causes—greater proportion of soft wood supplied by contractors, financial necessities causing stock to be low, and therefore necessitating the use of green wood; and the severe unusual cold of the winter of 1867-8, causing more wood to be burned to haul the same loads.

Very few complimentary passes are issued —the exceptions being the press and Americans whose interest as controllers of freight is important, and who are invariably passed on their own lines. No passes are given to M. P's or their families or other private parties.

A few rails in our own shops are repaired where it is economy to do so by our own men at day's wages. I have examined Baines' plan, and do not consider, after careful consideration, that it is desirable to adopt it. I can give my reasons, of course if necessary, but I suppose that an opinion is all that is now needed.

The volunteer corps has not cost the company anything, the whole of the outlay being borne by the Government and the men themselves. Drilling did not and does not come out of the company's time, nor did it ever interfere with a single train. Full particulars will be found in my letters to the London office.

Old rails vary in price according to the markets in the United States, the prices ranging from $18 to $25 a ton. The charge of re-rolling at Toronto is $25.50 a ton in gold, at Portland $40 in greenbacks, and at Detroit $38½ in greenbacks.

Cleveland coal laid down at Lake Ontario ports will cost from $5.80 to 6.20 a ton in gold. It is not economy to burn it at the present price of wood. Coal is being used in the Western States very partially, and only in prairie countries where no wood can be had and seams of coal can be met with.

Experiments have so far proved that Pictou coal is not suitable for locomotives. For stationary engines, it is at least 25 per cent. less profitable than English coal.

The subsequent action of Mr. Creak, and those who support him, has been strongly condemned by the English railway press. Herapath's Railway Journal, referring to Mr. Creak's action, denounces it as un-English, and likely to be detrimental to the company's fare. It inquires : "Since the meeting which Mr. Brydges attended and gave explanations, where he was very well and even lially received, what has occurred to jus- 'a renewal of the agitation against him ? r play is a jewel, and we will be no parto an agitation which will be simply aning, and can do no good." The *Railway les* says : "The circular is high-toned, l-written, but unfortunately not conclu- ... It takes up a few of the mischiefs that e been so fully and so frequently dested upon in these columns, but places in foreground its disapprobation of the results of Mr. Brydges' exertions to produce rofit to the shareholders." The *Railway os* says : "The portion of the circular to ch exception must be taken by every it-minded and honorable person, is that ch refers to Mr. Brydges, and the present annoyance to which Messrs. Creak, rtridge & Co. subject him. No sooner s he leave England to resume his duties Canada, than the attack is renewed, and ssrs. Creak, Hartridge & Co. are so insible to every feeling of fair-dealing and tlemanly conduct, that in their circular y denounce the directors for not supporta resolution calling upon Mr Brydges to ign."

ly way of answer to certain newspaper iments on a recent discussion in the New mpshire Legislature, Mr. Brydges has lished the following :

'I have a copy of the report made by the mmissioners, and after stating that they l two-thirds of the road 'in good running dition and safe running order,' and that other third needs repairs, they go on to te as follows :

"We also find the superstructure of the ad, the masonry and bridges are of the st workmanship, and we think cannot be rpassed in this State or the United States. his road has many disadvantages to connd against. Snow is upon the track nearly x months of the year, and at times in such antities as to nearly suspend travel. The ad has but one track, and with so many ng trains daily, leaves but little time to pair the track between trains. With all e contending elements incident to all ads, and especially to roads in this latide, we are of the opinion that there is no use for serious alarm, nothing which may ot be speedily remedied. We have the rongest assurance that the road will be it in a safe condition the present season. ie ties are already upon the line of the ad,' and the Managing Director assures 1 that the iron is negotiated for, and will laid immediately.'

'I may add, as a matter of fact, that the ins on the Portland line, since the snow appeared, have been, and are, running h perfect regularity ; that freight trains not continually off the track ; and that number of passengers and amount of ight that is now passing over the road is zely in excess of last year, and much ater than ever before since the line was med.

'There is no doubt about the fact that re are strong and powerful interests in ston and some parts of the New England tes who dislike to see the yearly increasbusiness which passes over the Grand nk Railway, and who try to check that ffic by making false statements as to the

condition of the "English Railway," as they call it.

"The New Hampshire Commissioners told me, after they had thoroughly inspected the line, that they found it in far better condition than the stories they had heard had led them to expect, and that in many important particulars it was far superior to any line in the New England States.

"I take the opportunity to add what are simple matters of fact, that the Grand Trunk Railway is throughout, at this moment, in a better condition than it has been at this time of the year since 1860 ; that its trains are throughout running with great regularity ; and that, notwithstanding the general dullness of trade in Canada, the receipts of the railway are increasing at the rate of $20,000 a week, which is the best evidence of its increasing usefulness to the country."

There is no doubt that the Grand Trunk had to contend with unusually great difficulties last winter, and that allowances must be made for other troubles, including the exaggerated reports which competition sets afloat respecting the state of the line. But the road is improving, traffic is extending, and the country's demands upon its carrying capacity are increasing every day. Even if such were not the case, we do not clearly see what is to be gained by persecuting the Managing Director. He went to England, gave an account of his stewardship, and was sustained. Instead of calling on him by circular to resign, or to do impossible things, it would be better for the dissatisfied to devote their attention, if there be mismanagement, to the proper object of attack—the Board of Directors. Mr. Brydges has his hands full on this side of the ocean.

Commercial.

Petrolia Oil Trade.

(From a Correspondent.)

PETROLIA, July 19, 1869.

There are at present in the oil district of Petrolia 50 wells in active operation, producing daily 600 brls. of crude oil ; among the best of which are:

McDougal, 1 well yielding	75 brls. per day.	
St. Catharines, 2 do. each........	40 "	"
Parsons & Ellwood, 2 do..........	50 "	"
Lancy, 3 do.	50 "	"
Noble, 2 do.	50 "	"
Marshall & Goodrich, 1 do.......	40 "	"

Besides these, we have the two new strikes, viz.: McGarry and Lancaster, neither of which have been fairly tested ; the rest will yield from 5 to 10 brls. per day each. There is a great difficulty in managing these wells, so that some of them are kept idle for three days in the week. We have also here four large refineries whose aggregate capacity amounts to 1,500 brls. per week ; all these are entirely devoted to the export trade. We have also to note the refineries of London.

Duffield & Bro.,.....capacity, 1,000 brls. per week.		
Spencer & Keenlyside, " ...	600 "	"
Waterman & Bro.	600 "	"

Together with the great works of Eagleheart & Co. (of New York), who have nearly completed a large refinery, capacity not given. All these have turned their attention to the export trade, adopting different treatments, some using Allan's, some Benjamin's, and some Nicol's. The Hamilton firm have already exported between 5,000 and 6,000 brls. with success ; excepting a little drawback in color, their oil will fairly compete with any American No. 1.

The crude oil market here is controlled by a

combination got up amongst the largest producers, who hold crude oil at $1.62½ per barrel, for home consumption, and $1.25 for export trade ; parties buying for export having to give bonds that the oil will be sent out of the country. In my next I will give you an account of all the new wells at present being drilled, and give you the statement of their production or failure, as the case may be. Refined oil can be bought here, at about 20c. per gallon for No. 1.
P.

Toronto Market.

PRODUCE.—The continued prospect of a bountiful harvest tends to bear down the market for breadstuffs. During the past week the gain in prices noted the previous week has been to some extent lost ; the general disinclination to operate in wheat and flour even at a concession on quoted rates shows that there is no confidence felt in the maintenance of prices. Still the ruling rates are very low rendering it probable that the influence of a large yield of breadstuffs upon the condition of the markets has already been discounted. With flour under $4 a barrel, farmers would find it more profitable to cultivate other products to the comparative neglect of wheat. *Wheat*—Receipts 7,220 bush. and 5,340 bush. last week. The market has ruled dull and weak the tendency of prices being downward ; very little business doing. *Oats*—Supply light and demand active ; as high as 57c. has been paid for western, and eastern sold at 53c. for car loads. *Peas*—Nothing whatever doing in lots ; 70c. is paid on the street. *Corn* is nominal at 65c., being a little firmer. *Flour*—Receipts 1,760 brls. and 1,425 brls. last week ; the market is dull and unsettled with few sales at reduced prices. There were some sales of No. 1 super. at $4.45 to $4.50 ; Fancy sold at $4.65 and extra at the same price. *Meal*—Oatmeal continues steady at $5.75 to $6 for small lots of choice ; cornmeal is firm at $3.75 to $4.

PROVISIONS.—*Butter* has been offered more freely and has met with a fair demand for the Montreal market at quotations. *Eggs*—The market is steady and the supply small. *Cheese* is weaker owing to advices of lower markets in England. *Pork*—nominal as quoted.

GROCERIES.—*Sugars* are firm and about ⅛c. higher on the week.

LIQUORS.—In consequence of the advance in corn spirits are somewhat dearer.

FREIGHTS—The Grand Trunk rates to Liverpool are:—Flour 4s. stg. per bbl. ; wheat 8s. 6d. stg., per quarter ; and boxed meats 55s. per ton.

The following are the Grand Trunk Railway Company's summer rates from Toronto to the undermentioned stations, which came into force on the 19th ult.:—Flour to all Stations from Belleville to Lynn, inclusive 25c.; grain, per 100 lbs., 13c ; flour to Prescott, 30c.; grain 15c ; flour to all stations between Island Pond and Portland, inclusive, 75c ; grain, 38c ; flour to Boston, 80c, gold ; grain 40c ; flour to Halifax, 90c ; flour to St. John, 85c.

Halifax Market.

BREADSTUFFS.—July 13.—Our markets for Flours, up to Friday of last week, continued inactive, with a downward tendency, and disposition on the part of holders to effect sales. Some lots of Supers changed hands at $5.60. The more favorable reports from the west have given tone to the markets, and have advanced the views of holders. Supers are now held at $6.00 without buyers. Our stocks of Canadian are very light. Extras are in limited demand at quotations ; Fancy inactive and nominal ; No. 2 dull and unchanged. We quote White Wheat Extra (Fall), $6.25 ; Fancy, $6.25 ; Superfine, $6.00 ; No. 2, $5.00 ; Cornmeal, (K.D.), $3.75 ; F.G., $3.00 ; Oatmeal, (N.S.) $5.50 to $6.00 ; Canada, $5.00 (dull).

Imports from January 1st to July 13th, 1868 and 1869.—

	Bbls. Flour.		Bbls. Cornmeal.
1869.........	80391		19145
1868.........	92979		30964

WEST INDIA PRODUCE.—Sugars and Molasses continue inactive at nominal rates. Several lots of the former offered at auction were withdrawn, buyers and sellers being too far apart in their views. The disposition of the holders of Sugar is to realize, and favors buyers. Molasses has not been pressed on the market recently, as no outlet is presented at present, and transactions are limited. Rum is in fair demand—prices unchanged.

FISH AND OIL.—Codfish continue in active demand for local wants, with light stocks. Pickled Fish are in request for shipment at full rates. The demand for Cod Oil continues active, and stocks are still light. Seal Oils are coming forward, and are offering at quotations without transactions. Petroleum dull and nominal, with large stocks.

EXCHANGE.—Bank Drafts, London, at 60 days, at 13 per cent. Montreal sight, 4 per cent. St. John, N.B., 3 per cent. prem.—*R. C. Hamilton & Co.'s Circular.*

Demerara Sugar Market.

The following is from Sandbach, Parker & Co's. Circular, dated, Georgetown, Demerara, 23rd June, 1869.

SUGAR.—We have no change to note in prices; since our last there has been a steady demand for America, and all good samples have been at once taken up; what little Sugar is coming forward is as a rule inferior, owing to the unfavorable weather we have had the past six months, which by stunting the growth of the Cane has injured the juice. Sales have been made at $7.25 for choice marks V.P., 18 D.S., and $4.75 for Muscovado, 12 D.S., no quantity of either, however, to be had.

MOLASSES.—There has not been a single good sample on offer during the fortnight; such as has been sold commanded 27 to 30 cents for Vacuum Pan, and 24 to 26 cents for Muscovado; but really good would command three to four cents more.

RUM.—No transactions in the Market to report.

Pennsylvania Oil Regions.

The following is from the monthly report of the Titusville *Herald*, for the month of June :—

The Production.—The production during the month under review, as ascertained from the shipments from the region, and the stocks on the first days of June and July, decreased about 100 barrels a day. This decrease was caused by the natural falling off in the product of the old wells having been greater than the enlargement occasioned by the striking of new and resuscitating of old wells.

The following table shows the production during June, the average per day, the production previously reported in 1869, and the average per day since January 1st; the product from January 1st to July 1st last year, and the average per day for the same time.

	BBLS.
Total shipment of Crude for June of bbls. of 45 galls. each	342,256
Add to reduce to bbls of 43 galls each.	15,918
Total shipment of bbls of 43 galls each	358,174
Stockton hand June 1st	365,484
Stock on hand July 1st	309,246
Deduct decrease on July 1st	56,238
Total production during June	301,936
Average per day for 30 days	10,064
Production previously reported	1,538,723
Total production since January 1st	1,840,659
Average per day for 182 days	10,174
Total production same time last year	1,689,565
Average per day same time last year, (181 days)	9,333
Average per day during June last year,	10,102

In most of the districts the production increased slightly, but the enlargement was more than counterbalanced by a falling off in other districts.

Stocks.—The annexed table shows the amount in iron tankage and the total stock at the dates named:—

	Amount in iron tanking	Total stock.
November 7, 1867, brls.	459,000	655,000
January " 1868, "	466,500	534,600
April " 1868, "	486,600	529,100
July 1, 1868, "	231,059	278,450
October " 1868, "	175,608	263,808
January " 1869, "	172,505	264,805
February " 1869, "	195,967	274,167
March " 1869, "	193,730	282,450
April " 1869, "	231,675	329,324
May " 1869, "	275,325	365,970
June " 1869, "	265,406	365,484
July " 1869, "	230,056	309,246

It will be seen by the above, that the stock on July this year was 31,000 barrels in excess of that on the same date last year.

The Shipments.—The shipments were larger during June than on any previous month this year. The daily average of crude, equivalent of 43 gallons per brl., was nearly 12,000 brls. against an average for the previous month of 10,000. The shipment of refined increased about 4,000 brls. The following were the shipments from January 1st to July 1st, 1869, and the crude equivalent:—

	Brls.
To New York	404,705
Cleveland	489,771
Boston	60,932
Philadelphia	87,970
Pittsburgh	404,667
Portland	16,844
Other points	113,208
Total	1,668,097
Difference between Crude and the Reshipped	45,705
Shipment of Crude equivalent	1,713,802

British America Assurance Company.

NOTICE IS HEREBY GIVEN that the Annual Court of proprietors of this Institution, at which the election of Directors for the ensuing year takes place, will be held in conformity with the Charter, at the House of Business of the Company, Church Street, city of Toronto, on MONDAY, the 2nd day of AUGUST, next.

The chair will be taken at twelve o'clock noon.

By order of the Board.

T. W. BIRCHALL,
Managing Director.
Per JOHN EVANS,
Accountant.

British America Assurance Office,
Toronto, 10th July, 1869.

Morton & Smith,

ACCOUNTANTS, REAL ESTATE AGENTS,

AND VALUATORS,

48 AND 50 CHURCH STREET,

TORONTO.

R. MORTON.   47-1y   J. LAMOND SMITH.

NOTICE.

Office of the Toronto, Grey and Bruce Railway Company.

A GENERAL Meeting of the Subscribers to the Capital Stock of the Toronto, Grey and Bruce Railway Company will be held at the office of the said Company, No. 46 Front Street, in the City of Toronto, on TUESDAY, the 10th day of August next, at TWELVE o'clock noon, for the purpose of electing Directors and organizing the said Company.

W. SUTHERLAND TAYLOR,
Secretary.

Toronto, July 7, 1869.

Western Assurance Company.

NOTICE is hereby given, that a dividend for the half-year, ending the 30th ult., at the rate of EIGHT per cent. per annum, upon the capital paid-up stock of this Company, has been declared, and will be payable at the Company's office, on and after Friday, the 9th inst.

By order of the Board.

BERNARD HALDAN,
Secretary.

Western Assurance Co.'s Office,
Toronto, 1st July, 1869.

Mercantile.

John Boyd & Co.,

E now in store, ex steamships "Peruvian," "North America," "Moravian," &c., their usual spring of

NEW SEASON TEAS;

CONSISTING

IG HYSONS,
UNPOWDERS,
IMPERIALS,
COLORED and UNCOLORED JAPANS,
CONGOUS,
SOUCHONGS,
TWANKEYS,
and PEKOES.

ALSO,

MORO CASTLE," "EAGLE," & "ELLA MARIA,

Direct from Havana,

[ES BRIGHT CENTRIFUGAL SUGAR.

AND 68 FRONT STREET
TORONTO.

nto, April 14th, 1869. 7-1y

Teas! Teas!! Teas!!!

FRESH ARRIVALS

NEW CROP TEAS,
VES, AND GENERAL GROCERIES,

Special Inducements given to
PROMPT PAYING PURCHASERS.

Goods sold at very Lowest Montreal Prices!
W. & R. GRIFFITH,
NTARIO CHAMBERS
of Front and Church Streets,
TORONTO
ONTARIO

E W CROP TEAS!

1,000 Half Chests

NEW CROP TEAS!

SUBSCRIBERS are now receiving a large and well lected Stock of NEW CROP TEAS, (to which they) call the attention of the Trade,) comprising.—
IG HYSONS AND HYSONS,
HYSON TWANKAYS,
TWANKAYS,
IMPERIALS,
GUNPOWDERS,
HONGS,
CONGOUS,
COLOURED JAPANS,
NATURAL LEAF JAPANS,
OOLONGS.

REFORD & DILLON.
2 & 14 WELLINGTON STREET, TORONTO.
7-1y

Robert H. Gray,
nufacturer of Hoop Skirts
AND
CRINOLINE STEEL,
IMPORTER OF
BERDASHERY, TRIMMINGS
AND
GENERAL FANCY GOODS,
43, YONGE STREET, TORONTO, ONT.

TORONTO PRICES-CURRENT.—JULY 22, 1869.

Name of Article	Wholesale Rates	Name of Article	Wholesale Rate	Name of Article	Wholesale Rates
Boots and Shoes. $ c. $ c.		**Groceries—Contin'd** $ c. $ c.		**Leather—Contin'd.** $ c. $ c.	
Mens' Thick Boots ...	2 05 2 50	Gunpowd'r c. to med..	0 55 0 70	Kip Skins, Patna	0 80 0 35
" Kip........	2 25 3 00	" med. to fine..	0 70 0 85	French	0 70 0 90
" Calf	3 20 3 70	" fine to fin'st..	0 85 0 95	English	0 65 0 80
" Congress Gaiters..	1 65 2 50	Hyson	0 45 0 80	Hemlock Calf (30 to 35 lbs.) per doz...	0 50 0 60
" Kip Cobourgs....	1 20 1 40	Imperial..........	0 42 0 80	Do. light	0 45 0 50
Boys' Thick Boots....	1 70 1 80	Tobacco, Manufact'd:		French Calf........	1 05 1 05
Youths' "	1 40 1 50	Can Leaf, ⅌ lb 5s & 10s..	0 26 0 30	Grain & Satn Cl'⅌ doz..	0 00 0 55
Women's Batts	0 95 1 90	Western Leaf, com...	0 25 0 26	Splits, large ⅌ lb.....	0 30 0 38
" Balmoral........	1 20 1 50	" Good......	0 27 0 32	" small	0 23 0 28
" Congress Gaiters..	0 90 1 50	" Fine.......	0 32 0 35	Enamelled Cow ⅌ foot..	0 20 0 21
Misses' Batts.......	0 75 1 00	" Bright fine...	0 40 0 50	Patent "	0 15 0 21
" Balmoral.......	1 00 1 20	" choice...	0 00 0 75	Pebble Grain	0 15 0 17
" Congress Gaiters..	1 00 1 30	**Hardware.**		Buff	0 14 0 16
Girls' Batts	0 65 0 85	Tin (usual prices)		**Oils.**	
" Balmoral........	0 90 1 05	Block, ⅌ lb......	0 35 0 00	Cod	0 65 0 70
" Congress Gaiters..	0 75 1 10	Grain............	0 30 0 00	Lard, extra	0 00 0 00
Children's C.T. Backs..	0 50 0 65	Pig	0 23 0 24	" No. 1.......	0 00 0 00
" Gaiters	0 65 0 90	" No. 1......	0 30 0 33	" Woollen.....	0 00 0 00
Drugs.		Cut Nails:		Lubricating, patent...	0 00 0 00
Aloes Cape.........	0 12½ 0 16	Assorted ¾ Shingles, ⅌ 100 lb. ...	2 95 3 00	" Mott's economic	0 00 0 00
Alum.............	0 05½ 0 08	Shingle alone do	3 15 3 25	Linseed, raw	0 76 0 89
Borax............	0 00 0 00	Lathe and 5 dy......	3 30 3 40	" boiled......	0 81 0 87
Camphor, refined...	0 65 0 70	Galvanised Iron:		Machinery	0 00 0 00
Castor Oil.........	0 10½ 0 23	Assorted sizes......	0 08 0 09	Olive, common, ⅌ gal..	1 00 1 60
Caustic Soda.......	0 04½ 0 05	Best No.	0 07½ 0 00	" salad	1 95 2 30
Cochineal........	0 90 1 00	" 26........	0 08 0 08½	" salad, in bots. qt. ⅌ case...	3 60 3 75
Cream Tartar......	0 30 0 35	" 28........	0 09 0 09½	Sesame salad, ⅌ gal...	1 60 1 75
Epsom Salts	0 03 0 04	Horse Nails:		Seal, pale........	0 75 0 85
Extract Logwood....	0 21 0 13	Guest'a or Griffin's assorted sizes.....	0 00 0 00	Spirits Turpentine....	0 12½ 0 00
Gum Arabic, sorts...	0 30 0 35	For W. and'l sizes....	0 18 0 19	Varnish	0 00 0 00
Indigo, Madras.....	0 90 1 00	Patent Hammer'd do..	0 17 0 18	Whale	0 90 0 90
Licorice	0 14 0 15	Iron (at 4 months):		**Paints, &c.**	
Madder...........	0 00 0 16	Pig—Gartsherrie No1..	24 00 25 00	White Lead, genuine in Oil, ⅌ 25lbs. ...	0 00 2 85
Galls	0 32 0 37	Other brands. No1...	22 00 24 00	Do. No. 1 " ...	0 00 2 00
Opium	13 00 13 50	" No2...	0 00 0 00	" 2 " ...	0 00 1 90
Oxalic Acid........	0 26 0 25	Bar—Scotch, ⅌100 lb..	2 25 2 50	" 3 " ...	0 00 1 65
Potash, Bi-tart.....	0 25 0 23	" Refined	3 00 3 85	White Zinc, genuine..	3 00 3 00
" Bichromate...	0 15 0 20	" Swedes	5 00 5 50	White Lead, dry	0 00 2 50
Potass Iodide	3 90 4 50	Hoops—Coopers...	3 00 3 25	Red Lead	0 07½ 0 08
Senna	0 12½ 0 60	" Band	3 00 3 25	Venetian Red, Eng'h..	0 0½ 0 08½
Soda Ash	0 02½ 0 04	Boiler Plates	3 25 3 50	Yellow Ochre, Fren'h..	0 0½ 0 08½
Soda Bicarb	0 00 4 00	Canada Plates	3 75 4 00	Whiting	0 85 1 25
Tartaric Acid.......	0 40 0 45	Union Jack	0 00 0 00	**Petroleum.**	
Verdigris	0 35 0 40	Pontypool........	3 25 4 00	(Refined ⅌ gal.)	
Vitriol, Blue........	0 08 0 10	Swansea	3 90 4 00	Water white, car'l'd....	0 20 0 21
Groceries.		Lead (at 4 months):		" small lots...	0 22 0 23
Coffee:		Bar, ⅌ 100 lbs.....	0 06½ 0 07	Straw, by car load....	0 00 0 00
Java, ⅌ lb.	0 22@0 28	Sheet "	0 00 0 00	" small lots....	0 00 0 00
Laguayra, "	0 17 0 18	Shot	0 7½ 0 07½	Amber, by car load...	0 00 0 00
Rio.., "	0 15 0 17	Iron Wire (net cash):		" small lots....	0 00 0 00
Fish:		No. 6, ⅌ bundle....	2 70 2 80	Benzine	0 00 0 00
Herrings, Lab. split..	0 00 0 00	" 9.........	3 10 3 20	**Produce.**	
" round......	0 00 0 00	" 12.......	3 40 3 50	Grain:	
" scaled.....	0 38 0 35	" 15.......	4 30 4 40	Wheat, Spring, 60 lb..	1 00 1 05
Mackerel, smallkitts..	0 00 0 00	Powder:		" Fall 60 "...	1 00 1 05
Loch. Her. wh's firks..	2 50 2 75	Blasting, Canada....	3 50 0 00	Barley..... 43 "...	0 00 0 00
" half " ...	1 25 1 50	FF "	4 25 4 50	Peas........ 60 "...	0 53 0 57
White Fish & Trout...	6 00 6 00	FFF "	4 75 5 00	Oats........ 34 "...	0 53 0 57
Salmon, saltwater....	14 00 15 00	Blasting, English ...	4 00 5 00	Rye......... 56 "...	0 56 0 00
Dry Cod, ⅌ 112 lbs...	4 50 5 00	FF " loose..	5 00 6 00	Seeds:	
Fruits:		FFF "	6 00 6 50	Clover, choice 60 "...	0 00 0 00
Raisins, Layers	1 90 2 00	Pressed Spikes (4 mos):		" com'n 68 "...	0 00 0 00
" M. R.......	1 90 1 50	IC Coke	7 50 8 50	Timothy, cho'e 4 "...	0 00 0 00
" Valentias....	0 8 0 6½	IC Charcoal.......	10 50 11 00	" in't to good 48 "...	0 00 0 00
Currants, new.......	0 4½ 0 0½	IX "	13 50 14 00	Flax .... 56 "...	0 00 0 00
Clayed, ⅌ gal.......	0 48 0 04	DC "	8 00 8 50	Flour (per brl.):	
Figs	0 11 0 12	DX "	9 50 0 00	Superior extra,.....	0 00 0 00
Molasses:		Tin Plates (net cash):		Extra superfine,....	4 80 4 70
Clayed, ⅌ gal.......	0 00 0 35	Regular sizes 100....	4 00 4 25	Fancy superfine,....	4 55 4 65
Syrups, Standard ...	0 55 0 60	Extra..........	4 50 5 00	Superfine No 1	4 45 4 50
" Golden	0 50 0 60	**Hides & Skins, ⅌lb.**		" No. 2.....	0 00 0 00
Rice:		Green rough	0 00 0 05	Oatmeal, (per brl.)....	5 50 6 00
Arracan	60 4 00	Green, salt'd & insp'd..	0 00 0 05½	**Provisions**	
Spices:		Cured	0 00 0 00	Butter, dairy tub ⅌ lb..	0 12½ 0 15
Cassia, whole, ⅌ lb...	0 00 0 45	Calfskins, green	0 00 0 10	" store packed...	0 12½ 0 14
Cloves	0 11 0 12	Calfskins, cured....	0 18 0 20	Cheese, new	0 11 0 12½
Nutmegs	0 00 0 00	" dry.....	0 18 0 20	Pork, mess, per brl ...	27 00 27 50
Ginger, ground	0 18 0 23	Sheepskins, ...	1 20 1 60	" prime mess,....	
" Jamaica, root..	0 20 0 25	" pelts.....	0 10 0 20	" pims	
Pepper, black.......	0 10½ 0 11	**Hops.**		Bacon, rough	0 12 0 12½
Pimento	0 08 0 09	Inferior, ⅌ lb.......	0 00 0 00	" Cumberl'd cut..	0 13 0 00
Sugars:		Medium............	0 00 0 00	" smoked.....	0 00 0 00
Port Rico, ⅌ lb.	0 9 0 9½	Good	0 00 0 00	Hams, in salt......	0 00 0 00
Cuba	0 9 0 9½	Fancy	0 00 0 00	" smoked.....	0 00 0 13
Barbadoes (bright)...	0 9½ 0 9½	**Leather, @ (4 mos.)**		Shoulders, in salt ...	0 00 0 11
Canada Sugar Refine'y, yellow No. 2, 60 ds...	0 9 0 9½	Spanish Sole, 1st qual'y heavy, weights ⅌ lb..	0 21 0 23	Lard, in kegs.......	0 14 0 15
Yellow, No. 2½......	0 9½ 0 9½	Do.1st qual middle do..	0 22 0 23	Eggs, packed	0 18 0 15
" No. 3.......	0 9½ 0 10	No. 2, light weights..	0 20 0 00	Beef Hams	0 00 0 00
Crushed X.........	0 10½ 0 11	Slaughter, heavy ...	0 00 0 00	Tallow	0 08 0 8½
" A.........	0 11½ 0 11½	Do. light.....	0 00 0 00	Hogs dressed, heavy..	0 00 0 00
Ground...........	0 12½ 0 12½	Harness, bent	0 25 0 27	" medium....	0 00 0 00
Dry Crushed	0 12 0 12½	" No. 2.....	0 00 0 00	" light.....	0 00 0 00
Extra Ground.......	0 13 0 12½	Upper heavy.......	0 30 0 33	**Salt, &c.**	
Teas:		" light....	0 33 0 34	American brls.......	1 85 1 87
Japan com'n to good..	0 48 0 50			Liverpool coarse	0 00 0 00
" Fine to choicest..	0 55 0 60			Goderich	0 00 1 53
Congou & Souch'ng..	0 60 0 75			Plaster...........	0 00 0 00
Oolong, good to fine..	0 50 0 65			Water Lime	1 50 4 C0
Y. Hyson, com to gd..	0 47½ 0 65				
Medium to choice ...	0 65 0 80				
Extra choice	0 85 0 95				

Soap & Candles.

	$ c.	$ c.
D. Crawford & Co.'s ..		
Imperial.........	0 07½	0 08
" Golden Bar	0 07	0 07½
" Silver Bar........	0 07	0 07½
Crown	0 05	0 05½
No. 1	0 03½	0 03¾
Candles	0 00	0 11

Wines, Liquors, &c.

Ale:		
English, per doz. qrts.	2 60	2 65
Guinness Dub Portr..	2 35	2 40
Spirits:		
Pure Jamaica Rum...	1 80	2 25
De Kuyper's H. Gin..	1 55	1 65
Booth's Old Tom.....	1 90	2 00
Gin:		
Green, cases.........	4 00	4 25
Booth's Old Tom, c...	6 00	6 25
Wines:		
Port, common	1 00	1 25
" fine old	2 00	4 00
Sherry, common	1 00	1 50
" medium........	1 70	1 80
"old pale or golden..	2 50	4 00
Brandy:	$ c.	$ c
Hennessy's, per gal..	2 30	2 50
Martell's " ..	2 30	2 50
J. Robin & Co.'s " ..	2 25	2 35
Otard, Dupuy & Cos..	2 25	2 35
Brandy, cases........	8 50	9 00
Brandy, com. per c...	4 00	4 50
Whiskey:		
Common 36 u. p......	0 58	0 60
Old Rye	0 77½	0 80
Malt	0 77½	0 80
Toddy	0 77½	0 80
Scotch, per gal........	1 90	2 10
Irish—Kinnahan's c...	7 00	7 50
" Dunnville's Belf't..	6 00	6 25

Wool.

Fleece, lb..............	0 30	0 31
Pulled "............	0 00	0 00

Furs.

Bear........	0 00	0 00
Beaver, ⅌ lb....	0 00	0 00
Coon	0 00	0 00
Fisher...............	0 00	0 00
Martin....	0 00	0 00
Mink.................	0 00	0 00
Otter................	0 00	0 00
Spring Rats..........	0 00	0 00
Fox.	0 00	0 00

INSURANCE COMPANIES.

ENGLISH.—*Quotations on the London Market.*

No. of Shares.	Last Dividend.	Name of Company.	Shares par val £	Amount paid.	Last Sale.
20,000		Briton Medical and General Life...	10	....	2½
50,000	7½	Commer'l Union, Fire, Life and Mar.	50	5	5½
24,000	8	City of Glasgow	25	2½	4½
5,000	9½	Edinburgh Life	100	15	33½
400,000	5—½ yr	European Life and Guarantee......	2½	11s6	4s. 0d
100,000	10	Etna Fire and Marine.............	10	1½	—
20,000	5	Guardian	100	50	53½
24,000	12	Imperial Fire.....................	500	50	352
7,500	9½	Imperial Life	100	10	17½
100,000	10	Lancashire Fire and Life.........	20	2	2⅜
10,000	11	Life Association of Scotland.......	40	7½	25
35,862	45s. p. sh	London Assurance Corporation ..	25	12½	48½
10,000	5	London and Lancashire Life	10	1	—
87,504	40	Liverp'l & London & Globe F. & L.	20	2	7½
20,000	5	National Union Life	5	1	1
20,000	12½	Northern Fire and Life	100	5	13
40,000	12 '68, bo 5s.	North British and Mercantile	50	6½	19½
40,000	50	Ocean Marine	25	5	17¾
2,500	£5 12s.	Provident Life....................	100	10	35
....	£4½ p. s.	Phœnix...........................	....	....	130½ x d
200,000	2½--h. yr.	Queen Fire and Life	10	1	21s.
100,000	3s. bo.4s	Royal Insurance..................	20	3	6½
20,000	10	Scottish Provincial Fire and Life ..	50	2½	5½
10,000	25	Standard Life	50	12	68 x d
4,000	5	Star Life	25	1½	—
		CANADIAN.			⅌ c.
8,000	4	British America Fire and Marine ..	$50	$25	53 54 x d
....	4	Canada Life	...	....	.....
4000	12	Montreal Assurance	£50	£5	135
10,000	3	Provincial Fire and Marine........	60	11	.....
....	....	Quebec Fire	40	32½	£22½ 23
....	7	" Marine..................	100	40	90
10,000	4 6 mo's.	Western Assurance................	40	9	50

RAILWAYS.	Sha's	Paid	Montr	London
Atlantic and St. Lawrence....................	£100	All.	....	58 60
Buffalo and Lake Huron	20½	"	....	2¾ 3
Do. do Preference	10	"	....	5 7
Buff., Brantf. & Goderich, 6⅌c., 1872-3-4....	100	"	....	60 70
Champlain and St. Lawrence	....	....	10 11	....
Do. do Pref. 10 ⅌ ct....	....	....	80 85	....
Grand Trunk	100	"	14 15	15 15½
Do. Eq.G. M. Bds. 1 ch. 6⅌c...........	100	"	....	85 87
Do. First Preference, 5 ⅌ c	100	"	....	54 55
Do. Deferred, 3 ⅌ ct..	100	"	....	....
Do. Second Pref. Bonds, 5⅌c...........	100	"	....	40 42
Do. do Deferred, 3 ⅌ ct...........	100	"	...	....
Do. Third Pref. Stock, 4⅌ct.	100	"	...	30 32
Do. do. Deferred, 3 ⅌ ct......	100	"	...	....
Do. Fourth Pref. Stock, 3⅌c...........	100	"	....	18 19
Do. do. Deferred, 3 ⅌ ct...........	100	"	....	....
Great Western	20½	"	14½ 15	15¾ 15⅞
Do. New	20½	18	....	....
Do. 6 ⅌ c. Bds, due 1873-76............	100	All.	....	100 102
5½⅌c Bds. due 1877-78....	100	"	....	94 96
Marine Railway, Halifax, $250, all.	$250	"	....	....
Northern of Canada, 6 ⅌c. 1st Pref. Bds.........	100	"	.. .	82 84

EXCHANGE.	Halifax.	Montr'l.	Quebec.	Toronto.
Bank on London, 60 days......				
Sight or 75 days date	12½ 13	9½ 9¾	9¾ 10¼	10⅜
Private do.	11½ 12	8½ 9	9 9½	9¾
Private, with documents..........	....	8 8½	....	....
Bank on New York..............	....	26 26½	25½ 25¾	26¾
Private do.	....	26½ 27	26½ 26¾	....
Gold Drafts do.	....	par.	par ¼ dis.	par ¼ dis.
Silver	....	4 4½	....	4 to 5½

STOCK AND BOND REPORT.

The dates of our quotations are as follows:—Toronto, July 21; Montreal, July 19; Quebec, July 17; London, July 8.

NAME.	Shares.	Paid up.	Divid'd last 6 Months	Dividend Day.	CLOSING PRICES. Toronto.	Montre'l	Quebec.
BANKS.			⅌ ct.				
British North America	$250	All.	3½ b½pc	July and Jan.	104 104½	104½ 105	104 104½
Jacques Cartier.........	50	"	4	1 June, 1 Dec.	108 108½	107½ 108½	107 107½
Montreal	200	"	6	"	160 160½	162½ 163	159¾ 160½
Nationale..................	50	"	4	1 Nov. 1 May.	107 108	107 107½	107½ 108
New Brunswick	100	"	......	......	....	....	....
Nova Scotia	200	—	7&b$3½	Mar. and Sept.	....	....	....
Du Peuple......	50	"	4	1 Mar., 1 Sept.	108½ 109	108½ 109½	108½ 109
Toronto	100	"	4	1 Jan., 1 July.	120½ 121	121 124	120 122
Bank of Yarmouth............	....	....	......	......	....	....	....
Canadian Bank of Com'e......	50	All.	......	......	102 102½	101 102	100 102
City Bank Montreal	80	"	4	1 June, 1 Dec.	99 99½	99 100	99½ 100
Commer'l Bank (St. John)....	100	"	⅌ ct.	. ...	....	..	....
Eastern Townships' Bank.....	50	"	4	1 July, 1 Jan..	....	98½ 100	98½ 100
Gore	40	...	none.	1 Jan., 1 July.	39 40	39 40	38 39
Halifax Banking Company....	...	....	......	. ....	...	...	...
Mechanics' Bank............	50	All.	4	1 Nov., 1 May.	92½ 93	93½ 94	93 93½
Merchants' Bank of Canada....	100	"	5	1 Jan., 1 July.	106½ 107	105 105½	105½ 106½
Merchants' Bank (Halifax)....	....	....	.....	.....	....	....	.. ..
Molson's Bank......	50	All.	4	1 Apr., 1 Oct.	100 109½	109 110	109 110
Niagara District Bank...	100	70	3½	1 Jan., 1 July.	...	....	....
Ontario Bank..............	40	All.	4	1 June, 1 Dec.	95 95½	94½ 95	94¾ 95
People's Bank (Fred'kton)....	100	"	......	......	....	...	. ..
People's Bank (Halifax)	20	"	7 12 m	......	....	....	....
Quebec Bank	100	"	3½	1 June, 1 Dec.	100½ 101	100 101	100½ 101
Royal Canadian Bank	50	60	4	1 Jan., 1 July.	49 50	45 50	45 50
St. Stephens Bank	100	All	.....	.....	....	....	....
Union Bank	100	"	4	1 Jan., 1 July.	104 105	105 105½	105 105½
Union Bank (Halifax)........	100	....	7 12 mo	Feb. and Aug.	....	....	.. .
MISCELLANEOUS.							
British America Land........	250	44	......	......	....	....	....
British Colonial S. S. Co....	250	32½	......	......	...	....	...
Canada Company	32½	All.	......	......	....	....	....
Canada Landed Credit Co.....	50	$50	3½	......	79 80	....	....
Canada Per. B'ldg Society....	50	All.	5	......	122½ 122¾	....	....
Canada Mining Company.....	4	90	......	......	....	....	....
Do. Inl'd Steam Nav. Co....	100	All.	15 12 m	......	....	99½ 100½	90 100½
Do. Glass Company.........	100	"	None.	......	....	35 45	....
Canad'n Loan & Investm't....	25	2½	......	......	....	....	....
Canada Agency	10	½	......	......	....	....	....
Colonial Securities Co........	...	....	.....	.....	....	....	....
Freehold Building Society....	100	All.	5	......	117 117½	....	....
Halifax Steamboat Co........	100	"	......	......	....	....	....
Halifax Gas Company........	....	....	......	. ..	....	...	....
Hamilton Gas Company......	....	....	.....	. ....	....	....	....
Huron Copper Bay Co........	4	12	20	. ....	....	30 40	....
Lake Huron S. and C........	5	102	......	......	....	...	....
Montreal Mining Consols.....	20	$15	......	. ....	....	3.00 3.25	...
Do. Telegraph Co....	40	All.	5	......	132 133	132 134	132 133
Do. Elevating Co...	00	"	5½	......	....	101 105	....
Do. City Gas Co.........	40	"	4	15 Mar. 15 Sep.	....	135 137	137 138
Do. City Pass. R,. Co....	50	"	2	......	....	111 112	111 112
Quebec and L. S.	8	84	......	.....	....	...	....
Quebec Gas Co.............	200	All.	4	1 Mar., 1 Sep.	....	...	120 125
Quebec Street R. R..........	50	25	None	......	....	....	Bks cl'd
Richelieu Navigation Co......	100	All.	7-12m	1 Jan., 1 July.	...	120 123	120 123
St. Lawrence Glass Company.	100	"	....	......	....	80 85	. ..
St. Lawrence Tow Boat Co....	100	"	......	3 Feb.	...	...	30 35
Tor'to Consumers' Gas Co....	50	"	½ m	1 My Au MarFe	107 107½	...	107 107½
Trust & Loan Co. of U. C.....	20	5	3	......	....	....	.. .
West'n Canada Bldg Soc'y....	50	All.	5	......	117½ 118	....	....

SECURITIES.	London.	Montreal	Quebec	Toronto.
Canadian Gov't Deb. 6 ⅌ ct. stg..................	....	103 104	102 103	104½ 105
Do. do. 6 do due Ja. & Jul. 1877-84........	104½ 105½	....	....	....
Do. do. 6 do. Feb. & Aug.........	102 104	....	.. .	....
Do. do. 6 do. Mch. & Sep.........	102 104	.. .	...	....
Do. do. 5 ⅌ ct. cur., 1883	93½ 94½	92½	91 92	92½ 93½
Do. do. 5 do. stg., 1885	93½ 94	91½ 92½	90 90½	92½ 93½
Do. do. 7 do. cur.,..................	....	....	......	....
Dominion 6 p. c. 1878 cy.....	....	106½ 107½	107 107½	106¾ 107½
Hamilton Corporation....	. ..	....	... ..	....
Montreal Harbor, 8 ⅌ ct. d. 1869................	..	....	......	....
Do. do. 7 do. 1870....	...	....	......	....
Do. do. 6½ do. 1883.......	....	102½ 107½	......	102 103
Do do. 6½ do. 1873..................	....	....	......	
Do. Corporation, 6 ⅌ c. 1891	....	96 96½	96½ 97	96 96½
Do. 7 p. c. stock...	....	109 110	108½ 109½	109 110
Do. Water Works, 6 ⅌ c. stg. 1878......... ..	....	96½ 97½	......	98 96½
Do. do. 6 do. cy. do.	....	....	......	96 97
New Brunswick, 6 ⅌ ct., Jan. and July	104 104½	....	.. ...	....
Nova Scotia, 6 ⅌ ct., 1875.......................	103 104	...	......	...
Ottawa City 6 ⅌ c. d. 1880	....	95 97	......	...
Quebec Harbour, 6 ⅌ c. d. 1883..................	....	....	60	....
Do. do. 7 do. do..................	....	....	65 70	....
Do. do 8 do. 1886.................	...	....	80 85	....
Do. City, 7 ⅌ c. d. 1½ years....	....	....	98 98½	....
Do. do. 7 do. 8 do.	....	....	91 92	....
Do. do. 7 do. 5 do.	....	....	96 96½	....
Do. Water Works, 7 ⅌ ct., 3 years..........	....	....	97 97½	....
Do. do. 6 do. 1½ do.	....	....	94 95	....
Toronto Corporation	....	92 94	...	....

EDINBURGH LIFE ASSURANCE COMPANY.

FOUNDED 1823.

AMOUNT OF ACCUMULATED AND INVESTED FUNDS—OVER ONE MILLION STERLING.

HEAD OFFICE—EDINBURGH.

PRESIDENT—The Rt. Hon. the Earl of Haddington.   MANAGER—D. Maclagan, Esq.   SECRETARY—Alex. H. Whytt, Esq.

CANADIAN OFFICE ESTABLISHED 1857.   WELLINGTON STREET, TORONTO.

CANADIAN BOARD—Hon. John Hillyard Cameron, M.P., Chairman.   J. W. Gamble, Esq., L. Moffatt, Esq., Hon J. B. Robinson, C. J. Campbell, Esq.   David Higgins, Secretary.

THE Edinburgh Life Assurance Company offer to the public the advantages of a Canadian as well as a British Company. They have invested a large amount of money on securities in this country, and the Toronto Local Board have full power, by an Imperial Statute, to take risks, make investments, and settle claims in Canada, without reference to the Head Office, Edinburgh. Some of the old Policies in the Company, which became claims during the past year, were settled by payment of amounts double of those originally insured, in consequence of the large bonuses that accrued on the Policies.

Every information that intending assurers may require can be obtained at the Company's Office in Toronto, or at any of the Agencies which have been established in the principal towns in Canada.

J. HILLYARD CAMERON, CHAIRMAN.   (33-1y)   DAVID HIGGINS, SECRETARY

NATIONAL LIFE INSURANCE COMPANY

OF THE

UNITED STATES OF AMERICA.

CHARTERED BY SPECIAL ACT OF CONGRESS.

CASH CAPITAL · $1,000,000, PAID IN FULL.

CANADIAN BOARD OF REFERENCE :

Hon. LUTHER H. HOLTON, M.P.

MICHAEL P. RYAN, Esq., M.P., Montreal.

GILMAN CHENEY, Esq., Manager Canadian Express Company.

H. A. NELSON, Esq., Messrs. Nelson & Wood.

JACKSON RAE, Esq., Cashier Merchants' Bank.

CHAMPION BROWN, Esq., of Messrs. Brown & Childs.

SOLICITORS.   MEDICAL REFEREE.   BANKERS.

Messrs. PERKINS & RAMSAY. | JOSEPH H. DRAKE, M.D. | THE BANK OF MONTREAL.

This company has deposited with the Canadian Government the required amount in GOLD, for benefit of Canadian Policyholders.

DOMINION OFFICE — 91 GREAT ST. JAMES STREET, MONTREAL

CHAS. A. PUTNEY,   WILLIAM DOUGLAS, Jr.,

SPECIAL AGENT.   GENERAL AGENT, CANADA.

The National Charter, the large Capital, the low rates, the common-sense plan, the definite contract, the honorable and fair dealings, the non-forfeiting policies, the perfect security, the liberal terms of the policies, the Gold Deposit in Canada, render the NATIONAL LIFE ASSURANCE COMPANY of the United States of America worthy of the patronage of every business man.

1-1y   C. G. FORTIER, AGENT, Toronto, Ont.

Insurance.   *Insurance.*   *Insurance.*

Briton Medical and General Life Association,

with which is united the

BRITANNIA LIFE ASSURANCE COMPANY.

Capital and Invested Funds............£750,000 Sterling.

ANNUAL INCOME, £220,000 STG. :

Yearly increasing at the rate of £25,000 Sterling.

THE important and peculiar feature originally introduced by this Company, in applying the periodical Bonuses, so as to make Policies payable during life, without any higher rate of premiums being charged, has caused the success of the BRITON MEDICAL AND GENERAL to be almost unparalleled in the history of Life Assurance. *Life Policies on the Profit Scale become payable during the lifetime of the Assured, thus rendering a Policy of Assurance a means of subsistence in old age, as well as a protection for a family,* and a more valuable security to creditors in the event of early death; and effectually meeting the often urged objection, that persons do not themselves reap the benefit of their own prudence and forethought.

No extra charge made to members of Volunteer Corps for services within the British Provinces.

☞ TORONTO AGENCY, 5 KING ST. WEST.

Oct 17—9-1yr   JAMES FRASER, Agent.

BEAVER
Mutual Insurance Association.

HEAD OFFICE—20 TORONTO STREET,
TORONTO.

INSURES LIVE STOCK against death from any cause. The only Canadian Company having authority to do this class of business.

E. C. CHADWICK, President.

W. T. O'REILLY, Secretary. ·   8-1y-25

HOME DISTRICT
Mutual Fire Insurance Company.

Office—North-West Cor. Yonge & Adelaide Streets,
TORONTO.—(UP STAIRS.)

INSURES Dwelling Houses, Stores, Warehouses, Merchandise, Furniture, &c.

PRESIDENT—The Hon. J. McMURRICH.
VICE-PRESIDENT—JOHN BURNS, Esq.
JOHN RAINS, Secretary.

AGENTS:
DAVID WRIGHT, Esq., Hamilton; FRANCIS STEVENS, Esq., Barrie; Messrs. GIBBS & BRO., Oshawa.   8-1y

THE PRINCE EDWARD COUNTY
Mutual Fire Insurance Company.

HEAD OFFICE,—PICTON, ONTARIO.

President, L. B. STINSON ; *Vice-President,* WM. DELONG. *Directors :* W. A. Richards, James Johnson, James Cavan, D. W. Ruttan, H. A. McFaul.—*Secretary,* John Twigg ; *Treasurer,* David Barker; *Solicitor,* R. J. Fitzgerald.

THIS Company is established upon strictly Mutual principles, insuring farming and isolated property, (not hazardous,) in *Townships only,* and offers great advantages to insurers, at low rates for *five years,* without the expense of a renewal.

Picton, June 15, 1869   9-1y

. Fire and Marine Assurance.

THE BRITISH AMERICA
ASSURANCE COMPANY.

HEAD OFFICE :

CORNER OF CHURCH AND COURT STREETS.
TORONTO.

BOARD OF DIRECTION :

Hon G. W. Allan, M L C.,	A. Joseph, Esq.,
George J. Boyd, Esq ,	Peter Paterson, Esq.,
Hon W. Cayley,	G. P. Ridout, Esq.,
Richard S. Cassels, Esq.,	E H. Rutherford, Esq.,
Thomas C. Street, Esq.	

Governor:
GEORGE PERCIVAL RIDOUT, Esq.

Deputy Governor:
PETER PATERSON, Esq.

Fire Inspector: *Marine Inspector:*
E. ROBY O'BRIEN.   CAPT. A. COURNEEN.

Insurances granted on all descriptions of property against loss and damage by fire and the perils of inland navigation.

Agencies established in the principal cities, towns, and ports of shipment throughout the Province.

THOS. WM. BIRCHALL,

23-1y   *Managing Director.*

Reliance Mutual Life Assurance Society

OF LONDON, ENGLAND. Established 1840.

Head Office for the Dominion of Canada:
131 ST. JAMES STREET, MONTREAL,

DIRECTORS—Walter Shanly, Esq., M.P.; Duncan Macdonald, Esq.; George Winks, Esq., W. H. Hingston, Esq., M.D., L.R.C.S.

RESIDENT SECRETARY—James Grant.

Parties intending to assure their lives, are invited to peruse the Society's prospectus, which embraces several entirely new and interesting features in Life Assurance. Copies can be had on application at he Head Office, or at any of the Agencies.

JAS. GRANT, Resident Secretary.

Agents wanted in unrepresented districts.   43-1y

The Gore District Mutual Fire Insurance Company

GRANTS INSURANCES on all description of Property against Loss or Damage by FIRE. It is the only Mutual Fire Insurance Company which assesses its Policies yearly from their respective dates ; and the average yearly cost of insurance in it, for the past three and a half years, has been nearly TWENTY CENTS IN THE DOLLAR less than what it would have been in an ordinary Proprietary Company.

THOS. M. SIMONS, Secretary & Treasurer.
ROBT. McLEAN, Inspector of Agencies.
Galt, 25th Nov., 1868.   15-1y

Canada Life Assurance Company.

ESTABLISHED 1847.

THE ONLY CANADIAN LIFE COMPANY AUTHORIZED BY GOVERNMENT FOR THE DOMINION,

Rates are lower than British or Foreign Offices.

A LARGER amount of Insurances and of Investments in Canada than any other Company, and its rapid progress is satisfactory evidence of the popularity of its principles and practice.

Last year there were issued

920 NEW POLICIES,

FOR ASSURANCE OF
$1,284,155,

WITH

ANNUAL PREMIUMS OF
$51,182.

· AGENCIES THROUGHOUT THE DOMINION, Where every information can be obtained, or at the Head Office, in Hamilton, Ont.

A. G. RAMSAY, Manager.

E. BRADBURNE, Agent,
May 25.   1y   Toronto Street.

Queen Fire and Life Insurance Company,

OF LIVERPOOL AND LONDON,

ACCEPTS ALL ORDINARY FIRE RISKS
on the most favorable terms.

LIFE RISKS

Will be taken on terms that will compare favorably with other Companies.

CAPITAL, - - £2,000,000 Stg.

CANADA BRANCH OFFICE—Exchange Buildings, Montreal.
Resident Secretary and General Agent,
A. MACKENZIE FORBES,
13 St. Sacrament St., Merchants' Exchange, Montreal.

WM. ROWLAND, Agent, Toronto.   1-1y

THE AGRICULTURAL
Mutual Assurance Association of Canada.

HEAD OFFICE ....LONDON, ONT.
A purely Farmers' Company. Licensed by the Government of Canada.

Capital, 1st January, 1869 .... $230,203 82
Cash and Cash Items, over $86,000 00
No. of Policies in force 30,892 00

THIS Company insures nothing more dangerous than a Farm property. Its rates are as low as any well-established Company in the Dominion, and lower than those of a great many. It is largely patronised, and continues to grow in public favor.

For insurance, apply to any of the Agents or address the Secretary, London, Ontario.

London, 2nd Nov., 1868.   12-1y.

The Waterloo County Mutual Fire Insurance Company.

HEAD OFFICE : WATERLOO, ONTARIO.
ESTABLISHED 1863.

THE business of the Company is divided into three separate and distinct branches, the

VILLAGE, FARM, AND MANUFACTURE

Each Branch paying its own losses and its just proportion of the managing expenses of the Company.

C. M. TAYLOR, Sec.   M. SPRINGER, M.M.P., Pres.
J. HUGHES, Inspector.   15-

Lancashire Insurance Company.

CAPITAL, - - - - - - - - £2,000,000 Sterlin

FIRE RISKS

Taken at reasonable rates of premium, and
ALL LOSSES SETTLED PROMPTLY,
By the undersigned, without reference elsewhere.

S. C. DUNCAN-CLARK & CO.,
General Agents for Ontario,
25-1y   N. W. Cor. of King & Church Sts., TORONT

Western Assurance Company,

INCORPORATED 1851.

CAPITAL ...... $400,000.

FIRE AND MARINE.

HEAD OFFICE....................TORONTO, ONTARIO

DIRECTORS.

Hon. JNO. McMURRICH. President.
CHARLES MAGRATH, Vice-Presiden
A. M. SMITH, Esq.   JOHN ISKEN, Esq.
ROBERT BEATY, Esq.,   ALEX. MANNING, Es
JAMES MICHIE, Esq.   N. BARNHART, Esq.

R. J. DALLAS, Esq.
B. HALDAN, Secretary.
J. MAUGHAN, JR., Assistant Secretary.
WM. BLIGHT, Fire Inspector.
CAPT. G. T. DOUGLAS, Marine Inspector.
JAMES PRINGLE, General Agent.

Insurances effected at the lowest current rates Buildings, Merchandise, and other property, against lo or damage by fire.

On Hull, Cargo and Freight against the perils of Inland Navigation.

On Cargo Risks with the Maritime Provinces by sail steam.

On Cargoes by steamers to and from British Ports.

WESTERN ASSURANCE COMPANY'S OFFICE, }
TORONTO, 1st April, 1869.   33-

The Victoria Mutual
FIRE INSURANCE COMPANY OF CANADA.

Insures only Non-Hazardous Property, at Low Rate

BUSINESS STRICTLY MUTUAL.

GEORGE H. MILLS, President.
W. D. BOOKER, Secretary.

HEAD OFFICE ....HAMILTON, ONTARI
aug 15-1yr

North British and Mercantile Insurance Company.

Established 1809.

HEAD OFFICE, - - CANADA ; - MONTREA

TORONTO BRANCH :

LOCAL OFFICES, Nos. 4 & 6 WELLINGTON STREET.
Fire Department, ...R. N. GOOCH, Agent.
Life Department, ...H. L. HIME, Agent.

Imperial Fire Insurance Company
OF LONDON.
No. 1 OLD BROAD STREET, AND 16 PALL MAL
ESTABLISHED 1803.
Canada General Agency,
RINTOUL BROS.,
24 St. Sacrament Street.

JAMES E. SMITH, Agen
Toronto, Corner Church and Colborne Streets.

PUBLISHED AT THE OFFICE OF THE MONETAR
TIMES, No. 60 CHURCH STREET.
PRINTED AT THE DAILY TELEGRAPH PUBLISHING HOUS
BAY STREET, CORNER OF KING

THE CANADIAN
MONETARY TIMES
AND
INSURANCE CHRONICLE,
DEVOTED TO FINANCE, COMMERCE, INSURANCE, BANKS, RAILWAYS, NAVIGATION, MINES, INVESTMENT, PUBLIC COMPANIES, AND JOINT STOCK ENTERPRISE.

| VOL, II—NO. 50. | TORONTO, THURSDAY, JULY 29, 1869 | SUBSCRIPTION $2 A YEAR. |

Mercantile.

Meetings.

QUEBEC BANK.

The following is the report of the directors to the shareholders at their fifty-first annual general meeting, held June 7th, 1869:

The directors have to report that the net profits for the year ending 1st of June last, after paying current expenses, amount to $149,626 36

From which have been paid
—Dividend, 1st December, 1868 .... $51,742 25
Dividend 1st June, 1869 .. 51,752 90
                                        ————— 103,495 15

Leaving $46,131 21
to be added to the account of profit and loss, which amounts to $120,665 95, and that sum the directors consider more than sufficient to cover any losses that may arise from debts overdue. In conformity with the wishes of the shareholders, the directors have made application to the Charter of the Dominion for a renewal of the Charter of the bank for a period of twenty-five years, from the termination of the existing charter. The branches of the bank have been duly inspected, and the directors have to report favourably of their progress. The directors deeply regret the loss they have recently sustained by the death of their much esteemed colleague, David D. Young, late President of the bank, and they cannot make this announcement without recording their sense of the valuable services he rendered in promoting the interests of the bank.

JAMES G. ROSS, Vice-President.

General Statement.

LIABILITIES.

To capital stock paid up	$1,478,800 00	
" Bank Notes in circulation	596,168 00	
" Semi-annual dividend, payable 1st June, 1869	51,752 90	
" Former dividends unpaid	5,104 02	
" Balances due to other banks....	42,354 63	
" Cash deposited	1,454,922 25	
Bearing interest $922,763 81		
Not bearing interest........... 532,158 44		
" Surplus fund	155,099 68	
At credit of profit and loss account 129,665 95		
Reserved for interest, &c...... 25,433 73		
		$3,784,201 48

ASSETS.

By coin, bullion and Provincial Notes $277,024 31		
Notes & cheques of other banks 86,674 84		
	363,699 15	
" Real estate belonging to the bank	88,912 00	
" Balances due from other banks	153,057 97	
" Government debentures..........	145,483 33	
" Amount of debts due to the bank on bills discounted and other securities.................	3,030,099 03	
	$3,784,201 48	

Proceedings of the Fifty-first Annual General Meeting of the Shareholders.

C. Delagrave, Esq., in the chair. After the report had been read, the following resolutions were put and carried unanimously.

Moved by the Rev. W. B. Clark, seconded by George Hall, Esq., that a committee be appointed to draw up a minute expressive of the high opinion of the stockholders regarding the worth of the deceased President of this bank, David Douglas Young, Esq., and the obligations under which they are for the able, disinterested and successful manner in which he discharged the duties of his office, and that such committee be composed of Messrs. W. H. Jeffery, W. White, and the mover and seconder.

Moved by John Laird, Esq., seconded by Vital Tetu, Esq., that the thanks of the meeting be given to the Vice-President and directors for their services during the year.

Moved by S. J. Shaw, Esq., seconded by Geo. Hall, Esq., that the thanks of the meeting be given to the cashier, the managers, agents, and other officers of the bank, for the efficient performance of their respective duties.

Moved by J. W. Henry, Esq., seconded by T. H. Grant, Esq., that the ballot-box be now opened and remain open till two o'clock this day, for the receipt of ballot tickets for the election of directors, and that Messrs. George Hall and William Petry do act as scrutineers.

The committee appointed to give expression to the feeling of the shoreholders on the occasion of the death of D. D. Young, Esq., late President of the bank, submitted as follows:—

The Shareholders cannot allow this meeting to separate without expressing their high sense of the character and worth of the deceased President of this Bank, the late David Douglas Young, Esquire, and whilst they would express their heartfelt sympathy with Mrs. Young and her family on the occasion of the irreparable loss which they have sustained in his death, they would record also the sense of the obligations under which they are to the departed for the disinterested zeal and unwearied attention which he manifested in the discharge of his duties as a Director and afterwards as President of the Bank.

It was then moved by His Worship the Mayor, seconded by H. S. Scott, Esq.:—That a copy of this expression of condolence and regard be transmitted to Mrs. Young.

The scrutineers, having made their report, the following gentlemen were declared duly elected Directors for the ensuing year, viz:—His Excellency Sir N. F. Belleau, J. G. Ross, Esq., Wm. Withall, Esq., Henry Fry, Esq., J. H. Dunn, Esq., R. H. Smith, Esq., A. F. A. Knight, Esq.,

At a subsequent meeting of Directors, James G. Ross, Esq., was elected President, and William Withall, Esq., Vice-President.

GUELPH BUILDING AND SAVINGS SOCIETY.— The annual meeting of the Guelph Building and Savings Society was held on Monday, July 19th George Elliott, Esq., president, in the chair. The annual report stated that the funds of the Society were in such a condition as to require no more calls upon the members, there being a surplus of about $1,000 on hand. The total assets are $37,002.60; and the liabilities $35,800. The directors were authorized to sell all matured securities, with a view to a final closing of the Society's business at an early date. A sum of $200 was voted to the President, and $200 to the Secretary, as a token of the Society's appreciation of their services. The directors appointed were Messrs. Grange, Elliott, Higinbotham, Hazelton, Loghrin, Sandilands, Hadden, Fergusson, Logan and Dow. At a subsequent meeting, Geo. Elliott, Esq., was re-lected president, and E. Newton, Esq., Secretary Treasurer.—*Advertiser.*

Financial.

TORONTO STOCK MARKET.

(Reported by Pellatt & Osler, Brokers.)

Business has been quiet for the past week, and not much improvement can be expected for the next month; prices, however continue firm.

Bank Stock.—Montreal advanced in the beginning of the week to 162½, but subsequently declined, the last sales being at 160½. British is asked for at 104½. Sales of Ontario were made during the week at 95½, 96, and 96½, closing in fair demand at 96. Small sales of Toronto are reported at 121; holders generally ask 124. No transactions in Royal Canadian during the week; buyers offer a small advance on 50, but there are no sellers. Commerce has further advanced; sales have been made at 102½, 103, 103½; buyers generally, however, do not offer more than 103. The shares of the Gore have been reduced from $40 to $24; stock may now be quoted as worth 62¼ to 65 on the reduced share. Merchants' declined early in the week from 106½ to 104; it has since revived, and there are no sellers under 106. Small sales of Quebec at 100½, which rate would still be paid. The last sales of Molsons' were at 109½. Buyers offer 99½ for City, with sellers at par. There are buyers of Du Peuple at 109, and no sellers. Nationale nominal at 107. There are inquiries for Jacques Cartier at 108. Nothing doing in Mechanics'. There are buyers of Union at 105, with sellers at 105½.

Debentures.—Canada 5's and 6's, both Sterling and Currency, are asked for, but there are none on market; Dominion Stock offers at 107¼. Toronto are offering to pay 7½ per cent. interest. County are in fair demand at about 99.

Sundries.—City Gas is much asked for at 107 and 107½; no sales for some time past. There are no sales of British America Assurance to report since our last. Small sales of Canada Permanent Building Society were made at 122½ and 123, and a slight advance might be paid for a round lot. Western Canada Building Society is in great request at 118 to 118½, but there is no stock offering. Freehold Building Society still continues in demand; there are no shares in market. Montreal Telegraph sold at 132, which would still be paid. Small sales of Canada Landed Credit at 80, at which rate there are sellers. Good mortgages are readily taken at from 8 to 9 per cent.

BANKING AND CURRENCY.

To the Editor of the Halifax Chronicle:

SIR,—When I formerly addressed you on the important subject of Banking and Currency, nothing was positively known as to the intentions of the Government. Much was surmised, but it was quite uncertain how far they would attempt to interfere with the existing bank note circulation. This state of uncertainty was removed when the resolutions of Mr. Rose were submitted to Parliament. Therein the policy of the Government was fully declared, and it was of a character so opposed to the best interests of the country that even staunch supporters of the Government felt compelled to oppose it. After the debate in which this opposition was so thoroughly and ably manifested, the resolutions were allowed to lie over; and it was only toward the close of the session, and after considerable discussion and difference of opinion in the Cabinet, that they were finally withdrawn. While thus reluctantly withdrawing his resolutions, Mr. Rose gave it to be understood that they were not abandoned, but only postponed; and he expressed the hope that they would yet receive the assent of the country. There can be very little doubt but that they will be brought forward next session, and that every influence will be used to secure their passage into law.

As is well known, the representatives of the banking interests gave to the resolutions of Mr. Rose their decided opposition. An attempt was made to shake their influence by endeavoring to create the impression that this was the result of entirely selfish motives, and that they were looking after their own interests alone, while indifferent to those of the public. On the other hand, Mr. Rose repeatedly assured Parliament, in the course of his speech, that the measure of the Government "was framed solely with a regard to the great interests of the country," and that they had no ulterior object in view. Mr. Tilley endeavored to prove that the public, as evidenced by the petitions presented, were, to a considerable extent, indifferent. Another member of the Government told me that whenever he saw so many bankers in opposition to the scheme, he was sure it was a good one for the country. Now I have no hesitation in asserting that it was because they thought the policy of the Government would be most injurious to our mercantile and industrial interests that the bankers were so unanimously opposed to it. True, there was a well grounded dislike to being compelled to invest a large portion of their capital in government securities of variable value, and which would not be available when required for the redemption of the notes. They also knew that whatever legislation might injuriously affect the mercantile community must react upon the banks. To this extent the bankers were selfish in their opposition. But it did not arise from any fear as regards their profits, as might be supposed, as these would be nearly, if not quite, as much under the Government scheme as they were at present, while some thought that if they had merely consulted their own interests they would have welcomed the proposed change.

The question in reality is one which mainly affects the merchant, the trader, the mechanic, the manufacturer, the lumberman, and the farmer, as it would be impossible for the banks under the proposed system to grant them anything like the same accommodation as they at present receive. The object of this letter is to draw attention again to the subject, and to show what the result would have been in Nova Scotia had the resolutions of Mr. Rose passed, and what there is in store for us should the Government hereafter succeed in forcing their policy through Parliament.

The plan of the Government, as explained by Mr. Rose, and embodied in his resolutions, was to compel the banks to purchase government bonds to an amount equal to their circulation, and to maintain besides a reserve of gold equal to twenty per cent of their circulation. The meaning of this is, that for every one hundred dollars of notes afloat the banks must originally possess one hundred and twenty dollars in gold, of which one hundred dollars were to be loaned to the Government, and twenty dollars held in their safe to meet any demand for specie payment. It will be seen at once that this was in reality, whatever it may have been in intention, a grand scheme for obtaining possession of a large amount of gold by a forced loan from the banks. The latter were also required to hold in gold, or legal tender notes, a further reserve equal to one-seventh of their call deposits. This was the entire reserve which Mr. Rose supposed to be necessary for safe banking; an opinion opposed to the views of most practical bankers. To show that this scheme would not be very detrimental to the commercial interests of the country, it was necessary for him to put the reserve at the very lowest point, which he accordingly did. And even with this very small reserve, he was obliged to confess that his scheme would withdraw at least $5,700,000 from the available banking funds of the Dominion.

The following calculation will show the effect on the banking funds of Nova Scotia. I have taken the figures as given in the returns of the chartered banks on the 31st July last, which is the latest date to which I have access, and have added one-fourth for the two private banks and the Bank of British North America. At that date the total circulation was $1,028,000, which, according to the Government proposal, was to be withdrawn, and other notes, based on government securities, substituted. The banks were required to hand over to the Government $1,028,000 in gold for their bonds. They were also to keep a reserve of 20 per cent. in gold, and a further reserve of one-seventh of their call deposits. The total amount of specie thus required would have been $1,358,000, to meet which the banks held $703,000 in gold and government bonds, the difference, amounting to $655,000, they could only obtain by permanently reducing their discounts to this extent. This, be it remembered, is according to Mr. Rose's own method of calculation; and yet it is equivalent to wiping out the capital of the Union Bank and half that of the People's Bank. But the calculations of Mr. Rose are defective in two particulars. He has not made provision for any reserve for deposits on interest, nor has he made any for the reserve of notes which banks must always hold in their tills, or which may be passing between the head offices and branches, and which are not in circulation. He has taken the amount of notes in the hands of the public alone as it stood on a particular day, or on the average; but there may be, and are, many days when it is considerably higher than on the day on which the returns are made up. A much larger amount than is made to appear in his calculations must be invested in government securities, and thus withdrawn from available banking funds. Adding to the $655,000 required to be withdrawn from discounts, according to Mr. Rose's mode of calculation, one-seventh say of the deposits on interest, or $225,000, and the very moderate allowance of one-seventh of the actual circulation for a reserve in the till, or $147,000 and we have, at the very lowest estimate consistent with necessity and prudence, $1,022,000 permanently withdrawn from the loanable banking funds in Nova Scotia, or more than the united capital of the Bank of Nova Scotia and the Union Bank. The following recapitulation will probably show the result more clearly:

Total circulation to be covered by Government bonds		$1,028,00
Reserve of 20 p. c. to be maintained in gold		205,00
Reserve of 1-7th of $877,000 call deposits		125,00
Total amount of gold required for circulation and deposits		$1,358,00
To meet this amount the banks held in specie	$620,000	
in government debentures	83,000	
		703,00
Making a deficiency to be taken out of discounts of		$665,00
To which add—		
Reserve in specie of 1-7th of $1,545,000 deposits on interest		220,00
Reserve of notes in till, viz., 1-7th of $1,028,000 actual circulation		147,00
Shewing the total amonnt to be withdrawn from discounts to be		$1,022,00

No scheme more injurious to the material interests of this Province could well be conceived than this with which we are still threatened. To conciliate the banks, if possible, and to prevent the damaging effects from being immediately felt, it was proposed to spread the operation over a peric five years. Although this would lessen the l for a time, it would go on growing year by r, until at the end of the five years the full righting influence would be experienced. And rade were to revive and increase in the mean. e, there would be a contraction of means con. ially going on side by side with a growing iand, which would necessarily cause embar. iment, tighten the money market, and raise the of discount.

he main object professedly of the resolutions to ensure the ultimate payment of bank notes r the suspension of a bank, and to make assur. r doubly sure, Mr. Rose, in addition to com. ing the banks to invest in government bonds, osed to make the notes a first lien on the ts of the bank, which of itself is a full and cient protection to the note holder . But, as is were not enough, he also proposed to render ediately available the clause in the charters which the stockholders are liable for double amount of their stock. For some reasons or er, by the way, which might be guessed at. bank of British North America was to have n exempted from the double liability. By this ans holders of notes of the Bank of British rth America would have not felt so secure as ders of other notes. Still if it were considered irable in the public interests to make the reholders in the local banks liable for double amount of their stock, there could be no valid son why those of this foreign institution should be equally liable. And if it were not consid. i necessary in the case of the latter, neither uld it have been in regard to the local banks. wever, these two provisions—the making the es a first lien on the assets of the bank, and dering the double liability of shareholders im. diately available after suspension—give un. bted and ample security without in any way ailing the power of the banks to assist trade commerce. And if Mr. Rose had merely ked at the interests of the public, he would ve stopped there. But he went very much then, and, in order to assure a certainty, pro. ied a plan by which the reserves of the banks uld have been reduced far below what the kers of the Dominion now consider necessary their own stability and the safety of the note. lder,—a plan which would not only have anged our present monetary system and largely tailed banking accommodation, but would have sorbed those resources which, if held by the ks themselves in times of difficulty, would ble them to meet their liabilities, and prevent pension from taking place.

PETER JACK.

—The Bank of Montreal has opened an agency Newcastle, N. B., for the convenience of the vernment. The principal business transacted this branch will be in connection with the In. colonial Railway. Of course, the bank will nnact any other business that may present itself. will be under the supervision of Mr. Winslow. —Mr. S. J. Scovil, the St. John banker, who de such a sensation some time ago in that city, i was held in custody in twelve cases, has been ing to obtain his release. The applications for ischarge under the insolvent act were granted in ven of the cases; in one it was refused, so that ren'si's 4n jail.

—The liquidation of Overend, Gurney & Co., oceeds most satisfactorily. The liabilities at the ie of suspension were about £18,000,000, the ole of which, with the exception of one shilling he pound has been paid to the creditors. The al payment has been deferred by arrangement till ac of next year, when the whole will be liqui. ed with-interest due at and since the stoppage. Brock Sale.—At W. M. Gray's stock sale in lifax July 17, by J. D. Nash, the following ces were realized: £100 stg. Provincial Deben. es 5¾ per cent prem. ; shares in Halifax Library, 50 @ $10 ; Nova Scotia Electric Telegraph

Company, $14 ; Strawberry Hill Gold Mining Company, 50c. and 51c.; Bank of British North America, £65 5s.; Acadia Fire Insurance Com. pany, $22.50.; Halifax Fire Insurance Company £10 5s.

STATEMENT of the Dominion Notes in circulation, 7th July, and of the Specie held against them at Montreal, Toronto and Halifax:

Dominion notes in circulation—
Payable at Montreal............ : $3,202,727
Payable at Toronto*....... 1,205,273
Payable at Halifax†............ 384,000

$4,792,000

Specie held—
At Montreal...................... $600,000
At Toronto...................... 500,000
At Halifax...................... 75,000

$1,175,000

Debentures held by the Receiver
Gen'l under the Dominion Note
Act.............................. $3,000,000

* Including $197,000 marked St. John.
† The Nova Scotia dollar not being equal in value to that of the other Provinces, the notes issued at Halifax are worth their face value in Nova Scotia only. They are stamp. ed "Payable at Halifax" and are numbered in black ink. None but $5 notes are yet in circulation.

BANK OF ENGLAND.—The return for the week ending the 7th of July, gives the following results when compared with the previous week:
Rest................£3,351,510...Increase....£173,805
Public deposits. 4,455,863...Decrease...4,306,513
Other deposits..21,091,460...Increase....1,941,734
On the other side of the account :
Gov't securities £15,702,999...Increase£1,5 48,626
Other securities 17,409,587...Decrease 3,142,622
Notes unemploy'd.9,748,680...Decrease 482,190
The amount of notes in circulation is £23,996,- 330, being an increase of £603,225; and the stock of Bullion in both departments is £19,810,598 showing an increase of £29,832, when compared with the proceeding return.

FIRE RECORD.—A St. John correspondent sends us the following:—Prince William, York County. N. B., July 18.—The Rectory occupied by Rev. E. N. Harrington, was totally destroyed by fire, at 12 o'clock noon. Supposed to have originated by a spark from the cooking stove. Most of the furniture was saved. Building insured in the "Central," for $400 ; the furniture in the "Queen," for $400.

Kars, King's County, N. B., July 19.—James Dunlop's dwelling house was destroyed by fire ; said to be partially insured.

Ashfield, Ont., July 7.—The house of James Mullen, with contents. The barn and stables, which were near the house, were also consumed, together with plows, harness, buggy, &c., &c. Total loss about $2,600 ; insured in the Agricul. tural Mutual for $1,300.

Brantford, July 21.—Oxley & Co.'s store, Mar. ket street, was damaged to to some extent ; cover. ed by insurance.

North Williamsburg, July 9.—The barn and sheds of D. McArthur were struck by lightning, and before the contents could be removed they, together with the buildings, were consumed. The loss amounts to some $750, made up of shoes, hogs, implements, &c., together with the build. ings. Insured in the Beaver Mutual of Toronto for $5,000.

West Garafraxa Township, July 10.—Barn of Robert Kerr, 2nd con., was struck by lightning during the tornado on the 10th, and partly burned; the heavy rain saved it from utter destruction.

Cæsarea, Ont., July 19.—An exchange says: the steam sawmill of Mr. Martin, was destroyed by fire together with four hundred thousand feet

of lumber. The mill was new. The origin of the fire is unknown, as everything was secure when left on Friday night. There is an insurance of $7,000 on mill and lumber. Loss, about $2,000 more.

Quebec, July 20.—A fire broke out in a one. storey wooden house in St. Croix Street, St. Lewis Suburbs, owned by J. Flanagan, and occupied by several families, the lower part by the proprietor as a grocery and tavern. Insurance in the Western of Canada for $600 on building; no insurance on stock or furniture.

A telegram says: a large part of the town of Canning, King's county, N. S., was destroyed by fire. The entire town was burned three years ago.

Victoria Barracks, Charlottetown, P.E.I., were destroyed by fire, which was the work of an in. cendiary ; the building was fully insured.

—The Canadian barque E. W. Head, went down at Windsor laden with lumber, and to all appearance is in a disabled condition. Her top. sail is badly split, while her square sail is by no means in a seaworthy condition.

—The barque John Braden, of Kingston, re. cently ashore near Port Washington, is found to be more damaged than it was at first supposed. Her bottom is "chawed" from stem to stern. She will require an entire new keel, and new bot. tom planking almost throughout. Her foremast is split, and foretopmast sprung, and her main gaff is broken. The work of repairing the hull and getting in the new spars will occupy two weeks time, and will cost in the neighbourhood of $5,- 000. The vessel is owned by the Folger Bros.

—Advices from Plymouth, 5th state that the ship Cavalier, Mansou master, from Quebec for London (timber), has put in there cut down sev. eral feet below the water's edge having been in collision the previous night, 15 miles S. W. of the Eddystone, with a brig-rigged steamer, bound up channel; the Cavalier filled immediately.

—Mr. F. W. Ballard, Secretary of the Security Insurance Company, New York, has proved a de. faulter to the extent of $63,000. A few years ago the same company suffered severely from the de. falcation of its president.

EDINBURGH LIFE.—At the annual meeting o the Edinburgh Life Assurance Company at Edin. burgh on Monday, 5th July, the report stated that during the year 750 new policies had been issued, assuring £353,219., and yielding in new premiums £10,841.

CHEAP INSURANCE.—The following is related as the experience of a farmer who insured in the Dumfries Mutual Insurance Company. If the in. suranc̀e was insurance at all, it was very cheap: A person who had been insured for $2,000, and had given his note for $100, had to pay $5.75 during the last ten years, which is between ¼ and ½ per cent. on the sum insured for ten years. I am in. sured for $1,176—premium note $88.30. It has cost me nearly $3 for eight years, including policy and survey. My brother Robert insured in this Company on the 9th of April, 1864, for $1,700, and gave his premium note for $85. It has cost him $1 for policy, fifty cents for survey, and $1.91 for assessment during five years. Mr. Edgar is insured for $4,400; he told me it had not cost him $5 during ten years.

CHANCES OF DEATH BY DIFFERENT DISEASES. —Men pray to be preserved from murder and from sudden death ; in other words, from what are called accidents and wilful injuries. The London Times states that the chances are as one to twenty-nine that a man will depart this life from such causes. That he will die of zymotic disease is as one to six ; that consumption will cause his-death is as one to nine. Out of every 1,000 deaths in 1867, 195 were caused by zymotic disease, 192 by constitutional diseases, 402 by local diseases, 167 by developmental diseases, and 36 by accidental and other violence. 113,003- out of every million deaths were the result of consumption.

CANADA LIFE ASSURANCE COMPANY.

Statement by the Canada Life Assurance Company, in terms of sec. 14 of the Act 31 Vic., c. 48:

Assets of the company	$988,140 89
Liabilities of the company	138,226 07
Amount of capital stock	1,000,000 00
Amount paid thereon	125,000 00

Of what the Assets of the Company consist, viz.:

Cash on hand in banks, and receipts on collection in hands of agents since paid	$47,303 14
Mortgages on real estate	203,354 95
Real estate	110,192 19
Municipal and other debentures, Dominion and other stock and accrued interest	439,020 22
Loans on policies, debentures, stock and bonds	33,100 80
Bills receivable	1,643 63
Half yearly and quarterly premiums secured on policies payable within nine months	44,100 38
Deferred half payments on half credit policies	30,512 89
Office furniture	1,648 71
Other assets	1,027 21
	$1,007,910 22
Deduct reserved on account of probable losses	19,718 53
	988,140 89

Total premiums received during the year	104,910 83
Number of policies issued during the year, 631.	
Amount of policies issued during the year	1,156,855 00
Number of claims from death during the year, 35.	
Amount of claims from death during the year	61,300 00
Expenses of management, agencies, &c	34,651 76
Amount at risk on total policies issued in Canada	5,475,358 86

I, Alexander Gillespie Ramsay, of the City of Hamilton, Manager of the Canada Life Assurance Company, make oath and say:—

That the above statement is true and correct in every particular, to the best of my knowledge and belief.—So help me God.

Sworn before me, at Hamilton,
this 22nd day of July, 1869.

Signed,)   ROBERT RAY, J.P.

(Signed,)
A. G. RAMSAY,
Manager.

THE CANADIAN MONETARY TIMES AND INSURANCE CHRONICLE *is printed every Thursday evening and distributed to Subscribers on the following morning.*

Publishing office, No. 60 Church-street, 3 doors north of Court-street.

Subscription price—

Canada $2.00 per annum.
England, stg. 10s. per annum.
United States (U.S.Cy.) $3.00 per annum.

Casual advertisements will be charged at the rate of ten cents per line, each insertion.

Address all letters to " THE MONETARY TIMES.*"*

Cheques, money orders, &c. should be made payable to J. M. TROUT, Business Manager, who alone is authorized to issue receipts for money.

☞ *All Canadian Subscribers to* THE MONETARY TIMES *will receive* THE REAL ESTATE JOURNAL *without further charge.*

THE CITIZENS' INSURANCE COMPANY
OF CANADA.)

Authorized Capital	$2,000,000
Subscribed Capital	1,050,000

HEAD OFFICE—MONTREAL.

DIRECTORS.

HUGH ALLAN,	· · · · PRESIDENT.
C. J. BRYDGES,	EDWIN ATWATER,
GEORGE STEPHEN,	HENRY LYMAN,
ADOLPHE ROY,	N. B. CORSE.

Life and Guarantee Department.

THIS Company—formed by the association of nearly 100 of the wealthiest citizens of Montreal—is prepared to transact every description of LIFE ASSURANCE; also, to grant Bonds of FIDELITY GUARANTEE, for Employees holding positions of trust. Applications can be made through any of the Company's Agents, or direct to

EDWARD RAWLINGS, Manager.

Agent for Toronto:	Agent for Hamilton ;
W. T. MASON.	H. BENNER.

The Canadian Monetary Times.

THURSDAY, JULY 29, 1869.

CANADIAN CANALS.

VIII.

The mode in which the proposers of the Caughnawaga Canal submitted the project to public notice is deserving of respect, and the clearness with which their views are stated furnishes the material by which those views may be criticised. The scheme has not been taken up as a matter of private speculation, it has been advocated on public grounds alone, and the attention of the government was claimed for it on purely commercial considerations. Its promoters obtained a survey of the ground in 1854, and in order to avoid local influence it was considered advisable to call in an engineer from the United States ; the ordinary duty of examination and surveying was properly enough done. In fact, it was hampered by no difficulty. The report by Mr. J. B. Jarvis on the canal as a question of commercial policy, is not so satisfactory. We must, for the moment, turn to the instructions given the latter by the Commissioner of Public Works. Although signed by Mr. Chabot, they were drawn up by the Hon. John Young, who in reality conducted the negotiations for the examination. A difference raised by Mr. Hincks having placed Mr. Young in the dilemma of accepting a commercial policy, which he had combatted for years, or of retiring from the ministry, he unhesitatingly accepted the latter course. Still the weight of his name turned the balance in favor of conducting the examination according to his views. In these instructions Mr. Young virtually shadowed forth the whole report of Mr. Jarvis, with the distinction, that Mr. Young states very clearly and in very few words, what Mr. J. B. Jarvis puts forth in an extended and confused form, combined with

much irrelevant and obscure "padding." For this report Mr. J. B. Jarvis asked a fee of ten thousand dollars, and it was paid to him.

The day is not distant when the whole canal policy of Canada must be considered, consequently it cannot be too earnestly or too frequently inculcated, that no scheme of secondary importance should be allowed to interfere in any way with the project of developing the St. Lawrence to the maximum extent of navigation practicable. If the attention of the country be divided between local projects, and its strength frittered away on schemes, clashing with each other, because each is considered by the light of private enterprise only, we can hope for nothing more than zealous and violent partizanship, often, we fear, not too scrupulously exercised. Unfortunately, all this energy, so far from forming a healthy condition of public opinion acts in opposition to its establishment. No one can, for a moment doubt, that if Ontario with one voice, demanded a commission to examine the St. Lawrence, it would be granted. Accepting the view that the Executive was desirous of satisfying the demand, and of arriving at the right solution of the problem, the danger is that parliamentary combinations would engraft on the main inquiry many of the irrelevant side issues privately entertained. It is with the hope of keeping the St. Lawrence navigation a question unencumbered by such views that further attention is drawn to the Caughnawaga Canal. Although of a totally different character to the several proposed new connections between lakes Erie and Ontario and to the Ottawa navigation which, as theory, is entirely to supersede the Saint Lawrence, it is advisable, clearly to establish that the Caughnawaga Canal is or is not quite distinct from the improvement of the St. Lawrence, and whether, if considered at all, it need be looked upon as a part of that scheme or as entirely subordinate to it. It is admitted that the canal would—

1. Extend very great facilities to the lumber trade.

2. That it is not impossible that western produce would seek its waters for the discharge of cargoes at Burlington on Lake Champlain.

The attempt has been made by the writer to argue these views with some closeness and, it is hoped, that if error exist in the conclusions drawn, that, at least, it cannot be said that the premises have been strained or misrepresented. Two distinct issues remain to be considered and all argument with regard to it is then exhausted.

The anticipated result, that the canal would connect Lake Champlain with the sea other words, would make Burlington and hitehall sea ports. It is proper to remark, at the interpretation of the letter of instructions may not go to this extent. They run to open the districts upon that lake [Champlain] to the sea via Quebec, and afford them a shorter and cheaper route for imports of coal, iron, salt fish, oil," &c. These articles can be generally purchased cheaply in ebec, in consequence of a large amount of pping entering in ballast, and accordingly ty can be profitably purchased in that market. Fifteen years, however, have elapsed ce this possibility was suggested, and if at advantages really presented themselves this branch of trade, to follow the direction indicated, it may be said that even the row limit of the present Chambly Canal uld have received some benefit from it.

find, however, by the returns published, e latest for reference being up to the 30th ne, 1867,] that of 364,609 tons of freight nsported from the St. Lawrence to Lake amplain; about 4,500 tons only did not sist of lumber in some form or other. It uld seem, therefore, that a canal having in w breakage of bulk at Quebec or Montreal, the supply of the Lake Champlain district, not called for, because the want is supplied by the Railway connecting with Boston. the other hand, were the Caughnawaga nal adapted to sea-going propellers, the estion is at once changed, and the argument ed on the possible benefit to the western e districts, applies with some modification the State of Vermont and eastern New rk. It is true that no return freight for rope, or the Atlantic sea-board of the ited States, is to be found in Lake Champlain itself. But the manufactures of Mashusets and New Hampshire, delivered by way on Lake Champlain, require transport to Chicago, and at that port the produce the lakes has to be moved eastward, to Atlantic sea-board or to some grain growing country. This view of the theoretical utility such a ship canal would confer, y be said to command a certain recognition, as to the extent of the trade, there must difficulty in defining its limit. The rerk, however, may be ventured, that its bable extent furnishes rather an incidental than a main ground of argument of the essity of the canal.

t now remains more succinctly to enter on the view already expressed, that it not possible to enlarge the Whitehall al to any extent. Until now the con- y fact has been assumed, and much e would have been saved if in answer to desire of the Canadian Government, "to l a more desirable route for the great trade ch passes between tide water in the Hud-

son River .... and the Western States," the simple answer had been given, that it could not be found by Whitehall. Mr. J. B. Jarvis, on the contrary, never enters into the consideration, he assumes it to be perfectly feasible. Throughout the report, not in one or two, but in fifty places, he deals with the possibility as a mere matter of expense. One sentence is worthy of preservation. The italics are the writers. The passage appears under the head "Champlain Canal of New York enlarged to a Ship Canal," so there is no mistake on the subject.

"*No examination has been made to ascertain the cost of such work.* From what I have seen, and from information obtained from intelligent persons who have been well acquainted with it and the country through which it passes, *there is believed to be no serious and not much expensive work required for its enlargement,* and that six millions of dollars would be sufficient for its completion. To this should be added, for *improving the Hudson River for twenty miles below Troy,* probably from *one to two millions.*"

One fact is learned from this sentence, that the Hudson River, for the distance of twenty miles below Troy, is exceedingly shallow, and requires very great improvement to be fitted for a deep navigation. It is of no benefit to imitate Mr. J. B. Jarvis' random mode of writing, but it is very certain that a formidable expense in the Hudson River itself lies in the way of any improvement of the water navigation between that river and Lake Champlain. When we turn to this canal* itself, everything is suggestive that it can be but little improved. At present the depth throughout is but four feet ; the locks are 110 feet long and 18 feet wide. Some few of them, however, require yet to be brought to these dimensions. It has three sources of supply. The first five miles from the junction with the Erie Canal at West Troy to a point one mile north of Waterford, are supplied from the Mohawk River at Cohoes ; the second distance, 25 miles to the crossing of the Hudson River, 2¼ miles south of Fort Miller, obtains the supply from the Hudson at Saratoga dam ; the remainder of the distance, 36 miles, is fed from Glen's Falls feeder and Wood Creek. From Fort Edward to Fort Ann, a reach of twelve miles, the summit of the canal proper is 81 feet above Lake Champlain. Fort Ann is twelve miles from Whitehall ; Fort Edward forty-two miles from the junction with the Erie at West Troy. Accordingly the whole supply is practically from the Hudson at Glen's Falls, brought by a feeder descending, in seven miles, the height of 132 feet. It is perfectly true that a very large tract of country in eastern New

* It was the writer's intention personally to have examined the Hudson at Glen's Falls. It is a matter of regret that, from circumstances, he has been unable to do so.

York, extending over the counties of Essex, Hamilton, Warren, Saratoga, and Fulton, is drained by the Hudson. But the physical geography of this district is suggestive of great variations in the flow of its rivers, and the map promises no mode by which an increased supply can be turned into the canal. As the strength of a whole chain is the power of resistance in its weakest part, so the capacity of a canal is to be determined at the most contracted point of its water supply. We have the Champlain Canal now with four feet of water. In 1860 the Legislature of the State of New York authorised that it should be deepened to five feet, but the work has not yet been carried out. What is essentially needed on the part of Canada is an examination, carefully and systematically made, as to the extent of improvement of which this canal is capable. Mr. J. B. Jarvis accepted the possibility that it could be deepened to 11 feet (pages 16, 4Cr) The inference to be gathered from the necessity of using three feeders in a navigation of sixty-six miles is, certainly, that the high level could not supply the water necessary for the present depth of four feet without this additional supply. Certainly it does not seem probable that it would be a wise policy for the navigation of the Hudson, in point of commerce the most considerable in the United States for its distance, to divert one-half of the supply from the most important of its head waters to Lake Champlain. Again, the physical aspect of the country is against the hope that the body of water could be increased. The evidence on which this opinion is grounded, it must be admitted, is sufficiently imperfect. Nevertheless, it throws the onus probandi on those who claim that the canal can be enlarged. It is they who must show that there is water sufficient for the purpose, for until that be done, the inference must remain that the present depth of four feet can be increased only in a very slight degree—a conclusion which at once puts all reasoning based on the enlargement to a ship canal out of court.

There is accordingly no ground for anticipating that the Caughnawaga Canal would have any bearing upon the commerce of Canada beyond exercising a moderate influence in the directions which we have pointed out. Accordingly it must be held to be a project in every way subordinate to the development of the Saint Lawrence navigation ; however, it may be considered to be to some extent supplemental to it, it is not to be looked on as a positive requirement, for no special reason exists for its immediate construction. Still, it presents so many favorable aspects, that it may be said that financial circumstances permitting, there are strong reasons why the canal should be regarded as a work hereafter to be executed.

THE INTERCOLONIAL RAILWAY LOAN.

When Mr. Holton and others in the Canadian House of Commons were led, by mere party spite, to make unpatriotic comments on what they were pleased to term the misapplication of trust funds by the Minister of Finance, we considered the explanation then afforded by the Government relative to the use made of the Intercolonial Railway loan so satisfactory as to call for no further remark. Although the strictures of the Opposition were calculated to do little except, perhaps, injure our credit, yet these were justifiable on constitutional grounds. We are, however, not disposed to extend the same leniency to those in the Imperial Parliament who undertook to lecture Canada on financial management. The speech of Mr. Monsell not only provoked an angry rejoinder from our Premier, but gave rise to a correspondence between the Dominion and Imperial Cabinets. Although the correspondence was not placed before the English House of Commons, a member of that body, Mr. Aytoun, thought fit again to bring the subject forward; and, forgetting that under the Act of 1867 Canada is not bound, in the slightest degree, to render an account of the way in which she manages her finances to Great Britain, moved a resolution—

"That this House is of opinion that the application of money raised under the Imperial guarantee, in pursuance of the Canada Railway Loan Act, 1867, to a redemption of a portion of the debt of the Canadian Dominion, is contrary to the intention of that Act; and that no further guarantee should be given by the Commissioners of Her Majesty's Treasury under the above Act, except in such form and manner as shall insure the direct application of the money so guaranteed to the construction of the Intercolonial Railway."

This resolution was intended to be a vote of censure on the Government of Canada. Mr. Hunt, in reply to Mr. Aytoun, put the matter in a clear light. He said:

"The Act imposed no duty on the Imperial Government to see to the *ad interim* investment of the money, and he maintained that it was no part of the Imperial Government's business to impose on the Canadian Dominion any conditions on that point beyond those contained in the Act. Supposing they were satisfied that all the prescribed conditions were fully complied with, it appeared to him that it was the duty of the Imperial Government to give an absolute guarantee. That was the view taken at the Treasury at the time, and he had no reason so suppose that it was not a sound one. What appeared to be the intention of the Act was, that there should be a separate account kept, and that all the money invested should be invested for the purposes of a railway; and if these investments were made in good securities until the money was wanted for the railway, and a proper account were kept, it

seemed to him that the Act would be satisfied."

Mr. Baring showed that when the loan for the making of the railway was proposed to be guaranteed by the Imperial Government, the idea was "scouted" that the Imperial Government should exercise any interference in the disposal of the money. He thought Mr. Rose had acted very judiciously in the way in which he had employed the money, and the whole amount had been placed in securities on which he could borrow again or sell, if desirable. If the guarantee had been accompanied by such restrictions as the mover of the resolution thought desirable, either the guarantee would have been declined, or, if accepted on those terms, it would have been made more onerous for Canada to carry the arrangements into effect, and more difficult to fulfil the objects of the Act. In consequence of the operations of Mr. Rose, the charge incurred in consequence of the loan would be much lightened, and the general result of the transactions was extremely successful. Mr. Gladstone said—

"He was extremely desirous of saying that as far as Canada was concerned, there was no imputation against her whatever in regard to the pecuniary operations. Indeed, he should no more think of casting doubt upon the good faith of the Government or Ministers of Canada than he should of casting doubt on the good faith of the Government or Ministers of this country. In that place both Governments ought to be recognized as standing on one and the same footing, and topics of such a nature ought to be excluded from discussions like the present. It was perfectly true, however, that there was such a thing as punctuality in complying with the provisions of an Act, and any neglect in such compliance might deserve the censure of the House."

The Imperial Government was made aware, as a matter of courtesy, of Mr. Rose's intentions, and had laid before it in May a statement showing the absolute safety of the loan, and that the whole guarantee fund could be repaid without the slightest inconvenience. Canada had $2,750,000 in the hands of their bankers, a further deposit of $1,500,000 at 4 per cent., $2,900,000 in the hands of Baring & Glynn; India bonds lodged with Barings worth $750,000, Great Western Preferential securities, $2,700,000; deposits by insurance companies, $1,500,000; receipts for postoffice savings banks, $600,000; bonds purchased in anticipation of the requirement of the Intercolonial sinking fund, $270,000. And over and above the foregoing means, special credits for the express purposes of meeting any possible call on Intercolonial account, rest with Messrs. Baring & Glynn, $1,250,000; the Bank of Montreal, $2,500,- 000. The entire guarantee fund only amounted to $10,431,983.18, from which must be deducted $388,739.68 expended on works

and negotiating loan ; so that to cover the balance of $10,000,000, the Dominion had assets readily convertible, or cash credits to the extent of $16,670,000.

PROVINCIAL INSURANCE COMPANY.

The annual meeting of this Company will be held shortly and every preparation is being made for a thorough overhauling of its affairs. There is great dissatisfaction with the management—no one who has read our remarks upon it will be surprised at that—and, so far as we can learn, there is a determination, in more than one quarter, to have a change or precipitate liquidation. When we think of the chances that the Provincial had, of the influence of its proprietary, of the large sections of country controlled by that influence, of the outrageous mistakes made from the outset of its career, of the absurd management which has characterized it up to the present moment, we can but attribute its misfortunes to an imbecility of the intensest character, an imbecility so astonishing as to be unique. In 1859, the Provincial had a subscribed capital of $1,986,080, in 1868 that amount had dwindled down to $470,760. We understand that its business has fallen off to a serious extent. No wonder. When we first appealed to the management to set their house in order, our advice was treated with affected contempt. Had a proper effort then been made, we should have a better state of affairs to-day. Although disposed to deal leniently with a local institution our motives were aspersed and when we were forced by the appearance of statements manifestly intended to hoodwink the public, to prick the bubble, we were answered by threats of prosecution for libel. Notwithstanding, we are not inclined to gloat over a falling antagonist. The consciousness of having performed a disagreeable duty will compensate for temporary misconstruction of motive, and if the shareholders will only take the trouble to attend the meeting about to be held and insist on a thorough investigation of the Company's affairs, we shall feel that we have not written in vain. The day of artificial figures and dissolving-view statements has gone by, and the public have been deceived too often of late to patronize an insurance company in which they cannot have confidence, no matter how respectable its directors may be. If the company has life in it, stir it up; if not close up at once. The half-dead and-alive system of doing things has brought a great deal of contempt on some Toronto undertakings.

THE annual meeting of the Gore Bank will be held next week. It is said that the question of immediate liquidation will be brought up for discussion and settlement.

THE CANADA LIFE.

/e give in another column the statement ɩished by this Company to the Govern- ɩt in terms of 31 Vic., cap. 48, sec. 14. we shall have occasion next week to ex- ne the annual report and chronicle the ɛeedings of the annual meeting, we reserve her comment until then. We understand report will shew that this Company has e the largest Life business in Canada; the interest upon its investments has ely exceeded the year's claims by death; the expenses of management have been 'eased, and that a dividend of five per :. may be declared. The results of the :'s business indicate great activity on the of the Company's officers and agents, testify to the excellence of Mr. Ramsay's ɩagement.

THE ETNA OF DUBLIN.

correspondent asks for information re- ting the affairs of the Etna. All the in- ɩation procurable has been published in columns. So far as we know the ted Ports has paid no losses in Canada. most tangible security claimants have ɩe. Etna's deposit with government, but n that will be distributed is a moot ɩt. If any of our English cotemporaries throw some light on this very dismal ect, claimants in Canada would be very h obliged by their doing so. We can advise patience, and more carefulness n about to insure.

: is not improbable that the Royal Cana- ɩ Bank will resume business in about a ɩight.

ARROW GAUGE RAILWAYS.—The Directors ɩe Toronto and Nipissing Railway have elected Robt. W. Elliot, one of our soundest mer- ts, to the office of President, and Mr. J. E. h, Collector of Customs, to the office of Vice- ident of the Company. The daily papers published a correspondence between Mr. Geo. law and Mr. C. J. Brydges, Managing Direc- ɔf the Grand Trunk. In response to the ation, by Mr. Laidlaw, to subscribe stock in ɩarrow gauge roads, Mr. Brydges, while :ting strongly to the gauge, has taken $2,500 in the stock of the Railways.

'ERATING IN WALL STREET.—The occasional gency of Wall Street affords such tempting rtunities for the profitable use of money, that bers of the country National Banks are re- nted there, and find that they can reap larger ts than by staying at home, and discounting ɩ for their customers. In a New York paper, :ing to the condition of the money market time ago, the following appears:—At a quar- ɔ three the scarcity of money became suddenly quite noticeable, and the interest rate advanced through the intermediate fractions of 1-32, 1-16, $\frac{1}{8}$, $\frac{1}{4}$, and $\frac{3}{8}$ until $\frac{1}{2}$ per cent. was paid, in order to get money with which to make accounts good at bank. This is the rate of 182½ per cent. per annum. It is the inducement of such rates as these that keeps so much money of the Bank of Montreal employed in Wall Street, Mr. King falling a victim to the same temptation that influences the managers of many of the United States country banks. The shareholders, no doubt, appreciate this sort of financing more highly than the customers of the banks. The recent usury prosecutions may somewhat restrict this class of operations, though the probabilities are that means will be found, as always hitherto, of evading the penalties of usury.

THE ENGLISH GOVERNMENT AND THE TELEGRAPH.—By the 1st of January next the telegraph wires of the United Kingdom will, it is expected, pass into the hands of the government. The necessary issue of securities to raise funds will be authorised by a bill now before Parliament. The amount of £5,715,047 will have to be paid the companies for their properties, and the extinction of their existing rights. It appears that the business of the companies is increasing, probably at an average rate of 10 per cent, though in the case of one company the rate was as high as 32 per cent per annum. The purchase of the lines is made on the basis of 20 years profits, nearly the whole amount of the purchase money being on account of these future profits, the existing plant costing less than half a million sterling. The government expect a gross revenue of £673,838, an expenditure of £359,484, and a profit of £314,354, which, after paying interest on the purchase money, would give a surplus of £60,000 to £75,000. The additional facilities to be given the public by the change, are claimed to be the creation of offices of deposit, so that every letter box, and every pillar box would be an office of deposit, where messages would be received to be sent to the telegraph office, to be forwarded to their destination. The next facility would be to bring the wires into the money-order office in every town, and district, thereby bringing the telegraph into the centre of a population, instead of its remaining, as it frequently did at present, in the outskirts. The third facility was the extension, in many places, of the number of hours during which the telegraph would be accessible to the public. It is expected that there will be an increase in the messages of 15 per cent. Telegraph messages are now divided into several prices: some are sent at 6d, others at 1s, others at 2s, at 3s, and at 4s. Those varying tariffs it is now proposed to assimilate to one uniform tariff of 1s. for 20 words. Taking the number of telegrams at 6,250,000, which was supposed to be the annual rate, from June this year the established number of messages in the first year would be 8,815,443. As a considerable number of these telegrams would consist of more than 20 words, each telegram had been estimated as producing 1s. 2d and at that price these 8,815,443 telegrams would yield a revenue of £514,234. The government would serve 3,376 places, instead of 1,882 now served by telegraphs and railroads, they would have 842 branch offices, as compared with 247 existing at present. There is now one telegraph office to every 13,000 of the population; the government would have an office to every 6,000 of the population.

The government will have an entire monopoly of the telegraph business of the United Kingdom.

Communications.

ETNA INSURANCE COMPANY.

Editor of the Canadian Monetary Times.

DEAR SIR,—The settlement of claims in Canada by the Etna insurance Company, of Dublin, is of much interest to the many claimants in Canada, who know literally nothing of the doings of the Company, or that the liquidators have taken the first step towards settling a claim or paid a first dividend. Could you make space for this letter or give us any information in the matter?

1. Has the Company paid a dividend?
2. Are the claims large at home?
3. How could the Company sell out to the United Ports when in the midst of liquidation and without funds to pay for taking existing risks off their hands?
4. Has the Canadian manager transmitted the funds he had at time of failure to the head-office, or does he by arrangement retain these to settle claims since the 30th October last, in the name of the United Ports Company?
5. Has the United Ports Company made any provision or arrangement to open a business in Canada, as advertised by the Canadian manager?
6. Has the United Ports Company paid any of the Etna losses since 30th October last, as advertised and guaranteed by the Canadian manager they would?
7. Did the United Ports Company pay Mrs. Trotter's loss of $3,000 at Ottawa, which has been stated is the case?
8. Have the liquidators no agent in Canada, or is Mr. Griffith their agent?
9. Is it true that the United Ports Company is substantially the Etna under a new name, with same officers, stockholders, &c. Yours truly,

Clinton, July 26, 1869. A CLAIMANT.

Railway News.

GREAT WESTERN RAILWAY.—Traffic for week ending July 9, 1869.

Passengers	$30,649 05
Freight	32,912 77
Mails and Sundries	1,865 25
Total Receipts for week	$65,427 07
Coresponding week, 1868	59,073 14
Increase	$6,353 93

NORTHERN RAILWAY.—Traffic receipts for week ending July 17, 1869.

Passengers	$2,709 32
Freight and live stock	11,091 28
Mails and sundries	347 69
	$14,148 29
Corresponding Week of '68	8,520 61
Increase	$5,627 68

NORTHERN RAILWAY.—Traffic Receipts of week ending July 24th 1869.

Passengers	$2,230 11
Freight	124 80
Mails and Sundries	246 36
Total Receipts for week	$14,956 66
Corresponding week 1868	7,534 07
Increase	$7,422 59

RAILWAY TRAFFIC RETURNS.
FOR THE MONTH OF JUNE, 1869.

NAMES OF THE RAILWAYS.	Passengers.	Mails and Sundries.	Freight.	Total 1869.	Total 1868.	Miles in Operation, 1869.	Miles in Operation, 1868.
Great Western Railway							
Grand Trunk Railway (3 weeks)							
London and Port Stanley Railway							
Welland Railway							
Northern Railway							
Port Hope, Lindsay, and Beaverton Railway, and Peterborough Branch							
Cobourg, Peterborough and Marmora Railway							
Brockville and Ottawa Railway							
St. Lawrence and Ottawa Railway							
Carillon and Grenville Railway*							
Stanstead, Shefford & Chambly Rail*							
St. Lawrence and Industry Railway							
New Brunswick and Canada Railway							
European & North American Railway							
Eastern Extension Railway*							
Nova Scotia Railway*							
Total.							

*No returns.

Rise in Grand Trunk.—*Herapath's Journal* says: "The whole of the Preferences of the Grand Trunk have sprung considerably in the week. The 1st Preference has gone up 2, the 2nd Preference 4, the 3rd Preference 3, and the 4th Preference 1½. The large increase in the traffic, and the fact of the Chairman going to Canada and devoting months of his time to looking closely into the management of the line, also the probable payment this year of the 1st Preference dividend in cash, are the causes of the spring in the prices. Indeed, we shall not be surprised to see the 1st Preference presently above 60, and the other Preferences advanced in proportion. If all go well the proper price of the 1st Preference is 80, at least, for after 1872 the interest rises from 5 to 6 per cent., and surely a six per cent. bond is worth 80.

A Wire Railway.—*Herapath's Journal* speaks of an invention now in use in Leicestershire, England, which obviates the necessity of cuttings, embankments, tunnels, viaducts or bridges, no matter how hilly the country to be travelled. It is a wire tramway, which consists of endless wire rope, supported on a series of pullies, carried by substantial posts, ordinarily about 150 feet apart, but which may be extended to 600 feet.' One of the ends of this rope passes round a Fowler's clip-drum, worked by a portable steam engine, and this drives the rope at a speed of six miles an hour. Boxes are hung on the rope at the loading end near the station by a pendant, which is ingeniously arranged to preserve a perfect equilibrium, and at the same time to pass without hindrance over the supports. Each of these boxes is loaded with a hundred weight, and the delivery is at the rate of two hundred boxes, or ten ton per hour, for a distance of three miles. This description applies to a wire extending that distance to some stone quarries in Lancashire. Already wire tramways on the same plan are said to be in course of erection in France, Italy, and Spain, and it is probable, (says the Journal) that this generation may see goods carried by wire as commonly as messages. The tramway is not unlike an exceedingly stout electrical telegraph; and there is something exceedingly droll in the sight of a regiment of well-laden trucks or boxes passing gravely along it at stated intervals and at a regular pace, much as if they were at aerial drill.

THE PATENT ACT OF 1869.

The new Act which makes the law respecting patents uniform throughout the Dominion took effect on the 1st of July. Any person, a resident of Canada for at least one year before his application, having invented or discovered any new and useful improvement on any art, machine, manufacture or composition, not known or used by others before his invention or discovery and not in public use or on sale in any of the Provinces, may obtain a patent granting an exclusive property therein. An original and true inventor or discoverer is not deprived of his right to a patent by reason of having taken out a patent for his invention or discovery in any other country at any time within six months and preceding his application here. The patent may be granted to any person to whom the inventor or discoverer has assigned his right of obtaining it.

Any person, having been a resident of Canada for at least one year next before his application, and who has invented or discovered any improvement on any patented invention or discovery, may obtain a patent for such improvement, but shall not thereby obtain the right of vending or using the original invention or discovery, nor shall the patent for the original invention or discovery confer the right of vending or using the patented improvement.

In cases of joint applications, patents shall be granted in the names of all the applicants; an assignment from one to the other shall be registered.

The applicant for a patent shall make oath or affirmation that he verily believes that he or his assignor is or was the true inventor or discoverer, that he is or the assignor was a resident of Canada for one year before the application. The petition shall specify the domicile of the applicant, the title of the invention or discovery, its object and a short description of it and distinctly allege all the facts necessary under the Act to entitle him to the patent and accompany it with a written specification in duplicate, describing the invention or discovery in such full and exact terms as to distinguish it from all contrivances or processes for similar purposes.

The application shall correctly and fully describe the mode of operating contemplated by the applicant; shall state distinctly the contrivances which he claims as new, and for the use of which he claims an exclusive privilege; shall bear the name of the place where it was made, the date, and be signed by the applicant and two witnesses —in the case of a machine the specification shall fully explain the principle and the several modes in which it is intended to apply and work out the same; in the case of a machine or in any other case where the invention or discovery admits of illustration by means of drawings, the applicant shall also, with his application send in drawings in duplicate showing clearly all parts of the invention or discovery; and each drawing shall bear the name of the inventor or discoverer and shall have written references, corresponding with the specification, and a certificate of the applicant that it is the drawing referred to in the specification; but the Commissioner may require any greater number of drawings than those above mentioned, or dispense with any of them, as he may see fit; one duplicate of the specifications and of the drawings, if any drawings, shall be annexed to the patent, of which it forms an essential part, and the other duplicate shall remain deposited in the Patent Office.

The applicant shall also deliver to the Commissioner, unless specially dispensed from so doing for some good reason, a neat, working model of his invention or discovery, whenever the invention or discovery admits of such model, and shall deliver to the Commissioner specimens of the ingredients, and of the composition of matter sufficient in quantity for the purpose of experiment, whenever the invention is a composition of matter.

An intending applicant for a patent who has not yet perfected his invention or discovery may file in the Patent office a description of his invention so far with or without plans. This document, called a *caveat*, is to be preserved in secrecy by the Commissioner until the patent issues. If application be made by any other person for a patent with which the *caveat* may interfere, the Commissioner shall give notice to him who filed the *caveat* and such person shall within three months after such notice take the other steps necessary in the application for a patent, unless the person filing a *caveat* shall within four years from the filing have made application for a patent the *caveat* shall be void. Under certain circumstances the Commissioner may object to grant a patent, but his decision is subject to appeal to the Governor in Council.

In case of interfering applications for any patent the same shall be submitted to the arbitration of three skilled persons one to be shewn by each of the applicants and the third by the Commissioner whose award shall be final. If either applicant shall fail to choose an arbitrator the patent shall issue to the opposite party.

No letters patent shall extend to prevent the use of any invention or discovery in any foreign ship or vessel, where such invention or discovery is not so used for the manufacture of any goods to be vended within or exported from Canada.

Every person who, before the issue of a patent, has purchased, constructed or acquired any invention or discovery for which a patent has been obtained under this Act, shall have the right to use and vend the specific article, but the patent shall not be invalid as regards other persons by reason of such purchase, &c., by the first named or those to whom he may have sold the same; unless the purchase, &c., was made more than one year before the application for the patent or the use extended for a longer period than a year.

Every patent shall be assignable either as to the whole interest or as to any part by an instrument in writing. Any grant and conveyance of an exclusive right to make and use and to grant to others the right to make and use the invention or discovery patented within the Dominion or throughout any one or more of the Provinces or any part of the Provinces shall be registered in the office of the Commissioner. Every assignment affecting a patent shall be void as against a subsequent assignee unless such instrument before prescribed is registered before the registering of the instrument under which such subsequent assignee may claim.

The fees payable to the Commissioner of Patents, are:—

On a petition for a patent for 5 years	$20 00
" " extension for 5 to 10 years	20 00
" " " 10 to 15 years	20 00
On lodging a caveat	5 00
On asking to register an assignment	2 00
" " attach a disclaimer to a patent	4 00
" " for a copy of a patent with specification	4 00
On petition to reissue a patent after demand and on petition to extend a former patent to the Dominion, for every unexpired year of duration of patent	4 00

The patent when granted shall be issued for five years, renewable for a second and third period of five years each; but every patent is subject to the condition that it shall cease at the end of three years unless the patentee shall within that period have commenced and shall after such commencement carry on in Canada the construction or manufacture of the invention or discovery patented in such manner that any person desiring to use it may obtain it or cause it to be made for him at easonable price at some manufactory or establ-ment for making or constructing it, in Canada, 1 that such patent shall be void if after the piration of eighteen months from the granting reof, the patentee or his assignee or assignees the whole or a part of his interest in the patent, ports or causes to be imported into Canada, the ention or discovery for which the patent is nted.

Patents granted under the laws of the various rvinces remain in force and may be extended er the whole Dominion on proper application 1 payment of fees.

Commercial.

Oil at Petrolia.
(From our own Correspondent.)

PETROLIA, July 26, 1869.

Since my last the well put down by Mr. Hill s struck a splendid show of oil. This is on lot 11th concession of Enniskillen.

The Reliable (Harry Prince's) enterprise, near a station, although drilled to the usual depth, s not as yet shown symptoms of being a strike, ly faint indications of oil showing themselves; is considered a failure. The same may be said the Spencer No. 1.

The Hyde well, near the station, has not turned t as well as was expected; and the Dunlop and lly, in which the tools were fastened, is not yet ar, but is nearly so. This well is close to the stern end of the station.

There is a new well going down near the famous ugheed, and another quite near the former, ing put down by Captain Tyler, the later by encer, Prince & Co. A Mr. Wallen is also put-g down a well nearly opposite these, which, gether with some three others, are all the wells present going down. I shall more particularly umerate and describe them as they mature.

The crude oil combination met last night, with full attendance of the producers, our most teemed and enterprising friend, Mr. Noble, in e chair. A very satisfactory statement of affairs ving been submitted and approved of, it was unimously agreed to place the price of crude oil $1.25 per barrel. This may appear to some a duction in price, but it really is not, as up to is time, although the price has been nominally .62½ per barrel, still, when we take into con-ieration the fact that a larger quantity had pre-ously been sold by said combination at 75 cents r barrel, the equalized price of the whole never ceeded $1.25.

The great still of Messrs. Duffield, Higgins & ., of this place, has been run off with perfect ccess, making a prime white distillate of the sest quality; and, in fact, coming up in every rticular to their most sanguine anticipations. I quote—Crude Oil, very firm at $1.25 per brl.; fined, 20c. per gallon.

The production of crude this week is about 500 barrels.
M. P.

Toronto Market.

PRODUCE.—Wheat—Receipts 2,090 bushs., and 230 bush. last week. The market has been un-ttled during the greater part of the week, but osed firm and 2 to 3 cents higher. There is a fair iquiry and sales are reported of a lot of Spring $1.03, early in the week, and a lot of 2,000 ishs. at about $1.05. 2,300 bushs. Fall sold at 1.07 f.o.b. Holders are firm in their views. he prospects of the crops continue good, although ie weather is too wet and greatly retards the in-ithering of the hay crop. Oats.—Receipts 1,800 ishs. Prices are firm and the demand active, dees closing with a downward tendency, Nu-ierous car loads of eastern have sold at 52 to 54c; o sales of western, they are worth 57c. Peas.— othing doing in lots, on the street 70c. would 3 paid.

FLOUR.—Receipts 1,410 bbls., and 1,760 bbls.

last week. The market is firm and tending up-wards. Sales were made of a number of lots at $4.55 to $4.80 of No. 1 Superfine, the market closing with holders asking $4.75. Spring wheat extra sold at $4.80, and 200 bbls. extra brought the same price at Weston. Meal.—Oatmeal is nomi-nal, car lots are probably worth $5.50 to $5.75; small lots of cornmeal sell at $4 to $4.25.

PROVISIONS.—Receipts are reported good and the demand fairly active with an upward tendency in prices. Cheese.—Considerable amount are to hand. Makers ask 10 to 11c.; shippers offering 9 to 10c; prices are easier. Eggs.—There are good supplies in market, packed are worth 14 to 15c. Pork.—Continues in good demand with light stocks, a lot 90 brls, extra prime, sold at $19. Salt.—There were two cargoes of American landed during the week.

WOOL.—The receipts were lighter and the mar-ket is dull; 9,000 lbs sold at 31c. which is now the ruling quotation.

FREIGHTS.—The rates for grain to Oswego is unchanged 3c. U.S. Currency; to Kingston 2c. gold. Flour to Montreal 20c. Lumber to Oswego $1.50 per M. Coal, Erie to Toronto, $1.35 to $1.40.

FREIGHTS—The Grand Trunk rates to Liverpool are:—Flour 4s. stg. per bbl.; wheat 8s. 6d. stg., per quarter; and boxed meats 55s. per ton.

The following are the Grand Trunk Railway Company's summer rates from Toronto to the un-dermentioned stations; which came into force on the 19th ult.:—Flour to all Stations from Belle-velle to Lynn, inclusive 25c; grain, per 100 lbs., 13c; flour to Prescott, 30c; grain 15c; flour to all stations between Island Pond and Portland, in-clusive, 75c; grain, 35c; flour to Boston, 80c, gold; grain 40c; flour to Halifax, 90c; flour to St. John, 85c.

Halifax Market.

BREADSTUFFS.—We have to report a modera-tively active market, for Flours during the past week, with considerable irregularity in prices. Several lots of Canada Extra, consigned to parties here outside the trade, were thrown on the mar-ket at from 30 to 40 cts. per bbl. below their actual value, (to the injury of the general trade). $5.90 was accepted for some lots of above. Supers are in light supply, with good demand. Fancy in limited request at quotations. Extras are without enquiry, with stocks in excess of require-ments. No. 2 inactive and nominal, with good supply of American. Imports from January 1st to July 20th, 1868 and 1869—

	Bbls. Flour.		Bbls. Cornmeal.
1869	82301		20407
1868	94336		33516

WEST INDIA PRODUCE.—Molasses continues unchanged, without transactions. Sugars are being pressed for offers, and continue nominal. No transactions of any moment, are reported; the trade being confined to retailers.

FISH AND OIL.—Codfish in active request for shipment and local wants. Receipts light. We have favorable reports from various outports of catch, both as to quantity and quality; and the general impression is that low prices will be seen this Fall. Pickled Fish unchanged. Cod Oil active and improved. Seal Oil unchanged.

EXCHANGE.—Bank Draughts, London, at 60 days, at 13½ per cent. Montreal sight, 4 per cent. St. John, N. B...3 per cent. prem.—R. C. Hamilton & Co's. Circular.

Imports of Groceries at Montreal.

Imports of following Groceries for fiscal year ending 30th June, 1869:

	Quantity.	Value.
Sugar, lbs.	38,943,044	$1,797,046
Molasses, gal.	13,075,492	296,865
Melada and Cane juice lbs.	10,236,532	281,399
Tea, Black lbs.	759,246	213,254
" Green "	4,495,053	1,508,921
Fruit Dried "	6,387,246	349,599

Imports of following Groceries for the half year ending 30th June, 1868, as compared with the same period in 1869:

	1868.	
	Quantity.	Value.
Sugar, lbs.	12,198,667	$580,758
Molasses, gal.	1,288,394	38,919
Melada, lbs.	5,609,182	255,603
Tea, Black lbs.	142,540	46,025
" Green "	1,727,766	608,563
Fruit, Dried "	1,704,790	65,495

	1869.	
	Quantity.	Value.
Sugar, lbs.	14,150,631	$690,119
Molasses, gal.	2,208,789	53,060
Melada, lbs.	5,166,865	142,609
Tea, Black lbs.	452,342	122,643
" Green "	2,824,621	961,205
Fruit, Dried "	2,868,064	94,486

—The barque Rothiemay has loaded at Mon-treal, with lumber for Buenos Ayres, South Ameri-ca. The lumber was bought in the Ottawa region by L. Barnes & Co., of Burlington, Vt. The Rothiemay is one of six vessels which will proba-bly be dispatched to the same country during the season.

STATEMENT OF BANKS

ACTING UNDER CHARTER, FOR THE MONTH ENDING 30TH JUNE, 1869, ACCORDING TO RETURNS FURNISHED BY THE BANKS TO THE AUDITOR OF PUBLIC ACCOUNTS.

NAME OF BANK	CAPITAL — Capital authorized by Act	CAPITAL — Capital paid up	LIABILITIES — Promissory Notes in circulation not bearing Interest	LIABILITIES — Balances due to other Banks	LIABILITIES — Cash Deposits not bearing Interest	LIABILITIES — Cash Deposits bearing Interest	LIABILITIES — TOTAL LIABILITIES	ASSETS — Coin, Bullion, and Provincial Notes	ASSETS — Landed or other Property of the Bank	ASSETS — Government Securities	ASSETS — Promissory Notes, or Bills of other Banks	ASSETS — Balances due from other Banks	ASSETS — Notes and Bills Discounted	ASSETS — Other Debts due the Bank, not included under foregoing heads	TOTAL ASSETS

ONTARIO AND QUEBEC

Montreal · Quebec · City · Gore · British North America · Banque du Peuple · Niagara District · Molson's · Toronto · Eastern Townships · Banque Nationale · Merchants' · Royal Canadian · Union Bk of Canada · Mechanics' · Bank of Commerce.

NOVA SCOTIA

Bank of Yarmouth · Merchants' Bank · People's Bank · Union Bank · Bank of Nova Scotia.

NEW BRUNSWICK

Bank of New Brunswick · Commercial Bank · St. Stephen's Bank · People's Bank.

Totals.

TORONTO PRICES CURRENT.—JULY 29, 1869.

Name of Article.	Wholesale Rates.	
	$ c.	$ c.
Boots and Shoes.		
Mens' Thick Boots	2 05	2 50
" Kip	2 25	3 00
" Calf	3 20	3 70
" Congress Gaiters	1 65	2 50
" Kip Cobourgs	1 20	1 40
Boys' Thick Boots	1 70	1 80
Youths' "	1 40	1 50
Women's Batts	0 95	1 30
" Balmoral	1 20	1 50
" Congress Gaiters	0 90	1 50
Misses' Batts	0 75	1 00
" Balmoral	1 00	1 20
" Congress Gaiters	1 00	1 30
Girls' Batts	0 65	0 85
" Balmoral	0 90	1 05
" Congress Gaiters	0 75	1 10
Children's C. T. Cacks	0 50	0 65
" Gaiters	0 65	0 90
Drugs.		
Aloes Cape	0 12½	0 16
Alum	0 02½	0 03
Borax	0 00	0 00
Camphor, refined	0 65	0 70
Castor Oil	0 16½	0 28
Caustic Soda	0 04½	0 05
Cochineal	0 90	1 00
Cream Tartar	0 30	0 35
Epsom Salts	0 03	0 04
Extract Logwood	0 11	0 12
Gum Arabic, sorts	0 30	0 35
Indigo, Madras	0 90	1 00
Licorice	0 14	0 15
Madder	0 00	0 16
Galls	0 32	0 37
Opium	12 00	13 50
Oxalic Acid	0 26	0 35
Potash, Bi-tart	0 25	0 28
" Bichromate	0 15	0 20
Potass Iodide	3 90	4 50
Senna	0 12½	0 60
Soda Ash	0 02½	0 04
Soda Bicarb	0 00	4 00
Tartaric Acid	0 40	0 45
Verdigris	0 35	0 40
Vitriol, Blue	0 08	0 10
Groceries.		
Coffees:		
Java, ℔ lb.	0 22@	0 23
Laguayra,	0 17	0 18
Rio	0 15	0 17
Fish:		
Herrings, Lab. split	0 00	0 00
" round	0 00	0 00
" scaled	0 33	0 35
Mackerel, small kitts	1 00	0 00
Loch. Her. wh'e firks	2 50	2 75
" half "	1 25	1 50
White Fish & Trout	0 00	3 50
Salmon, saltwater	14 00	15 00
Dry Cod, ℔ 112 lbs.	4 50	5 00
Fruit:		
Raisins, Layers	1 90	2 00
" M R.	1 90	2 00
" Valentias new	0 6	0 6½
Currants, new	0 4¾	0 05
" old	0 3¾	0 04
Figs	0 11	0 12
Molasses:		
Clayed, ℔ gal.	0 00	0 35
Syrups, Standard	0 55	0 56
" Golden	0 59	0 60
Rice:		
Arracan	60	4 00
Spices:		
Cassia, whole, ℔ lb.	0 00	0 45
Cloves	0 11	0 12
Nutmegs	0 50	0 55
Ginger, ground	0 18	0 23
" Jamaica, root	0 20	0 25
Pepper, black	0 10½	0 11
Pimento	0 08	0 09
Sugars:		
Port Rico, ℔ lb.	0 9	0 9¼
Cuba "	0 9	0 9¼
Barbadoes (bright)	0 9½	0 9¾
Canada Sugar Refine'y, yellow No. 2, 60ds	0 9¾	0 9½
Yellow, No. 2½	0 9¼	0 9¾
No. 3	0 9¾	0 10
Crushed X	0 10¾	0 11
" A	0 11¼	0 11½
Ground	0 12½	0 12¾
Dry Crushed	0 12	0 12½
Extra Ground	0 13	0 13½
Teas:		
Japan com'n to good	0 48	0 50
" Fine to choicest	0 55	0 60
Colored, com. to fine	0 60	0 70
Congou & Souch'ng	0 42	0 75
Oolong, good to fine	0 50	0 65
Y. Hyson, com to gd.	0 47½	0 55
Medium to choice	0 65	0 80
Extra choice	0 85	0 95

Name of Article.	Wholesale Rate.	
	$ c.	$ c.
Groceries—*Contin'd*		
Gunpowd'r c. to med.	0 55	0 70
" med. to fine.	0 70	0 85
" fine to fins't	0 85	0 95
Hyson	0 45	0 80
Imperial	0 42	0 80
Tobacco, Manufact'd:		
Can Leaf, ℔ lb 5s & 10s.	0 26	0 30
Western Leaf, com.	0 25	0 26
" Good	0 27	0 32
" Fine	0 32	0 35
" Bright fine	0 40	0 50
" " choice	0 60	0 75
Hardware.		
Tin (net cash prices)		
Block, ℔ lb	0 35	0 00
Grain	0 30	0 00
Copper:		
Pig	0 23	0 24
Sheet	0 30	0 33
Cut Nails:		
Assorted ¼ Shingles, ℔ 100 lb.	2 95	3 00
Shingle alone do	3 15	3 25
Lathe and 5 dy	3 30	3 40
Galvanized Iron:		
Assorted sizes	0 08	0 09
Best No. 24	0 07½	0 00
" 26	0 08	0 08½
" 28	0 09	0 09½
Horse Nails:		
Guest's or Griffin's assorted sizes	0 00	0 00
For W. ass'd sizes	0 18	0 19
Patent Hammer'd do	0 17	0 18
Iron (at 4 months):		
Pig—Gartsherrie No1	24 00	25 00
Other brands. No1	22 00	24 00
" No2	0 00	0 00
Bar—Scotch, ℔ 100 lb	2 25	2 50
Refined	3 00	3 25
Swedes	5 00	5 50
Hoops—Coopers	3 00	3 25
Band	3 00	3 25
Boiler Plates	3 25	3 50
Canada Plates	3 75	4 00
Union Jack	0 00	0 00
Pontypool	3 25	4 00
Swansea	3 90	4 00
Lead (at 4 months):		
Bar, ℔ 100 lbs.	0 06½	0 07
Sheet "	0 08	0 09
Shot	0 07½	0 07¾
Iron Wire (net cash):		
No. 6, ℔ bundle	2 70	2 80
" 9, "	3 10	3 20
" 12, "	3 40	3 50
" 16, "	4 30	4 40
Powder:		
Blasting, Canada	3 50	0 00
FF "	4 25	4 50
FFF "	4 75	5 00
Blasting, English	4 00	5 00
FF loose	5 00	6 00
FFF "	6 00	6 50
Pressed Spikes (4 mos):		
Regular sizes 100	4 00	4 25
Extra "	4 50	5 00
Tin Plates (net cash):		
IC Coke	7 50	8 50
IC Charcoal	8 50	9 00
IX "	10 50	11 00
IXX "	13 50	14 00
DC "	8 00	8 50
DX "	9 50	0 00
Hides & Skins, ℔ lb		
Green rough	0 00	0 05
Green, salt'd & insp'd	0 06	0 06½
Cured	0 00	0 00
Calfskins, green	0 00	0 10
Calfskins, cured	0 00	0 12½
" dry	0 18	0 20
Sheepskins,	1 20	1 60
" pelts	0 10	0 20
Hops.		
Inferior, ℔ lb	0 00	0 00
Medium	0 00	0 00
Good	0 00	0 00
Fancy	0 00	0 00
Leather, @ (4 mos.) In lots of less than 50 sides, 10 ℔ cnt higher.		
Spanish Sole, 1st qual'y heavy, weights ℔ lb	0 21	0 22
Do. 1st qual middle do	$0 22	0 23
Do. No. 2, light weights	0 20	0 00
Slaughter heavy	0 00	0 24
Do. light	0 00	0 00
Harness, best	0 25	0 27
" No. 2	0 00	0 00
Upper heavy	0 30	0 32
" light	0 33	0 34

Name of Article.	Wholesale Rates.	
	$ c.	$ c.
Leather—*Contin'd.*		
Kip Skins, Patna	0 30	0 35
French	0 70	0 90
English	0 65	0 80
Hemlock Calf (30 to 35 lbs.) per doz.	0 50	0 60
Do. light	0 45	0 50
French Calf.	1 03	1 06
Grain & Satn Clt ℔ doz.	0 00	0 55
Splits, large ℔ lb	0 30	0 38
" small	0 23	0 28
Enamelled Cow ℔ foot	0 20	0 21
Patent	0 20	0 21
Pebble Grain	0 15	0 17
Buff	0 14	0 16
Oils.		
Cod	0 65	0 70
Lard, extra	0 00	0 00
" No. 1	0 00	0 00
" Woollen	0 00	0 00
Lubricating, patent	0 00	0 00
" Mott's economic	0 30	0 00
Linseed, raw	0 76	0 82
" boiled	0 81	0 87
Machinery	0 00	0 00
Olive, common, ℔ gal.	1 00	1 60
" salad	1 95	2 30
" salad, in bots. qt. ℔ case	3 60	3 75
Sesame salad, ℔ gal.	1 60	1 75
Seal, pale	0 75	0 85
Spirits Turpentine	0 52½	0 60
Varnish	0 00	0 00
Whale.	0 00	0 90
Paints, &c.		
White Lead, genuine in Oil, ℔ 25 lbs.	0 00	2 35
Do. No. 1 "	0 00	2 10
" 2 "	0 00	1 90
" 3 "	0 00	1 65
White Zinc, genuine	3 00	3 50
White Lead, dry	0 05½	0 09
Red Lead	0 07½	0 08
Venetian Red, Eng'h	0 02½	0 03½
Yellow Ochre, Fren'h	0 02¾	0 03
Whiting	0 85	1 25
Petroleum. (Refined ℔ gal.)		
Water white, car l'd	0 20	0 21
" small lots	0 22	0 23
Straw, by car load	0 00	0 00
" small lots	0 00	0 00
Amber, by car load	0 00	0 00
" small lots	0 00	0 00
Benzine	0 00	0 00
Produce.		
Grain:		
Wheat, Spring, 60 lb	1 00	1 03
" Fall 60 "	1 00	1 05
Barley 48 "	0 00	0 70
Peas 60 "	0 00	0 00
Oats 34 "	0 53	0 57
Rye 56 "	0 56	0 00
Seeds:		
Clover, choice 60 "	0 00	0 00
" com'n 68 "	0 00	0 00
Timothy, cho'e 4 "	0 00	0 00
" inf. to good 48 "	0 00	0 00
Flax 56 "	0 00	0 00
Flour (per brl.):		
Superior extra	0 00	0 00
Extra superfine,	4 60	4 70
Fancy superfine	4 55	4 65
Superfine No 1	4 45	4 50
" No. 2	—	—
Oatmeal, (per brl.)	5 50	6 00
Provisions		
Butter, dairy tub ℔ lb.	0 13½	0 15
" store packed	0 12½	0 13
Cheese, new	0 11	0 12½
Pork, mess, per brl.	27 00	27 50
" prime mess	—	—
" prime	—	—
Bacon, rough	0 12	0 12½
" Cumberl'd cut	0 13	0 00
" smoked	0 00	0 00
Hams, in salt	0 00	0 00
" smoked	0 00	0 07
Shoulders, in salt	0 00	0 11
Lard, in kegs	0 16½	0 15½
Eggs, packed	0 13	0 15
Beef Hams	0 00	0 10
Tallow	0 08	0 8
Hogs dressed, heavy	0 00	0 00
" medium	0 00	0 00
" light	0 00	0 00
Salt, &c.		
American brls.	1 35	1 37
Liverpool coarse	0 80	0 90
Goderich	0 00	1 53
Plaster	0 00	0 00
Water Lime	1 50	0 00

Soap & Candles.	$ c.	$ c.
D. Crawford & Co.'s ..		
Imperial.........	0 07½	0 08
" Golden Bar	0 07	0 07½
" Silver Bar........	0 07	0 07½
Crown	0 05	0 05½
No. 1	0 03½	0 03¾
Candles	0 00	0 11
Wines, Liquors, &c.		
Ale:		
English, per doz. qrts.	2 60	2 65
Guinness Dub Portr..	2 35	2 40
Spirits:		
Pure Jamaica Rum...	1 80	2 25
De Kuyper's H. Gin..	1 55	1 65
Booth's Old Tom.....	1 90	2 00
Gin:		
Green, cases.........	4 00	4 25
Booth's Old Tom, c...	6 00	6 25
Wines:		
Port, common	1 00	1 25
" fine old	2 00	4 00
Sherry, common	1 00	1 50
" medium	1 70	1 80
"old pale or golden..	2 50	4 00

Brandy:	$ c.	$ c
Hennessy's, per gal..	2 30	2 50
Martell's " ..	2 30	2 50
J. Robin & Co.'s " ..	2 25	2 35
Otard, Dupuy & Cos..	2 25	2 35
Brandy, cases.........	8 50	9 00
Brandy, com. per c...	4 00	4 50
Whiskey:		
Common 36 u. p......	0 58	0 60
Old Rye	0 77½	0 80
Malt	0 77½	0 80
Toddy	0 77½	0 80
Scotch, per gal........	1 90	2 10
Irish—Kinnahan's c...	7 00	7 50
" Dunnville's Belf't..	6 00	6 25
Wool.		
Fleece, lb.............	0 30	0 31
Pulled "............	0 00	0 00
Furs.		
Bear..................	0 00	0 00
Beaver, ℘ lb..........	0 00	0 00
Coon	0 00	0 00
Fisher................	0 00	0 00
Martin................	0 00	0 00
Mink..................	0 00	0 00
Otter..................	0 00	0 00
Spring Rats	0 00	0 00
Fox.	0 00	0 00

INSURANCE COMPANIES.

ENGLISH.—*Quotations on the London Market.*

No. of Shares.	Last Dividend.	Name of Company.	Shares par val £	Amount paid.	Last Sale.
20,000		Briton Medical and General Life...	10	....	2½
50,000	7½	Commer'l Union, Fire, Life and Mar.	50	5	5¾
24,000	8	City of Glasgow	25	2½	4¾
5,000	9½	Edinburgh Life	100	15	33½
400,000	5—½ yr	European Life and Guarantee......	2½	11s6	4s. 0d
100,000	10	Etna Fire and Marine............	10	1½	—
20,000	5	Guardian	100	50	53½
24,000	12	Imperial Fire..................	500	50	352
7,500	9½	Imperial Life	100	10	17½
100,000	10	Lancashire Fire and Life..........	20	2	2⅝
10,000	11	Life Association of Scotland.......	40	7½	25
35,862	45s. p. sh	London Assurance Corporation ..	25	12½	48¾
10,000	5	London and Lancashire Life	10	1	—
87,504	40	Liverp'l & London & Globe F. & L.	20	2	7½
20,000	5	National Union Life	5	1	1
20,000	12½	Northern Fire and Life	100	5	13
40,000	12 '63, bo 5s.	North British and Mercantile	50	6¼	19½
40,000	50	Ocean Marine	25	5	17½
2,500	£5 12s.	Provident Life..................	100	10	35
....	£4½ p. s.	Phœnix.........................	....	....	139½ x d
200,000	2½—h. yr.	Queen Fire and Life	10	1	21s.
100,000	3s. bo. 4s	Royal Insurance..................	20	3	6½
20,000	10	Scottish Provincial Fire and Life ..	50	2½	5½
10,000	25	Standard Life	50	12	66 x d
4,000	5	Star Life	25	1¼	—
		CANADIAN.			℘ c.
8,000	4	British America Fire and Marine ..	$50	$25	53 54 x d
....	4	Canada Life	...	....	.....
4000	12	Montreal Assurance	£50	£5	135
10,000	8	Provincial Fire and Marine........	60	11	.....
....	....	Quebec Fire	40	32½	£22½ 23
....	7	" Marine..................	100	40	85 90
10,000	4 6 mo's.	Western Assurance...............	40	9	50

RAILWAYS.	Sha's	Paid	Montr	London
Atlantic and St. Lawrence.....................	£100	All.	....	58 60
Buffalo and Lake Huron	20½	"	....	2¾ 3
Do. do Preference	10	"	....	5 7
Buff., Brantt. & Goderich, 6℘c., 1872-3-4....	100	"	....	60 70
Champlain and St. Lawrence	....	....	10 11	....
Do. do Pref. 10 ℘ ct....	....	....	80 85	....
Grand Trunk	100	"	15 16	15 15½
Do. Eq. G. M. Bds. 1 ch. 6℘c...........	100	"	....	85 87
Do. First Preference, 5 ℘ c	100	"	....	54 55
Do. Deferred, 3 ℘ ct..	100	"	....	....
Do. Second Pref. Bonds, 5℘c..........	100	"	....	40 42
Do. do Deferred, 3 ℘ ct.	100	"	...	....
Do Third Pref. Stock, 4℘ct.	100	"	...	30 32
Do. do. Deferred, 3 ℘ ct......	100	"	...	....
Do. Fourth Pref. Stock, 3℘c...........	100	"	....	18 19
Do. do. Deferred, 3 ℘ ct............	100	"	....	....
Great Western	20½	"	15 15½	15⅝ 15⅞
Do. New	20½	18	....	....
Do. 6 ℘ c. Bds, due 1873-76............	100	All.	....	100 102
5½℘c Bds. due 1877-78....	100	"	....	94 96
Marine Railway, Halifax, $250, all......	$250	"	....	....
Northern of Canada, 6 ℘c. 1st Pref. Bds..........	100	"	.. ..	82 84

EXCHANGE.	Halifax.	Montr'l.	Quebec.	Toronto.
Bank on London, 60 days......				
Sight or 75 days date	12½ 13	9⅝ 9⅞	9¾ 10	10⅜
Private do.	11½ 12	8 9	9 9½	9⅞
Private, with documents.........	....	8 8½	....	....
Bank on New York..............	....	26½ 26¾	25½ 25¾	26½
Private do.	....	26¾ 27¼	26½ 26¾	....
Gold Drafts do.	....	par.	par ½ dis.	par ¼ dis.
Silver	....	4 4½	....	4 to 5½

STOCK AND BOND REPORT.

The dates of our quotations are as follows:—Toronto, July 28; Montreal, July 26; Quebec, July 24; London, July 8.

NAME.	Shares.	Paid up.	Divid'd last 6 Months.	Dividend Day.	CLOSING PRICES. Toronto.	Montre'l	Quebec.
BANKS.			℘ ct.				
British North America	$250	All.	3½ b½pc	July and Jan.	104 104½	104½ 105	104 104½
Jacques Cartier..............	50	"	4	1 June, 1 Dec.	107½ 108½	107½ 108½	107 107½
Montreal	200	"	6	"	160½ 161	161 162	160½ 161½
Nationale....................	50	"	4	1 Nov. 1 May.	107 107½	107 108	107½ 108
New Brunswick	100	"	......	......	....	....	....
Nova Scotia	200	—	7&b83½	Mar. and Sept.	....	....	....
Du Peuple......	50	"	4	1 Mar., 1 Sept.	109 109½	109 110	108½ 109
Toronto	100	"	4	1 Jan., 1 July.	121 124	121 123	120 122
Bank of Yarmouth...........	....	....	......	......	....	....	....
Canadian Bank of Com'c......	50	All.	......	......	103 103½	102 103	102 103
City Bank Montreal	80	"	4	1 June, 1 Dec.	99 99½	99 100½	99½ 100
Commer'l Bank (St. John)....	100	"	℘ ct.	. ...	....	..	....
Eastern Townships' Bank....	50	"	4	1 July, 1 Jan..	....	98½ 100	98 99
Gore	40	...	none.	1 Jan., 1 July.	62½ 65	60 62½	60 62½
Halifax Banking Company....	...	....	......	. ....	...	...	...
Mechanics' Bank.............	50	All.	4	1 Nov., 1 May.	93 95	93 94	93 93½
Merchants' Bank of Canada....	100	"	5	1 Jan., 1 July.	105 106	104 105	105½ 105
Merchants' Bank (Halifax)....	....	....	.....	.....	....	....	....
Molson's Bank......	50	All.	4	1 Apr., 1 Oct.	100 100½	109 110	100 109½
Niagara District Bank...	100	70	3½	1 Jan., 1 July.	...	....	..
Ontario Bank................	40	All.	4	1 June, 1 Dec.	95½ 96½	95 95½	95 95½
People's Bank (Fred'kton)....	100	"	......	......	....	...	. ..
People's Bank (Halifax)	20	"	7 12 m	......	....	....	....
Quebec Bank	100	"	3½	1 June, 1 Dec.	100½ 101	100½ 101	100½ 101
Royal Canadian Bank	50	60	4	1 Jan., 1 July.	50 55	50 60	45 50
St. Stephens Bank	100	All	.....	......	....	....	. .
Union Bank	100	"	4	1 Jan., 1 July.	105 105½	105 105½	105 105½
Union Bank (Halifax)........	100	....	7 12mo	Feb. and Aug.	....	....	....
MISCELLANEOUS.							
British America Land........	250	44	......	......	....	....	....
British Colonial S. S. Co......	250	32½	......	......	...	....	....
Canada Company	32½	All.	......	......	....	....	....
Canada Landed Credit Co.....	50	$50	8½	......	79 80	....	....
Canada Per. B'ldg Society....	50	All.	5	......	123 123½	....	....
Canada Mining Company.....	4	90	......	......	....	....	....
Do. Inl'd Steam Nav. Co....	100	All.	15 12m	......	....	99½ 100	90 100½
Do. Glass Company.........	100	"	None.	......	....	40 60	....
Canad'n Loan & Investm't....	25	2½	......	......	....	....	....
Canada Agency	10	¼	......	......	....	....	....
Colonial Securities Co........	...	....	......	......	....	....	....
Freehold Building Society....	100	All.	5	......	117½ 118	....	....
Halifax Steamboat Co........	100	"	......	......	....	....	....
Halifax Gas Company........	....	....	......	. .. .	....	...	....
Hamilton Gas Company......	....	....	.....	. ....	....	....	....
Huron Copper Bay Co........	4	12	20	. ....	....	30 45	....
Lake Huron S. and C.........	5	102	......	......	....	...	....
Montreal Mining Consols.....	20	$15	......	. ....	....	3.10 3.25	...
Do. Telegraph Co...	40	All.	5	......	132 133	131 133	132 133
Do. Elevating Co...	00	"	5½	......	....	105 107	....
Do. City Gas Co.........	40	"	4	15 Mar. 15 Sep.	....	138 140	137 138
Do. City Pass. R,. Co....	50	"	2	......	....	111 112	111 111½
Quebec and L. S.	8	84	......	......	....	...	....
Quebec Gas Co...............	200	All.	4	1 Mar., 1 Sep.	....	...	120 125
Quebec Street R. R..........	50	25	3	......	....	....	Bks cl'd
Richelieu Navigation Co......	100	All.	7-12m	1 Jan., 1 July.	....	120 123	120 123
St. Lawrence Glass Company.	100	"	....	......	....	50 90	. ..
St. Lawrence Tow Boat Co....	100	"	......	3 Feb.	....	...	30 35
Tor'to Consumers' Gas Co....	50	"	⅝ m	1 My Au Mar Fe	107 107½	...	107 107½
Trust & Loan Co. of U. C.....	20	5	3	......	....	....	.. .
West'n Canada Bldg Soc'y....	50	All.	5	......	118 118½	....	....

SECURITIES.	London.	Montreal.	Quebec.	Toronto.
Canadian Gov't Deb. 6 ℘ ct. stg..................	....	103 104	103 104	104½ 105
Do. do. 6 do due Ja. & Jul. 1877-84.......	104½ 105½	103 104	103 104	104 105
Do. do. 6 do. Feb. & Aug........	102 104	....	... .	....
Do. do. 6 do. Mch. & Sep.........	102 104	.. .	...	....
Do. do. 5 ℘ ct. cur., 1883	93¾ 94½	94 96	91 92	92½ 93½
Do. do. 5 do. stg., 1885	93½ 94	91½ 92½	90 90½	92½ 93½
Do. do. 7 do. cur.,......................	....	....	.....	....
Dominion 6 p. c. 1878 cy.....	....	106½ 107½	107 107½	107 107½
Hamilton Corporation....	. ..	....	... ..	....
Montreal Harbor, 8 ℘ ct. d. 1869.....................	..	....	......	....
Do. do. 7 do. 1870....................	...	....	......	....
Do. do. 6½ do. 1883....................	....	102½ 102½	......	102 103
Do. do. 6½ do. 1873....................	....	....	......	....
Do. Corporation, 6 ℘ c. 1891	....	96 96½	96½ 97	96 96½
Do. 7 p. c. stock...	....	108½ 110	108½ 109½	109 110
Do. Water Works, 6 ℘ c. stg. 1878.......... ..	....	96½ 97½	......	96 96½
Do. do. 6 do. cy. do.	....	....	......	96 97
New Brunswick, 6 ℘ ct., Jan. and July	104 104½	....	......	....
Nova Scotia, 6 ℘ ct., 1875.........................	103 104	...	......	....
Ottawa City 6 ℘ c. d. 1880	....	95 97	......	...
Quebec Harbour, 6 ℘ c. d. 1882......................	....	....	60	....
Do. do. 7 do. do..........................	....	....	65 70	....
Do. do 8 do. 1886........................	...	....	75 80	....
Do. City, 7 ℘ c. d. 1½ years.....	....	....	98 98½	....
Do. do. 7 do. 8 do.	....	....	91 92	....
Do. do. 7 do. 5 do.	....	....	96 96½	....
Do. Water Works, 7 ℘ ct., 3 years	....	....	97 97½	....
Do. do. 6 do. 1½ do.	....	....	94 95	....
Toronto Corporation	....	92 94	....	....

Insurance.	*Insurance.*	*Insurance.*

Briton Medical and General Life Association,

with which is united the

BRITANNIA LIFE ASSURANCE COMPANY.

Capital and Invested Funds............£750,000 *Sterling.*

ANNUAL INCOME, £220,000 STG. :

Yearly increasing at the rate of £25,000 Sterling.

THE important and peculiar feature originally introduced by this Company, in applying the periodical Bonuses, so as to make Policies payable during life, without any higher rate of premiums being charged, has caused the success of the BRITON MEDICAL AND GENERAL to be almost unparalleled in the history of Life Assurance. *Life Policies on the Profit Scale become payable during the lifetime of the Assured, thus rendering a Policy of Assurance a means of subsistence in old age, as well as a protection for a family,* and a more valuable security to creditors in the event of early death; and effectually meeting the often urged objection, that persons do not themselves reap the benefit of their own prudence and forethought.

No extra charge made to members of Volunteer Corps for services within the British Provinces.

☞ TORONTO AGENCY, 5 KING ST. WEST.

Oct 17—9-1yr   JAMES FRASER, *Agent.*

BEAVER

Mutual Insurance Association.

HEAD OFFICE—20 TORONTO STREET,
TORONTO.

INSURES LIVE STOCK against death from any cause. The only Canadian Company having authority to do this class of business.

E. C. CHADWICK, President.
W. T. O'REILLY, Secretary.   8-1y-25

HOME DISTRICT

Mutual Fire Insurance Company.

Office—North-West Cor. Yonge & Adelaide Streets,
TORONTO.—(UP STAIRS.)

INSURES Dwelling Houses, Stores, Warehouses, Merchandise, Furniture, &c.

PRESIDENT—The Hon. J. McMURRICH.
VICE-PRESIDENT—JOHN BURNS, Esq.
JOHN RAINS, Secretary.
AGENTS:
DAVID WRIGHT, Esq., Hamilton; FRANCIS STEVENS, Esq., Barrie; MESSRS. GIBBS & BRO., Oshawa.   8-1y

---

THE PRINCE EDWARD COUNTY

Mutual Fire Insurance Company.

HEAD OFFICE,—PICTON, ONTARIO.

President, L. B. STINSON ; *Vice-President,* WM. DELONG. *Directors :* W. A. Richards, James Johnson, James Cavan, D. W. Ruttan, H. A. McFaul.—*Secretary,* John Twigg ; *Treasurer,* David Barker; *Solicitor,* R. J. Fitzgerald.

THIS Company is established upon strictly Mutual principles, insuring farming and isolated property, (not hazardous,) in *Townships only,* and offers great advantages to insurers, at low rates for *five years,* without the expenses of a renewal.

Picton, June 15, 1869.   9-1y

Fire and Marine Assurance.

THE BRITISH AMERICA

ASSURANCE COMPANY.

HEAD OFFICE :
CORNER OF CHURCH AND COURT STREETS.
TORONTO.

BOARD OF DIRECTION :

Hon. G. W. Allan, M.L.C.,	A. Joseph, Esq.,
George J. Boyd, Esq.,	Peter Paterson, Esq.,
Hon. W. Cayley,	G. P. Ridout, Esq.,
Richard S. Cassels, Esq.,	E. H. Rutherford, Esq.,
Thomas C. Street, Esq.	

Governor :
GEORGE PERCIVAL RIDOUT, Esq.
Deputy Governor:
PETER PATERSON, Esq.
Fire Inspector: *Marine Inspector:*
K. ROBY O'BRIEN.   CAPT. R. OGUHNREN.

Insurances granted on all descriptions of property against loss and damage by fire and the perils of inland navigation.

Agencies established in the principal cities, towns, and ports of shipment throughout the Province.

THOS. WM. BIRCHALL,
23-1y   *Managing Director.*

Reliance Mutual Life Assurance Society

OF LONDON, ENGLAND. Established 1840.

Head Office for the Dominion of Canada :
131 ST. JAMES STREET, MONTREAL.

DIRECTORS—Walter Shanly, Esq., M.P.; Duncan Macdonald, Esq.; George Winks, Esq., W. H. Hingston, Esq., M.D., L.R.C.S.
RESIDENT SECRETAR—James Grant.

Parties intending to assure their lives, are invited to peruse the Society's prospectus, which embraces several entirely new and interesting features in Life Assurance. Copies can be had on application at the Head Office, or at any of the Agencies.

JAS. GRANT, Resident Secretary.

Agents wanted in unrepresented districts.   43-1y

The Gore District Mutual Fire Insurance Company

GRANTS INSURANCES on all description of Property against Loss or Damage by FIRE. It is the only Mutual Fire Insurance Company which assesses its Policies yearly from their respective dates ; and the average yearly cost of insurance in it, for the past three and a half years, has been nearly TWENTY CENTS IN THE DOLLAR less than what it would have been in an ordinary Proprietary Company.

THOS. M. SIMONS, Secretary & Treasurer.
ROBT. McLEAN, Inspector of Agencies:
Galt, 25th Nov., 1868.   15-1y

Canada Life Assurance Company.

ESTABLISHED 1847.

THE ONLY CANADIAN LIFE COMPANY AUTHORIZED BY GOVERNMENT FOR THE DOMINION.

Rates are lower than British or Foreign Offices.

A LARGER amount of Insurances and of Investments in Canada than any other Company, and its rapid progress is satisfactory evidence of the popularity of its principles and practice.

Last year there were issued

920 NEW POLICIES,

FOR ASSURANCE OF
$1,284,155,
WITH

ANNUAL PREMIUMS OF
$31,182.

AGENCIES THROUGHOUT THE DOMINION,
Where every information can be obtained, or at the HEAD OFFICE, IN HAMILTON, ONT.

A. G. RAMSAY, Manager.
E. BRADBURNE, Agent,
May 25.   1y   Toronto Street.

Queen Fire and Life Insurance Company,

OF LIVERPOOL AND LONDON,

ACCEPTS ALL ORDINARY FIRE RISKS
on the most favorable terms.

LIFE RISKS

Will be taken on terms that will compare favorably with other Companies.

CAPITAL, - - - £2,000,000 Stg.

CANADA BRANCH OFFICE—Exchange Buildings, Montreal.
Resident Secretary and General Agent,
A. MACKENZIE FORBES,
13 St. Sacrament St., Merchants' Exchange, Montreal.
WM. ROWLAND, Agent, Toronto.   1-1y

THE AGRICULTURAL

Mutual Assurance Association of Canada.

HEAD OFFICE .... LONDON, ONT.
A purely Farmers' Company. Licensed by the Government of Canada.

Capital, 1st January, 1869	$230,103 82
Cash and Cash Items, over	$80,000 00
No. of Policies in force	30,892 00

THIS Company insures nothing more dangerous than Farm property. Its rates are as low as any well-established Company in the Dominion, and lower than those of a great many. It is largely patronised, and continues to grow in public favor.

For insurance, apply to any of the Agents or address the Secretary, London, Ontario.
London, 2nd Nov., 1868.   12-1y.

The Waterloo County Mutual Fire Insurance Company.

HEAD OFFICE : WATERLOO, ONTARIO.
ESTABLISHED 1863.

THE business of the Company is divided into three separate and distinct branches, the

VILLAGE, FARM, AND MANUFACTURES.

Each Branch paying its own losses and its just proportion of the managing expenses of the Company.
C. M. TAYLOR, Sec.   M. SPRINGER, M.M.P., Pres.
J. HUGHES, Inspector.   15-y

Lancashire Insurance Company.

CAPITAL, - - - - - - - - £2,000,000 Sterling

FIRE RISKS

Taken at reasonable rates of premium, and
ALL LOSSES SETTLED PROMPTLY,
By the undersigned, without reference elsewhere.

S. C. DUNCAN-CLARK & CO.,
General Agents for Ontario,
25-1y   N. W. Cor. of King & Church Sts., Toronto

Western Assurance Company,

INCORPORATED 1851.

CAPITAL, ... $400,000.

FIRE AND MARINE.

HEAD OFFICE.................... TORONTO, ONTARIO

DIRECTORS.

Hon. JNO. McMURRICH, President.
CHARLES MAGRATH, Vice-President
A. M. SMITH, Esq.   JOHN ISKEN, Esq.
ROBERT BEATY, Esq.   ALEX. MANNING, Esq
JAMES MICHIE, Esq.   N. BARNHART, Esq.
R. J. DALLAS, Esq.
B. HALDAN, Secretary.
J. MAUGHAN, JR., Assistant Secretary.
WM. BLIGHT, Fire Inspector.
CAPT. G. T. DOUGLAS, Marine Inspector.
JAMES PRINGLE, General Agent.

Insurances effected at the lowest current rates on Buildings, Merchandize, and other property, against loss or damage by fire.
On Hull, Cargo and Freight against the perils of Inland Navigation.
On Cargo Risks with the Maritime Provinces by sail or steam.
On Cargo Risks by steamers to and from British Ports.

WESTERN ASSURANCE COMPANY'S OFFICE, }
Toronto, 1st April, 1869.   } 33-1y

The Victoria Mutual

FIRE INSURANCE COMPANY OF CANADA.

Insures only Non-Hazardous Property, at Low Rates

BUSINESS STRICTLY MUTUAL.

GEORGE H. MILLS, President.
W. D. BOOKER, Secretary.

HEAD OFFICE .... HAMILTON, ONTARIO
aug 15-1yr

North British and Mercantile Insurance Company.

𝕰stablished 1809.

HEAD OFFICE, - - CANADA¦ - MONTREAL

TORONTO BRANCH:

LOCAL OFFICES, Nos. 4 & 6 WELLINGTON STREET.
Fire Department, ...R. N. GOOCH, Agent.
Life Department, ...H. L. HIME, Agent.

Imperial Fire Insurance Company

OF LONDON.

No. 1 OLD BROAD STREET, AND 16 PALL MALL
ESTABLISHED 1803.

Canada General Agency,
RINTOUL BROS.,
24 St. Sacrament Street.
JAMES E. SMITH, Agent.
Toronto, Corner Church and Colborne Streets.

PUBLISHED AT THE OFFICE OF THE MONETARY TIMES, No. 60 CHURCH STREET.
PRINTED AT THE DAILY TELEGRAPH PUBLISHING HOUSE, BAY STREET, CORNER OF KING

THE CANADIAN
MONETARY TIMES
AND
INSURANCE CHRONICLE.

DEVOTED TO FINANCE, COMMERCE, INSURANCE, BANKS, RAILWAYS, NAVIGATION, MINES, INVESTMENT,
PUBLIC COMPANIES, AND JOINT STOCK ENTERPRISE.

| 'OL. II—NO. 51. | TORONTO, THURSDAY, AUGUST 5, 1869. | SUBSCRIPTION $2 A YEAR. |

Mercantile.

J. B. Boustead.
ROVISION and Commission Merchant.　Hops bought
and sold on Commission.　82 Front St. , Toronto.

John Boyd & Co.
7HOLESALE　Grocers and Commission Merchants,
Front St. , Toronto.

Childs & Hamilton.
TANUFACTURERS and Wholesale Dealers in Boots
　and Shoes, No. 7 Wellington Street East, Toronto,
tario.　28

L. Coffee & Co.
RODUCE and Commission Merchants, No. 2 Manning's
Block, Front St. , Toronto, Ont. Advances made on
asignments of Produce.

Candee & Co.,
ANKERS AND BROKERS, dealers in Gold and Silver
　Coin, Government Securities, &c., Corner Main and
xhange Streets, Buffalo, N. Y.　21-1v

John Fisken & Co.
OCK OIL and Commission Merchants, Yonge St.,
Toronto, Ont.

W. & R. Griffith.
IPORTERS of Teas, Wines, etc. Ontario Chambers,
cor. Church and Front Sts , Toronto.

Gundry and Langley,
RCHITECTS AND CIVIL ENGINEERS, Building Sur
　veyors and Valuators. Office corner of King and Jordan
eets, Toronto.
THOMAS GUNDRY.　　HENRY LANGLEY.

Lyman & McNab.
7HOLESALE　Hardware Merchants, Toronto, Ontario.

W. D. Matthews & Co.
RODUCE Commission Merchants, Old Corn Exchange,
16 Front St. East, Toronto Ont.

R. C. Hamilton & Co.
RODUCE Commission Merchants, 119 Lower Water
St., Halifax, Nova Scotia.

H. Nerlich & Co.,
IPORTERS of French, German, English and American
Fancy Goods, Cigars, and Leaf Tobaccos, No. 2 Adelaide
eet, West, Toronto.　15

Parson Bros.,
ETROLEUM Refiners, and Wholesale dealers in Lamps,
Chimneys, etc.　Warerooms 51 Front St. Refinery cor.
er and Don Sts., Toronto.

Reford & Dillon.
IPORTERS of Groceries, Wellington Street, Toronto,
Ontario.

C. P. Reid & Co.
IPORTERS and Dealers in Wines, Liquors, Cigars and
Leaf Tobacco, Wellington Street, Toronto.　28.

W. Rowland & Co.,
RODUCE BROKERS and General Commission Mer
hants. Advances made on Consignments.　Corner
irch and Front Streets, Toronto.

Sessions, Turner & Cooper.
ANUFACTURERS, Importers and Wholesale Dealer
　in Boots and Shoes, Leather Findings, etc. , 2 Wel
ton St. West, Toronto, Ont

Sylvester, Bro. & Hickman,
OMMERCIAL Brokers and Vessel Agents.　Office—No.
1 Ontario Chambers, [Corner Front and Church Sts.,
onto.　2-6m

Meetings.

CANADA LIFE ASSURANCE COMPANY.

The twenty-second annual meeting of this
Company was held in Hamilton, on the 3rd of
August, 1869.

REPORT.

It is gratifying to the directors to be able to intimate that the transactions of the past financial
year have been of the most satisfactory character.
The number and amount of new assurances have
been nearly twice as great as those of any former
year; and by its larger business in Canada than
any other life office there, the company continues
to maintain its lead among such institutions.
During last year, 993 applications, for assurances
of $1,390,655, were made to the company.　Of
these, it was thought advisable in the interests of
company to decline 73, for assurances of $106,500;
and of the balance of 920 policies which were issued for $1,284,155, 831 were taken up for $1,156,-
855 of assurances, yielding a new annual premium
income of $46,928.71.　The number of policies
which became claims by death during the year
was 35, upon 31 lives for assurances of $61,300, v
sum which is less than that of either of the previous two years, although the amount at risk last
year was very much larger than it was [during
these years.　The business in force at 30th April,
1869, amounted to $5,476,358.86 of assurances,
under 3,650 policies on 3,286 lives, yielding a
premium income of $164,670.58, with 3 annuities
for $842.33 and a deferred annuity of $9.50.　The
investments of the company continue to receive
the most careful attention of the directors and the
manager, and it will afford the shareholders satisfaction to notice by the accounts that they have
proved highly remunerative.　The interest account
is largely increased, having alone much exceeded
the year's claims by deaths, while the percentage
of the company's expenses is again this year materially reduced.　A dividend of 5 per cent upon
the paid-up capital is recommended, payable 1st
September next.　During the past year Mr.
Donald Murray, of Montreal, was appointed general agent for the company in the Province of Que
bec, and the directors have pleasure in saying that
that field has already been productive of considerable benefit to the institution, and it will without
doubt continue to add to the general success of
the company.　By the charter of incorporation,
the following gentlemen, being at the head of the
list of directors of the Co., vacate their seats at
the board, but are eligible for re-election:—Messrs
G. H.ᵗGillespie, Rev. G. M. Innes, D. McInnes,
John Ferrie, and F. W. Gates.
　(Signed)　　JOHN YOUNG, President.
　　　　　A. G. RAMSAY, Manager.

AUDITOR'S REPORT.

Gentlemen,—I have respectively to report the
completion of my audit of the financial affairs of
the company, for the year ending 30th April,

1869.　All the different securities in which your
assets are invested have been carefully examined
and verified—every debenture (with its coupons)
mortgage, or loan on a policy, has been checked
in detail—and the amount compared with the
figures in the company's books.　And bearing in
mind how large a proportion of your business
passes through the hands of agents, I have given
careful attention to this branch of my audit.　All
cash and bank transactions have been verified;
and the various books of the office have been
audited in detail. .As the result of my labors, I
submit herewith, duly certified, firstly, a statement
of receipts and expenditure for the past fiscal year;
and, secondly, a general abstract of the estimated
assets and liabilities of the company at 30th April,
1869, these returns exhibiting in a comprehensive
and plain form the position of the Company's
affairs at the close of the books for the year.　It
affords me much pleasure to observe the large and
healthy increase in the company's business during
the past twelve months; and I may well congratulate both shareholders and insurers on the marked
success which has attended your transactions
during that period, as well as on the sound foundation upon which the company rests.　I have to
acknowledge the attention which the manager has
shown to every request I have had, occasion to
make for information during the audit; and I have
to express my satisfaction with the accurate and
neat manner in which the books have been kept
by those in charge of that duty.　I remain, gentlemen, your obedient servant, (signed), G. A.
BARBER.

Statement of Receipts and Expenses.

RECEIPTS.

To Balance as at 30th April, 1868............		$909,532 39
" Premiums received on 881 new		
Policies and Renewals $164,670 58		
" Interest earned on Investments		
and Profits on sales of De-		
bentures	68,318 46	
" Extra Risks	239 74	
" Fines	53 66	
" Received on deposit and for		
accumulation	25 72	
		233,308 16
		$1,142,842 05

PAYMENTS.

By Expense Account............	$32,874 58	
" Vote for Board...............	1,500 00	
" 10 per cent. written off Office		
Furniture	188 18	
		$34,557 76
" Written off Investments......	$8,285 59	
" Company's Offices	1,200 00	
		9,485 59
" Unpaid Half Premiums written off (on		
Half Credit Policies suspended)........		794 71
" Re-Assurance Premiums		765 54
" Claims paid		70,738 33
" Cancelled (purchased) Policies		4,477 67
" Annuities paid (three)................		842 34
" Interest on Deposits..................		25 72
" Profits of Mutual Branch, paid		
as Bonus	$5,176 40	
" Profits of Mutual Branch, as		
Cash	2,217 97	
" Profits of Mutual Branch, per-		
manent reduction	1,559 72	
		8,954 09
" 21st Year's Dividend, paid on 2,500 shares		6,250 00
		$142,086 75
Leaving a balance—which is distributed		
as under :		990,855 30
		$1,142,842 05

Column 1

Cash in hand and in Bank $7,382 05
Cash in Agents and others' hands, including receipts held by them for Premiums since paid 30,870 34 $47,252 39

Investments $757,933 30
Real estate, Co.'s offices $55,311 39
" other property 60,886 80   116,192 19
  $874,125 58

Less reserved in Suspense on account of probable losses 8,004 12
  * $81,121 46

Interest accrued to 30th April, 1869 .... 10,123 47
Half-yearly and Quarterly Premiums, secured on Policies, and payable within 3 months. 44,192 38
Deferred Half-payments on half-credit Policies 30,512 89
Office Furniture 1,646 71
  $960,856 36

*This sum includes $11,714.41, being balance of reserve which may be required to meet losses arising upon old investments, and applicable to transactions not yet closed.

General Abstract.

ASSETS.

Cash in hand and in Bank $7,382 05
Cash in Agents and other hands, including receipts held by them for Premiums, which have since been paid 30,870 34 $47,252 39

Mortgages on Real Estate (Value in account) $293,204 96
Debentures (Value in account):
City $80,107 50
County 71,148 02
Township 19,731 71
Town (including City of Montreal $94,300 par) 144,874 06
Harbor (Montreal) .. 94,838 12
Village 3,459 34
  354,656 75
Dominion Stock 50,000 00
Montreal Consolidated Fund. ... 21 200 00
Stock in Hamilton Gas Company 3,040 00
Bills Receivable 1,643 68
Loans on Policies 29,800 80
Debentures 2,800 00
Stock 100 00
Bonds 400 00
Balance of sum paid on account of the Hamilton and Gore District Saving Bank 1,027 21
Real Estate—The Co.'s Offices..........$55,311 39
Other property........ 60,880 80
  116,192 19
  $874,125 58
Less—Reserved in suspense on account of probable losses...... $8,004 12
And Reserve on acco't of do 11,714 41
  19,718 53
  $854,407 05
Interest accrued on Debentures, &c 10,123 47
  $864,530 52
Half-yearly and Quarterly Premiums secured on Policies, and payable within 9 months $44,106 38
Deferred Half-payments on half-credit Policies 30,512 89
  74,709 27
Office Furniture 1,648 71
  $988,140 89
Value of Premium Income of $100,430.77, as at 30th April, 1865, that being the date of the last investigation 1,139,939 91
  $2,128,080 80

LIABILITIES.

Capital Stock paid up.............. $125,000 00
Balance of money lodged for accumulation $230 69
Balance of money unclaimed, at credit of Depositors in Hamilton Deposit and Savings' Bank. 223 87
  454 56
Claims not fully due, or for which claimants had not presented perfect discharges at 30th April, 1869, (nearly all since paid)... $12,056 67
Vested additions thereto 470 96
  $12,527 03
Cash profits on policies, remaining unpaid at 30th April, 1869 .... 198 43
Re-Assurance premiums unpaid (of 72nd year), at 30th April, 1869.. 35 45
Value of Assurances of $4,013,268.03, and Annuities of $851.83, as at 30th April,

Column 2

1865, that being the date of the last investigation 1,172,014 64
  $1,310,340 71
Balance, taking into account the value of the premium income on the one side, and the Assurance liabilities on the other, both as at 30th April, 1865, that being the date of the last investigation ; and including in it the value of certain lapsed Policies, which might than have been revived within 13 months *817,640 00
  $2,128,080 80

*NOTE.—In the valuations upon which the divisions of Profits are based, only the net or pure Premiums are taken into account.

The President, John Young, Esq., in moving the Report, said, the Report was of such an exceedingly favorable character that he felt it unnecessary for him to make any lengthened remarks. It might be well to briefly compare the figures of the year's business with those of the year before. The applications showed an increase from 539 in 1868 to 993 in 1869, an increase of 84 per cent., while the increase in amount was 105 per cent. The Policies issued showed an excess over the previous year of 86 per cent. and 103 per cent. in amount, while the income from Premiums had increased in the year 156 per cent. The interest income on investments had also very largely increased, and now reached the handsome sum of $68,318 per annum.

The claims from death had also this year been much lower than the estimated amount, and less than the year previous. They were in

1867......39 policies on 32 lives......$68,295
1868......40 " 37 " 62,200
1867......35 " 31 " 61,300
this year some $7,000 less than the interest earned by the Company on its investments.

The adoption of the Report was seconded by the Hon. John Hillyard Cameron, M.P., who said that the Report was remarkably satisfactory, and the statements so exceedingly clear that he felt it unnecessary to do more than second the Report, which he had much pleasure in doing.

Mr. John W. Bickle, seconded by Mr. Geo. A. Young, moved a vote of thanks to the Directors for their valuable services and attention to the interests of the Company.—Carried.

On motion of Mr. John Ferrie, seconded by Mr. G. H. Gillespie, a vote of thanks to the General Agents of the Company was passed.

Mr. Sheriff Thomas said he rose with much pleasure to move a vote of thanks to their Manager, Mr. H. Ramsay. His thorough capability for the duties of his position, and his unwearied devotion to the interests of the Company, were known to them all.

Mr. Tristram Bickle seconded the motion. He had never expected that a man so perfectly fitted in all respects for the situation could be found, and he could not think otherwise than that the Company was extremely fortunate in having the services of such a Manager.

The President, in putting the motion, said he heartily concurred in all that had been said by the Sheriff and Mr. Bickle. The interests of the Company could not be better served than they had been by Mr. Ramsay.—Carried.

Mr. Ramsay briefly thanked the meeting for the gratifying appreciation just given of his labors in their service, and said he hoped to merit their good opinion in the future as in the past. He felt it due to the other officers of the company to bear testimony to the diligence and ability of these gentlemen.

Mr. F. W. Gates moved, seconded by Dr. Hamilton, (West Flamborough,) that Messrs. George A. Young and John W. Bickle be scrutineers in taking the ballot for election of Directors, to fill the places of the five who retire this year. Carried.

Mr. Sheriff Thomas said that on a former occasion, when they had at their meeting a large attendance of policy-holders as well as shareholders, and when a long and animated discussion had

Column 3

taken place, the view had been expressed that gentlemen were holding the position of Directors while holding but small amounts of the Company's stock. The Board had duly considered this complaint, and had come to an arrangement amongst themselves by which ten shares of the Company's stock was made the minimum qualification for a Director, a change which he hoped would give every satisfaction.

The ballot was then taken, after which the scrutineers reported that the five retiring Directors had been re-elected, viz: Mr. G. H. Gillespie, Rev. G. M. Innes, Mr. D. McInnes, Mr. John Ferrie, and Mr. F. W. Gates.

On motion of Mr. Gates, the president left the chair, which was taken by Mr. Sheriff Thomas.

Dr. Hamilton then rose to move a vote of thanks to the President for his valuable services as the head of this Company. During many years his able conduct in that capacity, and his close attention in the company's business, had been well known.

The motion was seconded by Mr. Sheriff Thomas in putting it from the chair.

Mr. Young briefly expressed his thanks, after which the meeting adjourned. At the meeting of directors subsequently held, Mr. John Young was re-elected President, and Mr. John Ferrie, Vice-President.

BRITISH AMERICA ASSURANCE COMPANY.

The Annual Meeting of this Company was held on the 2nd instant, in Toronto, the Governor in the chair ; the Accountant read the following:

Annual Report, 1869.

The charter of the British America Assurance Company very properly providing for an annual meeting of shareholders on the first Monday of the month of August of each year, the Directors, in conformity with the Act, have much satisfaction in submitting to the proprietary, on this, the thirty-fifth anniversary of the institution, a full exposition of the affairs of the company for the twelve months ending 30th June.

The following particulars are embodied in the balance-sheet:

The Assets comprise,
Government deposit............$50,000
Accrued interest thereon........ 750
  $50,750 00
Debentures and mortgages on real estate.................. 161,485 27
Bills receivable 18,885 86
Office building and other real estate.. 18,128 18
Sundry accounts receivable, and other items 8,343 80
Cash in bank and agents' hands.... ... 29,948 11
  Total.............. $282,541 17
The paid up capital amounts to $200,000 00
Dividends unclaimed, and No. 51, not payable until July 9,981 63
Losses under adjustment, and other liabilities 25,519 52
  Total $235,501 15
  Balance.... .... $47,039 02

The profit and loss account shows :
Interest on investments ...$14,079 59
Premiums received in Fire Department...............116,659 77
Premiums received in Marine Department...... 41,958 20
Profit on investments redeemed..................... 697 90
  Total receipts...............$173,395 46

e losses............. ....$65,395 13
rine losses................. 26,838 01
ents' commissions and
:ther charges............. 35,673 15
miums on re-assurance 4,410 46

Total payments $132,316 75

Net profit of the year............ $41,078 71
The Rest, or surplus fund :
ance from last year's
tatement $21,961 31
fit of year ending 30th
une, 1869................ 41,078 71
$63,040 02
teith dividend at 4 per
ent $8,000 00
ty-first dividend at 4
er cent................ 8,000 00
$16,000 00

Balance at credit of fund......... $47,040 02
ly an examination of the foregoing items, it
l be seen that the transactions of the company
the past year have been of a very satisfactory
racter, enabling the Directors to declare the
al half-yearly dividends at the rate of eight
cent. per annum on the paid-up capital, be.
s adding the sum of $25,078.71 to the Rest,
surplus fund.
n the spring of the present year, an arrange-
nt was entered into between the Montreal As-
ance Company, the Western Assurance Com-
y, and the British America, for the prosecu-
a, share and share alike, of ocean insurance
iness from Canada to Great Britain, the West
ties and South America. Thus far the transac-
is have been of a satisfactory although limited
ure ; but there is good ground to infer that the
iness will in time become one of importance,
, in its results, profitable.
hanadian commerce having been greatly aug-
nted since confederation, and the intercourse
ween the various provinces much facilitated,
extension of the company's transactions, has
n commenced under certain well considered
ditions to and from the principal ports of the
minion.
. legal enactment having been obtained at the
: session of the Legislature, enlarging the
ers of the shareholders by By-Law, for the
ointment and regulation of the officers of the
pany, a draft of such By-law is herewith sub-
ted for their approval and adoption.
- All which is respectfully submitted,
(Signed)   GEO. PERCEVAL RIDOUT,
Governor.
(Signed)   T. W. BIRCHALL,
Managing Director.
per JOHN EVANS, Accountant.
he following Stockholders were elected to
'e the Office of Director for the ensuing year:—
P. Ridout, Esq., Toronto ; Peter Paterson,
., Scarboro ; E. H. Rutherford, Esq., To-
to ; Honorable William Cayley, Toronto ;
rge J. Boyd, Esq., Toronto ; Honorable George
Allan, Toronto ; Thomas C. Street, Esq., M.P.,
k Hill ; Peleg Howland, Esq., Toronto ; A.
ph. Esq., Quebec.
t the first Meeting of the Board, the under-
itioned were unanimously re-chosen for the
ective · Offices:—Governor, George Perceval
out, Esq. ; Deputy-Governor, Peter Paterson,
. Trustees:—E. H. Rutherford, Esq., Honor-
; William Cayley, G. J. Boyd, Esq.

GORE BANK.

he President, Edward Martin, Esq., was
d to the chair, and Thomas Mufr, Esq., was
ninted Secretary.
ort of the Directors for the year ending 30th
June, 1869.
The directors report that in accordance with
resolutions to that effect, passed at the special

meeting held on the 2nd Nov. last, they have obtained from the legislature the desired amendments to the bank's charter, and the paid up capital
of the bank is now reduced to $485,568, the shares
standing at $24 each, instead of $40, as heretofore ; the accompanying statements show the
manner in which the balances mentioned in the
statement submitted at the last annual meeting
have been dealt with, and the position of the bank
at the above date.
2 After mature consideration it was deemed advisable so close the branches at Woodstock, Galt
and Simcoe, which has been done and the amounts
transferred to the head office.
3. The assets of the bank have been recently
carefully valued, every debt deemed bad written
off and due allowance made for those considered
doubtful.   The whole of the Bank of Upper Canada certificates were disposed of and the Real Estate
reduced to $3,265.95; where it was deemed neces-
sary the value of mortgages and other items included in the statement submitted by the Board
in November last, have been reduced from the
sums at which they were valued in that statement.
Since the 30th of June sales of Real Estate have
been closed, which leave the balance at the debit
of this account at $1,900.
4. The charges for management during the
past year were materially increased by the expenses consequent on the realization within that
period of a large amount of doubtful assets, (the
accumulation of many former years' business) the
expenses of closing the six branches, the salaries
of the staff at these branches, for many months,
and other exceptional items are also included in
the amount at the debit of expenses.
5. The necessity for holding large sums to meet
the demand of depositors which existed when your
directors assumed office has passed away, but the
doubts which subsequently prevailed as to the
future operations of the bank prevented the realization of as large profits as would otherwise have
been secured.
6. Dr. McQuesten having resigned his position
as a director, Mr. G. J. Forster was selected to
fill the vacant seat.
7 In February last, Mr. Samuel Read, then
manager of the Bank of Montreal at Brantford,
was appointed cashier in place of Mr. Cassels,
who had previously resigned.
8. The amended act provides that the shareholders may change the name of the bank to that
of the Bank of Hamilton, reduce the number of directors from 7 to 5, and alter the scale of
voting so as to give a vote to each share. These
questions will no doubt be fully discussed at the
meeting. Signed on behalf of the Board.
EDWARD MARTIN, President.
Hamilton, July 19th, 1869.

General Statement of Liabilities and Assets to 30th
June, 1869.

LIABILITIES.
To Promissory Notes in
circulation $107,729 00
To balances due to other
banks..................... 96 85
" Current accounts...... 66,628 36
" Deposits at interest.... 37,330 99

Total liabilities to the public......... $211,785 20
To capital paid up............ 485,568 00
" Contingent Fund account............. 9,636 24
" Reserved for rebate of interest on
Current Discounts.................. 3,191 06
" Reserved for accrued interest on
Deposit Receipts.................. 1,716 71
" Reserved for discount on conver-
sion of American Funds held at
New York and Buffalo........... 3,377 86
" Dividends unclaimed............... 176 40
" Profit and loss account—balance
carried forward to next year...... 14,710 83
$730,162 30

ASSETS.
By specie and Provincial
Notes $78,807 29
By Notes and Cheques of
other banks............ 9,777 65
Balances due from other
banks 79,412 22
$167,997 16
By Government Securities (£17,000
stg.)............................ 76,114 66
" Hamilton Debentures ($97,000)... 63,050 00
" Notes discounted, current......... 285,331 46
" Notes discounted, overdue 26,116 71
" Other debts due to the bank....... 56,837 44
" Mortgages....................... 33,783 92
" Real Estate...................... 3,265 95
" Bank Premises and office Furniture 13,200 00
" Accrued interest on debentures and
Mortgages........................ 2,465 00
$730,162 30

PROFIT AND LOSS ACCOUNT.
DR.
To balance at debit of this account,
from 30th June, 1868 .... $9,865 34
To expenses for the year :
Gross charges at head offices and
branches...............$22,907 20
Expenses of Investigat-
ing Committee..........1,582 93
24,490 13
To bad debts and deprecia-
tion in securities, &c.,
written off during the
year ; loss on Bank of
Upper Can. certificates..$14,697 27
Depreciation of Govern-
ment debentures........ 6,618 67
Depreciation of City of
Hamilton debentures.... 40,969 00
Bank premises and office
furniture 10,819 11
Real estate............... 36,615 20
Mortgages................ 17,450 07
Past due bills............323,494 39
Sundry items.............. 26,341 93
377,005 64
To contingent fund account 9,636 24
" Interest reserved, rebate on bills
current 3,191 06
" Adjusting interest account—In-
terest on account of deposit re-
ceipts to date.................... 1,716 71
" Adjusting exchange account, dis-
count on current funds held at
New York and Buffalo............. 3,377 86
$429,282 98
" Balance (available)................. 14,710 83
$443,993 81

CR.
By gross profits for the year :
Interest $34,692 73
Commission.............. 4,006 06
Exchange................ 4,118 02
$42,816 81
By adjusting interest account :
Accrued interest on mort-
gages $1,515 00
Accrued debentures...... 950 00
2,465 00
By rest account transferred.............. 75,000 00
" reduction of capital stock 40 per
cent. of $809,280 written off..... 323,712 00
$443,993 81
S. READ, Cashier.

T. C. Street, Esq., moved the adoption of the
report, which motion was seconded by Dr. Clarke,
and carried.
The former gentleman addressed the meeting
in respect to a proposition made by other banks

to amalgamate their stock with that of this institution ; and in view of such proposition having been made, Mr. Street thought it would be well that the meeting should adjourn until the last Tuesday in August, which would be the 31st inst., in order that they might ascertain how much money they would get for their stock. He also advocated the appointment of a committee of the shareholders to confer with the Board, in the meantime, in regard to these negotiations—the whole matter, of course, to be ratified by the adjourned meeting of the shareholders. He advocated the re-election of the old Board of Directors until the expiration of the month, and that the election of directors could then take place at the adjourned meeting. By a recent Act of Parliament, the Board of Directors could legally be reduced from seven to five. He advocated the reduction. The expenses would thereby be materially reduced, and there would be as much efficiency as if there were seven on the Board. This question would not come up at present, but would be considered at the adjourned meeting. From the report of the bank it would be seen that the property of the bank is worth $500,000 ; consequently our assets are worth 62½ cents on the dollar on the old stock. This was not taking into consideration the outlying circulation, $107,000, of which a large amount would never come into the bank to be redeemed. Although this sum could not be fixed at any particular amount, it would undoubtedly be considerable, and should work in their favor in regard to negotiations with other banks. He was unfavorable to any lengthy discussion in regard to the property of the bank until the adjourned meeting, when the whole matter could be considered. Mr. Street closed his remarks by moving that the meeting stand adjourned until twelve o'clock, noon, of Tuesday, the 31st day of August, inst.

The resolution, after some discussion, was adopted.

It was moved by Mr. Æ. Irving, seconded by Mr. James Watson, that the following named gentlemen, Messrs. T. C. Street, J. Davidson, D. Campbell, Murray (of Montreal), by power of substitution by him in his own case ; Dr. McQuesten and Dr. Billings, be a committee to confer with the directors upon any changes of the affairs of the bank which may be proposed between this day and the adjourned meeting to be held on the 31st of August inst.

This motion was also carried.

Dr. Clarke gave notice that he would at the next meeting introduce a by-law to reduce the number of directors from seven to five, and that the necessary notice be given.

The following gentlemen were elected directors: Messrs. John Waldie, Edward Martin, Wm. Hendrie, G. J. Forster, Thos. McIlwraith, Hon. S. Mills, and Wm. McMillan, being the return of the old board. At a meeting of the board, Hon. Samuel Mills was elected president and Mr. Waldie, vice-president.

THE CITIZENS' INSURANCE COMPANY
OF CANADA.)

Authorized Capital..........................$2,000,000
Subscribed Capital............................ 1,000,000
        HEAD OFFICE—MONTREAL.

        DIRECTORS·

HUGH ALLAN, · · · - PRESIDENT.
C. J. BRYDGES,   EDWIN ATWATER,
GEORGE STEPHEN,   HENRY LYMAN,
ADOLPHE ROY,   N. B. CORSE.

Life and Guarantee Department.

THIS Company—formed by the association of nearly 100 of the wealthiest citizens of Montreal—is prepared to transact every description of LIFE ASSURANCE ; also, to grant bonds of FIDELITY GUARANTEE, for Employees holding positions of trust.
Applications can be made through any of the Company's Agents, or direct to
                EDWARD RAWLINGS, Manager.
Agent for Toronto : | Agent for Hamilton ;
W. T. MASON. | R. BENNER.

THE CANADIAN MONETARY TIMES AND INSURANCE CHRONICLE *is printed every Thursday evening and distributed to Subscribers on the following morning.*

Publishing office, No. 60 Church-street, 3 doors north of Court-street.

Subscription price—
        Canada $2.00 per annum.
        England, stg. 10s. per annum.
        United States (U.S.Cy.) $3.00 per annum.
Casual advertisements will be charged at the rate of ten cents per line, each insertion.
Cheques, money orders, &c. should be made payable to J. M. TROUT, Business Manager, who alone is authorised to issue receipts for money.
☞ All Canadian Subscribers to THE MONETARY TIMES *will receive* THE REAL ESTATE JOURNAL *without further charge.*

The Canadian Monetary Times.

THURSDAY, AUGUST 5, 1869.

ORILLIA RAILWAY.

A meeting was held at Barrie, on the 27th ult., to consider the project of continuing the Northern Railway to Orillia. Mr. Robinson, the President of the Northern, and Mr. Cumberland, the Manager, were present, and expressed their hearty approval of the proposed branch, and signified the readiness of the company to stock it, besides affording every encouragement in furthering an undertaking so full of promise. A resolution moved by Mr. McConkey, M.P., and seconded by Judge Gowan, was carried, appointing an influential committee to ascertain how far the municipalities interested would be disposed to assist such an undertaking. Barrie is therefore prepared to do its part, and it is assumed that Oro, Medonte, and Orillia townships will be favourable. Difficulty is anticipated with Orillia, as that village has in a measure committed itself to the Port Hope scheme. But as Mr. Cumberland shewed, the road from Orillia to Toronto viâ Barrie, is by many miles shorter than that by way of Port Hope. Port Hope and Barrie are about equal distances from Toronto. The tariff on the Northern Railroad, per 100 on first class goods, 94 miles, is 5 cents less than on the P. H. & L. Road of only 42 miles ; so that, in the same ratio, freight from Toronto to Orillia, via Port Hope, would cost double the amount of that via Northern Railway and Barrie to the same point. The speaker expressed himself in favour of a gravel road from Barrie, running through to the townships north, by which the trade now diverging to Stayner might be secured. The principal reason urged against the extension is, that villages would spring up along the line,

and absorb the business which Barrie now gets. But the *Advance* puts the matter with great fairness when it states that " there must be a give and take in such matters," and while there might be some loss, there would be manifold gain. Open up the country is the watchword of the party of progress. Let the farmer get free access to the best markets, and there is no fear that we shall all be the better off. Mr. Cumberland paid a high compliment to Barrie, when he stated: " H[e] did not believe there was a town in the Dominion where more real solid stability and prosperity were apparent than here." Th[e] country thereabouts is only beginning to be developed, and Barrie should look to it, that it be not deprived of the benefit of a traffi[c] which must rapidly extend.

THE CANADA LIFE.

The report of the Directors of this Company, which will be found in another column, presents many features of a very satisfactory character ; indeed, we think that a greate[r] degree of jubilance than the management thought fit to exhibit might have been indulged in with perfect propriety. We ar[e] not prepared to go into ecstacies over suc[h] cess, but we are ever ready to do it justice.

The business of the company has been steadily increasing. Last year, the larges[t] amount of life business done by any on[e] company in Canada was secured by it. A[n] increase of new business in one year of 8[?] per cent. in number of policies, and 105 per cent. in amount insured, is certainly not ba[d.] While the policies have increased both i[n] number and amount, the claims by deat[h] have decreased so that the interest on i[n]vestments has paid the claims, and le[ft] seven thousand dollars to spare. The i[n]vestments show a yield of over seven p[er] cent. One may fairly prophecy that, with [a] small a mortality such fertility in the i[n]vestments, and a steadily progressive bus[i]ness, the profits to be declared next yea[r] will be handsome. The cash liability of th[e] company, including the capital stock, bu[t] excluding the valuation of insurances [in] 1865, is placed at $138,226.07. It may b[e] noticed that the liability last year was $154[,]153, and the question may arise, why th[e] diminution in liability with an increase [of] business ? But in last year's account th[e] unsettled claims stood at $28,379, while the[y] are, this year, but $12,537.63. While, o[n] the one hand, the value of the assurances disregarded, on the other the value of th[e] premium income is omitted, and $088,1[?] stated as cash assets. This is done, we sup[?]pose, because a correct estimate cannot b[e] given of the value of the policies, as an a[n]nual valuation is not made, A valuatio[n] l be made next year, when the profits will divided. The item $138,226 does not, of rse, embrace the amount required to re- ire, and it would be useless to guess at sum required in the absence of proper 3.

'aking the statement as a whole, we think t policyholders will peruse it with great sfaction. The lives have apparently been cted with care, or life in Canada must 'e a great deal in its favor. The number apsed policies appears to be small. Not- hstanding the competition which exists e and the comparitively limited field for rations, the Canada has every reason to gratulate itself on the results it has ieved, owing no doubt to the zeal of its nts and the ability of its Manager. As a adian Company we wish it the greatest sible success. Were it not out of place make invidious comparisons, we might w considerable that would tend to the antage of the Canada, but as its agents doubtless, fully able and willing to do it mselves, we merely indicate the salient ures of the report and express our con- nce in the soundness of the Company.

THE BRITISH AMERICA.

'n the 2nd instant, the Directors of this opany presented their report to the stock- lers, on the year's business. The prem- is received in the fire department amounted $116,659.77, and the losses where $65,- .31, or 55 per cent. The premiums were ,958.20, and the losses $26,838, or 63 cent. During the year before, the ratis ire losses to fire premiums was about 63 cent.; and of marine premiums to marine es, 90 per cent.; while as large an amount usiness has not been done this year. What secured resulted in a greater profit. The profits of the year are placed at $41,078.71 against $17,355 of last year. Two divi- ds of four per cent., have been declared ing at the credit of reserve the sum of ,040. The arrangement between the Mon- l, the Western and the British America, reference to ocean marine, has been id to be satisfactory. The advantage of ose personal supervision on the part, of much respected Governor of this com- y is clearly seen, in the care with which iness is conducted and the confidence ch the company commands.

THE GORE BANK.

; will appear, on a comparison of this 's statement with the estimate of loss ved at on the investigation which took e at the instance of the shareholders, that 'e is difference between the two of $89,- 071. That amount has been written off over and above the estimate. From what occurred at the annual meeting we judge that the bank will not continue in business. The agencies have been closed, and the uncertainty that has prevailed, respecting the bank's future, of course, interfered seriously with its operations. Two offers have been made for the purchase of the institution; one by the Bank of Montreal, the other by the Bank of Commerce. On the 4th a deputation came to Toronto and had interviews on the subject, with one or both parties. The new board were elected on the understanding that they would resign, if required, on the 31st August. A great deal of substantial work has been done in realizing the assets, and matters are now in a fair way for any emergency.

MR. KING IN NEW YORK.

As the Bank of Montreal is the depositary of the Government and custodian of the gold held for the redemption of Dominion notes, it must expect to have the vagaries of its manager watched with considerable closeness. It appears that Mr. King has been operating pretty extensively in the New York gold market, and has, by some cool operations, gored severely, if we may judge by the press strictures, not a few of the bulls and bears The *World* of the 29th said :

"The price of gold has been advancing steadily, until it reached $137\frac{3}{4}$ yesterday, when the agent of a Canadian bank forced the price down by sales to the extent of $3,500,000. Besides forcing sales of this amount of gold, this Canada bank manager made forced sales of its sixty-day bills of exchange on London at $\frac{1}{8}$ to $\frac{1}{4}$ per cent. below the market quotations, and in round amounts to leading prime bankers, whom this speculative Canada agent had ascertained were about to ship specie to Europe. The Canada bank bills, being a cheaper remittance than specie, took its place, and the banks, at the last moment, withdrew the specie they would otherwise have shipped. Exchange was quoted weaker, although none of the prime bankers will draw sixty-day sterling under $110\frac{1}{8}$ to $110\frac{1}{4}$, and sight $110\frac{5}{8}$ to $110\frac{3}{4}$."

The *Express* takes up the cry, and is responsible for the following :

"In the Gold Room yesterday afternoon, it was freely reported that the steamer *Cuba*, sailing early to-day, would not take out any specie, whereupon the price of gold suddenly fell to $136\frac{1}{2}$. At this crisis came a counter report that the *Cuba* would take nearly $1,000,000, which started gold up again to $127\frac{1}{4}$. In proof of the last report, it was cited that $750,000 were already on a dray in front of one of the Wall-street banks, ready to go on board. This was actually the case, and the small kegs of double eagles were paraded up and down Wall street on the dray until the shades of evening threw its mantle over this "Kingly" *coup d'état*, when the gold was quietly returned to the bank vaults. The confiding community of speculators went home with golden visions of an advance in the premium on shipments to-day; but alas! they awoke only to find that they had been taken in by a shrewd, speculating "Kanuck" lately arrived from the Royal Dominion. This story formed the gossip of the street to-day, and is regarded as the sharpest piece of financiering, in a speculative way, that Wall street has witnessed for a long time."

On the 30th, the *World* again returned to the charge.

"The bills of the speculative Canada bank manager were offered freely through different brokers at 110 for sixty day sterling, while the manager was engaged in buying back the gold he had sold. There were no purchases, however, reported of the Canada bank's bills even at 110, although none of the prime bankers were willing to draw under $110\frac{1}{8}$ at the time.

"The average price at which the gold was sold was about $136\frac{1}{2}$, and it was all bought back again yesterday and to-day without any loss or profit. The profit or loss on a gold gambling transaction is not, however, the point for the stockholders in a bank to consider. The question is 'whether gold gambling in New York comes within the scope of a legitimate Canada banking business,' and, 'if so, how long will the capital of the bank remain intact?' Any departure from legitimate banking on the part of the manager of any bank will naturally injure its credit, and, as all experience has shown, generally ends in disastrous losses."

The *Times* of the 29th, gives its version of the affair:

"The Bank of Montreal agency made one of the shipments of gold coin of Saturday last, $500,000 in amount. The President (?) of the Bank, who is the city, made no further preparations to ship this week, as, by certain speculators in the Gold Room, it was supposed he would do. The story is that yesterday morning he turned his gold into currency, at $137\frac{1}{2}$ per cent., in place of shipping, and drawing against it on a more reluctant exchange market than he had anticipated. This would strike most people as a pretty shrewd banking operation, and the result, at all enters is, that he could now replace his gold at a good profit, if he chooses to do so, in place of waiting until the price runs down to 135 per cent. or less. But our very irascible neighbor of the *World* arraigns this 'first-class' exchange drawer as being no better than he should be; from which we infer that there was some disappointment yesterday somewhere in the neighborhood of the gold buying clique, around which our neighbor delights to revolve and to do knightly service for. Having of late broken a lance with the Browns and now another with the Bank of Montreal, we suppose he has one or more in rest for Belmont or Pickersgill, or our amiable friend of the Bank of British North America; these being the traditional 'five names' of the sterling market, against which, until the *World* took them in hand, there was believed to be no reproach."

We suppose that Mr. King has a good deal of exchange to disposo of just now, when he is drawing against the Intercolonial loan, and we cannot quarrel with him for seeking a market for it wherever he will do best with it. But, at the same time, we do not see clearly why he should go down to New York to measure wits with the speculators of the gold room, or demean himself by playing tricks, the parallels of which Chicago alone can furnish. Mr. King is certainly not above shrewd dodges if we may judge from the sly test he put on Mr. Paton's sagacity at one time, and the bold manœuvre he indulged in with the Merchants' Bank at another. If the story given above be true, we are disposed to credit Mr. King with a cool audacity, which, were it not so dangerous to his bank, might afford "Canucks" a good deal of amusement. We can scarcely afford to chuckle over the tale of the dray drawn pretentiously along Wall Street, when we remember that Canadian money was its load. The laugh might be rather turned against us if the mock shipment failed in its object. We have not too much money in Canada. There is use for every cent we can beg or borrow. Where banks are given great privileges by charter, or by favor, we do not expect that they will play at gambling in New York.

£1 NOTES.

In 1797, the Bank of England began to issue one pound notes, and the practice was immediately followed by the country banks, but in 1821 she withdrew them. In 1826 the circulation of these notes was prohibited in England and Wales, and since 1829, no notes for less than five pounds have been allowed to be issued. It was proposed at the same time to suppress one pound notes in Scotland, but the measure met with such opposition from the people there, that it was abandoned. They became unpopular in England, because they were in the hands of the poorer classes, and when the small issuers failed, during panic, much misery was caused. A Mr. Delaharty, an Irish member of the Imperial House of Commons, who considers that one pound notes are at the bottom of much of the Irish misery, recently gave the House the benefit of his views on the subject, justifying his opinion with a vast deal of economical authority. The Chancellor of the Exchequer not only differed with him but even said, that one pound notes were as good as other bank notes, and under good regulations, very good things indeed. If any bank notes are good, why not one pound notes? The question is not hard to answer, but Mr. Low's defence of the one pound note is regarded as a bold emancipation from an old and well established prejudice. He stated that the taste for metallic currency generated by former legislation had cost the country a great deal. This was proved by Prov. Jevons, who says:

"The sovereigns in circulation amount to £64,500,000 at the most, of which 31½ per cent. are below the legally current weight. In short, about 20,000,000 of sovereigns require to be withdrawn if we desire to maintain the credit of our currency on its present footing, together with 11,500,000 of half sovereigns, in all 31,500,000 coins. The cost of this recoinage may be estimated at £348,000.

His estimate of the total annual cost, without including the accidental loss of coins, is as follows:—

Annual wear of 64,500,000 sovereigns	£22,000
Annual wear of 24,000,000 half-sovereigns	13,000
Expenses of the Mint, including wear of silver coin	42,000
	77,000
Interest on £95,000,000 of gold, silver and copper coin, at 3 per cent	2,850,000
	£2,927,000

Financial.

TORONTO STOCK MARKET.

(Reported by Pellatt & Osler, Brokers.)

There were limited sales of Montreal Bank at 160½ to 162; British Bank enquired for at 104½ but none in the market; there were considerable sales of Ontario at 96 to 96¼, and buyers still ask for it at the latter rate; there were small sales of Toronto Bank at 123, and that price would still be paid. Early in the week a brisk demand arose for Royal Canadian and sales were made at 50½ 51 and 51½, there are now buyers at 52 with no stock in the market. Large transactions in Commerce at 103, 103½, 103¾ and 104. Gore is asked for at quoted rates but none offers. Merchants' has been sold at 104½ and 105. There are buyers of Quebec at par. Molsons' is nominal at 109 to 110. Buyers offer 99½ for City Bank but sellers want par. Du Peuple is in demand at 109, but no sellers. Nationale would command 107½, but none on market. Jacques Cartier is inquired for at 107½. Sales of Union at 105½ are reported. Toronto Gas is in demand at 108. British America Assurance has been largely dealt in at 55½, 56 and 56½ and there are still buyers at the latter rate. Buyers have advanced their offers to 119 for Western Building Society, but there is no stock procurable. Freehold is sought at 118½; a small lot sold at 120. Sellers want 133 for Montreal Telegraph; there have been small sales at 132. Large sales of Canada Landed Credit have been made at 79½ and 80, and buyers have advanced to 82. There are no Canada debentures in market. Dominion stock is heavy at 107. City of Toronto debentures have been sold to pay 7 per cent. interest, and are still in demand. 99½ is offered for many first class County debentures. A few good mortgages are offered at 8 per cent. For this season of the year, there has been a very large business done in most of our leading stocks, and, as a rule, at advancing prices. For all good securities, the demand far exceeds the supply.

The Provincial Accounts.—The settlement of the accounts between the Provinces of Quebec and Ontario and the Dominion is now in a fair way, it appears, of being completed soon. The Premier of Ontario, Mr. Sandfield Macdonald, and the Treasurer, Mr. Wood; the Premier of Quebec, Mr. Chauveau, the Treasurer, Mr. Dunkin, and the Attorney-General Mr. Ouimet, with Mr. Rose, the Finance Minister, and Mr. Langton, the Auditor of the Dominion, have been engaged on accounts at Montreal, and have made satisfactory progress; it was thought probable they would have completed their labors during last week.

Dominion Investments.—A correspondent of a Quebec journal writes respecting the application of the Intercolonial loan, as follows:—First, what fund is charged with the construction of the Intercolonial railway; Construction Fund with its trustees duly appointed, or the Consolidated Fund of the Dominion of Canada?

Answer,—The Consolidated Fund of Canada, with its three trustees, the ministers of the Dominion, for the time being. The money invested by Mr. Rose has therefore been rightly placed for construction purposes.

Next, what fund is charged with the duty of repayment of the money borrowed?

Answer,—The Consolidated Fund already named along with a sinking fund, to be gradually formed out of it.

As such sinking fund will be duly formed by its certain stipulated instalments, the Finance Minister in at once placing this cash to the credit of the Consolidated Fund, has given it its right destination, and observe, by the payments which he has made he has done neither more or less than place it to the credit of the fund. If the consolidated fund of Canada had not been considered trustworthy for the construction of the railway, and (in conjunction with its sinking fund to be formed,) for the subsequent repayment of the money borrowed, the requisite means would never have been lent, or guaranteed by the British Government. If a higher security than this consolidated fund had been required, it would certainly have been stipulated for. Neither men or government are in the habit of lending their money with a sentimental hope that better security will be afforded than the one asked for and put into the agreement accordingly.

The disposition of the money which has taken place has in practice only been the means of strengthening the very fund from which the repayment of the amount borrowed will in the due and ordinary course have to be made.

Express Business in the United States.—From reports in American papers, it would seem that the express business in that country, which heretofore has been considered profitable has for the last few years undergone material change, owing in part to rival companies, and in part to the high rates exacted by the railway companies. The stocks of the principal express companies are now selling in New York at from ten to fifty cents on the dollar; one large company after sinking over $5,000,000, being obliged to succumb, and the stockholders of another defunct concern are being sued individually for the debts of the company—thus demonstrating the fact that the business, although an important one, cannot be extended beyond a certain limit.

—Mr. Scovil, the St. John defaulter, broker, who has been imprisoned for about eight months in the jail at Kingston, N. B., has been released from custody after an examination before two judges of the Supreme Court. During the period of nearly eight months, Mr. Scovil did not set his foot outside the precincts of his prison.

—The Ontario Carbon Oil Company of Hamilton, have received from the Provincial Secretary letters patent of incorporation, with power to carry on business in the counties of Wentworth and Lambton, and with the nominal capital of $50,000.

—Mr. D. S. Eastwood, of the Ontario Bank, was presented with a very flattering address on the occasion of his removal from Peterborough to Ottawa.

—A Montreal paper asks why Mr. Rose sold out, recently, his two hundred shares of Bank of Montreal stock.

—Tenders were obtained for $80,000 of Halifax City Water Works, and $30,000 were allotted at rates ranging from 2¼ to 5 per cent. premium.

Railway News.

GREAT WESTERN RAILWAY.—Traffic for week ending July 16th 1869.

Passengers	28,526	86
Freight	30,564	03
Mails and Sundries	1,967	23

Total Receipts for week...... $61,059 12
Corresponding week, 1868... 56,103 73

Increase $4,954 39

PASSUMPSIC RAILWAY.—The net earnings for the year ending May 31st, 1869, exceeded any previous year by $8,500. Some 13,000 more tons freight and 5,000 more passengers were transported than last year.—Newport- Station, which is most of the Canadian freight, showed 1,313 ore tons than any other station, and St. Johnsbury the largest number of passengers. The lling stock, building and road bed have been added to and improved during the year and all ported in good condition. No fatal accidents ave occurred during the year. Two dividends of per cent. have been paid amounting to $129,- 50. The bonded debt was reduced by the sum $53,800 and notes payable $99,000 leaving outstanding in bonds and notes $795,000, which les not mature until 1876. In regard to Northn extension, the Directors say:

The necessity of a northern connection has en considered of vital importance to this corporation, and in accordance with a resolution ssed at the annual meeting of the stockholders, uly 31, 1867, the directors have entered into a ntract with the Massawippi Valley Railway mpany to lease, when completed, their road, nnecting ours with the Grand Trunk at Lennoxlle, Province of Quebec, for the term of 999 ars, on terms satisfactory to both corporations. e Massawippi Valley Railway is now under contract to be completed, ready for use, July 1, 1870. large force is now employed in grading and idging. The iron is all purchased, and some 800 tons delivered.

ILLINOIS CENTRAL RAILWAY.—The following the report of the Illinois Central Railroad Comny for the month of June, 1869:

Land Department.

res construction lands sold	5,157.51 for	$50,296.34
cres interest fund lands sold	79.32 for	820.10
cres free lands sold	1,009.52 for	14,172.76

otal sales during the month of June, 1869....6,246.35 for $65,289.20
which add town lot sales 435.00

otal of all ....6,246.35 for $65,724.20

ash collected in June $187,351.18

Traffic Department.

eceipts from freight	$390,796.00
eceipts from passengers	134,800.85
eceipts from mails	6,358.33
eceipts from rent of road	4,000.00
eceipts from other sources	80,000.00

otal receipts in month of June, 1869.$615,955.18
otal receipts in month of June, 1868. 543,018.60

stimated earnings in the month of June, on the D. & S. C. R. R., not included above $124,993.80
orresponding month of 1868 .... $3,271.38

PETERBORO' AND HALIBURTON RAILWAY.— he Peterboro' *Review* says that an appeal to the w townships on the Bobcaygeon road for aid to is enterprise has been so far encouraging. Four the councils applied to have already passed byws through the first and second readings, in der that they may at once be submitted to the vote of the ratepayers. The proposed bonuses are as follows: Dysart, &c., $25,000, Minden, $6,500, Snowden, $8,500, Lutterworth, Anson, &c., $4,000; total, $39,000. Besides these, the meetings in Stanhope and Harvey, each unanimously requested their councils to submit by-laws for in Stanhope, $1,000; Harvey, $10,000; making in all a total of $50,000.

—Mr. Hurlburt, builder of the Clifton wooden railway, N.Y., has been awarded the contract for the Quebec & Gosford Railway.

—The principal Prussian railway companies are about to raise a loan on joint account of 100 million thalers for the construction of new lines.

—The stock sheet of the Levis and Kennebec Railway, is being fast filled up, and the commencement of operations is looked forward to at an early date. An English company have offered to build the road for half in cash, and half in stock. The town of Levis will subscribe $50,000.

CHANGE OF GUAGE.

Thirteen hundred and fifty men were arranged along the three hundred and nine miles of the Missouri Pacific Road, on Saturday last, with orders to change the guage from 5 feet 6 inches to 4 feet 9 inches, during the interval of rest afforded to the regular traffic on the road by the occurrence of Sunday. The change was effected in sixteen hours, and on Monday morning the new rolling stock passed over the road as usual. This shows what the modern organization of railway labor can do on an emergency. Had the change been from 5 feet 8¼ inches or 5 feet 10 inches to 5 feet 9 inches this celerity would have been impossible. But the old spike holes were so far off from the new ones as not to interfere. As soon as the bridge at St. Louis is completed the same cars can pass from Philadelphia to the western borders of Kansas, and, in a few months more, to Denver City. The change of guage from 4 feet 8¼ inches to 4 feet 9 inches, and from 4 feet 10 inches to 4 feet 9 inches, is taking place on many roads to suit the so-called compromise wheels. The guage of 4 feet 9 inches will probably become universal. It is a great pity that President Lincoln did not decide for 5 feet when he fixed the guage of the Union Pacific, for it was understood by railroad men that the guage of that road would determine the future guage of the whole country. Since writing the above we learn by telegraph that the South Pacific Railway, which runs from St. Louis to the Southwest corner of Missouri, changed its guage on Thursday to conform with the Missouri Pacific, which runs from St Louis to Kansas City. The Kansas Pacific, from Kansas City and Leavenworth to the west Kansas line, retains its original guage of 4 feet 8¼ inches.—*U. S. R. R. Journal.*

—The Simcoe *Reformer* says a meeting of the Directors of the Norfolk Railway Company was held in this town on the 24th inst. We are not in possession of a report of the proceedings, but understand that arrangements are being made for opening stock books at once. George Laidlaw, Esq., of Toronto, was appointed Secretary of the company. The Directors express themselves as sanguine that the work of building the road will soon be in progress, and rapidly pushed forward to completion. We need not say that we sincerely trust their hopes would be realized.

Insurance.

FIRE RECORD.—Canning, Nova Scotia, July.— The *Chronicle* says the fire commenced in the store lately occupied by B. & I. Bigelow, and extended east to stores of Charles Dickie and G. E. Eaton & Co., and west to the stores of J. R. Kennedy, Sheffield & Wickwire and M. Reddy, burning in all eight buildings, three of them three stories in height. The loss in buildings is heavy; nearly covered by insurance. The goods were mostly saved, and mostly insured in the London, Liverpool and Globe and other offices. The fire engine purchased since the last fire, did good service, and saved a general conflagration, J. H. Clark's threestory store had caught fire, which was extinguished by it, and kept the devouring elements from crossing the street, as it did in the former fire of July, 1866. There may be other sufferers, but up to the hour of going to press we were unable to learn further particulars.

Fall river Bathrust 16th July.—The saw mill of Playfare & Steadman.

North Eastern Township, July 22.—The barns of Robert McLarty were struck by lightning. Both buildings were totally destroyed, together with all their contents, consisting of a mowing machine, farming implements, buggy, cutter, harness, &c. Mr. McLarty's loss is estimated at about $3,000, and he was only insured for $400.

Princeton, Ont., July 22.—The barn belonging to Mr. McCrow, near Princeton, was destroyed with its contents, by lightning. The property was insured for $1,000.

INTERNATIONAL LIFE OF LONDON.—The *Insurance Times* says:—Jay Cooke, Esq., the eminent Banker, has made a proposition to the receiver of this company, to re-insure its risks in the National Life of the United States of America, on a basis of 6 per cent. The terms have been submitted to the Prudential of London, which company assumed the risks of the International, and as there are sufficient funds in the department belonging to the International to re-insure at 6 per cent. the 400 policies still held by Americans in this company, it is to be hoped that Jay Cooke's offer will be accepted.

CAPTAINS vs. UNDERWRITERS.—"An Underwriter" in Halifax, has addressed the following letter to the editor of the *Chronicle* :—I may say that it has almost become a bye-word with underwriters, "what is to be done to protect our interests?" There is hardly a day but what the loss of some vessel is reported, and in many cases that losses are far from creditable to the masters, as gross carelessness, to say the least, is often the cause. I could give some of the most glaring instances, not only of carelessness, but actual fraud, which have come under my own notice, which should have sent the master to stand watch on the quarter deck of a ship that does not require a compass, but is navigated by a hammer and stone.

A day or two ago three vessels were reported lost on the coast, in one of which cases at least, gross carelessness to the interests of the underwriters was manifested. I allude to the brig *Foyle*, which got ashore at Bridgeport, and before an agent could be appointed by the underwriters even by telegraph, a notary and the captain had condemned and sold her, while with very little trouble, the purchaser got her afloat in a few hours. Now, I ask underwriters if nothing can be done to bring such a "captain" before them. A man who would abandon a fine vessel under such circumstances, counseled by a notary, who probably can hardly tell an anchor from a cooking stove, should never be allowed to take charge of another. Yet he, like many others before him, equally culpable, will probably take charge of another vessel, and will get insurance effected at as low rates as the best.

Now, were a board of underwriters formed, and a proper agent appointed, who would do his duty, and bring such men to book for every loss, I feel satisfied that the lead would go over the side a little oftener when vessels are standing in for the land in thick weather; and shipmasters might be taught to attend to their own business, instead of running off to the first notary they can find, to fix their papers to stand law. If his certificate were in danger, he would probably attend to running an anchor and chain out, and in many cases save his ship.

It is not an unusual case when a vessel is running off her class, to get her restored again, or paid for by the underwriters, and in some cases add a hurricane deck and call her new. When away from home, a master has great power, and can call as a survey on a vessel, many men who will report as he pays them, and thus defraud underwriters.

THE ÆTNA INSURANCE COMPANY was incorporated in 1819, with perpetual succession, and commenced business on the 17th August, in the same year. Its original capital was $150,000, which has been increased at different intervals, as follows: December 1822, $50,000; January, 1846, $50,000; October, 1849, $50,000; December, 1854, $200,-000; July 1857, $500,000; January, 1864, $750,-000; February, 1866, $750,000; aggregate, $3,-000,000. Of this existing three million capital, $2,805,000 represents savings from the company's business, or dividends which were paid in stock. The total cash dividends paid to stockholders of the company, since its organization, amounts to $4,189,950, which with the stock dividends, foots up $6,994,950, as the entire savings from $40,647,-317, the aggregate premium receipts. The total amount of losses paid by the company during the same period, is $24,389,453. From these figures we deduce the following average of results: Percentage of losses to premium receipts, 59.90; percentage of expenses to premium receipts 20.27. It should be observed, however, that this calculation takes no account of receipts from interest upon investments, or from appreciation of securities.—*Spectator.*

—An attempt was made one night last week to burn the Royal Hotel in Orillia. The fire was discovered in time and extinguished. The *Expositor* says that on examination it was found that the paper used by the incendiary consisted in whole or in part of a bundle of the circulars of an insurance agent named Colin Campbell, who was boarding at the Royal Hotel. It was subsequently ascertained that this individual having for some cause become incensed at Mrs. Johnson, had threatened that he would be revenged. At the excursion on Monday evening, he told a youth not to sleep at the hotel that night, "for he intended to make it warm for them before morning." It was also found that he was not in his room at t'e hotel. Campbell was arrested, and at the preliminary examination he has unabled to give a satisfactory account of his whereabouts during the night. There being a strong chain of circumstantial evidence against the prisoner, he was sent to Barrie for trial.

—A survey was held here yesterday upon the sch Lafayette Cook, damaged on the Charity Shoals, which resulted in an opinion that repairs upon her would be required to the amount of $1,200 to $1,500. She is insured in the British and Ætna companies.

—Mr Fackler, the Actuary, in a communication to the New York *Times*, says that some of the life companies have made fraudulent statements for years to Superintendent Barnes, and that the latter "shuts his eyes and publishes them without criticism." This is a charge of the gravest character, and we hope it has not much foundation.

MINERAL PAINTS.—Some excitement has been created in the village of Washington, in the county of Oxford, by the discovery near that place of a valuable and extensive mine of oxide of iron, from which several kinds of paints have been successfully manufactured. The paint mine was discovered last fall, and is now being worked by the lessee and proprietor, Mr. D. Winter. Five distinct colours are manufactured, namely—yellow ochre, light and dark red, and light and dark drab, umber. A trial of the manufactured article has been made by the painters of Washington and Plantsville, who pronounce it to be of a superior quality.

—It is stated that Mr. Cummins, of Brampton, has discovered a bed of soapstone on his lot, on the town line between Madoc and Elzevir.

MADOC MINING INTELLIGENCE.—The second cleaning up at the Gillen Co.'s mill was completed last week, the result being nearly 7½ oz. of gold. Although more than a week had elapsed since the first ingot was obtained, the above yield is estimated as equal to a week's actual work; the difference being accounted for by one of the stamps breaking down, and by some deficiency in the mill-dam impeding operations. We hear that owing to the promising aspect of affairs at the Gillen Co.'s property, it is in contemplation to remove the Caldwell mill for its present site to that neighbourhood; and also a rumour that the Toronto and Whitby Co.'s mill may be removed from Bannock-burn to Marmora.—*Mercury.*

—A St. John's paper says the Caledonia and the Budroe free stone quarries in Rockland, N. B., are in a flourishing condition, and are doing a very large business. The Caledonia Quarries owned by Messrs. Daniel & Boyd, of St. John, and Messrs. Smith & M'Kelvey, of Sackville, employ upwards of 75 men, and have manufactured and shipped to the United States, during the last five months, 800 tons of stone. The Budroe Quarry employs 96 men, besides horses, and turns out 2,500 tons of stone yearly. The latter quarry is owned by a New York Company, and it is larger than the Caledonia Quarry, and turns out more stone.

—Large quantities of spruce and pine wood are being shipped from Rockland, N. B., to Philadelphia, for the purpose of manufacturing it into paper. Mr. William Chapman has shipped during the summer 460 cords, and has orders for as much more.

Commercial.

The Harvest of 1868.

Arrived at the first week in August we should be well able to estimate the seasons crop of cereals, with some degree of certainty, but such has been the state of the weather that harvesting has been delayed a fortnight; it will therefore be necessary to wait that much longer before knowing what is in store for us. The subject is one of prime consequence, but unfortunately the information to be had is of the most vague and disjointed character. Even under favorable circumstances it is next to impossible to get reliable intelligence. It has to be derived from many separate sources, and each report partakes of the hopeful or desponding views of its compilers. In the United States, with a tolerably well organised corps of informants, the reports of the Bureau are looked upon as just about as valuable as the opinion of any single intelligent man on the same subject, and are so trusted. In Canada we cannot produce anything so authoritative as an official report; but from the collected information of leading mercantile firms, who watch the subject with the greatest interest, and who are regularly advised by their customers—men as capable of judging, and as deeply interested, as any class in the community—we can glean facts from which certain general conclusions may be drawn with great safety.

The bulk of the hay crop is now gathered, but the work has been uncommonly tedious and expensive, owing to the ever-interrupting showers; a good deal is yet out and will have to take its chance till the earlier wheat and barley is cared for; much of it will be inferior in quality from being badly saved or too ripe; still since it covered the earth as a thick carpet and yielded quantities almost without precedent, there will be a great abundance. The root crop has not been so good for many years; this is a universal tale. There is a tendency to grow too much to the tops, instead of filling out at the roots, but time will set this all right. With plenty of hay and roots comes also plenty of beef, mutton, butter, tallow, wool, &c.,—staples second only to our leading cereals and lumber.

Turning to the wheat crop, there is a great diversity of opinion. The most gloomy accounts

are from the newer and recently most productive sections of the country, and the most favorable from the older sections. The boot seems fairly to have got upon the other foot. Three years ago no wheat worth talking of could be found, near Toronto, because of the midge, which the north-western section of Ontario grew it in great abundance, and knew nothing of that pest; now it is unknown here, except by recollection, while there it is dealing deadly destruction over a wide area. With so much wet there must be, and is, rust, with plenty of it. A large breadth was sown and, taking all in all, a fine crop will be reaped; but not so large as was estimated a month ago, by the most reliable authorities; probably before all is over there will be still less than we now expect. A great growth of straw is liable to deceive, and this deception becomes apparent on thrashing day. Oats and barley, enough and to spare, will be harvested. Peas cannot yet be judged; the bug may take the conceit out of them before they are in the granary.

On the whole the prospect is delightful, "yellow fields of waving corn," full of promise and wealth, cover immense tracts of the most fertile soil, on the face of the broad earth; the shout of "harvest home." will soon ring throughout the land; millions of graineries will be filled as they have seldom been filled before. All this points to enhanced agricultural and commercial prosperity; it brings good news for the great carrying trade of the country; it will nourish and stimulate every other interest in the Dominion. And it is pleasant to add that the same hopeful story comes to us from almost every country the world over.

Boot and Shoe Trade.

The shoe business of Lynn, Mass., is steadily increasing. The total number of cases of boots and shoes manufactured in and sent away from Lynn during the six months ending July 1st, was 114,480—of which the first quarter of the year gave 62,911 cases, and the second 51,569 cases. For the first six months of 1868 the shipments were 98,361 cases, showing a gain of 16,089 cases this year. The total number of pairs of shoes manufactured and shipped during the past six months was 6,868,800, having a value of nearly if not quite ten million dollars.

Disasters on the Lakes.

The statistics of the passenger travel and the disasters during 1868 are as follows: Passengers carried 900,000; lives lost from fire, 73; from collision, 51; from wreck, 26; from explosion, 1⅞; making a total of 151. The accidents were 19 in number, as follows: Collisions, 8; fire, 6; striking on sandbars or rocks, 3; foundering, 2. Of the fires, five were of vessels burned at night, while lying at the dock.

Oil at Petrolia.

(From our own Correspondent.)

PETROLIA, Aug. 2, 1869.

A number of new wells are about being put down, viz.: Mr. Noble, near the large still, two wells; Mr. Shields, of Inland Revenue Department together with Frank Smith, near large still, one well; Samuel Stokes, north of Pithole station, 1 well; Mr. Walker, south do, one well; Col. C. B. Parsons, near his own well, one well; Mr. Laney, near his own well, one well; Mr. Woodward, in King Fencton, one well; besides some 8 or ten others. The old wells have done admirably this week and will average some 800 barrels per day. Sixteen car loads of crude oil left Petrolia station on Thursday last, and there were two more which could not be taken. Business is very brisk and there appears to be a certainty of an increased price for crude.

The export trade has now assumed an important item in Canadian commerce and it appears doubtful whether, after the accumulation of crude oil is worked off, we can supply enough to furnish the demands of the exporters. This, doubtless, will stimulate and has to a certain extent stimulated the production of oil, and caused the putting down of so many new wells. There is nothing to der Canadian competing successfully with American oil. At present our oils are shipped ough American ports, but I think, before long, St. Lawrence will prove a far more profitable nnel for exportation.

Petroleum.

he following shows the exports of Petroleum m the United States from January 1 to July 20:

	1869.	1868.
m New York......galls	34,321,892	26,687,876
Boston..................	1,241,003	1,286,606
Philadelphia	13,777,943	17,578,125
Baltimore..............	753,953	1,053,886
Cleveland...............	......	214,508

al export from the U. S.	50,194,796	46,820,501
ne time 1867...............		32,286,885
ne time 1866...............		29,159,711

Crude Oil Association.

At a special meeting of the Oil Producers' Association, held the 21st, a report was presented. wing the business done for the half year ended e 30th; as follows:—Oil delivered during the months, 69,313 brls. Sold for following prices:

322 brls.	Oil, at	$0 75	....	$23,491 50
164 "	"	1 07¼	....	2,326 40
116 "	"	for.....	....	1,464 00
857 "	"	at 1 00	....	23,857 00
208 "	"	1 25	....	9,010 00
146 "	"	1 62½	....	6,737 25

Amount received $66,886 05

id Producers........	$63,670 40
" Expenses...............	1,687 85
lance on hand.............	1,527 80

$66,886 05

Advance in Freights.

A meeting of the ship-brokers at Buffalo was d the other day, at which a union was formed, I the rates of freight advanced. The following he tariff for the present, as fixed by the union: al—Erie and Cleveland to Chicago, down town k, $1.25, free of handling; Erie and Cleveland up-town dock, Chicago, $1.91, free on board; ffalo to Chicago, $1 free; Buffalo to Milwaukee, ic., free; Erie and Cleveland to Milwaukee, 00 free; Buffalo to Toledo, Detriot and Cleved, 75c. f. o. b. and trimmed. Iron—Buffalo Chicago and Milwaukee $1, free. Water Lime— Toledo, Erie, Cleveland and Detroit . per brl.; slate $1 per ton; stone $3 per cord; rble $1 per ton, free.

Tobacco.

The cultivation of tobacco is increasing in Inna. It is stated that the weed is raised on nost every farm in Dubois, Orange, Green, vies, Pike, Gibson, and Martin counties. In uttingdim, Dubois county, there are four large acco stemmeries, which shipped last year 700 ds. of tobbacco, worth $350,000.

The Wine Trade.

The trade in Port wine for the past six months evinced by the shipments from Oporto, presents ery satisfactory increase upon the past two rs; some of the small shippers show most conciously by their increased trade. Trade at ne and abroad continues quiet. Advices from : wine-growing districts are of rather a grunng nature, but it is as yet premature to speak itively on the subject. Quotations—Common ing 22l. to 28l.; stout fair, 30l. to 40l.; vint- 1863, 45l. to 65l.; vintage 1864, 36l. to 50l.; tage 1865, 40l. to 55l.; superior old, 50l. to ; very fine, 65l. to 85l. The trade in brandy continues in a state of alst unprecedented dulness, which will not be proved whilst the present weather continues. ere is every prospect of an abundant, if not an ly, vintage. The absence of export demand ses brandy of the 1863 vintage to be neglected. ler vintages continue to hold their own, but slow of sale.—*London Grocer.*

Beet Root Sugar Crop.

The last issue of the Sugar Makers' *Journal* of France says that real autumn weather has set in and that the heat has proved favorable to the beet harvest. Reports of the crop continue to vary according to the locality. In a number of districts it is generally in fine condition, in others not so good, and in some places there are great complaints of the white worms which are attacking the beet with all their destructive powers. The smaller beets, which are expected to form the greater portion of the harvest, require frequent watering, and they must have very favourable weather if they are to turn out well. The fine promises of spring have vanished, and a good medium harvest is all that can be expected, but it will not nearly approach to the 300 million kilogrammes of sugar which we looked forward to at the commencement of the season. The temperature, which has greatly improved in Germany, has produced a radical change in the growth of the beet, and has quite dissipated all the fears which we entertained as to the approaching harvest. According to the more recent estimates taken in all sugar producing countries in Europe, the production on the quantity of beet sown will be 10 per cent. more than last year.

Crops in England.

Mr. A. K. Jackson, of Mark Lane, London, who has been traversing the great wheat-growing region of England, along the east coast, writes to the *Times* under date of June 16, that although May and June have been very wet and cold, the prospect is good for a reasonably fair crop of wheat; barley is not so good, while oats, with good weather, will yield very largely, and beans and peas are remarkably promising. He reports the crops in other European countries as "unseven but not small," and says that the Algerian harvest is begun. As the French barley-cutting has begun well. The price of wheat in England is less by one-third than it was one year ago, being then 69s 1½d a quarter, and now only 45s 8½d. Mr. Jackson says that the wheat in Cambridgeshire is expected to bloom by June 25, in average years; this year it was a week later, though many fields in Kent were in bloom at that date. Hot weather was much desired, as it has been here, showing that the cold rains we have had here prevailed also in England.

An English journal, believed to be well informed, says of the crops :—1. That the wheat is, on the whole, a deficient one. 2. That barley is also a deficient crop to, at least, the same extent as wheat. 3. That the crop of oats, though not so generally deficient as that of wheat and barley, is considerably below an average. 4. That beans and peas are an excellent crop, and very much above the average. 5. That potatoes are a good crop. 6. That mangolds and turnips give promise of being a good crop. 7. That clover is a fair crop, and hay an extraordinarily great crop. The great practical deduction to be drawn from the above is that there will be a short supply of the cereals which come most into use as the direct food of man, while there will be an abundance of those various making products which are consumed by our live stock. These reports will, in some degree, be affected by the certainty, which the report assures us of, that the harvest will be at least three weeks later than usual, and will be a prolonged one, owing to the backward districts being much more than three weeks behind the usual period with harvest. The stocks of grain will have to be drawn upon for about an additional month's consumption now; but, on the other hand, should we have harvest at the usual period next year, the crop of this year now growing will only be called upon to meet the demand for twelve instead of thirteen lunar months.

English Goods Markets.

Huddersfield.—Both English and foreign buyers of the fancy goods produced in this neighbourhood have shown a fair amount of activity. Almost every scrap of summer fabric being cleared out from the wholesale department, and merchants are storing themselves fully with the choicest novelties that are close at hand. Not less e per cent. sive have been the operations in the same departments of the Canadian buyers. The Continental buyers may have imitated them on but a small scale, yet the clearance of fancy trouserings and coatings for shipment has been satisfactory to the makers.

Leeds.—There has been a slight increase of business in some departments of the cloth-halls. So many out-town houses were not represented as earlier in the month, but the shipping trade shows a fair amount of animation. There is more buying in the way of speculation than has been noticeable since the beginning of the year, and there is a growing confidence as to the success of the fall and winter trade so soon to open. There has been in the coloured cloth-hall a fair inquiry for tweeds, meltons, and coatings. The former have changed hands to about an average extent, and there have been large deliveries to order. The market for plain cloths, as also for beavers and goods of that class, is steady, and not worse than it has been for two or three weeks past. There is more inquiry for black unions than for some time past, the medium and low-priced qualities forming the bulk of the sales. Hair lists and white mediums did not attract much attention in the white cloth-hall, but it is well known that the makers never were busier, having engagements for delivery to time at the warehouses.

Manchester.—Though there has been more activity, there is no substantial improvement to report. Early in the month, through the stronger tone in Liverpool, a marked improvement in the demand here was manifested, leading to an increased production, which has been fully absorbed. The middle of the month showed a lull, but during the last week, owing to the renewal of large transactions in cotton, this market has again become stronger, and the month closes with prices ruling, on the average, from 2½ per cent. to 5 per cent. higher than those current at the end of May. More failures have occurred during the month, showing further the disastrous position of the manufacturing interest here. Unless the new American cotton crop show a material increase—which cannot be ascertained for some time to come —we may have to pass through another year with the same unhappy results as have characterised the last twelve months. In Twist there has been rather an active business done during the greater part of the month, at hardening prices. The principal operations have been for East India and China, and in descriptions adapted for those markets, transactions of fair extent have been entered into. Buyers for the Home trade have also purchased pretty freely. The German merchants have operated cautiously, being discouraged by the poor accounts from the Continental markets, and their purchases have only been moderate. The general demand has absorbed the production, which has rather increased this month, and stocks continue very light. Prices have gradually advanced, and now rule about 1d per lb higher than at the close of last month. In the Goods market there have been few large transactions, but a fair general business has been done, and although buyers have been reluctant to follow any material advance, still current rates are higher than they were a month ago. Stocks generally are not heavy, and have rather diminished than increased during the month.

Condition of Trade in Great Britain.

The close of the half-year seems to be an appropriate period, not only for briefly reviewing that portion of 1869 which is believed by so many (whose wish was the father to the thought) would see a material improvement in commercial and monetary affairs generally, but also for looking forward into the future and endeavouring to form some opinion by the existing indications, of what we may reasonably expect to see during the second half of 1869. First, then, the six months that are drawing to a close have witnessed a lull in the activity in one department—and not the least important part of the business which is carried on between the nations of the earth—in that of borrowing and lending. England saves faster, and has more to lend, than any other country, because her people make profits quicker; and when a general stagnation sets in throughout Europe in consequence of a break down at the great centre, a vast deal of capital accumulates, as we have seen, independently of the savings, and is one of the greatest dangers in times of stagnation, as affording the most direct encouragement to engage in the kind of speculation which caused the collapse. The only approach to transactions of magnitude in any of the ramifications of trade beyond the importation of foreign bonds, has been in iron, and as part compensation for the loss which the country recently suffered by overshooting the mark as usual, our share in furnishing railway material to Russia, Austria and Hungary, America, and in a minor degree to some two or three other countries, may be mentioned. The extent to which this investment in foreign bonds was carried will be indirectly productive of good at least to this country, although it is not generally seen. Without the assistance which has thus been rendered to the Government of Russia more particularly, the lines of railway which it may safely be predicted will henceforth prevent the prices in Mark-lane ever reaching again what they have been could not have been constructed for years to come. Upon the completion of the lines which are being hurried forward, the produce of the great corn districts of the Baltic provinces will be no longer dependent upon the means of transport to Western Europe which hitherto have been barred by the ice, shortly after that period when the harvest yield of those nations which can pay the best price is accurately known. Beyond the partial revival in the iron districts which has thus been caused, we look in other directions in vain for indications of a similar nature; and the best proof that the immediate future prospects afford but little encouragement to the hundreds of unemployed is found in the stream of human beings which now sets in the direction of the United States and Canada from these shores.—*Morgan's Trade Journal.*

British Metal Market for the Quarter ended June 30.

A glance at the trade of the metal market during the last three months does not afford the satisfaction and encouragement which all had fairly looked for. Spring has come and gone, and in spite of peace everywhere, a low rate of discount, and other favourable circumstances, trade has been only steady—a steadiness, indeed, approaching dulness and inactivity. During the last part of the quarter there has been a slight movement for the better. In the early part of April, manufacturers were somewhat busy, owing, probably, more to the accumulation of orders during the Easter holidys than to any permanent revival in trade. In a week or two, business became dull again, and so it remained during the rest of the month, and also throughout May. Trade, the manufacturers reported, did not reach the average for that time of the year. During the early part of June, trade remained dull, but towards the end of the first fortnight, there came a better feeling. The reduction of the rate of discount from 4½ to 4 per cent. doubtless stimulated business, and gave rise to a hope that a better trade would soon be experienced. Nor has the expectation been altogether unrealized. The tone of the market is improving. Orders, of greater value than have lately found their way out, are now being regularly received; and as they embrace the general kinds of metals they lead to the inference that buyers are more disposed to enter into negotiations than they have been for some time. Prices are a little firmer, and there is every probability that they will become still more in favour of vendors.

Copper is decidedly improved, and prices are stiffer.

Iron.—In the general kinds of Staffordshire iron there is hardly so much doing, except in iron for constructive purposes, and for bridge and girder building. The demand for rails continues active, and other makers will, it is expected, enter the trade when they have watched how those makers succeed who have adapted their mills to this kind of work. The Welsh makers are well engaged upon Russian and American rail orders. Pigs are mostly firm.

For *Steel* there is a better foreign enquiry. Both English and Foreign *Tin* keeps in small demand. Only little is done in Straits at the price quoted, and English, saving refined, is sold under the price named.

Tin Plates are somewhat increasing in demand. The market is quiet for *Lead*; but for *Spelter* the market is firm, although the transactions have not been large.—*Morgan's Trade Journal.*

Stocks of Provisions at Liverpool.'

The following is a statement showing the stocks of provisions at Liverpool at the close of the half-year ending June 30, as compared with that of the two previous years:—On July 30, 1869, 25,881 tierces beef (including 17,348 tierces old and Texas), 3,812 barrels pork, 10,645 boxes bacon (including 3,284 hams and sholders), 350 tons lard, 11,274 boxes cheese, and 4,164 packages butter. On June 30, 1868, 16,636 tierces beef, 5,212 barells pork, 16,612 boxes bacon (including 616 hams and sholders), 1,100 tons lard, 9,116 boxes cheese, and 65 packages butter. On June 30, 1867, 3780 tierces beef, 5,390 barrels pork, 7813 boxes bacon, 253 tons lard, 11,461 boxes cheese, and 4580 packages butter.

Wool

A Buffalo paper says—There is danger that the Canadian buyers of combing wool will sustain heavy losses. Agents of the Pacific Mills, the largest establishment in the country, are said to be now in England, where they can obtain combing wool on more favorable terms than in the Canadian markets.

The Currant Crop.

A letter from Patras, dated July 8, says:—"Although this has been subject to many vicissitudes on account of the continued prevalence of unusually moist weather, yet we may, on the whole, expect a moderately abundant yield. The weather appears now fixedly hot and fine—facts most conducive to the maturity of the currants."

British America Assurance Company.

THE Thirty-fifth Annual Court of Proprietors of this Institution was held on Monday, the 2nd instant, as prescribed by the Act of Incorporation, when the following gentlemen were elected for the ensuing year, viz.:
 GEORGE PERCIVAL RIDOUT, Esq., of Toronto.
 PETER PATERSON, Esq. of Scarboro'.
 E. H. RUTHERFORD, Esq., of Toronto.
 HON. WM. CAYLEY, of Toronto.
 HON. G. W. ALLAN, of Toronto.
 GEORGE J. BOYD, Esq., of Toronto.
 THOS C. STREET, Esq., M.P.P., of Clark Hill.
 PELEG HOWLAND, Esq., of Toronto.
 A. JOSEPH, Esq., of Quebec.
 At a meeting of the Board, this day, the undermentioned were unanimously re-chosen for the respective offices :
 GOVERNOR—G. P. RIDOUT, Esq.
 Deputy-GOVERNOR—PETER PATERSON, Esq.
 Trustees—E. H. RUTHERFORD, Esq., HON. WM. CAYLEY, GEO. J. BOYD, Esq.
 By order of the Board.
   F. W. BIRCHALL, Manager,
   Per JOHN EVANS, Accountant
British America Assurance Office, }
 Toronto, 3rd August, 1869. }   aug 5-1t

Western Assurance Company.

NOTICE is hereby given that the Annual General Meeting of the Shareholders of this Company will be held at the Company's offices, Church Street, Toronto, on Tuesday the 31st day of August next, at 12 o'clock, noon, to receive the Directors' reports, with the Financial Statements for the year ending 30th June last, and also for the Election of Directors to serve during the ensuing year.
   By order of the Board,
     BERNARD HALDAN, Secretary.
Western Assurance Company's Office, }
 Toronto, 31st July, 1869. }

Arthur Jones,
Land Surveyor and Timber Agent.

IMPROVED and unimproved lands for sale, in the Counties of Kent, Essex, Lambton, Middlesex, and Elgin.
   Chatham County, Kent,
     Ontario

Northern Railway of Canada.

THE half yearly meeting of the proprietors of this Company will be held in their offices, Brock Street, on
WEDNESDAY, THE ELEVENTH DAY OF AUGUST,
   At TWELVE o'clock, noon, precisely,
when the Report of the Directors and the Financial Statements for the half year, ending 30th June last, will be submitted.
 By order.
       THOS. HAMILTON,
          Secretary.
Toronto, 27th July, 1869.

NOTICE.
Office of the Toronto, Grey and Bruce Railway Company.

A GENERAL Meeting of the Subscribers to the Capital Stock of the Toronto, Grey and Bruce Railway Company will be held at the office of the said Company, No. 46 Front Street, in the City of Toronto, on TUESDAY, the 10th day of August next, at TWELVE o'clock noon, for the purpose of electing Directors and organizing the said Company.
     W. SUTHERLAND TAYLOR,
        Secretary.
Toronto, July 7, 1869.

Western Assurance Company.

NOTICE is hereby given, that a dividend for the half-year, ending the 30th ult., at the rate of EIGHT per cent. per annum, upon the capital paid-up stock of this Company, has been declared, and will be payable at the Company's office, on and after Friday, the 9th inst.
 By order of the Board.
       BERNARD HALDAN,
          Secretary.
Western Assurance Co.'s Office,
 Toronto, 1st July, 1869.

Morton & Smith,
ACCOUNTANTS, REAL ESTATE AGENTS,
   AND VALUATORS,
 48 AND 50 CHURCH STREET,
     TORONTO.
R. MORTON.   47-1y   J. LAMOND SMITH.

Insolvent Act of 1864.

PROVINCE OF ONTARIO. }
COUNTY OF YORK. }
 In the County Court of the County of York.
 In the matter of THOMAS D. LEDYARD, an Insolvent
THE undersigned has filed a consent by his creditors to his discharge, and on Monday, the Twentieth day of September next, he will apply to the Judge of the said Court for a confirmation thereof.
 Dated at Toronto this fourteenth day of July, A.D. 1869.
46-10t   T. D. LEDYARD.

Insolvent Act of 1864

PROVINCE OF ONTARIO, }
COUNTY OF YORK. }
 In the County Court of the County of York.
 In the matter of HENRY S. LEDYARD, an Insolvent
THE undersigned has filed a consent by his Creditors to his discharge, and on Monday, the Thirteenth day of September next, he will apply to the Judge of the said Court for a confirmation thereof.
 Dated at Toronto, this Third day of July, A.D. 1869.
46-10t.   H. S. LEDYARD.

Montreal Telegraph Company,

NOTICE is hereby given, that a Dividend of FIVE per cent. for the half-year ending THIRTY-FIRST MAY, has been declared upon the Capital Stock of the Company, and the same will be payable at the offices of the Company, on and after FRIDAY, the NINTH JULY.
 The Transfer Book will be closed from 1st to 9th JULY.
   By order of the Board,
 (Signed)   JAMES DAKERS,
          Secretary

Mercantile.

TORONTO PRICES CURRENT.—AUGUST 5' 1869.

Name of Article.	Wholesale Rates.		Name of Article.	Wholesale Rate.		Name of Article.	Wholesale Rates.	
Boots and Shoes.	$ c.	$ c.	**Groceries**—*Contin'd*	$ c.	$ c.	**Leather**—*Contin'd.*	$ c.	$ c.
Mens' Thick Boots ...	2 05	2 50	Gunpowd'r c. to med..	0 55	0 7	Kip Skins, Patna	0 30	0 35
" Kip..........	2 25	3 00	" med. to fine.	0 70	0 8	French	0 72	0 90
" Calf	2 30	3 70	" fine to fin't ..	0 85	0 9	English	0 65	0 80
" Congress Gaiters..	1 65	2 50	Hyson	0 45	0 80	Hemlock Calf (30 to		
" Kip Cobourgs..	1 20	1 40	Imperial..........	0 42	0 80	35 lbs.) per dos ...	0 50	0 60
Boys' Thick Boots...	1 70	1 80	Tobacco, Manufac'd:			Do. light	0 45	0 50
Youths' "	1 40	1 50	Can Leaf, ♥ lb & 10s.	0 26	0 30	French Calf........	1 03	1 06
Women's Batts	0 95	1 30	Western Leaf, com..	0 25	0 26	Grain & Satin Cit'd dos ..	0 00	0 55
" Balmoral........	1 20	1 50	" Good....	0 27	0 32	Splits, large ♥ lb....	0 30	0.38
" Congress Gaiters..	0 90	1 50	" Fine	0 32	0 35	" small	0 20	0 28
Misses' Batts........	0 75	1 00	" Bright fine...	0 40	0 50	Enamelled Cow ♥ foot..	0 20	0 21
" Balmoral	1 00	1 30	" choice..	0 00	0 75	Patent	0 20	0 21
" Congress Gaiters..	1 00	1 30				Pebble Grain	0 15	0 17
Girls' Batts	0 65	0 85	**Hardware.**			Buff ..	0 14	0 16
" Balmoral........	0 90	1 05	*Tin (net cash prices)*			**Oils.**		
" Congress Gaiters..	0 75	1 10	Block, ♥ lb.......	0 35	0 00	Cod	0 65	0 70
Children's C. T. Cacks..	0 50	0 65	Grain..........	0 30	0 00	Lard, extra	0 00	0 00
" Gaiters....	0 65	0 90	*Copper:*			" No. 1	0 00	0 00
Drugs.			"	0 23	0 24	" Woollen	0 00	0 00
Aloes Cape..........	0 12½	0 16	"	0 30	0 33	Lubricating, patent..	0 00	0 00
Alum...............	0 02½	0 03	*Cut Nails:*			" Mott's economic	0 30	0 00
Borax	0 00	0 00	Assorted ½ Shingles,			Linseed, raw........	0 76	0 82
Camphor, refined...	0 65	0 70	♥ 100 lb......	2 95	3 00	" boiled....	0 81	0 87
Castor Oil..........	0 16½	0 23	Shingle alone do ..	3 15	3 25	Machinery	0 00	0 00
Caustic Soda........	0 04½	0 05	Lathe and 5 dy.....	3 30	3 40	Olive, common, ♥ gal..	1 00	1 30
Cochineal...........	0 90	1 00	*Galvanized Iron:*			" salad ...	1 95	2 30
Cream Tartar	0 30	0 35	Assorted sizes......	0 08	0 09	" salad, in bots		
Epsom Salts	0 03	0 04	Best No. 24.......	0 07½	0 00	qt. ♥ case...	3 60	3 75
Extract Logwood....	0 11	0 12	" 26........	0 08	0 08½	Sesame salad, ♥ gal..	1 65	1 75
Gum Arabic, sorts....	0 30	0 35	" 28......	0 09	0 09½	Seal, pale.........	0 75	0 85
Indigo, Madras.......	0 90	1 00	*Horse Nails:*			Spirits Turpentine...	0 55½	0 60
Liquorice	0 14	0 15	Guest's or Griffin's			Varnish	0 00	0 00
Madder.............	0 00	0 16	assorted sizes......	0 00	0 00	Whale.............	0 00	0 90
Galls	0 32	0 37	For W. as'd sizes...	0 18	0 19			
Opium..............	12 00	13 50	Patent Hammer'd do..	0 17	0 18	**Paints, &c.**		
Oxalic Acid.........	0 26	0 35	*Iron (at 4 months):*			White Lead, genuine		
Potash, Bi-tart......	0 25	0 28	Pig—Gartsherrie No1..	24 00	25 00	in Oil, ♥ 25lbs.......	0 00	2 35
" Bichromate...	0 15	0 20	Other brands. ...	23 00	24 00	Do. No. 1	0 00	1 90
Potass Iodide	4 40	4 60	No.3....	0 00	0 00	" 2	0 00	1 90
Senna	0 18½	0 60	Bar—Scotch, ♥ 100 lb..	2 25	2 50	" 3	0 00	1 65
Soda Ash	0 03½	0 04	Refined	3 40	3 50	White Zinc, genuine..	0 00	2 50
Soda Bicarb	0 00	4 00	Swedes	5 00	5 50	White Lead, dry.....	0 06½	0 09
Tartaric Acid.......	0 40	0 45	Hoops—Coopers.....	3 00	3 25	Red Lead..........	0 07½	0 08
Verdigris	0 35	0 40	Band	3 00	3 25	Venetian Red, Eng'h..	0 02½	0 03½
Vitriol, Blue........	0 08	0 10	Boiler Plates	3 25	3 50	Yellow Ochre, Fren'h..	0 02½	0 03½
Groceries.			Canada Plates......	3 75	4 00	Whiting...........	0 85	1 25
Coffees:			Union Jack	0 00	0 00			
Java, ♥ lb........	0 22	0 23	Pontypool.........	3 25	4 00	**Petroleum.**		
Laguayra, ...	0 17	0 18	Swansea	3 90	4 00	(Refined ♥ gal.)		
Rio................	0 15	0 17	*Lead (at 4 months):*			Water white, car'l'd..	0 20	0 21
Fish:			Bar, ♥ 100 lbs...	0 06½	0 07	" small lots ..	0 22	0 23
Herrings, Lab. split..	00	0 00	Sheet	0 08	0 09	Straw, by car load...	0 00	0 00
" round....	00	0 00	Shot.............	0 07½	0 07½	" small lots ..	0 00	0 00
" scaled...	0 35	0 33	*Iron Wire (net cash):*			Amber, by car load..	0 00	0 00
Mackerel, small kitts..	1 00	0 00	No. 6, ♥ bundle ...	2 70	2 80	" small lots ..	0 00	0 00
Louh. Har. wh'efish..	2 50	2 75	" 9, "	3 10	3 20	Benzine	0 00	0 00
" half " ..	1 25	1 50	" 12, "	3 40	3 50	**Produce.**		
White Fish & Trout...	0 00	3 50	" 16, "	4 30	4 40	*Grain:*		
Salmon, saltwater....	14 00	15 00	*Powder:*			Wheat, Spring, 60 lb..	1 00	1 02
Dry Cod, ♥112 lbs....	4 50	5 00	Blasting, Canada....	3 50	0 00	" Fall 60 "..	1 00	1 05
Fruit:			FF "	4 25	4 50	Barley........ 48 " ..	0 00	0 72
Raisins, Layers	1 90	2 00	FFF "	4 75	5 00	Peas.......... 60 " ..	0 00	0 00
" M R	1 90	2 00	Blasting, English ..	4 00	5 00	Oats.......... 34 " ..	0 53	0 57
" Valentiasnew...	0 6	0 6½	FF loose.	5 00	6 00	Rye .... 56 " ..	0 56	0 00
Currants, new........	0 4½	0 0½	FFF "	6 00	6 50	*Seeds:*		
" old......	0 3½	0 0½	*Pressed Spikes (4 mos):..*			Clover, choice 60 " ..	0 00	0 00
Figs	0 11	0 12	Regular sizes 100....	4 00	4 25	" com'n 68 " ..	0 00	0 00
Molasses:			Extra	4 50	5 00	Timothy, choice 4 " ..	0 00	0 00
Clayed, ♥ gal......	0 00	0 35	*Tin Plates (net cash):*			" inf. to good 48 " ..	0 00	0 00
Syrups, Standard	0 55	0 75	IC Coke	7 50	8 50	Flax............ 56 " ..	0 00	0 00
" Golden ..	0 09	0 60	IC Charcoal......	8 50	9 00	*Flour (per brl.):*		
Rice:			IX "	10 50	11 00	Superior extra.......	4 60	4 70
Arracan	60	4 00	IXX "	13 50	14 00	Extra superfine,.....	4 60	4 70
Spices:			DC "	8 00	8 50	Fancy superfine.....	4 55	4 65
Cassia, whole, ♥ lb..	0 00	0 45	DX "	9 50	0 00	Superfine No	4 45	4 50
Cloves	0 11	0 12	**Hides & Skins, ♥ lb**			" No. 2........		
Nutmegs	0 00	0 00	Green rough	0 00	0 05	Oatmeal, (per brl.)....	5 50	6 00
Ginger, ground	0 18	0 33	Green, salt'd & insp'd..	0 06	0 06½	**Provisions**		
" Jamaica, root..	0 30	0 25	Cured	0 00	0 00	Butter, dairy tub ♥ lb..	0 13½	0 15
Pepper, black........	0 18	0 20	Calfskins, green......	0 00	0 10	" store packed.	0 12½	0 13
Pimento	0 08	0 00	Calfskins, cured.....	0 18	0 26	Cheese, new	0 11	0 12½
Sugars:			" dry....	0 18	0 20	Pork, mess, per brl....	27 00	27 50
Port Rico, ♥ lb......	0 9	0 9½	Sheepskins,			" prime mess.....		
Cuba "	0 9	0 9½	pelts........	1 26	1 60	" prime		
Barbadoes (bright)...	0 9½	0 0½	" do........	0 10	0 20	Bacon, rough	0 12	0 12½
Canada Sugar Refine'y,			**Hops**			" Cumberl'd cut..	0 13	0 00
yellow No. 2, 30 ds..	0 9½	0 9½	Inferior, ♥ lb........	0 00	0 00	" smoked......	0 00	0 00
Yellow, No. 2½......	0 9	0 9½	Medium...........	0 00	0 00	Hams, in salt........	0 00	0 00
" No. 3......	0 9½	0 10	Good	0 00	0 00	" smoked......	0 00	0 07
Crushed X	0 11	0 11½	Fancy	0 00	0 00	Shoulders, in salt	0 00	0 11
A	0 11½	0 11¾	**Leather,** @ (4 mos.)			Lard, in kegs........	0 15½	0 16½
Ground.............	0 12½	0 12½	No.1st qual middle do..	0 21	0 23	Eggs, packed........	0 13	0 15
Dry Crushed	0 12	0 12½	Do. No. 2, light weights	0 20	0 00	Beef Hams	0 00	0 10
Extra Ground........	0 13	0 13½	" No. 3, light weights	0 20	0 00	Tallow	0 00	8
Teas:			higher.			Hogs dressed, heavy..	0 00	0 00
Japan, com'n to good..	0 48	0 50	Spanish Sole, 1st qual'y			" medium,	0 00	0 00
" Fine to choicest..	0 55	0 60	heavy, weights ♥ lb..	0 21	0 23	" light...	0 00	0 00
Colored, com. to fine..	0 55	0 65	Do.1st qual middle do..	0 20	0 00	**Salt, &c.**		
" good & Souch'ng..	3 42	0 75	Do. No. 2, light weights	0 20	0 00	American brls........	1 35	1 37
Oolong, good to fine..	0 60	0 65	" heavy	0 25	0 27	Liverpool coarse	0 00	1 28
Y. Hyson, com to gd..	0 47½	0 65	Harness, best	0 00	0 00	Goderich	0 00	1 53
Medium to choice	0 65	0 80	" No. 3	0 00	0 00	Plaster	0 00	0 00
Extra choice	0 85	0 95	Upper heavy.......	0 30	0 32	Water Lime	1 50	0 00
			" light.......	0 30	0 34			

Soap & Candles.

	$ c.	$ c.
D. Crawford & Co.'s ..		
Imperial..........	0 07½	0 08
" Golden Bar	0 07	0 07½
" Silver Bar........	0 07	0 07½
Crown	0 05	0 05½
No. 1	0 03½	0 03½
Candles	0 00	0 11

Wines, Liquors, &c.

Ale:		
English, per doz. qrts.	2 60	2 65
Guinness Dub Portr..	2 35	2 40
Spirits:		
Pure Jamaica Rum...	1 80	2 25
De Kuyper's H. Gin..	1 55	1 65
Booth's Old Tom.....	1 90	2 00
Gin:		
Green, cases.........	4 00	4 25
Booth's Old Tom, c...	6 00	6 25
Wines:		
Port, common	1 00	1 25
" fine old	2 00	4 00
Sherry, common	1 00	1 50
" medium........	1 70	1 80
"old pale or golden..	2 50	4 00

	$ c.	$ c
Brandy:		
Hennessy's, per gal..	2 30	2 50
Martell's " ..	2 30	2 50
J. Robin & Co.'s " ..	2 25	2 35
Otard, Dupuy & Cos..	2 25	2 35
Brandy, cases........	8 50	9 00
Brandy, com. per c...	4 00	4 50
Whiskey:		
Common 36 u. p......	0 58	0 60
Old Rye	0 77½	0 80
Malt	0 77½	0 80
Toddy	0 77½	0 80
Scotch, per gal.......	1 90	2 10
Irish—Kinnahan's c...	7 00	7 50
" Dunnville's Belf't..	6 00	6 25

Wool.

Fleece, lb.............	0 30	0 31
Pulled ".............	0 00	0 00

Furs.

Bear..................	0 00	0 00
Beaver, ℘ lb.........	0 00	0 00
Coon	0 00	0 00
Fisher...............	0 00	0 00
Martin...............	0 00	0 00
Mink................	0 00	0 00
Otter...............	0 00	0 00
Spring Rats	0 00	0 00
Fox.	0 00	0 00

INSURANCE COMPANIES.

ENGLISH.—*Quotations on the London Market.*

No. of Shares.	Last Dividend.	Name of Company.	Shares par val £	Amount paid.	Last Sale.
20,000		Briton Medical and General Life...	10	....	2½
50,000	7½	Commer'l Union, Fire, Life and Mar.	50	5	5½
24,000	8	City of Glasgow	25	2½	4½
5,000	9½	Edinburgh Life	100	15	33½
400,000	5—½ yr	European Life and Guarantee......	2½	11s6	4s. 0d
100,000	10	Etna Fire and Marine............	10	1½	—
20,000	5	Guardian	100	50	53½
24,000	12	Imperial Fire..................	500	50	352
7,500	9½	Imperial Life	100	10	17½
100,000	10	Lancashire Fire and Life.........	20	2	2¾
10,000	11	Life Association of Scotland.......	40	7½	25.10
35,862	45s. p. sh	London Assurance Corporation ..	25	12½	48¾
10,000	5	London and Lancashire Life	10	1	—
87,504	40	Liverp'l & London & Globe F. & L.	20	2	7½
20,000	5	National Union Life	5	1	1
20,000	12½	Northern Fire and Life	100	5	13
40,000	12 '68, bo 5s.	North British and Mercantile	50	6¼	19½
40,000	50	Ocean Marine	25	5	17¾
2,500	£5 12s.	Provident Life..................	100	10	35
....	£4½ p. s.	Phœnix......................	....	....	139½ x d
200,000	2½—h. yr.	Queen Fire and Life	10	1	21s.
100,000	3s. bo. 4s	Royal Insurance................	20	3	6½
20,000	10	Scottish Provincial Fire and Life ..	50	2½	5½
10,000	25	Standard Life	50	12	66 x d
4,000	5	Star Life	25	1¼	—
		CANADIAN.			℘ c.
8,000	4	British America Fire and Marine ..	$50	$25	56 56½
....	4	Canada Life	...	....	.....
4000	12	Montreal Assurance	£50	£5	135
10,000	3	Provincial Fire and Marine........	60	11	.....
....	....	Quebec Fire	40	32½	£22½ 23
....	7	" Marine..................	100	40	85 90
10,000	4 6 mo's.	Western Assurance..............	40	9	50 60

RAILWAYS.	Sha's	Paid	Montr	London
Atlantic and St. Lawrence......................	£100	All.	....	59 61
Buffalo and Lake Huron	20½	"	....	3 3½
Do. do Preference	10	"	....	5 7
Buff., Brantf. & Goderich, 6℘c., 1872-3-4....	100	"	....	60 70
Champlain and St. Lawrence	....	....	10 12	....
Do. do Pref. 10 ℘ ct....	....	....	80 84	....
Grand Trunk	100	"	13 15	15½ 15¾
Do. Eq.G. M. Bds. 1 ch. 6℘c..............	100	"	....	86 88
Do. First Preference, 5 ℘ c	100	"	....	54 55
Do. Deferred, 3 ℘ ct..	100	"	....	....
Do. Second Pref. Bonds, 5℘c..........	100	"	....	40 42
Do. do Deferred, 3 ℘ ct..........	100	"	...	....
Do Third Pref. Stock, 4℘ct...........	100	"	...	30 32
Do. do. Deferred, 3 ℘ ct......	100	"	...	....
Do. Fourth Pref. Stock, 3℘c..........	100	"	....	19 20
Do. do. Deferred, 3 ℘ ct..........	100	"	....	....
Great Western	20½	"	15 15½	15¾ 16
Do. New	20½	18	....	....
Do. 6 ℘ c. Bds, due 1873-76...........	100	All.	....	101 103
5½ ℘c Bds. due 1877-78...........	100	"	....	95 97
Marine Railway, Halifax, $250, all......	$250	"	....	....
Northern of Canada, 6 ℘c. 1st Pref. Bds..........	100	"	.. .	82 84

EXCHANGE.	Halifax.	Montr'l.	Quebec.	Toronto.
Bank on London, 60 days......				
Sight or 75 days date...........	12½ 13	9½ 9¾	9¾ 10	10½
Private do.	11½ 12	8 9	9 9½	9¾
Private, with documents..........	....	8 8½	....	....
Bank on New York...............	....	26 26½	25½ 25¾	26¼
Private do.	....	26½ 27	26½ 26¾	....
Gold Drafts do.	....	¼ dis.	par ⅛ dis.	par ¼ dis.
Silver	....	4 4⅝	....	4 to 5½

STOCK AND BOND REPORT.

The dates of our quotations are as follows:—Toronto, Aug. 3; Montreal, Aug. 3; Quebec, Aug. 2; London, July 22.

NAME.	Shares.	Paid up.	Divid'd last 6 Months	Dividend Day.	CLOSING PRICES. Toronto.	Montre'l	Quebec.
BANKS.			℘ ct.				
British North America	$250	All.	3½ b½ pc	July and Jan.	104½ 105	105 106	104 104½
Jacques Cartier..........	50	"	4	1 June, 1 Dec.	108 108½	108 109	107½ 108
Montreal	200	"	6	"	161 162	161 162	161½ 162½
Nationale..................	50	"	4	1 Nov. 1 May.	107½ 108	108	107½ 108
New Brunswick	100	"	......	......	....	....	....
Nova Scotia	200	—	7&b$3½	Mar. and Sept.	....	....	....
Du Peuple......	50	"	4	1 Mar., 1 Sept.	109½ 100	109 110	109 109½
Toronto	100	"	4	1 Jan., 1 July.	123 125	122 124	122 124
Bank of Yarmouth...........	....	....	......	......	....	....	....
Canadian Bank of Com'e.....	50	All.	......	......	103½ 104	100	102 103
City Bank Montreal	80	"	4	1 June, 1 Dec.	99½ 100	99 100½	99½ 100
Commer'l Bank (St. John)....	100	"	℘ ct.	......	...	..	....
Eastern Townships' Bank.....	50	"	4	1 July, 1 Jan..	....	99 100	98 99
Gore	40	...	none.	1 Jan., 1 July.	62½ 65	40 43	39 42
Halifax Banking Company....	..	....	......	......	...	...	...
Mechanics' Bank............	50	All.	4	1 Nov., 1 May.	93 95	93 95	92 93½
Merchants' Bank of Canada....	100	"	5	1 Jan., 1 July.	105 106	103 103½	104½ 104¾
Merchants' Bank (Halifax)....	....	....	......	......	....	....	....
Molson's Bank......	50	All.	4	1 Apr., 1 Oct.	100 109½	109 109½	109 109½
Niagara District Bank...	100	70	3½	1 Jan., 1 July.	...	....	....
Ontario Bank...............	40	All.	4	1 June, 1 Dec.	96 96½	95½ 96	95 95½
People's Bank (Fred'kton)....	100	"	......	......	....	...	...
People's Bank (Halifax)......	20	"	7 12 m	......	....	....	....
Quebec Bank	100	"	3½	1 June, 1 Dec.	100½ 101	100	100½ 104
Royal Canadian Bank	50	60	4	1 Jan., 1 July.	52 55	50 60	45 50
St. Stephens Bank	100	All	.....	......	....	....	....
Union Bank	100	"	4	1 Jan., 1 July.	105 105½	105 105½	105 105½
Union Bank (Halifax)........	100	....	7 12 mo	Feb. and Aug.	....	....	....
MISCELLANEOUS.							
British America Land........	250	44	......	......	....	....	....
British Colonial S. S. Co......	250	32½	......	......	...	....	...
Canada Company	32½	All.	......	......	....	....	....
Canada Landed Credit Co.....	50	$50	3½	......	80 81	....	....
Canada Per. B'ldg Society....	50	All.	5	......	123 123½	....	....
Canada Mining Company.....	4	90	......	......	....	....	....
Do. Inl'd Steam Nav. Co....	100	All.	15 12 m	......	....	99½ 101	...
Do. Glass Company........	100	"	None.	......	....	35 45	....
Canad'n Loan & Investm't....	25	2½	......	......	....	....	....
Canada Agency	10	¼	......	......	....	....	....
Colonial Securities Co........	...	....	......	......	....	....	....
Freehold Building Society....	100	All.	5	......	118 118½	....	....
Halifax Steamboat Co........	100	"	......	......	....	....	....
Halifax Gas Company.......	....	....	......	......	....	...	....
Hamilton Gas Company......	....	....	......	......	....	....	....
Huron Copper Bay Co........	4	12	20	......	....	30 40	....
Lake Huron S. and C.........	5	102	......	......	....	...	....
Montreal Mining Consols.....	20	$15	......	......	....	3.10 3.25	...
Do. Telegraph Co...	40	All.	5	......	132 133	132 133	132 133
Do. Elevating Co...	00	"	5½	......	....	101 105	....
Do. City Gas Co.........	40	"	4	15 Mar. 15 Sep.	....	138 140	138 139
Do. City Pass. R,. Co....	50	"	2	......	....	111½ 113	111 111½
Quebec and L. S.	8	$4	......	......	....	...	....
Quebec Gas Co..............	200	All.	4	1 Mar., 1 Sep.	....	...	124 125
Quebec Street R. R..........	50	25	3	......	....	....	85 90
Richelieu Navigation Co......	100	All.	7-12m	1 Jan., 1 July.	...	120 123	120 123
St. Lawrence Glass Company.	100	"	....	......	....	50 90	....
St. Lawrence Tow Boat Co....	100	"	......	3 Feb.	....	...	30 35
Tor'to Consumers' Gas Co....	50	"	⅔ m	1 My Au MarFe	107½ 108	...	107 107½
Trust & Loan Co. of U. C.....	20	5	3	......	....	....	..
West'n Canada Bldg Soc'y....	50	All.	5	......	118½ 119	....	....

SECURITIES.	London.	Montreal.	Quebec.	Toronto.
Canadian Gov't Deb. 6 ℘ ct. stg.....................	....	103 104	103 104	104½ 105
Do. do. 6 do due Ja. & Jul. 1877-84........	104 105	103 104	103 104	104 105
Do. do. 6 do. Feb. & Aug........	105 107	....	.. .	....
Do. do. 6 do. Mch. & Sep........	104 106	.. .	...	.. .
Do. do. 5 ℘ ct. cur., 1883	93 94	94 96	91 92	94 95
Do. do. 5 do. stg., 1885	92 94	91½ 92½	90 90½	92½ 93½
Do. do. 7 do. cur.,...................	....	....	......	....
Dominion 6 p. c. 1878 cy.....	....	107 107½	107 107½	106½ 107
Hamilton Corporation.....	. ..	....	... ..	....
Montreal Harbor, 8 ℘ ct. d. 1869......................	..	....	......	....
Do. do. 7 do. 1870..................	...	....	......	....
Do. do. 6½ do. 1883..................	...	102½	......	102 103
Do. do. 6½ do. 1873..................	....	....	......	....
Do. Corporation, 6 ℘ c. 1891	....	97 97½	96½ 97	96 97
Do. 7 p. c. stock...	....	109 110	108½ 109½	109 110
Do. Water Works, 6 ℘ c. stg. 1878...........	....	97 98	......	96 96½
Do. do. 6 do. cy. do.	....	....	......	96 97
New Brunswick, 6 ℘ ct., Jan. and July	102 104	....	......	....
Nova Scotia, 6 ℘ ct., 1875.........................	102 104	...	......	....
Ottawa City 6 ℘ c. d. 1880	....	95 97	......	...
Quebec Harbour, 6 ℘ c. d. 1883.....................	....	....	50	....
Do. do. 7 do. do.....................	....	....	65 70	....
Do. do 8 do. 1886..................	...	....	75 80	....
Do. City, 7 ℘ c. d. 1½ years....	....	....	98 98½	....
Do. do. 7 do. 8 do.	....	....	91 92	....
Do. do. 7 do. 5 do.	....	....	96 96½	....
Do. Water Works, 7 ℘ ct., 3 years	....	....	97 97½	....
Do. do. 6 do. 1½ do.	....	....	94 95	....
Toronto Corporation	....	94 95	...	....

Insurance.

Briton Medical and General Life Association,

with which is united the
BRITANNIA LIFE ASSURANCE COMPANY.

Capital and Invested Funds............£750,000 Sterling.

ANNUAL INCOME, £220,000 STG. : ·
Yearly increasing at the rate of £25,000 Sterling.

THE important and peculiar feature originally introduced by this Company, in applying the periodical Bonuses, so as to make Policies payable during life, without any higher rate of premiums being charged, has caused the success of the BRITON MEDICAL AND GENERAL to be almost unparalleled in the history of Life Assurance. Life Policies on the Profit Scale become payable during the lifetime of the Assured, thus rendering a Policy of Assurance a means of subsistence in old age, as well as a protection for a family, and a more valuable security to creditors in the event of early death; and effectually meeting the often urged objection, that persons do not themselves reap the benefit of their own prudence and forethought.

No extra charge made to members of Volunteer Corps for services within the British Provinces.

☞ TORONTO AGENCY, 5 KING ST. WEST.

Oct 17—9-1yr   JAMES FRASER, Agent.

BEAVER Mutual Insurance Association,

HEAD OFFICE—20 TORONTO STREET, TORONTO.

INSURES LIVE STOCK against death from any cause. The only Canadian Company having authority to do this class of business.

    E. C. CHADWICK, President.
W. T. O'REILLY, Secretary.   8-1y-25

HOME DISTRICT Mutual Fire Insurance Company.

Office—North-West Cor. Yonge & Adelaide Streets, TORONTO.—(UP STAIRS.)

INSURES Dwelling Houses, Stores, Warehouses, Merchandise, Furniture, &c.

PRESIDENT—The Hon. J. McMURRICH.
VICE-PRESIDENT—JOHN BURNS, Esq.
    JOHN RAINS, Secretary.
    AGENTS:
DAVID WRIGHT, Esq., Hamilton; FRANCIS STEVENS, Esq., Barrie; Messrs. GIBBS & BRO., Oshawa.   8-1y

THE PRINCE EDWARD COUNTY Mutual Fire Insurance Company.

HEAD OFFICE—PICTON, ONTARIO.

President, L. B. STINSON; Vice-President, WM. DELONG. Directors: W. A. Richards, James Johnson, James Cavan, D. W. Ruttan, H. A. McPaul.—Secretary, John Twigg; Treasurer, David Barker; Solicitor, R. J. Fitzgerald.

THIS Company is established upon strictly Mutual principles, insuring farming and isolated property, (not hazardous,) in Townships only, and offers great advantages to insurers, at low rates for five years, without the expense of a renewal.

Picton, June 1½, 1869   9-1y

Fire and Marine Assurance.

THE BRITISH AMERICA
ASSURANCE COMPANY.

HEAD OFFICE:
CORNER OF CHURCH AND COURT STREETS.
TORONTO.

BOARD OF DIRECTION:

Hon G. W. Allan, M L C.,	A. Joseph, Esq ,
George J. Boyd, Esq ,	Peter Paterson, Esq.,
Hon. W. Cayley,	G. P. Ridout, Esq.,
Richard S. Cassels, Esq.,	K H. Rutherford, Esq ,
Thomas C. Street, Esq.	

Governor:
GEORGE PERCIVAL RIDOUT, Esq.
Deputy Governor:
PETER PATERSON, Esq.

Fire Inspector: Marine Inspector:
E. ROBY O'BRIEN.   CAPT. R. COURNEEN.

Insurances granted on all descriptions of property against loss and damage by fire and the perils of inland navigation.

Agencies established in the principal cities, towns, and ports of shipment throughout the Province.

    THOS. WM. BIRCHALL,
33-1y   Managing Director.

Insurance.

Reliance Mutual Life Assurance Society

OF LONDON, ENGLAND. Established 1840.

Head Office for the Dominion of Canada:
131 ST. JAMES STREET, MONTREAL.

DIRECTORS—Walter Shanly, Esq., M.P.; Duncan Macdonald, Esq.; George Winks, Esq., W. H. Hingston, Esq., M.D., L.R.C.S.

RESIDENT SECRETAR—James Grant.

Parties intending to assure their lives, are invited to peruse the Society's prospectus, which embraces several entirely new and interesting features in Life Assurance. Copies can be had on application at he Head Office, or at any of the Agencies.

    JAS. GRANT, Resident Secretary.
Agents wanted in unrepresented districts.   43-1y

The Gore District Mutual Fire Insurance Company

GRANTS INSURANCES on all description of Property against Loss or Damage by FIRE. It is the only Mutual Fire Insurance Company which assesses its Policies yearly from their respective dates ; and the average yearly cost of insurance in it, for the past three and a half years, has been nearly TWENTY CENTS IN THE DOLLAR less than what it would have been in an ordinary Proprietary Company.

    THOS. M. SIMONS, Secretary & Treasurer.
ROBT. McLEAN, Inspector of Agencies.
Galt, 25th Nov., 1868.   15-1y

Canada Life Assurance Company.

ESTABLISHED 1847.

THE ONLY CANADIAN LIFE COMPANY AUTHORIZED BY GOVERNMENT FOR THE DOMINION,

Rates are lower than British or Foreign Offices.

A LARGER amount of Insurances and of Investments in Canada than any other Company, and its rapid progress is satisfactory evidence of the popularity of its principles and practice.

Last year there were issued
920 NEW POLICIES,
FOR ASSURANCE OF
$1,284,155,
WITH
ANNUAL PREMIUMS OF
$51,182.

AGENCIES THROUGHOUT THE DOMINION,
Where every information can be obtained, or at the
HEAD OFFICE, IN HAMILTON, ONT.

    A. G. RAMSAY, Manager.
    E. BRADBURNE, Agent,
May 25.   1y   Toronto Street.

Queen Fire and Life Insurance Company,
OF LIVERPOOL AND LONDON,
ACCEPTS ALL ORDINARY FIRE RISKS
on the most favorable terms.

LIFE RISKS
Will be taken on terms that will compare favorably with other Companies.

CAPITAL, · · · · **£2,000,000 Stg.**
CANADA BRANCH OFFICE—Exchange Buildings, Montreal.
Resident Secretary and General Agent,
    A. MACKENZIE FORBES,
13 St. Sacrament St., Merchants' Exchange, Montreal.
WM. ROWLAND, Agent, Toronto.   1-1y

THE AGRICULTURAL Mutual Assurance Association of Canada.

HEAD OFFICE...............................LONDON, ONT.
A purely Farmers' Company. Licensed by the Government of Canada.

Capital, 1st January, 1869....................	$230,193 82
Cash and Cash Items, over....................	$86,000 00
No. of Policies in force....................	30,892 00

THIS Company insures nothing more dangerous than Farm property. Its rates are as low as any well-established Company in the Dominion, and lower than those of a great many. It is largely patronised, and continues to grow in public favor.

For Insurance, apply to any of the Agents or address the Secretary, London, Ontario.

London, 2nd Nov., 1868.   12-1y.

Insurance. ·

The Waterloo County Mutual Fire Insurance Company.

HEAD OFFICE : WATERLOO, ONTARIO.
ESTABLISHED 1863.

THE business of the Company is divided into three separate and distinct branches, the
VILLAGE, FARM, AND MANUFACTURES.
Each Branch paying its own losses and its just proportion of the managing expenses of the Company.

C. M. TAYLOR, Sec.   M. SPRINGER, M.M.P., Pres.
    J. HUGHES, Inspector.   15-yr

Lancashire Insurance Company.

CAPITAL,- - - - - - - - - £2,000,000 Sterling

FIRE RISKS
Taken at reasonable rates of premium, and
ALL LOSSES SETTLED PROMPTLY,
By the undersigned, without reference elsewhere.

    S. C. DUNCAN-CLARK & CO.,
    General Agents for Ontario,
25-1y   N. W. Cor. of King & Church Sts., TORONTO.

Western Assurance Company,

INCORPORATED 1851.
CAPITAL, ... $400,000.
FIRE AND MARINE.
HEAD OFFICE................. TORONTO, ONTARIO.

DIRECTORS.
Hon. JNO. McMURRICH, President.
    CHARLES MAGRATH, Vice-President.
A. M. SMITH, Esq.   JOHN FISKEN, Esq.
ROBERT BEATY, Esq.   ALEX. MANNING, Esq.
JAMES MICHIE, Esq.   N. BARNHART, Esq.
    R. J. DALLAS, Secretary.
    B. HALDAN, Secretary.
J. MAUGHAN, Jr., Assistant Secretary.
    WM. BLIGHT, Fire Inspector.
    CAPT. G. T. DOUGLAS, Marine Inspector.
    JAMES PRINGLE, General Agent.

Insurances effected at the lowest current rates on Buildings, Merchandise, and other property, against loss or damage by fire.

On Hull, Cargo and Freight against the perils of Inland Navigation.

On Cargo Risks with the Maritime Provinces by sail or steam.

On Cargoes by steamers to and from British Ports.

WESTERN ASSURANCE COMPANY'S OFFICE, }
    TORONTO, 1st April, 1869. }   33-1y

The Victoria Mutual FIRE INSURANCE COMPANY OF CANADA.

Insures only Non-Hazardous Property, at Low Rates.

BUSINESS STRICTLY MUTUAL.

    GEORGE H. MILLS, President.
    W. D. BOOKER, Secretary.

HEAD OFFICE ....HAMILTON, ONTARIO
and 15-1yr

North British and Mercantile Insurance Company.

Established 1809.

HEAD OFFICE, - - CANADA, - MONTREAL,

TORONTO BRANCH :
LOCAL OFFICES, Nos. 4 & 6 WELLINGTON STREET.
Fire Department, ...R. N. GOOCH, Agent.
Life Department, ... H. L. HIME, Agent.

Imperial Fire Insurance Company
OF LONDON.
No. 1 OLD BROAD STREET, AND 16 PALL MALL.
ESTABLISHED 1803.
Canada General Agency,
    RINTOUL BROS.,
    24 St. Sacrament Street.
JAMES E. SMITH, Agen
    Toronto, Corner Church and Colborne Streets.

PUBLISHED AT THE OFFICE OF THE MONETARY TIMES, No. 60 CHURCH STREET.
PRINTED AT THE DAILY TELEGRAPH PUBLISHING HOUSE, BAY STREET, CORNER OF KING

THE CANADIAN
MONETARY TIMES
AND
INSURANCE CHRONICLE.

DEVOTED TO FINANCE, COMMERCE, INSURANCE, BANKS, RAILWAYS, NAVIGATION, MINES, INVESTMENT, PUBLIC COMPANIES, AND JOINT STOCK ENTERPRISE.

| OL. II—NO. 52. | TORONTO, THURSDAY, AUGUST 12, 1869. | SUBSCRIPTION $2 A YEAR. |

Mercantile.

J. E. Boustead.
ROVISION and Commission Merchant. Hops bought and sold on Commission. 82 Front St., Toronto.

John Boyd & Co.
WHOLESALE Grocers and Commission Merchants, Front St.. Toronto.

Childs & Hamilton.
MANUFACTURERS and Wholesale Dealers in Boots and Shoes, No. 7 Wellington Street East, Toronto, ario.   23

L. Coffee & Co.
PRODUCE and Commission Merchants, No. 2 Manning's Block, Front St., Toronto, Out. Advances made on signments of Produce.

Candee & Co.,
BANKERS AND BROKERS, dealers in Gold and Silver Coin, Government Securities, &c., Corner Main and hange Streets, Buffalo, Y. N.   21-1v

John Fisken & Co.
STOCK OIL and Commission Merchants, Yonge St, Toronto, Ont.

W. & R. Griffith.
PORTERS of Teas, Wines, etc. Ontario Chambers, cer. Church and Front Sts., Toronto.

Gundry and Langley.
ARCHITECTS AND CIVIL ENGINEERS, Building Sur reyors and Valuators. Office corner of King and Jordan sts, Toronto.
THOMAS GUNDRY.   HENRY LANGLEY.

Lyman & McNab.
WHOLESALE Hardware Merchants, Toronto, Ontario.

W. D. Matthews & Co.
PRODUCE Commission Merchants, Old Corn Exchange, 16 Front St. East, Toronto Ont.

R. C. Hamilton & Co.
PRODUCE Commission Merchants, 119 Lower Water St., Halifax, Nova Scotia.

H. Nerlich & Co.,
IMPORTERS of French, German, English and American ancy Goods, Cigars, and Leaf Tobaccos, No. 2 Adelaide et, West, Toronto.   15

Parson Bros.,
PETROLEUM Refiners, and Wholesale dealers in Lamps, Chimneys, etc. Wareroom 51 Front St. Refinery cor. ir and Don Sts., Toronto.

Reford & Dillon.
PORTERS of Groceries, Wellington Street, Toronto, Ontario.

C. P. Reid & Co.
PORTERS and Dealers in Wines, Liquors, Cigars and Leaf Tobacco, Wellington Street, Toronto.   38.

W. Rowland & Co.,
PRODUCE BROKERS and General Commission Mer mants. Advances made on Consignments. Corner roh and Front Streets, Toronto.

Sessions, Turner & Cooper.
MANUFACTURERS, Importers and Wholesale Dealer in Boots and Shoes, Leather Findings, etc., 8 Wel ton St West, Toronto, Out

Sylvester, Bro. & Hickman,
COMMERCIAL Brokers and Vessel Agents. Office—No. 1 Ontario Chambers, [Corner Front and Church Sts., nto.   2-6m

Meetings.

TORONTO, GREY AND BRUCE RAILWAY.

The first annual meeting of the Shareholders of the Toronto, Grey and Bruce Railway was held in Toronto on the 10th inst., the following gentlemen were present:—Messrs. Hon. D. L. McPherson, H. S. Howland, George Laidlaw, W. S. Lee, John Baxter, W. D. Mathews, A. R. McMaster, John Shedden, John Brown, James Bain, John McNab (Lyman McNab), John Gintey, John Burns and Wm. Thompson, of Thompson & Burns, C. J. Campbell, J. L. Blackie. John Canavan, James Bennett, James Graham, T. C. Chisholm, S. M. Jarvis, Wr. T. Mason, John Morrison, A. W. Lesuder, M.P.P., W. H. Beatty, Thomas Lailey, R. W. Elliott, Capt. Perry, Ald. Dickey, John Buchan, L. R. Boulton, J. H. Ince, Noah Barn hart, Isaac Harris, Caledon; Thos. Bell, Caledon; Nathan Clarke, Jackson Potter, Caledon; R. H. Brett, Mono; W. H. Hunter, Reeve, East Gara fraxa; Maitland McCarthy, Orangeville; Wm. Gillespie, do.; W. J. Middleton, do.; Patrick McGlauchlin, Mono Mills; L. R. Boulton, Boul ton Village; John Guardhouse, Boulton, and others.

On motion of Mr. A. R. McMaster, Mr. W. S. Taylor was then appointed Secretary, and Messrs. C. J. Campbell and John L. Blaikie were appoint ed Scrutineers.

The Chairman, J. G. Worts, Esq., then stated that he had great pleasure in taking the chair under such favorable auspices. They had most auspicious weather, bountiful crops, and every thing to help forward, the great project com menced to day. He was happy to say that stock to the amount of $311,511 had been subscribed, a sum considerable over that required by law to organize the company. He had also great pleasure to inform them that Mr. Fox had been as far as the Caledon Mountains and found that instead of having the difficulties he expected they were not one half what was expected, and he even told them that they were not half as serious an obstacle to be overcome as at the Rouge on the Eastern line. Mr. Fox still confidently assured them that $15,- 000 a mile will cover the whole expense of the road, and he need hardly tell them that the trade of the County of Bruce is well worth competing for; and if they had seen the papers lately, as they no doubt had, they would read of the exertions made by Hamilton to secure it. He had the op portunity of travelling through the county of Bruce on the business of the road some time ago, and a finer country he never saw. He felt per fectly satisfied that so far as the cutting the first section through was all the company could do at present, but they should, nor would they, he said rest satisfied till they went to Southampton. The railway would pay in one year in the difference between the getting of barley to market and leav ing it over till the spring, to be brought 80 or 90 miles slow travelling. He thought they would see that this of itself was an important item, and one that would induce us to build the road. They saw the exertions of the Hamiltonians, and there was no doubt that when they used such efforts they must anticipate some advantage. He thought the present fine weather would do more for the road than anything else. Every day would add to

the stores in the farmer's barns, and if the present weather continued for two or three weeks Canada would never see a more prosperous season. He had pleasure in telling them also that Mr. Laidlaw had consented to act on the board and still con tinue a working member. (Cheers.) This, he felt would be received with pleasure by everyone, for Mr. Laidlaw they knew was a modest man; (cheers) they all knew that if it was not for Mr. Laidlaw the project would never have been as far advanced as it is. The question was now open for the election of Directors, and he would be happy to hear any expression of opinion in regard to the matter.

The following gentlemen were elected Direc tors:—George Laidlaw, John Shedden John Gor don, George Gooderham, Thomas Lailey, Noah Barnhart, James E. Smith, A. R. McMaster, H. S. Howard.

NORTHERN RAILWAY.

The semi-annual meeting was held on the 11th; the President in the chair. The Managing Director submitted the following Report:

1. The Canadian Directors have the pleasure to submit their Report for the half-year ending 30th June, 1869, embracing the usual returns of Income and Expenditure, Details of Accounts, and Auditors' Reports.

2. The Gross Traffic Receipts, from all sources, have amounted to $310,012.66 (£63,701 4s 9d stg.) as against $275,073.34 (£56,521 18s 4d stg.) for the corresponding period of 1868, being an in crease of 12.70 per cent. in favor of 1869.

3. The ordinary Working Expenses of the half year have amounted to $168,094.89 (£34,640 0s. 11d., stg.) as against $173, 412.31 (£35,682 13s. 3d., stg.) in 1868, being at the rate of 54.22 per cent. of the gross earnings, as in comparison with 63.04 per cent. in 1868, or a decrease of 8.32 per cent. in in the half-year now reported.

4. The additional outlay for works of extension, as Rolling Stock, Buildings, Wharves, &c., neces sary to provide for the demands of an increasing traffic, has been $62,020.08 (£12,743 17s· 1d., stg.) as compared with $23,988.39 (£4,918 16s. 11d., stg.) for similar services in 1868.

5. The Net Revenue of the half-year, available for dividend, has amounted to $79,897.72 (£16,- 417 6s. 9d. stg.) as against $75,335.40 (£15,- 479 17s. 7d., stg.) in 1868. After payment of current Interest Dividends on both classes of the Company's bonds, a balance has been carried for ward of $36,458.34 (£7,491 8s. 10d. stg.) to the credit of Interest Dividend account.

6. Considerable additions have been made to the Rolling Stock and other equipment of the line, during the past half-year; but these provisions are yet wholly inadequate to the increasing traffic, and the Directors recognize the necessity for add ing more largely, and at the earliest possible mo ment, to the outfit, so that the transportation ser vice of next-year may be relieved of the embar rassments from which it has hitherto suffered.

7. The construction of the New Grain Elevator, Wharf, and approaches, at Toronto, is proceeding satisfactorily, and every effort is being made to ensure its completion in time for the winter storage of the present crop.

8. The Directors have been invited to consider the project of an extension of this Railway from

Barrie to Orillia. Such an enterprise, to be successful, must be initiated by the people themselves acting unitedly together, and contributing by Municipal and other aid such assistance as, with the cordial co-operation of this company, should secure an early, substantial and remunerative execution of the work. Awaiting such an efficient organization between all the local interests as will warrant practical measures, the Directors have expressed their entire approval of the project, and their readiness to promote it by whatever assistance or influence they can command.

(Signed) FRED. CUMBERLAND, Man'g Director.

(Signed) JOHN BEVERLEY ROBINSON, President.

The President moved the adoption of the report, which was seconded by J. D. Ridout, and unanimously carried.

Moved by G. H. Wyatt, seconded by D'Arcy Boulton, and unanimously carried, that Mr. E. Osler be appointed one of the auditors of this company in the place of Mr. James Brown, whose resignation is accepted with regret; and this meeting desires to express to Mr. Brown its appreciation of his faithful and efficient services as auditor of this company.

Insurance.

FIRE RECORD.—The saw mill with shingle and lathe machinery attached, belonging to Mr. Cane, fifth concession East Gwillimbury, was consumed on the 11th August, and between four and five thousand dollars worth lumber destroyed. Total loss about $15,000. No insurance.

Coverdale, Albert County, N.B.—The dwelling house of John Mitton, Esq., of Coverdale, was burned to the ground with all its contents; also a new house in the course of erection and nearly completed; together with all the tools of the contractor. Origin of the fire unknown. Loss estimated at $2,500. No insurance.

The Douglas Steam Saw Mill, owned by Z. Ring Esq., and others, situate on the Nashwaakisi River, N.B., was totally destroyed by fire, on the 3rd inst. There is little doubt that the incendiary has been at work, as the Mill, though in good order, has not been in operation these four or five years.

The dwelling house and barn of Mrs. Chapman, situated at North River Railway Crossing, Salisbury Parish, N.B., was destroyed by fire one night last week. The fire caught in the barn, and was said to be the result of drinking and smoking. No insurance.

The fire at Fredericton, on 31st ult., destroyed the M'Lean & Dowling Warehouse, occupied by Mr. Mearn; two houses belonging to Mrs. M'Lean, and occupied, one by Mrs. M'Manus, the other by Mrs. M'Leod and several tenements; and two dwellings and outbuildings occupied respectively by Mr. Wright and Mr. Tattersall. Much more damage would have been done, but for the steam fire engine, which was now fairly tried for the first time. The Central office loses $1,200—$400 on the M'Lean & Dowling Warehouse, and $800 on the Tattersall house. The Queen had risks amounting to $1,700—$1,200 on Mrs. M'Leod's two houses, and $500 on Mr. Wright's house. Mrs. M'Manus' loss in furniture is considerable. Mearn's loss in goods in Warehouse is about $250. Wright lost about $100 in harness, sleds, and furniture. Some others lost more or less.

LONDON ASSURANCE CORPORATION.—This Company has replaced its provisional deposit of British 3 per cent consols by the deposit of Cash, invested in Dominion Stock $99,873; Canada, 5 per cent consols held under the old Insurance Act, now transferred into the name of the Minister of Finance, in trust, under the new Act, 31 Vic., cap. 48, $56127; total, $150,000 and has been licensed to do a life as well as a fire business in Canada.

MARINE INSURANCE.

In writing upon the hulls of vessels, which for the most part is done by the year, though in some instances for a single voyage, the rate charged is governed largely by the place of building a vessel, and the name of the builders; for some firms build vessels to sell, and they are largely built of unsound or unseasoned timber; then the size or tonnage, and whether single, double or three decked; her model and draught of water, and fitness for the service in which she is engaged; mode of construction as relates to the manner of fastening, and metal used for that purpose; her age, and if old, when last overhauled, examined and re-coppered; the character of the owner or agent, and his reputation for keeping vessels in good sailing trim; his ability to pay for repairs when needed, at home or in a foreign port; the moral and professional reputation of the master; the number and efficiency of the crew—all these points enter into the determination of the rate of premium.

A few years ago the opinion prevailed among practical and scientific men, that the speed, as well as the safety of vessels on the ocean were in proportion to their size, and that the larger the ship the better; and this idea culminated in the Great Eastern; but lately, since pleasure yachts and a mere raft have crossed the Atlantic in safety, this idea has been materially modified; for their strength has not been increased in proportion to their size. Again the forces of nature in wind and wave are too great for feeble man to control; and the difficulty of handling a ship, and the constant liability to disaster, increase rapidly as her dimensions are increased beyond a certain point, and render the risks taken on them the least profitable to the underwriter.

Steamers, whether side-wheel or propellers, possess many advantages, in the estimation of the underwriter, over vessels propelled wholly by sails; the ease with which a steamer may be turned about, and thus enabled to shun a situation, which would prove inevitable destruction to a sailing vessel; the fact that the voyages are shorter; that the officers and men are of a superior grade to those commonly found on a sailing craft, need hardly be mentioned in proof of this point.

The nature of the cargo has a natural weight in determining the rate of premium; as the loss of the vessel by fire, or by foundering, almost necessarily involves the loss of the cargo. If bar or railroad iron form the cargo, up to or beyond the registered tonnage, it may strain and cause the vessel to leak and founder: hence the premium on this freight is from ¾ to even 7 per cent, according to the character of the vessel and amount of cargo and season of the year, Grain in full cargo in bulk is also considered very trying to a vessel, being liable to shift its position in heavy weather, and to choke the pumps; which occurrences may lead to the total loss of both vessel and cargo. Grain in sacks is a very desirable risk; but on grain in bulk the premium varies from ½ to 4 per cent. Articles likely to spontaneous combustion, or to be ignited by commotion or friction if stowed in the hold of a vessel, especially when the voyage is a long one, materially affect the hazard on all interests. The mode of packing merchandise, and the manner it is stowed away, have an important bearing upon the rate of premium charged. Matches, oil clothing and powder, placed in juxta-position, from their inherent nature, may at any moment produce combustion, and occasion an intanstaneous destruction of the entire vessel; and on this account it has been deemed of sufficient importance for the enactment of penal law concerning the stowing of such articles. Perishable articles, like green fruit and vegetables, are usually insured "free of particular average," or claim for depreciation in value, on account of damage; for no rate the owner might pay, would compensate the underwriter for the absence of this exemption. The facility with which a cargo may be saved, in

case of the stranding of a vessel, affects the premium. Heavy articles placed in the hold, are not often recovered, while lighter, though more valuable, articles are saved. An advanced rate is charged during the stormy seasons of the year, as well as that portion subject to epidemics in the latitudes to be visited.

A vessel is usually considered missing, after the lapse of twelve months from the date of the latest intelligence from her; but in short voyages, the loss is anticipated at the end of six months. The practice of insuring vessels out of time, at very high rates, is not so common in this country as in Europe. Missing vessels are insured at Lloyd's when even the chance of loss is so great, that 50 or 60 per cent. is charged; but such practices are considered illegitimate, and are rare in this country. As business becomes extended, and the number of vessels navigating the ocean multiplied; the danger of collision on the more frequented tracks of commerce is greatly enchanced; and since all vessels take the shortest and quickest route, they are frequently brought in dangerous proximity. However, the improvement of lights on the vessels, and fog signals have prevented many accidents, like that still so fresh in the memory of all, the "loss of the Arctic."—*Philadelphia Underwriter*.

THE MANAGEMENT OF LIFE INSURANCE COMPANIES.

(SUGGESTED BY J. HOOPER HARTNOLL.)

Most of our readers must be well acquainted with the nature of what is called a "Life Table." They are familiar with the title of the Northampton Table, prepared by Dr. Price—the first brought into use for life assurance purposes; but afterwards, from its defects, superseded in many offices by the Carlisle Table, compiled by Dr. Milne, which, in its turn, is being driven out of the field by the English Life Tables constructed by Dr. Farr, from the returns of births, marriages and deaths made to the Registrar-General relative to the entire population of the Kingdom. By these tables it is shown how many deaths will take place, year after year, out of so many born in any large community of persons. For example, according to the English Life Table No. 1, out of every 10,000 born, 5,585 will be alive at the age of 37. Of that number 66 will die during the next year; and consequently only 5,519 will reach age 38. Of the survivors, only 939 will reach the age of 80. At 90 there will be only 114 alive; and 2, possibly 1 only, will live to the age of 100.

Out of this table arises another, showing the "Expectation of life at all ages;"—that is to say, How many years an individual who has arrived at a particular age, say 37, and who is in good health, may expect to live. At that age the "Expectation" will be 29 years; and it is on the basis of such "Expectation" that the tables of rates of premiums are prepared.

Let us suppose 285 individuals who have arrived at age 37 to form themselves into a life assurance society, for the purpose of securing for the family of each assurant the sum of £500 to be paid at the member's death, out of the funds of the society. It has been carefully ascertained that, supposing the transactions of the association to be carried on without any expense whatever, an annual contribution of £12 10s. by each member, being at the rate of £2 10s. for every £100 assured (the money, as received, being invested at 3 per cent. compound interest), would be sufficient to provide for the several payments; and that at the death of the last member of the 285, the sum of £500 would be in hand available for payment to the person or persons entitled to receive it. This is life assurance pure and simple.

From what has been stated, it is beyond all doubt, or disputation, that if the fund arising out of these annual payments and invested at 3 r cent. is not tampered with, but is held safely the hands of responsible trustees, "and is not plied to any other purpose than that for which was created, nothing on earth can disturb the curity of the members." In the first year of e society's operations the premium receipts ould amount to £3,562 10s.; and during the ar three members would die, occasioning a withrawal of £1,500 in payment of claims. The nd in hand at the end of the first year would, erefore, be £2,062 10s. together with the sum ceived for interest. There would then be a cond year's premiums due by 282 members, oducing an addition to the fund of the sum of ,525, carrying interest; and at the end of the ar there would be a second withdrawal of £1,500 account of the like number of deaths; and so for the third and fourth years. In the fifth ar' the number of deaths that annually take ace will be increased to 4, and at that number ey will continue for twelve years, when they ill have increased to 5; in five years more to 6 aths annually; in four years more to 7; and in ven years more to 8; at which number the anial death-rate will be stationary for nine years, hen the rap will gradually diminish until the ciety has fulfilled its original purpose, and has come extinct, by the death of the whole of its embers.

But the business of a life assurance office is not rried on without expense; and in order to meet e charges of management, rent, taxes, &c., and provide for various contingencies, an addition neessarily made to the net premium. This dition is ordinarily at the rate of one-fifth, or per cent. on such net premium; so that at age the rate of premium charged by a company, ether mutual or proprietary, would be 3 per nt. instead of the £2 10s. mentioned in the preding example of a mutual society of 285 individual conducting their business among themlves without expense. This sum slightly varies different offices; but it may be adopted as the ndard rate. In a well-conducted office, the arginal charge above the net premium will alys be found sufficient not only to cover the anagement expenditure and to pay a liberal vidend to the shareholders in a proprietary comny, but to produce, from time to time, large rpluses applicable to appropriation among the licyholders, in proportion to their several interests.

We now come to our plan for the security of e last-named class of persons—the shareholders ay be left to take care of themselves. It is of e simplest possible kind; easy of accomplishent; as unimpeachable as an axiom in Euclid; d as safe in its results as the operations of the ink of England—namely,

"Never allow, under any pretext whatever, one illing of the net premium to be made use of for y other purpose than that of meeting policy ims."

And why should the principle not be acted on—honestly acted upon? Every pound withawn from the net insurance fund, except for e legitimate purpose of meeting death claims, a species of fraud against the policyholders. may eventually be restored, either out of the rplus percentage on the premiums, or by calls capital, if a proprietary company; but until at is done the abstraction would be a fraud, inmuch as that the shareholders, under such cirmstances, would be carrying on their business their own benefit with the policyholders' money. ie plea of liability to make repayment out of e unpaid-up capital of a company does not alter e character of the transaction. An apprehenm of approaching troubles may induce sharelders to get rid of their shares, and they may succeeded by men of straw, which has been own to be the case in hundreds of instances th public companies. It may therefore be asked, Who will there be to make restitution then? In order to show with what facility the plan we

have suggested may be acted upon we will give an example of its operation in the supposed case of a proprietary life assurance company being formed with a paid-up capital of £10,000; that 285 policies for £500 each are issued to new assurants every year, instead of a single issue of that number, as in the former example;—that the age at entry is, in every instance, 37;—that the net premium is £2 10s. per cent.;—and that the additional office charge, or, as it is sometimes called, loading, is 20 per cent. on that sum—raising it to a gross premium of £3 per cent. In practice, uniformity of age at entry would never occur; but it is adopted for convenience of explanation. The same results would arise, whatever might be the difference in ages and the consequent increase, or decrease, in the rate of premium. The death-rate at all ages may be ascertained by reference to pages 255 and 256 of the new edition of the "Insurance Guide and Hand-book." We have previously exhibited what that rate is, for any number of individuals arrived at age 37;—and now the reader is fully prepared to understand the details and object of the following table:—

Year.	A. No. of Policies.	B. No. of deaths.	C. Gross Premiums. (£)	D. Office Margin. (£ s.)	E. Net Premiums. (£ s.)	F. Interest on insurance fund. (£ s.)	G. Premiums and interest in hand. (£ s.)	H. Claims thereon. (£)	I. Fund after payment of claims. (£ s.)
1st	285	3	4,275	712 10	3,562 10		3,562 10	1,500	2,062 10
2nd	567	6	8,505	1,417 10	7,087 10	274 10	9,424 10	3,000	6,494 10
3rd	846	9	12,690	2,115 0	10,575 0	510 0	17,509 10	4,500	13,009 10
4th	1,122	12	16,830	2,805 0	14,025 0	810 0	27,844 10	6,000	21,844 10
5th	1,395	16	20,925	3,487 10	17,435 0	1,178 0	40,447 10	8,000	32,447 0
6th	1,664	20	24,960	4,160 0	20,775 0	1,596 13	54,818 0	10,000	44,818 0
					73,460 0	4,369 3		33,000	

Explanation of the several Columns in the preceding Table.

Column A.—Number of policies in force in each succeeding year, on the assumption of 285 new entrants in each year, of whom a certain number will die in that year, and in each succeeding year, increasing periodically with the age of the individuals up to a certain point, and then, from diminished numbers decrease in the manner previously shown.

Column B.—Number of assurants who die in each year.
" C.—Gross amount of premium received in each year.
" D.—One-sixth of gross premium applicable to management expenditure, payment of a dividend to shareholders and for appropriation for bonus to policyholders when a sufficient surplus arises for the purpose.
" E.—Net premium, to be added annually to the assurance fund; which is the sole property of the policyholders.
Column F.—Interest annually received on the amount available for investment after payment of the death-claims of the preceding year.
" G.—Amount of net premium and interest at end of each year.
" H.—Amount of claims in each year.
" I.—Amount of assurance fund that ought to be found safely invested at the end of each year. Upon the inviolability of the amounts in this column the security of the policyholders mainly depends.

The several sums in each of the columns E, F_1 and H, in the preceding table, have been added up for the purpose of testing the reliability of the plan. The fund in possession at the end of every year ought clearly to be the amount of the whole of the net premiums and interest thereon, minus the total amount of claims that have arisen and have been paid. By adding £78,450 (net premiums, col. E) to £4,369 (interest received, col. F_1) we get a total of £77,819; and by adding £33,000 (claims paid, col. H) to £44,818 (invested funds, col. I), we get a total, £77,818. The difference of £1 arises from neglecting shillings and pence in some of the items.

We have not yet dealt with the paid-up working capital. We have already supposed it to be £10,000, and we will further suppose, for convenience of argument, the annual expenditure of every kind with which it is chargeable—even payment of interest to which there could be no valid objection—to be £5,000. These annual payments would be reduced in amount by the sums in col. D, Table 1; the only column in which the shareholders have a present financial interest, and the only one over which the Directors ought to be permitted to exercise the slightest control, except as to the safe custody and judicious investment of the sums in cols. E, F and I. We will now exhibit, in a tabular form, the action of col. D on the capital:—

Year.	A Marginal Premium.	B Office Expenditure.	C Capital diminished to	Deficiency of Capital.
1	£712 10	£5,000	£5,712 10	......
2	1,417 10	5,000	2,130 0	......
3	2,115 0	5,000	......	£755 0
4	2,805 0	5,000	......	2,950 0
5	3,487 10	5,000	......	4,462 10
6	4,160 0	5,000	......	5,302 10

It will be seen by col. D that at the end of three years the £10,000 paid-up capital will be exhausted, and that there will be a deficiency of £755, to be provided for by a further call of capital. The deficiency, it will be observed, increases annually; and it will continue to do so up to the end of the eighth year, when it will begin to decrease rapidly, from the growing excess of the sums in col. D over the £5,000 annual expenditure.

It is to be borne in mind, however, that the sums in col. F, Table 1, are less than those that will arise in practice, from a rate of interest much higher than 3 per cent., and that the expenditure in the earlier years may be kept down to a much less sum than £5,000 per annum. The deficiencies in the proceeding table, to be provided for by the shareholders, will, consequently, be much diminished in amount, and the time for their being reduced and extinguished by the increasing marginal profits in col. A, will much sooner arrive.

REPORT ON INSURANCE BUSINESS.

The report of the Massachusetts legislative committee on insurance published in the *N. E. Insurance Gazette* reviews the history of insurance since the late war; speaks of the reckless competition as seen in the numerous fires which especially obtained from 1862 to 1867, and instances the great Portland fire of July 4, 1866. During this period many companies succumbed. Hazards are now increasing from the greater use of petroleum products, phosphorus, nitro-glycerine, and other chemicals. The increase of the crime of arson; the practice of over-insurance; the depression of trade and diminution of profits; are dwelt upon, as well as the bad system of brokerage in use. The fire losses from 1st January, 1859, to 31st December, 1868, amount to 59.26 of the premiums; the average running expenses being 30 per cent., leaving only a margin of 10 per cent. for profit, deducting the earning of vested capital, which is stated at 9 per cent.; the report concludes that only 1.23 per cent. is the real profit of insurance business.

Equally unfavorable, says the report, are the results of the insurance business in New York State, in which during the last three years, the 164 fire and fire-marine insurance companies, which do business in that State, received $110,-720,700.23 in premium receipts on fire and marine risks; and disbursed $111,519,470.26, or $799,-769.93 excess of disbursements over current receipts in a three years' business.

It is true that these companies during that period paid out $11,760,184 in the shape of dividends, or an annual average sum of $3,829,061. Their total assets for the three years exhibit an average of $72,902,576. Hence their net earnings, from all sources, were only 5.33 per cent., or but little more than one-half the general average. But even these small dividends were not derived from the profits of current business—which as we have seen was really a losing one—but were borrowed from the interest accruing on their surplus funds.

The following calculation of percentages will be interesting:

Percentages of total losses to total premium receipts	60.93
Percentage of total commissions to total premium receipts	11.81
Percentage of total management expenses, exclusive of commissions and taxes to total premium receipts	14.14
Percentage of total taxes to total premium receipts	5.14
Total	101.29
	100.00
Percentage of excess of current expenses to current receipts	1.29

The facts disclosed in the above tabular statement are both significant and suggestive. They show that 164 leading American insurance companies doing a fire and fire-marine business paid out, during the years 1865, 1866 and 1867, $12,-500,000 more than their premium receipts; that of $125,000,000 of total income for three years, less than $2,000,000 were reserved for additions to surplus, that the proportion of premium receipts saved for dividends is less than the amount thereof paid for taxes.

THE PRUDENTIAL AND INTERNATIONAL.

The whole of the revelations about the *Hercules* are of the most extraordinary nature. They disclose a course of business which might be deemed incredible. The company undertakes the liabilities of the *International*—a concern which for years was understood to be in a bankrupt state—

relying apparently solely on the judgment of Mr. Shrubb, general manager and secretary of the *Hercules*, one who is known to have had no actuarial knowledge whatever; and this they do on terms so monstrous that actuaries would have been aghast at the bare suggestion. True, the affairs of the *International* were valued by Mr. Woolhouse, the eminent mathematician, before the transfer took place; but he seems not to have acted on his own independent judgment, for he assumed a basis of five per cent. instead of the usual three or three and a half, and of course his valuation was in consequence utterly unsound. But nobody seems to have suspected this. Mr. Shrubb was not likely to find it out, and can hardly be suspected of having done so, especially if his assertion that he never received a penny over the transaction is correct; the board relied on their secretary, and so the whole mischief was done.

Yet it is marvellous that it could have been so. What were the directors about? Was it so small a matter, this buying up the business of another company, that it was not considered worth their attention, or was it so complicated that they could not fathom the mysteries of it? Mr. White, the official liquidator in the winding up of the Hercules, very properly points out, that had the effect of purchasing on a valuation, not of pure net premiums, but of gross premiums, at five per cent., been seen and considered by the board, they never could have been parties to such a transaction. "Yet," he adds, "it must be apparent to any shareholder (let alone a director) who has the least knowledge of insurance business, or of finance, in any form, that as it is nearly impossible to invest considerable sums of money so as to obtain more than £5 per cent.—and it is indeed very hard to invest large sums to obtain uniformly even that amount—that the Hercules must have realized a heavy loss year by year upon the business it had taken.

There was no margin out of which one penny of direct profit could be made by the investment of the International funds; and, indeed, was there any possibility of getting a single penny of margin to cover the whole expense of working that International business with its costly agencies in several parts of England, in Paris, Brussels, New York, Montreal, Halifax, Nova Scotia, and other places. Assuming (which is impossible in fact) that every shilling received from premiums, or otherwise, under the International transfer could have been invested at interest at £5 per cent., the moment it was received, so that not a fraction of interest was lost, the Hercules would then have had to bear, out of its own proper and independent resources, all the expenses incidental to the conduct of the International business.

Even this was not the worst of the case, for an attempt was made to show that the Hercules would, by profits on International policies bought on advantageous terms, be able wholly to turn the scale, which is mere moonshine. Looking at it altogether, it must be admitted that the Hercules has landed itself in a hole through one of the most amazing transactions in insurance history. The only parties who seem to have been benefited by the transfer are Mr. John Sheridan, the negotiator of the business, who netted £8,000 for his trouble, and Mr. Richardson, the Secretary of the International, who seems to have received £15,-000. This sum of £23,000 was paid away out of the assets of the International, reducing the funds by that amount, though its position was at the moment utterly hopeless. We question whether if the Court of Chancery were appealed to the whole of this money would not have to be refunded. If it be not, the unfortunate shareholders will have to make it good, besides a deficiency of some hundred thousands which they will have to subscribe to enable the Prudential, which has taken over the Hercules business, subject to certain conditions, to carry out this portion of the contract.

So far as the *Prudential* is concerned, it seems to have acted up to its name in the way in which it has set about acquiring the business of the two unfortunate companies. It has had their affairs valued by two competent actuaries, and has agreed to indemnify the policy holders of both companies in case the deficiency in the assets is subscribed. It could hardly have set to work in a more straightforward way. Meanwhile the whole affair in regard to the absorbed offices, now that it has been fully exposed by Mr. White, cannot be too closely scrutinised or strongly condemned. It reads more like a page in a novel than an incident in real business life. The *Hercules* directors appear to plunge into a difficult and delicate negotiation, wholly in the dark; they voluntarily "shoot Niagara," and elect to do so with their eyes shut. The thing affords a striking lesson to shareholders when called on to suffer their interests to be transferred from one company, to glide from comparative prosperity to ruin, from success to catastrophe at a single step, and especially in transactions of this sort. "But," it will be said, "the safety valve is the actuary's knowledge and experience. If he is not to be relied on, what security have we? How are simple shareholders to satisfy themselves and to secure their own interests unless by this means?" The question is far more easily asked than answered. The whole position of shareholders in public companies is, in truth, most unsatisfactory. They cannot all be suffered to take an active part in the transactions of business. That would never do. And even were it practicable in other respects, incompetency would furnish an effectual bar in nine cases out of ten. What are they to do then? Why, they must place reliance on those who are elected to sit at the board-table. The directors must have extensive powers and exercise a large discretion, under the advice of accredited and competent officers.

This state of affairs cannot be altered by any legislative or other device. Given complicated and extensive business arrangements on the one side, and a large body of interested but ignorant men on the other, and the present system is the only system which will work. There may, of course, be checks and counter-checks; Government actuaries may revise the calculations of private actuaries; accounts may be submitted to Government inspection or published for general information. Fifty different expedients may be resorted to; but the difficulties lying in the way will never be got over, and the more complicated the machinery, especially if there is to be a government spoke in the wheel, the more likely is the whole thing to get out of gear. All that the shareholders can do is to regard with suspicion and scrutinise as cautiously as possible all the propositions of an extraordinary nature submitted to them, demanding the fullest information, and insisting on the most stringent precautions their sagacity or experience may suggest. Let them not rely too surely on representations made to them, even when backed up by the advice of an actuary, who may not be a free agent, as we are willing to believe was the case in this instance.

The secret of the whole thing seems to be that the International was absolutely rotten—that it could not stand much longer; and that, therefore, at all hazards it must get rid of its liabilities to some unwary concern. For some years it had been in the market without finding a flat to purchase until the Hercules, utterly ignorant of actuarial science, and probably fearing the result of an investigation, entered into negotiations, on its own behalf, and bad as it was itself, actually consented to take over that which could only make it worse. The negotiator of this scandalous piece of business pocketed £8,000, and the officials of the Intercolonial netted an amount which seems almost fabulous. As these parties, excepting perhaps the lawyers, were the only ones that would be benefited by the transaction, their desire to carry out the transfer *per fas et nefas* is easily understood.—*Insurance Record*.

NEW EXPERIENCE TABLES.—Twenty Companies recently contributed their experience to the Institute of Actuaries. The total number of lives assured was discovered to be as follows:

	Entered.	Died.	Discontinued.	Existing Dec. 31, 1863.
healthy lives, male	130,243	20,521	35,024	74,698
" female	16,604	3,325	5,507	7,762
Both	146,847	23,857	40,531	82,400
diseased lives, male and female	11,146	2,456	3,365	5,825
lives exposed to extra risk from climate & occupation, male and female	2,433	400	1,480	544
Total	160,426	26,721	45,476	88,329

The average duration of each life was over nine years, which, taken into consideration with the total number of entries—160,426—was sufficient to allow of several valuable classes of tables being formed.

A volume has been published containing the whole results of the valuable data thus collected.

Railway News.

GREAT WESTERN RAILWAY.—Traffic for week ending July 23rd 1869.

Passengers	27,817 61
Freight	29,866 00
Mails and Sundries	2,078 00
Total Receipts for week	$59,261 61
Corresponding week, 1868	45,330 25
Increase	$13,931 36

CANADA CENTRAL RAILWAY.—The Ottawa *Times* urges that encouragement be given to this company to construct the section between Ottawa and Carleton Place; considering that if this were done the line would soon be extended east and west and Ottawa assured a good position in relation to the trade of the North-West.

WELLINGTON, GREY AND BRUCE RAILWAY.—The great quantity of rain which has fallen has kept back work on this road. Mr. Naismith has the contract for the heavy cutting between the Roman Catholic Church, in Elora, and the Grand River. The contract for building the road between Fergus and Harrison was let to Messrs. Robertson & Reekie, who are making the road from Guelph to Fergus. A correspondent of the Hamilton *Spectator* suggests that the Directors should include in their scheme a branch line from Durham through Normandy to some point near Harrison.

PORT HOPE, LINDSAY & BEAVERTON RAILWAY.—The official authorities of this road went to Orillia on the 3rd August to hear overtures regarding the extension to Beaverton. One speaker considered that rafted timber via Toronto for that was not sustained its greatest risk in the waters near that city, whereas by communication with Port Hope harbor that was avoided and the distance to Montreal and Quebec lessened; and further that the Port Hope line were extended to Orillia it must go to Hog bay. The meeting is said to have been enthusiastic.

—The surveyors on the Missisquoi Railroad from Newport to the Troy line, find the route a very feasable one.

—A meeting of the Directors of the Eastern Counties Junction Railway is called for the 17th instant, at Knowlton, when the result of the survey will be laid before them.

—Mr. O'Brien, agent of the Grand Trunk Railroad, has received a despatch from the Manager of the Union Pacific Railroad to reduce the fare. Passengers can go through from Montreal now in about seven days to San Francisco, and at a less rate, both first and second class than by steamer from New York.

RAILWAY TRAFFIC RETURNS
FOR THE HALF-YEAR ENDED JUNE 30, 1869.

RAILWAYS.	Passengers.	Mails and Sundries.	Freight.	Total 1863.	Total 1864.	Total 1865.	Miles 1860.	Miles 1865.
Great Western	673,577	61,221	1,290,000	1,906,798	1,774,785	351	351
Grand Trunk	1,093,583	185,207	1,927,591	3,146,381	3,291,971	1377	1377
Northern	66,011	5,576	155,788	209,279	246,169	95	95
Port Hope, Lindsay and Beaverton	6,881	4,709	15,759	27,349	17,517	97	97
London and Port Stanley	13,930	13,950	135,400	163,280	94,528	24½	24½
Welland							
Brockville and Ottawa	18,796	1,461	67,821	88,078	94,596	88	88
Carillon and Grenville (a)						12	12
Cobourg, Peterborough						28	28
St. Lawrence and Industry (a)	728	16	1,091	1,835	2,069	11½	11½
New Brunswick and Canada	19,905	900	47,660	68,465	71,718	116	116
European and North American	20,090	8	64,431	84,529	90,518	108	108
Eastern Extension	6,180	570	1,145	7,895		23	23
Nova Scotia Railway	4,150					93	93
Total	1,905,540	344,780	3,888,578	6,000,035	5,689,951	2302	2302

* No returns. § No returns for February, 1869. (a) May and June. (b) No return for June.

RAILWAY TRAFFIC RETURNS.
FOR THE MONTH OF JUNE, 1869.

NAMES OF THE RAILWAYS.	Passengers	Mails and Sundries	Freight	Total 1863.	Miles in Operation 1860.	Miles in Operation 1865.
Great Western Railway	123236	8316	151465	283527	351	351
Grand Trunk Railway (9 weeks)	345131	53153	325395	590211	1377	1377
London and Port Stanley Railway	1483	170	2154	3788	24½	24½
Welland Railway	985	900	8719	10616	55	55
Northern Railway	13007	3538	60900	94605	95	95
Port Hope, Lindsay and Beaverton Railway	5038	547	24694	30259	97	97
Cobourg, Peterborough and Marmora Railway	64		7401	7465	28	28
Brockville and Ottawa Railway	4148	988	12702	17113	88	88
Carillon and Grenville Railway*					12	12
St. Lawrence and Industry Railway		160	761	931	11½	11½
Stanstead, Shefford & Chambly Railway†						
New Brunswick and Canada Railway	2063	60	8586	10700	116	116
European & North American Railway	5059	130	6780	11969	108	108
Eastern Extension Railway	447	60	1232	1739	23	23
Nova Scotia Railway*					93	93
Total	405225	41160	623047	1069452	2302	2302

*No returns.

RAILWAY EXTENSION TO ORILLIA.—Mr. Cumberland, Manager of the Northern Railway, has addressed a resident of Orillia, substantially as follows: There are three possible projects now under consideration. 1st. The Nipissing narrow guage, in direct connection with Toronto, to which objection has been suggested on the ground that as it has only just been organized, and as all its strength will be required for and absorbed in the construction of its main line, any branches additional thereto would seem (for the present at least) to be difficult if not hopeless of attainment. 2nd. The proposed extension of the Port Hope, Lindsay and Beaverton Railway—and 3rd. The proposed extension of the Northern Railway from Barrie. Referring to these two latter projects it would seem to me that Orillia would prefer her own county town at Barrie—say 28 miles—to the county town of Victoria at Lindsay—say 54 miles, for public business will necessarily attract to Barrie, which, moreover, as a market and place of business, is also far superior in every way to Lindsay. Again, by the Beaverton route Orillia would be 151 miles from Toronto, while by the Barrie line it would only be 91 miles, and these differences of distances of course represent to passengers and freight a very large difference in the cost of transportation, even assuming (which is not the fact) that the tariffs on the two routes were similar mile for mile, of their lengths. But there is a very wide difference in the tariffs, that of the Northern being very low in comparison with the Port Hope and Lindsay. For instance, take the tariff from Port Hope to Lindsay for 43 miles in comparison with the tariff from Toronto to Bradford—which is the same distance—we find the following charges respectively on merchandise per 100 lbs:

	1st class.	2nd.	3rd.	4th.
Port Hope to Lindsay, 43 miles	35c.	20c.	15c.	nil.
Toronto to Bradford, 43 miles	20c.	16c.	14c.	9c.
Toronto to Barrie, 64½ miles	26c.	22c.	19c.	11c.
Toronto to Collingwood, 94 miles	30c.	25c.	20c.	12c.

Showing that we actually carry first class goods 94 miles, 5 cents less per 100 lbs. than is charged for 43 miles on the Port Hope line. Whilst it is also a fact that our present through rate (rail and boat) from Toronto to Orillia, is 36c. per 100, being only one cent. per 100 lbs. more than is charged on the same goods from Port Hope to Lindsay. Of course the sagacity of the Orillia people will lead them to compute the probable rate which would be charged for 93 miles if 35c. is now charged for 43 miles; and remembering that they now only pay us 36c. from Toronto, they will probably conclude that one cent. per 100 lbs. additional to the present Lindsay rate would scarcely pay for building and running 50 miles of road, from Lindsay to Orillia, and that even if competition kept the Port Hope rate just as it is, Port Hope is not Toronto, but 58 miles away from it.

SOREL & ARTHABASKA RAILWAY.—Mr. Hemming, M. P. P., has been elected President and J. B. Govement, Vice-President of this road. The Municipalities have subscribed $75,000 of the $300,000 required, and the government guarantees $120,000. Subscription books have been opened, and it is expected that the Directors will be in a position to commence operations early next spring, and to complete the road by the fall of 1870.

INTERCOLONIAL RAILWAY.

The line starts directly from the station of the Grand Trunk Railway, and at a very short distance crosses the Riviere du Loup by a bridge 300 feet in length, immediately above the falls at that place. Directly after crossing the river the line runs round a sharp curve, and through a heavy rock side hill cutting, after which, it descends to a level terrace, and runs through a well settled

French country. A good force of men are at work on the rock cutting, and gangs of men and horses all along this contract of twenty miles. In all about 500 men are at work upon this contract. Many culverts and water courses are already completed, and many in progress. A considerable quantity of grading is in active progress, several long cuttings and embankments being in a forward state. The next important structure to the bridge at Riviere du Loup is at Isle Verte, where the work is actively progressing.

Heavy work has to be done at Trois Pistoles. This is on contract No 2. The grading throughout the whole of contracts Nos 1 and 2 is in a forward state, and except at two or three heavy places will be completed it is expected this fall. Upwards of 500 men are employed upon No. 2 and Messrs. Worthington, who are the contractors for one and two, about 40 miles in all, are pushing forward the work with great energy. They have been fortunate in finding good stone for the culverts in close proximity to the work, and consequently they have already got a considerable part of this work in a forward state.—All the culvert work appears to be done in a very satisfactory manner. A large 15 foot arch culvert, about two miles east of Trois Pistoles, has one of its walls already completed up to the course from which the arch will spring and is as fine a piece of solid, well executed work as is to be found in Canada. The length of this culvert is about 75 feet. Competent inspectors are appointed to overlook the masonry, and from the character of the work executed so far, they appear to be thoroughly doing their duty.

The heaviest work upon contracts one and two is at the crossing of the Trois Pistoles river, about one mile and a half west of the village of that name. The river and the railway through which it runs are about 1,100 feet wide at the point where the line crosses them, and the railway will run at a height of about 70 feet from the bed of the river. This crossing is the heaviest work between Riviere du Loup and the Metis, a distance of about 90 miles. On the west side of the river the line is carried for nearly two miles across a number of gorges in which there will be several culverts and a number of side-hill embankments. The bridge, which will be 500 feet long will start at the west bank, and be carried nearly half-way across the flats, thus placing the bridge across the main channel, and allowing no check to the flow of the river. The bridge is approached on the west side by a heavy embankment about 40 feet deep, made from a cutting of the stiffest kind of blue clay. This bank will be about 800 feet long, and is being actively constructed, The material on both sides of the river is the same, and is very difficult to work, coming out in large blocks of blue clay. On the east side of the river the embankment will be about 1,400 feet long and about 65 feet high at the deepest point. Large gangs of men and horses are at work on both sides of the river, and the contractors are preparing to put in tramways and tip wagons, as soon as the haul gets long enough to use them with advantage. An excellent stone quarry for the piers of the bridge has been found on the St. Lawrence, about 9 miles from Trois Pistoles, to which point the stone is now being brought in scows. One of the Worthington's lives at Riviere du Loup, and the other at Trios Pistoles. They have now at work on these two contracts upwards of 1,000 men, and are pushing forward the work with great energy and skill.

Bic is the headquarters of contract No. 5, which was awarded to Mr. Haycock, of Ottawa. He took the contract about the end of April, and has already made considerable arrangements for carrying on the work, having now 350 men at work grading the line at several points. There is not much bridge or culvert work on this contract, but the larger part of the grading is rock. No. 5 ends at Rimouski. The village is large and prettily situated. Work is going on, on both sides of the river, which will be spanned by a bridge 300 feet

in length.—The country from Riviere du Loup is like a continuous village, very similar in its general characteristics, to that between Chaudiere and Riviere du Loup.

From Rimouski the line will run through a very level country for about 22 miles, to the Metis crossing, the Metapedia Road. The course of the line from Metis to the mouth of the Metapedia has been a source of considerable labor to the engineers, who after careful examination of the country, have found a moderately easy line, with favorable gradients throughout. The railway will cross the Metis about four miles from its mouth, and ascend by easy grades the highland between the St. Lawrence and the Restigouche. It then descends to the level of Lake Metapedia; then runs along the banks of the Metapedia river, which it crosses once instead of fourteen times as proposed originally by Major Robinson.

The scenery along the line through the valley of the Metapedia and Restigouche, and alone the shores of the Bay of Chaleurs will be the finest of any railway on this continent; about five miles from Bay of Metis the line will reach its highest level above the St. Lawrence.

Mining.

SEMI-ANNUAL REVIEW OF GOLD MINING IN CALIFORNIA.

Among the chief events in the gold mining industry of California in the last six months have been the general recognition of the superiority of giant over black powder for ordinary blasting purposes, the strike of Grass Valley league against the use of giant powder, and the consequent stoppage of some of the leading mines there. In the New Almaden Mine it was found that to cut a yard of one of the tunnels cost $65 with black and $45.45 with giant powder, showing a saving of 30 per cent.; in the Oaks and Reese Mine a hundred feet of drifts that would have cost $7,500 with black powder were made under contract for $4,437 50, a saving of $40 per cent.; and in the Empire Mine it was found on a long and fair trial that the extraction of a ton of ore cost $3.39 with black and $2.99 with giant powder, showing a saving of 61 per cent. by the use of the latter. These are a few of the most noteable results that have been obtained in cases where precise comparisons have been made. At Smartsville it was found that with giant powder derricks were no longer needed in the hydraulic claims for lifting large boulders, which can now be shattered at one blast into pieces small enough to be carried down through the sluices. The Cornish miners at Grass Valley refused to use giant powder, ostensibly because the fumes were poisonous, but the real reason is supposed to be because the single-hand drilling for giant powder requires only half the number of men, gives greater facilities for paying by the amount of work done instead of by the day, is not so fatiguing and demands less experience.

The Eureka Mine at Grass Valley has continued to yield munificently. It produced in June more than $47,000, of which, however, $4,500 were from sulphurets collected in previous months. The total yield of the first half of the year was $235,-109.14 from 9,000 tons of quartz, making an average of about $32 per ton. The expenses were $102,000, leaving $163,000, or more than $1,000 per day net, and $20 per ton net. The number of men employed is about one hundred and fifty. The Idaho Mine, which adjoins the Eureka on the east, although it had begun to do very well in November last, did not prove its value as a first class mine till this year. It is now paving from $15,000 to $20,000 per month in dividends, and has a large stock of ore in sight. The quartz yields $17 per ton gross. The North Star, the Empire and the Banner have been interrupted in their workings by the miners' strike, and we have no figures from them. Work has been resumed in pumping and clearing out the Allison Mine,

and preparing for the extraction of rock; and the mill has done well by working up selections from the old dump pile, thrown out as not rich enough to pay.

The Sierra Buttes Mine yielded $95,084 gross and $54,000 net in the five months, inclusive, from January to June. The average gross product per month is $19,000, the same as it was last year. The Independence Mine adjoining the Sierra Buttes claim, is yielding well, but is burthened with debts, resulting chiefly from the damage done by the snow slides of winter before last, and is paying no dividends. The Keystone of Sierra, on the mountain opposite the Sierra Buttes, also suffered severely by avalanches, but seems to have not only recovered but to have gained a much better position than it ever had before. It now promises to become one of the leading quartz mines of the State. The gross yield was $17,000 in May and $20,000 in June.

The returns of the Amador Mine for June have not yet been received, but the average gross yield had been about $63,000 per month from February to May, inclusive. At the present rate of production the mine will turn out nearly, if not quite $750,000 for 1869. The production for the first five months of this year was $47,861.53, $65,-670.98, $61,720.65, $66,346.52, and $61,576.70. The number of tons reduced averages about 2,950 per month, every ton yielding more than $20. The dividends for each of the last five months was $10 per share.

The working of the mines of the Mariposa Estate has been resumed. There are now 60 stamps crushing at the Benton Mills, and a new 60-stamp mill has been commenced. The Merced River furnishes abundant power to drive all the mills with little expense; and the supply of pay quartz in the Josephine and Pine Tree Mines is large. The average yield of the rock on which the mills are now at work is about $20 per ton. The Mariposa Mine has been pumped dry, and some good quartz has been taken out, in readiness for the mill which is being remodelled to crushing. Four Ryerson amalgamators are running at the Benton Mills, and they give such satisfaction that no other mode of separating the gold from the quartz is to be used on the estate. The Princeton Green Gulch and Bear Valley Mines are lying idle.

The Oaks and Reese Mill is yielding about $12,-000 gross, and $6,000 net per month, with sixteen stamps, and twelve more are being added. From September, 1866, to May, 1869, inclusive, $170,-000 were produced, and all that, and $60,000 additional, were expended, so that the mine was fully opened and the mill put in good condition.

The Oneida Mine of Amador has been incorporated; the Jefferson mill has been moved away from Brown's Valley and the mine abandoned, for a time at least. The Gimcrack, or Eric Mine, in Nevada County, was in a fair condition to pay well, but the mill was burned down by some villains who had been employed in the mine, and were angry with the owners for stopping work because the miners would not use giant powder. Some further experiments have been made with the Hagan furnace, but it is not in use anywhere, nor, so far as we know, is there any intention to use it. About the multitude of other quartz mines which are being worked we have no facts worthy of mention in this brief summary. In placer mining there has been little change since December, save that of the gradual exhaustion of the richer claims, the continuous decline in the total yield, and the consequent decrease in the value of property in the placer mining counties. The burden of taxation to pay debts incurred in flush times is very heavy. The opinion is gaining ground that the valuable unoccupied lands in the mineral districts should be sold without reference to its mineral or agricultural character.

THE FRENCH ATLANTIC CABLE.—The gutta-percha employed for insulation was brought direct from Singapore, as it left the hands of the natives, i the shape of unsightly idols, deformed quad-rupeds, caricatures of patriarchs, dogs, ships'-birds, nd was made into a paste for protecting the léctric core. The copper wire was received from he wire mills in hanks of fifteen or twenty pounds ach; each hank being tested on its arrival to scertain its conductivity, none below a certain andard being allowed to be used. The con-ductor consists of a strand of seven wires, 0.56 ich in diameter, or a little less than one-sixteenth f an inch, six being twisted round the central ire. The seven wires are rendered perfectly ompact by the coating of the central wire with n adhesive matter known as "Chatterton's Com-ound." The weight of the complete strand in our hundred pounds per nautical mile. It is is ngths of about one mile, and wound on reels eady to be covered with gutta-percha. The strand passed through a vessel of Chatterton's Com-ound, and through a die corresponding to the ize of the first coating of gutta-percha, which is reed round the strand as it passes through the ie. Four successive coats are thus applied, and etween each coating the wire receives a film of he compound, which improves the insulation and inds the coats together. The total weight of the ore is eight hundred pounds per nautical mile, qually divided between the copper and the gutta-ercha. The total length of the cable for the ection between Brest and St. Pierre is 2,788 nau-lcal miles, with smaller wire consisting of a onductor of one hundred and seven pounds per autical mile, and a covering of one hundred and fty pounds per mile. The cable thus prepared s finished with a serving of jute yarn and ten vires of homogeneous iron, each of which is covered vith manilla yarn steeped in tar.—*Mining Journal.*

GODERICH SALT WELLS.—The Goderich cor-espondent of the Guelph *Mercury* says:—"Since ey last our town has been quite excited over the alt question. I mentioned then that in a few lays Platt's Patent Evaporator would be thorough-y tested in two of the wells. Since then the test las taken place, and the result is that the Evap-rator is doing all that the inventor claimed for it efore it was applied. The Maitland well, with . pan of 94 feet in length by 8 or 9 feet in breadth s now producing, every twenty-four hours, 90 arrels of first-class salt, with a consumption of ix cords of wood, and the labour of seven hands, hey working 12 hours, that is, three hands for he day and one man to attend the engine while umping, which usually works from 12 to 14 ours in the twenty-four, and three hands for the ight. Under the new system a saving of at least ine cords of wood is effected, besides the labor of wo or three hands, in the production of 90 barrels f salt. In the Goderich well, as yet, the pan is failure, owing to the want of draught in the himney; but, doubtless, when the defect is emedied, the Evaporator will be as great a success n the Goderich as in the Maitland well. Mr. Platt, the patentee, gave, through the *Signal* the result of the working of his pan, claiming that by it salt could be produced at such a figure as to defy competition by our neighbors over the line in every place west of Kingston, and even to send it to Chicago, and pay the duty of 70 cents in gold."

PEAT.—The Hodge machine set to work at Wel-land by the Anglo-American Peat Company was found to be defective in some of its arrangements, and an engineer from Montreal is now engaged in putting it to rights. The machine takes the peat out clean five feet deep. The Ontario Peat Com-pany have a number of men at work and have made a large quantity of peat; as they press their peat into bricks, they are enabled to manufacture despite the wet season.

EUREKA, N. S. GOLD MINING COMPANY.—Mr. McDonald the Vice-President of this company has just returned from Halifax. He had a special blast made while he was on the company's property and had a crushing, the result of which was over 5 oz. to the ton.

THE CANADIAN MONETARY TIMES AND INSU-RANCE CHRONICLE *is printed every Thursday even-ing and distributed to Subscribers on the following morning.*

Publishing office, No. 60 Church-street, 3 doors *north of Court-street.*

Subscription price—
Canada $2.00 per annum.
England, stg. 10s. per annum.
United States (U.S.Cy.) $3.00 per annum.
Casual advertisements will be charged at the rate of ten cents per line, each insertion.
Address all letters to "THE MONETARY TIMES."
Cheques, money orders, &c. should be made pay-able to J. M. TROUT, *Business Manager, who alone is authorised to issue receipts for money.*

☞ *All Canadian Subscribers to* THE MONETARY TIMES *will receive* THE REAL ESTATE JOURNAL *without further charge.*

The Canadian Monetary Times.

THURSDAY, AUGUST 12, 1869.

ANNEXATION TO THE UNITED STATES.

Many of the writers for the press of the United States are fond of harping on the subject of the annexation of Canada to the republic which overshadows us with its great-ness. They break out, again and again, in thread-bare hyperbole over their greatness and our littleness, their progress, and our inertness, and express their astonishment at our stupid indifference to the glory we might achieve. The advantage of reciprocal trade will be conceded by all of us, and we do not deny but some parts of the Dominion would benefit greatly by such an arrangement as the old reciprocity treaty was based upon. But it has been shewn that we can get on very comfortably without reciprocity, and after an experience of several years, we find that our prosperity is not dependent on their forbear-ance or our existence endangered by their hostile tariffs. The closing of old channels of trade did affect various branches of indus-try, but taking everything into consideration,

we cannot consider that the lesson of self-reliance was too dearly purchased. We did not know our own strength, and the various provinces which now constitute the Dominion were as distinctly separated as if they lay in different quarters of the globe. Political economy has in it little of what is called sen-timent; but a desire for nationality begot confederation, produced sentimental results which cannot be ignored, and which the politi-cal economist, as well as others, must acknow-ledge. Interests clashed, selfishness ruled, the power which unity of purpose gives lay dormant. Now interests are reconciled, sel-fishness is swallowed up in the recognition of a common future, and we have got our hands on the rope, pulling all together at the car of progress. A provincial boundary surrounded ambition; now we talk without boasting, of a domain bathed by either ocean, and have visions of imperial greatness. This may be to some but an indication of folly, yet it cer-tainly proves that we have been awakened from lethargy and have received new ideas.

A country without enthusiastic hope is like a man lacking in respect for his own ability. We were kept in leading strings by the Mother Country, until we became a by-word. Travel-lers made comparisons between us and our neighbours, greatly to our prejudice, or ignor-ed us altogether. Shrewd go-a-head Yankees laughed us to scorn. While half the popula-tion were engaged in chopping down trees, the other half were either in office or trying to get in, afraid of sullying their gentility by work, but not ashamed to live on the hard earnings of the toilers of the forest. Many an immigrant who would, if landed in the States, have taken off his coat and gone to work, when he settled down in Canada ex-hausted more time and energy in finding out who his neighbour's grandfather was, than would have sufficed almost to earn a compe-tency. Then again, the political fever seized us, and for years our people tinkered the con-stitution of the country, until one day we woke up and discovered that the rivets were loose, and the whole political fabric so much out of joint as to be incapable of successful working. Politicians berated each other with such heartiness as to leave almost every one under the impression that his neighbour was a rogue, and the members of the Government unfaithful stewards. Instead of wholesome legislation, we were overwhelmed with speeches. According to one political party, the country was going to the dogs, it was bankrupt, it was ruined ; according to the other, everything was in perfect trim, our credit was good, our prosperity certain, so much, indeed, as to call for no useful mea-sures. However, when both sides united in a coalition and began to look around, it was ascertained that, although a great deal was to be done, things were not so irretrievably bad as they seemed. Such political squabbles may be regarded as the measles and whooping cough of nationality, but with us the attack was so severe as to do material injury to the country. However, of late years, legislation has pulled up wonderfully, and our politicians have, for the most part, seen the error of their ways.

Notwithstanding these adverse influences, Canada has not been sluggish in her movement. The statistics for Ontario and Quebec for the last twenty years exhibit evidence of prosperity. In 1850 the total value of exports and imports for these two Provinces was under thirty millions of dollars; for the year 1860 the amount was over sixty-eight millions; while for the year ended 30th June, 1867, it had risen to upwards of one hundred and seven millions of dollars. During nine years the imports into Ontario and Quebec increased upwards of 81 per cent.; into Nova Scotia, 62, and New Brunswick 38 per cent.; while the exports of Ontario and Quebec increased 44 per cent.; Nova Scotia 20 per cent. and New Brunswick 25 per cent. The deposits in banks increased from $8,358,437 in 1859 to $31,600,000 in 1868. During the last three years the deposits in banks and savings' banks increased from $32,600,000 to $37,500,000. The railway traffic shewed an increase from $4,620 per mile in 1866, to $5,020 in 1868. In one year the value of assessed property in Ontario increased $3,-588,000. The repeal of the Reciprocity Treaty did not work such great harm as some suppose. During the last year of the treaty the exports to the United States from all the Provinces of the Dominion, amounted to $21,340,000; in 1868, to $20,061,000, showing a decrease of a little over five per cent. But inter-provincial trade received a great impetus. In 1866-7 there were sent to Nova Scotia and New Brunswick 408,000 barrels of flour; in 1867-8 443,000 were sent, showing an excess of about 33 per cent. The demand for Nova Scotia coal is manifesting itself more strongly in Ontario and Quebec, and though the increase last year was about 17 per cent. over the previous year, the figures for the present year will be found to be much larger.

The average annual increase in population has been in Ontario 4½ per cent., Quebec 2½, New Brunswick 2½ and Nova Scotia 2. In 1868, a comparison was made as to the amount of debt the other British Colonies have to bear in proportion to population as well as annual charges with that of Canada. The result was, New Zealand, $6.02 per cent. per head; Queensland, $4.97; New South Wales, $3.21; Victoria, $2.88; Canada, $1.12½. The total taxation is an annual charge of a little over $5 per head instead of $45 per head as in New York and the debt less than $28 per head as compared with $158 in the State of New York.

Notwithstanding the enterprise of our cousins across the lines, despite their genius for competition and their high and hostile tariffs, we have done pretty well for "Britishers," and we can afford to hear with complacence their patriotic boasts, while our patriotism manifests itself in a quiet satisfaction and a determination to go ahead. We have but 3,900,000 of a population. Ere long we shall have a territory, at the least, over two millions of square miles in extent. While we bear rule over so much land we claim to rank third among the maritime countries of the world.

A great deal has been said about the number of people who leave Canada for the States. It is true a great many young men do go there, but it is also true that many come back. For that matter, a great many Americans come and settle in Canada; but this proves nothing more than that people will rove about. Canada never witnessed such an era of progress as at the present time. Railways are being built in all directions; new branches of industry are being developed; new territory is being opened up; and we have organized a system of immigration which has already borne good fruit. We have a new and fertile West for our young men, where their adventurous spirit can sate itself. Each Province is vieing with the other in economy. Our people are comfortable, and well satisfied with their political institutions. When we say that we have the freest country upon earth, it is no idle boast, for we challenge contradiction. Indeed, our American neighbors are the readiest to confess it; and none are more earnest in their advice that we should retain our identity than those who have experienced the evils which the better educated classes in the States labor under. On the whole, we think that Annexation, even as a topic of discussion, had better be postponed.

MARKED CHEQUES.

The paying teller of a bank which has an active business does not enjoy a sinecure. Not only is his honesty put to the test, but the nature of his duties places his good name and his prospects at the mercy of others, sometimes even at the mercy of chance. He, like everybody else, is liable to errors in calculation; but, unlike everybody else, he has to bear their full consequences. When he pays out two bank notes instead of one, or a roll of sovereigns instead of silver, the excess is not lost to the bank, but forms a set-off for so much against his own salary. Few will envy a teller who finds his cash in excess; certainly none will begrudge him the worry which results when his cash is short ; the weary retracing of the day's business—the anxious tax of memory—the fruitless search after a mistake which defies every effort at discovery—the hesitating confession—the meek acceptance of rebuke, and the submission to loss. The general rule respecting payments over the counter is, that mistakes must be rectified at the time, before the sufferer leaves the bank premises, but in practice it can scarcely be said to be strictly followed. Were it imperative and irrefragable, one could scarcely say that it is unjust ; for a teller has to do with a great number of people who are strangers to him, and might be cheated time and again, if liable to be called on to open up transactions, all trace of which has been obliterated in a multiplicity of payments.

The rule referred to is supposed by some to justify the keeping of all that one gets from a bank clerk, whether entitled to it or not. Such a conclusion savours little of morality, and we are glad to believe that but few act upon it. There are, however, persons, who can retain, with a chuckle of satisfaction, an extra five or ten dollars over the amount they are entitled to receive from a bank, and yet would repudiate the name of thief, and would consider their honesty unimpeachable.

The Quebec Gazette puts forward the following state of facts as the particulars of a case which recently occurred in Toronto :—A presented B's cheque to the ledger-keeper of the Ontario Bank, and it was marked good, in the usual manner; but before A left the premises, the ledger-keeper discovered that he had made a mistake, and requested him to return the cheque, in order that the acceptance might be corrected. A refused to do so, but brought his action, and got judgment, subject to a motion for non-suit. We quite agree with our contemporary when it says:—If a man occupying a respectable position in society is permitted to possess himself of $70. by the accident described, and to be declared legally entitled to retain the money, we do not see why another individual, who may see a person drop his pocket-book containing $700, and who picks it up, should not be allowed to keep it. The two things are very much alike ; and we do not see that the man who "found" the porte-monaie, and insisted upon appropriating its contents, would be more to blame than he who, by the miscalculation of a bank clerk (of which he was immediately informed), possessed himself of a sum of money, or of its equivalent, in the way we have stated. This view commends itself as the right and proper one to take of such a transaction.

But this is not a correct statement of the case. It appears that the cheque was drawn by a firm, one of whose members absconded on Saturday night; and on Monday morning the other member of the firm called at the Bank and forbade the payment of the cheque. The ledger-keeper did make the mistake mentioned, but the whole matter was referred to the cashier, who, under the circumstances, sustained the teller in his refusal to pay. This may not be all the particulars, but it embraces all those material at present. When the case came up in Court, the question arose whether the marking of the cheque constituted an acceptance, and whether there could be any such thing as an acceptance of a cheque. The presiding Judge ruled, we believe, that the ledger-keeper was the duly authorized agent of the bank, and that his marking the cheque was an acceptance, such as would bind the bank. There was evidence given by experts. The manager of the Montreal Bank, we think, considered that the ledger-keeper's initials on the cheque were of no value, as they were merely intended for the information of another officer of the same institution, and should not be taken as an absolute indication to the public that the cheque would be cashed. We can understand how such a conclusion is arrived at. If the ledger-keeper, by initialing cheques, is to bind the bank, then, certainly, we have a ledger-keeper who shares with the cashier and the president the power of acceptance. What is to prevent that clerk from issuing any number of such acceptances, and involving the bank in difficulties. Cheques so nearly resemble bills of exchange, that they are frequently spoken of without discrimination. Story, in pointing out the differences between cheques and bills, states that cheques require no acceptance, as distinct from prompt payment. It must be admitted that it has become a usage to receive marked cheques as cash, and unless it be decided that such marking by a bank ledger-keeper is an acceptance, the business community will have to look to it that they be not deceived for the future. If Mr. Yarker's right, a marked cheque is no more valuable than an unmarked one.

NORTHERN RAILWAY COMPANY.

It will be seen by reference to the semi-annual report that this company is again enabled to show a favorable balance sheet. The gross traffic receipts for the past half-year show an increase of 12.70 per cent. over the corresponding period of last year. The working expenses have decreased 8.82 per cent. and are now at the rate of 54.22 per cent. of the gross earnings. After providing for the demands of an increasing traffic, and payment of current returns on both classes of the company's bonds a balance of $36,458 has been carried forward to the credit of interest dividend account.

This number closes the second Volume of this Journal. An index of contents will be issued to subscribers. Those desirous of completing their file of the paper had better send in their orders.

PERSONAL.—Mr. Burnett Superintendent of the Foreign business of the North British and Mercantile Insurance Company of London, with Mr. Thomas Davidson, General Agent of the Company, Montreal, have arrived in this city, to inspect the Western Agencies of the Company. We observe that in Montreal the Fire Brigade was paraded for inspection by Mr. Burnett, who expressed himself in the highest terms as to its efficiency. This expression coming from a high London authority is certainly flattering to the fire organization of a Canadian city.

THE PHILADELPHIA UNDERWRITER.—We have received the first three numbers of this new insurance journal, and have to express great satisfaction with its typographical appearance and its contents. Mr. Cohen has our best wishes for its success.

COMMERCIAL BANK OF NEW BRUNSWICK.—A meeting of shareholders was held on the 3rd inst. at St. John. The liabilities had been reduced by $368,799, and the assets by $382,231. After some discussion, in which a Miss Ladd, of Halifax, distinguished herself by some severe comments on the management, the meeting adjourned.

Communications.

CANADA LIFE INSURANCE REPORT.

To the Editor of the Monetary Times.

DEAR SIR,—Official reports of insurance companies, in Canada or elsewhere, to be fair comparisons with each other, or of value to the public, should be made as uniform as possible, both in the character of the items and as to the date of the returns. It is a very great pity that the Canada Insurance Act did not provide for returns relating to the calendar years only, or that the several companies cannot all see the advisability of making their returns in that way. If some make returns of business for the year ending 31st December, and others choose to exercise the right of stringing their returns all the way along through the following year, the sooner the Act is either amended or repealed, the better for all concerned—except the Government printers.

Most of the offices, this year, complied with the request of the Finance Department, and sent in their returns at the commencement of the year, but there were some exceptions. The consequence is that instead of the Government report upon the returns being ready for distribution during the sitting of the Legislature, as it should have been, and as other departmental reports are, it has not yet made its appearance, and its contents are now nearly valueless through lapse of time.

As to the equity between the several companies, in placing their returns side by side, the want of uniformity in date could affect none of them favorably, or otherwise, except in relation to one item. viz.—"Total amount at risk in Canada." A company delaying its return until six months' additional business has been placed upon its books, must, of course, thereby place itself in the position of holding an unfair advantage over companies that made prompt and early returns. And if it be allowed always to thus delay its returns, it must continue to hold an undue advantage in reporting the "Total amount at risk," as well as in making "Memorandums"—if I may be allowed to coin a word—relating to this alone, out of all the other items composing the returns.

While on the subject of returns, and since your columns have given to the public the Auditor's Report and Government Return of the Canada Life Insurance Company, allow me to call the attention of those interested to some discrepancies upon the face of the two documents.

Both the Auditor's Report and the Government Return are evidently made up to the same date, and should, therefore, substantially agree with each other. They do agree as to most items, but but under the head of "Expenses of Management, &c., &c.," the "$34,657.76" found in the return is greatly exceeded by the actual disbursements reported by the Auditor. The following are the two statements as they appeared in your columns, omitting irrelevant matter:

AUDITOR'S REPORT.

By Expense Account.........$32,874 58		
" Vote for Board 1,600 00		
" Ten per cent written off Office Furniture......... 183 18		
		$34,657 76
" Written off Investments $8,285 59		
" Written off Company's Offices...................,...... 1,200 00		
		$9,485 59
" 21st year's Dividend paid on 2,500 Shares 6,250 00		

GOVERNMENT RETURN.

By expenses of Management, Agency, &c., &c................................$34,657 76

Now, if the Auditor's Report is correct, the amount that would seem to have been expended in management and agency charges was $50,393.35, instead of $34,657.76.

No doubt there are reasons, and perhaps very good ones, for not placing the last three items above quoted from the Auditor's Report in the return to the Government; but they are not reported as having been given at the annual meeting of the company, and in their absence the two statemements seem to seriously disagree.

Very truly yours,   I. C.
Montreal, Aug. 8.

PETROLIA OIL TRADE.

(From our own Correspondent.)

PETROLIA, Aug. 9, 1869.

The production of crude for the last week has not exceeded 4,000 brls., and this is owing to a partial failure of what is called the King Territory. The Hamilton export firm are still busily attending to their trade, and everything seems to be right with them, for they can now manufacture a distillate that will make an oil equal to if not better than than any American brand; they are now running their full capacity. Mr. Craise, of this place, has commenced running the High Well, which is yielding some 30 brls. per day. Things at present are just on the qui vive. A number of new wells are being drilled, and should the most of them strike oil, it is a comfort to know that they cannot over stock the crude market, for several new firms would engage in the exporting business if they could obtain the crude, and be sure of an ample after supply; for, as the refiners now stand, (there are some 60 of them spread over Western Canada)—the Standard, the Higgins, the Buffalo, and the Spencer, and the Waterman—could distil every drop of crude now produced, with ease.

The town of Petrolia looks very lively just now, and lots of new faces appear every day. I am preparing a description of the different oil territories near this, which I will send you for next week. The quotations are for crude... $1 25 per brl.
Refined .... 0 20 " gall.
Eagle & Hart are taking away a large amount of crude just now. I have not heard of any new sales effected this week.   M. P.

Financial.

TORONTO STOCK MARKET.
(Reported by Pellatt & Osler, Brokers.)

There has been a good business done during the week in favorite stocks, and, in most cases, prices have slightly advanced. The supply is still far short of the demand.

Bank of Montreal has been sold in small lots at 162, 161½ and 161, there being still buyers at the last-named rate. Small lots of British at 105½ have been offered. Ontario has been sold at 96 and 96½; there are buyers at the former rate, and sellers at 96½. Sales of Toronto Bank at 123½ are reported; but though that rate would now be given, there are no sellers. There is a demand for Royal Canadian at 52, with no sellers. Bank of Commerce has been largely dealt in at 103½, 103⅞ and 104, and there are now buyers at 104½. There have been considerable sales of Gore at 68 and 68½ on reduced stock. Sales of Merchants' at 104½ and 104⅝ have occurred; the market closed firm. There are buyers of Quebec at 100½ to 101. Sales of City at 100½ and 101 have been made, and there are buyers at the latter rate. Of Du Peuple there are buyers at 109½, with no sellers; of Jacques Cartier 108½; of Union at 104¼. There is no Toronto Gas Stock in the market; buyers would give 108. There have been sales of British America Assurance at 56½ and 57, and there are still buyers at the latter rate. Canada Permanent B. S. commands 123½. There is a demand for Western Canada B. S. at 119½; sales have occurred at 118½, 119 and 119½. Buyers would give 119 for Freehold, but there is none on market. There have been sales of Montreal Telegraph at 132 and 132½. Canada Landed Credit is in demand at 82. Short dated Sixes of Canada Debentures are offering at 103½, and Dominion Stock at 107· Fives and long-dated Sixes are in demand. Considerable sales of Toronto Debentures have been made to pay 7 per cent. interest, with a continued demand. County Debentures have sold during the week at 99 and 99½. Mortgages have been placed at from .8 to 9 per cent.

POST OFFICE SAVINGS' BANK STATEMENT FOR JUNE.—
In hands of the Receiver General as per last
    statement, 31st May, 1869 ....$771,380 83
Received from Depositors during
    June $98,506 00
Interest paid on closed ac-
    counts during June 326 58
Interest accrued during
    the year, made princi-
    pal on 30th June 19,008 67
                                   ———————$117,841 25
                                              ———————
Withdrawal cheques paid during June $2,416 82
                                              $85,424 43

In hands of Receiver General 30th June, 1869...$856,814 26

Bearing interest at 4 per cent....... $406,517 19
   "   "   5 " 352,300 00
Bearing no interest, being the amount
   in the hands of the Receiver General to meet outstanding cheques.   7,007 07
                                       ———————$856,814 26

DEPOSITORS' ACCOUNT, PROVINCIAL SAVINGS
BANK, HALIFAX, FOR JULY.—
In hands of the Receiver General, as per last
    statement, 31st May, 1869........$705,230 07
Balance received during June....   6,867 74

In hands of the Receiver General 30th June...$715,106 31
Rec'd from Depositors during July.. $31,081 40
Paid to Depositors during July...... 18,277 93
                                     ———————— 12,803 44
                                     ———————
In hands of Receiver General 24th July, 1869...$727,910 23

—The construction of a ship canal from New Orleans to Lake Pontchartrain, it is asserted, would diminish the port charges in pilotage and towage alone by the sum of $1,800 on a vessel of one thousand tons burden. At present it costs $2,555 to bring a vessel of that size from the mouth of The Mississippi to New Orleans. The charges to bring a vessel of one thousand tons burden from the ocean to the wharves amount to $570 at Boston and $676 at New York. It is argued, therefore, that a ship canal at New Orleans would place that port on an equality with Northern cities.

—A short time ago Mr. L. Shickluna launched, at St. Catherines, the bark Thomas C. Street. She is 148 feet long; depth of hold 11 feet 4 inches; breadth of beam 26 feet 3 inches; 400 tons burthen. The Journal says:—It is expected that she will carry 20,000 bushels of wheat through the canal. She will be commanded by Capt. Reuben Wynn, now of the St. Andrews, and her first trip will be to Chicago with a cargo of wood. Shickluna has another vessel and a propeller on the stocks, both of which will no doubt be afloat at the proper time.

—It is proposed to start a Gas Company in Peterborough.

—The Halifax Reporter advises Toronto to look sharp after the Coal trade with Nova Scotia, else Montreal will take the lead in it, and by consequence in the flour trade. Our contemporary adds:—If our coal-owners were to combine and appoint agents in Toronto and Montreal and other places, and then enter into the carrying trade themselves, a valuable impulse might be given to inter-provincial trade. Coal yards in Montreal and Toronto would help to introduce our coal among the people of the Upper Provinces.

—A telegram from Shanghai communicates the sailing of the first tea ships this season for England —namely, the Titania and Huntly Castle, sailing ships, and the Agamemnon and Erl King. Their cargoes in the aggregate amount to 6,000,000 lbs. of tea.

—The manufacture of wine in California is rapidly increasing. The vintage of 1867 is estimated at 3,500,000 to 4,000,000 gallons.

—The wheat crop in the county of Grey is suffering severely from the ravages of the midge; so we are informed by a reliable correspondent. As this is one of the largest wheat growing counties in Ontario, the failure of the crop there will materially lessen our exportable surplus, and go far to disappoint the high anticipations that have been formed of the harvest.

Commercial Travellers.

The number of commercial travellers in the United States is stated at fifty thousand. These are employed by firms in different parts of the country, divided as follows:—Boston and the New England States, 10,000; New York, 20,000; Cincinnati, Chicago and St. Louis, 10,000; Pennsylvania and Maryland, including Philadelphia, Pittsburg and Baltimore, 10,000.—Total, 50,000.

Intercolonial Railway.

Morton & Smith,
ACCOUNTANTS, REAL ESTATE AGENTS,
AND VALUATORS,
48 AND 50 CHURCH STREET,
TORONTO.
B. MORTON.   47-1y   J. LAMOND SMITH.

Insolvent Act of 1864.

Mercantile.

TORONTO PRICES CURRENT.—AUGUST 12, 1869.

Name of Article	Wholesale Rates	
Boots and Shoes.	$ c.	$ c.
Mens' Thick Boots ...	2 05	2 50
" Kip	2 25	2 00
" Calf	2 50	2 70
" Congress Gaiters ..	1 05	2 50
" Kip Cobourgs ..	1 90	1 40
Boys' Thick Boots..	1 70	1 80
Youths'	1 40	1 60
Women's Batts	0 95	1 20
" Balmoral..	1 20	1 50
" Congress Gaiters..	0 90	1 50
Misses' Batts	0 75	1 00
" Balmoral..	1 00	1 20
" Congress Gaiters..	1 00	1 30
Girls' Batts	0 65	0 85
" Balmoral..	0 40	1 05
" Congress Gaiters..	0 75	1 10
Children's C.T. Cacks..	0 50	0 65
" Gaiters..	0 05	0 90
Drugs.		
Aloes Cape..........	0 12½	0 16
Alum..............	0 02½	0 03
Borax..............	0 00	0 00
Camphor, refined....	0 65	0 70
Castor Oil..........	0 10½	0 13
Caustic Soda......	0 04½	0 05
Cream Tartar	0 90	0 35
Epsom Salts	0 00	0 00
Extract Logwood..	0 11	0 12
Gum Arabic, sorts..	0 30	0 35
Indigo, Madras....	0 90	1 00
Licorice	0 14	0 15
Madder............	0 00	0 16
Galls	0 32	0 37
Opium............	12 00	13 50
Oxalic Acid........	0 26	0 35
Potash, Bi-tart....	0 25	0 28
" Bichromate..	0 15	0 20
Potass Iodide	3 90	4 50
Rhubarb	0 12½	0 60
Senna	0 13½	0 60
Soda Ash	0 02½	0 04
Soda Bicarb	0 00	4 00
Tartaric Acid......	0 40	0 45
Verdigris	0 35	0 40
Vitriol, Blue......	0 08	0 10
Groceries.		
Coffees :		
Java, ℔.........	0 22	0 23
Laguayra, ...	0 17	0 18
Rio	0 15	0 17
Fish :		
Herrings, Lab. split..	00	0 00
" round..	00	0 00
" scaled..	0 88	0 35
Mackerel, smallkitts..	1 00	0 00
Louh. Her. wh'efrks..	2 50	2 75
" half ..	1 25	1 50
White Fish & Trout..	0 00	3 50
Salmon, saltwater..	14 00	15 00
Dry Cod, ℔112 lbs..	4 50	5 00
Fruit :		
Raisins, Layers ..	1 00	2 00
" M. R.	1 90	2 00
" Valentiasnew..	0 0	0 0½
Currants, new....	0 4½	0 0¼
" old.....	0 00	0 00
Figs	0 11	0 12
Molasses :		
Clayed, ℔ gal	0 00	0 35
Syrups, Standard ..	0 55	0 76
" Golden ..	0 59	0 60
Rice :		
Arracan	60	4 00
Spices :		
Cassia, whole, ℔ lb..	0 00	0 45
Cloves	0 11	0 12
Nutmegs	0 50	0 65
Ginger, gr'uud ...	0 18	0 23
" Jamaica, root..	0 20	0 25
Pepper, black......	0 10½	0 11
Pimento	0 08	0 09
Sugars:		
Port Rico, ℔ lb......	0 9	0 9½
Cuba	0 9	0 9½
Barbadoes (bright)..	0 9	0 9½
Canada Sugar Refine'y, yellow No. 2, 50 ds..	0 9½	0 9¾
Yellow, No. 3..	0 9	0 9½
" No. 3..	0 9½	0 10
Crushed X........	0 10	0 11
" X....	0 11	0 11½
Dry Crushed	0 12	0 12½
Extra Ground	0 13	0 13½
Teas:		
Japan com'n to good ..	0 48	0 50
" Fine to choicest..	0 55	0 60
Colored, com. to fine..	0 60	0 70
Congou & Souch'ng..	0 42	0 72
Oolong, good to fine..	0 50	0 65
Y. Hyson, com to gd..	0 47½	0 55
Medium to choice ..	0 65	0 80
Extra choice	0 85	0 95

Name of Article	Wholesale Rate	
Groceries—Contin'd	$ c.	c.
Gunpowd'r, to med...	0 5	70
" med. to fine..	0 7	85
" fine to fine't..	0 8	95
Hyson	0 44	80
Imperial.........	0 43	0 80
Tobacco, Manufac'd :		
Can Leaf, ℔ lbs & 10s..	0 26	30
Western Leaf, com..	0 25	20
" Good	0 27	32
" Fine	0 33	35
" Bright fine..	0 40	0 50
" choice..	0 60	0 75
Hardware.		
Tin (net cash prices)		
Block, ℔ lb........	0 35	0 00
Grain	0 30	0 00
Copper:		
Pig	0 23	0 24
Sheet............	0 30	0 33
Cut Nails:		
Assorted ⅜ Shingles, ℔ 100 lb.......	2 95	3 00
Shingle alone do ..	3 15	3 25
Lathe and ⅜ dy.....	3 90	3 40
Galvanized Iron:		
Assorted sizes....	0 08	0 09
Best No. ℔a......	0 07½	0 00
" 26......	0 08	0 08½
" 28......	0 09	0 09½
Horse Nails:		
Guest's or Griffin's assorted sizes....	0 00	0 00
For W. and C sizes..	0 13	0 19
Patent Hammer'd do..	0 17	0 18
Iron (at 4 months):		
Pig—Gartsherrie No1..	24 00	25 00
Other brands. No1..	22 00	24 00
" No 2..	0 00	0 00
Bar—Scotch, ℔100 lb..	2 85	2 60
Refined	3 00	3 50
Swedes	5 00	5 50
Hoops—Coopers..	3 00	3 25
" Band	3 00	3 25
Boiler Plates	3 25	3 50
Canada Plates	3 75	4 00
Union Jack	0 00	0 00
Pontypool........	3 25	4 00
Swansea	3 90	4 00
Lead (at 4 months):		
Bar, ℔ 100 lbs....	0 05½	0 07
Sheet "	0 08	0 09
Shot............	0 07½	0 07½
Iron Wire (net cash):		
No. 6, ℔ bundle...	2 70	2 80
" 9, " ..	3 10	3 20
" 12, " ..	3 40	3 50
" 15, " ..	4 30	4 40
Powder :		
Blasting, Canada....	3 50	0 00
FF	4 25	4 50
FFF	4 75	5 00
FF loose..	4 00	5 00
FFF " ..	6 00	6 50
Pressed Spikes (4 mos):		
Regular sizes 100..	4 00	4 25
Extra ..	4 50	5 00
Tin Plates (net cash):		
IC Coke	7 50	8 00
IC Charcoal......	8 00	9 00
IX " ..	10 50	11 00
IXX " ..	13 50	14 00
DC " ..	8 50	9 00
DX " ..	9 50	0 00
Hides & Skins, ℔ lb		
Green rough	0 00	0 05
Green, salt'd & insp'd..	0 06	0 06½
Cured	0 00	0 00
Calfskins, green ..	0 00	0 12½
Calfskins, cured....	0 00	0 00
" dry	0 18	0 20
Sheepskins, ...	1 90	1 60
" pelts....	0 10	0 90
Hops		
Inferior, ℔ lb......	0 00	0 00
Medium,..	0 00	0 00
Good	0 00	0 00
Fancy	0 00	0 00
Leather, (℔ ⅜ mos.)		
In lots of less than 50 sides, 10 ℔ cnt higher		
Spanish Sole, 1st qual'y heavy, weights ℔ lb..	0 21	0 22
Do.1st quai middle do..	0 20	0 23
Do. No. 2, light weights	0 20	0 00
Slaughter heavy ..	0 00	0 00
Do. light	0 26	0 29
Harness, best	0 25	0 37
" No. 2	0 00	0 00
Upper heavy......	0 30	0 32
" light..	0 33	0 34

Name of Article	Wholesale Rates	
Leather—Contin'd.	c.	$
Kip Skins, Patna	30	0 5
French	70	0 0
English .... ℔	05	0 90
Hemlock Calf (30 to 35 lbs.) per doz...	0 50	0 00
Do. light	0 45	0 50
French Calf........	1 03	1 06
Grain & Satn Cit'g doz..	0 00	0 55
Splits, large ℔ lb ...	0 30	0 38
" small ..	0 23	0 26
Enamelled Cow ℔ foot..	0 20	0 21
Patent	0 50	0 21
Pebble Grain	0 15	0 17
Buff..............	0 14	0 16
Oils.		
Cod	0 65	0 70
Lard, extra........	0 00	0 00
" No. 1	0 00	0 00
" Woollen......	0 00	0 00
Lubricating, patent..	0 00	0 00
" Mott's economic	0 30	0 00
Linseed, raw........	0 76	0 82
" boiled....	0 81	0 87
Machinery........	0 00	0 00
Olive, common, ℔ gal..	1 00	1 60
" salad	1 95	2 30
" salad, in bots.		
qt. ℔ case..	3 60	3 75
Sesame salad, ℔ gal..	1 60	1 75
Seal, pale........	0 75	0 85
Spirits Turpentine..	0 52½	0 00
Varnish	0 00	0 00
Whale............	0 00	0 90
Paints, &c.		
White Lead, genuine in Oil, ℔ 25lbs......	0 00	2 35
Do. No. 1	0 00	2 10
" 2	0 00	1 90
" 3	0 00	1 65
White Zinc, genuine..	3 00	3 50
White Lead, dry	0 00	0 07
Red Lead........	0 07½	0 08
Venetian Red, Eng'h..	0 02½	0 02¾
Yellow Ochre, Fren'h..	0 02½	0 03
Whiting ..,......	0 85	1 25
Petroleum.		
(Refined ℔ gal.)		
Water white, car'l'd..	0 20	0 21
" small lots..	0 23	0 23
Straw, by car load..	0 00	0 00
" small lots..	0 00	0 00
Amber, by car load..	0 00	0 00
" small lots..	0 00	0 00
Benzine	0 00	0 00
Produce.		
Grain :		
Wheat, Spring, 60 ℔..	1 00	1 08
" Fall ..	1 00	1 10
Barley 45	0 00	0 70
Peas.... 60	0 00	0 00
Oats.... 34	0 53	0 57
Rye 56	0 56	0 00
Seeds :		
Clover, choice 60 ℔..	0 00	0 00
" com'n 68 ..	0 00	0 00
Timothy, cho's ..	0 00	0 00
" Inf. to good 48 ..	0 00	0 00
Flax 00	0 00	0 00
Flour (per brl.) :		
Superior extra,..	0 00	0 00
Extra superfine,..	4 60	4 70
Fancy superfine..	4 55	4 65
Superfine No 1..	4 45	4 50
" No. 2..	0 00	0 00
Oatmeal, (per brl.)..	5 50	6 00
Provisions		
Butter, dairy tub ℔ lb..	0 13½	0 15
" store packed..	0 13½	0 15
Cheese, new	0 11	0 12½
Pork, mess, per brl...	27 00	27 50
" prime mess......		
" prime		
Bacon, rough......	0 13	0 13½
" Cumberl'd cut...	0 13	0 00
" smoked	0 00	0 00
Hams, in salt......	0 00	0 07
" smoked......	0 00	0 07
Shoulders, in salt ..	0 00	0 11
Lard, in kegs......	0 13½	0 13¾
Eggs, packed	0 12	0 15
Beef Hams	0 00	0 00
Tallow	0 08	0 9
Hogs dressed, heavy..	0 00	0 00
" medium...	0 00	0 00
Salt, &c.		
American brls.....	1 85	1 87
Liverpool coarse....	0 00	0 00
Goderich	0 00	1 53
Plaster............	0 00	0 00
Water Lime	1 50	0 00

Soap & Candles.	$ c.	$ c.
D. Crawford & Co.'s ..		
Imperial.........	0 07½	0 08
" Golden Bar	0 07	0 07½
" Silver Bar........	0 07	0 07½
Crown	0 05	0 05½
No. 1	0 03½	0 03¾
Candles	0 00	0 11
Wines, Liquors, &c.		
Ale:		
English, per doz. qrts.	2 60	2 65
Guinness Dub Portr..	2 35	2 40
Spirits:		
Pure Jamaica Rum...	1 80	2 25
De Kuyper's H. Gin..	1 55	1 65
Booth's Old Tom.....	1 90	2 00
Gin:		
Green, cases.........	4 00	4 25
Booth's Old Tom, c...	6 00	6 25
Wines:		
Port, common	1 00	1 25
" fine old	2 00	4 00
Sherry, common	1 00	1 50
" medium........	1 70	1 80
"old pale or golden..	2 50	4 00

	$ c.	$ c.
Brandy:		
Hennessy's, per gal..	2 30	2 50
Martell's " ..	2 30	2 50
J. Robin & Co.'s " ..	2 25	2 35
Otard, Dupuy & Cos..	2 25	2 35
Brandy, cases........	8 50	9 00
Brandy, com. per c...	4 00	4 50
Whiskey:		
Common 36 u. p......	0 58	0 00
Old Rye	0 77½	0 80
Malt	0 77½	0 80
Toddy	0 77½	0 80
Scotch, per gal........	1 90	2 10
Irish—Kinnahan's c...	7 00	7 50
" Dunnville's Belf't..	6 00	6 25
Wool.		
Fleece, lb.............	0 30	0 31
Pulled ".............	0 00	0 00
Furs.		
Bear..................	0 00	0 00
Beaver, ℘ lb.........	0 00	0 00
Coon	0 00	0 00
Fisher................	0 00	0 00
Martin................	0 00	0 00
Mink..................	0 00	0 00
Otter.................	0 00	0 00
Spring Rats..........	0 00	0 00
Fox	0 00	0 00

INSURANCE COMPANIES.

ENGLISH.—*Quotations on the London Market.*

No. of Shares.	Last Dividend.	Name of Company.	Shares par val £	Amount paid.	Last Sale.
20,000		Briton Medical and General Life...	10	....	2½
50,000	7½	Commer'l Union, Fire, Life and Mar.	50	5	5½
24,000	8	City of Glasgow	25	2½	4¼
5,000	9½	Edinburgh Life	100	15	33½
400,000	5—½ yr	European Life and Guarantee......	2½	11s6	4s. 0d
100,000	10	Etna Fire and Marine............	10	1½	—
20,000	5	Guardian	100	50	53¼
24,000	12	Imperial Fire...................	500	50	352
7,500	9½	Imperial Life	100	10	17½
100,000	10	Lancashire Fire and Life.........	20	2	2⅛
10,000	11	Life Association of Scotland.......	40	7½	25.10
35,862	45s. p. sh	London Assurance Corporation ..	25	12½	48¾
10,000	5	London and Lancashire Life	10	1	—
87,504	40	Liverp'l & London & Globe F. & L.	20	2	7½
20,000	5	National Union Life	5	1	1
20,000	12½	Northern Fire and Life	100	5	13
40,000	12 '68, bo 5s.	North British and Mercantile	50	6¼	19¼
40,000	50	Ocean Marine	25	5	17¾
2,500	£5 12s.	Provident Life..................	100	10	35
....	£4½ p. s.	Phœnix........................	....	....	139½ x d
200,000	2½--h.yr.	Queen Fire and Life	10	1	21s.
100,000	3s. bo.4s	Royal Insurance.................	20	3	6½
20,000	10	Scottish Provincial Fire and Life ..	50	2½	5½
10,000	25	Standard Life	50	12	66 x d
4,000	5	Star Life	25	1¼	—
		CANADIAN.			℘ c.
8,000	4	British America Fire and Marine ..	$50	$25	56 56½
....	4	Canada Life	...	....	.....
4000	12	Montreal Assurance	£50	£5	135
10,000	3	Provincial Fire and Marine........	60	11	.....
....	....	Quebec Fire	40	32½	£22½ 23
....	7	" Marine................	100	40	85 90
10,000	4 6 mo's.	Western Assurance..............	40	9	50 60

RAILWAYS.	Sha's	Paid	Montr	London
Atlantic and St. Lawrence..................	£100	All.	....	50 61
Buffalo and Lake Huron	20½	"	....	3 3½
Do. do Preference	10	"	....	5 7
Buff., Brantf. & Goderich, 6℘c., 1872-3-4....	100	"	....	60 70
Champlain and St. Lawrence	....	....	9 12	....
Do. do Pref. 10 ℘ ct....	....	....	80 85	....
Grand Trunk	100	"	13 15	15½ 15¾
Do. Eq.G. M. Bds. 1 ch. 6℘c..........	100	"	....	86 88
Do. First Preference, 5 ℘ c	100	"	....	54 55
Do. Deferred, 3 ℘ ct..	100	"	....	....
Do. Second Pref. Bonds, 5℘c........	100	"	....	40 42
Do. do Deferred, 3 ℘ ct..........	100	"	...	....
Do. Third Pref. Stock, 4 ℘ct..........	100	"	...	30 32
Do. do. Deferred, 3 ℘ ct...........	100	"	...	....
Do. Fourth Pref. Stock, 3℘c...........	100	"	....	19 20
Do. do. Deferred, 3 ℘ ct..........	100	"	....	....
Great Western	20½	"	15 15½	15¾ 16
Do. New	20½	18	....	....
Do. 6 ℘ c. Bds, due 1873-76..........	100	All.	....	101 103
5½ ℘c Bds. due 1877-78..........	100	"	....	95 97
Marine Railway, Halifax, $250, all......	$250	"	....	....
Northern of Canada, 6 ℘c. 1st Pref. Bds..........	100	"	....	82 84

EXCHANGE.	Halifax.	Montr'l.	Quebec.	Toronto.
Bank on London, 60 days......				
Sight or 75 days date	12½ 13	9½ 9¾	9¾ 10	10¾
Private do.	11½ 12	8½ 9	9 9½	9½
Private, with documents........	....	8 8¼	8½ 8¾	....
Bank on New York.............	....	25½ 26	25¾ 26¼	24
Private do.	....	26 26½	26¼ 26¾	....
Gold Drafts do.	....	½ dis.	par ⅛ dis.	par ½ dis.
ilver	....	4 4¾	....	4 to 5½

STOCK AND BOND REPORT.

The dates of our quotations are as follows:—Toronto, Aug. 10; Montreal, Aug. 10; Quebec, Aug. 9; London, July 29.

NAME.	Shares.	Paid up.	Divid'd last 6 Months	Dividend Day.	CLOSING PRICES. Toronto.	Montre'l	Quebec.
BANKS.			℘ ct.				
British North America	$250	All.	3½ b½ pc	July and Jan.	104½ 105	105 106	105 105½
Jacques Cartier.........	50	"	4	1 June, 1 Dec.	108 108½	108 108½	107½ 108
Montreal	200	"	6	"	160¼ 161	160¼ 160¼	160¼ 160¼
Nationale..................	50	"	4	1 Nov. 1 May.	107½ 108	108	107½ 108
New Brunswick	100	"	......	......	....	....	....
Nova Scotia	200	—	7 & b $3½	Mar. and Sept.	....	....	....
Du Peuple......	50	"	4	1 Mar., 1 Sept.	109½ 110	109¼ 110	109½ 110
Toronto	100	"	4	1 Jan., 1 July.	123½ 125	122½ 124	122 124
Bank of Yarmouth............	....	....	......	......	....	....	....
Canadian Bank of Com'e......	50	All.	......	......	104 104½	100	103 103½
City Bank Montreal	80	"	4	1 June, 1 Dec.	99½ 100	101 101½	100½ 101
Commer'l Bank (St. John)....	100	"	℘ ct.	. ...	...	..	....
Eastern Townships' Bank.....	50	"	4	1 July, 1 Jan..	....	99 100	99 100
Gore	40	...	none.	1 Jan., 1 July.	68 70	45 47	40 43
Halifax Banking Company....	...	....	......	. ....	...	...	....
Mechanics' Bank............	50	All.	4	1 Nov., 1 May.	93 95	93 95	92 93½
Merchants'Bank of Canada....	100	"	5	1 Jan., 1 July.	105 106	104 105	103½ 104
Merchants' Bank (Halifax)....	....	....	.....	.....	....	....	....
Molson's Bank..............	50	All.	4	1 Apr., 1 Oct.	109 109½	108¾ 109½	109 109½
Niagara District Bank...	100	70	3½	1 Jan., 1 July.	...	....	..
Ontario Bank...............	40	All.	4	1 June, 1 Dec.	96 96½	95½ 96	95½ 96
People's Bank (Fred'kton)....	100	"	......	......	....	...	...
People's Bank (Halifax)	20	"	7 12 m	......	....	....	....
Quebec Bank	100	"	3½	1 June, 1 Dec.	100½ 101	100	100½ 101½
Royal Canadian Bank	50	60	4	1 Jan., 1 July.	52 55	52 55	52 55
St. Stephens Bank	100	All	.....	.....	....	....	....
Union Bank	100	"	4	1 Jan., 1 July.	105 105½	105 105½	105½ 106½
Union Bank (Halifax)........	100	....	7 12 mo.	Feb. and Aug.	....	....	....
MISCELLANEOUS.							
British America Land........	250	44	......	......	....	....	....
British Colonial S. S. Co......	250	32½	......	......	...	....	...
Canada Company	32½	All.	......	......	....	....	....
Canada Landed Credit Co.....	50	$50	3½	......	80 81	....	....
Canada Per. B'ldg Society....	50	All.	5	......	123 123½	....	....
Canada Mining Company.....	4	90	......	......	....	....	....
Do. Inl'd Steam Nav. Co....	100	All.	15 12 m	......	....	100 101	...
Do. Glass Company.........	100	"	None.	......	....	35 45	....
Canad'n Loan & Investm't....	25	2½	......	......	....	....	....
Canada Agency	10	¼	......	......	....	....	....
Colonial Securities Co.........	...	....	.....	.....	....	....	....
Freehold Building Society....	100	All.	5	......	118½ 119	....	....
Halifax Steamboat Co........	100	"	......	......	....	....	....
Halifax Gas Company........	....	....	......	. ..	....	...	....
Hamilton Gas Company......	....	....	.....	. ....	....	....	....
Huron Copper Bay Co........	4	12	20	. ....	....	30 40	....
Lake Huron S. and C.........	5	102	......	......	....	...	....
Montreal Mining Consols.....	20	$15	......	. ....	....	3.10 3.25	...
Do. Telegraph Co....	40	All.	5	......	132 133	132 134	132½ 133
Do. Elevating Co....	00	"	5½	......	....	100	....
Do. City Gas Co.........	40	"	4	15 Mar. 15 Sep.	....	135	138 139
Do. City Pass. R. Co.....	50	"	2	......	....	112 113	111½ 111
Quebec and L. S.	8	$4	......	.....	....	...	....
Quebec Gas Co...............	200	All.	4	1 Mar., 1 Sep.	....	...	124 125
Quebec Street R. R..........	50	25	3	......	....	....	85 86
Richelieu Navigation Co......	100	All.	7-12m	1 Jan., 1 July.	...	120 122	120 122½
St. Lawrence Glass Company.	100	"	....	......	....	50 90	.. ..
St. Lawrence Tow Boat Co....	100	"	......	3 Feb.	...	...	20 35
Tor'to Consumers' Gas Co....	50	"	⅜ m	1 My Au Mar Fe	107½ 108	...	107 107½
Trust & Loan Co. of U. C....	20	5	3	......	....	....	..
West'n-Canada Bldg Soc'y....	50	All.	5	......	119 119½	....	....

SECURITIES.	London.	Montreal	Quebec	Toronto.
Canadian Gov't Deb. 6 ℘ ct. stg..................	...	103	102½ 103½	104½ 105
Do. do. 6 do due Ja. & Jul. 1877-84........	104 105	103 104	102 103	104 105
Do. do. 6 do. Feb. & Aug...	105 107	....	.. .	....
Do. do. 6 do. Mch. & Sep.........	104 106	.. .	...	.. .
Do. do. 5 ℘ ct. cur., 1883	93 94	94 95	91 92	94 95
Do. do. 5 do. stg., 1885	92 94	92	89½ 90	92½ 93½
Do. do. 7 do. cur.,....................	....	....	......	....
Dominion 6 p. c. 1878 cy.....	....	107 107½	106½ 107	106½ 107
Hamilton Corporation....	. ..	....	... ..	....
Montreal Harbor, 8 ℘ ct. d. 1869................	..	....	......	....
Do. do. 7 do. 1870....	...	....	......	....
Do. do. 6½ do. 1883..........	....	102½	......	102 103
Do. do. 6½ do. 1873................	....	....	......	....
Do. Corporation, 6 ℘ c. 1891	....	97 97½	96½ 97	96½ 97½
Do. 7 p. c. stock...	....	109 110	109 110	110 112
Do. Water Works, 6 ℘ c. stg. 1878.........	...	97½ 98	......	96½ 97
Do. do. 6 do. cy. do.	....	....	......	96 97
New Brunswick, 6 ℘ ct., Jan. and July	102 104	....	. ...	....
Nova Scotia, 6 ℘ ct., 1875........................	102 104	...	......	...
Ottawa City 6 ℘ c. d. 1880	....	95 97	......	...
Quebec Harbour, 6 ℘ c. d. 1883.	....	....	50	...
Do. do. 7 do. do..................	....	....	65 70	....
Do. do 8 do. 1886...............	...	....	75 80	....
Do. City, 7 ℘ c. d. 1½ years....	....	....	98 98½	....
Do. do. 7 do. 8 do.	....	....	91 92	....
Do. do. 7 do. 5 do.	....	....	96 96½	....
Do. Water Works, 7 ℘ ct., 3 years...........	....	....	97 97½	....
Do. do. 6 do. 1½ do.	....	....	94 95	....
Toronto Corporation	....	94 95	....	....

Insurance.

Insurance.

Insurance.

Briton Medical and General Life Association,
with which is united the
BRITANNIA LIFE ASSURANCE COMPANY.

Capital and Invested Funds..........£750,000 Sterling.

ANNUAL INCOME, £220,000 STG. :
Yearly increasing at the rate of £25,000 Sterling.

THE important and peculiar feature originally introduced by this Company, in applying the periodical Bonuses, so as to make Policies payable during life, without any higher rate of premiums being charged, has caused the success of the BRITON MEDICAL AND GENERAL to be almost unparalleled in the history of Life Assurance. *Life Policies on the Profit Scale become payable during the lifetime of the Assured, thus rendering a Policy of Assurance a means of subsistence in old age, as well as a protection for a family,* and a more valuable security to creditors in the event of early death; and effectually meeting the often urged objection, that persons do not themselves reap the benefit of their own prudence and forethought.

No extra charge made to members of Volunteer Corps for services within the British Provinces.

☞ TORONTO AGENCY, 5 KING ST. WEST.

Oct 17—9-1yr   JAMES FRASER, *Agent.*

BEAVER
Mutual Insurance Association.

HEAD OFFICE—20 TORONTO STREET,
TORONTO.

INSURES LIVE STOCK against death from any cause. The only Canadian Company having authority to do this class of business.
                    E. C. CHADWICK, President.
W. T. O'REILLY, Secretary.   8-1y-25

HOME DISTRICT
Mutual Fire Insurance Company.

Office—North-West Cor. Yonge & Adelaide Streets,
TORONTO.—(UP STAIRS.)

INSURES Dwelling Houses, Stores, Warehouses, Merchandise, Furniture, &c.
PRESIDENT—The Hon. J. McMURRICH.
VICE-PRESIDENT—JOHN BURNS, Esq.
                    JOHN RAINS, Secretary.
                    AGENTS:
DAVID WRIGHT, Esq., Hamilton: FRANCIS STEVENS, Esq.,
Barrie: Messrs. GIBBS & BRO., Oshawa.   3-1y

THE PRINCE EDWARD COUNTY
Mutual Fire Insurance Company.

HEAD OFFICE,—PICTON, ONTARIO.

President, L. B. STINSON ; *Vice-President,* WM. DELONG.
Directors: W. A. Richards, James Johnson, James CaVan, D. W. Ruttan, H. A. McFaul.—*Secretary,* John Twigg ; *Treasurer,* David Barker; *Solicitor,* R. J. Fitzgerald.

THIS Company is established upon strictly Mutual principles, insuring farming and isolated property, (not hazardous,) in *Townships only,* and offers great advantages to insurers, at low rates for *five years,* without the expense of a renewal.
Picton, June 15, 1869.   9-1y

Fire and Marine Assurance.

THE BRITISH AMERICA
A S S U R A N C E   C O M P A N Y .

HEAD OFFICE :
CORNER OF CHURCH AND COURT STREETS.
TORONTO.

BOARD OF DIRECTION :

Hon. G. W. Allan, M L.C.,	A. Joseph, Esq ,
George J. Boyd, Esq ,	Peter Paterson, Esq.,
Hon. W. Cayley,	G. P. Ridout, Esq.,
Richard S. Cassels, Esq.,	E H. Rutherford,Esq.,

Thomas C. Street, Esq.
                    Governor :
                GEORGE PERCIVAL RIDOUT, Esq.
                    Deputy Governor :
                    PETER PATERSON, Esq.
Fire Inspector: *Marine Inspector:*
E. ROBY O'BRIEN.   CAPT. R. COURNEEN.
Insurances granted on all descriptions of property against loss and damage by fire and the perils of inland navigation.
Agencies established in the principal cities, towns, and ports of shipment throughout the Province.
                    THOS. WM. BIRCHALL,
23-1y   *Managing Director.*

Reliance Mutual Life Assurance Society
OF LONDON, ENGLAND. Established 1840.

Head Office for the Dominion of Canada:
131 ST. JAMES STREET, MONTREAL.
DIRECTORS—Walter Shanly, Esq., M.P.; Duncan Macdonald, Esq.; George Winks, Esq., W. H. Hingston, Esq.,
M.D., L.R.C.S.
RESIDENT SECRETAR—James Grant.
Parties intending to assure their lives, are invited to peruse the Society's prospectus, which embraces several entirely new and interesting features in Life Assurance. Copies can be had on application at he Head Office, or at any of the Agencies.
                    JAS. GRANT, Resident Secretary.
Agents wanted in unrepresented districts.   43-1y

The Gore District Mutual Fire Insurance Company

GRANTS INSURANCES on all description of Property against Loss or Damage by FIRE. It is the only Mutual Fire Insurance Company which assesses its Policies yearly from their respective dates; and the average yearly cost of insurance in ft. for the past three and a half years, has been nearly TWENTY CENTS IN THE DOLLAR less than what it would have been in an ordinary Proprietary Company.
                    THOS. M. SIMONS, Secretary & Treasurer.
ROBT. McLEAN, Inspector of Agencies.
Galt, 25th Nov., 1868.   15-1y

Canada Life Assurance Company.

ESTABLISHED 1847.

THE ONLY CANADIAN LIFE COMPANY AUTHORIZED BY GOVERNMENT FOR THE DOMINION,

Rates are lower than British or Foreign Offices.

A LARGER amount of Insurances and of Investment in Canada than any other Company, and its rapid progress is satisfactory evidence of the popularity⁵of its principles and practice.

Last year there were issued
920 NEW POLICIES,
FOR ASSURANCE OF
$1,284,155,
WITH
A N N U A L   PREMIUMS   OF
$51,183.

AGENCIES THROUGHOUT THE DOMINION.
Where every information can be obtained, or at the
HEAD OFFICE, IN HAMILTON, ONT.
                    A. G. RAMSAY, Manager.
                    E. BRADBURNE, Agent,
May 25.   1y   Toronto Street.

Queen Fire and Life Insurance Company,
OF LIVERPOOL AND LONDON,
ACCEPTS ALL ORDINARY FIRE RISKS
on the most favorable terms.

L I F E   R I S K S
Will be taken on terms that will compare favorably with other Companies.
CAPITAL, · · · · £2,000,000 Stg.
CANADA BRANCH OFFICE—Exchange Buildings, Montreal.
Resident Secretary and General Agent,
                    A. MACKENZIE FORBES,
13 St. Sacrament St., Merchants' Exchange, Montreal.
WM. ROWLAND, Agent, Toronto.   1-1y

THE AGRICULTURAL
Mutual Assurance Association of Canada.

HEAD OFFICE ....LONDON, ONT.
A purely Farmers' Company. Licensed by the Government of Canada.

Capital, 1st January, 1869...................	$280,108 82
Cash and Cash Items, over.....................	$56,000 00
No. of Policies in force.......................	80,692 00

THIS Company insures nothing more dangerous than a Farm property. Its rates are as low as any well-established Company in the Dominion, and lower than those of a great many. It is largely patronised, and continues to grow in public favor.
For Insurance, apply to any of the Agents or address the Secretary, London, Ontario.
London, 2nd Nov., 1868.   12-1y

The Waterloo County Mutual Fire Insurance Company.

HEAD OFFICE : WATERLOO, ONTARIO.
ESTABLISHED 1863.

THE business of the Company is divided into three separate and distinct branches, the

VILLAGE, FARM, AND MANUFACTURES.
Each Branch paying its own losses and its just proportion of the managing expenses of the Company.
C. M. TAYLOR, Sec.   M. SPRINGER, M.M.P., Pres.
            J. HUGHES, Inspector.   15-yr

Lancashire Insurance Company.
CAPITAL.- - - - - - - - £2,000,000 Sterling

FIRE RISKS
Taken at reasonable rates of premium, and
ALL LOSSES SETTLED PROMPTLY,
By the undersigned, without reference elsewhere.
                    S. C. DUNCAN-CLARK & CO.,
                    General Agents for Ontario,
25-1y   N. W. Cor. of King & Church Sts., TORONTO.

Western Assurance Company.
INCORPORATED 1851.
CAPITAL, ... $400,000.
FIRE AND MARINE.
HEAD OFFICE.................TORONTO, ONTARIO.

DIRECTORS.
Hon. JNO. McMURRICH, President.
            CHARLES MAGRATH, Vice-President.
A. M. SMITH, Esq.   JOHN FISKEN, Esq.
ROBERT BEATY, Esq.   ALEX. MANNING, Esq.
JAMES MICHIE, Esq.   N. BARNHART, Esq.
            R. J. DALLAS, Esq.
            B. HALDAN, Secretary.
            J. MAUGHAN, JR., Assistant Secretary.
            WM. BLIGHT, Fire Inspector.
            CAPT. G. T. DOUGLAS, Marine Inspector.
            JAMES PRINGLE, General Agent.

Insurances effected at the lowest current rates on Buildings, Merchandize, and other property, against loss or damage by fire.
On Hull, Cargo and Freight against the perils of Inland Navigation.
On Cargo Risks with the Maritime Provinces by sail or steam.
On Cargoes by steamers to and from British Ports.
WESTERN ASSURANCE COMPANY'S OFFICE, }
TORONTO, 1st April, 1869.   } 33-1y

The Victoria Mutual
FIRE INSURANCE COMPANY OF CANADA.

Insures only Non-Hazardous Property, at Low Rates.

BUSINESS STRICTLY MUTUAL.

                    GEORGE H. MILLS, President.
                    W. D. BOOKER, Secretary.
HEAD OFFICE ....HAMILTON, ONTARIO
aug 15-1yr

North British and Mercantile Insurance Company.

Established 1809.

HEAD OFFICE, - - CANADA; - MONTREAL,

TORONTO BRANCH :
Local Offices, Nos. 4 & 6 WELLINGTON STREET.
Fire Department...............R. N. GOOCH, *Agent.*
Life Department...............H. L. HIME, *Agent.*

Imperial Fire Insurance Company
OF LONDON.
No. 1 OLD BROAD STREET, AND 16 PALL MALL.
ESTABLISHED 1803.
Canada General Agency,
                    RINTOUL BROS.,
                    24 St. Sacrament Street.
JAMES E. SMITH, Agent
Toronto; Corner Church and Colborne Streets.

PUBLISHED AT THE OFFICE OF THE MONETARY TIMES, No. 60 CHURCH STREET.
PRINTED AT THE DAILY TELEGRAPH PUBLISHING HOUSE, BAY STREET, CORNER OF KING

Lightning Source UK Ltd.
Milton Keynes UK
UKHW010322120219
337137UK00004B/367/P